Tolley's Corporation

Tolley's Corporation Tax 2011-12

by

Lisa-Jane Harper MA CTA ADIT

Mohammed Amin MA FCA AMCT CTA (Fellow)

Lee Holloway LLB (Hons) CTA ATT Barrister

Sarah Laing CTA

John Lindsay BA FCA FTII

Pete Miller CTA (Fellow)

Ruth Newman LLB (Hons) MA CTA

LexisNexis®

Members of the LexisNexis Group worldwide

United Kingdom	LexisNexis, a Division of Reed Elsevier (UK) Ltd, Halsbury House, 35 Chancery Lane, London, WC2A 1EL, and London House, 20–22 East London Street, Edinburgh EH7 4BQ
Australia	LexisNexis Butterworths, Chatswood, New South Wales
Austria	LexisNexis Verlag ARD Orac GmbH & Co KG, Vienna
Benelux	LexisNexis Benelux, Amsterdam
Canada	LexisNexis Canada, Markham, Ontario
China	LexisNexis China, Beijing and Shanghai
France	LexisNexis SA, Paris
Germany	LexisNexis Deutschland GmbH, Munster
Hong Kong	LexisNexis Hong Kong, Hong Kong
India	LexisNexis India, New Delhi
Italy	Giuffrè Editore, Milan
Japan	LexisNexis Japan, Tokyo
Malaysia	Malayan Law Journal Sdn Bhd, Kuala Lumpur
New Zealand	LexisNexis NZ Ltd, Wellington
Poland	Wydawnictwo Prawnicze LexisNexis Sp, Warsaw
Singapore	LexisNexis Singapore, Singapore
South Africa	LexisNexis Butterworths, Durban
USA	LexisNexis, Dayton, Ohio

Published by LexisNexis
This is a Tolley title

A CIP Catalogue record for this book is available from the British Library.

ISBN 9 780754 540434

Printed and bound by CPI Group (UK) Ltd, Croydon, CR0 4YY

Visit LexisNexis at www.lexisnexis.co.uk

About This Book

In 2010 we relaunched the Tolley's Tax Annuals to make them more practical and easier to use. They still contain the same trusted, valuable content but now you can find the answer you need even quicker than before.

What are the key changes?

- Key points – to direct you to matters that are of use in planning, or to areas of difficulty you may come across in practice.
- There are further practical examples – highly valued interpretation to help you understand the effects of the legislation on your day to day work. Examples are set in shaded boxes so they stand out if you need to go straight to practical interpretation.
- More contributions from practitioners using their own valuable experience.
- New, clearer text design – larger font and more white space for a more comfortable reading experience.
- Clearer contents – easier to read.
- The law and practice for the last four years is included and we have dispensed with any unnecessary historical text and statutory references.
- There are introductions for chapters – so that you can see quickly what is covered.
- We have split chapters where relevant – to break down the information into more manageable chunks and the structure of chapters has been improved.
- More headings have been introduced, with more distinct levels so that you can find the section that you want to read easily.
- Where appropriate, text has been converted to tables and lists to save you time and sentences shortened.

We hope that the new style meets your requirement for greater accessibility to the changing tax legislation and the ever increasing demands on you as a practitioner. We would be pleased to receive your feedback on the new style and any suggestions for further improvements. You can do this by e-mailing the Editor, Gemma Furniss at gemma.furniss@lexisnexis.co.uk. Technical queries will be dealt with by the author.

Contributors

Mohammed Amin MA FCA AMCT CTA (Fellow)

Mohammed Amin is an Islamic finance consultant and a member of HM Treasury's Islamic Finance Experts Group. He was previously a tax partner at PricewaterhouseCoopers LLP, being PwC's UK Islamic Finance leader and a member of their four-person Global Islamic Finance Leadership Team.

Lisa-Jane Harper MA CTA ADIT

Lisa-Jane specialises in corporate and international tax. A St Andrew's graduate, she obtained an MA in law at City University and was called to the Bar (Lincoln's Inn). She was in private practice before training in tax at KPMG's Tax Business School (ATT and CTA). Once qualified, Lisa-Jane worked as a tax lawyer in the City, undertaking predominantly cross-border transaction work and banking. Lisa-Jane moved to Ernst & Young in the Channel Islands in 2004 and whilst there took the Advanced Diploma in International Tax. Lisa-Jane moved back to the UK in December 2009 and has since been working with LexisNexis as a consultant.

Lee Holloway LLB (Hons) CTA ATT MCSI Barrister

Lee was called to the Bar by the Middle Temple before joining a Big 4 firm to complete the ATT and CTA qualifications. After spending over ten years in practice, six of which were in the M&A field, he took a role leading the UK tax function of a US owned multi-national group and has recently moved on to be Head of Tax and Corporate Finance at a leading FTSE 250 retailer. He has broad international tax experience but has mainly focused on UK corporation tax, re-organisations, vendor led M&A work (including vendor due diligence) and structuring corporate sales and acquisitions tax efficiently.

Sarah Laing CTA

Sarah Laing is a Chartered Tax Adviser and has been writing professionally since 1998 for the tax and accountancy professions. She has worked for both small and Big 5 firms. An established writer, she has contributed to a range of highly regarded tax publications. She is the news editor and a director of TaxationWeb.

John Lindsay BA FCA FTII

John Lindsay is a consultant in the tax department of Linklaters LLP where he advises on financing and M&A transactions. He has specialised in the taxation of loan relationships and derivative contracts for some years and is a member of the HMRC Working Group that is considering the ways in which tax legislation needs to be adapted to address proposed changes to the acccounting treament of loans and derivatives. He is also a contributor to Simon's Taxes.

Pete Miller CTA (Fellow), Partner, The Miller Partnership LLP

Pete Miller started with the Inland Revenue in 1988 and was an Inspector of Taxes before moving working in both Policy Division and Technical Division. Since leaving the Revenue, Pete worked for 11 years in 'Big 4' firms and specialised in reorganisations and reconstructions, the substantial shareholdings exemption, and the taxation of M&A transactions and of intangible assets. Pete is a member of the Editorial Boards of The Tax Journal and Simon's Taxes and a Consulting Editor to TolleyGuidance. He is co-author, with George Hardy, of Taxation of Company Reorganisations (Bloomsbury Professional, 3rd edition, December 2009).

Ruth Newman LLB (Hons), MA, CTA

Ruth Newman is a technical writer with LexisNexis. After working for many years with Ernst & Young and KPMG dealing with both corporate and capital taxes, she spent some time as an in-house tax manager with a major Plc.

Contents

Abbreviations and References

Abbreviations

ACT	Advance Corporation Tax.
APRT	Advance Petroleum Revenue Tax.
APRTA 1986	Advance Petroleum Revenue Tax Act 1986.
art	Article.
CAA	Capital Allowances Act.
CA	Court of Appeal.
CCA	Court of Criminal Appeal.
CCAB	Consultative Committee of Accountancy Bodies.
Ch D	Chancery Division.
CES	Court of Exchequer (Scotland).
Cf.	compare.
CFC	Controlled Foreign Company.
CGT	Capital Gains Tax.
CGTA 1979	Capital Gains Tax Act 1979.
CIR	Commissioners of Inland Revenue ('the Board').
CJEC	Court of Justice of the European Communities.
CRCA	Commissioners for Revenue and Customs Act.
CT	Corporation Tax.
CTA	Corporation Tax Act 2009.
CTT	Capital Transfer Tax.
CTTA 1984	Capital Transfer Act 1984.
EC	European Communities.
ECJ	European Court of Justice.
EEC	European Economic Community.
EU	European Union.

Ex D	Exchequer Division.
FA	Finance Act.
FII	Franked Investment Income.
FTT	First Tier Tribunal.
FY	Financial Year.
HC(I)	High Court (Ireland).
HL	House of Lords.
HMRC	Her Majesty's Revenue and Customs
ICAEW	Institute of Chartered Accountants in England and Wales.
ICTA	Income and Corporation Taxes Act.
IHTA 1984	Inheritance Tax Act 1984.
IR	Inland Revenue.
ITA	Income Tax Act 2007.
ITEPA 2003	Income Tax (Earnings and Pensions) Act 2003.
ITTOIA 2005	Income Tax (Trading and Other Income) Act 2005
KB	King's Bench Division.
NI	Northern Ireland.
OTA	Oil Taxation Act.
PC	Privy Council.
PDA	Probate, Divorce and Admiralty Division (now Family Division).
POCA 2002	Proceeds of Crime Act 2002
QB	Queen's Bench Division.
RI	Republic of Ireland (Eire).
s	Section.
SCS	Scottish Court of Session.
Sch	Schedule.
SI	Statutory Instrument.
SP	Revenue Statement of Practice.
Sp C	Special Commissioners.
SR&O	Statutory Rules and Orders.
TCGA 1992	Taxation of Chargeable Gains Act 1992.
TMA 1970	Taxes Management Act 1970.

VAT	Value Added Tax.
VATA 1994	Value Added Tax Act 1994.

References

(*denotes a series accredited for citation in court).

All E R	*All England Law Reports, (LexisNexis, Halsbury House, 35 Chancery Lane, London WC2A 1EL).
AC or App Cas	*Law Reports, Appeal Cases, (Incorporated Council of Law Reporting for England and Wales, 3 Stone Buildings, Lincoln's Inn, London WC2A 3XN).
Ch	*Law Reports, Chancery Division.
Ex D	*Law Reports, Exchequer Division (see also below).
IR	*Irish Reports, (Law Reporting Council, Law Library, Four Courts, Dublin).
LR Ex	*Law Reports, Exchequer Division.
SFTD	Simon's First Tier Decisions.
SSCD	Simon's Tax Cases Special Commissioners' Decisions, (LexisNexis as above).
STC	*Simon's Tax Cases, (LexisNexis as above).
STI	Simon's Tax Intelligence, (LexisNexis as above).
TC	*Official Reports of Tax Cases, (H.M. Stationery Office, PO Box 276, London, SW8 5DT.
WLR	*Weekly Law Reports, (Incorporated Council of Law Reporting, as above).

The first number in the citation refers to the volume, and the second to the page, so that [1999] 1 All ER 15 means that the report is to be found on page fifteen of the first volume of the All England Law Reports for 1999. Where no volume number is given, only one volume was produced in that year. Some series have continuous volume numbers.

Where legal decisions are very recent and in the lower courts, it must be remembered that they may be reversed on appeal. But references to the official Tax Cases (TC) and to the Appeal Cases (AC) may generally be taken as final.

In English cases, Scottish and Northern Irish decisions (unless there is a difference of law between the countries) are generally followed but are not binding, and Republic of Ireland Decisions are considered (and vice versa).

Acts of Parliament, Command Papers, 'Hansard' Parliamentary Reports and Statutory Instruments (SI) are obtainable from The Stationery Office Ltd (TSO), St Crispins, Duke Street,, Norwich NR3 1PD; telephone 01603 622211, http://www.tso.co.uk/). **Hansard** references are to daily issues and do not always correspond to the columns in the bound editions. **N.B.** Statements in the House, while useful as indicating the intention of enactments, have no legal authority and the Courts may interpret the wording of an Act differently, although they may in limited circumstances be prepared to consider evidence of parliamentary intent.

1

Introduction and Rates of Tax

Cross reference. See **67 SMALL PROFITS — REDUCED RATES.**

Simon's Taxes. See **D1.1, D1.12, D1.1312.**

The charge to tax

[1.1] Companies in the United Kingdom used to be assessed to income tax just like individuals. This changed in April 1966 with the introduction of corporation tax by the *Finance Act 1965*.

Corporation tax is charged on any company which is resident in the UK in respect of all its 'profits' *wherever arising, worldwide*. A non-resident company which carries on a trade in the UK through a permanent establishment is liable to corporation tax on the income and gains of the permanent establishment (see **65.6 RESIDENCE**). [*CTA 2009, ss 2(1), 5; ICTA 1988, ss 6(1), 8(1), 11; TCGA 1992, ss 10(3), 10B*]. See **27 CONTROLLED FOREIGN COMPANIES** for treatment of interests in certain non-resident companies.

Members of a group of companies are each dealt with independently, but there are a number of special provisions relating to the taxation of such members. Similar rules apply to the members of a consortium. See **39 GROUP RELIEF.**

'*Company*' for corporation tax purposes means 'any body corporate or unincorporated association' (including an authorised unit trust as defined in *CTA 2010, s 617; ICTA 1988, s 468(6)*). It does not include a partnership, a local authority or a local authority association. [*CTA 2009, Sch 1 para 272; CTA 2010, s 1121; ICTA 1988, s 832(1)(2)*]. See *Conservative and Unionist Central Office v Burrell* CA 1981, 55 TC 671 (in which the Conservative Party was held not to be an unincorporated association) and *Blackpool Marton Rotary Club v Martin* Ch D 1988, 62 TC 686 (Rotary Club was held to be an unincorporated association and not a partnership). For the treatment of income arising to certain unit trusts for the benefit of individuals, see **52.8 INVESTMENT FUNDS.**

'*Profits*' are defined as income and chargeable gains. [*CTA 2009, s 2(2); ICTA 1988, s 6(4)(a)*]. See **61 PROFIT COMPUTATIONS** and **17 CAPITAL GAINS.**

Corporation tax is charged on the profits of '*financial years*', which run from 1 April, e.g. the 'financial year 2011' means the year from 1 April 2011 to 31 March 2012. [*CTA 2009, s 8(1); ICTA 1988, ss 6(1), 834(1)*].

The profits of a company are calculated (and assessments are made) by reference to its **ACCOUNTING PERIODS** (**2**). The charge is on the full amount of profits arising in the accounting period. [*CTA 2009, s 8; ICTA 1988, s 8(3)*]. The profits of an accounting period on which corporation tax is chargeable (in *CTA 2010* referred to as the '*taxable total profits*') are found by adding together the amount chargeable under the charge to corporation tax on income (after any reductions required for reliefs) and the amount to be included in respect of chargeable gains (after reductions) to give the '*total profits*' of the period and then deducting any amounts which can be relieved against the total profits. [*CTA 2010, s 4; ICTA 1988, s 834C*].

Distributions received by a company on or after 1 July 2009 are subject to corporation tax, unless they are exempt. Distributions received prior to 1 July 2009 were either not taxable (if received from a UK-resident company) or were subject to the double tax relief regime for overseas dividends (if received from an overseas company). See **31 DISTRIBUTIONS** and **32 DOUBLE TAX RELIEF.**

Reduced rates of corporation tax apply to companies with 'small' profits. These are defined by reference to their profits in an accounting period. See **67 SMALL PROFITS — REDUCED RATES.**

Anything to be done by a company under the *Taxes Acts* must be done by the 'proper officer of the company' (usually the company secretary, except where a liquidator or an administrator has been appointed) or by any person having express, implied or apparent authority to act on its behalf (again, unless a liquidator or administrator has been appointed). [*TMA 1970, s 108(1)(3); FA 1993, Sch 14 para 7; FA 2003, Sch 41 paras 2, 5(1)*]. See also **59.14 PAYMENT OF TAX.**

Developments

Tax law rewrite

[1.2] A program of rewriting tax law was first announced in 1996. The intention was to redraft the various taxes acts into simpler language in order to make the legislation clearer. The project has issued *CAA 2001, ITEPA 2003, IT (PAYE) Regulations 2003, ITTOIA 2005, ITA 2007, CTA 2009, CTA 2010* and *TIOPA 2010*. With the commencement of the 2010 Acts, the Tax Law Rewrite project has now been completed, subject to the time-limited powers within each Act to make corrections. Details of any proposals and decisions in this regard can be found on the HMRC website.

The proposed new Management Act project has been postponed meantime, although *Finance Act 2008* introduces new powers for HMRC and further powers are included in *Finance Act 2009*. These powers have since been further amended and extended. See **43 HMRC INVESTIGATORY POWERS** and **60 PENALTIES.**

Tax Simplification

The Office of Tax Simplification (OTS) was set up by the new government in 2010 with a view to simplifying the UK's tax legislation, rather than re-writing it. The OTS has identified over 1,000 tax reliefs, allowances, and exemptions within the UK tax regime, and it is proposing to evaluate each one with a view to repeal or simplification.

An interim report was published on 13 December 2010, which reviewed 13 reliefs and gave provisional recommendations including: the abolition of some reliefs, such as the vaccine research relief, and certain income tax exemptions (the 15p luncheon voucher exemption); and the retention of reliefs such as the capital gains tax principal private residence relief. As commented by the OTS, the report acts as a test to gauge reaction to the OTS methodology for the rest of the review.

A final report was published on 3 March 2011 and made recommendations to the Chancellor some of which have been implemented in the Budget 2011, others will be included in the proposals for 2012.

The second task of the OTS was to review the tax position of small businesses and the intermediaries regime (under IR35). An interim report looking at small business taxation was published on 10 March 2011. Their initial recommendations included: merging income tax and national insurance; consideration of the future of IR35; updating HMRC's procedures and creating a simpler regime for the smallest businesses. The provisional recommendations are made with a view to simplifying the administrative burdens on small business.

Details of the work of the OTS can be found at: www.hm-treasury.gov.uk/ots.htm

Capital assets

In *FA 2007*, the phased withdrawal of industrial and agricultural buildings allowances began (see **15.9**, **15.12** and **15.14**). Further changes to these allowances and to plant and machinery allowances were included in *FA 2008* — a £50,000 per annum, 100% annual investment allowance per company or per group, a 20% writing down allowance on the pool in place of 25% and a new category of special expenditure qualifying for 10% writing down allowance. The rate of allowance on long-term assets was also increased to 10% (see **10 CAPITAL ALLOWANCES — INTRODUCTION**). *FA 2009* re-introduces a restricted first year allowance for one year only and introduces a new regime for cars.

FA 2010 introduced anti-avoidance provisions to counteract schemes involving capital allowance buying, and also increased the aforementioned annual investment allowance to £100,000 per annum.

FA 2011 confirms that the Annual Investment Allowance will be reduced to £25,000 per annum for expenditure incurred on or after 1 April 2012. Further changes to the capital allowance regime have been introduced by *FA 2011*, significantly from 1 April 2011 the short life asset pool will run for eight years instead of four, giving more opportunity for accelerated balancing allowances. As from 1 April 2012 the main writing down allowance rate will decrease to 18%, and to 8% for special rate expenditure.

Proposals for corporate tax reform and *FA 2011*

In the Autumn Statement of 29 November 2010 the government published its plans for corporate tax reform in the document 'Corporate Tax Reform: Delivering More Competitive System'. This document sets out proposals for the reform of the CFC regime and foreign branch taxation, along with changes to the interest deduction regime, a review of R&D tax credits and the introduction of a Patent Box regime which would provide a 10% tax on the income from new patents (from April 2013).

Part I of the document provides the Corporate Tax Road Map — which sets out the government's planned direction for tax policy. The Road Map outlines five principles for reform: lowering rates while maintaining the tax base; maintaining stability; being aligned with modern business practice; avoiding complexity; and maintaining a level playing field for tax payers.

A timetable for reform is set out as follows:

Year 1 — Autumn 2010: publish papers on: reforming CFC rules and interim arrangements; IP, the Patent Box and R&D credit reform; and changes to foreign branch taxation.

Year 2 — Spring 2011: introduce rate cuts and publish further details of the CFC reform and Patent Box proposals — Finance Bill 2011: legislate for capital allowance reductions, CFC interim changes, foreign branch reform — Autumn 2011: publish draft legislation on new CFC rules and the Patent Box regime.

Year 3 — Spring 2012: main CT rate down to 26%, reductions to capital allowances implemented — Finance Bill 2012: legislate following the consultations on CFCs and Patent Box.

Year 4 — Spring 2013: further cut to main CT rate to 25%, introduce Patent Box.

Year 5 — Spring 2014: further cut to main CT rate to 24%.

The budget of 23 March 2011 introduced some further changes to the plans outlined above, most notably the corporate tax rate has been reduced to 26% as from 1 April 2011, and will be reduced to 25% as from 1 April 2012, and a further 1% per year until the rate reaches 23% by 1 April 2014.

To offset this reduction in the main corporate tax rate, the supplementary charge on oil and gas production has been increased from 20% to 32% as from 24 March 2011. In addition the bank levy, which is introduced in *FA 2011* for periods of account ending on or after 1 January 2011, will be increased as from January 2012.

The CFC interim changes are found in *FA 2011* and will apply for accounting periods beginning on or after 1 January 2011, with the full reform to be undertaken in 2012. The foreign branch opt-in exemption from tax is included in *FA 2011*, with elections to opt-in being available for accounting periods beginning on or after the date of Royal Assent.

In addition *FA 2011* introduces an extension to R&D relief for small and medium sized enterprises (SMEs), their enhanced deduction for qualifying expenditure increases from 175% to 200% from 1 April 2011, and will increase further to 225% as from April 2012 (subject to EU State Aid approval). The rate at which losses may be surrendered for a payable tax credit is reduced from 14% to 12.5%. With regard to vaccine research relief the relief for SMEs is reduced from 40% to 20% as from 1 April 2011, with the intention to repeal this relief as from 1 April 2012.

Rates of tax

[1.3] The **full** and **small profits rates** of corporation tax for each financial year are enacted by Parliament and set out in the following table.

	Full rate	Small profits
Financial year 2012**	25%	20%
Financial year 2011*	26%	20%
Financial year 2010	28%	21%
Financial year 2009	28%	21%
Financial year 2008	28%	21%
Financial year 2007	30%	20%
Financial year 2006	30%	19%

* FY 2011 rates — the reduction of the main corporation tax rate to 27% was included in *F(No 2)A 2010*, however, the budget of 23 March announced a further reduction to 26% which is included in the *FA 2011*, along with a reduction in the small profits rate to 20%.

** FY 2012 rates — the reduction in the main rate to 25% was announced in the budget of 23 March 2011. In the absence of specific indication otherwise, it is assumed the small profits rate will remain at 20% for FY 2012.

The rates on 'ring fence profits' (see **67.2 SMALL PROFITS — REDUCED RATES**) are 30% for the full rate and 19% for the small profits rate for all of the above financial years. The small profits fraction for non-ring fenced profits is 3/200 for FY 2011.

[*CTA 2010, s 3; FA 2006, ss 24–26; FA 2007, ss 2, 3; FA 2008, ss 6, 7; FA 2009, ss 7, 8; FA 2010, ss 2, 3; FA 2011, ss 4, 5, 6*].

See **67 SMALL PROFITS — REDUCED RATES** for profit limits for the small profits rate to apply and for marginal relief limits.

Advance corporation tax. ACT was **abolished** after 5 April 1999 (see **3.1 ADVANCE CORPORATION TAX — SHADOW ACT**).

2

Accounting Periods

Simon's Taxes. See **D1.108, D1.309.**

Introduction

[2.1] An accounting period often, but not always, coincides with a company's period of account. It is the period in respect of which a company is charged to corporation tax. Per *CTA 2009, s 8*, corporation tax is charged on the full amount of profits arising in the accounting period, and there are specific rules with regard to when an accounting period starts and when it is treated as coming to an end.

In contrast, a period of account is the period for which a company makes up its accounts and the end of that period is the company's accounting date.

A self assessment return for the company is prepared for each accounting period.

[*CTA 2009, s 8(2), (3)*].

The start of an accounting period

[2.2] An accounting period of a company begins:

- when the company comes within the charge to corporation tax; or
- immediately after the end of the previous accounting period, if the company is still within the charge to corporation tax;
- when the company goes into liquidation;
- in the case of a company being wound up, when the winding up starts.

[*CTA 2009, s 9(1); ICTA 1988, s 12(2)*].

A UK resident company, if not otherwise within the charge to corporation tax, is treated as coming within the charge when it starts to carry on business.

[*CTA 2009, s 9(2); ICTA 1988, s 12(4)*].

If a company accrues a chargeable gain or allowable loss which is not otherwise in an accounting period, an accounting period then begins when the gain or loss accrues and it falls into that period.

[*CTA 2009, s 9(3); ICTA 1988, s 12(6)*].

As regards whether a company is 'within the charge to corporation tax' in the absence of income or gain, see *Walker (Inspector of Taxes) v Centaur Clothes Group Ltd* [2000] 2 All ER 589, [2000] 1 WLR 799, HL.

Apportionment

[2.3] Although assessments to corporation tax are made on the basis of accounting periods, the tax rate is fixed by reference to financial years (which run from 1 April to 31 March in any year — see **1.1 INTRODUCTION**). The financial year will therefore not always coincide with the accounting period. Where these periods do not coincide, apportionment is necessary to calculate the tax payable.

Apportionment is on a time basis, between the financial years which overlap the accounting period. Corporation tax is then charged on each proportion so computed at the rate fixed for the financial year concerned. [*CTA 2009, s 8(5); ICTA 1988, s 8(3)*].

Example

[2.4]

For the year ended 30 June 2011, the following information is relevant to A Ltd, a company with no associated companies.

	£
Trading income	200,600
Property income	25,000
Income from not-trading loan relationships	30,000

The small profits rate of corporation tax for the financial year 2010 is 21% and the rate for the financial year 2011 is 20%.

The corporation tax computation of A Ltd for the twelve-month accounting period ended on 30.6.11 is as follows.

		£	
Trading income		200,600	
Property income		25,000	
Income from non-trading loan relationships		30,000	
		255,600	
Total profits apportioned			
1.7.10 — 31.3.11	9/12 ×	£255,600	£191,700

1.4.11 — 30.6.11	3/12 ×	£255,600	£63,900
Tax chargeable			
21% × £191,700			40,257
20% × £63,900			12,780
Total tax charge			£53,037

The end of an accounting period

[2.5] An accounting period of a company ends on the first occurrence of any of the following:

(a) the expiration of twelve months from the beginning of the accounting period;
(b) an accounting date of the company;
(c) if there is a period for which the company does not make up accounts, the end of that period;
(d) the company's beginning or ceasing to trade;
(e) if the company carries on a single trade, its coming, or ceasing to be, within the charge to corporation tax in respect of that trade;
(f) if the company carries on more than one trade, its coming, or ceasing to be, within the charge to corporation tax in respect of all the trades;
(g) the company's becoming, or ceasing to be, UK resident;
(h) the company's ceasing to be within the charge to corporation tax;
(i) the company's entering administration; or
(j) the company's ceasing to be in administration under *Insolvency Act 1986, Sch B1* (or any corresponding event otherwise than under that Act).

[*CTA 2009, s 10*].

In addition an accounting period of a company ends immediately before a winding up starts and a new one begins when the winding up starts. Once the winding up has started then an accounting period ends after 12 months, or if earlier, when the winding up has been completed. [*CTA 2009, s 12; ICTA 1988, s 12(7), (9)*].

Where more than one trade is carried on with different accounting dates and the company does not prepare a set of accounts for the whole of its activities, the company may choose which of those accounting dates is to be used for the purpose of (b) above. HMRC may, however, select another of those dates if they think, on reasonable grounds, that the date selected by the company is inappropriate. [*CTA 2009, s 11; ICTA 1988, s 12(5)(5A)*].

Uncertainty

[2.6] Where the beginning or end of an accounting period is uncertain, HMRC may choose such period (not exceeding twelve months) as appears appropriate. If further facts come to their knowledge, HMRC may revise that period, but the company has rights of appeal. See *R v Ward, R v Special Commr (ex p Stipplechoice Ltd) (No 3)* QB 1988, 61 TC 391, where determination of an appeal was quashed because the company did not receive notification that HMRC intended to seek confirmation of the assessment under appeal after revision of the terminal date.

[*ICTA 1988, s 12(8)*].

The validity of extended time limit assessments made by virtue of the predecessor to *s 12(8)*, and subsequently varied by HMRC, was challenged in *Kelsall v Stipplechoice Ltd* CA 1995, 67 TC 349. It was held that the question of whether there was doubt as to the beginning or end of an accounting period at the time the assessment was made (so that the dates could subsequently be revised) is to be determined subjectively by reference to the state of mind of the inspector at that time. This reversed the decision in the High Court, where it was also held that no further leave of the General or Special Commissioners was required for the revision of an extended time limit assessment made by virtue of *s 12(8)* where the original leave to assess was given on the footing that it would be open to the company to contend for a different accounting date on appeal. The Court of Appeal expressed no view on this aspect of the decision.

Accounts for periods in excess of twelve months

[2.7] Where accounts are made up for a period in excess of twelve months, apportionments of profits or gains to different periods are, except where otherwise provided, made on a time basis [*CTA 2010, s 1172; ICTA 1988, s 834(4)*]. In the case of trading profits or miscellaneous profits it is specifically provided that apportionment is to be made on the basis of the number of days falling in each period.

[*CTA 2009, ss 52, 1307; ICTA 1988, s 72*].

Where, however, a more satisfactory basis of arriving at the profit of each accounting period is available, HMRC may apply that basis instead (*Marshall Hus & Partners Ltd v Bolton* Ch D 1980, 55 TC 539). Interest and foreign income is apportioned on an arising basis in accordance with income tax law and practice as if accounting periods were years of assessment [*CTA 2009, Sch 1 para 4; ICTA 1988, s 9(1)*], except that income from an overseas property business (see **62 PROPERTY INCOME**) is computed as if it were a property business (so that trading income principles apply).

[*CTA 2009, ss 206, 210; ICTA 1988, s 70A(5)*].

A charge in respect of a non-trading credit on loan relationships is calculated by reference to accounting periods (see **54.4**, **54.6 LOAN RELATIONSHIPS**). Chargeable gains are apportioned on an arising basis.

[*TCGA 1992, s 8(1)*].

Qualifying charitable donations are included in the period in which they are paid.

[*CTA 2010, s 189; ICTA 1988, s 338*].

Example

[2.8]

B Ltd prepares accounts for 16 months ending on 31 March 2010. The following information is relevant.

	£
Profit for 16 months	800,000
Income (in respect of non-trading loan relationships) received on 1 March and 1 September each year	50,000
Capital gain (after indexation) arising on 1.6.10	100,000
Tax written down value of plant pool at 1.12.09	40,000
Plant purchased 1.5.10	160,000
Plant purchased 1.2.11	246,000
Proceeds of plant sold 31.12.10 (less than cost)	4,000

B Ltd will be chargeable to corporation tax as follows.

	Accounting period 12 months to 30.11.10	Accounting period 4 months to 31.3.11
	£	£
Adjusted profits (apportioned 12:4)	600,000	200,000
Capital allowances (see note)	(106,667)	(53,466)
Trading income	493,333	146,534
Income from non-trading loan relationship	100,000	50,000
Chargeable gain	100,000	—
Chargeable profits	693,333	196,534

Note

Capital allowances are calculated as follows.

12 months to 30.11.10

	AIA	Pool	Allowances
	£	£	£
WDV b/f		40,000	
Additions	160,000		
AIA	(83,334)		83,334
	76,666		
Transfer to pool	(76,666)	(76,666)	
		116,666	
WDA at 20%		(23,333)	23,333
Total allowances			£106,667
WDV c/f		£93,333	

4 months to 31.3.11

	AIA	Pool	Allowances
	£	£	£
WDV b/f		93,333	
Additions	246,000		
AIA £100,000 × $^4/_{12}$	(33,333)		33,333
	212,667		
Transfer to pool	(212,667)	212,667	
		306,000	
Disposals		(4,000)	
		302,000	
WDA at 20% × $^4/_{12}$		(20,133)	20,133
Total allowances			£53,466
WDV c/f		£281,867	

It is assumed that the conditions for the annual investment allowance for the additions on 1.5.10 and 1.3.11 respectively are met. The AIA has been calculated on the proportions falling into FY2009 and FY2010, as the limit increased from £50,000 (1.4.08 to 31.3.10) to £100,000 (as from 1.4,10). So for the year ended 30.11.10 the AIA is calculated as 4/12(£50,000) + 8/12(£100,000) = 83,334.

The AIA is proportionately reduced for short accounting periods of less than twelve months.

Writing-down allowances are a proportionately reduced percentage of 20% where the accounting period is only part of a year. [*CAA 2001, s 56(3); CAA 1990, s 24(2)*].

Accounts made up to varying dates

[2.9] Where accounts are made up to slightly varying dates (eg the last Saturday in a specified month), provided the variation is not more than four days from a mean date, HMRC will (if the taxpayer agrees in writing) normally accept treatment of each period of account as if it were a twelve-month accounting period ending on the mean date. (HMRC Company Taxation Manual, CTM01560.)

See HMRC Extra-Statutory Concession, C12 for concessionary yearly accounting periods where a retail co-operative society prepares half-yearly or quarterly accounts.

Sale of lessors

[2.10] See also **5.27** *et seq.* **ANTI-AVOIDANCE** in relation to an accounting period ending and a new one starting on the change of ownership of a company leasing plant or machinery. *Finance Act 2010* has amended *CTA 2010* and has introduced a system for electing out of the charge on a qualifying change (with effect from 9 December 2009) see **5.27 ANTI-AVOIDANCE**.

[*CTA 2010, ss 383, 398A; CTA 2009, ss 9(5), 10(6), 1296; ICTA 1988, s 12(9); FA 2006, Sch 10 para 43*].

Key points

[2.11] Points to consider are as follows.

- An accounting period is usually the period for which a company makes up a set of accounts.
- An accounting period begins immediately after the end of the last accounting period or when the company comes within the charge to corporation tax. An accounting period also commences when a company enters liquidation or commences a winding up.
- An accounting period generally ends on the earliest of twelve months after the beginning of an accounting period or the company's accounting reference date. Accounting periods also come to an end when a company begins or ceases to trade; ceases to be within the charge to UK corporation tax; ceases to be UK resident or ceases to be in administration.
- An accounting period cannot exceed twelve months.
- If accounts are prepared for a period in excess of twelve months, profits and gains are required to be apportioned between the relevant accounting periods. Generally, profits (including trading income, property income and miscellaneous income) are required to be apportioned on a time basis. However, in some cases, a different apportionment is prescribed. For example, interest, foreign income and chargeable gains are apportioned on an arising basis.
- For accounts covering a period of more than twelve months, it may be possible to apportion profits and gains on a just and reasonable basis if time-apportionment would operate unjustly or unreasonably.

3

Advance Corporation Tax — Shadow ACT

Introduction

[3.1] Where a UK-resident company resident in the UK made a qualifying distribution (including the payment of a dividend — see **31 DISTRIBUTIONS**) before 6 April 1999, it became liable to pay advance corporation tax (ACT) [*ICTA 1988, s 14(1); FA 1998, Sch 3 para 8*] (subject to relief for franked investment income received — see **3.3** below). The ACT could then be offset against the company's liability to 'mainstream' corporation tax on its profits for that accounting period subject to a maximum set-off.

ACT was abolished from 6 April 1999, subject to a continuing 'shadow' system for relief of '*surplus ACT*' (ACT which could not be set-off against 'mainstream' corporation tax) prior to that date (see **3.2** *et seq.* below). For the provisions for computing ACT arising before this date and its offset against the liability to 'mainstream' corporation tax, see Tolley's Corporation Tax 2005–06 or earlier editions.

[*FA 1998, s 31*].

Distributions to non-resident companies

In the combined cases of *Metallgesellschaft Ltd v CIR: C-397/98*, [2001] Ch 620, [2001] ECR I-1727, ECJ, and *Hoechst AG v CIR: C-410/98*, [2001] Ch 620, [2001] ECR I-1727, ECJ, it was held that the requirement that both parties to a group income election under *ICTA 1988, s 247* be UK-resident contravened EC law.

Following this, it was held in *Pirelli Cable Holding NV and Others v CIR*, HL [2006] STC 548 (unanimously reversing the Court of Appeal's decision) that, had such a group income election been made (had it been available), the non-UK resident parent would not have been entitled to tax credits available under double tax agreements (see **32.3 DOUBLE TAX RELIEF**) in respect of the distributions made by the UK-resident subsidiary. Thus, such tax credits could be taken into account in calculating any compensation in a claim for restitution of ACT.

Shadow ACT

Introduction of shadow ACT

[3.2] Following the abolition of ACT for distributions made after 5 April 1999, a system of 'shadow ACT' was introduced to enable surplus ACT (see **3.5** below) as at that date to be relieved broadly in accordance with companies' expectations prior to abolition. The system, introduced under the enabling provisions of *FA 1998, s 32*, operates broadly as set out at **3.3** onwards. An accounting period straddling 5 April 1999 is treated as two separate accounting periods, ending on and commencing immediately after that date, with profits being time-apportioned between those accounting periods.

[*SI 1999 No 358, Reg 3*].

Computation of shadow ACT

[3.3] Shadow ACT is computed for the accounting period on a similar basis and at the same rate as applied before 6 April 1999. For the financial year 1999 onwards, shadow ACT is treated as having been paid at the rate of 25% of the amount or value of the 'relevant distributions' (i.e. 20% of the dividend etc. plus the shadow ACT).

'*Relevant distributions*'. The distributions in respect of which the shadow ACT computation is made include all distributions made on or after 6 April 1999 within *ICTA 1988, Pt VI* (see **31.2–31.7 DISTRIBUTIONS**), including both qualifying and non-qualifying distributions (see **31.17 DISTRIBUTIONS**), and also certain deemed distributions arising in respect of benefits provided to participators in close companies (see **31.20 DISTRIBUTIONS**), but *excluding* manufactured dividends within *ICTA 1988, Sch 23A* (as amended by *ITA 2007, Sch 1 para 238* and *CTA 2009, Sch 1 para 285*) (see **5.9 ANTI-AVOIDANCE**) and most intra-group distributions.

[*SI 1999 No 358, Regs 3, 11*].

Reduction for franked investment income

[3.4] Where franked investment income ('FII') is received in an accounting period, or surplus FII is brought forward (including a surplus arising before 6 April 1999), shadow ACT is *not* treated as having been paid in that period except to the extent that '*franked distributions*' (i.e. distributions plus the shadow ACT thereon) exceed the sum of nine-eighths of the FII received and the amount of any surplus FII brought forward.

'*Franked investment income*' ('FII') is the sum of the amount or value of dividends and other qualifying distributions (see **31.9 DISTRIBUTIONS**) received by a UK resident company from another UK resident company and such proportion of each distribution as corresponds to the 'tax credit fraction' in force when the distribution is made. From 6 April 1999, the tax credit fraction is one-ninth of the amount or value of the relevant distribution (i.e. 10% of the dividend etc. plus the tax credit). Thus, a dividend of £360 amounts to FII in the hands of a UK recipient company of £400.

Dividends or interest, or (from 6 April 2005) alternative finance return under **ALTERNATIVE FINANCE ARRANGEMENTS** (**4**), received from **BUILDING SOCIETIES** (**9**), are **not** included in the definition of franked distributions or FII. [*ICTA 1988, ss 476(3), 477A(3)(b); FA 2005, Sch 2 paras 5, 11–13*]. The definition of FII is, however, subject to a number of restrictions in relation to replacement of interest income by income consisting of distributions, arrangements to pass on the value of FII, distributions received by dealers, intra-group distributions and (from 1 April 2010, following the repeal of *CTA 2010, s 735*) abnormal dividends.

[*ICTA 1988, ss 231(1), 238(1), 832(1); F(No 2)A 1997, s 30; FA 1998, Sch 3 paras 11, 39; ITTOIA 2005, Sch 1 paras 113, 337, 602; SI 1999 No 358, Regs 3, 3A, 6A, 7–10A*].

Utilisation of shadow ACT and surplus ACT

[3.5] Shadow ACT which is treated as having been paid by a company in respect of any relevant distribution made by it in an accounting period is set against its liability to corporation tax on any profits charged to corporation tax for that accounting period, but no actual corporation tax relief is given for such amounts of shadow ACT. The capacity for offset against corporation tax available (see below) is allocated first to the shadow ACT so computed. Any balance of the offset capacity available for an accounting period is then allocated to surplus ACT brought forward at 6 April 1999, for which actual corporation tax relief is then given.

The *maximum* set-off is the amount of shadow ACT that would have been payable in respect of a franked distribution equal to the profits and made at the end of the accounting period (i.e. 20% of profits chargeable to corporation tax).

Surplus shadow ACT

If the shadow ACT exceeds the offset capacity for the period, it is treated as 'surplus shadow ACT', to be carried back and treated as shadow ACT in respect of distributions made in accounting periods beginning in the previous six years (but not before 6 April 1999), with any unused balance being carried forward to the next accounting period. Surplus shadow ACT is, however, not carried back so as to displace actual surplus ACT relieved in an earlier period except in the period beginning 24 months before the *end* of the accounting period in which the surplus shadow ACT arose and ending the day before the commencement of that period.

[*SI 1999 No 358, Regs 3, 12, 14, 15*].

For cases turning on whether there was an accounting period in relation to surplus ACT, see *Walker (Inspector of Taxes) v Centaur Clothes Group Ltd* [2000] 2 All ER 589, [2000] 1 WLR 799, HL, and *Aproline Ltd v Littlejohn* [1995] STC (SCD) 201.

Withdrawal from shadow ACT system

[3.6] A company may opt out of the shadow ACT system by notifying HMRC that it will not seek, or will cease to seek, recovery of unrelieved surplus ACT. Where such notice was given in the accounting period beginning on 6 April 1999 (as in **3.2** above) and related to that period, the company was thereby excluded from the shadow ACT arrangements from the start. Where it is given in any accounting period and indicates that the company wishes that accounting period to be the last for which it will seek recovery of unrelieved surplus ACT (the 'final accounting period'), then no further recovery will be possible after that period. In those circumstances, and also in relation to the accounting period in which all surplus ACT is exhausted, the shadow ACT computation continues to be made for (normally) the following accounting period, with any surplus shadow ACT arising in that period being carried back to displace surplus ACT relieved as under **3.5** above in the final accounting period (and in that case the accounting period from which the surplus shadow ACT is carried back becomes the final accounting period, i.e. the last period for which surplus ACT relief may be obtained). (These displacement provisions are more complex where accounting periods are not of twelve months' duration.) The latter prevents excessive relief being obtained by the restriction of dividends, and consequent ability to reclaim unrelieved surplus ACT, in the final period within the arrangements, followed by the payment of exceptional dividends in (normally) the following accounting period. There are special rules in relation to determination of the final accounting period for these purposes in the case of groups of companies (see generally **3.7** below).

[*SI 1999 No 358, Regs 4, 5*].

Special cases

Intra-group allocation of shadow ACT

[3.7] Special rules determine when and how shadow ACT generated within a group of companies is to be allocated, and the allocation of group surplus shadow ACT. Broadly, no company in a group gets relief for surplus ACT until all group shadow ACT has been offset.

Where a group member generates shadow ACT in excess of its maximum capacity to utilise it in the period in which it is generated, the excess is to be allocated by the parent company to another or other group member(s), but not so as to displace their own shadow ACT or to exceed their maximum capacity for using shadow ACT in the same period.

Where the total group shadow ACT exceeds the group capacity to use it, the balance remaining after the allocation to other group companies is to remain in the company in which it arose and to be carried forward.

Where the total group shadow ACT does not exceed the group capacity, the parent company determines which other group members are to receive the allocation and the amounts to be allocated to them, in accordance with their capacity to use that amount. HMRC may allocate the excess in accordance with the regulations where the company fails to do so, but such allocation can subsequently be overridden by an allocation made by the parent company.

There are also provisions dealing with a company joining or leaving a group, or being a member of more than one group. 'Group' for these purposes is broadly a company and its 51% subsidiaries, but is specially defined to take into account certain special rights.

[*SI 1999 No 358, Regs 6, 13*].

Changes in ownership of a company

[3.8] The provisions of *ICTA 1988, ss 245–245B* relating to changes in ownership of companies under the pre-April 1999 rules were imported, with appropriate modifications, into the shadow ACT rules.

Major change in business

If a 'major change in the nature or conduct of a trade or business' takes place within three years of (or at the same time as) a change in ownership of a company (see **55.13 LOSSES**), a new accounting period is deemed to commence at the time of the change in ownership. This applies for the purposes of setting off unrelieved surplus ACT against the company's liability to corporation tax on any profits charged to corporation tax for an accounting period ending after the change of ownership. For this purpose the profits of the company charged to corporation tax for the accounting period is to be apportioned to the revised accounting periods on a time basis.

In this case, unrelieved surplus ACT may not be carried forward from the accounting period ending with the change in ownership (such surplus ACT accordingly being lost). The prohibition on the carry forward of unrelieved surplus ACT also applies to ACT which had been surrendered to the company.

'*Major change in the nature or conduct of a trade or business*' includes:

(a) a major change in the type of property dealt in or services or facilities provided;
(b) a major change in customers, outlets or markets;
(c) the company's ceasing to be a 'trading company' and becoming an 'investment company' (or vice versa);
(d) where the company is an investment company, a major change in the nature of its investments.

The change may be the result of a gradual process which began outside the relevant period. See **55.13 LOSSES** for HMRC practice as regards what constitutes a major change in the nature or conduct of a trade or business.

'*Trading company*' means a company the business of which consists wholly or mainly of the carrying on of a trade or trades.

'*Investment company*' means a company (other than a 'holding company'), the business of which consists wholly or mainly of making investments whence the principal part of its income is derived.

'*Holding company*' means a company the business of which consists wholly or mainly in the holding of shares or securities of companies which are its 90% subsidiaries and which are trading companies.

Revival of business

Similar consequences ensue if, once the scale of the activities in its trade or business has become small or negligible, there is a change in the ownership of the company before any considerable revival of that trade or business.

Surrendered ACT

Where there is a change in the ownership of a company (see **55.13 LOSSES**) to which ACT had been surrendered in respect of a distribution made before the change, and in the period from three years before to three years after the change there is 'a major change in the nature or conduct of a trade or business' (see above) of the surrendering company, any unrelieved surplus ACT which had been so surrendered may not be carried forward to an accounting period ending after the change (the accounting period in which the change occurred being treated as two separate accounting periods, up to and after the change, for this purpose).

Assets acquired after change

Where there is a change in the ownership of a company (see **55.13 LOSSES**) which carries forward unrelieved surplus ACT of an accounting period beginning before the change to an accounting period ending after the change, and:

(i) after the change the company acquires an asset from a fellow group member under the no gain, no loss provisions of *TCGA 1992, s 171* (see **18.4 CAPITAL GAINS — GROUPS**); and

(ii) within three years of the change in ownership, a chargeable gain accrues to the company on its disposal of that asset (or of an asset deriving its value in whole or part from that asset),

the ACT set-off limit (in **3.5** above) for the period in which the chargeable gain arises is reduced by an amount equal to 20% of the gain.

Application of losses provisions

The provisions restricting the carry forward of losses following a change in ownership of a company are applied as if the benefit of losses were a reference to the benefit of unrelieved surplus ACT. For those provisions, see **55.13 LOSSES**.

[*SI 1999 No 358, Regs 16–18*].

In the case of *CIR v Aberdeen Milk Co Ltd* [1999] STC 787, 73 TC 563, Ct of Sess, surplus ACT arising to a successor company on privatisation could not be carried back to the period before the transfer.

Other provisions

[3.9] The profits against which unrelieved surplus ACT may be set include amounts chargeable on the company in respect of **CONTROLLED FOREIGN COMPANIES** (**27**) (see *SI 1999 No 358, Regs 3(3), 20*).

Where relief is available for a foreign tax credit, the income or gain subject to the foreign tax is excluded from profits for the purpose of determining the maximum shadow ACT set-off and the foreign tax credit is deducted from the corporation tax liability. Shadow ACT can be set against the corporation tax liability relating to the foreign income or gain limited to the maximum ACT credit that would have applied had the foreign income or gain been the only income or gain for the accounting period or, if lower, the corporation tax liability as reduced by the foreign tax credit (see *SI 1999 No 358, Reg 12(4)(5)*).

Any necessary assessment may be made to recover tax which ought to have been paid (including interest thereon) as a result of an excessive set-off of ACT, and to restore the tax position of those concerned (see *SI 1999 No 358, Reg 19*).

Simon's Taxes. See **D4.376, D5.201, D5.3.**

Examples

(A) Utilisation of surplus ACT

[3.10]

H Ltd, a company with no associated companies, has chargeable profits for the year ending 31 December 2009 of £1,600,000. During the year it pays a dividend of £500,000. At 1 January 2009, it has surplus ACT brought forward of £300,000.

H Ltd may obtain relief in the year ended 31.12.09 for surplus ACT as follows.

	£
Maximum ACT limit (£1,600,000 @ 20%)	320,000
Less Shadow ACT (£500,000 × 20/80)	125,000
ACT set-off	£195,000

Corporation tax for the y/e 31.12.09 is payable as follows.

	£
Corporation tax payable (£1,600,000 @ 28%)	448,000

Less ACT	195,000
Tax payable	253,000

Surplus ACT memorandum

	£
ACT brought forward at 1.1.09	300,000
Less Used y/e 31.12.09	195,000
ACT carried forward at 31.12.09	£105,000

(B) Shadow ACT and tax credits

J Ltd (which has no associated companies) pays a dividend of £1,000 on 30 June 2009 and receives a dividend of £800 on the same date.

J Ltd will have made a franked distribution as follows.

	£
Distribution	1,000
Shadow ACT (@ 20/80)	250
Franked distribution	£1,250

J Ltd will have received franked investment income

	£
Distribution	800
Tax credit (@ 10/90)	89
Franked investment income	889
Amount available to set against franked distribution: (FII × 9/8)	1,000
Shadow ACT treated as paid: ((1,250–1,000) × 20%)	50

(C) Allocation of shadow ACT among group members

A Ltd owns 51% of the share capital of both B Ltd and C Ltd. The following information is relevant.

	£	£	£
Year ended 31.3.09	*A Ltd*	*B Ltd*	*C Ltd*
(Loss)/Profits	(10,000)	80,000	110,000
Dividends paid (to companies other than to group companies)	80,000	70,000	16,000
Shadow ACT thereon	20,000	17,500	4,000
Year ended 31.3.10			
Profits	70,000	90,000	120,000

	£	£	£
Dividends paid (to companies other than to group companies)	60,000	80,000	40,000
Shadow ACT thereon	15,000	20,000	10,000

C Ltd has surplus ACT brought forward of £5,200 at 1 April 2008, not having been able to utilise it in prior years.

Year ended 31.3.09		*A Ltd*		*B Ltd*		*C Ltd*
	£	£	£	£	£	£
CT on profits at 21%		—		16,800		23,100
ACT capacity	—		18,800		23,100	
Shadow ACT	20,000		17,500		4,000	
Surplus shadow ACT	20,000		700		—	
Spare ACT capacity	—		—		19,100	
Allocation by parent company	(19,100)					
Surplus shadow ACT c/fwd	(900)		(700)		—	
Surplus ACT c/fwd					5,200	
					—	
Corporation tax liability		—		16,800		23,100

Year ended 31.3.10		*A Ltd*		*B Ltd*		*C Ltd*
	£	£	£	£	£	£
CT on profits at 21%		14,700		18,900		25,200
ACT capacity	14,700		18,900		25,200	
Shadow ACT in year	15,000		20,000		10,000	
Shadow ACT b/fwd	900		700		—	
Surplus shadow ACT	1,200		1,800		—	
Spare ACT capacity	—		—		15,200	
Allocation by parent company	(1,200)		(1,800)		(3,000)	(12,200)
Surplus ACT c/fwd		—		—		—
Corporation tax liability		14,700		18,900		3,000

4

Alternative Finance Arrangements

Cross references. See **9 BUILDING SOCIETIES, 46.2 INCOME TAX IN RELATION TO A COMPANY, 52.6 INVESTMENT FUNDS, 54 LOAN RELATIONSHIPS, 66.14 RETURNS.**

Simon's Taxes. See A1.3.

Introduction

[4.1] The provisions set out below provide for the taxation of finance arrangements that do not involve the receipt or payment of interest and respond to the development of financial products that embody such arrangements. The legislation took effect from 6 April 2005 for 'purchase and resale' and 'deposit' contracts, with detailed transitional rules that are not covered here as most affected transactions will have expired.

Customers who want access to the type of product referred to above include, in particular, individuals for whom it is important to adhere to Islamic law ('Shariah'). The Quran prohibits Muslims from the practice of 'riba' which is generally understood to mean the receipt or payment of interest. As a result, Muslims have devised other financing structures to facilitate commercial transactions such as:

- 'murabahah' (sale on deferred payment terms discussed in **4.3** below);
- 'diminishing musharaka' (co-ownership where one partner gradually buys out the other covered in **4.4** below);
- 'mudarabah' (providing finance to a venture in exchange for a share of the profits in **4.5** below);
- 'wakala' (an agent makes investments on behalf of a principal covered in **4.6** below).

The existing UK tax analysis of such transactions has in some areas been uncertain, and in other areas has produced anomalous results. These anomalies could put financial services providers at a commercial disadvantage, while customers could suffer a disadvantage if financial institutions charged proportionately more to cover the adverse impacts on them. The legislation described in **4.3–4.7** below sets out a definite tax treatment for certain specific types of contract used in Islamic finance, with economic returns equivalent to interest being treated in the same way as interest for all tax purposes.

It is a fundamental policy requirement that UK tax law apply equally to all taxpayers, irrespective of religion, and that the tax treatment of a transaction cannot depend on whether or not it is Shariah compliant. Accordingly, the legislation is applicable to all financing arrangements which fall within its definitions, regardless of whether undertaken by Muslims, non-Muslims, Islamic or conventional banks, and regardless of whether they are compliant with Shariah or not. For example it sets out a tax regime for a structure called an 'investment bond' (see **4.7** below) which corresponds to an Islamic finance structure called sukuk. However, to decide whether any particular transaction qualifies for the legislated tax treatment, one need consider only the tax law definition.

The legislation does not change the legal nature of the financial arrangements, nor does it deem interest to arise where there is none. Instead, it brings certain types of finance arrangements, and the returns from those arrangements, within the pre-existing tax regime for receipts and payments of interest.

The Treasury have wide powers to make provisions by statutory instrument. These include the power to designate arrangements further to those in **4.3–4.7** below as alternative finance arrangements and the introduction of new provisions relating to alternative finance arrangements. The provisions at **4.3–4.7** below are subject to the financial arrangements being entered into on an arm's length basis (see **4.9** below).

The provisions were originally enacted in *FA 2005, Pt 2 Ch 5, ss 46–57, Sch 2*. For corporation tax purposes, the provisions were rewritten in *CTA 2009, Pt 6 Ch 6, ss 501–521* for accounting periods ending on or after 1 April 2009. For individuals, trusts and companies outside the charge to corporation tax, the provisions were rewritten by *TIOPA 2010, Sch 2* and inserted into *ITA 2007* and *TCGA 1992*. Accordingly, except for provisions relating solely to income tax, this chapter cites only the rewritten provisions which apply for corporation tax.

[*CTA 2009, ss 508–520; TIOPA 2010, s 366*].

Definition

[4.2] A '*financial institution*' for the purposes of alternative finance arrangements is:

- a bank (within *ICTA 1988, s 840A*);
- a building society (within the meaning of the *Building Societies Act 1986*);

- a wholly-owned subsidiary of either of the above;
- a person authorised by a licence under the *Consumer Credit Act 1974, Pt 3* to carry on consumer credit business or consumer hire business within the meaning of that Act;
- a person authorised in a non-UK jurisdiction to receive deposits or other repayable funds from the public and to grant credits for its own account;
- from 15 October 2009 an insurance company as defined by *ICTA 1988, s 431(2)*;
- from 15 October 2009 a person who is authorised in a jurisdiction outside the United Kingdom to carry on a business which consists of effecting or carrying out contracts of insurance or substantially similar business but not an insurance special purpose vehicle as defined in *ICTA 1988, s 431(2)*;
- a bond-issuer but only in relation to any bond assets which are rights under purchase and resale arrangements or diminishing shared ownership arrangements and from 15 October 2009 extended to include rights under profit share agency arrangements.

In this context, a company is a wholly-owned subsidiary of another where it has no members apart from the parent, its wholly-owned subsidiaries and a person acting on their behalf.

[*CTA 2009, s 502; The Alternative Finance Arrangements (Amendment) Order 2009, SI 2009 No 2568*].

Alternative finance return

Purchase and re-sale

[4.3] A finance arrangement can, as an alternative to payment of interest, be structured as a purchase of an asset and its onward sale at a higher deferred price. This is illustrated in the following diagram, where the customer obtains the equivalent of a 24 month loan with all interest being paid on the repayment of the loan.

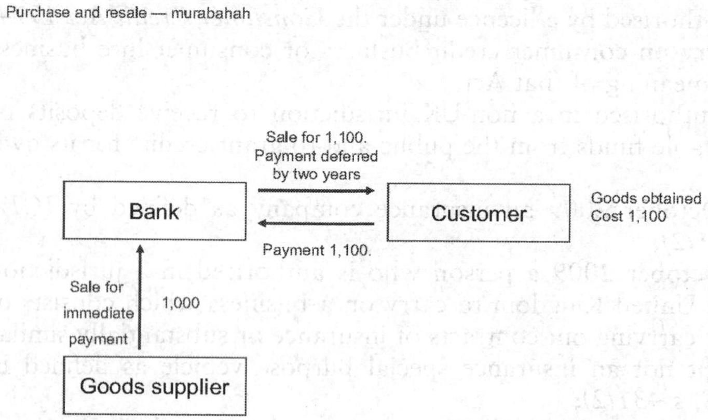

For these provisions to apply, arrangements must be entered into fulfilling the following conditions:

- the transaction must be between two persons;
- at least one of the persons must be a financial institution as defined — see **4.2** above;
- one person buys an asset and sells it to the other person, either immediately or in the case of a non-immediate sale where the seller is a financial institution which purchased the asset for the purposes of entering into purchase and resale arrangements;
- the consideration is deferred (or partly deferred);
- the consideration is greater than the purchase price; and
- the difference equates, in substance, to the return on an investment of money at interest.

Where the whole of the sale price is paid on one day, the alternative finance return is taken to be equal to the return included within the sale price. Where the sale price is to be paid by instalments, each instalment is taken to include alternative finance return equal to an amount of interest that would have been included in the instalment if:

(i) the effective return were interest payable on a loan equal to the first purchase price of the asset;
(ii) the total interest payable on the loan is equal to the amount by which the second purchase price exceeds the first purchase price;
(iii) the instalment were a part repayment of the principal with interest; and
(iv) the loan were made on arm's length terms and accounted for under generally accepted accounting practice.

In either case, the arrangements are treated for corporation tax purposes as a loan relationship to which the company is a party (see **54 LOAN RELATIONSHIPS**). The amount of the purchase price is treated as if it were a loan made to the company from the other party (or by the company to the other party as the case may be) and the alternative finance return is treated as if it were interest payable under the loan relationship. The effective return is ignored in determining the consideration for the purchase or sale of the asset for corporation tax or capital gains purposes. However, this does not override any corporation tax or capital gains provisions which provide for the consideration to be other than the actual consideration.

Alternative finane return in the form of an additional payment or any part of a redemption payment is not treated as a distribution.

Transactions other than at arm's length are excluded from these provisions.

Where a deduction is not available for an alternative finance return because the transaction is not at arm's length, the amount may not be surrendered under the group relief provisions.

[*CTA 2009, ss 503, 508–510, 514, 520, Sch 1 paras 124, 369, 660, 661; ICTA 1988, s 411ZA; TCGA 1992, ss 151H–151Y; SI 2009 No 2568*].

Diminishing shared ownership

[4.4] This is often used as a Shariah compliant alternative to a mortgage. It requires arrangements under which both a financial institution (see **4.2**) and another person (called the 'eventual owner') together acquire a beneficial interest in an asset. The eventual owner occupies the entire property, paying rent on the proportion not owned, and buys out the interest of the financial institution over time, either on a fixed schedule (corresponding to a repayment mortgage) or when desired (corresponding to an interest only mortgage.) It is illustrated below on the assumption that the eventual owner has 25% of the purchase price available.

Diminishing shared ownership — diminishing musharaka

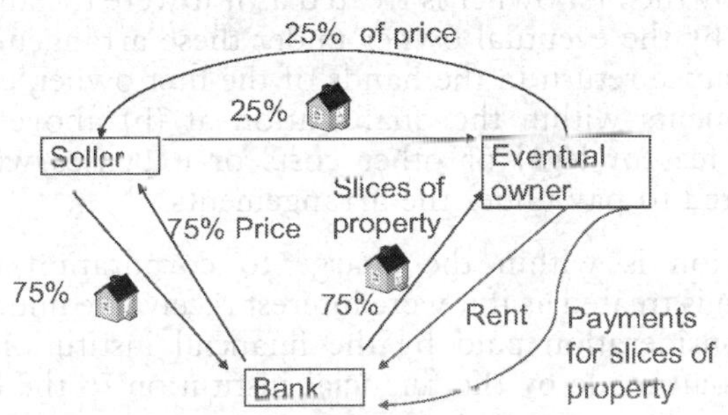

Eventual owner has sole occupancy and pays rent to Bank on proportion owned by Bank.

The requirements are that a financial institution (see **4.2** above) acquires a beneficial interest in an asset and another person ('the eventual owner'):

(a) also acquires a beneficial interest in the asset;
(b) is to make a series of payments to the financial institution amounting in total to the amount paid to acquire its beneficial interest;
(c) is to acquire (in stages or otherwise) the financial institution's beneficial interest as a result of those payments;

(d) is to make additional payments to the financial institution (whether under a lease or otherwise);

(e) has the exclusive right to occupy or otherwise use the asset; and

(f) is exclusively entitled to any income, profit or gain arising from or attributable to the asset, including, in particular, any increase in its value.

It is immaterial whether or not:

- the financial institution acquires its beneficial interest from the eventual owner (for example, in a case where there is an initial conveyance of real property to the eventual owner followed by a sub-sale from the eventual owner to the financial institution);
- whether the eventual owner (or another person other than the financial institution) also has a beneficial interest in the asset; or
- whether or not the financial institution has a legal interest in the asset.

The condition in (e) above does not preclude the eventual owner granting an interest or right in the asset to someone else, e.g. he may sub-let the asset. However, the person to whom the interest or right is granted cannot be the financial institution, a person controlled by the financial institution or a person controlled by a person who also controls the financial institution, and the grant must not be required by the financial institution or by arrangements to which the financial institution is a party.

The condition in (f) above does not prohibit arrangements under which the financial institution may bear any loss (or a share of any loss) resulting from a decrease in the asset's value.

The consideration paid by the first owner is treated as if it were the amount of a loan. Payments made by the eventual owner under these arrangements are treated as alternative finance return in the hands of the first owner, except in so far as they are payments within the qualification at (b) above or they constitute arrangement fees or legal or other costs or expenses which the eventual owner is required to pay under the arrangements.

If the financial institution is within the charge to corporation tax, the alternative finance return is treated as if it were interest receivable under a loan relationship and the consideration paid by the financial institution for its interest is treated as a loan made by the financial institution to the eventual owner.

Arrangements within these provisions are not to be treated as a partnership for tax purposes.

If these arrangements involve the sale of an asset by one party to the arrangements to another, the alternative finance return is excluded in determining the consideration for corporation tax or capital gains purposes (this not overriding any tax or capital gains provisions which provide for the consideration to be other than the actual consideration).

Where a deduction is not available for an alternative finance return because the transaction is not at arm's length, the amount may not be surrendered under the group relief provisions.

[*CAA 2009, ss 504, 508–510, 512, 514, 515, 520, Sch 1 paras 124, 369; ICTA 1988, s 411ZA; TCGA 1992, ss 151H–151Y; CTA 2009, s 504*].

Capital allowances

In HMRC Brief 26/07, HMRC state that where diminishing shared ownership ('DSO') arrangements are entered into to acquire assets which would qualify for capital allowances, then the buyer or lessee is entitled to claim capital allowances on capital payments for those assets when they are brought into use.

Capital gains

In HMRC Brief 26/07, HMRC state that, subject to there being any unusual conditions in the DSO arrangements, the buyer will be treated as acquiring the asset in full when unconditional contracts are entered into to acquire a beneficial interest. Indexation allowance is computed accordingly.

Deposit arrangements

[4.5] These are arrangements under which a person deposits money with a financial institution (see **4.2** above), which is invested by that institution, usually together money from other depositors, with a view to profit. The financial institution does not pay any interest to the depositors, but instead pays them a proportion of the profits it earns from investing their money.

This is illustrated in the diagram below.

Deposit — mudarabah

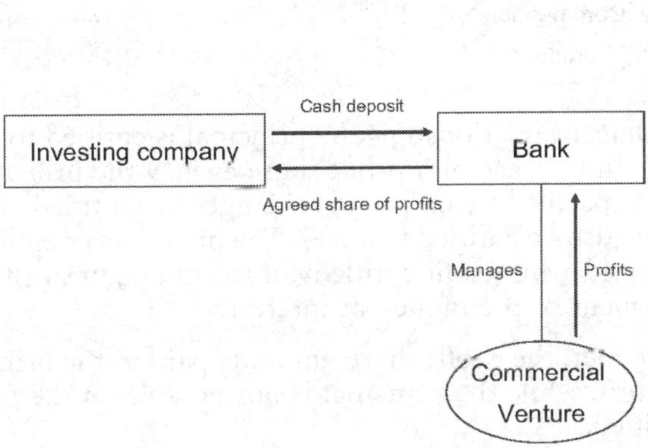

The amounts which the financial institution pays to its depositors equate in substance to the return on an investment of money at interest and constitutes alternative finance return. (Prior to *CTA 2009* it fell into a separate category called 'profit share return' which had identical tax consequences, but *CTA 2009, Sch 1* substituted 'profit share return' by 'alternative finance return' throughout the tax legislation.)

The arrangements are treated for corporation tax purposes as a loan relationship to which the company is a party (see **54 LOAN RELATIONSHIPS**). The amount of the deposit is treated as if it were a loan made by the company to the financial institution and the alternative finance return is treated as if it were interest payable under the loan relationship. The alternative finance return is not to be treated as a distribution under *ICTA 1988, s 209(2)(e)(iii)*.

Where a deduction is not available for an alternative finance return because the transaction is not at arm's length, the amount may not be surrendered under the group relief provisions.

[*CTA 2009, ss 505, 509, 510, 513, 520, Sch 1 paras 97, 124, 660, Sch 2 para 73; ICTA 1988, ss 209(6A), 411ZA*].

Profit share agency arrangements

[4.6] In the case of a 'profit share agency' as illustrated below, one party acts as agent of the other (the investor) and the agent uses the money provided by the principal with a view to producing a profit.

Profit share agency — wakala

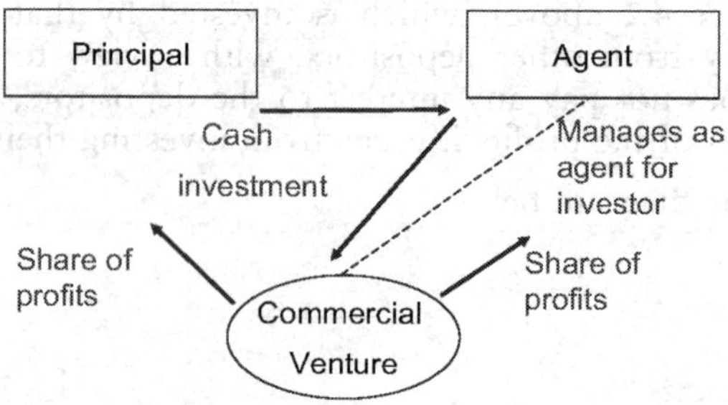

Whereas in most principal/agent relationships the principal is entitled to most of the rewards (and risks), in the case of a profit share agency the principal is entitled to the profits to a specified extent, while the agent is entitled to any additional profits (and may also be entitled to a fee). The provisions require the payments to the principal under his profit entitlement to equate, in substance, to the return on an investment of the money at interest.

If the above conditions are met, the profit share amounts paid to the principal are alternative finance return, while the principal is not taxable on the profits to which the agent is entitled.

The arrangements are treated for corporation tax purposes as a loan relationship to which the company is a party (see **54 LOAN RELATIONSHIPS**). Any amount provided under the arrangements is treated as a loan by the principal to the agent and the alternative finance return is treated as interest.

Alternative finance return in the form of a payment under a profit share agency is not treated as a distribution.

Where a deduction is not available for an alternative finance return because the transaction is not at arm's length, the amount may not be surrendered under the group relief provisions.

The provisions when first legislated by *FA 2006, s 95* (inserting *FA 2005, s 49A*) were asymmetric since only a financial institution could be the agent. With effect from 15 October 2009, *SI 2009 No 2568* makes the provisions symmetrical so they apply irrespective of the identity of the agent, provided that one or both of the principal and the agent is a financial institution. This change is interlinked with the extension to the definition of a financial institution discussed above, and makes it possible for an bond issuing company to be the agent in profit share agency transactions.

[*CTA 2009, ss 506, 509, 510, 513, 516, 520, 521; Sch 1 paras 97, 124; ICTA 1988, ss 209(6A), 411ZA; FA 2005, ss 46, 49A; FA 2006, s 95(1)(3)*].

Investment bond (IB) arrangements

[4.7] 'Sukuk' (plural of 'sakk' which is Arabic for 'certificate') are a form of tradable Islamic financial instrument that replicate the characteristics of conventional corporate bonds. They are usually structured by creating a special purpose vehicle to acquire assets, financing the acquisition by issuing participation certificates to investors. The assets so acquired are then used for the sponsoring group's business to generate income which is then paid out to the investors. The diagram below illustrates the most common structure, where land is sold to a special purpose vehicle and then rented back.

Alternative finance investment bond — sukuk

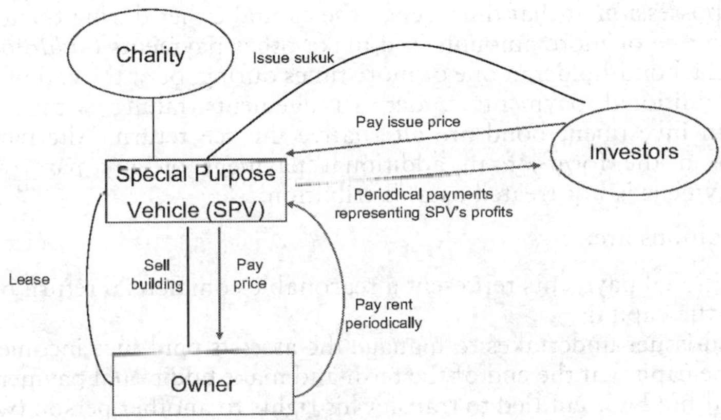

Specific legislation was needed to ensure UK issuers of, and investors in, sukuk receive a tax treatment which equates to the tax treatment of conventional bond issuers and investors.

The tax legislation now in *CTA 2009, s 507* defines for corporation tax purposes the arrangements which give rise to an 'investment bond'. Prior to the tax law rewrite, the legislation in *FA 2005, s 48A* referred to an 'alternative finance investment bond'. The name was changed by the tax law rewrite, perhaps to avoid confusion with the separate regulatory definition of an 'alternative finance investment bond' mentioned below. Following the tax law rewrite, the equivalent provisions for income tax purposes are contained in *ITA 2007, s 564G*. The corporation tax and income tax provisions are identical, so it should not be possible for an instrument to be an IB for income tax purposes without also being an IB for corporation tax purposes.

There is a regulatory provision in *The Financial Services and Markets Act 2000 (Regulated Activities) (Amendment) Order 2010, SI 2010 No 86* intended to exclude sukuk from constituting collective investment schemes. This order contains its own definition of an 'alternative finance investment bond' (AFIB) which, although similar to the definition of an IB in *CTA 2009, s 507* is not identical to it. Accordingly there is the risk that an instrument might fall within the tax provisions without falling within the regulatory provisions, or vice versa.

In passing *SI 2010 No 86*, which took effect on 24 February 2010, contained a drafting error which potentially changed the status of certain other instruments not connected with alternative finance arrangements. This was corrected by *SI 2011 No 133* which took effect on 16 February 2011. This second order could not itself be retrospective for tax purposes, but is given retrospective effect by *FA 2011, s 89*, along with a taxpayer election for the retrospection not to apply. This point is unlikely to be relevant to any alternative finance arrangements transactions.

The arrangements covered involve the bond-holder paying a sum of money (the '*capital*') to a bond-issuer, where the assets or class of assets to be acquired to generate income or gains, and the period of the arrangement, are specified. The bond-issuer undertakes to sell the assets at the end of the term, or any that are still in his possession at that time, repay the capital either during the term or at its end, in one or more amounts and make other payments ('*additional payments*') to the bond-holder at one or more times during, or at the end of the bond term. Additional payments under arrangements falling within the definition of an investment bond are alternative finance return. Alternative finance return in the form of an additional payment or any part of a redemption payment is not treated as a distribution.

The other conditions are:

- (a) the additional payments represent a reasonable commercial return on a loan of the capital;
- (b) the bond-issuer undertakes to manage the assets to produce income to repay the capital at the end of the term and make additional payments;
- (c) the bond-holder is entitled to transfer his rights to another person (who becomes the bond-holder);
- (d) the arrangements are listed on a recognised stock exchange; and
- (e) the arrangements are wholly or partly treated as a financial liability of the bond-issuer under international accounting standards, or would be if the issuer were to prepare financial statements under international accounting standards.

It is possible to designate a stock exchange only for the purposes of the IB rules. The clear intention is that this power can be used to designate certain foreign stock exchanges where existing sukuk are listed without the UK having to recognise those exchanges for all other tax purposes. On 20 July 2007,

HMRC issued an order under this provision, designating seven stock exchanges in the Middle East, Malaysia and Indonesia, which may be found at www.hmrc.gov.uk/legislation/rse-48a.pdf and has effect from 1 April 2007 in respect of arrangements entered into on or after that date.

Flexibility is allowed for in the terms of the 'arrangements', for example the bond-issuer may acquire the assets before or after the arrangements are in place, the arrangements may include provision for them to be terminated before the end of the term and the termination payment may be reduced should the value of the bond assets fall or the income on them be reduced.

[*CTA 2009, s 507(2), Sch 1 para 649; ITA 2007, s 564G*].

For the purpose of the Corporation Taxes Acts, the following applies. The effect of the arrangements is that the bond-holder is not treated as having the legal or beneficial interest in the bond assets, as trustee or otherwise, and any profits or gains arising on them is the income of the bond-issuer (otherwise than in a fiduciary capacity) not the bond-holder.

Redemption or additional payments to the bond-holder by the bond-issuer are treated for tax purposes as not made by him in a fiduciary capacity. The bond-holder is not entitled to tax relief on capital expenditure on the bond assets.

IB arrangements are securities for the purpose of the Corporation Tax Acts. A bond-issuer is not a securitisation company for the purpose of the special tax regime applicable to securitisation companies, unless it is one as a result of arrangements which are not investment bond arrangements. Provisions are made in *CTA 2009, s 519* as regards the treatment of a bond-holder for the close company and group relief provisions. The alternative finance return payable under the arrangements is treated as interest on a loan.

Where a deduction is not available for alternative finance return because the transaction is not at arm's length, the amount may not be surrendered under the group relief provisions.

The IB provisions were originally enacted by *FA 2007*. Although that created the tax framework for IBs, the legislation did not address a number of tax issues. Where a company transfers UK land to a special purpose vehicle which is to issue an IB, (as illustrated in the diagram at **4.7**) and then repurchases the land on the redemption of the IB, several undesirable tax consequences arise:

(1) The sale of the land from the company to the special purpose vehicle, and its eventual repurchase, are both subject to SDLT.
(2) Both the sale and the repurchase are disposals for the taxation of chargeable gains.
(3) The special purpose vehicle would be entitled to any available capital allowances on any assets it owns. However, as its taxable income from renting out or otherwise exploiting the assets will be matched by a deduction for the payments it makes to bond holders, the capital allowances will be of no value to the special purpose vehicle, and will not be available to any other party involved in the transaction.

None of the above tax disadvantages would arise if the company concerned were to issue a conventional bond secured on the land in question. Accordingly, the legislation did not give equality of tax treatment, and indeed no IBs were issued by any UK company between the royal assent to *FA 2007* and *2009*.

Accordingly, *FA 2009, s 123* and *Sch 61* eliminate the above tax disadvantages, by eliminating the SDLT charges and treating the sale and the repurchase as not being a disposal for capital gains tax purposes, and by continuing to give any capital allowances to the company which originally owns the land. There are a number of qualifying conditions set out in *Sch 61 para 5* that must be fulfilled. Following the *FA 2009* changes, the first UK based IB transaction took place during 2010.

[*CTA 2009, ss 507, 510, 513, 514, 517–520, Sch 1 paras 97, 124, 369, 650, 651, Sch 2 para 74; ICTA 1988, ss 209(6A), 411ZA; TCGA 1992, ss 151H–151Y; ITA 2007, s 564G; FA 2009, s 123*].

Other provisions

Non-residents

[4.8] Where a non-resident company is party to an alternative finance arrangement as in **4.3** or **4.6** above, the company is not treated as having a UK permanent establishment by virtue of anything done in relation to the arrangement.

[*CTA 2009, Sch 1 paras 560, 561; FA 2003, s 148(5A); ITA 2007, s 835J*].

Equally, where a UK-resident person is a party to or acts for a non-resident person, who is party to an alternative finance arrangement, that person is not regarded as the UK representative of the non-resident in relation to the arrangement.

[*FA 1995, s 127(1)(cb), (cc); ITA 2007, s 835J; CTA 2009, Sch 1 para 400*]

See **65.6 RESIDENCE**.

Arrangements not at arm's length

[4.9] The arrangements at **4.3–4.7** above are not treated as alternative finance arrangements if:

- they are not entered into at arm's length;
- the transfer pricing rules under in *TIOPA 2010, s 147* (which apply for corporation tax as well as income tax) require the alternative finance or profit share return (or amount representing it) to be recomputed on an arm's length basis;
- the affected person or persons is entitled to a return (the relevant return) which would be an alternative finance return or an amount representing an alternative finance return if the arrangements were alternative finance arrangements (the latter covers the situation where there is an intermediary in back to back arrangements); and

- the party receiving the return is not subject to income or corporation tax, or a corresponding tax under a foreign jurisdiction, on the return.

In this case, the person paying the return is not entitled to any deduction in respect of the return in computing profits or gains for corporation tax purposes or to any deduction against total income or profits. Nor can the prohibited deduction be surrendered by way of group relief.

[*CTA 2009, ss 508, 520, Sch 1 para 656; ITA 2007, s 564H; TIOPA 2010, s 147*].

Community investment tax relief

[4.10] References to a loan in the community investment tax relief ('CITR') legislation are taken to include references to alternative finance arrangements that involve purchase and re-sale, deposit or a profit share agency within the definitions given above. See **23 COMMUNITY INVESTMENT TAX RELIEF**.

[*CTA 2010, ss 256–259; ITA 2007, ss 372A–372D; CTA 2009, Sch 1 para 657*].

Deduction of income tax at source

[4.11] Alternative finance arrangements under which alternative finance return is payable (see **4.3–4.7** above and **51.4 INVESTMENT COMPANIES AND INVESTMENT BUSINESS**) are to be treated as deposits on which interest is payable for the purposes of deduction of income tax at source by deposit takers and building societies.

[*FA 2005, Sch 2 paras 11–13; ITA 2007, Sch 1 para 602; CTA 2009, Sch 1 para 663*].

5

Anti-Avoidance

Cross references. See **13.24**(C) **CAPITAL ALLOWANCES — PLANT AND MACHINERY: FIXTURES AND LEASING** for 'control' and 'main benefit' transactions, **17.36–17.46 CAPITAL GAINS** for value-shifting provisions, **17.4–17.8 CAPITAL GAINS** and **38.16 GAINS AND LOSS BUYING** for avoidance utilising losses, pre-entry losses and pre-entry gains; **22.20 CLOSE COMPANIES** in respect of close investment holding companies, **27 CONTROLLED FOREIGN COMPANIES** in relation to the apportionment of profits of controlled foreign companies in 'low tax' jurisdictions, **39.23, 31.28, 31.32 GROUP RELIEF** in respect of dual resident investing companies and exempt distributions, **54.52 LOAN RELATIONSHIPS** in relation to loan relationships for unallowable purposes, **55.11, 55.22, 55.23 LOSSES** in respect of company reconstructions, farming and market gardening and leasing, **58.12 PARTNERSHIPS** in relation to the realisation of capital from a partnership in a non-taxable form, and **72 TRANSFER PRICING.**

Introduction

[5.1] This chapter outlines the main anti-avoidance provisions with regard to the various Tax Acts, as they apply for corporation tax matters. Before outlining the different provisions, the approach of the Courts with regard to anti-avoidance transactions is considered.

For the **general approach of the Courts** to transactions entered into solely to avoid or reduce tax liability, leading cases are *Duke of Westminster v CIR* (1935) 19 TC 490, HL; *W T Ramsay Ltd v CIR, Eilbeck v Rawling* (1981) 54 TC 101, HL; *CIR v Burmah Oil Co Ltd* (1981) 54 TC 200, HL; *Furniss v Dawson (and related appeals)* (1984) 55 TC 324, HL; *Countess Fitzwilliam v CIR* [1993] STC 502, HL; and *CIR v McGuckian* (1997) 69 TC 1, HL. See also *Cairns v MacDiarmid* (1983) 56 TC 556, CA; *Ingram v CIR* [1985] STC 835; *Craven v White, CIR v Bowater Property Developments Ltd*, and *Baylis v Gregory* (1988) 62 TC 1, heard together in the HL; *Shepherd v Lyntress Ltd* (1989) 62 TC 495; *Moodie v CIR and Sinnett* (1993) 65 TC 610, HL; *Hatton v CIR* [1992] STC 140; *Ensign Tankers (Leasing) Ltd v Stokes* (1992) 64 TC 617, HL; *Pigott v Staines Investment Co Ltd* (1995) 68 TC 342; *MacNiven v Westmoreland Investments Ltd* (2001) 73 TC 1, HL; *Barclays Mercantile Business Finance Ltd v Mawson* [2005] STC 1 and *CIR v Scottish Provident Institution* [2005] STC 15, HL.

The classical interpretation of the constraints upon the Courts in deciding cases involving tax avoidance schemes is summed up in Lord Tomlin's statement in the *Duke of Westminster* case that '. . . every man is entitled if he can to order his affairs so that the tax attaching . . . is less than it otherwise would be'. The case concerned annual payments made under covenant by a taxpayer to his domestic employees, which were in substance, but not in form, remuneration. The judgment was thus concerned with the tax consequences of a single transaction, but in *Ramsay*, and subsequently in *Furniss v Dawson*, the Courts have set bounds to the ambit within which this principle can be applied in relation to modern sophisticated and increasingly artificial arrangements to avoid tax.

Ramsay concerned a complex 'circular' avoidance scheme at the end of which the financial position of the parties was little changed, but it was claimed that a large capital gains tax loss had been created. It was held that where a preconceived series of transactions is entered into to avoid tax, and with the clear intention to proceed through all stages to completion once set in motion, the *Duke of Westminster* principle does not compel a consideration of the individual transactions and of the fiscal consequences of such transactions taken in isolation.

The House of Lords' opinions in *Furniss v Dawson* are of outstanding importance, and establish, inter alia, that the *Ramsay* principle is not confined to 'circular' devices, and that if a series of transactions is 'preordained', a particular transaction within the series, accepted as genuine, may nevertheless be ignored if it was entered into solely for fiscal reasons and without any commercial purpose other than tax avoidance, even if the series of transactions as a whole has a legitimate commercial purpose.

In *Craven v White* the House of Lords indicated that for the *Ramsay* principle to apply all the transactions in a series have to be preordained with such a degree of certainty that, at the time of the earlier transactions, there is no practical likelihood that the transactions would not take place. It is not sufficient that the ultimate transaction is simply of a kind that was envisaged at the time of the earlier transactions.

However, the decision in this case was distinguished in the *Scottish Provident Institution* case where the HL held that 'it would destroy the value of the *Ramsay* principle' if the composite effect of transactions 'had to be disregarded simply because the parties had deliberately included a commercially irrelevant contingency, creating an acceptable risk that the scheme might not work as planned' and that 'the composite effect of such a scheme should be considered as it was intended to operate and without regard to the possibility that, contrary to the intention and expectations of the parties, it might not work as planned'.

The inheritance tax case *Fitzwilliam v CIR* appears to further restrict the application of the *Ramsay* principle, in that the HL found for the taxpayer in a case in which all their Lordships agreed that, once the scheme was embarked upon, there was no real possibility that the later transactions would not be proceeded with. There is, however, some suggestion that a decisive factor was that the first step in the transactions took place before the rest of the scheme had been formulated. Again, in the case of *MacNiven v Westmoreland Investments Ltd* it was held that the *Ramsay* principle did not apply where a company loaned money to a subsidiary to enable it to pay up outstanding interest and thus crystallise tax losses. The interest had been paid within the meaning of the legislation and the manner in which the payment was funded was irrelevant.

HMRC's Anti-Avoidance Group (AAG) is responsible for the development, maintenance and delivery of the department's anti-avoidance strategy. AAG co-ordinates anti-avoidance activity across HMRC and is responsible for anti-avoidance policy. AAG operates a risk assessment policy and in doing so has drawn up a list of common features of avoidance (or signposts). This list is not exhaustive, and a transaction featuring one or more of the signposts will not necessarily be classed as avoidance. The signposts are kept under review. A list of the signposts (at September 2007) is as follows:

- transactions or arrangements having little or no economic substance or whose effect on tax is disproportionate to the change in the taxpayers' economic position;
- transactions or arrangements which account for little or no pre-tax profit and rely wholly or mainly on anticipated tax savings for signification post-tax profit;
- transactions or arrangements which result in a mismatch;
- transactions or arrangements exhibiting little or no business, commercial or non-tax driver;
- transactions or arrangements involving contrived, artificial, transitory, pre-ordained or commercially unnecessary steps or transactions;
- transactions or arrangements where the income, gains, expenditure or losses falling within the UK tax net are not proportionate to the economic activity taking place or the value added in the UK. (This especially applies where the entities are within the same group and the transactions would not have arisen between parties acting at arm's length.); and
- transactions designed to side-step particular anti-avoidance legislation but to achieve the same result.

For examples see www.hmrc.gov.uk/avoidance/aag-risk-assessing.htm.

In March 2011, at the same time as the budget for the year, the government published a note on 'Tackling Tax Avoidance' which is a progress report highlighting the more strategic approach to the problems of tax avoidance, which was launched in June 2010 as part of the consultation document on tax policy making

The key elements of this new approach include: making the most of opportunities to make the tax system more watertight against avoidance, for example, as part of wider policy reform; reviewing areas of the tax system that have been under repeated avoidance attack, to get to the heart of the problem and develop sustainable solutions; and creating new generic defences against avoidance, going beyond closing identified avoidance loopholes, including considering the case for a General Anti-Avoidance Rule (GAAR).

HMRC's new anti-avoidance strategy focuses on three core elements: preventing avoidance at the outset where possible; detecting it early where it persists; and countering it effectively through challenge by HMRC.

In the document the Government launches two new pieces of work. Firstly new reviews of high risk areas of the tax code such as those areas which need frequent amendment to close loopholes. The first two areas under consideration are income tax losses and unauthorised unit trusts. The intention is for each budget to announce further areas for review as part of a rolling programme. Secondly there are plans for a consultation during the summer of 2011 on proposals to remove the cash flow advantage that tax avoiders can get by using high risk avoidance schemes. In addition the study group on a possible GAAR should produce their report by 31 October 2011.

The report then focuses on the progress made in HMRC's operational activities in support of their new strategic approach. With regard to large businesses, HMRC are seeking relationships based on greater openness and transparency. For the largest businesses, the report points to one-to-one Customer Relationship Managers (CRMs) who have been introduced to assist with understanding the tax and avoidance risks in the context of the operating commercial environment. Clearly the focus is particularly on large business cases and the wealthy, where it is perceived that the immediate tax at risk is greatest.

Whilst the report comments that HMRC aims to resolve any disputes with customers as quickly as possible, it indicates that they will, if necessary, litigate.

The last chapter of the document publishes the Government's Protocol on unscheduled announcements of tax changes. This provides a set of criteria to be observed when the Government is deciding whether to announce a change to tax law that has immediate effect. The Protocol reflects views from consultation on a draft text published in December 2010 and the Forum of Tax Professionals will monitor how the Protocol is applied in practice.

The document can be found at: http://cdn.hm-treasury.gov.uk/2011budget_taxavoidance.pdf.

Simon's Taxes. See A2.122.

Transactions in securities

[5.2] There are provisions for counteracting corporation tax advantages obtained or obtainable by companies in specified circumstances in respect of a transaction or transactions in securities. [*CTA 2010, Pt 15, Sch 2 para 84; ICTA 1988, ss 703–709 as amended*].

FA 2010 introduced an amendment to the corporation tax rules for transactions in securities which are outlined below. *CTA 2010, s 735* is repealed, as circumstance (A), involving abnormal dividends, has now been removed from both the income tax and corporation tax rules with regard to transactions in securities.

Subject to the exception below, the provisions apply where, in consequence of 'transaction(s) in securities', combined with any of the circumstances listed at (C)–(E) below, a company (or any body corporate) is able to obtain a 'corporation tax advantage'. 'Securities' includes shares and stock, and, in the case of a company not limited by shares, includes an interest of a member of the company in whatever form. (The provisions apply equally where the advantage is obtainable due to the combined effect of the transaction(s) and the liquidation of the company.) HMRC may make adjustments to counteract the tax advantage (see further below).

The provisions do *not* apply if the company shows that the transaction or transactions are made:

(i) for genuine commercial reasons or in the ordinary course of investment management, and
(ii) that enabling corporation tax advantages to be obtained is not a main object of the transaction or, as the case may be, any of the transactions.

[*CTA 2010, ss 733, 734, 751; ICTA 1988, ss 703(1)(2), 709(2)*].

For 'transactions in securities' see *CIR v Joiner* (1975) 50 TC 449, HL (in which a variation of rights prior to a liquidation was held to be such a transaction), and *CIR v Laird Group plc* [2003] STC 1349, HL (in which the payment of a dividend representing previously undistributed profits was held not to be).

For 'genuine commercial reasons' see *Laird Group* in the Ch D ([2001] STC 689) and *CIR v Brebner* (1967) 43 TC 705, HL; *Clark v CIR* [1979] 1 All ER 385, [1979] 1 WLR 416, HL, and *Marwood Homes Ltd v CIR* [1999] STC (SCD) 44. In *Lewis (trustee of Redrow Staff Pension Scheme) v CIR* [1999] STC (SCD) 349, a distribution by way of purchase of its own shares by a company from the trustees of its pension scheme, pursuant to legislation requiring the trustees to reduce their holding, was held to be a transaction carried out by the trustees both for genuine commercial reasons and in the ordinary course of investment management.

Specified circumstances

The circumstances mentioned above, only one of which needs to be met, are as follows.

(A) In connection with:
- a purchase of securities followed by the sale of the same or other securities; or
- a sale of securities followed by the purchase of the same or other securities; or
- the distribution, transfer or realisation of assets of a company; or
- the application of such assets in discharge of liabilities,

the company receives an 'abnormal amount by way of dividend' which is taken into account for purposes of the application of franked investment income in relation to 'shadow ACT' computations (see **3.4 ADVANCE CORPORATION TAX — SHADOW ACT**).

The *ICTA 1988* legislation also theoretically applied where the abnormal amount received was taken into account for the purposes of any corporation tax exemption, the setting-off of losses against profits or income or the giving of group relief, but this is no longer capable of having any practical effect for corporation tax purposes and was therefore not rewritten in *CTA 2010* (Explanatory Notes to *CTA 2010*).

[*CTA 2010, s 735*].

This circumstance has been repealed by *FA 2010* with effect in relation to corporation tax advantages obtained on or after 1 April 2010. This section contained circumstance (A) of *ICTA 1988, s 704*. This part of *s 704* has been deleted from both the income tax and corporation tax codes and therefore *s 735* is no longer required. Amendments to ensure that the shadow advance corporation tax (ACT) regime continues to work appropriately for abnormal dividends paid in these circumstances were made to *SI 1999 No 358* by *SI 2010 No 669*.

(B) In connection with any of the matters listed in (A) above, a company becomes entitled to a deduction from profits because of a decrease in value of securities held, formerly held, or sold which arises from payment by the company of a dividend thereon or from any other dealing with a company's assets (or where another company obtains the benefit of such a deduction by way of group relief). This circumstance was repealed with effect for transactions in securities on or after 1 April 2008.

(C) In consequence of a transaction whereby (see *CIR v Garvin* (1981) 55 TC 24, HL, and *Bird v CIR* (1988) 61 TC 238, HL, and contrast *Emery v CIR* (1980) 54 TC 607) another person has received or subsequently receives 'an abnormal amount by way of dividend', the company receives consideration which:

- is not otherwise taxable as income; and
- represents the value of:
  - (i) a company's trading stock or future receipts; or
  - (ii) assets which are, or would otherwise have been, available for distribution (see *CIR v Brown* (1971) 47 TC 217, CA) by a company as dividend, and which, in the case of a company incorporated abroad, do not represent a return of capital to subscribers.

For transactions entered into before 1 April 2008, the above applied equally if, instead of receiving an abnormal amount by way of dividend, the other person had become, or subsequently became, entitled to a deduction as in (B) above.

(D) In connection with the distribution, transfer or realisation of assets of a 'relevant company', or the application of such assets in discharge of liabilities, the company potentially within these provisions receives consideration which represents the value of:

(i) the relevant company's trading stock or future receipts, or

(ii) assets which are, or would otherwise have been, available for distribution (see *CIR v Brown* (1971) 47 TC 217, CA) by the relevant company as dividend, and which, in the case of a company incorporated abroad, do not represent a return of capital to subscribers,

and receives the consideration in such a way that it is not otherwise taxable as income.

(E) In connection with (i) the transfer of assets of a 'relevant company' to another such company, or (ii) a transaction in securities in which two or more relevant companies are concerned, the company potentially within these provisions receives consideration which:

- consists of any share capital or any security issued by a relevant company;
- is not otherwise taxable as income; and
- represents the value of:
  (i) a relevant company's trading stock, or
  (ii) assets which are, or would otherwise have been, available for distribution (see *CIR v Brown* (1971) 47 TC 217, CA) by a relevant company as dividend.

In so far as the consideration consists of non-redeemable share capital, it triggers these provisions only so far as the share capital is repaid (in a winding-up or otherwise, including any distribution made in respect of any shares in a winding-up or dissolution).

[*CTA 2010, ss 735–738, 751; ICTA 1988, ss 704, 709(2)(3); FA 2008, s 66(1)(5); CTA 2009, Sch 1 para 213*].

(C), (D) and (E) above are in practice unlikely to apply unless the company in question has (or has recently had) distributable reserves (HMRC Company Taxation Manual CTM36835–36845). For cases within (C) and (D) above, see *CIR v Cleary* (1967) 44 TC 399, HL; *Anysz v CIR* (1977) 53 TC 601; *Williams v CIR* (1980) 54 TC 257, HL; *CIR v Wiggins* (1978) 53 TC 639.

Abnormal amount of dividend

For the purposes of (A) (up to 1 April 2010) and (C) above, an '*abnormal amount by way of dividend*' is received if an officer of HMRC, the Commissioners of HMRC or the Tribunal (whichever is determining the question) is satisfied that the condition in (a) below is met and also, in relation to fixed rate dividends only, that the condition in (b) below is met.

(a) This condition is that the dividend substantially exceeds a normal return on the consideration provided by the recipient for the securities (or, if those securities are derived from securities previously acquired by the recipient, those securities). In determining 'normal return', regard must be had to the length of time the securities were held and to dividends paid and other distributions made in respect of them during that time. If the recipient acquired the securities for nil consideration or for greater than market value, the recipient is treated for the purposes of this test as having acquired them at market value.

(b) This condition is that the fixed rate dividend substantially exceeds the amount which the recipient would have received if the dividend had accrued from day to day and the recipient had been entitled to only so much of it as accrued while the recipient held the securities. But this condition is not met if during the six months beginning with the purchase of the securities the recipient does not dispose of them (or dispose of similar securities) or acquire an option to sell them (or to sell similar securities).

[*CTA 2010, ss 740–742; ICTA 1988, s 709(4)–(6); SI 2009 No 56, Sch 1 para 153*].

In any of (A)–(E) above, references to a dividend include any other qualifying distribution (see *CTA 2010, s 1136*) and also include interest.

[*CTA 2010, s 751; ICTA 1988, s 709(2)*].

'Dividend' includes interest and any other qualifying distribution. The amount of a qualifying distribution includes the related tax credit for these purposes (*CIR v Universities Superannuation Scheme Ltd* (1996) 70 TC 193). In the case of a purchase by a company of its own shares treated as a distribution under *ICTA 1988, s 209(2)(b)* (see **26.4 DISTRIBUTIONS**), it was held that the return was not abnormal (*CIR v Sema Group Pension Scheme Trustees* [2003] STC 95, CA).

In any of (C)–(E) above, references to consideration include money's worth. [*CTA 2010, ss 736(6), 737(6), 738(8); ICTA 1988, s 709(3)*].

Relevant company

For the purposes of (D) and (E) above, a '*relevant company*' is:

- a company under the control of five or fewer persons; or
- any other company none of whose shares or stocks (disregarding any debenture stock, preferred shares or preferred stock) is included in the Official UK list and dealt in on a recognised stock exchange in the UK (or before 19 July 2007 was listed in the Official List of the Stock Exchange, and dealt in on the Stock Exchange).

But a company is not a relevant company if it is under the control of one or more companies which are not themselves relevant companies. 'Control' is defined as in *CTA 2010, s 450* (see **22.6 CLOSE COMPANIES**). In determining 'under the control', the relevant date is the date of the dividend (*CIR v Garvin* (1981) 55 TC 24, HL).

During consultation on the transactions in securities legislation, HMRC raised the issue that this provision potentially constitutes unlawful discrimination under the EC Treaty. As a result, when the income tax rules were changed, the new regime was applied to close companies and companies that would be close, were they UK resident. However, no such change has been made or proposed to the corporation tax rules, which therefore remain potentially discriminatory.

[*CTA 2010, s 739, Sch 2 para 85; ICTA 1988, s 704; FA 2007, s 109, Sch 26 para 7(7)*].

Tax advantage

For these purposes, a '*corporation tax advantage*' means any of the following:

- a relief (or increased relief) from corporation tax;

- a repayment (or increased repayment) of corporation tax;
- the avoidance or reduction of a charge to corporation tax or an assessment to corporation tax; or
- the avoidance of a possible assessment to corporation tax.

As regards the last two items, it does not matter whether the avoidance or reduction is effected by receipts accruing in such a way that the recipient does not pay corporation tax on them or by a deduction in calculating profits or gains. For distributions made between 8 October 1996 and 31 March 2008 inclusive, it was made clear that, for this purpose, a relief included a dividend tax credit.

[*CTA 2010, s 732; ICTA 1988, s 709(1)(2A); FA 2008, s 66*].

For 'tax advantage' see *CIR v Cleary* (1967) 44 TC 399, HL (tax advantage obtained where taxpayers' company purchased shares from them), and contrast *CIR v Kleinwort, Benson Ltd* (1968) 45 TC 369 (no tax advantage where merchant bank purchased debentures with interest in arrear shortly before redemption). The decision in *Sheppard and another (Trustees of the Woodland Trust) v CIR (No 2)* (1993) 65 TC 724 that no tax advantage could arise where relief was obtained by virtue of charitable exemption was doubted in *CIR v Universities Superannuation Scheme Ltd* (1996) 70 TC 193, in which the opposite conclusion was reached.

Prior to the hearing of the latter case, HMRC had, in any event, indicated that they would continue to proceed under the above legislation on the footing that tax-exempt bodies obtain a tax advantage whenever they receive abnormal dividends, since they considered that there would have been good grounds for challenging the earlier decision had it not been for a defect in the assessment under appeal. This continues to be the HMRC approach. (HMRC Tax Bulletin August 1993 p 90, April 1998 p 537, October 1998 pp 590–592). For the quantum of the tax advantage, see *Bird v CIR* (1988) 61 TC 238, HL. On the question of whether a tax advantage was a 'main object' of a transaction, see *Marwood Homes Ltd v CIR* [1999] STC (SCD) 44. See also *Laird Group plc v CIR* [2001] STC 689; *Snell v Revenue and Customs Comrs* [2008] STC (SCD) 1094.

Procedure

(i) An officer of HMRC must notify the company that he has reason to believe that the above provisions may apply to it in respect of transaction(s) specified in the notification. [*CTA 2010, s 743; ICTA 1988, s 703(9)*]. See *Balen v CIR* (1978) 52 TC 406, CA.

(ii) The company notified may make a statutory declaration that in its opinion the above provisions do not apply, stating supporting facts and circumstances, and send it to the HMRC officer within 30 days. [*CTA 2010, s 744; ICTA 1988, s 703(9)*]. For acceptance of late statutory declarations, see HMRC Tax Bulletin April 1999 p 656.

(iii) The HMRC officer must then either take no further action or send the declaration together with a certificate that he sees reason to take further action (and any counter-statement he wishes to submit) to the Tribunal. The Tribunal will consider the declaration and certificate and counter-statement (if any) and decide whether there is a *prima facie* case for proceeding further. Such a determination does not affect the application of these provisions in respect of transactions including not only the ones to which the determination relates but also others. [*CTA 2010, s 745; ICTA 1988, s 703(10)*]. HMRC have no right of appeal if the determination goes against them and must take no further action. The taxpayer is not entitled to see HMRC's counter-statement nor to be heard by the Tribunal (*Wiseman v Borneman* (1969) 45 TC 540, HL). See also *Howard v Borneman* (1975) 50 TC 322, HL, and *Balen v CIR* (1978) 52 TC 406, CA.

(iv) If the Tribunal decides there is a case, or if no statutory declaration is made under (ii) above by the company, HMRC will make adjustments to counteract the corporation tax advantage. The adjustments required to be made, and the basis on which they are to be made, must be specified in a notice (a '*counteraction notice*') served on the company by an HMRC officer. The adjustments may take the form of an assessment, the cancellation of a tax repayment and/or a recalculation of profits or gains or liability to corporation tax. No assessment may be made later than six years after the accounting period to which the tax advantage relates. [*CTA 2010, s 746; ICTA 1988, s 703(3)(12)*]. If (E) above is in point, and is triggered by the repayment of share capital, the assessment must be for the accounting period in which that repayment occurs. [*CTA 2010, s 747; ICTA 1988, s 704*].

(v) A company on which a counteraction notice has been served may appeal, by giving notice to the Commissioners for HMRC within 30 days of the service of the notice, on the grounds that the provisions do not apply to the company in respect of the transaction(s) in question or that the stated adjustments are inappropriate. The Tribunal may then affirm, vary or cancel the counteraction notice or affirm, vary or quash an assessment made in accordance with the notice. [*CTA 2010, s 750; ICTA 1988, s 705(1)(5); SI 2009 No 56, Sch 1 para 151*].

(vi) HMRC used to have power to require of a company information (within 28 days of written notice) relevant to transaction(s) which it appears to them may give rise to a liability on that company under these provisions. [*ICTA 1988, s 708; SI 2009 No 2035, Sch para 19*]. For the way in which HMRC should exercise this powers, see *Preston v CIR* [1985] 2 All ER 327, [1985] STC 282, HL. With effect on and after 13 August 2009, this power is cancelled in view of HMRC's much wider powers at **43 HMRC INVESTIGATORY POWERS**.

(vii) The application of these provisions is outside self-assessment, so that returns should be made without having regard to a possible charge (although taxpayers may wish to draw the inspector's attention to any correspondence with the Clearance and Counteraction Team (see below) in connection with any particular transaction). Enquiries into the possible application of these provisions will accordingly be carried out independently of any enquiry into the self-assessment return (HMRC Tax Bulletin April 2000 pp 742, 743).

References above to the Tribunal are to the Appeal Tribunal described in **6 APPEALS**. Prior to 1 April 2009, there was a Section 703 Tribunal which specialised in the above matters but this was subsumed into the general Appeal Tribunals system.

Clearance

Taxpayers may take the initiative by submitting to HMRC particulars of any transaction effected or contemplated; HMRC may, within 30 days of receipt, call for further information (to be supplied within 30 days). Subject to this, they must notify their decision within 30 days of receipt of the particulars or further information, and if they are satisfied that no liability arises the matter is concluded as regards that transaction by itself, provided that all facts and material particulars have been fully and accurately disclosed. [*CTA 2010, ss 748, 749; ICTA 1988, s 707*].

HMRC is not obliged to give reasons for refusal of clearance but where the applicant has given full reasons for his transactions the main grounds for refusing clearance will be indicated. A refusal to give clearance indicates that counteraction would be taken if the transaction were completed. (HMRC Statement of Practice, SP 3/80).

Applications for clearance should be directed to the Clearance and Counteraction Team, First Floor, 22 Kingsway, London WC2B 6NR (if market-sensitive information is included, mark for the attention of Team Leader). Applications may be faxed to 020-7438 4409 or emailed to reconstructions@hmrc.gsi.gov.uk (in both cases after telephoning Team Leader (on 020-7438 6585) if market-sensitive information is included). A hard copy need not then be sent. Application may be made in a single letter to the same address for clearance under *CTA 2010, ss 748, 749*; *ICTA 1988, s 707* (transactions in securities), or under any one or more of *TCGA 1992, s 139* (reconstructions — see 11 capital gains); *CTA 2010, ss 1091, 1092*; *ICTA 1988, s 215* (demergers, see **31.37 GROUP RELIEF**), *CTA 2010, ss 1044, 1045*; *ICTA 1988, s 225* (see **63.8 PURCHASE BY A COMPANY OF ITS OWN SHARES**), *TCGA 1992, s 138(1)* (share exchanges, see Tolley's Capital Gains Tax under Anti-Avoidance), *TCGA 1992, s 140B* (transfer of a UK trade between EU member states, see **17.14** capital gains), *TCGA 1992, s 140D* (transfer of non-UK trade between EU member states, see **17.21** capital gains) and *CTA 2009, ss 831, 832; FA 2002, Sch 29 para 88* (see **48.27 INTANGIBLE ASSETS**).

HMRC 'Working Together' Bulletin August 2001 pp 8, 9 contain a checklist of the items of information whose omission from clearance applications most commonly causes delay in the processing of applications.

Simon's Taxes. See **D9.1**.

Rights to receive income from securities

[5.3] These provisions have been repealed with effect from 22 April 2009 by *FA 2009*, and replaced by the provisions in *FA 2009, Sch 25* — see **5.11** transfers of income streams, below.

Where the owner of securities sells or transfers the right to the interest, dividends, annuities etc. therefrom *but not to the securities themselves*, such interest etc. is treated for income or corporation tax purposes as income of that owner (or, where the owner is not the beneficial owner, of the beneficiary entitled to the income) for the chargeable period in which the right to receive the interest was sold. (In relation to sales or transfers before 2 December 2004, the income treated as that of the owner or beneficiary cannot be treated as the income of any other person.)

If the interest etc. on the securities is of such character that it may be paid gross, an assessment to income tax is made on the owner unless the owner shows that the proceeds of any sale etc. have otherwise been taxed. Credit is given in the assessment for any tax which the income is shown to have already borne. If income tax would have been chargeable on relevant foreign income on the remittance basis on the interest etc., the assessment is correspondingly limited to the amounts remitted. HMRC have power to obtain information.

For company accounting periods beginning after 30 September 2002, *s 730* does not have effect for the purposes of the loan relationships legislation (see **54 LOAN RELATIONSHIPS**).

In relation to sales or transfers **on or after 2 December 2004**, as a consequence of the introduction of separate legislation on corporate strips (see Tolley's Income Tax under Savings and Investment Income) and on transfers of rights to receive annuities and other annual payments (see **5.4** below), the above provisions no longer apply to interest and annuities but are instead restricted to sales or transfers of distributions (usually dividends) payable on company shares. The order of priority of charge is reversed, so that if the proceeds of sale or transfer are otherwise chargeable to tax there is no charge under these provisions.

In relation to subsequent sales or other realisations, **on or after 20 January 2006**, by the purchaser of a right to receive the distribution, the proceeds of the sale or realisation are treated as the income of the purchaser or person on whose behalf the right is otherwise realised. (HMRC will contest any losses claimed in transactions entered into before 20 January 2006. See Explanatory Notes to Finance (No 2) Bill 2006.)

[*ICTA 1988, s 730; FA 1996, Sch 7 para 23; FA 2002, Sch 25 para 51; ITTOIA 2005, Sch 1 para 300; F(No 2)A 2005, Sch 7 para 2; FA 2006, Sch 6 para 2; CTA 2009, Sch 1 para 214*].

Simon's Taxes. See D9.302–D9.309.

Transfers of rights to receive annual payments

[5.4] These provisions have been repealed with effect from 22 April 2009 by *FA 2009*, and replaced by the provisions in *FA 2009, Sch 25* — see **5.11** transfers of income streams, below.

If, on or after **16 March 2005**, a person sells or transfers the right to receive an annual payment and the consideration for the sale etc. would not otherwise be chargeable to tax, the seller or transferor is liable to corporation tax under

Schedule D, Case III, for the accounting period in which the sale etc. occurs, on an amount equal to the market value of the right to receive the annual payment. However, this does not apply in the case of a life annuity or pension annuity (both as defined) or (before 6 April 2007) an annual payment to which *ICTA 1988, s 347A* applies (annual payments that are not charges on income) or, for income tax purposes from 6 April 2005, an annual payment in respect of which, by virtue of *ITTOIA 2005, s 727* (annual payments made by individuals and arising in the UK), no liability to income tax arises under *ITTOIA 2005, Pt 5* (miscellaneous income).

These provisions also apply in relation to parts of annual payments as they apply in relation to the whole of an annual payment. The transfer of *all* the rights under an agreement to receive annual payments is also within the scope of the provisions.

Previously, there were provisions to counter the tax advantage of selling or transferring certain annuities, but those provisions do not apply in relation to any such sale or transfer on or after 2 December 2004 — see **5.3** above.

[*ICTA 1988, s 775A; F(No 2)A 2005, Sch 7 para 4; CTA 2009, Sch 1 para 230*].

Repos — new regime

[5.5] The current regime for sale and repurchase transactions ('repos'), introduced by *FA 2007*, applies to arrangements which come into force on or after 1 October 2007. The intention is that an arrangement involving the sale and repurchase of securities, which is, in substance, equivalent to a loan secured by those securities, is in effect treated as a loan for corporation tax purposes (except to the extent of charging corporation tax on capital gains on quasi-repos). [*CTA 2009, s 542(1), Sch 1 para 725(2), Sch 2 para 78(1); FA 2007, Sch 13 para 1(1); SI 2007 No 2483*].

It was announced on 9 February 2010 that legislation would be introduced to 'clarify' one aspect of the repo legislation (i.e. the new measures would be retrospective to 1 October 2007). The statement was issued persuant to a challenge that manufactured payments received by companies may not have to be taken into account for tax purposes if the securities to which they relate are not recognised on the companies' balance sheets. This could result in companies seeking to deduct for tax purposes manufactured payments that have contributed to their accounting profits. *FA 2010, s 45* introduces such legislation and clarifies that manufactured payments received by companies in the course of certain repo transactions must be taken into account in calculating profits chargeable to corporation tax if they are taken into account in computing accounting profits. This section of *FA 2010* made changes to both *FA 2007, Sch 13 para 4* and also the successor provisions in *CTA 2009, s 550* and applies retrospectively to repos entered into on or after 1 October 2007.

For HMRC guidance, see HMRC Corporate Finance Manual CFM17500 onwards.

For the purpose of this legislation, repos are analysed into debtor repos, debtor quasi-repos, creditor repos and creditor quasi-repos.

Debtor repos

A borrower company has a '*debtor repo*' if all the following conditions are met:

(a) under an 'arrangement', it receives an advance (in the form of money or an asset);
(b) under generally accepted accounting practice ('GAAP') it is obliged to bring a financial liability in respect of the advance into its accounts for the period in which it is received;
(c) under the arrangement, it sells 'securities' to the lender (i.e. the person making the advance) at any time;
(d) the arrangement confers a right, or imposes an obligation, on it to buy back the same or similar securities at any later time;
(e) under GAAP this repurchase would extinguish the financial liability in its accounts.

Where (c), (d) or (e) above are not satisfied, the repo legislation may still apply if the repo falls within the definition of a '*debtor quasi-repo*'.

For a '*debtor quasi-repo*' to exist, conditions (a) and (b) above must apply, in addition to the following:

(i) under the arrangement or any other arrangements, the borrower company or any other person sells any securities at any time;
(ii) either:
    (A) under the arrangement in (i) above, the borrower company is obliged to or has a right to buy any securities at any later time; or
    (B) the arrangement provides for such a right or obligation to apply to any other person and also provides for the borrower company to provide money or an asset to enable that other person to purchase the securities or provides for the discharge of any liability to the borrower company to enable the other person to make the purchase; and
(iii) under GAAP the financial liability in the accounts of the borrower company in respect of the advance would be extinguished by the purchase of securities, receipt of the asset or discharge of the liability in (ii) above.

In (a)–(e) and (i)–(iii) above, references to the borrower company include a 'firm' (i.e. a trading partnership) of which it is a member.

In the case of 'redemption arrangements' (see below), conditions (d) and (ii)(A) above are satisfied by a right or obligation for the borrower to receive an amount equivalent to the proceeds of redemption of the securities, and conditions (e) and (iii) above can be satisfied if a payment of an amount equivalent to those proceeds would, under GAAP, extinguish the financial liability in respect of the advance in the borrower's accounts.

[*CTA 2009, ss 548, 549; FA 2007, Sch 13 paras 2, 3; SI 2007 No 2485, Regs 1, 3*].

Where a company has a debtor repo or debtor quasi-repo or has a liability which is discharged under a 'relevant arrangement', it is treated for corporation tax purposes as if, throughout the period for which the arrangement was in force, it continued to hold the securities which it initially sold. No amount (such as interest or dividends) is charged to corporation tax as a result of this rule unless it is, in accordance with GAAP, recognised, or taken into account in calculating amounts which are recognised, in determining the company's profit or loss for any period. The company is also treated as not receiving in the period for which the arrangement was in force any amounts representative of income payable in respect of those securities (i.e. manufactured payments). Special rules apply where the securities initially sold are overseas securities. A '*relevant arrangement*' for this purpose is one which meets conditions (i) and (ii) above and of which a main purpose is the obtaining of a tax advantage.

Under the loan relationship rules (see **54 LOAN RELATIONSHIPS**), where the borrower company has a debtor repo or debtor quasi-repo, the advance is treated as a money debt of the borrower company (or, if the company is a member of a firm which receives the advance, of the firm) due to the person who originally bought the securities. The arrangement is treated, in the case of the company, as a transaction for the lending of money from which the debt is treated as arising. Any amount which is recorded under GAAP as a finance charge in respect of the advance in the company's (or the firm's) accounts is treated for corporation tax purposes and for the purposes of the deduction of income tax at source as interest paid at the earlier of the date on which the repurchase takes place or when it becomes apparent that there will be no repurchase.

FA 2010, s 45(1) amends *FA 2007, Sch 13 para 4* by inserting additional wording into the rules dealing with manufactured payments received by companies to put beyond doubt that where such amounts are received in the course of a repo, those payments must be taken into account for tax to the extent they are taken into account in accordance with generally accepted accounting practice (GAAP).

[*CTA 2009, ss 550, 551; FA 2007, Sch 13 paras 4, 5; FA 2010, s 45*].

The disposal and repurchase under a debtor repo are ignored for capital gains purposes if the borrower company is the only person with the right or obligation under the arrangement to make the repurchase. If, at a time after the initial sale, it becomes apparent that the repurchase will not take place or the accounting condition ceases to be met, the borrower company is treated for capital gains purposes as disposing of the securities at market value at that time. If this rule has applied as a result of the accounting condition ceasing to be met, any subsequent purchase of securities under the arrangement is not then ignored for capital gains purposes. For this purpose, the accounting condition ceases to be met if, in accordance with GAAP, the borrower's accounts for a period after that in which the advance is received, do not show a financial liability in respect of the advance (otherwise than because of repurchase of the securities).

In the case of a redemption arrangement, the borrower company is treated for capital gains purposes as having disposed of the securities on the date of redemption and for an amount equal to the proceeds of redemption.

[*FA 2007, Sch 13 para 6; SI 2007 No 2485, Reg 4*].

Creditor repos

'Creditor repos' look at the repo transaction from the point of view of the lender i.e. the party initially purchasing the securities forming the subject of the repo. A lender company has a '*creditor repo*' where:

(I) under an arrangement, the borrowing company receives from the lender money or other assets ('the advance');
(II) under GAAP the lender's accounts for the period in which the advance is made show a financial asset in respect of the advance;
(III) under the arrangement the borrower sells securities at any time to the lender;
(IV) under the arrangement, there is a right or obligation on the lender to sell the securities or similar securities at any later time;
(V) under GAAP the subsequent sale would extinguish the financial asset in the lender's accounts.

A '*creditor quasi-repo*' exists where (I) and (II) above are satisfied and, in addition:

(A) under that or any other arrangement a person sells securities to the lender or another person;
(B) either:
   (a) under the arrangement in (I) above, the lender is obliged to or has a right to sell any securities at any later time, or
   (b) the arrangement provides for such a right or obligation to apply to any other person and also provides for the lender to provide money, securities or other assets to enable that other person to sell the securities or provides for the discharge of any liability to the lender to enable the other person to make the sale; and
(C) under GAAP, the financial asset in the accounts of the lender company would be extinguished by the sale of securities, receipt of an asset or the discharge of a liability under the arrangement.

For the purposes of (I)–(V) and (A)–(C) above, the term '*lender*' includes a firm of which the lender is a member.

In the case of 'redemption arrangements' (see below), conditions (IV) and (B)(a) above are satisfied by a right or obligation for the lender to pay the proceeds of redemption of the securities, and conditions (V) and (C) above can be satisfied if a payment of an amount equivalent to those proceeds would, under GAAP, extinguish the financial asset in respect of the advance in the lender's accounts.

[*CTA 2009, ss 543, 544; FA 2007, Sch 13 paras 7, 8; SI 2007 No 2485, Regs 1, 3*].

Where a lender company has a creditor repo or a creditor quasi-repo, it is treated for corporation tax purposes on income as not holding the securities that are initially sold throughout the period for which the arrangement is in force. The company is also treated as not paying in that period any amounts representative of income payable in respect of those securities (i.e. manufactured payments). An amount (such as interest or dividends) or a manufactured payment is not ignored for corporation tax purposes as a result of these rules, however, if it is, in accordance with GAAP, recognised, or taken into account in calculating amounts which are recognised, in determining the company's profit or loss for any period (but this does not affect the question whether (apart from this rule) a manufactured payment can be deducted in calculating income or total profits for corporation tax purposes).

Under the loan relationship rules (see **54 LOAN RELATIONSHIPS**), where a lender company has a creditor repo or creditor quasi-repo, the advance is treated as a money debt owed to the lender (or a firm of which it is a member) by the person who initially sold the securities and the arrangement is treated, in the case of the company, as a transaction for the lending of money from which the debt is treated as arising. Any amount which is recorded under GAAP as a finance return in respect of the advance in the company's (or the firm's) accounts is treated for corporation tax purposes as interest received at the earlier of the date on which the repurchase takes place or when it becomes apparent that there will be no repurchase.

[*CTA 2009, ss 545, 546; FA 2007, Sch 13 paras 9, 10*].

The purchase and resale under a creditor repo are ignored for capital gains purposes if the lender (or firm of which it is a member) is the only person with the right or obligation under the arrangement to make the resale. If, at a time after the initial purchase, it becomes apparent that the resale will not take place or the accounting condition ceases to be met, the lender company is treated for capital gains purposes as acquiring the securities at market value at that time. If this rule has applied as a result of the accounting condition ceasing to be met, any subsequent sale of securities under the arrangement is not then ignored for capital gains purposes. For this purpose, the accounting condition ceases to be met if, in accordance with GAAP, the lender's accounts for a period after that in which the advance is made, do not show a financial asset in respect of the advance (otherwise than because of resale of the securities).

In the case of a redemption arrangement, the lender company is treated for capital gains purposes as having acquired the securities on the date of redemption and for an amount equal to the redemption proceeds.

[*FA 2007, Sch 13 para 11; SI 2007 No 2485, Reg 4*].

Anti-avoidance

Where, under an arrangement:

- a person receives an advance, in money or assets, from a company or a firm of which the company is a member;
- the company does not have a creditor repo or creditor quasi-repo under the arrangement but, on the 'applicable accounting assumption', would have one;
- the arrangement is intended to provide a return ('*quasi-interest*') which equates to interest on an investment; and

- the purpose or one of the main purposes of the arrangement is the realisation of a tax advantage,

the company is treated as having a creditor repo and the quasi-interest is treated as interest receivable. The '*applicable accounting assumption*' is that, under GAAP, the accounts of the company (or firm) for the period in which an advance is made, show the advance as a financial asset.

[*CTA 2009, s 547; FA 2007, Sch 13 para 12*].

Non-standard repos and redemption arrangements

The above provisions can be amended by regulations to apply, with modifications, to 'non-standard repos' or cases where 'redemption arrangements' are involved. There is a '*non-standard repo*' where:

(i) a company has a repo;
(ii) securities have been sold under the arrangement for the repo; and
(iii) one of the following is met:
  (A) the securities, or similar or other securities, are not subsequently repurchased under the repo;
  (B) under the arrangement, different or additional securities are to be substituted for or included with those which are to represent the securities originally sold;
  (C) provision is made for securities not to be so treated as included.

'*Redemption arrangements*' are involved where:

(1) arrangements, corresponding to those under a repo, are made for securities to be redeemed in the period after their sale; and
(2) a person has a right or obligation at a later time in respect of the benefits resulting from redemption.

[*CTA 2009, ss 554, 555; FA 2007, Sch 13 para 15*].

SI 2007 No 2485 contains regulations regarding redemption arrangements (for which, see above) and non-standard repos. The non-standard repo provisions apply where condition (iii)(B) above applies and securities ('*substituted securities*') are substituted for other securities. For the purposes of the definition of a debtor repo or creditor repo above and of the rules requiring a sale and subsequent purchase, or a purchase and subsequent sale, to be ignored for capital gains purposes, references to 'securities or similar securities' are to include substituted securities. [*SI 2007 No 2485, Reg 2*].

Definitions

For the purpose of the new repo regime:

'A*rrangement*' includes any legally binding, or non-enforceable agreement or understanding and an arrangement is in force from the date of sale of the securities until the earlier of the date of the relevant repurchase and when it becomes apparent that repurchase will not take place. It is immaterial whether or not a right or obligation to buy securities is subject to any conditions.

'*Securities*' are shares, stocks or other securities issued by the UK government, any UK public or local authority or any UK-resident company or other resident body, or 'overseas securities'. '*Overseas securities*' are shares, stocks or other securities issued by a government or public or local authority of a non-UK territory or by any other body or persons which is not UK-resident. Securities are similar if they entitle the holders to the same rights against the same persons as to capital, interest and dividends and provide the same remedies for the enforcement of those rights. Differences in total nominal amounts, form and the way in which they can be transferred are ignored for this purpose.

Reference to a person receiving an asset includes that person deriving the value of, or otherwise deriving any benefit from, an asset, whether directly or indirectly.

Where a person is acting as nominee in a purchase or sale of securities, or with regard to a right or obligation to buy securities, then the purchase or sale of the rights is treated as made by the person for whom he is acting.

In determining whether an amount is recorded in accounts as a financial liability or asset in respect of an advance, it is assumed that the period of account in which the advance is received or made ended immediately after it was received or made.

Where accounts are not drawn up in accordance with GAAP, for the purposes of taxing repo transactions it is assumed that they were so drawn up.

[*CTA 2009, ss 552, 553, 556–559; FA 2007, Sch 13 para 14*].

Legislation was introduced by *FA 2010, Sch 19* which amended *CTA 2009, ss 465A, 701A*, to respond to changes to be made to IAS 39 (and corresponding changes likely to be made to FRS 26 in the UK), which will affect the tax treatment of loans, derivatives and sale and repurchase agreements. The legislation provides a power to amend the loan relationships and derivative contracts rules through regulations. Any amendments will be limited to those necessary to ensure the rules continue to operate fairly and efficiently where companies adopt the modified accounting standards.

Regulations made under this power will generally have effect for accounting periods beginning on or after 1 January in the year in which the regulations are made.

The changes to IAS 39 that are being proposed by the International Accounting Standards Board (IASB) cover four main areas: the way that financial instruments are classified and measured for accounting purposes; when they are recognised on the balance sheet; how impairment losses are quantified; and how hedging arrangements should be accounted for.

See further **54 LOAN RELATIONSHIPS** and **30 DERIVATIVE CONTRACT LEGISLATION.**

[*FA 2010, s 62 Sch 19; CTA 2009, ss 465A, 701A*].

Repos — old regime

[5.6] This regime ceased to apply to transactions on or after 1 October 2007, the date the new repo regime (see **5.5** above) took effect.

Subject to the exception mentioned below, where a person (the 'original owner') has transferred securities to another person (the 'interim holder') under an agreement to sell them entered into on or after 1 May 1995 and before a date to be determined by statutory instrument, and the original owner or a **CONNECTED PERSON (25)** is required to buy them back under, or in consequence of the exercise of an option (whether a put or a call option) acquired under, the same or a 'related' agreement at a different price, the difference between the sale and repurchase price is treated for income and corporation tax purposes as a payment of interest which:

(a) where the repurchase price is greater than the sale price, is made by the repurchaser on a deemed loan from the interim holder of an amount equal to the sale price; and
(b) otherwise is made by the interim holder on a deemed loan from the repurchaser of an amount equal to the repurchase price.

In either case, the deemed interest is treated for income and corporation tax purposes as becoming due when the repurchase price becomes due and, accordingly, as paid when that price is paid. For income and corporation tax purposes (other than those of the current provisions and *ICTA 1988, ss 737A, 737C* — see **5.9** below), and for the purposes of *TCGA 1992* (unless *TCGA 1992, s 263A*, see below, applies), the repurchase price is treated as reduced by the amount of the deemed interest where (a) above applies or as increased by that amount where (b) above applies. For the purposes of *ICTA 1988, s 209(2)(d)* (interest treated as a distribution, see **31.5 DISTRIBUTIONS**) any deemed interest payment under (a) above is deemed to be interest in respect of securities issued by the repurchaser and held by the interim holder; for 2003/04 and earlier years, this also applied for the purposes of *ICTA 1988, s 209(2)(da)* (now repealed).

The repurchase price, in a case where *ICTA 1988, s 737A* (see **5.9** below) applies (or would apply were it in force in relation to the securities in question) is that price which is or would be applicable by virtue of *ICTA 1988, s 737C(3)(b), (9)* or *(11)(c)*. For agreements made after 8 April 2003, in cases involving the exercise of an option (whether a put or a call option), the sale price must be adjusted for any consideration given for the option (except where such consideration is brought into account under the derivative contracts provisions for companies (see **30 DERIVATIVE CONTRACTS LEGISLATION**).

For corporation tax purposes, deemed interest under these provisions is treated as payable under a loan relationship, in respect of which the debits and credits to be brought into account are trading or non-trading according to the extent to which the repurchase is in the course of activities forming an integral part of the company's trade. Any foreign exchange gain or loss arising on the original sale price over the period of the sale and repurchase agreement is to be similarly treated under the loan relationship rules; *ICTA 1988, s 730BB*, which applies to agreements made after 8 April 2003, is designed to provide clarity of treatment for such gains and losses. See **54 LOAN RELATIONSHIPS**.

For purposes other than corporation tax, HMRC generally accept that the deemed interest is short interest, except where it is clear that the transaction was entered into as a substitute for long term finance, and in particular where it is clear finance was arranged in this way specifically to avoid deduction of tax at source. (HMRC Tax Bulletin December 1995 p 266).

The exception referred to above disapplies these provisions (unless regulations under *ICTA 1988, s 737E*; see **5.9** below, otherwise provide) if the agreement(s) in question are non-arm's length agreements, or if all the benefits and risks arising from fluctuations in the market value of the securities accrue to, or fall on, the interim holder.

The Treasury has power to make regulations providing for an amount of deemed interest under these provisions to fall within the exemptions for pension business of insurance companies, for exempt approved pension schemes or superannuation funds or certain other such schemes, or for funds held for personal pension schemes or retirement annuity contracts. See *SI 1995 No 3036* (as amended).

See also *SI 1998 No 3177, Regs 16, 17* (as amended) as regards securities which, prior to their repurchase, are converted from currencies of States which have adopted the euro into euros.

[*ICTA 1988, ss 730A, 730BB; FA 2002, Sch 25 para 52; FA 2003, Sch 38 paras 5, 10–12, 16, 20, 21(2)(3); FA 2004, Sch 10 para 78, Sch 42 Pt 2(2); SI 2007 No 2485*].

Where the above provisions apply (or would apply were the sale and repurchase price different), the acquisition and disposal by the interim holder, and (except where the repurchaser is or may be different from the original owner) the disposal and acquisition (as repurchaser) by the original owner, are disregarded for capital gains tax purposes. This does not, however, apply:

(A) where the repurchase price falls to be computed by reference to provisions of *ICTA 1988, s 737C* (see **5.9** below) which are not in force in relation to the securities when the repurchase price becomes due; or

(B) if the agreement(s) in question are non-arm's length agreements, or if all the benefits or risks arising from fluctuations in the market value of the securities accrue to, or fall on, the interim holder; or

(C) in relation to any disposal or acquisition of qualifying corporate bonds (see Tolley's Capital Gains Tax under Qualifying Corporate Bonds) where the securities disposed of by the original owner, or those acquired by him or another person as repurchaser, are not such bonds.

See also *SI 1998 No 3177, Regs 14–18* (as amended) as regards conversions of securities from currencies of States which have adopted the euro into euros.

[*TCGA 1992, s 263A; FA 2007, Sch 14 paras 4, 5, 7, 8, 12*].

Interpretation

For the above purposes, the following apply.

(i) Agreements are 'related' if entered into in pursuance of the same arrangement.

(ii) References to buying back securities include buying back similar securities, and 'repurchase' is construed accordingly. Securities are 'similar' if they give entitlement to the same rights against the same persons as to capital, interest and dividends, and to the same enforcement remedies. Where securities are converted from the currency of a State which has adopted the euro into euros (a '*euroconversion*'), the new securities are treated as 'similar' (see *SI 1998 No 3177, Regs 3, 14*).

(iii) 'Securities' had the same meaning as in *ICTA 1988, s 737A* (see **5.9** below).

[*ICTA 1988, s 730B; FA 2007, Sch 14 para 7*].

The Treasury has broad powers to make regulations providing for the above provisions to apply with modifications (including exceptions and omissions) in relation to cases involving any arrangement for the sale and repurchase of securities where the obligation to repurchase is not performed, or the repurchase option not exercised, or where provision is made by or under any agreement:

(a) for different or additional securities to be treated as, or included with, securities which, for the purposes of the repurchase, are to represent securities transferred in pursuance of the original sale; or

(b) for any securities to be treated as not included with securities which, for repurchase purposes, are to represent securities transferred in pursuance of the original sale; or

(c) for the sale or repurchase price to be determined or varied wholly or partly by reference to fluctuations, in the period from the making of the agreement for the original sale, in the value of securities transferred in pursuance of that sale, or in the value of securities treated as representing those securities, or for any person to be required, where there are such fluctuations, to make any payment in the course of that period and before the repurchase price becomes due.

Regulations may also make such modifications in relation to cases where corresponding arrangements are made by an agreement, or by related agreements, in relation to securities which are to be redeemed in the period after their sale, those arrangements being such that the vendor (or a person connected with him), instead of being required to repurchase the securities or acquiring an option to do so, is granted rights in respect of the benefits that will accrue from their redemption. They may also provide for modifications in relation to cases involving any arrangement for the sale and repurchase of securities in relation to which there is an agreement which would not have been entered into by persons dealing at arm's length.

[*ICTA 1988, s 737E; FA 2003, Sch 38 paras 8, 13, 21(2); FA 2007, Sch 14, para 8*].

Although of wider general application, these provisions were introduced as part of a package of measures designed to facilitate an open market in the sale and repurchase of gilt-edged securities ('gilt repos'). See also **5.9** below, **46.11 INCOME TAX IN RELATION TO A COMPANY**. For a brief overview of the changes made by *FA 2003* to the tax provisions on sale and repurchase agreements, see HMRC Tax Bulletin August 2003 pp 1052, 1053.

Revenue and Customs Comrs v D'Arcy [2008] STC 1329 was found in favour of an individual, who had entered into a repo transaction to reduce her tax liability. The case turned on whether a person could cease to be entitled to securities before she had become entitled to them. It was found that she could not.

DCC Holdings (UK) Ltd v Revenue and Customs Comrs [2010] STC 80, CA, was also decided in favour of the taxpayer.

Simon's Taxes. See **D9.1015–D9.1018.**

Securities held for one month or less

[5.7] The following provisions are repealed where the purchase by the first buyer falls on or after 1 April 2008.

Prior to that date, they apply to income received on securities held for one month or less, or held for more than one month but not more than six months *and either* purchase or sale was not at current market price *or* agreement regarding sale was made at, or before, purchase (see *ICTA 1988, s 731(3)*). [*ICTA 1988, ss 731–735; FA 2007, Sch 14 para 6; FA 2008, s 66*].

Effects as regards various classes of recipient are as in (a) to (d) below.

In ascertaining whether the securities are held for more than one or six months, sale under prior option is regarded as a sale at option date [*ICTA 1988, s 731(4)*], and a sale of 'similar securities' is taken into account. [*ICTA 1988, s 731(5)(10)*]. A purchase or sale effected as a direct result of the exercise of a 'qualifying option' (broadly, a traded or financial option within *TCGA 1992, s 144(8)*) is treated as being at current market price (and so excluded from these provisions) if the first buyer acquired, or became subject to, the option on arm's length terms. [*ICTA 1988, s 731(4A)–(4C)*].

The '*appropriate amount*' is the pre-acquisition portion of the dividend, interest etc. calculated from last 'ex-div' day. [*ICTA 1988, s 735(3)*]. See *ICTA 1988, s 735(4)* if there is no last 'ex-div' day. In the case of (a) below, the portion taken is of net interest after deduction of tax and the amounts of actual dividends. In the case of (b), (c) and (d) below, it is the gross amount of interest and the amounts of dividends plus related tax credits. In all cases, special rules apply in relation to foreign income dividends within *ICTA 1988, Pt VI, Ch VA* (prior to their abolition after 5 April 1999). [*ICTA 1988, ss 731(9)–(9B), 735(1)(2); F(No 2)A 1997, Sch 6 para 14*].

These provisions do not apply where the purchaser is required by the purchase agreement to make to the vendor, before his re-sale of the securities, a payment representative of the interest, or where the purchaser is treated by *ICTA 1988, s 737A(5)* (see **5.9** below) as being required to make a payment representative of a dividend on them. [*ICTA 1988, s 731(2A)*].

Where there is a 'repo agreement' in relation to any securities, neither their purchase or repurchase, nor their sale or sale back, is taken into account under these provisions. The securities purchased by the original owner from the person to whom securities were sold under the agreement (the '*interim holder*') are instead treated under these provisions as the same securities, and as purchased at the same time, as his original holding. This does not, however, apply if the agreement(s) under which the arrangements are made are on non-arm's length terms, or if the interim holder bears any of the benefits or risks of market value fluctuations before the securities are repurchased. There is a '*repo agreement*' if the original owner sells the securities in pursuance of an agreement, and under the same or a related agreement either:

- is required to buy back the securities, either as a result of a straightforward obligation or the interim holder's exercise of an option; or
- acquires an option to buy them back which he subsequently exercises; or
- is entitled to receive from the interim holder an amount equal to any redemption proceeds.

See *ICTA 1988, s 730B* (under **5.6** above) for 'related agreements', 'securities' and the extended meaning of 'buying back' securities. From a date to be determined by statutory instrument, the references to 'related agreements' and the extended meaning of 'buying back' securities is in *ICTA 1988, s 731(2F),(2G); FA 2007, Sch 14 para 6*.

[*ICTA 1988, s 731(2B)–(2F); FA 2003, Sch 38 paras 6, 21(2); FA 2007, Sch 14 para 6*].

(a) **Share dealers.** The net 'appropriate amount' of the interest etc. is treated for all tax purposes as a reduction of the purchase price. This treatment does not apply if the interest falls to be taken into account in computing the first buyer's Schedule D, Case I or II profits (see **70.64 TRADE PROFITS — INCOME AND SPECIFIC TRADES**). It also does not apply to overseas securities if *ICTA 1988, s 732(4)* is complied with. [*ICTA 1988, s 732*].
See *ICTA 1988, s 731(7)(8)* regarding change in ownership, or commencement, of trade.
HMRC may make regulations by statutory instrument, effective from a day to be appointed therein, imposing conditions for the exclusion of market makers to apply, and making appropriate provision in regard to recognised investment exchanges other than the Stock Exchange. This power is repealed with effect from 1 April 2008. [*ICTA 1988, s 738(1); FA 2008, s 66*].

(b) **Person entitled to exemption from tax.** Exemption does not extend to the gross 'appropriate amount' of the interest etc. and any annual payment out of the interest etc. is treated as not paid out of taxed income. [*ICTA 1988, s 733*].

(c) **Traders other than share dealers** (whether company or not). The gross 'appropriate amount' of the interest etc. and tax thereon is ignored in calculating loss repayment claim under *ICTA 1988, s 380* or *s 381* (see Tolley's Income Tax under Losses). [*ICTA 1988, s 734(1)*].

(d) **Companies other than share dealers.** The gross 'appropriate amount' and tax thereon is ignored for tax purposes except that net equivalent is treated as capital distribution in calculation of chargeable gain. [*ICTA 1988, s 734(2)*].

'Securities' are defined to exclude those within the accrued income scheme (see Tolley's Income Tax under Accrued Income Scheme). [*ICTA 1988, s 731(9)*].

Simon's Taxes. See **D9.2.**

'Dividend stripping'

[5.8] The dividend stripping provisions are repealed with effect for distributions made on or after 1 April 2008.

Before that date, the 'dividend stripping' provisions of *ICTA 1988, s 736* apply where a **share dealing company holds shares or securities amounting to 10% of all the shares etc. of that class** issued by a company resident in the UK and, as a result of one or more distributions made in respect of that holding, the value at any accounting date (but see below) of any share or security comprised therein is materially reduced below its value at the time when it was acquired. So much of that reduction as is attributable to the distribution or distributions (the '*relevant reduction*'), is treated as a trading receipt of the dealing company when the holding is realised (or appropriated so that it is no longer dealing stock). Until such realisation or appropriation, the relevant reduction is treated as an addition to the value of the holding for valuation purposes.

Where only part of the holding is realised or appropriated, a proportionate part of the relevant reduction is brought into account as a trading receipt.

A reduction in value immediately before realisation or appropriation (as well as at an accounting date) is within this section.

Securities, shares, etc. having different entitlements or obligations are treated as being of different classes, and a company's holdings of different classes are treated as separate holdings. Subject to this, however, a company has a 10% holding in a particular class if the aggregate of its own holdings and those of persons connected with it (see **25 CONNECTED PERSONS**) amounts to 10%.

A company is a *dealing company* in relation to a holding if a profit on its sale would be taken into account in computing the company's trading profits.

Where *section 736* applies in relation to a distribution to which *ICTA 1988, s 732* (reduction in price of shares purchased by dealers) also applies, any reduction, under that section, in the purchase price of the shares is to be adjusted 'as seems appropriate to HMRC'.

[*ICTA 1988, s 736; FA 2008, s 66*].

Simon's Taxes. See **D9.1101.**

'Manufactured' payments

[5.9] The provisions of *CTA 2010, Pt 17, Chs 2–4* apply to certain arrangements for the transfer of securities under which a person is required to pay to the other party an amount representing a dividend.

The intention of the provisions is for both payer and recipient of the amount in question to be in the same position, for tax purposes, as if the payment had in fact been a dividend. See *CTA 2010, ss 783–787, 791–795* for the detailed mechanism by which this is achieved in each case.

The provisions apply separately to 'manufactured dividends' and 'manufactured overseas dividends'.

For this purpose, a '*manufactured dividend*' is an amount representative of a dividend on shares in a UK resident company which is required to be paid by one person to another under an arrangement between them for the transfer of the shares. [*CTA 2010, ss 782, 814(5); ICTA 1988, Sch 23A para 2(1)*].

A '*manufactured overseas dividend*' is an amount representative of an 'overseas dividend on overseas securities which is required to be paid by one person to another under an arrangement between them for the transfer of the securities'. An '*overseas dividend*' is defined as any interest, dividend or other annual payment payable in respect of overseas securities. '*Overseas securities*' are shares, stocks or other securities (including any loan stock or similar) issued by a government, local authority or other public authority of a territory outside the UK or any other non-UK resident body of persons.

[*CTA 2010, ss 790, 814(2)(3)(6); ICTA 1988, Sch 23A paras 1(1), 4(1)*].

See **54.78 LOAN RELATIONSHIPS** for the corporation tax treatment of manufactured interest. See also Tolley's Income Tax under Anti-Avoidance for the application of the manufactured dividends provisions to individuals and trusts. With regard to recent case law on anti-avoidance and individuals in this area, see *N Barnes v HMRC* (TC00972) [2011] UKFTT 95 (TC), [2011] SFTD 443. In this case an individual (B) entered into a complex scheme, devised by a firm of tax advisers, which sought to take advantage of a perceived mismatch between the accrued income legislation and the legislation governing the taxation of manufactured interest payments (*ICTA 1988, Sch 23A* re-enacted in *ITA 2007, ss 578–580*). He submitted a return claiming a deduction of £1,200,000. HMRC disallowed the claim, and B appealed. The First-Tier Tribunal reviewed the evidence in detail and dismissed the appeal. Judge Kempster observed that it was accepted that each and every one of the transactions upon which the taxpayer relied was part of a preordained series and that series had no purpose other than tax avoidance. He held that 'the end result taking each transaction step-by-step and applying a purposive construction to the relevant legislation is that (B) obtains the relief/allowance under *ss 713* and *714* (so that little or none of the £1.2 million interest receipt is chargeable on him) but any deduction under *Schedule 23A* is restricted to the amount (if any) of the interest after the relief/allowance under *ss 713* and *714*'. Accordingly B was not entitled to the deduction which he had claimed.

Guidance notes to help people in the financial markets to comply with the tax rules on manufactured payments are available on HMRC's website. See http://www.hmrc.gov.uk/mpgn/index.htm.

Manufactured payments exceeding or less than underlying payments

There are provisions to counteract any artificial allocation of a payment between the manufactured dividend or interest and any associated stock lending fee. The provisions apply both to manufactured dividends and manufactured overseas dividends where their amount exceeds the underlying payments, and to manufactured overseas dividends which are less than the underlying payments. [*CTA 2010, ss 796–798; ICTA 1988, Sch 23A para 7*].

Arrangements with an unallowable purpose

There are also provisions which deny tax relief for manufactured payments made by a company in pursuance of any arrangements that have an unallowable purpose, to the extent the relief is attributable (on a just and reasonable basis) to the unallowable purpose. Arrangements have an unallowable purpose where the purposes for which the company is a party to them include a purpose which is not among the business or other commercial purposes of the company.

[*CTA 2010, ss 799–801; ICTA 1988, Sch 23A para 7A*].

Treasury regulations

The Treasury may make 'dividend manufacturing regulations' for the purposes of these provisions which may, *inter alia*, extend the circumstances in which they may apply. [*CTA 2010, ss 802–804; ICTA 1988, Sch 23A para 8*]. See *SI 1993 No 2004* (as amended), *SI 1996 No 1826* (as amended), *SI 2007 No 2484* and *SI 2007 No 2487*.

Before 21 July 2008, the Treasury had power to make regulations providing for any manufactured payment to be treated as falling within the exemptions for pension business of insurance companies, for exempt approved pension schemes or superannuation funds or certain other such schemes, or for funds held for personal pension schemes or retirement annuity contracts. [*ICTA 1988, s 737D; FA 2008, Sch 17 para 35(1)*]. See *SI 1995 No 3036* (as amended) as regards payments.

Tax credits in respect of manufactured dividends

CTA 2010, Pt 17 Ch 5 introduces provisions with regard to manufactured dividends, tax credits, stock lending and certain repo transactions.

The legislation denies tax credits otherwise afforded under *CTA 2010, s 1109*, which provides for tax credits for certain recipients of exempt qualifying distributions (under the new distribution regime applicable from 1 July 2009).

The tax credits are denied with regard to a qualifying distribution made in respect of UK shares further to which a manufactured dividend payment is made with regard to the following transactions:

(i) stock lending arrangements in respect of UK shares;
(ii) creditor repo or creditor quasi-repo in respect of UK shares;
(iii) debtor repo or debtor quasi-repo in respect of UK shares.

'*Stock lending arrangement*' is defined within *CTA 2010, s 805* and refers to arrangements in respect of securities where a person has transferred the UK shares or UK securities to another person otherwise than by way of sale and under the arrangement the transferee is required to transfer the shares or securities back to the lender otherwise than by way of sale.

'*Creditor repo*', '*creditor quasi-repo*', '*debtor repo*', '*debtor quasi-repo*', are all as defined in *CTA 2009, Pt 6 Ch 10*, see **5.5** repos — new regime, above.

Stock lending arrangements

Special rules apply to stock lending arrangements. Where, under such an arrangement, interest or dividends on stock transferred is paid to a person other than the lender, with no provision for the lender to receive a payment representative of that interest or dividend, the legislation applies as if the borrower were required to make, and did make, such a payment on the date the interest or dividend it represents is paid. The borrower is not, however, entitled to any deduction in computing profits or gains for corporation tax purposes or against total profits. The treatment is different for overseas dividends paid before 22 April 2009.

[*CTA 2010, s 812, Sch 2 para 92; ICTA 1988, s 736B*].

Deemed interest on cash collateral. The following provisions were **repealed** with effect from 22 April 2009 on the introduction of the disguised interest provisions at **5.10** below.

Where a borrower is treated under the above provisions as paying an amount representative of interest on any securities ('*the relevant securities*') and also an amount ('*cash collateral*') is payable (under any arrangement) to the lender to secure the discharge of the requirement to transfer the relevant securities back to the lender, the borrower is treated as receiving an amount of interest payable in respect of the cash collateral.

Subject to the repeal of this provision noted above, this applies to stock-lending arrangements **made on or after 5 December 2005** which are designed to produce a return to the borrower which equates in substance to a return on an investment of money at interest and where the main purpose, or one of the main purposes, of the arrangement is the avoidance of tax.

Where an arrangement was entered into before 5 December 2005, the interest will be treated as received on any cash collateral computed from the date there is any substitution of securities under that arrangement. The interest is treated as payable on a money debt and taxable under the loan relationship rules, the credit to be brought into account using an amortised cost basis of accounting (see **54.3 LOAN RELATIONSHIPS**). (The measure effectively applies where a company swaps taxable interest on cash for income on the relevant securities such as dividends, the income being either not taxed or less highly taxed.)

The interest is to be computed at a commercial rate of interest and treated as if it is received on the date of the transfer back of the relevant securities and payable in respect of the period beginning with the date on which they were transferred to the borrower and ending with the return date. It is reduced by any interest which the borrower actually receives in respect of the collateral for the period. Where the stock-lending arrangement is made after 21 March 2006, it is payable on the amount of the cash collateral at the return date but if the amount of collateral varies at any time on or before the return date, it is taken as payable on the highest amount. Reference to the transfer of securities back has the same meaning as under *TCGA 1992, s 263B* (as amended by *FA 2007, Sch 14 para 12*) and if it becomes apparent that the borrower will not transfer any securities back, the borrower is treated as transferring them back on the date it becomes so apparent.

[*ICTA 1988, s 736C; FA 2006, Sch 6 para 3; CTA 2009, Sch 1 para 215; FA 2009, Sch 24 para 8(a)*].

Quasi-stock lending arrangements and quasi-cash collateral. The following provisions were **repealed** with effect from 22 April 2009 on the introduction of the disguised interest provisions at **5.10** below.

Subject to the above, where an arrangement, made after 21 March 2006, is not a stock-lending arrangement it is treated as if it were a stock-lending arrangement if, under the arrangement (a '*quasi-stock lending arrangement*'), a lender transfers securities to a borrower and a requirement is imposed on the borrower or other person to transfer any or all of the securities, or other property, back to the lender or other person. In relation to arrangements made after 21 March 2006, cash collateral (see above) under either stock-lending or quasi-stock lending arrangements includes '*quasi-cash collateral*' which is any money payable or any property transferable to or for the benefit of the lender under such an arrangement, or a person connected with that lender (see **25 CONNECTED PERSONS**), for the purpose of securing the discharge of the requirement to transfer any or all of the securities or other property back to the lender or other person. The amount of quasi-cash collateral relating to property other than money is determined by reference to its market value.

Where a quasi-stock lending arrangement involving cash collateral (see above) is designed to provide a tax advantage for a person other than the borrower, that other person is collateral. In any quasi-stock lending arrangement involving cash collateral, the references in *ICTA 1988, s 736C* (above) are widened such that a cash collateral payable to or for the benefit of a lender includes it being payable to a person connected with the lender, a return designed to benefit a borrower includes a return designed to benefit any other person and a transfer back of any or all securities or other property by the borrower to the lender includes such transfers by any person to the lender or any other person.

[*ICTA 1988, s 736D; FA 2006, Sch 6 para 4; FA 2009, Sch 24 para 8(a)*].

Sale and repurchase of securities

The following provisions were repealed for arrangements coming into force on or after 1 October 2007 (when the new regime for repos is introduced — see **5.5** above).

ICTA 1988, Sch 23A above and the dividend manufacturing regulations thereunder apply where a person (the 'transferor') agrees to sell any 'securities', and under the same agreement (or under another agreement under the same arrangement) he (or a person connected with him (within *ICTA 1988, s 839*)) is required to buy back the same or 'similar' securities (whether as a result of a straightforward obligation or the exercise of a put option), or acquires an option (which he subsequently exercises) to buy them back, and either of the following two sets of conditions is fulfilled. The first set of conditions is that:

(a) as a result of the transaction, a dividend on the securities is receivable by a person other than the transferor;
(b) the agreement(s) do not contain a requirement for an amount representative of the dividend to be paid to the transferor on or before the date the repurchase price becomes due; and
(c) it is reasonable to assume that the repurchase price took into account the fact that the dividend was receivable by a person other than the transferor.

The second set of conditions (relevant only to agreements made after 8 April 2003) is that:

(a) a dividend which becomes payable in respect of the securities is receivable otherwise than by the transferor;
(b) the transferor (or a person connected with him) is required to make a payment representative of the dividend;
(c) there is no requirement for a person to pay to the transferor an amount representative of the dividend on or before the date the repurchase price becomes due; and
(d) it is reasonable to assume that, in arriving at the repurchase price, account was taken of these circumstances.

The provisions apply (subject to below) as if the person from whom the securities are repurchased (or from whom the transferor has the right to repurchase them) were required under the arrangements for transfer of the securities to pay the transferor an amount representative of the dividend mentioned in (a) above, and a payment were accordingly made by that person to the transferor on the date the repurchase price of the securities becomes due. For the corporation tax treatment of such deemed payments, see **54.78 LOAN RELATIONSHIPS.**

In relation to agreements made after 26 June 2006 to sell securities, where the borrower is not the person to whom the transferor agreed to sell the securities, the borrower is not entitled to any deduction in computing profits or gains for income or corporation tax purposes or against total income or total profits, and no amount for which a deduction is so prohibited may be surrendered by way of group relief. This provision is intended to reverse the effect of the decision by the High Court (confirming the Special Commissioners' decision) in *Revenue and Customs Comrs v Bank of Ireland Britain Holdings Ltd* [2008] STC 398, CA. The case involved a repo agreement between an Irish bank, its UK subsidiary and a Cayman Islands company in which a deemed interest payment from the Cayman Islands company to the Irish bank was treated as arising under *ICTA 1988, s 730A(2)* (which was non-taxable in the UK) and a corresponding deemed dividend payment by the UK company to the Irish bank was treated as arising under *ICTA 1988, s 737A(5)* which was tax deductible. The Court of Appeal upheld the decision of the High Court in favour of the bank. The case is unusual in that the repo involved three parties.

'*Securities*' means UK equities and securities and overseas securities (as under *ICTA 1988, Sch 23A para 1(1)*), and securities are *'similar'* if they carry the same entitlement as to capital and interest (or dividends) and the same enforcement remedies. Where securities are converted from the currency of a State which has adopted the euro into euros (a '*euroconversion*'), the new securities are treated as 'similar' (see *SI 1998 No 3177, Regs 3, 14*). References in *ICTA 1988, s 737A* to dividends are, in the case of UK securities, to periodical payments of interest, and in the case of overseas securities, to overseas dividends (as under *ICTA 1988, Sch 23A para 1(1)*).

There are special provisions (in *ICTA 1988, s 737C*) for determining the amount of the deemed manufactured dividend or interest for these purposes, and for a corresponding adjustment to be made for tax purposes to the repurchase price of the securities.

Special provisions apply to dividends that represent payments of distributions of the tax-exempt profits of a REIT or principal company of a REIT group (see **53.11 INVESTMENT TRUSTS**).

See also *SI 1998 No 3177, Reg 17* as regards securities which, prior to their repurchase, are converted from currencies of States which have adopted the euro into euros.

[*ICTA 1988, ss 737A, 737B, 737C; FA 2006, s 139(5), Sch 6 para 5; FA 2007, Sch 14*].

Until 1 October 2007, see *SI 1995 No 3220* as regards such modification in cases where securities are redeemed rather than being repurchased, and where other securities are substituted for those originally transferred.

See also **5.7** above and, as regards application of accrued income scheme to such securities, Tolley's Income Tax under Accrued Income Scheme.

Simon's Taxes. See **D9.7**.

Disguised interest

[5.10] *FA 2009* introduces *Part 6 Chapters 2A* and *6A* into *CTA 2009*. This legislation is part of the new principles-based approach to anti-avoidance legislation and it replaces and repeals certain existing anti-avoidance provisions.

On or after 22 April 2009, the loan relationship rules in *CTA 2009, Pt 5* (**54 LOAN RELATIONSHIPS**), are to apply as if the company became a party to an arrangement where the income from it is 'economically equivalent to interest', subject to the exclusions below. An amortised cost basis of accounting must be used to determine the return. Where two or more persons are entitled to the return, the income is attributed to the companies on a just and reasonable basis. Exchange gains and losses are included in arriving at the return. Where a return is charged under these provisions, it is not also brought into account for corporation tax for other purposes (e.g. capital gains).

Exclusions

There are three categories:

(a) where the return is taxable as income under other provisions e.g. loan relationship, derivative contract or intangible asset rules, or would be so taxable were not for exceptions;

(b) where there is no tax avoidance purpose and it is not reasonable to assume that the purpose, or one of the main purposes, of the company's participation in the arrangement is the 'obtaining of a relevant tax advantage'. However, a company not within this provision may make an irrevocable election for the disguised interest provisions to apply. No election may be made if two or more persons are entitled to the return (see above). The election must be made before income arises from the arrangement. It might be advantageous to make an election if otherwise the return would be taxed under other provisions at a higher rate;

(c) where the return arises only on relevant shares (i.e. the return on the shares only reflects an increase in fair value of the shares) through the 'relevant period'.

Definitions

For the above purposes, terms are defined as follows:

An '*arrangement*' is widely drawn to include any agreement, understanding, scheme, transaction or series of transactions (whether or not legally enforceable). It does not include a finance lease.

A return is '*economically equivalent to interest*' only if it is reasonable to assume that if the return is determined by reference to the time value of money, it is reasonably comparable to a commercial rate of interest (taking account of the circumstances) and when the company becomes party to the arrangements or, if later, when income arises, there is no practical likelihood that it will cease unless the creditor defaults (e.g. due to insolvency).

'*Obtaining a relevant tax advantage*' is arranging for more favourable corporation tax treatment of the return than would have applied had it been brought into account under these provisions.

'*Fair value*' is the amount which the company would obtain from a knowledgeable and willing purchaser of the shares dealing at arm's length. There is an increase in the fair value even if the amount is used to pay a dividend or other distribution on the shares.

'*Relevant shares*' are shares which are fully paid up shares of a 'relevant company' throughout the relevant period or shares, not in a relevant company, which would be accounted for as a liability under generally accepted accounting practice and which produce a return economically equivalent to interest for the holding company.

A '*relevant company*' is a subsidiary of a company and that company and the holding company are connected, or the company is a relevant joint venture company (as defined) or it is a relevant controlled foreign company (as defined).

A '*relevant period*' begins with the later of the date the company enters the arrangement and the date the income is produced and ends with the earlier of the end of the relevant accounting period when the holding company leaves the arrangement and the income ceases.

Shares accounted for as liabilities

Where, on or after 22 April 2009, the following applies:

- the issuing company would account for a shareholding as a liability;

- the return on the share is 'economically equivalent to interest' (see above);
- the issuing company and the investing company are not connected;
- the share is not treated as a right under a creditor relationship of the investing company because of *CTA 2009, s 490*;
- the investing company holds the share for an 'unallowable purpose' but this does not apply if, in an accounting period, the investing company is an excluded controlled foreign company,

the shares are treated as if they were loan relationships so far as both the investing and issuing companies are concerned. A number of excepted shares are provided for, see *CTA 2009, s 521D*. Where shares come within the shares accounted for as liabilities regime or stop being within it, the investing company is treated as disposing and reacquiring the holding immediately before the scheme applies or ceases to apply for its notional carrying value at that time.

Definitions of terms used above are as follows.

An '*excepted share*' is a share issued as part of a public issue, other than to persons connected with the company and where less than 10% of the shares in that issue are held by the investing company or persons connected with it. The definition also encompasses chains of share issues between associated companies within seven days of a public issue. Companies are associated if they are within the same group for group relief purposes. See **39.3 GROUP RELIEF**.

An '*unallowable purpose*' is where the investing company's main purpose, or one of the main purposes, in holding the shares is to 'obtain a relevant tax advantage'. An election similar to that in (b) above may be made.

To '*obtain a relevant tax advantage*' means to arrange for the return on the investment to be received in such a way that it is more favourably treated for corporation tax than it would have been if taxed as, or brought into account for tax as, income of the investing company.

An '*excluded controlled foreign company*' is an investing company whose chargeable profits for the accounting period are to be apportioned under *ICTA 1988, s 752* or they are not apportioned as *ICTA 1988, s 748(1)* applies (being legislation on controlled foreign companies).

'*Notional carrying value*' is the value at which it would have been carried in the investing company's accounts had they been prepared to the date immediately before *CTA 2009, s 521B* began to or ceased to apply.

Transitional provisions are contained in *FA 2009, Sch 26 paras 13–16*.

[*FA 2009, s 48, Sch 24*].

Transfers of income streams

[5.11] With effect for transfers on or after 22 April 2009, a principles-based provision applies to tax lump sums received for the transfer of an income stream (i.e. a right to receive income) in the same way as the income would have been taxed. The provision applies where the income stream (which would have been charged to, or brought into account in calculating profits for the purposes of, corporation tax) is sold without the asset from which the income derives.

A sale and repurchase agreement is not regarded as the sale of an asset and is therefore within the provision. The provision also applies where the transfer of the income stream is a consequence of the transfer of all rights under an agreement for annual payments.

The amount of the consideration or market value (where consideration is substantially less than market value) for the transfer is treated as the transferor's income for corporation tax in the same way and to the same extent as if the company had received the income stream i.e. as if no transfer had taken place.

The income is treated as arising either when recognised under generally accepted practice, or, where market value is substituted for consideration, at the time it would have been so recognised if full market value had been received. If at any time it becomes reasonable to assume that the income would not be so treated as arising in an accounting period, it is treated as arising immediately before that time.

Exceptions

The above provision does not apply if the deemed income is otherwise charged to tax as income of the transferor, brought into account in calculating its profits or under *CAA 2001*. It also does not apply where the consideration for the transfer is an advance within the factoring of income provisions at **5.15** below.

The following transfers are treated as transfers of an asset and therefore outside the provision:

- the transfer of all or part of an interest in a partnership, provided either that the company's share in the partnership property and profits and losses does reduce or that tax avoidance is not a main purpose of the transfer;
- the grant, surrender or renunciation of a lease of land;
- the disposal of an interest in an oil licence;
- the grant or disposal of an interest in intellectual property which constitutes a pre-*FA 2002* asset; and
- any transactions which are to be treated as transfers of assets under a Treasury order.

[*CTA 2010, ss 752–757, Sch 2 para 86; FA 2009, s 49, Sch 25 paras 1–6*].

Treatment of transferee

The following applies to a company which is the recipient of an income stream as a result of a transfer to which the above provision or the equivalent income tax provision (see *ITA 2007, Pt 13 Ch 5A*) applies.

The consideration paid by the company for the transfer is treated as a money debt owed to it by the person who is due to pay the income stream and the transfer itself is treated as a transaction for the lending of money from which that debt arises. The loan relationship rules (see **54 LOAN RELATIONSHIPS**) apply accordingly.

[*CTA 2009, ss 486F, 486G; FA 2009, Sch 25 para 8; CTA 2010, Sch 1 paras 613, 614*].

International movements of capital

[5.12] With effect for events taking place and transactions carried out on or after 1 July 2009, the need to obtain Treasury consent for certain transactions outside Europe and to provide certain information about certain transactions involving movement of capital within Europe is removed. Instead, reporting requirements are introduced. Transitional provisions provide that, for transactions or events before 1 October 2009, the report is required to be made before 1 April 2010.

Where a company is a 'reporting body' when a 'reportable event' takes place or when it carries out a 'reportable transaction' it must make a report to HMRC within six months of the transaction (subject to transitional rules above). *SI 2009 No 2192, para 3* lays down the information to be provided in the report. The purpose of the report is to enable HMRC to judge if there is a tax advantage to any person. Special provision is made for the situation where there is more than one UK parent company.

Reportable events and transactions are those carried out by a reporting body and having a value of over £100 million, not being an excluded transaction (see below) and fulfilling a number of other conditions (see *FA 2009, Sch 17, para 8(2)*). HMRC may, by statutory instrument, amend the transaction value or otherwise amend the way in which the value of an event or transactions is determined. In general, the transaction value is market value. For the detailed provisions see *SI 2009 No 2192, para 4*.

A transaction is excluded if it is carried out in the ordinary course of trade, all parties are resident in the same country when the transaction is carried out, it is within regulations laid down by HMRC, it is the granting of security to a bank for borrowings of a foreign subsidiary obtained in the ordinary course of business or it consists of a foreign subsidiary giving an insurance company security in the course of a transaction entered into by that subsidiary in the ordinary course of business of investment of its funds.

An arrangement may be entered into when there is more than one 'UK corporate parent' and one of them has been chosen as the 'nominated reporting body' for the purposes of these provisions. HMRC has laid down the requirements for such an arrangement in *SI 2009 No 2192, para 6*.

A failure to report a transaction will give rise to a penalty (under *TMA 1970, s 98*) of £300 plus £60 per day of default.

Definitions

'*Reporting body*' is a UK resident company and one of the following conditions is met:

(A) the company is not controlled by a non-UK resident company;
(B) it is controlled by a non-UK resident company and no other relevant UK company is controlled by that parent;
(C) the company is controlled by a non-resident company as are one or more other UK parent companies are controlled by the foreign parent and the company is not party to an arrangement (see below);
(D) the company is controlled by non-resident company as are one or more other UK parent companies and the company is party to arrangement (see below) in respect of which it is the nominated reporting body.

A '*UK corporate parent*' is a UK resident company which controls one or more non-UK companies.

'*Control*' means the person's power to manage the company in accordance with that person's wishes, whether by a shareholding, voting or other powers (e.g. in the articles of association). Two or more persons may be taken together to have control. In a partnership, right to more than 50% of the assets or income is treated as control.

Guidance for the new provisions can be found in the International Manual, at INTM700000.

[*FA 2009, s 37, Sch 17; SI 2009 No 2192*].

Under the new legislation, some transactions which were covered by General Consents under the old provisions, will now have to be reported.

With effect for events taking place and transactions entered into on or after 1 July 2009, the following provisions no longer apply.

The pre-2009 regime

Before that date, consent had to be obtained from the Treasury for a body corporate resident in the UK:

(a) to cause or permit a non-resident body corporate over which it has 'control' to create or issue any share or debenture; or
(b) to transfer, or cause or permit to be transferred, to any person any share or debenture of a non-resident body corporate over which it has 'control' (or a beneficial interest in such share or debenture), if the resident body has an interest in such share or debenture. [*ICTA 1988, s 765(1)(c)(d)*].

'*Control*' was the power to secure that the affairs of a body corporate are conducted in accordance with the wishes of the resident body, whether by shareholding, voting power or powers given by Articles of Association etc., and whether directly or through another body corporate. If the non-resident body would be a partnership if resident in the UK, the resident body has control if it is entitled to more than half of the income or assets of the non-resident body. [*ICTA 1988, ss 767(5), 840*].

Exemptions applied as follows.

(i) The giving by a non-resident body corporate to its bankers of any security for moneys due or to become due from one to the other by reason of a transaction entered into between them in the normal course of the latter's business as bankers (see (a) above). [*ICTA 1988, s 765(2)*].

(ii) The giving by a non-resident body corporate to an 'insurance company' of any security for moneys due or to become due from one to the other by reason of a transaction entered into between them in the ordinary course of the latter's business by way of investment of its 'funds' (see (a) above). [*ICTA 1988, s 765(3)*].

(iii) For this purpose '*insurance company*' means a body corporate lawfully carrying on business as an insurer, and '*funds*' means the funds held by it in connection with that business. [*ICTA 1988, s 767(5)*].

(iv) The transfer of shares to qualify a person to act as a director (exempted from (b) above). [*ICTA 1988, s 765(1)(d)*].

(v) Neither (a) nor (b) above applies to a transaction which is a movement of capital within *Directive No 88/361/EEC, Article 1* (which includes such movements within the European Economic Area). Where but for this exemption a transaction would be unlawful (in particular, where it is not within the general consents), the UK resident company must:

 (A) within six months of the transaction give to HMRC such information relating to the transaction or to persons connected with it as HMRC may by regulation require (see *SI 1990 No 1671*); and

 (B) give to HMRC such further particulars as HMRC may by notice require, within 60 days.

 Penalties of up to £3,000 (and £600 per day for continued failure) could have been imposed under *TMA 1970, s 98* for failure to comply with the above requirements. [*ICTA 1988, s 765A; SI 1990 No 1671*].

 HMRC Statement of Practice, SP 2/92 (as revised) set out the views of the Treasury and HMRC where there may be doubt as to whether a transaction is a movement of capital to which *Article 1* relates, and gives guidance on the procedure for making a report as required under (A) above. See also HMRC Company Taxation Manual, CTM34490.

Granting of consent

The Treasury either gave a general consent or confined it to specified transactions of, or relating to, a specified body corporate ('special' consent). Conditions could be imposed in either case and a general consent may be revoked. [*ICTA 1988, s 765(4)*].

The Treasury was also empowered to give general consents (and see HMRC Company Taxation Manual, CTM34490 as regards the application in practice of their requirements). See also CTM34470 for the definitions of 'resident group', 'overseas group' and 'territorial group' in the General Consents.

Penalties

Any person who knowingly and actively participated in an offence under this section was liable to imprisonment for two years or to a fine of £10,000 or to both. If the offender was a body corporate, the maximum fine is £10,000 or three times the amount of tax attributable to the income, profits or gains (including chargeable gains) arising in the three years immediately preceding the commission of the offence, whichever was the greater. [*ICTA 1988, s 766(1)(3)*].

Proceedings under this section could not be instituted in England or Wales without the consent of the Attorney-General, or in Northern Ireland without the consent of the Attorney-General for Northern Ireland. In any proceedings against a director (or purported director) of the resident body corporate, he was assumed to be a party to any act of that body, unless he proved that it was done without his consent or connivance, and to have known that such an act would result in an offence under this section, unless he proved the contrary. [*ICTA 1988, s 766(2)(4)*].

See **60 PENALTIES.**

Company becoming non-resident. See **65.8, 65.9 RESIDENCE.**

Simon's Taxes. See **D6.502–D6.509.**

Transfer pricing

[5.13] *TIOPA 2010, Pt 4, ss 146 et seq*, formerly *ICTA 1988, Sch 28AA*, imposes a charge to eliminate a tax advantage gained where transactions are not carried out at arm's length prices.

The scope of the transfer pricing rules were extended by *FA 2004, ss 30–37, Sch 5*, with effect for accounting periods beginning on or after 1 April 2004, to include domestic transactions between UK parties. At the same time, the thin capitalisation rules under *ICTA 1988, s 209(2)(da)(8A)–(8F)* (see **31.6 DISTRIBUTIONS**) were repealed and subsumed within the transfer pricing regime.

See **72 TRANSFER PRICING.**

Certain dealing and non-dealing companies

[5.14] The provisions of *ICTA 1988, s 774* (as amended by *CTA 2009, Sch 1 para 225*) apply if a company dealing in securities, land or buildings is entitled to a deduction in computing its profits for a payment made to, or for depreciation of a right against, an associated company which does not deal in shares etc.

Where the amount of the payment or depreciation is not brought into account in computing the profits or gains of the non-dealing company, the non-dealing company is charged to corporation tax on an amount equal to such deduction as miscellaneous income, previously under *Sch D, Case VI*.

If the non-dealing company carries on a trade, the amount may be charged as part of its normal trading income, if the company so elects. If it carries on a number of trades, the amount may be allotted to whichever trade the non-dealing company chooses.

A payment made in respect of abortive expenditure of a non-dealing company carrying on (or formed to carry on) a trade is excluded.

The amount is deemed to have been received on the last day of the dealing company's accounting period.

Prior to *FA 2009* HMRC had powers under *s 774(5)* to require information of any person who may have incurred liability under this section. With effect from 13 August 2009 this subsection has been repealed. HMRC's information gathering powers under the *FA 2008, Sch 36* regime are in point and are outlined further at **43 HMRC INVESTIGATORY POWERS** (at **43.3**).

[*ICTA 1988, s 774; ITTOIA 2005, Sch 1 para 310; CTA 2009, Sch 1 para 225; FA 2009, Sch 47; CTA 2010, s 1177, Sch 1 para 103*].

Simon's Taxes. See **D7.401**.

Factoring of income receipts etc.

[5.15] The provisions described below are intended to counter, from **6 June 2006**, the situation in which a person enters into financing arrangements that equate in substance to his taking out a loan but which are structured in such a way as to effectively give him tax relief for repayment of principal as well as for finance charges.

Say, for example, a borrower (B) has the opportunity to take out a loan of £50,000, under which B would repay the loan to the lender (L) over five years together with total interest of £5,000. Tax relief might be available for the £5,000 interest but not for the repayment of the £50,000 principal. As an alternative, B transfers to L for £50,000 an asset that is fully expected to produce income of £55,000 over the next five years, at the end of which the asset will be transferred back to B for nothing. L receives £55,000 for an outlay of £50,000. B then claims that the transfer of the asset to L either gives rise only to a chargeable gain (which may be relatively small due to high base cost and available reliefs) or is not taxable at all, and that he is not chargeable on the income of £55,000 which is received not by him but by L. B effectively obtains tax relief on £55,000 (less any CGT payable).

Sometimes, instead of the borrower forgoing income, the arrangements generate a tax deduction for the borrower. Say B grants a long lease of freehold property to L for a premium of £50,000. L then grants a five-year sub-lease back to B at a rent of £11,000 per year. The arrangements will provide for the benefits of ownership to revert to B at the end of the five years. Again, L receives £55,000 for an outlay of £50,000. B obtains tax relief for rent payments of £55,000. For transactions entered into before 6 June 2006, this type of scheme may have been countered by the rent factoring legislation at *ICTA 1988, ss 43A–43G* (see Tolley's Corporation Tax 2010–2011, or earlier, at **62.16 PROPERTY INCOME**) (repealed by *FA 2006, Sch 6 para 1* as a consequence of the introduction of the wider provisions described below).

With effect for disposals on or after 6 March 2007 (whenever the arrangements were entered into) the legislation is amended to bring within it re-financing arrangements where an existing loan agreement is replaced by a structured financing arrangement and arrangements where the asset transferred does not produce an income flow immediately. However, where the arrangements were entered into prior to 6 March 2007, only amounts arising on or after that date are liable under these provisions.

Commencement and transitional

Except where otherwise indicated, the following provisions apply in relation to any arrangements whenever made. However, in relation to any arrangements made before 6 June 2006, any amount otherwise falling to be brought into account as a result of these provisions in determining taxable income is to be brought into account only if the amount arises on or after that date. In relation to the second type of arrangement described above, the following provisions do not apply in relation to a pre-6 June 2006 arrangement in so far as the (now repealed) rent factoring legislation applies to that arrangement (see 2010/11 version of Tolley's Corporation Tax (or earlier) at **62.16 PROPERTY INCOME**).

Type 1 finance arrangements: arrangements involving disposals of assets

The anti-avoidance provisions below apply where there is a '*type 1 finance arrangement*'. Such an arrangement exists where:

(i) under the arrangement a person ('the borrower') receives from another person ('the lender') any money or other asset ('the advance') in any period;
(ii) in accordance with generally accepted accounting practice (GAAP) the accounts of the borrower for that period record a financial liability in respect of the advance;
(iii) the borrower (or a person connected with the borrower) disposes of an asset ('the security') under the arrangement to or for the benefit of the lender (or a person connected with the lender);
(iv) the lender (or a person connected with the lender) is entitled under the arrangement to payments in respect of the security; and
(v) in accordance with GAAP those payments reduce the amount of the financial liability recorded in the borrower's accounts.

For the purposes of (ii) above, for transactions on or after 19 July 2007, it has to be assumed that the period in which the advance is received ended immediately after the receipt of the advance.

For these purposes, the provisions at **25 CONNECTED PERSONS** applies to determine whether persons are connected, except that the lender cannot be regarded as a person connected with the borrower and *vice versa*. If the borrower is a partnership (of which a company is a member), references above to accounts are to the accounts of any member of the partnership as well as the partnership itself. References to accounts also include consolidated group accounts of a group of which the borrower is a member. 'Arrangement' is widely defined for the purposes of these provisions to include any agreement or understanding (whether or not legally enforceable). 'Payments' is also widely defined to include any obtaining of value or benefit. Where it is not the case, these provisions apply as if the accounts in question had been prepared in accordance with GAAP.

Effect of provisions

If an arrangement is a type 1 finance arrangement as above, then:

(a) if, as a result of the arrangement, an amount of otherwise chargeable income would escape tax in the hands of the borrower (or a person connected with the borrower), it does not escape tax;

(b) if, as a result of the arrangement, any amount which would otherwise fall to be taken into account in computing income of the borrower (or a person connected with the borrower) for corporation tax purposes, is not so brought into account, that amount shall be so brought into account; and

(c) if, as a result of the arrangement, the borrower (or a person connected with the borrower) becomes entitled to a deduction in computing any taxable income, or a deduction from total profits, there shall be no such entitlement.

If the borrower is a partnership (of which a company is a member), the above have effect by reference to any member of the partnership.

If the arrangement would not in any event have had any of the effects in (a)–(c) above the payments in (iv) above are treated for corporation tax purposes as income of the borrower, provided that the borrower is a company within the charge to corporation tax or a partnership of which a member is such a company. This applies whether or not the payments are also taxable income of another person.

The advance is treated as a money debt owed by the borrower company and the arrangement as a loan relationship of the company (as a debtor relationship). Any amount which, in accordance with GAAP, is recorded in the accounts as a finance charge in respect of the advance is to be treated as interest payable under that relationship. The intended effect is to place the borrower in the same position for tax purposes as if he had taken out a loan instead of entering into the structured finance arrangement. (If the borrower is a partnership, it is the partnership itself that is deemed to be paying interest, even if the finance charge appears in the accounts of a member.) The time at which this notional interest is to be treated as having been paid depends on the timing of the payments made to the lender in respect of the security; each such payment is treated as if it were part repayment of principal and part interest.

[*CTA 2010, ss 758–762, 774–776; ICTA 1988, ss 774A, 774B, 774G; FA 2006, Sch 6 para 6; FA 2007, Sch 5 para 3; CTA 2009, Sch 1 para 226*].

See also below under Exceptions.

Simon's Taxes. See **D1.793.**

Arrangements involving partnership changes

More complex types of arrangement might be involved where the borrower (B) is a partnership. For example, B might transfer an income-producing asset ('the security') to a partnership of which it is a member. The lender (L) then joins the partnership for a capital contribution of £50,000 in return for the right to receive partnership profits of £55,000 over the next five years but no profits beyond that period. B claims not to be taxable on the £55,000 of partnership profits diverted to L. In another scenario, an established partnership may already hold an income-producing asset and the above steps then follow without the need for the initial transfer of an asset by B. In this case, the members of the partnership whose profits are thereby reduced claim not to be taxable on the partnership profits diverted to L.

There are similar anti-avoidance provisions to catch this type of arrangement. See now *CTA 2010, ss 763–769*. The provisions apply to 'Type 2 finance arrangements', where the security is transferred to the partnership under the arrangement and 'Type 3 finance arrangements' where the security is already held by the partnership. Broadly, the partnership change is treated for tax purposes as if it had not occurred. For this purpose, the partnership change might be the admission of the lender as a partner or a change in profit-sharing ratios affecting the lender's share. The provisions are widely drawn so as also to catch changes made indirectly and/or involving a person connected with the lender. Again, as above, there is provision for a finance charge to be treated as if it were interest paid on a loan.

See also below under Exceptions.

Simon's Taxes. See **D1.794**.

Exceptions

The above provisions are disapplied if the whole of the advance under the finance arrangement falls to be brought into account in determining the taxable income of a 'relevant person'. (However, the effect of the legislation relating to the rent factoring of leases of plant or machinery at **5.26** below, where relevant, is to be ignored for this purpose for transfers before 22 April 2009.) This includes a case where the advance falls to be brought into account as a disposal receipt or proceeds from a balancing or disposal event, for capital allowances purposes, but not if a balancing charge results and would fall to be restricted under the capital allowances legislation. In respect of amounts brought into account before 6 March 2007 under arrangements made before that date, a '*relevant person*' was a person otherwise affected by the provisions. On or after 6 March 2007, a '*relevant person*' means the borrower under the arrangements or a person connected with the borrower or, if the borrower is a partnership, another partner.

The provisions are also disapplied if the whole of the advance under the structured finance arrangement is a debtor relationship of the borrower under the loan relationship rules or would be if the borrower were a company within the charge to corporation tax. A debtor relationship in this case does not include a non-lending relationship within *CTA 2009, Pt 6 Ch 2* (see **54.3 LOAN RELATIONSHIPS**).

There are also exclusions in cases where certain other statutory provisions do in any case result in the arrangement being taxed as intended. These include, for example, certain repo and stock lending arrangements (see **5.6** above and **54.71 LOAN RELATIONSHIPS**), **ALTERNATIVE FINANCE ARRANGEMENTS** (**4**) and certain sale and finance leaseback transactions. The Treasury have power to specify further exclusions by statutory instrument, and any such exclusions may be given retrospective effect.

[*CTA 2010, ss 770–773, Sch 2 para 88; ICTA 1988, ss 774E, 774F; FA 2006, Sch 6 para 6; FA 2007, Sch 5 paras 5–7; FA 2008, Sch 20 para 12; CTA 2009, Sch 1 paras 228, 229; FA 2009, Sch 25 para 9*].

Miscellaneous

The lease premium rules at *CTA 2009, ss 217–221; ICTA 1988, s 34* (see **62.9 PROPERTY INCOME**) are disapplied where the grant of the lease constitutes the disposal of an asset for the purposes of these provisions.

In any case where, in relation to arrangements made before 6 June 2006, a person is treated as being a party to a loan relationship as a result of these provisions, a period of account is to be treated for loan relationship purposes as beginning on that date. For those purposes, the loan relationship is to be treated as being entered into for a consideration equal to the 'notional carrying value' of the liability representing the relationship.

The '*notional carrying value*' for this purpose is the amount that would have been the carrying value (as defined in *FA 1996, Sch 9 para 19A*) in the accounts if a period of account had ended immediately before 6 June 2006. (See **54.8 LOAN RELATIONSHIPS**.) In any case where, in relation to arrangements made before 6 March 2007, a person is treated as a party to a loan relationship as a result of the amendments made with effect from that date, a period of account is to be treated for loan relationship purposes as beginning on that date and the consideration for the transactions is the notional carrying value of the liability.

[*FA 2006, Sch 6 para 6; FA 2007, Sch 5 para 7*].

See *TCGA 1992, s 263E* as regards the CGT consequences of structured finance arrangements.

Transactions in land

[5.16] A charge to corporation tax on income applies to certain gains from disposals of land. The charge applies where:

(a) any of the following apply:
  (i) the land (or any property deriving its value from the land) is acquired with the sole or main object of realising a gain from disposing of all or part of it; or
  (ii) the land is held as trading stock; or
  (iii) the land is developed with the sole or main object of realising a gain from disposing of all or part of it when developed;

(b) the gain is a gain of a capital nature obtained from the disposal of all or part of the land;

(c) all or part of the land is situated in the United Kingdom; and

(d) the gain is obtained (for himself or 'another person') by the person acquiring, holding or developing the land (or by any connected person within **25 CONNECTED PERSONS**) or a person party to, or concerned in, any arrangement or scheme to realise the gain indirectly or by a series of transactions.

The gain from the disposal (computed as below) is within the charge to corporation tax on income for the accounting period of the company concerned in which the gain is realised. (Before *CTA 2009* took effect, the gain was assessable under *Sch D, Case VI*, but that label is now removed.) The company to which the charge applies is usually the company that realises the gain. Where, however, all or part of the gain is derived from value provided directly or indirectly by another person which is a company or from an opportunity of realising a gain provided directly or indirectly by another person which is a company, that company is chargeable.

For the purposes of (a) above, '*property deriving its value from land*' includes any shareholding in a company, partnership interest, or interest in settled property, deriving its value, directly or indirectly, from land, and any option, consent or embargo affecting the disposition of land. See, however, the exemptions below.

For the purposes of (b) above, a gain is of a capital nature if it does not (apart from these provisions or the equivalent income tax provisions) fall to be included in any computation of income for tax purposes. Land is '*disposed of*' if, by any one or more transactions or by any arrangement or scheme (whether concerning the land or any property deriving its value therefrom), the property in, or control over, the land is effectively disposed of. See also under 'General' below.

For the purposes of (d) above, any number of transactions can be regarded as a single arrangement or scheme if a common purpose can be discerned in them or there is sufficient other evidence of a common purpose. If, for example by a premature sale, one person ('A') directly or indirectly transmits the opportunity of realising a gain to another person ('B'), A obtains B's gain for B. '*Another person*' may include a partnership or partners in a partnership, the trustees of settled property and personal representatives, and for this purpose these are regarded as persons distinct from the individuals or persons who are for the time being partners, trustees or personal representatives.

[*CTA 2010, ss 815, 816, 818–821, 825, 833; ICTA 1988, s 776(1)–(5)(8)(13)(14); CTA 2009, Sch 1 para 231*].

Note that the charge applies where all or part of the land is situated in the UK, regardless of whether or not the company is UK-resident.

See *Yuill v Wilson* (1980) 52 TC 674, HL, and its sequel *Yuill v Fletcher* (1984) 58 TC 145, CA; *Winterton v Edwards* (1979) 52 TC 655; and *Sugarwhite v Budd* (1988) 60 TC 679, CA. *Bona fide* transactions, not entered into with tax avoidance in view, may be caught by the legislation — see *Page v Lowther* (1983) 57 TC 199, CA.

For the date of the capital gain where instalments are involved, see *Yuill v Fletcher* (1984) 58 TC 145, CA.

Computation of gain

Gains are to be computed 'as is just and reasonable in the circumstances', allowance being given only for expenses attributable to the land disposed of. The following may be taken into account:

- if a leasehold interest is disposed of out of a freehold, the way in which trading profits are calculated in such a case; and
- any adjustments under *CTA 2009, s 136* (previously *ICTA 1988, s 99(2)(3)*) (see **70.62 TRADE PROFITS — INCOME AND SPECIFIC TRADES**) for tax on lease premiums.

Valuations are to be made as appropriate and any necessary apportionments of expenditure, receipts, consideration or other amounts are to be made on a just and reasonable basis.

[*CTA 2010, ss 822, 826; ICTA 1988, ss 776(6), 777(6); CTA 2009, Sch 1 para 231(3)*].

Where the computation of a gain in respect of the development of land (as under (a)(iii) above) is made on the footing that the land or property was appropriated as trading stock, that land etc., is also to be treated for purposes of corporation tax on chargeable gains (under *TCGA 1992, s 161*) as having been transferred to stock. [*TCGA 1992, s 161(6); ICTA 1988, s 777(11); CTA 2010, Sch 1 para 238*].

Priority

The above provisions apply subject to *ITTOIA 2005, Pt 5 Ch 5* (amounts treated as income of settler) and to any other provision treating income as belonging to a particular person. [*CTA 2010, s 817; ICTA 1988, s 777(10)*].

Exemptions

A gain on the disposal of *shares in a company holding the land as trading stock* (or a company owning, directly or indirectly, 90% of the ordinary share capital of such a company) is exempt from the above provisions *provided that* the company disposes of the land by normal trade and makes all possible profit from it. The exemption does not apply if the person obtaining the gain is only a party to, or concerned in, an arrangement or scheme to realise the gain indirectly or by a series of transactions. See *Chilcott v CIR* (1981) 55 TC 446.

Where the liability arises solely under (a)(iii) above, any part of the gain fairly attributable to a period *before the intention was made* to develop the land is excluded from the above provisions.

[*CTA 2010, ss 827, 828; ICTA 1988, s 776(7)(10)*].

Recovery of tax

Where a company is assessed to tax under the above provisions in respect of consideration received by another person, the company is entitled to recover the tax from that person. HMRC will, on request, supply a certificate of income in respect of which tax has been paid. If the company fails to pay the tax within six months of it becoming due and payable, HMRC can collect the tax from the other person. [*CTA 2010, ss 829, 830; ICTA 1988, s 777(8)*].

Clearance

The company who made or would make the gain may (if it considers that (a)(i) or (iii) above may apply), submit to HMRC particulars of any completed or proposed transactions. If the company does so HMRC must, within 30 days of receiving those particulars, notify the taxpayer whether or not they are satisfied that liability under these provisions does not arise. If HMRC are so satisfied the company is not liable to corporation tax on that gain under the provisions, provided that all material facts and considerations have been fully and accurately disclosed. [*CTA 2010, s 831(1)(2); ICTA 1988, s 776(11)*].

General

See *CTA 2010, s 823* (previously *ICTA 1988, s 777(2)(3)*) for provisions to prevent avoidance by the use of indirect means to transfer any property or right, or enhance or diminish its value, e.g., by sales at less, or more, than full consideration, assigning share capital or rights in a company or partnership or an interest in settled property, disposal on the winding-up of any company, partnership or trust, creation of an option, consent requirement or embargo etc.

For ascertaining whether, and to what extent, the value of any property or right is derived from any other property or right, value may be traced through any number of companies, partnerships and trusts, at each stage attributing property held by the company, partnership or trust to its shareholders etc., in such manner as is appropriate to the circumstances. [*CTA 2010, s 824; ICTA 1988, s 777(5)*].

Information powers

For the above purposes HMRC may require, under penalty, any person to supply them with any particulars which they may reasonably require, including particulars of:

- transactions etc., in which he acts, or acted, on behalf of others; and
- transactions etc., which in the opinion of HMRC should be investigated; and
- what part, if any, he has taken, or is taking, in specified transactions etc. (Under this heading a lawyer (i.e. a barrister, advocate, solicitor or other legal representative with whom communications could be subject to professional privilege) who has merely acted as professional adviser is not compelled to do more than state that he acted and give his client's name and address.)

[*CTA 2010, s 832; ICTA 1988, s 778*].

The transactions of which particulars are required need not be identified transactions (*Essex v CIR* (1980) 53 TC 720, CA).

Simon's Taxes. See **B5.235–B5.246.**

Land sold and leased back — payments connected with transferred land

[5.17] The consequences described below ensue where land (or any interest or estate in land) is transferred (by sale, lease, surrender or forfeiture of lease etc.) and, as a result of:

- a lease of the land, or any part of it, granted at the time of transfer or subsequently by the transferee to the transferor; or
- another transaction or transactions affecting the land or interest or estate,

the transferor, or a company associated (see below) with the transferor, becomes liable to make a payment of rent under a lease of the land or part of it (including any premium treated as rent — see **62.9**, **62.16 PROPERTY INCOME**), or any other payment connected with the land or part of it (whether it is a payment of rentcharge or under some other transaction), which would be allowable as a deduction:

- in computing trading profits; or
- in computing the profits of a UK property business; or
- (for accounting periods ending on or after 1 April 2009) in computing profits or income under any of the provisions listed at *CTA 2010, s 1173* (miscellaneous income) or in computing losses for which relief is available under *CTA 2010, s 91* (see **55.9 LOSSES**); or
- (for accounting periods ended before 1 April 2009) in computing profits or losses under Schedule D, Case VI; or
- under *CTA 2009, s 1219* (management expenses of a company's investment business — see **51.3 INVESTMENT COMPANIES AND INVESTMENT BUSINESS**) (previously as a management expense under *ICTA 1988, s 75*); or
- under *ICTA 1988, s 76* (expenses of insurance companies).

A transfer of an estate or interest in land includes:

(a) the granting of a lease or another transaction involving the creation of a new estate or interest in the land;
(b) the transfer of the lessee's interest under a lease by surrender or forfeiture of the lease; and
(c) a transaction or series of transactions affecting land or an estate or interest in land, such that some person is the owner (or one of the owners) before and after the transaction(s) but another person becomes or ceases to be one of the owners.

With regard to (c), a person is to be regarded as a transferor for the purposes of these provisions if the person is an owner before the transaction(s) and is not the sole owner afterwards.

The consequences are that the deduction for tax purposes in respect of the rent or other payment is limited to the 'commercial rent' of the land to which it relates for the period for which the payment is made. In fact, the position is judged on a cumulative basis.

For any accounting period, amount E (which may be nil) is the expense or total expenses to be brought, in accordance with generally accepted accounting practice (GAAP), into account in the period in respect of the payments made (excluding any just and reasonable portion which relates to services, tenant's rates, or the use of assets other than land). Take the amount of E for the current accounting period and for every previous accounting period ending on or after the date of the transfer. Subtract from the aggregate amount the total deductions given for every such previous accounting period. What remains is the cumulative unrelieved expenses for the current period, and it is this figure which is then compared to the commercial rent for the period and restricted if necessary.

The cumulative unrelieved expenses cannot, however, be carried forward to an accounting period beginning after the payments have ceased; no deduction is available under these provisions for any such expenses. Different rules apply where the payments fall to be relieved under *ICTA 1988, s 76* (expenses of insurance companies) (see *CTA 2010, ss 839–842*).

In the case of a lease, '*commercial rent*' means the open-market rent, at the time the actual lease was created, under a lease whose duration and maintenance/repair terms are the same as under the actual lease but stipulating a rent payable at uniform intervals at a uniform rate, or progressively increasing proportionately to any increases provided by the actual lease. For other transactions, it is the open market rent which would be payable under a tenant's repairing lease (as defined by *CTA 2010, s 845(3)*) for the period over which payments are to be made (subject to a maximum of 200 years).

In these provisions, 'lease', as well as having its normal meaning, includes (i) an underlease, sublease, tenancy or licence, (ii) an agreement for a lease, underlease, sublease, tenancy or licence, and (iii) in the case of land outside the UK, an interest corresponding to a lease. 'Rent' includes any payment under a lease.

For the purposes of these provisions, the following persons are associated with one another:

(i) the transferor in an 'affected transaction' and the transferor in another affected transaction, if the two persons are acting in concert or if the two transactions are in any way reciprocal;

(ii) any person who is an associate of either of the associated transferors in (i);

(iii) two or more bodies corporate if they participate in, or are incorporated for the purposes of, a scheme the reconstruction, or amalgamation, of a body corporate or bodies corporate.

In addition, persons are associated with one another if they are associates as defined in *CTA 2010, s 882* (see **5.21** below). In (i) above, an '*affected transaction*' is a transfer within these provisions or within the corresponding income tax provisions.

[*CTA 2010, ss 834–848; ICTA 1988, s 779; CTA 2009, Sch 1 para 232*].

Simon's Taxes. See B5.247.

Land sold and leased back — new lease of land after assignment or surrender

[5.18] In certain circumstances where a lease of land is assigned or surrendered and another lease is granted or assigned, consideration received for the assignment or surrender of the first lease is chargeable to tax as income and tax relief is allowed for rent under the other lease. These provisions apply where all of the following conditions are met:

(a) a company (L) is a lessee of land under a lease which has 50 years or less to run ('the original lease') and is entitled to corporation tax relief on the rent;
(b) L assigns the original lease to another person or surrenders it to the landlord, and the consideration for the assignment or surrender would not be taxable except as capital in L's hands;
(c) another lease ('the new lease') for a term of 15 years or less is granted, or assigned, to L (or to a person linked to L);
(d) the new lease comprises or includes all or part of the land which was the subject of the original lease; and
(e) neither L (nor a person linked to L) had, before 22 June 1971, a right enforceable at law or in equity to the grant of the new lease.

The reference in (a) to corporation tax relief is to any of the allowable deductions listed in **5.17** above. For the purposes of (c) and (e), a person is linked to L if he is a partner of L, an associate of L or an associate of a partner of L. Persons are associated with one another if they are associates as defined in *CTA 2010, s 882* (see **5.21** below).

Appropriate proportion

A proportion of the consideration mentioned in (b) above (the 'appropriate proportion') is taxed as income (and not treated as a capital receipt). If it is received by L in the course of a trade and the rent payable under the new lease is allowable as a deduction in calculating the profits or losses of a trade, profession or vocation for tax purposes, the appropriate proportion is treated as a receipt of the trade. If not, it is treated as being within the charge to corporation tax on income; for accounting periods ended before 1 April 2009, it was chargeable under Schedule D, Case VI. The '*appropriate proportion*' is the proportion of the consideration found by applying to it the formula:

$$\frac{16 - N}{15}$$

where:

N = the term of the new lease expressed in years (taking part of a year as an appropriate proportion of a year).

If the consideration is paid in instalments, the formula is applied to each instalment. If the term of the new lease is one year or less, the appropriate proportion of the consideration or instalment is the whole of it. If the property which is the subject of the new lease does not include all the property which was the subject of the original lease, the consideration must be reduced as is reasonable before applying the formula.

Deductions

Provided the rent under the new lease is payable by a company within the charge to corporation tax, all provisions of *CTA 2009* or *ICTA 1988* providing for deductions or allowances by way of corporation tax relief in respect of payments of rent apply in relation to the rent payable under the new lease.

Relevant definitions

In these provisions, 'lease', as well as having its normal meaning, includes (i) an agreement for a lease, and (ii) any tenancy, but does not include a mortgage.

'Rent' includes a payment by a tenant for work to maintain or repair leased land or premises which the lease does not require the tenant to carry out.

There are provisions (see *CTA 2010, ss 854–858*) whereby for the above purposes the term of the new lease is deemed to end (i) on an earlier date if the rent is reduced or (ii) if the lessor or lessee has power to determine the lease or the lessee has power to vary its terms, on the earliest date on which it can be so determined or varied.

Not all conditions met

If conditions (a)–(d) above are met but condition (e) is not (such that the above provisions do not apply), and the rent under the new lease is payable by a person within the charge to corporation tax:

- no part of the rent paid under the new lease is to be treated as a payment of capital, and
- all provisions of *CTA 2009* or *ICTA 1988* providing for deductions or allowances by way of corporation tax relief in respect of payments of rent apply accordingly in relation to that rent.

Certain variations of a lease

Consequences ensue if all of the following conditions are met:

(A) a company (M) is a lessee of land under a lease which has 50 years or less to run ('the original lease') and is entitled to corporation tax relief on the rent;

(B) M varies the original lease by agreement with the landlord;

(C) under the variation, M agrees to pay a rent greater than that payable under the original lease and, does so in return for a consideration which would not be taxable except as capital in M's hands; and

(D) under the variation, the period during which the greater rent is to be paid ends not more than 15 years after the date on which the consideration is paid to M (or, where applicable, the final instalment of the consideration is paid to M).

The consequences are that M is treated as having surrendered the original lease for the consideration mentioned in (C) and as having been granted a new lease for a term of 15 years or less but otherwise on the terms of the original lease varied as mentioned in (B). The provisions described above are then applied accordingly.

[*CTA 2010, ss 849–862, Sch 2 para 95; ICTA 1988, s 780; CTA 2009, Sch 1 para 233*].

Simon's Taxes. See B5.248.

Changes to Lease Accounting Standards

[5.19] Provisions are introduced by *FA 2011, s 53* to ensure that the existing tax rules that rely on the accounting treatment of lease transactions continue to operate as they currently do. Much of the corporation tax code for lease transactions is based on accounting definitions with regard to accounts prepared in accordance with UK GAAP, or IAS.

Fundamental changes are expected with regard to IAS during 2011, and also in respect of UK GAAP (possibly in 2013). This will have an effect on the operation of the existing tax rules. The provision introduced as *FA 2011, s 53* requires businesses which account for lease transactions to treat them, for the purposes of the Taxes Acts only, as if the changes to accounting standards had not taken place. This will apply to any business, whether as lessee, lessor, or both, that accounts for lease transactions using a lease accounting standard that is newly issued or changed on or after 1 January 2011. It should therefore not change the existing tax treatment of leases and will ensure that such treatment continues.

The new rule does not apply where the change in a leasing standard is a change to UK GAAP that permits or requires businesses to account for a lease, or a transaction accounted for as a lease, in a manner equivalent to that provided for by IFRS for small and medium-sized entities issued by the IAS Board (ignoring any change that may be made to the leasing section of that Standard). This means that if the draft FRS for medium-sized entities which has been proposed by the UK Accounting Standards Board (on 29 October 2010) is issued, then this new standard will not constitute a change in a leasing accounting standard under this clause.

However, other changes will fall within the provisions of this clause. Therefore where a business prepares accounts using the old standard in their previous accounting period then they should use their old standard for their leasing transactions for the purpose of the Taxes Act instead of using the new standard (*s 53(8)*). Otherwise where a business is using a new standard for the first time in its accounts, then it should use the old standard which corresponds to the new standard with regard to their leasing transactions, for tax purposes (*s 53(9)*). The old standard for these purposes is either IAS disregarding any leasing change, or UK GAAP disregarding any leasing change (see *s 53(10)*).

[*FA 2011, s 53*].

Leased trading assets

[5.20] In certain circumstances where a payment is made under a lease of a trading asset, corporation tax relief for the payment is restricted. The provisions apply where:

- a payment is made by a company under a lease of an asset (other than land or an interest in land) created after 14 April 1964;
- a deduction is allowed for the payment in calculating trading profits for corporation tax purposes; and

- at a time before the lease was created the asset was used for the purposes of the trade or for the purposes of another trade carried on by the lessee, and was then owned by the person carrying on the trade in which it was used.

The deduction for the payment is limited to the 'commercial rent' of the asset to which it relates for the period for which the payment is made. In fact, the position is judged on a cumulative basis in similar manner to that described in **5.17** above, taking into account the payments for every previous accounting period ended on or after the date the lease was created. It is the cumulative unrelieved expenses for the current period which is then compared to the commercial rent for the period and restricted if necessary. The cumulative unrelieved expenses cannot, however, be carried forward to an accounting period beginning after the payments have ceased; no deduction is available under these provisions for any such expenses.

The '*commercial rent*' is the rent which might at the time the lease is created be expected to be paid under a lease of the asset if the lease were for the rest of the asset's 'expected normal working life' (as defined), the rent were payable at uniform intervals and at a uniform rate, and the rent gave a reasonable return for the asset's market value at that time, taking account of the terms and conditions of the actual lease. If the asset is used at the same time partly for the purposes of the trade and partly for other purposes, the commercial rent is to be determined by reference to what would be paid for such partial use.

For the above purposes, a lease is an agreement or arrangement under which payments are made for the use of, or otherwise in respect of, the asset. It includes an agreement or arrangement under which the payments (or any of them) represent instalments of, or payments towards, a purchase price.

The above provisions do not apply to payments due on or after 1 April 2006 under a lease which is a long funding finance lease as regards the lessee (see **13.4 CAPITAL ALLOWANCES — PLANT AND MACHINERY: FIXTURES AND LEASING**).

[*CTA 2010, ss 863–869; ICTA 1988, ss 782, 785; FA 2006, Sch 9 para 3; CTA 2009, Sch 1 para 235*].

Simon's Taxes. See B5.413.

Leased assets — capital sums

[5.21] In certain circumstances where a payment is made under a lease of an asset (other than one created on or before 14 April 1964), and a 'capital sum' is obtained in respect of an interest in the asset, corporation tax is chargeable. This does not apply if **5.20** above (or income tax equivalent) applies to the payment or would do so were it not for the exclusion in **5.20** of payments under long funding finance leases. A lease is defined as in **5.20** above.

A '*capital sum*' is any sum of money, or any money's worth, except in so far as it falls to be taken into account as a trading receipt or is chargeable to corporation tax as miscellaneous income (previously under Schedule D, Case VI).

The provisions apply where a payment is made under a lease of an asset (other than land or an interest in land), the payment is one for which a tax deduction is available (see below) and any one of the following conditions is met:

(a) the person making the payment (P) obtains a capital sum in respect of the lessee's interest in the lease;
(b) 'an associate' (see below) of P obtains a capital sum by way of consideration in respect of the lessee's interest in the lease;
(c) the lessor's interest in the lease, or any other interest in the asset, belongs to an associate of P, and the associate obtains a capital sum in respect of the interest; or
(d) the lessor's interest in the lease, or any other interest in the asset, belongs to an associate of P, and an associate of that associate obtains a capital sum by way of consideration in respect of the interest.

Conditions (a)–(d) may be met before, at or after the time when the payment is made, but can be met only if the person obtaining the capital sum is a company within the charge to corporation tax.

The conditions are not met if the lease is a hire-purchase agreement for plant or machinery and the capital sum has to be brought into account as the whole or part of the capital allowances disposal value of the plant or machinery (and provided, in the case of (c) or (d), that the capital sum is obtained in respect of the lessee's interest in the lease).

The reference above to a tax deduction is to a deduction allowable:

- in computing trading profits for corporation tax purposes; or
- (for accounting periods ending on or after 1 April 2009) in computing profits or income under any of the provisions listed at *CTA 2010, s 1173* (miscellaneous income) or in computing losses for which relief is available under *CTA 2010, s 91* (see **55.9 LOSSES**); or
- (for accounting periods ended before 1 April 2009) in computing profits or losses for corporation tax under *Sch D, Case VI*; or
- under *CTA 2009, s 1219* (management expenses of a company's investment business — see **51.3 INVESTMENT COMPANIES AND INVESTMENT BUSINESS**) (previously as a management expense under *ICTA 1988, s 75*); or
- under *ICTA 1988, s 76* (expenses of insurance companies); or
- in computing the profits of a trade, profession or vocation for income tax purposes; or
- in computing profits or income under any of the provisions listed at *ITA 2007, s 1016* (miscellaneous income) or in computing losses for which relief is available under *ITA 2007, s 152* (miscellaneous **LOSSES**); or
- against employment income under *ITEPA 2003, s 336* or in computing losses in an employment for income tax purposes.

The company obtaining the capital sum is treated as receiving, at the time the sum is obtained, an amount to which the charge to corporation tax on income applies. (For accounting periods ended before 1 April 2009, the amount was chargeable under *Sch D, Case VI*.)

The amount is equal to the amount(s) of the payment for which the above-mentioned tax deduction is made, but is not to exceed the capital sum. Where the lease is a hire-purchase agreement and the capital sum is obtained in respect of the lessee's interest in the lease, the recipient's capital expenditure on the asset is taken as reducing the capital sum for the purpose of applying this rule (see *CTA 2010, s 875*).

If a payment or part of a payment is taken into account in deciding the chargeable amount in respect of a capital sum, the payment or part must be left out of account in deciding whether a charge arises under these provisions in respect of another capital sum and, if so, the chargeable amount. This rule is applied in the order in which capital sums are obtained. If the capital sum is received before the payment is made, any necessary adjustment to the recipient's tax position can be made within six years after the accounting period in which the payment is made.

If a company disposes of an interest in an asset to a person who is the company's 'associate' (as below), it is regarded as obtaining the greatest of the actual sum obtained, the open market value and the value of the interest to the person to whom it is transferred.

Reference above to any sum obtained in respect of an interest in an asset includes any insurance money obtained in respect of the interest and any sum representing money or money's worth obtained in respect of the interest by a transaction or series of transactions disposing of it. Reference to any sum obtained in respect of the lessee's interest in a lease of an asset includes any sums representing consideration for a surrender of the interest to the lessor, an assignment of the lease, the creation of a sublease or another interest out of the lease or a transaction or series of transactions under which the lessee's rights are merged in any way with the lessor's rights or with any other rights as respects the asset.

There is provision for payments to be apportioned where made by persons in partnership and for sums to be apportioned where obtained by persons in partnership or by persons jointly entitled to the interest in an asset (see *CTA 2010, ss 880, 881*).

Meaning of 'associates'

For the above purposes, the following are associated with each other:

- an individual and the individual's spouse, civil partner or relative (meaning a brother, sister, ancestor or lineal descendant);
- an individual and a spouse or civil partner of a relative of the individual;
- an individual and a relative of the individual's spouse or civil partner;
- an individual and a spouse or civil partner of a relative of the individual's spouse or civil partner;
- a trustee of a settlement and an individual who is the settlor or any person associated with that individual;
- a person and a body of persons (which may be a partnership) of which he has control (within the meaning of *CTA 2010, s 1124*);
- a person and a body of persons of which persons associated with the person have control;

- a person and a body of persons of which the person and persons associated with the person have control;
- two or more bodies of persons associated with the same person;
- in relation to a disposal by joint owners, the joint owners and any person associated with any of them.

[*CTA 2010, ss 870–886; ICTA 1988, ss 781, 783–785; FA 1996, s 135, Sch 21 para 21; ITA 2007, Sch 1 paras 189, 190; CTA 2009, Sch 1 paras 234, 236; SI 2009 No 56, Sch 1 para 156*].

Simon's Taxes. See B5.410–B5.415A.

Leasing of plant or machinery

Leasing partnerships — restriction on use of losses

[5.22] Where a 'business of leasing plant or machinery' (as defined in **5.29** below), within the charge to corporation tax, is carried on by a company in partnership, certain losses derived from capital allowances are restricted as set out below. This provision has effect in relation to any business carried on by a company in partnership in any accounting period ending on or after 5 December 2005. In relation to accounting periods straddling that date, the provision applies only if the company starts to carry on the business in partnership, or a 'relevant change' in the company's interest in the business occurs, on or after that date. A '*relevant change*' in the company's interest in the business is a change to a basis of profit sharing which is not 'allowable'.

Where the company's interest in the leasing business during the accounting period of the partnership is not 'determined on an allowable basis', any loss incurred in its 'notional business' in its accounting period, comprised (wholly or partly) in the partnership accounting period, is restricted to the extent that it derives from any relevant capital allowances. The extent is determined on the basis that any relevant capital allowances are the final amounts to be deducted. The restricted part of the loss may be carried forward but can only be set off against income of the company's notional business deriving from a lease of plant or machinery which was entered into before the end of the accounting period in which the loss in the notional business was incurred. It is not available for group relief or relief against total profits of the company.

The interest of a company in the leasing business during the partnership's accounting period is 'determined on an allowable basis' if (for the purposes of *CTA 2009, ss 1262–1264* — see **58.3 PARTNERSHIPS**) the company's share in the profits (excluding chargeable gains) or loss of the leasing business and its share in any 'relevant capital allowances' for that period are both determined by reference to the same single percentage. '*Relevant capital allowances*' are capital allowances in respect of expenditure incurred on the provision of plant or machinery wholly or partly for the purposes of the leasing business. The company's '*notional business*' is the business the profits or losses of which are determined, in relation to the company, under *CTA 2009, s 1259* (see **58.3 PARTNERSHIPS**).

For the above purposes, a lease, as well as having its normal meaning, includes an underlease, sublease, tenancy or licence and an agreement for any of those things.

[*CTA 2010, ss 887–889; ICTA 1988, ss 785ZA, 785ZB; FA 2006, s 83; CTA 2009, Sch 1 paras 237, 238; SI 2009 No 2860, Art 3*].

Capital receipts to be treated as income

[5.23] If, under a lease of plant or machinery, there is an unconditional obligation, first arising after 12 December 2007, to make a 'relevant capital payment' or if such a payment is made after that date without obligation, the lessor is treated for corporation tax purposes as receiving income attributable to the lease of an amount equal to the amount of the 'capital payment'. The income is treated as income for the period of account in which the obligation first arose or, as the case may be, income for the period of account in which the payment is made. These provisions apply to long funding leases (see **71.55 TRADING EXPENSES AND DEDUCTIONS**) as well as to other plant or machinery leases. The provisions apply equally if the obligation arises, or the payment is made, under an agreement or arrangement relating to a lease of plant or machinery, whether made before, during or after the currency of the lease itself.

For these purposes, a payment includes the provision of value by whatever means. A '*capital payment*' is any payment other than one which, if made to the lessor, would fall to be included in the lessor's income for corporation tax purposes or which would fall to be included were it not for *CTA 2010, s 360* (which determines the amount to be brought into account as taxable income from a long funding finance lease — see **71.55 TRADING EXPENSES AND DEDUCTIONS**).

A capital payment is a '*relevant capital payment*' if either:

- it is payable by lessee to lessor in connection with the grant, assignment, novation or termination of the lease or with any provision of the lease or, as the case may be, the agreement or arrangement (including the variation or waiver of any such provision); or
- the lease rentals are less than (or payable later than) they might reasonably be expected to be if there were no obligation to make the capital payment and the capital payment were not made.

However, a capital payment is *not* a '*relevant capital payment*' if, or to the extent that:

- it reduces the lessor's expenditure for the purposes of plant and machinery capital allowances — see the rules on expenditure met another's contributions at **10.8 CAPITAL ALLOWANCES — INTRODUCTION** — or would do so if the circumstances were not such that the contributions rules are disapplied; or
- it represents compensation for damage to, or damage caused by, the plant or machinery in question.

Where a capital payment is an initial payment under a long funding lease (see **13.4 CAPITAL ALLOWANCES — PLANT AND MACHINERY: FIXTURES AND LEASING**) whose inception is on or after 22 April 2009 and the commencement of the term of the lease is an event that requires the lessor to bring a disposal value into account, the payment is a relevant capital payment but only to the extent (if any) that it exceeds the disposal value. If the inception of the lease is on or after 13 November 2008 but before 22 April 2009, the payment is not a relevant capital payment. Before 13 November 2008, a capital payment was not a relevant capital payment if, or to the extent that, it was a disposal value (see **12.24 CAPITAL ALLOWANCES — PLANT AND MACHINERY: POOLING AND DISPOSALS**) for the purposes of the lessor's plant and machinery capital allowances computations.

For these purposes, if the obligation to make the relevant capital payment arises, or the payment is made, after 11 March 2008, a lease of plant or machinery includes a lease of plant or machinery together with other property, in which case the payment is apportioned on a just and reasonable basis and only the amount apportioned to the plant or machinery is chargeable under these provisions. It does not, however, include a lease all the lessor's income from which (if any) would be chargeable as **PROPERTY INCOME (64)** or a long funding lease of plant or machinery on which the lessor would have been treated as having incurred qualifying expenditure for the purposes of plant and machinery capital allowances if it were not for *CAA 2001, s 34A* at **13.4 CAPITAL ALLOWANCES — PLANT AND MACHINERY: FIXTURES AND LEASING.** If the obligation to make the relevant capital payment arises, or the payment is made, on or before 11 March 2008, a lease of plant or machinery does not include a lease of plant or machinery together with other property, though it does include an equipment lease within **13.3**(b) **CAPITAL ALLOWANCES — PLANT AND MACHINERY: FIXTURES AND LEASING.**

There is bad debt relief if the above provisions have applied by virtue of an unconditional obligation and at any time the lessor reasonably expects that the relevant capital payment will not be paid (or will not be fully paid). The lessor is allowed a deduction for the expected shortfall in computing his profits for the period of account in which that time falls.

For the above purposes, a lease, as well as having its normal meaning, includes a licence and the letting of a ship or aircraft on charter or any other asset on hire.

[*CTA 2010, ss 890–894, Sch 2 paras 96, 97; ICTA 1988, ss 785B–785E; FA 2008, Sch 20 para 1; CTA 2009, Sch 1 paras 239, 240; FA 2009, Sch 32 paras 9, 11*].

Simon's Taxes. See **B5.415A.**

Restrictions with regard to the leasing of plant and machinery

[5.24] *FA 2010, Sch 5* introduces certain restrictions with regard to capital allowances claimed in respect of plant and machinery which is leased, and also with regard to deductions in respect of rental rebates for leased plant and machinery. The provisions have been introduced to combat two specific avoidance schemes which had been disclosed to HMRC.

The first scheme involved arrangements intended to create a company that is taxed on very little income from the leasing of an asset, but which is potentially able to claim capital allowances on the full cost of the asset, creating tax losses where there is a commercial profit. The first scheme may, alternatively or additionally, rely on obtaining a deduction for a rebate of rentals to generate a tax loss where there is a commercial profit.

The second scheme involved arrangements where a lessor that has claimed capital allowances in the initial loss-making phase of a lease of plant or machinery avoids tax on the income that arises once the lease moves into its tax-profitable phase. The intended effect is to turn a tax-timing advantage into a permanent loss of tax on a transaction that is commercially profitable.

These provisions have effect with regard to expenditure after 9 December 2009.

Amendments to *CAA 2001*

New *sections 228MA–228MC* are inserted into *CAA 2001*.

Where a lessor is treated as incurring capital expenditure under *CAA 2001, s 67* (hire purchase etc.) or under *CAA 2001, s 70A* (long funding leases) then the amount of capital expenditure that is treated as qualifying expenditure is limited where:

(i) there are arrangements under which plant or machinery is to be leased; and
(ii) there are arrangements under which the value of the asset to the lessor is reduced.

The amount of the lessor's qualifying expenditure is restricted to 'V'.

'V' is defined as the aggregate of the amount of the present value of the lessor's income from the asset and the amount of the present value of the residual value of the asset after any rental rebate.

For the purposes of calculating 'V', the lessor's income from the asset includes all amounts that it is reasonable to expect the lessor will receive in connection with the lease and which will be taxed as income (this includes amounts treated as income, for example under *CTA 2010, s 890*). The residual value is the market value (per *CAA 2001, s 577*) of the lessor's interest in the asset immediately after the termination of the lease. The reference to 'lessor's interest' covers the situation where the lessor is the beneficiary of a contract under *CAA 2001, s 67* or a lessee under a long funding lease.

Amounts which have been brought into account as disposal receipts for capital allowances purposes, charges made by the lessor for services supplied in connection with the leased asset and qualifying UK and foreign tax paid by the lessor are all excluded from the lessor's income amounts.

A 'lease' for these purposes includes any arrangements which provide for plant and machinery to be leased or otherwise made available by a person to another person.

[*CAA 2001, s 228MA*].

In the case of both the amounts receivable in connection with the lease and the residual value at the end of the lease term, the present value is calculated based on the interest rate implicit in the lease, but it provides for an alternative (London interbank offered rate plus 1%) if the rate cannot otherwise be established. [*CAA 2001, s 228MB*].

CAA 2001, s 228MC defines rental rebate for the purpose of *s 228MA*. The definition is largely based on the definition in *CAA 2001, s 70YH*.

[*FA 2010, Sch 5, para 1*].

Rental rebate for corporation tax purposes

Where the avoidance in the first scheme highlighted above is centered on, or includes, the amount of deduction claimed for rental rebate the amended legislation counters this. Broadly the effect of the new rules is that the amount of a rental rebate which may be claimed as a deduction in computing profits is limited to the amount receivable in connection with the lease that has been brought into account in computing the lessor's income.

In calculating this amount, however, the finance charge element of rentals paid under a finance lease is excluded, as are any elements that represent charges for service or tax (*CTA 2009, s 60A(1)(4)*).

[*FA 2010, Sch 5 para 2(2)*].

A further anti-avoidance provision is introduced by *FA 2010, Sch 5 para 3* in respect of arrangements reducing the disposal value of a leased asset. Where plant or machinery is leased and a disposal event occurs which falls within *CA 2001, s 61(2)* items 1, 2 or 7 (sale of plant or machinery) and arrangements have been entered into that have the effect of reducing the disposal value of the asset in so far as it is attributable to rentals payable under the lease, then the disposal value is to be determined as if arrangements had not been entered into.

The provision does not apply where the arrangements fall within the transfer of income stream provisions found at *ITA 2007, s 809AZA* or *CTA 2010, s 752* and the relevant amount has been treated as income under *ITA 2007, s 809AZB* or *CTA 2010, s 753*, respectively.

[*FA 2010, Sch 5 para 3*].

Further restrictions with regard to the leasing of plant and machinery

[5.25] Draft legislation has been published for inclusion in the Finance Bill 2011 which aims to counter an avoidance scheme involving capital allowances on plant and machinery. It is proposed the legislation will take effect for new arrangements relating to guarantees entered into on or after 9 March 2011, and for existing arrangements where payment under a guarantee has not been made before 9 March 2011.

As noted above, a lessee under a plant and machinery long funding lease is able to claim capital allowances on the expenditure incurred under the lease (even though they do not own the plant and machinery). The amount of the expenditure on which capital allowances can be claimed is the net present value of the minimum payments under the lease plus the amounts of guarantees made by the lessee as to the residual value of the leased plant and machinery at the end of the lease. Any actual payments made under the guarantee are then taken into account to reduce the disposal value of the plant and machinery at the end of the lease.

[*CAA 2001, ss 70A, 70C, 70E*].

The scheme which the new legislation aims to counter involves arrangements which have the effect of guaranteeing the value of the leased asset at the end of the lease but which then allow for any guarantee payment made to also be taken into account for tax relief purposes (i.e. a second time).

As noted in the Treasury Statement issued along with the draft legislation, some large businesses had entered into circular transactions, involving the sale, leaseback and reacquisition of their plant and machinery over a short period, with the aim of claiming tax relief twice on the one amount of expenditure. These schemes came to light under the disclosure rules, and the proposed legislation aims to prevent any benefits arising from such transactions.

The proposals introduce new *subsections 4A–4C* in *CAA 2001, s 70C*. Where the minimum lease payments include a 'relievable amount' then that amount is to be excluded in the present value calculation. A '*relievable amount*' is defined as an amount ('X') which is included within the minimum lease payments because of arrangements which are in place whereby all or part of any residual amount is guaranteed by the lessee or a person connected with the lessee, and, it is reasonable to assume that, if payment of X were to be made under the arrangements, relief would be available as a result (which is beyond the 'standard' relief given on the basis that X is within the minimum lease payments). When considering whether relief 'would be available as a result', account should only be taken of the element of the arrangements which guarantees the residual amount,

Amendments are also made to *CAA 2001, s 70D*, with new *sections 1A* and *1B* being inserted, which restrict the additional expenditure on which capital allowances may be claimed with respect to any increase in such expenditure attributable to the 'relievable amount'.

Changes are also made to *CAA 2001, s 70E* with regard to disposal events and values. New *sections 2DA* and *2DB* are added, inserting a definition of 'relievable payment', and *s 70E(2C)(b)* is amended so the calculation of the disposal value does not include any such payments. A '*relievable payment*' is defined as a payment ('X') which is included within the minimum lease payments because of arrangements which are in place whereby all or part of any residual amount is guaranteed by the lessee or a person connected with the lessee, and, it is reasonable to assume that, as a result of making payment X, relief would be available (which is beyond the 'standard' relief given on the basis that X is within the minimum lease payments).

The proposed changes ensure that a lessee under a long funding lease is not able to include an amount guaranteed by the lessee, or a person connected with them, in the capital allowance computation for the lease period, where it is reasonable to assume that tax relief would otherwise be available in respect of a payment under that guarantee.

Rent factoring of leases of plant and machinery

[5.26] The provisions described below are repealed with effect for transfers **on or after 22 April 2009** and are superseded by the more general provisions on transfers of income streams at **5.11** above.

Where a person enters into arrangements **after 1 July 2004** to transfer a right to receive some or all of his rentals from a lease of plant and machinery to which he is entitled and which would have been brought into account as his income for income or corporation tax purposes, the consideration for the transfer is to be treated as such income to the extent it would have been so treated (had the right not been transferred) and does not otherwise fall to be treated for tax purposes as his income or a capital allowances disposal receipt. The consideration so treated as income for tax purposes is taxable as rentals receivable under the lease in the period of account in which it is receivable.

The transfer of a right to receive rental income includes any arrangements which result in the rentals no longer being brought into account as the transferor's taxable income. Transfers of rights to receive rental income also includes transfers made by partners even if the partnership is a legal person or body corporate. This provision does not apply in so far as the structured finance arrangements provisions in **5.15** above (rent factoring of income receipts etc.) apply in relation to the above arrangements as a result of the transfer of the right to receive some or all of the rentals from a lease of plant or machinery. For arrangements or transfers of rights entered as income or as a capital allowances disposal receipt applies where the market value of the rights transferred at the time of transfer is treated as the income of the purchaser taxable as rentals under the lease. These provisions do not apply to capital receipts to be treated as income, see below. References to a person include a business partner where that person is a member of the partnership and trustees of any trust of which the person is a beneficiary.

[*ICTA 1988, s 785A; FA 2006, Sch 6 para 7; FA 2008, Sch 20 paras 2, 3; FA 2009, Sch 25 paras 9(1), 10*].

See also HMRC guidance on 'Plant or Machinery Rent Factoring' (available on their website) on the interaction of *ICTA 1988, s 785A* with *ss 43A–43G* (rent factoring — see **62.16** property income), *s 343* (company reconstruction without change of ownership) and *CAA 2001, ss 266, 267* (successions).

Simon's Taxes. See **B5.415**.

Sale of lessors

[5.27] The provisions at **5.28–5.33** below apply where a company, which carries on a 'business of leasing plant or machinery' on its own or in partnership, changes ownership, or changes its interest in a business carried on in partnership. See Explanatory notes to Finance Bill 2006 (and the HMRC Technical Note published on 31 March 2006) for background information on these provisions. See also HMRC Business Leasing Manual BLM80000 *et seq*.

The provisions are designed to ensure that on a change of ownership, or interest in a partnership, a charge is borne by the original owner and an equal and opposite relief is granted to the new owner. The charge applies in respect of long-leases where in the early years of a lease the capital allowances available to the lessor are greater than the rental income from the lease, giving rise to losses, the charge broadly equating to the tax benefit of such losses. This prevents the lessor making use of such losses, for example, by way of group relief, where the profits arising in the later years of the lease (when the rental income is greater than the capital allowances) are sheltered on the sale of the lessor company to a group with tax losses. The charge thus counters the losses available to the original owner and the corresponding relief counters the profits passed on to the new owner.

FA 2011, s 32 Sch 6 introduces changes to the regime with regard to the sale of lessors to resolve concerns as to the deferred tax charge in the companies involved in such arrangements. The new provisions apply: with regard to disposal values, where the event, transfer or succession takes place on or after 23 March 2011; with regard to the scope of the provisions, or the calculation of the income amount, where the relevant day is on or after 23 March 2011. The changes are highlighted below.

Leasing business carried on by a company alone

[5.28] If on any day (the '*relevant day*'):

- a company carries on a 'business of leasing plant or machinery' otherwise than in partnership;
- the company is within the charge to corporation tax in respect of the business; and
- there is a 'qualifying change of ownership' in relation to the company,

the accounting period of the company ends on the relevant day and a new accounting period begins on the following day. Also, the company is treated as receiving a taxable business receipt in the accounting period ending on the relevant day and as incurring a deductible business expense of an equal amount in the new accounting period. See below as to the amount of the taxable receipt. The expense potentially qualifies for the relief at **5.30** below. Any loss derived from the expense (to be calculated on the basis that the expense is the final amount to be deducted) cannot be carried back under *CTA 2010, s 37(3)(b)* (previously *ICTA 1988, s 393A(1)(b)*) as a trading loss for offset against profits of earlier accounting periods.

Business of leasing plant or machinery

A company carries on a '*business of leasing plant or machinery*' for this purpose if either:

(a) at least half of the 'relevant plant or machinery value' (or, where the relevant day fell before 13 November 2008, the 'accounting value' of the plant or machinery owned by the company on the relevant day) relates to 'qualifying leased plant or machinery'; or

(b) at least half of the company's income over the twelve-month period before the relevant day, derives from 'qualifying leased plant or machinery', with respect to a relevant day falling on or after 23 March 2011, at least half the company's income over the twelve months before the relevant day derives from plant or machinery falling within the definition at *CTA 2010, s 387(7)*, see below.

For the purposes of (a) above, '*relevant plant or machinery value*' is the total of (i) the value of plant and machinery in the company's balance sheet as at the start of the relevant day (see *CTA 2010, s 389*) and (ii) any such value which would be shown in the company's balance sheet drawn up at the end of the relevant day and would also have been shown in the balance sheet of an 'associated company' (as defined by *CTA 2010, s 408*) drawn up at the start of that day. The assumptions made as to the amount shown in the company's balance sheet are: that the balance sheet is drawn up in accordance with GAAP; and, that if the company acquired any plant or machinery from a connected person, then it is assumed the company acquired it for market value as at the relevant day. As from 23 March 2011, post-*FA 2011*, this latter assumption is amended to read that the company acquired the plant and machinery for the 'ascribed value' as at the relevant day.

In certain circumstances (see *CTA 2010, s 390*) where the company leases the plant or machinery under a long funding lease (and the relevant day falls on or after 13 November 2008), the market value of the plant or machinery on the relevant day must be used instead of its balance sheet value. For a relevant day falling on or after 23 March 2011, the reference to market value is replaced with 'ascribed value' [*FA 2011, Sch 6*].

The '*accounting value*' of the plant or machinery is broadly the amounts recorded in the company's balance sheet at the start of the relevant day together with the value of any plant or machinery transferred to the lessor company on that day by associated companies.

'*Qualifying leased plant or machinery*' is leased plant or machinery on which the company can claim capital allowances (or could have done so were it not for the long funding leasing rules at **13.4 CAPITAL ALLOWANCES — PLANT AND MACHINERY: FIXTURES AND LEASING**); the plant or machinery must have been subject to a plant or machinery lease (other than an excluded lease of background plant or machinery for a building — see **13.5**(1)(B) **CAPITAL ALLOWANCES — PLANT AND MACHINERY: FIXTURES AND LEASING**) at some time in the twelve months ending with the relevant day.

In determining the company's income for the purposes of (b) above, any necessary apportionment is to be made on a time basis or, where this leads to an unjust result, on a just and reasonable basis. The proportion of income that derives from qualifying plant or machinery is to be determined on a just and reasonable basis.

[*CTA 2010, ss 387–391*].

For a relevant day falling on or after 23 March 2011 this definition of 'qualifying leased plant or machinery' has been replaced. Reference is now made to plant and machinery which falls within the provisions of *CTA 2010, s 387(7)*. Plant and machinery falls within these provisions if: it is or has been leased out in the twelve months prior to the relevant day by the company or a qualifying associate (being a person connected with the company, on the relevant day or at any time in the prior twelve months); the lease is not an excluded lease of background plant or machinery for a building; and if the lessor is a qualifying associate, then the lessee under the lease is or was someone other than the company. Where the relevant company is owned by a consortium (or is a 75% subsidiary of such a company) then the reference to 'connected' person above includes any member of the consortium and any person connected with such a member.

The 'ascribed value' introduced by the provisions of *FA 2011, Sch 6*, is determined by reference to three new sections which are inserted into the sale of lessors legislation. New *sections 437A–437C* are added. Pursuant to *s 437A*, for plant and machinery which is subject to a lease at the relevant time, and the relevant company (partnership) is a lessor, and it does not fall into the exclusions, then the 'ascribed value' of such plant or machinery at the relevant time is the higher of: the market value at the relevant time; and the present value at that time of the lease.

The exclusion referred to is with regard to plant and machinery which is subject to an equipment lease (within the meaning of *CAA 2001, Ch 14 Pt 2* — fixtures), where the relevant company (or partnership) is the equipment lessor, and such lessor is treated at that time as the owner of the plant and machinery per an election made under *CAA 2001, s 177(1)(a)(i)*. In such cases the 'ascribed value' of the plant and machinery is the present value at the relevant time of the lease.

Where plant and machinery does not fall into either of these categories, then the 'ascribed value' is the market value. Market value is to be determined on the assumption of a disposal by an absolute owner free from all leases and other encumbrances. If plant and machinery is a fixture then its market value is so much of the market value of the relevant land (as defined in *CAA 2001, s 173(2)*) and the fixture together as is attributable to the fixture, on a just and reasonable apportionment.

The present value of a lease is the present value of: the amounts payable under the lease after the relevant time, and any residual amount. 'Amounts payable under the lease' does not include amounts payable by the lessor, or amounts that represent charges for services or qualifying UK or foreign tax to be paid by the lessor. Where a lessee has an option to continue the lease for a period after the end of its initial term, and it is reasonably certain that the lessee will exercise that option, then amounts payable under the continued lease are included. Where the lease relates to land or assets that are not plant or machinery, the present value of the lease is so much of the present value of the amounts above, as is attributable to the plant and machinery on a just and reasonable apportionment.

The present value is calculated using the interest rate implicit in the lease, which is the rate that would, in accordance with normal commercial criteria including GAAP, apply. Where a rate cannot be determined then it is taken as LIBOR plus 1%.

[*CTA 2010, ss 437A–437C, as inserted by FA 2011, Sch 6*].

Qualifying change of ownership

These provisions are supplemented by the provisions within *FA 2010* (see below) which provide for an election out of the charge on a change of ownership, where the relevant day is on or after 9 December 2009 and, further to *FA 2011* which withdraws such election out of charge, before 23 March 2011.

In addition *FA 2010, s 29* makes a number of changes to the operation of the rules determining whether a company is owned by a consortium. The requirement that the lessor company be a direct 90% subsidiary of the company owned by the consortium is removed, and replaced with a test of direct or indirect 75% shareholding. The effect of the change is that an indirect 75% subsidiary of a company owned by a consortium will be treated as 'a company owned by a consortium'.

Previously it was possible to prevent a *FA 2006, Sch 10* charge from arising on the change in ownership of 'a company owned by a consortium' by inserting an intermediate holding company between the lessor company and the company owned by the consortium. The insertion of the intermediate holding company does not itself trigger the charge because there is no change of economic ownership, but, as a consequence of the restructuring the lessor company is taken outside the definition of a company owned by a consortium. A subsequent change in ownership would then not be subject to a *Sch 10* charge.

The new definition of a company owned by a consortium includes a company that is a direct or indirect 75% subsidiary of a company owned by a consortium. As a consequence, a *Sch 10* charge will be triggered when there is a change in the economic ownership of such a lessor company owned by a consortium.

There is a '*qualifying change of ownership*' in relation to a company (A) on any day if there is 'a relevant change in the relationship' on that day between A and a 'principal company' of A.

Leaving aside consortium relationships, a company (B) is a '*principal company*' of A if A is its 'qualifying 75% subsidiary' (broadly as defined for group relief purposes) and B is not itself a qualifying 75% subsidiary of another company. There is a '*relevant change in the relationship*' between A and B on any day on which A ceases to be a qualifying 75% subsidiary of B. The same applies in the case of a chain of companies where the principal company is at the top of the chain, the '*relevant change in the relationship*' occurring whenever any of the links in the 75% chain are broken.

Prior to the changes in *FA 2010*, where the relevant day is before 9 December 2009, in the case of consortium relationships, a company (E) is the principal company of A if it is itself not a qualifying 75% subsidiary of any company and A is owned by a consortium, or is a 'qualifying 90% subsidiary' (broadly as defined for group relief purposes) of a company owned by a consortium, of which E is a member. Where the relevant day is on or after 9 December 2009, the above provisions are amended such that A is able to be a 75% subsidiary of another company, and that A is owned by a consortium or is a 'qualifying 75% subsidiary' of a company owned by a consortium — being a direct or indirect 75% subsidiary.

There is a '*relevant change in the relationship*' between A and E on any day if the 'ownership proportion' at the end of the day is less than it was at the start of the day.

The '*ownership proportion*' is whichever of these is the lowest: the percentage of A's ordinary share capital owned by E, the percentage to which E is beneficially entitled of profits available for distribution to equity holders of A and the percentage to which E would be entitled of any assets of A available for distribution to equity holders on a winding-up. But if A is a qualifying 90% subsidiary of a company, these three alternatives must be read as if references to that company were substituted for references to A. If E is a qualifying 75% subsidiary of another company (F), F would then be the principal company of A provided that F is not itself a qualifying 75% subsidiary of another company. See also comments above with regard to changes to the 90% consortium subsidiary provisions for a relevant day on or after 9 December 2009.

There is a '*relevant change in the relationship*' between A and F on any day if the ownership proportion at the end of the day is less than it was at the start of the day or if E ceases to be a qualifying 75% subsidiary of F. The same applies if F is a qualifying 75% subsidiary of another company and so on; the principal company of A is the company at the top of the chain and a '*relevant change in the relationship*' occurs whenever the ownership proportion falls or any of the links in the 75% chain are broken.

There is an exception to change of ownership rules in certain intra-group reorganisations (see *CTA 2010, s 395*) or (where the relevant day falls on or after 22 April 2009) if a principal company's interest in a consortium company remains unchanged despite a relevant change in the relationship (see *CTA 2010, s 396*).

Computing the amount of the taxable receipt

The basic amount of the taxable receipt is given by the formula PM – TWDV, which is broadly the net book value of the plant or machinery less its tax written-down value for capital allowances purposes. PM and TWDV are defined in more detail in the following paragraphs. The basic amount may then be subject to adjustment as described further below. If the basic amount given by the formula is a negative amount, the basic amount is taken instead to be nil.

PM is the aggregate of (i) amounts (if any) which would be shown in respect of plant and machinery in the company's balance sheet as at the start of the relevant day and (ii) any amount which would be shown in the company's balance sheet drawn up at the end of the relevant day and would also have been shown in the balance sheet of an 'associated company' (as defined by *CTA 2010, s 408*) drawn up at the start of that day. (Slightly different rules applied where the relevant day fell before 13 November 2008.)

As noted above the *FA 2011* introduces changes with regard to the use of market value, and in certain circumstances replaces this with 'ascribed value', with regard to a relevant day, or a transfer, which falls on or after 23 March 2011. These changes are further noted below.

For this purpose, the amounts shown in a company's balance sheet in respect of any plant or machinery are the amounts shown as the net book value (or carrying amount) in respect of the plant or machinery and the amounts shown in that balance sheet as the net investment in respect of finance leases of the plant or machinery. Where any of the plant or machinery is a fixture in land the amount of the net book value (or carrying amount) in respect of the fixture is determined on a just and reasonable basis. Where any of the plant or machinery, together with any other land or asset, is subject to a finance lease, the amount of the net investment in respect of the finance lease of that plant or machinery is similarly determined.

All amounts must be determined on the assumptions that balance sheets are drawn up in accordance with generally accepted accounting practice ('GAAP') and that, broadly if any plant or machinery has been acquired from connected parties, it was acquired at its market value on the relevant day. Further to the changes introduced as from 23 March 2011, market value is replaced with 'ascribed value'. A special rule applies (where the relevant day falls on or after 13 November 2008) if, at the start of the relevant day, the company is the lessee of plant or machinery under a long funding lease (see **13.4 CAPITAL ALLOWANCES — PLANT AND MACHINERY: FIXTURES AND LEASING**) or is treated as its owner under *CAA 2001, s 67* (hire-purchase and similar contracts — see **13.24**(A) **CAPITAL ALLOWANCES — PLANT AND MACHINERY: FIXTURES AND LEASING**). This rule also applies if the company acquired the plant or machinery from an associated company on the relevant day and either of those conditions are met at the end of that day. Under this rule, the amount included in the total in respect of the plant and machinery is replaced with market value. Post 23 March 2011 market value is replaced with 'ascribed value'.

'*Plant or machinery*' for the purpose of computing PM above means any plant or machinery (whether or not subject to a lease) apart from plant or machinery (i) on which the company has not incurred expenditure that is qualifying expenditure for capital allowances purposes; or (ii) of which the company is a lessor under a long funding lease; or (iii) treated as owned by other persons under *CAA 2001, s 67*; or (iv) which is to be ignored under the migration rule described below. Where the relevant day fell before 13 November 2008, (i) and (ii) did not apply but one could ignore plant or machinery on which the company had incurred expenditure which, by virtue of *CAA 2001, s 34A* (expenditure for long funding leasing) was not qualifying expenditure for capital allowances purposes.

Reference to 'ascribed value' per the changes implemented by *FA 2011* is as defined above.

TWDV is the total amount of unrelieved qualifying expenditure on plant or machinery in single asset pools, class pools and the main pool carried forward under normal capital allowances rules (see **12.1 CAPITAL ALLOWANCES — PLANT AND MACHINERY: POOLING AND DISPOSALS**) to the start of the new accounting period that begins the day after the relevant day (see above). Any expenditure incurred by the company on plant or machinery on the relevant day itself is to be left out of account unless it was acquired from an associated company. *FA 2011* amends *s 403* and extends the exclusion above for unrelieved qualifying expenditure, such that in addition any expenditure incurred on the relevant day but attributable to plant and machinery acquired by a company before that day is also left out of account.

An *adjustment* may fall to be made to the basic amount calculated above to reflect the degree to which the economic control of the company has changed. The adjustment is made where, on a company (A) ceasing to be a qualifying

75% subsidiary of another company (B) (the qualifying change of ownership referred to above), A becomes instead owned by a consortium (or a qualifying 90% subsidiary of a company owned by a consortium) of which B is a member. The taxable receipt is then limited to the 'appropriate percentage' of the basic amount.

The '*appropriate percentage*' is found by subtracting the 'ownership percentage' at the end of the relevant day from 100%.

The '*ownership percentage*' is whichever of these is the lowest: the percentage of A's ordinary share capital owned by B, the percentage to which B is beneficially entitled of profits available for distribution to equity holders of A and the percentage to which B would be entitled of any assets of A available for distribution to equity holders on a winding-up. But if A becomes a qualifying 90% subsidiary of a company, these three alternatives must be read as if references to that company were substituted for references to A.

Where the qualifying change of ownership arises from a change in a consortium relationship the adjustment is calculated as follows. If the change arises only because the 'ownership proportion' (see above) at the end of the day on which the change occurs is less than it was at the start of the day, the taxable receipt is limited to the 'appropriate proportion' of the basic amount. The '*appropriate proportion*' is found by subtracting the ownership proportion at the end of the day from the ownership proportion at the start of the day. In any other case, the taxable receipt is found by taking the ownership proportion at the start of the day on which the change occurs and applying it to the basic amount.

Migration to UK

If a company comes within the charge to corporation tax on any day as a result of migration into the UK and there is a qualifying change of ownership on that day in relation to that company, plant or machinery is to be ignored in calculating the amount of the taxable receipt if an amount would be shown in respect of it in a balance sheet of the company drawn up immediately before that day in accordance with GAAP. Where the relevant day fell before 13 November 2008, the plant or machinery to be ignored was simply that owned by the company immediately before the relevant day.

[*CTA 2010, ss 382–385, 387–408, 437, Sch 2 para 68(2)–(5); FA 2006, Sch 10 paras 3–22, 41; CTA 2009, Sch 1 para 695(2); FA 2009, Sch 10 paras 2–4, Sch 31 paras 2–7, 12; FA 2010, s 29*].

Election out of charge on qualifying change of ownership

FA 2010, s 61, Sch 18 provides for an election out of the charge on a qualifying change of ownership, and gives an option to elect for an alternative treatment. As outlined above, the sale of lessor companies legislation prevents a potential loss of tax when a lessor company changes hands. Tax could be lost if a lessor company with deferred tax profits is sold to a loss-making concern that is able to use its own losses against the deferred tax profits of the lessor company. The legislation counters such transactions by imposing a charge that is matched by a relief; the charge affecting the selling group and the relief benefiting the buying group.

However it should be noted that this election has been withdrawn by the provisions of *FA 2011, s 54* which amends *CTA 2010, s 398A* such that it applies only to a 'relevant day' before 23 March 2011.

Thus the relief is valuable to a buying group which is profit-making, so a purchaser is likely to be willing to pay for the relief (and to cover the seller's charge). However it is not valuable to a buying group which has losses, as the relief brings on benefit. However if the buyer is not loss-making normally, but is for a short period, perhaps as a consequence of a temporary dip in profitability, the rules operate to prevent the company from using the relief efficiently.

The new provisions give an option to elect for an alternative treatment which replaces the charge and relief with a ring fence that preserves the profits of the leasing business by restricting the set off of losses. The intention is to prevent the fragmentation of the business and the reduction of profits of the business through additional claims to capital allowances. As a consequence of these restrictions tax is collected on the deferred profits over time.

A 'qualifying change of ownership' is redefined at *s 394A* as being where there is a 'relevant change in the relationship' between A and a principal company of A, with the additional exception of where an election is made under the new provisions at *CTA 2010, ss 398A–398G*.

An election for an alternative treatment is available where a company (A) is carrying on a business of leasing plant or machinery alone, there is a relevant change in the relationship between A and a principal company and A elects for *s 398A* to apply. The effect of the election is that:

- there is no qualifying change of ownership in relation to the company, but *subsections (2)(b)* and *(4)(b)* of the existing *s 383* apply in bringing the accounting period of the company to a close and commencing a new accounting period on the day after the relevant day;
- *s 398D* (restrictions on the use of losses) applies during the relevant period; and
- *ss 398E* to *398G* apply during the relevant period and on the relevant day.

The restrictions on the use of losses which can be set against profits of the relevant activity are as follows:

(i) no loss may be deducted under *CTA 2010, Pt 4, Ch 2* (trade losses), *s 62* (losses made in UK property business) or *s 189* (charitable donations);

(ii) no group relief under *CTA 2010, Pt 5* is available;

(iii) no deficit may be set off under *CTA 2009, s 461* (non-trading deficit from loan relationship);

(iv) no loss may be set off under *CTA 2009, s 753* (non-trading loss on intangible fixed assets);

(v) no deduction under *CTA 2009, s 1219* (expenses of management of investment business) is allowed;

(vi) no sum may be set off under *ICTA 1988, Sch 26 para 1* if A is a controlled foreign company subject to an apportionment; and

(vii) if the company would otherwise be a tonnage tax company it is to be treated as not being a tonnage tax company.

Expenditure that has an unallowable purpose is taken out of account when computing the profits or losses of the relevant activity. Expenditure has an unallowable purpose if the main purpose, or one of the main purposes, of the lessor company in incurring it, is to obtain a relevant tax advantage.

A 'relevant tax advantage' is defined as:

(a) a reduction in the corporation tax profits attributable to the carrying on of the relevant activity;
(b) the creation of a corporation tax loss attributable to the carrying on of the relevant activity; or
(c) an increase in corporation tax losses attributable to the carrying on of the relevant activity.

The availability of capital allowances on expenditure incurred by the lessor company is limited by preventing expenditure incurred on the acquisition or creation of an 'independent asset' from qualifying for capital allowances. An 'independent asset' is defined as being an asset that, in the normal course of business, could be used individually, whether or not it could also be used as a constituent part of a single combined asset. Alternatively, an asset that could be used 'at different times' as a constituent part of different combined assets. A 'combined asset' is a single asset consisting of more than one asset.

Pursuant to *CTA 2010, s 398G*, where a transfer of assets into and out of the lessor company would fall within *CTA 2010, s 948* (modifies *CAA 2001* in certain circumstances) then such section will not apply and instead the plant or machinery belonging to the trade is treated as sold by the predecessor on cessation for market value. Where the lessor company is the predecessor and *CAA 2001, s 265* applies, then the transfer value is treated as equal to its market value being the value of the asset unencumbered by any leases or other encumbrances. *FA 2011, Sch 6* amends this section for disposal events taking place after 23 March 2011, including for elections made before that date. Where any event occurs which requires the company (as predecessor or successor) to bring the disposal value of plant or machinery into account under *CAA 2001*, then the disposal value is to be the higher of: the disposal value determined under *CAA 2001*, and the ascribed value of the plant or machinery.

With regard to these provisions, 'the relevant period' begins with the day after the relevant day and ends when there is next a relevant change in the relationship between A and a principal company of A. Where there is not such an event the relevant period continues.

The provisions apply where the relevant day is on or after 9 December 2009, and further to the provisions of *FA 2011* withdrawing the election, before 23 March 2011.

Provisions apply to prevent the relevant period from being brought to a close where *s 398A(4)* and *(5)* apply and the relevant day is before 24 March 2010. In addition the loss restriction with regard to CFCs and tonnage tax companies is disapplied in relation to accounting periods beginning before 24 March 2010, and until 24 March 2010, respectively.

[*FA 2010, s 61 Sch 18*].

Leasing business carried on by a company in partnership

[5.29] Similar changes as above, pursuant to *FA 2011, Sch 6*, with regard to the definition of 'qualifying plant and machinery' and the use of 'ascribed value' in place of 'market value' apply to leasing businesses carried on in partnership, for a relevant day, or transfer, falling on or after 23 March 2011.

If on any day (the '*relevant day*'):

- a company carries on a 'business of leasing plant or machinery' in partnership;
- the partner company is within the charge to corporation tax in respect of the business; and
- there is a qualifying change in the partner company's interest in the business,

the partner company is treated as receiving a taxable business receipt and any other company which carries on the business on that day and which is within the charge to corporation tax in respect of the business is treated as incurring a deductible business expense. See below as to the amount of the taxable receipt and deductible expense. Each such receipt is brought into account as a receipt of the notional business of the partner company in the accounting period in which it is treated as received. If, at the end of the relevant day, the other company is carrying on the business alone, the expense is treated as an expense of that company in its actual business and is allowed as a deduction for corporation tax purposes for the accounting period in which the expense is incurred.

This expense potentially qualifies for the relief at **5.30** below. In any other case, the expense is brought into account as a deductible expense of the notional business of the other company in the accounting period in which it is treated as incurred; the expense does not qualify for the relief at **5.30** below. A company's '*notional business*' is the business the profits or losses of which are determined, in relation to the company, under *CTA 2009, s 1259* (see **58.3 PARTNERSHIPS**). Where the relevant day falls on or after 22 April 2009, the above does not apply where:

- at the end of the relevant day none of the companies that carried on the business any longer has a share in the profits or loss of the business;
- as a result of what happens on the relevant day, the disposal value of all the business plant and machinery on which capital allowances were claimed is to be brought into account as in **12.24 CAPITAL ALLOWANCES — PLANT AND MACHINERY: POOLING AND DISPOSALS**; and
- the disposal value is the open market value of the plant and machinery.

Business of leasing plant or machinery

The question of whether a partnership is carrying on a '*business of leasing plant or machinery*' is determined as for a company in **5.28** above, but with the appropriate modifications. The provisions of *FA 2011* described at **5.28** above will equally apply in such a case. 'Associate' in this case means a person who is a partner in the partnership or connected with a partner in the partnership. A 'qualifying associate' is a person who is an associate at the start of the relevant day or at any earlier time in the prior twelve months.

Qualifying change in a partner company's interest in a business

There is a 'qualifying change in a partner company's interest in a business' if there is a fall on any day of its percentage share in the profits or loss of the business. The percentage share for this purpose is to be determined on a just and reasonable basis and with regard, in particular, to any matter that would be taken into account in determining the company's share of partnership profits or losses (see **58.3 PARTNERSHIPS**, but disregard for this purpose **58.6 PARTNERSHIPS**). 'Profits' for this purpose do not include chargeable gains or capital losses.

Computing the amount of the taxable receipt

The basic amount of the taxable receipt is given by the formula PM – TWDV where these have the meaning below. The basic amount may then be subject to adjustment as described further below. If the basic amount given by the formula is a negative amount, the basic amount is taken instead to be nil.

PM has the meaning given in **5.28** above but references to the company are to be read as references to the partnership and references to an associated company are to be read as references to a 'qualifying company'. '*Qualifying company*' means:

(a) the partner company or a company which is an 'associated company' (as defined by *CTA 2010, s 430*) of the partner company on the relevant day;
(b) any other partner company in relation to whose interest in the business there is a qualifying change on the relevant day;
(c) any other partner company in relation to which there is a qualifying change of ownership (as in **5.28** above) on the relevant day; any
(d) any company which is an associated company on the relevant day of any partner company mentioned in (b) or (c) above.

References in (b) and (c) to another partner company are to a company which carries on the business at the start of the relevant day and is within the charge to corporation tax in respect of it.

TWDV is the total amount of unrelieved qualifying expenditure on plant or machinery in single asset pools, class pools and the main pool that would be carried forward under normal capital allowances rules (see **12.1 CAPITAL ALLOWANCES — PLANT AND MACHINERY: POOLING AND DISPOSALS**) if a new chargeable period of the partnership began on the day after the relevant day. Any expenditure incurred by the partnership on plant or machinery on the relevant day itself is to be left out of account unless it was acquired from a qualifying company (as defined above). In addition pursuant to *FA 2011*, expenditure incurred on the relevant day but attributable to plant and machinery acquired by the partnership before that day is also left out of account.

An adjustment is made to the basic amount calculated above to reflect the fall in the partner company's percentage share in the profits or loss of the business. This is achieved by limiting the amount of the taxable receipt of the partner company to the appropriate percentage of the basic amount. The appropriate percentage is found by subtracting the company's percentage share at the end of the day on which the taxable receipt arises from its percentage share at the start of that day.

If another company's percentage share in the profits or loss of the business is greater at the end than at the start of the relevant day and the increase (or any part of it) is wholly attributable to the change in the partner company's interest in the business, the amount of the deductible expense it is treated as incurring is limited to the appropriate percentage of the amount of the taxable business receipt.

The appropriate percentage is found by the formula OCI/PCD, where OCI is the increase in that company's percentage share that is wholly attributable to the said change and PCD is the decrease in the partner company's percentage share. (Where the relevant day fell before 22 April 2009, the appropriate percentage was the percentage of the other company's percentage share in the profits or loss of the business immediately after the change that was wholly attributable to the change.) If, however, at the end of the relevant day the other company is carrying on the business alone, the deductible expense is equal to the amount of taxable business receipt.

Qualifying change of ownership of a corporate partner

If on any day (the '*relevant day*'):

- a company carries on a 'business of leasing plant or machinery' (as defined above) in partnership;
- the partner company is within the charge to corporation tax in respect of the business; and
- there is a 'qualifying change of ownership' (as in **5.28** above) in relation to the partner company,

the accounting period of the partner company ends on the relevant day and a new accounting period begins on the following day. Also, the partner company is treated as receiving a taxable business receipt (of its notional business) in the accounting period ending on the relevant day and as incurring a deductible business expense (of its notional business) of an equal amount in the new accounting period. See below as to the amount of the taxable receipt. The expense potentially qualifies for the relief at **5.30** below. A company's '*notional business*' is the business the profits or losses of which are determined, in relation to the company, under *CTA 2009, s 1259* (see **58.3 PARTNERSHIPS**). Any loss derived from the expense (to be calculated on the basis that the expense is the final amount to be deducted) cannot be carried back under *CTA 2010, s 37(3)(b)* (previously *ICTA 1988, s 393A(1)(b)*) as a trading loss for offset against profits of earlier accounting periods.

The amount of the taxable business receipt is calculated by first applying the formula above (PM – TWDV) to give the basic amount. This is then adjusted as described in **5.28** above. The taxable business receipt is then limited to the appropriate percentage' of this adjusted amount. If there is no qualifying change in the company's interest in the business on the relevant day, the appropriate percentage is the company's percentage share in the profits or loss of the business on the relevant day. If there is such a change, the appropriate percentage is the company's percentage share in the profits or loss of the business at the end of the relevant day.

See also comments in **5.28** above with regard to the amendments in respect of subsidiaries of consortiums and the change from 90% to a direct or indirect 75% subsidiary, post *FA 2010*, where the relevant day is on or after 9 December 2009.

[*CTA 2010, ss 409–418, 420–427, 429–431, 437, Sch 2 para 68(6)–(9); FA 2006, Sch 10 paras 23–37, 41; FA 2008, s 56(2)(3)(5); CTA 2009, Sch 1 para 695(3)(4); FA 2009, Sch 10 paras 5–7*].

Relief for expense in subsequent accounting period

[5.30] A special provision applies where:

(a) a company is treated under the provisions at **5.28** or **5.29** above as incurring an expense in an accounting period;

(b) the company also makes a loss in that accounting period or in a later accounting period;

(c) some or all of that loss would be carried forward to the accounting period after that in which the loss is made (the '*subsequent period*');

(d) some or all of that carried forward loss derives from the expense in (a) or from a notional expense (as below) which is allowed as a deduction for the accounting period in which the loss is made; and

(e) the subsequent period begins within the period of five years beginning immediately after the 'relevant day' (as in **5.28** or **5.29** above) and does not begin as a result of a subsequent application of **5.28** or **5.29** above.

To the extent that the loss derives from the expense, it is not carried forward but is instead treated as giving rise to a notional expense of an amount equal to:

$$DL + \frac{DL \times D \times R}{365}$$

where:

DL = the amount of the loss deriving from the expense,

D = the number of days in the accounting period in which the loss is incurred, and

R = the rate of INTEREST ON OVERPAID TAX (**50**).

The amount of that notional expense is allowed as a deduction in calculating profits for corporation tax purposes for the subsequent period. The extent to which a loss derives from an expense is determined on the basis that the expense is the final amount to be deducted.

In relation to losses incurred in accounting periods ended before 22 April 2009, these provisions applied only if the subsequent period began within the twelve months beginning with the 'relevant day'. The amount of the notional expense was equal to the amount of the expense in (a) above, i.e. the above formula did not apply.

[*CTA 2010, ss 386, 419, 428, Sch 2 paras 65–67; FA 2006, Sch 10 para 39; FA 2008, s 56(4)(5); FA 2009, Sch 10 paras 8, 9*].

Anti-avoidance

[5.31] Where a company enters into any 'arrangements' (as widely defined), a main purpose of which is to secure that it is treated as incurring an expense under **5.28** or **5.29** above, so much of any loss it incurs that derives from the expense may be carried forward but can only be set against 'relevant leasing income'. It is not available for group relief or relief against total profits of the company. '*Relevant leasing income*' is income deriving from any plant or machinery lease which was entered into before the day on which the company is treated as incurring the expense and which is not an excluded lease of background plant or machinery for a building (see **13.5**(1)(B) **CAPITAL ALLOWANCES — PLANT AND MACHINERY: FIXTURES AND LEASING**). The extent to which a loss derives from the expense is to be determined on the basis that the expense is the final amount to be deducted.

The following rules apply in relation to any qualifying change of ownership (**5.28** above) or qualifying change in a company's interest in a business (**5.29** above) occurring on or after 22 November 2006. They potentially apply where there is a question:

(a) as to whether a company is carrying on a business of leasing plant or machinery (whether alone or in partnership);
(b) as to the amount of the taxable receipt under **5.28** or **5.29** above; or
(c) where the relevant day falls on or after 23 March 2011 (per *FA 2011, Sch 6*), as to the amount of any disposal value to be substituted by *s 398G(3)*.

The first of these rules (*CTA 2010, s 435*) applies if:

(i) in determining the question at (a), (b) or (c) above, regard must be had to the amount (if any) which would fall to be shown in a company's balance sheet for plant or machinery, pursuant to *FA 2011* this is amended (for relevant days falling on or after 23 March 2011) and refers to situations where regard must be had to an amount as listed in new *s 435(1A)*;
(ii) there would be a reduction or increase in any such amount; and
(iii) the reduction or increase would arise in any way from any arrangements (as widely defined) a main purpose of which is to secure a 'relevant tax advantage'.

The new *s 435(1A)* lists the amounts to be considered:

(a) the relevant plant or machinery value;
(b) the value of plant or machinery falling within *s 387(7)* (for companies) or *s 410(6)* (for partnerships);

(c) the relevant company's or partnership's income in the period of twelve months ending with the relevant day;
(d) the amount of the PM;
(e) the amount of the TWDV;
(f) the amount of any disposal value to be substituted by *s 398G(3)*; and
(g) any underlying amount required to calculate or verify an amount mentioned above.

A '*relevant tax advantage*' arises if, disregarding this anti-avoidance rule:

- any company would not be regarded as carrying on a business of leasing of plant or machinery; or
- any taxable receipt of any company under **5.28** or **5.29** above is reduced; or
- any expense that any company is treated as incurring under **5.28** or **5.29** above is increased; or
- where the relevant day falls on or after 23 March 2011 (per *FA 2011, Sch 6*) the amount of any disposal value to be substituted by *s 398G(3)* would be reduced.

The rule is that, for the purpose of determining the question at (a), (b) or (c) above, the reduction or increase in the amounts shown in the balance sheet in respect of the plant or machinery, referred to at (ii) above must be ignored. Further to *FA 2011*, the reduction or increase referred to in (ii), with reference to the amounts identified at *subsection 1A*, and which is to be ignored, is 'to be ascertained' instead of as 'shown in the balance sheet'.

Secondly, (under *CTA 2010, s 436*), if a company owns any plant or machinery at any time on any day and, in determining the question at (a) or (b) above, regard must be had to the amount (if any) which would fall to be shown in its balance sheet in respect of that plant or machinery, the rule below applies if, disregarding this anti-avoidance rule:

(I) no amount would appear in the company's balance sheet in respect of that plant or machinery; or
(II) the amount which would appear is less than the amount which would appear on the assumption that the company had no liabilities of any kind (including share capital) in its balance sheet on the day in question.

The rule is that, for the purpose of determining the question at (a) or (b) above, the assumption referred to at (II) above must be made. *FA 2011* extends this section so as to apply equally to partnerships as it applies to companies, for relevant days falling on or after 23 March 2011.

[*CTA 2010, ss 432–437; FA 2006, Sch 10 paras 38, 38A, 38B, 41; FA 2007, Sch 6 para 2; CTA 2009, Sch 1 para 695(5)*].

Disposal of leased asset

[5.32] If, on the relevant day (where this fell before 13 November 2008), the company or the partnership of which it was a member disposed of any relevant plant or machinery subject to a lease while retaining a right to part of the income stream from the lease under *CAA 2001, s 228K* (see **13.24**(L) **CAPITAL**

ALLOWANCES — PLANT AND MACHINERY: FIXTURES AND LEASING), the provisions at **5.28–5.31** did not apply in so far as the taxable receipt and deductible expense arose by reference to the relevant leased plant or machinery disposed of which was subject to the charge under *CAA 2001, s 228K*. No accounting period was then treated as ending or beginning as a result of the qualifying change of ownership. (These rules applied in a modified form where the disposal was made before 2 June 2006.)

These rules were repealed with effect where the relevant day falls on or after 13 November 2008.

[*FA 2006, Sch 10 para 40; FA 2009, Sch 31 paras 8, 12*].

Reconstructions of companies with leasing trades

[5.33] An anti-avoidance measure has been introduced, with effect for cessations on or after 22 November 2006, to counter the use of reconstructions of companies with leasing trades to avoid tax. This section has now been rewritten to *CTA 2010, s 950*.

It applies only where the trade is part of a 'business of leasing plant or machinery' as in **5.28** above which the predecessor or the successor carries on on the day of cessation (as from 1 April 2010, on the day of transfer). Provided the business is carried on other than in partnership, the parties are not treated as the successor and predecessor.

Where the parties are carrying on the leasing trade in partnership and cessation occurs on or after 21 March 2007, the predecessor has to stop trading on the date of transfer for *CTA 2010, s 948; ICTA 1988, s 343(2)* to apply.

The effect of these provisions is that *CTA 2010, s 948; ICTA 1988, s 343(2)* do not apply unless the companies share the same principal company or companies for the purposes of **5.27–5.31** above.

If *CTA 2010, s 948; ICTA 1988, s 343(2)* do not apply to a transfer, for capital allowances purposes there is deemed to be a disposal by the predecessor of the leasing assets at market value and an acquisition by the successor at that value on the date of cessation of the trade. 'Market value' is to be determined (in accordance with *CTA 2010, s 437(9)*) on the assumption that there is a disposal by the absolute owner and that the asset has no leases or other encumbrances over it.

Pursuant to *FA 2011, Sch 6*, for transfers or successions taking place on or after 23 March 2011, *CTA 2010, s 950* is amended and the disposal above at 'market value' is replaced with the higher of: its ascribed value immediately before transfer of the trade; or the disposal value that the predecessor would be required to bring into account under *CAA 2001, Pt 2* as the result of a transfer of trade. 'Ascribed value' is as defined in **5.28** above, but with reference to predecessor instead of company or partnership.

[*ICTA 1988, s 343A; FA 2007, Sch 6 para 1; CTA 2010, s 950*].

Loan transactions

[5.34] Where, with reference to lending money or giving credit (or varying the terms of a loan or credit):

(i) A transaction provides for the payment of an *annuity or other annual payment* (other than interest) — that payment is treated as if it were a payment of interest.
(ii) Any person *surrenders, waives or forgoes* income on property (or, for transfers before 22 April 2009, assigns such income without a sale or transfer of the property) — that person is chargeable to corporation tax on income (before *CTA 2009* took effect, under *Sch D, Case VI*), on a sum equal to the income assigned, surrendered, waived etc. This does not apply where the person is chargeable to tax on that amount of income by virtue of the finance arrangements provisions in **5.15** above (factoring of income etc.).
(iii) If credit is given for the purchase price of property and during the life of the debt, the purchaser's rights to income from the property are suspended or restricted — he is treated for the purpose of (ii) above as if he had made a surrender of that income.

Transactions with **CONNECTED PERSONS** (**25**) are included.

[*CTA 2010, ss 777–779; ICTA 1988, s 786; FA 2006, Sch 6 para 8; CTA 2009, Sch 1 para 241; FA 2009, Sch 25 para 9*].

Simon's Taxes. See **E1.824.**

Relief by credit under double tax agreement

[5.35] Wide-ranging anti-avoidance provisions apply to certain schemes or arrangements in relation to relief by way of credit under a double tax agreement (see **32.5 DOUBLE TAX RELIEF**), where the main purpose or one of the main purposes of which is the avoidance of tax. The legislation applies in relation to any credit for foreign tax which is connected either with a payment of foreign tax **2005** or with income received from which foreign tax has been deducted (or treated as deducted) at source. For payments of foreign tax on or after 6 December 2006, income received on or after that date or any act or omission on or after that date, 'foreign tax' includes UK tax treated as foreign tax by *TIOPA 2010, s 63(5); ICTA 1988, s 801*.

These provisions, together known as the 'DTR anti-avoidance provisions' apply to any action (or failure of such action) taking place under a scheme or arrangement on or after 6 December 2006. *FA 2010* has introduced some amendments to the existing anti-avoidance rules as from 1 April 2010, to ensure that a person may only deduct foreign tax from any foreign income where he has not already reduced his income by reference to the foreign tax. A new *s 85A* is also added which is targeted at schemes involving deemed foreign tax (manufactured dividends).

HMRC may issue a notice (a '*section 804ZA notice*' or, since 1 April 2010, a '*counteraction notice*') to a company requiring that it make adjustments to or amend the company tax return to nullify the effects of any scheme or arrangement where they have reasonable grounds to believe that, in relation to any income or gains taken into account in determining the tax liability for a chargeable period:

(a) relief by way of credit against UK tax is available under a double tax agreement for the foreign tax suffered on the income or gain;
(b) there is a scheme or arrangement, which is a 'prescribed scheme or arrangement', the main purpose, or one of the main purposes, of which is to provide for an amount of foreign tax to be taken into account;
(c) the aggregate amount of credit relief which can be or has been claimed for the foreign tax by the company, and by any connected persons in a corresponding chargeable period (where the chargeable periods in question have at least one day in common), is more than a minimum amount i.e. at least £100,000 (see HMRCs manual INTM170120);
(d) the scheme or arrangement is either not a scheme or arrangement relating to underlying-tax and one or more of the five following conditions apply or it is an underlying-tax scheme or arrangement and, if it were assumed that the taxpayer company were resident in the UK, one of the five conditions would apply.

[*TIOPA 2010, s 81–83*].

The five conditions for a scheme or arrangement are as follows:

(i) A scheme enables foreign tax which is properly attributable to one source of income or gain to be shifted to a different source of income or gain.
(ii) It enables any scheme participant to claim credit for a payment of foreign tax that increases the total amount of foreign tax paid by all the scheme participants by less than the amount which that person can claim (for example, because the payment made by the claimant is matched by a tax saving for another scheme participant).
(iii) It involves a scheme participant making a claim or election etc. or omitting to make a claim or election etc. which in either case has the effect of increasing the credit for foreign tax available to any scheme participant. References here to claims and elections or suchlike are to claims etc. made under the law of any territory or under the terms of a double tax agreement.
(iv) It has the effect of reducing a scheme participant's total UK tax liability on income and chargeable gains to less than it would have been in the absence of the transactions made under the scheme. This will be the case, for example, where the credit for foreign tax on the scheme income covers not only the UK tax on that income but at least some of the UK tax on other income, thereby reducing total liability.
(v) Under the scheme, a tax deductible payment is made by a person, in return for which that person or a connected party (within the meaning of *CTA 2010, s 1122; ICTA 1988, s 839*) receives consideration which is taxable in a foreign territory (and thus on which credit relief can be obtained in respect of the foreign tax).

[*TIOPA 2010, ss 84–88*].

Where one of the main purposes of the scheme is to obtain relief for underlying tax in respect of a dividend paid by a foreign company, the above schemes are treated as prescribed schemes of the foreign company if they would be treated as such if the company were UK resident (without assuming its activities are carried on in a different place).

On or after 1 April 2010, changes to *TIOPA 2010, s 86* make it clear that it is immaterial whether a pre-execution step was under a scheme or arrangement — a step taken or not taken by a participant in a scheme or arrangement can be a step taken or omitted from being taken before a scheme or arrangement comes into existence. In addition, the reason for taking or not taking the step does not matter provided the effect is to increase, or give rise to, a credit claim by a participant.

TIOPA 2010, s 112 (deduction for foreign tax instead of credit) is amended, effective from 1 April 2010, such that a person may only deduct foreign tax where that person has not already reduced his income by reference to the foreign tax, so ensuring the foreign tax is only deducted once.

TIOPA 2010, s 85A — schemes involving deemed foreign tax

FA 2010, s 36, Sch 11 inserts into *TIOPA 2010* a new *s 85A* which prescribes a scheme or arrangement where there is an amount of deemed foreign tax and either condition A or condition B is met.

Condition A is met where it could reasonably be expected that, under the scheme or arrangement, no real foreign tax would be paid or payable by a participant in the scheme or arrangement. Condition B is met where it could reasonably be expected that, under the scheme or arrangement, real foreign tax would be paid or payable by a participant in the scheme or arrangement but the foreign-tax total would be increased by less than the amount of credit allowable to the claimant in respect of the amount of deemed foreign tax.

'*Real foreign tax*' is defined as including, in relation to *TIOPA 2010, s 10* (accrued income profits), the foreign tax chargeable in respect of the interest payable on the securities referred to in *s 10(1)(c)* and, in relation to the manufactured overseas dividend (MOD) rules, the foreign tax chargeable on the overseas dividend of which the MOD is representative. These provisions have effect for foreign tax paid or payable on or after 21 October 2009.

Counteraction notice

A counteraction notice will not be issued in the simple case of a company holding foreign shareholdings within an investment portfolio where the dividends are taxed as investment income (with credit for foreign tax deducted but no entitlement to underlying tax credit). Nor will a notice be issued in the case where a company holds intellectual property acquired or established in the course of its trade and tax is deducted from royalty income (but this exemption will not apply if intellectual property is created specifically for the purpose of creating an avoidance scheme or arrangement). These let-outs will not apply if income is received by a company for the purpose of benefiting from the let-out, for example if income is deliberately diverted to a non-trading company from a connected company in order to fall within the portfolio investment clearance. (See paras 27, 30 and 31 of HMRC's draft guidance).

There is no formal clearance procedure but HMRC will be prepared to give advice concerning actual or proposed transactions and, where appropriate, will confirm that no counteraction notice will be issued in respect of the disclosed transactions (see paras 23 to 25 of their draft guidance).

See *TIOPA 2010, s 89; ICTA 1988, s 804ZA* for the form of notice. Where a company tax return is made within 90 days after the issue of a counteraction notice, the notice may be disregarded when making the return, as long as the return is then amended in accordance with the notice before the end of that 90-day period.

Once a return has been made, HMRC may only issue a counteraction notice if a notice of enquiry has been issued in respect of the return, but an enquiry may be opened for just that purpose. If a counteraction notice is then issued, the company must then amend the return accordingly within the 90 days beginning with the date of issue of the notice.

Failure to make or amend a return in accordance with a counteraction notice results in the return becoming an incorrect return (so that penalties potentially apply). An enquiry cannot be closed until either the amendment is made or the 90-day period for making it expires. Disputes between HMRC and the taxpayer are settled under the normal self-assessment enquiry procedures and with the normal rights of appeal (see paras 15 to 17 of HMRC draft guidance referred to below).

Where an enquiry into a return has been completed, a counteraction notice can only be issued where HMRC could not have been reasonably expected to realise that a notice was required on the basis of the information supplied before the enquiry was completed, or, had requests for information by HMRC in the course of the enquiry been complied with, it is reasonable to suppose that they would have issued a notice at that time. Once a counteraction notice is issued in such circumstances, a related 'discovery' assessment cannot be made until either the necessary amendment is made to the tax return or the 90-day period for making it expires. The conditions at **7.3**(a) and (b) **ASSESSMENTS** for making a discovery assessment are disapplied (being replaced by the above conditions for issuing the notice).

[*TIOPA 2010, ss 90–95; ICTA 1988, ss 804ZA–804ZC, Sch 28AB; FA 2005, ss 87, 88, Sch 5; FA 2007, s 35*].

See generally HMRC's guidance at INTM170010–170140.

Restriction of deductions for annual payments

[5.36] In calculating a company's income from any source, no deduction is allowed for an annual payment to which the following apply.

- The payment is charged to income tax under *ITTOIA 2005, Pt V* (miscellaneous income) (otherwise than as relevant foreign income — see Tolley's Income Tax under Foreign Income) or, before 2005/06, under *Sch D, Case III*, or is charged to corporation tax under *CTA 2009, ss 976, 977* (see **61.13 PROFIT COMPUTATIONS**) or, for accounting periods ending before 1 April 2009, under Schedule D, Case III.
- The payment is made under a liability incurred for consideration in money or money's worth, all or any of which either (a) consists of, or of the right to receive, a dividend, or (b) is not required to be brought

into account in calculating for corporation tax purposes the income of the company making the annual payment. Condition (a) did not apply to annual payments made before 2 December 2004.

- The payment is not a payment of income which arises under a settlement made on divorce, annulment or separation and payable by one party to the marriage or civil partnership to or for the benefit of the other party.
- The payment is not made to an individual under a liability incurred in consideration of his surrendering, assigning or releasing in interest in settled property to, or in favour of, a person with a subsequent interest.
- The payment is not an annuity granted in the ordinary course of a business of granting annuities.

In calculating a company's income from any source for corporation tax purposes no deduction is allowed for interest except under the loan relationship provisions at *CTA 2009, Pt 5*. [*CTA 2009, s 1301A, as inserted by TIOPA 2010*].

In relation to Scotland, the reference to settled property is to property held in trust. For the position prior to the above, see *CIR v Plummer* (1979) 54 TC 1, HL, and *Moodie v CIR and Sinnett* (1993) 65 TC 610, HL, in which the decision in *Plummer* on similar facts was reversed on *Ramsay* principles (see **5.1** above).

[*CTA 2009, s 1301; ICTA 1988, s 125; FA 2005, s 91(2)(3)(7); ITTOIA 2005, Sch 1 para 107; F(No 2)A 2005, s 38(3)(7)(13), Sch 11 Pt 2(7); ITA 2007, Sch 1 para 125*].

Annual payments as above are made without deduction of tax at source. See **46.2**(a) **INCOME TAX IN RELATION TO A COMPANY**. Where made before 16 March 2005, such payments were excluded from being a charge on income; this specific exclusion is no longer necessary as all annual payments made on or after that date are so excluded. See **61.11 PROFIT COMPUTATIONS**.

Simon's Taxes. See **B8.428, D1.315, D1.317, E1.802.**

Pass on value of dividend tax credit

[5.37] Special provisions apply where:

(a) a person ('A') is entitled to a tax credit in respect of a qualifying distribution;
(b) arrangements (as widely defined) subsist such that another person ('B') obtains, whether directly or indirectly, a payment representing any of the value of the tax credit;
(c) the arrangements (whether or not made directly between A and B) were entered into for an 'unallowable purpose'; and
(d) had B been entitled to and received the distribution when it was made, he would not have been entitled to payment of the tax credit and, if a company, could not have used the income consisting of the distribution to frank a distribution made in the same accounting period (after using any actual franked investment income).

They apply equally where an amount representing any of the value of the tax credit is applied at the direction of, or otherwise in favour of, some other person, as if that other person had obtained a payment representing that value.

Where these provisions apply:

(i) no claim may be made for payment of the tax credit or for set-off against tax on other income;
(ii) the income consisting of the distribution is not regarded as franked investment income; and
(iii) no transitional charity relief payment may be claimed.

This does not, however, apply to the extent that the tax advantage otherwise obtained under the arrangements is cancelled or reduced by any other provision.

'Tax advantage' for this purpose is as under *CTA 2010, s 1139*; *ICTA 1988, s 709* (see **5.2** above), but also includes the obtaining of a payment representing any of the value of a tax credit where, had the person obtaining the payment been entitled to and received the distribution when it was made, that person would not have been entitled to payment of the tax credit and, if a company, could not have used the income consisting of the distribution to frank a distribution made in the same accounting period (after using any actual franked investment income).

Arrangements are entered into for an '*unallowable purpose*' if any person is a party to the arrangements for purposes which include a purpose other than a business or commercial purpose (which includes the efficient management of investments). The purpose of obtaining a tax advantage for any person is not a business or commercial purpose unless it is not a main purpose of entering into the arrangements.

[*ICTA 1988, s 231B; F(No 2)A 1997, s 28; ITTOIA 2005, Sch 1 para 116*].

Commodity futures — withdrawal of loss relief

[5.38] If, apart from *ICTA 1988, s 128(2)* (see **61.17 PROFIT COMPUTATIONS**) and *TCGA 1992, s 143(1)* (as amended by *CTA 2009, Sch 1 para 369*), gains arising in the course of dealing in financial futures or qualifying options would, for corporation tax purposes, constitute profits or gains chargeable as overseas income or miscellaneous income i.e. other than as profits of a trade, any loss arising in the course of that dealing is not allowable against profits or gains chargeable as overseas or miscellaneous income. [*ICTA 1988, s 399(1B)*].

Note that, following the rewriting of *ICTA 1988, s 128(2)(3)* as *CTA 2009, s 981* (which precludes such gains from the charge to corporation tax on income), *ICTA 1988, s 399(1B)* is repealed as unnecessary. [*CTA 2009, Sch 1 para 115*].

If a company carries on the trade of dealing in commodity futures in partnership, and a scheme has been effected or arrangements have been made whereby the sole or main benefit that might be expected to accrue to the company from its partnership interest is the making of a loss to be set off against general income under *ICTA 1988, s 393(2)* or *s 393A(1)* (see **55.3** and **55.4 LOSSES**), such relief is denied. Any relief already given is recouped by an assessment (under *Sche D, Case VI* for accounting periods beginning before 1 April 2009).

[*ICTA 1988, s 399; FA 2002, Sch 27 para 4; ITTOIA 2005, Sch 1 para 171; ITA 2007, Sch 1 para 76; CTA 2009, Sch 1 para 115*].

Simon's Taxes. See **D1.1110**.

Companies in partnership

[5.39] Where a company realises capital from a partnership such that the capital realised exceeds the company's contribution to the partnership and that excess results wholly or partly from an arrangement under which the partnership profits were not fully allocated to the company in accordance with its capital share, the company is chargeable to corporation tax on the lower of:

(a) the excess of the realised capital over contributions; and
(b) the amount by which the company's due share of allocated profits exceed the amount allocated to it where those profits would have otherwise been chargeable to corporation tax.

This section was repealed by *FA 2009, Sch 24*, the disguised interest provisions, with effect from 22 April 2009.

See **58.12 PARTNERSHIPS**. [*FA 2004, ss 131–133; CTA 2009, Sch 1 para 572*].

Change in ownership of a company

[5.40] There are a number of anti-avoidance provisions relating to the change in ownership of a company which are dealt with as indicated below.

3.8	**ADVANCE CORPORATION TAX — SHADOW ACT** [*SI 1999 No 358, Regs 16–18*].
5.27– 5.33	Sale of lessors
17.11	**CAPITAL GAINS** (reconstructions and amalgamations) [*TCGA 1992, ss 101, 101B*].
38.16, 38.18	**GAINS AND LOSS BUYING**
29.1– 17.45	**CAPITAL GAINS — GROUPS** (pre-entry losses, pre-entry gains and group transactions) [*TCGA 1992, ss 176–179*].
39.6	**GROUP RELIEF** (**39**) [*CTA 2010, ss 138–144, 154, 155; ICTA 1988, ss 403A–403C, 409, 410*].
51.9	**INVESTMENT COMPANIES AND INVESTMENT BUSINESS** [*CTA 2010, ss 677–691, 692–703; ICTA 1988, ss 768B, 768C, Sch 28A*].
55.2	**LOSSES** (restrictions on losses carried forward) [*CTA 2010, ss 673–676; ICTA 1988, ss 768–769*].

59.11 PAYMENT OF TAX (change in ownership of company) [*CTA 2010, ss 706–718; ICTA 1988, ss 767A, 767B*].

Disclosure of tax avoidance schemes

[5.41] There are obligations, as outlined below, on promoters of certain tax avoidance schemes, and in some cases on persons entering into transactions under such schemes, to disclose those schemes to HMRC. The primary legislation in *FA 2004, ss 306–319* provides the framework for these disclosure rules but the detailed provisions are mostly contained in regulations. Originally, the provisions required disclosure only of schemes connected with employment or involving financial products, but with effect, broadly, on or after 1 August 2006, the provisions are extended to cover the whole of income tax, capital gains tax and corporation tax. From that date, the disclosure requirements are triggered where arrangements feature one of eight hallmarks. Further amendments have been made by *FA 2007*, *FA 2008*, *FA 2010* and secondary legislation.

Disclosure can be made online via HMRC's Anti-Avoidance Group website (www.hmrc.gov.uk) or alternatively forms for making disclosures can be downloaded from the same location. For disclosures on or after 1 November 2008, information required **must** be provided on the appropriate forms, as follows:

(a) *FA 2004, s 308(1)* and *(3)* — forms AAG1 and AAG5;
(b) *FA 2004, s 309(1)* — forms AAG2 and AAG5;
(c) *FA 2004, s 310* — forms AAG3 and AAG5;
(d) *FA 2004, s 312(2)* — form AAG6;
(e) *FA 2004, s 312A(2)* — form AAG6;
(f) *FA 2004, s 313(1)* and *(3)(a)* — in the boxes provided for this purpose on the return;
(g) *FA 2004, s 313(1)* and *(3)(b)* — form AAG4,

unless notification is otherwise provided for (e.g. by notification in a corporation tax return).

Online disclosure may be made by clicking the relevant links on the Anti-Avoidance Group website at http://www.hmrc.gov.uk/aiu/index.htm or the forms may be downloaded and sent to:

Anti-Avoidance Group (Disclosure & Risk Team)
HM Revenue & Customs
1st Floor, 22 Kingsway
London
WC2B 6NR

The aim of the disclosure rules is to provide HMRC with early information about avoidance schemes and how they work, together with information about who has used them.

Arrangements requiring disclosure

[5.42] '*Notifiable arrangements*' requiring disclosure under the provisions are 'arrangements' which:

- fall within any description prescribed by Treasury regulations (see below);
- enable, or might be expected to enable, any person to obtain an 'advantage' in relation to any tax (which may include capital gains tax and corporation tax) that is so prescribed in relation to arrangements of that description;
- are such that the main benefit, or one of the main benefits, that might be expected to arise from the arrangements is the obtaining of that advantage; and
- it is a hallmarked scheme.

The provisions also require disclosure of '*notifiable proposals*', i.e. proposals for arrangements which would be notifiable arrangements if entered into, whether the proposal relates to a particular person or to any person who may seek to take advantage of it.

For these purposes, '*arrangements*' include any scheme, transaction or series of transactions. An '*advantage*', in relation to any tax, means:

- relief or increased relief from, or repayment or increased repayment of, that tax;
- the avoidance or reduction of a charge or assessment to that tax;
- the avoidance of a possible assessment to that tax;
- the deferral of any payment of tax;
- the advancement of any repayment of tax; or
- the avoidance of any obligation to deduct or account for any tax.

See also www.hmrc.gov.uk/aiu/disclosure-nov08.pdf for HMRC Guidance on Disclosure of Tax Avoidance Schemes, effective from 1 November 2008.

[*FA 2004, ss 306, 318(1)*].

Prescribed arrangements – on or after 1 August 2006. With effect as indicated below, any arrangements which fall within any of the descriptions (or '*hallmarks*') listed below are prescribed by the Treasury for the purposes of these provisions. The taxes covered are income tax, capital gains tax and corporation tax. These provisions apply with effect from 1 August 2006 but do not apply to notifiable proposals where the relevant date (see below) is before that date nor to notifiable arrangements, in relation to which the disclosure requirement falls on:

- a promoter, where the promoter first becomes aware of any transaction forming part of the arrangements before that date; or
- a person other than a promoter, where any transaction forming part of the arrangements is entered into before that date.

The hallmarks are as follows.

(1) **Confidentiality in cases involving a promoter.** Arrangements fall within this hallmark if it might be reasonably expected that a promoter would wish the way in which any element of the arrangements (including the way in which it secures a tax advantage or, from 1 January 2011, might secure a tax advantage) to be kept confidential from any other promoter at any time in the period beginning with the date of the first transaction

forming part of the arrangements and ending with the date by which the user of the arrangements must notify HMRC of the reference number (see below). From 1 January 2011 the hallmark applies in terms of confidentiality at *any date after the 'material date'*, which is broadly the relevant date for notification of a notifiable proposal (*SI 2010 No 2834, Reg 5*). These questions must be considered at the time the relevant trigger for disclosure arises. Arrangements also fall within this hallmark if either:

- the promoter would, but for these provisions, wish to keep the way in which the arrangements secure a tax advantage confidential from HMRC for some or all of that period (or, from 1 January 2011, from the material date) and a reason for doing so is to facilitate repeated or continued use of the element of the arrangements which secure the advantage or of substantially the same element; or
- where there is no promoter by virtue only of legal professional privilege ((C) below) or the promoter is not UK resident, the user of the arrangements wishes to keep confidential from HMRC the way that the arrangements secure a tax advantage for some or all of that period (or, from 1 January 2011, from the material date).

(2) **Confidentiality in cases not involving a promoter**. Arrangements fall within this hallmark if there is no promoter and:

- the intended user of the arrangements is a business (as defined) which is not a '*small or medium-sized enterprise*' (broadly, a micro, small or medium-sized enterprise as defined in the Commission Recommendation of 6 May 2003);
- the user wishes the way in which the arrangements secure a tax advantage to be kept confidential from HMRC for some or all of the period beginning with the date on which he enters into the first transaction forming part of the arrangements and ending with the latest date by which he must notify HMRC of the reference number (until 31 December 2010);
- from 1 January 2011 the user wishes the way in which the arrangements secure a tax advantage to be kept confidential from HMRC from the material date; and
- a reason for doing so is to facilitate repeated or continued use of the element of the arrangements which secure the advantage or of substantially the same element.

(3) **Premium fee.** Arrangements fall within this hallmark if they are such that it might reasonably be expected that a promoter or a person connected with a promoter of arrangements that are the same as, or substantially similar to, the arrangements in question, would, but for these provisions, be able to obtain a 'premium fee' from a person experienced in receiving services of the type being provided. Arrangements where there is no promoter or where the tax advantage is intended to be obtained by an individual or business which is a small or medium-sized enterprise are excluded. A '*premium fee*' for this purpose

is one chargeable by virtue of any element of the arrangements from which the tax advantage is expected to arise and which is to a significant extent attributable to, or to any extent contingent on the obtaining of, that advantage.

(4) **Off market terms.** This hallmark is repealed with effect from 1 January 2011.

Arrangements fell within this hallmark if:

- the tax advantage expected from the arrangements arises, to more than an incidental degree, from the inclusion of one or more 'financial products';
- a promoter or person connected with the promoter becomes party to one or more of those products; and
- the price of the product or products differs significantly from that which might reasonably be expected to apply in the open market.

For this purpose, the following are '*financial products*':

(a) loans (excluding finance leases);
(b) derivative contracts under *FA 2002, Sch 26*, including contracts otherwise excluded by virtue of their underlying subject matter (see **30 DERIVATIVE CONTRACTS LEGISLATION**);
(c) contracts which would be within (b) above if they were contracts of a company;
(d) agreements for the sale and repurchase of securities as described in *ICTA 1988, s 730A(1)* (see **5.6** above);
(e) arrangements which are debtor repos, a debtor quasi-repo, a creditor repo or a creditor quasi-repo (within the meanings given by *FA 2007, Sch 13*) *SI 2007 No 2484*;
(f) stock lending arrangements within *TCGA 1992, s 263B(1)* (see Tolley's Capital Gains Tax under Shares and Securities);
(g) shares; and
(h) any contract (other than the above) whether on its own or in combination with other contracts (including any of the above) which in accordance with UK generally accepted accounting practice is in substance and so treated as a loan or the advancing or depositing of money in whatever form (excluding finance leases).

Financial products held within an ISA are excluded.

(5) **Standardised tax products**. Arrangements fall within this hallmark if they are 'tax products' which are made available by a promoter for implementation by more than one person. A 'product' is a '*tax product*' for this purpose if it would be reasonable for an informed observer who had studied the arrangements to conclude that their main purpose was to enable a client to obtain a tax advantage. Arrangements are a '*product*' if:

- they have substantially standardised documentation to enable implementation of the arrangements by the client and the form of that documentation is determined by the promoter and not tailored to any material extent to the client;
- the client must enter into a specific transaction or series of transactions, which must be substantially standardised in form.

Arrangements which are the same, or substantially the same, as arrangements first made available for implementation before 1 August 2006 are excluded, as are arrangements consisting solely of one or more plant or machinery leases (see (7) below), an Enterprise Investment Scheme (see Tolley's Income Tax under Enterprise Investment Scheme) or ISA, arrangements using the **CORPORATE VENTURING SCHEME (28)** or **VENTURE CAPITAL TRUSTS (74)**, arrangements qualifying for **COMMUNITY INVESTMENT TAX RELIEF (23)**, specified approved employee share schemes, certain pension schemes and schemes to which *ITTOIA 2005, s 731* (periodical payments of personal injury damages) applies.

(6) **Loss schemes.** Arrangements are within this hallmark if the promoter expects more than one individual to implement them or to implement arrangements which are substantially the same and an informed observer, having studied them, could reasonably conclude that the main benefit of the arrangements for some or all of the participants would be the provision of losses which they would be expected to use to reduce their liability to income tax or capital gains tax.

(7) **Leasing arrangements.** Arrangements falling within this hallmark include a high value plant or machinery lease which is not a short-term lease where one of three additional conditions are met as set out below. A '*plant or machinery lease*' for this purpose is:

- any agreement or arrangement which, in accordance with generally accepted accounting practice, falls (or would fall) to be treated as a lease under which the lessor grants to the lessee the right to use the plant or machinery for a period;
- any other agreement or arrangement to the extent that, in accordance with generally accepted accounting practice, it conveys or falls (or would fall) to be regarded as conveying the right to use the plant or machinery; or
- a finance lease under *CAA 2001, s 221(1)(c)* where the plant or machinery is the subject of a sale and finance leaseback as defined under that section.

The lease is a '*high value*' lease if the lower of the cost to the lessor, or the market value, of either:

- any one asset forming part of the plant or machinery leased or to be leased under the arrangements is at least £10 million; or
- the aggregate of all the assets forming part of the plant or machinery leased or to be leased under the arrangements is at least £25 million.

The lease is a '*short-term lease*' if it has a term not exceeding two years. It will not be a short-term lease if the lessee can extend the term beyond two years by the exercise of an option or by some other arrangement entered into at the inception of the lease. Nor will it be a short-term lease if arrangements are entered into, at or about the time of the inception of the lease, for the assets to be leased to one or more other persons under one or more other leases and the aggregate of the terms of the lease to the lessee and to such other persons as are connected with the lessee exceed two years.

The three additional conditions, one of which must also be met, are as follows.

- Condition 1 is that the arrangements are designed such that one or more of the leases comprised in the arrangements are, or would be, entered into by one party who has the right to claim capital allowances on expenditure incurred on the plant or machinery and by another party (ignoring guarantors) who is not, or would not be, chargeable to corporation tax (whether or not there are other parties to the lease who satisfy neither of those conditions).
- Condition 2 is that the arrangements are designed to remove the whole or greater part of any risk of a loss which would otherwise fall directly or indirectly upon the lessor if the payments due under the lease are not made in accordance with its terms and the risk is so removed by the provision of money or a money debt (as defined in *ITEPA 2003, s 702(6)*).
- Condition 3 is that the arrangements are designed to consist of, or include, a sale and finance leaseback arrangement (within *CAA 2001, s 221*) or a lease and finance leaseback (within *CAA 2001, s 228F(5), CAA 2001, s 228A* for leases entered into on or after 9 October 2007). This does not apply where assets leased, or to be leased, under sale and finance leaseback arrangements are, or will be, unused and not second-hand at the time when the assets are acquired or created and where the interval between the acquisition or creation of the assets and their sale under the arrangements is not more than four months.

  Condition 3 does not apply if the plant or machinery is, or the promoter expects it to become, a fixture (as defined by *CAA 2001, s 173(1)*) which is leased with relevant land (as defined by *CAA 2001, s 173(2)*) unless it is used for storage or production (as defined). It will, however, apply if the qualifying expenditure incurred on that fixture amounts or will amount to more than 50% of the aggregate value of assets subject to the lease and the rent payable under the lease is directly or indirectly dependent on the availability of capital allowances on expenditure on any plant or machinery comprised in the lease. In determining the value of the assets subject to the lease, the value of the land is the market value of the lessor's interest and the value of plant or machinery is to be determined in the same manner as for a 'high value' lease above.

(8) **Pension arrangements.** This hallmark was introduced to target schemes that seek to avoid the pension contribution 'anti-forestalling' measures introduced in *FA 2009*. Pension arrangements are prescribed if they involve the accrual or expected accrual of pension scheme benefits to a person and the main benefit of the arrangements is that the person would not be subject to the special annual allowance charge (per *FA 2009, Sch 35*) or would suffer a reduced charge. *SI 2009 No 2033* amended *SI 2006 No 1543* with effect from 1 September 2009.

For the purpose only of determining whether arrangements are prescribed by (1)–(3) or (7) above, the provision that persons are not to be treated as promoters by virtue of legal professional privilege ((C) below) is disregarded.

[*SI 2006 No 1543*].

See also HMRC's guidance published on their website on 16 June 2006 and, from 1 November 2008, the new HMRC guidance at www.hmrc.gov.uk/aiu/disclosure-nov08.pdf.

Prescribed arrangements — prior to August 2006. Prior to the introduction of the hallmark system above, there were two types of arrangements prescribed by the Treasury. They were arrangements connected with employment (for details of which see Tolley's Income Tax), and arrangements related to financial products. The taxes covered were income tax, capital gains tax and corporation tax.

The arrangements in relation to financial products which had to be disclosed were those where the tax advantage was expected to derive to a significant degree from the inclusion of any financial products (defined as above).

Disclosure of arrangements relating to financial products was not required where:

- they (or similar arrangements) were not reasonably expected to generate premium fees for their promotion; and
- the tax advantage expected to be obtained did not arise from any element of the arrangements which the promoter might reasonably have expected to be kept confidential from other promoters.

Disclosure was also not required where:

- the only financial products involved in the arrangements were assets held within an ISA or a PEP; or
- the promoter (or person connected with the promoter) became a party to the financial product which did not differ significantly from that which might reasonably be expected to be offered in the open market.

[*SI 2004 No 1863, Sch paras 6–8; SI 2004 No 2429; SI 2006 No 1543, Reg 18*].

For examples of transactions which would and would not fall within these provisions, see HMRC's guidance material published on their website (www.hmrc.gov.uk) on 29 July 2004.

Disclosure by promoter

On or after 1 November 2008, the duty of a promoter to notify the reference number to the client is discharged where he has provided the client with the prescribed information relating to the reference number allocated to a notifiable proposal for the arrangements, provided that the proposal and the arrangements are substantially the same. On or after 1 April 2009, the prescribed information is that laid down in SI 2009 No 611. HMRC may, by notice, withdraw the obligation of a promoter to notify a reference number to a client. From the same date, a client who has been notified of a reference number must notify the reference number to any other person that he might reasonably be expected to know is or is likely to be a party to the arrangements and who might reasonably be expected to gain a tax advantage under the circumstances. This duty will not apply in circumstances to be prescribed or where HMRC give notice to that effect. [*FA 2004, ss 312, 312A; FA 2008, s 116, Sch 38 para 4; SI 2008 No 1935*].

A 'promoter' must provide HMRC with specified information on any 'notifiable proposal' within a prescribed period of five business days after the 'relevant date'. The '*relevant date*' is the date on which he makes the proposal available for implementation by any person or, if earlier, the date he first becomes aware of any transaction forming part of arrangements implementing the proposal or by 30 September 2004 if later. The time limit for disclosure is extended where the promoter reasonably expects to make a clearance application (see below) to HMRC under certain specified provisions.

There is a separate requirement for a 'promoter' to provide HMRC with specified information relating to notifiable arrangements and to do so within a prescribed period of five business days after the date on which he first becomes aware of any transaction forming part of those arrangements, or by 30 September 2004 if later; but this does not apply if the arrangements implement a proposal which has been notified as above.

The disclosure under these provisions must provide sufficient information as might be reasonably expected to enable an officer of HMRC to comprehend the manner in which the proposal or arrangements are intended to operate, including the details specified in *SI 2004 No 1864, Reg 3*.

Where two or more persons are promoters in relation to the same proposal or arrangements, notification by one promoter discharges the obligations of the others. If a promoter has discharged his obligations in relation to a proposal or arrangements, he is not required to notify proposals or arrangements which are substantially the same as those already notified (whether or not they relate to the same parties).

A case has been heard by the Special Commissioners on what are notifiable arrangements — *Revenue and Customs Comrs v Mercury Tax Group Ltd* [2009] SWTI 628. See now *Tax Avoidance Schemes (Prescribed Descriptions of Arrangements Regulations 2006* (*SI 2006 No 1543*), which came into force on 1 August 2006. It appears from the decision that the company accepted that the scheme fell within the 2006 Regulations, and notified it in September 2006.

Meaning of promoter

A person is a '*promoter*' in relation to a notifiable proposal if, in the course of a 'relevant business', he is to any extent responsible for the design of the proposed arrangements or he makes the notifiable proposal available for implementation by others. In addition, from 1 January 2011 (per *FA 2010, Sch 17*) a person is a promoter if he makes a firm approach to another person (C) in relation to a notifiable proposal with a view to making the proposal available for implementation by C or any other person.

A person is a '*promoter*' in relation to notifiable arrangements if, by virtue of his having made the proposal available for implementation or, from 1 January 2011, by making a firm approach to another person to do so, he is a promoter in relation to a notifiable proposal which is implemented by those arrangements or if, in the course of a 'relevant business', he is to any extent responsible for the design of the arrangements or the organisation or management of the arrangements.

A '*firm approach*' is where the person makes a marketing contact with another person in relation to the notifiable proposals at a time when the proposed arrangements have been substantially designed. '*Substantially designed*' means the transactions have been sufficiently developed for it to be reasonable to believe that a person might enter into them, or transactions not substantially different to them.

A '*marketing contact*' occurs when a person communicates information about the notifiable proposal to the other person, with a view to that person, or any other person, entering into transactions forming part of the proposed arrangements, and the information communicated includes an explanation of the advantage in relation to any tax that might be expected to be obtained from the proposed arrangements.

According to HMRC's guidance notes (see below), a scheme designer may not be a promoter if one of three tests is passed:

- the benign test — where the person's involvement falls short of responsibility for any element of the scheme — e.g. he gives specialist advice on some legal point not directly affecting the tax advantage;
- the non-adviser test — where the person is involved with the design of the scheme but does not contribute any tax advice; and
- the ignorance test — where the person does not have sufficient information to comply or might not reasonably be expected to know if the arrangements were disclosable.

Making a scheme available may involve more than one person, in which case each will have disclosure obligations to consider. HMRC will not consider a person who only introduces the scheme provider to a potential user as a promoter. He is not regarded as making the scheme available. A person who organises or manages a scheme that he did not design or make available is not a promoter, provided he is unconnected with a person who has marketed or designed it or similar schemes. Groups are treated as one entity in that they are obliged to disclose schemes supplied intra-group as 'in-house' schemes. A scheme is '*made available for implementation by another person*' if it has been developed to a stage where the promoter is confident in the tax analysis applying to it and it is passed to a potential user in the form that he could understand the tax advantages and decide whether or not to use it.

The regulations (*SI 2004 No 1865*, as amended by *SI 2004 No 2613*) exclude from the definition of promoter:

(A) a company providing taxation services to another company in the same 51% group;

(B) employees of employers who are promoters of or enter into transactions forming part of proposed arrangements;

(C) a person who is not required to provide the prescribed information by virtue of legal professional privilege (see below under legal professional privilege);

(D) persons not responsible for the design of any element of the proposals or arrangements giving rise to the expected tax advantage;
(E) persons who are to any extent responsible for the design of the proposals or arrangements but who do not provide tax advice in relation to them in a professional capacity;
(F) persons not responsible for the design of all the elements of the proposals or arrangements giving rise to the expected tax advantage, who could not reasonably be expected to have sufficient information so as to know whether the proposals or arrangements fall within these provisions or sufficient information to be able to comply with the duties of a promoter;
(G) a person not connected with a promoter in relation to the arrangements or arrangements which are substantially the same as those arrangements.

A '*relevant business*' is any trade, profession or business which involves the provision to other persons of taxation services or is carried on by a bank or a securities house. Where companies form a 51% group, anything done by one group company for the purposes of another company's relevant business is brought within the above disclosure requirements.

A 'marketed scheme' is one that is planned without a specific user in mind, other than, possibly, a certain class of taxpayer. The promoter may actively seek a user, or make the scheme available in response to a general request for taxation advice.

[*FA 2004, ss 307, 308, 319(3); SI 2004 No 1864, Regs 1, 3(1)(2), 4(1)–(3), 5, 6; SI 2004 No 1865; SI 2004 No 2613; FA 2010, s 56, Sch 17*].

Introducers

From 1 January 2011, *FA 2010, Sch 17* creates the role of 'introducer' in relation to notifiable proposals. A person is an introducer if that person makes a marketing contact with another person in relation to the notifiable proposal. An introducer is not a promoter but can be required to respond to pre-disclosure enquiries under *FA 2004, s 313A* or to give details of the person who has provided the introducer with any information relating to the proposal, under *FA 2004, s 313C*, both from 1 January 2011.

Disclosure by person dealing with non-UK promoter

A person who enters into any transaction forming part of notifiable arrangements in relation to which there is a non-UK resident promoter (and no UK resident promoter) must himself provide HMRC with specified information (similar to that which a promoter must provide) relating to those arrangements. He must do so within a prescribed period of five business days after entering into the transaction or by 30 September 2004 if later. This obligation is discharged if a promoter makes disclosure of the notifiable proposal for the arrangements in question. Similarly, where the promoter is a lawyer who is claiming that legal professional privilege prevents him from disclosing, the scheme user must disclose. Where there is no promoter (e.g. the user designs the scheme himself), the user is required to disclose within 30 days of the scheme being implemented.

This provision does not apply in relation to any notifiable arrangements which include transactions entered into before 23 April 2004. In the case of notifiable arrangements relating to financial products, the provision does not apply if the date on which any transaction forming part of the arrangements is entered into falls before 22 June 2004. The time limit for disclosure of all notifiable arrangements is extended to 31 October 2004 where the date on which any transaction forming part of the arrangements is entered into falls before 1 August 2004.

[*FA 2004, ss 309, 319(4); SI 2004 No 1864, Regs 1, 3(3), 4(4)(7), 6*].

Disclosure by parties to notifiable arrangements not involving a promoter

A person who enters into any transaction forming part of notifiable arrangements in respect of which neither he nor any other person in the UK has an obligation as above must himself provide HMRC with specified information (similar to that which a promoter must provide) relating to those arrangements. Such disclosure must normally be made within 30 days beginning with the day after the day in which he enters into the first transaction forming part of the arrangements. Reasonable and proportionate measures should be put in place to ensure that the date of the first transaction is identified and that notification is made within the time limit. However, if disclosure is made as soon as possible and there is a reasonable excuse for failing to notify in time, no penalty will be charged.

However, where a person is not to be treated as a promoter in relation to notifiable arrangements by virtue of legal professional privilege (see below under legal professional privilege), the disclosure must be made within five business days after entering into the transaction (subject to the transitional commencement provisions below). Before 1 August 2006, a disclosure under these provisions could, unless the five-day time limit applied, be made at any time after the date of the first transaction and before the person was first required to notify HMRC of the reference number for the arrangements (see below).

This does not apply in relation to any notifiable arrangements which include a transaction entered into before 23 April 2004. In the case of notifiable arrangements relating to financial products, the provision does not apply if the date on which any transaction forming part of the arrangements is entered into falls before 22 June 2004. The time limit for disclosure of all notifiable arrangements is extended to 31 October 2004 where the date on which any transaction forming part of the arrangements is entered into falls before 1 August 2004.

[*FA 2004, ss 310, 319(4); SI 2004 No 1864, Regs 1, 3(4), 4(5)(5A), 6; SI 2004 No 2613, Reg 2; SI 2006 No 1544, Reg 4*].

Mechanics of disclosure

The correct forms must be used (see above). The following information must be given:

- notifier's name and address;

- notifier's and promoter's name and address where non-UK promoter involved;
- details of the reason for the notification (normally the hallmark(s)) which apply;
- a summary of the scheme and its name;
- details of the steps involved and how the tax advantage arises;
- the statutory provisions on which the tax advantage is based.

Where more than one hallmark applies, it is only necessary to mention one, although HMRC would prefer that the main applicable hallmark was indicated.

The explanation of the scheme must be such that an HMRC officer may understand how the tax advantage arises. It should identify the steps and the applicable law. Common terms need not be explained in depth. It may be useful to provide any prospectus or scheme diagrams (anonomysed if necessary), but form AAG1 must still be completed. If any co-promoters are involved, they may be detailed in the application and they will not then have to disclose the scheme themselves.

Reference numbers allocated to arrangements

[5.43] Where a person has made a disclosure as above, HMRC may allocate a reference number to the arrangements in question and must notify the number to that person within 30 days after the disclosure. (The allocation of a reference number does not in itself indicate that HMRC consider the scheme will result in the successful avoidance of tax.) From a date to be appointed by statutory instrument, HMRC may allocate a reference number within 30 days of disclosure and thereafter notify it to the promoter and to any other person liable to notify under *FA 2004, s 308(1) or (3)* for whom they have a name and address. A reference number will still be issued if there is only purported compliance (i.e. all the conditions of disclosure are not met). [*FA 2008, Sch 38 para* 2].

A promoter who is providing services to a client in connection with notifiable arrangements must pass on to the client the reference number for those arrangements or for arrangements which are substantially the same as those arrangements. He must do so within 30 days after the date he first becomes aware of any transaction forming part of the arrangements or, if later, the date on which the reference number is notified to him by HMRC.

A company which is a party to any notifiable arrangements giving rise to a corporation tax or capital gains tax advantage must quote the allocated reference number in its company tax return for the accounting period in which the company is notified of the number (or, if earlier, the accounting period in which the tax advantage is expected to arise) or, on or after 1 November 2008, on form AAG4 (see below). If disclosure is made in the company's return, the number must be given in all subsequent returns until the advantage ceases to apply to the company. Form AAG4 should be used where the company is a party to a scheme but is not required to complete a return, or the return does not have a box for the information, or there are more numbers to be notified than there are spaces on the return. In the latter case, AAG4 should only be used to notify numbers which do not fit on the return.

Where an AAG4 is used, it must be filed not later than 12 months from the end of the accounting period in which the number is notified or, if earlier, the period in which the tax advantage is expected to arise. Where a scheme number has been notified to a company, but no tax advantage is expected (e.g. because it does not intend to use the scheme) the number does not need to be returned to HMRC. The company must also quote the accounting period in which, or the date on which, the advantage is expected to arise.

Comparable provisions apply for income tax. For arrangements under which a tax advantage is expected to arise by reason of a person's employment, the obligation falls on the employer to quote the reference number etc. on a return in such form as HMRC may specify. Where the arrangements are connected with employment under the pre-August 2006 regulations (see above), the employer must quote the reference number etc. in the annual return on form P35 for the appropriate tax year. Persons not required to file a tax return or, as the case may be, a P35 return, must instead provide HMRC with specified information no later than what would have been the filing date for such a return. HMRC have the power to remove, by notice, from a specified date a person's obligation to notify them of the avoidance scheme disclosure number.

From 1 January 2011, per *FA 2010, Sch 17*, if a promoter is under a duty to give the client information relating to the reference number, or if the promoter has not complied with the requirements to disclose relevant information about a notifiable arrangement to HMRC (such that he would be subject to the reference number requirement), such promoter must provide HMRC with prescribed information about the client.

A client of a promoter is obliged to pass on the reference number to third parties when there is sufficient commercial connection with that party to have a reasonable expectation that they will gain a tax advantage from the scheme.

Following consultation on how to improve the system of notification of reference numbers, legislation was included in *FA 2008*, and *SI 2008 No 1947* which provides that the prescribed information to be disclosed by the client is the scheme reference number allocated under *FA 2004, s 311* and the prescribed period under *FA 2004, s 312A* is 30 days of becoming aware of any transactions forming part of notifiable, or proposed notifiable arrangements or, if later, the day on which the prescribed information is notified to the client by the promoter. These amendments come into force on 1 November 2008. Further amendments to the time and manner of delivery were introduced with effect from 1 April 2009. In December 2009, HMRC gave notice that clients' duty to notify the scheme reference number to other parties to the arrangements would cease with effect from 9 December 2009.

[*FA 2004, ss 311–313, 316; FA 2008, Sch 38; SI 2004 No 1864, Reg 8; SI 2006 No 1544, Reg 6; SI 2009 No 611*].

Legal professional privilege

[5.44] These provisions do not require the disclosure of privileged information, i.e. information with respect to which a claim to legal professional privilege (or Scottish equivalent) could be maintained in legal proceedings. [*FA*

2004, s 314]. Where a person is not to be treated as a promoter for this reason, the party to the notifiable arrangements or notifiable proposals (the taxpayer making use of the scheme) must make the appropriate disclosure.

Penalties

[5.45] The maximum penalty for failure to comply with any of the disclosure obligations above is £5,000 (such penalty to be determined by the Special Commissioners). In the case of continuing failure after such a penalty is imposed, there is a daily penalty of up to £600 per day. Penalties of the same level apply if a promoter fails in his duty to notify a reference number to a client.

From 1 January 2011, the penalties imposed by *TMA 1970, s 98C* with regard to the disclosure regime are amended by *FA 2010, Sch 17 para 10(2)*.

The amendments add a new category to *s 98C(2)*, adding the new duties of promoters to provide client lists and of introducers to identify promoters to HMRC to the list of duties to which a penalty relates. The penalty in these cases is the existing single initial penalty not exceeding £5,000.

However, *s 98C(1)(a)* is also amended with regard to the failure to disclose a scheme. The initial single penalty of £5,000 for such a failure is replaced with an initial daily penalty not exceeding £600 for each day during the 'initial period', which is defined in new *s 98C(2ZA)*.

The 'initial period' begins with the 'relevant day' and ends on the day the penalty is determined by the Tribunal, or the day before the person complies with the duty in question, whichever is earlier. The 'relevant day' is defined in a table — in each case it is the day after the end of the period during which the person should have complied with the duty in question. Therefore the 'initial period' is the period of non-compliance beginning on the day after the deadline for complying, and ending when the penalty is determined, or when the person complies if earlier.

In determining the level of penalty for failure to disclose a scheme the Tribunal is also to take account of all relevant matters including the need for the penalty to be an adequate deterrent, having regard in particular to:

(i) in the case of a promoter's failure to make a disclosure within the prescribed period, to the fees received or likely to have been received in connection with the scheme; and
(ii) in the case of a taxpayer's failure to make a disclosure within the prescribed period, to the tax advantage obtained or sought from the scheme.

New *s 98C(2ZC)* provides that where the daily penalty determined above appears inappropriately low, then the Tribunal may increase the penalty to an amount, not exceeding £1 million.

HMRC may commence proceedings before the First-tier Tribunal for re-determination of a penalty where it appears that the 'relevant day' from which a penalty has been determined is incorrect. This may occur in cases where the Tribunal has made an order under *FA 2004, s 306A* that a scheme be treated as notifiable.

The new provisions also allow the Treasury to vary by secondary legislation the amounts of both the proposed initial daily penalty of £600 and the possible increase of penalty to £1 million in s *98C(2ZC)*. Such regulations are subject to an affirmative resolution of the House of Commons.

The initial penalty for failure to comply with other duties (duties imposed by the disclosure regime other than disclosing the scheme) mentioned in *TMA 1970, s 98C(2)* remains unchanged.

FA 2007, s 108 gives HMRC powers to deal with situations where they have grounds for believing that a disclosure should have been made, but either none has been made or that made is thought to be incomplete. This gives HMRC the right to apply to the Tribunal for an order to treat a scheme or arrangements as notifiable where there is doubt as to whether or not they are so notifiable. Although *FA 2004, s 306A(5)* sets out three factors which might make HMRC suspect a scheme is notifiable, these are not exclusive.

HMRC may, in writing, require a person suspected of being a promoter to provide by the tenth day after the date of the notice, his case for a specified scheme not being liable to be disclosed. In presenting his argument, the person must argue with reference to the legal tests. (A statement that a lawyer or other professional does not regard the scheme as disclosable is not sufficient.) Failure to answer by the tenth day will give rise to a penalty of up to £5,000, with the possibility of an additional penalty of £600 per day of default. In addition, HMRC may apply to the Tribunal for an order that a person supply information or documents supplementary to those already provided in any previous response. The promoter has 14 days from the date of the order to provide the details, and may be subject to a fixed penalty of up to £5,000 and a daily penalty of up to £600 for every day of default.

As above, HMRC may apply to the Tribunal for an order stating that a scheme is disclosable: to make such an order the Tribunal must be satisfied that the scheme is disclosable. Once such an order is made, HMRC may seek a penalty (up to £5,000) for late notification, subject to a defence of 'reasonable excuse'. When late disclosure continues after the tenth day from the date of the order, a daily penalty of up to £5,000 may be charged.

Alternatively, the Tribunal may give an order that the scheme is to be treated as disclosable. This order may be given, on application by HMRC, if the Tribunal is satisfied that HMRC have reasonable grounds for suspecting that the scheme is disclosable and have taken all reasonable steps to ascertain that it is so. After the order is granted, the promoter has ten days, from the tenth day from the date of the order, to disclose. If the promoter fails to do so within the time limit, a late disclosure penalty of £5,000 may be charged. Thereafter, a daily penalty of up to £5,000 may be charged until disclosure is made.

Where HMRC believe that the information disclosed is incomplete, they may apply to the Tribunal for an order that the promoter provide specified information and/or documents by the tenth day after the date of the order. The Tribunal must believe that HMRC has reasonable grounds for suspecting that the information requested will support or explain information already provided. Failure to provide the information specified in the order will result in a fine of up to £5,000, plus a daily penalty of up to £600 for each day of default.

The above powers are to be exercised only by officers in HMRC's Anti-Avoidance Group. To use these powers, HMRC must have reasonable grounds to suspect that the promoter is non-compliant with respect to a particular scheme. See Revenue & Customs Brief 57/07.

HMRC's Anti-Avoidance Group has issued an internet statement entitled: 'Risk assessing: factors which may indicate avoidance'. These factors, called signposts, may indicate avoidance (see **5.1** above.) The statement may be found at www.hmrc.gov.uk/avoidance/aag-risk-assessing.htm.

Although these provisions come into force on 19 July 2007, they may apply to events occurring before that date.

[*FA 2004, ss 306A, 308A, 313A, 313B, 314A, 317A; FA 2007, s 108; SI 2007 No 2153; SI 2007 No 3104*].

A party to notifiable arrangements who fails to give the reference number as required (for example, by including it in his tax return) is liable to a penalty of £100 for each scheme (i.e. each set of notifiable arrangements) to which the failure relates. A second such failure within a period of 36 months gives rise to a penalty of £500 per scheme. A third or subsequent failure within 36 months gives rise to a penalty of £1,000 per scheme. The pre-existing penalty regime for incorrect tax returns is, however, disapplied in relation to any such failure.

Statutory clearances

Special provisions apply where a promoter reasonably expects to make a clearance application on behalf of a client relating to:

- distributions and payments (*ICTA 1988, s 215* — see **31.37**);
- purchase of own shares (*ICTA 1988, s 225* — see **63.8**);
- the transfer of long-term insurance business (*ICTA 1988, s 444A*);
- transactions in securities (*ICTA 1988, s 707* — see **5.2** above); or
- share exchanges (*TCGA 1992, ss 138, 139, 140B, 140D* — see Tolley's Capital Gains under Anti-Avoidance).

If the promoter:

(i) reasonably expects to make such an application; and
(ii) must also disclose a notifiable proposal for which the relevant date is the date on which he makes the proposal available for implementation by any other person,

then the prescribed period for making the disclosure is the period beginning with the day after that relevant date and ending on the date on which the transaction first occurs in pursuance of the arrangements. But if the promoter ceases to hold a reasonable expectation of making the clearance application, the prescribed period ends five business days after he ceases to hold it.

Guidance on disclosure of tax avoidance schemes is on the HMRC website at: http://www.hmrc.gov.uk/aiu/disclosure-nov08.pdf. This applies from 1 November 2008.

[*SI 2004 No 1864, Reg 5*].

Simon's Taxes. See A7.2.

Tax arbitrage

[5.46] *F(No 2)A 2005* introduced anti-avoidance provisions to prevent the exploitation by companies of differences between or within national tax codes using hybrid entities or instruments (known as tax arbitrage). The provisions operate by reducing or disallowing deductions or by bringing receipts into charge, but apply only where HMRC issue a notice to the company. Separate provisions apply in relation to deductions cases and receipts cases. See below for the commencement rules.

The following apply for the purposes of the provisions. A '*scheme*' is any scheme, arrangements or understanding of any kind, whether or not legally enforceable, involving a single transaction or two or more transactions. The circumstances in which any two or more transactions are to be taken as forming part of a series of transactions or a scheme include any case in which it would be reasonable to assume that one or more of them would not have been entered into independently of the others or if entered into independently would not have taken the same form or have been on the same terms. It is immaterial in determining whether any transactions form part of a series of transactions that the parties to any of the transactions are different from the parties to another of the transactions. It does not matter if the parties to one or more of the transactions are different from the parties to another of the transactions.

[*TIOPA 2010, s 258*].

A scheme achieves a '*UK tax advantage*' for a person if in consequence of the scheme that person is in a position to obtain, or has obtained:

- a relief (including a tax credit) or increased relief from;
- a repayment or increased repayment of; or
- the avoidance or reduction of a charge to

corporation tax. Relief from corporation tax includes a tax credit on a qualifying distribution. In particular, avoidance or reduction of a charge to tax may be effected by receipts accruing in such a way that the recipient does not pay or bear tax on them or by a deduction in computing profits or gains. [*TIOPA 2010, s 234; F(No 2)A 2005, s 30*].

Deduction notices

HMRC may issue a deduction notice to a company if the company is within the charge to corporation tax and it is considered, on reasonable grounds, that the conditions for issue of a notice are or maybe satisfied.

The following provisions apply to a company which is resident in the UK, or a non-resident company which is within the charge to corporation tax, if the following conditions are satisfied in relation to a transaction to which the company is a party.

(a) The transaction forms part of a scheme which is a 'deduction scheme' (see below).

(b) The scheme is such that for corporation tax purposes the company is in a position to claim, or has claimed, an amount by way of deduction in respect of the transaction or is in a position to set off, or has set off, against profits in an accounting period an amount relating to the transaction.
(c) The main purpose, or one of the main purposes, of the scheme is to achieve a UK tax advantage for the company.
(d) The amount of the UK tax advantage is more than a minimal amount.

If the Commissioners for HMRC consider, on reasonable grounds, that the above conditions are or may be satisfied they may give the company a notice specifying the transaction involved, the accounting period in respect of which condition (b) above is or may be satisfied and informing the company that as a consequence the provisions apply. The Commissioners may issue such a notice to a company in respect of two or more transactions.

If a company receives a notice and conditions (a)–(d) above are in fact satisfied at the time it is given, the company must compute (or recompute) its income or chargeable gains for corporation tax purposes or its liability to corporation tax for the specified accounting period and any subsequent accounting period in accordance with the following two rules. The first rule is that no deduction is allowable in respect of the transaction specified in the notice to the extent that an amount in relation to the expense in question may be otherwise deducted or allowed in computing the income, profits or losses of any person for the purposes of any tax (including foreign tax but excluding petroleum revenue tax and tax chargeable under *ICTA 1988, s 501A(1); CTA 2009, Sch 1 para 171* in respect of ring fence trades), or would be so deductible or allowable but for a rule (whether a UK or non-UK tax provision) that has the same effect as this provision. The second rule applies where a transaction or series of transactions forming part of the scheme involves a payment which creates a deduction or allowance for tax purposes (including foreign tax purposes) for the payer or another party to the scheme but the payee is not liable to tax on the receipt or has its tax liability reduced as a result of the scheme. For this purpose, the circumstances in which a payee is treated as having its liability to tax reduced as a result of the scheme include where it can set-off against its income an expense or relief arising out of the scheme. A payee is not treated as not liable to tax on the receipt if it is not liable to tax on any income or gains under the tax law of any territory or if it is not liable to tax on the receipt because of a statutory exemption which exempts it from tax in respect of income or gains without providing that those income or gains are to be treated as those of another person.

Where the second rule applies, the aggregate of the amounts allowable as a deduction in computing profits for corporation tax purposes arising from the transaction specified in the notice and any other transactions forming part of the scheme and to which the company is party must be reduced. If the payee is not liable to tax on the receipt (as above), the aggregate is reduced to nil. If the payee is liable to tax on part of the receipt or its liability to tax is reduced as above, the aggregate is reduced proportionately to correspond to the payee's liability (treating the amount by which the payee's liability is reduced as an amount on which the payee is not liable to tax).

[*TIOPA 2010, s 248*].

The second rule applies if the following three conditions are met:

- a transaction or series of transactions form part of a scheme and provide for one person making a payment and the other entitled to a receipt;
- as a result of the payment, the payer or another party concerned in the scheme is allowed a tax deduction;
- the payee is not liable to tax on the receipt, or its tax liability is reduced.

However, a payee's tax exemption is not treated as a result of a scheme where either the payee is not liable to tax under the tax law of any territory or under a UK act of equivalent provision of a territory outside the UK without providing that the amount will be taxable on another person.

Instead of applying the above two rules, the company may choose to incorporate in its tax return for the specified accounting period any adjustments that are necessary to counteract the effects of the scheme that are referable to the purpose mentioned in (c) above. The adjustments to be made are to treat all or part of a deduction as not being allowable, or all or part of an amount which may be set off against profits as not falling to be set off. If the adjustments fully counteract the effects of the scheme the company is treated as having complied with the provisions. Clearance can be sought as to the amount of the necessary adjustment (see under 'Clearance' below).

See below for further provisions governing the effects of a notice under the above provisions.

[*TIOPA 2010, ss 232, 233, 243, 244, 245, 248; F(No 2)A 2005, ss 24, 25, 31(1)–(3)(5)*].

Qualifying scheme

A scheme is a '*qualifying scheme*' for the purposes of the above provisions if it is one of the following types.

(1) A scheme in which a party to a transaction forming part of the scheme is a 'hybrid entity', i.e. the party is regarded as a person under tax law of any territory and the profits in question are treated under the relevant tax law as being those of a party other than that mentioned before. For this purpose, an entity is a '*hybrid entity*' if under the tax law of any territory it is regarded as a person but its profits or gains are, for the purposes of a '*relevant tax*' (i.e. income tax, corporation tax or similar non-UK tax) under the law of any territory, treated as the profits of gains of a different person or persons. An entity is not so treated by reason only of its profits or gains being subject to a non-UK tax rule similar to that in *ICTA 1988, s 747(3)* (imputation of profits of **CONTROLLED FOREIGN COMPANIES** (**27**)).

(2) A scheme where one of the parties to the scheme is party to an instrument of which, under the law of a particular territory, a 'relevant characteristic' may be altered by any party to the instrument. A characteristic of an instrument is a '*relevant characteristic*' if, under the law of a particular territory, altering it has the effect of determining whether or not, for that territory's tax purposes, the instrument is taken

into account as giving rise to income or capital. For this purpose, an instrument is taken into account as giving rise to capital if a gain on disposal would be a chargeable gain, or would be if the person making the disposal were UK-resident.

(3) A scheme which includes the issuing by a company of shares subject to conversion or the amendment of rights attaching to shares issued by a company such that the shares become shares subject to conversion. Shares of a company are subject to conversion for this purpose if the rights attaching to them include provision by virtue of which a holder is entitled, on the occurrence of an event, to acquire securities (within the meaning of **31.13 DISTRIBUTIONS**) in that or another company by conversion or exchange and the occurrence of that event is within the reasonable expectation of the company either at the time when the shares are issued or at the time the rights attaching to the shares are amended.

(4) A scheme which includes the issuing by a company of securities subject to conversion or the amendment of rights attaching to securities issued by a company such that the securities become securities subject to conversion. Securities of a company are subject to conversion for this purpose if the rights attaching to them include provision by virtue of which a holder is entitled, on the occurrence of an event, to acquire shares in that or another company by conversion or exchange and the occurrence of that event is within the reasonable expectation of the company either at the time when the securities are issued or at the time the rights attaching to the securities are amended.

(5) A scheme which includes a 'debt instrument' issued by a company that is treated as equity in the company under generally accepted accounting practice (within *CTA 2010, s 1127; FA 2004, s 50*). A '*debt instrument*' for this purpose is an instrument issued by a company that represents a loan relationship (see **54.2 LOAN RELATIONSHIPS**), or would do if the company were UK-resident.

(6) A scheme which includes the issue by a company to a connected person (within *CTA 2010, s 1122; ICTA 1988, s 839*) of shares other than shares which, on their issue, are ordinary shares that are fully paid-up, which confer a 'qualifying beneficial entitlement' at all times in the accounting period in which they are issued and in respect of which there is no arrangement or understanding at the time of issue under which the rights attaching to the shares may be amended. A share in a company confers a '*qualifying beneficial entitlement*' if it confers a beneficial entitlement to the same proportion of any profits available for distribution to equity holders of the company, and of any assets available for distribution to equity holders on a winding-up, as the proportion of the issued share capital represented by that share. *CTA 2010, Ch 6 Part 5; ICTA 1988, Sch 18* (equity holders and profits or assets available for distribution — see **39.4 GROUP RELIEF**) applies for this purpose as it applies for the purposes of group relief.

(7) A scheme which includes a transaction or series of transactions under which a person transfers rights to receive a payment under a 'relevant security' to one or more other persons or otherwise secures that one or

more other persons are similarly benefited (i.e. that they receive a payment which would, but for the transaction or series of transactions, have arisen to the transferor), and:

- the transferor and at least one of the persons to whom a transfer of rights is made, or similar benefit is secured, are connected (within *CTA 2010, s 1122; ICTA 1988, s 839*); and
- following the transfer of rights or securing of the similar benefit, two or more persons either hold rights to receive a payment under the security or enjoy a similar benefit, and the rights held and benefits enjoyed by such of those persons as are connected have, taken together, a market value equal to or greater than the market value of any other such rights and benefits, taken together.

For this purpose, a '*relevant security*' is a security or any agreement under which a person receives an annuity or other annual payment (whether payable annually or at shorter or longer intervals) for a term which is not contingent on the duration of a human life or lives.

[*TIOPA 2010, ss 236–242; F(No 2)A 2005, Sch 3*].

Receipts cases

HMRC may issue a receipts notice if the company is UK resident and the officer considers on reasonable grounds that the receipt scheme conditions are or may be met by the company.

The provisions below apply to a company resident in the UK if the following conditions are satisfied.

(i) A scheme makes or imposes provision (the '*actual provision*') as between the company and another person (the '*paying party*') by means of a transaction or series of transactions.

(ii) The actual provision includes the making by the paying party, by means of a transaction or series of transactions, of a 'qualifying payment'. For this purpose, a '*qualifying payment*' is a contribution to the capital of the company made on or after 16 March 2005.

(iii) As regards the qualifying payment made by the paying party, there is an amount that is available for deduction for UK tax purposes or that may be deducted or otherwise allowable under the tax law of a territory outside the UK. (Such an amount is, however, disregarded for this purpose if or to the extent that it is set for tax purposes against any income arising to the paying party from the transaction or transactions forming part of the scheme.) This condition is not treated as satisfied if the paying party is a dealer (as defined) who incurs losses in the ordinary course of his business in respect of the transaction or transactions and the amount by reference to which this condition would otherwise be satisfied is an amount in respect of those losses.

(iv) At least part of the qualifying payment is not:

    (A) income or gains arising to the company in the accounting period in which the qualifying payment was made; or

(B) income arising to any other company resident in the UK in a 'corresponding' accounting period (i.e. an accounting period with at least one day in common with the accounting period in (A) above); or

(C) taken into account in determining the loan relationship credits or debits to be brought into account by a company as respects a share in another company under *CTA 2009, s 523* (previously *FA 1996, ss 91A, 91B* (shares treated as loan relationships — see **54.86 LOAN RELATIONSHIPS**).

(v) On entering into the scheme the company and the paying party expected that a benefit would arise as a result of (iv) above being satisfied (whether by reference to all or part of the qualifying payment).

If the Commissioners for HMRC consider, on reasonable grounds, that the above conditions are or may be satisfied they may give the company a notice specifying the qualifying payment involved, the accounting period in which the payment is made and informing the company that as a consequence the following provisions apply.

If a company receives a notice and conditions (i)–(v) above are in fact satisfied at the time it is given, the company must compute (or recompute) its income or chargeable gains for corporation tax purposes or its liability to corporation tax for the specified accounting period as if the part of the qualifying payment by reference to which (iii) and (iv) above are satisfied were an amount of income arising to the company in that period and chargeable as miscellaneous income. If (iii) and (iv) above are satisfied in relation to the whole of the qualifying payment, the whole of the payment is so chargeable.

See below for further provisions governing the effects of a notice under the above provisions.

[*F(No 2)A 2005, ss 26, 27, 31(4)(5); CTA 2009, Sch 1 paras 670(3), 671*].

Effects of a notice

A deductions notice must specify:

- the transactions which HMRC considers to be within these provisions;
- the accounting period in which the deduction scheme condition is or may be met;
- the provisions which will apply if each of the deduction scheme conditions is met in relation to the transaction.

A deduction notice may cover more than one transaction.

[*TIOPA 2010, s 235*].

If a notice under either of the above provisions is given before the company has made its return for the specified accounting period then, if the return is made in the period of 90 days beginning with the day on which the notice is given, it may disregard the notice, and at any time before the end of the 90 days the company may amend the return in order to comply with the notice.

If no notice has been given before the company's return has been made, a notice may only be given if the company has been given a notice of enquiry (see **66.19 RETURNS**) in respect of the return. After an enquiry has been completed, a notice may only be given if:

- at the time the enquiry was completed HMRC could not have reasonably been expected, on the basis of the information made available (within *FA 1998, Sch 18 para 44(2)(3)* — see **7.3**(b) **ASSESSMENTS**) to them or an officer of HMRC before that time, to have been aware that the circumstances were such that a notice could have been given; and
- the company was requested to provide information during the enquiry and, if it had been so provided, HMRC could reasonably have been expected to give the company a notice.

If the notice is given after the company has made its return, it may amend the return to comply with the notice within 90 days beginning with the day on which the notice is given. If the notice is given after an enquiry into the return has started, a closure notice (see **66.23 RETURNS**) may not be issued until the end of the period of 90 days beginning with the issue of the notice or, if earlier, an amendment is made to the return complying with the notice. If the notice is given after the completion of an enquiry, a discovery assessment (see **7.3 ASSESSMENTS**) in relation to the income or chargeable gain to which it relates may not be made until the end of the period of 90 days beginning with the issue of the notice or, if earlier, an amendment is made to the return complying with the notice.

Where a notice is issued and no amendment is made to the return for the purpose of complying with it, the above provisions do not prevent a return becoming incorrect if such an amendment should have been made.

[*TIOPA 2010, ss 254–257; F(No 2)A 2005, s 28*].

Clearance

Requests can be made to HMRC for advice about the legislation, including whether it will apply to a planned series of transactions that may constitute a scheme and, where possible, they will advise whether any notice will be issued in respect of the disclosed transactions. They will not give a clearance where the company seeking the clearance has not provided all the relevant information necessary for them to decide whether the legislation is applicable. Clearance applications and questions regarding the clearance procedures should be made to Martin Powell/ Margaret Kayse/ Michelle PallentAndrew Hoar, HMRC Business International, 3rd Floor, 100 Parliament Street, London, SW1A 2BQ (Tel: 020 7147 2719). The International Unit will aim to respond within 28 days provided all relevant information is included but if a request is made for a clearance decision to be given by a specific date, HMRC will try to meet that request. Certain information is required in all cases but the information required depends to some extent on the nature and characteristics of each case. HMRC will consider itself bound by a clearance given in accordance with the required procedure. Guidance can be found at INTM 596550.

Simon's Taxes. See **D4.701–D4.707**.

Financial arrangements avoidance

[5.47] In response to notified tax avoidance schemes, legislation is included in *FA 2009* to deny relief for interest if the loan is made as part of arrangements that are certain (ignoring insignificant risk) to enable the borrower to exit the arrangements with a profit by virtue of the interest being eligible for relief. Whilst the legislation is sufficiently wide-ranging to catch most likely variations to these schemes, it is not intended to catch genuine commercial investments in business where there is uncertainty as to the return that will be produced from the investment. The legislation applies to interest paid on or after 19 March 2009.

[*ITA 2007, s 384A; FA 2009, Sch 30 para 1*].

Capital allowances anti-avoidance

[5.48] *FA 2010, s 26 Sch 4* introduces provision to prevent capital allowance buying into *CAA 2001*, new *sections 212A–212S*.

When a company chooses not to claim allowances on plant and machinery (e.g. because it has trading losses, or other allowances to deduct from profits) the company may find that the written down value of the plant for capital allowance purposes is greater than the balance sheet value of the same plant — i.e. that it has latent capital allowances. The perceived avoidance arises where a company with latent capital allowances is sold to a profitable group.

That group may claim capital allowances and, by group relieving the resultant losses, obtain relief for the capital allowances earlier than the original company could have obtained them (or it might never have obtained relief had the losses been carried forward against the original company's future trading income only).

The new rules (similar to those which deter loss buying transactions) restrict the way in which capital allowances can be utilised following a transfer of entitlement to benefit from those capital allowances. Capital allowances or any loss attributable to a capital allowances claim will only be available to reduce the profits that they would have been able to reduce before the transaction took place.

The legislation applies when:

- The main purpose or one of the main purposes of the transaction is to obtain a tax advantage (Unallowable purpose).
- A company must carry on a trade or carry on a trade in partnership with others.
- That company (or partnership) must have an excess of capital allowances.
- There must be a 'qualifying change' in relation to the company.

Qualifying change (*CAA 2001, s 212C*)

A '*qualifying change*' could be any of the following:

- sale of a company or partial sale of a company;

- change in the ownership proportions of an exsiting consortium company;
- transfer of the trade with the excess of allowances in circumstances such that the Transfers of a trade provisions in *CTA 2010, Ch 1 Pt 22* apply.
- change in the profit sharing ratio of a partnership.

Condition A

For this to be satisfied, there must be a change in one or more principal companies on the relevant day.

The rules for deciding if any company is a principal company of C can be found in *s 212E* and are based on similar provisions in *CTA 2010, Pt 9 Chs 3–5* on the Sale of Lessors.

Notes to *FA 2010* provide some useful examples of when this condition is met:

- C is 100% owned by Y Group and is sold to the X Group;
- C is a consortium company owned 50:50 by Group Y and Group X. If Group Y sells its interest in C to the X Group or another Group;
- C is owned by the Jones family. On the relevant day the Jones family sell their shares to the X group. (Relevant day must be on or after 9 December 2009).

Condition B

This applies where a principal company of the company is a consortium principal company whose ownership proportion is greater at the end of the relevant day than it was at the beginning of that day.

CAA 2001, s 212F defines when a company is owned by a consortium and who the consortium members are. The company cannot be a 75% subsidiary of another company and at least 75% of the company's ordinary share capital must be owned by other companies and those other companies must each own 5% or more of the ordinary share capital.

Condition C

This applies where C ceases to carry on the whole or part of the relevant trade and the trade (or part of it) begins to be carried on in partnership by two or more companies in circumstances where *CTA 2010, Ch 1, Pt 22* applies.

Condition D

This applies where at the beginning of the relevant day the relevant trade is carried on by C in partnership and C's relevant percentage share in the relevant trade at the end of the day is less than at the beginning of the day or is nil.

Section 212I provides the rules for establishing C's 'relevant percentage share' in a partnership. Normally the profit sharing arrangements of the firm for the particular period will be followed but there may be instances where circumstances are such that to follow the profit sharing arrangements in force for the period would not be just and reasonable.

Excess of capital allowances

Where a company has deferred claiming capital allowances, it is likely that the tax written down value of its plant and machinery will exceed its balance sheet value.

Relevant tax written down value – balance sheet value = *Excess capital allowances*

CAA 2001, s 212J gives the calculation for establishing whether there are relevant excess of allowances in relation to the relevant trade but excludes plant and machinery if it is:

- leased out under a long funding lease;
- subject to a hire purchase contract where the person entitled to the benefit of the contract is deemed to be the owner.

In order to calculate the excess of allowances, the company's (or partnership's) accounting period ends on the day of a 'qualifying change' and a new accounting period begins the day after.

Relevant tax written down value (*CAA 2001, s 212K*)

This is based on the amounts that are actually in the capital allowances pools before the relevant date including the amounts in:

- single asset pools;
- class pools; or
- the main pool.

Unrelieved qualifying expenditure

Unrelieved qualifying expenditure contained in a pool is to be calculated on the basis of three assumptions:

- any qualifying expenditure that could have been allocated to the pool has been allocated to the pool by the end of the old period;
- the balance of any first-year qualifying expenditure incurred in the old period is allocated to a pool in the old period at the end of the old period;
- any transaction taking place on the relevant day that has the effect of reducing the amount of unrelieved qualifying expenditure in a pool is assumed not to have taken place.

Balance sheet values (*CAA 2001, s 212L*)

The balance sheet has to be drawn up in accordance with generally accepted accounting practice so as to reflect the position at the beginning of the relevant day but adjusted for the disposal.

The net book value or carrying amount of the relevant plant and machinery is added to any relevant plant and machinery that is leased to a lessee under one or more finance leases which are not long funding finance leases.

Any fixtures in land included in the net book value or carrying amount of the land must be included and determined on a just and reasonable basis.

The legislation operates by allocating an amount of expenditure equal to the excess of allowances in each pool to a new separate pool of the same type (i.e. a new single asset, class or main pool). Writing down allowances are calculated on the old and the new pools separately but at the same rate. If, however, in respect of another pool the balance sheet value of plant and machinery is greater than its tax written down value, then this difference can be used to reduce the excess of allowances in a pool. There are anti-avoidance rules to prevent the manipulation of the tax written down value and the balance sheet value used in the calculation to contrive a reduced excess of allowances.

To enable the excess of allowances to be calculated the company's (or the partnership's) accounting period is brought to an end on the day of a qualifying change and a new accounting period begins on the following day.

Capital allowances claimed in respect of expenditure in the new pools may only be used to reduce the profits (or increase the losses) from the trade as it was carried on, and to the extent that it was carried on, before the qualifying change. Any trading activities transferred in to the company or the partnership will be treated as a separate trade for these purposes. Any losses attributable to capital allowances on new pool expenditure may not be surrendered as group relief or set against other profits of the company for the year, unless they could have been used to reduce those profits before the qualifying change.

HMRC have issued guidance notes — see http://www.hmrc.gov.uk/avoidance/ca-technote.pdf.

The new rule takes effect for transactions on or after 21 July 2009.

Simon's Taxes. See **B3.364–B3.365**.

Gifts of qualifying investments to charities

[5.49] *FA 2010, s 31 Sch 7*, effective from 15 December 2009, counters avoidance exploiting gifts relief on qualifying investments to charities using *ICTA 1988, s 587B*.

The avoidance occurs in two circumstances — where the donor receives tax relief at its highest tax rate on the full market value of the qualifying investments at the date of the gift and either the donor acquired the assets at below market value as part of a scheme or arrangement or the market value of the investment is artificially inflated at the date of the gift to charity.

The new rules adjust the amount of relief to the donor to the economic cost of acquisition of the gift to the donor where: the qualifying investment gifted to the charity (or anything from which the investment derives) was acquired within four years of the date of disposal; and the main purpose, or one of the main purposes, of acquiring the qualifying investment was to dispose of it to a charity and claim the tax relief.

For corporation tax purposes the adjustments are made to *CTA 2010, Pt 6 Ch 3, s 209*, with the addition of a new *s 210A*.

Tainted charitable donations

[5.50] The provisions of *FA 2011* introduce a new anti-avoidance rule at *Sch 3* with regard to charitable donations, with effect from 1 April 2011. The rule prevents the usual tax reliefs from applying where donors enter into arrangements to obtain a financial advantage from the charity in return for their donation.

The provisions are aimed at substantial donors to charities, dealt with for corporation tax purposes at *CTA 2010, ss 512–510*. A new *Pt 21C (ss 939A–939I)* is inserted into *CTA 2010*. The new rule is based on the purpose test and considers the reason why the donor or someone connected with them entered into arrangements with a charity. A tainted donation is thus one which satisfies all three of the following conditions:

(A) the donor or person connected with them enter into arrangements and it is reasonable to assume that the donations and the arrangements would not have been made independently of each other;

(B) the donor or person connected with them enter into arrangements with the main purpose (or one of the main purposes) of obtaining a financial advantage directly or indirectly from the charity;

(C) the donor is not a qualifying company that is wholly owned by a charity or a relevant housing provider linked with the charity which received the donation. This allows for wholly owned trading companies of charities, which generally donate their profits to the parent each year, and relevant housing providers, to be outside of scope of the rules.

Certain financial advantages are ignored: where the person who receives the advantage applies it for charitable purposes; those which fall within the exceptions under the gift aid scheme; and where the benefits are already taken into account in computing the relief due on gifts of shares, securities, real property, trading stock etc. to charities.

Where a tainted charitable donation has been made then corporation tax relief is denied to the donor. Where more than one donation forms part of the arrangement, none of the donations ('associated donations') are eligible for tax relief (regardless of whether they are tainted in their own right).

In addition, the legislation with regard to substantial donors is then to be repealed as from 1 April 2013.

[*CTA 2010, Pt 21C ss 939A–939I*].

See further **20.10 CHARITIES** — transactions with substantial donors for more details.

Postponed capital gains charge

[5.51] *FA 2010* introduces amendments to *TCGA 1992, s 140*, with effect from 6 January 2010, to ensure that a postponed charge on gains arising where assets of an overseas branch are transferred to a non-resident company is brought back into charge on a deemed disposal of securities (with what would otherwise be exempt assets).

Thus for disposals on or after 6 January 2010, rather than add the deferred gain to the consideration received, *FA 2010* amends *s 140(4)* such that there shall be deemed to accrue to the transferor company as a chargeable gain on the disposal of the securities in question the whole or the appropriate proportion of the deferred gain (as above). A chargeable gain which is deemed to so accrue is in addition to any gain or loss which actually arises on the disposal.

A consequential amendment is made to the substantial shareholding exemption rules at *TCGA 1992, Sch 7AC*.
[*TCGA 1992, s 140; FA 2010, s 37*].

Risk transfer schemes

[5.52] *FA 2010, s 46* and *Sch 16* provide legislation that restricts the use of losses from overhedging and underhedging structures ('risk transfer schemes') to the real economic loss from those transactions.

Any losses from such arrangements, other than the real economic loss at group level, are ring-fenced and can only be offset against profits from the same risk transfer scheme. This will prevent such losses from reducing the group's tax liabilities except to the extent that the same scheme has generated previous taxable profits.

The new provisions apply to instruments that are treated, for tax purposes, as loan relationships or derivative contracts. Provisions also allow for regulations to be made in the future to include trading profits and losses made by certain types of business within the financial sector.

CTA 2010 is amended such that a new *Pt 21A* is added.

Group or single company scheme

A risk transfer scheme may be a group scheme or single company scheme. The risk transfer scheme provisions apply to single company schemes with modification. A 'group scheme' is where at least one other company is both associated with the relevant company and also party to the same scheme.

In order for two companies ('company A' and 'company B') to be 'associated with' each other at any time then any of the following five conditions need to be met:

(a) the financial results of company A and company B meet the 'consolidation condition'. The 'consolidation condition' is that the financial results of any two companies are required to be consolidated into accounts prepared under *Companies Act 2006, s 399* or, if they are not to be consolidated into such accounts, then this is due to the exemption at *Companies Act 2006, s 399(3)*;

(b) company A and company B should be connected for the accounting period of A in which the relevant time falls. As per new *subsection (8)*, the definition of connection used for the purposes of loan relationships at *CTA 2009, ss 466–471* will apply;

(c) company A has a major interest in company B, or vice-versa. The definition of 'major interest' used for the purposes of loan relationships at *CTA 2009, ss 473* and *474* will apply;
(d) company A and a third company must meet the 'consolidation condition' and that the third company has a major interest in company B; or
(e) company A and a third company are connected and that third company has a major interest in company B.

The definitions of 'connection' and 'major interest' are imported from the loan relationships legislation at *CTA 2009, ss 466–471* and *ss 473, 474* (respectively). 'The relevant group' for these provisions is the company that is party to the risk transfer scheme along with any other company that is associated with that company and is party to the same scheme.

Modifications are made to the risk transfer scheme provisions where the relevant scheme is a single company scheme. These are that all references to the 'relevant group', or members of the relevant group, are taken as being a reference to 'company A'.

Risk transfer scheme

In order for a company to be party to a 'risk transfer scheme' then the following three conditions must all be met:

Condition 1 — the main purpose, or one of the main purposes, of any member of the relevant group on entering into the scheme is to obtain a 'financial advantage' for the relevant group. It must be reasonable to assume that the 'financial advantage' could not otherwise have been obtained without the relevant group becoming subject to (or incurring the cost of avoiding) a relevant risk. A 'relevant risk' is where due to fluctuations in any sort of price or value (including rates of currency exchange between two currencies and the retail price index) the relevant group is subject to the risk of making an 'economic loss';

Condition 2 — the result of the scheme (ignoring the operation of these provisions) causes the relevant group not to be subject to the relevant risk, or is subject only to a negligible proportion of that risk; and

Condition 3 — is satisfied where the operation of the Corporation Tax Acts allows the relevant group not to be subject to (or only subject to a negligible proportion of) the relevant risk.

A 'financial advantage' occurs where combining the impact of the scheme on each member of the relevant group, the effect of the scheme is to increase returns on an investment, reduce the cost of borrowing or have an effect economically equivalent to either of those effects.

'Economic loss' includes losses that are unrealised as well as realised, and may be made by relevant group members. When calculating an economic profit or loss made by a group of companies that do not have coterminous accounting periods then the amounts are still to be calculated over the accounting period of the company whose scheme profit or loss is being considered. However, amounts are only to be taken into account to the extent that they relate to the times when the relevant company is party to the risk transfer scheme.

A loss or profit made by a company is a 'scheme loss' or 'scheme profit' in relation to a risk transfer scheme if the scheme loss or profit is from a loan relationship or derivative contract that is part of the scheme and would, apart from the operation of these rules, be brought into account under the loan relationship rules or derivative contract rules. The profit or loss must also have arisen due to fluctuations in the relevant rate, index or value pertaining to the scheme. Reference to a loss or profit from a loan relationship or derivative contract includes a loss or profit from a related transaction (as defined in the loan relationship or derivative contract rules) or one that is capital in nature.

Ring-fenced scheme losses and relevant scheme profits

Where a company makes one or more scheme losses in an accounting period in relation to a risk transfer scheme and, ignoring profits and losses made by the group not as a result of the scheme, the relevant group makes a pre-tax economic loss in the relevant period as a result of movements in the relevant rate, index or value pertaining to the scheme, then the loss is restricted — the relevant proportion of each scheme loss made by the company is a 'ring-fenced scheme loss'.

The 'relevant proportion' is the total of 'A' less 'B' less 'C' expressed as a proportion of 'A'. 'A' is the total of the scheme losses made in the period in relation to the scheme by members of the relevant group. 'B' is the total of the scheme profits made in the period in relation to the scheme by members of the relevant group. 'C' is the pre-tax economic loss.

If a company makes one or more scheme profits in an accounting period in relation to a risk transfer scheme and, ignoring profits and losses made by the group not as a result of the scheme, the relevant group makes a pre-tax economic profit in the relevant period as a result of movements in the relevant rate, index or value pertaining to the scheme then the relevant proportion of each scheme profit made by the company in the accounting period is a 'relevant scheme profit'.

The relevant proportion is the total 'A' less 'B' less 'C' expressed as a proportion of 'A'. 'A' is the total of the scheme profits made in the period in relation to the scheme by members of the relevant group. 'B' is the total of the scheme losses made in the period in relation to the scheme by members of the relevant group. 'C' is the pre-tax economic profit.

Treatment of ring-fenced scheme losses

With regard to the period in which they are made:

(a) no ring-fenced scheme loss can be brought into account if the company's profits pool, for the same scheme, at the start of the accounting period is nil;

(b) where there are amounts in the company's profits pool at the beginning of the relevant accounting period but that amount is less than the amount of the ring-fenced scheme losses made by the company in the relevant period in relation to the same scheme — then only the 'relevant proportion' of the ring-fenced scheme loss may be brought into account. The 'relevant proportion' being the amount of the company's profits pool at the start of the accounting period divided by the total of the ring-fenced scheme losses in the period made by that company that relate to the same scheme;

(c) the full amount of scheme loss will be brought into account in a period where the company's profits pool, at the beginning of the period, is greater than, or equal to, the total of ring-fenced scheme losses made by the company in that period in relation to the same scheme.

With regard to subsequent accounting periods, where there are amounts in a company's losses pool at the beginning of an accounting period, and where the company has made a scheme profit in relation to the same risk transfer scheme and (ignoring profits and losses made by the group not as a result of the scheme) the relevant group makes a pre-tax economic profit in the relevant period as a result of fluctuations in the relevant rate, index or value that pertains to the scheme, then the losses can be brought into account as follows:

(i) An amount of the losses pool at the beginning of the period can be brought into account as though it arose from a loan relationship — up to a maximum of the relevant scheme profits made in the period, in proportion to the amount of the relevant scheme profits in that period that arose from loan relationships.

(ii) An amount of the losses pool at the beginning of the period can be brought into account as though it arose from a derivative contract — up to a maximum of the relevant scheme profits made in the period, in proportion to the amount of the relevant scheme profits that arose from derivative contracts.

A company's losses pool for a risk transfer scheme, at the beginning of an accounting period, is the total of the amount of the loss pool at the beginning of the previous accounting period plus the scheme loss made in the previous accounting period that was not brought into account in that period. From this any scheme losses that were brought into account as a result of the rules relating to offsetting losses in later periods would be deducted. Where a risk transfer scheme starts in the current accounting period, it is assumed that the loss pool at the start of the period is nil.

A company's profits pool for a risk transfer scheme, at the beginning of an accounting period, is the total of the amount of the profits pool at the beginning of the previous accounting period plus the scheme profits made by the company in the previous accounting period that were not offset by a scheme loss in that previous period. From this any scheme losses that were brought into account in the previous accounting period as a result of the rules relating to offsetting loss in the period in which they arose would be deducted. Where a risk transfer scheme starts in the current accounting period, it is assumed that the profits pool at the start of the period is nil.

There are further provisions which deal with the assumption to be made that when calculating the economic profits and losses, when there is a scheme loss, it is assumed that the company obtained the 'full tax benefit' of the loss. The 'full tax benefit' being the reduction in corporation tax liability that would result if the scheme loss is fully deductible from an equivalent amount of taxable profits.

There are further provisions which deal with foreign currency accounting, and splitting accounting periods in relation to transitional rules in the application of these provisions.

These provisions apply to accounting periods beginning on or after 1 April 2010, with transitional provisions.

Authorised Investment Funds — CT anti-avoidance

[5.53] Further to the announcement in the Budget of 22 June 2010 legislation was introduced from that date to ensure that a corporate investor cannot make use of an authorised investment fund to create a credit for UK tax where no UK tax has been paid. *SI 2010 No 1642* amends the existing AIF regulations. The corporation tax deduction given for interest distributions is restricted so that the deduction is reduced to the extent that the distribution is derived from dividends that are exempt from corporation tax. Additionally where foreign tax is suffered by an authorised investment fund, the deemed tax credit in the hands of the corporate investor is treated as a foreign tax credit for all tax purposes (and a proportionate part of the income will be treated as foreign income).

[*The Authorised Investment Funds (Tax) (Amendment No 2) Regulations 2010 SI No 1642*].

Loan relationships — 'derecognition' provisions

[5.54] Pursuant to the Budget of 22 June 2010 legislation has been introduced to tackle avoidance schemes under which the profits arising to a company from a financial asset have been claimed to fall out of account for tax purposes as a result of the 'derecognition' of a loan or derivative. This has effect for credits or debits arising on or after 22 June 2010.

The legislation was introduced by *F(No 2)A 2010, Sch 5*, which amends *CTA 2009, ss 311, 132* and *599A*. It extends the circumstances in which amounts are to be fully recognised for tax purposes, to include cases where derecognition arises as a result of the acquisition or variation of a capital interest in a company, partnership or trust, or where derecognition is triggered by an event that occurs in a later accounting period to that in which the derecognition takes place.

The existing *s 311* of *CTA 2009* applies in three instances (conditions A to C) where a company is, or is treated as being, party to a creditor loan relationship in respect of which it does not fully recognise amounts in its accounts. Where one of the three conditions applies then the company is required to recognise for tax purposes the full amount of the credits and debits on the creditor loan relationship. The three conditions are: where the company is also a party to a debtor loan relationship; or has received a capital contribution; or has issued securities.

The amendment adds a new condition to this list, which specifies that the provisions of *s 311* apply where a company at any time acquires or varies a 'relevant interest' in a company, partnership or trust. A 'relevant interest' is an interest in a company's shares, or a partnership's profits or capital, or a trust's property.

In addition, the conditions are amended so that the provisions apply whenever one of the conditions is fulfilled (in 'any period'), and not just when the condition occurs in the same accounting period in which the creditor relationship is derecognised. *Section 312* is amended to take account of this.

CTA 2009, s 599A with regard to derivative contracts is similarly amended. The existing two conditions, being where the company has received a capital contribution, or has issued securities, are extended to include a new condition C. The new condition specifies that the provisions of *s 599A* to recognise the full amount of the credits and debits in respect of the derivative contract apply where a company at any time acquires or varies a 'relevant interest' in a company, partnership or trust. A 'relevant interest' is as above, being an interest in a company's shares, or a partnership's profits or capital, or a trust's property.

As with the loan relationship amendments, the conditions apply whenever the company receives the capital contribution, or issues securities.

Further amendments — Finance Act 2011

[5.55] Legislation amending the derecognition rules was published on 6 December 2010, included in the *Finance Act 2011*, to apply to accounting periods ending after that date. An accounting period which straddles that date is treated as if it were two separate periods, with the latter period staring on 6 December 2010.

The amendments to both the loan relationship and the derivative contract rules change the basis on which the legislation operates. The intention is for derecognition in the accounts to be overridden for tax purposes (and for losses arising from such derecognition not to be allowable), where a company is a party to tax avoidance arrangements. Thus these changes create a general rule that taxable amounts arising on loan relationships and derivatives are to be computed as if all profits and losses on derecognised financial instruments were fully recognised for accounting purposes, where the company is a party to tax avoidance arrangements.

Loan relationships

A new *CTA 2009, s 311(2)(b)* is inserted, which applies where there are amounts not fully recognised pursuant to tax avoidance arrangements which the company is a party to. The current conditions in *s 311* which require *s 312* to be applied are removed. A new *s 311(9)* is introduced so these provisions also apply where a company has disposed of its rights as part of a repo or stock lending relationship.

CTA 2009, s 312 is also amended to reflect these changes, so where *s 311* applies, credits arise on the creditor relationship as if amounts had been recognised in the accounts. Where there is a debtor relationship that corresponds to the creditor relationship then debits are brought into account up to the amount of the credits on the creditor relationship.

'*Tax avoidance arrangements*' are defined as arrangements for which the main purpose, or one of the main purposes, is the obtaining of a tax advantage. 'Tax advantage' has the meaning given by *CTA 2010, s 1139*.

In addition a new *s 455A* is added to *CTA 2009* with regard to tax avoidance provisions. Where a company is party to tax avoidance arrangements then no debit is to be brought into account if an amount is derecognised under GAAP as a result of those arrangements.

Derivative contracts

The rules for derecognition found at *CTA 2009, Pt 7* are similarly amended. Thus a new *s 599(2)(b)* is added which applies where there are amounts not fully recognised pursuant to tax avoidance arrangements which the company is a party to. The current conditions in *s 599A* which require *s 599B* to be applied are removed. The effect of *s 599B* remains the same in that where *s 599A* applies then for tax purposes credits arise on the derivative contracts as if amounts had been recognised in the accounts.

A new *s 599B(4)* ensures that any uplift in the value of the derivative contract cannot escape the anti-avoidance rule on the basis that the arrangements came into being in a later period. The section requires that where the fair value of the derivative contract is greater than its accounts value at the start of the period in which the arrangements came into being, then the difference is taxed as a credit. This section applies as from 23 March 2011.

A new *s 698A* is also inserted such that where a company is party to tax avoidance arrangements then no debit is to be brought into account if an amount is derecognised under GAAP as a result of those arrangements.

Group Mismatch Schemes

[5.56] Legislation is included in the *Finance Act 2011*, which is aimed at countering planning which uses the asymmetric treatment of loans and derivatives between group companies to generate tax advantages — 'Group Mismatch Schemes' ('GMS').

A new *Pt 21B* is inserted into *CTA 2010*, at new *ss 938A–938N*.

The new *s 938A* sets out the operative rule that if a company at any time in an accounting period is a party to a GMS and is a member of the scheme group, then any 'scheme losses and profits' made by the company are not to be brought into account as debits or credits for the purposes of the loan relationship or derivatives regimes.

This provision applies where two or more companies (that are members of a group) are party to a scheme, which is a 'Group Mismatch Scheme', where either of the following two conditions are met:

Condition A — when a company enters into the scheme (at the outset) there is no practical likelihood that the scheme will fail to produce a 'relevant tax advantage' of £2 million or more; or

Condition B — is that the purpose of one of the main purposes of any member of the group entering into the scheme is to obtain the chance of securing a relevant tax advantage, and at the time the scheme is entered into the expected value is a positive amount.

In determining whether the expected value is positive account should be taken of the likelihood of both a relevant tax advantage and disadvantage arising and the amount. In addition, hindsight is not to be used in assessing whether conditions A and B are met.

[*CTA 2010, ss 938A, 938B*].

'Scheme' is widely defined to include any scheme, arrangements or understanding of any kind whatsoever, whether or not legally enforceable, and involving a single or more transactions. [*CTA 2010, s 938H*].

'Group' is similarly widely defined, and includes company A and any associated company (B) — a company being associated where any of five conditions are met. Either: the financial results of companies A and B are required to be consolidated in group accounts (or would be but for the application of an exemption); there is a connection between companies A and B; either company has a major interest in the other; company A's financial results are consolidated with another company, which has a major interest in company B; or, there is a connection between company A and a third company, which has a major interest in company B.

The loan relationship definition of 'connected' and 'major interest' applies in this instance.

[*CTA 2010, s 938E*].

A '*relevant tax advantage*' is an economic profit (per *s 938D*) that is made by the scheme group over the whole scheme period, and arises because of asymmetries in the way different members of the scheme group either bring, or do not bring, debits and credits into account. A '*relevant tax disadvantage*' is an economic loss which similarly arises. References within the legislation to amounts being brought into account, or not, for the purposes of the loan relationship and derivative contracts rules include any amount brought into account as trading credits and debits.

In determining whether a scheme, will, or might, secure a relevant tax advantage the provisions, of *s 938G* will apply, which apply a 'tax capacity' assumption. In calculating the economic profits and losses made by the scheme group over the scheme period it is assumed that each company which is a party to the scheme obtains the full tax benefit of any loss made by that company in relation to loan relationships and derivatives during the period, and incurs the full tax cost of any profit made by that company in relation to a loan relationship or derivative contract. It is noted that this is to ensure that the tax advantage arises as a result of structurally asymmetrical tax treatment of the transactions and not because of circumstantial matters such as losses that might be available to shelter profits from the loan relationship or derivative contract.

[*CTA 2010, s 938G*].

'Asymmetries' is defined to include asymmetries in timing and also in quantification.

'Economic profit' or 'loss' is that made as a result of the Corporation Tax Acts with any adjustments to reflect the time value of money. With regard to the scheme group the economic profit or loss is as made in that period by the members of the group considered together.

A 'scheme loss' or 'scheme profit' is defined as a loss or profit made by a company in an accounting period in relation to a GMS if it arises: from a transaction(s) that forms part of the scheme; is, or is comprised in, an amount brought into account for the purposes of the loan relationship or derivative rules; and meets either of the asymmetry conditions in subsection (2) or (5). The first asymmetry condition at (2) is that the loss or profit affects the amount of the relevant tax advantage secured by the group. Where the scheme period is longer than the company's accounting period then it may not be clear at the end of the period whether the scheme that over its life will secure a relevant tax advantage, or not. Therefore *s 938(3)* states that where, at the end of an accounting period, it is not certain whether a tax advantage will be secured, or what amount will be secured, then the first asymmetry condition is treated as met, if there is a chance that the scheme will secure such an advantage and that the loss or profit will affect its amount.

The second asymmetry condition at (5) applies where the first condition is not met, but the loss or profit arises from a transaction(s) that might have given rise to a loss or profit that would have met that condition. This the second condition applies if it becomes clear that the scheme will not produce a relevant tax advantage — this is to ensure consistency over successive time periods, so earlier losses which have been disregarded can be 'matched' with later period non-taxation of profits.

The explanatory notes explain that the requirement for the profit to arise from asymmetries means that losses or profits on genuine third party loans or derivatives that might be part of a scheme cannot be 'scheme losses' or 'scheme profits'. These third party losses cannot affect the relevant tax advantage as they do not produce intra-group asymmetries, which is what the GMS legislation intends to catch.

[*CTA 2010, ss 938C, 938D, 938F, 938K*].

References to amounts not being brought into account for the purposes of the loan relationship and derivative contracts legislation do not include amounts that are not brought into account by virtue of the company being non-UK resident, or where an election has been made for the profits of a foreign permanent establishment to be exempt.

[*CTA 2010, s 938L*].

From the above it is evident that these provisions are aimed at companies within the charge to UK tax, but the rules are also extended to CFC companies. A CFC company's chargeable profits are calculated using the corporation tax rules, including the loan relationship and derivative contract provisions and are included within the GMS provisions where the CFC is a party to the scheme — thus the assumption that a CFC is not a member of a group for the purposes of the Taxes Acts does not apply for these purposes.

[*CTA 2010, s 938M*].

Repos, quasi-repos and structured finance arrangements are also caught within the GMS provisions — new *ss 938I* and *938J*.

The unallowable purpose rules within the loan relationship and derivative provisions, the transfer pricing provisions, the tax arbitrage rules, and the debt cap rules, have no effect for the purposes of the GMS rules, per *s 9378N* — the new GMS provisions applying in priority.

The provisions of *CTA 2009, Pt 21B* will have effect in relation to schemes entered into at any time (including any time before the commencement date, which is Royal Assent). However the regime does not apply to scheme losses or profits that relate to a time before Royal Assent or scheme profits that relate to a time on or after that date but are made in relation to a scheme entered into before that date. At the same time *CTA 2009, s 418/419* and *s 453* are repealed as from the commencement date (however amounts continue to be brought into account if they relate to a time before the commencement date).

Disguised remuneration rules

[5.57] Anti-avoidance provisions have been introduced in *FA 2011, s 26 Sch 2* in order to counter third party arrangements which allow an employee to enjoy the benefits of a sum of money or other assets provided but which at the same time are structured such that there is no legal right to such money or assets, thereby avoiding or deferring a charge to tax or national insurance. In particular the new legislation is aimed at the use of employee benefit trusts and employer funded unapproved retirement benefits schemes.

A new *Pt 7A* is inserted into *ITEPA 2003* which set out the scope of the arrangements which are caught within the provisions, and also provides gateways, which are exclusions from the regime. The drafting of arrangements which prima facie fall within the new regime is wide, and includes any agreement, scheme, settlement, transaction, trust or understanding whether or not it is legally enforceable.

The exclusions then limit the operation of the anti-avoidance provisions by providing for safe harbours, under certain specified conditions, in respect of: steps taken under HMRC approved SIPs, SAYE schemes, CSOPs, EMI options and certain pension schemes; loans made on commercial terms; transactions undertaken in the ordinary course of business; loans and benefits provided as a package of benefits in the ordinary course of the business; earmarked deferred remuneration which will vest within five years post the award date; incentive schemes with awards based on the market value of the shares; share awards linked to an exit event; shares earmarked for unapproved option schemes; options linked to an exit event; unapproved options, restricted securities and certain other acquisitions of employment related securities; employee car ownership schemes; exempt employment income; registered pension scheme contributions; non-UK resident duties of non-resident employees; consideration given by the employee; and non-domiciles and the remittance basis.

The charge to tax on the employee is triggered by a 'relevant step' which it is reasonable to suppose is taken wholly, or partly, pursuant to the arrangements or in connection (directly or indirectly) with them. The relevant step must be undertaken by a relevant third person and falls into three broad categories: the allocation of money or assets; the vesting of money or assets; or the making available of assets. A relevant third person could be the employer or the employee (acting as trustees) or some other person (whether or not as trustee). Generally an employer providing a benefit to the employee would not be within scope (where no third person is involved). Reference to a corporate employer includes all the group companies, where there is no connection with tax avoidance arrangements. The tax charge is the value of the relevant step.

The legislation imposes an income tax and NIC charge at the time of the earliest relevant event which falls outside of the gateways. Both the tax and NIC should be paid under PAYE and must be paid by the employer unless the person providing the reward deducts such tax at source and accounts for it to HMRC. The PAYE should be calculated by reference to the 'best estimate which can reasonably be made' (see *Sch 2 para 3* which introduces *ITEPA 2003, s 695A*), and paid on the normal PAYE due date. Where the relevant step takes place before Royal Assent, the payment is treated as made on the 30th day after the Act receives Royal Assent.

Corporate tax deductions

The provisions with regard to deductions for corporate employers for employee benefit contributions found at *CTA 2009, Pt 20* are also amended. *CTA 2009, s 1291* is amended to widen the definition of 'employee benefit scheme' to include relevant arrangements caught under *ITEPA 2003, Pt 7A*. *CTA 2009, s 1292* defines a qualifying benefit and is amended to include payments or transfers within the charge to tax under *ITEPA 2003, Pt 7A*. *CTA 2009, s 1293* as to the timing of benefits is amended to include the provision of benefits by a chargeable relevant step — provided at the date employment starts, if the step is before such date, or on the date the chargeable step is undertaken. The amount of the benefit provided will be the sum of money received as earnings (where the payment is money) otherwise with regard to benefits under *Part 7A*, it is the cost of the relevant step but so as not to exceed the amount charged under *ITEPA 2003* (or which would be so charged had not the employee been non-UK resident in any tax year).

The provisions of new *Pt 7A* and the amendments to *CTA 2009* have effect for relevant steps undertaken, and payments or transfers made, on or after 6 April 2011. For a detailed analysis of the new rules please refer to Tolley's Income Tax 2011/ 2012.

[*FA 2011, s 26 Sch* 2].

FA 2011 — group capital gains changes

[5.58] Various provisions have been introduced in by *FA 2011* which amend the provisions relating to capital gains for group companies, as follows:

Section 44 Sch 9 – value shifting – the value shifting rules, which are anti-avoidance provisions dealing with the group position where the capital gains proceeds on disposal are reduced because the value of an asset has been reduced, have been simplified.

Sections 31 and *45 Sch 10* – the de-grouping rules applicable when a company leaves a group whist holding an asset which has been the subject of a no gain no loss transfer in the prior six years, are firstly amended to catch a series of transactions undertaken to escape the de-grouping charge, and secondly the de-grouping rules are also simplified with regard to capital gains and intangible fixed assets.

Section 46, Sch 11 – the rules with regard to pre-entry losses are simplified, in particular the restrictions on the use of losses that arise after a company joins a group are removed.

See further **18 CAPITAL GAINS — GROUPS.**

Key points

[5.59] Points to consider are as follows.

- The approach of the courts to tax avoidance has developed over many years. Early cases, such as the *Duke of Westminster* case, dealt with the consequences of a single transaction, and the principle arising from that case was that a person is entitled to arrange his affairs so as to reduce his tax burden.
- More recent cases, such as *Furniss v Dawson* and *Craven v White*, have dealt with the treatment of transactions involving a number of steps, and whether circularity or steps inserted for no commercial purpose go beyond simply arranging one's affairs in a tax efficient manner.
- Latterly, HMRC have been active in introducing specific legislation to stop avoidance mechanisms, which has given rise to an enormous growth in anti-avoidance legislation.
- Transactions in securities have been the focus of anti-avoidance legislation for many years, and must be considered whenever shares are bought or sold, and will apply where a transaction is designed wholly or partly to gain a tax advantage.
- Whenever transactions involving shares in a company are dealt with under capital gains tax principles advisers should consider whether the transactions in securities legislation could be applied, as a result of which the transaction would be subject to income tax.
- Whenever a company disposes of an interest in land, in most situations it is clear whether the disposal should be treated as a capital gains or a trading transaction. However, where the transaction does not fall clearly within one or the other, HMRC may seek to apply the anti-avoidance provisions covering transactions in land. A transaction is particularly vulnerable where the land in question was acquired with the sole or main object of realising a gain either on resale or following redevelopment.
- Where a company enters into a sale and lease back in respect of land, the deduction for rent paid on the lease back is restricted to a commercial rent.

- There are wide ranging anti-avoidance provisions dealing with various aspects of leasing of property and plant and equipment, which should be borne in mind whenever a company is involved in these transactions either as lessor or as lessee.
- The new *Finance Act 2011* derecognition provisions in respect of loan relationships and derivatives are potentially very wide ranging, notwithstanding the 'tax advantage' condition. Derecognition events are not limited to schemes designed to achieve an accounting derecogniton for tax purposes, and could include a straightforward loan repayment, sub-participations and securitisations. Care will need to be taken to confirm whether such transactions fall within the new provisions.
- The new Group Mismatch Scheme provisions are widely drawn and could apply to normal commercial transactions between group companies which have no tax advantage purpose.
- Various changes have been made to the capital gains regime applying to groups of companies, see further **18 CAPITAL GAINS — GROUPS.**

6

Appeals

Cross-references. See **43 HMRC INVESTIGATORY POWERS**; **49 INTEREST ON OVERDUE TAX** as regards interest on tax becoming due where an appeal is made or determined; **60 PENALTIES**.

Simon's Taxes. See A5.1, A5.2, A5.3, A5.5, A5.6.

Introduction

[6.1] This chapter outlines the appeals process with regard to decisions made by HMRC. The tax appeals system underwent extensive reform with effect from 1 April 2009 with the introduction of the First-tier and Upper Tax Tribunals, which replaced the previous General and Special Commissioners regime. It covers the current basic appeals process, first to HMRC and then the procedure for appeals to the First-tier Tribunal, the Upper Tribunal, and finally considers when Judicial Review of a decision might be appropriate. The regime prior to 1 April 2009 is also outlined briefly.

A taxpayer who disagrees with an assessment or other decision made by HMRC can appeal against it. This is done by giving notice in writing to HMRC, stating the grounds of appeal. The notice must normally be given within 30 days after the date of issue of the assessment or decision, although late appeals can be made in some circumstances (see **6.3** below).

The appeal process has been dramatically changed with effect from 1 April 2009. Appeals made, but not concluded, before that date are generally dealt with under the new process, but there are some transitional rules, for which see **6.37** below.

After a taxpayer appeals there are three main options:

- a different HMRC officer can carry out a review of the decision;
- the taxpayer can ask the Tribunal to decide the matter in dispute;
- the appeal can be settled by agreement at any time.

Reviews are not compulsory, and where HMRC carry out a review but the taxpayer still disagrees with the decision, he can ask the Tribunal to decide the issue (or continue negotiations with HMRC in order to settle the appeal by agreement).

For HMRC reviews, see **6.7** below and for settlement by agreement, see **6.10** below.

Where the taxpayer asks the Tribunal to decide the appeal, the case is usually dealt with by the First-tier Tribunal. The appeal is allocated to one of four categories, default paper, basic, standard or complex, and the process differs according to the category. Basic, standard and complex cases are normally decided at a hearing at which the taxpayer (or his representative) and HMRC are able to present their cases.

Default paper cases can also be decided at a hearing where one of the parties requests a hearing. Complex cases may be transferred for hearing by the Upper Tribunal.

For the First-tier Tribunal process, see **6.14–6.26** below.

If either the taxpayer or HMRC disagree with a decision of the First-tier Tribunal, there is a further right of appeal to the Upper Tribunal, but only on a point of law. Permission to appeal must be obtained from the First-tier Tribunal, or where it refuses permission, from the Upper Tribunal.

For the Upper Tribunal process, see **6.27–6.35** below. Where either party disagrees with an Upper Tribunal decision, there is a similar right of appeal to the Court of Appeal. See **6.37** below.

Where there is no right of appeal or a taxpayer is dissatisfied with the exercise by HMRC or the Tribunal of administrative powers, he may in certain circumstances seek a remedy by way of application for judicial review. See **6.42** below.

Costs can be awarded to or against a taxpayer in cases dealt with by either tribunal or by the courts. See **6.26**, **6.35** and **6.43** below.

See generally HMRC Appeals, Reviews and Tribunals Guide.

It is notable that during the period February 2011 to July 2011 HMRC are proposing to run a alternative dispute resolution pilot scheme for small and medium size enterprises (SME), which aims to improve their understanding of SME tax disputes and to assist with finding alternative ways of resolving disputes which have gone past the formal HMRC decision stage.

Right of appeal

[6.2] Companies have similar rights to individuals with regard to an appeal made under the self-assessment regime. A taxpayer can appeal against:

(a) any assessment other than a self-assessment;
(b) any HMRC amendment of a company tax return following completion of an enquiry;
(c) any HMRC amendment (of a self-assessment) made, during an enquiry, to prevent potential loss of tax to the Crown (see **66 RETURNS**);
(d) any discovery determination (i.e. a determination by HMRC of an amount included in a company tax return which affects the tax payable for another accounting period or by another company).

An appeal within (d) above cannot be taken forward until the enquiry has been completed.

[*TMA 1970, s 31(1)(2); FA 1998, Sch 18 paras 30(3), 34(3), 48(1), 49; SI 2009 No 56, Sch 1 paras 19, 257*].

An appeal against an assessment to corporation tax is an appeal against the total amount of profits charged to tax in the assessment (*Owton Fens Properties Ltd v Redden* Ch D 1984, 58 TC 218).

It is notable that in *Hannigan v Revenue and Customs Comrs* [2009] UKFTT 334 (TC), [2010] SWTI 439, the First-tier Tribunal found that it did not have jurisdiction to hear appeals against income tax assessments that had been withdrawn.

Specific rights of appeal against HMRC decisions, notices or determinations are also included in a number of other provisions and, where relevant, such rights are referred to at the appropriate place in this work.

Unless otherwise stated or required by context, the remainder of this chapter applies to all appeals and all matters treated as appeals, and not only to appeals within (a)–(d) above. [*TMA 1970, s 48; SI 2009 No 56, Sch 1 para 28*].

Making an appeal

[6.3] An appeal is made by giving notice in writing, to the officer of Revenue and Customs concerned and specifying the grounds of appeal. Notice must normally be given within 30 days after the date of issue of the assessment or determination, the closure notice or the notice of amendment. [*TMA 1970, s 31A(1)–(5); FA 1998, Sch 18 paras 30(3)(4), 34(3)(4), 48(2), 92(2)*].

Late appeals

[6.4] If a taxpayer fails to make an appeal within the normal time limit, an appeal can still be made if HMRC agree or, where HMRC do not agree, the Tribunal gives permission.

HMRC must agree to a written request for a late appeal if they are satisfied that there was a reasonable excuse for not making the appeal within the time limit and that the request was made without unreasonable delay after the reasonable excuse ceased.

Before 1 April 2009, HMRC could accept a late appeal only if satisfied that there was such a reasonable excuse and no unreasonable delay. Otherwise, HMRC had to refer the application to the Commissioners (normally the General Commissioners) for their decision.

[*TMA 1970, s 49; SI 2009 No 56, Sch 1 para 29*].

In the event of refusal to accept a late appeal, the decision is not subject to further appeal (*R v Special Commrs (ex p. Magill)* QB (NI) 1979, 53 TC 135), but is subject to judicial review (see *R v Hastings and Bexhill General Commrs and CIR (ex p. Goodacre)* QB 1994, 67 TC 126, in which a refusal was quashed and the matter remitted to a different body of Commissioners).

In *R (oao Browallia Cal Ltd) v General Commissioners of Income Tax* QB 2003, [2004] STC 296, it was held that the Appeal Commissioners had a wider discretion than HMRC in considering a late appeal. The court held that the Commissioners in that case had misunderstood their powers and that the lack of any reasonable excuse was 'potentially relevant' but was 'not conclusive'. The decision was followed in *R (oao Cook) v General Commissioners of Income Tax* [2007] EWHC 167 (Admin), [2007] STC 499, [2007] All ER (D) 247 (Jan) in which the General Commissioners' refusal of a late appeal application was quashed because they had only considered the lack of a reasonable excuse and did not consider the possible merits of the appeal itself.

When the case was remitted to the General Commissioners, however, they again refused the late appeal, and the court upheld their decision — see *R (oao Cook) v General Commissioners of Income Tax (No. 2)* [2009] EWHC 590 (Admin), [2009] SWTI 683, [2009] STC 1212.

The First-tier Tribunal considered whether a fax stating intention to appeal was a valid notice of appeal in the case of *Greenoaks Pharmacy Ltd v HMRC* (TC01118) [2011] UKFTT 254 (TC). HMRC had commenced an enquiry into a company (G) which operated several retail pharmacies. On 23 July 2009 they issued jeopardy amendments to G's self-assessments, increasing its tax liability by more than £1,000,000. On 21 August G's accountant sent HMRC a fax stating that he would 'be sending appeal and postponement applications to those amendments in due course'. The HMRC officer dealing with the case treated this as an expression of intention rather than a formal appeal. Subsequently HMRC began action to collect the debt, and G sent a further fax indicating that it was appealing against the amendments. HMRC treated this as an application to make a late appeal, and rejected it on the grounds that there was no reasonable excuse for the delay. G lodged an application with the First-Tier Tribunal, contending firstly that the fax which it had sent on 21 August had been a valid notice of appeal (and was within the statutory time limit), and alternatively that it had a reasonable excuse for not having appealed with the statutory limit. The First-Tier Tribunal accepted these contentions and allowed the applications, finding that 'the fax of 21 August 2009 was sufficient to amount to a valid appeal against the amendments made'.

In *Pytchley Ltd v HMRC* (TC01139) [2010] UKFTT 277 (TC), the Tribunal considered the question of prejudice to the taxpayer's position with regard to a late appeal. A company (P) failed to respond to queries from HMRC concerning its tax return. In January 2009 HMRC issued an amendment to the return. In June 2009 P applied to lodge a late appeal against the amendment. HMRC opposed the application but the First-Tier Tribunal granted it. Judge Brannan held that 'the prejudice to the Appellant of being unable to advance an arguably meritorious appeal outweighed its dilatoriness and any prejudice to HMRC'.

Withdrawing an appeal

[6.5] An appeal once made cannot, strictly, be withdrawn unilaterally (see *R v Special Commissioners (ex p. Elmhirst)* CA 1935, 20 TC 381 and *Beach v Willesden General Commissioners* Ch D 1981, 55 TC 663). If, however, a taxpayer or his agent gives HMRC oral or written notice of his desire not to proceed with an appeal, the appeal is treated as if settled by agreement, so that the provisions at **6.10** below apply (and the appeal is settled without any variation). Agreement is effective from the date of the taxpayer's notification. This does not apply if HMRC give written notice of objection to such withdrawal within 30 days of the taxpayer's notice, in which case the proceedings will continue.
[*TMA 1970, s 54(4)(5)*].

For postponement of tax pending appeal and for payment of tax on determination of the appeal, see respectively **59 PAYMENT OF TAX**, and further **6.25** herein.

The appeal process after 31 March 2009

[6.6] When an appeal to HMRC is made, there are four options for the appeal to proceed:

(a) the appellant can require HMRC to review the matter in question;
(b) HMRC can offer to review the matter in question;
(c) the appellant can notify the appeal to the Tribunal for it to decide the matter in question; or
(d) the appeal can be settled by agreement between HMRC and the appellant.

Where the appellant requires an HMRC review, he can still notify the appeal to the tribunal if he disagrees with the review's conclusions or HMRC fail to complete a review within the required time.

If HMRC offer a review and the appellant does not accept the offer, he can likewise notify the appeal to the tribunal. Taking any of options (a) to (c) above does not prevent the appeal from being settled by agreement at any time. [*TMA 1970, s 49A; SI 2009 No 56, Sch 1 para 30*].

For details of the review process, see **6.7** below; for notifying an appeal to the tribunal, see **6.9** below; and for settlement of appeals by agreement, see **6.10** below.

All notices given under the appeal provisions must be made in writing. Notifications by the appellant can be made by a person acting on his behalf, but all HMRC notifications must be made directly to the appellant (although copies can be sent to his agent).

[*TMA 1970, s 49I; SI 2009 No 56, Sch 1 para 30*].

HMRC review

[6.7] HMRC implemented a new review procedure at the same time as the overhaul to the Tribunal system was being undertaken. As note above, the taxpayer has a statutory right to request an initial review of an HMRC decision, as a way of attempting to reach an agreement without the need to go to the Tribunal. A taxpayer is not obliged to request a review, and requesting a review does not stop the taxpayer from making an appeal to the Tribunal, as noted above.

As noted in HMRC's Appeals, Reviews and Tribunals Manual at ARTG4050, the following decisions are not reviewable:

(a) decisions where there is no right of appeal;
(b) decisions about whether to allow a late review;
(c) decisions about whether to allow late appeals;
(d) refusals to allow postponement or hardship applications; and
(e) conclusions of a review.

In addition there are a number of matters that the Tribunal considers on application or referral, for example applications for closure notices, information notice applications, applications for daily penalties (the latter two under *FA 2008, Sch 36*). Although these are considered by the Tribunal they are not appeals and they are not within the scope of the review provisions.

Where an appellant notifies HMRC that he requires them to review the matter in question, HMRC must first notify him of their view of the matter. They must do this within the 30 days beginning with the day on which they receive the notification from the appellant, or within such longer period as is reasonable. They must then carry out a review of the matter in question, as described at **6.8** below.

The appellant cannot request a second review of the matter in question and neither can he request a review if he has already notified the appeal to the tribunal.

If it is HMRC who offer to review the matter in question, they must, when they notify the appellant of the offer, also notify the appellant of their view of the matter. The appellant then has 30 days beginning with the date of the document notifying him of the offer to notify HMRC of acceptance of it. If the appellant does so, HMRC must then carry out a review of the matter in question, as described at **6.8** below. Alternatively, the appellant can, within the same 30-day period, notify the appeal to the tribunal for it to decide the matter in question.

If the appellant does not either accept the offer of review or notify the appeal to the tribunal within the 30-day period, then HMRC's view of the matter in question is treated as if it were contained in a written agreement for the settlement of the appeal, so that the provisions at **6.10** below apply (and the appeal is settled on the basis of HMRC's view). The appellant's normal right to withdraw from such agreements does not apply to the deemed agreement. The tribunal may, however, give permission for the appellant to notify the appeal to it after the 30-day period has ended.

HMRC cannot make a second offer of a review or make an offer if the appellant has already required a review or has notified the appeal to the tribunal.

[*TMA 1970, ss 49B, 49C, 49H; SI 2009 No 56, Sch 1 para 30*].

Conduct of the review

[6.8] The nature and extent of HMRC's review will be determined by them as seems appropriate in the circumstances, but they must take into account the steps taken before the start of the review both by them in deciding the matter in question and by anyone else seeking to resolve the disagreement. They must also take into account representations made by the appellant, provided that these are made at a stage which gives HMRC a reasonable opportunity to consider them.

The review must be completed and HMRC's conclusions notified to the appellant in writing within 45 days beginning with:

- where the appellant required the review, the day HMRC notified him of their view of the matter in question; or
- where HMRC offered the review, the day HMRC received notification of the appellant's acceptance of the offer.

HMRC and the appellant can, however, agree any other period for completion of the review.

If HMRC fail to notify the appellant of their conclusions within the required period, the review is treated as if the conclusion was that HMRC's original view of the matter in question were upheld. HMRC must notify the appellant in writing accordingly.

[*TMA 1970, s 49E; SI 2009 No 56, Sch 1 para 30*].

HMRC's notice stating the conclusions to the review is treated as a written agreement for the settlement of the appeal, so that the provisions at **6.10** below apply (and the appeal is settled on the basis of those conclusions). The appellant's normal right to withdraw from such agreements does not apply to the deemed agreement.

The appellant does, however, have a further opportunity to notify the appeal to the tribunal for them to determine the matter in question. This must normally be done within the period of 30 days beginning with the date of the document notifying the conclusions of the review. Where, however, HMRC have failed to notify the conclusions within the required period, the time limit is extended to 30 days after the date of the document notifying the appellant that the review is to be treated as if concluded on the basis of HMRC's original opinion. The tribunal may give permission for an appeal to be notified to them after the time limits have expired.

[*TMA 1970, ss 49F, 49G; SI 2009 No 56, Sch 1 para 30*].

HMRC practice

Reviews are carried out by HMRC officers who have experience of the subject matter of the appeal but are independent of the decision maker and the decision maker's line management. HMRC have published a factsheet on internal reviews as well as a new internal guidance manual (which replaces the existing Appeals Handbook (HMRC Decisions – what to do if you disagree, HMRC 1); HMRC Appeals, Reviews and Tribunals Guide, ARTG4310).

The review officer will consider whether the case is one which HMRC would want to defend before the tribunal, and in particular will consider:

- whether the facts have been established, and whether there is disagreement about the facts;
- the technical and legal merits of the case;
- whether it would be an efficient or desirable use of resources to proceed with an appeal that will cost more than the sum in dispute;
- the likelihood of success; and
- whether the appeal raises unusual questions of law or general policy or may in some other way potentially have an effect on future decisions.

(HMRC Appeals, Reviews and Tribunals Guide, ARTG4080).

Review officers are instructed generally to avoid discussing the case with the caseworker during the review in order to ensure that the review remains independent. If exceptionally it is necessary discuss a case with the caseworker in any depth during the review the review officer will tell the appellant and offer equivalent telephone or face to face contact with him or his agent, so the appellant has an equal opportunity to make representations. (HMRC Appeals, Reviews and Tribunals Guide, ARTG4620).

See further HMRC Appeals, Reviews and Tribunals Guide, ARTG4000–4860.

Appeal to the Tribunal

[6.9] A taxpayer who has appealed to HMRC can notify the appeal to the Tribunal without requesting an HMRC review first. If he does so, HMRC cannot then make an offer of a review. [*TMA 1970, s 49D; SI 2009 No 56, Sch 1 para 30*].

The aim of this two step approach (appeal to HMRC, then to the Tribunal) is to facilitate the resolution of issues with HMRC wherever possible, so the Tribunal considers only appeals which cannot be agreed by negotiation.

An appellant can also notify an appeal to the tribunal if he does not wish to accept an HMRC offer of a review or if he disagrees with the conclusions of a review. In both cases there are short time limits within which notification must be made, although the tribunal can give permission for notification to be made outside those limits: see **6.7** and **6.8** above.

There is no provision for HMRC to notify an appeal to the tribunal (unlike under the appeals system before 1 April 2009 where HMRC was responsible in most cases for listing appeals for hearing by the Commissioners — see **6.39** below).

Notice of appeal must include the appellant's details, details of the decision etc. appealed against, the result the appellant is seeking and the grounds of appeal. The notice must be accompanied by a copy of any written record of the decision and the reasons for it that the appellant has or can reasonably obtain. If the notice is made late it must also include a request for extension of time and the reason for lateness. [*SI 2009 No 273, Rule 20*].

Appeals should be notified to the tribunal by e-mail to taxappeals@tribunals.gsi.gov.uk or by post to the Tribunals Service, Tax, 2nd Floor, 54 Hagley Road, Birmingham B16 8PE. A Notice of Appeal form can be obtained from the Tribunals Service web site (www.tribunals.gov.uk) or by phoning 0845 223 8080.

With regard to a late appeal, in *G Lupson v HMRC* (TC00976) [2011] UKFTT 100 (TC), the First-tier Tribunal allowed an application to lodge a late appeal in a case where a former publican (L) had suffered brain damage following a heart attack, and had been evicted from the public house which he ran. The tribunal observed that there was serious doubt whether L had received some letters which HMRC had posted to him, and held that, in view of his medical history, it would be in the interests of justice to allow this application.

See **6.11** onwards below for the process by which an appeal notified to the tribunal is decided.

Settlement by agreement

[6.10] At any time before an appeal is determined by the tribunal, it may be settled by agreement between HMRC and the appellant or his agent. Where such an agreement is reached, in writing or otherwise, the assessment or decision as upheld, varied, discharged, or cancelled by that agreement, is treated as if it had been determined on appeal. Oral agreements are, however, effective only if confirmed in writing by either side (the date of such confirmation then being the effective date of agreement).

The taxpayer may withdraw from the agreement by giving written notice within 30 days of making it.

[*TMA 1970, s 54(1)–(3)(5); SI 2009 No 56, Sch 1 para 33*].

The agreement must specify the figure for assessment or a precise formula for ascertaining it (*Delbourgo v Field* CA 1978, 52 TC 225).

The agreement only covers the assessments (or decisions) which are the subject of the appeal, and does not bind HMRC for subsequent years, for example where relievable amounts are purported to be carried forward from the year in question (*MacNiven v Westmoreland Investments Ltd* HL 2001, 73 TC 1 and see also *Tod v South Essex Motors (Basildon)* Ltd Ch D 1987, 60 TC 598).

The issue of an amended notice of assessment cannot in itself constitute an offer for the purposes of a *section 54* agreement; nor can a lack of response by the taxpayer constitute acceptance of an offer (*Schuldenfrei v Hilton* CA 1999, 72 TC 167).

An agreement based on a mutual mistake of fact was as a result invalid, so that the taxpayer could proceed with his appeal (*Fox v Rothwell* [1995] STC (SCD) 336).

See *Gibson v General Commissioners for Stroud* Ch D 1989, 61 TC 645 for a case where there was held not to have been a determination and *R v Inspector of Taxes, ex p. Bass Holdings Ltd; Richart v Bass Holdings Ltd* QB 1992, 65 TC 495 for one where rectification of an agreement was ordered where a relief had been deducted twice contrary to the intention of Revenue and taxpayer.

See *CIR v West* CA 1991, 64 TC 196 for a case where the taxpayer was unsuccessful in seeking leave to defend a Crown action for payment of tax on the ground that the accountant who had entered into an agreement had no authority to do so given him by the taxpayer.

The Tribunal

[6.11] Under the unified tribunal system established by the *Tribunals, Courts and Enforcement Act 2007*, there are two tribunals; the First-tier Tribunal and the Upper Tribunal. The Tribunals are presided over by a Senior President of Tribunals. [*TCEA 2007, s 3*].

The First-tier Tribunal

[6.12] Tax appeals notified to the Tribunal are in most cases initially heard and decided by the First-tier Tribunal. [*TMA 1970, s 47C; SI 2009 No 56, Sch 1 para 27*].

The First-tier Tribunal is organised into separate chambers each with responsibility for different areas of the law and with its own Chamber President. This ensures the panel for any particular appeal has the relevant level of expertise.

With certain exceptions, the Tax and Chancery Chamber is responsible for all appeals, applications, references or other proceedings in respect of the functions of HMRC. It is also responsible for appeals etc. in respect of the exercise of HMRC functions by the Serious Organised Crime Agency (see **41.15 HMRC — ADMINISTRATION**). The exceptions relate to certain tax credit and national insurance matters and to matters for which the Upper Tribunal is responsible. [*TCEA 2007, s 7; SI 2008 No 2684, Arts 2, 5A; SI 2009 No 129, Arts 3, 5*].

The First-tier Tribunal tax appeals are managed by four offices: London, Manchester, Birmingham and Edinburgh. Hearings take place at a network of UK venues. The Upper Tribunal office is in London.

The Upper Tribunal

[6.13] The Upper Tribunal is a superior court of record, so that its decisions create legally binding precedents. [*TCEA 2007, s 3(5)*].

It is similarly divided into chambers, including the Tax and Chancery Chamber. The Chamber is responsible for:

(a) further appeals against decisions by the First-tier Tribunal Tax Chamber (see **6.29** below);
(b) applications by HMRC for a tax-related penalty under *FA 2008, Sch 36 para 50* in respect of failure to comply with an information notice or obstruction of an inspection (see **60 PENALTIES**);
(c) complex appeals, applications or references transferred from the First-tier Tribunal (see **6.14** below); and
(d) matters referred to the Upper Tribunal following a decision by the First-tier Tribunal Tax Chamber to set aside its own original decision (see **6.31** below).

[*SI 2008 No 2684, Arts 6, 8; SI 2009 No 196, Arts 6, 8; SI 2010 No 40*].

The Tribunal Procedure Rules which govern the operation of the Tribunals include an explicit statement of their overriding objective, which is to deal with cases fairly and justly. The Tribunals are required to deal with each case in ways proportionate to its importance, its complexity and the anticipated costs and resources of the parties to the appeal etc. They must avoid unnecessary formality and delay and seek flexibility in the proceedings. They must ensure that the parties are able to participate fully in the proceedings.

The parties to the appeal etc. are in turn required to help the Tribunal to further the overriding objective and to co-operate with the Tribunal generally.

[*SI 2008 No 2698, Rule 2; SI 2009 No 273, Rule 2*].

The Tribunals also have an explicit duty to point out to the parties the availability of any alternative procedure for resolving the dispute and to facilitate the use of the procedure if the parties wish. [*SI 2008 No 2698, Rule 3; SI 2009 No 273, Rule 3*].

Both the First-tier and Upper Tribunal consist of judges who have particular legal qualifications or experience, and other members who are not legally qualified but meet specified selection criteria. Judges of the Upper Tribunal are appointed by the Crown on the recommendation of the Lord Chancellor. Judges and members of the First-tier Tribunal, and members of the Upper Tribunal, are appointed by the Lord Chancellor. See *TCEA 2007, ss 4, 5, Schs 2, 3*.

First-tier Tribunal procedure

Case management

[6.14] The Tribunal has wide powers to regulate its own procedures and to give directions about the conduct or disposal of cases. In particular it can, by direction:

- consolidate or hear two or more cases together or treat a case as a lead case (see *SI 2009 No 273, Rule 18*);
- permit or require a party to the case or another person to provide documents, information or submissions to the tribunal or another party;
- hold a hearing to consider any matter, including a case management hearing;
- decide the form of any hearing;
- require a party to produce a bundle of documents for a hearing.

The Tribunal can also substitute a party to a case where necessary or add a person to the case as a respondent. A person who is not a party to the case can apply to the Tribunal to be added as a party.

Either party to a case can apply for the Tribunal to make a direction, either in writing or orally at a hearing, or the Tribunal can make a direction on its own initiative. Applications for a direction must include the reason for making it. Directions can be challenged by applying for a further direction.

Any action required to be done in relation to a case on or by a particular day must be done before 5pm on that day (or, if that day is not a working day, by 5pm on the next working day).

[*SI 2009 No 273, Rules 5, 6, 9, 12*].

Administration of cases referred to the Tribunal, including the categorisation of cases (see **6.16** below), is carried out by the Tribunals Service.

Starting proceedings

See **6.9** above for how to notify an appeal to the Tribunal. There are also rules for proceedings to be determined without notice to a respondent (*Rule 19*), and for proceedings started by originating application or reference (*Rule 21*).

Representation

A party to a case can appoint a representative to represent him in the proceedings. The representative does **not** need to be a lawyer or legal representative. The party has to notify the Tribunal and the other parties of the appointment of a representative and they will then treat the representative as authorised until notified otherwise.

Where no such person has been appointed, a party can, with the Tribunal's permission, nevertheless be accompanied at a hearing by another person who can act as a representative or assist in presenting the case.

SI 2010 No 43 (which came into force on 18 January 2010) widens the definition of 'legal representative' in this regard, to a person who, for the purposes of the *Legal Services Act 2007*, is an authorised person in relation to the exercise of a right of audience, or the conduct of litigation.

[*SI 2009 No 273, Rule 11*].

Withdrawal from a case

Subject to any legislation relating to withdrawal from or settlement of particular proceedings, a party can notify the Tribunal of the withdrawal of its case, or part of it. This can be done in writing before a hearing or orally at a hearing. If the case is to be settled without a hearing, written notice must be given before the Tribunal disposes of the case.

A party who has withdrawn its case can, however, apply (in writing) to the Tribunal to reinstate it. The application must be received by the Tribunal within 28 days after it received the withdrawal notice or the date of the hearing. It was held in the case of *St Annes Distributors v HMRC* [2010] UKUT 458 (TCC), [2011] STC 708, [2011] NLJR 102 that notification by email does not satisfy the 'written notice' requirement.

[*SI 2009 No 273, Rule 17*].

Failure to comply with rules

[6.15] An irregularity resulting from any failure to comply with the Tribunal Procedure Rules, a practice direction or a direction by the Tribunal does not in itself make the proceedings void.

Where a party fails to comply with the Rules etc. the Tribunal can take such action as it considers just. This could be to require compliance or waive the requirement, to strike the case out (see below) or, in certain cases, to refer the failure to the Upper Tribunal.

The Tribunal can refer to the Upper Tribunal any failure to:

- attend a hearing, or otherwise be available, to give evidence;
- to swear an oath in connection with giving evidence;
- to give evidence as a witness;
- to produce a document; or
- to facilitate the inspection of a document or other thing (including premises).

The Upper Tribunal then has the same powers as the High Court to deal with the failure (which may include financial penalties).

[*TCEA 2007, s 25; SI 2009 No 273, Rule 7*].

Striking out a case

A case will automatically be struck out if the appellant fails to comply with a direction which states that failure to comply will lead to striking out.

The Tribunal can also strike out a case if the appellant fails to comply with a direction which states that failure to comply may lead to striking out, if the appellant has failed to co-operate with the Tribunal to such an extent that the case cannot be dealt with fairly and justly, or if the Tribunal considers that there is no reasonable prospect of the appellant's case succeeding. In the last two cases, however, the Tribunal must first give the appellant an opportunity to make representations.

If the case is struck out because of the appellant's failure to comply with a direction, the appellant can apply for the case to be reinstated. This must be done in writing within 28 days after the date the Tribunal sent the notification of the striking out.

The above rules also apply to respondents except that, instead of the case being struck out, the respondent is barred from taking any further part in the case.

[*SI 2009 No 273, Rule 8*].

Categorisation of cases

[6.16] When an appeal, application or reference is notified to the Tribunal, the Tribunals Service allocate it to one of four categories of case:

(a) default paper;
(b) basic;
(c) standard; or
(d) complex.

Cases may be re-categorised by the Tribunal at any time either on the application of one of the parties or on the Tribunal's own initiative.

[*SI 2009 No 273, Rule 23(1)–(3)*].

The process by which the appeal etc. will be decided varies according to the category to which the case is allocated as described below.

Default paper cases

[6.17] Cases can be allocated to a different category if the Tribunal considers it appropriate to do so.

In a default paper case, the respondent (i.e., in an appeal, HMRC) must provide a statement of case to the Tribunal, the appellant and any other respondents to be received within 42 days after the Tribunal sends it notice of the proceedings (or by such time as the Tribunal directs). The statement must state the legislation under which the decision in question was made and set out the respondent's position. If the statement is late it must also include a request for a time extension and give the reason for lateness.

The statement can also contain a request for the case to be dealt with either at or without a hearing.

Once such a statement has been given to the appellant, he may send a written reply to the Tribunal. The reply must be received within 30 days after the date on which the respondent sent its statement to the appellant and must be sent also to each respondent. The reply may include the appellant's response to the respondent's statement of case, provide any further relevant information and contain a request for the case to be dealt with at a hearing. If the reply is late it must also include a request for a time extension and give the reason for lateness.

The Tribunal must hold a hearing before determining a case if any party has requested one in writing. Otherwise, on receipt of the appellant's reply or the expiry of the time limit for such a reply, the Tribunal will determine the case without a hearing, unless it directs otherwise.

[*SI 2009 No 273, Rules 25, 26*].

Default paper cases are decided by one judge or other member of the First-tier Tribunal. (Tribunals Practice Statement, 10 March 2009).

Basic cases

[6.18] The following types of cases must normally be allocated as basic cases (unless they must be allocated as default paper cases):

(a) appeals against penalties for late filing and late payment, including daily penalties;
(b) appeals against penalties under *FA 2007, Sch 24* (errors in documents and failure to notify HMRC of errors in assessments — see **60 PENALTIES**);
(c) appeals against indirect tax penalties on the basis of reasonable excuse and certain construction industry scheme decisions;
(d) appeals against information notices (including those at **43 HMRC INVESTIGATORY POWERS** and **66 RETURNS**);
(e) applications for permission to make a late appeal (see **6.2** above);
(f) applications for the postponement of tax pending an appeal (see **59 PAYMENT OF TAX**); and
(g) applications for a direction that HMRC close an enquiry (see **66 RETURNS**).

Appeals against penalties for deliberate action or where an appeal is also brought against the assessment to which the penalty relates are excluded from (b) above (as are indirect tax cases).

Cases can be allocated to a different category if the Tribunal considers it appropriate to do so.

(Tribunals Practice Direction, 10 March 2009).

Basic cases normally proceed directly to a hearing, without the need for the respondent to produce a statement of case. Where, however, the respondent intends to raise grounds at the hearing of which the appellant has not been informed, the appellant must be notified of those grounds as soon as is reasonably practicable. The respondent must include sufficient detail to enable the appellant to respond to the grounds at the hearing. [*SI 2009 No 273, Rule 24*].

A decision in a basic case that disposes of proceedings or determines a preliminary issue made at, or following, a hearing must be made by either one, two or, where the Chamber President so decides, three members. The members can be judges or other members as the Chamber President decides, and he will choose one of them to be the presiding member. Any other decision will be made by one judge or other member. (Tribunals Practice Statement, 10 March 2009).

Standard cases

[6.19] In a standard case, the respondent (i.e., in an appeal, HMRC) must provide a statement of case to the tribunal, the appellant and any other respondents to be received within 60 days after the Tribunal sends it notice of the proceedings (or by such time as the Tribunal directs). The statement must state the legislation under which the decision in question was made and set out the respondent's position. If the statement is late it must also include a request for a time extension and give the reason for lateness.

The statement can also contain a request for the case to be dealt with either at or without a hearing.

Within 42 days after the date on which the respondent sent the statement of case, each party to the case must send to the Tribunal and each other party a list of documents of which that party has possession (or the right to take possession or make copies) and on which the party intends to rely or to produce in the proceedings. The other parties must then be allowed to inspect or copy those documents, except for any which are privileged.

The case will then normally proceed to a hearing (see **6.21** below). [*SI 2009 No 273, Rules 25, 27*].

A decision in a standard case that disposes of proceedings or determines a preliminary issue made at, or following, a hearing must be made by one judge or by one judge and one or two members as determined by the Chamber President. The judge will be the presiding member, unless one or more of the other members is also a judge, in which case the Chamber President will choose the presiding member. Any other decision will be made by one judge. (Tribunals Practice Statement, 10 March 2009).

Complex cases

[6.20] A case can be classified as a complex case only if the Tribunal considers that it will require lengthy or complex evidence or a lengthy hearing, involves a complex or important principle or issue, or involves a large financial sum. [*SI 2009 No 273, Rule 23(4)*].

However, in complex cases the costs rule applies — so if the taxpayer loses they may be ordered to pay HMRC's costs of appeal as well as their own. The taxpayer may opt out of the costs regime by informing the Tribunal in writing (*SI 2009 No 273 Rule 10(1)(c)(ii)*). See further **6.26** below.

The procedures in a complex case are the same as those described at **6.19** above for standard cases. The same rules regarding the membership of the Tribunal also apply.

Transfer to Upper Tribunal

The Tribunal can, with the consent of the parties, refer a complex case to the Chamber President of the First-tier Tribunal with a request for transfer to the Upper Tribunal. The Chamber President can then, with the agreement of the President of the Tax and Chancery Chamber of the Upper Tribunal, direct that the case be so transferred. [*SI 2009 No 273, Rule 28 as amended by SI 2011 No 651; SI 2010 No 40*].

Costs

See **6.26** below for the taxpayer's option to request that a complex case be excluded from potential liability for costs.

The hearing

[6.21] Basic, standard and complex cases normally require a hearing before they are decided (and see **6.17** above for hearings in default paper cases).

This does not apply, however, if all of the parties consent to a decision without a hearing and the Tribunal considers that it is able to make a decision without a hearing. Hearings are also not required for the correction, setting aside, review or appeal of a tribunal decision (see **6.22–6.24** below) or where the Tribunal strikes out a party's case (see **6.15** above).

Each party to the proceedings is normally entitled to attend the hearing and the Tribunal must give reasonable notice of its time and place. Where the hearing is to consider disposal of the proceedings, at least 14 days' notice must be given except in urgent or exceptional circumstances or with the consent of the parties.

Hearings are normally held in public. The Tribunal may, however, direct that a hearing should be private if it considers that restricting access is justified in the interests of public order or national security, to protect a person's right to respect for their private and family life, to maintain the confidentiality of sensitive information, to avoid serious harm to the public interest or because not to do so would prejudice the interest of justice.

[*SI 2009 No 273, Rules 29–32*].

Failure to attend hearing

If a party fails to attend a hearing, the Tribunal can nevertheless proceed with the hearing if it considers that it is in the interests of justice to do so. The Tribunal must be satisfied that the party was notified of the hearing or that reasonable steps were taken to notify the party. [*SI 2009 No 273, Rule 33*].

The following cases were decided under the rather different provisions applicable before 1 April 2009 to failure to attend a hearing of the General Commissioners, but may be relevant to the above provision. Determinations in the absence of the taxpayer or his agent were upheld where notice of the meeting was received by the appellant (*R v Tavistock Commrs (ex p. Adams) (No 1)* QB 1969, 46 TC 154; *R v Special Commr (ex p. Moschi)* [1981] STC 465, CA, and see *Fletcher v Harvey (Inspector of Taxes)* [1990] STC 711, 63 TC 539, CA), but Commissioners were held to have acted unreasonably in refusing to re-open proceedings when the taxpayer's agent was temporarily absent when the appeal was called (*R & D McKerron Ltd v CIR* [1979] STC 815, 53 TC 28, Ct of Sess). Where the taxpayer was absent through illness, a determination was quashed because the Commissioners, in refusing an adjournment, had failed to consider whether injustice would thereby arise to the taxpayer (*R v Sevenoaks Commrs (ex p. Thorne)* QB 1989, 62 TC 341 and see *Rose v Humbles* CA 1971, 48 TC 103). See also *R v O'Brien (ex p. Lissner)* [1984] STI 710 where the determination was quashed when the appellant had been informed by the inspector that the hearing was to be adjourned.

Evidence and submissions

The Tribunal has wide powers to make directions as to issues on which it requires evidence or submissions, including the nature of such evidence or submissions, the way in which and time at which it must be provided and the need for expert evidence. It may also limit the number of witnesses whose evidence a party can put forward.

The Tribunal can accept evidence whether or not it would be admissible in a civil trial and can exclude evidence provided late or not in accordance with a direction.

[*SI 2009 No 273, Rule 15(1)(2)*].

The following cases relate to evidence given at hearings of the General Commissioners before 1 April 2009, but may be relevant to the above provision. A party to the proceedings could not insist on being examined on oath (*R v Special Commrs (in re Fletcher)* CA 1894, 3 TC 289). False evidence under oath would be perjury under criminal law (*R v Hood Barrs CA*, [1943] 1 All ER 665). A taxpayer was held to be bound by an affidavit he had made in other proceedings (*Wicker v Fraser* Ch D 1982, 55 TC 641). A remission to Commissioners to hear evidence directed at the credit of a witness was refused in *Potts v CIR* Ch D 1982, 56 TC 25. Rules of the Supreme Court under which evidence can be obtained from a witness abroad could not be used in proceedings before the Commissioners (*Leiserach v CIR* CA 1963, 42 TC 1). As to hearsay evidence under *Civil Evidence Act 1968*, see *Forth Investments Ltd v CIR* Ch D 1976, 50 TC 617 and *Khan v Edwards* Ch D 1977, 53 TC 597.

The Commissioners were under no obligation to adjourn an appeal for the production of further evidence (*Hamilton v CIR* CS 1930, 16 TC 28; *Noble v Wilkinson* Ch D 1958, 38 TC 135), and were held not to have erred in law in determining assessments in the absence abroad of the taxpayer (*Hawkins v Fuller* Ch D 1982, 56 TC 49).

Witnesses

The Tribunal, on the application of any party to the proceedings or its own initiative, can issue a summons (in Scotland, a citation) requiring any person either to attend the hearing of those proceedings to give evidence or to produce any relevant document in his possession or control. A witness required to attend a hearing must be given 14 days notice or a shorter period if the Tribunal so directs and, if the witness is not a party, the summons or citations must make provision for necessary expenses of attendance and state who is to pay them. If, before the summons or citation was issued, the witness did not have an opportunity to object, he may apply to the Tribunal for the summons to be varied or set aside. The application must be made as soon as reasonably practicable after the summons or citation is received.

A witness cannot be compelled to give evidence or produce documents which he could not be compelled to give or produce in an action in a court of law.

[*SI 2009 No 273, Rule 16*].

The Tribunal's decision

[6.22] In an appeal case, if the Tribunal decides:

(a) that the appellant is overcharged or undercharged by a self-assessment;
(b) that the appellant is overcharged or undercharged by an assessment other than a self-assessment,

the assessment or amounts are reduced or increased accordingly, but otherwise the assessment or statement stands good. The Tribunal is given the power to vary the extent to which a claim or election included in a tax return is disallowed following an enquiry. (Separate rules apply to claims and elections made outside returns.) In a case within (c) above, the Tribunal can normally only reduce or increase the amount assessed, and this determines the appeal; the Tribunal is not obliged to determine the revised tax payable.

The Tribunal's decision is final and conclusive, subject to:

(i) the correction of clerical mistakes etc. (see **6.23** below);
(ii) the setting aside of a decision (see **6.23** below); and
(iii) a further appeal against the decision (see **6.24** below).

[*TMA 1970, s 50(6)–(11); SI 2009 No 56, Art 31*].

See **60 PENALTIES** for the Tribunal's options in an appeal against a surcharge or a late filing penalty, which turns on the question of whether the appellant had a 'reasonable excuse' for his non-compliance.

The Tribunal can give its decision orally at a hearing or in writing. In either case it will give each party a decision notice in writing within 28 days after making a decision which finally disposes of all the issues in the case or as soon as practicable. The notice will also inform the party of any further right of appeal.

Unless each party agrees otherwise the notice should also include a summary of the findings of fact and the reason for the decision. If it does not, any party to the case can apply for full written findings and reasons, and must do so before applying for permission to appeal (see **6.24** below). The application must be made in writing so that the Tribunal receives it within 28 days after the date it sent the decision notice.

[*SI 2009 No 273, Rule 35*].

The following cases relate to decisions of the General Commissioners before 1 April 2009, but may be relevant to the above provisions.

In reaching their decision, the Commissioners could not take into account matters appropriate for application for judicial review (*Aspin v Estill* CA 1987, 60 TC 549). They did not generally have the power to review on appeal the exercise of a discretion conferred on HMRC by statute (see *Slater v Richardson & Bottoms Ltd* Ch D 1979, 53 TC 155; *Kelsall v Investment Chartwork Ltd* Ch D 1993, 65 TC 750).

The onus is on the appellant to displace an assessment. *See Brady v Group Lotus Car Companies plc* CA 1987, 60 TC 359 where the onus of proof remained with the taxpayer where the amount of normal time limit assessment indicated contention of fraud.

The general principle emerges in appeals against estimated assessments in 'delay cases', which, before self-assessment, made up the bulk of appeals heard by the General Commissioners. For examples of cases in which the Commissioners have confirmed estimated assessments in the absence of evidence that they were excessive, see *T Haythornthwaite & Sons Ltd v Kelly* CA 1927, 11 TC 657; *Stoneleigh Products Ltd v Dodd* CA 1948, 30 TC 1; *Rosette Franks (King St) Ltd v Dick* Ch D 1955, 36 TC 100; *Pierson v Belcher* Ch D 1959, 38 TC 387. In a number of cases, the courts have supported the Commissioners' action in rejecting unsatisfactory accounts (e.g. *Cain v Schofield* Ch D 1953, 34 TC 362; *Moll v CIR* CS 1955, 36 TC 384; *Cutmore v Leach* Ch D 1981, 55 TC 602; *Coy v Kime* Ch D 1986, 59 TC 447) or calling for certified accounts (e.g. *Stephenson v Waller* KB 1927, 13 TC 318; *Hunt & Co v Joly* KB 1928, 14 TC 165; *Wall v Cooper* CA 1929, 14 TC 552). In *Anderson v CIR* CS 1933, 18 TC 320, the case was remitted where there was no evidence to support the figure arrived at by the Commissioners (which was between the accounts figure and the estimated figure assessed), but contrast *Bookey v Edwards* Ch D 1981, 55 TC 486. The Commissioners were entitled to look at each year separately, accepting the appellant's figures for some years but not all (*Donnelly v Platten* CA(NI) 1980, [1981] STC 504). Similarly, the onus is on the taxpayer to substantiate his claims to relief (see *Eke v Knight* CA 1977, 51 TC 121; *Talib v Waterson* Ch D, [1980] STC 563).

For the standard of proof required in evidence, see *Les Croupiers Casino Club v Pattinson* CA 1987, 60 TC 196.

Consent orders. The case can also be settled by the Tribunal making a consent order where the parties have reached agreement. Such an order is made at the request of the parties but only if the Tribunal considers it appropriate to do so. No hearing is necessary if such an order is made. [*SI 2009 No 273, Rule 34*].

Amendment of a decision

[6.23] The Tribunal can correct any clerical mistake or other accidental slip or omission (such as spelling mistakes, or omitted words) in a decision at any time by notifying the parties of the amended decision. This rule applies also to directions and any other document produced by the Tribunal. [*SI 2009 No 273, Rule 37*].

The Tribunal can set aside a decision disposing of a case and re-make the decision if it considers that to do is in the interests of justice and one of the following applies:

- a relevant document was not sent to, or was not received at an appropriate time by, a party or his representative;
- a relevant document was not sent to the Tribunal at a relevant time;
- there was some other procedural irregularity; or
- a party or representative was not present at a hearing.

A party to a case can apply for a decision to be set aside. The application must be in writing and must be received by the Tribunal within 28 days after the date on which the Tribunal sent the decision notice.

[*SI 2009 No 273, Rule 38*].

Appeal against the Tribunal's decision

[6.24] A further appeal to the Upper Tribunal can be made against the First-tier Tribunal's decision. The appeal can be made only on a point of law. No appeal can be made against a decision on whether or not to review a decision (see below), to set aside a decision (see **6.23** above) or to refer a matter to the Upper Tribunal.

A person wishing to appeal must make a written application to the First-tier Tribunal for permission to appeal. Such an application must be received by the Tribunal no later than 56 days after the date the Tribunal sent full reasons for the decision to that person. Where a decision has been amended or corrected following a review (see below) or an application (other than a late application) for a decision to be struck out has been unsuccessful (see **6.23** above), the 56 day limit runs from the date on which the Tribunal sent the notification of amended reasons or correction of the decision or of the failure of the striking out application.

The application must identify the alleged errors in the decision and state the result sought. Late applications must include a request for extension of time and the reason for lateness.

On receiving an application, the Tribunal will first consider whether to review the decision. It can do so only if satisfied that there was an error in law in the decision. Unless it decides to take no action following the review, the Tribunal will notify the parties of the outcome and must give them an opportunity to make representations before taking any action.

If the Tribunal decides not to review the decision or, following a review, decides to take no action, it will then consider whether to give permission to appeal to the Upper Tribunal. It will send a record of its decision to the parties as soon as practicable together with, where it decides not to give permission, a statements of its reasons for refusal and details of the right to apply directly to the Upper Tribunal for permission to appeal (see **6.29** below). The Tribunal's permission can be in respect of part only of the decision or on limited grounds.

[*TCEA 2007, s 11; SI 2009 No 273, Rules 39–41*].

Payment of tax pending further appeal

[6.25] Tax is payable or repayable in accordance with the decision of the Tribunal even if a party appeals to the Upper Tribunal. If the amount charged in the assessment concerned is subsequently altered by the Upper Tribunal, any amount undercharged is due and payable at the end of the thirty days beginning with the date on which HMRC issue the appellant a notice of the amount payable in accordance with the Upper Tribunal's decision. Any amount overpaid will be refunded along with such interest as may be allowed by the decision.

This provision applies equally to any further appeal from a decision of the Upper Tribunal to the Courts.

Following the Budget 2009, HMRC announced on 12 March 2010 that where they receive a judgment in their favour they will collect the tax before the appeal is heard for all decisions made by the Tribunals or Courts on or after 1 April 2010. HMRC will not enforce payment in cases where an agreement not to do so had been made with the appellant before 9 December 2009. In addition, HMRC will not enforce payment in cases where to do so would be likely to drive the taxpayer into liquidation or bankruptcy.

[*TMA 1970, s 56; SI 2009 No 56, Sch 1 para 35*].

Award of costs

[6.26] The Tribunal can make an order awarding costs (or, in Scotland, expenses):

(a) under *TCEA 2007, s 29(4)* ('wasted costs');
(b) where it considers that a party or representative has acted unreasonably in bringing, defending or conducting the case; and
(c) in a complex case (see **6.20** above), where the taxpayer has not sent a written request that the case be excluded from potential liability for costs or expenses.

A request within (c) above must be sent within 28 days of the taxpayer receiving notice that the case has been allocated as a complex case.

'*Wasted costs*' are any costs incurred by a party because of an improper, unreasonable or negligent act or omission by any representative or employee of a representative, which the Tribunal considers it unreasonable for the party to pay.

Before making an order for costs, the Tribunal must give the person who will have to pay them the chance to make representations. If the payer is an individual, it must consider his financial means.

The Tribunal can make an order on its own initiative or on an application from one of the parties. Such an application must be sent both to the Tribunal and to the person from whom costs are sought, together with a schedule of the costs claimed. An application must be made no later than 28 days after the date on which the Tribunal sends a notice recording the decision which finally disposes of all the issues or notice of a withdrawal which ends the case.

The amount of costs will be decided either by agreement of the parties, by summary assessment by the Tribunal or, if not agreed, by assessment. Where the amount is to be decided by assessment, either the payer or the person to whom the costs are to be paid can apply to a county court, the High Court or the Costs Office of the Supreme Court for a detailed assessment of the costs on the standard basis or, where the tribunal's order so specifies, the indemnity basis.

[*TCEA 2007, s 29(4); SI 2009 No 273, Rule 10*].

Upper Tribunal procedure

[6.27] The powers of the Upper Tribunal to regulate its own proceedings are broadly the same as the powers of the First-tier Tribunal. See *SI 2008 No 2698, Rules 5, 6, 9, 12* and **6.14** above.

Representation

The same rights to representation in a case before the Upper Tribunal apply as in a case before the First-tier Tribunal. In addition it can also: (i) suspend the effect of a decision where a party has made an application for permission to appeal or whilst an appeal is on-going; and (ii) ask the First-tier Tribunal to provide documents in relation to any decision and the reasons for that decision. This power enables the Upper Tribunal to have all the information and reasons for decisions before it when it considers appeals and permissions to appeal.

The Upper Tribunal may give a direction itself or on written application by either or all of the parties (unless the application is made orally on the day of the hearing). Written notification of any directions will usually be sent to all parties, and any party may then ask for the direction to be amended, suspended or set aside.

See *SI 2008 No 2698, Rules 5, 6, 9, 12* and **6.14** above.

Withdrawal from a case

A party can notify the Upper Tribunal of the withdrawal of its case, or part of it. This can be done in writing before a hearing or orally at a hearing. If the case is to be settled without a hearing, written notice must be given before the Tribunal disposes of the case. The withdrawal only takes effect, however, if the Tribunal consents (but this requirement does not apply to the withdrawal of an application for permission to appeal).

A party who has withdrawn its case can, however, apply (in writing) to the Tribunal to reinstate it. The application must be received by the Tribunal within one month after it received the withdrawal notice or the date of the hearing.

[*SI 2008 No 2698, Rule 17*].

Failure to comply with rules

[6.28] An irregularity resulting from any failure to comply with the Tribunal Procedure Rules, a practice direction or a direction by the Upper Tribunal does not in itself make the proceedings void.

Where a party fails to comply with the Rules etc. the Upper Tribunal can take such action as it considers just. This could be to require compliance or waive the requirement, to strike the case out (see below) or to restrict a party's participation in the case.

The Upper Tribunal has the same powers as the High Court to deal with the failure (which may include financial penalties).

[*TCEA 2007, s 25; SI 2008 No 2698, Rule 7*].

The Upper Tribunal has similar powers to strike out a case as the First-tier Tribunal. See *SI 2008 No 2698, Rule 8* and **6.15** above. Note, however, that the Upper Tribunal cannot strike out an appeal from the decision of another tribunal or judicial review proceedings on the grounds that there is no reasonable prospect of the appellant's case succeeding.

Appeal against decisions of the First-tier Tribunal

Application for permission to appeal

[6.29] A party to a case who disagrees with a decision of the First-tier Tribunal can apply for permission to appeal against it. Applications must first be made to the First-tier Tribunal (see **6.24** above), but if that Tribunal refuses permission a further application can be made to the Upper Tribunal.

Applications to the Upper Tribunal must be in writing and must be received no later than one month after the date on which the First-tier Tribunal sent the notice refusing permission to appeal. An application must include the grounds for appeal and state whether the appellant wants the application to be dealt with at a hearing. It must be accompanied by copies of any written record of the decision being challenged, any statement of reasons for that decision, and the notice of the First-tier Tribunal's refusal of permission to appeal. Late applications must include a request for extension of time and the reason for lateness.

If the application to the First-tier Tribunal for permission to appeal was refused because it was made out of time, the application to the Upper Tribunal must include the reason for the lateness of the first application. The Upper Tribunal can then admit the application only if it considers that it is in the interests of justice to do so.

If the Tribunal refuses permission to appeal it will notify the appellant of its decision and its reasons. If the refusal is made without a hearing the appellant can apply in writing for the decision to be reconsidered at a hearing. The application must be received by the Tribunal within 14 days after the date that written notice of its decision was sent. This rule applies also where the Tribunal gives permission on limited grounds or subject to conditions without a hearing.

If the Tribunal grants permission, the application for permission is then normally treated as a notice of appeal, and the case will proceed accordingly. If all the parties agree, the appeal can be determined without obtaining any further response.

[*SI 2008 No 2698, Rules 21, 22; SI 2009 No 274, Rule 14*].

Notice of appeal

[6.30] If the First-tier Tribunal gives permission to appeal to the Upper Tribunal (or the Upper Tribunal gives permission but directs that the application for permission should not be treated as a notice of appeal) an appellant can appeal to the Upper Tribunal by providing a notice of appeal. This must be received by the tribunal within one month after the notice giving permission to appeal was sent.

The notice must include the grounds for appeal and state whether the appellant wants the application to be dealt with at a hearing. If, the First-tier Tribunal gave permission to appeal, the notice must be accompanied by copies of any written record of the decision being challenged, any statement of reasons for that decision, and the notice of permission to appeal. Late applications must include a request for extension of time and the reason for lateness.

A copy of the notice and the documents provided will then be sent by the Upper Tribunal to the respondents who can provide a written response. The response must be received by the Tribunal not later than one month after the copy of the notice of appeal was sent. (Where an application for permission to appeal stands as the notice of appeal (see **6.29** above), the response must be received not later than one month after the Tribunal sent to the respondent notice that if had granted permission to appeal.)

The response must indicate whether the respondent opposes the appeal, and if so, the grounds for opposition (which can include grounds which were unsuccessful before the First-tier Tribunal) and whether the respondent wants the case to be dealt with at a hearing. Late responses must include a request for extension of time and the reason for lateness.

A copy of the response and any documents provided will then be sent by the Tribunal to the appellant and any other parties to the case who can, in turn, provide a written reply. The reply must be received by the Tribunal within one month of the date the tribunal sent the copy of the respondent's response.

[*SI 2008 No 2698, Rules 23–25*].

Other cases before the Upper Tribunal

[6.31] Where a case has been transferred or referred to the Upper Tribunal from the First-tier Tribunal (see **6.2** above) or where a case is started by direct application to the Upper Tribunal, the Upper Tribunal will determine by direction the procedure for considering and disposing of the case.

[*SI 2008 No 2698, Rule 26A; SI 2009 No 274, Rule 16*].

The hearing

[6.32] The Upper Tribunal can make any decision with or without a hearing, but in deciding whether to hold a hearing, it must have regard to any view expressed by any party to the case.

Each party is normally entitled to attend the hearing and the Upper Tribunal must give reasonable notice of its time and place. At least 14 days' notice must normally be given except in urgent or exceptional circumstances or with the consent of the parties. In application for permission to bring judicial review cases, the notice period must normally be at least two days.

Hearings are normally held in public, but the Tribunal can direct that a hearing, or part of it, should be held in private.

[*SI 2008 No 2698, Rules 34–37; SI 2009 No 274, Rule 19*].

If a party fails to attend a hearing, the Upper Tribunal can nevertheless proceed with the hearing if it considers that it is in the interests of justice to do so. The Tribunal must be satisfied that the party was notified of the hearing or that reasonable steps were taken to notify the party. [*SI 2008 No 2698, Rule 38*].

Similar rules apply in relation to evidence, submission and witnesses as apply to the First-tier Tribunal. See *SI 2008 No 2698, Rules 15, 16* and **6.21** above.

The Upper Tribunal's decision

[6.33] If the Upper Tribunal decides that the First-tier Tribunal's decision involved an error on a point of law it can set aside that decision and either remit the case back to the First-tier Tribunal or remake the decision itself.

If it remits the case to the First-tier Tribunal, the Upper Tribunal can direct that the case is reheard by different members.

If it decides to remake the decision itself, the Upper Tribunal is free to make any decision that the First-tier Tribunal could make if it were rehearing the case (see **6.23** above) and can make such findings of fact as it considers appropriate.

[*TCEA 2007, s 12*].

The Upper Tribunal can give its decision orally at a hearing or in writing. In either case it will give each party a decision notice in writing as soon as practicable. The notice will include written reasons for the decision unless the decision was made with the consent of the parties or the parties have consented to the tribunal not giving written reasons. The notice will also inform the party of any further right of appeal. [*SI 2008 No 2698, Rule 40; SI 2009 No 274, Rule 21*].

The case can also be settled by the Upper Tribunal making a consent order where the parties have reached agreement. Such an order is made at the request of the parties but only if the Tribunal considers it appropriate to do so. No hearing is necessary if such an order is made. [*SI 2008 No 2698, Rule 39; SI 2009 No 274, Rule 20*].

Identical provisions to those applicable to decisions by the First-tier Tribunal apply to decisions of the Upper Tribunal. See *SI 2008 No 2698, Rule 42* and **6.23** above — amendments of a decision. With regard to setting aside a decision — virtually identical provisions to those applicable to decisions by the First-tier Tribunal apply to decisions of the Upper Tribunal. An application for a decision to be set aside must be received by the Upper Tribunal no later than one month after the date on which the Tribunal sent the decision notice. See *SI 2008 No 2698, Rule 43* and **6.23** above.

Appeal against the Tribunal's decision

[6.34] A further appeal to the Court of Appeal (in Scotland, the Court of Session) can be made against the Upper Tribunal's decision. The appeal can be made only on a point of law and the Tribunal will give permission to appeal only if the appeal would raise some important point of principle or practice or there is some other compelling reason for the Court to hear it.

A person wishing to appeal must make a written application to the Tribunal for permission to appeal. Such an application must be received by the Tribunal within one month after the date the Tribunal sent written reasons for the decision to that person. Where a decision has been amended or corrected following a review (see below) or an application (other than a late application) for a decision to be struck out has been unsuccessful (see **6.28** above), the one month limit runs from the date on which the tribunal sent the notification of amended reasons or correction of the decision or of the failure of the striking out application.

The application must identify the alleged errors of law in the decision and state the result sought. Late applications must include a request for extension of time and the reason for lateness.

On receiving an application, the Upper Tribunal will first consider whether to review the decision. It can do so only if either it overlooked a legislative provision or binding authority which could have affected the decision or if a court has subsequently made a decision which is binding on the Upper Tribunal and could have affected the decision.

The Tribunal will notify the parties of the outcome of a review. If it decides to take any action following a review without first giving every party an opportunity to make representations, the notice must state that any party not given such an opportunity can apply for the action to be set aside and for the decision to be reviewed again.

If the Tribunal decides not to review the decision or, following a review, decides to take no action, it will then consider whether to give permission to appeal. It will send a record of its decision to the parties as soon as practicable together with, where it decides not to give permission, a statements of its reasons for refusal and details of the right to apply directly to the court for permission to appeal (see **6.36** below). The Tribunal's permission can be in respect of part only of the decision or on limited grounds.

[*TCEA 2007, s 13; SI 2008 No 2698, Rules 44–46; SI 2008 No 2834*].

See **6.25** above for the payment of tax pending an appeal from a decision of the Upper Tribunal.

Award of costs

[6.35] The Upper Tribunal can make an order awarding costs (or, in Scotland, expenses):

(a) in proceedings on appeal from the Tax Chamber of the First-tier Tribunal;
(b) in judicial review cases (see **6.42** below);
(c) in cases transferred from the Tax Chamber of the First-tier Tribunal;
(d) under *TCEA 2007, s 29(4)* (wasted costs — see **6.26** above); or
(e) where the Tribunal considers that a party or representative has acted unreasonably in bringing, defending or conducting the case.

Before making an order for costs, the Tribunal must give the person who will have to pay them the chance to make representations. If the payer is an individual, it must consider his financial means.

The Tribunal can make an order on its own initiative or on an application from one of the parties. Such an application must be sent both to the tribunal and to the person from whom costs are sought, together with a schedule of the costs claimed. An application must be made no later than one month after the date on which the Tribunal sends the notice recording the decision which finally disposes of all the issues in the case.

The amount of costs will be decided either by agreement of the parties, by summary assessment by the Tribunal or, if not agreed, by assessment. Where the amount is to be decided by assessment, either the payer or the person to whom the costs are to be paid can apply to a county court, the High Court or the Costs Office of the Supreme Court for a detailed assessment of the costs on the standard basis or, where the Tribunal's order so specifies, the indemnity basis.

The Upper Tribunal has recently considered the matter of excessive costs claim. Following the Upper Tribunal decision in *HMRC v Taylor & Haimendorf (No 2)* [2010] UKUT 417 (TCC), [2011] STC 126, HMRC applied for costs of £17,990, including a claim for £8,010 in respect of 38 hours' attendance on documents. The shareholders objected to HMRC's claims, and in *HMRC v Taylor & Haimendorf (Costs) (No 3)* (UT 4 March 2011, FTC/43/2010) the Upper Tribunal held that HMRC were entitled to reasonable costs but that the claim for £8,010 was excessive and reduced the amount in question to £925. The tribunal therefore awarded HMRC total costs of £10,905.

[*SI 2008 No 2698, Rule 1; SI 2009 No 274, Rule 7*].

Appeal to the Court of Appeal

[6.36] As noted at **6.34** above, a party who disagrees with a decision of the Upper Tribunal can ask the Tribunal for permission to appeal to the Court of Appeal (in Scotland, the Court of Session). The appeal can be made only on a point of law.

If the Tribunal refuses permission, the party can seek permission to appeal directly from the Court. The Court will give permission only if the appeal would raise some important point of principle or practice or there is some other compelling reason for the Court to hear it.

[*TCEA 2007, s 13; SI 2008 No 2834*].

There are no tax-specific rules governing the making of applications for permission to appeal or for notifying appeals where permission has been given by the Court or Upper Tribunal. The *Civil Procedure Rules 1998, SI 1998 No 3132* therefore apply.

The Court's decision

If the Court finds that the decision of the Upper Tribunal involved an error on a point of law it can set aside the decision. It must then either remake the decision itself or remit the case back to either the Upper Tribunal or the First-tier Tribunal, with directions for its reconsideration. Those directions can include a direction that the case is to be re-heard by different tribunal members.

Where the case is remitted to the Upper Tribunal, it can itself decide to remit the case to the First-tier Tribunal.

If the Court decides to remake the decision itself, it can make any decision that the Upper Tribunal or first-tier Tribunal could have made, and can make such findings of fact as it considers appropriate.

[*TCEA 2007, s 14*].

Case law

The following cases relate to the pre-1 April 2009 appeal process (which involved initial appeal to the High Court rather than the Court of Appeal) but remain relevant to the new process.

Withdrawal etc.

Once set down for hearing, a case cannot be declared a nullity (*Way v Underdown* CA 1974, 49 TC 215) or struck out under *Order 18, Rule 19 of the Rules of the Supreme Court* (*Petch v Gurney (Inspector of Taxes)* [1994] 3 All ER 731, [1994] STC 689, 66 TC 743, CA), but the appellant may withdraw (*Hood Barrs v CIR (No 3)* CA 1960, 39 TC 209, but see *Bradshaw v Blunden (No 2)* Ch D 1960, 39 TC 73). Where the appellant was the inspector and the taxpayer did not wish to proceed, the Court refused to make an order on terms agreed between the parties (*Slaney v Kean* Ch D 1969, 45 TC 415).

Remission of cases to tribunal

In *Consolidated Goldfields plc v CIR* Ch D 1990, 63 TC 333, the taxpayer company's request that the High Court remit a case to the Commissioners for further findings of fact was refused. Although the remedy was properly sought, it would only be granted if it could be shown that the desired findings were:

(a) material to some tenable argument;
(b) reasonably open on the evidence adduced, and
(c) not inconsistent with the findings already made.

However, in *Fitzpatrick v CIR* CS 1990, [1991] STC 34, a case was remitted where the facts found proved or admitted, and the contentions of the parties, were not clearly set out, despite the taxpayer's request for various amendments and insertions to the case, and in *Whittles v Uniholdings Ltd (No 1)* [1993] STC 767n, remission was appropriate in view of the widely differing interpretations which the parties sought to place on the Commissioners' decision (and the case was remitted a second time (see [1993] STC 767) to resolve misunderstandings as to the nature of a concession made by the Crown at the original hearing and apparent inconsistencies in the Commissioners' findings of fact). If a case is remitted, the taxpayer had the right to attend any further hearing by the Commissioners (*Lack v Doggett* CA 1970, 46 TC 497) but the Commissioners could not, in the absence of special circumstances, admit further evidence (*Archer-Shee v Baker* CA 1928, 15 TC 1; *Watson v Samson Bros* Ch D 1959, 38 TC 346; *Bradshaw v Blunden (No 2)* Ch D 1960, 39 TC 73), but see *Brady v Group Lotus Car Companies plc* CA 1987, 60 TC 359 where the Court directed the Commissioners to admit further evidence where new facts had come to light suggesting the taxpayers had deliberately misled the Commissioners. Errors of fact in the case may be amended by agreement of the parties prior to hearing of the case (*Moore v Austin* Ch D 1985, 59 TC 110). See *Jeffries v Stevens* Ch D 1982, 56 TC 134 as regards delay between statement of case and motion for remission.

Appeal restricted to point of law

Many court decisions turn on whether the Commissioners' decision was one of fact supported by the evidence, and hence final. The courts will not disturb a finding of fact if there was reasonable evidence for it, notwithstanding that the evidence might support a different conclusion of fact. The leading case is *Edwards v Bairstow & Harrison* HL 1955, 36 TC 207, in which the issue was whether there had been an adventure in the nature of trade. The Commissioners' decision was reversed on the ground that the only reasonable conclusion from the evidence was that there had been such an adventure. For a recent discussion of the application of this principle, see *Milnes (Inspector of Taxes) v J Bean Group Ltd* [1975] STC 487, 54 ATC 156.

A new question of law may be raised in the courts on giving due notice to the other parties (*Muir v CIR* CA 1966, 43 TC 367) but the courts will neither admit evidence not in the stated case (*Watson v Samson Bros* Ch D 1959, 38 TC 346; *Cannon Industries Ltd v Edwards* Ch D 1965, 42 TC 625; *Frowd v Whalley* Ch D 1965, 42 TC 599, and see *R v Great Yarmouth Commrs (ex p. Amis)* QB 1960, 39 TC 143) nor consider contentions of which evidence in support was not produced before the Commissioners (*Denekamp v Pearce* Ch D 1998, 71 TC 213).

Use of Parliamentary material

Following the decision in *Pepper v Hart* HL 1992, 65 TC 421, the courts are prepared to consider the parliamentary history of legislation, or the official reports of debates in Hansard, where all of the following conditions are met.

- Legislation is ambiguous or obscure, or leads to an absurdity.
- The material relied upon consists of one or more statements by a Minister or other promoter of the Bill together if necessary with such other parliamentary material as is necessary to understand such statements and their effect.
- The statements relied upon are clear.

Any party intending to refer to an extract from Hansard in support of any argument must, unless otherwise directed, serve copies of the extract and a brief summary of the argument intended to be based upon the extract upon all parties and the court not less than five clear working days before the first day of the hearing (Supreme Court Practice Note, 20 December 1994) (1995 STI 98).

Status of decision

A court decision is a binding precedent for itself or an inferior court except that the House of Lords, while treating its former decisions as normally binding, may depart from a previous decision should it appear right to do so. For this see *Fitzleet Estates Ltd v Cherry* HL 1977, 51 TC 708. Scottish decisions are not binding on the High Court but are normally followed. Decisions of the Privy Council and of the Irish Courts turning on comparable legislation are treated with respect. A court decision does not affect other assessments already final and conclusive but may be followed, if relevant, in the determination of any open appeals against assessments and in assessments made subsequently irrespective of the years of assessment or taxpayers concerned (*Waring, Re, Westminster Bank Ltd v Burton-Butler* [1948] Ch 221, [1948] 1 All ER 257; *Gwyther v Boslymon Quarries Ltd* [1950] 2 KB 59, [1950] 1 All ER 384; *Bolands Ltd v CIR* SC(I) 1925, 4 ATC 526). Further, a court decision does not prevent the Crown from proceeding on a different basis for other years (*Hood Barrs v CIR (No 3)* CA 1960, 39 TC 209). A general change of practice consequent on a court decision may affect error or mistake relief (see **38.5 GAINS AND LOSS BUYING**).

For joinder of CIR in non-tax disputes, see In *re Vandervell's Trusts* HL 1970, 46 TC 341.

Appeals open on 1 April 2009

[6.37] Appeals made before 1 April 2009 are, in general, dealt with on and after that date under the process outlined at **6.6** onwards above. The following special rules apply, however, to deal with the transition to the new regime.

HMRC review

A review by HMRC of its decision (see **6.8** above) can be requested or sought if neither the appellant nor HMRC have served notice on the Appeal Commissioners requesting a hearing before 1 April 2009.

Where a review is required or offered before 1 April 2010, HMRC have 90 days within which to give notice of their conclusions (rather than the normal 45 days).

[*SI 2009 No 56, Sch 3 para 5*].

Hearing requested before 1 April 2009

Where either HMRC or the appellant notified the Appeal Commissioners requesting a hearing before 1 April 2009, the proceedings continue on and after that date before the Tribunal. (If a hearing was actually under way, but was not concluded, on 31 March 2009, it continued on 1 April 2009 as a Tribunal hearing, with the same Commissioners acting as members of the Tribunal.)

The Tribunal can give directions to ensure that the case is dealt with fairly and justly, in particular by applying the procedural rules applicable before 1 April 2009 and disapplying those applying from that date. Directions in force immediately before 1 April 2009 continue in force on and after that date. Any time period (such as for the delivery of particulars) which began but did not expire before 1 April 2009 continues to apply after that date.

The Tribunal can award costs only if, and to the extent that, costs could have been awarded before 1 April 2009. Costs cannot therefore be awarded where the appeal was to the General Commissioners and, if the appeal was to the Special Commissioners, can be awarded only against a party who has, in their opinion, acted wholly unreasonably in connection with the hearing (see **6.39** below).

[*SI 2009 No 56, Sch 3 paras 6, 7*].

Cases to be remitted by courts

Any case heard by the Appeal Commissioners before 1 April 2009 which is to be remitted by a court on or after that date is remitted to the Tribunal. [*SI 2009 No 56, Sch 3 para 8*].

Commissioners' decision made before 1 April 2009. Where a decision has been made by the Appeal Commissioners and immediately before 1 April 2009 there is a right of appeal to a court against that decision the same rights of appeal apply as apply in respect of a decision of the First-tier Tribunal (so that, initially, appeal will be to the Upper Tribunal).

Where, however, a party to a case decided by the General Commissioners before 1 April 2009 has, before that date, initiated an appeal to the High Court using the stated case procedure, the appeal will proceed to the High Court under that procedure (see **6.41** below). The General Commissioners concerned will be required to state and sign a case notwithstanding the general abolition of the Commissioners with effect from 1 April 2009.

Similarly the rules governing the correction of irregularities and the reviewing of a decision continue to apply to decisions of General Commissioners made before 1 April 2009. Again, the General Commissioners continue to function for that purpose notwithstanding their general abolition. See **6.40** below.

[*SI 2008 No 2696, Art 3; SI 2009 No 56, Sch 3 para 11*].

The appeal process before 1 April 2009

[6.38] As noted at **6.37** above, appeals made before 1 April 2009 but not concluded before that date generally transfer into the new system. The detailed procedures applying before 1 April 2009 are therefore not covered in this work. A brief summary of the rules is given at **6.39** below; for full details see the 2008/09 edition.

Certain provisions relating to decisions made by the General Commissioners before 1 April 2009 do, however, remain relevant in transitional cases. These provisions are covered in detail at **6.39–6.41** below.

Summary of process

[6.39] Before 1 April 2009 there was no HMRC review procedure, so that appeals were settled either by agreement (see **6.10** above) or by determination by the Appeal Commissioners. Appeals were normally to the General Commissioners, subject to specific statutory exceptions and subject also to the appellant's limited right of election to bring an appeal before the Special Commissioners.

The procedures for appeals hearings were governed by regulations: see *SI 1994 No 1812* for cases before the General Commissioners and *SI 1994 No 1811* for cases before the Special Commissioners.

General Commissioners

General Commissioners were appointed by the Lord Chancellor and required no legal qualifications. The Commissioners were appointed to local divisions, each with its own Clerk, usually a local solicitor, who attended meetings to take minutes and give advice. Proceedings in a particular case would be heard by between two and five Commissioners. Any party to the proceedings could serve notice on the Clerk that he wished a date for a hearing to be fixed, although in practice it was usually HMRC which did so.

The Commissioners' powers to make a decision in an appeal were broadly the same as those of the First-tier Tribunal — see **6.22** above. Their decision was final and conclusive, subject to the correction of irregularities, any application for review or any further appeal. [*TMA 1970, ss 46(2), 50 as previously enacted; SI 1994 No 1812, Regs 17, 24*].

Further appeal on a point of law was initially to the High Court (in Scotland the Court of Session) through the case stated procedure: see **6.41** below. Further appeal could then be made to the Court of Appeal and thence (with leave) to the House of Lords.

There was no provision for the award of costs in General Commissioners' cases.

Special Commissioners

Special Commissioners were appointed by the Lord Chancellor and were required to satisfy certain requirements as to legal qualifications and experience. They heard cases only in a small number of locations, each case being heard by one, two or three Commissioners.

Appeal against a decision of the Special Commissioners on a point of law was to the High Court (in Scotland the Court of Session). Further appeal could be made to the Court of Appeal and thence (with leave) to the House of Lords.

The Special Commissioners could make an order awarding costs (in Scotland expenses) of, or incidental to, the hearing of any proceedings against any party who had, in their opinion, acted wholly unreasonably in connection with the hearing, but not without giving that party the opportunity of making representations against the award. The award could be of all or part of the costs of the other party or parties, such costs to be taxed in the county court (in Scotland the sheriff court) if not agreed. [*SI 1994 No 1811, Reg 21*].

For this purpose an act 'in connection with the hearing' included any action taken once the appeal has been consigned by one or both parties to the Special Commissioners (*Carter v Hunt (Inspector of Taxes)* [2000] STC (SCD) 17). Failure by the taxpayer to attend or be represented at the hearing without giving prior notification could be a contributory factor in an award of costs, as could a failure to comply with a Commissioners' direction (*Phillips v Burrows (Inspector of Taxes)* [2000] STC (SCD) 17).

For cases in which costs/expenses were awarded against HMRC, see *Scott and another (trading as Farthings Steak House) v McDonald* [1996] STC (SCD) 381, *Robertson v CIR (No 2)* [2002] STC (SCD) 242, *Carvill v Frost* [2005] STC (SCD) 208 and *Oriel Support Ltd v HMRC* [2007] STC (SCD) 670.

In *McEwan v Revenue and Customs Comrs* [2005] STC (SCD) 681 the appellant was denied costs even though it was held that the Revenue had behaved wholly unreasonably, because the result of the appeal was that each party succeeded in roughly equal amounts. In *Salt v Young* [1999] STC (SCD) 249, the Revenue were refused costs on the grounds that although the taxpayer had, on an objective test, behaved unreasonably, he had not been wholly unreasonable, and his unreasonableness was connected with the hearing only to a very minor extent. Only in 'a very rare case' would the Court interfere with the Commissioners' decision as regards costs (see *Gamble v Rowe* Ch D 1998, 71 TC 190 in which a refusal of costs was upheld). For the basis for assessment of costs see *Carvill v Frost (No 2)* [2005] STC (SCD) 422.

General commissioners

General Commissioners' decisions — transitional provisions

[6.40] As indicated at **6.37** above, where a decision was made by the General Commissioners on or before 31 March 2009 certain provisions continue to apply after that date. The Commissioners must continue to operate their functions under the provisions, despite their general abolition with effect from 1 April 2009. The provisions are as follows.

The Commissioners' decision

Review of the Commissioners' final determination

[6.41] The Commissioners may review and set aside or vary a final determination made before 1 April 2009 on the application of any party or of their own motion where they are satisfied that either:

- it was wrongly made as a result of administrative error; or
- a party entitled to be heard failed to appear or be represented for good and sufficient reason; or
- relevant information had been supplied to the Clerk or to the appropriate inspector or other HMRC officer prior to the hearing but was not received by the Commissioners until after the hearing.

A written application for such a review must be made to the Commissioners no later than 14 days after the date of the notice of the determination (or by such later time as the Commissioners may allow), stating the grounds in full. Where the Commissioners propose of their own motion to review a determi nation, they must serve notice on the parties not later than 14 days after the date of the notice of the determination.

The parties are entitled to be heard on any such review or proposed review. If practicable, the review is to be determined by the Commissioners who decided the case, and if they set aside the determination, they may substitute a different determination or order a rehearing before the same or different Commissioners. A decision to vary or substitute a final determination is to be notified in the same way as the original determination (see above).

[*SI 1994 No 1812, Reg 17; SI 2008 No 2696, Art 4; SI 2009 No 56, Sch 3 para 11*].

Irregularities

Although irregularities resulting from failure to comply with regulations or with any Commissioners' direction did not of themselves, render the proceedings void, any of the Commissioners concerned (or the Clerk if all the Commissioners have died or ceased to be Commissioners) can correct clerical errors in any document recording a direction or decision by certificate under his hand. [*SI 1994 No 1812, Reg 24; SI 2008 No 2696, Art 4; SI 2009 No 56, Sch 3 para 11*].

Appeal to the High Court by case stated procedure

Within 30 days of the date of final determination before 1 April 2009 of an appeal any party dissatisfied with the determination as being erroneous in point of law may, before 1 April 2009, serve notice on the Clerk requiring the Commissioners to state and sign a case for the opinion of the High Court (in Scotland the Court of Session), setting forth the facts and final determination of the Commissioners. See *Grainger v Singer* KB 1927, 11 TC 704 as regards receipt of the case. The 30-day time limit for requesting a case does not apply to the payment of the fee (*Anson v Hill* CA 1968, 47 ATC 143). (Where no application for a stated case is made before 1 April 2009, the right of appeal against the Commissioners' decision is the same as that against a decision of the First-tier Tribunal — see **6.37** above.)

The Commissioners may serve notice on the person who required the stated case requiring him, within a specified period of not less than 28 days, to identify the question of law on which he requires the case to be stated. They may refuse to state a case until such notice is complied with, or if they are not satisfied that a question of law is involved, or if the requisite fee (see below) has not been paid. A requirement for a case to be stated becomes invalid if the determination to which it relates is set aside or varied.

The case stated procedure does not apply to a final determination by the General Commissioners of an appeal in which a question has been referred to another tribunal (the Lands Tribunal or the Special Commissioners) and all appeal rights have been exhausted. [*SI 1994 No 1812, Regs 20, 23; SI 1999 No 3293, Reg 6; SI 2008 No 2696, Art 4; SI 2009 No 56, Sch 3 para 11*].

A fee of £25 is payable to the Clerk by the person requiring the case before he is entitled to have it stated. [*TMA 1970, s 56(3) as previously enacted; SI 1994 No 1813; SI 2008 No 2696, Art 4; SI 2009 No 56, Sch 3 para 11*]. A single case may have effect as regards each of a number of appeals heard together (*Getty Oil Co v Steele and related appeals* Ch D 1990, 63 TC 376).

If the taxpayer dies, his personal representatives stand in his shoes (*Smith v Williams* KB 1921, 8 TC 321).

The case stated procedure is not open to a successful party to an appeal (*Sharpey-Schafer v Venn* Ch D 1955, 34 ATC 141), but where another party requires a case, the successful party may invite the Commissioners to include in the case an additional question relating to another ground on which the Commissioners had found against it (*Gordon v CIR* CS 1991, 64 TC 173). In the case of a partnership, the procedure is available to any one of the partners, with or without the consent of the others (*Sutherland & Partners v Barnes and Another* CA 1994, 66 TC 663).

Consideration of draft case

Within 56 days of receipt of a notice requiring a stated case (or of the Commissioners being satisfied as to the question of law involved), the Clerk must send a draft of the case to all the parties. Written representations thereon may be made to the Clerk by any party within 56 days after the draft case is sent out, with copies to all the other parties, and within a further 28 days further representations may similarly be made in response. Any party to whom copies of representations are not sent may apply to the Clerk for a copy. The validity of a case after it has been stated and signed, and of any subsequent proceedings, is not affected by a failure to meet these time limits or by a failure to send copies of representations to all parties. [*SI 1994 No 1812, Reg 21; SI 2008 No 2696, Art 4; SI 2009 No 56, Sch 3 para 11*].

An application for the taxpayer's name to be withheld was refused (In re *H Ch D 1964, 42 TC 14*) as was an application for the deletion of a passage possibly damaging the taxpayer (*Treharne v Guinness Exports Ltd* Ch D 1967, 44 TC 161). An application for judicial review on the ground that the case did not cover all matters in dispute was refused in *R v Special Commrs (ex p. Napier)* CA 1988, 61 TC 206. In *Danquah v CIR* Ch D 1990, 63 TC 526, an application for the statement of a further case was refused where the case did not set out all the questions raised by the taxpayer in the originating motion by which he had sought an order directing the Commissioners to state a case. See also *Consolidated Goldfields plc v CIR* Ch D 1990, 63 TC 333 in which a request to remit a case to the Commissioners for further findings of fact was refused.

Preparation and submission of final case

As soon as may be after the final date for representations, the Commissioners, after taking into account any representations, must state and sign the case. In the event of the death of a Commissioner, or of his ceasing to be a Commissioner, the case is to be signed by the remaining Commissioner(s) or, if there are none, by the Clerk. The case is then sent by the Clerk to the person who required it to be stated, and the other parties notified accordingly.

In England, Wales and Scotland, the party requiring the case must transmit it to the High Court (in Scotland, the Court of Session) within 30 days of receiving it, and at or before the time he does so must notify each of the other parties that the case has been stated on his application and send them a copy of the case. The 30 day time limit (under the similar earlier provisions of *TMA 1970, s 56(4)*) is mandatory (*Valleybright Ltd (in liquidation) v Richardson* Ch D 1984, 58 TC 290; *Petch v Gurney (Inspector of Taxes)* [1994] 3 All ER 731, [1994] STC 689, 66 TC 743, CA), may run from the date the case is received by the taxpayer's authorised agent (*Brassington v Guthrie* Ch D 1991, 64 TC 435), and requires the case to be *received* by the High Court within the 30 days (*New World Medical Ltd v Cormack* Ch D, [2002] STC 1245). The notification (and copy) to the other parties is required only to give 'adequate notice' of the appeal and not to be 'too long delayed' (*Hughes v Viner* Ch D 1985, 58 TC 437). In Northern Ireland, slightly different rules apply (and see *CIR v McGuckian* CA(NI) 1994, 69 TC 1).

[*SI 1994 No 1812, Regs 22, 23; SI 2008 No 2696, Art 4; SI 2009 No 56, Sch 3 para 11*].

Judicial review

[6.42] Principles have been developed by the Courts for the review of the legality of decisions made by public bodies and tribunals, which include HMRC, the First-tier Tribunal, Upper Tribunal and prior to 1 April 2009 the General and Special Commissioners. On the basis that a decision by HMRC will generally be of a public law nature, then judicial review (at the High Court) is the correct procedure, save in cases where the Upper Tribunal would itself have jurisdiction to hear an appeal.

TCEA 2007, s 18 states that the Upper Tribunal can determine applications for judicial review in specific circumstances where four conditions are satisfied:

(1) the application must solely be seeking relief that could be granted in judicial review proceedings;

(2) the application does not call into question anything done in a Crown Court;

(3) the application falls within the classes proscribed in directions. On 29 October 2008, the Lord Chief Justice made a direction stating that challenges could be made in relation to any decision of the First-tier Tribunal, unless the Lord Chancellor had made an order that the decision was an excluded decision for the purposes of *s 11(5)(f)*. However, the direction states that it does not apply to an application for a declaration of incompatibility under *HRA 1998, s 4*;

(4) the application must be heard by a High Court or Court of Appeal judge or a person authorised by the Lord Chief Justice.

In any other case the Upper Tribunal must transfer the application to the High Court.

Thus, a taxpayer who is dissatisfied with the exercise of administrative powers may in certain circumstances (e.g. where HMRC has exceeded or abused its powers or acted contrary to the rules of natural justice, or where the Tribunal has acted unfairly or improperly) seek a remedy in a mandatory or prohibiting order or a quashing order.

As noted, this is done by way of application for judicial review to the High Court under *Supreme Court Act 1981, s 31* and *Part 54 of the Civil Procedure Rules*. With effect from 1 April 2009, the High Court can in certain cases transfer an application for judicial review or for leave to apply for judicial review to the Upper Tribunal (see *Supreme Court Act 1981, s 31A*).

The issue on an application for leave to apply for judicial review is whether there is an arguable case (*R v CIR (ex p Howmet Corpn)* [1994] STC 413n). The procedure is generally used where no other, adequate, remedy, such as a right of appeal, is available. See *R v Special Commr (ex p. Stipplechoice Ltd) (No 1)* CA, [1985] STC 248 and *(No 3)* QB 1988, 61 TC 391, *R v HMIT (ex p. Kissane and Another)* QB, [1986] STC 152, *R v CIR (ex p. Goldberg)* QB 1988, 61 TC 403 and *R v Dickinson (ex p. McGuckian)* CA(NI) 1999, 72 TC 343.

There is a very long line of cases in which the courts have consistently refused applications where a matter should have been pursued through the ordinary channels as described earlier in this chapter. See, for example, *R v Special Commrs (ex p. Morey)* CA 1972, 49 TC 71; *R v Special Commrs (ex p. Emery)* QB 1980, 53 TC 555; *R v Walton General Commrs (ex p. Wilson)* CA, [1983] STC 464; *R v Special Commrs (ex p. Esslemont)* CA, 1984 STI 312; *R v Brentford General Commrs (ex p. Chan and Others)* QB 1985, 57 TC 651; *R v Special Commr (ex p. Napier)* CA 1988, 61 TC 206; *R v North London General Commrs (ex p. Nii-Amaa)* QB 1999, 72 TC 634.

See, however, *R v HMIT and Others (ex p. Lansing Bagnall Ltd)* CA 1986, 61 TC 112 for a successful application where the inspector issued a notice under a discretionary power on the footing that there was an obligation to do so, and *R v CIR (ex p. J Rothschild Holdings plc)* CA 1987, 61 TC 178 where the Revenue were required to produce internal documents of a general character relating to their practice in applying a statutory provision.

See also *R v CIR (ex p. Taylor) (No 1)* CA 1988, 62 TC 562 where an application for discovery of a document was held to be premature, and *R v Inspector of Taxes, Hull, ex p. Brumfield and others* QB 1988, 61 TC 589, where the court was held to have jurisdiction to entertain an application for judicial review of a failure by the Revenue to apply an established practice not embodied in an extra-statutory concession (cf. *R v Inspector of Taxes, Reading, ex p Fulford-Dobson* [1987] QB 978, [1987] 3 WLR 277 at **41.5 HMRC — ADMINISTRATION**, which see for 'care and management' powers of the Revenue). It was held that there had been no unfairness by the Revenue when it refused to assess on the basis of transactions that would have been entered into by the applicants had a Revenue Statement of Practice been published earlier (*R v CIR, ex p. Kaye* QB 1992, 65 TC 82). A similar view was taken in *R v CIR (ex p. S G Warburg & Co Ltd)* QB 1994, 68 TC 300 where the Revenue declined to apply a previously published practice because not only was it not clear that the taxpayer's circumstances fell within its terms but also the normal appeal procedures were available.

The underlying facts in *Carvill v CIR (No 2); R (oao Carvill) v CIR* Ch D, [2002] STC 1167 were that in two separate appeals relating to different tax years, income from an identical source had been held liable to tax for some years (the earlier years) but not others; an application for judicial review of the Revenue's refusal to refund tax, and interest on tax, paid for the earlier years was rejected; the assessments for those years were valid assessments which the Sp C in question had had jurisdiction to determine, and the taxpayer the right to challenge, and those assessments had not been set aside. See also *Davies and another v HMRC* CA, [2008] STC 2813, in which an application for judicial review was to be heard before any appeal to the Special Commissioners as it related to whether the taxpayers had a legitimate expectation that they would be treated in accordance with HMRC's published guidance.

The first step is to obtain leave to apply for judicial review from the High Court. Application for leave is made ex parte to a single judge who will usually determine the application without a hearing. The Court will not grant leave unless the applicant has a sufficient interest in the matter to which the application relates. See *CIR v National Federation of Self-Employed and Small Businesses Ltd* HL 1981, 55 TC 133 for what is meant by 'sufficient interest' and for discussion of availability of judicial review generally.

Applications must be made **within three months** of the date when the grounds for application arose. The Court has discretion to extend this time limit where there is good reason, subject to conditions, but is generally very reluctant to do so. Grant of leave for review does not amount to a ruling that application is made in good time (*R v Tavistock Commrs (ex p. Worth)* QB 1985, 59 TC 116).

Costs

[6.43] Prior to 1 April 2009, the costs position in the tax tribunals varied — the General Commissioners had no power to award costs, but the Special Commissioners had discretion to award costs where a party to an appeal had acted wholly unreasonably.

Costs may be awarded by the courts in the usual way. In suitable cases, e.g. 'test cases', HMRC may undertake to pay the taxpayer's costs. See **6.27** and **6.35** for the award of costs by the First-tier and Upper Tribunals. See **6.39** above as regards costs awarded by the Special Commissioners.

Costs awarded by the courts may include expenses connected with the drafting of the case stated (*Manchester Corporation v Sugden* CA 1903, 4 TC 595). Costs of a discontinued application for judicial review were refused where the Revenue were not informed of the application (*R v CIR (ex p. Opman International UK)* QB 1985, 59 TC 352).

Legal costs of appeals are not allowable for tax purposes generally (*Allen v Farquharson* KB 1932, 17 TC 59; *Smith's Potato Estates Ltd v Bolland* HL 1948, 30 TC 267; *Rushden Heel Co v Keene* HL 1948, 30 TC 298; *Spofforth & Prince v Golder* KB 1945, 26 TC 310).

With regard to the costs involved in pursuing judicial review proceedings which had been withdrawn, in *R (on the application of Valentines Homes & Construction Ltd) v HMRC* [2010] EWCA Civ 345, [2010] STC 1208, the Court of Appeal held that the taxpayer company should be awarded the costs of pursuing an application for judicial review.

A married couple were the sole directors of the taxpayer company, which was in the construction industry. Following a serious injury on the part of a director, the company failed to account for PAYE for the four months from May to August 2007. HMRC issued notices requiring payment of the deemed tax due under the PAYE regulations and instituted proceedings in the county court. The taxpayer calculated it owed less tax than was deemed due, but HMRC would not amend their figures. Agreement was not reached and the taxpayer applied for judicial review. The parties subsequently agreed to the withdrawal of the county court proceedings and the application for judicial review, but the taxpayer pursued the application for review when HMRC refused to pay the costs of the application. In the event, the taxpayer was ordered to pay to HMRC, the costs of preparation of the acknowledgment of service summarily assessed at £500, on the basis that it was not justified in pursuing the application for permission to apply for judicial review once the county court proceedings had been settled. The taxpayer appealed.

Allowing the appeal, the Court of Appeal held that it was not an abuse of process of the court or unreasonable for the appellant to resort to a public law claim. Despite the good sense and relevance of the equitable liability practice, HMRC had initiated, and despite all reasonable efforts by the taxpayer to settle for the sum actually due, persisted in their statutory claim for the amount deemed to be due. HMRC failed to respond to the appellants' proposals for over four months, notwithstanding reminders. They were then supplied with detailed and, it appears, scrupulous, calculations of the sum actually due but persisted in a claim for the sum deemed to be due. The taxpayer would be awarded £6,000 for the costs of commencing the judicial review.

7

Assessments

Cross references. See **6 APPEALS; 21.8 CLAIMS; 27.7 CONTROLLED FOREIGN COMPANIES; 58.3 PARTNERSHIPS; 61.15 PROFIT COMPUTATIONS** with regard to European Economic Interest Groupings; **65.6 RESIDENCE; 66.19, 66.27 RETURNS** for determination of tax liability where no return is delivered.

Simon's Taxes. See A6.705, D1.1315.

Introduction

[7.1] Self-assessment for corporation tax was introduced for accounting periods ending on or after 1 July 1999. Companies self-assess their profits chargeable to corporation tax by submitting returns which are processed by HMRC on receipt, with any queries being dealt with later by way of opening an enquiry (see **66.19 RETURNS** with regard to enquiries, now part of the compliance check process).

However, HMRC may also make assessments or determinations where necessary, for example where no return has been delivered, or where HMRC discover that profits have not been assessed. The following chapter provides details of the circumstances surrounding such assessments by HMRC, the discovery process, applicable time limits, and relevant case law with regard to fraudulent and negligent conduct.

Assessments

[7.2] Post-1 July 1999 a company must submit a return detailing its chargeable profits and including a self-assessment to tax. In addition to the self-assessment procedure, HMRC has retained the power to raise assessments in certain circumstances, for example, where no return has been made, or where it is considered profits have been under-declared. In the latter case HMRC is able to raise a 'discovery' assessment, relating to further facts or circumstances which have come to light with regard to the self-assessment within a return (see **7.3** below).

An assessment is made by an officer of HMRC by raising a notice of assessment for the relevant accounting period of the company. The notice must be served on the person assessed (normally by post) and must state its date of issue and the time limit for giving notice of appeal (**6.2 APPEALS**). Where any statutory provision gives the Commissioners for HMRC the power to make an assessment then such an assessment is also made by an officer in the same manner as above.

[*TMA 1970, s 30A(1)–(3)(5); FA 1998, Sch 18 para 47(1); ITTOIA 2005, Sch 1 para 370; CRCA 2005, ss 5, 7, Sch 4 para 68*].

Case law has had an impact on the various requirements as to an assessment, for example, an assessment must include a statement of the tax actually payable (*Hallamshire Industrial Finance Trust Ltd v CIR* (1978) 53 TC 631). An assessment defective in form or containing errors may be validated by *TMA 1970, s 114(1)*, or in some cases the court may choose to use its powers under *TMA 1970, s 56(6)* to alter an assessment on appeal (*Pickles v Foulsham* (1925) 9 TC 261, HL; *Bath & West Counties Property Trust Ltd v Thomas* (1977) 52 TC 20). However, *s 114(1)* does *not* extend to integral fundamental parts of the assessment such as an error in the year of assessment for which it is made (*Baylis v Gregory* (1988) 62 TC 1, HL).

Further, an officer's power of assessment is not limited to persons (or sources of income) within the area of his tax office (*R v Tavistock Commrs (ex p Adams) (No 2)* (1971) 48 TC 56, CA).

In *Gunn v HMRC* [2011] UKUT 59 (TCC), the First-Tier Tribunal had dismissed appeals by a company director, who then appealed to the Upper Tribunal, contending that the notices of assessment were invalid because they did not give details of the statutory provisions under which they were raised. The Upper Tribunal dismissed the appeal, holding that the notices of assessment were 'in substance and effect' in conformity with the Taxes Acts, and were therefore authorised by *TMA 1970, s 114*.

A taxpayer may authorise HMRC (on form 64-8) to automatically provide his agent with a copy of any assessment made on him. If an assessment is not dealt with promptly, interest (or additional interest) may arise on unpaid tax, and any appeal may be out of time.

See **7.10** below for the normal time limits within which an assessment may be made, including extended time limits.

See **66.27 RETURNS** for HMRC's power to make a determination of the tax liability in a case where a company tax return has been issued but not filed. Tax is payable as if the determination were a self-assessment, with no right of appeal, and the determination can only be displaced by the filing of a return and the making of a self-assessment based thereon.

See **34.5 EUROPEAN UNION LEGISLATION** regarding the application of the corporation tax provisions where a company ceases to be UK-resident in the course of the formation of an SE or where an SE becomes non-UK resident.

Discovery

Discovery assessments and determinations

[7.3] Under corporation tax self-assessment, if HMRC have any queries in respect of a return, they will open an enquiry as part of the compliance check process (see **66.19 RETURNS**). Once the time limit for an enquiry has passed, or an enquiry has been closed, then the only way HMRC can examine a chargeable period is by using the discovery process. Thus 'discovery' is the right of HMRC to re-open earlier periods which are otherwise considered closed.

However this right can only be used in specific instances — a 'discovery assessment' may be made where HMRC consider that an amount which ought to have been assessed to tax has not been assessed, or that an assessment has become insufficient, or that relief has been given which is, or has become, excessive. For example, this would occur where certain facts, or circumstances, which would have an impact on the tax payable have not been declared or disclosed, and HMRC discover this to be the case.

This additional assessment is made in the amount (or further amount) which HMRC consider, in their opinion, should be charged in order to make good the loss of tax.

Similarly, if HMRC discover that a return for an accounting period incorrectly states an amount that affects, or may affect, the tax payable for another accounting period or by another company, they may make a 'discovery determination' of the amount which, in their opinion, ought to have been stated in the return.

Notice of a discovery assessment or determination must be served on the company, stating the date of issue and the time limit for any appeal, and the assessment or determination may be altered after the notice has been served only under express provisions.

A *discovery assessment* will thus be appropriate where, for example, a discovery leads to an additional tax liability on the company for the period. A *discovery determination* would be appropriate where there is a discovery that losses carried forward or surrendered as group relief have been overstated. If such a determination reduces losses, etc. available for another period or to another company, and the time allowed for the required amendment has expired, a discovery assessment would be appropriate. (HMRC Company Taxation Manual, CTM95520 and CTM95530).

In practice, where a return has been filed and the time limit for opening an enquiry has not expired (nor an enquiry already been closed), HMRC normally deal with matters by opening an enquiry rather than by issuing a discovery assessment or determination. (HMRC Company Taxation Manual,

CTM95520). For the limited circumstances in which a discovery assessment may be made even though the deadline for opening an enquiry has not passed, see HMRC Enquiry Manual EM3255 and HMRC Tax Bulletin August 2001 pp 875, 876.

Required Circumstances

Subject to the exceptions below, a discovery assessment for an accounting period for which the company has delivered a return, or a discovery determination, may only be made in the following circumstances:

(a) where the discovery arose from a situation brought about carelessly or deliberately (from 1 April 2010), previous attributable to fraudulent or negligent conduct on the part of the company, a person acting on behalf of the company, or a partner of the company at the relevant time; or

(b) where the time limit to open an enquiry into the return has expired (see **66.19 RETURNS**), or where HMRC have completed their enquiries into the return, and HMRC could not reasonably have been expected, on the basis of the information made available to them before that time, to be aware of the situation giving rise to the discovery.
Information is for this purpose regarded as 'made available' to HMRC if it is contained:
 (i) in the company's returns (or accompanying documentation) for the period or the two immediately preceding accounting periods; or
 (ii) in a claim (or accompanying documentation) made by the company as regards the period; or
 (iii) in any documents, accounts or information produced to, or provided for, HMRC for the purposes of an enquiry into a return (as in (i)) or claim (as in (ii)),
or if it is information the existence and relevance of which are notified in writing to HMRC by the company (or a person acting on its behalf) or could reasonably be expected to be inferred by HMRC from information falling within (i)–(iii) above.

As regards (b) above, there is an onus on the company to draw attention to any important information relevant to a tax liability, particularly if there is some doubt as to the interpretation which could be placed on that information. Information made available by the company's agent on its behalf is made available by the company. However, where information is made available by, or on behalf of, someone other than the company, e.g. in the return of another member of the group, then HMRC may still make a discovery assessment or determination on the company. (HMRC Company Taxation Manual, CTM95550).

The above restrictions do not apply where a discovery assessment or determination gives effect to a discovery determination duly made in relation to another company's return.

Nor do these restrictions apply in relation to any income or gains in respect of which HMRC have given notice after completing an enquiry under certain anti-avoidance provisions, such as *TIOPA 2010, ss 81, 82; ICTA 1988, s 804ZA* (schemes and arrangements designed to increase double taxation relief — see **5.35 ANTI-AVOIDANCE**), *TCGA 1992, s 184G* or *s 184H* (avoidance utilising losses — see **17.4 CAPITAL GAINS**) or *TIOPA 2010, Pt 6; F(No 2)A 2005, s 24* or *s 26* as amended by *CTA 2009, Sch 1 para 670* (tax arbitrage — see **5.46 ANTI-AVOIDANCE**).

A discovery assessment or determination may in any event not be made if the discovery arose from a situation attributable to a mistake in the return as to the basis on which the company's liability ought to have been computed, and the return was in fact made on the basis of, or in accordance with, the practice generally prevailing at the time the return was made.

Any objection to a discovery assessment or determination on the grounds that the above conditions have not been complied with can only be made on an appeal against the assessment or determination.

The case of *DW Hankinson v HMRC (No 3)* [2010] UKUT 361 (30 September 2010) considered the interpretation of the similar income and capital gains tax provisions for discovery assessments found at *TMA 1970, s 29*. It is interesting to note that the Upper Tribunal rejected the taxpayer appellant's attempt to apply a restrictive interpretation to the discovery provisions. See also the case *M Jones v HMRC* (TC01023) [2011] UKFTT 149 (TC) (16 March 2011) below.

SP1/06 — providing HMRC with sufficient information

HMRC's Statement of Practice SP 1/06 on 'Self-Assessment: Finality and Discovery' clarifies how much information a taxpayer needs to provide in the tax return to remove the possibility of a discovery assessment.

The Statement is intended to provide more certainty for both individuals and companies following the decision in the case of *Langham v Veltema* (2004) 76 TC 259, CA, where it was held that a discovery assessment could be made once the enquiry window was closed even though HMRC was made aware of the possibility that a property valuation might have been insufficient.

The Statement provides three examples of where the taxpayer can rely on information in the tax return to provide against protection from a later discovery assessment provided the information is reasonable and true.

- In a valuation case, the information should state that a valuation has been used, by whom it has been carried out, that it was carried out by a named independent and suitably qualified valuer and, if that was the case, the appropriate basis of the valuation.
- In the case of an exceptional item in the accounts, for example concerning repairs, the information should state that a programme of work has been carried out, what it included, the total cost allocated to revenue and capital and the particular basis of allocation.
- In a case where the taxpayer adopts a different view of the law from that published as HMRC's view, the tax return should indicate that a different view had been adopted by providing comments to the effect that HMRC guidance has not been followed or that no adjustment has been made to take account of it.

The Statement stresses that only the minimum information necessary to make disclosure of an insufficiency should be submitted:

> 'Information will not be treated as being made available where the total amount supplied is so extensive that an officer "could not have been reasonably expected to be aware" of the significance of particular information and the officer's attention has not been drawn to it by the taxpayer or taxpayer's representative.'

It further states that the *Veltema* judgment does not require the provision of enough information to quantify the effect on the assessment.

[*FA 1998, Sch 18 paras 41–45; FA 2005, s 88(4)(5); F(No 2)A 2005, s 29(2); FA 2006, s 71(3); FA 2008, Sch 39 para 41; CTA 2009, Sch 1, para 671*].

Simon's Taxes. See **A6.702, A6.703, A6.705, A6.706.**

Over-repayments

[7.4] The discovery assessment provisions at **7.3** above also apply to an amount paid to a company by way of repayment of tax (or payment of tax credit), **INTEREST ON OVERPAID TAX** (**50**), 'land remediation tax credit' (see **61.14 PROFIT COMPUTATIONS**), research and development tax credits (see **64 RESEARCH AND DEVELOPMENT**), first-year tax credits (see **CAPITAL ALLOWANCES — PLANT AND MACHINERY: ELIGIBLE EXPENDITURE AND INITIAL ALLOWANCES 11.17**) or film tax credits (see **70.31 TRADE PROFITS — INCOME AND SPECIFIC TRADES**), to the extent that it ought not to have been paid, unless it is recoverable under *ICTA 1988, s 826(8A)* (interest recoverable as if it were **INTEREST ON OVERDUE TAX** (**49**)).

Any such assessment is on miscellaneous income, and **INTEREST ON OVERDUE TAX** (**49**) runs from the date when the payment being recovered was made. For these purposes amounts allowed by way of set-off are treated as paid, and an intended repayment which exceeds the tax paid is nonetheless treated as a repayment. In the case of an assessment to recover tax repaid in respect of an accounting period (or interest thereon), income tax repaid in respect of a payment received in an accounting period (or interest thereon), or land remediation or research and development tax credits paid for an accounting period, the assessment is treated as being for the accounting period in respect of which the repayment or credit was made.

Except in cases of careless or deliberate error (previously fraud or negligence) (for which see **7.7** below), the time limit for a discovery assessment by virtue of these provisions is (where relevant) extended to the later of the end of the accounting period following that in which the amount assessed was paid and the expiry of three months from the day on which HMRC complete an enquiry into a relevant company tax return (see **66.23 RETURNS**).

[*FA 1998, Sch 18 paras 52, 53; FA 2006, Sch 5 para 28; FA 2008, Sch 25 para 8, Sch 39 para 44; CTA 2009, Sch 1 paras 267, 454*].

Double assessment

[7.5] Where a company makes a written claim to HMRC that it has been assessed (including self-assessment) more than once for the same cause and for the same accounting period, and HMRC are satisfied, then HMRC must take the necessary steps to eliminate the double charge.

If the company does not agree with HMRC's decision on a claim then they may appeal to the relevant tribunal which has jurisdiction to hear an appeal relating to the assessment (or the later of the assessments) to which the claim relates. [*FA 1998, Sch 18 para 50*].

See also **6 APPEALS.**

Finality of assessments

[7.6] An assessment cannot be altered after the notice has been served except in accordance with the express provisions of the *Taxes Acts* (for example where the taxpayer appeals — see **6 APPEALS**).

[*FA 1998, Sch 18 paras 47(2), 49*].

Where over-assessment results from an *error or mistake* in a return, see **21.10 CLAIMS.**

Where an amount required to be included in a company tax return may affect tax payable for another accounting period or by another company, and that amount can no longer be altered (for which see *FA 1998, Sch 18 para 88(3)–(5)*), it is taken as conclusively determined in relation to the other period or company (without affecting HMRC's power to make assessments).

[*FA 1998, Sch 18 para 88; FA 2008, s 119*].

Extended time limits

[7.7] Except where specifically provided, the normal time limit for assessments is, from 1 April 2010, four (previously six) years after the end of the accounting period.

[*FA 1998, Sch 18 para 46(1), Sch 19 para 17; FA 2008, Sch 39 para 42(2)*]

In certain cases, however, as described below, extended limits apply to assessments for the purpose of making good a loss of tax.

An objection to the making of any assessment on the grounds that it is out of time can only be made on an appeal against the assessment. [*FA 1998, Sch 18 para 46(3)*].

From 1 April 2010, an assessment may be made on tax lost through:

- deliberate action of the company or a person related to the company;
- careless action not appropriately remedied; or

- failure to comply with the tax avoidance schemes legislation (see **5.41 ANTI-AVOIDANCE**)

The normal time limit is four years (from 1 April 2010). In the case of carelessness, the assessment may be made not more than six years after the accounting period to which it relates. Previous 'negligent' conduct now equates to careless behaviour.

In the case of deliberate action, the assessment may be up to 20 years from the end of the accounting period to which the loss of tax relates. The latter time limit applies where there is a failure to notify chargeability or failure to notify under the disclosure of anti-avoidance scheme provisions (see **5.41 ANTI-AVOIDANCE**). These rules replace the 20-year rule dealt with below. [*FA 1998, Sch 18 para 46(2)–(2B); FA 2008, Sch 39 para 42(3)*].

Assessments made after 26 July 1989 relating to accounting periods ending after 31 March 1983 and before 1 April 2010

Where the loss of tax arises due to the *fraudulent or negligent conduct* of a company (or of a person acting on behalf of the company), an assessment may be made at any time not later than 21 years after the end of the accounting period. If the company assessed so requires, the assessment may give effect to reliefs or allowances to which it would have been entitled had the necessary claims been made within the relevant time limits. [*FA 1998, Sch 18 paras 46(2), 65*].

For accounting periods ended before 1 July 1999, the equivalent time limit to those above was 20 years after the end of the accounting period.

An objection to the making of any assessment on the grounds that it is out of time can only be made on an appeal against the assessment. [*FA 1998, Sch 18 para 46(3)*].

Simon's Taxes. See **A4.321–A4.326**.

Contract settlements and closure notices

[7.8] Enquiries or compliance checks into company tax returns may be settled by either contract settlement or by formal closure notice.

Contract settlement

If the taxpayer is prepared to agree with the officer's findings, he is invited to enter into a contract settlement which is a contract between HMRC and the taxpayer to pay any additional tax resulting from the enquiry or investigation, together with interest and, where appropriate, penalties, without a formal assessment of all the tax.

A monetary offer may be made by the company taxpayer to HMRC in consideration for no formal proceedings being taken for any irregularities arising from the enquiry or investigation. If the offer is accepted by HMRC, it forms the basis of a binding contract under which proceedings can be taken for recovery of the amount offered. Such an agreement formally brings the enquiry or investigation to an end and HMRC are not able to make any further enquiries for the years concerned unless there is a new discovery.

Where a contract settlement is agreed, HMRC will usually not issue a closure notice, and it has been confirmed that the contract settlement will be treated for all purposes as a closure notice. [Leaflet IR 160 'Enquiries under self-assessment' p5, and HMRC Enquiry Manual EM6001].

Where appropriate, contract settlements are used as a way of closing a civil investigation of fraud under Code of Practice 9 (used where serious fraud is suspected), as a way of agreeing a monetary settlement without the need to proceed to formal prosecution.

See *CIR v Nuttall* (1989) 63 TC 148, CA, for confirmation of power to enter into such agreements. Amounts due under such an agreement which are unpaid may be pursued by an action for a debt, but the Crown does not rank as a preferential creditor in respect of the sums due (*Nuttall* above; *CIR v Woollen* [1992] STC 944, 65 TC 229, CA).

The importance of clarifying exactly what liabilities are to be included in a settlement can be seen in the recent case *S Hughes v HMRC* [2010] UKFTT 589 (TC) (23 November 2010). In this instance the taxpayer agreed a settlement covering personal income tax and Class 4 national insurance contributions. The officer conducting the enquiry noted payments were also required under the Construction Industry Scheme and HMRC subsequently issued determinations. The taxpayer appealed arguing these should have been included in the agreed settlement. The First Tier Tribunal dismissed the appeal noting the wording of the negotiated settlement stated specifically which taxes were being dealt with and that this would therefore not preclude HMRC from taking further action with regard to liabilities arising under a wholly separate regime which had not been the subject of the enquiry or the negotiations.

Closure Notice

In the case of a formal closure notice, HMRC notify the company in writing of any adjustments they consider to be necessary. With effect from 1 April 2010, the CTSA enquiry closure procedure is aligned with that for income tax in that the return is amended directly by the closure notice, without the need for the 30-day window which previously applied (see below), and the amount stated in the corporation tax return is conclusively amended when the closure notice is issued.

Prior to 1 April 2010, where adjustments were necessary following an enquiry, the company had 30 days to amend its self-assessment.

See also **60.15 PENALTIES** for mitigation of penalties.

Case law on fraudulent or negligent conduct

[7.9] The following cases relate to old legislation for 'fraud, wilful default or neglect' assessments which was replaced by 'fraudulent or negligent conduct' assessments. The latter expression is not defined, and the cases may be of continued assistance in this respect. As previously noted, the reference to fraudulent or negligent conduct has now been replaced by reference to 'deliberate' or 'careless' action — see **7.7** above.

The onus of proving fraud or wilful default is on the Crown (see e.g. *Hurley v Taylor* (1998) 71 TC 268, CA), but the onus is on the taxpayer to prove the assessments are excessive (*Johnson v Scott* (1978) 52 TC 383, CA; *Jonas v Bamford* (1973) 51 TC 1; *Nicholson v Morris* (1977) 51 TC 95, CA, and cf *Barney v Pybus* (1957) 37 TC 106 and *R v Spec Commrs (ex p Martin)* (1971) 48 TC 1, CA). For the standard of proof required, see *Les Croupiers Casino Club v Pattinson* (1987) 60 TC 196, CA.

Unexplained capital increases or admitted omissions may be held evidence of fraud or wilful default (*Amis v Colls* (1960) 39 TC 148; *Woodrow v Whalley* (1964) 42 TC 249; *Hudson v Humbles* (1965) 42 TC 380; *Hillenbrand* (1966) 42 TC 617, Ct of Sess; *Young v Duthie* (1969) 45 TC 624; *James v Pope* (1972) 48 TC 142; and cf *Brimelow v Price* (1965) 49 TC 41). Wilful default may be by agent (*Clixby v Pountney* (1967) 44 TC 515; *Pleasants v Atkinson* (1987) 60 TC 228).

'*Neglect*' means negligence or a failure to give any notice, to make any return or to produce or furnish any document or other information required by or under the Taxes Acts. [*TMA 1970, s 118 as previously enacted*]. Neglect may be by an agent (*Mankowitz v Special Commrs* (1971) 46 TC 707).

However, it is notable that the Special Commissioners decided that where no valid return had been made HMRC were still entitled to issue a discovery assessment without any finding of negligent conduct (*Osborne (dec'd) v Dickinson* [2004] STC (SCD) 104).

In *M Jones v HMRC*, [2011] UKFTT 149 (TC), an individual had been a member of two partnerships which carried on insurance business. In 2002 he sold his interests in these partnerships to one of the other partners. He did not declare the disposals on his tax return. HMRC issued a discovery assessment, and J appealed, contending that he had signed the sale agreement on behalf of a limited company. The First-Tier Tribunal rejected this contention and dismissed the appeal, finding that J had made the disposals in question and holding that his failure to declare them constituted negligent conduct and thus HMRC were entitled to issue a 'discovery' assessment.

Appeals

[7.10] An appeal may be brought against any discovery assessment or determination by written notice to HMRC within 30 days after issue of the notice of the assessment or determination. [*FA 1998, Sch 18 paras 48, 49*].

8

Banks

Cross-reference. **32.18 DOUBLE TAX RELIEF.**

Simon's Taxes. See D7.7.

Introduction

[8.1] In general, the term 'bank' is defined by reference to the carrying on of a *bona fide* banking business, but for certain purposes it is specially defined as:

(a) the Bank of England;
(b) a person who has permission under *Financial Services and Markets Act 2000, Pt 4* to accept deposits (excluding building and friendly societies, credit unions and insurance companies);
(c) an EEA firm within *Financial Services and Markets Act 2000, Sch 3 para 5(b)* which has permission under *para 15* of that Schedule (as a result of qualifying for authorisation under *para 12(1)*) to accept deposits;
(d) an international organisation of which the UK is a member and which is designated as a bank for the particular purpose by Treasury order; or
(e) on or after 6 April 2007, the European Investment Bank.

For what constitutes a bona fide banking business, see *Hafton Properties Ltd v McHugh* Ch D 1986, 59 TC 420.

See **8.9** below, **20.9**(F), **20.9**(3) **CHARITIES, 31.17 DISTRIBUTIONS, 46.2**(b) **INCOME TAX IN RELATION TO A COMPANY, 66.14, 66.16 RETURNS.**

[*CTA 2010, s 1120; ICTA 1988, s 840A; ITA 2007, s 991*].

Liability to corporation tax

[8.2] Banking businesses are assessable on their profits under normal taxation provisions with interest on advances to customers included in trading profits. The profits continue to be taxable as trading income where changes in the fair value of securities (held for the purpose of carrying on a banking or insurance business or a business consisting of dealing in securities) are accounted for in reserves (either in the statement of recognised gains and losses or statement of changes in equity). For the charge to corporation tax on income on certain net receipts arising during compulsory liquidation, see *CTA 2010, ss 634–641; F(No 2)A 1992, Sch 12; ITA 2007, ss 837A–837H.*

[*CTA 2009, s 128; ICTA 1988, s 472A*].

Agreements to forgo tax reliefs

[8.3] If part of any arrangements entered into are an agreement to forgo a right to tax relief (e.g. on losses), and the Treasury designates the arrangements as such, no tax relief is to be given to the company or any other party under the Corporation Taxes Acts. This provision applies to arrangements made on or after 22 April 2009, but it may affect tax reliefs for periods before that date. These rules were introduced in connection with the Asset Protection Scheme packages which the Government entered into with, principally, banks (although the provision is wide enough to cover other companies).

[*FA 2009, s 25*].

Overseas debts

[8.4] There is relief for certain receipts and debts the proceeds of which cannot be remitted to the UK but which form part of profits (see **71.74 TRADING EXPENSES AND DEDUCTIONS**). This relief applies to unremittable interest accrued on a loan made in the normal course of trade by a bank or other financial institution. It does not apply to the principal, or to a loan made in a currency other than the local currency of the country imposing currency restrictions where the interest is paid in the local currency and is available to be re-lent in that currency. [*CTA 2009, ss 172–179 formerly HMRC Extra-Statutory Concession, C34*].

Where a banking business is carried on in the UK by a person not resident or not ordinarily resident in the UK, the provisions of *ITTOIA 2005, s 154A; ICTA 1988, s 475* apply. See **65.10 RESIDENCE.**

Non-resident central banks

[8.5] Non-resident central banks as specified by Order in Council are exempt from tax on interest, public annuities and dividends paid out of UK public revenue (but may be taxable thereon if carrying on business in the UK) and also on chargeable gains. Profits, income and chargeable gains of the issue departments of the Reserve Bank of India and the State Bank of Pakistan are exempt.

[*CTA 2010, s 988; ITA 2007, ss 839, 840; ICTA 1988, ss 516, 517; TCGA 1992, s 271(8)*].

For security given in certain circumstances by a non-resident company to its bankers, see **5.12**(i) **ANTI-AVOIDANCE.**

Deduction of tax from interest

[8.6] The Taxes Acts contain several provisions under which a person making a payment to another person must deduct income tax from that payment. There are however specific exclusions and exemptions from this requirement such that payments can be made without deduction of tax (see **8.10**).

Net payment of interest

[8.7] Any 'deposit-taker' paying or crediting interest on a 'relevant investment' must deduct from it income tax (at the basic rate for the year of assessment in which the payment is made), unless the conditions for gross payment are met (see **8.10**).

[*ITA 2007, s 851; ICTA 1988, s 480A*].

ALTERNATIVE FINANCE ARRANGEMENTS (**4**) are treated as if they were investments and alternative finance return payable under those arrangements as if they were interest.

The deposit-taker must treat all investments as relevant investments unless satisfied to the contrary. In the latter case, he may treat an investment as not being a relevant investment until he receives information reasonably indicative that the investment is, or may be, a relevant investment.

[*ITA 2007, s 857; ICTA 1988, s 482*].

Deposit taker

For these purposes '*deposit-taker*' means:

- the Bank of England;
- a person who has permission under *FISMA 2000 Pt 4* to accept deposits which are relevant investments (and is not a Building Society, Friendly Society, Credit Union or Insurance company);
- persons authorised under the *Banking Act 1987* (or municipal bank within that Act);
- any local authority;
- an EEA firm which is of the kind mentioned *FISMA 2000, Sch 3 para 5(b)* of (EEA passport rights), and has permission under that Schedule to accept deposits;
- persons authorised under *FISMA 2000*;
- any other deposit-taker prescribed by Treasury order.

[*ITA 2007, s 853; ICTA 1988, s 481(2)*].

Relevant investment

A '*relevant investment*' (subject to the exclusions below) is an investment where either:

(a) the person beneficially entitled to any interest is an individual (or the persons so entitled are all individuals), or is a Scottish partnership all the partners of which are individuals;

(b) the person entitled to the interest receives it as the personal representative of a deceased individual (but note particularly the ordinary residence requirement at (xi) below); or

(c) the interest arises to the trustees of a discretionary or accumulation trust (see Tolley's Income Tax under Settlements).

[*ITA 2007, s 856; ICTA 1988, s 481(4)*].

Investments are not relevant investments (so interest is paid gross) if they are:

(i) (for corporation tax purposes) investments in respect of which a certificate of deposithas been issued for £50,000 or more (or foreign equivalent at the time the deposit is made) and which are repayable within five years [*ITA 2007, s 865; ICTA 1988, s 481(5)*];

(ii) (for income tax purposes), deposits in respect of which uncertificated eligible debt security units being a certificate or units (as defined in *ITTOIA 2005, s 552(2)*) have been issued for £50,000 or more (or foreign equivalent at the time the deposit is made) and which are repayable within five years [*ITA 2007, s 864; ICTA 1988, s 481(5)*];

(iii) non-transferable deposits of £50,000 or more (or foreign equivalent at the time the deposit is made) repayable at the end of a specified period of not more than five years [*ITA 2007, s 866; ICTA 1988, s 481(5)*];

(iv) debentures (as defined in *Companies Act 2006, s 738*) [*ITA 2007, s 870; ICTA 1988, s 481(5)*];

(v) loans made by a deposit-taker in the ordinary course of his business [*ITA 2007, s 870; ICTA 1988, s 481(5)*];

(vi) debts on securities listed on a recognised stock exchange [*ITA 2007, s 870; ICTA 1988, s 481(5)*];

(vii) deposits in a '*general client account deposit*', i.e. a client account, other than an account for specific clients, if the depositor is required by law to make payments representing interest to any of the clients whose money it contains [*ITA 2007, s 863; ICTA 1988, s 481(5)*];

(viii) Lloyd's underwriters' premiums trust funds [*ITA 2007, s 867; ICTA 1988, s 481(5)*];

(ix) deposits held at non-UK branches of UK resident deposit-takers [*ITA 2007, s 868; ICTA 1988, s 481(5)*];

(x) deposits with non-UK resident deposit-takers held other than in UK branches [*ITA 2007, s 868; ICTA 1988, s 481(5)*]; and

(xi) deposits in respect of which the 'appropriate person' has declared, in writing or by electronic means, to the deposit-taker that either:

  (1) where (a) above applies, the individual (or all of the individuals) concerned is (are), at the time of the declaration, not ordinarily resident in the UK;

  (2) where (b) above applies, the deceased, at the time of his death, was not ordinarily resident in the UK; or

(3) where (c) above applies, at the time of the declaration the trustees are not UK resident and do not have any reasonable grounds for believing that any of the beneficiaries (as defined for this purpose) is a UK ordinarily resident individual or a UK resident company.

The '*appropriate person*' is any person beneficially entitled to the interest, or entitled to receive it in his capacity as a personal representative or trustee, or to whom it is payable.

The declaration must be in such form, and contain such information, as is required by HMRC, and must include an undertaking to notify the deposit-taker should any individual concerned become ordinarily resident in the UK, or the trustees or any company concerned become resident in the UK, or any UK ordinarily resident individual or UK-resident company become a beneficiary of the trust to which the declaration relates.

HMRC have powers to review all declarations received by a deposit-taker.

[*ITA 2007, ss 858–861; ICTA 1988, s 481(5)*].

The collection procedure of *ITA 2007, s 946–960* as amended by *CTA 2009, Sch 1 para 714; ICTA 1988, Sch 16* (see **46.8 INCOME TAX IN RELATION TO A COMPANY**) applies, *mutatis mutandis*, to such payments whether or not the deposit-taker is UK-resident. In outline, returns are required at quarterly intervals, and tax is due without assessment within 14 days of the date for making the return. Income tax suffered by deduction in a return period may be set against liability of the period under these provisions.

HMRC have wide regulatory powers for giving effect to these provisions.

Gross payment of interest

[8.8] The requirement to deduct tax does not apply:

(a) to certain interest payable on an advance from a bank; or
(b) where the person beneficially entitled to the interest is UK ordinarily resident and has supplied the appropriate certificate confirming non-liability to income tax.

Interest paid by or to a bank

[8.9] The normal rules for deduction of tax from payments of **qualifying annual payments** that arise in the UK (see **46.2**(b) **INCOME TAX IN RELATION TO A COMPANY**) do not apply to interest payable on an advance from a bank where:

(a) the person beneficially entitled to the interest is within the charge to corporation tax in respect of it; or
(b) the interest is paid by such a bank in the ordinary course of its business.

[*ITA 2007, ss 878, 879, 899; ICTA 1988, s 349(3)(a)(b)(3AA)(3AB)*].

As regards whether interest is 'payable in the UK', see *Mistletoe Ltd v Flood (Inspector of Taxes)* [2003] STC (SCD) 66. See below as regards payments 'in the ordinary course' of business. The bank may be required to make a return of interest paid. For this purpose, 'interest' includes alternative finance returns. See **66.14 RETURNS**.

Interest paid by a bank is accepted by HMRC as being paid 'in the ordinary course of its business' unless either:

(i) the characteristics of the transaction giving rise to the interest are primarily attributable to an intention to avoid UK tax, or

(ii) the borrowing relates to the capital structure of the bank (and this includes borrowings conforming to any of the definitions of tier 1, tier 2 or (tier 3 capital, whether or not they count towards such capital).

Banks not recognised as such by HMRC before 29 April 1996 continue to have to deduct tax in certain cases. (HMRC Statement of Practice, SP 4/96).

Non-liability to income tax

[8.10] Gross payment may be made on relevant investments where the person beneficially entitled to the interest is UK ordinarily resident and has supplied the appropriate certificate to the deposit-taker to the effect that he is unlikely to be liable to income tax for the year of assessment in which the payment is made or credited. (For this purpose all interest arising in the year of assessment concerned which would, in the absence of such a certificate, be received under deduction of tax must be taken into account).

The certificate must be in prescribed form and must contain the name, permanent address, date of birth and (where applicable) national insurance number of the person beneficially entitled to the interest, and the name (and if necessary branch) of the deposit-taker and account number. It must also contain an undertaking to notify the deposit-taker if the person beneficially entitled to the payment becomes liable to income tax for the year in which the payment is made or credited. Form 85, on which to apply for gross payment, may be downloaded at www.hmrc.gov.uk/forms/r85.pdf. A claim may also be made electronically.

Such a certificate may only be given by:

(i) an investor aged 16 or over at the beginning of the year of assessment in which the payment is made or credited, or who attains age 16 during that year, who is beneficially entitled to the payment;

(ii) the parent or guardian of a person beneficially entitled to the payment who is under 16 at the beginning of that year;

(iii) a person authorised by power of attorney to administer the financial affairs of the person beneficially entitled to the payment;

(iv) the parent, guardian, spouse, civil partner, son or daughter of a mentally handicapped person, or any person appointed by a court to manage the affairs of a mentally handicapped person; or

(v) a person appointed by the Secretary of State to receive benefits on behalf of a person who is for the time being unable to act.

A certificate may not be given where the payment is treated as income of a parent of the person beneficially entitled to the payment, or where HMRC has issued a notice in relation to the account concerned requiring deduction of tax (see below).

The certificate must be supplied before the end of the year of assessment in which the payment is made or credited, or, in the case of a certificate given by a person who will reach 16 years of age during a year of assessment, before the end of that year.

A person who gives such a certificate fraudulently or negligently, or fails to comply with any undertaking contained in the certificate, is liable under *TMA 1970, s 99A* to a penalty up to £3,000.

Tax deducted from payments in a year prior to receipt of a certificate relating to that year may be refunded, and a like amount recovered by the deposit-taker from HMRC, provided that a certificate of deduction of tax has not been furnished to the investor prior to receipt of the gross payment certificate.

The fact that payments are made gross does not mean that the interest is thereby exempted from the charge to tax.

In HMRC's Guidance Notes for Deposit Takers (Tax Deduction Scheme for Interest) (November 2003), their position as regards incorrect certification for gross payment is explained. Paragraph 3.12 explains that where HMRC auditors are not satisfied that certificates are valid (because they contain other than trivial errors or omissions, which are described in Appendix 2 of the notes), they will seek recovery of basic-rate tax that should have been deducted (and interest and penalties — paragraphs 9.24 and 9.25). Paragraph 3.52 explains that such registrations will be cancelled.

A certificate becomes invalid:

(a) where the deposit-taker is notified (as above) that the person beneficially entitled to the payment is liable to income tax for the year in which the payment is made;
(b) where it was given by a parent or guardian, at the end of the year of assessment in which the person beneficially entitled to the payment attains 16 years of age;
(c) where it was given by a person who attained 16 years of age during the year of assessment in which a payment was made or credited, but who was not the holder of the account to which the certificate relates, and that person fails to become the holder before the first payment is made or credited after the end of that year of assessment;
(d) where the deposit-taker is notified that the person died; or
(e) where HMRC, having reason to believe that a person beneficially entitled to a payment of interest has become liable to income tax, give notice requiring the deposit-taker to deduct tax from payments of interest made, more than 30 days after the issue of the notice (or from earlier payments, if practicable), to or for the benefit of that person on a specified account held by or on behalf of that person.

A notice under (e) above must be copied to the person to whom it refers, and a further certificate in respect of the account referred to in the notice may not be given by or on behalf of that person (unless the notice is subsequently cancelled, see below).

A notice under (e) above may be cancelled (and the deposit-taker and person referred to in the notice so informed) if HMRC are satisfied that the person referred to in the notice was not at the date of the notice, and has not since become, liable to income tax, or is no longer so liable.

Certificates of non-liability given to a building society which converts to company status (see **9.4 BUILDING SOCIETIES**) are, by concession, treated as having been given to the successor company.

[*SI 2008 No 2682, HMRC Extra-Statutory Concession, A69*].

Administration

Joint accounts

[8.11] The position as regards certification by each of joint holders of an account is considered separately. Payments are apportioned equally to each joint holder, and tax deducted in respect of that part of a payment to which certification does not apply. The deposit-taker may, however, deduct tax from the whole of payments in respect of joint accounts where certification does not apply to all the joint holders, after giving notice to HMRC of its intention to do so (which notice the deposit-taker may subsequently cancel).

[*SI 2008 No 2682 Reg 13*].

Information

HMRC may by notice require any deposit-taker (within not less than 14 days) to furnish them with such information (including books, records etc.) as they require, in particular:

(i) payments made without deduction of tax and of the validity of certification for gross payment, and
(ii) the amount of tax deducted from payments of interest (but this does not include copies of books, records etc. from which the investor can be ascertained).

Copies of the deposit-taker's books, records etc. must be made available when required by HMRC. Certificates for gross payment must be retained for at least two years after they expire.

Subject to *FA 1989, s 182(5)*, information obtained under these provisions may not be used other than for gross payment or determining the tax liability of the deposit-taker or of the person beneficially entitled to interest paid without deduction of tax and to whom the information relates.

HMRC may also make regulations providing for the exclusion from its information powers of accounts held by non-UK ordinary residents.

[*SI 2008 No 2682 Regs 15–18*].

Simon's Taxes. See **A4.403–A4.411, D7.715** *et seq.*

Bank payroll tax

[8.12] A 50% tax, payable by the banks, was charged on all bonuses over £25,000 per annum paid from 9 December 2009 to 5 April 2010, unless the entitlement and amount was fixed prior to the announcement. The payroll tax paid is not an allowable deduction for corporation tax. HMRC guidance can be found at HMRC Bank Payroll Tax Manual.

[*FA 2010, s 22, Sch 1*].

Bank levy

[8.13] The Bank Levy came into force on 1 January 2011 and introduced a charge on specified liabilities reported in banks' balance sheets (excluding the first £20 billion). The levy is not an allowable deduction for corporation tax purposes.

The Bank Levy rate for 2011 is:

(a) 1 Jan — 28 Feb: 0.05% for short-term chargeable liabilities and 0.025% for long-term chargeable equity and liabilities;
(b) 1 Mar — 30 Apr: 0.1% for short-term chargeable liabilities and 0.05% for long-term chargeable equity and liabilities;
(c) 1 May — 31 Dec: 0.075% for short-term chargeable liabilities and 0.0375% for long-term chargeable equity and liabilities.

For 2012 the rate remains at 0.075% for short-term chargeable liabilities and 0.0375% for long-term chargeable equity and liabilities.

Regulations which deal with the collection and management of the Bank Levy have been made and came into force on 11 August 2011 (*The Corporation Tax (Instalment Payments) (Amendment) Regulations 2011* (*SI 2011 No 1785*).

[*FA 2011, s 73, Sch 19*].

9

Building Societies

Simon's Taxes. See D7.8.

Introduction

[9.1] A building society is one within the meaning of the *Building Societies Act 1986*. The tax treatment of such societies is outlined below.

[*CTA 2010, s 1119; ICTA 1988, s 832(1); Building Societies Act 1986, s 120, Sch 2*].

Liability to corporation tax

[9.2] A building society is liable to corporation tax on its profits. For the purposes of computing the taxable profits a building society is treated as though it were a company except with regard to dividends and interest payable to investors (and income tax thereon). Such interest, dividends or (from 6 April 2005) alternative finance return under alternative **FINANCE ARRANGEMENTS** (**4**), are treated as arising under a loan relationship, and so relievable under the **LOAN RELATIONSHIPS** (**54**) provisions. Interest under 'SAYE savings arrangements' within *ITTOIA 2005, s 702* and as defined by *ITTOIA 2005, s 703* are treated in the same way as dividends, and dividends and interest are not treated as distributions of the society.

The bank payroll tax and bank levy applies to building societies as well as banks. See **8.12** and **8.13**.

[*CTA 2010, s 1054; CTA 2009, ss 498, 1326; ICTA 1988, s 477A(3)–(4)*].

Simon's Taxes. See D7.820–D7.825 *et seq.*

Deduction of tax from interest and dividends

Treatment of payments to companies

[9.3] The Taxes Acts contain several provisions under which a person making a payment to another person must deduct income tax from that payment. There are however specific exclusions and exemptions from this requirement such that payments can be made without deduction of tax. From 2007, a uniform regime applies for the deduction of tax at source both by deposit-takers and building societies. The provisions as detailed at **8.6–8.10** therefore apply equally to building societies, with the following specific rules being applicable only to building societies:

(a) interest paid on a relevant investment also includes dividends paid by that society in respect of the investment;
(b) the following investments are expressly excluded from being relevant investments (**8.7**):
  (i) a loan made by a 'bank'; and
  (ii) a security (including a share) issued by a building society which is listed, or capable of being listed, on a recognised stock exchange.

[*ITA 2007, ss 851, 870(2)*].

Mergers and transfers

General rules

[9.4] There are various provisions that apply where there is a transfer of the whole of a building society's business to a successor company in accordance with the *Building Societies Act 1986*. A society can merge/transfer its business in a number of ways, as follows:

(a) in an amalgamation (under the *Building Societies Act 1986, s 93*) where two or more societies combine to establish a single new society which succeeds to their trades;
(b) in a transfer of engagements (under the *Building Societies Act 1986, s 94*) where one society transfers all or part of its business to another society; or
(c) on a transfer of its business (under the *Building Societies Act 1986, s 97*) where, with the consent of its members, a building society transfers its business to a public limited company — the successor company; (either one specially formed for the purpose or an existing company) or a mutual society.

The tax implications of such relevant transfers are set out in regulations and can be summarised as follows:

(i) for capital allowances purposes a trade will not be treated as ceasing and recommencing; all allowances etc that were available to the transferor will continue to be available to the transferee on the same basis;
(ii) loss relief that would have been available to the transferor if he had continued to carry on the trade, will generally continue to be available to the transferee on the same basis;
(iii) if the transferee carries on the transferred trade as part of its existing trade, the transferred trade will be treated as a separate trade carried on by the transferee. Similarly if part of a trade is transferred and the

transferee carries on the transferred trade as part of its existing trade, the transferor is treated as having carried on the transferred trade as a separate trade. In both situations, apportionments of expenses etc are to be made on a just and reasonable basis;

(iv) where a transferee replaces a transferor building society as a party to a loan relationship or a derivative contract and the closing value in the accounts of the building society in relation to the loan relationship or derivative contract is different from the opening value in the accounts of the transferee, the debits or credits in respect of the difference are to be brought into account; and

(v) where a loan relationship or derivative contract has been transferred intra-group to a company before a relevant transfer, the relevant transfer will not cause the degrouping provisions to apply (although they will apply if the company ceases to be a member of the same group as the transferee within six years whilst still a party to the relevant loan relationship or derivative contract).

In addition special rules apply where the relevant transfer is:

(1) within (c) above and there is a disposal of an asset (including an intangible fixed asset) by the transferor to the transferee. In such situations the disposal is treated as taking place on a no gain no loss basis;

(2) one that falls within (a) above, a transfer of all of a business within (b) above or a transfer within (c) above, which includes a transfer of assets (including intangible fixed assets) and:
   - the transferor and the recipient of the assets are not members of the same group at the time of the relevant transfer and, as a result of the transfer, a company leaves the transferor's chargeable gains group. In such situations, the degrouping provisions do not apply for any asset acquired by the company that leaves the group from the transferor or any other member of the transferor's group;
   - the transferor and recipient of the assets become members of the same chargeable gains group but later cease to be members of the same group. In such situations the degrouping provisions do not apply for any asset acquired by the transferee (or any other member of the same group as the transferee) as a consequence of the relevant transfer from the transferor or any other group company. Also, this regulation deals with the case where a company which was a member of the transferors group becomes a member of the transferee's group and subsequently ceases to be a member of that group. In these situations, the degrouping provisions apply to assets acquired from the transferor (or any other group company of the transferor) when the company ceases to be a member of the same group as the transferee;

(3) one that falls within (c) above and rights are conferred on members of a society to acquire shares in the successor company. In such situations, no capital gains liability arises in respect of rights, the issue of such

shares to trustees on behalf of the members and the subsequent disposal of such shares to members, or on the disposal by the society of shares in the successor company;

(4) one that falls within (c) above and distributions are made in connection with the transfer. In such situations, no liability to income tax (either on the society, the successor company or the members) arises in respect of the distributions, although such distributions may be capital receipts within *TCGA 1992, s 122*.

[*Mutual Societies (Transfers of Business) (Tax) Regulations 2009 SI 2009 No 2971; FA 1988 Sch 12, TCGA 1992, s 216*].

SAYE savings arrangements

The disregarding for income tax and capital gains tax purposes of certain sums payable under SAYE schemes within *ITTOIA 2005, s 702* (or before 2005/06 *ICTA 1988, s 326*) continues to apply to payments after the transfer under a scheme which was within that section in relation to the society immediately before the transfer, notwithstanding that it ceased to be so by reason of the transfer.

[*FA 1988, Sch 12 para 7; ITTOIA 2005, Sch 1 para 404*].

Declarations, etc. given to a society prior to incorporation

Declarations made as to the ordinary residence of depositors, and certificates of non-liability given to societies, in order that interest may be paid gross are treated as having been made or given to the successor company (see **8.7 BANKS**). (HMRC Extra-Statutory Concession, A69).

Costs of conversion

In *Halifax plc v Davidson (Inspector of Taxes)* [2000] STC (SCD) 251, (and associated cases), costs incurred by a building society on conversion to a public limited company were disallowed as capital expenditure to the extent that they related to payment of statutory cash bonuses to non-voting members of the society, but otherwise allowed.

Simon's Taxes. See **D7.830–D7.832.**

Permanent interest bearing shares

[9.5] Building societies are able to issue a type of perpetual share known as a 'permanent interest bearing share' ('PIBS'), which qualify as core (Tier 1) capital for regulatory purposes. The main tax implications relevant to PIBS (referred to in the legislation as 'qualifying shares') are summarised below.

Capital gains exemption

Building society shares which are qualifying shares expressed in sterling (and which are not convertible into, or redeemable in, a currency other than sterling) are *for purposes other than those of corporation tax* (and subject to

TCGA 1992, s 117(2)) 'qualifying corporate bonds' within *TCGA 1992, s 117*, and hence exempt from capital gains tax. As regards corporate holders, however, they are *not* qualifying corporate bonds and hence chargeable gains (or allowable losses) arise on disposal in the normal way.

[*TCGA 1992, s 117(A1)(4)–(6)(11)–(13)*].

Accrued income scheme

'Securities' for the purposes of *ITA 2007, ss 616–677*; *ICTA 1988, ss 711–728* (accrued income scheme) includes building society shares which are qualifying shares.

[*ITA 2007, s 619(1); ICTA 1988, s 710(2A)*].

Incidental costs of issue

A deduction is allowed, in computing the trading income of a building society for corporation tax purposes, for the incidental costs of obtaining finance by the issue of qualifying shares, provided that the amount of any dividend or interest on the shares is an allowable deduction. However, a deduction is not allowed where such costs are brought into account as debits under the **LOAN RELATIONSHIPS** (**54**) rules. The incidental costs allowed are expenditure (including abortive expenditure) on fees, commissions, advertising, printing and other incidental matters (but not stamp duty) wholly and exclusively for the purpose of obtaining the finance or of providing security for it or repaying it. Costs in consequence of, or for protection against, exchange rate losses, or of repayment of the shares that are attributable to their issue at a discount or repayment at a premium, are excluded.

[*CTA 2009, s 131; ICTA 1988, s 477B*].

Preferential rights of acquisition

Where a building society confers on members or former members priority rights to acquire shares in the society which are qualifying shares, the rights are regarded, for capital gains tax purposes, as options acquired for no consideration and having no value when acquired.

[*TCGA 1992, s 149*].

Simon's Taxes. See D7.803.

10

Capital Allowances — Introduction

Cross references. See **11 CAPITAL ALLOWANCES — PLANT AND MACHINERY: ELIGIBLE EXPENDITURE AND INITIAL ALLOWANCES; 12 CAPITAL ALLOWANCES — PLANT AND MACHINERY: POOLING AND DISPOSALS; 13 CAPITAL ALLOWANCES — PLANT AND MACHINERY: FIXTURES AND LEASING; 14 CAPITAL ALLOWANCES — MINERAL EXTRACTION; 15 CAPITAL ALLOWANCES — BUILDINGS; 16 CAPITAL ALLOWANCES — MISCELLANEOUS.**

Other sources. See Tolley's Capital Allowances.

Simon's Taxes. See B3.

Introduction

[10.1] The law relating to capital allowances was consolidated in *Capital Allowances Act 2001* (*CAA 2001*) as part of the Tax Law Rewrite programme.

Capital allowances (balancing charges) are a deduction from (addition to) the profits of trades and other qualifying activities in arriving at the taxable amount for the chargeable period to which they relate.

For a full list of qualifying activities in relation to which plant and machinery allowances are available, see **11.2 CAPITAL ALLOWANCES — PLANT AND MACHINERY: ELIGIBLE EXPENDITURE AND INITIAL ALLOWANCES.**

Certain allowances are given only in relation to trades, some only in relation to particular kinds of trade, and some additionally given against particular sources of non-trading income.

Details are given in the relevant sections of this chapter and **CHAPTERS 11–16** that follow.

For corporation tax purposes, a '*chargeable period*' is an accounting period. [*CAA 2001, s 6(1)*].

Matters of general application

[10.2] Matters of general application are as follows.

Claims

[10.3] A capital allowance claim under self-assessment must be included in the company tax return (or amended return) (see **66.4, 66.7 RETURNS**) for the accounting period for which the claim is made.

It must specify the amount claimed, which must be expressed in figures at the time the claim is made.

It must be made (and may be amended or withdrawn) at any time up to the latest of:

(a) the first anniversary of the filing date for the company tax return;
(b) 30 days after closure of any enquiry into that return (unless the enquiry, being otherwise out of time, was limited, as referred to in **66.21 RETURNS**, to matters to which a previous amendment making or withdrawing a capital allowance claim relates, or which are affected by the amendment);
(c) 30 days after notice of any amendment of that return by HMRC following such an enquiry; and
(d) 30 days after determination of any appeal against an amendment, or at a later time if HMRC allow it (for which see **55.3 LOSSES**).

These time limits override the normal time limits for amendment of a company tax return. Amendments or withdrawals of claims must be made by amending the return.

If the effect of a claim is to reduce the available capital allowances for another accounting period for which a return has already been made, the company has 30 days to make the necessary amendments of that return.

If it fails to do so, HMRC may, by written notice and subject to a right of appeal within 30 days of the issue of the notice, amend the return to correct the position (notwithstanding any time limit otherwise applicable).

[*CAA 2001, s 3; FA 1998, Sch 18 Pt IX para 82*].

Capital expenditure

[10.4] References in the capital allowances legislation to the incurring of capital expenditure and the paying of capital sums exclude any sums allowed as deductions in computing the payer's profits or earnings and sums payable under deduction of tax.

Corresponding rules apply as regards the receipt of such sums.

[*CAA 2001, s 4, Sch 3 para 9; ITEPA 2003, Sch 6 para 247; ITTOIA 2005, Sch 1 para 525*].

Time expenditure incurred

[10.5] Capital expenditure (other than that constituted by an 'additional VAT liability' — see **10.10** below) is generally treated, for capital allowances purposes, as incurred as soon as there is an unconditional obligation to pay it, even if all or part of it is not required to be paid until some later date.

However, expenditure is treated as incurred on a later date where:

- Any part of the expenditure is not required to be paid until a date more than four months after the date determined as above, it is treated as incurred on that later date.
- An obligation to pay becomes unconditional earlier than in accordance with normal commercial usage, with the sole or main benefit likely to be the bringing forward of the chargeable period in which the expenditure would otherwise be treated as incurred, it is instead treated as incurred on the date on or before which it is required to be paid.

As a result of an event such as the issuing of a certificate, an obligation to pay becomes unconditional within one month after the end of a chargeable period, but at or before the end of that chargeable period the asset concerned has become the property of, or is otherwise attributed under the contract to, the person having the obligation, the expenditure is treated as incurred immediately before the end of that chargeable period.

The above provisions do not override any specific rule under which expenditure is treated as incurred later than the relevant time given above.

[*CAA 2001, s 5*].

Simon's Taxes. See **B3.103, B3.104, B3.107**.

Exclusion of double allowances

[10.6] Where an allowance is made under one code, it cannot also be made under another of those codes.

So, for example, where expenditure has been allocated to a plant and machinery pool, it cannot also be allocated for research and development.

Additional rules apply under *CAA 2001, s 9* to prevent double allowances in relation to plant or machinery treated as fixtures (as at **13.1 CAPITAL ALLOWANCES — PLANT AND MACHINERY: FIXTURES AND LEASING**).

[*CAA 2001, ss 7–10, Sch 3 para 10*].

HMRC Brief 12/09

[10.7] This Brief (www.hmrc.gov.uk/briefs/company-tax/brief1209.htm) gives HMRC's view on re-classification of claims to capital allowances.

HMRC's view is that, once a business has chosen to claim one type of capital allowance rather than another, that choice may not be revisited and effectively reversed in respect of expenditure incurred in a closed year, or using and error or mistake claim.

An error or mistake claim may not be made in respect of a claim made in a return: the remedy is to amend the return.

Where the return has become final, the claim may no longer be amended.

Where the year is still open, it is open to the company to amend the claim.

CAA 2001 provides that if an allowance on expenditure is granted under one part of the Act, the expenditure does not qualify for relief under another part.

HMRC believe that it is not possible to use error or mistake provisions to, for example, substitute claims for plant and machinery allowances in place of industrial or agricultural buildings allowances on certain building fixtures after a year is closed.

Per HMRC Capital Allowances Manual at CA31800 'Once a choice has been made to claim one type of allowance, the taxpayer cannot change to another in later years.'

Simon's Taxes. See **B3.114.**

Expenditure met by another's contributions

[10.8] Subject to the exceptions below, a person is not regarded as incurring expenditure for capital allowances purposes (other than for dredging — see **16.1–16.4** in **CAPITAL ALLOWANCES — MISCELLANEOUS**) to the extent that it is met, or will be met, directly or indirectly by another person or by a '*public body*', i.e. the Crown or any government or public or local authority (whether in the UK or elsewhere).

For the scope of 'public authority', see *McKinney v Hagans Caravans (Manufacturing) Ltd* CA(NI) 1997, 69 TC 526.

Regional Development Grants

There is an exception where the expenditure is met by a Regional Development Grant or Northern Ireland equivalent (for which see *SI 1995 No 611; SI 1997 No 660; SI 1999 No 719; SI 2001 No 810* and predecessor orders).

Insurance and compensation

Expenditure met by insurance or other compensation money due in respect of a destroyed, demolished or defunct asset is not excluded from allowances (though this exception did not apply for the purpose of research and development (formerly scientific research) allowances before *CAA 2001* had effect).

As regards allowances for dredging (see **16.1–16.4 CAPITAL ALLOWANCES — MISCELLANEOUS**), the above is replaced by a rule to the effect that a person is not regarded as incurring expenditure for the purposes of a trade or future trade to the extent that it is met, or will be met, directly or indirectly by a public body or by capital sums contributed by another person for purposes other than those of the fore-mentioned trade.

Disapplying the rule

The main rule above (but not the rule for dredging) is disapplied, and allowances are thus available, if the contributor is not a public body and can obtain neither a capital allowance on contributions by virtue of **10.10** nor a deduction against profits of a trade, profession or vocation.

Where *CAA 2001* has effect, and for the purposes of plant and machinery allowances only, this is extended to cover profits of any qualifying activity within **11.2**(iii)–(vi) **CAPITAL ALLOWANCES — PLANT AND MACHINERY: ELIGIBLE EXPENDITURE AND INITIAL ALLOWANCES**. In relation to this particular change in law, the '*relevant chargeable period*' for the purposes of the election in **10.1** above (to defer the application of *CAA 2001*) is the earliest chargeable period for which the tax consequences of the transaction or event are altered — this exception to the rule recognises that a contribution might be made before the relevant date in **10.1** above to expenditure incurred in a chargeable period beginning after that date.

[*CAA 2001, ss 532–536, Sch 2 para 19, Sch 3 paras 106–108; ITTOIA 2005, Sch 1 para 570; CTA 2009, ss 147(5), 149(1), (3)–(5) and Sch 1 para 516*].

Repaid grants

Where a grant which has been deducted from expenditure qualifying for capital allowances (as above) is later repaid (in whole or part), the repayment will, by concession, be treated as expenditure qualifying for capital allowances.

Where allowances were restricted in respect of a contribution from a person (other than a public body) who himself obtained either a capital allowance under **10.10** or a trading deduction for his contribution (as above), this treatment is dependent upon the repayment falling to be taxed on the recipient through a balancing charge or as a trading receipt. (HMRC Extra-Statutory Concession B49 as revised. See also HMRC Capital Allowances Manual CA14300).

Simon's Taxes. See **B3.111**.

Contribution allowances

[10.9] Contributors towards another person's capital expenditure on an asset may receive '*contribution allowances*' where the contribution is for the purposes of a trade or '*relevant activity*' carried on (or to be carried on) by the contributor, and where the expenditure would otherwise have entitled the other person (assuming him not to be a public body) to agricultural buildings, industrial buildings, plant and machinery or mineral extraction allowances.

Contribution allowances are not available where the contributor and the other person are **CONNECTED PERSONS (25)**.

A '*relevant activity*' is a profession or vocation or, where *CAA 2001* has effect and for the purposes of plant and machinery allowances only, an activity within **11.2**(iii)–(vi) **CAPITAL ALLOWANCES — PLANT AND MACHINERY: ELIGIBLE EXPENDITURE AND INITIAL ALLOWANCES.**

Contribution allowances are such as would have been made if the contribution had been expended on the provision for the contributor's trade etc. of a similar asset and as if the asset were at all material times used for the purposes of the contributor's trade etc. (so that balancing adjustments do not apply to such contributions).

As regards plant and machinery, the contributor's deemed expenditure can only be allocated to a single asset pool (see **12.2 CAPITAL ALLOWANCES — PLANT AND MACHINERY: POOLING AND DISPOSALS**).

On a transfer of the trade etc., or part thereof, the allowances (or part) are subsequently made to the transferee.

In relation to agricultural buildings and industrial buildings allowances, the conditions are satisfied if the contribution is made for the purposes of a trade etc. carried on by a tenant of land in which the contributor has an interest. Entitlement to writing-down allowances passes to any person becoming entitled to the interest held by the contributor at the time of the contribution.

[*CAA 2001, ss 537–542, Sch 3 paras 109, 110; FA 2005, s 92, Sch 6 para 5*].

Capital contributions towards expenditure on dredging are treated as expenditure incurred by the contributor on that dredging.

[*CAA 2001, s 543*].

Simon's Taxes. See **B3.112.**

VAT capital goods scheme

[10.10] Under the VAT capital goods scheme, the input tax originally claimed on the acquisition of certain capital assets is subject to amendment within a specified period of adjustment in accordance with any increase or decrease in the extent to which the asset is used in making taxable, as opposed to exempt, supplies for VAT purposes.

The items covered by the scheme are limited to land and buildings (or parts of buildings) worth at least £250,000 and computers (and items of computer equipment) worth at least £50,000. See Tolley's Value Added Tax under Capital Goods Scheme for a full description.

Special capital allowances provisions apply where a VAT adjustment is made under the capital goods scheme. These affect allowances for industrial buildings, plant and machinery, business premises renovation and research and development (formerly scientific research), and the provisions specific to each are described in the appropriate sections of this chapter. General definitions and provisions are described below.

'*Additional VAT liability*' and '*additional VAT rebate*' mean, respectively:

- an amount which a person becomes liable to pay; or
- an amount which he becomes entitled to deduct,

by way of adjustment under the VAT capital goods scheme in respect of input tax.

Generally, such a liability or rebate is treated as incurred or made on the last day of the period:

- which is one of the periods making up the applicable VAT period of adjustment under the VAT capital goods scheme; and
- in which occurred the increase or decrease in use giving rise to the liability or rebate.

However, for the purpose of determining the chargeable period (see **10.1** above) in which it accrues, an additional VAT liability or rebate is treated as accruing on whichever is the relevant day below.

- Where the liability or rebate is accounted for in a VAT return, the last day of the period covered by that return.
- If, before the making of a VAT return, Customs assess the liability or rebate, the day on which the assessment is made.
- If the trade (or other qualifying activity — see **11.2 CAPITAL ALLOWANCES — PLANT AND MACHINERY: ELIGIBLE EXPENDITURE AND INITIAL ALLOWANCES**) is permanently discontinued before the liability or rebate has been accounted for in a VAT return and before the making of an assessment, the last day of the chargeable period in which the cessation occurs.

Where an allowance or charge falls to be determined by reference to a proportion only of the expenditure incurred or a proportion only of what that allowance or charge would otherwise have been, a related additional VAT liability or rebate is similarly apportioned.

[*CAA 2001, ss 546–551; FA 2005, s 92, Sch 6 para 6. See also HMRC Capital Allowances Manual CA11900 for guidance on ss 546–551*].

Simon's Taxes. See **B3.103, B3.104.**

Composite sales

[10.11] These may be apportioned by tribunal regardless of any separate prices attributed in the sale agreement. [*CAA 2001, ss 562–564*]. See *Fitton v Gilders & Heaton* Ch D 1955, 36 TC 233, and *Wood v Provan* CA 1968, 44 TC 701.

Finance leasing

[10.12] There are restrictions on capital allowances where certain finance leasing arrangements are involved (see **71.44 TRADING EXPENSES AND DEDUCTIONS**). These are disapplied from, broadly, 1 April 2006 in relation to long funding leases. See also **12.1 CAPITAL ALLOWANCES — PLANT AND MACHINERY: POOLING AND DISPOSALS, 13.4, 13.25** and **13.27 CAPITAL ALLOWANCES — PLANT AND MACHINERY: FIXTURES AND LEASING.**

Recovery of assets under Proceeds of Crime Act 2002, Pt 5

[10.13] *Proceeds of Crime Act 2002, Pt 5 Ch 2* provides for the recovery, in civil proceedings before the High Court (or, in Scotland, the Court of Session), of property which is, or represents, property obtained through 'unlawful conduct' (as defined in the Act).

If the Court is satisfied that any property is recoverable under the provisions, it will make a '*recovery order*', vesting the property in an appointed trustee for civil recovery.

Alternatively, the Court may make an order under *s 276* of the Act staying (or, in Scotland, sisting) proceedings on terms agreed by the parties.

The vesting of property in a trustee for civil recovery or any other person, either under a recovery order or in pursuance of a *s 276* order, is known as a *Pt 5* transfer.

A '*compensating payment*' may in some cases be made to the person who held the property immediately before the transfer. If the order provides for the creation of any interest in favour of that person, he is treated as receiving (in addition to any other compensating payment) a compensating payment equal to the value of the interest. [*Proceeds of Crime Act 2002, ss 240(1), 266(1)(2), 276, 316(1), 448, Sch 10 para 2*].

Where the property in question is plant or machinery, the relevant interest in an industrial building or in a flat (within **15.23 CAPITAL ALLOWANCES — BUILDINGS**), or an asset representing qualifying expenditure on research and development (within **16.12 CAPITAL ALLOWANCES — MISCELLANEOUS**), there are provisions to ensure that the *Pt 5* transfer has a tax-neutral effect, unless a compensating payment is made to the transferor in which case its amount and/or value must be brought into account as a disposal value or, as the case may be, as proceeds from a balancing event. [*Proceeds of Crime Act 2002, Sch 10 paras 12–29*].

Avoidance affecting proceeds of balancing event

[10.14] An anti-avoidance rule exists to prevent a balancing allowance being created or increased by means of any tax avoidance scheme that depresses an asset's market value and thus the amount to be brought into account on a balancing event (e.g. a sale) or as a disposal value.

The rule denies entitlement to a balancing allowance, though the unrelieved balance of expenditure immediately after the event must be computed as if the allowance had been made.

The rule applies to allowances for:

(i) business premises renovation;
(ii) flat conversion;
(iii) dwelling-houses let on assured tenancies;
(iv) mineral extraction.

The rule does not apply to plant and machinery allowances.

[*CAA 2001, s 570A; FA 2003, s 164(2); FA 2005, s 92, Sch 6 para 9*].

Simon's Taxes. See B3.244.

Key points

[10.15] Points to consider are as follows.

- For capital allowance purposes expenditure is incurred when there is an unconditional obligation to pay for it. This may be earlier than the payment or invoice date and could therefore present planning opportunities, especially given the fall in capital allowance rates legislated for in *Finance Act 2011, ss 10–12,* which generally apply from April 2012. Where payment is made more than four months after the unconditional obligation, however, that date becomes the date expenditure is incurred and there is also anti-avoidance legislation where the rules are manipulated to reduce tax.
- There is a time limit for claiming capital allowances (broadly one year after the due filing date) so for returns submitted late the tax liability may be higher than predicted. The capital allowances can be claimed in a later return but this may still lead to higher than expected interest payments and penalties.

11

Capital Allowances — Plant and Machinery: Eligible Expenditure and Initial Allowances

Simon's Taxes. Part B3.

Cross references. See **10 CAPITAL ALLOWANCES — INTRODUCTION; 12 CAPITAL ALLOWANCES — PLANT & MACHINERY: POOLING AND DISPOSALS; 13 CAPITAL ALLOWANCES — PLANT & MACHINERY: FIXTURES AND LEASING; 14 CAPITAL ALLOWANCES — MINERAL EXTRACTION; 15 CAPITAL ALLOWANCES — BUILDINGS; 16 CAPITAL ALLOWANCES — MISCELLANEOUS.**

Other sources. See Tolley's Capital Allowances.

Introduction

[11.1] Plant and machinery allowances are available in respect of 'qualifying expenditure' incurred by a person carrying on a trade or other 'qualifying activity'.

Expenditure incurred for the purposes of, and prior to the commencement of, a qualifying activity is treated as incurred on the first day on which the activity is carried on (see HMRC Capital Allowances Manual CA23020).

[*CAA 2001, s 12*].

Qualifying activity

[11.2] Any of the following is a '*qualifying activity*':

(i) a trade, profession or vocation;
(ii) an employment or office;
(iii) a property business or overseas property business (see **62 PROPERTY INCOME**);
(iv) a furnished holiday lettings business (see **62.6 PROPERTY INCOME**);
(v) any of the concerns listed in *CTA 2009, s 39(4)* (mines, quarries and sundry other undertakings);
(vi) managing the investments of a company with investment business (see **51 INVESTMENT COMPANIES AND INVESTMENT BUSINESS**);
(vii) special leasing, i.e. the hiring out of plant or machinery otherwise than in the course of another qualifying activity (see **13.23 CAPITAL ALLOWANCES — PLANT & MACHINERY: FIXTURES AND LEASING**).

[*CAA 2001, ss 15–18, 19(1), 20; ITEPA 2003, Sch 6 para 248; SI 2004 No 2310, Sch paras 52, 53; ITTOIA 2005, Sch 1 paras 526–529; CTA 2009, Sch 1 para 479*].

Simon's Taxes. See **B3.301–B3.305**.

Eligible expenditure

Meaning of plant or machinery

[11.3] *Plant* and *machinery* are not statutorily defined; instead we rely heavily on case law.

To qualify as plant and machinery, an item must be permanently employed in the qualifying activity and perform a *function* in the business operations rather than merely providing the place or *setting* in which these operations are performed.

If an item used for carrying on a business does not form part of the premises and is not stock-in-trade, then it is plant (*Wimpy International Ltd v Warland* (1988) 61 TC 51, CA).

J D Wetherspoon Ltd v HMRC [2008] STC (SCD) 460 — many items of expenditure were incurred on refurbishing a public house, and consideration was given to the treatment of three test categories, including preliminary expenditure. (*JD Wetherspoon plc v HMRC (No 2)*, FTT [2009] UKFTT 374 (TC)).

Permanent employment

Permanent employment demands some degree of durability.

Hinton v Maden & Ireland Ltd (1959) 38 TC 391, HL, (shoe manufacturer's knives and lasts, average life three years, held to be plant).

In practice, a life of two years or more is sufficient, and this applies equally as regards animals functioning as apparatus with which a trade is carried on (see HMRC Capital Allowances Manual CA21100, 21220).

Buildings

Under normal circumstances, a building is part of the setting in which a trade is carried on and therefore would not be eligible for plant and machinery capital allowances. However, the decision is not always so straight forward as case law has shown.

Not plant

Canopy over petrol-filling station (*Dixon v Fitch's Garage Ltd* (1975) 50 TC 509);

Ship used as floating restaurant (*Benson v Yard Arm Club Ltd* (1979) 53 TC 67);

False ceilings (*Hampton v Fortes Autogrill Ltd* (1979) 53 TC 691);

A football stand (*Brown (Inspector of Taxes) v Burnley Football and Athletic Co Ltd* [1980] 3 All ER 244, [1980] STC 424);

An inflatable tennis court cover (*Thomas v Reynolds* (1987) 59 TC 502);

Shop fronts, wall and floor coverings, suspended floors, ceilings and stairs etc. (*Wimpy International Ltd v Warland, Associated Restaurants Ltd v Warland* (1988) 61 TC 51, CA);

Permanent quarantine kennels (allowances having been granted for movable kennels) (*Carr v Sayer* (1992) 65 TC 15);

Prefabricated school buildings (*St. John's School v Ward* (1974) 49 TC 524, CA);

Access site and wash hall containing car wash equipment (*Anduff Carwash Ltd v Attwood (Inspector of Taxes)* (1997) 69 TC 575, CA);

Housing for underground electricity sub-station (*Bradley v London Electricity plc* (1996) 70 TC 155);

Golf putting greens (*Family Golf Centres Ltd v Thorne* [1998] STC (SCD)106);

An all-weather horse racing track (*Lingfield Park 1991 Ltd v Shove* (2004) 76 TC 363, CA);

Clothes bought by a BBC newsreader (*Williams* [2010] TC 00397).

Held to be plant

Dry docks, including cost of excavation, held to be plant (*CIR v Barclay, Curle & Co Ltd* (1969) 45 TC 221, HL);

Movable office partitions (*Jarrold v John Good & Sons Ltd* (1962) 40 TC 681, CA);

Mezzanine platforms installed in a warehouse (but not ancillary lighting) (*Hunt v Henry Quick Ltd* (1992) 65 TC 108);

Swimming pools for use on caravan site (*Cooke v Beach Station Caravans Ltd* (1974) 49 TC 514);

Grain silos (*Schofield v R & H Hall Ltd* (1974) 49 TC 538, CA(NI));

Building Society window screens (*Leeds Permanent Building Society v Proctor* (1982) 56 TC 293);

Light fittings (*Wimpy International Ltd v Warland* (1988) 61 TC 51, CA);

Synthetic grass football pitch (*Anchor International Ltd v CIR* [2005] STC 411, 2004 SCLR 1045, Ct of Sess);

Barrister's books (*Munby v Furlong* (1977) 50 TC 491, CA);

Gazebo in a pub garden (*Andrew* [2011] TC 00799).

Glasshouses

Glasshouses are likely to be accepted as plant only where, during construction, sophisticated environmental control systems are permanently installed, incorporating e.g. a computer system controlling heating, temperature and humidity control, automatic ventilation systems and automatic thermal or shade screens (HMRC Capital Allowances Manual CA22090).

Gray v Seymours Garden Centre (Horticulture) 67 TC 401, CA, where a 'planteria' was held to be premises.

See generally HMRC Capital Allowances Manual CA21000 *et seq*.

Always plant and machinery

Certain expenditure on buildings, as below, is treated for capital allowance purposes as being on plant and machinery.

(i) *Fire safety expenditure* incurred before 1 April 2008 in a trade or other qualifying activity in taking steps specified in a notice under *Fire Precautions Act 1971, s 5(4)* (or which might have been so specified but were in fact specified in a document from the fire authority on application for a fire certificate under that Act) and similarly for expenditure incurred in order to avoid restriction of use of premises by a prohibition notice under *s 10* of that Act. [*CAA 2001, ss 27, 29; FA 2008, s 72*].

Applies to Northern Ireland by concession (HMRC Extra Statutory Concession B16 as revised).

Applies by Order to hotels and boarding houses (*SI 1972 No 238*) and to premises of factories, offices, shops and railways with minimum of 10 employees (*SI 1976 No 2009*).

Lessors of such premises may claim allowances on contributions (see **10.9 CAPITAL ALLOWANCES — INTRODUCTION**) towards tenants' qualifying expenditure or own similar direct expenditure (HMRC Extra Statutory Concession B16 as revised).

(ii) Expenditure on *thermal insulation of existing building* (for expenditure incurred before 1 April 2008, an industrial building) by a person occupying the building for (in the case of expenditure incurred on or after 1 April 2008) the purposes of a qualifying activity or other than an ordinary property business or an overseas property business, or (in the case of expenditure before 12 March 2008), the purposes of a trade carried on by it or letting the building in the course of a UK property business or overseas property business.
Expenditure on plant and machinery for use in residential property does not qualify, nor does expenditure on which relief is available under *CTA 2009, s 251* (deduction for energy saving items).
[*CAA 2001, ss 27, 28; ITTOIA 2005, Sch 1 para 531; FA 2008, s 71*].

(iii) *Sports ground expenditure* incurred by a person carrying on a trade or other qualifying activity to comply with a safety certificate issued or to be issued under the *Safety of Sports Grounds Act 1975* or certified by local authority as falling within requirements if such certificates had been (or could have been) applied for. Also, expenditure incurred by a trade in respect of a 'regulated stand' (as defined by the *Fire Safety and Safety of Places of Sport Act 1987*) to comply with a safety certificate (as defined by that *Act*) issued for the stand or to take steps specified by the local authority as being necessary under the terms, or proposed terms, of such a safety certificate issued, or to be issued, by it. [*CAA 2001, ss 27, 30–32*]. See also **10.8–10.9 CAPITAL ALLOWANCES — INTRODUCTION** as regards certain contributions to expenditure.

(iv) *Hotels and restaurants*. HMRC regard as eligible for capital allowances expenditure on *apparatus* to provide electric light or power, hot water, central heating, ventilation or air conditioning, alarm and sprinkler systems. Also on cost of hot water pipes, baths, wash basins etc.
Also expenditure on alterations to *existing* buildings which is incidental to the installation of plant and machinery. (CCAB Statement, 9 August 1977.)
Cole Bros Ltd v Phillips (1982) 55 TC 188, HL, and *CIR v Scottish & Newcastle Breweries Ltd* (1982) 55 TC 252, HL.

Lighting

The extent to which lighting and lighting systems may qualify as plant, i.e. as part of the business apparatus as opposed to the setting, is discussed in the HMRC Capital Allowances Manual at CA211760ff.

An office lighting system incorporating anti-glare lighting throughout to enable effective use of personal computers may be plant.

Cole Bros Ltd v Phillips (1982) 55 TC 188, HL (electric wiring and fittings in department store held not to be plant).

CIR v Scottish & Newcastle Breweries Ltd (1982) 55 TC 252, HL (lighting and decor of licensed premises held to be plant).

Lighting ancillary to mezzanine platform installation qualifying as plant (*Hunt v Henry Quick Ltd* (1992) 65 TC 108).

Installing and relocating plant and machinery

The capital expenditure eligible for allowances includes that on alteration of existing buildings incidental to the installation of plant or machinery for the purposes of a trade or other qualifying activity [*CAA 2001, s 25*] and on demolition of plant or machinery which it replaces [*CAA 2001, s 26(1)(2)*].

Costs of moving plant from one site to another and re-erecting it, so far as not deductible in computing profits, qualify for allowances (HMRC Capital Allowances Manual CA21190).

Enterprise zones

Expenditure on plant or machinery which is to be an integral part of an industrial or commercial building in an enterprise zone may, until April 2011, qualify for 100% industrial buildings allowance. See **15.13 CAPITAL ALLOWANCES — BUILDINGS.**

Simon's Taxes. See **B3.305–B3.311, B3.341, B3.345.**

CAA 2001, ss 21–24

CAA 2001, ss 21–24 specifically excludes certain expenditure from the definition of plant and machinery for capital allowances purposes.

Assets which have been held to be plant under specific court decisions continue to qualify for plant and machinery allowances.

General exceptions

Expenditure falling within any of *CAA 2001, ss 28–33B, 71* and *F(No 2) A 1992, s 40D* or earlier equivalents relating to thermal insulation, fire safety, safety of sports grounds, security assets, computer software, films and sound recordings and integral features is not affected by the provisions described below.

Expenditure on buildings/structures

[11.4] Expenditure on the construction or acquisition of a building will not qualify for plant and machinery allowances where it is incurred after 29 November 1993 subject to the specific exceptions listed at (1)–(33) below.

For these purposes the expression 'building' includes:

- any assets incorporated in the building;
- any assets which, although not incorporated in the building (because they are movable or for some other reason), are nevertheless of a kind which are normally incorporated into buildings; and
- any of the following:
  - (i) walls, floors, ceilings, doors, gates, shutters, windows and stairs;
  - (ii) mains services, and systems of water, electricity and gas;
  - (iii) waste disposal systems;
  - (iv) sewerage and drainage systems;

(v) shafts or other structures in which lifts, hoists, escalators and moving walkways are installed; and
(vi) fire safety systems.

[*CAA 2001, s 21*].

Expenditure on structures which does not qualify for allowances

'*Structure*' means a fixed structure of any kind, other than a building. A structure is 'any substantial man-made asset' (see Revenue Press Release 17 December 1993).

Expenditure on the construction or acquisition of a structure or any other asset listed immediately below, or on any works involving the alteration of land, will not qualify for plant and machinery allowances where it is incurred after 29 November 1993 (subject to the above transitional provisions and general exceptions and to the specific exceptions listed at (1)–(33) below).

- A tunnel, bridge, viaduct, aqueduct, embankment or cutting.
- A way, hard standing (such as a pavement), road, railway, tramway, a park for vehicles or containers, or an airstrip or runway.
- An inland navigation, including a canal or basin or a navigable river.
- A dam, reservoir or barrage (including any sluices, gates, generators and other equipment associated with it).
- A dock, harbour, wharf, pier, marina or jetty, or any other structure in or at which vessels may be kept or merchandise or passengers may be shipped or unshipped.
- A dike, sea wall, weir or drainage ditch.
- Any structure not included above, except:
  (i) a structure (other than a building) within the definition of an 'industrial building' (see **15.3 CAPITAL ALLOWANCES — BUILDINGS**);
  (ii) a structure in use for the purposes of a gas undertaking; or
  (iii) a structure in use for the purposes of a trade consisting in the provision of telecommunications, television or radio services,

  and see *CIR v Anchor International Ltd* CS 2004, [2005] STC 411, in which a synthetic football pitch was held not to be within this exclusion.

[*CAA 2001, s 22, Sch 3 para 13*].

Specific exceptions

[11.5] The above exclusions do not affect the question as to whether expenditure on any of the items listed in (1)–(33) below qualifies for plant and machinery allowances.

Note that items (1)–(16) below do not include any asset whose principal purpose is to insulate or enclose the interior of a building or to provide an interior wall, floor or ceiling which (in each case) is intended to remain permanently in place.

(1) Any machinery (including devices for providing motive power) not within any other item in this list.

(2) Gas and sewerage systems provided mainly to meet the particular requirements of the qualifying activity, or provided mainly to serve particular plant or machinery used for the purposes thereof. For expenditure prior to 1 April 2008, electrical (including lighting) and cold water systems were also included.
(3) For expenditure prior to 1 April 2008, space or water heating systems; powered systems of ventilation, air cooling or air purification; and any ceiling or floor comprised in such systems.
(4) Manufacturing or processing equipment; storage equipment, including cold rooms; display equipment; and counters, checkouts and similar equipment.
(5) Cookers, washing machines, dishwashers, refrigerators and similar equipment; washbasins, sinks, baths, showers, sanitary ware and similar equipment; and furniture and furnishings.
(6) Hoists (and prior to 1 April 2008, lifts, escalators and moving walkways).
(7) Sound insulation provided mainly to meet the particular requirements of the qualifying activity.
(8) Computer, telecommunication and surveillance systems (including their wiring or other links).
(9) Refrigeration or cooling equipment.
(10) Fire alarm systems; sprinkler and other equipment for extinguishing or containing fires.
(11) Burglar alarm systems.
(12) Strong rooms in bank or building society premises; safes.
(13) Partition walls, where movable and intended to be moved in the course of the qualifying activity.
(14) Decorative assets provided for the enjoyment of the public in hotel, restaurant or similar trades.
(15) Advertising hoardings; signs, displays and similar assets.
(16) Swimming pools (including diving boards, slides and structures on which such boards or slides are mounted).
(17) Any glasshouse constructed so that the required environment for the growing of plants is provided automatically by means of devices forming an integral part of its structure.
(18) Cold stores.
(19) Caravans provided mainly for holiday lettings (see *CAA 2001, s 23(5)*).
(20) Buildings provided for testing aircraft engines run within the building.
(21) Movable buildings intended to be moved in the course of the qualifying activity.
(22) The alteration of land for the purpose only of installing plant or machinery.
(23) The provision of dry docks.
(24) The provision of any jetty or similar structure provided mainly to carry plant or machinery.
(25) The provision of pipelines, or underground ducts or tunnels with a primary purpose of carrying utility conduits.
(26) The provision of towers provided to support floodlights.

(27) The provision of any reservoir incorporated into a water treatment works or any service reservoir of treated water for supply within any housing estate or other particular locality.
(28) The provision of silos provided for temporary storage; or storage tanks.
(29) The provision of slurry pits or silage clamps.
(30) The provision of fish tanks or fish ponds.
(31) The provision of rails, sleepers and ballast for a railway or tramway.
(32) The provision of structures and other assets for providing the setting for any ride at an amusement park or exhibition.
(33) The provision of fixed zoo cages.

Before *CAA 2001* had effect, these rules operated slightly more restrictively.

Integral features

[11.6] Integral features do qualify as plant and machinery.

Relief is available on qualifying expenditure incurred by a company carrying on a qualifying activity at the special rate of 10% on the reducing balance basis (see **12.11 CAPITAL ALLOWANCES — PLANT & MACHINERY: POOLING AND DISPOSALS**). Note that the special rate of 10% will be reduced to 8% from 1 April 2012.

The following are integral features:

(a) an electrical system (including a lighting system);
(b) a cold water system;
(c) a space or water heating system, a powered system of ventilation, air cooling or air purification, and any floor or ceiling comprised in such a system;
(d) a lift, an escalator or a moving walkway; and
(e) external solar shading.

The above list does not include insulation or interior walls, floors or ceilings which are intended to remain permanently in place.

Expenditure on the replacement of an integral feature of a building or structure used for the qualifying activity acquired on or after 1 April 2008 will qualify for relief.

Expenditure incurred is treated as incurred on replacement of an integral feature either where:

- expenditure is incurred on an integral feature and the amount is more than 50% of the cost of replacing it at the time the expenditure is incurred; or
- where a person incurs initial expenditure of not more than 50% of the cost of replacement at the time the expenditure is incurred; and
- within a year of the initial expenditure, further expenditure on the feature is incurred; and
- the aggregate expenditure is more than 50% of the cost of replacement at the date of the earlier expenditure.

[*CAA 2001, ss 33A, 33B; FA 2011, s 10; FA 2008, s 73*].

Where it appears that any sums, not otherwise taxable, are to be payable, directly or indirectly, to the owner of plant or machinery in respect of, or to take account of, the *whole* of the **depreciation** of that plant or machinery, the expenditure incurred in providing that plant or machinery for the purposes of the qualifying activity is not qualifying expenditure. [*CAA 2001, s 37*]. As regards subsidies towards *partial* depreciation, see **13.33 CAPITAL ALLOWANCES — PLANT & MACHINERY: FIXTURES AND LEASING.**

Interests in land

[11.7] Expenditure on the provision of plant or machinery does not include expenditure incurred after 29 November 1993 on the acquisition of an interest in land, but this restriction does not apply to any asset which is so installed or otherwise fixed in or to any description of land as to become, in law, part of that land.

'Land' does not include buildings or other structures but is otherwise as defined in *Interpretation Act 1978, Sch 1*. 'Interest in land' for these purposes has the same meaning as in *CAA 2001, s 175* (allowances for fixtures — see **13.1CAPITAL ALLOWANCES — PLANT & MACHINERY: FIXTURES AND LEASING**). [*CAA 2001, s 24*].

Simon's Taxes. See B3.308.

Borrowings

[11.8] Interest etc. on money borrowed to finance purchases of plant and charged to capital, held not eligible for capital allowances (*Ben-Odeco Ltd v Powlson* HL 1978, 52 TC 459 and cf *Van Arkadie v Sterling Coated Materials Ltd* Ch D 1982, 56 TC 479).

It is understood that HMRC consider this exclusion to apply also to architects' fees and preliminary expenses on plant included in building works.

Computer software

[11.9] Where capital expenditure is incurred after 9 March 1992 on the acquisition of computer software for the purposes of a trade or other qualifying activity, the software, if it would not otherwise be plant, is treated as such for capital allowances purposes.

Similarly, where capital expenditure is incurred after that date in acquiring for such purposes a right to use or otherwise deal with computer software, both the right and the software are treated as plant provided for the purposes of the qualifying activity and (so long as entitlement to the right continues) as belonging to the person incurring the expenditure.

See also **48.4 INTANGIBLE ASSETS** for the extent to which computer software may be included in that regime (and hence excluded from the above provisions).

Film production

[11.10] Film production and acquisition expenditure incurred by a person carrying on a trade is treated for tax purposes as revenue expenditure.

In relation to certified films (broadly, British or European films), an election may be made to disapply this rule (and effectively to treat the expenditure as capital expenditure on plant) where the master version is expected to realise its value over a period of two years or more.

Ensign Tankers (Leasing) Ltd v Stokes HL 1992, 64 TC 617 for relief to investor in film production partnership.

Cable television

[11.11] The cost of provision and installation of ducting in connection with construction of cable television networks is regarded as expenditure on plant or machinery (Revenue Press Release 15 March 1984).

Animals in trade

[11.12] Capital expenditure on animals and other living creatures kept for the purposes of farming or any other trade, or on shares in such animals etc., is excluded. [*CAA 2001, s 38; ITTOIA 2005, Sch 1 para 534; CTA 2009, Sch 1 para 481*].

Stallions (*Earl of Derby v Aylmer* KB 1915, 6 TC 665) held to be plant;

First-year allowances

Introduction

[11.13] A person is entitled to a first-year allowance for a chargeable period in respect of any 'first-year qualifying expenditure' which he incurs in that period on plant and machinery which he owns at some time during that period.

He may claim the allowance in respect of the whole or a part of the first-year qualifying expenditure.

In determining for these purposes the time at which expenditure is incurred (**10.5 CAPITAL ALLOWANCES — INTRODUCTION**), *CAA 2001, s 12* (pre-commencement expenditure — see **11.1**) is disregarded.

First year allowances are given at varying rates depending on the type of expenditure that has been incurred.

100% FYAs

[11.14] 100% first allowances are available on:

(i) Plant and machinery qualifying for the **Annual investment allowance** (see below);
(ii) **energy saving plant and machinery** (boiler systems, certain motors etc); *CAA 2001, s 45A* (see below);
(iii) designated plant and machinery which meets strict **water saving or efficiency criteria** (e.g. meters, monitoring equipment, flow controllers, leakage detection, efficient toilets and taps);

(iv) expenditure by any person on plant or machinery installed at a '**gas refuelling station**' for use solely for or in connection with refuelling vehicles with natural gas or hydrogen fuel or with biogas (for expenditure incurred on or after 1 April 2008)); *CAA 2001, s 45E*;

(v) cars which are electrically propelled or have low carbon dioxide emissions currently 110g/km (after 16 April 2002 and before 1 April 2013); *CAA 2001, s 45D*;

(vi) zero-emission goods vehicles; *F(No 3)A 2010, s 18* and *Sch 7*. The expenditure must be incurred in the period of five years beginning on 1 April 2010 (corporation tax) or 6 April 2010 (income tax). The vehicle must be unused and not second-hand, and must be registered;

(vii) carbon efficient biofuels plant;

(viii) natural gas, biogas and hydrogen refuelling equipment; *CAA 2001, s 45E*;

(ix) **after 16 April 2002** by a company on plant or machinery for use wholly for the purposes of a '**ring fence trade**' within *ICTA 1988, s 501A; CTA 2009, Sch 1 para 171* (petroleum extraction activities), in which case the maximum FYA is **100%** (reduced to **24%** where the plant etc. is a long-life asset, see **12.12 CAPITAL ALLOWANCES — PLANT & MACHINERY: POOLING AND DISPOSALS**); (the relief is, however, withdrawn where the plant etc. is used for less than five years in such a trade, see *CAA 2001, s 45G*), or

the 100% first year allowance on energy saving plant and machinery and low emission cars is only available if these assets **are acquired unused** and are not second hand.

Annual investment allowance

Qualifying expenditure

[11.15] A company is entitled to the annual investment allowance (AIA) on qualifying expenditure on plant and machinery incurred on or after 1 April 2008 *but this excludes expenditure*:

(a) incurred in the period in which the qualifying activity is discontinued;
(b) on a car;
(c) incurred in connection with a ring fence trade;
(d) incurred for purposes other than a qualifying activity;
(e) on plant or machinery provided for long funding leasing.

The allowance

There is a 100% AIA on qualifying expenditure incurred in a 12 month period of account.

From 1 April 2010, there is an upper limit of £100,000 per annum (*FA 2010, s 5*). Previously, the limit was £50,000 (1 April 2008 to 31 March 2010). The upper limit will be reduced to £25,000 in relation to expenditure incurred on or after 1 April 2012 (6 April 2012 for income tax) (*FA 2011, s 11*). A company may choose to claim less than the maximum amount.

The annual allowance is proportionately reduced for periods shorter than 12 months.

Where a qualifying activity has more than one chargeable period ending in the same tax year, each such period must be considered separately, i.e. as if it were the only chargeable period for that activity ending in the tax year, in determining if the restriction applies.

Periods straddling 1st April 2010

Businesses which have a year-end other than 31 March must time apportion the old and new limits to arrive at a maximum potential allowance.

Example

Pringle Limited has a year ended 31 December 2010. The maximum AIA is calculated as:

	£
1 Jan 2010 – 31 Mar 2010 (£50,000 × 90/365)	12,328.77
1 April 2010 – 31 Dec 2010 (£100,000 × 275 /365)	75,342.47
	87,671.24

The maximum amount of qualifying expenditure falling before 1 April 2010 cannot exceed £50,000. Where it does, the excess may be eligible for other allowances. (See **11.13** for first year allowances and **12.7 CAPITAL ALLOWANCES — PLANT & MACHINERY: POOLING AND DISPOSALS** for writing down allowances).

Example

Assuming that the company incurs the following expenditure, AIA may be claimed as follows:

February 2010	£75,000	Claim limited to £50,000
May 2010	£20,000	Claim limited to £20,000
Total AIA	£70,000	

The excess of £25,000 spent in February 2010 may be eligible for first year allowances.

Single companies

A single AIA is available to a company for a chargeable period for all qualifying activities carried on by it.

It may be allocated to the qualifying expenditure as the company sees fit.

Groups of companies

Where there is a group, a single AIA is available to the group as a whole, which may be allocated to the expenditure of all companies as the group sees fit.

For this purpose, a group is a parent company and its subsidiaries as defined in *Companies Act 2006, s 1162*. A company is a parent of another if it is the parent at the end of the subsidiary's chargeable period ending in that financial year.

Common control and related

Where two or more groups are both under common 'control' and 'related' to one another, a single AIA is available to them, to be allocated as they see fit.

'*Control*' in this context means control by a person at the end of the financial year by means of shareholding or voting control or as a result of any powers conferred by the articles of association or other document.

Companies are '*related*' for a financial year if in that year, any member of one group is related to a member of a second group.

They are also related if they carry on the qualifying activity from the same premises and more than 50% of the turnover of one company is within the same NACE classification as more than 50% of the turnover of the other.

The shared premises condition is satisfied if, at the end of the financial year of one or both companies, they are carrying on the relevant activities from the same premises.

The NACE classifications are as follows:

- agriculture, hunting and forestry;
- fishing;
- mining and quarrying;
- mining and quarrying, except production of energy materials;
- manufacturing;
- electricity, gas and water supply;
- construction;
- wholesale and retail trade, repair of motor vehicles, motorcycles and personal and household goods;
- hotels and restaurants;
- transport, storage and communication;
- financial intermediation;
- real estate, renting and business activities;
- public administration and defence, compulsory social security;
- education;
- health and social work;
- other community, social and personal activities;
- activities of households;
- extra-territorial organisations and bodies.

Where there is more than one chargeable period in 12 months, each period is looked at separately in determining whether or not there is a group of companies under common control.

VAT — capital goods scheme

Where additional VAT is incurred in respect of the capital goods scheme, on AIA qualifying expenditure, it qualifies for AIA.

Anti-avoidance

Where there is a transaction between connected persons, or there is a transaction which appears to have the sole or main benefit of obtaining an AIA, no AIA is allowed, and if it has already been made, it is withdrawn. (*CAA 2001, s 218*).

[*CAA 2001, ss 38A, 38B, 51A–51L, 205, 218A; FA 2008, Sch 24*].

40% FYA

[11.16] Until 1 April 2010, where expenditure was incurred in excess of the annual investment allowance, it may be eligible for the 40% FYA.

Subject to the exclusions below, qualifying expenditure is '*first-year qualifying expenditure*' if it was incurred **after 31 March 2009 and before 1 April 2010** by any person within the charge to corporation tax incurring expenditure on plant and machinery not:

- within the general exclusions below;
- special rate expenditure;
- expenditure qualifying for FYAs under any other provision;
- expenditure in respect of which an AIA claim is made (see **11.15**).

The maximum FYA is 40% of the amount of qualifying expenditure incurred during the qualifying period.

Example

M Ltd prepares accounts to 31 December. During the year ended 31 December 2010 it spends £100,000 on plant and machinery (£80,000 pre 1 April 2010).

The capital allowances are as follows:

	£ Expenditure	£ FYAs (see 11.16)	£ Total allowances
Additions	100,000		
AIA [max pre 1 April 2010]	(50,000)		50,000
AIA [100K – 80k]	(20,000)		20,000
Transfer to pools	(30,000)	30,000	
FYA 40%		(12,000)	12,000
Total allowances			82,000

This example illustrates the apportionments necessary for AIA and for part of the period falling before and part on or after 1 April 2010.

'Small or medium-sized enterprise'

Prior to 1 April 2008, a 'small or medium-sized enterprise' was eligible for a 40% FYA for expenditure incurred **after 1 July 1998** (but long-life assets are excluded).

Prior to this date this was 50% (**12%** in the case of long-life assets — see **12.12 CAPITAL ALLOWANCES — PLANT & MACHINERY: POOLING AND DISPOSALS**); This is defined by reference to the *Companies Act 1985, s 247* (or Northern Ireland equivalent) definition of 'small or medium-sized company'.

Broadly, the requirement is that two of the following three conditions are fulfilled (Pre 30 January 2004 limits in brackets):

Employees-less than	250 employees
Turnover-not more than	£22.8 million (£11.2)
Balance sheet assets-not more than	£11.4 million (£5.6m)

If an enterprise which previously qualified fails to satisfy this requirement over two consecutive financial years, it will cease to qualify with effect from the second of those years.

An enterprise which did not previously qualify but which satisfies the requirement over two consecutive financial years will qualify with effect from the second of those years.

In the case of a company which is a member of a group of companies, the requirements apply to the group as a whole.

'Small enterprise'

In the case of a '**small enterprise**' only, **50%** FYA was available for expenditure incurred in the 24 months beginning 1 April 2006 and previously in the twelve months beginning 1 April 2004 (but long-life assets remain excluded).

A small enterprise is defined by reference to the *Companies Act 1985* definition of 'small company', i.e. where two of the following three conditions are fulfilled:

Employees-less than	50 employees
Turnover-not more than	£5.6 million (£2.8m)
Balance sheet assets-not more than	£2.8 million (£1.4m)

Exclusions

FYAs are not available in the circumstances listed below.

(i) The expenditure is incurred in the chargeable period in which the qualifying activity is permanently discontinued.

(ii) The expenditure is incurred on the provision of a '*car*' by *CAA 2001, s 81*:

Gurney v Richards Ch D 1989, 62 TC 287 (fire brigade car equipped with flashing light held within excluded class), decided on similarly worded legislation.

Bourne v Auto School of Motoring Ch D 1964, 42 TC 217 (driving school cars).

Roberts v Granada TV Rental Ltd Ch D 1970, 46 TC 295 (mini-vans etc.).

Mechanically-propelled road vehicles of a type commonly used as a hackney carriage are specifically included while motorcycles are excluded.

(iii) The expenditure is on a ship or railway asset of a kind excluded from being a long-life asset (see **12.12**(ii) **CAPITAL ALLOWANCES — PLANT & MACHINERY: POOLING AND DISPOSALS**).

(iv) The plant or machinery would be a long-life asset but for the transitional provisions of *CAA 2001, Sch 3 para 20* (see **12.12 CAPITAL ALLOWANCES — PLANT & MACHINERY: POOLING AND DISPOSALS**).

(v) The expenditure is on plant or machinery for leasing (whether or not in the course of a trade). For this purpose, 'leasing' expressly includes the letting of a ship on charter or of any other asset on hire.
Expenditure by a company on plant and machinery to be used by its subsidiary in return for an annual charge fell within the exclusion (*M F Freeman (Plant) Ltd v Jowett* [2003] STC (SCD) 423).
Supply by a business of plant or machinery with an operator: Where the equipment is to be operated solely by the operator provided, HMRC accept that this is the provision of a service and not merely plant hire. FYAs are not excluded.
Provision of building access services by the scaffolding industry: This is also accepted as the provision of a service provided it is not simply the supply of scaffolding poles etc. for use by others.
(Revenue Internet Statement 2 June 2003; HMRC Capital Allowances Manual CA23115).

(vi) The provision of the plant or machinery is connected with a change in the nature or conduct of a trade or business carried on by a person other than the person incurring the expenditure on its provision, and the obtaining of an FYA was the main benefit, or one of the main benefits, which could reasonably be expected to arise from the making of the change.

(vii) The provision of the plant of machinery is by way of gift (see **13.28 CAPITAL ALLOWANCES — PLANT & MACHINERY: FIXTURES AND LEASING**).

(viii) The plant or machinery was previously used by the owner for purposes other than those of the qualifying activity (see **13.29**), which includes the purposes of long funding leasing.

(ix) The plant or machinery is acquired by means of a transaction with a connected person (see **25 CONNECTED PERSONS**), or a sale and leaseback (or sale and finance leaseback) transaction, or a transaction the sole or main benefit of which would be the obtaining of a plant and machinery allowance (see *CAA 2001, ss 217, 223, 232* and note the definition of 'finance lease' at **13.27 CAPITAL ALLOWANCES — PLANT & MACHINERY: FIXTURES AND LEASING**).

(x) The *sub-licensing* of software rights.

(xi) Expenditure on long-life assets (see **12.12 CAPITAL ALLOWANCES — PLANT & MACHINERY: POOLING AND DISPOSALS**), on aircraft or hovercraft or on goods vehicles for use in a trade consisting primarily of the conveyance of goods, and unauthorised expenditure on plant or machinery for use primarily in agriculture, fishing or fish farming or in any transportation, storage, preparation, processing or packaging activities carried out in bringing any agricultural produce, fish or fish product to market (For Northern Ireland purposes).

Ownership

Before *CAA 2001* had effect the question of whether a person *owns* plant and machinery was expressed in terms of whether it *belonged* to him at some time during the chargeable period related to the incurring of the expenditure. [*CAA 1990, s 22(1)*].

'Belongs' has its ordinary meaning and normally entails a right of disposition over the thing possessed.

Bolton v International Drilling Co Ltd Ch D 1982, 56 TC 449,

Ensign Tankers (Leasing) Ltd v Stokes HL 1992, 64 TC 617,

Melluish v BMI (No 3) Ltd HL 1995, 68 TC 1,

BMBF (No 24) Ltd v CIR Ch D, [2002] STC 1450.

Specific provisions determine entitlement to allowances for:

(i) plant or machinery which are fixtures (**13.1 CAPITAL ALLOWANCES — PLANT & MACHINERY: FIXTURES AND LEASING**);
(ii) plant and machinery acquired on hire-purchase (**13.25 CAPITAL ALLOWANCES — PLANT & MACHINERY: FIXTURES AND LEASING**);
(iii) certain expenditure incurred by a lessee under the terms of a lease (**13.35 CAPITAL ALLOWANCES — PLANT & MACHINERY: FIXTURES AND LEASING**).

Ships (postponement of FYAs)

Where a ship qualifies for a FYA, the person entitled may, by written notice, *postpone* all or part of the allowance.

The notice must be given no later than two years following the end of the chargeable period for which the allowance is due.

Available qualifying expenditure for writing-down allowances (**12.2 CAPITAL ALLOWANCES — PLANT & MACHINERY: POOLING AND DISPOSALS**) is computed as if the postponed FYA had, in fact, been made.

Postponed FYAs may be claimed over one or more subsequent chargeable periods.

[*CAA 2001, ss 130(1)(3)–(6), 131(1)(2)(4)(7)*].

See **12.18 CAPITAL ALLOWANCES — PLANT & MACHINERY: POOLING AND DISPOSALS** for postponement of writing-down allowances and deferment of balancing charges.

Simon's Taxes. See **B3.320–B3.326, B3.350.**

First-year tax credits

[11.17] Loss making companies will be able to surrender the losses attributable to enhanced capital allowances (100% first year allowances) on designated energy-saving or environmentally-beneficial plant and machinery in exchange for a cash payment known as a first year tax credit from the Government — see *CAA 2001, Sch A1*. (See **55 LOSSES**.)

Expenditure incurred on or after 1 April 2008 and before 31 March 2013 may qualify for first-year tax credits, however, excluded organisations (co-operative housing associations, self-build societies, charities or scientific research organisations) may not claim first-year tax credits.

A company may claim a payable first-year tax credit for a chargeable period if it:

(i) incurs relevant first-year expenditure for a qualifying activity and has received an FYA in respect of that expenditure;
(ii) makes a loss in carrying on the qualifying activity and that loss, or part of that loss, is surrenderable;
(iii) is within the charge to corporation tax on the profits from that qualifying activity; and
(iv) is not an excluded company in that chargeable period.

A company may surrender all or part of its surrenderable loss but once a loss has been surrendered for a tax credit payment it is not available for relief in any other way.

Any losses carried forward to future accounting periods are reduced by the amount of loss surrendered for a first-year tax credit.

A first-year tax credit is not taxable income of the company.

Surrenderable loss

The surrenderable loss is the lesser of:

(i) the loss sustained in carrying on a qualifying activity in the chargeable period that is unrelieved; and
(ii) the amount of FYA given in the period in respect of relevant first-year expenditure on energy-saving and environmentally beneficial plant and machinery.

'Additional VAT liability' relating to the capital goods scheme is not eligible for a first-year tax credit claim.

For this purpose *CAA 2001, s 12* does not apply to deem that pre-trading expenditure is treated as incurred on the first day of trading, therefore such expenditure would not qualify for this relief.

Only unrelieved losses may be surrendered for a first-year tax credit.

The definition of unrelieved loss depends upon the qualifying activity. In each case, the loss incurred is reduced by:

(A) trade or a furnished holiday lettings business;
(B) property business;
(C) overseas property business;
(D) activity consisting of the management of investments, group relief and write off of government investment (see **55.26**).

A loss may not be surrendered as a first year tax credit if it could be set-off against its own taxable profits in the loss making period or surrendered as group relief.

Any losses available to carry forward will be reduced by the amount of the loss that has been surrendered under the new rules.

Amount of the tax credit

The tax credit will be 19% of the loss surrendered subject to an upper limit which will be the greater of:

- Total PAYE and NICs liabilities for period for which the loss is surrendered;
- £250,000.

In calculating the PAYE and NIC deductions, no deduction is to be made for child or working tax credits or, in the case of NIC, statutory sick pay or statutory maternity pay.

Interaction with other payable tax credits

A loss making company may make claims both for first-year tax credits and one of the other payable tax credits available (R&D tax credits for instance). See **64 RESEARCH AND DEVELOPMENT EXPENDITURE**.

A loss may only be surrendered once, but whether the surrender is solely for a first-year tax credit, solely for an R&D tax credit (say) or a combination of the two is for the company to decide; there is no prescribed order of surrender.

The company will need to make clear in its return which of the tax credit schemes it is claiming under and the quantum of each of the various claims.

Making the claim

A company must claim first year tax credits in a return or amended return.

The return (or amended return) must state the plant or machinery to which the relevant first-year expenditure relates, the amount of relevant first-year expenditure incurred and the date it was incurred.

Where appropriate, a certificate under *CAA 2001, s 45B* or *s 45I* must be produced.

A penalty will be charged if a fraudulent or negligent claim for tax credit is made, or subsequent to making a claim, a company finds that the claim it has made is incorrect (neither fraudulently or negligently) and fails to remedy the error without unreasonable delay.

The penalty is not more than the tax credit claimed in error.

First-year tax credits and interest thereon may be applied to meet a company's corporation tax liability.

Payment will be withheld if an HMRC enquiry is raised into the period in which the credit arises until the enquiry is complete.

However, HMRC have discretion to make a provisional payment. PAYE and NIC deductions for the period in question must be up to date before tax credits are paid.

Clawback

There will be a clawback of the tax credit if the qualifying plant and machinery for the enhanced capital allowances is sold within four years after the end of the period for which the tax credit was paid, in which case the loss will be reinstated.

The first-year tax credit which attached to the 'restored loss' is treated as if it ought never to have been paid.

Where the item has been disposed of to a connected person or there is a change of ownership of the item and the transferee stands in the shoes or the transferor company, the disposal value is treated as market value.

The proceeds of disposal are deducted from the capital allowances pool.

The '*restored loss*' is found by the formula (a negative amount being treated as nil):

$$(LS - OERPM) - (OE - DV) - ARL$$

where:

LS = the loss surrendered for the chargeable period under the first-year tax credit provisions and in respect of which a payment was made.

OERPM = the amount of original expenditure less the amount attributable to the plant and machinery disposed of.

OE = the total of the original qualifying expenditure on the item disposed of, less the original expenditure on any plant and machinery previously disposed of.

DV = the disposal value of the item disposed of and any previous items disposed of.

ARL = the restored losses for any previous disposal under these provisions.

Within three months from the date the company becomes aware that anything has happened to trigger a clawback, it must give notice to HMRC.

Interaction with other tax payable credits

A loss making company may make claims both for first-year tax credits and one of the other payable tax credits available (R&D tax credits for instance).

A loss may only be surrendered once, but whether the surrender is solely for a first-year tax credit, solely for an R&D tax credit (say) or a combination of the two is for the company to decide; there is no prescribed order of surrender.

The company will need to make clear in its return which of the tax credit schemes it is claiming under and the quantum of each of the various claims.

Anti-avoidance provisions

To the extent a transaction is entered into wholly or mainly for one of the following purposes, it is disregarded for first-year tax credit purposes:

(i) to obtain first-year tax credits to which it would not otherwise have been entitled; or
(ii) to obtain more first-year tax credits than that to which it would otherwise have been entitled.

There are no anti-avoidance provisions for groups.

[*FA 1998, Sch 18 para 83ZA; CAA 2001, s 262A, Sch A1; FA 2008, s 79, Sch 25; CTA 2009, Sch 1 para 551*].

Capital allowance buying

Introduction

[11.18] Anti avoidance legislation (*FA 2010, s 26, Sch 4*) aims to prevent a company or group obtaining relief for excess capital allowances against its existing profits by effectively acquiring capital allowances from:

- a company;
- an increased share in a company or partnership; or
- a trade.

The legislation is found at *CAA 2001, Ch 16A, ss 212A–212S*) and, unless otherwise stated, has effect from 21 July 2009.

The issue

Plant and machinery allowances are intended to give relief for the reduction in value of an asset while a company owns it and when deducted from profits, they may create or enhance a trading loss.

Trading losses may be utilised in several ways including being surrendered as group relief (See **39 GROUP RELIEF**) and so used to reduce the profits of companies other than the one that incurred the expenditure.

A company may claim restricted capital allowances in any period, carrying forward a higher tax written down value to future periods. This allows the company, and effectively its group, to defer allowances to future periods when deduction may be more beneficial.

When the legislation applies

Where no change in ownership is involved, this is not perceived to be a problem. However, where companies with large pools of unclaimed capital allowances are sold into a new group, principally to enable the new group to access the allowances in the form of group relief, this is potentially a problem. Hence the need for this legislation.

In such a situation, where a loss is created or enhanced by capital allowances, a group acquiring the company would not be able to use those losses within the group.

Such losses will only be available to reduce the profits that they would have been able to reduce before the transaction took place.

For these rules to be relevant, the following four conditions must apply:

(1) The main purpose or one of the main purposes of the transaction is to obtain a tax advantage (Unallowable purpose).
(2) A company must carry on a trade or carry on a trade in partnership with others.
(3) That company (or partnership) must have an *excess of capital allowances.*
(4) There must be a *'qualifying change'* in relation to the company.

Qualifying change (*CAA 2001, s 212C*)

A *qualifying change* could be any of the following:

- sale of a company or partial sale of a company;
- change in the ownership proportions of an exsiting consortium company;
- transfer of the trade with the excess of allowances in circumstances such that the Transfers of a trade provisions in *CTA 2010, Pt 22 Ch 1* apply. See **17 CAPITAL GAINS;**
- change in the profit sharing ratio of a partnership.

Condition A

For this to be satisfied, there must be a change in one or more *principal companies* on the relevant day.

The rules for deciding if any company is a principal company of C can be found in *s 212E* and are based on similar provisions in *CTA 2010, Pt 9 Chs 3–5* on the Sale of Lessors. See **5 anti-avoidance.**

Notes to *FA 2010* provide some useful examples of when this condition is met:

- C is 100% owned by Y Group and is sold to the X Group;
- C is a consortium company owned 50:50 by Group Y and Group X. If Group Y sells its interest in C to the X Group or another Group;
- C is owned by the Jones family. On the relevant day the Jones family sell their shares to the X group. (Relevant day must be on or after 9 December 2009).

Condition B

This applies where a principal company of the company is a consortium principal company whose ownership proportion is greater at the end of the relevant day than it was at the beginning of that day.

CAA 2001, s 212F defines when a company is owned by a consortium and who the consortium members are. The company cannot be a 75% subsidiary of another company and at least 75% of the company's ordinary share capital must be owned by other companies and those other companies must each own 5% or more of the ordinary share capital.

Condition C

This applies where C ceases to carry on the whole or part of the relevant trade and the trade (or part of it) begins to be carried on in partnership by two or more companies in circumstances where *CTA 2010, Pt 22 Ch 1* applies.

Condition D

This applies where at the beginning of the relevant day the relevant trade is carried on by C in partnership and C's relevant percentage share in the relevant trade at the end of the day is less than at the beginning of the day or is nil.

Section 212I provides the rules for establishing C's 'relevant percentage share' in a partnership. Normally the profit sharing arrangements of the firm for the particular period will be followed but there may be instances where circumstances are such that to follow the profit sharing arrangements in force for the period would not be just and reasonable.

Excess of capital allowances

Where a company has deferred claiming capital allowances, it is likely that the tax written down value of its plant and machinery will exceed its balance sheet value.

Relevant tax written down value-balance sheet value = *Excess capital allowances*

CAA 2001, s 212J gives the calculation for establishing whether there are relevant excess of allowances in relation to the relevant trade but excludes plant and machinery if it is:

- leased out under a long funding lease;
- subject to a hire purchase contract where the person entitled to the benefit of the contract is deemed to be the owner;

In order to calculate the excess of allowances, the company's (or partnership's) accounting period ends on the day of a '*qualifying change*' and a new accounting period begins the day after.

Relevant tax written down value (*CAA 2001, s 212K*)

This is based on the amounts that are actually in the capital allowances pools before the relevant date including the amounts in:

- single asset pools;
- class pools, or
- the main pool.

Unrelieved qualifying expenditure

Unrelieved qualifying expenditure contained in a pool is to be calculated on the basis of three assumptions:

- any qualifying expenditure that could have been allocated to the pool has been allocated to the pool by the end of the old period;
- the balance of any first-year qualifying expenditure incurred in the old period is allocated to a pool in the old period at the end of the old period;
- any transaction taking place on the relevant day that has the effect of reducing the amount of unrelieved qualifying expenditure in a pool is assumed not to have taken place.

Balance sheet values (*CAA 2001, s 212L*)

The balance sheet has to be drawn up in accordance with generally accepted accounting practice so as to reflect the position at the beginning of the relevant day but adjusted for the disposal.

The net book value or carrying amount of the relevant plant and machinery is added to any relevant plant and machinery that is leased to a lessee under one or more finance leases which are not long funding finance leases.

Any fixtures in land included in the net book value or carrying amount of the land must be included and determined on a just and reasonable basis.

What happens when Chapter 16A applies

CAA 2001, s 212N provides that when Chapter 16A applies, an accounting period ends and a new accounting period starts.

CAA 2001, s 212O explains how the amount of the excess of allowances in a pool (the relevant pool) is to be calculated. For each capital allowance pool or single asset computation, an amount of expenditure equal to the *excess of allowances* is reallocated to a new separate pool or computation. Where the balance sheet value of plant and machinery on a pool or computation exceeds its tax written down value, the difference is deducted from the *excess of allowances* in any relevant pool. The balance sheet values are apportioned to each pool on a just and reasonable basis.

WDAs are calculated on the relevant pools and the new pools separately but at the same rate.

CAA 2001, s 212P sets out what happens when there are excess allowances. New pool allowances may only be used to reduce the profits or increase the losses from the trade as it was carried on before the *qualifying change*.

Note: Any trading activities transferred in to the company or the partnership will be treated as a separate trade for these purposes.

Relief for losses against other income and group relief to other group companies is only allowed if they could have been claimed before the qualifying change.

CAA 2001, s 212R provides that disposal proceeds from the sale of any relevant plant or machinery is apportioned between the relevant pool and the new pool on a just and reasonable basis.

Ships

There are special capital allowances rules for ships that allow capital allowances to be claimed and then postponed so that the capital allowances are given in a subsequent year.

Postponed allowances that have not yet been relieved will be subject to the same rules as the amounts of excess allowances.

These rules are effective from 9 December 2009.

Key points

[11.19] Points to consider are as follows.

- Plant and machinery is not defined in the legislation. It is therefore necessary to look to case law which can be difficult to interpret. The basic starting point is whether the item in question performs a function in the business rather than merely being part of the setting.
- Many of the items which have been the subject of well known cases e.g. lighting in *CIR v Scottish & Newcastle Breweries Ltd* are now classified as integral features. Where, however, that item still performs a function — e.g. lighting adding to the ambience in a pub toilet, or a drainage system in a garden centre — it may still qualify as general plant and machinery.
- Integral features are a relatively new class of asset introduced to cover expenditure incurred on certain items after 31 March 2008. Integral features are limited to the items listed in *CAA 2001, s 33*. They don't include items which may be considered integral to a building e.g. doors.
- Where repairs on an integral feature total more than 50% of the cost to replace that item (at the time the repairs are incurred) over a twelve-month period the repairs are not fully deductible as revenue expenditure. Instead they are treated as an addition to the special rate pool and attract a 10% writing down allowance. Where possible it may be worth obtaining quotes before repairs are undertaken.
- Correct classification of expenditure is now even more important given the introduction of integral features and the repairs rule. Significant repairs to a lift, for example, are likely to be classified as an integral feature whereas the same repairs to a hoist should qualify as revenue expenditure and be fully tax deductible.
- First year allowances, where available, can only be claimed in the period in which the expenditure is incurred. This may mean that even if a company is loss making it is still advantageous to claim a first year allowance to build up additional losses to carry forward. The annual investment allowance is also a 'use it or lose it' relief.
- The Annual Investment Allowance is to be reduced to £25,000 for expenditure incurred after 31 March 2012. Where possible it may be worth considering bringing expenditure forward to make use of the current £100,000 allowance.
- First year allowances of 100% are available for expenditure on certain energy and water efficient items. In the majority of cases the item must be on the prescribed DEFRA issued list before the expenditure is incurred to qualify for the relief. It is worth reviewing the list before a major refurbishment to ascertain whether the relief could be claimed.

- Loss making companies are able to surrender the losses attributable to enhanced capital allowances in exchange for a 19% tax credit. There are many rules as to the quantum and type of loss which can be surrendered and in certain circumstances the credit may be clawed back but this can provide a real cash flow advantage. If a company does consider it is likely to be profitable in the next few years, however, it may be preferable to carry the losses forward as relief will be available at a potentially higher rate.
- Anti-avoidance legislation has been introduced to prevent companies with large capital allowance pools being acquired only to make use of the future capital allowances.

12

Capital Allowances — Plant and Machinery: Pooling and Disposals

Cross references. See **10** CAPITAL ALLOWANCES — INTRODUCTION; **11** CAPITAL ALLOWANCES — PLANT AND MACHINERY: ELIGIBLE EXPENDITURE AND INITIAL ALLOWANCES; **13** CAPITAL ALLOWANCES — PLANT AND MACHINERY: FIXTURES AND LEASING; **14** CAPITAL ALLOWANCES — MINERAL EXTRACTION; **15** CAPITAL ALLOWANCES — BUILDINGS; **16** CAPITAL ALLOWANCES — MISCELLANEOUS.

Other sources. See Tolley's Capital Allowances.

Simon's Taxes. See Part B3.

Introduction

Eligible expenditure

[12.1] Qualifying plant and machinery expenditure (**11.3 CAPITAL ALLOWANCES — PLANT AND MACHINERY: ELIGIBLE EXPENDITURE AND INITIAL ALLOWANCES**) that is not covered by a first year allowance (FYA), may be eligible for writing down allowances (WDAs).

It may be that the expenditure was not eligible for a FYA or, the FYA claimed does not cover all of the expenditure incurred (**11.13 CAPITAL ALLOWANCES — PLANT AND MACHINERY: ELIGIBLE EXPENDITURE AND INITIAL ALLOWANCES**).

Pooling

[12.2] Such unrelieved qualifying expenditure is allocated to its relevant pool; exactly which pool it is allocated to, is determined by the type of expenditure incurred.

Broadly, it will be allocated to one of the following pools:

(i) Main pool (**12.6, 12.13, 12.16**);
(ii) Special rate pool (**12.9, 12.13, 12.16**);
(iii) Single asset or class pool (**12.17–12.22**).

For each pool of qualifying expenditure, a **writing-down allowance** (**WDA**) is available for each chargeable period, other than the 'final chargeable period'. (See **12.24.**)

The allowance is calculated as a maximum of:

(i) 20% (25% for expenditure before 1 April 2008) for the main, single asset and class pools.
(ii) 10% for the special rate pool.

Finance Act 2011, s 10 provides that from 1 April 2012 the 20% WDA rate will be reduced to 18%, and the 10% rate will be reduced to 8%.

Having claimed capital allowances within the pool, the residual balance in the pool ('the tax written down value') is then carried forward as an opening balance in the next accounting period where it will be written-down again.

Interaction with annual investment allowance

[12.3] If an annual investment allowance (AIA) (**11.15 CAPITAL ALLOWANCES — PLANT AND MACHINERY: ELIGIBLE EXPENDITURE AND INITIAL ALLOWANCES**) is claimed for a chargeable period, the AIA qualifying expenditure in respect of which the allowance is made is added to the appropriate pool in that period, and the pool balance is then reduced by the amount of expenditure qualifying for AIA.

The balance of the expenditure that is not covered by the AIA, would be eligible for the WDA in the same period.

Example

Craggle Ltd draws accounts to 31 March 2011. In the year ended 31 March 2011, they incurred the following capital expenditure:

		Cost
		£
1 December 2010	Pressure washer	10,000
1 February 2011	Hydraulic car lift	110,000

The value on the main pool brought forward at 1 April 2010 was £12,000.

Craggle Ltd's capital allowances for the year ended 31 March 2011 are:

	AIAs @ 100%	General Pool	Total CAs
	£	£	£
Tax wdv b/fwd		12,000	
Additions:			
Pressure washer	10,000		
Hydraulic car lift	90,000	20,000	
	100,000	32,000	
AIA @ 100%	(100,000)		100,000
WDA @ 20%		(6,400)	6,400
C/fwd at 31.3.2011		25,600	
CA claim for year			£106,400

Short periods

[12.4] The WDA is proportionately reduced if the chargeable period is less than a year, or if the qualifying activity has been carried on for part only of the chargeable period.

Allocating to the correct pool

[12.5] Qualifying expenditure:

(a) Can be allocated to a pool for a chargeable period only to the extent that it has not been included in available qualifying expenditure for an earlier chargeable period.

(b) Cannot be allocated to a pool for a chargeable period earlier than that in which it is incurred.

(c) Can be allocated to a pool for a chargeable period only if the person concerned *owns* the plant or machinery at some time in that period.

Where an 'additional VAT liability' (**10.10 CAPITAL ALLOWANCES — INTRODUCTION**) is incurred in respect of qualifying expenditure, at a time when the plant or machinery in question is provided for the purposes of the qualifying activity, it is itself expenditure on that plant or machinery and may be taken into account in determining available qualifying expenditure for the chargeable period in which it accrues.

Demolition

The net cost of demolition of plant and machinery demolished during a chargeable period, and not replaced, is allocated to the appropriate pool for that chargeable period.

Main pool

Introduction

[12.6] Qualifying expenditure on plant and machinery (**11.3 CAPITAL ALLOWANCES — PLANT AND MACHINERY: ELIGIBLE EXPENDITURE AND INITIAL ALLOWANCES**) will be added to the main pool for WDA purposes, if it:

(i) Has not already been relieved by claiming the AIA (**11.17**) or another FYA (**11.13 CAPITAL ALLOWANCES — PLANT AND MACHINERY: ELIGIBLE EXPENDITURE AND INITIAL ALLOWANCES**).
(ii) Is not required to be recorded in one of the other pools (see **12.2**).

Writing down allowances

[12.7] Once recorded, WDAs are given at a rate of 20% per annum (25% for expenditure before 1 April 2008) for the main, single asset and class pools. Where an accounting period straddles 1 April 2008, a hybrid rate of writing-down allowance, worked out on a time basis, is to be used.

Interaction with FYAs

[12.8] If an FYA (**11.13 CAPITAL ALLOWANCES — PLANT AND MACHINERY: ELIGIBLE EXPENDITURE AND INITIAL ALLOWANCES**) is claimed in respect of an amount of first-year qualifying expenditure, none of that qualifying expenditure can be allocated to a pool for the chargeable period in which the expenditure is incurred.

However, the balance (after deducting the FYA) can be allocated to a pool for a subsequent chargeable period, when WDAs will be claimed.

However, expenditure which qualifies for an FYA for a chargeable period is not excluded from being allocated to a pool for that period it is incurred if either the FYA is:

(i) not claimed; or
(ii) claimed in respect of part only of the expenditure (in which case the remaining part can be so allocated).

Separate rules apply where the AIA applied (**12.3** above)

Special rate pool

Introduction

[12.9] The *Finance Act 2008* introduced a 'special rate pool' for qualifying expenditure incurred from 1 April 2008.

Assets that fall into the special rate pool will be eligible for the AIA (**11.15**) (but not the temporary 40% FYA, which applied for certain expenditure incurred before 1 April 2010) (**11.16 CAPITAL ALLOWANCES — PLANT AND MACHINERY: ELIGIBLE EXPENDITURE AND INITIAL ALLOWANCES**).

Any excess expenditure will be placed in a separate special rate pool where it will be eligible for a 10% writing down allowance, rather than the 20% allowance that is available to assets going into the main pool. Note that the 10% WDA rate will be reduced to 8% from 1 April 2012 (*FA 2011, s 10*).

Therefore when allocating the 100% AIA:

(i) first allocate the AIA to assets in the 'special rate' pool; then
(ii) allocate any remaining AIA to 'general' plant and machinery.

Example

J Ltd runs a business making aquariums and garden fish-ponds from a small factory in Colchester. They started trading on 1 May 2010 preparing their first set of accounts for the 12 months to 30 April 2011.

In the first year of trading J Ltd incurred the following capital expenditure:

		£
1 May 2010	Factory	300,000
1 May 2010	Air-conditioning units for factory	25,000
1 October 2010	Energy efficient motors	30,000
1 November 2010	2 delivery vans	56,000
1 December 2010	New roof on staff canteen	25,000

Solution

Expenditure on the factory does not qualify for plant and machinery allowances as it is as it is part of the setting in which the trade is carried on.

Expenditure on air conditioning qualifies as an integral feature and so falls into the special rate pool with a 10% WDA. However as we can choose what we allocate the AIA to, we will first allocate it to integral features. 100% relief will therefore be available.

The cost of the vans is covered by the £100,000 AIA limit, which applies from April 2010.

Expenditure on energy saving plant and machinery qualifies for FYAs at 100% (unaffected by the AIA).

The new roof is not an integral feature — it is part of a building and does not qualify.

None of the expenditure is allocated to the 'special rate pool' as the £25,000 expenditure on integral features in the period is covered by the AIA.

Qualifying expenditure

[12.10] Expenditure to be allocated to the 'special rate pool' consists of expenditure incurred on:

(i) provision or replacement of 'integral features' of a building or structure used for a qualifying activity (**12.11**);
(ii) 'long life assets' acquired from 1 April 2008 and the balance of the long-life asset pool in a chargeable period beginning on or after that date (**12.12**);
(iii) thermal insulation of buildings used in a business from 1 April 2008;
(iv) expenditure on certain cars from 1 April 2009 (**12.14**);
(v) expenditure on cushion gas incurred on or after 1 April 2010 (*FA 2010, s 28*).

Integral features

[12.11] For capital allowances purposes, the boundary between what is 'plant and machinery' and what is a 'commercial building' is not absolutely clear (**11.4 CAPITAL ALLOWANCES — PLANT AND MACHINERY: ELIGIBLE EXPENDITURE AND INITIAL ALLOWANCES**).

This has meant that certain assets which are 'integral' to a building (such as air conditioning systems and lifts etc.) previously qualified for writing down allowances at the 'old' rate (prior to April 2008) of 25% whereas other assets (such as electrical and water systems) were deemed to be part of the building and did not qualify for capital allowances.

From 6 April 2008, 'integral features' are separately identified in the special rate pool on which writing down allowances are given at 10%.

According to the government, assets such as lifts and air-conditioning systems have a longer economic life than other more 'productive equipment' used in the business, so the new special rate pool offers 'a more appropriate rate of write-off for these assets'.

FA 2008 introduced a list of features which are 'integral' to a building (**11.6 CAPITAL ALLOWANCES — PLANT AND MACHINERY: ELIGIBLE EXPENDITURE AND INITIAL ALLOWANCES**) and which will therefore only qualify for capital allowances at 10%.

Anti avoidance

In an anti-avoidance measure, where there is a sale of an integral feature which existed before 1 April 2008, the buyer and seller are connected and the buyer's expenditure would be special rate expenditure, the buyer does not qualify for relief in the special rate pool unless the original expenditure was qualifying expenditure or the buyer's expenditure would have been qualifying expenditure had it been incurred at the same time as the original expenditure.

Intra group transfers

There is provision for intra-group transfers of integral features which are 'pre-commencement', where the buyer and seller may jointly elect within two years of the date of the sale to transfer the integral feature at tax written-down value. The buyer is not entitled to put the balance transferred into the special rate pool. A group is defined as for *TCGA 1992, s 170(3)–(6)*. An integral feature is '*pre-commencement*' where the expenditure was incurred by the seller before 1 April 2008, or was incurred by it after that date and allocated to its main pool.

[*CAA 2001, ss 104A–104E; FA 2008, ss 82, 83; Sch 26*].

Simon's Taxes. See **B3.344**.

Long life assets

Introduction

[12.12] Like integral features, long life assets are taken to the special rate pool and are given writing down allowances at 10% on a reducing balance basis.

Long life assets are assets with a predicted useful life of at least 25 years. Typically this will apply to very specific trades such as large manufacturing trades, power stations, aircraft and shipbuilding etc., where some assets can be expected to be used in the business for a very long time.

For these purposes, the useful economic life of plant or machinery is the period from first use (by any person) until it ceases to be, or to be likely to be, used by anyone as a fixed asset of a business.

Where part only of capital expenditure on an item of plant or machinery falls within these provisions, that part and the remainder are treated as expenditure on separate items, any necessary apportionments being made on a just and reasonable basis.

Qualifying expenditure

Items are not treated as a long-life asset where total expenditure in the accounting period on such assets does not exceed £100,000 (*CAA 2001, s 99*).

For the purpose of applying the monetary limit, all expenditure under a contract is treated as incurred in the first chargeable period in which any expenditure under the contract is incurred.

If a sole trader or company buys assets with an expected useful life of over 25 years, but the expenditure on such assets in the period is less than £100,000, the asset is treated as a standard piece of plant and machinery and normal writing down allowances are available at a rate of 20%.

Excluded expenditure

The following *cannot* be long-life assets.

(i) Fixtures (**13.1 CAPITAL ALLOWANCES — PLANT AND MACHINERY: FIXTURES AND LEASING**) in, or plant or machinery provided for use in, a building used wholly or mainly as a dwelling-house, showroom, hotel, office or retail shop or similar retail premises, or for purposes ancillary to such use.

(ii) (In relation to expenditure incurred before 1 January 2011) ships of a seagoing kind, other than offshore installations (as now defined by *CTA 2010, s 1132*), and not of a kind used or chartered primarily for sport or recreation (which expression does not encompass passenger ships or cruise liners).

(iii) (In relation to expenditure incurred before 1 January 2011) 'railway assets' used only for a 'railway business' (as defined).

New versus second hand assets

The long-life asset rules only apply to new assets.

If an asset is acquired second-hand and had originally received a 20% writing down allowance, it will continue to obtain relief at 20%.

If an asset has been treated as a long life asset by a seller, the buyer (regardless of how much he buys the asset for) will also have to treat the asset as a long life asset.

[*CAA 2001, ss 56(5), 65(1), 90–104, Sch 3 para 20; FA 2004, Sch 27 paras 8, 11; FA 2008, s 73(3)*].

Short accounting periods

This £100,000 limit is adjusted for short accounting periods. For example, if a trader draws accounts for a six-month accounting period, the long life asset limit would be £50,000.

For a group of companies, the £100,000 limit is adjusted for the number of associated companies.

[*CAA 2001, s 99(2)*].

Expenditure incurred before 1 April 2008

Expenditure incurred on long life assets prior to the existence of the special rate pool was initially allocated to a long life asset pool where they received a 6% writing down allowance.

With the introduction of the special rate pool, the balance on that pool was brought into the special rate pool and qualifies for 10% writing-down allowance. [*CAA 2001, ss 101, 102; FA 2008, Sch 26 paras 9–10*].

Transitional period

Where expenditure on long-life assets was incurred before 1 April 2008 and allocated to a pool before that date, the writing-down allowance for the transitional period is calculated on a time apportionment basis using the days where the expenditure qualifies at 6% and those it qualifies at 10%.

Any unrelieved expenditure in a long-life asset pool at the end of the transitional period, or a chargeable period ending immediately before 1 April 2008 is carried forward into the special rate pool and treated as special rate expenditure thereafter.

Where the expenditure was in a single asset pool, it is carried forward as if it were special rate expenditure in the single asset pool. A transitional period is one which begins before and ends on or after 1 April 2008.

Example

B Ltd prepares trading accounts to 31 December.

In the year to 31 December 2006, the company has built new factory premises for use in its trade, which include a building mainly in use as offices (on which 20% of the cost of the premises is expended).

Industrial buildings allowances are available on the construction expenditure.

The main plant and machinery pool written-down value at 1 January 2006 is £800,000, and the disposal value to be brought into account in respect of plant and machinery in B Ltd's previous premises is £720,000.

Machines installed in the new factory cost £920,000.

No first-year allowances are available.

B Ltd also claims, for the year to 31 December 2006, plant and machinery allowances for expenditure of £520,000 incurred on fixtures integral to the new premises, which are agreed to have an expected life in excess of 25 years. Of this expenditure, it is agreed £120,000 should be apportioned to the offices.

On 1 May 2007 B Ltd incurs additional expenditure on upgrading the fixtures of £19,000, none of it relating to office fixtures.

On 1 October 2008 B Ltd moves to new premises, disposing of the old premises for a consideration including £425,000 relating to the integral fixtures (of which £95,000 relates to the office fixtures) and £510,000 relating to other plant and machinery.

Plant and machinery in the new premises costs £960,000, none of which relates to integral fixtures (which are included in the industrial buildings allowances claim for the new premises).

Small pools

[12.13] From 1 April 2008, companies can claim a writing down allowance of up to £1,000 when the tax written down value brought forward in either the general pool or the 'special rate pool' ('10% pool') is £1,000 or less. [*CAA 2001, s 56A*].

This means that businesses who have very small brought forward balances in the general pool will no longer have to calculate WDAs at 20% on such pools — instead where the pool is £1,000 or less, the full amount can be written down. This is intended to lessen the administration burden for small businesses.

This rule applies for accounting periods beginning on or after 1 April 2008.

The small pool limit of £1,000 is scaled up or down for short or long accounting periods.

It can apply to the 'special rate' (10%) pool but it does not apply to 'single asset' pools.

Disposals

[12.14] Where a person has incurred qualifying expenditure (**11.2 CAPITAL ALLOWANCES — PLANT AND MACHINERY: ELIGIBLE EXPENDITURE AND INITIAL ALLOWANCES**) on plant or machinery, a **disposal value** must be brought into account for a chargeable period in which any one of the following **disposal events** occurs (but normally only in relation to the first such event to occur in respect of that plant or machinery).

- (i) The person ceases to own the plant or machinery.
- (ii) The person loses possession of it, and it is reasonable to assume the loss is permanent.
- (iii) It has been in use for 'mineral exploration and access' (**14.2 CAPITAL ALLOWANCES — MINERAL EXTRACTION**) and the person abandons it at the site where it was so in use.
- (iv) It ceases to exist as such (by reason of its destruction, dismantling or otherwise).
- (v) It begins to be used wholly or partly for purposes other than those of the qualifying activity.
- (vi) It begins to be leased under a long funding lease (**13.4 CAPITAL ALLOWANCES — PLANT AND MACHINERY: FIXTURES AND LEASING**).
- (vii) The qualifying activity is permanently discontinued.

The amount to be brought into account depends upon the nature of the event.

- (a) On a sale (other than one within (b) below), it is the net sale proceeds plus any insurance or capital compensation received (by the person concerned) by reason of any event affecting the sale price obtainable.
- (b) On a sale at less than market value, it is market value, unless:
  - (i) the buyer (not being a dual resident investing company connected with the seller) can claim plant or machinery or research and development (formerly scientific research) allowances for his expenditure, or
  - (ii) the sale gives rise to a charge to tax under *ITEPA 2003* (i.e. on employment, pension or social security income),

  in which case (a) above applies.
- (c) On demolition or destruction, it is the net amount received for the remains, plus any insurance or capital compensation received.
- (d) On permanent loss (otherwise than within (c) above), or, where *CAA 2001* has effect, on abandonment as in (iii) above, it is any insurance or capital compensation received.
- (e) On commencement of a long funding lease, it is as stated in **13.4 CAPITAL ALLOWANCES — PLANT AND MACHINERY: FIXTURES AND LEASING.**

(f) On permanent discontinuance of the qualifying activity preceding an event in (a)–(d) above, it is whatever value would otherwise have applied on the occurrence of that event.

(g) On a gift giving rise to a charge to tax on the recipient under *ITEPA 2003* (i.e. on employment, pension or social security income), it is nil. See also HMRC Capital Allowances Manual CA23250.

(h) On any other event, it is market value at the time of the event.

However, the disposal value is in all cases limited to the qualifying expenditure incurred on the plant or machinery by the person in question.

In addition, where *CAA 2001* has effect, there is no requirement to bring a disposal value into account if none of the qualifying expenditure in question has been taken into account in determining the person's available qualifying expenditure (**12.1**) for any chargeable period up to and including that in which the disposal occurs. As regards both these rules, see also **13.27 CAPITAL ALLOWANCES — PLANT AND MACHINERY: FIXTURES AND LEASING** as regards certain transactions between connected persons.

Additional VAT rebates

Where an 'additional VAT rebate' (**10.10 CAPITAL ALLOWANCES — INTRODUCTION**) is made in respect of an item of qualifying expenditure, a disposal value of an equivalent amount must be brought into account (on its own or as an addition to any other disposal value brought into account for that item) for the chargeable period in which the rebate accrues.

Any disposal value brought into account for a subsequent chargeable period is limited to the original qualifying expenditure less all additional VAT rebates accrued in all chargeable periods up to (but not including) that chargeable period.

If the disposal value is itself the result of an additional VAT rebate, it is limited to the original qualifying expenditure less *any* disposal values brought into account as a result of earlier events.

[*CAA 2001, ss 60, 61, 62(1), 63(1), 64(1)(5), 238, 239; ITEPA 2003, Sch 6 paras 249, 250; FA 2006, Sch 8 para 5; CTA 2009, Sch 1 para 482*].

Simon's Taxes. See **B3.334**.

Cars

Introduction

[12.15] The rules for capital allowances on cars changed with effect from 1 April 2009.

As a general rule, cars do not qualify for the AIA (or the former temporary FYA).

There is an exception for cars with CO2 emissions of no more than 110 g/km on which FYAs are available at 100%. Subject to certain restrictions, 100% FYAs are also available from 1 April 2010 for a period of five years on zero-emission goods vehicles [*F(No 3)A 2010, Sch 7*].

Definition

The definition of a car for capital allowances purposes is a mechanically propelled vehicle except a vehicle:

(i) constructed in such a way that it is primarily suited for transporting goods of any sort; or
(ii) of a type which is not commonly used as a private vehicle and is not suitable for use as a private vehicle.

Lorries, vans, trucks are not therefore 'cars' for capital allowance purposes and will be treated as 'standard' pieces of plant and machinery.

Motorcycles are not cars.

Expenditure incurred from 1 April 2009

[12.16] The capital allowances available on expenditure on cars on or after 1 April 2009, or certain cars contracted for after 8 December 2009 (i.e. there was an unconditional written contract with no negotiable terms), depends on the vehicle's carbon dioxide emissions.

Categories of car

Cars are divided into 'main rate cars' and others.

A '*main rate car*' is defined as a car that:

(a) is first registered before 1 March 2001; or
(b) has a qualifying emissions certificate when first registered and emission =160 grams per kilometre driven; or
(c) is electrically propelled (as defined in *CAA 2001, s 268B; FA 2009, Sch 11 para 11*).

The CO2 figure may be changed by Treasury order.

'Qualifying emissions certificate' and other terms relating to emissions are defined in *CAA 2001, s 268C; FA 2009, Sch 11 para 11*.

Anti-avoidance

Where expenditure is incurred on a special-rate car and the company then permanently discontinues its qualifying activity and the other three conditions A to C below are satisfied, the balancing allowances available to the company is the balancing charges on the special rate pool less the excess of total of balancing charges of all pools over balancing allowances on all pools other than the special rate pool for the final period.

The effect of this is to ensure that the company is not denied a balancing allowance on the special rate pool while bringing balancing charges into charge to tax on other pools.

The conditions are:

(A) the qualifying activity of the company consisted (other than incidentally) of making cars available to other persons (e.g. a leasing company);

(B) within six months following discontinuance, any group company's qualifying activity consists of or includes (other than incidentally) the making of cars available to other persons;
(C) the special pool balancing allowance to which the company would normally be entitled is greater than the excess of the total balancing charges for all pools over balancing allowances on all pools other than the special rate pool for the final period. A negative answer is treated as nil.

The group relief company (or, if there is more than one, the group relief company nominated by the taxpayer company not more than six months after the end of the taxpayer company's final chargeable period, or as decided by HMRC in the absence of a nomination) is treated as incurring qualifying expenditure, on the day after the end of the taxpayer company's accounting period, equal to the excess of the taxpayer's balancing allowance on the special rate pool, over the excess of balancing charges on all pools over the balancing allowances on all pools other than the special rate pool. Where the group relief company's accounting period into which the expenditure falls overlaps with the taxpayer company's penultimate accounting period, a proportionate part of the expenditure is not qualifying expenditure for that period, but it may be taken into account by the group relief company in later periods.

[*CAA 2001, ss 104AA, 208F; FA 2009, s 30, Sch 11 para 9*].

Where a special rate car is disposed of and the anti-avoidance provisions in *CAA 2001, ss 217, 218* apply, the disposal value is taken as the lower of the market value of the car at date of disposal and the capital expenditure incurred, or treated as incurred on the provision of the car. The new owner qualifies for allowances on the disposal value brought into account by the disposing company.

Expenditure incurred prior to April 2009

Cars costing over £12,000

[12.17] Up to and including 31 March 2009, a different system operated for cars.

Qualifying expenditure (**11.2 CAPITAL ALLOWANCES — PLANT AND MACHINERY: ELIGIBLE EXPENDITURE AND INITIAL ALLOWANCES**) on a car costing over £12,000 could only be allocated to a single asset class pool.

Writing-down allowances (WDAs) were limited to a maximum of £3,000 per chargeable period (proportionately reduced or increased for chargeable periods of less or more than a year).

For expenditure incurred before 11 March 1992 or under a contract entered into before that date, these provisions apply to cars costing over *£8,000* and by reference to a maximum WDA of *£2,000*.

When an asset in its own pool is sold, the disposal proceeds are deducted from the pool. These proceeds are limited to original cost.

Where:

(i) Proceeds > tax written down value in the pool = Balancing charge
(ii) Proceeds < tax written down value in the pool = Balancing alowance

There are transitional provisions for cars or motorcycles forming single asset pools with a balance of expenditure on 1 April 2014. Until then, the same rules continue to apply.

Where a company's accounting period straddles that date, the balance on the single asset pool is transferred to the main pool (i.e. instead of being relieved by balancing allowance).

Where there is expenditure both before 1 April 2009 and on or after that date, the old and new expenditure is treated as incurred on separate assets, with just and reasonable apportionment, if necessary.

[*CAA 2001, ss 74–78, 81, 82, Sch 3 para 19; FA 2009, Sch 11; SI 1991 No 2874*].

See **13.27**(ii) **CAPITAL ALLOWANCES — PLANT AND MACHINERY: FIXTURES AND LEASING** for special rule determining the disposal value of a car within these provisions on a sale etc. to which the anti-avoidance provisions there mentioned apply.

See **71.9 TRADING EXPENSES AND DEDUCTIONS** as regards expenditure on *hiring* a car whose retail price when new exceeded £12,000 (previously £8,000) or, for expenditure on or after 1 April 2009, has CO2 emissions above 160 g/km.

Simon's Taxes. See **B3.342.**

Cars costing £12,000 or less

Cars costing £12,000 or less originally were included in a class pool of their own.

This requirement was abolished, for chargeable periods ending after 31 March 2000 (subject to election to defer this for one year), and qualifying expenditure on such cars was then allocated to the main pool

Under the new rules for cars brought inform 1 April 2009, cars that were already allocated to the main pool, remain so allocated.

Example

A company prepares accounts to 31 March. At 1 April 2010, the written down value brought forward is £100,000 on the general pool and £16,000 on a BMW car which had been owned for several years.

In the year the company bought an Audi car for £24,000 with CO2 emissions of 164g/km.

The capital allowances computation will be:

Y/e 31 March 2011	*General* Pool	BMW	*Special* Rate Pool	*Total* CAs
	£	£	£	£
Tax wdv b/f	100,000	16,000		
Addition – Audi CO2 > 160g/km			24,000	
WDA @ 20%	(20,000)			20,000
WDA @ 20% but restricted		(3,000)		3,000
WDA @ 10%			(2,400)	2,400
WDV c/f at 31.3.11	80,000	13,000	21,600	25,400

Note that the BMW originally cost more than £12,000 before April 2009, so it is kept in its own pool and the old rules apply.

The new Audi has emissions greater than 160g/km and so falls into the special rate pool with a writing down allowance of 10%.

Ships

[12.18] Qualifying expenditure (**11.2 CAPITAL ALLOWANCES — PLANT AND MACHINERY: ELIGIBLE EXPENDITURE AND INITIAL ALLOWANCES**) on the provision of a ship for the purposes of a trade or other qualifying activity can only be allocated to a *single asset pool* known as a *single ship pool*.

This does not apply if:

- an election is made to exclude such treatment (see below); or
- the qualifying activity is one of special leasing (**13.23 CAPITAL ALLOWANCES — PLANT AND MACHINERY: FIXTURES AND LEASING**); or
- the ship is otherwise provided for leasing (which expressly includes letting on charter), *unless* it is not used for 'overseas leasing' (other than 'protected leasing') at any time in the 'designated period' *and* it appears that it will be used only for a 'qualifying purpose' in that period (**13.14 CAPITAL ALLOWANCES — PLANT AND MACHINERY: FIXTURES AND LEASING** for meaning of expressions used here).

Disposal

When a disposal event occurs in relation to a single ship pool, the available qualifying expenditure in that pool for the chargeable period in question is transferred to the '*appropriate non-ship pool*' (i.e. the pool to which the expenditure would originally have been allocated in the absence of the single ship pool rules), and the single ship pool is brought to an end with no balancing allowance or charge.

The disposal value is brought into account in the pool now containing the qualifying expenditure.

In addition to the circumstances at **12.14**, a disposal event occurs if a ship is provided for leasing or letting on charter and begins to be used otherwise than for a 'qualifying purpose' at some time in the first four years of the 'designated period' (**13.17 CAPITAL ALLOWANCES — PLANT AND MACHINERY: FIXTURES AND LEASING**).

If the ship ceases to be used by the person who incurred the qualifying expenditure, without his having brought it into use for the purposes of the qualifying activity, then, in addition to any adjustments required as above, any writing-down allowances (WDAs) previously made (or postponed — see below) are withdrawn, and the amount withdrawn is allocated to the 'appropriate non-ship pool' for the chargeable period in question.

Election

A person who has incurred qualifying expenditure on a ship may elect, for any chargeable period, to disapply the single ship pool provisions in respect of:

- all or part of any qualifying expenditure that would otherwise be allocated to a single ship pool in that period; or
- all or part of the available qualifying expenditure already in a single ship pool,

with the result that the amount in question is allocated to the 'appropriate non-ship pool'.

The election must be made no later than two years after the end of the chargeable period in question.

Postponement of WDAs

A person entitled to a WDA for a chargeable period in respect of a single ship pool may, by written notice, postpone all or part of it to a later period.

The amount to be postponed must be specified in the notice.

Where a reduced WDA is claimed, all or part of the reduced amount may be postponed.

The time limits for giving notice are the same as for the election referred to immediately above.

Available qualifying expenditure is computed as if the postponed WDA had, in fact, been made.

Postponed WDAs may be claimed over one or more subsequent chargeable periods.

[*CAA 2001, ss 127–129, 130(2)(7), 131(1)(3)–(7), 132, 133, 157(1)*].

Deferment of balancing charges on qualifying ships

Balancing charges on ships may be deferred and set against subsequent expenditure on ships for a maximum of six years from the date of disposal. A claim for deferment of the whole or part of a balancing charge may be made by the shipowner where a disposal event within **12.14**(i)–(iv) above occurs after 20 April 1994 in relation to a 'qualifying ship' (the old ship).

A '*qualifying ship*' is, broadly, a ship of a sea-going kind of 100 gross registered tons or more, excluding offshore installations (as now defined by *CTA CTA 2010, s 1132*) and ships of a kind used or chartered primarily for sport or recreation (but passenger ships and cruise liners are not so excluded).

The provisions also apply to ships of less than 100 tons in cases where the old ship is totally lost or is damaged beyond worthwhile repair.

A ship brought into use in the trade on or after 20 July 1994 must within three months of first use (unless disposed of during those three months) be registered in the UK, the Channel Islands, Isle of Man, a colony (as to which see Revenue Tax Bulletin June 1998 p 553 and HMRC Capital Allowances Manual CA25230), a European Union State or a European Economic Area State and must continue to be so until at least three years from first use or, if earlier, until disposed of to an unconnected person.

It is a further condition that no amount in respect of the old ship has been allocated to an overseas leasing pool (**13.14 CAPITAL ALLOWANCES — PLANT AND MACHINERY: FIXTURES AND LEASING**), a 'partial use' single asset pool (**12.19**), a 'partial depreciation subsidy' single asset pool (**13.33**) or a pool for a qualifying activity consisting of special leasing (**13.23 CAPITAL ALLOWANCES — PLANT AND MACHINERY: FIXTURES AND LEASING**).

The balancing charge on the old ship is in effect calculated as if allowances had been granted, and the charge arises, in a single ship pool, with appropriate assumptions where that is not, in fact, the case (see *CAA 2001, s 139*, or for earlier chargeable periods *CAA 1990, s 33B*).

Deferment is achieved by allocating the amount deferred to the 'appropriate non-ship pool' (see above) for the chargeable period in question, so that it is effectively set against the disposal value brought into account in that pool (see above) as a result of the disposal event concerned.

Maximum deferment

The *maximum deferment* is the *lowest* of:

(i) the amount treated as brought into account in respect of the old ship under *CAA 2001, s 139* (see above);

(ii) the amount to be expended on new shipping (see below), so far as not already set against an earlier balancing charge, in the six years starting with the date of disposal of the old ship;

(iii) the amount which, in the absence of a deferment claim, would have been the total balancing charge for the chargeable period in question in the appropriate non-ship pool;

(iv) the amount needed to reduce the profit of the trade or other qualifying activity to nil (disregarding losses brought forward), no deferment being possible if no such profit has been made. If the amount actually expended within (ii) above turns out to be less than the amount deferred, the amount of the deficiency is reinstated as a balancing charge for the chargeable period to which the claim relates. (Before *CAA 2001* had effect (see **10.1 CAPITAL ALLOWANCES — INTRODUCTION**), the amount calculated at (iii) above could also include balancing charges in certain other pools and may therefore have been a larger amount.)

Where an amount is expended on new shipping within the six-year period allowed and is attributed by the shipowner, by notice to HMRC, to any part of an amount deferred, an amount equal to the amount so matched is brought into account as a disposal value, for the chargeable period in which the expenditure is incurred, in the single ship pool to which the expenditure is allocated, thus reducing the amount on which allowances may be claimed on the new ship.

No amount of expenditure can be attributed to a deferment if there is earlier expenditure on new shipping within the said six-year period which has not been attributed to that or earlier deferments. An attribution may be varied by the trader by notice to the inspector within a specified time (see *CAA 2001, s 142*, or for earlier chargeable periods *CAA 1990, s 33F(4)* and *FA 1995, s 98(6)(b)*).

For the purposes of these provisions, an amount is expended on new shipping if it is qualifying expenditure, incurred by the claimant wholly and exclusively for the purposes of a qualifying activity, on a ship (the new ship) which will be a qualifying ship (see above) for at least three years from first use or, if earlier, until disposed of to an unconnected person.

Expenditure is treated as incurred by the claimant if it is incurred by a successor following a partnership change or company reconstruction in consequence of which the qualifying activity was not treated as discontinued.

Expenditure incurred on a ship which has belonged to either the shipowner or a connected person within the previous six years or which is incurred mainly for tax avoidance reasons does not qualify.

The expenditure must be allocated to a single ship pool. If an election is made to disapply the single ship pool provisions, the expenditure is deemed never to have been expenditure on new shipping (but must nevertheless be treated as such in matching expenditure with deferments, so that the election prevents further matching of amounts already deferred).

Expenditure does not qualify if the overseas leasing provisions at **13.14 CAPITAL ALLOWANCES — PLANT AND MACHINERY: FIXTURES AND LEASING** come to apply to the new ship.

The claim

For corporation tax purposes, the claim for deferment must be made within two years after the end of the chargeable period of deferment.

Where a claim for deferment is found to be erroneous as a result of subsequent circumstances, the shipowner must, within three months after the end of the chargeable period in which those circumstances first arise, notify HMRC accordingly (failure to do so incurring a penalty under *TMA 1970, s 98*); consequential assessments may be made within twelve months after notice is given, notwithstanding normal time limits.

[*CAA 2001, ss 134–158, Sch 3 para 24; FA 2004, Sch 27 paras 9, 11; ITTOIA 2005, Sch 1 paras 542–544; SI 1996 No 1323; SI 1997 No 133*].

Simon's Taxes. See **B3.350–B3.353**.

Other plant and machinery

Partly used for non-trade

[12.19] Qualifying expenditure incurred partly for the purposes of the trade or other qualifying activity and partly for other purposes can only be allocated to a *single asset pool.*

Where in other cases plant or machinery *begins to be used* partly for other purposes, such that a disposal value falls to be brought into account (**12.14**(v) above) in a pool, an amount equal to the disposal value is allocated to a single asset pool for the chargeable period in question (but see **12.17** above as regards cars costing over £12,000 before 1 April 2009).

In respect of a single asset pool under these provisions, writing-down allowances and balancing allowances and charges are reduced to such amount as is just and reasonable (though the full amount is deducted in arriving at any unrelieved qualifying expenditure carried forward).

Where, after 20 March 2000, circumstances change such that the proportion of use for purposes other than those of the qualifying activity increases during a chargeable period, and the market value of the plant or machinery at the end of the period exceeds the available qualifying expenditure in the pool for that period by more than £1 million, then if no disposal value would otherwise fall to be brought into account for the period, a disposal value must be brought into account (equal to market value — see **12.14**(g) above) and, in the next or a subsequent chargeable period, an equivalent amount may be allocated to a new single asset pool as if it were qualifying expenditure newly incurred.

[*CAA 2001, ss 206–208, Sch 3 para 42*].

Kempster v McKenzie Ch D 1952, 33 TC 193.

G H Chambers (Northiam Farms) Ltd v Watmough Ch D 1956, 36 TC 711.

HMRC Capital Allowances Manual CA23530, 27100 as regards further adjustment for any element of personal choice.

Simon's Taxes. See B3.359.

Plant and machinery — partial depreciation subsidy

[12.20] In respect of which a **partial depreciation subsidy** is received, see **13.33 CAPITAL ALLOWANCES — PLANT AND MACHINERY: FIXTURES AND LEASING.**

Plant and machinery used for overseas leasing

[12.21] See **13.14 CAPITAL ALLOWANCES — PLANT AND MACHINERY: FIXTURES AND LEASING.**

Short-life assets

[12.22] A person who has incurred qualifying expenditure on an item of plant or machinery may elect for it to be treated as a short-life asset, provided it is not an excluded item.

Excluded items

Each of the following items of plant or machinery is excluded from being a short-life asset.

(i) A car, with the exception of cars hired out to persons receiving certain disability allowances or mobility supplements. For expenditure on or after 1 April 2009, a hire car for a disabled person is defined as a car wholly or mainly for hire to or use by a disabled person in the ordinary course of a trade. A 'disabled person' is a person in receipt of mobility allowance or supplement, disability living allowance or a similar payment.

(ii) A ship.

(iii) An item which is the subject of special leasing (**13.23 CAPITAL ALLOWANCES — PLANT AND MACHINERY: FIXTURES AND LEASING**).

(iv) An item acquired partly for the purposes of a trade or other qualifying activity and partly for other purposes.

(v) An item which is the subject of a partial depreciation subsidy (**13.33**).

(vi) An item received by way of gift or whose previous use by the person concerned did not attract capital allowances (**13.28, 13.29**) and, as regards long funding leasing, **13.4 CAPITAL ALLOWANCES — PLANT AND MACHINERY: FIXTURES AND LEASING**).

(vii) An item the expenditure on which is within the long-life asset provisions or, for expenditure incurred on or after 1 April 2008, special rate expenditure (**12.9**).

(viii) An item provided for leasing, unless it will be used within the 'designated period' for a 'qualifying purpose' (**13.18 CAPITAL ALLOWANCES — PLANT AND MACHINERY: FIXTURES AND LEASING**), and with the exception in any case of cars hired out to persons receiving certain disability allowances or mobility supplements.

(ix) An item leased overseas attracting only a 10% writing-down allowance (**13.15 CAPITAL ALLOWANCES — PLANT AND MACHINERY: FIXTURES AND LEASING**).

(x) An item leased to 2+ persons jointly such that *CAA 2001, s 116* applies (**13.20 CAPITAL ALLOWANCES — PLANT AND MACHINERY: FIXTURES AND LEASING**).

(xi) An item qualifying for a universal first-year allowance (**11.13 CAPITAL ALLOWANCES — PLANT AND MACHINERY: ELIGIBLE EXPENDITURE AND INITIAL ALLOWANCES**).

There is no requirement as to the expected useful life of the item, but short-life asset treatment will be of no practical benefit where the item remains in use for nine years or more. The election is irrevocable and must be made no later than two years after the end of the chargeable period in which the expenditure (or earliest expenditure) is incurred.

In general, HMRC will require sufficient information in support of an election to minimise the possibility of any difference of view at a later date (e.g. on a disposal) about what was and was not covered by the election, and to ensure that it does not incorporate any excluded items (see list below).

Where separate identification of short-life assets acquired in a chargeable period is either impossible or impracticable, e.g. similar small or relatively inexpensive items held in very large numbers, perhaps in different locations, then the information required in support of the election may be provided by reference to batches of acquisitions. (HMRC Statement of Practice 1/86).

The treatment

If a business acquires an asset and does not expect it to last for more than 8 years, the business can make an election to 'depool' that asset. For expenditure incurred prior to 1 April 2011 (for corporation tax) or 6 April 2011 (for income tax) the 8-year period was 4 years (*FA 2011, s 12*).

The effect of the election is that the asset is thereafter dealt with separately, i.e. the asset does not enter the general pool but instead stands on its own in a separate column. [*CAA 2001, s 85*].

The advantage of the asset being 'depooled' is that a balancing allowance will arise if the asset is sold at a loss within the 8-year period. This would not be the case if the asset was in the general pool. The short life asset election therefore has the effect of accelerating capital allowances into the year in which the asset is sold. [*CAA 2001, s 86*].

Strictly, each short-life asset should go into its own separate pool so that allowances on it are calculated separately. However this may not be practical where such assets are bought in large numbers. HMRC therefore accept that large numbers of short-life assets can be 'bunched' as long as the capital allowance computations give the correct statutory result and do not abuse the short life asset (SLA) provisions.

Example

BIG Industries plc is a large multinational company trading in the telecommunications sector. It draws accounts annually to 31 March.

In June 2010 the company bought 1,000 computer monitors for £200 each for use in its trade. The company expects the monitors to last for 21/2 years at which point it will sell them for £30 each. Its general pool at 1 April 2010 was £400,000.

BIG Industries plc is in a large group of companies. The AIA has already been used by other group companies hence no AIA is available to Big Industries plc.

Assuming no SLA election made

Expenditure (1,000 × £200 = £200,000) goes into the general pool and is written down as normal; and the sale in December 2012 (1,000 × £30 = £30,000) is treated as a disposal from the pool.

	General Pool	*CA claim*
Y/e 31.3.11:	£	£
WDV b/f	400,000	
Addition	200,000	
	600,000	
WDA @ 20%	(120,000)	120,000
WDV c/f	480,000	
Y/e 31.3.11:		
WDV b/f	480,000	
WDA @ 20%	(96,000)	96,000
WDV c/f	384,000	
Y/e 31.3.13:		
WDV b/f	384,000	
Disposal	(30,000)	
	354,000	
WDA @ 20%	(70,800)	70,800
WDV c/f	283,200	

Assuming SLA election made

Expenditure (1,000 × £200 = £200,000) goes into a separate 'short-life asset' pool and is written down; and the sale in December 2012 (1,000 × £30 = £30,000) is treated as a disposal from the SLA pool, giving rise to a balancing allowance.

	General Pool	*SLA*	*CA claim*
Y/e 31.3.11:	£	£	£
WDV b/f	400,000		
Addition		200,000	
WDA @ 20%	(80,000)	(40,000)	120,000
WDV c/f	320,000	160,000	
Y/e 31.3.12:			
WDV b/f	320,000	160,000	
WDA @ 20%	(64,000)	(32,000)	96,000
WDV c/f	256,000	128,000	
Y/e 31.3.13:			
WDV b/f	256,000	128,000	
Disposal		(30,000)	
Balancing Allowance		98,000	98,000
WDA @ 20%	(51,200)		51,200
WDV c/f	204,800		149,200

The effect of the SLA election has been to accelerate more capital allowances into the y/e 31 March 2013.

Choosing to make the election

If the asset is still in use more than eight years after the end of the year of acquisition (i.e. after **nine lots** of WDAs have been claimed on it), the **written down value is transferred to the general pool.**

Short-life asset elections are normally used by larger businesses incurring substantial expenditure since most smaller businesses will instead claim immediate tax relief by way of annual investment allowances. However, the reduction in the amount of AIA from £100,000 to £25,000 from April 2012 will make it likely that more businesses will wish to consider short-life asset elections.

Provided for leasing but used within designated period

The following applies where short-life asset treatment has been claimed on the basis that the item has been provided for leasing, but will be used within the 'designated period' for a 'qualifying purpose' (so is not excluded by (viii) above). (**13.14 CAPITAL ALLOWANCES — PLANT AND MACHINERY: FIXTURES AND LEASING**).

If, at any time in a chargeable period ending on or before the eight-year cut-off date (as above), the item begins to be used otherwise than for such a purpose, and that time falls within the first eight years of the 'designated period', the short-life asset pool is brought to an end at that time but with no balancing allowance or charge and no denial of a writing-down allowance for the final period.

The item ceases to be a short-life asset and the available qualifying expenditure in the pool is allocated, for the chargeable period in which that time falls, to the main pool (or, where appropriate and prior to its abolition, to the separate class pool for cars).

Disposal to a connected person

If at any time before the eight-year cut-off date, a short-life asset is disposed of to a connected person (within *CTA 2010, s 1122* — see **25 CONNECTED PERSONS**), short-life asset treatment continues in the connected person's hands (though the original eight-year cut-off date remains unchanged).

[*CAA 2001, ss 83–89, 240; ITEPA 2003, Sch 6 para 252*].

Simon's Taxes. See **B3.343**.

Disclaiming capital allowances

[12.23] There is no requirement for a company to claim all of the capital allowances due to them. In some instances it may be beneficial for a company to disclaim some (or all) of their capital allowances.

If a company disclaims capital allowances, this will lead to a higher tax written down value being carried forward which will, in turn, lead to higher capital allowances claims in future years.

Capital allowance claims can be timed to ensure that maximum relief is achieved for the expenditure incurred.

Final chargeable period

[12.24] For the 'final chargeable period', a balancing allowance is available, equal to the excess (if any) of (1) 'available qualifying expenditure' over (2) total disposal values.

If, for *any* chargeable period, (2) exceeds (1), there arises a liability to a balancing charge, equal to that excess.

The '*final chargeable period*', as regards the main pool and the special rate pool, is the chargeable period in which the trade or other qualifying activity is permanently discontinued.

As regards a single asset pool, it is normally the first chargeable period in which a disposal event (**12.14**) occurs.

As regards class pools, see **12.12** (long-life assets) and **13.14 CAPITAL ALLOWANCES — PLANT AND MACHINERY: FIXTURES AND LEASING** (overseas leasing).

Example

Caroline had owned a company that ran a gift card shop in Suffolk for many years. She drew accounts annually to 31 December.

On 31 October 2011 she sold her company to a major gift-card chain. As part of the total sales consideration she received £5,000 for her plant and machinery and £14,000 for her Lexus car.

The written down value brought forward on the general pool at 1 January 2011 was £6,000 and on the Lexus was £13,000. Business use of the Lexus was 60%. In May 2011 she had bought some new shelving for her shop at a cost of £1,500.

The capital allowances for the final period to 31 October 2011 are as follows:

	General Pool	*Lexus*	*CA claim*
P/e 31 October 2011	£	£	£
Tax wdv b/fwd	6,000	13,000	
Addition (shelving)	1,500		
	7,500		
Disposal of plant	(5,000)		
Disposal of car		(14,000)	
Balancing allowance	2,500		2,500
Balancing charge		(1,000)	(1,000)
Total for period			1,500

Note that no annual investment allowances at 100% are given on the shelving.

The balancing adjustment on the Lexus has not been apportioned for the private use as this only applies to unincorporated businesses.

Sale to connected person

Where on a cessation of trade the vendor sells his/her business to a 'connected person' the two parties can jointly elect to transfer all plant and machinery at its tax written down value (thereby avoiding a balancing adjustment on sale). This is most commonly seen when a sole trader incorporates his business [*CAA 2001, ss 266–267*].

Making of allowances and charges

[12.25] Plant and machinery allowances are treated as expenses of, and balancing charges are treated as receipts of, the trade, profession, vocation, property business, overseas property business, furnished holiday lettings business or *CTA 2009, s 39(4)* concern. [*CAA 2001, ss 247–252, 262; ITEPA 2003, Sch 6 para 253; ITTOIA 2005, Sch 1 paras 546, 547; CTA 2009, Sch 1 para 490; CTA 2009, Sch 1 para 475, 490*].

Allowances and charges are computed for corporation tax purposes by reference to events in accounting periods (see **10.1** CAPITAL ALLOWANCES — INTRODUCTION). [*CAA 2001, ss 2(1), 6(1)*].

See **13.23** CAPITAL ALLOWANCES — PLANT AND MACHINERY: FIXTURES AND LEASING as regards a qualifying activity of special leasing (as in **11.2**(vii) CAPITAL ALLOWANCES — PLANT AND MACHINERY: ELIGIBLE EXPENDITURE AND INITIAL ALLOWANCES).

See **10.3** CAPITAL ALLOWANCES — INTRODUCTION as regards the *claiming* of capital allowances.

Simon's Taxes. See B3.380–B3.386.

Comprehensive example

A Ltd is in business as a building and demolition contractor. Its business qualifies as a small business for the purposes of first-year allowances. The company makes up accounts to 31 March. The accounts for the year to 31 March 2010 reveal the following additions and disposals. A Ltd is not part of a group of companies and has no associates.

	£
Additions	
Plant	
Dumper Truck	5,000
Excavator	32,000
Bulldozer	30,000
	£67,000
Fittings	
Office furniture	£2,000

Motor Vehicles		
Land Rover		6,000
Van		5,000
Car 2 (CO2 emissions 150mg)		12,200
		£23,200

Disposals	Cost	Proceeds
	£	£
Excavator	32,000	25,000
Digger loader	15,000	2,500
Car 1	14,200	4,200
Fittings	3,500	500

The dumper truck was bought second-hand from Q Ltd, a company connected with A Ltd, but had not been used in a trade or other qualifying activity. The truck had originally cost Q Ltd £6,000, but its market value at sale was only £2,000.

The excavator was sold without having been brought into use.

The bulldozer was purchased from P Ltd, another connected company and had originally cost P Ltd £45,000. It had been used for the purposes of a qualifying activity, and the price paid by A Ltd was less than the market value.

The written-down values at 31 March 2009 of the main plant and machinery pool and Car 1 are £7,500 and £3,900 respectively.

The plant and machinery allowances for the accounting period ending on 31 March 2010 are:

	Expenditure qualifying for /AIA	Main Pool	Expensive car pools Car 1	Total allowances
	50%	25%		
	£	£	£	£
WDV b/f		7,500	3,900	
Additions				
Excavator (note (a))	32,000			
Dumper truck (notes (b)(c))		2,000		
Bulldozer (notes (b)(d))	5,000	25,000		
Furniture	2,000			
Land Rover and van	11,000			
Cars		12,200		
	50,000			
AIA (100%)	50,000			50,000
Disposals				
Excavator		(25,000)		
Digger		(2,500)		
Fittings		(500)		

Car 1		(4,200)	
	(18,700)	(£300)	
WDA (20%)	(3,740)		4,800
WDA (restricted)			3,000
WDV c/f	£14,960		
Total allowances			£57,800
Balancing charge			(£300)

Notes

(a) First-year allowances and writing-down allowances are available even though an item of plant or machinery is disposed of without being brought into use, always provided that the expenditure is qualifying expenditure.

(b) No AIA or first-year allowance is available in respect of an item of plant or machinery purchased from a connected person.

(c) Qualifying expenditure on the dumper truck is restricted to the lowest of:
  (i) market value;
  (ii) capital expenditure incurred by the vendor (or, if lower, by a person connected with him);
  (iii) capital expenditure incurred by the purchaser.

(d) Qualifying expenditure on the bulldozer is the lesser of A's actual expenditure and the disposal value brought into account in the vendor's computations. (The vendor's disposal value would have been market value but for the fact that the purchaser is himself entitled to claim capital allowances on the acquisition.) A's qualifying expenditure is thus equal to his actual expenditure.

(e) Car 2, as its emissions are less than 160 gm, is allocated to the main pool. By contrast, Car 1 was an expensive car and was in a single asset pool.

Key points

[12.26] Points to consider are as follows.

- From 1 April 2012 the rate of capital allowances in the main pool and the special rate pool will be reduced to 18% and 8% respectively. Where possible, it may be worth considering bringing expenditure forward to make use of the higher rates of relief.
- The Annual Investment Allowance should be allocated first to the special rate pool as this attracts the lowest writing down allowances.
- Where a main pool or special rate pool has a balance below £1,000 allowances can be claimed in one year to bring the balance to nil.

- The regime for cars underwent a significant overhaul for expenditure incurred after 31 March 2009. The rate of capital allowances is now based on how environmentally friendly a car is rather than its cost. Cars are no longer pooled separately (for companies) so balancing allowances are unlikely to be available upon a disposal unless the company ceases to trade. There are transitional rules which broadly cover situations where cars purchased prior to 1 April 2009 are still owned at 1 April 2014. At this date the cars are transferred to the general pool. If a company is expecting to sell a car for less than its written down value it is advisable to do so before the transfer to ensure the balancing allowance is still available.
- Where it is considered that a capital item which qualifies for capital allowances is likely to have a useful economic life of less than eight years (four years prior to 1 April 2011), that item should be pooled separately in order to claim balancing allowances on its disposal/scrappage. In order to make the most of short life asset elections a company should ensure that it tracks all disposals thoroughly to match them to the short life assets. It is not possible to elect for cars to be treated as short life assets.
- Capital allowances can be claimed in full, in part or not at all in a period. Where a trading company is expecting significant non-trading profits in a future year or where it is part of a group and may be able to surrender losses in a future year it is likely to be worth considering whether it is more tax advantageous to carry forward a higher pool to a future period.

13

Capital Allowances — Plant and Machinery: Fixtures and Leasing

Cross references. See **10 CAPITAL ALLOWANCES — INTRODUCTION; 11 CAPITAL ALLOWANCES — PLANT AND MACHINERY: ELIGIBLE EXPENDITURE AND INITIAL ALLOWANCES; 12 CAPITAL ALLOWANCES — PLANT AND MACHINERY: POOLING AND DISPOSALS; 14 CAPITAL ALLOWANCES — MINERAL EXTRACTION; 15 CAPITAL ALLOWANCES — BUILDINGS** and **16 CAPITAL ALLOWANCES — MISCELLANEOUS.**

Other sources. See Tolley's Capital Allowances.

Simon's Taxes. See Part B3.

Fixtures

Introduction

[13.1] There are special provisions to determine entitlement to allowances on fixtures. The issue of whether fixtures and fittings qualify as plant is discussed in the HMRC Capital Allowances Manual CA21200, but generally HMRC accept that they will qualify 'if they are of a permanent and durable nature ... and they were bought for the purposes of the trade'.

A dispute may arise as to whether fixtures have, in law, become part of a building or land.

Where two or more persons' tax liabilities are affected by the outcome of such a dispute, the question is determined for tax purposes by the tribunal, before whom all those persons are entitled to appear and be heard or to make written representations. [*CAA 2001, ss 172(1)(2), 173, 204(1)–(3)*].

Interest in land

[13.2] For the purposes of the fixtures provisions, an '*interest in land*' means:

(i) the fee simple estate in the land;
(ii) in Scotland, in the case of feudal property prior to abolition of feudal tenure, the estate or interest of the proprietor of the *dominium utile*, and in any other case, the interest of the owner;
(iii) a lease (defined for these provisions in relation to land as any leasehold estate in (or, in Scotland, lease of) the land (whether a head-lease, sub-lease or under-lease) or any agreement to acquire such an estate (or lease));
(iv) an easement or servitude;
(v) a licence to occupy land,

and any agreement to acquire an interest as in (i)–(iv) above. Where an interest is conveyed or assigned by way of security subject to a right of redemption, the interest is treated as continuing to belong to the person having the redemption right. [*CAA 2001, ss 174(4), 175, Sch 3 para 29*]. As regards (v) above, for the HMRC view of when a licence to occupy land exists for these purposes, see HMRC Capital Allowances Manual CA26100).

See generally HMRC Capital Allowances Manual CA26000 *et seq.*

Ownership of fixtures for capital allowances

[13.3] These provisions determine ownership for capital allowances purposes of plant or machinery that is or becomes a fixture and determine entitlement to allowances in each of the various circumstances described at (a)–(f) below.

(a) Expenditure incurred by holder of interest in land

Subject to the election in (b) or (f) below, the fixture is treated as belonging to the holder of the interest.

If there are two or more such persons, with different interests, the only interest to be taken into account for this purpose is:

(i) an easement or servitude, or any agreement to acquire same;
(ii) if (i) does not apply to any of those interests, a licence to occupy the land;
(iii) if neither (i) nor (ii) applies to any of those interests, that interest which is not directly or indirectly in reversion on any other of those interests in the land (in Scotland, that of whichever of those persons has, or last had, the right of use of the land).

[*CAA 2001, s 176*].

(b) Expenditure incurred by equipment lessor

An 'equipment lease' exists where:

- a person incurs capital expenditure on an item of plant or machinery for leasing;
- an agreement is entered into for the lease, directly or indirectly from that person (the '*equipment lessor*'), of the item to another person (the '*equipment lessee*');
- the item becomes a fixture; and
- the item is not leased as part of the land in relation to which it is a fixture.

Such an agreement, or a lease entered into under such an agreement, is an '*equipment lease*'.

Provided that:

(i) under the equipment lease, the plant or machinery is leased for the purposes of a trade or other qualifying activity carried on (or to be carried on in future) by the equipment lessee;
(ii) it is not for use in a dwelling-house;
(iii) the equipment lessor and equipment lessee are not **CONNECTED PERSONS (25)**;
(iv) if the expenditure on the fixture had been incurred by the equipment lessee, he would have been entitled to allowances under (a) above,

the lessor and lessee may jointly elect for the fixture to be treated, from the time the expenditure is incurred by the equipment lessor (or, if later, from the commencement of the lessee's qualifying activity), as owned by the lessor and not the lessee.

Conditions

Where the following conditions are met, (i) and (iv) above do not have to be satisfied (and the potentially later start date of the election is not relevant):

(1) the plant or machinery becomes a fixture by being fixed to land which is neither a building nor part of a building;
(2) the lessee has an interest in that land when he takes possession of the plant or machinery under the equipment lease;
(3) under the terms of the equipment lease the lessor is entitled, at the end of the lease period, to sever the plant or machinery from the land to which it is then fixed, whereupon it will be owned by the lessor;
(4) the nature of the plant or machinery and the way it is fixed to the land are such that its use does not, to any material extent, prevent its being used, after severance, for the same purposes on different premises; and
(5) the equipment lease is such as falls under generally accepted accounting practice to be treated in the accounts of the equipment lessor as an operating lease.

The election must be made within two years after the end of the equipment lessor's chargeable period in which the expenditure is incurred.

Where expenditure is incurred on or after 28 July 2000 and before 1 January 2008 on plant or machinery consisting of a boiler, heat exchanger, radiator or heating control installed in a building as part of a space or water heating system, and the equipment lease is approved under the Affordable Warmth programme by the Secretary of State (or the responsible Scottish, Welsh or Northern Ireland body), these provisions have effect without (i)–(ii) and (iv) above having to be satisfied.

If the approval is withdrawn, it is treated as never having had effect. The taxpayer must notify the inspector, within three months of his becoming aware that a return of his has become incorrect by reason of the withdrawal of approval, of the amendments to the return required in consequence of the withdrawal, subject to penalties for failure.

[*CAA 2001, ss 174(1)–(3), 177–180, 203, Sch 3 paras 30–33*].

(c) Expenditure in consideration for acquisition of existing land interest

Where a person acquires a pre-existing interest in land to which a fixture is attached, for a consideration in part treated for capital allowance purposes as being expenditure on provision of the fixture, the fixture is treated as belonging to the person acquiring the interest.

This applies equally where the fixture in question was previously let under an 'equipment lease' (see (b) above) and, in connection with the acquisition, the purchaser pays a capital sum to discharge the equipment lessee's obligations under that lease.

For accounting periods ending after 31 March 2001, it also applies where the fixture was provided under an energy services agreement (see (f) below) and, in connection with the acquisition, the purchaser pays a capital sum to discharge the client's obligations under that agreement.

[*CAA 2001, ss 181(1)(4), 182(1), 182A(1), Sch 3 paras 34, 35*].

Where the above provisions would otherwise apply, they are treated as not applying (and as never having applied) where:

(i) a person is treated as the owner of the fixture (other than under *CAA 2001, s 538* (contributions to expenditure — see **10.8 CAPITAL ALLOWANCES — INTRODUCTION**) immediately before the time of the above acquisition, in consequence of having incurred expenditure on its provision; and

(ii) that person is entitled to, and claims, an allowance in respect of that expenditure.
[*CAA 2001, ss 181(2)(3), 182(2)(3), 182A(2)(3), 203*].

(d) Costs incurred by incoming lessee — election to transfer entitlement

Where a person with an interest in land to which a fixture is attached grants a lease and that person would (or if chargeable to tax would) be entitled, for the chargeable period in which the lease is granted, to capital allowances in respect of the fixture, and the consideration given by the lessee falls, in whole or in part, to be treated for plant and machinery allowances purposes as expenditure on the provision of the fixture, an election is available to the lessor and lessee.

They may jointly elect (by notice to HMRC within two years after the date on which the lease takes effect) that, from the grant of the lease, the fixture is treated as belonging to the lessee and not to the lessor.

No such election is available if lessor and lessee are **CONNECTED PERSONS (25)**, or (where the lease was granted before 24 July 1996) if it appears that the sole or main benefit to the lessor from the grant of the lease and the election would be enhanced capital allowances or a reduced balancing charge; see now the anti-avoidance provision at *CAA 2001, s 197* below.

The instant provisions apply to the entering into of an agreement for a lease as they apply to a grant of a lease. [*CAA 2001, ss 174(4), 183, Sch 3 para 36*].

(e) Expenditure incurred by incoming lessee — lessor not entitled

Where:

- a person with an interest in land to which a fixture is attached grants a lease;
- the provisions at (d) above do not apply, because the lessor is not entitled to capital allowances in respect of the fixture;
- before the lease is granted, the fixture has not been used for the purposes of a trade or other qualifying activity by the lessor or a person connected with the lessor (see **25 CONNECTED PERSONS**); and
- the consideration given by the lessee includes a capital sum falling, in whole or in part, to be treated for plant and machinery allowances purposes as expenditure on the provision of the fixture,

the fixture is treated as belonging to the lessee from the time the lease is granted.

[*CAA 2001, s 184, Sch 3 para 37*].

(f) Expenditure incurred by energy services provider

An '*energy services agreement*' is an agreement entered into by an 'energy services provider' and his client that provides, with a view to the saving or more efficient use of energy, for:

- the design of plant or machinery or of systems incorporating it;
- the obtaining and installation of the plant or machinery; and
- its operation and maintenance,

and under which any payment by the client in respect of the operation of the plant or machinery is wholly or partly linked to the energy savings or increased energy efficiency.

An '*energy services provider*' is a person carrying on a qualifying activity consisting wholly or mainly in providing energy management services. [*CAA 2001, s 175A*].

For corporation tax accounting periods ending after 31 March 2001, where:

- an energy services agreement is entered into;
- the energy services provider incurs capital expenditure after 31 March 2001 under the agreement on an item of plant or machinery;
- the item becomes a fixture;
- at the time the item becomes a fixture, the client has an interest in the land in relation to which it is a fixture but the provider does not;
- the item is neither leased nor used in a dwelling-house;
- the operation of the item is carried out wholly or substantially by the provider or a person connected with him; and
- provider and client are not **CONNECTED PERSONS (25)**,

the energy services provider and the client may jointly elect for the fixture to be treated, from the time the expenditure is incurred, as owned by the former and not the latter.

This opens the way for the energy services provider to claim 100% first-year allowances where his expenditure is within **11.13 CAPITAL ALLOWANCES — PLANT AND MACHINERY: ELIGIBLE EXPENDITURE AND INITIAL ALLOWANCES.**

The election must be made no later than two years after the end of the accounting period in which the expenditure is incurred.

If the client would not have been entitled to allowances under (a) above if he had incurred the expenditure himself, the election is available only if the item belongs to the:

(i) technology class 'Combined Heat and Power' in the Energy Technology Criteria List, as specified by Treasury order *SI 2001 No 2541* and *SI 2007 No 2165*; or
(ii) any other class of plant or machinery specified for this purpose by Treasury order.

The intention is that, in such specified cases, allowances to the provider are not to be denied only because the client is a non-taxpayer. [*CAA 2001, s 180A*]. See also HMRC Capital Allowances Manual CA23150.

Cessation of ownership

(A) If a person is treated as owning a fixture under *CAA 2001, s 176* (see (a) above) *ss 181, 182* or *182A* (see (c) above), *s 183* (see (d) above) or *s 184* (see (e) above), that person is treated as ceasing to be the owner if and on ceasing to have the 'qualifying interest'.
The '*qualifying interest*' is the interest in the land in question, except that where (d) or (e) above apply it is the lease there referred to. There are rules (see *CAA 2001, s 189*) for identifying the qualifying interest in special cases.

(B) Where, under (d) above, the lessee begins to be treated as owning the fixture, the lessor is treated as ceasing to own it at that time.

(C) Where a fixture is permanently severed from the building or land, such that it is no longer owned by the person treated as owning it, that person is treated as ceasing to own it at the time of severance.

(D) Where an equipment lessor is treated as owning a fixture (see (b) above) and either the lessor assigns the rights under the equipment lease or the financial obligations of the equipment lessee (or the assignee etc.) are discharged, the equipment lessor is treated as ceasing to own the fixture at that time (or the earliest of those times).

(E) Where an energy services provider is treated as owning a fixture (see (f) above) and either the provider assigns the rights under the energy services agreement or the financial obligations of the client (or the assignee etc.) are discharged, the energy services provider is treated as ceasing to own the fixture at that time (or the earliest of those times).

[*CAA 2001, ss 188–192A*].

Disposal value

The *disposal value* to be brought into account in relation to a fixture depends upon the nature of the event.

(1) On cessation of ownership under (A) above due to a sale of the qualifying interest (other than where (2) below applies), and subject to the election below, it is that part of the sale price that falls (or would, if there were an entitlement, fall) to be treated for plant and machinery allowances purposes as expenditure by the purchaser on the provision of the fixture.

(2) On cessation of ownership under (A) above due to a sale of the qualifying interest at less than market value (unless the buyer (not being a dual resident investing company connected with the seller) can claim plant or machinery or research and development (formerly scientific research) allowances for his expenditure, in which case (1) above applies), it is the amount that, if that interest were sold at market value (determined without regard to the disposal event itself) at that time, would be treated for plant and machinery allowances purposes as expenditure by the purchaser on provision of the fixture.

(3) On cessation of ownership under (A) above where neither (1) or (2) above applies but the qualifying interest continues (or would do so but for being merged with another interest), it is an amount determined as in (2) above.

(4) On cessation of ownership under (A) above due to the expiry of the qualifying interest, it is any capital sum received by reference to the fixture, or otherwise nil.

(5) On cessation of ownership under (B) above, and subject to the election below, it is that part of the capital sum given by the lessee for the lease as qualifies for plant and machinery allowances as the lessee's expenditure on the fixture.

(6) On cessation of ownership under (C) above, it is market value at time of severance.

(7) On cessation of ownership under (D) above, it is the consideration for the assignment or, as the case may be, the capital sum, if any, paid to discharge the equipment lessee's financial obligations.

(8) On cessation of ownership under (E) above, it is the consideration for the assignment or, as the case may be, the capital sum, if any, paid to discharge the client's financial obligations.

(9) On permanent discontinuance of the trade or other qualifying activity followed by the sale of the qualifying interest, it is an amount determined as in (1) above.

(10) On permanent discontinuance of the qualifying activity followed by demolition or destruction of the fixture, it is the net amount received for the remains, plus any insurance or capital compensation received.

(11) On permanent discontinuance of the qualifying activity followed by permanent loss (other than as in (10) above) of the fixture, it is any insurance or capital compensation received.

(12) On the fixture's beginning to be used wholly or partly for purposes other than those of the qualifying activity, it is that part of the sale price that would fall to be treated for plant and machinery allowances purposes as expenditure by the purchaser on the provision of the fixture if the qualifying interest were sold at market value.

'Notional written down value' and avoidance

Fixtures are treated as disposed of at their 'notional written-down value' (if greater than would otherwise be the case) where the disposal event is part of a scheme or arrangement having tax avoidance (whether by increased allowances or reduced charges) as a main object.

The '*notional written-down value*' is qualifying expenditure on the item in question less maximum allowances to date, computed on the assumption that all allowances have been made in full. [*CAA 2001, s 197*].

Election

A special election is available where the disposal value of fixtures falls to be determined under (1) or (5) above at a time on or after 19 March 1996.

Subject as below and to *CAA 2001, ss 186, 187* (see below) and *s 197* (above), the seller and purchaser (or, where (5) above applies, the lessor and lessee under (d) above) may jointly elect to fix the amount so determined at a figure not exceeding either the capital expenditure treated as incurred on the fixtures by the seller (or lessor) former owner or the actual sale price (or capital sum). The remainder (if any) of the sale price (or capital sum) is attributed to the other property included in the sale.

The notice of election must be given within two years after the interest is acquired (or the lease granted), and is irrevocable.

A copy must also accompany the return of the persons making the election.

The notice must contain prescribed information and must quantify the amount fixed by the election, although if subsequent circumstances reduce the maximum below that fixed, the election is treated as being for that reduced maximum amount.

Where a person has made a tax return and becomes aware that it has become incorrect because of such an election (or because of subsequent circumstances affecting the election), the necessary amendments to the return must be notified to HMRC within three months of his becoming so aware, subject to penalties for failure. [*CAA 2001, ss 198–201, 203, 204(4)–(6)*].

In practice, HMRC normally accept an election covering a group of fixtures, or all the fixtures in a single property, but not one covering fixtures in different properties (e.g. where a portfolio of properties is sold) (HMRC Capital Allowances Manual CA28600).

Acquisition of ownership in certain cases

If, on the termination of a lease, the outgoing lessee is treated under (A) above as ceasing to own a fixture, the lessor is thereafter treated as the owner. This applies in relation to a licence as it does in relation to a lease. [*CAA 2001, s 193*].

The following apply where an election is made under (b) above (election to treat fixture as owned by equipment lessor), and either:

- the equipment lessor assigns his rights under the equipment lease; or
- the equipment lessee's financial obligations under the lease (or those of his assignee etc.) are discharged (on the payment of a capital sum).

If the former applies, then, from the time of the assignment, the fixture is treated as belonging to the assignee for capital allowance purposes, and the consideration for the assignment treated as consideration given by him on provision of the fixture. If the assignee makes any further assignment, he is treated under this provision as if he were the original lessor.

If the latter applies, the capital sum is treated as consideration for the fixture, and the fixture is treated from the time of the payment as belonging to the equipment lessee (or to any other person in whom his obligations under the lease have become vested).

[*CAA 2000, ss 194, 195*].

The same applies, with appropriate modifications, where the election in question was under (f) above (election to treat fixture as owned by energy services provider). [*CAA 2001, ss 195A, 195B*].

Restriction of qualifying expenditure where allowance previously claimed

Where:

(i) a fixture is treated under these provisions as belonging to any person (the current owner) in consequence of his incurring capital expenditure on its provision;

(ii) the plant or machinery is treated (other than under *CAA 2001, s 538* — contributions to expenditure, see **10.8 CAPITAL ALLOWANCES — INTRODUCTION**) as having belonged at a 'relevant earlier time' to a person (who may be the same as the person within (i) above) in consequence of his incurring expenditure other than that within (i) above; and that person, having claimed a plant and machinery allowance for that expenditure, must bring a disposal value into account *by reason of an event occurring after 23 July 1996*,

so much (if any) of the expenditure referred to in (i) above as exceeds the 'maximum allowable amount' is left out of account in determining the current owner's qualifying expenditure or, as the case may be, is taken to be expenditure which should never have been so taken into account.

Relevant earlier time

A '*relevant earlier time*' is any time before the earliest time when the plant or machinery is treated as belonging to the current owner in consequence of the expenditure referred to in (i) above.

The relevant earlier time does not, however, include any time before an earlier sale of the plant or machinery other than as a fixture and other than between **CONNECTED PERSONS (25)**.

Maximum allowable amount

The '*maximum allowable amount*' is the sum of the disposal value referred to in (ii) above and so much (if any) of the expenditure referred to in (i) above as is deemed under *CAA 2001, s 25* (installation costs, **11.3 CAPITAL ALLOWANCES — PLANT AND MACHINERY: ELIGIBLE EXPENDITURE AND INITIAL ALLOWANCES**) to be on provision of the plant or machinery.

Where (ii) above is satisfied in relation to more than one disposal event, only the most recent event is taken into account for this purpose.

Where a person has made a return and becomes aware that it has become incorrect because of the operation of this provision, the necessary amendments to the return must be notified to HMRC within three months of his becoming so aware, subject to penalties for failure.

[*CAA 2001, ss 185, 203, Sch 3 para 38*].

Restriction

Where:

(I) a person has claimed industrial buildings allowances for expenditure partly on the provision of plant or machinery, and transfers the relevant interest in the building concerned; and

(II) the transferee, or any other person to whom the plant or machinery is subsequently treated under these provisions as belonging, claims plant and machinery allowances for expenditure incurred thereon *at a time after 23 July 1996* when it is a fixture in the building, the qualifying expenditure in respect of which the claim in (II) above is made is restricted to the '*relevant amount*', i.e. the proportion of the consideration for the transfer referred to in (I) above attributable to the fixture.

It is assumed for this purpose that the transfer was a sale for an amount equal to the residue of expenditure (**15.7 CAPITAL ALLOWANCES — BUILDINGS**) immediately after the transfer.

A similar restriction applies where research and development (formerly scientific research) allowances have previously been claimed.

[*CAA 2001, ss 186, 187, Sch 3 paras 39, 40*].

Simon's Taxes. See **B3.355–B3.358.**

Finance leasing

See **71.44 TRADING EXPENSES AND DEDUCTIONS** as regards restrictions on capital allowances where certain finance leasing arrangements are involved.

Long funding leasing

Introduction

[13.4] The rules on leasing of plant and machinery were reformed by *FA 2006, s 81, Sch 8* as set out below with effect from, broadly, **1 April 2006.**

A new regime was brought in for 'long funding' leases from 1 April 2006.

FA 2011, s 33 introduced legislation to counter a tax avoidance scheme which had the claimed effect of giving a lessee of plant and machinery tax relief of up to twice the actual cost (**13.8** *FA 2011* changes).

Broadly, '*long funding*' leases are leases of more than 5 years and the rules cover both operating and finance leases.

The substance of a long funding finance lease is that the lessor (the legal owner of the plant and machinery) is effectively lending money to the lessee (the person using the asset) to enable the lessee to buy the plant and machinery.

The way in which a long funding lease is taxed is therefore to treat the lessee as the owner of the plant and machinery who has purchased the plant and machinery by way of a loan. The lessor is effectively the finance provider.

Therefore the lessee claims capital allowances as if he owned the plant and machinery.

Consequently, any deductions the lessee has made for depreciation expense must be added back for tax purposes, since capital allowances are given to the lessee instead.

[*CAA 2001, s 70A*].

Definitions

[13.5] The following definitions apply for these purposes.

(1) 'Long funding lease'

This is a 'funding lease' (see (2) below) that is not:

- a 'short lease' (see (A) below);
- an 'excluded lease of background plant or machinery for a building' (see (B) below);
- excluded under the *de minimis* provision at (C) below for plant or machinery leased with land.

Change in activity

Where, at the 'commencement' (see *CAA 2001, s 70YI(1)*) of the term of a plant or machinery lease (as widely defined by *CAA 2001, s 70K*), the plant or machinery is not being used for the purposes of a qualifying activity, but subsequently is so used, the lease is a long funding lease if it would otherwise have been a long funding lease at its 'inception' (see *CAA 2001, s 70YI(1)*); this covers, for example, the situation where either the lessor or the lessee is originally non-UK resident and subsequently becomes UK resident.

Conditions

However, the treatment of a lease as a long funding lease as regards the *lessee* is always subject to the following two conditions.

(1) The lessee must treat the lease as a long funding lease in his first tax return (and thus his first accounts) the profits declared by which are affected by the question of whether or not the lease is a long funding lease. That tax return cannot be altered in this respect by a subsequent error or mistake claim.

(2) A lease is not a long funding lease as regards the lessee if either the lessor or any superior lessor under a chain of leases (as defined) is entitled, at the commencement of the term of the lease, to any capital allowance (not necessarily a plant or machinery allowance) in respect of the leased plant or machinery. This also applies if such entitlement would have arisen but for *CAA 2001, s 70V* (see below under Miscellaneous: Tax avoidance involving international leasing). It also applies if the entitlement arose at an earlier time but no requirement has yet arisen to bring into account a disposal value as described below under Lessors. These conditions are applied on the assumption that the lessor in question is within the charge to UK tax, even if that is not, in fact, the case. However, where the inception of the lease is before 28 June 2006 and the lessor remains entitled to capital allowances by virtue only of the exception under (2)(iii) below the lease is still regarded as a long funding lease as regards the lessee.

Certain leases held by tonnage tax companies are not to be treated as being long funding leases (see **70.76 PROFIT COMPUTATIONS**).

[*CAA 2001, ss 70G, 70H, 70Q; FA 2006, Sch 8 para 7*].

Exclusions from long funding leases

The above-mentioned exclusions from long funding lease treatment are defined in (A)–(C) below.

Exclusion (A)

A '*short lease*' is defined as a lease whose term is five years or less or, if three conditions are met, a lease whose term is more than five years but no more than seven. (The 'term' of a lease is defined by *CAA 2001, s 70YF*.)

The first two conditions are that the:

(i) lease falls to be treated under GAAP as a finance lease; and
(ii) residual value of the plant or machinery implied in the terms of the lease must not be more than 5% of its market value at commencement of the lease term.

The third condition compares the lease rentals due in each year of the lease term (ignoring any variations resulting from changes in published interest rates); the total rentals due in Year 1 must not be more than 10% less than those due in Year 2, and the total rentals due in any of Years 3 to 7 must not be more than 10% greater than those due in Year 2.

There is an anti-avoidance rule at *s 70I(9)* (effective for leases entered into on or after 7 April 2006) aimed at preventing arrangements between **CONNECTED PERSONS (25)** being used to create artificially short leases. [*CAA 2001, ss 70I, 70YI(4); FA 2006, Sch 8 para 7*].

Exclusion (B)

An '*excluded lease of background plant or machinery for a building*' occurs where 'background plant or machinery' is affixed to (or otherwise installed in or on) land that consists of (or includes) a building and is leased with that land under a 'mixed lease' (as defined by *CAA 2001, s 70L* — broadly a lease of plant or machinery plus other assets — see also below under Miscellaneous — Mixed leases).

'*Background plant or machinery*' is plant or machinery of such description as might reasonably be expected to be installed in various buildings and whose sole or main purpose is to contribute to the functioning of the building or its site as an environment in which activities can be carried on. The Treasury has supplemented this definition in *SI 2007 No 303*.

Background plant and machinery

The following are examples of plant and machinery that may fall within the definition of background plant and machinery in the building:

(i) heating and air conditioning installations;
(ii) ceilings which are part of an air conditioning system;
(iii) hot water installations;
(iv) electrical installations that provide power to a building, such as high and low voltage switchgear, all sub-mains distribution systems and standby generators;
(v) mechanisms, including automatic control systems, for opening and closing doors, windows and vents;
(vi) escalators and passenger lifts;
(vii) window cleaning installations;

(viii) fittings such as fitted cupboards, blinds, curtains and associated mechanical equipment;
(ix) demountable partitions;
(x) protective installations, such as lightning protection, sprinkler and other equipment for containing fires, fire alarm systems and fire escapes; and
(xi) building management systems.

Not background plant and machinery

However, the above is subject to the list of plant or machinery *not* deemed to be background plant or machinery if it is used as follows:

(i) for storing, moving or displaying goods to be sold in the course of a wholesale or retail trade;
(ii) manufacturing goods or materials;
(iii) processing goods or materials;
(iv) storing goods or materials for manufacture or storing manufactured or imported goods pending delivery.

Deemed background plant and machinery

The following are deemed to be background plant or machinery:

(i) lighting installations including all fixed light fittings and emergency lighting systems;
(ii) telephone, audio-visual and data installations incidental to the occupation of the building;
(iii) computer networking facilities incidental to the occupation of the building;
(iv) sanitary appliances and other bathroom fittings including hand driers, counters, partitions, mirrors, shower and locker facilities;
(v) kitchen and catering facilities for producing and storing food and drink for the occupants of the building;
(vi) fixed seating;
(vii) signs;
(viii) public address systems; and
(ix) intruder alarm systems and other security equipment including surveillance equipment.

[*SI 2007 No 303*].

There are anti-avoidance provisions to prevent this exclusion from applying if a main purpose of the mixed lease (or of transactions of which it is part) is to entitle the lessor to capital allowances on the background plant or machinery or if the rentals vary according to the value of allowances available to the lessor. [*CAA 2001, ss 70R–70T; FA 2006, Sch 8 para 7*].

Exclusion (C)

The *de minimis* provision referred to above applies in a case in which relatively small amounts of plant and machinery are leased with land and the exclusion at (B) above would have applied but for the plant or machinery not being 'background plant or machinery'. The lease is excluded from long funding lease treatment if, at commencement of its term, the aggregate market value of all such plant or machinery does not exceed 10% of the aggregate market value of any 'background plant or machinery' leased with the land *and* does not exceed 5% of the market value of the land (including buildings and fixtures and assuming an absolute interest). [*CAA 2001, s 70U; FA 2006, Sch 8 para 7*].

A '*funding lease*'

This is a plant or machinery lease (as widely defined by *CAA 2001, s 70K*) which does not fall within one of the exceptions below and meets one or more of the:

(i) 'finance lease test'; or
(ii) 'lease payments test'; or
(iii) 'useful economic life test'.

A plant or machinery lease whose inception is on or after 1 April 2010 is automatically a funding lease if the plant or machinery is cushion gas, i.e. gas that functions, or is intended to function, as plant in a particular gas storage facility. [*FA 2010, s 28*].

Finance lease test

A lease meets the '*finance lease test*' as regards any person if it is one that, under GAAP, falls (or would fall) to be treated in that person's accounts as either a finance lease or a loan.

A lease also meets the finance lease test as regards *the lessor* if it is one that, under GAAP, falls (or would fall) to be so treated in the accounts of a person connected with him (within **25 CONNECTED PERSONS**).

The Treasury has power to vary the finance lease test by statutory instrument.

Lease payment test

A lease meets the '*lease payments test*' if the present value of the 'minimum lease payments' (see (5) below) is not less than 80% of the 'fair value' of the leased plant or machinery.

Present value is calculated using the interest rate implicit in the lease (applying normal commercial criteria including GAAP or, in default, the temporal discount rate contained in *FA 2005, s 70* or amending regulations).

'*Fair value*' means market value less any grants receivable towards the purchase or use of the plant or machinery.

Useful economic life test

A lease meets the '*useful economic life test*' if the term of the lease exceeds 65% of the remaining useful economic life (see *CAA 2001, s 70YI(1)*) of the leased plant or machinery. (The 'term' of a lease is defined by *CAA 2001, s 70YF*.)

***Exceptions* to being a funding lease**

The following are not funding leases:

(i) A contract within **13.24**(A) (hire-purchase contracts etc.).

(ii) If, before the 'commencement' (see *CAA 2001, s 70YI(1)*) of its term, the lessor has leased the same plant or machinery under one or more other plant or machinery leases, none of which were funding leases, and the aggregate term of those other leases exceeds 65% of the remaining useful economic life of the plant or machinery at the commencement of the earliest lease (for this purpose only, any person who was a lessor under a pre-1 April 2006 lease is treated as the same person as the lessor under the first post-1 April 2006 lease).

(iii) A lease is not a funding lease as regards the lessor if, before 1 April 2006, the plant or machinery had, for a period or periods totalling at least ten years, been the subject of one or more leases and the lessor was also the lessor of the plant or machinery on the last day before 1 April 2006 on which it was leased.

[*CAA 2001, ss 70J, 70N–70P, 70YI(4), 70YJ; FA 2006, Sch 8 para 7*].

(3) A '*long funding operating lease*'

This is any long funding lease that is not a long-funding finance lease within (4) below. [*CAA 2001, s 70YI(1); FA 2006, Sch 8 para 7*].

(4) A '*long funding finance lease*'

This is a long funding lease that meets the *finance lease test* at (2) above (disregarding the connected persons rule). [*CAA 2001, s 70YI(1); FA 2006, Sch 8 para 7*].

(5) Minimum lease payments

The '*minimum lease payments*' are the minimum payments under the lease over the term of the lease (including any initial payment).

In the case of the lessee, they also include so much of any 'residual amount' as is guaranteed by him or a person connected with him. In the case of the lessor, they also include so much of any 'residual amount' as is guaranteed by the lessee or a person who is not connected with the lessor.

Any payment representing charges for services or representing 'taxes' to be paid by the lessor must be excluded from 'minimum payments' for the purposes of this definition. ('*Taxes*' means UK or foreign taxes or duties, but not income tax, corporation tax or foreign equivalents.)

'*Residual amount*' means so much of the 'fair value' (see the 'lease payments test' in (2) above) of the plant or machinery subject to the lease as cannot reasonably be expected to be recovered by the lessor from the payments under the lease. [*CAA 2001, s 70YE; FA 2006, Sch 8 para 7*].

This definition of 'minimum lease payments' is based on GAAP (Treasury Explanatory Notes to Finance Bill 2006).

(6) Market value

For the purposes of these provisions, the *market value* of any plant or machinery at any time is to be determined on the assumption of a disposal by an absolute owner free from all leases and other encumbrances. [*CAA 2001, s 70YI(2); FA 2006, Sch 8 para 7*].

Lessees — Treatment of long funding leases

[13.6] Where a person carrying on a qualifying activity (**11.2 CAPITAL ALLOWANCES — PLANT AND MACHINERY: ELIGIBLE EXPENDITURE AND INITIAL ALLOWANCES**) incurs expenditure (whether or not capital expenditure) on the provision of plant or machinery for the purposes of that activity under a 'long funding lease', the plant or machinery is treated as owned by him at all times whilst he is the lessee for the purposes of capital allowances.

He is then treated as having incurred *capital expenditure* on the provision of the plant or machinery, of an amount determined as below depending on whether the lease is a 'long funding operating lease' (see (3) above) or a 'long-funding finance lease' (see (4) above), at the 'commencement' (see *CAA 2001, s 70YI(1)*) of the term of the lease.

Long funding operating lease

If the lease is a 'long funding operating lease', the capital expenditure is equal to the market value of the plant or machinery as at the commencement of the term of the lease or, if later, the date on which the plant or machinery is first brought into use for the purposes of the qualifying activity.

Long funding finance lease

If the lease is a 'long funding finance lease', then, subject to the possible addition and restriction described below, the capital expenditure is equal to the present value, as at the commencement of the term of the lease or, if later, the date on which the plant or machinery is first brought into use for the purposes of the qualifying activity, of the 'minimum lease payments'.

Present value is computed as it would be if accounts were prepared in accordance with generally accepted accounting practice (GAAP) on the date on which that value is first recognised in the lessee's books or other financial records.

If the lessee paid rentals under the lease before its term commenced, the capital expenditure also includes the amount of any such rentals for which tax relief is otherwise unavailable (and would still have been unavailable even if the plant or machinery had been used pre-commencement).

If a main purpose of entering into the lease (or arrangements that include the lease) was to obtain capital allowances on an amount materially greater than the market value of the leased asset at the commencement of the term of the lease, the capital expenditure is restricted to that market value.

If the *lessor* under the long funding finance lease subsequently incurs additional expenditure such that the lease rentals increase, the *lessee* is treated as incurring further capital expenditure on the plant or machinery.

The further expenditure is equal to the increase (if any) in the present value of the minimum lease payments and is treated as incurred on the date it is first recognised in the lessee's books or other financial records.

Disposal events and values

Disposal event

[13.7] A '*relevant event*' occurs if the:

(i) lease terminates;
(ii) qualifying activity is permanently discontinued; or
(iii) plant or machinery starts to be used wholly for purposes other than the qualifying activity.

Where the relevant event occurs on or after 13 November 2008, the following applies in relation to disposal value.

Disposal value

The amount of the disposal value is the excess of qualifying expenditure over the 'qualifying amount' less any relevant rebate.

Qualifying amount

For a long funding operating lease, this is the total of deductions made under *CTA 2010, s 379*.

For a long funding finance lease, this is the sum of the payments made under the lease (including the initial payment) and any payments to the lessor by a guarantor, but where charges are shown in the lessee's accounts, prepared under generally accepted accounting practice, representing charges for services and any amount in respect of UK or foreign tax, these are excluded.

Where the lease is not at arm's length, only amounts or rebates which would reasonably have been paid had the transaction been at arm's length are taken into account.

The disposal value may not be a negative.

[*FA 2009, s 64, Sch 32*].

Where the event occurs before 13 November 2008, as regards long funding finance leases, the same principles apply whether the lease is accounted for as a lease or as a loan.

Termination of a lease

The termination of a long funding lease is a disposal event, and a **disposal value** (**12.14 CAPITAL ALLOWANCES — PLANT AND MACHINERY: POOLING AND DISPOSALS**) must be brought into account by the lessee for the chargeable period in which that event occurs, computed as follows.

Long funding operating lease

The disposal value is equal to the sum of elements A and B where:

- element A is the excess (if any) of the original amount of capital expenditure (computed as above) over the total *reductions* falling to be made under *CTA 2010, s 379* (see **71.55 TRADING EXPENSES AND DEDUCTIONS** under Lessees) (and its income tax equivalent) for periods of account in which the person concerned was the lessee; and

- element B is the total of any amounts payable to the lessee that are calculated by reference to 'termination value' (as defined by *CAA 2001, s 70YH*), e.g. lease rental refunds.

Long funding finance lease

The disposal value is equal to the sum of Elements C and D less any amount payable by the lessee to the lessor in consequence of the termination, where:

- element C is the total of any amounts payable to the lessee that are calculated by reference to 'termination value' (as defined by *CAA 2001, s 70YH*), e.g. lease rental refunds; and
- element D is, if the lease terminates short of its full term, the present value, immediately before the termination, of the excess of the original amount of the 'minimum lease payments' (see (5) above), over what would have been the amount of the minimum lease payments had the lease had been designed to expire when it did.

If the termination would also give rise to a disposal event within **12.14 CAPITAL ALLOWANCES — PLANT AND MACHINERY: POOLING AND DISPOSALS** in the case of the lessee, that disposal event is ignored.

Additional rules

Where the term of the lease begins on or after 13 November 2008, additional rules apply in determining the allowances available on transfer and long funding leaseback.

Where a person transfers plant or machinery to another person at any time and after the date of the transfer the transferor, or a connected person of the transferor enters a long funding lease of the machinery, no annual investment or first year allowance is given to the leasee or a person connected to the lessee in respect of the plant or machinery.

Qualifying expenditure for capital allowances purposes is calculated by leaving out of account the excess of the lessee, or a connected person of the lessee's capital expenditure on the plant or machinery less the disposal value the lessee is obliged to bring into account. If there is no disposal value to be brought into account, the amount to be taken in is the smallest of the market value, the amount of the lessee's capital expenditure or the amount of capital expenditure incurred by the person connected with the lessee on the provision of the plant and machinery.

For this purpose, a transfer involving the grant of a lease takes place on the commencement of the term of the lease. [*FA 2009, s 64, Sch 32*].

[*CAA 2001, ss 70A–70E; FA 2006, Sch 8 para 6; FA 2009, Sch 32*].

FA 2011 changes

[13.8] Under the disclosure rules HMRC have received notice of a tax avoidance scheme which has the claimed effect of giving to a lessee of plant and machinery tax relief of up to twice for the actual cost. Therefore *FA 2011* introduces legislation to counter such a scheme. *FA 2011, s 33* has amended the provisions of *CAA 2001, ss 70C–70E*, with regard to payments made on or after 9 March 2011.

CAA 2001, s 70C provides how to calculate the amount of capital expenditure for a lessee under a long funding finance lease. New *subsections (4A), (4B)* and *(4C)* are inserted into *s 70C*.

Section 70C(4) defines the 'commencement PVMLP', the present value of lease payments, which is an amount to be included in such capital expenditure. Per the new *s 70C(4A)* the present value of a 'relievable amount' is to be excluded from commencement PVMLP. An amount is a 'relievable amount' if three conditions (in *s 70C(4B)*) are met:

(a) that as a result of an arrangement being in place the lessee, or a person connected with the lessee, has guaranteed all or part of the residual amount (the residual value of the leased asset as determined at the commencement of the lease). (The residual amount for a lessee is defined in *s 70YE(3)*);
(b) that the amount must be within the minimum lease payments, as defined in *s 70YE(1)*, because of the arrangement;
(c) that it is reasonable to assume that, were the amount to be incurred, relief would be available as a result. It further provides that relief in this context does not include relief under *s 70C* or *s 70E* where relief under those two sections is available because the amount is within minimum lease payments.

With regard to condition (c) above, in deciding whether relief would be available as a result of incurring the amount, no account is to be taken of any part of the arrangement other than the part by virtue of which all or part of the residual amount is guaranteed, or any other arrangement connected with the arrangement, or forming part of a set of arrangements that includes the arrangement. [*s 70C(4C)*].

New *sections (1A)* and *(1B)* are inserted into *s 70D*, which deals with additional capital allowances for the lessee under a long funding finance lease, where:

- the lessor incurs additional expenditure on plant or machinery; and
- there is consequently an increase in the present value of the minimum lease payments of the lessee.

Pursuant to the new *subsection (1A)* if any increase in the minimum lease payments is attributable to a 'relievable' amount then it is to be ignored with regard to the possible increase in the present value of the minimum lease payments (above).

Subsection (1B) provides for new *sections 70C(4B)* and *70C(4C)* to be used for the purposes of determining whether or not new *s 70D(1A)* above applies.

CAA 2001, s 70E considers disposal events and disposal values for a lessee under a long funding lease. It is amended and the words 'other than any relievable payment' are inserted into *s 70E(2C)(b)*. The 'qualifying amount' (QA) used in the formula for disposal value in *s 70E(2A)* is restricted, for long funding finance leases. The restriction is that a payment under a guarantee of a residual amount does not include a 'relievable payment'. Residual amount is defined in *s 70YE(3)*.

A new *s 70E(2DA)* defines when a payment is a 'payment'. This replicates the provisions at *s 70C(4B)* above, save that some references in the new *s 70C(4B)* to 'amount' are replaced in new *s 70E(2DA)* by references to 'payment', and the new *s 70E(2DA)* excludes from the meaning ofs relief any relief which only arises under *ss 70E, 70C* or *70D* where relief under those sections is available because the payment is within minimum lease payments. In addition a payment is a relievable payment if it is reasonable to assume that relief would be available as a result of making the payment, except for the exclusions in the new *ss 70C–70E*.

'Relief' in this section has the meaning given in *s 70C* — relief can be relief by way of an allowance under *CAA* or a deduction in computing profits for corporation tax or income tax purposes or a deduction from total profits or total income for corporation tax or income tax purposes.

For the purposes of new *s 70E(2DA)(c)*, no account is to be taken of certain matters, as detailed in *s 70C(4C)* (above), in deciding whether a payment is a relievable payment,

[*FA 2011, s 33*].

Lessors — Treatment of long funding leases

[13.9] Expenditure incurred on the provision of plant or machinery for leasing under a long funding lease is not qualifying expenditure for the purposes of plant and machinery capital allowances. [*CAA 2001, s 34A; FA 2006, Sch 8 para 3*].

Where expenditure on plant or machinery is already included in qualifying expenditure and the plant or machinery begins to be leased under a long funding lease, a disposal event then occurs and a disposal value must be brought into account as follows.

Long funding operating lease

The disposal value is the market value of the plant or machinery at commencement of the lease.

Long funding finance lease

The disposal value is the amount that would fall to be recognised as the lessor's net investment in the lease if accounts were prepared in accordance with GAAP on the date on which the lessor's net investment in the lease is first recognised in the lessor's books or other financial records ('the relevant date').

For leases granted on or after 13 December 2007, any rent paid or falling due on or before the relevant date is treated as due the day after the relevant date.

For leases granted on or after 12 March 2008, the lessee is to be treated as having no liabilities (including share capital treated under generally accepted acconting practice as a liability), if the effect of this would be to increase the disposal value. [*CAA 2001, s 61(1)(ee), (2); FA 2006, Sch 8 para 5; FA 2008, Sch 20 para 4*]. (See **12.14 CAPITAL ALLOWANCES — PLANT AND MACHINERY: POOLING AND DISPOSALS** as regards disposal events and disposal values generally.)

Notional capital expenditure — cessation of long funding lease

Where the owner of plant or machinery has been leasing it under a long funding lease and ceases to do so but continues to use it for the purposes of a qualifying activity (see **11.2 CAPITAL ALLOWANCES — PLANT AND MACHINERY: ELIGIBLE EXPENDITURE AND INITIAL ALLOWANCES**), writing-down allowances are available to him as if he had, on the day after the cessation, incurred capital expenditure on the acquisition of that plant or machinery and as if he owned it as a result of that notional capital expenditure.

The plant or machinery is thereafter treated as if it were not the same plant or machinery that existed previously.

The amount of the notional capital expenditure is equal to the 'termination amount' in relation to the long funding lease under which the plant or machinery was last leased.

First-year allowances are not, however, available on the notional capital expenditure, and nor can it qualify for short-life asset treatment. [*CAA 2001, ss 13A, 46(2), 84; FA 2006, Sch 8 paras 2, 4, 8*].

Termination amount

The '*termination amount*' is determined as follows.

- If that lease terminated as a result of a disposal event or if a disposal event is triggered by the termination, the termination amount is the disposal value that would have fallen to be brought into account by the lessor on the fictional assumptions that he had been entitled to capital allowances on the plant or machinery and had claimed his full entitlement. 'Disposal event' is itself to be construed in accordance with those assumptions. See generally **12.14 CAPITAL ALLOWANCES — PLANT AND MACHINERY: POOLING AND DISPOSALS** as regards disposal events and disposal values.
- If the above does not apply and the lease is a 'long funding operating lease', the termination amount is the market value of the plant or machinery immediately after the termination.
- If the above does not apply and the lease is a 'long funding finance lease', the termination amount is the value at which, immediately after the termination, the plant or machinery is recognised in the lessor's books or other financial records.

[*CAA 2001, s 70YG; FA 2006, Sch 8 para 7*].

Note that where plant or machinery either begins or ceases to be leased under a long funding lease, there is also, by virtue of *TCGA 1992, s 25A*, a deemed disposal and reacquisition, at similar values as above, for CGT purposes. See Tolley's Capital Gains Tax under Assets.

Fixtures

[13.10] The fixtures rules at **13.1** above do not apply to determine either ownership or entitlement to allowances of either the lessee or the lessor, where plant or machinery that is (or becomes) a fixture is the subject of a long funding lease.

If the lessee under the long funding lease himself leases out all or any of the plant or machinery under a lease that is not a long funding lease, the provisions at **13.1–13.3** are similarly disapplied as regards both the lessor and the lessee under that sub-lease. (Thus, the allowances (for expenditure on fixtures) available to any such lessors and lessees are to be determined under the rules applicable to long funding leases, rather than the rules applicable to fixtures.) [*CAA 2001, ss 172(2A), 172A; FA 2006, Sch 8 para 9*].

Mixed leases

There is provision for a situation where plant or machinery is leased with other types of asset (whether plant or machinery or not). In such case, different leases are deemed to exist so that the above rules (and those at **71.55 TRADING EXPENSES AND DEDUCTIONS**) can be applied to each such notional lease ((known as a '*derived lease*'). [*CAA 2001, ss 70L, 70M; FA 2006, Sch 8 para 7*].

Transfers and assignments

[13.11] Where a *lessor* of plant or machinery transfers it to a new lessor (other than by granting him a lease), it is treated for the purposes of these provisions (as regards lessors) as the termination of the existing lease and the creation of a new lease commencing at the date of transfer (which may or may not be the case in reality).

Provided there is effectively no change to the term of the original lease or to the payments due under it, then, as regards the new lessor, the new lease retains the classification of the original lease (i.e. as a long funding lease or as a lease other than a long funding lease, as the case may be) and, as regards the lessee, the old and new leases are treated as a single continuing lease. [*CAA 2001, s 70W; FA 2006, Sch 8 para 7*].

The above also applies, with the appropriate modifications, where a *lessee* of plant or machinery transfers it to a new lessee. [*CAA 2001, s 70X; FA 2006, Sch 8 para 7*].

Extension of the term of a lease

[13.12] Where the term of a *long funding operating lease* is extended as a result of one or more specified events (involving variations to the provisions of the lease, the granting or exercise of options etc.), a new lease is deemed to begin. [*CAA 2001, s 70YB; FA 2006, Sch 8 para 7*].

Where the term of a lease that is *not* a long funding lease is extended as a result of one or more specified events (as above), it is necessary to consider whether or not it thereby becomes a long funding lease.

If, were it to be assumed that the lease has then terminated and a new lease commenced, the new lease would be a long funding lease, that assumption is made, and the 'new' lease is a long funding lease as regards the lessor, If not, the term of the lease is taken to be the term as extended. [*CAA 2001, s 70YC; FA 2006, Sch 8 para 7*].

Other points

Tax avoidance involving international leasing

[13.13] There are anti-avoidance rules aimed at arrangements such that a non-UK resident leases plant and machinery to a UK resident who then leases it back to a non-UK resident (other than under a long funding lease) in order to obtain the benefit of UK capital allowances. The rules deem the leasing by the UK resident to be long funding leasing, so that capital allowances are not available to him.

They apply where the provision of the asset by the non-UK resident is itself long funding leasing as regards the UK resident or is under a contract within **13.25** (hire-purchase contracts etc.), such that the UK resident would otherwise be entitled to capital allowances.

They are not aimed at normal commercial arrangements (see also Treasury Explanatory Notes to Finance Bill 2006). [*CAA 2001, s 70V; FA 2006, Sch 8 para 7*].

Sale and leaseback/lease and leaseback arrangements

Where an existing long funding lessor transfers (e.g. by selling or leasing) the plant or machinery that is the subject of the existing lease to another person and leases the plant or machinery back from that other person, the leaseback is a long funding lease as regards both of them.

Similar treatment is applied where the leaseback is via a series of leases. [*CAA 2001, s 70Y; FA 2006, Sch 8 para 7*].

Change in the accountancy classification of a long funding lease

There are rules to cater for changes in generally accepted accounting practice (GAAP) such that an operating lease falls to be reclassified as a finance lease for accounting purposes or *vice versa*. [*CAA 2001, s 70YA; FA 2006, Sch 8 para 7*].

Increase in proportion of residual amount guaranteed

The following applies as regards the lessor if, in the case of a lease other than a long funding lease and as a result of arrangements, there is an increase in the proportion of the residual amount that is guaranteed by the lessee (or by a person not connected with the lessor) (as to which see (5) above) and the lease would have been a long funding lease if those arrangements had been made before its 'inception' (see *CAA 2001, s 70YI(1)*).

The lease is treated as terminated, and a new lease treated as commenced, as at the time of the arrangement (or the latest arrangement if more than one). [*CAA 2001, s 70YD; FA 2006, Sch 8 para 7*].

Commencement/transitional provisions

The long funding leasing rules above (and those at **71.55** TRADING EXPENSES AND DEDUCTIONS) apply in respect of a lease where one of the conditions at (a) and (b) below is met.

However, regardless of these conditions, a lease 'finalised' (see below) before 21 July 2005 cannot be a long funding lease but this let-out is itself disapplied if the lessor does not come within the charge to UK tax until after 17 May 2006.

(a) Condition 1 is that the lease is not an 'excepted lease' and that it is 'finalised' on or after 1 April 2006 or the 'commencement' (see *CAA 2001, s 70YI(1)*) of its term is on or after that date.

(b) Condition 2 applies if the commencement of the term of the lease was before 1 April 2006 but the plant or machinery is not brought into use by the person concerned for the purposes of a qualifying activity (**11.2 CAPITAL ALLOWANCES — PLANT AND MACHINERY: ELIGIBLE EXPENDITURE AND INITIAL ALLOWANCES**) until on or after that date.
This covers, for example, the situation where the person concerned becomes UK resident on or after that date, such that his activity becomes a qualifying activity. The person concerned may be the lessor or the lessee depending on from whose point of view one is applying the provisions.

Lessor election

The Treasury has made regulations (*SI 2007 No 304*) enabling a *lessor* to elect for a lease to be treated, as regards him only, as a long funding lease if it would not otherwise be such a lease.

The election applies to all of the lessor's eligible leases and 'qualifying incidental leases'.

The election must be made, in the case of an individual or partnership, within the period commencing with the end of the year of assessment to which the election relates and ending a year after 31 January next following that year of assessment.

For corporation tax, the election must be made in the period between the end of the accounting period to which the election relates and ending two years later.

Where an election is made, it applies to all eligible leases and qualifying incidental leases finalised on or after the later of 1 April 2006 and the beginning of the year of assessment or accounting period to which the election applies, and the leases are treated as if they had been long funding leases since they were finalised.

A lease is eligible if:

- it is a lease of plant or machinery;
- it is not otherwise a long funding lease;
- it is finalised on or after 1 April 2006;
- it is for 12 months or more;
- the plant etc. was unused and not second hand at the start of the lease;
- the plant or machinery was leased previously, the last lease was a long funding lease and a valid election under *CAA 2001, s 227* was made before the lessor made a return for the period covering the commencement of the lease or replaces similar plant or machinery;

- the subject of the lease is not a car (*CAA 2001, s 81*);
- the asset leased is not valued at more than £10m at the start of the lease;
- the plant is not background plant or machinery (*CAA 2001, s 70R*) or does not have a low percentage value (*CAA 2001, s 70U*); and
- any assignment of the lease was made within four months of the commencement of its term and no other lessor must have claimed capital allowances in respect of the plant or machinery.

Qualifying incidental lease

A qualifying incidental lease is one of plant and machinery where the lease is wholly incidental to an eligible lease, and would itself be an eligible lease under the above criteria, except that the condition that the lease be for a year or more need not be satisfied.

[*SI 2007 No 304*].

'Finalised'

For these purposes, a lease is '*finalised*' when there is a written contract for it between lessor and lessee, the contract is unconditional (or any conditions have already been met) and there are no terms still to be agreed.

Excepted lease

For the purposes of (a) above, a lease is an '*excepted lease*' if it meets *all* the following conditions.

(i) Condition 1 is that before 21 July 2005 there was written evidence of an agreement or common understanding (the '*pre-existing heads of agreement*') between (or effectively between) the lessor and lessee as to the 'principal terms of the lease' (as defined).

(ii) Condition 2 is that the leased plant or machinery was 'under construction' (as defined) before 1 April 2006.

(iii) Condition 3 is that the lease is 'finalised' (see above) before 1 April 2007 (but see below).

(iv) Condition 4 is the commencement of the term of the lease is before 1 April 2007 (but see below).

(v) Condition 5 is that the lessee is the person(s) identified as such in the 'pre-existing heads of agreement' (within (i) above).

(vi) Condition 6 is that the principal terms of the lease are not materially different from those in the 'pre-existing heads of agreement' (within (i) above).

The date in (iii) and (iv) above is deferred to 1 April 2009 if construction of the asset proceeds continuously from 1 April 2006 (and at the normal pace for an asset of its type) and the lease commences as soon as is practicable after construction is substantially complete. There is provision to treat this condition as satisfied if it is failed only by reason of unforeseen events beyond the control of the parties (including the main constructor).

There are rules (see *FA 2006, Sch 8 paras 20, 25*) as to how these transitional provisions are to be applied in a case where the 'pre-existing heads of agreement' (see (i) above) relates to two or more assets.

If a person incurs expenditure before 19 July 2006 for leasing under a long funding lease which does not meet all the conditions in (i)–(vi) above but in respect of which there was a 'pre-existing heads of agreement' before 21 July 2005 (as in (i) above), such expenditure (the '*old expenditure*') is treated as separate from any expenditure incurred on or after date (the '*new expenditure*').

FA 2006, Sch 8 para 22 provides rules, for this purpose only, as to the time at which an amount of expenditure is treated as being incurred. The old and new expenditure are treated as if incurred on separate assets leased under separate leases; the notional lease relating to the old expenditure is then deemed to be an excepted lease. The lease rentals are apportioned between the two notional leases in just and reasonable manner. These splitting provisions apply in determining the income tax or corporation tax liability of anyone who is at any time the lessor or the lessee under the actual lease.

Mixed leases

Where a lease is a mixed lease, it is first necessary to consider whether the mixed lease is itself an 'excepted lease' for the purposes of these transitional provisions. If it is not, one can then consider separately, in the case of each derived lease, whether that lease is an 'excepted lease'.

Transfers

There is provision to ensure that a lease that is outside the long funding leasing regime (by virtue of the commencement/transitional provisions) remains outside that regime if it is transferred from one lessor to another or from one lessee to another.

For this to have effect, there must be no effective change to the term of the lease or to the payments due under it, and the lessor or lessee (as the case may be) must be within the charge to UK tax immediately before the transfer.

Leases of cushion gas

Cushion gas in a gas storage facility that constitutes plant and it may be leased under a plant and machinery lease. However, cushion gas is different from most other plant and machinery in that it does not wear out.

It would, therefore, have been possible to write very long operating leases of cushion gas, without ever triggering the application of the long funding lease rules. This could have meant that leases of cushion gas would have been taxed by reference to their legal form, rather than commercial substance, which would have been at variance with the 2006 leasing reforms.

The legislation therefore specifies that all leases of cushion gas are to be funding leases. This means that, from the perspective of the lessor, any lease of cushion gas for five years or more will be taxed by reference to the commercial substance rather than the legal form.

The lessee, where UK resident, will have the choice of claiming a deduction for the lease rentals in accordance with the accounting treatment, or of opting to claim capital allowances with a restricted deduction in respect of the lease rentals.

Overseas lessees will be entitled to claim under the rules applicable to their particular jurisdiction and will not be affected by these changes.

[*FA 2010, s 28*].

Anti-avoidance

For transactions on or after 13 November 2008, legislation in *FA 2009* to counters avoidance involving the sale of an intermediate company in a chain of leases in order to avoid a 'sale of lessors' charge.

[*FA 2006, Sch 8 paras 15–27*].

Overseas leasing

Introduction

[13.14] For the purposes of the provisions described below, plant or machinery is used for overseas leasing if it is leased to a person who:

(1) is not resident in the UK; and
(2) does not use the plant or machinery exclusively for earning profits chargeable to UK tax (which includes profits from exploration or exploitation activities carried on in the UK or its territorial sea).

However, in determining whether plant or machinery is used for overseas leasing, no account is to be taken of any lease finalised on or after **1 April 2006** (see **13.13** under Commencement/transitional provisions).

For the purpose of (2) above, profits chargeable to UK tax do not include profits in respect of which the trader is entitled to tax relief under a double taxation agreement. This does not apply in the case of leases entered into before 16 March 1993 for which, in addition, the use of the plant or machinery does not have to be *exclusively* for the purposes stated.

[*CAA 2001, s 105(2)–(4), Sch 3 para 21; FA 2006, Sch 9 para 13; CTA 2009, Sch 1 para 483*].

Terminology

For the purposes of the provisions described below, a 'lease' includes a sub-lease, with 'lessor' and 'lessee' being construed accordingly, and 'leasing' is regarded as including the letting of any asset on hire or of a ship or aircraft on charter (and see *Barclays Mercantile Industrial Finance Ltd v Melluish* [1990] STC 314, 63 TC 95). [*CAA 2001, s 105(1)*].

New and old expenditure

The provisions apply in relation to 'new expenditure'.

'*New expenditure*' means expenditure incurred after 31 March 1986 on plant and machinery other than certain cars costing £12,000 or less (see **12.17 CAPITAL ALLOWANCES — PLANT AND MACHINERY: POOLING AND DISPOSALS**), provided that it is not 'old expenditure'.

'*Old expenditure*' means, broadly, expenditure incurred before 1 April 1986, although certain post-31 March 1986 expenditure was included in the term under transitional provisions, as was post-31 March 1986 expenditure qualifying for a universal (as opposed to targeted) first-year allowance (see **11.13 CAPITAL ALLOWANCES — PLANT AND MACHINERY: ELIGIBLE EXPENDITURE AND INITIAL ALLOWANCES**) other than the temporarily reinstated 40% allowance for expenditure in the twelve months to 31 October 1993.

[*CAA 1990, s 50(3); FA 1993, Sch 13 para 11(1); F(No 2)A 1997, s 42(6); FA 1998, s 85(4)*].

Chain of leases

Where there is a chain of leases, HMRC consider that the provisions apply where any lessee in the chain falls within (1) and (2) above.

HMRC used to be of the opinion that in determining whether or not overseas leasing is 'protected leasing' (see **13.15** and **13.19** below), it was necessary to consider only the end lease in a chain. HMRC now take the view that every lease in the chain must be considered; if the leasing under any of the leases is not 'protected leasing', the overseas leasing restrictions apply to the whole chain.

HMRC will apply their earlier view to leasing arrangements entered into before 3 February 2005, or within three months after that date where the principal terms were agreed in writing before that date and did not materially alter in the intervening period. (HMRC Internet Statement 3 February 2005).

Separate pooling and restriction of writing-down allowances

[13.15] Separate pooling provisions apply to qualifying expenditure (**11.2 CAPITAL ALLOWANCES — PLANT AND MACHINERY: ELIGIBLE EXPENDITURE AND INITIAL ALLOWANCES**) if it is incurred on the provision of plant or machinery for leasing and if that plant or machinery is at any time in the 'designated period' (see **13.17** below) used for overseas leasing other than 'protected leasing' (see **13.19** below).

They do not apply to long life asset expenditure (see **12.12**) or to expenditure which can only be allocated to a single asset pool (see **12.2 CAPITAL ALLOWANCES — PLANT AND MACHINERY: POOLING AND DISPOSALS**).

Qualifying expenditure meeting the above conditions can only be allocated to a *class pool*, known as the *overseas leasing pool*.

The final chargeable period (see **12.24**) of the overseas leasing pool is the chargeable period at the end of which circumstances are such that no further disposal values (see **12.14 CAPITAL ALLOWANCES — PLANT AND MACHINERY: POOLING AND DISPOSALS**) could fall to be brought into account.

Writing-down allowances on qualifying expenditure meeting the above conditions are restricted to **10% p.a.** The restriction applies whether such expenditure falls to be allocated to the overseas leasing pool or to a single asset pool.

The 10% rate does not, however, displace the 6% rate applicable to long-life asset expenditure (see **12.12 CAPITAL ALLOWANCES — PLANT AND MACHINERY: POOLING AND DISPOSALS**).

The 10% allowance is proportionately reduced or increased if the chargeable period is less or more than a year, or if the qualifying activity has been carried on for part only of the chargeable period. A claim for a writing-down allowance may require it to be reduced to a specified amount.

[*CAA 2001, ss 56(5), 65(4), 107, 109*].

When plant or machinery in the overseas leasing pool is disposed of to a **CONNECTED PERSON (25)** (otherwise than on a change in the members of a partnership or a company reconstruction in circumstances such that, in each case, the qualifying activity is treated as continuing) the disposal value to be brought into account (see generally **12.14 CAPITAL ALLOWANCES — PLANT AND MACHINERY: POOLING AND DISPOSALS**) is its market value or, if lower, its original cost, and the person acquiring it may claim allowances on the same value. [*CAA 2001, s 108; ITTOIA 2005, Sch 1 para 537; CTA 2009, Sch 1 para 485*].

Cars costing £12,000 or less, and which are not leased so as to be otherwise within these provisions, previously had to be included in a similar class pool, but *not* the same pool as that used for overseas leasing.

This car pool also included certain 'old expenditure' on plant or machinery provided for leasing.

The separate pooling requirement is, however, abolished for periods of account ending after 5 April 2000, except that an election may be made to treat the abolition as deferred by one year in any particular case. Any unrelieved qualifying expenditure brought forward from the immediately preceding chargeable period in the separate pool is included in the main pool of qualifying expenditure for the chargeable period for which abolition has effect. [*CAA 1990, s 41(1)(b)(c)(4); FA 2000, s 74*].

Prohibition of allowances

[13.16] No writing-down or balancing allowances are available in respect of qualifying expenditure meeting the conditions in **13.15** if the plant or machinery is used other than for a 'qualifying purpose' (see **13.18**) *and*:

(i) there is more than one year between consecutive payments due under the lease; or
(ii) any payments other than periodical payments are due under the lease or under any collateral agreement; or
(iii) any payment expressed monthly under the lease or any collateral agreement is not the same as any other such payment, but disregarding variations due to changes in rates of tax, capital allowances, interest which is linked with rates applicable to inter-bank loans or changes in premiums for insurances of any kind by a person not connected with the lessor or lessee; or
(iv) either the lease is for a period exceeding 13 years or there is any provision for its extension or renewal or for the grant of a new lease such that the leasing period could exceed 13 years; or

(v) at any time, the lessor or **CONNECTED PERSON** (**25**) could be entitled to receive from the lessee or any other person a payment (not insurance money) of an amount determined before expiry of the lease and referable to the value of the plant or machinery at or after that expiry (whether or not the payment relates to a disposal of the plant or machinery).

Where allowances (including any first-year allowance) have been made but by reason of any event in the 'designated period' (**13.17**) the expenditure is brought within the above provisions, the net allowances are clawed back by means of a balancing charge.

For this purpose only, the allowances made are determined as if the item of plant or machinery in question were the only item, i.e. as if it had not been pooled. A disposal value equal to the balance of the expenditure is also brought into account so as to effectively remove the item from the pool.

Connected person

Where the item was acquired from a **CONNECTED PERSON** (**25**), or as a part of a series of transactions with connected persons, allowances made to those persons are also taken into account in computing the balancing charge, with any actual consideration on a connected persons transaction being ignored and with the amount of such allowances being adjusted 'in a just and reasonable manner' where balancing allowances/charges have already been made in respect of the item in question.

This does not apply in the case of transactions between connected persons which are treated as not involving a cessation of the quality activity, i.e. where there is a change in the members of a partnership but there is at least one continuing partner or where the activity is treated as continuing by virtue of *CTA 2009, s 1259* (partnership changes involving companies) or *CTA 2010, Pt 22, Ch 1* (transfers of trade without a change of ownership). [*CAA 2001, ss 114, 115; ITTOIA 2005, Sch 1 para 539*].

'Designated period'

[13.17] For the purposes of these provisions, the '*designated period*' is the period of ten years after the item of plant or machinery in question is first brought into use by the person who incurred the expenditure.

It is, however, brought to an end at any time within that ten-year period at which that person ceases to own the item, disregarding any disposal to a **CONNECTED PERSON** (**25**) or on a change in members of a partnership where there is at least one continuing individula or corporate partner.

For leases entered into before 16 March 1993, the ten-year period was reduced to one of four years if the plant or machinery was used for a 'qualifying purpose' (**13.18**). [*CAA 2001, s 106; ITTOIA 2005, Sch 1 para 536; CTA 2009, Sch 1 para 484*].

'Qualifying purpose'

[13.18] Plant or machinery on which a person (the buyer) has incurred expenditure is used for a '*qualifying purpose*' at any time if, at that time:

(i) the lessee uses it for the purposes of a qualifying activity without leasing it; and had the lessee bought the plant or machinery himself at that time, his expenditure would have fallen to be wholly or partly included in his available qualifying expenditure for a chargeable period; or

(ii) the buyer uses it for 'short-term leasing' (**13.19**); or

(iii) the lessee uses it for 'short-term leasing' and is either UK resident or so uses it in the course of a qualifying activity carried on in the UK; or

(iv) the buyer uses it for the purposes of a qualifying activity without leasing it.

For the purposes of (ii) and (iv) above, where the plant or machinery is disposed of to a connected person, or on a change in the members of a partnership where there is at least one continuing individual or corporate partner, the new owner is treated as the 'buyer'.

[*CAA 2001, ss 122, 125; ITTOIA 2005, Sch 1 paras 540, 541; CTA 2009, Sch 1 paras 488, 489*].

As regards the reference to 'leasing' in (i) above, the word is to be construed in accordance with the narrow test applicable to leases of land, so that distribution agreements entered into by film lessee companies were not leases for these purposes but arrangements entered into in the ordinary course of their businesses (*Barclays Mercantile Industrial Finance Ltd v Melluish* [1990] STC 314, 63 TC 95).

Ships, aircraft and transport container

Without prejudice to (i)–(iv) above, a ship is also used for a 'qualifying purpose' at any time when it is let on charter in the course of a trade of operating ships if the lessor is resident, or carries on the trade, in the UK and is responsible as principal (or appoints another person to be responsible as principle) for navigating and managing the ship and for defraying substantially all its expenses except those directly incidental to a particular voyage or charter period.

The same applies with necessary modifications in relation to aircraft.

However, neither ship nor aircraft chartering qualifies if the main object, or one of them, of the chartering (or of a series of transactions of which the chartering was one) was the obtaining by any person of an unrestricted writing-down allowance.

A transport container is also used for a '*qualifying purpose*' at any time when it is leased in the course of a trade carried on in the UK or by a UK resident if either the trade is one of operating ships or aircraft and the container is at other times used by the trader in connection with such operation, or the container is leased under a succession of leases to different persons who, or most of whom, are not connected with each other. [*CAA 2001, ss 123, 124, Sch 3 para 23*].

'Protected leasing'

[13.19] This means 'short-term leasing' (see below) or, in the case of a ship, aircraft or transport container, its use for a qualifying purpose (see **13.18** above). [*CAA 2001, s 105(5)*].

'*Short-term leasing*' means leasing an item of plant or machinery in such a manner that:

(A) the number of consecutive days for which it is leased to the same person will normally be less than 30; and

(B) the total number of days to the same person in any period of 12 months will normally be less than 90.

Or alternatively that:

(A) the number of consecutive days for which it is leased to the same person will not normally exceed 365; and

(B) the aggregate of the periods for which it is leased to lessees not falling within **13.18**(i) above in any period of four consecutive years within the 'designated period' will not exceed two years.

For the above purposes, persons who are connected with each other (see **25 CONNECTED PERSONS**) are to be treated as the same person. Where plant or machinery is leased from a group of items of similar description and not separately identifiable, all the items in the group may be treated as used for short-term leasing if substantially the whole of the items in the group are so used.

[*CAA 2001, s 121*].

Joint lessees

[13.20] The following applies where an item of plant or machinery is leased (otherwise than by 'protected leasing') to two or more persons jointly, and at least one of the joint lessees is a person within (1) and (2) above (definition of overseas leasing).

An unrestricted writing-down allowance is due if the lessees use the item for the purposes of a qualifying activity or activities (but not for leasing) but only to the extent that it appears that the profits therefrom throughout the 'designated period', or the period of the lease if shorter, will be chargeable to UK income tax or corporation tax.

The part of the expenditure so qualifying for unrestricted allowances is treated as if it were expenditure on a separate item of plant or machinery (outside the overseas leasing pool) with the remaining part treated as expenditure within the overseas leasing provisions, with such apportionments as are necessary.

Excess relief is recoverable under **13.21** below if at any time in the designated period while the item is so leased, no lessee uses it for the purposes of a qualifying activity the profits of which are chargeable to UK tax as above (referred to below as '*eligible use*') or if, at the end of the designated period, it appears that the actual extent of eligible use was less than anticipated.

In the latter case the amount of excess relief recoverable is in proportion to the reduction in eligible use and any disposal value subsequently brought into account is apportioned to the extent of the eligible use as determined at the end of the designated period.

[*CAA 2001, ss 116, 117, Sch 3 para* 22].

Recovery of excess relief

[13.21] Where expenditure has qualified for a normal writing-down allowance (or for a first-year allowance) and the plant or machinery is used for overseas leasing (other than 'protected leasing') at any time in the 'designated period', any 'excess relief' is recovered.

This is achieved by means of a balancing charge of an amount equal to the excess relief, to be made on the person who owns the item when it is first so used, for the chargeable period in which it is first so used.

The item is removed from its existing pool by means of a disposal value equal to the item's written-down value for capital allowances purposes at the end of that period.

Excess relief

The '*excess relief*' is the excess, if any, of the allowances made, up to and including the chargeable period in question, over the maximum allowances that could have been made if the expenditure had been within **13.15** or **13.16** from the outset.

The allowances made are determined for this purpose as if the item in question were the only item, i.e. as if it had not been pooled with any other item of plant or machinery. The sum of the excess relief and the disposal value is then allocated to the appropriate pool (usually the overseas leasing pool) for the following chargeable period.

Connected persons transactions

Where the person on whom the balancing charge falls to be made acquired the item in question from a **CONNECTED PERSON** (**25**), or as part of a series of transactions with connected persons, the allowances taken into account in computing the excess relief include the allowances made to such person(s), any consideration passing between them for the item being ignored.

The amount of excess relief is adjusted 'in a just and reasonable manner' where balancing allowances/charges have been made on any of the transactions. However, these modifications do not apply in the case of transactions between connected persons which are treated as not involving a cessation of the quality activity, i.e. where there is a change in the members of a partnership but there is at least one continuing individual or corporate partner or where the activity is treated as continuing by virtue of *CTA 2010, Pt 22, Ch 1* (transfers of trade without a change of ownership).

In the case of a ship, any allowance previously postponed (**12.18 CAPITAL ALLOWANCES — PLANT AND MACHINERY: POOLING AND DISPOSALS**) cannot be made for any chargeable period in or after that in which the ship is first used for overseas leasing (other than protected leasing) within the designated period. The total of any such allowances is instead allocated to the appropriate pool for the following chargeable period as if it were itself qualifying expenditure.

[*CAA 2001, ss 111–113; ITTOIA 2005, Sch 1 para 538; CTA 2009, Sch 1 para 486*].

Information to be provided

[13.22] *Information* must be provided to HMRC, by the then owner, where expenditure on plant or machinery has qualified for a normal writing-down allowance (or for a first-year allowance) and the item is subsequently used for overseas leasing (other than 'protected leasing') at any time in the 'designated period'.

Information must also be provided to HMRC, by the lessor, where plant or machinery is leased to joint lessees as described in **13.20** and, in addition, if circumstances occur such that excess relief is recoverable.

In all cases, the time limit for providing the information is three months after the end of the chargeable period in which the item is first so used (or the said circumstances occur), extended to 30 days after the informant came to know that the item was being so used (if the informant could not reasonably have been expected to know earlier).

Where expenditure has not yet qualified for a normal writing-down allowance or a first-year allowance or for either and the item is used for overseas leasing which is protected leasing, a claim for a first-year allowance or writing-down allowance thereon must be accompanied by a certificate describing the protected leasing.

[*CAA 2001, ss 118–120, 126*].

Examples

Separate pooling

L Ltd has a leasing business preparing accounts annually to 31 May. In the year to 31 May 2011, its expenditure included the following.

		£
(i)	Machine 1, leased to M Ltd, a UK-resident company for the purposes of its trade	20,000
(ii)	Machine 2, leased to N, a UK-resident individual, for private use	8,000
(iii)	Machine 3, leased to P, a non-UK resident, for his overseas trade	16,000
(iv)	Fixtures and fittings for use in L Ltd's business	2,000
(v)	Car used by L Ltd for business	6,000

At 1 June 2010, there is a written-down value of £40,000 brought forward in L Ltd's main plant and machinery pool.

The leasing in (iii) above is not 'protected leasing' (see **13.19** above), but neither does it fall within **13.16** above (prohibition of allowances). All leases were finalised before 1 April 2010. None of the expenditure qualifies for first-year allowances.

L Ltd's plant and machinery allowances for the year ended 31 May 2011, assuming no capital expenditure other than as listed above, are as follows.

	Main Pool	Overseas leasing pool	Total allowances
	£	£	£
WDV b/f	40,000		
Additions	36,000	16,000	
WDA 20%	(15,200)		15,200
WDA 10%		(1,600)	1,600
WDV c/f	£60,800	£14,400	
Total allowances			£16,800

Notes

(a) Machines 1 and 2 go into the main plant and machinery pool, as do the fixtures and fittings and the car. Machine 3 goes into an overseas leasing pool under **13.15**.

(b) The writing-down allowance for Machine 3 is restricted to 10%.

Recovery of excess relief

M Ltd, which has a 30 September accounting date, incurred expenditure of £16,000 in October 2005 on a machine leased to Q Ltd, a company trading in the UK. In December 2007, Q Ltd terminated the lease and M Ltd then leased the machine, with effect from January 2008, to P Ltd, a company resident in Panama, for the purposes of its trade there. The leasing was not 'protected leasing' (see **13.19**).

A balancing charge arises in the accounting period to 30.9.08 as follows.

Actual allowances

		Total allowances
	£	£
Expenditure (y/e 30.9.06)	16,000	
WDA 25% for y/e 30.9.06	4,000	4,000
	12,000	
WDA 25% for y/e 30.9.07	3,000	3,000
	9,000	
WDA 25% for y/e 30.9.08	2,250	2,250
Balance of expenditure	£6,750	
	Total allowances claimed	£9,250

Notional allowances

		Total allowances
	£	£
Expenditure (y/e 30.9.06)	16,000	

WDA 10% for y/e 30.9.06 note (a)	1,600	1,600
	14,400	
WDA 10% for y/e 30.9.07	1,440	1,440
	12,960	
WDA 10% for y/e 30.9.08	1,296	1,296
	£11,664	
Notional allowances		£4,336
Balancing charge, equal to the excess of actual allowances over notional allowances, for y/e 30.9.08		£4,914

M Ltd will then be deemed to have incurred qualifying expenditure of £11,664 (equal to the balance of expenditure plus the balancing charge) for the year ended 30.9.09, i.e. the chargeable period following that in which the change of use arose, and will then be entitled to writing-down allowances of 10% for that and subsequent chargeable periods. The expenditure will constitute, or form part of, an overseas leasing pool under **13.15**.

Notes

(a) Notional writing-down allowances are restricted to 10% notwithstanding the fact that the machine was used for a qualifying purpose up to December 2007. It is used for overseas leasing (other than protected leasing) at some time in the 'designated period' (see **13.15**).

(b) In practice, the machine would originally have been included in the main plant and machinery pool. For the purpose of calculating the balancing charge, it is assumed to have been the only item of plant and machinery qualifying for writing-down allowances. For the year ended 30 September 2008, a disposal value equal to the residue of expenditure (£6,750) must be brought into account in the main pool, so as to effectively remove the item from that pool.

(c) If the expenditure had qualified for a first-year allowance, this also enters into the calculation of excess relief and is thus effectively clawed back.

Special leasing

Introduction

[13.23] '*Special leasing*' is the hiring out of plant or machinery otherwise than in the course of a trade or other qualifying activity.

It is itself a qualifying activity for the purpose of claiming plant and machinery allowances.

However, plant or machinery provided for use in a dwelling-house or flat is excluded from being qualifying expenditure.

Where a person hires out more than one item of plant and machinery, that person has a *separate qualifying activity* in relation to each item.

A qualifying activity of special leasing begins when the plant or machinery is first hired out.

It is permanently discontinued if the lessor permanently ceases to hire it out.

Making allowances and charges for special leasing

A plant and machinery allowance is given effect by deduction from the company's income for the accounting period in question from qualifying activities of special leasing.

If, however, the plant or machinery was not used for the whole (or for a part) of the accounting period for the purposes of a qualifying activity carried on by the *lessee*, the allowance (or a proportionate part) can only be set against the lessor's income from that particular qualifying activity of special leasing.

Any excess of allowances over the income for an accounting period against which they may be set may be:

(a) carried forward against such income in succeeding accounting periods; or
(b) deducted from profits generally.

A claim for relief under (b) above may, if the allowances exceed the profit of the accounting period, require the excess to be relieved (as far as possible) against the profits of an immediately preceding period of equal length.

Relief under (b) above is only available where the lessee does not use the assets concerned for the purposes of a trade, and group relief is similarly restricted in such circumstances (see **39.5 GROUP RELIEF**).

A claim must be made within two years of the end of the accounting period in which the excess allowances arose.

A balancing charge is taxed as income from special leasing and is included in the income against which an allowance may be set as above.

Partnerships

The above provisions for allowances and charges do not apply in the case of a company:

(i) which carries on, in partnership with other persons in a chargeable period of the partnership, a 'business of leasing plant or machinery' (as defined in **5.28 ANTI-AVOIDANCE**); and
(ii) which is entitled to such special leasing allowances in any chargeable period comprising (wholly or partly) the partnership accounting period,

where the company's interest in the leasing business during the partnership's chargeable period is not determined on an 'allowable' basis.

Interest in leasing business

A company's interest in the leasing business is determined on an '*allowable*' basis if (for the purposes of *CTA 2009, ss 1262–1264* — see **58.3 PARTNERSHIPS**) the company's share in the profits (excluding chargeable gains) or loss of the leasing business and its share in any 'relevant capital allowances' for that period are both determined by reference to the same, single percentage.

Relevant capital allowances

'*Relevant capital allowances*' are capital allowances in respect of expenditure incurred on the provision of plant or machinery wholly or partly for the purposes of the leasing business.

When it applies

This provision has effect in relation to any business carried on by a company in partnership in any accounting period ending on or after 5 December 2005.

In relation to accounting periods straddling that date, the provision applies only if the company starts to carry on the business in partnership, or a 'relevant change' in the company's interest in the business occurs, on or after that date.

Relevant change

A '*relevant change*' in the company's interest in the business is a change to a basis of profit sharing which is not allowable.

Where the company's share in profits for a chargeable period is not the same as its share of capital allowances for that period, there are restrictions on how it may set off excess capital allowances.

Excess capital allowances from special leasing may not be set against profits of the current or any previous accounting period within the carry back period (ie a period the same length as the current accounting period, ending when that period starts).

Where an accounting period is partly within the carry back period the excess allowances may be set off proportionately. See HMRC Capital Allowances Manual CA29450.

[*CAA 2001, ss 3(4), 258–260, 261A; ITTOIA 2005, Sch 1 para 548; FA 2006, s 83; CTA 2009, Sch 1 para 237; CTA 2010, ss 887–888*].

Simon's Taxes. See B3.385.

Miscellaneous

[13.24] The following also apply for the purposes of capital allowances on plant and machinery.

Hire-purchase and similar contracts

Introduction

[13.25] The following applies where a person incurs capital expenditure, on the provision of plant or machinery for the purposes of a trade or other qualifying activity, under a contract providing that that person shall or may become the owner of it on performance of the contract. One example of such a contract is a hire-purchase agreement.

That person is treated for the purposes of plant and machinery allowances as the sole owner of the plant or machinery for as long as that person is entitled to the benefit of the contract.

When the plant or machinery is brought into use for the purposes of the qualifying activity, the full outstanding capital cost (i.e. excluding the hire or interest element) attracts capital allowances immediately.

Any such capital payments made before it is brought into use attract allowances as they fall due.

Contracts finalised on or after 1 April 2006

As regards any such contract finalised on or after 1 April 2006 (as to which see **13.13** under Commencement/transitional provisions) that, in accordance with generally accepted accounting practice (GAAP), falls to be treated as a lease (or would so fall if the person prepared accounts), the person mentioned above is treated as owning the plant or machinery only if the contract falls (or would fall) under GAAP to be treated by that person as a *finance lease*.

At any time at which, by virtue only of the preceding rule, the lessee is *not* treated as owning the plant or machinery, no-one else is treated as owning it either; so, in these circumstances, neither lessee nor lessor are entitled to capital allowances. (According to the Treasury Explanatory Notes to Finance Bill 2006, the treatment of ordinary hire-purchase contracts, with a nominal option fee payable to acquire the plant or machinery at the end of the lease, remains unaltered as such contracts will fall to be accounted for as finance leases.)

Also as regards contracts finalised on or after 1 April 2006, these provisions are extended so as to apply where the plant or machinery is used for the purposes of any overseas activity that would be a qualifying activity within **11.2 CAPITAL ALLOWANCES — PLANT AND MACHINERY: ELIGIBLE EXPENDITURE AND INITIAL ALLOWANCES** if the person carrying it on were UK resident.

Also as regards contracts finalised on or after 1 April 2006, any two or more agreements (or undertakings) are treated for these purposes as a single contract if, when taken together, they have the effect that the person concerned will (or may) become the owner of the plant or machinery on performance of the 'contract'.

Contract not completed

If the person mentioned above is treated as owning the plant or machinery but the contract is not completed so that he does not, in fact, become the owner of the plant or machinery, he is treated as ceasing to own it on ceasing to be entitled to the benefit of the contract.

The resulting disposal value depends on whether the plant or machinery has been brought into use for the purposes of the qualifying activity.

If it has, the disposal value is:

(i) the total of any capital sums received by way of consideration, compensation, damages or insurance in respect of the person's rights under the contract or the plant or machinery itself; plus

(ii) the capital element of all instalments treated as paid (see above) but not, in fact, paid.

This is subject to the over-riding rule that the disposal value cannot exceed the qualifying expenditure brought into account (see **12.14 CAPITAL ALLOWANCES — PLANT AND MACHINERY: POOLING AND DISPOSALS**).

If the plant or machinery has not been so brought into use, then where *CAA 2001* has effect, the disposal value is the total in (i) above (but see below as regards assignments). Previously, no specific rule was provided in such a case, so disposal value was equal to market value.

[*CAA 2001, ss 67, 68, Sch 3 para 15; FA 2006, Sch 9 para 12*].

See **71.9 TRADING EXPENSES AND DEDUCTIONS** as regards hire-purchase agreements relating to cars whose retail price when new exceeded £12,000.

Fixtures

The above rules do not apply to expenditure incurred on 'fixtures' within *CAA 2001, ss 172–204* (see **13.1**), and if (at a time on or after 28 July 2000) plant or machinery which has been treated under the above rules as owned by a person becomes such a fixture, that person is treated as ceasing to own it at that time (unless it is treated as belonging to that person under *ss 172–204*). [*CAA 2001, s 69, Sch 3 para 16*].

With effect for chargeable periods ending on or after 2 July 1997, the above rules similarly do not apply (except in relation to deemed ownership of the asset concerned) to expenditure incurred after 1 July 1997 (unless it is incurred before 1 July 1998 under a contract entered into on or before 1 July 1997) if the person mentioned above acquires the plant or machinery for leasing under a 'finance lease', and note the exclusion of long funding leases from that definition from, broadly, 1 April 2006).

[*CAA 2001, s 229(3), Sch 3 para 44*].

See HMRC Tax Bulletin June 1998 pp 539–544 for a general article on how these and associated capital allowance restrictions are intended to operate. In particular it is noted that the commencement rules for the fore-mentioned restriction apply before the rule above for bringing in capital costs before they are actually incurred, so that where the asset is brought into use by the lessor in a chargeable period ending on or after 2 July 1997, only expenditure actually incurred before that date (or before 2 July 1998 under an existing contract) can be brought into account at that time. See **13.4** as regards long funding leasing.

Assignment

If the person entitled to the benefit of a hire-purchase or similar contract assigns that benefit before the plant or machinery is brought into use, and the assignee's allowances fall to be restricted under the anti-avoidance provisions at **13.27**(ii) below, both the disposal value and the expenditure against which it is set are increased by the capital expenditure he would have incurred if he had wholly performed the contract.

The same applies in finance lease cases. This is to protect the assignee against an undue repression of qualifying expenditure by reference to the assignor's disposal value (see **13.27**)(ii) below). [*CAA 2001, s 229*].

Transfers between parties

For contracts entered into on or after 13 November 2008, where plant or machinery is transferred between parties but at any time after the transfer the plant etc. is available for the transferor or his connected person under a hire purchase contract and either of those parties incur capital expenditure on the provision of the plant or machinery under the hire purchase contract, no annual investment allowance or first-year allowance is available in respect of that expenditure.

Qualifying expenditure for capital allowances purposes is calculated by leaving out of account the excess of the lessee, or a connected person of the leasee's capital expenditure on the plant or machinery less the disposal value the lessee is obliged to bring into account. If there is no disposal value to be brought into account, the amount to be taken in is the smallest of the market value, the amount of the lessee's capital expenditure or the amount of capital expenditure incurred by the person connected with the lessee on the provision of the plant and machinery.

Simon's Taxes. See **B3.340A.**

Abortive expenditure

[13.26] The rules at **13.25** for hire-purchase and similar contracts can equally be applied to expenditure under other contracts which proves to be abortive.

A disposal value falls to be brought into account as in **13.25** when the contract fails to be completed.

Thus, for example, plant and machinery allowances can be obtained in respect of a non-refundable deposit paid on an item of plant or machinery which is never actually supplied, notwithstanding the fact that the item is never owned by the person incurring the expenditure.

Connected persons and other anti-avoidance measures

[13.27] See **25 CONNECTED PERSONS** for the definition of that term for these purposes.

(i) For disposals of plant or machinery acquired as a result of transaction(s) between connected persons, the limit on the disposal value (see **12.14 CAPITAL ALLOWANCES — PLANT AND MACHINERY: POOLING AND DISPOSALS**) is to the greatest amount of qualifying expenditure incurred on it by any of the participants in the transaction(s) (after deducting any 'additional VAT rebates' made — see **10.10 CAPITAL ALLOWANCES — INTRODUCTION**)).
The normal absence of any requirement to bring a disposal value into account if none of the qualifying expenditure in question has been taken into account in determining available qualifying expenditure does not

apply if the person concerned acquired the plant or machinery as a result of such transaction(s) as are mentioned above *and* any earlier participant was required to bring a disposal value into account. Instead, the current participant's qualifying expenditure is deemed to be allocated (if this is not actually the case), for the chargeable period in which the current disposal event occurs, to whichever pool is appropriate, thus requiring the bringing into account of a disposal value (which is then subject to the above-mentioned limit).
[*CAA 2001, ss 62(2)–(4), 64(2)–(5), 239(5)(6)*].

(ii) Where plant or machinery is purchased from a connected person, or (before 9 October 2007) in a 'sale and leaseback transaction', or in transaction(s) from which the sole or main benefit appears to be the obtaining of a plant and machinery allowance, no first-year allowances (where otherwise relevant) are available (see **11.13 CAPITAL ALLOWANCES — PLANT AND MACHINERY: ELIGIBLE EXPENDITURE AND INITIAL ALLOWANCES**), and, in determining the buyer's qualifying expenditure, there is disregarded any excess of his expenditure (including any 'additional VAT liability' incurred in respect thereof — see **10.10 CAPITAL ALLOWANCES — INTRODUCTION**) over the disposal value to be brought into account by the seller.
Where no such disposal value is to be brought into account (e.g. where the seller is non-UK resident), the buyer's qualifying expenditure (if otherwise greater) is restricted to the lesser of:
(a) market value at time of sale; and
(b) capital expenditure, if any, incurred by the seller or any person connected with him,
with modifications to allow for 'additional VAT liabilities' and 'rebates' — see **10.10 CAPITAL ALLOWANCES — INTRODUCTION**. However, this provision does not apply to plant and machinery subject to a sale or lease back where the transaction is on or after 9 October 2007.

Sale and leaseback
For these purposes, a sale is a '*sale and leaseback transaction*' if the plant or machinery:
(A) continues to be used for the purposes of a 'qualifying activity' carried on by the seller or, for contracts entered into on or after 22 April 2009, a person connected with the seller; or
(B) is used at some time after the sale for the purposes of a 'qualifying activity' carried on by the seller (or by a connected person other than the buyer) without having been used in the meantime for the purposes of any other 'qualifying activity' except that of leasing the plant or machinery.

Qualifying activity
For the purposes of these provisions, a '*qualifying activity*' is any activity within **11.2 CAPITAL ALLOWANCES — PLANT AND MACHINERY: ELIGIBLE EXPENDITURE AND INITIAL ALLOWANCES** regardless of whether or not profits therefrom are within the charge to UK tax.

These restrictions do not apply to the supply of unused plant or machinery in the ordinary course of the seller's business. Also, for chargeable periods ending before 12 May 1998, where the plant or machinery had not before the sale been used in a qualifying activity carried on by the seller or any person connected with the seller, first-year allowances (where otherwise relevant) were available, on the lesser of (a) and (b) above (if less than actual expenditure).

The above provisions apply to contracts for future delivery, hire-purchase etc. contracts, and hire-purchase etc. contract assignments as they apply to direct sales.

[*CAA 2001, ss 213(1)(2), 214–218, 230–233, 241, 242; FA 2008, Sch 20 para 6(10)*].

'Sole or main benefit' restriction

The 'sole or main benefit' restriction referred to above does not generally apply to straightforward finance leasing transactions (*Barclays Mercantile Industrial Finance Ltd v Melluish* [1990] STC 314, 63 TC 95).

However, with effect for expenditure incurred on or after 2 July 1997 (unless incurred before 2 July 1998 under a pre-2 July 1997 contract), the above rules are extended to further restrict allowances in the case of 'sale and finance leasebacks'.

A '*sale and finance leaseback*' is a transaction which either:

- meets one of the conditions at (A) and (B) above; or
- in which the plant or machinery is used at some time after the sale etc. for the purposes of a non-qualifying activity carried on by the seller (or by a connected person other than the buyer) without having been used in the meantime for the purposes of a 'qualifying activity' (defined as above) except that of leasing the plant or machinery,

where the availability of the plant or machinery for the use in question is a direct or indirect consequence of its having been leased under a 'finance lease'.

Where before 9 October 2007 an item of plant or machinery is the subject of a sale and finance leaseback, the buyer's qualifying expenditure (*and* in this case the seller's disposal value, if any) is further limited to the item's notional written-down value, computed on the assumption that all available allowances have been made in full. There are also restrictions on the qualifying expenditure of any future owner of the item. Where the finance lessor has substantially divested himself of any risk that the lessee will default, the lessor's expenditure does not qualify for plant and machinery allowances at all (and this applies regardless of any election as below). Modifications to these rules allow for any 'additional VAT liabilities' and 'rebates' — see **10.10 CAPITAL ALLOWANCES — INTRODUCTION**.

Finance lease

A '*finance lease*' is any arrangements for plant or machinery to be leased (from 9 October 2007, which are not long-funding leases) or made available such that the arrangements (or arrangements in which they are comprised) would fall, in accordance with generally accepted accounting practice (see **61.9 PROFIT COMPUTATIONS**), to be treated in the accounts of one or more of those companies as a finance lease or as a loan.

However, with effect, broadly, from 1 April 2006 (but see **13.13** under Commencement/transitional provisions), any arrangements which are a long funding lease as regards the lessor are not within the definition of 'finance lease' for these purposes (and for the purposes of (iv) below).

With effect from 28 July 2000, in the case of sale and leaseback (and sale and finance leaseback) transactions within the above provisions, a joint (irrevocable) election may be made by the seller (or assignor) and the lessor (within two years of the sale etc.) provided that:

- the seller (or assignor) incurred capital expenditure on acquiring the plant or machinery unused (and not second-hand) and not under a transaction itself within the above provisions;
- the sale etc. takes place not more than four months after the plant or machinery is first brought into use for any purpose; and
- the seller (or assignor) has not claimed capital allowances for the expenditure or included it in a pool of qualifying expenditure.

The effect of the election is that no allowances are made to the seller (or assignor) in respect of the expenditure, and that allowances which are accordingly available to the lessor are given by reference to the lesser of his expenditure and the amount in (b) above, i.e. disregarding the current market value at the time of the sale etc. (and, in the case of sale and finance leasebacks, the item's notional written-down value).

[*CAA 2001, ss 219, 221–228, 243–245, Sch 3 paras 45, 51; FA 2005, s 80, Sch 4 para 33; FA 2006, Sch 9 para 14; FA 2008, Sch 20 paras 9–12*].

(iii) Where a disposal value is required to be brought into account in respect of a car costing over £12,000on a sale (or on the performance of a contract) within any of the provisions in (ii) above, the disposal value is equal to the lesser of market value at the time of the event and the capital expenditure incurred (or treated as incurred) on it by the person disposing of it.

The new owner is treated as having incurred capital expenditure on the car of the same amount. These provisions will continue to apply for a transitional period of around five years, pending transfer over to the emissions-based system. [*CAA 2001, s 79*].

(iv) In a case where an item of plant or machinery is the subject of a sale and finance leaseback (as defined in (ii) above) and the seller's disposal value falls to be restricted as in (ii) above, further anti-avoidance provisions apply in relation to periods ending after 16 March 2004 (but subject to the transitional provisions below) so as to limit the amount of lease rentals deductible in computing the lessee's income or profits.

The amount deductible is limited to the aggregate of the finance charges shown in the accounts and the depreciation that would have been charged if the value of the item at the beginning of the leaseback had been taken for this purpose to be equal to the restricted disposal value.

In the accounting period in which the leaseback terminates:

- the above restriction on deductible lease rentals does not apply to any refund of lease rentals;
- the aforementioned aggregate is increased by a proportion of the net book value of the item immediately before the termination, such proportion to be computed in accordance with a formula in *CAA 2001, s 228B(4)*;
- (other than where a pre-17 March 2004 leaseback terminates before that date) the lessee's income/profits from the qualifying activity for the purposes of which the leased item was used immediately before the termination are increased by a proportion of the original consideration on the sale less the restricted disposal value, such proportion to be computed in accordance with a formula in *CAA 2001, s 228C(3)*.

The above rules do not apply to a lessee who became the lessee by means of an assignment of the lease.

For the above purposes and those below, a '*termination*' of a leaseback includes an assignment of the lessee's interest, the making of any other arrangements under which a person other than the lessee becomes liable to make payments under the leaseback and any variation as a result of which the leaseback ceases to be a finance lease.

In any case in which the above restriction on the lessee's deductible lease rentals potentially applies (or would do so if he had not obtained his interest by way of assignment), the following apply in computing the income/profits of the *lessor* for an accounting period. Amounts receivable by the lessor under the leaseback are included as income without netting off any amounts due by the lessor to the lessee.

However, amounts receivable are not included as income to the extent that they exceed the aggregate of the gross earnings under the leaseback as shown in the lessor's accounts (effectively the finance charge element of the lease rentals) and a proportion of the restricted disposal value, such proportion to be computed in accordance with a formula in *CAA 2001, s 228D(4)*. These rules do not apply if the lessee became the lessee by means of an assignment of the lease made before 17 March 2004.

Where the leaseback terminates and the lessor disposes of the plant or machinery in circumstances such that the resulting disposal value is limited under the general rule in **12.14 CAPITAL ALLOWANCES — PLANT AND MACHINERY: POOLING AND DISPOSALS** (disposal value of plant or machinery to be limited to qualifying expenditure incurred on its acquisition) or by that rule as modified under (i) above, then, in computing the lessor's income/profits for the accounting period in which termination occurs, any amount refunded to the lessee is deductible only to the extent that it does not exceed the limited disposal value. This does not apply in the case of a pre-17 March 2004 leaseback terminating before that date.

Special provision is made for cases in which accounts are not drawn up in accordance with generally accepted accounting practice (GAAP). Additionally, the above rules are adapted, in so far as they relate to the lessee, in a case where the leaseback does not fall under GAAP to be treated in the lessee's accounts as a finance lease but does fall to be so treated in the accounts of a person connected with the lessee. If the leaseback falls to be so treated in the accounts of neither the lessee nor a person connected with him, those rules are disapplied. In that case, however, where the term of the leaseback begins after 17 May 2004, the lessee's income/profits for the accounting period during which it begins are increased by the sale consideration less the restricted disposal value. Where plant or machinery, whilst continuing to be the subject of a sale and finance leaseback, is leased to the original owner, or a person connected with him, under an operating lease (meaning, for this purpose, a lease that does not fall under GAAP to be treated in the lessee's accounts as a finance lease) commencing after 17 May 2004, the following apply. In computing the income/profits of the lessee (i.e. the lessee under the operating lease), the deduction for operating lease rentals is restricted to the 'relevant amount'. In computing the income/profits of the lessor (i.e. the lessor under the operating lease), amounts receivable by the lessor under the operating lease are included as income without netting off any amounts due by the lessor to the lessee. However, amounts receivable are not included as income to the extent that they exceed the 'relevant amount'. In each case, the '*relevant amount*' is the maximum amount of finance lease rentals deductible in computing the finance lessee's income/profits (see above). In applying these rules, such apportionments are to be made as are just and reasonable where only some of the plant or machinery subject to the sale and finance leaseback is also subject to the operating lease.

Lease and finance leasebacks

The above rules also apply, again in relation to periods ending after 16 March 2004 (subject to the transitional provisions below), to a 'lease and finance leaseback' but with appropriate modifications; in particular, depreciation is disregarded in computing the finance lessee's lease rentals and the above limitation on the finance lessor's income/profits applies by reference only to the gross earnings under the leaseback. A '*lease and finance leaseback*' occurs if a person leases plant or machinery to another in circumstances such that, had it been a sale, the transaction would have been a sale and finance leaseback as defined in (ii) above (except that the availability of the plant or machinery for the use in question must in this case be a *direct* consequence of its having been leased under a finance lease). For this purpose, a person is regarded as leasing an item of plant or machinery to another person only if he grants that other person rights over the item for consideration and is not required to bring all of that consideration into account under the plant and machinery capital allowances code; there is a let-out where the last condition is met only because a joint election under *CAA 2001, s 199* was made by lessor and lessee before 18 May 2004 in relation to a fixture (see **13.1** under Cessation of ownership).

Transitional provisions

In relation to any leasebacks whose term commenced before 17 March 2004, transitional rules seek to preserve the pre-existing treatment of lease rentals payable before that date or in respect of any period ending before that date and a time proportion of lease rentals payable for periods straddling that date. For the effect on the lease rental deductions due to the lessee, see *FA 2004, Sch 23 paras 2, 3*; for the equivalent rules affecting computation of the lessor's income/profits, see *FA 2004, Sch 23 paras 7, 8*.

The increase in the lessee's income/profits for the accounting period in which the leaseback terminates is capped, in accordance with a formula in *FA 2004, Sch 23 para 5*, if a pre-17 March 2004 leaseback terminates early, i.e. other than by expiry of its term.

The increase in the lessee's income/profits for the accounting period in which the leaseback terminates is abated if a pre-17 March 2004 leaseback terminates early, the lessee reacquires ownership of the plant or machinery and the lessee's capital expenditure on reacquisition is itself restricted under (ii) above. If the restriction equals or exceeds the increase in profits/income, the increase is cancelled; in other cases, the increase is reduced by the restriction. However, the increase is reinstated in modified form if a disposal event (see **12.14 CAPITAL ALLOWANCES — PLANT AND MACHINERY: POOLING AND DISPOSALS**) occurs in relation to the whole or part of the plant or machinery within six years after the leaseback terminates. See *FA 2004, Sch 23 para 6*.

Where a pre-17 March 2004 lease and finance leaseback terminates and the finance lessee then disposes of the plant or machinery, there is provision for his chargeable gain to be reduced for capital gains tax purposes. See *FA 2004, Sch 23 para 10*.

See Tolley's Capital Allowances for more detail on these transitional provisions.

[*CAA 2001, ss 228A–228J; FA 2004, s 134, Sch 23*].

Simon's Taxes. See **B3.334, B3.340H–B3.340S, B3.342, B3.365, B3.366, B3.375, B3.377.**

(v) In relation to capital expenditure incurred on or after 9 December 2009, a lessor's qualifying expenditure for the purposes of plant and machinery allowances may fall to be restricted to the 'value of the asset to the lessor'.

The restriction applies if, at the time the lessor incurs the capital expenditure on the asset (i.e. the plant or machinery):

- the asset is leased or arrangements exist under which it is to be leased; and
- arrangements have been entered into in relation to payments under the lease that reduce the value of the asset to the lessor.

The '*value of the asset to the lessor*' is the sum of (i) the present value of the lessor's anticipated taxable income from the lease of the asset and (ii) the present value of the residual value of the asset (reduced by the amount of any rental rebate).

In calculating the lessor's anticipated taxable income from the lease, one excludes any amount brought into account as a disposal value and any amounts that represent charges for services or 'taxes' to be paid by the lessor. ('*Taxes*' means UK or foreign taxes or duties, but not income tax, corporation tax or foreign equivalents.)

Present value is calculated by using the 'interest rate implicit in the lease' (see *CAA 2001, s 228MB*).

A rental rebate means any sum payable to the lessee that is calculated by reference to the value of the plant or machinery at or about the time when the lease terminates (see *CAA 2001, s 228MC*).

Where the lessor has previously incurred capital expenditure on the same asset, the qualifying expenditure falling to be restricted is his total qualifying expenditure on that asset. This covers the possibility that the lessor may incur the capital expenditure in instalments.

For the above purposes, a 'lease' includes any arrangements which provide for plant or machinery to be leased or otherwise made available by one person to another.

[*CAA 2001, ss 228MA–228MC; FA 2010, Sch 5 para 1*].

Plant or machinery received by way of gift

[13.28] Where plant or machinery received by way of gift is brought into use for the purposes of a trade or other qualifying activity carried on by the donee, the donee is entitled to writing-down allowances as if he had purchased it from the donor at the time it is brought into use and at its market value at that time.

Where the gift was brought into use between 1 November 1992 and 31 October 1993 inclusive, the donee's deemed expenditure qualified for the temporarily reinstated 40% first-year allowance (**11.13 CAPITAL ALLOWANCES — PLANT AND MACHINERY: ELIGIBLE EXPENDITURE AND INITIAL ALLOWANCES**), but such deemed expenditure cannot qualify for any of the targeted first-year allowances introduced subsequently. [*CAA 2001, ss 14, 213(3), Sch 3 paras 12, 43*]. See **Simon's Taxes**. See **B3.303**.

Previous use outside trade etc.

[13.29] Where a person brings into use, for the purposes of the trade or other qualifying activity, plant or machinery which that person previously owned for purposes not providing entitlement to plant and machinery allowances in respect of that activity, writing-down allowances are calculated as if the trader etc. had, at the time of bringing it into use, incurred expenditure on its acquisition equal to its market value at that time.

Actual cost, if less, is substituted for market value where the plant or machinery is brought into trade etc. use after 20 March 2000. The actual cost for this purpose is reduced to the extent that it would have been reduced under the anti-avoidance provisions of *CAA 2001, s 218* or (where the date of the sale and finance leaseback is before 9 October 2007) *s 224* or earlier equivalents (see **13.27**) had it been expenditure on plant or machinery for use in the qualifying activity.

Where the plant or machinery was brought into use between 1 November 1992 and 31 October 1993 inclusive, the deemed expenditure qualified for the temporarily reinstated 40% first-year allowance (**11.13 CAPITAL ALLOWANCES — PLANT AND MACHINERY: ELIGIBLE EXPENDITURE AND INITIAL ALLOWANCES**); such first-year allowances were not, however, available where plant or machinery was transferred from one qualifying activity to another carried on by the same person and was brought into use in the second activity after 13 April 1993. Expenditure deemed to be incurred under these provisions does not qualify for any of the targeted first-year allowances introduced subsequently.

[*CAA 2001, s 13, Sch 3 para 11; FA 2008, Sch 20 para 6(2)*].

See also **13.4** as regards an asset ceasing to be used for long funding leasing but being retained by the lessor for use in a qualifying activity.

Simon's Taxes. See **B3.303**.

Partnerships

[13.30] Partnerships are entitled to allowances in respect of an item of plant or machinery used for the trade or other qualifying activity carried on by the partnership, and owned by one or more partners without being partnership property.

Any transfer of the item between partners, whilst it continues to be so used, does not require a disposal value to be brought into account. These provisions do not apply if such an item is *let* by one or more partners to the partnership or otherwise made available to it in consideration of a tax-deductible payment. [*CAA 2001, s 264*].

Following a change in the persons carrying on a trade or other qualifying activity, other than one resulting in the activity being treated as permanently discontinued, allowances are subsequently given and balancing charges subsequently made as if the new partnership etc. had carried on the activity before the change.

For this purpose, a '*qualifying activity*' does not include an office or employment but otherwise includes any of the activities at **11.2** (i)–(vii) **CAPITAL ALLOWANCES — PLANT AND MACHINERY: ELIGIBLE EXPENDITURE AND INITIAL ALLOWANCES** regardless of whether or not the profits therefrom are within the charge to UK tax. [*CAA 2001, s 263; CAA 1990, s 78(3)(4); ITTOIA 2005, Sch 1 para 549*]. See **13.31** as regards partnerships treated as discontinued and successions to trades generally.

Simon's Taxes. See **B3.390**.

Successions

[13.31] Following a change in the persons carrying on a trade or other qualifying activity, such that the activity is treated as permanently discontinued, any plant or machinery transferred, without being sold, to the new owner for continuing use in the qualifying activity is treated as sold at market value on the date of change, although no first-year allowance or, for expenditure on or after 1 April 2008, annual investment allowance (where otherwise applicable) is available to the new owner.

Qualifying activity

For this purpose, a '*qualifying activity*' does not include an office or employment but otherwise includes any of the activities at **11.2**(i)–(vii) **CAPITAL ALLOWANCES — PLANT AND MACHINERY: ELIGIBLE EXPENDITURE AND INITIAL ALLOWANCES** regardless of whether or not the profits therefrom are within the charge to UK tax.

These provisions apply equally to plant or machinery not in use but provided and available for use for the purposes of the qualifying activity.

Where *CAA 2001* has effect (see **10.1 CAPITAL ALLOWANCES — INTRODUCTION**), they apply only to plant and machinery actually owned by the predecessor. [*CAA 2001, s 265; ITTOIA 2005, Sch 1 para 550; CTA 2009, Sch 1 para 496*].

Joint election by connected persons

Where:

(i) a person succeeds to a trade or other qualifying activity carried on by a person 'connected' with that person;
(ii) each is within the charge to UK tax on the profits; and
(iii) the successor is not a dual resident investing company,

they may jointly elect, within two years after the date of change, for plant or machinery to be treated as transferred at a price giving rise to neither a balancing allowance nor a balancing charge.

This applies to plant or machinery which immediately before and after the succession is owned by the person concerned and either in use, or (where *CAA 2001* has effect — see **10.1 CAPITAL ALLOWANCES — INTRODUCTION**) provided and available for use, for the purposes of the qualifying activity, and regardless of any actual sale by the predecessor to the successor. Allowances and charges are subsequently made as if everything done to or by the predecessor had been done to or by the successor. Where *CAA 2001* has effect, it is expressly provided that the deemed sale takes place when the succession takes place.

Connected

For this purpose, persons are '*connected*' if:

(a) they are **CONNECTED PERSONS** (**25**) within *CTA 2010, s 1122*; or
(b) one of them is a partnership in which the other has the right to a share of assets or income, or both are partnerships in both of which some other person has the right to such a share; or

(c) one of them is a body corporate over which the other has control (within *CAA 2001, s 574*), or both are bodies corporate, or one a body corporate and one a partnership, over both of which some other person has control.

An election in relation to a succession occurring after 26 July 1989 precludes the application of *CAA 2001, s 104E* (disposal value of special rate assets) for expenditure incurred on or after 1 April 2008 and long-life asset expenditure incurred before that date but allocated to a pool in a chargeable period beginning on or after that date and *s 104* for previous expenditure or periods, *CAA 2001, s 265* (see above) and the similar provisions in *CAA 2001, s 108*, and their forerunners. First-year allowances would appear to be precluded.

In relation to successions occurring after 4 December 2005, the above election does not have effect in relation to qualifying leased plant or machinery where the transferee succeeds to a trade carried on by the transferor which is a 'business of leasing plant or machinery' as defined in **5.28 ANTI-AVOIDANCE**.

For transfers under *CTA 2010, Pt 22, Ch 1* (transfers of trade without a change in ownership) see **55.11 LOSSES**. For transfers between companies and co-operative societies (SCEs) in different EU member states *under CAA 2001, s 560*, see **17.14 CAPITAL GAINS**, and between such companies on the formation of an SE by merger under *CAA 2001, s 561A*, see **17.27 CAPITAL GAINS**.

[*CAA 2001, ss 266–267A, Sch 3 para 52; FA 2006, s 85; FA 2008, Sch 24 para 14; Sch 26 para 12*].

Simon's Taxes. See B3.390.

A renewals basis

[13.32] A renewals basis is generally available as an alternative to capital allowances.

A deduction is allowed in computing profits of the cost of a replacement item less the proceeds of sale (or scrap value) of the item replaced.

Where, however, the replacement item is an improvement on that replaced, the deduction is restricted to the cost of replacing like with like. See *Caledonian Railway Co v Banks* CES 1880, 1 TC 487; *Eastmans Ltd v Shaw* HL 1928, 14 TC 218; *Hyam v CIR* CS 1929, 14 TC 479.

Cost of renewals of trade implements, utensils etc. are allowed as a deduction under *CTA 2009, Pt 3*, but cf. *Hinton v Maden & Ireland Ltd* HL 1959, 38 TC 391 and also see *Peter Merchant Ltd v Stedeford* CA 1948, 30 TC 496 (provision for future renewals not allowable). Replacement of parts is allowed under general principles so far as identity of plant or machinery is retained.

For further details of 'renewals basis' and change from renewals basis to normal capital allowances and *vice versa*, see HMRC Extra-Statutory Concession B1 as revised and HMRC Business Income Manual BIM46935, 46950, 46955.

Simon's Taxes. See B3.312.

A **valuation basis** is a variation of renewals basis in which a class of assets, for example spare parts for plant and machinery, are dealt with in a similar way to trading stock, involving opening and closing valuations. For further detail, and for change from capital allowances to valuation basis, see HMRC Business Income Manual BIM46940, 46960.

Partial depreciation subsidies

[13.33] Partial depreciation subsidies, i.e. sums, not otherwise taxable on the recipient, are payable to him, directly or indirectly, by any other person in respect of, or to take account of, *part* of the depreciation of plant or machinery resulting from its use in the recipient's trade or other qualifying activity.

Where it appears that a partial depreciation subsidy will be payable, a first-year allowance and annual investment allowance can nevertheless be given, but must be scaled down as is just and reasonable (though the full amount is deducted in arriving at the balance of expenditure available for writing-down allowances).

Qualifying expenditure (**11.2 CAPITAL ALLOWANCES — PLANT AND MACHINERY: ELIGIBLE EXPENDITURE AND INITIAL ALLOWANCES**) which has been the subject of a partial depreciation subsidy can only be allocated to a *single asset pool*.

Where qualifying expenditure has otherwise been allocated to a pool and a partial depreciation subsidy is received for the first time in respect of it, it must be transferred to a single asset pool. This is achieved by bringing in a disposal value (equal to market value) in the original pool for the chargeable period in which the subsidy is paid and allocating an equivalent amount to the single asset pool.

Writing-down allowances and balancing allowances and charges in respect of the single asset pool are reduced to such amounts as are just and reasonable (though the full amount is deducted in arriving at any unrelieved qualifying expenditure carried forward).

[*CAA 2001, ss 209–212*].

See **11.3 CAPITAL ALLOWANCES — PLANT AND MACHINERY: ELIGIBLE EXPENDITURE AND INITIAL ALLOWANCES** as regards subsidies towards the whole of such depreciation. See **10.2 CAPITAL ALLOWANCES — INTRODUCTION** as regards contributions by others towards *expenditure* qualifying for plant and machinery and other capital allowances.

Simon's Taxes. See B3.360.

A lessee required to provide plant or machinery

[13.34] A lessee required to provide plant or machinery under the terms of the lease (including any tenancy), and using it for the purposes of a trade or other qualifying activity, is treated as if he owned it (for as long as it is used for those purposes), but is not required to bring in a disposal value (**12.14 CAPITAL ALLOWANCES — PLANT AND MACHINERY: POOLING AND DISPOSALS**) on termination of the lease. If:

- the plant or machinery continues to be so used until termination of the lease;
- the lessor holds the lease in the course of a qualifying activity; and
- on or after termination, a disposal event occurs at a time when the lessor owns the plant or machinery,

the *lessor* is required to bring in a disposal value, for the chargeable period in which the disposal event occurs, in the pool to which the expenditure would have been allocated if incurred by the lessor.

These rules do not, however, apply where the plant or machinery becomes, by law, part of the building in which it is installed or attached (**13.1**) under a lease entered into after 11 July 1984 unless pursuant to an agreement made on or before that date. [*CAA 2001, s 70, Sch 3 para 17*].

Disposal of leased asset where income retained

[13.35] Where, after 4 December 2005, a lessor sells or disposes of plant or machinery which is subject to a lease but remains entitled immediately after the disposal to some or all the rental income payable after that date in respect of the lease, the disposal value to be brought into account by the lessor is determined as follows.

Where the disposal consideration exceeds the limit imposed in **12.14 CAPITAL ALLOWANCES — PLANT AND MACHINERY: POOLING AND DISPOSALS** (broadly, the original cost) the disposal value is to equal the consideration received and that limit does not apply.

In any other case, but subject to that limit, the disposal value is to equal the sum of the consideration received plus the 'net present value' of the rentals payable (after 4 December 2005) to which the lessor remains entitled immediately after the disposal. In so far as any such future rentals receivable by the lessor are brought into account in determining the disposal value, the amount of the rentals equal to their value so brought into account is to be excluded in calculating the lessor's leasing business income for corporation tax purposes (any necessary apportionment to be made on a just and reasonable basis).

The '*net present value*' of the rentals is the amount as determined under *CA 2001, s 228L* using a discount rate of 3.5% (which can be varied by regulation). If any land or asset other than plant or machinery is subject to the lease, the net present value of the rentals relating to the plant or machinery is to be determined using a just and reasonable basis.

Any rentals receivable by the lessor before 22 March 2006 are to be excluded in calculating the lessor's leasing business income for corporation tax purposes.

This provision applies to a lessor which carries on a '*business of leasing plant or machinery*' as defined in **5.28 ANTI-AVOIDANCE** and the disposal of plant or machinery for this purpose is that on whose provision expenditure is incurred wholly or partly for the purposes of the business. A '*lease*' in this case includes an underlease, sublease, tenancy or licence or an agreement for any of those things.

[*CAA 2001, ss 228K–228M; FA 2006, s 84*].

Transfers of trade to obtain balancing allowance

[13.36] The following provision applies to the transfer of a trade on or after 12 March 2008 which fulfils the following conditions:

(i) a company ceases to carry on a trade or part of a trade;
(ii) another company begins to carry on the trade or part;
(iii) the first company would be entitled to a balancing allowance (where the whole trade is transferred only);
(iv) the cessation of the trade or part is part of a scheme or arrangement the main purpose, or one of the main purposes of which is to entitle the first company to an allowance.

In the case of a transfer within *CTA 2010, Pt 22, Ch 1*, the trade or part discontinued is treated as a separate trade for both companies, with apportionment of expenses, assets and liabilities so far as just.

The trade is treated as continuing and no balancing adjustment arises. For transfers under *CTA 2010, Pt 22, Ch 1* (transfers of trade without a change in ownership) see **17.14 CAPITAL GAINS**, and between such companies on the formation of an SE or SCE by merger under *CAA 2001, s 561A*, see **17.27 CAPITAL GAINS.**

This anti-avoidance provision does not apply where there is a company reconstruction within *CTA 2010, Pt 22, Ch 1* with no change in ownership of the assets. [*CTA 2010, ss 954–957*].

Key points

[13.37] Points to consider are as follows.

- In order to claim capital allowances on fixtures the owner of the qualifying asset is generally required to have an interest in the land on which it is affixed. Elections may be possible where, for example, expenditure is incurred by an equipment lessor and in the absence of such an election nobody would be entitled to the allowances.
- Where fixtures are disposed of it is often advisable for the seller and purchaser to enter into a joint election (*CAA 2001, s 198*) to fix the disposal proceeds for capital allowance purposes. Such an election clarifies the situation and should reduce the likelihood of questions from HMRC. Elections can be entered into between connected parties but there is anti-avoidance legislation to prevent values being set only for the purpose of mitigating tax and where there are no bona fide commercial reasons.
- The long funding lease rules were introduced for leases entered into from 1 April 2006 to correct a long standing distortion between borrowing via a third party loan and leasing. Broadly

where the legislation applies the entitlement to capital allowances is transferred from the lessor to the lessee (even though legal ownership remains with the lessor).

- The long funding lease rules will generally apply to operating or finance leases which are for more than five years and not excluded (see **13.5**). The rules were not intended to apply to property investors.
- Where an operating lease meets the definition of a long funding lease the rental income and expenses for the lessor and lessee respectively are adjusted for tax purposes to compensate for the loss/gain of the capital allowances. In the absence of such adjustments the operating lessee would be entitled to both capital allowances and full rental deductions.
- Partnerships are also entitled to capital allowances. Each partner is entitled to its corresponding share of the allowances based on the profit share ratio. A partnership is only entitled to an Annual Investment Allowance if all of the members are individuals.
- Where plant and machinery is transferred to a connected party a joint election may be entered into to treat the asset, for tax purposes, as being transferred at tax written down value rather than market value.

14

Capital Allowances — Mineral Extraction

Cross references. See **10 CAPITAL ALLOWANCES — INTRODUCTION; 11 CAPITAL ALLOWANCES — PLANT AND MACHINERY: ELIGIBLE EXPENDITURE AND INITIAL ALLOWANCES; 12 CAPITAL ALLOWANCES — PLANT AND MACHINERY: POOLING AND DISPOSALS; 13 CAPITAL ALLOWANCES — PLANT AND MACHINERY: FIXTURES AND LEASING; 15 CAPITAL ALLOWANCES — BUILDINGS** and **16 CAPITAL ALLOWANCES — MISCELLANEOUS.**

Other sources. See Tolley's Capital Allowances.

Simon's Taxes. See B3.4.

Mineral extraction

Introduction

[14.1] Mineral extraction allowances are available in respect of qualifying expenditure incurred by a person carrying on a 'mineral extraction trade'.

A '*mineral extraction trade*' is a trade consisting of or including the working of a source of '*mineral deposits*', i.e. such deposits of a wasting nature including any natural deposits or geothermal energy capable of being lifted or extracted from the earth.

A '*source of mineral deposits*' includes a mine, oil well and a source of geothermal energy. [*CAA 2001, s 394*].

A *share* in an asset may qualify for mineral extraction allowances. [*CAA 2001, s 435*].

Simon's Taxes. See B3.4.

Qualifying expenditure

[14.2] '*Qualifying expenditure*' means capital expenditure, incurred for the purposes of a mineral extraction trade, on:

(a) '*mineral exploration and access*' (i.e. searching for or discovering and testing the mineral deposits of any source, or winning access to any such deposits);
(b) acquisition of a '*mineral asset*' (i.e. any mineral deposits or land comprising mineral deposits, or any interest in or right over such deposits or land) (subject to the limitations in **14.5** below);
(c) construction of works, in connection with the working of a source of mineral deposits, which are likely to become of little or no value when the source ceases to be worked;
(d) construction of works which are likely to become valueless when a foreign concession under which a source of mineral deposits is worked comes to an end.

Included in (a) above is abortive expenditure (including appeal costs) on seeking planning permission for the undertaking of mineral exploration and access or the working of mineral deposits.

Expenditure on the acquisition of, or of rights over, mineral deposits or the site of a source of mineral deposits falls into (b) rather than (a) above.

Expenditure that does not qualify includes expenditure on:

- the provision of plant or machinery (except certain pre-trading expenditure — see below), and see **14.11**;
- the acquisition of, or of rights in or over, the *site* of any works in (c) or (d) above;
- works constructed wholly or mainly for processing the raw products, unless the process is designed to prepare the raw products for use as such;
- (subject to *CAA 2001, s 415* — see below) buildings and structures for occupation by, or welfare of, workers;
- a building constructed *entirely* for use as an office;
- the office part of a building or structure constructed *partly* for use as an office, where such expenditure exceeds 10% of the capital expenditure on construction of the whole building.

[*CAA 2001, ss 395–399, 400(1), 403(1)(2), 414*].

Qualifying expenditure also includes capital contributions, for the purposes of a mineral extraction trade carried on outside the UK, to the cost of accommodation buildings, and certain related utility buildings and welfare works, for employees engaged in working a source, provided that the buildings or works are likely to be of little or no value when the source ceases to be worked, that the expenditure does not result in the acquisition of an asset, and that relief is not due under any other tax provision. [*CAA 2001, s 415*].

Net expenditure incurred on the restoration of the site of a source of mineral deposits (or land used in connection with working such a source) within three years after the cessation of the trade is also qualifying expenditure, treated as incurred on the last day of trading, unless relieved elsewhere. [*CAA 2001, s 416*].

Pre-trading expenditure

[14.3] *Pre-trading expenditure* for the purposes of a mineral extraction trade is treated as incurred on the first day of trading.

This applies equally to pre-trading expenditure on mineral exploration and access, but in determining whether such expenditure is qualifying expenditure within (a) above, the following limitations apply.

(i) In the case of pre-trading expenditure on plant or machinery which is used at a source but is sold, demolished, destroyed or abandoned before commencement of the mineral extraction trade, qualifying expenditure is limited to net expenditure after taking account of sale proceeds, insurance money or capital compensation.

(ii) In the case of pre-trading exploration expenditure other than on plant or machinery, qualifying expenditure is limited to net expenditure after taking into account any reasonably attributable capital sums received before the first day of trading.

In either case, if mineral exploration and access is not continuing at the source on the first day of trading, qualifying expenditure is further limited to net expenditure incurred in the six years ending on that day.

[*CAA 2001, ss 400(2)–(5), 401, 402, 434*].

First year qualifying expenditure

[14.4] Qualifying expenditure (as above) incurred by a company **after 16 April 2002** is '*first-year qualifying expenditure*' if it is incurred wholly for the purposes of a 'ring fence trade' within *CTA 2010, s 330*, subject to the exclusion of expenditure on:

(A) acquisition of mineral assets (see (b) above); and

(B) acquisition of an asset representing expenditure incurred by a connected company (within *CTA 2010, s 1122*, see **25 CONNECTED PERSONS**), including any results obtained from any search, exploration or enquiry on which mineral exploitation and access expenditure was incurred.

For this purpose, *CAA 2001, ss 400(4), 434* (see above), which treat certain expenditure as having been incurred on the first day of trading, do not apply.

[*CAA 2001, ss 416A–416C*].

Simon's Taxes. See **B3.405–B3.414**.

Limitations on qualifying expenditure

[14.5] Qualifying expenditure within **14.2**(b) above (acquisition of mineral asset) is limited in the following circumstances.

If the mineral asset is an interest in land, an amount equal to the 'undeveloped market value' of the interest is excluded.

'*Undeveloped market value*' is the market value of the interest at the time of acquisition ignoring the mineral deposits and assuming that development of the land (other than that already lawfully begun or for which planning permission has already been granted) is, and will remain, unlawful.

Where the undeveloped market value includes the value of buildings or structures which, at any time after acquisition, permanently cease to be used, their value at acquisition (exclusive of land and after deducting any net capital allowances received in respect of them) is treated as qualifying expenditure incurred at the time of cessation of use.

These provisions operate by reference to the actual time of acquisition, regardless of any different time given by the pre-trading expenditure provisions at **14.3** above. They do not apply where an election is made under *CAA 2001, s 569* or its forerunner (election to treat connected persons transactions as made at written-down value). [*CAA 2001, ss 403(3), 404, 405, Sch 3 para 84*].

Where a deduction has been allowed under *CTA 2009, ss 62–67* or their predecessors (or, for income tax purposes, under *ITTOIA 2005, ss 60–67* or their predecessors) in respect of a premium under a lease (see **70.62 TRADE PROFITS — INCOME AND SPECIFIC TRADES**), the qualifying expenditure allowable in respect of the acquisition of the interest in land to which the premium relates is correspondingly reduced. [*CAA 2001, s 406; ITTOIA 2005, Sch 1 para 561; CTA 2009, Sch 1 para 508*].

Simon's Taxes. See **B3.410**.

Second-hand assets

[14.6] Where:

(a) an asset is acquired from another person; and
(b) either that person or any previous owner incurred expenditure on it in connection with a mineral extraction trade,

the buyer's qualifying expenditure is restricted to the seller's qualifying expenditure on the asset less net allowances given to him.

If an oil licence (or an interest therein) is acquired, the buyer's qualifying expenditure is limited to the amount of the original licence fee paid (or such part of it as it is just and reasonable to attribute to the interest).

However, these restrictions do not affect amounts *treated* under rules below as qualifying expenditure on mineral exploration and access.

In relation to a mineral asset situated in the UK, the restrictions do not apply to an acquisition under a pre-16 July 1985 contract, and the reference above to previous owners excludes any person who has not been the owner at any time after 31 March 1986.

Where:

(i) the purchased asset above is a mineral asset; and
(ii) part of its value is properly attributable to expenditure on mineral exploration and access incurred as in (b) above,

so much if any of the buyer's expenditure as it is just and reasonable to attribute to the part of the value in (ii) above (not exceeding the amount of original expenditure to which it is attributable) is treated as qualifying expenditure on mineral exploration and access, with the remainder treated as expenditure on acquisition of a mineral asset. In relation to an asset situated in the UK, this rule does not apply to an acquisition under a pre-16 July 1985 contract, and the reference to previous owners excludes any person who has not been the owner at any time after 31 March 1986. In relation to claims made after 25 November 1996, expenditure deducted by a previous owner in computing taxable profits is excluded for these purposes from the original expenditure.

Where:

- capital expenditure is incurred in acquiring assets for a mineral extraction trade from a person (the seller) who did *not* carry on a mineral extraction trade; and
- the assets represent expenditure on mineral exploration and access incurred by the seller,

the buyer's qualifying expenditure is limited to the amount of the seller's expenditure.

Assets include any results obtained from any search, exploration or inquiry on which the expenditure was incurred.

This restriction does not apply if the asset is an interest in an oil licence acquired by the buyer after 12 September 1995; in this case, so much if any of the buyer's expenditure as it is just and reasonable to attribute to the part of the value of the licence attributable to the seller's expenditure (but limited to the amount of that expenditure) is treated as qualifying expenditure on mineral exploration and access, with the cost of the oil licence being reduced by the buyer's expenditure so attributable (without limitation).

Where a mineral asset is transferred between companies under common control, and no election is made under *CAA 2001, s 569* or its forerunner (election to treat connected persons transactions as made at written-down value), the buyer's expenditure is limited to that of the seller.

However, this does not affect amounts *treated* under rules above as qualifying expenditure on mineral exploration and access.

Where the asset is an interest in land, the limitations at **14.5** above generally apply as if the buyer acquired the interest when the seller acquired it (or, in the case of a sequence of such transactions, when the first seller acquired it).

[*CAA 2001, ss 407–413, Sch 3 paras 85–87*].

Simon's Taxes. See **B3.411–B3.414** *et seq.*

Allowances and balancing adjustments

First Year Allowance (FYA)

[14.7] For each item of first-year qualifying expenditure (see **14.2–14.4** above), a **FYA** of up to **100%** is available for the chargeable period in which the expenditure is incurred.

No FYA is available, however, to the extent that a transaction is attributable to any scheme, agreement or understanding, whether or not legally enforceable, a main purpose of which is the obtaining of a first-year allowance which would not otherwise have been available (or of a greater allowance than would otherwise have been available).

Writing Down Allowance (WDA)

For each item of qualifying expenditure (see **14.2–14.4** above), a **WDA** is available for each chargeable period (see **10.1 CAPITAL ALLOWANCES — INTRODUCTION**) and is equal to a set percentage (as below) of the amount (if any) by which 'unrelieved qualifying expenditure' exceeds the total of any disposal values falling to be brought into account as in **14.8**.

The WDA is proportionately reduced or increased if the chargeable period is less or more than a year, or if the mineral extraction trade has been carried on for part only of the chargeable period.

Balancing adjustments

In the circumstances listed at **14.9** below, a **balancing allowance** is available, instead of a WDA, equal to the excess (if any) of (1) 'unrelieved qualifying expenditure' over (2) total disposal values. (This is subject to the anti-avoidance rule at **10.14 CAPITAL ALLOWANCES — INTRODUCTION.**)

If, for any chargeable period, (2) exceeds (1), there arises a liability to a **balancing charge**, normally equal to that excess but limited to net allowances previously given (including, where a balancing charge arises in respect of first-year qualifying expenditure incurred in the period, any FYA given on that expenditure).

A claim for a WDA *or* a balancing allowance may require it to be reduced to a specified amount.

Rates of WDAs

Rates of WDA are as follows:

Acquisition of a mineral asset (see **14.2**(b) above)	**10% p.a.**
Other qualifying expenditure	**25% p.a.**

Unrelieved qualifying expenditure

'*Unrelieved qualifying expenditure*' means qualifying expenditure (other than first-year qualifying expenditure) incurred in the chargeable period and the tax written-down value brought forward (i.e. net of allowances and any disposal values) of qualifying expenditure (including first-year qualifying expenditure) incurred in a previous chargeable period.

If a disposal receipt falls to be brought into account in the case of first-year qualifying expenditure for the chargeable period in which it was incurred, any balance of that expenditure after deducting any FYA given in respect of it is treated as unrelieved qualifying expenditure *but only* for the purpose of determining whether there is a balancing allowance or charge for that period and, if so, the amount of such an allowance or charge.

[*CAA 2001, ss 416D–419*].

The net demolition costs (i.e. the excess, if any, of demolition costs over money received for remains) of an asset representing qualifying expenditure is added to that expenditure in determining the amount of any balancing allowance or charge for the chargeable period of demolition, and is not then treated as expenditure incurred on any replacement asset. [*CAA 2001, s 433*].

Pooling

There is no provision for pooling expenditure (cf. plant and machinery at **12.2 CAPITAL ALLOWANCES — PLANT AND MACHINERY: POOLING AND DISPOSALS**).

In practice, HMRC do not object to the grouping together of assets for computational convenience, provided individual sources are kept separate and assets attracting different rates of WDA are not grouped with each other.

However, where a disposal value falls to be brought into account or a balancing allowance arises, it will sometimes be necessary to reconstruct separate computations for individual items of expenditure previously grouped. (HMRC Capital Allowances Manual CA50410).

Simon's Taxes. See **B3.419–B3.422.**

Disposal events and values

[14.8] A disposal value must be brought into account by deduction from unrelieved qualifying expenditure (see **14.7** above), for the chargeable period in which the event occurs, on the occurrence of any of the following events.

(i) An asset representing qualifying expenditure (see **14.4** above) is disposed of or permanently ceases to be used for the purposes of a mineral extraction trade (whether because of cessation of trade or otherwise).

(ii) A mineral asset begins to be used (by the trader or another person) in a way which constitutes development which is neither 'existing permitted development' nor development for the purposes of a mineral extraction trade. Development is '*existing permitted development*' if, at the time of acquisition, it had already lawfully begun or the appropriate planning permission had already been granted.

(iii) In a case not within (i) or (ii) above, a capital sum is received which, in whole or in part, it is reasonable to attribute to qualifying expenditure.

The amount to be brought into account depends upon the nature of the event.

(a) On an event within (i) or (ii) above, it is an amount determined in accordance with the list at **12.14 CAPITAL ALLOWANCES — PLANT AND MACHINERY: POOLING AND DISPOSALS** (disregarding (f), the reference to abandonment at (d) and the text immediately following the list). However, if the asset is an interest in land, the amount so ascertained is then restricted by excluding the '*undeveloped market value*', determined as in **14.5** above but by reference to the time of disposal.

(b) On an event within (iii) above, it is so much of the capital sum as is reasonably attributable to the qualifying expenditure.

[*CAA 2001, ss 420–425; ITEPA 2003, Sch 6 para 254*].

In relation to sales at other than market value, the connected person and other anti-avoidance provisions, and election potential, of *CAA 2001, ss 567–570* (and forerunners) apply with appropriate modifications for mineral extraction allowances as they do for industrial buildings allowances.

Simon's Taxes. See B3.420.

Balancing allowances

[14.9] A person is entitled to a balancing allowance (instead of a writing-down allowance) for a chargeable period if:

- the chargeable period is that in which the first day of trading falls, and either the qualifying expenditure is pre-trading expenditure on plant or machinery within **14.3** above or it is pre-trading exploration expenditure within **14.3** above where mineral exploration and access is not continuing at the source on the first day of trading; or
- the qualifying expenditure was on mineral exploration and access, and in that chargeable period that person gives up the exploration, search or inquiry to which the expenditure related, without subsequently carrying on a mineral extraction trade consisting of or including the working of related mineral deposits; or
- in that chargeable period that person permanently ceases to work particular mineral deposits and the qualifying expenditure was on mineral exploration and access relating solely to those deposits or on the acquisition of a mineral asset consisting of those deposits or part of them; but where two or more mineral assets are comprised in, or derive from, a single asset, the above applies only when *all* the relevant mineral deposits cease to be worked; or
- the qualifying expenditure falls within *CAA 2001, s 415* (capital contributions to certain buildings or works for benefit of employees abroad — see **14.2** above), and in that chargeable period, the buildings or works permanently cease to be used for the purposes of or in connection with the mineral extraction trade; or
- the qualifying expenditure was on the provision of any assets, and in that chargeable period, any of those assets is disposed of or otherwise permanently ceases to be used for purposes of the trade; or
- the qualifying expenditure is represented by assets, and in that chargeable period those assets are permanently lost or cease to exist (due to destruction, dismantling or otherwise) or begin to be used wholly or partly for purposes other than those of the mineral extraction trade; or
- the mineral extraction trade is permanently discontinued in that chargeable period.

[*CAA 2001, ss 426–431*].

Simon's Taxes. See B3.421.

Making of allowances and charges

[14.10] Mineral extraction allowances (or balancing charges) are given (or made) as trading expenses (or trading receipts) in calculating the profits of the mineral extraction trade. [*CAA 2001, s 432*].

Simon's Taxes. See B3.423.

Plant and machinery allowances

[14.11] Plant and machinery is normally excluded from relief under the current provisions, but certain pre-trading expenditure may qualify (see **14.3** above).

The normal plant and machinery rules (see **11.2** *et seq*. **CAPITAL ALLOWANCES — PLANT AND MACHINERY: ELIGIBLE EXPENDITURE AND INITIAL ALLOWANCES**) apply to plant and machinery provided for mineral exploration and access in connection with a mineral extraction trade. [*CAA 2001, ss 159, 160*].

Where such expenditure (limited to capital expenditure where *CAA 2001* has effect — see **10.1 CAPITAL ALLOWANCES — INTRODUCTION**) is incurred prior to the date of commencement of a mineral extraction trade and the plant or machinery is still owned at that date, it is treated as if sold immediately before that date and re-acquired on that date.

The capital expenditure on re-acquisition is deemed to be equal to the actual expenditure previously incurred. [*CAA 2001, s 161, Sch 3 para 25; CTA 2009, Sch 1 para 177*].

Example

X Ltd operates a mining business with two mineral sources, G and S. Accounts are prepared to 30 September.

On 31 December 2010 the mineral deposits and mineworks at G are sold at market value to Z Ltd for £80,000 and £175,000 respectively.

A new source, P, is purchased on 30 April 2011 for £170,000 (including land with an undeveloped market value of £70,000) and the following expenditure is incurred before the end of the accounting period ended 30 September 2011.

	£
Plant and machinery	40,000
Construction of administration office	25,000
Construction of mining works which are likely to have little value when mining ceases	50,000
Staff hostel	35,000
Winning access to the deposits	150,000
	£300,000

During the year to 30 September 2011, X Ltd also incurred expenditure of £20,000 in seeking planning permission to mine a further plot of land, Source Q. Permission was refused.

Residue of expenditure brought forward (based on accounts to 30 September 2010)		£
Mineral exploration and access	– Source G	170,000
	– Source S	200,000
Mineral assets	– Source G	95,250
	– Source S	72,000

The mineral extraction allowances due for the year ending 30 September 2011 are as follows.

		£	£
Source G			
Mineral exploration and access			
WDV b/f		170,000	
Proceeds		175,000	
Balancing charge		£5,000	(5,000)
Mineral assets			
WDV b/f		95,250	
Proceeds		80,000	
Balancing allowance		£15,250	15,250
Source S			
Mineral exploration and access			
WDV b/f		200,000	
WDA 25%		(50,000)	50,000
WDV c/f		£150,000	
Mineral assets			
WDV b/f		72,000	
WDA 10%		(7,200)	7,200
WDV c/f		£64,800	
Source P			
Mineral exploration and access			
Expenditure		150,000	
WDA 25%		(37,500)	37,500
WDV c/f		£112,500	
Mineral assets			
Expenditure	note (c)	100,000	
WDA 10%		(10,000)	10,000
WDV c/f		£90,000	

		£	£
Mining works			
Expenditure		50,000	
WDA 25%		(12,500)	12,500
WDV c/f		£37,500	
Source Q			
Mineral exploration and access			
Expenditure	note (b)	20,000	
WDA 25%		(5,000)	5,000
WDV c/f		£15,000	
Total allowances (net of charges)			£132,450

Notes

(a) Allowances are not due on either the office or staff hostel. The plant and machinery qualify for plant and machinery allowances (see **11.2 CAPITAL ALLOWANCES — PLANT AND MACHINERY: ELIGIBLE EXPENDITURE AND INITIAL ALLOWANCES**) rather than for mineral extraction allowances (see **14.11**).

(b) Abortive expenditure on seeking planning permission is qualifying expenditure as if it were expenditure on mineral exploration and access (see **14.2** above).

(c) The undeveloped market value of land is excluded from qualifying expenditure (see **14.5** above).

Transition to current code of allowances

[14.12] The current code of allowances, as described at **14.1–14.10** above was introduced for expenditure incurred after 31 March 1986 (though a trader could elect to continue to apply the old code to certain expenditure incurred in the twelve months to 31 March 1987).

Any unrelieved balance of expenditure at 1 April 1986 (or 1 April 1987 where applicable) under the old code was treated for the purposes of the current code as expenditure incurred on that day for the purposes for which the original expenditure was actually incurred.

If expenditure had been fully relieved under the old code but the assets remained in use, the current code applies as if the expenditure had been incurred on 1 April 1986 and had been fully relieved under the current code (thus enabling balancing charges to accrue subsequently).

Expenditure on mineral exploration and access, or on acquisition of mineral assets, or on construction of certain works, which did not qualify for allowances under the old code because either the trade, or output from the source, had not commenced, or for some other reason, was treated as incurred on 1 April 1986 and relieved as appropriate under the new code.

Special rules apply where the old code expenditure on a mineral asset included the acquisition of an interest in land. The undeveloped market value of that interest was not excluded from the relievable expenditure where some relief had already been given under the old code, but nor is such value excluded under **14.8**(a) above from any disposal value to be brought into account.

In making balancing charges where old code expenditure has been brought under the new code, allowances given under the old code will be taken into account together with those given under the new code.

[*CAA 2001, Sch 3 para 88*].

Simon's Taxes. See **B3.401**.

15

Capital Allowances — Buildings

Cross references. See **10 CAPITAL ALLOWANCES — INTRODUCTION; 11 CAPITAL ALLOWANCES — PLANT AND MACHINERY: ELIGIBLE EXPENDITURE AND INITIAL ALLOWANCES; 12 CAPITAL ALLOWANCES — PLANT AND MACHINERY: POOLING**

AND DISPOSALS; 13 CAPITAL ALLOWANCES — PLANT AND MACHINERY: FIXTURES AND LEASING; 14 CAPITAL ALLOWANCES — MINERAL EXTRACTION and 16 CAPITAL ALLOWANCES — MISCELLANEOUS.

Other sources. See Tolley's Capital Allowances.

Introduction

[15.1] In this chapter we consider the various capital allowances that are available for expenditure on buildings including:

- Industrial buildings (**15.2**)
- Agricultural buildings (**15.14**)
- Business premises renovation (**15.18**)
- Dwelling-houses let on assured tenancies (**15.28**)
- Flat conversion (**15.23**)

Industrial buildings

Introduction

[15.2] Allowances are given in respect of certain capital expenditure incurred before 1 April 2011 [*FA 2008, s 84(1)(4)*] (**15.5**) on industrial buildings (**15.3**), and are available to traders and to lessors and licensors of industrial buildings for use by traders.

However, the allowances are abolished for chargeable periods beginning on or after 1 April 2011. [*FA 2008, s 84(2)–(4)*].

Simon's Taxes. See **B3.2**.

Qualifying buildings

[15.3] An '*industrial building*' is a building or structure, or part of a building or structure, in use either:

(a) for the purposes of a trade, or part of a trade, consisting of:
 (i) the manufacture or processing of goods or materials; or
 (ii) the maintaining or repairing of goods or materials (but not goods etc. employed by the person carrying out the repair or maintenance in any trade or undertaking unless that trade etc. itself qualifies the building as an industrial building); or
 (iii) the storage of (a) raw materials for manufacture, (b) goods to be processed, (c) goods manufactured or processed but not yet delivered to any purchaser, or (d) goods on arrival in the UK from a place outside the UK; or
 (iv) the working of mines, oil wells etc. or foreign plantations; or
 (v) agricultural operations on land not occupied by the trader; or
 (vi) catching fish or shellfish; or

(b) for the purposes of:
  (i) a transport, dock, inland navigation, water, sewerage, electricity, hydraulic power, bridge or tunnel undertaking; or
  (ii) a toll road or 'highway undertaking'; or

(c) for the welfare of workers employed in a trade or undertaking within (a) or (b) above; or

(d) as a sports pavilion for the welfare of workers employed in any trade; or

(e) as a qualifying hotel (see **15.12**).

Exclusions

[15.4] Certain buildings or structures are excluded if in use as, or as part of:

(i) dwelling-houses;
(ii) retail shops;
(iii) showrooms;
(iv) offices (Capital Allowances Manual at CA32312).

Provided the excluded part of the building is less than or equal to 25% of the total cost of the building or structure, then the whole building or structure continues to qualify.

Note that when alterations, extensions etc. or changes in use result in the 25% limit being exceeded, no amendment is made to allowances for chargeable (or basis) periods before that of the change, and allowances continue to be available in respect of that part of the building or structure not excluded.

Similarly, where the 25% condition commences to be met, allowances are available for the whole of the building or structure only for the chargeable (or basis) period of the change and subsequent periods.

Case law — IBAs refused

Vibroplant Ltd v Holland (1981) 54 TC 658, CA (depots of plant hire contractor);

Copol Clothing Co Ltd v Hindmarch (1983) 57 TC 575, CA (inland storage of goods imported in containers);

Carr v Sayer (1992) 65 TC 15 (quarantine kennels, claimed under (a)(iii)(d) above);

Girobank plc v Clarke (1998) 70 TC 387, CA (bank document and data processing centre);

Bestway (Holdings) Ltd v Luff (1998) 70 TC 512 (cash-and-carry wholesale warehouse);

Sarsfield v Dixons Group plc (1998) 71 TC 121, CA (warehouse used by retail group distribution company for receiving, storing and delivering goods);

Maco Door & Window Hardware (UK) Ltd v HMRC [2008] STC 2594, HL (building used for part of trade consisting of storage was held to be an activity in the course of a trade, not a part of a trade and thus the expenditure was not eligible for industrial buildings allowance).

Case law — IBAs granted

CIR v Lambhill Ironworks Ltd (1950) 31 TC 393, Ct of Sess (drawing office);

Kilmarnock Equitable Co-operative Society Ltd v CIR (1966) 42 TC 675, Ct of Sess (coal packing not ancillary to retail shop);

CIR v Saxone Lilley & Skinner (Holdings) Ltd [1967] 1 All ER 756, [1967] 1 WLR 501, HL (warehouse for shoes both bought and manufactured).

Qualifying expenditure

[15.5] Qualifying expenditure is the cost of construction of the building or structure.

It includes the cost of preparing, cutting, tunnelling or levelling land, but excludes expenditure on the land itself or on rights therein. [*CAA 2001, ss 272(1), 294*].

A just and reasonable apportionment is required to exclude unallowable expenditure. [*CAA 2001, s 356*].

The fees of professionals involved in the design and construction of a building or structure (e.g. architects, quantity surveyors and engineers) are also included. (HMRC Capital Allowances Manual CA31400).

Where, for the purpose of erecting a new building or structure on the same site, costs are incurred in demolishing an existing building or structure, and the costs cannot be taken into account in calculating a balancing adjustment (**15.9**) on the demolished building or structure (e.g. because more than 25 (or 50) years has elapsed since it was first used), the demolition costs may be treated as expenditure on construction of the new building or structure. (HMRC Capital Allowances Manual CA31400).

Roads on an industrial trading estate, where most of the buildings on which are industrial buildings, will themselves be treated as industrial buildings. [*CAA 2001, s 284*].

Excluded expenditure

The following are considered by HMRC to be excluded from being qualifying expenditure:

(i) expenditure on obtaining planning permission (although if a builder's costs are inclusive of such expenditure, no apportionment will be made);
(ii) capitalised interest;
(iii) public enquiry costs;
(iv) land, land drainage, reclamation and landscaping;
(v) legal expenses (HMRC Capital Allowances Manual CA31400);
(vi) certain expenditure treated as plant or machinery (**11.3 CAPITAL ALLOWANCES — PLANT AND MACHINERY: ELIGIBLE EXPENDITURE AND INITIAL ALLOWANCES**);
(vii) expenditure (including professional fees) incurred on the construction of a building or structure which never becomes an industrial.

Example

Mr Major is in business making garden gnomes. He draws accounts annually to 31 March. He incurred the following expenditure:

	£
Land	190,000
Levelling and cutting the land	20,000
Legal fees	10,000
Architects fees	20,000
Factory construction (including offices £170,000)	660,000
Total expenditure	900,000

The qualifying expenditure for IBA purposes is as follows:

	£
Construction (see Note)	660,000
Levelling and cutting	20,000
Architects' fees	20,000
	700,000

Note

£700,000 × 25% = £175,000

Offices cost £170,000. This is < 25% of total qualifying cost, so the offices are eligible.

Buildings bought unused

The purchaser is treated as having incurred the lower of the:

(i) actual cost of construction;
(ii) net purchase price of the interest.

Where the original expenditure was incurred by a builder as part of their trade with a view to sale, the purchaser's construction cost is taken as the lower of the:

(i) net purchase price paid by the purchaser;
(ii) net price paid to the builder on previous sales.

The net purchase price includes acquisition costs such as legal fees, surveyors' fees and stamp duty. (HMRC Capital Allowances Manual CA33520).

Appropriation from trading stock

A building or structure appropriated by a builder from trading stock to capital account (with a corresponding market value credit to profit and loss) and let as an industrial building, is eligible for writing-down allowances based on the construction cost (rather than on the transfer value).

Relevant interest

IBAs will be available to the person who has the 'relevant interest' in the particular property. This is normally the freeholder.

If a freeholder owns a factory and leases it to a trader who uses the building for manufacturing, processing or industrial storage, the freeholder will claim the IBAs (not the trader). The freeholder will set the IBAs against his rental income from the factory.

The availability of IBAs therefore depends on what the tenant is using the building for. If the tenant uses the building for a qualifying trade, IBAs can be claimed by the freeholder.

Accordingly, clauses are often inserted into rental agreements by landlords to ensure that their tenants use the building for a qualifying trade.

When a long lease is granted, the freeholder and lessee may jointly elect to transfer the relevant interest from the freeholder to the lessee.

The lessee is deemed to have acquired an industrial building for the purchase price of £200,000 – the lease premium. Therefore the lessee will obtain IBAs on this £200,000 – he now owns the relevant interest by election and can claim IBAs to set against trading profits.

Initial allowances

[15.6] Initial allowances may be available to a person incurring qualifying expenditure (**15.5**) on a building which is to be in use as an 'industrial building' (**15.3**) for a trade carried on by that person or by his lessee or, for licences granted after 9 March 1982, by his licensee. [*CAA 2001, s 305, Sch 3 para 64*].

Initial allowances apply at a rate of:

(i) 100% for certain expenditure in enterprise zones (**15.13**);
(ii) 20% for general expenditure incurred in the year ended 31 October 1993.

An initial allowance is given for the chargeable period in which the expenditure is incurred. [*CAA 2001, s 306(3)*] and may be claimed in whole or part. [*CAA 2001, s 306(2)*].

Expenditure taken into account for the purposes of certain grants or payments specified by the Treasury for the purpose are excluded from initial allowances. [*CAA 2001, s 308, Sch 3 para 65*].

Writing-down allowances

Available when

[15.7] WDAs are available where a qualifying building or structure (**15.3**) is in use as such (or in temporary disuse following such use, **15.3** at the end of a chargeable period.

An initial allowance and WDA may be claimed on the same expenditure in the same period.

Qualifying expenditure

The allowances are calculated on the qualifying expenditure (**15.5**) incurred, and continue until the 'residue of expenditure' is nil.

Where an 'additional VAT liability' (**10.10 CAPITAL ALLOWANCES — INTRODUCTION**) is incurred in respect of any qualifying expenditure, the amount of the liability qualifies for writing-down allowances as if it were additional capital expenditure incurred on the construction in question; the 'residue of expenditure' is increased by that amount at the time the liability accrues.

Short periods

The annual writing-down allowance is available in full where the expenditure is incurred during the chargeable period, but is proportionately reduced where the chargeable period is less than twelve months. [*CAA 2001, ss 309, 310, 312, Sch 3 para 66*].

The rate available

For expenditure incurred after 5 November 1962, the rate of allowance was 4% p.a. or such smaller amount as may be claimed.

Non industrial use

If a building is in non-industrial use at the end of the accounting period, no IBA will be given. Instead a *notional writing-down allowance* is deducted from the pool of qualifying expenditure. The notional WDA does not reduce taxable profits for that year — it merely reduces the balance of qualifying expenditure going forward.

Temporary disuse

Empty periods (i.e. when the building is vacant and not being used for any purpose) take on the same form as the immediate preceding use. Therefore if on the last day of an accounting period the building was empty, we look back to the immediately preceding use and treat the 'empty' period exactly the same as that preceding use. [*CAA 2001, s 285*].

All disuse other than that preceding demolition or dereliction is in practice regarded as temporary.

Simon's Taxes. See **B3.203–B3.213.**

Year of sale

There is no writing-down allowance in the year of sale.

Phasing out of writing-down allowances

[15.8] On Budget day in March 2007, the Chancellor announced that WDAs on industrial buildings would be phased out from 2008/09 onwards, with a final withdrawal of all IBAs after 2010/11.

To prepare the way for the abolition of IBAs, balancing adjustments on the sale of an industrial building were withdrawn from 21 March 2007. The sale of an industrial building on or after 21 March 2007 will not therefore give rise either to a balancing allowance or balancing charge. This does not apply to qualifying enterprise zone expenditure (**15.13**).

During the transitional period from 1 April 2008 to 31 March 2011, writing-down allowances are granted at a percentage of the total allowance which would otherwise be due. This excludes buildings in an enterprise zone which continue as before (**15.13**).

The percentages are:

Year ended	% of IBA available	Effective rate of IBA
31 March 2008	100%	4%
31 March 2009	75%	3%
31 March 2010	50%	2%
31 March 2011	25%	1%
31 March 2012	NIL	NIL

Example

Leon Ltd built a factory in 2000 at a cost of £2m. The factory is used for manufacturing. Leon Ltd draws accounts annually to 31 December.

The IBAs in the transitional period will be as follows:

Year ended		IBA claim
		£
31 December 2007	£2m x 4%	80,000
31 December 2008	(£2m x 4% x 3/12) + (£2m x 3% x 9/12)	65,000
31 December 2009	(£2m x 3% x 3/12) + (£2m x 2% x 9/12)	45,000
31 December 2010	(£2m x 2% x 3/12) + (£2m x 1% x 9/12)	25,000
31 December 2011	(£2m x 1% x 3/12)	5,000
31 December 2012		NIL

Note: as the accounting period spans 31 March, the IBA rates are time apportioned on a monthly basis.

Balancing event

Before 21 March 2007

[15.9] Where a balancing event (normally a disposal) takes place on or after 21 March 2007 (a post-commencement relevant event) and neither:

(i) involves qualifying enterprise zone expenditure; nor
(ii) arises from a relevant pre-commencement contract,

no balancing allowance or charge will arise and the purchaser will be entitled to capital allowances on the vendor's balance of unrelieved expenditure.

Post commencement balancing event

A post-commencement balancing event includes a 'relevant event' (as defined in *CAA 2001 s 311)* taking place on or after 21 March 2007, but does not include an event occurring on or after 21 March 2007 and before 1 April 2011 under a relevant pre-commencement contract.

Such a contract must be:

(a) made in writing before 21 March 2007;
(b) unconditional or its conditions have been satisfied before that date;
(c) final before 21 March 2007 — i.e. no terms had to be agreed on or after that date; and
(d) not significantly varied on or after that date.

[*FA 2007, s 36*].

Events before 21 March 2007

Prior to this date, and providing that that the event occurred with 25 years of the building or structure first being used, a balancing allowance or charge could arise where a relevant interest in a building or structure was:

(i) sold;
(ii) destroyed;
(iii) permanently put out of use.

Also when the relevant interest is lost on termination of a lease or foreign concession, or when a highway concession is brought to or comes to an end.

Calculating the balancing adjustment

A *balancing allowance* arises if 'residue of expenditure' immediately before the sale etc. exceeds the proceeds of any sale, insurance, salvage or compensation.

A *balancing charge* arises if the 'residue of expenditure' immediately before the sale etc. is less than the proceeds of any sale, insurance, salvage or compensation.

Residue of expenditure before sale

'*Residue of expenditure*' is original capital expenditure:

- *minus* all industrial buildings and research and development (or scientific research) allowances (see **16.12 CAPITAL ALLOWANCES — MISCELLANEOUS**) granted, including balancing allowances; and
- *minus* 'notional writing-down allowances' for periods, following first use of the building or structure for any purpose, at the end of which the building or structure was not in use as an 'industrial building' (**15.7**); and
- *plus* any balancing charges made; and
- *plus* or *minus* any 'additional VAT liability' or 'additional VAT rebate' (**10.10 CAPITAL ALLOWANCES — INTRODUCTION**) incurred or made in respect of that expenditure.

Example

Writing-down allowances and balancing adjustments

(A) Prior to commencing business on 1 April 1998 P Ltd incurred the following expenditure.

	£
10.12.98 Plot of land	50,000
20.1.99 Clearing and levelling site	20,000
20.3.99 Construction of factory	500,000
	£570,000

The factory was brought into use for a qualifying purpose on commencement of trade, and remained in such use until 31 January 2010, when it was sold for £550,000, being £480,000 for the factory and £70,000 for the land.

P Ltd drew up accounts annually to 31 March.

The allowances available to P Ltd are as follows.

Accounting period ended			Residue of expenditure £
31 March 1999	Qualifying expenditure		520,000
	Writing-down allowance	4% × £520k	(20,800)
			499,200
31 March 2000 to 31 March 2008 incl	9 years	4% × £520k × 9	(187,200)
31 March 2009	Phasing out (Yr 1)	3% × £520k × 1	(15,600)
			296,400
	Sale proceeds		(480,000)
Sale (Jan 2010) No balancing adjustment as sold after 22 March 2008			£183,600

Disposal after non industrial use

Where a building or structure has been in non industrial use and notional allowances deducted from the tax written down value, the balancing adjustment calculation is more complex.

Where proceeds of sale, insurance, salvage or compensation are equal to or exceed the 'starting expenditure' of the building or structure, a balancing charge will be made to recover all allowances given.

Where those proceeds are nil or less than the 'starting expenditure', a balancing adjustment is calculated by comparing the actuall allowances claimed with the adjusted net cost.

(i) Adjusted net cost < allowances claimed = balancing allowance

(ii) Adjusted net cost > allowances claimed = balancing charge

Starting expenditure

'*Starting expenditure*' means the expenditure incurred on the construction of the building or structure (less any balancing charge made in respect of an 'additional VAT rebate' — see below) or, in the case of a second-hand building or structure, the residue of expenditure (see **15.7**) at the beginning of the relevant period, together (in either case) with the net cost of demolition if appropriate.

Adjusted net cost

In essence, this is the fall in value of the building or structure over the period which it was used for industrial purposes:

$$(\text{Starting expenditure} - \text{Proceeds}) \times \frac{\text{Period of industrial use}}{\text{Total use}}$$

[*CAA 2001, ss 314(1)–(4), 315, 316, 318–324, 343, 350(5), Sch 3 paras 68–70*].

The new owner

If the 'relevant interest' in a building or structure is sold, and the sale is a balancing event giving rise to a balancing allowance or charge, subsequent writing-down allowances are given to the purchaser.

These are calculated on the 'residue of expenditure' immediately after the sale, spread over the period from the date of sale to the 25th anniversary of the first use of the building or structure for any purpose (50th anniversary for expenditure incurred before 6 November 1962). [*CAA 2001, s 311, Sch 3 para 67*].

If, following a sale after non-qualifying use, a balancing charge arises on the excess of allowances given over adjusted net cost, the residue after the sale is restricted to the net sale proceeds.

However, remember that the new owner's WDA will be phased-down and finally withdrawn after 2010/11.

Successive sales etc. during non-use as industrial building

Where there are two or more sales etc. in a period during which a building or structure is not an 'industrial building', a balancing adjustment arises only on the first such sale etc. [*CAA 2001, s 314(5); CAA 1990, s 4(2); FA 1991, Sch 14 para 4(2)*].

Additional VAT rebate

Where an 'additional VAT rebate' (**10.10 CAPITAL ALLOWANCES — INTRODUCTION**) is made in respect of qualifying expenditure, and this exceeds the residue of expenditure (**15.7**), a balancing charge, equal to the excess, will be made. [*CAA 2001, s 350; CAA 1990, s 4(1)(e)(2A); FA 1991, Sch 14 para 4(1)(3)*].

Demolition

The net cost (after crediting sales of materials and scrap) of demolition borne by the person on whom a balancing adjustment arises is added to 'residue of expenditure' (**15.7**) for balancing allowance and balancing charge calculations (and those costs are then not taken into account for capital allowance purposes except in the case of dwelling-houses let on assured tenancies, **15.28**). [*CAA 2001, s 340*].

Where this is not possible (e.g. because more than 25 years has elapsed since the building or structure was first used), and if the holder of the relevant interest demolishes the building or structure for the purpose of erecting a new building or structure on the same site, the demolition costs may be treated as expenditure by the holder on construction of the new building or structure. (HMRC Capital Allowances Manual CA31400).

Simon's Taxes. See **B3.237–B3.239.**

Temporarily unused buildings

[15.10] Where an allowance or charge falls to be made in a period during which a building or structure is temporarily out of use but deemed still to be an industrial building (**15.3**) and, since it was last used as such, the trade in question has ceased (or, where the relevant interest was subject to a lease, or the building or structure used under licence, the lease or licence has come to an end), such allowances and charges are dealt with in the same way as those falling to be made to or on lessors.

Where a balancing charge falls to be made on any person following such a period of temporary disuse, and the most recent use was as an industrial building for the purposes of a trade carried on by that person which has since ceased, the same deductions can be made from the charge as can be made under *CTA 2009, s 196* (formerly *ICTA 1988, s 105*) from a post-cessation receipt (without prejudice to the deduction of any amounts allowable against the balancing charge under other provisions). [*CAA 2001, s 354; ITTOIA 2005, Sch 1 para 556*].

Lessors

[15.11] *Lessors* (and licensors) of industrial buildings may claim allowances for an accounting period. Allowances and balancing charges are treated as expenses and receipts of a property business (see **62.1** property income) or, if the lease or licence is an asset of an overseas property business (see **62.19** property income), of that business. Where it is not an asset of any property business, allowances and charges are treated as expenses and receipts of a notional property business. [*CAA 2001, s 353; ITTOIA 2005, Sch 1 para 555; CTA 2001, Sch 1 para 501*].

Simon's Taxes. See **B3.236, B3.241.**

Hotels

[15.12] Provided a hotel satisfies a number of conditions, expenditure on the construction or extension of that hotel is eligible for IBAs. [*CAA 2001, s 279*].

Those conditions are that is should:

(i) have at least 10 letting bedrooms; and
(ii) be open for at least 4 months during the period April to October; and
(iii) provide a service of the making of beds, cleaning of rooms and offering breakfast and dinner as a normal part of the hotel's business.

Certain expenditure on fire safety and thermal insulation may be treated as on plant and machinery, see **11.3 CAPITAL ALLOWANCES — PLANT AND MACHINERY: ELIGIBLE EXPENDITURE AND INITIAL ALLOWANCES.**

Simon's Taxes. See B3.251–B3.254.

Enterprise zones

[15.13] An 'enterprise zone' is an area designated as such by the Secretary of State (or by Scottish Ministers, the National Assembly for Wales or, for Northern Ireland, the Department of the Environment). [*CAA 2001, s 298(3)*].

Advantageous provisions apply to expenditure on the construction of an industrial building, which for this purpose includes a 'qualifying hotel' or a 'commercial building or structure', which is incurred (or contract entered into) within ten years of the inclusion of the site in an enterprise zone.

Expenditure incurred more than 20 years after a site was first included in an enterprise zone does not attract enterprise zone allowances, regardless of when the contract for the expenditure was entered into. [*CAA 2001, ss 271(1)(b), 298*].

'*Qualifying hotel*' has the same meaning as in **15.12**. (Note that any hotel not qualifying under this heading will qualify as a commercial building.)

'*Commercial building or structure*' means a building or structure which is used for the purposes of a trade, profession or vocation or as an office for any purpose, but does not include any building in use as, or as part of, a dwelling house. [*CAA 2001, s 281*].

Allowances

An initial allowance of 100% is given but the full amount need not be claimed.

If any part of the initial allowance is not claimed, then writing-down allowances at 25% p.a. of cost on the straight line basis will apply to the unclaimed balance. [*CAA 2001, ss 306(1)(2), 310(1)(a)*].

Allowances will not be available on or after 1 April 2011, but the phasing out provisions detailed in **15.8** do not apply to enterprise zone expenditure.

If an accounting period straddles 1 April 2011, only a time-apportioned allowance is available in respect of the time before that date. [*FA 2008, s 86*].

Date expenditure incurred

As regards buildings or structures bought unused, the normal rules under *CAA 2001, ss 294–296* apply (**15.5**), except that:

(a) where some or all of the actual construction expenditure is incurred (or incurred under a contract entered into) within ten years of the inclusion of the site in an enterprise zone, a corresponding proportion of the purchaser's deemed expenditure is treated as giving rise to entitlement to enterprise zone allowances, notwithstanding that it may be deemed to have been incurred outside that ten-year period;

(b) where (a) does not apply, the purchaser's deemed expenditure is treated as not giving rise to entitlement to enterprise zone allowances, notwithstanding that it may be deemed to have been incurred during the ten-year period.

Where some of the actual construction expenditure fell within (a) above and some or all of the balance could qualify for a 20% initial allowance by virtue of the provisions in **15.5**, the above provisions and those in **15.5** interacted. The purchaser could thus obtain a 100% enterprise zone initial allowance on part of his deemed expenditure and the 20% initial allowance on another part or, where appropriate, on the balance.

[*CAA 2001, ss 300, 302, Sch 3 para 61*].

Buildings purchased within two years of first use

Where some or all of the construction expenditure on a building or structure is incurred within ten years of the inclusion of the site in an enterprise zone, and the 'relevant interest' is sold during the two years following its first use, then on the first such sale the:

(i) normal balancing allowance or charge rules apply to the vendor;

(ii) purchaser is deemed to have incurred expenditure on purchase of a building or structure bought unused.

A proportion of the deemed expenditure corresponding to the proportion of the actual construction expenditure which was incurred within ten years of the inclusion of the site in the enterprise zone is treated as giving rise to entitlement to enterprise zone allowances, notwithstanding that it may be deemed to have been incurred outside the ten-year period.

The balance of the deemed expenditure does not attract enterprise zone allowances.

If the purchase is directly from a person who constructed the building or structure in the course of a trade of constructing such buildings or structures for sale, the part of the purchaser's deemed expenditure which does *not* attract enterprise zone allowances is calculated by reference to the actual expenditure of the vendor if that is less than the price actually paid by the purchaser. [*CAA 2001, ss 301, 303, 304, Sch 3 para 62*].

Plant and machinery forming an integral part

This was not subject to the restriction of first-year allowances to lessors under *CAA 1990, s 22(4)* (**13.14 CAPITAL ALLOWANCES — PLANT AND MACHINERY: FIXTURES AND LEASING**). [*CAA 1990, s 22(5)*].

Balancing charge on realisation of capital value

Where capital expenditure on construction of a building or structure in an enterprise zone has been incurred (or is deemed to have been incurred) under a contract entered into after 12 January 1994 (or which becomes unconditional after 25 February 1994), and 'capital value' is received in respect of the building or structure, a balancing charge (but not a balancing allowance) may arise.

This applies generally where the payment is made (or an agreement to make it made) seven years or less after the date of the agreement relating to the expenditure (or the date on which that agreement became unconditional). Where, however, there are certain guaranteed exit arrangements, it applies throughout the normal balancing adjustment period (i.e. 25 years from first use, see **15.9**).

'*Capital value*' is realised when a sum is paid which is attributable to an interest in land to which the relevant interest in the building or structure in question is or will be subject, e.g. where a lease is granted out of the relevant interest, unless *CAA 2001, s 290* (see **15.7**) applies to the grant of that interest.

There are detailed provisions as to the form and amount of the capital value, and as to its attribution to the grant of the interest. See HMRC Capital Allowances Manual CA37730 *et seq.*

[*CAA 2001, ss 327–331, Sch 3 para 71; ITTOIA 2005, Sch 1 para 554; CTA 2009, Sch 1 para 500*].

Additional VAT liability

An 'additional VAT liability' (**10.10 CAPITAL ALLOWANCES — INTRODUCTION**) incurred in respect of qualifying expenditure, within ten years of the inclusion of the site in the enterprise zone, is itself qualifying expenditure for the chargeable period in which the liability accrues. [*CAA 2001, s 346*].

Where a 100% initial allowance was not claimed on the expenditure to which the additional VAT liability relates, a 100% allowance may nevertheless generally be claimed for the additional VAT liability.

If less than the full 100% allowance is claimed for the additional VAT liability, writing-down allowances for the whole of the expenditure on the building or structure in question will be recomputed as under **15.7**, resulting in a substantial reduction in the rate of annual allowance.

Plant or machinery

Expenditure on plant or machinery, or on thermal insulation treated as plant or machinery under **11.3 CAPITAL ALLOWANCES — PLANT AND MACHINERY: ELIGIBLE EXPENDITURE AND INITIAL ALLOWANCES**, which is to be an integral part of an industrial or commercial building in an enterprise zone may be treated as part of the expenditure on construction of the building or structure, and so attract the 100% initial allowance.

A claim for expenditure on plant or machinery to be so treated does not prevent a subsequent purchaser of the building or structure from claiming plant and machinery allowances on that expenditure and industrial buildings allowances on the fabric of the building. (This commentary is not included in the current HMRC Capital Allowances Manual, but was previously at CA1060 and is presumed still to be of application.)

Simon's Taxes. See **B3.261–B3.265.**

Example 1

In 2005, J, a builder, incurred expenditure of £400,000 on the construction of a building in a designated enterprise zone. The whole of the expenditure was incurred (or contracted for) within ten years of the site's first being included in the zone.

In January 2007, he sold the building unused to K Ltd for £600,000 (excluding land).

In February 2007, K Ltd let the building to a trader who immediately brought it into use as a supermarket. K Ltd claims a reduced initial allowance of £50,000.

In March 2009, it sells the building to L Ltd for £750,000 (excluding land). K Ltd draws up accounts to 31 March each year.

K Ltd's allowances are as follows.

Accounting period ended		£	Residue of expenditure £
31 March 2007	Qualifying expenditure		600,000
	Initial allowance (maximum 100%)	50,000	
	Writing-down allowance 25% of £600,000	150,000	
	Total IBA due	200,000	(200,000)
31 March 2008	Writing-down allowance	150,000	(150,000)
			250,000
31 March 2009	Writing-down allowance	—	—

No balancing charge as sale took place on or after 22 March 2007

Notes

(a) K Ltd's qualifying expenditure would normally be the lesser of cost of construction and the net price paid by it for the building. However, on purchase from a builder, whose profit on sale is taxable as a trading profit, the qualifying expenditure is equal to the net price paid for the relevant interest (excluding the land). **15.5, 15.13.**

(b) Providing the building continues to be used for a qualifying purpose, L Ltd can claim writing-down allowances until 31 March 2011 when the relief is abolished. Its qualifying expenditure is £250,000, i.e. K Ltd.'s written down value.

(c) In this example, the first sale after the building was first used took place just over two years after the date of first use. If the sale had taken place within two years after first use, L Ltd could have claimed an initial allowance and 25% writing-down allowances as if it had bought the building unused. L Ltd's qualifying expenditure would again have been restricted to £600,000, being the lesser of the price paid by it for the relevant interest in the building and that paid on the original purchase by K Ltd from the builder.

Example 2

The facts are as above, except that, of the £400,000 construction expenditure actually incurred, only £360,000 is incurred (or contracted for) within ten years of the site's first being included in an enterprise zone, and the first sale occurred after the expiry of that ten-year period.

K Ltd's qualifying expenditure of £600,000 is divided into an enterprise zone element and a non-enterprise zone element.

The enterprise zone element is

$$£\,600{,}000 \times \frac{360{,}000}{400{,}000} = £\,540{,}000$$

The non-enterprise zone element is £600,000 − £540,000 = £60,000

The non-enterprise zone element does not qualify for enterprise zone allowances. (It could have qualified for normal IBAs if the building had been an industrial building.)

K Ltd's allowances are as follows.

Accounting period ended		£	Residue of expenditure £
31 March 2007	Qualifying expenditure (enterprise zone element)		540,000
	Initial allowance (maximum 100%)	50,000	
	Writing-down allowance (25% of £540,000)	135,000	
		185,000	(185,000)
31 March 2008	Writing-down allowance	135,000	(135,000)
			220,000
31 March 2009	Writing-down allowance		

No balancing charge as sale took place on or after 22 March 2007. L Ltd's qualifying expenditure is £220,000, i.e. K's residue of £220,000.

Connected persons and other anti-avoidance provisions

Special provisions apply to sales of industrial buildings where the:

(a) sale results in no change of control, including sales between connected persons; or

(b) sole or main benefit arising is the obtaining of an industrial buildings allowance.

Normally, where these provisions apply, market value is substituted for purchase price.

This also applies to transfers other than by way of sale.

However, provided that (b) above does not apply, for sales within (a) above and other transfers the parties may elect for the substitution of the residue of expenditure if this is lower than market value, and for any subsequent balancing charge on the buyer to be calculated by reference to allowances etc. of both buyer and seller.

Such an election is *not* available if the circumstances are such that an allowance or charge which otherwise would or might fall, in consequence of the sale, to be made to or on *any* of the parties to the sale cannot fall to be made.

The election must be made within two years after the sale. The election also covers qualifying hotels and commercial buildings etc. in enterprise zones. [*CAA 2001, ss 567–570, 573, 575(1), 577(4)*].

Balancing allowances are restricted on sales after 13 June 1972 where the relevant interest in an industrial building is sold subject to a subordinate interest (e.g. in a sale and lease-back) and either the:

(1) seller, the purchaser of the interest, and the grantee of the subordinate interest (or any two of them) are **CONNECTED PERSONS (25)**; or
(2) sole or main benefit appears to be the obtaining of an industrial buildings allowance.

In such cases the net sale proceeds are increased, in determining any balancing allowance, by:

(A) where less than a commercial rent is payable under the subordinate interest, the difference between actual sale proceeds and market value had a commercial rent been payable; and
(B) the amount of any premium receivable for the grant of the subordinate interest and not chargeable under *CTA 2009, s 217, ICTA 1988, s 34*,

but not by more than is required to eliminate any balancing allowance.

Special provisions apply if the terms of the subordinate interest are varied before the sale.

The residue of expenditure following the sale is, however, calculated as if the balancing allowance had been made without the application of these provisions.

[*CAA 2001, ss 325, 326; ITTOIA 2005, Sch 1 para 553; CTA 2009, Sch 1 para 499*].

Partnerships

Partnerships, including partnerships of which companies are members, are entitled to industrial buildings allowances in respect of qualifying expenditure on industrial buildings.

Following a change in the persons carrying on the trade, other than one resulting in the activity being treated for tax purposes as permanently discontinued, unexhausted allowances are carried forward, and subsequent balancing adjustments made as if the new partnership had carried on the trade before the change. [*CAA 2001, ss 557, 558; ITTOIA 2005, Sch 1 para 571*].

Successions

Following a change in the persons carrying on the trade, such that the activity is treated for tax purposes as permanently discontinued, any asset transferred without being sold to the new owner for continuing use in the trade is treated as sold at market value on the date of change.

No initial allowance is available to the new owner.

No company carrying on the activity immediately before the change may continue carrying it on after the change. [*CAA 2001, ss 557, 559; CAA 1990, s 152(1)(2); ITTOIA 2005, Sch 1 para 572; CTA 2009, Sch 1 para 519*].

For transfers under former *ICTA 1988, s 343* (company reconstructions without a change in ownership) see **55.11 LOSSES**.

For transfers between companies in different EU member states *under CAA 2001, s 560*, see **17.14 CAPITAL GAINS**, and between such companies on the formation of an SE or SCE by merger under *CAA 2001, s 561A*, see **17.27 CAPITAL GAINS**.

Anti-avoidance

Where there is a sale of a relevant interest on or after 12 March 2008 which is a balancing event, the buyer and seller have different chargeable periods, the control test in *CAA 2001, s 567* is met and the purpose, or one of the main purposes, of the sale is the obtaining of a tax advantage by the buyer, the writing-down allowance is restricted by the following fraction:

$$\frac{\text{number of days buyer held the relevant interest in the chargeable period}}{\text{total number of days in the chargeable period}}$$

This provision does not apply to sales under an unconditional written contract, or one becoming unconditional before 12 March 2008 which remains in force at that date and the terms of which are not varied significantly on or after that date. [*FA 2008, s 87*].

Agricultural buildings and works

Introduction

[15.14] Like Industrial Buildings Allowances, Agricultural Buildings Allowances (ABAs) are abolished for chargeable periods beginning on or after 1 April 2011.

[*FA 2008, s 87(2)–(4)*].

The code of capital allowances for agricultural buildings and works (as described below) applied to expenditure incurred on or after 1 April 1986 (1 April 1987 where it was incurred under a contract entered into before 14 March 1984). [*CAA 2001, Sch 3 para 82*].

Available to who?

[15.15] Until 1 April 2011, allowances were available where a person who had a 'freehold' or 'leasehold' interest in land in the UK occupied wholly or mainly for the purposes of husbandry incurred capital expenditure on qualifying buildings for the purposes of husbandry on that land.

Qualifying buildings

ABAs are available on construction costs of agricultural buildings in the UK which include:

(i) farmhouses;
(ii) farm buildings;
(iii) cottages occupied by farm workers;
(iv) construction costs of fencing and other works (such as drainage, irrigation, walls, farm roads, water and electricity installations etc). (HMRC Capital Allowances Manual CA40100, 40200).

A building used by a farmer as a retail shop is an agricultural building to the extent that it sells farm produce. It is not an agricultural building if it sells bought-in produce.

[*CAA 2001, s 361*].

The rules are similar to those for Industrial Buildings Allowances (IBAs) although there are some important differences.

Qualifying activities

Farming or 'husbandry' for allowable purposes includes:

(i) Intensive rearing of livestock or fish on a commercial basis for the production of food for human consumption;
(ii) '*Short rotation coppice*' (i.e. a perennial crop of tree species planted at high density, the stems of which are harvested above ground level at intervals of less than ten years). [*CAA 2001, s 362; ITTOIA 2005, Sch 1 para 481*].

Market gardening, whether of plants or flowers or for the production of food should also qualify.

If the buildings come to be first used other than for the purposes of husbandry, no writing-down allowance can be made in respect of the related expenditure and any allowance previously given is withdrawn.

Qualifying expenditure

The expenditure is '*qualifying expenditure*' except that:

(a) expenditure on the acquisition of the land or rights over the land is excluded;

(b) a maximum of one-third of expenditure on the construction of a farmhouse may qualify (reduced as is just and reasonable where the accommodation and amenities are disproportionate to the nature and extent of the farm).
For the meaning of 'farmhouse', see *Lindsay v CIR* (1953) 34 TC 289, Ct of Sess, *CIR v Whiteford & Sons* (1962) 40 TC 379, Ct of Sess; *Korner v CIR* [1969] 1 All ER 679, [1969] 1 WLR 554, HL; HMRC Capital Allowances Manual CA40100 (including the circumstances in which it may be accepted that a farm has two farmhouses); and

(c) only a just and reasonable proportion of expenditure on assets (other than the farmhouse) only partly used for the purposes of husbandry on the land in question may qualify.

[*CAA 2001, ss 361(1)(2), 363, 369, 393, Sch 3 para 81*].

As regards *buildings bought unused*, similar provisions apply as in the case of industrial buildings (**15.5**), modified to take account of the restrictions and exclusions referred to above. [*CAA 2001, ss 370, 374*].

Relevant interest

Allowances are available to the person with the relevant interest.

If there is more than one such interest and one was reversionary on all the others, that one is the relevant interest.

The creation of a lease to which the relevant interest is subject is disregarded for these purposes.

Where an interest in land has been conveyed or assigned by way of security subject to a right of redemption, it will still be treated as belonging to the person with the right of redemption. [*CAA 2001, ss 361(3), 364–366*].

When a leasehold relevant interest is surrendered or reverts, the interest into which it merges becomes the relevant interest, unless a new lease takes effect on the extinguishment.

Otherwise, on a leasehold relevant interest coming to an end, if a new lease is granted to the former lessee, the lessee is treated as continuing to have the same relevant interest.

If the new lease is granted to a person other than the former lessee, the relevant interest is treated as acquired by the new lessee if he makes a payment to the former lessee for the assets representing the expenditure in question. In any other case, the interest of the landlord under the former lease is treated as becoming the relevant interest. [*CAA 2001, ss 367, 368*].

Writing-down allowances

[15.16] Subject to the phasing out rules, ABAs are writing-down allowances given at 4% on a straight line basis.

ABAs are only given on buildings in their 'tax life'. The tax life for an agricultural building is 25 years from the first day of the accounting period in which the expenditure was incurred.

[*CAA 2001, ss 372, 373*].

Phasing out of writing-down allowances

During the transitional period from 1 April 2008 to 31 March 2011, writing-down allowances are granted at a percentage of the total allowance which would otherwise be due.

The percentages are:

Year ended	% of ABA available	Effective rate of ABA
31 March 2008	100%	4%
31 March 2009	75%	3%
31 March 2010	50%	2%
31 March 2011	25%	1%
31 March 2012	NIL	NIL

Where an accounting period straddles the end of a financial year as mentioned above, a hybrid percentage is calculated on a time basis by reference to the number of days in the period for which the person held a relevant interest in the expenditure.

The written down value is calculated by deducting 100% of the allowance which would have been available but for this provision. [*FA 2008, s 85*].

Example

Jack, a dairy farmer, started trading on 1 October 1998 when he incurred the following expenditure on new agricultural buildings:

	£
Farmhouse	300,000
Cow shed	50,000
Milking parlour	30,000

He draws accounts annually to 30 September.
Annual ABAs for periods up to 30 September 2007 have been as follows:

Qualifying expenditure:	£
Farmhouse £(300,000 × 1/3)	100,000
Cow shed	50,000
Milking parlour	30,000
	180,000

Annual ABAs @ 4%		£7,200

Jack's ABAs in future periods will be as follows:

Year ended		ABA claim £
30 Sept 2008	(£7,200 × 6/12 × 100%) + (£7,200 × 6/12 × 75%)	6,300
30 Sept 2009	(£7,200 × 6/12 × 75%) + (£7,200 × 6/12 × 50%)	4,500
30 Sept 2010	(£7,200 × 6/12 × 50%) + (£7,200 × 6/12 × 25%)	2,700
30 Sept 2011	(£7,200 × 6/12 × 25%) + (£7,200 × 6/12 × 0%)	900
30 Sept 2012		NIL

Note

As the accounting period spans 31 March, the ABA rates are time apportioned on a monthly basis.

Ceasing to own relevant interest

[15.17] Where a person ceases to own the relevant interest in the land (or part of the land), and another person acquires that interest, the right to the writing-down allowances (or appropriate part) is transferred to the new owner of the interest.

Allowances are time apportioned where the transfer falls during a chargeable period of either the former or the new owner.

If, by virtue of a transfer of the relevant interest, the total allowances which were or could have been claimed (disregarding any anti-avoidance etc. restrictions on balancing allowances) during the writing-down period would otherwise be less than the amount of the expenditure, then the difference is made up in the chargeable period in which the writing-down period ends. [*CAA 2001, s 379*].

Balancing events

A '*balancing event*' occurs when the relevant interest in land (or part) is acquired by another person or when the building (or part) on construction of which the expenditure was incurred is demolished, destroyed, or otherwise ceases altogether to be used.

A balancing event will not give rise to a balancing adjustment where the event takes place on or after 21 March 2007, except where the event occurs before 1 April 2011 under a relevant pre-commencement contract.

Such a contract must be:

(i) made in writing before 21 March 2007;
(ii) unconditional or its conditions have been satisfied before that date;
(iii) final before 21 March 2007 — i.e. no terms had to be agreed on or after that date; and

(iv) not significantly varied on or after that date.

When there is a 'post-commencement balancing event', the amount on which the purchaser may claim writing-down allowances is the balance of unrelieved expenditure immediately before that event (i.e. the seller's written down value).

A '*post-commencement balancing event*' is a sale or other event which would have given rise to a balancing adjustment under legislation in force before 21 March 2007.

Prior to 21 March 2007

Prior to 21 March 2007, there was potentially a balancing event giving rise to a balancing adjustment *but only where* a written election to that effect was made.

Where no election was made, the WDA would be apportioned as described above.

The election must be made:

(i) no later than two years after the end of the chargeable period in which the balancing event occurs;
(ii) jointly in the case of acquisition of the relevant interest, but otherwise by the former owner only.

An election may not be made by a person outside the charge to income tax or corporation tax, nor if the sole or main benefit of an acquisition was the obtaining of an allowance or greater allowance (but ignoring *CAA 2001, ss 568, 573* (previously *CAA 1990, s 157*), see below).

[*CAA 2001, ss 381, 382; FA 2007, s 35(4)–(7)*].

No WDA is given is the period in which a balancing adjustment arises.

Where the residue of expenditure immediately before the balancing event exceeds any sale, compensation etc. receipts, a balancing allowance arises.

Where any sale, compensation etc. receipts exceed that residue, a balancing charge arises but limited to the allowances previously given to the person on whom the charge arises.

[*CAA 2001, ss 377, 380, 383–388, Sch 3 para 80*].

New owner

Where a balancing event occurs on the transfer of the relevant interest, the writing-down allowances available to the new owner consist of the residue of expenditure immediately before the balancing event, plus any balancing charge or less any balancing allowance consequent on that event, spread over the period from the balancing event to the end of the original 25-year writing-down period.

For this purpose, any balancing allowance which (on that or any previous balancing event) has been reduced or denied under *CAA 2001, s 389* or *CAA 1990, s 130* (see below) is treated as having been made in full.

[*CAA 2001, ss 376, 378*].

Making of allowances and charges

Allowances and balancing adjustments for a chargeable period are given effect by treating allowances as expenses, and charges as receipts, of the trade.

If no trade is carried on in that chargeable period, then allowances and charges are treated as expenses and receipts of a property business (see **62.1 PROPERTY INCOME**) or, where the taxpayer is not, in fact, carrying on such a business, of a notional property business.

[*CAA 2001, ss 391, 392; ITTOIA 2005, Sch 1 para 558; CTA 2009, Sch 1 para 504*].

See also **10.2 CAPITAL ALLOWANCES — INTRODUCTION.**

There are connected person and anti-avoidance provisions in respect of certain balancing events, similar to those applicable to industrial buildings allowances (**15.2**).

[*CAA 2001, ss 389, 390, 567, 568, 570(1), 573; ITTOIA 2005, Sch 1 para 557; CTA 2009, Sch 1 para 503*].

Business premises renovation allowances

Introduction

[15.18] For expenditure incurred on or after 11 April 2007, 100% capital allowances (are available for qualifying expenditure incurred by companies, whether as landlords or tenants, on the conversion or renovation of vacant business premises in any of the disadvantaged areas of the UK designated as 'Enterprise Areas' for the purpose of *bringing those premises back into business use.*

The scheme is expected to run for five years from date of commencement, but is capable of being extended.

[*CAA 2001, ss 360A–360Z4; FA 2005, s 92, Sch 6 para 1; SI 2007; No 949; CTA 2009, Sch 1 para 506, 507*].

Available to who?

[15.19] Business premises renovation allowances (BPRAs) are available to the person who incurred the qualifying expenditure and has the 'relevant interest' in the 'qualifying building'. [*CAA 2001, s 360A(2)*].

The '*relevant interest*' in relation to qualifying expenditure is determined in similar manner, with appropriate modifications, as for industrial buildings allowances (**15.7**), except that it cannot be transferred by the grant of a lease.

[*CAA 2001, ss 360E, 360F*].

As regards termination of leases, provisions similar to those of *CAA 2001, s 359* apply (**15.7**).

[*CAA 2001, s 360Z3*].

Qualifying expenditure

This means capital expenditure incurred before the 'expiry date' on, or in connection with:

- the conversion of a 'qualifying building' into 'qualifying business premises';
- the renovation of a 'qualifying building' if it is or will be 'qualifying business premises'; or
- repairs to a 'qualifying building' (or to a building of which the 'qualifying building' forms part), to the extent that they are incidental to either of the above (and for this purpose repairs are treated as capital expenditure if disallowable in computing the taxable profits of a property business or of a trade, profession or vocation),

other than expenditure incurred on, or in connection with the:

- acquisition of, or of rights in or over, land;
- extension of a qualifying building (except to the extent necessary to provide access to 'qualifying business premises');
- development of adjoining or adjacent land; or
- provision of plant and machinery, unless it is, or it becomes, a fixture as in **13.1 CAPITAL ALLOWANCES — PLANT AND MACHINERY: FIXTURES AND LEASING.**

Qualifying building

A '*qualifying building*' is any building or structure (or part thereof) which:

(a) is situated in an area which, on the date the renovation work begins, is a 'disadvantaged area';
(b) was unused for at least one year before the date the work begins;
(c) was last in use for the purposes of a trade, profession or vocation or as an office(s); or
(d) was not last in use as a dwelling or part of a dwelling; and
(e) (in the case of part of a building or structure) had not last been occupied and used in common with another part of the building or structure which was last in use as a dwelling or which does not meet itself the one-year rule in (b) above.

Once premises are qualifying business premises, they do not cease to be so by reason only of *temporary* unsuitability for use, or for letting, for qualifying purposes.

[*CAA 2001, s 360D(1)–(3)*].

Relevant trade

However, if the person entitled to claim is carrying on a relevant trade or the premises are wholly or partly used for such a trade, the buildings do not qualify for business premises renovation allowances.

A relevant trade for this purpose is a trade in any of the following sectors: fisheries and aquaculture, shipbuilding, coal, steel, synthetic fibres, the primary production of certain agricultural products, and the manufacture or marketing of products which imitate or substitute for milk and milk products. [*SI 2007 No 945*].

Disadvantaged area

A '*disadvantaged area*' is an area specified as a development area by the *Assisted Areas Order 2007* or Northern Ireland.

Any such regulations may designate an area for a limited time only.

The areas targeted by the legislation are the 1,997 (at time of writing) most deprived areas of the UK, originally announced in the 2002 Pre-Budget Report and often known as 'Enterprise Areas' (Treasury Explanatory Notes to the 2005 Finance (No 2) Bill).

If a building or structure is situated partly in a designated area and partly outside it, expenditure is to be apportioned on a just and reasonable basis in determining how much of it is qualifying expenditure. Where the postcode is known, it is possible to see whether or not a building lies within an assisted area using the site at www.dtistats.net/regional-aa/aa2007.asp.

[*CAA 2001, s 360C(1)–(6); SI 2007 No 945*].

Initial allowances

[15.20] Provided that the conditions above are met when the building is first used by the person with the relevant interest or, if not so used, are first suitable for letting for qualifying purposes, the initial allowance is **100%** of the qualifying expenditure.

This may be claimed in whole or in part, and is made for the chargeable period in which the expenditure is incurred.

[*CAA 2001, ss 360G, 360H*].

Writing-down allowances (WDAs)

[15.21] These allowances are available where the expenditure has not been wholly relieved by an initial allowance.

The annual WDA is **25%** of the qualifying expenditure, on a straight line basis, proportionately reduced or increased if the chargeable period is less or more than a year, and may be claimed in whole or in part.

The person who incurred the expenditure is entitled to a WDA for a chargeable period if *at the end of that period* the:

- person is still entitled to the relevant interest in the qualifying building;
- person has not granted, out of the relevant interest, a long lease (exceeding 50 years) of the qualifying building for a capital sum; and
- qualifying building is qualifying business premises.

There is nothing to prevent a WDA being given in the same chargeable period as an initial allowance for the same expenditure.

[*CAA 2001, ss 360I–360K, 360Q, 360R*].

Effect of grants on entitlement to allowances

No initial allowance or WDA is available to the extent that the qualifying expenditure is taken into account for the purposes of a relevant grant or a relevant payment made towards that expenditure; any allowance already made is withdrawn to the appropriate extent.

To the extent that a relevant grant or payment is repaid by the grantee, it is treated as having never been made.

Any assessments, or adjustments of assessments, necessary to give effect to these rules are not out of time if made within three years after the chargeable period in which the grant or payment was made or, as the case may be, repaid.

A grant or payment is '*relevant*' if it is a State aid notified to, and approved by, the European Commission or any other grant or subsidy nominated by Treasury order for these purposes.

[*CAA 2001, s 360L*].

Balancing allowances and charges

[15.22] If a 'balancing event' occurs, a balancing allowance or charge is made to or on the person who incurred the qualifying expenditure and for the chargeable period in which the event occurs.

If the unrelieved balance of qualifying expenditure immediately before the event exceeds the proceeds of the event, a balancing allowance arises, equal to the excess. (This is subject to the anti-avoidance rule at **10.14 CAPITAL ALLOWANCES — INTRODUCTION**.)

If the proceeds exceed the residue, a balancing charge arises, normally equal to the excess but limited to the total initial allowances and WDAs previously given to the person concerned in respect of the expenditure.

[*CAA 2001, ss 360M–360P*].

If more than one balancing event occurs, a balancing adjustment is made only on the first of them.

No balancing adjustment is made in respect of a balancing event occurring more than seven years after the time the premises were first used, or suitable for letting, for qualifying purposes.

Balancing event

Any of the following is a '*balancing event*':

(i) sale of the relevant interest in the qualifying building;
(ii) grant of a long lease (exceeding 50 years) of the qualifying building for a capital sum;

(iii) coming to an end of the lease otherwise than on the person entitled to it acquiring the reversionary interest;
(iv) death of the person who incurred the qualifying expenditure;
(v) demolition or destruction of the qualifying building;
(vi) qualifying building's otherwise ceasing to be qualifying business premises.

Proceeds of a balancing event

The proceeds of a balancing event depend upon the nature of the event and are as follows.

(1) On a sale of the relevant interest, the net sale proceeds receivable by the person who incurred the qualifying expenditure.
(2) On the grant of a long lease, the capital sum involved or, if greater, the premium that would have been paid in an arm's length transaction.
(3) In an event within (iii) above, where the persons entitled to, respectively, the lease and the superior interest are **CONNECTED PERSONS (25)**, the market value of the relevant interest in the qualifying building at the time of the event.
(4) On death, the residue (see below) of qualifying expenditure.
(5) On demolition or destruction, the net amount received for the remains by the person who incurred the qualifying expenditure, plus any insurance or capital compensation received by him.
(6) On the qualifying building's otherwise ceasing to be qualifying business premises, the market value of the relevant interest in the qualifying building at the time of the event.

Note that, by virtue of *CAA 2001, s 572*, a surrender for valuable consideration of a leasehold interest is treated as a sale (for equivalent proceeds), and thus falls within (1) above (if not caught by (3) above).

Any proceeds of sale of the relevant interest or other proceeds of a balancing event are, if attributable to both, apportioned on a just and reasonable basis between assets representing qualifying expenditure and other assets, and only the first part taken into account as above.

[*CAA 2001, s 360Z2*].

Demolition costs

Where a qualifying building is demolished, the net cost (after crediting any money received for remains) of demolition borne by the person who incurred the expenditure is added to the residue of qualifying expenditure immediately before the demolition.

No amount included in gross demolition costs can then be included for any capital allowances purposes as expenditure on replacement property.

[*CAA 2001, s 360S*].

Making of allowances and charges

If the person entitled to allowances or liable to charges under these provisions carries on a trade or occupies the qualifying building for the purposes of a trade, profession or vocation, the allowances/charges are treated as expenses/receipts of the trade, profession or vocation.

If the company's interest in the qualifying building is an asset of a property business (see **62.1** property income) carried on by it at any time in the accounting period in question, allowances/charges under these provisions are treated as expenses/receipts of that business.

If the above is not the case but the company's interest in the building is nevertheless subject to a lease or a licence, it is deemed to be carrying on a property business anyway, and allowances/charges given effect accordingly.

[*CAA 2001, ss 360Z, 360Z1*].

Additional VAT liabilities and rebates

See **10.10 CAPITAL ALLOWANCES — INTRODUCTION** as regards these generally.

The initial allowance above is also available in respect of any additional VAT liability incurred at a time when the qualifying building is, or is about to be, qualifying business premises; the allowance is made for the chargeable period in which the liability accrues.

For the purposes of WDAs, the residue of qualifying expenditure is treated as increased by the amount of an additional VAT liability at the time it accrues.

The making of an additional VAT rebate is a balancing event, but it does not give rise to a balancing allowance and gives rise to a balancing charge only if it exceeds the residue (including a nil residue) of qualifying expenditure at the time the rebate accrues; otherwise the residue is treated as reduced by the amount of the rebate at the time it accrues.

[*CAA 2001, ss 360T–360Y*].

Connected persons and other anti-avoidance provisions

The provisions at **15.2** for industrial buildings allowances apply equally to business premises renovation allowances, *except* that the election to treat a sale etc. as being at tax written-down value is *not* available in the instant case.

[*CAA 2001, ss 567–570, 573, 575(1), 577(4); FA 2005, s 92, Sch 6 paras 7, 8, 10*].

Flat conversion

Introduction

[15.23] For expenditure incurred **on or after 11 May 2001,** 100% capital allowances (known as flat conversion allowances) is available for qualifying expenditure on converting former residential space above shops and other commercial premises in the UK into flats for letting or on renovating such flats. [*CAA 2001, ss 393A–393W*].

The allowances are available only in computing the profits of a property business (see **62.1 PROPERTY INCOME**).

Available to who?

[15.24] Flat conversion allowances are available to a company which incurred qualifying expenditure and has the 'relevant interest' in the flat. [*CAA 2001, s 393A(2)*].

For these purposes, a '*flat*' is a separate set of premises (covering one or more floors) forming part of a building and divided horizontally from another part. [*CAA 2001, s 393A(3)*].

The part of the building being converted, or the flat being renovated, must have been unused, or used only for storage, throughout the 12 months immediately preceding the commencement of the work.

[*CAA 2001, s 393B(1)–(4); ITTOIA 2005, Sch 1 para 559; CTA 2009, Sch 1 para 505*].

Relevant interest

The '*relevant interest*' in relation to qualifying expenditure is determined in similar manner, with appropriate modifications, as for industrial buildings allowances (**15.7**), except that for the present purposes it cannot be transferred by the grant of a lease.

In its simplest form, the relevant interest is the interest in the flat to which the person incurring the expenditure was entitled when it was incurred. [*CAA 2001, ss 393F, 393G*].

As regards termination of leases, provisions similar to those of *CAA 2001, s 359* apply (**15.7**). [*CAA 2001, s 393V*].

'*Lease*' is defined (as are related expressions) accordingly, and in particular includes an agreement for a lease whose term has begun and a tenancy. [*CAA 2001, s 393W*].

Qualifying expenditure

This means capital expenditure incurred on, or in connection with:

- the conversion of part of a 'qualifying building' into a 'qualifying flat';
- the renovation of a flat in a 'qualifying building' if the flat is, or will be, a 'qualifying flat'; or
- repairs to a 'qualifying building', to the extent that they are incidental to either of the above (and for this purpose repairs are treated as capital expenditure if disallowable in computing the profits of a UK property business),

other than expenditure incurred on, or in connection with:

- the acquisition of, or of rights in or over, land;
- the extension of a qualifying building (except to the extent necessary to provide access to a 'qualifying flat');
- the development of adjoining or adjacent land; or
- furnishings or chattels.

Qualifying building

For a building to be a '*qualifying building*':

- all or most of its ground floor must be 'authorised for business use';

- its construction must have been completed before 1 January 1980 (disregarding any extension completed on or after that date but before 1 January 2001);
- it must have no more than four storeys above ground floor (disregarding an attic storey, unless used, or previously used, as a dwelling or part of a dwelling); and
- at time of construction, all such storeys must have been primarily for residential use.

[*CAA 2001, s 393C(1)(3)(4)*].

Authorised for business use

'*Authorised for business use*' is defined by reference to specified uses designated in the relevant ratings rules for England and Wales, Scotland and NI. [*CAA 2001, s 393C(2)*].

Included are retail shops, food and drink outlets, premises offering financial and professional services, other offices, medical and dental practices, and premises used for research and development and industrial processes which can be carried out in residential.

Qualifying flat

For a flat to be a '*qualifying flat*' it must:

(a) be in a qualifying building;
(b) be suitable for letting as a dwelling (disregarding any temporary unsuitability where previously suitable);
(c) be held for short-term letting, i.e. on leases of five years or less;
(d) be accessible by some means other than via the ground floor business area;
(e) have no more than four rooms (disregarding kitchens and bathrooms of whatever area, and closets, cloakrooms and hallways of no more than five square metres in each case);
(f) not be a 'high value flat';
(g) not be (or have been) created or renovated as part of a scheme involving the creation etc. of one or more 'high value flats'; and
(h) not be let to a person connected (within *CTA 2010, s 1122* (*ITA 2007, s 993* for income tax purposes) — see **25 CONNECTED PERSONS**) with the person who incurred the conversion or renovation expenditure.

[*CAA 2001, s 393D(1)–(4)*].

A flat is a '*high value flat*' if the 'notional rent' exceeds the relevant limit below.

No. of rooms (as in (e) above)	*Greater London*	*Outside Greater London*
1 or 2	£350 per week	£150 per week
3	£425 per week	£225 per week
4	£480 per week	£300 per week

The '*notional rent*' is the rent that could reasonably have been expected, at the time expenditure on the conversion etc. work is first incurred, if the work had been completed and the flat was then let furnished, on a shorthold tenancy (not applicable in NI), other than to a **CONNECTED PERSON** (**25**), and otherwise than for any additional payment, such as a premium.

[*CAA 2001, s 393E(1)–(5)(7)*].

The above definitions of qualifying expenditure, qualifying building and qualifying flat and the above notional rent limits may be amended by Treasury regulations. [*CAA 2001, ss 393B(5), 393C(5), 393D(5), 393E(6)*].

Initial allowances

[15.25] The initial allowance is **100%** of the qualifying expenditure, may be claimed in whole or in part, and is made for the chargeable period in which the expenditure is incurred.

The initial allowance is not available if:

(i) the flat is not a qualifying flat at the time it is first suitable for letting as a dwelling; or
(ii) the person who incurred the expenditure sells the relevant interest before that time. [*CAA 2001, ss 393H, 393I*].

Writing-down allowances

[15.26] Writing-down allowances (WDAs) are available where the expenditure has not been wholly relieved by an initial allowance.

The annual WDA is 25% of the qualifying expenditure, on a straight line basis, proportionately reduced or increased if the chargeable period is less or more than a year, and may be claimed in whole or in part.

The person who incurred the expenditure is entitled to a WDA for a chargeable period if *at the end of that period*:

- he is entitled to the relevant interest in the flat;
- he has not granted, out of the relevant interest, a long lease (exceeding 50 years) of the flat for a capital sum; and
- the flat is a qualifying flat.

There is nothing to prevent a WDA being given in the same chargeable period as an initial allowance for the same expenditure.

[*CAA 2001, ss 393J–393L, 393Q, 393R*].

Balancing allowances and charges

[15.27] If a 'balancing event' occurs, a balancing adjustment, i.e. a balancing allowance or balancing charge, is made to or on the person who incurred the qualifying expenditure and for the chargeable period in which the event occurs.

If the unrelieved balance of qualifying expenditure immediately before the event exceeds the proceeds of the event, a balancing allowance arises, equal to the excess. (This is subject to the anti-avoidance rule at **10.14 CAPITAL ALLOWANCES — INTRODUCTION**.)

If the proceeds exceed unrelieved balance of qualifying expenditure, a balancing charge arises, normally equal to the excess but limited to the total initial and writing-down allowances previously given to the person concerned in respect of the expenditure.

[*CAA 2001, ss 393M–393P*].

If more than one balancing event occurs, a balancing adjustment is made only on the first of them.

No balancing adjustment is made in respect of a balancing event occurring more than seven years after the time the flat was first suitable for letting as a dwelling.

Balancing event

Any of the following is a '*balancing event*':

(i) sale of the relevant interest (see above) in the flat;
(ii) grant, out of the relevant interest, of a long lease (exceeding 50 years) of the flat for a capital sum;
(iii) coming to an end of the lease otherwise than on the person entitled to it acquiring the reversionary interest;
(iv) death of the person who incurred the qualifying expenditure;
(v) demolition or destruction of the flat;
(vi) flat's otherwise ceasing to be a qualifying flat.

Proceeds of a balancing event

The proceeds of a balancing event depend upon the nature of the event and are as follows.

(1) On a sale of the relevant interest, the net sale proceeds receivable by the person who incurred the qualifying expenditure.
(2) On the grant of a long lease, the capital sum involved or, if greater, the premium that would have been paid in an arm's length transaction.
(3) In an event within (iii) above, where the persons entitled to, respectively, the lease and the superior interest are **CONNECTED PERSONS (25)**, the market value of the relevant interest in the flat at the time of the event.
(4) On death, the residue (see below) of qualifying expenditure.
(5) On demolition or destruction, the net amount received for the remains by the person who incurred the qualifying expenditure, plus any insurance or capital compensation received by him.
(6) On the flat's otherwise ceasing to be a qualifying flat, the market value of the relevant interest in the flat at the time of the event.

Note that, by virtue of *CAA 2001, s 572*, a surrender for valuable consideration of a leasehold interest is treated as a sale (for equivalent proceeds), and thus falls within (1) above (if not caught by (3) above).

Any proceeds of sale of the relevant interest or other proceeds of a balancing event are, if attributable to both, apportioned on a just and reasonable basis between assets representing qualifying expenditure and other assets, and only the first part taken into account as above. [*CAA 2001, s 393U*].

Demolition costs

Where a qualifying flat is demolished, the net cost (after crediting any money received for remains) of demolition borne by the person who incurred the expenditure is added to the residue of qualifying expenditure immediately before the demolition, and is thus taken into account in computing the balancing adjustment; no amount included in gross demolition costs can then attract capital allowances of any kind. [*CAA 2001, s 393S*].

Making of allowances and charges

If the company is within the charge to corporation in respect of the allowance and it's interest in the flat is an asset of a property business (see **62.1** property income) carried on by it at any time in the chargeable period in question, allowances/charges under these provisions are treated as expenses/receipts of that business.

If the above is not the case, the company is deemed to be carrying on a property business anyway, and allowances/charges given effect accordingly. [*CAA 2001, s 393T; ITTOIA 2005, Sch 1 para 560*].

Connected persons and other anti-avoidance provisions

The provisions at **15.2** for industrial buildings allowances applied equally to flat conversion allowances, *except* that the election to treat a sale etc. as being at tax written-down value was *not* available in the instant case. [*CAA 2001, ss 567–570, 573, 575(1), 577(4)*].

HMRC guidance

See generally HMRC Capital Allowances Manual CA43000 *et seq.*

Simon's Taxes. See B3.10.

Dwelling-houses let on assured tenancies

Introduction

[15.28] Legislation was introduced by *FA 1982* to give capital allowances on capital expenditure incurred by an '*approved body*' (i.e. a body specified by the Secretary of State under *Housing Act 1980, s 56(4)*), on the construction of buildings consisting of, or including, dwelling-houses let on assured and certain other tenancies, after 9 March 1982 and before 1 April 1992.

[*CAA 2001, ss 490(1), 491, 492*].

The provisions were substantially modified following repeal of the relevant sections of the *Housing Act 1980* by the *Housing Act 1988*.

Qualifying dwelling house

[15.29] A dwelling-house is a '*qualifying dwelling-house*' when it is let on a tenancy being an assured tenancy within *Housing Act 1980, s 56* (or, not being an assured shorthold tenancy, within *Housing Act 1988*) and continues to qualify at any time when:

(i) it is subject to a regulated tenancy or a housing association tenancy (as defined in the *Rent Act 1977*); and
(ii) the landlord under the tenancy either is or has been an approved body.

[*CAA 2001, s 490(2)–(5)*].

A dwelling-house does not qualify:

(a) unless the landlord is a company (applicable to expenditure contracted and incurred after 4 May 1983, or where a person other than a company becomes entitled to the 'relevant interest' after that date) and either is entitled to the relevant interest in the dwelling-house or is the person who incurred the capital expenditure on the construction of the building containing it; or
(b) if the landlord is a housing association approved under *CTA 2010, Pt 13, Ch 7* (co-operative housing association) or is a self-build society under the *Housing Associations Act 1985*; or
(c) if the landlord and tenant, or a company of which the tenant is a director, are connected persons (**25**); or
(d) if the landlord is a close company and the tenant is a participator, or associate of a participator, in that company; or
(e) if the tenancy is part of a reciprocal arrangement between the landlords or owners of different dwelling-houses designed to counter the restrictions in (c) or (d) above.

[*CAA 2001, ss 504, 505*].

Qualifying capital expenditure

Capital expenditure attributable to a dwelling-house is limited to £60,000 if it is in Greater London and £40,000 elsewhere.

Single qualifying dwelling-house

The whole of the expenditure on its construction qualifies.

Dwelling-house forms part of a building

The amount qualifies is:

(i) the proportion of capital expenditure attributable to that dwelling-house, and
(ii) such proportion of the capital expenditure on any common parts of the building as is just and reasonable, but not exceeding one-tenth of the amount in (i).

[*CAA 2001, s 511*].

The acquisition of, or of rights in or over, any land is not included in expenditure incurred on the cost of construction of a building for these purposes. Any capital expenditure incurred on repairs is treated as if incurred on the construction for the first time of that part of the building.

[*CAA 2001, s 493*].

Buildings bought unused

The provisions in *CAA 2001, ss 502, 503* are similar to those for former industrial buildings in *CAA 2001, ss 295, 296*, for which see **15.5, 15.6**.

Allowances

[15.30] Initial allowances were, and writing-down allowances are, given in a similar manner, at similar rates and under similar conditions as for former industrial buildings, for which see **15.6, 15.7**. [*CAA 2001, ss 507–510, 519*].

References to 'temporary disuse' [*CAA 2001, s 506(2)*], 'residue of expenditure' [*CAA 2001, ss 512, 523–528*], and 'relevant interest' [*CAA 2001, ss 495–498, 500*] should be taken as they apply for former industrial buildings allowances, but it should be noted that the creation of a subsidiary interest (e.g. leasehold out of freehold) does not transfer the relevant interest.

Balancing allowances and charges are made in a similar manner and under similar conditions as for former industrial buildings in *CAA 2001, s 314 et seq.* (see **15.9**). [*CAA 2001, s 513 et seq.*].

If *cessation of qualifying use occurs* otherwise than by sale or transfer of the relevant interest, that interest is treated as having been sold at the time of cessation at the open market price. [*CAA 2001, s 506(1)*].

Making of allowances and charges

Allowances and charges are made in a similar way as they apply to lessors and licensors of former industrial buildings, for which see **15.10**. [*CAA 2001, s 529; ITTOIA 2005, Sch 1 para 569; CTA 2009, Sch 1 para 515*].

Holding over by lessee etc.

Where the relevant interest in relation to the capital expenditure incurred on the construction of a building is an interest under a lease, the following provisions apply. The lease will be treated as continuing where:

(i) with the consent of the lessor, a lessee remains in possession of any building after his lease ends and without a new lease being granted;
(ii) where a lease ends and a new lease is granted to the same lessee under an option available in the first lease; and
(iii) where a lease ends and another lease is granted to a different lessee who pays a sum to the first lessee (i.e. the transaction is treated as an assignment).

However, where a lease ends and the lessor pays any sum to the lessee in respect of the building, the transaction is treated as if the lease had come to an end by reason of its surrender in consideration of the payment. [*CAA 2001, s 499*].

Connected persons and other anti-avoidance provisions

The provisions of *CAA 2001, ss 567–570* (and forerunners) apply to certain sales as they apply to sales of industrial buildings (see **15.2**) but an election is only available if both the seller and the buyer are, at the time of the sale (or were at any earlier time), approved bodies. Any transfer of relevant interest which is not a sale will be treated as a sale other than at market price under these provisions but there is no balancing allowance or charge if the dwelling-house is treated as having been sold for a sum equal to the residue of expenditure before the sale. [*CAA 2001, ss 569(5), 570(4), 573*]. See also the anti-avoidance rule at **10.14 CAPITAL ALLOWANCES — INTRODUCTION.**

Simon's Taxes. See B3.9.

Student residences

[15.31] On 29 December 2008, HMRC published Brief 66/08 which sought comments on certain proposed revisions to guidance in the Capital Allowances Manual. One of the proposed revisions concerned an update to guidance on the meaning of 'dwelling-house' for the purposes *CAA 2001, s 35*. Broadly, *s 35* provides that expenditure on plant or machinery 'for use in a dwelling-house' does not qualify for capital allowances in certain cases, for example, in the case of an ordinary or overseas property business. In the subsequent Brief 45/10, HMRC provided the following details of how they intend to apply the developing rules in practice:

> 'The updated view, as expressed in the revised guidance will apply in all circumstances in relation to capital expenditure incurred on or after 22 October 2010.
>
> In relation to capital expenditure incurred on or after 29 December 2008 but before 22 October 2010 HMRC will either accept capital allowances claims in returns made in respect of communal areas on the basis of the view as set out in HMRC Brief 66/08 or on the basis of the view as previously set out in CA 11520 and CA 23060.
>
> In relation to capital expenditure incurred before 29 December 2008 claims made in returns for open years and filed before 22 October 2010 relying on HMRC Brief 66/08 will also be accepted.'

Whilst there has been no change to the underlying legislation, the differing views are open to challenge and a tribunal hearing may be needed to determine whether or not the latest HMRC view is deemed correct.

Key points

[15.32] Points to consider are as follows.

- Capital allowances on industrial buildings, hotels and agricultural buildings have now been phased out. For the year to 5 April 2011 they only attract 1% writing-down allowance (previously 4%). Given the loss of this relief it may be advantageous, if possible, for companies to reclassify certain items of historic expenditure as plant and machinery or integral features.

- Since April 2007 balancing allowances/charges have not crystallised on disposal of industrial or other qualifying buildings even when the property has been sold for more than its tax written down value (residue value).
- It is never too late to review historic expenditure to check that the maximum capital allowances have been claimed. As long as a company still owns the property it can make capital allowance claims on historic expenditure through any open returns.
- Business premises renovation allowances entitle companies to claim 100% capital allowances on qualifying expenditure incurred in bringing a disused property back into commercial use (provided all of the conditions are met). The relief is currently expected to be available only until April 2012 so it may be worth considering bringing any projects forward.

16

Capital Allowances — Miscellaneous

Other sources. See Tolley's Capital Allowances.

Cross references. See **10** CAPITAL ALLOWANCES — INTRODUCTION; **11** CAPITAL ALLOWANCES — PLANT AND MACHINERY: ELIGIBLE EXPENDITURE AND INITIAL ALLOWANCES; **12** CAPITAL ALLOWANCES — PLANT AND MACHINERY: POOLING AND DISPOSALS; **13** CAPITAL ALLOWANCES — PLANT AND MACHINERY: FIXTURES AND LEASING; **14** CAPITAL ALLOWANCES — MINERAL EXTRACTION and **15** CAPITAL ALLOWANCES — BUILDINGS.

Dredging

Introduction

[16.1] Writing-down, balancing and, previously, initial allowances may be claimed for capital expenditure on **dredging** incurred for the purposes of a *qualifying trade* (provided that neither industrial buildings allowances (see **15.2** CAPITAL ALLOWANCES — BUILDINGS) nor plant and machinery allowances (see **11.2** CAPITAL ALLOWANCES — PLANT AND MACHINERY: ELIGIBLE EXPENDITURE AND INITIAL ALLOWANCES) are available in respect of the same expenditure).

'*Dredging*' must be done in the interests of navigation, and either:

(i) the qualifying trade must consist of the maintenance or improvement of navigation of a harbour, estuary or waterway; or
(ii) the dredging must be for the benefit of vessels coming to, leaving or using docks or other premises used in the qualifying trade.

It includes removal, by any means, of any part of, or projections from, any sea or inland water bed (whether then above water or not), and the widening of any inland waterway.

The HMRC interpretation of the definition is that dredging includes 'the deepening or widening of a channel for the passage of ships, whether in tidal waters or in an inland waterway. Dredging does not include normal maintenance work on an existing channel' (HMRC Capital Allowance Manual CA80200).

Qualifying trade

[16.2] A '*qualifying trade*' is one either within (i) above or within the industrial buildings allowance definitions at **15.3**(a)–(c) **CAPITAL ALLOWANCES — BUILDINGS**. Expenditure only partly for a qualifying trade is apportioned as may be just and reasonable, and for this purpose, where part only of a trade qualifies, the qualifying and non-qualifying parts are treated as separate trades.

[*CAA 2001, ss 484, 485*].

Writing down allowances

[16.3] Initial allowances were abolished for expenditure incurred after 31 March 1986, unless incurred before 1 April 1987 under a contract entered into before 14 March 1984 by the person incurring the expenditure. [*FA 1985, s 61*].

Writing-down allowances are given to the person carrying on the trade during a writing-down period of 25 years beginning with the first day of the chargeable period in which the expenditure was incurred, subject to an overall restriction on allowances (initial and writing-down) of the amount of the expenditure.

No allowance is given for a chargeable period in which a balancing allowance arises.

The rates of allowance, fixed by the date expenditure was incurred, are as follows (although a lesser amount may be claimed).

Before 6 November 1962 — 2% p.a.
From 6 November 1962 — 4% p.a.

[*CAA 2001, ss 487, 489, Sch 3 para 103*].

Pre trading expenditure

Expenditure incurred for a trade before it is carried on attracts allowances as if it were incurred on the first day on which the trade was carried on.

Similarly, expenditure incurred in connection with a dock etc. with a view to occupying it for the purposes of a qualifying trade other than one within (i) above attracts allowances as if it were incurred when the dock etc. is first so occupied. [*CAA 2001, s 486*].

Slightly different rules applied before *CAA 2001* came into effect (see **10.1 CAPITAL ALLOWANCES — INTRODUCTION** and Change 57 listed in Annex 1 to the Explanatory Notes to the 2001 Capital Allowances Bill).

[*CAA 1990, ss 134(7), 135(2)*].

Balancing allowances

[16.4] A balancing allowance is given for the chargeable period of *permanent discontinuance* of the trade, equal to expenditure incurred less initial and writing-down allowances given, to the person last carrying on the trade.

Permanent discontinuance includes sale of the business (unless it is a sale between **CONNECTED PERSONS (25)**, or without change of control, or one the sole or main benefit of which appears to be a capital allowance advantage), but not deemed discontinuance under *ICTA 1988, s 337(1); CTA 2009, Sch 1 para 514*.

[*CAA 2001, s 488, Sch 3 para 104; ITTOIA 2005, Sch 1 para 568*].

Example

D Ltd operates an estuary maintenance business preparing accounts to 30 June. Expenditure qualifying for dredging allowances is incurred as follows.

	£
Year ended 30.6.10	4,000
Year ended 30.6.11	5,000

On 2 January 2012, D Ltd sells the business to an unconnected third party. The allowances available are

Date of expenditure	Cost	Residue brought forward	Allowances WDA 4%	Residue carried forward
	£	£	£	£
Accounting period ended 30.6.10				
2010	4,000	—	160	£3,840
Accounting period ended 30.6.11				
2010	4,000	3,840	160	3,680
2010	5,000	—	200	4,800
			£360	£8,480

Six months ending 2.1.12	
Balancing allowance	£8,480

'Know-how'

Introduction

[16.5] Expenditure on acquiring 'know-how' (so far as not otherwise deductible for corporation tax purposes) gives rise to writing-down and balancing allowances (and balancing charges) where the company acquiring it either:

(i) is then carrying on a trade for use in which it is acquired; or
(ii) subsequently commences such a trade (in which case the expenditure is treated as incurred on commencement); or
(iii) acquires it with a trade (or part) in which it was used, and either the parties to the acquisition make the appropriate joint election under *CTA 2009, s 178(7)* or *ITTOIA 2005, s 194* (election for disposal of know-how on disposal of trade not to be treated as disposal of goodwill), or corporation tax equivalent, or the trade was carried on wholly outside the UK before the acquisition.

The same expenditure may not be taken into account in relation to more than one trade.

Expenditure is, however, *excluded* where the buyer and seller are bodies of persons (which includes partnerships) under common control.

[*CAA 2001, ss 452(1), 454, 455; CTA 2009, ss 178(7), 179(1)–(3), 909(5), (6), 1316(2); ITTOIA 2005, Sch 1 paras 207, 562, 563; CTA 2009, Sch 1 para 509, 510*].

Allowances are not available where know-how falls within the regime for intangible assets. **48.36 INTANGIBLE ASSETS.**

'*Know-how*' means any industrial information and techniques of assistance in:

(a) manufacturing or processing goods or materials;
(b) working, or searching etc. for, mineral deposits; or
(c) agricultural, forestry or fishing operations.

[*CTA 2009, s 908(4); CAA 2001, s 452(2)(3)*].

For expenditure on offshore divers' training courses treated as on know-how, see HMRC Capital Allowances Manual CA74000.

Allowances

[16.6] All qualifying expenditure of a trade is pooled, and:

(1) if the 'available qualifying expenditure' exceeds the 'total disposal value', a writing-down allowance is available of 25% of the excess, proportionately reduced or increased where the period is less or more

than one year, or if the trade has been carried on for part only of a chargeable period (and subject to any lesser amount being claimed), *except that* if the chargeable period is that of permanent discontinuance of the trade, a balancing allowance of **100%** of the excess is available;

(2) if the 'total disposal value' exceeds the 'available qualifying expenditure', a balancing charge arises of **100%** of the excess.

Available qualifying expenditure

'*Available qualifying expenditure*' in a pool for a chargeable period consists of qualifying expenditure allocated to the pool for that period and any unrelieved qualifying expenditure brought forward in the pool from the previous chargeable period (usually referred to as the written-down value brought forward).

In allocating qualifying expenditure to the pool, rules identical to those for patent rights at **16.7** must be observed.

Total disposal value

The '*total disposal value*' is the aggregate of any disposal values to be brought into account for the period, i.e. the net sale proceeds (being capital sums) from any disposal of know-how on which qualifying expenditure was incurred (but excluding any sale the consideration for which is treated as a payment for goodwill under *CTA 2009, s 178* or *ITTOIA 2005, s 194(2)*. (The restriction to capital sale proceeds is introduced by *CAA 2001* (see **10.1 CAPITAL ALLOWANCES — INTRODUCTION**) — see Change 55 in Annex 1 to the 2001 Capital Allowances Bill.)

The allowances and charges are given effect as deductions or receipts of the relevant trade.

[*CAA 2001, ss 456–463; ITTOIA 2005, Sch 1 para 564; CTA 2009, Sch 1 para 511*].

For receipts arising from sales of know-how, see also **70.55 TRADE PROFITS — INCOME AND SPECIFIC TRADES.**

Patent rights

Introduction

[16.7] Subject to the application of the regime for **INTANGIBLE ASSETS (48)**, allowances are available, and balancing charges made, in respect of 'qualifying expenditure' on the purchase of patent rights, i.e. the right to do or authorise the doing of anything which would, but for that right, be a patent infringement.

The obtaining of a right to acquire future patent rights and the acquisition of a licence in respect of a patent are each treated for these purposes as a purchase of patent rights.

Allowances are not available where the intangible assets regime applies to the patent rights. See in particular the commencement and transitional provisions for that regime at **48.36 INTANGIBLE ASSETS**.

Qualifying expenditure

[16.8] '*Qualifying expenditure*' may be either:

- '*qualifying trade expenditure*', i.e. capital expenditure incurred by a person on purchase of patent rights for the purposes of a trade carried on by him and within the charge to UK tax; or
- '*qualifying non-trade expenditure*', i.e. capital expenditure incurred by a person on purchase of patent rights if the above does not apply but any income receivable by him in respect of the rights would be liable to tax.

Pre trading expenditure

Expenditure incurred by a person for the purposes of a trade he is about to carry on is treated as if incurred on the first day of trading, unless all the rights in question have been sold before then. The same expenditure cannot be qualifying trade expenditure in relation to more than one trade.

Grant of licence

The grant of a licence in respect of a patent is treated as a sale of part of patent rights. The grant by a person entitled to patent rights of an exclusive licence, i.e. a licence to exercise the rights to the exclusion of the grantor and all others for the remainder of their term, is, however, treated as a sale of the whole of those rights.

[*CAA 2001, ss 464–469*].

Allowances

Pooling

[16.9] Qualifying expenditure incurred after 31 March 1986 is pooled for the purpose of determining entitlement to writing-down allowances and balancing allowances and liability to balancing charges. A separate pool applies for each separate trade and for all qualifying non-trade expenditure.

Writing down allowance

For each pool of qualifying expenditure, a writing-down allowance (WDA) is available for each chargeable period other than the 'final chargeable period'.

It is calculated as 25% of the amount (if any) by which 'available qualifying expenditure' exceeds the total of any disposal values falling to be brought into account.

The WDA is proportionately reduced or increased if the chargeable period is less or more than a year, or if (where relevant) the trade has been carried on for part only of the chargeable period.

A claim for a WDA may require it to be reduced to a specified amount.

Final period

For the 'final chargeable period', a balancing allowance is available, equal to:

Excess (if any) of (1) 'available qualifying expenditure' over (2) total disposal values.

If, for *any* chargeable period, (2) exceeds (1), there arises a liability to a balancing charge, equal to that excess.

The '*final chargeable period*', as regards a pool of qualifying trade expenditure, is the chargeable period in which the trade is permanently discontinued.

As regards a pool of non-qualifying trade expenditure, it is the chargeable period in which the last of the patent rights in question either comes to an end (without any such rights being revived) or, where *CAA 2001* has effect (see **10.1 CAPITAL ALLOWANCES — INTRODUCTION**), is wholly disposed of.

Available qualifying expenditure

'*Available qualifying expenditure*' in a pool for a chargeable period consists of qualifying expenditure allocated to the pool for that period and any unrelieved qualifying expenditure brought forward in the pool from the previous chargeable period (usually referred to as the written-down value brought forward).

Allocating to a pool

In allocating qualifying expenditure to a pool, the following must be observed.

(i) Qualifying expenditure can be allocated to a pool for a chargeable period only to the extent that it has not been included in available qualifying expenditure for an earlier chargeable period.
(ii) Qualifying expenditure cannot be allocated to a pool for a chargeable period earlier than that in which it is incurred.
(iii) Qualifying expenditure cannot be allocated to a pool for a chargeable period if in any earlier period the rights in question have come to an end (without any of them being revived) or have been wholly disposed of.

[*CAA 2001, ss 470–475*].

Disposal

[16.10] A *disposal value* falls to be brought into account for a chargeable period in which a person sells the whole or part of any patent rights on the purchase of which he has incurred qualifying expenditure.

The disposal value is equal to the net sale proceeds (limited to *capital* sums where *CAA 2001* has effect (**10.1 CAPITAL ALLOWANCES — INTRODUCTION**), except that:

(1) it cannot exceed the qualifying expenditure incurred on purchase of the rights in question; and

(2) where the rights were acquired as a result of a transaction between **CONNECTED PERSONS** (**25**) (or a series of such transactions), (1) above shall have effect as if it referred to the greatest capital expenditure incurred on the purchase of those rights by any of those connected persons.

[*CAA 2001, ss 476, 477*].

Connected persons and anti-avoidance

[16.11] Anti avoidance rules apply where a person incurs capital expenditure after 26 July 1989 on the purchase of rights either:

(i) (from a connected person (see **25 CONNECTED PERSONS**); or
(ii) so that it appears that the sole or main benefit from the sale and any other transactions would have been the obtaining of an allowance under these provisions.

In these circumstances, the amount of that expenditure taken into account as qualifying expenditure may not exceed an amount determined as follows:

(a) where a disposal value falls to be brought into account, an amount equal to that value;
(b) where no disposal value falls to be brought into account, but the seller receives a capital sum chargeable under *CTA 2009, s 912* or *ITTOIA 2005, s 587* (see **61.18 PROFIT COMPUTATIONS**), an amount equal to that sum;
(c) in any other case, an amount equal to the smallest of:
  - market value of the rights;
  - the amount of capital expenditure, if any, incurred by the seller on acquiring the rights;
  - the amount of capital expenditure, if any, incurred by any person connected with the seller on acquiring the rights.

[*CAA 2001, s 481, Sch 3 para 102; ITTOIA 2005, Sch 1 para 566; CTA 2009, Sch 1 para 512*].

Previously, the restriction was by reference to the disposal value only. See also (2) above.

Making of allowances and charge

An allowance (or balancing charge) in respect of qualifying *trade* expenditure is given effect as a trading expense (or trading receipt). [*CAA 2001, s 478*].

An allowance in respect of qualifying *non-trade* expenditure is set against the company's 'income from patents' for the same accounting period, with any excess being carried forward without time limit against such income for subsequent accounting periods. A balancing charge is treated as income from patents. For these purposes, '*income from patents*' embraces royalties and similar sums, balancing charges under these provisions, and receipts from the sale of patent rights taxable under *CTA 2009, s 912* or *s 918*. [*CAA 2001, ss 479, 480, 483; ITTOIA 2005, Sch 1 paras 205, 209, 565, 56; CTA 2009, Pt 9, Ch 3, Sch 1 para 513*].

For expenditure incurred before 1 April 1986, a different set of rules applied, for which see the 2004/05 and earlier editions of Tolley's Income Tax.

Simon's Taxes. See **B3.601–B3.609.**

Example

P Ltd, who prepares accounts to 31 December, acquires two new patent rights for trading purposes.

	Date	Term	Cost
Patent 1	19.4.010	15 years	£4,500
Patent 2	5.10.011	5 years	£8,000

On 1.12.010 P Ltd sold part of the rights under patent 1 for £2,000.

The allowances for each patent are:

	Pool	WDA
Y/e 31.12.10		
	£	£
Expenditure (patent 1)	4,500	
WDA 25%	(1,125)	£1,125
	3,375	
Y/e 31.12.11		
Expenditure (patent 2)	8,000	
Disposal proceeds (patent 1)	(2,000)	
	9,375	
WDA 25%	(2,344)	£2,344
WDV c/f	£7,031	

Research and development

Introduction

[16.12] 'Qualifying expenditure' incurred by a trader on 'research and development' (R&D) attracts an allowance equal to 100% of the expenditure.

A claim for an allowance may require it to be reduced to a specified amount (but the part of the allowance thus forgone cannot be claimed for a later chargeable period).

References below to R&D, except in the definition thereof, also embrace scientific research.

Qualifying expenditure

[16.13] '*Qualifying expenditure*' is capital expenditure incurred by a trader on R&D related to the trade and undertaken directly or on his behalf (i.e. by an agent or other person in a similar contractual relationship, see *Gaspet Ltd v Elliss* [1987] 1 WLR 769, 60 TC 91, CA).

It includes such expenditure incurred before commencement of the trade (pre-commencement expenditure).

Expenditure potentially leading to or facilitating an extension of the trade is related to that trade, as is expenditure of a medical nature specially related to the welfare of workers in the trade.

A just and reasonable apportionment may be made of capital expenditure only partly qualifying.

Expenditure on R&D includes all expenditure incurred for carrying out (or providing facilities for carrying out) R&D.

Expenditure on the acquisition of rights in, or arising out of, R&D is, however, excluded.

Also excluded is expenditure on provision of a *dwelling*, except where not more than 25% of the expenditure (disregarding any 'additional VAT liability' or 'rebate' (**10.10 CAPITAL ALLOWANCES — INTRODUCTION**) on a building consisting partly of a dwelling and otherwise used for R&D is attributable (on a just and reasonable apportionment) to the dwelling, in which case the dwelling can be ignored and the whole of the building treated as used for R&D.

Additional VAT liability

An 'additional VAT liability' (**10.10 CAPITAL ALLOWANCES — INTRODUCTION**) incurred in respect of qualifying expenditure is itself qualifying expenditure, provided the same person still owns the asset in question and it has not been demolished or destroyed.

Land

Expenditure on the acquisition of, or of rights in or over, land cannot be qualifying expenditure, except in so far as, on a just and reasonable apportionment, such expenditure is referable to a building or structure already constructed on the land, or to plant or machinery which forms part of such a building or structure, and otherwise qualifies as R&D expenditure.

Making of allowances

The allowance is given as a trading expense of the chargeable period in which the expenditure is incurred (or, in the case of pre-commencement expenditure, the chargeable period in which the trade commences).

An allowance in respect of an additional VAT liability is similarly given, but by reference to the time the *liability* is incurred.

[*CAA 2001, ss 437(1), 438–441, 447, 450, Sch 3 paras 89, 90*].

Definitions

'*Research and development*' is, from 6 April 2007, as defined by *ITA 2007, s 1006* and, before that date, as defined by *ICTA 1988, s 837A* and supporting regulations (see **64.1 RESEARCH AND DEVELOPMENT EXPENDITURE**), but also includes oil and gas exploration and appraisal (within *CTA 2010, s 1134*). [*CAA 2001, s 437(2); CAA 1990, s 139(1)*].

Disposal events and balancing charges

[16.14] Where *CAA 2001* has effect (**10.1 CAPITAL ALLOWANCES — INTRODUCTION**), if a disposal value falls to be brought into account for the same chargeable period as that for which the related allowance falls to be given, the allowance is given on the excess (if any) of the expenditure over the disposal value.

If a disposal value falls to be brought into account for the chargeable period after that for which the related allowance is given, liability to a balancing charge arises for that later chargeable period.

Effect is given to the charge by treating it as a trading receipt.

The charge is equal to disposal value (or, where a reduced allowance was claimed, the excess, if any, of disposal value over unrelieved expenditure), except that it cannot exceed the allowance given (less any earlier balancing charges arising from 'additional VAT rebates').

A disposal value falls to be brought into account for a chargeable period in which a disposal event occurs, or, if such an event occurs later, for the chargeable period in which the trade is permanently discontinued.

If, exceptionally, a disposal event occurs *before* the chargeable period for which the related allowance falls to be given, it is brought into account for the later chargeable period; before *CAA 2001* had effect (**10.1 CAPITAL ALLOWANCES — INTRODUCTION**), the resulting net allowance was given for the chargeable period *in which the disposal event occurred.*

Disposal event

Either of the following is a disposal event (unless it gives rise to a balancing charge under the rules for industrial buildings or plant and machinery allowances).

(a) The trader ceases to own the asset representing the qualifying expenditure.
(b) An asset representing the qualifying expenditure is demolished or destroyed before the trader ceases to own it.

On the sale of an asset, the seller is treated for these purposes as ceasing to own it at the earlier of the time of completion and the time when possession is given.

Disposal value

The amount of the disposal value depends on the nature of the disposal event, as follows.

- If the event is a sale of the asset at not less than market value, it is the *net* sale proceeds; (before *CAA 2001* had effect, **10.1 CAPITAL ALLOWANCES — INTRODUCTION**, it was the sale proceeds).
- If the event is the demolition or destruction of the asset, it is the net amount received for the remains, plus any insurance or *capital* compensation received (but see below as regards demolition costs); (before *CAA 2001* had effect, *any* compensation received had to be taken into account).

- In any other event, it is the market value of the asset at the time of the event.

An 'additional VAT rebate' (**10.10 CAPITAL ALLOWANCES — INTRODUCTION**) made in respect of qualifying expenditure, before the asset in question ceases to belong to the trader or has been demolished or destroyed, must be brought into account as a disposal value (or as an addition to a disposal value otherwise arising) for the chargeable period in which the rebate accrues or, if later, the chargeable period in which the trade commences.

[*CAA 2001, ss 441(1), 442–444, 448, 449–451*].

Demolition costs

On demolition of an asset (within (b) above), the disposal value is reduced (or extinguished) by any demolition costs incurred by the trader.

If the demolition costs exceed the disposal value, then, provided the asset had not begun to be used for non-qualifying purposes, the excess is itself treated as qualifying R&D expenditure, incurred at time of demolition (or, if earlier and where relevant, immediately before cessation of the trade).

The demolition costs cannot be treated for any capital allowances purposes as expenditure on any replacement asset.

[*CAA 2001, s 445*].

Anti-avoidance provisions

[16.15] Market value is substituted for sales consideration on certain 'sole or main benefit' transactions, sales without change of control and sales between connected persons.

For most sales, the election referred to at **15.30 CAPITAL ALLOWANCES — BUILDINGS** is available, with the result that an asset representing expenditure for which an R&D allowance has been made as above will be treated as transferred for nil consideration. [*CAA 2001, ss 567–570*].

For R&D expenditure of an HMRC nature, see **71.64 TRADING EXPENSES AND DEDUCTIONS**.

For enhanced tax reliefs, see **64 RESEARCH AND DEVELOPMENT EXPENDITURE.**

Simon's Taxes. See **B3.7**.

Example

C Ltd is in business manufacturing and selling cosmetics, and prepares accounts annually to 30 June.

For the purposes of this trade, the company built a new laboratory adjacent to its existing premises, incurring the following expenditure.

		£
April 2008	Laboratory building	50,000
June 2008	Technical equipment	3,000
March 2009	Technical equipment	4,000
July 2009	Plant	2,500
August 2010	Extension to existing premises comprising 50% further laboratory area and 50% sales offices.	30,000

In September 2009 a small fire destroyed an item of equipment originally costing £2,000 in June 2007; insurance recoveries totalled £3,000. In March 2010, the plant costing £2,500 in July 2009 was sold for £1,800.

The allowances due are as follows.

		£
Y/e 30.6.08		
Laboratory building		50,000
Technical equipment		3,000
		£53,000
Y/e 30.6.09		
Technical equipment		4,000
		£4,000
Y/e 30.6.10		
Net allowance on plant sold	(note (a))	£700
Balancing charge on equipment destroyed	(note (b))	(£2,000)
Y/e 30.6.011		
Extension (qualifying R&D expenditure only)		£15,000

Notes

(a) As the plant is sold in the accounting period in which the expenditure is incurred, the disposal value of £1,800 is set against the expenditure of £2,500, resulting in a net allowance of £700.

(b) The destruction of the equipment in the year to 30 June 2010 results in a balancing charge limited to the allowance given. The charge accrues in the accounting period in which the event occurs.

Key points

[16.16] Points to consider are as follows.

- Allowances are available for capital expenditure on dredging incurred for the purposes of a qualifying trade.
- Expenditure on know-how and patent rights may qualify for capital allowances but its eligibility depends on whether it falls within the intangible assets regime and is therefore entitled to relief for amortisation.
- Capital expenditure incurred on research and development relating to a trade may qualify for 100% writing down allowances.

17

Capital Gains

Cross-references. See also **18 CAPITAL GAINS — GROUPS; 19 CAPITAL GAINS — SUBSTANTIAL SHAREHOLDINGS; 35 EXEMPT ORGANISATIONS; 54.86 LOAN RELATIONSHIPS.**

Other sources. See Tolley's Capital Gains Tax.

Simon's Taxes. See **C3.1, D1.9.**

Introduction

[17.1] Companies resident in the UK are liable to corporation tax on their chargeable gains (i.e. capital gains chargeable to tax) and accordingly do not pay 'capital gains tax'. The chargeable gains are included in their profits subject to corporation tax as described in **17.2** below. [*CTA 2010, s 4; CTA 2009, s 4; ICTA 1988, s 6(3)*].

This applies equally to non-resident companies in respect of assets of a UK permanent establishment (see **65.6 RESIDENCE**). [*TCGA 1992, s 10B; FA 2003, s 149(4)(6)*].

This chapter considers the application of the capital gains legislation to a company in respect of capital transactions which might be undertaken. The following chapter considers the capital gains position with regard to groups of companies (see **18 CAPITAL GAINS — GROUPS**).

Although companies do not pay capital gains tax as such, their chargeable gains less allowable losses are computed in accordance with the provisions relating to capital gains tax (for which see Tolley's Capital Gains Tax) with certain exceptions, as follows:

(i) computations are made by reference to accounting periods instead of years of assessment [*TCGA 1992, s 8(3)*];
(ii) provisions in the legislation confined solely to individuals do not apply to companies [*TCGA 1992, s 8(4)(5)*];
(iii) the indexation allowance rules applied (subject to transitional provisions) to disposals after 31 March 1982, and not 5 April 1982 as for individuals, and the *FA 1985* rules operated similarly after 31 March 1985 instead of 5 April 1985 [*FA 1982, s 86(1)(a); FA 1985, s 68, Sch 19*]. Whilst indexation no longer applies to individuals, it continues to apply to companies see **17.50**;

(iv) special provisions apply after 31 March 1996 to gilts, loan stock etc. acquired by companies (see **54 LOAN RELATIONSHIPS**);
(v) taper relief, applicable to individuals, trustees etc. post 6 April 1998 (up to 5 April 2008 when it was abolished for individuals and replaced with a flat rate of 18%, from 23 June 2010 the flat rate is 28%), does not apply to companies, for which, however, as mentioned above, indexation continues to apply, [*FA 2008 s 8, Sch 2*; *FA 1998, ss 121, 122*];
(vi) identification rules for shares and securities acquired after 5 April 1998 are different for companies [*FA 1998, ss 123, 124*];
(vii) gains and losses on **48 INTANGIBLE ASSETS** created or acquired by companies after 31 March 2002 are taxed as income (under the intangible fixed assets regime, see *CTA 2009, Pt 8*) rather than under the chargeable gains regime; and
(viii) as further indicated below.

See *TCGA 1992, ss 284A, 284B* for anti-avoidance legislation bringing into charge certain gains deferred under extra-statutory concessions.

European single currency (the 'euro'). Under *FA 1998, s 163*, the Treasury has power to make regulations to implement tax changes needed as a result of the introduction of the single currency. See *SI 1998 No 3177* as amended, in particular *Regs 36–39*.

Substantial shareholdings exemption

For the exemption of substantial shareholdings of companies, see **19 CAPITAL GAINS — SUBSTANTIAL SHAREHOLDINGS.**

Rate of corporation tax on capital gains

[17.2] The whole of the chargeable gains (less allowable losses under **17.3** below) of a company is included in the profits chargeable to corporation tax (i.e. the '*taxable total profits*').

The rate of corporation tax applicable will either be the full rate as in **1.3 INTRODUCTION AND RATES OF TAX** or the starting rate or small profits rate (see **67 SMALL PROFITS — REDUCED RATES**) (with marginal relief as appropriate) but the rate so determined applies to both income and chargeable gains included in the chargeable profits.

If the company's accounting period straddles different financial years, chargeable profits are apportioned on a time basis between the years.

[*CTA 2010, ss 4, 18–33; CTA 2009, s 8(5); ICTA 1988, ss 8(3), 13, 13AA*].

See **9 BUILDING SOCIETIES** and **52 INVESTMENT FUNDS** for special provisions in relation to these organisations.

Capital losses

[17.3] The amount of chargeable gains assessable for an accounting period is the total chargeable gains accruing to the company in that period less allowable losses in that period and allowable losses brought forward from any previous period. The resulting net figure is treated as chargeable to corporation tax as in **17.2** above.

Allowable losses include short-term losses accruing under Schedule D, Case VII (as was) for years before 1971/72 which remain unrelieved. This is the only instance where losses incurred before 6 April 1965 can be carried forward.

[*TCGA 1992, s 8(1), Sch 11 para 12*].

For corporation tax on chargeable gains purposes an allowable loss does not include:

(a) any loss which, if it had been a gain, would have been exempt from corporation tax in the hands of the company; or
(b) any loss accruing on a disposal on or after 5 December 2005 directly or indirectly in consequence of, or otherwise in connection with, any 'arrangements' the main purpose of which, or one of the main purposes of which, is to secure a 'tax advantage'.

For the purposes of (b) above, it does not matter whether the loss accrues at a time when there are no chargeable gains against which it could be set or whether the tax advantage would be secured for the company incurring the loss or for another company.

'*Arrangements*' include any agreement, understanding, scheme, transaction or series of transactions, whether or not legally enforceable.

'*Tax advantage*' means relief or increased relief from, or repayment or increased repayment of, corporation tax or the avoidance or reduction of a charge or assessment to corporation tax or the avoidance of a possible assessment to corporation tax.

[*TCGA 1992, ss 8(2), 16A, 184D; FA 2006, ss 69, 70(2); FA 2007, s 27*].

HMRC consider that interdependence of transactions or of the terms on which transactions take place is a strong indicator (although not a necessary condition) of the existence of an arrangement. In their view, if, on the facts, any participant in arrangements is found to have a main purpose of achieving a tax advantage, that is sufficient to demonstrate that one of the main purposes of the arrangements is the securing of a tax advantage.

HMRC is likely to examine carefully any relevant case in which a normal commercial objective is lacking, or where commercial objectives are not being sought in a genuine and straightforward manner. Where there is more than one way of achieving a commercial objective and a course of action is chosen on commercial grounds, any incidental tax advantage is not relevant. However, where the tax advantage was material to the choice, the anti-avoidance legislation may be in point, but HMRC have indicated that this is unlikely to be the case unless there is evidence of additional, complex or costly steps included solely for tax reasons. (HMRC Guidance 'Avoidance through the creation and use of capital losses by companies', 27 July 2006).

Allowable capital losses cannot normally be offset against trading profits or other income (but see **55.17 LOSSES**). However, trading losses can be offset against chargeable gains within the same accounting period and, if unexhausted, against chargeable gains arising in earlier periods (**55.3, 55.4 LOSSES**). Management expenses of a company with investment business (for accounting periods beginning before 1 April 2004, an investment company) may be offset against chargeable gains within the same or a succeeding accounting period (**51 INVESTMENT COMPANIES AND INVESTMENT BUSINESS**).

[*CTA 2010 s 37; CTA 2009, ss 1219, 1223; ICTA 1988, s 75(9) (previously ICTA 1988, s 75(3)); FA 2004, s 38(1)*].

Capital losses are generally computed in the same way as capital gains. A capital loss is not an allowable loss unless it is claimed in a quantified amount. The time limit for such claims is four years (prior to 1 April 2010, six years) after the end of the accounting period in which the loss was incurred. Where unused losses are brought forward and set against chargeable gains in a later accounting period, losses incurred after the start of self-assessment are used before earlier ones.

[*TCGA 1992, s 16; FA 1995, s 113; F(No 2)A 2005, Sch 4 para 7; FA 2008, s 118 Sch 39*].

Avoidance utilising losses

[17.4] There are a number of anti-avoidance provisions relating specifically to corporate capital losses. In particular, *FA 2006* introduced three targeted provisions attacking arrangements entered into which have as a main purpose the obtaining of a tax advantage.

For details of the provisions, see this paragraph, **17.7** and **17.8** below and **38.5 GAINS AND LOSS BUYING**.

See also **38.6–38.19 GAINS AND LOSS BUYING** for the restriction (where the provisions at **38.1–38.5 GAINS AND LOSS BUYING** do not apply) on the set-off of pre-entry losses where a company joins a group.

As part of a general initiative countering various avoidance schemes (see **17.3** above) provisions were introduced by *FA 2006* to ensure that capital losses cannot be used against income profits. HMRC have indicated that the provisions are intended to affect only companies that deliberately and knowingly enter into arrangements to avoid tax (HMRC Guidance 'Avoidance through the creation and use of capital losses by companies', 27 July 2006).

Two strategies to utilise capital losses are targeted by the provisions. The first is to turn an income receipt into capital (see **17.7** below). The second is to generate a deduction from income as part of arrangements to crystallise a capital gain (see **17.8** below). The effect is to restrict the use of capital losses. In both cases, the provisions apply only where HMRC issue a notice to the company concerned (see below).

Both sets of provisions require that there be 'arrangements', the main purpose, or one of the main purposes, of which is to secure a 'tax advantage' (although each contains a qualification of the definition of tax advantage given below — see **17.7** and **17.8** below). [*TCGA 1992, ss 184G(2)(5), 184H(2)(4); FA 2006, s 71(1)*].

'*Arrangements*' for this purpose include any agreement, understanding, scheme, transaction or series of transactions, whether or not legally enforceable.

A '*tax advantage*' means obtaining or increasing relief from, or repayment of, corporation tax, the avoidance or reduction of a corporation tax charge or assessment or the avoidance of a possible assessment to corporation tax. [*TCGA 1992, ss 184D, 184G(10), 184H(10); FA 2006, ss 70(2), 71(1)*].

For HMRC's view on the application of the terms 'arrangements', 'tax advantage' and 'main purpose', see **17.3** above and HMRC Guidance 'Avoidance through the creation and use of capital losses by companies', 27 July 2006, available on their website (www.hmrc.gov.uk).

HMRC notices

[17.5] As noted above, the application of the provisions is contingent upon the issue of a notice to the company by HMRC. Such a notice may be issued if HMRC have reasonable grounds for considering that the statutory conditions triggering the legislation are present. It must specify the arrangements in question, the accounting period (or periods) involved and the effect of the anti-avoidance provisions.

If the company has not yet made a return for the accounting period it may, if it makes a return within the 90-day period beginning with the day on which the notice is given, make the return disregarding the notice and make any necessary amendment later within the same 90-day period.

If the company has already made a return for the accounting period, HMRC may only issue a notice if a notice of enquiry (see **66.19 RETURNS**) has been given in respect of that return. The company may amend its return in light of the notice at any time within the 90-day period beginning with the day on which the notice is given. A closure notice in respect of the enquiry may not be issued before the earlier of the company amending its return or the end of the 90-day period.

If enquiries into the return have been completed, HMRC's power to issue a notice is subject to two requirements, both of which must be met:

(1) at the time enquiries were completed HMRC could not, on the basis of information made available to them (within *FA 1998, Sch 18 para 44(2)(3)* — see **7.3 ASSESSMENTS**) before that time, reasonably have been aware of circumstances indicating that a notice could have been issued; and
(2) a request for information was made during the enquiry which, if duly complied with, would have resulted in a reasonable expectation that HMRC would issue a notice.

If a notice is issued in these circumstances no discovery assessment may be made before the earlier of the company amending its return or the end of the 90-day period beginning with the day on which the notice is given. However, the normal restrictions on making discovery assessments in *FA 1998, Sch 18 paras 43, 44* do not apply (see **7.3 ASSESSMENTS**).

On receiving a notice containing HMRC's view of the position, it is up to the company to decide if it needs to amend its self-assessment. If it fails to make an amendment which ought to have been made its return will be incorrect (with all the resulting implications for penalties, etc.).

[*TCGA 1992, ss 184G(6)(8)(9), 184H(6)(8)(9), 184I; FA 2006, s 71(1)*].

Clearances

[17.6] HMRC operate an informal clearance procedure and will give advice on actual or proposed transactions. Applications for clearance procedure should be sent to HM Revenue & Customs, Clearance & Counteraction Team, Anti Avoidance Group Intelligence, First floor, 22 Kingsway, London WC2B 6NR.

HMRC will aim to give a response within 30 days of receipt of a clearance application. A clearance will state the terms on which it has been given and HMRC will regard itself bound by a clearance provided that all relevant facts are accurately given. Where the clearance is sought in advance, the transaction must be executed in accordance with the proposals set out in the clearance application. Where a clearance cannot be given HMRC will state the reasons, but taxpayers are not bound by their decision.

For details of the information required by HMRC in clearance applications see HMRC Guidance 'Avoidance through the creation and use of capital losses by companies', 27 July 2006, available on their website (www.hmrc.gov.uk).

Schemes converting income into capital

[17.7] HMRC may issue a notice (see **17.5** above) invoking anti-avoidance measures where it has reasonable grounds for considering that the following four conditions are, or may be, satisfied:

- any receipt arises to a company (the '*relevant company*') on the disposal of an asset and that receipt arises directly or indirectly in consequence of, or otherwise in connection with, any arrangements (see **17.4** above);
- a chargeable gain (the '*relevant gain*') accrues to the relevant company on the disposal and that company has allowable losses available;
- but for the arrangements an amount would have been taken into account wholly or partly instead of the capital receipt as income of the relevant company (or as the income of a company in the same capital gains tax group (see **18.2 CAPITAL GAINS — GROUPS**) at any time in the period beginning with the time at which the arrangements were made and ending when the matters, other than the tax advantage, intended to be secured by the arrangements are secured); and
- the main purpose, or one of the main purposes, of the arrangements was the obtaining of a tax advantage (see **17.4** above) involving the deduction of the capital losses from the relevant gain.

If all these conditions are satisfied when the HMRC notice is given, the relevant company may not deduct any loss from the relevant gain.

[*TCGA 1992, s 184G(1)–(5)(7)(10); FA 2006, s 71(1)*].

Schemes securing deductions

[17.8] HMRC may issue a notice (see **17.5** above) invoking anti-avoidance measures where it has reasonable grounds for considering that the following four conditions are, or may be, satisfied:

- a chargeable gain (the '*relevant gain*') accrues to a company (the '*relevant company*') directly or indirectly in consequence of, or otherwise in connection with, any arrangements (see **17.4** above) and that company has capital losses available;
- the relevant company, or a company connected with it, incurs expenditure in connection with the arrangements which is deductible in calculating total profits but not in calculating chargeable gains;
- the main purpose, or one of the main purposes, of the arrangements was the obtaining of a tax advantage (see **17.4** above) involving both the deduction of the expenditure in calculating total profits and the deduction of losses from the relevant gain; and
- the arrangements are not 'excluded arrangements' (see below).

It does not matter whether the tax advantage is secured for the relevant company or any other company.

'*Excluded arrangements*' are certain arm's length sale and leaseback transactions involving land within *CTA 2010, s 835(1)* or *s 835(1)* (previously *ICTA 1988, s 779(1)(2)* — see **5.17 ANTI-AVOIDANCE**) where there is no connection between the lessor and the lessee.

If all the above conditions are satisfied when the HMRC notice is given, the relevant company may not deduct any loss from the relevant gain.

[*TCGA 1992, s 184H(1)–(5)(7)(10)(11); FA 2006, s 71(1); CTA 2010, Sch 1 para 245*].

Liquidation

[17.9] The vesting of a company's assets in a liquidator is disregarded. All the acts of the liquidator in relation to such assets are treated as acts of the company. [*TCGA 1992, s 8(6)*].

See also **76 WINDING UP**.

Recovery from shareholders

[17.10] Where a person connected with a UK resident company (see **25 CONNECTED PERSONS**):

- receives, or becomes entitled to receive, in respect of shares in that company;
- a capital distribution which is not a reduction of capital but which constitutes, or is derived from, a disposal of assets from which a chargeable gain accrues to the company; and
- the company does not pay, within a specified time (see below), the corporation tax due from it for the accounting period in which the gain accrues,

the recipient of the distribution may, by assessment within two years of the due date, be required to pay so much of that corporation tax as relates to chargeable gains but not exceeding the lesser of:

(i) a part of that tax, at the rate in force when the gain accrued, proportionate to his share of the total distribution made by the company; and
(ii) the value of the distribution he received or became entitled to receive.

The person then has a right of recovery against the company, including any interest charged on him under *TMA 1970, s 87A* (see **49.2 INTEREST ON OVERDUE TAX**).

The time specified (as above) is the date the tax became payable by the company or, if later, the date the assessment was made on the company.

[*TCGA 1992, s 189*].

See also **59.11 PAYMENT OF TAX** as regards recovery of tax from third parties generally.

Simon's Taxes. See **D1.904.**

Reconstructions involving transfer of business

[17.11] The provisions found at *TCGA 1992, s 139* allow for the deferral of the capital gains charge where two companies are involved in a reconstruction which includes the transfer of a business, in specific circumstances, and where the transaction has been undertaken for bona fide commercial reasons.

Under these provisions (and subject to the following conditions) where a 'scheme of reconstruction' takes place which involves the transfer of a company's business to another company for no consideration (other than the assumption of liabilities of the business), the capital assets (not used as trading stock by either company) are regarded as being transferred at a 'no gain, no loss' price, and the acquiring company takes over the disposing company's acquisition date.

Thus no gain or loss arises at the time of the reconstruction – a gain (or loss) only arises when the acquiring company subsequently disposes of any capital assets transferred with the business (such gain or loss being the 'full' amount – calculated with a base cost as at the original acquisition date of the disposing company).

The provisions *TCGA 1992, s 139* apply where:

(i) any scheme of reconstruction involves the transfer of the whole or part of a company's business to another company; and
(ii) the conditions at (A) and (B) below are met in relation to the assets included in the transfer; and
(iii) the first-mentioned company receives no part of the consideration for the transfer (otherwise than by the acquiring company taking over the whole or part of the liabilities of the business).

The *FA 2011* rules on degrouping charges may apply to deem a degrouping charge to be added to the consideration for the main disposal on such a business transfer (see **29.1**). Where this is so, *TCGA 1992, s 139(1B)* operates so that this deemed consideration is ignored for the purposes of *TCGA 1992, s 139(1)*.

The application of these provisions is conditional on:

(A) either the transferee company being UK resident at the time of acquisition or the assets being 'chargeable assets' in relation to that company immediately after that time; and

(B) either the transferor company being UK resident at that time or the assets being 'chargeable assets' in relation to that company immediately before that time.

For the purpose of the test at (B), above, an asset is a '*chargeable asset*' in relation to a company at a particular time if, on a disposal by the company at that time, any gain would be a chargeable gain and within the charge to corporation tax by virtue of *TCGA 1992, s 10B* (non-UK resident company trading through UK permanent establishment, see **65.6 RESIDENCE**).

Scheme of reconstruction

A '*scheme of reconstruction*' is as defined within *TCGA 1992, s 136*, which refers to the meaning given by *TCGA 1992, Sch 5AA*. Pursuant to this schedule, a 'scheme of reconstruction' is a scheme of merger, division or other restructuring meeting both of conditions (a) and (b) below and either condition (c) or condition (d) below.

(a) **Issue of ordinary share capital.** The scheme must involve the issue of 'ordinary share capital' of a company or companies (the 'successor company' or 'successor companies') to holders of ordinary share capital of another company or companies (the 'original company' or 'original companies'). Or, if the original company or any of the original companies has more than one class of ordinary shares, the issue to holders of one or more classes of ordinary share capital of any such company. The scheme must not involve the issue of ordinary share capital of the successor company or companies to anyone else.
'*Ordinary share capital*' of a company is all the issued share capital of the company other than capital the holders of which have a right to a dividend at a fixed rate but no other right to share in company profits. It also includes interests possessed by members in a company which has no share capital, and rights in unit trust schemes which are treated as shares under *TCGA 1992, s 99(1)(b)*.

(b) **Equal entitlement to new shares.** The entitlement of any person to acquire ordinary share capital of the successor company or companies by virtue of holding ordinary share capital (or any class of such capital) of the original company or companies which is involved in the scheme (as in (a) above) must be the same as that of any other person holding such shares (or shares of that class). (See the example in HMRC's Capital Gains Manual at CG52707b.)

Where a reorganisation (within *TCGA 1992, s 126*) of the share capital of the original company, or of any of the original companies, is carried out for the purposes of the scheme, (a) and (b) above apply in relation to the position after the reorganisation.

An issue of shares in or debentures of the successor company, or any of the successor companies, after the latest date on which any ordinary share capital of the successor company, or of any of them, is issued in consideration of the transfer of any business (or part) under the scheme, or in pursuance of the compromise or arrangement referred to in (d) below, is disregarded for the purposes of (a) and (b) above.

As referred to above, both (a) and (b) above and either (c) or (d) below must be satisfied.

(c) **Continuity of business**. The effect of the restructuring must be either:
   (i) if there is one original company, that the business or substantially the whole of the business carried on by the original company is carried on by a successor company (which must not be the original company) or successor companies (which may include the original company); or
   (ii) if there is more than one original company, that all or part of the business(es) carried on by one or more of the original companies is carried on by a different company, and the whole or substantially the whole of the business(es) carried on by the original companies are carried on by the successor company (which may be one of the original companies) or successor companies (which may be the same as or include the original companies).

   The requirement in (i) and (ii) above that the whole or substantially the whole of a business or businesses be carried on by two or more companies is satisfied where the activities of those companies taken together embrace the whole or substantially the whole of the business or businesses concerned. See HMRC Capital Gains Manual, CG52709 as regards the meaning of 'business' for these purposes.

   A business carried on by a company under the control (within *ICTA 1988, s 840*) of another company is for these purpose treated as carried on by both the controlling and the controlled company.

   The holding and management of assets retained by the original company (or by one of the original companies) for the purpose of making a capital distribution (within *TCGA 1992, s 122*) in respect of shares in the company is disregarded for these purposes.

(d) **Compromise or arrangement with members**. The scheme must be carried out in pursuance of a compromise or arrangement under *Companies Act 2006* (or NI or foreign equivalent), and no part of the business of the original company, or any of the original companies, must be transferred under the scheme to any other person.

[*TCGA 1992, s 139(1)(1A)(2)(9), Sch 5AA; FA 2003, Sch 27 para 2(3)*].

For practical illustrations of 'schemes of reconstruction', see HMRC Capital Gains Manual, CG52720–52729.

Anti-avoidance, disapplication of relief and advance clearance

[17.12] *TCGA 1992, s 139* does not apply unless the scheme is for *bona fide* commercial reasons and not to avoid corporation tax, capital gains tax or income tax, or where HMRC, on written application by the acquiring company, has notified its satisfaction with the scheme before the transfer is made.

Applications for such clearance should be addressed to Clearance and Counteraction Team, Anti-Avoidance Group Intelligence, First Floor, 22 Kingsway, London WC2B 6NR (or, if market-sensitive information is included, to the Team Leader, at that address). Applications may be faxed to 020–7438 4409 or emailed to reconstructions@hmrc.gov.uk (after calling the team leader on 020–7438 7215 if market-sensitive information is included).

Application may be made in a single letter to the same address for clearance under *TCGA 1992, s 139* and under any one or more of *CTA 2010, ss 1091, 1092*; *ICTA 1988, s 215* (demergers, see **31.37 GROUP RELIEF**), *CTA 2010, ss 1044, 1045*; *ICTA 1988, s 225* (see **63.8 PURCHASE BY A COMPANY OF ITS OWN SHARES**), *CTA 2010, ss 748, 749*; *ICTA 1988, s 707* (transactions in securities, see **5.2 ANTI-AVOIDANCE**), *TCGA 1992, s 138(1)* (share exchanges, see Tolley's Capital Gains Tax under Anti-Avoidance), *TCGA 1992, s 140B* (transfer of a UK trade between EU member states, see **17.14** below), *TCGA 1992, s 140D* (transfer of non-UK trade between EU member states, see **17.21** below) and *CTA 2009, ss 831, 832; FA 2002, Sch 29 para 88* (see **48.27 INTANGIBLE ASSETS**).

The application should give full details of the transactions and of all the companies directly involved, their tax districts and references. Copies of accounts for the last two years for which accounts have been prepared should accompany the application. HMRC may, within 30 days of receipt, call for further particulars (to be supplied within 30 days, or longer if HMRC allows; if the information is not supplied, the application lapses). Subject to this, HMRC must notify its decision within a further 30 days. If not so notified, or if dissatisfied with the decision, the applicant may within a further 30 days require HMRC to refer the application to the tribunal for their decision. All material facts and considerations must be disclosed, otherwise any decision is void.

If any tax arising on the transfer is not paid by the disposing company within six months of a specified date, then, within two years of that date, the tax may be assessed on any person who:

(a) holds all or any of the assets to which the tax relates; and
(b) is either the acquiring company or any other group member to which the assets have been subsequently transferred.

From 9 October 2007 applications for advance clearance may be made to HMRC's Advance Agreement Unit (AAU) for reconstructions and inward investment of at least £250 million. Applicants can rely on the advance agreement provided that all relevant facts and issues have been disclosed and the law is not subsequently changed by legislation or case decision.

The date specified (as above) is the date the tax became payable by the company or, if later, the date the assessment was made on the company.

The tax charge will be proportionate to the assets held and the paying company has the right of recovery against the original disposing company of the tax charged and any interest thereon under *TMA 1970, s 87A* (see **49.2 INTEREST ON OVERDUE TAX**). Where the disposing company has been wound up, any tax due from it may be recovered from the acquiring company. [*TCGA 1992, s 139(5)–(8)*].

The provisions of *TCGA 1992, s 139* do not apply to the transfer of the whole or part of a company's business to a unit trust scheme (where it is either within *TCGA 1992, s 100(2)* or an authorised unit trust, see **52.3 INVESTMENT FUNDS**), to an investment trust (see **53.1 INVESTMENT TRUSTS**) or to a venture capital trust (see **74.2 VENTURE CAPITAL TRUSTS**). [*TCGA 1992, s 139(4); FA 1998, s 134(1)(4)*].

Where *s 139* has applied in relation to a transfer to a company which was not then an investment trust but which subsequently becomes one for an accounting period, then any assets of the business transferred which are still owned by the company at the beginning of that accounting period are deemed to have been sold and immediately reacquired by the transferee company, immediately after the transfer, at their market value at that time. The resulting chargeable gain or allowable loss is deemed to accrue to the transferee company immediately before the end of the accounting period preceding that in which the company becomes an investment trust. Notwithstanding normal time limits, a corporation tax assessment in respect of any resulting liability can be made within six years after the end of the accounting period in which the company becomes an investment trust.

Similar provisions apply where, after a transfer to which *s 139* applied, the transferee company becomes a venture capital trust (within *ITA 2007, Pt 6, ss 258 et seq*; *ICTA 1988, s 842AA*, see **74.2 VENTURE CAPITAL TRUSTS**). They apply by reference to the time at which HMRC's approval for the purposes of the VCT legislation comes into effect, and the resulting gain or loss is deemed to accrue immediately before that time rather than at the time of the deemed disposal. In a case in which HMRC's approval has effect as from the beginning of an accounting period, any consequential corporation tax assessment can be made, notwithstanding normal time limits, within six years after the end of that accounting period. These provisions do not apply if those above relating to investment trusts have already applied (in relation to the same transfer of assets) and *vice versa*.

[*TCGA 1992, ss 101, 101B*].

See **17.48** below as regards disapplication of *s 139* in relation to certain dual resident companies.

Simon's Taxes. See **D1.359, D6.450.**

Transfer of assets to non-resident company

[17.13] A UK resident company may be trading overseas through a permanent establishment. If the company decides to transfer this trade to a non-UK resident company, *TCGA 1992, s 140* gives relief with regard to chargeable gains which might arise — the provisions allow the UK company to postpone the gains arising on the transfer.

Certain conditions need to be met, as follows:

(a) a UK resident company has to have been carrying on a trade outside the UK through a permanent establishment;
(b) the whole or part of that trade together with its assets (excluding cash) are transferred to a company that is not UK resident;
(c) the transfer is wholly or partly in exchange for securities (shares or shares and loan stock) issued by the transferee to the transferor;
(d) following the issue of the shares, the transferor holds at least 25% of the ordinary share capital of the transferee; and
(e) a net chargeable gain arises on the assets transferred.

Where these conditions are met, the proportion of the resulting net chargeable gains relating to the shares (and not any cash received — thus in proportion that the market value of the shares at the time of the transfer bears to the market value of the whole consideration received) may be claimed by the transferor company as being deferred.

The gain will only be treated as arising when one of the following events occurs:

(i) The *transferor company disposes* of all or any of the shares received. For disposals prior to 6 January 2010, the appropriate proportion of the deferred gain (in so far as not already charged under this specific provision or under (ii) below) is then added to the consideration received on the disposal. The '*appropriate proportion*' is the proportion which the market value of the shares disposed of bears to the market value of the shares held immediately before the disposal. However, deferred gains relating to events occurring before 1 April 1982 are disregarded for this purpose.
For disposals on or after 6 January 2010, rather than add the deferred gain to the consideration received, *FA 2010* amends *s 140(4)* such that there shall be deemed to accrue to the transferor company as a chargeable gain on the disposal of the securities in question the whole or the appropriate proportion of the deferred gain (as above). A chargeable gain which is deemed to so accrue is in addition to any gain or loss which actually arises on the disposal.

(ii) The *transferee company disposes*, within six years of the transfer, of the whole or part of the assets on which chargeable gains were deferred. The gain chargeable (in so far as it has not already been charged under this provision or under (i) above) is the proportion which the deferred gain on the assets disposed of bears to the total deferred gains on assets held immediately before the disposal.

The following disposals are disregarded.

- For the purposes of (i) above, intra-group transfers within *TCGA 1992, s 171* (see **18.2** onwards CAPITAL GAINS — GROUPS). A charge will arise when a subsequent owner makes a disposal outside the group.

- For the purposes of (i) above, securities transferred by a transferor as part of the process of a merger to which *TCGA 1992, s 140E* applies (see **17.27** below). In relation to a subsequent disposal of the shares or disposal by the transferee company of assets within (ii) above, the transferee is treated as if it were the transferor company.
- For the purposes of (i) above, securities transferred on or after 1 January 2007 by a transferor company as part of the process of the transfer of a business to which **17.14** or **17.21** below applies. In relation to a subsequent disposal of the securities or disposal by the transferee company of assets within (ii) above, the transferee is treated as if it were the transferor company.
- For the purposes of (ii) above, intra-group transfers which would be within *TCGA 1992, s 171* if for those purposes a group included (without qualification) non-UK resident companies. A charge will arise when a subsequent owner makes a disposal outside the group.

No claim may be made under these provisions as regards a transfer in relation to which a claim is made under *TCGA 1992, s 140C* (see **17.21** below).

[*TCGA 1992, s 140, Sch 4 para 4; F(No 2)A 2005, s 64(2); SI 2007 No 3186, Sch 1 para 7, Sch 2 para 5*].

For the interaction between (i) above and the substantial shareholdings exemption, see **19.8 CAPITAL GAINS — SUBSTANTIAL SHAREHOLDINGS.**

Simon's Taxes. See **D6.523.**

UK business divided between companies in different EU states

Transfer of UK business

[17.14] A special relief may be claimed pursuant to *TCGA 1992, s 140A* where a company resident in one EU member state transfers the whole or part of a business carried on by it in the UK to a company resident in another member state wholly in exchange for shares or debentures (for issues effected before 1 April 2005, securities (including shares)) in the latter company, provided that the further conditions below are satisfied.

It is notable that the transferor or transferee may be resident in the UK, provided the further conditions below are still met.

For transfers before 1 January 2007, the relief could only be claimed in respect of a transfer of a trade, and both the transferor and transferee had to be a body incorporated under the law of a member state. For such transfers, it was specifically provided that a company was regarded as resident in a member state under the laws of which it was chargeable to tax because it was regarded as so resident (unless it was regarded under **DOUBLE TAX RELIEF (32.17)** arrangements entered into by the member state as resident in a territory not within any of the member states).

Division of UK business

[17.15] The relief under *TCGA 1992, s 140A* may also be claimed where a company resident in one EC member state transfers, on or after 1 January 2007, part of its business to one or more companies at least one of which is resident in another member state.

The part of the transferor's business which is transferred must be carried on by the transferor in the UK and the transferor must continue to carry on a business after the transfer.

The transfer must be made in exchange for the issue of shares in or debentures of each transferee to the holders of shares in or debentures of the transferor, except where, and to the extent that, a transferee is prevented from meeting this requirement by reason only of *Companies Act 2006, s 658* (rule against limited company acquiring its own shares) or a corresponding provision in another member state.

The further conditions below must also be satisfied.

Further conditions

[17.16] A claim for relief must be made by both the transferor and the transferee (or each of the transferees). The anti-avoidance provision below must not apply, and either:

(i) if the transferee company is, or each of the transferee companies are, non-UK resident immediately after the transfer, any chargeable gain accruing to it, or them, on a disposal of the assets included in the transfer would form part of its, or their, corporation tax profits under *TCGA 1992, s 10B* (see **65.6 RESIDENCE**); or

(ii) if it is, or they are, UK resident at that time, none of the assets included in the transfer is exempt from UK tax on disposal under double tax relief arrangements.

Effect of relief

[17.17] Any assets included in the transfer are treated for the purposes of corporation tax on chargeable gains as transferred for a no gain/no loss consideration. In addition, the transfer is taken not to be a deemed disposal by non-resident on ceasing to trade in the UK through a permanent establishment or a branch or agency (thus *TCGA 1992, s 25(3)* does not apply to the assets transferred — see further Tolley's Capital Gains Tax under Overseas Matters).

In the case of a division of a UK business, where the transfer is not made wholly in exchange for the issue of shares in or debentures of each transferee only by reason of the *Companies Act 2006, s 658* applying, neither *TCGA 1992, s 24* (deemed disposal where asset lost, destroyed or becoming of negligible) nor *TCGA 1992, s 122* (capital distributions) apply to the transfer.

Also in the case of a division of a UK business, where the transferor and transferee (or each of the transferees) are all resident in EU member states, but are not all resident in the same state, the transfer of assets is treated as if it were a scheme of reconstruction within *TCGA 1992, s 136* if it would not otherwise be so treated. Where *s 136* applies as a result of this provision, the anti-avoidance provision at *s 136(6)* does not apply (and neither does *s 137* (restrictions on company reconstructions)). [*TCGA 1992, s 140DA*].

Anti-avoidance

[17.18] The above provisions do not apply unless the transfer is effected for *bona fide* commercial reasons and not as part of a scheme or arrangement a main purpose of which is avoidance of income, corporation or capital gains taxes. Advance may be obtained from HMRC on the application of the companies, subject to the same conditions and appeal procedures as apply to clearances under *TCGA 1992, s 138* (see Tolley's Capital Gains Tax under Anti-Avoidance).

Applications for clearance should be addressed to Clearance and Counteraction Team, First Floor, 22 Kingsway, London WC2B 6NR (or, if market-sensitive information is included, to the Team Leader at that address). Applications may be emailed to reconstructions@gtnet.gov.uk (after calling the Team Leader on 020–7438 7215 if market-sensitive information is included).

As per **17.12** above, application may be made in a single letter to the same address for clearance under this and other sections of *TCGA 1992* (such as *s 140B* etc.) and other relevant provisions of the Taxes Acts.

[*TCGA 1992, ss 140A, 140B, 140DA; FA 2003, Sch 27 para 2; F(No 2)A 2005, s 59(3)(7); FA 2007, s 110; SI 2007 No 3186, Sch 1 paras 2, 3, 6*].

Capital allowances

[17.19] Where the above provisions apply and, immediately after the transfer, either the transferee or one or more of the transferees, is resident in the UK, or at that time carries on a business (or pre 1 January 2007 a trade) in the UK through a permanent establishment (or branch or agency), consisting of, or including, the business (or part) transferred, then the transfer or division does not give rise to any allowances or charges in respect of the *Capital Allowances Act 2001*.

Furthermore, in relation to the assets included in the transfer, anything done by or to the transferor before the transfer is treated, after the transfer, as having been done to or by the transferee or each transferee.

This treatment does not apply if the successor is a dual resident investing company (as defined) in the accounting period in which the transfer takes place.

The provisions of *CTA 2010, ss 948, 949* (*ICTA 1988, s 343(2); CTA 2009, Sch 1 para 107*) (see **55.11 LOSSES**) do not apply where a claim is made under these provisions.

[*CAA 2001, s 561; SI 2007 No 3186, Sch 1 para 25*].

Mergers Directive

[17.20] The above provisions were introduced to comply with *EEC Directive No 90/434/EEC*. Where the directive applies, the host country of the permanent establishment is not permitted to tax any capital gain arising on the transfer except where the state of the transferring company applies a worldwide system of taxation. In that case, the state of the transferring company may tax any profits or capital gains of the permanent establishment resulting from a merger, division or transfer of assets (as defined in the directive) provided it gives relief for the tax which would, but for the provisions of the directive, have been charged on those profits or capital gains in the host country of the permanent establishment as if that tax had been actually charged and paid.

The changes to the above provisions applying on or after 1 January 2007 were made to comply with *Directive No 2005/19/EC*.

Simon's Taxes. See D6.522.

Transfer or division of non-UK business

Transfer of non-UK business

[17.21] Pursuant to Mergers Directive 90/434/EEC (as implemented in this respect in the UK by way of *TCGA 1992, s 140C* – see also **17.20** above – and *TIOPA 2010, s 122; ICTA 1988, s 815A*) a form of tax relief applies where a non UK trade is carried on in a member state and is then transferred to another company resident in a member state. Gains on an applicable transfer are aggregated and set off against aggregated losses to give a single gain. Further relief is then given by way of a credit against the UK tax charge for any foreign tax that would have been payable in the EU State, were it not for the operation of the directive.

A claim can be made for relief under this section where the following conditions are satisfied with regard to the transfer:

(a) the transferor company is resident in the UK and the transferee company is resident in another member state;
(b) the transfer includes the whole or part of a business carried on by the UK company immediately before the transfer through a permanent establishment (or, for accounting periods beginning before 1 January 2003, through a branch or agency) in a member state other than the UK;
(c) the transfer is wholly or partly in exchange for shares or debentures (for issues effected before 1 April 2005, securities (including shares)) in the non-UK transferee company; and
(d) the further conditions below are satisfied.

For transfers before 1 January 2007, the provisions only applied in respect of a transfer of a trade, and both the transferor and transferee had to be a body incorporated under the law of a member state. For such transfers, it was specifically provided that a company was not regarded as resident in the UK if it were regarded under any **DOUBLE TAX RELIEF** (**32.17**) arrangements to which the UK was a party as resident in a territory not within any of the member states.

A company was regarded as resident in another member state under the laws of which it was chargeable to tax because it was regarded as so resident (unless it was regarded under a double tax relief arrangement entered into by the member state as resident in a territory not within any of the member states).

Simon's Taxes. See **D6.524**.

Division of non-UK business

[17.22] The provisions may also apply where a company resident in the UK transfers, on or after 1 January 2007, part of its business to one or more companies at least one of which is resident in another member state other than the UK. The part of the transferor's business which is transferred must be carried on by the transferor immediately before the transfer in a member state other than the UK through a permanent establishment and the transferor must continue to carry on a business after the transfer.

The transfer must be made in exchange for the issue of shares in or debentures of each transferee to the holders of shares in or debentures of the transferor, except where, and to the extent that, a transferee is prevented from meeting this requirement by reason only of *Companies Act 2006, s 658* (rule against limited company acquiring its own shares) or a corresponding provision in another member state.

The further conditions below must also be satisfied.

Further conditions

[17.23] The further conditions are that:

(i) The transfer must include all the UK company's assets used in the business or part (with the possible exception of cash) and the anti-avoidance provision below must be satisfied; and

(ii) The aggregate of the chargeable gains accruing to the UK company on the transfer must exceed the aggregate of the allowable losses so accruing.

The UK company must make a claim for the provisions to apply. Any claim is subject to the anti-avoidance provisions below.

No claim may, however, be made where a claim is made under *TCGA 1992, s 140* at **17.13** above in relation to the same transfer.

Effect of provisions

[17.24] The transfer is treated as giving rise to a single chargeable gain of the excess of the aggregate of the chargeable gains accruing to the UK company on the transfer, over the aggregate of the allowable losses so accruing. The tax on such gain can then be reduced by the notional foreign tax credit applicable under the provisions of *TIOPA 2010, s 122; ICTA 1988, s 815A* — see **17.26** below.

In the case of a division of a non-UK business, where the transferor and transferee (or each of the transferees) are all resident in EU member states, but are not all resident in the same state, the transfer of assets is treated as if it were a scheme of reconstruction within *TCGA 1992, s 136* if it would not otherwise be so treated.

Where *s 136* applies as a result of this provision, the anti-avoidance provision at *s 136(6)* does not apply (and neither does *s 137* (restrictions on company reconstructions)).

Anti-avoidance

[17.25] The transfer must be effected for *bona fide* commercial reasons and not as part of a scheme or arrangement a main purpose of which is avoidance of income, corporation or capital gains taxes. Advance clearance may be obtained from HMRC on the application of the UK company, to the same address and subject to the same conditions and appeal procedures as apply to clearances under *TCGA 1992, s 140B* (see **17.14** above).

From 9 October 2007 applications for advance clearance may be made to HMRC's Advance Agreement Unit (AAU) for reconstructions and inward investment of at least £250 million. Applicants can rely on the advance agreement provided that all relevant facts and issues have been disclosed and the law is not subsequently changed by legislation or case decision.

[*TCGA 1992, ss 140C, 140D, 140DA; FA 2003, s 153(1)(b)(4); F(No 2)A 2005, s 59(4)(7); FA 2007, s 110; SI 2007 No 3186, Sch 1 paras* 4–6].

The above provisions were introduced to comply with *EEC Directive No 90/434/EEC* (the 'Mergers Directive'). The changes applying on or after 1 January 2007 were made to comply with *Directive No 2005/19/EC*. See **17.14** above.

Double tax relief

[17.26] As noted above, where these provisions apply, where gains accruing to the UK company would have been chargeable to tax under the law of the member state in which the trade was carried on immediately before the transfer but for the Mergers Directive, the amount of tax is treated for double tax relief purposes as tax paid in that other member state. In calculating the amount of the tax so treated it is assumed that, so far as permitted under the law of the member state, any losses arising on the transfer are set against the gains, and that the UK company claims any available reliefs.

These provisions apply also where *TCGA 1992, s 140F* (European cross-border merger: assets not left within UK tax charge — see **17.27** below) applies.

[*TIOPA 2010, s 122; ICTA 1988, s 815A(3); FA 2003, s 153(1)(4); F(No 2)A 2005, s 59(1)*].

European cross-border mergers

[17.27] The following provisions (*TCGA 1992, ss 140E–G*) were originally introduced to facilitate the tax-neutral formation of SEs (see **34.5 EUROPEAN COMMUNITY LEGISLATION**) by merger, but have since been extended to apply also to the formation of SCEs (European Co-operative Societies) by merger and other mergers of companies resident in different EU member states.

Accordingly, the provisions apply to:

(a) the formation of an SE on or after 1 April 2005 by the merger of two or more companies in accordance with *Council Regulation (EC) No 2157/2001, Arts 2(1), 17(2)*;
(b) the formation of an SCE on or after 18 August 2006 by the merger of two or more 'co-operative societies', at least one of which is a society registered under *Industrial and Provident Societies Act 1965*, in accordance with *Council Regulation (EC) No 1435/2003*;
(c) a merger on or after 1 January 2007 effected by the transfer by one or more companies or co-operative societies of all their assets and liabilities to a single existing company or co-operative society; and
(d) a merger on or after 1 January 2007 effected by the transfer by two or more companies of all their assets to a single new company (which is not an SE or SCE) in exchange for the issue by the transferee company of shares or debentures to each person holding shares in or debentures of a transferee company.

For the purposes of (b) and (c) above, a '*co-operative society*' is a society registered under the *Industrial and Provident Societies Act 1965* or a similar society established under the law of a member state other than the UK.

Each of the merging companies or co-operative societies must be resident in a member state but they must not all be resident in the same state and the other conditions must be satisfied. For mergers before 18 August 2006, it was specifically provided that a company was resident in a member state for this purpose if it was within a charge to tax under the law of the State as being resident and it was not regarded, for the purposes of any **DOUBLE TAX RELIEF** (**32.17**) arrangements to which the state was a party, as resident in a territory not within a member state.

In the case of a merger, the other conditions are that:

- in the course of the merger, a UK resident company transfers to a non-UK resident company (but which is resident in another member state) a business which the UK resident carried on in another member state through a permanent establishment;
- in the case of a merger to which (a), (b) or (c) applies, either the consideration is an issue of shares or debentures to the shareholders in the resident company or the only reason this is not satisfied is that the transferee is prohibited by law from issuing shares or debentures to itself; and
- in the course of the merger to which (c) or (d) applies, the transferors cease to exist without being liquidated. [*TCGA 1992, s 140F; SI 2007 No 3186; SI 2008 No 1579*].

Where there is a merger which involves the transfer by the transferor of all its assets and liabilities to a single company which holds all the share capital of the transferor and the following conditions apply:

- all the merging countries are EU resident;
- they are not all resident in the same state;
- *TCGA 1992, s 139* (reconstruction) does not apply; and
- the effect of the merger is that the transferor ceases to exist without being liquidated,

then *TCGA 1992, s 24* (asset becoming of negligible value) and *TCGA 1992, s 122* (distribution not a new holding) do not apply. [*SI 2008 No 1579*].

If it does not constitute or form part of a scheme of reconstruction within the meaning of *TCGA 1992, s 136* (see Tolley's Capital Gains Tax under Shares and Securities), the merger is nevertheless treated as if it were a scheme of reconstruction for the purposes of that section, but the anti-avoidance provision at *s 136(6)* does not apply (and neither does *s 137* (restrictions on company reconstructions)). See, however, the anti-avoidance provision below.

Assets left within UK tax charge

No gain no loss treatment to apply

[17.28] Further to the conditions highlighted at **17.27** above, where the following apply:

(i) *TCGA 1992, s 139* (reconstruction involving transfer of business — see **17.11** above) does not apply to the merger;
(ii) where the merger is within **17.27**(b) or (c) above, or is within (a) above and takes place on or after 18 August 2006, the transfer of assets and liabilities is made in exchange for the issue of shares in or debentures of the transferee to the holders of shares in or debentures of a transferor, except where, and to the extent that, the transferee is prevented from meeting this requirement by reason only of *Companies Act 2006, s 658* (rule against limited company acquiring its own shares) or a corresponding provision in another member state; and
(iii) where the merger is within **17.27**(d) above, in the course of the merger each transferor ceases to exist without being in liquidation (within the meaning of *Insolvency Act 1986, s 247*),

then any 'qualifying transferred assets' are treated for chargeable gains purposes as acquired by the transferee (i.e. the SE, SCE or merged company) for a consideration resulting in neither gain nor loss for the transferor company or co-operative society.

For this purpose, an asset transferred to the transferee as part of the merger process is a '*qualifying transferred asset*' if:

- either the transferor was resident in the UK at the time of the transfer or any gain accruing on disposal of the asset immediately before that time would have been a chargeable gain forming part of the transferor's chargeable profits by virtue of *TCGA 1992, s 10B* (trade carried on via UK permanent establishment — see **65.6 RESIDENCE**); and

- either the transferee is resident in the UK at the time of the transfer or any gain accruing to it on disposal of the asset immediately after the transfer would have been a chargeable gain forming part of its chargeable profits by virtue of *TCGA 1992, s 10B*.

Where the condition at (ii) above applies, but the transfer is not made wholly in exchange for the issue of shares in or debentures of each transferee, neither *TCGA 1992, s 24* (deemed disposal where asset lost, destroyed or becoming of negligible value) nor *TCGA 1992, s 122* (capital distributions) apply to the transfer.

[*TCGA 1992, s 140E*].

Assets not left within UK tax charge

Single chargeable gain

[17.29] Further to the conditions highlighted at **17.27** above, where the following apply:

- in the course of the merger a company or co-operative society resident in the UK (company A) transfers to a company or co-operative society resident in another member state all the assets and liabilities relating to a business carried on by company A in a member state other than the UK through a permanent establishment;
- the aggregate chargeable gains accruing to company A on the transfer exceed the aggregate allowable losses; and
- where the merger is within (b) or (c) above, or is within (a) above and takes place on or after 18 August 2006, the transfer of assets and liabilities is made in exchange for the issue of shares in or debentures of the transferee to the holders of shares in or debentures of a transferor, except where, and to the extent that, the transferee is prevented from meeting this requirement by reason only of *Companies Act 2006, s 658* (rule against limited company acquiring its own shares) or a corresponding provision in another member state,

then the allowable losses are treated as set off against the chargeable gains and the transfer is treated as giving rise to a single chargeable gain equal to the excess.

See **17.21** above for special double tax relief provisions applying where this provision applies.

[*TCGA 1992, s 140F; TIOPA 2010, s 122; ICTA 1988, s 815A*].

Anti-avoidance

[17.30] The above provisions do not apply if the merger is not effected for *bona fide* commercial reasons or if it forms part of a scheme or arrangements of which the main purpose, or one of the main purposes, is avoiding liability to UK tax. The advance clearance provisions at **17.18** above apply for this purpose.

[*TCGA 1992, ss 140E–140G; F(No 2)A 2005, s 51; FA 2007, s 110; SI 2007 No 3186, Sch 2 para* 2].

Capital allowances

[17.31] Where there is a merger leaving assets within the charge to UK tax to which the above provisions apply (or would apply but for *TCGA 1992, s 139* applying), the transferee takes over the capital allowance position of the transferor company in relation to any 'qualifying assets' transferred as part of the merger, so that no allowances or charges arise from the transfer in respect of the *Capital Allowances Act 2001*.

Any necessary apportionments are made in a reasonable manner. *ICTA 1988, s 343(2)* (see **55.11 LOSSES**) does not apply where this provision applies. An asset is a '*qualifying asset*' if it is transferred to the transferee as part of the merger, either the transferor is resident in the UK at the time of transfer or the asset is an asset of the transferor's UK permanent establishment, and either the transferee is resident in the UK on formation or the asset is an asset of the transferee's UK permanent establishment on formation.

[*CAA 2001, s 561A; F(No 2)A 2005, s 56; SI 2007 No 3186, Sch 2 para 14*].

Held-over gains

[17.32] Provision is made for continuity of group membership following a merger for the purposes of certain hold-over reliefs. See **17.13** above and **29.1 DEGROUPING CHARGES**. See also Tolley's Capital Gains Tax under Qualifying Corporate Bonds and Rollover Relief.

[*F(No 2)A 2005, s 64*].

Transparent entities

[17.33] Certain of the rules at **17.14–17.32** above do not apply where one of the parties is a 'transparent entity'. For the rules applying in such circumstances, see Tolley's Capital Gains Tax under Overseas Matters.

A '*transparent entity*' for this purpose is an entity which is resident in a member state other than the UK and is listed as a company in the Annex to the Mergers Directive, but which does not have an ordinary share capital and, if resident in the UK, would not be capable of being registered as a company under *Companies Act 2006*.

[*TCGA 1992, ss 140H–140L; SI 2007 No 3186, Sch 3 para 1*].

Interest charged to capital

[17.34] In relation to interest referable to an accounting period ending **before 1 April 1996**, before the introduction of the **LOAN RELATIONSHIPS (54)** provisions, interest on money borrowed by a company for the construction of any building, structure or works, and referable to a period before disposal, could be added to the expenditure allowable as a deduction under *TCGA 1992, s 38* in computing the gain on the disposal by the company of the building etc. This was subject to the proviso that the expenditure on the construction itself was allowable, and that the interest was neither allowable as a deduction in computing any profits or gains for corporation tax purposes (nor would have been so but for an insufficiency of profits or gains) nor a charge on income (see **61.11 PROFIT COMPUTATIONS**). [*TCGA 1992, s 40; CTA 2009, Sch 1 para 362*].

Government securities and QCBs

[17.35] See the general taxation provisions relating to **LOAN RELATIONSHIPS** (**54**).

Value-shifting

[17.36] For the provisions of general application to individuals, etc. as well as companies, see Tolley's Capital Gains Tax under Anti-Avoidance. *FA 1989, ss 135–137* introduced various extensions to the scope of *CGTA 1979, s 26* which apply to companies disposing of assets, and these, now contained in *TCGA 1992, ss 30–34*, are described below.

There is a special regime for taxation of **INTANGIBLE ASSETS** (**54**) (now at *CTA 2009, Pt 8*), taking assets chargeable under that regime out of chargeable gains taxation, the appropriate modifications are applied to *TCGA 1992, ss 30–33* to ensure that those provisions continue to apply to such assets.

[*TCGA 1992, s 33A*].

The value-shifting provisions at *ss 30–34* are specifically aimed at preventing tax free benefits arising as a result of schemes or arrangements being entered into either before or after a disposal whereby the value of an asset has been materially reduced and a tax free benefit arises as a result of a person making the disposal, or a person connected to him or any other person. The provisions are widely drawn and can apply to the person making the disposal, to a person connected with that person or to any other person. Hhowever, they only apply to any other person where tax avoidance was one of the main purposes of the scheme or arrangements.

A value shifting adjustment is made on a just and reasonable basis and can decrease a loss, increase a gain or turn a loss into a gain.

TCGA 1992, s 30 applies to the disposal of an asset if a scheme has been effected or arrangements made (whether before or after the disposal) whereby the value of the asset, or of a 'relevant asset', has been materially reduced and a 'tax-free benefit' is conferred at any time on:

(a) the person making the disposal or a person connected with him (see **25 CONNECTED PERSONS**); or

(b) any other person, unless tax avoidance was not a main purpose of the scheme or arrangements.

Where the disposal of the asset precedes its acquisition, references to a reduction include references to an increase.

The consideration for the disposal in the capital gains computation is increased by a just and reasonable amount having regard to the scheme or arrangements and the 'tax-free benefit'. Where the consideration for the disposal of one asset has been so increased and the 'tax-free benefit' was an increase in the value of another asset, the consideration for the first subsequent disposal of that other asset is reduced by a just and reasonable amount. (There is no provision for the acquirer's cost to be correspondingly adjusted.)

These provisions do not apply to, *inter alia*, disposals between companies in a group (see **18.2 CAPITAL GAINS — GROUPS**).

[*TCGA 1992, s 30(1)(4)–(7)(9)*].

Reference to a 'relevant asset' was repealed by *FA 2011, Sch 9, para 1*. Previously, an asset ('the second asset') was a '*relevant asset*' if:

(a) the disposal of an asset (here called 'the first asset')was made by a company ('the disposing company');
(b) the first asset comprised shares in, or securities (within *TCGA 1992, s 132*) of, a company; and
(c) the second asset was owned at the time of disposal of the first asset by a company 'associated' (see **17.42** below) with the disposing company.

A reduction in value of a relevant asset was not taken into account for the purposes of a value shifting adjustment except in a case where:

(A) during the period from the reduction in value to the time immediately before the disposal of the first asset there was no disposal of it other than one within *TCGA 1992, s 171(1)* (see **18.4 CAPITAL GAINS — GROUPS**);
(B) no disposal of that asset was treated as occurring during that period under *TCGA 1992, s 179* (see **29.1**) **DEGROUPING CHARGES**; and
(C) if the reduction had not occurred, but any consideration given for the relevant asset and any other material circumstances (including any consideration given before the disposal for the first asset disposed of) were unchanged, the value of the first asset would have been materially greater at the time of its disposal.

[*TCGA 1992, s 30(2)*].

A '*tax-free benefit*' arises to a person if he becomes entitled to money or money's worth, or his interest in the value of any asset is increased, or he is wholly or partly relieved of any liability to which he is subject, *and* none of the foregoing benefits, when conferred, is otherwise liable to income tax, capital gains tax or corporation tax.

[*TCGA 1992, s 30(3)*].

It is understood that HMRC do not regard ordinary group relief transactions (e.g. the purchase of group relief) as falling within *TCGA 1992, s 30*.

Where a disposal within *TCGA 1992, s 30* forms the basis of a claim for relief under *ICTA 1988, ss 573, 574* (see **55.17 LOSSES**), *s 30* applies if *any* benefit is conferred, whether tax-free or not.

[*ICTA 1988, s 576(2)*].

See HMRC Capital Gains Manual, CG46800 *et seq*.

Simon's Taxes. See **D2.353**.

Certain disposals of shares by companies — post-FA 2011

[17.37] New rules were introduced by *FA 2011, Sch 9*, for the disposal by a company of shares in, or securities of, another company. These rules will apply from 19 July 2011 and introduce a motive-based rule for these disposals. *TCGA 1992, ss 31–34* were replaced by a new *TCGA 1992, s 31*.

Under the new rule, an adjustment is only made where there is a disposal by a company of shares in, or securities of, another company and there are arrangements whereby the value of those shares or securities, or of any relevant asset, is materially reduced, and where the main purpose or one of the main purposes of the arrangements is obtaining a tax advantage. Where the rule applies, the consideration for the disposal will be treated as increased by an amount that is just and reasonable bearing in mind both the arrangements themselves and the charge to or relief from corporation tax that would otherwise arise were *TCGA 1992, s 31* not in place.

Where the disposal of the shares or securities precedes their acquisition then the references to a material reduction in value are to be read as including material increases in value.

These provisions will also apply to deemed disposals under *TCGA 1992, s 29(2)*.

A relevant asset is any asset owned by a company which is a member of the same group as the disposing company and it does not matter for the purposes of this legislation whether the tax advantage is obtained for the disposing company or any other person.

The rules do not apply if the arrangements consist solely of the making of an exempt distribution. An exempt distribution means, broadly, any dividend that is derived from transactions not designed to reduce tax. Specifically, an exempt distribution is a distribution which would fall within an exempt class by virtue of *CTA 2009, s 931H*, or would be such a dividend but for the recipient company being a small company as defined by *CTA 2009, s 931S*.

Certain disposals of shares by companies — pre-FA 2011

[17.38] The following provisions apply where a disposal within **17.36** above ('the *s 30* disposal') is of shares ('the principal asset') which are owned by a company ('the first company') in another company ('the second company'). These rules were repealed with effect from 19 July 2011 (*FA 2011*).

[*TCGA 1992, s 30(8)*].

Distributions within a group followed by a disposal of shares

[17.39] If a reduction in the value of an asset is attributable to the payment of a dividend by the second company while the two companies are 'associated' (see **17.42** below), it is not treated as a reduction for the purposes of **17.36** above except to the extent (if any) that the dividend is attributable (see below) to 'chargeable profits' of the second company; and, in such a case, the tax-free benefit is ascertained without regard to any part of the dividend that is not attributable to such profits.

'*Chargeable profits*' are:

(a) the 'distributable profits' of a company, to the extent that they arise from a 'transaction caught by this *section*'; and
(b) the 'distributable profits' of a company, to the extent that they represent so much of a distribution received from another company as was attributable to chargeable profits of that company (including ones similarly representing a distribution).

'*Distributable profits*' are such profits computed on a commercial basis as, after allowance for any provision properly made for tax, the company is empowered, assuming sufficient funds, to distribute to persons entitled to participate in its profits. So far as possible, in ascertaining distributable profits, losses and other amounts to be set against profits must be set against profits other than ones which could be chargeable profits.

Profits arising on a '*transaction caught by this section*' are profits of a company ('company X') where the following three conditions are met but the three exceptions to them (see below) do not apply.

The three conditions to be met are:

(1) The transaction is:
   (i) a no gain/no loss disposal by company X to another group company within *TCGA 1992, s 171(1)* (see **18.4 CAPITAL GAINS — GROUPS**); or
   (ii) an exchange, or deemed exchange, of shares in or debentures of a company held by company X for shares in or debentures of another company which, immediately after the transaction, is 'associated' (see **17.42** below) with company X, being a transaction treated by virtue of *TCGA 1992, s 135* or *s 136* as a reorganisation of share capital; or
   (iii) a revaluation of an asset in the accounting records of company X.
(2) No disposal of the 'asset with enhanced value':
   (i) occurs, other than one within *TCGA 1992, s 171(1)*, during the period beginning with the transaction within (1) above and ending immediately before the *s 30* disposal; or
   (ii) is treated as having occurred during that period by virtue of *TCGA 1992, s 179* (see **29.1 DEGROUPING CHARGES**).
(3) Immediately after the *s 30* disposal the asset with enhanced value is owned by a person other than the disposing company or a company 'associated' with it (see **17.42** below).

'*Asset with enhanced value*' is defined as follows, according to which transaction within (1)(i), (1)(ii) or (1)(iii) above occurs, respectively: the asset acquired from company X; the shares or debentures acquired by company X as a result of the exchange; and the revalued asset.

The three exceptions to the foregoing three conditions are as follows.

(A) At the time of the transaction within (1) above, company X carries on a trade, and a profit on a disposal of the asset with enhanced value would form part of the trading profits.
(B) By reason of the nature of the asset with enhanced value, there could be no chargeable gain or allowable loss on its disposal.
(C) Immediately before the *s 30* disposal, the company owning the asset with enhanced value carries on a trade, and a profit on disposal would form part of the trading profits.

Attribution of profits to a distribution is made by determining the total distributable profits and chargeable profits which remain at the time of distribution, after allowing for all earlier distributions and distributions to be made then or subsequently in respect of other classes of shares, etc., and so far as possible attributing distributable profits other than chargeable profits.

Chargeable profits are treated as arising to shareholders etc. proportionately to their holdings of shares etc.

[*TCGA 1992, s 31*].

See generally HMRC Capital Gains Manual, CG46805–CG46834.

Asset-holding company leaving the group

[17.40] The following provisions apply wherever profits of a company would be profits on a transaction caught by *TCGA 1992, s 31* (see above) but for the fact that condition (3) in **17.39** above is not satisfied. In those circumstances, the profits are treated as arising on a transaction caught by *s 31* (with the result that *TCGA 1992, s 30* (see **17.36** above) has effect) if, at any time during the period of six years beginning with the date of the *s 30* disposal, either:

(a) an event occurs which consists of the 'asset-holding company' ceasing to be a member of the 'disposal group' (otherwise than by virtue of the principal company of the group becoming a member of another group, i.e. the group being taken over); or
(b) the 'asset-holding company' ceases to be a member of the 'disposal group' by virtue only of the principal company of the group becoming a member of another group *and* an event occurs as a result of which either:
    (i) there is no member of the 'disposal group' of which the 'asset-holding company' is a 75% subsidiary; or
    (ii) there is no member of the 'disposal group' of which the 'asset-holding company' is an effective 51% subsidiary (see **18.2 CAPITAL GAINS — GROUPS**).

These provisions do not, however, apply (and there is thus no double charge), if, during that six-year period but prior to the occurrence of an event within (a) or (b) above, a disposal of the asset with enhanced value has been treated as having occurred by virtue of *TCGA 1992, s 179* (company leaving a group after acquiring an asset intra-group, see **29.1 DEGROUPING CHARGES**).

The '*asset-holding company*' at any time is the company holding the asset with enhanced value at that time. The '*disposal group*' is the group of which the company which made the *s 30* disposal was a member at the time of that disposal (or a group regarded as being the same as that group under *TCGA 1992, s 170(10)*, see **18.2 CAPITAL GAINS — GROUPS**).

Where *TCGA 1992, s 30* has effect as above, the consideration for the *s 30* disposal is not adjusted, but a chargeable gain is treated as accruing to the 'chargeable company' immediately before the event within (a) or (b) above.

The '*chargeable company*' is normally the company which made the disposal. If, however, that company is, immediately before the event within (a) or (b) above, no longer a member of the disposal group, the chargeable company is any member of the group immediately before the event which is so designated for the purpose by HMRC by notice served on the company.

The amount of the imputed gain is the shortfall between the allowable loss or chargeable gain which accrued on the *s 30* disposal and the allowable loss or chargeable gain which would have accrued on that disposal if the consideration had been treated as increased as in **17.36** above.

If an allowable loss arose on the *s 30* disposal and has not been otherwise utilised, it may be set against the imputed gain arising as above, notwithstanding the connected persons rule in *TCGA 1992, s 18(3)*.

TCGA 1992, s 31A will continue to apply to *s 30* disposals that occurred before the commencement date of the new rule introduced by *FA 2011, Sch 9* (see **17.36**).

[*TCGA 1992, s 31A*].

Distributions within a group followed by a share disposal under s 32

[17.41] A reduction in the value of an asset is not treated as a reduction for the purposes of **17.36** above if it is attributable to the disposal of any asset ('the underlying asset') by the second company while the two companies are 'associated' (see **17.42** below), and the disposal is within *TCGA 1992, s 171(1) or s 211* (with reference to long term insurance business), unless:

(I) the actual consideration for the disposal of the underlying asset is less than both its market value and its 'cost';

(II) the disposal is not effected for *bona fide* commercial reasons and forms part of a scheme or arrangements of which a main purpose is the avoidance of a corporation tax liability; and

(III) the first company is not treated as disposing of an interest in the principal asset by virtue of a distribution in a dissolution or winding-up of the second company.

For the purpose of (I) above, the '*cost*' of an asset is the aggregate of any capital expenditure incurred by the company in acquiring or providing it, or in respect of it while owned after its acquisition.

In the case of a part disposal of an underlying asset:

(A) the market value in (I) above is the market value of the asset acquired by the transferee; and
(B) the amounts attributed to the cost of the underlying asset are reduced to the '*appropriate proportion*' thereof; i.e.
  (i) the proportion of capital expenditure properly attributed in the company's accounting records to the asset acquired by the transferee; or
  (ii) if (i) does not apply, such proportion as is just and reasonable.

[*TCGA 1992, s 32*].

Interpretation

[17.42] The following interpretational provisions apply.

As regards any asset ('the original asset'), the provisions in (1)–(5) below apply in relation to the enactments mentioned in (a) and (b) below.

(a) The enactments concerning relevant assets in *TCGA 1992, s 30(2)*.
(b) The enactments concerning distributions within a group followed by a disposal of shares in *TCGA 1992, s 31(7)–(9)*.

The provisions in (1)–(5) below also apply in connection with *TCGA 1992, s 31A* for the purpose of determining any question in relation to the asset with enhanced value.

(1) In (A) and (B) in **17.36** above and in condition (2) in **17.39** above, references to the disposal of an asset do not include a part disposal.
(2) For the purposes of the enactments referred to in (a) and (b) above, references to an asset are to the original asset, except that if subsequently one or more assets are treated under (4) or (5) below as the same as the original asset:
  (i) if there has been no disposal falling within (A) or (B) in **17.36** above or (2) in **17.39** above, the references are to the asset(s) so treated; and
  (ii) in any other case, the references are to the asset(s) representing that part of the value of the original asset remaining after allowing for earlier disposals within the relevant provision.

  For the above purposes a disposal includes a part disposal which would have been within (A) or (B) in **17.36** above or (2) in **17.39** above if it had not been excluded by (1) above.

  For the purposes of *TCGA 1992, s 31A* at **17.40** above, the following apply where one or more assets is treated under (4) or (5) below as the same as the asset with enhanced value.
  (I) If, in the period beginning with the transaction in **17.39**(1) above, there is no disposal of the asset with enhanced value to any person other than on a no gain/no loss intra-group disposal

within *TCGA 1992, s 171(1)* (see **18.4 CAPITAL GAINS — GROUPS**), and no disposal of that asset is treated as having occurred by virtue of *TCGA 1992, s 179* (see **29.1 DEGROUPING CHARGES**), then references to the asset with enhanced value are to the asset(s) treated under (4) or (5) below as the same as that asset.

(II) In any other case, references to the asset with enhanced value are to the asset(s) representing that part of the value of the asset with enhanced value remaining after allowing for disposals of either kind referred to in (I) above.

(3) If, by virtue of (2) above, a reference to an asset is treated as a reference to two or more assets:
   (i) the assets are treated as a single asset;
   (ii) a disposal of any of them is a part disposal; and
   (iii) the reference to the second asset in (3) in **17.36** above, to the asset in condition (3) in **17.39** above and to the asset in the definition of 'asset-holding company' in **17.40** above is in each case a reference to all or any of those two or more assets.

(4) If there is a part disposal of an asset, that asset and the asset acquired by the transferee are treated as the same.

(5) Where:
   (i) the value of an asset is derived from another asset owned by the same or an 'associated' company (see below); and
   (ii) assets have been merged or divided or have changed their nature, or rights or interests in or over assets have been created or extinguished,

   the two assets are treated as the same.

Where a reduction in the value of a relevant asset is to be taken into account under *TCGA 1992, s 30(2)* (see (1)–(3) and (A)–(C) in **17.36** above) and at the time of the disposal of the first asset in **17.36**(1) by the disposing company:

(A) references to the relevant asset are treated under (1)–(5) above as references to two or more assets treated as a single asset; and
(B) one or more, but not all, of those assets is owned by a company 'associated' (see below) with the disposing company,

the amount of the reduction in the value of the relevant asset to be taken into account is reduced to such an amount as is just and reasonable.

For the purposes of the provisions in TCGA 1992, s 31 concerning distributions within a group followed by a disposal of shares (see **17.39** above), the reduction in value of the principal asset (see **17.41** above) is to be reduced to such amount as is just and reasonable if:

(a) a dividend paid by the second company is attributable to that company's chargeable profits; and
(b) the criterion in (2), (3) or (C) in **17.39** above is satisfied by reference to an asset, or assets treated as a single asset, treated under (2)(ii) above as the same as the asset with enhanced value.

Where *TCGA 1992, s 31A* (see **17.40** above) treats profits as arising on a transaction caught by *TCGA 1992, s 31* and either condition (2) or condition (a) or (b) in **17.39** above is satisfied by reference to an asset (or assets treated as a single asset) treated by virtue of (2)(II) above as the same as the asset with enhanced value, the reduction in value of the principal asset (see **17.41** above) is to be reduced to such amount as is just and reasonable.

The definitions relating to groups of companies in TCGA 1992, s 170(2)–(11) apply as in **18.2 CAPITAL GAINS — GROUPS**; and companies are '*associated*' if they are members of the same group.

[*TCGA 1992, s 33*].

Transactions treated as a reorganisation of share capital

[17.43] If the following conditions apply, a 'disposing company' is treated as receiving the amount specified in (b) below on a part disposal within *TCGA 1992, s 128(3)* of the 'original holding'.

(a) But for the rules whereby shares, etc. held after a reorganisation, reconstruction, etc. are treated as the same as those held beforehand, *TCGA 1992, s 30* in **17.36** above would apply on an exchange by a company (the 'disposing company') of shares, etc. in another company (the 'original holding') for shares, etc. in a further company which immediately afterwards is not in the same group (as defined in *TCGA 1992, s 170(2)–(11)*, see **18.2 CAPITAL GAINS — GROUPS**) as the disposing company.

(b) If *TCGA 1992, s 30* had applied, any allowable loss or chargeable gain on the disposal would have been calculated as if the consideration had been increased by an amount.

Similarly if, but for the rules referred to in (a) above, *s 30* would have applied by virtue of *TCGA 1992, s 31A* (see **17.38** above) on an exchange of the kind referred to in (a) above, *s 31A* is applied (with appropriate modification) as if the said rules did not apply. In the computation of the shortfall under that *section*, an allowable loss is in this case regarded as a chargeable gain of nil.

These provisions are interpreted as if *TCGA 1992, s 136* had effect generally for the capital gains tax legislation.

[*TCGA 1992, s 34*].

Depreciatory transactions

[17.44] Where two or more group companies are parties to a disposal of assets at other than market value, and such a disposal **materially reduces the value of the shares or securities of one of those companies** (a '*depreciatory transaction*'), any loss arising on the ultimate disposal of those shares by a member or former member of the group (having been a member when the transaction took place) is to be allowable only so far as is 'just and reasonable'.

This applied where the depreciatory transaction was after 31 March 1982 (or 6 April 1965 if the 31 March 1982 market value is not substituted for cost under *TCGA 1992, s 35(2)*). Following *FA 2011*, the depreciatory transaction must now be within the period of six years ending with the disposal.

Account may be taken of any other transaction which may have:

(i) enhanced the value of the assets of the company the shares in which are being disposed of; *and*

(ii) depreciated the value of the assets of any other member of the group.

The restriction is applied to the allowable loss after indexation, rather than to the unindexed loss before indexation (*Tesco plc v Crimmin* (1997) 69 TC 510), and in arriving at the amount by which it was 'just and reasonable' to reduce the allowable loss, indexation should be applied to the value of the depreciatory transaction(s) from the date(s) of the transaction(s) to the date of the ultimate disposal (*Whitehall Electric Investments Ltd v Owen* [2002] STC (SCD) 229). See, however, **17.50** as regards prohibition on indexation allowance creating or enhancing a loss.

Where such a reduction is made, any chargeable gain accruing on the disposal within 6 years of the transaction of the shares etc. in any other party thereto is to be reduced as is 'just and reasonable' (but not so as to exceed the reduction in the allowable loss). Regard may also be had to the effect of the depreciatory transaction on the value of the shares at the date of disposal.

A 'depreciatory transaction' also includes any other transaction where:

(a) the company, the shares or securities in which are the subject of the ultimate disposal, or any 75% subsidiary of that company, was party to that transaction; and

(b) the parties to the transaction were, or included, two or more companies which, when the transaction occurred, were in the same group.

A transaction is not depreciatory to the extent that it is a payment which is brought into account in computing a chargeable gain or allowable loss of the company making the ultimate disposal. Cancellation within *Companies Act 2006, s 641* of shares or securities of one group member which are owned by another is deemed to be a depreciatory transaction unless it falls within this exemption.

Claims under *TCGA 1992, s 24(2)* that shares or securities have become of negligible value also come within this section.

References to the disposal of assets include appropriation by one member of a group of the goodwill of another.

'*Securities*' includes loan stock or similar securities, whether secured or unsecured.

'*Group of companies*' includes non-resident companies (before, on and after 1 April 2000).

[*TCGA 1992, s 176; FA 2000, Sch 29 para 24; FA 2011, Sch 9, para 3*].

As regards distributions out of post-acquisition profits, see HMRC Capital Gains Manual, CG46580 et seq.

Simon's Taxes. See **D2.350.**

Depreciatory distributions

[17.45] The restriction on capital losses because of 'depreciatory transactions' (see **17.44** above) also applies where a 'first company' has a holding in a 'second company' which amounts (with or without the addition of holdings by **CONNECTED PERSONS** (**25**)) to 10% of all the holdings of the same class in the second company (and the first company is not a dealing company in relation to the holding) and a distribution is, or has been, made in respect of the holding which materially reduces the value of the holding. Distributions brought into account in computing a chargeable gain or allowable loss accruing to the ultimate disponor are ignored. [*TCGA 1992, s 177; FA 2000, Sch 29 para 25*].

Simon's Taxes. See **D2.352**.

Close company transferring asset at undervalue

[17.46] Where, after 5 April 1965 (31 March 1982 where, on the ultimate disposal after 5 April 1988, market value at that date is substituted for cost), a close company transfers an asset to any person otherwise than at arm's length for a consideration less than market value, the difference is apportioned among the issued shares of the company so as to reduce the deductible cost in the capital gains tax computation on disposal of those shares; but this does not apply to transfers within a group. [*TCGA 1992, s 125*].

By concession, *s 125* is not applied where the transferee is a participator (or associate) and the transfer is treated as an income distribution under *CTA 2010, ss 1000, 1020; ICTA 1988, s 209(2)(b)(4)* (see **31.3, 31.9 DISTRIBUTIONS**) or as a capital distribution under *TCGA 1992, s 122* (see Tolley's Capital Gains Tax under Shares and Securities), or where the transferee is an employee and is assessed as employment income on the excess of the market value of the asset over any amount paid for it. (HMRC Extra-Statutory Concession, D51).

Where the transfer is to a trust for the benefit of the employees of the transferring company, the difference that is apportioned is limited (where it would otherwise be greater) to any excess of allowable expenditure over the transfer consideration. [*TCGA 1992, s 239*].

Simon's Taxes. See **C1.430, D1.919**.

Companies in partnership

[17.47] A charge to corporation applies under *FA 2004, s 131* where a company realises capital from a partnership on or after 17 March 2004 by disposing of all or part of it's partnership interest on or after that date in connection with certain anti-avoidance schemes which shelter taxable profits within a partnership structure. The provisions ensure that any amounts subject to the charge under *s 131* are taken into account in computing gains under the chargeable gains legislation so as to avoid double taxation and it specifically sets out the amounts which will fall within *TCGA 1992*. See **58.12 PARTNERSHIPS**.

From 12 March 2008, the charge to corporation tax under these provisions does not arise where such transactions or arrangements are also caught by the loan relationship anti-avoidance rules in *CTA 2009, ss 537, 538* (formerly *FA 1996, ss 91H, 91I*). Instead, these amounts are subject to corporation tax under the loan relationship provisions.

The provisions in *FA 2004* and *CTA 2009* above were repealed with effect from 22 April 2009 by *FA 2009* as a result of the introduction of the disguised interest legislation and the shares accounted as liabilities provisions.

[*FA 2004, ss 131, 133; CTA 2009, Sch 1 para 572; FA 2009 s 48, Sch 24*].

Dual resident companies

[17.48] Special provisions applied **before 30 November 1993** to '*dual-resident companies*', i.e. companies resident both in the UK and, under any double taxation relief arrangements, in a territory outside the UK. From that date, they were replaced by *FA 1994, s 249* (now *CTA 2009, s 18*), which has effect to treat companies otherwise regarded as UK-resident as non-resident where they are so treated under such arrangements. See **65.2 RESIDENCE**.

Privatisation

[17.49] British Telecommunications plc ('British Telecom') is treated for all purposes of corporation tax as being the same person as British Telecommunications, to whose business it succeeded on privatisation, except that it is not regarded as a nationalised undertaking within *TCGA 1992, s 170(12)*. [*Telecommunications Act 1984, s 72*]. Similar provisions apply in relation to the successor companies to the British Airways Board and the National Freight Corporation [*ICTA 1988, s 513* repealed by *CTA 2010*, as spent], the British Airports Authority [*British Airports Act 1986, s 77* as amended by *CTA 2009, Sch 1 para 321*], the British Gas Corporation [*Gas Act 1986, s 60* as amended by *CTA 2009, Sch 1 para 327*], the British Steel Corporation [*British Steel Act 1988, s 11* as amended by *CTA 2009, Sch 1 para 329*], the General Practice Finance Corporation [*Health and Medicines Act 1988, s 6*], statutory port undertakings [*Ports Act 1991, s 35*], the National Research Development Council and National Enterprise Board [*British Technology Group Act 1991, s 12*], milk marketing boards [*Agriculture Act 1993, Sch 2 Pt I; FA 1996, s 203*], Northern Ireland Airports Ltd [*FA 1994, s 253, Sch 25*] and the Atomic Energy Authority [*Atomic Energy Authority Act 1995, Sch 3*]. See also *Water Act 1989, s 95, Electricity Act 1989, s 90, Sch 11, Environmental Protection Act 1990, ss 6–9, Coal Industry Act 1994, Sch 4, Broadcasting Act 1996, Sch 7 as amended by CTA 2009, Sch 1 para 446, Transport Act 2000, Sch 26* and *Scottish Water (Transfer of Functions, etc.)(Tax Provisions) Order 2002* (*SI 2002 No 653*), and, as regards the *Railways Act 1993, FA 1994, s 252, Sch 24*.

Surplus ACT arising to the successor company on privatisation may not be carried back to a period before the transfer (*CIR v Aberdeen Milk Co Ltd*) [1999] STC 787, 73 TC 563, Ct of Sess.

Indexation allowance

[17.50] The basic indexation provisions applicable to individuals up to 5 April 1998 continue to apply to companies. For companies, however, they applied initially to disposals after 31 March 1982 instead of 5 April 1982, and the revised rules introduced by *FA 1985* applied to disposals after 31 March 1985 instead of 5 April 1985. The rules introduced by *FA 1988* apply only to disposals after 5 April 1988. See Tolley's Capital Gains Tax for full details.

Key points

[17.51] Points to consider are as follows.

- Where it is intended that a capital loss will be used, ensure that the claim to use the loss is submitted on time.
- There are a number of restrictions on the use of capital losses. Where a company is to rely upon the use of losses, ensure that the losses have been identified and their availability for use analysed before they are needed.
- When analysing the likely availability of capital losses, consider carefully the targeted anti-avoidance rules. The broad meaning of the term 'arrangements' and the purpose test are designed to give these provisions a relatively low threshold for application.
- Where anti-avoidance provisions are potentially in point (whether in relation to capital losses, value shifting or otherwise), the taxpayer should consider taking advice to limit potential penalties under the new penalties regime.
- Make use of the clearance regime for reorganisations and reconstructions, but remember that the statutory regime is only concerned with the question of whether the transactions involved are being carried out for bona fide commercial reasons. Where there is doubt as to a technical issue, the HMRC non-statutory business clearance service may be used. In each case, submit the clearance application as soon as possible once the likely structure is settled, to allow time to deal with any questions HMRC raises.
- Bear in mind the potential for secondary chargeable gains liabilities. It may be prudent to consider the need for indemnities if external investors are involved or all or part of a business is to be sold.
- If assets are to be transferred to a non-resident company under *TCGA 1992, s 140* or *s 140A et seq*, ensure that the relevant claim is made on time. Remember also that a claim made under one such provision may preclude a claim being made under a similar provision (as is the case with, for example, *ss 140* and *140C*).
- If a transaction within *TCGA 1992, s 140* is in contemplation, consider carefully the events that could bring the deferred gain into charge. In particular, while there is a six-year period during which the disposal of the relevant assets can crystallise the gain

(with exceptions for certain intra-group disposals), the disposal of the shares issued in consideration for the transfer of the business will bring the gain into charge at any time in the future. Therefore, care must be taken to ensure that a disposal of those shares is not triggered, even accidentally, in the future.

18

Capital Gains — Groups

Cross-references. See also **19 CAPITAL GAINS — SUBSTANTIAL SHAREHOLDINGS, 35 EXEMPT ORGANISATIONS, 54.86 LOAN RELATIONSHIPS.**

Other sources. See Tolley's Capital Gains Tax.

Simon's Taxes. See C3.1, D2.3.

Introduction

[18.1] Groups of companies are able to benefit from beneficial reliefs with regard to capital gains. For example, a key relief allows the transfer of assets between group companies to happen without giving rise to a chargeable gain. In addition, rollover relief (see further Tolley's Capital Gains Tax) is extended to other members of a capital gains group, so a gain in one company can be 'rolled over' into the acquisition of an appropriate asset made by another group company.

In addition to the various reliefs described below, there are certain anti-avoidance provisions applicable to transactions between companies within a capital gains group. For example, the provisions restricting the use of losses (or set off of gains) arising before a company joins a group, the application of a charge when an asset which has been transferred intra-group is sold to a third party, the rules regarding appropriations to and from stock, and transactions undertaken which lead to an artificial reduction in the value of a group member's shares before a share sale.

This chapter outlines the rules regarding membership of a capital gains group, the reliefs available to such members, and the anti-avoidance provisions applicable. A more detailed analysis of capital gains provisions in general can be found in Tolley's Capital Gains Tax.

Definitions

[18.2] As highlighted above, there are certain beneficial reliefs afforded companies within a capital gains group. There are rules which govern when a company can be treated as being a member of a capital gains group, found at *TCGA 1992, s 170*, similar in some respects (but not all) to the rules with regard to a group for group relief purposes (see **39 GROUP RELIEF**).

With regard to these provisions, and for the purposes of this chapter, the following definitions are applicable.

Definition of company

'*Company*' for the purposes of the capital gains group provisions means one within the meaning of the *Companies Act 2006* or the corresponding enactment in Northern Ireland or which is constituted under any other Act, Royal Charter, or letters patent (other than a limited liability partnership) or under the law of a country outside the UK. It also includes a registered **INDUSTRIAL AND PROVIDENT SOCIETY (47)**, a building society (see **9.2 BUILDING SOCIETIES**) and (from 17 March 1998) an incorporated friendly society (see **37.3 FRIENDLY SOCIETIES**). [*TCGA 1992, s 170(9)*].

Residence

From (broadly) 1 April 2000, any company, whatever its country of residence, can be a member of a group (previously a company had to be UK-resident), and can be taken into account in establishing the existence of a group, for the purposes of corporation tax on chargeable gains. See **39.2 GROUP RELIEF** for the corresponding group relief provisions. For transitional measures which ensure continuity of treatment as regards a pre-existing group of companies, see (iii) below.

[*TCGA 1992, s 170(1A)(9)*].

Definition of group

The definition of a group for capital gains purposes is found at *TCGA 1992, s 170*.

A '*group*' comprises:

(a) a company ('*the principal company of the group*'); and
(b) that company's '75% subsidiaries' (i.e. where not less than 75% of the 'ordinary share capital' is beneficially owned directly or indirectly by the principal company), and those subsidiaries' 75% subsidiaries (and so on), except that any 75% subsidiary which is not 'an effective 51% subsidiary' of the principal company is excluded. Beneficial ownership is not affected by the existence of an option which may require disposal of shares at a future date (see *J Sainsbury plc v O'Connor* (1991) 64 TC 208, CA).

This definition is subject to the following rules.

(i) A company ('the subsidiary') which is a 75% subsidiary of another company cannot be a principal company of a group, unless:

- (A) because of the exclusion in (b) above (with regard to the 51% subsidiary requirement), the two companies are not in the same group;
- (B) the requirements of the definition of a group in (a) and (b) are otherwise satisfied; and
- (C) no further company could, under this provision, be the principal company of a group of which the subsidiary would be a member.

(ii) A company can only be a member of one capital gains group. Therefore if a company would otherwise belong to more than one group (the principal company of each of which is below called the '*head of a group*'), it belongs only to the group which can first be determined under the following tests.

- (A) The group to which it would belong if the exclusion of a company which is not an 'effective 51 per cent subsidiary' in (b) above were applied without the inclusion of any amount to which the head of a group:
  - (a) is entitled of any profits available for distribution to equity holders of a head of another group; or
  - (b) would be entitled of any assets of a head of another group available for distribution to its equity holders on a winding-up.
- (B) The group the head of which is entitled to a greater percentage than any other head of a group of its profits available for distribution to equity holders.
- (C) The group the head of which would be entitled to a greater percentage than any other head of a group of its assets available for distribution to equity holders on a winding-up.
- (D) The group the head of which owns (as in *CTA 2010, s 1154(2); ICTA 1988, s 838(1)(a)*) directly or indirectly more of its ordinary share capital than any other head of a group.

The provisions of *CTA 2010, Ch 6 Pt 5, previously ICTA 1988, Sch 18* (group relief: equity holders and profits or assets available for distribution, see **39.4 GROUP RELIEF**) apply with minor modification for (ii) and (A) and (B) above. One modification to the *CTA 2010* provisions (formerly *Sch 18*) for these purposes disapplies the requirement that certain arrangements for changes in profit or asset shares are assumed to take place in applying the 50% test. The anti-avoidance measures of *CTA 2010, ss 171(1)(b) and (3), 173, 174* and *176–178*, formerly *paras 5B–5E* of *Sch 18* (introduced by *F(No 2)A 1992, Sch 6*, see **39.4 GROUP RELIEF**, with effect from 15 November 1991) do **not** apply for these purposes.

[*TCGA 1992, s 170(2)–(8); ICTA 1988, s 838; FA 2000, Sch 29 para 46(4)–(6)*].

Example

For group capital gains purposes, the 'A' group is formed with A Ltd being the ultimate holding company (the principal company). A Ltd owns 75% of B Ltd and 56.25% (75% × 75%) of C Ltd so both B Ltd and C Ltd can be included in A Ltd's gains group.

However, A Ltd only owns 42% of D Ltd (75% × 75% × 75%), and therefore as this is below 50%, D Ltd is not part of A Ltd's group. Consequently, the A Ltd's capital gains group comprises companies A Ltd, B Ltd and C Ltd.

C Ltd and D Ltd cannot be linked for group gains purposes. The reason for this is that a company which is a 75% subsidiary of another company cannot be a principal company unless it fails the effective subsidiary test. In other words a company cannot be a member of more than one group for group gains purposes — as in (ii) above.

However, D Ltd can be a principal company in its own right and form its own group with E Ltd.

Thus for group gains, there are two groups:

(a) the A group comprising A Ltd, B Ltd and C Ltd; and
(b) the D group, comprising D Ltd and E Ltd.

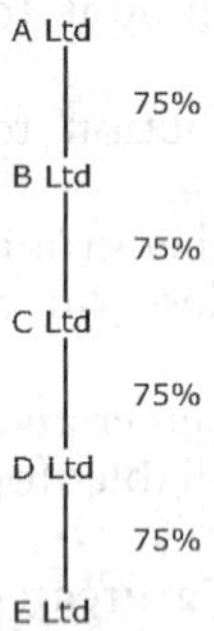

OEICs

With effect for disposals on or after 1 April 2006, it is specifically provided that an open-ended investment company (see **52 INVESTMENT FUNDS**) cannot be the principal company of a group [*TCGA 1992, s 170(4A) treated as inserted by SI 2006 No 964, Reg 107*] or a member of a group (see HMRC Capital Gains Manual, CG45173).

Ordinary Share Capital

'*Ordinary share capital*' means all issued share capital of a company except shares carrying a fixed rate of dividend only. [*CTA 2010, s 1119; ICTA 1988, s 832(1)*]. Any share capital of a registered industrial and provident society is treated as ordinary share capital. 'Issued share capital' does not include founder members' deposits in a company limited by guarantee (*South Shore Mutual Insurance Co Ltd v Blair* [1999] STC (SCD)296).

HMRC has issued Brief 54/07 (now CG/APP 11) which sets out HMRC's interpretation of 'ordinary share capital' in *ICTA 1988, s 832* (now *CTA 2010, s 1119*), with special regard to foreign entities. The advice given with regard to UK companies was updated for changes in the law following the coming into force of *Companies Act (CA) 2006* on 1 October 2008.

When looking at overseas companies, a number of factors may be taken into account in deciding if a foreign 'company' has 'issued share capital'. Firstly, there are a number of documents which should be considered. These are the corporate law of the country in question, the body's equivalent of a Memorandum and Articles of Association, any general legal and commercial commentaries on the commercial status of the body in question and the company's accounts (in particular in relation to status of capital).

As an essential, the foreign 'company' must be a distinct legal entity, separate from its members and able to hold assets. If this condition is met, other factors to be considered are:

- Is the member's interest like shares or debt?
- Did the member pay for his interest?
- Does the amount subscribed become the company's property or does ownership remain with the member?
- What responsibilities and proprietary rights does the member have?
- Can the right be legally evidenced in accordance with local law?
- Is the 'capital' divided into fixed units of a stated value?
- Is the subscription part of a fixed and certain amount of capital to which creditors may look for security?
- Are the subscriptions allocated to fixed capital?
- Can the member's interest be transferred as a transfer of rights rather than as a transfer of money or loan?
- Are there any other factors which would indicate that the member's interest is issued in the form of ordinary share capital?

Factors may be given different weight and not all need necessarily be present.

Simon's Taxes. See **D2.305–D2.307**.

Companies deemed not to change group

Principal becomes member of another group

[18.3] A group remains the same group so long as the same company remains the principal company of the group. If at any time the principal company of a group becomes a member of another group, the first group and the other group are regarded as the same, and the question whether or not a company has ceased to be a member of a group is determined accordingly. [*TCGA 1992, s 170(10)*].

Becoming a European Company — Societas Europaea

Where the principal company of a group:

- becomes an SE (see **17.27 CAPITAL GAINS**) on or after 1 April 2005 by reason of being the acquiring company in the formation of an SE by merger by acquisition (in accordance with *Council Regulations (EC) No 2157/2001, Arts 2(1), 17(2) and 29(1)*);
- becomes a subsidiary of a holding SE (formed on or after 1 April 2005 in accordance with *Art 2(2)*); or
- is transformed on or after 1 April 2005 into an SE (in accordance with *Art 2(4)*),

the group and any group of which the SE is a member on formation are regarded as the same, and the question whether or not a company has ceased to be a member of a group is determined accordingly. [*TCGA 1992, s 170(10A); F(No 2)A 2005, s 62*].

Winding up

The passing of a resolution, or the making of an order, or any other act for the winding-up of a member of a group is not treated as an occasion on which any company ceases to be a member of the group. [*TCGA 1992, s 170(11)*].

Transfers within a group

[18.4] A key benefit from being in a capital gains group is that transfers of chargeable assets between members of the same group are treated as no gain, no loss transfers. Thus the transfer happens at the disposing company's base cost plus indexation to the date of transfer. (See further Tolley's Capital Gains Tax under Indexation). This rule (*TCGA 1992, s 171*) applies automatically and is mandatory for such transfers (assuming the conditions for it to apply are met).

The conditions for intra-group transfers of assets to be treated as no gain, no loss disposals are:

(a) that either the transferor company is UK resident at the time of disposal or the asset is a 'chargeable asset' in relation to that company immediately before that time; and

(b) that either the transferee company is UK resident at that time or the asset is a 'chargeable asset' in relation to that company immediately after that time.

For these purposes, an asset is a '*chargeable asset*' in relation to a company at a particular time if, on a disposal by the company at that time, any gain would be a chargeable gain and within the charge to corporation tax by virtue of *TCGA 1992, s 10B* (non-UK resident company trading through UK permanent establishment, see **65.6 RESIDENCE**).

[*TCGA 1992, s 171; FA 2003, Sch 27 para 2(3); F(No 2)A 2005, Sch 7 para 9; FA 2007, Sch 5 para 10; CTA 2009, Sch 1 paras 375, 673*].

Example

A Ltd owns 100% of B Ltd. In September 1992 A Ltd purchased a property at a cost of £500,000. In January 2010 A Ltd decided to transfer the property to B Ltd. This transaction will automatically be treated as taking place at no gain no loss.

The cost is £500,000, if it is assumed indexation is approximately 50% (therefore £250,000) the proceeds of the transaction are deemed to be £750,000, in order to give rise to no gain no loss:

	£
Proceeds	750,000
Cost	(500,000)
Indexation	(250,000)
Gain/loss	NIL

After the transfer B Ltd will have a base cost of this particular property of £750,000 which it will index in a future disposal calculation from January 2010, the date of the intra-group transfer.

Such intra-group transfers are subject to anti-avoidance provisions where the company which acquired the asset leaves the group within six years of the transfer, see further **29.1 DEGROUPING CHARGES**.

Exceptions to no gain no loss transfer

[18.5] There are various exceptions to the intra group 'no gain no loss' transfer relief detailed above — the provisions of *TCGA 1992, s 171(1)* do not apply to:

- (i) *assumed* (as opposed to actual) transfers;
- (ii) a disposal of a *debt* due from a group member effected by satisfying it (or part of it);
- (iii) a disposal on redemption of *redeemable shares*;
- (iv) a disposal of an interest in shares in consideration of a *capital distribution*;
- (v) the receipt of *compensation* for destruction etc. of assets (in that the disposal is treated as being to the insurer or other person who ultimately bears the burden of furnishing the compensation);
- (vi) a disposal by or to an investment trust (and see **29.7** below);
- (vii) a disposal to a 'dual resident investing company' (see **39.23 GROUP RELIEF**);
- (viii) a disposal by or to a real estate investment trust (see **69.4 UNIT TRUSTS ETC.**);
- (ix) a disposal by one member of a group to another in fulfilment of its obligations under an option granted to that other member at a time when the two companies were not members of the same group; this applies where the option is exercised on or after 6 March 2007 (even if the option is granted before that date);
- (x) a disposal by or to an incorporated friendly society entitled to tax exemptions under *ICTA 1988, s 461B* (see **37.3** *et seq.* **FRIENDLY SOCIETIES**);
- (xi) a disposal by or to a venture capital trust (and see **29.8** below);
- (xii) a disposal on or after 16 March 2005 where *CTA 2009, s 524* (previously *FA 1996, s 91A* (certain shares subject to outstanding third party obligations — see **54.86 LOAN RELATIONSHIPS**)) does not apply to the asset in relation to the company making the disposal ('the vendor') immediately before the disposal but does apply in relation to the acquiring company ('the buyer') immediately after its acquisition, or where that section applies in relation to the vendor immediately before the disposal but not to the buyer immediately afterwards – note this provision repealed by *FA 2009, s 48*, with effect from 22 April 2009.

As regards (iv), the assets acquired in the capital distribution are nevertheless treated as transferred at a 'no gain, no loss' price (see *Innocent v Whaddon Estates Ltd* Ch D 1981, 55 TC 476). Where an exchange of securities for those in another company is, under *TCGA 1992, ss 127, 135*, not treated as involving a disposal of the original shares or the acquisition of a new holding, it is not treated as a 'no gain, no loss' transfer as above. [*TCGA 1992, s 171(3)*]. Where the consideration given for shares consists of qualifying corporate bonds, see Revenue Tax Bulletin December 1996 p 372 for an analysis of the consequences.

Where it is assumed, for any purpose, that a group member has acquired or sold an asset, it is also assumed that it was not prima facie a sale to, or acquisition from, a group member. [*TCGA 1992, s 171(1) as originally enacted; TCGA 1992, s 171(6) as introduced by FA 2000, Sch 29 para 2(5)*].

HMRC have indicated that they will not seek to apply the '*Ramsay* principle' (see **5.1 ANTI-AVOIDANCE**) where straightforward transfers of assets between members of the same group enable asset sales to be routed through group members with allowable capital losses. Where the effect of a series of transactions is to transfer the benefit of capital losses from one group to another, the *Ramsay* principle may be applicable, depending on the relationship between the amounts of the loss involved, the period for which the company with the loss has been within the group and on the circumstances in which the losses have arisen.

Simon's Taxes. See **D2.314–D2.317**.

Election for deemed intra-group transfers

[18.6] A joint election may be made under *TCGA 1992, s 171A* which allows a gain or loss arising to one group company to be transferred to another group company. This allows the group to utilise capital losses and also to ensure gains are taxed at the lowest marginal rate. This election can only be made if the no gain, no loss transfer rules would apply between the two companies which make the election.

Prior to *FA 2009* (for disposals prior to 21 July 2009) an election under *s 171A* resulted in a notional transfer within the group of an asset, or part of it, prior to the subsequent third party disposal. However this was considered inflexible, not least as the relief was only available in respect of actual disposals to third parties, and amendments were made to the rule in *FA 2009*.

Post-FA 2009 position

Where two companies ('X' and 'Y') are members of a group, and X disposes of an asset to a person outside the group, on or after 21 July 2009, the chargeable gain or allowable loss, or such part of it as is specified, may be treated as accruing to Y rather then X at the date of the actual disposal. A joint election must be made and it must be shown that had an actual disposal from X to Y taken place before the disposal to the outside party it would have been a no gain no loss disposal under *TCGA 1992, s 171*.

The election must be made in writing to an officer of HMRC within two years after the end of the accounting period of X in which the actual disposal was made. If Y is not UK resident for tax purposes, it is regarded as having owned a chargeable asset in respect of which the gain or loss arose. Any payment between X and Y in respect of the transfer is ignored for tax purposes, unless it exceeds the chargeable gain or allowable loss.

There is an anti-avoidance provision to ensure that, by using two or more elections, relief is not obtained for more than the actual gain or loss.

These provisions do not apply in a de-grouping situation prior to 19 July 2011 (*FA 2011*). Following 19 July 2011, *TCGA 1992, s 171A(7)* is repealed and these provisions can apply to a degrouping situation. If an early commencement election is made under *FA 2011, Sch 10, para 9*, the repeal of *TCGA 1992, s 171A(7)* is treated as being effective from 1 April 2011. This is part of the wider simplification of the degrouping charge (see **29.1**).

Pre-FA 2009 position

For disposals to a third party before 21 July 2009, where two companies, X and Y, are members of a group, and X disposes of an asset to a person outside the group, X and Y and may jointly elect to the effect that, for the purposes of corporation tax on chargeable gains:

(a) the asset (or a specified part of it) is deemed to have been transferred by X to Y immediately before the actual disposal;
(b) that transfer is deemed to be a no gain, no loss disposal within *TCGA 1992, s 171* (see **18.2** above);
(c) the actual disposal (or the part of it to which the election relates) is deemed to have been made by Y; and
(d) X's actual incidental disposal costs are deemed to be such costs to Y of making the deemed disposal.

The election must be made in writing to an officer of HMRC within two years after the end of the accounting period of X in which the actual disposal was made. It can only be made if an actual transfer of the asset (or part) from X to Y would have been a no gain, no loss disposal within *s 171* (although, in relation to disposals on or after 23 December 2002, this does not apply where Y is an insurance company and *s 171* is precluded from applying by *ICTA 1988, s 440(3)*, the asset (or part) involved then being treated for these purposes as not being part of Y's long-term insurance fund).

Any payment agreed between X and Y in connection with the election is ignored in computing profits or losses for corporation tax purposes, and is not regarded as a distribution or (for payments before 16 March 2005) a charge on income (see **61.11 PROFIT COMPUTATIONS**), provided that it does not exceed the amount of the chargeable gain or allowable loss treated, as a result of the disposal, as accruing to Y.

For disposals on or after 16 March 2005, where Y is not resident in the UK but is carrying on a trade in the UK through a permanent establishment there, the asset deemed to be transferred by X to Y is treated for the purposes of these provisions as having been acquired by Y for use by or for the purposes of the permanent establishment (so that, if the asset is situated in the UK, the deemed transfer is a no gain/no loss disposal and the deemed disposal by Y is a deemed disposal of a chargeable asset). This treatment is not taken to affect the question of whether the asset or part is situated in the UK.

This provision is intended to facilitate the bringing together of chargeable gains and allowable losses within one group company.

[*TCGA 1992, s 171A; FA 2001, s 77; FA 2003, Sch 33 para 17; F(No 2)A 2005, s 36, Sch 11 Pt 2(7); FA 2009 s 31, Sch 12*].

Simon's Taxes. See **D2.329**.

Appropriation to or from trading stock

[18.7] Companies may transfer assets between group members which were not held as trading stock in one company, but will be so held by the other company (and vice versa). Provisions are in place to prevent such transfers from happening without giving rise to an appropriate chargeable gain, or trading profits or loss (as applicable), when the intra-group transfer occurs.

Thus, where a company ('company A') acquires an asset as trading stock of a trade from another member of the group ('company B'), and the asset did not form part of the trading stock of a trade carried on by company B, company A is treated as acquiring the asset otherwise than as trading stock and immediately appropriating it as trading stock (for the purposes of *TCGA 1992, s 161* or *Sch 7AC para 36*).

The effect is that, subject to an election being made under *s 161(3)*, a chargeable gain or allowable loss accrues to company A based on the difference between market value and the no gain, no loss transfer value (which applies to the transfer of the asset from B to A, before A then appropriates the asset to stock) (see **18.4** above).

Similarly, where a company ('company C') disposes of an asset forming part of the trading stock of a trade to another member of the group ('company D'), and the asset is acquired by company D otherwise than as trading stock of a trade carried on by it, company C is treated as appropriating the asset immediately before the disposal for a purpose other than use as trading stock (for the purposes of *TCGA 1992, s 161* or *Sch 7AC para 36*).

The effect is that company C is treated as making a disposal from trading stock at market value prior to the transfer and is then deemed to have acquired the asset (for capital gains purposes) at that time at the amount brought into the accounts of the trade for tax purposes on the deemed appropriation. Company D will then receive the asset at that market value, and indexation will run from the date the property is transferred.

Although a non-UK resident company can be a member of a group (see **18.2** above), references above to a trade do not include a trade carried on by a non-UK resident company unless it is carried on in the UK through a permanent establishment (see **65.6 RESIDENCE**).

[*TCGA 1992, s 173*].

Acquisition 'as trading stock' implies a commercial justification for the acquisition, see *Coates v Arndale Properties Ltd* (1984) 59 TC 516, HL, *Reed v Nova Securities Ltd* (1985) 59 TC 516, HL, *N Ltd v Inspector of Taxes* [1996] STC (SCD) 346 and *Property Dealing Company v Inspector of Taxes* [2003] STC (SCD) 233.

Simon's Taxes. See D2.313.

Rollover relief

[18.8] Rollover relief on the *replacement of business assets* is granted under *TCGA 1992, ss 152–158* (see Tolley's Capital Gains Tax under Rollover Relief) is extended to groups such that a gain made by one company can be rolled over into the purchase of an appropriate asset by another group company.

With regard to the requirements for the application of rollover relief and groups:

(i) all the trades carried on by group members are treated as a single trade (except as regards intra-group transfers);

(ii) *TCGA 1992, s 154* (special rules for depreciating assets) applies as if all group members were the same person.

A disposal by a company when it is a member of a group, and an acquisition by another company when it is a member of the same group, are treated as made by the same person.

Claims to relief must be made by both companies concerned. It is not necessary for the companies making the disposal and acquisition to be members of the group throughout the period between the transactions, as long as each is a member at the time of its own transaction.

Where a non-trading group member disposes of or acquires assets used only for the trades within (i) above (ie. trades of other group members), relief is given as if it were carrying on a trade.

The relief is not available in respect of consideration applied in the acquisition of new assets by a 'dual resident investing company' (see **39.23 GROUP RELIEF**). See also **17.48 CAPITAL GAINS** as regards other dual resident companies.

Relief is also denied where the acquisition of the new asset is one to which any of the no gain/no loss provisions applies (for disposals before 6 April 2008 reference was to the no gain/ no loss provisions found in *TCGA 1992, s 35(3)(d)* — generally this is to prevent rollover relief where the new asset has been acquired from another group member) or where the new asset is a chargeable intangible asset.

In determining whether a company is a member of a group for the these purposes with regard to either the acquisition or the disposal (or both), see **18.2** above.

However, the reference above to 'trade' does not include a trade carried on by a non-UK resident company otherwise than through a permanent establishment in the UK (see **65.6 RESIDENCE**). Where either the acquisition or the disposal (but not both) was before 1 April 2000, this applies also to that acquisition or disposal.

Where the disposal or the acquisition, or both, occur on or after 1 April 2000 and are made by different group companies:

(i) either the company making the disposal must be UK resident at the time of the disposal or the assets must be 'chargeable assets' (see **18.4** above) in relation to that company immediately before that time; and
(ii) either the company making the acquisition must be UK resident at the time of the acquisition or the assets must be chargeable assets in relation to that company immediately after that time.

Compulsory acquisitions of land

[18.9] For the purposes of the rollover relief under *TCGA 1992, s 247* (see Tolley's Capital Gains Tax under Land), a disposal by a company when it is a member of a group, and an acquisition by another company when it is a member of the same group, are treated as made by the same person, provided that relief is claimed by both companies. Relief is, however, denied where the acquisition of the new land is one to which any of the no gain/no loss provisions applies.

[*TCGA 1992, ss 175, 247(5A); CTA 2009, Sch 1 para 372*].

Where (i) above applies in a case where one member of a group makes the disposal and a second the acquisition, it may happen that the disposal takes place after the first company has ceased to trade, or the acquisition takes place before the second company commences trading. Relief will then be restricted in respect of the period during which the assets disposed of were not used for business purposes, and will be conditional on the replacement assets not being used or leased for any purpose prior to the second company's commencing trading, and being taken into use for the purposes of the trade on its commencement. (HMRC Statement of Practice, SP 8/81).

For the *interaction of rollover relief with the exemption for substantial shareholdings*, see **19.19 CAPITAL GAINS — SUBSTANTIAL SHAREHOLDINGS**. For the *transitory interaction with relief on reinvestment in fixed intangible assets*, see *CTA 2009, FA 2002, Sch 29 para 132* (as amended by *F(No 2)A 2005, s 41(4)(1)*).

Simon's Taxes. See **D2.340, D2.341.**

Assets held on 31 March 1982

[18.10] See Tolley's Capital Gains Tax under Assets held on 31 March 1982 for details of these provisions generally, and in particular for the election under *TCGA 1992, s 35(5)* for all disposals by a person after 5 April 1988 of assets held on 31 March 1982 to be subject to the general re-basing rule of *TCGA 1992, s 35(1)(2)*. This election is subject to the following special provisions in relation to groups of companies.

Election by principal company

No group member other than the 'principal company' of a group (for which see *TCGA 1992, s 170* as in **18.2** above) may make an election under *TCGA 1992, s 35(5)* unless the company did not become a group member until after the 'relevant time'.

An election by the principal company does, however, have effect as an election by any other company which is a group member at the 'relevant time', except that this does not apply to a company which, in some period after 5 April 1988 and before the 'relevant time', makes a disposal, at a time when it is not a group member, of an asset held on 31 March 1982, and does not itself make the election within the prescribed time limit.

The time limit for the making of the election by the principal company is two years (or such longer time as HMRC may allow) from the end of the accounting period in which occurs the first disposal after 5 April 1988 of an asset held on 31 March 1982 by a company which is a group member (other than an 'outgoing company' in relation to the group) or which is an 'incoming company' in relation to the group.

See, however, HMRC Statement of Practice, SP 4/92 as regards certain disposals which are ignored for this purpose. See HMRC Capital Gains Manual, CG46374 for the circumstances in which a late election may be accepted.

An election by the principal company of a group continues to apply to a company leaving the group after the 'relevant time', unless it is an 'outgoing company' in relation to the group and the principal company election is made after it ceases to be a group member.

The '*relevant time*' is the earliest of:

(i) the first time when a group member (other than an 'outgoing company' in relation to the group) makes a disposal after 5 April 1988 of an asset held on 31 March 1982;
(ii) the time immediately after the first occasion on which an 'incoming company' in relation to the group becomes a group member; and
(iii) the time when the principal company makes the election.

An '*outgoing company*', in relation to a group, is a company which ceases to be a group member before the end of the period during which an election could be made which would apply to it, and at a time when no such election has been made.

An '*incoming company*', in relation to a group, is a company which makes its first disposal after 5 April 1988 of an asset held on 31 March 1982 at a time when it is not a group member, and which becomes a group member before the expiry of the time limit for making an election which would apply to it without that election having been made.

In relation to a determination as to whether a company is a member, or the principal member, of a group, see **18.2** above.

[*TCGA 1992, s 35(5), Sch 3 paras 8, 9; FA 2000, Sch 29 para 38*].

Collection of unpaid tax from group members and directors

[18.11] Where a chargeable gain accrues to a company (the 'taxpayer company') and either:

(i) that company is UK resident at the time the gain accrues; or
(ii) the gain is within the charge to corporation tax by virtue of *TCGA 1992, s 10B* (non-UK resident company trading in the UK through a permanent establishment — see **65.6 RESIDENCE**),

the following rules apply where all or part of the corporation tax assessed on the taxpayer company for the accounting period in which the gain accrues remains unpaid six months after it became payable.

HMRC may serve on any of the following persons a notice requiring that person to pay, within 30 days, the unpaid tax or, if less, an amount equal to corporation tax on the chargeable gain at the rate in force when the gain accrued:

(a) if the taxpayer company was a member of a 'group' at the time when the gain accrued, the 'principal company' of the 'group' at that time and any other company which was, at any time in the twelve months before the gain accrued, a member of the same 'group' and owned the asset disposed of, or any part of it, or where that asset is an interest or right in or over another asset, owned either asset or any part of either asset;
(b) if the gain forms part of the chargeable profits of the taxpayer company for corporation tax purposes by virtue of *TCGA 1992, s 10(3)* (see (ii) above), any person who is, or during the twelve months before the gain accrued was, a 'controlling director' of the taxpayer company or of a company which has, or within that twelve-month period had, 'control' over the taxpayer company.

For the purpose of (a) above, '*group*' and '*principal company*' are as defined as in **18.2** above but as if references there to 75% subsidiaries were to 51% subsidiaries. In determining whether a company is a member of a group at any time in the twelve-month period referred to in (a) and (b) above, see **18.2** above. As regards (b) above, '*control*' is as under *CTA 2010, ss 450, 451* (previously *ICTA 1988, s 416* — see **22.6 CLOSE COMPANIES**), and a '*controlling director*' is a 'director' (within the extended meaning under the employment income benefits legislation and *CTA 2010, s 452(1)* (previously *ICTA 1988, s 417(5)(6)* — see **22.8 CLOSE COMPANIES**) with such control.

The notice must state the amount of tax assessed, the original due date and the amount required from the person on whom it is served. It has effect, as regards collection, interest and appeals, as if it were a notice of assessment on that person. The notice must be served within three years beginning with the date on which the liability of the taxpayer company for the accounting period in question was finally determined (including a determination under *FA 1998, Sch 18 para 36* or *37* in the absence of a full return, see **66.27 RETURNS**). In the case of a self-assessed liability, including one superseding a determination, the date of determination of the liability is taken as the last date on which notice of an enquiry into the return may be given (see **66.19 RETURNS**), or, if such notice is given, 30 days after the action which concludes the enquiry process. In the case of a discovery assessment (see **7.3 ASSESSMENTS**), it is the due and payable date or (if there is an appeal against the assessment) the date the appeal is finally determined.

A person paying an amount under these provisions may recover it from the taxpayer company, but such an amount is not deductible for any tax purpose.

[*TCGA 1992, s 190; FA 2000, Sch 29 para 9; FA 2003, Sch 27 para 2(3); CTA 2010, Sch 1 para 246*].

See also **65.6 RESIDENCE** as regards tax unpaid by non-resident companies.

Simon's Taxes. See D2.345.

Depreciatory transactions

[18.12] Where two or more group companies are parties to a disposal of assets at other than market value, and such a disposal **materially reduces the value of the shares or securities of one of those companies** (a '*depreciatory transaction*'), any loss arising on the ultimate disposal of those shares by a member or former member of the group (having been a member when the transaction took place) is to be allowable only so far as is 'just and reasonable'.

This applied where the depreciatory transaction was after 31 March 1982 (or 6 April 1965 if the 31 March 1982 market value is not substituted for cost under *TCGA 1992, s 35(2)*). Following *FA 2011*, the depreciatory transaction must now be within the period of 6 years ending with the disposal.

Account may be taken of any other transaction which may have:

(i) enhanced the value of the assets of the company the shares in which are being disposed of; *and*
(ii) depreciated the value of the assets of any other member of the group.

The restriction is applied to the allowable loss after indexation, rather than to the unindexed loss before indexation (*Tesco plc v Crimmin* (1997) 69 TC 510), and in arriving at the amount by which it was 'just and reasonable' to reduce the allowable loss, indexation should be applied to the value of the depreciatory transaction(s) from the date(s) of the transaction(s) to the date of the ultimate disposal (*Whitehall Electric Investments Ltd v Owen* [2002] STC (SCD) 229). See, however, **17.50 CAPITAL GAINS** as regards prohibition on indexation allowance creating or enhancing a loss.

Where such a reduction is made, any chargeable gain accruing on the disposal within six years of the transaction of the shares etc. in any other party thereto is to be reduced as is 'just and reasonable' (but not so as to exceed the reduction in the allowable loss). Regard may also be had to the effect of the depreciatory transaction on the value of the shares at the date of disposal.

A 'depreciatory transaction' also includes any other transaction where:

(a) the company, the shares or securities in which are the subject of the ultimate disposal, or any 75% subsidiary of that company, was party to that transaction; and
(b) the parties to the transaction were, or included, two or more companies which, when the transaction occurred, were in the same group.

A transaction is not depreciatory to the extent that it is a payment which is brought into account in computing a chargeable gain or allowable loss of the company making the ultimate disposal. Cancellation within *Companies Act 2006, s 641* of shares or securities of one group member which are owned by another is deemed to be a depreciatory transaction unless it falls within this exemption.

Claims under *TCGA 1992, s 24(2)* that shares or securities have become of negligible value also come within this section.

References to the disposal of assets include appropriation by one member of a group of the goodwill of another.

'*Securities*' includes loan stock or similar securities, whether secured or unsecured.

'*Group of companies*' includes non-resident companies (before, on and after 1 April 2000, see **18.2** above).

[*TCGA 1992, s 176; FA 2000, Sch 29 para 24; FA 2011, Sch 9 para 3*].

As regards distributions out of post-acquisition profits, see HMRC Capital Gains Manual, CG46580 *et seq*.

Simon's Taxes. See D2.350.

Distributions as depreciatory transactions

[18.13] The restriction on capital losses because of 'depreciatory transactions' (see **17.44** above) also applies where a 'first company' has a holding in a 'second company' which amounts (with or without the addition of holdings by **CONNECTED PERSONS** (**25**)) to 10% of all the holdings of the same class in the second company (and the first company is not a dealing company in relation to the holding) and a distribution is, or has been, made in respect of the holding which materially reduces the value of the holding. Distributions brought into account in computing a chargeable gain or allowable loss accruing to the ultimate disponor are ignored. [*TCGA 1992, s 177; FA 2000, Sch 29 para 25*].

Simon's Taxes. See D2.352.

Key points

[18.14] Points to consider are as follows.

- When assessing the position of a chargeable gains group, the status of overseas entities can be important. In particular, consider whether such entities are likely to be respected as companies and whether ownership interests in those entities will be treated as ordinary share capital.
- Bear in mind the priority rules where transactions have more than one potential interpretation. For example, a reorganisation under *TCGA 1992, s 135* will take priority over the no-gain/no-loss rules in *s 171*.
- If reliance is to be placed on relief under *TCGA 1992, s 171A*, ensure that an election is made on time.
- Where a company is to rely upon the use of losses, ensure that the losses have been identified and their availability for use analysed before they are needed.

- Where anti-avoidance provisions are potentially in point (for example in relation to capital losses), the taxpayer should consider taking advice to limit potential penalties under the new penalties regime.
- If roll-over relief is to be claimed on the replacement of business assets, ensure that the transactions take place within the time scales required by the legislation and claims are submitted by the parties on time.
- Consider the potential for secondary chargeable gains liabilities. It may be prudent to consider the need for indemnities if external investors are involved or all or part of a business is to be sold.

19

Capital Gains — Substantial Shareholdings

Simon's Taxes. See D1.10.

Introduction

[19.1] With the introduction of the substantial shareholding exemption ('SSE') from capital gains in 2002, share sales have become more popular, as they can provide a tax efficient means of disposal and also of reorganisation. At a basic level, the provisions of *TCGA 1992, Sch 7AC* allow a gain on a disposal by a company of shares to be exempt for capital gains tax purposes (with the corresponding proviso that any loss is not allowable).

This exemption applies where the gain arises from the disposal of shares and throughout a continuous twelve-month period beginning not more than two years before the disposal, the company (the '*investing company*') held a '*substantial shareholding*' (broadly, at least a 10% interest) in the company (the '*investee company*') whose shares are the subject of the disposal. There is no requirement for the proceeds of the sale of the shareholding to be used in any particular way.

The exemption extends to assets 'related to shares' (as in **19.5** below).

The provisions within *Sch 7AC* are very prescriptive and therefore care should be taken with regard to the various conditions and requirements which need to be satisfied in order to obtain the exemption, in respect of both the investing and the investee company.

For example, the investing company must be a trading company or a member of a trading group and the investee company must be a trading company or the holding company of a trading group (or subgroup). Details of what it means to be 'trading' are found at **19.11** below.

This chapter thus outlines the details of the conditions and requirements for the SSE to apply, and provides an overview of the interaction between this exemption and other provisions within the chargeable gains legislation.

[*TCGA 1992, s 192A, Sch 7AC*].

See generally HMRC Capital Gains Manual, CG53000–53240.

Application of the exemptions under the SSE

[19.2] It should first be noted that where the disposal does not give rise to a chargeable gain (or an allowable loss) by virtue of some other enactment, then the exemptions described in this chapter are of no application.

Neither do they apply to a disposal which, by virtue of any chargeable gains enactment, is a 'no gain/no loss' disposal.

[*TCGA 1992, Sch 7AC para 6(1)*].

Definition of company and group

[19.3] For the purposes of the SSE provisions, a '*company*' is as defined at **18.2 CAPITAL GAINS — GROUPS**.

A '*group of companies*' is also as defined at **18.2** but as if each reference there to '75%' were a reference to '51%'. Thus, subject to the detailed rules there, a '*group*' comprises a company and its 'effective 51% subsidiaries' (within *CTA 2010, s 1154; ICTA 1988, s 838*), and may include non-UK resident companies.

A '*holding company*' of a group is the principal company of the group (within the meaning given in **18.2**).

A '*subgroup*' is a number of companies that *would* form a group were it not for the fact that one of them (the '*holding company*' of the subgroup) is itself a 51% subsidiary.

Shares held by members of a worldwide group are aggregated in determining whether a company holds a substantial shareholding — see further **19.8** below.

[*TCGA 1992, Sch 7AC para 26; FA 2002, Sch 8 para 1*].

The exemptions

Exemptions for shares — the main SSE

[19.4] A gain accruing to a company (the '*investing company*') on a disposal of shares (or an 'interest in shares' — see **19.21** below) in another company (the '*investee company*') is not a chargeable gain if:

(a) the investing company held a 'substantial shareholding' (see **19.8** below) in the investee company throughout any continuous period of twelve months beginning not more than two years prior to the disposal (see **19.9** below);
(b) the investing company meets the requirements at **19.10** below; and
(c) the requirements at **19.12** below are met in relation to the investee company.

See also the anti-avoidance rule at **19.7** below.

[*TCGA 1992, Sch 7AC paras 1, 7, 28*].

By virtue of *TCGA 1992, s 16(2)* (see **17.3 CAPITAL GAINS**), a loss on a disposal is not an allowable loss if a gain on that disposal would not have been a chargeable gain.

The nature of the condition at (a) above is such that part disposals out of a once-substantial shareholding can continue to attract the exemption for up to a year after the shareholding has ceased to be substantial (i.e. has dropped below the 10% threshold).

The exemption is available even where the shares disposed of are not the shares that meet the substantial shareholding requirement at (a) above. If (a) above is met in relation to ordinary shares (and (b) and (c) are also met), a disposal of a holding of, say, fixed-rate preference shares in the investee company will qualify for the exemption, irrespective of the size and duration of that holding. (HMRC Capital Gains Manual, CG53155).

The exemption is automatic and does not require the making of a claim.

Exemption for assets related to shares

[19.5] *Schedule 7AC para* 2 includes a subsidiary exemption, which allows the SSE to be extended to cover assets which are 'related to shares', such as share options or convertible securities, where the main exemption conditions are met.

A gain accruing to a company (company A) on a disposal of an asset 'related to shares' in another company (company B) is not a chargeable gain (and a loss is not an allowable loss) if:

(i) at the time of the disposal, company A holds shares (or an 'interest in shares' — see **19.21** below) in company B; and
(ii) any gain on a disposal at that time of those shares (or that interest) would be exempt under **19.4** above (disregarding **19.2** above).

This exemption also applies where:

(a) the shares etc. are held not by company A itself but by another member of a group of companies (see **19.3** above) of which company A is a member; and
(b) any gain on a disposal at that time of those shares etc., on the assumption that they were held by company A, would be exempt under **19.4** above (disregarding **19.2** above).

Where assets of a company are vested in a liquidator, the above applies as if they were vested in the company and as if the acts of the liquidator were the acts of the company (disposals by the company to the liquidator, and *vice versa*, being disregarded).

See also the anti-avoidance rule at **19.7** below.

[*TCGA 1992, Sch 7AC paras 2, 6(2)*].

The exemption is automatic and does not require the making of a claim.

For this purpose, an asset is '*related to shares*' in a company if it is:

(1) an option to acquire or dispose of shares (or an 'interest in shares' — see **19.21** below) in that company; or
(2) (broadly) a security that is convertible or exchangeable into shares (or an interest in shares) in that company, or into an option within (1) above, or into another security within this definition; or
(3) an option to acquire or dispose of a security within (2) above (or an interest in any such security); or
(4) an interest in, or option over, any option or security within (1)–(3) above; or
(5) an interest in, or option over, any interest or option within (4) above (or an interest in, or option over, any interest or option within this sub-paragraph).

As regards (2) above, a convertible or exchangeable security is not an asset related to shares if, when the conversion etc. rights were granted, there was no more than a negligible likelihood that they would be exercised to any significant extent. It is therefore not possible to bring a security within the scope of the exemption by attaching some spurious or extremely remote rights to convertibility in the event of some unlikely occurrence. (HMRC Capital Gains Manual, CG53010).

Certain securities, options etc. are outside the scope of corporation tax on chargeable gains, and thus outside the exemptions in this chapter, due to their falling within the special **LOAN RELATIONSHIPS (54)** or **DERIVATIVE CONTRACTS LEGISLATION (30)** rules. (HMRC Capital Gains Manual, CG53010).

An '*interest*' in a security or option has a similar meaning to an 'interest in shares' at **19.21** below.

[*TCGA 1992, Sch 7AC para 30; FA 2002, Sch 8 para 1*].

Exemption where main conditions previously met

[19.6] A further possibility of exemption is provided under *Sch 7AC para 3* where the exemption at either **19.4** or **19.5** above does not apply because some of the conditions were not satisfied at the time of the disposal even though they had been satisfied at a time in the two years immediately preceding the disposal.

If the conditions at either **19.4** or **19.5** above are not fully met (with the result that a chargeable gain or allowable loss would arise on the disposal), then a gain accruing to a company (company A) on a disposal of shares (or an interest in shares — see **19.21** below), or an asset 'related to shares' (see **19.5** above), in another company (company B) is still not a chargeable gain (and a loss is not an allowable loss) where *all* of the following conditions *are* met:

(a) At the time of disposal, company A had held a 'substantial shareholding' (see **19.8** below) in company B throughout any continuous period of twelve months beginning not more than two years prior to the disposal (see also **19.9** below).

(b) At the time of disposal, either company A is UK-resident or any chargeable gain accruing to it on the disposal would form part of its corporation tax profits by virtue of *TCGA 1992, s 10B* as amended by *CTA 2009, Sch 1 para 360* (trade carried on through UK permanent establishment — see **65.6 RESIDENCE**).

(c) There was a time within the two years ending with the disposal (the '*relevant period*') when a gain on a hypothetical disposal by:
    (i) company A; or
    (ii) a company that at any time in the relevant period was a member of the same group (see **19.3** above) as company A,

    being a disposal of shares (or an interest in shares) in company B that the disposing company then held, would have been exempt under **19.4** above (disregarding **19.2** above, and see also below).

(d) If, at the time of disposal, the requirements at **19.12** below as to the investee company are not met in relation to company B, there was a time within the relevant period (as defined at (c) above) when company B was controlled by:
    (i) company A; or
    (ii) company A together with any persons connected with it (within *TCGA 1992, s 286* — see **25.4 CONNECTED PERSONS**); or
    (iii) a company that at any time in the relevant period was a member of the same group (see **19.3** above) as company A; or
    (iv) any such company together with persons connected with it.

'Control' is to be construed in accordance with *CTA 2010, ss 450, 451 (previously ICTA 1988, s 416* — see **22.6 CLOSE COMPANIES**).

If the exemption at **19.4** or **19.5** above is not available for the *sole* reason that the investing company fails to meet the requirement at **19.10**(b) below (as to its trading company status immediately after the time of the disposal), this further possibility of exemption is available only if the failure to meet that requirement is due to the actual or imminent winding-up or dissolution of the investing company (provided that, in a case where this is imminent, it actually takes place as soon as is reasonably practicable in the circumstances).

For the purpose only of determining the 'relevant period' for the purposes of (c) or (d) above, the time of disposal is taken as the time the contract is made, notwithstanding that the contract may be conditional. In determining whether the gain on the hypothetical disposal in (c) above would have attracted the exemption at **19.4** above, the requirements at **19.10**(b) below and **19.12**(b) below as to the status of the investing and investee companies immediately after the time of disposal are taken to be satisfied.

See also the anti-avoidance rule at **19.7** below.

[*TCGA 1992, s 288(1), Sch 7AC paras 3(1)–(4)(7)(8), 6(2); F(No 2)A 2005, Sch 4 para 9; CTA 2010, Sch 1 para 264(2)(b)*].

Thus, for example, where the investee company ceases to trade on being put into liquidation, so that it can no longer meet the requirements at **19.12** below, disposals by the investing company (including capital distributions) can continue to attract the exemption for a further two years.

Anti-avoidance

It should be noted, however, that the above exemption also contains an anti-avoidance element in that if, for example, the investee company's trade is transferred elsewhere (within a group, for instance) and the conditions above are all met, a loss on a disposal by the investing company within the two years following the transfer will not be an allowable loss.

A further anti-avoidance measure applies as follows to prevent the exemption from applying to a gain (but not a loss) where value has been transferred into the investee company within the said two-year period and a claim made for gift relief. Otherwise it would be possible to put a valuable asset into a company, which had ceased trading, under the protection of a gift relief hold-over claim, then dispose of the shares and claim no chargeable gain arises under the SSE rules.

Thus, where the above exemption would otherwise apply but:

(1) immediately before the disposal by company A, company B holds an asset, and
(2) the allowable expenditure attributable to that asset has been reduced by a claim for gifts hold-over relief under *TCGA 1992, s 165* (see Tolley's Capital Gains Tax under Hold-Over Reliefs) on an earlier disposal of the asset within the relevant period (as defined above),

a gain on the disposal by company A does not attract the exemption *but* a loss on the disposal is not an allowable loss. (Where assets of company B are vested in a liquidator, (1) above applies as if they were vested in the company.)

[*TCGA 1992, Sch 7AC para 3(5)(6)*].

The exemption is automatic and does not require the making of a claim.

Example

Swallow Ltd acquired 1,500 shares in Summer Ltd in April 1998 Swallow Ltd holds no other investments in any company, has been a trading company throughout its existence, and is not a member of a group. Summer Ltd has 10,000 issued shares and has been a trading company since its formation. Swallow Ltd makes the following disposals of Summer Ltd shares.

31 May 2008	600 shares
30 April 2009	400 shares
30 June 2009	500 shares

The effect of the disposals for the purpose of corporation tax on chargeable gains is as follows.

31 May 2008 disposal

Swallow Ltd held at least 10% of the ordinary share capital of Summer Ltd throughout the two years prior to the disposal. The disposal is therefore part of a substantial shareholding and no chargeable gain or allowable loss arises on the disposal.

30 April 2009 disposal

Although Swallow did not hold at least 10% of the shares in Summer Ltd immediately before the disposal (the minimum holding being only 900 of 10,000 shares), there is a twelve-month period beginning within two years prior to the disposal throughout which it did hold at least 10%. The period is 1 June 2007 to 31 May 2008. Accordingly, the substantial shareholding exemption applies and no chargeable gain or allowable loss arises on the disposal.

30 June 2009 disposal

Swallow Ltd holds only 5% of the share capital of Summer Ltd immediately before the disposal. In the two year period prior to the disposal, from 1 July 2007 to 30 June 2009, the company held at least 10% of Summer Ltd's shares only from 1 July 2007 to 31 May 2008. This is not a continuous twelve-month period beginning two years prior to the disposal, and therefore the substantial shareholding exemption will not apply. A gain on the disposal of 500 shares will be a chargeable gain, and a loss an allowable loss.

General anti-avoidance

[19.7] *Schedule 7AC para 5* excludes the application of the SSE where arrangements have been put in place from which the sole or main benefit is obtaining the exemption from chargeable gains.

Therefore none of the exemptions in **19.4–19.6** above are available where:

(a) an 'untaxed' gain accrues to an investing company (Company A) on a disposal of shares (or an interest in shares, see **19.21** below), or an asset related to shares (see **19.5** above), in another company (Company B);

(b) before the accrual of that gain, either:

(i) Company A acquired control of Company B, or the same person(s) acquired control of both companies; or
(ii) there was a 'significant change of trading activities affecting Company B' at a time when it was controlled by Company A or when both companies were controlled by the same person(s); and

(c) these circumstances occur in pursuance of arrangements (including any scheme, agreement or understanding, whether or not legally enforceable) from which the sole or main benefit that could be expected is that the gain would be exempt under any of **19.4–19.6** above.

For the above purposes:

(A) a gain is '*untaxed*' if it (or all but an insubstantial part of it) represents profits that have not been brought into account (in the UK or elsewhere) for the purposes of tax on profits for a period ending on or before the date of the disposal. Profits in respect of which an amount is apportioned to a UK resident company under the **CONTROLLED FOREIGN COMPANIES (27)** rules are brought into account for this purpose. '*Profits*' means income or gains (whether or not realised);

(B) 'control' is to be construed in accordance with *CTA 2010, ss 450, 451* (previously *ICTA 1988, s 416* — see **22.6 CLOSE COMPANIES**); and

(C) there is a '*significant change of trading activities affecting Company B*' if:
(i) there is a 'major change in the nature or conduct of a trade' carried on by Company B or a '51% subsidiary' (within *CTA 2010, s 1154*; *ICTA 1988, s 838*) of Company B; or
(ii) there is a major change in the scale of the activities of a trade carried on by Company B or a 51% subsidiary; or
(iii) Company B or a 51% subsidiary begins to carry on a trade.

By virtue of *CTA 2010, Pt 14, s 672 et seq*; *ICTA 1988, s 768*, a '*major change in the nature or conduct of a trade*' includes a major change in the type of property dealt in or services or facilities provided, or in customers, outlets or markets. See **55.13 LOSSES**.

[*TCGA 1992, s 288(1), Sch 7AC para 5; CTA 2010, ss 450, 451*].

HMRC expect cases where this anti-avoidance rule is in point to be unusual and infrequent. It is a question of fact as to whether a gain wholly (or wholly but for an insubstantial part — interpreted by HMRC as 20% or less) represents untaxed profits; this involves looking at how the consideration obtained for the disposal by Company A is derived from assets held directly or indirectly by Company B. Profits are not 'untaxed' if they are simply covered by a specific relief or if they represent dividends which are themselves paid out of taxed profits. If a gain represents both taxed and untaxed profits, it should be taken as first representing taxed profits, with only any remaining balance representing untaxed profits. (HMRC Statement of Practice SP 5/02).

'Substantial shareholding' requirement

Meaning of substantial shareholding

[19.8] For the purposes of these provisions, a company holds a '*substantial shareholding*' in another company if it holds shares (or 'interests in shares' — see **19.21** below) in that company by virtue of which:

(a) it holds **at least 10%** of the company's ordinary share capital;
(b) it is beneficially entitled to at least 10% of the profits available for distribution to equity holders of the company; and
(c) it would be beneficially entitled on a winding-up to at least 10% of the assets of the company available for distribution to equity holders.

CTA 2010, Pt 5 Ch 6 (s 157 et seq), formerly *ICTA 1988, Sch 18* applies, with suitable modifications, to define an 'equity holder' and to determine the profits or assets available for distribution (see **39.4, GROUP RELIEF**).

[*TCGA 1992, Sch 7AC para 8*].

For the purposes of deciding whether the 'substantial shareholding' test is satisfied, holdings of shares (and interests in shares) by members of the same group of companies (which may be a worldwide group — see **19.3** above) are aggregated. [*TCGA 1992, Sch 7AC para 9(1)*].

When a company goes into liquidation it loses beneficial interest of its assets as a result of those assets being vested in the liquidator. However, the SSE rules protect an investing company from this outcome (as far as the SSE rules are concerned) so that it can continue to satisfy the necessary conditions for exemption.

Therefore where assets of the investing company, or of a member of the same group as the investing company, are vested in a liquidator, they are treated for the purposes of the substantial shareholding requirement (and those of **19.15**, **19.16** below) as if they were vested in the company and as if the acts of the liquidator were the acts of the company (disposals by the company to the liquidator, and *vice versa*, being disregarded). [*TCGA 1992, Sch 7AC para 16*].

Insurance companies

Special rules apply in relation to assets of long-term insurance funds where the investing company is an insurance company, or in certain cases a 51% subsidiary of an insurance company, or a member of the same group as an insurance company. [*TCGA 1992, Sch 7AC paras 9(2), 17*].

Holding period

[19.9] As stated at **19.4**(a) above, the investing company must have held a substantial shareholding in the investee company throughout a continuous period of twelve months beginning not more than two years prior to the disposal. Shares are treated as having been held for such a period if, for example, they were acquired at any time on 15 June 2002 and sold at any time on 14 June 2003; they do not have to be held on the anniversary of the acquisition. (HMRC Capital Gains Manual, CG53008).

With regard to the holding period, the following special rules apply.

No gain/no loss transfers

Where the investing company acquired any shares from another company by means of a 'no gain/no loss' transfer, i.e. under any chargeable gains enactment that states that a disposal is to be treated as made for such consideration that no gain or loss accrues, the period during which it is treated as holding those shares is extended to include the period during which the previous owner held them.

The period is further extended back through any series of no gain/no loss transfers by which the shares arrived in the hands of the present owner. The present owner is thus treated as having had the same entitlements, to shares and to any rights enjoyed by virtue of holding shares, as the company or companies by which they were held at any earlier time in the extended period.

These include any entitlements etc. arising from the aggregation rule for groups of companies in **19.8** above. These rules also cover 'interests in shares' (see **19.21** below), and the extension also covers any period during which the asset held by any of the previous companies concerned in the no gain/no loss series consisted of shares (or an interest in shares) from which the current shares (or interest) are 'derived'.

For the above purposes, any transfer which, by virtue of *TCGA 1992, s 171(3)*, is not treated as a no gain/no loss transfer (intra-group share exchanges, see **18.4 CAPITAL GAINS — GROUPS**), and which would otherwise have been so, is treated as if it had been a no gain/no loss transfer.

Shares (or interests in shares) are '*derived*' from other shares (or interests) only where:

(a) a company becomes co-owner of shares previously owned by it alone, or *vice versa*;
(b) a company's interest in shares as co-owner changes (but co-ownership continues);
(c) a shareholding is treated by virtue of *TCGA 1992, s 127* (including its application by virtue of another enactment) as the same asset as another shareholding; or
(d) there is a sequence of two or more of the above occurrences.

[*TCGA 1992, Sch 7AC para 10*].

Deemed disposals and reacquisitions

Where, under any corporation tax enactment, shares have been deemed to be disposed of and immediately reacquired by a company, the company is regarded as not having held the shares during any part of the holding period falling before the deemed disposal and reacquisition. This rule extends to 'interests in shares' (see **19.21** below) and to shares (or interests) from which the current shares (or interest) are 'derived' (as above).

[*TCGA 1992, Sch 7AC para 11*].

Sale and repurchase agreements (repos)

Where the company that holds shares transfers them under a repo (as defined), such that, by virtue of *FA 2007, Sch 13 para 6* or *TCGA 1992, s 263A* (see Tolley's Capital Gains Tax under Shares and Securities), the disposal falls to be disregarded, it is similarly disregarded for the purposes of the provisions in this chapter.

Thus, during the period covered by the repo, the ownership of the shares, and the entitlement to any rights attached to them, rests with the original owner and not the interim holder.

If, at any time during that period, the original owner, or a member of the same group as the original owner, becomes the *actual* holder of any of the shares transferred (or any shares directly or indirectly representing them), this rule ceases to have effect at that time in relation to the shares concerned.

[*TCGA 1992, Sch 7AC para 12; FA 2003, Sch 38 para 9; FA 2007, Sch 14 para 13*].

Stock lending arrangements

Rules identical to those above for repos apply where shares are transferred under a stock lending arrangement (as defined), such that, by virtue of *TCGA 1992, s 263B(2)* (see Tolley's Capital Gains Tax under Shares and Securities), the disposal falls to be disregarded. [*TCGA 1992, Sch 7AC para 13*].

FA 2009, Sch 13 — borrower becomes insolvent

With regard to stock lending arrangements, *FA 2009, Sch 13* applies where the borrower becomes insolvent on or after 24 November 2008, (or, by election, for insolvencies during the period from 1 September 2008 up to 23 November 2008), the securities cannot be returned, and the lender uses collateral to directly or indirectly acquire replacement securities within 30 days of the borrower's insolvency.

In these circumstances, the transaction is not treated as a disposal by the lender for capital gains purposes. The borrower is treated as acquiring the securities on the date of insolvency for their market value at that date. The general rule may not apply in an insolvency situation as the securities may not be available. The acquisition of replacement securities, using the collateral, is not treated as an acquisition for capital gains purpose by the lender.

However, if the number of replacement securities is less than the original number, the lender is treated as having disposed of the securities representing the difference. The consideration for the disposal is treated as nil, if all the collateral is used and where it is not all used, the difference between the market value of the number of securities which could have been acquired using the security and the market value of those acquired, both at their value at the date of insolvency. Any amount recovered by the lender in respect of these transactions is treated as a chargeable gain realised by the lender.

An election must cover all stock lending between a lender and borrower and must be made within two years of the end of the accounting period of the lender in which 23 November 2008 falls, and in any case no later than 31 January 2011.

Under *TCGA 1992, s 263B* transfers and re-transfers of securities under stock lending arrangements are disregarded for tax on capital gains purposes (see above).

[*TCGA 1992, ss 263B, 263CA; FA 2009, s 32, Sch 13*].

Requirements

To be met by investing company

[19.10] The requirements to be met by the investing company for the purposes of the exemption at **19.4** above are that:

(a) it must have been a sole 'trading company' (see **19.11** below) or a member of a 'qualifying group' (see below) throughout the period:
  (i) beginning with the start of the latest twelve-month period (within the two years prior to disposal) for which the substantial shareholding requirement (see **19.4**(a) above) was met; and
  (ii) ending with the time of the disposal; and

(b) it must be a sole 'trading company' or a member of a 'qualifying group' immediately after the time of the disposal.

A '*qualifying group*' is a 'trading group' (see **19.11** below) or a group that would be a trading group if the activities of any group member not established for profit were disregarded to the extent that they are carried on otherwise than for profit. In determining whether a company is established for profit, any object or power which is merely incidental to the company's main objects is to be ignored.

The requirement at (a) above is met if the company was a sole trading company for part of the said period and a member of a qualifying group for the rest of it.

Where the disposal is made under a contract and, by virtue of *TCGA 1992, s 28* (see Tolley's Capital Gains Tax under Disposal), the time of disposal for tax purposes precedes the conveyance or transfer of the asset disposed of, the requirements at both (a) and (b) above must be met by reference to the time of conveyance or transfer as well the time of the disposal.

The requirement at (a) above is treated as met if, at the time of the disposal (and, where relevant, the time of the conveyance or transfer):

(1) the investing company is a member of a group (as in **19.3** above); and

(2) the requirement is not met by that company but would have been met by another group member if, immediately before the disposal, the subject matter of the disposal had been transferred to that member under the no gain/no loss provisions of *TCGA 1992, s 171* (see **18.4 CAPITAL GAINS — GROUPS**) and that member had then made the disposal.

[*TCGA 1992, Sch 7AC para 18*].

Trading company and trading group

[19.11] For the purposes of this chapter, a '*trading company*' is a company whose activities do not include to a 'substantial' extent activities other than 'trading activities'.

A '*trading group*' is a group (as in **19.3** above), one or more of whose members carry on 'trading activities' and the activities of whose members, taken together, do not include to a 'substantial' extent activities other than 'trading activities'.

'*Substantial*' in this connection is taken by HMRC to mean 'more than 20%'. (HMRC Capital Gains Manual, CG53116).

In relation to a single company, '*trading activities*' means 'activities' carried on by the company:

(a) in the course of, or for the purposes of, a 'trade' being carried on by it; or
(b) for the purposes of a 'trade' that it is preparing to carry on; or
(c) with a view to its acquiring or starting to carry on a trade; or
(d) with a view to its acquiring a 'significant interest' in the share capital of another company that is itself a trading company or the 'holding company' (as in **19.3** above) of a trading group or 'trading subgroup' (see **19.13** below) and that is not already a member of the same group as the acquiring company.

'*Activities*' is interpreted by HMRC to mean what a company does, so that the expression in itself includes engaging in trading activities, making and holding investments, planning, holding meetings and so on. (HMRC Capital Gains Manual, CG53113).

'*Trade*' means any trade, profession or vocation (within the meaning of the *Income Tax Acts*) conducted on a commercial basis with a view to profit. It also comprises the commercial letting of furnished holiday accommodation (see **62.2**(C) **PROPERTY INCOME**). Activities qualify under (c) or (d) above only if the acquisition is made, or the trade commenced, as soon as is reasonably practicable in the circumstances. A company acquires a '*significant interest*' (see (d) above) if it acquires sufficient ordinary share capital in the other company to make that company its '51% subsidiary' within *ICTA 1988, s 838*, or to give the acquiring company a 'qualifying shareholding' in a 'joint venture company' (see **19.17** below) without making the two companies members of the same group.

In relation to a group, '*trading activities*' means activities carried on by a member of the group, being activities that would fall within (a)–(d) above if these were interpreted by reference not only to that member but also to any other member of the group. The activities of group members are regarded as a single business, so that intra-group activities are disregarded for the purposes of determining whether the group is a trading group. Thus, for example, where one group company lets a property to another group company, the letting activity would be disregarded for this purpose.

A group member acquires a '*significant interest*' (see (d) above) if it acquires sufficient ordinary share capital in the other company to make that company a member of the same group as the acquiring company, or to give the acquiring company a 'qualifying shareholding' in a 'joint venture company'.

[*TCGA 1992, Sch 7AC paras 20, 21, 26(4), 27; FA 2002, Sch 8 paras 1, 3*].

Many of the expressions used above are considered further in the HMRC Capital Gains Manual, CG53110 to CG53119. A company could, prior to 19 July 2006, ask its tax district to give a view on its status for the above purposes under Code of Practice 10, but any opinion expressed is subject to revision to the extent that it relates to a time for which the full facts are not yet available. (HMRC Capital Gains Manual, CG53120 and HMRC Tax Bulletin August 2006 p 1308).

See **19.17** below as regards the treatment of holdings in joint venture companies.

Relating to investee company

[19.12] The requirements to be met in relation to the investee company for the purposes of the exemption at **19.4** above are that:

(a) it must have been a 'qualifying company' (see below) throughout the period:
   (i) beginning with the start of the latest twelve-month period (within the two years prior to disposal) for which the substantial shareholding requirement (see **19.4**(a) above) was met; and
   (ii) ending with the time of the disposal; and

(b) it must be a 'qualifying company' immediately after the time of the disposal.

A '*qualifying company*' is a 'trading company' (see **19.11** above) or the 'holding company' (as in **19.3** above) of a 'trading group' (see **19.11** above) or 'trading subgroup' (see **19.13** below).

Where the disposal is made under a contract and, by virtue of *TCGA 1992, s 28* (see Tolley's Capital Gains Tax under Disposal), the time of disposal for tax purposes precedes the conveyance or transfer of the asset disposed of, the requirements at both (a) and (b) above must be met by reference to the time of the conveyance or transfer as well as the time of the disposal.

See also the position outlined at **19.6** with regard to the subsidiary exemptions where the condition at (b) above is not satisfied.

[*TCGA 1992, Sch 7AC para 19*].

[19.13] For the purposes of this chapter, a '*trading subgroup*' is a 'subgroup' (as in **19.3** above), one or more of whose members carries on 'trading activities' and the activities of whose members, taken together, do not include to a 'substantial' extent (see **19.11** above) activities other than 'trading activities'.

'*Trading activities*' are defined in relation to a subgroup as they are in relation to a group (for which see **19.11** above), with the appropriate modifications. [*TCGA 1992, Sch 7AC para 22*]. Thus intra-subgroup activities are disregarded in the same way as intra-group activities when determining whether there is a 'trading subgroup'. However, intra-group activities between a member of a subgroup and another group company that is not within the subgroup are not disregarded in considering the status of the subgroup.

See **19.17** below as regards the treatment of holdings in joint venture companies.

Share reorganisations etc.

Treatment of certain events as disposals

[19.14] Without the special rules below, the exemptions at **19.4–19.6** above would be of no relevance to any of the following events (in relation to shares held by the investing company in the investee company).

(a) A reorganisation of share capital, company take-over/reconstruction or conversion of securities which, by virtue of *TCGA 1992, s 127*, does not constitute a disposal (see Tolley's Capital Gains Tax under Shares and Securities), the 'new holding' standing in the shoes of the original shares.

(b) An event which would have been within (a) above but for the fact that the 'new asset' consists of a qualifying corporate bond and which, by virtue of *TCGA 1992, s 116(10)* (see Tolley's Capital Gains Tax under Qualifying Corporate Bonds), is not treated as a disposal.

(c) A tax-exempt distribution on a demerger which, by virtue of *TCGA 1992, s 192* (see **31.31 GROUP RELIEF**), does not constitute a capital distribution.

To the extent that a gain would thereby be exempt (or a loss non-allowable) under **19.4–19.6** above, the enactment mentioned in (a), (b) or (c) above, whichever is relevant, is disapplied, so that an event in (a) or (b) is treated as a disposal, a distribution in (c) is treated as a capital distribution and the new shares or securities are normally treated as acquired at market value. This disapplication does not, however, have effect if the result would be a withdrawal or reduction (under *FA 2000, Sch 15 para 46*) of investment relief under the **CORPORATE VENTURING SCHEME** (**28.11**). Where it does have effect, the provisions at **28.24 CORPORATE VENTURING SCHEME**, where relevant, are modified accordingly.

[*TCGA 1992, Sch 7AC para 4*].

Example

A Ltd owns 35% of B Ltd. Both are trading companies. X plc intends to take over B Ltd; X plc offers all the shareholders in B Ltd three X plc shares for each B Ltd share that they own. As a result of this offer A Ltd will receive 10,500 X plc shares which have a market value of £126,000. A Ltd acquired the B Ltd shares for £3,500 in January 1999. Following the share exchange there will be a total of 500,000 X plc shares in issue.

The take over above falls within the reorganisation provisions at *TCGA 1992, s 135* and thus *TCGA 1992, s 127* operates such that the shares in B Ltd will not be treated as being disposed of and the X plc shares will not be treated as being acquired — instead the B Ltd and X plc shares will be treated as the same asset with the X plc shares taking on the base cost of the B Ltd shares (of £3,500) and the original acquisition date (January 1999).

Thus A Ltd has a relief from tax at this point, which applies until such time the X plc shares are sold. However, if *TCGA 1992, ss 135/127* were disapplied, the disposal of the B Ltd shares would give rise to a chargeable gain, which would qualify for SSE under the exemptions at **19.4–19.6** above.

Therefore pursuant to *TCGA 1992, Sch 7AC para 4*, the reorganisation provisions are not used and the disposal of the B Ltd shares is treated as giving rise to a chargeable gain, which is covered by the SSE. This means that A Ltd acquires the X plc shares on the day it receives them in exchange for the B Ltd shares, with a base cost of £126,000.

Effect of earlier company reconstruction etc.

[19.15] The following applies where:

(a) shares held by the investing company in the investee company were acquired as a result of either:
   (i) an exchange of securities within *TCGA 1992, s 135*; or
   (ii) a scheme of reconstruction within *TCGA 1992, s 136*; and

(b) *TCGA 1992, s 127* applied, such that the event was not treated as a disposal and the 'new holding' stood in the shoes of the original shares; and

(c) *TCGA 1992, s 127* did not fall to be disapplied by **19.14** above (because, for example, the conditions for the exemptions at **19.4–19.6** above were not satisfied or the event took place before 1 April 2002).

The question of whether, at any time *before* the event in (a)(i) or (ii) above, the substantial shareholding requirement at **19.8** above was met, or the requirements relating to the investee company at **19.12** above were met, is determined by reference to the shares held by the investing company at that time. This rule can apply more than once, i.e. where there has been more than one event within (a)(i) or (ii) above, and it can apply in combination with the rule at **19.16** below where there have been one or more transfers within that paragraph as well as one or more events within (a)(i) or (ii) above.

[*TCGA 1992, Sch 7AC paras 14, 25; FA 2002, Sch 8 para 1*].

Effect of earlier demerger

[19.16] The following applies where:

(a) shares held by the investing company in the investee company were acquired as a result of a transfer by a parent company of shares in its subsidiary; and

(b) the demerger provisions of *TCGA 1992, s 192* (see **31.31 GROUP RELIEF**) applied, such that the transfer was not treated as a capital distribution and the transferred shares in the subsidiary fell to be treated as received as a result of a reorganisation of share capital and thus (by virtue of *TCGA 1992, s 127*) as standing in the shoes of the shares previously held in the parent company.

The question of whether, at any time *before* the transfer, the substantial shareholding requirement at **19.8** above was met, or the requirements relating to the investee company at **19.12** above were met, is determined by reference to the shares held by the investing company at that time. This rule can apply more than once, i.e. where there has been more than one such transfer, and it can apply in combination with the rule at **19.15** above where there have been one or more events within that paragraph as well as one or more transfers within this paragraph.

[*TCGA 1992, Sch 7AC paras 15, 25*].

Treatment of holdings in joint venture companies

[19.17] The legislation sets out rules for disregarding and looking through shares where a company has a qualifying shareholding in a joint venture company, as detailed below.

For the following purposes, a company is a '*joint venture company*' ('JVC') if (and only if):

(i) it is a 'trading company' (see **19.11** above) or the 'holding company' (as in **19.3** above) of a 'trading group' (see **19.11** above) or 'trading subgroup' (see **19.13** below); and

(ii) there are five or fewer persons who between them hold **75% or more** of its ordinary share capital (within *ICTA 1988, s 832(1)*, see **18.2 CAPITAL GAINS — GROUPS**) (counting members of a group of companies, as in **19.3** above, as if they were a single company).

The following provisions apply only where a company has a 'qualifying shareholding' in a JVC. A company has a '*qualifying shareholding*' in a JVC if (and only if):

(a) it is a sole company (i.e. not a member of a group) and it holds shares, or an 'interest in shares' (see **19.21** below), in the JVC by virtue of which it holds **10% or more** of the JVC's ordinary share capital; or

(b) it is a member of a group, the group members between them hold 10% or more of the ordinary share capital of the JVC and the company itself holds part of that ordinary share capital.

Where the above conditions are satisfied, definitions of 'trading company', 'trading group' and 'trading subgroup' have effect with the modifications in (1)–(3) below. Where the JVC is itself a 'holding company' (as in **19.3** above), the references in (1), (2) and (3) below to its activities are to the activities (other than intra-group activities) of the JVC and its '51% subsidiaries' (within *CTA 2010, s 1154; ICTA 1988, s 838*). Each reference below to a holding of shares in a JVC includes securities of the JVC or an interest in shares in, or securities of, the JVC.

(1) In determining whether a company with a qualifying shareholding in a JVC is a 'trading company' (see **19.11** above), its holding of shares in the JVC is disregarded. It is treated as carrying on a share of the JVC's activities proportionate to its percentage shareholding in the JVC. This does not apply if the company and the JVC are members of the same group of companies.

(2) In determining whether a group, of which a company with a qualifying shareholding in a JVC is a member or is the holding company, is a 'trading group' (see **19.11** above), there is disregarded any holding of shares in the JVC by any member of the group which has a qualifying shareholding in the JVC. Each such member is treated as carrying on a share of the JVC's activities proportionate to its percentage shareholding in the JVC. This does not apply if the JVC is itself a member of the group.

(3) In determining whether a company with a qualifying shareholding in a JVC is the holding company of a 'trading subgroup' (see **19.13** above), there is disregarded any holding of shares in the JVC by the company and by any of its 51% subsidiaries which itself has a qualifying shareholding in the JVC. The company and each such subsidiary is treated as carrying on a share of the JVC's activities proportionate to its percentage shareholding in the JVC. This does not apply if the JVC is a member of the same group as the company.

[*TCGA 1992, Sch 7AC paras 23, 24, 26(4)*].

Disposal of trades

Finance Act 2011 introduced a new extension to the substantial shareholdings exemption for situations where a company is disposing of a trade or part of a trade. The new relief permits a company to do so by transferring that trading activity into a new company which can be sold as a clean vehicle to the purchaser. Prior to the enactment of *Finance Act 2011*, such a transaction would have left the target company (the new company) susceptible to a degrouping charge under *TCGA 1992, s 179(3)* and the disposal of the new company would not have qualified for the substantial shareholdings exemption.

Under the new rules, this degrouping charge will, instead, be added to the consideration for the disposal of the new company by the vendor, under *TCGA 1992, s 179(3A)* (see **29.1**) and the disposal of the new company by the vendor will, itself, be exempt under *TCGA 1992, Sch 7AC*, as amended, subject to certain conditions being satisfied. The conditions for the extension of the substantial shareholdings exemption are that:

- immediately before the disposal the vendor company holds a substantial shareholding in the new company;
- an asset which, at the time of the disposal is being used for the purposes of a trade carried on by the new company, has been transferred to it by the vendor or another company in the group at a time when all the relevant companies were members of the same group; and
- the asset was previously used by a member of the group (other than the new company itself) for the purposes of a trade carried on by that other company.

If these conditions are satisfied the vendor company is treated as having held the substantial shareholding in the new company for the period of twelve months ending with the time of the disposal, so long as, during the whole of that period, the relevant asset had been in use for the purposes of a trade carried on by a company in the group. Furthermore, if these conditions are satisfied then the requirement at *TCGA 1992, Sch 7AC para 19*, that the new company has been a trading company for at least twelve months prior to the disposal, is also treated as being satisfied.

As a result, this relief is available for the 'packaging' of trading activities by a vendor company, with the disposal itself and any additional degrouping element, both being exempt.

It is to be noted, however, that the changes detailed here are not mirrored in the degrouping rules for chargeable intangible assets under *CTA 2009, Pt 8* (see **48 INTANGIBLE ASSETS**).

[*TCGA 1992, Sch 7AC paras 15A, 19(2A)–(2C)*].

Consequential rules

Degrouping charge

[19.18] See **29.28 DEGROUPING CHARGES** for interaction between the exemptions in this chapter and the charge where a company ceases to be a member of a 75% group of companies and has had an asset transferred to it by another group member within the preceding six years.

Negligible value claims

Where:

(a) a company makes a negligible value claim under *TCGA 1992, s 24(2)* (see Tolley's Capital Gains Tax under Losses) in respect of an asset; and
(b) by virtue of the provisions in this chapter, a loss on a disposal of that asset at the time of the claim would not be an allowable loss,

the consequent deemed disposal and reacquisition is regarded as taking place at the time of the claim and cannot be backdated to an earlier time. Thus, in these circumstances, a negligible value claim cannot result in an allowable loss. [*TCGA 1992, Sch 7AC para 33; FA 2002, Sch 8 para 1*].

Reorganisation involving qualifying corporate bond

Where, on a reorganisation of share capital, the 'new asset' consists of a qualifying corporate bond (see Tolley's Capital Gains Tax under Qualifying Corporate Bonds), the exemptions in this chapter do not apply to or affect the chargeable gain or allowable loss deemed to accrue under *TCGA 1992, s 116(10)(b)* on a subsequent disposal of the whole or part of the new asset. This does not apply if the 'reorganisation' was, in fact, a deemed disposal and reacquisition within *FA 1996, s 92(7)* (asset ceasing to be a 'convertible security' but continuing to be a creditor relationship of the company). [*TCGA 1992, Sch 7AC para 34; FA 2002, Sch 8 para 1*].

Note that the above is of no application where the reorganisation has itself been treated as an exempt disposal by virtue of **19.14** above.

UK resident company transferring assets to overseas company

Where in specified circumstances a UK resident company transfers its non-UK trade to a non-UK resident company in exchange (or part exchange) for securities, the whole (or part) of any resulting gain may be deferred under *TCGA 1992, s 140* (see **17.13 CAPITAL GAINS**). If, subsequently:

(a) the UK resident company disposes of any securities received in exchange for the transfer, such that all or part of the deferred gain would normally become chargeable; but
(b) by virtue of the provisions in this chapter, any gain on the disposal would not be a chargeable gain,

the provisions at **17.13**(i) **CAPITAL GAINS** are disapplied. Instead, the deferred gain, or the 'appropriate proportion' of it (as there defined), is treated as a gain accruing to the company at the time of the disposal in (a) above and as being a gain which is outside the exemptions in this chapter. Any gain on the disposal of the securities themselves may still attract the exemptions in this chapter (and, equally, any loss may be non-allowable). [*TCGA 1992, Sch 7AC para 35; FA 2002, Sch 8 para 1*].

FA 2010, s 37 has now amended *TCGA 1992, s 140* to ensure that the postponed charge on gains arising where assets of an overseas branch are transferred to a non-resident company is brought back into charge at the appropriate time, with regard to disposals of securities on or after 6 January 2010.

FA 2010, s 37(2) provides a consequential amendment by omitting *TCGA 1992, Sch 7AC para 35*. Where a company disposes of shares that are exempt from chargeable gains under the SSE rules, and which were received in exchange for a transfer of overseas assets to which *s 140* applied, a gain is now deemed to accrue to the transferor under the amended *TCGA 1992, s 140(4)*. *Schedule 7AC para 35* achieved this same result and is no longer required.

[*FA 2010, s 37*].

Appropriation of asset to trading stock

Where an asset acquired by a company otherwise than as trading stock is appropriated by the company for the purposes of its trade as trading stock (whether on the commencement of the trade or otherwise) and, if the company had then sold the asset for its market value, a chargeable gain or allowable loss would have accrued to the company but for the exemption under the current provisions, the company is treated for chargeable gains purposes as if it had thereby disposed of the asset for its market value. *TCGA 1992, s 173* applies for this purpose as it does for the purposes of *TCGA 1992, s 161* (see **18.7 CAPITAL GAINS — GROUPS**). [*TCGA 1992, Sch 7AC para 36*].

Held-over gains on gifts of business assets

[19.19] Where:

(a) a company disposes of an asset;

(b) the allowable expenditure attributable to that asset would have been greater were it not for a claim for gifts hold-over relief under *TCGA 1992, s 165* (see Tolley's Capital Gains Tax under Hold-Over Reliefs) having been made in respect of an earlier disposal; and

(c) by virtue of the provisions in this chapter, any gain on the disposal in (a) above would not be a chargeable gain,

the amount of the held-over gain is treated as a gain accruing to the company at the time of the disposal in (a) above and as being a gain which is outside the exemptions in this chapter. If the disposal in (a) above is a part disposal, only an appropriate proportion of the held-over gain becomes chargeable on that occasion. [*TCGA 1992, Sch 7AC para 37*].

FOREX matching regulations

No gain or loss is treated as arising under *SI 1994 No 3227* on a disposal on which any gain would be exempt under the provisions in this chapter. [*TCGA 1992, Sch 7AC para 39*].

Miscellaneous

[19.20] The question of whether an asset is a chargeable asset for the purposes of corporation tax on chargeable gains generally is to be determined without regard to the availability, or potential availability, of the exemptions covered in this chapter, and references elsewhere to 'chargeable assets' should be read accordingly.

For the purposes of this chapter, an '*interest in shares*' is an interest as a co owner of shares (whether they be owned jointly or in common and whether the interests of the co-owners are equal or disparate). [*TCGA 1992, Sch 7AC para 29*].

From 1 June 2007, the Code of Practice ('COP') facility to obtain clearance for transactions will be reinstated (having been discontinued for transactions on or after 19 July 2006). The applications will be handled by specialist teams in the Large Business Office ('LBO'). Where a company's affairs are not dealt with by an LBO, they should send the application to their usual HMRC officer in the first instance. Those companies whose affairs are dealt with by an LBO should send the application to the officer who deals with their affairs. Applications should be marked on the envelope and the covering letter with 'compliance – Code of Practice 10 application – substantial shareholding exemption'. See HMRC Brief 41/2007 1 June 2007.

The First-tier Tribunal decision in *Williamson Tea Holdings Ltd v HMRC* [2010] SFTD 1101 looked at whether the consideration given in a transaction was wholly in respect of the sale of shares, to which the substantial shareholdings exemption could apply. The case arose because part of the consideration was described in the contract as a payment for a non-competition agreement and HMRC sought to tax that element as a disposal of goodwill. The Tribunal found as a fact that the whole sum paid was for the disposal of shares but this case emphasises the practical importance of being able to demonstrate that consideration is clearly paid for the disposal of shares, to which the exemption can apply.

Key points

[19.21] Points to consider are as follows.

- Each case must be analysed in detail, working through the various conditions for the substantial shareholding exemption (SSE) to apply; the legislation is very complex and can give rise to some odd and unexpected results.
- The grouping provisions for SSE purposes cover companies which are incorporated and/or resident outside the UK as well as UK companies. Take particular care when dealing with overseas entities; they may not be treated as companies for UK tax purposes, or may be respected as companies but may not be treated as having ordinary share capital. If that is the case, UK companies within the group may not qualify for the SSE.
- The requirement that the substantial shareholding condition be met by virtue of the holding of shares or interests in shares can cause difficulties. An example might be where a company has issued ordinary shares and convertible loan notes to its parent company but the rights of the parent under the loan notes swamp its rights under the shares. It is possible that such a loan note holding could dilute the parent's rights by virtue of its shareholding to less than 10%.
- Bear in mind the distinctions between the investing company and investee company trading tests. While it is enough for an investing company to be a member of a trading group, an investee company that is not a trading company will need to be a holding company of a trading group or sub-group. Split shareholdings within a group can cause problems here. For example, the shares of a trading company, X, are held as to 60% by Company A, and the remaining 40% by Company B. On a disposal of the shares in Company B, Company B may not satisfy the investee company trading condition because it is not a holding company of a trading group — it does not hold in excess of 50% of Company X.
- The trading conditions often give rise to questions in practice; the legislation does not clearly indicate when non-trading activities will be regarded as 'substantial' and reliance must be placed on the guidance given by HMRC in its capital gains manual. If there is doubt, it is possible to ask HMRC to confirm the position under its non-statutory business clearance procedure.
- Where a scenario appears to lend itself to the application of the SSE, ensure that no other chargeable gains reliefs may apply instead. The interaction between the SSE and other such reliefs (for example, no-gain/no-loss transfers under *TCGA 1992, s 171* and no disposal fictions such as *TCGA 1992, s 135*) must always be considered carefully.

- Remember that a deemed disposal and reacquisition of shares will restart the SSE 'clock', i.e. a disposal of the shares within the following twelve months may not qualify for the SSE. Where there is a step up in base cost (in a gain scenario) or a disposal in the following twelve months crystallises a loss, this may not give rise to significant issues.
- Where a disposal of shares is thought to qualify for the SSE but the consideration for the sale includes deferred consideration, bear in mind that the deferred consideration will not qualify for the SSE (on the basis that an earn-out right is a separate capital gains asset, per *Marren (Inspector of Taxes) v Ingles* [1979] STC 58). Consider whether it may be possible commercially to structure the consideration in a different way to enable the seller to benefit more fully from the application of the SSE.

20

Charities

Cross-references. See **35 EXEMPT ORGANISATIONS** and **71.49 TRADING EXPENSES AND DEDUCTIONS.**

See also Detailed Guidance at www.hmrc.gov.uk/charities/chapter_1.htm, www.hmrc.gov.uk/businesses/giving/assets.htm, www.hmrc.gov.uk/charities/guidance-notes/annex4/sectiona.htm, and CWL 4, www.hmrc.gov.uk/charities/fund-raising-events.htm. See also 'A guide to tax incentives for corporate giving', published jointly by the Treasury and Home Office (and available at www.hm-treasury.gov.uk/spend_ccr_corporategiving.htm).

Other sources. See Tolley's Charities Manual.

Simon's Taxes. See **C5.1, D7.2.**

Introduction

[20.1] UK charitable tax reliefs are extended to organisations equivalent to charities in the EU and the EEA countries. This involves a new definition of a 'charity' for tax purposes, in the form of a four stage test. The stages are:

- The company must be established for charitable purposes only (per *Charities Act 2006, s 2*);

- It must be located in the UK or an EU member state or a specified country (as specified by SI). Norway and Iceland (EEA countries) will be specified as soon as possible;
- The charity must be registered with the Charity Commission or similar body;
- All persons with control or management responsibilities must be fit and proper persons.

The fourth stage may be relaxed in certain circumstances, at HMRC's discretion. There is a right of appeal against HMRC's decision.

HMRC may publish a list of charities names and addresses that appear to be eligible for relief, but this is a guide only, not definitive. The new definition applies on or after 6 April 2010.

[*FA 2010, s 30, Sch 6*].

Prior to 1 April 2010, in general '*charitable company*' means a body of persons established for charitable purposes only.

The following are '*eligible bodies*' which qualify as charities:

- a scientific research association;
- the Trustees of the National Heritage Memorial Fund;
- the Historic Buildings and Monuments Commission for England;
- the National Endowment for Science, Technology and the Arts; or, for the purposes of charitable companies;
- the Trustees of the British Museum, and
- the Trustees of the National History Museum.

Under the law in England and Wales, '*charity*' means a body of persons or trust resident in the UK and established for the public benefit in one of the following areas:

(a) the advancement of education;
(b) the prevention or relief of poverty;
(c) the advancement of religion;
(d) the advancement of health or the saving of lives;
(e) the advancement of citizenship or community development;
(f) the advancement of the arts, culture, heritage or science;
(g) the advancement of amateur sport;
(h) the advancement of human rights, conflict resolution or reconciliation or the promotion of religious or racial harmony or equality and diversity;
(i) the advancement of environmental protection or improvement;
(j) the relief of those in need by reason or youth, age, ill-health, disability, financial hardship or other disadvantage;
(k) the advancement of animal welfare;
(l) the promotion of the efficiency of the armed forces of the Crown, or of the efficiency of the police, fire and rescue services or ambulance services;
(m) any other purposes, not within (a)–(l) above but recognised as charitable purposes under previous law, or *Recreational Charities Act 1958, s 1* or otherwise reasonably recognised as within the spirit of charity law.

[*Charities Act 2006, s 2*].

Charities are regulated by the Charities Commissioners, and in Scotland by the Office of the Scottish Charities Regulator. Under *Charities Act 1993, s 10*, HMRC may disclose information regarding charities to the Charity Commission.

A scientific research association is defined in *CTA 2010, ss 469, 470*.

HMRC Charities provides guidance on the HMRC website (at www.hmrc.gov.uk/charities) and may be contacted at local call rates on 08453 020203. [*CTA 2010, ss 466–470*].

Simon's Taxes. See **C5.101–C5.114**.

Specific exemptions and reliefs from tax

[20.2] Apart from the exemptions at **20.3–20.8** below, charities are subject to tax on investment and rental income and gains and on profits from trades carried on in order to raise funds. The exemptions at **20.3**, **20.4** and **20.5** below are not general exemptions. Therefore, they do not extend to trades not falling within **20.5** below or to miscellaneous income generally (cf. *Grove v Young Men's Christian Association* (1903) 4 TC 613 and *Governors of Rotunda Hospital, Dublin v Coman (Surveyor of Taxes)* (1920) 7 TC 517, HL).

The exemptions are subject to the restrictions at **20.9** below.

Claims can be made, generally within four years (six years before 1 April 2010) of the end of the accounting period to which they relate, to HMRC Charities, St John's House, Merton Road, Bootle, Merseyside L75 1BB (tel: 08453020203). Separate claims for exemptions are provided for in the legislation for that class of claim. In each case, the claim must be made to HMRC, normally in the appropriate corporation tax return.

[*CTA 2010, Pt 11; ICTA 1988, s 505(1); CTA 2009, Sch 1 para 174*].

HMRC have powers to require the production of books, documents etc. relevant to any claim for exemption under *CTA 2010, Pt 11 Ch 2–4*; *ICTA 1988, ss 505(1), 507 or 508* (see **35.4**, **35.9**, **35.12 EXEMPT ORGANISATIONS**) leading to the repayment of income tax or the payment of tax credits. [*F(No 2)A 1992, s 28*].

Further guidance is available on the HMRC website (www.hmrc.gov.uk/charities).

Simon's Taxes. See **C5.117A–C5.125**.

Rents

[20.3] UK or overseas rents or other receipts from an estate, interest or right in or over any land vested in any person for charitable purposes, and otherwise chargeable to corporation tax as property or trading income (or to income tax under *ITTOIA 2005, Pt 2* (trading income) or *Pt 3* (property income)), are exempt to the extent they are applied for charitable purposes only.

Distributions from REITs which are liable to corporation tax, are exempt to the extent that they arise in respect of a person who holds them for charitable purposes and the income is applied for those purposes.

[*CTA 2010, s 485; CTA 2009, Pts 3 and 4, Sch 1 para 173; ICTA 1988, s 505(1)(a); FA 1996, s 146(2)(5); ITTOIA 2005, Sch 1 para 198(2); CTA 2009, Sch 1 para 174*].

Interest, distributions, etc.

[20.4] Income of a charitable company, or applicable for charitable purposes under an Act of Parliament, charter, decree, deed of trust or will, is exempt so far as applied for charitable purposes and consisting of:

- income from non-trading loan relationships; or
- distributions from unauthorised unit trusts;
- dividends from UK or overseas resident companies.

To qualify for exemption, the income must be applied for charitable purposes only, and a claim is required.

Exemption for corporation tax also applies to tax in respect of non-trading gains of companies on intangible fixed assets under *CTA 2009, ss 745–753; FA 2002, Sch 29* (see **48.7 INTANGIBLE ASSETS**).

Income of trustees arising from public revenue dividends, and which is applicable towards repairs of any cathedral, college, church, chapel etc., being income otherwise chargeable to corporation tax on trading profits (or to income tax under *ITTOIA 2005, Pt 4 Ch 2* (interest)), is also exempt so far as applied to those purposes only.

[*CTA 2010, ss 486, 487; ICTA 1988, s 505(1)(c)(d), (1AA); FA 1996, s 146(3)(5), Sch 7 para 19; ITTOIA 2005, Sch 1 para 198(2)(3); FA 2009, Sch 14 para 4*].

Trading profits

[20.5] A charitable trade is a trade carried on by a charitable company where:

(a) the trade is exercised in the course of carrying out a primary purpose of the charity; or

(b) the work is mainly carried on by its beneficiaries.

Profits of a charitable trade carried on by a charitable company or post-cessation receipts of such a trade which it receives or to which it is entitled are exempt from corporation tax provided that the profits or receipts are applied for charitable purposes only and that a claim is made.

Where the trade is exercised partly in the course of carrying out a primary purpose of the charity and partly otherwise, each part is treated as a separate trade. Where the work is carried out partly but not mainly by beneficiaries, the part carried on by the beneficiaries and the other part are treated as separate trades. Expenses and receipts are to be apportioned on a just and reasonable basis between the separate trades.

[*CTA 2010, ss 478, 479, Changes 32, 33 in Annex 1V; ICTA 1988, s 505(1)(e)(1B); FA 1996, s 146(4)(5); ITTOIA 2005, Sch 1 para 198(2); FA 2006, s 56*].

For trades held to fall within the exemption, see *Glasgow Musical Festival Association* (1926) 11 TC 154, Ct of Sess; *Royal Choral Society v CIR* (1943) 25 TC 263, CA, and *Dean Leigh Temperance Canteen Trustees v CIR* (1958) 38 TC 315. For regular trading see *British Legion, Peterhead Branch Remembrance and Welcome Home Fund v CIR* (1953) 35 TC 509, 32 ATC 302, Ct of Sess. (In practice, HMRC may in such cases allow a reasonable deduction for services etc. provided free.) For annual shows of agricultural societies, see **35.2 EXEMPT ORGANISATIONS**.

Detailed guidance notes are available from HMRC Charities (see **20.1** above for details), which includes guidance on 'Trading by Charities' (at www.hmrc.gov.uk/charities/tax/trading/basics.htm#6) giving advice on the tax treatment of particular types of trade commonly carried on by charities. It includes guidance as to the type of fund-raising activities originally covered by extra-statutory concession C4 (see (ii) below) and the conditions the activities must satisfy, the kind of profits covered by the concession and the consequences if an event is not covered by it. Advice can also be given on the Charities helpline, 08453 020203.

Other exemptions

Small trades and certain miscellaneous income

[20.6] Subject to the following conditions, a tax exemption applies, on a claim being made to HMRC, to trading profits and other income which is chargeable to corporation tax as miscellaneous income under any of the provisions listed in *CTA 2010, s 1173; ICTA 1988, s 834A*.

The conditions are that it is not otherwise exempted from tax and the income is applied solely for the purposes of the charity and either:

(a) the trading incoming resources do not exceed the 'requisite limit'; or
(b) the charity had, at the beginning of the chargeable period, a reasonable expectation that the requisite limit would be met.

The '*requisite limit*' is that:

(1) 25% of the charitable company's total incoming resources for the accounting period; but
(2) must not be less than £5,000 or more than £50,000.

The monetary limits are proportionately reduced for chargeable periods of less than twelve months. The extension of the exemption to miscellaneous income is intended to cover miscellaneous fund-raising activities not being trading activities (or treated as trading). Certain specified tax charges on miscellaneous income (listed in *CTA 2010, s 1173; ICTA 1988, s 834A*) are excluded from the exemption.

[*CTA 2010, ss 480–482, Change 34 of Annex 1; FA 2000, s 46; ITTOIA 2005, Sch 1 para 514; CTA 2009, Sch 1 para 463*].

HMRC's guidance is that they will consider any evidence to satisfy the reasonable expectation test in (b) above. Such evidence may include minutes of meetings at which the expectations were discussed, copies of cash-flow forecasts and business plans prepared for these meetings and copies of the previous year's accounts.

Small-scale fund-raising events

Profits from events such as bazaars, jumble sales, gymkhanas, carnivals etc., arranged by voluntary organisations or charities, held for, and promoted as being held for, the purpose of raising funds for charity, are not taxed if a claim is made and:

(a) the organisation or charity is not regularly carrying on these trading activities;
(b) it is not competing with other traders; and
(c) the profits are transferred to charities or otherwise applied for charitable purposes.

The exemption covers up to 15 of each type of event in any one location in any financial year of the charity etc. and includes events accessed electronically. Small events, e.g. jumble sales or coffee mornings, do not count toward the limit to the extent that the gross takings from these events do not exceed £1,000 in any week. The limit of 15 is increased or reduced proportionately for financial years of more or less than 12 months.

The exemption corresponds with the VAT exemption for fund-raising events, for which see the corresponding chapter of Tolley's Value Added Tax. Any event meeting the criteria for the VAT exemption will automatically qualify for the corporation tax exemption if the condition at (c) above is satisfied.

[*CTA 2010, s 483; Change 35 in Annex IV to CTB 2010; HMRC Extra-Statutory Concession, C4*].

Lotteries

Lottery profits applied solely to the charity's purposes, being profits otherwise chargeable to corporation tax as trading income (or to income tax under *ITTOIA 2005, Pt 2* (trading income) or *Pt 5* (miscellaneous income)), are exempt, provided that the lottery is promoted and conducted in accordance with *Lotteries and Amusements Act 1976, s 3 or s 5* (or NI equivalent).

[*CTA 2010, s 484; ICTA 1988, s 505(1)(f); FA 1995, s 138; ITTOIA 2005, Sch 1 para 198(2)*].

Property income

Property income, whether chargeable as trading or property income, is exempt from corporation tax if the income is vested in any person for charitable purposes. REIT distributions are also exempt to the extent the shares from which they derive are similarly held for charitable purposes. In each case a claim must be made.

[*CTA 2010, s 485*].

Estate income

Where a charitable company is liable to corporation tax on estate income, that income is not brought into account in calculating total profits of that company, provided that the estate income is applied for charitable purposes only and a claim is made.

[*CTA 2010, s 489; Change 37 of Annex IV*].

Investment income and non-trading profits from loan relationships

Such income is exempt from corporation tax if it is income of a charitable company or it is required by legislation, court judgment, charter, trust deed or will be used for charitable purposes only and is so used. A claim is required.

Where public revenue dividends are received on securities by trustees and the income is applicable and applied only for the repair of a cathedral, college, church, chapel or other building used for divine worship, the income is exempt from corporation tax provided a claim is made. For distributions paid before 1 July 2009, the conditions are amended.

[*CTA 2010, ss 486, 487, Sch 2 para 71*].

Miscellaneous income

Where income is received by a charitable company or is required by statute to be applied for charitable purposes only and is so applied, it is exempt provided a claim is made. The income covered by this provision is non-trading gains on intangible fixed assets, annual payments, qualifying income from intangible fixed assets and, for distributions paid before 1 July 2009, 'relevant foreign distributions'. '*Relevant foreign distributions*' are distributions of a non-UK resident company which are not chargeable as dividends of non-UK resident companies.

[*CTA 2010, s 488, Sch 2 para 72, Change 36 of Annex 1*].

Capital gains

[20.7] Charities are exempt from corporation tax on capital gains applicable, and applied, for charitable purposes. Where property held on charitable trusts ceases to be subject to those trusts without actually being disposed of, the trustees are deemed to have disposed of, and immediately reacquired, the property at its market value at that time. The notional gain arising is taxable. To the extent that the property represents, directly or indirectly, gains which have accrued to the trustees from disposals made during the currency of the charity, tax is chargeable as if the exemption had never applied. Tax on such gains may be assessed within three years after the year of assessment or accounting period in which the cessation occurs.

[*TCGA 1992, ss 256, 256A–256D; CTA 2010, Sch 1 paras 254, 257*].

The exemption applies to capital payments made to UK charities as beneficiaries of an offshore settlement, in respect of which a chargeable gain would be treated as accruing to the trust under *TCGA 1992, s 87*. The exemption applies only to the extent that the payment is applicable and is applied for charitable purposes. (HMRC Tax Bulletin Issue 36, August 1998 pp 573, 574).

See also *TCGA 1992, s 257; CTA 2010, Sch 1 para 258* as regards gifts to charities treated as made for a 'no gain, no loss' consideration.

There is a concession, which operates as follows, but which will be withdrawn with effect from 1 April 2010. There is a deemed disposal and reacquisition where land given for educational and certain other charitable purposes ceases to be used for such purposes and the following applies. Under the *Reverter of Sites Act 1987*, the property is held by the trustees on a trust for sale for the benefit of the revertee and the revertee is not known to be a charity. A chargeable capital gain may arise. Any income from the property will be liable to income tax, and a chargeable gain may also arise on a subsequent sale of the land.

Where the revertee is subsequently identified as a charity or disclaims all entitlement to the property (or where certain orders are made by the Charity Commission or the Secretary of State), provided that charitable status is re-established within six years of the date on which the land ceased to be held on the original charitable trust, any capital gains tax paid as above in the interim period will be discharged or repaid (with repayment supplement where appropriate). Any income tax will also be discharged or repaid (provided that the income charged was used for charitable purposes).

Partial relief will be given where the above conditions are only satisfied in respect of part of the property concerned. A request by the trustees for postponement of the tax payable will be accepted by HMRC where the revertee has not been identified and this concession may apply. (HMRC Extra-Statutory Concession, D47 — was in operation up to 31 March 2010).

In respect of covenanted donations by companies, the Trustees of the National Heritage Memorial Fund, The Historic Buildings and Monuments Commission for England and the National Endowment for Science, Technology and the Arts are treated as established for charitable purposes only.

[*CTA 2010, s 202; ICTA 1988, s 339(9)*].

As regards the time at which charitable purposes arise, see *Guild and Others (as Trustees of the William Muir (Bond 9) Ltd Employees' Share Scheme) v CIR* (1993) 66 TC 1, Ct of Sess (trustees of share scheme required to repay loans out of proceeds of distribution and to apply balance to charitable purposes; held not to apply proceeds of distribution for charitable purposes).

See, however, **20.10** below as regards restrictions on relief.

HMRC Charities provides guidance on the HMRC website (at www.hmrc.gov.uk/charities) and may be contacted at local call rates on 08453 020203.

Simon's Taxes. See **C5.105**

Miscellaneous

[20.8] Charities are exempt from tax on offshore income gains if applicable and applied for charitable purposes (see **57 OFFSHORE FUNDS**).

[*ICTA 1988, s 761(6)*].

Charitable unit trust schemes are excluded from the normal income tax treatment of unauthorised unit trusts, and are thus able to pass on their income to participating charities without deducting tax.

[*SI 1988 No 267; SI 1994 No 1479*].

Employee secondment

For a deduction in arriving at trading profits for employees seconded by companies to charities, see **71.49 TRADING EXPENSES AND DEDUCTIONS**.

Restrictions on exemptions

[20.9] If a charity incurs (or is treated as incurring) 'non-charitable expenditure' (a 'non-exempt amount') in a chargeable period, relief for 'attributable income' is restricted to the amount by which it exceeds the non-charitable expenditure.

If a charity's non-charitable expenditure exceeds its 'total income and gains', the excess is treated as non-charitable expenditure of the previous period for this purpose. Excess non-charitable expenditure may arise in a chargeable period wholly or partly as result of the carry back in which case the excess is to be carried back to the previous period and so on, but only to chargeable periods ending not more than six years before the end of the period in which the expenditure was actually incurred. Any necessary adjustments are to be made accordingly by assessment or otherwise. Where a charity's attributable income and gains are so restricted, the charity may specify (by notice to HMRC) which items of income or gains are to be disallowed. If such a notice is required by HMRC and the charity fails to comply within 30 days from the date the requirement is imposed, HMRC will determine which items to disallow.

A charity has a '*non-exempt amount*' for an accounting period if it has both non-charitable expenditure for the period and attributable income and gains and it is the lesser of these amounts.

'*Attributable income*' for an accounting period is exempt income and attributable gains are those which are not chargeable.

[*CTA 2010, ss 492–495*].

Where a charitable company has a non-exempt amount, attributable gains of that company for the period may be allocated to the non-exempt amount, so far as not already used up. Attribution may be by specification by the charitable company or determination by an officer of HMRC.

Non-charitable expenditure

'*Non-charitable expenditure*' is expenditure falling into one of the following categories:

(a) any trading loss other than in charitable trade or it qualifies under the small trade, fund raising or lotteries exemptions;

(b) any loss relating to land where income from the land would not qualify for exemption;
(c) any miscellaneous loss not arising as a result of charitable activities;
(d) expenditure not incurred for charitable purposes only and not required to be taken into account in calculating the profits of a trade or property business carried on by the charitable company or the profit or loss on any miscellaneous transaction carried on by such a company;
(e) any payment to a substantial donor (see **20.10** below) treated as non-charitable expenditure;
(f) any non-charitable expenditure treated as incurred as a result of a transaction between the charitable company and a substantial donor;
(g) the amount of the charitable company funds invested in an investment other than an approved charitable investment;
(h) loans made by the company in an accounting period which are neither investments nor approved charitable loans.

When expenditure is treated as incurred depends on UK GAAP.

[*CTA 2010, ss 496–501, Sch 1 para 257; Changes 38, 39 Annex 1*].

Where the investment or loan is realised or repaid in whole or in part in the chargeable period in which it was made, any further investment or lending of the sum realised or repaid in that period is, to the extent that it does not exceed the sum originally invested or lent, ignored in arriving at non-charitable expenditure of the period.

'*Approved charitable investments and loans*' are the following:

(A) investments in securities:
  (a) issued or guaranteed by an EU government;
  (b) issued or guaranteed by the government or a governmental body of any territory or part;
  (c) issued by an international entity listed in the Annex to Council Directive 2003/48/EC or an entity meeting the four criteria set out at the end of that Annex;
  (d) issued by a building society;
  (e) issued by a mutual credit institution authorised by the appropriate governmental body in the territory in which the securities are issued;
  (f) issued by an open ended investment trust;
  (g) issued by an open-ended investment company;
  (h) issued by a company and listed on a recognised stock exchange; or
  (i) issued by a company but not listed on a recognised stock exchange,
(B) an investment in a common investment fund established under the *Charities Acts 1960* (or NI equivalent) or *1993*;
(C) an investment in a common deposit fund established under the *Charities Acts 1960 and 1993*;
(D) an investment in a fund which is similar to those in (i) or (ii) above, which is established for the exclusive benefit of charities or class of charities;

(E) Northern Ireland Treasury bills;
(F) deposits with a banks (as defined in *CTA 2010, s 1120*) in respect of which interest is payable at a commercial rate, but excluding a deposit made as part of an arrangement whereby the bank, etc. makes a loan to a third party;
(G) an interest in land, other than as security;
(H) certificates of deposit including uncertificated eligible debt security units as defined in *ITA 2007, s 986;*
(I) units in a unit trust scheme or in a recognised scheme within *FISMA 2000, s 237*;
(J) loans or other investments as to which HMRC are satisfied, on a claim, that the loans or other investments are made for the benefit of the charity and not for the avoidance of tax (whether by the charity or by a third party);
(K) a deposit with the National Savings Bank, a building society or a credit institution operating on mutual principles and duly authorised in the territory in which the deposit is taken;
(L) bills, certificates of tax deposit, savings certificates and tax reserve certificates issued by the UK government.

(A)(a), (b) or (c) do not apply to an investment unless:

(i) the securities are traded or quoted on a recognised investment exchange or an exchange being the principal or only market in a territory where the securities are listed; and
(ii) (if the securities are shares or debenture stock):
- the securities are fully paid up or the terms of issue require them to be fully paid up within nine months of issue; or
- the shares do not have a nominal value.

In the case of an investment in a company which is incorporated, (A) above does not apply unless conditions (i) and (ii) above are met and throughout the last business day before the investment day the company has issued and paid up share capital of at least £1 million (or its equivalent in some other currency) and dividends were paid in every year from 5 years before the calendar year in which the investment day falls on all shares in issue at that time.

[*CTA 2010, ss 511–513, Change 40 Annex 1*].

'Approved charitable loans'

A loan which is not made by way of investment is a qualifying loan if it is one of the following:

(1) A loan made to another charity for charitable purposes only.
(2) A loan to a beneficiary of the charity which is made in the course of carrying out the purposes of the charity.
(3) Money placed on a current account with a recognised bank or licensed institution (as in (F) above) otherwise than under arrangements under which a loan is made to another person.
(4) A loan, not within (1) to (3) above, as to which HMRC are satisfied, on a claim, that the loan is made for the benefit of the charity and not for the avoidance of tax (whether by the charity or by a third party).

[*CTA 2010, s 514; ICTA 1988, s 506, Sch 20; ITTOIA 2005, Sch 1 para 347; FA 2006, s 55(2)(3), Sch 26 Pt 3(5)*].

Payments between charities

Any payment received by one charity from another, other than in return for full consideration, which would otherwise not be chargeable to tax (and which is not of a description within any of the relieving provisions of *CTA 2010, s 515; ICTA 1988, s 505*, see **20.2** *et seq.* above), is chargeable to corporation tax as income from non-trading loan relationships, but is eligible for relief, on making a claim, if it is applied for charitable purposes only.

[*CTA 2010, s 474*].

Simon's Taxes. See **C5.127–C5.127B.**

Transactions with substantial donors

Payments made before 1 April 2011

[20.10] In relation to payments made prior to 1 April 2011 by a charity in the course of, or for the purposes of, the transactions in (a)–(e) below between a charity and its 'substantial donors' are treated as non-charitable expenditure (see **20.9** above).

The transactions are:

(a) the sale or letting of property by (or to) a charity to (or by) a substantial donor;
(b) an exchange of property between a charity and a substantial donor;
(c) the provision of services by (or to) a charity to (or by) a substantial donor;
(d) the provision of 'financial assistance' by (or to) a charity to (or by) a substantial donor; and
(e) investment by a charity in the business of the donor.

As regards (d) above, '*financial assistance*' includes the provision of a loan, guarantee or indemnity or entering into **ALTERNATIVE FINANCE ARRANGEMENTS (4)**.

A payment made by a charitable company to a substantial donor during a substantial donor transaction is treated as non-charitable. Also, at the same time or on its own, if the terms of a transaction are less beneficial to the charity than would be expected if made at arm's length, the charity will be treated as incurring non-charitable expenditure at such time (or times) as determined by HMRC and equal to an amount determined by HMRC as the cost to the charity of the difference in terms. In this case, an amount will be deducted from the amount so determined equal to any payment by the charity treated as above as non-charitable expenditure in respect of the same transaction.

[*CTA 2010, ss 502–506*].

A payment of remuneration to a substantial donor will also be treated as non-charitable expenditure unless it is for remuneration for services as a trustee (duly approved by the Charity Commission, a court or other body with regulatory responsibility under UK legislation). Where the payment is other than a monetary payment, this provision applies to the cash equivalent of the payment, calculated in accordance with the benefit in kind rules (see Tolley's Income Tax under Employment Income).

The above provisions apply where a transaction is entered into in a chargeable period with a donor who is a substantial donor in respect of that period, even if the donor does not fall within the definition of a 'substantial donor' until after the transaction is entered into.

A '*substantial donor*' is a person who provides the charity with 'relievable' gifts of at least £25,000 in a twelve-month period, or at least £150,000 in a six-year period (including non-monetary gifts of that value), in which the chargeable period wholly or partly falls (such amounts and time periods being variable by Treasury order). £100,000 is substituted for £150,000 prior to 23 April 2009.

[*CTA 2010, Sch 2 para 75*].

If a person falls within the definition of a substantial donor under these rules, that person continues to be a substantial donor to the charity for the following five chargeable periods. A person may satisfy the definition of substantial donor by reference to gifts made at any. A gift is 'relievable' if it falls within the provisions set out in **20.12**, or **20.17** below or the provisions for individual gift aid (*CTA 2009, s 105* — see **71.49 TRADING EXPENSES AND DEDUCTIONS** — and *FA 1990, s 25*), gifts of chargeable assets (*TCGA 1992, s 257; CTA 2010, Sch 1 para 258*), gifts of trading stock (*ITTOIA 2005, s 108*), payroll giving (*ITEPA 2003, ss 713–715*) or gifts from settlor-interested trusts *(ITTOIA 2005, ss 628, 630)*. A company wholly owned by a charity will not be treated as a substantial donor in relation to that charity or any charities which own it. Charities which are connected (in matters relating to the structure, administration or control of a charity) are treated as a single charity. (Accordingly, relievable gifts made to those charities by a donor will be aggregated for the purpose of the substantial donor test.)

Appeals

An appeal against an assessment to tax under the above provisions can be reviewed by the First Tier Tribunal.

Exceptions

The above provisions do not apply:

(i) where a substantial donor sells or lets property, or provides services, to a charity which HMRC determine to be on arm's length terms in the course of a business and not as part of an arrangement to avoid tax;

(ii) to the provision of services to a substantial donor if HMRC determines that they are provided on arm's length terms in the course of the actual carrying out of a primary purpose of the charity;

(iii) to the provision of financial assistance to a charity by a substantial donor if HMRC determines that it is provided on arm's length terms and not as part of an arrangement to avoid tax;

(iv) to an investment by a charity in the business of a substantial donor where the investment takes the form of the purchase of shares or securities listed on a recognised stock exchange; or
(v) to disposals at an undervalue of gifts to charity under *TCGA 1992, s 257(2)* or *ICTA 1988, s 587B* (see **20.17** below).

Payments by a charity, or benefits arising to a substantial donor from a transaction, are disregarded to the extent they relate to a gift aid payment and do not exceed the permitted limits (see **20.12** below) or *FA 1990, s 25* (donations by individuals, see Tolley's Income Tax under Charities).

References above to substantial donors or other persons include persons connected with them (see **25 CONNECTED PERSONS**). A registered social landlord or housing association will not be treated as a substantial donor in relation to a charity with which it is connected.

[*CTA 2010, ss 502–510, Sch 2 para 75; ICTA 1988, ss 506A–506C; FA 2006, s 54*].

Payments made after 31 March 2011

[20.11] Charities have claimed that the anti-avoidance legislation on substantial donors to charities referred to in **20.10** above has been burdensome in its application. As a result, *Finance Act 2011* introduces new rules that will deny tax relief on donations only where the donor is party to arrangements, the main purpose or one of the main purposes of which is to obtain an advantage for the donor or a connected person, directly or indirectly, from the charity (known as 'tainted donations'). The legislation has effect in relation to charity donations made on or after 1 April 2011 irrespective of when the arrangements were entered into. The previous legislation ceases to have effect in respect of donations received on or after 1 April 2011. Under the new rules there are no thresholds on the size of a donation that must be exceeded before the legislation can apply and consequently the concept of a 'substantial donor' disappears. Another key change in approach is that where a donation is deemed tainted under the new rules, tax relief is denied and the donor (as opposed to the charity) will be the primary target for recovery of any relief that, under these rules, should not have been given.

[*FA 2011, s 27, Sch 3*].

Charitable donations relief

[20.12] A company may claim relief by deduction from total profits (after all other deductions other than group relief of the period in which the donation is made for a 'qualifying charitable donation'). However, the donation cannot create a loss. A '*qualifying charitable donation*' for corporation tax purposes is a qualifying payment i.e. one which is:

- a payment of a sum of money;
- a sum which is not repayable (but see below for exception);

- not made by a company which is a charity;
- not disqualified as an 'associated acquisition, etc.' by the charity;
- not disqualified as a certain distribution;
- not disqualified as having an 'associated benefit'.

Where the company is wholly owned by the charity, or that charity and a number of others, the payment was designed to reduce the company's taxable profits to nil and the repayment, made within the year after the end of the period in which the donation was made, was intended to make such adjustment as was necessary to reduce the taxable profits to nil, the payment is not treated as a repayment of the original donation.

An '*associated acquisition*' is a donation which is conditional on an acquisition of property by the charity from the donor company or an associate and the donation and the acquisition are associated or form part of an arrangement. Where the acquisition is for no consideration (i.e. it is a gift) it is to be ignored for this purpose.

In the case of *Noved Investment Co v Revenue and Customs Comrs* [2006] STC (SCD) 120, the Special Commissioners held that *ICTA 1988, s 209(4)* was not restricted to bilateral transactions and that transfers of assets or liabilities by a company to its members at an undervalue can include cash. Accordingly, such cash transfers were qualifying donations. This is in contradiction of HMRC's view (announced in the course of this case) that such transfers do not include cash, having changed their view from that previously adopted that such assets could include cash. See HMRC's Corporate Tax Manual CTM15250 and 15350.

'*Charity*' for this purpose is as defined in **20.1** above. A payment is not a qualifying donation if the company, or a connected person (**25 CONNECTED PERSONS**), or a person connected with such a person, receives a benefit in consequence of the gift, and either:

(A) the aggregate value of the benefits received in relation to the gift exceeds the variable limit, which is:
  (1) 25% of a donation of up to £100;
  (2) £25 where the donation is more than £100 but not more than £1,000; or
  (3) from 6 April 2007, 5% (prior to 6 April 2007 2½%) of a donation of more than £1,000; or

(B) the sum of the total value of the benefits received in relation to the gift and the total value of any other benefits (if any) received in relation to qualifying donations made by the company to the charity earlier in the accounting period exceeds £500 (from 6 April 2007) or £250 (prior to 6 April 2007).

Where (A) above applies, the treatment of a payment is modified if (i) to (iv) below applies. These are:

(i) the related benefit applies to a period of less than a year;
(ii) the benefit relates to a right to receive payments at intervals over less than a year;
(iii) the benefit is one of a series received at intervals over less than a year;

(iv) the payment is not associated with benefits received at intervals, but is one of a series of payments made at intervals of less than a year.

In the cases of (i) to (iii), the benefit and the payment are annualised and for (iv) the payment is annualised. The annualised amount, in the case of (i) and (ii) (where (iii) and (iv) do not also apply) is found by multiplying the amount by 365 and dividing the result by the number of days in the period of time referred to in (i) or (ii). Where (iii) or (iv) applies, the denominator is the average number of days in the intervals of less than a year.

Where a benefit:

(1) consists of the right to receive a benefit or benefits at intervals over a period of less than twelve months;
(2) is an associated benefit which relates to a period of less than twelve months; or
(3) is one of a series of benefits, received at intervals, in consequence of making a series of gifts at intervals of less than twelve months;
(4) the benefit is not received at intervals, but the payment is one of a series of payments made at intervals of less than 12 months,

the value of the benefit and the amount of the gift are 'annualised' for the purposes of (ii) above. Where a one-off benefit is received in consequence of making a gift which is one of a series of gifts made at intervals of less than twelve months, the amount of the gift is likewise 'annualised'. Acknowledgement of a donor in the charity's literature does not amount to a benefit *provided that* it does not take the form of an advertisement for the donor's business (see para 3.27 of the HMRC guide referred to below).

Charity trading subsidiaries

Where a qualifying payment is made by a company that is wholly owned by a charity, the company can claim that the donation, or any part of it, is to be treated as made in an earlier accounting period falling wholly or partly within the nine months prior to the date of the donation. A claim to have the payment treated as paid in an earlier accounting period must be made within two years from the end of the accounting period in which the payment is made, or such longer period as HMRC may allow.

A company is treated as wholly owned by a charity if all its ordinary share capital is directly or indirectly owned by one or more charities, or if it is limited by guarantee and every person beneficially entitled to participate in its divisible profits, or to share in the net assets available for distribution in a winding-up, is a charity or a company wholly owned by a charity.

Where a charity-owned company makes an estimated gift aid payment, which subsequently proves to exceed its profits for the accounting period in which the payment is made, so that a repayment is made within 12 months, solely as adjustment, the donation is not made 'subject to a condition as to repayment' and such repayment is not treated as non-charitable expenditure for corporation tax purposes. These provisions do not apply to payments to a charity made before 1 April 2010.

[*CTA 2010, ss 189–202, Sch 2 paras 56–58; Change 27 in Annex 1 to CTA 2010; ITA 2007, Sch 1 para 125*].

Simon's Taxes. See D1.321.

Gift Aid donation to charity

[20.13] When a charitable company receives a donation under the Gift Aid scheme, it is treated as receiving an amount under deduction of tax at the basic rate for the tax year in which it is made. Therefore, its income is the grossed up amount of the gift. This amount is exempt from corporation tax to the extent that it is applied for charitable purposes only. A claim must be made for this exemption, unless the gift is made though a self assessment return by reallocation of a tax repayment.

[*ITA 2007, ss 429, 472*].

Gifts of money to charities

[20.14] Cash payments, when made by non-charities, are exempt from corporation tax in the hands of the charity if they are used for charitable purposes only and a claim is made.

Where cash payments are made to a charity by a company, the gift is not liable to corporation tax, provided a claim is made.

Where there is a gift of money to a scientific research association in an accounting period for which the exemption is claimed, the payment is exempt from corporation tax provided a claim is made.

[*CTA 2010, ss 473, 475–477, Change 31 of Annex 1*].

Other gifts

[20.15] Where the payment is made by another charity other than for full consideration and it is not chargeable to corporation tax apart from *CTA 2010, s 474*, if the amount is applied for charitable purposes only and a claim is made the company may claim exemption.

[*CTA 2010, s 474*].

Gift Aid supplement

[20.16] Where a charitable company or community amateur sports club receives a gift aid payment in a transitional year (tax years 2008/09 to 2010/11) and makes a claim for gift aid exemption within two years of the end of the accounting period to which the claim relates, gift aid supplement will be payable with the gift aid repayment. The supplement is compensation for the effect of the reduction in the basic rate of tax from 22% to 20%. The amount of the supplement is the difference between the actual basic rate tax on the grossed up amount of the donation and the notional basic rate tax on the same amount for the transitional year. The notional rate is the actual rate plus the transitional supplement for the year. If the total rate is greater than 22%, the notional rate is taken to be 22%. The rate of supplement cannot exceed 2%. Gift aid supplement is not liable to corporation tax. There is provision for HMRC to recover any supplement paid in error.

[*FA 2008, s 53, Sch 19*].

Gifts of shares, securities and real property

[20.17] Relief is available to companies other than charities which dispose of the whole of the beneficial interest in the 'qualifying investments' listed below, otherwise than at market value and which make a claim. For this purpose, a charity must fall within on of the following categories:

(i) a body of persons or trust established for charitable purposes only;
(ii) the Trustees of the National Heritage Memorial Fund;
(iii) the Historic Buildings and Monuments Commission for England; or
(iv) the National Endowment for Science, Technology and the Arts.

'*Qualifying investments*' are:

(a) shares and securities listed or dealt in on a recognised stock exchange or on or after 6 April 2007 dealt in on any designated market in the UK;
(b) units in authorised unit trusts (see **52.3 INVESTMENT FUNDS**);
(c) shares in open-ended investment companies (see **52.2 INVESTMENT FUNDS**);
(d) interests in offshore funds (see **57 OFFSHORE FUNDS**); and
(e) a 'qualifying interest in land'.

Where a valid claim is made, relief for the 'relievable amount,' is available as a qualifying charitable donation for the accounting period in which the disposal is made. Where relief is claimed under *CTA 2010, s 205*, no relief can be claimed under *CTA 2009, s 105* (see **71.49 TRADING EXPENSES AND DEDUCTIONS**) or any other provision for the same disposal.

For disposals to a charity, the '*relievable amount*' is the value of the 'net benefit to the charity' either at the time the disposal is made or immediately after that time (whichever gives the lower value), plus 'incidental costs' of the disposal minus the total value of any benefits by the company as a result of the disposal, or (where the disposal is at an undervalue) the excess (if any) of that value over any consideration given for the disposal.

'*Incidental costs*' are defined as:

(A) payments for services of a surveyor, valuer, auctioneer, accountant, agent or legal adviser, incurred wholly and exclusively by the company for the purposes of the disposal;
(B) costs wholly and exclusively incurred by the company in connection with transfer or conveyance;
(C) costs of advertising to find a buyer; and
(D) reasonable costs of valuation or apportionment required for these provisions.

The '*net benefit to the charity*' is normally the market value of the investment. Where, however, the charity is, or becomes, subject to a 'disposal-related obligation' to any person (whether or not the donor or a connected person), the net benefit is the market value of the investment reduced by the aggregate 'disposal-related liabilities' of the charity.

An obligation is a '*disposal-related obligation*' if it is reasonable to suppose that the disposal would not have been made in its absence or if it relates to, or is framed by reference to, or is conditional upon the charity receiving, the investment in question or a related investment.

A charity's '*disposal-related liability*' is its liability under the disposal-related obligation. Contingent obligations are taken into account if the contingency actually occurs.

The market value of the investment is determined as for capital gains tax purposes. In computing the amount deductible, any consideration receivable at a future time, contingently or otherwise, is brought fully into account as it is for capital gains tax purposes (see Tolley's Capital Gains Tax under Disposal).

The amount deductible is reduced by the value of any benefits received by the donor company or any connected person (see **25 CONNECTED PERSONS**). The amount deductible is increased by any incidental costs of disposal (construed as for capital gains tax purposes) incurred by the person making it. Where consideration is received for the disposal, this increase is limited to the excess, if any, of the deemed consideration for capital gains tax purposes (disposal deemed to be at no gain/no loss) over the actual consideration. The cost of the asset to the charity for capital gains tax purposes is reduced by the amount deductible as above, or, if it is less than that amount, is reduced to nil.

[*CTA 2010, ss 203–212; ITA 2007, Sch 1; FA 2007, Sch 26 para 7; FA 2004, ss 139, 145, Sch 26 para 10; ITTOIA 2005, Sch 1 para 249; CTA 2009, Sch 1 para 199*].

A payment made, or to be made to a foreign charity is non-charitable expenditure if it is incurred for charitable purposes only but a charity has not taken such steps as are reasonable in the circumstances to ensure that the payment will be applied for charitable purposes.

[*CTA 2010, s 500*].

Special rules applicable to gifts of real property

[20.18] A '*qualifying interest in land*' is a freehold interest (or a leasehold interest which is for a term of years absolute) in UK land (but not an agreement to acquire freehold land or for a lease). The following two circumstances are additionally brought within the relief.

(i) Where there is a disposal of the beneficial interest in a qualifying interest in land to a charity, and there is also a disposal to the charity of any easement, servitude, right or privilege so far as benefiting that land, the disposal of the easement etc is regarded as a separate disposal from the disposal of the land.
[*CTA 2010, s 205(2)(3)*].

(ii) Where a person with a freehold or leasehold interest in UK land grants to a charity a lease, for (except in Scotland) a term of years absolute, of the whole or part of that land, this is regarded as a disposal for which the relief is available.

In the application of the above in Scotland:

(1) references to a freehold interest in land are to the interest of the owner;
(2) references to a leasehold interest in land which is a term of years absolute are to a tenant's right over or interest in a property subject to a lease; and
(3) references to an agreement for a lease do not include missives of let that constitute an actual lease.

[*CTA 2010, s 205(6)*].

The following supplementary provisions apply to disposals of qualifying interests in land.

(A) Where two or more persons are entitled jointly or in common to a qualifying interest in land, the relief applies only if each person disposes of the whole of his beneficial interest in the land to the charity. Relief is then allowed to each of those persons, being apportioned between or amongst them as they may agree.
(B) The relief is dependent on the receipt by the person disposing of the interest of a certificate given by or on behalf of the charity specifying the description of the interest concerned and the date of the disposal, and stating that the charity has acquired the interest.
(C) If a 'disqualifying event' occurs at any time in the period from the date of the disposal to the sixth anniversary of the end of the accounting period of the disposal ('*the provisional period*'), the person (or each of the persons) making the disposal is treated as never having been entitled to the relief in respect of the disposal (and HMRC has the necessary assessment, etc. powers). A '*disqualifying event*' occurs if the person (or any one of the persons) who made the disposal, or any connected person (see **25 CONNECTED PERSONS**), either becomes entitled to an interest or right in relation to all or part of the land to which the disposal relates, or becomes party to an arrangement under which he, or a person connected with him, enjoys some right in relation to all or part of that land, otherwise than for full consideration in money or money's worth. This does *not* apply if the person became so entitled as a result of a disposition of property on death, whether by will, by intestacy or otherwise.

[*CTA 2010, ss 203–216; FA 2004, ss 139, 145, Sch 26 para 10; ITTOIA 2005, Sch 1 para 249; CTA 2009, Sch 1 para 199*].

Foreign charities are currently excluded from *ICTA 1988, s 506* by virtue of *ICTA 1988, s 506(3)* and the European Commission has sent a formal request to the UK under Article 226 of the EC Treaty to end what it considers to be discrimination against foreign charities which is contrary to the EC Treaty (see IP/06/964, 10 July 2006).

[*CTA 2010, ss 213–217; ICTA 1988, s 587BA; ITA 2007, Sch 1 para 138; FA 2007, Sch 26 para 7*].

Key points

[20.19] Points to consider are as follows:

- Does the body fall within the definition of a charity for tax purposes?
- Does company law permit the company to make the charitable gift?
- Exemptions from tax on charities' income are specific, not general. Therefore if a charity has income not within the specific exemptions it will be liable to tax on that income.
- Companies receive relief for charitable donations against profits of the year in which they are made, except where the donor is owned by the charity, in which case the donation may be made up to nine months after the end of the accounting period to which it relates.
- Charities should avoid making investments in or substantial loans to their trading companies from which they have received donations financed by trading profits.

21

Claims

Cross references. See **10.2**(i) CAPITAL ALLOWANCES — INTRODUCTION; **17.3** CAPITAL LOSSES for requirement to notify loss; **28.4** CORPORATE VENTURING SCHEME; **32.5** DOUBLE TAX RELIEF.

Simon's Taxes. See **A4.202, D1.1345–D1.1352.**

Introduction

[21.1] The Taxes Acts provide for a number of claims and elections. With effect from 1 April 2010, these must be made within four years of the end of the accounting period to which they relate, unless a different time limit is prescribed within the legislation for that particular claim or election. Before 1 April 2010, the standard time limit was six years.

Amendments may be made to claims within the same time limit for the original claim or election. All claims must be expressed in figures at the time the claim is made.

Certain claims must be made in the tax return of the company in question, such as claims with regard to group relief, capital allowances, research and development tax credits, film tax relief, land remediation tax credits and vaccine research tax credits. Other claims do not need to be made in the return but may not be made before the return for the period to which the claim relates is delivered.

This chapter examines these claims in more detail and considers appeals and other relief in respect of such claims.

[*FA 2008, Sch 39 para 42; SI 2009 No 403*].

Claims and elections

[21.2] Generally claims or elections should be made in writing (whether within the tax return, or otherwise). *CTA 2009* and *CTA 2010* specifically state this is to be the case with regard to claims and elections made under those acts. [*CTA 2010, s 1175; CTA 2009, s 1315; FA 1998, Sch 18 paras 54–56*].

Subject to any express provision to the contrary:

(a) claims and elections affecting only one accounting period, and which are made after notice has been given requiring the delivery of a company tax return for that period, must be made in the return, or by amendment of the return, if they can be so made. This requirement does not apply with regard to a claim for an amount to be exempt from tax under the provisions for gifts qualifying for gift aid relief in respect of charitable companies and certain eligible bodies (within *CTA 2010, ss 472, 475*). [*FA 1998, Sch 18 para 57*].
A claim, etc. made after the return has been delivered is treated as an amendment of the return (as under **66.9 RETURNS**).
Group relief, first-year tax credit and capital allowance claims (see further below) and claims to research and development tax credits (see **64 RESEARCH AND DEVELOPMENT**) may only be made by inclusion in a tax return;

(b) claims and elections which affect an accounting period (or periods) other than that in which the event or occasion giving rise to the claim (etc.) occurs are treated as amending the return for that period (or for the period affected), as under **66.9 RETURNS**, where that return has already been delivered and can be so amended [*FA 1998, Sch 18 para 58*];

(c) otherwise, *TMA 1970, Sch 1A* (as amended by *FA 1998, Sch 19 para 42*) provides the procedure for claims etc. (see **21.7** below).

(a)–(c) above do not, however, affect the time limit or any other condition for making a claim or election.

A joint claim or election may be made in a return. The written claim etc. signed by the appropriate person(s) need be delivered with only one of the returns to which it applies, the return(s) of the other party or parties being required to reveal its existence and be prepared in accordance with it. (HMRC Guide to Self-Assessment, para 7.6.6).

Certain claims not required to be made in a company tax return may not be made before the return for the period to which the claim relates is delivered. This applies to claims for payment of tax credits, where still available, excluding claims by companies entitled to certain corporation tax exemptions unless *ICTA 1988, Sch 19AB* applies, to certain claims for income tax repayments, and to claims for relief under *FA 2000, Sch 15 Pt V* (**CORPORATE VENTURING SCHEME** (**28**)).

As noted at (c) above a claim not included in a company tax return must be in such form as HMRC require and must contain a declaration that the particulars in it are correct to the best of the information and belief of the claimant. See further **21.7** below.

Consequential claims

For consequential claims, elections etc. arising out of HMRC assessments or amendments to self-assessments, see **21.6** below.

[*TMA 1970, Sch 1A para 2; FA 1998, Sch 18 paras 9, 10(2), 57–60; FA 2008, Sch 25 para 8(2); CTA 2009, Sch 1 para 454*].

Simon's Taxes. See **D1.1345** *et seq.*

Group relief

Claimant company

[21.3] A claim to group relief must be included in the company tax return (or amended return) for the accounting period for which the claim is made. It must specify the quantum of the amount claimed and the name of the surrendering company.

It should also state whether any of the following:

(a) the claimant company;
(b) the surrendering company; or
(c) any other company by reference to which either those companies are members of the same group or the conditions for consortium relief are satisfied,

was not UK resident in either or both of the surrendering company's accounting period to which the surrender relates and the corresponding accounting period of the claimant company.

[*FA 1998, Sch 18 para 68*].

The claim must be made (and may be withdrawn) at any time up to the latest of:

(i) the first anniversary of the filing date for the claimant company tax return;
(ii) 30 days after closure of any enquiry into that return (unless the enquiry, being otherwise out of time, was limited, as referred to in **66.21 RETURNS**, to matters to which a previous amendment making or withdrawing a group relief claim relates, or which are affected by the amendment);
(iii) 30 days after notice of any amendment of that return by HMRC following such an enquiry; and
(iv) 30 days after determination of any appeal against an amendment within (iii),

or at a later time if HMRC allow it (for which see **55.3 LOSSES**).

[*FA 1998, Sch 18 para 74*].

These time limits override the normal time limits for amendment of a company tax return. Withdrawals of claims must be made by amending the return, and a claim can only be amended by withdrawal and replacement by another claim.

A claim may be made after the surrendering company has left the group (*A W Chapman Ltd v Hennessey* (1981) 55 TC 516).

A claim may:

- be for the full amount available or for less than the full amount available for surrender at the time of the claim;
- be ineffective if it is for more than the full amount available for surrender;

and in addition withdrawals are given effect before any claims made on the same day.

Where claims are made on the same day for an aggregate amount in excess of the amount available for surrender, HMRC determines which of the claims is to be ineffective to prevent an excess arising. In practice, they will treat as ineffective the claim(s) in the lowest amount(s) consistent with achieving this objective (see HMRC Company Taxation Manual, CTM97070).

The amount available for surrender at any time is the total amount available under *CTA 2010, Part 5*, formerly *ICTA 1988, s 403; CTA 2009, Sch 1 para 118* (see **39.5 GROUP RELIEF**) on the basis of the surrendering company's tax return, disregarding any amendment whose effect is deferred pending completion of an enquiry (see **66.21 RETURNS**), less all amounts for which notices of consent (see below) have been given and not withdrawn.

Claims may be made by more than one company in respect of the same surrendering company accounting period.
[*FA 1998, Sch 18 para 69*].

Consent — surrendering company

A claim for group relief or for consortium relief requires the written consent of the surrendering company or in a claim for consortium relief, the consent of all consortium members. The consent form must be given to the officer of HMRC to whom the company makes its tax returns at, or before, the time the claim is made, and a copy of the consent form must accompany the claim.

The consent notice must give:

- the names and tax district references of the surrendering company and the company or companies to which relief is being surrendered;
- the amount of the relief; and
- the surrendering company accounting period to which the surrender relates.

It may not be amended, but may be withdrawn (by notice to the officer to whom the consent was notified) and replaced within the normal time limits (as above). Notice of withdrawal must be accompanied by the written consent of the claimant company, unless the withdrawal is the result of a reduction in the amount available for surrender (for which see below). The claimant company must, so far as it may do so, amend its return accordingly.

There are simplified claim and surrender procedures — see further below.

Where the surrendering company has filed its return for the period to which the surrender relates, it must, at the same time as giving its consent, amend its return to reflect that consent.

Where the consent relates to a trading loss for which relief has already been obtained by carry-forward, the surrendering company must (notwithstanding any time limits otherwise applicable) amend its return(s) for the subsequent period(s) in which relief was given for the loss to reflect the consent (relief for such periods being treated as given for carry-forward losses of earlier accounting periods before later ones).

Where there is a reduction in the total amount available for surrender (as above) below the amount for which consent to surrender has already been given, the company must, within 30 days, withdraw its consent (and may issue new notices of consent) so as to bring the total of amounts for which consent is given within the total amount available. Copies of the withdrawal notices and any new consents must be sent to the companies affected and to HMRC.

If the company fails to take such corrective action, HMRC may by written amend and reallocate the consents to the extent necessary to achieve that objective (subject to appeal in writing by the company within 30 days of the notice to the officer by whom it was given). HMRC must copy the notice to any claimant company affected by those directions. A claimant company notified of any withdrawal or new consent or HMRC direction must, so far as it may do so, amend its return for the period in question accordingly.

[*FA 1998, Sch 18 paras 70–75*].

Unpaid tax and HMRC assessments

Any tax arising as a result of the above which is unpaid six months after the company's 'time limit for claims' (see below), HMRC may, up to two years after that time limit, make an assessment in the name of the claimant company on any other company which has obtained group relief as a result of the surrender. The amount of the assessment is limited to the lesser of the amount of the unpaid tax and the amount of tax the other company saves by virtue of the surrender. The other company may recover the tax (and any interest thereon) from the claimant company.

The company's '*time limit for claims*' for this purpose is the latest of the dates in (i)–(iv) above on which the company could make or withdraw a group relief claim for the accounting period for which the claim in question was made.

An assessment may be made to recover group relief which in the opinion of HMRC is, or has become, excessive. This is without prejudice to the making of a discovery assessment (see **7.3 ASSESSMENTS**) or to the making of adjustments by way of discharge or repayment of tax. As regards notices of assessment, time limits and appeals, the same conditions apply as in relation to discovery assessments. Where a claimant company fails, or is unable, to amend its return following receipt of a notice of withdrawal or new consent or HMRC direction (as above), an assessment may be made (if otherwise out of time) up to one year after the date of the notice (the date of the new notice if a new notice of consent follows a withdrawal notice).

[*FA 1998, Sch 18 paras 75A–76*].

Simplified group relief procedures

These are contained in *The Corporation Tax (Simplified Arrangements for Group Relief) Regulations 1999* (*SI 1999 No 2975*) (as amended). A group of companies all, or substantially all, of whose tax returns are made to the same tax office, may enter into special arrangements. These enable an authorised company within the group to act for the group in relation to group relief claims. The authorised company may then provide a written statement containing the information necessary for the amendment of tax returns of the companies covered by the arrangements for the purpose of making or withdrawing group relief claims and surrenders. The statement must be in a form provided or authorised by HMRC.

Group companies remain liable for any incorrect claim or return arising from the authorised company's statement.

Consortium companies which can claim or surrender group relief may be included in the arrangements (and the authorised company may be a consortium company).

For the detailed requirements as to the making of an application by an authorised company, and the consequences of entering into such arrangements, see *SI 1999 No 2975* (as amended).

[*FA 1998, Sch 18 para 77; SI 1999 No 2975*].

Overseas losses of non-resident companies

The above provisions apply to claims (from 1 April 2006) in respect of overseas losses of non-resident companies (*FA 1998, Sch 18 para 77A*; see further **39.2**(b) and **39.10 GROUP RELIEF**) with the following modifications. References to the relief being surrendered is to the 'EEA amount' (see **39.10 GROUP RELIEF**). References to the surrendering company's accounting period are to its deemed accounting period under **39.10**(iii) **GROUP RELIEF**. Notice of consent of the surrendering company is to be given by the claimant company to the officer of HMRC to whom that company makes its returns and the requirement for the notice to contain details of tax district reference does not apply.

Notice of withdrawal of consent is to be given by the claimant company and not the surrendering company. A notice of withdrawal and any new notice of consent under *FA 1998, Sch 18 para 75* (reduction in amount available for surrender) is to be sent to an officer of HMRC by the claimant rather than the surrendering company and any notice containing directions by an officer of HMRC is to be given to the claimant company. The claimant company rather than the surrendering company can appeal against such directions and the rest of *Sch 18* is to be similarly read with appropriate modifications.

Where a notice to produce documents is given to the claimant company for the purposes of an enquiry, the notice may require the claimant company to explain why the EEA amount meets the conditions for it to be treated as a qualifying loss and to provide details of the recalculation required (see **39.10 GROUP RELIEF**). The claimant company may also be required to explain why the EEA amount is not prevented from being surrendered by virtue of the unallowable losses provision in **39.12 GROUP RELIEF**.

[*CTA 2010, ss 111–128; ICTA 1988, s 402(5); FA 1998, Sch 18 paras 10(2), 66–77A; FA 2006, Sch 1 para 8*].

See HMRC Company Taxation Manual, CTM97600 onwards.

Capital allowances

[21.4] A capital allowance claim under self-assessment must be included in the company tax return (or amended return) for the accounting period for which the claim is made. It must specify the quantum of the amount claimed. It must be made (and may be amended or withdrawn) at any time up to the latest of:

- the first anniversary of the filing date for the company tax return;
- 30 days after closure of any enquiry into that return (unless the enquiry, being otherwise out of time, was limited, as referred to in **66.21 RETURNS**, to matters to which a previous amendment making or withdrawing a capital allowance claim relates, or which are affected by the amendment);
- 30 days after notice of any amendment of that return by HMRC following such an enquiry; and
- 30 days after determination of any appeal against an amendment within (iii),

or at a later time if HMRC allow it (for which see **55.3 LOSSES**).

These time limits override the normal time limits for amendment of a company tax return. Amendments or withdrawals of claims must be made by amending the return.

If the effect of a claim is to reduce the available capital allowances for another accounting period for which a return has already been made, the company has 30 days to make the necessary amendments of that return. If it fails to do so, HMRC may, by written notice and subject to a right of appeal within 30 days of the issue of the notice, amend the return to correct the position (notwithstanding any time limit otherwise applicable).

[*FA 1998, Sch 18 paras 10(2), 78–83; CAA 2001, Sch 2 para 103*].

Other claims

[21.5] For claims for payment of research and development tax credits, see **64 RESEARCH AND DEVELOPMENT**. For claims for payment of film tax credits see **70.31 TRADE PROFITS — INCOME AND SPECIFIC TRADES**. For claims for first-year tax credits, see **11.17 CAPITAL ALLOWANCES — PLANT AND MACHINERY: ELIGIBLE EXPENDITURE AND INITIAL ALLOWANCES**.

For consequential claims, elections etc. arising out of HMRC assessments or amendments to self-assessments (which may generally be made within one year from the end of the accounting period in which the assessment was made or the enquiry into the relevant return closed), or where an assessment is made in a case involving careless or deliberate acts (previously fraud or negligence), see **21.6** below.

Consequential claims

[21.6] Where:

(a) a company tax return is amended by HMRC under *FA 1998, Sch 18 para 34(2)(b)* (i.e. an amendment, following closure of an enquiry, to a return other than the return which was the subject of the enquiry) so that the tax payable is increased (see **66.24 RETURNS**); or
(b) a discovery assessment (see **7.3 ASSESSMENTS**) is made; or
(c) an assessment to recover excessive group relief (see **21.2** above) is made,

the following provisions apply to allow certain claims, elections, applications and notices to be made, given, revoked or varied. However, where an assessment is made in a case involving, from 1 April 2009, careless or deliberate conduct (see **7.3 ASSESSMENTS**), the more restricted relief described in the final paragraph below applies instead.

A claim or election, as above, which:

- relates to the accounting period in respect of which the amendment or assessment was made; or
- was made or given by reference to an event occurring in that period,

and the making of which has or could have the effect of reducing a 'relevant liability' of the company, may be made or given at any time within one year from the end of the '*relevant accounting period*', i.e. that in which the closure notice was issued or the assessment made.

Similarly, if previously made or given, it may be varied or (unless irrevocable) revoked in the same manner as it was made or given, and by or with the consent of the same person(s) who made it, gave it or consented to it (or their personal representatives).

A '*relevant liability*' is the increased liability arising from the amendment or assessment, or any other liability of the company for the accounting period to which the amendment or assessment relates or any subsequent accounting period ending not later than one year after the end of the relevant accounting period.

If the effect of a consequential claim, etc. as above would be to alter the tax liability of another person, the written consent of that person (or their personal representative) to the claim, etc. is required. If the effect is to increase that person's liability, neither the above provisions nor *TMA 1970, s 43A* (the corresponding income and capital gains tax provisions) apply in relation to any amendment or assessment made because of the increased liability.

Where one or more claims etc. as above are made in consequence of an amendment or assessment, the combined tax liability of the company and any other persons affected cannot be reduced by more than the additional tax liability resulting from that amendment or assessment. Where this limitation involves more than one period or more than one person, the limited amount available is apportioned between the periods or persons concerned. The manner in which the apportionment is to be made is specified by HMRC by written notice to the person(s) concerned, who may, however, within 30 days from the date of the notice (where more than one person is concerned, the last notice), give (or jointly give) written notice substituting a different manner of apportionment.

The claims appeals provisions are appropriately modified in relation to revocations or variations of claims under the above provisions.

Assessments involving careless or deliberate acts

Where an assessment is made in a case, from 1 April 2009, involving careless or deliberate acts (previously fraudulent or negligent conduct), the above provisions for consequential claims are disapplied. Instead, the company may require that in arriving at the tax assessed, any relief or allowance is given to which the company would have been entitled for the accounting period had a claim or application been made within the normal time limits. The claims or applications must be made either before the assessment is made or within the time provided for an appeal against the assessment (see HMRC Company Taxation Manual, CTM90665).

[*FA 1998, Sch 18 paras 61–65; FA 2008, Sch 39 paras 46, 47*].

Simon's Taxes. See **D1.1348.**

Claims etc. not included in returns

[21.7] A claim not included in a company tax return must be in such form as required by HMRC and must contain a declaration that the particulars contained therein are correct to the best information and belief of the claimant. HMRC do not generally provide a standard form for claims but may set certain requirements for any such claims.

For example, subject to any specific provision otherwise, a claim or election made otherwise than in a return must be made to an officer of HMRC. As noted, the claim etc. must include a declaration by the claimant that all particulars are correctly stated to the best of his information or belief. No claim requiring a tax repayment can be made unless the claimant has documentary proof that the tax has been paid or deducted. The claim must be made in a form determined by HMRC and may require, *inter alia*, a statement of the amount of tax to be discharged or repaid and (except as below) supporting information and documentation.

In practice, HMRC do not generally determine the particular form in which a claim must be made. In the case of a claim by or on behalf of a person who is not resident in the UK, HMRC may require a statement or declaration in support of the claim to be made by affidavit.

A person who may wish to make a claim must keep all records that may be required for the purpose and must preserve them until such time as HMRC may no longer enquire into the claim or such enquiries are treated as completed. Following *FA 2008*, HMRC have the power to make regulations specifying records which are required to be kept. There is a maximum penalty of £3,000 for non-compliance in relation to any claim *actually made*. Similar provisions and exceptions apply as in **66.18 RETURNS** as to the preservation of the information contained in documents and other records instead of originals and the exception from penalty for non-compliance in relation to dividend vouchers, interest certificates etc.

A claimant may, at any time within twelve months of making a claim, amend the claim by notice to an officer of HMRC. An officer of HMRC may similarly, at any time within nine months of the claim being made, amend the claim to correct any obvious errors or mistakes (including errors of principle and arithmetical mistakes).

No such amendments may, however, be made while the claim is under enquiry (see below). HMRC have powers to enquire into a claim etc. (or amendment thereof) similar to those relating to company tax returns (see **66.19 RETURNS**), but these powers are to be replaced by the unified powers at **43.3–43.10 HMRC INVESTIGATORY POWERS** with effect from a date to be appointed. Notice of intention to enquire must be given by the first anniversary of the end of the accounting period to which the claim relates or, if later, by the quarter day (meaning 31 January, 30 April etc.) next following the first anniversary of the date of claim etc. In the event of such an enquiry, they have powers to call for documents, etc. similar to those relating to enquiries into company tax returns (see **66.20 RETURNS**). Where an enquiry is in progress, an officer of HMRC may give provisional effect to the claim etc. (or amendment thereof) to such extent as he thinks fit.

An enquiry is complete when HMRC's officer issues a closure notice informing the claimant of his conclusions. If the claim is for discharge or repayment of tax, the notice must either state that, in the officer's opinion, no amendment of the claim is required or amend the claim so as to make good or eliminate any deficiency or excess which in the officer's opinion has arisen (the latter only applying, in the case of an enquiry into an amendment of a claim, so far as the deficiency or excess is attributable to that amendment). In the case of any other claim, the notice must either allow the claim or disallow it wholly or to the extent the officer considers appropriate. The claimant may apply to the Commissioners for a direction to issue a closure notice in the same way as applies to enquiries into returns (see **66.23 RETURNS**).

For earlier enquiries, the provisions for amendment of claims on completion of an enquiry were similar to those which apply to amendment of a company's return on completion of an enquiry (see **66.24 RETURNS**).

HMRC must give effect to such an amendment, by assessment if necessary, within 30 days after issue of the closure notice (or, before 11 May 2001, of the amendment being made).

An appeal may be made against an amendment by HMRC to a claim following an enquiry, written notice of appeal to be given normally within 30 days after the amendment is made (extended to three months where questions of residence are involved). If an amendment is varied on appeal, HMRC have a further 30 days to give effect to the variation. Where a claim etc. does not give rise to a discharge or repayment of tax (for example, a claim to carry forward trading losses), there are provisions as to disallowance of such claims on completion of the enquiry, with appeal procedures similar to those above.

Appeals against amendments to claims are normally made to the First-tier Tribunal.

Where these provisions apply to a claim, etc. which results in an increase in the tax payable, all necessary adjustments, by way of assessment or otherwise, may be made so as to give effect to it.

[*TMA 1970, s 42(11), Sch 1A; FA 1998, Sch 18 para 60(3); FA 2008, ss 113, 115, Sch 36 para 77, Sch 37 para 3; SI 2009 No 571*].

Simon's Taxes. See **D1.1346.**

Time limits

[21.8] Unless otherwise specified, claims for relief from corporation tax must be made, from 1 April 2010, within four years (before that date, six years) of the end of the accounting period to which they relate.

[*FA 1998, Sch 18 para 55; FA 2008, Sch 39 para 45; SI 2009 No 403*].

See **69 TIME LIMITS** and Tolley's Income Tax under Time Limits — Fixed Dates and Time Limits — Miscellaneous. See also **21.11** below with respect to recovery of tax paid under mistake of law.

Appeals in respect of claims

[21.9] Appeals have to be made in writing within 30 days of the issue of:

- a notice of amendment to a self-assessment; or
- a notice of an assessment which is not a self-assessment.

See **7.3 ASSESSMENTS, 66.24 RETURNS, 6.2 APPEALS.**

As regards claims etc. to which *TMA 1970, Sch 1A* applies (see below), appeals against amendments to claims etc. must be made within 30 days of the amendment being made, extended to three months where the appeal relates to certain residence etc. claims or to pension funds for overseas employees.

Any notice of appeal in connection with the self-assessment provisions must state the grounds of appeal.

[*TMA 1970, Sch 1A para 9; FA 1998, Sch 18 para 92*].

TMA 1970, Sch 1A (as amended) deals with all aspects of claims not within *FA 1998, Sch 18 paras 57, 58* (mainly those not included in the company tax return (or amended return), see **21.1** above).

[*FA 1998, Sch 18 para 59*].

TMA 1970, ss 46B–46D (as amended) have effect as respects the Tribunal to which an appeal under that *Schedule* lies.

Error or mistake relief

[21.10] With effect from 1 April 2010, *FA 2009* replaces error or mistake relief with a relief for overpaid tax which applies where, in the taxpayer's view, tax has been overpaid, or the liability has been determined at a figure higher than the taxpayer believes is due.

To obtain repayment, a claim must be made to HMRC within four years from the end of the accounting period to which the return relates, where the error is connected with a corporation tax return and the end of the accounting period of payment in other cases. No account can be taken of tax paid by a third party in arriving at a repayment (e.g. in a status dispute where the assessment is on the company but it is believed that the tax was paid by the worker).

HMRC do not have to accept a claim if it falls within any of the following:

- regarding a claim, election or notice or certain allocations under the *CAA 2001*;
- there are other remedies under the Taxes Acts;
- the company did not claim within a deadline which has passed and he should reasonably have known to claim before the deadline;
- the claim has already been considered by a tribunal or court or by HMRC in the course of an agreed appeal;
- the company knew or ought reasonably to have known the grounds of appeal when a claim could have been made in time;
- proceedings were brought by HMRC against the claimant for recovery of the amount;
- the amount at issue arose from a calculation, and the basis of calculation was that generally prevailing at the time.

Where a party acts on behalf of another, that other company may make a claim under these provisions. For partnership returns, the claim must be made by the partner nominated by all the other partners.

[*FA 1998, Sch 18 para 51 (as amended) and paras 51A–51G; FA 2009, s 100, Sch 52*].

Where a company believes it has paid too much tax under an assessment (or self-assessment) due to an error or mistake in a return, it may claim relief by written notice to HMRC not more than four years, from 1 April 2010, (previously six years) after the end of the accounting period to which the return relates.

After enquiring into the matter, and having regard to all the relevant circumstances, HMRC may make a tax repayment that is just and reasonable. In determining the claim they will, in particular, consider whether the granting of relief would result in amounts being excluded from the charge to tax, taking into consideration accounting periods of the company other than that to which the claim relates.

Where the return was made on the basis of, or in accordance with, the practice generally prevailing at the time, an error or mistake claim may not amend it in respect of a change of basis. Nor may relief be given where the mistake was in a claim or election included in the return.

An appeal against a decision of HMRC on a claim lies to the First-tier Tribunal, which determine the claim in accordance with the same principles as apply to HMRC's decision. An appeal to the Upper Tribunal against a decision of the First-tier Tribunal can only be made on a point of law in connection with the computation of profits (including amounts chargeable under *ICTA 1988, s 419* (loans to participators, see **22.12** *et seq.* **CLOSE COMPANIES**) and *ICTA 1988, s 747* (**CONTROLLED FOREIGN COMPANIES** (**27**)). [*FA 1998, Sch 18 para 51; FA 1998, Sch 18 para 51(4)(b) (post FA 2009 amendment) which applies TMA 1970, Sch 1A para 9*].

A claim to error or mistake relief may still be made in relation to an amendment to a self-assessment notwithstanding an agreement with the inspector preceding that amendment (*Wall v CIR* [2002] STC (SCD) 122).

In *G Allen v HMRC* (TC00903) [2011] UKFTT 26 (TC), a dentist had formed the opinion that his accounts had overstated his profits, because of errors by his previous accountant. He submitted a claim for error or mistake relief. The Revenue accepted the claim for 1993/94 onwards, but rejected the claim for 1992/93 and earlier years on the grounds that it was outside the six-year time limit of *TMA 1970, s 33(1)* as then in force. In 2009 the dentist lodged an appeal to the First-Tier Tribunal. The tribunal struck out the appeal, holding that it had no jurisdiction under *SI 2009 No 273*. Whilst this case refers to an income tax claim, and *FA 2009* applies since 1 April 2010 with regard to error or mistake claims, it does illustrate the point that claims must be lodged within the applicable time limits.

See also **21.11** below for recovery of tax paid under mistake of law.

Simon's Taxes. See **A4.206–A4.208, D1.1350**.

Restitution — tax paid under mistake of law

[21.11] For claims brought before 22 July 2004 see Tolley's Corporation Tax 2009–10 under Claims.

Pursuant to *FA 2004, s 320*, where an action for restitution is brought after 7 September 2003 which is based on mistake of law, it must generally be brought within six years of the tax having being paid. This derogates (with regard to claims relating to taxes administered by HMRC) from the provisions within the *Limitation Act 1980, s 32(1)(c)* whereby the six-year limitation runs from the date a mistake is discovered. See further below.

FA 2007, s 107 extends this existing treatment (under *FA 2004*) of claims for restitution of tax paid under mistake of law to apply to past transactions as well as future transactions. It provides that the *Limitation Act 1980, s 32(1)(c)* does not apply to an action for restitution of direct tax due to a mistake of law brought before 8 September 2003, whether the action relates solely to a claim for restitution or otherwise.

However, this rule does not apply to actions on which judgment on the application of the *Limitation Act 1980, s 32(1)(c)* had been given by the House of Lords in favour of the taxpayer (or another party in a group litigation order) before 6 December 2006, the date of the pre-budget report 2006 when the proposed provisions of *FA 2007* were first announced.

Where a court has decided in favour of a taxpayer on or after 6 December 2006 but before 19 July 2007 (the date *FA 2007* received Royal Assent) and tax has been repaid, the judgment is reversed so far as restitution is concerned and the amount received is repayable with interest.

There was a body of case law on this subject. It was held in *Woolwich Equitable Building Society v CIR* [1993] AC 70, [1992] 3 All ER 737, HL (see **50.7 INTEREST ON OVERPAID TAX**), that tax paid pursuant to an *ultra vires* demand was recoverable as of right at common law and without need to invoke mistake of law by the taxpayer.

It was held by the House of Lords in *Deutsche Morgan Grenfell Group plc v CIR (and cross appeal)* [2006] UKHL 49, HL, that English law recognised a restitution claim for tax paid under a mistake of law and that the limitation period (under the *Limitation Act 1980*) ran from the date the mistake at law was discovered, which, in Deutsche Morgan's case, was the date of the CJEC decision which made it clear that a mistake in law had occurred (8 March 2001). Therefore the decision was in favour of the taxpayer. This confirmed the ruling by the High Court, following which provisions were introduced by *FA 2004, s 320*.

Under the *Limitation Act 1980, s 32(1)(c)* (or in Northern Ireland *Article 71(1)(c)* of the *Limitation (Northern Ireland) Order 1989 (SI 1989 No 1339)*), the six-year period of limitation in the case of mistake of law does not begin to run until the claimant discovers the mistake (or could with reasonable diligence have discovered it). However, under provisions introduced by *FA 2004, s 320*, this does not apply in relation to a mistake of law relating to taxes administered by HMRC where the action for restitution is brought after 7 September 2003. The effect is that court actions for restitution based on mistake of law must generally be brought within six years of the tax having been paid.

[*FA 2007, s 107*].

22

Close Companies

Simon's Taxes. See Part **D3**.

Introduction

[22.1] There are many UK resident companies that are defined as 'small' for various parts of the Corporation Taxes Acts. In addition, many private limited companies are owner managed businesses and are controlled by a limited number of individuals. These companies may therefore be defined as 'close'. There are special tax rules that apply to 'close' companies. This stems from the fact that the directors and shareholders are often the same people, and there are concerns that, because of this link, it is easier for the company's affairs to be arranged to give tax advantages to the company, its directors and shareholders.

The following paragraphs describe these special rules and the effects that may arise as a result.

For HMRC's guide to close companies see CTM60100 *et seq*.

Close company — definition

[22.2] Subject to the exceptions at **22.3** below, a company is a '*close company*' if *either* Condition A or Condition B below is met.

Condition A is that the company:

- is under the 'control' (**22.6** below) of five or fewer 'participators' (**22.7** below); or
- is under the control of participators who are 'directors' (**22.8** below).

Condition B is that five or fewer participators, or participators who are directors, together possess or are entitled to acquire:

(a) such rights as would, in the event of a winding-up, entitle them to receive the greater part of the assets available for distribution among participators; or
(b) such rights as would, in the event of a winding-up, so entitle them if one were to disregard any rights which any of them (or any other person) has as a loan creditor (**22.11** below), whether of that company or any other company.

For the purpose of applying Condition B, participators in and directors of any company (a 'company participator') entitled to receive assets in the notional winding-up are themselves treated as participators in or directors of the company under consideration. Company participators are disregarded for that purpose, unless acting in a fiduciary or representative capacity.

[*CTA 2010, ss 439, 441; ICTA 1988, s 414(1)(2)(2C)(2D)*].

CTA 2010, s 440 (previously *ICTA 1988, s 414(2A)(2B)*) determines the part of the assets available for distribution among the participators which a person is treated as being entitled to receive in the notional winding-up envisaged by Condition B above. In particular, the assumption is made that any company participator will also be wound up and that the assets distributed to it will be distributed onwards to its own participators.

For the purposes of Condition B, a person is treated as entitled to acquire anything which he is entitled to acquire at a future date or will, at a future date, be entitled to acquire, with reference to both contractual rights and any rights under a trust deed, for example. See further CTM60120.

If a person (B) possesses any rights or powers on behalf of another person (A), or may be required to exercise any rights or powers on A's direction or on A's behalf, those rights or powers are to be attributed to A. There can also be attributed to a person (P) all the rights and powers:

(i) of any company of which P has control, or of which P and his 'associates' (**22.9** below) have control;
(ii) of any two or more companies within (a) above;
(iii) of any associate of P; or
(iv) of any two or more associates of P.

Any rights or powers already attributed to A, where A is a company or an associate of P, may in turn be attributed to P under any of (i)–(iv) above. However, any rights or powers attributed under (i)–(iv) to an associate cannot consequently be attributed under (i)–(iv) to another associate.

Any such attributions that *can* be made under (i)–(iv) above *will* be made if they result in the company being treated as under the control of five or fewer participators and thus a close company.

[*CTA 2010, s 451; ICTA 1988, s 416(4)–(6)*].

The first-mentioned holder of shares in joint ownership is treated as able alone to exercise the rights attaching thereto (*Harton Coal Co Ltd* [1960] Ch 563, [1960] 3 All ER 48). For circumstances in which HMRC are bound to attribute rights and powers as in (a)–(d) above, see *R v CIR (ex p Newfields Developments Ltd)* [2001] UKHL 27, [2001] 4 All ER 400, [2001] 1 WLR 1111.

Simon's Taxes. See **D3.101–D3.112, D3.121.**

Exceptions

[22.3] Notwithstanding **22.2** above, none of the following can be a close company.

(a) A non-UK resident company.
(b) A registered industrial and provident society (within *CTA 2010, s 1119*).
(c) A building society.
(d) A company controlled by the Crown or by persons acting on behalf of the Crown and independently of any other person. But this exception applies only for the purposes of Condition A at **22.2** above. It does not apply at all if the company is a close company as a result of its being under the control of persons acting independently of the Crown.
(e) A company 'involved' with a non-close company (see below).
(f) Subject to the conditions set out at **22.4** below, a quoted company.

For the purposes of (e) above, a company is '*involved*' with a non-close company if:

(i) it is controlled by one or more non-close companies and cannot be treated as a close company except by taking, as one of its five or fewer participators, a non close company; or
(ii) it would not be a close company were it not for **22.2**(a) above or **22.6**(d) below and would still not be a close company if the term 'participators' did not include loan creditors (**22.11** below) which are non-close companies.

For the purposes only of applying (i) and (ii) above, the term 'close company' includes a company that would be a close company if it were UK resident; and 'non-close company' must be construed accordingly. If shares in a company (C) are held on trust for a registered pension scheme, the persons holding the shares are generally treated as the beneficial owners, so that the shares are held by a non-close company. However, this is not the case if the scheme is established for the benefit of (or for the benefit of dependants of) present or former directors or employees of C or of certain companies related to C (for which see *CTA 2010, s 445(3)*).

[*CTA 2010, ss 442–447; ICTA 1988, ss 414(1)(2), (4)–(7), 415*].

Quoted companies

[22.4] The circumstances under which a quoted company cannot be a close company at a particular time are summarised below. All three of conditions (a)–(c) must be met.

(a) Shares carrying at least 35% of the voting power in the company must have been allotted unconditionally to, or acquired unconditionally by, and at that time be beneficially held by, the public. For this purpose, 'shares' include stock but do not include shares entitled to a fixed rate of dividend. See below as regards 'voting power' and see **22.5** below as regards shares 'beneficially held by the public'.

(b) Such shares must, within the twelve months before that time, have been dealt in on, and listed on, a 'recognised stock exchange'.

(c) The voting power possessed by 'principal members' of the company must not at that time exceed 85% of the total voting power in the company.

In determining for these purposes the voting power which a person possesses, there is to be attributed to the person any voting power that would be attributed to him if the attribution rules at **22.2** above applied.

A '*principal member*' of a company is a person possessing more than 5% of the voting power. If, however, there are more than five such persons, a person is a principal member of the company only if he is one of the five persons possessing the greatest percentages. If there are no such five persons because two or more persons possess equal percentages, a person is a principal member of the company only if he is one of the six or more persons (including the two or more who are equal) who possess the greatest percentages.

[*CTA 2010, s 446; ICTA 1988, s 415(1)(2)(6)–(8); FA 2007, s 109, Sch 26 para 7(4)*].

Example

A holds 10% of the voting power of X Ltd. B and C hold 8% each, D and E hold 7% each and F holds 6%. No other member holds more than 5%. A, B, C, D and E each hold more than 5% and are principal members of the company, as they are the five persons holding the greatest percentages. F is not a principal member, as he does not meet the latter requirement. If, with the facts as above, G acquires a 10% holding, he will also become a principal member of the company. Since D and E have equal shareholdings, both will remain principal members, making six in total.

On and after 19 July 2007, a '*recognised stock exchange*' means:

- any market of a recognised investment exchange designated by HMRC; and
- any market outside the UK which is designated by HMRC.

HMRC publish a current list of recognised stock exchanges on their website at www.hmrc.gov.uk/fid/rse.htm.

Before 19 July 2007, '*recognised stock exchange*' meant The Stock Exchange (or such other recognised investment exchange as may be prescribed by HMRC for this purpose) and any non-UK stock exchange designated by HMRC. See HMRC Company Taxation Manual, CTM60310. The position may be affected by a double taxation agreement (see **32 DOUBLE TAX RELIEF**).

[*CTA 2010, s 1137; ICTA 1988, s 841; ITA 2007, s 1009; FA 2007, s 109, Sch 26 para 1*].

HMRC issued a guidance note on 29 March 2007 on the treatment of AIM shares and the designation of recognised investment exchanges as recognised stock exchanges — see SWTI Issue 14, 13 April 2007.

Simon's Taxes. See **D3.113, D3.114.**

Shares beneficially held by the public

[22.5] For the purposes of **22.4**(a) above, shares are beneficially held by the public if:

- they are beneficially held by a UK resident company which is not a close company, or by a non-UK resident company which would not be a close company if it were UK resident; or
- they are held on trust for a registered pension scheme; or
- they are not comprised in the holding of a 'principal member' (see **22.4** above).

A principal member's holding consists of the shares which carry the voting power possessed by him.

But shares in a company (C) are *not* beneficially held by the public if they are held:

(a) by a director (**22.8** below) of C;
(b) by an associate (**22.9** below) of a director of C;
(c) by a company which is under the control (**22.6** below) of one or more persons each of whom is such a director or associate;
(d) by an associated company (**22.10** below) of C; or
(e) as part of a fund the capital or income of which is applicable or applied wholly or mainly for the benefit of:
  - individuals who are employees, directors, past employees or past directors of C or of any company within (c) or (d) above, or
  - dependants of any such individuals.

In determining (a)–(e) above, if a person (B) (a nominee) possesses any rights or powers on behalf of another person (A), or may be required to exercise any rights or powers on A's direction or on A's behalf, any shares to which those rights or powers are attached are attributed to A.

[*CTA 2010, s 447; ICTA 1988, s 415(3)–(5)*].

Control

[22.6] A person (P) is treated as having '*control*' of a company (C) if P exercises, is able to exercise, or is entitled to acquire, direct or indirect control over C's affairs. It includes the possession of, or right to acquire:

(a) the greater part of the share capital or issued share capital of C; or
(b) the greater part of the voting power of C; or
(c) so much of the issued share capital of C as would give the right to receive the greater part of the company's income, were all that income distributed; or
(d) rights to the greater part of C's assets in a distribution on a winding-up or in any other circumstances.

Any rights that P or any other person has as a loan creditor (**22.11** below) are disregarded for the purposes of the assumption inherent in (c) above.

If two or more persons together satisfy any of the above conditions, they are treated as having control of C.

For the above purposes, a person is treated as entitled to acquire anything which he is entitled to acquire at a future date or will, at a future date, be entitled to acquire. The attribution rules at **22.2** above also apply for these purposes.

It should be noted that the control test found at (d) above with regard to a winding-up is distinct from the winding-up test found at *s 439(3)* described at **22.2** above.

[*CTA 2010, ss 450, 451; ICTA 1988, s 416(2)–(6)*].

See also **67.4 SMALL PROFITS — REDUCED RATES.**

Participator

[22.7] '*Participator*' means a person having a share or interest in the capital or income of the company and includes:

(a) any person possessing, or entitled to acquire, share capital or voting rights;
(b) any 'loan creditor' (**22.11** below);
(c) any person possessing a right to receive, or to participate in, distributions or any amount payable by the company (in cash or in kind) to loan creditors by way of premium on redemption;
(d) any person entitled to acquire such a right as in (c) above; and
(e) any person entitled to ensure that present or future income or assets of the company will be applied directly or indirectly for his benefit.

In (c) above, with reference to the definition of participator, 'distribution' is not to be given the extended meaning explained in **31.20 DISTRIBUTIONS.**

For the above purposes, a person is treated as entitled to do anything which he is entitled to do at a future date or will, at a future date, be entitled to do.

It should be noted that for the purposes of determining whether a company is controlled by five or fewer participators the definition of 'participator' is effectively widened by the attribution to such a persons of the rights and powers of their associates, etc. see **22.2** above. Thus a person may be treated as a participator even though they do not fall into any of the categories (a) to (e) above by virtue of being an associate of a participator — see **22.9** below.

[*CTA 2010, s 454; ICTA 1988, s 417(1)(2)*].

A recognised money broker is not treated as a participator in a stock-jobbing company solely by reason of short-term loans or advances arising in the ordinary course of their respective trades. (HMRC ESC C8).

Director

[22.8] '*Director*' includes any person:

(a) who occupies the position of director (by whatever name called); or

(b) in accordance with whose directions or instructions the directors are accustomed to act; or

(c) who is a manager of the company (or otherwise concerned in the management of the company's trade or business) and who is the beneficial owner of, or able directly or indirectly to control, at least 20% of the ordinary share capital of the company. For this purpose, the holdings and powers of his associates (**22.9** below) may be attributed to him.

[*CTA 2010, s 452; ICTA 1988, s 417(5)(6)*].

As regards (b) above, whilst not specifically stated for the purposes of this definition, HMRC do not normally regard a professional adviser as a director merely because the directors act on advice given by that person in a professional capacity. See, for example, *ITEPA 2003, s 67(2)*.

Associate

[22.9] '*Associate*' in relation to a person (P) means:

(a) any spouse or civil partner of P, any parent or remoter forebear of P, any child or remoter issue of P, or any brother or sister of P;

(b) any partner of P;

(c) the trustee(s) of any settlement of which P, or any relative (as in (a) above) of P (living or dead), is or was a settlor; see **25.2 CONNECTED PERSONS** for the definitions of 'settlement' and of 'settlor';

(d) if P has an interest in any shares or obligations of a company which are subject to a trust, the trustee(s) concerned;

(e) if P is itself a company and has an interest in any shares or obligations of a company which are subject to a trust, any other company which has an interest in those shares or obligations;

(f) if P has an interest in any shares or obligations of a company which are part of a deceased person's estate, the personal representatives of the deceased; and

(g) if P is itself a company and has an interest in any shares or obligations of a company which are part of a deceased person's estate, any other company which has an interest in those shares or obligations.

[*CTA 2010, s 448; ICTA 1988, s 417(3)(4)*].

Note that (a) above also does not include the spouse or civil partner of another relative of P; this is in contrast to the definition of 'connected person' (see **25.1 CONNECTED PERSONS**). Trustees have an interest in shares comprised in the settlement (*CIR v J Bibby & Sons Ltd* [1945] 1 All ER 667, 29 TC 167, HL).

Associated company

[22.10] A company is an '*associated company*' of another company at a particular time if, at that time or at any other time within the preceding twelve months:

- one of them has control of the other, or

- both are under the control of the same person or persons.

[*CTA 2010, s 449; ICTA 1988, s 416(1)*].

Loan creditor

[22.11] A '*loan creditor*' is a person to whom money is owed by the company in respect of:

- any money borrowed by the company; or
- any capital assets acquired by the company; or
- any right to receive income created in the company's favour; or
- any redeemable loan capital issued by the company; or
- any debt the value of which (to the company) at the time the debt was incurred (including any premium thereon) substantially exceeded the consideration given for it.

The definition is extended to include any person, other than the creditor himself, who has a beneficial interest in the debt or loan capital.

A person carrying on a banking business is not deemed to be a loan creditor in respect of any loan capital issued or debt incurred by the company for money lent by him to the company in the ordinary course of that business.

[*CTA 2010, s 453; ICTA 1988, s 417(7)–(9)*].

As to what constitutes a *bona fide* banking business, see *Hafton Properties Ltd v McHugh* (1986) 59 TC 420.

Example

A plc is a quoted company whose ordinary share capital is owned as follows.

		%
B	a director	10
C	wife of B	5
D	father of B	4
E		17
F	business partner of E	2
G	a director	10
H		8
I Ltd	a non-close company	30
J		7
100	other shareholders	7
		100

It can be shown that A plc is a close company by considering the following three steps.

(i) Is A plc controlled by five or fewer participators or by its directors?

		%	%
I Ltd			30
B	own shares	10	
	C's shares	5	
	D's shares	4	
			19
E	own shares	17	
	F's shares	2	
			19
			68

As A plc is controlled by three participators, the initial conclusion is that the company is close.

(ii) Is A plc a quoted company, with at least 35% of the voting power owned by the public?

	%
I Ltd	30
J	7
100 other shareholders	7
	44

As at least 35% of the share capital is owned by the public it appears that A plc is exempt from close company status, subject to step (iii).

(iii) Is more than 85% of the voting power in A plc owned by its principal members?

	%
I Ltd	30
B	19
E	19
G	10
H	8
	86

Although J owns more than 5% of the share capital, he is not a principal member because five other persons each hold more than J's 7% and so themselves constitute the principal members.

Because the principal members own more than 85% of the share capital A plc is a close company.

Loans to participators

[22.12] A tax charge arises if a close company makes any loan or advances any money to an individual who is either:

- a 'participator' in the company; or
- is an 'associate' of a participator.

There is due from the company, as if it were an amount of corporation tax chargeable on the company for the accounting period in which the loan or advance is made, an amount equal to 25% of the amount of the loan or advance.

The tax is due and payable in accordance with *TMA 1970, s 59D* (see **59.2 PAYMENT OF TAX**) on the day following the end of the period of nine months from the end of the accounting period in which the loan or advance was made (for companies not within the instalment payment regime — see **59.3**), and that is the date from which interest is chargeable for late payment.

'*Participator*' and '*associate*' are generally as defined in **22.7** and **22.9** above. If, however, a company (C) controls another company (D), a participator in C is to be treated for these purposes as being also a participator in D.

These provisions apply to a loan or advance made by a close company to a company receiving it in a fiduciary or representative capacity as they do to a loan or advance made to an individual.

[*CTA 2010, s 455(1)–(3), (5)(6), Sch 1 para 158; TMA 1970, s 109(3); ICTA 1988, s 419(1)–(3), (6)(7)*].

See **22.13** below as regards circumstances in which a close company is to be *treated* as making a loan, and **22.14** below for exceptions to the above provisions. See **22.15** below as to what happens when the loan or advance (or part of it) is repaid, released or written off.

HMRC do not accept that separate accounts with the same participator may be aggregated or 'netted off' for these purposes (HMRC Company Taxation Manual, CTM61550).

HMRC have appropriate information powers. [*CTA 2010, s 465; FA 1989, Sch 12 Pt I*].

In *Earlspring Properties Ltd v Guest* (1995) 67 TC 259, CA, it was held that a failure to notify liability under these provisions constituted neglect and gave rise to a liability to interest and penalties. See also *Joint v Bracken Developments Ltd* (1994) 66 TC 560.

Simon's Taxes. See **D3.401–D3.407**.

Matters treated as loans

[22.13] The circumstances in which, for the purposes of these provisions, a close company is to be *treated* as making a loan to a person are listed below.

(a) The person incurs a debt to the close company. This does not apply if the debt is for goods or services supplied by it in the ordinary course of the company's trade or business and on credit not exceeding six months and no longer than that normally given to the company's customers.

(b) A debt due from the person to a third party is assigned to the close company.

(c) Under arrangements made by any person:

- a close company makes a loan or advance not otherwise within **22.12** above, and
- some person other than the close company makes a payment or transfers property to, or releases or satisfies (in whole or in part) a liability of, an 'individual' who is a participator, or the associate of a participator, in the lending company. ('*Individual*' includes fiduciary or representative companies as mentioned in **22.12** above.)

The above does not apply if:

- the arrangements are made in the ordinary course of a business carried on by the person making them, or
- an amount not less than the loan or advance falls to be included for tax purposes in the total income of the participator or associate.

If a company (C) controls another company (D), a participator in C is to be treated for the above purposes as being also a participator in D.

(d) A company (C) which is controlled by a close company makes a loan or advance not otherwise within **22.12** above; the provisions apply as if the loan or advance had been made by the close company. If C is not controlled by a close company at the time of making the loan or advance but a close company subsequently acquires control of it, the provisions apply as if the loan or advance had been made by the close company immediately after the time it acquired control. See also below.

[*CTA 2010, ss 455(4), 456(2), 459, 460(1)–(3); ICTA 1988, ss 419(2)(5)(6)(7), 420(1), 422(1)(2)(6)*].

As regards (a) above, in *Grant v Watton (Inspector of Taxes)* [1999] STC 330, 71 TC 333, the company supplied services to a partnership in which it was a limited partner, and of which its controlling director was the general partner, under an agreement for reimbursement of the amounts charged in the company's accounts (plus a mark up), but with no formal or implied agreement as to the time payment would be made. It was held that, for these purposes, the debt was incurred when the debtor became legally committed to expenditure in relation to the services supplied to the partnership.

The misappropriation of a close company's money by a participator may give rise to a debt within (a) above (*Stephens (Inspector of Taxes) v T Pittas Ltd* [1983] STC 576, 56 TC 722).

The rules in (d) above apply equally where two or more close companies control, or acquire control of, C. The loan is apportioned between them in proportion to the nature and amount of their respective interests in C. [*CTA 2010, s 460(4); ICTA 1988, s 422(3)(6)*].

References in (d) above to a company making a loan or advance include the company being treated under (a) or (b) above as making a loan or advance. [*CTA 2010, s 460(7); ICTA 1988, s 422(6)*].

The rules at (d) above *do not apply* if it is shown that there are no arrangements (otherwise than in the ordinary course of business) connecting the making of the loan with:

- the acquisition of control; or
- the making of any payment or the transfer of any property (whether directly or indirectly) by the close company to C; or
- the releasing or satisfying by the close company (in whole or in part) of any liability of C.

[*CTA 2010, s 461; ICTA 1988, s 422(4)(6)*].

Exceptions

[22.14] The charge in **22.12** above does not apply to a loan or advance made in the ordinary course of a business carried on by a company if the business includes the lending of money. [*CTA 2010, s 456(1); ICTA 1988, s 419(1)*]. For a case in which a loan by an investment company to its chairman was held not to have been made in the ordinary course of its business, so that the charge to tax applied, see *Brennan v Deanby Investment Co Ltd* (2001) 73 TC 455, CA(NI).

Loans and advances are excluded from the charge in **22.12** above if they are made to a director (**22.8** above) or employee of a close company (or of an associated company (**22.10** above) of the close company) and:

(a) the loan or advance does not exceed £15,000;
(b) the loan/advance and any other outstanding loans/advances from the close company and any of its associated companies to the borrower do not together exceed £15,000;
(c) the borrower works 'full-time' for the close company or any of its associated companies; and
(d) the borrower does not have a 'material interest' in the close company or in any of its associated companies. If the borrower acquires a material interest whilst any part of the loan or advance remains outstanding, the company is to be regarded as making to him at that time a loan or advance equal to the amount outstanding.

The reference in (b) above to other outstanding loans/advances does not include one made before 31 March 1971 unless it was made for the purpose of purchasing an only or main residence. The condition in (b) is not to be treated as met if any such outstanding pre-31 March 1971 loans/advances together exceed £10,000. The reference in (d) above to an outstanding loan or advance does not include one made before 31 March 1971.

A '*material interest*' is defined by *CTA 2010, s 457* and broadly means a 5% interest. The interests of any associates (**22.9** above) of the borrower must be taken into account in determining whether the borrower has a material interest.

[*CTA 2010, ss 456(3)–(7), 457, Sch 2 para 69; ICTA 1988, s 420(2)*].

For the above purposes, a director or employee is treated as working '*full-time*' if his hours are at least three-quarters of the company's normal working hours (HMRC Company Taxation Manual CTM61540).

For the exclusion from the charge in **22.12** above of loans to Scottish partnerships or to partnerships of which the lending company is itself a member, see HMRC Company Taxation Manual, CTM61515.

Loan repaid, released or written off

[22.15] If a close company has made a loan/advance which gave rise to a charge to tax under **22.12** above, relief is given from that tax (i.e. by repayment, discharge or set-off), or a proportionate part of it, if the whole or part of the loan/advance is repaid, released or written off. The relief is given on a claim, which must be made no later than four years after the end of the financial year in which the repayment is made or the release or writing off occurs. (Before 1 April 2010, the time limit was six years after the end of the financial year concerned — see 68 time limits.)

If the event giving rise to the relief occurs after the tax has become due and payable, the relief cannot be given before the end of the period of nine months after the end of the accounting period in which that event occurred.

TMA 1970, Sch 1A (claims etc. not included in returns — see **21.7 CLAIMS**) applies to the above claim unless it is included (by amendment or otherwise) in the return for the period in which the loan/advance was made *and* the relief is capable of being given at the time the claim is made.

If a loan/advance is repaid, released or written off, any **INTEREST ON UNPAID TAX** (**49**) in respect of the related tax ceases to accrue from the date of the repayment, release or writing off. However, any liability to interest accrued up to that date still stands.

[*CTA 2010, s 458, Sch 1 para 158; ICTA 1988, s 419(4)–(4B); TMA 1970, s 109(1)(3A)(4)*].

As long as the company was a close company at the time of making the loan/advance, the above treatment is followed even if the company is not a close company when the loan/advance etc is released or written off (HMRC Company Taxation Manual CTM61605, 61630).

Where, under the terms of a deed, a company accepted the replacement of the participator by a third party as its debtor, this amounted to the release of the debt (*Collins v Addies; Greenfield v Bains* (1992) 65 TC 190, CA).

It should be noted that with regard to a release or write off on or after 24 March 2010 the company cannot claim a debit under the loan relationship provisions for the amount released or written off on a loan to a participator.

[*FA 2010, s 43*].

Effect on the borrower

[22.16] Where a close company that is chargeable to tax under **22.12** above, in respect of a loan/advance releases or writes off the debt, the amount released or written off is grossed up by reference to the dividend ordinary rate and included in the taxable income of the borrower. That person is deemed to have paid the notional tax but it is not repayable. See Tolley's Income Tax under Savings and Investment Income.

Where the borrower is also an employee (or a relative of an employee), this charge to tax takes priority over any potential charge under the beneficial loan provisions of *ITEPA 2003, s 188* (see Tolley's Income Tax under Employment Income), so that the same amount will not give rise to a charge under both sets of rules (HMRC Company Taxation Manual CTM61630).

With regard to the position of a controlling director, in *Stewart Fraser Ltd v HMRC* (TC00923 – 1 February 2010), a close company waived a loan to its director. It was accepted the waiver gave rise to a charge to income tax under (now) *CTA 2010, s 455* and that this took precedence over the employment income charge at *ITEPA 2003, s188*. HMRC ruled that this waiver gave rise to a Class 1 NIC liability. The company appealed. This was dismissed by the First Tier Tribunal which held that the waiver was in respect of the director's employment and not his shareholding, on the basis the shareholders had not been consulted on the waiver. It was therefore remuneration which was subject to Class 1 contributions.

If:

- a company (X) was chargeable to tax under **22.12** above in respect of a loan/advance made to the trustees of a settlement;
- X releases or writes off the whole or part of the debt;
- the person from which the debt was due at the time of the release or writing off is a company (Y); and
- the release or writing off takes place after the settlement has ended,

Y is treated as receiving (at the time of the release or writing off) an amount within the charge to corporation tax on income. That amount is the amount released or written off grossed up at a rate equivalent to the dividend ordinary rate for the tax year in which the release or writing off takes place.

[*CTA 2010, ss 463, 464; ICTA 1988, ss 421(1), 422(5)*].

Example

T is a participator in V Ltd, a close company. V Ltd loaned T £100,000 on 10 May 2009. On 2 March 2010, T repays £73,000 and on 11 February 2011, V Ltd agrees to waive the balance of the loan. V Ltd has a year end of 31 March and is not a large company for instalment payment purposes.

The effect of these transactions is as follows.

V Ltd

On 1.1.11	The company becomes liable to pay corporation tax of (£100,000 – £73,000 =) £27,000 × 25%	£6,750
On 31.12.11	The company is due a repayment of £27,000 × 25%	£6,750

T

On 11.2.11	T's 2010/11 taxable income is increased by £27,000 × $^{10}/_{9}$	£30,000

And	
he is credited with dividend ordinary rate tax paid of £30,000 at 10%	£3,000
If T pays tax at the higher rate, the deemed income will be subject to tax at the dividend upper rate of 32.5% on £30,000	9,750
Less: tax credit (as above)	3,000
T's tax liability	£6,750

Additional items treated as distributions

[22.17] As regards certain benefits provided by close companies to participators and/or directors, which are classed as distributions, see **31.10**, **31.12**, **31.19 DISTRIBUTIONS**. See also **31.14**(g)(i) **DISTRIBUTIONS** for items *not* treated as distributions.

Close company transferring assets at undervalue

[22.18] See **17.46** capital gains.

Demergers

[22.19] For treatment of certain 'chargeable payments' made following an 'exempt distribution', see **31.32 GROUP RELIEF**.

Close investment-holding companies

[22.20] The **SMALL PROFITS — REDUCED RATES** (**67**) provisions do not apply to a company for any accounting period in which the company is a 'close investment-holding company'.

A close company is a '*close investment-holding company*' in an accounting period unless throughout the period it exists wholly or mainly for one or more of the following purposes.

(a) The carrying on of trade(s) on a commercial basis.
(b) The making of investments in land, or estates or interests in land, let, or intended to be let, other than to **CONNECTED PERSONS** (**25**) of the company or to certain individuals related to such connected persons.
(c) The holding of shares in and securities of, or making loans to, a company or companies which, or each of which, is either:

   (i) a 'qualifying company'; or
   (ii) a company under its 'control', or under the 'control' of the same company as it, which itself exists wholly or mainly for the purpose of holding shares in or securities of, or making loans to, one or more 'qualifying companies'.

(d) The co-ordination of the administration of two or more 'qualifying companies'.

(e) The purposes of trade(s) carried on on a commercial basis by one or more 'qualifying companies', or by a company which has 'control' of the company in question.

(f) The making, by one or more 'qualifying companies' or by a parent company, of investments within (b) above.

A '*qualifying company*' in relation to the company in question is a company which is under its 'control', or under the 'control' of the same company as it, and which exists wholly or mainly for either or both of the purposes in (a) or (b) above.

'*Control*' for all these purposes is as under *CTA 2010, s 450* (previously *ICTA 1988, s 416*) — see **22.6** above.

With regard to condition (b) above, in *Herts Photographic Bureau Ltd v HMRC* (TC00868 – 23 December 2010) although a company had sold its rental property, it argued that it was entitled to the small companies' rate (as was) on the basis that it intended to reinvest the sale proceeds in another property, therefore it existed 'for the purpose of making investments in land'. The First Tier Tribunal accepted the company's evidence and held it was not a close investment holding company.

A company is not treated as a close investment-holding company in the accounting period beginning at the commencement of its winding-up if it was not such a company in the immediately preceding period. If, however, there is an interval between cessation of trading and commencement of winding-up, this will obviate the relief but HMRC will review the position where a company has not been able to avoid a short gap and would suffer significantly without the relief (see HMRC Company Taxation Manual, CTM60780).

[*CTA 2010, ss 18, 19(1), 34; ICTA 1988, ss 13(1)(a), 13A; FA 2006, s 26(3), Sch 27 Pt 3(1)*].

HMRC have appropriate information powers. [*CTA 2010, s 31; FA 1989, Sch 12 Pt I; SI 2009 No 2035, Sch para 25*].

Simon's Taxes. See **D3.2.**

Key points

[22.21] Points to consider are as follows.

- The majority of owner managed companies will fall within the definitions of a close company so for most practitioners the points in this chapter will be of direct relevance to their clients.
- Only UK resident companies can be close companies. If a company is not UK resident the rules for close companies cannot apply.
- Close companies under common control are treated as associated for the purposes of the small profits rate. The effect is to divide the profit limits between the number of associated companies.
- The attribution of rights to and from associates can result in a person controlling a company where they are associated in the current period.
- A close company owning a property which is only let to connected parties will be treated as a close investment holding company (CIHC) and will be taxed at the full corporate tax rates.
- Where loans are made to participators a tax charge of 25% will be payable by the company if the loan is still outstanding nine months following the end of the accounting period. Where the loan is released/repaid the tax is refunded/relieved but not before the end of the period of nine months following the accounting period in which it is released/repaid. The refund/relief must be claimed no later than four years from the end of the accounting period in which the loan is released/repaid.
- The charge on a loan to a participator cannot be avoided by routing the loan through another person or entity. There are specific provisions to catch this.
- Where there are two separate loans with a shareholder they are treated separately in determining the tax due. Care should be exercised in dealing with the bookkeeping.
- Where the repayment of a loan is dealt with via book entries the repayment date is the date the book entries are made.
- If there are a number of loans and a repayment is made it can be offset against a particular debt. If no assignment is made the repayment is set against the earliest debt first.
- Where a bed and breakfast arrangement is carried out in relation to a loan HMRC will scrutinise the arrangement closely so care should be exercised to ensure all the transactions are carried out in the right order on the correct dates.

23

Community Investment Tax Relief

Introduction

[23.1] The Community Investment Tax relief scheme provides tax relief to companies and individuals investing in Community Development Finance Institutions ('CDFIs') which have been accredited by the Government under the rules of the scheme. The intention is that CDFIs will use investors' funds to finance small businesses and social enterprises in disadvantaged communities.

The relief takes the form of a reduction in the investor's corporation tax or income tax liability. The quantum of the relief is a maximum of 25% of the amount invested (which may be by way of loan or by subscription), spread over five years, (although note that the investment term need not be limited to five years). Relief cannot in any year exceed the amount needed to reduce the investor's tax liability to nil.

The relief is available for investments made on or after 17 April 2002. Claims for relief may be made after 22 January 2003. A CDFI which is accredited at any time before 6 April 2003 is to have its accreditation backdated to 17 April 2002. (Treasury Explanatory Notes to Finance Bill 2002). [*CTA 2010, ss 218–269, Sch 2 para 59; FA 2002, s 57, Sch 16; SI 2003 No 88*].

No exemption is provided for chargeable gains on disposals of investments in CDFIs.

This chapter concentrates on the relief due to investors who are companies. For coverage of the relief due to individual investors, see the corresponding chapter of Tolley's Income Tax.

The European Commission has determined that the scheme is outside the scope of, or compatible with, EU state aid rules.

References in this chapter to the '*investment date*' are to the day on which the investment in the CDFI is made, and references to the '*five-year period*' are to the five years beginning with that day. [*CTA 2010, s 223; FA 2002, Sch 16 para 3*].

Guidance is available in HMRC Community Investment Tax Relief Manual and on HMRC's website.

The relief

Eligibility for relief

[23.2] Relief will be available to a qualifying investor (see **23.3** below) who makes a qualifying investment (see **23.4** below) in a body that is accredited as a CDFI at the time the investment is made.

[*CTA 2010, s 219; FA 2002, Sch 16 para 1*].

Qualifying investor

No control of CDFI by investor

[23.3] The investor must not control the CDFI at any time in the five-year period. 'Control' is construed in accordance with *CTA 2010, s 1124* (previously *ICTA 1988, s 840*) where the CDFI is a body corporate, with similar rules applying in other cases, with any potential future rights and powers of the investor, and any rights and powers held or exercisable by another on his behalf, taken into account. References to 'the investor' include any person connected with it (within **25 CONNECTED PERSONS**).

Beneficial ownership

The investor must be the sole beneficial owner of the investment when it is made (which in the case of a loan means sole beneficial entitlement to repayment).

Investor not to be accredited

The investor must not itself be accredited as a CDFI as at the investment date. See **23.11** below as regards denial of relief where an investor company subsequently becomes a CDFI.

No acquisition of share in partnership

Where the CDFI is a partnership, the investment must not consist of or include any capital contributed by the investor on becoming a member of the partnership. This includes the provision of loan capital treated as partners' capital in the partnership accounts.

No tax avoidance purpose

The investment must not be made as part of a scheme or arrangement a main purpose of which is the avoidance of tax.

[*CTA 2010, ss 231–235; FA 2002, Sch 16 paras 14–18, 51(3)*].

Qualifying investment

[23.4] An investment is a '*qualifying investment*' in a CDFI if:

(a) the investment consists of a loan, securities or shares satisfying the conditions at **23.5** or, as the case may be, **23.6** below;
(b) the investor receives from the CDFI a valid tax relief certificate (see **23.20** below); and
(c) the conditions at **23.7** below (no pre-arranged protection against risks) are met.

[*CTA 2010, s 225; FA 2002, Sch 16 para 8*].

For implications for alternative finance arrangements see **4.10 ALTERNATIVE FINANCE ARRANGEMENTS**.

Conditions to be satisfied in relation to loans

[23.5] There are three such conditions.

(1) Either the CDFI receives from the investor, on the investment date, the full amount of the loan or, in the case of a loan made under a drawdown facility, the loan agreement provides for the CDFI to receive the full amount of the loan within 18 months after the investment date. Where a loan agreement authorises the body to draw down amounts of the loan over a period of time, the loan is treated as made when the first amount is drawn down.
(2) The loan must not carry any present or future right to be converted into, or exchanged for, a loan, securities, shares or other rights, any of which are redeemable within the five-year period.
(3) The loan must not be made on terms that allow any person to require:
    (a) repayment within years one and two (of the five-year period) of any of the loan capital advanced during those two years; or
    (b) repayment within year three of more than 25% of the balance of loan capital outstanding at the end of year two; or
    (c) repayment before the end of year four of more than 50% of the balance of loan capital outstanding at the end of year two; or
    (d) repayment before the end of year five of more than 75% of that balance.

Any of the above percentages may be altered by Treasury order, but only in relation to loans made on or after a date specified in the order. For the above purposes, there is disregarded any requirement to repay that may arise as a consequence of certain standard commercial default provisions in the loan agreement.

[*CTA 2010, s 226; FA 2002, Sch 16 para 9*].

Conditions to be satisfied in relation to securities or shares

[23.6] There are two such conditions.

(1) The securities or shares must be subscribed for wholly in cash and fully paid for (in the case of shares, fully paid up) on the investment date and with no undertaking for any further payment in connection with the acquisition.

(2) The second is that they must not carry:
   (a) any present or future right to be redeemed within the five-year period; or
   (b) any present or future right to be converted into, or exchanged for, a loan, securities, shares or other rights, any of which are redeemable within the five-year period.

[*CTA 2010, ss 227, 228; FA 2002, Sch 16 paras 10, 11*].

Pre-arranged protection against risks

[23.7] Any arrangements (as very broadly defined) under which the investment in the CDFI is made (or arrangements preceding the investment but relating to it) must not include arrangements a main purpose of which is to provide (by means of any insurance, indemnity, guarantee or otherwise) complete or partial protection for the investor against the normal risks attaching to the investment. Arrangements are, however, allowed if they do no more than provide the kind of commercial protection, e.g. the use of property as security for a loan, that might be expected if the investment were made by a bank. [*CTA 2010, s 230; FA 2002, Sch 16 para 13*].

Form of corporation tax relief

[23.8] Where a company which is eligible for relief makes a claim for relief for any one of the 'relevant accounting periods', its corporation tax liability for that period falls to be reduced by the lesser of:

(a) 5% of the 'invested amount' (see **23.10** below) in respect of the investment in question; and
(b) an amount sufficient to reduce that liability to nil.

The reduction in corporation tax liability is made after any reduction in respect of investment relief under the **CORPORATE VENTURING SCHEME** (**28**) but before any double tax relief.

The '*relevant accounting periods*' are the accounting period in which the investment date falls, and each of the accounting periods in which the subsequent four anniversaries of that date fall.

Attribution of relief

[23.9] Community investment tax relief is 'attributable' to any investment in respect of an accounting period if relief as in **23.8** above has been obtained in respect of that investment and has not been withdrawn (as opposed to reduced).

Where for any accounting period relief has been obtained by reason of a single investment (i.e. one loan, or securities or shares comprised in one issue), the relief attributable to it is the reduction made in the investor's tax liability. Where the relief has been obtained by reason of two or more investments, it is attributed to those investments in proportion to the invested amounts (see **23.10** below) for the period.

Relief attributable to any one issue of securities or shares is attributed *pro rata* to each security or share in that issue, and any reduction of relief is similarly apportioned between the securities or shares in question. For these purposes, any bonus shares, issued in respect of the original shares and being shares in the same company, of the same class and carrying the same rights, are treated as if comprised in the original issue, and relief is apportioned to them accordingly. This applies only if the original shares have been continuously held (see **23.25** below) by the investor (as sole beneficial owner) since their issue, and, where it does apply, the bonus shares are themselves treated as having been continuously held since the time of the original issue.

[*CTA 2010, ss 240, 241, 269(1)(2); FA 2002, Sch 16 paras 26, 51(2)*].

Claims

The company is entitled to make a claim for a relevant accounting period if it appears to the company that the conditions for the relief are for the time being satisfied. The company *must* also have received a tax relief certificate from the CDFI. No claim can be made before the end of the accounting period to which it relates. Otherwise, by default, the general time limit for making claims applies. See **23.11** below for specific circumstances in which no claim for relief can be made.

[*CTA 2010, s 220; FA 1998, Sch 18 para 8(1); FA 2002, Sch 16 para 20, Sch 17 para 5*].

Meaning of the 'invested amount'

[23.10] For the purposes of **23.8** above, in respect of a **loan**, the '*invested amount*' is as follows.

(a) In the accounting period in which the investment date falls, it is the 'average capital balance' (see below) for the first year of the five-year period (see **23.1** above).

(b) In each subsequent accounting period (subject to (c) below), it is the average capital balance for the one year beginning with the anniversary of the investment date falling in that tax year.

(c) For any accounting period after that in which the first anniversary of the investment date falls, it is initially determined as in (b) above but is restricted to, if less, the average capital balance for the six-month period beginning eighteen months after the investment date.

For the purposes of (a)–(c) above, the '*average capital balance*' of a loan for any period of time is the mean of the daily balances of capital outstanding during that period.

In respect of **securities or shares**, the '*invested amount*' for any accounting period is the amount subscribed for them (not necessarily in that accounting period).

[*CTA 2010, s 222; FA 2002, Sch 16 para 21*].

See **23.12** below as regards receipt of value which may lead to restriction of the invested amount.

Circumstances in which no claim for relief can be made

[23.11] In the circumstances listed below, no claim for community investment tax relief can be made.

Loans — disposals and excessive repayments/receipts of value

No claim can be made for an accounting period in respect of a loan if:

(a) the investor disposes of all or any part of the loan (disregarding any repayment of the loan) before the 'qualifying date' relating to that period; or
(b) at any time after the investment is made but before that 'qualifying date', the amount of the capital outstanding on the loan is reduced to nil; or
(c) before that 'qualifying date', cumulative loan repayments (or receipts of value treated as repayments) trigger the withdrawal of relief provisions (see **23.12** below).

The '*qualifying date*' relating to an accounting period is the anniversary of the investment date next occurring after the end of that period.

[*CTA 2010, s 236; FA 2002, Sch 16 para 22*].

Securities or shares — disposals and excessive receipts of value

No claim can be made for an accounting period in respect of any securities or shares other than those held by the investor (as sole beneficial owner) continuously (see **23.25** below) throughout the period beginning when the investment is made and ending immediately before the 'qualifying date' (as in (a) above) relating to that period. In addition, no claim can be made for an accounting period if, before the 'qualifying date' (as above) relating to that period, cumulative receipts of value trigger the withdrawal of relief provisions (see **23.12** below). [*CTA 2010, s 237; FA 2002, Sch 16 para 23*].

Loss of accreditation by the CDFI

Where the CDFI ceases to be accredited as such during the first year of the five-year period, no claim for relief can be made. Where accreditation is lost at any later time within the five-year period, no claim can be made for the accounting period in which falls the most recent anniversary of the investment date preceding (or coinciding with) the date the accreditation is lost, or for any subsequent accounting period. (There is no withdrawal of relief for any earlier accounting period). [*CTA 2010, s 238; FA 2002, Sch 16 para 24*].

Accreditation of the investor

Provisions similar to those applying on loss of CDFI accreditation (as above) apply if the investor becomes accredited as a CDFI within the five-year period. [*CTA 2010, s 239; FA 2002, Sch 16 para 25*]. This does not apply to individual investors.

Withdrawal or reduction of relief

[23.12] Community investment tax relief may fall to be withdrawn or reduced on:

(a) a disposal of the investment (see **23.13** below);
(b) a repayment of an investment consisting of a loan (see **23.15** below);
(c) a return of value to the investor in respect of the investment (see **23.16–23.19** below); or
(d) relief subsequently being found not to have been due.

Where relief given falls to be withdrawn or reduced, and also where it is found not to have been due in the first place, the withdrawal etc. is achieved by means of an assessment to corporation tax for the accounting period for which the relief was obtained. An assessment to recover relief may be made up to six years after the end of the accounting period for which the relief was obtained (without prejudice to powers of recovery where loss of tax has been brought about deliberately). [*CTA 2010, ss 254, 255; FA 2002, Sch 16 para 27*].

Disposals

[23.13] An investment is regarded as being disposed of if it is so regarded for the purposes of tax on chargeable gains, and see also **23.24** below (certain company reconstructions treated as disposals). [*CTA 2010, s 266; FA 2002, Sch 16 para 48*].

Loans

Where the investment consists of a loan, and the investor disposes of the whole of it within the five-year period (see **23.1** above), otherwise than by way of a 'permitted disposal', or disposes of part of it during that period, any relief attributable to the investment (see **23.9** above), for any accounting period, is withdrawn. Repayment of the loan does not count as a disposal. A disposal is a '*permitted disposal*' if it is:

(a) by way of a distribution in the course of dissolving or winding up the CDFI; or
(b) a disposal within *TCGA 1992, s 24(1)* (entire loss, destruction etc. of asset — see Tolley's Capital Gains Tax under Computation of Gains and Losses); or

(c) a deemed disposal under *TCGA 1992, s 24(2)* (assets of negligible value — see Tolley's Capital Gains Tax under Losses); or
(d) made after the CDFI has ceased to be accredited as such.

[*CTA 2010, s 243; FA 2002, Sch 16 para 28*].

Securities or shares

Where the investment consists of securities or shares, and the investor disposes of the whole or any part of the investment within the five-year period, any relief attributable to the investment (see **23.9** above), for any accounting period, is withdrawn or reduced. This does not apply if the CDFI has ceased to be accredited before the disposal or if the disposal arises from the repayment, redemption or repurchase by the CDFI of any of the securities or shares.

In the case of a 'permitted disposal' (defined as for Loans above) or a disposal by way of a bargain made at arm's length, the relief attributable to the investment for any accounting period is withdrawn, or is reduced by 5% of the disposal consideration (if such reduction would not amount to full withdrawal). If the relief initially obtained for any accounting period was less than 5% of the invested amount (see **23.8** above), i.e. because the investor's tax liability was insufficient to fully absorb the available relief, the reduction is correspondingly restricted. In the case of any other disposal, the relief for all accounting periods is withdrawn.

[*CTA 2010, s 244; FA 2002, Sch 16 para 29*].

Identification rules on disposal of securities or shares

[23.14] Special rules apply on the disposal of shares if community investment tax relief is attributable (see **23.9** above) to the shares disposed of and they have been held continuously (see **23.25** below) since the time of issue. The rules apply for the purposes of **23.13** above and this chapter generally and for the purposes of taxing chargeable gains. The rules apply to securities as they apply to shares.

Where shares comprised in the holding have been acquired on different days, a disposal is identified with acquisitions on a first in/first out basis. In matching the shares disposed of with shares acquired on a particular day, shares to which relief is attributable, and which have been held continuously since issue, are treated as being disposed of after any other shares included in the holding and acquired on that day. If, on a reorganisation of share capital (e.g. a scrip issue), a new holding falls, by virtue of *TCGA 1992, s 127* (or any other chargeable gains enactment which applies that section — see Tolley's Capital Gains Tax under Shares and Securities, and see also **23.23** below), to be equated with the original shares, shares comprised in the new holding are deemed for these purposes to have been acquired when the original shares were acquired.

[*CTA 2010, ss 264, 269(2), Sch 1 para 234; TCGA 1992, s 151BA; FA 2002, Sch 16 paras 47, 51(2)*].

Excessive repayments of loan capital

[23.15] Where the investment consists of a loan, and the 'average capital balance' for the third, fourth or final year of the five-year period (see **23.1** above) is less than the 'permitted balance' for the year in question (other than by an amount of 'insignificant value'), any relief attributable to the investment (see **23.9** above), for any accounting period, is withdrawn.

For these purposes, the '*average capital balance*' of the loan for any period of time is the mean of the daily balances of capital outstanding during that period, disregarding any 'non-standard repayments' made in that period or at any earlier time. The '*permitted balance*' of the loan is as follows:

(a) for the third year of the five-year period, 75% of the average capital balance for the six months beginning eighteen months after the investment date;
(b) for the fourth year, 50% of that balance; and
(c) for the final year, 25% of that balance.

For these purposes, an amount is of '*insignificant value*' if it does not exceed £1,000 or if it is insignificant in relation to the average capital balance for whichever year of the five-year period is under consideration.

'*Non-standard repayments*' are repayments made:

(i) at the choice or discretion of the CDFI and not under any obligation under the loan agreement; or
(ii) as a consequence of certain standard commercial default provisions in the loan agreement.

[*CTA 2010, s 245; FA 2002, Sch 16 para 30*].

Value received by investor — loans

[23.16] Where the investment consists of a loan, and the investor 'receives value' (see **23.18** below), other than an amount of 'insignificant value', from the CDFI during the 'six-year period', (i.e. the period of six years beginning one year before the investment date) the investor is treated as having received a repayment equal to the amount of value received.

This may have consequences for **23.10** above (determination of invested amount) and **23.15** above (withdrawal of relief where excessive repayments made). Where the value is received in the first or second year of the six-year period, the repayment is treated as made at the beginning of that second year. Where the value is received in a later year, the repayment is treated as made at the beginning of the year in question. The repayment is not treated as a 'non-standard repayment' for the purposes of **23.15** above.

An amount is of '*insignificant value*' if it does not exceed £1,000 or if it is insignificant in relation to the 'average capital balance' for the year of the six-year period in which the value is received (treating any value received in the first year as received at the beginning of the second). There are provisions to aggregate a receipt of value, whether insignificant or not, with amounts of insignificant value received previously, and treating that aggregate, if it is not itself an amount of insignificant value, as an amount of value received at the time of the latest actual receipt. The '*average capital balance*' of the loan for any year is the mean of the daily balances of capital outstanding during that year, disregarding the receipt of value in question.

[*CTA 2010, ss 246, 248; FA 2002, Sch 16 paras 31, 33, 34*].

These provisions apply equally to receipts of value by and from persons connected (within **25 CONNECTED PERSONS**), at any time in the six-year period, with the investor or, as the case may be, the CDFI. [*CTA 2010, s 253; FA 2002, Sch 16 para 39*].

Value received by investor — securities or shares

[23.17] Any relief attributable (see **23.9** above) to the 'continuing investment' (see (b) below), is withdrawn where the investment consists of securities or shares, and the following circumstances are present, for any accounting period:

(a) the investor 'receives value' (see **23.18** below), other than an amount of 'insignificant value', from the CDFI during the six-year period (defined as in **23.16** above);
(b) the investment or a part of it has been continuously held (see **23.25** below) by the investor (as sole beneficial owner) since the investment was made (the '*continuing investment*'); and
(c) the receipt wholly or partly exceeds the permitted level of receipts (see below) in respect of the continuing investment (other than by an amount of insignificant value).

The permitted level of receipts is exceeded where:

(i) any value is received by the investor (disregarding any amounts of insignificant value) in the first three years of the six-year period; or
(ii) the aggregate value received by the investor (disregarding any amounts of insignificant value) exceeds:
    (A) before the beginning of the fifth year of the six-year period, 25% of the amount subscribed for the securities or shares comprising the continuing investment;
    (B) before the beginning of the final year of that period, 50% of that amount;
    (C) before the end of that period, 75% of that amount.

Where a receipt of value in (a) above is not an amount of 'insignificant value' but is nevertheless insufficient to trigger any withdrawal of relief under the above rules, any tax relief subsequently due is computed as if the amount subscribed for the securities or shares comprising the continuing investment (and thus the invested amount at **23.10** above) were reduced by the amount of value received. This restriction applies for accounting periods ending on or after the anniversary of the investment date falling immediately before (or coinciding with) the receipt of value.

For the above purposes, an amount is of '*insignificant value*' if it does not exceed £1,000 or if it is insignificant in relation to the amount subscribed by the investor for the securities or shares comprising the continuing investment.

There are provisions to aggregate a receipt of value, whether insignificant or not, with amounts of insignificant value received previously, and treating that aggregate, if it is not itself an amount of insignificant value, as an amount of value received at the time of the latest actual receipt.

[*CTA 2010, ss 247, 248, 252; FA 2002, Sch 16 paras 32, 34, 38*].

These provisions apply equally to receipts of value by and from persons connected (within **25 CONNECTED PERSONS**), at any time in the six-year period, with the investor or, as the case may be, the CDFI. [*CTA 2010, s 253; FA 2002, Sch 16 para 39*].

Meaning of, and amount of, value received

[23.18] For the purposes of **23.16** and **23.17** above, the investor may '*receive value*' from the CDFI in a number of situations, as follows (and see **23.16, 23.17** above re connected persons):

Type of value received	Quantification of value received
Repayment, redemption or repurchase by the CDFI of any securities or shares included in the investment	The amount received
Release or waiver by the CDFI of any liability of the investor to the CDFI (which it is deemed to have done if discharge of the liability is twelve months or more overdue) or discharge (or agreement to discharge) of any liability of the investor to a third party	The amount of the liability
Making of a loan or advance by the CDFI to the investor which has not been repaid in full before the investment is made; for this purpose a loan includes any debt incurred, other than an ordinary trade debt (as defined), and any debt due to a third party which is assigned to the CDFI	The amount of the loan etc. less any amount repaid before the making of the investment
Provision of a benefit or facility by the CDFI for the investor, or for any associates (as defined) of the investor — except in circumstances such that, if a payment had been made of equal value, it would have been a 'qualifying payment'	The cost to the CDFI of providing the benefit etc. (net of any consideration given for it by the investor, its associate, a director or employee or an associate of a director or employee)
Disposal of an asset by the CDFI to the investor for no consideration or for consideration less than market value (as defined), or acquisition of an asset from the investor for consideration exceeding market value	The difference between market value and the consideration received (if any)

Type of value received	Quantification of value received
Making of a payment by the CDFI to the investor other than a 'qualifying payment'	The amount of the payment

References above to a debt or liability do not include one which would be discharged by making a qualifying payment. References to a benefit or facility do not include one provided in circumstances such that, had a payment been made of an amount equal to its value, that payment would have been a qualifying payment. References to a payment or disposal include one made indirectly to, or to the order of, or for the benefit of, the person in question.

Each of the following is a 'qualifying payment':

(i) a reasonable (in relation to their market value) payment for any goods, services or facilities provided by the investor in the course of trade or otherwise;
(ii) the payment of interest at no more than a reasonable commercial rate on money lent;
(iii) the payment of a dividend or other distribution which represents no more than a normal return on investment;
(iv) a payment to acquire an asset at no more than its market value;
(v) a payment not exceeding a reasonable and commercial rent for property occupied;
(vi) a payment discharging an ordinary trade debt.

[*CTA 2010, ss 249, 250, 268, 269(3); FA 2002, Sch 16 paras 35, 36, 50, 51(4)*].

Value received where more than one investment

[23.19] Where the investor makes more than one investment in the CDFI for which relief is claimed, any value received (other than value within **23.18** above, in the first row of the table) is apportioned between the investments by reference to the average capital balances of loans and the amounts subscribed for securities or shares. [*CTA 2010, s 251; FA 2002, Sch 16 para 37*].

Administration

Tax relief certificates

[23.20] Before an investment in a CDFI can qualify for tax relief, the CDFI must issue to the investor a tax relief certificate (see **23.8**, **23.4**(b) above) in a specified form. In relation to an accreditation period, a CDFI may issue tax relief certificates in respect of investments made in it within that period of an aggregate value of up to £20 million in the case of a 'wholesale CDFI' (i.e. one whose objective is to finance other, generally smaller, CDFIs) or £10 million in the case of a 'retail CDFI' (i.e. one whose objective is to invest directly in enterprises). The Treasury may substitute other figures by order but not so as to reduce them for periods beginning before the order takes effect. Any tax relief certificate issued wholly or partly in contravention of these limits is invalid (and thus the investment in question does not satisfy **23.4**(b) above and does not attract tax relief). A CDFI is liable to a penalty of up to £3,000 for the issue of a tax relief certificate made fraudulently or negligently. [*CTA 2010, s 229; FA 2002, Sch 16 paras 4(6)(7),* 12].

Disclosure

Notification to HMRC

[23.21] Certain events giving rise to withdrawal or reduction of investment relief must be notified to HMRC by the investor. Such notice must be given no later than twelve months after the end of the accounting period in which the event occurs. If the requirement arises from the receipt of value by a connected person, the above deadline is extended to, if later, the end of the period of 60 days beginning when the investor comes to know of the event. The penalty provisions of *TMA 1970, s 98* apply in the event of non-compliance. [*CTA 2010, s 260; FA 2002, Sch 16 para 42, Sch 17 para 1*].

CASCs can appoint a tax adviser to deal with HMRC regarding their tax affairs. A completed form 64-8 should be sent to HMRC Charities at:

HMRC Charities
St Johns House
Merton Road
Liverpool
L75 1BB

Exchange of information

[23.22] There are provisions for the exchange of information between the Secretary of State and HMRC in so far as this is necessary to enable them both to discharge their functions appertaining to community investment tax relief. Information thus obtained cannot be further disclosed except for the purposes of legal proceedings arising out of those functions. [*CTA 2010, s 261; FA 2002, Sch 16 para 43*].

Miscellaneous

Company restructuring

[23.23] For the attribution of relief to any loan, securities or shares for these purposes, see **23.9** above.

Reorganisations of share capital

The following apply where the CDFI is a company and the investment consists of shares or, in the case of **23.24** below, shares or securities.

Rights issues etc.

The share reorganisation rules of *TCGA 1992, ss 127–130* are disapplied where:

(a) a reorganisation (within *TCGA 1992, s 126*) involves an allotment of shares or debentures in respect of, and in proportion to, an existing holding of shares of the same class in the CDFI held by the investor in a single capacity;
(b) community investment tax relief is attributable to the shares in the existing holding or to the allotted shares; and
(c) if the relief is attributable to the shares in the existing holding, those shares have been held continuously (see **23.25** below) by the investor since they were issued.

The effect is that the allotted shares are treated as a separate holding acquired at the time of the reorganisation. This does not, however, apply in the case of bonus shares where these are issued in respect of shares comprised in the existing holding and are of the same class and carry the same rights as those shares. (For *TCGA 1992, ss 126–130*, see Tolley's Capital Gains Tax under Shares and Securities.)

Reorganisation involving issue of QCB

The general deferral treatment on a reorganisation involving an issue of QCBs is disapplied if, in a case otherwise within *TCGA 1992, s 116(10)* (see Tolley's Capital Gains Tax under Qualifying Corporate Bonds):

(i) the old asset consists of shares to which community investment tax relief is attributable and which have been held continuously (see **23.25** below) by the investor since they were issued; and
(ii) the new asset consists of a qualifying corporate bond.

The effect is that the investor is deemed to have disposed of the shares at the time of the reorganisation, and the resulting chargeable gain or allowable loss crystallises *at that time*.

[*TCGA 1992, s 151BB; FA 2002, Sch 16 paras 40, 51(2); ITA 2007, Sch 1 para 317; CTA 2010, Sch 1 para 235*].

Company reconstructions

[23.24] *TCGA 1992, s 135* (exchange of securities for those in another company) and *s 136* (schemes of reconstruction involving issue of securities), which normally equate the new holding with the original shares, are disapplied in the following circumstances:

(a) an investor holds shares in or debentures of a company (company A);
(b) community investment tax relief is attributable to those shares;
(c) those shares have been held continuously (see **23.25** below) by the investor since they were issued; and
(d) there is a reconstruction whereby another company issues shares or debentures in exchange for, or in respect of, company A shares or debentures.

The result is that the transaction is treated, both for the purposes of this chapter and for the purposes of taxing chargeable gains, as a disposal of the original securities or shares (and an acquisition of a new holding). (For *TCGA 1992, ss 135, 136*, see Tolley's Capital Gains Tax under Shares and Securities.)

[*TCGA 1992, s 151BC; CTA 2010, s 266; FA 2002, Sch 16 para 48(2)*].

Circumstances in which investment not held 'continuously'

[23.25] An investor is not treated as having held an investment (or a part of an investment) continuously throughout a period if:

(a) under any provision of *TCGA 1992*, the investment (or part) has been deemed to be disposed of and immediately reacquired by the investor at any time in that period; or
(b) there has been at any time in that period a transaction treated, by virtue of **23.24** above (company reconstructions etc.), as a disposal by the investor.

[*CTA 2010, s 267; FA 2002, Sch 16 para 49*].

Nominees and bare trustees

[23.26] For the purposes of this chapter, actions of a person's nominee or bare trustee in relation to loans, shares or securities are treated as actions of that person. [*CTA 2010, s 262; FA 2002, Sch 16 para 44*].

24

Compensation and Damages

Simon's Taxes. See **A1.210–A1.215, B2.204, B2.213, B2.417, B2.419, C2.5.**

Introduction

[24.1] The following paragraphs deal with the treatment of all types of compensation received or paid with the exception of capital sums received as compensation for damage or injury to, or the destruction or depreciation of, assets and compensation for loss of office.

These issues are dealt with in Tolley's Capital Gains Tax under Disposal and Tolley's Income Tax under Compensation for Loss of Employment.

Paragraphs **24.2–24.8** cite case law which determines whether compensation and damages received or paid in various situations is treated:

- as a trading receipt/expense;
- on capital account; or
- under a different basis e.g. as employment income.

Compensation for compulsory acquisition

[24.2] Following *Stoke-on-Trent City Council v Wood Mitchell & Co Ltd* [1979] STC 197, any element of compensation, paid by an authority possessing compulsory purchase powers for the acquisition of property used for a trade or profession, representing temporary loss of profits, will be treated as a trading receipt.

Compensation for losses on trading stock and to reimburse revenue expenditure, such as removal expenses and interest, will be similarly treated. (HMRC Statement of Practice, SP 8/79. See HMRC Capital Gains Manual CG72150.)

Cancellation or variation of trading agreements

[24.3] Compensation etc. received on the cancellation or variation of contracts which, if completed, would have given rise to trading receipts, is normally also treated as a trading receipt of the accounting period in which the cancellation or variation took place.

See *Short Bros Ltd v CIR* (1927) 12 TC 955, CA (cancellation of shipbuilding contract); *CIR v Northfleet Coal & Ballast Co Ltd* (1927) 12 TC 1102 (cancellation of contract for minerals extraction); *Jesse Robinson & Sons v CIR* (1929) 12 TC 1241 and *Creed v H & M Levinson Ltd* (1981) 54 TC 477 (cancellation of contract for sale of goods); *Greyhound Racing Association (Liverpool) Ltd v Cooper* (1936) 20 TC 373 (surrender of hiring agreement); *Bush, Beach & Gent Ltd v Road* (1939) 22 TC 519 (cancellation of merchanting franchise); *Shove v Dura Manufacturing Co Ltd* (1941) 23 TC 779 (cancellation of commission agreement); *Shadbolt v Salmon Estate (Kingsbury) Ltd* (1943) 25 TC 52 (withdrawal of building rights); *Sommerfelds Ltd v Freeman* (1966) 44 TC 43 (breach of contract for sale of goods — rights assigned).

For further cases on this point, see Tolley's Tax Cases. See also **24.6** below.

Termination of agencies

[24.4] Compensation received on the termination of agencies is a trading receipt (unless the agency, by reason of its relative size, etc., is part of the 'whole structure of the recipient's profit-making apparatus', see **24.7** below).

See *Kelsall Parsons & Co v CIR* (1938) 21 TC 608, CS (manufacturers' agency); *Fleming v Bellow Machine Co Ltd* (1965) 42 TC 308 (distributors' sub-agency); *Anglo-French Exploration Co Ltd v Clayson* (1956) 36 TC 545, CA, and *Blackburn v Close Bros Ltd* (1960) 39 TC 164 (provision of agency, managerial and secretarial services).

In all these cases, compensation was held to be a trading receipt, but compare *Ellis v Lucas* (1966) 43 TC 276 where a certified accountant, who was auditor to a number of companies and carried out related accountancy work, was paid compensation on his agreeing to relinquish his post as auditor. In the absence of a finding by the Commissioners that the auditorship did not constitute an asset of the taxpayer's profession, except in so far as it included general accountancy work, so much of the payment as did not relate to general accountancy work was compensation for loss of office and therefore within the charge to tax as employment income (although exempt under what is now *ITEPA 2003, Pt 6 Ch 3*) (see Tolley's Income Tax under Compensation for Loss of Employment and Damages) and only the balance constituted a trading receipt.

For further cases on this point, see Tolley's Tax Cases. See also **24.5** below.

For payments received on termination of building society agencies, see HMRC Capital Gains Tax Manual, CG13050 *et seq*.

Ex gratia payments

[24.5] In *Walker v Carnaby, Harrower, Barham & Pykett* (1969) 46 TC 561, a sum equivalent to the audit fee was paid to a firm of accountants as a solatium on their agreeing not to seek re-election as auditors to a group of companies. It was held that, but for being voluntary, the payment would have been taken into account as part of the firm's profits, but that 'ordinary commercial principles' did not require the bringing into account of a voluntary payment not made as consideration for past services, but in recognition of such services or by way of consolation for the termination of a contract.

Voluntary payments were also held not to be assessable as trading receipts in *Brander & Cruickshank* [1971] 1 All ER 36, [1971] 1 WLR 212, HL (loss of company secretaryships by firm of advocates); *Chibbett v Joseph Robinson & Sons* (1924) 9 TC 48 (loss of office as ship-managers on liquidation); *Simpson v John Reynolds & Co (Insurances) Ltd* (1975) 49 TC 693, CA (loss of client by insurance brokers) and *Murray v Goodhews* (1977) 52 TC 86, CA (termination of caterers' tenancies).

However, ex gratia payments to an estate agent who, contrary to local custom, had not been given an agency which he expected were held to be assessable as additional remuneration for work already carried out (*McGowan v Brown & Cousins* (1977) 52 TC 8), and a non-contractual payment to a diamond broker by a fellow-broker, as compensation for transfer of a client's business after substantial work had been done on the client's behalf but before any corresponding benefit had been gained from purchases by the client, was held to be a trading receipt (*Rolfe v Nagel* (1981) 55 TC 585, CA).

See also *Falkirk Ice Rink Ltd* [1975] STC 434, 51 TC 42, Ct of Sess, where the payment related to future services, and for further cases on this point, see Tolley's Tax Cases.

Other receipts assessable as income

[24.6] Damages awarded to producers for breach of a sole licence to perform a play were held assessable in *Vaughan v Parnell & Zeitlin Ltd* (1940) 23 TC 505 as was statutory compensation for the restriction of development rights (*Johnson v W S Try Ltd* (1946) 27 TC 167, CA). Retrospective compensation for requisitioned trading stock was held to be a trading receipt of the year of requisition in *Newcastle Breweries Ltd* (1927) 12 TC 927, HL, as were compensation to a shipping company for delay in the overhaul of a ship (*Burmah Steam Ship Co v CIR* (1930) 16 TC 67, Ct of Sess) and to a jetty owner for loss of use (*London & Thames Haven Oil Wharves Ltd v Attwooll* (1966) 43 TC 491, CA). For further cases on this point, see Tolley's Tax Cases. See also **24.7** below.

Compensation relating to capital assets

[24.7] An agreed sum received on the termination of 'pooling agreements' between two companies was held to be a capital receipt on the ground that the agreements '*related to the whole structure of the appellants' profit-making* *apparatus*' in *Van Den Berghs v Clark* (1935) 19 TC 390, HL. This was followed in *Barr, Crombie & Co Ltd v CIR* (1945) 26 TC 406, 1945 SC 271, Ct of Sess (terminating ship-managers' agreement) and *Sabine v Lookers Ltd* (1958) 38 TC 120, CA (variation of car distributor's agreement). See also *British-Borneo Petroleum Syndicate Ltd v Cropper* (1968) 45 TC 201 (cancellation of royalty agreement).

Compensation paid to a company making fireclay goods for refraining from working a fireclay bed was held to be capital in *Glenboig Union Fireclay Co Ltd v CIR* (1922) 12 TC 427, HL, but cf. *Waterloo Main Colliery Co Ltd v CIR (No 1)* (1947) 29 TC 235 where compensation for the requisition of part of a mining area was held to be a trading receipt. Reimbursement for restoration expenditure on a ship which had deteriorated whilst requisitioned was held to be a capital receipt in *CIR v West* (1950) 84 Ll L Rep 284, 31 TC 402, Ct of Sess, but compensation for loss of use of a requisitioned ship was assessable as a trading receipt in *Ensign Shipping Co Ltd v CIR* (1928) 12 TC 1169, CA. For further relevant cases, see Tolley's Tax Cases. See also **24.6** above.

Payment of compensation

[24.8] Payment of compensation is treated as follows:

(a) Deductible as revenue expenditure. A substantial payment by a principal for the cancellation of an expensive agency agreement was held deductible in *Anglo-Persian Oil Co Ltd v Dale* (1931) 16 TC 253, CA, on the grounds that it was made not only to commute revenue expenditure but also to rationalise the principal's working arrangements. The decision was applied in *Croydon Hotel & Leisure Co Ltd v Bowen* [1996] STC (SCD) 466, in which a payment for the termination of a hotel management agreement was held to be allowable.
Contrast *Mallett v Staveley Coal & Iron Co Ltd* (1928) 13 TC 772, CA, where a payment to surrender certain onerous mining leases was held to secure an advantage for the enduring benefit of the trade and therefore to be capital expenditure. For other items held to be revenue expenditure, see *Commr of Taxes v Nchanga Consolidated Copper Mines Ltd* [1964] AC 948, PC, and *United Steel Companies* (below), *BW Noble Ltd v Mitchell (Inspector of Taxes)* 11 TC 372, 43 TLR 102, CA (payment to get rid of director), and *O'Keeffe v Southport Printers Ltd* (1984) 58 TC 88 (payments on cessation in lieu of notice). See also *G Scammell & Nephew v Rowles* (1939) 22 TC 479, CA.

(b) Capital expenditure. A payment by the operator of a single ship for cancelling an order for a second was held to be on capital account (*'Countess Warwick' Steamship Co Ltd v Ogg* (1924) 8 TC 652) as were payments by a steel company to secure the closure of railways steelworks (*United Steel Companies Ltd v Cullington (Inspector of Taxes)* [1940] AC 812, [1940] 2 All ER 170, HL, which also involved payments by sub-contractors on revenue account); for cessation of mining to prevent subsidence (*Bradbury v The United Glass Bottle*

Manufacturers Ltd (1959) 38 TC 369, CA); for the cancellation of an electricity agreement on the closure of a quarry (*William Sharp & Son* (1959) 38 TC 341, Ct of Sess) and as compensation on the termination of tied tenancies by a brewery company (*Watneys London Ltd v Pike* (1982) 57 TC 372).

(c) Other expenditure not deductible. Damages paid by a brewery to a hotel guest injured by a falling chimney were held to have been incurred as a property owner and not as a trader (*Strong & Co of Romsey Ltd v Woodifield* (1906) 5 TC 215, HL). Penalties for the breach of war-time regulations (and associated costs) were disallowed in *Alexander von Glehn & Co Ltd* (1920) 12 TC 232, CA, and damages for breach of American anti-trust law (but **not** the associated legal expenses) in *Cattermole v Borax & Chemicals Ltd* (1949) 31 TC 202. See also *Fairrie v Hall* (1947) 28 TC 200 (damages for libel) and *Knight v Parry* (1972) 48 TC 580 (damages for breach of contract of employment).

(d) Date of payment. Where damages awarded by a court against a solicitor were later compounded, the compounded amount (accepted as allowable) was held to be an expense of the year in which the court award was made (*Simpson v Jones* (1968) 44 TC 599). See also *CIR v Hugh T Barrie Ltd* (1928) 12 TC 1223, CA (NI).

For further relevant cases, see Tolley's Tax Cases.

Key points

[24.9] Points to consider are as follows.

- As a general rule, where compensation is in respect of a trade it will usually be taxed as a trading receipt. This includes compensation for loss of profits, cancellation of trading contracts etc. Compensation for the permanent loss of a capital asset is a capital receipt but compensation for the temporary loss of a capital asset is an income receipt. A compensation receipt can be apportioned between capital and income elements.
- Where the payment is voluntary there may be scope for it not to be treated as a trading receipt.
- For the payer the payment is usually tax deductible where it relates to the trade or business and is not a capital payment. The question is whether the payment is made wholly and exclusively for business purposes.

25

Connected Persons

Introduction

[25.1] Transactions between connected persons are deemed to be made other than by way of an arm's length bargain. Therefore, the transaction is deemed to be made for consideration equal to market value.

This chapter sets out the definition of 'connected persons' under the general provision of *CTA 2010, s 1122* [*previously ICTA 1988, s 839*]. Reference is made to this section throughout the Corporation Taxes Acts. It should be noted that a modified definition may be applied in relation to any specific legislation. In these cases, reference is made as appropriate in the text describing that legislation. The definition of connected persons was modified by the Tax and Civil Partnership Regulations 2005 to cover civil partners from 5 December 2005.

[*SI 2005 No 3229, Reg 100*].

Simon's Taxes. See **A1.156, C2.110.**

Definition of connected persons

[25.2] An individual is connected with:

- his spouse or (from 5 December 2005) civil partner;
- any 'relative' of himself or of his spouse or civil partner; and
- with the spouse or civil partner of any such relative.

'*Relative*' means brother, sister, ancestor or lineal descendant.

It appears that a widow or widower is no longer a spouse (*Vestey's Exors and Vestey v CIR* HL 1949, 31 TC 1). Spouses divorced by decree nisi remain connected persons until the divorce is made absolute (*Aspden v Hildesley* Ch D 1981, 55 TC 609).

A trustee of a 'settlement', in his capacity as such, is connected with:

(a) the 'settlor' (if an individual) (see below); and

(b) any person connected with the settlor (if within (a)); and
(c) a 'body corporate connected with the settlement' (see below).

Partners are connected with each other and with each other's spouses or civil partners and relatives except in connection with acquisitions and disposals of partnership assets made 'pursuant to *bona fide* commercial arrangements'.

A 'company' (see below) is connected with another company if:

(a) the same person 'controls' both;
(b) one is controlled by a person who has control of the other in conjunction with persons connected with him;
(c) a person controls one company and persons connected with him control the other;
(d) the same group of persons controls both; or
(e) the companies are controlled by separate groups which can be regarded as the same by interchanging connected persons.

A company is connected with a person who (either alone or with persons connected with him) has control of it. It is understood that HMRC will accept that a partnership and a company under common control are connected in relation to the treatment for capital allowances of assets transferred on a succession.

Persons acting together to secure or exercise control of a company are treated in relation to that company as connected with each other and with any other person acting on the direction of any of them to secure or exercise such control. For the meaning of 'acting together to secure or exercise control', see *Steele v EVC International NV (formerly European Vinyls Corp (Holdings) BV)* CA 1996, 69 TC 88. Control may be 'exercised' passively. (See *Floor v Davis* HL 1979, 52 TC 609).

Interpretation of definitions

[25.3] '*Company*' includes any body corporate, unincorporated association or unit trust scheme. It does not include a partnership.

'*Control*' is as defined in *CTA 2010, ss 450, 451* [*previously ICTA 1988, s 416*] (see **22.6 CLOSE COMPANIES**).

'*Settlement*' includes any disposition, trust, covenant, agreement, arrangement or transfer of assets (but not a charitable loan arrangement).

[*ITTOIA 2005, s 620, Sch 1 para 273; ICTA 1988, s 660G(1)*].

'*A body corporate connected with the settlement*' is a close company (or one which would be close if resident in the UK) the participators in which include the trustees of the settlement, or a company of which such a close company etc. has control (as defined by *CTA 2010, s 1124, previously ICTA 1988, s 840*).

[*ITTOIA 2005, s 637(8), Sch 1 para 276; CTA 2010, s 1122(6), previously ICTA 1988, s 839(3A)*].

'*Settlor*' is any person by whom the settlement was made or who has directly or indirectly (or by a reciprocal arrangement) provided, or undertaken to provide, funds for the settlement.

[*ITTOIA 2005, s 620, Sch 1 para 273; ICTA 1988, s 660G(1)(2)*].

Group of companies

[25.4] The same definitions are applied for the purposes of corporation tax on chargeable gains by *TCGA 1992, s 286*. In a 2009 case, *Kellogg Brown & Root Holdings Ltd v HMRC* ChD [2009], the taxpayer company was a subsidiary of a US parent. In the course of a re-organisation, two of the company's subsidiaries were transferred to another group company and the shares were subsequently distributed in kind. The company claimed that the loss on transfer of the subsidiaries was available for set off against subsequent gains. It was held that the effect of *TCGA 1992, s 286(5)(b)* was that the companies were connected at the time of the sale of the shares.

26

Construction Industry Scheme

HMRC guidance on the post-2007 Construction Industry Scheme can be found in the HMRC Construction Industry Reform Manual, which is available on their website (see www.hmrc.gov.uk/manuals/cismanual/index.htm). Guidance on the scheme is also available on the HMRC website at www.hmrc.gov.uk/cis/index.htm.

Simon's Taxes. See E5.5.

Introduction

[26.1] The construction industry scheme (CIS) sets out how payments to sub-contractors by contractors in the construction industry for construction work are treated for tax purposes. In the main, the CIS applies to sub-contractors and contractors engaged in mainstream construction work. However, its remit also extends to businesses in other sectors that have a high annual spend on construction.

The present scheme commenced on 6 April 2007, replacing the previous CIS scheme that operated from 1999 until 5 April 2007. However, HMRC remain concerned about potential misclassification of workers within the construction industry. In the 2009 Budget, the then Chancellor announced that the Government would be addressing the issue false self-employment in the construction industry. A consultation published in July 2009 outlined HMRC's concern that too many workers in the construction industry were treated as being self-employed when in reality they were employees. The document proposed a legislative solution based around a test to deem construction workers to be in receipt of employment income unless certain conditions were met. A summary of responses to the consultation was published in March

2010, which concluded that further work on the test was needed before the proposals could became law. A report commissioned by HMRC and published in October 2010 gave some insight into the operation of the CIS (see the HMRC website at www.hmrc.gov.uk/research/eval-cis.pdf), but there are no changes to the current scheme at this time.

Overview of the CIS

[26.2] The current construction industry scheme (CIS) applies from 6 April 2007. The scheme sets out the rules for taxing payments made to sub-contractors in the construction industry by contractors. The framework for the scheme is provided for in *FA 2004*, but much of the detail is contained in regulations (see *Income Tax (Construction Industry Scheme) Regulations 2005* (*SI 2005 No 2045*)). HMRC are given wide powers to make regulations governing the scheme as they consider necessary or expedient.

[*FA 2004, ss 73, 76, 77(1), Sch 12 para 9; ITA 2007, Sch 1 para 461*].

Various transitional measures applied on the introduction of the scheme (see **26.11** below).

Outline of the scheme

The purpose of the CIS is to target tax evasion by sub-contractors working in construction who are unknown to HMRC. Under the scheme payments made to sub-contractors suffer deduction of tax at one of two rates. The amount deducted must be paid over by the contractor to HMRC. A sub-contractor can only be paid gross if certain conditions are met. Key features of the scheme include:

- a verification service to enable contractors to check whether sub-contractors are registered for gross or net payment (see **26.10** below); and
- periodic returns by contractors to replace the voucher system (see **26.10** below).

The scheme imposes various obligations on both sub-contractors and contractors. Sub-contractors must register with HMRC. Sub-contractors who do not register with HMRC are subject to a higher rate of deduction. Sub-contractors who registered are automatically registered for net payment. However, where a sub-contractor can show that the eligibility conditions for gross payment have been met, HMRC will grant gross payments status, allowing payments to the sub-contractor to be made gross without deduction of tax.

Contractors are obliged to verify their sub-contractors with HMRC and to ensure that sub-contractors are paid correctly in accordance with their deduction status. Amounts deducted from sub-contractors must be paid over to HMRC by the contractor. From 2010/11 onwards penalties apply where payments are made late more than once during the tax year. The penalty rate depends on the number of late payments during the year. The contractor must also make periodic returns to HMRC concerning contract payments, as well as providing information about such payments to the sub-contractor.

Definitions

[26.3] The CIS scheme applies to payments under a '*construction contract*'. This is a contract relating to 'construction operations' and involving a 'sub-contractor' and a 'contractor'. A contract of employment is specifically excluded from the definition of a construction contract. [*FA 2004, s 57(2)*]. For a discussion of the indicators of employment status, see Tolley's Income Tax under Employment Income.

Construction operations

The following operations are '*construction operations*':

(a) construction, alteration, repair, extension, demolition or dismantling of buildings or structures, including offshore installations and temporary structures;
(b) construction, alteration, repair, extension or demolition of works forming part of the land, and this specifically includes walls, road-works, power-lines, electronic communications apparatus, aircraft run ways, docks and harbours, railways, inland waterways, pipe-lines, reservoirs, water-mains, wells, sewers, industrial plant and installations for purposes of land drainage, coast protection or defence;
(c) installation of heating, lighting, air-conditioning, ventilation, power supply, drainage, sanitation, water supply or fire protection;
(d) internal cleaning if carried out during construction, alteration, repair, extension or restoration; and
(e) painting or decorating (internal and external).

Operations which are an integral part of operations in the above list are also included; for instance, site clearance, earth-moving, excavation, tunnelling and boring, laying of foundations, erection of scaffolding, site restoration, land-scaping and the provision of roadways and other access works.

Specifically excluded from the definition of construction operations are:

(i) operations outside the UK and its territorial sea;
(ii) drilling for, or extraction of, oil or natural gas, and extraction of minerals;
(iii) manufacture of building or engineering components or equipment and delivery of these to site;
(iv) manufacture of components for heating, ventilation etc. systems and delivery to site;
(v) the work of architects, surveyors and consultants;
(vi) making, installing or repairing artistic works;
(vii) signwriting and erecting, installing or repairing signboards and adver-tisements;
(viii) installation of seating, blinds and shutters;
(ix) installation of security systems and public address systems.

The Treasury may, by order, amend the definition of construction operations. [*FA 2004, s 74*].

Sub-contractor

A person is a 'sub-contractor' if the contract imposes on him a duty to:

(A) carry out construction operations; or
(B) furnish his own labour or the labour of others in carrying out construction operations; or
(C) arrange for the labour of others to be furnished in carrying out construction operations.

Alternatively, a person may be a sub-contractor if, under the construction contract, he is answerable to the contractor for construction operations carried out by others who are working for him (whether under a contract or other arrangements).
[*FA 2004, s 58*].

Contractor

A '*contractor*' in relation to a construction contract is a body or person falling within one of the following categories.

(1) Persons who are automatically classed as contractors. These are:
  (a) any person carrying on a business which includes construction operations; and
  (b) the Secretary of State if the contract is made by him under the *Housing Associations Act 1985, s 89*.
(2) Persons carrying on a business at any time which exceeds a set level of expenditure is more than:
  (a) £1,000,000 per year on average over the period of three years ending at the same time as the last period of account; or
  (b) where the business was not being carried on at the beginning of that three-year period, total expenditure in the truncated period exceeds £3,000,000.

  Where a person is classed as a contractor by virtue of this test, they remain a contractor for the purposes of the CIS until HMRC are satisfied that expenditure on construction operations has been less than £1,000,000 for each of three successive years beginning in or after the period of account in which contractor status was acquired. For the purposes of all these limits, where a trade is transferred from one company to another and there is no change of ownership under *CTA 2010, Pt 22, Ch 1*, the transferor's expenditure is treated as the transferee's, with apportionment by HMRC (subject to appeal) when only part of the trade is transferred.
(3) The following are deemed to be contractors for the purpose of the CIS, provided that their average annual expenditure on construction operations in any three-year period ending on 31 March exceeds £1,000,000:
  (a) any public office or department of the Crown (including any Northern Ireland department and any part of the Scottish Administration);
  (b) the Corporate Officer of the House of Lords, the Corporate Officer of the House of Commons, and the Scottish Parliamentary Corporate Body;

(c) any local authority;
(d) any development corporation or new town commission;
(e) the Commission for the New Towns;
(f) the Housing Corporation, a housing association, a housing trust, Scottish Homes, and the Northern Ireland Housing Executive;
(g) any NHS trust; and
(h) any HSS trust.

Contractor status ceases to apply if, subsequently, there are three successive years (ending on 31 March) in which expenditure was less than £1,000,000.

[*FA 2004, ss 57(2), 59*].

Contract payments

'*Contract payments*' are payments under a construction contract from the contractor to:

- a sub-contractor;
- a nominee of the sub-contractor or the contractor; or
- a nominee of a person who is a sub-contractor under another construction contract relating to the construction operations.

Where the contractor makes a payment to a third party which discharges his obligation to pay a person within the above list, that payment is deemed to have been made directly to that person.

However, the following are not contract payments.

(I) Payments to agency workers (i.e. earnings under *ITEPA 2003, Pt 2 Ch 7*).
(II) Payments where the recipient is registered for gross payment (see **26.5** below) when the payment is made (but see below for certain qualifications in the case of nominees and partnerships).
(III) Payments excepted by regulations as follows:
- small payments, i.e. payments made by contractors within **26.3**(1)(b), (2) or (3) above and approved for this purpose, in a case where the total payments under the construction contract (excluding direct cost of materials) do not, or are not likely to, exceed £1,000;
- payments made by a contractor within **26.3**(1)(a) above, and approved for this purpose, to a body or person for work carried out on land owned by that body or person or on agricultural property (as defined) of which that body or person is a tenant, in a case where the total payments under the construction contract (excluding direct cost of materials) do not, or are not likely to, exceed £1,000;
- reverse premiums (within the meaning of *FA 1999, Sch 6* or *CTA 2009, s 96* — see **70.62 TRADE PROFITS — INCOME AND SPECIFIC TRADES** — as modified for this purpose);
- payments by local authority maintained schools under devolved budgets;

- payments made by contractors within **26.3**(2) above in respect of construction operations relating to property used (as defined) in their own or another group company's business;
- payments made by public bodies within **26.3**(1)(b) or (3) above under a private finance transaction (as defined); and
- payments made by any body of persons or trust established for charitable purposes only.

The qualifications to the exception at (II) above are as follows:

(a) where the recipient is a nominee, then the nominee, the person who nominated him and the person for whose labour the payment is made (employee's labour in the case of a company) must all be registered for gross payment when the payment is made;

(b) where the recipient is registered for gross payment as a partner in a firm, the exception only applies to payments under contracts where the firm is a sub-contractor or, where the firm has been nominated to receive payments, the person who nominated the firm is a sub-contractor. Note that, in such a case, the person nominating the firm must also be registered for gross payment;

(c) where the recipient is registered for gross payment other than as a partner in a firm but is or becomes a partner in a firm, the exception does not apply to payments under contracts where the firm is a sub-contractor or, where the firm has been nominated to receive payments, the person who nominated the firm is a sub-contractor.

[*FA 2004, s 60; SI 2005 No 2045, Regs 18–24*].

Payments from which tax must be deducted

[26.4] A key feature of the CIS is the deduction of tax from payments made to sub-contractors who are not registered for gross payment status.

Where a contractor makes a contract payment to a sub-contractor, the contractor must make a deduction on account of tax. Tax is deducted at the 'relevant percentage' of the contract payment after excluding the cost of materials (exclusive of VAT) used (or to be used) in carrying out the construction operation. The 'relevant percentage', is set by *SI 2007 No 0046* and depends on the registration status of the contractor:

Registration status of sub-contractor	Relevant percentage
Registered under deduction	20%
Not registered	30%
Registered for gross payment	Nil

The amount deducted from a contract payment by the contractor must be paid to HMRC. The sub-contractor's income for tax purposes includes any deduction made under the CIS.

> *Example*
>
> A contactor makes payment of £5,400 to a sub-contractor. The sub-contractor is registered under deduction. The sub-contractor spends £1,500 on materials in carrying out the construction contract.
>
> The amount paid to the sub-contractor excluding materials is £3,900 (£5,400 – £1,500).
>
> The contractor must deduct £780, being 20% of £3,900, and pay the amount deducted over to HMRC.

Where the sub-contractor is not a company, the amounts deducted are treated as income tax paid in respect of the profits of the trade, with any excess being treated as Class 4 National Insurance contributions.

Where the sub-contractor is a company, the amount deducted is applied in the following order:

(1) against payment due under the contractor's obligations as an employer or contractor in respect of PAYE, Class 1 NIC, deductions under the CIS or student loan deductions, whether arising before or after the deduction in question;
(2) against corporation tax,

any excess is repaid.

HMRC have extensive powers to make regulations governing the treatment of sums deducted.

[*FA 2004, ss 61, 62*].

Registration

[26.5] Sub-contractors are required to register with HMRC. Those who fail to register suffer a higher rate of deduction. The registration requirement aims to tackle tax avoidance by ensuring sub-contractors are 'known' to HMRC.

A sub-contractor can register under deduction of tax or, if the gross payment conditions are met, for gross payment.

In order to be registered, an applicant must provide sufficient documents, records and information to establish, to the satisfaction of HMRC, his identity and address. If HMRC are not satisfied with the information provided, they may refuse to register the person and issue a refusal notice advising him of this decision. Where a refusal notice is issued, a person can appeal against the decision to refuse registration (see below).

Where the sub-contractor wishes to register for gross payment (see **26.6** below), he must also supply sufficient evidence that gross payment registration conditions are met.

An application for registration under deduction may be made on form CIS301 and an application for registration for gross payment is made on form CIS302. The forms are available to download from the HMRC website (www.hmrc.g

ov.uk). It is also possible to register online via the HMRC website. HMRC also produce extensive guidance for contractors and sub-contractors in booklet CIS340 (http://www.hmrc.gov.uk/forms/cis340.pdf). Where an application for gross payment is refused (or gross payment registration cancelled), the sub-contractor has a right of appeal (see below).

A penalty of up to £3,000 applies for knowingly or recklessly making a statement, or supplying a document, for the purpose of becoming registered which is false in a material particular.

[*FA 2004, ss 63, 72; SI 2005 No 2045, Reg 25(3)*].

Registration for gross payment

A sub-contractor who meets certain conditions can register for gross payment. This enables the contractor to pay the sub-contractor gross without making a deduction on account of tax.

The requirements for registration for gross payment vary, depending upon whether the applicant is:

(a) an individual (see **26.6** below);
(b) a company (see **26.7** below); or
(c) an individual or company applying as a partner in a firm (see **26.8** below).

The rules governing the documents, records and information that must be provided to HMRC in support of an application for registration are set out in *SI 2005 No 2045*. The regulations also provide for appeals against a notice of cancellation of, or a refusal to grant, registration. The Treasury is specifically empowered to alter, by order, the conditions relating to registration for gross payment.

[*FA 2004, s 64, Sch 11 para 13; SI 2005 No 2045, Regs 25, 26*].

Cancellation of registration for payment under deduction

Where a person has registered for payment under deduction, HMRC can issue a determination cancelling that registration where they have reasonable grounds to suspect that the person:

- has provided incorrect information in support of the application for registration;
- has fraudulently made an incorrect return or provided incorrect information under the CIS scheme, whether as a contractor or a sub-contractor; or
- knowingly failed to comply with any provision of the CIS, whether as a contractor or as a sub-contractor.

Where such a determination is made, the registration is cancelled with immediate effect by issuing a cancellation notice to the person stating the reasons for the cancellation.

[*SI 2005 No 2045, Reg 25(4)*].

Cancellation of gross payment registration

A person's registration may be cancelled where that person fails to comply with the requirements of the construction industry scheme. HMRC have the power to make a determination cancelling a person's registration for gross payment where it appears to them that:

- if an application for gross payment registration were to be made by a sub-contractor at that time, HMRC would refuse to register him;
- an incorrect return has been made or incorrect information provided by that person under the CIS, whether as a contractor or a sub-contractor; or
- he has failed to comply with any provision of the CIS, whether as a contractor or a sub-contractor.

Where such a determination is made, a person's registration is cancelled with effect from 90 days after the date of notice of cancellation (see below). However, the effective date may be delayed by an appeal (see below). Where an appeal is made, the cancellation date is the latest of:

- the abandonment of the appeal;
- determination of the appeal by the Tribunal; or
- determination of the appeal by the Upper Tribunal or a court.

Where a person's gross payment registration is cancelled, that person becomes registered under deduction of tax (and is liable to deduction at the rate of 20%).

More seriously, HMRC can also make a determination cancelling a person's gross payment registration where they have reasonable grounds to suspect that the person:

- became registered for gross payment on the basis of false information;
- fraudulently made an incorrect return or provided incorrect information under the CIS scheme; or
- knowingly failed to comply with any provision of the CIS scheme, whether as a contractor or a sub-contractor.

Where a determination is made in these circumstances, the person's gross payment registration is cancelled with immediate effect. Where gross payment registration is cancelled, HMRC must issue without delay a notice stating the reasons for the cancellation. It is up to HMRC's discretion whether that person is then registered for payment under deduction.

The person whose gross payment registration is cancelled may not re-apply for gross payment registration for at least a year after the cancellation takes effect.

Numerous cases have reached the tax tribunals and courts concerning the granting or withdrawal of gross payment status. The case of *Westview Rail Ltd* (TC00215) [2009] UKFTT 269 (TC) tested whether there were grounds for an appeal against cancellation of gross payment status. *Enderby Properties Ltd* (TC00396) [2010] UKFTT 85 (TC) and *GC Ware Electrics* (TC00499) [2010] UKFTT 197 tested whether insufficient funds constituted a reasonable excuse for late payments. *Grosvenor* (TC00227) [2009] UKFTT

283 (TC), *Ductaire Fabrications Ltd* (TC00288) [2009] UKFTT 350 (TC), *Pollard* (TC00563) [2010] UKFTT 269 (TC) and *Burns (t/a TK Fabrications)* (TC00371) [2010] UKFTT 58 (TC) are examples of cases where the consequences of cancelling gross payment status.

[*FA 2004, ss 66, 67(5), 68; SI 2005 No 2045, Regs 25, 26*].

Appeals

A right of appeal exists against:

- the refusal to register a person for payment under deduction (appeal against a refusal notice);
- the cancellation of registration for payment under deduction (appeal against a cancellation notice);
- the refusal to register a person for gross payments;
- the cancellation of gross payment registration; or
- the refusal to register a person for payment under deduction where gross payment registration has been cancelled.

As far as appeals against a refusal to register for payment under deduction (whether after cancellation of a gross payment registration or otherwise) and the cancellation of registration for payment under deduction, the appeal must be made within 30 days of the 'timing event' stating the reason for the appeal. The 'timing event' in relation to each type of appeal is, respectively:

- the issue of the refusal notice;
- the issue of the cancellation notice; and
- the cancellation of the gross payment registration

The following table summarises the position for each type of appeal.

Nature of appeal	Deadline for making appeal	Reason for appeal
Appeal against a refusal notice	30 days from issue of the refusal notice	Reasons for believing that the application should not have been refused
Appeal against a cancellation notice	30 days from the issue of the cancellation notice	Reasons for believing that the registration should not have been cancelled
Refusal to register for payment under deduction after cancellation of gross payment registration	30 days from cancellation of gross payment registration	Reasons for believing that the person should have been registered for payment under deduction

[*SI 2005 No 2045, Reg 25(5)*].

Where the appeal concerns the refusal to register for gross payment or the cancellation of gross payment registration, it must be made by giving notice to HMRC within 30 days of the decision. The notice must state the reasons why the decision is believed to be unjustified. Appeal is to the Tribunal.

[*FA 2004, ss 67, 68; SI 2005 No 2045, Reg 25*].

Registration for gross payment — individuals

[26.6] For an individual to qualify for registration for gross payment, he must satisfy three tests:

- the business test;
- the turnover test; and
- the compliance test.

The business test

In order to meet the business test, the individual must satisfy HMRC that he or she is carrying on a business in the UK that:

- consists of or includes the carrying out of construction operations or the furnishing of labour or arranging for the furnishing of labour for the carrying out of construction operations; and
- that the business is, to a substantial extent, be carried on using an account with a bank.

The individual must provide the following evidence to HMRC to demonstrate that the business test is met:

- the business address;
- invoices, contracts or purchase orders for construction work;
- the books and accounts of the business; and
- details of the business bank account, including bank statements.

[*FA 2004, Sch 11, para 2; SI 2005 No 2045, Reg 27*].

The turnover test

To pass the turnover test, the individual must satisfy HMRC that the likely receipt of 'relevant payments' in the year following the application is not less than the relevant turnover threshold. For individuals, the turnover threshold is set at £30,000.

Relevant payments' for this purpose are payments under contracts relating to 'construction operations' (see **26.3** above) or contracts relating to the work of individuals in the carrying out of construction operations. Payments representing the cost of materials are excluded.

The following evidence is required to satisfy the turnover test:

(a) evidence of the turnover during the twelve months prior to the application (the '*qualifying period*') (this is the net turnover excluding VAT and cost of materials);

(b) evidence of relevant payments which may include bank statements and paid cheques;

(c) evidence that total relevant payments received in the 12 months prior to the application equalled or exceeded the relevant turnover threshold (£30,000) (or, for the purposes of cancellation of registration for gross payment (under *FA 2004, s 66*), evidence that the relevant payments in the qualifying period equalled or exceeded the relevant turnover threshold, or the average amount of relevant payments received in the qualifying period and two previous years equalled or exceeded the relevant turnover threshold);

(d) documentary evidence that construction operations were carried out during the qualifying period.

A business that does not meet the turnover test can be treated as if it did if:

(i) the business does not consist mainly of construction operations;
(ii) overall turnover in the year prior to making the application exceeds the relevant turnover threshold; and
(iii) any relevant payments likely to be received in the year following the application will relate to construction operations which are an ancillary part of the business.

This is designed to cover the situation where overall turnover exceeds the threshold but relevant payments derive from an ancillary part of the business and are less than the threshold.

[*FA 2004, Sch 11 para 3; SI 2005 No 2045, Reg 29*].

The compliance test

The final test that must be met by individuals is the compliance test. To meet the compliance test, the individual must have complied with all tax obligations (i.e. imposed by the *Tax Acts*, *TMA 1970* or regulations there under including the construction industry scheme itself) in the 12 months prior to the application. This period is known as the '*qualifying period*'. In addition, there must be reason to expect that the applicant will continue to comply with tax obligations and requests for documents, etc. after the end of that period.

During the qualifying period, the application must have supplied HMRC with all requested information and accounts concerning the applicant's business. These requirements also apply to any company controlled (within *CTA 2010, ss 449–451*) by the applicant, in respect of periods falling within the qualifying period. Compliance for this purpose must be within any required time limits or at the required time.

The above compliance requirements are relaxed in two respects, as follows:

- HMRC are of the opinion that the applicant or company had a reasonable excuse for the failure and that the failure has been remedied without unreasonable delay after the excuse ceased to apply; or
- the obligation or request is of a kind prescribed in column 2 of Table 3 in *SI 2005 No 2045, Reg 32*.

In the event that an applicant was not subject to any compliance obligations because of absence abroad, unemployment, or being in full-time education, HMRC require evidence in support of this. In the case of absence abroad, the applicant must also show evidence of compliance with comparable obligations under the tax laws of the country of residence.

The applicant must have paid any National Insurance contributions as they fell due. This is not subject to the 'reasonable excuse' defence.

Finally, there must be reason to expect that the applicant will continue to comply with compliance obligations and requests for documents etc., and continue to pay his national insurance contributions, after the qualifying period.

[*FA 2004, s 64, Sch 11 paras 1–4, 14; SI 2005 No 2045, Regs 27–29, 31–37*].

Registration for gross payment — partners

[26.7] An individual applying for registration for gross payment as a partner in a firm must first meet the compliance test laid down for individuals (see **26.6** above). A company applying for such registration must first meet all the tests for companies (see **26.8** below) as appropriate. In addition, the firm itself must meet the following business, turnover and compliance tests.

The business test

The firm's business must be carried on in the UK. It must include either the carrying out of construction operations, or the furnishing of, or arranging for the furnishing of, labour for construction operations. It must, to a substantial extent, be carried on using an account with a bank. The evidence required to satisfy HMRC that these conditions are satisfied is as prescribed for individuals by *SI 2005 No 2045*, see **26.6** above.

The turnover test

The partners must satisfy HMRC that the likely receipt of relevant payments (see **26.6** above) in the year following the application is not less than the smaller of:

(a) the relevant turnover threshold which, in the case of partnerships, is £200,000; and
(b) the 'multiple turnover threshold'.

The '*multiple turnover threshold*' is obtained by adding together:

(i) the number of individuals in the partnership multiplied by the threshold for individuals (£30,000, see **26.6** above); and
(ii) in respect of each company (if any) in the partnership, the threshold that would obtain were the company to be applying in its own behalf (see **26.8** below).

Where the number of partners in (i) above has fluctuated over the twelve-month period prior to the application, the number is taken to be the maximum number of partners at any one time in that period. In calculating the figure in (ii) above, it is necessary to ignore companies whose only shareholders are other companies which are limited by shares and registered for gross payment.

The evidence required to satisfy the turnover test (prescribed by *SI 2005 No 2045, Reg 29*) includes the evidence as prescribed for individuals in **26.6** above by reference to the above turnover threshold for partnerships. In the case of a new business carried on by the firm where there is no evidence as prescribed in (a), (c) or (d) in **26.6** above, the following evidence can be given instead, but only in relation to one application for registration for gross payment:

(A) evidence of relevant payments which may include bank statements and paid cheques;
(B) evidence of turnover of partners during the qualifying period;

(C) evidence of construction contracts entered into by the firm including payment schedules where the aggregate value of contracts exceeds £200,000 and payments have been made of at least £30,000.

A firm that does not meet this test may be treated as if it did (as in the case of individuals — see **26.6** above).

The compliance test

Each of the partners at the time of the application must, during the qualifying period (see **26.6** above), have complied with all tax obligations in relation to any income tax or corporation tax charge which was computed by reference to the firm's business. Over the same period, the applicant must have supplied all requested information and accounts concerning the firm's business or his share of that business. Compliance must be within any required time limits or at the required time. Similar provisions as for individuals at **26.6**(A), (B) above apply to treat a person as not having failed a compliance obligation in certain circumstances.

There must be reason to expect that, following the qualifying period, each of the persons who are from time to time partners in the firm will continue the record of compliance.

[*FA 2004, s 64, Sch 11 paras 5–8, 14; SI 2005 No 2045, Regs 27–37*].

Registration for gross payment — companies

[26.8] In order to register for gross payment, a company must pass the business, turnover and compliance tests described below. However, HMRC may, in addition to these tests, make a direction applying the conditions relating to individuals (see **26.6** above) to the directors of the company. If the company is a close company, this is extended to include the beneficial owners of shares in the company. Rather than apply all the conditions to all of the directors or shareholders, the direction may specify which conditions are to apply, and to which directors or shareholders.

In particular, HMRC may make such a direction where there has been a change in control (within *CTA 2010, s 1124(1)–(3)*) of a company that either is, or is applying to be, registered for gross payment. HMRC are empowered to make regulations requiring the submission of information concerning changes in control of such companies.

The business test

The company's business must be carried on in the UK. It must include either the carrying out of construction operations, or furnishing of, or arranging for the furnishing of labour for construction operations. It must, to a substantial extent, be carried on using an account with a bank. The evidence required to satisfy HMRC that these conditions are satisfied is prescribed for individuals by *SI 2005 No 2045* in **26.6** above.

The turnover test

A company may pass this test by:

(a) satisfying HMRC that its only shareholders are companies limited by shares and registered for gross payment; or
(b) providing HMRC with evidence that relevant payments (see **26.6** above) received in the year following the application are likely to equal or exceed a set threshold.

The set threshold is the smaller of:

(i) the relevant turnover threshold which, in the case of companies, is £200,000; and
(ii) the individual threshold (£30,000, see **26.6** above) multiplied by the number of 'relevant persons'. A '*relevant person*' is a director (within *ITEPA 2003, s 67*) or, for close companies, a director or a beneficial owner of shares. Where the number of relevant persons has fluctuated over the twelve-month period prior to the application, the number is taken to be the maximum number of such relevant persons at any one time in that period.

The evidence required to satisfy the turnover test (prescribed by *SI 2005 No 2045, Reg 29*) includes the evidence as prescribed for individuals in **26.6** above but by reference to the above set threshold for companies. In the case of a new business carried on by the company where there is no evidence as prescribed in (a), (c) or (d) in **26.6** above, the following evidence may be given instead, but only in relation to one application for registration for gross payment:

(A) evidence of relevant payments which may include bank statements and paid cheques;
(B) evidence of turnover of relevant persons during the qualifying period;
(C) evidence of construction contracts entered into by the company including payment schedules where the aggregate value of contracts exceeds £200,000 and payments have been made of at least £30,000;
(D) where the business was acquired from another person, firm or company, similar evidence as above in relation to the transferor.

A company that does not meet this test may be treated as if it did (as in the case of individuals — see **26.6** above).

The compliance test

The provisions relating to companies mirror those relating to individuals (see **26.6** above). However, in addition to this a company must have complied with certain *Companies Act 2006* (or the Northern Ireland equivalent) obligations during the qualifying period. Those obligations are under:

- *sections 394, 395, and 437–451* (contents, laying and delivery of annual accounts);
- *sections 167(1) and (2), and 276(1) and (2)* (return of directors and secretary and notification of changes therein);
- *sections 854–859* (annual returns);
- *Part 34* (accounts of overseas company).

[*FA 2004, s 64 and Sch 11 paras 9–12, 14; SI 2005 No 2045, Regs 27–37*].

Charities

[26.9] For the purposes of the CIS, a payment under a construction contract is not regarded as a contract payment if the payment is made by a charity. [*SI 2006 No 2045, Reg 24*].

Procedures and administration

[26.10] Detailed procedures and administrative arrangements for the operation of the scheme applying from April 2007 are contained in *The Income Tax (Construction Industry Scheme) Regulations 2005* (*SI 2005 No 2045*), as amended. The regulations specify the procedures governing verification of contractors, returns by contractors, payments and recovery of amounts deducted, electronic communications and methods of payment, and HMRC powers to inspect records.

[*FA 2004, ss 69–71, 73; ITA 2007 Sch 1 para 461*].

General guidance on the CIS, including compliance obligation imposed by the scheme is available on the HMRC website (see www.hmrc.gov.uk/cis/).

Multiple contractors

A contractor may elect to be treated as different contractors for each of any specified group of sub-contractors. The election must be made (or revoked) by notice to an officer of HMRC before the beginning of the tax year for which it is to have effect. There are special provisions which apply where a contractor acquires the business of another contractor. [*SI 2005 No 2045, Reg 3*].

Verification of status of sub-contractors

Anyone making contract payments must verify with HMRC the registration status of the recipient. Verification is not necessary if the recipient has been included in the contractor's returns (see below) in the current or previous two tax years. Where the contractor is a company, the exclusion from the need to verify the status of the sub-contractor also applies where the sub-contractor has, within current or previous two tax years, been included in a return made by another company in the same group. Likewise, where multiple contractors election has been made (see above), the return may include one from a different specified group of sub-contractors. Where this condition is met and the business is transferred as a going concern, no further verification is required by the transferee provided the contractor has notified HMRC of the transfer.

HMRC must notify a contractor if a person registered for gross payment becomes registered for payment under deduction, or vice versa, or if a registered person has ceased to be so registered. Once a person has been verified as being registered (whether for gross payment or payment under deduction) the contractor is entitled to assume that the person has not subsequently ceased to be so registered.

[*SI 2005 No 2045, Reg 6*].

The verification system removes the need for the sub-contractor to present documents which the contractor must inspect, and thus reduces some of the bureaucratic burden.

Monthly returns by contractors

A contractor must make monthly returns to HMRC within 14 days after the end of every tax month and written information must also be provided to sub-contractors who are registered for payment under deduction or who are not registered. Where a return has been made, or should have been made, and no contract payments are made in the tax month following that return, the contractor must make a nil return for that month unless the contractor has notified HMRC that no further contract payments are to be made within the following six months. From 2010/11 penalties are charged where the monthly returns are made late on more than one occasion during the tax year. The penalty charged depends on the number of late returns in the year (see **60.9** penalties). [*SI 2005 No 2045, Reg 4*].

Scheme representative

A contractor company may appoint another company in the same group ('a scheme representative') to act on its behalf in relation to the requirement to make a return or other such requirements under the regulations. [*SI 2005 No 2045, Reg 5*].

Collection and recovery of sums deducted

The arrangements for accounting for tax deductions and for interest on unpaid and overpaid tax broadly follow those for PAYE (see Tolley's Income Tax under Pay as You Earn and HMRC publication CIS340). There are detailed provisions governing methods of payment and electronic communications. [*FA 2004, s 71; ITTOIA 2005, Sch 1 para 630; SI 2005 No 2045, Regs 7–17, 44–49, 58; SI 2007 No 672; CTA 2009, Sch 1 para 570*].

Late filing penalties

[26.11] A new regime of penalties for late filing of CIS returns will apply from October 2011 (*FA 2009, Sch 55*; see www.hmrc.gov.uk/cis/penalties-late-returns.htm). Although the new regime will take effect from October 2011, special rules apply where this will result in a lower penalty being charged (see below).

The penalties that may be charged are as follows (*FA 2009, Sch 55 paras 7–13*):

(1) a fixed penalty of £100 as soon as a return is late;
(2) a second fixed penalty of £200 if the return is still outstanding two months after the filing date;
(3) a tax-geared penalty for returns still outstanding six months after the filing date, which will be 5% of the deductions shown on the outstanding return or, if greater, £300; and
(4) a second tax-geared penalty for returns still outstanding after 12 months, the amount depending on the degree of culpability:
    (a) if HMRC consider that the return information has been deliberately withheld and concealed then the penalty will be 100% of the deductions shown on the outstanding return or, if greater, £3,000;

(b) if HMRC consider that the return information has been deliberately withheld but not concealed then the penalty will be 70% of the deductions shown on the outstanding return or, if greater, £1,500;

(c) in any other case, the penalty will be five per cent of the deductions shown on the outstanding return or, if greater, £300.

For new contractors who have not previously filed any returns, there will be an upper limit of £3,000 on the total amount of £100 and £200 fixed penalties. There is no cap for tax-geared penalties, but the lower limit of £300 will not be applied if the tax-geared penalty would otherwise have been less than that amount.

Earlier application of the rules

HMRC guidance on the new penalty regime applying from October 2011 advises that there will be cases where a penalty calculated under the new regime will be lower than if it were calculated under the old rules. Any contractor who has already paid a penalty, or who is asked to pay a penalty in relation to any earlier period, may ask for it to be recalculated on the new basis if that new basis will result in a lower charge. This applies to any CIS penalty charged under *TMA 1970, s 98A(2)*. Where appropriate, penalties already paid will be reimbursed to the extent that the newly calculated charge is lower.

Pre-existing certificates and registration cards

Where a sub-contractor had a tax certificate under the predecessor scheme that was in force immediately before 6 April 2007, the sub-contractor was treated as if he had been registered for gross payment on 6 April 2007. Similarly, where a registration card under the old scheme was in force immediately before 6 April 2007, the sub-contractor was treated as having been registered for payment under deduction on 6 April 2007. [*FA 2004, s 77(2)(3)*].

Existing relationships

On the introduction of the current CIS, a contractor was not required to verify the status of a particular sub-contractor if:

(a) he had already paid that sub-contractor under a construction contract before 6 April 2007;

(b) the last such payment was within either the same tax year as the first payment under the current scheme or the preceding two tax years;

(c) at the time of the last payment under the old scheme, a tax certificate or registration card was in force; and

(d) at the time of the first payment under the current scheme the contractor had no reason to believe that the sub-contractor did not benefit from automatic registration on the appointed day under the rules described above, and was still unregistered.

Where these conditions applied, the contractor could continue to assume the sub-contractor is registered unless HMRC notify him of a change in status. [*FA 2004, s 77(4)–(6)*].

Key points

[26.12] The key points are as follows:

- The current construction scheme was introduced with effect from 6 April 2007.
- The scheme sets out how payments by contractors to sub-contractors are treated for tax purposes.
- Although the scheme applies predominantly to those in main-stream construction work, its remit also extends to businesses in other sectors with a high annual spend on construction.
- The scheme aims to tackle tax evasion in the construction industry by sub-contractors who are not known to HMRC.
- Sub-contractors must register with HMRC, either for payment under deduction or, if certain conditions are met, for gross payment status.
- Unless a sub-contractor is registered for gross payment status, the contractor must make a deduction on account of tax when making a payment to a sub-contractor under a construction contract.
- The rate of deduction depends on whether the sub-contractor is registered with HMRC. Contractors registered under deduction with HMRC suffer deduction at a rate of 20%. A higher rate of deduction of 30% applies to unregistered sub-contractors.
- Contractors must verify the registration status of sub-contractors they engage with HMRC.
- Contractors must make monthly returns to HMRC and pay over amounts deducted on account of tax. Penalties are charged for late returns.
- HMRC remain concerned about tax evasion in the construction industry and are consulting on false self-employment in the construction industry with a view to introducing legislation deeming construction workers to be employees unless certain conditions are met.

27

Controlled Foreign Companies

Cross-references. See also **32.13 DOUBLE TAXATION RELIEF**, **36 EXCHANGE GAINS AND LOSSES**.

Simon's Taxes. See D4.3 *et seq*.

Introduction

[27.1] The '*controlled foreign company*' provisions are anti-avoidance legislation which aims to prevent UK resident companies setting up subsidiaries abroad with a view to keeping low taxed profits outside the UK tax net. The income would normally only be taxable in the UK when a dividend is paid to the UK company (but see also the new dividend regime at **31 DISTRIBUTIONS**). Therefore if the profits are not needed in the UK they could be retained overseas with the lower overseas tax charge only being applied. The legislation thus brings these profits back within the charge to UK tax by attributing such overseas profits to the UK company, in certain circumstances.

The provisions described in this chapter apply in relation to an accounting period (see **27.8** below) of a company which was, in that accounting period, a 'controlled foreign company' (a 'CFC') (see **27.2** below). [*ICTA 1988, ss 747(1)(2), 751(4)*]. A charge (see **27.8** below) may then arise on certain companies having an 'interest' (see **27.7** below) in the CFC.

For limitations on direction-making powers and clearances, see **27.11** below.

Under self-assessment, UK companies are required to include details of significant interests in CFCs in their tax returns and to self-assess any CFC tax due. [*FA 1998, s 113, Sch 17*]. Guidance notes are provided in HMRC International Manual, INTM200000 *et seq.* These are referred to below where HMRC interpretation or practice is explained in the guidance. Guidance on particular cases may be sought (provided that it is not with a view to facilitating tax avoidance) from HMRC, Revenue Policy International, 100 Parliament Street, London SW1A 2BQ. Clearances may be sought from the same source (see HMRC International Manual, INTM214120–214150). See generally INTM214000 *et seq.* as regards completion of the self-assessment return.

On 26 January 2010 the Government issued a discussion document which sets out the Government's proposals for reform of the new regime for taxation of controlled foreign companies. The intention is to enhance the competitiveness of UK companies while protecting the UK tax base. The new regime will focus on artificial diversion of UK profits. Objective exemptions will exclude companies where there is a low risk of diversion, and a new motive test is to be introduced. Profits from trading activities, including group treasury operations and actively managed intellectual property should be exempt. A new presumption would be introduced with regard to excess cash, which is treated as belonging in the UK and therefore where it is held offshore it would be taxed under the new proposals. Group finance companies would be exempt where appropriately funded. Further to this and as part of the wider proposals for Corporate Tax Reform announced on 29 November 2010, details of the proposals for long term CFC reform were published, along with a set of interim measures. These are included in the Finance Act 2011.

The proposals for new CFC rules are mainly entity based and will operate in a targeted fashion by bringing within the CFC charge only the proportion of overseas profits that have been artificially diverted from the UK, a number of exemptions will also apply. Where needed it is intended to design rules which address specific sectors such as banking, insurance and property.

A 'partial finance company' exemption is proposed, which will consider the finance company's debt:equity ratio, where this is more than the set minimum then excess equity funding would be subject to the CFC charge. Currently a minimum debt:equity ratio of 1:2 has been mooted. For trading companies incidental or ancillary interest income would be exempt, with the finance company proposals then applying to any excess cash held in the trading company. The proposals envisage further discussion with regard to the position of treasury companies.

New targeted rules with regard to intellectual property ('IP') companies are proposed, which target high risk cases where: the IP has been developed in the UK and transferred to a low tax jurisdiction; the IP held offshore is effectively managed in the UK; and where UK funds are used to invest in offshore IP but the UK does not receive a return on that investment. For the first two scenarios an exempt sae harbour rate is proposed, in excess of which a detailed transfer pricing analysis would be undertaken to identity the profits which have been artificially diverted from the UK. For the latter scenario a debt:equity ratio test would be applied and a charge imposed above a minimum ratio.

Comments are invited on the above by 22 February 2011, with a view to these proposals being legislated in the Finance Bill 2012.

In the meantime specific interim measures have been implemented in the Finance Act 2011, as follows:

- an exemption for a CFC carrying on trading activities with minimal UK connection;
- an exemption for a CFC whose main business is the exploitation of IP with a minimal UK connection;
- an exemption for up to three years for foreign subsidiaries which first come within the scope of the UK CFC rules through a reorganisation or change to UK ownership;
- a new additional de minimis exemption;
- deferral of the end of the transitional period for holding companies for the changes introduced by *FA 2009*.

Save for the *FA 2009* transitional relief deferral, which will treated as always having had effect, the interim measures will have effect in relation to accounting periods of a CFC beginning on or after 1 January 2011.

Details of the proposals can be found at:

www.hm-treasury.gov.uk/controlled_foreign_companies.htm

Compatibility with EU law

The High Court granted an application for a CFC and EU Dividend Group Litigation Order on 30 July 2003, to manage claims which seek to challenge the UK CFC provisions, and provisions which make dividends received by UK companies from non-UK resident companies subject to corporation tax, on the basis they are contrary to EU law.

In the case of *Cadbury Schweppes plc v CIR (Order for reference to the ECJ)* [2004] STC (SCD) 342, 6 ITLR 1060n, the question was referred to the European Court of Justice as to whether the application of the CFC legislation to Cadbury Schweppes Irish financing subsidiaries constitutes a breach of the freedom of establishment under *Article 43* of the EC Treaty, of the freedom to provide services under *Article 49* and of the freedom of movement of capital and payments under *Article 56*. The ECJ ruled in *Cadbury Schweppes plc v Revenue and Customs Comrs: C-196/04* [2007] Ch 30, [2006] ECR I-7995 on 12 September 2006 that the UK CFCs legislation constitutes a restriction on the freedom of movement in the case where companies could be objectively judged to be established in a host member state and carrying on genuine economic activities there. Subject to the existing exceptions (as set out in **27.11** *et seq*. below), the legislation should apply only to 'wholly artificial' arrangements entered into to escape the national tax normally payable. The fact that a CFC's activities could equally well have been carried out in the parent's member state does not imply 'wholly artificial arrangements'.

The ECJ has said that it was up to the UK courts to decide whether the motive test (see **27.11** below) can be interpreted as limiting the CFC legislation to wholly artificial arrangements intended to circumvent national tax law (in which case it would be compatible with EU law), or whether the motive exception does not apply if the CFC had been incorporated with the central intention of reducing UK tax even if there was no artificial arrangement in place (in which case, the legislation would not comply with EU law and would have to be changed). The ECJ decision does not include a time limit on the making of claims. (See also the European Commission press release of 14 September 2006 and Tax Journal 25 September 2006 p 7.)

As a result of the decision of the ECJ in the *Cadbury Schweppes* case the CFC rules have been amended with effect from 6 December 2006 (see **27.6**, **27.7**, **27.13**). In addition, the publicly quoted condition is withdrawn.

An additional 'exemption' has been introduced for CFCs resident in the EU or EEA states, where the entity is undertaking genuine economic activity. However, to fulfil this condition, such concerns must have sufficient staff, with the appropriate skills, working for the CFC in the state in which the company is resident, to be able to undertake all, or substantially all, of that company's business. If they are not employees of the CFC, they must work in the CFC's state of residence, have decision making powers and work separately for the CFC, not as part of a job for another employer.

HMRC's view is that profits from capital, or intellectual property or from intra-group transactions will not normally qualify as 'genuine economic activity'.

In the case of *Vodafone 2 v Revenue and Customs Comrs* [2009] EWCA Civ 446, [2010] Ch 77, [2010] 2 WLR 288 the Court of Appeal (in a judgment of 22 May 2009) held that the UK's CFC legislation could be interpreted in such a way as to conform with EU fundamental freedoms and in particular the right to freedom of establishment. This was a long running case concerning the application of the CFC rules to a Luxembourg finance company which was a subsidiary of the UK-incorporated and UK-tax resident company, Vodafone 2. HMRC enquired into the tax return for the year ended 31 March 2001 and requested documentation and information on the Luxembourg subsidiary to determine whether a CFC apportionment was required. The company argued that the legislation did not apply and that it was an unlawful restriction on the company's freedom of establishment (under Article 43 EC, as was). The Commissioners referred the case to the ECJ but withdrew this referral when the Court handed down its decision on *Cadbury Schweppes* (see above). The parties agreed the *Cadbury Schweppes* decision has direct effect and thus the UK courts needed to consider whether it was possible to interpret the UK's CFC's legislation in such a way that it did not create a restriction on the company's freedom of establishment, and if not, to what extent the CFC legislation should be disapplied.

The Commissioners' were divided but ultimately decided in favour of HMRC. In the High Court it was held that the motive test was not compatible with *Article 43* EC and therefore the CFC rules should not be applied. HMRC appealed. The Court of Appeal considered the CFC rules in their entirety and did not limit themselves to a consideration only of the motive test (see **27.11** below). The Court of Appeal reversed the High Court decision and decided that when considering the legislation as a whole it can be interpreted in accordance with the ECJ ruling in *Cadbury Schweppes*, provided that an additional exemption is read into the legislation such that where the CFC, in the relevant accounting period, is actually established in another Member State of the EEA and carries out genuine economic activities there, then no apportionment under the CFC rules is required. Leave to appeal was refused the company.

Controlled foreign company

[27.2] A '*controlled foreign company*' is a company which is:

(a) resident outside the UK (see **65.3 RESIDENCE**);
(b) 'controlled' by persons resident in the UK; and
(c) subject to a 'lower level of taxation' (see **27.4** below) in the territory in which it is 'resident' (see **27.3** below).

[*ICTA 1988, s 747(1)(2)*].

Any company which is resident both in the UK and, under double taxation relief arrangements, in a territory outside the UK is treated by *CTA 2009, s 18* (previously *FA 1994, s 249*) as resident outside the UK and as not resident in the UK (see **65.2 RESIDENCE**). However, from 1 April 2002, in determining for any purposes of the CFC provisions, *other than* (a) above, whether a company is a person resident in the UK, that *section* is disregarded (thus, a UK resident company deemed to be non-resident by virtue of a double tax treaty, remains subject to the CFC provisions).

The CFC rules do not apply to any company that, by virtue of *CTA 2009, s 18* (previously *FA 1994, s 249*), was treated immediately before 1 April 2002 as resident outside the UK, and not UK-resident, and which has not subsequently ceased to be so treated. However there are two exceptions to this, where either of the following events occurs in relation to the non-resident company at any time after 21 March 2006:

(i) the non-resident company, which immediately before 22 March 2006 does not own (directly or indirectly) any subsidiary companies, acquires (directly or indirectly) a UK-resident subsidiary company; or
(ii) the non-resident company, which immediately before 22 March 2006 owns (directly or indirectly) any subsidiary companies, acquires (directly or indirectly) a UK-resident subsidiary company as a consequence of, or in connection with, which there is a major change in the nature, conduct or scale of the activities of either the non-resident company or the group of companies of which the non-resident company is a member,

then the company will become treated as resident in the UK for the purposes of the CFC rules.

[*ICTA 1988, s 747(1B); FA 2006, s 78; CTA 2009, Sch 1 para 217*].

'Control'

'*Control*' of a company is defined for these purposes as the power of a person to secure that the affairs of the company are conducted in accordance with their wishes, either by means of shareholding or voting power in or in relation to the company or any other company, or by virtue of any powers conferred by the articles of association or other document regulating the company or any other company. Two or more persons together having such power are taken as controlling the company.

In determining whether a person or persons have such control, a wide range of rights and powers is attributed to them, in so far as not already so attributed (see *ICTA 1988, s 755D(5)–(11)*). These include future rights and powers and rights and powers of certain connected and other persons. [*ICTA 1988, s 755D*].

Where a company would not otherwise be treated as controlled by UK-resident persons, it is so treated if there are two persons, one of whom is UK resident, who together control the company, and a '40% test' is satisfied in relation to each of them. This requires that each of them has interests, rights and powers representing at least 40% of the holdings, rights and powers in respect of which they fall to be taken as together controlling the company (after a similar attribution of rights and powers as applies in determining that control), and that in the case of the non-UK resident such holdings etc. do **not** exceed 55%.

Example 1

In both the following examples control is held to be in the UK:

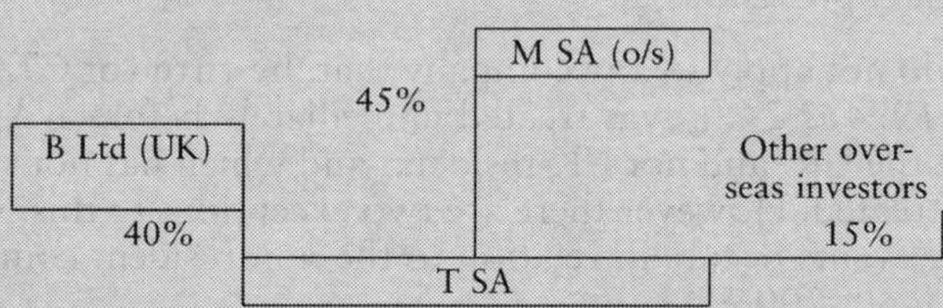

Applying the control test there are two companies (B Ltd and M SA (overseas)) who taken together control T SA. Both own at least 40% and M SA does not own more than 55%. Thus T SA is controlled in the UK.

Example 2

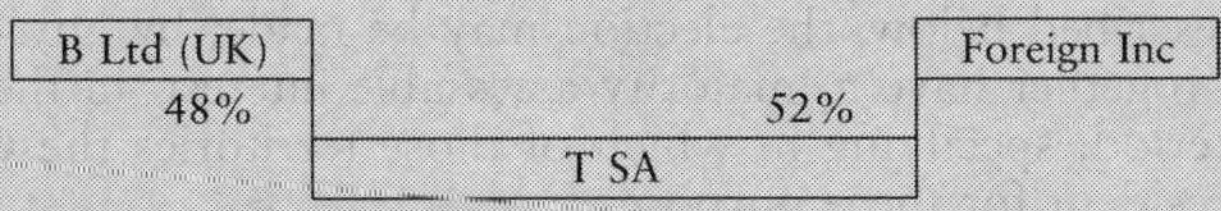

Looking at the control test, irrespective of the fact Foreign Inc owns 52% of the shares, applying the 40% test: one party is UK resident, both parties own at least 40% and neither holds more than 55%, thus T SA is controlled in the UK for the purposes of *ICTA 1988, s 747(1A)*.

On or after 12 March 2008, a person is also treated as having control if he has or is entitled to acquire rights to the greater part of the company's income, were that all distributed, capital distribution on a sale or on a winding up.

[*ICTA 1988, ss 747(1A), 755D(3)–(11); FA 2008, s 64(3)*].

The advice of HMRC International Division may be sought (see **27.1** above) where there is doubt as to whether an overseas entity is a company.

Simon's Taxes. See D4.301–D4.303.

'Residence'

[27.3] For the purposes of these provisions, a company is regarded, in any accounting period in which it is resident outside the UK (see **65.3 RESIDENCE**), as '*resident*' in the territory in which, throughout that period, it is liable to tax by reason of domicile, residence or place of management.

'Territory' includes jurisdictions which do not have full independent status, such as the Channel Islands, but not individual states of a federal state (e.g. in the USA), and 'tax' in this context means a tax similar in nature to UK income tax or corporation tax, and not e.g. turnover or payroll taxes or flat-rate levies. (For these and for the interpretation of 'domicile, residence or place of management', see HMRC International Manual, INTM202050).

If there are two or more such territories and no election or designation is made (see below), the company is regarded as resident in only one of them, namely:

(i) the company's place of effective management (for which see HMRC International Manual, INTM202050) throughout the period or, if two or more territories would still be the territory of residence under this definition, the one from those territories in which the greater amount of the company's assets is situated at the end of the period, determined by reference to their market value at that time;
(ii) if (i) does not apply, the territory in which the greater amount of the company's assets is situated at the end of the period (determined as in (i));
(iii) if (i) and (ii) do not apply to determine a single territory of residence, the territory which may be specified in an election (for which see below) or if no timeous election is made, HMRC may designate in which of those territories the CFC is to be regarded as resident on a just and reasonable basis.

Election or designation

As regards (iii) above, subject to the continuing application of an earlier election as described below, the election may be made, by any one or more persons who together have a 'majority assessable interest' in the CFC in the accounting period, specifying in which of those territories the CFC is to be regarded as resident for these purposes.

One or more persons have such a '*majority assessable interest*' in a CFC in an accounting period if it is likely that, were an apportionment of chargeable profits to be made for the period, more than 50% of the aggregate amounts so chargeable would be chargeable on him or on them together. For this purpose an application under *ICTA 1988, s 751A*; and for periods ending on or after 1 January 2010 *s 751AA*; and for periods beginning on or after 1 January 2011 *ss 751AB*, or *751AC*; are disregarded (see **27.6**). Where such an election or HMRC designation has effect for an accounting period, the CFC continues to be regarded as resident in the same territory for subsequent accounting periods up to (but not including) the next one in which the territories in which the CFC is liable to tax by reason of domicile, residence or place of management are different.

An election under this provision, which is irrevocable, must be made to HMRC within twelve months after the end of the CFC accounting period in relation to which it is made, must be signed by the persons making it, and must state, as regards each of those persons, the percentage of chargeable profits and creditable tax (if any) of the CFC for that period which would be likely to be apportioned to them in the event of an apportionment being made. A designation by HMRC as above is irrevocable, and must be notified to every UK-resident company which it appears to HMRC would be chargeable under these provisions were an apportionment of chargeable profits of the accounting period in question to be made.

[*ICTA 1988, ss 749, 749A; FA 2007, Sch 15 para 2*].

See generally HMRC International Manual, INTM202050.

Territories with a 'lower level of taxation'

[27.4] A company regarded as resident in a particular territory outside the UK (see **27.3** above) is considered to be subject to a '*lower level of taxation*' (see **27.2** above) for an accounting period if the tax paid under the law of that territory in respect of profits (other than capital profits) from that period (the 'local tax') is less than three-quarters of the 'corresponding UK tax' on those profits, basically the UK tax that would be payable on its profits if the company were UK resident.

The '*corresponding UK tax*' on the profits of an accounting period is the corporation tax (at the small companies rate where appropriate) which would be chargeable, on the assumptions set out in *ICTA 1988, Sch 24* (see **27.9** below), on the CFC's 'chargeable profits' (see **27.9** below) for that period.

For this purpose:

(a) it is assumed that an apportionment of chargeable profits falls to be made under these provisions (see **27.7** below);

(b) (for periods on or after 6 December 2006) any application under *ICTA 1988, s 751A*; and for periods ending on or after 1 January 2010 *s 751AA*; and for periods beginning on or after 1 January 2011 *ss 751AB*, or *751AC*; are to be disregarded (see **27.6** below);

(c) double taxation relief in respect of the local tax is disregarded; and

(d) a deduction is made from the corporation tax calculated as above in respect of:
   - any amount which would be set off under *CTA 2010, s 967; ICTA 1988, s 7(2)* (sums received under deduction of income tax, see **46.9 INCOME TAX IN RELATION TO A COMPANY**) on the assumptions set out in *ICTA 1988, Sch 24* (see **27.9** below); and
   - any income or corporation tax actually charged in respect of the chargeable profits,

   provided that such amounts have not been, and do not fall to be, repaid to the company.

Tax paid in third countries is relieved against both local tax and corresponding UK tax, according to the rules applicable in each jurisdiction (see HMRC International Manual, INTM202030).

Groups of companies have attempted to distort the comparison of UK and foreign tax by diverting income into the overseas company that is not subject to UK tax, thus making the foreign tax a greater proportion of the UK tax that would be payable. An alternative technique was for the tax paid by the overseas company to be repaid in some way to an associated person. These issues were addressed by the *F(No 2)A 2005*. For accounting periods of non-UK resident companies beginning on or after 2 December 2004, subject to the anti-avoidance provision below, in determining the amount of local tax paid by those companies for the above purposes, a reduction in the amount of the local tax is to be made:

(i) by discounting any income or expenditure which has been brought into account by the overseas company in computing its profits for local tax purposes which would not be so brought into account in computing profits chargeable to UK tax under these provisions (see **27.9** below); and

(ii) to the extent of any tax which has been paid by the company but which has been repaid, or paid by way of tax credit, directly or indirectly to a person other than the company.

Where the overseas company's accounting period would have ended on or after 2 December 2004 but is amended on or after that date so as to end before that date, it will be deemed to have ended on 1 December 2004.

[*ICTA 1988, s 750(1)–(4); FA 1993, s 119; F(No 2)A 2005, s 44; FA 2007, Sch 15 para 4*].

See generally HMRC International Manual, INTM202030.

See **27.11** below as regards countries in which a company will be excluded from charge under these provisions.

Designer rate regimes

Where a company would be treated under the above rules as subject to a lower level of taxation in a territory in an accounting period but for the local tax not being less than three-quarters of the corresponding UK tax, but where that local tax is determined under 'designer rate tax provisions', the company *is* treated as being subject to a lower level of taxation in that territory in that period.

'*Designer rate tax provisions*' are provisions which appear to HMRC to be designed to enable companies to exercise significant control over the amount of tax they pay, and which are specified in regulations (which may make different provision for different cases or with respect to different territories, and may contain supplementary, incidental, consequential or transitional provisions). The first such regulations (see below) may take effect for accounting periods beginning up to 15 months before the date the regulations are made. [*ICTA 1988, s 750A*].

The regulations apply to the following.

- Guernsey — bodies with international tax status;
- Jersey — international business companies;
- Isle of Man — international companies; and
- Gibraltar — income tax qualifying companies.

[*SI 2000 No 3158*].

It should be noted that between 2007 and 2009 the above regimes have changed, with regard to Jersey, Guernsey and the Isle of Man. The international companies regimes have been abolished. However in all instances the new regimes impose a general corporate tax rate of zero per cent, with derogations for certain types of business or income which are subject to tax at either 10% or 20%.

In Gibraltar the qualifying company regime was abolished in 2005. Whilst there are no new exempt companies from 2007, certain existing exempt companies are grandfathered until 2010. During 2010 Gibraltar introduced a flat 10% tax rate for companies.

Further regimes may in future be added to this list.

Simon's Taxes. See **D4.307, D4.308.**

Example

[27.5]

CC Co, an unquoted company, is incorporated and resident in Blueland and carries on business there as a wholesaler. It obtains the majority of its goods from associated companies although 10% is obtained from local suppliers. The goods are exported to UK customers — the major one of which is ADE Co Ltd. CC Co has a share capital of 1,000 ordinary shares which are owned as follows:

SS Co Ltd (non-UK resident company)	50

ADE Co Ltd (UK incorporated and resident company)	150
John James (UK domiciled and resident individual)	300
Mrs James (wife of John James)	300
Caroline James (daughter of Mr & Mrs James) living in France	200
	1,000

The shareholders of SS Co Ltd are all non-UK residents. The shareholders of ADE Co Ltd are Mr & Mrs Andrew James (parents of John James).

The following figures (converted into sterling) have been obtained for CC Co for the year to 31 March 2011.

	£
Profit before tax	7,000,000
Depreciation	1,000,000
Dividend proposed for year	500,000
Blueland tax paid on profits of year	1,200,000
Market value of plant and machinery at 1.4.10	2,500,000
Additions to plant and machinery in year	1,800,000

There were no disposals of fixed assets during the year.

The company is not a CFC with respect to any earlier accounting period.

CC is a controlled foreign company because:

(i) it is resident outside the UK;
(ii) it is controlled by persons resident in the UK, as follows:

	UK residents Ordinary shares	Non-UK residents Ordinary shares
ADE Co Ltd	150	
John James	300	
Mrs James	300	
SS Co Ltd		50
Caroline James		200
	750	250
Percentage holding	75%	25%

(iii) it is subject to a lower level of taxation in the country where it is resident, as follows:

Notional UK chargeable profits

Year ended 31 March 2011	£
Profit before tax	7,000,000
Add Depreciation	1,000,000
	8,000,000
Capital allowances (see note below)	940,000
	7,060,000
£7,060,000 @ 28%	1,976,800
75% thereof	1,482,600
Overseas tax paid	£1,200,000

The overseas tax paid is less than three-quarters of the 'corresponding UK tax' so the company is regarded as being subject to a lower level of taxation.

Note

Capital allowances:

Plant and machinery	Pool	Allowances
	£	£
Market value at 1.4.10	2,500,000	
Additions (less annual investment allowance claim)	1,700,000	100,000
	4,200,000	
WDA (20%)	(840,000)	840,000
WDV c/f	£3,360,000	
Total allowances		£940,000

Activities of EEA businesses

[27.6] Post *Cadbury Schweppes* (see above) an 'exemption' was introduced for CFCs with business establishments within the EEA. Where an apportionment falls to be made for such a CFC, then the UK company can apply to have the apportioned profits reduced on a just and reasonable basis, to the extent such profits represent genuine economic activity within the EEA state — i.e. 'net economic value' generated by the CFC.

Thus, for accounting periods beginning on or after 6 December, 2006 (subject to transitional provisions for accounting periods straddling that date, where the following conditions are satisfied):

(a) a controlled foreign company is liable to apportionment in an accounting period;
(b) the company has had a business establishment in an 'EEA territory' throughout that period;
(c) it has employees working for it in the 'EEA territory' throughout the period; and
(d) a UK resident company has a 'relevant interest' (see **27.8** below) in it in the period,

the UK resident may apply to HMRC (in a form laid down by HMRC and attaching any relevant information and documentation) for a reduction in the CFC's chargeable profits for that period.

If the application is granted, the CFC's chargeable profits for that period will be reduced by the amount specified in the application and its creditable tax will be reduced on a just and reasonable basis. The reductions are made for the purposes only of determining the sum chargeable on the UK company.

HMRC may only grant the application if they are satisfied that the specified amount does not exceed the economic value arising to the CFC, persons who have an interest in it and other group companies directly from 'qualifying work'. This is work done by individuals directed by the CFC to perform duties on its behalf in a particular EEA territory in which the CFC had a business throughout the accounting period in question. In addition to the above, for accounting periods beginning on or after 1 January 2011, they may only grant the application where they have not previously granted an application made by the UK resident company in respect of *s 751AB* (relating to claims where the company has failed the UK connection exemption or the IP exploitation exemption) or *s 751AC* (relating to claims by a company where the temporary exemption following a reorganisation, etc. is terminated early).

The application must be made on or before the filing date of the company's corporation return for the accounting period to which it relates. It may be amended or withdrawn at any time before HMRC accept it. If an application is accepted after the company has filed its corporation tax return for the period, it has 30 days (commencing with the date of acceptance) within which to amend the return. For accounting periods beginning on or after 1 January 2011, the period during which an application may be made is the period within which an amendment to the relevant company tax return may be made under *FA 1998, Sch 18 para 15* (one year after the filing date) or if the tax return has been amended post an enquiry under *para 34* of that schedule, the period of 30 days beginning when the amendment was notified to the company (or where this is appealed, the period of 30 days following determination of such appeal).

Where an application is refused, the taxpayer company has a right of appeal to the Tribunal: an appeal must be made to HMRC in writing within 30 days of the refusal. If the Tribunal find that the amount applied for is the correct amount, they must direct HMRC to accept the application; if the amount in respect of which the application should have been made differs from those specified in the application, they must direct HMRC to accept the application for that amount and in other cases the appeal must be dismissed.

An '*EEA territory*' at any time is a territory which is an EEA state at that time, other than the UK.

[*ICTA 1988, ss 751A, 751B; FA 2011; FA 2007, Sch 15 paras 5, 6, 10*].

Companies chargeable in respect of CFC

[27.7] Where these provisions apply in respect of an accounting period of a CFC (see **27.1** above), the 'chargeable profits' (see **27.9** below) and 'creditable tax' (see **27.10** below) are apportioned amongst all the persons (whether UK resident or not) having an 'interest' (see below) in the CFC at any time in the accounting period.

Any UK resident company which has sufficient interest in the CFC (the threshold being 25%), and to which those sums are apportioned, is then chargeable on a sum as if it were corporation tax (see **27.8** below).

[*ICTA 1988, s 747(3)(4)(5)*].

The following have an '*interest*' in a CFC with regard to apportionment:

(a) any person possessing, or entitled to acquire, share capital or voting rights in the CFC;
(b) any person possessing, or entitled to acquire, a right to receive or participate in distributions of the CFC ('distribution' not being limited by reference to UK resident companies, see **31 DISTRIBUTIONS**) or (except as below) any amounts payable (in cash or kind) by the CFC to loan creditors (as defined in *CTA 2010, s 453; ICTA 1988, s 417*, see **22.7 CLOSE COMPANIES**) by way of premium on redemption;
(c) any person entitled to secure (other than on a default of the CFC or any other person, which has not occurred, under an agreement) that income or assets, present or future, of the CFC will be applied directly or indirectly for his benefit; and
(d) any other person who, with or without others, has control (see **27.2**(b) above) of the CFC.

In (a), (b) and (c), the entitlement to do anything includes present entitlement to do it at a future date and future entitlement. [*ICTA 1988, s 749(5)–(7)*]. See HMRC International Manual, INTM210040–210070.

Where an apportionment is made to a UK resident company which has made a successful application under *ICTA 1988, s 751A* (the EEA reduction) or for accounting periods ending on or after 1 January 2010 under *s 751AA* (reduction for certain financing income), or for accounting periods beginning on or after 1 January 2011 under *s 751AB* (relating to claims where the company has failed the UK connection exemption or the IP exploitation exemption) or *s 751AC* (relating to claims by a company where the temporary exemption following a reorganisation, etc. is terminated early), its apportionment is to be governed by that section. Where that company has associates or persons connected with it, it is assumed that they all had made successful applications under *ss 751A, 751AA, 751AB or 751AC.*

[*ICTA 1988, s 747(3A), (5A); FA 2011; FA 2007 Sch 15(1)*].

A person or persons having an interest in a company which has an interest in a CFC are treated themselves as having a corresponding interest in the CFC. Joint interests (other than in a fiduciary or representative capacity) are treated as being in equal shares. [*ICTA 1988, s 749B*].

HMRC determinations

Any determination by HMRC of the amounts of chargeable profits and creditable tax for a CFC accounting period which fall to be apportioned under these provisions requires the sanction of HMRC.

There is, however, an exception, in relation to a notice of closure of an enquiry into a company tax return or a discovery assessment, where those amounts are the subject of an agreement with HMRC (for the requirements for which see *ICTA 1988, s 754B(6)–(9)*). Where a determination thus requiring the sanction of HMRC is made for the purpose of giving a closure notice or making a discovery assessment, and the notice of the closure or discovery assessment is given without the determination, so far as taken into account in the notice or assessment, having been approved by HMRC, or without notification of such approval having been served at or before the time the notice was given, the closure notice or discovery assessment is deemed to have been given or made as if the determination had not been taken into account.

Notification of HMRC's approval must be in writing, and must state that HMRC have given approval on the basis that stated amounts of chargeable profits and creditable tax (which may be nil) fall to be apportioned under these provisions for the accounting period in question. The approval must apply specifically to the case in question and the amount determined, but may otherwise be given (either before or after the making of the determination) in any such form or manner as HMRC may determine. An appeal relating to a determination approved by HMRC may not question HMRC's approval except to the extent that the grounds for questioning the approval are the same as the grounds for questioning the determination itself. [*ICTA 1988, s 754B*].

See generally HMRC International Manual, INTM214060–214090 as regards HMRC enquiries into CFC returns.

Simon's Taxes. See **D4.311, D4.323–D4.325, D4.365, D4.368.**

Basis of charge

[27.8] Where a part of a CFC's 'chargeable profits' (see **27.9** below) is apportioned (as below) to a UK resident company (see **27.7** above), a sum equal to corporation tax at the 'appropriate rate' on those profits, less the part of the CFC's 'creditable tax' (see **27.10** below) (if any) so apportioned, is chargeable on the company as if it were corporation tax.

No charge arises, however, unless at least 25% of the CFC's 'chargeable profits' for the period in question is apportioned either to the UK resident company or to persons 'connected' (see **25 CONNECTED PERSONS**) or 'associated' (as defined *in CTA 2010, s 882; ICTA 1988, s 783(10)*) with it.

The '*appropriate rate*' is the full corporation tax rate (or average rate) applicable to the accounting period in which ends the CFC's 'accounting period' (see below) whose 'chargeable profits' are the subject of the apportionment. [*ICTA 1988, s 747(4)(5)*]. The small companies rate does not apply (INTM210010).

Apportionment

An apportionment of chargeable profits and creditable tax for an accounting period is to be made as follows. Where:

(A) the persons with 'relevant interests' in the CFC at any time in the period have those interests by virtue only of direct or indirect holdings of ordinary shares in the CFC;
(B) each of those persons is either UK-resident throughout the period or not UK-resident at any time in the period; and
(C) no company has an 'intermediate interest' in the CFC at any time in the period other than by virtue of a direct or indirect holding of ordinary shares in the CFC,

the apportionment is made amongst the persons within (A) above in direct proportion to the percentage holding of the CFC's issued ordinary shares which their relevant interests represent (see below).

Otherwise, the apportionment is made on a just and reasonable basis amongst the persons who have a 'relevant interest' in the CFC at any time in the period (and see **27.20** below for HMRC's right to determine a basis different from that selected by the company in certain cases).

The charge to tax in respect of a CFC apportionment is made in the tax calculation for the company as computed under *FA 1998, Sch 18 para 8*. The tax is calculated on the normal profits of the company under the first step of *para 8*, any reliefs or set-offs are given effect under the second step, and then under the third step any amounts assessable as if they were corporation tax are included which includes the *s 747(4)(a)* CFC charge. The fourth step then allows for set-offs against the total liability such as income tax suffered.

An '*accounting period*' of a CFC begins whenever:

(a) the company comes under the control (see **27.2**(b) above) of persons resident in the UK; or
(b) the CFC, not having previously been subject to an apportionment under these provisions (see **27.7** above), commences business; or
(c) an accounting period ends without the CFC ceasing either to carry on business or to have any source of income at all,

and ends when:

(i) it ceases to be under the control (as above) of persons resident in the UK; or
(ii) it becomes, or ceases to be, liable to tax by reason of domicile, residence or place of management in a territory; or
(iii) it ceases to have any source of income at all.

In addition, the normal rules at **2.5 ACCOUNTING PERIODS** (relating to the end of accounting periods, and to the winding-up, of UK resident companies) apply, with the omission of the provisions relating to a company's coming or ceasing to be within the charge to corporation tax. Also, where it appears to HMRC that the beginning or end of an accounting period is uncertain, they may specify an appropriate period not exceeding twelve months as an accounting period, and the period specified may subsequently be amended in the light of further facts.

[*ICTA 1988, s 751(1)–(5); CTA 2009, Sch 1 para 218*].

'Relevant Interest' in a CFC

A UK-resident company with a direct interest in a CFC has a '*relevant interest*' in the CFC by virtue of that interest. This applies similarly to an indirect interest in the CFC unless it arises by virtue of a direct or indirect interest in another UK-resident company.

A '*related person*' (i.e. a person, other than a UK-resident company, who is connected or associated (as above) with a UK-resident company which has a relevant interest in the CFC) with a direct or indirect interest in a CFC has a '*relevant interest*' in the CFC by virtue of that interest, except:

(I) to the extent that a UK-resident company has the whole or any part of the same interest indirectly (by virtue of a direct or indirect interest in the related person), and itself has a relevant interest in the CFC by virtue of that indirect interest; and

(II) in the case of an indirect interest, if it is held by virtue of a direct or indirect interest in a UK-resident company or another related person.

A direct interest in a CFC which does not give rise to a relevant interest under the above rules is nonetheless a '*relevant interest*' except to the extent that another person has the whole or a part of the same interest indirectly and itself has a relevant interest in the CFC by virtue of that indirect interest.

No '*relevant interest*' arises in a CFC except as above. The percentage of the issued ordinary shares of a CFC which a relevant interest (by virtue of a holding of those shares) represents for an accounting period is determined under *ICTA 1988, s 752B*, broadly by taking successive proportions in the case of indirect holdings and by averaging where holdings vary over the period.

See *ICTA 1988, s 752C* as regards nominee or bare trustee holdings and other holdings in a fiduciary or representative capacity, and as regards interpretation generally.

[*ICTA 1988, ss 752–752C*].

See generally HMRC International Manual, INTM210000 *et seq.*

Simon's Taxes. See **D4.304, D4.311, D4.365.**

Example

Following the example at **27.5** above, CC Co's notional UK chargeable profits and creditable tax are apportioned among the persons who had an interest in the company during its accounting period.

Shareholder	% shareholding	Attributable profits £	Creditable tax £
SS Co Ltd	5	353,000	60,000
ADE Co Ltd	15	1,059,000	180,000
John James	30	2,118,000	360,000
Mrs James	30	2,118,000	360,000

Caroline James	20	1,412,000	240,000
	100%	£7,060,000	£1,200,000

ADE Co Ltd is the only UK resident company to which chargeable profits and creditable tax are apportioned. As ADE Co Ltd shareholders are Mr and Mrs James, the company is connected with them, and therefore ADE Co Ltd's interest is greater than the 25% threshold. Thus ADE Co Ltd is chargeable to corporation tax on a sum equal to the profits of CC Co which are apportioned to it in relation to its own interest, and this corporation tax charge is then reduced by the apportioned amount of creditable tax. The corporation tax rate applicable is the rate (or average rate) applicable to ADE Co Ltd's own profits for the accounting period in which CC Co's accounting period ends. ADE Co Ltd has a 31 March year end.

ADE Co Ltd

Year to 31 March 2011

Tax calculations — before apportionment

	£
Trading income	8,000,000
Losses brought forward	
	8,000,000
Income from non-trading loan relationships	50,000
Overseas income (assume not exempt)	1,250,000
Chargeable gains	250,000
Taxable Total Profits	£9,550,000
	£
UK tax at 28% on £9,550,000	2,674,000
DTR on overseas income	(350,000)
Mainstream CT liability	£2,324,000

Tax calculations — after CFC apportionment

		£
Taxable Total Profits		£9,550,000
UK tax at 28% on £9,550,000		2,674,000
DTR on overseas income		(350,000)
CFC charge under *s 747*:		
CFC profits apportioned:	1,059,000	
Charged at 28%:	296,520	
Less: creditable tax:	(180,000)	
ICTA 1988, s 747 CFC charge:		116,520
Mainstream CT liability		£2,440,520

'Chargeable profits'

[27.9] '*Chargeable profits*' of a CFC for an accounting period are the total profits (but excluding chargeable gains), as defined for corporation tax purposes, on which, on the assumptions set out in *ICTA 1988, Sch 24* (see below) and after allowing for any available deductions from those profits, it would be chargeable to corporation tax for the period.

On or after 12 March 2008, chargeable profits include income accruing to trustees of a settlement where the company is a settlor or beneficiary, unless that income is otherwise taken into account, e.g. as a dividend received. Where there is more than one settlor or beneficiary, profits are apportioned on a just and reasonable basis. The *Schedule 24* assumptions do not, however, affect the corporation tax liability of any non-UK resident company in respect of any trade carried on in the UK through a permanent establishment (see **65.6 RESIDENCE**). [*ICTA 1988, s 747, Sch 24 para 1(5); FA 2008, s 64*].

Where (under (ii) below) a company is deemed to become, or cease to be, resident during a period of account, profits will generally be time-apportioned, but if the true profit of the period of deemed residence can be established by reference to transactions, etc. of that period at reasonable cost, then it should be used instead (see HMRC International Manual, INTM209030).

Except as otherwise provided in *Sch 24*, it is assumed that, for the purpose of calculating chargeable profits or corresponding UK tax under that *Schedule* for any accounting period, such a calculation has been made for all previous accounting periods which did not precede the first such period for which an apportionment has been made under these provisions (see **27.7** above), or is treated as having been made (see (i) below). [*ICTA 1988, Sch 24 para 2(2)*].

Additional reduction — *FA 2009*

For accounting periods of CFCs ending on or after 1 January 2010, a reduction in chargeable profits may be available for certain financing income. This applies if:

(i) an apportionment has to be made for an accounting period;
(ii) the chargeable profits of the CFC for that period would include the receipt of a payment by another company (the paying company);
(iii) the paying company's corporation tax relief for the payment is restricted (by virtue of *FA 2009, Sch 15*, tax treatment of financing costs and income);
(iv) and a UK resident company has a relevant interest in the CFC in the accounting period.

In these circumstances, the UK resident company may apply to HMRC for the CFC's chargeable profits to be reduced by an amount specified in the application. The profits may be reduced to nil.

If the application is accepted, profits and creditable tax are reduced accordingly for the purposes of determining the chargeable profits for apportionment only. HMRC must be satisfied that the amount of the reduction does not exceed the amount it is just and reasonable should be adjusted for having regard to the provisions of *FA 2009, Sch 15*.

[*ICTA 1988, s 751AA; FA 2009, Sch 16, paras 21–25*].

Double tax treaty exemptions which may have applied to income of the CFC are of no application in relation to the computation of chargeable profits (*Bricom Holdings Ltd v CIR* (1997) 70 TC 272, CA).

Finance Act 2011 — partial application of new exemptions

The *Finance Act 2011* introduces new exemptions from the CFC regime (see **27.15** below) and new *s 751AB* and *s 751AC* allow for an application for a reduction of the CFC charge where not all the conditions for the full exemptions are met. See further **27.19**.

For the treatment in determining chargeable profits of debits and credits in respect of intangible fixed assets, see **48.34 INTANGIBLE ASSETS**.

Schedule 24 — assumptions

The assumptions set out in *Sch 24* are as follows.

(i) For the purpose of determining the chargeable profits of an accounting period at a time when no apportionment has been made under these provisions (see **27.7** above) for that or any earlier accounting period, it is assumed (for the purposes of any provision of *Sch 24* which refers to the first accounting period for which an apportionment has been made) that an apportionment has made for that period.
Similarly where an apportionment has not been made for that or any earlier accounting period and where it has not been established that that or any earlier accounting period is an 'ADP exempt period', that accounting period is treated, for the purposes of any provision of *Sch 24*, as one for which an apportionment has been made or which is an ADP exempt period. An '*ADP exempt period*' is an accounting period beginning after 27 November 1995 in respect of which the company pursued an acceptable distribution policy (NB. the ADP exemption was repealed by *FA 2009* for accounting periods beginning on or after 1 July 2009 — see further **27.12** below).

(ii) The CFC is UK resident with effect from the beginning of the first accounting period in respect of which an apportionment has been made under these provisions or which is an ADP exempt period (as above), and remains UK resident until it ceases to be controlled by UK residents. This assumption does not, however, require any assumption to be made of a change in the place(s) at which the CFC's activities are carried on.

(iii) The CFC is not a close company (see **22 CLOSE COMPANIES**).

(iv) The CFC has made all relevant claims and elections so as to obtain maximum relief, subject to a right of the UK resident company which has a 'majority interest' in the CFC to modify or cancel such claims and elections (by notifying HMRC). This applies for accounting periods in respect of which an apportionment has been made under these provisions or which are ADP exempt periods (as above). See HMRC International Manual, INTM209110 as regards form of notice of disclaimer.
Such notice must be given within 20 months of the end of the accounting period (for periods prior to the commencement of self-assessment (see **27.1** above), within the normal time limit for making

appeals under these provisions (see **27.20** below) for an accounting period for which a direction is given, or within 20 months of the end of the accounting period if it is an ADP exempt period). In either case, HMRC may allow a longer period (and see HMRC International Manual, INTM209130).

'*Majority interest*' for this purpose is by reference to chargeable profits of the CFC (for the period, or first period, for which the relief in question is available) apportioned to a company or companies as a proportion of such profits apportioned to *all* UK resident companies and giving rise to any liability on such companies (see **27.8** above) (in the case of an ADP exempt period, on the assumption that an apportionment has been made for the period).

As regards disclaimers and variations, see HMRC International Manual, INTM209100.

(v) The CFC is not a member of a group or consortium (see **39 GROUP RELIEF**). Notwithstanding this assumption, where there is in fact a surrender by the CFC by way of group relief (see **39.2 GROUP RELIEF**), the CFC's chargeable profits are to be increased to the extent of the relief surrendered and allowed.

(vi) (For payments made on or before 11 May 2001) the conditions for an election by the CFC under *ICTA 1988, s 247* are not fulfilled.

(vii) Except in so far as the CFC may carry on a trade in the UK through a permanent establishment (see **65.6** residence), it can never be the 'successor' to another company within *CTA 2010, s 938 et seq; ICTA 1988, s 343* (company reconstructions, see **55.11 LOSSES**).

(viii) Where trading losses have been incurred by the CFC in an accounting period during which it was non-UK resident (and which is not an ADP exempt period for which it is assumed to be UK resident under (ii) above) and which ended less than six years before the start of the first accounting period for which an apportionment has been made under these provisions, the UK resident company or companies having a majority interest (see (iv) above) in the CFC may claim to have chargeable profits of the CFC computed for any such period as is specified in the claim (and for subsequent accounting periods) on the assumption that an apportionment has been made in respect of the period specified in the claim. The claim must be made in writing to HMRC within 20 months after the end of the first accounting period for which an apportionment has been made.

(ix) Writing-down allowances and balancing adjustments are given or charged as if machinery or plant on which expenditure was incurred before the 'starting period' (i.e. the first accounting period for which an apportionment has been made under these provisions or which is an ADP exempt period) was not brought into use for trade purposes before the starting period, and is thus brought in at market value at the beginning of that period.

Where the chargeable profits for an accounting period are to be computed and expressed in a currency other than sterling (see below), any amount relevant to the computation of capital allowances for the period which was arrived at in relation to accounting periods before the first one beginning on or after 23 March 1995 is converted into the relevant foreign currency at the London closing rate on the first day of the period. The amounts referred to in *CTA 2009, ss 56–58, 1251; ICTA 1988, ss 578A, 578B* and *CAA 2001, ss 74–76* (relating to expensive motor cars) and *CAA 2001, s 511* (relating to dwelling-houses) are, for such a period, converted into the relevant foreign currency at the London closing rate for the day the expenditure in question was incurred.

It is not possible to disclaim or postpone plant and machinery allowances under (iv) above for periods for which an apportionment under these provisions has not been made and which are not ADP exempt periods, since the right to disclaim applies only to such periods. Capital allowances other than plant and machinery allowances are given according to the normal rules (see HMRC International Manual, INTM209140).

(x) Relief for unremittable overseas income is extended to include inability to remit to the territory of residence, and notice of desire for such relief may be given by the UK resident company or companies having a majority interest in the CFC (see (iv) above).

(xi) For accounting periods beginning before 1 April 2004 and to which self-assessment applies (see **27.1** above), the application of the transfer pricing provisions (see **72 TRANSFER PRICING**) to the computation of CFC chargeable profits is modified (see *ICTA 1988, Sch 24 para 20*). Broadly, a compensatory adjustment is made to CFC profits where, as a result of transactions between the CFC and a UK company, the latter's profits have been increased under the transfer pricing rules. Also, subject to certain conditions, those rules do not apply to transactions between CFCs. This provision was repealed for chargeable periods beginning after 31 March 2004.

[*ICTA 1988, Sch 24; CAA 2001, Sch 2 para 66; FA 2004, s 37(2), Sch 5 para 4; ITTOIA 2005, Sch 1 para 349; CTA 2009, Sch 1 para 286*].

Computation of chargeable profits in a currency other than sterling

Where, for accounting periods beginning before 16 March 2005, a company's chargeable profits fall to be determined for the 'first relevant accounting period' of the company or any subsequent accounting period, then notwithstanding any other rule (statutory or otherwise), they are computed and expressed for any such period in the currency used in the accounts for the 'first relevant accounting period'.

Where, as a result of the adoption of the euro by a State, the currency used for the 'first relevant accounting period' is to be replaced by the euro, there is provision for the euro to be substituted (although the local currency may continue to be used for accounting periods during any part of which it continues to be a legal sub-unit of the euro).

The '*first relevant accounting period*' is the first accounting period for which an apportionment has been made, or for which it can reasonably be assumed that an apportionment would have been made but for its pursuing an 'acceptable distribution policy' (see **27.12** below).

Similarly, where a company's chargeable profits fall to be determined for any accounting period falling before its first relevant accounting period, they are computed and expressed for any such period in the currency used in the accounts for the accounting period concerned.

In either case, the 'accounts' concerned are those the company is required to keep by the law of the country or territory under whose law it is incorporated or formed, or if it is not required under that law to keep accounts, those which most closely correspond to those required under UK law.

The chargeable profits computed and expressed in a currency other than sterling (as above) for an accounting period are converted into sterling by reference to the London closing rate for the last day of the accounting period for the purposes of:

(1) determining the apportioned amount thereof under *ICTA 1988, s 747(4)* (see **27.7** above);
(2) the exception under *ICTA 1988, s 748(1)(d)* (see **27.11**(iv) below); and
(3) the calculation of corresponding UK tax under *ICTA 1988, s 750(2)(3)* (see **27.4** above).

This provision is repealed for accounting periods beginning on or after 16 March 2005 following the introduction of the corporation tax currency provisions for periods of account beginning on or after 1 January 2005 (see **36.4–36.7 EXCHANGE GAINS AND LOSSES**).

[*ICTA 1988, ss 747(4A)(4B), 747A, 748(4)(5), 750(5)–(8); SI 1998 No 3177, Reg 40; FA 2005, s 80, Sch 4 para 24*].

See generally HMRC International Manual, INTM209060.

Simon's Taxes. See D4.315–D4.322.

'Creditable tax'

[27.10] '*Creditable tax*' of a CFC's accounting period is the aggregate of:

(i) the double taxation relief, in respect of tax on income brought into account in determining chargeable profits of the period (see **27.9** above), which would be available on the assumptions set out in *ICTA 1988, Sch 24* (see **27.9** above and **32.2 DOUBLE TAX RELIEF**) and assuming the company to be liable to corporation tax on those chargeable profits;
(ii) the set-off available under *CTA 2010, s 967; ICTA 1988, s 7(2)* (sums received under deduction of income tax, see **46.9 INCOME TAX IN RELATION TO A COMPANY**) against those chargeable profits on the assumptions in (i) above; and
(iii) the amount of any income or corporation tax actually charged in respect of those chargeable profits, less any such tax which has been or falls to be repaid to the CFC.

[*ICTA 1988, s 751(6)*].

Tax spared in the overseas territory, and for which provision is made in the relevant double tax agreement, may be included in creditable tax up to the limit specified in the agreement. Foreign taxes are converted into sterling for these purposes at the exchange rate prevailing at the time the taxes become payable. (See HMRC International Manual, INTM209220).

Simon's Taxes. See D4.323.

Exceptions

[27.11] Subject to the territorial exclusions described below, a CFC is excepted from an apportionment under these provisions (see **27.7** above) for an accounting period if:

(i) it pursues an 'acceptable distribution policy' (see **27.1** above and **27.12** below) in respect of the period. This exception is deleted for accounting periods of controlled foreign companies beginning on or after 1 July 2009. Where a CFC's accounting period straddles this date, the period is treated as split and profits and creditable tax are to be apportioned on a just and reasonable basis. Dividends paid on or after 1 July 2009 out of profits earned before that date are dealt with under the pre-1 July 2009 regime [*FA 2009, Sch 16 para 8*]; or

(ii) throughout the period it is engaged in 'exempt activities' (see **27.13** below). For accounting periods beginning on or after 1 July 2009, this exception is amended to remove references to superior holding companies and non-local holding companies. This exception now only applies to local holding companies; or

(iii) for accounting periods of CFCs beginning on or before 5 December 2006, it meets the 'public quotation' condition (*FA 2007, Sch 15 para 8(1)*. See **27.14** below); or

(iv) its chargeable profits for the period do not exceed £50,000 or pro rata for periods of less than twelve months; or

(v) The *Finance Act 2011* provisions retain the exemption at (iv) above and include a further *de minimis* exemption with regard to accounting periods beginning on or after 1 January 2011 (new paragraph *ICTA 1988, s 748(1)(da)* is inserted). The de minimis amount is increased to £200,000 (pro rata for periods of less than a year) based upon profits calculated in accordance with GAAP ignoring exempt distributions and chargeable gains (rather then the CFC chargeable profits). The profits include any amounts accruing to the CFC under a settlement of which it is a settlor or beneficiary and also any income accruing to the CFC as a partner in a partnership. The profits are subject to the provisions of the transfer pricing rules found at *TIOPA 2010, Pt 4* of (for adjustments of more than £50,000). Anti-avoidance provisions are also introduced at a new *s 748ZA* to deny the benefit of the exemption where: a scheme has been implemented the main purposes, or one of the main purposes, is to secure the de minimis exemption; or where the loan relationship provisions at *CTA 2009, s 418(5)* affect the CFC so as to bring into account a credit for the period; or where the group mismatch scheme (under *CTA 2010, Pt 21B*) has effect; or

(vi) it is, as respects the period, resident (within the meaning of regulations made for these purposes) in a territory specified in those regulations (the 'Excluded Countries' regulations *SI 1998 No 3081*), and meets such conditions with respect to its income or gains, and any other conditions, as may be specified in those regulations (see below); or

(vii) in that period:
  (a) in so far as any transaction(s) reflected in the profits of the period achieved a 'reduction in UK tax', either it was minimal or that reduction was not a main purpose of the CFC, or of any person having an interest (see **27.7** above) in it in that period, in carrying out the transaction(s); and
  (b) it was not a main reason for the CFC's existence to achieve a 'reduction in UK tax' by a 'diversion of profits' from the UK.

  This is known as the 'motive test'. For a case in which a captive insurance company was held to have failed the test in (b) (although passing that in (a)), see *Association of British Travel Agents Ltd v CIR* [2003] STC (SCD) 194.

[*ICTA 1988, s 748(1)(3), Sch 25 para 18*].

None of the above exceptions applies, however, for an accounting period beginning **on or after 24 July 2002** where either:

(I) the CFC is incorporated in a territory specified for the purpose as respects that accounting period in Treasury regulations; or
(II) it is at any time in that accounting period liable to tax in such a territory by reason of domicile, residence or place of management; or
(III) at any time in that accounting period it carries on business through a permanent establishment (see **65.6 RESIDENCE**) in such a territory (unless the business it carried on in that period through permanent establishments (or branches or agencies) in such territories, taken as a whole, is only a minimal part of the whole of the business it carried on in that period).

The Treasury regulations prescribing such territories may make different provision for different cases or with respect to different territories, and may contain such incidental, supplemental, consequential or transitional provision as the Treasury may think fit. [*ICTA 1988, s 748A*].

Clearances

HMRC will be prepared to confirm, on the facts provided, whether the CFC meets any of the exemption tests and will thus not be subject to these provisions. It should in most cases be possible for HMRC to give an advance ruling covering a number of years, provided that all the relevant facts have been accurately disclosed and there is no change in the nature and conduct of the CFC's business. Details of how to make a clearance application and guidance on the information which will be required can be obtained from CT & VAT (International CT), 100 Parliament Square, London SW1A 2BQ. (See HMRC International Manual, INTM214120–214150 for clearance procedures).

Excluded countries

As regards (v) above, see *The Controlled Foreign Companies (Excluded Countries) Regulations 1998* (*SI 1998 No 3081* as amended). These exclude territories specified in *Sch 2* to the Regulations (for accounting periods in which self-assessment applies) where:

- in the case of a company resident in a territory specified in *Part I* of the Schedule, the company satisfies the income and gains requirement set out in the Regulations; and
- in the case of a company resident in a territory specified in *Part II* of the Schedule, the company satisfies the income and gains requirement and is not entitled to any tax benefit, or does not fall within any condition, specified in *Part II* of the Schedule in relation to the territory concerned.

The income and gains requirement is that the 'non-local source income' (as defined) does not exceed the greater of £50,000 (on an annual basis) and 10% of its 'commercially quantified income' (as defined). See generally HMRC International Manual, INTM203000 *et seq.*

The regulations were amended by *SI 2002 No 2406* to remove the Republic of Ireland from the list of excluded countries. Regulations *SI 2005 No 185* make further amendments to the above regulations to counter avoidance with effect for accounting periods of non-UK resident companies beginning on or after 3 December 2004 by making changes to the tests for residence and control, by restricting certain income from connected persons from inclusion in 'commercially quantified income' and by including certain income from connected persons in 'non-local source income'. Regulations *SI 2005 No 186* introduce an additional requirement that controlled foreign companies, with effect for accounting periods beginning on or after 31 March 2005, should not be involved in a scheme or arrangement one of the main purposes of which is the reduction of UK tax.

[*SI 1998 No 3081; SI 2002 No 2406; SI 2005 No 185; SI 2005 No 186*].

Motive test

For HMRC's view of the 'motive test' in (vi) above, see (A)–(I) below.

The motive test applies if the company can satisfy HMRC that it is non UK resident for reasons other than gaining a tax advantage — essentially that the reason for the CFC existing is not to divert profit away from the UK. There are two legs to this test as identified at (vi)(a) and (b) above — firstly, a transactions leg, whereby it must be shown that the transactions involving the CFC were not designed to reduce tax and secondly, a diversion of profits leg.

As regards the first test, a transaction (or two or more transactions taken together) achieves a '*reduction in UK tax*' if, had it not been effected, any person would have been liable for, or for more, UK tax, or would have been entitled to a smaller (or no) relief from or repayment of UK tax. For these purposes, UK tax means income, corporation and capital gains taxes.

As regards the second test, there is a reduction in UK tax by a '*diversion of profits*' from the UK in an accounting period resulting from a CFC's existence if it is reasonable to suppose that (1) and (2) below would have applied had it not been for the CFC's existence (or for the existence of a company resident outside the UK, 'connected' (see **25 CONNECTED PERSONS**) or 'associated' (as defined in *CTA 2010, s 882*; *ICTA 1988, s 783(10)*) with the CFC, which fulfils or could fulfil, directly or indirectly, substantially the same function as the CFC in relation to any UK resident company or companies):

(1) the whole or substantial part of the CFC's receipts in the period would have been received by a UK resident individual or company, or by such a company it is reasonable to suppose would have been established in those circumstances; and

(2) that company or individual (or any other person resident in the UK) would have been liable for (or for more) UK tax or entitled to a lesser (or no) relief from or repayment of UK tax.

[*ICTA 1988, Sch 25 paras 16, 17, 19*].

HMRC have provided guidance on the application of the 'motive test' at (vi) above in their International Manual, INTM200000 *et seq*. The following points are of particular interest.

(A) The motive test is entirely separate from the tests at (i) to (v) above, and failure to satisfy those other tests will not prejudice consideration of the motive test, except that where there is a marginal and isolated failure to satisfy those other tests this is regarded as an indication that the CFC is not being used to reduce tax liabilities (HMRC International Manual, INTM208170, HMRC International Manual, INTM208180).

(B) In determining what the tax position would have been had a transaction not been carried out, hypothetical transactions which might have taken place instead are not taken into account (HMRC International Manual, INTM208060).

(C) Tax consequences remote from the transaction are not regarded as resulting from it (e.g. a fee received for giving tax planning advice to an unconnected UK resident would not lead to failure of the motive test merely because that person achieved a tax reduction by acting on that advice) (HMRC International Manual, INTM208060).

(D) A reduction in tax which is substantial in absolute terms will not be regarded as 'minimal' merely because it represents a relatively small proportion of the total liability of the company concerned (HMRC International Manual, INTM208070).

(E) The motives of a CFC's customers have no relevance to the motive test (HMRC International Manual, INTM208080).

(F) As regards (1) above, it would be rare for this not to apply, as it is unlikely that a group would allow the diversion of receipts within the group to an outsider, and any claim that the law of the territory in which the CFC is resident would prevent a UK company from acquiring the CFC's receipts 'would have to be looked at very carefully' (HMRC International Manual, INTM208140).

(G) The transfer of the activities of an overseas branch to a non-resident subsidiary will often be made for predominantly commercial reasons, e.g. as a necessary preliminary to expanding the overseas business or attracting local capital, and in such cases the motive test will often be satisfied as tax considerations will normally be only a subsidiary reason for the transfer. HMRC will, however, wish to consider in depth the reasons for incorporation (HMRC International Manual, INTM208200).

(H) HMRC will, on receipt of a satisfactory clearance application (see above), accept that the motive test is satisfied in the case of newly-acquired overseas subsidiaries up to the end of the first full twelve-month accounting period following acquisition. This applies only to CFCs not previously under UK control and whose main business remained unchanged throughout the period in question (HMRC International Manual, INTM208210).

(I) The UK holder of an interest in a CFC may also be treated as having a creditor relationship with the CFC (see **54.2 LOAN RELATIONSHIPS**). Where this is so and the increase in value under the loan relationships provisions reflects the chargeable profits arising for an accounting period, the motive test is accepted as applying for that period. This is because the reduction in UK tax is fully compensated for by the tax charge on the UK parent, indicating that the achievement of that reduction is not a main reason for the CFC's existence (HMRC International Manual, INTM208270).

For the circumstances in which holding companies (and in particular 'brass plate' holding companies) may satisfy the motive test, see HMRC International Manual, INTM208220–208250.

A number of examples of different aspects of the motive test are included at HMRC International Manual, INTM208280–208350.

See **27.1** above under 'Compatibility with EU law' with regard to the ECJ judgment in the case of *Cadbury Schweppes* in which the ECJ has said that it was up to the UK courts to decide whether the motive test can be interpreted as limiting the CFC legislation to wholly artificial arrangements intended to circumvent national tax law (in which case it would be compatible with EU law), or whether the motive exception does not apply if the CFC had been incorporated with the central intention of reducing UK tax even if there was no artificial arrangement in place (in which case, the legislation would not comply with EU law and would have to be changed). See further *Vodafone 2 at* **27.1** *above*.

Legislation was introduced post the ECJ decision above to provide an additional exception to a possible CFC apportionment in respect of companies established in EEA territories, see further **27.6** above.

[*FA 2009, s 36, Sch 16*].

'Acceptable distribution policy'

[27.12] As highlighted above, this exception applied with regard to periods beginning before 1 July 2009, per **27.11**(i) above. A CFC pursues an '*acceptable distribution policy*' in respect of an accounting period if, and only if, the amount of all dividends paid for the accounting period during, or within 18 months of the end of, that period, other than out of specified profits, which is paid to UK residents is not less than 90% of the CFC's 'net chargeable profits' for that period. (The 18-month limit may be extended, exceptionally, at HMRC's discretion and an extension is normally agreed where, following an enquiry, amendments are made to profits such that further distributions would be required to meet the test — see HMRC International Manual, INTM204030.)

A dividend which is not paid for the period(s) the profits of which are, in relation to the dividend, 'relevant profits' for the purposes of *ICTA 1988, s 799* (see **32.11 DOUBLE TAX RELIEF**) is treated as so paid, and where a dividend is paid for a period which is not an accounting period but which falls wholly within an accounting period, it is treated as paid for that accounting period. A dividend paid for a period falling within two or more accounting periods is apportioned and treated as separate dividends paid for each accounting period.

A dividend paid by a CFC is disregarded for these purposes to the extent that the relevant profits in relation to the dividend (see *ICTA 1988, s 799(3)(4)*) derive from dividends or other distributions paid to the CFC at any time to which *CTA 2009, s 1285*, formerly *ICTA 1988, s 208* (UK company distributions not chargeable to UK corporation tax, see **31.16 DISTRIBUTIONS**) applied, or would have applied had the CFC then been UK-resident.

A dividend paid by a CFC *to* a company is also disregarded for these purposes unless it is taken into account in computing the recipient company's income for corporation tax and, in relation to a dividend paid after 6 March 2001 for an accounting period ending after that date, it is not so chargeable under *Case I* of *Schedule D* or, if so chargeable, the payment is not involved in a UK tax avoidance scheme (as specially defined, see *ICTA 1988, Sch 25 para 2B*).

Where the CFC accounts are drawn up in a foreign currency, they do not have to be translated into sterling for these purposes. A dividend equalling 90% of the appropriate foreign currency profits will meet the test. (See HMRC International Manual, INTM204140.)

'*Net chargeable profits*' of an accounting period are the chargeable profits for that period (see **27.9** above) less the amount of any creditable tax (see **27.10** above) which would arise for the period were an apportionment to be made (see **27.7** above) if the restriction of *ICTA 1988, s 797; CTA 2009, Sch 1 para 246* did not apply to limit relief to the attributable corporation tax (see **32.5 DOUBLE TAX RELIEF**). Where the CFC pays a dividend out of specified profits representing dividends received, directly or indirectly, from another CFC, so much of those profits as is equal to the dividend paid out of them is left out of account in determining chargeable profits.

The gross amount of the dividend (i.e. the amount before deduction of any tax withheld on payment to the UK recipient) is taken into account for the purposes of the acceptable distribution test (see HMRC International Manual, INTM204150).

The above 90% test is applied by reference to a part only of the net chargeable profits where, throughout the accounting period, the CFC has either:

(a) only one class of shares in issue; or
(b) only two classes of shares in issue, being either fixed rate preference shares (as defined in *ICTA 1988, Sch 18 para 1*, see **39.4 GROUP RELIEF**) carrying no voting rights (or only carrying such a right, contingent upon non-payment of a dividend on the shares, which has not become exerciseable prior to payment of a dividend for the period in question) (the 'non-voting shares') or shares carrying the right to vote at general meetings (the 'voting shares');

and

(i) at the end of the period, some of the issued shares are held by persons resident outside the UK; and

(ii) no person has an interest in the CFC (see **27.7** above) other than one derived from issued shares.

Where (a) above applies, the fraction of net chargeable profits considered is that fraction of the issued shares at the end of the period which gives rise to interests in the CFC at that time by persons resident in the UK.

If such persons hold both immediate and indirect interests in the CFC, and the immediate interests do not reflect the proportion of issued shares by virtue of which they have those interests (e.g. where they hold shares in a company having a direct or indirect interest in the CFC), the number of shares held by them is treated for this purpose as reduced to such number as is appropriate having regard to the immediate interests held by persons resident in the UK and any intermediate shareholdings between those interests and the shares in the CFC. Where (b) above applies, the amount of net chargeable profits considered is:

$$\frac{P \times Q}{R} + \frac{(X - P) \times Y}{Z}$$

where:

P is the amount of dividends (as above) paid in respect of non-voting shares;

Q is the number of non-voting shares by virtue of which UK residents have interests in the CFC at the end of the period;

R is the number of non-voting shares in issue at that time;

X is the net chargeable profits for the period;

Y is the number of voting shares by virtue of which UK residents have interests in the CFC at the end of the period; and

Z is the number of voting shares in issue at that time.

The number of shares under Q and Y may be reduced in the same way as where (a) above applies (see above) where UK resident persons hold both immediate and indirect interests in the CFC.

See HMRC International Manual, INTM204080–204130.

Dividends taken into account

Where the main condition detailed below is satisfied in relation to a particular accounting period (the '*relevant accounting period*'), dividends to be taken into account, in addition to those paid for that period, are any paid (other than out of specified profits) for the immediately preceding accounting period and (if the condition is satisfied for that period) for the accounting period before that and so on.

There is an additional condition in each case, that the dividend is not an '*excluded dividend*', i.e. it is not paid, in whole or part, out of total profits from which are derived the chargeable profits for an '*excluded period*', i.e. a period in respect of which an apportionment under these provisions falls to be made.

The main condition in relation to any such accounting period is that either there were no 'relevant profits' for the period or:

(A) a dividend or dividends is (are) paid for the period to UK residents;
(B) the amount or aggregate amount of such dividends is not less than the relevant profits for the period (or, where only a part of the net chargeable profits is taken into account, a corresponding part of those relevant profits); and
(C) any dividends to be taken into account are paid not later than the time by which dividends paid for the relevant accounting period are required to be paid.

The following provision applies to dividends paid on or after 12 March 2008. In determining a company's acceptable distribution policy, income from a settlement of which the company is a beneficiary or a settlor or which accrues for the company or to which the company is entitled during the period (whether or not the company receives it) is taken into account. However, there is no double counting for tax purposes where the income attributed to the company is later distributed or apportioned. Where both the settlor and the beneficiary would fall to include profits, only the beneficiary is to include them. Where there is more than one settlor or beneficiary, the trust income is apportioned on a just and reasonable basis. Where an accounting period straddles 12 March 2008, the parts before and after that date are treated as separate accounting periods for this purpose. [*FA 2008, s 64*].

'*Relevant profits*' are the profits which would be the relevant profits for the purposes of *ICTA 1988, s 799* (as was, see **32.11 DOUBLE TAX RELIEF**) if a dividend were actually paid for the period. See also HMRC International Manual, INTM204070 for the calculation of relevant profits.

Where no apportionment could be made under these provisions for an earlier period because the company pursued an acceptable distribution policy for that period, dividends are excluded from treatment as above to the extent that they are required to be taken into account for that purpose.

A dividend paid by a CFC to a non-UK resident company is regarded as paid to a UK resident and as meeting the requirements as regards chargeability in the UK (see above) to the extent that it is represented by a subsequent dividend paid to that UK resident by that other company (or by a 'related' company) out of profits derived, directly or indirectly, from the whole or part of the initial dividend paid by the CFC.

The subsequent dividend must be taken into account in computing the recipient company's income for corporation tax and, in relation to a dividend paid after 6 March 2001 for an accounting period ending after that date, must not be chargeable under *Case I of Schedule D* (or, in the case of certain insurance companies, under *Case VI* but on profits computed as under Case I) or, if so chargeable, the payment must not be involved in a UK tax avoidance scheme (as specially defined, see *ICTA 1988, Sch 25 para 4A*).

A company is '*related*' to another if at least 10% of its voting power is 'controlled' (see **27.2**(b) above) by that other company or its parent company, or where there is a chain of such relationships, and, in relation to dividends paid after 6 March 2001 for an accounting period ending after that date, neither company is UK-resident.

[*ICTA 1988, s 748(1)(a)(2), Sch 25 Pt I; CTA 2009, Sch 1 para 287*].

See generally HMRC International Manual, INTM204000 *et seq.*

Returns where not established if acceptable distribution policy applies

Where a UK-resident company has an interest in a CFC at any time during an accounting period of the CFC, and at the time when the company delivers its company tax return it is not established whether or not the CFC has pursued an acceptable distribution policy in relation to that period, then:

(i) if the company considers that the CFC is likely to do so, it must make the return on the basis that it does so;
(ii) otherwise, it must make the return on the basis that it does not do so.

HMRC do not object to a company erring on the side of caution by acting as under (ii) above even though it thinks it likely that an acceptable distribution policy will be pursued (see HMRC International Manual, INTM214050).

If (i) above applies but in the event the CFC does not do so, or if (ii) above applies but in the event the CFC does do so, the company must amend the return accordingly. Any such amendment must be made within 30 days after the end of the period allowed for establishing an acceptable distribution policy in relation to the CFC accounting period, i.e. the period ending 18 months after the end of the accounting period or at such later time as HMRC allows for payment of a dividend (see above).

Otherwise, the normal return amendment provisions apply. If it has not been established by the end of the period allowed that the CFC pursued an acceptable distribution policy in relation to an accounting period, it is for these purposes assumed that it did not do so.

Failure to make a timeous amendment where (i) above applies but the CFC did not in the event pursue an acceptable distribution policy in relation to the period renders the company liable to a penalty not exceeding the amount of tax understated. [*ICTA 1988, s 754A*].

Simon's Taxes. See **D4.330–D4.338.**

See **32.13** double tax relief for the separate streaming for double tax credit relief purposes and for restriction of underlying tax relief in respect of certain dividends paid in pursuit of an acceptable distribution policy.

Example

The ADP exemption applied to periods beginning before 1 July 2009. DEF Co Ltd, a UK incorporated and resident company with two associated companies, holds 35% of the shares of LNB Co, an unquoted non-trading controlled foreign company resident in Pinkland, where tax is levied at only 10%.

LNB Co has chargeable profits (see **27.9** above) for the year ended 31 March 2008 of £500,000. No withholding tax is applicable in Pinkland.

The following information is available in respect of DEF.

Year to 31 March	2007	2008
	£	£
Trading profits	600,000	780,000
Income from a non-trading loan relationship	10,000	10,000
Chargeable gains	90,000	—
Overseas income (gross) (tax suffered £30,000)	100,000	—

LNB Co

Calculation of profits apportioned to DEF Co Ltd and dividend required to avoid apportionment.

	£
Chargeable profits for the year ended 31 March 2008	500,000
Deduct Creditable tax (10% tax rate in Pinkland)	50,000
Net chargeable profits	£450,000
Amount of distribution required to avoid apportionment 90% × £450,000	£405,000

	Apportionment of profit	Dividend
DEF share	£	£
35% × £500,000: 35% × £405,000	175,000	141,750
Creditable/underlying tax	17,500	15,750
		157,500

DEF Co Ltd

With apportionment

Year to 31 March	2007	2008
	£	£
Trading income	600,000	780,000
Income from a non-trading loan relationship	10,000	10,000
Chargeable gains	90,000	—
Overseas income	100,000	—
	£800,000	£790,000

Year to 31 March		2007	2008
		£	£
UK tax thereon at 30% / 28%		240,000	221,200
Less			
DTR on Case V income	(30,000)	(30,000)	
Plus			
CFC tax on apportionment	52,500		
less: creditable tax	(17,500)	35,000	
Mainstream tax payable		£245,000	£221,200

If dividend paid in y/e 31.3.2009

Year to 31 March	2007	2008
	£	£
Trading income	600,000	780,000
Income from a non-trading loan relationship	10,000	10,000
Chargeable gains	90,000	—
Overseas income	100,000	157,500
	£800,000	£947,500
UK tax thereon at 30% / 28%	240,000	265,300
Less DTR	(30,000)	(15,750)
Mainstream tax payable	£210,000	£249,550
Tax saving (cost)	£35,000	£(28,350)

DEF Co Ltd will make a net tax saving of £3,500 in tax if LBN Co pays the required dividend for the year ended 31 March 2008 by 31 March 2009.

'Exempt activities'

The exempt activities test

[27.13] As regards the exempt activities exclusion, highlighted at **27.11**(ii) above, a CFC is engaged in '*exempt activities*' in an accounting period if, and only if, throughout that accounting period, it has a 'business establishment' in the territory in which it is 'resident' (see below), its business affairs in that territory are 'effectively managed' there, and either (1), (2), (3) or (4) below is satisfied.

It should be noted the provisions with regard to holding companies was amended in *FA 2009* for accounting periods beginning on or after 1 July 2009, see further below with regard to the changes and the transitional provisions.

(1)

(a) At no time in the accounting period does the company's main business (for which see HMRC International Manual, INTM205060) consist of either investment business (see INTM205070), including the holding of intellectual property (see *ICTA 1988, Sch 25 para 9*) or of dealing in goods (i.e. buying and selling goods in unchanged form, see INTM205080) for delivery to or from the UK or to or from connected or associated persons (see **27.11** above) which are not actually delivered to the territory in which it is resident, and

(b) in the case of a company mainly engaged in the period in wholesale, distributive or financial or (for accounting periods beginning after 20 March 2000, service) business (as exemplified in *ICTA 1988, Sch 25 para 11(1)*), less than 50% of its gross trading receipts from that business (net of the cost of any description of property or rights, sale proceeds of which are included therein) is derived, directly or indirectly, from connected or associated persons (see **27.11** above) or persons with an 'interest' in the company.

For accounting periods beginning on or after 27 November 2002, this is extended to other persons being companies either UK-resident or carrying on business through a UK permanent establishment (see **65.6 RESIDENCE**), by reference only to receipts derived from that permanent establishment, or individuals habitually resident in the UK (although this extension does *not* apply to certain CFCs engaged in insurance business, see *ICTA 1988, Sch 25 paras 6(2B), 11A, 11B*). Guidance on the extended provision is included in HMRC International Manual, INTM205090.

A person has an '*interest*' for this purpose if, on an apportionment under these provisions, at least 25% of the CFC's chargeable profits of the period would be apportioned to that person. For accounting periods beginning after 20 March 2000, where a company is a CFC only by virtue of joint control by two persons within *ICTA 1988, s 747(1A)* (see **27.2** above), the connected or associated persons to be considered also include persons connected or associated with either of those two persons.

Special provisions apply as regards application of the requirement to banking or similar concerns and to insurance business of any kind (see *ICTA 1988, Sch 25 para 11(3)–(9)* and INTM205100, 205110).

(2) The company is a 'local holding company', i.e. a 'holding company' 90% of whose gross income in the accounting period is derived directly from companies it controls (see **27.2**(b) above) and which, throughout that period, are resident in the territory in which the holding company is 'resident' (see below) and are not themselves holding companies or 'superior holding companies' but either are engaged in exempt activities or are 'exempt trading companies'. In addition, the income must, (for accounting periods beginning after 20 March 2000) be received by the 'holding company' in its territory of residence.

(3) The company is a 'holding company' other than a local holding company (see (2) above) 90% of whose gross income during the accounting period is derived directly from companies it controls (see **27.2**(b) above) and which are themselves throughout the period either local holding companies or not themselves 'holding companies' or 'superior holding companies' but either engaged in exempt activities or 'exempt trading companies'. In addition, (for accounting periods beginning after 20 March 2000) either 90% of the gross income of the 'holding company' must consist of 'qualifying dividends', or the company from which the 'holding company' directly derives 90% of its gross income must, throughout the accounting period in question, be resident in the territory in which the 'holding company' is resident and in which it must receive that income. A '*qualifying dividend*' is any dividend other than one for which the paying company is entitled to a deduction against its profits for tax purposes under the law of the territory in which it is resident.

(4) The company is a 'superior holding company', 90% of whose gross income during the accounting period represents 'qualifying exempt activity income of its subsidiaries' and is derived directly from companies it controls (see **27.2**(b) above) and each of which, throughout that accounting period, either:

   (a) not itself being a 'superior holding company', is otherwise either engaged in exempt activities or an 'exempt trading company'; or

   (b) is itself a 'superior holding company' 90% of whose gross income during the accounting period represents 'qualifying exempt activity income of its subsidiaries' and is derived directly from companies which it controls (see **27.2**(b) above) and which themselves fall within this subparagraph or within (a) above.

   In addition, (for accounting periods beginning after 20 March 2000) either 90% of the gross income of the 'superior holding company' (under either leg of the test) must consist of 'qualifying dividends' (as in (3) above), or the company from which the 'superior holding company' directly derives 90% of its gross income must, throughout the accounting period in question, be resident in the territory in which the 'superior holding company' is resident and in which it must receive that income.

In (2), (3) and (4) above, a 'holding company' or 'superior holding company' is treated as controlling any trading company in which it holds the maximum amount of ordinary share capital permitted under the law of the territory in which that trading company is resident, and from whose laws it derives its status as a company.

A trading company for this purpose includes (for accounting periods beginning after 20 March 2000) any trading company which is a CFC under the 40% joint control test (see **27.2** above) where the non-UK resident joint owner also controls the 'holding company' or 'superior holding company'.

For the 90% of gross income test, see *ICTA 1988, Sch 25 para 12(4)–(6)* as amended by; *CTA 2009, Sch 1 para 287* and INTM205170–205200.

See INTM205160 for the circumstances in which a holding company may be deemed to pass the motive test where its subsidiaries carry on broadly commercial activities along the lines of the exempt activities test, or where it controls a holding company which is not a local holding company.

For income accruing on or after 12 March 2008, the gross income of a holding company will include any income accruing during an accounting period from a settlement of which the company is a settlor or beneficiary (whether or not it is received by the company during the period). Where there is more than one settlor or beneficiary, the income is to be apportioned on a just and reasonable basis. Where an accounting period straddles 12 March 2008, the parts before and after that date are treated as separate accounting periods for this purpose. [*FA 2008, s 64*].

As regards (4) above, see *ICTA 1988, Sch 25 para 12A(3)(4)* as amended by *CTA 2009, Sch 1 para 287* as regards the profits out of which dividends are regarded as paid, and see also INTM205190.

Relevant definitions

A '*business establishment*' means 'premises' from which the company's business in the territory in which it is 'resident' (see below) is wholly or mainly carried on, and which are, or are intended to be, occupied and used with a reasonable degree of permanence. HMRC's interpretation of this requirement is set out at INTM205030. An office building, or even a single office, shared by a number of companies can be the 'business establishment' of each company.

The requirement that the premises be '*occupied and used with a reasonable degree of permanence*' depends on the nature of the company's business. Thus a holding company's business might need only occasional attendance of its staff at the premises, and the use of an office on such occasions would suffice, provided that it was retained by the company for its use for a considerable period of time. Continuous occupation of the office during normal working hours would not be required. The occasional hiring of, say, a hotel room for meetings would not qualify as having a 'business establishment'.

Again, a company (e.g. a bank) purporting to do business with the general public would be expected to have an office, shop, etc. actually occupied by its staff for at least a substantial part of each working day.

'*Premises*' includes an office, shop, factory or other building (or part); a mine, oil well, gas well or quarry or other place of extraction of natural resources; or a building, construction or installation site where the project has a duration of at least twelve months. A company whose business in the territory of residence is carried on from a number of sites in the territory will be treated as having a business establishment there even if no one site can be identified as the main place of business in the territory (see INTM205030).

'*Resident*' in this context is as defined in **27.3** above. However, a non-UK resident company which, for the accounting period in question, is not liable to tax in any territory by reason of domicile, residence or place of management, but whose affairs are 'effectively managed' in a territory outside the UK in which companies are not liable to tax by reason of domicile, residence or place of management, is treated for this purpose as resident in the latter territory or, if there is more than one, in such a territory as is notified to HMRC for this purpose by the UK resident company or companies having a majority interest in the CFC (see **27.9**(iv) above).

Where, however, the territory in which it is 'effectively managed' is either the Hong Kong or the Macao Special Administrative Region of the People's Republic of China, and it is liable to tax for the period in that Region, it is instead treated as resident in that Region.

'*Effectively managed*' — the requirement that the CFC's business affairs be '*effectively managed*' in the territory of residence is not regarded as satisfied unless the number of employees in the territory is adequate to deal with the volume of the company's business, and unless any services provided for persons resident outside the territory (other than through a permanent establishment (or branch or agency) liable to UK tax on its profits or gains, or for arm's length consideration through any other person so liable) are not in fact performed in the UK (or are merely incidental to services performed outside the UK). Employees in the territory include persons engaged in the company's business but paid by a person connected (see **25 CONNECTED PERSONS**) with, and resident in the same territory as, the CFC, provided that they are engaged in the CFC's business (wholly or mainly so engaged in the case of a company other than a 'holding company' or 'superior holding company').

The requirement as to the number of employees does not mean that every person involved in the company's business must be located in the territory of residence, but the staff employed there must be sufficient, in numbers and in qualifications and experience, to supervise and control profit-making activities of the company (see INTM205040).

For accounting periods beginning on or after 6 December 2006, the '*effectively managed*' condition will not be fulfilled unless there are sufficient employees of that company in the company's country of residence who have the skills and authority to conduct all, or substantially all, of the company's business. Where an accounting period straddles 6 December 2006, the accounting period is treated as if it were two periods, one comprising the period ending on 5 December and the other runnning on and after 6 December 2006. Profits and creditable tax are apportioned on a just and reasonable basis.

Holding company definitions

A '*holding company*' is a company whose business consists wholly or mainly in holding shares or securities in companies which are either its 90% subsidiaries and local holding companies (see (2) above) or its 51% subsidiaries and trading companies or companies in which it holds the maximum permitted amount of ordinary share capital (see below); or a company which would satisfy that condition if so much of its business were disregarded as consists in holding property or rights wholly or mainly for use by fellow resident companies controlled by it (see **27.2**(b) above).

However, in determining whether a company is a local holding company for this purpose, the reference in the definition of holding company to companies which are 90% subsidiaries and local holding companies is omitted. Determination of 51% or 90% subsidiary status is by reference to direct ownership, of more than 50% or not less than 90% respectively, of ordinary share capital.

For the purposes of (2) and (3) above, income of a holding company is treated as *not* being derived directly from a company it controls where:

(a) the controlled company from which it derives the income is not itself a holding company or 'superior holding company' but either is engaged in exempt activities or is an 'exempt trading company'; and
(b) the income was, or could have been, paid out of any non-trading income (i.e. income which would not be chargeable on a UK resident company on trading income on normal corporation tax principles) of the controlled company derived, directly or indirectly, from a third company connected or associated with it (see **27.11** above).

For the purpose of (2), (3) and (4) above, in the case of a holding company or 'superior holding company' part of whose business consists of activities other than holding shares, securities, property or rights, gross income of an accounting period is determined by:

(i) leaving out of account any part derived from any activity which, of itself, would satisfy (1) above; and
(ii) to the extent that the company's receipts from any other activities included proceeds of sale of any description of property or rights, deducting the cost of the property or rights (up to the amount of the receipts therefrom), and making no other deduction in respect of that activity.

A '*superior holding company*' is a company whose business consists wholly or mainly in holding shares or securities in holding companies or local holding companies or other superior holding companies, or which would satisfy that condition if so much of its business were disregarded as consists in holding property or rights wholly or mainly for use by fellow resident companies controlled by it (see **27.2**(b) above).

A company is an '*exempt trading company*' throughout a period if it is a trading company throughout each of its accounting periods falling wholly or partly within the period, and in each of those accounting periods:

(A) it is not subject to a lower level of taxation (see **27.4** above) in the territory in which it is resident;
(B) it is within **27.11**(v) above; and
(C) it satisfies the conditions in **27.11**(vi) above,

and income of a company during a period represents '*qualifying exempt activity income of its subsidiaries*' if it is derived directly or indirectly from companies which it controls (see **27.2**(b) above) and which, throughout that period, fall within (4)(a) above, but which are not holding companies other than local holding companies.

On or after 6 December 2006, companies resident in an EEA territory are liable under the CFC legislation in the same way as companies resident elsewhere.

[*ICTA 1988, s 748(1)(b), Sch 25 Pt II; FA 2003, ss 200, 201, Sch 42; FA 2007, Sch 15 para 7, 10; CTA 2009, Sch 1 para 287*].

FA 2009 — accounting periods beginning after 1 July 2009

FA 2009 introduced a change in the legislation with regard to the exempt activities exclusion, applicable to certain CFCs which are holding companies for periods beginning on or after 1 July 2009.

As noted above, where a CFC undertakes exempt activities it is considered outside the apportionment rules described above. CFCs which are holding companies of subsidiaries (undertaking exempt activities) also receive the benefit of the exclusion, as: 'local' holding companies (with subsidiaries in its own territory undertaking exempt activities); holding companies (with subsidiaries which are 'local' holding companies, or CFCs directly undertaking exempt activities); or superior holding companies (with subsidiaries which are either local holding companies, other holding companies). See further the definitions above.

It was considered that the changes brought about by the new participation exemption regime meant that the exemption for non-local holding companies and superior holding companies was no longer required. Therefore *FA 2009* introduced new rules whereby the exclusion for non-local and superior holding companies was removed, for accounting periods beginning on or after 1 July 2009. The provisions will therefore in future refer only to local holding companies.

However, the transitional provisions mean that in some cases the abolition of the exemption for these holding companies will be delayed until 1 July 2012 (as extended by the Finance Act 2011, and applicable as if it had always been so drafted).

Where a CFC has an accounting period which straddles 1 July 2009 then for the CFC rules such period will be split into two separate accounting periods and the CFC's gross income, chargeable profits and creditable tax will be apportioned between the two periods. A similar approach will be taken for periods straddling 1 July 2012.

To qualify for transitional relief a company must be a 'qualifying holding company' for the duration of the last accounting period to end before 1 July 2009 (excluding any straddle period). A 'qualifying holding company' is one that meets the requirements for an 'exempt holding company' for this last accounting period — see further the definition below.

Where a qualifying holding company has an accounting period beginning on or after 1 July 2009 and ending on or before 1 July 2012, the provisions of *ICTA 1988, Sch 25 para 6(4)* and *(4A)* (which outline the requirements for a CFC to be a non-local holding company or superior holding company, see below) apply so far as gross income is concerned, but only if at all material times:

(i) the company was a member of a group with the same ultimate parent; and

(ii) the company's gross income in the accounting period that is non-qualifying gross income does not exceed the company's non-qualifying gross income in the 'specified period', determined by how many reference periods there are in relation to the company. Where the length of the accounting period is not the same as the length of the reference period, the amount of such profits for the reference period is multiplied by the fraction of number of days in the accounting period over number of days in the reference period.

There is an anti-avoidance provision to cover the situation where a company alters its accounting date on or after 9 December 2008 to enable any period which would otherwise have fallen into an accounting period ending on or after 9 December 2008 to fall into an accounting period ending before that date.

A '*qualifying holding company*' is a CFC which was an exempt holding company in relation to the last accounting period to end before 1 July 2009. An exempt holding company is a company which throughout a particular accounting period was engaged in exempt activities under the rules applying to non-local and superior holding companies (see above).

A '*reference period*' is an accounting period which is one of the last three accounting periods of the company to end before 9 December 2008 and is an accounting period in relation to which the company is an exempt holding company.

'*Non-qualifying gross income*' is gross income not satisfying the test in *ICTA 1988, Sch 25 paras 6(3), (4) or (4A)*.

The '*material time*' is as 'the beginning of 9 December 2008 and all times during the accounting period in question'. [*FA 2009, s 36, Sch 16*].

See generally HMRC International Manual, INTM205000 *et seq.*

Simon's Taxes. See **D4.340–D4.348.**

'Public quotation' exclusion

[27.14] CFCs which fulfilled the 'public quotation condition' were exempt from apportionment under the CFC rules. It should be noted that for accounting periods commencing on or after 6 December 2006, the public quotation condition does not apply. Where an accounting period straddles 6 December 2006, the period is apportioned into two periods for CFC purposes.

The 'public quotation condition' is met by a CFC in an accounting period if:

(i) shares or stock (other than that entitled to a fixed rate of dividend, whether also participating in profits or not) have, within the twelve months to the end of the accounting period, been dealt in on, and listed in the official list of, a recognised stock exchange (i.e. one designated as such by HMRC, see HMRC International Manual, INTM206010–206050) in its territory of residence; and

(ii) such shares, etc. carrying at least 35% of the total voting power in the company have been 'beneficially held by the public' throughout the accounting period, and have been acquired unconditionally by the public; and

(iii) the voting power possessed by 'principal members' of the company (including that attributed to shares entitled to a fixed rate of dividend) has not at any time in the accounting period exceeded 85% of the total voting power in the company.

Shares etc. are '*beneficially held by the public*' if held by any person other than a person connected or associated with the CFC (see **27.8** above) or a 'principal member' of the company.

A '*principal member*' of a company is a person possessing more than 5% of the voting power in the company or, where there are more than five such persons, those five persons holding the highest percentages. Where more than one person possesses a percentage which would, if held by only one person, be the fifth largest percentage holding, each of those persons is a principal member in addition to the four persons possessing higher percentage holdings.

Any person's holding of shares for these purposes includes all nominee holdings for him, and a person's voting power includes that of his associates (see **22.9 CLOSE COMPANIES**), of any company which he controls (see **27.2**(b) above) with or without his associates, and of any nominees for him, his associates or such companies. Voting power of associates' associates and of companies controlled only by associates is disregarded.

[*ICTA 1988, Sch 25 paras 13–15; FA 2007 Sch 15 paras 8, 10*].

See generally HMRC International Manual, INTM206000 *et seq.*

Simon's Taxes. See D4.360.

Finance Act 2011 — Interim Measures

[27.15] The additional de minimis exemption, and the extension to the transitional period for holding companies have been outlined above. Further measures are outlined below. The measures to be introduced by the *Finance Act 2011* apply to accounting periods beginning on or after 1 January 2011.

Exemption for trading companies with limited UK connection

[27.16] *ICTA 1988, s 748(1)* is amended to include this exemption at new *subparagraph (ba)*, with the details found at new *Part 2A* of *Sch 25 paras 12B–12G*. The new exemption applies to CFCs that carry on trading activities where there is limited connection with the UK, irrespective of the extent of intra-group transactions. Full exemption is available where the CFC meets the required conditions with regard to all of the following: business establishment; business activities; the amount of finance income and IP income; and the extent of its UK connection.

The business establishment condition requires the CFC to have a business establishment in its territory of residence — the provisions mirror that of the exempt activities test requiring sufficient substance in that territory.

[*ICTA 1988, Sch 25 para 12C*].

The business activities condition requires the majority of the CFCs business to be trading activity — it must not include to a substantial extent non-exempt activities.

The provisions set out those activities which are considered 'non-exempt' activities: the holding or managing of shares or securities; the holding of intellectual property; dealing in securities (other than as broker); leasing of property or rights of any description; investing in funds which would otherwise be invested in by a person that controls the CFC; where the CFC is not a member of an insurance group, entering into contracts of insurance with related parties (to catch captive insurance companies).

A person is '*related*' to the company if: the person is connected or associated with the company; or the person has a 25% assessable interest in the company; or the company is a CFC and the person is connected or associated with the two parties that control the CFC under the 40% test (see **27.2** above).

[*ICTA 1988, Sch 25 para 12D*].

Finance income and income from intellectual property condition: the new provisions introduce a separate limitation in respect of this income set at 5% of the CFC's gross income. Finance and relevant IP income in excess of this amount will be subject to a CFC charge.

'*Finance income*' is any amount which arises from financial assets under UK GAAP; and any return which is economically equivalent to interest (being any amount which would be recognised as income under the loan relationship disguised interest rules).

'*Relevant IP income*' is income arising from the exploitation of IP, such as royalties and receipts of a similar nature.

[*ICTA 1988, Sch 25 para 12F*].

UK business connection condition: the proposals limit the extent to which the CFC can have transactions or business connections with the UK — the CFC should not have a significant connection with the UK during the accounting period. It will have a significant connection if it meets either condition A or B. The approach is to test the gross income and the business expenditure of the CFC to measure to what extent that income arises from, or expenditure is incurred with, the UK.

Under condition A there is a significant connection with the UK if more than 10% of the gross income or expenditure of the CFC arises from a UK connection.

However, if there is a connection with the UK of more than 10%, but not more than 50%, full exemption will be available to CFCs whose overall level of profitability is low (the relevant profits do not exceed 10% of the relevant staffing costs in respect of directors and employees resident in the CFC's territory), and which is effectively managed in that territory. For this purpose, effective management means sufficient individuals working in the territory of residence, or in any other territory outside the UK, who have the competence and authority to undertake all, or substantially all, of the CFC's business.

Under condition B there is a significant connection where the UK-connected related-party business expenditure of the period exceeds 50% of the company related-party business expenditure and during the period the company has been involved in a scheme the main purpose, or one of the main purposes, of any party to the scheme was to achieve a reduction in corporation tax (or any tax chargeable as if it were such tax). 'Related-party business expenditure' is any expenditure (other than capital), which gives rise to income of a person related to the company. 'UK-connected related-party business' is related party business which gives rise to income of a person within the charge to UK tax in respect of that income.

If these conditions are not satisfied, then the UK company with a relevant interest in the CFC may apply to HMRC for a reduction in the CFC charge (the partial exemption application, see further below). If the level of UK connection exceeds 50%, this exemption will not be available.

[*ICTA 1988, Sch 25 para 12E*].

'Gross income' for the purposes of the above is defined with *para 12G*. It does not include dividends that would be exempt under the UK's dividend exemption regime (under *CTA 2009, Pt 9A*, see further **31 DISTRIBUTIONS**) nor chargeable gains. However, it does include income that accrues to a settlement of which the CFC is a settlor or beneficiary and it does include income arising in a partnership of which the CFC is a partner.

[*ICTA 1988, Sch 25 para 12G*].

Non-UK Intellectual Property Exemption

[27.17] Whilst the treatment of CFCs which receive income from IP is the subject of the main reform provisions, in the interim, a new exemption excludes profits from intellectual property with little or no connection to the UK. *ICTA 1988, s 748(1)* is amended and new *subsection (bb)* added, referring to new *Part 2B* of *Sch 25* of the Act. The draft legislation inserts into *Sch 25* new *paras 12H–12N* and imposes requirements as to all of the following: business establishment; IP business; other business activities; UK connection; finance income.

The business establishment test is as in *para 12C* highlighted above.

[*ICTA 1988, Sch 25 para 12I*].

The business activities conditions at *12J* and *12K* require that the main business of the CFC is the exploitation of IP. Any other business activities should be secondary activities which do not constitute a substantial part of the CFC's business and which would, if treated as the main business, satisfy either the existing exempt activities test, or the new intra-group exempt activities test.

In addition, the IP business should not have a relevant UK connection. In this context, the IP will have a relevant UK connection if:

(a) it has been held by a person resident in the UK at any time within the accounting period or within the preceding six years; or

(b) the activities in relation to the creation, development, maintenance or enhancement of the IP have been carried on by a person related to the CFC and within the charge to UK tax.

Failure of either condition will mean that the exemption is not available.

[*ICTA 1988, Sch 25 para 12J and 12K*].

The UK connection condition: the CFC should not have a significant connection to the UK during the accounting period. There is a significant connection if:

(a) all or substantial proportion of the CFC's gross income is derived from persons within the charge to UK tax; or
(b) the CFC incurs expenditure on R&D subcontractor payments or on the creation, development or maintenance of the IP, which expenditure forms part of the gross income of a person related to the CFC and within the charge to UK tax. Incidental or insignificant expenditure is disregarded.

[*ICTA 1988, Sch 25 para 12L*].

The finance income condition: not more than 5% of the CFC's gross income should consist of finance income (as defined in *para 12F*), with the excess subject to a CFC charge.

A partial exemption claim may be made — see below.

[*ICTA 1988, Sch 25 para 12M*].

A person is related to the CFC is the person is connected or associated with the CFC, or has a 25% assessable interest in the CFC, or the person is connected or associated with either or both of the two persons satisfying the 40% test of control of the CFC under *ICTA 1988, s 747(1A)*.

[*ICTA 1988, Sch 25 para 12N*].

Temporary exemption following acquisition or reorganisation

[27.18] Currently there is a concessionary one year 'period of grace' provided with regard to foreign subsidiaries which are acquired and which fall within the CFC regime. The new provisions formalise and expand this period in respect of acquisitions and reorganisations.

The CFC rules will not apply to relevant companies for a period starting on the date of acquisition or reorganisation and ending 24 months after the end of the accounting period in which the acquisition takes place. In practice, this will be a period of up to three years.

A new *subsection (f)* is added to *ICTA 1988, s 748(1)*, exempting CFCs where the accounting period ends during an exempt period per a new *Part 3A* to *Sch 25* of that Act.

The exempt period begins when a company becomes a CFC (being that it is resident outside the UK and is controlled by UK resident persons) and where there is at least one relevant UK corporate investor in the company, and either the requirements of s 15C or s 15D (see below) are met.

A 'relevant UK corporate investor' is a UK resident company to which a CFC apportionment would be made, assuming the CFC had chargeable profits, and assuming no reductions would be made in respect of the EEA exemption, or with regard to certain finance income, or for a failure to qualify for the limited UK connection test or relevant IP exemptions.

The requirements of s 15C specify that: no company was at any earlier time a relevant UK corporate investor in the CFC; no asset owned by the CFC or part of its business was previously owned or carried on by a company under UK control and related to the CFC; one of the four conditions A to D are met; and a disqualifying relevant transaction does not occur at the time the company becomes a CFC.

Condition A — is that immediately before becoming a CFC the company was in existence and not a member of the same group of companies acquiring it.

Condition B — is that when the company becomes a CFC it is controlled by a UK resident company; and that immediately before such time if the CFC was controlled by the same company, that company was not UK resident.

Condition C — is that when the company becomes a CFC it is controlled by a UK resident company and this intermediate parent is controlled by a non-UK resident company, and immediately before becoming a CFC the company was controlled by the parent but not the intermediate parent.

Condition D — is that when the company is formed it is a CFC and it is formed by one or more persons for the purpose of controlling one or more companies in such circumstances that an exempt period under these provisions is expected to start with regard to those companies when the CFC begins to control them.

The alternative requirements of s 15D provide that the exempt period will apply where the time at which the company becomes a CFC falls after 23 March 2011, and no company was a relevant UK corporate investor during the accounting period in which 23 March 2011 falls, or immediately before the time the company became a CFC. When the company becomes a CFC it should be controlled by a company which is UK resident but which is not under the control of another company or two or more companies. In respect of control, a company holding less than 10% of the issued ordinary shares of the CFC is disregarded. No disqualifying relevant transaction should occur.

A '*relevant transaction*' is one where: the CFC is making, or increasing, or changing the conditions of (affecting the interest payable), a loan or advance to a person related to the CFC and subject to UK tax; or one which is referable to any non-exempt activities carried on by the CFC, the results of which are not negligible and are reflected in the CFC's profits, and which transaction alone or together with others, achieves a reduction in UK tax. Whether a person is related to the CFC is determined by *para 15G(2)* and is the same as in *para 12N* above.

A '*disqualifying relevant transaction*' is a relevant transaction which occurs at the time the company becomes a CFC, or which occurs on or after 9 December 2010 but before the time the company becomes a CFC and that transaction forms part of an avoidance scheme.

[*ICTA 1988, Sch 25 paras 15B–15E*].

The exempt period will end immediately after 24 months, commencing after the end of the first accounting period during which the company becomes a CFC, which could mean and exemption of up to three years.

The exempt period also ends if an early termination event occurs. An early termination event is when a relevant transaction (as defined above) occurs, or where the exempt period began because condition D was met, the CFC's business is not that of solely holding shares in companies which it controls (together with activities incidental to such holding).

[*ICTA 1988, Sch 25 para 15F*].

For the accounting period in which a termination event occurs, a partial CFC charge may arise in order to deal with the reduction in UK tax identified. For accounting periods outside this exemption period, the other CFC exemptions will apply in the usual way.

See below with regard to the partial exemption mechanism which has been introduced.

Partial exemption mechanism

[27.19] A new *s 751AB* is introduced to enable a partial CFC exemption for entities which do not meet the conditions for full exemption under the non-UK trading activities and non-UK IP company exemptions outlined above.

The UK resident company with a relevant interest in the CFC will make an application to HMRC, and will specify the amount of the CFC apportionment.

Applications may be required where there is a '*relevant failure*' which means with regard to any of the following circumstances:

- for non-UK IP CFCs where finance income exceeds 5% of gross income;
- for non-UK trading activity CFCs where the combined financial and IP income exceeds 5% (but where the relevant IP income does not exceed 5% of the gross income);
- for non-UK trading activity CFCs where the level of UK connection exceeds 10% but not 50%.

[*ICTA 1988, s 751AB(1)–(4)*].

For the application to be granted the specified amount cannot be less than 'the relevant amount' and no previous adjustment under *ss 751A* or *751AC* can have been agreed.

The 'relevant amount' for a non-UK trading activity CFC is the excess combined finance and IP income which is over 5% of its total gross income (ignoring negligible amounts), to which is added a charge for UK transactions if the UK connection test is failed.

Thus for the non-UK trading activity CFCs, where the level of UK connection exceeds 10% but not 50%, an assessment of the economic value added by the CFC and the extent to which the profits of the CFC have arisen as a result of transactions with the UK is required.

For non-UK IP CFCs the 'relevant amount' is the amount of finance income in excess of 5% of its total gross income (ignoring negligible amounts).

The 'relevant amount' does not include: profits which represent economic value added by work carried out for the CFC in its territory by individuals working there; or profits which are not attributable to transactions with persons within the charge to UK tax (any transactions undertaken with non-UK resident companies which are within the charge to UK corporation tax are only taken into account to the extent they are undertaken with the UK permanent establishment).

For the purposes of determining 'net chargeable profits' and 'qualifying work' the provisions of *s 751A(5),(6)* and *(9)* also apply, which reduce the profits for certain activities of EEA businesses. The residence rules at *Sch 25 para 5* also apply.

[*ICTA 1988, s 751AB(5)–(11)*].

A new *s 751AC* is also introduced to allow for a partial exemption in respect of the temporary exemption after a reorganisation provisions above. It applies for CFC's whose exempt period ends due to an early termination event and an apportionment becomes due. It does not apply if the early termination event is given by *para 15F(3)(b)* (the exempt period began because condition D was met, and the CFC's business is not that of solely holding shares in companies which it controls — see above).

The UK resident company can apply to the Commissioners under a new *ICTA 1988, s 751AC* for a just and reasonable apportionment taking into account the relevant transaction(s) which triggered the end of the exempt period.

[*ICTA 1988, s 751AC(1)–(6)*].

Assessment, recovery and postponement of tax

[27.20] Whilst the tax payable under the CFC apportionment rules is not corporation tax, it is charged as if it were corporation tax. Therefore the normal corporation tax provisions apply to the charge to tax of a sum under these provisions as under **27.8** above, including those relating to company tax returns, to the assessment, collection and receipt of corporation tax, and to appeals, administration, penalties, interest and priority in insolvency (including the provisions under *FA 1998, Sch 18*). The provisions of *TMA 1970* apply as if references to corporation tax referred also to amounts charged under these provisions, and as if references to company profits referred also to chargeable profits apportioned to a company under these provisions. A sum chargeable under these provisions is chargeable for the accounting period in which ends the CFC accounting period whose chargeable profits were apportioned.

Just and reasonable apportionments

Where an apportionment of chargeable profits for an accounting period of a CFC falls to be made on a just and reasonable basis (see **27.8** above), and a company uses a particular basis in its tax return, HMRC may determine that a different basis is to be used, and require the company to provide such documents and information as are reasonably required for this purpose. A basis so determined is then treated as if it were the only basis permissible. A determination may be questioned (in an appeal against an amendment to the company's tax return) only on the ground that the basis determined is not just and reasonable.

Appeals against amendments to company tax returns (or against discovery assessments or determinations) relating to charges under these provisions are heard by the Tribunal. Where their determination of a particular question is likely to affect the liability of more than one person under these provisions in relation to the CFC concerned, every such person is entitled to appear, or to make written representations to them, and their determination of that question is treated as separate from any other determination on the appeal and as if each of those persons were a party to the appeal on that question.

The *reliefs* which may be claimed against a liability under these provisions are as follows:

(a) **Trading losses, etc.** Where a company is regarded as liable to corporation tax in respect of chargeable profits apportioned to it (as above), it may claim to set against its liability a sum equal to corporation tax, at the rate (or average rate) applicable to profits of the accounting period, on all or part of a loss. (which is then treated as having been set off against profits of the company). Such a loss may be a trading loss, a loss in a property business charge on income, management expense, excess capital allowance, group relief claim or non-trading loan relationship deficit.

(b) **Surplus ACT**. Surplus ACT (from accounting periods beginning before 6 April 1999) (see **3.2** et seq. ADVANCE CORPORATION TAX — SHADOW ACT) of an accounting period for which a company is regarded as liable to corporation tax in respect of chargeable profits apportioned to it (as above) may, on a claim, be set against that liability (so far as it is not relieved, and could not be relieved, under (a) above), and is then treated as having been set against a corporation tax liability of the period. The maximum set-off allowed is the amount of shadow ACT on a distribution made at the end of the accounting period, where the amount of the distribution plus the shadow ACT in respect of it is equal to the apportioned chargeable profits in respect of which the company is chargeable for the period less any deduction under (a) above. [*SI 1999 No 358, Reg 20*].

(c) **Dividends from the CFC**. The total of assessments on UK resident companies under these provisions in respect of a CFC's chargeable profits (the '*gross attributed tax*') is treated as underlying tax for double taxation relief purposes (see **32.11** DOUBLE TAX RELIEF) where a dividend is paid by the CFC wholly or partly out of profits from which those chargeable profits derive. The gross attributed tax is *not*, however, treated as increasing the amount of the dividend income in determining liability on that income.

Special recovery powers

Where the same interest in a CFC is held directly by one person and indirectly by another, and the company to be treated as holding the interest is defined by **27.8**(1) to (3) above, special recovery powers apply to any overdue tax chargeable on that company. HMRC may serve notice of liability to that overdue tax on another UK resident company (the '*responsible company*') which holds or has held, directly or indirectly, the same interest in the CFC as the chargeable company. Interest both up to the date of the notice and thereafter is then payable by the responsible company. If tax and interest is not paid by the responsible company within three months of the date of HMRC's notice, it may be recovered from either the responsible company or the company originally chargeable.

[*ICTA 1988, s 754, Sch 26*].

HMRC guidance. See generally HMRC International Manual, INTM214000 *et seq*.

Simon's Taxes. See **D4.366–D4.369, D4.375–D4.377.**

Miscellaneous

[27.21] Corporation tax on chargeable gains on disposal of shares: relief may be claimed where:

(i) an apportionment is made under these provisions (see **27.7** above) in respect of a CFC's accounting period;
(ii) a UK resident company (the 'claimant company') disposes of shares, acquired before the end of that accounting period, in either the CFC or another company whose shares give rise to the claimant company's interest in the CFC (see **27.7** above); and
(iii) chargeable profits (see **27.8** above) of the CFC are apportioned to the claimant company, and a sum accordingly becomes chargeable on it as if it were corporation tax (see **27.7** above).

Where a claim is made, in the computation of the chargeable gain accruing on the disposal in (ii) above, a deduction is allowed of the sum chargeable to tax as in (iii) above, reduced to the proportion thereof that the average market value (in the period for which the apportionment was made) of the interest in the CFC bears to the average market value in that period of the shares disposed of. A sum chargeable to tax as at (iii) above may only be relieved once in this way.

Relief may, however, be restricted where, before the disposal, a dividend is paid by the CFC out of profits from which the chargeable profits in (iii) above derived. If either:

(a) the effect of the payment of the dividend is to reduce the value of the shares disposed of as in (ii) above; or
(b) the claimant company obtains relief as under **27.20**(c) above in respect of a dividend paid on the shares disposed of as in (ii) above, by reference to sums including that referred to in (iii) above,

then relief is denied in respect of so much of the sum chargeable to tax as corresponds to the part of the chargeable profits in (iii) above corresponds to the profits which the dividend represents.

Claims for relief must be made within three months of the later of the end of the accounting period in which the disposal occurs and the date the charge to tax in (iii) above becomes final and conclusive.

Identification of shares disposed of for this purpose is with those acquired earlier before those acquired later.

[*ICTA 1988, Sch 26 para 3*].

Simon's Taxes. See **D4.378.**

See generally HMRC International Manual, INTM211120.

See **27.20**(c) above as regards restriction of dividend relief following relief under this provision.

***ICTA 1988, s 739* (transfer of assets abroad)**

Where a sum forming part of a CFC's chargeable profits (see **27.9** above) would otherwise be deemed income of an individual under *ITA 2007, s 716 et seq; ICTA 1988, s 739* (see Tolley's Income Tax under Anti-Avoidance) that deemed income is reduced by the proportion of those chargeable profits which gives rise to a liability to tax on UK resident companies by virtue of an apportionment under these provisions (see **27.8** above). [*ICTA 1988, s 747(4)(b)*].

Key points

[27.22] Points to consider are as follows.

- The controlled foreign company (CFC) rules seek to cancel any tax advantage of placing subsidiaries into low tax jurisdictions. If a UK holding company has a subsidiary in, say, Jersey, which has a zero rate of tax, any profits diverted to that company would escape UK corporation tax. In order to negate this possible leakage of tax the CFC rules impute these profits back to the UK parent company. Many of the more sophisticated jurisdictions operate similar rules for the same reasons.
- Before an overseas company is deemed to be a CFC it is necessary to determine if it breaches the definition. In order to be categorised as a CFC it is necessary to calculate the taxable profits in the overseas company along UK corporation tax lines. Once the 'taxable' profits are determined any overseas tax paid is compared to the UK equivalent corporation tax that would be payable on those profits. If the overseas tax is less than three quarters of the UK equivalent tax the company is deemed to be a CFC.
- There is no imputation of the profits of a CFC if it can fall into certain exemptions. A CFC that carries out exempt activities through a real base in the overseas territory is exempted from the

rules. Also CFCs that have an acceptable distribution policy and distribute 90% of their profits of any accounting period are exempt. Any CFC that is quoted on a Stock Exchange is also exempt.

- A motive test also applies. If it can be demonstrated to the satisfaction of HMRC that the CFC has been established for bona fide commercial reasons and the avoidance of UK tax is purely coincidental then the imputation of the profits may also be avoided. In practice HMRC is very sceptical of claims along these lines.
- CFCs in other EU territories may avoid being caught under EU law, but this has been challenged through the Courts. In the UK both Cadbury Schweppes and Vodafone have tested HMRC's policy relating to CFC's in other EU countries. With Cadbury Schweppes the CFC in question was in Ireland and in the case of Vodafone the CFC was in Luxembourg.
- HMRC may also seek to test the residency of a CFC if is situated in a 'tax haven' and appears to carry out no real business there. By challenging the residency of the CFC under the central management and control test the CFC may be brought into the UK corporation tax net completely.
- On a practical level if there is a CFC within a group, it may now be worthwhile pursing an acceptable distribution policy as from 1 July 2009 many dividends received by UK corporates are exempt from corporation tax following the introduction of the 'Taxation of Foreign Profits' rules. The paying of a dividend results in tax free income in the UK parent rather than imputed CFC profits which continue to be taxable if retained in the CFC.
- Consultation is under way between HMRC and interested parties reviewing possible changes to the CFC regime in the UK. A consultation document has been published by HMRC with various proposals for consideration. As noted above there are two main proposals with regard to finance and IP companies with interim measures brought in by the Finance Act 2011, to have effect for accounting periods beginning on or after 1 January 2011.
- Under the interim measures: an additional de minimis exemption is included based on accounting profits up to £200,000; the one-year period of grace is extended to up to three years for a 'new' CFC, post a reorganisation; two new exemptions are introduced for trading companies with limited UK connections and for companies exploiting IP with limited UK connections.

28

Corporate Venturing Scheme

See HMRC guidance 'The Corporate Venturing Scheme' (www.hmrc.gov.uk/guidance/cvs.htm).

Simon's Taxes. See **D8.3**.

Introduction

[28.1] For shares issued on or after 1 April 2000 but before 1 April 2010, a scheme applied whereby most trading companies were able to obtain corporation tax relief at 20% ('*investment relief*') on corporate venturing investments, i.e. acquisitions (by cash subscription) of minority shareholdings in 'small higher risk' trading companies.

In addition, investing companies were able to postpone chargeable gains ('*deferral relief*') on disposals of corporate venturing investments where they reinvested in other shares attracting investment relief. Also, an allowable capital loss on the disposal of a corporate venturing investment, computed net of investment relief, could be relieved against *income* of the accounting period in which the loss arises and accounting periods ending in the previous 12 months (but could alternatively be relieved against chargeable gains in the normal way). [*FA 2000, s 63(1)(4), Sch 15 para 1*].

Investee companies were limited to those with gross assets not exceeding £7 million immediately before the investment and £8 million immediately afterwards. Such companies had to exist for the purpose of carrying on trading activities other than the kind of 'lower risk' activity excluded under the Enterprise Investment Scheme (see Tolley's Income Tax) or the provisions for **VENTURE CAPITAL TRUSTS (74)**.

Potential investee companies could request advance clearance from HMRC.

The maximum investment qualifying for relief was 30% of the issued ordinary share capital of the investee company, and no minimum investment was stipulated. It was at least 20% of the ordinary share capital of the investee company had to be held by individuals (other than directors and employees of the investing company). To qualify for the relief, the investing company had to retain the shares acquired for at least three years. Investing companies carrying on financial trades (e.g. banking, share dealing etc.) were not eligible.

See generally HMRC Venture Capital Schemes Manual, VCM10000–17320, VCM50000 *et seq.*

Investment relief

Eligibility

[28.2] An investing company was eligible for investment relief (see **28.3** below) in respect of an amount subscribed by it for shares in an investee company (the '*issuing company*') if:

(a) the shares (the '*relevant shares*') were issued to the investing company;
(b) the investing company was a 'qualifying investing company' (see **28.5** below);
(c) the issuing company was a 'qualifying issuing company' (see **28.6** below) in relation to the relevant shares; and
(d) the general requirements at **28.8** below were met.

For advance clearance as regards (c) and (d) above, see **28.9** below.

Qualification period

In these provisions, the '*qualification period*' was normally the three-year period beginning with the date of issue of the relevant shares. If, however, the money raised by the issue was employed wholly or mainly for the purposes of a qualifying trade (or trades) (see **28.7** below) which, on the date of issue, was not being carried on by the issuing company or a qualifying 90% subsidiary, the qualification period begins on the date of issue and ends immediately before the third anniversary of the date of commencement of the trade (or the latest such date where there was more than one such trade). In determining when the trade begins for this purpose, the carrying on of any trade by a subsidiary before it became a qualifying 90% subsidiary was to be disregarded.

[*FA 2000, Sch 15 paras 2, 3, 102(8); FA 2004, s 95, Sch 20 paras 3, 13, 15*].

Form of relief

[28.3] Where an investing company was eligible for investment relief (see **28.2** above) in respect of amounts subscribed by it for shares, its corporation tax liability for the accounting period in which the shares were issued was reduced, on a claim (see **28.4** below), by the lesser of:

(a) 20% of the amount (or aggregate amount) subscribed; and
(b) the amount which reduced the liability to nil.

The reduction in corporation tax liability was made before any deduction for **COMMUNITY INVESTMENT TAX RELIEF (23)** or **DOUBLE TAX RELIEF (32)**.

[*FA 2000, Sch 15 para 39, Sch 16 para 5(1)(2); FA 2002, Sch 17 para 5*].

Investment relief was said to be 'attributable to shares' if relief as above has been obtained in respect of those shares and has not been withdrawn — see **28.10** below. Where for any one accounting period relief has been obtained by reason of more than one issue of shares, the relief was attributed to those issues in proportion to the amounts subscribed. Relief attributable to any one issue of shares was attributed *pro rata* to each share in that issue, and any reduction of relief (see **28.10** below) was similarly apportioned between the shares in question. For these purposes, any bonus shares, issued in respect of the original shares and being shares in the same company, of the same class and carrying the same rights, were treated as if comprised in the original issue, and relief was apportioned to them accordingly. This applies only if the original shares have been held continuously since issue (as in **28.20**(a) below), and, where it does apply, the bonus shares were themselves treated as having been held continuously since the time of the original issue.

[*FA 2000, Sch 15 para 45*].

Claims for relief

[28.4] No deadline was specified for making a claim, so the general six-year time limit applies as in **21.8 CLAIMS**. A claim for relief cannot be made in respect of any investment until the 'funded trade' has been carried on by no person other than the issuing company or a qualifying 90% subsidiary for at least four months and the investing company has received from the issuing company a 'compliance certificate' (see below). In determining whether the 'funded trade' has been carried on for four months, the time spent *preparing* to carry on the trade and, where the funded trade was carried on by a partnership or joint venture, the other partners or parties to the joint venture, were to be disregarded.

No postponement of tax pending appeal (see **59.10 PAYMENT OF TAX**) could be made on the grounds of eligibility for investment relief until a claim for that relief could be and had been made. The '*funded trade*' was the trade or trades by reference to which the requirement at **28.8** below as to 'use of money raised' was met (or, where applicable, the notional trade of research and development therein mentioned). A claim *could* be made if the funded trade was carried on as above for less than four months by reason of the winding-up or dissolution of any company (or, for shares issued before 17 March 2004, the issuing company or subsidiary concerned) or its going into administration or receivership (both as defined), provided that this was for commercial reasons and not part of tax avoidance arrangements.

A '*compliance certificate*' was a certificate issued, with the authority of HMRC and in such form as they could direct, by the issuing company in respect of the relevant shares and confirming that, from the issuing company's point of view, the requirements for investment relief were for the time being met in relation to the shares. To obtain authority for the issue of a certificate, the issuing company had to provide HMRC with a 'compliance statement' in respect of the issue of shares which includes the relevant shares. Where notice of an event giving rise to withdrawal etc. was given to HMRC by or in relation to the issuing company (see **28.10** below), any authority already given was invalid unless renewed.

A '*compliance statement*' was a statement, in respect of an issue of shares, to the effect that, from the issuing company's point of view, the requirements for investment relief were for the time being met in relation to the shares and had been met at all times since the shares were issued. The statement had to be in required form and had to contain any additional information HMRC reasonably require, a declaration that it was correct to the best of the company's knowledge and belief, and such other declarations as HMRC reasonably require. A compliance statement cannot be made until such time as the funded trade has been carried on for at least four months (or such shorter time as is specified above). It *had to* be made within two years after the end of the accounting period in which the shares were issued or, if later, two years after the minimum period of trading condition was satisfied.

The issuing company could give notice of appeal, within 30 days, against a refusal by HMRC to authorise a compliance certificate (as if that refusal were the disallowance of a claim other than for discharge or repayment of tax — see **21.9 CLAIMS**).

The issuing company was liable to a penalty of up to £3,000 for issuing a compliance certificate which was made fraudulently or negligently or without HMRC authority, or for making a compliance statement fraudulently or negligently.

[*FA 2000, Sch 15 paras 40–44, 102(4); FA 2004, Sch 20 paras 12, 15*].

Qualifying investing company

[28.5] The investing company was a '*qualifying investing company*' (see **28.2**(b) above) in relation to the relevant shares if it meets all the requirements below as to absence of material interest, reciprocal arrangements, control and tax avoidance, the nature of its activities, and the relevant shares being a chargeable asset. [*FA 2000, Sch 15 para 4*].

No material interest requirement

At no time in the qualification period (see **28.2** above) had the investing company to have a material interest in the issuing company. For this purpose, a person had a material interest in a company if he (alone or together with any person connected with him (within *ICTA 1988, s 839*, see **25 CONNECTED PERSONS**)) directly or indirectly possesses, or was entitled (or would in future be entitled) to acquire (at present or at a future date), more than **30%** of:

(a) the 'ordinary share capital' of; or
(b) the voting power in,

the company or any 51% subsidiary. In applying the test, there had to be attributed to a person any rights or powers of any associate of his (as defined by *FA 2000, Sch 15 para 99*). For these purposes, a company's '*ordinary share capital*' comprises:

(i) all of its issued share capital other than 'relevant preference shares'; and
(ii) all of its loan capital (as widely defined but excluding a bank overdraft or an ordinary business debt) that carried a right to convert into, or to acquire, shares which would fall within (i) above.

'*Relevant preference shares*' were, broadly, non-voting, non-convertible shares issued for new consideration and carrying no right to dividends other than dividends which:

(A) were of a fixed amount or at a rate which was fixed or which varies according to a standard published interest rate, a tax rate, a retail price index or an official share price index; and
(B) which were not dependent on the company's business results or asset values and did not represent more than a reasonable commercial return on the investment.

[*FA 2000, Sch 15 paras 5, 7, 9, 102(3)*].

No reciprocal arrangements requirement

The investing company's subscription for the relevant shares had not to be part of any arrangements which provide for any other person to subscribe for shares in a 'related company'. A '*related company*' was a company in which the investing company, or any other person who was party to the arrangements, has a 'material interest' (as defined immediately above). Arrangements were disregarded to the extent that they provide for the issuing company to subscribe for shares in any qualifying subsidiary (see **28.6** below). [*FA 2000, Sch 15 para 6*].

No control requirement

At no time in the qualification period (see **28.2** above) had to the investing company 'control' the issuing company. '*Control*' was determined in accordance with *ICTA 1988, s 416(2)–(6)* (see **22.6 CLOSE COMPANIES**) as modified for this purpose. [*FA 2000, Sch 15 para 8*].

No tax avoidance requirement

The relevant shares had to be subscribed for by the investing company for commercial reasons and not as part of a tax avoidance scheme or arrangement. [*FA 2000, Sch 15 para 14*].

Non-financial activities requirement

Throughout the qualification period (see **28.2** above), the investing company:

(a) if a '*single company*' (i.e. a company which was not a parent company or a 51% subsidiary), had to exist wholly for the purpose of carrying on one or more 'non-financial trades'; and
(b) if a '*group company*' (i.e. a parent company and any of its subsidiaries), had to be part of a 'non-financial trading group' and had to either exist wholly for the purpose of carrying on one or more 'non-financial trades' or businesses other than trades or be the parent company of the group.

In determining the purpose for which a company exists, purposes having no significant effect (other than in relation to incidental matters) on the extent of the company's activities were disregarded. Purposes for which a company exists were also disregarded to the extent that they consist of:

(i) (as regards a single company) the holding and managing of property used by the company for one or more 'non-financial trades' carried on by it;
(ii) (as regards a group company) any activities within (I) or (II) below; or
(iii) (as regards any company) holding shares to which investment relief was attributable (see **28.3** above) unless the holding of such shares was a substantial part of the company's business.

A trade was a '*non-financial trade*' if:

(A) it was conducted on a commercial basis and with a view to profit; and
(B) it did not consist, wholly or as to a substantial part, in the carrying on of 'financial activities'.

'*Financial activities*' include for this purpose:

(1) banking, or money-lending, carried on by a bank, building society or other person;
(2) debt factoring, finance-leasing or hire-purchase financing;
(3) insurance;
(4) dealing in shares, securities, currency, debts or other assets of a financial nature; and
(5) dealing in commodity or financial futures or options.

A group was a '*non-financial trading group*' unless the business of the group (treating the activities of the group companies, taken together, as a single business) consists, wholly or as to a substantial part, in the carrying on of trades other than non-financial trades (as above) and/or businesses other than trades. Activities of a group company were disregarded to the extent that they consist of:

(I) holding shares in or securities of, or making loans to, another group company;

(II) holding and managing property used by a group company for the purposes of one or more non-financial trades carried on by a group company; or

(III) holding shares to which investment relief was attributable (see **28.3** above), unless the holding of such shares was a substantial part of the company's business.

Amendments to the non-financial activities requirement could be made in the future by Treasury Order.

[*FA 2000, Sch 15 paras 10–12, 101, 102(1)*].

Requirement as to shares being a chargeable asset

The relevant shares had to be a 'chargeable asset' of the investing company immediately after they were issued to it. For this purpose, an asset was a '*chargeable asset*' at a particular time if, on a disposal at that time, a gain would be a chargeable gain. [*FA 2000, Sch 15 para 13*].

Qualifying issuing company

[28.6] The issuing company was a '*qualifying issuing company*' (see **28.2**(c) above) in relation to the relevant shares if it met all the requirements below as to unquoted status, independence, individual-owners, partnerships and joint ventures, qualifying subsidiaries, property managing subsidiaries, gross assets, trading activities and, on or after **19 July 2007** or later, number of employees. [*FA 2000, Sch 15 para 15; FA 2004, Sch 20 para 3*].

Unquoted status requirement

At the time of issue of the relevant shares, none of the issuing company's shares, debentures or other securities had to be listed on a recognised stock exchange or a 'designated' exchange outside the UK or be dealt in outside the UK by 'designated' means, and there had to be no arrangements in existence for such a listing or such dealing. This applies whether or not the company was UK-resident. '*Designated*' means designated by order of HMRC for the purposes of *ICTA 1988, s 312(1B)* (enterprise investment schemes, see Tolley's Income Tax). The company does not fail to meet the requirement simply because a designation order was made, or a stock exchange obtained recognition, after the time of issue of the shares.

If, at the time of issue of the relevant shares, arrangements were in existence for the issuing company to become a wholly-owned subsidiary of a new holding company by means of a share exchange within **28.24** below, there had to be no arrangements made for any of the new company's shares, debentures or other securities to be listed or dealt in as above.

[*FA 2000, Sch 15 para 16*].

Independence requirement

At no time in the qualification period (see **28.2** above) had the issuing company to be a 51% subsidiary of another company or otherwise under the control (within *ICTA 1988, s 840*) of another company or of another company and persons connected with it (within *ICTA 1988, s 839*, see **25 CONNECTED PERSONS**). No arrangements had to exist at any time during the qualification period whereby the company could become such a subsidiary or fall under such control (whether during that period or otherwise). Arrangements with a view to a company reconstruction within **28.24** below were disregarded for this purpose. [*FA 2000, Sch 15 paras 17, 102(3)*].

Individual-owners requirement

Throughout the qualification period (see **28.2** above), at least **20%** of the issued ordinary share capital of the issuing company had to be beneficially owned by one or more 'independent individuals'. An '*independent individual*' was one who was not, at any time during the qualification period when he holds ordinary shares in the issuing company, a director or employee of the investing company or of any company connected with it (within *ICTA 1988, s 839*, see **25 CONNECTED PERSONS**), or a relative (i.e. spouse or (from 5 December 2005) civil partner, forebear or issue) of such a director or employee. Where an independent individual owned shares immediately prior to his death, they were treated for these purposes as continuing to be owned by an independent individual until they cease to form part of the deceased's estate. [*FA 2000, Sch 15 paras 18, 102(3); SI 2005 No 3229, Reg 132*].

Partnerships and joint ventures requirement

At no time in the qualification period (see **28.2** above) had the issuing company or any qualifying subsidiary (see below) been a member of a partnership or a party to a joint venture where:

(a) a trade by reference to which the trading activities requirement (see below) was met by the issuing company was being carried on, or was to be carried on, by the partners in partnership or, as the case could be, by the company or a qualifying subsidiary (see below) as a party to the joint venture;
(b) the other partners or parties to the joint venture include at least one other company; and
(c) the same person(s) was/were the beneficial owner(s) of more than 75% of the issued share capital or the ordinary share capital of both the issuing company and at least one of the other partners/parties.

For these purposes, there had to be attributed to any person any share capital held by an associate of his (within *FA 2000, Sch 15 para 99*).

[*FA 2000, Sch 15 para 19*].

Qualifying subsidiaries requirement

At no time in the qualification period (see **28.2** above) had the issuing company to have a 'subsidiary' other than a 'qualifying subsidiary'. For this purpose, a '*subsidiary*' of a company was any company which it controls (within *ICTA 1988, s 416(2)–(6)*, see **22.6 CLOSE COMPANIES**), with or without the aid of **CONNECTED PERSONS** (**25**). A subsidiary was a '*qualifying subsidiary*' of another company (the '*relevant company*') if the following conditions were met:

(i) *in relation to shares issued on or after 17 March 2004*, the subsidiary was a 51% subsidiary (within *ICTA 1988, s 838*) of the relevant company;

(ii) *in relation to shares issued before 17 March 2004*, the relevant company, or another of its subsidiaries, possesses at least 75% of the issued share capital of, and the voting power in, the subsidiary, and was beneficially entitled to at least 75% of the assets available for distribution to shareholders on a winding-up etc. and of the profits available for distribution to shareholders; and

(iii) in either (i) or (ii) above, no other person has control (within *ICTA 1988, s 840*) of the subsidiary; and no arrangements exist whereby any of these conditions could cease to be satisfied (though see also below).

The fact that a subsidiary or another company was wound up or otherwise dissolved or went into administration or receivership (both as defined) did not mean the subsidiary ceased to be a qualifying subsidiary, provided that the winding-up etc., and anything done as a consequence of administration or receivership, was for genuine commercial reasons and not part of a tax avoidance scheme or arrangements. Similarly, the fact that arrangements could exist to dispose of the entire interest held in the subsidiary did not prevent the subsidiary from being a qualifying subsidiary of the relevant company if the disposal was to be for commercial reasons and was not to be part of a tax avoidance scheme or arrangements.

[*FA 2000, Sch 15 paras 20, 21, 102(3)(4); FA 2004, s 95, Sch 20 paras 4, 5, 15, Sch 42 Pt 2(12)*].

Property managing subsidiaries requirement

In relation to shares issued after 16 March 2004, the issuing company had not to have, at any time in the qualification period, a 'property managing subsidiary' other than one which was its 'qualifying 90% subsidiary'. For this purpose, a '*property managing subsidiary*' was a qualifying subsidiary (see above) whose business consists wholly or mainly in the holding or managing of land or any property deriving its value from land (and the terms 'land' and 'property deriving its value from land' have the same meaning as in *ICTA 1988, s 776*, see **5.16 ANTI-AVOIDANCE**). [*FA 2000, Sch 15 para 21A; FA 2004, Sch 20 paras 6, 15*].

Qualifying 90% subsidiary

A subsidiary was a '*qualifying 90% subsidiary*' of the issuing company if the following conditions were met.

(1) The issuing company possesses at least 90% of the issued share capital of, and the voting power in, the subsidiary, and was beneficially entitled to at least 90% of the assets available for distribution to shareholders on a winding-up etc. and of the profits available for distribution to shareholders;

(2) No other person had control (within *ICTA 1988, s 840*) of the subsidiary; and

(3) No arrangements existed whereby (1) or (2) could cease to be satisfied (though see also below).

The fact that a subsidiary or another company was wound up or otherwise dissolved or went into administration or receivership (both as defined) did not mean the subsidiary ceased to be a qualifying 90% subsidiary of the issuing company, provided that the winding-up etc., and anything done as a consequence of administration or receivership, was for genuine commercial reasons and not part of a tax avoidance scheme or arrangements. Similarly, the fact that arrangements could exist to dispose of the entire interest held in the subsidiary did not prevent the subsidiary from being a qualifying 90% subsidiary of the issuing company if the disposal was to be for commercial reasons and was not to be part of a tax avoidance scheme or arrangements.

On or after 6 April 2007, a company (company A) was also a qualifying 90% subsidiary of the issuing company if:

- company A would be a qualifying 90% subsidiary of another company (company B) if company B were the issuing company, and company B was a 'qualifying 100% subsidiary' of the issuing company; or
- company A was a qualifying 100% subsidiary of company B and company B was a qualifying 90% subsidiary of the issuing company.

No account was taken for this purpose of any control the issuing company could have of company A. The definition of a qualifying 90% subsidary was used to define a 'qualifying 100% subsidiary', replacing the references in that definition to 'at least 90%' with references to '100%'.

[*FA 2000, Sch 15 para 23(10)(11); FA 2004, Sch 20 paras 7(d), 15; FA 2007, Sch 16 para 14*].

Gross assets requirement

The value of the company's gross assets had not to exceed £7 million immediately before the issue of the relevant shares or £8 million immediately afterwards. If the company was the parent company of a group, those limits apply by reference to the aggregate value of the gross assets of the group (disregarding certain assets held by any member of the group which correspond to liabilities of another member). The limits could be amended in the future by Treasury Order. [*FA 2000, Sch 15 paras 22, 101; FA 2006, Sch 14 para 3*].

The general approach of HMRC was that the value of a company's gross assets was the sum of the value of all the balance sheet assets. Where accounts were actually drawn up to a date immediately before or after the issue, the balance sheet values were taken provided that they reflect usual accounting standards and the company's normal accounting practice, consistently applied. Where accounts were not drawn up to such a date, such values will be taken from the most recent balance sheet, updated as precisely as practicable on the basis of all the relevant information available to the company. Values so arrived at might need to be reviewed in the light of information contained in the accounts for the period in which the issue was made, and, if they were not available at the time of the issue, those for the preceding period, when they become available. The company's assets immediately before the issue did not include any advance payment received in respect of the issue. Where shares were issued partly paid, the right to the balance was an asset, and, notwithstanding the above, would be taken into account in valuing the assets immediately after the issue regardless of whether it was stated in the balance sheet. (HMRC Statement of Practice, SP 2/06 — which supercedes SP2/00).

Trading activities requirement

Throughout the qualification period (see **28.2** above), the issuing company had to meet the trading activities requirement, which was as follows. If the company was a single company (i.e. neither the parent company of a group nor a subsidiary), it had to exist wholly for the purpose of carrying on one or more 'qualifying trades' (see **28.7** below) and had to actually be carrying on such a trade or preparing to do so. Purposes having no significant effect (other than in relation to incidental matters) on the extent of the company's activities were disregarded. For the ascertainment of the purposes for which a company exists, see HMRC Venture Capital Schemes Manual, VCM15070, VCM50140.

If the company was a parent company, the business of the group (treating the activities of the group companies, taken together, as a single business) had to not consist wholly or as to a substantial part (i.e. broadly 20%, but see HMRC Venture Capital Schemes Manual, VCM17040, VCM50140) in any 'non-qualifying activities', and at least one company in the group had to satisfy the above trading activity requirement for a single company. '*Non-qualifying activities*' means 'excluded activities' (as in **28.7** below, and with similar exceptions in relation to the letting of ships and the receiving of royalties or licence fees) and non-trading activities.

Where the trading activities requirement would otherwise be met by reason of the company *preparing* to carry on a qualifying trade, the requirement was treated as not having been met at any time if that trade does not commence within two years after the issue of the relevant shares. In determining when the trade begins for this purpose, the carrying on of any trade by a subsidiary before it became a qualifying 90% subsidiary was to be disregarded.

Purposes for which a company exists were disregarded to the extent that they consist of:

(A) (as regards a single company) the holding and managing of property used by the company for one or more qualifying trades carried on by it;
(B) (as regards a group company) any activities within (1), (2) or (4) below; or
(C) (as regards any company) holding shares to which investment relief was attributable (see **28.3** above), unless the holding of such shares was a substantial part of the company's business.

For the purposes of determining the business of a group, activities of a group company were disregarded to the extent that they consist of:

(1) holding shares in or securities of, or making loans to, another group company;
(2) holding and managing property used by a group company for the purposes of one or more qualifying trades carried on by a group company;

(3) holding shares to which investment relief was attributable (see **28.3** above), unless the holding of such shares was a substantial part of the company's business; or

(4) incidental activities of a company which met the above trading activities requirement for a single company.

A company does not cease to meet the trading activities requirement purely by reason of it or a qualifying subsidiary (see above) being wound up or otherwise dissolved, provided that the winding-up or dissolution was for commercial reasons and not part of a tax avoidance scheme or arrangements. A similar let-out applies in relation to a company or its qualifying subsidiary going into administration or receivership (both as defined) and to anything done as a consequence thereof.

Amendments to the trading activities requirement (including the provisions at **28.7** below) could be made in the future by Treasury Order.

[*FA 2000, Sch 15 paras 23, 24, 101, 102(1)(4)(8); FA 2004, Sch 20 paras 7, 8, 13, 15, Sch 27 para 6(2), Sch 42 Pt 2(12)*].

The corporation tax liability of a qualifying issuing company, and the monitoring of the company during the qualifying period, will be dealt with by the Small Company Enterprise Centre, Ty Glas, Llanishen, Cardiff CF14 5ZG (tel. 029–2032 7400; fax 029–2032 7398; e-mail enterprise.centre@ir.gsi.gov.uk).

Number of employees requirement

When the shares were issued and the company was not part of a group, it had to have a full-time equivalent of less than 50 employees. Where the company was the parent company of a group, the total full-time equivalent employees of it and all its subsidiaries had to be less then 50 when the shares were issued. For this purpose, directors were included as employees but those on maternity or paternity leave or students on vocational training were not included. Full-time equivalents were to be calculated by adding to the number of full-time employees a just and reasonable fraction for each part-time employee.

[*FA 2000 Sch 15 para 22A; FA 2007 Sch 16 para 1*].

Qualifying trades

[28.7] A trade was a '*qualifying trade*' if it was conducted on a commercial basis with a view to the realisation of profits and it does not, at any time in period B (as defined) consist to a substantial extent in the carrying on of 'excluded activities'. '*Period B*' for these purposes was broadly the period beginning with the date of issue of the shares and ending three years after that date. For these purposes, 'trade' (except in relation to the trade mentioned in (p) below) does not include a venture in the nature of trade. '*Excluded activities*' were:

(a) dealing in land, commodities or futures, or in shares, securities or other financial instruments;

(b) dealing in goods otherwise than in an ordinary trade of wholesale or retail distribution (see below);

(c) banking, insurance or any other financial activities;
(d) (before 7 March 2001) oil extraction activities (but without prejudice to relief in respect of oil exploration above) for which the activities would otherwise qualify);
(e) leasing or letting or receiving royalties or licence fees;
(f) providing legal or accountancy services;
(g) 'property development';
(h) farming or market gardening;
(i) holding, managing or occupying woodlands, any other forestry activities or timber production;
(j) operating or managing hotels or comparable establishments (i.e. guest houses, hostels and other establishments whose main purpose was to offer overnight accommodation with or without catering) or property used as such;
(k) operating or managing nursing homes or residential care homes (both as defined) or property used as such;
(l) shipbuilding (as defined for the EU Framework on state aid to shipbuilding (2003/C 317/06)) — where the shares were issued on or after 6 April 2008;
(m) producing and extracting coal (per Article 2 of Council Regulations (EC) No 1407/2002) — where the shares were issued on or after 6 April 2008;
(n) producing steel (per Annex 1 to guidelines on national regional aid 2006/C54/08) — where the shares were issued on or after 6 April 2009; or
(o) providing services or facilities for any trade, profession or vocation concerned in (a) to (o) and carried on by another person (other than a parent company), where one person has a 'controlling interest' in both trades.

However, these three exclusions were not retrospective and a company with trades comprising of shipbuilding, coal or steel production could still qualify if the funds were raised before 6 April 2008.

As regards (f) above, the provision of the services of accountancy personnel was the provision of accountancy services (*Castleton Management Services Ltd v Kirkwood* (Sp C 276), [2001] SSCD 95).

Exclusions (k) and (l) applied only if the person carrying on the activity in question has an estate or interest (e.g. a lease) in the property concerned or occupies that property.

HMRC regarded as 'substantial' for the above purposes a part of a trade which consisted of 20% or more of total activities, judged by any reasonable measure (normally turnover or capital employed). (HMRC Venture Capital Schemes Manual VCM17040). As regards (a) above, dealing in land includes cases where steps were taken, before selling the land, to make it more attractive to a purchaser; such steps might include the refurbishment of existing buildings. (HMRC Venture Capital Schemes Manual VCM17050).

As regards (b) above, a trade of wholesale distribution was a trade consisting of the offer of goods for sale either to persons for resale (or processing and resale) (which resale had to be to members of the general public for their use or consumption) by them. A trade of retail distribution was a trade in which goods were offered or exposed for sale and sold to members of the general public for their use or consumption. A trade was not an ordinary wholesale or retail trade if it consists to a substantial extent of dealing in goods collected or held as an investment (or of that and any other activity within (a)–(p) above), and a substantial proportion of such goods was held for a significantly longer period than would reasonably be expected for a vendor trying to dispose of them at market value. Whether such trades were 'ordinary' was to be judged having regard to the following features, those under (A) supporting the categorisation as 'ordinary', those under (B) being indicative to the contrary.

(A)

- (i) The breaking of bulk.
- (ii) The purchase and sale of goods in different markets.
- (iii) The employment of staff and incurring of trade expenses other than the cost of goods or of remuneration of persons connected (within *ICTA 2007, s 839*) with a company carrying on such a trade.

(B)

- (i) The purchase or sale of goods from or to persons connected (within *ICTA 1988, s 839*) with the trader.
- (ii) The matching of purchases with sales.
- (iii) The holding of goods for longer than would normally be expected.
- (iv) The carrying on of the trade at a place not commonly used for wholesale or retail trading.
- (v) The absence of physical possession of the goods by the trader.

As regards the application of (e) above in relation to shares issued after 5 April 2000, a trade was not excluded from being a qualifying trade solely because at some time in period B it consists to a substantial extent in the receiving of royalties or licence fees substantially attributable (in terms of value) to the exploitation of 'relevant intangible assets'.

A '*relevant intangible asset*' was an 'intangible asset' the whole or greater part of which (by value) had been created by the issuing company or by a company which was a qualifying subsidiary (as defined) of the issuing company throughout the period during which it created the whole or greater part (by value) of the asset. For this purpose only, '*issuing company*' included a company all of whose shares were acquired by the issuing company at a time when the only shares issued in the issuing company were subscriber shares and the consideration for the acquisition consisted wholly in the issue of shares in the issuing company. Before 6 April 2007, the whole or greater part of the asset had to be created by the company carrying on the trade or by a company which throughout the creation of the asset was the 'holding company' of that company or a qualifying subsidiary of that holding company. In relation to shares issued before 6 April 2007, an activity was not treated as an excluded activity if it would otherwise have become such an activity on or after that date by reason only of the change in this definition.

A '*holding company*' was for these purposes a company with one or more 51% subsidiaries which was not itself a 51% subsidiary. Where the asset was 'intellectual property', it was treated as created by a company only if the right to exploit it vests in that company (alone or with others). The term '*intellectual property*' incorporates patents, trade marks, copyrights, design rights etc. and foreign equivalents. An '*intangible asset*' was an asset falling to be treated as such under generally accepted accounting practice, including all intellectual property and also industrial information and techniques (see HMRC Venture Capital Schemes Manual VCM17310).

As regards the application of (e) above in relation to shares issued before 6 April 2000, a company engaged throughout period B in the production of original master films, tapes or discs was not excluded from the scheme by reason only of its receipt by way of trade of royalties or licence fees, provided that all royalties and licence fees received by it in the relevant period were in respect of films etc. produced by it in that period or in respect of by-products arising therefrom. The company could also be engaged in the distribution of films produced by it in period B. Similarly, royalties and licence fees attributable to research and development which a company carrying on a trade has engaged in throughout the period B do not prevent the trade being a qualifying trade.

Also as regards (e) above, a trade would not be excluded by reason only of its consisting of letting ships, other than offshore installations (previously oil rigs) or pleasure craft (as defined), on charter, provided that:

(i) the company beneficially owns all the ships it so lets;
(ii) every ship beneficially owned by the company was UK-registered;
(iii) throughout period B, the company was solely responsible for arranging the marketing of the services of its ships; and
(iv) in relation to every letting on charter, certain conditions as to length and terms of charter, and the arm's length character of the transaction, were fulfilled,

and if any of (i)–(iv) above was not fulfilled in relation to certain lettings, the trade was not thereby excluded if those lettings and any other excluded activities taken together do not amount to a substantial part of the trade.

For HMRC's views on the scope of the exclusions in relation to (e) above, see Revenue Tax Bulletin August 2001 pp 877, 878.

'*Property development*' in (g) above meant the development of land by a company, which has (or has had at any time) an 'interest in the land' (as defined), with the sole or main object of realising a gain from the disposal of an interest in the developed land.

As regards (m) above, a person has a '*controlling interest*' in a trade etc. carried on by a company if:

- he controls (within *ICTA 1988, s 416*) the company; or
- if the company was close and he or an 'associate' was a director of the company and the owner of, or able to control, more than 30% of its ordinary share capital; or
- if at least half of its ordinary share capital was directly or indirectly owned by him.

In any other case a controlling interest was obtained by such a person being entitled to at least half of the assets used for, or income arising from, the trade etc. In either case, the rights and powers of a person's 'associates' were attributed to him. An '*associate*' of any person was any 'relative' (i.e. spouse, civil partner, ancestor or linear descendant) of that person, the trustee(s) of any settlement in relation to which that person or any relative (living or dead) was or was a settler and, where that person has an interest in any shares or obligations of a company which were subject to any trust or were part of a deceased estate, the trustee(s) of the settlement or the personal representatives of the deceased and, if that person was a company, any other company which has an interest in those shares or obligations. For this purpose, 'settlor' was defined as in *ICTA 1988, ss 685A–D*.

[*ICTA 1988, ss 297, 298, 312; FA 2004, Sch 27 para 4; FA 2007, Sch 16 paras 11(1)(7), 13, 14; FA 2008, Sch 11 paras 1–3, 10, 11*].

The Treasury could, by statutory instrument, amend any of the above provisions.

[*ICTA 1988, s 298(4)*].

General requirements

[28.8] For investment relief to be available in respect of the relevant shares (see **28.2** above), the following requirements (see **28.2**(d) above) had to be met as to the shares, the use of money raised by the issue, the absence of pre-arranged exits, the absence of a tax avoidance motive and the maximum amount raised annually through risk capital schemes. [*FA 2000, Sch 15 para 34*].

The shares

The relevant shares had to be ordinary, fully paid up shares and had to be subscribed for wholly in cash. Shares were not fully paid up for this purpose if there was any undertaking to pay cash to the issuing company at a future date or, in relation to shares issued on or after 17 March 2004, to any person at a future date in respect of the shares (i.e. the whole of the subscription price had to actually have been paid at the time of issue, see HMRC Venture Capital Schemes Manual, VCM50020). At no time in the qualification period (see **28.2** above) had the shares to carry any present or future preferential right to dividends or to assets on a winding-up, or any present or future right to be redeemed. [*FA 2000, Sch 15 para 35; FA 2004, Sch 20 paras 10, 15*].

Use of money raised

For shares issued on or after 22 April 2009, 100% of the money raised by the share issue had to be wholly employed (disregarding any insignificant amount) within two years of the date of issue or, if later, of beginning to carry on the relevant trade. For shares issued before that date, at least 80% of the money raised by the 'relevant issue of shares' had to be employed wholly (disregarding any insignificant amount) for the purposes of a 'relevant trade' not later than

12 months from the date of issue or, if later, 12 months from the commencement of the relevant trade by the issuing company or a 90% subsidiary. The balance must have been used within 24 months. In determining when the trade begins for this purpose in relation to shares issued on or after 17 March 2004, the carrying on of any trade by a subsidiary before it became a qualifying 90% subsidiary was to be disregarded.

For these purposes, employing money for the purposes of *preparing* to carry on a trade (other than a notional trade of research and development — see **28.7** above) was equivalent to employing it for the purposes of a trade. Money whose retention could reasonably be regarded as necessary or advisable for financing current trade requirements was regarded as employed for trade purposes (see HMRC Venture Capital Schemes Manual, VCM12080, VCM50030).

The '*relevant issue of shares*' means the issue of shares which includes the relevant shares. A '*relevant trade*' was a trade by reference to which the issuing company meets the trading activities requirement in **28.6** above. Where the trade by reference to which the trading activities requirement was met was a notional trade of research and development (see **28.7** above), the term 'relevant trade' also refers to any qualifying trade which was derived or benefits from that notional trade and was carried on by the issuing company or a qualifying 90% subsidiary (or, in relation to shares issued before 17 March 2004, a qualifying subsidiary, see **28.6** above); in this case, the 80% requirement referred to above does not apply, and all the money raised by the issue had to be employed for the purposes of that trade before the third anniversary of the date of issue of the shares, notwithstanding that a later date could be given by virtue of (b) above.

[*FA 2000, Sch 15 paras 36, 102(8); FA 2004, Sch 20 paras 11, 13, 15; FA 2009, s 27, Sch 8 paras 4, 8*].

No pre-arranged exits

The arrangements (as very broadly defined) under which the relevant shares were issued to the investing company (including arrangements preceding the issue but relating to it and, in certain cases, arrangements made on or after the issue and within the qualification period) had not to:

(i) provide for the eventual disposal by the investing company of the relevant shares or other shares or securities of the issuing company;
(ii) provide for the eventual cessation of a trade of the issuing company or a person connected with it;
(iii) provide for the eventual disposal of all, or a substantial part of, the assets of the issuing company or of a person connected with it; or
(iv) provide (by means of any insurance, indemnity, guarantee or otherwise) partial or complete protection for investors against the normal risks attaching to the investment (but excluding commercial arrangements which merely protect the issuing company and/or its subsidiaries against normal business risks).

Arrangements with a view to a company reconstruction within **28.24** below were excluded from (i) above. Arrangements applicable only on an unanticipated winding-up of the issuing company for commercial reasons were excluded from (ii) and (iii) above.

[*FA 2000, Sch 15 paras 37, 102(1)*].

No tax avoidance motive

The relevant shares had to be issued for commercial reasons and not as part of a tax avoidance scheme or arrangement. [*FA 2000, Sch 15 para 38*].

For the year up to the date of the current issue, the amount of 'relevant investments' made in the issuing company (or in any company which was a subsidiary at any time in the year) had not to exceed £2 million. A '*relevant investment*' in a company was one which was made by a VCT or under a corporate venturing or EIS arrangement. VCT investments made before 6 April 2007 or from 'protected money' were not included. '*Protected money*' was money raised by an issue of shares or securities of the VCT before 6 April 2007, or money derived from the investment of such money.

[*FA 2000 Sch 15 para 35A; FA 2007 Sch 16 paras 4, 8*].

Advance clearance

[28.9] A *potential* qualifying issuing company (see **28.6** above) could apply to HMRC for an advance clearance notice in respect of an issue of shares. An application had to contain particulars, declarations and undertakings as required and had to disclose all material facts and circumstances. An advance clearance notice states that, on the basis of the particulars etc. provided by the applicant, HMRC were satisfied that, at the time the shares were issued, the requirements of **28.6–28.8** above would be met (or, in the case of a requirement that could only be met in the future, will for the time being be met).

Applications for clearance had to be sent to: Small Company Enterprise Centre, Centre for Research and Intelligence (CRI), Ty Glas, Llanishen, Cardiff CF14 5ZG; telephone: 02920 327400; e-mail: Enterprise.centre@hmrc.gsi.gov.uk. For guidance on HMRC requirements as to content of applications for advance clearance, the information and documents needed and the undertakings required, see HMRC Statement of Practice, SP 1/00. Where subscribers to the same issue of shares were expected to include individuals who could wish to claim relief under the Enterprise Investment Scheme (see Tolley's Income Tax under Enterprise Investment Scheme), any request for informal clearance under that scheme should accompany the application under the Corporate Venturing Scheme.

Within 30 days after receiving an application (or within 30 days after an 'information notice' was complied with), HMRC had to either issue an information notice (or further information notice), issue an advance clearance notice, or refuse the application. An '*information notice*' was a notice requiring further particulars to be provided within such time, not being less than 30 days, as was stated therein. If the applicant fails to comply timeously with an information notice, HMRC need not proceed further with the application. If the shares in question were issued before the advance clearance notice was given or the application refused, then again HMRC need not proceed further.

Within 30 days after a refusal of an application, or a failure to give a decision, the applicant could require HMRC to transmit the application, together with any information notices given and further particulars provided, to the Special Commissioners, whose approval, if given, has effect as if it were an advance clearance notice given by HMRC.

An advance clearance notice was rendered void if it transpires that any particulars provided did not fully and accurately disclose all facts and circumstances material for the decision, or if the applicant or any subsidiary (including any new subsidiary) fails to act in accordance with any declaration or undertaking given as part of the application.

[*FA 2000, Sch 15 paras 89–92*].

Withdrawal or reduction of investment relief

[28.10] Investment relief falls to be withdrawn or reduced on a disposal of the relevant shares (see **28.11** below), if value was received in respect of the shares (see **28.12–28.15** below), or on the grant of certain options relating to the shares (see **28.16** below).

Where investment relief given falls to be withdrawn or reduced, and also where it was found not to have been due, the withdrawal etc. was achieved by means of an assessment for the accounting period of the investing company *in which the relief was given*. For relief to be withdrawn on the grounds that the issuing company was not a qualifying issuing company (see **28.6** above), or that the general requirements at **28.8** above were not met, or by virtue of value received by the investing company (see **28.12** below) or other persons (see **28.15** below), certain statutory notice procedures had to be followed. The investing company could give notice of appeal, within 30 days, against an HMRC notice pending withdrawal of relief on such grounds (as if the giving of that notice were the disallowance of a claim other than for discharge or repayment of tax — see **21.9 CLAIMS**).

HMRC cannot make an assessment to withdraw (or reduce) investment relief, or give statutory notice pending withdrawal of relief on the above-mentioned grounds, more than six years after the end of whichever was the later of the following accounting periods:

(a) the accounting period in which falls the deadline for employing money raised by the issue of the shares (see **28.8** above); and
(b) the accounting period in which occurs the event giving rise to withdrawal (or reduction) of relief.

The above was subject to the extended time limit for assessments in cases of fraud or negligence (see **7.7 ASSESSMENTS**).

In most cases, interest on overdue tax runs from the date of the event giving rise to withdrawal (or reduction) of relief, if this was later than the normal due date, or the latest such date, for payment of corporation tax for the accounting period for which the assessment was made (see **59.3 PAYMENT OF TAX**).

[*FA 2000, Sch 15 paras 60–63; CTA 2009, Sch 1 para 463*].

Information

Certain events giving rise to withdrawal or reduction of investment relief had to be notified to HMRC, generally within 60 days, by the investing company or the issuing company (or any person connected with the issuing company and having knowledge of the matter), as the case could be. HMRC have power to require information from such persons where they have reason to believe that such notice should have been given or from a person whom they believe to have given or received value which would have triggered a requirement to give such notice but for the amount of value being insignificant (see **28.12** below). The penalty provisions of *TMA 1970, s 98* apply in the event of non-compliance with these information provisions. [*FA 2000, Sch 15 paras 64–66, Sch 16 para 1*].

Disposal

[28.11] Where, during the qualification period (see **28.2** above), the investing company disposes of any shares to which relief was attributable (see **28.3** above) and which it has held continuously since their issue (see **28.20**(a) below), relief was withdrawn or reduced as set out below. See **28.10** above re consequences of withdrawal etc.

If the disposal was either:

(a) by way of bargain at arm's length for full consideration; or
(b) by way of a distribution on a dissolution or winding-up of the issuing company; or
(c) a disposal within *TCGA 1992, s 24(1)* (entire loss, destruction etc. of asset); or
(d) a deemed disposal under *TCGA 1992, s 24(2)* (assets of negligible value),

the relief attributable to the shares disposed of was withdrawn, or was reduced by 20% of the disposal consideration (if such reduction would not amount to full withdrawal). If the relief initially obtained was less than 20% of the amount subscribed for those shares (i.e. because the company's corporation tax liability was insufficient to fully absorb the available relief), the reduction was correspondingly restricted.

In the case of any other disposal, for example a transaction not at arm's length, the relief attributable to the shares disposed of was withdrawn.

[*FA 2000, Sch 15 para 46*].

For the above purposes, shares were regarded as being disposed of if they were so regarded for the purposes of corporation tax on chargeable gains, and see also **28.23** below (certain company reconstructions and amalgamations treated as disposals). [*FA 2000, Sch 15 para 96*]. In the case of a part disposal, see **28.17** below for the rules for identifying shares disposed of.

Value received by investing company

[28.12] Subject to **28.14** below (replacement value), where during the 'period of restriction' the investing company 'receives value' (see **28.13** below), other than an 'amount of insignificant value', from the issuing company, investment relief attributable to the relevant shares was withdrawn, or was reduced by 20% of the amount of value received (if such reduction would not amount to full withdrawal). If the relief initially obtained was less than 20% of the amount subscribed for those shares (i.e. because the company's corporation tax liability was insufficient to fully absorb the available relief), the reduction was correspondingly restricted. These provisions apply equally to receipts of value by and from persons connected (within *ICTA 1988, s 839*, see **25 CONNECTED PERSONS**), at any time in the period of restriction, with the investing company or, as the case could be, the issuing company. See **28.13** below for the meaning of 'value received' and the determination of the amount of value received. See **28.10** above re consequences of withdrawal etc.

The '*period of restriction*' in relation to the relevant shares was the period beginning one year before their issue and ending at the end of the qualification period in **28.2** above.

Where two or more issues of shares have been made by the same issuing company to the same investing company, in relation to each of which investment relief was claimed, and value was received during a period of restriction relating to more than one such issue, the value received was apportioned between them by reference to the amounts subscribed for each of those issues.

An '*amount of insignificant value*' was an amount of value which:

(a) did not exceed £1,000; or
(b) was insignificant in relation to the amount subscribed by the investing company for the relevant shares.

If at any time in the period beginning one year before the date of issue of the relevant shares and ending with the date of issue, there were in existence arrangements (as very broadly defined) providing for the investing company to receive, or become entitled to receive, any value from the issuing company at any time in the period of restriction (see above), no amount of value received by the investing company was treated as an amount of insignificant value.

There were provisions to aggregate a receipt of value, whether insignificant or not, with amounts of insignificant value received previously, and treating that aggregate, if it was not itself an amount of insignificant value, as an amount of value received at the time of the latest actual receipt.

Where relief was withdrawn or reduced by reason of a disposal (see **28.11** above), the investing company was not treated as receiving value from the issuing company in respect of the disposal.

[*FA 2000, Sch 15 paras 47, 48, 51–53, 102(1)*].

Meaning of, and amount of, value received

[28.13] The investing company '*receives value*' from the issuing company if the latter (and see **28.12** above re connected persons):

(a) repays, redeems or repurchases any part of the investing company's holding of the issuing company's share capital or securities, or makes any payment to the investing company in respect of the cancellation of any of the issuing company's share capital or any security;

(b) repays, in pursuance of any arrangements for or in connection with the acquisition of the relevant shares, any debt owed to the investing company other than one incurred by the issuing company on or after the date of issue of the shares and otherwise than in consideration of the extinguishment of a debt incurred before that date;

(c) makes any payment to the investing company in respect of the cancellation of any debt owed to it;

(d) releases or waives any liability of the investing company to the issuing company (which it was deemed to have done if discharge of the liability was twelve months or more overdue) or discharges, or undertakes to discharge, any liability of the investing company to a third person;

(e) makes a loan or advance to the investing company which has not been repaid in full before the issue of the relevant shares; for this purpose a loan includes any debt incurred, other than an ordinary trade debt (as defined), and any debt due to a third person which was assigned to the issuing company;

(f) provides a benefit or facility for the directors or employees of the investing company or any of their associates (as defined), except in circumstances such that, if a *payment* had been made of equal value, it would have been a 'qualifying payment';

(g) disposes of an asset to the investing company for no consideration or for consideration less than market value (as defined), or acquires an asset from the investing company for consideration exceeding market value; or

(h) makes a payment to the investing company other than a 'qualifying payment'.

References above to a debt or liability do not include one which would be discharged by making a 'qualifying payment'. References to a payment or disposal include one made indirectly to, or to the order of, or for the benefit of, the person in question.

Each of the following was a '*qualifying payment*':

(i) a reasonable (in relation to their market value) payment for any goods, services or facilities provided by the investing company in the course of trade or otherwise;

(ii) the payment of interest at no more than a reasonable commercial rate on money lent;

(iii) the payment of a dividend or other distribution which represents no more than a normal return on investment;

(iv) a payment to acquire an asset at no more than its market value;

(v) a payment not exceeding a reasonable and commercial rent for property occupied; and

(vi) a payment discharging an ordinary trade debt.

The *amount of value received* was:

(A) in a case within (a), (b) or (c) above, the amount received or, if greater, the market value of the shares, securities or debt in question;
(B) in a case within (d) above, the amount of the liability;
(C) in a case within (e) above, the amount of the loan etc. less any amount repaid before the issue of the relevant shares;
(D) in a case within (f) above, the cost (net of any consideration given for it by the recipient or his associate) of providing the benefit etc.;
(E) in a case within (g) above, the difference between market value and the consideration received (if any); and
(F) in a case within (h) above, the amount of the payment.

[*FA 2000, Sch 15 paras 49, 50, 99, 102(5)*].

Replacement value

[28.14] The provisions at **28.12** above were disapplied if the person from whom the value was received (the '*original supplier*') receives, by way of a 'qualifying receipt' and whether before or after the original receipt of value, at least equivalent replacement value from the original recipient. From 7 March 2001, any reduction in the value originally received by virtue of its having been received during a period of restriction relating to more than one issue was disregarded for this purpose. Thus in any case where there was a receipt of value at a time which falls in two or more periods of restriction relating to investments made in the issuing company, investment relief will be withdrawn in respect of all those investments unless restitution was made of the whole amount of the value received. A receipt was a '*qualifying receipt*' if it arises by reason of:

(a) a payment by the original recipient to the original supplier other than an 'excepted payment' (before 7 March 2001, such a payment other than a qualifying payment as in **28.13** above or a payment for any shares or securities in any company in circumstances not within (c) below);
(b) (where the original receipt of value falls within **28.13**(d) above) an event having the effect of reversing the original event; or
(c) the acquisition of an asset by the original recipient from the original supplier for consideration exceeding market value (as defined), or the disposal of an asset by the original recipient to the original supplier for no consideration or for consideration less than market value. (Before 7 March 2001, this applied only where the original receipt of value fell within **28.13**(g) above.)

An '*excepted payment*' was:

(I) a reasonable (in relation to their market value) payment for any goods, services or facilities provided (in the course of trade or otherwise) by the original supplier;
(II) a payment of interest at no more than a reasonable commercial rate on money lent to the original recipient;
(III) a payment not exceeding a reasonable and commercial rent for property occupied by the original recipient;
(IV) a payment within **28.13**(iii), (iv) or (vi) above; or

(V) a payment for any shares or securities in any company in circumstances not within (c) above.

References in (I)–(III) above to the original supplier or recipient include a reference to any person who at any time in the period of restriction was an 'associate' of his (within *FA 2000, Sch 15 para 99*) or, in the case of an original supplier, was 'connected' with him (within *ICTA 1988, s 839*).

The amount of replacement value was:

(i) in a case within (a) above, the amount of the payment;
(ii) in a case within (b) above, the same as the amount of the original value; and
(iii) in a case within (c) above, the difference between market value and the consideration received (if any).

The receipt of replacement value was disregarded if:

(A) it occurs before the start of the period of restriction (see **28.12** above);
(B) there was an unreasonable delay in its occurrence; or
(C) it occurs more than 60 days after the relief falling to be withdrawn (or reduced) has been determined on appeal.

It was also disregarded if it has previously been set against a receipt of value for these purposes.

Where:

(1) the receipt of replacement value was a qualifying receipt (as above), and
(2) the event giving rise to the receipt was (or includes) a subscription for shares by the investing company or a person connected (within *ICTA 1988, s 839*, see **25 CONNECTED PERSONS**) with it at any time in the period of restriction,

the subscriber was not eligible for investment relief, enterprise investment scheme income tax relief (see Tolley's Income Tax) or enterprise investment scheme capital gains deferral relief (see Tolley's Capital Gains Tax) in relation to those shares or any other shares in the same issue.

[*FA 2000, Sch 15 paras 54, 55, 102(3)(5)*].

Value received by other persons

[28.15] Investment relief was withdrawn (or reduced) in certain cases of value received by persons other than the investing company (see **28.10** above re consequences of withdrawal etc.). This applied where, during the period of restriction (as in **28.12** above), the issuing company or a 'subsidiary':

(a) repays, redeems or repurchases any part of its share capital from a member (other than the investing company) unless the member thereby suffers a withdrawal or reduction of any investment relief, enterprise investment scheme income tax relief (see Tolley's Income Tax) or enterprise investment scheme capital gains deferral relief (see Tolley's Capital Gains Tax) attributable to his shares (or, from 7 March 2001, is only prevented from suffering such a withdrawal or reduction under the 'insignificant value' rules); or

(b) makes any payment to any such member in respect of the cancellation or extinguishment of any of the share capital of the issuing company or subsidiary.

The investment relief attributable to the relevant shares held by the investing company was withdrawn, or was reduced by 20% of the amount received by the member (if such reduction would not amount to full withdrawal). If the relief initially obtained was less than 20% of the amount subscribed for those shares (i.e. because the company's corporation tax liability was insufficient to fully absorb the available relief), the reduction was correspondingly restricted. The amount received was also apportioned between investing companies (by reference to amounts subscribed) where the receipt of value causes a withdrawal or reduction of more than one such company's investment relief. Where the receipt of value falls into overlapping periods of restriction in relation to more than one issue of shares which included shares to which investment relief was attributable, the value received was similarly apportioned between issues.

If the amount received by the member in question was insignificant in relation to the remaining share capital (from 7 March 2001, the remaining issued share capital) of the issuing company or, as the case might be, subsidiary, it was disregarded. In applying this test, the market value, immediately before the event concerned, of the shares to which the event relates was substituted for the amount received if this would give a greater amount. The assumption was made that the shares in question were cancelled at the time of the event. This let-out does not apply if at any time in the period beginning one year before the date of issue of the relevant shares and ending with the date of issue, there were in existence arrangements (as very broadly defined) providing for a payment within these provisions to be made, or entitlement to such a payment to come into being, at any time in the period of restriction.

For the above purposes, a '*subsidiary*' was a company which was a 51% subsidiary of the issuing company at any time in the period of restriction, whether or not at the time of receipt of value.

The above provisions do not apply to the redemption, within twelve months of issue, of any share capital of nominal value equal to the authorised minimum issued to comply with *Companies Act 1985, s 117* (or NI equivalent).

[*FA 2000, Sch 15 paras 56–58, 102(1)*].

Put options and call options

[28.16] Where there was granted during the qualification period (see **28.2** above):

(a) an option, the exercise of which would bind the grantor to purchase any of the relevant shares from the investing company; or
(b) an option, the exercise of which would bind the grantor, in this case the investing company, to sell any of the relevant shares,

investment relief attributable (see **28.3** above) to those of the relevant shares which would (on given assumptions) be treated as disposed of on exercise of the option was withdrawn. See **28.10** above re consequences of withdrawal.

[*FA 2000, Sch 15 para 59*].

Identification rules

[28.17] The rules below apply, for the purpose of identifying shares disposed of, where a company makes a part disposal of a holding of shares of the same class in the same company, and the holding includes shares to which investment relief was attributable (see **28.3** above) and which have been held continuously (see **28.20**(a) below) since the time of issue. The rules apply for the purposes of the corporate venturing scheme and for the purposes of corporation tax on chargeable gains generally. As regards the latter, the normal rules (see Tolley's Capital Gains Tax under Shares and Securities) were disapplied.

Where shares comprised in the holding have been acquired on different days, a disposal was identified with acquisitions on a first in/first out basis. In matching the shares disposed of with shares acquired on a particular day, shares to which investment relief was attributable and which have been held continuously were treated as being disposed of *after* any other shares acquired on that day.

If, on a reorganisation of share capital (e.g. a scrip issue), a new holding falls, by virtue of *TCGA 1992, s 127*, to be equated with the original shares (see Tolley's Capital Gains Tax under Shares and Securities, and see also **28.22** below), shares comprised in the new holding were deemed for the above purposes to have been acquired when the original shares were acquired.

[*FA 2000, Sch 15 para 93; FA 2006, s 72(2)(e)*].

Chargeable gains and allowable losses

[28.18] A gain on the disposal at any time by the investing company of shares to which investment relief was attributable (see **28.3** above) was a chargeable gain, though see **28.21** below as regards possibility of deferral relief. A loss on such a disposal was an allowable loss — see **28.19** below as to the computation of the loss and **28.20** below as regards possibility of setting the loss against income rather than gains. For the rules for identifying disposals with acquisitions, see **28.17** above.

Computation of allowable loss

[28.19] If a loss would otherwise accrue on a disposal by the investing company of shares to which investment relief was attributable, and the investment relief does not fall to be withdrawn (as opposed to reduced) as a result of the disposal (see **28.10** above), the company's acquisition cost for the purposes of corporation tax on chargeable gains was reduced by the amount of investment relief attributable to the shares immediately after the disposal, but not so as to convert the loss into a chargeable gain. This applied only if the condition at **28.20**(a) below (shares held continuously) was met from issue to disposal.

[*FA 2000, Sch 15 para 94*].

Set-off of allowable loss against income

[28.20] Subject to all the conditions at (a)–(c) below being satisfied and a claim being made, an allowable loss, on a disposal by the investing company of shares to which investment relief was attributable (see **28.3** above), could be set against *income* (as an alternative to setting it against chargeable gains in the normal way — see **17.3 CAPITAL GAINS**). The loss was as computed after applying the reduction at **28.19** above. The conditions were as follows.

(a) The shares had to have been held continuously by the company from time of issue to time of disposal. If, during any period:
   (i) the company was deemed under any provision of *TCGA 1992* to have disposed of and immediately reacquired the shares; or
   (ii) following a scheme of reconstruction or amalgamation within *TCGA 1992, s 136* (or which would have been within that *section* but for the provisions of *TCGA 1992, s 137(1)*, which excludes schemes effected other than for *bona fide* commercial reasons or for tax avoidance), the company was deemed by virtue of **28.23** below to have made a disposal of shares which it retained under the scheme,

   it was not treated for the purposes of the corporate venturing scheme provisions as having held the shares continuously throughout that period.
(b) The investment relief had to not fall to be withdrawn in full as a result of the disposal.
(c) The disposal had to be either:
   (i) by way of bargain at arm's length for full consideration; or
   (ii) by way of a distribution on a dissolution or winding-up of the issuing company; or
   (iii) a disposal within *TCGA 1992, s 24(1)* (entire loss, destruction etc. of asset); or
   (iv) a deemed disposal under *TCGA 1992, s 24(2)* (assets of negligible value).

The set-off was against income of the accounting period in which the loss was incurred. As regards any unrelieved balance, the claim could be extended to income of accounting periods ending within the 12 months immediately preceding the accounting period in which the loss was incurred. Income of an accounting period beginning before, and ending within, that 12 months was apportioned on a time basis so as to exclude income thereby deemed to have accrued prior to that 12-month period. The income of each accounting period included in the claim was treated as reduced by the loss, or by so much of it as cannot be relieved in a later accounting period. Where claims were made to relieve two or more losses, they were relieved in the order in which they were incurred. Relief was given before any relief claimed under *ICTA 1988, s 573* (loss incurred by investment company on disposal of unlisted shares — see **55.17 LOSSES**) and before any deduction for charges on income or other amounts which could be deducted from or set against or treated as reducing profits of any description. Once relief has been obtained under these provisions for an amount of loss, that amount cannot be relieved under *s 573(2)* or against chargeable gains.

Claims had to be made within two years after the end of the accounting period in which the loss was incurred.

Where a claim was made under these provisions, *TCGA 1992, s 30* (value shifting to give tax-free benefit, see **17.36 CAPITAL GAINS**) has effect in relation to the disposal if *any* benefit was conferred, whether tax-free or not. No loss relief against income was available if the disposal was the result of a scheme of reconstruction effected for tax avoidance rather than commercial reasons. [*FA 2000, Sch 15 paras 67–72, 97*].

Deferral relief

[28.21] Deferral relief was available where a chargeable gain would otherwise accrue to the investing company:

(a) on a disposal of shares to which investment relief was attributable (see **28.3** above) immediately before the disposal and which satisfy the condition at **28.20**(a) above (shares held continuously) from issue to disposal; or

(b) on the occurrence of a chargeable event under these provisions (see below),

and the company makes a 'qualifying investment'. A '*qualifying investment*' was a subscription for shares ('*qualifying shares*') on which investment relief was obtained under the corporate venturing scheme, other than shares issued by a 'prohibited company'. The qualifying shares had to be issued to the investing company within the one year immediately preceding or the three years immediately following the time the chargeable gain in question accrues. If the qualifying shares were issued *before* the gain accrued, they had to have been held continuously (see **28.20**(a) above) by the investing company from issue until the time the gain accrues, and investment relief had to still be attributable to them. A '*prohibited company*' means either:

(i) the company whose shares were disposed of (as in (a) above) or, or as the case could be, in relation to whose shares the chargeable event occurred (as in (b) above); or

(ii) a company which, when the gain accrues or when the qualifying shares were issued, was a member of the same group as the company in (i) above.

Deferral relief was said to be 'attributable to shares' if expenditure on those shares has been used to defer the whole or part of a chargeable gain and no chargeable event has occurred resulting in the deferred gain being brought back into charge.

The following themselves become qualifying shares:

(A) any bonus shares, issued in respect of the qualifying shares and being shares in the same company, of the same class and carrying the same rights;

(B) any shares issued on a company reconstruction within **28.24** below in exchange for qualifying shares.

Postponement of the original gain

On a claim by the investing company, the whole or part of the chargeable gain could be deferred. The amount to be deferred was the lower of:

(I) the amount of the gain (or the amount remaining in charge after any previous deferral relief claim);
(II) the amount subscribed for the qualifying shares (to the extent that it has not been used in previous deferral relief claims); and
(III) the amount specified by the company in the claim.

No time limit was specified for making a claim, so the general six-year time limit applies as in **21.8** claims.

Deferred gain becoming chargeable

The deferred gain will become chargeable on the occurrence of, *and at the time of*, one of the following chargeable events:

(1) a disposal of qualifying shares by the investing company; or
(2) any other event giving rise to a withdrawal of, or reduction in, the investment relief attributable to qualifying shares (see **28.10** above).

If the qualifying investment was made before the gain accrues, there was disregarded for the purposes of (2) above any reduction made by reason of an event occurring before the gain accrues.

The chargeable gain accruing to the investing company at the time of the chargeable event was equal to so much of the deferred gain as was attributable to the shares in relation to which the chargeable event occurs. For these purposes, a proportionate part of the net deferred gain (i.e. the deferred gain less any amount brought into charge on an earlier chargeable event, e.g. a part disposal) was attributed to each of the qualifying shares held immediately before the chargeable event. Thus, a part disposal of qualifying shares brought into charge a proportionate part of the deferred gain.

Provision was made to ensure that a previously deferred gain accruing as above was brought into charge under *TCGA 1992, s 10B* (see **65.6 RESIDENCE**) in the case of a non-UK resident company carrying on a trade or vocation through a permanent establishment in the UK.

[*FA 2000, Sch 15 paras 73–79; FA 2003, Sch 27 para 8*].

Company restructuring

Reorganisations of share capital

[28.22] The following applies where a company holds shares in another company, being shares of the same class, held in the same capacity and forming part of the ordinary share capital of that other company, and there was a reorganisation within the meaning of *TCGA 1992, s 126*. If the shares fall within two or more of the categories below, *TCGA 1992, s 127*, or, where appropriate, *TCGA 1992, s 116*, applies separately to each category. (This was subject to the disapplication of those provisions in the circumstances set out below.) The categories were:

(a) shares to which deferral relief was attributable (see **28.21** above);
(b) shares to which investment relief, but not deferral relief, was attributable (see **28.3** above) and which have been held continuously (see **28.20**(a) above) by the company since they were issued; and
(c) shares in neither of the categories above.

[*FA 2000, Sch 15 para 80*].

Rights issues etc. Where:

(i) a reorganisation (within *TCGA 1992, s 126*) involves an allotment of shares or debentures in respect of and in proportion to an existing holding;
(ii) investment relief was attributable (see **28.3** above) to the shares in the existing holding or to the allotted shares; and
(iii) if investment relief was attributable to the shares in the existing holding, those shares have been held continuously (see **28.20**(a) above) by the company since they were issued,

the share reorganisation rules of *TCGA 1992, ss 127–130* were disapplied. The effect was that the allotted shares were treated as a separate holding acquired at the time of the reorganisation. This does not apply in the case of bonus shares where these were issued in respect of shares comprised in the existing holding and were of the same class and carry the same rights as those shares.

If, in a case otherwise within *TCGA 1992, s 116(10)* (see Tolley's Capital Gains Tax under Qualifying Corporate Bonds):

(A) the old asset consists of shares to which investment relief was attributable and which have been held continuously (see **28.20**(a) above) by the company since they were issued; and
(B) the new asset consists of a qualifying corporate bond,

the usual treatment was disapplied. The effect was that the investing company was deemed to have disposed of the shares at the time of the relevant transaction, and the resulting chargeable gain or allowable loss crystallises *at that time*.

[*FA 2000, Sch 15 para 81*].

Company reconstructions and amalgamations

[28.23] Subject to **28.24** below, *TCGA 1992, s 135* and *s 136*, which equate the new holding with the original shares, were disapplied in the following circumstances:

(a) a company holds shares in another company (Company A);

(b) investment relief was attributable (see **28.3** above) to those shares;
(c) those shares have been held continuously (see **28.20**(a) above) by the investing company since they were issued; and
(d) there was a reconstruction or amalgamation whereby a third company issues shares or debentures in exchange for, or in respect of, Company A shares or debentures.

The result was that the transaction was treated, both for the purposes of the corporate venturing scheme provisions and for the purposes of corporation tax on chargeable gains generally, as a disposal of the original shares (and an acquisition of a new holding).

[*FA 2000, Sch 15 paras 82, 96*].

Issuing company becoming wholly-owned subsidiary of new holding company

[28.24] Notwithstanding **28.23** above, *TCGA 1992, s 135* was not disapplied (and there was thus no disposal and acquisition) where, by means entirely of an exchange of shares, all the shares in one company (the '*old shares*') were acquired by another company, and the conditions below were satisfied. Following such a share exchange, the shares thereby issued by the acquiring company (the '*new shares*') stand in place of the old shares, so that:

(i) any investment relief or deferral relief attributable to the old shares (see, respectively, **28.3**, **28.21** above) was attributed to the new shares for which they were exchanged;
(ii) the new shares were treated as having been issued at the time the old shares were issued and as having been held continuously (see **28.20**(a) above) by the investing company since that time (provided the old shares had been so held);
(iii) generally speaking, anything done, or required to be done, by or in relation to the acquired company was treated as having been done etc. by or in relation to the acquiring company; and
(iv) certain of the requirements of **28.5**, **28.6** above which were met to any extent in relation to the old shares were deemed to be met to the same extent in relation to the new shares.

The conditions to be satisfied were as follows.

(a) The consideration for the old shares consisted entirely of the issue of the new shares.
(b) New shares were issued only at a time when the issued shares in the acquiring company consist entirely of subscriber shares (and any new shares already issued in consideration of old shares).
(c) The consideration for new shares of each description consisteds entirely of old shares of the 'corresponding description'.
(d) New shares of each description were issued to holders of old shares of the 'corresponding description' in respect of, and in proportion to, their holdings.
(e) Before any exchange of shares took place, HMRC have given an 'approval notification'.

For the purposes of (c) and (d) above, old and new shares were of a '*corresponding description*' if, assuming they were shares in the same company, they would be of the same class and carry the same rights. All references above to 'shares' (other than to 'subscriber shares') include references to 'securities'. An '*approval notification*' (see (e) above) was given by HMRC, on an application by either company involved, if they were satisfied that the share exchange will be effected for commercial reasons and does not form part of a scheme or arrangements to avoid liability to corporation tax or capital gains tax.

The provisions of *FA 2000, Sch 15 para 80* (see **28.22** above) were applied to a reconstruction within the above provisions where a company's holding of 'old shares' fell within more than one of the categories there mentioned.

[*FA 2000, Sch 15 paras 83–87*].

For interaction between these provisions and the exemptions relating to substantial company shareholdings, see **19.14 CAPITAL GAINS — SUBSTANTIAL SHAREHOLDINGS.**

29

Degrouping Charges

Cross-references. See also **19 CAPITAL GAINS — SUBSTANTIAL SHAREHOLDINGS**, **35 EXEMPT ORGANISATIONS**, **54.86 LOAN RELATIONSHIPS**.

Other sources. See Tolley's Capital Gains Tax.

Simon's Taxes. See C3.1, D2.3.

The pre-*FA 2011* degrouping rules

[29.1] These rules apply to all degrouping events prior to the commencement date for *FA 2011*, or prior to 1 April 2011 if an early commencement election has been made by the group. These rules also apply to any degrouping event after commencement that is not the result of a disposal of shares of the asset-holding company or of another member of that company's group.

Where a company ceasing to be a member of a group owns a chargeable asset which has been transferred to it by another group member within the preceding six years, the company leaving the group is treated as if, immediately after its acquisition of the asset, it had sold, and immediately reacquired, the asset at its then market value. There will thus be a liability on the market value at the date of the intra-group transfer less the sum of the 'no gain, no loss' transfer price and any indexation allowance due under **18.4** or, conversely, an allowable loss.

The provisions also apply to a company leaving a group holding property to which a gain on the disposal of the original asset has been carried forward under rollover relief or an asset the value of which is wholly or partly derived from the original asset. And the provisions also apply where, when the company leaves the group, an associated company also leaves the group holding the asset, property to which a gain on the disposal of the original asset has been carried forward under rollover relief or an asset the value of which is wholly or partly derived from the original asset.

For these purposes, prior to *FA 2011*, companies were associated if, by themselves, they formed a group. The definition was amended by *FA 2011, Sch 10 para 3(12)*, so that two companies are associated with each other if one is a 75% subsidiary of the other or both are 75% subsidiaries of another company.

[*TCGA 1992, s 179(3)(10)*].

Any chargeable gain or allowable loss arising is treated as accruing immediately after the beginning of the company's accounting period in which (or at the end of which) the company ceases to be a member of the group, or (if later) the time when the company actually acquires the asset from a fellow group member. See **29.17–29.28** below for certain relieving provisions.

The companies involved in the asset transfer did not, until *FA 2011*, both have to be members of the group at the time of the original transfer for this degrouping charge to apply. It was sufficient that the transferee company left the group of which the transferor company was a member at the time of transfer. Following Royal Assent to *FA 2011* (19 July 2011), the original transfer must be between companies in the same group. This is unlikely to have any practical effect as, in practice a charge could only arise under the old rules if the transfer was other than at market value and in particular if it was at no gain/no loss. (HMRC Capital Gains Manual CG45411).

In relation to assets acquired by intra-group transfer on or after 1 April 2000, the degrouping charge can apply only if the asset is a chargeable asset. Prior to *FA 2011*, this meant an asset within the charge to UK corporation tax both before and after the transfer, the precise conditions being similar to those for intra-group transfers at **18.4**. This definition was repealed by *FA 2011* and replaced by a definition that only requires the asset to be one whereby if it were disposed of, the gain would be a chargeable gain, or would have been a chargeable gain but for the substantial shareholdings exemption.

[*TCGA 1992, s 179(1A)(10A), FA 2011, Sch 10 para 3(3)*].

Where the transfer occurred before 1 April 2000 and the degrouping charge would otherwise arise on or after that date, there can be no such charge where the transferee company leaves the group whilst remaining in a wider worldwide group of which it became a member by virtue of the relaxation in the residence rules from 1 April 2000 (see **18.2**). The fact that the company may not be an effective 51% subsidiary of the principal company of the worldwide group does not prevent it being a member of that group *for so long as* it remains an effective 51% subsidiary of the company which, prior to the change in the residence requirement, was the principal company of the narrower group. (See for example HMRC Capital Gains Manual, CG45406, CG45407).

[*TCGA 1992, s 179(1)(1A)(2)(3)(4); FA 2000, Sch 29 paras 4(2)(6), 47; FA 2001, s 79; FA 2003, Sch 27 para 2(3); FA 2011, Sch 10 para 3(2)*].

The time limit for electing for 6 April 1965 value (normally two years from the end of the accounting period in which the disposal took place, *TCGA 1992, Sch 2 para 17*) is concessionarily extended. Otherwise, gains deemed to accrue under *TCGA 1992, s 179(3)* more than two years before the degrouping event would be out of time for the election. (HMRC Statement of Practice D21).

The FA 2011 rules

Commencement of the FA 2011 rules

[29.2] In general, the new rules apply to degrouping events from 19 July 2011 (i.e. a company ceases to be a member of a group after that date or ceases to satisfy the conditions in *TCGA 1992, s 179(7)* after that date). However, there are provisions whereby a group can elect that the provisions apply from 1 April 2011 (i.e. a company ceases to be a member of a group after 1 April 2011 or ceases to satisfy the conditions in *TCGA 1992, s 179(7)* after 1 April 2011).

This 'early commencement election' must be made by the principal company of the group on or by 31 March 2012 and can also be revoked on or before that date. If an election is revoked it is treated as never having been made. But if a company ceases to be a member of a group between 1 April 2011 and 19 July 2011 (*FA 2011*), an early commencement election can only be made or revoked with the consent of that company, too. That consent must accompany the election or revocation.

[*FA 2011, Sch 10 para 9(4)–(8)*].

The degrouping charge, post-FA 2011

[29.3] If the company ceases to be a member of the group by virtue of a disposal of shares (of that company, or of another group member), the basic rule does not apply and the deemed gain is, instead, added to the consideration for the main disposal (or a deemed loss deducted from that consideration). This has the effect that the impact is on the vendor company, not the target, and also means that any reliefs, such as the substantial shareholdings exemption or the reorganisation reliefs, which would apply to the vendor's chargeable gain on the disposal will now apply to that chargeable gain, as enhanced by the degrouping charge.

The new rules apply where a company ceases to be a member of a group by virtue of one or more disposals of shares of the target company of another member of the group, referred to as 'the group disposal'. The company making the disposal must either be resident in the United Kingdom or the shares must be chargeable assets of that company immediately before the disposal or the company must be subject to a gain treated as accruing under *TCGA 1992, s 13(2)*.

If none of these conditions apply, i.e. the group disposal is outside the scope of UK corporation tax, a degrouping charge might nevertheless still arise in a UK resident target company. If, had the group disposal been within the charge to UK corporation tax, that disposal would have been exempt under the substantial shareholdings exemption, then the new rules will apply to the deemed disposal and reacquisition by the target company, even though the group disposal is outside the scope of UK corporation tax.

The effect of the new rule is that, instead of the target company being subject to the chargeable gain arising on the deemed disposal or reacquisition, that gain is added to the consideration for the group disposal by the vendor company. If the result of the computation is an allowable loss, this is treated as an allowable expense of the group disposal, under *TCGA 1992, s 38* and effectively deducted from the gain arising on the group disposal.

The major impact of this is that any reliefs or exemptions which apply to the chargeable gain arising on the group disposal will apply to that chargeable gain as augmented (or reduced) by the degrouping element. While the legislation is reasonably complex, this is a practical simplification in that, prior to *FA 2011*, it was very easy to have a commercial disposal where the main disposal would be exempt under, say, the substantial shareholdings exemption but a degrouping charge would nevertheless apply in the target company in respect of assets previously transferred to it.

Interaction with Reorganisations Provisions

[29.4] A degrouping charge can arise where a company leaves a group by way of a share-for-share exchange or reconstruction transaction to which *TCGA 1992, s 127* would apply, deeming there to have been no disposal for tax purposes. In such a case, the 'no disposal' fiction is ignored in deciding whether there is a disposal to which the new rules at TC*GA 1992, s 179(3A)–(3B)* might apply.

Where, however, there is a degrouping event and *TCGA 1992, s 127* applies to the group disposal, the no disposal fiction means that there will be no chargeable gain to which the degrouping charge can be applied under the new rules. Instead, the degrouping gain is effectively held over and will enhance the chargeable gain on the eventual disposal of the new assets. Where the degrouping charge gives rise to a loss, the relevant amount will, instead, be deducted from the chargeable gain on disposal of the new holding, as if it were an allowable expense of the group disposal, under *TCGA 1992, s 38*.

Multiple Group Disposals

[29.5] Where the degrouping charge arises as a result of more than one group disposal, the vendor companies can make a joint election to allocate the degrouping charge between them. The election must be made no later than two years after the end of the first accounting period of a company in which any chargeable gain or allowable loss on a group disposal accrues and must specify the appropriate proportion of the gain in respect of each group disposal. If no election is made then the amount is divided equally between the group disposals.

Where the group disposals are of shares of more than one class, then the company may apportion any increase or deduction to the chargeable gains on the group disposal as it chooses.

[*TCGA 1992, s 179(3A)–(3H)*].

Claim for adjustment of degrouping gains

[29.6] *FA 2011* introduced a new provision whereby a claim can be made for the adjustment of the degrouping charge in cases where it would be unreasonable for such a charge to apply. The provision, at *TCGA 1992, s 179ZA*, applies where there is a gain that accrues either to the target company or to one or more vendor companies. The company to which the gain would accrue (either the vendor company or the target company) may make a claim for the gain to be reduced for all purposes of the Act by an amount that must be specified in the claim.

Where a claim is made, HMRC is required to reduce the gain by such amount as is just and reasonable, taking into account, in particular, any transaction whereby the asset holding company or an associated company acquired the asset directly or indirectly. Where a claim is admitted, the gain is treated as reduced for all purposes of the Act and the difference is also applied to the deemed disposal and reacquisition of the asset concerned, so that references to its market value are replaced by references to its market value less the amount deducted under *TCGA 1992, s 179ZA*.

The claim is to be made by the company on which the gain accrues. This is the vendor company or companies where *TCGA 1992, s 179(3A)* or *(7A)* apply, or the target company where *TCGA 1992, s 179(3)* or *(6)* apply.

Company becoming an investment trust after acquiring asset intra-group

Becoming an investment company after intra-group transfer

[29.7] Similar treatment as in **29.1** above (company leaving group) applies where a company (the '*acquiring company*') becomes an investment trust (within *CTA 2010 s 1158 et seq*; *ICTA 1988, s 842*, see **53.1 INVESTMENT**

TRUSTS) had acquired an asset from another company in its group in the previous six years, the corresponding disposal having been treated by virtue of *TCGA 1992, s 171* (intra-group transfers, see **18.4**) as a no gain/no loss disposal.

The provisions apply where, at the beginning of the accounting period in which it became an investment trust, the acquiring company owns, otherwise than as trading stock, either the asset itself or replacement property (i.e. property into which a chargeable gain on disposal of the asset has been rolled over, see **18.8**). An asset acquired is deemed for these purposes to be the same as an asset owned subsequently if the value of the latter asset is derived, wholly or partly, from the original asset (in particular where the original was a leasehold and the lessee has acquired the freehold reversion). The provisions do not apply if the acquiring company was an investment trust at the time of the corresponding disposal (in which case the no gain/no loss treatment would not have applied, see **18.4**(vi)) nor if it has been an investment trust for any intervening accounting period.

The acquiring company is treated as if, immediately after the corresponding disposal, it had sold and immediately reacquired the asset at its market value at that time. The resulting chargeable gain or allowable loss is treated as accruing immediately before the end of the acquiring company's accounting period which immediately preceded that in which it became an investment trust.

Notwithstanding normal time limits, any consequential corporation tax assessment may be made at any time within six years after the end of the accounting period in which the company became an investment trust. These provisions are disapplied if, prior to the company becoming an investment trust, the above treatment has already applied to the asset by virtue either of **29.1** or **29.8** below (company becoming a venture capital trust).

[*TCGA 1992, s 101A; FA 1998, s 133(1)(3)*].

Simon's Taxes. See **D2.315.**

Company becoming a venture capital trust after acquiring asset intra-group

Becoming a VCT after intra-group transfer

[29.8] The same treatment as in **29.7** above (company becoming an investment trust) applies where the acquiring company was granted approval as a venture capital trust (VCT) (within *ITA 2007, s 258 et seq*, *ICTA 1988, s 842AA*, see **74.2 VENTURE CAPITAL TRUSTS**) and within the previous six years it had acquired an asset intra-group by means of a no gain/no loss disposal under *TCGA 1992, s 171* (see **18.4**). The provisions apply where, at the time the approval became effective, the acquiring company owned, otherwise than as trading stock, either the asset itself (with the same rules as in **29.7** above as to derivation of assets) or replacement property (as in **29.7** above). The provisions do not apply if the acquiring company was a VCT at the time of the intra-group disposal (in which case the no gain/no loss treatment would have applied only if that disposal occurred before 17 March 1998, see **18.4**(vii)) nor if it has been a VCT at any time in the intervening period. Nor do they apply if, prior to the company becoming a VCT, the said treatment has already applied to the asset by virtue either of **29.7** above or **29.1** above (company leaving group).

The chargeable gain or allowable loss resulting from the deemed disposal at market value immediately after the intra-group transfer is treated as accruing to the acquiring company immediately before the time approval as a VCT became effective.

Notwithstanding normal time limits, any consequential corporation tax assessment may, in a case in which HMRC's approval has effect as from the beginning of an accounting period, be made at any time within six years after the end of that accounting period.

[*TCGA 1992, s 101C; FA 1998, s 135(2)(5)*].

Simon's Taxes. See **D2.316.**

Interaction with group relief

[29.9] The rules for the general limitation on the amount of group relief (*CTA 2010, ss 138–142, ICTA 1988, ss 403A, 403B* see **39.6 GROUPS OF COMPANIES**) apply as if the deemed disposal and reacquisition were a real disposal and reacquisition. [*TCGA 1992, s 179(4)*].

Exceptions from the degrouping charge

Associated companies leaving the group

[29.10] There are a number of situations where the degrouping charge is specifically disapplied by the legislation.

The degrouping provisions did not apply in relation to transfers of assets between associated companies which then leave the group at the same time. [*TCGA 1992, s 179(2)*]. Companies were '*associated*' if they would form a group by themselves. [*TCGA 1992, s 179(10)(a) before FA 2011*].

The companies also had to be associated immediately after leaving the group at the same time, on the authority of *Dunlop International AG v Pardoe* [1999] STC 909, (1999) 72 TC 71, CA. This was a case where the principal company of the group ceased to be UK resident (before *FA 2000*), so that all of its subsidiaries ceased to be members of a UK group at the same time, but were not associated with each other, as they did not form a group by themselves.

In *Johnston Publishing (North) Ltd v HMRC* [2008] EWCA Civ 858, [2008] STC 3116, CA, which turned on the construction of *TCGA 1992, s 179(2)*, the Court of Appeal found, against the company, that the transferor and transferee companies must be associated at the time of the original transfer of the asset as well as at the time of leaving the group, in order to avoid the degrouping charge. The taxpayer was refused the right of appeal to the House of Lords, so the Court of Appeal decision is final.

Following the *Johnston* case, HMRC issued Brief 59/08 to clarify what they thought it meant to be 'associated companies' for the capital gains degrouping charge, although this point was not directly covered in the case. Where the transferor and transferee can only be considered to form a group by reference to some other company at the time of transfer, then all three companies also had to form a group at the time they left the main group. For example, the transferor and transferee may both be subsidiaries of a third company.

The rules were eventually changed by *FA 2011*. The associated companies rule now applies if either:

- both companies are 75% subsidiaries and effective 51% subsidiaries of another company on the date of the acquisition and both remain 75% subsidiaries and effective 51% subsidiaries of that other company until immediately after they cease to be members of the group; or
- one of the companies is both a 75% subsidiary and an effective 51% subsidiary of another company on the date of the acquisition and remains a 75% subsidiary and effective 51% subsidiary of that other company until immediately after they cease to be members of the group.

These changes resolve the concerns raised in the *Johnston* case (particularly the arguments raised in front of the Special Commissioner) but they are particularly restrictive in the context of groups of companies and the frequency with which assets are moved around within groups, given the new requirement that the relationship between the companies remain largely the same throughout a period starting with the intra-group transfer and ending with the degrouping event.

[*FA 2011, Sch 10 para 3(4) and (12); TCGA 1992, s 179(2)(2ZA)(2ZB)(10)(a)*].

Where, however, the company which acquired the asset subsequently leaves another group which has a 'connection' with the first, the provisions apply as if it was the second group of which both companies were members at the time of the acquisition. There is a '*connection*' between the two groups if, when the company leaves the second group, the 'principal company' (see **18.2**) of that group is under the 'control' of the principal company of the first group (or, if the first group no longer exists, of the principal company at the time the company left the first group), or of certain other companies exercising higher levels of 'control' or where common control of the two groups is exercised by any person or persons (which includes natural persons as well as companies). These provisions were amended by *FA 2011, s 31* to counter a specific tax avoidance scheme, although the changes should not have any impact on normal commercial transactions. However, they do incorporate a new motive test, which might be helpful if the provisions are inadvertently triggered by normal commercial transactions.

'*Control*' in this context is as under *CTA 2010, ss 450, 451* (previously *ICTA 1988, s 416* — see **22.6 CLOSE COMPANIES**) but disregarding control by banks deriving from loan capital or debt issued or incurred in the normal course of the banking business.

[*TCGA 1992, s 179(2A)(2AA)(2B)(9A); FA 2000, Sch 29 para 4(3)(4)(6); CTA 2010, Sch 1 para 244(3)*].

Companies ceasing to exist

[29.11] The degrouping provisions also do not apply where a company ceases to be a member of a group in consequence of another group member ceasing to exist. [*TCGA 1992, s 179(1); F(No 2)A 1992, s 25*]. HMRC take the view that this 'liquidation let out' only applies to the case of a parent company ceasing to be a member of a group on the occasion of its only subsidiary ceasing to exist on dissolution (or all its subsidiaries ceasing to exist simultaneously on dissolution). (HMRC Capital Gains Manual, CG45441–45445).

Principal company joins another group

[29.12] There are certain provisions which apply where the only reason a company is treated as leaving a group is because the principal company of that group has become a member of a new group (thus the old group has been subsumed into a new one). This might occur where the company in question is only just an effective 51% subsidiary of the original principal company. If that principal company joins another group, by virtue of, say, only 75% of its shares being sold, the company in question would no longer be an effective 51% subsidiary of the new principal company and would, therefore be treated as having left a group.

Where this happens, the rules apply so that the company in question is not treated as selling the asset at any time. Instead, if it ceases to be a 75% subsidiary and an effective 51% subsidiary of one or more members of the group (see **18.2**) and still owns (otherwise than as trading stock) the asset, or property to which a chargeable gain has been rolled over from the asset, the company in question is treated as if, immediately after acquiring the asset, it had sold and reacquired it at its market value at the time of acquisition.

The rules were amended by *FA 2011* to ensure that the new mechanism for the degrouping charge applies to the subsequent disposal under *TCGA 1992, s 179(6)* as it would apply to any degrouping gain. It applies the new rule for adding degrouping gains to the consideration for the group disposal, if the degrouping charge under *TCGA 1992, s 179(6)* arises because of the disposal of shares of the company in question or of another member of the original group (i.e. the group in existence before the principal company in that group became a member of another group).

[*TCGA 1992, s 179(5)–(8), before and after amendment by FA 2011, Sch 10 para 3(7)–(10)*].

EU Mergers

[29.13] Where, as part of a process of merger to which *TCGA 1992, s 140E* (European cross-border merger: assets left within UK tax charge — see **17.27 CAPITAL GAINS**) applies, a company which is a member of a group ceases to exist and as a consequence, assets or shares in one or more companies which were also members of the group, are transferred to the transferee, the company which has ceased to exist and any company whose shares have been transferred to the transferee are, for the purposes of these provisions, not treated as having left the group. The transferee and the company which ceased to exist are treated as the same entity and, if the transferee is itself a member of a group following the merger, any company which was a member of the first group and became a member of the transferee's group as a result of the merger is treated as if the two groups were the same.

[*TCGA 1992, s 179(1B)–(1D); F(No 2)A 2005, s 64(4); SI 2007 No 3186, Sch 2 para 7*].

Business transfer

[29.14] Where shares in a company are transferred on or after 1 January 2007 as part of the process of the transfer of a business to which *TCGA 1992, s 140A* (see **17.14 CAPITAL GAINS**) or *s 140C* (see **17.21 CAPITAL GAINS**) applies, and as a result, the company ceases to be a member of a group, it is treated as not having left the group. If the company becomes a member of a second group, of which the transferee company is a member, as a result of the transfer, the company is treated as if the two groups were the same.

[*TCGA 1992, s 179(1AA); SI 2007 No 3186, Sch 1 para 9*].

Mergers

[29.15] Certain mergers are exempt from this provision if the merger was carried out for '*bona fide* commercial reasons' and that the avoidance of liability to tax was not a main purpose of the merger. [*TCGA 1992, s 181; FA 2000, Sch 29 para 28*].

Value Shifting

Interaction with Value Shifting rules

[29.16] If, under any of the foregoing provisions, a deemed sale arises, and on an actual sale at market value at that time any loss or gain would, under the value shifting provisions of *TCGA 1992, s 30* (see **17.36 CAPITAL GAINS**), have been calculated as if the consideration were increased by an amount, the market value at the time of the deemed sale is treated as having been greater by that amount.

[*TCGA 1992, s 179(9)*].

See **9.4 BUILDING SOCIETIES** as regards application of these provisions where a building society's business is transferred to a company.

Simon's Taxes. See D2.330–D2.334.

Example

A Ltd had the following transactions.

1.3.80	Purchased a freehold property £100,000.
31.3.82	Market value £250,000.
1.12.04	Sold the freehold to B Ltd (a wholly-owned subsidiary) for £250,000 (market value £620,000).
31.7.10	Sold its interest in B Ltd (at which time B Ltd continued to own the freehold property).

Both companies prepare accounts to 30 April.

Relevant values of the RPI are: March 1982: 79.44, December 2004: 189.9

(i) A Ltd's disposal of the property to B Ltd is to be treated as one on which, after taking account of the indexation allowance, neither gain nor loss arises.

Indexation factor:

$$\frac{189.9 - 79.44}{79.44} = 1.39$$

	£
Cost to A Ltd	100,000
Indexation allowance £250,000 × 1.39 (see note (a))	347,500
Deemed cost to B Ltd	£447,500

(ii) Following the sale of A Ltd's shares in B Ltd on 31.7.10 (i.e. within six years after the transaction in (i) above), B Ltd will have a deemed disposal as follows.

Deemed disposal on 1.12.04			
	£	£	£
Market value at 1.12.04		620,000	620,000
Cost (as above)	447,500		
Less indexation to date	347,500		
		100,000	
Market value at 31.3.82			250,000
Unindexed gain		520,000	370,000
Indexation allowance	£250,000 × 139	347,500	347,500
Indexed gain		£172,500	£22,500
Chargeable gain subject to CT			£22,500

B Ltd's new base cost for future gains	£620,000

Although the deemed disposal occurs on 1 December 2004, i.e. immediately after B Ltd's acquisition, the gain is treated as accruing on 1 May 2010, i.e. the beginning of the accounting period in which B Ltd left the group, being later than the date of the deemed disposal. The gain thus forms part of B Ltd's profits for the year ended 30 April 2011.

Notes

(a) The indexation allowance on the no gain/no loss transfer is calculated by reference to the market value at 31 March 1982 as this is higher than the original cost. [*TCGA 1992, s 55(1)(2)*].

(b) For re-basing purposes, B Ltd is deemed to have held the asset at 31 March 1982. [*TCGA 1992, Sch 3 para 1*]. *TCGA 1992, s 55(5)(6)* apply in the computation of B Ltd's chargeable gain.

Transfer of degrouping charge to another company in the group

[29.17] This provision was repealed by *FA 2011, Sch 10 para 5(a)* with effect from 19 July 2011. However, the restriction in *TCGA 1992, s 171A(7)* was also repealed (by *FA 2011, Sch 10 para 2*), so that the election under *TCGA 1992, s 171A* can now be made in respect of degrouping charges, too (see **18.6**).

Where, **after 31 March 2002**, a company (company A) ceased to be a member of a group such that the provisions of *TCGA 1992, s 179* in **29.1** apply, the company could jointly elect with another company (company C) for the resultant gain or loss to be treated as accruing to company C instead of company A.

Where the degrouping charge arose under *TCGA 1992, s 179(3)*, the two parties to the election had to be members of the same group at the 'time of accrual'; for this purpose the '*time of accrual*' is the time at which the gain or loss is treated as accruing under *TCGA 1992, s 179(4)* and not, if earlier, the time at which the deemed sale and reacquisition in **29.1** above is treated as occurring.

Where the charge arises under *TCGA 1992, s 179(6)*, company C must be a member of the second group referred to at *TCGA 1992, s 179(5)*, i.e. the group that the principal company of the first group joined above at the 'time of accrual'; for this purpose the '*time of accrual*' is the latest time at which company A satisfies the conditions at *TCGA 1992, s 179(7)*, i.e. company A was a 75% subsidiary of a member of the new group and an effective 51% subsidiary of a member of that group (see **29.12** above).

In either case, the following further conditions all had to be met at the relevant time of accrual.

(a) Company C had either to be UK-resident or own assets that were chargeable assets in relation to it. For this purpose, an asset was a chargeable asset in relation to a company at a particular time if, on a disposal by that company at that time, any gain would have been a chargeable gain and would have been within the charge to corporation tax by virtue of *TCGA 1992, s 10B* (non-UK resident company trading in the UK through a permanent establishment — see **65.6 RESIDENCE**).

(b) Company C could not be an investment trust (within *ICTA 1988, s 842* see **53.1 INVESTMENT TRUSTS**), a venture capital trust (within *ICTA 1988, s 842AA*, see **74.2 VENTURE CAPITAL TRUSTS**) or a dual resident investing company (within *ICTA 1988, s 404*, see **39.24 PAYMENTS AND COLLECTIONS OF TAX**).

(c) Neither company A nor company C could be a qualifying friendly society (as at **18.4**(viii) above).

On the making of a joint election by company A and company C, the chargeable gain or allowable loss on the deemed sale under *TCGA 1992, s 179*, or such part of that gain or loss as was specified in the election, was treated as accruing to company C, not to company A. The election had to be made by notice in writing to HMRC within two years after the end of the accounting period of company A in which the time of accrual fell. More than one election could be made, with more than one other company, within the time limit, each specifying part of the gain or loss. Of course, the sum of the elections could not exceed the whole gain.

If company C was a non-UK resident company, the gain or loss was treated as accruing in respect of a chargeable asset held by it and thus remained within the charge to UK corporation tax.

Any payment made by company A to company C, or *vice versa*, in connection with the election was not to be taken into account in computing profits or losses of either company or treated as a distribution or (for payments made before 16 March 2005) a charge on income (see **61.11 PROFIT COMPUTATIONS**), provided it did not exceed the chargeable gain or allowable loss thereby treated as accruing to company C.

[*TCGA 1992, s 179A; FA 2002, s 42(1)(4); F(No 2)A 2005, Sch 4 para 8; Sch 11 Pt 2(7)*].

The above provisions could be applied in combination with those at **29.18** below.

Rollover of degrouping charge into new business assets

[29.18] This provision was repealed by *FA 2011, Sch 10, para 5(b), (c)* with effect from 19 July 2011.

Where, after 31 March 2002, a company ceased to be a member of a group such that a gain arose under *TCGA 1992, s 179* (see **29.1** above) on a deemed sale and reacquisition of an asset, and the asset was a qualifying asset for rollover relief purposes (see **18.8**), the company could claim rollover relief if it acquired a new qualifying asset.

The normal rollover relief rules applied, subject to minor modifications, described below.

[*TCGA 1992, s 179B(1)(2)*].

The relief

[29.19] Relief under *TCGA 1992, s 152* (see **18.8**) was available to the company leaving the group (company A), where all of the following conditions were satisfied.

(a) Company A was deemed to have sold and immediately reacquired an asset ('*the old asset*'), and the company from which the asset was transferred (company B) was carrying on a trade at the time of transfer.
(b) Throughout its ownership by company B, the asset was used, and used only, for the purposes of that trade.
(c) A gain (as opposed to a loss) accrued to company A on the deemed sale.
(d) An amount equivalent to the deemed sale proceeds was applied by company A in acquiring other assets or an interest in other assets ('*the new assets*') within the time limit below (but see below as regards partial relief).
(e) On acquisition, the new assets were taken into use, and used only, for the purposes of a trade carried on by company A.
(f) Both the old and new assets were within the classes of assets listed in *TCGA 1992, s 155* (see under *Qualifying assets* below).

On a claim by company A to that effect, the deemed sale proceeds (if otherwise of a greater amount) were reduced by the amount necessary to secure that neither a gain nor a loss accrued on the deemed sale. The consideration given by company A for the new assets was treated as reduced by the same amount. This did not affect the treatment for the purposes of *TCGA 1992* of the other party to the transaction involving the new assets. There was no reduction in the amount for which company A was deemed to have reacquired the old asset.

The acquisition of the new assets had to take place **within one year before, or three years after**, the 'time of accrual' (though HMRC have discretion to extend the specified period in either direction). It is sufficient if an unconditional contract for acquisition is entered into within the specified period, but adjustments can be made to the tax position, without time limit, if the contract is not completed.

The '*time of accrual*' is explained at **29.17** above.

The other provisions of *TCGA 1992, s 152* apply as modified. This applies equally to the provisions of *s 152(6)(7)(9)(11)* (partial non-trade use); in particular, references there to the 'period of ownership', in so far as they relate to the old asset, are to be taken as references to the period during which that asset was owned by company B.

[*TCGA 1992, ss 152, 179B, Sch 7AB paras 1, 2*].

Partial relief

[29.20] Where the above conditions were satisfied except that the amount applied by company A in acquiring the new assets was less than the deemed sale proceeds, the provisions of *TCGA 1992, s 153* (see Tolley's Capital Gains

Tax under Rollover Relief) applied with similar modifications as above. The part of the deemed proceeds not so applied had to be less than the amount of the gain on the deemed sale. The relief then operated by reducing the gain to the amount of the said part and treating the consideration given for the new assets was reduced by the same amount.

[*TCGA 1992, ss 153, 179B, Sch 7AB paras 1, 3*].

Claims for relief

[29.21] By virtue of *FA 1998, Sch 18 para 55* and HMRC Capital Gains Manual CG60600, the time allowed for making a claim under *TCGA 1992, s 152* or *s 153* above was four years (from 1 April 2010, following changes to *FA 1998, Sch 18 para 55* per *SI 2009 No 403*, previously time limit was six years) after the later of:

(i) the end of the accounting period of company A in which the 'time of accrual' (as defined at **29.17** above) fell; and

(ii) the end of the accounting period of company A in which the new assets were acquired.

It is considered that (i) above applied by reference to an accounting period of company A even if it was company C (see above) that claims the relief.

The procedure in *TCGA 1992, s 153A* for making *provisional claims* (see Tolley's Capital Gains Tax under Rollover Relief) applied as suitably modified. The 'relevant day' for the purpose of such claims was the fourth anniversary of the last day of the accounting period of company A (not of company C, see above, even if it was that company that provisionally claims the relief), in which the 'time of accrual' fell (**29.17** above).

[*TCGA 1992, ss 153, 179B, Sch 7AB paras 1, 4*].

Qualifying assets

[29.22] The classes of assets qualifying for the relief are listed in *TCGA 1992, s 155* (see Tolley's Capital Gains Tax under Rollover Relief). Note that certain of the classes listed are of no relevance to companies where the post-31 March 2002 intangible assets regime has effect (see **48 INTANGIBLE ASSETS**). As regards Class 1, Head A (land, buildings etc.), the trade there referred to is, in relation to the old asset, the trade carried on by company B and, in relation to the new asset, the trade carried on by company A. [*TCGA 1992, ss 155, 179B, Sch 7AB paras 1, 5*].

Qualifying activities

[29.23] The provisions of *TCGA 1992, s 158* (see Tolley's Capital Gains Tax under Rollover Relief) had effect to the extent that these were relevant to companies.

New assets acquired by another group member

[29.24] The provisions of *TCGA 1992, s 175* (see Tolley's Capital Gains Tax under Rollover Relief) were adapted to make the relief available where company A was a member of a group at the time of accrual (**29.17** above), the acquisition of the new assets was made by another member of that group (judged at the time of acquisition) and the claim was made by both companies. The conditions to be met were that:

(A) *either* company A was UK-resident at the time of accrual *or* the old asset (or, where relevant, the replacement property referred to in **29.1** above) was a chargeable asset in relation to that company immediately before that time; and

(B) *either* the acquiring company was UK-resident at the time of acquisition *or* the new assets were chargeable assets in relation to that company immediately after that time.

The relief was also available where:

(1) company B was not carrying on a trade when it transferred the old asset to company A but was a member of a group at that time; and

(2) immediately before that time, the old asset was used, and used only, for the purposes of the trade treated by *TCGA 1992, s 179(1)* as a single trade carried on by all the trading members of the group.

The relief could similarly be claimed where the acquiring company was a non-trading company but the new assets were taken into use, and used only, for the purposes mentioned in (2) above. In no case was relief available where the acquisition of new assets resulted from a no gain/no loss disposal, e.g. where the assets are acquired from another group member.

[*TCGA 1992, ss 175, 179B, Sch 7AB paras 1, 7; FA 2003, Sch 27 para 2(3)*].

Wasting assets

[29.25] The depreciating asset provisions of *TCGA 1992, s 154* (see Tolley's Capital Gains Tax under Rollover Relief) applied equally in relation to the relief described above.

Overseas matters

[29.26] Under a modified version of *TCGA 1992, s 159* (see Tolley's Capital Gains Tax under Overseas Matters), the above rollover relief was not available if the old asset (or, where relevant, the replacement property referred to in **29.1** above) was a chargeable asset in relation to company A at the time of accrual (as defined above) unless the new assets were chargeable assets in relation to company A immediately after they were acquired. This did not, however, apply where company A acquired the new assets after the time of accrual and was UK resident immediately after acquiring them (unless it was then dual resident and the assets were prescribed assets). The exclusion of rollover relief where a company became non-UK resident between the time of accrual and the acquisition of the new assets also applied in suitably adapted form.

[*TCGA 1992, ss 159, 179B, 185, Sch 7AB paras 1, 6, 8; FA 2003, Sch 27 para 2(3)*].

Interaction with TCGA 1992, s 179A

[29.27] These provisions could be applied in combination with those at **29.17** above. Thus, where a joint election had been made under *TCGA 1992, s 179A* by company A and company C at **29.17** above to allocate the whole of the degrouping charge to company C, and that company acquired a new qualifying asset and took it into use for the purpose of its trade, a rollover relief claim could be made by company C (but not by company A).

In these circumstances, references in **29.1** above to company A should be read as references to company C where appropriate. Where the *s 179A* election covered only part of the gain, rollover relief wass potentially available to each company, in relation to its proportion of the gain, as if the deemed sale under *TCGA 1992, s 179* had been of two separate assets.

[*TCGA 1992, s 179B(3)–(6)*].

Exemption for substantial shareholdings

[29.28] Where a company ceases to be a member of a group and is deemed under *TCGA 1992, s 179* to have sold and immediately reacquired at market value an asset transferred to it by another group member, then normally the time of the deemed sale is immediately after the transfer (see **29.1** above). However, where:

(a) a company ceases to be a member of a group at any time (the '*time of degrouping*') after 31 March 2002; and
(b) a degrouping charge arises in relation to an asset; and
(c) a gain on a disposal of that asset (by the company then owning it) immediately before the time of degrouping would have been exempt under the provisions at **19 CAPITAL GAINS — SUBSTANTIAL SHAREHOLDINGS,**

the deemed sale and reacquisition is instead treated as taking place immediately before the time of degrouping.

A comparable rule applies where the degrouping charge arises under *TCGA 1992, s 179(5)–(8)* and the 'relevant time' (see **29.1**(B)(i) above) falls after 31 March 2002. In this case, the rule applies by reference to the 'relevant time' rather than the 'time of degrouping'.

[*TCGA 1992, Sch 7AC para 38*].

Key points

[29.29] Points to consider are as follows.

- If roll-over relief is to be claimed on the replacement of business assets, ensure that the transactions take place within the time scales required by the legislation and claims are submitted by the parties on time.
- Remember that degrouping charges for the purposes of corporation tax on chargeable gains can crystallise losses as well as gains.
- Bear in mind that all degrouping charges are not the same. Where the substantial shareholding exemption applies, the timing of the deemed disposal and reacquisition is altered to the time immediately before the time of the degrouping. Also, while the intangible fixed asset regime rules are very similar to the capital gains provisions, the loan relationships and derivative contracts rules are different in some important respects, not least timing and the inability to realise a loss.
- Where it is intended to rely upon the pre-*FA 2011* 'associated companies' exception in the degrouping charge provisions, check that the companies were associated at the time of the transfer of the asset as well as the time of degrouping.
- Where it is intended to rely upon the post-*FA 2011* 'associated companies' exception in the degrouping charge provisions, check that the companies satisfied the new rules for being associated from the time of the transfer of the asset up to the time of degrouping.
- If a degrouping charge is to be treated as accruing to a member of a chargeable gains group other than the company leaving the group, ensure that an election to do so is submitted on time.

30

Derivative Contracts Legislation

Cross references. See **36 EXCHANGE GAINS AND LOSSES** and **54 LOAN RELATIONSHIPS.**

Other sources. See generally, HMRC Corporate Finance Manual.

Simon's Taxes. See **D1.8.**

Introduction

[30.1] The original aim of the derivative contracts legislation was that profits and losses on derivative contracts that fall within its scope would be brought into account for tax purposes on the basis that they are recognised in a company's accounts in accordance with generally accepted accounting practice. Where a company prepares its accounts in accordance with UK Generally Accepted Accounting Practice (UK GAAP) and has not adopted Financial Reporting Standard (FRS) 26 such treatment continues to apply.

Where a company prepares its accounts in accordance with International Financial Reporting Standards (IFRS) or UK GAAP incorporating FRS 26 it has since been necessary to introduce, by regulation, a special basis for recognising the profits and losses arising on derivative contracts that are used for hedging purposes and these rules are contained in the *Loan Relationships and Derivative Contracts (Disregard and Bringing into Account of Profits and Losses) Regulations 2004 (SI 2004 No 3256)*. Such regulations are commonly referred to as the *Disregard Regulations* and they are considered at **30.18–30.21** below.

The intention is that the derivative contracts legislation will pick up all derivatives to which a company is a party. There are certain limited exceptions to this rule which involve derivative contracts over shares. Where certain conditions are satisfied such derivatives are excluded from the derivative contracts legislation. These exceptions are considered further at **30.3**.

Equally where an embedded derivative is separated from a contract other than a loan relationship the bifurcation of the contract is generally ignored for tax purposes and thus profits and losses arising on the embedded derivative are generally disregarded for the purposes of the derivative contracts legislation. This is considered further at **30.2**.

A number of anti-avoidance provisions apply including cases where a company is a party to a derivative contract for an unallowable purpose. These provisions are considered further at **30.22, 30.23, 30.25, 30.28, 30.29, 30.30, 30.33** and **30.34**.

Generally, any profits and losses arising on a derivative contract are treated either as trading or as non-trading profits and losses depending on whether or not a company is a party to the derivative contract for the purposes of its trade. In certain cases any profits and losses arising on a derivative contract are treated as giving rise to chargeable gains or allowable losses for the purposes of the *TCGA 1992*. The circumstances in which such treatment applies are considered at **30.53**.

For accounting periods ending on or after 1 April 2009, the legislation is contained in *CTA 2009, Pt 7* and statutory instruments. The provisions are described in detail in **30.2–30.60** below. The general rule is that all profits, including exchange gains and losses, arising to a company on its derivative contracts are chargeable to corporation tax as income. This is subject to *CTA 2009, Pt 7 Ch 7* (see **30.53** below) which sets out when such profits are chargeable as capital gains. Profits and losses are calculated in accordance with the derivative contract rules, except for issuers of securities with embedded derivatives that are deemed options or contracts for differences that meet certain requirements, see **30.59** below.

[*CTA 2009, ss 571, 572*].

Except where otherwise indicated, the derivative contracts rules take priority over other legislation in respect of the tax treatment of derivative contracts to which the rules apply. This includes, e.g. priority over the capital gains rules in *TCGA 1992* and the provisions dealing with financial futures and commodities in *CTA 2009, s 981; ICTA 1988, s 128*.

The loan relationship rules take precedence over the derivative contract rules except where:

(a) an embedded derivative has been bifurcated from a loan relationship (in this case the derivative contracts legislation applies to the embedded derivative); and
(b) an amount only falls to be dealt with under the loan relationships legislation as it represents interest or discount arising on a money debt that has not arisen as a result of a transaction for the lending of money. [*CTA 2009, s 700*].

[*CTA 2009, ss 699, 700, 981; FA 2002, ss 83, 101, Sch 26 para 1, Sch 27 para 19*].

Simon's Taxes. See D1.8.

Derivative contracts

[30.2] A company's '*derivative contracts*' are those of its 'relevant contracts' which meet the 'accounting condition' for the accounting period in question and are not prevented from being derivative contracts by virtue of their underlying subject matter (see **30.3** below) or by any other corporation tax provision.

A '*relevant contract*' is:

(a) an 'option';
(b) a 'future'; or
(c) a 'contract for differences'.

Effectively, these definitions were intended to cover all types of derivative contract (which met certain accounting and other tests), broadly following the classification in the *Financial Services and Markets Act 2000 (Regulated Activities) Order SI 2001 No 544* at *Articles 83–85*. A company acquires a relevant contract when it becomes a party to such a contract, with consequent rights or liabilities.

The '*accounting condition*' is that the relevant contract is treated as a derivative for the purposes of the relevant accounting standard for the accounting period in question or would be so treated for accounting purposes were the relevant accounting standard used.

'*Relevant accounting standard*' is FRS 25 issued in December 2004, for any accounting period in relation to which it is required or permitted to be used. FRS 25 in turn cross refers to the FRS 26 meaning of derivative.

[*CTA 2009, s 579(1)(a), (3), (5); FA 2002, Sch 26 para 3*].

A relevant contract which does not satisfy the accounting test solely because it fails to satisfy the requirements of FRS 26, para 9(b) (essentially this prevents prepaid or substantially prepaid contracts from falling within the definition of a derivative for the purposes of FRS 26) is brought within the derivative contracts legislation. The profits and losses arising on the derivative contract for the purposes of the derivative contracts legislation have to be determined using a fair value basis of accounting

[*CTA 2009, ss 579(1)(b), (4), 600; FA 2002, Sch 26 paras 3(1)(b), (4), 17A(1A)*].

Derivative contracts that do not satisfy the accounting condition

Where a relevant contract does not satisfy the accounting condition it is nevertheless brought within the derivative contracts legislation if:

(a) the underlying subject matter of the contract is commodities; or

(b) the contract is a contract for differences whose underlying subject matter is: land; tangible movable property other than commodities which are tangible assets; intangible fixed assets; weather conditions; or creditworthiness.

[*CTA 2009, s 579(2); FA 2002, Sch 26 para 3(1)(b), (c)*].

A company becomes a party to a relevant contract when it enters into or acquires such a contract. It acquires a relevant contract on becoming entitled to the rights, and subject to the liabilities, under the contract, whether by assignment or otherwise.

Meaning of Option, future and contract for differences

An '*option*' includes any instrument (a 'warrant'). A '*warrant*' is an instrument which gives the holder a right to subscribe for shares or loan stock in a company, whether or not the shares or assets exist or are identifiable. However, the term '*option*' does not include a contract which provides that, after setting off their obligations to each other under the contract, a cash payment of the difference is made by one party to the other or each party has a duty to make a cash payment to the other in respect of all their obligations under the contract and no property passes. These conditions do prevent a contract with currency as the subject matter from being an option.

[*CTA 2009, s 580; FA 2002, Sch 26, paras 12(1), (8), 10*].

A '*future*' is a contract for the sale of property under which delivery is to be made at a future date agreed when the contract is made, and at a price so agreed. A price is taken to be so agreed whether it is for a determined amount, or left to be determined by reference to a future market or exchange price, or so expressed as to allow for variations to take account of changes in quality and quantity on delivery. As in the case of an option, a future that can only be cash settled (except where the underlying subject matter of the future is currency) is treated as a contract for differences.

[*CTA 2009, s 581; FA 2002, Sch 26, para 12(1)(6)(7)(10)*].

A '*contract for differences*' is a contract which has the purpose or pretended purpose of securing a profit or avoiding a loss by reference to fluctuations in the value or price of property described in the contract or in an index or in other factors designated in the contract. A contract for differences does *not* include a future or option (as above), an insurance contract, a capital redemption policy effected in the course of a capital redemption business within the meaning of *ICTA 1988, s 458*, a contract of indemnity, a guarantee, a warranty or a loan relationship. As noted above, however,where an option or a future can only be cash settled (i.e. there is no provision for physical settlement to take place) and the underlying subject matter of the option or future is not currency, the option or future will be treated as a contract for differences for the purposes of the derivative contracts legislation.

[*CTA 2009, s 582; FA 2002 Sch 26, para 12(1)(3)(4)(5)*].

Embedded derivatives that are separated from loan relationships

An embedded derivative which is separated from a loan relationship in a company's accounts is brought within the derivative contracts legislation. According to its characteristics the embedded derivative is treated as an option, future or contract differences. For example, where an option to acquire shares is separated from a convertible security the embedded derivative will be treated as an option. In the case of an index-linked loan relationship where the embedded derivative is separated from the loan relationship, the embedded derivative will, typically, be treated as a contract for differences. In certain cases a special treatment applies to:

(a) certain options to acquire shares which are separated from a creditor relationship;
(b) certain contracts for differences that are separated from a creditor relationship and are linked to movements in the value of certain shares;
(c) certain options to acquire shares that are separated from a debtor relationship; and
(d) certain contracts for differences that are separated from a debtor relationship and are linked to movements in the value of shares.

This is considered further in **30.53** onwards.

[*CTA 2009, s 585; FA 1996, s 94A*].

Embedded derivatives that are separated from other contracts, including derivative contracts

An embedded derivative which is separated from a derivative contract or from a non-financial contract is brought within the derivative contracts legislation. Typically, such bifurcation is ignored for tax purposes and, instead, the profits and losses arising on the contract (including a derivative contract) have to be determined using an amortised cost basis of accounting.

It is possible in certain cases for a company to elect for the bifurcation of the contract to be respected for tax purposes. No such an election, however, can be made if the contract is a contract of long-term insurance or the underlying subject matter of the embedded derivative is, or includes, commodities. Such an election must be made before the end of the first accounting period in which the contract is bifurcated in the company's accounts. Where such an election is made the election continues to apply if the derivative contract is later transferred to another company in the same CGT group.

[*CTA 2009, ss 584, 586, 616, 617, 618; FA 2002, Sch 26 paras 2A, 2B, 45L, 45LA, 45M*].

The bifurcation of a contract will not be ignored for tax purposes where *Reg 9* of the *Disregard Regulations* (*SI 2004 No 3256*) applies to the embedded derivative. The reason for this is to enable a company to use an embedded derivative to hedge an asset or liability to which the company is a party.

[*CTA 2009, s 616(1)(d); FA 2002, Sch 26 para 45L(1)(b)*].

It is also not possible for a company to elect to disregard the bifurcation where *CTA 2009, s 592* applies. This section applies where an embedded derivative is separated from a derivative contract and the underlying subject matter of the embedded derivative consists, or is treated as consisting wholly, of shares in a company. In such cases under *CTA 2009, s 592* the embedded derivative is excluded from the derivative contracts legislation and is treated as being a chargeable asset whilst the host contract is taxed under the provisions of the loan relationships legislation.

[*CTA 2009, ss 592, 616(1)(c); FA 2002, Sch 26 para 45L(1)(ab)*].

Excluded contracts

[30.3] A relevant contract is not a derivative contract if its underlying subject matter consists wholly of, or is treated as consisting wholly of, any one or more of the following types of excluded property. '*Excluded property*' is intangible fixed assets or shares in a company, (but, in the former case, only for relevant contracts which are options or futures). In the case of shares, the exclusion applies only where any of the conditions A to E below apply and the transaction is not designed to produce a return equating in substance to a return on a money investment at a commercial rate of interest.

Further the exclusion for shares does not apply to shares in an open ended investment company or units in a unit trust which are treated for tax purposes as being creditor relationships under *CTA 2009, s 490*.

The conditions are as follows:

(A) the relevant contract is a 'plain vanilla contract' entered into or acquired by a life assurance company or is an approved derivative for the purposes of Rule 3.2.5 of the Insurance Prudential Sourcebook and is not prevented from being treated as a derivative for the purposes of FRS 26 because it has been prepaid in whole or in part; or

(B) the relevant contract is entered into or acquired otherwise than in the course of a trade, as part of a hedging transaction where shares or rights of a unit holder or the company's share capital or a liability related to the share capital of the company are the subject matter of the contract, and the company is not treated as a party to a derivative contract under the loan relationships with embedded derivatives rules (see **30.53**); or

(C) the relevant contract is entered into or acquired otherwise than in the course of a trade and is a quoted option to subscribe for shares in a company; or

(D) the contract, an option or future, is entered into or acquired otherwise than as an integral part of a company's trade, *CTA 2009, s 585(2)* does not require the company to be treated as a party to an embedded derivative and the shares to be acquired or delivered under the terms of the option or future amount to 10% or more of the ordinary share capital of the company (as defined for the purposes of *CTA 2010, s 1119*), or would do so if acquired or delivered; or

(E) the company has a hedging relationship between the derivative contract and a loan relationship that has been bifurcated in the company's accounts into a host contract and an embedded derivative and one of *CTA 2009, ss 645, 648, 653–655, 658* apply to the embedded derivative.

[*CTA 2009, ss 589, 591; FA 2002, Sch 26, para 4(1)(2)(2ZA)(2A)–(2D)(4)*].

A '*plain vanilla contract*' is a contract which is a relevant contract that has not been separated from another contract (see **30.2**).

Underlying subject matter

The underlying subject matter of a relevant contract is:

(1) in the case of an option, the property to be delivered on the exercise of the option;

(2) in the case of a future, the property which, if the future were to run to delivery, would fall to be delivered at the date and price agreed when the contract was made;

(3) in the case of a contract for differences, where the contract relates to fluctuations in the value or price of property described in the contract, it is the property so described, and where an index or factor is designated in the contract, it is the matter by reference to which the index or factor is determined. This may for example include interest rates, weather conditions or creditworthiness.

As regards (1) and (2) above, there is no requirement that the property actually has to be delivered, and if the property to be delivered is itself a derivative contract, the underlying subject matter is the underlying subject matter of that other contract. As regards (3) above, interest rates are not the underlying subject matter of a contract where they are used merely in a formula to determine the amount of the payment where the date of payment may vary and the amount varies according to the date of payment.

Where the underlying subject matter of a relevant contract consists of or includes income from shares in a company or rights of unit trust holder or unit trust scheme (for example dividends), the underlying subject matter is not to be treated as shares by reason only of that income.

[*CTA 2009, ss 583, 589–593; FA 2002, Sch 26 para 11*].

Mixed derivatives

[30.4] Special provisions apply where the underlying subject matter of a relevant contract consists of any one or more of the excluded types of property within **30.3** above in addition to property which is not so excluded, and which satisfies the accounting requirements.

Where the non-excluded property is not 'subordinate' or 'small', then in the case of a derivative contract which is an option or a future, it is to be treated as two separate contracts using a just and reasonable apportionment, i.e. a relevant contract whose underlying subject matter consists of one or more of the excluded properties and a relevant contract whose underlying subject matter consists of the non-excluded property. In the case of a contract for differences where the non-excluded subject matter is not 'subordinate' or 'small', the entire contract will not be excluded from the derivatives contracts legislation.

[*CTA 2009, s 593; FA 2002, Sch 26 paras 9, 46, 47*].

Contract which becomes or ceases to be a relevant contract

[30.5] This provision applies if a company is a party to a chargeable asset which becomes a derivative contract, the company must bring into account any chargeable gain or allowable loss for the period during which it ceases to be a party to the contract, for example where the contract ceases to satisfy the necessary conditions for it to be excluded from the derivative contracts legislation. The gain or loss is calculated on the assumption that the company disposed of the contract immediately before the time when the contract became a derivative contract and the consideration was the notional carrying value of the contract at that time.

These provisions do not apply if the contract became a derivative contract before 30 December 2006.

[*CTA 2009, s 661, Sch 2 para 89*].

Where a relevant contract ceases to fall within the derivative contracts legislation the company is treated as having become a party to the contract for chargeable gains purposes for a consideration equal to the value at which it would have been carried in the company's accounts had a period of account ended immediately before that time.

[*CTA 2009, s 662*].

Taxation of derivative contracts

[30.6] The taxation implications of derivative contracts is as laid out below.

The credits or debits for an accounting period arising from a derivative contract

[30.7] These (as computed below) are brought into account as follows.

(a) **Trading credits and debits.** Where the company enters into a derivative contract for trading purposes, credits or debits arising from the contract are treated as receipts or expenses of the trade for that period (in the case of expenses, overriding anything to the contrary in *CTA 2009, ss 53, 54 or 59; ICTA 1988, s 74* (allowable deductions).

(b) **Non-trading credits and debits.** Any credits or debits arising from derivative contracts *not* entered into for trading purposes are treated as if they were non-trading credits or debits arising under the loan relationships rules in *CTA 2009, Pt 5; FA 1996, Pt 4 Ch 2*, and effectively aggregated with other non-trading loan relationship credits and debits, the net amount being chargeable as non-trading income (formerly under *Schedule D, Case III*) or relievable as a non-trading deficit, as the case may be.

[*CTA 2009, ss 573, 574; FA 2002, Sch 26, para 14(2)(3)(4)*].

Credits and debits to be brought into account comprise amounts which fairly represent all profits and losses arising to or incurred by the company from its derivative contracts and related transactions including exchange gains and losses (see below) arising from derivative contracts or related transactions (but see exception below) and all expenses incurred by the company under or for the purposes of those contracts and transactions.

[*CTA 2009, s 595; FA 2002, Sch 26 paras 15, 17A(1)*].

'*Expenses*' also include those incurred directly in bringing derivative contracts or related transactions into existence, entering into or giving effect to them, making payments under them or securing receipt of payments in accordance with them, including where they are incurred before the contract is entered into.

[*CTA 2009, s 595(4); FA 2002, Sch 26 para 15(4)*].

'*Related transactions*' include any acquisition or disposal (in whole or part) of rights or liabilities under the contract, including where such rights or liabilities are transferred or extinguished by a sale, gift, surrender or release, and where the contract is discharged by performance in accordance with its terms.

[*CTA 2009, s 596; FA 2002, Sch 26 para 15(7), (8)*].

Pre-contract or abortive expenses

Where a company is considering entering a derivative contract or related transaction but has not done so, and it incurs expenses in connection with entering the contract or regarding a liability which may arise under it, the debits may be brought into account in the same way as they would be taken in had the contract been completed.

[*CTA 2009, s 607; FA 2002, Sch 26 para 15(5)*].

'Post-cessation' debits or credits

If a company ceases to be a party to a derivative contract and in its accounts in accordance with generally accepted accounting practice it spreads any profit or loss arising from the termination over future periods the post cessation debits or credits as recognised in the company's accounts are brought into account in computing its derivative contract profits for the accounting period in which they are recognised in its accounts. In determining whether the debit or credit is trading or non-trading, has a particular purpose post-cessation or whether the company and any other party is connected, reference must be made to the circumstances immediately before the company ceased to be a party to the derivative contract.

[*CTA 2009, s 608; FA 2002, Sch 26 para 53(2)–(6)*].

Exchange gains and losses

[30.8] Profits and losses arising to a company from its derivative contracts and related transactions include exchange gains and losses arising from such contracts. They do not, however, include an exchange gain or loss of a company to the extent that it:

(A) arises on a derivative contract whose underlying subject matter consists wholly or partly of currency; or
(B) results from the translation from one currency to another of the profit or loss of part of the company's business,

and it is recognised in the company's:

(a) statement of total recognised gains and losses;
(b) statement of recognised income and expense;
(c) statement of changes in equity; or
(d) statement of income and retained earnings.

Nor does it include, for periods of account beginning on or after 1 April 2011, any exchange movements that are recognised in an investment company's accounts in respect of a derivative contract as a result of a change to its functional currency.

For accounting periods ending before 1 April 2009 exchange gains and losses were left out of account where they were recognised in the company's statement of recognised gains and losses (which would apply where it prepared its accounts in accordance with UK GAAP) or statement of changes in equity (which would apply where it prepared its accounts in accordance with IFRS).

[*CTA 2009, s 606(2A)(3)(4)(4A)(4B); FA 2002, Sch 26 para 16(3)*].

The rules discussed above were introduced in order to enable a company to use a forward currency contract or a cross currency swap to hedge the exchange exposure on shares in subsidiaries and associates (where the subsidiary or associate prepares its accounts in a different currency), a net investment in an overseas branch and ships and aircraft. Under UK GAAP excluding FRS 26 (and thus FRS 23), where a company uses a forward currency contract or a cross currency swap to hedge such assets it is possible for the company to take exchange movements on the derivative contract to reserves in its accounts and thus the exchange movements will fall to be disregarded under the above provisions.

Matching using currency forward contracts — UK GAAP excluding FRS 23 and FRS 26

Where a company:

(a) prepares its accounts in accordance with UK GAAP excluding FRS 23 and FRS 26; and
(b) uses a forward currency contract to match its exchange exposure arising on a particular asset or assets,

the exchange movements arising in respect of the forward currency contract that are eligible for matching treatment have to be determined by reference to the spot rate between the two currencies covered by the contract at the date that the company entered into the contract and the spot rate prevailing at the end of the relevant accounting period, or the date that the company ceases to be a party to the contract. This treatment applies for exchange movements arising on or after 22 April 2009. The effect of this provision is that it is no longer possible for profits or losses that are attributable to the forward points arising on a currency contract (these represent the difference between the forward exchange rate implied in the contract and the spot rate at the date that the contract is concluded) to be left out of account for the purposes of the derivative contracts legislation.

[*CTA 2009, s 606(4C)(4D), as inserted by FA 2009, Sch 21 para 6*].

Derivative contract carried at fair value — determination of exchange gains and losses

Where a derivative contract is carried at fair value in a company's accounts, as generally would be the case where a company prepares its accounts in accordance with IFRS or UK GAAP incorporating FRS 23 and FRS 26, exchange movements arising on the contract would not be separately recognised in its accounts. In such cases the exchange movement arising on the contract is determined for tax purposes by comparing the spot value of the contract, as translated into the currency by reference to which the company's taxable profits (excluding chargeable gains) are computed, at the start of the accounting period in question (or, if later, the date that it became a party to the contract) and the spot value of the currency or currencies covered by the contract, again as translated into the company's functional currency, at the end of the accounting period (or if earlier, the date that it ceased to be a party to the contract).

[*SI 2005 No 3422, Reg 7*].

Matching — Disregard Regulations

[30.9] Where a company prepares its accounts in accordance with IFRS or UK GAAP incorporating FRS 26, is not possible for the company to take exchange movements on a derivative contract that it uses to hedge shares in subsidiaries or associates, or ships or aircraft, to reserves in its individual, as opposed to consolidated, accounts. Accordingly, therefore, it was necessary to introduce special provisions to permit a company to continue to use forward currency contracts and cross currency swaps to hedge exchange movements arising on shares, ships and aircraft. These provisions are contained in *Regs 4, 4A–4C* and *5* of the *Disregard Regulations* (*SI 2004 No 3256*) and are considered below.

Under *Reg 4* of the *Disregard Regulations* exchange movements arising on a currency contract or a cross currency swap that is used to hedge exchange movements on shares, ships or aircraft are disregarded where certain conditions are satisfied.

Exchange movements are not disregarded however to the extent that movements in the fair value of, or profits or losses arising on the disposal of, the shares, ships, or aircraft are taken into account in computing the company's profits for the purposes of a trade carried on by it where this trade consists of, or includes, dealing in shares, ships or aircraft
[*SI 2004 No 3256, Reg 4(2)*].

Under *Reg 4* of the *Disregard Regulations* shares, ships or aircraft are treated as matched with a derivative contract where either of the following conditions are satisfied:

(a) Condition 1: for the accounting period the shares, ships or aircraft are a hedged item under a designated hedge of exchange rate risk in which the derivative contract is the hedging instrument. This is designed to cover cases where a forward currency contract or a cross currency swap is designed as a fair value hedge of the relevant asset in the company's individual (as opposed to consolidated) accounts;

(b) Condition 2: the subject matter of the derivative contract is such that the company intends, by entering into or continuing to be a party to the derivative contract, to eliminate or substantially reduce the economic risk of holding the asset, or part of the asset, which is attributable to fluctuations in exchange rates. In this case a derivative contract is treated as matched with an asset only to the extent that the value of obligation under the derivative contract does not exceed the unmatched carrying value of the asset. The normal rule is that the carrying value of the asset is the value of the asset as shown in the company's accounts at the time at which the company becomes a party to the derivative contract or, if later, the time at which the asset is acquired. In the case of shares it is open to a company to elect for accounting periods beginning on or after 1 January 2008 to match the higher of the carrying value of the shares in its accounts and the net asset value underlying such shares.

[*SI 2004 No 3256, Regs 4(3)(4), 4A(1)(2)(4B)(5)*].

Election to match net asset value of shares

The reason why an election was introduced to permit a company to match the net asset value of shares, as opposed to the cost of the shares, is that, prior to the introduction of IFRS and of FRS 23 and FRS 26, certain companies had been revaluing shareholdings in subsidiaries, joint ventures and associates in their accounts to reflect the net asset value underlying such shareholdings from time to time and had been hedging the exchange exposure attributable to the carrying value of such shareholdings in their accounts. Where a company prepares its accounts in accordance with IFRS or with FRS 26 (and thus FRS 23) such accounting treatment is not possible. Despite this change in accounting treatment however, certain groups still wished to hedge the net asset value of shares in subsidiaries, joint ventures and associates as if they had continued to apply their former accounting treatment and this is why such an election has been introduced.

The election had to be made by the later of 31 March 2008 and 30 days from the start of a company's first accounting period beginning on or after 1 January 2008 where a company held shares on or before the start of that accounting period.

A later election can be made in respect of shares acquired after the start of a company's first accounting period beginning on or after 1 January 2008.

HMRC will also be prepared to accept a later election in respect of shares that a company held at the start of its first accounting period beginning on or after 1 January 2008 where the company first seeks to match shares in accordance with *SI 2004 No 3256, Regs 3(3)(b)* or *4(3)(b)* after the start of that period (see Corporate Finance Manual at CFM62730).

In each case the later election must be made within 30 days of the date that the company first matches the shares with a derivative contract or a debtor relationship in accordance with the provisions of *SI 2004 No 3256, Regs 3* or *4*.

Where an election is made it has effect for all shareholdings held by the company, whenever acquired, it takes effect from the start of the accounting period in which it is made and it is irrevocable.

[*SI 2004 No 3256, Reg 4A(1)(a)(2)–(8)*].

Where a company makes such an election it has to designate a review period. For accounting periods that began before 1 April 2011 the life of a review period could not exceed 92 days. For accounting periods beginning on or after 1 April 2011 a company is able to elect to have a review period of whatever length it chooses provided that a review period starts with the start of an accounting period and a review period ends with the end of an accounting period (where a company had elected to apply net asset matching for accounting periods beginning before 1 April 2011, it was able to elect to vary the length of its review periods by giving notice in writing to HMRC 1 July 2011). The company is required to determine the net asset value of the shares in question at the start of each review period and this becomes the value which is eligible to be treated as matched during that period. For accounting periods beginning on or after 1 April 2011, where during a review period (current review period) there is an increase or decrease of 10% or more in the net asset value underlying any shares that the company is matching, a new review period is deemed to start in respect of those shares at that time and will end at the end of the current review period. This is to permit a company to vary its hedging in respect of the shares in question at the time that the variation in the net asset value occurs.

For accounting periods beginning both before and on or after 1 April 2011, where a company begins to match shares in a company for the first time a new review period will start at that time in respect of those shares and will end at the end of the current review period in which the shares were first matched.

[*SI 2004 No 3256, Regs 4A(1)(a)(i), 4B, 4C*].

Identification rules

Where a company holds a number of assets in the same currency and has debtor relationships or derivative contracts which are eligible to be treated as matched against such assets, identification rules apply to determine the extent to which an asset is to be treated as matched.

The extent to which an asset is matched is determined in accordance with the following rules:

(a) Rule 1: Debtor relationships and currency contracts are regarded as matched to the greatest extent possible with assets which are ships or aircraft;

(b) Rule 2: Subject to Rule 1: Debtor relationships and currency contracts are regarded as matched to the greatest possible extent with assets on the disposal of which a chargeable gain would accrue if a disposal were made on a date falling more than 12 months after the date of acquisition of the asset. This is designed to exclude shares and assets related to shares which are eligible for substantial shareholding relief (*TCGA 1992, Sch 7AC*);

(c) Rule 3: Subject to Rules 1 and 2, debtor relationships and currency contracts are regarded as matched with assets on the disposal of which no chargeable gain would be treated as accruing by virtue of the substantial shareholding legislation.

[*SI 2004 No 3256, Reg 5*].

Partial matching

Where a currency contract is treated as matched by virtue of Condition 2 and only part of a currency contract could be regarded as matching an investment in shares, ships or aircraft, matching treatment will only apply to the relevant portion of the currency contract.

[*SI 2004 No 3256, Reg 5(2)*].

Currency contract matched with company's own share capital

Provision is also made for exchange movements arising on a forward currency contract or a cross currency swap which is matched with the whole or part of a company's share capital to be disregarded for tax purposes. The regulations do not specify the conditions which have to be satisfied in order for such treatment to apply. Rather, they provide that such treatment will apply, in particular, where the exchange movements arising on the shares and the derivative contract were taken to reserves in the company's accounts for its last accounting period beginning before 1 January 2005. HMRC provide guidance in the Corporate Finance Manual at CFM62850 as to the circumstances in which they consider that this provision will apply. They suggest that this is most likely where share capital is treated as a liability in a company's accounts. HMRC have announced that amendments would be made to the matching own share capital provisions to limit their scope for accounting periods beginning on or after 1 January 2012 to redeemable preference shares that are treated as a liability in the issuing company's accounts and that are issued to persons who are not connected with the issuer. It was also proposed that matching of own shares would be possible for accounting periods beginning on or after 1 January 2012 in other cases by obtaining prior approval from HMRC.

[*SI 2004 No 3256, Reg 4(4A), (4B)*].

Bringing into account of matched exchange gains and losses

[30.10] Any matched exchange gains and losses are only brought into account for tax purposes when a company ceases to own the matched asset. The treatment that applies depends on the nature of the asset.

Shares

In the case of shares the matched exchange movement is treated as a chargeable gain or an allowable loss for the purposes of the *TCGA 1992*. For disposals that take place on or after 6 April 2010 the base cost of the shares is adjusted and is increased where a net gain has arisen and is reduced where a net loss has arisen. If the amount of the net loss exceeds the base cost of the shares the excess is treated as additional consideration for the disposal of the shares.

For disposals that took place before this date a freestanding chargeable gain or allowable loss arose except where the shares qualified for the substantial shareholding exemption, in which case the held over exchange movement was left out of account for tax purposes.

[*SI 2002 No 1970, Regs 2, 4*].

It is possible for the time of recognition of the matched exchange movements to be deferred where a company disposes of shares and the disposal is treated as a no gain no loss disposal for the purposes of the *TCGA 1992*, or for disposals that took place before 6 April 2010, the *TCGA 1992* reorganisation provisions applied to the disposal.

[*SI 2002 No 1970, Regs 8–12 and SI 2010 No 809*].

Ships and aircraft

Where the matched asset is a ship or an aircraft, the matched exchange gain or loss will be brought into account as a loan relationship debit or credit when the company disposes of the asset in question.

[*SI 2002 No 1970, Reg 6*].

Net investment in a branch

Where the matched asset is a net investment in a branch the matched exchange movement is not brought into account for tax purposes. This is because there is no provision to bring such deferred exchange movements within the charge to tax.

One way matching anti-avoidance measure

[30.11] The measures discussed below were introduced in *FA 2009* to counter arrangements between companies in the same group that were designed to achieve 'one-way' matching. These arrangements typically took the form of one company (company X) in a group advancing a loan or entering into a currency forward contract or cross currency swap with another group company (company Y). Company Y would in turn use the debtor relationship or derivative to match an investment in shares or other assets eligible for matching treatment.

If an exchange gain arose to company Y on the debtor relationship or derivative contract, the exchange gain would be treated as matched (and thus would be left out of account for tax purposes), whereas company X would be able to obtain tax relief for the loss. If, however, an exchange loss arose to company Y this would produce the wrong result on a group basis. This is because the loss arising to company Y would be treated as matched, whereas the corresponding exchange gain arising to company X would be taxable.

Accordingly, arrangements were devised so that in such circumstances company Y could avoid any exchange loss arising on the loan relationship or derivative contract. For example, in the case of a loan company Y might have the option of repaying the loan at the spot rate of exchange prevailing at the date that the loan was advanced.

These anti-avoidance measures apply to prevent exchange gains arising on or after 22 April 2009 from being treated as matched where 'one way' matching arrangements exist. In such cases any exchange loss, however, continues to be treated as matched.

The anti-avoidance measures apply to an exchange gain arising to a company in an accounting period to the extent that:

(I) the derivative contract's underlying subject matter is wholly or partly currency;
(II) the derivative forms part of arrangements with a 'one-way exchange effect'; and
(III) the company that is party to the contract, or any other company, gains a tax advantage which is not a negligible tax advantage.

A '*one-way exchange effect*' in relation to a company arises if two conditions are fulfilled. These are that the arrangement includes an option or 'relevant contingent contract' and the second involves the comparison of relevant exchange gains and losses of the company and its connected companies for accounting periods ending on the test day with what those gains and losses would have been using counterfactual currency movement assumptions.

A '*relevant contingent contract*' is a contract to which the taxpayer company or a company connected with it is a party and which includes a condition which if met alters a right or liabililty under the contract and operates, directly or indirectly, by reference to the exchange rate of between the operating and another currency

A '*relevant exchange gain or loss*' for this purpose is one which arises in relation to an asset or liability representing a loan relationship or a relevant contract to which the company is a party where these are part of the arrangement and the exchange gain or loss is to be brought into account for corporation tax. In deciding if a relevant gain or loss exists, the one-way exchange effect and unallowable purpose rules are ignored.

A '*test day*' is, where the arrangements include one or more options, a day on which an option is exercised, is varied, is capable of being exercised, the company or a connected company ceased to be a party or the last day of the accounting period. Where the arrangements include one or more relevant contingent contracts, a test day is a day on which an operative condition is satisfied, the contract is varied, the company or a connected company ceased to be a party to the contract or the last day of the accounting period.

A '*relevant foreign currency*' is a foreign currency in which the loan relationships or relevant contracts giving rise to the gain or loss is denominated. There may be more than one such currency.

A '*counterfactual currency movement*' requires the company to assume that the transactions took place as they actually occurred (e.g. exercise of an option on a test day), but that a currency movement of the same size arose in the opposite direction.

Special rules apply when the arrangements include an option. There are provisions for determining when a currency appreciates or depreciates in relation to another and the percentage appreciation or depreciation.

[*CTA 2009, ss 606(4E), 606A–606H, introduced by FA 2009, Sch 21 paras 4, 6 with effect for exchange gains arising on or after 22 April 2009*].

Intra-group hedging arrangements — exchange movements arising before 22 April 2009

[30.12] This anti-avoidance provision applied where a group of companies entered into arrangements that were designed to ensure that on a group basis an exchange gain arising on an external loan or currency contract would be treated as matched against a net investment in a foreign operation of the group (see below), whereas if an exchange loss arises arose on the external loan or currency contract, the loss would not be treated as matched so that the group would be able to obtain relief for the loss. This provision applied where the following conditions were satisfied:

(a) one company (the first company) in a group entered into a debtor relationship or a derivative contract, the subject matter of which included currency (the specified instruments);

(b) another company in the same group (the second company) had a 'net investment in a foreign operation' (that is a branch or a shareholding in another company where the functional currency of the branch or of the other company differed from that of the second company). For these purposes the first company and the second company were treated as being members of the same group where they were treated as connected with each other for the purposes of *FA 1996, s 87* (under this provision two companies were treated as connected with each other for an accounting period where at any time during that accounting period one of the companies had control over the other, or both companies were under the control the same third person (not necessarily a company));

(c) if the assets constituting the net investment in the foreign operation were held instead by the first company, it is likely that there would have been a hedging relationship between the specified instruments and the net investment in the foreign operation; and

(d) the second company was a party to a loan relationship or a derivative contract directly or indirectly with the first company and it, or another company which was a party directly or indirectly to a loan relationship or derivative contract with the first company, could, by exercising an option, determine that an exchange gain or loss that would otherwise have arisen on a loan relationship or derivative contract to which it was a party did not arise.

In such circumstances the first company was denied relief for any exchange loss arising on the specified instruments, to the extent that relief for this loss is was not already denied under the unallowable purposes provisions of the loan relationships legislation (see **54 LOAN RELATIONSHIPS**) or of the derivative contracts legislation (see **30.25**) This measure applied for accounting periods beginning on or after 22 March 2006 except where the company had ceased to be a party to the loan relationship or derivative contract before that date (*SI 2006 No 843, Reg 4*). It was repealed by *FA 2009, Sch 21* with effect for exchange movements arising on or after 22 April 2009.

Hedging using option arrangements — exchange movements arising before 22 April 2009

[30.13] This anti-avoidance provision applied where a company was applying UK GAAP excluding FRS 23 and FRS 26 and it was a party to two or more derivative contracts that were together intended to act as a hedge of currency risk: the arrangements were such that if an exchange profit arose on one of the derivative contracts the profit would have been taken to reserves and thus would be left out of account in computing the company's derivative contract profits under *FA 2002, Sch 26 para 16(3)* (see above), whereas if an exchange loss arose this would not have been taken to reserves and would thus not have fallen within *FA 2002, Sch 26 para 16(3)*. In such circumstances where the exchange loss arose under an option the loss was disregarded in determining the company's taxable profits for any accounting period. This measure took effect for accounting periods beginning on or after 1 January 2006 and ending after 28 March 2006 except where the company had ceased to be a party to the derivative contracts in question before that latter date (*SI 2006 No 843, Reg 5*). It was repealed by *FA 2009, Sch 21* with effect for exchange movements arising on or after 22 April 2009.

[*CTA 2009, ss 579, 600, 607*].

Risk transfer schemes

[30.14] Anti-avoidance legislation was introduced by *FA 2010* for exchange losses that arise on or after 1 April 2010 to counter so-called risk transfer or over hedging transactions. The scheme typically involved, in a derivative contracts context, one company in a group entering into a cross currency swap in order to hedge exchange exposure arising on an asset owned by another group company. As exchange movements on the cross currency swap were not left out of account for tax purposes, the amount of the swap was grossed up so that, on an after-tax basis, exchange movements on the swap would be equal to exchange movements on the asset. For example, where the rate of corporation tax was 30% and the asset had a cost of US$100, the amount of the US dollar leg of the swap would be $143. The arrangements are called risk transfer schemes as the effect of the over hedging is that the risk of loss is transferred to the Exchequer through tax relief being available for the grossed up loss.

Such transactions had been accepted by HMRC for many years but in recent years a number of groups had suffered significant exchange losses on such transactions which in turn significantly reduced their corporation tax liabilities. Accordingly a policy decision was taken to prevent the use of such schemes.

The effect of the legislation is that where a company or a group (an extended definition applies — see *CTA 2010, s 937K*) enters into a risk transfer or over hedging scheme, any exchange losses arising on a derivative contract that forms part of the scheme will be ring fenced to the extent that the loss exceeds the economic loss suffered by the group. Such ring fence losses can only be relieved against future gains which arise to the same company on derivative contracts or loan relationships that form part of the scheme and then only to the extent that the exchange gains exceed the economic profit realised by the group. The economic profit or loss is, in effect, the amount by which the exchange movement on the derivative contract or loan relationship exceeds the exchange movement on the asset which is being hedged as part of the scheme.

Whilst the transactions undertaken were transactions to hedge foreign exchange risk, the anti-avoidance legislation will also catch transactions which are 'grossed up' to hedge the RPI or other index or any price or other value (*CTA 2010, ss 937A–O* as inserted by *FA 2010, Sch 16*).

Computation in accordance with generally accepted accounting practice

[30.15] The general rule is that the amounts to be brought into account are the credits and debits recognised for the period for accounting purposes in arriving at the company's profit or loss computed using generally accepted accounting practice. The debits and credits are those amounts which fairly represent for the accounting period all profits or losses arising on derivative contracts and 'related transactions' and all expenses incurred under or in connection with those transactions, subject to any other provision of the derivative contract rules.

If a company does not draw up its accounts in accordance with generally accepted accounting practice, or does not draw up accounts at all, the amounts to be brought into account are those that would be recognised had the company done so. This applies equally to amounts derived from earlier periods for which accounts were not drawn up in accordance with generally accepted accounting practice.

Expenses are brought into account as above only if they are incurred directly in bringing any of the derivative contracts into existence, entering into or giving effect to any of the related transactions, in making payments under any of the contracts or in taking steps to ensure the receipt of payments under any of the contracts or transactions.

'*Related transactions*' means any whole or part disposal or acquisition of rights or liabilities under a derivative contract.

'*Amounts recognised in determining a company's profit or loss*' for accounting periods ending after 31 March 2009 means amounts recognised in a company's:

(a) profit and loss account, income statement, or statement of comprehensive income for the period;

(b) statement of total recognised gains and losses, statement of recognised income and expense, statement of changes in equity, or statement of income and retained earnings for the period; or
(c) any other statement of items recognised in calculating the company's profits and losses for the period.

For accounting periods that ended before 1 April 2009, profits, losses and expenses arising on derivative contracts and related transactions were normally recognised for tax purposes on the basis in which they were recognised in a company's profit and loss account, statement of recognised gains and losses (where the accounts were prepared in accordance with UK GAAP incorporating FRS 26) or income statement or statement of changes in equity (where the accounts were prepared in accordance with IFRS), or any other statement of items brought into account in computing the company's profits and losses for the period.

Where a company's accounts are not prepared in accordance with IFRS or UK GAAP (whether or not incorporating FRS 26) the profits and losses that are to be brought into account for the purposes of the derivative contracts legislation are to be determined on the basis that it had prepared its accounts in accordance with UK GAAP.

The Treasury may, by regulation, provide for a different means of recognising profits, losses and expenses and using such powers the Treasury have introduced the Disregard Regulations (*SI 2004 No 3256* — see below).

[*CTA 2009, ss 597, 598, 599; FA 2002, Sch 26 paras 17A, 17B, 17C*].

Prior period adjustment

An amount which is recognised in a company's accounts in respect of a prior period adjustment will normally be brought into account in computing the company's derivative contracts profits for the accounting period in which it is recognised, subject to two exceptions. These are:

(a) where the amount arises as a result of a change in accounting treatment. In this latter case the adjustment will be spread over a ten-year period subject to certain exceptions (see below); or
(b) where the adjustment arises as a result of the correction of a fundamental error. In such cases HMRC will require that the company's corporation tax profits for the relevant accounting are computed as if the correct accounting treatment had applied for that period.

[*CTA 2009, s 597; FA 2002, Sch 26 para 17B; SI 2004 No 3271, Reg 4*].

Background to the Disregard Regulations — accounting for derivatives contracts under IFRS or UK GAAP incorporating FRS 26

Change of accounting policy

[30.16] The derivative contracts legislation picks up any movements in the value of a derivative contract arising as a result of a change in accounting policy, for example a company beginning to prepare its accounts in accordance with IFRS or UK GAAP incorporating FRS 26. Such amounts will be picked up either where they are taken to reserves in the accounts as a result of a prior year adjustment in arriving at the opening numbers for the company's first accounting period following the change in accounting treatment, or in other cases under special provisions contained within the debt contracts legislation itself (for example where the company restates the comparative figures for the previous period using the new basis).

[*CTA 2009, ss 597, 598, 612–614; FA 2002, Sch 26 paras 17B, 17C, 50A*].

Any debits or credits arising as a result of a change in accounting policy will normally be spread in equal instalments over a ten-year period. Where a company began to prepare its accounts in accordance with IFRS or UK GAAP incorporating FRS 26 with effect from its first accounting period beginning on or after 1 January 2005, the ten-year spreading began with effect from its first accounting period beginning on or after 1 January 2006. Where a company began to prepare its accounts in accordance with IFRS or UK GAAP incorporating FRS 26 at a later date, the ten-year spreading started from the start of the company's first accounting period for which it adopted its new accounting treatment.

There are a number of cases where additional adjustments arising as a result of the change in accounting treatment will not be brought into account for tax purposes. These are:

(a) where a company had issued a convertible or an exchangeable security before the start of its first accounting period beginning on or after 1 January 2005 and when the company begins to prepare its accounts in accordance with IFRS or UK GAAP incorporating FRS 25 and FRS 26, the security is separated into a host contract and an embedded derivative. In such cases any debits or credits arising in respect of the embedded derivative are ignored for tax purposes [*SI 2004 No 3271, Reg 3C(2)(a)*];

(b) where a debtor relationship to which the former *FA 1996, s 93* (securities linked to chargeable assets — see **30.59**) applied immediately before the start of a company's first period of account beginning on or after 1 January 2005 and the loan relationship is bifurcated in the company's accounts into a host contract and an embedded derivative, any transitional adjustment arising in respect of that embedded derivative is ignored for tax purposes [*SI 2004 No 3271, Reg 3C(2)(aa)*];

(c) where the derivative contract is an embedded derivative which is separated from a contract other than a loan relationship and the embedded derivative is not brought within the scope of the derivative contracts legislation (see **30.2**). In this case any transitional adjustment arising in respect of the embedded derivative is ignored for tax purposes [*SI 2004 No 3271, Reg 3C(2)(b)*];

(d) where *Reg 7* or *8* of the Disregard Regulations applies to a derivative contract (see **30.19**), any transitional adjustments are brought into account on the same basis as the other profits or losses arising on the contract are brought into account for these purposes [*SI 2004 No 3256, Regs 7(1)(b), (c), 8(1)(b), (c), 10*];

(e) where *Reg 9* of the Disregard Regulations (interest rate contracts) applies (see **30.20**), any transitional adjustment arising in respect of the derivative contract is ignored for tax purposes. This is because such contracts are required to be brought into account for tax purposes using an appropriate accruals basis which is designed to track the way in which the contract would previously have been accounted for under former UK GAAP. The effect of such treatment is that all profits and losses arising on the contract should be brought into account for tax purposes over its life [*SI 2004 No 3271, Reg 3C(2)(c)*];

(f) where a company has elected to apply *Reg 9A* of the Disregard Regulations (cash flow hedging — see **30.21**) in respect of its currency, commodity and debt contracts which are used to hedge forecast transactions or firm commitments and/or in respect of its interest rate contracts where such contracts are accounted for as cash flow hedges, any transitional debits or credits are disregarded for tax purposes to the extent that they will be brought into account under the provisions of *Reg 9A* when they are recycled from the statement of changes in equity (where the company prepares its accounts in accordance with IFRS) or the statement of recognised gains and losses (where the company prepares its accounts in accordance with UK GAAP incorporating FRS 25 and FRS 26) and are taken to profit or loss [*SI 2004 No 3271, Reg 3C(2)(e)*]; and

(g) any transitional adjustments arising in respect of a derivative contract:
   (i) where there is a hedging relationship between that contract and a loan relationship and the Disregard Regulations [*SI 2004 No 3256*] do not apply to the contact; or
   (ii) where the derivative contract is an embedded derivative that was separated from a loan relationship,

   are recognised in full in the company's first accounting period beginning on or after 1 January 2005 for which it prepares its accounts in accordance with IFRS or UK GAAP incorporating FRS 26 where the transitional debits or credits arising in respect of the loan relationship are recognised for tax purposes in that period. The transitional debits and credits arising in respect of the loan relationship will be recognised in full in this accounting period where the latest date on which the loan relationship falls to be fully discharged (i.e. repaid) falls in that accounting period [*SI 2004 No 3271, Reg 4(3), (4)*]; and

(h) any exchange gains or losses arising to a company in respect of a derivative contract, the underlying subject of which consists of currency, are disregarded where those exchange gains or losses represent the reversal of exchange gains or losses arising to the company in periods of account before it began to prepare its accounts in accordance with FRS 26 or IAS 39 and such exchange gains or losses had been taken to reserves and had been treated as matched for tax purposes. This provision applies where, following the change in accounting treatment, the net exchange gain or loss that had been taken to reserves was reversed out. It applies in respect of accounting periods beginning on or after 1 January 2009. Where an accounting period straddled

1 January 2009, an adjustment was made to eliminate debits or credits, which on a time apportionment basis, were attributable to times on or after 1 January 2009 [*SI 2004 No 3271, Regs 3A(7A), 3C(2)(ca)*].

Contracts ceasing to be within or beginning to fall within the derivative contracts legislation

[30.17] Where a company is a party to a derivative contract that ceases to fall within the derivative contracts legislation it is treated as if it had disposed of the contract for a consideration equal to the value at which it would have been carried in the company's accounts had an accounting period of the company ended immediately before the derivative contract ceased to be within the derivative contracts legislation. The company is deemed to have acquired the contract for the purposes of the *TCGA 1992* for the same consideration. This situation is most likely to arise where a derivative contract begins to satisfy one of the conditions for it to be treated as an excluded contract (see **30.3**).

[*CTA 2009, ss 622, 662; FA 2002, Sch 26 para 43B*].

Where a derivative contract was previously dealt with under the *TCGA 1992* (for example where the derivative has excluded subject matter — see **30.3**) and the derivative contract later comes within the derivative contracts legislation, the company is required to bring into account when it ceases to be a party to the contract the amount of any chargeable gain or allowable loss which would have arisen had the company disposed of the derivative contract at the value it would have been shown in the company's accounts had an accounting period ended immediately before the contract came within the derivative contracts legislation.

[*CTA 2009, s 661; FA 2002, Sch 26 para 43A*].

Background to the Disregard Regulations — accounting for derivatives contracts under IFRS or UK GAAP incorporating FRS 26

[30.18] In order to understand the *Disregard Regulations* it is necessary to have some understanding of the accounting treatment of a derivative under IFRS or UK GAAP incorporating FRS 26. Under IAS 39 and FRS 26 a derivative contract is normally required to be accounted for on a fair value basis with any movements in the fair value of the contract being taken to the company's profit and loss account (IAS 39, para 9 and FRS 26, para 9). Where certain conditions are satisfied it is possible for a derivative contract to be accounted for as a hedge. IAS 39 and FRS 26 recognise three types of hedge.

(a) A cash flow hedge. This is a hedge of the exposure to variability of cash flows that is attributable to a specific risk that could affect profit or loss. Under a cash flow hedge, the movements in fair value of the hedging instrument, in so far as the derivative is an effective hedge, are deferred in equity (IFRS) or reserves (UK GAAP) and the fair value movements of the ineffective portion are recorded in the profit or loss. The amount which is deferred in equity or reserves is released to profit or loss in line with the impact which the hedged item has on profit or loss. An example of a cash flow hedge would be where a company which has borrowed on floating rate terms enters into an interest rate swap under the terms of which it is obliged to make fixed or fixed rate payments and is entitled to receive floating rate payments (IAS 39, paras 86, 95–101 and FRS 26, paras 86, 95–101);

(b) A fair value hedge. This is a hedge of the exposure to changes in value of a specific risk (the hedged risk) which could affect profit or loss. An example of a fair value hedge would be where a company has borrowed on fixed rate terms and wants floating rate exposure and accordingly enters into an interest rate swap, under the terms of which it is entitled to receive fixed or fixed rate payments and is obliged to make floating rate payments.

In the case of a fair value hedge movements in the fair value of the contract are taken to profit or loss. A company, however, is permitted to adjust the carrying amount of the hedged item by the gain or loss attributable to the hedged risk, to the extent that the contract is considered to be an effective hedge. For example, where a company has a fixed rate borrowing and it wishes to switch this into a floating rate borrowing, provided that the IAS 39 or FRS 26 hedging criteria are satisfied (see below) and the derivative is a fully effective hedge, it would be possible for the company to revalue the interest rate element of the loan only (i.e. no other factors will be reflected in the market value, such as a change in the credit rating of the borrower). The effect of this is that the movements in the fair value of the derivative contract should be offset by equal and opposite movements in the value of the hedged risk.

If the contract is not a fully effective hedge, any movements in the fair value of the ineffective portion of the derivative contract will still have to be taken to profit and loss account but insofar as the contract is not an effective hedge the company may not revalue the risk attributable to the item which is being hedged. Thus the fair value movements on the ineffective portion of the hedge will not be matched by equal and opposite movements in the value of the item that is being hedged (IAS 39, paras 86, 89–94 and FRS 26, paras 86, 89–94);

(c) An hedge of a net investment in a foreign operation. Such hedges must be accounted for in a way similar to a cash flow hedge (see (a) above). The portion of the hedge which is an effective hedge is taken to equity and is released from equity to profit or loss on the disposal of the foreign operation (IAS 39, paras 86, 102 and FRS 26, paras 86, 102). Where a derivative contract is being used to hedge an investment in an overseas subsidiary, associate or joint venture it is only possible for amounts to be taken to equity on consolidation (IAS 21, para 32 and FRS 23, para 32). Thus, in the absence of specific provision to the contrary, where a company prepares its accounts in accordance with IFRS or UK GAAP incorporating FRS 23 and FRS 26, it would not be possible to defer the time of recognition of any exchange movements arising on the derivative. HMRC have introduced a regulation to permit a company to use a foreign currency derivative to hedge a net investment in shares (see **30.9**).

In order for a derivative contract to qualify for hedging treatment under IAS 39 or FRS 26, the following conditions have to be satisfied:

(a) at the inception of the hedge there is a formal designation and documentation of the hedging relationship and the entity's risk management objective and strategy for undertaking the hedge. This documentation must include identification of the hedging instrument, the hedged item or transaction, the nature of the risk being hedged and how the entity will assess the hedging instrument's effectiveness in offsetting the exposure to changes in the hedged item's fair value or cash flows attributable to the hedged risk;
(b) the hedge is expected to be highly effective in achieving offsetting changes in fair value or cash flows attributable to the hedged risk, consistently with the originally documented risk management strategy for that particular hedging relationship;
(c) the effectiveness of the hedge can be reliably measured, i.e. the fair value or cash flows of the hedged item that are attributable to the hedged risk and the fair value of the hedging instrument can be reliably measured;
(d) the hedge is assessed on an ongoing basis and determined actually to have been highly effective throughout the financial reporting period for which the hedge was designated; and
(e) where the derivative contract is used as a cash flow hedge of a forecast transaction, this transaction must be highly probable and must present an exposure to variations in cash flows that could ultimately affect profit or loss.

[*IAS 39, para 88 and FRS 26, para 88*].

The result of the accounting treatment discussed above is that in all cases where a company prepares its accounts in accordance with IFRS or UK GAAP incorporating FRS 26, any profits or losses arising on its derivative contracts would, ordinarily, have to be brought into account for tax purposes on a fair value basis. Where a derivative contract has been designated as a fair value hedge in a company's accounts this would not give rise to a tax mismatch, so long as profits and losses on the hedged item are brought into account for tax purposes in the accounting period in which they are so recognised. In all other cases, however, the effect is that, in the absence of provision to the contrary, it would not be possible to use derivative contracts for hedging in a tax efficient manner.

In order to enable companies to continue to use derivative contracts as a hedge for tax purposes special provisions have been introduced by regulations. These regulations are the *Loan Relationships and Derivative Contracts (Disregard and Bringing into Account of Profits and Losses) Regulations 2004 (SI 2004 No 3256)*. Such regulations are generally referred to as the *Disregard Regulations* and are considered below.

Disregard Regulations — hedging forecast transactions and firm commitments

[30.19] *Regulation 7* of the *Disregard Regulations* applies where a company uses a currency contract to hedge a firm commitment or a forecast transaction whilst *Reg 8* applies where a company uses a commodity contract or a debt contract to hedge a forecast transaction or a firm commitment.

A currency contract is defined as a contract whose underlying subject matter consists wholly of currency. This in effect means that the scope of *Reg 7* is limited to contracts for the forward purchase and sale of foreign currency (including contracts which are settled by a cash payment equal to the difference between the contract rate and the exchange rate between the two currencies covered by the contract at the date of settlement). It does not extend to cross currency swaps since these also involve periodic payments over the life of the contract that are determined by reference to interest rates. Where a company uses a cross currency swap as a hedge the swap will normally fall within the scope of *Reg 9* of the *Disregard Regulations* (interest rate contracts — see below).

[*SI 2004 No 3256, Reg 7(1)*].

A commodity contract is defined as a derivative contract whose underlying subject matter is commodities. Where the underlying subject matter of a derivative contract also includes interest rates the contract will normally fall within *Reg 9* of the *Disregard Regulations* (interest rate contracts — see below) where the contract is used as a hedge.

[*SI 2004 No 3256, Reg 8(2)*].

A debt contract is defined as a derivative contract whose underlying subject matter is an asset or liability representing a loan relationship. Where the underlying subject matter of the contract also includes interest rates the derivative will normally fall within *Reg 9* of the *Disregard Regulations* (interest rate contracts — see below) where the contract is used as a hedge.

[*SI 2004 No 3256, Reg 8(2)*].

The terms '*forecast transaction*' and '*firm commitment*' are defined as having the meaning that they have for accounting purposes. A forecast transaction is defined in IAS 39 and FRS 26, para 9 as an uncommitted but anticipated future transaction. A firm commitment is defined in IAS 39 and FRS 26 at para 9 respectively as a binding agreement for the exchange of a specified quantity of resources at a specified price on a specified future date or dates.

[*SI 2004 No 3256, Reg 2(2)*].

In order for *Reg 7* or *8* of the *Disregard Regulations* to apply for an accounting period:

(a) there must be a hedging relationship between the contract or part of the contract and the forecast transaction or firm commitment; and
(b) any fair value profits or losses arising on the hedged item must not be brought into account for corporation tax purposes.

The reason why *Regs 7* and *8* are disapplied where fair value profits and losses arising on the hedged item are brought into account for corporation tax purposes is because in such cases any fair value movements on the hedge should be matched by fair value profits and losses arising on the hedged item. [*SI 2004 No 3256, Regs 7(1)(a), 8(1)(a)*].

Meaning of hedging relationship

There will be a hedging relationship where:

(a) the contract is designated as a hedge in the company's accounts; or

(b) the contract is intended to act as a hedge of the exposure to changes in fair value of a hedged item which is an unrecognised firm commitment or an identified portion of such a commitment that is attributable to a particular risk and could affect profit or loss of the company; or

(c) the exposure to variability in cash flows is attributable to a particular risk associated with a hedged item that is a forecast transaction and could affect profit or loss of the company.

[*SI 2004 No 3256, Reg 2(5)*].

Recognition of profits and losses for tax purposes

Where *Reg 7* or *8* applies to a derivative contract, as mentioned above, the normal rule is that any profits or losses arising on the contract (including any transitional or prior period adjustments arising as a result of the company beginning to prepare its accounts in accordance with IFRS or UK GAAP incorporating FRS 26) will be brought into account for tax purposes on the earlier of:

(a) the time that the company ceases to be a party to the contract (unless it enters into a replacement contract to hedge the same forecast transaction or firm commitment); or

(b) the time when the hedged item begins to affect the company's profit or loss.

[*SI 2004 No 3256, Reg 10(1), (2), (10), (11)*].

The above rule is modified where the forecast transaction or firm commitment is a transaction or commitment in relation to expenditure which would be taken into account for tax purposes in computing the profits of a trade or a property business, or which would be so deducted but for a provision prohibiting the deduction of capital expenditure in relation to the depreciation of an asset. In such cases the net profit or loss arising on the contract is brought into account for tax purposes on the same basis as the hedged expenditure is taken into account in computing the company's taxable profits, or in the case of capital expenditure on the basis in which the asset is depreciated in the company's accounts.

[*SI 2004 No 3256, Reg 10(3)(3A)*].

Where a company partially terminates a contract, or where part of the hedged item is recognised in determining the company's profit or loss, a proportionate amount of the net profit or loss that has arisen on the contract will be brought into account for tax purposes.

[*SI 2004 No 3256, Reg 10(5), (6)*].

Where a company ceases to be a party to a contract and immediately enters into a replacement contract to hedge the same forecast transaction or firm commitment, any net profit or loss which has arisen on the contract will be deferred and will be brought into account for tax purposes on the same basis as profits and losses arising on the replacement contract. The profits and losses arising on the replacement contract will be subject to the same recognition rules as are discussed above.

[*SI 2004 No 3256, Reg 10(7)*].

Intra-group transfers

It is possible for any net profit or loss which has arisen on a currency, commodity or debt contract to which *Reg 7* or *8* applies to continue to be deferred where the contract is transferred to another company within the same CGT group which is within the charge to the derivative contracts legislation in respect of the contract. Such treatment applies provided that the transferee uses the contract to hedge the same forecast transaction or firm commitment.

Where the transferee has elected to disapply *Regs 7* and *8* of the *Disregard Regulations*, or that *Reg 9A* should apply instead of *Regs 7* and *8* (see below) it is deemed not to have made that election as regards that derivative contract.

Where any profit or loss arising on a currency, commodity or debt contract is deferred as a result of an intra-group transfer, the net profit or loss that has arisen on the contract up to the time of the transfer will be brought into account when the transferee ceases to be a party to the contract (unless it enters into a replacement contract to hedge the same forecast transaction or firm commitment, when the time of recognition will be further deferred) or when the forecast transaction or firm commitment begins to affect the transferee company's profit or loss.

[*SI 2004 No 3256, Reg 10(8), (9)*].

Election to disapply Regs 7 and 8 of the Disregard Regulations

There are two ways in which a company can elect that *Regs 7* and *8* of the *Disregard Regulations* shall not apply to its currency, commodity and debt contracts which it uses to hedge forecast transactions and firm commitments.

In the first case a company may simply elect that *Regs 7* and *8* shall not apply. In such cases the effect of the election is that any profits or losses arising on such contracts (including amounts which are taken to reserves) will be brought into account for tax purposes on the basis in which they are reflected in the company accounts in accordance with generally accepted accounting practice. In effect, this means that profits and losses arising on the contract will be recognised for tax purposes on a fair value basis.

Such an election normally had to be made on or before 1 October 2005, or, if later within 90 days of the start of the company's first statutory accounting period to which the *Disregard Regulations* apply.

[*SI 2004 No 3256, Reg 6(3), (4), (6)*].

Where a company was not a party to a currency, commodity or debt contract to which *Reg 7* or *8* applied before the start of its first statutory accounting period beginning after 31 December 2004 it may elect that these regulations shall not apply to currency, commodity or debt contracts which it uses to hedge forecast transaction or firm commitments provided that this election is made within 90 days of the date that it becomes a party to a currency, commodity or debt contract to which *Reg 7* or *8* applies.

[*SI 2004 No 3256, Reg 6(7)*].

Where a company did not account for its derivative contracts for its first statutory period beginning on or after 1 January 2005 using a fair value basis but it begins to use fair value accounting for its derivative contracts for a subsequent accounting period, it may elect that *Regs 7* and *8* of the *Disregard Regulations* shall not apply to its currency, commodity and debt contracts which it uses to hedge a forecast transaction or a firm commitment, provided that such election is made before the start of that subsequent accounting period.

[*SI 2004 No 3256, Reg 6(6A)*].

Where a company has elected that *Reg 7* and *8* of the *Disregard Regulations* shall not apply to its currency, commodity and debt contracts, it may revoke the election at a later date. Any contracts to which it was party at the date on which it revoked the election, however, continue to remain outside the scope of those regulations.

[*SI 2004 No 3256, Reg 6(8)*].

An alternative approach is for a company to elect that *Reg 9A* of the *Disregard Regulations* (see below) should apply in place of *Regs 7* and *8* to currency, commodity and debt contracts which the company uses to hedge forecast transactions and firm commitments, to the extent that such contracts are accounted for as cash flow hedges in its accounts. Such an election, once made, is irrevocable. The reason for this election is to enable a company's accounting treatment to be followed for tax purposes, thus minimising its compliance burden.

Where such election is made and a derivative contract is not designated as a cash flow hedge in the company's accounts, any profits or losses arising on the contract will be brought into account on the basis in which these are recognised in the company's accounts. This treatment applies even if the corresponding gains and losses on the hedged item are not brought into account for tax purposes, or are not brought into account on the basis on which they are recognised in the company's accounts. As this election is irrevocable a company will need to think very carefully before making it.

A company normally had to elect before 1 April 2007 for *Reg 9A* of the *Disregard Regulations* to apply in place of *Reg 7* and *8*. If a company made such an election the election took effect from the start of its first accounting period beginning on or after 1 January 2006. In such cases an appropriate adjustment was made under *Reg 9A* to ensure that no amount was brought into account more than once or that no amount ceased to brought into account as a result of the change in the tax treatment of a contract (the reason for this is that *Reg 9A* took effect one year after *Regs 7* and *8* came into force). Such an adjustment was brought into account at the start of a company's first accounting period beginning on or after 1 January 2006.

Where a company elected that *Reg 9A* of the *Disregard Regulations* should apply to its currency, commodity and debt contracts this election revoked any earlier election that the company may have made to disapply *Regs 7* and *8* in respect of such contracts.

[*SI 2004 No 3256, Reg 6(3A), (4), (7A), (7B)*].

It is possible for a company to make an election to disapply *Regs 7* and *8* at a later date where it had not begun to prepare its accounts in accordance with IFRS or FRS 26 before 1 April 2007. In such cases a company may make an election before the start of its first accounting period for which it begins to prepare its accounts in accordance with IFRS or FRS 26.

Where a company was not a party to any currency, commodity or debt contracts to which *Regs 7* and *8* applied at the start of its first accounting period for which it began to prepare its accounts in accordance with IFRS or FRS 26 it is able to make a later election to apply *Reg 9A* in place of *Regs 7* and *8*. Such an election must be made within 90 days of the date that the company becomes a party to its first derivative contract to which *Reg 7* or *8* would apply.

[*SI 2004 No 3256, Reg 6(7)*].

Effect of election on group counterparty

Special provisions apply where a company elects to disapply *Reg 7* or *8* of the *Disregard Relations*, or to apply *Reg 9A* in place of *Regs 7* and *8*, and the counterparty to a contract, which would otherwise fall within the scope of *Reg 7* or *8*, is another company that is a member of the same CGT group and is within the charge to UK corporation tax in respect of the contract. In such cases where the counterparty has not made the same election its profits and losses arising on that derivative contract are computed for the purposes of the derivative contracts legislation on the assumption that it had made the election. This rule does not apply where either party to the contract entered into it in the ordinary course of a banking business or a business as a securities house.

[*SI 2004 No 3256, Reg 6(10), (11)*].

Disregard Regulations — hedging using interest rate contracts

[30.20] As noted above, where a company prepares its accounts in accordance with IFRS or UK GAAP incorporating FRS 26, absent any provision to the contrary, any profits and losses arising on derivative contracts to which it is a party will be brought into account for tax purposes on a fair value basis. In order to enable such companies to continue to use derivative contracts to hedge in a tax efficient way *Reg 9* of the *Disregard Regulations* was introduced, as an alternative to *Reg 9* applying to its interest rate contracts, a company can elect for *Reg 9A* to apply to such contracts. *Regulation 9A* and the reason why it was introduced is considered further below.

Regulation 9 was introduced to preserve the tax treatment which previously applied (and still applies) where a company prepared its accounts in accordance with UK GAAP excluding FRS 26 (Old UK GAAP). Under Old UK GAAP where an interest rate contract (e.g. an interest rate swap) is used as a hedge it is accounted for on an accruals basis and profits and losses arising on the contract are recognised in the company's accounts on a basis that matches the profits and losses arising on the item being hedged. For example, where a company borrows on fixed rate terms but wishes to obtain floating rate funding it would typically enter into an interest rate swap under the terms of which it would make floating rate payments and it would receive fixed rate payments. In its accounts, typically, the swap would not appear separately and, in effect, the company would treat itself as having a floating rate cost of funding (i.e. the fixed rate payments on the loan would be set against the fixed rate receipts on the swap). The tax treatment would in turn follow the accounting treatment.

Regulation 9 applies where a company uses all or part of an interest rate contract in order to hedge an underlying transaction. An interest rate contract is defined as:

(a) a derivative contract whose underlying subject matter is, or includes, interest rates. It will thus be noted that the definition goes far wider than what would generally be considered to be an interest rate contract, for example an interest rate swap, forward rate agreement or an interest rate future; or

(b) in a case not falling within (a) above, a swap contract in which payment falls to be made by reference to a rate of interest or to an index determined by reference to income or retail prices (e.g. an RPI swap).

[*SI 2004 No 3256, Reg 9(4)*].

Regulation 9 only applies provided that:

(a) there is a hedging relationship between the contract, or a portion of the contract, and any of the risks arising in respect of an asset, liability, receipt or expense (the hedged item); and

(b) the fair value profits or losses arising on the hedged item or in relation to any of the risks, in relation to which the contract was intended to act as a hedge, arising in respect of the hedged item, or any portion of the hedged item, are not brought into account for the purposes of corporation tax for that period.

The intention of the wording in (b) above is that *Reg 9* will not apply where:

(i) a derivative contract is designated as a fair value hedge in a company's accounts and revaluations of the hedged item are taken into account for corporation tax purposes; or

(ii) the hedged item is accounted for on a fair value basis and such fair value profits and losses are brought into account in computing the company's taxable profits.

[*SI 2004 No 3256, Reg 9(1)*].

Hedging relationship

There will be a hedging relationship between an interest rate contract (hedging instrument) and an asset, liability, receipt or expense (the hedged item) if and to the extent that:

(a) the hedging instrument and the hedged item are designated by the company as a hedge;

(b) in any other case the hedging instrument is intended to act as a hedge of:

  (i) the exposure to changes in fair value of a hedged item which is a recognised asset or liability or an unrecognised firm commitment, or an identified portion of such an asset, liability or commitment that is attributable to a particular risk and could affect profit or loss of the company;

  (ii) the exposure to variability in cash flows that is attributable to a particular risk associated with a hedged item that is a recognised asset or liability or a forecast transaction and could affect profit or loss of the company; or

  (iii) a net investment in a foreign operation of the company. In this case *Reg 9* of the *Disregard Regulations* will apply to the fair value profits or losses arising on a currency contract other than in respect of exchange movements, which will be dealt with under *Reg 4* of the *Disregard Regulations* (see **30.9**). [*SI 2004 No 3256, Reg 2(5)*].

Effect of *Reg 9*

Where a *Reg 9* applies to an interest rate contract, any fair value profits or losses arising in respect of the contract (or the relevant portion of such fair value profits or losses where a derivative contract is only partially used for hedging purposes) as recognised in the company accounts will be disregarded for the purposes of the derivative contracts legislation. Similarly, any amounts which are recycled from a company's statement of changes in equity or statement of recognised gains and losses to profit or loss will also be disregarded. Instead, any profits and losses arising in respect of the interest rate contract, or where the contract is only partially used for hedging purposes, the relevant proportion of the contract, will be recognised for tax purposes on an appropriate accruals basis.

[*SI 2004 No 3256, Reg 9(1), (5), (6)*].

Appropriate accruals basis

The intention of the definition of an appropriate accruals basis is to track the accounting treatment which applied for UK GAAP for accounting periods that ended on or before 31 December 2004 (i.e. UK GAAP excluding FRS 26). The accounting treatment which applied to a derivative contract which was used as a hedge was more a question of practice, as opposed to being set out clearly in an accounting standard. In view of this HMRC decided by regulation to prescribe the basis on which profits and losses should be brought into account for tax purposes, as opposed to merely stating that such amounts should be recognised on the same basis as they would have been recognised had the company still continued to prepare its accounts in accordance with UK GAAP excluding FRS 26.

An appropriate accruals basis is defined as one where:

(a) the contract is shown in the company's accounts at cost (which may be nil) and the cost is adjusted for any cumulative amortisation of any premium or other amount falling to be recognised in arriving at the cost of the contract; and

(b) the aggregate of:
   (i) the amount of periodical payments under the contract, or in the case of a swap contract under which only a single payment is to be made, the value of the payment; and
   (ii) the credits and debits representing interest arising, on the assumption that an effective interest method is used, in respect of the asset or liability representing a loan relationship which is a hedged item,

   represent the credits or debits that would be given by generally accepted accounting practice in relation to an asset or liability representing a loan relationship whose terms include those of both the hedged item and the interest rate contract;

(c) exchange gains and losses are recognised as a result of the translation of the contract at the balance sheet date. This means, in the case of a currency contract, that the contract has to be revalued by translating the currency or currencies to which the contract relates into the company's functional currency (defined as 'the currency of the primary environment in which the company operates'), or in the case of an investment company that has elected for a currency to be its designated currency for tax purposes, that currency, using the relevant spot rate of exchange at the end of the accounting period in question; and

(d) profits or losses which arise as a result of the contract coming to an end before its stated maturity date are amortised and brought into account over the unexpired term of the hedged item.

[*SI 2004 No 3256, Reg 9(4)*].

Contract comes within or ceases to be within the scope of Reg 9

Where an interest rate contract begins or ceases to fall within *Reg 9* of the *Disregard Regulations* an adjustment is required for tax purposes to reflect the fact that under this regulation the taxable profits arising on the derivative contract have to be determined on an appropriate accruals basis (see below), whereas otherwise the taxable profits arising on the contract would be determined on a fair value basis. The amount of this adjustment has to be determined on a just and reasonable basis with a view to ensuring that as a result of the change no amounts are double counted or are left out of account for tax purposes. *Regulation 9* may cease to apply to a derivative contract, for example, where a company ceases to use the derivative contract as a hedge but it continues to be a party to the contract.

[*SI 2004 No 3271, Reg 9(2A)*].

Disregard of transitional adjustments

Where *Reg 9* of the *Disregard Regulations* applies to an interest rate contract, any transitional adjustments arising in respect of the interest rate contract will be left out of account for tax purposes. The reason for this is that regulation 9 continues the accruals treatment which previously applied for tax purposes. Thus any amount representing the difference between the carrying value of the derivative contract on an accruals basis immediately before it began to prepare its accounts in accordance with IFRS or UK GAAP incorporating FRS 26 will be brought into account for tax purposes under *Reg 9* over the remaining life of the contract.

[*SI 2004 No 3256, Reg 3C(2)(c)*].

Intra-group transfers

It is possible for a derivative contract to which *Reg 9* of the *Disregard Regulations* applies to be transferred at its carrying value for the purposes of *Reg 9* to another company in the same CGT group as the transferor provided that the transferee company is within the charge to the derivative contracts legislation in respect of the contract that is transferred. This is because *Reg 6(12)* of the *Disregard Regulations* disapplies the provisions of *CTA 2009, s 628; FA 2002, Sch 26 para 30* which otherwise prevents the intra-group transfer provisions of *CTA 2009, s 625; FA 2002, Sch 26 para 28* from applying where a derivative contract is accounted for on a fair value basis in a company's accounts (as would be the case where the company prepares its accounts in accordance with IFRS or UK GAAP incorporating FRS 26).

[*SI 2004 No 3256, Reg 6(12)*].

Election to disapply *Reg 9*

Where *Reg 9* applies to a derivative contract, the company has to account for the derivative contract for tax purposes on an appropriate accruals basis. Many banks and financial traders were proposing electing out of *Reg 9* as they considered that it would be simpler to follow their accounting treatment for tax purposes where they had large numbers of interest rate contracts, only some of which were used hedging purposes. Originally, therefore, *Reg 9* contained a provision whereby a company could elect that this regulation should not apply to its interest rate contracts.

Some banks, however, wished to be able to use interest rate contracts as cash flow hedges and for amounts which were taken to reserves to be disregarded until they were recycled to profit or loss. To address this *Reg 9A* of the *Disregard Regulations* was introduced (see below). As is discussed in more detail below, *Reg 9A* applies, inter alia, to interest rate contracts which are designated as cash flow hedges in a company's accounts. Where *Reg 9A* applies any amounts which are taken to equity (IFRS) or reserves (UK GAAP) are ignored for tax purposes and instead such amounts are brought into account for tax purposes when they are recycled from equity or reserves or are taken to the carrying value of an asset or liability where the profits or losses on the asset are not taken into account for tax purposes on the basis in which they are recognised in the company's accounts.

First election

The election which was originally introduced under *Reg 6(5)* of the Disregard Regulations provides that *Reg 9* shall still continue to apply to:

(a) interest rate contracts that are designated as a fair value hedge in the company's accounts where fair value profits and losses arising on the hedged item are not brought into account for tax purposes on the same basis as that in which they are recognised in its accounts; and

(b) all interest rate contracts that are used to hedge connected companies relationships. This includes cases where a derivative contract is designated as a cash flow hedge of a connected companies relationship in a company's accounts.

Second election

As mentioned above, *Reg 9A* was introduced at the request of the banks. Certain banks lobbied HMRC pointing out that it would involve too much internal compliance to keep track of *all* interest rate contracts which might be regarded as hedging connected companies loan relationships. In response to this HMRC introduced the second election which is contained in *Reg 6(5B)* of the *Disregard Regulations*.

As in the case of the first election, where a company makes such an election *Reg 9* continues to apply to derivative contracts that are designated as a fair value hedge in the company's accounts where profits and losses arising on the hedged item are not brought into account for tax purposes on the same basis as they are recognised in its accounts.

In addition, *Reg 9* continues to apply to interest rate contracts which are used to hedge connected companies creditor relationships which are carried at fair value in the company's accounts. On the basis that such relationships will have to be accounted for tax purposes on an amortised cost basis, it was felt that it would not be too burdensome for companies to keep track of such derivative contracts and, further, it would ensure that profits and losses arising on such contracts are recognised on the same basis as that in which profits and losses on the underlying loan relationship are brought into account for tax purposes.

Deadline for election to apply Reg 9A in place of Reg 9

The first election normally had to be made before 31 March 2006 and it took effect from the start of a company's first statutory accounting period beginning on or after 1 January 2005. It is possible, however, for a company to make a later election (see below) where it had not begun to prepare its accounts in accordance with IFRS or FRS 26 by this date.

[*SI 2004 No 3256, Reg 6(5), (6)(b)*].

The second election normally had to be made before 1 April 2007 and took effect for accounting periods beginning on or after 1 January 2006.

[*SI 2004 No 3256, Reg 6(5B), (7A)*].

In both cases it is possible for a company to make a later election provided that the election is made:

(a) before the start of its first accounting period for which it begins to prepare its accounts in accordance with IFRS or UK GAAP incorporating FRS 26; or

(b) where a company was not a party to any interest rate contracts to which *Reg 9* would have applied at the start of that accounting period, within 90 days of the date on which it becomes a party to its first interest rate contract to which *Reg 9* of the *Disregard Regulations* would otherwise apply.

[*SI 2004 No 3256, Reg 6(6A), (7)*].

Where a company made the second election (but not the first) and previously *Reg 9* had applied to its interest rate contracts an adjustment was made on a just and reasonable basis to ensure that no amount fell out of account from tax or was double counted for tax purposes as a result of the change in tax treatment. This adjustment had to be brought into account in computing the company's derivative contract profits for its first accounting period beginning on or after 1 January 2006.

Effect of election on group counterparty

Special provisions apply where a company elects to apply *Reg 9A* of the *Disregard Relations* in place of *Reg 9* to an interest rate contract and the counterparty to the contract is another company that is a member of the same CGT group and is within the charge to UK corporation tax in respect of the contract. In such cases where the counterparty has not made the same election its profits and losses arising on that contract are computed for the purposes of the derivative contracts legislation on the assumption that it had made the election. This rule does not apply where either party to the contract entered into it in the ordinary course of a banking business or a business as a securities house.

[*SI 2004 No 3256, Reg 6(10), (11)*].

Cash flow hedging — Reg 9A

[30.21] As has been discussed above, it is possible for a company to elect that *Reg 9A* should apply instead of *Regs 7* and *8* to its currency, commodity and debt contracts which it uses to hedge forecast transactions or firm commitments. It is also possible for a company to separately elect for *Reg 9A* to apply to its interest rate contracts to which *Reg 9* would otherwise apply.

Regulation 9A applies to a derivative contract that has been designated as a cash flow hedge in a company's accounts. In such cases any amounts which are taken to equity (IFRS) or reserves (FRS 26) are left out of account for tax purposes. Instead such amounts are brought into account for tax purposes when they are recycled from equity or reserves and are included in arriving at the company's accounting profit or loss or are taken to the carrying value of an asset or liability, in cases where the profits and losses arising on the asset or liability are not determined for corporation tax purposes in accordance with generally accepted accounting practice (i.e. the tax treatment of the asset does not follow its accounting treatment).

[*SI 2004 No 3256, Reg 9A*].

It should be noted that *Reg 9A* will not apply to an interest rate contract that has been used to hedge a connected companies relationship and has been designated as a cash flow hedge in the company's accounts where a company has made an election under *Reg 6(5)* to apply *Reg 9A*. Instead *Reg 9* continues to apply to such contracts.

[*SI 2004 No 3256, Reg 6(5)*].

Transitional adjustments

Where a derivative contract falls within *Reg 9A* of the *Disregard Regulations* any transitional adjustments arising in respect the change in the accounting treatment of the derivative contract are disregarded to the extent that such amounts will be brought into account when they are recycled from equity to profit or loss.

[*SI 2004 No 3271, Reg 3C(2)(e)*].

Special computational provisions

Amounts not fully recognised for accounting purposes

[30.22] This anti-avoidance provision applies for times on or after 6 December 2010 where profits and losses arising on a derivative contract are not fully recognised in a company's accounts in accordance with generally accepted accounting practice as a result of tax avoidance arrangements to which the company is at any time a party. For these purposes arrangements are tax avoidance arrangements if the main purpose, or one of main purposes, of any party to the arrangements, in entering into them, is to obtain a tax advantage (the *CTA 2010, s 1139* definition applies). Arrangements in turn are defined as including any arrangements, scheme or understanding of any kind, whether or not legally enforceable, involving a single transaction or two or more transactions. Where this provision applies the company is required to recognise the full amount of the credits arising on the derivative for an accounting period in computing its derivative contract profits and a fair value basis has to be used to determine the credits and debits that are brought into account in respect of the contract. Where a company becomes a party to the tax avoidance arrangements on or after 23 March 2011 it is not permitted to bring any net debits into account in respect of the derivative contract for the relevant period.

Where the company is a party to the derivative contract at the start of the first accounting period to which the provisions apply and the fair value of the contract is greater that its carrying value in the company's accounts at that time, the company is required to recognise a credit equal to the difference in computing its derivative contract profits for that period. This measure applies where a company becomes a party to the tax avoidance arrangements in question on or after 23 March 2011.

[*CTA 2009, ss 599A, 599B, as amended by FA 2011, Sch 4, paras 8, 13 with effect for times on or after 6 December 2010*].

For times before 6 December 2010 the anti-avoidance provision applied where profits and losses arising in respect of a derivative contract were not fully recognised in a company's accounts for an accounting period as a result of the derivative contract being treated as linked for accounting purposes with an amount that had at any time been contributed to the company and which formed part of its capital for the period, or with securities that the company had issued that again formed part of its capital for the period. In such cases the company was required to recognise all the debits and credits arising in respect of the derivative contract for that accounting period and the debits and credits which were brought into account in respect of the contract for that accounting period had to be determined using a fair value basis of accounting.

This anti-avoidance provision was extended by *F(No 2)A 2010* so that it applied where a company acquired an interest in shares in another company, an interest in a partnership or interest in property in a trust or where such an interest that the company held was varied and in consequence profits and losses were not fully recognised in the company's accounts in accordance with generally accepted accounting practice in respect of a derivative contract to which it was a party. In such cases it was required to bring into account for tax purposes the full profit or loss arising on the derivative contract for the relevant accounting period. This amendment had effect for times on or after 22 June 2010 and applied until the *FA 2011* amendment discussed above took effect.

[*CTA 2009, ss 599A, 599B, as introduced by FA 2009, Sch 30, para 3, with effect for debits and credits arising on or after 22 April 2009 and as amended by F(No2)A 2010, s 8, Sch 5*].

Debits arising from the derecognition of derivative contracts

[30.23] Where a company prepares its accounts in accordance with IFRS or UK GAAP incorporating FRS 26, in certain cases it is possible for a company to derecognise a derivative contract in its accounts even though the company remains a party to the contract. Following an amendment introduced by the *Finance Act 2011*, which took effect for times on or after 6 December 2010, a company will not be able to claim any relief in computing its derivative contract profits for any debits it recognises in its accounts in respect of the derecognition of a derivative contract if the company remains a party to the derivative contract and the derecognition is a result of tax avoidance arrangements to which the company is a party. Arrangements are tax avoidance arrangements if the main purpose, or one of the main purposes, of any party to the arrangements, in entering into them, is to obtain a tax advantage (the *CTA 2010, s 1139* definition applies). Arrangements in turn are defined as including any arrangements, scheme or understanding of any kind, whether or not legally enforceable, involving a single transaction or two or more transactions.

[*CTA 2009 s 698A, as introduced by FA 2011, Sch 4, paras 11, 13*].

Special provision for a release of a liability under a derivative contract

[30.24] Where a company's liability to pay an amount under the contract is released, no credit is required to be brought into account in respect of the release if it is part of a statutory insolvency arrangement within the meaning given by *CTA 2009, s 1319 (ICTA 1988, s 834(1))* or, for periods of account beginning before 1 January 2005, a relevant arrangement or compromise within the meaning given by *ICTA 1988, s 74(2)*.

[*CTA 2009, s 611; FA 2002, Sch 26 para 22; FA 2004, s 52, Sch 10 paras 52, 53; FA 2005, s 80, Sch 4 paras 1, 8, 19*].

Unallowable purposes

[30.25] Where, in any accounting period, a company is a party to a derivative contract, or a related transaction (defined as any acquisition or disposal in whole or in part of the contract) in respect of the contract, for an unallowable purpose, any '*exchange credits*' (i.e. credits attributable to exchange gains arising on the contract) and any debits in respect of the contract which, on a just and reasonable apportionment, are attributable to the unallowable purpose are not to be brought into account for that period, except as detailed below.

A company will be regarded as being a party to a derivative contract for an unallowable purpose where at any time during the accounting period the company is a party to, or enters into a related transaction in respect of, the contract:

(a) otherwise than for its business or other commercial purposes;
(b) in respect of activities for which it is not within the charge to corporation tax;
(c) for a tax avoidance purpose.

A company will be regarded as being a party to a derivative contract for a tax avoidance purpose where the main purpose, or one of the main purposes, for which the company was a party to the contract at that time, or for which it entered into the related transaction, was to secure a tax advantage for itself or any other person. '*Tax advantage*' is defined by reference to *CTA 2010, s 1139* (*ICTA 1988, s 840ZA*) for accounting periods ending on or after 6 April 2007 and *ICTA 1988, s 709* (transactions in securities — as it stood before it was amended by *ITA 2007* for accounting periods which ended before that date).

Where, in the case of a derivative contract, the debits relating to the unallowable purpose for an accounting period exceed the exchange credits relating to it in the same accounting period, the difference (the '*net loss*') may be brought into account as a debit to the extent that the 'accumulated net losses' for the period do not exceed the 'accumulated credits'. The '*accumulated net losses*' are the amount of any net loss arising from the derivative contract, either for that accounting period or for an earlier accounting period, less any amount already brought into account under this provision in an earlier accounting period. The '*accumulated credits*' are:

(A) the amount of any credits, other than exchange credits, arising from the derivative contract, either for that accounting period or for an earlier accounting period; less
(B) the amount of:
  (i) any debits arising on the derivative contract for that accounting period or any earlier accounting period, which are not referable to the unallowable purpose; and
  (ii) any net loss arising on the same derivative contract already brought into account under this provision in an earlier accounting period.

Amounts not brought into account by virtue of this provision are not to be brought into account in any other way for corporation tax purposes. There is a net loss on a contract if the total debits on that contract which are not brought into account for the period exceeds the sum of exchange credits on that contract which are excluded under *CTA 2009, s 690(2)*.

The net loss on a contract for an accounting period is found as follows:

(I) find the sum of net losses for the period and any preceding period;
(II) deduct any part of I which has been dealt with in previous periods;
(III) find the sum of credits (others than exchange credits) for the period and any previous periods;
(IV) deduct any part of III which has been dealt with in any previous periods and any part of the credits not excluded under *CTA 2009, s 690(3)*;
(V) compare the result of II with that of IV — the lower amounts gives the amount of the excess accumulated net losses for the period.

[*CTA 2009, ss 690–692; FA 2002, Sch 26 paras 23, 24*].

Capitalised expenditure

[30.26] Where, in accordance with generally accepted accounting practice, a company capitalises debits or credits arising in respect of a derivative contract as part of the cost of a fixed capital asset or project, such debits or credits will be brought into account for tax purposes in the accounting period in which they are capitalised in the same way as if the debits or credits had been recognised in arriving at the company's accounting profit for that period in accordance with generally accepted accounting practice. Such treatment does not apply to a debit where the debit is taken into account in determining a company expenditure on intangible fixed assets for the purposes of the intangible fixed assets legislation in *CTA 2009, Pt 8; FA 2002, Sch 29* (see INTANGIBLE ASSETS (**48**)).

Where such treatment applies any debits arising from the writing down of the capital asset or project, including any amortisation or depreciation, are disregarded for the purposes of the derivative contracts legislation.

[*CTA 2009, s 604; FA 2002, Sch 26, para 25*].

Amounts recognised in equity or shareholders' funds

[30.27] Where debits or credits in respect of a derivative contract are, under generally accepted accounting practice, recognised in equity or shareholders' funds but not in any of the company's statements of items brought into account in computing profits or losses for the period, they are to be brought into account as if they were treated as profit and loss items. [*CTA 2009, ss 597, 605; FA 2002, Sch 26 para 25A; FA 2005, s 80, Sch 4 para 35; F(No 2)A 2005, Sch 6 para 4(3)(6)*].

Disposals for consideration not fully recognised by accounting practice

[30.28] An anti-avoidance provision applies where, in an accounting period (the 'relevant accounting period') a company, with the intention of eliminating or reducing the credits to be brought in under the Derivative Contract rules, disposes of rights or liabilities under a derivative contract wholly or partly in exchange for a consideration which is not wholly in money or a debt to be settled in money and is not fully recognised in its accounts for that or any other period. A consideration is not fully recognised if it does not fall to be taken into account, in whole or in part, in determining the company's profit or loss, computed in accordance with generally accepted accounting practice. If *TIOPA 2010 Pt 4* (*ICTA 1988, Sch 28AA para 1(2) as amended by CTA 2009, Sch 1 para 291*) applies to increase the liability of the company in respect of the disposal, these provisions will not apply. Otherwise, the full consideration is brought into account.

[*CTA 2009, s 698; FA 2003, Sch 26 para 27A, introduced by FA 2008, Sch 22 para 4(2) with effect for disposals on or after 16 May 2008*].

Transfers of value to connected companies

[30.29] Where, on or after 6 March 2007, a company fails to exercise in full its rights under an option which was a derivative contract and there is a transfer of value by the company which held the option (the 'transferor') to a connected company (the 'transferee') which is not otherwise chargeable to corporation tax, a credit is brought into account by the transferor. The credit has to be brought into account in the accounting period in which the option expires, or would have expired had the rights under it been exercised. The amount of the credit is, where the option expired, the amount paid by the transferor for it and where any of the rights were exercised, an amount representing a just and reasonable proportion of the amount paid. In determining whether or not there is a transfer of value, it is assumed that if there had not been a connection between the companies, all rights would have been exercised in full on the latest date they could be exercised.

Before 6 March 2007, where a company failed to exercise it rights in full under an option which was a derivative contract, there was a transfer of value by the company which held the option (the 'transferor') to a 'connected' company (the 'transferee') which was not otherwise chargeable to corporation tax in respect of the contract, a credit had to be brought into account by the transferor in the accounting period in which the option expired, or would have expired had the rights under it been exercised. The credit that had to be brought into account was, where the option expired on or after 6 March 2007, the amount paid by the transferor for it and, where any of the rights were exercised, an amount representing a just and reasonable proportion of the amount paid. Where the option expired before 6 March 2007, the credit to be brought into account was the amount (if any) paid by the transferor to the transferee for the grant of the option by the transferee. In determining whether there was a transfer of value, it was assumed that, if the parties had not been connected, the option would not have expired and would have been exercised on the date it expired.

An option is within these provisions if it falls within the definition in **30.2** above, but without the exclusion of cases involving cash settlement.

Companies are '*connected*' for these purposes in an accounting period if, at any time in that period, one company controls the other or both companies are under the control of the same person. The *CTA 2009, s 472; FA 1996, ss 87(3)(4), 87A* definition of contol (see **54.31 LOAN RELATIONSHIPS**).

[*CTA 2009, s 695; FA 2002, Sch 26 para 26; FA 2007, Sch 5 para 18*].

For transfers of value in general, see **72 TRANSFER PRICING**.

Exchange gains and losses where derivative contract not at arm's length

[30.30] Where, in an accounting period, a company is party to a derivative contract the provisions of which are not at arm's length, so that the transfer pricing provisions of *TIOPA 2010, Pt 4; ICTA 1988, Sch 28AA* (see **72 TRANSFER PRICING**) apply to treat the company as not being party to the contract, any exchange gains and losses arising in that accounting period as regards the derivative contract are to be disregarded in determining the related credits and debits. Where the transfer pricing provisions instead require profits and losses to be computed as if the contract had been on arm's length terms, any such exchange gain or loss is instead adjusted for those purposes to the amount which would have arisen if the contract had been on such terms. Apart from this provision, nothing in *TIOPA 2010, Pt 4; ICTA 1988, Sch 28AA* is to require exchange gains and losses from derivative contracts to be computed as though the contracts had been on arm's length terms.

[*CTA 2009, s 694; FA 2002, Sch 26 para 27*].

Transactions within groups

[30.31] There are provisions requiring adjustments to ensure that intra-group transactions under the derivative contracts regime are tax neutral. Anti-avoidance provisions aim to prevent the rules from being used to obtain a tax benefit. The provisions apply where, as a result of a related transaction (see **30.7** above) between two members of a group (both being within the charge to corporation tax in respect of the transaction), one of those companies (the 'transferee company') directly or indirectly replaces the other (the 'transferor company') as a party to a derivative contract, or becomes party to a contract equivalent to one to which the other company has ceased to be party. The provisions similarly apply where a series of transactions, having the same effect as a related transaction between two companies each of which has been a member of the same group at some time in the course of those transactions, results in such a replacement.

In determining the credits and debits to be brought into account, the transferor company is treated as having entered into the transaction (or the first of a series of transactions, as the case may be) in the accounting period in which the transaction takes place for a consideration equal to the 'notional carrying value' of the derivative contract. The transferee is treated as having acquired the contract for a consideration equal to that amount for any accounting period in which it is party to the contract. (This means that where the transferee uses fair value accounting the movement in fair value in the accounting period of transfer will be the difference between the fair value at the end of that period and the carrying value to the transferor of the contract and where the transferee uses an amortised cost, then the carrying value of the transferor will be used as the cost to the transferee.) The '*notional carrying value*' is the amount that would have been the carrying value (see **30.15** above) of the contract in the transferor's accounts had a period of account ended immediately before the company ceased to be party to the contract.

Where:

(a) payment of the transfer consideration is deferred;
(b) the amount payable exceeds the amount which would have been payable had payment been made at the time of the transfer; and
(c) some or all of the excess can reasonably regarded as representing a return on an investment of money at interest (and thus as a discount arising on the money debt),

the transferor's disposal consideration is increased by the amount of the discount. No adjustment, however is made to the price at which the transferee is deemed to have acquired the derivative contract. Such treatment applies for transfers that take place after 21 March 2006.

There are anti-avoidance provisions where there are transactions which would fall to be treated as above, but the purpose or one of the main purposes of the arrangements is to secure a tax advantage for the transferor or a person connected with him. *CTA 2009, s 629; FA 2002, Sch 26 para 28(3ZB)–(3ZD)* as introduced by *FA 2008, Sch 22 para 5(2)* with effect in relation to transactions taking place, or a series of transactions of which the first takes place on or after 16 May 2008.

A '*relevant transaction*' is a related transaction (as in **30.7** above) or the first of a series of related transactions or a transfer by virtue of which these provisions apply or would apply but for the transferor company using fair value accounting (see below).

The transfer pricing provisions in *TIOPA 2010, Pt 4; ICTA 1988, Sch 28AA* (see **72 TRANSFER PRICING**) do not apply to debits or credits determined as above.

'Group' for these purposes is as under *TCGA 1992, s 170* (see **18.2 CAPITAL GAINS — GROUPS**).

The meaning of '*company replacing another as party to derivative contract*' includes a company becoming a party to a derivative contract which confers rights, imposes liabilities or does both, equivalent to those held or owed by the original party to the contract.

Fair value accounting: These provisions do not apply where the transferor's profits and losses arising on the contract are determined for the purposes of the derivative contracts legislation using a fair value basis of accounting. In this case, the amount to be brought into account by the transferor company is the fair value (as defined by *CTA 2009, s 710*) of the contract as at the date the transferee company becomes a party to the contract.

As above, where:

(a) payment of the transfer consideration is deferred;
(b) the amount payable exceeds the amount which would have been payable had payment been made at the time of the transfer; and
(c) some or all of the excess can reasonably be regarded as representing a return on an investment of money at interest (and thus as a discount arising on the money debt),

the transfer is consideration is increased by the amount of the discount. No adjustment, however, is made to the price at which the transferee is deemed to acquire the derivative contract. Such treatment applies for transfers that take place after 21 March 2006.

Where the transferor accounts for the derivative contract on a fair value basis the amount to be brought into account by the transferee company is:

(i) for relevant transactions after 21 March 2006, the same as the amount brought into account by the transferor company ignoring any discount required to be brought into account by that company;
(ii) for relevant transactions on or after 16 March 2005 and before 22 March 2006, the notional carrying value of the contract in the accounting period in which it becomes party to the contract or, for relevant transactions before that date, the same amount as brought into account by the transferor company.

Where a company accounts for a derivative contract using a fair value basis of accounting and *Regs 7, 8* or *9* of the *Disregard Regulations* (see **30.19–30.20**) applies to the derivative contract *CTA 2009, s 625* is not prevented from applying to the derivative contract.

[*SI 2004 No 3256, Reg 6(12)*].

In *HBOS Treasury Services plc (now HBOS Treasury Services Ltd) v Revenue and Customs Comrs* [2009] UKFTT 261 (TC), [2010] SFTD 134 the bank entered a scheme to monetise interest rate swaps by a transfer to a subsidiary followed by a later sale of the subsidiary (at a time before a degrouping charge applied). The scheme involved the novation of the swaps. The Tribunal Judge held that in order for the intra-group transfer provisions to apply in the case of a novation there must not be any amendments to the terms of the contract as a result of the novation that have any meaningful financial consequences. In the present case there were amendments to the terms of the contract and, accordingly, the Tribunal Judge concluded that *FA 2002, Sch 26 para 28* (now *CTA 2009, s 625*) did not apply to the novation of the contract.

[*CTA 2009, ss 624–629; FA 2002, Sch 26 paras 28–30*].

Degrouping charge

[30.32] A degrouping charge applies where after replacing the transferor company as party to a derivative contract as in **30.31** above, the transferee company ceases within the 'relevant six-year period' to be a member of the group. The '*relevant six-year period*' is the period of six years following a related transaction between two members of a group of companies or following the last of a series of transactions between two companies each of which has been a member of the same group at some time in the course of those transactions.

In this case, the transferee company is treated (subject to the conditions below) as having assigned the rights and liabilities under the derivative contract immediately before degrouping for consideration equal to their fair value at that time and as having immediately reacquired them for the same amount. (Thus, any gain is brought into charge to tax under the derivative contract provisions immediately before the transferee leaves the group.)

Where a deemed disposal and reacquisition as above applies, the degrouping charge only applies if a credit would be brought into account by the transferee company on the assignment of the rights and liabilities under the derivative contract. Where a loss would arise in such circumstances the loss may only be brought into account where there is a hedging relationship (as defined in *CTA 2009, s 707*) between the derivative contact and a creditor relationship in respect of which a degrouping charge arises under the equivalent degrouping provisions that apply for the purposes of the loan relationships legislation (*CTA 2009, ss 344, 345*). In such cases the amount of the loss that may be brought into account is not limited to the amount of the degrouping charge that arises on the creditor relationship.

The degrouping charge does not apply where the transferee company ceases to be a member of the group by reason only of an exempt distribution within *CTA 2010, s 1075; ICTA 1988, s 213(2)* or *s 213A*. However, if there is a chargeable payment (within the meaning of *CTA 2010, s 1088(1); ICTA 1988, s 214(2)*) within five years after making the exempt distribution, a degrouping charge arises as above but the transferee company is treated as having assigned the rights and liabilities under the derivative contract immediately before making the chargeable payment for a consideration equal to their face value at the time that it left the group. As above, the degrouping charge only applies if a credit would be brought into account by the transferee company or merging companies on the assignment of the rights and liabilities under the derivative contract or, if that is not the case, a credit would be brought into account under the loan relationship rules (under *CTA 2009, s 346; FA 1996, Sch 9 para 12A*) in respect of a creditor loan relationship where the company has a hedging relationship (as defined by *CTA 2009, s 707; FA 2002, Sch 26 para 12(14)*) between the derivative contract and the creditor relationship.

[*CTA 2009, ss 630–632; FA 2002, Sch 26 para 30A; F(No 2)A 2005, Sch 7 para 24; SI 2007 No 3186; SI 2008 No 1579*].

Company ceasing to be UK-resident etc.

[30.33] Where a company ceases to be UK-resident, it will be deemed to have assigned its rights and liabilities under its derivative contracts immediately before and to have reacquired them immediately after it ceased to be UK-resident, at their fair value, unless the rights and liabilities under the contract continue to be held or owed for the purposes of the company's UK permanent establishment (see **65.6** residence). The provision similarly applies where rights or liabilities under a derivative contract cease to be held for the purposes of a UK permanent establishment of a non-UK resident company in any circumstances not involving a related transaction. (Thus, any profit or loss on the rights or liabilities will be brought into account as a derivative contract credit or debit.) This provision does not apply to a derivative contract that has been transferred to the transferee under the group transfer provisions contained in *CTA 2009, s 625 (FA 2002, Sch 26 para 28)* within the previous six years and the time at which the transferee migrates from the UK is the same as that at which it leaves the group. There is no requirement that a degrouping charge arises.

[*CTA 2009, ss 609–610, Change 66 listed in Annex l to CTA 2009; FA 2002, Sch 26 para 22A; FA 2004, Sch 9 para 3, Sch 10 para 54*].

Derivative contracts with non-residents

[30.34] Special provisions apply (except as below) where either:

(a) a company and a non-resident both become party to a derivative contract; or
(b) a company becomes party to a derivative contract to which a non-resident is party or *vice versa*.

For each accounting period for any part of which the company and a non-resident are both parties to a derivative contract which makes provision for 'notional interest payments' (e.g. interest-based payments under an interest rate or currency swap), no 'excluded debits' arising to the company from the derivative contract may be brought into account by the company.

An '*excluded debit*' is the excess of the aggregate of 'notional interest payments' made by the company to the non-resident while they are both party to the contract over the aggregate of such payments made by the non-resident to the company. A '*notional interest payment*' is any payment of an amount determined (wholly or mainly) by applying a rate equal to a specified rate of interest to a specified notional principal amount for a specified period.

These special provisions do not apply:

(i) to a company which is a bank, a building society, a financial trader (see below) or a recognised clearing house (within *Financial Services and Markets Act 2000, s 285*) holding the derivative contract (otherwise than as agent or nominee) solely for the purposes of a UK trade (or part);
(ii) where the non-resident holds the derivative contract (otherwise than as agent or nominee) solely for the purposes of a *UK* trade (or part) carried on through a permanent establishment (or branch or agency — see **65.6 RESIDENCE**); or

(iii) where arrangements made under *TIOPA 2010, s 2(1); ICTA 1988, s 788* (see **32.3 DOUBLE TAX RELIEF**) with the government of the territory in which the non-UK resident is resident (or, if the non-resident is party to the contract as agent or nominee of another person, with the government of the territory in which that other person is resident) make provision, whether for relief or otherwise, in relation to interest.

As regards (i) above, for the guidelines used by HMRC in deciding whether a company should be approved as a financial trader, see HMRC Statement of Practice SP 4/02, 30 September 2002.

[*CTA 2009, ss 696, 697; FA 2002, Sch 26 para 31*].

Provisions not at arm's length — amounts imputed

[30.35] Where, under the provisions of *TIOPA 2010, Pt 4* (formerly *ICTA 1988, Sch 28AA*) (see **72 TRANSFER PRICING**), any amounts fall to be treated as profits or losses arising to, or expenses incurred by, a company in respect of any of its derivative contracts or related transactions, those provisions will have effect so as to require credits or debits relating to the deemed amounts to be brought into account to the same extent as if they were actual amounts. [*CTA 2009, s 693; FA 2002, Sch 26 para 31A*].

Group mismatch scheme legislation

[30.36] The group mismatch scheme legislation was introduced by *FA 2011 (Sch 5)* and took effect for times on or after 19 July 2011. In the case of a group mismatch scheme entered into before that date where the legislation applies any losses arising on loan relationships or derivative contracts will be disregarded but the profits will remain within the charge to tax. [*FA 2011, Sch 5, para 6(2), (3)*].

The aim of this legislation is to counter transactions that seek to exploit an asymmetry in the accounting (and hence tax) treatment of transactions involving loan relationships or derivatives in order for a group (see below) to obtain a tax advantage. Where this legislation applies (subject to the transitional rule discussed above) any profits or losses arising on loan relationships or derivative contracts that form part of the scheme are disregarded for tax purposes. The legislation also applies to transactions that are deemed to be loan relationships for tax purposes including repos and quasi repos and transactions treated as financing arrangements under *CTA 2010, ss 758, 763 and 767* (see *CTA 2010, ss 938I, 938J*).

Scheme profit or loss

[30.37] The legislation applies to a scheme profit or a scheme loss. This is a profit or loss that forms part of the group mismatch scheme, which, but for this legislation, would be brought into account as a debit or credit for the purposes of the loan relationships or derivative contracts legislation and meets the first or second asymmetry condition.

The first asymmetry condition is that the loss or profit affects the amount of any relevant tax advantage secured by the scheme. Where at the end of an accounting period it is not certain whether the scheme will secure a relevant tax advantage or what the amount of the relevant tax advantage secured by the scheme will be, the first asymmetry condition is regarded as being met if there is a chance that the scheme will secure a relevant tax advantage and the loss or profit will affect its amount.

The second asymmetry condition applies where the loss or profit does not meet the first asymmetry condition but arises from a transaction, or series of transactions, that might (if events had turned out differently) have given rise to a loss or profit that would have met the first asymmetry condition. [*CTA 2010, s 938C*].

Meaning of group mismatch scheme

[30.38] A scheme is defined as including any scheme, arrangements or understanding of any kind whatever, whether or not legally enforceable, involving a single transaction or two or more transactions. [*CTA 2010, s 938H*]. A scheme is a group mismatch scheme if the parties to the scheme are, or include, members of the same group (see below) and condition A or condition B is met.

Condition A is that at the time that the scheme is entered into there is no practical likelihood that the scheme will fail to secure a relevant tax advantage (see below) of £2 million or more.

Condition B is that:

(a) the purpose, or one of the main purposes, of any member of the scheme group in entering into the scheme is to obtain the chance of securing a relevant tax advantage (of any amount); and
(b) at the time the scheme is entered into:
  (i) there is no chance that the scheme will secure a relevant tax disadvantage (see below); or
  (ii) there is such a chance but the expected value of the scheme is nevertheless a positive amount.

If at the time the company enters into the scheme, there are chances that the scheme would, if carried out, secure different relevant tax advantages or disadvantages in different circumstances, the amount and probabilities of each must be taken into account in determining the expected value of the scheme. Where at the time that the scheme is entered into the length of the scheme is uncertain condition A or condition B will be regarded as being met where they would be met on any reasonable assumption as to the length of the scheme period.
[*CTA 2010, s 938B*].

Relevant tax advantage and relevant tax disadvantage

[30.39] A relevant tax advantage is defined in relation to a scheme as an economic profit:

(1) that is made by the scheme group over the scheme period (defined as the period over which the scheme has effect) which arises as a result of asymmetries in the way different members of the group bring, or do not bring, amounts into account as debits and credits for the purposes of *CTA 2009, Pt 5 or 7* (or for the purposes of *Pt 3* of that Act, where the relevant member the group is a party to the loan relationship or derivative for the purposes of its trade); and
(2) is not negligible.

A relevant tax disadvantage is in turn defined in relation to a scheme as an economic loss that:

(1) is made by the scheme group over the scheme period and arises as a result of asymmetries in the way different members of the scheme group bring, or do not bring, amounts into account as debits and credits for the purposes of *CTA 2009, Pt 5 or 7* (or for the purposes of *Pt 3* of that Act, where the relevant member the group is a party to the loan relationship or derivative for the purposes of its trade); and
(2) is not negligible.

Asymmetries are defined in as including, in particular, asymmetries relating to quantification and asymmetries relating to timing.

The reference to an economic profit includes an increase in an economic profit and a decrease in an economic loss. Similarly the reference to an economic loss includes an increase in an economic loss and a decrease in an economic profit.

[*CTA 2010, ss 938D, 938K*].

The reference to amounts being not brought into account for the purposes of the loan relationships legislation or the derivative contracts legislation do not include:

(a) a company not bringing amounts into account because the company is not UK resident and the amounts are not attributable to a permanent establishment that the company has in the UK; or
(b) amounts attributable to an overseas permanent establishment of a UK resident company that has made an election to exclude the profits of its foreign permanent establishments from tax under *CTA 2009, s 18A*.

[*CTA 2010, s 938L*].

Economic profit or loss

[30.40] Whether an economic profit or loss arises to the scheme group as a whole for the purposes of the group mismatch scheme legislation is to be determined by taking into account, in particular:

(1) profits and losses made as a result of the operation of the *Corporation Tax Acts*; and
(2) any adjustments required to reflect the time value of money.

For these purposes any profits or losses made by a member of the scheme group are only to be taken into account to the extent that they are attributable to times at which the member is a party to the scheme.

In determining the economic profits and losses made by the scheme group as a whole over the scheme period it is to be assumed that each company that is a party to the scheme:

(1) is in a position to fully relieve any losses; and
(2) incurs the full tax cost of any profit made by that company,

where such losses or profits arise in respect of loan relationships or derivative contracts. The full tax cost is defined as the profit that would be brought into account as a credit (or as a reduction of a debit) if the company had no other profits for the period.

[*CTA 2010, ss 938, 938G*].

Priority over other anti-avoidance measures

[30.41] The group mismatch scheme legislation takes precedence over the following anti-avoidance provisions that are treated as having no effect:

- *CTA 2009, s 441* (loan relationships for unallowable purposes);
- *CTA 2009, s 690* (derivative contract unallowable purposes);
- *TIOPA 2010, Pt 4* (transfer pricing);
- *TIOPA 2010, Pt 6* (tax arbitrage); and
- *TIOPA 2010, Pt 7* (worldwide debt cap legislation).

[*CTA 2010, s 938N*].

Meaning of group

[30.42] For the purposes of the group mismatch legislation a company (company A) is treated as being a member of a group in relation to a scheme if any other company is associated with company A at any time during which the scheme has effect. The group consists of company A and each company with which it is associated. For these purposes another company (company B) is associated with company A at a time (the relevant time) if any of the following conditions is met:

(1) the first condition is that the financial results of company A and company B for a period that includes the relevant time:
    (a) are required to be comprised in group accounts;
    (b) would be required to be comprised in such accounts but for the application of an exemption; or
    (c) are included in group accounts,
(2) the second condition is that there is a connection between company A and company B for the accounting period of company A in which the relevant time falls. There will be a connection for these purposes where one company controls the other or both companies are under the control of the same person (the *CTA 2009, s 472* definition of control applies);
(3) the third condition is that at the relevant time company A has a major interest in company B or company B has a major interest in company A (major interest has the meaning of *CTA 2009, ss 473, 474*);
(4) the fourth condition is that:

(a) the financial results of company A and a third company, for a period that includes the relevant time:
  (i) are required to be comprised in group accounts;
  (ii) would be required to be comprised in such accounts but for the application of an exemption; or
  (iii) are comprised in such accounts; and
(b) at the relevant time the third company has a major interest in company B (within the meaning of *CTA 2009, ss 473, 474*);

(5) the fifth condition is that:
(a) there is a connection between company A and a third company for the accounting period of company A in which the relevant time falls; and
(b) at the relevant time the third company has a major interest in company B (within the meaning of *CTA 2009, ss 473, 474*).

[*CTA 2010, s 938E*].

European cross-border mergers

[30.43] The following provisions apply to:

(a) the formation of an SE on or after 18 August 2006 by the merger of two or more companies in accordance with *Council Regulation (EC) No 2157/2001, Arts 2(1), 17(2)*;
(b) the formation of an SCE on or after 18 August 2006 by the merger of two or more 'co-operative societies', at least one of which is a society registered under *Industrial and Provident Societies Act 1965*, in accordance with *Council Regulation (EC) No 1435/2003*;
(c) a merger on or after 1 January 2007 effected by the transfer by one or more companies or co-operative societies of all their assets and liabilities to a single existing company or co-operative society; and
(d) a merger on or after 1 January 2007 effected by the transfer by two or more companies of all their assets to a single new company (which is not an SE or SCE) in exchange for the issue by the transferee company of shares or debentures to each person holding shares in or debentures of a transferor company.

Each of the merging companies must be resident in a member state, but not all can be resident in the same state. A company is resident in a member state for this purpose if it is within a charge to tax under the law of the State as being resident for that purpose and it is not regarded, for the purposes of any **DOUBLE TAX RELIEF (32)** arrangements to which the State is a party, as resident in a territory not within a member state. In the case of merger under (c) or (d) above, the transferor must cease to exist without being in liquidation.

For the purposes of (b) and (c) above, a '*co-operative society*' is a society registered under the *Industrial and Provident Societies Act 1965* or a similar society established under the law of a member state other than the UK.

Where:

(i) immediately after the merger the transferee is either resident in the UK and within the charge to corporation tax or is not resident in the UK but is within the charge to corporation tax as a consequence of carrying on a trade in the UK through a permanent establishment; and

(ii) for mergers within (a), (b) or (c) above, the transfer of assets and liabilities is made in exchange for the issue of shares in or debentures of the transferee to the holders of shares in or debentures of a transferor, except where, and to the extent that, the transferee is prevented from meeting this requirement by reason only of *Companies Act 2006, s 658* (rule against limited company acquiring its own shares) or a corresponding provision in another member state,

then, in determining the debits and credits to be brought into account in respect of a derivative contract, if the rights and liabilities under the contract are transferred in the course of the merger, the transfer is treated as having been made for a consideration equal to the notional carrying value (see **30.31** above). This does not apply where the transferor uses fair value accounting for the contract. Instead, the transfer must be treated by both companies as being at fair value.

Where:

(A) in the course of the merger, a company resident in the UK transfers all the assets and liabilities relating to a business it carries on through a permanent establishment in a member state other than the UK to a company resident in the another member state;

(B) the transfer includes the transfer of rights and liabilities under a derivative contract; and

(C) for mergers within (a), (b) or (c) above, the transfer of assets and liabilities is made in exchange for the issue of shares in or debentures of the transferee to the holders of shares in or debentures of a transferor, except where, and to the extent that, the transferee is prevented from meeting this requirement by reason only of *Companies Act 2006, s 658* (rule against limited company acquiring its own shares) or a corresponding provision in another member state,

then, if tax would have been chargeable under the law of the other member state in respect of the transfer of rights or liabilities under the derivative contract but for the Mergers Directive (*90/431/EEC*), double tax relief (whether unilateral or by agreement) is available as if the amount of tax which would have been so payable but for the Directive were payable. For this purpose, it is to be assumed that, to the extent permitted by the law of the other member state, losses arising on the transfer are set against gains so arising and that any relief due to the UK company under that law is claimed.

The above provisions do not apply unless the merger is effected for *bona fide* commercial reasons and is not part of a scheme or arrangements of which the main purpose or one of the main purposes is avoiding a liability to tax. Advance clearance can be obtained that this condition is met.

[*CTA 2009, ss 682–686; FA 2002, Sch 26 paras 30B, 30C, 30I; F(No 2)A 2005, s 55; SI 2007 No 3186, Sch 2 para 10; SI 2008 No 1579, para 3*].

Cross border transfers of business

[30.44] Where a UK resident company transfers the whole or part of a business that it previously carried on through a permanent establishment in another EEA member state and a derivative contract is included as part of the assets that are transferred, and certain conditions are satisfied, the UK resident company is able to claim double tax credit relief for the overseas tax that would have been payable in respect of the merger, but for the operation of the mergers directive.

[*TIOPA 2010, ss 118, 119*].

Transparent entities

[30.45] The cross border merger and cross border transfer of business provisions are varied apply where one of the parties is a 'transparent entity'. See *CTA 2009, s 687 and TIOPA 2010, ss 120, 121; FA 2002, Sch 26 para 30H.*

A '*transparent entity*' for this purpose is an entity which is resident in a member state other than the UK and is listed as a company in the Annex to the Mergers Directive, but which does not have an ordinary share capital and, if resident in the UK, would not be capable of being registered as a company under *Companies Act 2006*. [*CTA 2009, ss 687, 688; TIOPA 2010, s 120(6); FA 2002, Sch 26 para 30I(1); SI 2007 No 3186, Sch 3 para 4*].

Derivative whose underlying subject matter is an interest in a unit trust, open ended investment company or offshore

[30.46] *CTA 2009, ss 587, 601, 602, 660; FA 2002, Sch 26 Pt 7* make special provision in relation to such schemes. Broadly, these are as follows.

Where a contract does not otherwise qualify as a derivative contract, it is to be treated as such if its underlying subject matter is wholly or partly comprised of a holding in an open ended investment company, unit trust or an offshore fund and that company, unit trust or offshore fund does not satisfy the 'qualifying investments' test.

[*CTA 2009, ss 587, 601, Change 63 listed in Annex l of the Explanatory Notes to CTA 2009*].

Where a company has, for two successive years, a relevant contract which is a contract relating to a holding in an OEIC, unit trust or offshore fund that does not satisfy the qualifying investments test for the second year but not the first and immediately before the beginning of the second period it was a chargeable asset, any chargeable gain or allowable loss has to be brought in by the company in the year in which it ceases to be a party to the contract, using the following assumptions:

(i) the company disposed of the relevant contract immediately before the beginning of the second accounting period;
(ii) the consideration for the disposal was the accounting value (if any) according to the company's accounts at the end of the first year.

[*CTA 2009, s 660*].

Investment trusts and venture capital trusts

[30.47] Any capital profits or losses arising to an investment trust or a venture capital trust from a derivative contract must not be brought into account in determining derivative contract credits or debits. Capital profits or losses in this case are those which, in preparing accounts in accordance with UK generally accepted accounting practice, are carried to or sustained by a capital reserve in accordance with the relevant Statement of Recommended Practice (SORP). The relevant SORP is that relating to the Financial Statements of Investment Trust Companies issued by the Association of Investment Trust Companies in January 2003 as from time to time modified or revised.

The excess of relevant credits over relevant debits from derivative contracts is to be treated as income from shares and securities for the purposes of determining whether or not a company may be approved as an investment trust or a venture capital trust under *CTA 2010, s 1160(3); ICTA 1988, s 842* or *ITA 2007, s 276(3); ICTA 1988, s 842AA* respectively. (See generally **53.1 INVESTMENT TRUSTS** and **74 VENTURE CAPITAL TRUSTS**.)

Treasury powers

The Treasury may by order amend the above provisions so as to alter the definition of capital profits or losses following the modification, amendment, revision or replacement of a SORP.

[*CTA 2009, ss 637, 638, Sch 1 para 669; FA 2002, Sch 26 paras 32–40; FA 2004, s 145, Sch 10 paras 59–63, Sch 26 para 2, Sch 42 Pt 2(5); FA 2005, Sch 4 para 36; F(No 2)A 2005, ss 17–19; ITA 2007 Sch 1 para 605*].

Authorised unit trusts and open ended investment companies

[30.48] Capital profits, gains or losses arising to authorised unit trusts and open ended investment companies in respect of derivative contracts to which they are a party are excluded in computing their profits chargeable to corporation tax. These are defined as such profits, gains or losses that fall to be dealt with under the heading 'net gains/losses', in the statement of total return for the accounting period. This is in turn defined as the statement of total return which, in accordance with the Statement of Recommended Practice (SORP) used for the accounting period, must be included in the accounts contained in the annual report of the authorised investment fund. The SORP is in turn defined as, in relation to any accounting period for which it is required or permitted to be used, the SORP relating to authorised investment funds issued by the Investment Management Association in November 2008.

It is not possible for an authorised unit trust or open ended investment company to carry back a loss on a derivative contract that is not excluded in calculating its taxable profits for set off against its taxable profits of earlier periods.

[*SI 2006 No 964, Regs 10–14*].

Miscellaneous provisions

Amounts brought into account after company ceases to be party to a contract

[30.49] Where a company ceases to be party to a derivative contract in an accounting period and profits or losses arise to the company from the contract or a related transaction (see **30.7** above) in that period, then if the derivative contract credits or debits brought into account in that period do not represent the whole of those profits or losses, credits or debits in respect of the balance of profits or losses continue to be brought into account in any subsequent accounting periods as if the company had not ceased to be a party to the contract. [*CTA 2009, s 608; FA 2002, Sch 26 para 53(3)–(5)*].

Partnerships involving companies

[30.50] Where any of the partners in a partnership which carries on a trade, profession or business, and which is a party to a derivative contract, is a company, no account is taken of debits or credits in relation to the contract in calculating the profits of the partnership for corporation tax purposes. Each company partner is instead required to bring into account a share of the credits and debits in respect of the contract as follows. The credits and debits are determined separately for each company partner as if the contract was entered into or acquired by the company for the purposes of its own trade or business, and as if any transactions carried out by the firm in relation to the contract were carried out by the company. To the extent that any exchange gains or losses are recognised in the firm's statement of recognised gains and losses or statement of changes in equity, they are treated as recognised in the corresponding statement of the company partner (such that they fall to be disregarded in computing the derivative contract profits of that company partner). The company is then required to bring into account a share of the credits and debits so determined corresponding to its share in partnership profits.

Where the company partner uses fair value accounting in relation to its interest in the firm the credits and debits determined as above must be determined on a fair value basis of accounting.

[*CTA 2009, ss 620, 621; FA 2002, Sch 26 paras 49, 50; FA 2004, s 52, Sch 10 paras 65, 66*].

Prevention of deduction of tax

[30.51] A company is not required to deduct income tax from any payment made under a derivative contract to which these provisions apply. [*ITA 2007, s 980; FA 2002, Sch 26 para 51*].

Index-linked gilt-edged securities with embedded contracts for differences

[30.52] Credits and debits arising on a derivative contract are not to be brought into account where:

(a) the rights and liabilities arising under a contract are split into two parts as set out in **30.53** below (under 'embedded derivatives'), with respect to a creditor relationship;

(b) the creditor relationship is an index-linked gilt-edged security giving rise to non-trading credits and debits in respect of the equivalent deemed loan relationship; and

(c) the 'embedded derivative' contract is a contract for differences.

[*CTA 2009, s 623; FA 2002, Sch 26 para 45I; SI 2004 No 2201, Arts 1, 15*].

Derivative contracts and chargeable gains basis

[30.53] For the purpose of these provisions, a '*chargeable asset*' is any asset on which a gain would be a chargeable gain. '*Asset*' includes any obligations under futures contracts which are regarded as assets under *TCGA 1992, s 143*.

In four circumstances, a derivative contract is charged under the capital gains regime. These are:

(a) the contract relates to land or certain tangible moveable property;

(b) the company has a creditor relationship with an embedded derivative which is an option;

(c) the company has a creditor relationship with an embedded derivative which is an exactly tracking contract for differences, the underlying subject matter of which is certain shares;

(d) the contract is a property based total return swap.

Any profits or losses that are recognised in the company's accounts in respect of such derivatives in accordance with generally accepted accounting practice are treated as chargeable gains or allowable losses for the purposes of corporation tax on chargeable gains and are brought into account for tax purposes in the accounting period in which they are so recognised. There is one exception to this rule and this is where, were the embedded derivative an actual option which was disposed at the end of that accounting period, any gain arising on the option would be ignored for tax purposes under the substantial shareholding legislation that is contained in *TCGA 1992, Sch 7AC* (see **19.5 CAPITAL GAINS — SUBSTANTIAL SHAREHOLDINGS**). In such cases any gains or losses arising on the embedded derivative contract are ignored in computing the company's profits for the purposes of derivative contracts legislation.

[*CTA 2009, ss 640, 641, 642; FA 2002, Sch 26 para 45A*].

Carry back of losses

[30.54] Where there is a 'net loss' under the provisions in **30.53** above in an accounting period (the '*loss period*') and, in a previous accounting period falling wholly or partly within 24 months immediately preceding the start of the loss period, there is a 'net gain' under the above provisions, a claim can be made for the loss to be wholly or partly carried back and set against part or all of the gain (but not so as to reduce either the loss or the gain below nil). The claim must be made within two years of the end of the period in which the net loss arose. Losses must be set against gains of a later period before those of an earlier period. Where a gain period falls partly before the 24-month period mentioned above, the loss can only be offset against the proportion of the gain falling within the 24-month period (time-apportioned based on the number of days).

A'*net loss*' in this case is the sum of any allowable losses arising under *CTA 2009, s 641* in a period less the sum of any chargeable gains arising under the above provisions in the same period, in both cases in respect of the company's derivative contracts. A'*net gain*' is the excess of *CTA 2009, s 641* gains over *s 641* losses, further reduced by any non-*s 641* allowable losses. Any non-*s 641* allowable losses must be set against any non-*s 641* gains before the remainder is deducted from *s 641* gains.

[*CTA 2009, ss 663–664; FA 2002, Sch 26 para 45B; SI 2004 No 2201, Art 15*].

Derivative contracts relating to land etc.

[30.55] For contracts entered into on or after 1 August 2004 in an accounting period ending on or after 17 September 2004, non-trading increases and decreases in the value of derivative contracts are not treated as non-trading credits and debits under the derivative contracts regime but instead are treated as chargeable gains or allowable losses within the capital gains regime where conditions A, B and C are met:

(A) the underlying subject matter relates to land (wherever situated) or tangible movable property other than commodities which are tangible assets (*CTA 2009, ss 643, 644; FA 2002, Sch 26 para 45C*);
(B) the company is not a party to the derivative contract at any time in the accounting period for trading purposes; and
(C) the company is not an excluded body.

Where the derivative includes income from land or tangible moveable property (see above) and that income is subordinate income, it is left out of account. Whether or not income is subordinate is determined at the time the company enters into or acquires the contract. There are also special provisions allowing carry back losses (see below).

[*CTA 2009, ss 643, 644; FA 2002, Sch 26 paras 45A, 45C, 45G; SI 2004 No 2201, Arts 1, 15; SI 2004 No 3270, Arts 1, 8; SI 2005 No 2082; SI 2005 No 3440, Art 8*].

Creditor relationships — embedded derivatives which are options to acquire shares

[30.56] Where in a company's accounts in accordance with generally accepted accounting practice a derivative contract is separated from a creditor relationship:

(i) the contract is treated as an option by *CTA 2009, s 585(3)*;
(ii) the underlying subject matter is qualifying ordinary shares or mandatorily convertible preference shares;
(iii) the creditor relationship is not a trading relationship at any time in the accounting period;
(iv) the company is not an open ended investment company, investment trust, venture capital trust or a unit trust; and
(v) the company was not a party to the loan relationship immediately before the start of its first statutory accounting period beginning on or after 1 January 2005.

the asset representing the creditor relationship is not treated as a qualifying corporate bond, under *TCGA 1992, s 117(A1)* and so is not prevented from falling within the chargeable gains rules by virtue of the exemption for QCBs under *TCGA 1992, s 115(1)(b)*. Therefore gains and losses on a disposal of the loan relationship are subject to capital gains tax rules. This treatment does not apply if either:

(a) the creditor relationship provides that the shares to be acquired on conversion or exchange will have a specified cash (i.e. market) value at the time of conversion or exchange or:
   (i) the rights and liabilities in the derivative contract are such that the company is entitled or obliged to accept cash instead of the underlying shares; and
   (ii) the amount of the payment differs by a not insignificant amount from the value of the shares which it would be entitled or obliged to acquire under the contract.

'*Mandatorily convertible preference shares*' are shares which represent the creditor relationship, are not qualifying ordinary shares and are issued on terms that stipulate they must be converted into or exchanged for qualifying ordinary shares within 24 hours after the time that they are acquired.

'*Qualifying ordinary shares*' are listed shares or those in a holding company or a trading company, where the shares form all or part of the issued share capital (other than, in either case, capital which carries a right to a fixed rate dividend but no other right to share in profits or capital where the holders have no right to dividends or to share in profits in any other way). [*CTA 2009, ss 645–647; FA 2002 Sch 26 paras 45D, 45E*].

Prevention of double counting

Where the option to acquire shares is exercised and the transaction is treated as a no gain/no loss reorganisation for the purposes of *TCGA 1992, s 127* in order to avoid any double counting an adjustment will be made on the subsequent disposal of the shares that are acquired. The adjustment is determined on a formula basis and, very broadly, is designed to secure that the base cost of the shares is increased by any chargeable gains that have been brought into charge to tax in respect of the embedded derivative and any profits that have been brought into account in respect of the host contract (including any discount that is recognised in the company accounts) and is reduced by any allowable losses that are brought into account in respect of the embedded derivative.

A further adjustment applies where an exchangeable security is exchanged for shares or a convertible security is disposed of otherwise than for shares. In such cases the acquisition cost of the security is increased to the extent that the sum of the discount that has been brought into account in respect of the loan relationship host contract and any chargeable gains that have been brought into account in respect of the embedded derivative exceed any allowable losses that have been so brought into account. The acquisition cost of the security is reduced to the extent that the allowable losses that have been brought into account in respect of the embedded derivative exceed the sum of any chargeable gains that have been so brought into account and any discount that has been recognised in respect of the host contract. Where the amount of this adjustment exceeds the cost of the asset the excess is added to the disposal consideration.

[*CTA 2009, ss 670, 671; FA 2002, Sch 26 para 45H*].

Transitional rules — existing assets

The above rules do not apply where a company was a party to the underlying loan relationship immediately before the start of its first statutory accounting period beginning on or after 1 January 2005. In such cases where the loan relationship is bifurcated in the company's accounts into a host contract and an embedded derivative and *CTA 2009, s 645* would otherwise have applied to the embedded derivative, any profits or losses arising on the embedded derivative are disregarded for the purposes of the derivative contracts legislation. Further, the loan relationship as a whole is treated as not being a QCB for the purposes of *TCGA 1992*.

On a disposal of the loan relationship the disposal proceeds for the purposes of the *TCGA 1992* are reduced by any interest which has accrued up to the time of the disposal and which as result of the disposal will not be payable to the company. At the same time the disposal proceeds are increased by any exchange losses which have arisen on the loan relationship during the company's period of ownership and which have been brought into account in computing its loan relationship profits. Where an exchange gain has arisen over this period the amount of the disposal consideration is reduced (but not below nil) by the amount of this loss. Any excess of such exchange gains over the disposal consideration is treated as being an incidental cost of making the disposal.

[*CTA 2009, Sch 2 paras 82–84; FA 2002, Sch 26 paras 45FA*].

Where the security is disposed of in exchange for shares and the reorganisation provisions of *TCGA 1992, ss 126–132* apply (such that the exchange is not treated as being a disposal) the adjustments discussed above will be made on a disposal of the replacement shares that the company acquires as a result of the reorganisation.

[*CTA 2009, Sch 2 para 84; FA 2002, Sch 26 para 45H*].

Embedded derivatives — exactly tracking contracts for differences

[30.57] In certain cases where a company holds an index-linked loan or loan note that is bifurcated in its accounts into a host debt contract and an embedded derivative which falls to be treated as a contract for differences for the purposes of the derivative contracts legislation, any profits or losses arising on the embedded derivative will be treated as giving rise to chargeable gains or allowable losses for the purposes of corporation tax on chargeable gains on the basis on which such profits or losses are recognised in the company's accounts.

For such treatment to apply the following conditions have to be satisfied:

(a) the company must not be a party to the underlying creditor relationship for the purposes of its trade, unless the company is a mutual trading company or it is a party to the creditor relationship for the purposes of its life assurance business;
(b) the company is not an authorised unit trust, investment trust, open ended investment company or venture capital trust;
(c) the underlying subject matter of the derivative contract is qualifying ordinary shares which are listed on a recognised stock exchange. '*Qualifying ordinary shares*' are defined as shares other than those which entitle the holder to a dividend at a fixed rate and to no other right to share the profits of the company or which do not entitle the holder to receive dividends or to otherwise share in the profits of the company;
(d) the contract must be an exactly tracking contract. This means that the amount which must be paid to discharge the non-bifurcated loan or loan note must be exactly linked to movements in the value of the relevant index or asset from the time at which the loan or loan note came into existence until its redemption. It is permissible however for there to be a very slight variation to the period for which the indexation applies provided that such deviation is only required for valuation purposes; and
(e) the company was not a party to the creditor relationship before the start of its first statutory accounting period beginning on or after 1 January 2005.

[*CTA 2009, ss 633, 634, 635, 648, 649, Sch 2 para 86; FA 2002, Sch 26 para 45F*].

As the loan relationship as a whole is not treated as a QCB in such cases anti-double counting provisions apply for the purposes of the *TCGA 1992* on a disposal of the security. In such cases the disposal proceeds of the security are reduced to the extent that the discount that has been brought into account in respect of the host contract and the chargeable gains that have been brought into account in respect of the embedded derivative exceed the allowable losses that have been so brought into account. Where the amount of the allowable losses exceeds the amount of the discount and the chargeable gains, the cost of the asset is reduced by this amount and to the extent that the amount of the reduction exceeds the cost of the asset, the disposal consideration of the asset is increased by the excess.

[*CTA 2009, ss 672–673; FA 2002, Sch 26 para 45HZA*].

CTA 2009, s 648; FA 2002, Sch 26 para 45F does not apply where a company was a party to the underlying loan relationship immediately before the start of its first statutory accounting period beginning on or after 1 January 2005. In such cases where the loan relationship is bifurcated in the company's accounts into a host contract and a contract for differences, and *CTA 2009, s 648* would otherwise have applied, any debits and credits arising on the embedded derivative are disregarded in computing its profits and losses for the purposes of the derivative contracts legislation. Further, the loan relationship as a whole is not treated as a QCB for the purposes of the *TCGA 1992*. When the company disposes of the loan relationship the disposal proceeds are adjusted for any accrued interest which as a result of the disposal will not be payable to the company.

[*CTA 2009, Sch 2 paras 86, 87; FA 2002, Sch 26 para 45FA*].

Property-based total return swaps

[30.58] This applies to a contract for differences where one or more indices are specified in the contract, at least one being the index of changes to the value of land and the underlying subject matter also includes interest rates. The contract is not at any time held by the company for trading purposes and the company is not an excluded body. They are to be taxed on a capital gains basis per *CTA 2009, s 641* (see below).

[*CTA 2009, s 650*].

Special treatment for derivatives that are separated from a debtor loan relationship

[30.59] The following transactions are not to be brought into account for corporation tax under the derivative contract rules.

Debtor relationships with embedded derivatives — options

Where a debtor relationship is bifurcated in a company's accounts into a host contract and an embedded option, any gains or losses that the company recognises in its accounts in respect of the embedded option are left out of account for the purposes of the derivative contracts legislation where the following conditions are satisfied:

(a) the embedded derivative is separated from the host loan relationship and is treated as an option;
(b) the underlying subject matter is shares;
(c) either the company was not carrying on a banking or securities business or the contract was not entered into in the ordinary course of such business;
(d) the company is not an open ended investment company, investment trust, venture capital trust or a unit trust;
(e) the company was not a party to the loan relationship immediately before the start of its first statutory accounting period beginning on or after 1 January 2005.

[*CTA 2009, Sch 2 para 94; FA 2002, Sch 26, para 45J(1), (2), (10)*].

Where profits or losses arising in respect of an embedded option are disregarded for the purposes of the derivative contracts legislation and the option is an option to acquire shares in the issuer and the option is exercised,

TCGA 1992, s 144(2) will apply so that the grant of the option and the issue of the shares are treated as a single transaction. Since the issue by a company of its own shares is not a disposal for the purposes of the *TCGA 1992*, this means that no chargeable gain or allowable loss will arise as a result of the exercise of the option.

When the option is exercised and the issuer makes a cash payment to discharge its obligations in respect of the option, in essence, the issuer will be treated as realising a chargeable gain to the extent that the amount of the payment made to redeem the security that is attributed to the embedded option is less than the initial carrying value of the option and as realising an allowable loss where the payment that is attributed to the embedded option exceeds the initial carrying value of the option. The payment made to redeem the security is split as follows. An amount equal to the fair value of the loan relationship host contract (i.e. the loan relationship after the option has been separated from it) at the date that the option is exercised is allocated to the loan relationship host contract with the balance being deemed to be payable in respect of the embedded derivative. This follows the accounting treatment that a company would adopt in its accounts.

[*CTA 2009, s 654; FA 2002, Sch 26 para 45J(3), (6)*].

Where a loan relationship is redeemed in circumstances where the option is not exercised, in essence, the same approach is followed as discussed in the preceding paragraph to determine whether a chargeable gain or an allowable loss arises in respect of the redemption or novation of the security.

[*CTA 2009, s 655; FA 2009, Sch 26 para 45J(3), (9)*].

Where a company was a party to the underlying debtor relationship immediately before the start of its first accounting period beginning on or after 1 January 2005 the treatment discussed above does not apply. Any profits or losses that the company recognises in its accounts in respect of the option are disregarded for the purposes of the derivative contracts legislation. If the option is exercised and the issuer makes a cash payment to discharge its obligations in respect of the option, the issuer is entitled to claim a capital loss for the proportion of the redemption payment that is attributable to the embedded option.

[*CTA 2009, Sch 2 para 94; FA 2002, Sch 26 para 45JA*].

Debtor relationships with embedded derivatives — contracts for differences

Any debits or credits that a company recognises in its accounts in respect of a contract for differences that has been separated from a debtor relationship are left out of account for the purposes of the derivative contracts legislation where the following conditions are satisfied:

(A) the contract is a relevant contract and the company is a party to it because of a debtor relationship;

(B) the contract is treated as a contract for differences and is not a deemed option under *CTA 2009, s 652*;

(C) the contract is an exactly tracking contract;
(D) the underlying subject matter is shares;
(E) when the company became a party to the contract, it was not trading as a bank or securities house, or, if it was, it did not become a party to the contract in the ordinary course of such business;
(F) the company is not an open ended investment company, investment trust, venture capital trust or a unit trust;
(G) the company was not a party to the underlying debtor relationship immediately before the start of its first statutory accounting period beginning on or after 1 January 2005.

In such cases a chargeable gain or allowable loss can arise for the purposes of the *TCGA 1992* when a company ceases to be a party to the loan relationship. A chargeable gain will arise if the amount paid to redeem the loan relationship is less than its issue price whereas if the redemption amount exceeds the issue price an allowable loss will arise.

[*CTA 2009, Sch 2, para 88; FA 2002, Sch 26 para 45K*].

An '*exactly tracking contract*' means a contract where the amount to be paid to discharge the rights and liabilities is equal to R% of C where R% is the percentage change (if any) over the relevant period in the value of the underlying subject matter and the consideration, determined using generally accepted accounting practice, being the proceeds of the issue giving rise to the debtor relationship. The '*relevant period*' is usually the time between the issue of the securities and their redemption, or otherwise the relationship comes to an end but this can change if there is a delay in obtaining the valuation of the rights and liabilities under the liability representing the debtor relationship. Where the debtor relationship comes to an end and an amount is paid to discharge the company's obligations under the relationship (discharge amount), the gain or loss is treated as a capital gain or loss and the following assumptions are made:

(i) the derivative contract is an asset of the company;
(ii) there is a disposal at the time the relationship ends;
(iii) the consideration is equal to the 'relevant amount'; and
(iv) the cost of the asset is equal to the discharge amount.

For this purpose, the '*relevant amount*' means the proceeds of issue of the security representing the loan relationship or, if the company was not a party to the original loan relationship, the carrying value of the host contract when the company became a party. The '*host contract*' means the loan relationship to which the company is a party because of a debtor relationship.

A '*securities house*' means a person authorised under *FISMA 2000* and whose business consists wholly or mainly of dealing, as a principal, in financial instruments within the meaning of *ITA 2007*.

[*CTA 2009, ss 656–658, 709; FA 2002, Sch 26 para 45K; SI 2006 No 3269*].

Such treatment does not apply where a company was a party to the underlying debtor relationship immediately before the start of its first statutory accounting period beginning on or after 1 January 2005.

[*CTA 2009, Sch 2 para 88; FA 2002, Sch 26 para 45KA*].

Loan relationship bifurcated into a host contract and an equity instrument

Where a debtor relationship is bifurcated in a company's accounts in accordance with generally accepted accounting practice into a host contract and an equity instrument, the equity instrument will fall outside the derivative contracts legislation. Any profits and losses arising on the host contract will be dealt with under the loan relationships legislation.

Where a company ceases to be a party to the debtor relationship it is possible for the company to claim an allowable loss for the purposes of the *TCGA 1992* to the extent that the amount that it pays to redeem the loan relationship as a whole (i.e. ignoring the bifurcation), as reduced by an amount equal to the fair value of the host contract at that date, exceeds the initial carrying value of the equity instrument. The initial carrying value of the equity instrument is the value at the time at which it was separated from the loan relationship. Where an embedded option is treated as an equity instrument it is never revalued for accounting purposes.

It is not possible for a company to claim an allowable loss where it was a party to the underlying debtor relationship at the start of its first accounting period beginning on or after 1 January 2005.

[*CTA 2009, ss 665, 666, Sch 2 para 90; FA 2002, Sch 26 para 45JA*].

Plain vanilla options and futures over shares — prevention of double counting

Anti-double counting provisions apply where a company is a party to a plain vanilla (or stand alone) option or future, i.e. an option or future that has not been separated from another contract, and it acquires shares under the terms of the option or future. In such cases an adjustment is made to the base cost of the shares for the purposes of the *TCGA 1992*. The base cost of the shares is increased for any net gain that has arisen to the company on the option or future and which has been brought into account in computing its derivative contract profits. Where a net loss has arisen on the option or future the base cost of the shares acquired is reduced. Where the amount of the net loss exceeds the base cost of the shares acquired the excess is added to the disposal proceeds of the shares on a subsequent disposal of the shares

[*CTA 2009, ss 667–669; FA 2002, Sch 26 para 45HA*].

Power to amend by regulation

[30.60] The Treasury may by order amend most provisions of the derivative contracts legislation and such amendment may have effect for statutory accounting periods beginning at any time in the calendar year in which the order is made. For further information see *CTA 2009, s 701*. In addition the Treasury has the power to amend the derivative contracts legislation by regulation where there is a change in accounting standards which affects the way in which profits and losses arising on a derivative contract are recognised in a company's accounts. Such changes may be made with retrospective effect to the date that a company began to apply the new accounting treatment if th change in accounting treatment takes effect before the necessary legislative changes have been made (see *CTA 2009, s 701A*).

[*CTA 2009, ss 701, 701A*].

Key points

[30.61] Points to consider are as follows:

1. The derivative contracts legislation covers virtually all derivative contracts to which a company is a party. There are certain limited cases where derivative contracts the underlying subject matter of which consists, or is deemed to consist wholly of shares are excluded from the derivative contracts legislation (see **30.3**).

Recognition of profit

2. Where a company prepares its accounts in accordance with UK GAAP excluding FRS 26 profits and losses arising on derivative contracts will generally be recognised for the purposes of the derivative contracts legislation on the basis in which these are recognised in the company's accounts.

3. Where a company prepares its accounts in accordance with IFRS or UK GAAP incorporating FRS 26 profits and losses on derivative contracts will generally be brought into account for tax purposes on a fair value basis. Where a derivative contract is used as a hedge, in certain cases profits and losses might be brought into account for tax purposes on a different basis under the provisions of the Disregard Regulations.

4. When advising companies that prepare their accounts in accordance with IFRS or UK GAAP incorporating FRS 26 it will be necessary to ascertain whether the contract falls within the scope *of Regs 4, 7, 8*, or *9* of the *Disregard Regulations* [*SI 2004 No 3256*]. In the case of contracts falling within *Regs 7* or *8* (see **30.19**) it will be necessary to ascertain whether a company has made an election to disapply these regulations or to apply *Reg 9A* in place of these regulations.

5. In the case of contracts falling within *Reg 9* of the *Disregard Regulations* it will be necessary to ascertain whether a company has made an election to apply *Reg 9A* in place of *Reg 9* and, if so, which of the two possible elections it has made. This will determine the extent to which interest rate contracts that are used to hedge connected companies loan relationships still fall within the scope of *Reg 9* (see **30.20**).

Contracts with non-residents

6. Where a company is a party to an interest rate swap, a cross currency swap or any other contract which provides for payments to be made by the company that are based on applying a specified interest rate to a notional principal amount, the company will need to ensure that the counterparty to the contract meets one of the following conditions:

(a) it is a UK resident company;
(b) it is a party to the contract solely for the purposes of a trade carried on through a UK permanent establishment; or
(c) it is resident for tax purposes in a territory that has a double tax treaty with the UK that contains an interest article (see **30.34**).

Where these conditions are not satisfied the UK company will be denied tax relief for any net interest-based payments that it makes under the terms of the contract unless it is a bank, building society or financial trader. It is normal for companies to cover against this exposure by requiring representations to be given by the counterparty to the contract that it will satisfy one of the above conditions and by providing that the counterparty may only transfer or novate the contract to a person who satisfies one of these conditions.

Intra-group transfers

7. Where it is desired to transfer a derivative contract from one group company to another under the intra-group transfer provisions of *CTA 2009, s 625* (see **30.31**), and the transfer is taking place by way of a novation it will be important to ensure that there are no changes to the terms of the contract as a result of the novation which might have material financial consequences. If this is not the case such changes might prevent the transfer from falling within *CTA 2009, s 625* based on the Tribunal's decision in *HBOS Treasury Services plc (now HBOS Treasury Services Ltd) v Revenue and Customs Comrs* [2009] UKFTT 261 (TC), [2010] SFTD 134.

Anti-avoidance provisions

8. The derivative contracts legislation contains a number of anti-avoidance provisions, including cases where a company is a party to a derivative contract, or a related transaction in respect of the derivative contract, for an unallowable purpose. This provision is modelled on that of *CTA 2009, s 441* of the loan relationships legislation (see **30.25**).

9. Other anti-avoidance provisions include cases where a company allows an in the money option to lapse, or it is only partially exercises an in the money option, and it is connected with the counterparty (see **30.29**), as well as cases where a company disposes of a derivative contract and does not recognise the full disposal consideration in its accounts (see **30.28**).

31

Distributions

Cross-references. See **9.4** BUILDING SOCIETIES; **39** GROUP RELIEF; **54.86** LOAN RELATIONSHIPS and **63** PURCHASE BY A COMPANY OF ITS OWN SHARES.

Simon's Taxes. See Part D5.

Introduction

[31.1] The term 'distribution' within the Corporation Tax Acts is more widely drawn and includes some payments and other transactions which would not normally be treated as 'distributions' within the normal meaning of the term — for example, some payments of interest on securities of a company may be treated as distributions in certain circumstances.

The following chapter considers the scope and treatment of distributions within the Corporation Tax Acts.

It is also notable that as part of the tax law rewrite programme, the provisions in respect of distributions made by companies have been rewritten to *CTA 2010, Pt 23*. The rewrite generally replicates the provisions contained within *ICTA 1988, s 209 et seq*, with a few changes in terminology. For example, reference in *CTA 2010* is made to 'special securities' which were not defined as a term within *ICTA 1988*, but were found within *s 209(2)(e)*.

In addition *CTA 2009*, as amended by *FA 2009*, introduces a new regime for the taxation of dividends, providing an exemption from corporation tax for certain specific classes of dividends received by a company. This regime is outlined further at **31.15**.

Legislation was introduced in *F(No 3)A 2010* to ensure certain distributions (mainly of a capital nature) fall within the general rule that all distributions are exempt under the distributions legislation in this chapter. Although a distribution is exempt under the distribution regime, it may still be taken into account in computing a capital gain. These changes in the definition of a distribution take effect retrospectively to 1 July 2009. However, a company may elect for this change to have no effect on specified distributions made before 22 June 2010.

Scope of distributions

[31.2] The term 'distribution' is widely defined in *CTA 2010, s 1000; ICTA 1988, ss 209–211*. Subject to the exceptions listed at **31.14** below, it includes any of the items listed below as follows. See also the additional items at **31.19**, **31.20** below.

(a) Dividends (including capital dividends). [*CTA 2010, s 1000(1)A; ICTA 1988, s 209(2)(a)*].

(b) Any distribution in respect of shares (except for repayments of share capital or where there is equivalent new consideration). The distribution may be in cash or otherwise (see **31.3** below).

(c) Issue of redeemable share capital or any security (otherwise than for new consideration) (see **31.4** below).

(d) Interest or other distribution exceeding a reasonable commercial return in respect of non-commercial securities of the company and any such amount which exceeds the principal secured by the security. No amount is regarded as part of the principal of a security in so far as it exceeds new consideration received by the borrowing company (see **31.5** and **31.9** below).

(e) Interest or other distribution paid in respect of 'special securities' except to the extent it represents repayment of principal or falls within (d) above (see **31.6** and **31.9** below).
(f) The excess over new consideration arising on transfers of assets or liabilities by a company to its shareholders or to a company by its shareholders. [*CTA 2010, s 1020*].
(g) where a company makes a bonus issue following a repayment of share capital, it may be treated as having made a distribution.

The following definitions are provided at **31.13**.

- 'new consideration';
- 'shares';
- 'security'; and
- 'in respect of shares'.

An extended meaning of distribution is applicable to close companies and in 90% groups.

See also HMRC Tax Bulletin Issue 76, April 2005 p 1199 for HMRC's view that, in the majority of cases, where goodwill is transferred by a sole trader (or partnership) to a company on the incorporation of a business, before the company has commenced trading, at a value higher than its market value, the excess is to be treated as a distribution for the purposes of *ICTA 1988, s 209(2)(b)* (as was, see further **31.3** below) or *s 209(4)* (as was, see **31.10** below). If it is clear that there was no intention to transfer the goodwill at excess value and that reasonable efforts were made to carry out the transfer at market value by using a professional valuation, the distribution can be 'unwound'. For discussion of valuation of goodwill of property-based business (e.g. public houses, hotels, care homes etc.) see 'Taxation' 23 October 2008 p 445.

[*CTA 2010, ss 1000, 1002, 1006, 1019, 1064, 1072*].

Simon's Taxes. See **D5.1**.

Distribution (other than cash) in respect of shares

[31.3] As noted above a distribution can be made in cash or otherwise. Thus a transfer of assets may also be treated as a distribution in certain circumstances.

A transfer of assets (other than cash) or of liabilities made between companies resident in the UK is not to be treated as a distribution provided that neither company is the '51% subsidiary' of a non-resident company and that the companies are not under the control of the same person or persons either at the time of, or as a result of, the transfer. [*CTA 2010, ss 1002, 1021; ICTA 1988, s 209(6)*].

A company is a '*51% subsidiary*' if more than 50% of its ordinary share capital is owned directly or indirectly by another. [*CTA 2010, s 1154; ICTA 1988, s 838(1)(a)*].

See also, however, **31.10** below and **63 PURCHASE BY A COMPANY OF ITS OWN SHARES**.

Issue of redeemable share capital or any security

[31.4] A distribution includes the issue in respect of shares in the company of redeemable share capital in so far as it is not referable to 'new consideration', see **31.13** below. It also includes the issue of securities only partly for new consideration. The value of any redeemable share capital (or security) is the amount of the share capital (or principal) together with any premium payable on redemption (or maturity), or in a winding-up, or in any other circumstances. The paying-up of issued share capital by the company also falls under this head. See also **31.17** below.

[*CTA 2010, ss 1003–1004; ICTA 1988, ss 209(2)(c)(8), 254(10)*].

Interest or other distribution exceeding a reasonable commercial return

[31.5] With reference to **31.2**(d) above a non-commercial security is one where the consideration given by the company for the use of the principal represents more than a reasonable commercial return for its use. Thus a distribution includes any interest or other distribution borne by the company in respect of securities (except any part representing principal), to the extent that the interest etc. exceeds a reasonable commercial return for the use of the principal secured. A distribution is not treated as representing the principal of the security to the extent it exceeds new consideration.

[*CTA 2010, ss 1005, 1006; ICTA 1988, s 209(2)(d)*]. See also **31.9** below.

Where a security is issued by a company for new consideration in excess of the amount of the principal secured by the security, the amount of the principal so secured is treated for this purpose as increased to the amount of the new consideration, subject to the further provisions below: where there is a link between the security and the value of shares of the issuing company (or an associated company); or where hedging arrangements are in place.

[*CTA 2010, s 1008; ICTA 1988, s 209(3AA)*].

Link to shares of company or associated company (i.e. where one company 'controls' the other or both are under common control)

CTA 2010, s 1008; ICTA 1988, s 209(3AA) does not apply where the security is one which to a significant extent reflects dividends or other distributions in respect of, or fluctuations in the value of, shares in one or more companies each of which is either the issuing company or an associated company.

There is, however, an exception (so that *CTA 2010, s 1008; ICTA 1988, s 209(3AA)* does apply) if the security is issued in the ordinary course of its business by a bank (within *CTA 2010, s 1120; ICTA 1988, s 840A*, see **8.1 BANKS**) or 'securities house' (as defined) and the link to shares is by reason only that the security reflects fluctuations in an index whose underlying subject matter is shares in other companies as well as the issuing company (or associated companies — as defined in *CTA 2010, s 1010*), those other companies' shares representing a significant proportion of the underlying market value.

Where a company issues a security at a premium representing new consideration, references to the part of the distribution representing principal secured on the security is to be taken as a reference to the sum of the part of the distribution as represents the principal and the part representing the premium. The reasonable commercial return for this purpose is taken as the sum of the part of the distribution representing a reasonable commercial return for the use of the principal and that for the use of the premium.

'*Control*' for this purpose is held by a person who exercises, is able to exercise or who is entitled to acquire control over a company's affairs, whether directly or indirectly. In particular, there is control where the greater part of issued share capital, voting power, income on a distribution or assets on a winding up is held by a company. Rights held as a loan creditor are ignored and two or more companies together may satisfy the conditions and have control.

[*CTA 2010, ss 450, 451*].

Shares held by a company (and voting or other powers arising from such shares) are left out of account for this purpose if a profit on sale of the shares would be treated as a trading receipt of the company's trade and the shares are not assets of an insurance company's long-term insurance fund.

[*CTA 2010, ss 1007–1011; ICTA 1988, s 431(2)*].

Hedging arrangements

CTA 2010, s 1008; ICTA 1988, s 209(3AA) also does not apply at any time at which there are (or have been after 16 April 2002) 'hedging arrangements' (as defined in *CTA 2010, s 1010*) relating to some or all of the issuing company's liabilities under the security. There is, however, an exception (so that *CTA 2010, s 1008; ICTA 1988, s 209(3AA)* does apply) where each of the following four conditions are met at that time *and* at all earlier times after 16 April 2002 when there have been such hedging arrangements.

(i) The hedging arrangements must not constitute, include or form part of any scheme or arrangement a main purpose of which is avoidance of tax, stamp duty or stamp duty land tax.

(ii) They must be such that where, at any time, a corporation tax deduction falls to be made by the issuing company in respect of the security, then at that time (or within a reasonable time before or after it) any offsetting amounts under the arrangements arise to the issuing company or to a fellow group member (see **39.3 GROUP RELIEF**).

(iii) The whole of every offsetting amount under (ii) above must be brought into charge to corporation tax by a company (or together by companies) within (ii) above.

(iv) Any corporation tax deduction for expenses of establishing or administering the hedging arrangements must be reasonable in proportion to the amounts required to be brought into charge under (iii) above.

'Hedging arrangements' means any scheme or arrangement for the purpose of securing that an offsetting amount of income or gain accrues or is received/receivable.

[*CTA 2010, ss 1012, 1013, 1014; ICTA 1988, ss 209A, 209B; FA 2003, Sch 18 para 3(2)*].

Distribution paid in respect of 'special securities'

[31.6] *CTA 2010* introduces the term 'special securities' at *s 1015*, which generally replicates the provisions found previously within *ICTA 1988, s 209(2)(e)*, see further **31.7** below.

For the purpose of (e) in **31.2** above, '*special securities*' are such securities as fulfil any of the following conditions:

(a) they are issued otherwise than for new consideration;
(b) the securities are (i) convertible, directly or indirectly into shares or securities; or (ii) carry a right to receive shares in or securities of the company; and (iii) are not quoted or issued on terms comparable to listed securities;
(c) the return on the security depends to any extent on the results of the company's business or any part of it (but not merely if the return increases if results deteriorate or decreases if results improve);
(d) the securities are 'connected with' shares in the company;
(e) the securities are equity notes held by a company associated with the issuing company or which is a funded company.

For this purpose, an 'equity note' is a security in respect of which any of the following tests are satisfied so far as the whole or part of the principal is concerned:

- no redemption date is given;
- the redemption date, or the latest date for redemption, falls after the end of the permitted period;
- the redemption date is after a particular event occurs and it is probable or certain that the event will occur;
- the issuing company can secure that there is no specified redemption date and that the redemption date falls after the end of the permitted period.

The permitted period is 50 years after the issue date of the security.

Relevant alternative finance return is not treated as a distribution under the above provisions.

Per *CTA 2010, Sch 2 para 103*: shares issued before 6 April 1965 or securities issued before 6 April 1972 do not meet condition (a). Similarly securities issued before 6 April 1972 do not meet condition (b)(ii) above.

See further the exception listed at **31.9** below.

[*CTA 2010, ss 1015–1017*].

In *HBOS Treasury Services plc v HMRC* [2009] UKFTT 261 (TC) the bank entered a scheme to remonetise interest rate swaps in such a way as to avoid the normal incidence of tax on such a transaction. The scheme involved the novation of the swaps. It was held that the scheme did not work.

Interest in respect of certain securities

[31.7] This refers to the provisions in *ICTA 1988, s 209(2)(e)*, now rewritten as above. A distribution includes any interest or other distribution not representing principal or exceeding a reasonable commercial return per **31.5** above, the cost of which is borne by the company, in respect of:

(i) bonus securities issued under **31.4** above in respect of shares (for issues after 5 April 1965) or securities (for issues after 5 April 1972) of the company;

(ii) securities convertible directly or indirectly into shares in the company which are neither listed on a recognised stock exchange nor issued on terms reasonably comparable to those on which securities so listed were issued;

(iii) securities issued after 5 April 1972 carrying a right to receive shares in, or securities of, the company (being neither quoted nor issued on comparable terms, see (ii) above);

(iv) securities the interest on which varies with the results of the company's business. This does not apply by reason only of the terms of a security providing for the interest to be reduced if the results improve or increased if they deteriorate (commonly known as 'ratchet loans');

(v) securities carrying rights such that it is 'necessary or advantageous' for the holder, disposer, or acquirer of those securities to hold, dispose of, or acquire, a proportionate holding of shares. Such securities are '*connected with*' the shares; or

(vi) 'equity notes' held by a company which either is '*associated with*' the issuing company (i.e. one is a '75% subsidiary' of the other or both are such subsidiaries of a third company) or is a '*funded company*' (i.e. there are arrangements involving the company being put in funds (directly or indirectly) by the issuing company or by a company associated with the issuing company).

Where an accounting period of a company straddles 1 April 2004, it is treated, for the purposes of calculating the company's profits and losses, as two separate accounting periods, the first ending on 31 March 2004 and the second, to which the new rules apply, beginning on 1 April 2004.

[*ICTA 1988, ss 209(2)(e)(10)(11), 254(2); FA 2004, ss 34(1), 37*].

Exceptions with regard to certain securities, and to 'special securities'

[31.8] Interest within (i)–(vi) above on securities issued by a company to another company within the charge to corporation tax is *not* treated as a distribution *provided that* the recipient company is neither exempt from tax in respect of the interest, etc. (other than under the general corporation tax exemption of UK company distributions) nor (where **31.6** above applies) otherwise outside the matters in respect of which that company is within the charge to corporation tax. This exception also applies under *CTA 2010* to 'special securities' which are not 'non-commercial' securities, see further **31.6** above, on the same conditions.

These provisions do not apply where the securities are within (iv) above, or 'special securities' within **31.6**(c) above, and:

(a) the principal does not exceed £100,000;
(b) the principal and interest must be repaid within five years of the principal being paid to the borrower; and
(c) the obligation was entered into before 9 March 1982, or was entered into before 1 July 1982 pursuant to negotiations in progress on 9 March 1982, the borrower having before that date applied for the loan and supplied any documents required in support of his application.

Where the repayment period of either principal or interest is extended after 8 March 1982 (but is still within (b) above), (i)–(vi) above and **31.6** above do not apply to any interest etc. paid after the repayment period in force at that date.

[*CTA 2010, s 1032, Sch 2 para 107; ICTA 1988, s 212; CTA 2009, Sch 1 para 99*].

As regards (vi) in **31.7** above, a security is an '*equity note*' if, as regards the whole or any part of the principal, any of the following apply:

(1) under the terms of issue, either there is no particular redemption date, or the latest (or only) redemption date falls more than 50 years after the date of issue;
(2) under the terms of issue, redemption is to occur more than 50 years after the date of issue if a particular event occurs, and (judged at the time of issue) that event is certain or likely to occur; or
(3) the issuing company can secure that there is no particular redemption date or that the redemption date falls more than 50 years after the date of issue.

For *CTA 2010*, an 'equity note' is similarly defined, see **31.6** above.

[*CTA 2010, s 1016; ICTA 1988, s 209(9)*].

HMRC have confirmed that ownership of shares in the company holding the security will not of itself be treated as bringing the issuing company within (3) above, and that a demand loan is not regarded as an equity note. The word 'arrangements' in relation to the definition of a funded company implies a purposive connection, and would not for example apply were a bank group to loan money to a company which, as a separate matter, happened to acquire equity notes issued by the group.

In HMRC Brief 47/2008, HMRC set out their policy on deduction of tax at source from interest which is treated as a distribution. In their view, income tax is only deductible from payments that have the character of interest, i.e. which fall to be treated as interest under UK tax rules. If the payments are classed as a distribution, that test is no longer satisfied and therefore no withholding tax is required. This will mainly apply to companies that issue securities.

See HMRC Tax Bulletin May 1993 p 68 as regards the definition of an equity note.

See also **31.9** below.

'Principal'

[31.9] As regards **31.5**, **31.6** and **31.7** above:

(i) no amount is regarded as representing principal secured by a security in so far as it exceeds 'new consideration' (see **31.13** below) received by the company for its issue; and

(ii) where a security is issued at a premium consisting of 'new consideration', references to the principal represented by a distribution are taken as referring to the aggregate of the principal and the premium represented by the distribution (and a similar rule applies as regards **31.5** above in relation to the reasonable commercial return for the use of principal represented by a distribution). This does *not* have effect as regards **31.5** above where (as referred to in **31.5** above) *ICTA 1988, s 209(3AA)* applies (and is not disapplied by *ICTA 1988, ss 209A, 209B*).

Where an accounting period of a company straddles 1 April 2004, it is treated, for the purposes of calculating the company's profits and losses, as two separate accounting periods, the first ending on 31 March 2004 and the second, to which the new rules apply, beginning on 1 April 2004.

[*CTA 2010, ss 1007, 1008, 1018; ICTA 1988, s 209(3)(3A); FA 2004, ss 34(1), 37*].

Transfer of assets or liabilities between company and members

[31.10] The transfer of assets or liabilities between a company and its members is treated as a distribution in so far as the market value of any benefit received by a member exceeds that of any 'new consideration' (see **31.13** below) given by him.

As noted at **31.3** above, such a transfer is not, however, to be treated as a distribution if it is made between companies resident in the UK and *either*:

(i) the transferor company is a 51% subsidiary (see below) of the transferee company; *or*

(ii) both are 51% subsidiaries of a company resident in the UK.

For this purpose, shares held directly or indirectly as trading stock and shares owned directly or indirectly in a company which is not UK resident are ignored.

[*CTA 2010, ss 1020, 1021; ICTA 1988, s 209(4)(5)*].

In the case of *Noved Investment Co v HMRC* (2006) Sp C 521, the Special Commissioners held that transfers of assets or liabilities by a company to its members at an undervalue under *ICTA 1988, s 209(4)* can include cash. Distributions are excluded from being treated as qualifying charitable donations under *ICTA 1988, s 339(1)(a)* apart from such transfers (see **20.12**(a) CHARITIES) and therefore, the decision in this case allows such cash transfers to be treated as qualifying donations. This contradicts HMRC's view (in a change to their previously adopted view, as announced in the course of this case) that such transfers do not include cash. (HMRC Internet Notice 3 November 2005). See HMRC Company Tax Manual CTM15250 and CTM15350.

In determining whether a company is a 51% subsidiary of another, that other's holding (whether direct or indirect) of shares in a non-resident company or of shares any profit on the sale of which would be a trading receipt, are disregarded.

[*CTA 2010, s 1021; ICTA 1988, s 209(7)*].

Transfers of assets (other than cash) or of liabilities are excluded if they fall within *CTA 2010, ss 1002, 1021*; *ICTA 1988, s 209(6)*, see **31.3** above, where '51% subsidiary' is defined without the restriction on shareholdings to which regard is to be had.

Repayment of share capital followed by a bonus issue

[31.11] Certain repayments of share capital which are then followed by a bonus issue are treated as distributions of the company. Where a company repays share capital (and see **31.12** below), and at the same time or later issues any share capital as paid up (otherwise than by the receipt of 'new consideration', see **31.13** below), the amount so paid up is treated as a distribution.

Such a distribution is treated as made in respect of the bonus shares and is limited to the total amount of share capital repaid less any amount previously treated as a distribution under this provision. [*ICTA 1988, s 210(1) now CTA 2010, s 1022*].

Where the bonus share capital is issued after 5 April 1973, this provision only applies if the issue is made within ten years of the repayment or is of redeemable share capital. [*ICTA 1988, s 210(3) now CTA 2010, s 1023*].

The original rules apply unaltered, however, if the company is under the control of not more than five persons or is unquoted (disregarding debentures and preference shares), unless it is under the control of a company (or companies) which is (or are) neither controlled by five or fewer persons nor unquoted.

[*CTA 2010, ss 1022, 1023, Sch 2 para 105; ICTA 1988, ss 210(3), 704D*].

'Control' is as defined in **22.6 CLOSE COMPANIES**.

> *Example*
> In 2000 X Ltd, a close company, redeemed £50,000 worth of variable-rate preference shares. In 2003 it made a bonus issue of one ordinary share of £1 for every ten held, which amounted to £20,000. In 2005 it made a further bonus issue of ordinary shares on a 1:11 basis, which also amounted to £20,000. X Ltd is treated as having made a distribution of £20,000 in each of the financial years 2003 and 2005. If X Ltd makes a similar bonus issue of 1:12 in 2010, the amount treated as a distribution (assuming that there has been no further repayment of share capital) will be limited to £10,000, being the balance of the £50,000 repaid in 2000.

These provisions do not apply to the repayment of fully-paid 'preference shares' which:

(i) existed as such on 6 April 1965, or
(ii) were issued as such after 6 April 1965 wholly for 'new consideration not derived from ordinary shares'

and in either case remained fully-paid preference shares until the date of repayment.

[*CTA 2010, ss 1022, 1023, Sch 2 para 105; ICTA 1988, s 210(2)*].

'*Preference shares*' are defined for this purpose as shares carrying the right to a dividend at a fixed percentage of the nominal value only and such other rights in respect of dividends and capital as are comparable with those general for fixed-dividend shares listed in the Official List of the Stock Exchange. Thus variable-rate preference shares (as in the example above) are outside this definition.

'*New consideration not derived from ordinary shares*' means 'new consideration' (see **31.13** below) except in so far as it consists of:

(a) the surrender, transfer or cancellation of 'ordinary shares' in the company or any other company;
(b) the variation of rights in such shares; or
(c) consideration derived from a repayment made in respect of such shares.

'*Ordinary shares*' are all shares except preference shares as defined above.

[*CTA 2010, s 1023; ICTA 1988, s 210(4); FA 1996, Sch 38 para 7*].

Repayment of share capital

[31.12] Where a company issues (or has issued at any time after 6 April 1965) any 'share capital' as paid up (otherwise than by the receipt of 'new consideration', for example a bonus issue, and the amount 'paid up' is not treated as a qualifying distribution), then any subsequent distribution in respect of that share capital is not treated as a repayment of share capital up to the amount treated as 'paid up' (so that the exclusion from distribution treatment in **31.2**(b) does not apply). This does not apply to that part of the repayment which exceeds the amount so 'paid up' — the excess is generally a distribution as under **31.3** above.

[*CTA 2010, ss 1025–1027; ICTA 1988, s 211(1)(3)*].

'Share capital' for this purpose includes:

(a) all the shares of the same class;
(b) shares issued in respect of any shares under (a) above;
(c) shares exchanged for any shares under (a) above (whether directly or indirectly);
(d) shares into which any shares under (a) above have directly or indirectly been converted.

[*CTA 2010, s 1027; ICTA 1988, s 211(4)*].

Where shares have been issued at a premium representing new consideration, the premium (less any amount that has been applied in paying up share capital) is treated as part of the share capital in determining whether any repayment is to be treated as a distribution. [*CTA 2010, s 1025; ICTA 1988, s 211(5)(6)*] Subject to this, premiums paid on the redemption of share capital are not to be treated as repayments of share capital. [*CTA 2010, ss 1024, 1025; ICTA 1988, s 211(7)*].

A distribution is outside these provisions if it is made:

(i) more than ten years after an issue of shares within that subsection;
(ii) otherwise than in respect of redeemable share capital; and
(iii) by a company which is neither under the control of five or fewer persons nor unquoted (disregarding debentures and preference shares), or which is controlled by a company (or companies) which is or are neither controlled by five or fewer persons nor unquoted.

[*CTA 2010, s 1026(3); ICTA 1988, ss 211(2), 704D*].

Draft provisions have been published which introduce a new *s 1027A* into *CTA 2010*, to counteract issues arising with regard to capital distributions and the new exemption regime (see further **31.15** below under 'Capital Distributions'). The new *s 1027A* prevents a distribution from being excluded from the tax definition of a distribution solely on the grounds that it is made out of a reserve arising from a reduction of share capital. Included in the definition of share capital for this purpose is the amount of any premium which represents new consideration.

Definitions

[31.13] A company is a '*75% subsidiary*' if not less than 75% of its ordinary share capital is owned directly or indirectly by another. [*CTA 2010, s 1154; ICTA 1988, s 838*].

A company is a '*51% subsidiary*' if not less than 51% of its ordinary share capital is owned directly or indirectly by another. [*CTA 2010, s 1154; ICTA 1988, s 838*].

'*New consideration*' means consideration provided otherwise than out of the assets of the company (i.e. where the cost does not fall on the company). Amounts retained by the company by way of capitalising a distribution do not constitute new consideration, but a premium paid on the issue of shares which is later applied in paying up further share capital may be treated as new consideration (except in so far as it has been taken into account to enable a distribution to be treated as a repayment of share capital (see **31.12** above)).

Consideration derived from the value of any share capital or security of, or from voting or other rights in, a company is new consideration only if it represents:

(i) money or value received from the company as a qualifying distribution (see **31.16** below);
(ii) money received from the company which, for the purposes of *Pt 23* of *CTA 2010*; *Pt VI* of *ICTA 1988*, constitute a repayment of share capital (see **31.12** above) or of the principal of the security; or
(iii) the giving up of the right to the share capital or security on its cancellation, extinguishment or acquisition by the company.

But in so far as any amount under (ii) or (iii) exceeds any payment made to the company for the issue of the share capital or security or, in the case of share capital which constituted a qualifying distribution (see **31.17** below), exceeds the nominal value of that share capital, it is not to be treated as new consideration. [*CTA 2010, s 1115; ICTA 1988, s 254(1)(5)(6)(7)*].

'*Shares*' includes stock and any other interest of a member in a company.

[*CTA 2010, s 1117; ICTA 1988, s 254(1)*].

'*Security*' includes securities not creating or evidencing a charge on assets. Interest paid, or other consideration given, by a company for money advanced without the issue of a security is nevertheless treated as if paid or given in respect of a security issued for that advance by the company. Where securities are issued at a discount, and are not listed on a recognised stock exchange, the principal secured is to be taken as not exceeding the issue price, unless the terms of issue are reasonably comparable with those of securities so listed.

[*CTA 2010, s 1117; ICTA 1988, s 254(1)(11); FA 1996, Sch 38 para 6*].

A thing is to be regarded as done '*in respect of*' shares or securities if it is done to the holder or former holder thereof (as such), or in pursuance of a right granted or offer made in respect of a share. Anything so done by reference to shareholdings at a particular time is regarded as done to the then holder or his personal representatives. If reciprocal arrangements are entered into among companies to make distributions to each other's members, the acts of one may be attributed to another. In relation to a group of companies, anything done to a UK resident 90% member of the group is treated as being in respect of securities of that company or any other company in the group.

[*CTA 2010, ss 1112, 1114, 1117; ICTA 1988, s 254(8)(12)*].

Items not treated as distributions

[31.14] Items not treated as distributions are:

(a) Distributions made in respect of share capital on winding up (see **76 WINDING UP**) [*CTA 2010, ss 1029, 1030; ICTA 1988, s 209(1)*], or (in most circumstances) on dissolution under *Companies Acts* [*ICTA 1988, s 652 or s 652A*]. (HMRC Extra-Statutory Concession, C16 — currently under consideration to be given legislative effect).

(b) A distribution as part of a merger to which *TCGA 1992, s 140E* or s *140F* applies (cross border mergers) where the company ceases to exist as a result of the merger without being wound up, is treated as a distribution in respect of share capital in a winding up. [*CTA 2010, ss 1029, 1031*].

(c) Small distributions to members on dissolution of an unincorporated association which is of a social or recreational nature and has not carried on a trade or investment business. (HMRC Extra-Statutory Concession, C15).

(d) Payments for group relief (or for the surrender of ACT on dividends paid prior to 6 April 1999) (see **39.16 GROUP RELIEF**) [*CTA 2010, s 183; ICTA 1988, ss 240(8), 402(6); FA 1998, Sch 3 para 13*], except in so far as they exceed the amount surrendered.

(e) *Share or loan interest* paid by registered **INDUSTRIAL AND PROVIDENT SOCIETIES** (**47**) or certain co-operative associations. [*CTA 2010, ss 1029, 1055; ICTA 1988, s 486(1)(8)(9); CTA 2009, Sch 1 para 163*].

(f) *Dividends or bonuses* deductible in computing the income of registered **INDUSTRIAL AND PROVIDENT SOCIETIES** (**47**) or **MUTUAL COMPANIES** (**56**). [*CTA 2010, ss 1029, 1056; ICTA 1988, s 486(10)–(12) (ss 10 repealed by CTA 2009, Sch 1 para 163)*].

(g) *Dividends or interest* payable in respect of shares in, deposits with, or loans to, **BUILDING SOCIETIES** (**9**). [*CTA 2010, ss 1029, 1054; ICTA 1988, ss 476(3)(c), 477A(3)(b); FA 1990, Sch 5 para 4*].

(h) *Stock dividends* (see Tolley's Income Tax under Savings and Investment Income). [*CTA 2010, ss 1029, 1049; ICTA 1988, s 230; ITTOIA 2005, Sch 1 para 112*].

(i) *Interest on securities* not within **31.5–31.7** above i.e. interest etc. paid in respect of certain securities, provided the securities are 'special securities', both companies are within the charge to corporation tax and the terms are commercial. However, this exemption does not apply to securities falling within the exceptions outlined at **31.9** above, for securities within *CTA 2010, Sch 2 para 107* [*CTA 2010, ss 1029, 1032*].

(j) Money provided by a close company for the *purchase of its shares by trustees of its profit sharing scheme.* (CCAB Memorandum TR 308, June 1978).

(k) Certain *purchases by a company of its own shares* (see **PURCHASE BY A COMPANY OF ITS OWN SHARES** (**63**)). [*CTA 2010, ss 1029, 1033–1047; ICTA 1988, ss 219–229*].

(l) Any 'relevant alternative finance' return within *CTA 2009, ss 507* or *513* is not treated as a distribution for corporation tax purposes. (See **4.7 ALTERNATIVE FINANCE ARRANGEMENTS** with effect from 1 April 2007.) [*CTA 2009, ss 507, 513; ICTA 1988, s 209; CTA 2009, Sch 1 para 97*].

(m) transfer of a building society's business to a company [*FA 1998, Sch 12 para 6*].

(n) interest and share dividends paid by a UK agricultural or fishing co-operative. [*CTA 2009, ss 1029, 1057*].

HMRC will give 'sympathetic consideration' to cases where a terminal payment is made by a continuing company to an arm's length director or employee, where the sum is both reasonable in amount (having regard to past services and length of service), and an admissible deduction for corporation tax purposes. (CCAB Memorandum TR 127, 19 February 1974).

A bonus issue of non-redeemable share capital does not constitute a distribution unless it follows a repayment of share capital (see **31.11** above).

Distributions on or after 1 July 2009

2009 regime

[31.15] For distributions on or after 1 July 2009, a new tax treatment is introduced for dividends. HMRC have made draft guidance available at www.hmrc.gov.uk/guidance/dist-exempt-dr-guidance.pdf. The effect of this regime is that most dividends, whether received from a UK company or a foreign company, are exempt from UK corporation tax.

FA 2009, Sch 14 amends *CTA 2009* and inserts a new *Pt 9A*. This provides for a different treatment for distributions by different categories of company — small and medium-sized or large.

A company is a 'small company' for this purpose if it is a micro or small enterprise as defined in the Annex to *Commission Recommendation 2003/361/EC* of 6 May 2003. However, a company is not small for this purpose if at any time in an accounting period it is an open-ended investment company, an authorised unit trust scheme, an insurance company or a friendly society. [*CTA 2009, s 931S*].

Distributions are prima facie subject to corporation tax, unless they fall within one of the exemptions detailed below.

Capital distributions were originally excluded from this treatment but this was an error in drafting and represented an inadvertant move away from the previous practice. Amendments were made to the legislation in *F(No 3)A 2010* and were deemed always to have had effect, although companies are entitled to elect for the 'old' treatment to apply, so that they are not adversely affected by the retrospective change.

Small companies

A distribution received by a small company is exempt if:

(i) the paying company is a UK resident or resident in a 'qualifying territory' at the time the small company receives the distribution;
(ii) the distribution is not interest that is treated as a distribution by *paras E or F* of *CTA 2010, s 1000(1)*, see **31.2** above;
(iii) the receipt is a dividend in respect of which no tax deduction is given for the distribution outside the UK; and
(iv) the distribution is not made as part of a tax advantage scheme.

Definitions

For the purposes of the small companies' exemption, a country is a '*qualifying territory*' if the UK has a double tax agreement containing a non-discrimination provision with the territory.

However, the Treasury may, by statutory instrument, provide that a country fulfilling these conditions is not a qualifying territory or that a country not fulfilling these conditions is a qualifying territory. *SI 2009 No 3314*, issued under this power, provides that a territory which would otherwise qualify, is not a qualifying territory if the payer of the distribution is an 'excluded company'. An '*excluded company*' is one excluded from one or more benefits of any double taxation relief arrangements in force in relation to that territory.

A '*non-discrimination provision*' is a clause in a double taxation agreement which provides that a national of one state is not to be less favourably treated in tax matters than a national of the other contracting state.

For this purpose, a company is '*resident*' if, under the laws of a state, it is resident because of its domicile, residence or place of management but not only on its income from sources in that territory or capital situated there.

Wide powers are given to the Treasury to amend these provisions by statutory instrument.

[*CTA 2009, s 931C*].

Companies that are not small

A dividend paid on or after 1 July 2009 and received by a large or medium-sized company is exempt if it falls into an exempt class, is not interest treated as a distribution (per para E or F of *CTA 2010, s 1000(1)*) and no tax deduction is given for the distribution outside the UK.

[*CTA 2009, s 931D*].

The following five classes of dividend are exempt:

(a) **Distributions from controlled companies:** a dividend is exempt where the recipient, or the recipient together with another person controls the payer company and, in the latter case, one of the parties holds at least 40% and not more than 55% of the share capital, rights and powers. However, the dividend is not exempt if it is paid as part of a tax avoidance scheme one of the purposes of which is to arrange for the dividend to fall into an exempt class and the dividend is paid out of pre-control profits [*CTA 2009, ss 931E, 931J*];

(b) **Distributions in respect of non-redeemable, ordinary shares:** a dividend on an ordinary, non-redeemable share is exempt. There is an anti-avoidance provision which provides that if a dividend is paid as part of an avoidance scheme and the shares are not true ordinary shares or are in fact redeemable shares, they do not fall into the exempt class [*CTA 2009, ss 931F, 931K*];

(c) **Distributions in respect of portfolio holdings:** a dividend on a holding (a portfolio holding) carrying a right to less than 10% of the profits, or assets on a winding up of all the share capital of that class of share (if more than one). Where not all shares in a class are paid up to the same extent, the shares are not all of one class (share premiums being disregarded for this purpose). There is an anti-avoidance provision which attacks schemes to manipulate holdings so as to come within this exempt class [*CTA 2009, ss 931G, 931L*];

(d) **Dividends derived from transactions not designed to reduce tax:** refers to a dividend paid in respect of 'relevant profits'. '*Relevant profits*' means any profits available for distribution when the dividend was paid, other than profits from avoidance transactions [*CTA 2009, s 931H*].

The order in which dividends are treated as derived is firstly where the dividend falls under another exempt class, it is treated as paid first out of relevant profits, any other dividend is treated as paid out of other than relevant profits (i.e. it is non-exempt) and when the non-relevant profits are exhausted, the balance is treated as paid out of relevant profits. No transaction is taken into account if it was entered into before 1 July 2008. Where a transaction falling before 1 July 2009 has to be taken into account, it is assumed that the 2009 regime was in force at that time;

(e) **Dividends in respect of shares accounted for as liabilities:** a dividend is exempt if it fulfils the conditions to be accounted for as a liability per the provisions of *CTA 2009, s 521C* except for condition (1)(f) of that section, not being a share held for an unallowable purpose. If such share is held for an unallowable purpose it would be treated as within the loan relationship rules [*CTA 2009, s 931I*].

Where a dividend is not exempt under (a) above, but would qualify under one of the other exemptions and it is paid as part of a tax avoidance scheme, is part of the return for such a scheme, the return is economically equivalent to interest and there is a connection between the payer and recipient, then the dividend is not treated as exempt. [*CTA 2009, s 931M*].

In addition to the specific anti-avoidance provisions identified for certain exemptions above, there are four further general anti-avoidance provisions, not specifically linked to the exempt classes, which apply to prevent a distribution from falling into an exempt class if it would otherwise do so. The main aim of these provisions is to ensure that dividends paid as part of a tax avoidance scheme remain taxable in the UK. These are that the distribution is part of a tax advantage scheme and:

(i) a non-UK resident receives a tax deduction in respect of it [*CTA 2009, s 931N*];

(ii) the scheme involves making a payment or giving up a right to income and all or part of the consideration is the distribution and *CTA 2009, s 1301(2), (4)* to *(7)* applies to the payment [*CTA 2009, s 931O*];

(iii) the scheme involves the giving up of a right to payment for goods or services, and in return the receipt of the income given up as a distribution. This provision does not apply when the transfer pricing provisions apply [*CTA 2009, s 931P*];

(iv) the scheme has diverted a payment which would be trading income of a company to another person and one of the main purposes of the scheme was to achieve exemption on the distribution [*CTA 2009, s 931Q*].

It is open to a company to elect, within two years of the end of the accounting period in which the distribution is received, for the distribution not to be exempt [*CTA 2009, s 931R*].

Manufactured dividends and manufactured overseas dividends

CTA 2010 amends the exempt distribution provisions of *CTA 2009, Pt 9A* with regard to manufactured dividends and manufactured overseas dividends.

Manufactured dividends: If a person pays a manufactured dividend to another person the Corporation Tax Acts apply to the recipient (and companies claiming title through or under such recipient) as if the manufactured dividend were a dividend on shares. Thus such a dividend may be treated as exempt if it falls into one of the exempt classes within *Pt 9A* of *CTA 2009*, as modified such that references to the payer are taken as references to the company that pays the dividend for which the manufactured dividend is representative. [*CTA 2010, ss 787, 784*].

Manufactured overseas dividends: If a person pays a manufactured overseas dividend to another person and the amount of income tax required to be accounted for and paid under *ITA 2007, s 923(1)* has been so accounted for and paid, then the dividend is treated as an overseas dividend for the purposes of *CTA 2009*. Thus such a dividend may be treated as exempt if it falls into one of the exempt classes within *Pt 9A* of *CTA 2009*, as modified such that references to the payer are taken as references to the company that pays the dividend for which the manufactured overseas dividend is representative. [*CTA 2010, s 795*]. The amount treated as exempt is taken to be an amount equal to the gross manufactured overseas dividend, but assuming such dividend has been paid after the deduction from it of overseas tax (being the amount of income tax accounted for and paid as a result of *ITA 2007, s 923*). [*CTA 2010, s 794*].

Capital distributions

Uncertainty arose about the treatment of capital distributions under the new regime, as originally enacted. Legislation would be introduced in *F(No 3)A 2010* to remove the exception for capital distributions, so that the legislation was once again in accordance with accepted practice before the tax law rewrite.

The main change was to remove the provision in *CTA 2009, s 931A* that excluded capital distributions from the new regime. However, a number of consequential changes were also made.

- New *CTA 2010, s 1027A* ensures that a distribution made out of a reserve arising from a reduction of share capital, including share premium, is treated as an income distribution. What is unclear is whether a reduction of capital per se, without the conversion of share capital and premium into distributable form, can still qualify as a capital distribution.
- A new *s 931RA* preserves the position following the case of *Strand Options & Futures Ltd v Vojak* CA 2004, 76 TC 220 (see **31.16**), so that dividends or other distributions that are exempt from taxation as income can still be charged to tax as a chargeable gain of a company.
- *TCGA 1992, s 22* was amended, so that neither a capital distribution nor a distribution within *CTA 2009, Pt 9A*, whether it is taxable or exempt, cannot fall within the ambit of *TCGA 1992, s 22*.
- *TCGA 1992, s 122* was amended, so that a distribution within *CTA 2009, Pt 9A*, whether it is taxable or exempt, cannot fall within the ambit of *TCGA 1992, s 122*. The impact of this provision and *CTA 2009, s 931RA* is that any gains arising should be taxed exclusively under the basic provisions of *TCGA 1992, s 1*, as was the case in *Strand Options & Futures Ltd v Vojak*.

It is not entirely clear why some of these provisions were considered to be necessary, although HMRC suggested that they arose out of some of the queries received when the problem with capital distributions was first identified.

The above amendments are to have retrospective effect and therefore apply to distributions made on or after 1 July 2009. A company can elect to opt out of the new provisions with regard to distributions made before 22 June 2010.

Definitions

A '*relevant person*' in relation to a distribution is the company which receives the distribution and any person connected with that company [*CTA 2009, s 931T*].

A '*scheme*' includes any scheme, arrangements or understanding of any kind whatever, whether or not legally enforceable, involving a single transaction or two or more transactions.

A '*tax advantage scheme*' is a scheme with a main purpose of obtaining a tax advantage (other than a negligible tax advantage) [*CTA 2009, s 931V*].

[*CTA 2009, Pt 9A; FA 2009, Sch 14 Pt 1*].

The provisions *of CTA 2009* dealing with trading profits and property income take priority over the above.

In *First Nationwide v The Commissioners for HMRC* [2010] UKFTT 24 (TC) the First Tier Tax Tribunal held that certain dividends paid by a Cayman company out of share premium were income in nature, on the basis that following the payment of the dividends the corpus of the shares was still intact. This decision therefore has an impact with regard to the application of the dividend exemption described above, which currently excludes capital distributions. Whilst UK companies are not permitted to pay dividends in this way, the case will have an impact with regard to similar dividends paid by companies incorporated outside the UK. However, see also the comments above with regard to proposals to amend *CTA 2009, Pt 9A*.

The previous tax treatment of distributions

[31.16] A UK distribution was not chargeable to corporation tax in the hands of a UK-resident recipient company, nor taken into account in computing the income of the paying company for corporation tax purposes. [*CTA 2009, s 1285; ICTA 1988, s 208*]. But see **31.17** below.

Where the special rules in *CTA 2010, ss 1033–1048; ICTA 1988, ss 219–229* do not apply on the occasion of a **PURCHASE BY A COMPANY OF ITS OWN SHARES** (**63**), so that the purchase is treated as a distribution, and the shareholder is itself a company, the transaction is subject to tax as a chargeable gain and the distribution is included in the consideration which, for the purposes of corporation tax on chargeable gains, the shareholder company is treated as receiving for disposal of the shares. This treatment was confirmed in *Strand Options & Futures Ltd v Vojak* CA 2004, 76 TC 220, where it was held that *ICTA 1988, s 208* exempted the consideration from the charge on the dividends but not on the distribution element of the chargeable gain.

Tax credits

[31.17] Where, on or after 1 July 2009, a company, wherever resident, makes an 'exempt distribution' to a UK resident company, the recipient is entitled to a tax credit of 10%, equal to one-ninth of the dividend. Where a UK-resident company makes a 'qualifying distribution' on or after 6 April 1999 and before 1 July 2009, to another UK-resident company, the recipient of such a distribution is entitled to a 10% tax credit, equivalent to one-ninth of the dividend. The distribution, together with the tax credit, is franked investment income (see earlier edition of this book for more information on this) in the hands of a UK-resident recipient company. [*CTA 2010, s 1109, Sch 2 para 111; ICTA 1988, ss 231, 832(1)*].

Returns of non-qualifying distributions must be made under *CTA 2010, s 1100; ICTA 1988, s 234(5)–(9)*. See **66.11 RETURNS**.

Any company making a payment of dividend or interest to any person must, within a reasonable period, send a written statement giving details of the payment to that person or, if the payment is made direct to a bank (within *CTA 2010, s 1120; ICTA 1988, s 840A*, see **8.1 BANKS**) or building society, either to the bank or building society or to the account holder. Nominee recipients are similarly obliged to provide a statement when passing on the payment. The statement must include:

(i) in the case of interest (not being a qualifying distribution or part), the gross amount, the rate and amount of income tax deducted from the gross amount, the net amount actually paid and the date of payment;
(ii) in the case of a dividend or interest which is a qualifying distribution or part, the amount paid, the date of payment and the related tax credit.

[*CTA 2010, s 1104*].

HMRC have powers by regulation to provide alternative rules for compliance. [*CTA 2010, s 1108; ICTA 1988, s 234A*].

For dividends payable to non-residents, see **32.14 DOUBLE TAX RELIEF.**

Simon's Taxes. See **D5.140, D5.410, D5.501–D5.505, E1.414.**

Stock dividends

[31.18] For this purpose, a stock dividend is either one issued in lieu of cash, or a bonus issue of shares in respect of shares of a 'qualifying class'. In both cases, the issuing company must be UK resident. In the case of bonus shares, shares are of a '*qualifying class*' if shares of that class carry the right to bonus shares of that or another class under the terms of original issue or those terms as subsequently amended.

There are special rules for the situation where bonus share capital (as defined) is converted into or exchanged for shares of a different class.

'*Bonus share capital*' means the share capital or part of it not issued for new consideration.

There is provision for returns to be made to HMRC where stock dividends or bonus issues are made and rules for determining the return periods.

[*CTA 2010, ss 1049–1053; ICTA 1988, s 250*].

Close companies — additional distributions

[31.19] Certain payments made and benefits given to participators and their associates by close companies are treated as distributions, see **31.20** below. Unless otherwise stated, terms have the same meaning as in **22.2–22.9 CLOSE COMPANIES**. The exceptions listed in **31.14** above apply. [*CTA 2010, s 1064; ICTA 1988, s 418*].

Benefits to participators and their associates

[31.20] Where a close company incurs expense in, or in connection with, the provision for any 'participator' (or an associate of his) of living or other accommodation, entertainment, domestic or other services, or of other benefits or facilities of whatever nature, so much of that expense as is not made good by the participator is treated as a distribution.

The distribution treatment does not apply to benefits provided to a participator who is an employee to whom the earnings and benefit code under *ITEPA 2003, Pt 3* applies in the case of: the provision of benefits given, on that person's death or retirement, to the spouse, children or dependants; the provision of living accommodation (under *ITEPA 2003, ss 97–113*) and the benefits under *ITEPA 2003, ss 114–215* (cars and vans, loans, etc.) and *s 223* (payments of director's tax) ignoring the exclusion for lower paid employees in *s 216*. (See HMRC Company Taxation Manual CTM60510).

[*CTA 2010, ss 1064, 1065; ICTA 1988, s 418(1)–(3); ITEPA 2003, Sch 6 para 55*].

'*Participator*' includes an associate of a participator and a participator in a company which controls the company providing the benefit. [*CTA 2010, s 1069; ICTA 1988, s 418(8)*].

Reciprocal arrangements whereby each of a number of companies makes a payment etc. to a participator in another are included. [*CTA 2010, s 1067; ICTA 1988, s 418(7)*].

The measure of the distribution is the cash equivalent of the benefit or expense as defined in the employment benefits legislation (see Tolley's Income Tax under Employment Income) less any amount made good to the company.

[*CTA 2010, s 1064; ICTA 1988, s 418(4)*].

These provisions do not apply where the company and the participator are resident in the UK and:

(a) one is a '51% subsidiary' of the other or both are 51% subsidiaries of a third company so resident; and

(b) the benefit arises on or in connection with the transfer of assets or liabilities between the company and the participator.

'*51% subsidiary*' is as defined in **31.10** above.

[*CTA 2010, s 1066; ICTA 1988, s 418(5)(6)*].

Simon's Taxes. See **D3.301.**

Example

[31.21]

R is a participator in S Ltd, a close company, but he is neither a director nor an employee earning £8,500 a year or more. For the whole of 20010/11, S Ltd provided R with a new car of which the 'price' for tax purposes (i.e. under *ITEPA 2003, ss 122–124*) was £23,200, and which had a carbon dioxide emissions figure of 235 g/km. R was required to, and did, pay S Ltd £500 a year for the use of the car. The cost of providing the car, charged in S Ltd's accounts for its year ended 31 March 2011, was £5,000.

Deemed distribution

If the benefit of the car had been assessable as employment income, the cash equivalent would have been:

	£
£23,200 @ 35%	8,120
Less contribution	500
	£7,620

S Ltd is treated as making a distribution of £7,620 to R.

Income of R for 2010/11 £7,620× 100/90	£8,467

Tax credit for R for 2010/11 £8,467@ 10%	£847

The income is dividend income and thus taxable at 10% (satisfied by the tax credit) except to the extent that it falls within R's higher rate band, in which case it would be taxable at the dividend upper rate of 32.5%.

S Ltd's taxable profits

In computing S Ltd's profits chargeable to corporation tax, the actual expenditure charged (£5,000) must be added back.

Mutual and non-trading companies

[31.22] Payments made to members of:

(a) MUTUAL COMPANIES (**56**) (other than those carrying on life assurance business); or

(b) companies which were not formed to carry on, and which have never carried on, a trade or the business of holding investments,

are within the above provisions only if made out of income chargeable to corporation tax or out of franked investment income.

[*CTA 2010, ss 1070, 1071; ICTA 1988, s 490*].

Friendly societies

[31.23] Payments made by certain **FRIENDLY SOCIETIES** (**37**) are qualifying distributions.

[*ICTA 1988, s 461(3)*].

Companies not carrying on a business

[31.24] Dividends paid by companies not carrying on a trade or investment business are also within the Corporation Tax Acts with regard to distributions made by them, pursuant to *CTA 2010, s 1071*.

Therefore, where a company:

(i) does not carry on, and has never carried on a trade, or a business of holding investments;
(ii) does not hold, and has never held, an office; and
(iii) is not established for purposes which include either carrying on a trade, carrying on a business of holding investments, or holding an office,

then the provisions of the Corporation Tax Acts (as described above, etc.) apply to distributions made by the company which are made out of profits of the company which are within the charge to corporation tax or which are franked investment income.

[*CTA 2010, s 1071; ICTA 1988, s 490(4)*].

Discretionary payments from trusts

[31.25] Where trustees of a settlement make a discretionary distribution to a company, other than a charity (within *CTA 2010, s 467*), an eligible body within *CTA 2010, s 468* or a scientific research association (within *CTA 2010, s 469*) the payment is disregarded in calculating the company's income for corporation tax purposes, and no credit is given, or repayment made, of the tax deducted at the trust income tax rate. In the case of non-UK resident companies, this applies to so much (if any) of the payment as is income of the company for corporation tax purposes.

[*CTA 2010, s 610; ICTA 1988, ss 687, 687A*].

Dividends from non-resident companies

[31.26] With effect on and after 1 July 2009, all dividends, whether arising in the UK or overseas, are taxable in the UK unless they fall within one of the exemptions. See **31.15**. In practice, most distributions will be exempt.

Dividends receivable by a UK company from a non-UK resident company are within the charge to corporation tax on income. For accounting periods ending before 1 April 2009, the charge was under Schedule D, Case IV or V. Dividends of a capital nature are excluded from the charge.

[*CTA 2009, s 933; ICTA 1988, ss 9(1)(2)(2B)(2C)(3), 18(1)–(3)*].

HMRC considered that a non-UK resident company could not claim repayment of tax credits under section 242, notwithstanding the existence of a non-discrimination clause in a double taxation convention between the UK and the country in which the company was resident. (HMRC Statement of Practice 2/95, now obsolete).

A number of UK companies applied to the Chancery Division for a declaration that the UK corporation tax rules, under which dividends from UK companies were not taxed (*ICTA 1988, s 208*) but dividends from companies resident in other EC member states were subject to tax, contravened the *EC Treaty*. This is subject to a Franked Investment Income (Group Litigation Order) case involving the UK treatment of dividends received from non-resident companies and is currently awaiting a decision from the CJEC. In *Test Claimants in the FII Group Litigation v CIR* (Case C-446/04) the CJEC decided that, on the application of *Articles 43* and *56* to the UK treatment of franked investment income:

- for companies holding 10% or more of the foreign subsidiary's share capital, the UK system was not, in principle, unacceptable, although some questions have been remitted to the UK courts for decision; and
- where there is less than a 10% holding, the UK rules which tax receipts without allowance for underlying tax are unacceptable.

The CJEC also held that payment of ACT on foreign dividends and the prohibition of surrender of ACT to overseas companies contravened the *EC Treaty*, while the restriction on offset of ACT against UK tax did not.

Following the CJEC decision, the case was referred back to the Chancery Division, where it was held that 'the UK system of taxation of dividends received from member states has at all material times infringed Article 43EC' and that the rules governing foreign income dividends also infringed *Article 43EC*. However, there would need to be a further reference to CJEC to consider the question whether the inability to surrender surplus ACT for set-off (or equivalent relief) against the foreign profits of a foreign subsidiary also infringed *Article 43EC*. See *Test Claimants in the FII Group Litigation v CIR* [2008] STC [2009] 254.

Decision on the FID regime and any claim for consequential loss has been left to the UK courts.

See also *Manninen v Finland, CJEC Case C-319/02*; [2004] STC 1444 in which the CJEC held that the Finnish legislation, allowing for dividends from Finnish companies to attract a tax credit but not dividends from companies established outside Finland, contravened *Article 56EC* of the *EC Treaty*.

In the case of *UBS AG v HMRC* [2006] EWHC 117 (Ch D), the court (in reversing the Special Commissioners' decision), allowed the claim made by a London branch of a Swiss bank for a payment of tax credits under *ICTA 1988, s 243* in respect of dividends received during 1993 to 1996. The court held that reference to a tax credit in this case included a tax credit under *ICTA 1988, s 231* as embraced by *ICTA 1988, s 788(3)(d)*. As such, it covered the payment of a tax credit to a foreign company.

Demergers

[31.27] A group may have grown without much planning and a point may be reached where it is considered that the group could be run more efficiently by separating out various parts. There are three main ways to carry out a demerger: the statutory route (which is examined further below); via liquidation; and by way of a Companies Act reconstruction (which requires court approval).

The statutory route depends on the provisions found in *CTA 2010, ss 1073–1099 (formerly ICTA 1988, ss 213–218)* which are intended to facilitate the breaking-up of large companies and groups of companies by exempting certain distributions of assets from the normal tax treatment (see **31 DISTRIBUTIONS**).

General enquiries concerning the demerger legislation should be addressed to HMRC, Clearance and Counteraction Team, First Floor, 22 Kingsway, London WC2B 6NR. Market sensitive issues should be addressed to the Team Leader.

Simon's Taxes. See **D6.420–D6.424**.

Exempt distributions — Demergers

[31.28] Generally, in a demerger the holding company transfers its subsidiaries, either directly to its shareholders, or indirectly to new companies set up by the shareholders. Such transfer by the holding company would normally be treated as a distribution of its assets to its shareholders. However, if the conditions for an exempt demerger are met, then no distribution will arise.

Subject to **31.32** below, the following are exempt distributions (i.e. they are not distributions for the purposes of the Taxes Acts) provided that they would otherwise have been distributions under the Corporation Tax Acts (see **31 DISTRIBUTIONS**). (HMRC Statement of Practice, SP 13/80 as revised).

(a) The transfer is to all or any of its 'members' by a company ('the distributing company') of 'shares' in a '75% subsidiary' which:
   - (i) are irredeemable;
   - (ii) constitute the whole or 'substantially the whole' of the distributing company's holding of the subsidiary's 'ordinary share capital';
   - (iii) confer the whole or 'substantially the whole' of the distributing company's voting rights in the subsidiary;
   - (iv) unless the distributing company is a 75% subsidiary after the distribution, the distributing company must be a trading company or the holding company of a trading group; and

- (v) similarly unless the transfer relates to two or more 75% subsidiaries and the distributing company is dissolved without having any residual net assets for distribution on a winding up or otherwise then the distributing company must be a trading company or the holding company of a trading group. [*CTA 2010, ss 1076, 1082*].

(b) The transfer is by the distributing company to another company or companies of:

- (i) a 'trade' or trades (provided that no, or only a minor, interest in any such trade is retained); or
- (ii) shares in one or more of its 75% subsidiaries. (In this case, the shares may be redeemable, but must otherwise meet the requirements set out in (a) above.)

To qualify for exemption, the transfer must be coupled with the issue by the transferee company (or companies) to all or any of the members of the distributing company of shares which:

- (A) are irredeemable;
- (B) constitute the whole or 'substantially the whole' of the transferee company's issued ordinary share capital; and
- (C) confer the whole or 'substantially the whole' of the voting rights in that company.

The distributing company must not retain more than a minor interest in the transferred trade.

Shares issued by the transferee must be irredeemable, constitute the whole or substantially the whole of the issued ordinary share capital and confer the whole or substantially the whole of the voting rights in the company. After the making the distribution, the distributing company must be a trading company or a holding company of a trading group — however this condition does not apply if the distributing company is dissolved without making a further distribution (and having no assets).

[*CTA 2010, ss 1077, 1083*].

The carrying on of the transferred trade or trades or the holding of the transferred shares must constitute the only or main activity of each and every transferee company after the distribution. This is not construed as meaning 'for ever after', but an intention that the conditions should cease to be satisfied at some later time would require consideration under the anti-avoidance provisions (see below). (HMRC Statement of Practice, SP 13/80 as revised).

The group, or the largest group must be a trading group after the transfer.

All companies must be resident in a member state and must either be a trading company or a member of a trading group at the time the distribution is made.

The distribution must be made wholly or mainly to benefit some or all of the trading activities carried on before the distribution by a single company or group and afterwards by two or more companies or groups.

The distribution must not be part of a scheme or arrangement for a prohibited purpose.

The distribution must be made wholly or mainly for the purpose of benefiting some or all of the 'trading activities' which before the distribution are carried on by a single company or 'group' and after the distribution will be carried on by two or more companies or groups.

[*CTA 2010, ss 1074, 1081*].

A distribution cannot be exempt if it forms part of a scheme or arrangements the main purpose or one of the main purposes of which is:

(i) the avoidance of tax (including stamp duty or stamp duty land tax);
(ii) the making of a 'chargeable payment' (see **31.32** below) (or what would be a chargeable payment if any of the companies were an unquoted company);
(iii) the acquisition (other than by members of the distributing company) of 'control' of that or of any other 'relevant company' or of any company in the same group as a relevant company;
(iv) the cessation of a trade; or
(v) the sale of a trade after the distribution.

[*CTA 2010, s 1081; ICTA 1988, ss 213(1)–(11), 218(1)*].

HMRC's interpretation of several of these requirements is contained in HMRC Statement of Practice, SP 13/80 as revised. In brief:

(i) the question of whether what is transferred constitutes a trade is considered from the transferee's point of view, and without regard to minor assets linked with trading assets. Whether only a part of the transferor's trade, or merely some of his assets, are transferred is not conclusive;
(ii) a 'minor interest in a trade' means around 10% or less, and does not include indirect involvement conferring no measure of control;
(iii) 'substantially the whole' means 90% or more;
(iv) the concurrent transfer of ordinary share capital to ordinary shareholders for consideration, or to preference shareholders, or of other shares or securities to ordinary shareholders, does not prevent relief being given under these provisions;
(v) 'after' in (5) means 'at any time after'.

For the treatment for income and capital gains tax purposes of trustees and beneficiaries where the trustees hold shares in a company which carries out an exempt distribution, see HMRC Tax Bulletin October 1994 pp 162–165 and HMRC Capital Gains Tax Manual, CG33900 onwards.

Simon's Taxes. See **D6.421, D6.422.**

Transactions involving entities in EU member states

[31.29] The following is also an exempt distribution if:

(a) it is a distribution consisting of:
  (i) the transfer of part of a business by a company to one or more other companies; and
  (ii) the issue of shares by the transferees to the members of the transferor;

(b) the requirements of either *TCGA 1992, s 140A(1A) or s 140C(1A)* (See **17.33**) are satisfied.

[*CTA 2010, s 1078; ICTA 1988, s 213A(1)*].

Definitions

[31.30] From 1 January 2007, 'distributing company' means a company to which *CTA 2010, s 1079; ICTA 1988, s 213(3)(b)* or s *213A(1)(a)* applies. Prior to that date, the '*distributing company*' must at the time of the distribution be a 'trading company' or a 'member of a trading group' and resident in the UK. After the distribution (again not meaning 'for ever after' — see **31.28** above), it must continue to be a trading company or the 'holding company' of a trading group except where the distributing company is itself the 75% subsidiary of another, when the following conditions must be satisfied instead.

(a) The group (or, if more than one, the largest group) to which it belongs at the time of the distribution must be a trading group.

(b) The distribution must be followed by other exempt distributions within **31.28**(a) or (b)(ii) above, as a result of which members of the holding company of the 'group' (or the largest group) to which the distributing company belonged at the time of the distribution become members of:
   (i) each and every transferee company to which a trade was transferred by the distributing company;
   (ii) each and every subsidiary shares in which were transferred by the distributing company; or
   (iii) a company (other than that holding company) of which a company falling within (i) or (ii) above is a 75% subsidiary.

[*CTA 2010, ss 1082, 1083, 1085; ICTA 1988, s 213(6)(b)(8)(e)(12)*].

See also **31.34** below.

A '*member*' of a company means a holder of ordinary share capital of that company. [*CTA 2010, s 1099; ICTA 1988, s 218(1)*].

'*Shares*' includes stock. [*CTA 2010, s 1099; ICTA 1988, s 218(1)*].

In determining whether a company the shares in which are transferred by the distributing company is a '75% subsidiary' of that company, shares therein owned indirectly by the distributing company are to be disregarded. The subsidiary must, at the time of transfer, be either a trading company or the holding company of a trading group.

For all the purposes of these provisions, the parent company is to be treated as not owning shares held as trading stock either directly, or indirectly through another body corporate. [*ICTA 1988, ss 213(5), 218(2)(3)*].

'*Ordinary share capital*' is all the issued share capital of the company except that carrying a fixed dividend only. [*CTA 2010, s 1119; ICTA 1988, s 832(1)*]. 'Issued share capital' does not include founder members' deposits in a company limited by guarantee (*South Shore Mutual Insurance Co Ltd v Blair (Inspector of Taxes)* [1999] STC (SCD) 296). See **18.2 CAPITAL GAINS — GROUPS.**

'*Trade*' does not include dealing in shares, securities, land, trades or commodity futures, and '*trading activities*' are to be construed accordingly. [*CTA 2010, s 1099; ICTA 1988, s 218(1)*].

A '*group*', except for the purposes of **31.28**(3) above, means a company and its 75% subsidiaries.

In **31.28**(3) above, the term means a company and its 51% subsidiaries.

[*ICTA 1988, ss 213(11), 218(1)*].

See also below regarding a 'trading company'.

'*Unquoted company*'. A company is unquoted if no class of shares or securities therein (disregarding debenture or loan stock or preferred shares) is listed in the Stock Exchange Official List and dealt in on the Stock Exchange. A company under the sole control of one or more companies which are not unquoted is outside this definition. [*CTA 2010, s 1098; ICTA 1988, s 218(1)*].

'*Control*' is as defined in *CTA 2010, s 1099; ICTA 1988, s 416(2)–(6)*, see **22.6 CLOSE COMPANIES.**

A '*trading company*' is one the business of which consists wholly or mainly in the carrying on of a trade or trades, and a '*trading group*' is a group the business of the members of which (taken together) consists wholly or mainly in the carrying on of a trade or trades.

[*CTA 2010, s 1099; ICTA 1988, s 218(1)*].

A '*holding company*' means a company the business of which (disregarding any trade that it carries on) consists wholly or mainly in the holding of shares or securities of one or more companies which are its 75% subsidiaries.

[*CTA 2010, s 1099; ICTA 1988, s 218(1)*].

Relief from tax on capital gains

[31.31] Any exempt distribution within **31.28**(a) above is not a capital distribution for the purposes of *TCGA 1992, s 122*, and will not, therefore, give rise to a deemed disposal.

The distribution is treated as if it were a reorganisation of the distributing company's share capital for the purposes of *TCGA 1992, ss 126–130*. [*TCGA 1992, s 192(2)*]. See Tolley's Capital Gains Tax under Shares and Securities.

For distributions before 17 April 2002, an exempt distribution within **31.28**(b)(ii) above was regarded as a scheme of reconstruction for the purpose of relief under *TCGA 1992, s 139* (see **17.11 CAPITAL GAINS**), so that the transfer of assets to the transferee company was, in relation to corporation tax on capital gains, treated as giving rise to neither gain nor loss. (HMRC Statement of Practice, SP 5/85). See now **17.11 CAPITAL GAINS.**

Where a company ceases to be a member of a group solely because of an exempt distribution (within **31.28**(a) or (b) above), no charge arises under *TCGA 1992, s 179* (see **29.1 DEGROUPING CHARGES**). This relief is withdrawn if a chargeable payment (see **31.32** below) is made within five years after the exempt distribution; the time limit for making assessments is extended (where necessary) to three years after the making of the chargeable payment. [*TCGA 1992, s 192(3)(4)*].

For the treatment of trustees and beneficiaries where the trustees hold shares in a company which carries out an exempt distribution, see HMRC Capital Gains Manual CG33900.

Chargeable payment connected with exempt distribution

[31.32] If within five years after an exempt distribution there is a 'chargeable payment', it is treated as:

(a) miscellaneous income (chargeable to corporation tax);
(b) an annual sum payable otherwise than out of profits or gains chargeable to income tax for the purposes of *ITA 2007, ss 449, 901, 946, 962–964* (formerly *ICTA 1988, ss 349(1), 350*) (requiring the payer to deduct and account for income tax at the basic rate) unless it is a transfer of money's worth; and
(c) a distribution for the purposes of *CTA 2009, s 1305(1)* (previously *ICTA 1988, s 337A(1)*) (distributions not deductible in computing income).

In no case is the payment to be treated as a repayment of capital for the purposes of *CTA 2010, ss 1022, 1026; ICTA 1988, s 210* or *s 211* (see **31.11**, **31.12 DISTRIBUTIONS**).

A '*chargeable payment*' is any 'payment' made by a 'company concerned in an exempt distribution':

(i) directly or indirectly to a member of that company or of any other such company;
(ii) in connection with, or with any transaction affecting, the shares of that or any other such company;
(iii) which is neither a distribution nor an exempt distribution nor made to a member of the same group as the paying company; and
(iv) which is not made for *bona fide* commercial reasons or forms part of a scheme or arrangements a main purpose of which is the avoidance of tax (including stamp duty and stamp duty land tax).

[*CTA 2010, s 1088*].

Where a company concerned in an exempt distribution is an 'unquoted company' (see **31.30** above), (i) above is extended to payments made by or to any other person in pursuance of a scheme or arrangements made with the unquoted company. If the unquoted company is:

(A) under the control of five or fewer persons; and
(B) not under the sole control of a company not within (A) above,

payments made in pursuance of a scheme or arrangements made with any of the persons referred to in (A) above are chargeable payments.

'*Payment*' includes a transfer of money's worth including the assumption of a liability.

A '*company concerned in an exempt distribution*' includes every relevant company and any company connected with a relevant company (or with any other company which is so connected) at any time between the exempt distribution and the chargeable payment. In establishing connection, *CTA 2010, s 1122; ICTA 1988, s 839* (see **25 CONNECTED PERSONS**) applies.

Where a chargeable payment is made within five years of an exempt distribution, the chargeable payment is treated as a distribution within *CTA 2009, s 1305* therefore it does not qualify for a corporation tax deduction.

[*CTA 2010, ss 1087, 1089; ICTA 1988, ss 214, 218(1); FA 2003, Sch 18 para 3(4); ITTOIA 2005, Sch 5 para 111; CTA 2009, Sch 1 para 99(2)*].

See also **31.31** above.

Simon's Taxes. See **D6.423**.

Consequences of demerger

[31.33] The types of demerger detailed at **31.28**(a) and (b)(ii) above result in a change of ownership of the subsidiary company demerged.

If this is accompanied by a major change in the nature or conduct of the trade (which may result from those management changes the legislation is designed to bring about), the provisions of *CTA 2010, ss 673–676; ICTA 1988, ss 768, 768A* (see **55.13 LOSSES**), and *CTA 2010, ss 704, 705; CTA 2009, Sch 1 para 223* (see **62 PROPERTY INCOME**) may be triggered.

Briefly, these act to prohibit the carry-forward of losses arising before the change of ownership to be used in periods after the change of ownership. Since such restrictions contradict the intention of the demerger legislation, HMRC will consider sympathetically the application of *CTA 2010, ss 673–676, et seq; ICTA 1988, ss 768, 768A, 768D* and *245* where they apply as a result of an exempt distribution, and the underlying ownership of the trade is unchanged.

Winding-up etc.

[31.34] The requirement for a distribution company to be a trading company or the holding company of a trading group after the distribution (see **31.30** above) is removed in the following circumstances.

(a) Distributions within **31.28**(a) above
Where the transfer relates to two or more 75% subsidiaries of the distributing company which is then dissolved without there having been, after the exempt distribution, net assets of the company available for distribution in a winding-up or otherwise. A company will, concessionally, not be regarded as failing to meet these conditions merely because it retains, after the distribution, sufficient funds to meet the cost of liquidation and to repay a negligible amount (i.e. £5,000 or less) of share capital remaining. (HMRC Extra-Statutory Concession, C 11).

(b) Distributions within **31.28**(b) above

Where there are two or more transferee companies, each of which receives a trade or shares in a separate 75% subsidiary of the distributing company, and the distributing company is dissolved without there having been, after the exempt distribution, net assets of the company available for distribution in a winding-up or otherwise.

[*CTA 2010, s 1082; ICTA 1988, s 213(7)(9)*].

Returns

[31.35] Within 30 days after an exempt distribution, the distributing company must make a return to the inspector giving particulars of the distribution and the reasons why it is exempt. Where a clearance (see **31.37** below) has been given in respect of the distribution, the return need only refer to the clearance notification and confirm that the distribution is precisely that for which clearance application was made. (HMRC Statement of Practice, SP 13/80 as revised).

If a chargeable payment is made consisting of the transfer of money's worth, the payer must, within 30 days of the payment, make a return to the inspector giving particulars of:

(a) the transaction effecting the transfer;
(b) the name and address of each and every recipient and the value of what is transferred to him; and
(c) any chargeable payment in money which accompanied the transfer.

In the case of a payment which is not a chargeable payment solely because it is made for *bona fide* commercial reasons and otherwise than for tax avoidance purposes (see **31.32** above), a return must be made within 30 days of the payment giving particulars of:

(i) in the case of a transfer of money's worth, the transaction by which it is effected;
(ii) the name and address of each and every recipient and the value of the payment made to him; and
(iii) the circumstances by reason of which the payment is not a chargeable payment.

[*CTA 2010, ss 1095, 1096; ICTA 1988, s 216*].

See, however, **31.37** below.

Power to obtain information

[31.36] If the inspector has reason to believe that a distribution which is otherwise exempt may form part of a scheme or arrangements within *CTA 2010, s 1081; ICTA 1988, s 213(11)* (see **31.28**(1)–(5) above) he may give written notice to any relevant company or any person controlling such a company to supply the following information within such time as may be specified in the notice (but not less than 30 days).

(a) A written declaration stating whether or not, according to information which the company or that person has or can reasonably obtain, any relevant scheme or arrangements exist or have existed.

(b) Such other information as the inspector may reasonably require for the purposes of *CTA 2010, s 1081; ICTA 1988, s 213(11)* and the company or that person has or can reasonably obtain.

Similar powers exist, *mutatis mutandis*, if the inspector has reason to believe that a payment which is not otherwise a chargeable payment has been made in pursuance of such a scheme or arrangements as are outlined in **31.32** above. In addition, the inspector may require from any recipient of such payment the name and address of anyone on whose behalf it was received. [*CTA 2010, s 1097; ICTA 1988, s 217*].

If the inspector has reason to believe that a person has not delivered an account or made a return in accordance with the provisions outlined above, he may give written notice to that person to supply such information as the inspector may reasonably require for the purposes of *CTA 2010, s 1096; ICTA 1988, s 214(1)(b) or s 216(2)–(4)*.

[*CTA 2010, ss 1081, 1096, 1097; ICTA 1988, s 217(2); SI 2007 No 3506*].

Clearance

[31.37] Application may be made for advance determination that a distribution is exempt or that a payment is not chargeable.

Applications for clearance should be addressed to Clearance and Counteraction Team, First Floor, 22 Kingsway, London WC2B 6NR (or, if market-sensitive information is included, to Team Leader at that address). Applications may be faxed to 020–7438 4409 or emailed to reconstructions@gtnet.gov.uk (after advising Team Leader if market-sensitive information is included). Application may be made in a single letter to the same address for clearance under *CTA 2010, ss 1091–1094; ICTA 1988, s 215* and under any one or more of *CTA 2010, ss 1044, 1045; ICTA 1988, s 225* (see **63.8 PURCHASE BY A COMPANY OF ITS OWN SHARES**), *CTA 2010, ss 748, 749; ICTA 1988, s 707* (transactions in securities, see **5.2 ANTI-AVOIDANCE**), *TCGA 1992, s 138(1)* (share exchanges, see Tolley's Capital Gains Tax under Anti-Avoidance), *TCGA 1992, s 139(5)* (reconstructions involving the transfer of a business, see **17.11 CAPITAL GAINS**), *TCGA 1992, s 140B* (transfer of a UK trade between EU member states, see **17.14 CAPITAL GAINS**), *TCGA 1992, s 140D* (transfer of non-UK trade between EU member states, see **17.21 CAPITAL GAINS**) and *CTA 2009, s 832; FA 2002, Sch 29 para 88* (see **48.27 INTANGIBLE ASSETS**).

The application must fully and accurately disclose all facts and circumstances material for the decision of HMRC, failing which any clearance granted is void. In general, it should include the following.

(i) The name of each relevant company (see **31.30** above), its tax district and reference, residence status, whether it is a distributing, subsidiary or transferee company (see **31.28** above) in relation to the proposed transactions, and whether it is a trading company or holding company (see **31.30** above) under the demerger provisions definitions, or some other type of company.
(ii) Details of the group structure where appropriate.

(iii) A statement of the reasons for the demerger, the trading activities to be divided, the anticipated trading benefits and any other benefits expected to accrue.

(iv) A detailed description of all the proposed transactions, including any prior transactions or rearrangements in preparation for the demerger, making it clear why it is considered that all the relevant conditions are satisfied.

(v) Confirmation, together with all relevant information, that the distribution is not excluded from relief as part of a scheme (see **31.28** above), and a statement of the circumstances (if any) in which it is envisaged that control of a relevant company might be acquired by someone other than a member of the distributing company, or that a trade carried on by one of those companies before or after the demerger might cease or be sold.

(vi) The latest available balance sheets and profit and loss accounts of the existing companies (as listed at (i) above), and, where appropriate, a consolidated group balance sheet and profit and loss account, with a note of any material relevant changes between balance sheet date and the proposed demerger.

Where, exceptionally, it is not possible to explain the purpose of a demerger adequately in writing, HMRC will invite the applicants to an interview.

(HMRC Statement of Practice, SP 13/80 as revised).

HMRC may call for further particulars within 30 days of the receipt of the application, or of particulars previously requested, and if these are not supplied within a further 30 days (or such longer period as HMRC may allow) HMRC need not proceed further on the application. Subject to this, HMRC must notify its decision to the applicant within 30 days of the receipt of the application or of the particulars last requested. If the decision is unfavourable, or not communicated to him within the time limit, the applicant may, within 30 days after the receipt of the decision or after the expiry of the time limit, require HMRC to place the matter before the tribunal. The decision of the tribunal is then treated as that of HMRC.

Where a clearance has been given in respect of a payment which would otherwise be a chargeable payment, there is no obligation to make a return under these provisions (see **31.35** above).

[*CTA 2010, ss 1091–1094; ICTA 1988, ss 215, 216(4)*].

A company which becomes or ceases to be connected (see **25 CONNECTED PERSONS** and **31.32** above) with another company may seek clearance for any payment which may be made at any time after it became, or ceased to be, so connected (whether or not there is any present intention to make any payment). No payment to which a clearance relates is to be treated as chargeable merely by reason of the company's being, or having been, connected with the other company.

[*CTA 2010, s 1092; ICTA 1988, s 215*].

Simon's Taxes. See **D6.429**.

Key points

[31.38] Points to consider are as follows.

- A distribution from a company can take many forms, and can include not only normal dividends in respect of shares in the company, but also interest on securities that exceeds a normal commercial return. Most types of payment in respect of shares are likely to be treated as a distribution.
- A return of capital will usually not be treated as a distribution. This is important in the context of a purchase of own shares or a capital reduction. For this to apply it is important to check that the shares were acquired for valuable consideration. A bonus issue created out of distributable reserves will not be regarded as having been acquired for valuable consideration.
- Care must be taken where a purchase of own shares follows or is followed by a bonus issue, as this could give rise to a distribution. It is important to look at the history of a company before proceeding with a purchase of own shares or other capital reduction.
- Where a close company provides benefits to shareholders, and those benefits are not taxed as benefits arising from employment, they can be taxed on the shareholders as distributions.
- Bonus shares in the form of stock dividends are taxed on the shareholder as distributions. These occur usually where the shareholder is offered a choice between receiving a cash dividend or additional shares of broadly equivalent value.

32

Double Tax Relief

Cross-references. See **5.13, 5.35 ANTI-AVOIDANCE; 17.48 CAPITAL GAINS; 27 CONTROLLED FOREIGN COMPANIES; 31.15 DISTRIBUTIONS 39.23 GROUP RELIEF; 65 RESIDENCE.**

Other sources. See Tolley's Double Taxation Relief.

Simon's Taxes. See D4.8, D4.9, D4.10, E6.4, Parts F1, F2, F4.

Introduction

[32.1] This chapter considers the provisions within UK tax law that provide relief for double taxation suffered (as a tax charge in the UK and overseas) by a UK company on the same source of income.

With regard to dividends, the exempt dividend regime was introduced by *FA 2009*. This regime broadly provides that most dividends received by a UK company on or after 1 July 2009 (from the UK or overseas) will be exempt from corporation tax, see further **31.15 DISTRIBUTIONS**.

Therefore the double tax relief provisions in this chapter will no longer apply to overseas income in the form of a distribution or dividend, where the dividend exemption applies. However, the provisions outlined herein will apply to overseas dividends received on or after 1 July 2009 that are not exempt, and to all other overseas dividends received before 1 July 2009.

Thus in the case of non-dividend income or where the exemption does not apply and the same income is liable to be taxed in both the UK and another country, relief may be available in the following ways:

(a) under the specific terms of a double tax agreement between the UK and that other country — see **32.3** below [*TIOPA 2010, s 2; ICTA 1988, s 788*];
(b) under special arrangements with Ireland — see Tolley's Income Tax under Double Tax Relief; or
(c) under the unilateral double tax relief provisions contained in UK tax legislation — see **32.2** below. [*TIOPA 2010, s 18; ICTA 1988, s 790*].

An exemption from UK tax is included in the *Finance Act 2011* for the profits of foreign permanent establishments of UK resident companies. Companies will be able to make an irrevocable election for the exemption to apply. See further **32.7** below.

Unilateral relief

[32.2] Unilateral relief applies to taxes other than those for which credit is available under the bilateral double tax agreements in **32.17** below. The taxes are those payable under the law of any territory outside the UK and computed by reference to income or gain arising in that territory. They are allowed (to the extent defined below) as a credit against UK income tax or corporation tax paid on that income or gain by UK residents. Unilateral relief is not available if relief is available under a double tax agreement.

Relief is only available against UK tax chargeable under the same category of income or gain under which the foreign income is chargeable (*George Wimpey International Ltd v Rolfe* (1989) 62 TC 597). Where appropriate an apportionment must be made to determine what part of income may be regarded as 'arising in' the overseas territory, and in making that apportionment it is the principles of UK tax law which are to be applied (see *Yates (Inspector of Taxes) v GCA International Ltd* [1991] STC 157, 64 TC 37 and HMRC Statement of Practice, SP 7/91, 16 July 1991).

The machinery and limits (with modifications as below) are substantially the same as those under which the bilateral agreements operate and the credit given is, basically, such as would be allowable were a double taxation agreement in force with the territory concerned.

A limit is placed on relief available for corporation tax where a non resident incurs overseas tax on the profits or capital gains of a UK permanent establishment. Relief is limited to the amount which would have been relieved if the permanent establishment had been a UK resident liable to tax on the income or gains.

[*TIOPA 2010, ss 8, 9, 11, 18, 30, Change 3 in Annex 1; ICTA 1988, ss 790(1)–(4), 794*].

As highlighted, unilateral relief is not allowed where credit could be claimed under a double tax agreement under **32.3** below, or in cases or circumstances in which such an agreement made on or after that date specifically prohibits relief.

[*TIOPA 2010, s 25; ICTA 1988, s 793A(2)(3)*].

Unilateral relief under *TIOPA 2010, ss 8–18; ICTA 1988, s 790* is available on dividends received from overseas companies (which do not fall within the exemption regime) with regard to:

(a) overseas tax directly charged on the dividend which would not have been charged if the dividend had not been paid; and
(b) tax in respect of the overseas company's profits paid under the law of the country in which it is resident where:
 (i) the dividend is paid by a company resident overseas to a company resident in the UK, or to a company resident outside the UK but forming part of the profits of a UK permanent establishment (see **65.6 RESIDENCE**) of the company; and
 (ii) the recipient company (or a company of which it is a 'subsidiary') controls (directly or indirectly) at least 10% of the voting power in the overseas company (but see also **32.10** below).

In (b)(i) above, in the case of a company resident outside the UK but forming part of the profits of a UK permanent establishment, relief is limited to the amount which could be claimed in the same circumstances by a UK-resident company. The taxes concerned must correspond to income tax, capital gains tax or corporation tax on income or capital gains. Municipal taxes qualify, provided they meet these criteria.

'*Subsidiary*' means a company of which 50% or more of the voting power is controlled, directly or indirectly, by the other.

[*TIOPA 2010, ss 12–17*].

A credit for tax on income or gains which is paid under the other territory's law and corresponds to UK tax is available as a credit against UK tax unless a credit is available for tax on those income or gains under a double taxation agreement.

[*TIOPA 2010, ss 9, 18; ICTA 1988, ss 790(4)–(6A), 794(2)(bb), 800–802; FA 2001, Sch 27 paras 3, 7*].

For the scope of 'dividends', see *Memec plc v CIR* (1998) 71 TC 77, CA (in which receipts under a silent partnership agreement were held not to attract relief). See also HMRC Tax Bulletin June 2006 p 1295 for an article on the classification of foreign entities for UK tax purposes and for a list of overseas business entities on whose classification for UK tax purposes HMRC has been asked to express a view. See also Revenue Interpretation (RI) 279 with regard to entity classification.

Where no credit is available for foreign tax, relief is available by deduction of foreign tax paid on the non-UK source income from that income, in computing the income liable to UK corporation tax. If part or all of the foreign tax is repaid to the company by the foreign tax authorities, the company's income is increased by that amount.

To be eligible for relief, the taxes must be charged on income or capital gains and correspond to income tax, capital gains tax or corporation tax in the UK but, subject to this, provincial, state and municipal taxes are included.

See *Yates (Inspector of Taxes) v GCA International Ltd* [1991] STC 157, 64 TC 37 where a tax imposed on gross receipts less a fixed 10% deduction was held to correspond to UK income tax or corporation tax. Following that decision, HMRC amended their practice. (HMRC Statement of Practice, SP 7/91, as revised.) Foreign taxes are examined to determine whether, in their own legislative context, they serve the same function as UK income and corporation taxes in relation to business profits, and are thus eligible for unilateral relief. As regards those overseas taxes which HMRC consider admissible (or inadmissible) for relief, these are listed by country in HMRC Double Taxation Relief Manual, DT2100 *et seq*. See also HMRC Business Income Manual, BIM45905. Current information may be obtained from the HMRC website (www.hmrc.gov.uk/international).

[*TIOPA 2010, ss 112, 113; ICTA 1988, ss 790, 811*].

Simon's Taxes. See **D4.801, E6.414, F4.104.**

Relief by agreement

[32.3] Relief from double taxation may be available under the provisions of an applicable double taxation agreement. A list is given in **32.17** below of the bilateral agreements made by the UK which are currently operative. Subject to the following general provisions, the extent of such relief depends on the terms of the relevant double tax agreement, which should be carefully studied.

Arrangements under such an agreement may provide for:

(i) relief from income or corporation tax in respect of income or chargeable gains;
(ii) charging UK income to non-UK residents;
(iii) determining income to be attributed to non-UK residents or their agencies, etc., or to UK residents who have special relationships with non-UK residents;
(iv) granting non-UK residents the right to set-off or repayment of the tax credit in respect of distributions made to them by UK resident companies; or
(v) exchange of information concerning taxes covered by the agreement, particularly in relation to the prevention of fiscal evasion.

[*TIOPA 2010, ss 6, 18; ICTA 1988, s 788(3); ITTOIA 2005, Sch 1 para 321; FA 2006, ss 173–175 (previously ICTA 1988, s 788(2) as amended by FA 2003, s 198)*].

It should be noted that following the changes in 2007 to HMRC's double tax treaty process and the introduction of the treaty passport scheme, the provisional treaty relief scheme ('PTRS') with regard to one to one loan transactions has been discontinued as from 1 September 2010. The PTRS allowed interest payments to be made without the deduction of income tax (or at a reduced treaty rate) pursuant to a double tax treaty, pending the issue of a Direction on the treaty position by HMRC. The part of the PTRS dealing with syndicated loans has been retained under the name syndicated loan scheme. This scheme applies only where the borrower and the lenders are unconnected and the transaction is on arm's length terms.

As regards (i) above, it was held, in the case of *NEC Semi-Conductors Ltd v Revenue and Customs Comrs* [2006] EWCA Civ 25, [2006] STC 606, 8 ITLR 819, that the phrase 'corporation tax in respect of income or chargeable gains' in *ICTA 1988, s 788(3)(a)* did not include ACT. Thus, the restriction of the group income election to UK-resident companies was not contrary to the non-discrimination article of double tax convention concerned (between UK and Japan).

As regards (iv) above, the general abolition of the repayment of tax credits after 5 April 1999 does not affect the entitlement of a non-UK resident to payment in respect of a tax credit under such arrangements (although it should be noted that in practice, with the reduction after that date to one-ninth in the rate of tax credit, such repayments will be very limited). [*F(No 2)A 1997, s 30(9)(10); ITTOIA 2005, Sch 1 para 496*]. Similarly, the tax credit payment restrictions applicable to pension funds in relation to distributions made after 1 July 1997 do not apply to non-residents' entitlements under such arrangements. [*ICTA 1988, s 231A(6)(b); as repealed by F(No 2)A 1997, s 19(2), Sch 8 Pt II(9)*].

Also as regards (iv) above, in the combined cases of *Metallgesellschaft Ltd v CIR* and *Hoechst AG v CIR* [2001] STC 452, it was held that the requirement that both parties to a group income election under *ICTA 1988, s 247* (for the payment of dividends prior to the abolition of ACT on 6 April 1999) be UK-resident, contravened EU law. Following this, it was held in *Pirelli Cable Holding NV v CIR* [2006] STC 548, HL (unanimously reversing the Court of Appeal's decision), that, had such a group income election been made (had it been available), the non-UK resident parent would not have been entitled to tax credits in respect of the distributions made by the UK-resident subsidiary. The ECJ, in *Test Claimants in Class IV of the ACT Group Litigation v CIR: C-374/04* ([2006] ECR I-11673, [2007] All ER (EC) 351, [2010] All ER (D) 247) held that EC Treaty (as was, now TFEU) Articles 43 and 56 did not preclude a member state from granting a tax credit to a company resident within it on dividends received from other resident companies, although no such credit was available on dividends from companies resident in other member states. The granting of the tax credit was linked with a charge to tax on the dividend and therefore the non-resident company (that did not receive the tax credit but equally did not suffer UK tax on the dividend) was not in a comparable position to the resident company. Where the two states have a double taxation agreement in force between them and a third state does not, granting of a tax credit on a dividend paid by a company in the first state to one in the second state, but not to one in the third state, is not precluded. The case was returned to the UK courts and judgment in the most recent appeal was handed down on 21 December 2010. The Court of Appeal ruled that the judge in the lower court had been entirely correct to grant the claimant groups of companies only a partial tax credit and in finding that the claimants were not entitled to a repayment of the 5% income tax charge.

In the case of *UBS AG v HMRC* [2007] STC 588, CA, it was held by the Court of Appeal that it was not discriminatory to deny the UK branch of a Swiss bank the benefit of a claim under *ICTA 1988, s 243* (for accounting periods beginning before 2 July 1997, set off of surplus franked investment income against trading losses brought forward) in respect of entitlement to repayment of tax credits under *ICTA 1988, s 788(3)(d)*. In *Hill Samuel Investments Ltd v Revenue and Customs Comrs* [2009] STC (SCD) 315, 11 ITLR 734 the point at issue was to what extent was the UK claimant required to take reasonable steps to reduce the foreign tax on the transaction. It was held that 'taking reasonable steps' did not involve entering an entirely different transaction whether or not it had the same economic effect.

In the case of *Bayfine UK v HMRC* [2011] EWCA Civ 304, [2010] EWHC 609 (Ch), [2010] STC 1379, where more than one state taxes the same profits, which state is to give credit is determined according to the state of source, which has the primary taxing right. This involved a UK recipient of US source income, which had 'checked the box' in the US and so its income was included in the US profits of its parent. In the High Court it was held that the US was the state of source and had the primary taxing rights, thus the UK had to give relief under the US-UK treaty. However this was overturned in the Court of Appeal and it was held the UK had primary taxing rights and that HMRC was not obliged to give relief for US tax either under the treaty or unilaterally.

As regards the concept of 'permanent establishment' on which taxation rights are based under most treaties, HMRC take the view that a website, or a server on which e-commerce is conducted through a website, is not of itself a permanent establishment. (See HMRC International Manual, INTM266100 and **65.6 RESIDENCE**).

For the circumstances in which HMRC will certify that a company is UK resident for the purposes of double tax agreements, see Revenue Tax Bulletin December 2002 pp 989–991. See also INTM120130 for revised guidance in respect of instances when HMRC will not review a company's residence, and also INTM120070 for revised guidance on the operation of the residence tie-breaker clause in double tax treaties, and a list of treaties with the UK which have such a clause.

For the scope of 'dividends' attracting treaty relief, see *Memec plc v CIR* (1998) 71 TC 77, CA (in which receipts under a silent partnership agreement were held not to attract relief), and see also Revenue Tax Bulletin February 1999 p 627 for an article on the classification of foreign entities for UK tax purposes. See also Revenue Tax Bulletin December 2000 pp 809–812 for a list of overseas business entities on whose classification for UK tax purposes HMRC has been asked to express a view. See also RI 279 on entity classification.

In *R v CIR (ex p Commerzbank AG)* (1991) 68 TC 252, interest on unpaid tax was held not to fall within the scope of double tax agreements, but on a reference to the European Court of Justice (see 68 TC 264), the Court upheld the view that, in the case of EU member states, such discrimination against non-UK resident companies was prevented by the relevant Articles of the EC Treaty (now TFEU). See HMRC Double Taxation Relief Manual, DT1950 *et seq*. for HMRC's approach to non-discrimination claims generally.

See, however, HMRC Statement of Practice, SP 2/95 for HMRC's view of the restricted operation of non-discrimination clauses in double tax treaties.

Mutual agreement procedure

Double tax agreements normally contain a 'mutual agreement procedure' provision enabling a taxpayer who considers that the action of a tax authority has resulted, or will result, in taxation not in accordance with the agreement to present his case to the competent authority in his state of residence.

The UK competent authority is HMRC, and the address to which all relevant facts and contentions should be sent is Revenue Policy International, 100 Parliament Street, London SW1A 2BQ. For the presentation of such cases, and for giving effect to solutions and agreements reached under such procedures, see *TIOPA 2010, ss 124, 125*; *ICTA 1988, s 815AA*. Details of the procedures can be found in the HMRC Double Taxation Relief Manual. See also SP1/11 which outlines HMRC's approach to the operation of the MAP, in particular with reference to transfer pricing disputes (outlined at **72.16 TRANSFER PRICING**).

Anti-avoidance

The case of *Bayfine UK v HMRC* [2011] EWCA Civ 304, [2010] EWHC 609 (Ch), [2010] STC (SCD) 43, has been highlighted above. In that case two UK resident companies (both subsidiaries of a US company) entered forward contracts. One made a loss and the other a profit of the same amount. Group relief was claimed on the loss and double tax relief on the profit. It was found by the Special Commissioners that no DTR was due as the profit arose in the UK. The High Court did not agree, but the decision of the Commissioners was upheld in the Court of Appeal on 23 March 2011 who applied a purposive construction to the interpretation of the treaty. Arden LJ commented (at para 40) that the primary purpose of double tax treaties is both to eliminate double taxation and 'to prevent fiscal evasion which would include the avoidance of taxation' and thus the Treaty should be interpreted to avoid the grant of double relief as well as to confer relief against double taxation.

An anti-avoidance provision was introduced by *FA 2008* aimed at the use of double taxation agreements to obtain a tax advantage. A double tax agreement may provide that the trading profits of a non-resident company which is controlled or managed outside the UK are not taxable in the UK except to the extent that they are attributable to a permanent establishment in the UK. Where this clause is included, nonetheless, the UK profits will be taxable on any company resident in the UK which is entitled to those profits. Residence is determined according to the relevant double tax agreement. This provision does not apply to partnership profits chargeable to tax in the UK. This provision applies to income arising on or after 12 March 2008.

[*TIOPA 2010, s 130; ICTA 1988, s 815AZA; FA 2008, s 59*].

Simon's Taxes. See D4.802, E6.411–E6.413.

Specific matters

Relief by deduction

[32.4] An election can be made not to claim relief by way of credit (see **32.5** below), for example where there is no or insufficient UK tax payable on the foreign income against which the foreign tax can be credited. Where such an election is made or where a credit for foreign tax is not taken under treaty or unilateral relief, or is not otherwise allowable in respect of foreign income (see also **32.5** below under Relief for disallowed credit), any foreign tax paid on that income is generally deductible from that income for purposes of UK assessment.

This does not apply to underlying tax excluded from a claim for relief under *TIOPA 2010, s 60; ICTA 1988, s 799(1B)* (to prevent the application of the 'mixer' cap in certain cases — see **32.12** below). Where foreign tax for which such a deduction has been given is subsequently adjusted, the UK tax charge may be revised within six years from date of the foreign tax adjustment. Where, by reason of the adjustment, relief has become excessive, written notice of that fact must be given to HMRC within one year of the date of the adjustment subject to a penalty for failure to comply not exceeding the amount of the additional UK tax payable.

FA 2010 amends *TIOPA 2010, s 112* to ensure that a person may only deduct foreign tax from any foreign income where he has not already reduced his income by reference to the foreign tax.

[*TIOPA 2010, ss 27, 79, 80, 112; ICTA 1988, ss 805, 811; CTA 2009, para 263*].

Foreign tax levied by reference to the value of assets employed to produce income chargeable to UK tax may, in practice, be allowed as a business expense under normal trading income rules. (HMRC International Tax Handbook, ITH602).

Simon's Taxes. See D4.801, E6.416.

Prevention of double relief

Credit may not be given for foreign tax for which relief is available in the territory in which it would otherwise be payable, either under double tax arrangements or under the law of that territory in consequence of any such arrangements. It is also made clear that unilateral relief will not be allowed where credit could be claimed under a double tax agreement, or in cases or circumstances in which such an agreement made after 20 March 2000 specifically prohibits relief.

[*TIOPA 2010, s 25; ICTA 1988, s 793A*].

Simon's Taxes. See **D4.801, E6.414, E6.433.**

Tax sparing relief

Under *TIOPA 2010, ss 4, 20; previously ICTA 1988, s 788(5)* it may be provided in a double tax agreement that any tax which would have been payable in a foreign country but for a relief under the law of that territory given with a view to promoting industrial, commercial, scientific, educational or other development therein is nevertheless treated for purposes of credit against UK tax as if it had been paid. (It is not available for unilateral relief or where relief is given by way of deduction from dividend income.)

See, for example, HMRC Double Taxation Relief Manual at DT12758 in the case of Malaysia and at DT16911 in the case of Singapore.

Matching credit for tax spared below immediate overseas subsidiary

Where:

(a) an amount of tax would, but for a relief, have been payable by a company ('company A'), in respect of any of its profits, under the law of its territory of residence;

(b) company A pays a dividend out of those profits to another company ('company B') resident in the same territory;

(c) company B, out of profits consisting of or including all or part of that dividend, pays a dividend to a UK-resident company ('company C'); and

(d) had company B been UK resident, it would have been entitled under a double tax agreement with its actual territory of residence to relief for the spared tax,

then the spared tax is taken into account for the purposes of unilateral relief for underlying tax as if it had been payable and paid. If these conditions are not fulfilled, unilateral relief is not available for spared tax in respect of any dividend paid by a non-UK resident company to a UK-resident company, notwithstanding any double tax agreement with the territory concerned providing any relief for spared tax.

Without prejudice to the above specific relief, treaty relief for underlying tax which is spared below the level of the immediate non-resident subsidiary is denied unless it is specifically provided for in a double tax agreement.

[*TIOPA 2010, ss 4, 17, 20; ICTA 1988, ss 788(5), 790(10A)–(10C)*].

Simon's Taxes. See **D4.936, E6.436.**

Acquisitions and disposals of loan relationships

Special provision is made for the relief of foreign tax relating to accrued interest in relation to which a non-trading credit (or, if the Treasury so provides by order before 12 March 2008, a trading credit) is brought into account (see **54.4 LOAN RELATIONSHIPS**), and for foreign tax to be disregarded where it is attributable to interest accruing under a loan relationship (see **54.2 LOAN RELATIONSHIPS**) at a time when the company concerned was not a party to the relationship (unless it ceased to be a party under certain repo or stock-lending arrangements).

Foreign tax attributable to 'relevant payments' within *ICTA 1988, s 807A(7)* (now *'notional interest payment'* within *TIOPA 2010, s 107(3))* are to be disregarded where it is attributable to a time when the company was not a party to the derivative contract (or, for accounting periods beginning before 1 October 2002, to the interest rate or currency contract) concerned.

[*TIOPA 2010, s 107*].

Where shares are treated as loan relationships (see **54.86 LOAN RELATIONSHIPS**), the above provisions have effect for share distributions as they would for interest under a loan relationship.

With regard to loan relationships, the foreign tax is disregarded where it is attributable to the distribution accruing in respect of such shares, or to interest accruing under a loan relationship, at a time when the company does not hold the shares, or is not a party to the relationship (unless it ceased to hold the shares under certain repo or stock-lending arrangements).

[*TIOPA 2010, s 108; ICTA 1988, s 807A; F(No 2)A 2005, Sch 7 para 5; FA 2007, Sch 14 para 10*].

Simon's Taxes. See **D4.807**.

Special arrangements — interest

Double tax agreements under *TIOPA 2010, s 6; ICTA 1988, s 788* making provision in relation to interest may also have a provision dealing with cases where, owing to a special relationship, the amount of interest paid exceeds the amount which would have been paid in the absence of that relationship, and requiring the interest provision to be applied only to that lower amount.

Any such special relationship provision has to be construed:

(a) as requiring account to be taken of all factors, including whether, in the absence of the relationship, the loan would have been made at all, or would have been in a different amount, or a different rate of interest and other terms would have been agreed. This does not apply, however, where the special relationship provision expressly requires regard to be had to the debt on which the interest is paid in determining the excess interest, and accordingly expressly limits the factors to be taken into account, and in the case of a loan by one company to another, the fact that it is not part of the lending company's business to make loans generally is disregarded; and

(b) as requiring the taxpayer either to show that no special relationship exists or to show the amount of interest which would have been paid in the absence of that relationship.

[*TIOPA 2010, s 131; ICTA 1988, s 808A*].

With regard to (a) above, see HMRC International Manual, INTM501010 for a further discussion of the tax considerations of intra-group funding, the special relationship provision and transfer pricing.

Special relationships — royalties

Double tax agreements may make similar provision in relation to royalties. Where royalties are payable on or after 28 July 2000, any special relationship provision, unless it expressly requires regard to be had to the use, right or information for which royalties are paid in determining the excess royalties, has to be construed as requiring account to be taken of all factors. These include:

(A) in the absence of the relationship, whether the royalty agreement would have been made at all, or the rate or amount of royalties and other terms which would have been agreed; and

(B) if the asset in respect of which the royalties are paid (or any asset which it represents or from which it is derived) had previously been in the beneficial ownership of:

- (i) the person liable to pay the royalties;
- (ii) a person who has at any time carried on a business which, when the royalties fall due, is carried on in whole or part by the person liable to pay the royalties; or
- (iii) a person who is or has been an 'associate', as specially defined, of a person within (i) or (ii),

the amounts paid under the transaction(s) which resulted in the asset falling into its present beneficial ownership, the amounts which would have been so paid in the absence of the special relationship, and the question as to whether the transaction(s) would have taken place at all in the absence of that relationship.

The taxpayer must also show either that no special relationship exists, or the amount of royalties which would have been paid in the absence of the relationship, and if he cannot show that (B) above does not apply, he must show that the transaction(s) mentioned therein would have taken place in the absence of a special relationship, and the amounts which would then have been paid under those transaction(s).

The taxpayer must also show either that no special relationship exists, or the amount of royalties which would have been paid in the absence of the relationship, and if he cannot show that (B) above does not apply, he must show that the transaction(s) mentioned therein would have taken place in the absence of a special relationship, and the amounts which would then have been paid under those transaction(s).

[*TIOPA 2010, ss 132, 133; ICTA 1988, s 808B*].

Simon's Taxes. See **E1.570.**

Royalties and 'know how' payments

Notwithstanding that credit for overseas tax is ordinarily given only against income which arises (or is deemed to arise) in the overseas territory concerned, HMRC treatment (per ESC B8) as regards this class of income is as follows.

Income payments made by an overseas resident to a UK trader for the use, in that overseas territory, of any *copyright, patent, design, secret process or formula, trade mark etc.*, may be treated, for credit purposes (whether under double tax agreements or by way of unilateral relief) as income arising outside the UK — *except* so far as they represent consideration for services (other than merely incidental) rendered in the UK by the recipient to the payer (HMRC Extra Statutory Concession B8).

For the treatment of sales of 'know-how' etc., see **70.55 TRADE PROFITS — INCOME AND SPECIFIC TRADES** and **61.18 PROFIT COMPUTATIONS**.

Relief by way of credit

[32.5] Relief is to be allowed by way of credit against attributable corporation tax (i.e. UK tax otherwise chargeable) on any income or chargeable gain ('the relevant income or gain') up to the amount of that tax (see below in relation to trade receipts). The foreign tax on the overseas income can only be set against the corresponding UK tax in respect of the same income (see **32.8** below). The credit for tax must not exceed corporation tax at the rate payable by the company on the income or gain which is the subject of the claim, less specified deductions. The rules regarding permanent establishments apply for determining how much of the UK resident company's profits is attributable to the company's permanent establishment outside the UK.

For the purposes of *TIOPA 2010, s 42*, tax on non-trading loan relationships is taken as tax on income from total non-trading credits with regard to the period, and not the company's non-trading profits it has on its non-trading loan relationships. Similarly, with regard to intangible fixed assets.

[*TIOPA 2010, ss 18, 42, 43, 50, 51; CTA 2009, Pt 2 Ch 4; ICTA 1988, s 797(1)(2)*].

This applies both to unilateral relief and to relief by agreement, though it is confined in the latter case to those UK taxes which are covered by the agreement. Relief is only available against UK tax chargeable under the same class of income as that under which the foreign tax was chargeable on the foreign income. (*George Wimpey International Ltd v Rolfe* (1989) 62 TC 597).

Both reliefs apply to corporation tax on chargeable gains as they do to income. [*TIOPA 2010, ss 2, 18; ICTA 1988, ss 788(1), 790(1)*].

Relief for overseas tax paid is available against UK tax on chargeable gains provided that both liabilities relate to the same source, i.e. notwithstanding that they may arise at different times or be charged on different persons. (HMRC International Manual, INTM161040 and HMRC Statement of Practice, SP 6/88).

Relief under an agreement is limited to that which would be allowed if all reasonable steps had been taken, including all relevant claims, elections, etc., under the law of the territory concerned or under double tax arrangements with that territory, to minimise the foreign tax payable.

[*TIOPA 2010, s 33; ICTA 1988, s 795A*].

As regards what HMRC considers taxpayers can and cannot reasonably be expected to do, the former is likely to include appeals against excessive assessments, claims for reliefs generally known to be available, and selection of any option which produces a lower tax liability, and the latter is likely to include claims to reliefs whose availability is uncertain, and where disproportionate expenditure would be required to pursue a claim, substituting carry-forward claims for carry-back claims and *vice versa*, and attempting to exercise influence the taxpayer does not have on the underlying tax paid by a subsidiary. See the brief note on HMRC's website (www.hmrc.gov.uk/international/dtr26.htm).

Trade income

The following restriction applies in relation to a credit for foreign tax in connection either with a payment of foreign tax or with income received in respect of which foreign tax has been deducted at source.

The meaning of 'relevant income or gain' under *ICTA 1988, s 797(1), TIOPA 2010, s 42* (see above) is amended in relation to 'trade income' to refer only to so much of the income arising or gains accruing out of transactions in connection with which the foreign tax arises.

For this purpose, '*trade income*' includes:

(a) income or profits chargeable as UK or overseas trading income (see **70 TRADE PROFITS — INCOME AND SPECIFIC TRADES**); or
(b) of a property business (see **62.4 PROPERTY INCOME**); or
(c) post-cessation receipts chargeable to corporation tax (see **70.16 TRADE PROFITS — INCOME AND SPECIFIC TRADES**); or
(d) income arising outside the UK which is charged to tax as income not otherwise charged (under *CTA 2009, s 979*); and
(e) any other instance where the trading rules are used to calculate profits (but this does not apply to income of an insurance company to which *TIOPA 2010, s 99; ICTA 1988, s 804C* applies).

In determining the corporation tax attributable to any income or gain, account is to be taken of deductions or expenses etc. that would be allowable and are directly attributable to the income and also a reasonable proportion of expenses etc. that are only partly attributable, e.g. overheads. Connected company (within *ICTA 1988, s 839; CTA 2010, ss 1122, 1123*) expenses are also to be taken into account in so far as they are reasonably attributable to the income or gain. There are anti-avoidance provisions the purpose of which is to catch arrangements which divert income for credit relief purposes to other persons.

[*TIOPA 2010, ss 44, 45*].

Special cases

Where a foreign tax payment is made in connection with an asset which is in a 'hedging relationship' (as defined) with a derivative contract, the reference to 'relevant income or gain' (or 'income or gain' in *TIOPA 2010*) for these purposes is extended to include the income arising out of the assets and the derivative contract taken together (but only so as to include the income or loss from the derivative contract as is reasonably attributable to the hedging relationship).

Where royalties from different non-UK jurisdictions are paid in respect of the same asset, the royalty income in an accounting period (before 1 April 2010 — in a year of assessment) in respect of that asset is to be treated as arising from a single transaction and the foreign tax credits in respect of such income are to be aggregated.

Where a person ('A') carrying on a trade enters into a scheme or arrangement with another person ('B') in order to circumvent the above provisions in relation to A, any income received in pursuance of the scheme or arrangement is to be treated as trade income of B.

Where there is a series or group of transactions, arrangements or assets (a 'portfolio') and a number of tax credits arise in respect of that portfolio, the income or gains arising from the portfolio or part of the portfolio may be aggregated and apportioned in a fair and reasonable manner. This is provided it is not reasonably practicable to prepare separate computations for each transaction etc. or separate computations would not, when compared with an aggregate computation, make a material difference to the amount of allowable credit for foreign tax.

Relief under *TIOPA 2010, s 44(2)* is restricted in the case of a bank or a company connected with a bank.

[*TIOPA 2010, ss 44–49; ICTA 1988, ss 798A, 798B; FA 2005, s 86(1)(3)–(5); CTA 2009, Sch 1 paras 249, 662*].

See HMRC guidance 'Double Taxation Relief: Trade Receipts' issued on 6 May 2005 (available on their website at www.hmrc.gov.uk/budget2005/dtr tr.pdf).

See also **32.18** below in relation to banks and other financial traders regarding the case of *Legal & General Assurance Society Ltd v HMRC* [2006] STC 1763 (which preceded the above changes made by *FA 2005*).

Relief for disallowed credit

Where an amount of credit for foreign tax is disallowed because of the application of *ICTA 1988, s 797, TIOPA 2010, s 42; CTA 2009, Sch 1 para 246* above, relief may be available instead as a deduction in computing taxable profits.

This has effect in relation to a credit for foreign tax in connection with either a payment of foreign tax on or after 16 March 2005 or with income received on or after that date in respect of which foreign tax has deducted at source, and has effect notwithstanding the general rule in *ICTA 1988, s 795(2); TIOPA 2010, s 31* that relief may be by credit or deduction but not a mixture of the two. The amount that can be deducted is the lower of the disallowed credit and the amount of any loss, *after* deducting foreign tax, that is attributable to the income in respect of which the foreign tax was paid; if there is no such loss, no deduction is available.

[*TIOPA 2010, s 35; ICTA 1988, s 798C; FA 2005, s 86(1)(3)(4)*].

See HMRC's draft guidance (available at www.hmrc.gov.uk/budget2005/dtrt r.pdf).

Anti-avoidance

See **5.35** for wide-ranging anti-avoidance provisions introduced by *FA 2005* applying to schemes or arrangements the main purpose or one of the main purposes of which is to obtain credit relief for foreign tax. This legislation was extended in *FA 2007*. These provisions are replicated in *TIOPA 2010* post the rewrite.

Further anti-avoidance legislation was introduced in *FA 2010, s 36* and *Sch 11*, generally to counter certain schemes entered into by financial traders. The provisions amend *ICTA 1988, Sch 28AB para 3, TIOPA 2010, s 86* and *s 112*, and introduce a new *s 85A* into *TIOPA 2010* in order to:

(i) prevent the use of manufactured payments instead of real overseas dividends in order to sidestep existing anti-avoidance defences in the double tax relief legislation, These changes will prevent credits for notional overseas tax from being treated more favourably than tax credits on real dividends. This will not result in the automatic denial of relief in relation to deemed overseas tax, since it will still be necessary for that tax to arise as part of a scheme or arrangement one of the main purposes of which is to cause that tax to be taken into account for double tax relief purposes;

(ii) ensure that a person may only deduct foreign tax from any foreign income where he has not already reduced his income by reference to the foreign tax.

See **5.35 ANTI-AVOIDANCE**.

[*TIOPA 2010, ss 81–95; ICTA 1988, ss 804ZA–804ZC, Sch 28AB; FA 2005, s 87, Sch 5; FA 2007, s 35*].

Simon's Taxes. See **D4.801, D4.805, E6.415, E6.430–E6.438**.

Claims

Relief must be claimed within six years after the end of the accounting period for which the income or gains are chargeable or, if later, within one year after the end of the accounting period in which the foreign tax is paid. Where the amount of foreign tax payable is adjusted subsequent to a claim for relief, with the result that the tax credit becomes excessive, the taxpayer must give written notice to HMRC of this fact within one year of the date on which the adjustment is made, subject to a penalty for failure to comply which may not exceed the excess relief. Certain cases where the adjustment is taken into account under regulations relating to Lloyd's underwriters are excluded from this requirement. For this, and for HMRC view of what constitutes an 'adjustment', see HMRC International Manual, INTM162120.

[*TIOPA 2010, ss 79, 80; ICTA 1988, s 806*].

Where a company claimed double tax relief arising from two US partnerships, HMRC denied the relief on the grounds that the company had not taken 'all reasonable steps' to minimise the US tax. The Special Commissioners found there were no other reasonable steps open to the company which would reduce the US tax, therefore there was no restriction on the ability to claim relief. *Hill Samuel Investments Ltd v Revenue and Customs Comrs* [2009] STC (SCD) 315, 11 ITLR 734.

FA 2009, s 59 introduces an anti-avoidance provision which applies when a company qualifies for a credit for foreign tax and it, or a person connected with it, receives a payment by reference to that credit. The credit is reduced by the amount of the payment. The *CTA 2010, s 1122; ICTA 1988, s 839* definition of a connected person is adopted for this purpose. The provision applies whether the relief is under treaty or unilateral.

[*TIOPA 2010, s 34; ICTA 1988, ss 804G, 811; FA 2009, s 59*].

Simon's Taxes. See **D4.901, E6.453.**

Overseas PE — Finance Act 2011: exemption for foreign permanent establishment profits

[32.6] The amendments in the Finance Act 2011 at *s 48, Sch 13* give an optional exemption from UK corporation tax for profits arising from foreign permanent establishments of a UK company. If an election is made under these provisions to exempt such profits, then any losses of foreign permanent establishments will also be excluded (subject to a transitional rule). The election becomes irrevocable at the start of the first accounting period to which it applies. In addition there are various exceptions (see further below).

The provisions of *CTA 2009* are amended, with a new *Chapter 3A* of *Part 2* being inserted. A new *CTA 2009, s 18A* provides that where a UK resident company makes an election then for each 'relevant accounting period' of the company 'exemption adjustments' will be made to the calculation of taxable total profits. These adjustments ensure that exempt branch profits (the 'foreign permanent establishments amount') are left out of account in computing the company's chargeable profits.

New *CTA 2009, ss 18B–18E* provide the details as to the effect of the election with regard to chargeable gains, capital allowances, payments subject to deduction, and employee share acquisitions; *s 18F* provides that the election is irrevocable; *ss 18G–18I* detail the anti-diversion rules including a motive test; *ss 18J–18O* provide details of how to deal with a PE which has been loss making in the periods prior to exemption; *ss 18P* and *18Q* cover special cases; and *ss 18R* and *18S* provide interpretation. *Part 2* of the *Schedule* deals with applicable amendments to other Acts.

A 'relevant accounting period' is one: in relation to which the company has made an election; these periods are those which follow the one in which the election has been made.

'Exemption adjustments' are any such adjustments that are appropriate to ensure that any profits and losses taken into account in arriving at the foreign permanent establishments amount are not included in the company's calculation of chargeable profits.

The 'foreign permanent establishments amount' is defined as the aggregate of the relevant profits amount for each relevant foreign territory (being a territory where the company carries on business through a permanent establishment), less the aggregate of the relevant losses amount for each such territory. Thus by way of the exemption adjustments, the net profits from all the company's overseas permanent establishments will be exempt.

[*CTA 2009, s 18A(1)–(5)*].

The 'relevant profits amount' in relation to a permanent establishment in a foreign territory is defined as:

- where there is a full treaty (i.e. a double tax treaty with a relevant non-discrimination article) the relevant profits as defined by reference to that treaty;
- where there is not a full treaty, the relevant profits amount is defined by reference to the 2010 version of the OECD Model Convention.

With reference to both the above cases, the relevant profits amount is the amount which would be attributable to the permanent establishment in the foreign territory for the purpose of ascertaining the amount for which credit would be allowed under the UK's double tax credit regime pursuant to *TIOPA 2010*. It is assumed the permanent establishment is a distinct and separate enterprise, reflecting the treaty approach, see below with regard to the updated *TIOPA 2010, s 43*.

Where a full treaty allows a foreign territory to tax profits of a non-resident without any requirement that such profits be attributable to a permanent establishment in that territory, a relevant profits amount will include the profits on which such tax would be paid to the extent that the profits were attributable to that permanent establishment, similarly for losses.

If a treaty does not provide for the foreign tax credit to be calculated by reference to the same profits that the foreign territory treated as taxable, then the relevant profits and losses amounts must be calculated as if there were such a provision.

Similarly with regard to the definition of 'relevant losses amount', reference must be made to whether there is a full treaty in place, or the OECD Model Convention should be used, and similarly the UK measure of the losses should be used under the rules and principles applicable per *TIOPA 2010*.

The new *s 18F* provides that the election will apply to all accounting periods beginning after that in which the election is made. The election can be revoked at any time before the first accounting period of the company for which the election would have effect, thereafter it is irrevocable.

[*CTA 2009, ss 18A(6)–(11), 18F*].

Companies are expected to minimise the profits which are taxed in the permanent establishment jurisdiction and so all claims and elections (other than those for capital allowances, see below) that would reduce any relevant profits amount, or increase the relevant losses amount, are assumed to have been made in calculating the profits to be exempted.

[*CTA 2009, s 18C(5)*].

Chargeable gains

The exempt profits will include the permanent establishment's capital gains. Exemption adjustments should be made to the UK company's profits to remove the effect of any gains or losses relating to assets taken into account in computing the foreign permanent establishment amount.

Consider an example where an asset has not been held by the overseas permanent establishment for the entire period of ownership of the UK company. Part of the gain arising on disposal of the asset will be exempt, and part will not. The exemption adjustment will need to reflect this.

Example (ignoring indexation)

An asset is acquired for £300 in 2011 and used exclusively in a foreign permanent establishment until 2014 when it is transferred back to the UK head office to be used there. At the time of the transfer its market value is £2,100 and the other state taxes a gain of £1,800. The asset is eventually sold to an unconnected party in 2019 for £4,300.

The gain in the corporation tax computation will be £4,000 but this will be reduced to £2,200 by the exemption adjustment of £1,800 in relation to the gain arising in 2014.

The legislation does not prescribe how the adjustment is calculated and HMRC draft guidance on the matter states time apportionment would also be an appropriate method.

Under a double tax treaty gains in respect of immovable property are normally taxed in the state of situs of the asset irrespective of any permanent establishment therefore such gains are not attributed to the permanent establishment for credit relief purposes. However, by virtue of *s 18B(2)* such gains or losses on immovable property which is used by the permanent establishment are to be included in the relevant profits or losses amount of the permanent establishment.

There is a limitation with regard to the exemption of foreign gains or losses realised before the exemption has effect in that an earlier gain or loss can only be taken into account to the extent that the foreign tax was paid in respect of an accounting period that is within the election.

[*CTA 2009, s 18B*].

Capital allowances

Capital allowances are to be taken into account in the foreign permanent establishment profits calculation to an appropriate extent. Therefore provisions are introduced such that notional plant and machinery allowances (and charges) that would be available to a company, if the election had not been made, are automatically included in calculating the permanent establishment profits or losses for all accounting periods after the election. To achieve this the *CAA 2001* is amended (a new *s 15(2A)* is inserted) and is assumed to apply as if the separate permanent establishment activity was a qualifying activity for capital allowances purposes, provided that it would be but for the effect of the election.

A further amendment is made, with a new *CAA 2001, s 62A* inserted, such that in calculating the notional allowances (and charges), the qualifying expenditure attributable to the permanent establishment on the same plant and machinery being used for the separate activity under these provisions is its tax-written down value.

Profits or losses from plant or machinery leases are to be disregarded in the calculation of relevant profits or losses where any allowance (other than a notional allowance as above) has been claimed on the expenditure by the company (or a connected company) as lessor (see *CAA 2001, s 70K*).

[*CTA 2009, s18C*].

Payments subject to deduction

Anti-avoidance provisions are introduced to prevent the use of permanent establishments in order to avoid withholding tax obligations under *ITA 2007, Pt 15*. The profits or losses of a permanent establishment will therefore be excluded from the relevant profits and losses calculations, and thus the exemption, where: they are referable to any transaction between a UK resident person and an exempt permanent establishment; and the UK resident would be required under *ITA 2007* to deduct income tax from payments in respect of the transaction if those payments were made to a company resident in the permanent establishment's territory, having regard to any relevant treaty provisions.

This does not apply to banks unless the transaction is part of arrangements the main purpose (or one of the main purposes) of which is to avoid such a withholding obligation.

[*CTA 2009, s 18D*].

Employee share acquisitions

Any corporation tax relief for employee share acquisitions as provided for under *CTA 2009, Pt 12, Chs 2* or *3* is taken into account in determining the relevant profits or losses amounts of the exempt foreign permanent establishment in a relevant territory to the extent that the relief is linked to the business carried on by the permanent establishment in that territory.

The extent to which any relief is so linked must be determined on a just and reasonable basis having regard to the extent to which the work of the employees concerned contributes to the purposes of the branch business.

[*CTA 2009, s 18E*].

Transitional rule — pre-exemption losses

A transitional rule is included in order to defer exemption for permanent establishments that have generated more losses than profits in the previous six years (being any accounting period ending not more than six years before the accounting period in which the election is made). When a company elects into the regime it will match these permanent establishment losses with profits arising in the first loss-making period or subsequent periods.

More losses than profits have been generated in the prior six year period where there is a 'total opening negative amount', which is a loss arising that has not been matched by any subsequent profit — based on the profits of the foreign permanent establishment determined without including any chargeable gains or allowable losses ('adjusted foreign permanent establishments amount').

To determine whether there is such an opening amount three steps should be followed:

Step 1 — take the earliest negative adjusted foreign permanent establishments amount arising in the prior six year period. This negative amount is carried forward to the following period.

Step 2 — this amount is added to the adjusted foreign permanent establishments amount of the next affected prior accounting period, (but not to give a result which exceeds nil);

Step 3 — repeat for each affected prior accounting period.

An '*affected prior accounting period*' is the period of the company in which an election is made, and any earlier accounting period ending less than six years before the end of that accounting period.

If (after the application of step 3) there remains a negative amount for the last such period, this is the 'total opening negative amount'.

Example

The overseas permanent establishment of Zed Ltd has the following results for the six years prior to the operation of the election:

Year	Profit/(loss)	Loss carried forward (if any)
-6	2,000	0
-5	(1,000)	1,000
-4	4,000	0
-3	(5,000)	5,000
-2	1,500	3,500
-1	1,000	2,500

The total opening negative amount is 2,500.

Under the transitional rules this total opening negative amount is reduced by the amount of any aggregate relevant profits in the relevant accounting periods, until it is extinguished (it cannot be reduced to below nil), thereby deferring operation of the exemption until such time that there is no total opening negative amount left. The first accounting period to which the exemption applies is the one in which the residual negative amount is finally extinguished, with the remainder of any foreign 'profits' for that period being within the exemption. In this final period the company can specify which part of the unused profits the exemption applies to and which are used up to reduce these losses.

The application of the exemption is further delayed where the permanent establishment losses exceed £50 million in an accounting period beginning up to six years before the date of Royal Assent. Where this is the case then that period, and every later period before the first relevant accounting period that would not otherwise be subject to the matching requirement, are subject to the matching requirement.

In addition where the provisions of *s 18O* apply in relation to a transfer of a business and the effect of the section is such that a relevant losses amount which forms part of the £50 million referred to above would be ignored for the purposes of calculating the total opening negative amount, then, in the accounting period in which the transfer took place, such relevant losses amount is to be added to the adjusted foreign permanent establishments amount, as a negative amount.

[*CTA 2009, ss 18J, 18K; FA 2011, Sch 13 para 33*].

These transitional rules are subject to provisions relating to streaming and to transfers of the business of foreign permanent establishments.

Territorial streaming

Provisions are introduced which allow a company to apply the transitional rule above separately to losses in a particular territory so that they do not delay the application of exemption to other territories in relation to which the company would otherwise have no (or a shorter) transitional period — thus to 'stream' the losses in a territory. An election is required which should be made at the same time as the election into the main regime. The transitional rule above will therefore apply separately to each streamed territory. The remaining 'unstreamed' territories are aggregated.

The streaming election becomes irrevocable at the start of the first accounting period to which it applies. It must state which territories are to be streamed and the company must state in its tax return for the first exempt accounting period how much of the opening negative amount is to be streamed for each territory. The amount which can be streamed to a territory is what the opening negative amount of the company would be if the territory were the only territory in which the company has carried on business through a permanent establishment.

Example

A company with three foreign permanent establishments elects into the exemption regime in 2015. The profits and losses arising in the three territories in the preceding six years are as follows:

Year	Territory 1	Territory 2	Territory 3	Aggregate
2010	2,000	0	(6,000)	(4,000)
2011	1,000	(2,000)	1,000	0
2012	(5,000)	(2,000)	2,000	(5,000)
2013	2,000	4,000	(3,000)	3,000
2014	(10,000)	1,000	2,000	(7,000)

2015	2,000	2,000	2,000	6,000
Total	(8,000)	3,000	(2,000)	(7,000)
ONA	8,000	nil	2,000	7,000

If the company elects for territory 1 to be streamed, then the streamed loss for that territory is the lower of 8,000 or 7,000 (being the aggregate total opening negative amount), i.e. 7,000. The company streams no other territory, so the unstreamed loss is the difference between the aggregate pool of losses of 7,000 and the streamed pool of 7,000, which is nil.

Therefore this company has a streamed opening loss of 7,000 for territory 1 and no other opening negative amount.

This means that the first 7,000 of profits arising in territory 1 after exemption are excluded from the exemption. These profits will be matched with the streamed opening loss. All other profits and losses in the other territories are included in exemption (and once the 7,000 has been matched, then the profits in territory 1 can also be included in the exemption).

Permanent establishment business transfers

Anti-avoidance provisions are introduced with regard to the transitional rules when a business or part of a business carried on through a foreign permanent establishment is transferred to a connected company that is (or later becomes) UK resident. If the effect of such a transfer is to tax the profits of the companies (taken together) less under the transitional rule above and the streaming rules [*CTA 2009, ss 18K–18N*] than the transferee would be taxed if the business were at all material times carried on by the transferee, then the provisions apply (to the transferor, and transferee if appropriate) such as to cancel any such advantage.

[*CTA 2009, s 18O*].

Exclusions and restrictions

A new *s 18P* and *s 18Q* of *CTA 2009* sets out any applicable exclusions and restrictions.

For small companies ('micro' or 'small' per the definition in the Annex to Commission Recommendation 203/361/EC) the exemption is restricted to permanent establishments in full treaty territories only. [*s 18P(1)*].

In addition, the profits of a close company that are derived from gains which are chargeable gains (for the purposes of corporation tax) are not profits for the purposes of applying the exemption. [*s 18P(2)*].

The exemption does not apply to any profits or losses arising from basic life assurance and general annuity business [*CTA 2009, s 18Q(1)*]. This section also contains further provisions with regard to insurance companies and the investment return of the business carried on through a permanent establishment (per *ICTA 1988, s 432E*).

[*CTA 2009, ss 18P, 18Q*].

Anti-diversion rule and motive test

New *ss 18G* and *18H* of *CTA 2009* introduce an anti-diversion rule and provide for a motive test.

Where the permanent establishment is based in a jurisdiction with a lower level of tax then, if there is an 'adjusted relevant profits amount' in relation to the foreign territory (the 'adjusted relevant profits amount' is calculated without including any chargeable gains or losses, as above), then that amount is taken to be nil – therefore there are no profits to fall within the exemption – unless one of the two exceptions apply.

Similarly to the CFC test, a foreign permanent establishment is subject to a lower level of tax for this purpose if the foreign tax paid in respect of its profits is less than 75% of the corporation tax that would be payable on those profits if they were chargeable to corporation tax (ignoring any credit which would be allowed for foreign tax under *TIOPA 2010*) and assuming where there is more than one rate of corporation tax applicable to the period, that it were chargeable at the average rate.

The two exceptions are:

(i) where the adjusted relevant profits amount is less than the amount defined as the 'entry limit'; and
(ii) where 'the motive test' is satisfied.

The entry limit is £200,000 reduced proportionately if the accounting period is less than 12 months.

[*CTA 2009, s 18G*].

The 'motive test' is met where both conditions A and B are satisfied.

Condition A is met where the reduction in United Kingdom tax achieved by any relevant transaction is minimal or the achievement of that reduction was not the main purpose or one of the main purposes of the transaction. The persons to be considered in this regard are the purposes of the company, or a person who has an interest in the company (per *ICTA 1988, s 749B*) at any time during the relevant accounting period.

A 'relevant transaction' is one the results of which are reflected in the permanent establishment's profits. A 'reduction in United Kingdom tax' is achieved if, had the transaction not been effected, any person would have been liable for UK tax, or for a greater amount of UK tax, or would not have been entitled to a relief from, or a repayment of, UK tax, or becomes entitled to a greater relief or repayment.

Condition B is satisfied where it was not the main reason or one of the main reasons for the UK resident company carrying on business through a permanent establishment to achieve a reduction in UK tax by a diversion of profits from the UK.

A permanent establishment achieves a reduction in UK tax where it is reasonable to suppose that if the trade were not carried on through that permanent establishment (or any related company) the whole or a substantial part of the receipts reflected in its profits would have been received (otherwise than through the permanent establishment) by the UK resident company, or another UK resident person, who would thereby have been liable for a greater amount of UK tax or would not have been entitled to as large (or any) relief from or repayment of UK tax.

A 'related' company is one which is not UK resident, is connected with or is an associate (per *CTA 2010, s 882*) of the UK company, and which fulfils, or could fulfil the same functions as the permanent establishment.

Where condition B is satisfied but condition A is not, then the adjusted relevant profits amount is reduced by an amount that is just and reasonable to reflect transactions that achieve a UK tax reduction (other than those for which achieving the reduction was not the main purpose, or one of the main purposes).

Motive test — transitional rules

There are two transitional rules introduced with regard to the motive test above and the position of existing permanent establishments. Where they are satisfied condition B of the motive test is assumed to be met in relation to an 'affected accounting period' which is an accounting period that is the first exempt period (or an accounting period beginning less than 12 months after the beginning of the first exempt period). This means that achieving a reduction in UK tax by diverting profits out of the UK was not a main reason in carrying on the business through the permanent establishment.

First transitional rule — the first rule applies in relation to a company carrying on business through a permanent establishment in an affected relevant accounting period if the company carried on the business through the permanent establishment throughout the period of 12 months ending with the day before Royal Assent.

The transitional provision is satisfied if the following conditions are fulfilled:

(a) the gross income attributable to the permanent establishment for the exempt period is no more than 10% greater than the gross income attributable to the permanent establishment for the period of 12 months immediately preceding the exempt period. If the exempt period is shorter than 12 months, the comparison will be with the appropriate proportion of the income for the immediately preceding 12-month period;

(b) there has been no 'major change in the nature or conduct of the business' carried on through the permanent establishment in the period (relevant period) beginning with the pre-commencement year and ending with the end of the affected relevant accounting period; and

(c) no asset attributable to the permanent establishment was previously owned, and no part of the permanent establishment's business in the affected relevant accounting period was previously carried on, by a company whose chargeable profits and creditable tax (if any) for any accounting period ending within the relevant period were (or, but for an agreement made or undertaking given, would have been) apportioned under the CFC rules.

'Major change in the nature or conduct of the business' includes a major change in the type of property dealt in, or services or facilities provided, in the business, as well as in customers, outlets or markets of the business. For these purposes, a change can be achieved gradually as a result of a series of transfers.

[*FA 2011, Sch 13, paras 31(1)–(4)*].

Second transitional rule — the second rule applies in relation to a company (A) carrying on business through a permanent establishment in an affected relevant accounting period if a company (B) that was non-UK resident and was controlled by A (within *CTA 2010, s 1124*) carried on the business throughout the pre-commencement year.

The second transitional provision is satisfied if the following conditions are fulfilled:

(a) the gross income attributable to the permanent establishment for the affected relevant period is no more than 10% greater than the level of gross income of the business for the period of 12 months immediately preceding the first relevant accounting period. If the period is shorter than 12 months, the comparison will be with the appropriate proportion of the income for the immediately preceding 12 month period;
(b) there has been no 'major change in the nature or conduct of the permanent establishment's business' in the period (relevant period) beginning with the pre-commencement year and ending with the end of the affected relevant accounting period;
(c) company B was not a company whose chargeable profits and creditable tax (if any) for any accounting period ending within the relevant period were (or, but for an agreement made or undertaking given, would have been) apportioned under the CFC rules; and
(d) no asset attributable to the permanent establishment was previously owned, and no part of the business carried on through the permanent establishment in the affected relevant accounting period was previously carried on, by such a company.

'Major change in the nature or conduct of the permanent establishment's business' has the same meaning here as it does for the first transitional rule.

[*FA 2011, Sch 13 para 32(1)–(4)*].

Amendments to other Acts

Various amendments are made to other acts to take account of these new rules:

- *TCGA 1992* is amended, a new *s 276A* is inserted, such that when a gain or loss is taken into account when calculating a relevant profit or loss for the exemption, and it is a no gain/ no loss disposal, then the consideration used is that which (taking into account the exemption) secures neither a gain nor a loss for the transferor company. This means the no gain/ no loss value will now include the overseas permanent establishment amount which would be attributable to the disposal if it were not a no gain/ no loss transfer;

> ***Example (ignoring indexation)***
>
> An asset costing £2,000 is used in the exempt permanent establishment of group company X. It is transferred to group company Y when its value is £2,400. *TCGA 1992, s 171* applies such that this is a no gain/ no loss transfer. However, *TCGA 1992, s 276A* requires the no gain/ no loss value to be £2,400 rather than £2,000.
>
> If company Y then used the asset in the UK before disposing of it for £3,000 its chargeable gain would be £600 (instead of £1,000) which preserves the value of the exemption for the transferee company – which is not taxed on company X permanent establishment's £400 gain.

- *CAA 2001* is amended and a new *s 15(2A)* is inserted, as noted above. If a company carries on a business through permanent establishments outside the UK and makes an exemption election then, from the beginning of the first accounting period after the election is made, the business carried on in the permanent establishment is treated for capital allowances purposes as a separate activity the profits and gains of which are not chargeable to tax. As highlighted above, 'notional' capital allowances are used in the calculation of the exempt permanent establishment profits.
  Where this section applies then a disposal event must be brought into account, with the value being the tax written down value (new *CAA 2001, s 62A*). This does not apply if: the qualifying expenditure on the plant or machinery (or on the group of plant and machinery with which it is used and forms part at any time during a relevant accounting period), exceeds £5 million; and the plant or machinery has been used otherwise than for the purposes of a foreign permanent establishment at any time during such a period. A 'relevant accounting period' is the period during which an exemption election is made or an earlier period ending not more than six years before the end of that period. For the purposes of *s 62A* there is a further de minimis spend on qualifying expenditure: where such expenditure does not exceed £50 million then an accounting period ending more than 12 months before Royal Assent is not a relevant accounting period; and where it does exceed this amount, then any accounting period beginning within the period of six years ending with the day before such date and which would not be a relevant preceding accounting period (apart from this paragraph) is treated as a relevant accounting period;
- *CTA 2009, ss 1007(2)(b)* and *1015(2)(b)* are amended so a deduction can be given for the cost of providing an employee share scheme irrespective of an exemption election;
- *CTA 2009, s 775* which allows for tax neutral intra-group transfers of intangible fixed assets is amended and does not apply where the exemption election has been made by the transferor and the asset has at any time been held for the purposes of a permanent establishment of the transferor. Where this applies and the asset has not been held wholly for the purposes of a permanent establishment at all times during which an

exemption election applied, then the transferee is treated as having acquired the asset for such amount as is appropriate having regard to the operation of the exemption (new *CTA 2009, s 776A*);

- *ICTA 1988, Sch 24* is amended, such that CFC's are assumed not to have made an election under *CTA 2009, s 18A*;
- *ITA 2007* is amended modifying the rules applicable to manufactured overseas dividends (MODs) (per *ss 922* and *923*);
- *ITA 2007, s 879(1)* is amended such that the exception from withholding tax on interest payable on an advance from a bank is extended to situations where the recipient is a bank that would be within the charge to corporation tax in respect of the interest but for the operation of the exemption;
- *TIOPA 2010, s 43* is replaced with a new version to give clarification on determining how much of a UK resident company's profits which are, or would be, chargeable to corporation tax is attributable to a foreign permanent establishment;
- *TIOPA 2010, ss 263(4A)* and *317A* are inserted such that any amounts excluded under this exemption are not taken into account for the purposes of the debt cap provisions.

Amended TIOPA 2010, s 43

A new *s 43* replaces the existing section and applies for the purposes of establishing how much of a UK resident company's profits are to be attributed to the foreign permanent establishments of UK resident companies.

Certain assumptions must be made in order to attribute profits to a permanent establishment, as follows:

- the permanent establishment is treated as a distinct and separate enterprise engaged in the same or similar activities under the same or similar conditions and dealing wholly independently with the company of which it is a permanent establishment;
- the permanent establishment has the same credit rating as the company of which it is part;
- regardless of any allocation per the books of the company, the permanent establishment has the equity and loan capital it would have on an allocation made on a just and equitable basis of the company's capital amongst its foreign permanent establishments, on the basis they were distinct and separate entities from the company, subject to the provisions of any full double taxation treaty, in force between the UK and the state in which the permanent establishment is situated;
- any 'free assets' of an insurance company are to be attributed to its permanent establishment on this same basis, HMRC may make provision as to the meaning of free assets, until such provision is made 'free assets' has the meaning given by *Reg 3* of *SI 2003 No 2714* (*The Non-resident Insurance Companies Regulations 2003*).

The above provisions with regard to foreign permanent establishments are to take effect from Royal Assent.

Utilisation of unrelieved foreign tax

[32.7] The provisions in **32.5** above apply, in the case of profits from an 'overseas permanent establishment' to 'unrelieved foreign tax'.

'*Unrelieved foreign tax*' on any income is the excess of the amount of the credit for foreign tax which would (disregarding the limitation to corporation tax on that income under *TIOPA 2010, s 42*) be available under any double tax arrangements against corporation tax in respect of the income over the amount which is actually so allowed. (There are no comparable provisions for unilateral relief (see **32.2** above).)

For this purpose, every gain is a chargeable gain. If relief for foreign capital gains tax is available by carry back or carry forward (see below) double tax relief is not also available for UK corporation tax.

[*TIOPA 2010, s 105*].

An '*overseas permanent establishment*' for this purpose is a 'permanent establishment' through which a company carries on a trade in a territory outside the UK, and '*permanent establishment*' has the meaning given by any double tax agreement with that territory or, in the absence of such a definition, the meaning given by *FA 2003, s 148*, now *CTA 2010, s 1141* (see **65.6 RESIDENCE**).

Where an amount of unrelieved foreign tax arises in respect of any UK-resident company 'qualifying income', the unrelieved foreign tax may, on a claim, be treated as if it were paid in respect of, and computed by reference to, income of the same description and from the same source in either:

(a) the next accounting period (and successive accounting periods), whether or not there is any income from that source in that accounting period; or
(b) such one or more preceding accounting periods, beginning not more than three years before that in which the unrelieved foreign tax arises, as results from applying the rules described below. Set off is against the latest year first (and current years credits are set off first),

or partly in one way and partly in the other (i.e. a mix of (a) and (b)).

Where the company ceases to have a permanent establishment, no further relief is given for any balance of excess.

The rules referred to in (b) above require that the unrelieved foreign tax must be so treated that:

(1) credit for it (or for any remaining balance) is allowed against corporation tax in respect of income of a later period before an earlier one; and
(2) before allowing credit for it against corporation tax in respect of any income of an accounting period, credit for foreign tax must be allowed first for foreign tax in respect of the income of that period (other than unrelieved foreign tax of another period), and then for unrelieved foreign tax arising in an earlier accounting period before a later one.

The claim must be made not more than four years after the end of the accounting period in which the excess arose or, if later, one year after the end of the accounting period in which the foreign tax concerned is paid.

Where unrelieved foreign tax of an accounting period is treated as paid in respect of income of another accounting period, no further application of these provisions may be made in relation to that tax.

Where there is more than one permanent establishment in the same territory and their profits are charged to tax together, such establishments are treated as if they were a single establishment for these purposes. However, where there was one establishment, which has ceased, and a new establishment is started in the same territory, they are treated as separate establishments.

'*Qualifying income*' of a permanent establishment is those of its profits which are chargeable as a trade carried on partly, but not wholly, outside the UK, under *CTA 2009, Ch 2 Pt 3* (or certain other such profits e.g. of life insurance companies).

If a particular permanent establishment ceases in an accounting period, unrelieved foreign tax relating to it may not be carried forward from that period. If the company subsequently in the same period has a permanent establishment in the same territory, it is treated as a new and different source. However, two or more overseas permanent establishments in the same territory which are taxed as one under the law of that territory are treated for the purposes of these provisions as a single permanent establishment.

Claims to relief under (a) or (b) above must be made within four years (*per TIOPA 2010, s 77(3)*), previously six years of the end of the accounting period in which the unrelieved foreign tax arose (or, if later, within one year of the end of the accounting period in which the foreign tax in question is paid) and must specify the amounts to be dealt with under each of (a) and (b) above.

[*TIOPA 2010, ss 72–78; ICTA 1988, ss 806L, 806M; FA 2003, Sch 27 para 1(3); FA 2008, Sch 39 para 26*].

There are similar provisions relating to underlying tax relief on dividend income as utilised in the onshore pooling rules (see **32.11** below). See *ICTA 1988, ss 806D–806G*. These provisions have been repealed with effect in relation to distributions paid on or after 1 July 2009, when the new dividend exemption regime commenced.

Simon's Taxes. See **D4.809, E6.416.**

Allocation of charges

[32.8] In arriving at corporation tax attributable to the relevant income or gain for a relevant accounting period, the following is to be taken into account.

(i) Any amount that for corporation tax purposes is deductible from or allowable against profits of more than one description may be allocated as the company thinks fit.
[*TIOPA 2010, s 52; ICTA 1988, s 797(3); SI 2004 No 2310, Art 34*].
Charges so allocated may not, however, exceed the income against which they are set (*Commercial Union Assurance Co plc v Shaw* (1999) 72 TC 101, CA).

(ii) Where a non-trading credit is brought into account as regards a loan relationship (see **54.4 LOAN RELATIONSHIPS**), special provision is made for the attribution of corporation tax to such credits for the purposes of relief of any foreign tax on the item. A similar provision applies from 1 April 2002 in relation to non-trading credits on intangible fixed assets (see **48.7 INTANGIBLE ASSETS**). Non-trading deficits brought forward may only be set against subsequent non-trading loan relationship gains, but may be allocated among such gains as the company thinks fit. [*TIOPA 2010, ss 50–55; ICTA 1988, ss 797A, 797B; FA 1998, s 82(2), Sch 30 para 5(4); CTA 2009, Sch 1 paras 247, 248*].

Where, as regards loan relationships, this does not apply, and there is a non-trading deficit (see **54.5 LOAN RELATIONSHIPS**) on the company's loan relationships, the deficit is allocated for foreign tax relief purposes in the same way as relief is claimed or is available under *FA 1996, s 83; CTA 2009, Pt 5 Ch 16, s 456 et seq.*

[*TIOPA 2010, ss 42, 53, 55; ICTA 1988, s 797(3A)(3B); FA 1998, s 82(2)*].

(iii) Where there are non-trading debits on intangible assets, these have to be analysed for double tax relief purposes. The amount eligible for double tax relief is the excess of the total amount of the company's non-trading deficits for the period less those carried forward (if any) [*TIOPA 2010, s 56*].

(iv) *CTA 2009, ss 19–32* (or earlier equivalents) (profits attributable to permanent establishments — see **65.6 RESIDENCE**), and regulations thereunder, apply (with the necessary modifications) for these purposes. [*TIOPA 2010, s 43; ICTA 1988, s 797(2A); FA 2003, s 154; CTA 2009, Sch 1 para 246(2)*].

Simon's Taxes. See **D4.806, D4.807, E6.434.**

Example

The following information about A Ltd (which owns 20% of the voting power of B Ltd, a non-resident company) for the year ended 31 March 2011 is relevant.

	£
UK income	1,200,000
UK chargeable gains	300,000
Overseas income (tax rate 40%) from B Ltd (gross)	300,000
Charges paid (qualifying charitable donations)	15,000

A Ltd may allocate charges as it wishes in order to obtain maximum double tax relief. The following calculation shows how this is best done.

	UK income and gains	Overseas income	Total
	£	£	£
Income and gains	1,500,000	300,000	1,800,000
Deduct Charges	15,000	—	15,000
	£1,485,000	£300,000	£1,785,000

	UK income and gains	Overseas income	Total
	£	£	£
CT at 28%	415,800	84,000	499,800
Deduct Double tax relief	—	(84,000)	(84,000)
CT liability	£415,800	—	£415,800

If charges were set off against overseas income first, the following tax would be payable.

	UK income and gains	Overseas income	Total
	£	£	£
Income and gains	1,500,000	300,000	1,800,000
Deduct Charges	—	15,000	15,000
	£1,500,000	£285,000	£1,785,000
CT at 28%	420,000	79,800	499,800
Deduct Double tax relief	—	(79,800)	(79,800)
CT liability	£420,000	—	£420,000

This gives a maximum double tax relief of £79,800.

Compared with the recommended allocation, £4,200 of double tax relief (£90,000 – £85,500) is lost, representing an increase in the corporation tax liability of £4,200 (£415,800 – £420,000).

Shadow ACT

[32.9] Where relief is available for a foreign tax credit, the income or gain subject to the foreign tax is excluded from profits for the purpose of determining the maximum set-off of shadow ACT and surplus ACT (from accounting periods beginning before 6 April 1999, see **3.2** *et seq.* **ADVANCE CORPORATION TAX — SHADOW ACT**) and the foreign tax credit is deducted from the corporation tax liability. Shadow ACT can be set against the corporation tax liability relating to the foreign income or gain limited to the maximum ACT credit that would have applied had the foreign income or gain been the only income or gain for the accounting period or, if lower, the corporation tax liability as reduced by the foreign tax credit (see *SI 1999 No 358, Reg 12(4)(5)*).

Underlying tax

Underlying tax attributable to dividends

[32.10] Where a non-exempt dividend is paid to a UK resident company or to a non-resident company but forming part of the profits of a UK permanent establishment (see **65.6 RESIDENCE**) by a 'related company' in the circumstances set out in **32.2**(b) above (ie. the recipient controls at least 10% of the voting power of the overseas company), relief is given for the following taxes payable by the overseas company in respect of its profits:

(a) any UK income or corporation tax; and
(b) any tax imposed by the law of any other territory,

being underlying tax, which is any tax not chargeable directly on, or by deduction from, the dividend.

Where the overseas company has received a dividend from a third company similarly related to the overseas company, relief may similarly be claimed (subject to certain restrictions on the taxes to be taken into account) for underlying tax payable by the third company, to the extent that it would have been taken into account had it been paid (at the time when the relevant dividend was received) direct to a UK-resident company entitled to relief.

Dividends payable through a chain of related companies may similarly be relieved. While relief is given only for underlying tax (and not withholding tax), it is given for withholding tax arising on dividends paid between foreign companies in a chain, which is treated as part of the underlying tax charge, under (b) above, in the recipient companies.

For this purpose, the 'related company' criteria in **32.2**(b) above (where companies are treated as related where one company, or a company of which it is a subsidiary, controls at least 10% of the voting power in the other company) are amended where the dividend is paid on or after 1 January 2005 (for the purpose of implementing the amended Parent/Subsidiary Directive (see **32.14** below)). The companies in this case are also related where one company, or a company of which it is a subsidiary, controls at least 10% of the ordinary share capital of the other company.

See, however, **32.12** below as regards a general restriction on the amount of relief applicable where dividends are paid through so-called 'mixer' companies. See also **32.13** below as regards a restriction on the relief applicable where the overseas company is a controlled foreign company which is exempt from apportionment by virtue of an acceptable distribution policy.

[*TIOPA 2010, ss 57, 62; ICTA 1988, s 801; FA 2005, s 91(4)–(6)(8), Sch 11 Pt 9; F(No 2)A 2005, s 43*].

Simon's Taxes. See **D4.905–D4.907**.

Restriction of relief

Where an 'avoidance scheme' is involved, and underlying tax relating to a dividend includes an amount in respect of tax payable (by reference to the profits which bear that tax) at a rate in excess of the full corporation tax rate in force at the time the dividend was paid, relief is restricted as if tax had been payable at the corporation tax rate.

An '*avoidance scheme*' for this purpose is a scheme or arrangement of any kind, a main purpose of which is to claim relief for an amount of underlying tax, and the parties to which include the company claiming the relief (or a related company or a connected person within *ICTA 1988, s 839, CTA 2010, s 1122*) and a person not under the control (as specially defined) of that company at any time before anything is done in relation to the scheme etc. [*TIOPA 2010, ss 67, 68; ICTA 1988, s 801A*].

For an indication of Revenue practice as to the circumstances in which *section 801A* may be applied, see Revenue Tax Bulletin June 1997 p 441. Note that for dividends paid to the UK after 30 March 2001 this provision is largely redundant due to the introduction of the 'mixer' cap rules (see **32.12** below).

Example — TIOPA 2010, ss 67, 68; ICTA 1988, s 801A

T Ltd, a UK-resident company liable to corporation tax at the full 28% rate for the year ended 31 March 2011, receives a non-exempt dividend on 1 June 2010 of £18,500 gross (tax withheld £825) from X inc, a non-UK resident company in which it holds 20% of the voting power. It claims relief for underlying tax of £6,000 as follows.

£1,500 tax at 10% on profits of £15,000 out of which a £13,500 dividend paid.

£4,500 tax at 50% on profits of £9,000 of Y pty (a subsidiary of X inc) from whom a dividend was received by X Inc, out of which a £5,000 dividend was paid.

T Ltd computes relief as follows.

	£	£
Gross dividend received		18,500
plus underlying tax		6,000
		£24,500
Tax thereon at 28%		6,860
less underlying tax	6,000	
tax withheld	825	6,825
Corporation tax payable		£35

It transpires, however, that the dividend from Y pty was bought in as part of a tax avoidance scheme, so that the provisions of *TIOPA 2010, ss 67, 68; ICTA 1988, s 801A* apply. The computation is therefore revised as follows.

	£	£
Gross dividend received		18,500
plus underlying tax (see below)		3,250
		£21,750
Tax thereon at 28%		6,090

less	underlying tax	3,250	
	tax withheld	825	4,075
Corporation tax payable			£2,015

Underlying tax

The relief for underlying tax in respect of the dividend from Y pty is recalculated as if the tax rate on the underlying profits had been the corporation tax rate of 28% applicable at the time of receipt of the dividend from X inc by T Ltd.

£4,500 × $^{100}/_{72}$ = £6,250 on which 28% tax is £1,750.

The total underlying tax is thus (£1,750 + £1,500 =) £3,250.

Simon's Taxes. See **D4.940.**

Foreign mergers

In relation to dividends received by a UK-resident company from an overseas company, relief for underlying tax also includes cases where profits of an overseas company ('company A'), which have borne foreign tax, become profits of another overseas company ('company B') other than by payment of a dividend (e.g. following a merger), and company B then pays a dividend to another company out of those profits.

For the purposes of underlying tax relief, company B is treated as having paid the tax paid by company A in respect of those of its profits which have become profits of company B. However, the amount of relief accordingly available to a UK-resident company is limited to that which would have been available had the profits been transferred from company A to company B by way of dividend. [*TIOPA 2010, s 69; ICTA 1988, s 801B*].

Simon's Taxes. See **D4.929.**

Group treated as a single entity

There are provisions enabling two or more overseas companies which are taxed as a single entity in the country or territory in which they are resident to be treated as a single company for underlying tax relief purposes in relation to the payment of a dividend to another company by any one of the overseas companies. [*TIOPA 2010, s 71; ICTA 1988, s 803A*].

For this and for HMRC response to various questions on other aspects of the application of *section 803A* (with several examples), see Revenue Tax Bulletin August 2001 pp 870–874, now superseded by HMRC International Manual, INTM164150. For the implications of their application in various countries, see Revenue Tax Bulletins February 2002 pp 911–913, February 2003 p 1007 and October 2003 pp 1063–1064.

With effect for dividends paid on or after 16 March 2005, the single company treatment does not apply to a controlled foreign company to which exemption applies under the 'acceptable distribution policy' test (see **27.12 CONTROLLED**

FOREIGN COMPANIES). [*ICTA 1988, s 803A(1A); FA 2005, s 90*]. This treatment is no longer applicable with the abolition of the acceptable distribution policy exemption for accounting periods of CFCs beginning on or after 1 July 2009.

Simon's Taxes. See **D4.928**.

Calculation of underlying tax relief

[32.11] The underlying tax is calculated in accordance with *TIOPA 2010, ss 57–60; ICTA 1988, s 799*, by reference to the paying company's 'relevant profits'.

Thus the underlying tax is:

(a) if a relevant dividend is received in an accounting period of the recipient in which it is a medium-sized or large company (ie. where the dividend exemption rules apply), the foreign tax borne on the appropriate proportion of 'relevant profits', which, for these purposes, are those profits out of which the dividend is treated as being paid under *CTA 2009, s 931H* (being profits out of which a non exempt dividend is paid) [*TIOPA 2010, s 59(2),(3)*];

(b) when (a) above does not apply, the foreign tax attributable to the proportion of the 'relevant profits' represented by the dividend;

(c) in both (a) and (b) above, such foreign tax as does not exceed (for claims made *on or after 31 March 2001*) the formula of M% × (D+PA) (prior to *TIOPA 2010* the formula was M% x (D+U)), this being the corporation tax rate applicable to the profits of the recipient in the accounting period in which the dividend is paid (M) (or the average rate over the period) applied to the sum of the dividend (D) and the underlying tax (PA) (as calculated per (a) and (b) above — formerly (U)). The formula has come to be known as the 'mixer cap' formula (see **32.12** below). Prior to 1 April 2008 'M' was the corporation tax rate in force at the time the dividend was paid.

'*Small company*' is as defined for the *FA 2009* legislation on company distributions (see **31.16** DISTRIBUTIONS).

A '*relevant dividend*' is a dividend paid other than on 'relevant profits' per *CTA 2009, s 931H*.

With effect for dividends paid *on or after 16 March 2005*, no relief for underlying tax is given if a deduction is allowed in a foreign jurisdiction in respect of an amount determined by reference to the dividend.

The meaning of '*relevant profits*' was considered, in the case of *Bowater Paper Corporation Ltd v Murgatroyd* (1969) 46 TC 37, HL, to be the profits available for distribution as shown by the accounts and not as computed for foreign tax purposes. This is added to any tax chargeable directly on, or deducted from, the dividend, and the total is deducted from the UK tax as under **32.5** above.

'*Relevant profits*' are specifically defined in *TIOPA 2010, s 59(8); ICTA 1988, s 799(5)–(7)* (as amended by *FA 2005, s 80, Sch 4 para 7*) as profits of any period shown as available for distribution in the accounts of the company paying the dividend. The 'accounts' in this case are those drawn up in accordance with the law of the country or territory in which the distributing company is incorporated or formed, with no provision for reserves, bad debts, impairment losses or contingencies except as required under that law.

The '*relevant profits represented by the dividend*' are the profits of the specified period covered by the dividend or, if not paid for a specified period, the profits of the last period of account made up to the date before the dividend became payable. Where the total dividend exceeds the profits available for distribution of that period, the relevant profits are the profits of that period plus so much of the profits remaining available for distribution of preceding periods equal to the excess, taking the most recent preceding period before the next most recent preceding period and so on.

[*TIOPA 2010, ss 57–59; ICTA 1988, s 799*].

Where the paying company has *accumulated losses*, HMRC consider that the 'relevant profits' for this purpose are the undistributed profits of the most recent period available at the time of payment. Computations in line with a previous practice will, however, continue to be accepted for dividends paid between 31 March 2000 and 31 December 2001 inclusive. (HMRC Statement of Practice SP 3/01; Revenue Press Release 27 November 2001 and Annex D to Technical Note 'An Exemption for Substantial Shareholdings').

Rates of underlying tax are calculated by HMRC, Revenue Policy International (Underlying Tax Group), PO Box 46, Fitz Roy House, Nottingham NG2 1BD (tel. 0115–974 2033) in accordance with the following formula.

$$\frac{\text{actual tax paid} \times 100}{\text{actual tax paid} + \text{relevant profit}}$$

This formula automatically takes into account any deferred taxation charged plus under- and over-provisions for tax in previous years. (CCAB Memorandum 19 October 1979).

Example

A Ltd, a company resident in the UK, receives a dividend of £1,000 gross from B Ltd, an overseas company in which it controls 10% of the voting power. Overseas tax of £100 is deducted from the dividend on payment. The underlying tax rate for the dividend is agreed at 18%.

			£
Gross dividend			1,000.00
Underlying tax @ 18%			219.51
Underlying assessable income			£1,219.51
Corporation tax thereon @ 28%			341.46
Overseas tax suffered:	Direct tax	100.00	

Underlying tax	219.51	
Tax credit relief due		319.51
Corporation tax payable		£21.95

If the corporation tax liability were at 21% (small profits rate) being £256.10, the double tax relief would be restricted to this amount.

The underlying tax for which relief is given is limited in certain cases to the amount of the tax actually paid by the overseas company on the particular profits out of which the dividend is paid. This applies in particular to dividends declared by and from a company resident in Belize, the Gambia, Malaysia, Malta or Singapore (where relief is given under an agreement) or Guernsey or Jersey (where the relief is unilateral), each of which operates a 'company tax deducted' system whereby tax is deducted from the dividend at the standard corporate rate and accounted for to the tax authorities, but subject to subsequent adjustment. In so far as that tax is refunded or found not to be due, double tax relief is denied. (SP 12/93, 27 July 1993). But note further the changes to the tax systems in Guernsey and Jersey applicable from 2008 and 2009 respectively.

Credit for underlying tax along a chain of shareholdings is concessionally given to:

(i) portfolio shareholders (where relief is given under the relevant double tax agreement for underlying tax); or
(ii) resident insurance companies carrying on part of their business through an overseas branch or agency; or
(iii) resident companies controlling at least ten per cent of the voting power of an overseas company carrying on insurance business. Credit under this last head is subject to apportionment.

(HMRC Extra-Statutory Concession, C1).

General guidance on computing an underlying rate and information about underlying tax in overseas countries, is available from HMRC International, address as above. See also HMRC International Manual, INTM 164100 *et seq.* and INTM164400 *et seq.* For calculation of relief for tax in overseas countries, see HMRC Double Taxation Manual, DT2140 onwards (for example, for the calculation of relief for Californian corporate franchise tax, see DT19855).

For underlying tax generally see *Barnes v Hely-Hutchinson* (1939) 22 TC 655, HL; *Canadian Eagle Oil Co Ltd v R* (1945) 27 TC 205, HL; *Brooke Bond & Co Ltd v Butter* (1962) 40 TC 342.

Split rate taxes

Where foreign tax on profits is dependent on how much of the profits is distributed, HMRC consider that the underlying tax in relation to a dividend should reflect the rate of tax on distributed profits rather than the average rate.

For dividends paid between 31 March 2000 and 31 December 2001 inclusive, however, HMRC will in practice accept computations on either basis. (SP 3/01, 27 November 2001 and Annex D to Technical Note 'An Exemption for Substantial Shareholdings').

Simon's Taxes. See **D4.905–D4.910**.

Mixing and onshore pooling

Restriction of relief — 'mixer' companies

[32.12] Provisions which effectively eliminate the tax advantage of routing overseas dividends through 'mixer' companies in favourable foreign jurisdictions (such as the Netherlands) apply to claims for credit relief made on or after 31 March 2001, unless the dividend concerned was paid to the UK-resident company before that date. As a result of the reduction in the main rate of corporation tax from 30% to 28%, some problems arose with the mixer cap. *FA 2009* included provisions designed to sort out these problems.

For the purposes of claims made on or after 1 April 2008, where the credit is to be given to a company, the rate of corporation tax to be used is the rate paid by the recipient of the dividend in the accounting period in which the dividend was received or, if relevant, the average rate for that period. For claims made before that date, the corporation tax rate was the rate in force when the dividend was paid.

The relievable underlying tax in respect of any dividend paid up through an overseas subsidiary (including a lower-tier subsidiary) is restricted by the formula of M% × (D+PA) (see also **32.11**(c) above), the restriction being to the rate of corporation tax determined as above (M), applied to the sum of the dividend (D) and the underlying tax (PA) to be taken into account (apart from these provisions).

The claim for relief may, however, be so framed as to exclude any specified amounts of underlying tax from being taken into account for this purpose (which may prevent the application of the cap in certain cases and so allow for onshore pooling — see below. Onshore pooling was applicable with regard to dividends paid before 1 July 2009).

The 'mixer cap' restriction does not, however, apply where the overseas companies paying and receiving the dividend are 'related' (in the circumstances described at **32.2**(b) above). Neither does it apply where the companies are both resident in the same overseas territory (subject to Treasury regulations which may prescribe cases where this exclusion will not apply, for which see *SI 2001 No 1156* which prevents certain dual-resident companies resident in the same overseas territory from obtaining the benefit of mixing).

Like other income, dividends are apportioned on a time basis between financial years with different rates of corporation tax. The effect is that profits are taxed for the whole period at an average rate. Therefore the rate above which relief will cut off will be lower as a result of the rate cut. This difference may not be covered by eligible unrelieved foreign tax (if any is applicable to that period).

[*TIOPA 2010, ss 57, 58, 60; ICTA 1988, ss 799(1)(b)(1A)(1B), 801; FA 2009, s 57*].

Examples

A corporation tax rate of 26% is assumed throughout.

(A) Simple mixer company

UK plc wholly owns Dutch Holding BV which in turn wholly owns Low Tax Co which pays tax at 10% and High Tax Co which pays tax at 40%. Both subsidiaries make pre-tax profits of £100 and make full distributions to the UK via Dutch Holding BV which does not pay any tax on the dividends. Low Tax Co is a trading company which is exempt from the CFC rules otherwise than through pursuing an acceptable distribution policy. All three subsidiaries are resident in different countries. The tax position for UK plc is as follows.

	£
Net dividend (60 + 90)	150
Underlying tax (40 + 10)	50
Overseas income	200
Corporation tax @ 26%	52
Double tax relief (Low Tax Co £10 and High Tax Co £26 as restricted by the mixer cap)	(36)
UK tax liability	16
Unused tax credits (foreign tax paid of 50)	14

(B) Simple mixer company with withholding tax

The position is as in (A) above but the dividend paid by High Tax Co to Dutch Holding BV suffers withholding tax of £9.

Dividend from:	Low Tax Co	High Tax Co	Dutch Holding BV	
	£	£	£	£
Net dividend	90	60	141	
Underlying tax	10	40	50	
Withholding tax (see note below)			9	
Overseas income	100	100		200

Dividend from:	Low Tax Co	High Tax Co	Dutch Holding BV	
	£	£	£	£
Corporation tax @ 26%	26	26		52
Double tax relief (as restricted)	(10)	(26)	(9)	(45)
UK tax liability				7
Unused tax credits				14

Note that under *ICTA 1988, s 801(1)(b), TIOPA 2010, s 65*, credit relief is given for any tax paid by an overseas company under the law of any other territory. Thus the withholding tax of £9 paid by Dutch Holding BV (via deduction at source) is treated as underlying tax in respect of its own profits (see **32.10** above).

(C) Chain of subsidiaries — high into low tax mixing

UK plc wholly owns Low Tax Co which pays tax at 20% and which in turn wholly owns High Tax Co which pays tax at 40%. Both subsidiaries (which are resident in different countries) make pre-tax profits of £100 and make full distributions. Low Tax Co is a trading company which is exempt from the CFC rules otherwise than through pursuing an acceptable distribution policy. The dividend from High Tax Co is exempt from tax in the hands of Low Tax Co. The tax position for UK plc is as follows.

	£
Net dividend	140
Underlying tax	60
Overseas income	200
Corporation tax @ 26%	52
Double tax relief (Low Tax Co £20 and High Tax Co £26 as restricted by the mixer cap)	(46)
UK tax liability	6
Unused tax credits	14

(D) Chain of subsidiaries — low into high tax mixing

UK plc wholly owns High Tax Co which pays tax at 40% and which in turn wholly owns Low Tax Co which pays tax at 20%. Both subsidiaries (which are resident in different countries) make pre-tax profits of £100 and make full distributions. Low Tax Co is a trading company which is exempt from the CFC rules otherwise than through pursuing an acceptable distribution policy. The dividend from Low Tax Co is exempt from tax in the hands of High Tax Co. The tax position for UK plc is as follows.

	£
Net dividend	140
Underlying tax	60
Overseas income	200
Corporation tax @ 26%	52
Double tax relief (see below)	(52)
UK tax liability	—

The mixer cap restriction does not apply to the dividend paid by Low Tax Co to High Tax Co because the tax paid on the dividend from Low Tax Co of £20 is lower than £26 which is 26% of the sum of the dividend (£80) and the underlying tax (£20). Whilst, the mixer cap restriction does apply to the dividend paid by High Tax Co to UK plc because the total tax paid of £60 (£20 + £40) is higher than 26% of the sum of the dividend of £140 (£80 + £60) and the underlying tax of £60 (£20 + £40) — the restriction only reduces the underlying tax to the level of UK tax which means the UK tax liability is off-set in full.

See HMRC International Manual at INTM164220, 164230 and 164235 for a summary (with example) of these provisions. See also below for provisions which permit a degree of 'onshore pooling' of dividend income against the tax on which relief at a rate of up to 45% may be obtained for underlying tax so capped in certain cases.

Simon's Taxes. See **D4.915**.

Onshore pooling and utilisation of eligible unrelieved foreign tax

In relation, broadly, to dividends paid on or after 31 March 2001, relief for underlying tax on dividends paid up through overseas subsidiaries is generally restricted to corporation tax, at the full rate in force when the dividend is paid, on the gross amount of the dividend (the 'cap' aimed at avoidance through the use of so-called 'mixer' companies, see above).

However, a partial relief from this capping restriction was provided by the concurrent introduction of a system of 'onshore pooling' of certain foreign dividends, against the tax on which may be set the excess tax over the cap, allowing relief up to a maximum of 45% in total. Essentially the onshore pooling provisions relaxed the source by source principle and allowed excess foreign tax to be offset against the UK tax on certain low tax dividends, as if such dividends were a single pool of income.

Relief may similarly be obtained up to the same overall 45% limit for unrelieved withholding and underlying tax on dividends received directly from overseas subsidiaries.

The onshore pooling provisions were repealed by *FA 2009, s 34, Sch 14* with regard to payments made on or after 1 July 2009 (subject to transitional provisions), as it was considered such provisions were no longer required, with the commencement of the new dividend exemption regime from that date.

Therefore the details which follow in respect of the onshore pooling regime are only applicable to overseas dividends paid before 1 July 2009.

The scheme provides for the set-off of '*eligible unrelieved foreign tax*' against the UK tax arising on '*qualifying foreign dividends*'.

Eligible unrelieved foreign tax (EUFT) is the excess, subject to the 45% maximum limit, of:

(i) the credit for the foreign tax, excluding any underlying tax which has been restricted by the 30% cap, of a foreign dividend over the UK tax charged on the dividend (this being referred to as 'Case A' EUFT); and
(ii) the underlying tax of a foreign dividend which has been restricted by the mixer cap (this being referred to as 'Case B' EUFT).

Qualifying foreign dividends (QFDs) are foreign dividends other than:

- dividends paid by controlled foreign companies to satisfy the acceptable distribution policy test (see below), or dividends representing such dividends; and
- dividends for which relief is itself restricted (and so gives rise to EUFT — referred to as '*tainted dividends*'. Under *ICTA 1988, s 799(1B)*, a claim for relief can exclude a specific amount of underlying tax from being taken into account so as to prevent a dividend from becoming 'tainted'.

Other exclusions, both from pooling and from the categories of dividend on which unrelieved tax may be treated as eligible for relief under these provisions, are dividends treated (or which could be treated) as trading income under *ICTA 1988, s 393* (see **55.5 LOSSES**), dividends the underlying tax on which is subject to restriction under *ICTA 1988, s 801A* (see **32.10** above) or *ICTA 1988, s 803* (see **32.18** below), and dividends treated under *ICTA 1988, s 811* as reduced by foreign tax paid for which no credit is allowable (see **32.4** above).

Relief for EUFT

For the purpose of giving relief, the following totals are aggregated (for any accounting period) and are treated as a single dividend or a single item of tax, as the case may be:

(a) 'related QFDs';
(b) 'unrelated QFDs';
(c) underlying tax on related QFDs; and
(d) withholding tax on both related and unrelated QFDs.

A '*related QFD*' is any QFD paid to a UK resident company by a foreign company which, at the time the dividend is paid, is related to the UK company (under the circumstances set out in **32.2**(b) above). An '*unrelated QFD*' is a QFD paid by any other foreign company.

Credit relief is then given:

- firstly, for the aggregate underlying tax on related QFDs ((c) above) against the UK tax arising on the single related QFD ((a) above) (which must be grossed up for the underlying tax); and

- secondly, for the aggregate withholding tax ((d) above) against the UK tax arising on the single related QFD ((a) above) or against that arising on the single unrelated QFD ((b) above) or partly against both.

Any remaining UK tax arising on the QFDs (under (c) and (d) above) may then be reduced or eliminated by any EUFT, which is aggregated into:

(1) relievable underlying tax which can be set off against UK tax arising on the single related QFD ((a) above); and then
(2) relievable withholding tax which may be set off against UK tax arising on the single related QFD ((a) above) or the single unrelated QFD ((b) above) or partly against both.

Utilisation of EUFT

Provision is made for relief to be given in the same accounting period or in accounting periods beginning not more than three years before that in which the relievable tax arises, or to be carried forward, broadly in the same way as applies in relation to foreign tax on income other than dividend income (see **32.7** above).

Repayment supplement is restricted where relief is carried back to an earlier accounting period, in the same way as applies in relation to the carry back of losses, loan relationship deficits, etc. (see **50.2 INTEREST ON OVERPAID TAX**). Regulations allow the surrender of foreign tax relievable as above between members of groups of companies (**39 GROUP RELIEF**).

[*ICTA 1988, ss 806A–806J, 826(7BB)(7BC); SI 2001 Nos 1163, 3873; SI 2003 No 1829; SI 2008 No 2681; CTA 2009, Sch 1 paras 252–256*].

These provisions are applied to UK permanent establishments (or branches or agencies) of non-UK residents as they are to UK resident companies. This provision is superceded by the FA 2009 regime for all dividends with effect for distributions paid on or after 1 July 2009, subject to transitional provisions. [*ICTA 1988, s 806K; FA 2000, Sch 30 para 22*].

Controlled foreign company dividends

See **32.13** below as regards separate streaming and the restriction on relief for underlying tax where the overseas company is a controlled foreign company which is exempt from apportionment by virtue of an acceptable distribution policy.

Examples

(E) Pooling

UK plc has two wholly owned foreign subsidiaries, High Tax Co which pays tax at 40% and Low Tax Co which pays tax at 10%. Both subsidiaries (which are resident in different countries) make pre-tax profits of £100 and make full distributions to the UK. Low Tax Co is a trading company which is exempt from the CFC rules otherwise than through pursuing an acceptable distribution policy.

High Tax Co suffers underlying tax of £40 and withholding tax of £3, which is restricted by the mixer cap, giving rise to Case B EUFT of £12 and Case A EUFT of £3. Low Tax Co suffers underlying tax of £10, leaving a UK tax liability of £18. This can be relieved by the EUFT of £15 leaving a net liability of £3.

	High Tax Co	Low Tax Co	Pool
	£	£	£
Net dividend	60	90	150
Underlying tax	40	10	50
Overseas income	100	100	200
Corporation tax @ 28%	28	28	56
Double tax relief (High Tax Co £28 restricted – mixer cap)	(28)	(10)	(38)
UK tax liability	—	18	18
Case B EUFT	12		(12)
Case A EUFT	3		(3)
Net liability			3

Note in the example above, the EUFT is set off against the tax arising in respect of the Low Tax Co dividend, as this is a QFD (as no restriction under *ICTA 1988, s 799* applied to it).

Had High Tax Co been subject to tax at 50%, the Case B EUFT would have been restricted to £17 (maximum relievable tax at 45% (£45) less the underlying tax as restricted by the mixer cap at 28% (£28)), leaving £7 of foreign tax which could not be used, and a net UK tax liability of nil.

(F) 'Tainted' dividends

UK plc wholly owns Dutch Holding BV which in turn wholly owns High Tax Co A which pays tax at 40% and Low Tax Co which pays tax at 10%. UK plc also wholly owns High Tax Co B which pays tax at 50%. All the subsidiaries make pre-tax profits of £100 and make full distributions (High Tax Co A and Low Tax Co via Dutch Holding BV). Low Tax Co is a trading company which is exempt from the CFC rules otherwise than through pursuing an acceptable distribution policy. All three subsidiaries are resident in different countries.

High Tax Co A suffers underlying tax of £40 which is restricted by the 28% mixer cap giving rise to Case B EUFT of £12. The dividend paid up to UK plc is a blend of this capped dividend and the 10% taxed dividend from Low Tax Co. Since EUFT has arisen on it, the dividend is not a QFD and so does not qualify for onshore pooling.

UK tax of £18 arises (after relief for the underlying tax) on the Low Tax Co element of the blended dividend but the Case B EUFT of £12 cannot be relieved against it and can only be carried back or carried forward (assuming there is no other UK tax liability on low taxed dividends against which it could be relieved).

High Tax Co B suffers underlying tax of £50 which is restricted by the 28% mixer cap giving rise to Case B EUFT of £17 (limited by the 45% cap). Since the blended dividend from Dutch Holding BV is not a QFD and cannot be pooled, the EUFT can only be carried back or carried forward, leaving a net UK tax liability of £16.

	Dutch Holding BV	High Tax Co B	Total
	£	£	£
Net dividend	150	50	200
Underlying tax	50	50	100
Overseas income	200	100	300
Corporation tax @ 28%	56	28	84
Double tax relief (restricted by mixer cap)	(40)	(28)	(68)
UK tax liability	16	—	16
Unused Case B EUFT	12	17	

(G) Excluding underlying tax from a claim to avoid 'tainting'

The above situation in (F) could be mitigated by limiting the claim to High Tax Co A's underlying tax to 28%. In this case, the blended dividend from Dutch Holding BV would then become a QFD and qualify for onshore pooling. The UK tax of £16 which arises in respect of the Dutch BV dividend could be relieved by the Case B EUFT of £17 suffered by High Tax Co B, leaving a net UK tax liability of nil. The Case B EUFT of £12 arising on the dividend from High Tax Co A would be lost.

	Dutch Holding BV	High Tax Co B	Pool
	£	£	£
Net dividend	150	50	200
Underlying tax	50	50	100
Overseas income	200	100	300
Corporation tax @ 28%	56	28	84
Double tax relief (as per limited claim)	(40)	(28)	(68)
UK tax liability	16	—	16
Case B EUFT (restricted to 45%)	—	17	(16)
Net UK tax liability			nil

See HMRC International Manual at INTM164210–164340 for summaries of the provisions for onshore pooling and relief for eligible unrelieved foreign tax ('EUFT'), and of the CFC dividend provisions, together with a number of examples.

Simon's Taxes. See **D4.920–D4.925**.

Foreign income dividends

The High Court, to which the case was remitted by the ECJ, found in favour of the taxpayers that dividends paid out of taxed overseas profits were not subject to ACT (before April 1999) when paid to the UK company's shareholders. The treatment of the dividends where no overseas corporation tax had been paid required a further reference to ECJ. See *Claimants in the FII Group Litigation v Revenue and Customs Comrs* [2008] EWHC 2893, [2009] STC 254.

Controlled foreign company dividends

ADP exemption applying to a period ending before 1 July 2009

[32.13] The following two paragraphs refer to a CFC which is exempt from the CFC attribution regime by virtue of following an 'acceptable distribution policy' ('ADP') — by distributing 90% of its net chargeable profits (see further **27.12** controlled foreign companies). The ADP exemption was abolished for accounting periods of CFCs beginning on or after 1 July 2009. Where an accounting period straddles this date then it is treated as split and profits and creditable tax are apportioned on a just and reasonable basis.

Separate streaming of dividend

Where a controlled foreign company ('CFC') is exempt from a profit apportionment under *ICTA 1988, s 747* solely by virtue of the payment of a dividend or dividends satisfying the 'acceptable distribution policy' test (see **27.12 CONTROLLED FOREIGN COMPANIES**), and any dividend by virtue of which that test is met (an 'ADP dividend') is a dividend paid by the CFC to another non-UK resident company and subsequently paid on to a UK resident, there are provisions for the separate streaming of the dividend for all credit relief purposes, thus in effect preventing the avoidance of tax on dividends paid in order to gain exemption from CFC apportionment. (See HMRC International Manual, INTM204010 *et seq*.) These provisions have effect as above, broadly for dividends paid on or after 31 March 2001. [*ICTA 1988, s 801C*].

Restriction of relief for underlying tax

Where a dividend is paid on or after 2 December 2004 by an overseas company which is a CFC which is exempt from a profit apportionment under *ICTA 1988, s 747* solely by virtue of the payment of a dividend or dividends satisfying the ADP test (as above), and the dividend in question is an ADP dividend, anti-avoidance provisions apply to prevent the ADP dividend from attracting double tax relief in excess of that which would have been due in respect of an apportionment had the CFC not paid a dividend. A modified version of the 'mixer cap' formula (see **32.12** above) applies to restrict relief for underlying tax on dividends paid to the CFC by related companies (whether or not they are resident in the same overseas territory as the CFC). In this case, the relievable underlying tax in respect of any dividend paid up to the CFC is restricted by the formula of $X \times (D \div (1-X))$ where X is the corporation tax rate in force at the time the dividend was paid (expressed as a decimal fraction) and D is the amount of the dividend. The effect is that credit relief in relation to dividends paid to the CFC is restricted to the amount of the current rate of corporation tax applied to the gross dividend, or the actual foreign tax paid if lower. [*ICTA 1988, s 801; FA 2005, s 89*].

See generally HMRC's draft guidance on 'Double Taxation Relief: Underlying Tax' (at www.hmrc.gov.uk/budget2005/dtrutc.pdf).

Dividends, interest, etc. paid to non-residents

Dividends

[32.14] Before the abolition of ACT on 6 April 1999, HMRC could make arrangements with a UK resident company whereby it could pay to a non-resident shareholder that part of the tax credit relating to a dividend to which he was entitled under the terms of a double tax agreement (see **32.3** above). Such payment by the company discharged a corresponding amount of its liability to ACT. Under most agreements, half of the tax credit attached to a dividend, less a deduction by reference to a percentage of the sum of the dividend and the tax credit (see below), could be paid to the non-resident or set off against UK liabilities.

See *Steele v EVC International NV (formerly European Vinyls Corp (Holdings) BV)* (1996) 69 TC 88, CA, for refusal of tax credit in the case of certain 'connected' companies. See also *Océ Van Der Grinten NV v CIR: C-58/01* [2003] ECR I-9809, [2003] 3 CMLR 1104, ECJ, where a challenge to the deduction from the payment of the half tax credit was dismissed by the European Court of Justice. See also **32.3** above for cases in connection with the various ACT group litigation orders in which it was found that UK legislation contravened EU law and regarding the restitution of ACT.

Where a treaty provides for an overseas recipient of distributions from a UK resident company to receive a tax credit determined by reference to the credit a UK resident individual would receive, subject to a deduction calculated by reference to the sum of the distribution and the tax credit paid, the deduction is to be calculated without any allowance for the deduction itself. [*FA 1989, s 115*].

Where set-off or repayment of a sum in respect of a tax credit would be available under an agreement, it may nevertheless be denied where the non-resident recipient is, or is an 'associated company' of, a company with a 'qualifying presence' in a 'unitary state'. A company has such a '*qualifying presence*' if it is a member of a 'group' 7½% or more of whose property, payroll or sales in the territory of which the state is a part are in that state.

The Treasury may instead provide by order either that a company has a qualifying presence in a 'unitary state' if it is liable to tax on income or profits in that state, or alternatively that it has such a presence if its principal place of business is in that state, including the place(s) where central management and control and immediate day-to-day management are exercised.

A '*unitary state*' is broadly a state, etc. which reserves the right to tax companies with sources of income within the state by taking into account the company's activities outside the territory of which the state is a part. The Treasury has powers to prescribe states, etc. as unitary states.

A fine may be imposed where a tax credit is repaid despite its being within these provisions, and there are provisions for claiming tax credits following remedial legislation effective before 1 January 1987 in the unitary state, and to prevent avoidance by the payment of interest or the allowing of a discount in substitution for a distribution.

Other terms are specifically defined in *ICTA 1988, s 812(5)*. These provisions, if applied, will take effect for distributions on or after a date to be appointed by the Treasury by statutory instrument, although implementation has now been indefinitely deferred. [*ICTA 1988, ss 812–815; FA 1998, Sch 3 para 37; ITTOIA 2005, Sch 1 para 326*].

Withholding tax

Since the abolition of the ACT regime, there is generally no withholding tax deducted on payments of dividends made by a UK company to another company, whether resident within the UK or overseas.

In the Dutch case of *Amurta SGPS v Inspecteur van de Belastingdienst/Amsterdam: C-379/05* [2007] ECR I-9569, [2008] 1 CMLR 851, the ECJ held that the Dutch law under which Dutch residents qualified for an exemption on domestic dividends on holdings of 5% or more, but the exemption did not apply to non-resident recipients, infringed the EC Treaty (as was, now TFEU) articles on free movement of capital. However, it might comply by having a bilateral DTA with another member state – it is for the national court to decide whether such an agreement should be taken into account and if it does neutralise the restriction on free movement of capital.

In the case *Commission of the European Communities v Italian Republic: C-540/07* OJ C24, 30.01.2010, p.5, ECJ, in a decision of 19 November 2009, the ECJ held that the Italian withholding tax regime constituted a restriction on the free movement of capital (*Art 56(1)* EC Treaty, as was, now *Art 63* TFEU). The regime exempted (in the amount of 95%) dividends distributed to Italian resident companies, but subjected dividends paid to companies established in other member states to a withholding tax at a rate of 27%, subject to any reduction by operation of a double tax agreement. No justifications put forward by the Italian government were considered sufficient, and it was held that the Italian Republic had failed to fulfil its obligations under the EC Treaty. This case is likely to have wide ranging implications with regard to member states' dividend withholding regimes.

The European 'Parent-Subsidiary' Directive 90/435/EEC, which came into force on 1 January 1992, applies where the parent company holds a specified minimum of the capital of a company in another member state (or, by bilateral agreement, a specified minimum of the voting rights). The *Directive* provides that dividends paid to such a parent company are to be exempt from withholding tax in the country of the paying company, that the country of the parent company is equally not to charge withholding tax on the dividend received, and that the recipient country must either exempt the dividend from corporation tax or give credit for the proportion of the subsidiary's corporation tax relating to the dividend. Where the *Directive* applies and gives more favourable treatment than the dividends article in a double taxation agreement, the *Directive* is to take precedence over the agreement. The *Directive* applied (before 1 January 2005) where the parent company held a minimum of 25% of the capital of a company in another member. It was amended by *Directive 2003/123/EC*, which came into force on 2 February 2004 to be implemented with effect from 1 January 2005. The amended *Directive* gradually reduces the minimum capital holding to 20% from 1 January 2005, 15% from 1 January 2007 and 10% from 1 January 2009. A member state can instead, by means of a bilateral agreement, substitute a voting power test such as the 10% test used by the UK (see **32.2** above).

The *Directive* is extended to cover all companies subject to tax within the European Union regardless of their legal form (including the new European Company — see **34.5 EUROPEAN COMMUNITY LEGISLATION**), and the amendments extend double taxation relief by making a tax credit available for underlying tax paid by second-tier and lower-tier subsidiaries.

Interest etc.

[32.15] Where payments required or authorised to be made under deduction of UK income tax are made to non-UK residents, the payer may be authorised by HMRC, International — Centre for Non-Residents, by a notice under *SI 1970 No 488*, to make payments without deduction of tax, or under deduction of tax at a specified or maximum rate (but see below under European member states and also **46.5 INCOME TAX IN RELATION TO A COMPANY**).

Payments may normally only be so made once the notice has been given by HMRC following application by the overseas recipient, and there may be a substantial delay in HMRC being in a position to issue a notice in response to such an application. Accordingly, a Provisional Treaty Relief scheme provides for two types of loan, the one to one company loan (provided that there is no common shareholding or ownership) and the syndicated loan, where there is a syndicate manager. This allows the UK borrower to apply for immediate authority to make payments incorporating the treaty relief, pending a decision by HMRC on the issue of a formal notice. It is a condition of the scheme that the recipient's application for relief (certified by the overseas tax authority) is received by HMRC within three months of the provisional authority, and if that condition is not met, or the relief is found not to be due, HMRC will look to the payer for the tax that should have been deducted (and any interest thereon). In the case of a syndicated loan, a composite application for relief (which does not need overseas tax authority certification) must be made by the syndicate manager within three months of the provisional authority. The borrowers in respect of the loan should not be connected with the lenders and the loan should be on arm's length terms.

Following the changes announced in 2007 to HMRC's double tax treaty relief processes (in response to the changes in the thin capitalisation query procedure) and following the introduction of the double tax treaty passport scheme, it was considered the one-to-one loan aspect of the provisional treaty relief scheme was no longer needed and has been discontinued.

The part of the scheme that deals with syndicated loans remains and has been renamed the syndicated loan scheme.

Application for provisional relief is made on form PTR PAY 1 (in the case of one-to-one loans) or forms PTR SM 1 or PTR SM 1A (in the case of syndicated loans), which may be obtained from HMRC's website (www.hmrc.gov.uk/cnr/dtt_inter.htm) or from HMRC, International — Centre for Non-Residents, Fitz Roy House, PO Box 46, Nottingham NG2 1BD (tel. 0115–974 1940). Explanatory 'Guidelines' may be obtained from the same address. For a summary of the scheme, see Revenue Tax Bulletin June 1999 pp 668–670.

The double tax treaty passport scheme was introduced as from 1 September 2010 for overseas corporate lenders.

An overseas corporate lender applies for a 'Treaty Passport' from HMRC — it can do so where it is resident in a country with which the UK has a double taxation treaty that includes an interest or income from a debt-claims Article. When the treaty passport is granted then the passport holder is entered onto a publicly available register with a unique DTTP number.

Potential UK resident corporate borrowers can then check this online register to verify the lender's Treaty Passport status. Where a UK borrower enters into a loan agreement with a DTTP lender who is registered, the lender notifies them of their passport holder status and reference number. The UK borrower must then notify HMRC within 30 working days of the 'passported' loan. The notification should be made using form DTTP2 that can be completed and sent to HMRC online (or returned to HMRC by post). HMRC uses these notification details to issue a 'Direction' to the UK borrower to pay the interest with income tax deducted at the rate set out in the relevant double taxation treaty.

Where a lender does not have a passport then the usual application rules above apply.

European member states

With effect for payments made **on or after 1 January 2004**, FA 2004 implements the European *Directive 2003/49/EC* adopted by the EU on 3 June 2003 whereby certain payments of interest and royalties between associated companies of different EU member states are exempt from income tax. See **46.5 INCOME TAX IN RELATION TO A COMPANY**. [*FA 2004, ss 97–106; ITTOIA 2005, ss 757–767, Sch 1 paras 631–639*].

There is a limited discretion available to UK companies or permanent UK establishments of EU companies, which believe that a royalty payment is exempt from deduction of tax at source. Payment may be made gross to an EU company. However, tax will be due if payment is made gross but it subsequently appears that exemption was not available. [*ITA 2007, s 758, Sch 1 paras 576, 577*].

Beneficial ownership

One of the most important conditions for treaty relief is that the recipient must be the 'beneficial owner' of the interest or dividend, etc.

In determining whether the recipient of dividends, interest or royalties is the 'beneficial owner', HMRC will, as far as UK double taxation conventions are concerned, interpret 'beneficial ownership' using the 'international fiscal meaning'.

In the case of *Indofood International Finance Ltd v JP Morgan Chase Bank* [2006] EWCA Civ 158, the Court of Appeal supported the view (in the OECD Model Convention on Income and on Capital) that, under an 'international fiscal meaning', beneficial ownership is to be determined by reference to a test which requires that the recipient 'enjoy the full privilege to directly benefit from the income'. It added that where recipients are bound in commercial and practical terms to pass on the income, they will not be the beneficial owner of the income and so not entitled to treaty relief. HMRC guidance provided in their Internet Statement of 9 October 2006 followed the *Indofood* case and discussed their practice in relation to existing treaty clearances.

Simon's Taxes. See **E6.461**.

European cross-border transfers of business

[32.16] This provision applies either where a UK resident company transfers the whole or part of a business carried on by it in another member state and a loan relationship, derivative contract or intangible fixed asset is part of the transfer.

Or it applies if a UK resident company transfers part of its business to one or more companies. The transfer must be for genuine commercial reasons and must not be part of tax avoidance arrangements. At least one of the transferees must be resident in a member state other than the UK. The transferee must continue to carry on a business after the transfer. The transfer must be made in exchange for shares or debentures, unless this is precluded by UK or other country's legal prohibition on purchase of own shares.

In these cases, notional tax is treated as having been incurred and is eligible for double tax relief. Any losses or reliefs are assumed to be claimed in calculating the notional tax charge.

Similar rules apply for mergers of SEs or SCEs, subject to an additional condition which is that, in the course of the merger, each transferor ceases to exist without going into liquidation.

[*TIOPA 2010, ss 116–121, 123; ICTA 1988, ss 807B–807G; CTA 2009, Sch 1 paras 257–262*].

Agreements in force

[32.17] Double tax agreements with the following countries came into force from the date specified in each agreement and remain so until further notice. *Statutory Instrument* dates and numbers are given in round brackets. For the agreement relating to the Republic of Ireland, see Tolley's Income Tax. For details of agreements, see **Simon's Taxes**, Part **F1**.

Antigua and Barbuda (1947/2865, 1968/1096); **Argentina** (1997/1777); **Australia** (1968/305, 1980/707, 2003/3199)(new treaty applies from 1 April 2004 (UK) and from 1 July 2004 (Australia)); **Austria** (1970/1947, 1979/117, 1994/768, 2010/2688); **Azerbaijan** (1995/762);

Bahrain, signed 10 March 2010, not in force as yet; **Bangladesh** (1980/708); **Barbados** (1970/952, 1973/2096); **Belarus** (1986/224 – see note below); **Belgium** (1987/2053) – 2009 protocol not in force as yet; **Belize** (1947/2866, 1968/573, 1973/2097); **Bolivia** (1995/2707); **Bosnia-Hercegovina** (1981/1815 – see note below); **Botswana** (1978/183, 2006/1925) (new treaty applies from 1 April 2007 with respect to corporation tax, from 6 April 2007 with respect to income tax and capital gains tax (UK) and 1 July 2007 (Botswana)); **Brunei** (1950/1977, 1968/306, 1973/2098); **Bulgaria** (1987/2054); **Burma** (see Myanmar);

Canada (1980/709, 1980/1528, 1985/1996, 2003/2619) (new protocol to take effect from 1 April 2005 (UK) and 1 January 2005 (Canada)), (1980/780, 1987/2071, 1996/1782 revoked from 1 January 2001 – see 2000/3330); **Chile** (2003/3200) (from 1 April 2005 (UK) and 1 January 2005 (Chile)); **Cayman Islands** (2010/2973) in force 20 December 2010, effective UK 1 April 2011; **China** (1984/1826, 1996/3164) (see also note below , new treaty was signed on 27 June 2011 but is not in force as yet); **Croatia** (1981/1815 – note below); **Cyprus** (1975/425, 1980/1529); **Czech Republic** (1991/2876 – see note below);

Denmark (1980/1960, 1991/2877, 1996/3165);

Egypt (1980/1091); **Estonia** (1994/3207); **Ethiopia** (new treaty signed 9 June 2011, not in force as yet);

Falkland Islands (1997/2985); **Faroe Islands** (2007/3469) in force 3 June 2008, effective UK 1 April 2009; **Fiji** (1976/1342); **Finland** (1970/153, 1980/710, 1985/1997, 1991/2878, 1996/3166); **France** (2009/226);

Gambia (1980/1963); **Georgia** (2004/3325) (from 1 April 2006 (new treaty applies from 6 April 2006 with respect to income tax and capital gains tax) (UK) and 1 January 2006 (Georgia)) (see also note below) protocol to the treaty signed 3 February 2010 entered into force 17 December 2010; **Germany** (1967/25, 1971/874– new treaty 2010/2975 in force 30 December 2010, effective UK 1 April 2011); **Ghana** (1993/1800); **Greece** (1954/142); **Grenada** (1949/361, 1968/1867); **Guernsey** (1952/1215, 1994/3209); **Guyana** (1992/3207);

Hong Kong (2010/2974) in force 20 December 2010, effective UK 1 April 2011; **Hungary** (1978/1056);

Iceland (1991/2879); **India** (1993/1801); **Indonesia** (1994/769); **Ireland** (Republic of) (1976/2151, 1976/2152, 1995/764, 1998/3151); **Isle of Man** (2009/228); **Israel** (1963/616, 1971/391); **Italy** (1990/2590); **Ivory Coast** (1987/169);

Jamaica (1973/1329); **Japan** (1970/1948, 1980/1530, 2006/1924) (new treaty applies from 1 January 2007 with respect to taxes withheld at source, from 1 April 2007 with respect to corporation tax, from 6 April 2007 with respect to income tax and capital gains tax (UK) and 1 January 2007 (Japan)); **Jersey** (1952/1216, 1994/3210); **Jordan** (2001/3924) (from 1 April 2003 (UK) and 1 January 2003 (Jordan));

Kazakhstan (1994/3211, 1998/2567); **Kenya** (1977/1299); **Kiribati and Tuvalu** (1950/750, 1968/309, 1974/1271); **Korea (South)** (1996/3168); **Kuwait** (1999/2036) (from 1 April 2001 (UK) and 1 January 2001 (Kuwait)); **Kyrgyzstan** (see note below);

Latvia (1996/3167); **Lesotho** (1997/2986) from 1 April 1998; **Libya** (2010/243) in force 8 March 2010; **Lithuania** (2001/3925, 2002/2847) (from 1 April 2002 (UK) and 1 January 2002 (Lithuania) (subject to protocol)) (and see note below); **Luxembourg** (1968/1100, 1980/567, 1984/364, 2009 protocol effective 1 April 2011);

Macedonia (1981/1815 – note below, 2007/2127); **Malawi** (1956/619, 1964/1401, 1968/1101, 1979/302); **Malaysia** (1997/2987 – protocol to treaty entered into force 28 December 2010); **Malta** (1995/763); **Mauritius** (1981/1121, 1987/467, 2003/2620 – protocol to treaty signed 11 January 2011); **Mexico** (1994/3212); **Moldova** (2008/1795 see note below); **Mongolia** (1996/2598); **Montserrat** (1947/2869, 1968/576); **Morocco** (1991/2881); **Myanmar** (1952/751);

Namibia (1962/2352, 1967/1490); **Netherlands** (2009/227, in force 25 December 2010, effective in UK from 1 April 2011); **New Zealand** (1984/365, 2004/1274, 2008/1793); **Nigeria** (1987/2057); **Norway** (1985/1998, 2000/3247)(new treaty applies from 1 April 2001 (UK) and 1 January 2001 (Norway));

Oman (1998/2568) protocol to treaty entered into force 9 January 2011;

Pakistan (1987/2058); **Papua New Guinea** (1991/2882); **Philippines** (1978/184); **Poland** (2006/3323); **Portugal** (1969/599);

Qatar (2010/241) in force 15 October 2010, effective UK 1 January 2011, protocol signed 20 October 2010;

Romania (1977/57); **Russian Federation** (1994/3213);

St. Christopher (St. Kitts) and Nevis (1947/2872); **Saudi Arabia** (2008/1770); **Serbia and Montenegro** (1981/1815 – see note below); **Sierra Leone** (1947/2873, 1968/1104); **Singapore** (1997/2988, 2010/2685; protocol to treaty entered into force 8 January 2011); **Slovak Republic** (1991/2876 – see note below); **Slovenia** (2008/1796 see note below); **Solomon Islands** (1950/748, 1968/574, 1974/1270); **South Africa** (1969/864, 2002/3138) (new treaty applies from 1 April 2003 (UK) and 1 January 2003 (South Africa) – protocol signed 8 November 2010); **Spain** (1976/1919, 1995/765); **Sri Lanka** (1980/713); **Sudan** (1977/1719); **Swaziland** (1969/380); **Sweden** (1984/366) (1961/619 revoked from 1 January 2001 – see 2000/3330); **Switzerland** (1978/1408, 1982/714, 1994/3215, 2007/3465, protocol to treaty entered into force 15 December 2010);

Taiwan (2002/3137) from 1 April 2003 (UK) and 1 January 2003 (Taiwan); **Tajikistan** (1986/224 – see note below); **Thailand** (1981/1546); **Trinidad and Tobago** (1983/1903); **Tunisia** (1984/133); **Turkey** (1988/932); **Turkmenistan** (1986/224 – see note below);

Uganda (1993/1802); **Ukraine** (1993/1803); **USA** (1980/568; 2002/2848) (from 1 April 2003 (UK) (1 May 2003 with respect to taxes withheld at source) and 1 January 2004 (US) — 1946/1331, 1955/499, 1961/985, 1980/779, 1994/1418, 1996/1781 all revoked from 1 January 2001 (see 2000/3330) and see note below); **USSR** (see note below); **Uzbekistan** (1994/770);

Venezuela (1996/2599); **Vietnam** (1994/3216);

Yugoslavia (see note below);

Zambia (1972/1721, 1981/1816); **Zimbabwe** (1982/1842).

Shipping & Air Transport only — Algeria (Air Transport only) (1984/362), Argentina (but see now above), Belarus (but see now above), Brazil (1968/572) (new air crew agreement signed 2 September 2010, not in force as yet), Cameroon (Air Transport only) (1982/1841), China (Air Transport only) (1981/1119), Ethiopia (Air Transport only) (1977/1297), Hong Kong (Air Transport only) (1998/2566), Hong Kong (Shipping only) (2000/3248) from 1 April 2002, Iran (Air Transport only) (1960/2419), Jordan (1979/300), Kuwait (Air Transport only) (1984/1825), Lebanon (1964/278), Russia (but see now above), Saudi Arabia (Air Transport only) (1994/767), Venezuela (but see now above), USSR (but see now above), Ukraine (but see now above), Uzbekistan (but see now above), Zaire (1977/1298).

Notes

China. The Convention published as *SI 1984 No 1826* does not apply to the Hong Kong or Macao Special Administrative Regions. (Revenue Tax Bulletin October 1996 p 357). See above as regards Hong Kong Air Transport and Shipping agreements. A new double tax agreement was signed on 27 June 2011, not in force as yet.

Czechoslovakia. The Convention published as *SI 1991 No 2876* is treated as remaining in force between the UK and, respectively, the Czech Republic and the Slovak Republic. (HMRC Statement of Practice, SP 5/93).

Montserrat. A draft amendment order to the existing agreement was published on 21 February 2011, most notably to update the information exchange article and to introduce a mutual agreement article, both in line with the OECD standard.

USA. For an article setting out the understanding of HMRC on how certain of the provisions of the new USA treaty will be interpreted and applied, see Revenue Tax Bulletin Special Edition April 2003.

USSR. Following the dissolution of the USSR, new agreements have come into force with Azerbaijan, Estonia, Kazakhstan, Latvia, Lithuania (subject to protocol), Moldova, the Russian Federation, Ukraine and Uzbekistan (see above). *SI 1986 No 224* (the former USSR agreement) is treated as continuing to apply to Belarus, Tajikistan and Turkmenistan (in the case of Belarus until the coming into force of *SI 1995 No 2706*). It was similarly so treated by the UK until 31 March 2002 in the case of Armenia, Georgia, Kyrgyzstan, Lithuania and Moldova (none of which considered itself bound by that convention) but as ceasing so to apply after that date (although new treaties are in force with Lithuania (subject to protocol) and with Georgia). (HMRC Statement of Practice, SP 4/01, as revised).

Yugoslavia. The Convention published as *SI 1981 No 1815* is treated as remaining in force between the UK and, respectively, Bosnia-Herzegovina, Croatia, Macedonia, Serbia and Montenegro. Negotiations for a new double taxation convention are taking place with Croatia, Serbia and Montenegro. New agreements have been entered into with Macedonia and Slovenia. (HMRC Statement of Practice 3/2004 (superseding SP 6/93), Revenue Press Release, 29 September 2004).

Banks and other financial traders

Restriction of credit relief

[32.18] Special provisions restrict the amount of double taxation relief which can be claimed by banks or other financial concerns involved in overseas lending. These were extended in *FA 2008* for payments of foreign tax on or after 6 April 2008 or income received on or after that date under deduction of foreign tax. Where there is a payment of foreign tax or income received in respect of which foreign tax has been deducted at source, see **32.5** above for the restrictions which apply to credit relief for foreign tax in connection with trade income.

Provisions also restrict underlying tax which a UK bank (or a company connected with the bank) can claim on dividends received from a foreign related company. The restriction applies where the underlying tax is (or includes) foreign tax on interest or dividends earned or received by the foreign related company (or by a third, fourth or successive company); and where the restrictions set out in **32.5** above in relation to trade income would have applied to that company if it were UK resident.

The credit for underlying tax is not to exceed the UK corporation tax, at the rate in force at the time when the foreign tax was chargeable, on the amount of interest or dividends less the company's 'relevant expenditure' which is properly attributable to the earning of the interest or dividends.

The 2005 rules were amended by *FA 2009, s 60* in respect of credits relating to payments of foreign tax, or income received under deduction of foreign tax, on or after 22 April 2009. This is an anti-avoidance measure targeted at a scheme used by banks — other companies are not affected by the changes. Banks have to include the 'notional funding costs' in calculating the credit, where this is significantly different from the funding costs used in the calculation. '*Notional funding costs*' means the funding costs that the bank would incur in order to wholly fund the transaction (on the basis of the bank's average funding costs).

[*TIOPA 2010, ss 36, 37, 42, 44–49; ICTA 1988, ss 798–798C, 803; FA 2005, s 86; FA 2009, s 60*].

See *Legal & General Assurance Society Ltd v Revenue and Customs Comrs* [2006] STC 1763 (which preceded the changes made by *FA 2005*), where the High Court confirmed (in dismissing HMRC's appeal) that the legislation did not require the identification of the UK profit which corresponded exactly with the foreign taxable income for the purpose of determining the credit available for foreign tax paid.

See HMRC's guidance 'Double Taxation Relief: Trade Receipts' issued on 6 May 2005 (available on their website at www.hmrc.gov.uk/budget2005/dtr tr.pdf).

See Revenue Tax Bulletin April 1996 p 306.

Foreign residents

Non-UK resident persons (whether companies or individuals) trading in the UK through permanent establishments (or branches or agencies) may claim tax credit relief for tax withheld by a third country from interest on a loan to a resident of that country where the unilateral relief arrangements in their state of residence allow for such relief.

[*TIOPA 2010, s 30; ICTA 1988, s 794(2)(bb); FA 2001, Sch 27 para 7*].

See *CIR v Commerzbank AG; CIR v Banco Do Brasil* (1990) 63 TC 218 for a case on interest exemption under the UK/USA Agreement.

See also **55.27 LOSSES**.

Simon's Taxes. See **D4.1001–D4.1008.**

Key points

[32.19] Points to consider are as follows.

- Where a treaty is in force the treaty relief must be taken. Before any income is received from an overseas jurisdiction or any payments are made from the UK the taxpayer should ensure that the necessary clearances have been obtained from the appropriate Fiscal Authorities. This process may vary between jurisdictions. For example when receiving income from a US payer the completion of the form W8-BEN by the recipient and its subsequent filing with the payer of the income in the US is sufficient to operate treaty rates. However in the UK it is necessary for HMRC forms to be completed. These forms normally require the overseas recipient to obtain confirmation of their fiscal residence status in the other territory by having their home tax authorities certify their residence status. Once completed, HMRC will ratify to the UK payer operation of the treaty rate.
- Relief for foreign taxes in excess of the treaty rate are not allowed; instead a repayment must be sought from the overseas authority. It is recommended that this situation is avoided (if possible) as obtaining these refunds can be a difficult process including filing foreign tax returns leading to delays.

- Foreign taxes suffered but not credited against UK tax liabilities, for example, because there is no UK liability, cannot be carried forward.
- By election foreign taxes may be claimed as a deduction from income rather than a credit. This offers some relief from the loss of credit relief. For example if a taxpayer has UK trading losses to cover their foreign income so that there is no UK tax liability then the foreign taxes are lost. By electing to deduct the foreign taxes from the overseas income as an 'expense' the losses required to offset that income is reduced by an amount equal to the foreign tax. This loss is then available for relief in future years. This effectively gives an indirect partial carry forward of the foreign taxes suffered.
- The Finance Act 2011 contains provisions for an exemption from UK tax for the profits of foreign permanent establishments of UK resident companies. It is considered the new regime will be most beneficial to industry sectors which have to operate overseas through branches due to regulatory reasons, such as the banking and insurance sectors (save for long term business which is excluded). Companies with loss making branches overseas would not make the election (it is an opt-in regime) and would therefore be able to continue with the existing treatment.
- The local tax treatment of some entities as against HMRC's treatment can give rise to double taxing even in treaty countries. A typical example of this is US Limited Liability Corporations (LLCs). With LLCs the US treat them as transparent entities and tax the income and gains as if they were the shareholder's income and gains, thus paying US tax on these sources. However, if the shareholder is UK resident then they are treated as only receiving a dividend on actual distributions. HMRC take the view that the US tax paid has been paid on behalf of the LLC and not as the shareholder's own liability and deny any form of double tax relief. This leads to a double charge on effectively the same income. This is particularly a problem for individuals rather than corporates resident in the UK. The recent case of *Swift* TC 00399 heard in the First-tier Tribunal has overturned HMRC's view, however, HMRC has appealed this decision and has indicated that it intends to continue with its current general practice in relation to US LLCs. In addition, it was apparent from the case report that this decision was reached solely on the facts of the case and should not be treated as a precedent.

33

Estate Income

Introduction and definitions

Introduction

[33.1] Corporate beneficiaries of deceased person's estates in administration are within the charge to corporation tax on income treated as arising from their interest in the residue of the estate (referred to in *CTA 2009* as '*estate income*'). Where a company has an interest in different parts of an estate, each interest is treated as a separate estate.

[*CTA 2009, s 934; ICTA 1988, ss 695(2)–(4), 696(3)(6), 698(3), 701(11)*].

Liability under these provisions depends on the type of interest that the company has (an 'absolute interest' (**33.4** below), a 'limited interest' (**33.5** below) or a 'discretionary interest' (**33.6** below)) and whether the estate is a 'UK estate' or a 'foreign estate' (as defined at **33.2** below).

Definitions

[33.2] The following definitions apply for the purposes of these provisions.

The '*personal representatives*' of a deceased person mean, in the UK, the persons responsible for administering his estate and, outside the UK, the persons having equivalent functions under the law of the territory concerned.

[*CTA 2010, s 1119; ICTA 1988, s 701(4)*].

A person has an '*absolute interest*' in the whole or part of the residue of an estate if the capital of the residue (or part) is properly payable to that person or would be so payable if the residue had been ascertained.

A person has a '*limited interest*' in the whole or part of the residue of an estate during any period if the person does not have an absolute interest and the income from the residue (or part) would be properly payable to the person if it had been ascertained at the beginning of the period.

A person has a '*discretionary interest*' in the whole or part of an estate if a discretion may be exercised in the person's favour so that any income of the residue during the whole or part of the administration period would be properly payable to the person if the residue had been ascertained at the beginning of that period. For this purpose, an amount is only treated as properly payable to a person (A) if it is properly payable to A, or to another person in A's right, for A's benefit (whether directly or through a trustee or other person). The personal representatives of a deceased person (B) are treated as having an absolute or limited interest in the whole or part of the estate of another deceased person (C) if they have a right in their capacity as B's personal representatives and, were the right vested in them for their own benefit, they would have that interest in C's estate.

[*CTA 2009, s 935; ICTA 1988, ss 698(1)(3), 701(2)(3)*].

An estate is a '*UK estate*' in relation to a tax year if either:

(i) as regards the income of the estate:
   - all of the income of the estate (disregarding any life assurance gains and any sums *treated as* bearing income tax at the dividend ordinary rate) has either borne UK income tax by deduction or is income in respect of which the personal representatives are directly assessable to UK income tax for the year; and
   - none of the income of the estate (disregarding any life assurance gains and any sums *treated as* bearing income tax at the dividend ordinary rate) is income for which the personal representatives are not liable to UK income tax for the year by virtue of being not resident or not ordinarily resident in the UK; or

(ii) the income of the estate for the year consists only of life assurance gains and/or sums treated as bearing income tax at the dividend ordinary rate.

If an estate is not a UK estate in relation to a tax year it is a '*foreign estate*' in relation to that year.

[*CTA 2009, s 936; ICTA 1988, ss 699A(1B), 701(9)(10)(10A)*].

The '*aggregate income*' of an estate for a tax year is the total of:

(a) the income of the personal representatives in that capacity which is charged to income tax for the year, less any allowable deductions;
(b) the income of the personal representatives in that capacity which would have been chargeable to income tax if it were income from a UK source of a person resident and ordinarily resident in the UK, less any deductions which would have been allowable;
(c) any stock dividends that would be chargeable on the personal representatives if such income were so chargeable;
(d) any amount that would be chargeable on the personal representatives on release of a loan to a participator in a close company if such amounts were so chargeable; and

(e) any gain from a life insurance contract that would have been treated as income of the personal representatives in that capacity if the condition for such gains to be so treated were met.

Income from property devolving on the personal representatives otherwise than as assets for payment of the deceased's debts and income to which any person is or may become entitled under a specific disposition (as defined) is, however, excluded.

[*CTA 2009, s 947; ICTA 1988, ss 701(5)(8), 702*].

The '*residuary income*' of an estate for a tax year is the aggregate income of the estate for the year less deductions for:

- all interest (or, before *CTA 2009* came into effect (see **70 TRADE PROFITS — INCOME AND SPECIFIC TRADES**), annual interest) paid in the year by the personal representatives in that capacity (other than interest on unpaid inheritance tax under *IHTA 1984, s 233*);
- all annual payments for the year which are properly payable out of residue;
- all expenses of management of the estate paid in the year (but only where, ignoring any specific direction in a will, properly chargeable to income); and
- any excess of allowable deductions for the previous year over the aggregate income of the estate for that year.

No deduction is allowed for any amount allowable in calculating the aggregate income of the estate.

[*CTA 2009, s 949; ICTA 1988, s 697(1)(1A)*].

A transfer of assets or the appropriation of assets by personal representatives to themselves is treated for the purposes of these provisions as the payment of an amount equal to the assets' value at the date of the transfer or appropriation.

The set off or release of a debt is treated as the payment of amount equal to it. If at the end of the administration period there is an obligation to transfer assets to any person or the personal representatives are entitled to appropriate assets to themselves, an amount equal to the assets' value at that time is treated as payable then. If at that time there is an obligation to release or set off a debt owed by any person or the personal representative are entitled to release or set off a debt in their own favour, a sum equal to the debt is treated as payable then.

[*CTA 2009, s 964; ICTA 1988, s 701(12)*].

Grossing-up of estate income

[33.3] In the case of a UK estate, in arriving at the amount of estate income, the basic amounts treated as income of the beneficiary are 'grossed up' by the basic rate of tax or the dividend ordinary rate, depending on the type of income and the tax year in which it arose. (Certain income arising before 2008/09 fell to be grossed up at the 20% savings rate of tax.) The estate income is then treated as having borne income tax at that rate or rates.

In determining the rate applicable, it is assumed first that amounts are paid to beneficiaries out of the different parts of the aggregate income of the estate in such proportions as are just and reasonable for their different interests. Secondly, it is assumed that payments are made from those parts bearing tax at the basic rate before they are made from those parts bearing tax at the dividend ordinary rate. (Before 2008/09, payments were assumed to be made firstly from income bearing tax at the basic rate, then from income bearing tax at the savings rate and lastly from income bearing tax at the dividend ordinary rate.)

If some of the aggregate income of the estate is income *treated as* having suffered tax at source, e.g. life assurance gains and UK stock dividends, it is assumed that an amount is paid from other income in priority to that income. The above assumptions are then made in relation to each part of the payment.

Grossing up is applicable to payments out of a foreign estate only in respect of certain sums *treated as* having suffered tax at source, so that, for example, life insurance gains are grossed up at the basic rate (before 2008/09 at the savings rate) and UK stock dividends are grossed up at the dividend ordinary rate. No repayment of such notional tax can be made.

See Tolley's Income Tax for the rates of income tax applicable to different types of income.

[*CTA 2009, ss 941, 942, 946, 962, 963; ICTA 1988, ss 695(2)–(4)(7), 696(3)(4)(6)(9), 698(3), 699A, 701(3A)*].

Classes of interest

Absolute interests

[33.4] A corporate beneficiary with an absolute interest is chargeable to corporation tax on income treated as arising in an accounting period from the interest if:

(a) it has an 'assumed income entitlement' for that accounting period; and
(b) a payment is made in respect of the interest in the accounting period and before the end of the administration period.

For the accounting period in which the administration period ends (the '*final accounting period*'), income is treated as arising if the company has an assumed income entitlement for that accounting period (whether or not any payments are made).

Subject to the grossing-up provisions in **33.3** above, the amount so treated as income for an accounting period is the lower of the:

(i) total amount of all sums paid in the accounting period in respect of the interest; and

(ii) company's assumed income entitlement for the accounting period.

For the final accounting period, the amount is the company's assumed income entitlement for that accounting period. Where, however, the residuary income of the estate for the '*final tax year*' (i.e. the tax year in which the administration period ends) is nil as a result of the allowable deductions exceeding the aggregate income of the estate, the amount for the final accounting period is reduced by the excess (or, where the interest is in part of the residue only, a just and reasonable part of that excess).

A company's '*assumed income entitlement*' for an accounting period is the excess of the total of the company's share of the residuary income of the estate (less, in the case of a UK estate, income tax on that amount at the appropriate rate) for that accounting period and for each previous accounting period for which it held the interest over the total of the amounts (before grossing-up) relating to the interest in respect of which the company was liable to tax for all previous accounting periods (or would have been liable had it been within the charge to corporation tax).

A company's share of the residuary income of an estate is determined firstly by reference to a tax year and then apportioned to the accounting periods (if more than one) coinciding with that tax year.

If the total of all sums paid during or payable at the end of the administration period in respect of the interest (grossed-up, in the case of a UK estate, at the basic rate for the tax year of payment or, where applicable, the final tax year) are less than the total of the company's shares of the residuary income for all tax years, the deficiency is applied to reduce its share of the residuary income, firstly for the final accounting period, then for the previous accounting period and so on.

[*CTA 2009, ss 937, 938, 943, 948, 950–952; ICTA 1988, ss 695(1), 696(2)(3)(3A)(3B)(4)(5)(8), 697(2)(3), 701(3A)(13), 702*].

Limited interests

[33.5] Subject to the grossing-up provisions in **33.3** above, sums paid (including assets transferred, debts released etc.) to a corporate beneficiary with a limited interest *during administration* are treated as its income for the accounting period of payment and are chargeable to corporation tax accordingly. Any amount which remains payable in respect of the limited interest *on completion of administration* is treated as income of the company for the accounting period in which the administration period ends. If the interest ceases earlier, any amount then remaining payable is treated as income for the accounting period in which the interest ceased.

[*CTA 2009, ss 939, 944; ICTA 1988, s 695(2)–(4)*].

Discretionary interests

[33.6] The company in whose favour the discretion is exercised is charged to corporation tax on the total payments made in an accounting period in exercise of the discretion, grossed up, where appropriate, as indicated at **33.3** above.

[*CTA 2009, ss 940, 945; ICTA 1988, s 698(3)*].

This applies whether the payments are out of income as it arises, or out of income arising to the personal representatives in earlier years and retained pending exercise of the discretion. See HMRC SP 4/93.

Foreign estates

[33.7] Where UK corporation tax is charged for an accounting period on estate income from a foreign estate and UK income tax has already been borne by part of the aggregate income of the estate for the 'relevant tax year', the company may make a claim for the corporation tax charged to be reduced in accordance with the formulae in *CTA 2009, ss 960, 961*. The *'relevant tax year'* is the tax year in which the estate income would be treated as arising if the company were within the charge to income tax rather than corporation tax.

[*CTA 2009, ss 946(5), 960, 961; ICTA 1988, ss 695(5)(7), 696(7)(9), 698(3)*].

Successive interests

[33.8] Special rules apply to the calculation of estate income where there are two or more successive absolute or limited interests during the period of administration.

[*CTA 2009, ss 953–959; ICTA 1988, s 698(1A)(1B)(2)(4)–(6)*].

Adjustments etc. after administration period

[33.9] If, after the administration period ends, it is clear that a company's liability under the above provisions for an accounting period is greater or less than previously appeared, all necessary assessments, adjustments etc. can be made. Assessments may be made or adjusted, and relief may be claimed, at any time on or before the third anniversary of 31 January following the accounting period in which the administration period ended.

[*CTA 2009, s 965; ICTA 1988, s 700(1)–(3)*].

Information

[33.10] A personal representative has a duty to supply a corporate beneficiary on request with a statement of income and tax borne for an accounting period.

[*CTA 2009, ss 966, 967; ICTA 1988, s 700(5)–(6)*].

34

European Union Legislation

Introduction

[34.1] The UK became a member of the European Economic Community (EEC) (as was, now European Union) in 1972, on ratification of the Treaty of Rome (termed the 'EC Treaty'), and with the commencement of the *European Communities Act 1972*.

The main purpose of the EC Treaty was to bring about the gradual integration of the states within Europe and to establish a common market founded on the four freedoms of movement (for goods, services, people and capital). In order to pursue these goals the member states surrendered part of their sovereignty and gave the Community institutions (now institutions of the Union) the power to adopt legislation that would be directly applicable in the member states and take precedence over national law.

Since joining, the UK, along with the other member states, has entered into various additional treaties, which have developed the role of the Community and its institutions, the most recent being the Treaty of Lisbon. Post this treaty the European Community has become the European Union, and the areas where the Union has competence to legislate have been widened. In addition, the old treaties of the Communities were consolidated. The EC Treaty has now become the Treaty on the Functioning of the European Union ('TFEU') and, along with the updated Treaty on European Union ('TEU'), it establishes the Union, the internal market, the fundamental freedoms, and the Union's institutions, functions and legislative powers.

The following chapter provides an overview of EU Law as it applies to direct tax matters, and highlights some current key issues relevant to company taxation.

The judgments of the European Court of Justice ('ECJ') are extensive and wide ranging. They examine the principles and application of EU Law, and there is a considerable body of case law dealing with the application of EU Law to direct tax matters. Such case law is not considered herein.

EU Jurisdiction

[34.2] European Union law is effective in the UK by virtue of *European Communities Act 1972, s 2.*

EU law consists of the Treaties (the TEU and the TFEU), Regulations, Directives and Decisions made under delegated powers, together with the general principles of interpretation developed by the ECJ. The primacy of EU law is one of the general principles underpinning the foundation of the EU, and the ECJ has ruled that national courts must apply EU law 'in its entirety . . . and must accordingly set aside any provision of national law which may conflict with it, whether prior or subsequent to the community rule' (*Simmenthal* (C-106/77) [1978] ECR 629).

With regard to the application of a Directive, similarly the ECJ has held that 'wherever the provisions of a Directive appear . . . to be unconditional and sufficiently precise, those provisions may . . . be relied upon as against any national provision which is incompatible with the Directive in so far as the provisions define rights which individuals are able to assert against the State' (*Becker v Finanzamt Munster-Innenstadt* [1982] 1 CMLR 499).

Under these principles judgments of the ECJ have supremacy over domestic decisions, even if the proceedings commenced in another member state.

Whilst indirect taxes, such as VAT, are specifically within the competence of the EU, direct taxes are not. However, under the provisions as to the approximation of laws, Directives which have an impact on direct tax matters can be adopted, where they are necessary to ensure the functioning of the internal market. However, an extensive body of case law has developed in relation to direct tax, which deals with instances where such matters contravene or infringe a fundamental freedom enshrined in the Treaties.

EU Statements

[34.3] The primary law consists of the EU Treaties and the general principles, as highlighted in **34.3** above. Secondary law is made up of laws which give effect to the aims of primary law. Secondary legislation comprises statements of the European Council and European Commission and are graded under the EU Treaties as follows.

(a) **Regulations** are binding in their entirety and have general effect in all member states. They are directly applicable in the legal systems of member states and do not have to be implemented by national legislation.

(b) **Directives** are binding as to result but their general effect is specific to named member states. The form and methods of compliance are left to individual member states, which are normally given a specific period in which to implement the necessary legislation.

(c) **Decisions** are binding in their entirety and are specific to a member state, commercial enterprise or private individual. They take effect on notification to the addressee.

(d) **Recommendations and opinions** are not binding and are directed to specific subjects on which the Council's or Commission's advice has been sought.

Applicable Regulations and Directives

[34.4] As highlighted above, in contrast to the extensive application of EU legislation in the VAT sphere, as direct taxes are not within the competency of the EU, the Union only has limited powers to issue legislation in this sphere, such powers being based on ensuring the correct functioning of the internal market. Therefore direct taxes are currently subject to only the following specific measures.

(a) *Council Regulation 2137/85* (25 July 1985) concerning European Economic Interest Groupings.
(b) *Directive 90/434/EEC* (23 July 1990) concerning deferral of tax on income and gains on mergers, divisions, transfers of assets and exchanges of shares between companies of different member states (as amended by *Directive 2005/19/EC*, adopted on 17 February 2005 concerning the transfer of registered offices of European companies between member states).
(c) *Directive 90/435/EEC* (23 July 1990) as amended by *Directive 2003/123/EC* (2 February 2004) concerning distributions of profits to parent companies.
(d) *Directive 2003/48/EC* (3 June 2003) concerning the taxation of savings income.
(e) *Directive 2003/49/EC* (3 June 2003) concerning interest and royalty payments.
(f) *Directive 2005/19/EC* (17 February 2005) concerning mergers.

However, as noted above, the case law of the ECJ considers the application of EU law to direct taxes in the member states where a possible infringement is in point. As often repeated by the ECJ: 'although direct taxation falls within their competence, the Member States must nonetheless exercise that competence consistently with Community law' (*Manninen* C-319/02 para 19) [2004] ECR I-7477.

See also **34.5** below on the European Company.

As regards (a), see the related UK legislation at **61.15 PROFIT COMPUTATIONS**, and as regards (b), **17.14, 17.21 CAPITAL GAINS**. As regards (c), see **32.14 DOUBLE TAX RELIEF**. As regards (d), see **66.14 RETURNS** and as regards (e), see **46.2 INCOME TAX IN RELATION TO A COMPANY**. As regards (f), see **17.14** and **17.21**

For a case on the application of *Directive 90/434/EEC*, see *Leur-Bloem v Inspecteur der Belastingdienst/Ondernemingen Amsterdam 2: C-28/95* [1998] QB 182, [1997] ECR I-4161, ECJ. For a case on the application of *Directive 90/435/EEC* see joined cases *Denkavit International BV: C-283/94, VITIC Amsterdam BV: C-291/94 and Voormeer BV v Bundesamt fur finanzen: C-292/94* [1996] ECR I-5063.

On 16 March 2011 proposals for a new directive introducing a common consolidated corporate tax base (CCCTB) were released. The draft directive is currently being reviewed by the Member States. Such a directive would need to be agreed upon unanimously by all Member States before becoming law. See further Future Directions at **34.6** below.

The *Finance Act 2011* includes provisions in *Sch 25* for the implementation of the 2010 updated Directive on the mutual assistance for the recovery of taxes, *Directive 2010/24/EU*. Pursuant to this Directive member states will assist each other in the recovery of tax claims, including exchanging information as to such claims and pursuing recovery at the other state's request.

In addition to the above, *Convention 90/436/EEC* (23 July 1990), concerning arbitration in double taxation disputes, came into force on 1 January 1995. See **5.13 ANTI-AVOIDANCE.**

The European Company/Cooperative

[34.5] In order to achieve an internal market (and a level playing field for businesses within the EU) there is a need for companies to be able to undertake activities such as mergers, and relocation of corporate seats, without having to consider restrictions imposed by the company law of each member state. In the absence of full harmonisation of such law across member states, it was considered a legal form at EU level would be beneficial.

The European Public Limited-Liability Company Regulations 2004 (SI 2004 No 2326) give effect to *The European Company Statute Regulation (Council Regulation (EC) No 2157/2001) and Directive 2001/86/EC*, which was adopted on 8 October 2001 (see European Commission Press Release IP/01/1376), and applies to all member states with effect from 8 October 2004. It creates the legal framework for a new corporate entity, the European Company or 'Societas Europaea' (SE), to facilitate cross-border activities within the European Union including cross-border mergers.

The new form of company, which is entirely voluntary and available to commercial bodies which operate in more than one member state, is a European public limited-liability company registered in one of the member states, with a minimum share capital of 120,000 euros. The company can be formed in a number of ways as set out in the *Regulations* (broadly formation by merger, formation of a holding SE or a subsidiary SE, or by conversion of a public limited company into an SE). (DTI Press Release 13 September 2004.)

On 22 July 2003 *Council Regulation 1435/2003/EC* was adopted, along with an associated Directive 2003/72/EC which creates a European Cooperative Society — 'Societas Cooperative Europaea' (SCE). Similarly to an SE the SCE is a capital company limited by shares. It has legal personality after it has been registered in the national company register of a Member State. Its subscribed capital is at least 30,000 euros. The SCE provisions were implemented in the UK by the *European Cooperative Society Regulations 2006 (SI 2006 No 2078)*.

The SE and SCE Council Regulations do not contain any provisions relating to the taxation of an SE/SCE, nor do the applicable Directives. Therefore the direct tax position of the SE/SCE should be no different from the direct tax position of a plc or cooperative under national law, save for any specific requirements under the direct tax directives, such as the deferral of tax required under the *Mergers Directive* (see **34.4** above).

The provisions of *F(No2)A 2005* (*ss 51–65*) (which applied on the formation of an SE occurring after 31 March 2005) were replaced (via regulations, see below) to comply with EU Mergers Regulations. The new legislation, essentially reiterates the old rules applying to the formation of an SE but then extends these provisions to cover cross-border mergers forming SCE's (as from 18 August 2006).

CTA 2009 now includes the provisions dealing with the tax consequences of the formation of an SE by merger of two or more companies resident in different member states, and an SCE by merger of two or more cooperative societies, one of which is registered under the Industrial and *Provident Societies Act 1965*.

The provisions cover the deferral of tax charges on the formation of the SE/SCE that would otherwise arise in respect of:

- capital gains and capital allowances (see **17.27 CAPITAL GAINS**);
- intangible assets (see **48.24**, **48.25 INTANGIBLE ASSETS**);
- loan relationships (see **54.67 LOAN RELATIONSHIPS**); and
- derivative contracts.

Anti-avoidance provisions ensure that the rules apply only to the formation of an SE/SCE by merger effected for *bona fide* commercial reasons and which is not part of a scheme or arrangements of which the main purpose (or one of the main purposes) is avoiding a liability to tax and where the merging parties (one or more of them) are not transparent for tax purposes.

There are provisions for obtaining advance clearance from HMRC that the transactions satisfy the anti-avoidance provision. The provisions have effect in relation to the formation of SEs occurring on or after 1 April 2005, or for SCEs occurring on or after 18 August 2006.

[*CTA 2009, merger provisions within Part 5 Loan Relationships, Part 7 Derivatives, Part 8 Intangible Assets; TCGA 1992, ss 140E–140G; F(No2)A 2005, ss 51–65 as amended by the Corporation Tax (Implementation of the Mergers Directive) Regulations 2007 and 2008 (SI 2007 No 3186 and SI 2008 No 1579)*].

Residence

For the residence for tax purposes of an SE/SCE transferring its registered office to the UK, see **65.2 RESIDENCE**.

Continuity on ceasing to be UK resident

If at any time a company ceases to be resident in the UK in the course of the formation of an SE by merger (whether or not the company continues to exist following the merger), *FA 1998, Sch 18* (company **RETURNS (66)**, **ASSESSMENTS (7)**, **APPEALS (6)**, etc.) applies after that time in relation to liabilities accruing and other matters arising before that time as if the company were still UK-resident and, if the company has ceased to exist, as if the SE were the company.

Where an SE transfers its registered office outside the UK and ceases to be UK-resident, *FA 1998, Sch 18* applies after that time in relation to liabilities accruing and other matters arising before that time as if the SE were still UK-resident.

[*F(No 2)A 2005, s 61*].

Future Directions of EU Law

Home state taxation and the CCCTB

Home State Taxation for SMEs

[34.6] The European Commission adopted a Communication in 2005 proposing that EU member states allow small and medium-sized enterprises (SMEs) to compute their taxable corporate profits according to the tax rules of the home state of their parent company or head office ('Home State Taxation'). The different national tax rates would then apply to the share of profits allocated to each member state according to an agreed allocation mechanism.

The system, which would apply to SMEs which establish subsidiaries or permanent establishments in another member state, would be voluntary for member states and would initially run as a pilot scheme for five years.

An SME would be defined in accordance with the general EU definition in *Commission Recommendation 2003/361/EC* familiar in all member states, that is, a company with less than 250 employees and having a turnover not exceeding €50 million and/or a balance sheet total not exceeding €43 million. The Commission suggests that member states may restrict the application of the scheme to small enterprises (companies with less than 50 employees and having a turnover not exceeding €10 million and/or a balance sheet total not exceeding €10 million).

The '*home state*' of a participating SME-group is defined as the country of tax residence of the lead company. In the case of doubt or dual residence, it would be the country in which the place of effective management (or central management and control) of the lead company is located and where this company is subject to corporation tax before entering the pilot scheme.

The Commission suggested a simple formula be used for apportioning the tax base between participating member states. It recommends using the respective share in a combination of the total payroll and overall turnover.

The scheme would apply to corporation taxes only but member states could apply national or local profit-related surcharges on the member state's share of corporation tax. Non-profit related local or regional taxes could also be levied under the rules of the member states involved.

However, notwithstanding the communication, the proposals appear to have stalled. Although Home State Taxation continues to be examined as a possible way forward with regard to the harmonisation of corporate taxes within the EU, the introduction of a common consolidated corporate tax base (CCCTB) has taken precedence with the adoption of a draft Directive in March 2011 — see further below.

See COM/05/702 and also European Commission Press Release IP/06/11 of 10 January 2006 (SWTI 2006 p 171).

CCCTB — Common Consolidated Corporate Tax Base

The CCCTB refers to a common tax base and a common profit determination system for tax purposes across the EU. Thus it is required to be designed and agreed upon at EU level.

The basic premise is that a group of companies operating in several member states would be taxed only once on the group's consolidated profits irrespective of the legal form of the entities within the group, and irrespective of their location. The group's consolidated EU income would be split amongst the member state in which the group entities operated. This allocation of income would be based on a predetermined formula, based on information such as turnover, asset value and payroll. Thereafter the member state would apply its own corporate tax rate to the allocated tax base. This approach would be aimed at large (quoted) groups of companies.

A public consultation was held in 2003 concerning the use of IAS/IFRS as a possible starting point for a common EU tax base, however, further research is currently been undertaken in this regard. Agreement would also be needed with regard to the position on losses, non-deductible items and the apportionment factors.

In July 2004 a non-paper on the common tax base was presented by the Commission and discussed at the informal ECOFIN meeting in September 2004. The discussions revealed broad support for the creation of a Commission Working Group to progress work on the common tax base.

On 2 May 2007 the Commission adopted a Communication on 'Implementing the Community Programme for improved growth and employment and the enhanced competitiveness of EU business: Further Progress during 2006 and next steps towards a proposal on the Common Consolidated Corporate Tax Base (CCCTB).'

For the meeting on 27–28 September 2007 the Commission Services prepared a working paper on 'CCCTB: possible elements of a technical outline' which sets out a possible outline of the principles of a Common Consolidated Corporate Tax Base by beginning to bring the various structural elements of the base together into a coherent set of rules.

The CCCTB continued to be the subject of further research and discussion until a draft Directive was finally published by the Commission on 16 March 2011.

Per the press release, in practical terms:

> 'the CCCTB would make it possible for companies or groups of companies to consolidate all profits and losses across the EU, thereby recognising their cross-border activity. The single consolidated tax return would be used to establish the tax base of the company, after which all Member States in which the company is active would be entitled to tax a certain portion of that base, according to a specific formula based on three equally-weighted factors (assets, labour and sales). This

would all be done through the tax authorities of the company's principal Member State (i.e. through a one-stop-shop system).

Under the proposed Directive, clear procedural rules are set out on how companies should opt-in to the CCCTB system, how they should submit their tax returns, how the relevant forms should be harmonised and how audits should be coordinated. For each company or group, the tax return for the whole of their activities within the EU would be filed through the tax authorities in their principle Member State, and this same Member State would be responsible for coordinating the appropriate checks and follow up on the return.'

The proposals make it clear that this is not an attempt to coordinate direct tax rates across the Union.

The draft directive is now being scrutinised by the Member States, which would need to agree unanimously to its implementation. However, in the absence of unanimity, it is possible that the Council (by qualifying majority) could invoke the enhanced co-operation procedure under the TEU/TFEU which would allow a group of member states (minimum of nine) to move forward with implementation, with the possibility of other member states following suit in the future.

35

Exempt Organisations

Introduction

[35.1] Certain companies, societies and other bodies are treated as exempt from corporation tax for the purposes of UK tax law. The benefit of such exemption is generally afforded organisations with charitable, social policy or international purposes. The position with regard to certain statutory bodies is considered at **68 STATUTORY BODIES**. The main exempt entities are listed below.

Agricultural societies

[35.2] Agricultural societies established to promote the interests of agriculture, horticulture, livestock breeding or forestry are exempt from tax on profits or gains 'from an exhibition or show held for the purposes of the society . . . applied solely to the purposes of the society'.

[*CTA 2010, s 989; ICTA 1988, s 510*].

See *Peterborough Royal Foxhound Show Society v CIR* KB 1936, 20 TC 249; *Glasgow Ornithological Association* CS 1938, 21 TC 445. An agricultural society may also qualify for relief as a charity.

Non-resident central banks

[35.3] Non-resident central banks as specified by Order in Council are exempt from tax on certain classes of income. The issue departments of the Reserve Bank of India and the State Bank of Pakistan are exempt from corporation taxes.

[*CTA 2010, s 988; ICTA 1988, s 517; TCGA 1992, s 271(8); ITA 2007, Sch 1 para 104*].

See **8.5** BANKS.

The British Museum, The Natural History Museum

[35.4] The British Museum and The Natural History Museum are defined as 'eligible bodies' within the charities provisions and are, on a claim, exempt from tax, including in respect of chargeable gains, as CHARITIES (**20**).

[*CTA 2010, ss 468, 475–477A, 490; ICTA 1988, s 507; TCGA 1992, s 271(6); Museums and Galleries Act 1992, Sch 8 para 1(8)(9)*].

Charities

[35.5] CHARITIES (**20**) are generally exempt.

The Crown

[35.6] The Crown is not within the taxing Acts. In addition it is specifically not subject to tax in respect of stock or dividends belonging to it (*ICTA 1988, s 49(2)*) see relevant case law *Bank voor Handel v Administrator of Hungarian Property* HL 1954, 35 TC 311, and *Boarland v Madras Electric Supply Corpn Ltd* HL 1955, 35 TC 612. But see also *ITA 2007 s 978; ICTA 1988, s 829(1)*) as to instances of assessment, deduction and payment of tax by public offices and departments of the Crown.

International organisations

[35.7] International organisations (e.g. the United Nations (*SI 1974 No 1261*)) may be specified by Order in Council as exempt from certain taxes (*International Organisations Act 1968*), as may certain financial bodies under the *Bretton Woods Agreement Act 1945* (e.g. the International Monetary Fund (*SI 1946 No 36*)) and other bodies under the *European Communities Act 1972* (e.g. the North Atlantic Salmon Conservation Organisation (*SI 1985 No 1773*)).

The International Development Association is exempt [*International Development Association Act 1960, s 3 and SI 1960 No 1383*] as is the International Finance Corporation [*International Finance Corporation Act 1955, s 3 and SI 1955 No 1954*].

Prior to repeal by *ITA 2007* on the grounds the exemption had become redundant the International Maritime Satellite Organisation was exempt from income and corporation tax on payments received under the agreement. [*ICTA 1988, s 515; TCGA 1992, s 271(5)*]. The exemption from capital gains tax for signatories remains.

The Treasury may also designate any of the international organisations of which the UK is a member (e.g. The European Bank for Reconstruction and Development (*SI 1991 No 1694*)) for the purpose of exemption from various requirements for the deduction of tax from payments made in the UK. [*ITA 2007, s 979(1); ICTA 1988, s 582A*].

Friendly societies

[35.8] **FRIENDLY SOCIETIES** (**37**) within *ICTA 1988, ss 460–463* are generally exempt.

The Historic Buildings and Monuments Commission for England

[35.9] The Historic Buildings and Monuments Commission for England is exempt from tax as an 'eligible body' under the charities provisions, on a claim, as if it is a charity the whole of whose income is applied only for charitable purposes. It is also exempt from tax on chargeable gains (without claim).

[*CTA 2010, ss 468, 475–477A, 490; ICTA 1988, ss 339(9), 507(1), 577(9); TCGA 1992, s 271(7)*].

Housing Associations and self-build societies

[35.10] Housing Associations and self-build societies have certain exemptions. See **45 HOUSING ASSOCIATIONS.**

Local authorities, etc.

[35.11] The income and gains of local authorities, local authority associations and health service bodies (as defined by *CTA 2010, ss 984–987; ICTA 1988, ss 842A, 519(3), 519A* are exempt from corporation tax. The Treasury may by order disapply the exemption for a specified activity, or class of activity, of an NHS foundation trust. See further **68 STATUTORY BODIES**.

[*CTA 2010, s 984; ICTA 1988, s 519; TCGA 1992, s 271(3); National Health Service and Community Care Act 1990, s 61(1); FA 2004, s 148; ITA 2007, Sch 1 para 235*].

HMRC guidance for NHS Foundation Trusts on the tax treatment of non-core health care commercial activities is available on the HMRC website (at www.hmrc.gov.uk/specialist/ct-nhs.htm).

For payments of interest by local authorities, see **46.12 INCOME TAX IN RELATION TO A COMPANY**.

National Heritage Memorial Fund

The National Heritage Memorial Fund is classed as an 'eligible body' under the charities provisions and has the same exemptions as **CHARITIES (20)**. A claim must be made, except in relation to chargeable gains.

[*CTA 2010, ss 468, 475–477A, 490; ICTA 1988, s 507(1); TCGA 1992, s 271(7)*].

Scientific research associations

[35.12] A scientific research association is granted the same exemptions from tax as a charity (see **20 CHARITIES**). It is exempted from corporation tax on capital gains if it falls within the requirements set out at *CTA 2010, s 469*:

(a) the Association has as its object the undertaking of scientific research which may lead to or facilitate an extension of any class(es) of trade (and prior to 1 January 2008, is approved for these purposes by the Department of Trade and Industry (DTI)); and

(b) it is prohibited by its Memorandum or similar instrument from distribution of its income or property, in any form, to its members (other than as reasonable payments for supplies, labour, power, services, interest and rent).

In relation to any accounting period of a scientific research association beginning on or after 1 January 2008:

- the above requirement for approval by the DTI was dropped;
- the reference in (a) above to 'scientific research' changed to 'research and development' (within the meaning given by *CTA 2010, s 1138; ICTA 1988, s 837A* — see **64.1 RESEARCH AND DEVELOPMENT EXPENDITURE**);
- it is clarified that the exemptions will relate to the accounting period for which the claim is made;
- the Treasury has issued *SI 2007 No 3426* which specifies:
  - (i) what is and is not an Association for these purposes;
  - (ii) circumstances in which an association is to be deemed to have, or not to have, research and development as its object;
  - (iii) circumstances in which research and development is to be deemed capable or incapable of achieving the objectives in (a) above; or
  - (iv) what is to be deemed to be, or not to be, a class of trade for these purposes.

[*CTA 2010, ss 469–470, et seq; ICTA 1988, s 508; TCGA 1992, s 271(6)(b); F(No 2)A 2005, s 13; SI 2007 No 3424; SI 2007 No 3426*].

See also **64.10 RESEARCH AND DEVELOPMENT EXPENDITURE** and **71.64 TRADING EXPENSES AND DEDUCTIONS** as regards relief for contributions to scientific research organisations.

Simon's Taxes. See C5.135.

Statutory bodies

[35.13] Some **STATUTORY BODIES** (**68**) receive a measure of exemption.

Pension schemes

[35.14] Registered pension schemes from 6 April 2006. A new pension schemes tax regime, introduced by *FA 2004*, came into force on 6 April 2006. It fully replaces the pre-existing rules for occupational pension schemes, personal (and stakeholder) pension schemes and retirement annuity schemes.

[*TCGA 1992, s 271(1A); FA 2004, ss 186, 187(4); ITTOIA 2005, Sch 1 para 644*].

For details of this regime, including charges made on scheme administrators and charges and surcharges for unauthorised payments, and the changes brought in by *FA 2011*, see Tolley's Income Tax under Pension Provision for 2006–07 onwards. A brief overview of the provisions is outlined below.

A registered pension scheme is exempt from income tax on income derived from investments (including futures contracts and option contracts) or deposits held for the purposes of the scheme. [*FA 2004, s 186; FA 2006, s 158, Sch 21 para 7*]. In addition a gain accruing on a disposal of scheme investments is not a chargeable gain for capital gains tax purposes. [*TCGA 1992, s 271(1A)*]. This is subject to exceptions where income is derived from certain property held by self-directed schemes or where gains are realised from such property.

An individual aged under 75 is entitled to tax relief on the contributions made to a registered pension scheme during a tax year if they are, in general, resident in the UK during the year (at some point) and have relevant UK earnings. '*Relevant UK earnings*' means employment income; income from a trade, profession or vocation; income from a furnished holiday lettings business; or patent income charged to tax under *ITTOIA 2005*. The individual is entitled to relief on contributions up to the total amount of their relevant UK earnings chargeable to income tax for the year — and relief for contributions up to £3,600 applies in any event.

The annual allowance is the amount by which pension savings in a registered pension scheme (the 'total pension input') are allowed to increase each year. 'Pension input' broadly means the employee's plus employer's pension contributions in the tax year. The annual allowance for 2010/11 is £255,000. The *Finance Act 2011* reduces this allowance to £50,000 for 2011/12.

However, annual increases in the capital value of a pension over and above this limit will be subject to a tax charge — the annual allowance charge of 40% (the *FA 2011* changes this rate to the appropriate income tax rate for the taxpayer). The charge is payable by the individual member and is declared on the self-assessment return — per *FA 2011* changes the taxpayer can elect for the charge to be paid by the pension scheme out of their pension benefits.

Further restrictions are placed on the total value of the pension fund over the individual's lifetime – the lifetime allowance – for 2010/11 and 2011/12 this is £1.8m. The *Finance Act 2011* reduces this for 2012/13 to £1.5m (subject to transitional provisions). Where pension funds have been built up and the capital value exceeds the lifetime allowance, a tax charge will be levied on the excess — the 'lifetime allowance charge'.

The charge is triggered by a 'benefit crystallisation event', for example where payments are made from the retirement fund, such as the payment of a pension or a lump sum. There will be a charge on the amount crystallised to the extent that payments from the fund exceed the lifetime allowance at the date of the benefit crystallisation event. The excess is charged at 25% to the extent that it is used to buy a pension and at 55% where it is taken as a lump sum.

The liability for the lifetime allowance charge is jointly and severally on the individual member and the scheme administrator. In practice, the scheme administrator will deduct the relevant tax from the fund and pay it over to HMRC.

Further details as to the pension provisions and how the changes in *FA 2011* will affect such provision, can be found in Tolley's Income Tax.

Pension Protection Fund

The Pension Protection Fund (PPF) (set up by *Pensions Act 2004* to assume responsibility for final salary occupational pension schemes (and other pension schemes with defined benefit elements) whose sponsoring employers have become insolvent, leaving insufficient assets in the scheme) is to be given broadly equivalent tax treatment to that of an HMRC-approved occupational pension scheme for 2005/06 (see Tolley's Income Tax under Retirement Schemes) and that of a registered pension scheme for 2006/07 onwards (see Tolley's Income Tax under Pension Provision after 5 April 2006).

Simon's Taxes. See E7.1–E7.5.

Trade Unions

[35.15] Registered trade unions which are precluded from assuring more than £4,000 by way of gross sum or £825 p.a. by way of annuity for any one person and which make a claim, are exempt from corporation tax on qualifying income or gains. An annuity contract which is a registered pension scheme is ignored for these purposes, as is an annuity contract issued and held in connection with a registered pension scheme (other than an occupational scheme). The limits may be increased by Treasury order.

The exemption is granted in respect of non-trading income and chargeable gains which are applicable and applied for the purpose of 'providing benefits', i.e. sickness, injury and superannuation payments, payments for loss of tools, etc. This includes legal expenses incurred in representing members at Industrial Tribunal hearings of cases alleging unfair dismissal, or in connection with a member's claim in respect of an accident or injury he has suffered, and general administrative expenses of providing such benefits. (HMRC Statement of Practice, SP 1/84).

The exemption also applies to employers' associations registered as trade unions and to the Police Federations for England and Wales, Scotland, and Northern Ireland, and other police organisations with similar functions.

[*CTA 2010, ss 981–983; ICTA 1988, s 467*].

Simon's Taxes. See D7.635.

Unit trusts, investment trusts and VCTs

[35.16] Unit trusts (**52.5 INVESTMENT FUNDS**) and investment trusts (**53.1 INVESTMENT TRUSTS**) and **VENTURE CAPITAL TRUSTS** (**74**) are exempt from corporation tax on their capital gains.

[*TCGA 1992, s 100(1)*].

Clubs and societies

[35.17] For the concessionary exemption of certain clubs and societies, see **66.5 RETURNS**, and for the principle that a person cannot derive a taxable profit from trading with itself, see **56 MUTUAL COMPANIES**.

London Organising Committee of the Olympic Games Limited

[35.18] The London Organising Committee of the Olympic Games Limited (LOCOG), incorporated on 22 October 2004, is exempt from corporation tax with effect from that date. The provisions for the deduction of income tax at source in relation to annual payments (under *ITA 2007, Pt 15; ICTA 1988, s 349(1)*) do not apply to payments to LOCOG and a claim may be made for the repayment of income tax.

The Treasury may provide, by order, for the exemption to apply to a wholly owned subsidiary of LOCOG. They may also make further provision to restrict the application of the exemptions where it appears to the Treasury that LOCOG is acting in concert with a third party or is undertaking activities other than those in pursuance of the '*Host City Contract*' (under the *London Olympic Games and Paralympic Games Act 2006, s 1*). The Treasury may also repeal this provision by order. [*FA 2006, ss 65, 66*].

Similar exemptions may also be made, by order, in relation to the International Olympic Committee (IOC) and certain persons owned or controlled by it, and in relation to non-UK resident athletes and other non-resident persons temporarily in the UK to carry out Olympic-related business.

[*FA 2006, ss 67, 68*].

National Endowment for Science, Technology and the Arts

[35.19] The National Endowment for Science, Technology and the Arts from 2 July 1998, is an 'eligible body' under the charities provisions and is exempt from tax — see **20 CHARITIES**.

[*CTA 2010, ss 468, 475–477A, 490; ICTA 1988, s 507*].

36

Foreign Currency

Simon's Taxes. See D4.2.

Introduction

[36.1] Companies do not always prepare their accounts in the same currency as they operate in, and in addition neither of these may be sterling. The Taxes Acts make provision for the translation of these amounts into sterling for the purposes of UK corporation tax.

These currency provisions were introduced with effect for accounting periods beginning of or after 23 March 1995 and have been regularly updated since. Most recently the provisions have been re-written into the *CTA 2010*. The *Finance Act 2011* has introduced provisions with regard to UK resident investment companies providing an election for a specific currency to be used for tax purposes, along with targeted anti-avoidance provisions aimed at changes in functional currency.

This chapter outlines the current provisions, as updated, which apply to accounting periods beginning on or after 1 January 2005. Reference only is made to the provisions which applied to previous periods (at **36.8**).

Corporation tax currency provisions

[36.2] The *Finance Act 2000* updated and replaced earlier provisions for accounting periods beginning on or after 1 January 2000 and ending on or after 21 March 2000. For accounting periods beginning **on or after 1 October** 2002, these provisions were further modified by the *Finance Act 2002*.

These rules were replaced (and to an extent simplified) in *FA 2004* for periods of account beginning on or after 1 January 2005. The *FA 2009* introduced amendments for the carry forward and back of losses. The provisions have since been re-written into the *CTA 2010*.

[*FA 1993, s 95(6); FA 2000, s 105(4)(5); FA 2004, s 52, Sch 10 para 77; FA 2005, Sch 4 para 50*].

Simon's Taxes. See D4.2.

Post-FA 2009 rules

Changes to 2004 regime — sterling equivalents

[36.3] The purpose of the 2009 amendments is to enable companies accounting in a foreign currency to carry losses forward and back against profits, both the losses and the profits being expressed in the foreign currency. See **55.16** LOSSES for details of the provisions.

Post-FA 2004 rules

Periods of account beginning on or after 1 January 2005

The basic rule — sterling to be used

[36.4] For corporation tax purposes, a company's income and chargeable gains for an accounting period must be computed and expressed in sterling. This basic rule is subject to the exceptions outlined at **36.5** and **36.7** below. The position with regard to losses is also outlined therein.

[*CTA 2010, s 5; FA 1993, s 92(1); FA 2004, Sch 10 para 77*].

Operating and accounting currencies

[36.5] The application of the rule in **36.4** above is modified with regard to its application to certain profits or losses falling to be computed in accordance with generally accepted accounting practice. The rules consider three main circumstances:

(a) **Company operating in sterling and preparing accounts in another currency.** Where for a period of account a UK-resident company, in accordance with generally accepted accounting practice, prepares its accounts in a currency other than sterling but identifies sterling as its 'functional currency' in those accounts, then, for corporation tax purposes, sterling must be used to compute its profits or losses which fall to be calculated in accordance with generally accepted accounting practice as if the company prepared its accounts in sterling. [*CTA 2010, s 6*].

(b) **Company operating in currency other than sterling and preparing accounts in another currency.** Where for a period of account a UK-resident company, in accordance with generally accepted accounting practice, prepares its accounts in one currency but identifies another currency other than sterling as its 'functional currency', then, for corporation tax purposes, sterling must be used to compute its profits or losses which fall to be calculated in accordance with generally accepted accounting practice by:

(i) computing those profits or losses in the functional currency as if the company prepared its accounts in that currency; and
(ii) taking the sterling equivalent of those profits or losses. (see **36.7** below). [*CTA 2010, s 7*].

(c) **Company preparing accounts in currency other than sterling.** If, for a period of account a UK-resident company prepares its accounts in a currency other than sterling (the '*accounts currency*') and neither (a) nor (b) above applies, then, for corporation tax purposes, sterling must be used to compute its profits or losses which fall to be calculated in accordance with generally accepted accounting practice by:
(i) computing those profits or losses in the accounts currency; and
(ii) taking the sterling equivalent of those profits or losses (see **36.7** below).

This also applies to a non-UK resident company, if for a period of account the company prepares the accounts of its UK permanent establishment in a currency other than sterling. [*CTA 2010, ss 8, 9*].

'*Functional currency*' means the currency of the primary economic environment in which the company operates.

Where (b) above applies, it is assumed that any sterling amount mentioned in any other provision is its equivalent expressed in the company's functional currency. Where (c) above applies, it is assumed that any such sterling amount is its equivalent expressed in the company's accounts currency.

[*CTA 2010, ss 6–9, 16(4); FA 1993, ss 92(2), 92A–92C, 92E*].

Finance Act 2011

[36.6] The Finance Act 2011 amends *CTA 2010, Part 2 Ch 4* with regard to investment companies, applicable to periods of account beginning on or after 1 April 2011. The amendments counter avoidance involving changes in the functional currency of an investment company as applied to the loan relationship and derivatives regimes. In addition investment companies may elect prospectively for a different functional currency for tax purposes other than that used in the accounts.

A new *s 9A* is inserted into *CTA 2010*, providing for a UK resident investment company to elect for a currency to be its designated currency for tax purposes, if at the time the election is made either a significant proportion of the company's assets and liabilities are denominated in that currency, or the currency is the functional currency of another company and both companies meet the consolidation condition. The consolidation condition is met where the financial results of the UK resident investment company are required to be consolidated into accounts prepared under acceptable accounting practice by the other company or would be so required if such accounts were prepared.

The election has effect until the end of the period of account where the company makes another election, or the start of the period of account in which it is not the case that a significant proportion of the assets and liabilities of the company are denominated in the elected currency, or the consolidation condition is failed.

An election may be made or revoked at any time on or after 9 December 2010.

New *subsections (1A)* are inserted into *CTA 2010, ss 6* and *7* which allow for the elected currency of the investment company to be used for tax purposes. Under *s 6*, where the company has prepared its accounts in a currency other than sterling and has elected for sterling to be its designated currency, then the profits or losses for the period are calculated in sterling. Under *s 7*, where the company has prepared its accounts in one currency and had elected for a different non-sterling currency to be its designated currency, then the profits or losses for the period are first calculated in the designated currency and the sterling equivalent then taken. Where no election has been made then *sections 6* and *7* apply as normal.

Anti-avoidance provisions have also been introduced amending *CTA 2009, s 328* (loan relationships) and *CTA 2009, s 606* (derivative contracts) such that any exchange gain or loss arising in the first period of account under a new currency, which has changed as a result of an election under the new *s 9A* (above), or from a change in the company's functional currency, is not brought into account for tax purposes.

Sterling equivalents

[36.7] Where an amount is to be translated into its sterling equivalent as required by **36.5**(b) or (c) above or a sterling amount is to be translated into its equivalent in another currency, the translation is made as follows. The translation must be made:

- by reference to the average exchange rate for the accounting period; or
- if the amount to be translated relates to a single transaction, an appropriate spot exchange rate; or
- for accounting periods beginning on or after 29 December 2007, where the amount to be translated relates to more than one transaction, an exchange rate derived on a just and reasonable basis from appropriate spot exchange rates for those transactions.

This provision is subject to special rules where a translation into sterling is made for the purposes of calculating carried-forward or carried-back amounts: see **55.16 LOSSES**.

[*CTA 2010, ss 10, 11; FA 1993, ss 92B(4), 92C(5), 92D, 92E(4); FA 2009, s 38, Sch 18*].

Transitional provision

[36.8] Any trading losses, losses from an overseas property business, management expenses or non-trading deficits on loan relationships carried forward to a company's first period of account beginning on or after 1 January 2005, are to be translated to sterling using the London closing exchange rate for the last day of the previous period of account. [*FA 2004, Sch 10 para 79; FA 2005, Sch 4 para 51*].

Post-FA 2000 rules

[36.9] These rules applied to accounting periods beginning on or after 1 January 2000, as amended by *FA 2002*, such amendments being applicable to accounting periods beginning on or after 1 October 2002.

As above the basic rule is that sterling is to be used. However, there were rules applicable to the position where the accounts as a whole were in a foreign currency or the accounts were partly from statements in a foreign currency. Special provisions applied to the translation into sterling of a receipt or expense, or the value of any asset, liability or derivative contract.

See further the relevant sections within the applicable finance acts.

[*FA 1993, ss 92, 93, 93A, 94, 94AA, 94AB; FA 2000, s 105(1); FA 2003, Sch 27 para 3*].

For accounting periods beginning on or after 1 October 2002 the provisions dealing with partnerships which include companies have been included within the rules on **LOAN RELATIONSHIPS** (**54.72**) and **DERIVATIVE CONTRACTS LEGISLATION** (**30.49**).

37

Friendly Societies

[*ICTA 1988, ss 459–466*].

Simon's Taxes. See D7.601–D7.619.

Introduction

[37.1] There is no definition of a friendly society. However, to qualify as such, a new registered and incorporated society must have among its objects the conducting of insurance business with its members in return for voluntary contributions. When insurance business is not carried on, there is no requirement to be incorporated or registered.

Unregistered societies

[37.2] On making a claim, those with incomes not exceeding £160 p.a. are wholly exempt from corporation tax on both income and chargeable gains.

[*ICTA 1988, s 459*].

Registered and incorporated societies

Tax exemption

[37.3] On making a claim, registered and incorporated societies are exempt from corporation tax (on both income and chargeable gains) on profits from 'life or endowment business' (see below) where the necessary conditions are met. In addition where a policy is a 'qualifying policy' chargeable gains events do not arise. In certain situations business other than life or endowment business may be exempt (referred to as 'other business').

[*ICTA 1988, ss 460(1), 461(1), 461B(1), 462(2), Sch 15 para 3*].

'*Life or endowment business*' means any business of effecting or carrying out contracts of insurance which fall within *SI 2001 No 544, Sch I Pt II, paras I, II or III* (before 1 December 2001, any business within *Friendly Societies Act 1992, Sch 2 Head A, Classes I–III*); any pension business; and the issue of, or undertaking of liability under, policies of insurance on human life and the granting of annuities on human life ('life assurance business'); but, for contracts made before 1 September 1996, excluding sickness benefit policies unless at least 60% of the premiums is attributable to the sickness provision and the policy also assures a gross sum, independent of sickness, on which no bonus or addition may be declared. Also excluded is the granting of annuities bought with the proceeds of maturity or surrender of any other policy issued by the same society in the course of its tax exempt life or endowment business. For contracts made before 1 September 1996, and those made on or after that date where the effecting and carrying out of the contract also constitutes business within *SI 2001 No 544, Sch I Pt II, paras I, II or III*, business within *Pt II, para IV* is also included (and before 1 December 2001 a similar rule applied to business within *Friendly Societies Act 1992, Sch 2 Head A, Class IV*).

[*ICTA 1988, s 466(1)–(2); SI 2001 No 3629, Art 37*].

Incorporated societies

The *Friendly Societies Act 1992* enables friendly societies to incorporate and take on new powers, and to provide a wider range of financial services through subsidiaries. *F(No 2)A 1992, s 56, Sch 9* introduced a large number of amendments and additional provisions to ensure that registered societies which incorporate, and societies newly established as incorporated societies, receive the same treatment as regards tax exemption as existing registered societies and that the incorporation of a registered society neither affects those exemptions nor results in any tax charges as a result of the incorporation, either on the society or on its members.

Declining exemption

The general exemption from tax does not in any event apply in relation to profits attributable to contracts expressed at the outset not to be made in the course of tax-exempt 'life or endowment business', and either:

(i) made on or after 20 March 1991 for the assurance of gross sums; or
(ii) made before that date, where the society so elected.

A society could also elect for the exemption not to apply to profits attributable to contracts where, at the outset of the contract, it was assumed by the society not to be made in the course of tax-exempt life or endowment business (without being expressed either to be or not to be so), and the policy issued in pursuance of it was in the required form of a 'qualifying policy'.

[*ICTA 1988, ss 460(2)(ca), 462A*].

Conditions for exemption

Life or endowment business

[37.4] The funds underlying life policies and annuities constituting life or endowment business are exempt from tax, provided the relevant investment limits are not exceeded. These limits state that the exemption does not apply to profits from pension or individual savings account business, or from other life or endowment business consisting of the granting of annuities exceeding £156 p.a., or of the assurance of gross sums under contracts under which the total premiums payable in any twelve-month period exceed a maximum figure as follows:

for contracts made after 30 April 1995	£270
for contracts made after 24 July 1991 and before 1 May 1995	£200
for contracts made after 31 August 1990 and before 25 July 1991	£150
for contracts made after 31 August 1987 and before 1 September 1990	£100

Where the premium under a contract made after 31 August 1987 and before 1 May 1995 was increased by a variation after 24 July 1991 and before 1 August 1992, or after 30 April 1995 and before 1 April 1996, the contract is treated for these purposes as having been made at the time of the variation.

In determining these limits, no account is taken of any bonus or addition declared upon an assurance or accruing thereon by reference to an increase in the value of any investments, and, in relation to premium limits, so much of any premium as relates to exceptional risk of death or disability is disregarded, as is 10% of premiums payable more frequently than annually. [*ICTA 1988, s 460(2)–(12)*].

Other business

A registered friendly society may claim tax exemption in respect of business other than life or endowment business if it is within one of the following categories:

(a) a society registered before 1 June 1973 which is not subject to a direction withdrawing such exemption (see below);

(b) a society registered after 31 May 1973 whose business is limited to the provision of benefits for employees of a particular employer or for any other group of persons approved by HMRC for this purpose.

If a society registered before 1 June 1973 begins life or endowment business (see **37.3**), or enlarges the scale or changes the character of such business, HMRC may direct that it is to be treated as registered after 31 May 1973.

Similar provisions are made also for incorporated societies which were, before incorporation, registered friendly societies that were entitled to exemption in respect of 'other business'. [*ICTA 1988, ss 461–461C; SI 2001 No 3629, Arts 33, 36*].

Exclusions from exemption

[37.5] Profits arising from 'life or endowment business' (see **37.3** above) are not within the exemption if:

(a) the society was registered after 31 December 1957 and issued a single premium policy during the three months to 3 May 1966, or is an incorporated successor to such a society;

(b) the profits relate to profits from gross roll-up business;

(c) the profits are attributable to contracts made on or after 20th March 1991 and expressed at the outset not to be made in the course of tax exempt life or endowment business.

[*ICTA 1988, s 460(2)*].

Where the rules are altered or there are amalgamations or acquisitions of societies, the exemption or non-exemption of previous contracts is unaffected. [*ICTA 1988, s 460(7)–(10)*].

Conditions for qualification

[37.6] For qualifying policies, taxable chargeable events only arise in the case of early termination, or discontinuance of premiums (note, non-qualification does not prevent application of the exemption enjoyed by a society unless the loss of qualification arises from a breach of limits through aggregation of policies with the particular society). [*ICTA 1988, s 462(1)(a)*]. The following conditions must be satisfied in respect of all policies issued by a society under contracts made after 3 May 1966.

(a) the interval (the 'term' of the policy) between the making of the insurance (or, if the term started within the previous three months, the commencement of the term) and payment of the sum assured (or of the first instalment of the annuity) is at least ten years, with a saving for sums payable on the death or retirement due to ill health of the life insured or the person liable to pay the premiums. This requirement is reduced to five years from the beginning of the term if the payment is made to an infant and the premium payable in any year does not exceed £13, or if the payment is one of a series payable at intervals of five years or more, each of which (other than the final payment) does not exceed four-fifths of the premiums paid since the preceding payment.

(b) the premiums are of equal or rateable amounts, payable at intervals not exceeding one year over the whole term of the policy. For this purpose, the term of the policy excludes any period after the life insured or person liable to pay the premiums attains a specified age, provided that at least ten years of the term has then elapsed. A policy providing for commutation of future premiums after the expiration of ten years or of half the term (whichever occurs earlier), or when the person liable to pay the premiums becomes non-resident, is nevertheless deemed to satisfy these conditions. Premiums may also be paid by surrendering a sum which has become payable on the maturity of any other policy issued by the same society (or by a predecessor of it), in the course of its tax-exempt 'life or endowment business', to the person liable to pay the premiums or to his parent, and they may be waived by reason of disability.

(c) the total premiums and benefits applicable to the member from all societies in respect of exempt business must not exceed the limits detailed at **37.4**.

[*ICTA 1988, Sch 15 para 3(2)–(4)*].

A policy issued by a friendly society is a '*qualifying policy*' only if it meets the conditions at (a), (b) and (c) above, and if in addition the minimum sum assured is at least 75% of the total premiums payable and (in relation to contracts with a 'new society' made before 25 July 1991) it is with a member over the age of 18 years. [*ICTA 1988, Sch 15 para 3(1)*]. A health insurance policy ceases to be a qualifying policy if the rights conferred by it are surrendered in whole or part. For the detailed application of the 75% test, see *ICTA 1988, Sch 15 paras 3(5)–(11), 4*. In the case of a society which is not a 'new society', a policy can be a qualifying policy even if it was made with a person under 18 years of age or the rights have been wholly or partly surrendered. Where a society which is not a 'new society' begins carrying on tax exempt life or endowment business, or carrying on such business on an enlarged scale or of a new character, HMRC may direct that it be treated, in respect of new business, as if it were a 'new society'. [*ICTA 1988, s 465*].

'*Policy*' includes an instrument evidencing a contract to pay an annuity on human life. [*ICTA 1988, s 466(2)*].

A '*new society*' is a society registered after 3 May 1966, or one registered in the previous three months which did not carry on any life or endowment business during that period, or an incorporated society, provided that it was not, before incorporation, excluded from being a new society. [*ICTA 1988, s 466(2)*].

A friendly society includes all its branches. A society formed on the amalgamation of others is treated as being different from those others. However, if each of those others was within the exemption, and at least one was not a 'new society', the society resulting from the amalgamation is treated as having been registered before 4 May 1966.

[*ICTA 1988, s 466*].

Before 19 March 1985, broadly similar conditions applied, except for the requirement that policies be 'qualifying policies' (which was not necessary as all friendly society policies were qualifying policies) and absence of provision for a waiver of the requirement as to regular rateable premiums in cases of disability.

There are transitional provisions under which profits arising from certain policies issued in respect of insurances made after 31 May 1984 and before 19 March 1985, which either do not meet the 75% test under *ICTA 1988, Sch 15 para 3(5)–(11)* (see above) or fail to satisfy the conditions in *para 3(2)* (see above), are excluded from the exemption. The conditions in *section 460(1)* (see above) do not apply in respect of such policies. [*ICTA 1988, s 462(1)*].

Simon's Taxes. See **D7.613**.

Taxable societies

[37.7] Life and endowment business which is not exempt is treated in the same way as mutual insurance business, or other long term business, carried on by insurance companies, subject to regulations made by the Treasury. Transfers (in whole or part) of the business of a friendly society to another society or to a company which is not a friendly society are treated in the same ways as transfers of long term business between insurance companies. Amalgamations of friendly societies and their conversion into companies which are not friendly societies, and transfers of long term business of insurance companies to friendly societies, are also treated in the same ways as transfers of long term business between insurance companies. In each case, the transfers are subject to Treasury regulations (see below).

[*ICTA 1988, s 463*].

The Treasury regulations are consolidated in *SI 2005 No 2014 (Friendly Societies (Modification of the Corporation Tax Acts) Regulations 2005*, as modified by *SI 2007 No 2134* and *SI 2008 No 1942 (The Friendly Societies (Transfers of Other Business) (Modification of the Corporation Tax Acts) Regulations 2008)*. The 2005 Regulations modify the life assurance tax provisions to take into account changes made by *F(No 2)A 2005* and by the Financial Services Authority ('FSA') to their Handbook. See **56 MUTUAL COMPANIES.**

Societies deregistering

[37.8] Where a society ceases to be registered under *Friendly Societies Act 1992, s 91*, its existing tax exempt life and endowment business and any other exempt business, in so far in each case as it relates to contracts already entered into, continue to be exempt from corporation tax on income or chargeable capital gains arising from the exempt business. Life and endowment and other exempt business are each treated as a separate business. In the latter case, the exemption is lost if the benefits are increased. [*ICTA 1988, ss 460(11)(12), 461(4), 461B(5)–(7); SI 2001 No 3629, Art 33(3)*].

On or after 19 July 2007, when a friendly society's tax exempt business is transferred to an insurance company, the business transferred will be treated as a separate trade from the company's other insurance business and will remain exempt from corporation tax on income and chargeable gains. However, the favourable tax treatment is lost if premiums on policies transferred are increased above specified limits. HMRC are given wide powers to make regulations, which may affect periods before their date.

On or after 21 July 2008, where a friendly society which is exempt from corporation tax on its business other than life or endowment business transfers that business to another friendly society, the transferee will also be exempt on that business, unless there is an increase in the scale of benefits, in which case exemption is lost for that and subsequent accounting periods. The Treasury has introduced regulations to implement these provisions. [*FA 2008, s 44, Sch 18; SI 2008 No 1942*]. Where business, other than life assurance business, is transferred from a registered friendly society to an insurance company and the friendly society was exempt from corporation tax in respect of that business, the insurance company shall also have exemption on the contracts transferred. However, if the benefits are increased, the exemption will be lost for that accounting period and for future accounting periods. There is provision for modification of this legislation by statutory instrument.

Similar rules apply to incorporated friendly societies.

[*ICTA 1988, ss 460(11)(12), 461, 461B, 461D; SI 2001 No 3629, Art 33(3); FA 2008, s 44, Sch 18*].

38

Gains and Loss Buying

Cross-references. See also **19 CAPITAL GAINS — SUBSTANTIAL SHAREHOLDINGS, 35 EXEMPT ORGANISATIONS, 54.86 LOAN RELATIONSHIPS**.

Other sources. See Tolley's Capital Gains Tax.

Simon's Taxes. See C3.1, D2.3.

Buying gains or losses

[38.1] There are three sets of anti-avoidance provisions designed to prevent groups of companies buying and selling companies in order to make use of capital losses suffered by another company or group.

The first set of provisions, introduced in 1993 and described at **38.6–38.19** below, applies to prevent 'loss buying' where a group of companies with unrealised gains would acquire a company with realised or unrealised losses. The assets in question would then be transferred to the new group company at no gain/no loss as in **18.4** above, and the gain would then realised by that company, thus enabling the losses to be utilised against the gain. The provisions operate by restricting the deduction of losses accruing to a company before the time it becomes a member of a group or which accrue on assets held by it at such a time.

These provisions were supplemented in 1998 by provisions countering 'gain buying', where a group of companies with unrealised capital losses would acquire a company with a realised gain. The assets in question would then be transferred to the new group company, and the losses then realised by that company in the same accounting period as it realised the gain, thus enabling the losses to be utilised against the gain. Under the 1998 provisions the losses that can be set against a gain realised before a company joins a group are restricted to those that arose before it joined the group and those that arise after it joins the group on assets which that company held at the time of its joining the group. These provisions were repealed in their entirety by *FA 2006*, as below.

The last set of provisions was introduced in *FA 2006* as part of a package of anti-avoidance provisions relating to capital losses of companies (see **17.3** and **17.4 CAPITAL GAINS**). The provisions restrict the use of losses in both loss buying and gain buying situations where there is a change of ownership of a company as a result of arrangements with a tax avoidance purpose and are described below. The provisions apply in priority to the original loss buying provisions and replace the original gain buying provisions, which are repealed. The provisions are wide in scope and can apply in certain cases where there is no group of companies involved (see (c) below).The stated intention of the provisions is to ensure that relief for a company's capital losses should only be available against its own capital gains or those of companies that were under the same economic ownership both when the capital loss was realised and when the loss is used to reduce other gains. (Treasury Explanatory Notes to the Finance Bill 2006). Some companies were using the limited set off allowed under the *FA 2006* provisions to sell a company with a capital gain or loss, along with its subsidiaries, the shares in which were pre-change assets. *FA 2007, s 32* counteracts such arrangements by amending *TCGA 1992* (see **38.2** below).

Tax avoidance schemes

[38.2] Subject to the commencement provisions below, the provisions described below to restrict loss buying and gain buying apply where:

(A) there is a 'qualifying change of ownership' of a company (the '*relevant company*'); and

(B) the change occurs directly or indirectly in consequence of, or otherwise in connection with, any 'arrangements' the main purpose, or one of the main purposes, of which is to secure a 'tax advantage'.

For this purpose, there is a '*qualifying change of ownership*' of a company if any of the following occur.

(a) The company joins a group of companies. Whether a company is a member of a group is determined as in **18.2** above except that nothing in *TCGA 1992, s 170(10)* or *(10A)* is treated as preventing all the companies of one group from being regarded as joining another group when the principal company of the first group becomes a member of the other group at any time unless:

(i) the same persons own the 'shares' of the principal company of the first group immediately before that time and the shares of the principal company of the other group immediately after that time;

(ii) the principal company of the other group was not the principal company of any group immediately before that time; and

(iii) immediately after that time the principal company of the other group had assets consisting entirely (or almost entirely) of shares of the principal company of the first group.

References above to '*shares*' of a company are to the shares comprised in the company's issued share capital.

(b) The company ceases to be a member of a group.

(c) The company becomes subject to different control, i.e. one or more of the following occur:

(i) a person who did not previously have control (within *ICTA 1988, s 416*, now *CTA 2010, s 450*) of the company (whether alone or together with one or more others) comes to have control;

(ii) a person who previously had control of the company alone comes to have control of the company together with one or more others; or

(iii) a person ceases to have control of the company (whether the person had control alone or together with one or more others).

A company is not, however, treated as becoming subject to different control where it joins a group of companies in circumstances in which (a)(i)–(iii) above apply or where, although there is a change in the direct ownership of the company, it continues to be a 75% subsidiary of the same company.

'*Arrangements*' include any agreement, understanding, scheme, transaction or series of transactions, whether or not legally enforceable.

'*Tax advantage*' means relief or increased relief from, or repayment or increased repayment of, corporation tax or the avoidance or reduction of a charge or assessment to corporation tax or the avoidance of a possible assessment to corporation tax.

[*TCGA 1992, ss 184A(1)(4), 184B(1)(4), 184C, 184D, 288(1); FA 2006, s 70(2); CTA 2010, s 450*].

For HMRC's views on the application of the terms 'arrangements', 'tax advantage' and 'main purpose', see **17.4 CAPITAL GAINS** and HMRC Capital Gains Manual CG47024–47029. For HMRC's views generally, see HMRC Capital Gains Manual CG47020–47338.

Loss buying

[38.3] The loss buying provisions apply where conditions (A) and (B) above are met and the tax advantage under the arrangements involves the deduction from any chargeable gains of a loss (a '*qualifying loss*') accruing to the relevant company on a disposal of a 'pre-change asset' (see below).

In these circumstances, the qualifying loss is not deductible from a company's chargeable gains except where the gains arise on the disposal before 21 March 2007 of a pre-change asset.

It is immaterial whether the loss accrues before, after or at the time of the qualifying change of ownership, whether the loss accrues at a time when there are no gains from which it could be deducted, whether the tax advantage also involves something other than the deduction of a qualifying loss or whether the advantage would be secured for the company to which the loss accrues or any other company.

[*TCGA 1992, s 184A(1)(2)(5); FA 2006, s 70(2); FA 2007, s 32(2),(7)*].

Example

A Ltd is a company with realised by unrelieved capital losses. It has an issued share capital of 600 shares.

A Ltd issues 400 new shares with limited rights to X. The original shareholders sell their shares in A Ltd to group B, but because of the holding of X, A Ltd does not become a member of the B group.

The B group has just acquired assets that are expected to rise in value. The assets are transferred at cost to A Ltd in the expectation that when the assets are sold the gains arising will be reduced by the losses in A Ltd.

The issue of shares with limited rights and the sale of the remaining shares to the B group is an arrangement designed to obtain a tax advantage. The loss is a qualifying loss and therefore cannot be deducted from the post-change gains.

Gain buying

[38.4] The gain buying provisions apply where conditions (A) and (B) above are met and the tax advantage under the arrangements involves the deduction of a loss from a gain (a '*qualifying gain*') accruing to the relevant company or any other company on a disposal before 21 March 2007 of a pre-change asset. In these circumstances, only a loss arising on a disposal of a pre-change asset can be deducted from a qualifying gain.

It is immaterial whether the gain accrues before, after or at the time of the qualifying change of ownership, whether the gain accrues at a time when there are no losses which could be deducted from it, whether the tax advantage also involves something other than the deduction of a loss from a qualifying gain or whether the advantage would be secured for the company to which the gain accrues or any other company. [*TCGA 1992, s 184B(1)(2)(5); FA 2006, s 70(2); FA 2007, s 32(3)(8)*].

For HMRC examples of the operation of the provisions, see HMRC Guidance 'Avoidance through the creation and use of capital losses by companies', 27 July 2006, available on their website (www.hmrc.gov.uk).

Commencement

The above provisions apply for the purpose of determining the chargeable gains to be included in a company's total profits for accounting periods ending on or after 5 December 2005. Transitional rules apply, however, where the change does occur before that date and:

- the change occurs because the relevant company ceases to be a member of a group (whether or not it also occurs for any other reason);
- the principal company of the group continues to have control of the relevant company;
- (for disposals before 21 March 2007) the principal company does not, at or after the time of the change, join another group other than in circumstances in which (a)(i)–(iii) above apply;
- for disposals on or after 9 May 2007, there is no qualifying change of ownership of the principal company of the group directly or indirectly in consequence of, or in connection with, any arrangements with a main purpose of securing a tax advantage involving the deduction of a qualifying loss from a chargeable gain; and
- a qualifying loss or, for disposals before 21 March 2007, qualifying gain accrues to the relevant company or any other company on a pre-5 December 2005 disposal.

For disposals on or after 21 March 2007, where the transitional rules apply, the gain buying provisions have effect:

- so that a loss arising on a disposal of a pre-change asset can be deducted from a qualifying gain; and
- as if any asset held before the time of the change of ownership by any company meeting the following conditions were a pre-change asset. The conditions are that the company must have been a member of the relevant company's group immediately before the time of the change of ownership and that the company must, throughout the period beginning with that time and ending immediately after the asset's disposal, have remained under the control of the company which was the principal company of that group at that time.

For disposals before 21 March 2007, the provisions apply to the qualifying loss or gain as if any asset held before the time of the change of ownership by any company which was a member of the relevant company's group immediately before that time were a pre-change asset.

[*FA 2006, s 70(6)–(11); FA 2007, s 32(5),(6),(9)*].

Pre-change assets

[38.5] For the purposes of the above provisions, a '*pre-change asset*' is an asset held by the relevant company before the qualifying change of ownership occurs.

An asset ceases to be a pre-change asset on disposal by a company other than the relevant company if, after the qualifying change of ownership, it has been disposed of otherwise than by an intra-group no gain/no loss transfer within **18.4** above. If the company making the latter disposal retains an interest in or over the asset, that interest continues to be a pre-change asset.

If the relevant company or any other company holds an asset (*'the new asset'*) at or after the time of the qualifying change of ownership, the value of which derives in whole or in part from a pre-change asset, the new asset is also treated as a pre-change asset provided that the company concerned did not acquire the asset as a result of a transfer other than an intra-group no gain/no loss transfer. For this purpose, the cases in which the value of an asset is derived from another asset include any case where assets have been merged or divided or have changed their nature and where rights or interests in or over assets have been created or extinguished.

Where a pre-change asset is the 'old asset' for the purposes of *TCGA 1992, s 116*, (reorganisation of share capital involving qualifying corporate bonds (see Tolley's Capital Gains Tax)) the 'new asset' under that section is also a pre-change asset. Where a pre-change asset is the 'original shares' for the purposes of *TCGA 1992, ss 127–131* (reorganisation of share capital — see Tolley's Capital Gains Tax under Shares and securities), the 'new holding' under those provisions is also a pre-change asset.

Where one of the deferral provisions listed below applies to defer a gain on the disposal of a pre-change asset, so much of any gain or loss accruing on a subsequent occasion as accrues in consequence of the application of the deferral provision is treated as a gain or loss on the disposal of a pre-change asset. The provisions are:

- *TCGA 1992, s 139* (reconstruction involving transfer of business — see **17.11 CAPITAL GAINS**);
- *TCGA 1992, s 140* (transfer of assets to non-resident company — see **17.13 CAPITAL GAINS**);
- *TCGA 1992, s 140A* (transfer or division of UK business between companies in different EC member states — see **17.14 CAPITAL GAINS**);
- *TCGA 1992, s 140E* (cross-border merger leaving assets within UK tax charge — see **17.27** capital gains);
- *TCGA 1992, ss 152, 153* (rollover relief on the replacement of business assets — see **18.8** below); and
- *TCGA 1992, s 187* (postponement of charge on deemed disposal on company ceasing to be UK resident — see **65.8 RESIDENCE**).

If a pre-change asset is transferred by the relevant company to another company directly or indirectly in consequence of, or in connection with the arrangements in (A) above, and any of *TCGA 1992, ss 139*, *140A* or *140E* apply to the transfer, the asset is a pre-change asset in the hands of the transferee company. The above provisions for determining when an asset ceases to be a pre-change asset then apply as if the transferee company were the relevant company.

Pooled assets

Special identification rules apply where a pre-change asset (whether held by the relevant company or, as a consequence of an intra-group no gain/no loss transfer, by another company) consists of a 'section 104 holding' or '1982 holding' (see Tolley's Capital Gains Tax under Shares and securities — identification rules) of shares, securities or other assets dealt in without identifying the particular asset disposed of or acquired.

Such a holding (a '*pre-change pooled asset*') cannot be added to as a result of any disposal or acquisition taking place after the qualifying change of ownership. Any shares etc. that would otherwise be added to the pre-change pooled asset instead form or are added to a separate *s 104* holding (the '*other pooled asset*').

Shares etc. of the same class as those comprised in the other pooled asset which are disposed of at or after the time of the qualifying change of ownership are identified:

- first with shares etc. forming part of the other pooled asset;
- next with shares etc. forming part of the pre-change pooled asset; and
- finally, in accordance with the normal identification rules (see Tolley's Capital Gains Tax under Shares and securities — identification rules).

These identification rules apply even if some or all of the assets disposed of are separately identified by the disposal or by a transfer or delivery giving effect to it. Shares etc. disposed of by a company in one capacity are not identified with shares etc. which are held, or which can only be disposed of, in some other capacity. Shares or securities of a company are not treated as being of the same class unless they are so treated by the practice of a recognised stock exchange or would be if dealt with on such an exchange.

[*TCGA 1992, ss 184A(3), 184B(3), 184E, 184F; FA 2006, s 70(2)*].

Pre-entry losses — the 1993 rules

General outline and commencement

[38.6] Where the loss buying provisions at **38.2** above do not apply, *TCGA 1992, Sch 7A* restricts losses accruing to a company before the time it becomes a member of a group of companies and losses accruing on assets held by any company at such a time. The restriction is described in detail at **38.7–38.19** below.

The restrictions apply for the calculation of the amount to be included in respect of chargeable gains in a company's total profits for any accounting period ending after 15 March 1993. However, the restrictions apply only in relation to the deduction from chargeable gains accruing after 15 March 1993 of amounts in respect of, or of amounts carried forward in respect of:

(a) 'pre-entry losses' accruing, before it became a member of a UK capital gains group, to a company whose membership of that group began or begins after 31 March 1987; and
(b) losses accruing on the disposal of any assets so far as it is by reference to such a company that the assets fall to be treated as being or having been 'pre-entry assets' or assets incorporating a part referable to pre-entry assets.

The restriction does not apply where the loss buying provisions at **38.3** above apply.

[*TCGA 1992, s 177A, Sch 7A; FA 1993, s 88, Sch 8; FA 2006, s 70(3)*].

The restriction is widely drawn, and whilst its stated principal intention is to prevent the fiscal effectiveness of an acquisition of a 'capital loss' company (i.e. a company that has a *realised* allowable loss as its only commercial feature) it may also impinge on an acquisition of a company solely for commercial reasons where it becomes a member of a group whilst holding an asset which is later disposed of (whether by the company itself, or by another group member to whom the asset has been transferred) outside the group at a loss. Further restrictions are imposed by *FA 1994, s 94* in relation to the deduction of a loss from a chargeable gain where either the gain or the loss accrues after 10 March 1994. See **18.2** above as regards the definition of a group of companies for the purposes of these provisions.

The regime was partially relaxed by *FA 2011, Sch 11*, with effect from 19 July 2011 ('commencement'). The changes have effect regardless of whether a loss accrued before commencement and regardless of whether the company that had accrued the loss became a member of a relevant group before commencement. [*FA 2011, Sch 11, para 11*].

See HMRC Capital Gains Manual CG47500 *et seq*.

Simon's Taxes. See **D2.410–D2.455**.

Application and construction of TCGA 1992, Sch 7A

[38.7] *Schedule 7A* has effect, in the case of a company which is or has been a member of a group of companies (within *TCGA 1992, s 170*, see **18.2** above, and referred to as '*the relevant group*'), in relation to any 'pre-entry losses'.

A '*pre-entry loss*', in relation to a company, means any allowable loss that accrued to it at a time before it became a member of the relevant group or, prior to 19 July 2011, the 'pre-entry proportion' (see **38.8–38.11** below) of any allowable loss accruing to it on the disposal of any 'pre-entry asset'. [*TCGA 1992, Sch 7A para 1(1)(2)*].

A '*pre-entry asset*', in relation to any disposal, means any asset that was held, at the time immediately before the 'relevant event' occurred in relation to it, by any company (whether or not the one which makes the disposal) which is or has at any time been a member of the relevant group.

This definition was repealed by *FA 2011, Sch 11* from 19 July 2011. The new definition, which is effectively the same is at *TCGA 1992, Sch 7A para 7(4)*: a 'pre-entry asset' is an asset held by a company immediately before the entry date.

The '*relevant event*' occurs in relation to a company when it becomes a member of the relevant group provided that either the company is UK resident at that time or the asset is then a 'chargeable asset' in relation to it. If the company is an SE (see **17.27 CAPITAL GAINS**) resident in the UK and the asset was transferred to the SE as part of the process of its formation on or after 1 April 2005 by the merger by acquisition of two or more companies in accordance with *Council Regulation (EC) No 2157/2001, Arts 2(1)* and *17(2)*, the relevant event occurs when the asset becomes a chargeable asset in relation to the SE or, if at the time of the formation of the SE the asset was a chargeable asset in relation to a company which ceased to exist as part of the process of the formation of the SE, when the asset became a chargeable asset in relation to that company. In any other case a relevant event subsequently occurs when the company becomes UK resident or the asset become a chargeable asset in relation to it (whichever is the earlier).

For these purposes, an asset is a '*chargeable asset*' in relation to a company at a particular time if, on a disposal by that company at that time, any gain would be a chargeable gain and would be within the charge to corporation tax by virtue of *TCGA 1992, s 10* or *s 10B* (non-UK resident company trading in the UK through a permanent establishment (previously a branch or agency) — see **17.1 CAPITAL GAINS**) or, if the company is an SE formed on or after 1 April 2005, by virtue of the asset having been transferred to the SE on its formation.

[*TCGA 1992, Sch 7A para 1(3)(3A); FA 2000, Sch 29 para 7(2)(3)(6)–(9); FA 2003, Sch 27 para 2(3); F(No 2)A 2005, s 65(2)(3)(6)*].

These rules were repealed by *FA 2011, Sch 11* from 19 July 2011.

Subject to **38.9** below, an asset is not, however, a pre-entry asset if the company which held the asset at the time the relevant event occurred in relation to it is not the company which makes the disposal and since that time the asset has been disposed of otherwise than on the no gain, no loss basis of *TCGA 1992, s 171* (see **18.4** above), except where the company making the disposal retains an interest in or over the asset (when the interest is treated as a pre-entry asset). [*TCGA 1992, Sch 7A para 1(4); FA 2000, Sch 29 para 7(4)(6)–(8)*].

This rule was repealed by *FA 2011, Sch 11* from 19 July 2011 and replaced by an identical rule at *TCGA 1992, Sch 7A para 7(4A), (4B)*.

Subject to **38.9** below, an asset ('*the second asset*'), which derives its value wholly or partly from another asset ('*the first asset*') acquired or held by a company at any time, is treated as the same asset if it is held subsequently by the same company, or by any company which is or has been a member of the same group of companies as that company (e.g. a freehold derived from a leasehold where the lessee acquires the reversion). Where this treatment applies, whether under this provision or otherwise (e.g. under *TCGA 1992, s 43*, for which see Tolley's Capital Gains Tax), the second asset is treated as a pre-entry asset in relation to a company if the first asset would have been. [*TCGA 1992, Sch 7A para 1(8)*].

This rule was repealed by *FA 2011, Sch 11* from 19 July 2011 and replaced by an identical rule at *TCGA 1992, Sch 7A para 7(4C)*.

In relation to a pre-entry asset, references in *Schedule 7A* to '*the relevant time*' are references to the time when the relevant event occurred in relation to the company by reference to which that asset is a pre-entry asset. Where a relevant event has occurred in relation to a company more than once, an asset is a pre-entry asset in relation to that company if it would be a pre-entry asset in relation to that company in respect of any of those occasions, but in these circumstances any reference to the time when a relevant event occurred in relation to the company is a reference to the last such occasion. [*TCGA 1992, Sch 7A para 1(5); FA 2000, Sch 29 para 7(5)–(8)*].

This rule was repealed by *FA 2011, Sch 11* from 19 July 2011.

Subject to so much of *para 9(6)* (see **38.15** below) as requires groups of companies to be treated as separate groups for the purposes of *TCGA 1992, Sch 7A para 9*, if:

(a) the principal company of a group (the '*first group*') has at any time become a member of another group (the '*second group*') so that the two groups are treated as the same under *TCGA 1992, s 170(10)* or *(10A)* (see **18.2** above); and
(b) the second group, together (in pursuance of *TCGA 1992, s 170(10)* or *(10A)*) with the first group, is the relevant group,

then except where the circumstances are as in *TCGA 1992, Sch 7A para 1(7)* (below), the members of the first group are treated for the purposes of *Sch 7A* as having become members of the relevant group at that time, and not (by virtue of *TCGA 1992, s 170(10)* or *(10A)*) at the times when they became members of the first group. [*TCGA 1992, Sch 7A para 1(6); F(No 2)A 2005, s 65(4)*]. See *HMRC v Limitgood Ltd* [2009] EWCA Civ 177, [2009] STC 980 and *HMRC v Prizedome Ltd* [2009] EWCA Civ 177, [2009] STC 980.

The circumstances mentioned in *para 1(6)* are where:

(1) the persons who immediately before the time when the principal company of the first group became a member of the second group owned the shares comprised in the issued share capital of the principal company of the first group are the same as the persons who, immediately after that time, owned the shares comprised in the issued share capital of the principal company of the relevant group; and
(2) the company which is the principal company of the relevant group immediately after that time:
    (i) was not the principal company of any group immediately before that time; and
    (ii) immediately after that time had assets consisting entirely, or almost entirely, of shares comprised in the issued share capital of the principal company of the first group.

[*TCGA 1992, Sch 7A para 1(7)*].

Where an allowable loss accrues to a company under *TCGA 1992, s 116(10)(b)* (crystallisation of gain or loss on shares exchanged on reorganisation, etc. for qualifying corporate bonds, see Tolley's Capital Gains Tax and **38.13** below), that loss is deemed to accrue at the time of the reorganisation etc. for the purposes of deciding whether a loss accrues before a company becomes a member of the relevant group. [*TCGA 1992, Sch 7A para 1(9)*]. Likewise, the annual deemed disposals of unit trust etc. holdings of a life assurance company's long-term insurance fund under *TCGA 1992, s 212* are deemed to occur for this purpose without regard to the 'spreading' provisions of *TCGA 1992, s 213*. [*TCGA 1992, Sch 7A para 1(10)*].

Pre-entry proportion of losses on pre-entry assets

[38.8] This legislation (*TCGA 1992, Sch 7A, paras 2–5*), was repealed from 19 July 2011 (*FA 2011*). The previous rules are explained below.

Subject to **38.9–38.11** below, the '*pre-entry proportion*' of an allowable loss accruing on the disposal of a pre-entry asset is the allowable loss that would accrue on that disposal if that loss were the sum of the amounts determined, for every item of '*relevant allowable expenditure*' (i.e. expenditure within *TCGA 1992, s 38(1)(a)* or *(b)*), according to the following formula:

$$A \times \frac{B}{C} \times \frac{D}{E}$$

where:

A is the total amount of the allowable loss;
B is the amount of the item of relevant allowable expenditure concerned;
C is the sum of the total amount of all such relevant expenditure;
D is the length of the period beginning with 'the relevant pre-entry date' and ending with the relevant time or, if that date is after that time, nil (i.e. there is no pre-entry proportion if the relevant time precedes the relevant pre-entry date); and
E is the length of the period beginning with the relevant pre-entry date and ending with the day of disposal.

[*TCGA 1992, Sch 7A para 2(1)(2)(9); FA 1994, s 93(8)(a)*].

'*The relevant pre-entry date*', in relation to any item referred to above, is the later of 1 April 1982 and the date the asset was acquired or provided or, as the case may be, improvement expenditure became due and payable (such date being subject to the assumptions of *TCGA 1992, Sch 7A para 2(4)(5)* (below) and additionally, in relation to the deduction of a loss from a chargeable gain where either the gain or the loss accrues after 10 March 1994, to those of *para 2(6A)(6B)*). [*TCGA 1992, Sch 7A para 2(3); FA 1994, s 94(1)(2)(4)*].

Where any 'original shares' are treated as the same asset as a 'new holding' (within *TCGA 1992, s 127*), the above formula and (where applicable) the provisions in **38.9** below are applied:

(a) as if any item referred to above consisting in consideration given for the acquisition of the new holding had been incurred at the time the original shares were acquired; and
(b) where there is more than one such time, as if that item were incurred at those different times in the same proportions as the consideration for the acquisition of the original shares.

[*TCGA 1992, Sch 7A para 2(4); FA 1994, s 93(8)(b)*].

Without prejudice to (a) and (b) above, the formula is applied to any asset which:

(i) was held by a company at the time when it became a member of the relevant group; and

(ii) is treated as having been acquired by that company on *any* no gain/no loss corresponding disposal,

as if the company and every person who acquired that asset or 'the equivalent asset' at a 'material time' had been the same person and, accordingly, as if the asset had been acquired by the company when it or the equivalent asset was acquired by the first of those persons to have acquired it at a material time, and the time at which any expenditure had been incurred were to be determined accordingly. [*TCGA 1992, Sch 7A para 2(5)*].

A '*material time*' is any time before an acquisition of an asset in circumstances as in (ii) above and is, or is after, the last occasion before the occasion on which any person acquired that asset or the equivalent asset otherwise than on an acquisition which is within (ii) above, or is an acquisition by virtue of which any asset is treated as the equivalent asset; and the formula is applied in relation to any asset within (i) and (ii) above without regard to *TCGA 1992, s 56(2)* (consideration on no gain/no loss disposal deemed to include indexation allowance). [*TCGA 1992, Sch 7A para 2(6)*].

In relation to the deduction of a loss from a chargeable gain where either the gain or the loss accrues after 10 March 1994, and notwithstanding anything in *TCGA 1992, s 56(2)* (see above), where in the case of the disposal of any pre-entry asset any company has, between the relevant time and the time of the disposal, acquired that asset or 'the equivalent asset', and the acquisition was either an acquisition in pursuance of a no gain/no loss disposal under *TCGA 1992, s 171* (see **18.4** above) or an acquisition by virtue of which an asset is treated as 'the equivalent asset', the items of relevant allowable expenditure in the above formula, and the times they are treated as having been incurred, are determined on the assumption that the company by reference to which the asset in question is a pre-entry asset, and the company which acquired the asset or the equivalent asset as above (and every other company which has made such an acquisition), were the same person and, accordingly, that the pre-entry asset had been acquired by the company disposing of it at the time when it or the equivalent asset would have been treated as acquired by the company by reference to which the asset is a pre-entry asset. [*TCGA 1992, Sch 7A para 2(6A)(6B); FA 1994, s 94(1)(2)(4)*].

In relation to the deduction of a loss from a chargeable gain where either the gain or the loss accrues after 10 March 1994, for the purposes of the provisions in *TCGA 1992, Sch 7A para 2(5)(6)(6A)(6B)* (above), '*the equivalent asset*', in relation to another asset acquired or disposed of by any company, is any asset which falls in relation to that company to be treated (whether under *TCGA 1992, Sch 7A para 1(8)* (see **38.7** above) or otherwise) as the same as the other asset or which would fall to be so treated after applying, as respects other assets, the assumptions for which those provisions provide.

In relation to the deduction of a loss from a chargeable gain where both the gain and the loss accrue before 11 March 1994, for the purposes of the provisions in *para 2(5)(6)* (above), '*the equivalent asset*', in relation to the acquisition of any asset by any company, is any asset which (whether under *para 1(8)* or otherwise) would be treated in relation to that company as the same as the asset in question. [*TCGA 1992, Sch 7A para 2(7); FA 1994, s 94(1)(2)(4)*].

The above provisions and (where applicable) those in **38.9** below have effect where a loss accrues to a company under *TCGA 1992, s 116(10)(b)* (crystallisation of gain or loss on shares exchanged on reorganisation, etc. for qualifying corporate bonds; see **38.7** above), and the shares are treated under **38.9** below as including pre-entry assets, as if the disposal on which the loss accrues were the disposal of the shares assumed to be made by *section 116(10)(a)* at the time of reorganisation etc. [*TCGA 1992, Sch 7A para 2(8)*].

Where, by virtue of *TCGA 1992, s 55(8)*, the allowable loss (or part) accruing on the disposal of a pre-entry asset is attributable to an amount of rolled-up indexation, the total relevant allowable expenditure is treated for the purposes of *TCGA 1992, Sch 7A para 2* as increased by that rolled-up amount, each item of expenditure being treated as increased by the attributable proportion of the total. [*TCGA 1992, Sch 7A para 2(8A); FA 1994, s 93(8)(c)*].

Where *TCGA 1992, s 56(3)* applies to reduce the total allowable expenditure on the disposal of a pre-entry asset on which an allowable loss accrues, the amount of each item of relevant allowable expenditure is treated for the purposes of *para 2* as reduced by so much of that reduction as is attributable to it. [*TCGA 1992, Sch 7A para 2(8B); FA 1994, s 93(8)(c)*].

Disposals of pooled assets

[38.9] This legislation (*TCGA 1992, Sch 7A, paras 2–5*), was repealed from 19 July 2011 (*FA 2011*). The previous rules are explained below.

Subject to **38.10** and **38.11** below, the provisions below apply where any assets acquired by any company fall to be treated with other assets as indistinguishable parts of the same asset ('*a pooled asset*') and the whole or part of that asset is referable to pre-entry assets.

For the purposes of *Sch 7A*, where a pooled asset has at any time contained a pre-entry asset, the pooled asset is treated, until on the assumptions below all the pre-entry assets included in the asset have been disposed of, as incorporating a part which is referable to pre-entry assets, the size of that part being determined as below. [*TCGA 1992, Sch 7A para 3(1)(2)*].

Where there is a disposal of any part of a pooled asset and the proportion of the asset which is disposed of does not exceed the proportion of that asset which is represented by any part of it which is not referable to pre-entry assets (at the time of disposal), then that disposal is treated for the purposes of *Sch 7A* as confined to assets which are not pre-entry assets. Consequently, no part of any loss accruing on that disposal is treated as a pre-entry loss (except where *para 4(2)*, see **38.10** below, applies), and the part of the pooled asset which after the disposal is treated as referable to pre-entry assets is correspondingly increased (without prejudice to the effect of any subsequent acquisition of assets to be added to the pool in determining whether, and to what extent, any part of the pooled asset is to be treated as referable to pre-entry assets). [*TCGA 1992, Sch 7A para 3(3)(11)*].

Where such a disposal does give rise to such an excess, the disposal is treated for the purposes of *Sch 7A* as relating to pre-entry assets only so far as required for the purposes of the excess. Consequently:

(a) any loss accruing on that disposal is treated for the purposes of *Sch 7A* as an allowable loss on a pre-entry asset;
(b) the pre-entry proportion of that loss is deemed (except where *para 4(3)*, see **38.10** below, applies) to be the amount (in so far as it does not exceed the amount of the loss actually accruing) which would have been the pre-entry proportion under **38.8** above of any loss accruing on the disposal of the excess if the excess were a separate asset, and
(c) the pooled asset is treated after the disposal as referable entirely to pre-entry assets (without prejudice to the effect of any subsequent acquisition of assets to be added to the pool in determining whether, and to what extent, any part of the pooled asset is to be treated as referable to pre-entry assets).

[*TCGA 1992, Sch 7A para 3(4)(11)*].

Where there is a disposal of the whole or part of a pooled asset at a time when the asset is referable entirely to pre-entry assets, (a) and (b) above apply to the disposal of the asset or the part as they apply in relation to the assumed disposal of the excess (mentioned in the preamble to (a) and (b)). However, where the whole of an asset, only part of which is referable to pre-entry assets, is disposed of, the reference in (b) above to the excess is taken as a reference to that part. [*TCGA 1992, Sch 7A para 3(5)*].

In applying (b) above, for the purposes of determining what would have been the pre-entry proportion of any loss accruing on the disposal of any assets as the separate asset mentioned in (b) above, it is assumed that none of the assets treated as comprised in that separate asset has ever been comprised in a pooled asset with any assets other than those which are taken to constitute that separate asset. [*TCGA 1992, Sch 7A para 3(6)*].

Assets comprised in any asset which is treated as separate are identified on the following assumptions:

(i) that assets are disposed of in the order of the relevant pre-entry dates in relation to the acquisition consideration as under **38.8** above;
(ii) subject to (i), that assets with earlier relevant times are disposed of before those with later ones;
(iii) that disposals made when a company was not a member of the relevant group are made in accordance with *para 3(1)–(6)* and (i) and (ii) above, as they have effect in relation to the group of companies of which the company was a member at the time of disposal or, as the case may be, of which it had most recently been a member before that time; and
(iv) subject to (i)–(iii) above, that a company disposes of assets in the order in which it acquired them.

[*TCGA 1992, Sch 7A para 3(7)*].

Where there is more than one relevant pre-entry date in relation to the consideration for any acquisition, the date in (i) above is the earlier or earliest of those dates if any such date relating to an option to acquire the asset is disregarded. [*TCGA 1992, Sch 7A para 3(8)*].

Where a second asset falls to be treated as acquired at the same time as a first asset which was acquired earlier (whether under *para 1(8)*, see **38.7** above, or otherwise), and the second asset is either comprised in a pooled asset partly referable to pre-entry assets, or is or includes an asset which is to be treated as so comprised, (i)–(iv) above apply not only in relation to the second asset as if it were the first asset but also, in the first place, for identifying the asset which is to be treated as the first asset under the above provisions. [*TCGA 1992, Sch 7A para 3(10)*].

Where the formula in **38.8** above is applied to an asset treated as above as a separate asset, the amount or value of the asset's acquisition or disposal consideration and any related incidental costs are determined, not under *TCGA 1992, s 129* or *s 130*, but by apportioning the consideration or costs relating both to that asset, and to other assets acquired or disposed of at the same time, according to the proportion that is borne by that asset to all the assets to which the consideration or costs related. [*TCGA 1992, Sch 7A para 3(9)*].

'Anti-flooding'

[38.10] This legislation (*TCGA 1992, Sch 7A, paras 2–5*), was repealed from 19 July 2011 (*FA 2011*). The previous rules are explained below.

There are rules which prevent pre-entry losses on pooled assets from being treated as post-entry losses ('*anti-flooding*'). These are described below and they apply if:

(a) there is a disposal of any part of a pooled asset which under **38.9** above is treated as including a part referable to pre-entry assets;
(b) the assets disposed of are or include assets ('*the post-entry element of the disposal*') which for the purposes of **38.9** above are treated as having been included in the part of the pooled asset which is not referable to pre-entry assets;
(c) an allowable loss ('*the actual loss*') accrues on the disposal; and
(d) the amount which in computing the allowable loss is allowed as a deduction of relevant allowable expenditure ('*the expenditure actually allowed*') exceeds such expenditure attributable to the post-entry element of the disposal.

[*TCGA 1992, Sch 7A para 4(1)*].

Anti-flooding rules

Where the post-entry element of the disposal comprises all of the assets disposed of, the actual loss is treated for the purposes of *Sch 7A* as a loss accruing on the disposal of a pre-entry asset; and the pre-entry proportion of that loss is treated as being the amount (in so far as it does not exceed the amount of the actual loss) of the excess referred to in (d) above. This is subject to an election under *TCGA 1992, Sch 7A para 4(6)* below. [*TCGA 1992, Sch 7A para 4(2)*].

In addition, where the actual loss is treated under **38.9** above as a loss accruing on the disposal of a pre-entry asset, and the expenditure actually allowed exceeds the actual cost of the assets to which the disposal is treated as relating, the pre-entry proportion of the loss is treated as being the amount which (in so far as it does not exceed the amount of the actual loss) is equal to the sum of that excess and what would, apart from these provisions and those in **38.11** below, be the pre-entry proportion of the loss accruing on the disposal. This is also subject to an election under *TCGA 1992, Sch 7A para 4(6)* below.

For this purpose, the actual cost of the assets to which the disposal is treated as relating is taken to be the sum of:

(i) the relevant allowable expenditure attributable to the post-entry element of the disposal; and

(ii) the amount which, in computing the pre-entry proportion of the loss under *para 3(4)(b)* and *para 3(6)*, for which see **38.9** above, would be treated for the purposes of C in the formula in **38.6** above as the total amount allowable as a deduction of relevant allowable expenditure in respect of such of the assets disposed of as are treated as having been incorporated in the part of the pooled asset referable to pre-entry assets.

[*TCGA 1992, Sch 7A para 4(3)(4)*].

Without prejudice to *para 4(6)* below, where *para 4(2)* or *(3)* above applies for the purpose of determining the pre-entry proportion of any loss, no election can be made under **38.11** below for the purpose of enabling a different amount to be taken as the pre-entry proportion of that loss. [*TCGA 1992, Sch 7A para 4(5)*].

Election under *TCGA 1992, Sch 7A para 4(6)*

Where:

(A) the pre-entry proportion of the loss accruing to any company on the disposal of any part of a pooled asset falls to be determined under the anti-flooding rules at *para 4(2)* or *(3)* above;

(B) the amount determined thereunder exceeds the amount determined under *para 4(7)* below ('the alternative pre-entry loss'); and

(C) the company makes an election for the purpose,

the pre-entry proportion of the loss determined as specified in (A) above is reduced to the amount of the alternative pre-entry loss. [*TCGA 1992, Sch 7A para 4(6)*].

For this purpose '*the alternative pre-entry loss*' is whatever, apart from these provisions, would have been the pre-entry proportion of the loss on the disposal in question, if the identification of the assets disposed of for the purposes of *Sch 7A* were to be made disregarding the part of the pooled asset which was not referable to pre-entry assets, except to the extent (if any) by which the part referable to pre-entry assets fell short of what was disposed of. [*TCGA 1992, Sch 7A para 4(7)*].

An election for the purposes of (C) above with respect to any loss must be made by the company incurring the loss by notice to the inspector given within the period of two years beginning with the end of the accounting period of that company in which the disposal giving rise to the loss is made, or within such longer period as HMRC may by notice allow. The provisions in **38.11** below may be taken into account under *para 4(7)* in determining the amount of the alternative pre-entry loss as if an election had been made under **38.11**, but only if the election under (C) above contains an election corresponding to the election that, apart from this provision, might have been made under **38.11** below. [*TCGA 1992, Sch 7A para 4(8)*].

Relevant allowable expenditure

For the purposes of the above, the relevant allowable expenditure attributable to the post-entry element of the disposal is the amount which, in computing any allowable loss accruing on a disposal of that element as a separate asset, would have been allowed as a deduction of relevant allowable expenditure if none of the assets comprised in that element had ever been comprised in a pooled asset with any assets other than those which are taken to constitute that separate asset for the purposes of this provision. [*TCGA 1992, Sch 7A para 4(9)*]. To identify the assets which are to be treated for this purpose as comprised in the post-entry element of the disposal, a company is taken to dispose of assets in the order in which it acquired them. [*TCGA 1992, Sch 7A para 4(10)*].

TCGA 1992, Sch 7A para 3(9), for which see **38.9** above, is applied as suitably modified for the purposes of *para 4(9)* above, as is *para 3(10)*, for which see **38.9** above, for the purposes of this provision in relation to *para 4(10)* above. [*TCGA 1992, Sch 7A para 4(11)*].

In the above provisions, references to an amount allowed as a deduction of relevant allowable expenditure are references to the amount falling to be so allowed in accordance with *TCGA 1992, 38(1)(a)* and *(b)* and (so far as applicable) *s 42*. Nothing in the above provisions affects the operation of the rules contained in **38.9** above for determining, for any purposes other than those of *para 4(7)* above, how much of any pooled asset at any time consists of a part which is referable to pre-entry assets. [*TCGA 1992, Sch 7A para 4(12)–(14); FA 1994, s 93(9)*].

Alternative calculation by reference to market value

Election for market value disposal

[38.11] This legislation (*TCGA 1992, Sch 7A, paras 2–5*), was repealed from 19 July 2011 (*FA 2011*). The previous rules are explained below.

Subject to *TCGA 1992, Sch 7A para 4(5)*, see **38.10** above, and the following provisions, if an otherwise allowable loss accrues on the disposal by any company of any pre-entry asset, and that company makes an election accordingly, the pre-entry proportion of that loss (instead of being the amount determined under the preceding provisions of *Sch 7A*) is to be whichever is the smaller of:

(a) the amount of any loss which would have accrued if that asset had been disposed of at the relevant time at its market value at that time; and
(b) the amount of the otherwise allowable loss accruing on the actual disposal of that asset.

[*TCGA 1992, Sch 7A para 5(1)(2)*].

In determining the amount of any notional loss under (a) above, it is assumed that the prohibition on indexation allowance enhancing an allowable loss under *FA 1994, s 93* has effect for disposals on or after the day on which the relevant time falls. [*TCGA 1992, Sch 7A para 5(2A); FA 1994, s 93(10)*].

Where no loss would have accrued on the deemed disposal assumed in (a) above, the loss accruing on the disposal mentioned in (b) above is deemed not to have a pre-entry proportion. [*TCGA 1992, Sch 7A para 5(3)*]. The election mentioned above must be made by the company incurring the loss by notice to the inspector given within the period of two years beginning with the end of its accounting period in which the disposal giving rise to the loss is made, or within such longer period as HMRC may by notice allow. [*TCGA 1992, Sch 7A para 5(8)*].

Interaction with 'pooled assets' provisions

The provisions in *para 5(5)* below apply where an election is made in relation to any loss accruing on the disposal ('*the real disposal*') of the whole or any part of a pooled asset, and the case is one in which (but for the election) the provisions in **38.9** above would apply for determining the pre-entry proportion of a loss accruing on the real disposal. [*TCGA 1992, Sch 7A para 5(4)*]. In these circumstances, these provisions have effect as if the amount specified in (a) above were to be calculated:

(i) on the basis that the disposal which is assumed to have taken place was a disposal of all the assets falling within (1)–(3) below; and
(ii) by apportioning any loss that would have accrued on that disposal between:
    (A) such of the assets falling within (1)–(3) below as are assets to which the real disposal is treated as relating; and
    (B) the remainder of the assets so falling,

    according to the proportions of any pooled asset whose disposal is assumed which would have been, respectively, represented by assets mentioned in (A) above and by assets mentioned in (B) above.

Where assets falling within (1)–(3) below have different relevant times there is assumed to have been a different disposal at each of those times. [*TCGA 1992, Sch 7A para 5(5)*].

Assets fall to be included within (A) and (B) above if:

(1) immediately before the time which is the relevant time in relation to those assets, they were comprised in a pooled asset which consisted of or included assets which fall to be treated for the purposes of **38.9** above as:
    (a) comprised in the part of the pooled asset referable to pre-entry assets; and

(b) disposed of on the real disposal;

(2) they were also comprised in such a pooled asset immediately after that time; and

(3) the pooled asset in which they were so comprised immediately after that time was held by a member of the relevant group.

[*TCGA 1992, Sch 7A para 5(6)*].

Interaction with 'anti-flooding' rules

Where:

(A) an election is made under *para 4(6)*, see **38.10** above, requiring the determination by reference to these provisions of the alternative pre-entry loss accruing on the disposal of any assets comprised in a pooled asset; and

(B) under that election any amount of the loss that would have accrued on an assumed disposal is apportioned in accordance with (i) and (ii) above to assets ('*the relevant assets*') which:

(I) are treated for the purposes of that determination as assets to which the disposal related; but

(II) otherwise continue after the disposal to be treated as incorporated in the part of that pooled asset which is referable to pre-entry assets,

then, on any further application of these provisions for the purpose of determining the pre-entry proportion of the loss accruing on a subsequent disposal of assets comprised in that pooled asset, that amount (without being apportioned elsewhere) is deducted from so much of the loss accruing on the same assumed disposal as, apart from the deduction, would be apportioned to the relevant assets on that further application of these provisions. [*TCGA 1992, Sch 7A para 5(7)*].

Restrictions on the deduction of pre-entry losses

[38.12] In the calculation of the amount to be included in respect of chargeable gains in any company's total profits for any accounting period:

(a) if in that period there is any chargeable gain from which the whole or any part of any pre-entry loss accruing in that period is deductible in accordance with the provisions in **38.13** below, the loss or, as the case may be, that part of it, is deducted from that gain;

(b) if, after all the deductions in (a) above have been made, there is in that period any chargeable gain from which the whole or any part of any pre-entry loss carried forward from a previous accounting period is deductible in accordance with the provisions in **38.13** below, the loss or, as the case may be, that part of it is deducted from that gain;

(c) the total chargeable gains (if any) remaining after all the deductions in (a) or (b) above is subject to deductions in accordance with *TCGA 1992, s 8(1)* (chargeable gains less allowable losses of company to be included in chargeable profits) in respect of any allowable losses that are not pre-entry losses; and

(d) any pre-entry loss which has not been the subject of a deduction under (a) or (b) above (as well as any other losses falling to be carried forward under *s 8(1)*) are carried forward to the following accounting period of that company.

[*TCGA 1992, Sch 7A para 6(1)*].

Prior to *FA 2011*, and subject to (a)–(d) above, any question as to which or what part of any pre-entry loss has been deducted from any particular chargeable gain was decided:

(i) where it falls to be decided in respect of the setting of losses against gains in any accounting period ending before 16 March 1993 as if:
   (A) pre-entry losses accruing in any such period had been set against chargeable gains before any other allowable losses accruing in that period were set against those gains;
   (B) pre-entry losses carried forward to any such period had been set against chargeable gains before any other allowable losses carried forward to that period were set against those gains; and
   (C) subject to (A) and (B) above, the pre-entry losses carried forward to any accounting period ending after 15 March 1993 were identified with such losses as may be determined in accordance with such elections as may be made by the company to which they accrued;

   and
(ii) in any other case, in accordance with such elections as may be made by the company to which the loss accrued,

and any question as to which or what part of any pre-entry loss has been carried forward from one accounting period to another shall be decided accordingly. [*TCGA 1992, Sch 7A para 6(2)*].

An election under (i)(C) above must be made by the company by notice to the inspector within two years of the end of its accounting period which was current on 16 March 1993. An election under (ii) above must similarly be made within two years of the end of the company's accounting period in which the gain in question accrued. [*TCGA 1992, Sch 7A para 6(3)*].

From 19 July 2011 (*FA 2011*), any question as to which or what part of any pre-entry loss has been deducted from any particular chargeable gain is decided in accordance with such elections as may be made by the company to which the loss accrued. The election must be made within two years of the end of the company's accounting period in which the gain in question accrued. [*TCGA 1992, Sch 7A para 6(2) and (3), as amended*].

For the purposes of *Sch 7A*, where any matter falls to be determined under these provisions by reference to an election, but no election is made, it shall be assumed, so far as consistent with any elections that have been made, that losses are set against gains in the order in which the losses accrued; and that the gains against which they are set are also determined according to the order in which they accrued with losses being set against earlier gains before they are set against later ones. [*TCGA 1992, Sch 7A para 6(4)*].

See *Kellogg Brown & Root Holdings Ltd v HMRC* [2009] EWHC 584 (Ch) for pre-entry losses where there is a transfer between connected persons as part of a group reorganisation.

Gains from which pre-entry losses are to be deductible

Set against gains of same company

[38.13] A pre-entry loss that accrued to a company before it became a member of the relevant group is deductible from a chargeable gain accruing to that company if the gain is one accruing:

(a) on a disposal made by that company before the date on which it became a member of the relevant group ('*the entry date*');
(b) on the disposal of an asset which was held by that company immediately before the entry date; or
(c) on the disposal of any asset which:
  (i) was acquired by that company on or after the entry date from a person who was not a member of the relevant group at the time of the acquisition; and
  (ii) since its acquisition from that person has not been used or held for any purposes other than those of a trade which was being carried on by that company at the time immediately before the entry date and which continued to be carried on by that company until the disposal.

This last condition is modified by *FA 2011, Sch 11* with effect from 19 July 2011. A pre-entry loss can now be deducted from a chargeable gain arising on the disposal of an asset that:

(i) was acquired, on or after the entry date, by the company to which the pre-entry loss accrued (company A), or a company which, at the time of the acquisition, was a group company of company A, from a person who at the time of the acquisition was not a group company of company A;
(ii) so long as the asset has not, since its acquisition, been used or held for any purposes other than those of a trade or business which was carried on by company A. The trade or business must have been carried on by company A immediately before the entry date and must have been carried on by company A or a company in the same group as company A up to the time of the disposal of the asset.

The two important relaxations of the rules are the application to gains on assets used in a trade or business, not just in a trade, and to the fact that the trade or business can now be transferred within the group.

Conversely, once a loss has become subject to restriction under these rules, then the same restriction continues to apply should the company subsequently join another group. This is intended to 'clarify' the position following the cases of *Revenue and Customs Comrs v Limitgood Ltd* [2009] EWCA Civ 177, [2009] STC 980, [2009] SWTI 689 and *Revenue and Customs Comrs v Prizedome Ltd* [2009] EWCA Civ 177, [2009] STC 980, [2009] SWTI 689 (see **38.7**).

[*TCGA 1992, Sch 7A para 7(1), (1A)–(1C)*].

The pre-entry proportion of an allowable loss accruing to any company on the disposal of a pre-entry asset is deductible from a chargeable gain accruing to that company if:

(A) the gain is one accruing on a disposal made, before the date on which it became a member of the relevant group, by that company and that company is the one ('*the initial company*') by reference to which the asset on the disposal of which the loss accrues is a pre-entry asset;

(B) the pre-entry asset and the asset on the disposal of which the gain accrues were each held by the same company at a time immediately before it became a member of the relevant group; or

(C) the gain is one accruing on the disposal of an asset which:
   (i) was acquired by the initial company (whether before or after it became a member of the relevant group) from a person who, at the time of the acquisition, was not a member of that group; and
   (ii) since its acquisition from that person has not been used or held for any purposes other than those of a trade which was being carried on, immediately before it became a member of the relevant group, by the initial company and which continued to be carried on by the initial company until the disposal.

This rule was repealed by *FA 2011, Sch 11* with effect from 19 July 2011.

[*TCGA 1992, Sch 7A para 7(2)*].

Member of pre-entry group

Where two or more companies become members of the relevant group at the same time and those companies were all members of the same group of companies immediately before they became members of the relevant group, then, without prejudice to the provisions in **38.15** below:

(1) an asset is treated for the purposes of (b) above as held, immediately before it became a member of the relevant group, by the company to which the pre-entry loss in question accrued if that company is one of those companies and the asset was in fact so held by another of those companies;

(2) two or more assets are treated for the purposes of (B) above as assets held by the same company immediately before it became a member of the relevant group wherever they would be so treated if all those companies were treated as a single company; and

(3) the acquisition of an asset is treated for the purposes of (c) and (C) above as an acquisition by the company to which the pre-entry loss in question accrued if that company is one of those companies and the asset was in fact acquired (whether before or after they became members of the relevant group) by another of those companies.

[*TCGA 1992, Sch 7A para 7(3)*].

TCGA 1992, Sch 7A para 1(4) (see **38.7** above – regarding an asset previously disposed of other than on a no gain no loss basis) is applied as suitably modified for determining, for the purposes of the above provisions, whether an asset on the disposal of which a chargeable gain accrues was held at the time when a company became a member of the relevant group. [*TCGA 1992, Sch 7A para 7(4)*].

Subject to *para 7(6)* (below), where a gain accrues on a disposal of the whole or any part of:

(1) any asset treated as a single asset but comprising assets only some of which were held at the time mentioned in (b) or (B) above; or

(2) an asset which is treated as held at that time by virtue of a provision requiring an asset which was not held at that time to be treated as the same as an asset which was so held (see **38.7** above),

a pre-entry loss is deductible under (b) or (B) above from the amount of that gain to the extent only of such proportion of that gain as is attributable to assets held at that time or, as the case may be, represents the gain that would have accrued on the asset so held. [*TCGA 1992, Sch 7A para 7(5)*].

Where:

(AA) a chargeable gain accrues under *TCGA 1992, s 116(10)* on the disposal of a qualifying corporate bond which has been exchanged for shares etc. (see Tolley's Capital Gains Tax under Qualifying Corporate Bonds and **38.7** above);

(BB) that bond was not held as required by (b) or (B) above at the time mentioned respectively in (b) or (B); and

(CC) the whole or any part of the asset which is the 'old asset' for the purposes of *TCGA 1992, s 116* (as amended by *CTA 2009, Sch 1 para 366*) was so held,

the question as to whether that gain is one accruing on the disposal of an asset the whole or any part of which was held by a particular company at that time is determined for the purposes of *para 7* as if the bond were deemed to have been so held to the same extent as the old asset. [*TCGA 1992, Sch 7A para 7(6)*].

Change of a company's nature

[38.14] These rules were amended by *FA 2011, Sch 11* from 19 July 2011, so that all references to a trade are now references to a trade or business.

Where a company's trading activities change, there will be an impact with regard to **38.1**(c) and C above, which require a trade to have been carried on before and after entry into the relevant group. The following provisions allow a previous trade to be disregarded in certain circumstances.

Thus if:

(a) within any period of three years, a company becomes a member of a group of companies and there is (either earlier or later in that period, or at the same time) a major change in the nature or conduct of a trade (or business, post-*FA 2011*) carried on by that company; or

(b) at any time after the scale of the activities in a trade (or business, post-*FA 2011*) carried on by a company has become small or negligible, and before any considerable revival of the trade (or business, post-*FA 2011*), that company becomes a member of a group of companies,

the trade (or business, post-*FA 2011*) carried on before that change, or which has become small or negligible, is disregarded for the purposes of **38.13**(c) and (C) above in relation to any time before the company became a member of the group in question.

A '*major change in the conduct of a trade*' includes:

- a major change in the type of property dealt in, or services or facilities provided, in the trade (or business, post-*FA 2011*);
- a major change in customers, markets or outlets of the trade (or business, post-*FA 2011*);
- post-*FA 2011*, in the case of a company with investment business (within the meaning of *CTA 2009, s 1218*), a major change in the nature of the investments held.

This rule applies even if the change is the result of a gradual process which began outside the period of three years mentioned above.

Regard will also be had to appropriate changes in other factors such as the location of the company's business premises, the identity of the company's suppliers, management or staff, the company's methods of manufacture, or the company's pricing or purchasing policies to the extent that these factors indicate that a major change has occurred. Efficiency changes and technological advancements would not in themselves indicate that a major change in the nature or conduct of a trade has occurred.

HMRC will compare any two points in three years which include the date of change of ownership of the company. This applies even if the change is the result of a gradual process which began outside the period of three years mentioned in (a) above. They take note of both qualitative and quantitative issues, as discussed in the cases of *Willis v Peeters Picture Frames Ltd* (1982) 56 TC 436, CA(NI), and *Purchase v Tesco Stores Ltd* (1984) 58 TC 46 respectively. (HMRC Statement of Practice, SP 10/91). See also **55.13 LOSSES**.

Where the operation of the above provisions depends on circumstances or events at a time after the company becomes a member of any group of companies (but not more than three years after), an assessment to give effect to the provisions may be made within six years from that time or the latest such time. [*TCGA 1992, Sch 7A para 8*].

The above provisions are similar to those in *ICTA 1988, s 768 (now CTA 2010 s 673 et seq.)* regarding the disallowance of trading losses on a change in ownership of a company. See **55.13 LOSSES** for coverage of these provisions.

Identification of the 'relevant group'

[38.15] These rules were repealed by *FA 2011, Sch 11* from 19 July 2011.

The provisions below apply where there is more than one group of companies which would be the relevant group in relation to any company.

Where any loss has accrued on the disposal by any company of any asset, *Sch 7A* does not apply by reference to any group of companies in relation to any loss accruing on that disposal unless:

(a) that group is a group in relation to which that loss is a pre-entry loss because it is an allowable loss that accrued to that company at a time before it became a member of the group or, if there is more than one such group, the one of which that company most recently became a member;

(b) that group, in a case where there is no group falling within (a) above, is either:
  (i) the group of which that company is a member at the time of the disposal; or
  (ii) if it is not a member of a group of companies at that time, the group of which that company was last a member before that time;

(c) that group, in a case where there is a group falling within (a) above or, in relation to the deduction of a loss from a chargeable gain where either the gain or the loss accrues after 10 March 1994, (b) above, is a group of which that company was a member at any time in the accounting period of that company in which it became a member of the group falling within (a);

(d) that group is a group the principal company (see **18.2** above) of which is or has been, or has been under the control (within *ICTA 1988, s 416, CTA 2010, s 450*) of:
  (i) the company by which the disposal is made; or
  (ii) another company which is or has been a member of a group by reference to which *Sch 7A* applies in relation to the loss in question under (a), (b) or (c) above; or

(e) that group is a group of which either:
  (i) the principal company of a group by reference to which *Sch 7A* applies; or
  (ii) a company which has had that principal company under its control,

  is or has been a member.

In the case of a loss accruing on the disposal of any asset where, under (a)–(e) above, there are two or more groups ('*connected groups*') by reference to which *Schedule 7A* applies, the further provisions in *para 9(3)–(5)* below apply. [*TCGA 1992, Sch 7A para 9(1)(2); FA 1994, s 94(1)(3)(4)*].

Connected groups considered separately

These rules were repealed by *FA 2011, Sch 11* from 19 July 2011.

Schedule 7A is applied separately in relation to each of the connected groups (so far as they are not groups in relation to which the loss is a pre-entry loss because it is a loss that accrued to a company at a time before it became a member of the group) for the purpose of determining whether the loss on the disposal of any asset is a loss on the disposal of a pre-entry asset, and calculating the pre-entry proportion of that loss. [*TCGA 1992, Sch 7A para 9(3)*].

Subject to *para 9(5)* below, the provisions in **38.12** above have effect:

(A) as if the pre-entry proportion of any loss accruing on the disposal of an asset which is a pre-entry asset in the case of more than one of the connected groups were the largest pre-entry proportion of that loss as calculated under *para 9(3)* above; and

(B) so that, where the loss accruing on the disposal of any asset is a pre-entry loss because it is an allowable loss that accrued to a company at a time before it became a member of a group in the case of any of the connected groups, the pre-entry loss for the purposes of **38.12** above is that loss, and not any amount which is the pre-entry proportion of that loss in relation to any of the other groups.

[*TCGA 1992, Sch 7A para 9(4)*].

Where, on the separate application of *Sch 7A* in the case of each of the groups by reference to which *Sch 7A* applies, there is, in the case of the disposal of any asset, a pre-entry loss by reference to each of two or more of the connected groups, no amount in respect of the loss accruing on the disposal is to be deductible under **38.13** above from any chargeable gain if any of the connected groups is a group in the case of which, on separate applications of the provisions in **38.13** above in relation to each group, the amount deductible from that gain in respect of that loss is nil. [*TCGA 1992, Sch 7A para 9(5)*].

Notwithstanding that the principal company of one group ('*the first group*') has become a member of another ('*the second group*'), those two groups are not treated for the purposes of the above provisions as the same group by virtue of *TCGA 1992, s 170(10)* or *(10A)* (see **18.2** above) if the principal company of the first group was under the control, immediately before it became a member of the second group, of a company which at that time was already a member of the second group.

In addition, in relation to accounting periods ending after 16 March 1998, again where the principal company of the first group has become a member of the second group, the two groups are not for those purposes treated, in relation to any company that is (or has become) a member of the second group, as the same group if the time at which that company became a member of the first group falls in the same accounting period as that in which the principal company of the first group became a member of the second group. [*TCGA 1992, Sch 7A para 9(6); FA 1998, s 138; F(No 2)A 2005, s 65(5)*]. For an example, see HMRC Capital Gains Manual, CG47944.

Where, in the case of the disposal of any asset:

(aa) two or more groups which but for *para 9(6)* above would be treated as the same group are treated as separate groups because of the treatment therein; and

(bb) one of those groups is a group of which either:
  - (i) the principle company of a group by reference to which *Sch 7A* applies by virtue of (a), (b) or (c) above in relation to any loss accruing on the disposal; or
  - (ii) a company which has had that principal company under its control,

  is or has been a member,

the above provisions have effect as if that principal company had been a member of each of the groups mentioned in (aa) above.
[*TCGA 1992, Sch 7A para 9(7)*].

Appropriations to stock in trade

[38.16] Where, but for an election under *TCGA 1992, s 161(3)*, there would be deemed to have been a disposal at any time by any company of any asset, the amount by which the market value of the asset may be treated as increased in pursuance of that election does not include the amount of any pre-entry loss that would have accrued on that disposal; and *Sch 7A* has effect as if the pre-entry loss of the last mentioned amount had accrued to that company at that time. [*TCGA 1992, Sch 7A para 10*].

Continuity provisions

[38.17] The provisions below apply where provision has been made by or under any enactment ('*the transfer legislation*') for the transfer of property, rights and liabilities to any person from:

(a) a body established by or under any enactment (as defined) for the purpose, in the exercise or statutory functions (as defined), of carrying on any undertaking or industrial or other activity in the public sector or of exercising any other statutory functions;
(b) a subsidiary of such a body; or
(c) a company wholly owned by the Crown (as defined).

A loss is not a pre-entry loss for the purposes of *Sch 7A* in relation to any company to whom a transfer has been made by or under the transfer legislation if that loss:

(i) accrued to the person from whom the transfer has been made; and
(ii) falls to be treated, in accordance with any enactment made in relation to transfers by or under that legislation, as a loss accruing to that company.

For the purposes of *Sch 7A*, where a company became a member of the relevant group by virtue of the transfer by or under the transfer legislation of any shares in or other securities of that company or any other company;

(A) a loss that accrued to that company before it so became a member of that group is not a pre-entry loss in relation to that group; and

(B) no asset held by that company when it so became a member of that group shall by virtue of that fact be a pre-entry asset (this measure was repealed by *FA 2011, Sch 11* from 19 July 2011).

[*TCGA 1992, Sch 7A para 11*].

Companies changing groups on certain transfers of shares

[38.18] For the purposes of *Sch 7A*, and without prejudice to the provisions in **38.17** above, where:

(a) a company which is a member of a group of companies becomes at any time a member of another group of companies as the result of a disposal of shares in or other securities of that company or any other company; and
(b) that disposal is one on which neither a gain nor a loss would accrue, by virtue of any of the no gain/ no loss provisions,

then *Sch 7A* has effect in relation to the losses that accrued to that company before that time and the assets held by that company at that time as if any time when it was a member of the first group were included in the period during which it is treated as having been a member of the second group.

[*TCGA 1992, Sch 7A para 12*].

Example

[38.19]

C Ltd has a 100% subsidiary, D Ltd. D Ltd acquired a 100% subsidiary, E Ltd, on 1 April 2005 and a 75% subsidiary, F Ltd, on 1 April 2007. All the companies prepare their accounts to 31 March. The following information is relevant (neither E Ltd nor F Ltd having realised any gains or losses except as stated).

(i) At 1 April 2005, E Ltd had unrelieved capital losses of £120,000 and its assets included a freehold property which it had acquired on 1 July 2001 for £700,000 and on which it had incurred enhancement expenditure of £100,000 on 1 October 2002. The property was valued at £700,000 at 1 April 2005. During the year ended 31 March 2009, E Ltd realised chargeable gains of £30,000 on assets held at 1 April 2005 and it also realised an allowable loss of £10,000 on an asset purchased on 31 May 2005. On 1 October 2009, the company sold the above-mentioned freehold property for £550,000.

(ii) F Ltd had no capital losses brought forward at 1 April 2007. At that date, it held 100,000 ordinary shares in XYZ plc, a quoted company. It had acquired 60,000 of these on 1 May 2001 for £100,000 and 40,000 on 1 June 2005 for £70,000. The shares had an indexed pool value of £186,790 at 1 April 2007, and their market value at that date was £110,000. On 1 November 2007, F Ltd acquired a further 50,000 XYZ ordinary shares for £30,000 and on 31 August 2009 it sold 120,000 such shares for £60,000.

F Ltd also made two disposals other than of XYZ shares during the year to 31 March 2010, realising chargeable gains on each. The first disposal, on which the gain was £55,000, was of an asset acquired by transfer from C Ltd (at no gain/no loss by virtue of *TCGA 1992, s 171*). The second, on which the gain was £35,000, was acquired from outside the group in December 2007 and used since that time in F Ltd's trade, which has continued unchanged since 31 March 2007.

The provisions restricting set-off of pre-entry losses have the following effects.

(i) E Ltd

For the year to 31.3.10, E Ltd can elect (before 1 April 2012) for the whole of the £30,000 gain to be regarded as covered by pre-entry losses. The £100,000 losses carried forward at 31.3.09 then comprise pre-entry losses of £90,000 and other losses of £10,000. In the absence of an election, losses are set against gains on a first in/first out basis for these purposes, so the same result would accrue in this case. See **38.12** above.

The £90,000 pre-entry losses are carried forward and may be set only against gains on other assets held by E Ltd immediately before 1.4.05 or gains on assets acquired by it on or after that date from outside the group and not used or held for any purposes other than those of the trade carried on by E Ltd immediately before that date and which continued to be carried on by it up to the date of disposal. See **38.13** above.

The overall loss on the disposal of the freehold property is as follows.

	£	£
Proceeds (1.10.09)		550,000
Cost (1.7.01)	700,000	
Enhancement expenditure (1.10.02)	100,000	800,000
Allowable loss		£250,000

The pre-entry proportion of the allowable loss is calculated as follows.

		£
$£250{,}000 \times \frac{700{,}000}{800{,}000} \times \frac{3y9m(1.7.01 - 1.4.05)}{8y3m(1.7.01 - 1.10.09)}$	=	99,432
$£250{,}000 \times \frac{100{,}000}{800{,}000} \times \frac{2y6m(1.10.02 - 1.4.05)}{7y0m(1.10.02 - 1.10.09)}$	=	11,161
Pre-entry proportion		£110,593
Balance of allowable loss		£139,407

See **38.8** above.

E Ltd may elect (before 1 April 2012) to use an alternative method of computing the pre-entry proportion of the allowable loss, as follows.

	£	£
Market value (1.4.05)		700,000
Cost (1.7.01)	700,000	
Enhancement expenditure (1.10.02)	100,000	800,000

Pre-entry proportion of allowable loss	£100,000
Balance of allowable loss (£250,000 – £100,000)	£150,000

See **38.11** above.

The whole of the loss of £250,000 is available for carry-forward but the pre-entry proportion of the allowable loss (£100,000 on the assumption that the election referred to above is made) can be set only against the same types of gain against which the pre-entry losses of £90,000 can be set (see above).

(ii) F Ltd

Allowable loss on XYZ plc ordinary shares

	Number of shares	Qualifying expenditure	Indexed pool
		£	£
Acquisition 1.5.01	60,000	100,000	
Acquisition 1.6.05	40,000	70,000	
At 1.4.07	100,000	170,000	187,380
Indexed rise to 1.11.07: £187,380 × say 0.018			3,373
Acquisition 1.11.07	50,000	30,000	30,000
	150,000	200,000	220,753
Indexed rise to 31.8.09: £220,753 × say 0.070			15,453
			236,206
Disposal 31.8.09	(120,000)	(160,000)	(188,965)
Pool carried forward	30,000	£40,000	£47,241

	£
Proceeds 31.8.09	60,000
Cost	160,000
Allowable loss	£100,000

Indexation allowance would be £28,965 (£188,965 – £160,000), but indexation allowance cannot increase an allowable loss.

Pre-entry proportion of allowable loss

Stage 1 (see ***38.9*** *above)*

The proportion of the pool disposed of (120,000 shares) exceeds the proportion *not* referable to pre-entry assets (50,000 shares). The excess of 70,000 shares is regarded as a separate asset made up as follows.

		Cost
		£
60,000 shares acquired 1.5.01		100,000
10,000 shares acquired 1.6.05	(£70,000 × $^1/_4$)	17,500
		£117,500
Proceeds of 70,000 shares £60,000 × $^7/_{12}$		35,000
Cost as above		117,500
Notional allowable loss on pre-entry assets		£82,500

The pre-entry proportion of the allowable loss is calculated as follows.

		£
$£82{,}500 \times \dfrac{100{,}000}{117{,}500} \times \dfrac{5y11m(1.5.01 - 1.4.07)}{8y4m(1.5.01 - 31.8.09)}$	=	49,851
$£82{,}500 \times \dfrac{17{,}500}{117{,}500} \times \dfrac{1y10m(1.6.05 - 1.4.07)}{4y3m(1.6.05 - 31.8.09)}$	=	5,300
Pre-entry proportion of allowable loss (subject to below)		£55,151

Stage 2 (see 38.10 *above)*

		£
The amount deductible in computing the allowable loss is	(I)	160,000
The amount deductible which is attributable to the post-entry element of the disposal (50,000 shares acquired on 1.11.07) is	(II)	30,000

As (I) exceeds (II), an adjustment is required to the figure calculated at *Stage 1* above, as follows.

	£	£
Expenditure actually allowed		160,000
Deduct Actual cost of assets disposed of:		
pre-entry element (see *Stage 1* above)	117,500	
post-entry element (see (II) above)	30,000	147,500
Excess		£12,500

The excess is added to the pre-entry proportion as calculated at *Stage 1* above. The pre-entry proportion of the allowable loss is thus

£55,151 + £12,500 =	£67,651

Because an adjustment is required under *Stage 2*, the election for the alternative method (see **38.11** above) is *not* available. If the election *had been* available, the calculation would have been as follows.

	£
Market value of 100,000 shares held at 1.4.07	110,000
Unindexed pool value at 1.4.07	170,000
Notional loss on 100,000 shares	£60,000

As only 70,000 of the 100,000 shares held at 1.4.07 are regarded as included in the disposal on 31.8.07 (see *Stage 1* above), the pre-entry proportion of the allowable loss would have been £60,000 × $^7/_{10}$ = £42,000.)

Stage 3 (see **38.10** *above)*

As the adjustment at *Stage 2* applies, F Ltd may elect (before 1 April 2012) that the pre-entry proportion of the loss calculated at *Stage 2* (£67,651) be reduced to the amount of the 'alternative pre-entry loss', if lower. In calculating the alternative pre-entry loss, *Stage 1* is re-computed as if the disposal was primarily of pre-entry assets, as follows.

	Cost £
60,000 shares acquired 1.5.01	100,000
40,000 shares acquired 1.6.05	70,000
	£170,000

	£
Proceeds of 100,000 shares £60,000 × $^{10}/_{12}$	50,000
Cost as above	170,000
Notional allowable loss on pre-entry assets	£120,000

The pre-entry proportion of the allowable loss is calculated as follows.

$$£120{,}000 \times \frac{100{,}000}{170{,}000} \times \frac{5y11m(1.5.01 - 1.4.07)}{8y4m(1.5.01 - 31.8.09)} = £\ 50{,}118$$

$$£120{,}000 \times \frac{70{,}000}{170{,}000} \times \frac{1y10m(1.6.05 - 1.4.07)}{4y3m(1.6.05 - 31.8.09)} = 21{,}315$$

Alternative pre-entry loss (subject to below)	£71,433

The alternative loss is higher than the pre-entry proportion of the allowable loss calculated at *Stage 2* (£67,651), so, subject to *Stage 4* (below), the election would not be made.

Stage 4 (see **38.10, 38.11** *above)*

In making an election under *Stage 3*, F Ltd may specify that the alternative method (see **38.11** above) be used, as follows.

	£
Market value of 100,000 shares held at 1.4.07	110,000
Unindexed pool value at 1.4.07	170,000
Notional loss on 100,000 shares	£60,000

As all the 100,000 shares held at 1.4.07 are regarded as included in the disposal on 31.8.09 (see *Stage 3*), the alternative pre-entry loss is £60,000. It is therefore beneficial for F Ltd to make the election mentioned at *Stage 3*, imputing an election as under **38.11** above.

The pre-entry proportion of the allowable loss is then reduced from £67,651 (Stage 2) to	£60,000
Balance of allowable loss is £100,000 – £60,000 =	£40,000

Utilisation of losses (see **38.12, 38.13** *above)*

The pre-entry loss may be set against the gain of £35,000. It may not be set against the gain of £55,000. The balance of the allowable loss can be set against the gain of £55,000. F Ltd's chargeable gains for the year ended 31.3.10 are therefore as follows.

	£	£
Total gains		90,000
Deduct Pre-entry losses	35,000	
Other allowable losses	40,000	75,000
Chargeable gains		£15,000

Losses carried forward (all pre-entry losses) £(60,000 – 35,000)	£25,000

Key points

[38.20] Points to consider are as follows.

- When assessing the position of a chargeable gains group, the status of overseas entities can be important. In particular, consider whether such entities are likely to be respected as companies and whether ownership interests in those entities will be treated as ordinary share capital.
- Bear in mind the priority rules where transactions have more than one potential interpretation. For example, a reorganisation under *TCGA 1992, s 135* will take priority over the no-gain/no-loss rules in *s 171*.
- If reliance is to be placed on relief under *TCGA 1992, s 171A*, ensure that an election is made on time.
- Where a company is to rely upon the use of losses, ensure that the losses have been identified and their availability for use analysed before they are needed.
- Where anti-avoidance provisions are potentially in point (for example in relation to capital losses), the taxpayer should consider taking advice to limit potential penalties under the new penalties regime.
- If roll-over relief is to be claimed on the replacement of business assets, ensure that the transactions take place within the time scales required by the legislation and claims are submitted by the parties on time.
- Consider the potential for secondary chargeable gains liabilities. It may be prudent to consider the need for indemnities if external investors are involved or all or part of a business is to be sold.
- Remember that degrouping charges for the purposes of corporation tax on chargeable gains can crystallise losses as well as gains.
- Bear in mind that all degrouping charges are not the same. Where the substantial shareholding exemption applies, the timing of the deemed disposal and reacquisition is altered to the time immediately before the time of the degrouping. Also, while the intangible fixed asset regime rules are very similar to the capital gains provisions, the loan relationships and derivative contracts rules are different in some important respects, not least timing and the inability to realise a loss.
- Where it is intended to rely upon the 'associated companies' exception in the degrouping charge provisions, check that the companies were associated at the time of the transfer of the asset as well as the time of degrouping.

- If a degrouping charge is to be treated as accruing to a member of a chargeable gains group other than the company leaving the group, ensure that an election to do so is submitted on time.

39

Group Relief

Cross-references. See **18.2–17.45** CAPITAL GAINS — GROUPS; **27** CONTROLLED FOREIGN COMPANIES; **76.4** WINDING UP; **59.3** PAYMENT OF TAX.

Simon's Taxes. See D2.1, D2.2.

Introduction

[39.1] There are certain benefits afforded groups of companies under UK tax law. In some respects this means a group of companies is treated in a similar fashion to one corporate entity, as the intention of the legislation is to minimise or extinguish certain tax charges on transactions between group entities, and to allow losses within a group to be used in the most tax efficient manner (subject to any appropriate anti-avoidance provisions).

Group income elections was one example of such a benefit, whereby payments of certain intra-group charges, such as interest, or dividends, could be made without any deduction for income tax or ACT respectively (on ACT see further **1 INTRODUCTION AND RATES OF TAX** and **3 ADVANCE CORPORATION TAX — SHADOW ACT**). Such elections were discontinued post 6 April 1999, when ACT mainly disappeared. However there is ongoing litigation (see below) arising from the fact that no election was available to non-UK resident group companies.

One of the main tax advantages of membership of a group is that certain losses etc. of one company within the group may be relieved against the profits of another (**39.2–39.4** below). This is known as group relief, or, where a consortium exists, it may be consortium relief. For these reliefs, the definition of 'group' may vary.

See also **55.26 LOSSES** as regards restriction of losses where a fellow group member is the subject of a write-off of Government investment.

With regard to the benefits afforded groups of companies in respect of capital gains on transfers of assets between group members, see further **18.2 CAPITAL GAINS — GROUPS.**

Demergers aim to qualify to have the distribution of shares treated as an exempt distribution. There is a clearance procedure to enable companies to have certainty, provided they make complete disclosure and the actual procedure does not differ from that disclosed.

Each of the above matters is considered further, in turn, below.

Changes have been implemented by the *Finance (No 3) Act 2010*, with regard to EEA based link companies under the consortium rules, pursuant to EU case law, and also some further restrictions as to the proportion of losses which may be claimed from or surrendered to a consortium company.

Group relief

[39.2] Where companies form part of a group (as defined below) then losses and other amounts for an accounting period may be surrendered by one company to another within this same group — this is known as '*group relief*'. Where companies are part of a consortium, then certain relief is available as between the consortium company and the consortium member. This is known as 'consortium' relief — see further **39.19**.

Relief from corporation tax may be obtained by surrendering the items specified in **39.5** below (in whole or in part) by one member of a group (the 'surrendering company') and claimed by another (the 'claimant company') against its own profits chargeable to corporation tax. The relief is also available to and from certain consortium companies, see **39.19** below.

Claims may be made:

(a) for trading losses and other amounts eligible for corporation tax relief (as set out in **39.5** below) where both the claimant and surrendering companies are resident in the UK or carrying on a UK trade through a permanent establishment (see **65.6 RESIDENCE**); or

(b) for accounting periods beginning on or after 1 April 2006, for losses and other amounts not eligible for corporation tax relief (effectively for 'qualifying overseas losses', see further the 'EEA amount', as set out in **39.10** and **39.11** below) arising to an 'EEA company'. An '*EEA company*' is a non-resident company within the charge to tax under the law of any European Economic Area (EEA) territory and which is either resident in any EEA territory or not so resident but carrying on a trade through a permanent establishment in any EEA territory. Accounting periods straddling 1 April 2006 are treated for this purpose as two separate periods. The amount of the claimant company's profits and the amount of the loss or other amount of the non-resident, surrendering company are apportioned to the two periods on a just and reasonable basis.

[*CTA 2010, s 99; ICTA 1988, s 402(1)–(3B); FA 2006, s 27, Sch 1 paras 1, 9*].

Losses of EEA group members

The change in legislation to bring in losses arising within the EEA was in response to the case of *Marks and Spencer plc v Halsey (Inspector of Taxes): C-446/03* [2006] STC 237 (see below), in which the UK company claimed group relief in respect of losses incurred by its European subsidiaries.

The ECJ ruled (on 13 December 2005) that, although *Articles 43 EC* and *48 EC* on freedom of establishment and discrimination do not preclude the residence requirements, which prevent resident parent companies from deducting losses of non-resident subsidiaries, it is an infringement of those EC Treaty rights to deny group relief to a resident parent company where the non-resident subsidiary has exhausted all possibilities in its member state of residence of utilising the losses in question. This followed the referral to the ECJ of the case by the High Court which stayed proceedings on the appeal of the company against the decision of the Special Commissioners (*Marks and Spencer plc v Halsey (Inspector of Taxes)* [2003] STC (SCD) 70, 5 ITLR 536).

The High Court then ruled (in *Marks and Spencer plc v Halsey (Inspector of Taxes)* [2006] STC 1235) that, on the basis of the ECJ judgment, group relief was not available in the case of the French subsidiary. Claims in respect of the German and Belgian subsidiaries were remitted to the Special Commissioners to hear further evidence and submissions and to determine the appeals in light of this and the ECJ decision.

Both parties appealed to the Court of Appeal, which ruled that the UK group relief rules should not be struck out in their entirety, that what was meant by 'no possibility of use of losses locally' was 'a real possibility' rather than 'no real likelihood' and that that test can be met at or up to the time when the claimant company makes its claim for group relief. (*Marks and Spencer plc v Halsey (Inspector of Taxes)* [2007] EWCA Civ 117, [2007] 2 CMLR 499, [2008] STC 526.)

The case was then heard by the First-tier Tribunal, which had to consider if Marks & Spencer fulfilled the requirements for relief laid down by the ECJ. The point at issue concerned the 'no possibility of relief' in the member state of residence test. The Tribunal held that this test was satisfied in the respect of all claims made while the overseas company was in liquidation or had been dissolved. The Tribunal also considered the correct method to be used to compute the losses relievable. One of the methods put forward by the company was accepted. Under this method, a UK tax computation was prepared, based on the local accounting loss per the annual accounts. The case went to the Upper Tribunal and judgment was given on 21 June 2010 where the losses of the foreign subsidiaries were allowed, except with regard to the years where the 'no possibility' test of other set off were not satisfied at the date of the original claims and the later claims were outside the time limits. Both parties have applied for leave to appeal. (*Marks & Spencer plc v Revenue and Customs Comrs* [2009] UKFTT 64 (TC), [2009] SFTD 1; [2010] UKUT 213 (TCC).)

In *Phillips Electronics UK Ltd v Revenue and Customs Comrs* [2009] UKFTT 226 (TC), [2010] 1 CMLR 511 the Tribunal accepted the company's claim that *ICTA 1988, ss 403D* and *406(2)* (which restricted consortium relief with regard to UK resident investors in joint ventures, and UK branches of overseas companies) contravened EC law and therefore could not prohibit the taxpayer company from claiming consortium relief. The case is likely to go to appeal.

Simon's Taxes. See **D2.2** *et seq.*

Group companies

Definition of a 'group'

[39.3] Companies are members of a 'group' of companies if one is a '75% subsidiary' of the other or both are 75% subsidiaries of a third company. This requires 75% of the company's ordinary share capital to be beneficially held directly or indirectly, and entitlement to 75% of the profits on a distribution and 75% of the assets available to equity holders on a winding up (see below with regard to 'equity holders').

[*CTA 2010, ss 151, 152, 1154; ICTA 1988, s 413(3)(a)*].

The residence of the companies constituting the group is not relevant although only UK-resident companies and companies carrying on a UK trade through a permanent establishment (or branch or agency) may claim group relief (see **39.2** above). See, however, **39.8** below as regards limitation of the application of the definition of 'group'.

Illustration of a group for group relief purposes:

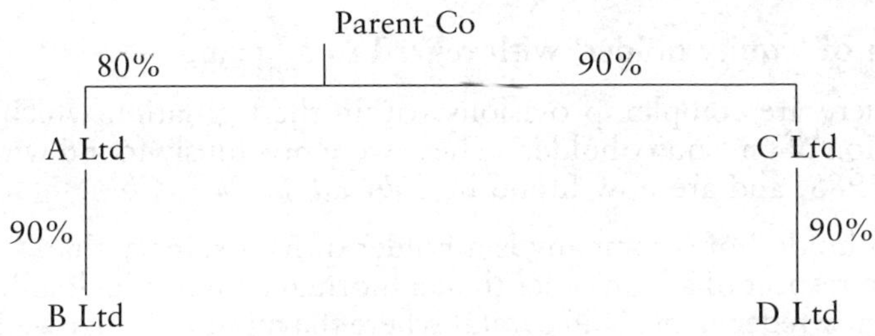

In the above scenario Parent Co and A Ltd are in a 75% group.

However, Parent Co and B Ltd are not in the same group for group relief purposes, as Parent Co holds 80% of the shares in A Ltd, which in turn holds 90% of the shares in B Ltd – which gives an indirect shareholding to Parent Co of only 72% (80% of 90% gives 72%). This is less than the required 75% so a group is not formed by Parent Co, A Ltd and B Ltd, therefore B Ltd is not able to surrender losses to Parent Co, or vice versa.

B Ltd and A Ltd are within a 75% group, so trading losses can be surrendered between them.

There are thus two group relief groups in the above scenario:

Parent Co + A Ltd + C Ltd + D Ltd

and

A Ltd + B Ltd

It can therefore be seen that a company can participate in more than one group for group relief purposes.

For the purposes of group relief, however, a company is treated as not owning:

(a) any share capital held as trading stock; or
(b) any share capital which it owns indirectly and which is directly held by another body corporate as trading stock.

[*CTA 2010, s 151(3); ICTA 1988, s 413(5)*].

Any share capital of registered **INDUSTRIAL AND PROVIDENT SOCIETIES** (**47**) is treated as ordinary share capital. [*CTA 2010, s 151(2); ICTA 1988, s 413(4)*].

As noted above, the company owning the shares must also be beneficially entitled to **at least 75%** of profits available for distribution to equity holders as such of the subsidiary **and** of assets similarly available in a winding-up. [*CTA 2010, s 151(4); ICTA 1988, s 413(7)*]. There are various provisions which provide the rules with regard to an analysis of these two additional conditions, and these are considered further in detail below.

It is provided that an open-ended investment company or authorised unit trust (see **52 INVESTMENT FUNDS**) can not be treated as a member of a group by *ICTA 1988, s 413(3A)* treated as inserted by *SI 2006 No 964, Reg 94(4)*.

Simon's Taxes. See D2.205–D2.207 *et seq*.

'Equity holders'

Definition of 'equity holder' with regard to a 'group'

[39.4] There are complex provisions within the legislation which deal with the definition of an 'equity holder'. These were previously found within *Sch 18* of *ICTA 1988*, and are now found in *CTA 2010, Pt 5, Ch 6*.

An 'equity holder' of a company is a holder of its 'ordinary shares' or a 'loan creditor' in respect of a loan other than a 'normal commercial loan'. The latter applies to any redeemable loan capital where the money is borrowed or capital assets transferred in return for any right of the company to receive income or in return for consideration, the value to the creditor company being at the time of transfer substantially less than the amount of the debt (including any debt premium).

[*CTA 2010, s 158; ICTA 1988, Sch 18 para 1(1)*].

Definition of 'ordinary shares' with regard to an 'equity holder'

'*Ordinary shares*' means, for this purpose, all shares other than certain preference shares: special provision was necessary to prevent companies (in particular banks), which received funding in exchange for shares, failing the test for a group for group relief purposes. For periods beginning on or after 1 January 2008, the shares must be restricted preference shares, defined as follows:

(i) issued for consideration, which is or includes new consideration, received by the company in respect of the issue of the shares;
(ii) carrying no rights to conversion into other shares or securities (subject to certain exclusions);
(iii) carrying no rights to acquire shares or securities;
(iv) not carrying rights to dividends, or carrying a restricted right to dividends; and
(v) not carrying a right to repayment of more than the consideration given for the shares, except in so far as the rights are comparable to those attaching to fixed interest shares quoted on the Stock Exchange.

Dividends carry a 'restricted right' to dividends if the dividends are no more than a reasonable commercial return on the new consideration; and one of the following applies:

(1) the dividends are fixed as to amount or rate of the nominal value of the shares and the company has no entitlement to reduce or not pay any of the dividends;
(2) the rate of dividend on the nominal value of the shares is a standard published rate or varies with RPI or similar index and the company has no entitlement to reduce or not pay any of the dividends; or
(3) (1) or (2) would be met but for the requirement that the company has no entitlement to reduce or not pay any of the dividends and either the company is only entitled to reduce the dividend 'in relevant circum-

stances' or having regard to all circumstances it is only likely that the company will reduce the amount of or fail to pay dividends if the company is in severe financial difficulties or does not pay on the recommendation of a regulatory body.

The Treasury may prescribe the circumstances in which a company is to be treated as in severe financial difficulties.

A company may make an irrevocable election, in its tax return, or by amending its tax return if it has already been filed, for the post 1 January 2008 provisions not to have effect in relation to shares issued before 18 December 2008 or on or after that date under an agreement entered into before it.

[*CTA 2010, ss 158–164; FA 2009, s 28, Sch 9*].

For periods beginning before 1 January 2008, fixed rate preference shares were defined as:

(a) issued for consideration which is or includes new consideration (as defined in *ICTA 1988, s 254*, see **31.13 DISTRIBUTIONS**);
(b) carrying no rights to conversion into other shares or securities or acquisition of additional shares or securities;
(c) on which any dividends are limited to a fixed amount, or to a fixed percentage of the nominal value, and represent no more than a reasonable commercial return on the new consideration received by the company for the issue of the shares; and
(d) on which any repayment right is limited to such consideration or is reasonably comparable with rights generally attached to listed fixed-dividend shares.

As regards (b) above, rights of conversion into shares or securities of the company's 'quoted parent company' are disregarded, as are rights of conversion into shares satisfying (a), (c) and (d) above, or securities satisfying (ii) and (iii) below, not themselves carrying conversion (other than into shares or securities in the 'quoted parent company') or acquisition rights.

[*ICTA 1988, Sch 18 para 1(2)(3)(5A)(5B)(8)*].

A company is another company's '*quoted parent company*' for these purposes if and only if:

(A) the other company is its 75% subsidiary (see **39.3** above), for which purpose it is assumed that the company is the 'quoted parent company' of the other;
(B) the parent is not itself a 75% subsidiary; and
(C) the parent's ordinary shares (or each class thereof) are listed on a recognised stock exchange or dealt in on the Unlisted Securities Market.

[*CTA 2010, s 164; ICTA 1988, Sch 18 para 1(5C)(5D); ITA 2007, s 1005; FA 2007, Sch 26*].

Definition of 'loan creditor'

As highlighted above, an 'equity holder' of a company is also a 'loan creditor' in respect of a loan other than a 'normal commercial loan'.

'*Loan creditor*' is as defined in *CTA 2010, s 453*, previously *ICTA 1988, s 417(7)* (see **22.7 CLOSE COMPANIES**) except that banks are specifically included.

[*CTA 2010, ss 158, 453; ICTA 1988, Sch 18 para 1(4)*].

'*Normal commercial loan*' is one representing (in whole or in part) new consideration (as defined in *ICTA 1988, s 254, see also CTA 2010, s 162*) and:

(i) which carries no right of conversion into other shares or securities or acquisition of additional shares or securities;
(ii) the interest on which is dependent neither on the results of the company's business (or part thereof) nor on the value of its assets, and represents no more than a reasonable commercial return on the new consideration lent; and
(iii) on which any repayment right is limited to such consideration or is reasonably comparable with the amount generally repayable (in respect of an equal amount of new consideration) under the terms of issue of listed securities.

As regards (i) above, rights of conversion into shares or securities of the company's quoted parent company (as above) are disregarded, as are rights of conversion into shares satisfying (a), (c) and (d) above, or securities satisfying (ii) and (iii) above, not themselves carrying conversion (other than into shares or securities in the quoted parent company) or acquisition rights.

A loan is not within (ii) above by reason only of the fact that:

(I) the terms of the loan provide for a reduction in the rate of interest in the event of an improvement in that business (or part) or an increase in the value of any of those assets, or for an increase in the rate of interest in the event of a deterioration in the business (or part) or a diminution in the value of any of those assets; or
(II) where the loan was to be applied in the acquisition of land other than with a view to resale at a profit (or to incidental loan costs), and was secured only on that land, the terms of the loan are such that the only way the loan creditor can enforce payment is by exercising rights granted as security over that land.

A loan on which the amount of interest depends to an extent on the results of the company's business as above, covers a limited recourse loan. (HMRC Company Taxation Manual, CTM81010.)

[*CTA 2010, s 162; ICTA 1988, Sch 18 para 1(5)(5A)(5B)(8)*].

Where any person has, directly or indirectly, provided new consideration for shares or securities in the company and that person (or any person connected with him, see **25 CONNECTED PERSONS**) uses in his trade assets belonging to the company which have been the subject of certain capital allowances, that person and no other is treated as an equity holder in respect of those shares or securities and as beneficially entitled to any distribution of profits or assets attributable to those shares or securities.

[*CTA 2010, ss 159, 1122, 1123; ICTA 1988, Sch 18 para 1(6)*].

Where this provision applies to a bank which has provided new consideration solely by way of a normal commercial loan in the normal course of its banking business, and the cost of the assets so used is less than such new consideration, the bank is treated as a loan creditor for an amount equal to that cost and therefore as an equity holder in respect of that amount.

[*CTA 2010, s 159; ICTA 1988, Sch 18 para 1(7)*].

Definition of 'profits available for distribution'

Profits available for distribution represent the total profits of the subsidiary for the 'accounting period' or, if there is no such profit, £100 (the 'profit distribution'). It does not matter that there are no profits. All payments not otherwise treated as **DISTRIBUTIONS (31)** are included. In the case of a non-resident company trading through a UK permanent establishment (or branch or agency) (see **39.2** above), the total profits are determined as if it were UK-resident.

[*CTA 2010, s 165; ICTA 1988, Sch 18 para 2*].

'Profits' for this purpose are the 'commercial' distributable profits (having regard to company law requirements), rather than those computed for tax purposes (see HMRC Company Taxation Manual, CTM81035) and only the company's interest as an equity holder is taken into account [*CTA 2010, s 167*].

Assets available on a winding up

The assets available for distribution in a winding-up comprise any excess of assets over liabilities as shown in the subsidiary's balance sheet at the end of the accounting period, or (if there is no such excess or the balance sheet is prepared to a different date) £100. Any such asset received by the equity holder on a winding-up is treated as a distribution to him, notwithstanding that it would not otherwise be so treated.

[*CTA 2010, s 166*].

Any new consideration provided by an equity holder for its shares which is then loaned to, or used to acquire shares in, that equity holder or any person connected with it (see **25 CONNECTED PERSONS**) is to be deducted from the total distributable assets and from those distributable to that equity holder.

[*CTA 2010, s 166; ICTA 1988, Sch 18 para 3*].

The percentage of the profits or assets to which an equity-holding company is, or would be, beneficially entitled includes any indirect entitlement through another body corporate.

[*CTA 2010, s 167; ICTA 1988, Sch 18 para 6*].

'*Accounting period*' (or post 1 April 2010, 'relevant accounting period') means any which is current at a time relevant to the group relief claim.

[*CTA 2010, s 168; ICTA 1988, Sch 18 para 7*].

There are detailed anti-avoidance provisions relating to the calculation of the relevant percentages in relation to equity holders of shares or securities with restricted or terminable rights. There are special rules where the surrendering or claimant company is non-UK resident.

[*CTA 2010, ss 170–182; ICTA 1988, Sch 18 paras 4, 5–5F; FA 2006, Sch 1 para 6*].

See **39.15** below for HMRC's interpretation of 'option arrangements'.

Kinds of group relief

[39.5] Group relief applies to various losses, deficits and excess management expenses. The following can be surrendered as group relief by a company for an accounting period:

(a) **Trading losses** computed as under *CTA 2009, s 47; CTA 2010, ss 37, 45; ICTA 1988, s 393(2)* or *s 393A(1)* except losses:
   (i) from trades carried on wholly overseas;
   (ii) from trades not carried on on a commercial basis and with a view to the realisation of gain (with an exception for statutory functions) (*CTA 2010, s 44*; see **55.2 LOSSES**); and
   (iii) which are denied relief by *CTA 2010, s 48* (losses from farming or market gardening); *ICTA 1988, s 397; CTA 2009, Sch 1 para 113* (see **55.22 LOSSES**).

(b) **Capital allowance excess** — refers to the excess allowances which have been deducted from or set against income from special leasing of plant and machinery. Such excess allowances may be surrendered in so far as they exceed such income for an accounting period (before deduction of losses or capital allowances brought forward) and the machinery or plant is not used by the lessee for a non-qualifying purpose (*CTA 2010, s 101*; see Note (2) under **13.23 CAPITAL ALLOWANCES — PLANT AND MACHINERY: FIXTURES AND LEASING**). See **55.3 LOSSES**.

(c) Non-trading deficits on loan relationships (see **54.5 LOAN RELATIONSHIPS**), these include non-trading debits on derivative contracts.

(d) **Amounts allowable as charitable donations.**

(e) **Losses in a UK property business**, excluding losses brought forward from earlier periods and losses incurred in a property business which was not carried on either on a commercial basis or in the exercise of statutory functions (*CTA 2010, s 102*, see further **62 PROPERTY INCOME**).

(f) **Management expenses** of companies with investment business (not brought forward from an earlier accounting period) *CTA 2010, s 103* and see further **51 INVESTMENT COMPANIES AND INVESTMENT BUSINESS.**

(g) **Non-trading losses on intangible fixed assets** (from 1 April 2002) (*CTA 2010, s 104*, see further **48.7 INTANGIBLE ASSETS**), excluding any brought forward from an earlier accounting period.

Amounts within (a) to (c) above are eligible for surrender regardless of whether the surrendering company has other profits of the same accounting period against which they could be set.

Amounts within (d), (e), (f) and (g) (relevant amounts) above are available for surrender only to the extent that the total available for surrender exceeds the surrendering company's gross profits of the accounting period, the order of set off for surrender purposes being taken to consist first of qualifying charitable donations, then of losses in a UK property business, then of management expenses and finally of non-trading losses on intangible assets.

The profits taken into account as 'gross' profits are those without any deduction in respect of amounts within (a)–(f) above or of 'any losses' etc. of other periods. The term '*any losses*' for this purpose does not include capital losses brought forward from a previous period and deducted as part of the computation of chargeable gains. Capital losses are not taken into account for this purpose (see **17.3 CAPITAL GAINS**). (*Taylor v MEPC Holdings Ltd* [2004] STC 123, HL.)

Where a non-UK resident company carries on business through a permanent establishment in the UK and has 'non-UK profits', relief will be available if three conditions are met. These are:

- the loss etc. must derive from activities within the charge to corporation tax in the surrender period;
- relief must not be available for the loss etc. under a double tax agreement for the surrender period;
- relief must not be available for such loss for non-UK tax purposes.

If these conditions are fulfilled, the loss etc. is treated as allowable (by deduction or otherwise) for UK tax purposes. See further **39.10** and **39.11** below.

The availability of group relief as above is subject to restriction in the case of dual resident investing companies (see **39.23** below), certain ring-fenced activities (see **55.3 OIL COMPANIES**), certain transactions in relation to the sale of lessor companies (see **5.27 ANTI-AVOIDANCE**) and certain transactions by leasing partnerships (**5.20 ANTI-AVOIDANCE**).

[*CTA 2010, ss 97–109; ICTA 1988, ss 403–403ZE; CAA 1990, s 61(7); CAA 2001, s 260(7), Sch 2 para 36; FA 2006, ss 82, 83, Sch 10 para 43; SI 2004 No 2310, Arts 14, 15; CTA 2009, Sch 1 paras 118–121*].

Simon's Taxes. See **D2.215–D2.225.**

Limits on group relief

[39.6] In order for a valid claim for group relief to be made both the surrendering and claimant company must apply to HMRC: a company may surrender its surrenderable amounts for the surrender period; the claimant company may make a claim for group relief for the claim period for all or part of the amounts.

The following conditions must be met:

(i) the surrendering company must consent to the claim (see **39.13** below);
(ii) there is a common period (the overlapping period); and
(iii) the surrendering and the claimant company are 75% subsidiaries of each other or both are 75% subsidiaries of a third company and both are UK-related, i.e. each company is either UK resident or the non-UK resident carries on a trade through a permanent establishment in the UK.

The amount for which group relief may be claimed against total profits may not exceed the lesser of:

(a) the 'unused part of the surrenderable amount for the overlapping period'; and
(b) the 'unrelieved part of the claimant company's total profits for the overlapping period'.

[*CTA 2010, s 138; ICTA 1988, s 403A(1)*].

The amount referred to in (a) above is so much of the total amount available for surrender for the accounting period of the surrendering company as is attributable (see below) to the 'overlapping period' and has not been the subject of any prior surrenders attributable to the 'overlapping period'.

The amount referred to in (b) above is so much of the total profits of the claimant company for the accounting period of the claim as is attributable (see below) to the 'overlapping period', reduced by any previously claimed group relief attributable to the 'overlapping period'.

The '*overlapping period*' is the period common to the accounting periods of both the claimant company and the surrendering company to which the claim relates, but excluding any part of the common period when:

- those companies are not both members of the same group and in the case of a non-UK resident company, carrying on a UK trade through a permanent establishment (or branch or agency); or
- (from 1 April 2006), in the case of a 'qualifying overseas loss' (see **39.10** below), the surrendering company is not a member of the same group as the claimant company (as defined for this purpose in **39.3** above) and is not resident or not carrying on a trade through a permanent establishment within an EEA territory.

There are detailed rules for determining the surrenderable amount for the overlapping period and the unrelieved part of the claimant company's total profits.

[*CTA 2010, ss 139, 140*].

For the above purposes the group relief allowable on any claim is determined as at the time when it becomes final (i.e. when it can no longer be withdrawn), as if every claim which had previously become final were a prior claim, and every claim which has not become final were a subsequent claim. Under self assessment this is impracticable as assessments are not final until the enquiry window is ended. The legislation has been changed in the rewrite to *CTA 2010* to put the current practice onto a statutory footing. Claims which would otherwise be treated as having been made at the same time are deemed to have been made in such order as the company or companies making them elect or jointly elect, or in the absence of such an election in such order as HMRC may direct. See the example at **39.7** below.

[*CTA 2010, ss 129–131, 134, 135, 141; ICTA 1988, s 403A; FA 2006, Sch 1 paras 2, 9*].

Attribution to overlapping periods

Where an apportionment falls to be made as above, to determine how much of an amount for a period falls to be attributed to a part of the period, the apportionment is generally made on a time basis according to how much of the whole period coincides with the part.

However, if some or all of the apportionments to be made in any particular case would lead to an unjust or unreasonable result, in relation to any person, the apportionments are to be made in such other manner as may be just and reasonable.

[*CTA 2009, ss 139–141; ICTA 1988, s 403B*].

For 'just and reasonable' apportionment, see HMRC Company Taxation Manual, CTM80260.

De-grouping charge

See **29.1 DEGROUPING CHARGES** for the effect on *CTA 2010, ss 138–142; ICTA 1988, ss 403A, 403B* of the application of the de-grouping provisions of *TCGA 1992, s 179*.

Consortia

The above rules apply with appropriate modifications to consortium group relief claims. Limitations also apply with regard to such relief claims. See further **39.19** below.

For provisions dealing with companies joining or leaving a group prior to the commencement of the above provisions (which apply broadly for accounting periods ending after 1 July 1997), see previous editions of Tolley's Corporation Tax.

Example

[39.7]

X Ltd incurs a trading loss in the year ending 31 December 2010 of £120,000. Throughout that period, it has two wholly-owned subsidiaries Y Ltd and Z Ltd. Y Ltd prepares accounts to 31 March, and has profits of £100,000 in the year ending 31 March 2010. Z Ltd prepares accounts to 30 September and has profits of £400,000 in the year ending 30 September 2010. No group relief claims or surrenders have been made other than those referred to below.

Y Ltd claims the maximum relief for the year ending 31 March 2010 by surrender from X Ltd.

Overlapping period three months to 31 March 2010

Maximum loss available for surrender

$^{3}/_{12} \times £120{,}000 = £30{,}000$

Maximum profits against which loss surrendered may be set

$^{3}/_{12} \times £100{,}000 = £25{,}000$

Thus X Ltd surrenders losses of £25,000 to Y Ltd.

Z Ltd then claims the maximum relief for the year ending 30 September 2010 by surrender from X Ltd.

Overlapping period nine months to 30 September 2010

Maximum loss available for surrender

	£
$^9/_{12}$ × £120,000 =	90,000
less amount previously surrendered (note (*a*))	25,000
	£65,000

Maximum profits against which loss surrendered may be set

$^9/_{12}$ × £400,000 = £300,000

Thus X Ltd surrenders losses of £65,000 to Z Ltd.

The balance of X Ltd's loss (£30,000) may be surrendered against losses of subsequent periods of Y Ltd and Z Ltd which overlap with X Ltd period to 31 December 2010.

Note

(a) As the overlapping period in relation to the surrender to Y Ltd falls entirely within the overlapping period in relation to the surrender to Z Ltd, the whole of the loss surrendered in relation to the earlier period is deducted from that available for the later period.

Overseas losses

UK losses of non-resident companies

[39.8] In relation to group relief for UK losses of non-resident companies carrying on a UK trade through a permanent establishment (see **39.2** and **39.5** above), relief attributable to the UK permanent establishment is broadly restricted as follows. Amounts available for surrender under these provisions, in addition to any losses or other amounts available for surrender (from 1 April 2006) by non-resident companies, are as set out in **39.10** below.

As highlighted above, losses, etc. available for surrender by the non-resident company for an accounting period are those which:

(i) are attributable to activities the income or gains from which for that period are or (if there were any) would be brought into account in computing chargeable profits for corporation tax purposes;

(ii) are not attributable to activities which are exempt under any double taxation relief arrangements (see **32.17 DOUBLE TAX RELIEF**), disregarding any claim requirement; and

(iii) do not correspond to, or are represented by, an amount which is allowable for foreign tax purposes against any 'non-UK profits', although this does not apply to amounts which are, or are an element in computing, profits exempted from that foreign tax.

'Foreign tax' for this purpose means any tax corresponding to income or corporation tax (including local and regional taxes), and any foreign tax provision by virtue of which the deductibility of an amount is dependent on whether or not it is deductible for UK tax purposes is disregarded.

'*Non-UK profits*' are amounts (or elements in computing amounts) charged to foreign tax and not included in corporation tax total profits of any person for any accounting period.

Similarly the total profits for an accounting period against which relief may be claimed by a non-resident company are restricted to amounts comprised in the company's corporation tax chargeable profits for the period and not arising from activities exempt from corporation tax under any double taxation relief arrangements (and this restriction on the scope of total profits applies also for the purposes of the definition of 'non-UK profits' as above).

For these purposes, amounts are exempt under double tax relief arrangements if their effect is to cause any income or gains arising from the activities to be disregarded in computing chargeable profits.

[*CTA 2010, ss 107, 108, 186, 187; ICTA 1988, s 403D; FA 2006, Sch 1 paras 3, 9*].

Overseas losses of UK-resident companies

[39.9] A loss, etc. of a UK-resident company is not available for surrender by way of group relief if it is 'attributable' to a permanent establishment through which the company carries on a trade outside the UK, and all or any part of it is, or represents, an amount allowable against 'non-UK profits' (as above) of any other person for the purposes of 'non-UK tax' under the law of the territory where the permanent establishment is situated. 'Non-UK tax' for this purpose means any tax corresponding to income or corporation tax (including local and regional taxes.

A loss, etc. is 'attributable' to a permanent establishment for this purpose if it would be available for surrender by way of group relief if it were computed only by reference to that permanent establishment and by the application of the same principles as apply to a permanent establishment through which a non-UK resident company carries on a trade in the UK (as above).

[*CTA 2010, ss 106, 187; ICTA 1988, s 403E*].

Simon's Taxes. See D2.224.

Allowable overseas losses of non-resident companies

Periods beginning on or after 1 April 2006

Losses of EEA group members

[39.10] Group relief may be available for a 'qualifying overseas loss' of a company resident in an EEA territory or carrying on a trade in an EEA territory through a permanent establishment (see **39.2** above). The relief attributable to the non-resident company is restricted as set out below and in **39.12** below.

The relief applies to accounting periods beginning on or after 1 April 2006. Accounting periods straddling 1 April 2006 are treated for this purpose as two separate periods, the amount of the claimant company's profits and the amount of the loss or other amount of the non-resident, surrendering company being apportioned to the two periods on a just and reasonable basis. These provisions were rewritten to *CTA 2010* for periods ending on or after 1 April 2010, see **39.11** below.

A loss or other amount is treated as a '*qualifying overseas loss*' available for surrender as group relief by the non-resident company only where all the following conditions are met in relation to the EEA territory.

(a) **The equivalence condition.** The amount must correspond (in all material respects) to the amount that would be available for surrender as group relief under *ICTA 1988, s 403* (see **39.5** above) if the company were resident in the UK.

(b) **The EEA tax loss condition.** This condition is met if the loss or other amount eligible for relief from tax under the relevant territory is calculated in accordance with the applicable rules under the law of that territory and, in the case of a non-resident company resident in any EEA territory, the amount is not attributable to a permanent establishment through which the company carries on a trade in the UK. In the case of a non-resident company that is not resident but carries on a trade through a permanent establishment in any EEA territory, the amount must not be attributable to activities which are exempt from tax under any double taxation arrangements (which would have the effect, if a claim were made, that income and gains arising from those activities are ignored in calculating the company's taxable profits, income or gains under the relevant territory).

(c) **The qualifying loss condition.** In the case of a non-resident company that is resident, or not resident but carrying on a trade through a permanent establishment, in any EEA territory, a loss or other amount qualifies for group relief if it cannot be given relief in any EEA territory in any period and has not been given any other qualifying relief in any other territory outside the UK. The circumstances in which an amount qualifies for relief in any EEA territory, or qualified for relief in any other territory outside the UK, is widely defined and includes amounts which can be set off against chargeable profits, income or gains arising to persons other than the non-resident company and also amounts which can be relieved by the payment of a credit, elimination or reduction of a tax liability or 'by any other means of any kind'. Whether an amount can be relieved in a future period is to be determined immediately after the end of the current period. All possible steps must be taken by the company or any other person to obtain the relief so that, effectively, the amount will not qualify for group relief if there was a way in which relief could have been obtained.

(d) **The precedence condition.** In the case of a non-resident company ('the relevant company') that is resident, or not resident but carrying on a trade through a permanent establishment, in any EEA territory, a loss or other amount qualifies for group relief if it cannot be relieved in any other territory outside the UK which is a qualifying territory in relation to that company. A territory is a qualifying territory in relation to the relevant company if another company resident in that territory owns (directly or indirectly) any of its ordinary share capital or if a third company resident in the UK owns (directly or indirectly) any ordinary share capital of that other company. The relevant company in this case must be a 75% subsidiary of the third company or a 75% subsidiary of a fourth company resident in the UK.

Where the above conditions are met so that a loss or other amount is available for surrender by way of group relief, the following provisions apply with respect to the calculation of the loss or other amount ('the EEA amount') arising to a non-resident company ('the EEA company') in any period ('the loss period').

The EEA amount must be recalculated in accordance with applicable UK tax rules, i.e. any applicable provision made by or under the Corporation Tax Acts.

The EEA amount available for surrender by way of group relief is so much of the amount meeting the above conditions that does not exceed the relevant proportion of the amount given by that recalculation. (In other words, where only a proportion of the losses are available for surrender, because some of the losses are relievable elsewhere, that proportion of the UK recomputed amount will be available for surrender.)

If the amount given by that recalculation is an amount of income or profits then none of the EEA amount will be available for surrender. The Treasury is given powers to modify such provisions, by regulation, for the purpose of recalculating the EEA amount.

The assumptions made with regard to the recalculation of the EEA amount can be found at *ICTA 1988, s 403F* and *Pts 1* and *2* of *Sch 18A*. They were rewritten to *CTA 2010, ss 111–128*, as follows. The provisions of *CTA 2010* apply with regard to accounting periods ending on or after 1 April 2010.

CTA 2010 rewrite

[39.11] As highlighted above, companies resident in or carrying on a trade in an EEA territory may surrender certain losses and other amounts to other group members within the UK. The definition of an EEA group can be found at *CTA 2010, s 136*.

The EEA amount which may be surrendered

Five steps have to be taken in order to determine the amount which may be surrendered. The steps are:

(1) find out how much is eligible for corporation tax relief (ignoring these provisions). Only the eligible amount will be available for relief — it is called the EEA amount.
(2) find the 'qualifying part of the EEA amount' by finding out if the extent to which the EEA amount satisfies the equivalence, EEA tax loss, qualifying loss and precedence conditions. (See below.)
(3) recalculate the EEA amount using the certain assumptions. (See below.) This will produce the recalculated EEA amount. The recalculation is done using corporation tax computational rules for determining losses or other amounts. (The Treasury has power to amend these rules for this purpose.)

(4) determine the amount which may be surrendered i.e. the lesser of the EEA amount and the 'relevant proportion' of the recalculated EEA amount. The relevant proportion is the qualifying part of the EEA amount to the EEA amount. There is an anti-avoidance provision which applies if there are arrangements with the main purpose, or one of the main purposes, of obtaining group relief;

(5) if any of this amount is excluded as mentioned below, deduct the excluded amount.

The conditions mentioned in (2) above are as follows:

(a) the equivalence condition is that the EEA amount is made up of items which would be surrenderable if the company had been UK resident, i.e. items within **39.5** (see also (a) at **39.10** above).

(b) the tax loss condition differs according to whether the companies are resident in the EEA country or not. In the former case, this condition is met by identifying the EEA amount as the amount calculated under the overseas tax law. However, amounts attributable to permanent establishments in the UK are excluded. Where the company is not resident in an EEA country but is carrying on trade through a permanent establishment within the EEA, the EEA amount is the amount determined for tax purposes in an EEA territory. However, there are exclusions to the extent that the EEA amount is subject to 'relieving arrangements'.

'*Relieving arrangements*' are double tax relief arrangements which have such effect that the income of gains would be ignored for UK tax purposes.

(c) the qualifying loss condition is fulfilled if the surrendering company or any other company cannot relieve the EEA amount in an EEA territory for overseas tax purposes by:

- set off against profits or gains in the current or a previous period;
- obtaining a repayment, tax deduction or any other relief against such tax or set off against future profits or gains of the surrendering company or any other company.

A similar exclusion applies, for relief that has been given, to the extent the EEA amount has been set against profits of the surrendering company in any period and were chargeable to tax for the period.

(d) the precedence condition addresses the situation where relief could be claimed in more than one country. It applies where the surrendering company is resident in an overseas country (not the EEA territory) and, by virtue of the UK parent holding ordinary share capital, is a 75% subsidiary of that UK resident company, other than as a result of it being a 75% subsidiary of another UK resident company.

In recalculating the EEA amount using UK tax rules, four assumptions have to be made. These are:

(i) residence — the surrendering company is assumed to become UK resident at the beginning of the EEA accounting period and to remain UK resident throughout that period. This does not involve assuming that there is a change in residence for the purpose of assumption (ii) below, or that it loses UK residence at the end of the EEA accounting period;

(ii) place the activities carried on — a trade is assumed to be carried on in the UK, as is any property business. Regarding interests in property, they have to be treated as being, so far as possible, the UK equivalents;

(iii) accounting periods — the UK accounting period is treated as beginning at the beginning of the EEA accounting period and ending at the earlier of the end of the EEA accounting period and 12 months after the beginning. Thereafter, if the EEA accounting period continues, it ends at the earlier of 12 months or when the EEA accounting period ends;

(iv) capital allowances — if the EEA company incurred any capital expenditure on the provision of plant or machinery for the purposes of any activity before the beginning of the loss period, it is treated as incurred for a non-qualifying activity and then brought into use for a qualifying activity at the beginning of the loss period under *CAA 2001, s 13* (see **13.24**(E)).

[*CTA 2010, ss 111–128; ICTA 1988, s 403F, Sch 18A; FA 2006, Sch 1 paras 4(1), 7, 9; CTA 2009, Sch 1 para 281*].

See HMRC Company Tax Manual, CTM81502 onwards which details how the extension to the group relief rules work.

Unallowable overseas losses of non-resident companies

[39.12] There are anti-avoidance provisions to prevent losses arising in EEA territories from being available for group relief in the UK where they have been purposefully created for such relief.

In the case of a non-resident company that is resident in any EEA territory, or if not resident is carrying on a trade in such territory through a permanent establishment, where a loss or other amount (as set out in **39.10** above) arising to that company is not attributable for corporation tax purposes to any UK permanent establishment, then it is not available for surrender by way of group relief under the provisions identified at **39.10** and **39.11** above if:

(a) it qualifies for group relief or arises to the non-resident company by reason only of 'relevant arrangements'; and

(b) the main purpose or one of the main purposes of the relevant arrangements was to secure that the amount would qualify for group relief.

'*Relevant arrangements*' are arrangements made on or after 20 February 2006 or arrangements made before that date where the amount arises or would (but for this provision) first qualify for group relief on or before that date. '*Arrangements*' includes any agreement, understanding, scheme, transaction or series of transactions (whether or not legally enforceable) made. See Company Tax Manual, CTM81502.

[*CTA 2010, s 127; Sch 2 para 52; ICTA 1988, s 403G; FA 2006, Sch 1 para 4(2)*].

Claims

Claimant company

[39.13] A claim for group relief under self-assessment must be included in the company tax return (or amended return) (see **66.4, 66.9 RETURNS**) for the accounting period for which the claim is made. It must specify the amount claimed (which must be expressed in money at the time the claim is made) and the surrendering company.

It must also state whether any of the following:

(a) the claimant company;
(b) the surrendering company; or
(c) any other company by reference to which either those companies are members of the same group or the conditions for consortium relief are satisfied,

was not UK resident in either or both of the surrendering company's accounting period to which the surrender relates or the corresponding accounting period of the claimant company.

The claim must be made (and may be withdrawn) at any time up to the latest of:

(i) the first anniversary of the filing date for the claimant company tax return;
(ii) 30 days after closure of any enquiry into that return (unless the enquiry, being otherwise out of time, was limited (see **66.21 RETURNS**) to matters to which a previous amendment making or withdrawing a group relief claim relates, or which are affected by the amendment);
(iii) 30 days after notice of any amendment of that return by HMRC following such an enquiry; and
(iv) 30 days after determination of any appeal against an amendment within (iii),

or at a later time if HMRC allow it (for which see **55.3 LOSSES**).

These time limits override the normal time limits for amendment of a company tax return. Withdrawals of claims must be made by amending the return, and a claim can only be amended by withdrawal and replacement by another claim.

A claim may be made after the surrendering company has left the group (*A W Chapman Ltd v Hennessey* (1981) 55 TC 516).

A claim may be made for less than the full amount available for surrender at the time of the claim, but is ineffective if it is for more than that amount. The amount available for surrender at any time is the total amount available (see **39.5** above) on the basis of the surrendering company's tax return, disregarding any amendment whose effect is deferred pending completion of an enquiry (see **66.21 RETURNS**), *less* all amounts for which notices of consent (see below) have been given and not withdrawn. Withdrawals are given effect before any claims made on the same day.

Where claims are made on the same day for an aggregate amount in excess of the amount available for surrender, HMRC determines which of the claims is to be ineffective to prevent an excess arising. In practice, they will treat as ineffective the claim(s) in the lowest amount(s) consistent with achieving this objective (see HMRC Company Taxation Manual, CTM97015, CTM97070).

Claims may be made by more than one company in respect of the same surrendering company accounting period. [*CTA 2010, s 135; ICTA 1988, s 402(5)*].

Consent — surrendering company

A claim requires the written consent of the surrendering company (and a consortium claim also that of each member of the consortium), which must be given to the officer of HMRC to whom the company makes its tax returns at or before the time the claim is made, and a copy of which must accompany the claim.

The consent notice must give the names and tax district references of the surrendering company and the company to which relief is being surrendered, the amount of the relief, and the surrendering company accounting period to which the surrender relates. It may not be amended, but may be withdrawn (by notice to the officer to whom the consent was notified) and replaced within the normal time limits (as above). Notice of withdrawal must be accompanied by the written consent of the claimant company, unless the withdrawal is the result of a reduction in the amount available for surrender (for which see below), and the claimant company must, so far as it may do so, amend its return accordingly.

See, however, below as regards simplified claim and surrender procedures.

Where the surrendering company has already made its return for the period to which the surrender relates, it must, at the same time as giving its consent, amend its return to reflect that consent. Where the consent relates to a trading loss for which relief has already been obtained by carry-forward, the surrendering company must (notwithstanding any time limits otherwise applicable) amend its return(s) for the subsequent period(s) in which relief was given for the loss to reflect the consent (relief for such periods being treated as given for carry-forward losses of earlier accounting periods before later ones).

Where there is a reduction in the total amount available for surrender (as above) below the amount for which consent to surrender has already been given, the company must, within 30 days, withdraw its consent (and may issue new notices of consent) so as to bring the total of amounts for which consent is given within the total amount available. Copies of the withdrawal notices and any new consents must be sent to the companies affected and to HMRC. If the company fails to take such corrective action, HMRC may by written notice to the company give directions as to which consents are to be treated as reduced or eliminated to the extent necessary to achieve that objective (subject to appeal in writing by the company within 30 days of the notice to the officer by whom it was given), and must copy the notice to any claimant company affected by those directions. A claimant company notified of any withdrawal or new consent or HMRC direction must, so far as it may do so, amend its return for the period in question accordingly.

Unpaid tax and HMRC assessments

Where a claimant company becomes liable to tax in consequence of receiving a notice of withdrawal or new consent or HMRC direction (as above), and any of the tax is unpaid six months after the company's 'time limit for claims' (see below), HMRC may, up to two years after that time limit, make an assessment in the name of the claimant company on any other company which has obtained group relief as a result of the surrender. The amount of the assessment is limited to the lesser of the amount of the unpaid tax and the amount of tax the other company saves by virtue of the surrender. The other company may recover the tax (and any interest thereon) from the claimant company.

The company's 'time limit for claims' for this purpose is the latest of the dates in (i)–(iv) above on which the company could make or withdraw a group relief claim for the accounting period for which the claim in question was made.

An assessment may be made to recover group relief which in the opinion of HMRC is or has become excessive. This is without prejudice to the making of a discovery assessment (see **7.3 ASSESSMENTS**) or to the making of adjustments by way of discharge or repayment of tax. As regards notices of assessment, time limits and appeals, the same conditions apply as in relation to discovery assessments. Where a claimant company fails, or is unable, to amend its return following receipt of a notice of withdrawal or new consent or HMRC direction (as above), an assessment may be made (if otherwise out of time) up to one year after the date of the notice (the date of the new notice if a new notice of consent follows a withdrawal notice).

[*FA 1998, Sch 18 paras 66–76*].

Simplified group relief procedures

Simplified arrangements

The *Corporation Tax (Simplified Arrangements for Group Relief) Regulations 1999* (*SI 1999 No 2975*) (as amended) provide for a group of companies all, or substantially all, of whose tax returns are made to the same tax office to enter into special arrangements enabling an authorised company within the group to act for the group in relation to group relief claims. The authorised company may then, in a form provided or authorised by HMRC, provide a written statement containing the information necessary for the amendment of company tax returns of the companies covered by the arrangements for the purpose of making or withdrawing group relief claims and surrenders.

Group companies are liable for any incorrect claim or return arising from the authorised company's statement. Consortium companies which can claim or surrender group relief may be included in the arrangements (and the authorised company may be a consortium company).

For the detailed requirements as to the making of an application by an authorised company, and the consequences of entering into such arrangements, see *SI 1999 No 2975* (as amended) and HMRC Company Taxation Manual, CTM97600 onwards. Note that it is not necessary for all the companies included in the arrangements to have identical accounting periods.

[*FA 1998, Sch 18 para 77; SI 1999 No 2975*].

Losses of non-resident companies

Overseas losses of non-resident companies

The above provisions apply to claims (from 1 April 2006) in respect of overseas losses of non-resident companies (see **39.2**(b), **39.10** and **39.11** above) with the following modifications. References to the relief being surrendered is to the EEA amount. References to the surrendering company's accounting period are to its deemed accounting period under **39.10**(iii) above. Notice of consent of the surrendering company is to be given by the claimant company to the officer of HMRC to whom that company makes its returns and the requirement for the notice to contain details of tax district reference does not apply.

Notice of withdrawal of consent is to be given by the claimant company and not the surrendering company. A notice of withdrawal and any new notice of consent under *FA 1998, Sch 18 para 75* (reduction in amount available for surrender) is to be sent to an officer of HMRC by the claimant rather than the surrendering company and any notice containing directions by an officer of HMRC is to be given to the claimant company. The claimant company rather than the surrendering company can appeal against such directions and the rest of *Sch 18* is to be similarly read with appropriate modifications.

Where a notice to produce documents is given to the claimant company for the purposes of an enquiry, the notice may require the claimant company to explain why the EEA amount meets the conditions for it to be treated as a qualifying loss and to provide details of the recalculation required (see **39.10** and **39.11** above). The claimant company may also be required to explain why the EEA amount is not prevented from being surrendered by virtue of the unallowable losses provision in **39.12** above.

[*CTA 2010, s 97 et seq; FA 1998, Sch 18 paras 66–77A; FA 2006, Sch 1 para 8*].

A claim may be made after the surrendering company has left the group (*A W Chapman Ltd v Hennessey* (1981) 55 TC 516).

See **39.5** above as regards amounts available for relief.

Simon's Taxes. See D2.240–D2.244.

Claims by non-UK resident companies trading in the UK

[39.14] As noted above, non-UK resident companies who are trading in the UK through a permanent establishment and who fulfil the conditions for group relief may make a claim for such relief.

Such claims must fulfil the following conditions:

- the surrendering company must consent to the claim;
- there must be an overlapping period;
- either, the surrendering company is a 75% subsidiary of the claimant and the latter is UK resident; or both the claimant and surrendering companies are 75% subsidiaries of a third company and that company is UK resident.

[*CTA 2010, ss 135, 136*].

Arrangements for transfer of company to another group or consortium

[39.15] Relief is denied where two companies are members of a group and 'arrangements' are in existence by virtue of which one company could leave the group and join another group, or any person could gain control of one company but not the other, or a third company could succeed to the trade of one of the companies.

Similar restrictions apply to consortium relief. There are also provisions to cover the situation where there are arrangements under which the consortium-owned company could leave the group or where the company could come under the control of a third company.

[*CTA 2010, ss 154, 155; ICTA 1988, s 410*].

Definition of 'arrangements'

'*Arrangements*' for this purpose are those of any kind, whether in writing or not (*CTA 2010, s 156*), which are in existence during the relevant period, irrespective of when they came into existence (*Pilkington Bros Ltd v CIR* (1982) 55 TC 705, HL) and without regard to the extent of their implementation (*Irving v Tesco Stores (Holdings) Ltd* (1982) 58 TC 1, HL).

Arrangements which could not legally be carried out without variation of the underlying agreement were ineffective for these purposes (*Scottish and Universal Newspapers Ltd v Fisher* [1996] STC (SCD) 311).

The restriction of relief applies only to accounting periods or parts thereof during which the arrangements subsisted (*Shepherd v Law Land plc* (1990) 63 TC 692, HL).

Exceptions under SP 3/93 and ESC C10

'Arrangements' (and 'option arrangements', see **39.4** above) are the subject of HMRC practice and concession (see HMRC Statement of Practice, SP 3/93 and HMRC Extra-Statutory Concession C10 as revised). Under these, the special rules relating to 'arrangements' are not applied to the following cases:

(I) Certain types of agreement regulating the affairs of companies which hold shares or securities in a commercial joint venture company, under which those shares or securities could be transferred following certain triggering events, until such a triggering event occurs. Such agreements will be of a kind under which remaining members are allowed or required to acquire the holding of a departing company, or a departing company is allowed or required to transfer its holding to remaining members. For detailed guidance on the manner in which shares will be transferred under such an agreement, and of the triggering events which may apply, see HMRC Extra-Statutory Concession C10 as revised.

(II) The use of shares or securities as security for a loan, e.g. a mortgage. The mortgage etc. will not constitute 'arrangements' until an event occurs which allows the mortgagee to exercise his rights against the mortgagor, provided that, prior to the occurrence of such an event, the mortgagee possesses only such control over the shares etc. as is required to protect his interest. If a default is remedied before the mortgagee exercises his rights, the default will not be regarded as having brought 'arrangements' into existence.

(III) Straightforward negotiations for the disposal of shares or securities in a company, before the point at which an offer is accepted subject to contract or on a similar conditional basis.

(IV) An offer to the public at large of shares in a business, unless there are exceptional features.

(V) Operations leading towards the disposal of shares or securities in a company, until any necessary approval by shareholders has been given, or the company's directors become aware that it will be given.

(VI) Where, following negotiations with a number of potential purchasers, the vendor concentrates on one, unless there were an understanding between them in the character of an option, e.g. if the offer, whether or not formally made, were allowed to remain open for an appreciable period, allowing the potential purchaser to choose the moment to create a bargain.

(VII) Company reconstructions requiring the approval of shareholders, until the necessary approval is given or the directors are aware that it will be given.

(I) and (II) above do not apply where the person standing to acquire shares, securities or control could (alone or with **CONNECTED PERSONS** (**25**)) dictate the terms or timing of the acquisition in advance of the triggering event. Membership of the joint venture company will not of itself result in members being 'connected'.

'Arrangements' (but not 'option arrangements') may exist even though not enforceable. If an agreement provides for the creation of specified option rights exerciseable at some future time, 'option arrangements' come into existence when the agreement is entered into.

(HMRC Statement of Practice, SP 3/93 and HMRC Extra-Statutory Concession C10 as revised). (SP 3/93 supersedes SP 5/80, published on 26 March 1980, but states that, although some features of SP 5/80 are omitted or revised, 'this does not indicate a more restrictive approach on the part of the Inland Revenue'.)

The power of a Minister to direct a statutory body as to the disposal of its (or any subsidiary's) assets is not an arrangement for this purpose. [*CTA 2010, s 156; ICTA 1988, s 410(7)*].

See also HMRC Company Taxation Manual, CTM80175–CTM80205.

Simon's Taxes. See **D2.251, D2.252.**

Payment for group relief

[39.16] Payments may be made for group relief and, in certain circumstances, will be tax neutral. If, by agreement, the claimant company pays the surrendering company an amount equal to, or less than, the relief surrendered by it as above, that payment is ignored in the corporation tax computations of both payer and payee and is not treated as a distribution (see **61.11 PROFIT COMPUTATIONS**).

[*CTA 2010, s 183; ICTA 1988, s 402(6); F(No 2)A 2005, s 38, Sch 11 Pt 2(7)*].

Other limitations on relief

[39.17] Relief may not be given more than once in respect of the same amount. [*CTA 2010, s 137(7); ICTA 1988, s 411(1)*].

In the case where it is discovered that too much relief has been given, see **39.13** above.

See also **39.5** above.

No group relief is available where a deduction is denied for the relevant return under alternative finance arrangements where the provision is not at arm's length and *CTA 2009, s 520* applies.

[*CTA 2009, Sch 1 para 124*].

Relationship to other reliefs

[39.18] Group relief is deducted from the claimant company's total profits (see **39.5** above) before reduction by any losses etc. carried back, but as reduced by any other relief from tax (including relief in respect charitable donations under *ICTA 1988, s 338* or in respect of non-trading deficits on loan relationships (see **54.5 LOAN RELATIONSHIPS**). Total profits for this purpose are calculated on the assumption that that company makes all relevant claims to set trading losses and capital allowances against total profits under *CTA 2010, s 37; ICTA 1988, s 393A(1)* and *CAA 2001, s 260(3)* (or *CAA 1990, s 145(3)*) respectively. See **55.3 LOSSES** and **10.2 CAPITAL ALLOWANCES — INTRODUCTION**.

'*Losses etc carried back*' means trading losses carried back under *CTA 2010, s 37; ICTA 1988, s 393A(1)(b)*, capital allowances carried back under *CAA 2001, s 260(3)*, and non-trading deficits carried back under *FA 1996, s 83(2)* (see **54.4 LOAN RELATIONSHIPS**) or a deficit under *CTA 2009, s 459* for a later year than the year of claim.

[*CTA 2010, s 137; ICTA 1988, s 407; CAA 2001, Sch 2 para 37; CTA 2009, Sch 1 para 123*].

Example

A Ltd (a group member) has the following, for the accounting periods shown.

	To 31 December 2009	To 31 December 2010
Trading (loss) brought forward	(£500)	—
Trading income/(loss)	£1,000	(£1,000)
Income from non-trading loan relationships	£500	£500
Charges paid (charitable donations)	(£200)	(£200)

Group relief available to A Ltd will be subject to the following options and restrictions.

(a) *For the accounting period ended 31 December 2009*

(i) The loss brought forward and the charges paid must be relieved in priority to group relief. The maximum amount of group relief claimable will accordingly be the amount of profits on which corporation tax would otherwise be borne, i.e. £800.

(ii) If relief for this period is claimed under *s 393A(1)* for so much of the trading loss of the following period as cannot be relieved in that period, i.e. £500, such relief would be displaced by a group relief claim, and would then be available for carrying forward.

(b) *For the accounting period ending 31 December 2010*

Whether or not the company claims relief under *s 393A(1)* (*now CTA 2010, s 37*), no group relief is obtainable.

Simon's Taxes. See D2.202.

Consortia

[39.19] Consortium relief is a variation of group relief where losses of a consortium company can be transferred to consortium members and vice versa. The transfer of losses will be in proportion to the consortium member's interest in the consortium.

Definition of consortium

A consortium company is a company which is owned, to the extent of 75% (at least) by consortium members (each of which owns at least 5% of the shares of the consortium company). There are other requirements, see further below.

Available consortium relief

Group relief is available where either the surrendering company or the claimant company is a member of a consortium and the other company (the consortium company) is:

(a) a 'trading company' which is 'owned by the consortium' and which is not a 75% subsidiary (see **39.3** above) of any company, or

(b) a trading company which:
  (i) is a '90% subsidiary' of a 'holding company' which is owned by the consortium, and
  (ii) is not a 75% subsidiary of any other company, or
(c) a holding company which is owned by the consortium and which is not a 75% subsidiary of any company;

and both companies are UK related, i.e. each is UK resident or a non-resident company carrying on a trade in the UK through a permanent establishment (see **39.6** above).

For accounting periods beginning on or after 12 July 2010, legislation was introduced in *F(No 3)A 2010* to allow the relief to be available even if the link company is not UK related, as long as it is a company established in the European Economic Area (EEA).

CTA 2010, s 133 is amended to allow for an EEA established link company and a new *s 134A* has been inserted defining a company established in the EEA as one which is constituted under the law of the UK or an EEA territory and which has its registered office, central administration or principal place of business within the EEA.

Consortium relief is also available where the claimant or the surrendering company is not a member of a consortium, but is a member of the same group as a third company (the link company) which itself is a member of the consortium and the claimant, surrendering and link companies are all UK related.

[*CTA 2010, ss 132, 133, 153; ICTA 1988, s 402(3)*].

Where the surrendering company consents to the claim, there is an overlapping period and one of the undernoted conditions applies, then consortium relief is available. More than one company may make a claim against a surrenderable amount.

The conditions are:

(1) either (when surrendering up) the surrendering company is a trading company or a holding company which is owned by a consortium and the claimant is a member of the consortium and both are UK related (see above), or (when surrendering down) the claimant company is a trading or holding company owned by a consortium, the surrendering company is a member of the consortium and both are UK related;
(2) the above similarly applies where the consortium company is surrendering and there is a link company, which is a member of the consortium, but the claimant company is not;
(3) the above similarly applies where the consortium company is the claimant company and there is a link company, which is a member of the consortium, but the surrendering company is not.

No claim may be made where the shares in the other company (or its holding company) are held by the member of the consortium as trading stock.

[*CTA 2010, ss 130, 132, 133; ICTA 1988, s 402(4)*].

The residence of the companies is not relevant in determining whether the consortium relationship requirement is satisfied (and see further below), although the claimant and surrendering companies must each either be resident in the UK or carry on a UK trade through a permanent establishment.

[*CTA 2010, s 134; ICTA 1988, s 402(3A)(3B); FA 2006, Sch 1 para 1(4)*].

Relief may also be restricted by reference to the surrendering company's losses, and the claimant company's profits, of the corresponding accounting period (see below for more details).

With effect for accounting periods beginning *on or after 1 October 2002*, relief may also be restricted where a company which is a consortium member claims consortium group relief and also claims bad debt relief in respect of a loan to the consortium company. See **54.42 LOAN RELATIONSHIPS**.

See also **64.6 RESEARCH AND DEVELOPMENT EXPENDITURE** for a restriction on surrendering losses by a small or medium-sized company which is owned by a consortium and is entitled to research and development relief.

A '*holding company*' is a company the business of which consists wholly or mainly in the holding of shares or securities in trading companies which are its 90% subsidiaries. [*CTA 2010, s 185; ICTA 1988, s 413(3)*]. A single subsidiary will constitute its parent a holding company.

Prior to *FA 2000*, the group relief rules applied only to UK-resident companies. The House of Lords held in *ICI plc v Colmer* [1996] STC 352, HL, that the UK legislation clearly required the subsidiaries to be considered to be UK-resident for this purpose, but on a reference to the European Court of Justice ([1998] STC 874) it was held that, in relation to EU subsidiaries, this requirement was incompatible with Community law. Following the ECJ decision, the House of Lords reconsidered and affirmed its decision in relation to companies resident outside the EU and EEA ([1999] STC 1089). (See HMRC Company Taxation Manual, CTM80300–CTM80370 regarding international groups and changes made by *FA 2000*.)

A '*trading company*' is a company the business of which consists wholly or mainly of the carrying on of a trade or trades or the holding company of a trading group. [*CTA 2010, s 90; ICTA 1988, s 413(3)*].

A company is '*owned by a consortium*' if at least 75% of its 'ordinary share capital' is directly and beneficially owned amongst them by companies each owning at least one-twentieth, which are the 'members of the consortium'. [*CTA 2010, s 154; ICTA 1988, s 413(6)*].

For this purpose, '*ordinary share capital*' means all the issued share capital of a company other than restricted preference shares. Restricted preference shares are those fulfilling all the following conditions:

- shares issued for, or which include, new consideration;
- no conversion rights attached to loan stock or shares or stock in the parent company;
- no right to acquisition of shares or securities attached to the shares;
- no right to dividends or restricted right to dividends;

- no right to repayment in excess of new consideration, except so far as the rights are reasonably comparable with those generally carried by fixed dividend shares listed on a recognised stock exchange.

'Issued share capital' does not include founder members' deposits in a company limited by guarantee (*South Shore Mutual Insurance Co Ltd v Blair (Inspector of Taxes)* [1999] STC (SCD) 296).

A company is the '*90% subsidiary*' of another if not less than 90% of its ordinary share capital is directly owned by that other. The definition of 'ordinary share capital' given above applies. The parent company must also be beneficially entitled to at least 90% of profits available for distribution to the equity holders as such of the subsidiary and of assets similarly available in a winding-up.

[*CTA 2010, ss 154–157; ICTA 1988, s 838*].

See **39.4** above, and note that a holder of 'ordinary share capital' of a company may not qualify as an 'equity holder', for which a different definition of 'ordinary shares' applies. [*CTA 2010, ss 153, 1154; ICTA 1988, ss 413(7), 832(1), 838, Sch 18*].

For the definition of a 75% subsidiary, see **39.3** above.

A claim for group relief requires the consent of all other members of the consortium.

[*ICTA 1988, Sch 17A para 10(2); FA 1998, Sch 18 para 70(2)*].

Restrictions on consortium relief

Claims for consortium relief are restricted as follows:

(i) Where the claimant company is a member of a consortium, the amount which may be set off against its total profits for the overlapping period is the lowest in that period of the following percentages of the surrenderable amount:
   (A) the percentage (or average percentage) of the surrendering company's ordinary share capital which is beneficially owned by the claimant company;
   (B) the percentage (or average percentage) of any profits available for distribution to the surrendering company's equity holders to which the claimant company is beneficially entitled; and
   (C) the percentage (or average percentage) of any assets of the surrendering company available for distribution to its equity holders on a winding-up to which the claimant company would be beneficially entitled.

(ii) Where the surrendering company is a member of a consortium, the amount which may be set off against the total profits of the claimant company for the overlapping period is the lowest in that period of the following percentages of those total profits:
   (A) the percentage (or average percentage) of the claimant company's ordinary share capital which is beneficially owned by the surrendering company;

(B) the percentage (or average percentage) of any profits available for distribution to the claimant company's equity holders to which the surrendering company is beneficially entitled; and

(C) the percentage (or average percentage) of any assets of the claimant company available for distribution to its equity holders on a winding-up to which the surrendering company would be beneficially entitled.

(iii) Where the claimant (or surrendering) company is a subsidiary of a holding company owned by a consortium, (i) (or (ii)) above applies by reference to the holding company rather than the claimant (or surrendering) company.

Terms used in (i)–(iii) are defined as above and as in **39.3–39.4** above.

In determining the average percentage of a member's interest in a consortium, a weighted average taking into account the length of time involved will be used. (HMRC Company Taxation Manual, CTM80540).

Finance (No3) Act 2010 has introduced further restrictions (at *Sch* 6) as to the losses which may be claimed from or surrendered to a consortium with regard to accounting periods beginning on or after 12 July 2010.

An additional test of directly held voting power on the part of the surrendering or claimant company has been added to the tests outlined above with *CTA 2010, ss 143 and 144* amended accordingly.

As noted at **39.15** above, there are restrictions under *CTA 2010, s 155* where arrangements are in place such that a person (or persons) with less than 50% of the ordinary share capital of a trading company together control (or who could obtain control) of the company, in such a case the company is not treated as a consortium company. Pursuant to *F(No 3)A 2010* further, anti-avoidance provisions have been introduced (*CTA 2010, ss 146A and 146B*) which limit the amount of relief available on a consortium claim where arrangements have been put in place which allow a member (or members) access to a proportion of losses in excess of that which they are entitled to under the above rules.

Where a claimant company or link company would control the surrendering company (being the consortium company), but for the existence of arrangements which prevent such control (either by those companies alone, or together with other consortium members), then the available relief is halved. Similarly with regard to the position of a surrendering company or link company which might control the claimant company, but for the existence of arrangements which prevent such control. The provisions apply where those arrangements are part of a scheme, the main purpose, or one of the main purposes, of which is to enable the claimant company to obtain a tax advantage per *CTA 2010, s 1139*.

[*CTA 2010, ss 143, 144, 146A, 146B; ICTA 1988, s 403C*].

Simon's Taxes. See **D2.208, D2.230, D2.231**.

Examples

(A) Loss by company owned by consortium

[39.20]

On 1 April 2009 the share capital of E Ltd was owned as follows.

	%
A Ltd	40
B Ltd	40
C Ltd	20
	100

All the companies were UK resident for tax purposes.
During the year ended 31 March 2010 the following events took place.
On 1.7.09 D Ltd bought 20% from A Ltd
On 1.10.09 C Ltd bought 10% from B Ltd
The companies had the following results for the year ended 31 March 2009.

		£
A Ltd	Profit	40,000
B Ltd	Profit	33,000
C Ltd	Profit	10,000
D Ltd	Profit	18,000
E Ltd	Loss	(100,000)

Consortium relief for the loss sustained by E Ltd would be available as follows.

	A Ltd	B Ltd	C Ltd	D Ltd
	£	£	£	£
Profits for the year ended 31.3.10	40,000	33,000	10,000	18,000
Deduct Loss surrendered by E Ltd	(25,000)	(33,000)	(10,000)	(13,500)
Chargeable profits	£15,000	—	—	£4,500

E Ltd		Losses
	£	£
Loss for the year ended 31.3.10		100,000
Deduct Loss surrendered to A Ltd	(25,000)	
B Ltd	(33,000)	
C Ltd	(10,000)	
D Ltd	(13,500)	(81,500)
Not available for consortium relief		£18,500

Notes

(a) Loss relief for each member of the consortium is the lower of its share of the loss and its own profit for the overlapping period.
(b) The maximum share of losses of E Ltd appropriate to each member is:

	%	£
A Ltd 40% × 3/12 + 20% × 9/12	25	25,000
B Ltd 40% × 6/12 + 30% × 6/12	35	35,000
C Ltd 20% × 6/12 + 30% × 6/12	25	25,000
D Ltd 20% × 9/12	15	15,000
	100	£100,000

(B) Loss by consortium member

A Ltd, B Ltd, C Ltd and D Ltd have for many years held 40%, 30%, 20% and 10% respectively of the ordinary share capital of E Ltd. All five companies are UK resident and have always previously had taxable profits. However, for the year ended 30 June 2010, D Ltd has a tax loss of £100,000, followed by taxable profits of £40,000 for the subsequent year. E Ltd's taxable profits are £80,000 and £140,000 for the two years ending 31 December 2009 and 31 December 2010 respectively.

With the consent of A Ltd, B Ltd and C Ltd, D Ltd can (if it wishes) surrender the following part of its loss of £100,000 to E Ltd.

	£
Common period 1.7.09 to 31.12.09	
E Ltd's profit 6/12 × £80,000 × 1/10	4,000
D Ltd's loss 6/12 × £100,000	(50,000)
Common period 1.1.10 to 30.6.10	
E Ltd's profit 6/12 × £140,000 × 1/10	7,000
D Ltd's loss 6/12 × £100,000	(50,000)

The lower common figures for the two periods are £4,000 and £7,000.

Therefore, E Ltd can claim £4,000 of D Ltd's loss against its own profits for the year ended 31.12.09 and £7,000 against its profits for the year ending 31.12.10.

Group/consortium relief interaction

[39.21] Special provisions apply where both consortium group relief ('consortium relief') (see **39.19** above) and other group relief ('group relief') (see **39.2** onwards above) may be claimed in respect of the same losses, etc, i.e. where either the member of a consortium or a company owned by a consortium is a member of a group, or both are members of separate groups. Restrictions apply to the consortium relief available as follows.

Company owned by consortium also a member of a group

(i) Consortium relief is available on the ownership proportion to members of the consortium in respect of losses, etc. of the company owned by the consortium only after deduction of all possible group relief claims thereon (but taking into account any claims made by group companies in respect of other losses within the group).

(ii) The profits of the company owned by the consortium against which (or against a fraction of which) relief for losses, etc. of members of the consortium may be claimed are first reduced by any group relief claims it could make in respect of losses, etc. of other companies in the group (but taking into account any claims made by other group companies in respect of such losses).

(iii) the ownership proportion is the lowest of:

- (A) the proportion of the ordinary share capital of the surrendering company which is beneficially owned by the claimant company;
- (B) the proportion of profits of the surrendering company available for distribution to equity holders of that company to which the claimant is beneficially entitled;
- (C) the proportion of the surrendering company's assets available for distribution to such equity holders on winding up to which the claimant would be beneficially entitled.

The proportions are those for the overlapping period, and if they vary during that period, the average is taken.

Similar rules apply where the claimant company is owned by the consortium and where there is a link company (see below).

An '*equity holder*' for this purpose is any person holding ordinary shares in the company or is a loan creditor in respect of a loan which is not a normal commercial loan. For this purpose, loan creditor and ordinary shares are specially defined (*CTA 2010, ss 158(1)(b)–160*).

[*CTA 2010, ss 143–147, 157–168*].

Member of consortium also a member of a group (referred to as the 'link company')

(a) Any consortium relief claim the link company could make (disregarding any deficiency of profits) may be made by any other company in the group (provided that it is not itself a member of the consortium). The provisions at **39.6** above (which limit relief by reference to overlapping periods of the claimant and surrendering companies) apply as if any period during which the claimant company was not a group member were not comprised in the overlapping period and were a part of the claimant company's accounting period which did not coincide with any part of the surrendering company's accounting period. The total consortium relief of the link company and other companies in the same group may not exceed that claimable by the link company (but disregarding any deficiency of profits in the link company).

(b) Consortium relief may be claimed by a company owned by the consortium in respect of losses, etc. of members of the same group as the link company, which are not themselves members of the consortium, as if the surrendering company were a member of the consortium at all times at which the link company is a member. The fraction of the profits against which the losses, etc. may be claimed is determined by reference to the consortium member's share in the claimant company in the surrendering company's overlapping period of loss, etc. The provisions at **39.6** above (which limit relief by reference to overlapping periods of the claimant and surrendering companies) apply as if any period during which the surrendering company was not a group member were not comprised in the overlapping period and were a part of the claimant company's accounting period which did not coincide with any part of the surrendering company's accounting period. The total relief which may be claimed by the company owned by the consortium in an accounting period from the link company and other members of the same group may not exceed what it could have claimed from the link company if the link company's accounting period was the same as that of the company owned by the consortium.

Where a *company owned by a consortium* has trading losses and other profits against which the losses could be set under *CTA 2010, s 37; ICTA 1988, s 393(2)* or *s 393A(1)* (see **55.3 LOSSES**), the losses, etc. available for consortium relief are reduced by the amount of any such set-off which could be claimed. This operates in priority to (i) above where applicable.

[*CTA 2010, ss 147–149; ICTA 1988, ss 403ZA(3)(4), 405, 406*].

The *Finance (No3) Act 2010* has introduced provisions in respect of link companies within the EEA. *CTA 2010, s 133* has been amended, with new *subsections 133(5) to 133(8)* being inserted. A link company may now be established in the EEA Where it is not UK related, the link company must be a member of the same group as the claimant or surrendering company without the involvement of a company not established in the EEA.

A company is established in the EEA if it is constituted under the law of the UK or an EEA territory and has its registered office, central administration or principal place of business within the EEA. The link company is then assumed to be UK related for the purpose of establishing the amount of relief that the link company's group is able to claim.

These provisions have effect in relation to accounting periods beginning on or after 12 July 2010.

Simon's Taxes. See D2.232.

Example

[39.22]

A Ltd owns 100% of the share capital of B Ltd

B Ltd owns 40% of the share capital of D Ltd

C Ltd owns 60% of the share capital of D Ltd

D Ltd owns 100% of the share capital of E Ltd

D Ltd owns 100% of the share capital of F Ltd

There are two groups, A and B, and D, E and F.

D is owned by a consortium of B and C. This relationship has existed for a number of years with all companies having the same accounting periods. None of the companies has any losses brought forward.

The companies have the following results for year ended 31 July 2010.

A Ltd	£100,000	profit
B Ltd	£(30,000)	loss
C Ltd	£Nil	
D Ltd	£(20,000)	loss
E Ltd	£10,000	profit
F Ltd	£(3,000)	loss

E Ltd claims group relief as follows.

		£	£
Profit			10,000
Deduct Group relief: loss surrendered by F Ltd	note (a)	3,000	
Group relief: loss surrendered by D Ltd	note (a)	7,000	(10,000)
			—

A Ltd can claim group relief and consortium relief as follows.

		£	£
Profit			100,000
Deduct Group relief: loss surrendered by B Ltd	note (b)	30,000	
Consortium relief: loss surrendered by D Ltd	note (c)	5,200	(35,200)
Chargeable profit			£64,800

Notes

(a) Where a loss of a company owned by a consortium or of a company within its group may be used both as group relief and consortium relief, group relief claims take priority. In determining the consortium relief available, it is assumed that the maximum possible group relief is claimed after taking account of any other actual group relief claims within the consortium-owned company's group. As F Ltd has surrendered losses of £3,000 to E Ltd, D Ltd can only surrender £7,000 to E Ltd. Consortium relief is restricted to the balance of D Ltd's loss, i.e. £13,000. If E Ltd had not claimed £3,000 group relief for F Ltd's loss, D Ltd could have surrendered £10,000 to E Ltd by way of group relief and this would have reduced D Ltd's loss for consortium relief purposes to £10,000.

(b) Group relief available to A Ltd is the lower of £100,000 and £30,000.

(c) Consortium relief available to A Ltd is the lower of £70,000 (its profit as reduced by group relief) and £5,200 (40% of £13,000, see note (a) above). The relief available to A Ltd is the same as that which B Ltd could have claimed if it had had sufficient profits. A Ltd could also have claimed

> consortium relief in respect of F Ltd's loss if that had exceeded the £10,000 necessary to cover E Ltd's profit.

Dual resident investing companies

[39.23] Group relief is not available for a loss, etc. of the company which would otherwise have been the surrendering company, if that company is a 'dual resident investing company'.

A UK resident company is a '*dual resident company*' if it is within the charge to tax under the laws of a territory outside the UK, whether it derives its company status under those laws, or because its place of management is in that territory, or because it is for any other reason regarded as resident in that territory, for the purposes of that charge. A dual resident company is a '*dual resident investing company*' in an accounting period if either:

(a) throughout that period it is not a '*trading company*', i.e. a company whose business consists wholly or mainly of the carrying on of a trade or trades; or
(b) although it is a trading company in that period, either:
  (i) it carries on in that period a trade of which a main function is:
    (A) acquiring and holding, directly or indirectly, investments of any kind, including interests in companies which are **CONNECTED PERSONS** (**25**) within *CTA 2010, ss 1122, 1123*; formerly *ICTA 1988, s 839*; or
    (B) making payments which are similar to those in (C) below but which are deductible in computing the surrendering company's profits for corporation tax; or
    (C) making payments which are qualifying charitable donations; or
    (D) making payments in relation to which debits fall to be brought into account under the **LOAN RELATIONSHIPS** (**54**) provisions as regards loan relationships; or
    (E) obtaining funds in connection with any activity within (A)–(D) above; or
  (ii) although not within (i) above, it carries on any of the activities within (i)(A)–(E) above:
    (A) to an extent which does not appear justified by any trade which it does carry on; or
    (B) for a purpose which does not appear to be appropriate to any such trade.

[*CTA 2010, s 109; ICTA 1988, s 404; CTA 2009, Sch 1 para 122; SI 2004 No 2310, Article 16*].

Certain capital allowance restrictions apply to transactions between **CONNECTED PERSONS** (**25**) one of which is a dual resident investing company, as above. See also **13.24 CAPITAL ALLOWANCES — PLANT AND MACHINERY: FIXTURES AND LEASING, 18.4, 18.8 CAPITAL GAINS — GROUPS**, and **55.11 LOSSES**.

Simon's Taxes. See **D4.133**.

Arrangements for payment of tax

[39.24] HMRC may enter into arrangements with some or all of the members of a group of companies for one of those members to discharge the liabilities of each of those members to pay corporation tax for the accounting period(s) to which the arrangements relate. The arrangements may also cover interest and penalties and certain amounts treated as corporation tax liabilities. They do not affect the liability of any company to which the arrangements relate.

A 'group' for this purpose is a company and all its 51% subsidiaries (i.e. companies more than 50% of whose ordinary share capital it beneficially owns, either directly or indirectly), together with 51% subsidiaries of those subsidiaries and so on.

[*FA 1998, s 36*].

See **59.3 PAYMENT OF TAX** for the detailed arrangements.

Simon's Taxes. See **D1.1321**.

Surrender of tax refund, etc. within group

[39.25] Where two companies within a group (defined as for group relief purposes — see **39.3** above) jointly give notice to an HMRC officer, a corporation or income tax refund relating to an accounting period which falls to be made to one of them may be surrendered in whole or part to the other. The companies must be members of the same group throughout the period starting with the date the accounting period for which the refund arises and ending with the date the election is made. The notice must be made before the refund is made and must specify the amount to be surrendered. It must be in such form as is specified by HMRC.

The surrendering company is then treated as having received on the 'relevant date' a payment equal to the refund (or part), and the recipient company as having paid on that date corporation tax equal to the amount of the refund (or part) (except that in relation to tax-based penalties under *TMA 1970, s 94(6)* or *FA 1998, Sch 18 para 18* for excessive delay in rendering corporation tax returns (see **60.5 PENALTIES**, **66.7 RETURNS**) the corporation tax is treated as having been paid on the date of the notice referred to above). If the refund is of corporation tax and interest relating to that tax has been paid by the surrendering company, it is treated as having been paid by the recipient company.

Where the repayment to the surrendering company would not have carried interest ('*the interest-free period*') for part of the period, so that interest on tax repaid to the surrendering company would have been restricted (see **50.2 INTEREST ON OVERPAID TAX**), a corresponding restriction applies in relation to the deemed payment by the claimant company.

The surrendering company accounting period to which the refund relates must also be an accounting period of the recipient company. Both companies must be members of the group from the beginning of the relevant accounting period until the date of the notice referred to above.

The '*relevant date*' is the date on which corporation tax for the relevant accounting period became due and payable or, if later and if the refund is of corporation tax, the date on which the corporation tax was paid.

Any agreed payment by the recipient company to the surrendering company for a surrender as above (not exceeding the amount of the refund) is disregarded for tax purposes and is not treated as a distribution.

[*CTA 2010, ss 183, 963–966; FA 1989, s 102*].

For the effect on these provisions of group payment arrangements (see **59.3 PAYMENT OF TAX**), see HMRC Tax Bulletin April 2001 pp 834, 835 and also HMRC Company Taxation Manual, CTM97400 *et seq*.

Example

[39.26]

V Ltd has had, for some years, a 75% subsidiary, W Ltd, and both prepare accounts to 30 April. On 1 February 2010 (the due date), both companies make payments on account of their CT liabilities for the year ended 30 April 2009 V Ltd pays £250,000 and W Ltd pays £150,000. In January 2011, the liabilities are eventually agreed at £200,000 and £180,000 respectively.

Before any tax repayment is made to V Ltd, the two companies jointly give notice that £30,000 of the £50,000 tax repayment due to V Ltd is to be surrendered to W Ltd. W Ltd makes a payment of £20,000 to V Ltd in consideration for the tax refund surrendered.

It is assumed for illustrative purposes that the rates of interest on overdue tax and overpaid tax are, respectively, 3.5% and 1% throughout.

If no surrender had been made, and all outstanding tax payments/repayments made on, say, 1 February 2011, the interest position would have been as follows.

		£
V Ltd		
Interest on CT repayment of £50,000 for the period 1.2.10 to 1.2.11	£50,000 × 1% =	500
W Ltd		
Interest on late paid CT of £30,000 for the period 1.2.10 to 1.2.11	£30,000 × 3.5% =	1,050
Net interest payable by the group		£550

The surrender has the following consequences.

(i) Only £20,000 of the repayment (the unsurrendered amount) is actually made, and is made to V Ltd together with interest of £200 (at 1% for one year).

(ii) V Ltd, the surrendering company, is treated as having received a CT repayment of £30,000 (the surrendered amount) on the 'relevant date' which in this case is the normal due date of 1.2.10 V Ltd having made its CT payment on time. V Ltd is thus not entitled to any interest on this amount.

(iii) W Ltd, the recipient company, is deemed to have paid CT of £30,000 on the 'relevant date', 1.2.10 as above. It thus incurs no interest charge.

(iv) The group has turned a net interest charge of £550 into a net interest receipt of £200, a saving of £750. This arises from the differential in the rates of interest charged on unpaid and overpaid tax. (The surrendered amount £30,000 × 2.5% (3.5 – 1) × 1 year = £750.)

(v) The payment of £20,000 by W Ltd to V Ltd, not being a payment in excess of the surrendered refund, has no tax effect on either company.

V Ltd could have given notice to surrender its full refund of £50,000 to W Ltd, instead of just £30,000. There would, in fact, have been no point in doing so, but if W Ltd had made its original CT payment later than the due date, so as to incur an interest charge on the £150,000 originally paid, a full surrender would have produced a saving as the amount surrendered would be treated as having been paid on the due date.

Key points

[39.27] Points to consider are as follows.

- For group relief purposes subsidiaries must be effective 75% subsidiaries. It is important to establish which companies are part of a group for group relief, and it is possible to have more than one group within a larger group where shareholdings are complex and fragmented.
- Group relief can be claimed so as to maximise the availability of the small profits rate of corporation tax. Group relief is not an all or nothing claim, unlike certain other loss reliefs.
- The time limit for making a group relief claim is usually two years from the end of the accounting period of the company using the loss.
- Group relief can be comprised of a number of elements, for example trading losses, non-trading loan relationship deficits, surplus management expenses. Rules differ in terms of the computation of each of these elements, and it may be possible to surrender only certain types of loss.
- Any payment to a fellow subsidiary for the use of surrendered losses is not taxable and no tax deduction is given to the paying company.
- Losses incurred by overseas resident group companies can be claimed by UK resident group companies if those losses cannot be used in the overseas territory either in the year of loss or in any other year in which those losses can be claimed. In practice claims for such losses are likely to be rare, but should not be forgotten.

- Groups can bc formed relatively easily, but it is harder to split up a group. The exempt distribution demerger provisions allow groups to be split up, but there are a number of requirements that must be met in order to make use of these provisions (see **39.18**). For example, the exempt distribution route cannot be used where the demerger involves investment companies. The shareholders would have to consider more complex methods to separate the activities of the group, for example an *Insolvency Act 1986, s 110* liquidation demerger.

40

Groups of Companies — Financing Costs and Income

Introduction

[40.1] New rules with regard to the taxation of foreign profits for companies were introduced by *FA 2009, Sch 14* (see **31.15**), applicable as from 1 July 2009. As part of these changes provisions were also made to restrict interest relief in the UK for large groups (a finance cap), by introducing a mechanism to compare the level of UK debt within the group to the level of worldwide debt. In essence where the level of UK to worldwide debt exceeds a certain limit then a disallowance of interest and other financing expenses will arise. The rules have now been transposed into *TIOPA 2010, Pt 7* (as part of the tax law rewrite) and are applicable to accounting periods beginning on or after 1 January 2010 (subject to anti-avoidance measures see **40.9** below).

These worldwide debt cap rules are an integral part of the new foreign profits rules. However, it should be noted that they do not form a safe harbour for thin capitalisation purposes or replace the need for an advance thin capitalisation agreement, where this is appropriate.

In addition, these rules only apply to large groups with at least one UK resident member. A group is 'large' at any time if (and only if) any member of the group is not at the time within the category of micro, small and medium-sized enterprises as defined in the Annex to Commission Recommendation *2003/361/EC* of 6 May 2003 [*TIOPA 2010, s 344; FA 2009, Sch 15 paras 79, 85*].

This chapter provides an overview of the worldwide debt cap rules as they apply to large groups of companies, including details of the various exclusions and exemptions which may apply. Applicable definitions have been included at the end of the chapter, in section **40.17**, unless the text requires them to be defined where they are referred to. Draft guidance has been issued and is located at http://www.hmrc.gov.uk/guidance/anti-avoidance-rules.pdf, in addition details of how the debt cap rules are applied by HMRC can be found in HMRC's Corporate Finance Manual.

Legislation was introduced in *F(No 3)A 2010*, effective from 1 January 2010, the start of the worldwide debt cap rules, which amended the details of those rules, although the basic workings of the debt cap remained unaltered. Such changes have been indicated in the text below.

It was announced as part of the 2011 Budget that an informal consultation will be conducted with regard to the operation of the worldwide debt cap rules in June 2011. This will focus on practical issues previously identified, for example, the application of the de minimis rule (which disregards companies with net financing income or expense of less than £500,000). The plan is for legislation to be published for consultation in Autumn 2011 with a view to inclusion in the Finance Bill 2012.

The worldwide debt cap

[40.2] As noted above, the broad intention of the new provisions is to restrict the UK companies' tax deductions for intra-group financing costs to the external gross worldwide finance charge.

The legislation included in *FA 2009* and *TIOPA 2010* (as discussed below), has been amended by *F(No 3)A 2010* as from the start of the regime. The changes are highlighted below.

UK member of a worldwide group

The worldwide debt cap rules apply to large groups, as above. A worldwide group is any large group which has at least one relevant UK member. Group is as defined in International Accounting Standards, and is based on control of more than 50% of voting power. A relevant UK member is a company that is resident in the UK or is trading in the UK through a permanent establishment in the UK and is either the ultimate parent or a subsidiary of the ultimate parent.

F(No 3)A 2010 amends *TIOPA 2010, s 345* and excludes group securitisation companies from the definition of 'relevant group company' and 'UK group company', although such securitisation companies are still taken into account for the purpose of the Gateway test.

In considering groups the rules allow for the ultimate parent company being a transparent body or dual listed structure. Collective investment schemes are excluded from the definition. The rules do not apply to qualifying financial service groups and certain group treasury companies can be excluded per *s 261(2)* (see **40.10** herein).

Regulation making powers have been inserted by *F(No 3)A 2010* to allow a company to jointly elect to have another group company discharge its tax liability, where such company is party to capital market arrangements and is subject to tax by operation of the debt cap rules.

[*F(No 3)A 2010, Sch 5 paras 31–33; TIOPA 2010, ss 261, 266, 275, 338–341; FA 2009, Sch 15 paras 57, 78, 79, 80–84, 86*].

The Gateway Test

For periods of account of the worldwide group beginning on or after 1 January 2010 where the 'UK net debt' of the group exceeds 75% of the 'worldwide gross debt' of the group, the restriction applies and this is determined as detailed below. This is known as the 'Gateway test'. From the definitions below it can be seen that this a balance sheet test, based on the average of the opening and closing figures found in the financial statements.

The Treasury has power to vary the percentage by statutory instrument. Any such change may not have retrospective effect. As noted above the restriction does not apply to a group which is a 'qualifying financial services group' in the accounting period, nor does the restriction apply to securitisation companies post *F(No 3)A 2010*. A new *TIOPA 2010, s 273A* provides the definition of 'group securitisation company' which should either be within the temporary regime for such companies (*FA 2005, s 83*) or the permanent regime (*CTA 2010, s 623*). There is an anti-avoidance provision which may apply if a group changes its accounting date with a main purpose of removing the period from the debt cap where otherwise it would have fallen within a period covered by these provisions. There are also transitional provisions concerning *CTA 2009, ss 373, 409* and *SI 2009 No 3271, Reg 3A*. It should be noted that whilst the restriction itself does not apply to group securitisation companies, per the amended *TIOPA 2010, s 262* group securitisation companies are included as relevant companies for the purposes of the gateway test and the calculation of UK net debt.

When considering whether a group is a qualifying financial services group, consideration is given to the qualifying activities of the group, per *TIOPA 2010, s 267*. This includes lending activities, insurance activities and relevant dealing in financial instruments (within *s 270*). *F(No 3)A 2010* expands the definition of 'financial instruments' to include an option, a future, or a contract for differences, as defined within the derivative contracts regime (*CTA 2009, Pt 7*).

[*TIOPA 2010, ss 260–353; FA 2009, Sch 15 paras 97–99*].

The test is applied each accounting period. For any company with a net debt of less than £3 million, the net debt is treated as nil. Companies which are dormant throughout the accounting period are also treated as having a net debt of nil. The figure of £3 million may be changed by statutory instrument. There are special rules for determining the appropriate balance sheet where a UK company does not draw up accounts to the group's balance sheet date, or where a non-UK company trades through a permanent establishment in the UK.

There are special rules for group with oil extraction, shipping or property rental interests within special tax regimes.

[*TIOPA 2010, ss 333–335*].

The '*net debt*' of a company is the total of relevant liabilities and relevant assets as at a specific date. *F(No 3)A 2010* widens this definition (found at *TIOPA 2010, s 263*). A new category of relevant liabilities and assets has been included, which brings into the calculation any liability or asset which yields a return economically equivalent to interest (and which is not short term, i.e., less than twelve months). Such alternative finance arrangements include Shari'a compliant finance, repos and PFI contracts which are accounted for as financial assets.

'*Relevant liabilities*' are all borrowings, plus liabilities arising from finance leases, plus any alternative finance arrangements, plus any amount designated by HMRC.

'*Relevant assets*' are cash and cash equivalents, loans and assets arising from finance leases, any alternative finance arrangements and any amount designated by HMRC.

Shares or other equity interests held by a company which are being accounted for as financial assets are excluded for these purposes, pursuant to the amended *TIOPA 2010, s 263(5)*.

'*Worldwide gross debt*' is the average of the sum of 'relevant liabilities' of the group on the last day of the previous accounting period and as at the last day of that period. Relevant liabilities are borrowings (long or short-term), finance lease liabilities, alternative finance arrangements (per the amended legislation) and other amounts laid down by statutory instrument, disclosed in the consolidated balance sheet of the ultimate parent and its subsidiaries at the relevant date.

There is provision in *TIOPA 2010, ss 347, 348; FA 2009, Sch 15, paras 88, 89; SI 2009 No 3217* for the situation when financial statements of the group are non-compliant with generally accepted accounting practice or where they do not exist. Any balances in group pension schemes or a non-group company (e.g. a consortium company) are not taken into account. As noted per the amendments to *TIOPA 2010, s 266* group securitisation companies are included when considering this calculation for Gateway test purposes.

'*Relevant accounting period*' for this purpose is an accounting period that falls wholly or partly within the period of account of the worldwide group. [*TIOPA 2010, ss 260–272; FA 2009, Sch 15 paras 1–13*].

Acceptable or compliant financial statements for this purpose if they meet one of the following conditions:

- they are drawn up in accordance with IAS, as modified on 19 July 2002;
- they are drawn up in accordance with UK generally accepted accounting practice;
- they are drawn up in accordance with generally accepted principles or practice of Canada, China, Japan, South Korea, USA or India.

Under the new *TIOPA 2010, s 265A*, where a group and a company use different accounting treatments and this gives rise to different amounts within the group's consolidated figures, and those of the individual company, then for the purposes of computing the UK net debt the amount of the 'company level relevant liability' is adjusted to be equal to the amount derived from the consolidated accounts.

A company may elect that the operation of the changes to the Gateway test, (per *F(No 3)A 2010, Sch 5 paras 4* and *5(3), (4)*), which bring in alternative finance arrangements, be delayed and will only apply in periods of account of the worldwide group beginning on or after Royal Assent of the Act being 16 December 2010.

Example — the Gateway Test

The A Group is a large worldwide group with consolidated gross debt of £40m as at 31.12.2010 and £38m as at 31.12.2011. There are three UK resident companies with net debt amounts as follows:

	31.12.2010	31.12.2011	Average
X Ltd	10m	14m	12m
Y Ltd	2m	1m	1.5m
Z Ltd	18m	18m	18m

In performing the Gateway test we do not take account of Y Ltd as it has a net debt of less than £3m. The total of the UK net debt amounts is £30m.

The gross debt figure for the group per the consolidated accounts is £39m.

The UK net debt is almost 77% of the worldwide debt and the gateway test is failed — therefore the group must apply the worldwide debt cap rules to their financing costs and expenses.

Foreign currency accounting

[40.3] Unless otherwise stated, financing costs and income expressed in a currency other than sterling, are to be converted to sterling at the spot rate on the balance sheet date or any other day.

However, where all the balance sheets are expressed in the same currency, which is not sterling, the currency is not converted and, for the purpose of the £3 million de minimis, that limit is to be translated to the foreign currency at the start and closing dates at the spot rate of exchange on those dates.

[*TIOPA 2010, s 273; FA 2009, Sch 15 para 14*].

The disallowance

[40.4] Where the group has failed the Gateway test then a disallowance of interest and other financing expenses will arise where the 'tested expense amount' exceeds the 'available amount' — this difference is the total disallowed amount.

The 'tested expense amount' is, briefly, the sum of the net financing deductions of each 'relevant group company' (being a company which is UK resident, but including the UK PE of a non resident company, and is either the ultimate parent of the group or a 75% subsidiary of the ultimate parent — *TIOPA 2010, s 345*). Where financing income exceeds the finance expense the figure used is nil. Similarly, if the net amount is less than £500,000 it is nil. The 'available amount' is the amount disclosed in the financial statements of the group in respect of finance costs. Per the *F(No 3)A 2010* amendments this does not include amounts with respect to a group securitisation company. See further **40.17** with regard to definitions of tested expense amount and available amount. Certain intra-group short term financing expense may be excluded by election within 36 months of the end of the period of account for the worldwide group. Where a member of the worldwide group is a member of a partnership then see further **40.16** with regard to amounts to be taken into account.

A new *s 331A* has been inserted by *F(No 3)A 2010*, which provides a new regulation making power with regard to the tested expense amount and the available amount. Such regulations may be made with regard to any situation where, in respect of the same debt there is a mismatch between the 'account amount' which contributes to the available amount, and the 'tax amount' which is taken into account in computing a company's net financing deduction. Regulations may provide that the tested expense amount be calculated in such a way to correct any such mismatches.

Regulations have been introduced which:

(a) amend the definition of 'available amount' (*SI 2010 No 2929* — in force 1 January 2011); and
(b) provide clarification with regard to the figures to be included in the 'available amount' where there is a mismatch between the amounts disclosed in the financial statements of the worldwide group in respect of a liability and the amounts accounted for in respect of the same liability by the UK member of the worldwide group (*SI 2010 No 3025* — in force 13 January 2011, applicable to accounting periods beginning on or after 1 January 2010).

See further **40.17** and **40.18** below.

Example 1

P Ltd a UK member of a worldwide group has the following finance income and expenses:

Finance Expense		Finance Income	
Interest on loan from Parent company	150,000	Interest on loan to fellow subsidiary	18,000
Interest payable on bank loan	50,000	Bank interest receivable	42,000
Finance Lease interest	12,000		
	212,000		60,000

P Ltd has a net finance expense of £152,000 for the purposes of calculating the tested expense amount.

Example 2

The companies below are all 100% subsidiaries of a common parent. The following is a table of the expenses and income with regard to company UK 1 and its transactions with the rest of the group, both UK and overseas companies, and third parties. For example, it can be seen that UK 1 has entered into a transaction with UK 2, which gives rise to finance income in UK 1 of 3m, which is a finance expense for UK 2 of the same amount.

	UK 1 – Expense £	UK 1 – Income £
UK 1	-	-
UK 2	-	3m
UK 3	4m	-
UK 4	2.5m	-
O/S 1	-	5m
O/S 2	5m	-
O/S 3	-	2m
Bank	15m	-

In addition UK 4 pays interest of £3.5m to the bank.

For the purpose of the tested expense amount calculations only 'relevant group company' figures are included:

- UK 1 has net finance expense of £16.5m;
- UK 2 has net finance expense of £3m;
- UK 3 has net finance income of £4m, which is not considered further for purposes of the tested expense amount; and
- UK 4 has net finance expense of £1m.

The total tested expense amount is therefore £20.5m.

Where there is a disallowance a return needs to be made to HMRC. The statement of allocated disallowances must be submitted within 12 months of the end of the accounting period. The group may appoint a group company ('the *reporting body*') to act for it in relation to these provisions on financing expense and income, but to do so a signature on behalf of all affected companies must be obtained. Where such an appointment has been made, the appointed company is the reporting body. In other cases, the companies affected are together jointly liable.

The reporting company must make a written application to an HMRC officer at least three months before a statement of allocated allowances is due. In other cases, the companies affected are together jointly liable to comply. The statements to be included in an application to be a reporting company must apply in are listed in *SI 2009 No 3173, Reg 4* and a specimen copy of the statement of allocated disallowances for the relevant period of account must also be enclosed. The appointment takes effect three months from the date of application ('the three month date') and runs for an indefinite period, until revoked, the company is no longer within *FA 2009, Sch 15* or until reporting company leaves the group.

Where such an appointment has been made, the appointed company is the reporting body. In other cases, the companies affected are together jointly liable. Where a company has a relevant liability that is also such liability for the group, the amount is quantified in the same way for both purposes. Shares or other equity interests in another entity are excluded from the definition of relevant liability or relevant asset.

[*TIOPA 2010, ss 274–277; FA 2009, Sch 15 paras 15–18, 70–73, 60–62; SI 2009 No 3173, Regs 1–9*].

Allocation of the disallowance

[40.5] As noted above the reporting company must submit a statement of allocated disallowances in relation of a period within one year of the end of the relevant period of account, but it may submit a revised statement within three years of the end of the period. The statement must be signed on behalf of the reporting body or on behalf of each company where no reporting body has been appointed. The statement must be filed with the reporting company's tax district or, if there is no reporting company, the tax district of the ultimate parent, if resident in the UK, and the UK ultimate parent's tax office in any other case.

The statement must show the tested expense amount, the available amount and the total disallowed amount, together with a list of the companies and an allocation of the total disallowed amount to them. In addition the following would be taken into account — which of conditions (a)–(c) (see **40.17**, **40.18** under financing expense amount) applies and which corporation tax computation would be adjusted for the allocated disallowed expense. See *SI 2009 No 3173, Regs 11–13* for details of the contents of a statement of allocated disallowance and what is accepted as being received by HMRC by the deadline.

Where the corporation tax return for the period has not been filed, the effect of the statement of disallowances is that the amounts shown against the various companies are financing expenses which are not allowable as deductions in arriving at profits chargeable to corporation tax. Where the corporation tax return for the period has been filed, the statement is treated as amending the filed corporation tax return for a period affected by the allocated disallowance. There are provisions to treat a statement of allocated disallowances, or a revision of such a statement, as having been received on time.

Where a statement of disallowances is not submitted then HMRC will undertake the allocation by way of a set formula. The total deductions for the group must equal the amount calculated by the fraction:

$$\frac{NFD}{TEA} \times TDA$$

where NFD stands for net finance deduction, TDA for total disallowed amount and TEA the tested expense amount. Therefore, the fraction given by the net finance deduction of the company over the tested expense amount is applied to the total disallowed amount. The financing expense amounts which must be reduced will be determined in accordance with statutory instruments issued by HMRC, including *SI 2009 No 3173, Regs 15–18*.

F(No 3)A 2010 has amended the provisions with regard to the allocation of disallowance in respect of dual resident investing companies ('DRICs'). These are defined in a new *s 275A* as those companies prevented from surrendering losses as group relief by *CTA 2010, s 109(2)*. A new *s 280A* sets out how a disallowance can be allocated where one or more group companies are DRICs. The overall disallowance must first be allocated to each non-DRIC within a group. Where a default allocation applies to a group with one or more DRICs then a new allocation formula per *TIOPA 2010, s 284A* is to be applied.

[*TIOPA 2010, ss 278–285; FA 2009, Sch 15 paras 19–26*].

Exemption of financing income

[40.6] Where a company within a worldwide group has suffered a disallowance of financing charges for corporation tax purposes, then there is an adjustment mechanism whereby corresponding financial income may be left out of account and not taxed. A UK group company which is also part of a worldwide group must calculate the '*total disallowed amount*' for the group: this is the excess of the 'tested expense amount' over the 'available amount'. (See above and **40.18**). They will then be able to calculate the relevant compensating adjustments — up to the value of the lower of the total disallowed amount and tested income amount.

A calculation similar to that for the 'tested expense amount' above is performed but considering the income of each company. Thus the net 'financing income amount' (see definitions at **40.17**) of each group company is calculated and aggregated to give the 'tested income amount'. It should be noted in this calculation all UK group companies are considered, which means all UK resident companies which are members of the worldwide group as defined under international accounting standards (the 75% test applicable to 'relevant group companies' does not apply in this case). This is then compared to the total disallowed amount. The excess of the total disallowed amount over the tested income amount (if there is an excess) represents the financing expense restriction which will not have a compensating adjustment and will therefore be suffered by the group.

The companies affected may choose to appoint one of their number as the reporting body in relation to a period of account. Once appointed, the reporting body must submit a statement of allocated exemptions within one year of the end of the period of account — although it may submit a revised statement within three years of the end of the period of account. The duties of the reporting body are the same as duties under **40.6** above, substituting statement of allocated exemptions for statement of allocated disallowances. The effect of this compensating adjustment is that the amount of income allocated is excluded from the company's corporation tax computation.

Where a reporting body fails to submit a statement of allocated exemptions, then HMRC will make an allocation by way of a set formula, and each unrestricted reduction is reduced by:

$$\frac{\text{UR}}{\text{TUR}} \times X$$

i.e. where UR is the unrestricted reduction, TUR is the total of the unrestricted reductions and X is the excess of the total disallowed amount over the tested income amount.

[*TIOPA 2010, ss 286–297; FA 2009, Sch 15 paras 27–38*].

Exemptions for certain EEA companies

[40.7] As the new rules need to be EU compliant it was provided that intra-group financing income received from a company resident in the EEA, excluding the UK, would be exempt from corporation tax.

Therefore, where a company is a member of a worldwide group, the following financing income amounts are not brought into account for corporation tax for a period of account, where:

(a) it arises from a payment by another company which is a member of the same worldwide group;
(b) the payment arises in a period of account of the worldwide group;
(c) when the payment is received the payer is the parent, a 75% subsidiary or a 75% of a parent of the recipient;
(d) when the payment is received, the payer is resident in the an EEA territory and the payer is liable to tax there based on profits, income or gains;
(e) no tax relief (as defined) in the EEA territory is available to the payer in the current period, a previous period or in the future.

For the purpose of these provisions, financing income amounts of a company are defined as any amount which fulfils one of three conditions. These relate to the amount taxed under loan relationship legislation, a receipt derived from the finance element of a finance lease and a receipt corresponding to the finance element of a debt factoring arrangement.

The definition of financing income per *TIOPA 2010, s 305* has been amended by *F(No 3)A 2010*, and will include a new category. A new condition D is introduced which is the amount that would be brought into account for the purposes of corporation tax which derives from another company and which represents consideration for guaranteeing the company's borrowing, including amounts brought into charge by the operation of the transfer pricing rules at *TIOPA 2010, Pt 4*. This amendment is to provide symmetry between the company paying the guarantee fee (which is a financing expense) and the company receiving it. See also **40.17**.

There are detailed rules for what is qualifying EEA tax relief in current, previous or future periods.

[*TIOPA 2010, ss 299–305; FA 2009, Sch 15 paras 40–46*].

Balancing payments

[40.8] Any payment made by a company to another solely in connection with disallowances or exemptions under these provisions is ignored for corporation tax purposes in the cases of both companies.

[*TIOPA 2010, s 298; FA 2009, Sch 15 para 39*].

Anti-avoidance

[40.9] Targeted anti-avoidance provisions were also enacted at the same time as the introduction of the worldwide debt cap rules. They are split into three parts:

I – schemes aimed at circumventing the Gateway test: if at any time during a period of account, a company enters a scheme (not an excluded scheme), any party to which has as one of the main purposes to arrange that the period of account is not within these provisions, is treated as having a period of account where the UK net debt of the group exceeds 75% of the worldwide gross debt of the group and is therefore within *Sch 15*;

II – schemes aimed at manipulation of the disallowance deduction or the exemption of income;

III – schemes aimed at manipulating the rules that give an exemption form UK tax for finance income received from a group member resident in the EEA.

A '*scheme*' is defined as including any scheme, arrangements or understanding of any kind, whether or not legally enforceable and involving any number of transactions.

[*TIOPA 2010, ss 306–312; FA 2009, Sch 15 paras 47–53*].

Group treasury companies

[40.10] There are special provisions for group treasury companies. A group treasury company may elect, within three years of the end of the period of account for all financing expense and financing income amounts to be treated as not being such amounts of the company. Where there is more than one treasury company, all must make elections for them to be valid.

A treasury company should be a member of a worldwide group, it should undertake treasury activities in the relevant period and if the company is the only treasury company (or the only such company resident in the UK) then at least 90% of the company's relevant income for the relevant period is group treasury income. Currently where there are two such group treasury companies within the UK then the 90% test is applied to their aggregate income.

Pursuant to *F(No 3)A 2010, s 316* has been amended and an amended *subsection 8* inserted. Where there is more than one UK resident treasury company, the 90% test is to be applied to each company separately.

There are exclusions for REITs and oil extraction companies carrying on a ring fence trade.

[*TIOPA 2010, ss 316–318; FA 2009, Sch 15 para 57–59*].

Intra-group short-term financing expense

[40.11] Where, in the relevant period, a company has income or an expense which is a financing income amount or financing expense amount, the company and the other party to the loan may jointly elect within three years of the end of the period of account to exclude it from the financing expense provided that the other party to the loan is a member of the same worldwide group and the loan is short-term. The election is irrevocable.

A loan is short-term for this purpose if it has been settled within the relevant period and within 12 months of the debt's creation or the loan relationship or other finance arrangement provides for settlement within 12 months. Alternatively, HMRC may provide by statutory instrument for certain finance arrangements to be treated as short-term loan relationships and may also make other regulations in this area.

HMRC exercised this power in *SI 2009 No 3313*. It provides that a finance relationship is not to be regarded as a short-term financing arrangement if it, or any part of it, is for a 'long-term funding purpose' (as defined) or the arrangement is a long-term aggregated loan relationship.

The *F(No 3)A 2010* changes remove this regulation making power (*s 321(7)* is omitted). It is not considered practicable to exercise such powers as there is no provision to allow for the set up of appropriate regulations for the use of such powers, such as an appeal structure.

[*TIOPA 2010, ss 319–321; FA 2009, Sch 15 paras 60–62*].

Stranded deficits

[40.12] In some instances one party to a loan relationship has a non-trading deficit on the loan within its accounts which it is unable to set off for tax purposes against any income. The parties to a loan relationship may jointly elect within three years of end of the period of account of the worldwide group that a non-trading loan relationship financing expense should not be treated as a financing expense amount. To qualify to make this election, the following conditions must be fulfilled:

(1) both companies must be in the same worldwide group;
(2) the other party to the loan must either be UK resident or carry on a trade in the UK through a permanent establishment;
(3) the other party is carrying forward a non-trading deficit from the arrangement and sets it off against non-trading profits which coincides with or overlaps with the worldwide group's period of account;
(4) the amount of non-trading deficit carried forward is equal to or greater than the relevant amount excluded under this provision.

Correspondingly, the same amount is not treated as a financial income amount of the other party.

[*TIOPA 2010, ss 322–325; FA 2009, Sch 15 paras 63–66*].

Charities, educational and public bodies

[40.13] Where the creditor (or recipient of the amount under a finance lease or the finance element of a debt factoring agreement) is a charity, a designated educational establishment, a health service body, a local authority or other designated person, a relevant amount is not a financing expense amount where otherwise it would be such amount. *Section 327* has been amended and 'relevant public bodies' has been added to the list of entities to which this treatment applies.

[*TIOPA 2010, ss 326, 327; FA 2009, paras 67, 68*].

Dual resident investment companies

[40.14] Provisions have been made, with regard to dual resident investment companies (DRICs) and any disallowance to be allocated to such companies is restricted, see **40.5** above. Any disallowance must first be allocated to all non-DRICs within the group.

Late interest rules

[40.15] Where the 'late interest' rules (see **54 LOAN RELATIONSHIPS**) apply, the tested amount is reduced by the amount not allowed for tax. When the interest is paid, the amount allowed for tax purposes will increase the tested amount.

Partnerships

[40.16] Where a UK company is a member of a partnership, a proportionate share of the loan relationship debits and credits of the partnership are deemed to be those of the company for debt cap purposes. However, the amount taken into account in the group accounts may be different, depending on the accounting convention used. Changes to the legislation per *F(No 3)A 2010* deal with this situation.

This mismatch is addressed by *s 332B*, by providing that where the partnership has financing costs, any actual amounts disclosed by the consolidated accounts regarding those costs are ignored. In computing the available amount, it is assumed that the consolidated accounts were prepared on the basis that each member of the partnership owed the 'appropriate proportion' of the partner ship liability – i.e., the figure will be arrived at by allocating the partnership borrowing between all of the partners in the partnership on the basis of their profit-sharing ratios.

A new *s 332C* makes the same provisions in relation to the expenses of finance leases or debt factoring incurred by a partnership.

Where the company in partnership, which has deemed borrowings, is a member of a group and the borrowings are not intra-group, these are included in arriving at the available amount.

LLPs are excluded from being treated as a corporate entity under the debt cap provisions.

[*TIOPA 2010, ss 332B, 332C*].

Definitions

[40.17] '*UK net debt*' is the average of the total of all the UK group companies' opening and closing net debts for an accounting period. The net debt is the sum of the company's 'relevant liabilities' less the sum of its 'relevant assets'. Alternative finance arrangements are included within this calculation.

The '*worldwide group*' is one that is large and contains one or more relevant companies. '*Group*' is interpreted as in international accounting standards from time to time.

A '*large group*' is one which, at any time, does not include a company within the EC definition of a micro, small or medium-sized enterprise (see Annex to *2003/361/EC* of 6 May 2003).

The '*financing expense amount*' of a company is the amount which, in respect of a relevant accounting period, satisfies (a), (b) or (c) below:

(a) it is a debit brought into account under the loan relationship rules and is not an impairment loss, an exchange loss or a related transaction; or
(b) it is a debt brought into account in respect of a finance lease; or
(c) it is a financing cost on debt factoring or any similar transaction.

Where part of an accounting period in which an expense is incurred as above does not fall within the period of account of the worldwide group, the amount is to be reduced by time apportionment. Where the amount is negative, the net financing deduction is nil.

Payments to health service bodies, charities, educational establishments and relevant public bodies which are tax exempt and non-profit making, are to be ignored for the purposes of the debt cap rules.

[*TIOPA 2010, ss 313, 329, 344*].

Except as otherwise provided, the '*financing income amount*' of a company is the amount which in respect of a relevant accounting period satisfy (i), (ii), (iii) or (iv) below:

(i) it is a credit brought into account under the loan relationship rules, which is not a reversal of an impairment loss, an exchange gain or a profit from a related transaction; or
(ii) it is an amount which would be brought into account in respect of a finance lease; or
(iii) it is financing income receivable on debt factoring or any similar transaction; or
(iv) it is an amount that is receivable from another company and is in consideration of the provision of a guarantee of any borrowing of that other company (per the amended *s 314*, see also **40.7** above).

Deemed loan relationships (such as those under the alternative finance provisions) are treated as loan relationships for this purpose.

There is a similar reduction as for finance expense amounts where part of the relevant of accounting period is not within the period of account of the worldwide group. If the financing income amount is 'small', the net financing income of the company for the period is nil. '*Small*' in this context is less than £500,000. This figure may be amended, for later periods only, by statutory instrument.

[*TIOPA 2010, ss 314, 330, 331*].

'Exchange gain', 'exchange loss', impairment loss' and 'related transaction' have the same meaning as in **LOAN RELATIONSHIPS (54)**.

The '*tested expense amount*' is the total of net financing deductions of each relevant group company in the worldwide group.

[*TIOPA 2010, s 329*].

The '*net financing deduction*' is the excess of financing expense amounts less financing income amounts for the period. Transactions which took place when a company was not a member of the worldwide group are not taken into account. Where the answer is a negative figure, it is taken as nil. The 'tested income account' is similarly calculated, substituting income for expense. Where the excess of expense or income is less than £500,000, it is treated as 'small'. The limit may be amended by Treasury statutory instrument. [*TIOPA 2010, s 329; FA 2009, Sch 15 paras 70–72*].

The '*available amount*' is broadly the gross worldwide finance expense of the group for a period of account as disclosed in the group's financial statements. *F(No 3)A 2010* changes to *s 332(1)(d)* mean the term 'ancillary costs' is more precisely defined as those expenses incurred directly in bringing the borrowing into existence or altering its terms or making payments. A new *s 332(1B)* means abortive expenditure in bringing borrowing into existence will also qualify. Dividends on preference shares are excluded, even if the shares are treated as a liability in the accounts. Special rules also apply to groups with oil, property (REITs) or shipping interests. See also special cases below.

Regulations in force from 1 January 2011 extend the definition of 'available amount' found at *s 332* to include:

(i) interest payable in respect of relevant non-lending relationships (per *CTA 2009, ss 479(4)* and *480*);
(ii) alternative finance returns (per *CTA 2009, ss 511–513*) for alternative finance arrangements (as defined in *CTA 2009, s 501*);
(iii) manufactured interest (per *CTA 2009, s 539(5)*);
(iv) finance charges treated as interest payable under a debt (per *CTA 2009, s 551(4)*); and
(v) finance charges arising from structured finance arrangements and treated as interest payable under a transaction or loan relationship (per *CTA 2010, ss 761(3), 762(2), 766(3)* or *769(3)*).

The regulations have effect for periods of account of the worldwide group beginning on or after 1 January 2011.

With regard to the 'available amount', see also the 'Correction of Mismatches Regulations' below.

[*TIOPA 2010, s 332; SI 2010 No 2929; FA 2009, Sch 15 para 73–77*].

There are special rules for groups with income from oil extraction, shipping or property rental subject to taxation in the UK.

[*TIOPA 2010, ss 333–335*].

'*Qualifying activities*' means lending and and ancillary activities, insurance and insurance-related activities and relevant dealing in financial instruments (i.e. otherwise than as a broker and where the profits and losses fall into trading profits or losses). [*FA 2009, Sch 15 paras 8–10*].

'*Qualifying financial services group*' is a group where all or substantially all the UK trading income of the worldwide group or of its worldwide trading income is derived from lending and ancillary activities, insurance and related activities and dealing in financial instruments other than as a broker and profits and losses from dealing fall into trading profits. There are special rules for the computation of UK and worldwide trading income of the worldwide group.

'*Entity*', '*parent*', '*subsidiary*' and '*effective interest method*' are as defined by international accounting standards. However, per the amended *s 351*, the definition of 'subsidiary' does not affect the meaning of the expression '75% subsidiary', which is defined in *CA 2010, s 1154*.

A '*group*' is as defined for international accounting standards purposes and a '*worldwide group*' is any large group with one or more relevant group companies.

'*Relevant non-corporate entity*' is a company incorporated in the UK or elsewhere or a body in which the capital is divided into shares, or similar interests, and a decision on the allocation of profits depends on a decision of the entity or its members and is taken after profits for the period have arisen.

[*TIOPA 2010, s 340*].

An '*immediate parent*' is a company which directly owns more than 50% of the ordinary share capital of another company.

An '*ultimate parent*' is an entity that is: a member of the group; is a corporate entity or a relevant non-corporate entity, but not a limited liability partnership (per the amendment to *s 339(1)(b)*; not a subsidiary (direct or indirect) of a corporate entity, relevant non-corporate entity, or collective investment scheme; and not a collective investment scheme (as defined by *FSMA 2000*, and per the amended *s 339(1)(c)*, does not fall outside the FSMA definition solely because it is a body corporate).

Regulations

[40.18] The Treasury and HMRC are given wide powers under *FA 2009, Sch 15* to introduce regulations in connection with the debt cap regime and various provisions within *TIOPA 2010, Pt 7* allow for further regulations to be introduced.

The Mismatch Regulations *SI 2010 No 3025*

In addition to the regulations outlined above with regard to the 'available amount', new regulations came into force on 13 January 2011 to deal with the issues surrounding the different amounts which might be disclosed in the financial statements of the worldwide group in respect of a liability and those amounts accounted for (in respect of the same liability) by the UK group member.

The 'Tax Treatment of Financing Costs and Income (Correction of Mismatches) Regulations 2010' clarify the treatment of such amounts, and apply to periods of account beginning on or after 1 January 2010, subject to certain elections which the group can make.

The regulations provide for adjustments to be made to the 'available amount' as follows:

Fair value adjustments

The mismatch might arise due to the use of fair value or hedge accounting. Under such instances, where the amount disclosed in the worldwide group accounts and included in the available amount ('Amount A') is greater than the amount that would be brought into account by the relevant group company for the purposes of the loan relationship provisions (per *CTA 2009*) for the same financial relationship ('Amount B'), then the available amount is decreased by the fair value adjustment made or the excess (whichever is the lower). The fair value adjustment is the adjustment made by the relevant group company in that period which brings into account a profit or loss for the loan relationship in question, where fair value accounting is used. Where Amount A is less than Amount B then the available amount is increased by the fair value adjustment or the excess (whichever is the lower). Amount B is treated as zero under the regulations if it would otherwise be a negative amount.

[*SI 2010 No 3025, Regs 3 and 4*].

Late paid interest

Where an interest payment of a relevant group company falls into the late paid interest provisions (at *CTA 2009, s 373*), and relief is only given under the loan relationship rules when the interest is paid (and not accrued), then the debit is excluded in the calculation of the available amount in the period it accrues. Instead it is included in the available amount in the period it is paid (to the extent it has not been included in this amount for this period by virtue some other provision). This applies to interest payments that have accrued in accounting periods beginning on or after 1 January 2010.

[*SI 2010 No 3025, Regs 5, 6, 7 and 8*].

Deeply discounted securities

Where a debit in respect of debtor relationship of a relevant group company which is a deeply discounted security is brought into account at redemption under the rules at *CTA 2009, ss 407, 409*, then the available amount excludes any debits which might accrue in respect of the discount in the periods prior to redemption. Instead the available amount includes such a debit in the period in which the security is redeemed (to the extent it has not already been included for that period by virtue of some other provision). This applies to deeply discounted securities any debits for which would accrue (ignoring the restriction to relief only at redemption) in accounting periods beginning on or after 1 January 2010.

[*SI 2010 No 3025, Regs 9, 10, 11, and 12*].

Loan relationships with embedded derivatives

Where a debit is brought into account by the relevant group company under the embedded derivative provisions of the loan relationship rules, and is included as a financing expense of the company (and an amount is included in this regard in the available amount) then the amount of the debit which is directly attributable to the use of IAS and the measurement under amortised cost using the effective interest rate method, is also to be included in the available amount.

[*SI 2010 No 3025, Regs 13 and 14*].

Debt restructuring

An amount equal to such part of the debit that is directly attributable to the requirement that it be measured at amortised cost is to be included in the available amount. This applies where:

- the relevant group company stands in the position of debtor with regard to a loan relationship, or with regard to a relationship which is treated as a loan relationship (per *CTA 2009, Pt 6*), or with regard to a deemed loan relationship (per *CTA 2010, ss 761(2) or 762(2)*);
- a debit in respect of such relationship is a financing expense of the company;
- an amount in respect of such relationship is included in the available amount;
- the relationship has been recognised under IAS using fair value accounting as a new financial liability, due to an exchange for an existing liability in substantially different terms, or due to the substantial modification of an existing liability, and the existing liability is treated as extinguished; and
- after the initial recognition of the relationship using fair value accounting, the debit is required under IAS to be measured at amortised cost using the effective interest rate method.

[*SI 2010 No 3025, Regs 15 and 16*].

Elections

A worldwide group may make an irrevocable election that certain regulations or pairs of regulations will not apply to it, or that the regulations as a whole are not to apply to periods of account beginning before 21 December 2010. Any such election must be made by the later of one year from the end of the accounting period beginning on or after 1 January 2010, and 31 March 2011.

[*SI 2010 No 3025, Regs 17–19*].

Key points

[40.19] Points to consider are as follows.

- The worldwide debt cap was introduced in 2009 to restrict loan interest relief in the UK for large groups where there is an international involvement. These rules are very complex but must not be ignored.
- The key 'gateway test' serves to measure whether UK net debt of the group exceeds 75% of the worldwide gross debt of the group. Where the gateway test is failed there will be a disallowance of interest deducted in the UK.
- The rules allow for a compensating adjustment where there is equivalent financing income, so, where possible, the disallowance is effectively set-off against the finance income of the UK group.
- A company's financing by way of loan or other debt instrument will be treated for corporation tax purposes under loan relationship rules. Broadly these follow accounting treatment, with certain exceptions principally with regard to companies with a connection.
- The usual capital/revenue divide that governs much of UK tax legislation does not apply to loan relationships.

41

HMRC — Administration

Simon's Taxes. See **A3.3, A3.4, D1.1304A.**

Introduction

[41.1] Her Majesty's Revenue and Customs (HMRC) was formed by the merger of the Inland Revenue and HM Customs and Excise, following the coming into force of the *Commissioners for Revenue and Customs Act 2005* on 7 April 2005.

This chapter examines how HMRC undertakes the administration of tax and provides an outline of the structure and powers of HMRC, the Commissioners and its officers. In addition it provides an overview of various administrative matters including the taxpayer's Charter, how a taxpayer may go about making a complaint when HMRC make an error, electronic communication provisions, HMRC's international obligations, and the new requirements as to the duties of senior accounting officers.

Structure of HMRC

[41.2] The collection and management of corporation tax is administered by the **Commissioners** for Her Majesty's Revenue and Customs (HMRC). [*TMA 1970, s 1; Commissioners for Revenue and Customs Act 2005, Sch 4 para 12*].

Previously, this tax was administered by the Commissioners of Inland Revenue (normally referred to as 'the Board'). [*TMA 1970, s 1(1) as originally enacted*]. All the functions vested in the Board before 7 April 2005 (with the exception of prosecutions for tax offences — see below) are now vested in the Commissioners for HMRC.

[*Commissioners for Revenue and Customs Act 2005, s 5; SI 2005 No 1126*].

The Commissioners also have the important function of advising the Treasury and the Chancellor of the Exchequer on proposals for new or amending legislation, in particular to stop avoidance of tax, and for alterations in the law deemed advisable in view of adverse decisions of the courts. Therefore the practical day to day administration of tax is undertaken by officers of Revenue and Customs, who are civil servants appointed by the Commissioners.

Such HMRC officers may undertake the functions previously vested in either Inland Revenue officers or Customs and Excise officers, but not both at the same time. In relation to corporation tax, these officers have broadly taken over the functions previously vested in officers of the Board of Inland Revenue, inspectors of taxes and collectors of taxes.

As such they are responsible for processing returns, making assessments, dealing with claims and allowances, carrying out enquiries and collection and recovery of tax. HMRC officers may issue notices to taxpayers to make returns and notices of appeal have to be given to them. Disputes may be resolved through the Tribunal structure (the vast majority of cases being heard by the First-tier Tribunal) with subsequent appeals limited to points of law being available to the Upper Tribunal and thence to the Court of Appeal (or in Scotland, to the Court of Session) and then the Supreme Court (see further 6 appeals).

[*Commissioners for Revenue and Customs Act 2005, ss 2, 6, 7, Sch 1; FA 1998, Sch 18, para 48*].

Criminal prosecutions of tax offences in England and Wales are conducted by an independent Revenue and Customs Prosecutions Office, whose director is appointed by the Attorney General.

[*Commissioners for Revenue and Customs Act 2005, ss 34–42, Sch 3*].

In this publication, 'HMRC' means Her Majesty's Revenue and Customs, and any references to 'HMRC' are to both HMRC and the Inland Revenue.

HMRC maintains an internet website (www.hmrc.gov.uk/index.htm) which provides access to detailed information on many aspects of corporation tax including legislation, forms and publications, and the Revenue Manuals.

Small businesses

Proposals to integrate and streamline services to small businesses were published in March 2005 as 'Working towards a new relationship: small business'.

The work of the Office of Tax Simplification ('OTS') set up in 2010 is outlined further below. One task appointed the OTS was to review the tax position of small businesses and the intermediaries regime (under IR35). An interim report looking at small business taxation was published on 10 March 2011. Their initial recommendations included: merging income tax and national insurance; consideration of the future of IR35; updating HMRC's procedures and creating a simpler regime for the smallest businesses. The provisional recommendations are made with a view to simplifying the administrative burdens on small business.

Appeal Commissioners (prior to 1 April 2009)

[41.3] Both the General and Special Commissioners were abolished with effect from 1 April 2009. (See **6 APPEALS** for details of the new tribunal regime highlighted above). Prior to that date, appeals against assessments or amendments of self-assessments were heard by:

(a) the General Commissioners (local persons appointed on a voluntary basis by the Lord Chancellor or, in Scotland, by the Secretary of State) [*TMA 1970, s 2*]; or

(b) the Special Commissioners (full-time civil servants, being barristers, advocates or solicitors etc. of at least ten years' standing, appointed for this purpose) [*TMA 1970, s 4; Courts and Legal Services Act 1990, Sch 10 para 30*].

[*TMA 1970, ss 2A, 3A; Access to Justice Act 1999, ss 102, 103; SI 2001 No 916*].

Statutory effect for concessions

[41.4] Extra-statutory Concessions, ESCs, are derogations from an applicable statutory tax treatment, as published by HMRC. Such concessionary treatment has been a feature of the UK's tax system for many years. However, the House of Lords' decision in the *Wilkinson* case clarified the scope of HMRC's administrative discretion to make concessions that depart from the strict statutory position.

In light of that decision, HMRC is in the process of undertaking a review of its published concessions. In anticipation of the need to legislate the effect of some ESCs *Finance Act 2008, s 160* provided an enabling power allowing the tax treatment afforded by existing published concessions (ones granted before 21 July 2008) to be given statutory effect.

A concession in this context is eligible whether it is described as an extra-statutory concession, a statement of practice, an interpretation, a decision or a press release or in any other way. The order may modify the existing concession, may include supplementary, incidental, consequential or transitional provision and may amend any Act or statutory instrument.

A consultation process was undertaken during 2009 and many of the concessions will continue in their current form, as they are within the scope of HMRC's administrative discretion. However, where an existing concession exceeds the scope of HMRC's administrative discretion, as clarified in the

Wilkinson judgment, such concession will be put onto a legislative basis as appropriate. The work of the Office of Tax Simplification ('OTS') should also be noted with regard to concessions, as part of their review of the reliefs available within UK tax law.

The OTS was set up in 2010 with a view to simplifying the UK's tax legislation, rather than re-writing it. The OTS has identified over 1,000 tax reliefs, allowances, and exemptions within the UK tax regime, to be evaluated. An interim report was published on 13 December 2010, which reviewed 13 reliefs and gave provisional recommendations including: the abolition of some reliefs, such as the vaccine research relief, and certain income tax exemptions (the 15p luncheon voucher exemption); and the retention of reliefs such as the capital gains tax principal private residence relief. A final report was published on 3 March 2011 which made recommendations to the Chancellor. Some of these recommendations are being enacted in *FA 2011, s 91 Sch 26* — redundant reliefs.

Details of the work of the OTS can be found at: www.hm-treasury.gov.uk/ots.htm.

See further **42 HMRC EXTRA-STATUTORY CONCESSIONS** for the results of such consultations.

[*FA 2008, s 160; R (oao Wilkinson) v CIR* [2005] UKHL 30, [2006] 1 All ER 529].

'Care and management' powers

[41.5] As noted at **41.2** above, the Commissioners for HMRC have responsibility for the 'collection and management' of taxes, including corporation tax. The courts have stated that HMRC's general duties of 'care and management' of the tax system have further ramifications and impose an implied duty to treat taxpayers fairly and to use their discretionary powers to ensure discrimination does not arise. See *R v CIR (ex p National Federation of Self-employed and Small Businesses Ltd)* (1981) 55 TC 133, HL in which the validity of amnesties by the Board was considered.

These powers and duties have been further considered by the courts on a number of occasions. HMRC extra statutory concessions (**41.4** above) have been the subject of frequent judicial criticism (see Lord Edmund-Davies' opinion in *Vestey v CIR (No 1)* (1979) 54 TC 503, HL, for a review of this and the *Wilkinson* decision above). In *R v Inspector of Taxes, Reading, ex p Fulford-Dobson* [1987] QB 978, [1987] 3 WLR 277, a claim that the Revenue had acted unfairly in refusing a concession where tax avoidance was involved was rejected, but the taxpayer's right to seek judicial review of a Revenue decision to refuse the benefit of a concession was confirmed in *R v HMIT (ex p Brumfield)* (1988) 61 TC 589.

A decision by the Revenue to revoke its authorisation to pay a dividend gross was upheld in *R v CIR (ex p Camacq Corporation)* (1989) 62 TC 651, CA.

For a general discussion of the HMRC's care and management powers, and an example of a ruling by the Court that HMRC had exercised a discretionary power reasonably, see *Preston v CIR* [1985] 2 All ER 327, [1985] STC

282, HL. Where a discretionary power is given to the Revenue, it is an error in law to proceed on the footing that the power is mandatory (*R v HMIT and Others (ex p Lansing Bagnall Ltd)* (1986) 61 TC 112, CA). See also *R v CIR (ex p J Rothschild Holdings plc)* (1987) 61 TC 178, CA, where the Revenue were required to produce internal documents of a general character relating to their practice in applying a statutory provision.

HMRC policy of selective prosecution for criminal offences in connection with tax evasion did not render a decision in a particular case unlawful or *ultra vires*, provided that the case was considered on its merits fairly and dispassionately to see whether the criteria for prosecution were satisfied, and that the decision to prosecute was then taken in good faith for the purpose of collecting taxes and not for some ulterior, extraneous or improper purpose (*R v CIR (ex p Mead and Cook)* (1992) 65 TC 1).

The making of a 'forward tax agreement', by which the Inland Revenue (as was) renounced their right and duty to investigate the true financial and other circumstances of the other party during the period of the agreement in return for payments of money, was not a proper exercise of the Inland Revenue's care and management powers, and was accordingly *ultra vires* and illegal. As such, it was not unfair of the Revenue to end the agreement. (*Al Fayed v A-G for Scotland* [2004] STC 1703).

HMRC rulings

[41.6] Taxpayers can apply to HMRC for guidance as to HMRC's interpretation of tax law, and may also request a formal ruling from HMRC on specific facts and transactions, where appropriate.

HMRC may provide a post-transaction ruling for a transaction after it has occurred but before the tax return is submitted. Rulings will only be given where the tax treatment of a transaction is in doubt, for example in relation to unusual transactions or transactions entered into in usual circumstances. See Code of Practice 10 for the types of transactions on which a ruling can be given, the extent to which HMRC will be bound by the ruling, the effect of the ruling on interest and penalties and the procedures in obtaining such a ruling.

For the extent to which taxpayers may rely on guidance given by HMRC, see further the letter from the Deputy Chairman to the various professional bodies following the decision in *Matrix-Securities Ltd v IRC* [1994] 1 All ER 769, [1994] 1 WLR 334, HL. HMRC have also issued guidance alongside COP 10 (above), as to reliance on advice provided by them.

From 9 October 2007 advance agreements for reconstructions and inward investments will be offered by an Advance Agreements Unit. The inward investments must amount to at least £250 million.

A non-statutory clearances pilot ran from January 2008 to 31 March 2008, available to businesses in the retail sector dealt with by the Large Business Service and also all businesses whose tax affairs are dealt with by HMRC offices in the North West & Midlands group of Local Compliance. The results of the pilot were taken into account in the service offered from 1 April 2008.

From this date, HMRC will give views to business taxpayers on the tax consequences (across all taxes) of tax legislation. There is additional guidance to COP 10 for such business taxpayers, with regard to non-statutory clearances.

Where the legislation in question is more than four years old, there must be significant commercial implications. The opinion may be relied upon provided that all relevant facts and issues have been disclosed by the applicant and there has not been a change in legislation or case law since HMRC gave their opinion.

Applications should be sent to the Large Business Service by taxpayers whose affairs are dealt with by them, and to the HMRC Clearances Team, Alexander House, 21 Victoria Avenue, Southend-on-Sea, Essex SS99 1BD by other taxpayers.

Advanced Pricing Agreements (APAs) and Advanced Thin Capitalisation Agreements (ATCAs) are considered at **71 TRANSFER PRICING**.

Taxpayer charter

[41.7] As required by *FA 2009*, HMRC produced a taxpayer charter before the end of 2009. The charter includes standards of behaviour and values to which HMRC will be required to aspire when dealing with taxpayers. The charter must be regularly reviewed and the reviews must be published. An annual review of standards and actual behaviour is required. [*FA 2009, s 92*].

The charter, which can be found at www.hmrc.gov.uk/charter, sets out nine rights and three obligations of companies in their dealing with HMRC. In return for a taxpayer undertaking to be honest, respecting HMRC staff and taking care to get things right, HMRC undertake to:

(a) respect the company;
(b) help and support it to get things right;
(c) treat its officers as honest;
(d) treat it even-handedly;
(e) be professional and act with integrity;
(f) tackle people who deliberately break the rules and challenge those who bend the rules;
(g) protect taxpayer information protect taxpayer privacy;
(h) accept that someone else can represent the company; and
(i) do all they can to keep the cost of dealing with HMRC as low as possible.

The charter also provides pointers to further information on taxpayer's rights and how taxpayer companies can access help and support and HMRC's role in this.

HMRC publish a series of factsheets and codes of practice setting out the standards of service people can expect in relation to specific aspects of HMRC's work, including advice on how to complain. Most of these are available on the HMRC website.

See: www.hmrc.gov.uk/complaints-appeals/how-to-complain/make-complaint.htm.

HMRC error

[41.8] HMRC factsheet 'Complaints' (see **41.7** above), has replaced the previous Code of Practice 1, as from July 2007. The factsheet outlines the complaints procedure and points to the Redress Guidance Manual with regard to advice on the circumstances in which payment may be claimed from HMRC as a consequence of Revenue mistake or unreasonable delay. These fall into three general categories.

(a) **Claiming back costs.** Any reasonable costs paid as a direct result of Revenue error, such as postage, telephone calls, travelling expenses, professional fees, financial charges, and interest on overpaid tax and national insurance, may be reclaimed. If the extra costs arose because of HMRC delay in dealing with the taxpayer's affairs, interest normally charged on overdue tax or national insurance owed by the taxpayer may be waived, or interest paid on money owed by HMRC, during the unreasonable delay.

(b) **Compensation for worry and distress.** If HMRC's actions have affected the taxpayer particularly badly, HMRC may pay compensation (usually in the range £25–£500) to acknowledge and apologise for the way the taxpayer was treated.

(c) **Further mistakes or delays in dealing with complaint.** If HMRC handle a complaint badly, or take an unreasonable time to deal with it, compensation (usually in the range £25–£500) may be paid, on top of any reasonable costs, to reflect this.

HMRC Adjudicator

[41.9] A taxpayer who is not satisfied with HMRC's response to a complaint has the option of putting the case to an independent Adjudicator. The Adjudicator's Office considers complaints about HMRC's handling of a taxpayer's affairs, e.g. excessive delays, errors, discourtesy or the exercise of HMRC discretion. Matters subject to existing rights of appeal are excluded.

Complaints normally go to the Adjudicator only after they have been considered by, firstly, the Customer Relations or Complaints Manager and, secondly, a senior officer of the relevant HMRC office, and where the taxpayer is still not satisfied with the response received. The alternatives of pursuing the complaint to an MP, or (through an MP) to the Parliamentary Ombudsman continue to be available.

The Adjudicator reviews all the facts, considers whether the complaint is justified, and, if so, settles the complaint by mediation or makes recommendations as to what should be done. HMRC normally accept the recommendations.

The adjudicator also investigates complaints about the Valuation Office Agency (now part of HMRC).

The address is The Adjudicator's Office, Eighth Floor, Euston Tower, London NW1 3US (tel. 0300 057 1111 or 020 7667 1832).

The Adjudicator publishes an annual report.

See also HMRC leaflet AO1 'The Adjudicator's Office'.

Leave to apply for judicial review of the rejection by the Adjudicator of a complaint concerning the use of information from unidentified informants was refused in *R v Revenue Adjudicator's Office (ex p Drummond)* (1996) 70 TC 235.

Communications

Open Government

[41.10] Information on HMRC policies and decisions is widely available. Most internal HMRC guidance manuals are available on the HRMC website (at www.hmrc.gov.uk/manuals/index.htm).

Telephone Helplines

[41.11] An employers' telephone helpline on 08457 143 143 can be used for general enquiries about PAYE, national insurance and value added tax registration. The service is available from 0800 to 2000 on working days and 0800 to 1600 on Saturdays. Calls will be charged at local rates. See also **26.8 CONSTRUCTION INDUSTRY SCHEME.**

There is also a helpline for **new employers** on 0845 607 0143 (0800 to 2000 weekdays, 1000 to 1600 Saturdays), where the employer may register for PAYE, order an information pack on the operation of payroll tax and national insurance, and obtain help and information on payroll queries. Arrangements may also be made for access to business support teams and workshops providing further assistance.

A range of other helplines for general and specific enquiries is available on the HMRC website (at www.hmrc.gov.uk/contactus/by-phone.htm).

Use of electronic communications

[41.12] The Commissioners for HMRC have broad powers to make regulations, by statutory instrument, to facilitate two-way electronic communication in the delivery of information, e.g. tax returns (and see **66.29 RETURNS**), and the making of tax payments. The regulations may allow or require the use of intermediaries such as internet service providers. They will have effect notwithstanding any existing legislation requiring delivery or payment in a manner which would preclude the use of electronic communications or intermediaries. [*FA 1999, ss 132, 133*]. The intention is to provide a range of electronic services which taxpayers can use as an alternative to paper if they so wish.

HMRC's Corporation Tax Online service allows company tax returns, including tax computations and accounts, to be filed over the Internet. For filing dates post 1 April 2011 the electronic filing of corporate tax returns and the electronic payment of corporation tax has become mandatory (see **66 RETURNS**).

Mandatory e-filing

The Commissioners of HMRC have been given extremely wide powers to make regulations requiring the use of electronic communications for the delivery of information required or authorised to be delivered under tax legislation.

The powers have been further extended by *FA 2007*. [*FA 2002, ss 135, 136; FA 2003, ss 204, 205; FA 2007, ss 93, 94*]. The *Income Tax (Employments) Regulations 1993* (*SI 1993 No 744*), as amended by *SI 2003 No 2494* to provide for mandatory electronic payroll e-filing, provide that, where an e-filing notice has been issued by 31 December following a 'specified date':

(a) employers with 250 or more employees ('large employers') are required to file electronically from 2004/05; and
(b) employers with 50 or more employees ('large or medium-sized employers') are required to file electronically from 2005/06.

The '*specified date*' is the date on which the employer is treated as a 'large employer' or a 'large or medium-sized employer'. The specified date is to be announced annually by means of a direction by the Board but is to be no later than 30 November of the year preceding that in which the relevant PAYE payments are made.

For small employers with less than 50 employees, see below for incentives for voluntary electronic payroll e-filing.

The regulations provide for a default surcharge for payments not received by the collector in accordance with the regulations by the applicable due date rising from 17% of the PAYE payable for the third default to 83% for the twelfth and subsequent defaults. Penalties are also chargeable where PAYE returns and accompanying information are not delivered electronically by the applicable due date. The penalties rise on a sliding scale from £900 for 'large employers' with 250 to 399 employees, and from £600 for 'large or medium-sized employers' with 50 to 249 employees, to £3,000 for 1,000 or more employees in both cases. Interest is payable on unpaid penalties under *TMA 1970, s 103A*. See **69.26 TIME LIMITS** for the applicable due dates.

See also the HMRC Tax Bulletin February 2003 pp 995, 996 for an article summarising the e-filing requirements.

e-filing of Corporate Tax returns

Over recent years HMRC have promoted the e-filing of income and corporation tax self assessment returns, for example, by moving the filing date for paper returns for income tax to 30 September after the end of the tax year in question (returns filed online have the usual 31 January filing date). The ultimate intention is for all income and corporation tax returns to be filed solely in electronic format.

This is now the case for corporate tax with regard to accounting periods ending on or after 31 March 2010. The returns (and supporting documentation) for these periods have to be filed electronically in iXBRL format). This applies to corporation tax returns with a filing date from 1 April 2011 onwards.

A list of HMRC recognised software which can be used for e-filing can be found at:

www.hmrc.gov.uk/efiling/ctsoft_dev.htm.

For further details see also: www.hmrc.gov.uk/ct/mandatory-online-filing.pdf.

[*SI 2009 No 3218*].

(See further **66.29 ELECTRONIC FILING OF TAX RETURNS.**)

HMRC disclosure of information

[41.13] A memorandum of understanding has been agreed between HMRC and the Financial Reporting Review Panel (FRRP) on the principles underlying the provision of information that may be disclosed by HMRC to the FRRP under the *Companies (Audit, Investigations and Community Enterprise) Act 2004*. (HMRC Statement 24 June 2005, SWTI (2005) 1197.)

The information gathering powers of HMRC are outlined in **43 INVESTIGATORY POWERS.**

International co-operation

[41.14] Further to global moves to combat fraud and tax evasion the UK has been pursuing a policy of entering into international agreements with regard to mutual assistance in tax enforcement, covering exchange of information foreseeably relevant to the administration, enforcement or recovery of UK or foreign tax, the recovery of debts and the service of documents relating to UK or foreign tax. The *FA 2006, ss 173–175* makes certain provisions in respect of such arrangements, applicable post 19 July 2006.

Any information that can be disclosed to another territory under this provision can be disclosed to HMRC by any other Government department. Such information can then be disclosed by HMRC to an authorised officer of any territory with whom arrangements have been made. Information may not, however, be disclosed under any such arrangements unless HMRC are satisfied that the counterparty is bound by, or has undertaken to observe, rules of confidentiality at least as strict as those applying in the UK.

HMRC are able to use their existing information gathering powers regarding domestic taxes (pursuant to *FA 2008, Sch 36* formerly under *TMA 1970, s 20(1)–(8)(8C)–(9)*) to obtain information in respect of foreign tax liabilities covered by the international arrangements. For the procedural rules governing recovery of foreign taxes under these provisions, see *SI 2007 No 3507*. Pursuant to the *Finance Act 2011* there have been amendments to the information gathering powers under *Sch 36* with regard to information from third parties (termed data-holders). See further **43 INVESTIGATORY POWERS.**

The above provisions replace and widen similar provisions under *ICTA 1988, s 815C* and *FA 2003, s 198* and *ICTA 1988, s 788(2)*. Any provisions in existing Orders made prior to 19 July 2006 are to have effect from that date as if they were included (where they could have otherwise been so included) in an Order made under *FA 2006, s 173*. This also applies to arrangements covering UK or foreign taxes other than those in relation to which such Orders had effect.

The above provision similarly applies in relation to inheritance tax (replacing the provision in *IHTA 1984, s 220A*).

On 21 February 2011 a draft order was published with regard to the implementation of the protocol to the joint Council of Europe and OECD Convention on Mutual Administrative Assistance in Tax Matters. The UK signed the convention on 24 May 2007 and it entered into force on 1 May 2008 (*SI 2007 No 2126*). The protocol amending the convention was signed by the UK on 27 May 2010 .The convention includes provisions for: exchange of information on request; automatic exchange of information; spontaneous exchange of information; simultaneous tax examinations; tax examination abroad; assistance in recovery of tax; and service of documents.

The *Finance Act 2011* (*s 87* and *Sch 25*) contains provisions implementing the 2010 EU Directive on Mutual Assistance in the Recovery of Taxes 2010/24/EU which updates and amends previous directives, see below.

Co-operation between tax authorities of EU member states

The Mutual Assistance Directive (*Directive 77/799/EEC* as amended) provides for the exchange of information between tax authorities of EU member states to enable them to correctly assess liabilities to the taxes covered by the *Directive* (which include taxes on income and capital). The requirements of the *Directive* are transposed into UK domestic law by *FA 1978, s 77; FA 1990, s 125(5)(6); FA 2003, s 197(1)–(6), Sch 43 Pt 5(1)*. By virtue of amending *Directive 2004/56/EC*, the *Mutual Assistance Directive* now extends to the notification of instruments and decisions by the tax authority of a member state, to persons residing in that State, at the request of the tax authority of the member state from which the instrument or decision emanates. This requirement is transposed into UK domestic law by *F(No 2)A 2005, s 68* with effect in relation to requests received by HMRC (and its predecessors) on and after 1 January 2005.

Recovery of taxes etc. due in other EU member states

Provision is made for the recovery in the UK of amounts in respect of which a request for enforcement has been made in accordance with the *Mutual Assistance Recovery Directive* (*Directive 2010/24/EU, which replaces Directive 2008/55/EC, previously Directive 76/308/EEC* as amended by *Directive 2001/44/EC*) by an authority in another EU member state. *Finance Act 2011, s 87* and *Sch 25* has introduced provisions with regard to the implementation of the 2010 version of the Directive – 2010/24/EU – mentioned above. Further details of these provisions can be found at **43 INVESTIGATORY POWERS**.

Obligations of secrecy will not generally prevent disclosure of information by a UK tax authority (i.e. the Commissioners of HMRC, the Commissioners of Inland Revenue, the Commissioners of Customs and Excise or, in relation to certain agricultural levies, the relevant Minister) for these purposes (or for the purposes of a request for enforcement by the UK). There are transitional provisions to deal with requests for assistance outstanding at 28 November 2008.

Broadly, the UK tax authority has the same powers it would have for a corresponding claim in the UK, in particular in relation to penalties and interest. Treasury regulations may make provision as to what UK claim corresponds to a foreign claim, and for other procedural and supplementary matters (for which see *SI 2004 No 674* as amended by *SI 2005 No 1709* and *SI 2007 No 3508*). Regulations may also be made by the relevant UK tax authority for the application, non-application or adaptation of the law applicable to corresponding UK claims, without prejudice to its application when not dealt with by such regulations.

No proceedings may be taken against a person under these provisions if he shows that proceedings relevant to the liability in question are pending (i.e. still open to appeal), or about to be instituted, before a competent body in the member state in question. This does not apply if the foreign proceedings are not prosecuted or instituted with reasonable expedition, or if regulations made by the UK tax authority apply a UK enactment that permits proceedings in the case of a corresponding UK claim. If a final decision on the foreign claim (i.e. one against which no further appeal lies or would be in time), or a part of it, has been given in favour of the taxpayer by a competent body in the member state in question, no proceeding may be taken under these provisions in relation to the claim (or part).

The Treasury may amend, replace or repeal any of the above provisions by regulations for the purpose of giving effect to future amendments to the Directive.

[*FA 2002, s 134, Sch 39; SI 2004 No 674; SI 2005 No 1479; SI 2005 No 1709; SI 2008 No 2871*].

Assets Recovery

[41.15] See also **59.8 PAYMENT OF TAX — ENFORCEMENT.**

There are provisions within the *Proceeds of Crime Act 2002* (*Pt 6*) in respect of certain serious crimes which allow the functions of HMRC to be undertaken by a specific investigatory body — the Serious Organised Crime Agency ('SOCA').

Such powers were originally given to the Asset Recovery Agency, however, on 1 April 2008 this Agency was merged with SOCA, (see the *Serious Crime Act 2007, s 74, Sch 8*) and the undernoted powers are now exercisable by SOCA.

In order to carry out HMRC functions, SOCA must have reasonable grounds to suspect that:

(a) income arising or a gain accruing to a person in respect of a chargeable period is chargeable to income tax or is a chargeable gain and arises or accrues as a result (whether wholly or partly, directly or indirectly) of the 'criminal conduct' of that person or another; or

(b) a company is chargeable to corporation tax on its profits arising in a chargeable period and the profits arise as a result (whether wholly or partly, directly or indirectly) of the criminal conduct of the company or another person,

and must serve a notice on HMRC specifying the person or company, the period or periods concerned, and the functions which they intend to carry out. The periods involved may include periods beginning before the *Act* was passed.

Where SOCA is acting in such a capacity it is immaterial that a source cannot be identified for any income. Thus an assessment made by SOCA under *TMA 1970, s 29* (discovery assessment) in respect of income charged to tax under *ITTOIA 2005, Pt 5 Ch 8* (income not otherwise charged — see Tolley's Income Tax under Miscellaneous Income), or, before 2005/06, under Schedule D, Case VI cannot be reduced or quashed only because it does not specify (to any extent) the source of the income.

SOCA may cease carrying out the functions specified in the notice (originally served on HMRC) at any time, but *must* so cease where the conditions allowing the original notice to be made are no longer satisfied. Any assessment made under *TMA 1970, s 29* is subsequently invalid to the extent that it does not specify a source for income.

For the above purposes, '*criminal conduct*' is conduct which constitutes an offence anywhere in the UK or which would do so if it occurred there, but does not include conduct constituting an offence relating to a matter under the care and management of HMRC.

It should be noted that the vesting of a function in SOCA under these provisions does not divest HMRC or its officers of their functions (so that, for example, HMRC can continue to carry out routine work). Certain functions, as listed in *Proceeds of Crime Act 2002, s 323(3)*, cannot be carried out by SOCA. For example, if SOCA serves notice in relation to a company and in respect of a chargeable period or periods, the general HMRC functions vested in SOCA do not include functions relating to any requirement which is imposed on the company in its capacity as an employer and relates to a tax year which does not fall wholly within the chargeable period(s).

Appeals in respect of actions carried out by SOCA in the exercise of HMRC functions may be made to the appropriate tribunal. In hearing such appeals, the tribunal may be assisted by one or more assessors selected for their special knowledge and experience of the matter to which the appeal relates from a panel appointed for the purpose by the Lord Chancellor.

[*Proceeds of Crime Act 2002, ss 317, 318(1)(2), 319, 320(1)–(3), 323(1)(3), 326(1)(2); SI 2003 No 120; ITTOIA 2005, Sch 1 para 582*].

A company whose tax affairs are being investigated by the Serious Organised Crime Agency should check the SOCA website (www.soca.gov.uk) for guidance on how their cases will be dealt with.

Confidentiality

[41.16] For the confidential treatment of information supplied to HMRC see Tolley's Income Tax under HMRC — Confidentiality of Information.

Duties of senior accounting officers

[41.17] For accounting periods beginning on or after 21 July 2009, a new type of anti-avoidance provision is introduced in the form of a duty on senior accounting officers of qualifying companies to certify that the company has taken reasonable steps to ensure that it has 'appropriate tax accounting arrangements'. The legislation is not retrospective, but the SAO will be expected to take reasonable steps to have measures in place to ensure the brought forward balances are correct.

For this purpose, the *Companies Act 2006* definition of company, director and officer are adopted. Charities, mutual societies and dormant companies are all potentially within the scope, if the conditions are fulfilled.

Excluded, or potentially excluded companies are:

- bodies incorporated other than under the *Companies Act 2006* e.g. industrial and provident societies;
- partnerships;
- private equity structures — these will not be held responsible for the tax accounting arrangements of a target;
- foreign companies — only UK incorporated companies are caught. Therefore, CFCs, UK permanent establishments and overseas companies resident in the UK due to the location of central management and control are all outside the SAO provisions;
- companies incorporated in the UK but not resident there — such a company will be within the SAO legislation only to the extent that they are trading in, or have a taxable activity in the UK;
- dormant companies — although strictly within the SAO legislation, they are unlikely to have a tax charge or any tax accounting arrangements. They should be included in the certificate, with a note to the effect that they are dormant.

Foreign branches of UK companies are within the SAO legislation. Provided the responsibility for foreign tax has been delegated to a reasonably competent and qualified individual, reasonable steps would not include an in depth check of the foreign tax position. However, a check that the foreign tax had been paid would be expected.

Where a company or group is in liquidation or is insolvent, there may be no SAO and therefore the legislation will not apply.

A qualifying company must, for every financial year, notify HMRC of the name or names of the senior accounting officer for that year in a form laid down by HMRC by the deadline for filing the company's accounts for that year, or such longer period as HMRC may allow. The notification should be sent to the company's Client Relationship Manager at HMRC. A notification may apply to more than one company.

The main duty of the SAO is to take reasonable steps to ensure the company establishes, maintains and monitors appropriate tax accounting arrangements. This involves monitoring the accounting arrangements and identifying the ways in which the arrangements are deficient. As evidence of these steps, the officer must complete a certificate stating that the company had appropriate tax accounting arrangements or give an explanation as to the respects in which it was deficient. Guidance is available as to the extent to which entries and balances in earlier years come within the scope of the provisions. The certificate must be filed within the time limit for filing accounts, or such longer period as HMRC may allow.

The taxes and duties covered by this legislation are:

- corporation tax (including any amount assessable or chargeable as if it were CT for example in connection with loans to participators);
- VAT;
- PAYE;
- insurance premium tax;
- stamp duty land tax;
- stamp duty reserve tax;
- petroleum revenue tax;
- customs duties;
- excise duties (including air passenger duty).

Note that National Insurance is not included in the list. What are appropriate and reasonable steps will vary with the tax in question (e.g. stamp duty may be a one off while corporation tax is continuous). Typically, a company's tax accounting arrangements will be discussed in the course of the company's business risk review. Where third parties are used, an assessment of their competence, qualification and system of monitoring is needed. Special care is needed where there is an acquisition or merger. However, HMRC are only interested in significant transactions, taxes or systems relative to the size of the business. The guidance states: 'HMRC are not interested in small or insignificant errors and this fits with our policy of focusing on significant risks'. The following link is to HMRC's Tax Compliance Risk Management Process ('TCRM'): http://www.hmrc.gov.uk/manuals/tcrmanual/index.htm The TCRM involves three activities:

- the Business Risk Review;
- the risk assessment;
- risk working.

Penalties are provided for under these provisions. They are as follows:

(a) failure of the senior accounting officer to take reasonable steps to maintain appropriate tax accounting arrangements, £5,000;
(b) failure of senior accounting officer to provide a certificate or to provide a certificate with a careless or deliberate inaccuracy, £5,000;
(c) failure of a qualifying company to notify name of senior accounting officer for a year, £5,000.

Where there is more than one senior accounting officer liable to the penalty, the latest is responsible for paying it. If such an officer, either in post or having left it, complies with the requirements under these provisions, no-one else is liable for a penalty in respect of that financial year. No penalty will be charged where HMRC are satisfied that there is reasonable excuse. HMRC may issue an assessment in respect of the penalty to the person liable, but must do so not more than 6 months after the behaviour resulting in the penalty first comes to HMRC's notice or more than 6 years after the filing date. The person then has 30 days during which to appeal. Otherwise the person has 30 days to pay the penalty. Where an appeal is made and determined or withdrawn, the 30 days run from the date of withdrawal or determination. There is provision to avoid double assessment when the senior accounting officer holds that capacity for more than one company in a group. There are provisions for appeals against penalty notices.

The HMRC guidance may be found at: http://www.hmrc.gov.uk/largecompanies/duties-sen-acc-officer.pdf

Definitions

'*Appropriate tax accounting arrangements*' are arrangements to keep accounting records which enable the company to calculate accurately in all material respects its liability to a specified list of direct and indirect taxes.'

Subject to an overriding power of the Treasury to specify by statutory instrument that a company or class of company is not a qualifying company, a '*qualifying company*' is one which satisfies both or either of the following conditions:

(1) relevant turnover more than £200 million. (Turnover is as defined in *CA 2006, s 474* and shown in the statutory accounts i.e. adjustments in the corporation tax computation are not taken into account.) Where no turnover is shown in the statutory accounts (e.g. in the case of banks and insurance companies) the test at (2) below applies on its own;

(2) relevant '*balance sheet total*' more than £2 billion.

Where the company is a member of a group, these figures relate to the whole group. If the group companies' year ends are not co-terminous, the latest accounts ending before the group's balance sheet date are to be used.

'*Balance sheet total*' is the gross total of assets in the balance sheet.

'*Senior accounting officer*' for a non-group company is the director or officer who, in the company's reasonable opinion, has overall responsibility for the company's financial accounting arrangements. In a group situation, it is the group director or officer with overall responsibility for the accounting function, as above. One person may be senior accounting officer for more than one company. In determining if a group exists, a test of 51% ownership applies.

'*Director*' or '*officer*' are taken to have their *Companies Act 2006* meaning.

[*FA 2009, s 93, Sch 46*].

42

HMRC Extra-Statutory Concessions

Introduction

[42.1] Extra Statutory Concessions (ESCs) are relaxations of the strict letter of the law which give taxpayers a reduction in tax liability to which they would not otherwise be entitled. Most ESCs are made to deal with what are, generally, minor or transitory anomalies under the legislation and to meet cases of hardship at the margins of the code where a statutory remedy would be difficult to implement.

ESCs are of general application, however, it should be borne in mind that in a particular case there may be special circumstances which will require to be taken into account in considering the application of a concession.

A concession will not be given in any case where an attempt is made to use it for tax avoidance.

Following the House of Lords' decision in the *Wilkinson* case ([2006] STC 270) the scope of HMRC's discretion to make ESCs was clarified and since then HMRC has undertaken reviews of its ESCs, with a view to putting them onto a legislative footing where the existing ESC exceeds the scope of its discretion. The provisions of *FA 2008, s 160* allow the tax treatment afforded by existing ESCs to be legislated by Treasury order.

Further to various consultations, this and other enabling powers have been used to legislate nearly 30 ESCs to date. A fourth consultation document was released in December 2010 which sets out proposed draft legislation for several ESCs, including the following:

B11 Compensation for compulsory slaughter of animals

C10 Groups of companies: arrangements

C16 Dissolution of companies under *s 652* and *s 652A Companies Act 1985*

It is envisaged these will be legislated during 2011.

[42.2] The following is a summary of the concessions applicable to companies published by HMRC and as amended to date (available on HMRC's website), or subsequently announced. The published list of ESCs can be found at www.hmrc.gov.uk/specialist/esc.pdf.

See also **41.5 HMRC — ADMINISTRATION.**

A37 **Tax treatment of directors' fees received by partnerships and other companies.** Under certain conditions, such fees may be included in computing partnership profits or in the corporation tax assessment of the other company. See Tolley's Income Tax under Employment Income.

A69 **Building societies: conversion to company status.** Certain declarations made to a building society are treated as having been made to the successor company following conversion to company status. See **8.7 BANKS, 9.4 BUILDING SOCIETIES.**

B1 **Machinery or plant: changes from 'renewals' to the capital allowances basis.** Capital allowances may be claimed on expenditure which has been the subject of a renewals allowance, provided that all items of the same class are changed to the new basis. See **13.24 CAPITAL ALLOWANCES — PLANT AND MACHINERY: FIXTURES AND LEASING.**

B7 **Benevolent gifts by traders** may be allowable trading expenses. This has been given legislative effect by *ITTOIA 2005, s 47* and *CTA 2009, s 1300*, and is considered obsolete as from 9 December 2010. See **71.41, 71.67 TRADING EXPENSES AND DEDUCTIONS.**

B8 **Double taxation relief: income consisting of royalties and know-how payments.** Payments made by an overseas resident to a UK trader for the use of copyright etc. are treated as arising outside the UK except in so far as they represent consideration for services (other than merely incidental services) rendered in the UK by the recipient to the payer. See **32.4 DOUBLE TAX RELIEF.**

B10 **Income of contemplative religious communities,** or of their members, which is paid into the common fund of such communities which are not charities, is regarded as income of each member up to the amount of the basic personal allowance for the year. Where the aggregate of 'allowable figures' exceeds income of the community, the excess may be set against chargeable gains of that year. This has been given legislative effect.

B11 **Compensation for the compulsory slaughter of farm animals.** Provided that no election for the Herd Basis (see **70.42 TRADE PROFITS — INCOME AND SPECIFIC TRADES**) is in force in respect of the animals, the profit attributable to the compensation (calculated as required in the Concession) may be spread over the three years following that in which the slaughter took place. See **70.29 TRADE PROFITS — INCOME AND SPECIFIC TRADES.**

B16 **Fire safety: capital expenditure incurred on certain trade premises (a) in Northern Ireland and (b) by lessors:**

(a) Notwithstanding that *Fire Precautions Act 1971* (and, consequently, *CAA 2001, s 29*) does not apply to NI, relief is generally given on the same basis as in Great Britain. Where the expenditure qualifies for relief under *CAA 2001, s 271* (hotel buildings allowance), it may nevertheless be treated as above, provided that the claimant renounces his relief under *s 271*.

(b) Relief is allowed where the lessor incurs the expenditure himself, if similar expenditure by the tenant or licensee would have qualified for relief.

See **11.3 CAPITAL ALLOWANCES — PLANT AND MACHINERY: ELIGIBLE EXPENDITURE AND INITIAL ALLOWANCES.**

B41 **Claims to repayment of tax.** Where an over-payment of tax has arisen because of official error, and there is no doubt or dispute as to the facts, claims to repayment of tax are accepted outside the statutory time limit (generally six years from the end of the year concerned). See Tolley's Income Tax under Claims.

B42 **'Free gifts' and insurance contracts.** Certain incentive gifts offered in connection with the issue of insurance policies are disregarded. See Tolley's Income Tax under Life Assurance Policies.

B46 **Automatic penalties for late company and employers' and contractors' end-of-year returns.** A short period of grace is allowed for submission of annual returns. See **60.5 PENALTIES, 66.7 RETURNS** and Tolley's Income Tax under Penalties. From 1 April 2011, company tax returns must be filed online and all forms P35 and P14 are already filed online. Contractors are no longer required to file end-of-year Construction Industry Scheme returns. ESC B46 has therefore become redundant thus it ceases to apply as from 31 March 2011.

B47 **Furnished lettings of dwelling houses — wear and tear of furniture.** As an alternative to the renewals basis, an allowance of 10% of rent may be claimed. See **62.5 PROPERTY INCOME.**

B49 *CAA 2001, s 532* **— repaid grants.** Capital allowances will be given for repayments of grants which were deducted from expenditure qualifying for capital allowances. See **10.2 CAPITAL ALLOWANCES — INTRODUCTION.**

B54 **Tax relief for expenditure on films, tapes and discs confirmed.** Notwithstanding the changes made by *FA 2000, s 113(2)*, expenditure on the production of master audio tapes and discs will continue to be treated as of a revenue nature. Replaced by legislation under the *FA 2006* regime. See **70.31 TRADE PROFITS — INCOME AND SPECIFIC TRADES.**

C1 **Credit for underlying tax: dividends from trade investments in overseas companies.** Credit is given along a chain of shareholdings in certain circumstances. See **32.11 DOUBLE TAX RELIEF.**

C4 **Trading activities for charitable purposes** are exempt subject to certain conditions. See **20.6 CHARITIES.**

C5 **Industrial and provident societies** carrying on trades may treat certain income as trading income for the purposes of loss relief under *ICTA 1988, s 393(8)* (see **55.5 LOSSES**). See **47.6 INDUSTRIAL AND PROVIDENT SOCIETIES.**

C9 **Associated close and small companies.** The rights and powers of a person's relatives (other than spouse and children) are not attributed to him in certain circumstances, and various other concessions made as regards associated status. See **67.4 SMALL COMPANIES — REDUCED RATES.**

C10 **Groups of companies: arrangements.** Certain agreements etc. will not constitute 'arrangements' for the various purposes of the legislation relating to groups of companies. See **39.15 GROUP RELIEF.**

C11 **Demergers:** ***ICTA 1988, s 213(7).*** The conditions imposed following a distribution are relaxed. See **31.34 GROUP RELIEF.**

C12 A **retail co-operative society** which prepares half-yearly or quarterly accounts can be treated as having yearly accounting periods ending on an agreed date. See generally **2.9 ACCOUNTING PERIODS.**

C13 **'Second and third tier'** agricultural co-operative associations are treated as if members of the basic level associations were members of them. Considered redundant so withdrawn as from 1 April 2010. See generally **47.5 INDUSTRIAL AND PROVIDENT SOCIETIES.**

C15 **Dissolution of unincorporated associations: distributions to members.** Small distributions by social or recreational associations which have not carried on a trade or business are not treated as distributions under *ICTA 1988, s 209*. See **31.14**(b) **DISTRIBUTIONS.**

C16 **Dissolution of companies under *Companies Act 1985, ss 652, 652A*: distributions to shareholders.** Distributions of assets to members on such a dissolution will in most circumstances not be treated as distributions under *ICTA 1988, s 209*. See **31.14**(a) **DISTRIBUTIONS.**

C30 **Authorised unit trusts and open-ended investment companies — waivers of distributions.** Distribution treatment is disapplied in the case of certain *de minimis* waivers of distributions (or accumulations). See **52.6 INVESTMENT FUNDS.**

C31 **Scientific research associations.** Tax exemptions will temporarily continue under the previous practice following a change in the DTI guidance on the qualification requirements. See **35.12 EXEMPT ORGANISATIONS.**

C36 **Treatment of income from caravan sites where there is both trading and associated letting income.** In such circumstances, letting income from caravans and caravan pitch sites may be treated as income of the trade. Formerly ESC B29. Now put onto a statutory footing by *CTA 2009, s 43*. See **62.2 PROPERTY INCOME.**

D10 **Unquoted shares acquired before 6 April 1965: disposal following reorganisation of share capital.** Where, in consequence of a reorganisation of share capital before 6 April 1965, a valuation at that date is required, or time apportionment is limited, under *TCGA 1992, Sch 2 para 19*, the gain chargeable to corporation tax on a disposal of the entire holding (whether in a single transaction or in separate transactions in the same accounting period) is limited to the actual gain realised. See Tolley's Capital Gains Tax under Assets held on 6 April 1965.

D15 **Relief for the replacement of business assets: unincorporated associations.** Relief is available in respect of assets owned by companies whose shares are wholly (or apart from a very small proportion) held by or on behalf of such an association or its members. See Tolley's Capital Gains Tax under Rollover Relief. Now put onto a statutory footing from 5 April 2009.

D16 **Relief for the replacement of business assets: repurchase of same asset** will give rise to relief where for purely commercial reasons. See Tolley's Capital Gains Tax under Rollover Relief.

D18 **Default on mortgage granted by vendor.** In such circumstances and where the vendor regains beneficial ownership of the asset and so elects, the chargeable gain is limited to the net proceeds obtained from the transactions and the loan treated as never having existed. See Tolley's Capital Gains Tax under Disposal.

D22 **Relief for the replacement of business assets: expenditure on improvements to existing assets** may attract relief provided that the existing assets are used only for trade purposes, or are so used on completion of the improvements. See Tolley's Capital Gains Tax under Rollover Relief.

D23 **Relief for the replacement of business assets: partition of land on the dissolution of a partnership.** Partitioned assets are treated as new assets provided that the partnership is immediately dissolved. See Tolley's Capital Gains Tax under Rollover Relief.

D24 **Relief for the replacement of business assets: asset not brought immediately into trading use** may attract relief provided that:

(a) it is proposed to incur expenditure on work for the purpose of enhancing its value;
(b) the work begins as soon as possible after acquisition, and is completed within a reasonable time;
(c) on completion of the work, the asset is taken into use for trade purposes only; and
(d) the asset is not let or used for non-trade purposes between acquisition and being taken into use for trade purposes.

See Tolley's Capital Gains Tax under Rollover Relief.

D25 **Relief for the replacement of business assets: expenditure on acquisition of an interest in an asset already used for the purposes of a trade** will attract relief as if the further interest acquired was a new asset taken into use for trade purposes. See Tolley's Capital Gains Tax under Rollover Relief.

D26 **Relief for exchange of joint interests** in land will apply to exchanges after 19 December 1984, on the lines of that available on compulsory purchase. After 29 October 1987, the relief is further extended to exchanges of joint interests in milk or potato quota in parallel with such exchanges of land. The concession applies to disposals made before 6 April 2010. This has been given legislative effective by *TCGA 1992, ss 248A–248E*, which apply after this date. See Tolley's Capital Gains Tax under Land.

D32 **Transfer of a business to a company.** Liabilities taken over on a transfer of business will not be treated as consideration for the rollover provisions of *TCGA 1992, s 162* and no capital gain will arise on the transfer. See Tolley's Capital Gains Tax under Rollover Relief.

D33 **Capital gains tax on compensation and damages.** Damages derived from underlying assets will be treated as exempt where the asset is exempt, and where there is no underlying asset damages will be exempt. See Tolley's Capital Gains Tax under Assets.

D34 **Rebasing and indexation: shares held at 31 March 1982.** A single holding treatment will apply even if the shares were acquired before 7 April 1965. See Tolley's Capital Gains Tax under Assets held on 31 March 1982.

D39 **Extensions of leases.** Relief is given where a lessee surrenders an existing lease and is granted a new, longer lease at arm's length on the same property at a different rent, but otherwise on the same terms. See Tolley's Capital Gains Tax under Land.

D42 **Mergers of leases.** Indexation allowance may be given on the costs of acquisition of a lease by reference to the date on which it was acquired, even though it ceased to exist on the acquisition of a superior interest in the property, such as the freehold reversion. This replaces an earlier practice for disposals after 28 June 1992. See Tolley's Capital Gains Tax under Land.

D44 **Rebasing and indexation: shares derived from larger holdings held at 31 March 1982.** A more favourable basis of valuation at 31 March 1982 for rebasing and indexation purposes may be available in relation to shares and securities acquired intra-group. See Tolley's Capital Gains Tax under Assets held on 31 March 1982.

D47 **Temporary loss of charitable status due to reverter of school and other sites.** Liabilities which may arise in the period before charitable status is re-established will be discharged or repaid. Considered obsolete so withdrawn as from 1 April 2010. See **14.1 CHARITIES**.

D50 **Capital gains tax treatment of compensation.** Gains arising on compensation from foreign governments may in certain circumstances be exempt. This has been given legislative effect by *TCGA 1992, s 268B*, as from 1 April 2010. See Tolley's Capital Gains Tax under Disposal.

D51 **Transfer from a close company at undervalue.** *TCGA 1992, s 125* is not applied in certain cases where the transfer gives rise to a charge under other provisions. See **17.46 CAPITAL GAINS**. Now put onto a statutory footing by *SI 2009 No 730*.

D52 **Share exchanges, company reconstructions and amalgamations — incidental costs of acquisition and disposal and warranty payments** may be treated as consideration given for the new holding. See Tolley's Capital Gains Tax under Shares and Securities.

D53 ***TCGA 1992, s 50*: grants repaid.** Government, public or local authority grants for acquiring assets which are then repaid on disposal of the asset will reduce the value of the consideration received for capital gains purposes.

I3 ***Oil Taxation Act 1975, Sch 3 para 9*.** Certain time limits are extended.

I4 ***Oil Taxation Act 1983, s 9(5)*: tariff receipts allowance in respect of foreign 'user' fields** may be backdated to the date on which tariffs were first received or receivable.

I5 **PRT instalments** may be withheld where production ceases following catastrophic loss or damage.

43

HMRC Investigatory Powers

Cross-references. See **60 PENALTIES**; **66 RETURNS**.

Introduction

[43.1] HMRC have wide powers to enforce compliance with tax legislation. In most cases, the powers used are those for enquiries (HMRC now refer to compliance checks, however this term includes the enquiry process) into self-assessment returns, for which see **43.2** below and **66.19–66.23 RETURNS**. Those powers do, however, operate in tandem with further powers to obtain evidence both directly from the taxpayer and from third parties, which are described in this chapter.

FA 2008, Sch 36, as amended and extended by *FA 2009, Schs 47* and *48*, introduces a common set of information and inspection powers for HMRC covering income tax, capital gains tax, corporation tax and VAT. The powers apply from 1 April 2009 (or 1 April 2010 in the case of powers included in *FA 2009, Sch 48*). See **43.3–43.10** below.

The *FA 2008* powers replace the existing powers at **43.14, 43.15** below to obtain documents and particulars and the existing power to call for documents during self-assessment enquiries (see **43.2** below).

HMRC can require a tax accountant who has been convicted by or before any UK court of a tax offence or incurred a penalty under *TMA 1970, s 99* (see **60.8 PENALTIES**) to deliver 'documents' in his possession or power relevant to any tax liability of any of his clients. See **43.16** below.

With effect from 1 December 2007, HMRC are able to exercise certain powers under the *Police and Criminal Evidence Act 1984* when conducting direct tax criminal investigations. See **43.17** below. As a result of the availability of those powers, the pre-existing search and seizure powers are no longer needed and are repealed. The pre-existing power to seek judicial authority to require the delivery of documents at **43.19** below is restricted to circumstances where the equivalent police power cannot be used.

There are special provisions relating to computer records (see **43.18** below).

The Finance Act 2011 updates HMRC's information powers with regard to certain classes of person who hold information on taxpayers as from 1 April 2012. The changes introduce a single set of general rules covering the form of a notice, how it may be complied with, and penalties. HMRC will be able to specify the format for data to be provided to them, and a right of appeal is introduced. In addition the legislation contains a single set of general provisions which will, firstly, bring the existing legislation with regard to 'data-holders' (from whom HMRC can request information) into one place, and secondly specify in regulations what data may be required from each group. These proposals are outlined further at **43.12** below.

The new updated EU Mutual Assistance for the Recovery of Taxes Directive (MARD) is also implemented by *FA 2011, Sch 25*. These provisions are outlined at **43.13** below.

Self-assessment enquiries

[43.2] The self-assessment enquiry procedures are explained at **66.19–66.23 RETURNS**; these operate in tandem with the provisions below.

The enquiry procedures incorporate a separate power to call for documents but, from 1 April 2009, that power is repealed and replaced by the powers at **43.3–43.10** below.

See in particular **43.6** below for restrictions on HMRC's power to issue an information notice where a tax return has been made.

FA 2008 — information and inspection powers

[43.3] *FA 2008, Sch 36* introduces a common set of information and inspection powers for HMRC covering income tax, capital gains tax, corporation tax and VAT. The powers will apply from 1 April 2009, and are covered at **43.4–43.10** below only to the extent that they apply for the purposes of corporation tax. The powers replace those at **43.14** below and the existing power to call for documents during self-assessment enquiries (see **66.19 RETURNS**).

Definitions

For the purposes of the provisions at **43.4–43.10** below, the following definitions apply.

'*Checking*' includes carrying out an investigation or enquiry of any kind. '*Document*' includes a part of a document (unless the context requires otherwise).

An '*authorised HMRC officer*' is an HMRC officer who is, or who is a member of a class of officers, authorised by the Commissioners for HMRC for the particular purpose.

The carrying on of a business includes the letting of property and the activities of a charity, a government department, a local authority (within *ITA 2007, s 999*), a local authority association (within *ITA 2007, s 1000*) or any other public authority. HMRC can make regulations specifying activities as businesses.

'*Tax*' means any or all of income tax, capital gains tax, corporation tax and VAT. It also includes taxes of EU member states in respect of which information can be disclosed and taxes of territories to which a tax enforcement agreement apply.

A company's '*tax position*' is its position at any time and in relation to any period as regards any tax, including its position as to past, present and future liability to any tax, penalties and other amounts which have been paid or are, or may be, payable by or to him in connection with any tax, and any claims, elections, applications and notices that have or may be made or given in connection with any tax.

'*Parent undertaking*', '*subsidiary undertaking*' and '*undertaking*' have the same meanings as in *Companies Act 2006, ss 1161, 1162, Sch 7*.

[*FA 2008, Sch 36 paras 33(7), 58–60, 63, 64*].

Responsibility of company officers

Everything to be done by a company under the provisions at **43.4–43.10** below must be done by it through the '*proper officer*' (i.e. the secretary of a corporate body, except where a liquidator or administrator has been appointed when the latter is the proper officer, or the treasurer of a non-corporate body) or, except where a liquidator has been appointed, any authorised officer. The service of a notice on a company may be effected by serving it on the proper officer. [*TMA 1970, s 108; FA 2008, Sch 36 para 56*].

Information and documents

[43.4] With effect from 1 April 2009, an HMRC officer may by notice in writing require a person to provide information or to produce a document if it is reasonably required by him:

(a) for the purpose of checking that person's tax position;

(b) for the purpose of checking the tax position of another person whose identity is known to the officer; or
(c) for the purpose of checking the UK tax position of a person whose identity is not known to the officer or of a class of persons whose individual identities are not known to the officer.

Such a notice (an '*information notice*') may require either specified information or documents or information or documents described in the notice (so that a notice is not restricted to information or documents which HMRC can specifically identify). Where it is given with the approval of the tribunal (see further below), the notice must say so.

The information or documents must be provided or produced within the time period and at the time, by the means and in the form (if any) reasonably specified in the notice.

Documents must be produced for inspection either: at a place agreed to by the recipient of the notice and an HMRC officer; or at a place (other than one used solely as a dwelling) that an HMRC officer reasonably specifies.

Subject to any conditions or exceptions set out in regulations made by HMRC, copies of documents can be produced unless the notice requires the production of the original document or an HMRC officer in writing subsequently requests the original document. Where an officer makes such a request, the document must be produced within the period and at the time and by the means reasonably requested by the officer.

An HMRC officer may take copies of, or make extracts from, a document (or copy) produced to him, and if it appears necessary to him, he may remove the document at a reasonable time and retain it for a reasonable period. The officer must, without charge, provide a receipt for a document which is removed where this is requested and must also provide, again without charge, a copy of the document, if the person producing it reasonably requires it for any purpose. Where a document which has been removed is lost or damaged, HMRC are liable to compensate the owner for expenses reasonably incurred in replacing or repairing it.

The production or removal of a document under these provisions does not break any lien (i.e. any right) claimed on it.

In the case of *P Whight v HMRC* [2011] UK FTT 60(TC) the First Tier Tribunal held that HMRC have a right to see the original documentation which supported schedules forwarded on behalf of the taxpayer. The case related to capital gains tax on a share disposal, and the determination of residence of the taxpayer, who claimed to have been non-UK resident for five tax years. The tribunal held that the taxpayer in this case had not shown as a matter of fact that the documents were not reasonably required for the purpose of checking the taxpayer's position, and also that the request was not disproportionate or onerous in these particular circumstances.

Notices

Taxpayer notice

[43.5] An information notice under (a) above can be given without the approval of the tribunal (see **6 APPEALS**), but where such approval is obtained the taxpayer has no right of appeal against the notice or a requirement in it.

Where approval is sought from the tribunal, the application for approval must be made by, or with the agreement of, an authorised HMRC officer. The taxpayer must normally have been told that the information or documents are required and have been given a reasonable opportunity to make representations to HMRC, and the tribunal must be given a summary of any such representations. Where, however, the tribunal is satisfied that informing the taxpayer would prejudice the assessment or collection of tax, it can approve the giving of the notice without the taxpayer having been informed.

Third party notice

A notice within (b) above cannot be given without either the agreement of the taxpayer (i.e. the person whose tax position is to be checked) or the approval of the tribunal and must normally name the taxpayer. The appeal may be heard without giving notice to the taxpayer i.e. the application will be heard in his absence. Where approval is obtained from the tribunal, there is no right of appeal against the notice or a requirement in it.

Where approval is sought from the tribunal, the application for approval must be made by, or with the agreement of, an authorised HMRC officer. The taxpayer must normally have been given a summary of the reasons why an officer requires the information or documents. The person to whom the notice is to be given must normally have been told that the information or documents are required and have been given a reasonable opportunity to make representations to HMRC and the tribunal must be given a summary of any such representations. These requirements can, however, be disapplied where the tribunal is satisfied that informing the recipient of the notice or giving a summary of reasons to the taxpayer would prejudice the assessment or collection of tax.

The tribunal can also disapply the requirement to name the taxpayer in the notice if it is satisfied that the officer has reasonable grounds for believing that naming him might seriously prejudice the assessment or collection of tax. There is no appeal against the grant of a notice.

A copy of the notice must normally be given to the taxpayer. The tribunal can, however, disapply this requirement if an application for approval is made by, or with the agreement of, an authorised HMRC officer. The tribunal must be satisfied that the officer has reasonable grounds for believing that giving a copy of the notice to the taxpayer might prejudice the assessment or collection of tax.

Where a third party notice is given for the purpose of checking the tax position of a parent undertaking and any of its subsidiary undertakings, the above provisions apply as if the parent undertaking were the taxpayer. The requirement for the notice to name the taxpayer is satisfied by stating in the notice that its purpose is checking the tax position of the parent and subsidiary undertakings and naming the parent undertaking. Where a notice is given to a parent undertaking for the purpose of checking the tax position of one or more subsidiary undertakings, neither the agreement of the parent undertaking or the approval of the tribunal is required and a copy does not have to be given to the parent undertaking.

Where a third party notice is given for the purpose of checking the tax position of more than one of the partners in a business carried on in partnership, in their capacity as such, the above provisions apply as if the taxpayer were at least one of the partners. The requirement for the notice to name the taxpayer is satisfied by stating in the notice that its purpose is checking the tax position of more than one of the partners and giving a name in which the partnership is registered for any purpose. Where a third party notice is given to one of the partners for the purpose of checking the tax position of any of the other partners, neither the agreement of any of the partners nor the approval of the tribunal is required and a copy does not have to be given to any other partners.

Notice about persons whose identity is not known

The giving of a notice under (c) above requires the approval of the tribunal. No notice need be given of the hearing. The tribunal can approve the giving of the notice only if it is satisfied that:

- there are reasonable grounds for believing that the person or class of persons to whom the notice relates may have failed, or may fail, to comply with any provision of the *Taxes Acts* or any other enactment relating to UK tax;
- any such failure is likely to have led, or to lead, to serious prejudice to the assessment or collection of UK tax; and
- the information or document is not readily available from another source.

Where a third party notice or a notice about persons whose identity is not known is given to an 'involved third party' (see **43.10** below) to check a person's corporation tax position and refers only to 'relevant information' or 'relevant documents', certain provisions regarding approval and copying of notices to the taxpayer are disapplied. Appeals are permitted on any grounds, save with regard to the involved this party's statutory records (for which no appeal lies).

From 1 April 2010, where a third party notice or a notice about persons whose identity is not known refers only to information or documents that relate to any pensions matter, being registered pension schemes, certain purchased annuities or employer financed retirement benefits schemes, then certain provisions regarding approval and copying of notices to the taxpayer are disapplied. Appeals are permitted on any grounds, save with regard to any person's statutory records (for which no appeal lies).

The approval of the tribunal is not required for a notice to be given to a parent undertaking for the purpose of checking the tax position of one or more subsidiary undertakings whose identities are not known to the HMRC officer giving the notice.

Such approval is also not required for a notice to be given to a partner in a business carried on in partnership for the purpose of checking the tax position of partners whose identities are not known to the officer giving the notice. There is no appeal against the grant of a notice. Appeals are however permitted on any grounds, save with regard to the parent's or subsidiary undertakings' statutory records (for which no appeal lies).

Such approval is also not required for a notice to be given to a partner in a business carried on in partnership for the purpose of checking the tax position of partners whose identities are not known to the officer giving the notice. Appeals are however permitted on any grounds, save with regard to any of the partner's statutory records (for which no appeal lies).

Inaccurate information and documents in reply to a notice

Where, in complying with an information notice, a company provides inaccurate information or a document carelessly or deliberately and, on later discovering the mistake, does not take reasonable steps to inform HMRC, the company will incur a penalty of £3,000 in respect of each such inaccuracy.

[*FA 2008, s 40A, Sch 36 paras 1–9, 13, 14, 33, 35; FA 2009, Sch 47 paras 2–4, 15, Sch 48 para 11*].

For further restrictions on the above powers, see **43.6** below. For appeals against information notices, see **43.8** below.

See HMRC Compliance Handbook 220000 onwards, third party notices 225000 onwards.

Restrictions on information notice powers

[43.6] An information notice does not require a person to:

- (i) produce a document if it is not in his possession or power;
- (ii) provide or produce information that relates to the conduct of a pending tax appeal or any part of a document containing such information;
- (iii) provide journalistic material (within *Police and Criminal Evidence Act 1984, s 13*) or information contained in such material;
- (iv) subject to the exceptions below, provide or produce 'personal records' (within *Police and Criminal Evidence Act 1984, s 12*); or
- (v) produce a document the whole of which originates more than six years before the giving of the notice, unless the notice is given by, or with the agreement of, an authorised officer.

With regard to (iv) above, an information notice may require a person to produce documents (or copies) that are personal records, omitting any personal information (i.e. information whose inclusion in the documents makes them personal records) and to provide any information in personal records that is not personal information.

[*FA 2008, Sch 36 paras 18–20*].

Notice where tax return made

Where a person has made a tax return under *TMA 1970, ss 8, 8A* or *12AA* or *FA 1998, Sch 18 para 3* (see **66.5** and **66.9 RETURNS**) in respect of a tax year or accounting period, a taxpayer notice (see **43.4**(a) above) can be given for the purpose of checking the income tax, capital gains tax or corporation tax position for that year or chargeable period only if:

(a) an enquiry notice under *TMA 1970, ss 9A, 12AC, Sch 1A para 5* or *FA 1998, Sch 18 para 24* (see **66.5** and **66.9 RETURNS**) has been given in respect of either the return or a claim or election for the year or period to which the return relates and the enquiry has not been completed;

(b) an HMRC officer has reason to suspect that an amount that ought to have been assessed to tax may not have been assessed, that an assessment for the period may be or have become insufficient or relief from tax for the period may be or have become excessive;

(c) the notice is given for the purpose of obtaining information or a document that is also required to check the taxpayer's position as regards any tax other than income tax, capital gains tax or corporation tax (with effect from 1 April 2010, previously 'VAT position'); or

(d) the notice is given for the purpose of obtaining information or a document that is required to check the taxpayer's position as regards his obligation to make deductions or repayments under PAYE, the construction industry scheme or any other provision.

However, this provision does not prevent a notice being given for the provision of information or documents relating to the animals subject to a herd basis election or the products of those animals. In addition, it does not apply where a counteraction provision under *CTA 2010, s 733; ICTA 1988, s 703* or *ITA 2007, s 684* (transactions in securities) applies.

From 1 April 2010, if a person has made a stamp duty land tax return, claim or amendment of a claim for a chargeable period, a taxpayer notice can be given to check the person's stamp duty land tax for that period only if one or more of the following conditions apply:

(i) there is an open enquiry into the return, claim or amendment to a claim; or

(ii) an HMRC officer has reason to suspect that:
   - an amount that ought to have been assessed to stamp duty land tax in respect of the transaction may not have been assessed; or
   - an assessment to stamp duty land tax in respect of the transaction may be or have become insufficient; or
   - relief from stamp duty land tax given in respect of the transaction may be or have become excessive; or

(iii) the notice is given for the purpose of obtaining any information or document that is also required for the purpose of checking that person's position regarding a tax other than stamp duty land tax.

Where a third party notice is given to a parent undertaking for the purpose of checking the tax position of one or more subsidiary undertakings, the above provisions apply as if the notice were a taxpayer notice or taxpayer notices given to the subsidiary undertaking or each of them.

Where a business is carried in partnership and a partnership return (see **64 RETURNS**) has been made by one of the partners, the above provisions apply as if the return had been made by each of the partners, and condition (a) above can be met in relation to a partner by reference to either the partnership return or his personal, trustee or company return for the period concerned.

Where it appears to HMRC that there has been a change in ownership of a company (within *CTA 2010, Pt 14 Ch 7* (previously *ICTA 1988, s 769*)) and, in connection with that change, a person (the '*seller*') may be or become liable to corporation tax under *CTA 2010, ss 710* or *713* (previously *ICTA 1988, ss 767A* or *767AA*) (recovery of unpaid corporation tax from persons controlling company), the above restriction does not apply to a taxpayer notice given to the seller.

[*FA 2008, Sch 36 paras 21, 35(4), 36, 37(1)(2); FA 2009, Sch 47 para 12; CTA 2010, Sch 1 para 573(2)*].

Legal professional privilege

An information notice cannot require a person to provide information, or to produce any part of a document, in respect of which a claim to legal professional privilege (or, in Scotland, a claim to confidentiality of communications) could be maintained in legal proceedings.

HMRC can make regulations providing for the resolution of disputes as to whether information or a document is privileged by the tribunal.

In the recent case *R (oao Prudential plc) v Special Commissioner of Income Tax* [2010] STC 161 the High Court considered whether legal professional privilege could be extended to cover advice on tax law given by tax accountants (legal advice, rather than litigation privilege). Whilst it was recognised by the Court that it is slightly anomalous that tax lawyers and tax accountants should be in a different position in this regard, they concluded that legal professional privilege should not be granted to tax accountants — it was closely linked to the legal profession and was a reflection of the necessarily close relationship of lawyers with the administration of justice and their professional duties. On 13 October 2010 the Court of Appeal confirmed this decision ([2010] STC 2802).

See also cases referred to at **43.15**.

[*FA 2008, Sch 36 para 23*].

Auditors

An information notice does not require an auditor (i.e. a person appointed as an auditor for the purpose of an enactment) to provide information held in connection with the performance of his functions under that enactment or to produce documents which are his property and which were created by him, or on his behalf, for or in connection with the performance of those functions.

This restriction does not apply to any information, or any document containing information, which explains any information or document which an auditor has, as tax accountant, assisted any client in preparing for, or delivering to, HMRC. Where the notice is given under **43.4**(c) above, the restriction also does not apply to information giving the identity or address of a person to whom the notice relates or of a person who has acted on behalf of such a person or to a document containing such information. Where the restriction is so disapplied, only that part (or parts) of a document which contains the relevant information has to be produced. The restriction is not disapplied if the information concerned, or a document containing the information, has already been provided or produced to an HMRC officer.

[*FA 2008, Sch 36 paras 24, 26, 27*].

Tax advisers

An information notice does not require a 'tax adviser' to provide information about, or to produce documents which are his property and which consist of, communications between him and a person in relation to whose tax affairs he has been appointed or between him and any other tax adviser of such a person, the purpose of which is the giving or obtaining of advice about any of those tax affairs. For this purpose, a '*tax adviser*' is a person appointed (directly or by another tax adviser) to give advice about the tax affairs of another person.

This restriction is disapplied in the same circumstances as the restriction applying to auditors is disapplied.

[*FA 2008, Sch 36 paras 25–27*].

Obtaining contact details for debtors

[43.7] HMRC are given power to issue a written notice requiring a third party which is a company or local authority etc. or otherwise has a business relationship with the debtor named in the notice to provide the address or other contact details for that debtor who owes money to HMRC. The third party has a right of appeal on the grounds that the requirement would be unduly onerous. The penalty for non-compliance is £300, but this amount may be changed by statutory instrument where there is a change in the value of money. [*FA 2009, s 97, Sch 49*].

Appeals against information notices

[43.8] A taxpayer can appeal to the tribunal against a taxpayer notice (see **43.4**(a) above) or any requirement in such a notice unless the notice was given with the approval of the tribunal. No appeal can be made against a requirement to provide information or to produce a document which forms part of his 'statutory records'.

Third party notices

A person given a third party notice (see **43.4**(b) above) can appeal to the tribunal against the notice or any requirement in it on the ground that compliance would be unduly onerous. No appeal can be made, however, where the notice was given with the approval of the tribunal or against a requirement to provide information or produce a document forming part of the taxpayer's statutory records.

Where a third party notice is given for the purpose of checking the tax position of a parent undertaking and any of its subsidiary undertakings, no appeal can be made against a requirement to provide information or produce a document forming part of the statutory records of the parent undertaking or any of its subsidiaries. No appeal can be made against a requirement, in a third party notice given to a parent undertaking for the purpose of checking the tax position of one or more subsidiary undertakings, to produce a document forming part of the statutory records of the parent undertaking or any of its subsidiary undertakings.

Where a third party notice is given for the purpose of checking the tax position of more than one of the partners in a business carried on in partnership, no appeal can be made against a requirement to provide information or produce a document forming part of the statutory records of any of the partners. No appeal can be made against a requirement, in a notice given to a partner for the purpose of checking the tax position of other partners, to produce a document forming part of the statutory records of the partner receiving the notice.

A person given a notice about persons whose identity is not known (see **43.4**(c) above) can appeal to the tribunal against the notice or any requirement in it on the ground that compliance would be unduly onerous. No appeal can be made against a requirement, in a notice given to a parent undertaking for the purpose of checking the tax position of one or more subsidiary undertakings, to produce a document forming part of the statutory records of the parent undertaking or any of its subsidiary undertakings. Likewise, no appeal can be made against a requirement, in a notice given to a partner in a business carried on in partnership for the purpose of checking the tax position of other partners, to produce a document forming part of the statutory records of the partner receiving the notice.

Definitions

For this purpose, '*statutory records*' are information and documents which a taxpayer is required to keep and preserve for tax purposes (see **66.18 RETURNS**) and VAT purposes. To the extent that information or documents do not relate to the carrying on of a business and are not required to be kept or preserved for VAT purposes, they only form part of a taxpayer's statutory documents to the extent that the tax year or accounting period to which they relate has ended. Information and documents cease to be statutory records when the period for which they are required to be preserved ends.

Time limit for appeal

Notice of appeal under the above provisions must be given in writing to the HMRC officer who gave the information notice within the period of 30 days beginning with the date on which the information notice was given. A decision on an appeal by the tribunal is final. Where the tribunal confirms the notice or a requirement in it, the person to whom the notice was given must comply with the notice or requirement within the period specified by the tribunal. If the tribunal does not specify such a period, compliance must be within such period as an HMRC officer reasonably specifies in writing.

Subject to the above, the appeal provisions of *TMA 1970, Pt 5* (see **6 APPEALS**) apply to an appeal against an information notice as they apply to an appeal against an income tax assessment.

[*FA 2008, Sch 36 paras 29–33, 35, 37, 62*].

Concealing, destroying or disposing of documents

[43.9] A person to whom an information notice is addressed must not conceal, destroy or otherwise dispose of, or arrange for the concealment, destruction or disposal of, a document that is the subject of the notice. This does not apply if he does so after the document has been produced to HMRC in accordance with the notice, unless an HMRC officer has notified him in writing that the document must continue to be available for inspection (and has not withdrawn the notification). It also does not apply if a copy of the document was produced in compliance with the notice and the destruction, etc. takes place after the end of the period of six months beginning with the day on which the copy was produced unless within that period an HMRC officer makes a request for the original document.

Similarly, where a person has been informed that a document is, or is likely to be, the subject of an information notice addressed to him, he must not conceal, destroy or otherwise dispose of, or arrange for the concealment, destruction or disposal of, the document. This does not apply if he acts more than six months after he was so informed (or was last so informed).

[*FA 2008, Sch 36 paras 42, 43*].

Failure to comply with the above provisions may be a criminal offence or result in penalties. See **43.11** below.

Inspection of business premises and other property

[43.10] With effect from 1 April 2009, an HMRC officer may enter a person's 'business premises' and inspect the premises and any 'business assets' and 'business documents' that are on the premises if the inspection is reasonably required for the purpose of checking that person's tax position. The officer may not enter or inspect any part of the premises used solely as a dwelling.

From 1 April 2010, HMRC also have the power to enter the business premises on two other occasions. Firstly, where the premises are those of an 'involved third party', defined for corporation tax as a person who is or has been a managing agent at Lloyd's in relation to a Lloyd's syndicate. Secondly, where HMRC need to inspect the premises for the purposes of valuation for the purposes of corporation tax on chargeable gains. In this case, the officer may be accompanied by a person needed to assist with the valuation (e.g. a valuer). In the latter case, the occupier or controller of the premises must agree the time of the inspection and be given written notice of the agreed time or the tribunal must approve the inspection and the occupier, etc. must be given seven days' notice. Evidence of authority must be produced if the occupier etc. requests it.

Agreed time for inspection

An inspection must normally be carried out at a time agreed to by the occupier of the premises. It can, however, be carried out at any reasonable time if:

(i) the occupier has been given at least seven days' notice (in writing or otherwise) of the time of the inspection; or
(ii) the inspection is carried out by, or with the agreement of, an authorised HMRC officer.

Where (ii) above applies, the officer carrying out the inspection must provide a notice in writing stating the possible consequences of obstructing the officer in the exercise of the power. If the occupier is present when the inspection begins, the notice must be given to him. If he is not present, the notice must be given to the person who appears to be the officer in charge of the premises, but if no such person is present, the notice must be left in a prominent place at the premises. The giving of such a notice does not require the approval of the tribunal, but such approval can be applied for by, or with the agreement of, an authorised HMRC officer. No notice of an application for approval of inspection need be given to the taxpayer and there is no appeal against the decision. A penalty for deliberate obstruction of an officer in the course of an inspection can only be charged where such approval has been obtained (see **43.11** below).

An officer may not inspect a business document if or to the extent that an information notice (see **43.4** above) given at the time of the inspection to the occupier of the premises could not require him to produce the document (see **43.6** above).

Marking assets, copying documents etc.

The officer may mark business assets and anything containing business assets to indicate that they have been inspected. He may obtain and record information (electronically or otherwise) relating to the premises, assets and documents inspected. He may take copies of, or make extracts from, a document (or copy) which he inspects, and if it appears necessary to him, he may remove the document at a reasonable time and retain it for a reasonable period. He must, without charge, provide a receipt for a document which is removed where this is requested and must also provide, again without charge, a copy of the document, if the person producing it reasonably requires it for any purpose. Where a document which has been removed is lost or damaged, HMRC are liable to compensate the owner for expenses reasonably incurred in replacing or repairing it.

Definitions

For the above purposes, '*business premises*' are premises (including any land, building or structure or means of transport), or a part of premises, that an HMRC officer has reason to believe are used in connection with the carrying on of a business by or on behalf of the taxpayer concerned.

'*Business assets*' are assets, other than documents, that an HMRC officer has reason to believe are owned, leased or used in connection with the carrying on of any business. They do not include documents, other than documents that are trading stock or plant.

'*Business documents*' are documents, or copies of documents, relating to the carrying on of any business that form part of any person's statutory records.

[*FA 2008, Sch 36 paras 10–17, 32, 62; FA 2009, Sch 47, paras 5–8, Sch 48 paras 3–5*].

Offences and penalties under *FA 2008, Sch 36*

[43.11] For penalties for failure to comply with an information notice within **43.4** above or deliberately obstructing an HMRC officer in the course of an inspection of business premises under the power at **43.10** above that has been approved by the tribunal, see **60.4 PENALTIES**.

It is an offence for a person required to produce a document by an information notice within **43.4** above which has been approved by the tribunal to conceal, destroy or otherwise dispose of the document or to arrange for its concealment, destruction or disposal. This does not apply if he does so after the document has been produced to HMRC in accordance with the notice, unless an HMRC officer has notified him in writing that the document must continue to be available for inspection (and has not withdrawn the notification). It also does not apply if a copy of the document was produced in compliance with the notice and the destruction, etc. takes place after the end of the period of six months beginning with the day on which the copy was produced unless within that period an HMRC officer makes a request for the original document.

It is also an offence for a person to conceal, destroy or otherwise dispose of, or to arrange for the concealment, destruction or disposal of, a document after an HMRC officer has informed him in writing that the document is, or is likely to be, the subject of an information notice approval for which is to be obtained from the tribunal. This does not apply if the person so acts more than six months after he was so informed (or was last so informed).

On summary conviction of either of the above offences the offender is liable to a fine not exceeding the statutory maximum. On conviction on indictment the punishment is imprisonment for a maximum of two years and/or a fine.

[*FA 2008, Sch 36 paras 53–55*].

Updated information powers from 1 April 2012

[43.12] The Finance Act 2011 contains new legislation at *Sch 23* aimed at modernising further HMRC's information powers by updating the existing legislation with regard to: bulk information powers used by HMRC to gather information about groups of taxpayers (for use in risk analysis); and specialist 'unnamed taxpayer' powers, which are narrowly defined, to be used in very specific circumstances during a compliance check. The legislation is to come into force as from 1 April 2012.

The legislation also contains provisions that:

- allow HMRC to apply to the tribunal for increased daily penalties where data is not supplied;

- cover data about certain foreign taxes;
- update *FA 2008, Sch 36* to mirror these two provisions;
- and amend *FA 2008, Sch 36* to provide a penalty if a person is aware of an inaccuracy when providing information or documents.

As noted above, the legislation brings together into one place a single set of rules with regard to the form of a Notice, how it may be complied with, penalties for failure to so comply, details as to a requested format of any data, and a right of appeal.

Data gathering from third parties

The new schedule provides information powers for collecting data from certain third parties for use by HM Revenue & Customs (HMRC) in its compliance activities. The provisions which can currently be found within various of the Taxes Acts, arebrought together into this one set of rules. The provisions relate specifically to information gathering from classes of persons identified as 'data-holders'.

This brings together powers from various statutes into one place. With regard to *FA 2008, Sch 36*, the provisions of *s 34A* which deal with information gathering from 'involved parties' are replaced by these new rules.

FA 2011, Sch 23 is split into seven parts.

Part 1: Power to obtain data

An officer of HMRC may issue a 'data-holder notice' to a relevant data-holder requiring the provision of relevant data. The categories of data-holder are specified in Part 2, outlined below. The data that may be required is to be specified in Treasury regulations.

The power may be used for:

- collecting data for the purposes of risk assessment; and
- for obtaining third-party data in connection with specific tax checks.

It cannot be used for the purpose of checking the tax position of the data-holder themselves (*FA 2008, Sch 36* should be used in this regard), except where the notice is aimed at finding the beneficial owner of securities, which exception applies where it is not known whether or not the recipient of the notice is the taxpayer. The schedule covers a wide range of taxes, as defined in *Part 5*, including income tax, corporation tax, capital gains tax, VAT, IPT, inheritance tax, stamp tax, SDLT and also 'relevant foreign tax'.

The notice must specify the data required and only data that an officer has reason to believe may be relevant to a chargeable or other period ending within the last four years may be specified. In addition the notice can only require documents to be provided if they are in the data-holder's possession and power.

HMRC may specify in the notice (or in a document referred to in the notice) the means and form in which the data must be provided and the address to which the data must be sent. If the notice requires the data to be provided by making documents available for inspection then the documents must be made available as is reasonably specified therein, or as agreed between HMRC and the data holder. The venue where documents are to be made available may not include a place used solely as a dwelling.

HMRC may ask the tribunal for approval to issue a data-holder notice, although it is not obliged to. The tribunal needs to be satisfied that in the circumstances the officer is justified in giving the notice, and the data holder has been told that the information is required and has been given an opportunity to make representations to HMRC. However, HMRC may also request the tribunal to formally approve the issue of a data-holder notice in an 'ex-parte' hearing, where it is considered that giving the data-holder an opportunity to make representations before the issue of the notice might prejudice any purpose for which the data is required. Where the notice has been approved by the tribunal the data-holder may not appeal against the notice itself.

HMRC may make copies of or make extracts from any document pursuant to the notice. In addition HMRC may retain any document provided for a reasonable period and if requested must give the data-holder a copy. The retention of a document is not regarded as breaking any lien claimed on the document and HMRC must compensate the owner if a document is lost or damaged.

[*FA 2011, Sch 23 paras 1–7*].

Part 2: Relevant data-holders

The previous legislation referred to various third parties from whom data may be requested. Such persons are now called data-holders. *Part 2* sets out broad categories of data-holders to whom these rules apply, including persons identified as 'involved' third parties under *FA 2008, Sch 36*. Each paragraph or group of paragraphs sets out a particular category of data-holder. The provisions are taken from the earlier legislation, which this schedule is to replace. It is considered there are no significant changes from the existing information powers.

Per *para 9*, with regard to salaries, fees, commission etc, each of the following is a relevant data-holder:

(a) an employer;
(b) a person who is concerned in making payments to or in respect of another person's employees with respect to their employment with that other person;
(c) an approved agent within the meaning of *ITEPA 2003, s 714* (which relates to payroll giving); and
(d) a person who carries on a business in connection with which relevant payments are or are likely to be made.

'*Relevant payments*' are: payments for or in connection with services provided by persons who are **not** employed in the business, or periodical or lump sum payments in respect of any copyright, public lending right, right in a registered design or design right.

Payments are taken to be made in connection with a business if they are made in the course of carrying on the business or a part of it, or in connection with the formation, acquisition, development or disposal of the business or a part of it. A reference to the making of payments includes the provision of benefits, and the giving of any other valuable consideration.

Where services that an individual provides, or is obliged to provide, under an agency contract are treated as the duties of an employment with the agency (per *ITEPA, s 44*), or, remuneration receivable under arrangements per *ITEPA, s 45* is treated as earnings from an agency, then the individual is treated as being employed by the agency, and payments made to the individual do not count as relevant payments which could be the subject of a notice.

Where a non-UK resident person (A), employed by a person resident outside the UK, performs duties of employment within the UK for a UK resident person (B) carrying on a trade, profession or vocation, then the UK resident person B is treated as person A's employer and may be required to provide the name and place of residence of A.

This replicates the provisions with regard to certain overseas employments at *TMA 1970, s 15A*.

Under *para 12*, with regard to interest payments, a person by or through whom interest is paid or credited is a relevant data-holder. '*Interest*' is defined as: a dividend in respect of a share in a building society; an amount to which a person holding a deeply discounted security is entitled on the redemption of that security; a foreign dividend; and an alternative finance return.

With regard to income, assets etc. belonging to others, a person who (in whatever capacity) is in receipt of money or value of or belonging to another is a relevant data-holder.

With regard to payments derived from securities the following persons are relevant data-holders:

(a) a person who is the registered or inscribed holder of securities;
(b) a person who receives a payment derived from securities or would be entitled to do so if a payment were made;
(c) a person who receives a payment treated by the company as a purchase of own shares (by an unquoted trading company); and
(d) a person who receives a chargeable payment under the company distributions: demergers provisions.

For these relevant data-holders, data may only be specified where it concerns the following matters:

- whether the relevant data-holder is the beneficial owner (or sole beneficial owner) of the securities or payment in question;
- if not, details of the beneficial owner (or other beneficial owners);
- and, if those details are not known or if different, details of the person for whom the securities are held or to whom the payment is or may be paid on;
- and if there is more than one beneficial owner or more than one person for whom the securities are held, their respective interests in the securities or payment.

'Payment derived from securities' includes in particular: an amount (whether of income or capital) that is payable out of or in respect of securities or rights attaching to securities, and a payment that is representative of any such amount.

In addition, a person who makes a payment derived from securities that has been received from or is paid on behalf of another is also a relevant data-holder.

With regard to grants and subsidies out of public funds, a person by whom a payment out of public funds is made by way of grant or subsidy is a relevant data-holder. A person by whom licences or approvals are issued or a register is maintained is also a relevant data-holder.

In addition, a relevant data-holder may be a lessee or occupier of land; a person having the use of land; and a person who, as agent, manages land or is in receipt of rent or other payments arising from land.

Relevant data-holder for these provisions also includes persons involved with dealing (etc.) in securities; dealing in other property; a managing agent at Lloyds; investment plan managers (see *ITTOIA 2005, s 696*); child trust fund account providers; persons involved with an insurance business; holders of Petroleum Act licences; persons involved with certain environmental activities such as landfill disposal; settlors/beneficiaries of a trust and the trustees; and charities.
[*FA 2011, Sch 23 paras 8–27*].

Part 3: Appeals against data-holder notices

Provisions regarding appeals against notices have been introduced. A person receiving a notice may appeal on the basis that it is: unduly onerous to comply with; the data-holder is not the relevant data-holder; or the data specified in the notice is not the relevant data. There are two exceptions: firstly with regard to data that forms part of the data-holder's statutory records (in such a case there is no defence of compliance being unduly onerous); and secondly where the tribunal has approved the giving of the notice. The term 'statutory records' is defined in *Part 5* and is data the data-holder is under a duty to keep and preserve for tax purposes.

Notice of appeal must be given to the HMRC officer who issued the data notice, in writing, within 30 days of receiving the notice, stating the grounds. On an appeal referred to the tribunal, the tribunal is given wide powers to confirm, vary a requirement in a notice (including the deadline for compliance), or set aside the notice. A decision by the tribunal is final. The general rules in *TMA 1970, Pt 5* relating to appeals apply to appeals against data-holder notices.

[*FA 2011, Sch 23 paras 28–29*].

Part 4: Penalties

There is an initial fixed penalty of £300 for failing to comply with a notice. 'Failing to comply' includes concealing, destroying or otherwise disposing of a document that is required by notice, or that the data-holder has been told (within the prior six months) will be required. The provisions are similar to those applying to information notices under *FA 2008, Sch 36*.

A daily penalty of up to £60 may also apply for a failure that continues after the award of an initial penalty. An alternative increased daily penalty of up to £1,000 may also be imposed by the tribunal, on application by HMRC, where the notice has still not been complied with, within 30 days of the daily penalty being notified. HMRC would apply for such an increased penalty where it is not expected that a daily penalty of up to £60 will encourage compliance. HMRC must notify the data-holder of the amount of the daily penalty imposed and the date from which it applies.

A penalty of up to £3,000 may also be imposed for deliberately or carelessly providing inaccurate information or documents. The penalty applies if the data-holder submits information or a document knowing about an inaccuracy attributable to another person and fails to tell HMRC at the time. It also applies in cases where an inaccuracy comes to light later and the data-holder does not then take reasonable steps to tell HMRC.

No late-filing penalty arises if HMRC or the tribunal is satisfied that there is a reasonable excuse for the failure. Reasonable excuse is defined in the same terms as at *FA 2008, Sch 36 para 45*, it does not include: an insufficiency of funds or where reliance has been placed on another person (except where the data-holder took reasonable care to avoid the failure).

HMRC may assess a penalty for failure to comply within 12 months of the latest of the following: the date on which the data-holder became liable to the penalty; the end of the period in which notice of appeal could have been given; and if notice of appeal has been given, the date on which the appeal the appeal is determined or withdrawn. HMRC may asses a penalty for providing inaccurate information within the period of 12 months beginning with the date on which the inaccuracy first came to the attention of HMRC and within 6 years of the date on which the data-holder became liable to the penalty.

A data-holder may appeal, in writing, against a decision of HMRC to impose a penalty within 30 days from the date the notification of penalty was given, stating the grounds for appeal.

Any penalty imposed under these provisions is payable within 30 days of the date that it is notified or if appealed, the date on which the appeal is determined or withdrawn. No penalty may be charged for anything in respect of which the data-holder has been convicted of an offence. Penalties are treated like income tax for enforcement purposes.

The Treasury may make regulations to change the fixed and maximum penalty levels in this Schedule if there is a change in the value of money.

[*FA 2011, paras 30–42*].

The above provisions come into force for Financial Year 2012 and are under effective in relation to notices issued after 1 April 2012. *Parts 5, 6* and *7* of the proposed schedule contain miscellaneous provisions, definitions, and consequential amendments and repeals in respect of the schedule. The sections of the *TMA 1970* which included details as to third parties from whom information might be sought are repealed, as the definitions of data-holder within *Sch 23* replace them. Where provisions had already been rewritten to *CTA 2010* or

TIOPA 2010, the rewritten and original provisions are repealed. The sections of *FA 2008, Sch 36* which relate to the information gathering powers in respect of 'involved third parties' are repealed. The 'data-holder' regime above replaces these information powers.

FA 2011, Sch 24 — changes to FA 2008, Sch 36

FA 2011, Sch 24, amends *FA 2008, Sch 36* as follows.

FA 2008, Sch 36 para 5 is amended such that all of the information powers in *Sch 36* may now be used to obtain information in relation to relevant foreign tax of a territory outside the UK. These amendments come into force on 1 April 2012.

Schedule 36, para 40A is amended to introduce a new category for which a penalty may be charged: where a person knowingly provides information containing an inaccuracy but does not notify HMRC at the time. This relates to inaccuracy of information, or documents produced, after 1 April 2012.

New *paras 49A–49C* are inserted into *FA 2008, Sch 36* which allow for a daily penalty to be charged up to £1,000 per day. This applies where there is a continuing failure to comply with a notice under *para 5* of *Sch 36*. The increased penalty must be approved by the tribunal and the person involved must be given prior warning and may attend the hearing. This applies to failure to comply with a notice on or after 1 April 2012.

Schedule 36 para 50 is also amended to clarify the relevant date for the purpose of charging a tax-related penalty under *para 39*.

[*FA 2011, Sch 24*].

The Mutual Assistance for Recovery Directive

[43.13] *Finance Act 2011, s 87* and *Sch 25* implement the new mutual assistance recovery Directive (MARD) which was agreed by the EU in 2010, which replaces the older 2008 Directive. Under this Directive EU Member States can provide each other with assistance in the recovery of tax debts and duties, including the service of documents and exchanging information.

Clause 87 allows for regulations to be made to implement the Directive and to give effect to any amendments or extensions of the Directive, or any EU instrument that may replace it.

The details of implementation of the latest Directive are found in *Sch 25*. The Directive itself sets out the rules that should be applied, leaving the detail of how to transpose these into domestic law up to the Member States.

Certain matters are excluded from these provisions: outbound requests for assistance with a devolved tax, defined as agricultural levies in Scotland, or any tax or duty for which the competence to legislate rests with the devolved governments of Scotland and Northern Ireland; and inbound requests for assistance with agricultural levies in Scotland.

Pursuant to the provisions of *Sch 25* a public authority or anyone acting on their behalf, is permitted to disclose information to other EU Member States for the purpose of the MARD. In certain circumstances the information may be further shared in pursuance of a court order, with regard to civil or criminal proceedings, with the consent of the person to whom it relates, or with the consent of the Commissioners. Wrongful disclosure on the part of the public authority, or on the part of its employees, agents, service providers, or those authorised to receive information on its behalf, is an offence. A person found guilty may be subject to a fine, a term of imprisonment or both. However, a defence is afforded such persons if they believed that the wrongful disclosure was lawful.

With regard to the enforcement of foreign claims in the UK, any legal provisions relating to the similar UK claim will apply, including those relating to penalties and interest, with any necessary adaptations. Where possible the UK should match foreign claims to the UK tax equivalent and recover the foreign claim in the same way they would a UK debt. Where there is no equivalent then the UK income tax provisions will apply.

The Treasury is provided with regulation making powers to set out any differences in treatment for foreign claims from the UK equivalent, and to deal with any appropriate procedural or other supplementary matters.

Where a taxpayer shows that the claim has been, or will, disputed in the Member State where the debt arose, then the enforcement action in the UK should be suspended. The debtor should begin or progress the dispute proceedings reasonably quickly, otherwise the suspension is lifted. However, if the enforcement action would be continued in the UK for a disputed equivalent, then such action may continue. The enforcement action should not be taken or continued where a final decision on the foreign claim has been given in the taxpayer's favour.

Previous provisions in relation to the 2008 Directive are repealed as from 1 January 2012, and outstanding requests under the current version of the Directive will be treated as being made under the new MARD provisions when they come into force.

[*FA 2011, s 87 Sch 25*].

Calling for documents before 1 April 2009

[43.14] The following provisions are to be repealed with effect from 1 April 2009 (see **43.3–43.10** above) and replaced by the provisions in *FA 2008*, *Sch 36* (see above).

For the purposes of the provisions, a '*document*' is anything in which information of any description is recorded, but does not include personal records or journalistic material (within *Police and Criminal Evidence Act 1984, ss 12, 13*) (and those exclusions apply also to particulars contained in such records or material). The documents concerned are those in the possession or power of the person receiving the notice. Photographic, etc. facsimiles may be supplied provided the originals are produced if called for, and documents relating to any pending tax appeal need not be delivered. In practice, the latter also applies to documents relating to a pending referral of questions during an enquiry (Hansard Standing Committee A, 8 May 2001, Cols 172–174). There are special provisions relating to computer records (see **43.18** below). Documents in a person's 'possession or power' are those actually in existence at the time the notice is given, and not any which would have to be brought into existence in order to satisfy the notice.

Note that, before 18 April 2005, the functions of the Commissioners for HMRC referred to below were vested in the Board of Inland Revenue. Functions to be carried out by an HMRC officer were to be carried out by an inspector (or, in certain cases, an officer of the Board).

(a) Where an HMRC officer is of the reasonable opinion that documents contain, or may contain, information relevant to the tax liability of a person, he may (with the authority of the Commissioners for HMRC and the consent of a tribunal) by notice in writing require that person to deliver such documents to him (but only after that person has been given reasonable opportunity to produce them).
The officer must give a written summary of his reasons for applying for consent to the giving of the notice. He is not required to identify any informant in the summary and no summary need be provided if the tribunal giving consent so directs, and the tribunal concerned must not so direct unless it is satisfied that the officer has reasonable grounds for believing that disclosure of the information in question would prejudice the assessment or collection of tax. The tribunal concerned must not take part in or be present at any subsequent proceedings concerning an appeal made by the person if the tribunal concerned has reason to believe that any of the documents which were the subject of the notice is likely to be adduced in evidence in those proceedings.
For an unsuccessful challenge to the validity of a notice, see *Kempton v Special Commrs & CIR* (1992) 66 TC 249. In *R v CIR (ex p. Banque International à Luxembourg SA)* (2000) 72 TC 597, an application for judicial review based *inter alia* on the protections afforded by the European Convention on Human Rights was refused. In *R (oao Morgan Grenfell & Co Ltd) v Special Commr* [2002] STC 786, the HL quashed a notice on the grounds that the Revenue were not entitled to require delivery of documents subject to legal professional privilege, a fundamental human right not expressly overridden by *TMA 1970, s 20(1)*.

(b) An HMRC officer may similarly by notice in writing require a person to furnish him with such particulars as he may reasonably require as being relevant to any tax liability of that person.
The notice is subject to the same authority and giving of consent requirements as at (a) above, and the requirements there relating to the giving of a written summary and the obligation imposed on the tribunal giving consent apply similarly in relation to particulars as they do there to documents.

(c) An HMRC officer may similarly by notice in writing require any other person (including the Director of Savings) to deliver to him (or, if the person so elects, make available for inspection by a named officer) documents relevant to any tax liability of a 'taxpayer'. A copy of the notice must be given to the taxpayer concerned unless, in a case involving suspected fraud, a tribunal so directs. Production of documents originating more than six years before the notice cannot be required (unless the tribunal which gave consent to the notice specifically allows it on being satisfied that there is reasonable ground for believing loss of tax through fraud).
'*Taxpayer*' includes a company which has ceased to exist.
The notice is subject to the same authority and giving of consent requirements as at (a) above, and the requirements there relating to the giving of a written summary and the obligation imposed on the tribunal giving consent apply similarly, except that the summary must be given to, and the obligation imposed relates to an appeal brought by, the taxpayer rather than the person to whom the notice is given, and no summary need be given if the taxpayer is not, as above, given a copy of the notice.
A notice cannot require the production by a statutory auditor of his audit papers, nor by a tax adviser of communications with a client (or with any other tax adviser of his client) relating to advice about the client's tax affairs. This exemption does not, however, apply to explanatory documents concerning any other documents prepared with the client for, or for delivery to, HMRC, unless HMRC already has access to the information contained therein in some other document. Where the exemption is so disapplied, either the document must be delivered or made available to HMRC or a copy of the relevant parts must be supplied (which parts must be available if required for inspection).
HMRC's application of these provisions relating to papers of a statutory auditor or client communications of a tax adviser is set out in HMRC Statement of Practice 5/90. In particular, it is made clear that accountants' working papers will be called for only where voluntary access has not been obtained and it is considered absolutely necessary in order to determine whether a client's accounts or returns are complete and correct. Requests for access may on occasion extend to the whole or a particular part of the working papers, rather than just to information explaining specific entries, and HMRC will usually be prepared to visit the accountants' or clients' premises to examine the papers and to take copies or extracts.
For an unsuccessful challenge to the validity of a notice, see *R v CIR (ex p TC Coombs & Co.)* (1991) 64 TC 124, HL.

(d) An HMRC officer may similarly, on an application authorised by the Commissioners for HMRC, give a notice in writing as under (c) above without naming the taxpayer concerned. Consent to the application must be obtained from a Special Commissioner, who must be satisfied that: it relates to a taxpayer or class of taxpayers whose identity(ies) is (are) not known; there are reasonable grounds to believe the taxpayer(s) to have failed to comply with the *Taxes Acts*, with the likelihood of serious prejudice to the assessment or collection of tax; and the information is not reasonably available from elsewhere. The recipient can object (with a right of appeal to the tribunal), by notice in writing, within 30 days on the ground that it would be onerous for him to comply.

The requirements at (a) above relating to the giving of a written summary and the obligation imposed on the tribunal giving consent do not apply. The exemption, and disapplication of the exemption, from the requirements of a notice under (d) above relating to the production of the papers of a statutory auditor or client communications of a tax adviser apply similarly, except that the exemption does not apply to any document giving the identity or address of any taxpayer to whom the notice relates or of any person who has acted on behalf of any such person, unless HMRC already has access to the information contained therein in some other document.

The power of the Commissioners for HMRC to authorise an application may be delegated to one of their officers, and the authorisation may be given orally (*R v Special Commr (ex p CIR); R v CIR (ex p Ulster Bank Ltd)* (2000) 73 TC 209).

(e) The Commissioners for HMRC may require, by notice in writing, a person to deliver or furnish to a named officer of theirs documents or information as specified in (a) and (b) above relevant to the tax liability of that person.

The requirements at (a) above relating to the giving of consent and a written summary do not apply. However, notices cannot be given on or after 26 July 1990 under this power unless there are reasonable grounds for believing that that person may have failed, or may fail, to comply with any provision of the *Taxes Acts*, and that any such failure is likely to have led, or to lead, to serious prejudice to the proper assessment or collection of tax.

For procedural matters in relation to such a notice, see *R v CIR (ex p Taylor) (No 1)* (1988) 62 TC 562, CA; *(No 2)* (1990) 62 TC 578, CA.

The notice must specify or describe the documents or particulars required, the time limit for production (generally not less than 30 days) and, except as above, the name of the taxpayer or client, as appropriate; and the person to whom they are delivered may take copies.

The penalty for failure to comply with a notice is given by *TMA 1970, s 98*. In addition there are severe penalties (in summary proceedings, a fine of the statutory maximum, and on indictment, imprisonment for two years and/or an unlimited fine) for the falsification, concealment, destruction or disposal of a document which is the subject of a notice, unless strict conditions and time limits are observed.

[*TMA 1970, ss 20, 20B(1)(1A)(1B)(2)(4)–(7)(9)–(14), 20BB, 20D; CRCA 2005, ss 5, 7; FA 2008, s 113, Sch 36 paras 67–70*].

The person to whom notice is to be given is not entitled to attend or be legally represented at the meeting at which HMRC seek the consent of a tribunal (*Applicant v Inspector of Taxes* [1999] STC (SCD) 128).

Notices other than those under (d) above may relate to tax liabilities in EU member states other than the UK [*FA 1990, s 125(1)(2)(6); FA 2008, Sch 36 para 83*], or in any other territory with which the UK has entered into a tax enforcement agreement or other arrangements providing for the obtaining of information. [*FA 2006, s 174, Sch 26 Pt 8(2); FA 2008, Sch 36 para 91*].

For an article setting out HMRC's view on the question of claims to legal or professional privilege in relation to requests for information under these provisions (other than where tax evasion or tax fraud is suspected), see Revenue Tax Bulletin April 2000 pp 743–746 (updated by Revenue Tax Bulletin December 2002 p 993 following the *Morgan Grenfell* case at (a) above) (and see **43.15** below).

Barristers, advocates or solicitors

[43.15] A notice under **43.14**(a), (b) or (c) above to a barrister, advocate or solicitor can be issued only by the Commissioners for HMRC (or, before 18 April 2005, the Board of Inland Revenue), although they may nevertheless delegate their powers (see *R v CIR (ex p. Davis Frankel & Mead)* (2000) 73 TC 185). The requirements at **43.14**(a) above relating to the giving of consent and a written summary do not apply. The barrister etc. cannot (without his client's consent) be required to deliver under **43.14**(c) or (d) documents protected by professional privilege but, subject to that, the exemption, and disapplication of the exemption, from the requirements of a notice under, as the case may be, **43.14**(c) or (d) relating to the production of the papers of a statutory auditor or client communications of a tax adviser apply similarly. [*TMA 1970, s 20B(3)(8); FA 2008, Sch 36 para 68(6)(9)*].

See *R v CIR (ex p Goldberg)* (1988) 61 TC 403 and cf *Dubai Bank Ltd v Galadari* [1989] 3 WLR 1044, CA (a non-tax case).

In *R (oao Prudential Plc) v Special Commissioner of Income Tax* [2010] STC 161, the taxpayer company tried to extend the principle of legal or professional privilege to accountants giving legal advice on tax matters so as to avoid complying with notices for information. The company was unsuccessful. On 13 October 2010 the Court of Appeal confirmed this decision ([2010] STC 2802). The court considered that legal professional privilege was a fundamental condition for the administration of justice and not a mere rule of evidence. Any change in this regard would need to be made by statute and not by the courts.

In an attempt to avoid delays due to legal or professional privilege claims, *SI 2009 No 1916* has been introduced setting down a procedure to be followed where there is a dispute over whether information is entitled to legal or professional privilege or not. Two articles on this subject may be found in Tax Journal 10 August 2009 p 6 and 21 September 2009 p 13.

For an article setting out HMRC's view on the question of claims to legal or professional privilege in relation to requests for information under these provisions (other than where tax evasion or tax fraud is suspected), see Revenue Tax Bulletin April 2000 pp 743–746 (updated by Revenue Tax Bulletin December 2002 p 993 following the *Morgan Grenfell* case at **43.14**(a) above).

Power to call for papers of tax accountant

[43.16] An HMRC officer may (with the authority of the tribunal and the consent of a Circuit judge in England and Wales, a sheriff in Scotland or a county court judge in Northern Ireland) by notice in writing require a '*tax accountant*' (i.e. a person who assists another in the preparation of returns, etc. for tax purposes) who has been convicted by or before any UK court of a tax offence or incurred a penalty under *TMA 1970, s 99* (see **66.7 PENALTIES**) to deliver 'documents' in his possession or power relevant to any tax liability of any of his clients. The tax accountant must be given an opportunity to deliver the documents in question before a notice is issued.

The notice must be issued within twelve months of the final determination of the conviction or penalty award and must specify or describe the documents required and the time limit for production (generally not less than 30 days).

A '*document*' is anything in which information of any description is recorded, but does not include personal records or journalistic material (within *Police and Criminal Evidence Act 1984, ss 12, 13*). Photographic etc. facsimiles may be supplied provided the originals are produced if called for, and documents relating to any pending tax appeal need not be delivered.

A notice to a barrister, advocate or solicitor can be issued only by the Commissioners for HMRC, although they may nevertheless delegate their powers (see *R v CIR (ex p Davis Frankel & Mead)* (2000) 73 TC 185). The barrister etc. cannot (without his client's consent) be required to deliver documents protected by professional privilege [*TMA 1970, s 20B(3)(8)*].

The penalty for failure to comply with a notice is given by *TMA 1970, s 98*. In addition there are severe penalties (in summary proceedings, a fine of the statutory maximum, and on indictment, imprisonment for two years and/or an unlimited fine) for the falsification, concealment, destruction or disposal of a document which is the subject of a notice, unless strict conditions and time limits are observed.

See also the comments above at **43.15** with regard to the *Prudential* case and the question of tax accountants and legal professional privilege.

[*TMA 1970, ss 20A, 20B(1)(2)–(4)(8), 20BB, 20D as amended by FA 2008, Sch 36 paras 68–70; SI 2009 No 56*].

The references above to the Commissioners for HMRC and HMRC officers were, before 18 April 2005, references to the Board of Inland Revenue and inspectors.

Police and Criminal Evidence Act 1984 powers

[43.17] With effect from 1 December 2007, HMRC are able to exercise certain powers under the *Police and Criminal Evidence Act 1984* when conducting direct tax criminal investigations. Previously, such powers were available to HMRC only in relation to matters that were handled by HM Customs and Excise before the merger with the Inland Revenue in 2005. The powers involved include those concerning search warrants and arrest. Only HMRC officers authorised by the Commissioners for HMRC are able to exercise the powers. Similar powers are available to HMRC in Scotland and Northern Ireland.

As a result of the availability of the above police powers, the search and seizure powers are no longer needed and are repealed with effect from 1 December 2007. The power to seek judicial authority to require the delivery of documents at **43.19** below is restricted to circumstances where the equivalent police power cannot be used because the material concerned is outside its scope.

[*Police and Criminal Evidence Act 1984, s 114; FA 2007, ss 82–87, Schs 22, 23; SI 2007 Nos 3166, 3175*].

See HMRC Technical Note 'Criminal investigation powers and safeguards', 30 November 2007.

Computer records etc.

[43.18] The following applies to any tax provisions requiring a person to produce a document or cause a document to be produced, furnished or delivered, or requiring a person to permit HMRC to inspect a document, to make copies of or extracts from, or remove, a document (i.e. including the provisions at **43.4**, **43.11**, **43.14**, **43.16** and **43.19**).

For the purposes of such provisions, a reference to a document is a reference to anything in which information of any description is recorded, and a reference to a copy of a document is to anything onto which information recorded in the document has been copied, by whatever means and whether directly or indirectly.

Where a document has been, or may be, required to be produced, inspected etc. under any such provisions, a person authorised by the Commissioners for HMRC (previously the Board of Inland Revenue) can obtain access to any computer and associated apparatus or material used in connection with the document at any reasonable time in order to inspect it and check its operation. Reasonable assistance can be required from the person by whom or on whose behalf the computer has been so used or any person in charge of the computer etc. or otherwise concerned with its operation.

A penalty of £300 (£500 before 21 July 2008) applies for obstruction of such access or refusal to provide assistance.

[*FA 1988, s 127; FA 2008, s 114*].

HMRC's practice in cases of serious tax fraud

[43.19] From 18 April 2005 to 2010, criminal prosecutions for serious tax fraud in England and Wales were conducted by the Revenue and Customs Prosecutions Office ('RCPO'), independent of HMRC. The Office had its own investigatory powers under *Serious Organised Crime and Police Act 2005, ss 60–62*. In January 2010 the RCPO merged with the Crown Prosecution Service to become a specialist Revenue and Customs Division within the CPS. The RCD works with HMRC investigators in the same way that the CPS operates with the police.

Cases of serious fraud not expected to result in prosecution are worked in accordance with HMRC's Civil Investigation of Fraud procedure and under the terms in Code of Practice 9 (see further below).

For new cases opened from 1 September 2005, the policy of the Commissioners of HMRC in cases of suspected serious tax fraud, as set out in Code of Practice COP 9 (2005), is as follows.

(1) The Commissioners reserve complete discretion to pursue a criminal investigation with a view to prosecution where they consider it necessary and appropriate.
(2) Where a criminal investigation is not considered necessary or appropriate the Commissioners may decide to investigate using the civil investigation of fraud procedure.
(3) Where the Commissioners decide to investigate using the civil investigation of fraud procedure they will not seek a prosecution for the tax fraud which is the subject of that investigation. The taxpayer will be given an opportunity to make a full and complete disclosure of all irregularities in their tax affairs.
(4) However, where materially false statements are made or materially false documents are provided with intent to deceive, in the course of a civil investigation, the Commissioners may conduct a criminal investigation with a view to a prosecution of that conduct.

If the Commissioners decide to investigate using the civil investigation of fraud procedure the taxpayer will be given a copy of the above statement by an authorised officer.

Previously, the practice of the Board of Inland Revenue (and, after 18 April 2005, of HMRC) in cases of suspected serious tax fraud was set out in the so-called 'Hansard Statement' (last revised on 7 November 2002). This practice continues for investigations commenced before 1 September 2005. The practice was as follows.

(i) The Board reserve complete discretion to pursue prosecutions in the circumstances they consider appropriate.
(ii) Where serious tax fraud has been committed, they may accept a money settlement instead of pursuing a criminal prosecution.
(iii) They will accept a money settlement, and will not pursue a criminal prosecution, if the taxpayer, in response to being given a copy of the Hansard Statement by an authorised officer (meaning a current serving member of Inland Revenue Special Compliance Office), makes a full and complete confession of all tax irregularities.

(Revenue Internet Statement 8 November 2002; Revenue Tax Bulletin December 2002 pp 979–981).

This replaced the previous Hansard Statement of 18 October 1990, which did not include the undertaking in (iii) above. Instead, the Board retained full discretion as to the course they would pursue. In considering this, it was the Board's practice to be *influenced* by the taxpayer having made a full confession and given full co-operation during the investigation, but they gave no explicit assurance that they would not prosecute in such cases.

See also Revenue Code of Practice COP 9 referred to above and reissued to cover the new civil investigations of fraud procedure.

HMRC's policy is to use the civil investigation of fraud procedure wherever possible. Criminal investigation is reserved for cases where HMRC needs to send a strong deterrent message or where the conduct involved is such that only a criminal sanction is appropriate. Circumstances in which HMRC will usually consider commencing a criminal, rather than civil, investigation include:

- cases of organised or systematic fraud including conspiracy;
- where an individual holds a position of trust or responsibility;
- where materially false statements are made or materially false documents are provided in the course of a civil investigation;
- where deliberate concealment, deception, conspiracy or corruption is suspected;
- cases involving the use of false or forged documents;
- cases involving money laundering;
- where the perpetrator has committed previous offences or there is a repeated course of unlawful conduct or previous civil action;
- cases involving theft, or the misuse or unlawful destruction of HMRC documents;
- where there is evidence of assault on, threats to, or the impersonation of HMRC officials; and
- where there is a link to suspected wider criminality, whether domestic or international, involving offences not under the administration of HMRC.

When considering whether a case should be investigated under the civil investigation of fraud procedure or will be the subject of a criminal investigation, one factor considered by HMRC is whether the taxpayer has made a complete and unprompted disclosure of the offences committed.

(HMRC Internet Statement 20 December 2005, see www.hmrc.gov.uk/prosecutions/crim-inv-policy.htm).

See also **41.6 HMRC — ADMINISTRATION.**

Statements made or documents produced by or on behalf of a taxpayer are admissible as evidence in proceedings against him notwithstanding that reliance on the Board's practice above or on their policy for mitigating penalties (see **60.15 PENALTIES**) may have induced him to make or produce them. [*TMA 1970, s 105; FA 2003, s 206(1)(2)(5)*].

Simon's Taxes. See **A6.1007, A6.1008.**

Case law on fraudulent or negligent conduct

[43.20] The following cases relate to old legislation for 'fraud, wilful default or neglect' assessments which has now been replaced by 'fraudulent or negligent conduct' assessments. The latter expression is not defined, and the cases may be of continued assistance in this respect. As noted in **7 ASSESSMENTS**, reference to 'fraudulent or negligent conduct' has now been replaced by reference to 'deliberate' or 'careless' action.

The onus of proving fraud or wilful default is on the Crown (see e.g. *Hurley v Taylor* (1998) 71 TC 268, CA), but the onus is on the taxpayer to prove the assessments are excessive (*Johnson v Scott* (1978) 52 TC 383, CA; *Jonas v Bamford* (1973) 51 TC 1; *Nicholson v Morris* (1977) 51 TC 95, CA, and cf *Barney v Pybus* (1957) 37 TC 106 and *R v Spec Commrs (ex p Martin)* (1971) 48 TC 1, CA). For the standard of proof required, see *Les Croupiers Casino Club v Pattinson* (1987) 60 TC 196, CA.

Unexplained capital increases or admitted omissions may be held evidence of fraud or wilful default (*Amis v Colls* (1960) 39 TC 148; *Woodrow v Whalley* (1964) 42 TC 249; *Hudson v Humbles* (1965) 42 TC 380; *Hillenbrand* (1966) 42 TC 617, Ct of Sess; *Young v Duthie* (1969) 45 TC 624; *James v Pope* (1972) 48 TC 142; and cf *Brimelow v Price* (1965) 49 TC 41). Wilful default may be by agent (*Clixby v Pountney* (1967) 44 TC 515; *Pleasants v Atkinson* (1987) 60 TC 228).

'*Neglect*' means negligence or a failure to give any notice, to make any return or to produce or furnish any document or other information required by or under the *Taxes Acts*. [*TMA 1970, s 118* as previously enacted]. Neglect may be by an agent (*Mankowitz v Income Tax Special Comrs and CIR* (1971) 46 TC 707, 50 ATC 75).

Publishing details of deliberate tax defaulters

[43.21] With effect from a date to be appointed by statutory instrument, HMRC are given the power to publish, in any manner they think appropriate, information about a company. The power may be exercised where, following an investigation, one or more 'relevant tax penalties' are due and the total lost revenue in respect of all penalties exceeds £25,000. (This amount may be varied by statutory instrument.) A '*relevant tax penalty*' is one which falls into one of the following categories:

- a penalty in respect of a deliberate inaccuracy in a taxpayer's document;
- a penalty in respect of an inaccuracy in a taxpayer's document due to the deliberate supply of false information or withholding of information; or
- a deliberate failure to notify chargeability.

The details which may be published, in manner at the discretion of HMRC, is intended to be such as to make the taxpayer company's identity clear, including the name of the taxpayer, registered address, and nature of any business.

Before publishing, the company must be informed of HMRC's intention and be given reasonable opportunity to make representations. Publication may only take place after a penalty becomes final. It may not occur more than one year after the day the penalty becomes final. Where the maximum reduction in penalty has been given for unprompted disclosure or the maximum reduction has been given for prompted disclosure (and in this case only, at HMRC discretion having regard to circumstances) publication may not take place. A penalty becomes final when the appeal period has expired, or, if there is a contract settlement, the date of the contract.

[*FA 2009, s 94*].

44

HMRC Statements of Practice

Introduction

[44.1] Statements of Practice (SOP) explain HM Revenue and Customs interpretation of legislation and the way HMRC applies the law in practice. They do not affect a taxpayer's right to argue for a different interpretation, if necessary in an appeal to an independent tribunal.

The following is a summary of those Statements of Practice published by HMRC as updated which are relevant to companies and, where applicable, referred to in this book. These can be found at www.hmrc.gov.uk-practitioners-sop.pdf.

Statements are divided into those originally published before 18 July 1978 (which are given a reference letter (according to the subject matter) and consecutive number, e.g. A34) and later Statements (which are numbered consecutively in each year, e.g. SP 6/94).

Certain Statements marked in SOP as obsolete continue to be referred to in the text (having been relevant within the last four years), and the original source is quoted in such cases, as it is where the Statement awaits inclusion in SOP.

As regards HMRC internal guidance manuals, see **41.10 HMRC — ADMINISTRATION.**

B1	**Treatment of VAT.** Guidance on the general principles applied in dealing with VAT in the computation of corporation tax liabilities. See **73 VALUE ADDED TAX.**
B6	**Goods sold subject to reservation of title.** Goods treated as purchases in the accounts of the buyer will be similarly treated for tax purposes. See **71.66 TRADING EXPENSES AND DEDUCTIONS.**
C1	**Lotteries and football pools.** Where part of the cost of a ticket is to be donated to a club, etc., that part is, in certain circumstances, not treated as a trading receipt. See **70.5 TRADE PROFITS — INCOME AND SPECIFIC TRADES, 75.6 VOLUNTARY ASSOCIATIONS.**
C6	**Group relief:** ***ICTA 1988, s 403C.*** Consortium relief — in determining the average percentage of a consortium member's interest in the consortium company HMRC's position is to take weighted average over the relevant time period. See **39.19 GROUPS.**

C10 **Valuation fees.** Costs related to *Companies Act 1985* compliance are regarded as allowable expenses. See **70.57 TRADE PROFITS — INCOME AND SPECIFIC TRADES.**

D21 **Capital gains tax — 6 April 1965 valuation time limit: company leaving group: *TCGA 1992, ss 178, 179*.** HMRC will exercise discretion to extend the time limit as appropriate. See **29.1 DEGROUPING CHARGES.**

SP 8/79 **Compensation for acquisition of property under compulsory powers.** Guidance as to the treatment of compensation for temporary loss of profits and expenses. See **24.2 COMPENSATION, DAMAGES, ETC.**

SP 4/80 **Industrial Buildings Allowance — industrial workshops constructed for separate letting to small businesses.** Claims for estates consisting of small industrial workshops can be made on a global rather than individual basis. It should be noted that IBAs have been phased out and will not apply after 1 April 2011 (for corporation tax purposes), 6 April 2011 (for income tax purposes). See further **15 CAPITAL ALLOWANCES — BUILDINGS.**

SP 13/80 **Demergers — *ICTA 1988, ss 213–218*.** Guidance on the application of the provisions and on clearance procedures. See **31.28** et seq. **GROUP RELIEF.**

SP 5/81 **Expenditure on farm drainage.** Certain expenditure to restore drainage is permitted as revenue expenditure. See **70.29 TRADE PROFITS — INCOME AND SPECIFIC TRADES.**

SP 8/81 **Replacement of business assets: groups of companies.** Conditions for relief explained where assets are disposed of or acquired by group companies after cessation or before commencement of trading. See **18.8.**

SP 11/81 **Additional redundancy payments — *ICTA 1988, s 90*.** The provisions for allowance as a deduction of such payments extended to partial discontinuances. Superseded by *CTA 2009, s 79*. See **71.23 TRADING EXPENSES AND DEDUCTIONS.**

SP 12/81 **Construction industry tax scheme — carpet fitting** is considered to be outside the scope of the scheme. See **26.3 CONSTRUCTION INDUSTRY SCHEME.**

SP 2/82 **Company purchasing own shares — *ICTA 1988, ss 219–229*.** The conditions for relief are clarified. See **63.4**(2), **63.8 PURCHASE BY A COMPANY OF ITS OWN SHARES.**

SP 1/84 **Trade unions — provident benefits: legal and administrative expenses.** See **35.15 EXEMPT ORGANISATIONS.**

SP 6/84 **Non-resident lessors — *ICTA 1988, s 830*.** The factors governing liability to tax on profits or gains of such lessors of mobile drilling rigs etc. are outlined. See **65.12 RESIDENCE.**

SP 2/86 **Offshore Funds.** Various aspects of the legislation are clarified. See **57.24–57.26 OFFSHORE FUNDS.**

SP 1/87 **Exchange rate fluctuations.** HMRC practice following the *Marine Midland* decision is explained. (Replaced by SP 2/02 below.)

SP 6/88 **Double taxation relief — capital gains tax.** The conditions under which relief is available are clarified. See **32.5 DOUBLE TAX RELIEF.**

SP 4/89 **Company purchase of own shares — CGT treatment.** This confirms capital gains treatment for a corporate shareholder where a company buys back shares. See also *Strand Options and Futures Ltd v Vojak* [2003] EWCA Civ 1457, [2004] STC 64, 76 TC 220.

SP 6/89 **Delay in rendering tax returns — interest on overdue tax: *TMA 1970, s 88*.** The circumstances in which interest will be sought are clarified.

SP 1/90 **Company residence.** HMRC's interpretation of the application of the case law on company residence is explained. See **65.2, 65.3 RESIDENCE.**

SP 2/90 **Guidance notes for migrating companies — notice and arrangements for payment of tax.** See **65.9 RESIDENCE.**

SP 3/90 **Stocks and long-term contracts.** Revenue practice as regards bases of valuation and changes therein. Obsolete. See **71.14 TRADING EXPENSES AND DEDUCTIONS.**

SP 1/91 **Small companies' rate of corporation tax and corporation tax starting rate.** The claims procedure is explained. See **67.2 SMALL COMPANIES — REDUCED RATES.**

SP 3/91 **Finance lease rental payments.** See **71.43 TRADING EXPENSES AND DEDUCTIONS.**

SP 7/91 **Double taxation — business profits: unilateral relief.** Revenue practice as regards admission of foreign taxes for relief is revised. See **32.2 DOUBLE TAX RELIEF.**

SP 10/91 **Corporation tax — a major change in the nature or conduct of a trade.** HMRC's interpretation of that expression is explained. See **38.14 GAINS AND LOSS BUYING, 55.13 LOSSES.**

SP 12/91 **Income tax — 'in the ordinary course' of banking business.** HMRC's interpretation of this expression is explained. (Superseded by SP 4/96 below.) See **8.9 BANKS.**

SP 16/91 **Accountancy expenses arising out of accounts investigations.** Revenue practice on the allowance of such expenses. Superseded by Tax Bulletin 37, see also EM9010 See **71.54 TRADING EXPENSES AND DEDUCTIONS.**

SP 2/92 **Transactions within *ICTA 1988, s 765A*: movements of capital between residents of EC member states.** Guidance as to when the relevant provisions apply and on procedural matters. See **5.12 ANTI-AVOIDANCE.**

SP 4/92 **Capital gains re-basing elections.** Certain disposals are ignored in relation to the time limit for such elections. See **18.10 CAPITAL GAINS — GROUPS.**

SP 3/93 **Groups of companies — arrangements.** Guidance on HMRC's interpretation of 'arrangements' for the various purposes of the group legislation. See **39.4, 39.15, 39.19 GROUP RELIEF.**

SP 4/93 **Deceased persons' estates — discretionary interests in residue.** Payments out of income of the residue are treated as income of the recipient for the year of payment, whether out of income as it arises or out of income arising in earlier years. See **33.6 ESTATE INCOME.**

SP 5/93 **UK/Czechoslovakia double taxation Convention.** The Convention is regarded as applying to the Czech and Slovak Republics. See **32.17 DOUBLE TAX RELIEF.**

SP 6/93 **UK/Yugoslavia double taxation Convention.** The Convention is regarded as applying to Croatia, Slovenia, Macedonia and the former Republic of Yugoslavia. Now replaced and superseded by SP 3/04 which in turn is superseded by SP 3/07 (see below). See **32.17 DOUBLE TAX RELIEF.**

SP 12/93 **Double taxation — dividend income — tax credit relief** for dividends paid under a 'company tax deducted' arrangement may be restricted. See **32.11 DOUBLE TAX RELIEF.**

SP 15/93 **Business tax computations rounded to nearest £1,000** will be accepted in certain cases. See **66.32 RETURNS.**

SP 5/94 **Associated companies for small companies' relief and corporation tax starting rate — holding companies.** The circumstances in which a holding company is disregarded in calculating profits limits are explained. See **67.4 SMALL PROFITS — REDUCED RATES.**

SP 2/95 **Payment of tax credits to non-resident companies.** HMRC consider that a claim for repayment of tax credits under *ICTA 1988, s 242* may not be made by a non-resident company notwithstanding the existence of a non-discrimination clause in the relevant double tax treaty. Obsolete. See **32.3 DOUBLE TAX RELIEF.**

SP 8/95 **Venture capital trusts — default terms in loan agreements.** Certain event of default clauses will not disqualify a loan from being a security for the purposes of approval. See **74.2 VENTURE CAPITAL TRUSTS.**

SP 4/96 **Income tax — interest paid in the ordinary course of a bank's business.** HMRC's interpretation of this requirement is explained. See **8.9 BANKS.**

SP 1/97 **The electronic lodgement service.** HMRC's operation and detailed requirements of the scheme are explained. See **66.29 RETURNS.**

SP 3/97 **Investment trusts investing in authorised unit trusts or open-ended investment companies.** The conditions under which such investments may be made are clarified. See **52 INVESTMENT FUNDS** and **53.1 INVESTMENT TRUSTS.**

SP 4/97 **Taxation of commission, cashbacks and discounts.** HMRC's views are outlined. See **70.26 TRADE PROFITS — INCOME AND SPECIFIC TRADES.**

SP 3/99 **Advance pricing agreements (APAs).** The detailed administration of the scheme of APAs relating to transfer pricing issues is explained. This statement has been updated and is now superseded by SP2/10. See **72 TRANSFER PRICING.**

SP 1/00 **Corporate venturing scheme — applications for advance clearance under *FA 2000, Sch 15 Pt X*.** The requirements for such applications are set out. See **28.9 CORPORATE VENTURING SCHEME.**

SP 2/00 **Venture capital trusts, the enterprise investment scheme, the corporate venturing scheme and enterprise management incentives — value of 'gross assets'.** HMRC's general approach to the valuation of gross assets is explained. Replaced SP 5/98 and superseded by SP2/06. See **28.6 CORPORATE VENTURING SCHEME, 74.4**(e) **VENTURE CAPITAL TRUSTS.**

SP 3/00 **Enterprise investment scheme, venture capital trusts, corporate venturing scheme, enterprise management incentives and capital gains tax reinvestment relief — location of activity.** The requirement that trade(s) be carried on 'wholly or mainly in the UK' is clarified. Replaces SP 7/98. See **28.7 CORPORATE VENTURING SCHEME, 74.4**(2)(b) **VENTURE CAPITAL TRUSTS.**

SP 4/00 **Tonnage tax.** Detailed administrative practice for the entire tonnage tax regime is set out. See **70.76 TRADE PROFITS — INCOME AND SPECIFIC TRADES.**

SP 1/01 **Treatment of investment managers and their overseas clients.** Guidance is given on the application of the *FA 1995* rules. See **65.6 RESIDENCE.**

SP 3/01 **Relief for underlying tax.** The treatment of foreign dividends paid out of profits subject to variable rates of tax or where there are accumulated losses is clarified. (Revenue Press Release 27 November 2001; Annex D to Technical Note 'An Exemption for Substantial Shareholdings.) See **32.11 DOUBLE TAX RELIEF.**

SP 4/01 **Double taxation relief — status of the UK's double taxation conventions with the former USSR and with newly independent states.** The current position is clarified. See **32.17 DOUBLE TAX RELIEF.**

SP 5/01 **Loss relief, capital allowances and group relief.** The conditions for acceptance of late claims for relief are set out. See **55.3 LOSSES.**

SP 1/02 **Corporation tax self-assessment and chargeable gains valuations.** Certain enquiries remaining open solely because of an unagreed chargeable gains valuation will be limited to outstanding matters relating to the valuation. See **66.19 RETURNS.**

SP 2/02 **Exchange rate fluctuations.** Revenue practice is explained. (Replaces SP 1/87 above, but does not apply to companies within the charge to corporation tax.) (Revenue Internet Statement 30 September 2002.)

SP 3/02 **Tax treatment of transactions in financial futures and options.** Sets out HMRC views on the tax treatment of such transactions as defined in *TCGA 1992, s 143*.

SP 4/02 **Definition of financial trader for the purposes of *FA 2002, Sch 26 para 31*.** The guidelines used by HMRC in deciding whether a company should be approved as a financial trader are explained. (Replaces SP 3/95 above.) (Revenue Internet Statement 30 September 2002.) See **30.34 DERIVATIVE CONTRACTS LEGISLATION.**

SP 5/02 **Exemptions for companies' gains on substantial shareholdings: sole or main benefit test — *TCGA 1992, Sch 7AC para 5*.** Revenue guidance is given on the application of the anti-avoidance rule. (Revenue Internet Statement 29 October 2002.) See **19.7 CAPITAL GAINS — SUBSTANTIAL SHAREHOLDINGS.**

SP 3/04 **Double taxation relief — Status of the UK's double taxation conventions with the former Socialist Federal Republic of Yugoslavia.** This replaces and supersedes Statement of Practice 6/93. It confirms that the provisions of the UK/Yugoslavia Double Taxation Convention will be treated as remaining in force between the UK and respectively, Bosnia-Herzegovina, Croatia, Macedonia, Serbia and Montenegro and Slovenia. Superceded by 3/07 (see below). See **32.17 DOUBLE TAX RELIEF.**

SP 1/06 **Self-Assessment — Finality and Discovery.** This clarifies how much information a taxpayer needs to provide in the tax return to remove the possibility of a discovery assessment. See **7.3 ASSESSMENTS.**

SP 2/06 **Venture Capital Trusts, Corporate Venturing Schemes.** This clarifies the gross assets rule, valuation of assets and payments in respect of shares and securities. See **28 CORPORATE VENTURING; 74 VENTURE CAPITAL TRUSTS.**

SP 2/07 **Advance Agreements Unit.** This gives advice on the support that HMRC will provide to inward investors and businesses involved in corporate reconstructions. See **17.21 CAPITAL GAINS.**

SP 3/07 **Double Taxation Relief — Yugoslavia.** This replaces SP 3/04.

SP 4/07 **Advance Thin Capitalisation Agreements under the APA legislation.** This gives detailed guidance about how HMRC will operate the advance pricing agreements legislation in practice. See **72.3 TRANSFER PRICING.**

SP 2/10 **Advance pricing agreements (APAs).** This was released in December 2010 and it provides up to date details of the administration of the APA scheme relating to transfer pricing issues. It supersedes the earlier SP 3/99. See **72 TRANSFER PRICING.**

SP 1/11 **Transfer pricing, mutual agreement procedure and arbitration.** Issued on 15 February 2011 this describes the UK's practice in relation to methods for reducing or preventing double taxation and supersedes Tax Bulletins 25 and 31. It considers the use of mutual agreement procedure (MAP) under the relevant UK Double Taxation Convention and/or the EU Arbitration Convention and also describes the UK's approach to the use of arbitration where MAP is unsuccessful.

45

Housing Associations

Simon's Taxes. See D7.637 *et seq.*

Introduction

[45.1] This chapter looks at the tax treatment of housing associations and self-build societies. Housing associations which are approved for the purpose can claim tax exemptions for rent received from its members and for gains made on disposal of their properties. Similar reliefs apply to self-build societies.

'*Housing association*', according to the *Housing Associations Act 1985*, means a society, body of trustees or company:

(a) which is established for the purpose of, or amongst whose objects or powers are included those of, providing, constructing, improving or managing, or facilitating or encouraging the construction or improvement of, housing accommodation; and

(b) which does not trade for profit or whose constitution or rules prohibit the issue of capital with interest or dividend exceeding such rate as may be prescribed by the Treasury, whether with or without differentiation as between share and loan capital.

Further provision may be made, by statutory instrument, for the purposes of the reliefs for housing associations and self-build societies.

[*CTA 2010, ss 649, 657; ICTA 1988, ss 488(8), 489(6)*].

Tax treatment

Rental income

[45.2] Housing associations may claim to have rents, which they are entitled to receive from their members, disregarded for tax purposes, provided that the associations are approved as in **45.8** below.

[*CTA 2010, s 642(1)(2); ICTA 1988, s 488(1)*].

Interest paid

[45.3] Where an approved housing association claims exemption from tax (see **45.2**), interest paid that is attributable to the properties subject to a tenancy is ignored for tax purposes. However, if the interest is attributable to a property not subject to a tenancy, the amount of interest attributable to that property is treated as so paid.

[*CTA 2010, s 642(1)(3)(4); ICTA 1988, s 488(1)(2)*].

Example

A housing association pays yearly interest of £4,000. It has three properties, two of which are occupied and one vacant. The last rent charged for this latter property was £400 p.a.

Rents		£
Property A		400
Property B		800
Property C (unoccupied)		400
Total rents		£1,600
Interest attributable to		
Property A	$\frac{400}{1,600} \times £4,000$	£1,000
Property B	$\frac{800}{1,600} \times £4,000$	£2,000
Interest attributable to let properties treated as not paid		£3,000

The balance of £1,000 interest paid by the association is treated as so paid for tax purposes.

Chargeable gains

[45.4] An approved housing association within **45.5** may also claim exemption from corporation tax on chargeable gains accruing on the sale of any property which is or has been occupied by a tenant of the association. A claim is made as under **45.6**.

[*CTA 2010, s 643; ICTA 1988, s 488(5), (9)–(11)*].

Disposals of land and other assets by a housing association to the Regulator of Social Housing, the Secretary of State or Scottish Homes under a scheme within *Housing Act 1964, s 5* or *Housing Associations Act 1985, Sch 7 para 5*, and subsequent disposals of those assets by the Regulator of Social Housing, etc. to a single housing association, are treated as taking place on a no gain, no loss basis. The same applies to:

(a) transfers of land between the Regulator of Social Housing and relevant housing providers (essentially non-profit registered providers of social housing);
(b) transfers of land between relevant housing providers; and
(c) transfers under a direction from the Regulator of Social Housing of property other than land between relevant housing providers.

Similar relief applies to NI housing associations from 6 April 1984.

[*TCGA 1992, ss 218–220*].

A non-arm's length disposal of an estate or interest in land to a relevant housing provider may, on a joint claim being made, be treated as that of the association on a subsequent disposal. [*TCGA 1992, s 259*].

Approved associations

[45.5] Housing associations are approved, for the purposes of the tax exemptions in this chapter, by the Secretary of State for the Environment, the Scottish Ministers, the Welsh Ministers or the Department for Social Development for NI (or under delegated authority). A housing association may only be approved if certain conditions are satisfied.

(a) The association is a housing association within the meaning of the *Housing Associations Act 1985* or its NI equivalent.
(b) The association must be (or be deemed to be) a society registered under *Industrial and Provident Societies Act 1965* or its NI equivalent.
(c) Membership must be restricted to tenants or prospective tenants, and the grant or assignment of tenancies must be restricted to members.
(d) The association must satisfy such other requirements and comply with such other conditions as may be laid down by the approving authority.

Approval has effect from the date specified by the approving authority (which may be earlier or later than the date approval is given).

[*CTA 2010, ss 644–646; ICTA 1988, s 488(6)*].

Administration

[45.6] A claim for exemption from tax must be made within two years of the end of the accounting period to which it relates.

A housing association must not make a claim unless the following requirements are substantially complied with for the period to which the claim relates:

(a) none of its properties were occupied other than by a member (or, for a maximum period of six months after a member's death, by another person in accordance with his will or intestacy); and
(b) the association satisfied the conditions at **45.5** above and observed any covenants required under those conditions to be included in grants of tenancies.

If an adjustment to an association's corporation tax liability is required as a result of a claim, the adjustment can be made by assessment, repayment of tax or otherwise. Such adjustments can also be made where, following an enquiry, the association's claim or company tax return is amended.

[*CTA 2010, ss 647, 648; ICTA 1988, s 488(4)(9)–(11A)*].

Special situations

[45.7] The following are governed by special rules.

Relief by grant

[45.8] Housing associations, which are not approved under **45.5** and do not trade for profit, may claim relief from corporation tax, by means of a grant. The claim must be made to the Secretary of State for the Environment or the Secretary of State for Scotland or Wales. It must show that, throughout the period for which the claim is made, the association provided or maintained houses for letting or hostels, and its other activities were incidental thereto. The form of the claim and its supporting evidence are as required by the Secretary of State from time to time, and HMRC are authorised to disclose information to him. The terms and conditions of the grant are within the Minister's discretion, save that no relief is available for tax attributable to activities other than those specified above. A housing association must be registered to be eligible for relief. Identical provisions (with necessary modifications) apply for Northern Ireland. [*Housing Act 1988, s 54*].

Approved self-build societies

[45.9] A self-build society (within the meaning of *Housing Associations Act 1985* or NI equivalent) which is registered (or deemed to be registered) under *Industrial and Provident Societies Act 1965* and which is approved by the Secretary of State, Welsh Ministers or Department for Social Development in NI (or under delegated authority) may claim relief from corporation tax on rent receivable from its members and on chargeable gains arising on the disposal of any land to a member, provided that none of its land is occupied by a non-member. Claims are made as outlined in **45.4** above.

[*CTA 2010, ss 650–656; ICTA 1988, s 489*].

Disposals of land by unregistered self-build societies to the Regulator of Social Housing are treated as being for such consideration that no chargeable gain or allowable loss arises.

[*TCGA 1992, s 219*].

46

Income Tax in relation to a Company

Cross-reference. See **39 GROUP RELIEF**.

Introduction

[46.1] Historically the corporation tax liability of a company was computed by reference to income tax principles, pursuant to *ICTA 1988, s 9*, which were applicable to the particular source of income (and subject to any special corporation tax provisions, such as the loan relationship rules). This changed with the tax law rewrite and from 1 April 2009 is no longer the case, post *CTA 2009*, which contains provisions specifically applicable to corporation tax.

[*CTA 2009, s 8(3); ICTA 1988, s 9; ITTOIA 2005, Sch 1 para 7*].

See **61.10 PROFIT COMPUTATIONS**.

Income tax is not charged on the income of a company resident in the UK (or if the company is resident abroad, on any income which is chargeable to corporation tax), other than income received in a fiduciary or representative capacity. Such companies are charged to corporation tax on their profits.

However, certain payments by a company must be made under deduction of basic rate income tax, and the company is required to account for this tax to HMRC.

[*CTA 2009, s 3; ICTA 1988, s 6(2)*].

See also **65 RESIDENCE**.

This chapter considers the rules applicable with regard to the deduction of income tax from payments made by a company and any exemptions available, along with special cases such as gilts and local authority securities.

In March 2010, HMRC issued a consultation document entitled 'Changes to the rules on deduction of income tax'. This consultation document invited comments (before the end of May 2010) on possible changes to the tax rules on the deduction of income tax at source from interest, annual payments and similar payments, as they currently apply to companies, amongst others. The document may be found on HMRC's website. No changes to the current regime have been put in place to date.

Payments by a company etc.

[46.2] As highlighted above, certain payments made by a company have income tax deducted from them. The treatment of such payments is detailed as follows:

(a) **Annual payments.** Income tax at the basic rate is deductible from annuities, annual payments and patent royalties (and this applies whether the payments are made by a company or any other person, but see below as regards inter-company payments). [*ITA 2007, ss 449, 898, 901, 903; ICTA 1988, s 349(1)*].

But annual payments within **5.36** **ANTI-AVOIDANCE** do not have tax deducted. (See **61.11**(v) **PROFIT COMPUTATIONS**.) [*ITA 2007, s 904; ICTA 1988, s 125; FA 2005, s 91; F(No 2)A 2005, s 38(3)(7)(13), Sch 11 Pt 2(7)*].

(b) **Interest.** Income tax at the basic rate is deductible from yearly interest of money chargeable to tax under *ITTOIA 2005, Pt 4 Ch 2* (as it applies for income tax purposes, regarding which see Tolley's Income Tax, under Savings and Investment Income) if such interest is paid:
   (i) by a company or local authority (otherwise than in a fiduciary or representative capacity);
   (ii) by or for a partnership of which a company is a member; or
   (iii) to a person whose usual place of abode is outside the UK (subject to **46.5** below).

[*ITA 2007, ss 449, 874; ICTA 1988, s 349(2); FA 2004, s 105(5); ITTOIA 2005, Sch 1 para 148(3)*].

'Yearly' interest is not defined, however a discussion of the case law with regard to this term can be found at HMRC manual SAIM9075 and 9076. Yearly interest is interest arising on loans or debts capable of existing for more than 12 months. The rule is not mechanical and will depend on the facts, but the intention of the parties as to the length of the loan will be a determining factor (see *Cairns v MacDiarmid* [1982] STC 226, 56 TC 556).

However, where all or part of interest paid by the issuer of a security is treated as a distribution for corporation tax purposes, it is taxed in the recipient's hands as if it were a dividend, not interest and income tax should not be deducted by the company from that payment or part of it. See HMRC Brief 47/08.

See, however, below as regards certain payments by companies and local authorities.

For payments by a company which is a financial institution, the above rules with regard to income tax to be deducted from a payment (pursuant to *ITA 2007*) have effect in relation to alternative finance return (see **4 ALTERNATIVE FINANCE ARRANGEMENTS**) as they have effect in relation to interest. This applies to alternative finance arrangements entered into on or after 6 April 2005 subject to commencement rules for arrangements entered into before that date where an alternative finance return is payable on or after that date.

[*ITA 2007, Pt 10A as inserted by TIOPA 2010, Sch 2; FA 2005, s 56, Sch 2 para 3; ITA 2007, Sch 1 paras 452, 602; CTA 2009, Sch 1 para 660*].

Interest under the *Late Payment of Commercial Debts (Interest) Act 1998* (or under a contractual right but for which that Act would have applied) is *not* 'yearly interest'. (Revenue Tax Bulletin August 1999 pp 686, 687.)

Interest payable on an advance from a bank (within *ITA 2007, s 991(1)–(4); ICTA 1988, s 840A*, see **8.1 BANKS**) is excluded where the person beneficially entitled to the interest is within the charge to corporation tax in respect of it, as is interest paid by such a bank in the ordinary course of its business. See **8.9 BANKS** for earlier provisions and generally. See also **8.7 BANKS** as regards certain payments of interest by banks and certain other borrowers. Interest paid to **BUILDING SOCIETIES (9)** is payable gross, including (for payments on or after 6 April 2005) alternative finance return and under **ALTERNATIVE FINANCE ARRANGEMENTS (4)** treated as interest.

[*ITA 2007, ss 449, 876, 879, 881–886, 898, 889, 901; ICTA 1988, ss 349(3)(3A), 476(9), 477A(7); FA 2005, Sch 2 para 5; CTA 2009, Sch 1 para 659*].

For other specific exclusions from the deduction requirement, see Tolley's Income Tax (under Deduction of Tax at Source).

'*UK public revenue dividends*' (i.e. any income from securities which is paid out of the UK or NI public revenue, but excluding interest on local authority stock (see (i) above)) are, from 1 April 2001, payable under deduction of tax, subject to any provision to the contrary in the *Taxes Acts* (and see in particular **46.11** below as regards gilt-edged securities). See further *ITA 2007, Ch 5 Pt 15*. HMRC have wide powers to make regulations governing the accounting arrangements and modifying *ITA 2007, ss 449, 899, 901, 903, 946, 962–964* (*CTA 2009, Sch 1 para 707; ICTA 1988, ss 349, 350*) in their application to UK public revenue dividends.

Manufactured interest on UK securities paid by UK residents are also subject to deduction at source under *ITA 2007, s 919(2)*.

[*ITA 2007, ss 889, 892, 919; ICTA 1988, ss 349(3C)(4), 350A*].

(c) Interest paid on '*quoted Eurobonds*' (i.e. listed securities issued by a company and carrying a right to interest) is excluded from the above provisions for deduction of tax from interest.

[*ITA 2007, ss 882, 987; ICTA 1988, s 349(3)*].

(d) **Copyright and design royalties and public lending rights.** Subject to the special rules for inter-company payments (see below) and to the exemption for payments between associated companies in EU member

states (see **46.5** below), income tax must be deducted at the basic rate from such payments to an owner whose usual place of abode is outside the UK as if they were annual payments. A paying agent must deduct his commission (if any) before the tax is computed.
[*ITA 2007, ss 906–909; ICTA 1988, ss 536, 537, 537B*].

But see **39 GROUP RELIEF** for elections to pay charges without deducting income tax.

Certain payments excepted from the deduction

Excepted payments

[46.3] Certain payments made by companies and local authorities do not need to have income tax deducted, where certain conditions are satisfied — they are 'excepted payments'. The provisions which require tax to be deducted, and to which these exceptions relate, are listed below at (i) to (iv).

For payments made after 30 September 2002, where a company or local authority reasonably believes that any one of (a)–(e) may be satisfied at the time the payment is made, then no income tax need be deducted:

(a) The person beneficially entitled to the income in respect of which the payment is made is a UK-resident company [*ITA 2007, s 933*].

(b) The person beneficially entitled to the income in respect of which the payment is made is a non-UK resident company which carries on a trade in the UK through a permanent establishment (see **65.6 RESIDENCE**) and the payment falls to be brought into account when computing the 'chargeable profits' of such permanent establishment. [*ITA 2007, s 934*].

(c) The payment is made to one of the following or its nominee:
   - (i) a local authority;
   - (ii) a health service body within *CTA 2010, s 986; ICTA 1988, s 519A(2)*;
   - (iii) a public officer or department of the Crown within *ITA 2007, s 978; ICTA 1988, s 829(1)* (other than one within *ITA 2007, s 978(2)*);
   - (iv) a charity (see **20.1 CHARITIES**);
   - (v) a body mentioned in *CTA 2010, s 468; ICTA 1988, s 507(1)* (bodies afforded the same tax exemptions as charities, see **35.9**);
   - (vi) a scientific research organisation within *CTA 2010, s 469; ICTA 1988, s 508*;
   - (vii) (for accounting periods ending before 1 April 2005) the United Kingdom Atomic Energy Authority;
   - (viii) (for accounting periods ending before 2 April 2005) the National Radiological Protection Board;
   - (ix) the trustees of a Parliamentary pension fund within *ICTA 1988, s 613(4)*;
   - (x) the persons entitled to receive the income of certain colonial, etc. pension funds within *ICTA 1988, s 614(3)*;
   - (xi) scheme administrator of a registered pension scheme.

   [*ITA 2007, s 936*].

(d) The person to whom the payment is made is (or is the nominee of) the plan manager of an individual investment plan under *ITTOIA 2005, Pt 6 Ch 3*, and receives the payment in respect of plan investments [*ITA 2007, s 935*].

(e) The person beneficially entitled to the income in respect of which the payment is made is a partnership each member of which is either:
   (i) a body within (c) above;
   (ii) a UK-resident company;
   (iii) a non-UK resident company which carries on a trade in the UK through a permanent establishment (or branch or agency) and in computing whose 'chargeable profits' (see **65.6 RESIDENCE**) the company's share of the payment falls to be brought into account; or
   (iv) the European Investment Fund.

The Treasury has powers by order to amend the persons and bodies to whom (c) and (e)(ii)–(iv) above apply. [*ITA 2007, s 936*].

This applies equally to payments by a partnership of which a company or local authority is a member, but not where a company makes a payment acting as trustee or agent for another person. [*ITA 2007, s 930(1)*].

Provisions to which excepted payments apply

The provisions concerned are:

(i) *ITA 2007, ss 900, 901, 903, 906(5), 910, 928, 942, 944; ICTA 1988, s 349(1)* (certain annuities and other annual payments and royalties and other sums paid for the use of UK patents);

(ii) *ITA 2007, ss 874, 875, 919; ICTA 1988, s 349(2)(a)(b)* (UK interest);

(iii) *ITA 2007, ss 878, 879; ICTA 1988, s 349(3A)* (dividends or interest on securities issued by building societies); and

(iv) *ITA 2007, s 910; ICTA 1988, s 349ZA(2)* (before 6 April 2005 *ICTA 1988, s 524(3)(b)*) (proceeds of sale of UK patent rights).

(i)–(iii) above do not apply to those provisions as applied under *ITA 2007, s 944(1)–(3); ICTA 1988, s 777(9)* (certain payments to non-residents) or *ICTA 1988, Sch 23A para 4(2)); CTA 2009, Sch 1 para 285* (manufactured overseas dividends). See above and **5.9 ANTI-AVOIDANCE** for the general application of these provisions.

Disapplication of relief and penalties

Where HMRC have reasonable grounds for believing that none of the relevant conditions above will be satisfied in relation to any payment at the time the payment is made, they may give a direction to a company or local authority (or a partnership of which a company or local authority is a member) disapplying the above relief in relation to any such payment. The direction may refer to either a particular payment or a specified description of payment, but may not apply to payments made before the giving of the direction.

A company or local authority (or a partnership of which a company or local authority is a member) may make a payment without deduction of tax if they have a reasonable belief that one of the relevant conditions above applies.

However, if none of the relevant conditions was in fact met, then the right to make the payment without deduction of income tax is treated as never having applied to the payment. Thus the provisions of *ITA 2007, Ch 15 Pt 15, s 945 et seq; ICTA 1988, s 350* and *Sch 16* (see **46.8** below) then apply as if tax was deductible under *ITA 2007, ss 449, 899, 901, 903; ICTA 1988, s 349.*

Penalties of up to £3,000 (and £600 per day for continuing failure) may be imposed under *TMA 1970, s 98* for failure to deduct and account for tax where the conditions for the relief described above are not satisfied.

[*ITA 2007, ss 910, 930–940; ICTA 1988, ss 349A–349D; TMA 1970, s 98(4A)–(4C); SI 2002 No 2931; ITTOIA 2005, Sch 1 paras 133, 141, 150, 151; F(No 2)A 2005, s 22, Sch 11 Pt 2(3)*].

Deduction of tax from annual payments does not apply to payments to the London Organising Committee of the Olympic Games Limited (see **35.18 EXEMPT ORGANISATIONS**).

See Revenue Tax Bulletin August 2001 pp 867, 868 for a brief summary of the provisions and an indication of HMRC's approach to the 'reasonable belief' requirement.

Simon's Taxes. See **A4.460.**

Cross-border royalties

[46.4] With reference to payments of royalties made by companies within *ITA 2007, ss 449, 901; ICTA 1988, s 349(1)*, if the company reasonably believes that, at the time the payment is made, the 'payee' (i.e. the person beneficially entitled to the income in respect of which the payment is made) is entitled to relief under any double tax arrangements, then the company may calculate the sum to be deducted from the payment under *ITA 2007, ss 449, 901* by reference to the rate of income tax applicable under the arrangements (and, if appropriate, pay the interest gross).

If the payee was not so entitled, the company must account for the tax as if the above rule had never applied, and HMRC have powers to direct the company that it is not to apply to a particular payment or payments.

'Royalty' for this purpose includes any payment received as consideration for the use of, or the right to use, any copyright, patent, trade mark, design, process or information, and any proceeds of sale of all or any part of any patent rights. Information about such payments may be required in a company's tax return (subject to a penalty of up to £3,000 under *FA 1998, Sch 18 para 20* (see **66.16 RETURNS**) for failure). Penalties of up to £3,000 (and £600 per day for continuing failure) may be imposed under *TMA 1970, s 98* for failure to deduct and account for tax where the conditions for the relief described above are not satisfied.

[*ITA 2007, ss 911, 913; ICTA 1988, s 349E; TMA 1970, s 98(4D); FA 2002, s 96*].

See also **46.5** below.

Simon's Taxes. See **A4.4, A4.445**.

Interest and Royalties Directive — exemption from income tax

[46.5] The EU Directive 2003/49/EC of 3 June 2003 on a common system of taxation applicable to interest and royalty payments made between associated companies of EU member states (the 'Interest and Royalties Directive') is implemented in the UK (within *ITTOIA 2005, ss 757–767*) for payments made on or after 1 January 2004 unless indicated otherwise below. The Treasury may amend by order the provisions set out below for the purpose of implementing any amendment to or replacement of the Directive adopted after 8 April 2004.

[*ITTOIA 2005, s 757, Sch 1 paras 631, 639; FA 2004, ss 97, 106*].

See *SI 2005 No 2899* dealing with the accession of new member states to the EU and various transitional arrangements.

Exemption from income tax

[46.6] Except as detailed below, payments of interest or royalties are not liable to income tax provided that at the time the payment is made:

(a) it is made by a UK company or a UK permanent establishment of an EU company (but not a UK company's permanent establishment in a territory other than the UK);
(b) the person beneficially entitled to the income is an EU company (but not such a company's UK or non-EU permanent establishment);
(c) the companies referred to in (a) and (b) above are 25% associates (see below); and
(d) if the payment is one of interest, HMRC has issued an exemption notice.

As regards (a) above, a payment is treated as made by a permanent establishment in a territory of a company resident in another territory (and not by the company) if and to the extent that it represents a tax-deductible expense for that permanent establishment.

As regards (b) above, the person beneficially entitled to the income is an EU company's UK or non-EU permanent establishment (rather than the company) if and to the extent that the payment is directly connected to the permanent establishment's business and is subject to corporation tax (or foreign equivalent) in the State where the permanent establishment is situated.

As regards (c) above, two companies are '25% *associates*' if one of them holds directly 25% or more of the capital or voting rights in the other or a third company holds directly 25% or more of the capital or voting rights in each of them.

As regards (d) above, the procedures governing the issue of exemption notices are set out in the *Exemption from Tax for Certain Interest Payments Regulations 2004* (*SI 2004 No 2622*). The regulations also make provision for the cancellation of an exemption notice where the conditions are not satisfied and also for the recovery of tax.

[*ITTOIA 2005, ss 758–762, Sch 1 paras 632–634; FA 2004, ss 98–100; SI 2004 No 2622; ITA 2007, s 758, Sch 1 paras 576, 577*].

Payment of royalties without deduction at source

[46.7] For payments made of royalties within *ITA 2007, ss 449, 901; ICTA 1988, s 349(1)* in respect of which the company reasonably believes that, at the time the payment is made, the payment falls within the above exemption under the provisions implementing the Interest and Royalties Directive, i.e. *ITTOIA 2005, s 758* (or, before 6 April 2005, *FA 2004, s 98*), then the company may, if it thinks fit, make the payment without deduction of tax.

If the exemption did not in fact apply to the payment, the company must account for the tax as if the above rule had never applied, and HMRC have powers to direct the company that it is not to apply to a particular payment or payments (and such directions may be varied or revoked by subsequent directions).

If, before the royalty payment is made, the company beneficially entitled to the payment believed the exemption would apply but has subsequently become aware that it would not, it must without delay notify HMRC and the company making the payment.

Information about such payments may be required in a company's tax return (subject to a penalty of up to £3,000 under *FA 1998, Sch 18 para 20* (see **66.16 RETURNS**) for an incorrect or uncorrected return). Penalties of up to £3,000 (and £600 per day for continuing failure) may be imposed under *TMA 1970, s 98* for failure to deduct and account for tax where the exemption does not apply and the company did not believe or could not reasonably have believed that it would apply.

Where the exemption applies but a payment has been made subject to deduction of tax source, a claim for relief may be made to HMRC.

[*ITTOIA 2005, Sch 1 paras 379, 635(2)–(4), 636; TMA 1970, s 98(4DA); FA 2004, ss 101, 102, 105*].

The above exemption does not apply to so much of any interest or royalties paid between parties in a 'special relationship' as exceeds the amount that would have been paid in the absence of such relationship (i.e. payments exceeding an arm's length amount (which may be nil)).

'*Special relationship*' in this case is construed in the same way as under *ICTA 1988, ss 808A* (in the case of interest) and *808B* (in the case of royalties) as set out in **32.4 DOUBLE TAX RELIEF.** This provision does not affect any claim for double taxation relief under *ICTA 1988, s 788* (see **32.3 DOUBLE TAX RELIEF**).

[*ITTOIA 2005, ss 763, 764, Sch 1 paras 635(5), 637; FA 2004, s 103*].

The above exemption does not apply to a payment of interest or royalties made on or after 8 April 2004 where the main purpose or one of the main purposes for the creation or assignment of the debt-claim in the case of interest, or the right in respect of royalties, is to take advantage of the exemption.

[*ITTOIA 2005, s 765, Sch 1 para 638; FA 2004, s 104*].

(This might apply for example where a loan from a non-EU resident company is routed through an EU-resident associate.)

Guidance notes on the implementation of the EU Directive and on how HMRC, Centre for Non-Residents deal with applications for relief from UK tax are available on HMRC's website (www.hmrc.gov.uk/cnr/form_crossborder.htm).

The Centre for Non-Residents has published guidance notes, CNR DT 6 and 7, dealing with the above changes, the accession of 10 additional states to the European Union on 1 May 2004, and how this affects claims for relief.

Income tax deductions from payments

[46.8] Where income tax is deducted from relevant payments then a UK-resident company must make a return to the Collector of Taxes of:

(i) payments from which it was liable to deduct income tax and the income tax for which it is accountable; and
(ii) credits that it claims for income tax deducted from payments received.

[*ITA 2007, ss 946, 949, 950, 952, 953, 962; ICTA 1988, s 350(4), Sch 16 paras 3, 5; ITA 2007, ss 946, 962*].

Returns (form CT61) must be made for 'return periods' which end on 31 March, 30 June, 30 September, 31 December and at the end of an accounting period of the company. Such returns must be made within 14 days of the end of the return period. If a company's year end is different from any of these dates then there will be five return periods, to the accounting date of the company.

[*ITA 2007, s 949; ICTA 1988, Sch 16 para 2*].

If a relevant payment is made outside an accounting period, a return must be made within 14 days of the payment. If a company becomes aware of an error in the return, it must submit an amended return for that period.

[*ICTA 1988, Sch 16 paras 7A, 9*].

Credit can be claimed in a return for income tax deducted from payments received in the accounting period in which the return period falls.

Income tax which has been suffered in a return period will be refunded to the maximum of income tax deducted and paid by the company in the return periods up to that point. Any excess not repaid is carried forward as a credit to the following return period. At the end of the accounting period if there is a cumulative excess of tax suffered (which has not been repaid) then this will be set off against the company's corporation tax liability.

[*ITA 2007, ss 952, 953; ICTA 1988, Sch 16 para 5*].

The company is liable to pay to HMRC the income tax it deducted (or was liable to deduct) from payments (against which it may claim credit for income tax deducted from payments received) at the time by which the return is to be made, i.e. 14 days after the end of the return period (or 14 days after a payment which is not made in an accounting period). An officer of HMRC has power to assess the company if he considers that a return is incorrect, or believes that a payment has not been returned.

[*ITA 2007, ss 951–953, 956; ICTA 1988, Sch 16 paras 4, 5*].

See **8.7 BANKS** as regards returns of tax deducted from bank interest payments and **9.3 BUILDING SOCIETIES** as regards building society interest.

See **49.8 INTEREST ON UNPAID TAX** for the position if such income tax is not paid by the due date. The raising of an assessment on the company does not affect the due date of payment of the tax for interest purposes.

[*ITA 2007, ss 951, 956; ICTA 1988, Sch 16 para 4(2)*].

Return form CT61 is used for making returns required as above.

For the information which must be provided by the payer in relation to a distribution, see **31.17 DISTRIBUTIONS**.

Non-UK resident companies (and non-corporates) are directly liable to assessment under *ITA 2007, ss 963, 964 therefore ITA 2007, s 945 et seq; ICTA 1988, s 350* does not apply. See **49.8 INTEREST ON UNPAID TAX** as regards interest on late paid tax under such assessments.

Simon's Taxes. See **D5.510–D5.513** *et seq.*

Income tax suffered by a company

[46.9] Few UK resident companies receive income under deduction of income tax. Where a company does receive such income, the income tax suffered is to be set off against any corporation tax due by the company for the accounting period into which the receipt falls for corporation tax purposes.

Where the receipt is exempt from corporation tax, the income tax is taken into account in the accounting period into which it would have fallen had it been liable to corporation tax.

Payments made to another party on behalf of or in trust for the company are taken into account but receipts by a company on behalf of or in trust for another person are not.

[*CTA 2010, s 967(1)–(3); ICTA 1988, s 7(2)*].

No payment received *from* another company resident in the UK is to be treated as made out of profits or gains brought into charge to income tax, and the obligation to deduct income tax is not affected by the fact that the recipient company is not chargeable to income tax.

[*CTA 2010, s 967(4); ICTA 1988, s 7(4)*].

Example

[46.10]

S Ltd, a company with nine associated companies, prepares accounts each year to 31 October. During the two years ending 31 October 2011 it makes several payments (not being interest) from which basic rate income tax is deducted and receives several sums under deduction of basic rate income tax. The payments are taxable/ deductible for corporation tax purposes.

The following items are shown net.

	Receipts	Payments
	£	£
21.12.09		7,800
4.1.10	3,900	
9.8.10	7,800	
24.10.10	11,700	
25.3.11		7,800
14.8.11		9,360

The adjusted profits (*before* taking account of the gross equivalents of the above amounts) were as follows.

	£
Year ended 31.10.10	630,000
Year ended 31.10.11	860,000

S Ltd will use the following figures in connection with the CT61 returns rendered to HMRC and will also be able to set off against its corporation tax liability the income tax suffered as shown.

	£	£	£	£
Return period	Payments	Receipts	Cumulative payments less receipts	Income tax paid/ (repaid) with return
Year ended 31.10.10				
1.11.09 to 31.12.09	7,800		7,800	1,950
1.1.10 to 31.3.10		3,900	3,900	(975)
1.4.10 to 30.6.10 (No return)			3,900	
1.7.10 to 30.9.10		7,800	(3,900)	(975)*
				(975)*
1.10.10 to 31.10.10		11,700	(15,600)	(2,925)
				(3,900)*

Year ended 31.10.11

1.11.10 to 31.12.10 (No return)			
1.1.11 to 31.3.11	7,800	7,800	1,950
1.4.11 to 30.6.11 (No return)		7,800	
1.7.11 to 30.9.11	9,360	17,160	2,340
1.10.11 to 31.10.11 (No return)		17,160	
			£4,290

* for the period 1.7.10 to 30.9.10 during the year ended 31 October 2010, of the total income tax suffered of £1,950, £975 will be refunded (as £1,950 has been paid to date and £975 repaid so far) and the remaining £975 will be carried forward. As no further income tax is deducted by the company and paid to HMRC during this accounting period, at the end of the year the net tax suffered of £3,900 will be set off against the company's corporation tax liability.

Taxable profits

	Year ended 31.10.10	Year ended 31.10.11
	£	£
Adjusted profits as stated	630,000	860,000
Add Cumulative receipts £15,600 + net tax £3,900	19,500	
Deduct Cumulative payments £17,160 + tax of £4,290		21,450
Taxable profits	£649,500	£838,550

Tax payable

	Year ended 31.10.10	Year ended 31.10.11
	£	£
CT @ 28% / 26% (as apportioned)	181,860	225,011
Deduct Income tax suffered	3,900	
Net liability	£177,960	£225,011

Gilt-edged securities

[46.11] See Tolley's Income Tax under Savings and Investment Income for provisions of general application, and in particular for the general availability of gross payment of interest on gilt-edged securities. For the general corporation tax treatment of gilts, see **54 LOAN RELATIONSHIPS**.

Local authority securities

[46.12] A local authority (as defined in *ITA 2007, s 999; ICTA 1988, s 842A*) must (except as below) deduct income tax from payments of yearly interest at the basic rate (for tax year 2008/09 onwards, previously lower/starting rate as appropriate) for the year in which the payment is made.

[*ITA 2007, s 874; ICTA 1988, s 349(2); ITA 2007, s 449*].

Interest on local authority securities issued in foreign currency is, if the Treasury so directs, paid without deduction of income tax and exempt from income tax (but not corporation tax) in the hands of a non-resident beneficial owner. Where for repayment of the principal amount due under a security there is an option between sterling and one or more foreign currencies, these provisions apply only if that option is exercisable solely by the holder of the security. Income from such securities is not exempt merely because it is deemed to be income of a non-resident.

[*ITTOIA 2005, ss 755, 756; ICTA 1988, s 581(1)–(3)*].

For securities issued before 6 April 1982, similar provisions apply where the securities were issued in the currency of a country outside the scheduled territories at the time of issue.

[*ITTOIA 2005, ss 755, 756; ICTA 1988, s 581(6); ITTOIA 2005, s 755(1), Sch 1 paras 241, 242*].

47

Industrial and Provident Societies

Cross-references. **45 HOUSING ASSOCIATIONS; 56.1 MUTUAL COMPANIES.**
Simon's Taxes. See D7.625–D7.630.

Introduction

[47.1] The legislation sets out the tax treatment which applies to industrial and provident societies registered or deemed to be registered under *Industrial and Provident Societies Act 1965* or its NI equivalent.

[*CTA 2010, ss 1055, 1056; ICTA 1988, s 486(12)*].

Share or loan interest paid

[47.2] Share or loan interest paid by a society is not a distribution (see **31 DISTRIBUTIONS**).

Dividends, bonuses, interest payments etc. payable to a shareholder by a society are treated as interest under a loan relationship (see **54.2 LOAN RELATIONSHIPS**). The society must make a return to HMRC within three months of the end of the relevant accounting period. The return must show the name and place of residence of every recipient of more than £15 and the amount paid to him.

The shareholder is treated as holding the loan relationship for trading or non-trading purposes according to the purpose for which his holding in the society is held. Before *CTA 2009* had effect, the dividends etc. were chargeable to corporation tax on the shareholder under *Schedule D, Case III* (whether or not the holding was held for trade purposes).

Interest is paid by a society without deduction of income tax (unless paid to a person whose usual place of abode is abroad, when income tax is deductible under *ITA 2007, ss 449, 899, 901, 903; ICTA 1988, s 349*).

[*CTA 2009, ss 499, 500; ICTA 1988, s 486(1)–(4)(6)(7)*].

Note this treatment applies equally to co-operative associations established and resident in the UK provided the primary objective of the association is to assist their members in the carrying on of agricultural or horticultural businesses on land occupied by them in the UK or of fishery businesses. A 'co-operative association' is a body of persons with a written constitution, which the Secretary of State (or the Department of Agriculture and Rural Development for NI, as the case may be) is satisfied is 'in substance' a co-operative association.

[*CTA 2009, ss 499, 500; ICTA 1988, s 486(9)(12); see also HMRC Extra-Statutory Concessions, C12 and C13 (which is to be withdrawn and enacted in legislation)*].

Deductions in computing trading profits

[47.3] Certain deductions are available in computing the profits of a trade carried on by a society which either does not sell to non-members or does not by its rules or practice limit the number of shares in the society. A deduction is allowed if:

- it represents a discount, rebate, dividend or bonus granted by the society to a member or non-member in connection with his transactions with the society. The transactions must be taken into account in computing the society's trading profit; and
- the sum is calculated by reference to the size of the transaction or the amounts paid or payable by or to the person concerned. It must not be calculated by reference to any share or interest in the capital of the society.

If a dividend or bonus is deductible under these provisions it is not treated as a distribution (see **31 DISTRIBUTIONS**).

[*CTA 2009, s 132; ICTA 1988, ss 230A, 486(10)*].

Amalgamations, transfers etc.

[47.4] Where one of a number of transactions takes place on or after 1 December 2009 in relation to an industrial and provident society (e.g. amalgamation and transfer to a new industrial and provident society or transfer of an industrial and provident society's whole business to another industrial and provident society) the transaction is a 'relevant transfer' and *SI 2009 No 2971 Mutual Societies (Transfers of Business) (Tax) Regulations* applies. Assets disposed of by one society to another on a union, amalgamation or transfer of engagements are treated as disposed of, for the purpose of capital gains computations, at such a consideration as would secure that no gain or loss accrues on the disposal. [*TCGA 1992, s 217D*].

Note this treatment applies equally to co-operative associations established and resident in the UK provided the primary objective of the association is to assist their members in the carrying on of agricultural or horticultural businesses on land occupied by them in the UK or of fishery businesses.

A '*co-operative association*' is a body of persons with a written constitution, which the Secretary of State (or the Department of Agriculture and Rural Development for NI, as the case may be) is satisfied is 'in substance' a co-operative association.

[*CTA 2009, ss 499, 500; ICTA 1988, s 486(9)(12); see also HMRC Extra-Statutory Concessions, C12 and C13 (which is to be withdrawn and enacted in legislation)*].

Co-operative associations

[47.5] A '*co-operative association*' is a body of persons with a written constitution which the Secretary of State (or the Department of Agriculture and Rural Development for NI, as the case may be) is satisfied is 'in substance' a co-operative association.

The provisions outlined in **47.2**, **47.4** above apply to co-operative associations established and resident in the UK provided the primary objective of the association is to assist their members in the carrying on of agricultural or horticultural businesses on land occupied by them in the UK or of fishery businesses.

[*CTA 2009, ss 499, 500; ICTA 1988, s 486(9)(12)*].

See also HMRC Extra-Statutory Concessions, C12 and C13 (which is to be withdrawn and enacted in legislation).

Trading losses

[47.6] Trading losses brought forward under *CTA 2010, s 45* (see **55.3 LOSSES**) may be set off against:

(a) non-trading loan relationship profits; and
(b) amounts assessable as overseas income (other than from an overseas trade).

[*CTA 2010, s 47*].

Note that, before *CTA 2010* took effect, this relief applied by concession (HMRC Extra-Statutory Concession, C5).

48

Intangible Assets

Cross reference. See **54 LOAN RELATIONSHIPS.**

Simon's Taxes. See D1.6.

Introduction

[48.1] A regime for the treatment of expenditure and receipts in respect of intangible assets was introduced by *FA 2002, s 84, Schs 29, 30*. It was rewritten in *CTA 2009, Pt 8*. It applies *only to companies* and only to assets acquired or created on or after 1 April 2002 (subject to transitional arrangements, see **48.36** below).

The regime deals with expenditure on the creation, acquisition and enhancement of intangibles (including abortive expenditure) as well as on their preservation and maintenance. It also applies to payments for the use of such assets, e.g. royalties. Profits on disposal of such assets are taxed as income. Losses on disposal and payments are relievable against income. The tax treatment of amortisation normally follows the accounts treatment.

A form of rollover relief (similar to, but not to be confused with, capital gains tax rollover relief) is available where realisation proceeds of intangibles are reinvested in new intangibles. See **48.9**. In general, amounts brought into account under the intangible asset regime, are not brought into account for corporation tax under any other provisions unless the legislation expressly states otherwise. See generally HMRC Corporate Intangibles Research and Development (CIRD) Manual, CIRD10000 *et seq*.

[*CTA 2009, s 906*].

Intangible fixed assets

[48.2] Except as otherwise indicated, transactions involving gains or losses in respect of 'intangible fixed assets' are dealt with for corporation tax purposes as described in this chapter. No other charges or reliefs apply in respect of those transactions.

An '*intangible asset*' for this purpose has the meaning it has under 'generally accepted accounting practice'. In particular it includes 'intellectual property', other assets such as agricultural quota, franchises and telecommunication rights and, except as otherwise indicated, is extended to include 'goodwill' (as defined under 'generally accepted accounting practice' and excluding goodwill which appears only in consolidated accounts).

For accounting periods beginning on or after 22 April 2009, the definition is specifically extended to include internally-generated intangible assets (*CTA 2009, ss 712(1)* and *715(3)*, amended by *FA 2009, s 70*). This followed the case of *Greenbank Holidays Ltd v HMRC* [2010] SFTD 653. Where an accounting period straddles 22 April 2009, the periods before and after are treated as separate accounting periods for this purpose. All goodwill is treated as created in the course of carrying on the business i.e. for this purpose it cannot be created by purchase. Goodwill is treated as created on or after 1 April 2002, unless the business was carried on at any time before that date by the company or by a related company.

Definitions

[48.3] An asset is an '*intangible fixed asset*' if it is acquired or created for use on a continuing basis in the course of the company's activities. This includes an option or other right either to acquire an intangible asset which, if acquired, would be a fixed asset, or to dispose of an intangible fixed asset. It is generally irrelevant whether or not the asset is capitalised in the company's accounts.

'*Intellectual property*' is:

(a) any patent, trade mark, registered design, copyright or design right, plant breeders' rights or rights under *Plant Varieties Act 1997, s 7*, or corresponding or similar right under foreign law;
(b) any economically valuable information or technique not protected by a right within (a); or
(c) any licence or other right in respect of anything within (a) or (b).

'*Royalty*' means a royalty in respect of the enjoyment or exercise of rights that constitute an intangible fixed asset.

'*Generally accepted accounting practice*' is as defined by *FA 2004, s 50*. Accounts drawn up in accordance with generally accepted accounting practice are referred to in this chapter as 'GAAP-compliant accounts'. Where non-GAAP-compliant accounts are drawn up, or accounts are not drawn up at all, these provisions are applied to amounts as they would have appeared had GAAP-compliant accounts been drawn up. This applies equally to amounts derived from earlier periods with non-GAAP-compliant accounts.

In determining whether a company's accounts are GAAP-compliant, reference may be made to consolidated group accounts as regards the useful life or economic value of any asset. Resort cannot be made to such accounts if prepared under the law of a foreign jurisdiction on a basis that diverges substantially from generally accepted accounting practice in relation to the useful life or economic value of any assets. Nor, for periods of account beginning on or after 1 January 2005, can resort be made to the consolidated accounts if they are drawn up using a different accounting framework from that used for the company's individual accounts and as a result they are prepared on a basis that differs substantially from that of the individual accounts in relation to the useful life or economic value of any assets.

[*CTA 2009, ss 712–719; FA 2002, s 102(1)(2), Sch 29 paras 1–6; FA 2005, s 80, Sch 4 para 38; FA 2009, s 709*].

Excluded assets

[48.4] Where (or to the extent that) an asset is excluded (see below), any option or other right to acquire or dispose of it is similarly excluded. Assets which are partly excluded are treated as two separate assets, one within the current provisions, the other subject to the normal corporation tax provisions, with any necessary apportionments being made on a just and reasonable basis.

The following assets are **excluded entirely** from the current provisions.

(a) An asset representing rights enjoyed through an estate, interest or right in or over land, or rights in relation to tangible movable property (see *CTA 2009, s 805; FA 2002, Sch 29 para 73*).

(b) An asset treated in the company accounts as an intangible asset but which in a previous accounting period was treated as a tangible asset on which capital allowances (on plant and machinery) were claimed (see *CTA 2009, s 804; FA 2002, Sch 29 para 73A*). This applies for periods of account beginning on or after 1 January 2005.

(c) Certain oil licences (see *CTA 2009, s 809; FA 2002, Sch 29 para 74*).

(d) Financial assets (including loan relationships, derivative contracts and insurance or capital redemption policies) (see *CTA 2009, s 806; FA 2002, Sch 29 para 75* as amended by *FA 2002, Sch 23 para 24, Sch 27 para 26*), subject to special provision in relation to finance leases under *FA 2002, Sch 29 para 104(2)(a)* (see **48.34** below).

(e) An asset representing:
   (i) shares or other rights in relation to the profits, governance or winding up of a company;
   (ii) rights under a trust (other than a right which is treated for accounting purposes as representing an interest in trust property which is an intangible fixed asset within these provisions); or

(iii) the interest of a partner in a partnership (other than an interest which falls, for accounting purposes, to be treated as representing an interest in partnership property which is an intangible fixed asset within these provisions).

(f) An asset to the extent it is held either for a non-commercial purpose or for the purpose of activities in respect of which the company is not within the charge to corporation tax.

(g) An asset held by a film production company to the extent it represents production expenditure on a film under the *FA 2006* regime (see **70.30** and **70.31 TRADE PROFITS — INCOME AND SPECIFIC TRADES**).

The following assets are excluded except as regards *'royalties'*, i.e. any payment in respect of the enjoyment or exercise of rights that constitute an intangible fixed asset.

(i) An asset to the extent that it is held for the purposes of any mutual trade or business (other than life assurance business) or by an insurance company (but excluding computer software) for the purposes of its life assurance business within *ICTA 1988, Pt 12 Ch 1*. See *CTA 2009, ss 810, 902*.

(ii) An asset held by a company to the extent that it represents expenditure by the company on:

- the production of the original master version (as defined) of a film that commenced principal photography before January 2007;
- the acquisition before 1 October 2007 of the original master version of a film that commenced principal photography before 1 April 2006; or
- the production or acquisition of a 'master version' (as defined) of a sound recording.

(iii) An asset held by a company to the extent that it represents expenditure by the company on computer software falling to be treated for accounting purposes as part of the costs of the related hardware.

The following assets are excluded to the extent specified.

(A) An asset held by a company to the extent that it represents expenditure by the company on research and development (within *CTA 2009, ss 1039–1142; ICTA 1988, s 838*, see **64 RESEARCH AND DEVELOPMENT**) is excluded from the provisions as follows.

(i) The provisions at **48.5**, **48.6** below for the computation of tax debits and credits do not apply, *except for* credits in respect of receipts recognised as they accrue and debits reversing such credits.

(ii) The provisions at **48.8** below for debits and credits on the realisation of intangible fixed assets apply as if the cost of the asset did not include any of the research and development expenditure.

(B) An asset held by a company to the extent that it represents capital expenditure (as determined for capital allowance purposes) by the company on computer software in respect of which the company has so elected is excluded from the provisions as follows.

(i) The provisions at **48.5**, **48.6** below for the computation of tax debits and credits do not apply, except *for* credits in respect of receipts recognised as they accrue and debits reversing such credits.

(ii) The provisions at **48.8** below for debits and credits on the realisation of intangible fixed assets apply as if the cost of the asset did not include any expenditure in respect of which the election was made.

(iii) A credit is brought in under the current provisions only to the extent that the receipts to which the credit relates do not fall to be taken into account in computing disposal values for capital allowance purposes under *CAA 2001, s 72*.

Such an election must specify the expenditure to which it relates, must be made in writing to HMRC within two years after the end of the accounting period in which the expenditure was incurred, and is irrevocable.

[*CTA 2009, ss 800–816; FA 2002, Sch 29 paras 72–83, 138, 139; FA 2004, s 52, Sch 10 para 71; FA 2005, Sch 4 para 50; FA 2006, ss 51, 77(4)(5)*].

Computation of tax debits

[48.5] Debits are brought into account for tax purposes in respect of three types of loss relating to intangible fixed assets. These are:

(a) expenditure on an intangible fixed asset that is written off for accounting purposes as it is incurred;

(b) writing down an intangible fixed asset on an accounting or fixed rate basis; or

(c) reversal of a previous accounting gain,

other than on realisation of intangible fixed assets see **48.8** below.

Expenditure on an asset includes;

- expenditure (including abortive expenditure) incurred to acquire, create or establish title to an asset, as a royalty for use of an asset; or
- in maintaining, enhancing or defending title to it.

Capital expenditure on tangible assets is not taken into account.

Expenditure written off as it is incurred

Where expenditure is recognised in determining the profit or loss (and does not relate to previously capitalised expenditure, see below), a corresponding debit is brought into account for tax purposes. This debit is equal in amount to the accounting debit except in so far as the further provisions described in this chapter otherwise require. This applies to expenditure for the purpose of acquiring, creating, or establishing title to, the asset, by way of royalty in respect of use of the asset, or on maintaining, preserving or enhancing, or defending title to, the asset, and includes abortive expenditure. However, capital expenditure on tangible assets is excluded in determining expenditure on intangible assets.

[*CTA 2009, ss 59, 726–728; ICTA 1988, ss 74(1)(m)(p), 817(1)(b) (regarding annual payments and royalties) do not prevent relief being given for such debits*].

Writing-down of capitalised cost

Where a loss is recognised in determining the profit or loss in respect of capitalised expenditure, a corresponding debit is brought into account for tax purposes, equal in amount to the accounting debit unless other provisions described in this chapter otherwise require. This is subject to the election described below. The loss may arise though amortisation, or as a result of an impairment review. However, the valuation of an asset to determine the initial amount to be capitalised is not included.

Where the amount of the expenditure on the asset (the 'accounting expenditure') is adjusted for tax purposes (the 'tax expenditure'), e.g. where the cost is reduced as a result of reinvestment relief (see **48.10** below), then for the period of account in which the expenditure is first capitalised the tax debit is the amount which bears the same relation to the accounting debit as the tax expenditure bears to the accounting expenditure. For subsequent periods, the accounting debit is adjusted in the ratio which the 'tax written-down value' immediately before the accounting write-down bears to the accounting value. The '*tax written-down value*' of an asset for this purpose is the expenditure as adjusted for tax purposes *less* the debits previously brought into account (as above) (taking account of any debits brought into account on a change of accounting policy, see **48.35** below). On a part realisation of the asset, the previous written-down value is reduced to the proportion which the carrying values for accounting purposes immediately after the part realisation represent of those immediately before it, and subsequent allowances are based on this amount.

A company may, however, elect instead to write down the cost of an asset at a fixed rate for tax purposes. This applies whether or not the asset is written down for accounting purposes. The election, which is irrevocable, must be made in writing within two years after the end of the accounting period in which the asset was acquired or created by the company. It has effect in relation to all capitalised expenditure on the asset. The debit is at an annual rate of 4% of the capitalised tax expenditure on the asset (see above), but limited to the balance of the 'tax written-down value'. For this purpose this is the expenditure as adjusted for tax purposes less the fixed rate allowances previously given. An adjustment is made as above in the case of a part realisation and taking account of any debits or credits brought into account on a change of accounting policy, see **48.35** below. After a part realisation the allowance is given by reference to the accounting value of the part retained immediately after the part realisation and of any subsequent expenditure (subject to any adjustments required for tax purposes).

Reversal of earlier accounting gain

A loss may be recognised in determining the profit or loss which reverses (in whole or part) a gain previously recognised and in respect of which a credit was brought into account for tax purposes (see **48.6** below). In such a case, a corresponding debit is brought into account for tax purposes, the amount bearing the same relation to the accounting loss as the previous tax credit bore to the accounting gain (or part) reversed.

This does not apply to a loss recognised by way of amortisation, or as a result of an impairment review, of an asset previously revalued (see **48.6** below).

[*CTA 2009, ss 726–732, 742–744; FA 2002, Sch 29 paras 7–12, 27–29, 133–136; FA 2004, Sch 10 para 76; FA 2005, Sch 4 paras 39, 40, 42, 43, 46*].

Example A

A company acquires an intangible fixed asset in year 1 at a capitalised cost of £2,000, amortised on a straight-line basis over 10 years. As a result of a reinvestment relief claim (see **48.9** below), the cost for tax purposes is reduced to £1,600. The charge in the accounts in each of years 1 to 10 (£200) is thus reduced to a tax debit of (£200 × £1,600/2,000) = £160.

In year 2 further expenditure of £700 on the asset is capitalised. The revised book value of (£2,000 – £200 + £700) = £2,500 is amortised over a further 10 years at £250 a year. The tax written-down value is (1,440 + 700) = £2,140, so that the charge in the accounts becomes (£250 × £2,140/2,500) = £214.

Example B

A company acquires an intangible fixed asset with an indefinite life for £1,000 in year 1. There is no amortisation charge in the accounts. It elects for the fixed-rate write-down for tax purposes. No adjustment is required to the cost for tax purposes, and the tax debit is thus 40 a year.

In year 10 the asset is partly realised for £700, 600 of the book value of the asset being set against the disposal in the accounts, giving a profit on disposal of 100 and a revised book value of £400.

The tax written-down value at the end of year 9 is (£1,000 - (9 × 40)) = £640. The remaining tax expenditure set against the disposal proceeds is (£600/1,000 × £640) = £384, resulting in a taxable profit on sale of 316. The tax written-down value is reduced to (£400/1,000 × 640) = £256. The fixed rate deduction is reduced to £400 @ 4%, i.e. 16 over the following 16 years.

Example C

Writing-down on accounting basis

On 1 April 2007, Oval Ltd purchased an intangible asset from an unrelated company, Edgbaston Ltd, for £100,000. The asset is to be used for trading purposes and has a remaining useful economic life of 15 years. The cost of the asset is capitalised in Oval Ltd's accounts and in accordance with generally accepted accounting practice is amortised on a straight-line basis over the remaining 15 year life. On 1 April 2010, the company sells the asset to another unrelated company, Riverside Ltd, for £150,000.

Oval Ltd will bring into account for tax purposes the following debits and credits in respect of the intangible asset.

	£
Y/e 31.3.08	
Cost of asset	100,000
Debit for year (1/15 of cost)	(6,667)

	£
WDV at 31.3.08	93,333
Y/e 31.3.09	
Debit for year (1/15 of cost)	(6,667)
WDV at 31.3.09	86,666
Y/e 31.3.10	
Debit for year (1/15 of cost)	(6,667)
WDV at 31.3.10	£80,000
Y/e 31.3.11	
Proceeds of realisation	150,000
Less Tax written-down value	80,000
Taxable credit	£70,000

As the asset was held for trading purposes, the debits of £6,667 for each of the years ended 31 March 2008, 2009 and 2010 are allowable trading deductions, and the credit of £70,000 for the year ended 31 March 2011 is a trading receipt.

Example D

Non-Trading Loss on Intangible Assets

A Ltd is an investment company drawing up accounts each year to 31 March. The following figures are relevant for the two years ended 31 March 2010 and 2011.

	Y/e 31.3.10	Y/e 31.3.11
	£	£
Schedule A profits	15,000	16,000
Schedule D, Case III	5,000	20,000
Schedule D, Case V (foreign tax paid £4,000)	20,000	—
Management expenses	5,000	5,000
Non-trading profit/(loss) on intangible fixed assets	(55,000)	11,000

A Ltd wishes to make the most tax-efficient use of the non-trading loss, and so makes a claim to set off £15,000 against profits of the year ended 31 March 2010 under *CTA 2009, s 753(1); FA 2002, Sch 29 para 35(1)*. The corporation tax computations for the two years ended 31 March 2011 are as follows.

	£
Y/e 31.3.10	
UK Property income	15,000
Income from non-trading loan relationships	5,000
Overseas income	20,000
	40,000
Deduct Management expenses	5,000

Non-trading loss	15,000
Profits chargeable to CT	£20,000
Corporation tax: £20,000 @ 21%	4,200
Deduct Double tax relief	4,000
Corporation tax payable	200
	£
Y/e 31.3.11	
Schedule A	16,000
Schedule D, Case III	20,000
Schedule D, Case VI (see below)	—
	36,000
Deduct Management expenses	5,000
Non-trading loss	29,000
Profits chargeable to CT	£2,000
Corporation tax: £2,000 @ 21%	£420

Use of non-trading loss

	£
Loss y/e 31.3.10	55,000
Set-off against profits for y/e 31.3.010	15,000
Carry-forward as non-trading debit	£40,000
Y/e 31.3.11	
Non-trading profit of period	11,000
Deduct Non-trading debit brought forward	10,000
Non-trading loss set off against profits for y/e 31.3.11	£29,000

Computation of tax credits

[48.6] Five types of credits relating to intangible fixed assets are brought into account for tax purposes. Amounts brought into account in connection with the realisation of an intangible fixed asset do not give rise to a credit (see **48.8** below). Where the following provisions require an amount to be a '*recognised amount*' for a period, this is an amount recognised (including prior-year adjustments apart from corrections of fundamental errors) in the company's profit and loss account or income statement, in its statement of recognised gains and losses or statement of changes in equity, or in any other statement of items brought into account in determining the company's profits and losses for that period. It also includes an amount which would have been so recognised if the profit and loss or other such statement as mentioned above had been drawn up in accordance with generally accepted accounting practice (see **48.2** above).

Receipts recognised as they accrue

Where a gain representing a receipt in respect of an intangible asset is recognised in determining the profit or loss, a corresponding credit is brought into account for tax purposes, equal in amount to the accounting gain except in so far as the further provisions described in this chapter otherwise require.

Revaluations

Where the accounting carrying value of an intangible fixed asset is increased on a revaluation (including a valuation of an asset which has a balance sheet value but has not previously been valued, and the restoration of past losses), a credit is brought into account for tax purposes of the lesser of:

(a) an amount bearing the same relation to the increase in value as the tax written-down value immediately before the revaluation bears to the accounting book value by reference to which the revaluation is carried out; or

(b) the 'net total of relevant tax debits' previously brought into account.

The '*net total of relevant tax debits*' is the difference between the total debits (in respect of the writing-down of capitalised cost, see **48.2** above) and total credits (under the current revaluations provision) previously brought into account for tax purposes in respect of the asset concerned. Such debits and credits also take account of any adjustments on a change of accounting policy as described at **48.35** below.

'Revaluation' includes the valuation of an asset shown at a value in the company's balance sheet, but which has previously been valued and a revaluation representing the restoration of past losses.

The above does not apply to an asset in respect of which an election has been made for tax write-down at a fixed rate (see **48.5** above).

Negative goodwill

Where an accounting gain is recognised in determining the profit or loss in respect of negative goodwill arising on an acquisition of a business, a corresponding tax credit is brought into account, equal in amount to so much of the accounting gain as, on a just and reasonable apportionment, is attributable to intangible fixed assets.

Reversal of earlier accounting debit

A gain may be recognised in determining the profit or loss which reverses (in whole or part) a loss previously recognised and in respect of which a debit was brought into account for tax purposes (see **48.5** above). In such a case, a corresponding credit is brought into account for tax purposes, the amount bearing the same relation to the accounting gain as the previous tax debit bore to the accounting loss (or part) reversed. This does not apply to a gain on a revaluation (as above).

Receipts in respect of royalties

A credit is to be brought into account for a receipt in respect of a royalty in so far as it does not give rise to a credit which (as above) is taken into account as a receipt recognised as it accrues (whether in the period of account in which it is received or a subsequent period of account). The credit is to equal so much of the amount as does not give rise to such a credit and is to be brought into account in the period the receipt is recognised in the accounts. This provision is deemed to have always had effect in relation to any credits so brought into account. [*CTA 2009, ss 720–725; FA 2002, Sch 29 paras 13–17, 134, 135; FA 2004, Sch 10 para 74; FA 2005, Sch 4 paras 40, 41, 46; FA 2006, s 77(2)(3)(10(11)*].

Giving effect to credits and debits

[48.7] Credits and debits under the current provisions are given effect according to the purpose for which the asset concerned is used, as follows, with any necessary apportionment where an asset is held for more than one of the following purposes being made on a just and reasonable basis.

Assets held for trade purposes

Credits and debits are given effect as receipts and expenses of the trade in computing the profits of the trade carried on in that period.

Assets held for property business purposes

Credits and debits are given effect as receipts and expenses of the property business in computing business profits. A '*property business*' for this purpose is a 'UK property business' (other than a 'furnished holiday lettings business' or an 'overseas property business' (see **62 PROPERTY INCOME**). Commercial lettings of furnished holiday accommodation which are treated as a trade under *CTA 2009, s 265; ICTA 1988, s 503; CTA 2009, Sch 1 para 172* are similarly so treated for these purposes.

Assets held for mines, transport undertakings, etc. purposes

Credits and debits are given effect as receipts and expenses of the concern in computing trading profits. This applies to concerns listed in *CTA 2009, s 749; ICTA 1988, s 55(2)*.

Assets held for other purposes

Credits and debits in respect of assets used for purposes other than the above (described as 'non-trading credits and debits') are aggregated, and the aggregate 'non-trading gain' or 'non-trading loss' given effect as follows.

A non-trading gain is chargeable to corporation tax as income

Relief for a non-trading loss may be claimed, in whole or part, by set-off against total profits. Such a claim must be made within two years after the end of the accounting period to which it relates, or within such further period as

HMRC may allow. To the extent that the loss is neither so relieved nor surrendered by way of group relief, it is carried forward as a non-trading debit of the following accounting period. See **55.3 LOSSES** and, as regards group relief claims generally, **39.5 GROUP RELIEF**.

[*CTA 2009, ss 745–753; FA 2002, Sch 29 paras 30–36, Sch 30 paras 2, 4; SI 2004 No 2310, Art 67; FA 2007, Sch 8 para 27*].

See **51.9 INVESTMENT COMPANIES AND INVESTMENT BUSINESS** for restrictions on relief for non-trading losses following a change of ownership of an investment company.

Realisation of intangible fixed assets

[48.8] '*Realisation*' of an intangible fixed asset for this purpose means a transaction (including any event giving rise to an accounting gain) which results, in accordance with generally accepted accounting practice (see **48.2** above), in its ceasing to be recognised in the balance sheet or in its carrying value being reduced (the latter being referred to as a 'part realisation'). This applies to an asset that has no balance sheet value (or no longer has one) as if it had one.

Where there is a realisation of an intangible fixed asset in respect of which tax debits have been brought into account under *CTA 2009, ss 729, 730; FA 2002, Sch 29 para 9* or *para 10* (writing-down of capitalised cost, see **48.5** above), or under *CTA 2009, s 871* (adjustment on change of accounting policy, see **48.35** below) a tax credit (or debit) is brought into account equal to the amount by which the 'proceeds of realisation' (if any) exceed (or are less than) the 'tax written-down value' of the asset (see **48.5** above) immediately before the realisation.

If no tax debits have been brought into account in respect of the asset, the same applies by reference to the cost of the asset recognised for tax purposes, i.e. (subject to any adjustment for tax purposes) the amount of the capitalised expenditure for accounting purposes. Otherwise, a tax credit is brought into account equal to the full amount of the 'proceeds of realisation'. In the case of a part realisation, the tax written-down value (or cost) is for these purposes reduced in the same proportion as that by which the accounting carrying value is reduced as a result of the realisation. Thereafter, the cost of the asset (where no tax debits have been brought into account in respect of it) is that immediately after the part realisation plus any subsequent expenditure.

The '*proceeds of realisation*' are those recognised for accounting purposes reduced by amounts so recognised as incidental realisation costs, subject to any adjustment required for tax purposes (e.g. under transfer pricing rules).

The above provisions are subject to the reinvestment relief rules in **48.9** below.

Abortive realisation expenditure

A loss recognised in determining the profit or loss in respect of abortive expenditure on realisation of an intangible fixed asset gives rise to a corresponding tax debit which, subject to any adjustment required for tax purposes, is equal in amount to the accounting loss.

A '*chargeable realisation gain*' is a gain on realisation of an asset which gives rise to a credit to be taken into account as above and a chargeable intangible asset is an asset giving rise to such a gain.

[*CTA 2009, ss 733–741; FA 2002, Sch 29 paras 18–26, 135, 136; FA 2004, Sch 10 para 75; FA 2005, Sch 4 para 40*].

> *Example*
>
> A company realises part of an intangible fixed asset with accounting book value of £5,000 and tax written-down value of £4,000 for £3,750, the book value of the part retained being £1,875. The amount to be set against the sale proceeds in arriving at the tax credit to be brought into account is (£4,000 × (£5,000 – £1,875)/£5,000) = £2,500, so that the tax credit is (£3,750 – £2,500) = £1,250.

Relief in case of reinvestment

[48.9] Where a company invests the proceeds of realisation of an intangible asset (the 'old asset') in other such assets, and the proceeds exceed the capitalised cost (if any) for accounting purposes (so far as recognised for tax purposes) of the old asset, it may claim relief as below. In the case of a part realisation, the cost for this purpose is reduced to the same proportion as the reduction in accounting value as a result of the part realisation bears to that value immediately before the part realisation (and so on for subsequent part realisations).

Full relief is available if the old asset was a 'chargeable intangible asset' of the company throughout the period of its ownership by the company, but if this condition was met for a substantial part, but not the whole, of that period (including the time of realisation), relief is available as if a corresponding part of the asset were a separate asset in respect of which the relief is available (any necessary apportionments being made on a just and reasonable basis). The other assets in which the proceeds are invested must also be 'chargeable intangible assets' immediately after the expenditure on them was incurred, and the expenditure must have been incurred in the period beginning one year before, and ending three years after, the date of realisation of the old asset (which period may be extended as HMRC may by notice allow in any particular case), and must be capitalised by the company for accounting purposes. Expenditure is for this purpose treated as incurred when recognised for accounting purposes. Reacquisition of the old asset is treated as acquisition of a different asset for these purposes. Deemed realisations and reacquisitions are disregarded for these purposes (except as detailed in **48.19**, **48.20** below). An asset is a '*chargeable intangible asset*' in relation to a company at any time if, were it to be realised at that time, any gain on realisation would give rise to a credit within **48.8** above (disregarding the availability of relief under this provision or by virtue of the transfer being treated as 'tax-neutral'). References to a transfer being treated as '*tax-neutral*' mean that it is not regarded in relation to the current provisions as involving any realisation by the transferor or acquisition by the transferee, with anything done by the transferor in relation to the asset being treated as having been done by the transferee.

The relief is given by reducing both the proceeds of realisation of the old asset and the cost of the other assets acquired (so far as recognised for tax purposes) by the amount available for relief. The amount available for relief is the amount by which the lesser of the proceeds of realisation of the old asset and the cost of the other assets acquired exceeds the cost of the old asset (adjusted as referred to above in the case of part realisation). Other parties to the transactions are not affected by the relief claim.

Where, in periods of account beginning on or after 1 January 2005, there is a change in accounting policy which results in an intangible fixed asset that was treated as one asset ('*the original asset*') in the earlier period, being treated as two or more assets ('*the resulting assets*') in the later period (see **48.35** below), the cost of each of the resulting assets for the purposes of reinvestment relief is taken as a proportion of the cost of the original asset. The proportion is arrived at by multiplying the cost by the same fraction as is applied in arriving at the tax written down value of the asset on a disaggregation of assets on a change of accounting policy (the opening accounting value of the resulting asset in the later period over the aggregate opening accounting values of the resulting assets at that time).

Where an asset is disposed of and subsequently re-acquired, it is treated as a different asset from that disposed of for the purpose of these provisions. Deemed disposals and re-acquisitiions are ignored for the purpose of these provisions.

The relief must be claimed in the company's return for the period (see **15.1 CLAIMS**), and must specify the old asset(s) to which the claim relates, the expenditure on other assets by reference to which relief is claimed and the amount of relief claimed. Relief is given on a provisional basis where the company declares, in its return for a period in which it has realised an intangible fixed asset, that it proposes to reinvest the proceeds so as to give rise to relief of a specified amount and therefore is provisionally entitled to relief of a specified amount. The provisional relief lapses four years after the end of the accounting period in which the realisation occurred if it has not already been superseded by an actual claim to relief or withdrawn, and on its ceasing to have effect all necessary adjustments are made, notwithstanding any time limits on assessments, etc.

[*CTA 2009, ss 754–763; FA 2002, Sch 29 paras 37–45, 137, 140; FA 2005, s 80, Sch 4 para 44*].

Example A

An intangible fixed asset with cost (for accounting and tax purposes) of £1,000 is part realised for £900, its book value thereby being reduced from £500 to £400. The proceeds of realisation (£900) exceed the appropriate proportion of the cost (£1,000 × (£500 – £400)/£500=) £200, so that full relief is available on reinvestment of £900 or more.

If a further part realisation for £600 reduces the book value from £300 to £150, the original cost of £1,000 is reduced by the part taken into account on the earlier part realisation (£200) to £800. Since the realisation proceeds (£600) exceed the appropriate proportion of the balance of the cost (£800 × (£300 – £150)/£300=) £400, full relief is available on reinvestment of £600 or more.

If full reinvestment relief is claimed, then on a subsequent disposal of the asset, in arriving at the tax credit or debit to be taken into account, the original cost of £1,000 is reduced by £600, the cost taken into account on the earlier part realisations.

Groups of companies

[48.10] For the purposes of the current provisions, the capital gains tax definition of a group of companies is adopted (see **18.2 CAPITAL GAINS — GROUPS**). A company cannot be a member of more than one group. There are rules for determining which group a company is a member of where it would otherwise be a member of more than one group. A group of companies remains the same group for these purposes so long as it has the same principal company. Where the principal company becomes a member of another group, the old and new groups are treated as the same group. Going into liquidation does not cause a company to leave a group for these purposes. Where the principal company in a group becomes (by acquisition, merger or otherwise) an SE, the original group of which it was a member and the SE group are treated as the same group.

If the principal company becomes a member of another group, the two groups are treated as the same and the question of whether a company has left the group is determined accordingly. Where a winding up order is passed on any member of the group, it ceases to be a member.

A company is an 'effective 51% subsidiary' of another if that other is entitled to more than 50% of profits available for distribution to equity holders on a and that company would be beneficially entitled to more than 50% of any assets of the subsidiary available for distribution to equity holders on a winding up. *ICTA 1988, Sch 18* applies for this purpose. Share capital of an industrial and provident society is treated as ordinary share capital.

[*CTA 2009, ss 764–771; FA 2002, Sch 29 paras 46–54; F(No 2)A 2005, s 63*].

The following modifications apply in the application of the current provisions to such groups.

Transfers within a group

[48.11] The transfer intra-group of an intangible fixed asset is treated as 'tax-neutral' (see **48.9** above) provided the asset is a 'chargeable intangible asset' (see also **48.9** above) in relation to the transferor company before and the transferee company after the transfer. This does **not**, however, apply where either the transferor or the transferee is an incorporated friendly society within *ICTA 1988, s 461A* (see **37.3 FRIENDLY SOCIETIES**) or the transferee is a dual-resident investing company within *ICTA 1988, s 404; CTA 2009, Sch 1 para 122* (see **39.23 GROUP RELIEF**). The provisions of *ICTA 1988, Sch 28AA* (see **72 TRANSFER PRICING**) do not apply to such intra-group transfers treated as 'tax neutral'.

'*Tax neutral*' in relation to the transfer of an asset means that the transaction is not treated as being either an acquisition or a realisation of the asset. The transferee stands in the shoes of the transferor.

Interaction with treatment of company reconstructions or amalgamations. These rules take precedence over the company reconstruction and amalgamation rules at **48.23** below.

[*CTA 2009, ss 774–776; FA 2002, Sch 29 paras 55, 84(3); FA 2004, Sch 5 para 16(2)*].

Roll-over relief on reinvestment

Application to group member

[48.12] Rollover relief is not available where the other assets are acquired from another member of the same group. For the purposes of the rules at **48.9** above, where the realisation of the old asset is by one company in a group and the reinvestment in other assets by another (not being a dual resident investing company (see **39.23 GROUP RELIEF**)), then provided that the other assets are 'chargeable intangible assets' in relation to the latter company immediately after the expenditure is incurred, and are not acquired from another group member by a 'tax-neutral transfer' (see **48.11** above), the companies may jointly claim to be treated as the same person.

[*CTA 2009, s 777; FA 2002, Sch 29 para 56*].

Acquisition of company becoming group member

[48.13] For the purposes of the rules at **48.9** above, expenditure by a company ('A') on the acquisition of a 'controlling interest' in a company ('B'), where company B (or one or more other companies not in the same group as company A before it acquired that interest but which become so immediately after (and as a result of) that acquisition) holds intangible fixed assets (the 'underlying assets'), is treated as equivalent to expenditure on acquiring the assets themselves. The 'chargeable intangible assets' requirement under **48.9** above has then to be met by reference to the company by which they are held immediately after that acquisition.

Company A acquires a '*controlling interest*' in company B by acquiring shares in company B such that they become members of the same group immediately after the acquisition, having not been so immediately before the acquisition. The amount of expenditure treated as incurred by company A on the underlying assets is then the lesser of the 'tax written down value' (see **48.5** above) of the underlying assets immediately before the acquisition and the amount or value of the consideration for the acquisition of the controlling interest. In these circumstances, relief under **48.9** above must be claimed jointly by company A and the company or companies holding the underlying assets, and the tax written down value of the underlying assets in the hands of the company or companies holding the underlying assets is reduced by the amount available for relief (see **48.9** above). Any necessary allocation of the reduction between different underlying assets is made by the company which holds them (or, if there is more than one such company, as they agree between them).

[*CTA 2009, ss 778, 779; FA 2002, Sch 29 para 57*].

Degrouping

Company ceasing to be group member

[48.14] Despite extensive changes to the capital gains rules for degrouping charges (see **29.1** *et seq.*) by *FA 2011*, no similar changes were made to the legislation relating to chargeable intangible assets.

Where:

(i) a company which is a member of a group transfers to another company an intangible fixed asset (the 'relevant asset') which is a 'chargeable intangible asset' (see above) in relation to the former company before the transfer and the latter company after the transfer, and
(ii) the transferee company, having been a member of the group at the time of the transfer or having subsequently become so, ceases to be a member after the transfer but within six years after the date of the transfer at a time when it (or an 'associated company' (see **48.15** below) leaving the group at the same time) still holds the relevant asset,

then for the purposes of the current provisions, the transferee company is treated as if, immediately after the relevant asset was transferred to it, it had disposed of and reacquired it at its then market value. Any resulting adjustments to be made for tax purposes by the transferee company (or by a company to which the relevant asset has subsequently been transferred) in relation to the period between the transfer of the relevant asset to the transferee company and that company ceasing to be a group member is made by bringing in the aggregate net credit or debit as if it had arisen immediately before the transferee company left the group.

To determine how effect is to be given to debits and credits in these circumstances (see **48.7** above), it is the purposes for which the relevant asset was held by the transferee company immediately after the transfer which are considered, except that if it was then held by that company for the purposes of a trade, a property business or a mine or transport undertaking, etc. which ceased before it left the group, any debit or credit is instead treated as a non-trading debit or credit.

These provisions are subject to *CTA 2009, ss 780–791; FA 2002, Sch 29 paras 59–62* (see **48.15–48.18** below).

Where a relevant asset is transferred as part of the process of a transfer on or after 1 January 2007 to which the provisions at **48.24** below apply, then if as a result of the transfer the transferee ceases to be a member of a group, the above provisions are disapplied by deeming the transferee not to have left the group. If, as a consequence of the transfer, the transferee ceases to be a member of one group and becomes a member of another, the two groups are treated as the same group for the purposes of the above provisions.

[*CTA 2009, ss 780–784; FA 2002, Sch 29 para 58; SI 2007 No 3186, Sch 1 para 23*].

In these and the following degrouping provisions:

(a) companies are '*associated*' if, by themselves, they would form a group of companies (see **48.10** above);
(b) an asset acquired by a company is treated as the same as an asset owned at a later time by the company (or by an associated company) if the second asset derives its value in whole or part from the first; and
(c) references to a company leaving a group do not include cases where it does so in consequence of another group member ceasing to exist.

[*CTA 2009, s 788; FA 2002, Sch 29 paras 63, 64*].

Associated companies leaving group at same time

[48.15] The provisions in **48.14** above do not apply where the transferor and transferee companies are 'associated companies' and leave the group at the same time. Following the decision in *Johnston Publishing (North) Ltd v HMRC* [2008] EWCA Civ 858, [2008] STC 3116, CA, (see **29.1**), *FA 2011* amended the rules for this exception. The provisions in **48.14** above now do not apply if either:

- both companies are 75% subsidiaries and effective 51% subsidiaries of another company on the date of the acquisition and both remain 75% subsidiaries and effective 51% subsidiaries of that other company until immediately after they cease to be members of the group; or
- one of the companies is both a 75% subsidiary and an effective 51% subsidiary of another company on the date of the acquisition and remains a 75% subsidiary and effective 51% subsidiary of that other company until immediately after they cease to be members of the group.

These changes resolve the concerns raised in the *Johnston* case (particularly the arguments raised in front of the Special Commissioner). But they are particularly restrictive in the context of groups of companies and the frequency with which assets are moved around within groups, given the new requirement that the relaitionship between the companies remain largely the same throughout a period starting with the intra-group transfer and ending with the degrouping event.

[*FA 2011, Sch 10, para 3, CTA 2010, ss 780, 783, 788*].

Where the transferee company subsequently leaves another group which has a 'relevant connection' with the first (for which see the corresponding capital gains provisions of *TCGA 1992, s 179* at **29.1 DEGROUPING CHARGES**), **48.14** above applies as if it was the second group of which both companies were members at the time of the transfer. This is subject to **48.18** below where a merger was carried out for genuine commercial reasons.

There is a '*relevant connection*' between two groups if, at the time the transferee leaves the second group, the principal company of that group is under the control of the principal company of the first group (at that time or which was the principal company when the transferee ceased to be a member) or of a person or persons who at present, or at any time since the transferee ceased to be a member of the first group had control of it or such a person who would have had control had the company continued to exist. For this purpose, control is as defined in *ICTA 1988, s 416(2)*, subject to limitations where a bank would be treated as having control.

[*CTA 2009, ss 783–784, 788; FA 2002, Sch 29 para 59*].

Principal company becoming member of another group

[48.16] The provisions in **48.14** above do not apply where a company leaves a group by reason only of the fact that the 'principal company of the group' (see **18.2 CAPITAL GAINS — GROUPS**) joins another group (the 'second group'). If, however, within six years after the transfer to it of the relevant asset, the transferee company at any time ceases to satisfy the condition that it is both a '75% subsidiary' and an 'effective 51% subsidiary' (for both of which again see **18.2 CAPITAL GAINS — GROUPS**) of one or more members of the second group, and at that time the asset is held by either the transferee company or another company in the same group, the following applies. The transferee company is treated for the purposes of the current provisions as if, immediately after the transfer to it of the asset, it had realised and immediately reacquired it at its market value at the time of the transfer. Any resulting adjustments to be made for tax purposes by the transferee company (or by a company to which the relevant asset has subsequently been transferred) in relation to the period between the transfer of the relevant asset to the transferee company and that company ceasing to satisfy the condition referred to above are made by bringing in the aggregate net credit or debit as if it had arisen immediately before the transferee company ceased to satisfy that condition.

To determine how effect is to be given to debits and credits in these circumstances (see **48.7** above), it is the purposes for which the relevant asset was held by the transferee company immediately after the transfer which are considered. However, if it was then held by that company for the purposes of a trade, a property business or a mine or transport undertaking, etc. which ceased before it ceased to satisfy the condition referred to above, any debit or credit is instead treated as a non-trading debit or credit.

These provisions are subject to **48.18** below.

[*CTA 2009, ss 785, 786, 788; FA 2002, Sch 29 para 60*].

Company ceasing to be a member of a group by reason of exempt distribution

[48.17] **48.14** and **48.16** above do not apply where a company ceases to be a member of a group by reason only of an 'exempt distribution' within *ICTA 1988, s 213(2)* (see **31.28 GROUP RELIEF**), unless there is a 'chargeable payment' within *ICTA 1988, s 214(2)* (see **31.32 GROUP RELIEF**) within five years after the making of the exempt distribution. (In this case all necessary adjustments for tax purposes may be made within the three years after the making of the chargeable payment.)

For the purposes of the '75% subsidiary' test in **31.30 GROUP RELIEF**, a company is not treated as owning any share capital in a company if a profit on sale of the shares would be treated as a trading receipt, by the company itself if it owns them directly or, if it owns them indirectly, by the company which owns them directly.

[*CTA 2009, ss 787, 788; FA 2002, Sch 29 para 61*].

Merger carried out for bona fide commercial reasons

[48.18] The provisions in **48.14–48.17** above do not apply where the transferee company leaves the group as part of a 'merger' carried out for *bona fide* commercial reasons and not having avoidance of liability to tax as a main purpose. '*Merger*' is specially defined for this purpose in *CTA 2009, ss 789(2)–(6), 790; FA 2002, Sch 29 para 62(2)–(5)*.

[*CTA 2009, ss 789, 790; FA 2002, Sch 29 para 62*].

Application of relief on reinvestment in relation to degrouping charge

[48.19] The provisions described at **48.9** above apply with the following modifications where, under **48.14** or **48.16** above, the transferee company is treated as having realised (and immediately reacquired) an asset immediately after the transfer by the transferor company.

(a) The requirement for the old asset to be a chargeable intangible asset applies in relation to the transferor company.
(b) The period within which expenditure on the other assets must be incurred applies by reference to the date the transferee company ceased to be a group member (in **48.14** above) or ceased to satisfy the requisite condition (in **48.16** above) rather than the date of realisation of the asset.
(c) References to the proceeds of realisation of the old asset are read as referring to the amount (market value) for which the transferee is treated as having realised it.

Any reduction of the deemed realisation proceeds as a result of a claim to reinvestment relief does not, however, affect the deemed cost of reacquisition by the transferee company.

[*CTA 2009, s 791; FA 2002, Sch 29 para 65*].

Reallocation of degrouping charge within group

[48.20] Where, by virtue of the provisions in **48.14** or **48.16** above, a realisation gain giving rise to a charge under **48.8** above accrues to a company ('company X'), the gain (or any part of it) may be treated as accruing to any other company ('company Y') which, at the 'relevant time', is a member of the 'relevant group', if both companies jointly so elect, provided that, at the 'relevant time', company Y:

(a) is either UK-resident or carrying on a UK trade through a UK permanent establishment (see **65.6 RESIDENCE**) in respect of the profits or gains of which it is not exempt from corporation tax under double tax arrangements; and

(b) is not either an incorporated friendly society within *ICTA 1988, s 461A* (see **37.3 FRIENDLY SOCIETIES**) or a dual-resident investing company within *ICTA 1988, s 404; CTA 2009, Sch 1 para 122* (see **39.23 GROUP RELIEF**).

The gain (or part) is then treated as a non-trading credit (see **48.7** above) accruing to company Y at the 'relevant time' (and as so accruing in respect of an asset held for the purposes of a UK permanent establishment (or branch or agency) where it is not UK-resident).

The '*relevant time*' is immediately before company X ceased to be a group member (in **48.14** above) or ceased to satisfy the requisite condition (in **48.16** above), and the '*relevant group*' is the group of which it ceased to be a member (in **48.14** above) or the second group (in **48.16** above).

The election must be made by written notice to HMRC within two years after the end of the accounting period (of company X) in which the relevant time falls.

Where such an election has been made, company Y may claim relief on reinvestment (see **48.9** above) as if the deemed realisation had been made by company Y and not company X, the conditions as regards the old asset being treated as met if they would have been had there been no election and had the claim had been made by company X. The proceeds of realisation and the cost of the old asset are similarly what they would have been on a claim by company X. Where the election relates to only part of the gain on the deemed realisation, relief may be claimed as if a corresponding part of the asset had been the subject a separate deemed realisation, with any necessary apportionments being made accordingly.

[*CTA 2009, ss 792–794; FA 2002, Sch 29 paras 66, 67*].

Recovery of degrouping charge from another group company or controlling director

[48.21] Where a degrouping charge falls to be brought into account on a company for an accounting period under **48.14** or **48.16** above, or following an election under **48.20** above, and corporation tax assessed on the company for that period remains unpaid six months after the due date, provision is made for recovery from the following persons of the amount referable to the degrouping charge (or the outstanding tax if less).

(a) If the defaulting company was a member of a group at the 'relevant time', a company which was at that time the principal company of the group and any other company which at any time in the period of twelve months ending with the 'relevant time' was a member of that group and owned the asset or part of it in respect of which the degrouping charge arose (or any part of it).
(b) If at the 'relevant time' the defaulting company is non-UK resident but carries on a UK trade through a permanent establishment (see **65.6 RESIDENCE**), any person who is, or during the period of twelve months

ending with the 'relevant time' was, a 'director' (as widely defined) having 'control' (within *ICTA 1988, s 416*) of the defaulting company or of a company that has, or within that period had, control of the defaulting company.

Somewhat wider definitions of 'group' and 'principal company' apply for these purposes (by reference to 51% subsidiaries rather than 75% subsidiaries). The '*relevant time*' is when the defaulting company ceased to be a group member (in **48.14** above) or ceased to satisfy the requisite condition (in **48.16** above), or whichever of those times would have applied had there been no election (in **48.20** above).

An HMRC notice requiring payment from another person as above (within 30 days from the date of the notice) has effect (as regards recovery, interest and appeals) as if it were a notice of assessment. It must be served within three years after the date of final determination (for which see *FA 2002, Sch 29 para 70(2)–(4)*) of the corporation tax liability of the defaulting company for the accounting period for which the degrouping charge fell to be brought into account. The company paying the tax may recover it from the defaulting company, but the payment is not an allowable deduction for tax purposes.

[*CAA 2009, ss 795–798; FA 2002, Sch 29 paras 68–70*].

Intra-group payments in respect of reliefs

[48.22] A payment either for group rollover relief (see **48.12**, **48.13** above) or for the reallocation of a degrouping charge (see **48.20** above) is not taken into account for corporation tax purposes as regards the payer or the payee provided that it does not exceed the amount of the relief.

A payment for group rollover relief means a payment made in connection with a claim for relief under **48.9** above by virtue of the provisions in **48.12** or **48.13** above, by the company whose proceeds of realisation are reduced as a result of that claim, to a company whose acquisition costs are thereby reduced (in **48.12** above), or the tax written-down value of whose assets is thereby reduced (in **48.13** above), under an agreement between the companies. The amount of the relief in such a case is the amount of the reduction as a result of the claim in the acquisition costs, or the tax written-down value of the assets, as the case may be, of the company to which the payment is made.

A payment for the reallocation of a degrouping charge means a payment made in connection with an election under the provisions in **48.20** above, by the company to which the chargeable realisation gain accrues to the company to which, as a result of the election, the whole or part of that gain is treated as accruing, under an agreement between the companies. The amount of the relief in such a case is the amount treated as a result of the election as accruing to the company to which the payment is made.

[*CTA 2009, s 799; FA 2002, Sch 29 para 71*].

Transfer of business or trade

Company reconstruction involving transfer of business

[48.23] Where a scheme for the reconstruction of any company or companies within *TCGA 1992, s 136*:

(a) involves the transfer of the whole or part of the business of one company to another, and
(b) the transferor company receives no part of the consideration for the transfer (otherwise than by the transferee company taking over liabilities of the business),

the following provisions apply. This is, however, conditional on the reconstruction being effected for genuine commercial reasons and not as part of a scheme or arrangements a main purpose of which is avoidance of liability to income tax, corporation tax or capital gains tax (although advance clearance may be obtained that this condition is met, see **48.27** below).

If:

(i) the assets transferred include intangible fixed assets which are chargeable intangible assets (see **48.9** above) in relation to the transferor company immediately before the transfer, and
(ii) in relation to the transferee company immediately thereafter,

the transfer of those assets is treated for the purposes of the current provisions as tax-neutral (see **48.9** above). This does not, however, apply where the transfer is within a group or either company is an incorporated friendly society within *ICTA 1988, s 461A* (see **37.3 FRIENDLY SOCIETIES**) or a dual-resident investing company within *ICTA 1988, s 404* (see **39.23 GROUP RELIEF**).

See **48.11** above for the interaction between these provisions and those dealing with transfers within a group.

[*CTA 2009, s 818; FA 2002, Sch 29 para 84*].

Companies resident in different EU member states

[48.24] Special provisions apply where an '*EU company*' (i.e. a body incorporated under the law of a member state) resident in one member state transfers the whole or part of a business (trade before 1 January 2007) carried on in the UK to an EU company resident in another member state in exchange for securities (including shares) in the latter company, and both companies make a claim.

The provisions also apply where an EU company transfers on or after 1 January 2007 part of a business to one or more EU companies and the following conditions apply. Where the business transferred is carried on in the UK, at least one transferee must be resident in a member state other than that in which the transferor is resident, and the transferor must remain in business after the transfer. A claim must be made by all parties and either the transfer must be made in exchange for an issue of shares or debentures of the transferees to the holders of shares and debentures in the transferor, or the only reason that this is not done is a legal prohibition on purchase of own shares.

The application of the provisions is, however, conditional on the reconstruction or amalgamation being effected for genuine commercial reasons and not as part of a scheme or arrangements a main purpose of which is avoidance of liability to income tax, corporation tax or capital gains tax (although advance clearance may be obtained that this condition is met, see **48.27** below).

A company is regarded for these purposes as '*resident in a member state*' under the laws of which it is chargeable to tax because it is regarded as so resident (unless it is regarded under double tax arrangements entered into by the member state as resident in a territory not within any of the member states).

Where such a claim is made, if the transfer includes intangible fixed assets which are chargeable intangible assets (see **48.9** above) in relation to the transferor company immediately before the transfer and in relation to the transferee company immediately thereafter, the transfer of those assets is treated for the purposes of the current provisions as tax-neutral (see **48.9** above).

These provisions do not apply if the transferor is a 'transparent entity'. [*CTA 2009, ss 819, 820, Sch 2 para 102; FA 2002, Sch 29 para 85; SI 2007 No 3186, Sch 1 para 21; SI 2008 No 1579, para 11*].

Transparent entities

Special provisions apply where one of the parties is a 'transparent entity'. [*ICTA 1988, ss 807F, 807G; CTA 2009, Sch 1 paras 260, 261; FA 2002, Sch 29 para 85B*].

A '*transparent entity*' for this purpose is an entity which is resident in a member state other than the UK and does not have an ordinary share capital. [*CTA 2009, 820(4); FA 2002, Sch 29 para 85D(1); SI 2007 No 3186, Sch 3 para 5*].

European cross-border mergers

[48.25] The following provisions were originally introduced to facilitate the tax-neutral formation of SEs (see **34.5 EUROPEAN COMMUNITY LEGISLATION**) by merger, but have since been extended to apply also to the formation of European co-operative societies (SCEs) by merger and other mergers of companies resident in different EU member states. Accordingly, the provisions apply to:

(a) the formation of an SE on or after 1 April 2005 by the merger of two or more companies in accordance with *Council Regulation (EC) No 2157/2001, Arts 2(1), 17(2)*;
(b) the formation of an SCE on or after 18 August 2006 by the merger of two or more 'co-operative societies', at least one of which is a society registered under *Industrial and Provident Societies Act 1965*, in accordance with *Council Regulation (EC) No 1435/2003*;
(c) a merger on or after 1 January 2007 effected by the transfer by one or more companies or co-operative societies of all their assets and liabilities to a single existing company or co-operative society; and

(d) a merger on or after 1 January 2007 effected by the transfer by two or more companies of all their assets to a single new company (which is not an SE or SCE) in exchange for the issue by the transferee company of shares or debentures to each person holding shares in or debentures of a transferee company.

Each merging company must be resident in a member state, and not all in the same member state. In the cases of (a), (b) and (c) above either the transfer taking place as part of the merger is in exchange for the issue of shares or debentures by the transferee to each person holding shares in or debentures of a transferor or the only reason this condition is not fulfilled is that purchase of own shares is prohibited by law. In the cases of (c) and (d) it is required that, in the course of the merger, each transferor ceases to exist without being put into liquidation. Where the requisite conditions are fulfilled, the transfer of qualifying assets in the course of a merger is tax-neutral.

For the purposes of (b) and (c) above, a '*co-operative society*' is a society registered under the *Industrial and Provident Societies Act 1965* or a similar society established under the law of a member state other than the UK.

A company is resident in a member state for this purpose if it is within a charge to tax under the law of the state as being resident for that purpose and it is not regarded, for the purposes of any **DOUBLE TAX RELIEF (32)** arrangements to which the state is a party, as resident in a territory not within a member state.

The assets must be chargeable intangible assets (see **48.9** above) both in the hands of the transferor immediately before the transfer and in the hands of the transferee immediately afterwards.

These provisions do not apply unless the merger is for genuine commercial reasons and is not part of a scheme or arrangements of which the main purpose or one of the main purposes is avoiding liability to tax. Advance clearance can be obtained that this condition is met (see **48.27** below).

These provisions do not apply if one or more of the parties is a transparent entity and the assets and liabilities of a transparent entity are transferred to another company as a result of the merger.

[*CTA 2009, ss 821–823; FA 2002, Sch 29 para 85A; F(No 2)A 2005, s 52; SI 2007 No 3186, Sch 2 para 11; SI 2008 No 1579, para 17*].

Transfer of non-UK trade.

(A) Where:
   (i) in the course of the merger a company or co-operative society resident in the UK (company A) transfers to a company or co-operative society resident in another member state all the assets and liabilities relating to a business carried on by company A in a member state other than the UK through a permanent establishment; and
   (ii) the transfer includes intangible fixed assets:
      (I) which are chargeable intangible assets (see **48.9** above) in relation to the company A immediately before the transfer; and

(II) in the case of one or more of which the proceeds of realisation exceed the cost recognised for tax purposes; **or**

(B) where a UK resident company transfers part of a business (carried on in a member state other than the UK through a permanent establishment immediately before the transfer) to one or more companies and at least one transferee is resident in a member state other than the UK, the transferor continues to carry on a business after the merger; and

(C) no claim is made under the provisions at **48.26** below in relation to those assets; and

(D) where the merger is within (b) or (c) above, or is within (a) above and takes place on or after 18 August 2006, the transfer of assets and liabilities is made in exchange for the issue of shares in or debentures of the transferee to the holders of shares in or debentures of a transferor, except where, and to the extent that, the transferee is prevented from meeting this requirement by reason only of *Companies Act 2006, s 658* (rule against limited company acquiring its own shares) or a corresponding provision in another member state,

then, if tax would have been chargeable under the law of the other member state in respect of the transfer of those assets but for the Mergers Directive (*90/434/EEC*), double tax relief (whether unilateral or by agreement) is available as if the amount of tax which would have been so payable but for the Directive were payable.

These provisions do not apply unless the merger is for genuine commercial reasons and is not part of a scheme or arrangements of which the main purpose or one of the main purposes is avoiding liability to tax. Advance clearance can be obtained that this condition is met (see **48.27** below).

[*CTA 2009, ss 821–825; FA 2002, Sch 29 para 87A; F(No 2)A 2005, s 53; SI 2007 No 3186, Sch 2 para 12; SI 2008 No 1579, para 12*].

Transparent entities. Special provisions apply where one of the parties is a 'transparent entity'. See *FA 2002, Sch 29 para 85C.*

A '*transparent entity*' for this purpose is an entity which is resident in a member state other than the UK and is listed as a company in the Annex to the Mergers Directive, but which does not have an ordinary share capital and, if resident in the UK, would not be capable of being registered as a company under *Companies Act 2006*. [*FA 2002, Sch 29 para 85D(1); SI 2007 No 3186, Sch 3 para 5*].

Claims to postpone charge on transfer of assets to non-resident company

[48.26] Special provisions apply where a UK-resident company carrying on a non-UK trade through a permanent establishment (see **65.6 RESIDENCE**) transfers the whole or part of that trade together with its assets, or its assets other than cash, to a non-UK resident company in exchange, wholly or partly, for shares (or shares and loan stock) in that company, so that thereafter it holds one-quarter or more of the transferee company's ordinary share capital. This is, however, conditional on the transfer being effected for genuine commercial reasons and not as part of a scheme or arrangements a main purpose of which is avoidance of liability to income tax, corporation tax or capital gains tax (although advance clearance may be obtained that this condition is met, see **48.27** below). For this purpose, transfers within a group are ignored.

If such a transfer includes intangible fixed assets which are chargeable intangible assets (see **48.9** above) in relation to the transferor company immediately before the transfer ('*relevant assets*'), that company may claim as follows.

(a) If the proceeds of realisation of a relevant asset exceed the cost recognised for tax purposes, they are treated as reduced by the excess or, if the securities are not the whole of the consideration for the transfer, by a proportion of the excess corresponding to the proportion that the market value of the securities at the time of the transfer bears to the market value of the whole of the consideration at that time.

(b) If at any time after the transfer the transferor company realises the whole of the securities held by it immediately before that time, it must bring into account for tax purposes a credit equal to the aggregate of the amounts by which proceeds of realisation were reduced under (a) above (so far as not already recovered under this provision or (c) below). If it realises part only of the securities, this applies to a proportion of that aggregate corresponding to the proportion that the market value of the part of the securities disposed of bears to the market value of the securities held immediately before the disposal. Disposals within *TCGA 1992, s 171* (no gain, no loss disposals, see **18.6 CAPITAL GAINS — GROUPS**) are disregarded for this purpose, but the first subsequent disposal of the securities not so disregarded is then treated as a disposal by the transferor company.

(c) If at any time within six years after the transfer the transferee company realises all of the relevant assets held by it immediately before that time, the transferor company must bring into account for tax purposes a credit equal to the aggregate of the amounts by which proceeds of realisation were reduced under (a) above (so far as not already recovered under (b) above or under this provision). If only part of the relevant assets so held is disposed of at that time, the credit is reduced to the proportion applicable to the relevant assets disposed of. Intra-group disposals are disregarded for this purpose, but the first subsequent disposal of the relevant assets not so disregarded is then treated as a disposal by the transferee company.

[*CTA 2009, ss 827–830; FA 2002, Sch 29 para 86*].

Clearance

[48.27] Application may be made for clearance that the transactions in **48.23** above (reconstruction, transfer or merger) are genuine commercial transactions and not for tax avoidance purposes. The condition is treated as satisfied if, prior to the transaction taking place, the company has applied to HMRC and received clearance. The applicant must be, in the case of transactions within **48.22** or **48.23** above, the transferee, and within **48.24** and **48.25**, the transferor. The provisions are similar to those in *TCGA 1992, s 138* (see **17.13 CAPITAL GAINS** and Tolley's Capital Gains Tax under Anti-Avoidance). [*FA 2002, Sch 29 para 88; F(No 2)A 2005, s 59(5); SI 2007 No 3186, Sch 2 para 13*].

A clearance application must be made in writing and details of the transactions must be given. HMRC may request further information by notice issued within 30 days of receipt of the application or of receiving information previously requested. If the company does not provide information within 30 days, HMRC need not proceed with the application.

HMRC must give their decision within 30 days of receiving the application or 30 days of receiving information requested in a notice. The applicant has a right of appeal to the tribunal if clearance is refused or HMRC do not meet the 30 day time limit. The tribunal's decision on clearance is treated as a decision by HMRC under these provisions. Where the information provided by the applicant is not full and accurate, and clearance is granted, it is void.

Applications for clearance should be addressed to Clearance and Counteraction Team, Anti-Avoidance Group, First Floor, 22 Kingsway, London WC2B 6NR (or, if market-sensitive information is included, to the Team Leader at that address). Applications may be faxed to 020–7438 4409 or emailed to reconstructions@hmrc.gsi.gov.uk (after advising the Team Leader (on 020–7438 6585) if market-sensitive information is included). Application may be made in a single letter to the same address for other clearances. [*CTA 2009, ss 831–833*].

Transfer of business of building society to company

[48.28] Provisions equivalent to those relating to capital gains in *TCGA 1992, s 216* (see **9.4 BUILDING SOCIETIES**) apply in relation to the current provisions to treat the transfer of chargeable intangible assets as tax-neutral (see **48.9** above). [*CAA 2009, ss 824, 825; FA 2002, Sch 29 para 90*].

Amalgamation of, or transfer of engagements by, certain societies and associations

[48.29] Provisions equivalent to those relating to capital gains in *TCGA 1992, s 215* (see **9.2 BUILDING SOCIETIES**) and *CTA 2010, s 1057; ICTA 1988, s 486(8)(9)* (see **47.4, 47.5 INDUSTRIAL AND PROVIDENT SOCIETIES**) apply in relation to the current provisions to treat the transfer of chargeable intangible assets as tax-neutral (see **48.9** above) on the amalgamation of, or transfer of engagements by, building societies, industrial and provident societies and co-operative associations. [*CAA 2009, s 826; FA 2002, Sch 29 para 91*].

Transactions between related parties

[48.30] A person ('B') is a '*related party*' in relation to a company ('A') in the following circumstances.

(a) B is a company, and either A controls or has a major interest in C or *vice versa*.

(b) B is a company and B and A are both under the control of the same person (other than the Crown or certain governmental or international institutions).

(c) A is a close company (see **22 CLOSE COMPANIES**) and B is a 'participator' (or an 'associate' of a 'participator') in A or, in relation to transfers or accounting periods beginning on or after 16 March 2005 (see below), a 'participator' in a company that controls, or has a major interest in, C. ('*Associate*' and '*participator*' are as defined at **22.7**, **22.9 CLOSE COMPANIES**) except that for these purposes 'participator' excludes certain loan creditors.)

(d) P is a company and C is another company in the same group (see **48.10** above).

For determining whether a party is related to a company on or after 12 March 2008, where they would be related under the above rules but for one party (other than an individual) being the subject of 'insolvency arrangements' or equivalent, they are treated as related for the purposes of debits and credits to be brought into account. An accounting period straddling 12 March 2008 is split into two separate accounting periods for this purpose. [*FA 2008, s 65*].

For these purposes:

(i) '*control*' in relation to a company is the power of a person to secure that the company's affairs are conducted in accordance with their wishes, either through shareholding or voting power (in or in relation to any company) or through powers conferred by the articles of association or other regulatory document of any company;

(ii) a person has a '*major interest*' in a company if it and any other person together control the company, with each of them having at least 40% of the rights and powers by means of which they have such control;

(iii) insolvency arrangements include arrangements under which a liquidator, provisional liquidator, receiver, administrator or administrative receiver of a company or partnership act.

'*Connected persons*' are specially defined in *CTA 2009, ss 842–843; FA 2002, Sch 29 para 101*, broadly as under *ICTA 1988, s 839* (see **25 CONNECTED PERSONS**) but with the omission of the 'partners' and 'persons acting together' provisions at **25.2**.

The rights and powers of a partner are ignored unless the partner has control of or a major interest in the firm. 'Control' is determined as for a company (see (i) above). Rights and powers held, or to be held, jointly are taken into account.

[*CTA 2009, ss 835–841, Sch 2 para 100; FA 2002, Sch 29 paras 95–101; FA 2003, s 184; ITTOIA 2005, Sch 1 para 580; (F(No 2)A 2005, s 41(3)(7)–(9); FA 2008, s 65; CTA 2010, Sch 1 para 657*].

Transfer between company and related party

[48.31] Where an intangible asset is transferred by a company to a related party or *vice versa* and the asset is a chargeable intangible asset (see **48.9** above) in relation to the transferor immediately before the transfer or in relation to the transferee immediately thereafter, the transfer of those assets is treated for all tax purposes, as regards both transferor and transferee, as being at market value, *except* in any of the following circumstances.

(a) The transfer pricing provisions of *CTA 2010, ss 146–259; ICTA 1988, Sch 28AA* (see **72 TRANSFER PRICING**) apply (whether or not the consideration for the transfer falls to be adjusted under that *Schedule*).

(b) The transfer is, under any of the current provisions, tax-neutral (see **48.9** above).

(c) **In relation to transfers on or after 16 March 2005**, an asset is transferred from the company to a related party at less than market value or to the company by the related party at more than its market value and:
   - the related party is not a company, or is a company in relation to which the asset is not an intangible asset falling within these provisions; and
   - the transfer results in an amount being taken into account (or to an amount which would be taken into account but for the market value rule) in computing any person's taxable income, profits or losses by virtue of *ICTA 1988, s 209* (see **31 DISTRIBUTIONS**) or *ITEPA 2003, Pt 3* (see Tolley's Income Tax under Employment Income). In this case, the market value rule above does not apply for the purposes of those provisions.

(d) In relation to transfers on or after 16 March 2005, the asset is transferred to the company by a related party who makes a claim for hold-over relief on gifts for business assets under *TCGA 1992, s 165* (see Tolley's Capital Gains Tax under Hold-Over Reliefs). In this case, the transfer is treated as being at market value less the amount of the held-over gain and any necessary adjustments may be made to the company's tax position as a result of the claim.

As regards (a) above, the consideration falls within the transfer pricing provisions without falling to be adjusted in a case where the conditions in *CTA 2010, s 148(2), Sch 28AA para 1(1)* as amended by *CTA 2009, Sch 1 para 291* are met (see **72.2**(a)(b) **TRANSFER PRICING**) but the actual and arm's length provisions do not differ.

As regards (c) above, an example is given by the Explanatory Notes to the Finance (No 3) Bill 2005 of a controlling shareholder transferring an intangible asset to the company for £10,000 when the asset is worth only £1,000 where the market value rule does not prevent the shareholder from being taxed on a distribution representing the consideration received for the asset in excess of its value.

[*CTA 2009, ss 844–849; FA 2002, Sch 29 para 92; FA 2004, s 37(2), Sch 5 para 16(3); F(No 2)A 2005, s 41(2)(6)*].

Reinvestment relief in case of part realisation involving related party

[48.32] Reinvestment relief (see **48.9** above) does not apply in relation to the part realisation of an intangible fixed asset by a company if, as a result of or in connection with the part realisation, a related party acquires an interest of any description in the asset or in another asset deriving all or part of its value from that asset.

[*CTA 2009, s 850; FA 2002, Sch 29 para 93*].

Delayed payment of royalty to related party

[48.33] Where a royalty (see **48.4** above) payable by a company to or for the benefit of a related party is not paid in full by twelve months after the end of the period of account in which a debit in respect of it is recognised by the company for accounting purposes (see **48.5** above), and credits representing the full amount of the royalty are not brought into account under the current provisions (see **48.6** above) in any accounting period by the person to whom it is payable, the royalty is brought into account under the current provisions only when it is paid.

[*CTA 2009, s 851; FA 2002, Sch 29 para 94*].

Supplementary provisions

Research and development

[48.34] With effect for accounting periods beginning on or after 1 January 2005, where a deduction is allowed for revenue expenditure on research and development (see **64 RESEARCH AND DEVELOPMENT EXPENDITURE**), which is brought into account in determining the value of an intangible asset, no deduction for tax purposes will be allowed in respect of the writing down of so much of the value of the intangible asset as is attributable to that expenditure.

[*CTA 2009, s 1308(4)(5); FA 2004, s 53; SI 2004 No 3268*].

Treatment of grants etc.

Where a grant or other payment is intended by the payer to meet, directly or indirectly, a company's expenditure on an intangible fixed asset, any gain recognised in determining the company's profit or loss in respect of the grant etc. is treated as representing a receipt in respect of the asset (and hence as within **48.6** above). This does not, however, apply to grants under *Industrial Development Act 1982, Pt 2* or corresponding NI grants, any profit and loss account gain in respect of which is disregarded for the purposes of the current provisions. Where the bringing of such an exempt grant into account by a company results in a reduction in the amount of a loss recognised in determining the profit or loss, or in the amount of expenditure on an intangible fixed asset capitalised for accounting purposes, the amount of the reduction is added back for the purposes of the current provisions.

[*CTA 2009, ss 852, 853; FA 2002, Sch 29 paras 102, 103; FA 2005, Sch 4 para 40*].

Finance leasing etc.

The Treasury has wide regulatory powers to make provision for the application of the current provisions in relation to a company which is a finance lessor of an intangible asset which is the subject of a finance lease. The term 'finance lease' has the meaning for this purpose that it has for accounting purposes, including hire-purchase, conditional sale and other like arrangements, and 'finance lessor' and 'finance lessee' have a corresponding meaning.

[*CTA 2009, ss 854, 855; FA 2002, Sch 29 para 104*]. For the initial regulations under this provision, see *SI 2002 No 1967*.

Assets acquired or realised together

Assets acquired of or disposed of in a single bargain are treated as acquired or disposed of together, notwithstanding any separate pricing or separate acquisitions or disposals. Where assets are acquired together, values allocated in accordance with generally accepted accounting practice (see **48.2** above) to particular assets are accepted for the purposes of the current provisions, and in the absence of such allocation a just and reasonable apportionment is made. Where assets are disposed of together, a just and reasonable apportionment of the disposal proceeds is made.

[*CAA 2009, s 856; FA 2002, Sch 29 para 105*].

Deemed market value acquisition — adjustment of amounts in case of nil accounting value.

Where a company is treated under the current provisions as acquiring an asset at market value, but the accounting value of the asset transferred, in the hands of the transferee, is nil, then:

(a) the cost of the asset recognised for accounting purposes;
(b) the accounting value of the asset; and
(c) the amount of any loss recognised for accounting purposes in respect of capitalised expenditure on the asset,

are all taken to be such as would have been recognised had the asset been acquired at market value. Any revaluation of the asset (see **48.6** above) is disregarded.

[*CTA 2009, s 857; FA 2002, Sch 29 para 106*].

Fungible assets

Assets of a nature to be dealt in without identifying the particular assets involved, and which are of the same kind and held by the same person in the same capacity (e.g. milk quotas), are treated for the purposes of the current provisions as indistinguishable parts of a single asset which grows or diminishes as assets of the same kind are added or realised.

[*CTA 2009, s 858; FA 2002, Sch 29 para 107*].

See also **48.36** below for transitional rules.

Assets ceasing to be chargeable intangible assets

Where an asset ceases to be a chargeable intangible asset in relation to a company (see **48.9** above) either:

(a) on the company's ceasing to be UK-resident; or
(b) on the asset beginning to be held for the purposes of a mutual trade or business; or
(c) (in the case of a non-UK resident company) in any circumstances not involving the realisation of the asset by the company,

the current provisions have effect as if the company had, immediately before the triggering event, realised and immediately reacquired the asset at its market value at that time. An election may be made for a gain arising by virtue of (a) above to be postponed in certain cases where the asset concerned is held for the purposes of a non-UK trade carried on through a permanent establishment (see **65.6 RESIDENCE**).

[*CTA 2009, ss 859–862; FA 2002, Sch 29 paras 108, 109*].

Asset becoming chargeable intangible asset

Where an asset becomes a chargeable intangible asset in relation to a company (see **48.9** above) either:

(a) on the company's becoming UK-resident; or
(b) on the asset ceasing to be held for the purposes of a mutual trade or business; or
(c) (in the case of a non-UK resident company) on its beginning to be held for the purposes of a trade carried on in the UK through a permanent establishment (see **65.6 RESIDENCE**),

the current provisions have effect as if the company had, immediately after the triggering event, acquired the asset at its book value at that time.

[*CTA 2009, s 863; FA 2002, Sch 29 paras 110, 135*].

Tax avoidance

Arrangements (as widely defined) a main object of which are to enable a company to obtain a debit (or a greater debit) under **48.5** above or to avoid (or reduce) a credit under **48.8** above are disregarded in determining such debits and credits.

[*CTA 2009, s 864; FA 2002, Sch 29 para 111; FA 2003, s 184*].

Expenditure not generally tax-deductible

No debit may be brought in under the current provisions (see **48.5** above) in respect of expenditure which would not be an allowable trade deduction under:

(a) *ICTA 1988, s 577* (business entertainment or gifts);
(b) *ICTA 1988, s 577A* (crime-related expenditure);
(c) *ICTA 1988, s 578A* (expensive hired cars or motorcycles); or

(d) *FA 1989, s 76(1)–(3)* (certain retirement benefits).

[*CTA 2009, s 865; FA 2002, Sch 29 para 112*].

Delayed payment of pension contributions

Where a company includes in its accounts a debit in respect of pension contributions, but they are not paid until after the end of the period in which the debit is recognised, the contributions are brought into account only when paid. Any necessary allocations must be made on a just and reasonable basis.

[*CTA 2009, s 868*].

Delayed payment of employees' remuneration

Where a debit in respect of employees' remuneration is recognised by a company for accounting purposes but the remuneration is not treated as received as employment income within nine months after the end of the period of account in which the debit is recognised, the remuneration is brought into account under the current provisions (see **48.5** above) only when it is paid.

This applies equally to '*potential remuneration*', i.e. amounts reserved in the employer's accounts with a view to it becoming remuneration, which is regarded as received when it becomes remuneration so treated as above. Any necessary apportionment for these purposes is made on a just and reasonable basis.

If a tax calculation has to be made before the nine months has expired and when remuneration (as above) has not been paid, it is to be assumed that it will not be paid before the end of the nine-month period. If it is subsequently paid before the end of that period, and a claim was made to HMRC within two years after the end of the period of account concerned, the calculation may be adjusted. A change, effective for accounting periods ending after 31 March 2009, removes the requirement to make a claim. Instead the corporation tax return is amended. Remuneration is treated as paid when it is treated as received by the employee under *ITEPA 2003*, or would be so treated if it were not exempt income.

[*CTA 2009, ss 886, 887, Change 68 in Annex 4 to CTA 2009; FA 2002, Sch 29 paras 113, 114; FA 2003, Sch 24 para 10(2); FA 2004, Sch 17 para 8*].

Bad debts etc.

For the purposes of the current provisions, no debit may be brought into account in respect of a debt (monetary or otherwise) except by way of impairment loss or to the extent the debt is released as part of a statutory insolvency arrangement. Any gain brought into account for accounting purposes by the debtor in respect of a release as part of a statutory insolvency arrangement is disregarded. Otherwise, any gain relating to an unpaid debt in respect of an intangible fixed asset which is brought into account for accounting purposes by the debtor is treated as regards credits in respect of receipts recognised as they accrue (see **48.8** above) as a gain in respect of the asset. Any necessary apportionment for these purposes is made on a just and reasonable basis. [*CTA 2009, s 869; FA 2002, Sch 29 para 115; FA 2005, s 80, Sch 4 para 20*].

Controlled foreign companies ('CFCs')

In computing the chargeable profits of a CFC (see **27.9 CONTROLLED FOREIGN COMPANIES**), the following assumptions are made in applying the current provisions.

(a) Subject to the commencement rules for the current provisions (see **48.36** below), any intangible fixed asset acquired or created by the company before the first accounting period for which an apportionment has been made under the CFC provisions, or which is an ADP exempt period (see **27.9**(i) **CONTROLLED FOREIGN COMPANIES** for a definition) under those provisions, is assumed to have been acquired or created by the company at the beginning of that accounting period at a cost equal to its value for accounting purposes at that time.

(b) It is assumed that the company has not claimed any reinvestment relief or made any provisional declaration of entitlement to such relief (see **48.9** above), notwithstanding the general assumption referred to in **27.9**(iv), although notice may be given as described in **27.9**(iv) modifying or disapplying this assumption.

[*CTA 2009, s 870; FA 2002, Sch 29 para 116*].

Change of accounting policy

[48.35] Where there is a change in accounting policy in preparing a company's accounts from one period of account to the next in accordance with the law and practice applicable in relation to those periods, then if there is any accounting difference between the closing accounting value of the assets concerned in the earlier period and their opening value in the later period, a corresponding debit or credit (as the case may be) is to be taken into account for tax purposes in the later period. This applies in particular where a company prepares its accounts for one period in accordance with UK generally accepted accounting practice and for the next period in accordance with international accounting standards, or vice versa.

Change of value

Where, as a result of the change of accounting policy, there is a difference between the closing accounting value of an intangible fixed asset in the earlier period and its opening accounting value in the later period, the amount of the debit or credit to be brought into account (subject to the cap as noted below) is the proportion of the accounting difference that the tax written down value of the asset at the end of the earlier period bears to the accounting value at that time.

The tax written down value of the asset at the beginning of the later period is then taken to be the tax written down value at the end of the earlier period as reduced by the debit or increased by the credit (as the case may be). Subsequently, the cost of the asset for tax purposes is the tax written down value (as reduced or increased) together with the cost recognised for tax purposes of any subsequent expenditure that is capitalised for accounting purposes and the tax written down value is to be determined taking account only of subsequent debits and credits.

This does not apply to an intangible fixed asset in respect of which an election for writing down at a fixed-rate has been made (see **48.5** above). Nor does it apply where, in respect of the accounting difference, a debit or credit is brought into account for tax purposes on the reversal of an earlier accounting credit or debit, or in respect of a revaluation gain (see **48.5** and **48.6** above).

Disaggregation

A change of accounting policy may result in an intangible fixed asset that was treated as one asset ('*the original asset*') in the earlier period, being treated as two or more assets ('*the resulting assets*') in the later period. In this case, where, as a result of the change of accounting policy, there is a difference between the closing accounting value of the original asset in the earlier period and the opening accounting value of the resulting assets in the later period, the amount of the debit or credit to be brought into account (subject to the cap noted below) is the proportion of the accounting difference that the tax written down value of the original asset at the end of the earlier period bears to the accounting value of that asset at that time.

The tax written down value of each resulting asset at the beginning of the later period is then taken to be the proportion of the tax written down value of the original asset at the end of the earlier period (as reduced by the debit or increased by the credit as the case may be) that the opening accounting value of that asset in the later period bears to the aggregate opening accounting values of the resulting assets at that time. Subsequently, the cost of each resulting asset for tax purposes is the tax written down value (as above) together with the cost recognised for tax purposes of any subsequent expenditure that is capitalised for accounting purposes and the tax written down value is to be determined taking account only of subsequent debits and credits. However, where a credit is to be taken into account, it must not exceed the excess of debits previously brought into account for tax purposes over previous credits.

This does not apply where an election for writing down at a fixed-rate has been or is subsequently made (see **48.5** above) in respect of the original or resulting assets (see below). Nor does it apply where, in respect of the accounting difference, a debit or credit is brought into account for tax purposes on the reversal of an earlier accounting credit or debit, or in respect of a revaluation gain (see **48.5** and **48.6** above).

Original asset subject to fixed-rate writing down

Where a change in accounting policy results in the disaggregation of assets (as above) and an election for writing down at a fixed-rate (see **48.5** above) has been or is subsequently made in respect of the original asset, the election applies to the original asset for periods up to and including the earlier period, and to the resulting assets for the later and subsequent periods. The tax written down value of each resulting asset at the beginning of the later period is then taken to be the proportion of the tax written down value of the original asset at the end of the earlier period that the opening accounting value of that asset in the later period bears to the aggregate opening accounting values of the resulting assets at that time. Subsequently, the cost of each resulting asset for tax purposes is the tax written down value (as above) together with the cost recognised for tax purposes of any subsequent expenditure that is capitalised for accounting purposes and the tax written down value is to be determined taking account only of subsequent debits and credits.

Resulting assets subject to fixed-rate writing down

Where a change in accounting policy results in the disaggregation of assets (as above) and no election for writing down at a fixed-rate (see **48.5** above) has been made in respect of the original asset, such an election may be made in respect of any of the resulting assets provided it is made within two years after the end of the accounting period in which the original asset was acquired or created.

The effect of the election is that the original asset is treated as consisting of as many assets ('notional original assets') as there are resulting assets, each notional original asset being treated as the same asset as one of the resulting assets (its 'corresponding resulting asset'). An appropriate proportion of every amount falling to be taken into account in relation to the original asset is to be attributed to each notional original asset, the 'appropriate portion' being ascertained by reference to its corresponding resulting asset. The '*appropriate proportion*' in this case is the amount which the opening accounting value of that asset in the later period bears to the aggregate opening accounting values of all the resulting assets at that time. The provisions of this chapter apply to each of the notional original assets and its corresponding resulting asset accordingly.

Cap on credit to be brought into account

Where a change in accounting policy results in a difference between the closing accounting value of the asset (or, in the case of disaggregation, the original asset) in the earlier period and the opening accounting value of the asset (or the resulting assets) in the later period, the amount of any credit to be brought into account for tax purposes is limited to the net aggregate amount of relevant tax debits previously brought into account, this being the total debits previously brought into account in respect of the asset (or, in the case of disaggregation, the original asset at the end of the earlier period) less the total credits previously brought into account in respect of that asset.

Subsequent events

Where there is a further change in accounting policy affecting an asset to which these provisions have already applied, these provisions are to apply again. Where there is a subsequent part realisation affecting an asset to which these provisions have already applied, the provisions of *CTA 2009, s 744; FA 2002, Sch 29 para 29* apply. In this case the tax written-down value of the intangible asset immediately after the subsequent part realisation is found by reducing its written-down value immediately before the subsequent part realisation by the fraction equal to its carrying value (for accounting purposes) immediately after the part realisation divided by that immediately before it. Subsequent allowances are based on that amount.

[*CTA 2009, ss 872–879; FA 2002, Sch 29 paras 116A–116H; FA 2004, s 52, Sch 10 para 72; FA 2005, s 80, Sch 4 para 45*].

Commencement and transitional provisions

[48.36] The commencement date for the purposes of the current provisions was 1 April 2002.

[*CTA 2009, ss 880, 882; FA 2002, Sch 29 para 117*].

Assets created or acquired after commencement

Except as below, the current provisions apply only to intangible fixed assets of a company which are:

(a) created by the company after commencement; or
(b) acquired by the company after commencement other than from a related party (see **48.30** above); or
(c) acquired by the company after commencement from a related party (see **48.30** above) where either:
   (i) the asset is acquired from a company in relation to which the asset was a chargeable intangible asset (see **48.9** above) immediately before the acquisition; or
   (ii) the asset is acquired from an intermediary who acquired the asset after commencement from a third person. Neither the company and the third person nor the intermediary and the third person can be related parties (see **48.30** above) for this to apply; or
   (iii) the asset was created by any person after commencement.

For these purposes (except in the case of certain internally-generated assets, see below) an asset is regarded as acquired or created after commencement to the extent that expenditure on its acquisition or creation is so incurred, and acquisition expenditure is generally treated as incurred when it is recognised for accounting purposes. There are, however, two special cases.

(A) Acquisition expenditure which does not qualify for any form of tax relief against income under the law as it was before 1 April 2002, and which would be treated as incurred after commencement under the general rule, is treated as incurred before commencement if the asset is (or would be) treated as disposed of and acquired before commencement for chargeable gains purposes.
(B) Creation or acquisition expenditure which under law as it was before 1 April 2002 qualifies for any capital allowance is treated as incurred when an unconditional obligation to pay it comes into being (notwithstanding that all or any part of the expenditure may not be required to be paid until a later date).

If only part of the expenditure on an asset is incurred after commencement, the expenditure is treated as being on two separate assets, one within and one outside the current provisions, with any necessary apportionment being made on a just and reasonable basis.

Intangible fixed assets not within (a)–(c) above are referred to as '*pre-FA 2002 assets*'. As regards application of certain of the current provisions to certain pre-*FA 2002* assets, see further below.

[*CAA 2009, ss 880–889; FA 2002, Sch 29 paras 118, 120, 123–125; FA 2006, s 77(6)(7)(10)(11)*].

Royalties

A '*royalty*' is defined as any payment in respect of the enjoyment or exercise of rights that are an intangible fixed asset. The current provisions apply to royalties only where they are recognised for accounting purposes after commencement, and royalties brought into account for tax purposes before commencement are not brought into account again after commencement.

To the extent that royalties would have been brought in before commencement had the current provisions been in force, but were not, they are brought in immediately after commencement. A royalty is brought into account for these purposes if it would have been had the person concerned been within the charge to corporation tax. These rules are not affected by the above rules determining whether assets are within the current provisions.

These rules cannot be interpreted as allowing or requiring an amount to be brought into account in connection with the realisation of an existing asset within **48.8** above. [*CTA 2009, ss 714, 896; FA 2002, Sch 29 paras 118(6), 119, 139; FA 2006, s 77(6)(7)(10)(11)*].

Internally-generated assets

Internally-generated *goodwill* is regarded as created before (and not after) commencement of the current provisions if the business in question was carried on at any time before commencement by the company or a related party (see **48.30** above). Other internally-generated assets representing expenditure which under existing law does not qualify for any capital allowance ('*non-qualifying expenditure*') are regarded as created before (and not after) commencement if the asset in question was held at any time before commencement by the company or a related party (see **48.30** above). If only part of the expenditure on an asset is non-qualifying expenditure, the expenditure is correspondingly treated as being on two separate assets, with any necessary apportionment being made on a just and reasonable basis. [*CTA 2009, ss 884, 885; FA 2002, Sch 29 paras 121, 122*].

Fungible assets

The commencement provisions apply to fungible assets (see **48.34** above) as if pre-*FA 2002* assets (see above) and other intangible fixed assets were assets of different kinds, the single asset consisting of pre-*FA 2002* assets itself being an existing asset and the single asset consisting of other intangible fixed assets being subject to the current provisions. Realisation of an intangible fixed asset which, apart from this special treatment, would form part of a single asset comprising both types of asset are regarded as diminishing the pre-*FA 2002* asset component in priority to the component consisting of assets subject to the current provisions. Intangible fixed assets acquired by a company which would not otherwise be pre-*FA 2002* assets are treated as such to the extent that, under the following rules, they are identified with existing assets realised by the company.

(1) Assets acquired are identified with pre-*FA 2002* assets of the same kind realised by the company within 30 days either side of the acquisition.
(2) Assets realised earlier are identified before assets realised later.
(3) Assets acquired earlier are identified before assets acquired later.

[*CTA 2009, ss 890, 891; FA 2002, Sch 29 para 126*].

Assets acquired on transfer of business

Where a pre-*FA 2002* asset (see above) in the hands of a company is transferred to another company, and the transfer is one to which *TCGA 1992, s 139* (company reconstruction or amalgamation), *TCGA 1992, s 140A* (transfer of UK business (trade before 1 January 2007) to company resident in another member state) or *TCGA 1992, s 140E* (merger leaving assets within UK tax charge) applies (see **17.11, 17.14, 17.27 CAPITAL GAINS**), so that the transferor company is treated as disposing of the asset for a no gain, no loss consideration, the asset is treated as a pre-*FA 2002* asset in the hands of the transferee company. [*FA 2002, Sch 29 para 127; F(No 2)A 2005, s 59(6)*].

Assets treated as pre-FA 2002 assets

Assets whose value derives from pre-FA 2002 assets

This anti-avoidance provision is aimed at the type of scheme which commonly involves the grant of a long-term licence over an intangible asset for a lump sum. Where a company acquires an intangible fixed asset from a related party after the commencement of the intangible fixed assets regime and the asset is created after the commencement of the intangible asset regime, it will be treated as a pre-*FA 2002* asset in the hands of the company (and so excluded from the regime) in so far as its value is derived in whole or in part from another asset which:

- has not at any time after 4 December 2005 been a chargeable intangible asset in the hands of the company or related transferor or another related party of the company or transferor; and
- has been a pre-*FA 2002* asset in the hands of the related transferor or in the hands of another related party of the company or transferor.

The value of an asset is derived from another asset where assets have been merged or divided or have changed their nature, or where rights or interests in or over assets have been created or extinguished. Where only part of the value of the acquired asset is derived from the existing asset, it is treated as a separate existing asset to the extent that its value is so derived, any necessary apportionment being made on a just and reasonable basis.

Assets acquired in connection with disposals of pre-FA 2002 assets

Where a company acquires an intangible fixed asset it will be treated as an existing asset where the acquisition is made directly or indirectly in consequence of or otherwise in connection with a disposal of a pre-*FA 2002* asset by a person who at the time of the disposal is a related party in relation to the company. This provision applies where the asset acquired would otherwise be a chargeable intangible asset in the hands of the company at the time of the acquisition, and a disposal of an existing asset can include a part disposal or any other disposal of the asset (under the capital gain tax rules). It does not matter whether the asset disposed of is the same as the one acquired, whether the acquisition and disposal take place at the same time or whether the acquired asset is acquired by the merging of two or more assets or by any other way. This anti-avoidance provision applies to transactions such as where a company grants a licence out of an existing trademark and claims to have made a part-disposal of the trade mark to which the 'no loss, no gain' rule under *TCGA 1992, s 171* applies while the company to whom the licence was granted claims it is a newly created intangible fixed asset. (Explanatory notes to draft legislation published on 5 December 2005.)

[*CTA 2009, ss 893–895; FA 2002, Sch 29 paras 127A, 127B; FA 2006, s 77(8)(10)(11)*].

Where relief is available under these provisions, the consideration for disposal for capital gains purposes is treated as reduced by the amount qualifying for relief. The purchaser is unaffected by this adjustment for tax purposes. [*TCGA 1992, s 156ZA; CTA 2009, Sch 1 para 372*].

Application of relief on reinvestment in relation to pre-FA 2002 assets

Where a company realises an existing asset after commencement, the rules for relief on reinvestment (see **48.9** above) apply with the necessary modifications. [*CTA 2009, ss 898–900; FA 2002, Sch 29 paras 130, 131*]. For the transitory interaction with capital gains roll-over relief, see *FA 2002, Sch 29 para 132* (as amended by *F(No 2)A 2005, s 41(4)(10)*).

Special provisions

See *CTA 2009, ss 897; FA 2002, Sch 29 paras 128, 129* for special provisions relating to *telecommunications rights* within *FA 2000, Sch 23* (as replaced by *ITTOIA 2005, Pt 2 Ch 10*, see **70.74 TRADE PROFITS — INCOME AND SPECIFIC TRADES**) and *Lloyd's syndicate capacity*.

Key points

[48.37] Points to consider are as follows:

Scope

1. The intangible fixed assets legislation applies, with certain limited exceptions (see **48.4**), to assets which are treated as intangible assets for accounting purposes and which are capitalised in a company's accounts. It is specifically provided that the legislation applies to goodwill and intellectual property (see **48.2**).

2. The legislation only applies to intangible fixed assets which were acquired or created by a company on or after 1 April 2002. Assets that were acquired or created by a company (or a related party) before this date are referred to as pre-*FA 2002* assets and fall outside the legislation, subject to transitional rules that bring expenditure post-31 March 2002 on certain pre-*FA 2002* assets within the legislation (see **48.36**).

3. Anti-avoidance provisions apply to prevent a company from arranging to bring a pre-*FA 2002* asset held by the company, or a person related with the company, within the intangible fixed assets legislation. Profits or losses arising on a disposal of pre-*FA 2002* assets (to the extent that such assets are excluded from the legislation) are normally treated as chargeable gains or allowable losses for the purposes of the *TCGA 1992*.

Relief for expenditure

4. Where an intangible asset is within the intangible fixed assets legislation a company is able to obtain relief for the amortisation which is recognised in its accounts in respect of the intangible fixed asset. Adjustments are made for tax purposes where there is a difference between the expenditure on the asset which is recognised for tax purposes and the amount capitalised in a company's accounts (see **48.5**).

5. As an alternative to claiming relief for an intangible fixed asset on the basis on which it is amortised in a company's accounts, a company may elect to claim relief for the expenditure at the rate of 4% per annum on a straight line basis. This election has to be made within two years of the end of the accounting period in which the asset was created or acquired. The election would be beneficial where expenditure on an asset has been capitalised but the asset is not being written down in the company' accounts, or possibly where an asset is being written down over a period of more than 20 years (this will depend on the rate at which the asset is being written down) (see **48.5**).

6. Where a company does not capitalise expenditure on an intangible fixed asset it is able to obtain relief for expenditure which is charged to profit or loss (e.g. royalties or licence fees for the use of an intangible fixed asset or expenditure that is written off as it is incurred) (see **48.5**).

Non-deductible expenditure

7. No relief may be claimed in respect of expenditure (whether or not it is capitalised) which relates to business entertaining and gifts, crime related expenditure, expensive hired cars or motorcycles or certain retirement benefits — see **48.34** (expenditure not generally deductible).

Revaluations

8. A company is liable to tax on any revaluation gains recognised in its accounts in respect of an intangible fixed asset. The gain which is brought into charge to tax, however, is limited to the amortisation for which the company has claimed tax relief in respect of the asset. A revaluation charge does not arise where a company has elected to write the asset down at 4% per annum on a straight line basis (see **48.6**).

Disposals

9. When an intangible fixed asset is sold a company is liable to tax on the difference between the disposal proceeds of the asset and the tax written down value of the asset. It is possible for a company to elect to roll over

the disposal proceeds against the purchase of a replacement asset (otherwise than from another group company) either by it or by another company in its group (the intangible fixed asset legislation group definition tracks the *TCGA 1992, s 170* group definition) that is within the charge to the intangible fixed assets legislation in respect of the replacement asset. A company, however, may only claim rollover relief to the extent that the disposal proceeds exceed the original tax cost of the asset (as opposed to its tax written down value). This thus means that even where rollover relief is claimed that there will be a clawback of the tax relief which has been claimed in respect of the amortisation of the asset (see **48.9, 48.11** and **48.12**).

10. Where a company in the group acquires a new group member it is possible for an intangible fixed asset gain to be rolled over against the cost of intangible fixed assets held by the new group member where certain conditions are satisfied (see **48.13**).

Intra-group transfers and degrouping charge

11. It is possible for an intangible fixed asset to be transferred between group companies at its tax written down value. The definition of a group for the purposes of the intangible fixed assets legislation tracks the *TCGA 1992, s 170* definition. A degrouping charge applies if the transferee leaves the group within six years of the transfer and in such cases the transferee is deemed to have disposed of and immediately reacquired the intangible fixed asset at its market value at the time of the transfer (see **48.11**).

12. The taxable profit arises in the accounting period in which the transferee company leaves the group. At the same time the transferee company is entitled to claim additional amortisation from the time of the transfer representing the difference between the amortisation for which relief has been claimed and the amount which would have been claimed had the calculations been based on the market value of the asset at the time of the transfer (see **48.14**).

Anti-avoidance

13. An anti-avoidance provision applies where a company enters into arrangements which have as their main object, or one of the main objects, to increase the debits or to reduce the credits which are taken into account under the intangible fixed assets legislation. Where this provision applies the arrangements are disregarded in determining the debits or credits which are brought into account for the purposes of the intangible fixed assets legislation (see **48.34**).

Treatment of debit and credits

14. Where a company is a party to an intangible fixed asset for the purposes of its trade any debits and credits arising in respect of the asset are included in computing its trading profits.

15. Where an intangible fixed asset is held for a property business any debits and credits are treated as expenses and receipts of the business.

49

Interest on Overdue Tax

Cross-reference. See **73.5 VALUE ADDED TAX**.

Introduction

[49.1] Legislation was included in *F(No 3)A 2010* bringing corporation tax into the new harmonised interest regime introduced by the *Finance Act 2009*. The introduction of the regime will be phased in by statutory instrument over a number of years. However, it should be noted the rules for quarterly instalment payments remain unchanged and do not form part of the harmonised rules. These provisions came into force for the purposes of bank payroll tax on 31 August 2010 and will come into force for income tax self-assessment purposes on 31 October 2011. Corporation tax will follow in due course.

Interest is charged on overdue corporation tax by virtue of *TMA 1970, s 87A*. The existing rules with regard to interest have evolved over time and there are various regimes with regard to both interest on overdue tax, and interest on tax overpaid. The *Finance Act 2009* created a harmonised interest regime for all taxes and duties administered by HMRC, initially with the exception of corporation tax and petroleum revenue tax.

As a prelude to the forthcoming changes, *FA 2009, s 103* provided for HMRC to set the rate of interest on tax repayments by statutory instrument. On or after 22 July 2009, interest rates are harmonised across the taxes within the Act.

For details with regard to accounting periods ending before 1 July 1999 please refer to earlier versions of Tolley's Corporation Tax.

Accounting periods ending on or after 1 July 1999

[49.2] In relation to accounting periods ending on or after 1 July 1999 to which self-assessment applies, corporation tax carries interest from the due and payable date (nine months and one day after the end of the accounting period, see **59.2 PAYMENT OF TAX**), even if it is a non-business day, until payment.

Where corporation tax assessed on a company may be assessed on other persons in certain circumstances, the due and payable date is that which refers to the company's liability. An assessment to recover excessive tax credit and interest thereon carries interest from the date of payment of the tax credit.

Interest payable under these provisions is deductible in computing income, profits or losses under the loan relationship rules (see **54.3 LOAN RELATIONSHIPS**).

In the case of interest on tax assessable under *ICTA 1988, Sch 13 (Collection of ACT, repealed for periods beginning after 5 April 1999)* or *Sch 16 (rewritten to ITA 2007, s 945 et seq for periods ending on or after 6 April 2007)*, these provisions apply in relation to return periods which fall within a self-assessment accounting period.

Details of interest rates are set out at **49.5** below.

Interest on tax subsequently discharged is adjusted or repaid so as to secure that the total is as it would have been had the tax discharged never been charged.

Large companies — instalment payments

In the case of certain 'large' companies which are required to make instalment payments in respect of their corporation tax liabilities (see **59.3 PAYMENT OF TAX**), a special rate of interest (see **49.5** below) applies to unpaid instalments until nine months after the end of the accounting period. This is calculated as base rate plus 1%. After this date the normal rate of interest applicable to overdue corporation tax applies, until the tax is paid.

Return to be filed

Interest is not calculated until a return is made or some other charge to tax arises. (HMRC Pamphlet 'A Guide to Corporation Tax Self Assessment' para 5.4.4).

In the case of quarterly instalment payments, interest (and penalties) is only calculated after the company has filed its return (or HMRC have determined the liability in the absence of a return) *and* the normal due date has passed. (HMRC Tax Bulletin April 1999 p 647). See also HMRC Tax Bulletin April 2001 pp 833, 834.

Carry back of losses etc.

Generally a trading loss of an accounting period can only be carried back twelve months and set against the profits of such a preceding period (*CTA 2010, s 37; ICTA 1988, s 393A(1)*). However, in certain situations the trading loss can be set against profits arising up to three years previously (see further **55.4 LOSSES**).

Where the losses are set-off in an accounting period falling wholly within that prior twelve-month period, and some or all of the tax for that period is unpaid, interest is calculated on the net amount after set-off.

However, where the losses are carried back to an accounting period not falling wholly within the preceding twelve months, interest on the unpaid tax for that earlier period which is cancelled by the loss relief will run up to the normal due date for payment of tax for the period in which the loss incurred (so it will only be relieved for the period arising after the due date to payment (i.e. the period arising after nine months post the end of the loss making period).

Similar restrictions also apply where a non-trading deficit on a company's loan relationships is carried back on a claim under *CTA 2009, s 389(1)* or *s 459(1)(b)*; *FA 1996, s 83(2)* (see **54.4 LOAN RELATIONSHIPS**). Where relief is given by repayment, the amount repaid is, as far as possible, treated as if it were a discharge of the corporation tax charged for that period.

Similarly, where the discharge arises from the set-off (prior to its abolition) of surplus ACT of a later accounting period, calculation of any interest payable takes account of that set-off only from nine months after the end of the accounting period in which the surplus ACT arose. A claim for carry-back of any surplus ACT for the earlier period resulting from the loss relief claim is disregarded for this purpose, but the provisions described above in relation to interest for the period to which the surplus ACT is carried back are then amended so that interest continues to run until nine months after the end of the accounting period in which the loss was incurred (rather than that in which the surplus ACT arose).

See **49.8** below as regards ACT for accounting periods beginning before 6 April 1999.

Close companies

Interest on tax charged on certain loans by close companies (see **22.12** *et seq* **CLOSE COMPANIES**) is not, however, refunded when tax is repaid following repayment, release or writing off of the loan, and any relief from tax under **22.12** is, for the purposes of refund of interest under *TMA 1970, s 91*, set only against tax assessed under **22.12**. Interest ceases to run, however, from the date of the repayment, etc. and for this purpose any tax unpaid at that time is assumed, as far as possible, to be tax under **22.12** (see HMRC Pamphlet 'A Guide to Corporation Tax Self Assessment', para 5.4.2).

[*TMA 1970, ss 87A, 90, 91(1A)(1B)(2A), 109(3A)–(5); FA 1998, Sch 3 para 4, Sch 4 para 4; ITTOIA 2005, Sch 1 para 378; CTA 2009, Sch 1 para 305; CTA 2010, Sch 1 para 158; SI 1998 No 3175, Reg 7*].

Simon's Taxes. See **A4.623, A4.624, D1.1322.**

Foot and mouth outbreak — relief from interest on unpaid tax

Where HMRC have agreed that payment of any tax be deferred because of the foot and mouth outbreak in 2001, no interest is chargeable on the amount so deferred for the period from 31 January 2001 (or, if HMRC so direct, any later date from which the deferral agreement has effect) to the date on which the deferral agreement ceases to have effect (subject to any agreed extension of the deferral period because of the continued outbreak). If the agreement is for payment by instalments, the deferral period in relation to each instalment ends on the date by which the instalment is to be paid. However, if an instalment is not paid by the agreed date (without HMRC agreement to a further deferral), the whole agreement ceases to have effect on that date. Provision is also made for a deferral agreement to be assumed to have been made, with the like consequences to an actual agreement, where it was not made but HMRC are satisfied that it could have been made. The terms of such a notional agreement are assumed to be such as HMRC are satisfied would have been agreed in the circumstances.

This relief applies until ended by the Treasury order, such cessation not to affect its continued operation in relation to deferral agreements already in effect. A deferral agreement is effective whether made before or after the enactment of this provision or before or after the due date for the tax concerned. [*FA 2001, s 107*]. For the full range of measures relating to the foot and mouth outbreak, see HMRC Tax Bulletin Special Edition May 2001. *FA 2001, s 107* is repealed by *FA 2008, s 135*, but any company still receiving relief under that provision will continue to be eligible under *s 135*.

Disaster etc. of national significance

No interest is chargeable on unpaid tax where HMRC agree that payment may be deferred by reason of circumstances arising from a disaster or emergency specified by order in a statutory instrument made for the purpose. The provision is to be first used to waive interest on tax paid late due to the severe floods in the UK in June and July 2007.

Where no actual agreement is made, but HMRC are satisfied that one could have been made, this paragraph applies as if there were a notional agreement. The relief period is that beginning with a date specified in the order, or such later date as HMRC direct and ending when the agreement for deferment, or an extension of it, ceases to have effect or the date the order is revoked, if earlier. These provisions apply to disasters before as well as after an order is made. If, under the agreement, payment is to be by instalments, the agreement comes to an end if any instalment is not paid by the due date.

[*FA 2008, s 135*].

Examples

(A) General

[49.3]

S Ltd (which has no associated companies) prepares accounts to 31 July. On 31 May 2011, it makes a payment of £120,000 on account of its corporation tax liability for the year to 31 July 2010, the due date being 1 May 2011. On completing its corporation tax return, the company ascertains its total CT liability for that year to be £142,500 and makes a further payment of £22,500 on 16 July 2011. Following an enquiry by HMRC, various adjustments are made and the final CT liability is agreed at £145,500 on 25 November 2011. The company pays a further £3,000 on 5 January 2012.

It is assumed that interest rates remain unchanged after 29 September 2009.

Interest on overdue tax will be payable as follows.

		£
1.05.11 to 31.05.11	£120,000 × 3% × $^{31}/_{366}$ =	304.92
1.05.11 to 16.07.11	£22,500 × 3% × $^{76}/_{366}$ =	140.16
1.05.11 to 5.01.12	£3,000 × 3% × $^{250}/_{366}$ =	61.48
Total interest charge		£506.56

(B) Refund of interest charged

On 1 November 2011 T Ltd pays CT of £100,000 for its year ended 31 December 2010. The due date for payment was 1 October 2011. The liability is finally agreed at £80,000 and a repayment of £20,000 is made to T Ltd on 1 March 2012.

Assuming that interest rates remain unchanged after 29 September 2009, the interest position will be as follows.

(i) T Ltd will be charged interest on £100,000 for the period 1.10.11 to 1.11.11 (31 days). The charge will be raised following payment of the £100,000 on 1.11.11.

£100,000 × 3% × $^{31}/_{366}$ = £254.10

(ii) The company will be entitled to interest on overpaid tax of £20,000 for the period 1.11.11 (date of payment) to 1.3.12 (date of repayment) (120 days).

£20,000 × 0.5% × $^{120}/_{365}$ = £0

(iii) T Ltd will also receive a refund of interest charged on £20,000 for the period 1.10.11 to 1.11.11.

£20,000 × 3% × $^{31}/_{366}$ = £50.82

(C) Instalment payments

R Ltd has no associated companies and had taxable profits in excess of £1,500,000 for the year ended 31 March 2009. It was therefore large in the prior year.

For the year ended 31 March 2010, R Ltd makes instalment payments of £110,000 (this being equivalent to a quarter of its estimated corporation tax liability of £440,000) on the first three due dates. The last instalment is not paid until 24 July 2010. On 3 September 2010, the tax liability is finally agreed at £524,800. R Ltd pays the balance due of £84,800 on 10 September 2011.

The rates of interest are assumed for the purposes of this example to remain unchanged after 16 March 2009 for quarterly payments and after 29 September 2009 otherwise.

The interest on tax unpaid is calculated as follows.

Instalments due on quarter dates £524,800 × $^1/_4$ = £131,200

	£
1st instalment	
14 October 2009 to 14 January 2010	
131,200 – 110,000 = £21,200 @ 1.5% × $^{93}/_{366}$ =	80.80
1st and 2nd instalment	
15 January 2010 to 13 April 2010	
262,400 – 220,000 = £42,400 @ 1.5% × $^{89}/_{366}$ =	154.66
1st, 2nd and 3rd instalments	
14 April 2010 to 13 July 2010	
393,600 – 330,000 = £63,600 @ 1.5% × $^{91}/_{366}$ =	237.20
14 July 2010 to 23 July 2010	
524,800 – 330,000 = £194,800 @ 1.5% × $^{10}/_{366}$ =	79.85
24 July 2010 to 31 December 2010	
524,800 – 440,000 = 84,800 @ 1.5% × $^{161}/_{366}$ =	559.54
Normal due date for payment — 1 January 2011	
1 January 2011 to 10 September 2011	
524,800 – 440,000 = 84,800 @ 3% × $^{252}/_{366}$ =	1,751.60
Interest on unpaid tax	2,863.65

New harmonised regime

[49.4] The new rules apply a consistent interest charge to late payments across all taxes and duties, which replaces the current range of different interest regimes. The general rule remains the same for corporation tax, in that interest on overdue corporation tax ('late payment interest') will run from the due date of payment to the day before the actual date of payment of the tax (or the date it is satisfied by set-off).

There will be a number of exceptions to the general rules and special provisions detail how the charge will apply specific circumstances. With regard to corporation tax special rules will apply with regard to certain loss carry back claims. These are detailed in *F(No 3)A 2010, Sch 9*. The new rules are similar to the previous rules outlined above,

Late payment interest will be charged on such amounts in the earlier period as if no carry back claim had been made, but only up to the normal due date for tax in the later period in which the loss arises (i.e. nine months and one day post the end of the accounting period), with regard to the following loss carry back claims:

(i) non-trading loan relationship deficit claims under *CTA 2009, ss 389(1), 459(1)(b)*;
(ii) loss claims under *CTA 2010, s 37* or *s 42*, which are not wholly carried back to the preceding twelve-month period;
(iii) claim under *TIOPA 2010, s 77* to carry back unrelieved foreign tax for an overseas branch or agency per *TIOPA 2010, s 72*; or
(iv) loss carry back under *CTA 2010, s 37* or *s 42* which generates or increases excess unrelieved foreign tax which is then carried back under a *TIOPA 2010, s 77* claim.

With regard to payment of corporation tax by persons other than the company assessed, under: *TCGA 1992, ss 137(4), 139(7)* or *190; FA 1998 Sch 18 para 75A(2); CTA 2009, s 795(2);* and *CTA 2010, Ch 7 Pt 22*; the late payment interest start date in respect of such amount is the date when the tax became due and payable.

Under the new harmonised regime, where there is a 'common period' then neither late payment interest nor repayment interest will arise. A 'common period' arises where there is an amount of corporation tax payable by the company at the same time there is an amount of corporation tax repayable to the company by HMRC [*new FA 2009, Sch 54A, as inserted by F(No 3)A 2010, Sch 9*]. In addition, this new schedule sets out the conditions to apply for HMRC to recover repayment interest which ought not to have been paid as if it were late payment interest.

Whilst the new regime with regard to income tax self assessment will come into operation as from 31 October 2011, pursuant to SI 2011 No 701, the Treasury Order with regard to corporation tax self assessment has not yet been made.

Interest rates

[49.5] As noted above, as part of the changes to harmonise the interest rate regimes changes have been made to how the interest rate is set. New regulations, as amended, took effect on 12 August 2009 state that the rates will be based on the official bank rate as determined by the Monetary Policy Committee of the Bank of England. Revisions will take effect 13 working days after any change of base rate is announced, and will be published on the HMRC website. Reference to a minimum rate was repealed with effect from 12 August 2009.

Interest charged on late payment of tax generally is the base rate as above plus 2.5%, but a special rate of interest on overdue tax applies to instalment payments paid by large companies (base rate plus 1%).

The first rate set under the new regime was on 29 September 2009.

Prior to September 2009, the rate of interest was adjusted by reference to the rounded-down average of base lending rates of certain clearing banks, the formula being such average base rate plus 2.5%. A statutory instrument was required to put any rate changes into effect. Where an interest rate of below zero was calculated, a rate of zero was to be used.

[*SI 2008 No 3234; SI 2009 No 2032*].

It is understood that a denominator of 366 is used in calculations of such interest regardless of whether or not a leap year is involved.

Self-assessment

Overdue corporation tax payments

[49.6] For underpayments of corporation tax for accounting periods ending on or after 1 July 1999, the following rate of interest applies, changes being announced in HMRC Press Releases.

- **3.00% p.a. from 29 September 2009**
- 2.50% p.a. from 24 March 2009 to 28 September 2009
- 3.50% p.a. from 27 January 2009 to 23 March 2009
- 4.50% p.a. from 6 January 2009 to 26 January 2009
- 5.50% p.a. from 6 December 2008 to 5 January 2009
- 6.50% p.a. from 6 November 2008 to 5 December 2008
- 7.50% p.a. from 6 January 2008 to 5 November 2008
- 8.50% p.a. from 6 August 2007 to 5 January 2008
- 7.50% p.a. from 6 September 2006 to 5 August 2007
- 6.50% p.a. from 6 September 2005 to 5 September 2006
- 7.50% p.a. from 6 September 2004 to 5 September 2005
- 6.50% p.a. from 6 December 2003 to 5 September 2004
- 5.50% p.a. from 6 August 2003 to 5 December 2003
- 6.50% p.a. from 6 November 2001 to 5 August 2003
- 7.50% p.a. from 6 May 2001 to 5 November 2001
- 8.50% p.a. from 6 February 2000 to 5 May 2001
- 7.50% p.a. from 6 March 1999 to 5 February 2000

- 8.50% p.a. from 7 January 1999 to 5 March 1999

Overdue instalment payments

For accounting periods ending on or after 1 July 1999, a special rate of interest applies in the case of certain 'large' companies, which are required to make instalment payments in respect of their corporation tax liabilities (see **59.3** PAYMENT OF TAX). The special rate of interest (which is generally from 1 to 1.75% lower than the normal interest rates above from 20 April 2000 onwards) applies to any unpaid instalments until nine months after the end of the accounting period (whereafter the normal interest rate (above) applies). The special rate changes more frequently than the normal rate, and changes are announced in Revenue Press Releases. Details are as follows.

- **1.50% p.a. from 16 March 2009**
- 2.00% p.a. from 16 February 2009 to 15 March 2009
- 2.50% p.a. from 19 January 2009 to 15 February 2009
- 3.00% p.a. from 15 December 2008 to 18 January 2009
- 4.00% p.a. from 17 November 2008 to 14 December 2008
- 5.50% p.a. from 20 October 2008 to 16 November 2008
- 6.00% p.a. from 21 April 2008 to 19 October 2008
- 6.25% p.a. from 18 February 2008 to 20 April 2008
- 6.50% p.a. from 17 December 2007 to 17 February 2008
- 6.75% p.a. from 16 July 2007 to 16 December 2007
- 6.50% p.a. from 21 May 2007 to 15 July 2007
- 6.25% p.a. from 22 January 2007 to 20 May 2007
- 6.00% p.a. from 20 November 2006 to 21 January 2007
- 5.75% p.a. from 14 August 2006 to 19 November 2006
- 5.50% p.a. from 15 August 2005 to 13 August 2006
- 5.75% p.a. from 16 August 2004 to 14 August 2005
- 5.50% p.a. from 21 June 2004 to 15 August 2004
- 5.25% p.a. from 17 May 2004 to 20 June 2004
- 5.00% p.a. from 16 February 2004 to 16 May 2004
- 4.75% p.a. from 17 November 2003 to 15 February 2004
- 4.50% p.a. from 21 July 2003 to 16 November 2003
- 4.75% p.a. from 17 February 2003 to 20 July 2003
- 5.00% p.a. from 19 November 2001 to 16 February 2003
- 5.50% p.a. from 15 October 2001 to 18 November 2001
- 5.75% p.a. from 1 October 2001 to 14 October 2001
- 6.00% p.a. from 13 August 2001 to 30 September 2001
- 6.25% p.a. from 21 May 2001 to 12 August 2001
- 6.50% p.a. from 16 April 2001 to 20 May 2001
- 6.75% p.a. from 19 February 2001 to 15 April 2001
- 7.00% p.a. from 20 April 2000 to 18 February 2001
- 8.00% p.a. from 21 February 2000 to 19 April 2000
- 7.75% p.a. from 24 January 2000 to 20 February 2000
- 7.50% p.a. from 15 November 1999 to 23 January 2000
- 7.25% p.a. from 20 September 1999 to 14 November 1999
- 7.00% p.a. from 21 June 1999 to 19 September 1999
- 7.25% p.a. from 19 April 1999 to 20 June 1999
- 7.50% p.a. from 15 February 1999 to 18 April 1999

- 8.00% p.a. from 18 January 1999 to 14 February 1999
- 8.25% p.a. from 7 January 1999 to 17 January 1999

[*SI 1989 No 1297, Regs 3ZA, 3ZB; SI 1998 No 3175, Reg 7; SI 1998 No 3176, Regs 4–6; SI 2000 No 893*].

Effective date of payment of tax

[49.7] From 1 April 2011, companies have to submit their tax returns online and pay all corporation tax and related payments electronically. Related payments include interest charges on overdue corporation tax and penalties for not filing on time.

The only way a company will be able to pay by cheque after March 2011 is by taking their cheque and HMRC payslip to their bank or building society or to a participating Post Office and paying it in over the counter. HMRC have confirmed this would count as electronic payment.

It should also be noted that where, exceptionally, payment is accepted by cheque after March 2011, the funds will be treated as being received by HMRC on the date when cleared funds reach HMRC's bank account — not the date when HMRC receive the cheque.

HMRC take the date of payment in respect of each payment method to be as follows.

(1) *Cheques, cash, and postal orders* handed in at an HMRC office or received by post. Prior to 1 April 2011, , the date of payment was the day of receipt of such cheques etc. by HMRC *unless* received by post following a day on which the office was closed for whatever reason, in which case it is the day on which the office was first closed. (Under *FA 2007, s 95*, HMRC had the power to provide that payments made by cheque are 'made' for tax purposes at the date the cheque is cleared.)
(2) *Electronic funds transfer* — payment by BACS (transfer over two days) or CHAPS (same day transfer) — one day prior to receipt by HMRC.
(3) *Bank giro or Girobank* — the date on which payment was made at the bank or post office.

(HMRC Special 'Working Together' Tax Bulletin July 2000 p 3).

For the purposes of *TMA 1970* and *ICTA 1988, ss 824, 825* and *826* (see **50 INTEREST ON OVERPAID TAX**), where any payment to an officer of HMRC or HMRC itself is received by cheque and the cheque is paid on its first presentation to the bank on which it is drawn, the payment is treated as made on the date of receipt of the cheque by the officer or HMRC, subject to the provisions of *FA 2007, s 95*, see above, and the treatment post 1 April 2011. [*TMA 1970, s 70A*].

[*SI 2009 No 3218*].

Income tax deducted from payments

[49.8] As regards income tax payable by companies that they have deducted from yearly interest and other payments, interest arises if payment is made after the due date. The interest will run until the date of payment, but see further below where the income tax due for an earlier return period is discharged by items received in a later return period.

The rates of interest for payments due on or after 14 October 1999 (i.e. under self-assessment) are as under **49.2**(ii) above.

[*TMA 1970, s 87; FA 1989, s 178; FA 1998, Sch 3 para 3; SI 1989 No 1297, Regs 3, 3AA, 3AC; SI 1999 No 2637, Reg 4*].

For *UK-resident companies*, the due dates are 14 days after the expiry of the return periods (ending 31 March, 30 June, 30 September, 31 December and with the ending of an accounting period) in which the relevant dividends or other payments were made and interest will run from these dates even if they are non-business days.

[*ICTA 1988, Schs 13 (ACT — now repealed), 16 (rewritten to ITA 2007, s 945 et seq); FA 1998, Sch 3 para 41*].

Where ACT is assessed on a qualifying distribution which is not a payment, or on a payment of an uncertain nature, the due date is 14 days after the issue of the notice of assessment.

[*ICTA 1988, Sch 13 para 10(2) (now repealed); FA 1998, Sch 3 para 41*].

If a payment is made by a company on a date not falling within an accounting period of the company, tax is due 14 days after the payment.

[*ICTA 1988, Sch 13 para 9 (now repealed), Sch 16 para 9 (rewritten to ITA 2007, s 956 et seq); FA 1998, Sch 3 para 41*].

Where ACT or income tax paid is repaid or discharged following the receipt in a later return period of FII or income suffering tax by deduction, interest will nevertheless be chargeable where the original payment was late. The interest charged in such a case will, cease to run at the earliest of:

- the date the income tax was paid;
- 14 days after the end of the later return period; or,
- if the return for that period was made within those 14 days, from the date of the return.

[*TMA 1970, s 87(2)(3); FA 1998, Sch 3 para 3; ITA 2007, s 1025, Sch 1 paras 242, 258; FA 2009, Sch 53 para 6*].

See **46.8 INCOME TAX IN RELATION TO A COMPANY.**

The new regime under *FA 2009* replicates these provisions — *FA 2009, Sch 53 para 13.*

For *non-UK resident companies* (and non-corporates), assessment is directly under *ITA 2007, ss 946, 962–964; ICTA 1988, s 350* (see **46.8 INCOME TAX IN RELATION TO A COMPANY**). Interest under *TMA 1970, s 86* runs from

31 January following the end of the year of assessment. See HMRC Tax Bulletin February 2001 p 827 for the application of these provisions (and for the omission in practice of any interest charge on assessments issued before 1 February 2001 or for 1998/99 or earlier years).

In the case of *Mellham Ltd v Burton (Collector of Taxes)* HL [2006] STC 908, interest was held not to be payable on overdue ACT to the extent that, if paid, it would have been repaid or set off against mainstream corporation tax.

Simon's Taxes. See **A4.626, D5.511.**

Exchange restrictions

[49.9] Where corporation tax is payable in respect of income or chargeable gains arising abroad which cannot be remitted to the UK due to action of the foreign government, HMRC may allow the tax to remain uncollected. If so, interest ceases to run from the date on which HMRC were in possession of the information necessary to make their decision. No interest is payable if that date is within three months of the due and payable date.

Where a demand for payment is subsequently made by the Collector, interest begins to run again unless the tax is paid within three months. [*TMA 1970, s 92*]. See **65.4 RESIDENCE.**

HMRC error

[49.10] HMRC factsheet 'Complaints and putting things right' has replaced Code of Practice No 1 as from July 2007. The factsheet sets out the circumstances in which they will consider waiving a charge to interest on unpaid tax where there has been undue delay on the part of HMRC. See **41.8 HMRC — ADMINISTRATION.**

50

Interest on Overpaid Tax

Introduction

[50.1] Legislation was included in *F(No 3)A 2010* bringing corporation tax into the new harmonised interest regime introduced by the *Finance Act 2009*. The introduction of the regime will be phased in by statutory instrument over a number of years. However, it should be noted the rules for quarterly instalment payments remain unchanged and do not form part of the harmonised rules. These provisions came into force for the purposes of bank payroll tax on 31 August 2010 and will come into force for income tax self-assessment purposes on 31 October 2011. Corporation tax will follow in due course.

The existing rules with regard to interest have evolved over time and there are various regimes with regard to the interest paid out on overpayments of tax. For example, where repayment interest applies at the present time it may be called a repayment supplement, credit interest or statutory interest, and it may be based on differing rates.

The *FA 2009* created a harmonised interest regime for all taxes and duties administered by HMRC, initially with the exception of corporation tax and petroleum revenue tax (which have now been included under *F(No 3)A 2010*).

As a prelude to the forthcoming changes, *FA 2009, s 103* provided for HMRC to set the rate of interest on tax repayments by statutory instrument. On or after 22 July 2009, interest rates are harmonised across the taxes within the Act. There is a new minimum interest rate on tax repayments of 0.5%, so that even when the Bank of England base rate falls below 1.5%, interest will be paid on repayments. Interest will be paid on repayments from the date the tax was due to be paid, or, if later, the date the payment was actually received, to the date the repayment is made. For details with regard to accounting periods ending before 1 July 1999 please refer to earlier versions of Tolley's Corporation Tax.

Accounting periods ending on or after 1 July 1999

[50.2] For accounting periods ending on or after 1 July 1999, to which self-assessment applies, a repayment of tax or payment of credit carries interest from the 'material date' until the payment order is issued, where the repayment or payment falls to be made in respect of any of the following:

(a) corporation tax for the period;
(b) surplus advance corporation tax in respect of distributions made in accounting periods beginning before 6 April 1999 under the foreign income dividend scheme (see Tolley's Corporation Tax 2004–05 or earlier editions);
(c) income tax in respect of a payment received in the period;
(d) a tax credit comprised in any franked investment income received in such a period falling to be wholly or partly paid to the company;
(e) research and development tax credits (see **64 RESEARCH AND DEVELOPMENT**) for accounting periods ending after 31 March 2000 (or, in the case of vaccine research, in relation to expenditure incurred after 21 April 2003);
(f) land remediation tax credits (see **61.14 PROFIT COMPUTATIONS**) or life assurance company tax credits for accounting periods ending after 31 March 2001;
(g) film tax credits payable under the *FA 2006* regime (see **70.31 TRADE PROFITS — INCOME AND SPECIFIC TRADES**);
(h) first-year tax credits payable under the *FA 2008* regime (see **11.17**).

Details of the rates, including those for instalment payments by 'large companies', are as set out in **50.4** below.

Interest under these provisions is paid without deduction of tax. Where interest is payable under these provisions to a company within the charge to corporation tax, it is brought into account in computing profits or income under the loan relationship rules (see **54.3 LOAN RELATIONSHIPS**).

The '*material date*' is:

(i) for corporation tax, the later of the date the corporation tax was paid and the date on which it became (or would have become) due and payable, i.e. nine months after the end of the accounting period (see **59.2 PAYMENT OF TAX**);
(ii) for income tax repayments and payments of tax credit in relation to (c) or (d) above, the day after the end of the accounting period in which the payment was received by the company;
(iii) (in relation to accounting periods beginning before 6 April 1999) for repayments of surplus ACT, the date on which corporation tax for the period became (or would have become) due and payable, i.e. nine months after the end of the accounting period;
(iv) in the case of a tax repayment on a claim under *CTA 2010, s 458* (previously *ICTA 1988, s 419(4)*) in respect of repayment, release or writing off of a close company loan or advance (see **22.15** close companies), the later of:

- the date the entitlement to the tax repayment accrued (i.e. the date nine months after the end of the accounting period in which the loan etc. was made or, if the loan had not been repaid, released or written off at that date, the date nine months after the end of the accounting period in which it was repaid, released or written off); and
- the actual date of payment of the tax to be repaid.

(For a loan made in an accounting period ending before 31 March 1996, it is the later of the date the loan (or part) was repaid and the actual date of payment of the tax);

(v) in the case of research and development, land remediation and film tax credits, the filing date (see **66.4 RETURNS**) for the company tax return for the accounting period for which the credit is claimed (or if later the date of receipt by HMRC of the return (or amended return) containing the claim);

(vi) in the case of first-year tax credits, the later of the filing date of the company's return for the chargeable period and the date the return, or amended return is filed with HMRC.

In relation to repayments within (iv) above, the repayment is treated as if it were a repayment of corporation tax for the accounting period in which the loan (or part) was repaid, released or written off.

Corporation tax repayments are as far as possible treated as repayments of tax paid on a later rather than an earlier date.

Large companies — Instalment Payments

In the case of certain 'large' companies, which are required to make instalment payments in respect of their corporation tax liabilities (see **59.3 PAYMENT OF TAX**), a special rate (see **50.4** below) applies to any excess instalment payments until nine months after the end of the accounting period concerned and a lower rate applies to repayments made after that time.

The special higher rate also applies to corporation tax payments made by a company, which is *not* a large company, before the day following the expiry of nine months after the end of an accounting period. Interest is payable from the date of payment until that day although not for periods before the first instalment date which would apply if the company were a large company.

As noted above, interest on instalment payments will not be included within the new *FA 2009* regime as amended to apply to corporation tax.

Restrictions on interest

Interest is restricted where losses of an accounting period are carried back under *CTA 2010, s 37*; previously *ICTA 1988, s 393A(1)* (see **55.4 LOSSES**) to an accounting period not falling wholly within the twelve months preceding the period in which the loss was incurred. Interest on any repayment of corporation tax paid for the earlier period, or on any payment of income tax or tax credit in respect of payments received in that period, is only payable from nine months after the end of the accounting period in which the loss arose.

To the extent that a repayment of corporation tax, or of income tax in respect of a payment received, arose from surplus ACT carried back from a subsequent accounting period beginning before 6 April 1999, interest as above is only payable from nine months after the end of the accounting period in which the surplus ACT arose.

Where, as a result of the loss being carried back, surplus ACT arises in the earlier period (beginning before 6 April 1999) which is itself carried back, the provisions described above in relation to interest in relation to the period in which the surplus ACT is applied are amended to prevent such interest being payable for any time before nine months after the end of the accounting period in which the loss arose (rather than the period in which the surplus ACT arose). (These provisions do not apply where the period to which the loss or surplus ACT is carried back ended before 1 October 1993, but the provisions of *ICTA 1988, s 825* have similar effect.)

See HMRC Tax Bulletin April 1996 pp 304, 305 for an example illustrating the point that *ICTA 1988, s 826* only applies to repayments of tax paid for accounting periods ending after 30 September 1993, regardless of whether a repayment for an earlier period may arise from surplus ACT carried back from such a period.

See also **32.7 DOUBLE TAX RELIEF** as regards similar provisions relating to relief for excess unrelieved foreign tax.

Similar restrictions also apply where a non-trading deficit on a company's loan relationships is carried back on a claim under *CTA 2009, s 389(1)* or *s 459(1)(b); FA 1996, s 83(2)* (see **54.4 LOAN RELATIONSHIPS**).

Recovery of interest paid

For accounting periods ending on or after 1 July 1999, where, solely as a result of a change in a company's corporation tax liability, it appears to HMRC that any interest paid under these provisions ought not to have been paid, it is recoverable without assessment as if it were **INTEREST ON OVERDUE TAX (49)**.

[*ICTA 1988, ss 826, 826A; FA 1998, s 34, Sch 3 para 38, Sch 4 paras 1–3, 5; FA 1999, s 90; FA 2000, Sch 30 para 29; FA 2006, Sch 5 para 26; FA 2008, Sch 25 para 7; SI 1998 No 3175, Reg 8; CTA 2009, Sch 1 para 267; CTA 2010, Sch 1 para 117(2)*].

Simon's Taxes. See **A4.632–A4.634, D1.1323.**

Repayment supplement is not paid in respect of out of date claims, since the amount repaid is regarded as an *ex gratia* payment made without acceptance of any legal liability. (HMRC Repayment Claims Manual, RM5104).

In the case of *Sempra Metals Ltd v CIR* [2007] UKHL 34, HL, (following the finding by the CJEC that the requirement that both parties to an election under *s 247* be UK-resident contravened EC law), it was held that in providing for compensation, interest should be calculated on the basis of compound.

Examples

(A) Self-assessment

X Ltd prepares accounts to 31 December. On 15 June 2011 it submits its tax return for the year ended 31 December 2010 showing a corporation tax liability for the period of £14,000, and accompanied by a payment of £7,000. On 1 October 2011 it makes a further payment of £7,000. It subsequently submits an amended return showing a reduced liability of £12,500, and £1,500 is repaid to the company on 1 December 2011.

It is assumed that interest rates for corporation tax repayments other than by instalment, and for tax paid before the due date, remain unchanged after 29 September 2009 and 21 September 2009 respectively.

X Ltd will be entitled to interest on overpaid tax, calculated as follows.

		£
15.6.11 to 30.9.11	£7,000 × 0.5% × $^{108}/_{365}$ =	10.35
1.10.11 to 30.11.11	£1,500 × 0.5% × $^{61}/_{365}$ =	1.25
Total interest		£11.60

(B) Instalment payments

Z Ltd has no associated companies and had taxable profits in excess of £1,500,000 for the year ended 31 March 2010. For the year ended 31 March 2010, Z Ltd pays £143,000 for the first instalment on 30 September 2009 (early payment of instalment due on 14 October) this being equivalent to a quarter of its estimated corporation tax liability of £572,000.

The same amount is paid on the due dates for the second and third instalments and on 5 July 2009 for the fourth instalment (early). On 3 September 2011, the tax liability is agreed at £506,800 and £65,200 is repaid to the company on 22 September 2011.

As above, the rates of interest are assumed for the purposes of this example to remain unchanged after 29 September and 21 September 2009.

The interest on tax overpaid is calculated as follows.

Instalments due on quarter dates £506,800 × $^{1}/_{4}$ = £126,700

	£
1st instalment	
14 October 2009 to 13 January 2010	
143,000 – 126,700 = £16,300 @ 0.5% × $^{91}/_{365}$ =	20.32
1st and 2nd instalments	
14 January 2010 to 13 April 2010	
286,000 – 253,400 = £32,600 @ 0.5% × $^{90}/_{365}$ =	40.19
1st, 2nd and 3rd instalments	
14 April 2010 to 5 July 2010	
429,000 – 380,100 = £48,900 @ 0.5% × $^{83}/_{365}$ =	55.60

Plus early payment 4th instalment	
6 July 2010 to 13 July 2010	
572,000 – 380,100 = £191,900 @ 0.5% × 8/365 =	21.03
14 July 2010 to 31 December 2010	
£572,000–506,800 = £65,200 @ 0.5% × 169/365 =	150.94
Normal due date 1 January 2011	
1 January 2011 to 21 September 2011	
572,000 – 506,800 = £65,200 @ 0.5% × 264/365	235.79
Interest on overpaid tax	523.87

New harmonised regime

[50.3] Interest will be paid from the 'start date', as defined, to the date of repayment (including set-off).

The general rule found at *FA 2009, Sch 54* is that the repayment start date is the later of: the date on which the amount was paid to HMRC; and, where the payment is in connection with a liability to make a payment to HMRC and is to be repaid by them, the date payment of the tax became due and payable. For corporation tax purposes the general due and payable date is nine months and one day after the end of the accounting period. [*TMA 1970, s 59D*].

The instalment payment regime is to remain outside the new provisions.

The provisions in *F(No 3)A 2010* with regard to the new harmonised regime clarify the position with regard to loss set off further where non-trade loan relationship deficits, losses and excess unrelieved foreign tax are carried back.

Repayment interest on the corporation tax to be repaid for the earlier periods will only arise from the day after the expiry of nine months following the end of the period in which the deficit, loss, or excess arose, with regard to the following:

(i) non-trading loan relationship deficit claims under *CTA 2009, ss 389(1), 459(1)(b)*;
(ii) loss claims under *CTA 2010, s 37* or *s 42*, which are not wholly carried back to the preceding twelve-month period;
(iii) claim under *TIOPA 2010, s 77* to carry back unrelieved foreign tax for an overseas branch or agency per *TIOPA 2010, s 72*; or
(iv) loss carry back under *CTA 2010, s 37* or *s 42* which generates or increases excess unrelieved foreign tax which is then carried back under a *TIOPA 2010, s 77* claim.

In addition, the provisions clarify the position as to the start date of repayment interest for a repayment of income tax or tax credit within FII — the date is the day after the end of the accounting period in which the repayment is received.

With regard to close companies, where relief is claimed following the repayment of a loan to a participator, the start date is the later of: (a) nine months after the end of the accounting period in which the loan date falls, or if the loan repayment date is on or after the tax due date, nine months after the end of the accounting period in which the loan is repaid; or (b) the date on which the tax which is to be repaid was paid to HMRC.

Under the new harmonised regime, where there is a 'common period' then neither late payment interest nor repayment interest will arise. A 'common period' arises where there is an amount of corporation tax payable by the company at the same time there is an amount of corporation tax repayable to the company by HMRC [*new FA 2009, Sch 54A, as inserted by F(No 3)A 2010, Sch 9*]. In addition, this new schedule sets out the conditions to apply for HMRC to recover repayment interest which ought not to have been paid as if it were late payment interest.

Whilst the new regime with regard to income tax self assessment will come into operation as from 31 October 2011, pursuant to SI 2011/ 701, the Treasury Order with regard to corporation tax self assessment has not yet been made.

[*F(No 3) A 2010, s 25 Sch 9*].

Interest rates

[50.4] As noted above, as part of the changes to harmonise the interest rate regimes changes have been made to how the interest rate is set. New regulations, as amended, which took effect on 12 August 2009 state that the rates will be based on the official bank rate as determined by the Monetary Policy Committee of the Bank of England. Revisions will take effect 13 working days after any change of base rate is announced, and will be published on the HMRC website.

The standard repayment interest rate is base rate less 1%.

Prior to September 2009 the rate was determined by reference to the average of base lending rates of certain clearing banks. Prior to September 2009, where an interest rate of below zero was calculated, a rate of zero was to be used. A minimum rate of 0.5% now applies. A statutory instrument was required to put any rate changes into effect.

A special rate applies to quarterly instalment repayment interest — calculated as base rate less 0.25%. However, currently the quarterly instalment payment, and main repayment, rates are the same as the bank interest rate is sufficiently low that the minimum rate applies.[*FA 1989, ss 178, 179; SI 1989 No 1297 as amended; SI 2008 No 3234; SI 2009 No 2032*].

It is understood that a denominator of 365 is used in calculations of repayment interest regardless of whether or not a leap year is involved.

Self-assessment

Corporation tax repayments

[50.5] For corporation tax repayments for accounting periods ending on or after 1 July 1999, the following rate of interest applies, changes being announced in HMRC Press Releases.

0.50% p.a. from 29 September 2009
0.00% p.a. from 27 January 2009 to 28 September 2009
1.00% p.a. from 6 January 2009 to 26 January 2009
2.00% p.a. from 6 December 2008 to 5 January 2009
3.00% p.a. from 6 November 2008 to 5 December 2008
4.00% p.a. from 6 January 2008 to 5 November 2008
5.00% p.a. from 6 August 2007 to 5 January 2008
4.00% p.a. from 6 September 2006 to 5 August 2007
3.00% p.a. from 6 September 2005 to 5 September 2006
4.00% p.a. from 6 September 2004 to 5 September 2005
3.00% p.a. from 6 December 2003 to 5 September 2004
2.00% p.a. from 6 August 2003 to 5 December 2003
3.00% p.a. from 6 November 2001 to 5 August 2003
4.00% p.a. from 6 May 2001 to 5 November 2001
5.00% p.a. from 6 February 2000 to 5 May 2001
4.00% from 6 March 1999 to 5 February 2000
5.00% p.a. from 7 January 1999 to 5 March 1999

The rates listed below in relation to pre-self-assessment accounting periods ending before 1 July 1999 continue to apply in relation to other interest payments.

Instalment payments and other tax paid early

For accounting periods ending on or after 1 July 1999, a special rate of interest applies in the case of certain 'large' companies, which are required to make instalment payments in respect of their corporation tax liabilities (see **59.3 PAYMENT OF TAX**). The special rate (which is generally from 0.25% to 1.25% higher than that referred to above) applies to any excess instalment payments until nine months after the end of the accounting period concerned. The lower rate referred to above applies to repayments made after that time.

The special rate also applies to corporation tax payments made early by a company, which is *not* a large company, early being before the day following the expiry of nine months after the end of an accounting period. Interest is payable from the later of: (a) the date on which the tax was paid, and (b) the date on which, if the company had been a large company, the first instalment of tax for the accounting period would have been due; up to the normal due date.

The special rate changes more frequently than the normal rate, and changes are announced in HMRC Press Releases. Details are as follows.

0.50% p.a. from 21 September 2009
0.25% p.a. from 16 March 2009 to 20 September 2009
0.75% p.a. from 16 February 2009 to 15 March 2009
1.25% p.a. from 19 January 2009 to 15 February 2009
1.75% p.a. from 15 December 2008 to 18 January 2009
2.75% p.a. from 17 November 2008 to 14 December 2008
4.25% p.a. from 20 October 2008 to 16 November 2008
4.75% p.a. from 21 April 2008 to 19 October 2008
5.00% p.a. from 18 February 2008 to 20 April 2008

5.25% p.a. from 17 December 2007 to 17 February 2008
5.50% p.a. from 16 July 2007 to 16 December 2007
5.25% p.a. from 21 May 2007 to 15 July 2007
5.00% p.a. from 22 January 2007 to 20 May 2007
4.75% p.a. from 20 November 2006 to 21 January 2007
4.50% p.a. from 14 August 2006 to 19 November 2006
4.25% p.a. from 15 August 2005 to 13 August 2006
4.50% p.a. from 16 August 2004 to 14 August 2005
4.25% p.a. from 21 June 2004 to 15 August 2004
4.00% p.a. from 17 May 2004 to 20 June 2004
3.75% p.a. from 16 February 2004 to 16 May 2004
3.50% p.a. from 17 November to 15 February 2004
3.25% p.a. from 21 July 2003 to 16 November 2003
3.50% p.a. from 17 February 2003 to 20 July 2003
3.75% p.a. from 19 November 2001 to 16 February 2003
4.25% p.a. from 15 October 2001 to 18 November 2001
4.50% p.a. from 1 October 2001 to 14 October 2001
4.75% p.a. from 13 August 2001 to 30 September 2001
5.00% p.a. from 21 May 2001 to 12 August 2001
5.25% p.a. from 16 April 2001 to 20 May 2001
5.50% p.a. from 19 February 2001 to 15 April 2001
5.75% p.a. from 21 February 2000 to 18 February 2001
5.50% p.a. from 24 January 2000 to 20 February 2000
5.25% p.a. from 15 November 1999 to 23 January 2000
5.00% p.a. from 20 September 1999 to 14 November 1999
4.75% p.a. from 21 June 1999 to 19 September 1999
5.00% p.a. from 19 April 1999 to 20 June 1999
5.25% p.a. from 15 February 1999 to 18 April 1999
5.75% p.a. from 18 January 1999 to 14 February 1999
6.00% p.a. from 7 January 1999 to 17 January 1999

[*SI 1998 No 3175, Reg 8; SI 1998 No 3176, Regs 4, 7, 8*].

HMRC error

[50.6] HMRC factsheet 'Complaints and putting things right' has replaced the previous Code of Practice No 1 as from July 2007. This factsheet sets out the circumstances in which they will consider paying a repayment supplement on money owed to the taxpayer for any period during which there has been undue delay on the part of HMRC. See **41.9 HMRC — ADMINISTRATION**.

Unauthorised demands for tax

[50.7] There is a general right to interest under *Supreme Court Act 1981, s 35A* in a case where a taxpayer submits to such an unauthorised demand, provided that the payment was not made voluntarily to close a transaction. (*Woolwich Equitable Building Society v CIR* HL 1992, 65 TC 265).

Value added tax

[50.8] Value added tax repayment supplements under *VATA 1994, s 79* are disregarded for corporation tax purposes. [*CTA 2009, s 1286; ICTA 1988, s 827(2); ITTOIA 2005, Sch 1 para 332*].

Over-repayments

[50.9] See **59.17 PAYMENT OF TAX, 7.4 ASSESSMENTS** as regards assessment of overpaid interest under these provisions.

51

Investment Companies and Investment Business

Cross-reference. See **22.20 CLOSE COMPANIES** as regards close investment-holding companies.

Simon's Taxes. See D7.301–D7.324.

Introduction

[51.1] Companies with investment business, and investment companies, should be distinguished from trading companies. Whilst the basic approach to the calculation of their profits within the charge to corporation tax is the same, in that you consider the separate sources of income (each trade for example being such a source), there is key difference with regard to the deductions for expenses which are allowed. Unlike trading companies, companies with investment business can obtain relief for management expenses that are not otherwise relievable, subject to certain restrictions. [*CTA 2009, s 1217(2)(3)*].

The broad definition of what constitutes management expenses is examined further below, along with any restrictions applicable to their deduction.

The position with regard to certain types of receipt is then examined at **51.7**, and the specific relief for investment companies with regard to unquoted shares, at **51.8**.

The updated anti-avoidance provisions relating to a change in ownership, post the tax law rewrite which was completed with *CTA 2010*, is then considered at **51.9**.

Companies with investment business

A '*company with investment business*' is a company whose business consists wholly or partly of making investments. It is not simply a company that holds investments or receives interest income, it must have a business of making investments. A credit union is not a company with investment business. [*CTA 2009, s 1218; ICTA 1988, s 130; FA 2004, s 38(2)–(5)*]. However, it will include, for example, a trading company with shares in subsidiary companies, as this is a distinct business of making investments.

Investment companies

An '*investment company*' is a company whose business consists wholly or mainly in the making of investments and the principal part of whose income is derived therefrom. [*CTA 2009, Sch 1 para 94; ICTA 1988, s 130*]. It accordingly will include unit trusts and open-ended investment companies (**52 INVESTMENT FUNDS**) and investment trusts (**53.1 INVESTMENT TRUSTS**). '*The making of investments*' does not require turning them over (*Tyre Investment Trust Ltd* (1924) 12 TC 646). For treatment of income from land as investment income, see *Webb v Conelee Properties Ltd* (1982) 56 TC 149.

It appears that a company's status as an 'investment company' is to be based on its activities over a representative period, see *FPH Finance Trust Ltd v CIR* [1944] AC 285, [1944] 1 All ER 653, 26 TC 131, HL.

A company formed to run a family estate was held not to be an investment company (under similar Irish legislation) in *Casey v Monteagle Estate Co* [1962] IR 106. A similar decision was reached by the Special Commissioner in *Tintern Close Residents Society Ltd v Winter* [1995] STC (SCD) 57, in which a company formed to 'acquire, hold, manage and deal with' common land and buildings on a residential estate (whose income consisted of members' subscriptions and ground rent) was held not to be an investment company as its main function and activity was the management and maintenance of the property. See Revenue Tax Bulletin October 1995 pp 253, 254 for an appreciation of this decision and for HMRC's view of the scope of *s 130*, for which see also HMRC Company Taxation Manual, CTM08050. In *Cook v Medway Housing Society Ltd* (1996) 69 TC 319, however, the business of a society formed to acquire and manage local authority housing stock was held to consist in the making of investments.

It can be seen that the definition of a company with investment business is much wider than that of an investment company and that all investment companies are also companies with investment business. The term investment company is now only relevant when considering which companies may claim relief against income for capital losses on sales of certain shares, see further **51.8** below.

For accounting periods beginning before 1 April 2004, savings banks (other than trustee savings banks or successor companies) are considered to be investment companies. [*ICTA 1988, s 130; FA 2004, ss 38, 42*].

Finance Act 2011

[51.2] The Finance Act 2011 introduces legislation to counter avoidance with regard to loan relationships and derivatives involving changes in the functional currency of an investment company.

An election is also provided for investment companies to elect for a different functional currency for tax purposes than the currency used in the accounts.

A new *s 9A* is inserted into *CTA 2010*, providing for a UK resident investment company to elect for a currency to be its designated currency for tax purposes, if at the time the election is made either a significant proportion of the company's assets and liabilities are denominated in that currency, or the currency is the functional currency of another company and both companies meet the consolidation condition. The consolidation condition is met where the financial results of the UK resident investment company are required to be consolidated into accounts prepared under acceptable accounting practice by the other company, or would be so required if such accounts were prepared.

The election has effect until the end of the period of account where the company makes another election, or the start of the period of account in which it is not the case that a significant proportion of the assets and liabilities of the company are denominated in the elected currency, or the consolidation condition is failed.

The provisions apply to accounting periods beginning on or after 1 April 2011. An election may be made or revoked at any time on or after 9 December 2010.

New *subsections (1A)* are inserted into *CTA 2010, ss 6 and 7* which allow for the elected currency of the investment company to be used for tax purposes.

See further **36 FOREIGN CURRENCY**, **54 LOAN RELATIONSHIPS** and **30 DERIVATIVE CONTRACTS**.

Management expenses

[51.3] As highlighted above, the ability to claim management expenses has been extended (as from 1 April 2004) to include companies with investment business – not just those qualifying as investment companies – and also to include non UK resident companies. The extension to companies with an investment business is important for companies who hold shares in subsidiaries as well as having their own trade.

Management expenses of a company's investment business which are 'referable' to a particular accounting period (i.e. when they are debited in the accounts, see further below) are allowed as a deduction in computing the company's total profits for corporation tax purposes for that period.

For this purpose, management expenses are management expenses of the company's investment business so far as they are incurred in respect of the business of making investments and so far as the investments concerned are not held for an 'unallowable purpose' during the accounting period. Any apportionment of expenses necessary to meet these requirements is to be made on a just and reasonable basis. See **51.4** below for certain expenses which are treated as management expenses.

No deduction is allowed for expenses which are otherwise deductible from total profits or in computing any component of total profits. Therefore where the expenses relate to a particular source of income, such as UK property income, then they will be deducted in calculating the profits of such source, and not as a general management expense of the company.

Subject to certain exceptions, no deduction is allowed for expenses of a capital nature. The exceptions are amounts treated as management expenses under:

- *CTA 2009, ss 1232–1246* (see **51.4**(i)–(x) below);
- *CTA 2009, s 985(3)* (share incentive plans);
- *CTA 2009, s 999(4)* (deduction for costs of setting up certain employee share schemes);
- *CTA 2009, s 1000(3)* (deduction for costs of setting up employee share ownership trust);
- *CTA 2009, s 1013(3)* (employee share acquisitions: relief if shares acquired by employee or other person);
- *CTA 2009, s 1021(3)* (employee share acquisitions: relief if employee or other person acquires share option);
- *ICTA 1988, Sch 24 para 4(1A)* — this has been repealed for accounting periods ending or after 1 April 2010 (manufactured dividends and interest);
- *FA 2004, s 196* (employers' contributions to pension scheme);
- *CTA 2010, s 791(4)* (treatment of payer of manufactured overseas dividends) — applicable to accounting periods ending on or after 1 April 2010; or
- any other provision of the Corporation Tax Acts.

[*CTA 2009, ss 1219, 1221(1); ICTA 1988, s 75(1)(2)(3)(4); FA 2004, s 38(1)*].

Accounting period to which management expenses are referable

Where management expenses are debited to a company's accounts (be it charged in the profit and loss account or income statement, the statement of recognised gains or losses or statement of changes in equity, or other statement) in accordance with generally accepted accounting practice for a period of account which coincides with an accounting period, the expenses are '*referable*' to that accounting period.

Where the company's period of account does not coincide with an accounting period (for example where the company's period of account exceeds twelve months), the expenses are to be apportioned between any accounting periods falling within the period of account on a time basis unless that would give an unjust or unreasonable result in which case a just and reasonable method is to be used.

If a company draws up accounts for a period of account but management expenses are not debited in accordance with generally accepted accounting practice, the expenses are referable to the accounting period to which they would have been referable had they been debited in accordance with the above provisions.

Where management expenses are not referable to an accounting period by virtue of the above provisions because the company has not drawn up accounts, they are referable to the accounting period to which they would have been referable on the assumption that there is a period of account coinciding with that accounting period (where it does not otherwise coincide), and so much of the expenses are debited for any such deemed period of account as would fall to be debited in accordance with generally accepted accounting practice.

These provisions do not take precedence over any other provision of the Corporation Tax Acts which provides for amounts to be treated as management expenses referable to an accounting period.

[*CTA 2009, ss 1224–1227, 1255(1); ICTA 1988, s 75A; FA 2004, s 39; FA 2005, s 80, Sch 4 para* 22].

Unallowable purpose

Investments are held for an '*unallowable purpose*' so far as they are held for a purpose that is not a business or other commercial purpose of the company or for the purpose of activities in respect of which the company is not within the charge to corporation tax. This will therefore exclude investments held for social or recreational purposes and investments of a non resident company with a permanent establishment in the UK, if the investment is not part of the business of that permanent establishment.

For accounting periods beginning on or after 20 June 2007, investments are treated as not being held for a business or other commercial purpose if they are held directly or indirectly in consequence of, or otherwise in connection with, 'arrangements' the main purpose, or one of the main purposes, of which is to obtain a deduction or increased deduction for management expenses or any other tax advantage (within *CTA 2010, s 1139; ICTA 1988, s 804ZA*).

Where an accounting period straddles 20 June 2007, the accounting period is treated for this purpose only as split into two accounting periods, the first ending on 19 June 2007 and the second beginning on 20 June 2007.

'*Arrangements*' include any agreement, understanding, scheme, transaction or series of transactions, whether or not legally enforceable. An expense which is only partly allowable must be apportioned on a 'just and reasonable' basis.

[*CTA 2009, s 1220; ICTA 1988, s 75(5)(5A)(11); FA 2004, s 38(1); FA 2007, s 28(3)–(6)*].

HMRC consider that the test would not be failed solely because the company's investments generate dividends exempt from tax under *CTA 2009, s 1285; ICTA 1988, s 208*, or capital gains covered by the substantial shareholdings exemption or exempt under *TCGA 1992, s 100(1)* (in the case of authorised unit trusts etc.), or because the investment is in a company which itself is not within the charge to corporation tax (for example, a non-UK resident subsidiary). See HMRC Company Taxation Manual CTM08210–08230.

Reduction for income derived from non-taxable sources

Management expenses must be reduced by any income derived from non-taxable sources (other than franked investment income) held in the course of a company's investment business or, in the case of a non-UK resident company, non-taxable sources held in the course of its investment business carried on through a UK permanent establishment which is property or rights used by, or held by or for that establishment (see **65.6 RESIDENCE**). [*CTA 2009, s 1222; ICTA 1988, s 75(6); FA 2004, s 38(1)*].

Claw back of relief where credits reverse management expense debits

Accounts prepared in accordance with generally accepted accounting practice could include a deduction for management expenses made for a period of account earlier than that in which payment of the expense is made. This arises where the accounts include a debit for expenses accrued in the period. If some, or all, of the sum represented by the debit is paid, and then wholly or partly repaid (or the sum is never paid) the accounts for a later period of account will include a credit for the amount accrued and not paid. There are rules to deal with such a situation and to claw back any relief given.

Pursuant to such provisions, a claw back of relief for management expenses applies where a 'credit' is 'brought into account' by a company in a period of account ending on or after 1 April 2004 (the '*period of the credit*') that 'reverses' some or all of a 'debit' brought into account in an earlier period of account and that debit represents management expenses deductible for an accounting period ending before, or at the same time as, the period of the credit.

For this purpose, a credit '*reverses*' a debit if it is made because the sum represented by the debit (i.e. the expenses in question) is paid and then repaid, or is never paid. A credit or debit is '*brought into account*' if it is brought into account in the company's profit and loss account or income statement, the statement of recognised gains or losses or statement of changes in equity, or other statement. A '*credit*' is an amount which increases or creates a profit or reduces a loss, and a '*debit*' is an amount which reduces a profit or increases or creates a loss, for accounting purposes for a period of account.

Where the period of the credit coincides with an accounting period beginning on or after 1 April 2004, the 'reversal amount' is applied to reduce any management expenses (excluding any brought forward expenses) deductible for that accounting period. Any amount remaining after reducing those management expenses to nil is treated as a receipt of the company chargeable for that period under the charge to corporation tax on income (or, before *CTA 2009* took effect (see **70.2 TRADE PROFITS — INCOME AND SPECIFIC TRADES**) charged to tax under *Schedule D Case VI* for that period).

Where the reversal period does not coincide with an accounting period, the reversal amount is apportioned between any accounting periods falling within the reversal period and only that amount apportioned to an accounting period is dealt with for that period in accordance with the above provisions. The apportionment is to be made on a time basis unless that would give an unjust or unreasonable result in which case a just and reasonable method is to be used. Where an accounting period does not coincide with, or fall within, any period of account of the company, a period of account is to be deemed to coincide with that accounting period and it is assumed that, in calculating for accounting purposes the company's profits and losses for that period of account, amounts were brought into account in accordance with UK generally accepted accounting practice.

The '*reversal amount*' is however much of the credit reverses the part of the debit that represents deductible management expenses. Any amount of the credit that represents sums otherwise taken into account in calculating the company's corporation tax profits or losses, whether in the relevant accounting period or any earlier accounting period, is excluded. The '*relevant accounting period*' for this purpose is the latest accounting period of the company falling wholly or partly in the period of the credit.

[*CTA 2009, ss 1228–1230, 1231(1)(2), 1255(2)(3); ICTA 1988, s 75B; FA 2004, s 45*].

Carry forward of excess management expenses etc.

Management expenses are automatically set against the investment income and gains in the current accounting period. Where the management expenses exceed the gross income and gains in the current period they are 'excess' and if the company is part of a group these excess management expenses may be transferred to a fellow 75% owned company, upon making the relevant claim (see further **39 — GROUP RELIEF**).

Any management expenses which remain unrelieved in an accounting period may be carried forward and treated as management expenses of the next succeeding accounting period and may continue to be so carried forward until relieved.

Any qualifying charitable donations made (for accounting periods ending before 1 April 2010, charges on income paid) in the accounting period, to the extent they are paid for the purpose of the company's investment business, may similarly be carried forward as management expenses. [*CTA 2009, s 1223; ICTA 1988, s 75(8), (9); FA 2004, s 38(1)*]. See also **51.6** below with regard to losses of a property business.

Anti-avoidance

For accounting periods beginning on or after 20 June 2007, no deduction is given for any particular management expenses (including any amount treated as a management expense — see **51.4** below) if any part of them is incurred directly or indirectly in consequence of, or in connection with, any 'arrangements for securing a tax advantage'. This rule does not apply to an expense if, under *CTA 2010, s 799; ICTA 1988, Sch 23A para 7A* (manufactured payments under arrangements with unallowable purpose — see **5.9 ANTI-AVOIDANCE**), the company is not entitled to a relevant tax relief (within the meaning of that provision) in respect of all or part of the expense.

For this purpose, '*arrangements for securing a tax advantage*' are arrangements (including any agreement, understanding, scheme, transaction or series of transactions, whether or not legally enforceable) the main purpose, or one of the main purposes, of which is to secure a deduction or increased deduction for management expenses or any other tax advantage (within *CTA 2010, s 1139; ICTA 1988, s 840ZA*).

Where an accounting period straddles 20 June 2007, the accounting period is treated for the purpose only of the above provision as split into two accounting periods, the first ending on 19 June 2007 and the second beginning on 20 June 2007.

[*CTA 2009, s 1248; ICTA 1988, s 75(1)(2)(2A)–(2C)(4)(10); FA 2004, ss 38(1), 42; FA 2007, s 28(2),(5),(6)*].

Accounting period straddling 1 April 2004

Where an accounting period begins before and ends on or after 1 April 2004, that accounting period is deemed to consist of two separate accounting periods, the first beginning with the straddling period and ending on 31 March

2004 and the second beginning on 1 April 2004 and ending with the straddling period. However, in the case of an investment company, this does not have effect in determining the amounts deductible in the straddling period of management expenses carried forward from accounting periods beginning before 1 April 2004, or sums treated as management expenses under any other provision. [*FA 2004, s 43(5),(6)*].

Transitional provisions — management expenses carried forward

Where management expenses have been disbursed in an accounting period beginning before 1 April 2004 and have been carried forward so that they would have been treated under the old rules (*ICTA 1988, s 75(3)* as originally enacted) as disbursed in the first accounting period beginning on or after 1 April 2004, they are to be treated as if they were management expenses deductible for that period under the new rules (now *CTA 2009, s 1223*). To the extent that the expenses are deductible by an investment company in an accounting period beginning before 1 April 2004 (excluding any unrelieved excess carried forward to a later accounting period), they may not be deducted in an accounting period beginning on or after 1 April 2004. Where management expenses incurred by an investment company in an accounting period beginning before 1 April 2004:

(a) were not deductible in that period (because they had not been disbursed); but
(b) would have been deductible had the new rules been in force for that accounting period (because they were properly charged to the company's accounts in that accounting period),

they are treated as deductible in the first accounting period beginning on or after 1 April 2004. [*FA 2004, s 43(1)–(4)*].

Amounts treated as management expenses

[51.4] Generally expenses will only qualify for a deduction as a management expense to the extent that they are made in respect of the company's investment business and to the extent they are not made for an unallowable purposes, as highlighted above. There has been considerable case law on this subject, some of which is discussed further below.

Certain types of management expenses now have a statutory footing. The amounts listed at (i)–(x) below are treated as management expenses, so far as they would not otherwise be so treated, if they are not otherwise deductible from total profits or in calculating a component of total profits. [*CTA 2009, s 1232*].

(i) **Excess capital allowances.** Capital allowances on plant and machinery to which a company with investment business is entitled in respect of a qualifying activity consisting of managing its investments (see **11.1 CAPITAL ALLOWANCES — PLANT AND MACHINERY: ELIGIBLE EXPENDITURE AND INITIAL ALLOWANCES**) are treated as management expenses so far as they cannot be deducted from the income of the business. The deemed expenses are referable to the accounting period for which the company is entitled to the allowances. [*CTA 2009, s 1233; ICTA 1988, s 75(7)* (as introduced by *FA 2004, s 38(1)*; previously *ICTA 1988, s 75(4)*); *CAA 2001, ss 15(1)(g), 18, 253, Sch 1 paras 476, 479; SI 2004 No 2310, Sch paras 52–54*].

(ii) **Payments for restrictive undertakings.** A payment for a restrictive undertaking which is treated as earnings of an employee under *ITEPA 2004, s 225* is treated as a management expense if it is made, or treated under *ITEPA 2003, s 226* (valuable consideration given for restrictive undertaking) as made, by a company with investment business. [*CTA 2009, s 1234; FA 1988, s 73(3)*].

(iii) **Employees seconded to charities and educational establishments.** Where a company carrying on a business consisting wholly or partly of making investments makes the services of an employee employed for the purposes of that business available to a charity or educational establishment (within *CTA 2009, s 70*), the company's expenses attributable to the employment during the secondment are treated as management expenses. The secondment must be both stated and intended to be temporary. [*CTA 2009, s 1235; ICTA 1988, s 86; ITTOIA 2005, Sch 1 para 60; SI 2004 No 2310, Sch paras 2, 7*].

(iv) **Payroll deduction scheme — contributions to agents' expenses.** Where a company with investment business withholds sums from payments to an individual under an approved payroll deduction scheme (see *ITEPA 2003, s 714*) and pays those sums to an approved agent (within *ITEPA 2003, s 714(3)*), expenses the company incurs in making a payment to the agent for expenses incurred by him in connection with his scheme functions are treated as management expenses. [*CTA 2009, s 1236; ICTA 1988, s 86A; ITTOIA 2005, Sch 1 para 61*].

(v) **Counselling and outplacement services.** 'Counselling expenses' incurred by a company with investment business in relation to an employee or office-holder of the company are treated as management expenses if certain conditions are met. For this purpose, '*counselling expenses*' are expenses incurred in the provision of services to the employee in connection with the cessation of the office or employment or incurred in the payment or reimbursement of fees for, or travelling expenses in connection with, such provision. The conditions to be met are conditions A–D and, for travelling expenses, condition E in *ITEPA 2003, s 310*. [*CTA 2009, s 1237; ICTA 1988, s 589A; ITTOIA 2005, Sch 1 para 251; SI 2004 No 2310, Sch paras 2, 29*].

(vi) **Retraining expenses.** Expenses incurred by a company with investment business in the payment or reimbursement of 'retraining course expenses' (within *ITEPA 2003, s 311(2)*) for an employee or office-holder are treated as management expenses if the conditions in *ITEPA 2003, s 311(3)(4)* and, for travelling expenses, those in *s 311(5)*, are met. If the company's corporation tax liability for an accounting period has been determined on the assumption that a deduction for such expenses is allowable but the deduction is not in fact allowable, the recovery of tax provisions at *CTA 2009, s 75(2)–(6)* (see **71.25 TRADING EXPENSES AND DEDUCTIONS**) apply. [*CTA 2009, s 1238; ICTA 1988, s 588(1)–(4); ITTOIA 2005, Sch 1 para 250; SI 2004 No 2310, Sch paras 2, 28*]. Before *CTA 2009* had effect (see **70.2 TRADE PROFITS — INCOME AND**

SPECIFIC TRADES), it was a requirement that the employee be exempt under *ITEPA 2003, s 311* from income tax on the benefit of the payment or reimbursement (see Change 16 in Annex 1 to the Explanatory Notes to *CTA 2009*).

(vii) **Redundancy payments etc.** Where a company with investment business makes a 'redundancy payment' or an 'approved contractual payment' to an employee, and management expenses are deductible by the company, then, if the payment is in respect of the employee's employment wholly in the investment business, it is treated as management expenses. In the case of an approved contractual payment, the deduction cannot exceed the amount which would have been due to the employee if a redundancy payment had been payable. If the payment is in respect of employment which is only partly in the investment business, the payment is apportioned on a just and reasonable basis.

Where the payment is referable to an accounting period beginning after the investment business has ceased, it is treated as referable to the last accounting period in which the business was carried on.

For this purpose, a '*redundancy payment*' is a redundancy payment payable under *Employment Rights Act 1996, Pt 11* (or Northern Ireland equivalent) and a '*contractual payment*' is one which, under an agreement, an employer is liable to make to an employee on the termination of his employment contract. Such a payment is '*approved*' if, in respect of the agreement, an order is in force under *Employment Rights Act 1996, s 157* (or Northern Ireland equivalent).

If the company's business, or part of it, permanently ceases and the company makes a payment to the employee in addition to the redundancy payment or, if an approved contractual payment is made, the amount that would have been due if a redundancy payment had been payable, the additional payment is treated as management expenses if it would not otherwise be so treated because of the cessation of the business or part of the business. The deduction is limited to three times the amount of the redundancy payment or, if an approved contractual payment is made, the amount that would have been due if a redundancy payment had been payable. If the additional payment is referable to an accounting period beginning after the investment business, or part of it, has ceased, it is treated as referable to the last accounting period in which the business or part was carried on.

A payment made by the Secretary of State under *Employment Rights Act 1996, s 167* (or an equivalent Northern Ireland payment) is treated as a redundancy payment or approved contractual payment by the company for the purpose of the above provisions to the extent that the company reimburses the government.

[*CTA 2009, ss 1239–1243; ICTA 1988, ss 90, 579, 580; ITTOIA 2005, Sch 1 paras 66, 239; SI 2004 No 2310, Sch paras 2,10, 26*].

(viii) **Contributions to local enterprise organisations or urban regeneration companies.** Contributions, in cash or in kind, by a company with investment business to a 'local enterprise organisation' or an 'urban regeneration company' are treated as management expenses. If, however, the company or a connected person receives, or is entitled to receive, a 'disqualifying benefit', whether from the local enterprise organisation, urban regeneration company or anyone else, the management expenses are reduced by the value of the benefit. For this purpose, a '*disqualifying benefit*' is a benefit the expenses of obtaining which, if incurred directly by the company at arm's length, would not be deductible as management expenses. '*Local enterprise organisation*' and '*urban regeneration company*' are defined as for the purposes of *CTA 2009, s 82* — see **71.67** TRADING EXPENSES AND DEDUCTIONS. [*CTA 2009, s 1244; ICTA 1988, ss 79–79B; ITTOIA 2005, Sch 1 paras 48–50; SI 2004 No 2310, Sch paras 2, 3*].

(ix) **Payments to Export Credit Guarantee Department**. Sums payable by a company with investment business to the Export Credits Guarantee Department under an agreement entered into under arrangements made under *Export and Investment Guarantees Act 1991, s 2*, or with a view to entering into such an agreement, are treated as management expenses. [*CTA 2009, s 1245; ICTA 1988, s 88; ITTOIA 2005, Sch 1 para 64; SI 2004 No 2310, Sch paras 2, 9*].

(x) **Levies under *Financial Services and Markets Act 2000*.** Sums spent by a company with investment business in paying certain levies, or as a result of an award of costs, under *Financial Services and Markets Act 2000* are treated as management expenses. See *CTA 2009, s 92(2)(3)* for the full list of qualifying payments. [*CTA 2009, s 1246; ICTA 1988, s 76B; Financial Services and Markets Act 2000, s 411(2); SI 2001 No 3629, Art 16(7)(8); FA 2004, Sch 6 para 1*].

Amounts within (i), (iii)–(viii) or (x) above are deductible as management expenses without having to satisfy the requirement that they be incurred in respect of so much of the company's investment business as consists of making investments and for the investments concerned not to be held for an 'unallowable purpose' (see **51.3** above). This rule applies also to amounts treated as management expenses under *CTA 2009, ss 993–998* (costs related to approved share incentive plans), *CTA 2009, s 999(4)* (deduction for costs of setting up approved employee share option schemes), *s 1000(3)* (deduction for costs of setting up qualifying employee share ownership trusts) or any of *CTA 2009, ss 1001–1038* (tax relief in connection with employee share acquisitions). [*CTA 2009, s 1221(2)(3)*]. Amounts within (ii) or (ix) above, or otherwise treated as management expenses (see the remaining entries in the list at **51.3** above), must satisfy the requirements.

Costs incurred on an acquisition by merger or takeover of another company were held to be allowable as management expenses in *Camas plc v Atkinson (Inspector of Taxes)* [2004] EWCA Civ 541, [2004] 1 WLR 2392, [2004] STC 860, CA, on the grounds that the activities on which the expenditure was incurred were part of the process of managerial decision-making and it was further held that capital expenditure was not excluded by the legislation in force at the time. In that case the company had incurred substantial expenditure in evaluating a proposed acquisition, which did not go ahead. It should be noted, however, that *CTA 2009, s 1219(3)(a)* (previously the new *ICTA 1988, s 75(3)* introduced by *FA 2004, s 38(1)*) specifically excludes expenditure of a capital nature from deduction as management expenses from 1 April 2004 (see

51.3 above). A distinction should be drawn between the costs of a change in a company's investments (including its share portfolio) and the acquisition of share capital of a new subsidiary.

In *Holdings Ltd v CIR* [1997] STC (SCD) 144, a Special Commissioner held that fees for professional advice concerning an investment company's potential liabilities under letters of assurance given to the bankers of a trading subsidiary were allowable. For the interaction of management expenses and double tax relief, see *Jones v Shell Petroleum Co Ltd* (1971) 47 TC 194, HL.

Where an investment company provides relocation packages for its employees who are obliged to relocate, reasonable costs may be allowed as management expenses. However, where the company acquires the beneficial interest in the employee's property, the purchase and subsequent sale of the property will normally fall to be dealt with under the **CAPITAL GAINS** (**17**) provisions. (Revenue Tax Bulletin May 1994 p 124).

Other items which generally qualify as management expenses include audit and accountancy costs, share register and annual general meeting costs; reasonable salaries and staff costs; premises costs; registered office expenses; stock exchange quotation cost; and valuation costs. Commitment fees and guarantee commissions are part of the cost of raising loans and so will be deductible under the loan relationship rules and not as management expenses.

Any expenses relating to specific income must be set against that source only, for example a UK property business. Expenses relating to properties being let out must be set against the UK property business income, and not treated as a management expense.

See generally HMRC Company Taxation Manual, CTM08150 *et seq.*

Restrictions on deductions for management expenses

Unpaid remuneration

[51.5] Employees' 'remuneration' must be paid within the nine months following the end of the period of account for which it is charged in a company's accounts to be deductible as a management expense for that period. Otherwise, the amount is deductible only for the period of account in which it is paid. No deduction is allowable for any amount not paid at all.

This rule applies also to a provision made in accounts with a view to its becoming employees' remuneration and to an amount paid in respect of employee benefit contributions (within what is now *CTA 2009, ss 1290–1296*) before 27 November 2002 and held by an intermediary with a view to becoming remuneration. It is immaterial whether an amount is charged for particular employments or employments generally. '*Remuneration*' is an amount which is, or is treated as, earnings for the purposes of *ITEPA 2003, Pts 2–7*. It is paid when treated as received by an employee for the purposes of *ITEPA 2003, s 18* or *s 19*, or would be if it were not exempt income. '*Employee*' includes an office-holder.

If the company's profits are calculated before the end of the nine-month period, it must be assumed that any unpaid remuneration will not be paid before the period ends. If the remuneration is then in fact paid before the period ends, this rule does not prevent the revision of the calculation and the amendment of the tax return accordingly.

[*CTA 2009, ss 1249, 1250, Sch 2 para 133; FA 1989, s 44; ITEPA 2003, Sch 6 para 158; FA 2003, Sch 24 para 10; SI 2004 No 2310, Art 42*].

Car or motor cycle hire

With respect to expenses incurred prior to 1 April 2009, where a deduction for management expenses incurred on the hiring of a 'car or motor cycle' of which the retail price when new (i.e. unused and not second-hand) exceeded £12,000 was allowed, the amount of that deduction was reduced for tax purposes by multiplying it by the fraction:

(12,000 + RP) = 2RP

where RP was the retail price when new. If the price paid for the car by the lessor when new was known, it could be used as the retail price when new, but otherwise the manufacturer's list price, net of any discount generally available but inclusive of extras and VAT, was used (HMRC Business Income Manual BIM47717).

The restriction did not apply to 'qualifying cars or motor cycles' nor to cars with low carbon dioxide emissions or electrically-propelled cars hired before 1 April 2013. These exclusions were identical to those applicable to the corresponding provision restricting trading expenses: for the detailed provisions, and for the meaning of 'car or motorcycle', see **71.9 TRADING EXPENSES AND DEDUCTIONS**.

Where the above restriction, or a 'corresponding restriction' has applied, any subsequent rental rebate (or debt release other than as part of a statutory insolvency arrangement) is reduced for the purposes of the claw back provisions at **51.3** above in the same proportion as the hire charge restriction. For this purpose, the '*corresponding restrictions*' are those under *CTA 2009, s 56(2)* (see **71.9 TRADING EXPENSES AND DEDUCTIONS**), *ITTOIA 2005, s 48(2)* (income tax trading income restriction) and *ICTA 1988, s 76ZN(2)* (insurance company expenses).

With respect to expenditure incurred on or after 1 April 2009, where a car, not falling into one of the following categories is hired, the hire charges are restricted by 15%. The reference to motor-cycles has been repealed.

The excepted categories are:

(a) a car first registered before 1 March 2001;
(b) a car with low CO_2 omissions (not more than 160 gm per kilometre driven);
(c) an electrically propelled car; or
(d) a qualifying hire car.

(b) and (c) are defined as for capital allowances.

The legislation at *CTA 2009, s 1251* states the provisions under *CTA 2009, s 58A* (short term hiring in and long-term hiring out) also apply. The restriction above in deductible hire charges does not apply if A or B applies:

(i) the hire period does not exceed 45 consecutive days; and
(ii) the hire period and any linked period do not together exceed 45 days 'the sub-hire period'

or if:

(i) the company makes the car available to a customer for more than 45 days; or
(ii) a car is so made available and the linked periods exceed 45 days.

Condition B does not apply if the customer is an employee of the taxpayer company, or connected with it and there must be no reciprocal arrangements. The exceptions do not apply if there is an avoidance motive. Where there is a sub-hire period, expenditure must be apportioned between it and the remainder of the period on a time basis. If the contract provides for a replacement car in the event of the original car being unavailable, both cars are treated as if they were the same car.

Where there is a rebate post a reduction in expenses, or a debt in respect of the hire charges is released (save where the release is part of statutory insolvency agreements), and the credit representing the rebate reverses a debit representing the expenses, then the calculation of the reversal amount includes the reduction of the amount given by step 1 of *CTA 2009, s 1230* by 15% (instead of applying step 2).

[*CTA 2009, s 1251; ICTA 1988, ss 578A, 578B; CAA 2001, Sch 2 para 52, Sch 3 para 113; ITTOIA 2005, Sch 1 para 238*].

Other restrictions

In addition to the above provisions, those listed below (and, where relevant, their predecessors) prohibit or restrict the deduction of management expenses:

- *CTA 2009, s 1290* (employee benefit contributions);
- *CTA 2009, s 1298* (business entertaining and gifts);
- *CTA 2009, s 1302* (social security contributions);
- *CTA 2009, s 1303* (penalties, interest and VAT surcharges);
- *CTA 2009, s 1304* (crime-related payments);
- *FA 2004, s 200* (no other relief for employers in connection with pension contributions); and
- *FA 2004, s 246* (restriction of deduction for non-contributory pension provision).

See also *FA 2004, s 196A* (power to restrict employer's pension contributions relief).

[*CTA 2009, s 1247*].

Case law

Management expenses do not include an exchange loss on the payment of interest (*Bennet v Underground Electric Railways Co of London Ltd* (1923) 8 TC 475); or brokerage and stamp duty on investment changes (*Capital and National Trust Ltd v Golder* (1949) 31 TC 265, CA); or payments to the guarantor of loan stock capital by the investment company issuing the stock (*Hoechst Finance Ltd v Gumbrell* (1983) 56 TC 594, CA). In *L G Berry Investments Ltd v Attwooll* (1964) 41 TC 547, the Special Commissioners' finding that part of the directors' remuneration was not allowable was upheld.

Miscellaneous

UK property business losses

[51.6] Where a company with investment business (or, for accounting periods beginning before 1 April 2004, an investment company) continues to carry on an investment business (or continues to be an investment company) but ceases to carry on a UK property business (see **62 PROPERTY INCOME**), any unrelieved losses from that business may be carried forward and treated as management expenses of the following accounting period. [*CTA 2010, s 63; ICTA 1988, s 392A(3); CTA 2009, Sch 1 para 108; SI 2004 No 2310, Art 12*].

Appeals

Appeals on management expense matters can be made under the general rules in *TMA 1970*, and the First Tier Tribunal will adjudicate, see further **6.1 APPEALS.**

Claims

Claims may be made to set off unrelieved management expenses of an accounting period as **GROUP RELIEF** (**39.5**) under *CTA 2010, ss 99, 103; ICTA 1988, s 403.*

Simon's Taxes. See **D1.1116, D2.220, D7.312.**

Example

XYZ Ltd, an investment company, rents out rooms, halls and equipment to conference providers. It makes up accounts to 31 March.

The following details are relevant.

	31.3.09	31.3.10
	£	£
Rents received	38,000	57,000
Interest receivable accrued (gross)	10,000	5,000
Chargeable gains	18,000	15,000
Management expenses		
attributable to property	20,000	25,000
attributable to management	50,000	40,000
Capital allowances		
attributable to property	1,000	500
attributable to management	2,000	1,000

The corporation tax computations are as follows.

Year ended 31.3.09

	£	£
Property income		
Rents		38,000

Deduct	Capital allowances	1,000	
	Management expenses	20,000	(21,000)
			17,000
Income from non-trading loan relationships			10,000
Chargeable gains			18,000
			45,000
Deduct	Management expenses	50,000	
	Capital allowances	2,000	(52,000)
			(7,000)
As at 31.3.09			
Unrelieved balance carried forward			£(7,000)

Year ended 31.3.10		£	£
Property income			
Rents			57,000
Deduct	Capital allowances	500	
	Management expenses	25,000	(25,500)
			31,500
Income from non-trading loan relationships			5,000
Chargeable gains			15,000
			51,500
Deduct	Management expenses	40,000	
	Capital allowances	1,000	
	Unrelieved balance from previous accounting period	7,000	(48,000)
			3,500

On 1 April 2010, XYZ Ltd diversified and began to provide conference services itself.

The following details are relevant for its accounting period ending 31 March 2011.

	31.3.11
	£
Income from conferences	65,000
Rents received	40,000
Interest receivable accrued (gross)	5,000
Conference costs	22,000
Management expenses attributable to property	20,000

			31.3.11
			£
attributable to management			73,000
Capital allowances			
attributable to conferences			2,000
attributable to property			400
attributable to management			800

The corporation tax computations are as follows.

Year ended 31.3.11				
		£	£	£
Trading income				65,000
Deduct	Conference costs		22,000	
	Capital allowances		2,000	
				(24,000)
				41,000
Property income				
Rents			40,000	
Deduct	Capital allowances	400		
	Management expenses	20,000	(20,400)	
				19,600
Income from non-trading loan relationships				5,000
Deduct	Management expenses	73,000		
	Capital allowances	800		(73,800)
Unrelieved balance carried forward				(8,200)

Receipts

Industrial development grants

[51.7] A grant received by a company with investment business under *Industrial Development Act 1982, ss 7* or *8* (or Northern Ireland equivalent) is an amount to which the charge to corporation tax on income applies (or, before *CTA 2009* took effect (see **70.2 TRADE PROFITS — INCOME AND SPECIFIC TRADES**), an amount chargeable to tax under *Schedule D, Case VI*).

This rule does not apply if the grant is designated as made towards specified capital expenditure or as compensation for the loss of capital assets, or if the grant is for all or part of a corporation tax liability (including one already paid). It also does not apply if the grant is taken into account in calculating corporation tax profits under another provision.

For accounting periods beginning before 1 April 2004, and subject to the transitional rule at **51.3** above for periods straddling that date, this provision applies only to investment companies.

[*CTA 2009, s 1252; ICTA 1988, s 93; ITTOIA 2005, Sch 1 para 72; SI 2004 No 2310, Sch paras 2, 11*].

Contributions to local enterprise organisations or urban regeneration companies — disqualifying benefits

If a management expenses deduction has been made by a company under **51.4**(viii) above and the company or a connected person receives a 'disqualifying benefit' which is attributable in any way to the contribution, the company is treated as receiving an amount equal to the value of the benefit and to which the charge to corporation tax on income applies (or, before *CTA 2009* took effect (see **70.2 TRADE PROFITS — INCOME AND SPECIFIC TRADES**), chargeable to tax under *Schedule D, Case VI*).

For this purpose, 'disqualifying benefit' has the same meaning as at **51.4**(viii) above. So far as the value of a benefit is taken into account in determining the amount of the original deduction it is excluded from this provision.

[*CTA 2009, s 1253; ICTA 1988, ss 79(9), 79A(4), 79B(4); ITTOIA 2005, Sch 1 paras 48–50*].

Repayments under Financial Services and Markets Act 2000

A payment made to a company with an investment business, as a result of a repayment provision made either under *Financial Services and Markets Act 2000, s 136(7)* or *s 214(1)* or by scheme rules (i.e. the rules referred to in *Financial Services and Markets Act 2000, Sch 17 para 14(1)*) for fees to be refunded in certain cases, is treated as an amount to which the charge to corporation tax on income applies (or, before *CTA 2009* took effect (see **70.2 TRADE PROFITS — INCOME AND SPECIFIC TRADES**), as an amount chargeable to tax under *Schedule D, Case VI*). Payments treated as trading or property business receipts are ignored for this purpose.

For accounting periods beginning before 1 April 2004, and subject to the transitional rule at **51.3** above for periods straddling that date, this provision applies only to investment companies.

[*CTA 2009, s 1254; ICTA 1988, s 76(2)(5); FA 2004, s 41, Sch 6 para 1*].

Losses on unquoted shares

[51.8] Where an investment company makes a capital loss on the disposal of shares in certain qualifying companies (unquoted shares in certain trading companies, as defined by the EIS rules) then it may claim to set that loss against income, under *CTA 2010, s 68 et seq; ICTA 1988, s 573*. This relief can only be claimed by investment companies — it does not extend to companies with investment business.

For details see further **55.17 LOSSES**.

Change in ownership

Restrictions on relief

Prescribed circumstances

[51.9] Anti-avoidance provisions apply to restrict the carry forward of management expenses, loan relationship and intangible assets deductions where there is a change in the ownership of a company with an investment business, in prescribed circumstances.

The restrictions mirror those for trading losses at **55.13 LOSSES** and apply where:

(a) after the change there is a 'significant increase' in the company's capital; or

(b) within the period from three years before to three years after the change there is a major change in the nature or conduct of the company's business. This includes a change in the nature of the company's investments, even if it is the result of a gradual process which began before that period; or

(c) the change occurs after the scale of business activities carried on by the investment company has become small or negligible and before any considerable revival.

[*CTA 2010, ss 677, 729; ICTA 1988, s 768B(1)–(3)*].

As regards (b) above, see further **55.13 LOSSES** as regards what constitute a change in ownership of a company and a 'major change' in the nature or conduct of a trade or business.

As regards (a) above, there is a '*significant increase*' in the company's capital if 'amount B' is more than twice 'amount A' or exceeds it by at least £1 million, where:

- 'amount A' is the lower of (I) the amount of its capital immediately before the change and (II) the 'highest 60 day minimum amount' for the year immediately preceding the change; and
- 'amount B' is the highest 60 day minimum amount for the three years beginning with the change.

The '*highest 60 day minimum amount*' for a period is found by taking the highest of the daily amounts of the company's capital over the period and determining whether there was a period of at least 60 days within the overall period in which there was no daily amount lower than the amount taken. If there was no such period, the next highest of the daily amounts is taken and the same test carried out, and so on until the highest 60 day minimum amount is found.

For this purpose, the amount of the company's capital (expressed in sterling) is the aggregate of (I) its paid up share capital (including any share premium account), (II) any outstanding debts (including interest due) incurred by the company for any money borrowed or capital assets acquired by the company, for any right to receive income created in favour of the company, or for consideration the value of which to the company (at the time the debt was incurred) was substantially less than the amount of the debt (including any premium thereon), and (III) any outstanding redeemable loan capital.

[*CTA 2010, ss 688–691; ICTA 1988, Sch 28A paras 1–5*].

Apportionment between accounting periods

Where these provisions apply the accounting period in which the change occurs is treated (for the purposes only of the provisions) as two separate accounting periods, up to and after the change.

The amounts listed below are then apportioned as specified below between those periods. The amounts are:

(A) the amount for the accounting period being divided of any adjusted non-trading loan relationship profits (as defined);
(B) any adjusted non-trading loan relationship deficit for that period (as defined);
(C) any non-trading debit falling to be brought into account for that period in respect of any debtor relationship;
(D) any non-trading loan relationship deficit carried forward to that period;
(E) any non-trading intangible fixed assets credits or debits for that period (other than any amount within (F) below;
(F) any non-trading loss on intangible fixed assets carried forward to that period;
(G) any management expenses referable to that period, but excluding any amounts which would be disallowed because of *CTA 2009, s 1219(3)(b)* (expenses otherwise allowable in computing total profits);
(H) any excess management expenses carried forward to that period;
(I) any capital allowances which would (apart from these provisions) be added to the management expenses of that period; and
(J) any other amounts by reference to which the profits or losses of that period would (apart from these provisions) be calculated.

The basis of apportionment of amounts within (A)–(J) above is as follows.

- Amounts within (A), (B), (I) and (J) above are apportioned on a time basis.
- Amounts within (C) above, where an amortised cost basis applies, are apportioned by reference to the time of accrual of the amount to which the debit relates *except* in the case of certain late interest payments where interest is brought into account when paid, or where an adjustment is required under *CTA 2009, ss 407, 409* (certain debits relating to discounted securities to be brought into account on redemption, see **54.46 LOAN RELATIONSHIPS**), where the debit is apportioned to the pre-change part of the period in full.
- Amounts within (D), (F) and (H) above are apportioned to the pre-change part of the period in full.
- Amounts within (E) and (G) above are apportioned in accordance with generally accepted accountancy principles as if accounts were drawn up for each part of the period.

If in any case such apportionment would work unreasonably or unjustly, a just and reasonable method of apportionment may be substituted.

[*CTA 2010, ss 678, 685, 686; ICTA 1988, ss 768B(4)(5), 768D(3)(4)(9), 768E(2)(3), Sch 28A paras 6–8*].

Restrictions applicable

The following restrictions apply to the various debits and expenses identified:

(i) **Loan relationship debits.** 'Relevant non-trading debits' may not be carried forward beyond the change of ownership date to the extent to which the aggregate of those debits (including any amounts brought into account for any previous period ending after the change in ownership) exceed the total taxable profits for the accounting period ending with the change in ownership.
'*Relevant non-trading debits*' are non-trading debits which are determined on an amortised cost basis of accounting (see **54.1 LOAN RELATIONSHIPS**) to which one of the following applies:
  (I) *CTA 2009, ss 407 or 409* (postponement until redemption of debits for connected or close companies' deeply discounted securities — see **54.46 LOAN RELATIONSHIPS**) applies and, were it not for those sections, the debit would have been brought into account for an accounting period ending before or with the change in ownership;
  (II) *CTA 2009, s 373* (late interest not treated as accruing until paid — see **54.43 LOAN RELATIONSHIPS**) applies and, were it not for that section, the debit would have been brought into account for an accounting period ending before or with the change in ownership: or
  (III) the debit is not within (I) or (II) above but is in respect of a debtor relationship and relates to an amount which accrued before the change in ownership.

(ii) **Non-trading loan relationship deficits.** A brought-forward non-trading loan relationship deficit which is apportioned to the notional accounting period ending at the time of the change in ownership under (D) above cannot be carried forward to any accounting period ending after the change.

(iii) **Non-trading loss on intangible fixed assets.** Relief for such a loss (see **48.7 INTANGIBLE ASSETS**) against the total profits of the same accounting period is available only in relation to each of the notional accounting periods considered separately. A loss for an accounting period ending before the change in ownership cannot be carried forward to an accounting period ending after the change or treated as if it were a non-trading debit of that period.

(iv) **Management expenses.** Management expenses and capital allowances which are apportioned to either of the notional accounting periods as in (H) and (I) above, are treated as management expenses referable to that notional period. In computing the taxable total profits of the company for an accounting period ending after the change, no deduction can be made for management expenses deductible, or allowances falling to be made for, an accounting period beginning before the change.

(v) **UK property business losses.** Relief for losses under *CTA 2010, s 62(3)* (relief for loss against total profits of accounting period of loss — see **62 PROPERTY INCOME**) is available only in relation to each of the notional accounting periods considered separately. A loss made in an accounting period beginning before the change in ownership cannot be carried forward to an accounting period ending after the change.

(vi) **Overseas property business losses.** A loss made in an accounting period beginning before the change in ownership cannot be carried forward to an accounting period ending after the change.

Where deductions have been restricted because of (i), (ii) or (iv) above, in applying the *CAA 2001* provisions relating to balancing charges by reference to any event after the change, any allowance falling to be made in taxing the company's trade for any period before the change is disregarded in so far as the profits of that and any subsequent chargeable period before the change are insufficient to give effect to it (assuming that it is relieved in priority to any loss not attributable to such an allowance).

[*CTA 2010, ss 679–684, 687, 730; ICTA 1988, ss 768B(6)–(13), 768D, 768E, Sch 28A paras 9A, 11, 12*].

Assessment

Where these provisions are triggered by circumstances or events at any time in the three years after the change, an assessment to give effect to them may be made within six years of that time (or the latest such time). [*CTA 2010, s 727; ICTA 1988, ss 768B(12), 768D(7), 768E(6)*].

Information

For the purposes of these provisions HMRC may, by notice in writing, require any person who is the registered owner of shares, stock or securities of a company to state whether he is the beneficial owner thereof and, if not, to supply the name and address of the person(s) on whose behalf he holds them. [*CTA 2010, s 728; ICTA 1988, ss 768B(12), 768D(7), 768E(6)*].

Asset transferred within group

Where there is a change in ownership of a company with investment business and none of the prescribed circumstances in (a)–(c) above applies, restrictions similarly apply where:

(1) after the change the company acquires an asset from another company in the same group so that *TCGA 1992, s 171* (transaction treated as giving rise to neither gain nor loss, see **18.4 CAPITAL GAINS — GROUPS**) or *CTA 2009, s 775* (tax-neutral transfer of intangible fixed asset, see **48.11 INTANGIBLE ASSETS**) applies, and

(2) a chargeable gain or a non-trading chargeable realisation gain on an intangible fixed asset (the 'relevant gain') arises to the company on disposal or realisation of the asset (or of an asset deriving its value wholly or partly from that asset — in particular where the original asset was a leasehold, the lessee has acquired the reversion and the freehold is disposed of) within three years of the change.

[*CTA 2010, s 692; ICTA 1988, ss 768C(1)(2)(13), 768D(1), 768E(1)*].

See **55.13 LOSSES** as regards what constitute a change in ownership of a company.

The accounting period of the change is divided in two as above and the amounts listed at (A) to (J) above are then apportioned as specified above between those periods.

In addition, the chargeable gains and the non-trading chargeable realisation gains included, in accordance with *TCGA 1992, s 8(1)* and *Sch 7A* (see **17.3 CAPITAL GAINS, 38.6 GAINS AND LOSS BUYING**) and *CTA 2009, Pt 8 Ch 6* (see **48.8 INTANGIBLE ASSETS**), in the total profits for the period being divided are also apportioned. The total of those amounts, in so far as it exceeds the relevant gain, is apportioned to the pre-change part of the divided period, and an amount equivalent to the relevant gain (or, if less, the total itself) is apportioned to the post-change part of the divided period.

Management expenses and capital allowances which are apportioned to either of the notional accounting periods as in (H) and (I) above, are treated as management expenses referable to that notional period. [*CTA 2010, ss 694, 695, 699(2)(3), 702, 703; ICTA 1988, ss 768D(3)–(5)(12)(13), 768D(3)(4), 768E(2)(3), Sch 28A paras 13–17*].

If the total profits of the company for the accounting period in which the relevant gain accrues include, in accordance with *TCGA 1992, s 8(1)* and *Sch 7A* and *CTA 2009, Pt 8 Ch 6*, an amount in respect of chargeable gains or non-trading chargeable realisation gains, the following restrictions apply:

- **Loan relationship debits.** The debits which can be brought into account in any accounting period beginning after the change in ownership do not include 'relevant non-trading debits' (see (i) above) to the extent that those debits exceed the 'modified total profits' of the accounting period. If debits are excluded in this way, they can nevertheless be carried forward to the next accounting period, subject to the application of this rule for that period.
  The '*modified total profits*' of an accounting period are the total profits less the relevant gain if it accrues in the period and after deducting any amounts which can be relieved against the profits (other than a non-trading deficit of the period falling to be deducted under *CTA 2009, s 461* (see **54.4 LOAN RELATIONSHIPS**)).
- **Non-trading loan relationship deficit.** If a non-trading deficit is apportioned to the first of the notional accounting periods, none of it may be carried forward to a subsequent accounting period.
- **Non-trading loss on intangible fixed assets.** Relief for such a loss (see **48.7 INTANGIBLE ASSETS**) against the total profits of the same accounting period is available only in relation to each of the notional accounting periods considered separately. A loss for an accounting period beginning before the change in ownership may not be relieved in the accounting period in which the relevant gain arises against so much of the total profits of that period as 'represent the relevant gain'.
  The amount of any profits that '*represent the relevant gain*' is the amount of the relevant gain or, if less, the amount included in the profits in respect of chargeable gains or, as the case may be, non-trading chargeable realisation gains for the accounting period concerned.

- **Management expenses.** In calculating the taxable total profits for the accounting period in which the relevant gain arises, no deduction for management expenses may be made for such expenses or capital allowances carried forward from an accounting period beginning before the change in ownership from so much of the total profits as represents the relevant gain.
- **UK property business losses.** Relief for losses under *CTA 2010, s 62(3)* (relief for loss against total profits of accounting period of loss — see **62 PROPERTY INCOME**) is available only in relation to each of the notional accounting periods considered separately. A loss made in an accounting period beginning before the change in ownership may not be deducted from so much of the profits of an accounting period ending after the change as represents the relevant gain.
- **Overseas property business losses.** A loss made in an accounting period beginning before the change in ownership may not be deducted from so much of the profits of an accounting period ending after the change as represents the relevant gain.

[*CTA 2010, ss 693, 696–701; ICTA 1988, ss 768C(6)–(9)(13), 768D(2)(5)–(7)(9), 768E(1)(4)(5), Sch 28A paras 10, 10A*].

The assessment and information powers relating to the deductions provisions above apply equally under these provisions.

Simon's Taxes. See D7.320–D7.324.

Key points

[51.10] Points to consider are as follows.

- The parent company of a group will be a 'company with investment business', regardless of whether it also has trading operations. It will therefore be able to claim as management expenses a deduction for costs it incurs in relation to managing its investments in its subsidiaries.
- Care is needed when considering how unrelieved management expenses for an accounting period can be utilised. It is not possible to carry back management expenses to a prior period. Management expenses may only be group relieved to the extent that current period management expenses exceed current period profits of the surrendering company (i.e. profits before offset of losses (current year or brought forward), charges on income and management expenses).
- Management expenses carried forward are treated as management expenses arising in the following accounting period.
- Brought forward management expenses are deductible in the next accounting period in which the company has investment business. Excess management expenses cannot however be carried forward after the company ceases to carry out investment business. In the event that a company has excess management expenses and is to

sell all its investments but intends to recommence its business, consideration should be given to maintaining an investment business. Holding surplus cash on deposit does not comprise an investment business.

- It is not possible to claim a management expense deduction for expenses of a capital nature. As a result, expenses incurred in relation to the acquisition or disposal of investments will not be deductible as management expenses, although they may be deductible in calculating any chargeable gain arising on disposal of the investment. It may however be possible to claim a management expense deduction for expenses incurred before a decision to proceed with an acquisition or disposal is made. For example, costs incurred in appraising and investigating investments should generally be deductible.
- Given the broad application of the loss restriction provisions on a change of ownership of a company (see **51.9**), in most cases it is unlikely that a purchaser would ascribe value to tax losses in the target company.

52

Investment Funds

Cross-references. See **17.11**, **17.50** CAPITAL GAINS; **18.4**, CAPITAL GAINS — GROUPS; **30.46** DERIVATIVE CONTRACTS LEGISLATION; **54.96** LOAN RELATIONSHIPS; **61.11** PROFIT COMPUTATIONS.

Simon's Taxes. See D8.1 *et seq*.

Authorised investment funds

[52.1] The legislation applying to 'authorised investment funds' ('AIFs'), which includes open-ended investment companies ('OEICs') and authorised unit trusts ('AUTs') (see **52.2** and **52.3** below) is contained in *SI 2006 No 964* (as amended by *SI 2011 No 244*) and *SI 2009 No 2036* (as amended by *SI 2009 No 2199*) under powers in *F(No 2)A 2005, ss 17, 18*. The former regulations have effect for accounting periods beginning on or after 1 April 2006 (and for disposals and distributions made on or after that date) and the latter regulations from 1 September 2009.

[*SI 2006 No 964, Regs 1, 3; SI 2006 No 982; SI 2006 No 3239; SI 2007 No 683; SI 2009 No 2036; SI 2011 No 244*].

Collective investment schemes

Authorised unit trusts and open-ended investment companies are the most common forms of 'collective investment schemes'. A '*collective investment scheme*' is an arrangement with respect to property of any description, including money, the purpose or effect of which is to enable persons taking part in the arrangements (whether by becoming owners of all or part of the property or otherwise) to participate in or receive profits or income arising from the acquisition, holding, management or disposal of the property or sums paid out of such profits or income. [*Financial Services and Markets Act 2000, s 235; FA 2004, s 118(4); SI 2001 No 3629, Arts 62(2), 70; SI 2006 No 964, Regs 6, 8*]. The object of such a scheme is to enable a large number of investors to pool their money by investing in a professionally managed fund of investments, thus spreading risk. A body corporate (other than an open-ended investment company) is not regarded as a collective investment scheme, so that **INVESTMENT TRUSTS (53)**, **VENTURE CAPITAL TRUSTS (74)**, **INDUSTRIAL AND PROVIDENT SOCIETIES (47)** and **FRIENDLY SOCIETIES (37)** are not collective investment schemes.

Individual savings accounts (ISAs)

The *Individual Savings Accounts Regulations 1998* (*SI 1998 No 1870*) as amended by The Individual Savings Accounts Regulations (Amendments) 2011 (*SI 2011 No 782*) enable investments in authorised investment funds to be held in individual savings accounts (see Tolley's Income Tax under Exempt Income) and similar rules applied to personal equity plans (*SI 1997 No 1716* as amended).

Open-ended investment companies

[52.2] OEICs are investment companies in which shares are continuously created or redeemed, according to investor demand. An OEIC is defined in *CTA 2010, s 613* as a company incorporated in the UK to which the *Financial Services and Markets Act 2000, s 236* applies.

The taxation of OEICs and their shareholders are covered partly by primary legislation but mainly by *SI 2006 No 964* (the new regulations for authorised investment funds) set out in **52.5–52.10** below. With effect from 6 April 2008 regulations were introduced to deal with property authorised investment funds ('PAIFs'). (*SI 2008 No 705*).

[*CTA 2010, ss 613–615; ICTA 1988, s 468A; FA 1995, s 152; F(No 2)A 2005, ss 16–19; SI 2006 No 964, Reg 4; ITA 2007 Sch 1 para 605*].

Regulations also deal with VAT (*Value Added Tax (Finance) Order 1997* (*SI 1997 No 510*)) and stamp duty and stamp duty reserve tax (*Stamp Duty and Stamp Duty Reserve Tax (Open-ended Investment Companies) Regulations 1997* (*SI 1997 No 1156*), *(Amendment) Regulations 1999* (*SI 1999 No 1467*) and *(Amendment No 2) Regulations 1999* (*SI 1999 No 3261*)) in relation to OEICs.

Simon's Taxes. See **D8.140, D8.141.**

Authorised unit trusts

[52.3] As defined in *CTA 2010, s 616(1)*, an AUT is a 'unit trust scheme' where the property is held for the beneficiaries by a trustee and it is authorised by the FSA to sell to the public (subject to an order set out in the *Financial Services and Markets Act 2000, s 243*, for the whole or part of an accounting period). The investors are issued with units that represent their entitlement to profit, losses and gains in the AUT. The primary objective of an AUT is to provide income or capital return to the investor by reducing investment risk through holding a range of different investments.

There are some exclusions to the general definition of a 'unit trust scheme' for Capital Gains Tax purposes as outlined in *SI 1988 No 266, SI 1988 No 267, SI 1988 No 268* as amended. These include unit trust schemes which are:

- a limited partnership scheme;
- a profit sharing scheme which has been approved as an approved share option scheme; and
- an employee share ownership plan.

The same exclusions apply for Income Tax purposes but in addition, an enterprise zone property scheme or a charitable unit trust scheme are also excluded.

See also **52.21** below as regards court investment funds.

Umbrella companies and umbrella schemes

[52.4] An '*umbrella company*' is an OEIC which provides for separate pooling of shareholder contributions and of the profits or income out of which payments are made to those shareholders and under which they may exchange rights in one pool for those of another. Each of the parts of an umbrella company is regarded for the purpose of these provisions as an OEIC unless expressly provided for elsewhere in any other tax provisions, but the umbrella company as a whole is not to be regarded as an OEIC nor as a company. [*CTA 2010, s 615; ICTA 1988, s 468A; SI 2006 No 964, Reg 7*].

'*Umbrella schemes*' are authorised unit trust schemes which provide for separate pools of contributions and of the profits or income out of which payments are made to the participants and under which they may exchange rights in one pool for those of another. Each of the parts of an umbrella scheme is regarded for the purpose of these provisions as an authorised unit trust but the scheme as a whole is not to be regarded as an authorised unit trust or any other form of collective investment scheme. [*CTA 2010, s 619; ICTA 1988, s 468(7)–(9); SI 2006 No 964, Reg 7*].

Tax treatment of authorised investment funds

Corporation tax

[52.5] *CTA 2010, s 614* has effect as if the trustees of an AUT were a company resident in the UK, and the rights of unit holders were shares in the company. [*CTA 2010, s 617; ICTA 1988, s 468(1)*].

A special rate of corporation tax applies to OEICs and to the trustees of an AUT, equal to the basic rate of income tax in that financial year. [*CTA 2010, ss 614, 618; ICTA 1988, ss 468(1A), 468A*].

SI 2006 No 964, Reg 94(2)–(4) makes it clear that AIFs cannot form part of any arrangements for group relief purposes.

Capital gains

For capital gains purposes, any unit trust scheme is treated as if the scheme were a company and the rights of the unit holders were shares in the company and, in the case of an authorised unit trust, as if the company were UK resident and ordinarily resident. [*TCGA 1992, s 99(1)*]. Capital gains, accruing to OIECs or AUTs (including umbrella companies or umbrella schemes see **52.4** above), for the benefit of investors, are not chargeable gains. [*TCGA 1992, s 100(1); SI 2006 No 964, Reg 100*]. For company reorganisations involving authorised unit trusts, see **17.11 CAPITAL GAINS**.

See Tolley's Capital Gains Tax under Unit Trusts and Other Investment Vehicles for the capital gains tax treatment of disposals, amalgamation with or conversion of an AUT to an OEIC, accumulation units and monthly savings schemes.

Loan relationships and derivative contracts

'Capital profits, gains or losses' arising to an AIF from a derivative contract or (with effect for accounting periods beginning on or after 1 January 2009 (*SI 2008 No 3159*)) from a debtor or creditor relationship are to be disregarded under these provisions. '*Capital profits, gains or losses*' in this case are those which, in preparing accounts in accordance with UK generally accepted accounting practice, fail to be dealt with in the statement of total return (under the heading of 'net gains/losses on investments during the period' or 'other gains/losses') in accordance with the relevant Statement of Recommended Practice (SORP). Interest distributions paid by an AIF are taxable under the loan relationship rules (see **54 LOAN RELATIONSHIPS**) as if they were interest payable on a loan. A deficit on a loan relationship of an AIF cannot be carried back to set against profits of an earlier accounting period under *CTA 2009, ss 456–460*.

[*SI 2006 No 964, Regs 8, 10–14; replacing ICTA 1988, s 468L(5)–(7)*].

Diversely owned AIFs

Tax treatment of diversely owned AIFs

[52.6] An AIF that carries out an 'investment transaction' (see below) and meets the 'genuine diversity of ownership condition' (see **52.13**) in respect of an accounting period is referred to as a 'diversely owned AIF'.

SI 2009 No 2036 inserted *Part 2B* to *SI 2006 No 964* and these regulations prevent defined financial transactions carried out by diversely owned AIFs from being characterised as trading transactions for tax purposes. The rules give diversely owned AIFs certainty that gains on the realisation of certain types of investments cannot be re-characterised as profits arising from a trade, which would then be taxable as income.

Where an AIF is diversely owned, all capital profits, gains or losses arising from investment transactions are treated as non-trading and the corporation tax provisions under which trading profits and losses are computed and charged do not apply to these transactions.

Capital profits, gains and losses for this purpose are any profits, gains or losses treated as capital for accounting purposes under the Statement of Recommended Practice (SORP) which applies to AIFs.

The regulations prevent capital gains being re-characterised as trading profits (and therefore revenue), but they do not prevent revenue profits from investment transactions being taxable as income. For example, interest receivable in respect of a loan relationship will be taxable as income even where the regulations apply to prevent any capital profit on disposal of the loan relationship being characterised as trading income.

Where the regulations do not apply, it remains a question of fact whether or not activities carried out by an AIF amount to trading for tax purposes. In such cases, the normal principles for determining whether or not there is a trade will apply however, there is no automatic assumption that transactions which are not investment transactions will be trading transactions by default.

Whilst it is possible that some activities carried out by an AIF might, based on the facts, amount to trading, there is a general and prevailing assumption that an AIF will not be conducting a trade.

These provisions apply to transactions carried out on or after 1 September 2009.

Meaning of investment transaction

Regulations 14F–14N of *SI 2006 No 961* specify the types of transactions that are investment transactions for the purposes of the regulations, commonly referred to as the '*white list*'. The regulations provide that an investment transaction is any transaction:

- in stocks or shares;
- in a 'relevant contract';
- which results in the diversely owned AIF becoming party to a loan relationship or related transaction;
- in units in a collective investment scheme;
- in securities;
- consisting of the buying or selling of foreign currency; or
- in a carbon emission trading product.

Any transaction that is not specified in *Regs 14F–14N* of *SI 2006 No 964* will not be an investment transaction for the purposes of the regulations. However, this does not mean that the transaction will be a trading transaction by default. Such a transaction may still be non-trading on first principles.

Under the regulations, any transaction in a relevant contract is deemed to be an investment transaction, with a 'relevant contract' defined as an option, a future or a contract for differences.

Transactions in a wide range of derivative contracts are encompassed in the regulations. The definitions are widely-drawn and, importantly, there is no requirement for options, futures or contracts for differences to be accounted for as a derivative financial instrument in order to be a relevant contract.

[*SI 2009 No 2036; SI 2006 No 964*].

The practical effect of the introduction of the white list is that significant volumes of transactions can be undertaken by the AIFs (in respect of items included in the white list) without the risk of the fund being regarded as trading in these investments. In a situation where an AIF undertakes a transaction which is not on the white list, and is subsequently found to be trading, only that particular transaction would be taxed as a trading item, and it would not result in the entire AIF activity being treated as trading. It is important to note, however, that this certainty would only apply to those AIFs which satisfy a genuine diversity of ownership condition (see **52.13**).

Distributions made by authorised investment funds

[52.7] The total amount available for distribution to participants is to be shown in the distribution accounts as available for distribution either as dividends (a 'dividend distribution'), or as yearly interest (which may not include any amount chargeable to corporation tax as income of a UK or an overseas property business — an 'interest distribution'). These provisions do not apply to an AIF which is a registered pension scheme within the meaning of *FA 2004, Pt 4* or is treated as having become such a scheme under *FA 2004, Sch 36*. They also do not apply for Tax Elected Funds (TEFs) or Property Authorised Investment Funds (PAIFs). [*SI 2006 No 964, Regs 16, 17; SI 2006 No 982; SI 2009 No 2036, Reg 11*].

For these purposes, the making of a distribution includes the investment of an amount on behalf of the participant in respect of his accumulation units (this being subject to the treatment of de minimis amounts — see below). [*SI 2006 No 964, Regs 15, 18(4)(b), 22(4) replacing ICTA 1988, s 468H(2) and SI 1997 No 1154 (as amended) from 1 April 2006*].

Interest distributions

An '*interest distribution*' is treated as a payment of yearly interest made on the '*distribution date*' (i.e. the date specified or in accordance with the terms of the trust or instrument of incorporation of the company or, if there is no such date, the last day of the distribution period), to the participants in proportion to their rights, including interest paid to a participant not liable to income tax. No amount may be shown as an interest distribution unless the AIF satisfies a 'qualifying investments test' throughout the distribution period. This requires that, at all times in the period, at least 60% of the market value of the fund's investments are represented by 'qualifying investments'.

'*Qualifying investments*' are funds invested within any of the following categories.

(1) Money placed at interest.

(2) Securities (excluding shares in a company).
(3) Shares in a building society.
(4) Qualifying units in another AIF (which itself satisfies the qualifying investments test in relation to 1–3 above and 5–8 below).
(5) Derivative contracts (for accounting periods beginning on or after 1 October 2002) whose underlying subject matter consists wholly of any one or more of 1–4 above or (for accounting periods beginning on or after 1 April 2006) currency.
(6) Contracts for differences (for accounting periods beginning on or after 1 October 2002) whose underlying matter consists wholly of any one or more of the following; interest rates, creditworthiness or (for accounting periods beginning on or after 1 April 2006) currency.
(7) Derivative contracts (for accounting periods beginning on or after 1 April 2006) not within 5 or 6 above where there is a hedging relationship (as defined) between the derivative contract and an asset within 1–4 above. Or;
(8) Alternative finance arrangements. Funds invested in alternative finance arrangements are qualifying investments under *SI 2006 No 964, Reg 20* from 1 April 2006. For interest distributions before that date and broadly on or after 6 April 2005, qualifying investments of money placed at interest includes money invested under alternative finance arrangements. [*FA 2005, s 56, Sch 2 para 4 as repealed by SI 2006 No 964, Reg 92; CTA 2009, Sch 1 para 660*].

[*SI 2006 No 964, Regs 15, 18–21 replacing ICTA 1988, s 468L and SI 1997 No 1154 (as amended) from 1 April 2006; SI 2006 No 982*].

Dividend distributions

A '*dividend distribution*' is treated as a dividend on shares paid on the distribution date (as above), to the participants in proportion to their rights, including dividends paid to a participant not liable to corporation tax. [*SI 2006 No 964, Regs 15, 22 replacing ICTA 1988, s 468J and SI 1997 No 1154 (as amended) from 1 April 2006; ITTOIA 2005, Sch 1 para 179; SI 2006 No 982*].

De minimis amounts

An AIF is not treated as making an interest or dividend distribution if:

- the fund has (in accordance with FSA rules) an agreed '*de minimis limit*' (an amount in respect of which a distribution of fund income is not required if the amount shown in the fund's distribution accounts as available for distribution does not exceed that limit);
- the fund has a de minimis amount shown in the distribution accounts as available for distribution to participants but waives distribution of that amount and carries it forward as an amount available for distribution in the next distribution period; and
- none of the fund's units in issue on the 'distribution date' (as above) are in bearer form.

[*SI 2006 No 964, Reg 23*].

Tax treatment of participants

[52.8] These provisions do not apply to an AIF which is a registered pension scheme within the meaning of *FA 2004, Pt 4* or is treated as having become such a scheme under *FA 2004, Sch 36*. [*SI 2006 No 964, Reg 25*].

Participants chargeable to income tax

Interest distributions

[52.9] For interest distributions made to a participant chargeable to income tax, basic rate tax is deductible under *ITA 2007, s 874* (formerly *ICTA 1988, s 349(2)*) unless either:

- the participant is a company or the trustee of a unit trust scheme; or
- the 'residence condition' or the 'reputable intermediary condition' is met with respect to the participant on the distribution date.

However, if the participant is a company which is a trustee of the trust to which (or under which) the distribution is made (or received), the obligation to deduct tax is not excluded by virtue of the fact that the participant is a company and one of the other conditions would have to be satisfied for the exemption to apply. In the case of accumulation units, the obligation to deduct tax is an obligation to deduct a sum out of the amount being credited to scheme capital on the participant's behalf.

[*SI 2006 No 964, Reg 26; ICTA 1988, ss 468L, 468M; FA 2003, s 203, Sch 43 Pt 5(3); ITTOIA 2005, Sch 1 para 180, SI 1997 No 1154; SI 2003 No 1830 and SI 2003 No 1831*].

The '*residence condition*' requires broadly that a valid declaration is made to the legal owner of the AIF, in the prescribed form, that either the participant is not ordinarily resident in the UK or, if the units are held by the participant as the personal representative of a deceased holder, the deceased was not ordinarily resident in the UK at the time of his death. [*SI 2006 No 964, Regs 30–33, 75; ICTA 1988, ss 468O, 468P FA 2003, s 203(4)–(8) and SI 1997 No 1154 (as amended)*].

The '*reputable intermediary condition*' requires broadly that the interest distribution is paid on behalf of the participant to a company which is subject to certain money laundering controls, and that the legal owner has reasonable grounds for believing the participant to be not ordinarily resident in the UK. If it subsequently transpires that the participant was in fact ordinarily resident, the tax which should have been deducted is payable by the legal owner under *ICTA 1988, s 350, Sch 16*. See *TMA 1970, s 98(4E)* for penalty provisions. [*SI 2006 No 964, Regs 27–29; ICTA 1988, ss 468O(1A)–(1B), 468PA; FA 2003, s 203(6)(9) and SI 1997 No 1154 (as amended)*].

Where interest distributions are made without the deduction of tax, the fund is required to notify HMRC under *SI 2006 No 964, Regs 71–74* within 14 days of the end of the tax year. This notice must be given in writing and has effect for the tax year in which it is given and for subsequent tax years until the notice is withdrawn. Failure to do so will result in the fund being liable to a maximum penalty of £3,000.

HMRC may, by notice, require that a fund provide them with information for the purpose of determining whether interest distributions were properly made without deduction of tax. This information will include copies of any relevant books, documents, residence declarations or other records, and must be provided within the timescale as specified in the notice.

Guidance notes are available on HMRC's website (at www.hmrc.gov.uk/specialist/auth-unit-trust-notes.htm) for managers and operators of AUTs and OEICs about the circumstances in which interest distributions of such funds can be paid without deduction of income tax. Various forms are also available including forms for individuals who are not ordinarily resident and companies (where they have joint holdings with individuals) which are non-resident, to make a declaration to obtain payment without deduction of income tax.

Dividend distributions

A dividend distribution from an AIF is treated in the same way as other UK company dividends and bears a notional tax credit of 10% that may be used to reduce the investor's liability to tax on the income.

For non-taxpayers, the fact that the credit is only notional means that they cannot claim a repayment of the credit, and they are in exactly the same position as a basic rate taxpayer.

Participants chargeable to corporation tax

Interest distributions

[52.10] Where, on the distribution date, the participant is within the charge to corporation tax, the obligation to deduct tax does not apply to interest distributions unless the participant is a company which is a trustee of the trust to which (or under which) the distribution is made (or received). In the case of accumulation units, the obligation to deduct tax is an obligation to deduct a sum out of the amount being invested on the participant's behalf.

[*SI 2006 No 964, Reg 47*].

SI 2006 No 964, Regs 71–74 lays out the requirements to notify HMRC in writing within 14 days of the end of the tax year where interest distributions are made without deduction of tax and the powers of HMRC in this respect.

Dividend distributions

Where, on the distribution date, the participant is within the charge to corporation tax, then (unless the participant is the manager of the AIF in the ordinary course of business) for the purpose of computing the unit holder's corporation tax liability, the 'unfranked' part of a dividend distribution is treated as:

(i) an annual payment and not as a dividend distribution or interest distribution; and
(ii) having been received by the participant after deduction of income tax at the basic rate for the tax year in which the distribution date falls.

If there is any foreign element to the tax treated as deducted in (ii) a corresponding proportionate part of the distribution is treated as if it were income from the respective territory and the tax suffered treated as if it were tax equivalent to UK corporation tax, payable under the law of the territory. [*SI 2010 No 1642*].

Where tax is deemed to have been deducted under (ii) above, repayment to the participant may not exceed the participant's portion (by reference to the participants' rights in the fund in the distribution period in question) of the legal owner's net liability to corporation tax in respect of that gross income, as reduced by any double tax relief, whether under an agreement or by way of credit under *TIOPA 2010, s 18; ICTA 1988, s 790(1)* (see **32.2, 32.3 DOUBLE TAX RELIEF**). In calculating the amount repayable, tax treated as having been deducted by virtue of (ii) above is set off in priority to any other tax subject to deduction under *ITA 2007, Pt 15*. The statement sent to the participant relating to the distribution must show the legal owner's net liability to corporation tax in respect of the gross income.

The '*unfranked*' part of the dividend distribution is found by the formula:

$$U = \frac{A \times C}{D}$$

where:

U is the unfranked part of the dividend distribution to the participant;
A is the amount of the dividend distribution;
C is such amount of the gross income as does not derive from franked investment income, as reduced by the amount of the legal owner's net liability to corporation tax in respect of that gross income less any double tax relief, whether under an agreement or by way of credit under *TIOPA 2010, s 18; ICTA 1988, s 790(1)* (see **32.2, 32.3 DOUBLE TAX RELIEF**); and
D is the gross income as in C (and similarly reduced), but including any part deriving from franked investment income.

[*TIOPA 2010, s 18; SI 2010 No 1642; SI 2006 No 964, Regs 48–52, 70; ICTA 1988, s 468Q and SI 1997 No 1154 (as amended); SI 2006 No 981*].

Qualified investor schemes

[52.11] A 'qualified investor scheme' (QIS) is a fund, authorised by the Financial Services Authority, in which a statement that the fund is a qualified investor scheme is included in the instrument constituting the scheme. [*SI 2006 No 964, Reg 53(3)*]. Only institutional and certain sophisticated investors are eligible to participate in such schemes.

Prior to 1 January 2009 a special tax regime applied to participants with a 'substantial holding' in a QIS, whereby the participants were required to ascertain the market value of the holding at specified measuring dates, and then were charged to tax by reference to the difference in the market value of the holding between the two specified measuring dates. The aggregate of these differences in market value for an accounting period (or tax year) was taken, and where the aggregate was a positive amount, that amount was charged to either income or corporation tax as miscellaneous income (and a negative amount is an income loss).

As increases in the value of a holding were taxed under the regime as income, no chargeable gain arose on disposals of all or part of the holding. However, on the first measuring date, the participant was required to calculate the chargeable gain or loss which would have accrued on the disposal of the substantial holding at its market value at that time. This was not immediately chargeable (or allowable), but deferred until any subsequent disposal (or part disposal) of the substantial holding. See Tolley's Capital Gain Tax under Unit Trusts and Other Investment Vehicles for full details.

SI 2008 No 3159 introduced a new regime from 1 January 2009, removing the specific corporate ownership condition, the 10% test, and allowing all investors in a QIS to benefit from the tax regime applying to AIFs, subject to the condition that investment in the QIS will not be limited to specific individuals or companies ('the genuine diversity of ownership condition' — see **52.13**).

Property Authorised Investment Funds

[52.12] Following the successes of the UK-Real Estate Investment Trust (REIT) regime, introduced in January 2007, regulations came into force from 6 April 2008 under which Property Authorised Investment Funds (PAIFs) can be set up. A PAIF is an AIF that has an investment portfolio primarily comprising of real property or shares in UK REITs or certain other similar entities.

The PAIF regime was introduced to provide an open-ended equivalent of the UK-REIT regime that aims to provide a UK tax efficient vehicle for investments in real estate. It does this by shifting the point of tax for property income from the AIF level to the investor (i.e. the effect is broadly the same as if the investor had owned the property or REIT shares directly).

Entry into and membership of the PAIF regime

[52.13] *SI 2008 No 705* inserted *Part 4A* to *SI 2006 No 964*, which outlines the conditions that are to be met in order to be treated as a PAIF from 6 April 2008. In order to be within the PAIF regime, an AIF must be constituted as an OEIC. The PAIF regime is an elective regime where an Authorised Corporate Director (ACD), or proposed ACD, must give advance notice in writing to HMRC if it wants the PAIF rules to apply from a given date. For existing OEICs, notice must be given at least 28 days before the beginning of the accounting period for which the PAIF regime is to apply, whilst this notification period is extended to 42 days for new OEICs.

In addition to being an OEIC, to be eligible to be treated as a PAIF there are six conditions that have to be met throughout each accounting period. These conditions are:

- the property investment business condition;
- the genuine diversity of ownership condition;
- the corporate ownership condition;
- the loan creditor condition;
- the balance of business conditions; and
- the notification condition.

[*SI 2006 No 964, Pt 4A, paras 69D–69O*].

The property investment business condition

In order to meet the property investment business condition:

- the OEIC's instrument of incorporation and prospectus (including supplements) must include a statement that the company's investment objectives are to carry on 'property investment business' and to manage cash raised from investors for that purpose; and
- the OEIC must carry on such a business.

The term '*property investment business*' means a business consisting of one or more of the following:

- 'property rental business' (see below);
- owning shares in UK REITs; or
- owning shares or units in foreign entities that are equivalent to UK REITs.

For this purposes a 'property rental business' (as defined in *SI 2006 No 964, Pt 4A, para 69H*) is:

- a UK or overseas property business; and
- the relevant business of an intermediate holding vehicle (IHV). An entity is an IHV in an accounting period if:
  - (a) it is a company, trust or partnership and not a collective investment scheme;
  - (b) it is wholly owned either by the PAIF or another IHV or series of IHVs which are wholly owned by the parent, unless this is prohibited by local laws or regulations that require a proportion of local ownership;
  - (c) the function of the IHV is solely to enable the holding of real estate based outside of the UK;
  - (d) the IHV has its accounts consolidated with those of the parent; and
  - (e) all property rental income of the IHV (or the full proportion of that income representing the interest of the parent in the IHV) must be reflected in the distribution accounts of the parent at the same time as the income is reflected in the accounts of the IHV.

The genuine diversity of ownership condition

[*SI 2006 No 964, Reg 9A*].

The genuine diversity of ownership condition is met if condition A–C are satisfied:

Condition A

The fund documents (meaning the instrument constituting the fund and its prospectus) must contain a statement that units in the fund will be widely available, must specify the intended categories of investor and must specify that the manager of the fund must market and make available the units in accordance with condition C below.

Condition B

Neither the specification of the intended categories of investor, nor any other terms or conditions governing participation in the fund (whether or not specified in the fund documents), has the effect of limiting investors to a limited number of specific persons or specific groups of connected persons, or deters a reasonable investor within the intended categories of investor from investing in the fund.

Condition C

Units in the fund must be marketed and made available sufficiently widely to reach the intended categories of investor in a manner appropriate to attract those categories of investors. In addition, a person who is an intended category of investor can, upon request to the manager of the fund, obtain information about the fund and acquire units in it.

This condition shall be treated as being met even if, at the relevant time, the fund has no capacity to receive additional investments, unless the capacity of the fund to receive investments in it is fixed by the fund documents, and a pre-determined number of specific persons or specific groups of connected persons make investments in the fund which collectively exhaust all, or substantially all, of that capacity.

A PAIF also meets the genuine diversity of ownership condition if:

- an investor in the fund is a unit trust scheme (a 'feeder fund');
- conditions A–C above are met in relation to the PAIF after taking into account the fund documents relating to the feeder fund and the intended investors in the feeder fund; and
- the PAIF and the feeder fund have the same manager (or proposed manager).

Prior to 1 September 2009, the following additional conditions were also in place:

- where there was a qualified investor scheme, a person qualified to invest could obtain information without difficulty;
- the minimum investment was not unreasonably high in view of the risk profile of the company or the intended categories of investors; and
- where charges were imposed on larger investors, charges on smaller investors must not have been greater than was commercially normal and reasonable.

An advance clearance in relation to the genuine diversity of ownership condition may be made in writing to the Tax Tribunal by the manager (or proposed manager) of an AIF. An application for clearance must be accompanied by the fund documents in the form in which it is proposed that those documents will apply at the beginning of the first accounting period of the fund for which clearance is sought.

The corporate ownership condition — the 10% test

The aim of this condition is to prevent a corporate body from owning 10% or more of a PAIF, so ensuring the fund's income from UK property stays within the remit of UK taxation. The corporate ownership condition must be met upon entering the regime, and throughout each accounting period within which the AIF is within the PAIF regime, and is met if conditions A–D are satisfied:

Condition A

No body corporate is beneficially entitled (directly or indirectly) to 10% or more of the net asset value of the fund. This condition is treated as met in cases where the body corporate has taken reasonable steps to prevent it from acquiring a holding of 10% or more and, on becoming aware that it does in fact hold 10% or more, it takes steps to ensure that the holding is reduced;

Condition B

The instrument of incorporation and prospectus of the PAIF must include provisions under which any corporate shareholder must undertake not to acquire 10% or more of the share capital of the PAIF and undertake that should its holding exceed 10%, it would be reduced to below 10%;

Condition C

The instrument of incorporation and prospectus of the PAIF must include provisions under which any company acquiring shares must provide a certificate stating that it holds the shares as beneficial owner or, that it does not hold them as beneficial owner but has obtained undertakings from the beneficial owners; and

Condition D

The investing company must undertake to disclose certain information about its ownership to the manager of the PAIF, if so required.

There are special rules and circumstances that apply to feeder funds.

The loan creditor condition

The purpose of this condition is to restrict the way in which a PAIF can borrow money so as to prevent income, or capital growth of the fund from being extracted through a profit-related loan. A PAIF must meet three conditions throughout each accounting period in respect of any loan relationship in which the PAIF is the debtor party, these being that:

- no interest is due which is calculated by reference to the results of the PAIF business or the value of any of its assets;

- the creditor in respect of any debt is not entitled to interest which exceeds a reasonable commercial return on any amount lent; and
- the amount due to the creditor on repayment does not exceed the amount lent or it is reasonably comparable with the amount generally repayable under the terms of issue of securities listed on a recognised stock exchange.

The balance of business conditions — the 60% test

(a) no less than 60% of a PAIF's net income must come from property investment assets; and
(b) at least 60% of the PAIF's assets, at fair value, must be property investment assets.

Throughout the accounting period, conditions (a) and (b) above are relaxed for those newly set up PAIFs, where a reduced level of at least 40% will be allowed in their first period of account. This relaxation does not apply to PAIFs that are created as a result of a conversion.

For the purposes of the 60% test (or the 40% test if relaxed in the first period of account), assets must be valued in accordance with generally accepted accounting practice. If there is a choice of accounting method, then a fair value option must be used. No account should be taken of liabilities secured against or otherwise relating to assets of any property investment business when determining net assets for the purposes of this condition.

The notification condition

The manager has to elect by giving notice that the PAIF regime will apply or, if it is proposed to incorporate an OEIC, that the person expected to become the manager of the OEIC on its incorporation has given notice for it to apply to the company and such notice has taken effect.

Notice must be given in writing to HMRC. For an existing company, notice must be given at least 28 days before the first accounting period for which the PAIF regime is going to apply, and for a new company notice must be given at least 42 days before the date of expected incorporation and authorisation. The notice may be amended or withdrawn at any time before it takes effect.

HMRC may issue a 'quashing notice' in prescribed circumstances and the procedure for this is laid down in *Reg 69S* of *SI 2006 No 964, Pt 4A, 69S*. There is a right of appeal to the Tax Tribunal against a quashing notice within 28 days beginning with the date of the notice. In this case, the Tax Tribunal will decide whether HMRC's action was just and reasonable and the date from which the PAIF regime is to apply, subject to certain restrictions.

Consequences of entry

On entering the PAIF regime, a new accounting and distribution period begins for the fund (*SI 2006 No 964, Reg 69V*). Any pre-entry property rental business shall be treated for the purposes of corporation tax as ceasing on entry into the regime. The assets of the pre-entry property rental business will be treated as being sold immediately before entry, and reacquired immediately after entry, at their market value at that time. Any property investment business carried on afterwards will be tax exempt.

Under *SI 2006 No 964, Reg 69V* assets which were used in any pre-entry property business are treated, for capital allowances purposes, as being sold immediately after entry at a value which does not give rise to any balancing allowances or charges.

Tax treatment of PAIFs

[52.14] A PAIF is exempt from UK corporation tax on its net Property Investment Business (PIB) income, but the other non-PIB (or 'residual business') is theoretically still subject to tax at the rate applicable to open-ended investment companies (although in practice no tax should apply due to tax deductions being available in respect of distributions made out of this income). UK dividend income receipts are not subject to UK corporation tax in the hands of a PAIF.

To arrive at the net PIB income, the calculation should be made in accordance with the current Statement of Recommended Practice (SORP) as issued by the Investment Management Association (IMA). Essentially the net PIB income computation follows the rules for the computation of property income.

However, loan relationship adjustments, hedging derivative contracts and embedded derivatives are taken into account so far as they relate to the tax-exempt business. Any capital allowances that the tax-exempt business would claim if it were taxable, should be claimed in full.

Residual income comprises of UK dividends and income arising from the residual business. In arriving at the taxable income, the residual income is reduced by any deduction allowable for corporation tax purposes along with PAIF interest distributions.

There is a charge to corporation tax where a PAIF is also a QIS and the net PIB income divided by financing cost of the exempt business gives a figure of less than 1.25.

There may also be a charge to corporation tax if HMRC considers that the arrangements have been designed to obtain a 'tax advantage' that qualifies as tax avoidance.

Where distributions are made to a 'holder of excessive rights' and the PAIF has not taken sufficient care to avoid making such a distribution, it is treated as receiving an amount of income equal to the percentage held by the holder applied to the net tax exempt income of the PAIF. Such income is subject to corporation tax as if it were residual net income arising in the accounting period in which the distribution was made by the company.

A '*holder of excessive rights*' is a company which is a participant in a PAIF and is beneficially entitled to shares representing the right to 10% or more of the net asset value of the PAIF.

Tax compliance

A PAIF must file a corporation tax return complimented by:

- a calculation of its tax exempt net income and residual income; and

- a reconciliation between the net income of the company and the total income shown in the distribution accounts, as attributed to the three different categories of distribution (see distributions made by PAIFs below).

There is an obligation to make a quarterly return (CT61 return) in respect of PIB income or PAIF interest income (relevant income). The return must be filed during a period ending within 14 days of the day immediately following the end of the return period in question, with any tax due payable with the return.

The relevant PAIF must issue a certificate of tax deducted to the recipients. HMRC have the power to assess if payment is not made on the due date or where HMRC think a relevant distribution has been omitted or a return is otherwise incorrect.

Distributions made by PAIFs

PAIFs are required to distribute all their income to investors. Distributions are treated first as coming out of tax exempt income, secondly out of PAIF distributions of interest (up to the pre-distribution amount) and thirdly out of PAIF distributions (dividends). All distributions are treated as paid to fund-holders in proportion to their rights [*SI 2006 No 964, Regs 69Z15(2), 69Z16(2) and 69Z17(2)*].

Tax treatment of participants

Distributions of property income by a PAIF are chargeable to corporation tax as property income in the hands of a company recipient. In the case of a recipient within the charge to income tax, the distributions are treated as profits of a UK property business (within the meaning of *ITTOIA 2005, s 264*).

Where the participant is not resident in the UK, similar charging provisions apply and the non-resident landlords rules do not apply.

There are exclusions for dealers in respect of distributions, e.g. dealers in securities and members of Lloyd's.

For participants within the charge to UK corporation tax, PAIF interest distributions should be treated as though they were payments of yearly interest usually without deduction of tax. Participants are treated as receiving a gross amount of yearly interest arising from a loan relationship.

In the case of participants within the charge to income tax, PAIF interest distributions should be treated as though they were net of tax receipts of yearly interest in the hands of UK income tax payers [*ITTOIA 2005, Pt 4, Ch 2*].

No tax credit is available under *CTA 2010, Pt 23, Ch 7* in respect of interest distributions for corporate recipients and non-corporate recipients [*ITTOIA 2005, s 397*].

PAIF dividend distributions received by participants shall be treated as if they were a dividend on shares (i.e. they are exempt from corporation tax, *SI 2006 No 964, Reg 69Z20(1)*). In the case of participants within the change to UK income tax, PAIF dividend distributions should be treated in the same manner as any other UK company dividend and carry a 1/9 non-repayable tax credit.

Breaches

Where a PAIF becomes aware that it no longer satisfies any one of the PAIF conditions highlighted above (except in the case of excessive rights — see below), it must provide to HMRC the date of the breach and the date the condition became satisfied again (if appropriate). It must also give details of the condition that was breached and what, if anything, the company has done to prevent the breach recurring.

In the event of the excessive rights condition being breached, as soon as it is reasonably practicable, the company must provide the name and address of the person who received the distribution, its value, details of the recipient's interest in the company, the steps the company took to prevent the acquisition of any excessive holdings, and steps the company has taken (or is taking) to ensure there is no longer any excessive holding in the company.

Leaving the PAIF regime

[52.15] An OEIC may leave the PAIF regime in four ways:

- optional exit — a PAIF must notify HMRC in writing specifying the final day on which the regime is to apply, which must be after the date that HMRC receives any notice;
- HMRC have power to issue a termination notice, but only in specified circumstances, and there is a right of appeal against the notice (*SI 2006 No 964, Reg 69Z37*);
- a PAIF may cease to be authorised by the Financial Services Authority, or cease to carry on property investment business;
- the PAIF may be the subject of a merger or take-over.

In these circumstances, the tax exempt property business of the PAIF is treated as ceasing and, immediately before cessation, the assets are deemed to be sold and re-acquired at market value (for corporation tax but not for capital gains tax purposes). The OEIC's accounting period is treated as coming to an end on the date of the cessation and a new one will begin immediately post cessation. For the purposes of capital allowances, the assets are treated as being sold immediately before cessation and re-acquired by the OEIC after the cessation, at the tax written down value. [*SI 2006 No 964, Reg 69Z41(5)*]. No balancing allowance or charge will arise and the provisions for successions (*CAA 2001, ss 198, 199*) do not apply.

[*SI 2008 No 705*].

Tax elected funds

[52.16] The tax elected funds (TEF) regime is an elective regime which is open to AIFs meeting certain conditions. Similar to the PAIF regime above, the TEF regime moves the point of taxation from the fund to the investor and as such, investors in a TEF will broadly be taxed in the same way as if they owned the underlying assets directly.

Entry into and membership of the TEF regime

[52.17] On or after 1 September 2009, an AIF that meets the following conditions, contained in *SI 2006 No 964, Regs 9A, 69Z45–69Z48*, may elect to become a TEF:

- the property condition;
- the genuine diversity of ownership condition;
- the loan creditor condition; and
- the scheme documentation condition.

The property condition

The AIF must not have a UK or overseas property business.

The genuine diversity of ownership condition

The three conditions described in **52.13** for PAIFs must be met throughout the accounting period. Similar to the PAIF regime, an advance clearance in relation to the genuine diversity of ownership condition may be made in writing to the Tax Tribunal by the manager (or proposed manager) of the AIF.

The loan creditor condition

The conditions to be met in terms of the loan creditor condition are similar to those described in **52.13** for PAIFs.

The scheme documentation condition

The instrument constituting the AIF and its prospectus must include terms which require the AIF to meet the property condition and the loan creditor condition on entry and throughout each accounting period.

Application process

[52.18] Either the manager, or the prospective manager (where the fund is not yet established), is required to apply in writing to HMRC to enter the TEF regime, at least 28 days before the beginning of the specified accounting period for an existing AIF, and at least 42 days before the expected authorisation date for a new fund.

Before making an application in relation to an existing AIF, shareholder or unit holder approval must be obtained and the fund must have applied for any necessary regulatory approval. The contents of the application are described in *SI 2009 No 2036, Reg 69Z51*.

Tax treatment of TEFs

[52.19] For the purpose of corporation tax, the income arising to a TEF will be categorised under one of the following:

(a) dividend income;

(b) property investment income (e.g. REITs tax-exempt distributions and property income distributions in relation to shares held in a PAIF);
(c) property business income (arising as a result of a breach of the property condition) being profits of a UK property business that are not within (b) above and income from an overseas property business; and
(d) other income.

Distributions made by TEFs

[52.20] Distributions by TElFs shall be attributed as follows:

- TEF distributions (dividends):
  - (a) dividend income;
  - (b) property investment income; and
  - (c) property business income.
- TEF distributions (non-dividends).

Where a distribution is made from TEF distributions (dividends), it is treated as paid to fund-holders in proportion to their rights on the distribution date by the fund (*SI 2009 No 2036, Reg 69Z60*) and subject to a de minimis amount (*SI 2009 No 2036, Reg 69Z66*).

In the case where a distribution is made from TEF distributions (non-dividend), the distributions are treated as being a payment of yearly interest made on the distribution date and subject to the treatment of de minimis amounts.

Breach of TEF conditions

Provisions within *SI 2009 No 2036, Reg 69Z65* apply if one or more of the TEF conditions are breached. Within 28 days of becoming aware of the breach, the fund must provide designated information to HMRC, including the date of the breach, details of the condition that was breached and the steps the fund proposes to take to rectify the breach.

Leaving the TEF regime

Optional exit

In the event that the manager decides to take its AIF outside of the TEF regime, then the manager must give notice to HMRC in writing, specifying the reasons for the fund leaving the TEF regime and the final accounting period for which the regulations are to apply.

Forced exit

HMRC can, in certain circumstances, issue a termination notice to the manager of an OEIC. A TEF may appeal against any termination notice within 28 days, beginning with the day on which the termination notice is given.

[*SI 2009 No 2036, Reg 69Z70*].

Court investment funds

[52.21] Court investment funds (CIFs) are a form of authorised unit trust set up by the Lord Chancellor under the *Administration of Justice Act 1982, s 42(1)*. They are available only for individuals whose money is under control of certain courts, e.g. road accident victims and the mentally incapacitated. The Public Trustee as Accountant General of the Supreme Court holds all units in the fund on the investors' behalf. CIFs are treated for tax purposes as authorised unit trusts, the investment manager being treated as the trustee. Persons whose interests entitle them, as against the Accountant General (or other authorised person), to share in the fund's investments and persons authorised to hold shares in the fund on their own behalf are treated as unit holders.

[*CTA 2010, s 620; ICTA 1988, s 469A*].

Simon's Taxes. See **D8.164.**

Unauthorised unit trusts

[52.22] Special provisions apply to the income of a unit trust scheme (other than one within **52.3** above) unless the trustees are non-UK resident. Such a trust is outside the rules in **52.5** above (tax treatment of AIFs) and its income is treated for tax purposes as the income of the trustees and not of the unit holders.

The unit holders (including corporate unit holders) of an unauthorised unit trust (within the meaning of *ITA 2007, s 989*) are treated as receiving an amount of income that has been taxed at the basic rate of income tax [*CTA 2009, s 973*]. The date the payment is treated as having been received by the unit holder is the specific date or latest date for distribution under the terms of the trust deed, except, if there is no such date or it is more than twelve months after the end of the distribution period, then the last day of the distribution period is taken as the date of receipt. An amount thereby treated as received by a company is within the charge to corporation tax on income. [*CTA 2010, ss 621, 622; CTA 2009, ss 971–973; ICTA 1988, s 469; ITA 2007, s 941, Sch 1 para 87*].

See **46.9 INCOME TAX IN RELATION TO A COMPANY** as regards relief available for income tax deducted at source from payments received by a company.

Pension fund pooling scheme (PFPS)

[52.23] A PFPS is an authorised unit trust where special provisions apply to ensure that certain international pooled pension funds (registered as 'pension fund pooling vehicles') are transparent for UK tax purposes, by disapplying the tax rules for unauthorised unit trusts (as above). An application must be made to HMRC to participate in the scheme. The participants in a PFPS are treated for income tax, capital allowances and capital gains tax purposes as though they themselves own a share of each of the trust assets directly.

There is also relief from stamp duty reserve tax on the transfer of assets by participants into the scheme. Participation in PFPS is restricted to registered pension schemes which are occupational pension schemes, UK-based superannuation funds used primarily by companies employing British expatriates working overseas (as defined in *ICTA 1988, s 615(6)*), and pension funds established outside the UK broadly equivalent to UK registered pension schemes. [*SI 1996 Nos 1583, 1585 as amended*]. The position in the country in which any overseas participator is based will of course be crucial to the operation of such schemes.

Simon's Taxes. See **D8.130–D8.133**.

Unit trusts for exempt unit holders

[52.24] If, for any reason other than non-residence, any of the holders of units in a unit trust scheme would not be liable to capital gains tax (or to corporation tax on chargeable gains) on a disposal of units, any gains accruing to the trust itself are also not chargeable gains. In determining whether this exemption applies, no account is taken of units which are disposed of by a unit holder and are held by the fund managers pending disposal. Also, no account is to be taken of the possibility of a corporation tax charge on income arising in respect of a gain accruing on a disposal by an insurance company or an incorporated or registered friendly society (see **37.3 FRIENDLY SOCIETIES**).

[*TCGA 1992, s 100(2–2B); F(No 2)A 2005, s 20*].

This exemption applies whenever the gains accrue, and is of practical importance in relation to unit trust schemes which have not been designated as authorised unit trusts (in **52.3** above).

53

Investment Trusts

Cross-references. See **17.11** CAPITAL GAINS; **18.2** CAPITAL GAINS — GROUPS; **29.7** DEGROUPING CHARGES; **51.3** INVESTMENT COMPANIES AND INVESTMENT BUSINESS; **54.96** LOAN RELATIONSHIPS.

Investment trusts

[53.1] Investment trust companies are the closed ended form of collective investment schemes available in the UK. Investment trusts are not in fact trusts in any legal sense, but limited companies incorporated under UK company law and listed on the official UK list. Investment trusts are subject to corporate tax legislation, however, they are exempt from tax on chargeable gains provided they are approved by HMRC. In order to obtain approval from HMRC, the company must fulfil certain conditions.

Approval as an investment trust

The definition of an investment trust has been amended significantly by the *Finance Act 2011* to increase certainty for investors and remove certain restrictions.

Previously an investment trust had to fulfil the following conditions:

(a) It was not a close company.
(b) It was resident in the UK.
(c) It derived its income wholly or mainly (in practice, 70% or more) from shares or securities.
(d) No 'holding' in any one company represented more than 15% of the value of its investments, unless that company was itself an investment trust or would be so but for being unquoted. This requirement was waived in respect of investments which, when acquired, represented no more than 15% of the value of the investments, and in respect of an investment held on 6 April 1965, provided that the holding represented not more than 25% of the overall value of the investments at that date. There was no waiver in either case where there has been an 'addition' to the holding.
(e) Its 'ordinary share capital' (and every class thereof, if there was more than one) was listed in the Official UK List.
(f) Its Memorandum or Articles prohibit the distribution by way of dividend of gains arising from the sale of investments.
(g) It did not retain an amount greater than 15% of its income derived from shares and securities in any accounting period.
(h) It was approved by HMRC.

As regards (c) above, in determining the amount of the company's income, no account was to be taken of the income chargeable under *CTA 2009, s 1229(3)(b)* on reversal of expenses of management previously deducted.

For accounting periods beginning on or after 1 January 2008 (the date having been originally set at 1 January 2006), offshore income gains (computed under *ICTA 1988, s 761; CTA 2009, Sch 1 para 220*), arising from disposals of material interests in offshore funds not qualifying for 'distributing or reporting fund' status (see **57 OFFSHORE FUNDS**), no longer qualify as eligible investment income. This was a change of interpretation by HMRC who considered that the disposal of a material interest was a disposal of a capital asset (notwithstanding the treatment under *ICTA 1988, s 761* as income) and that the deemed income could not be said to derive from shares or securities. The gains were ignored in the calculation of both total income and income from shares and securities. (See HMRC Tax Bulletin, Issue 79, October 2005 pp 1242–1243 as amended by HMRC Internet Notice 23 November 2005.)

Any excess of relevant credits over relevant debits arising in a period was treated as income derived from shares or securities. '*Relevant debits*' and '*relevant credits*' are those brought into account under the loan relationship rules. .

Where investment trusts had received a refund of VAT charged on management fees, both the VAT and any interest arising on the refunded VAT were not regarded as income for the purposes of (c) above. As such, the amounts were not included in the calculation of eligible income, notwithstanding that the VAT and interest were likely to be treated as taxable income.

As regards (c) and (g) above:

- in determining the amount of the company's income or the amount of its income derived from shares and securities, the amount to be brought into account in respect of the company's loan relationships was to be determined without reference to any of its debtor relationships;
- stock lending fees, underwriting commission and bank deposit interest were not regarded as income from securities; and
- units in an authorised unit trust were treated as shares in a company.

When considering condition (d) above in relation to a holding in an open-ended investment company or a unit trust, that condition was regarded as being satisfied provided that, during any accounting period in which units in the unit trust or shares in the OEIC were held by the investment trust, the unit trust or OEIC itself satisfied the condition at (c) above. This was always considered to be the case where the unit trust was a securities fund under the relevant regulations or the OEIC was a securities company under the corresponding OEIC regulations (and for certain similarly constituted sub-funds). (HMRC Statement of Practice SP 3/97).

Condition (g) above did not apply if the amount the company would be required to distribute to meet the 15% requirement for a period was less than £10,000 (proportionately reduced for periods of less than twelve months), or if the company was required by law to retain income in excess of the 15% limit for the period. The latter exclusion only applied, however, if the aggregate of the excess of retentions over those required by law and any distribution for the period was less than £10,000 (proportionately reduced for periods of less than twelve months).

FA 2009 gives the Treasury wide powers to provide by statutory instrument for the designation by an investment trust of a dividend (in specified circumstances and in respect of specified persons) as an interest payment within the loan relationship rules. [*FA 2009, s 45*].

Finance Act 2011 changes

The changes outlined below seek to remove unnecessary restrictions on the commercial activities of investment trusts, reduce cost to the business and also provide further certainty for the investors.

The Finance Act rewords *CTA 2010, s 1158*, and *s 1159* in particular.

Under the Finance Act changes the company will need to fulfil the following rules:

(a) The business of the company consists of investing its funds in shares, land or other assets with the aim of spreading investment risk and giving members of the company the benefit of the results of the management of its funds.
(b) The shares making up the company's ordinary share capital (or, if there are such shares of more than one class, those of each class) are admitted to trading on a regulated market. A regulated market has the same meaning as Directive 2004/39/EC.
(c) The final condition is that the company is not a company UK REIT or venture capital trust.

The Finance Act makes amendment to *CTA 2010, s 1159* that includes granting specific provisions enabling HM Treasury to make regulations to provide a regime under which a company can be approved as an investment trust and the process for this approval.

Capital gains

Investment trusts are exempt from tax on capital gains realised on disposals. [*TCGA 1992, s 100(1)*].

For the treatment of forward currency transactions as being of a capital or revenue nature, and their effect on the test in (c) above, see HMRC Company Taxation Manual, CTM47210. For loan relationships of investment trusts, see **54.96 LOAN RELATIONSHIPS**.

For company reorganisations involving investment trusts, see **17.11 CAPITAL GAINS**. For the transfer of assets within a group of companies to a company which subsequently becomes an investment trust, see **29.7 DEGROUPING CHARGES.**

Treatment of investment trust interest dividends

[53.2] On and after 1 September 2009, the tax treatment of investment trust dividends may be altered where three conditions are fulfilled:

- a company is an investment trust or prospective investment trust in the relevant accounting period;
- the company pays a dividend in respect of that period; and
- the dividend is paid on or before the first anniversary of the end of that period of account.

Where a dividend is paid for a period of account containing more than one accounting period, the body must be an investment trust or prospective investment trust for the whole of the accounting period. The trust may designate all or part of the dividend (not to exceed the trust's qualifying interest income for the period) as an 'interest distribution'. The designation is irrevocable once the interest distribution is made.

Where a distribution is paid for a period of account which includes more than one accounting period, the following formula should be applied to attribute the distribution to a particular accounting period:

$$\frac{A \times I}{T}$$

Where A is the amount of 'qualifying interest income' for the accounting period, I is the total distributed as interest distributions for the period of account and T is the total qualifying interest income for all accounting periods in the period of account.

'*Qualifying interest income*' is, broadly, the excess of the company's relevant credits over its relevant debits for a year — e.g. interest income over interest payments. Loan relationship transactions and certain transactions in derivatives and contracts for differences are taken into account. See *SI 2009 No 2034, Regs 8, 9*.

Interest distributions are not treated as dividend distributions for the purposes of the Taxes Acts. The effect on the trust or prospective trust is that the distribution is treated as if it were an interest payment under a loan relationship, and therefore a deduction is allowable in arriving at the company's profits chargeable to corporation tax. However, where the interest distribution exceeds the trust's qualifying interest income for the period, the excess is not allowed as a deduction.

Similarly, the recipient of the interest distribution is treated as interest received.

The trust must deduct tax at the basic rate from the interest distribution, except to the extent it is paid to:

(a) a UK or overseas company (but not where the company is acting as a trustee);
(b) the trustees of a unit trust; or
(c) the reputable intermediary condition is met; or
(d) the residence condition is met.

In the cases of (c) and (d), the conditions must be met on the date the distribution is made. Three conditions must be fulfilled to meet the reputable intermediary condition:

- the interest distribution must be made to an intermediary which is a company;
- there must be reasonable grounds for the paying trust to believe the recipient is not ordinarily resident in the UK; and
- the intermediary is subject to the EC Money Laundering Directive or the equivalent non-EC provisions, is resident in a regulated country and is associated with a company to which the above conditions apply.

Further conditions for this test are contained in *SI 2009 No 2034, Regs 15, 16*.

The residence condition requires one of the following to be met:

- where no trust is involved, the recipient declares that it is not ordinarily resident in the UK;
- where the recipient is deceased, the deceased had made such a declaration of non-ordinary residence prior to his death which was valid at the date of death;
- the personal representative makes a similar declaration as to the deceased's residence status at date of death;
- in the case of a distribution to be received under a trust and where the interest distribution is deemed to be the income of someone other than the trustees, that person makes a valid declaration of non-ordinary residence, or, if it is a company, of non-residence; or
- where trustees receive the income for tax purposes, there is a valid declaration that the trustees are not resident in the UK and all beneficiaries are either not ordinarily resident, or in the case of a company not resident, in the UK.

SI 2009 No 2034, Reg 18 gives details of the form of the declarations mentioned above.

[*SI 2009 No 2034*].

There is further guidance available in HMRC Corporate Tax Manual, CTM47000 *et seq.*

Real estate investment trusts

[53.3] With effect for accounting periods beginning on or after 1 January 2007, UK resident, property companies or groups which carry on a 'property rental business' may opt to become real estate investment trusts (REITs). UK REITs must distribute at least 90% of net taxable profits on rental income to investors, withholding tax at the basic rate. Provided a company meets the eligibility criteria for a REIT, the qualifying profits and gains from the 'property rental business' will not be subject to corporation tax, but profits on any other business will be subject to corporation tax at the main rate of corporation tax (whether or not the REIT would otherwise qualify for the small profits rate). To the extent that dividends paid by the trust derive from the profits and gains of the 'property letting business' they are taxed in the hands of the recipient as property income rather than as distributions. Companies wishing to enter the regime must pay an entry charge.

Separate, but similar rules are laid down for groups and single companies.

[*CTA 2010, ss 523–609; ITA 2007, ss 973, 974*].

Property rental business

[53.4] A '*property rental business*' is a business forming part of a UK property business or overseas property business (see **62 PROPERTY INCOME**). For accounting periods ending on or after 22 April 2009, where a REIT has receipts and expenses relating to tied premises, these may be regarded as part of a UK property business. [*CTA 2010, s 519*]. However, the following type of business is not a property rental business:

- incidental letting of property (wherever situated) held in connection with a property trade;
- letting of property used for administrative purposes of the property rental business, but temporarily not required for those purposes, where it is let for a term of not more than three years and the space let is comparatively small compared to that occupied for administrative purposes;
- letting of property if the property would fall within generally accepted accounting practice to be described as owner-occupied. *CTA 2010* does not define 'owner-occupied', however, HMRC guidance states that IAS 40 defines 'owner-occupied' as property held by the owner for use in the production or supply of goods or services or for administrative purposes. A property should not be treated as being owner-occupied merely because the company is providing services to an occupant who is in exclusive occupation of the property and is not connected with a member of the group;
- provision of services in connection with overseas property where the services would not be taxed as property income if provided in connection with a UK property;

- entering into structured finance arrangements in connection with factoring of rent and other income receipts (see **5.15 ANTI-AVOIDANCE**).

In relation to any time before 6 July 2009, the condition regarding owner-occupied property will only apply if the property is let by one member of a group to another member of a group, or to a company the shares in which are 'stapled' to the shares of a group member. The shares of one company are treated as '*stapled*' to those of another where the rights attaching to the shares of the first company contain terms that make it beneficial or necessary for those shares to be sold or acquired with the shares of the other company.

CTA 2010, s 604 is amended by *CTA 2010, Sch 2 Pt 13 para 79* in respect of dates before 6 July 2009.

A business is not a property rental business in so far as it gives rise to the following type of income or profits:

- income in connection with a caravan site treated as trading receipts under *ITTOIA 2005, s 20(1)*;
- rent in respect of an electric-line wayleave;
- rent in respect of the siting of a gas or oil pipeline or of a wind turbine;
- rent in respect of the siting of a mast or similar structure for use in a mobile telephone network or other system of electronic communication;
- dividends from shares in a company within the REIT regime; or
- income from an interest in a limited liability partnership on a winding-up under *CTA 2009, s 1273(4)*.

HMRC may, by order, amend the above exclusions.

[*CTA 2010, s 605*].

A business carried on by a non UK group company is a property rental business for REIT purposes if the business would be a property rental business if carried on in the UK. References to a non-UK company's UK property rental business are to the company's property rental business in the UK. Income from such a business would normally be chargeable to income tax. For REIT purposes, however, the income is treated as chargeable to corporation tax.

[*CTA 2010, ss 519(4), 520*].

Qualifying conditions — single companies

[53.5] In order to qualify for REIT status, a number of conditions must be met by the company itself and by the business activities of the company.

Conditions for company

[53.6] A company may give notice to become a UK REIT provided it meets the following conditions:

(a) the company is a UK company;
(b) the company is not an open-ended investment company (see **52.2 INVESTMENT FUNDS**);

(c) the company's ordinary share capital is listed on a recognised stock exchange;

(d) the company is not a close company (see **22 CLOSE COMPANIES**) or is so only by virtue that a limited partnership, which is a collective investment scheme (see **52.1 INVESTMENT FUNDS**), is a participator of the company. For this purpose, a company will be treated as a close company even if prevented from being close by virtue of *ICTA 1988, ss 414(5), 415(4)(a)*;

(e) there must be no more than one class of ordinary shares issued by the company and issued shares must either form part of the company's ordinary share capital or be non-voting fixed-rate preference shares (as set out in **27.12**(b) **CONTROLLED FOREIGN COMPANIES**). For accounting periods ending on or after 22 April 2009, preference shares must be preference shares. Such shares are shares as defined for group relief purposes but which carry a right of conversion into shares or securities of the company. Such shares must also carry no voting rights; and

(f) in the case of any borrowings, the interest payable to the loan creditor must not exceed a reasonable commercial return nor be contingent upon the results of all or any part of the company's business or on the value of any of its assets. On repayment of the loan, the creditor must not be entitled to an amount exceeding the amount lent, or if repayment is made by way of listed securities, the amount must be reasonably comparable with the amount generally repayable. However, a loan is not treated as dependent on the company's results only due to the interest under the contract being reduced if the results improve or being increased should the results deteriorate.

The effect of the notice is that the company is a UK REIT from the date specified in the notice. The requirements of the notice are laid down in *CTA 2010, s 525*, as amended by *CTA 2010, Sch 2 Pt 13 para 78* for accounting period beginning before 22 April 2009.

Once a company is accepted as a UK REIT, it will remain a UK REIT until notice is given by the company to HMRC, notice is given to the company by HMRC, or there is an automatic termination due to the breach of certain conditions (see below **53.26**).

[*CTA 2010, ss 528, 529; FA 2009, s 65, Sch 34*].

Conditions for property rental business

[53.7] In order to qualify for REIT status the company must have a qualifying property rental business (whether or not it has any other business) throughout an accounting period. A property rental business qualifies as such if the conditions (a) and (b) below are met and if at least 90% of the profits of the property rental business (see **53.10** below) arising in an accounting period are distributed by way of dividend on or before the filing date for the company's tax return for the accounting period.

For distributions on or after 16 December 2010 a REIT can issue stock dividends in lieu of cash dividends in order to meet the distribution requirement, as amended by *F(No 3)A 2010*.

The distribution condition does not apply to the extent it would be unlawful. Where part of a distribution has been withheld to avoid, or reduce, a tax charge which may be imposed if the REIT makes a distribution to investors with a shareholding of 10% or more (see **53.20** below), it will nevertheless count as having been made.

Where the 90% condition is not satisfied, the REIT regime shall continue to apply, provided that corporation tax will be charged on an amount calculated as follows, as if it were miscellaneous income:

$$P - D$$

Where:

P = 90% of the profits of the property rental business in the accounting period; and

D = total profits of the property rental business distributed before the filing date for that accounting period.

No deduction is permitted from the taxable amount for this purpose. However, no tax will be due if the company pays an additional dividend within three months of the date that the profits from the rental business for the period are finalised, and the additional dividend means the distribution condition is met. Such a dividend must be ignored for calculating whether the condition has been met in any other accounting period.

[*CTA 2010, ss 530, 564, 565; SI 2006 No 2864, Reg 6*].

In addition, the following conditions must be met throughout the accounting period.

(a) The property rental business must involve at least three properties. A property is treated as a single property if it is rented or available for rent as a commercial or residential unit separate from any other such unit (for example, a shop within a shopping complex or a flat within an apartment block).

(b) No one property is to have a value of more than 40% of the total value of all the properties involved in the property rental business.

For these purposes, the property rental businesses of all members of a group are treated as one business.

A property involved in a business includes any estate or interest in land which is exploited in earning income for that business.

[*CTA 2010, s 529*].

Conditions for the balance of business

[53.8] The following conditions must also be met in relation to the proportion of a company's qualifying property rental business relative to its other business.

(a) The 'profits' arising from the company's property rental business in the accounting period must amount to at least 75% of the aggregate of the profits arising from that business and from any other business in that period. '*Profits*' in this case are those before deduction of tax as calculated in accordance with international accounting standards, excluding realised and unrealised gains and losses on property disposals and, excluding changes in the fair value of hedging derivative contracts (as defined) and amounts out of the company's normal business over its history, however they are treated in the accounts.

(b) The value of the assets involved in the property rental business at the beginning of the accounting period must be at least 75% of the total value of assets held by the company.

As regards the valuation of assets in (a) and (b) above, they must be valued in accordance with international accounting standards and, where the valuation can be made on either a cost or fair value basis, a fair value basis must be used. Any liabilities secured against or relating to the assets are ignored for this purpose. Where the property is used as security for borrowings, those liabilities are ignored for valuation purposes. If a non-group company holds an interest in a group company, its percentage interest of profits, expenses, gains, losses, assets and liabilities are excluded for REIT purposes.

[*CTA 2010, ss 531, 533(3)*].

Qualifying conditions — groups

[53.9] A group for these purposes is a company (the principal company) and all of its 75% subsidiaries held directly or indirectly, provided that the principal company has at least a 51% interest in each other company. Insurance companies and open-ended investment companies cannot form part of a REIT group. Subject to the rules for joint ventures (see **53.34** below), a company cannot be a member of more than one group.

The principal company of a group may give notice to become a UK REIT group, provided all of the relevant conditions are fulfilled.

The conditions in **53.6**(a) to (f) must be fulfilled by the principal company. In addition, the group as a whole must have a property rental business which must have at least three properties and no single property must account for more than 40% of the total value of properties in that property rental business.

Finally, the principal company must produce financial statements for the accounting period and file them with HMRC, showing:

(a) all the group's property rental business;
(b) the group's UK property business; and
(c) the group's other (or 'residual') business.

The group's UK property business includes the property rental business of UK members of the group and the UK property rental business of other, non-UK members.

The statements for (a) and (c) above must specify for each member, in accordance with international accounting standards, the income, expenses, profits before tax (excluding gains or losses on property, whether realised or not) and assets (valued at the beginning of the accounting period using fair value, where there is a choice), ignoring liabilities secured against or relating to those assets. The statement in relation to (b) above must specify, for each member, profits calculated in accordance with **53.14** below. Where a subsidiary company is not wholly owned, the income, expenses, gains, losses, assets and liabilities of that subsidiary are to be reduced by the proportion of the subsidiary owned by non-group members. Further provisions in relation to the financial statements are contained in *SI 2006 No 2865*.

[*CTA 2010, ss 532, 533, 606; SI 2006 No 2865; SI 2007 No 3536*].

Conditions for business

[53.10] The property rental businesses of the group members are treated as a single business.

With respect to the 90% distribution condition at **53.7** above, at least 90% of the 'UK profits' of the property rental business arising in an accounting period must be distributed by the principal company by way of dividend on or before the filing date for the principal company's tax return for the accounting period. The principal company of a REIT group can issue stock dividends in lieu of cash dividends in order to meet the distribution requirement, as amended by *F(No 3)A 2010*.

'*UK profits*' for this purpose are those in the financial statements of the property rental businesses in the UK.

The distribution condition does not apply to the extent that compliance with the condition would be unlawful. Where part of a distribution has been withheld to avoid or reduce a tax charge which may be imposed if the principal company makes a distribution to investors with a shareholding of 10% or more (see **53.20** below), it will nevertheless count as having been made.

Therefore if a property is rented out by a member of the group to another member of the group, the property could be treated as being owner-occupied. There is further guidance available on owner-occupation in HMRC Guidance and Real Estate Investment Trusts Manual, GREIT01030.

With regard to the conditions in relation to the proportion of a company's property rental business relative to its other business in **53.9** above, the income and assets tests are applied to determine the balance of business between the group's property rental business, based on the financial statements for (a) above, and the group's residual business, based on the financial statements for (c) above.

[*CTA 2010, ss 530, 531, 532, 552*].

Entry into the regime

Notice of entry

[53.11] A company or a group of companies can enter into the REIT regime from a date specified by written notice to HMRC. Notice must be given to HMRC by the company or principal company of the group before the date specified. The notice must be accompanied by a statement by the company that the conditions set out in **53.6** above for the single company, or **53.9** above for a group of companies, are reasonably expected to be satisfied throughout the specified accounting period.

There is a special facility for new companies or groups seeking to qualify. Where the company or principal company of a REIT group does not expect to satisfy condition (c) in **53.6** on the first day of its accounting period, the statement in the company or principal company's notice must indicate the following:

- that condition (c) is reasonably expected to be satisfied for at least part of the first day of, and throughout the rest of, the accounting period; and
- that the other conditions are reasonably expected to be satisfied throughout the period.

Similarly, where the company or group does not expect to satisfy condition (d) in **53.6** on the first day of the accounting period, the statement in the company or principal company's notice must indicate the following:

- that condition (d) is reasonably expected to be satisfied for at least part of the first day of, and throughout the rest of, the accounting period; and
- that the other conditions are reasonably expected to be satisfied throughout the period.

For accounting periods beginning before 22 April 2009, where the company or principal company of a REIT group does not expect to satisfy condition (d) in **53.6** on the first day of the accounting period, because the company's shares have not been listed and dealt on a recognised stock exchange within the preceding twelve months, then the company or principal company's notice must indicate the following:

- that conditions (a), (b), (e) and (f) set out in **53.6** are reasonably expected to be met throughout the accounting period;
- that condition (c) is reasonably expected to be met for at least part of the first day and throughout the remainder of the accounting period; and
- that condition (d) is reasonably expected to be met throughout the accounting period apart from the first day.

HMRC may prescribe (by order) any other information or documents to be given in or with the notice. Once a company enters the regime, it will remain within the regime until it ceases to be so as a result of a termination event set out in **53.28** below.

[*CTA 2010, ss 523–526*].

Effects of entry

[53.12] On entry into the regime, the company or group's existing property rental business is treated as ceasing to exist at the point of entry and for corporation tax purposes, one accounting period ends immediately before entry and another begins on entry for the new, property rental business. The assets involved in that business are treated for corporation tax purposes as sold immediately before the entry, and reacquired immediately after the entry, at their market value and any gains arising as a result are not chargeable gains. On any subsequent disposal (apart from one following an early exit from the regime — see **53.31** below) of such an asset (whether actual or deemed), that deemed consideration at market value is to be used as its base cost. For capital allowances purposes, the new business is treated as acquiring the assets at their written-down value as though the pre-entry business had not ceased and no election may be made under *CAA 2001, ss 198, 199*.

The reference to the pre-entry business of a group is to be read as a reference to the pre-entry business of the UK property business of the group (or UK pre-entry business of a non-UK resident member of the group). The deemed disposal and re-acquisition of assets has effect in relation to each UK resident member and the UK property business of any non-UK members of the group. References to the pre-entry or post-entry property rental business of the company is to be read as a reference to the company as a group member. The cessation of an accounting period before entry, and the beginning of a new accounting period on entry, applies to each UK resident member.

If a company becomes a member of a REIT group, the effects of entry apply to the company at the time it joins the group. References to the pre-entry business of the company are to be read as references to its business before it joins the group and references to the property rental business of the company as references to the company as a member of the group's property rental business of the group with property rental business.

Where a subsidiary company is not wholly owned, and a proportion of the assets of a group member's property rental business are excluded from a financial statement (see **53.9** above), the excluded amount is to be ignored for the purposes of these provisions.

[*CTA 2010, ss 536, 537*].

Entry charge

[53.13] On entry into the regime, the company or principal company is charged on a notional amount of income which is treated as arising in respect of the company's residual business. The notional income is 2% of the aggregate market value of the assets treated as sold and reaquired on entry to the property rental business divided by the main rate of corporation tax applicable to the company's property rental business. No loss, deficit, expense or allowance may be set off against the notional income or the tax charge arising on it.

The company can elect to spread the notional income over four years. In this case, the first instalment is treated as arising on the date of entry and the other three on the first three anniversaries of that date and, for this purpose, the percentage referred to above is 0.5% for the first instalment, 0.53% for the second, 0.56% for the third and 0.6% for the fourth instalment. The election must be given to HMRC with the notice for entry and is irrevocable. If the company ceases to be a REIT before the third anniversary of entry, any remaining instalments become chargeable immediately. The specified percentage rates may be amended by Treasury order (but not retrospectively) to reflect a change in interest rates.

The rules apply to each member of a group and the notional income is treated as arising separately on each member of the group's residual business. In determining the market value of assets treated as sold and re-acquired, where a subsidiary company is not wholly owned, and a proportion of the assets of a group member's property rental business are excluded from a financial statement (see **53.9** above), the excluded amount is to be ignored for this purpose.

For non-UK resident members of the group, the effects of entry are to apply to the UK property rental business carried on by them. The references to corporation tax are to be read as a reference to income tax on miscellaneous income. Reference to the rate at which the company pays tax on the notional income is to be read as a reference to the non-resident company's basic rate of UK income tax.

Where a company joins a REIT group, the entry charge applies to a company on joining a group as if it were entering into the REIT regime. In this case, reference to the residual business of a company is to be read as a reference to the residual business of the company as a group member.

[*CTA 2010, ss 538–540*].

Calculation of profits

[53.14] The profits arising from the property rental business (as calculated above) are not chargeable to corporation tax. The exemption is extended to the profits of a UK property rental business of a non-UK member of a UK REIT group.

Those profits arising from the residual business are chargeable to corporation tax at the main rate of corporation tax. The small profits rate of corporation tax does not apply to REITs.

Where a percentage of profits are excluded from the financial statements of a UK REIT group, (see **53.7**), those profits are treated as being profits of the residual business for the relevant member of the group. Such profits may be chargeable to corporation tax in the hands of the member company.

[*CTA 2010, s 534*].

For the purposes of attributing distributions (in **53.19** below) or determining whether the REIT meets the 90% distribution test (in **53.10** above) or the debt financing ratio (in **53.25** below), profits are calculated as follows.

The profits of a UK property rental business are calculated using the property income rules in *CTA 2009, s 210; ITTOIA 2005, s 272* (see **62 PROPERTY INCOME**) whether the profits relate to a UK or a non-UK company.

However, the exclusion for property income purposes relating to debits and credits arising from loan relationships, embedded derivatives and hedging derivative contracts does not apply in respect of loan relationships, certain embedded derivative contracts and certain hedging relationships entered into for the purpose of the property rental business.

Income and expenditure relating partly to the property rental business and partly to the residual business is to be apportioned on a just and reasonable basis. Any capital allowances available will automatically be taken into account in the calculation of profits of the property rental business without the requirement for a claim under *CAA 2001, s 3*.

[*CTA 2010, s 599*].

Ring-fencing and offset of losses

[53.15] The new business is effectively ring-fenced and treated as a separate business distinct from the pre-entry business, any residual business and the business after cessation of the regime ('the post-cessation business') (see **53.28** below). *'The post-cessation business'* relates to the property rental business after the group or company ceases to be a UK REIT.

A loss incurred by the property rental business cannot be set off against profits of the residual business and vice versa. A loss incurred by the pre-entry business cannot be set off against profits of the property rental business and a loss incurred by the property rental business cannot be set against the profits of any post-cessation business. Receipts accruing after entry to the REIT regime, relating to the pre-entry business, cannot be treated as receipts of the property rental business. '*Loss*' in this case also includes a deficit, expense, charge or allowance.

The provisions regarding ring-fencing and offset of losses apply to the UK property business of a non-UK member of a UK REIT group.

For the purpose of calculating the amount of profits, *CTA 2010, s 66* is disapplied so that losses arising from an overseas part of the property rental business can be set off against the UK part of the business. Also for this purpose, the exemption from the transfer pricing rules for small and medium-sized enterprises (see **72.6 TRANSFER PRICING**) does not apply to either the company's property rental or residual business.

[*CTA 2010, ss 66, 541, 542*].

Distributions

Treatment of shareholders' dividends from REITs

[53.16] REITs can offer investors a stock dividend as an alternative to, or in combination with, a cash dividend, in meeting the 90% of profits from tax exempt property business distribution requirement for distributions made on or after 16 December 2010, as amended by *F(No 3)A 2010*. Distributions made from a REIT, or the principal company of a REIT group, of the property rental business' profits (including gains) are taxable on the shareholder (whether or not UK resident) as income from a UK property business.

In the case of a group REIT, the property rental business' profits includes profits and gains in respect of the UK property rental business of non-UK members (see **53.1**).

A non-resident shareholder is not subject to taxation as a non-resident landlord in respect of the distributions. In the case of certain traders where distributions would normally be taxable as trading income, such as financial traders and members of Lloyd's, the REIT distribution will continue to be taxable under those rules.

'*Property income dividends*' (distributions from property rental income of REITs, commonly known as 'PIDs') do not fall to be treated as property income for double tax treaty purposes. They derive from shares, therefore they are dividends and the dividend article applies. However, where a REIT pays a dividend, not derived from property income and with a one-ninth tax credit attached, no tax credit repayment claim may be made (as a UK shareholder would not be entitled to claim a repayment).

The property income treatment applies in the case of companies which are members of a partnership. A tax credit does not apply to these distributions. Distributions from one or more REITs are treated, in the hands of the shareholder, as the profits of a single business separate from any other UK or overseas property business. This applies equally, in the case of a shareholder which is a partnership, to receipts by a partner of a share of any distribution.

Property income treatment continues to apply to distributions, made by a company or principal company, deriving from the profits of a property rental business after that company or group has left the REIT regime.

[*CTA 2010, ss 548, 549*].

Deduction of tax

[53.17] Where a REIT makes a distribution from its property rental profits (including gains), the rules for the assessment, collection and recovery of tax are to be prescribed by Treasury regulations. In particular, the regulations may require the company or principal company of a REIT group to deduct income tax at source at the basic rate and may specify classes of shareholder to whom distributions can be made gross. The regulations may also contain detailed provisions for the calculation and payment of tax, claims and appeals, payment of interest, notices and returns, etc. The regulations may also apply to distributions deriving from the profits of a property rental business after a company or group has left the REIT regime.

[*ITA 2007, ss 973, 974; CTA 2010, s 548*].

Non-residents

[53.18] Double taxation treaties contain a variety of ways for dealing with dividends. It is necessary to consider in each case how the treaty provisions affect PIDs. Details of any relief available to a resident of another country who is paid a PID can be found at http://www.hmrc.gov.uk/cnr/dtdigest.pdf. A claim must be made in respect of each dividend, but any number of PIDs may be included in each claim.

The first claim must be sent for certification to the tax authority in which the claimant is resident. It should then be sent to HMRC. Subsequent claims should be sent direct to HMRC, unless the country of residence is Switzerland, in which case all claims must first be sent to the tax authority there for certification. Some country-specific claim forms will be issued in due course.

Attribution of distributions

[53.19] In identifying which distributions derive from the REIT's property rental business (and which, therefore, are liable to deduction of tax at source and treatment as property income in the hands of the recipient), the distributions are to be attributed in the following order:

(1) payments made to meet the 90% distribution requirement in **53.7** above;
(2) to the extent that the company determines, distributions deriving from activities chargeable to corporation tax in relation to income (excluding gains on capital assets);
(3) distributions of profits of the company's property rental business (up to the amount of such profits not yet identified as having been distributed);
(4) distributions of gains arising from the property rental business which, by virtue of **53.21** below, are not chargeable gains;
(5) other distributions.

The provisions above dealing with the attribution of distributions applies to the principal company of a group, and in identifying the part of the distribution relating to the property rental business, reference to the company's property rental business is to the group's property rental business.

[*CTA 2010, s 550*].

Example

In its first period as a REIT a company has the following profits:

	£000
Property rental business	
Net rental income	5,500
Less: capital allowances	(500)
Property rental income	5,000
Property rental gains on disposal of rental property	250
Residual business	
Investment income	200
Gain on sale of fixed asset	150

The REIT distributes £5,500,000 in respect of that year's profits. This can be attributed to profits in the following ways.

A: Attributing as much as possible to property rental business

		£000
90% distribution requirement	((1) above)	4,500
Balance of property rental income	((3) above)	500
Property rental gain	((4) above)	250
Other activities	((5) above)	250
		5,500

B: Attributing as much as possible to the residual business

		£000
90% distribution requirement	((1) above)	4,500
Investment income	((2) above)	200
Other income*	((2) above)	500
Profits of property rental income	((3) above)	300
		5,500

* £500,000 is the difference between the tax measure of property rental business income (£5m) and the accounting measure (£5.5m) represented by capital allowances.

Distributions to holders of excessive rights

[53.20] A charge may be imposed, by Treasury regulation, on a REIT, or the principal company of a UK REIT group, if it makes a distribution to or in respect of a person who is beneficially entitled (directly or indirectly) to 10% or more of the company's share capital or dividends or controls 10% or more of its voting rights. For these purposes a person is a company, or person treated as a body corporate, in a territory outside the UK.

Where a REIT, or principal company of a UK REIT group, distributes to a person with more than the maximum holding and it has not taken reasonable steps to avoid so doing, the REIT company, or principal company, is treated as receiving an amount of income equivalent to:

$$\left(DO \times SO \times \frac{(BRT)}{(MCT)}\right) + \left(DP \times SP \times \frac{(BRT)}{(MCT)}\right)$$

where:

DO = the total amount of the company's property rental profits distributed in respect of ordinary shares.

SO = is the lesser of:

- excessive shareholder's percentage interest; and
- percentage interest of recipient of distributions.

BRT = the basic rate of tax at the time of the distribution.

DP = the REIT's total property rental profits distributed in respect of preference shares.

SP = the lesser of the percentage of rights:

- in respect of preference shares by the holder of the excessive rights; and
- held by the distribution recipient in respect of which the distribution was made.

MCT = the UK corporation tax rate on residual profits.

The amount arrived at is charged to corporation tax at the main rate as if it were profits of the residual business of the REIT for the accounting period in which the distribution was made. No loss, deficit, expense or allowance may be offset from the amount chargeable.

There are regulations requiring a REIT which makes a distribution to a holder of excessive rights to provide information to HMRC.

[*CTA 2010, ss 551–554; SI 2006 No 2864, Regs 10, 11*].

Capital gains

[53.21] Where a company is a REIT or is a member of a UK REIT group, a gain arising on the disposal of an asset used wholly and exclusively for the purpose of the property rental business is not a chargeable gain. Nor is an asset chargeable if it has been used partly for the property rental business and partly for the residual business during one or more periods of which in aggregate amounts to less than one year.

Where an asset has been used partly for the property rental business and partly for the residual business during one or more periods of at least one year in total, the gain is not chargeable to the extent that it can reasonably be attributed to the property rental business. The gain should be attributed on the basis of the length of time and extent to which the asset has been used in each business. Gains arising in respect of the residual business are chargeable to corporation tax at the main rate, and the small profits rate does not apply.

Where a proportion of the gains of a group member's property rental business are excluded from a financial statement (see **53.9** above), the excluded amount is to be treated for corporation tax purposes as gains of the relevant member's residual business. With respect to transfers out of the ring-fence (see **53.22** below) in relation to property developed by the company and sold within three years of completion, such property being treated as if it were never part of the property rental business, reference to the company is a reference to the group member.

[*CTA 2010, ss 533, 535*].

Movement of assets out of ring-fence

[53.22] An asset used wholly and exclusively for the purpose of the property rental business which begins to be used (otherwise than by being disposed of in the course of a trade) wholly and exclusively in the residual business is treated as disposed of by the property rental business and immediately re-acquired by the residual business for a consideration equal to the market value of the asset. On any subsequent disposal (apart from one following an early exit from the regime — see **53.31** below) of such an asset (whether actual or deemed), the deemed consideration at that market value is to be used as its base cost. This treatment excludes assets disposed of in the course of a trade (see below). For capital allowances purposes, the assets are not treated as having been transferred, the residual business being treated as standing in the shoes of the property rental business.

Where a percentage of a gain relating to the property rental business is excluded, that part is treated as a gain of the residual business. These provisions apply to non-UK group members as well as UK group members.

[*CTA 2010, s 555*].

Where an asset which has been used wholly and exclusively for the purpose of the property rental business is disposed of in the course of a trade for the purposes of the residual business, there is no deemed sale and re-acquisition but the asset is treated as disposed of in the course of the residual business. This applies in particular where a company develops property, where the cost of development exceeds 30% of the fair value of the property at entry or acquisition, whichever is the later, and where the property is disposed of within three years from the completion of the development. Where an asset held by the property rental business at entry is disposed of in the course of a trade, the company can claim repayment of a proportion of the entry charge (at **53.13** above) relating to that asset. The proportion is the market value of the asset at entry divided by the aggregate market value of assets treated as sold and re-acquired on entry, ignoring any assets of negative market value.

[*CTA 2010, s 556*].

Movement of assets into ring-fence

[53.23] An asset used wholly and exclusively for the purpose of the residual business which begins to be used wholly and exclusively in the property rental business, is treated as disposed of by the residual business and immediately re-acquired by the property rental business for a consideration equal to the market value of the asset. For capital allowances purposes, the assets are not treated as having been transferred, the property rental business being treated as standing in the shoes of the residual business.

Where a percentage of a gain of property rental business is excluded, that part is treated as a gain of the residual business. These provisions apply to non-UK group members as well as UK group members.

[*CTA 2010, s 557*].

Disposal proceeds awaiting re-investment

[53.24] Where a company or a member of a UK REIT group disposes of an asset used wholly and exclusively for the purposes of the property rental business and holds the proceeds in 'cash', the proceeds will count as an asset of the property rental business for the purpose of the 75% rule in **53.8**(a) above for the period of 24 months from the date of the disposal.

Any income derived from those proceeds is treated as income from the residual business. Where the proceeds are used to enter into a loan relationship (such as a bank deposit) any profits or losses arising from that relationship (such as bank interest) is not treated as part of the profits of the property rental business but are taxable under the loan relationship rules as arising in the residual business.

'*Cash*' in this case includes any currency held on deposit or gilt stocks or bonds or other investments as specified by HMRC regulations. Where the asset disposed of was used partly for the property rental business and partly for the residual business this treatment applies to the proportion of the disposal proceeds that may reasonably be attributed to the property rental business on the basis of the length of time and extent to which the asset has been used in each business.

[*CTA 2010, s 547*].

Debt financing

[53.25] The Treasury may make regulations for a tax charge to be imposed on a REIT that does not meet a minimum financing cost ratio. The charge may be imposed where, for an accounting period, the profits from the property rental business (or in the case of a REIT group, the sum of the property rental profits for members of the group) as set out in the financial statements (see **53.9**), divided by the property finance costs is less than 1.25.

In this case, the property rental profits are taken before the offset of capital allowances, losses brought forward from a previous accounting period or the disregarding of debits and credits arising from loan relationships, embedded derivatives and hedging derivative contracts (see **53.14**).

Finance costs in this case mean the amount of financing costs incurred in respect of the property rental business, or in the case of a REIT group, the amount of financing costs incurred in respect of the property rental business excluding any financing costs owed by one member of the group to another member. In calculating finance costs, the following should be included:

- debtor relationship debits other than those in respect of exchange losses from such relationships;
- exchange gains or losses from a debtor relationship in relation to debt finance;
- debits or credits arising from derivative contracts in relation to debt finance;
- financing costs arising under finance leases; and
- any other costs that under generally accepted accounting practice are considered to arise from a financing transaction.

Where the ratio of the REIT's financing cost ratio is less than 1.25, the company is charged to corporation tax on the difference between the actual financing costs for the period and the amount of financing costs that would have caused the calculation outlined above to equal 1.25. The difference will be treated as profits of the residual business of the company, or the principal company in the case of a REIT group. No deductions or reliefs may be set against these chargeable profits.

HMRC may waive this charge if they consider that the company was in severe financial difficulties at a time in the accounting period, the financial cost ratio is less than 1.25 for that accounting period because of unexpected circumstances and the company could not reasonably have taken action to avoid the ratio being below 1.25. HMRC has power to make regulations regarding waiver of a charge to corporation tax.

[*CTA 2010, ss 543, 544, 599; SI 2006 No 2864*].

Breach of conditions

[53.26] A company or principal company which has given notice of entry into the regime (**53.14** above) must notify HMRC as soon as reasonably practicable if the following conditions cease to be satisfied:

- conditions (c) and (d) of the conditions for the company (see **53.6**);
- conditions (a) and (b) of the conditions for the business (see **53.7**);
- the distribution condition (see **53.7**); or
- conditions (a) and (b) for the balance of business (see **53.8**).

The company or principal company must provide HMRC with details of the date on which the breach occurred and when the breach was rectified (if at all), a description of the breach and details of the steps taken (if any) to prevent the breach happening again.

Breach of conditions for company

The REIT regime will continue to apply if the breach is the result of a REIT becoming a member of a REIT group or as the result of the principal company of a REIT group becoming a member of another REIT group.

In addition, the REIT regime will also continue to apply if the breach is due to the actions (or lack of actions) by a person other then the REIT company or principal company. However, the company must remedy the breach no later then the end of the accounting period after the breach occurred. If the breach is not remedied within that time frame, the company or group will be treated as ceasing to be a REIT or REIT group at the end of the accounting period in which the breach occurred.

If there is a breach of condition (c) or (d) of the conditions of the company (see **53.6**) and the provisions above do not apply, the company or group will be treated as ceasing to be a REIT or REIT group from the end of the previous accounting period.

Breach of conditions for the business

The REIT regime will continue to apply if a company or principal company does not meet the conditions throughout the accounting period. However, HMRC may issue a notice of termination where the conditions are breached more than twice in a ten-year period, beginning with the date that the first breach occurred. If a breach of condition (b) is a necessary consequence of a breach of condition (a) in the same accounting period, then the breach of condition (b) is to be ignored. If the breach of either condition lasts for more than one, but not more than two accounting periods, the breach is treated as only occurring once.

HMRC may also issue a notice of termination if there is a breach of conditions (a) and (b) for three consecutive accounting periods (see **53.7**).

Breach of the distribution condition

The REIT provisions will continue to apply if there is a breach of the distribution condition, but the company will be chargeable to corporation tax on an amount determined to be profits of the residual business. The amount is calculated as 90% of the company or group's property rental profits less the amount distributed before the filing date (see **53.7**).

However, no charge to corporation tax will arise if the company or principal company make a dividend distribution within a three-month period (beginning on the date on which the company or group's profits can no longer be altered) which is sufficient to meet the distribution condition.

Breach of balance of business condition

Where a company does not comply with condition (b) in **53.8** at the beginning of its initial accounting period in the REIT regime, that regime will apply provided that condition (b) is met at the beginning of the second accounting period.

However, there is a charge to tax on the company, or the principal company of a REIT group. The amount added to corporation tax profits of the residual business is the notional income, calculated as follows:

$$\frac{\text{Market Value of assets} \times 2\,\% - \text{Entry charge notional income}}{\text{Tax rate}}$$

Where:

'Market value of assets' = the aggregate market value of assets involved in the UK property rental business of the REIT, individual company or group, plus the proportion of the value of the property rental business assets of a joint venture company or group corresponding to the REIT's interest. Market value is to be determined at the end of the initial period and negative values are to be ignored.

Tax rate = the percentage rate at which the company, or principal company of a group, is chargeable to tax on profits from the residual business.

For entry charge notional income see **53.13**. To this figure is added the proportion of the joint venturing company or group's entry charge notional income.

Where a company holds an asset when it becomes a REIT, but not at the end of the initial period, the entry charge notional income is reduced by an amount calculated as follows:

$$\frac{\text{Asset market value} \times \text{entry charge notional income}}{\text{Aggregate market value}}$$

Where:

Asset market value = the market value when the company becomes a REIT.

Aggregate market value = the aggregate market value of assets deemed to be sold and reacquired on entry into the regime (ignoring any negative value).

No loss, deficit, expense or allowance may be set off against notional income or tax.

The REIT regime will cease to apply if condition (b) is not met at the beginning of the second accounting period and HMRC consider the breach so fundamental that the regime should not apply.

Where conditions (a) or (b) of the balance of business conditions are not satisfied after the initial accounting period, the REIT regime will continue to apply where, in the case of (a), the profits from the property rental business are at least 50% of the total profits for the accounting period and in the case of (b), the assets of the property rental business are at least 50% of the total assets.

A company or principal company may rely on the relaxation of condition (a) and condition (b) for up to two times in a ten-year period beginning with the first date the relaxation was relied on. But, if the conditions are breached in three consecutive accounting periods, the breach will no longer qualify for this relaxation. However, where a breach lasts for one, but not more than two accounting periods, it is treated as one breach.

Condition (a) is treated as breached on the last day of the accounting period for which its profit are assessed.

[*CTA 2010, ss 561–569; SI 2006 No 2864, Reg 7; SI 2007 No 3540*].

Cancellation of tax advantage

[53.27] If HMRC consider that a company or a company in a UK REIT group has tried to obtain a 'tax advantage' under these provisions for itself or another person, they may, by notice to the company, counteract the advantage and assess the company to an additional amount of corporation tax equivalent to the value of the tax advantage. The tax advantage may be counteracted by adjustment by way of an assessment, amendment of a tax return, cancellation of a right of repayment or a requirement for the return of a repayment already made. A 'tax advantage' has the meaning given under *CTA 2010, s 1139* from 1 April 2010, (formerly *ICTA 1988, s 840ZA* from 6 April 2007 to 31 March 2010, and prior to that *ICTA 1988, s 709*) and includes in particular entering into arrangements to avoid or reduce the entry charge under **53.13** above. A tax advantage does not, however, include benefits arising from the REIT regime unless the sole or main purpose of joining the regime is to create or inflate a loss, deduction or expense or to have another effect which may be specified by Treasury regulation. An appeal against a notice to cancel a tax advantage may be made to the tribunal by written notice to HMRC within 30 days from the date of the notice to the company. The tribunal may quash the notice, confirm it or vary it.

[*CTA 2010, ss 545, 546*].

Leaving the regime

Termination by notice

[53.28] A company REIT or the principal company in a REIT group can give notice in writing to HMRC specifying a date (to be later than that on which HMRC receives the notice) at the end of which the REIT regime is to cease to apply to the company or group.

[*CTA 2010, s 571*].

HMRC may give written notification to a company REIT or to the principal company in a REIT group, giving the reasons for the issue of the notice, that the regime is to cease to apply to it if:

(a) the company has relied on the breach provisions on the specified number of occasions in the specified period (see **53.26** above);
(b) the company has been given two notices in relation to the cancellation of a tax advantage in a specified period (see **53.27** above); or
(c) HMRC consider that the breach of the company conditions (see **53.6** above), property rental business conditions (see **53.7**), the balance of business conditions (see **53.8** above) or an attempt by the company to obtain a tax advantage is so great that it no longer qualifies for REIT status.

The regime will cease to apply (subject to the early exit provisions below) at the end of the accounting period before that in which the event occurs (or the last event occurs) which caused HMRC to give the notice. An appeal against such a notice may be made to the tribunal, by notice in writing from the company or the principal company to HMRC within 30 days from the date on which the notice is given to the company.

[*CTA 2010, ss 572–576*].

HMRC may also give a notice of termination where there are multiple breaches of conditions. A notice of termination may be issued where there has been a breach of at least two of the conditions at **53.6**, **53.7** and **53.8** above during the ten-year period beginning on the day on which the company first fails to satisfy a condition, at least one of the conditions breached is contained in a different section from that containing another and the company has relied on the breach provisions more then four times in the ten-year period. For this purpose, a company is treated as having first failed to satisfy the condition at **53.7**(a) above on the last day of the accounting period in which its profits are assessed. The following types of breach are not taken into account in determining the number of breaches:

- a breach of either of the conditions at **53.6**(c) and (d) above in consequence of a REIT becoming a member of a REIT group;
- a breach of either of the conditions at **53.6**(c) and (d) above in respect of which the company used the special facility for new companies at **53.11** above;
- a breach of the condition at **53.7**(a) above in the company's initial accounting period within the REIT regime; and
- a breach of the condition at **53.7**(b) above at the beginning of the company's initial accounting period within the regime.

[*CTA 2010, s 577*].

Automatic termination

[53.29] If any of the company conditions (a), (b), (e) or (f) in **53.6** above are not satisfied in an accounting period, the REIT regime is treated as ceasing to apply to the company at the end of the previous accounting period. The company which gave notice of entry, as set out in **53.11** above, must notify HMRC as soon as is reasonably practicable if any of those conditions cease to be satisfied. [*CTA 2010, s 578*].

Effects of cessation

[53.30] The effect of cessation will apply where a company or group ceases to be a UK REIT or where a company ceases to be a member of a UK REIT group. The effects will apply to each member of a UK REIT group.

On leaving the regime, the company's property rental business is treated as ceasing to exist immediately before the cessation and for corporation tax purposes, an accounting period of the residual business ends on cessation and a new accounting period of the company (in respect of the '*post-cessation*' business) begins.

The assets involved in the property rental business immediately before cessation are treated for corporation tax purposes as sold immediately before cessation by the property rental business and reacquired immediately after cessation by the post-cessation business at their market value. On any subsequent disposal (apart from one following an early exit — see below) of such an asset (whether actual or deemed), the deemed consideration at that market value is to be used as its base cost. Where a subsidiary company is not wholly owned, and a proportion of the profits of a group member's property rental business are excluded from a financial statement (see **53.9** above), the excluded amount is to be ignored for the purpose of these provisions.

For capital allowances purposes, the post-cessation business is treated as acquiring the assets at their written-down value as though the property rental business had not ceased. [*CTA 2010, ss 579, 580, 602*].

Effects of early exit

Notice by the company or group

[53.31] The following rule applies if a company leaves the REIT regime, a company leaves a UK REIT group, or a group leaves the REIT regime by notice from HMRC or automatic termination and that company or group has been within the regime for a continuous period of less than ten years immediately before the cessation.

Where the company disposes of an asset that was part of the property rental business within a period of two years beginning with the date of cessation, any deemed disposals that applied to that asset on entry to the regime (under **53.12** above), on transfer out of the ring fence (under **53.22** above) or on exit from the regime (as above), are ignored in calculating the gain on the disposal.

[*CTA 2010, s 581*].

Notice by HMRC

The following rules apply if the company leaves the REIT regime as a result of an HMRC termination notice or an automatic termination and has been within the regime for a continuous period of less than ten years immediately before the cessation. An HMRC termination notice or an automatic termination may relate to the group as a whole or to one or more members and may, in particular, alter the effects of the provisions relating to groups.

HMRC may direct that:

(i) the effects of a regime provision are modified. In particular, they may alter the time the company or group is treated as leaving the REIT regime as a result of the termination notice or automatic termination and they may disapply or alter the effect of the provisions which exempt the profits and gains of the REIT's property rental business from corporation tax; or
(ii) the effects of other corporation tax provisions are applied, disapplied or modified, in particular to prevent all or part of a loss, deficit or expense from being set off or otherwise used at all or in a specified manner.

An appeal against such a direction may be made by the company or principal company of the group to the tribunal, who may quash HMRC's direction, confirm it or vary it.

[*CTA 2010, s 582*].

Groups

[53.32] In relation to the following group reliefs, the property rental businesses of the group members are treated as a separate group distinct from the pre-entry businesses of those companies, the residual businesses and the post-cessation businesses:

- actual or notional transfers within a group under *TCGA 1992, ss 171, 171A–171C*;
- reallocation of rolled-over gains within a group under *TCGA 1992, ss 179A, 179B*;
- group relief under *CTA 2010, Pt 5*;
- loan relationships under *CTA 2009, Pt 5 Chs 4, 6–8;*
- derivative contracts under *CTA 2009, Pt 7*; and
- intangible fixed assets under *CTA 2009, Pt 8*.

[*CTA 2010, s 601*].

Anti-avoidance

The changes to *TCGA 1992, s 171A* in *FA 2009, Sch 12* counter arrangements by groups which aimed to use the REIT's exemption from tax in a way HMRC view as unacceptable. The legislation designed to prevent such abuse of the REIT legislation will take effect on chargeable gains and allowable losses accruing on or after 21 July 2009.

[*FA 2009, s 31, Sch 12*].

Demergers

[53.33] Where a REIT leaves a group and either the company, or where the REIT has become a member of a new group, the new group satisfies certain conditions immediately after it leaves the group, the company or principal company of the new group may give notice of entry to HMRC by the day the company leaves the existing REIT group. The conditions to be satisfied are as follows:

- conditions (a) and (b) of the conditions for the company (see **53.6**);
- conditions (a) and (b) of the conditions for the business (see **53.7**);
- the distribution condition (see **53.7**); and
- conditions (a) and (b) of the conditions for the balance of business (see **53.7**).

The date of entry given in the notice must be the day the company leaves the existing group. The company will qualify as a REIT from that date even if it does not expect to satisfy the conditions in paragraphs (c) to (f) at **53.6** above throughout the first accounting period. The company has six months to qualify, during which it will be treated as a REIT. If it fails to satisfy all the conditions by the time six months has expired, it will be treated as if it had not been a REIT from the date it left the group.

Where there is a demerger, involving a REIT transferring a property rental business asset to a 75% subsidiary and a subsequent disposal of that subsidiary by the REIT, and the acquiring company subsequently gives a notice of entry (see **53.9**) specifying an accounting period commencing within six months of the date of transfer, the REIT provisions apply to the group that the subsidiary is now a member of from the beginning of that accounting period. The purchasing company may give notice of entry even if conditions (c) to (f) in **53.6** are not complied with throughout the period stated in the notice.

The provisions concerning the effects of entry, the entry charge and the movement of assets out of ring fence (see **53.9** and **53.12** respectively) do not apply to the transfer of the property rental business asset by the existing REIT provided conditions (c) to (f) in **53.6** are met by the acquiring company within six months of the date of transfer.

[*CTA 2010, ss 558, 559*].

Joint ventures

[53.34] A joint venture for this purpose means a company or group carrying on a property rental business where an interest in the joint venture is held by a REIT or one or more members of a REIT group.

A REIT or principal company of a REIT group, known as the venturing company or group, may apply for a joint venture look through notice to apply to the joint venture company if the following conditions are satisfied:

- the venturing company or group is beneficially entitled to 40% or more of the profits available for distribution; and

- the venturing company or group is beneficially entitled to 40% or more of the assets on a winding up.

The notice must specify the joint venture company, the date from which the notice will apply and be given in writing to HMRC before the date on which the notice will apply.

A REIT or principal company of a REIT group may also give notice for a joint venture look through notice to apply in relation to property rental business carried on by one or more members of a joint venture group. The conditions above will apply in so far as they relate to the principal company of the joint venture group.

[*CTA 2010, ss 583–587*].

Once notice has been given by a venturing company, the property rental business carried on by the joint venture company will be treated as if it had formed a new REIT group with the venturing company. Where notice has been given by a venturing group, the property rental business carried on by the joint venture company will be treated as if it were a member of the venturing group. These provisions apply where a joint venture look through notice has been issued in respect of a joint venture group.

The notice will continue to apply until the venturing company or group ceases to fulfil the conditions above as to entitlement to profits or assets. However the early exit rules (see **53.18**) will continue to apply to a joint venture company or group.

The conditions regarding the balance of business (see **53.7**) must be met by the joint venture company or group at the beginning of each accounting period for which the notice has effect.

The venturing company's accounts are prepared in accordance with *SI 2006 No 2865*, as amended for the joint venture situation. The principal company of a joint venture group must prepare accounts for the group for each accounting period in much the same way as for a REIT group (see **53.7**).

The joint venture company or members of a joint venture group may be chargeable to tax on an entry charge (see **53.9**) in certain circumstances. In particular, this may apply where the venturing company becomes the principal company of a REIT group and increases its holding in the joint venture company or group or where the venturing company or group increases its shareholding in the joint venture company or group to at least 75%.

[*CTA 2010, ss 588–597; SI 2006 No 2865*].

Where the principal company of a UK REIT group gives notice in relation to members of a joint venture group, the above apply in relation to a property rental business carried on by the members of the joint venture UK REIT group. Similar provisions apply where a company UK REIT and the members of a joint venture group become members of a new UK REIT group.

[*CTA 2010, s 589*].

Penalties

[53.35] Penalties under *TMA 1970, s 98* will apply for failure to comply with:

- the requirement to provide a notice of a breach of conditions or with any requirements imposed by regulations in relation to such breaches under **53.26** above;
- requirements imposed by regulations in connection with deduction of income tax from distributions under **53.17** above;
- the requirement to provide notice of a breach of company conditions in relation to automatic termination under **53.29** above; and
- the requirement to meet the company conditions and for the principal company to send in financial statements as part of those conditions under **53.6** and **53.9** above.

An initial penalty will apply of up to £300 and if the failure continues after this penalty has been imposed, a further penalty of up to £60 per day can be imposed for each day the failure continues.

[*TMA 1970, s 98; FA 2006, s 140*].

Administration

[53.36] When a company makes a distribution from its property letting business it must deduct tax at the basic rate in force for the year of payment unless the conditions for gross payment are made.

[*SI 2006 No 2867, Regs 2, 3*].

Where a REIT or principal company of a REIT group makes a distribution from property rental income, it must submit a return to HMRC for each quarter in which a distribution is made plus a return to the accounting date if that does not fall on a calendar quarter. The returns should be delivered within 14 days after the end of the period.

A reconciliation of the payments for the year also has to be delivered within 14 days of the accounting date, with the distributions attributed as to source (see **53.11**). The tax deducted from the distribution must be paid over to HMRC, without assessment, with the same deadlines as for the returns. The company has to give the recipient a statement showing the gross payment, tax deducted and net amount paid.

No tax is to be deducted if the payee is a company resident or trading through a permanent establishment in the UK, a local authority, NHS Trust, public office or department of the Crown, charity or similarly treated body, the EIF, scientific research organisation, various pension funds, ISAs, CTF, PEP funds which are to apply the payment for permitted purposes or a partnership otherwise qualifying.

[*SI 2006 No 2867, Regs 2, 4, 6, 7*].

HMRC has power to assess where it believes that tax due has not been paid. [*SI 2006 No 2867, Reg 9*].

Miscellaneous provisions

Manufactured dividends

[53.37] Special provisions apply to dividends that represent payments of distributions of the property rental profits of a REIT or principal company of a REIT group.

[*CTA 2010, ss 785, 786*].

Charities

For charitable companies and REITs see **20.3 CHARITIES.**

Connected persons

The Treasury are given powers to regulate, by statutory instrument, the operation of the REIT legislation in the public interest where there are transactions between connected persons.

[*CTA 2010, ss 598, 600*].

Anti-avoidance

[53.38] *SI 2009 No 3315* introduces anti-avoidance provisions aimed at artificially manipulated commercial arrangements where the purpose or main purpose of the arrangements is to enable the party or parties of the arrangement to meet the conditions to qualify as a REIT, where it or they would not otherwise have qualified.

Key points

[53.39] Points to consider are as follows.

- When calculating the value of assets used in the property rental business for the purposes of the asset balance of business test, all assets used in that business should be included, not just properties. For example, the value of company cars used by those who work in the property rental business should be included.
- Where a UK REIT relies on the Day 1 breach concession (i.e. where the UK REIT fails the asset balance of business test on entry to the regime), the additional entry charge payable at the end of the first accounting period will cover not only assets acquired since entry to the regime, but also any increase in the value of properties held on entry to the regime.
- Note that the 10% test only applies to corporate shareholders.
- Where a group of companies wishes to hold more than 10% of a UK REIT, it could do so by fragmenting its shareholding in the UK REIT between a number of sister subsidiaries, each holding less than 10%. This is generally accepted by HMRC as the 10% rule and was introduced to prevent tax treaties removing the withholding tax requirements for dividends paid by UK REITs.
- The non-UK property business of non-UK group members can be taken into account for the purposes of the profit and asset balance of business tests and the property business tests.
- The purpose of the UK REIT regime is to tax shareholders on a similar basis to holding the underlying property directly. The treatment is not directly comparable however as gains arising

from the property rental business distributed to shareholders by way of dividend are treated as property income in the hands of shareholders rather than as gains.

- On a takeover of a UK REIT by a non-REIT, the UK REIT will at some point breach the close company condition and the listed company condition, with the result that the UK REIT will leave the regime. A UK REIT is deemed to leave the regime at the end of the accounting period in which the company becomes close or at the end of the accounting period before that in which the company ceased to be listed. In order to maximise the time during which the REIT is within the regime, consideration could be given to amending the accounting reference date of the UK REIT to a date shortly before the company ceases to be listed.
- Where a UK REIT and a non-REIT enter into a joint venture, the UK REIT will need to ensure that profits and losses are shared on a pre-tax basis since the UK REIT's share of the joint venture's income is not subject to tax. If returns are shared equally after tax, the UK REIT will suffer a loss.
- When determining whether profits are required to be distributed as property income distributions, the measure of profits to use is calculated on the same basis as if they were taxable profits. As such, whilst capital allowances are not relevant in reducing a UK REIT's charge to tax, they are relevant in reducing the amount required to be distributed by the UK REIT and taxed as property income in the hands of shareholders.
- When acquiring UK properties, UK REITs will need to weigh up the cost of stamp duty land tax (at a maximum rate of 4%) with, generally, a more straightforward acquisition of property, against stamp duty (at 0.5% on shares), a UK REIT entry charge (a fixed 2%) with a more complex corporate acquisition involving due diligence, warranties and indemnities.
- Certain conditions for being within the UK REIT regime are required to be met throughout an accounting period, including the company conditions, the property business conditions (being at least three properties with no one property worth more than 40% of the total portfolio value), the profit balance of business test and the profit: financing cost ratio. Compliance with these tests will need to be monitored on an ongoing basis. In particular, UK REIT operations managers will need to assess commercial proposals alongside their internal or external tax advisers to ensure that the proposals do not result in a breach of any of the conditions.

54

Loan Relationships

Cross-references. See **4 ALTERNATIVE FINANCE ARRANGEMENTS; 46.11 INCOME TAX IN RELATION TO A COMPANY.**

Other sources. See HMRC Company Taxation Manual, CTM50000 *et seq.* and HMRC Corporate Finance Manual.

Simon's Taxes. See D1.7.

Introduction

[54.1] The rules for the taxation of loan relationships were introduced by *FA 1996* with effect from 1 April 1996 to treat all profits and losses made by companies on debtor or creditor relationships as income items. A company will be a party to a debtor relationship where it is a debtor in respect of the underlying money debt and will be a party to a creditor relationship where it is a creditor in respect of the underlying money debt.

Loan relationship debits and credits are based on the profits and losses that are reflected in a company's accounts in respect of its loan relationships where its accounts are prepared in accordance with UK generally accepted accounting practice or international accounting standards.

Trading items are dealt with as trading receipts or deductions and non-trading items are within the charge to corporation tax on income from non-trading loan relationships). Whether a company is treated as being a party to a debtor relationship for trading or non-trading purposes depends on the purposes for which it is a party to the loan relationship. In the case of a creditor relationship a company will only be treated as being a party to the loan relationship for the purposes of its trade where it is a party to the loan relationship in the course of activities forming an integral part of its trade. In practice this means that such treatment will normally only apply where the company is carrying on a financial trade for tax purposes.

See also **30 DERIVATIVE CONTRACTS**, over which the current provisions generally take priority.

Taxation of loan relationships

[54.2] All profits arising to a company from 'loan relationships' are (subject to the exception for certain distributions at **54.74** below) chargeable to corporation tax as income as described at **54.4** below.

Unless otherwise specified, a charge or relief under the loan relationship provisions precludes any other charge to or relief from corporation tax in respect of the same matter.

[*CTA 2009, ss 295, 464; FA 1996, s 80(1)(5)*].

Where interest is charged to tax as a trading receipt, this does not affect any requirement for deduction of tax by the payer (see **46.2**(b) **INCOME TAX IN RELATION TO A COMPANY**). See Revenue Tax Bulletin, issue 42 (August 1999): www.hmrc.gov.uk/bulletins/tb42.htm.

A company has a '*loan relationship*' wherever it is a creditor or debtor as respects any 'money debt' which arises from a transaction for the lending of money, i.e. any debt which is, under general law, a loan. A debt is not taken to arise from such a transaction to the extent that it arises from rights conferred by 'shares' in a company. For this purpose, a 'share' is any share in a company under which an entitlement to receive distributions may arise, but does not include a share in a building society. Subject to this, a money debt is taken to arise from such a transaction where an instrument is issued by any person for the purpose of representing security for, or the rights of a creditor in respect of, the debt. Where a company is a party to a loan relationship as a debtor it is a party to a debtor relationship and where it is a party to a loan relationship as a creditor it is a party to a creditor relationship.

A '*money debt*' is a debt falling to be settled by:

(a) payment of money;
(b) the transfer of a right to settlement under a debt falling to be so settled; or
(c) in relation to loan relationships to which a company is a party, the issue or transfer of any shares in any company (mandatory convertibles).

The settlement as above may be at the option of the debtor or creditor and any other option exercisable by either party is to be disregarded. This reverses the decision in *HSBC Life (UK) Ltd v Stubbs and related appeals* (Sp C 295) 2001, [2002] SSCD 9 in which certain financial futures contracts entered into with derivatives dealers, involving both an option for cash settlement and one for settlement in a non-cash form, were held not to constitute loan relationships.

Certain types of interest and other amounts arising from a money debt which is not a loan relationship are treated as if they did so arise as regards credits and debits relating to those amounts (see **54.3** below). In addition, there are a number of provisions treating certain transactions or amounts as loan relationships or as rights, payments or profits under loan relationships. For details see:

- **54.96** below (holdings in OEICS, unit trusts and offshore funds);
- **9.3 BUILDING SOCIETIES** (building society interest and dividends);

- **47 INDUSTRIAL AND PROVIDENT SOCIETIES;**
- **4 ALTERNATIVE FINANCE ARRANGEMENTS;**
- **54.78** below (manufactured interest etc.);
- **54.80** below (for times on or after 22 April 2009 shares treated as liabilities);
- **54.79** below (for times on or after 22 April 2009 disguised interest);
- **5.5 ANTI-AVOIDANCE** (repos); and
- **54.86** below (for times before 22 April 2009 shares with guaranteed returns etc. and returns from partnerships).

[*CTA 2009, ss 294, 302, 303, 476(1); FA 1996, ss 81(1)–(4), 103(1); FA 2002, s 82, Sch 25 paras 2, 14; FA 2006, Sch 6 para 10*].

Any payment or interest paid or payable in pursuance of any of the rights or liabilities under a loan relationship, or under the arrangement(s) by virtue of which the relationship exists (including a security representing the relationship), are treated as made or payable under that relationship.
[*CTA 2009, s 305; FA 1996, s 81(5)*].

See also **54.12** below regarding the treatment of the loan relationship as continuing where a company ceases to be a party to a loan relationship and in accordance with generally accepted accounting practice it spreads any resulting profit or loss over one or more future periods.

Money debts etc. not arising from the lending of money

[54.3] Certain money debts which do not arise from a loan relationship (such as trade debts, unpaid or overpaid tax) are nevertheless effectively treated as payable under a loan relationship. This applies where the money debt is one of the following (referred to in *CTA 2009* as '*relevant non-lending relationships*').

(a) A debt on which interest is payable by or to a company. Where a company has such a relevant non-lending relationship and it enters into a related transaction in respect of the right to receive interest, and as a result interest is no longer payable to the company, the company nevertheless continues to be treated as having a relevant non-lending relationship.

(b) A debt in relation to which exchange gains or losses arise to a company.

(c) A debt in relation to which an impairment loss (or credit in respect of a reversal of an impairment loss) arises in relation to a trading receipt or a receipt of a UK or overseas property business (this means that where the creditor is connected with the debtor (see **54.31**) the creditor will be denied relief for any impairment loss).

(d) A debt in respect of which a company has been entitled to relief for the underlying expense represented by the debt in calculating the profits of a trade, UK property business, or overseas property business. This provision was introduced by *FA 2009* for cases where a debt is released on or after 22 April 2009. This was designed to ensure that the release of the debt would not give rise to a taxable profit where the debtor was connected with the creditor for the purposes of the loan relationships legislation. This is because the creditor was already denied relief for any impairment provisions or release debits arising in respect of such debts.

(e) A debt from which a discount (of an income or capital nature) arises to a creditor company in respect of a money debt to which the company is party where:
- the money debt would not be treated as a trading receipt if it is consideration (or part-consideration) for the disposal a disposal of property;
- the money debt arises from the disposal of property which is not an asset representing a loan relationship or derivative contract the disposal of which is a 'relevant disposal'; and
- the discounts would be accounted for as an alternative finance return (see **4 ALTERNATIVE FINANCE ARRANGEMENTS**).

A discount will arise, in particular, where the company disposes of a property for consideration which is wholly or partly deferred, the amount of the total consideration is greater than that which the purchaser would have paid if payment was required in full at the time of the disposal and some or all of the excess can reasonably be regarded as being a return on an investment of money at interest (and, thus, as being a discount arising from the money debt).

In relation to the disposal of property which is a loan relationship or a derivative contract, a '*relevant disposal*' is one as respects which the whole consideration is brought into account under the loan relationship or derivative contract rules or it is one to which the group provisions at **54.58** above, or at **30.31** derivative contracts legislation, apply or would apply but for the use of fair value accounting. Note that where a disposal of a loan relationship or derivative is a 'relevant disposal' the above provision is applied where the payment of the transfer consideration is deferred and the conditions above are satisfied (see *CTA 2009, s 340(5)* and *s 341(7)* — the equivalent provisions that apply for the purposes of the derivative contracts legislation are discussed in **30.31 DERIVATIVE CONTRACTS LEGISLATION**).

Interest payable on a money debt includes payments which fall under *TIOPA 2010, Pt 4*, previously *ICTA 1988, Sch 28AA* (see **72 TRANSFER PRICING**) to be treated as interest on a money debt or an amount treated as a money debt.

Where a company has a relevant non-lending relationship, the loan relationship provisions apply to the matters listed below as they apply to such matters in relation to actual loan relationships but the only debits or credits to be brought into account under these provisions in respect of the relationship are those relating to those matters and any references in other provisions to loan relationships is taken to include a relevant non-lending relationship. For relationships within (a)–(c) above, the matters in relation to which this applies are:

(A) the interest, exchange gains or losses, impairment or reversal as appropriate; and

(B) with effect for money debts which are assets and in respect of which interest is payable to the company, profits (but not losses) arising to the company from any 'related transaction' (see **54.6** above) in respect of the right to receive interest (i.e. where the company disposes of the rights without disposing of the associated asset).

For relationships within (d) above, the matters in relation to which the above rules apply are:

(I) matters within (A) or (B) above;
(II) the discount arising from the debt;
(III) profits (but not losses) arising from any related transaction; and
(IV) any impairment, or reversal of an impairment, in respect of the discount.

Credits in respect of a discount are determined using an amortised cost basis of accounting.

These provisions do not apply to profits, gains or losses arising on money debts, which fall within the derivative contracts regime or the intangible assets regime.

See **54.4** above with respect to the determination of the trading or non-trading nature of the associated debits.

Any debits or credits which relate to interest on **OVERPAID TAX (50)** or **INTEREST ON UNPAID TAX (49)** are treated as non-trading debits or credits.

Exchange gains and losses arising on money debts are not to be taken into account under this provision where they relate to:

(i) UK tax; or
(ii) foreign tax (unless deductible under *TIOPA 2010, s 112*, previously *ICTA 1988, s 811*);
(iii) amounts which would, but for any statutory provision (other than *CTA 2009, s 53* (previously *ICTA 1988, s 74(1)(f)* or *(g)*), which relates to capital expenditure) or rule of law prohibiting such deduction, be deductible in computing trading profits, or as a management expense; or
(iv) expenses of insurance companies within Step 1 of *ICTA 1988, s 76(7)*.

The money debts owed to a company on which exchange gains and losses arising are taken into account by virtue of this provision include any currency held by the company and certain deferred acquisition costs of an insurance company. The money debts owed by a company to which this applies include any provision for future liabilities in the company's statutory accounts which would be incurred and fall to be taken into account in computing the profits or losses of a trade, a UK property business or an overseas property business and, in the case of an insurance company, certain provisions for unearned premiums and unexpired risks.

In relation to arrangements coming into force before 1 October 2007, these provisions do not apply to exchange gains and losses in relation to a money debt arising from an obligation to repurchase securities under *ICTA 1988, s 730A(1)(b)* (see **5.6 ANTI-AVOIDANCE**) where the company stands, or has stood, in the position of a creditor or debtor as respects that debt.

[*CTA 2009, ss 478–486, Sch 2 para 72; FA 1996, s 100; FA 1998, s 108(4)(5), Sch 4 para 7; FA 2002, Sch 23 para 6; FA 2003, Sch 38 para 14; FA 2005, s 80, Sch 4 para 9; F(No 2)A 2005, Sch 7 para 12; FA 2006, Sch 6 para 17; FA 2007, Sch 14 paras 14, 17; FA 2009, s 42; SI 2004 No 2310, Art 49; SI 2007 No 2483, Art 3*].

Simon's Taxes. See D1.743.

Charge to, and relief from, tax

[54.4] The credits or debits for an accounting period in respect of any loan relationship (including interest, discount, impairment and foreign exchange movements arising on a money debt not resulting from a transaction for the lending of money — see **54.3**) (computed as described at **54.6** onwards below) are brought into account as follows.

(a) Where the loan relationship is for trading purposes, they are treated as receipts or expenses of the trade for that period (in the case of expenses, notwithstanding *CTA 2009, ss 53, 54* or *59* (*ICTA 1988, s 74* — restrictions on allowable deductions)). (This does not affect any requirement for deduction of tax by the payer (see **46.2**(b) **INCOME TAX IN RELATION TO A COMPANY**), see HMRC Tax Bulletin, issue 42 (August 1999); www.hmrc.gov.uk/bulletins/tb42.htm.)

(b) Where there are credits and/or debits in respect of a non-trading relationship (i.e. '*non-trading credits*' and/or '*non-trading debits*'), they are aggregated, and the net amount is chargeable to corporation tax on income (or, before *CTA 2009* took effect (see **70.2 TRADE PROFITS — INCOME AND SPECIFIC TRADES**) under *Schedule D, Case III*) or relievable as a non-trading deficit (see below) as the case may be.

For a creditor company, a loan relationship is taken to be for trade purposes only if it is a party to the relationship in the course of activities forming an integral part of that trade. Mutual trading, mutual insurance or other mutual business which is not life assurance business, and, for periods of account beginning on or after 1 January 2007, any basic life assurance and general annuity business are treated for this purpose as not constituting the whole or any part of a trade.

[*CTA 2009, ss 296–301; FA 1996, ss 82, 103(3); FA 2007, Sch 10 paras 6, 17*].

Non-trading deficits

[54.5] A non-trading deficit of an accounting period (the '*deficit period*') may be claimed, to the extent not already surrendered as group relief (under *CTA 2010, s 99; ICTA 1988, s 403; CTA 2009, Sch 1 para 118*, see **39.2** onwards **GROUP RELIEF**), either:

(A) by set-off against profits of the deficit period; or

(B) by carry-back and set-off against profits of earlier accounting periods arising from non-trading loan relationships.

Any non-trading deficit for which relief is not claimed under (A) or (B) above, or surrendered as group relief, is carried forward and set against non-trading profits (i.e. so much of the company's profits as does not consist of trading income for the purposes of *CTA 2010, s 37; ICTA 1988, s 393A*) for succeeding accounting periods.

The carried forward non-trading deficit is set against the non-trading profits of the accounting period immediately following the deficit period (the 'first later period'). This is subject to a claim for any amount of that deficit to be excepted from being set against non-trading profits of the first later period (to allow, for example, for any double taxation relief to be used that would otherwise be wasted). Where such a claim is made, or where there are insufficient non-trading profits in the first later period for the whole of the deficit to be set off in that period, the amount not set off in that period is treated as a non-trading deficit of that period to be carried forward for offset against non-trading profits of succeeding accounting periods.

Relief under (A) or (B) above is not available if the company is a charity.

Claims under (A) and (B) above must be made within two years of the end of the deficit period or within such further period as HMRC may allow. A claim for a part or the whole of the deficit to be treated as a non-trading deficit of the first later period, to be carried forward for offset against non-trading profits of succeeding accounting periods, must be made within two years of the end of that first later period.

A claim under (A) above is given effect after relief for brought forward trading losses, but before relief under *CTA 2010, ss 37* or *62; ICTA 1988, s 392A(1)* or *s 393A(1)* (losses relieved against profits of current or earlier accounting periods, see **55.3, 55.4 LOSSES, 62 PROPERTY INCOME**) or under (B) above. Relief against oil companies' ring-fenced profits is prohibited. Different claims may be made as respects different parts of a non-trading deficit, but not so as to give relief more than once.

A claim under (B) above must exclude any amount claimed under (A) above or surrendered as group relief. Only profits for the accounting periods (or parts) falling within a twelve-month period immediately preceding the deficit period may be relieved and relief is given for later accounting periods before earlier ones. Profits of an accounting period straddling the start of the twelve-month period are apportioned for this purpose on a time basis. Relief is given after any relief under (A) above and after any relief for losses or deficits of accounting periods before the deficit period, for trade charges, for trading losses of the same or subsequent periods, or, for companies with investment business (**51 INVESTMENT COMPANIES AND INVESTMENT BUSINESS**), for plant and machinery capital allowances, management expenses or business charges.

[*CTA 2009, ss 456–463; FA 1996, ss 83, 103(2), Sch 8*].

Simon's Taxes. See **D1.739, D1.740.**

Examples

(A) Loan relationship for trading purpose

A Ltd requires additional trade finance, and on 1 January 2010 enters into an agreement with Bank plc to borrow £100,000 for three years. Interest at 6% p.a. is payable at six-month intervals commencing 1 July 2010. The company's accounting reference date is 31 March, and it adopts an authorised accruals basis of accounting for all its loan relationships.

A Ltd's accounts for the year ended 31 March 2010 show the following:

	£	£
Turnover		1,400,000
Purchases and expenses (all allowable for tax purposes)	900,000	
Finance charges		
Bank plc interest to 31 March 2010	1,500	
Depreciation*	120,000	1,024,300
Net profit per accounts		£375,700

* Capital allowances for the year are £95,000.

A Ltd's corporation tax computation for the same period is as follows.

	£
Net profit per accounts	375,700
Add: Depreciation	120,000
Less: Capital allowances	(95,000)
Corporation tax adjusted profit	£400,700

The accrued interest on the bank loan taken for trading purposes will be treated for corporation tax purposes as a trade expense.

The profit and loss charge for each relevant accounting period will be as follows.

Year ended	31.3.10	31.3.11	31.3.12	31.3.13
	£	£	£	£
Interest payable	1,500	6,000	6,000	4,500

This conforms to an amortised cost basis of accounting as interest will be allocated to the period to which it relates.

(B) Loan relationship for non-trading purpose

T Ltd, a trading company, bought £10,000 nominal gilt-edged securities at £94 per £100 nominal stock as a speculative venture on 1 January 2010. The securities will be redeemed on 1 January 2013 at par. Interest at 5% is payable annually on 31 December. The company uses an amortised cost basis of accounting for all its loan relationships. The accounting reference date is 31 March.

As the purchase does not relate to the company's trade, the income will be assessed as income from non-trading loan relationships. In addition to the interest, the company will be taxable on the discount, spread over three years.

Year ended	31.3.10	31.3.11	31.3.12	31.3.13
	£	£	£	£
Interest received	125	500	500	375

Discount	50	200	200	150
Income from non-trading loan relationships	175	700	700	525

(C) Non-trading deficit on a loan relationship

C Ltd, which is not a member of a group, made a loan to X Ltd, outside its normal trading activities. X Ltd defaults on the loan on 1 October 2011, leaving a balance of £8,500 due to C Ltd. The accounting reference date is 31 March.

C Ltd's computations for relevant years are as follows.

Year ended	31.3.10	31.3.11	31.3.12	31.3.13
	£	£	£	£
Trading income	10,000	11,000	800	12,000
Income from non-trading loan relationships	2,000	2,000	100	400

The £8,500 debit is set against the non-trading loan relationship credit of £100 in the year ending 31 March 2012, and the remaining deficit of £8,400 may be relieved in whole or in part in three different ways (group relief not being available), as follows.

	£
Non-trading deficit	8,400
(1) Set against total profits for year ended 31 March 2012	(800)
(2) Carry back against profits from non-trading loan relationships of the preceding accounting period	(2,000)
(3) Carry forward and set against non-trading profits for year ended 31 March 2013	(400)
Net deficit to carry forward against subsequent non-trading profits	£5,200

Computation of debits and credits

[54.6] The credits and debits to be brought into account by a company in respect of its loan relationships are sums which, when taken together, fairly represent, for the accounting period in question:

(a) all profits and losses (capital or otherwise) which (disregarding interest and any expenses) arise to the company from its loan relationships and 'related transactions'; and

(b) all interest under its loan relationships and all expenses incurred under, or for the purposes of, those relationships and transactions.

Subject to the exception at **54.71** below, a '*related transaction*' is any disposal or acquisition (in whole or part) of rights or liabilities under a relationship. This includes the transfer or extinguishment of any such rights or liabilities by any sale, gift, exchange, surrender, redemption or release. Certain transfers under *Proceeds of Crime Act 2002, Part 5*, known as 'Part 5 transfers' (by which property obtained through unlawful conduct is vested in an appointed trustee for civil recovery), which would otherwise be 'related transactions', are, however, disregarded for this purpose except for the purpose of identifying the person for whom debits or credits not related to the transfer are to be brought into account.

Expenses within (b) above include only those incurred directly:

(i) in bringing any of the loan relationships into existence;
(ii) in entering into or giving effect to any of the related transactions;
(iii) in making payments under any of the relationships or in pursuance of any of the related transactions; or
(iv) in taking steps for ensuring the receipt of payments under any of the relationships or in pursuance of any of the related transactions.

They do, however, include expenses connected with entering into, or giving effect to any obligation under, a prospective loan relationship or related transaction into which the company has not entered at the time they are incurred. See HMRC Corporate Finance Manual, at CFM33060 for examples of the expenses allowed.

[*CTA 2009, ss 293, 304, 307(3)(4), 329; FA 1996, s 84; FA 2002, Sch 25 para 4; FA 2004, Sch 10 para 1*].

Costs directly incurred in varying the terms of a loan relationship may be brought into account as a debit under the above provisions. Guarantee fees are included where the loan would not have been advanced without the provision of a guarantee (see HMRC Corporate Finance Manual at CFM33060). It should be noted that HMRC do not consider that premiums payable for key man insurance are deductible even in cases where such insurance was required in order to obtain a loan (see HMRC Corporate Finance Manual at CFM33060).

There is a special relief for debits which are pre-trading expenditure. A company can elect for a non-trading debit not to be brought into account in the period in which it arises, within two years of the end of that period. If the company then begins to carry on a trade within seven years after the end of that period, and the debit would have been a trading debit if it had been given in the accounting period in which the trade commenced, it is brought into account as a trading debit in that period.

[*CTA 2009, s 330; ICTA 1988, s 401(1AB)(1AC)*].

Simon's Taxes. See **D1.715**.

Imputed interest and other amounts

[54.7] Where, under *TIOPA 2010, Pt 4* previously *ICTA 1988, Sch 28AA* (see **72 TRANSFER PRICING**), any amount falls to be treated as interest payable under a loan relationship of a company, the loan relationship provisions have effect as if the amounts were actual interest. [*CTA 2009, s 446; FA 1996, Sch 9 para 16*].

Generally accepted accounting practice

[54.8] The debits and credits to be brought into account for the purposes of the loan relationships legislation are those 'recognised in determining the company's profit or loss' for the period in accordance with generally accepted accounting practice (the definition of generally accepted accounting practice covers accounts prepared in accordance with IFRS, or UK GAAP including or excluding FRS 26 (*CTA 2010, s 1127(1), (3); FA 2004, s 50*)). The amounts can generally be determined on any accounting basis that is in accordance with generally accepted accounting practice and, in particular, an 'amortised cost basis' or 'fair value accounting'. This is subject to any other provisions of the loan relationship rules, in particular the computation of debits and credits in **54.6** above. If a company does not draw up its accounts in accordance with generally accepted accounting practice, or does not draw up accounts at all, the amounts to be brought into account are those that would be recognised had the company done so. This applies equally to amounts derived from earlier periods for which accounts were not drawn up in accordance with generally accepted accounting practice.

Amounts in this case that are 'recognised in determining the company's profit or loss' for an accounting period are amounts recognised (including prior-year adjustments apart from corrections of fundamental errors) in the company's profit and loss account, income statement or statement of comprehensive income, in its statement of recognised gains and losses, statement of recognised income and expense, statement of changes in equity or statement of income and retained earnings, or in any other statement of items brought into account in determining the company's profits and losses for the period. Where the debit or credit represents a prior year adjustment, *SI 2004 No 3271* defers such debits and credits (see below under change of accounting practice) and instead they are brought into account for tax purposes over a 10 year period.

[*CTA 2009, ss 307(2), 308–310, 313(1)(2), Sch 2 para 71; FA 2004, s 52, Sch 10 para 3; FA 2005, s 80, Sch 4 para 26; FA 2006, Sch 6 para 11*].

Held to maturity assets

[54.9] Regulations have been introduced to permit creditor loan relationships that have been accounted for as held to maturity assets and that are required for accounting purposes to be reclassified as available for sale assets, to continue to be treated as held to maturity assets for tax purposes. This is to enable the profits and losses arising on such assets for tax purposes to continue to be determined on an amortised cost basis (where assets are accounted for as available for sale assets a fair value basis has to be used for tax purposes). Such regulations apply where the reclassification did not arise from the disposal of more than 10% of the company's then held to maturity assets. It is possible for a company to elect that this provision should not apply so that its accounting treatment can be followed for tax purposes.

[*SI 2004 No 3271, Reg 5*].

Revaluation of debts

[54.10] Where a creditor company does not use fair value accounting and revalues an asset representing a loan relationship:

(a) no debits can be brought into account for loan relationship purposes except an impairment loss or a debit resulting from the release of any liability under the relationship; and
(b) no credits can be brought into account in respect of a reversal of any debits disallowed under (a) above or because exceptions for write-offs and provisions in the case of insolvency, etc. did not apply.

A '*revaluation*' of an asset for these purposes includes any provision or allowance made by the company reducing the carrying value of the asset (or group of assets including the asset in question).

This provision does not affect debits to be brought into account in respect of exchange gains and losses.

[*CTA 2009, ss 324, 325, Sch 2 para 61; FA 1996, Sch 9 para 6D; FA 2005, s 80, Sch 4 para 16*].

Company ceasing to be a party to a loan relationship

[54.11] Where a company has ceased to be a party to a loan relationship in an accounting period and the whole of the profits or losses arising in that period have not been accounted for as loan relationship credits or debits in that period (for example, where in accordance with generally accepted accounting practice the company is spreading the resulting profit or loss over a number of future accounting periods), then any amounts not yet brought into account and which are recognised in the company's accounts in future periods continue to be brought into account as credits or debits in those subsequent accounting periods as if the company had not ceased to be a party to that loan relationship, by reference to the circumstances in the period in which the company ceased to be a party to the relationship. [*CTA 2009, s 331; FA 1996, s 103(6)–(8); FA 2002, Sch 25 para 16*].

Repos, stock lending and other transactions

[54.12] Subject to the commencement provisions below, where a company has ceased to be a party to a loan relationship (for example, because of the disposal of rights or liabilities under a repo or stock lending arrangement) in an accounting period but, in accordance with generally accepted accounting practice, the company treats itself as continuing to be a party to the loan relationship, the company must bring into account under the loan relationship provisions the amounts that it continues to recognise in its accounts in respect of the loan relationship. Any question about the company's purpose for being a party to the loan relationship is to be determined by reference to the circumstances immediately before it ceased to be a party to the loan relationship. This provision does not apply to any amount brought into account under *CTA 2009, s 331* above or under *CTA 2009, s 550* (effect of borrower under repo etc. ignored; see **5.5 ANTI-AVOIDANCE**).

This provision applies to repos coming into force on or after 1 October 2007, to stock lending arrangements where the transfer takes place on or after that date and in any other case to disposals on or after that date.

[*CTA 2009, s 332, Sch 2 para 66; FA 1996, Sch 9 para 15; FA 2007, Sch 14 para 10; SI 2007 No 2483*].

Amounts not fully recognised for accounting purposes

[54.13] For times on or after 6 December 2010 an anti-avoidance provision applies where a company is, or is treated as being, a party to a creditor relationship in an accounting period and as a result of tax avoidance arrangements to which the company is at any time a party, in accordance with generally accepted accounting practice, an amount is not fully recognised for the period in respect of the creditor relationship in the company's accounts. Arrangements are tax avoidance arrangements if the main purpose, or one of the main purposes, of any party to the arrangements, in entering into them is to obtain a tax advantage (the *CTA 2010, s 1139* definition applies). Arrangements in turn are defined as including any arrangements, scheme or understanding of any kind, whether or not legally enforceable, involving a single transaction or two or more transactions.

For the purposes of this provision an amount is regarded as not being fully recognised in a company's accounts where either no amount is recognised in respect of the creditor relationship or an amount is only recognised in respect of part of the relationship. Under this provision a company is treated as remaining a party to a creditor relationship in cases where the company has disposed of its rights under the creditor relationship under a repo or stock lending transaction, or under a transaction which is treated as not involving any disposal by virtue of *TCGA 1992, s 26* (*CTA 2009, s 311*, as amended by *FA 2011, Sch 4 paras 1, 2, 13,* with effect for times on or after 6 December 2011).

Where the above conditions are satisfied the company is required to recognise the full amount of the credits arising in respect of the creditor relationship during the accounting period. Where a company partially recognises credits arising in respect of the creditor relationship in its accounts, the credits that are recognised under this provision have to be determined using the same basis of accounting. In other cases an amortised cost basis of accounting has to be used to determine the credits to be brought into account under this provision. Where this provision applies, however, a company is not permitted to bring any debits into account in respect of the creditor relationship where the company became a party to the tax avoidance arrangements in question on or after 23 March 2011.

Where pursuant to the tax avoidance arrangements the company becomes, or is treated as becoming, a party to a debtor relationship and in accordance with generally accepted accounting practice an amount is not fully recognised in respect of the debtor relationship, the company is required to recognise the full amount of any credits arising on the debtor relationship. The debits that it is permitted to recognise under this provision may not exceed the credits that are brought into account under this provision in respect of the creditor relationship. Again, where the debtor relationship is partially recognised in the company's accounts the accounting treatment adopted in its accounts will be used to determine the credits and debits to be brought into account under this provision. In other cases an amortised cost basis of accounting has to be used (*CTA 2009, s 312* as amended by *FA 2011, Sch 4 paras 1, 3, 13,* with effect for times on or after 6 December 2011).

For times before 6 December 2010 the provision applied where all the following conditions were satisfied:

(a) the company was, or was treated as being, a party to a creditor loan relationship in an accounting period;

(b) an amount was not fully recognised for the period in respect of the creditor loan relationship — as a result of the application of generally accepted accounting practice to the creditor loan relationship and items falling within any of (c)(i)–(iv) below;

(c)

  (i) the company was, or was treated as being, a party to a debtor loan relationship in the period; or

  (ii) an amount had been contributed to the company (*relevant capital contribution*) which formed part of its capital (whether share capital or otherwise) for the period. This rule applied for periods of account ending on or after 9 May 2007 and in respect of amounts accruing on or after that date where a period of account straddled that date. For periods of account that ended before that date the provision applied where the company had issued share capital which fell to be treated for accounting purposes as a liability (*relevant accounting liability*) for the accounting period; or

  (iii) for periods of account that began on or after 22 April 2009, where the company had issued securities that formed part of its capital for the accounting period in question (if a period of account straddled this date for the purposes of this provision a new period was deemed to start on that date); or

  (iv) for times on or after 22 June 2010, where a company acquired an interest in the shares or other capital of another company, a right to share in the profits or capital of a partnership or an interest under a trust in any property which was subject to the rules of the trust, or where an interest which the company had in the shares or capital of another company, or in a partnership or a trust, was varied; and

(d) in the case of (c)(i)–(iii) above, where an amount was not recognised for the accounting period in respect of the debtor loan relationship, securities (for periods of account beginning or that are deemed to begin) on or after 22 April 2009, or relevant capital contribution or (for accounting periods ending before 9 May 2007) relevant capital contribution, securities issued by the company or relevant accounting liability.

[CTA 2009, s 311 as amended by FA 2009, Sch 30 para 2 and by F(No 2)A 2010, Sch 5].

Where these conditions were satisfied the full amount of the debits and credits arising on the creditor loan relationship were required to be brought into account in computing the company's taxable profits. In the case of the debtor loan relationship the full amount of any credits arising were required to be brought into account for tax purposes. The total amount of debits that were brought into account in respect of the debtor loan relationship under this provision could not exceed the credits which were brought into account for tax purposes for that accounting period under this provision in respect of the creditor loan relationship (*CTA 2009, s 312*).

Where a company partially recognised credits and debits in its accounts in respect of the creditor loan relationship and/or of the debtor loan relationship, the credits and debits which were required to be brought into account for tax purposes followed the accounting treatment adopted in the company's accounts. In other cases the company was required to bring such debits and credits into account using an amortised cost basis of accounting.

The provision in its original form had effect for periods of account ending on or after 22 March 2006. Where a period of account straddled that date it applied to debits and credits arising on or after that date.

[*CTA 2009, ss 311, 312; FA 2006, Sch 6 para 12; FA 2007, Sch 5 para 11; FA 2009, Sch 20 para 2; F(No 2)A 2010, Sch 5*].

Debits arising from the derecognition of a creditor loan relationship

[54.14] For times on or after 6 December 2010 a company is denied relief under the loan relationships legislation (and cannot otherwise obtain relief for tax purposes) for any debits arising from the derecognition in whole or in part of a creditor loan relationship where:

(a) the company continues to be a party to the creditor loan relationship; and
(b) the derecognition results from tax avoidance arrangements to which the company is a party at any time.

Arrangements are tax avoidance arrangements if the main purpose, or one of the main purposes, of any party to the arrangements, in entering into them, is to obtain a tax advantage (the *CTA 2010, s 1139* definition applies). Arrangements in turn are defined as including any arrangements, scheme or understanding of any kind, whether or not legally enforceable, involving a single transaction or two or more transactions.

A company is treated as continuing to be a party to a creditor loan relationship where it has disposed of the loan relationship under a repo or stock lending transaction or under a transaction which is treated as not involving any disposal as a result of *TCGA 1992, s 26* (mortgages and charges not to be treated as disposals).

[*CTA 2009, s 455A as inserted by FA 2011, Sch 4 para 5 with effect for times on or after 6 December 2010*].

Change of accounting practice

[54.15] The following provisions apply where a company changes its accounting policy from one period (the '*earlier period*') to the next (the '*later period*') if the accounting policy in each period is in accordance with the law and practice applicable to that period. In particular, the provisions apply where the company switches from UK generally accepted accounting practice to international accounting standards or vice versa.

(a) Any difference between the closing 'carrying value' of an asset or liability representing a loan relationship in the earlier period and the opening 'carrying value' in the later period, is treated as a debit or credit (as the case may be) in the later period. *SI 2004 No 3271* (as amended by *SI 2005 No 3383; SI 2006 No 3238; SI 2007 Nos 950, 3432*), however, defers any such debits and credits so that they are brought into account over a ten-year period. Broadly, one-tenth of the applicable amount is brought into account for each of the ten years. Special rules apply in the case of debits and credits in respect of dormant accounts of banks and building societies. Deferment does not apply to debits and credits in relation to loan relationship assets or liabilities falling to be fully discharged at the latest on a date within the later period. (Deferment is to bring the tax treatment in line with the mandatory adoption of FRS 26 and IAS 39 by companies using fair value accounting, the ten-year period for the deferral being chosen because of the uncertainty as to the size and direction of the transitional adjustments (see HMRC guidance, available on its website, on international accounting standards).)

(b) Where the company ceases to be party to a loan relationship in an accounting period (the '*cessation period*') and *CTA 2009, s 331* (previously *FA 1996, s 103(6)*) provides for debits and credits to be accounted for as though the relationship had not ceased (see **54.3** below), then any difference between 'the amount outstanding' in respect of the loan relationship at the end of the earlier period and 'the amount outstanding' at the beginning of the later period is treated as a debit or credit (as the case may be) in the later period.

As regards (a) above, '*carrying value*' means the carrying value of the assets or liabilities recognised for accounting purposes and includes accruals, prepayments and impairment losses (including provisions for bad and doubtful debts). In order to stop a number of avoidance schemes, certain specified provisions apply in determining the carrying value for this purpose (for example, the use of the amortised cost basis where parties are connected as required by *CTA 2009, s 349(2)*) as they apply for the purpose of determining loan relationship debits and credits. As regards (b) above, '*the amount outstanding*' means so much of the amount recognised in the company's balance sheet as deferred income or loss arising in the cessation period as has not yet brought into account.

These change of accounting practice provisions do not apply if the differences as detailed above are brought into account in computing a company's loan relationship profits (for example as a result of a prior year adjustment — see above). However, amounts that are brought into account as a prior year adjustment have to be spread over a ten year period, subject to the same exceptions as are discussed above. This is because *SI 2004 No 3271* applies to prior year adjustments, whether or not they arise from a change of accounting policy.

[*CTA 2009, ss 315–318, Sch 2 para 62; FA 1996, Sch 9 para 19A; FA 2004, s 52, Sch 10 para 36; FA 2005, s 80, Sch 4 para 31; F(No 2)A 2005, Sch 6 para 4(2)(6); SI 2004 No 3271; SI 2004 No 3347*].

Change in accounting standards

[54.16] The International Standards Board is in the process of rewriting IAS 39 on a phased basis and it is likely that equivalent changes will be made to FRS 26. In view of this, provision has been made for the loan relationships legislation to be amended by regulation to accommodate changes in accounting treatment. Such changes may be made retrospectively to the date that a particular change in accounting treatment was adopted. Any regulations that are introduced under this provision are subject to affirmation by the House of Commons (*CTA 2009, s 465A as inserted by FA 2010, Sch 19, para 1*).

Exchange gains and losses

[54.17] The reference to profits, gains and losses arising to a company from its loan relationships includes a reference to exchange gains and losses. However, exchange gains or losses will not be brought into account as credits or debits for accounting periods ending on or after 1 April 2009 where the exchange gains and losses arise:

(a) on an asset or liability representing a loan relationship of the company; or
(b) as a result of the translation from one currency to another of the profit or loss of part of the company's business,

and are recognised in the company's:

(i) statement of total recognised gains and losses;
(ii) statement of recognised income and expense;
(iii) statement of changes in equity; or
(iv) statement of income and retained earnings.

For earlier accounting periods exchange gains and losses were left out of account where they were recognised in the company's statement of recognised gains and losses (which applied where it prepared its accounts in accordance with UK GAAP) or statement of changes in equity (which applied where it prepared its accounts in accordance with IFRS).

For periods of account beginning on or after 1 April 2011 any exchange movements that are recognised in an investment company's accounts as a result of a change to its functional currency are disregarded.

[*CTA 2009, s 328(2A)(3); FA 1996, s 84A(3)*].

The rule in (a) above was introduced, inter alia, in order to enable a company to use a debtor relationship that is repayable in an appropriate currency to hedge the exchange exposure on shares in subsidiaries and associates (where the subsidiary or associate prepares its accounts in a different currency), a net investment in an overseas branch and ships and aircraft. Under UK GAAP excluding FRS 26 (and thus FRS 23), where a company uses a debtor relationship to hedge such assets it is possible for the company to take exchange movements on the loan to reserves in its accounts and thus the exchange movements will fall to be disregarded under the above provisions.

Where a company prepares its accounts in accordance with IFRS or UK GAAP incorporating FRS 26, it is not possible for the company to take exchange movements on a debtor relationship that it uses to hedge shares in subsidiaries or associates, or ships or aircraft, to reserves in its individual, as opposed to consolidated accounts. Accordingly, therefore, it was necessary to introduce special provisions to permit a company to continue to be able to use debtor relationships to hedge exchange movements arising on shares, ships and aircraft. These provisions are contained in *Regs 3, 4A–4C* and *5* of the *Disregard Regulations* (*SI 2004 No 3256*) and are considered below.

Matching — Disregard Regulations

[54.18] Under *Reg 3* of the *Disregard Regulations* exchange movements arising on a debtor relationship that is used to hedge exchange movements on shares, ships or aircraft are disregarded where certain conditions are satisfied.

Exchange movements are not disregarded however to the extent that movements in the fair value of, or in profits or losses arising on the disposal of the shares, ships, or aircraft are taken into account in computing the company's profits for the purposes of a trade carried on by it where this trade consists of, or includes, dealing in shares, ships or aircraft.

[*SI 2004 No 3256, Reg 3(2)*].

Under *Reg 3* of the *Disregard Regulations* shares, ships or aircraft are treated as matched with a debtor relationship where either of the following conditions are satisfied:

(a) Condition 1: for the accounting period the shares, ships or aircraft are a hedged item under a designated hedge of exchange rate risk in which the debtor relationship is the hedging instrument. This is designed to cover cases where a debtor relationship is designed as a fair value hedge of the relevant asset in the company's individual (as opposed to consolidated) accounts;

(b) Condition 2: the currency in which the liability is expressed is such that the company intends, by entering into and continuing to be a party to that liability, to eliminate or substantially reduce the economic risk of holding the asset, or part of the asset, which is attributable to fluctuations in exchange rates. In this case a debtor relationship is treated as matched with an asset only to the extent that the carrying value of the debtor relationship does not exceed the unmatched carrying value of the asset. The normal rule is that the carrying value of the asset is the value of the asset as shown in the company's accounts at the time at which the company becomes a party to the debtor relationship or, if later, the time at which the asset is acquired. In the case of shares it is open to a company to elect for accounting periods beginning on or after 1 January 2008 to match the higher of the carrying value of the shares in its accounts and the net asset value underlying such shares.

[*SI 2004 No 3256, Regs 3(3)(4)(7), 4A(1)(2)(4B)*].

Election to match net asset value of shares

[54.19] The reason why an election was introduced to permit a company to match the net asset value of shares, as opposed to the cost of the shares, is that, prior to the introduction of IFRS and of FRS 23 and FRS 26, certain companies had been revaluing shareholdings in subsidiaries, joint ventures and associates in their accounts to reflect the net asset value underlying such shareholdings from time to time and had been hedging the exchange exposure attributable to the carrying value of such shareholdings in their accounts. Where a company prepares its accounts in accordance with IFRS or with FRS 26 (and thus FRS 23) such accounting treatment is not possible. Despite this change in accounting treatment however, certain groups still wished to hedge the net asset value of shares in subsidiaries, joint ventures and associates as if they had continued to apply their former accounting treatment and this is why such an election has been introduced.

The election had to be made by the later of 31 March 2008 and 30 days from the start of a company's first accounting period beginning on or after 1 January 2008 where a company held shares on or before the start of that accounting period.

A later election can be made in respect of shares acquired after the start of a company's first accounting period beginning on or after 1 January 2008.

HMRC will also be prepared to accept a later election in respect of shares that a company held at the start of its first accounting period beginning on or after 1 January 2008 where the company first seeks to match shares in accordance with *SI 2004 No 3256, Regs 3(3)(b)* or *4(3)(b)* after the start of that period (see Corporate Finance Manual at CFM62730).

In each case the later election must be made within 30 days of the date that the company first matches the shares with a derivative contract or a debtor relationship in accordance with the provisions of *SI 2004 No 3256, Regs 3* or *4*.

Where an election is made it has effect for all shareholdings held by the company, whenever acquired, it takes effect from the start of the accounting period in which it is made and it is irrevocable.

[*SI 2004 No 3256, Reg 4A(7), (8)*].

Where a company makes such an election it has to designate a review period. For accounting periods that began before 1 April 2011 the life of a review period could not exceed 92 days. For accounting periods beginning on or after 1 April 2011 a company is able to elect to have a review period of whatever length it chooses provided that a review period starts with the start of an accounting period and a review period ends with the end of an accounting period (where a company had elected to apply net asset matching for accounting periods beginning before 1 April 2011, it was able to elect to vary the length of its review periods by giving notice in writing to HMRC 1 July 2011). The company is required to determine the net asset value of the shares in question at the start of each review period and this becomes the value which is eligible to be treated as matched during that period. For accounting periods beginning on or after 1 April 2011, where during a review period (current review period) there is an increase or decrease of 10% or more in the net asset value underlying any shares that the company is matching, a new review period is deemed to start in respect of those shares at that time and will end at the end of the current review period. This is to permit a company to vary its hedging in respect of the shares in question at the time that the variation in the net asset value occurs.

For accounting periods beginning both before and on or after 1 April 2011, where a company begins to match shares in a company for the first time a new review period will start at that time in respect of those shares and will end at the end of the current review period in which the shares were first matched.

[*SI 2004 No 3256, Regs 4A(1)(a)(i), 4B, 4C*].

Identification rules

[54.20] Where a company holds a number of assets in the same currency and has debtor relationships or derivative contracts which are eligible to be treated as matched against such assets, identification rules apply to determine the extent to which an asset is to be treated as matched.

The extent to which an asset is matched is determined in accordance with the following rules:

(a) Rule 1: Debtor relationships and currency contracts are regarded as matched to the greatest extent possible with assets which are ships or aircraft;
(b) Rule 2: Subject to Rule 1, debtor relationships and currency contracts are regarded as matched to the greatest possible extent with assets on the disposal of which a chargeable gain would accrue if a disposal were made on a date falling more than 12 months after the date of acquisition of the asset. This is designed to exclude shares and assets related to shares which are eligible for substantial shareholding relief (*TCGA 1992, Sch 7AC*);
(c) Rule 3: Subject to Rules 1 and 2, debtor relationships and currency contracts are regarded as matched with assets on the disposal of which no chargeable gain would be treated as accruing by virtue of the substantial shareholding legislation.

[*SI 2004 No 3256, Reg 5*].

Partial matching

[54.21] Where a debtor relationship is treated as matched by virtue of Condition 2 and only part of the debtor relationship could be regarded as matching an investment in shares, ships or aircraft, matching treatment will only apply to the relevant portion of the debtor relationship.

[*SI 2004 No 3256, Reg 5(2)*].

Creditor relationship matched with share capital

[54.22] Provision is also made for exchange movements arising on a creditor relationship which is matched with the whole or part of a company's share capital that is denominated in a foreign currency to be disregarded for tax purposes. The regulations do not specify the conditions which have to be satisfied in order for such treatment to apply. Rather, they provide that such treatment will apply, in particular, where the exchange movements arising on the shares and the creditor relationship were taken to reserves in the company's accounts for its last accounting period beginning before 1 January 2005. HMRC provide guidance in the Corporate Finance Manual at CFM62850 as to the circumstances in which they consider that this provision will apply. They suggest that this is most likely where share capital is treated as a liability in a company's accounts. HMRC have announced that amendments would be made to the matching own share capital provisions to limit their scope for accounting periods beginning on or after 1 January 2012 to redeemable preference shares that are treated as a liability in the issuing company's accounts and that are issued to persons who are not connected with the issuer. It was also proposed that matching of own shares would be possible for accounting periods beginning on or after 1 January 2012 in other cases by obtaining prior approval from HMRC.

[*SI 2004 No 3256, Reg 3(5)(6)*].

Bringing into account of matched exchange gains and losses

[54.23] Any matched exchange gains and losses are only brought into account for tax purposes when a company ceases to own the matched asset. The treatment that applies depends on the nature of the asset.

Shares

In the case of shares the matched exchange movement is treated as a chargeable gain or an allowable loss for the purposes of the *TCGA 1992*. For disposals that take place on or after 6 April 2010 the base cost of the shares is adjusted and is increased where a net gain has arisen and is reduced where a net loss has arisen. If the amount of the net loss exceeds the base cost of the shares the excess is treated as additional consideration for the disposal of the shares.

For disposals that took place before this date a freestanding chargeable gain or allowable loss arose except where the shares qualified for the substantial shareholding exemption, in which case the held over exchange movement was left out of account for tax purposes.

[*SI 2002 No 1970, Regs 2, 4*].

It is possible for the time of recognition of the matched exchange movements to be deferred where a company disposes of shares and the disposal is treated as a no gain no loss disposal for the purposes of the *TCGA 1992*, or for disposals that took place before 6 April 2010 the *TCGA 1992* reorganisation provisions apply to the disposal.

[*SI 2002 No 1970, Regs 8–12 as amended by SI 2010 No 809*].

Ships and aircraft

Where the matched asset is a ship or an aircraft, the matched exchange gain or loss will be brought into account as a loan relationship debit or credit when the company disposes of the asset in question.

[*SI 2002 No 1970, Reg 6*].

Net investment in a branch

Where the matched asset is a net investment in a branch the matched exchange movement is not brought into account for tax purposes. This is because there is no provision to bring such deferred exchange movements within the charge to tax.

One way matching

[54.24] The measures discussed below were introduced in *FA 2009* to counter arrangements between companies in the same group that were designed to achieve 'one-way' matching. These arrangements typically took the form of one company (company X) in a group advancing a loan or entering into a currency forward contract or cross currency swap with another group company (company Y). Company Y would in turn use the debtor relationship or derivative contract to match an investment in shares or other assets eligible for matching treatment.

If an exchange gain arose to company Y on the debtor relationship or derivative contract, the exchange gain would be treated as matched (and thus would be left out of account for tax purposes) whereas company X would be able to obtain tax relief for the loss. If, however, an exchange loss arose to company Y this would produce the wrong result on a group basis. This is because the loss arising to company Y would be treated as matched, whereas the corresponding exchange gain arising to company X would be taxable. Accordingly, arrangements were devised so that in such circumstances company Y could avoid any exchange loss arising on the loan relationship or derivative contract. For example, in the case of a loan company Y might have the option of repaying the loan at the spot rate of exchange prevailing at the date that the loan was advanced.

These anti-avoidance measures apply to prevent exchange gains arising on or after 22 April 2009 from being treated as matched where 'one way' matching arrangements exist. In such cases any exchange loss, however, continues to be treated as matched.

A '*one-way exchange effect*' in relation to a company arises if two conditions are fulfilled. The first condition that the arrangement includes an option or relevant 'contingent contract'. The second condition involves the comparison of relevant exchange gains and losses of the company and its connected companies for accounting periods ending on the test day that would be brought into account for corporation tax if the currency moved in one direction (Amount A) with what those gains and losses would have been using counterfactual currency movement assumptions (i.e. if the currency moved one way and the exchange gain moved the other) (Amount B). The anti-avoidance provisions will apply only if the amounts are not equal. In addition, the difference must not be the same as it would be if Amount A and Amount B were calculated ignoring the matching rules.

A '*relevant contingent contract*' is a contract to which the taxpayer company or a company connected with it is a party and which includes a condition which if met alters a right or liability under the contract and operates, directly or indirectly, by reference to the exchange rate between the operating and another currency.

A '*relevant exchange gain or loss*' for this purpose is one which arises in relation to an asset or liability representing a loan relationship or a relevant contract to which the company is a party where these are part of the arrangement and the exchange gain or loss is to be brought into account for corporation tax. In deciding if a relevant gain or loss exists, the one-way exchange effect and unallowable purpose rules are ignored.

A '*test day*' is, where the arrangements include one or more options, a day on which an option is exercised, is varied or is capable of being exercised and the company or a connected company ceased to be a party or the last day of the accounting period. Where the arrangements include one or more relevant contingent contract, a test day is a day on which an operative condition is satisfied, the contract is varied, the company or a connected company ceased to be a party or the last day of the accounting period.

A '*relevant foreign currency*' is a foreign currency in which the loan relationships or relevant contracts giving rise to the gain or loss is denominated. There may be more than one such currency.

A '*counterfactual currency movement*' requires the company to assume that the transactions took place as they actually occurred (eg exercise of an option on a test day), but that a currency movement of the same size arose in the opposite direction. Special rules apply when the arrangements include an option.

'*Part of arrangements*' is widely defined to include part of agreements, understandings, schemes, transactions, whether or not legally enforceable. Such factors as the circumstances when the deal was entered into and the currency in which it is denominated are taken into account.

In the context of foreign exchange matching, '*tax advantage*' is defined as in *CTA 2010, s 1139; ICTA 1988, s 840ZA*. There is no requirement that the advantage arises in the same accounting period being self assessed. There is a de minimis rule in the Corporate Finance Manual at CFM63170. HMRC state that they will generally accept that a tax advantage is negligible if the increase in losses or decrease in taxable losses is likely to be less than £50,000 in any twelve month period (pro-rated for periods of less than twelve months). However, the relative size of the transaction needs to be considered as well. £50,000 may not be 'negligible' where very large sums are involved.

There are provisions for determining when a currency appreciates or depreciates in relation to another and, the percentage appreciation or depreciation.

[*CTA 2009, ss 328(4A), 328A–328H, as introduced by FA 2009, Sch 21 paras 1–3, 11 with exchange movements arising on or after 22 April 2009*].

One way matching — times before 22 April 2009

[54.25] A different anti-avoidance provision applied to counter one-way matching for foreign exchange movements which arose before 22 April 2009. This provision applied where a group of companies entered into arrangements that were designed to ensure that on a group basis an exchange gain arising on an external loan or currency contract would be treated as matched against a net investment in a *foreign operation* (see below) whereas if an exchange loss arose on the external loan or currency contract, the loss would not be treated as matched such that the group would be able to obtain tax relief for the loss.

The provision applied where all the following conditions were satisfied:

(a) one company (*the first company*) in a group entered into a debtor loan relationship or a derivative contract, the subject matter of which included currency (*the specified instruments*);
(b) another company in the same group (*the second company*) had a net investment in a *foreign operation* (that is a branch, or a shareholding in another company, where the functional currency of the branch or of the other company differed from that of the second company). For these purposes the first company and the second company were treated as being members of the same group where they were treated as connected with each other for the purposes of *FA 1996, s 87* (see **54.31**);
(c) if the assets that constituted the net investment in the foreign operation were held instead by the first company, it is likely that there would have been a hedging relationship between the specified instruments and the net investment in the foreign operation; and
(d) the second company was a party to a loan relationship or a derivative contract, directly or indirectly with the first company and it, or another company which was a party directly or indirectly to a loan relationship or derivative contract with the first company, could, by exercising an option, determine that an exchange gain or loss that would arise on a loan relationship or derivative contract to which it is a party did not arise.

In such circumstances the first company was denied relief for any exchange loss arising on the specified instruments, to the extent that relief for this loss was not already denied under the unallowable purposes provisions of the loan relationships legislation (see **54.52**) or of the DERIVATIVE CONTRACTS LEGISLATION (see **30**).

This provision applied for accounting periods ending on or after 22 March 2006. It did not apply to deny a company relief for losses arising on a loan relationship or a currency contract where the company had ceased to be a party to the loan relationship or currency contract before 22 March 2006 (*SI 2006 No 843, Reg 4*).

Risk transfer schemes

[54.26] For exchange losses that arise on or after 1 April 2010 anti-avoidance legislation was introduced by *FA 2010* to counter so-called risk transfer or over hedging transactions. The scheme typically involved one company in a group entering into a cross currency swap in order to hedge exchange exposure arising on an asset owned by another group company. As exchange movements on the cross currency swap were not left out of account for tax purposes, the amount of the swap was grossed up so that, on an after-tax basis, exchange movements on the swap would be equal to exchange movements on the asset. For example, where the rate of corporation tax was 30% and the asset had a cost of US$100, the amount of the US dollar leg of the swap would be $143. The arrangements are called risk transfer schemes as the effect of the over hedging is that the risk of loss is transferred to the Exchequer through tax relief being available for the grossed up loss.

Such transactions had been accepted by HMRC for many years but in recent years a number of groups had suffered significant exchange losses on such transactions which in turn significantly reduced their corporation tax liabilities. Accordingly a policy decision was taken to prevent the use of such schemes.

The effect of the legislation is that where a company or a group (an extended definition applies — see *CTA 2010, s 937K*) enters into a risk transfer or over hedging scheme, any exchange losses arising on a loan relationship or derivative contract that forms part of the scheme will be ring fenced to the extent that the loss exceeds the economic loss suffered by the group. Such ring fence losses can only be relieved against future gains which arise to the same company on loan relationships or derivative contracts that form part of the scheme and then only to the extent that the exchange gains exceed the economic profit realised by the group. The economic profit or loss is, in effect, the amount by which the exchange movement on the loan relationship or derivative contract exceed the exchange movement on the asset which is being hedged as part of the scheme.

Whilst the transactions undertaken were transactions to hedge foreign exchange risk, the anti-avoidance legislation will also catch transactions which are 'grossed up' to hedge the RPI or other index or any price or other value (*CTA 2010, ss 937A–O as inserted by FA 2010, Sch 16*).

Debt releases and Impairment losses

[54.27] The general rule is that any profit arising to a debtor company from the release in whole or in part of a liability to which it is subject under the terms of a debtor relationship should be included in computing its taxable profits. Equally, the general rule is that a creditor company is able to obtain tax relief for any impairment provision for release debits that it recognises in its accounts in accordance with generally accepted accounting practice. The following paragraphs consider exceptions to these general rules.

Debt releases where credit need not be brought into account

[54.28] Where a liability under a debtor relationship is released in an accounting period for which the debtor company uses an amortised cost basis of accounting as respects the relationship in question, no credit is required to be brought into account in respect of the release in any of the following circumstances.

(i) The release is part of a statutory insolvency arrangement (see **76.5 WINDING UP**).

(ii) Where the release is in consideration of shares (or an entitlement to shares) forming part of the ordinary share capital of the debtor company.

(iii) Where the debtor company is in one of the forms of insolvency procedure noted at **54.35** below and the debtor relationship is not a 'connected companies relationship' (see **54.31** below).

(iv) The relationship is a connected companies relationship. However, this does not apply in the case where a credit is required to be brought into account on a deemed release within **54.38** below.

(v) Where the creditor company is in one of the forms of insolvency procedure noted at **54.35** below and the relationship between the parties immediately before but not immediately after the company enters into the insolvency procedure, is a connected companies relationship.

[*CTA 2009, ss 322, 358, 359; FA 1996, Sch 9 para 5(3)–(8); FA 2002, Sch 23 para 8; FA 2004, s 52, Sch 8 para 3, Sch 10 para 20; FA 2005, s 80, Sch 4 para 11*].

Connected companies creditor relationships

[54.29] A company is not permitted to claim relief for any impairment losses or release debits arising on a connected companies creditor relationship unless the creditor company is in insolvent liquidation etc (see further **54.35**). There is a further exception to this rule where a creditor company only becomes connected with the debtor company as a result of agreeing to treat the debt as discharged in return for ordinary shares, or an entitlement to ordinary shares, in, the borrower. In such cases the lender is not treated as being connected with the borrower at any time before it acquired the ordinary shares, or rights to such shares, and thus it is able to obtain relief for any losses that have been suffered on the loan that is so discharged. It should be noted that this relieving provision will not prevent the connected party rules from applying to any other loan relationships to which the creditor is a party with the debtor in the accounting period in which the share for debt swap takes place, even if the creditor ceases to be a party to the other loans before the share for debt swap takes place.

[*CTA 2009, ss 354, 356*].

Release of loans to participators

[54.30] Where a loan to a participator, which has given rise to a charge under *CTA 2010, s 455*, is released or written off in whole or in part, the amount written off may not be treated as a loan relationship debit for loan relationship purposes. This applies for releases or write offs on or after 24 March 2010. The background to the amendment to the legislation from 24 March 2010 is that HMRC became aware of schemes that sought to exploit the fact that a close company was able to obtain relief for the release in computing its loan relationship profits whereas the participator was taxed as if he had received a dividend from the company, the net amount of which was equal to the amount of the loan that had been released.

[*CTA 2009, s 321A, as inserted by FA 2010, s 43*].

Connected parties

[54.31] If a loan relationship is a 'connected companies relationship', the debits and credits brought into account must be determined on an amortised cost basis of accounting.

For this purpose, there is a '*connected companies relationship*' for an accounting period if there is a 'connection' at any time in that period between the company and a company which is the other party to the relationship (including any company standing indirectly in that position by reference to a series of loan relationships, or money debts which would be loan relationships were the company a debtor or creditor).

Where in any period a related transaction (see **54.6** above) takes place in relation to a creditor relationship which is a connected companies relationship, the debits in respect of the relationship for that period shall be no more, and the credits no less, than they would have been had the transaction not taken place (disregarding any amounts which would have accrued after the transaction took place). These provisions do not affect the debits and credits to be brought into account in respect of exchange gains and losses arising from the debt.

[*CTA 2009, ss 348–352; FA 1996, s 87(1)–(2C)(5); FA 2004, Sch 10 para 4*].

See also **54.57** as regards loan relationships carrying rights to acquire shares in the debtor company that were treated differently by a connected creditor and debtor for times before 19 July 2011.

Subject to the exception below, there is a '*connection*' between two companies for an accounting period if at any time in the period one company controls the other or both are under the control of the same person (other than the Crown, a Minister of the Crown, a government or NI department, a foreign sovereign power or an organisation of which two or more sovereign powers, or their governments, are members).

Where a partnership which carries on a trade or a business has a loan relationship with a company, any connection between companies, and the effect of any such connection, is to be determined as though each of the partners (excluding the general partner of a limited partnership which is a collective investment scheme within *Financial Services and Markets Act 2000, s 235*) holds a separate loan relationship with the company equivalent to that partner's share of the partnership's loan relationship. The partner's share is that corresponding to its share in partnership profits.

[*CTA 2009, ss 466, 467; FA 1996, s 87(3)(4)(5A)(5B); FA 2002, Sch 25 para 7; FA 2004, s 52, Sch 10 paras 4, 8*].

Meaning of 'control'

[54.32] '*Control*' in relation to a company means the power of a person to secure:

(i) by means of the holding of shares or possession of voting power in, or in relation to, the company or any other company; or
(ii) by virtue of any powers conferred by the articles of association or other document regulating the company or any other company,

that the affairs of the company are conducted in accordance with his wishes.

'*Shares*' for this purpose do not include those held by companies where a profit on sale would be a trading receipt (e.g. banks or financial traders), and powers arising from such shares are similarly excluded. This does not apply where such shares are assets of an insurance company's long-term insurance fund.

Where a partnership has property, rights or powers in a company, these are attributed to company partners in proportion to their share in the partnership profits. This excludes a general partner of a limited partnership which is a collective investment scheme within *Financial Services and Markets Act 2000, s 235* (so that it cannot be regarded as controlling the partnership for the purposes of this provision).

[*CTA 2009, s 472; FA 1996, s 87A; FA 2002, Sch 25 para 8*].

Exemption

[54.33] Where a company is party to a creditor relationship, any connection in an accounting period with another company which (directly or indirectly) stands in the position of the debtor is disregarded where the conditions below are met. This does not apply in relation to the other company in relation to its debtor relationship. The conditions are that:

(A) in the course of carrying on activities forming an integral part of a trade carried on in that period the creditor company disposes of or acquires assets representing creditor relationships;
(B) the asset representing the creditor relationship in question was acquired in the course of those activities and is either listed on a recognised stock exchange at the end of that period or a security which must be redeemed within twelve months of issue;

(C) at some time in that period assets of the same kind as the asset representing the creditor relationship in question are in the beneficial ownership of persons other than the company; and

(D) in not more than three months (in aggregate) in that period is the equivalent of 30% or more of the assets of that kind in the beneficial ownership of connected companies (and a connected company is taken as having beneficial ownership of an asset wherever there is (apart from the current exemption) a connection between the company having beneficial ownership of the asset and a company which (directly or indirectly) stands in the position of debtor as respects the debt by reference to which any loan relationship represented by that asset exists).

As regards (C) and (D) above, assets are taken to be of the same kind where they are so treated by the practice of any recognised stock exchange (or would be if dealt with on such an exchange).

See *CTA 2009, s 471* for the operation of the exemption in the case of an insurance company carrying on basic life and general annuity business.

[*CTA 2009, ss 468–470; FA 1996, s 88; FA 2004, s 52, Sch 10 para 5*].

Simon's Taxes. See **D1.720**.

Release of connected companies relationship

[54.34] The restrictions for relief for impairment losses detailed in **54.35** below apply equally in relation to a debit in respect of a release of a liability of a creditor company as they apply in relation to an impairment loss. At the same time the release of a liability in respect of a connected companies debtor relationship will be tax free for the debtor company unless the anti-avoidance provision that is discussed at **54.37** applies and a taxable deemed release was only avoided under that provision because the corporate rescue or debt-for-debt exception applied (see **54.38**).

[*CTA 2009, ss 354, 358; FA 1996, Sch 9, paras 5(3), (5), 6(1)–(3), (8)*].

Exclusion of debits for connected companies' debts

[54.35] Where *CTA 2009, s 348* ((parties to relationship having connection — previously *FA 1996, s 87*), see **54.31** above) requires an amortised cost basis of accounting to be applied for an accounting period as regards a creditor relationship of a company, no 'impairment loss' may be recognised except in one of the following circumstances:

(a) where the creditor company is in insolvent liquidation etc. (see below); and

(b) where the company treats the liability as discharged in consideration of shares (or an entitlement to shares) forming part of the ordinary share capital of the debtor company, and was no connection between the companies before the shares (or entitlement) were acquired (*CTA 2009, s 356; FA 1996, Sch 9, para 6(4), (5)*).

An '*impairment loss*' is a debit relating to an uncollectable amount of the loan or financial asset (i.e. a bad debt). A '*release debit*' is a debit in respect of a release by a company of liability under a creditor relationship. [*CTA 2009, s 476(1); FA 2009, s 42*].

If an impairment loss is not allowed under the above provisions, no credit is to be brought into account for the reversal of the impairment.

These provisions do not affect the debits and credits to be brought into account in respect of exchange gains and losses arising from the debt.

Where in accordance with generally accepted accounting practice a creditor company does not accrue interest or discount on a connected companies creditor relationship in its accounts it will not be required to recognise such interest or discount in computing its loan relationship profits. This is because there is nothing in the definition of an amortised cost accounting treatment that requires interest or discount to be recognised (see *CTA 2009, s 313(4); FA 1996, s 103(1)*).

As mentioned above a company is permitted to claim relief for an impairment loss suffered on a connected companies creditor relationship where it is in insolvent liquidation or administration or insolvent administrative receivership, under the *Insolvency Act 1986* or NI equivalent, or a provisional liquidator has been appointed under that Act or NI equivalent, or corresponding processes under foreign law are in place, the departure is allowed at a time in the course of the winding up or administration, or when the appointment of the administrative receivership or provisional liquidator is in force, or at a corresponding time under the foreign process.

[*CTA 2009, ss 323, 357; FA 1996, Sch 9, paras 6(4), (5), 6A*].

Cessation of connection

[54.36] Where relief for an impairment loss or release debit has been denied in an accounting period due to a connection between the parties as above, and the connection ceases in a subsequent accounting period, no debits are to be brought into account in that or any later accounting period to the extent that they represent the loss or release debit. On or after 22 April 2009, 'release debit' is as defined in *CTA 2009, s 476(1)* (as substituted by *FA 2009*). [*FA 2009, s 42*].

[*CTA 2009, s 355; FA 1996, Sch 9, para 6C(1), (3)*].

Connected party loan relationship purchased at a discount

[54.37] An anti-avoidance provision applies to prevent a group of companies from avoiding a tax charge arising on the release of an unconnected party loan relationship by first arranging for the loan relationship to be acquired by a connected company and then arranging for it to be released. This provision is required because a connected party creditor is not required to assume that all amounts which are payable under the terms of the creditor loan relationship will be paid in full as and when they fall due for payment (*CTA 2009,* *ss 361–363; FA 1996 Sch 9 para 4A*). The provision applies where the purchaser is connected with the borrower or becomes connected with the borrower in the accounting period of the borrower in which the purchase takes place.

In such cases where the purchase price of the creditor loan relationship is less than the carrying value of the corresponding debtor loan relationship, there is deemed to be a release of an amount owed in respect of the debtor relationship equal to that difference and the debtor company is required to include the amount of the deemed release in computing its loan relationship profits. The carrying value of the debtor loan relationship is determined on the assumption that an accounting period of the debtor company had ended immediately before the time at which the creditor loan relationship was acquired and in determining the carrying value of the debtor loan relationship any accrued amounts or amounts that have been paid or received in advance are ignored.

For acquisitions which take place on or after 14 October 2009 no charge will arise under this provision where one of the following three exceptions is satisfied:

(a) The corporate rescue exception

This applies where *all* the following conditions are met:

(i) the acquisition of the creditor relationship is an arm's length transaction;
(ii) there has been a change in the ownership of the debtor company at any time in the period beginning one year before and ending 60 days after the date of the acquisition;
(iii) it is reasonable to assume that, but for the change in ownership, the debtor company would, within one year of the date of the change in ownership, have gone into insolvent liquidation etc. (see **54.35**);
(iv) it is reasonable to assume that, but for the change in ownership, the acquisition of the creditor relationship would not have been made.

[*CTA 2009, s 361A as inserted by FA 2010 Sch 15 para 2(5)*].

In the Corporate Finance Manual HMRC have stated that they will accept that the condition in (iii) is satisfied where insolvency is avoided not only by the change in ownership but also by steps taken following that change (See CFM35540).

(b) The debt-for-debt exception

This applies if one of the following two conditions is met.

The first condition applies in respect of the acquisition of a creditor relationship that is represented by a security (*the old security*) where:

(i) the acquisition of the old security is an arm's length transaction; *and*
(ii) the consideration given by the purchaser for the acquisition consists only of a security (*the new security*) representing a loan relationship to which the purchaser is a party as a debtor; *and*
(iii) the new security has the same nominal value as the old security and at the time of the acquisition has substantially the same market value as the old security.

In the Corporate Finance Manual at CFM35550 HMRC have stated that they would accept that the requirement in (ii) is satisfied where the issuer of the new security agrees to pay any accrued but unpaid interest on the old security when it acquires it in exchange for the new security.

The second condition applies in respect of the acquisition of a creditor relationship that is represented by an asset other than a security (*the old unsecured loan*) where:

(i) the acquisition of the creditor relationship is an arm's length transaction; *and*
(ii) the consideration given by the purchaser for the acquisition consists only of an asset other than a security (*the new unsecured loan*) representing a loan relationship to which the purchaser is a party as a debtor; *and*
(iii) the amount of the new unsecured loan and its terms are substantially the same as those of the old unsecured loan.

[*CTA 2009, s 361B as inserted by FA 2010, Sch 15 para 2(5)*].

In the Corporate Finance Manual at CFM35550 HMRC have stated that they will accept that either condition is satisfied where a proportion of the old debt is released in exchange for new debt and a proportion in exchange for the issue of shares.

(c) The equity-for-debt exception

This applies where the following two conditions are met:

(i) the acquisition is an arm's length transaction; *and*
(ii) the consideration given by the purchaser for the acquisition consists only of *either* shares forming part of the ordinary share capital of the purchaser or of a company connected with the purchaser; *or*
(iii) an entitlement to shares in the purchaser or in a company connected with the purchaser.

[*CTA 2009, s 361C as inserted by FA 2010, Sch 15 para 2(5)*].

Debtor loan relationship is later released

[54.38] Where a deemed release has been avoided by virtue of the corporate rescue or debt-for-debt exceptions (see (a) or (b) above) a taxable profit will arise if the debtor relationship is later released (including cases where the debt is released in exchange for the issue of shares by the debtor company). The amount of the deemed release will be equal to the deemed release which would have arisen at the time of the acquisition, but for the availability of the exception, as reduced by any of the discount which has been taken into account in computing the loan relationship profits of the purchaser and any connected company to which the creditor relationship was later transferred (*CTA 2009, ss 322(4), 358 as amended by FA 2010 Sch 15 paras 1, 2(3)*).

Transitional provisions in respect of debtor buybacks which were under way at 14 October 2009

[54.39] These applied where either the acquisition was made pursuant to an agreement entered into before 14 October 2009 or the acquisition was made in the period 14 October 2009 – 31 January 2010 (both dates inclusive) and certain conditions were satisfied. [*FA 2010, Sch 14 para 4*].

Purchases which took place before 14 October 2009

[54.40] The anti-avoidance provision did not apply where the purchaser acquired the loan relationship as a result of an arm's length transaction and it was not connected with the debtor company at any time during a three-year period ending 12 months before the time at which it purchased the loan relationship. This particular exception was designed to assist corporate rescues where often a purchaser might acquire shares in the target company as well as a debt owed by the target company to other members of its group. It was open to abuse as it enabled groups to use a newly-incorporated company to buy back debt; for this reason it was replaced with the measures discussed above. [*CTA 2009, s 361(1), (2); FA 1996, Sch 9, para 4A*].

Creditor company becomes connected with debtor company

[54.41] The anti-avoidance provision discussed at **54.37** above also applies where a creditor company becomes connected with the company that is a party to the corresponding debtor relationship. In this case a deemed release will arise to the debtor company, in the accounting period in which the two companies become connected, equal to the amount of the impairment loss which the creditor company would have recognised in its accounts immediately before the two companies became connected, had its accounting period ended at that time and had no prior impairment provision been made. [*CTA 2009, s 362; FA 1996, Sch 9 para 4A*].

Impairment losses, debt releases and consortium relief

[54.42] The following provision applies to restrict relief where an impairment loss or a debit in respect of a release of liability, has been brought into account in respect of a 'relevant consortium creditor relationship'. For this purpose, a '*relevant consortium creditor relationship*' is a creditor relationship of a company which is a member of a consortium (the '*member company*'), or of any fellow group member (not being a member of the consortium), where a company owned by the consortium (the '*consortium company*') or, where it is a holding company, a consortium company which is its subsidiary, is the debtor. Membership of a group is determined for these purposes as under *CTA 2010, Pt 5; ICTA 1988, Pt 10 Ch 4* (see **39.3 GROUP RELIEF**) and ownership of the consortium company as under *CTA 2010, s 153; ICTA 1988, s 413(6)* (see **39.19 GROUP RELIEF**). (Note that this provision does not affect ordinary group relief, since impairment relief is restricted where the parties to the loan relationship are connected under *CTA 2009, s 354; FA 1996, s 86* as detailed in **54.35** above.)

The restriction of relief (which effectively allows for relief to be given to the higher of the impairment provision or the group relief claim) works as follows.

(a) **Restriction of impairment loss debits.** The 'net consortium debit' is reduced (but not below nil) by the amount of any group relief which may be surrendered by the consortium company and which is claimed in the same 'group accounting period' by the member company or by any fellow group member. Where a reduction is to be made to more than one debit (where impairment relief is claimed by more than one company), it is to be apportioned between the debits in proportion to their respective amounts.

The '*net consortium debit*' is the excess of the total impairment losses and release debits brought into account for that accounting period by the member company or by any fellow group members in respect of relevant consortium creditor relationships over the total of any credits so brought into account in that period in respect of debt recoveries from consortium companies in respect of those relationships.

A '*group accounting period*' means any accounting period of the member company or any accounting period of a fellow group member 'corresponding' to such a member company accounting period. Such periods are regarded as the same accounting period for the purposes of this provision. An accounting period of a group member '*corresponds*' to an accounting period of a member company if:

(i) the two accounting periods coincide;

(ii) the accounting period of the member company includes more than half of the accounting period of the group member; or

(iii) the accounting period of the member company includes part of the accounting period of the group member, but the remainder of that period does not fall within any accounting period of the member company.

(b) **Reduction of credits exceeding impairment losses.** Where, in any group accounting period, the total credits brought into account by the member company and any fellow group member in respect of relevant consortium creditor relationships exceed the impairment losses and release debits brought into account by those companies for that period under the relevant relationships, the credits are reduced (but not below nil) as follows. The total cumulative reduction made in earlier group accounting periods to the debits in (a) above (so far as not previously apportioned under this provision) is apportioned between the credits in proportion to their respective amounts.

(c) **Restriction of group relief based on earlier debits.** Any claim for group relief for a group accounting period by the member company or a fellow group member, in respect of amounts available for surrender by debtor consortium companies, is to be reduced (but not below nil) by the cumulative net amount of the net consortium debits for earlier group accounting periods (as reduced under (a) above) in respect of the relevant consortium creditor relationships (i.e. the claim for group relief is to be reduced by the actual amount of debt relief claimed). If there is more than one such group relief claim, the reduction is to be apportioned between them in proportion to their respective amounts.

(d) **Group relief claim to restrict future impairment loss.** Where there is a claim for group relief as in (c) above, but there is no net consortium debit in the same group accounting period in respect of the relevant consortium creditor relationships, the amount of the claim is taken into account when considering restrictions under (a) above in subsequent accounting periods. Thus, the claim for group relief is treated as carried forward for the purposes of this provision to the next accounting period, and, in addition to any actual claim for that period, is used to restrict impairment losses and release debits as under (a) above.

Where any credit is brought into account by the consortium company in respect of the release of a debt owed to the member company, the released amount is not to be treated as a debit by the member company for the purposes of these provisions.

When determining the amount of group relief which can be claimed, *CTA 2010, ss 143, 144; ICTA 1988, s 403C* has priority over this provision. See generally **39.19** *et seq.* GROUP RELIEF for consortium and group relief claims.

[*CTA 2009, ss 364–371; FA 1996, Sch 9 paras 5ZA, 5A; FA 2004, s 52, Sch 10 para 21; FA 2005, s 80, Sch 4 para 12*].

See also HMRC Corporate Finance Manual, CFM35610–CFM35710.

Late interest

[54.43] The rules for late interest were substantially amended by *FA 2009* so that they only apply in the case of interest payable to a company where the recipient of the interest is either resident for tax purposes in a non-qualifying territory (within the meaning of *TIOPA 2010, s 173*), or is effectively managed in a non-qualifying territory under whose laws companies are not liable to tax by reason of domicile, residence or place of management, at any time in the accounting period in which the interest accrued. The effect of these changes is that, broadly, the late paid interest rules will only apply in such cases where the recipient is resident, or is effectively managed, in a tax haven. These rules normally took effect for accounting periods beginning on or after 1 April 2009. A company could, however, elect that any of the *FA 2009* amendments should not have effect for its first accounting period (not ending after 31 March 2011) for which they would otherwise apply. The election had to be made in the corporation tax return for the period for which it is to apply.

[*FA 2009, Sch 20*].

Where any of (i)–(iv) below applies in respect of a loan relationship, then if:

(a) interest payable under the relationship is not paid within twelve months of the end of the accounting period (the '*actual accrual period*') in which it would otherwise be treated as accruing; and
(b) credits representing the full amount of the interest are not brought into account for any accounting period in respect of the corresponding creditor relationship,

debits relating to interest payable under the relationship are not brought into account until the interest is paid. This rule applies where:

(i) there is, for the actual accrual period, a connection within **54.31** above between the debtor company and the creditor;

(ii) at any time in the actual accrual period, the debtor company is a 'close company' and the creditor is either:
- a 'participator' in the debtor company or a person who controls a company which is such a participator (a 'participator company');
- an 'associate' of a person who is a participator in the debtor company at that time or an associate of a person who controls a participator company at that time;
- a company controlled by a participator in the debtor company or a person who controls a participator company; or
- a company in which a participator in the debtor company has a 'major interest'.

However, the restriction does not apply where:
- either:
  - — the debtor company is a 'CIS-based close company' and a 'small or medium-sized enterprise' (as defined by *TIOPA 2010, s 172; ICTA 1988, Sch 28AA para 5D*), and the creditor is not 'resident' (as defined by *TIOPA 2010, s 172; ICTA 1988, Sch 28AA para 5B(6)*) in a 'non-qualifying territory' (as defined by *TIOPA 2010, s 173; ICTA 1988, Sch 28AA para 5E*); or
  - — the debt is owed to (or to persons acting for) a 'CIS limited partnership' no member of which is resident in a non-qualifying territory (this to be confirmed in writing by the partnership to the debtor company) and the debtor company is a small or medium-sized enterprise;

(iii) the creditor is a company in which the debtor company has a 'major interest' (see below) at any time in the actual accrual period; or *vice versa;* or

(iv) the loan is made by the trustees of a occupational pension scheme (within *FA 2004, s 150(5)*) and, at any time in the actual accrual period, the debtor company is the employer operating the scheme, or is connected with the employer (see **54.31** above), or the employer is a company in which the debtor company has a 'major interest' or which itself has a major interest in the debtor company.

This provision also applies to indirect creditors where there is a series of loan relationships, or money debts which would be loan relationships if a company directly stood in the position of creditor or debtor. In this case, the reference to the corresponding creditor relationship in (b) above includes a person who indirectly stands in the position of a creditor.

A '*CIS-based close company*' is a company that would not be close apart from the attribution under *CTA 2010, s 451(4)–(6)* (previously *ICTA 1988, s 416(6)*) of the rights and powers of a partner in a 'CIS limited partnership' to other partners by virtue of *CTA 2010, s 448(1)(a)* (previously *ICTA 1988, s 417(3)(a)*). A '*CIS limited partnership*' is a limited partnership which is a collective investment scheme or would be a collective investment scheme if not a body corporate, within the meaning of the *Financial Services and Markets Act 2000, s 235* (see **54.96** below).

For these purposes, a '*close company*' is as defined at **22.2 CLOSE COMPANIES** but, notwithstanding **22.3**, includes non-resident companies. An '*associate*' is as defined at **22.9 CLOSE COMPANIES**. '*Control*' is as defined in *CTA 2009, s 472* (see **54.32** above). A '*participator*' in relation to a company is a person who, by virtue **22.7 CLOSE COMPANIES,** is treated as such for the purposes of the close company legislation other than by reason only of being a loan creditor. A person who is a participator in a company which controls another company is treated as also being a participator in that other company.

For a discussion of when interest can be treated as paid (under (a) above), see HMRC Corporate Finance Manual, CFM5610. See also CFM5616 for HMRC's view of when credits (under (b) above) should be treated as being 'brought into account' by the creditor.

Major interest

[54.44] A company ('company A') has a '*major interest*' in another company ('company B') if company A and one other person ('C') together control (within *CTA 2009, s 472*, see **54.31** above) company B, and each of C and company A have at least 40% of the total interests, rights and powers subsisting in company B giving that control. Connected companies' interests, rights and powers are attributed to company A and (if it is a company) C for this purpose (companies being connected if one controls the other or they are under common control).

Where interests, rights or powers are held in partnership, these are apportioned to company partners in proportion to their share in partnership profits. Where a partnership which carries on a trade or a business stands as debtor or creditor in relation to a money debt, each company partner is for the purposes of this test treated as holding a separate money debt corresponding to their share in partnership profits. A general partner of a limited partnership which is a collective investment scheme within the meaning of the *Financial Services and Markets Act 2000, s 235* is disregarded for these purposes.

[*CTA 2009, ss 372–379, 473, 474, 476(1); FA 1996, Sch 9 paras 2, 20; FA 2002, Sch 25 paras 22, 36; FA 2003, Sch 37 para 2; FA 2004, s 52, Sch 8 paras 2, 7; Sch 42 Pt 2(4); F(No 2)A 2005, Sch 8 paras 2, 4; FA 2009, s 41, Sch 20; CTA 2010, Sch 1 paras 610, 624(a)*].

Funding bonds issued in respect of interest on certain debts

[54.45] Funding Bonds etc. issued in respect of a liability to pay interest on a debt incurred by any Government, public authority or institution, or company are treated as income the payment of interest equal to bonds' value when issued; but their eventual redemption is not treated as a payment of the interest. '*Funding bonds*' include 'stocks, shares, securities or certificates of indebtedness'.

[*CTA 2009, ss 413, 414; ICTA 1988, s 582(1)(3)–(4); FA 1996, s 134, Sch 6 para 14, Sch 20 para 32; FA 2002, Sch 25 para 50; ITTOIA 2005, Sch 1 para 243*].

Deeply discounted securities

General

[54.46] The rules for discount payable on deeply discounted securities were substantially amended by *FA 2009* in cases where such securities are held by a company. Now they only apply in such cases where the corporate holder is either resident for tax purposes in a non-qualifying territory (within the meaning of *TIOPA 2010, s 173*), or is effectively managed in a non-qualifying territory under whose laws companies are not liable to tax by reason of domicile, residence or place of management, at any time in the accounting period in which the discount accrued. The effect of these changes is that, broadly, these rules will only apply in such cases where the holder is resident, or is effectively managed, in a tax haven. These rules normally took effect for accounting periods beginning on or after 1 April 2009. The election must be made in the corporation tax return for the period for which it is to apply. [*FA 2009, Sch 20 paras 7–9*].

The deeply discounted securities provisions deal with the situation where, for any accounting period (the 'relevant period'):

(a) a debtor relationship of a company is represented by a 'deeply discounted security' issued by the company;
(b) at any time in that period another company stands in the position of creditor in respect of that security;
(c) there is a 'connection' between the companies for that period; and
(d) the credits representing the full amount of the discount referable to that period are not brought into account for any accounting period in respect of the corresponding creditor relationship.

As regards (b) above, this applies to a company which indirectly stands in the position of a creditor by reference to a series of loan relationships or money debts which would be loan relationships if a company directly stood in the position of creditor or debtor. Where these provisions apply, the debits to be brought into account in respect of the relationship are adjusted so that every debit which relates to the amount of the discount and which is referable to the relevant period is brought into account instead for the accounting period of redemption. The amount of the discount referable to the relevant period for this purpose is the amount which would otherwise be brought into account for the relevant period relating to the difference between the issue price and the amount payable on redemption. That difference is determined on the basis that 'redemption' does not include any redemption which may be made before maturity otherwise than at the option of the holder, and refers to the earliest occasion on which the holder may require redemption, and that the amount payable on redemption excludes any interest.

Companies are '*connected*' for these purposes for the relevant period if, at any time in that period, one 'controls' (see **54.32** above) or has a 'major interest' (see **54.44** above) in, the other, or both are under the control of the same person (other than the Crown, a Minister of the Crown, a government or NI department, a foreign sovereign power or an organisation of which two or more sovereign powers, or their governments, are members).

A '*deeply discounted security*' for these purposes is as defined for the purposes of the income tax rules under *ITTOIA 2005, s 430*. It means, broadly, any security which is such that, as at the time of issue, the amount payable on maturity or any other possible occasion of redemption exceeds (or may exceed) the issue price by more than 0.5% of that amount payable on maturity etc. for each year in the 'redemption period' up to a maximum of 30 years.

Exclusions include:

(A) shares in a company;
(B) gilt-edged securities which are not strips;
(C) excluded indexed securities (broadly, where the amount payable on redemption is linked to the value of capital gains tax chargeable assets);
(D) life assurance policies and capital redemption policies (see **54.77** below).

Close companies

[54.47] A similar restriction applies where:

(I) a debtor relationship of a close company is represented by a deeply discounted security issued by the company;
(II) at any time in the accounting period in question (the 'relevant period') the creditor as respects that security was either:
  (i) a 'participator' in the issuing company (within **22.7 CLOSE COMPANIES** but see also below) or a person who controls a company which is such a participator (a 'participator company'); or
  (ii) an 'associate' (within **22.9 CLOSE COMPANIES**) of a participator in the debtor company or an associate of a person who controls a participator company; or
  (iii) a company 'controlled' by a participator in the debtor company or by a person who controls a participator company. '*Control*' is as defined in *CTA 2009, s 472* (see **54.32** above).

However, the restriction does not apply in relation to the debtor relationship in the case of the following exceptions.

- The discounted security is held by a creditor which is a company and brings into account credits representing the full amount of the discount referable to the period in respect of the corresponding creditor relationship.
- The discounted security is held by a company that is not resident for tax purposes in a non-qualifying territory within the meaning of *TIOPA 2010, s 173* or is effectively managed in a non-qualifying territory under whose laws companies are not liable to tax by reason of domicile, residence or place of management at any time in the accounting period in which the discount accrued. The effect of these changes is that, broadly, these rules will only apply in such cases where the deeply discounted security is held by a company where the holder is resident in

a tax haven. These rules normally took effect for accounting periods beginning on or after 1 April 2009. The election must be made in the corporation tax return for the period for which it is to apply. [*FA 2009, Sch 20 paras 7–9*].

- The issuing company is a 'CIS-based close company' and is a small or medium-sized enterprise (as defined by *TIOPA 2010, s 172; ICTA 1988, Sch 28AA para 5D*), and the creditor is not 'resident' (as defined by *TIOPA 2010, s 172; ICTA 1988, Sch 28AA para 5B(6)*) in a 'non-qualifying territory' (as defined by *TIOPA 2010, s 173; ICTA 1988, Sch 28AA para 5E*).
- The debt is owed to (or to persons acting for) a 'CIS limited partnership' no member of which is resident in a non-qualifying territory at any time in the period where the creditor is connected with the debtor (this to be confirmed in writing by the partnership to the debtor company) and the issuing company is a small or medium-sized enterprise.

A '*CIS-based close company*' is a company that would not be close apart from the attribution under *CTA 2010, s 451(4)–(6)* (previously *ICTA 1988, s 416(6)*) of the rights and powers of a partner in a 'CIS limited partnership' to other partners by virtue of *CTA 2010, s 448(1)(a)* (previously *ICTA 1988, s 417(3)(a)*). A '*CIS limited partnership*' is a partnership which is a collective investment scheme or would be if not a body corporate.

'Participator' excludes a person who is such by reason only of being a loan creditor of the company, and in the case of a banking business, securities acquired in the ordinary course of the business are disregarded. A participator in a company which controls another company is treated for this purpose as a participator in that other company.

This provision applies to a company which indirectly stands in the position of a creditor by reference to a series of loan relationships or money debts which would be loan relationships if a company directly stood in the position of creditor or debtor.

[*CTA 2009, ss 406–412, 476(1); FA 1996, Sch 9 paras 17, 18*].

Simon's Taxes. See **D1.755.**

Anti-avoidance provisions

Imported losses

[54.48] Special rules apply for an accounting period (the '*loss period*') of a company (the '*chargeable company*') where:

(a) there is a loss arising in connection with a loan relationship of the company which would fall to be brought into account under these provisions; and
(b) that loss is wholly or partly referable to a time when the chargeable company (or any predecessor in the same position as respects the loan relationship at that time) would not have been liable to UK tax on any profits arising from the relationship.

In those circumstances, the amounts brought into account in the loss period in respect of that relationship are adjusted to ensure that no part of the loss referable to such a time is treated for the purposes of the current provisions as arising in any accounting period of the chargeable company or as otherwise available to be brought into account for corporation tax purposes.

This provision does not apply where a fair value basis of accounting is used.

[*CTA 2009, s 327; FA 1996, Sch 9 para 10; FA 2002, Sch 25 para 28; FA 2004, s 52, Sch 10 para 28*].

Simon's Taxes. See **D1.790**.

Transactions not at arm's length

[54.49] Where debits or credits falling to be brought into account in respect of a loan relationship relate to amounts arising from a non-arm's length 'related transaction' (as in **54.6** above), they are determined on the assumption that the transaction was entered into on the same terms it would have been if at arm's length between knowledgeable and willing independent persons. This does not, however, apply to:

(A) debits arising from the acquisition of rights under a loan relationship for less than market value; or
(B) any related transaction where the transaction is one, or part of a series of transactions, to which **54.58** (continuity of treatment to provide for tax neutral intra-group transactions) below applies or would apply but for the fact that the transferor uses fair value accounting; or
(C) any of a series of transactions by a member of a group which together have the same effect as a related transaction between members of a group; or
(D) exchange gains or losses (but see further below); or
(E) amounts falling within the scope of *TIOPA 2010, Pt 4; ICTA 1988, Sch 28AA* (see **72 TRANSFER PRICING**) whether or not the amounts fall to be adjusted.

The exclusion at (C) above applies only if both group members are within the charge to corporation tax in respect of the transaction. See **18.2 CAPITAL GAINS — GROUPS** with regard to the residence requirements for groups of companies.

[*CTA 2009, ss 444, 445; FA 1996, Sch 9, para 11*].

Transactions not at arm's length — Exchange gains and losses

[54.50] Similar treatment applies to exchange gains and losses as follows.

(a) Where a company has a debtor relationship in an accounting period, and either:
  (i) the whole or part of any interest or other distribution paid in respect of securities of the company representing that relationship falls to be regarded as a distribution under *CTA 2010, s 1015(6); ICTA 1988, s 209(2)(e)(vii) (equity notes)* — (see **31.6, 31.7 DISTRIBUTIONS**); or

(ii) the profits and losses of the company fall by virtue of *TIOPA 2010, s 147(3) or (5); ICTA 1988, Sch 28AA para 1* (transactions not made at arm's length) to be computed as if the loan had not, or had not in part, been made,

the whole, or a proportionate part, of any exchange gains or losses arising in respect of a liability representing the debtor relationship are to be left out of account in determining the loan relationship debits and credits.

(b) Where a company has a creditor relationship in an accounting period, and, had the parties been dealing at arm's length, either the transaction giving rise to the loan would not have been entered into at all or the loan would have been smaller, any exchange gains or losses arising in respect of an asset representing the relationship, or in the case of a reduced arm's length loan the non-arm's length proportion thereof, are to be ignored in determining the loan relationship debits and credits. This does not, however, apply to the extent that the same amount of exchange gains or losses is brought into account (or would be brought into account apart from *CTA 2009, s 328(2)–(7); FA 1996, s 84A(2)–(10)*, see **54.17** above) by a person having a corresponding debtor relationship.

Where a company would be treated as having a debtor relationship if a claim were made under *TIOPA 2010, s 192(1), (2), (4) previously ICTA 1988, Sch 28AA para 6D(2)* (see **72.7 TRANSFER PRICING**) and the company is 'connected' (see **54.31** above) with the company which would have the corresponding creditor relationship, in determining the exchange gains and losses to be brought into account in respect of the debtor relationship, it is assumed that such a claim has been made. Where, because of such a claim (whether an actual claim or one deemed to be made under these provisions) more than one company is treated as having a debtor relationship in respect of the same liability, the total credits in respect of exchange gains from those debtor relationships must not exceed the total debits in respect of exchange losses from the corresponding creditor relationship, and the total debits in respect of exchange losses from those debtor relationships must not exceed the total credits in respect of exchange gains from the corresponding creditor relationship.

[*CTA 2009, ss 447–452; FA 1996, Sch 9, para 11A*].

Consideration not fully recognised by accounting practice

[54.51] Where a company which intends to eliminate or reduce the credits to be brought into account disposes of rights under a creditor relationship on or after 16 May 2008, and the consideration is not wholly in the form of money or a debt falling to be settled by payment of money and is not fully recognised (see below), the credits which the company must bring into account for the accounting period of the disposal are calculated on the assumption that the whole of the consideration is so recognised for that period.

For this purpose, consideration is not fully recognised if, under generally accepted accounting practice, its full amount or value is not recognised in determining the company's profit or loss for any accounting period.

This rule does not apply if *TIOPA 2010, s 147(3) or (5); ICTA 1988, Sch 28AA para 1(2)* (see **72 TRANSFER PRICING**) operates in respect of the disposal to increase the company's tax liability.

[*CTA 2009, s 455, Sch 2 para 68; FA 1996, Sch 9 para 11B; FA 2008, s 62, Sch 22 para 4*].

Loan relationships for unallowable purposes

[54.52] Any debits which, on a just and reasonable apportionment, are attributable to an 'unallowable purpose' of a loan relationship in an accounting period are not to be brought into account for that period as loan relationship debits or for any other corporation tax purposes. This also applies to both debits and credits in respect of exchange gains and losses. Amounts so excluded are not to be brought into account for corporation tax purposes under any other provision.

A company will be regarded as being a party to a loan relationship for an unallowable purpose where it is a party to the loan relationship at any time during an accounting period, or enters into a related transaction in respect of that loan relationship (essentially an acquisition or disposal of that loan relationship in whole or in part):

(a) otherwise than for its business or other commercial purposes; or
(b) in respect of activities for which it is not within the charge to corporation tax; or
(c) for a tax avoidance purpose.

Paragraph (b) would catch a loan relationship entered into by a UK permanent establishment of a non-resident company where the loan relates to the company's non-UK operations. It could also apply for example where a mutual trading company borrows money to finance its non-taxable mutual activities.

In the case of (c), a company will be regarded as being a party to a loan relationship or a related transaction for a tax avoidance purpose where the main purpose or one of the main purposes for which it was a party to the loan relationship at that time or for which it entered into the related transaction was to secure a tax advantage, whether for itself or for any other person. '*Tax advantage*' is defined by reference to *CTA 2010, s 1139* (formerly *ICTA 1988, s 840ZA*) for accounting periods ending on or after 6 April 2007 and *ICTA 1988, s 709* (transactions in securities — as it stood before its amendment by *ITA 2007*) for accounting periods ending before that date and thus has a very wide meaning.

[*CTA 2009, ss 441, 442; FA 1996, Sch 9 para 13; FA 2002, Sch 23 para 13, Sch 25 para 30; FA 2004, Sch 10 para 32*].

For guidance on the application of the unallowable purposes rule in *CTA 2009, ss 441, 442; FA 1996, Sch 9 para 13*, see HMRC Corporate Finance Manual, at CFM38110 et seq.

Simon's Taxes. See **D1.787**.

Rate of interest reset

[54.53] This provision applies where the object, or one of the main objects, of a company in entering into or becoming a party to a creditor loan relationship was to secure a tax advantage (within the meaning of *CTA 2010, s 1139; ICTA 1988, s 840ZA*), whether for itself or another person, and the difference between the issue price of the asset representing the relationship and its fair value after a change in either:

(i) the rate of interest;
(ii) the amount payable to discharge the debt; or
(iii) the time at which any payments relating to the asset (whether interest or otherwise) fall due,

is at least 5% of the issue price. With effect from the day on which those conditions are satisfied, a fair value basis of accounting must be used in determining the credits and debits to be brought into account in respect of the loan relationship.

This provision applies even if the relationship is a connected companies relationship (*CTA 2009, s 349(3)*).

The fair value of an asset for these purposes is to be determined on the assumption that all amounts payable by the debtor will be paid in full as they fall due.

[*CTA 2009, ss 349(3), 454; FA 1996, s 88A; FA 2004, s 52, Sch 10 para 6*].

Restriction of relief for interest payable

[54.54] A debit in respect of interest will not be a loan relationship debit (whether a payment or not) if, at any time, a scheme has been effected or arrangements made in relation to the transaction giving rise to the interest whereby the sole or main benefit which might be expected to accrue to the payer was a reduction in a tax liability through bringing the debit into account. Any question as to whether a benefit might be expected to accrue from a transaction, where group relief is claimed under *CTA 2010, Pt 4 Ch 4; ICTA 1988, s 403; CTA 2009, Sch 1 para 118* for trading or non-trading debits, is to be determined by reference to the claimant company and the surrendering company taken together. The restriction of relief has effect in relation to payments of alternative finance return or profit share return under **ALTERNATIVE FINANCE ARRANGEMENTS** (4) as it has effect in relation to payments of interest.

[*CTA 2009, s 443; ICTA 1988, s 787*].

Company ceasing to be UK-resident etc.

[54.55] Where a company ceases to be UK-resident, it will be deemed to have assigned the assets and liabilities representing its loan relationships immediately before and to have reacquired them immediately after it ceased to be UK-resident, at their fair value, unless the assets or liabilities continue to be held or owed for the purposes of the company's UK permanent establishment (see **65.6 RESIDENCE**). The provision similarly applies where an asset or liability ceases to be held for the purposes of a UK permanent establishment of a non-UK resident company in any circumstances not involving a related transaction. (Thus, any profit or loss on an asset or liability will be brought into account as a loan relationship credit or debit.) This does not apply, however, if the provisions in **54.61** below apply (application of degrouping charge where a transferee company leaves the group within six years) and the company leaves the group under those provisions at the same time as it ceases to be UK-resident or the asset or liability ceases to be held for the purposes of the UK permanent establishment, whether or not a degrouping charge arises.

[*CTA 2009, ss 333, 334; FA 1996, Sch 9 para 10A*].

Benefits derived by connected persons

[54.56] This provision was repealed by *FA 2011, Sch 5 paras 6, 8*, with effect for times on or after 19 July 2011. Where it applied in the case of a creditor relationship to which a company was a party, the creditor company had to use fair value accounting for any credits brought into account where:

- the return to the creditor company from the relationship was less than a 'commercial return' (a return on an investment of money at a commercial rate of interest);
- another company connected with the creditor (the *CTA 2010, s 1139; ICTA 1988, s 839* definition of connection applies — see **25 CONNECTED PERSONS**) derived any benefit (including value in any form) as a result of any arrangements made in consequence of, or otherwise in connection with, the relationship; and
- the benefit derived by the connected company was designed to make up for part or all of the amount lost to the creditor company as a result of the return being less than a commercial return.

The definition of '*arrangements*' included any agreement or understanding (whether or not legally enforceable). In determining the return to the creditor company from the relationship any benefit, which it derived directly or indirectly from the above benefit derived by the connected company, had to be disregarded. [*CTA 2009, s 453; FA 1996, s 93C*].

Convertible and exchangeable securities issued between connected companies

[54.57] An anti-avoidance provision applied for times before 19 July 2011 where a security that carried rights to acquire or an obligation to acquire shares in a company (whether by conversion, exchange, or otherwise) was held directly or indirectly (via a series of loan relationships or money debts) by a company that was connected with the issuer. For these purposes a debtor and creditor company were treated as connected where they were connected for the purposes of *CTA 2010, s 1139* (formerly *ICTA 1988, s 839*), or where their accounting results were reflected in the consolidated group accounts of a group of companies. The provision applied where the debits which the debtor company recognised in respect of the debtor relationship exceeded the credits which the creditor company recognised in respect of the corresponding creditor relationship. In such cases the creditor company was required to recognise credits on the corresponding creditor relationship equal to the debits that the debtor company had recognised. Where a loan relationship was bifurcated in a debtor or a creditor company's accounts, the credits and debits that were recognised in respect of the debtor or creditor relationship for the purposes of this anti-avoidance provision were the credits or debits that were recognised in respect of the loan relationship host contract.

Where a creditor company that was treated as connected with the debtor company for these purposes became a party to an existing creditor relationship the provision only had effect for debits accruing on the corresponding debtor relationship on or after the time that the creditor company became a party to the creditor relationship.

For times on or after 6 December 2010 until 19 July 2011 the measure applied where a person connected with the creditor company (as opposed to the creditor company itself) had the right to acquire or could be required to acquire shares in any company. Also for such times it was provided that the debits and credits that fell to be taken into account under this provision included debits and credits arising to a CFC [*CTA 2009, ss 418, 419, as amended by FA 2011, s 29*].

The above measure applied for debits and credits arising on or after 22 April 2009 and before 19 July 2011, when it was repealed by *FA 2011, Sch 5, paras 6, 7*.

[*CTA 2009, ss 418, 418A (as amended and introduced respectively by FA 2009, Sch 30, para 4) and s 419*].

A similar anti-avoidance provision applied on an accounting period by accounting period basis for debits and credits arising on or after 12 March 2008 and before 22 April 2009 where a debtor company bifurcated a debtor relationship in its accounts, a connected company was a party directly or indirectly (via a series of loan relationships, or money debts which would be treated as a loan relationship were a company a debtor or creditor in respect of that money debt) to the corresponding creditor relationship, and that connected company did not bifurcate the creditor relationship in its accounts. In such circumstances the creditor company was required to recognise additional credits in respect of the creditor relationship equal to the debits (discount on the host contract and interest payable) which the debtor company recognised in its accounts, to the extent that the credits which the creditor company recognised in its accounts in respect of that loan relationship were less than this amount. Where the creditor company was only a party to a creditor relationship for part of an accounting period it was only required to recognise such credits as, on a just and reasonable basis, were attributable to the part of the accounting period for which it was a party to the loan relationship.

This measure was introduced primarily to counter an arrangement whereby a debtor company issued a convertible security to a group company and it bifurcated the security in its accounts, whereas the creditor company (which typically was preparing its accounts in accordance with UK GAAP excluding FRS 26) did not and carried the loan relationship at cost in its accounts. In such cases the group company received a 'free' deduction for the discount arising on the host contract.

The *ICTA 1988, s 839* definition of connection applied for these purposes. In addition the two companies were treated as connected where their accounting results were reflected in the consolidated accounts of a group of companies.

[*CTA 2009, s 418 (as it stood before it was amended by FA 2009, Sch 30 para 4), formerly FA 1996, s 94B, as introduced by FA 2008, Sch 22, para 18*].

Continuity of treatment — groups

[54.58] The following provisions apply to ensure that intra-group transactions are tax neutral under the loan relationships regime. The provisions apply where:

(i) as a result of a 'related transaction' (as in **54.6** above) between two members of a group (both being within the charge to corporation tax in respect of the transaction), one of those companies (the '*transferee*') directly or indirectly replaces the other (the 'transferor') as a party to a loan relationship or becomes party to a loan relationship which is 'equivalent' (for which see *CTA 2009, s 338*) to a loan relationship to which the other company has ceased to be a party;

(ii) a series of transactions, having the same effect as a related transaction between two companies each of which has been a member of the same group at some time in the course of those transactions (and would be within the charge to corporation tax in respect of such a relevant transaction), results in such a replacement; or

(iii) *TCGA 1992, ss 127–130* (equation of original shares and new holding — reorganisation of share capital; see Tolley's Capital Gains Tax) apply (or would apply but for *TCGA 1992, s 116(5)*) as a result of *section 135(3)* (which permits an exchange of securities to be treated as a reorganisation) to an exchange taking place on or after 1 January 2007 and the 'original shares' consist of or include an asset representing a loan relationship. The two companies involved must be resident in different EU member states and the provisions at **54.63** and **54.67** must not apply to the exchange.

A company is resident in a member state for this purpose if it is within a charge to tax under the law of the State as being resident for that purpose and it is not regarded, for the purposes of any DOUBLE TAX RELIEF (**32**) arrangements to which the State is a party, as resident in a territory not within a member state.

The provisions also apply to certain transfers between insurance companies which result in one replacing the other as a party to a loan relationship (and (i) and (ii) above are correspondingly disapplied to certain such transfers). See *CTA 2009, s 337*.

Where (i) or (ii) above apply, the transferor company is treated as having entered into the transaction (or the first of a series of transactions, as the case may be) in the accounting period in which the transaction takes place for a consideration equal to the 'notional carrying value' of the loan relationship asset or liability. The transferee is treated as having acquired the loan relationship asset or liability for a consideration equal to that amount for any accounting period in which it is party to the relationship.

The '*notional carrying value*' is the amount that would have been the carrying value of the asset or liability in the transferor's accounts had a period of account ended immediately before the company ceased to be party to the loan relationship. Where a discount arises in respect of the transaction (or series of transactions or transfer), the consideration treated as payable by the transferor company is to be increased by the amount of the discount.

A '*relevant transaction*' is a related transaction (as in **54.6** above) or the first of a series of related transactions or a transfer by virtue of which these provisions apply or would apply but for the transferor company using fair value accounting (see below).

Where the payment of the transfer consideration is deferred, the amount of the consideration exceeds what the purchaser would have paid if payment had been required in full at the time of sale and it is reasonable to regard some or all of the excess as representing a return on an investment of money at interest, this element of the purchase price will be included in computing the transferor's profits but the transferee will be unable to obtain relief for this amount. [*CTA 2009, s 340(5)*].

The transfer pricing provisions of *TIOPA 2010, Pt 4; ICTA 1988, Sch 28AA* (see **72 TRANSFER PRICING**) do not apply to amounts so determined as above for accounting periods beginning on or after 1 April 2004 (subject to transitional rules for periods straddling that date).

'Group' for these purposes is as under *TCGA 1992, s 170* (see **18.2 CAPITAL GAINS — GROUPS**).

Where (iii) above applies, debits and credits are brought into account as if the transaction had been a disposal of the loan relationship constituting or included in the original shares at its notional carrying value.

[*CTA 2009, ss 335–340, 342; FA 1996, Sch 9, paras 12, 12G*].

Fair value accounting

[54.59] The above provisions do not apply where (i) or (ii) above applies. Instead, where (i) or (ii) above applies, the amount to be brought into account by the transferor company is the fair value of the asset (or rights under or interest in the asset) or liability as at the date on which the transferee becomes a party to the loan relationship. Where the payment of the transfer consideration is deferred, the amount of the consideration exceeds what the purchaser would have paid if payment had been required in full at the time of sale and it is reasonable to regard some or all of the excess as representing a return on an investment of money at interest, this element of the purchase price will be included in computing the transferor's profits but the transferee will be unable to obtain relief for this amount. [*CTA 2009, s 341(4)*].

The transferee is treated as acquiring the asset or liability for a consideration equal to the same amount as that brought into account by the transferor company ignoring any deemed interest element of the consideration that is required to be brought into account by the transferor (see above).

Where (iii) above applies, the amount to be brought into account by the transferor is the fair value of the asset (or rights under or interest in the asset) as at the date of the exchange. The company acquiring the loan relationship is treated as acquiring it for the same amount as that brought into account by the transferor.

For these purposes, a company is regarded as using fair value accounting as respects a loan relationship only if the debits and credits brought into account in respect of the relationship are determined for the purposes of the loan relationships legislation on a fair value basis, whether or not it otherwise uses fair value accounting as respects the relationship.

[*CTA 2009, ss 341, 343; FA 1997, Sch 9, paras 12(2A), (2B), (2C), 12G*].

Anti-avoidance

[54.60] The above provisions do not apply, where (i) or (ii) above applies and the relevant transaction occurs on or after 16 May 2008, if:

- the transferor is a party to 'arrangements' under which there is likely to be a 'transfer' of rights or liabilities under the loan relationship by the transferee to another person in circumstances under which neither (i) nor (ii) above would apply and the purpose, or a main purpose, of the arrangements is to secure a tax advantage for the transferor or a connected person; or
- *CTA 2009, s 455* (previously *FA 1996, Sch 9 para 11B* — see **54.49** above) applies in relation to the disposal.

For this purpose, '*arrangements*' include any scheme, agreement, understanding, transaction or series of transactions, and '*transfer*' includes any arrangement which equates in substance to a transfer (including any acquisition or disposal of, or increase or decrease in, a share of the profits of a partnership).

[*CTA 2009, s 347; FA 1996, Sch 9, para 12(2E), (2F)*].

Degrouping charge

[54.61] A degrouping charge applies where, after replacing the transferor as party to a loan relationship as in **54.58**(i) or (ii) above, the transferee ceases within the 'relevant six-year period' to be a member of the group. The '*relevant six-year period*' is the period of six years following the related transaction or the last of the series of transactions.

In this case, the transferee company is treated (subject to the conditions below) as having assigned the loan relationship asset or liability immediately before the cessation for consideration equal to its fair value at that time and as having immediately reacquired it for the same amount where a gain would arise. (Thus, any gain is brought into charge to tax under the loan relationship provisions immediately before the transferee leaves the group.)

No disposal is deemed to take place where the deemed disposal would give rise to a loss unless:

(a) the loan relationship is a creditor relationship and there is a hedging relationship (within the meaning of *CTA 2009, s 707*) between the creditor relationship and a derivative contract; and
(b) a degrouping charge arises in respect of the derivative contract under the equivalent provisions of the derivative contracts legislation (*CTA 2009, ss 630, 631*).

Where such conditions are satisfied a deemed disposal of the creditor relationship will take place and the amount of the loss that may be brought into account is not restricted to the amount of the degrouping charge that arises on the derivative contract.

Where an asset or liability is transferred in the course of a transfer or merger to which **54.63** or **54.67** below applies and as a result the transferee leaves a group, the transferee is not treated for these purposes as leaving the group. If the transferee becomes the member of another group, it is treated for the purposes of these provisions as if that group and the original group were the same.

The degrouping charge does not apply where the transferee company ceases to be a member of the group by reason only of an exempt distribution within *CTA 2010, s 1075; ICTA 1988, s 213(2)* or *s 213A*. However, if there is a chargeable payment (within the meaning of *CTA 2010, s 1088(1); ICTA 1988, s 214(2)*) within five years after making the exempt distribution, a degrouping charge arises as above but the transferee company is treated as having assigned the loan relationship asset or liability immediately before making the chargeable payment for a consideration equal to its fair value at the time the company left the group. As above, the degrouping charge only applies if a credit would be brought into account by the transferee company on the assignment of the asset or liability or, if that is not the case, a credit would be brought into account under the degrouping provisions of the derivative contract rules where the loan relationship is a creditor relationship and the company has a hedging relationship between a derivative contract and the creditor relationship.

[*CTA 2009, ss 344–346; FA 1996, Sch 9 para 12A*].

Group mismatch scheme legislation

[54.62] The group mismatch scheme legislation was introduced by *FA 2011, Sch 5* and took effect for times on or after 19 July 2011. In the case of a group mismatch scheme entered into before that date where the legislation applies any losses arising on loan relationships or derivative contracts will be disregarded but the profits will remain within the charge to tax. [*FA 2011, Sch 5, para 6(2), (3)*].

The aim of this legislation is to counter transactions that seek to exploit an asymmetry in the accounting (and hence tax) treatment of transactions involving loan relationships or derivatives in order for a group (see below) to obtain a tax advantage. Where this legislation applies (subject to the transitional rule discussed above) any profits or losses arising on loan relationships or derivative contracts that form part of the scheme are disregarded for tax purposes. The legislation also applies to transactions that are deemed to be loan relationships for tax purposes including repos and quasi repos and transactions treated as financing arrangements under *CTA 2010, ss 758, 763 and 767* (see *CTA 2010, ss 938I, 938J*).

Scheme profit or loss

The legislation applies to a scheme profit or a scheme loss. This is a profit or loss that forms part of the group mismatch scheme, which, but for this legislation, would be brought into account as a debit or credit for the purposes of the loan relationships or derivative contracts legislation and meets the first or second asymmetry condition.

The first asymmetry condition is that the loss or profit affects the amount of any relevant tax advantage secured by the scheme. Where at the end of an accounting period it is not certain whether the scheme will secure a relevant tax advantage or what the amount of the relevant tax advantage secured by the scheme will be, the first asymmetry condition is regarded as being met if there is a chance that the scheme will secure a relevant tax advantage and the loss or profit will affect its amount.

The second asymmetry condition applies where the loss or profit does not meet the first asymmetry condition but arises from a transaction, or series of transactions, that might (if events had turned out differently) have given rise to a loss or profit that would have met the first asymmetry condition.

[*CTA 2010, s 938C*].

Meaning of group mismatch scheme

A '*scheme*' is defined as including any scheme, arrangements or understanding of any kind whatever, whether or not legally enforceable, involving a single transaction or two or more transactions. [*CTA 2010, s 938H*]. A scheme is a group mismatch scheme if the parties to the scheme are, or include, members of the same group (see below) and condition A or condition B is met.

Condition A is that at the time that the scheme is entered into there is no practical likelihood that the scheme will fail to secure a relevant tax advantage (see below) of £2 million or more.

Condition B is that:

(a) the purpose, or one of the main purposes, of any member of the scheme group in entering into the scheme is to obtain the chance of securing a relevant tax advantage (of any amount); and
(b) at the time the scheme is entered into:
    (i) there is no chance that the scheme will secure a relevant tax disadvantage (see below); or
    (ii) there is such a chance but the expected value of the scheme is nevertheless a positive amount.

If at the time the company enters into the scheme, there are chances that the scheme would, if carried out, secure different relevant tax advantages or disadvantages in different circumstances, the amount and probabilities of each must be taken into account in determining the expected value of the scheme. Where at the time that the scheme is entered into the length of the scheme is uncertain condition A or condition B will be regarded as being met where they would be met on any reasonable assumption as to the length of the scheme period.

[*CTA 2010, s 938B*].

Relevant tax advantage and relevant tax disadvantage

A relevant tax advantage is defined in relation to a scheme as an economic profit:

(a) that is made by the scheme group over the scheme period (defined as the period over which the scheme has effect) which arises as a result of asymmetries in the way different members of the group bring, or do not bring, amounts into account as debits and credits for the purposes of *CTA 2009, Pt 5* or *7* (or for the purposes of *CTA 2009, Pt 3*, where the relevant member the group is a party to the loan relationship or derivative for the purposes of its trade); and
(b) is not negligible.

A relevant tax disadvantage is in turn defined in relation to a scheme as an economic loss that:

(a) is made by the scheme group over the scheme period and arises as a result of asymmetries in the way different members of the scheme group bring, or do not bring, amounts into account as debits and credits for the purposes of *CTA 2009, Pt 5* or *7* (or for the purposes of *CTA 2009, Pt 3*, where the relevant member the group is a party to the loan relationship or derivative for the purposes of its trade); and
(b) is not negligible.

Asymmetries are defined in as including, in particular, asymmetries relating to quantification and asymmetries relating to timing.

The reference to an economic profit includes an increase in an economic profit and a decrease in an economic loss. Similarly the reference to an economic loss includes an increase in an economic loss and a decrease in an economic profit.

[*CTA 2010, ss 938D, 938K*].

The reference to amounts being not brought into account for the purposes of the loan relationships legislation or the derivative contracts legislation do not include:

(a) a company not bringing amounts into account because the company is not UK resident and the amounts are not attributable to a permanent establishment that the company has in the UK; or
(b) amounts attributable to an overseas permanent establishment of a UK resident company that has made an election to exclude the profits of its foreign permanent establishments from tax under *CTA 2009, s 18*.

[*CTA 2010, s 938L*].

Economic profit or loss

Whether an economic profit or loss arises to the scheme group as a whole for the purposes of the group mismatch scheme legislation is to be determined by taking into account, in particular:

(a) profits and losses made as a result of the operation of the Corporation Tax Acts; and
(b) any adjustments required to reflect the time value of money.

For these purposes any profits or losses made by a member of the scheme group are only to be taken into account to the extent that they are attributable to times at which the member is a party to the scheme.

In determining the economic profits and losses made by the scheme group as a whole over the scheme period it is to be assumed that each company that is a party to the scheme:

(1) is in a position to fully relieve any losses; and
(2) incurs the full tax cost of any profit made by that company,

where such losses or profits arise in respect of loan relationships or derivative contracts. The full tax cost is defined as the profit that would be brought into account as a credit (or as a reduction of a debit) if the company had no other profits for the period.

[*CTA 2010, ss 938, 938G*].

Priority over other anti-avoidance measures

The group mismatch scheme legislation takes precedence over the following anti-avoidance provisions that are treated as having no effect:

- *CTA 2009, s 441* (loan relationships for unallowable purposes);
- *CTA 2009, 690* (derivative contract unallowable purposes);
- *TIOPA 2010, Pt 4* (transfer pricing);
- *TIOPA 2010, Pt 6* (tax arbitrage); and
- *TIOPA 2010, Pt 7* (worldwide debt cap legislation)

[*CTA 2010, s 938N*].

Meaning of group

For the purposes of the group mismatch legislation a company (company A) is treated as being a member of a group in relation to a scheme if any other company is associated with company A at any time during which the scheme has effect . The group consists of company A and each company with which it is associated. For these purposes another company (company B) is associated with company A at a time (the relevant time) if any of the following conditions is met:

(1) the first condition is that the financial results of company A and company B for a period that includes the relevant time:

(a) are required to be comprised in group accounts;
(b) would be required to be comprised in such accounts but for the application of an exemption; or
(c) are included in group accounts:

(2) the second condition is that there is a connection between company A and company B for the accounting period of company A in which the relevant time falls. There will be a connection for these purposes where one company controls the other or both companies are under the control of the same person (the *CTA 2009, s 472* definition of control applies — see **54.32** above);

(3) the third condition is that at the relevant time company A has a major interest in company B or company B has a major interest in company A (major interest has the meaning of *CTA 2009, ss 473, 474* — see **54.44** above);

(4) the fourth condition is that:
(a) the financial results of company A and a third company, for a period that includes the relevant time:
(i) are required to be comprised in group accounts;
(ii) would be required to be comprised in such accounts but for the application of an exemption; or
(iii) are comprised in such accounts; and
(b) at the relevant time the third company has a major interest in company B (within the meaning of *CTA 2009, ss 473, 474*);

(5) the fifth condition is that:
(a) there is a connection between company A and a third company for the accounting period of company A in which the relevant time falls; and
(b) at the relevant time the third company has a major interest in company B (within the meaning of *CTA 2009, ss 473, 474*).

[*CTA 2010, s 938E*].

European cross-border mergers

[54.63] The following provisions apply to:

(a) the formation of an SE on or after 18 August 2006 by the merger of two or more companies in accordance with *Council Regulation (EC) No 2157/2001, Arts 2(1), 17(2)*;

(b) the formation of an SCE on or after 18 August 2006 by the merger of two or more 'co-operative societies', at least one of which is a society registered under *Industrial and Provident Societies Act 1965*, in accordance with *Council Regulation (EC) No 1435/2003*;

(c) a merger on or after 1 January 2007 effected by the transfer by one or more companies of all their assets and liabilities to a single existing company or co-operative society; and

(d) a merger on or after 1 January 2007 effected by the transfer by two or more companies of all their assets to a single new company (which is not an SE or SCE) in exchange for the issue by the transferee company of shares or debentures to each person holding shares in or debentures of a transferee company.

Each of the merging companies must be resident in a member state, but not all can be resident in the same state. A company is resident in a member state for this purpose if it is within a charge to tax under the law of the State as being resident for that purpose and it is not regarded, for the purposes of any **DOUBLE TAX RELIEF** (**32**) arrangements to which the State is a party, as resident in a territory not within a member state.

For the purposes of (b) above, a '*co-operative society*' is a society registered under the *Industrial and Provident Societies Act 1965* or a similar society established under the law of a member state other than the UK.

Where:

(i) immediately after the merger the transferee is within the charge to corporation tax; and

(ii) for mergers within (a), (b) or (c) above, the transfer of assets and liabilities is made in exchange for the issue of shares in or debentures of the transferee to the holders of shares in or debentures of a transferor, except where, and to the extent that, the transferee is prevented from meeting this requirement by reason only of *Companies Act 2006, s 658* (rule against limited company acquiring its own shares) or a corresponding provision in another member state,

then, in determining the debits and credits to be brought into account in respect of a loan relationship, if an asset or liability representing the loan relationship is transferred in the course of the merger, the transfer is treated as having been made for a consideration equal to the notional carrying value (see **54.58** above). For mergers falling within (d) above, and in the case of mergers falling within (c) above where the transfer is not made in exchange for shares in the transferee, in the course of the merger the transferor must cease to exist without being liquidated. Where the transferor's profits and losses arising on loan relationships that are transferred are determined for the purposes of the loan relationship legislation using a fair value basis of accounting. Instead, the amount to be brought into account by the transferor is the fair value of the asset (or rights under or interest in the asset) or liability as at the date on which the transferee becomes a party to the loan relationship. The transferee is treated as acquiring the asset or liability for a consideration equal to the amount brought into account by the transferor.

[*CTA 2009, ss 431–434, 439, Sch 2 para 70; FA 1996, Sch 9 paras 12B(1)–(4)(9), 12J; SI 2007 No 3186; SI 2008 No 1579, Sch 2 para 3*].

Reorganisations involving loan relationships

[54.64] Where *TCGA 1992, ss 127–130* (equation of original shares and new holding — reorganisation of share capital; see Tolley's Capital Gains Tax) apply, or would apply but for *s 116(5)* (reorganisations involving a qualifying corporate bond), to a reorganisation taking place on or after 1 January 2007 and the 'original shares' consist of or include an asset representing a loan relationship, then, if the above provisions apply to a transfer in the course of the merger in which the reorganisation occurs, debits and credits are brought into account as if the reorganisation had been a disposal of the asset representing the loan relationship at its notional carrying value (see **54.58** above).

This rule also applies if the above provisions do not apply only because (i) above is not satisfied if in the course of the merger a UK-resident company transfers to a company resident in another member state all assets and liabilities relating to a business which it carried on in a member state other than the UK through a permanent establishment and the transfer includes the transfer of an asset or liability representing a loan relationship.

Where the original holder of the original shares is regarded (as above) as using fair value accounting in respect of the loan relationship constituting or included in the original shares, the above rule does not apply. Instead, the amount to be brought into account by the original holder is the fair value of the asset (or rights under or interest in the asset) representing the loan relationship as at the date of the reorganisation. The successor creditor company (i.e. the company which holds the creditor relationship immediately after the reorganisation) is treated as acquiring the asset for a consideration equal to the amount brought into account by the original holder.

[*CTA 2009, ss 435, 436; FA 1996, Sch 9 para 12G; SI 2008 No 1579, Sch 2 para 8*].

Anti-avoidance

[54.65] The above provisions do not apply unless the merger is effected for genuine commercial reasons and is not part of a scheme or arrangements of which the main purpose or one of the main purposes is avoiding a liability to tax. Advance clearance can be obtained that this condition is met.

[*CTA 2009, s 437; FA 1996, Sch 9 para 12B(6)–(8); SI 2007 No 3186*].

Transparent entities

[54.66] The above provisions do not apply to a transfer, resulting from a merger, of the assets and liabilities of a 'transparent entity' to another company. The reorganisation provisions above do not apply to the new holding if as a result of a merger the assets and liabilities of one or more other companies are transferred to a transparent entity. as a result of a merger.

A '*transparent entity*' for this purpose is an entity which is resident in a member state other than the UK and is listed as a company in the Annex to the Mergers Directive, but which does not have an ordinary share capital.

[*CTA 2009, s 438; FA 1996, Sch 9 paras 12I(1)(2), 12J(1); SI 2007 No 3186, Sch 3 para 2*].

Cross-border transfers of business within the EC

Transfer of UK business

[54.67] Special provisions apply where:

(i) a company resident in one member state transfers on or after 1 January 2007 the whole or part of a business carried on in the UK to a company resident in another member state in exchange for shares or debentures issued by the latter company, and both companies make a claim; or

(ii) a company resident in a member state transfers on or after 1 January 2007 part of a business that is carried on in the UK is transferred to one or more companies all of which are resident in member states and at least one transferee is resident in a member state other than that in which the transferor is resident, the transferor continues to carry on a business after the transfer, and either the transfer is made in exchange for an issue of shares or debentures of the transferees to the holders of shares and debentures in the transferor, or the only reason that this is not done is a legal prohibition on acquisition of own shares.

In either case, the transferee, or each of the transferees must be within the charge to corporation tax immediately after the transfer.

Where the above conditions are satisfied, a claim is made by all the parties and an asset or liability representing a loan relationship is transferred during the transfer, that asset or liability is treated as transferred at its notional carrying value (see **54.58** above).

This does not apply where the transferor is regarded as using fair value accounting in respect of the loan relationship. Instead, the amount to be brought into account by the transferor is the fair value of the asset (or rights under or interest in the asset) or liability as at the date on which the transferee becomes a party to the loan relationship. The transferee is treated as acquiring the asset or liability for a consideration equal to the amount brought into account by the transferor. For this purpose, a company is regarded as using fair value accounting as respects a loan relationship only if the debits and credits brought into account in respect of the relationship for the purposes of the loan relationships legislation are determined on a fair value basis, whether or not it otherwise uses fair value accounting as respects the relationship.

A company is resident in a member state for the above purpose if it is within a charge to tax under the law of the State as being resident for that purpose and it is not regarded, for the purposes of any DOUBLE TAX RELIEF (**32**) arrangements to which the State is a party, as resident in a territory not within a member state.

[*CTA 2009, ss 421–423, 430, Sch 2 para 70; FA 1996, Sch 9 paras 12D, 12J; SI 2007 No 3186, Sch 1 para 16, Sch 3 para 2*].

Reorganisations involving loan relationships

[54.68] Where *TCGA 1992, ss 127–130* (equation of original shares and new holding — reorganisation of share capital; see Tolley's Capital Gains Tax) apply, or would apply but for *s 116(5)* (reorganisations involving a qualifying corporate bond), to a reorganisation taking place on or after 1 January 2007 and the 'original shares' consist of or include an asset representing a loan relationship, then, if (ii) above applies to the transfer in the course of which the reorganisation occurs, debits and credits are brought into account as if the reorgansiation had been a disposal of the asset representing the loan relationship at its notional carrying value (see **54.58** above).

This rule also applies if a UK-resident company transfers part of its business which is carried on in a member state other than the UK through a permanent establishment to one or more companies all of which are resident in member states, if at least one transferee is resident in a member state other than that in which the transferor is resident, the transferor continues to carry on a business after the transfer, and either the transfer is made in exchange for an issue of shares or debentures of the transferees to the holders of shares and debentures in the transferor, or the only reason that this is not done is a legal prohibition on acquisition of own shares.

Where the original holder of the original shares is regarded (as above) as using fair value accounting in respect of the loan relationship constituting or included in the original shares, the above rule does not apply. Instead, the amount to be brought into account by the original holder is the fair value of the asset (or rights under or interest in the asset) representing the loan relationship as at the date of the reorganisation. The successor creditor company (i.e. the company which holds the creditor relationship immediately after the reorganisation) is treated as acquiring the asset for a consideration equal to the amount brought into account by the original holder.

[*CTA 2009, ss 424, 425; FA 1996, Sch 9 para 12G; SI 2008 No 1579, Sch 2 para 8*].

Anti-avoidance

[54.69] The provisions discussed at **54.67–54.68** above do not apply if the transfers are not executed for genuine commercial reasons or if they form part of a scheme or arrangements a main purpose of which is to avoid income tax, corporation tax or capital gains tax. However, if advance clearance has been sought and given, these exclusions will not apply. See *CTA 2009, ss 427, 428* for the clearance procedures.

[*CTA 2009, s 426; FA 1996, Sch 9 para 12F; SI 2007 No 3186, Sch 1 para 16*].

Transparent entities

[54.70] The cross border transfer of business and reorganisation provisions that have been discussed at **54.63–54.68** above do not apply if the transferor is a 'transparent entity'. In addition the reorganisation provisions that have been discussed at **54.68** above do not apply if the transferee is a transparent entity.

A '*transparent entity*' for this purpose is an entity which is resident in a member state other than the UK and is listed as a company in the Annex to the Mergers Directive, but which does not have an ordinary share capital.

[*CTA 2009, s 429; FA 1996, Sch 9 paras 12H, 12J(1); SI 2007 No 3186, Sch 3 para 2; SI 2008 No 1579, Sch 2 para 9*].

Transfer of non-UK business

See **32 DOUBLE TAX RELIEF**.

Repo transactions and stock-lending

[54.71] The following provisions apply to repo arrangements coming into force before 1 October 2007 and to stock lending arrangements where the lender transfers securities to the borrower before that date. See **54.12** below for replacement provisions which apply where a company ceases to be a party to a loan relationship as a result of entering into a repo or a stock lending transaction.

Subject to the above, a 'related transaction' (as in **54.6** above) does not include a disposal or acquisition of rights or liabilities under a loan relationship made in pursuance of any 'repo or stock-lending arrangements'. In consequence, the transferor ('A') does not cease to be a party to the loan relationship.

(Thus, the provisions allow for any profits arising under the loan relationship, rather than just the interest, to be taxed.)

'*Repo or stock-lending arrangements*' were arrangements consisting in or involving an agreement or series of agreements under which provision is made:

(a) for the transfer from A to B of any rights under that relationship;
(b) for A (the transferor) subsequently to be entitled, or to become entitled, or to be required, to have the same or equivalent (as above in relation to *FA 1996, Sch 9 para 12*) rights transferred back to him, or to have rights in respect of benefits accruing in respect of that relationship on redemption.

As regards the transfer back to A in (b) above, the transfer had to be made by B so that the two parties to the agreement to buy and sell the rights are the same two parties to the agreement to resell and repurchase the rights. This applies to transfers back to A under arrangements consisting in or involving an agreement made after 26 June 2006 for the transfer of rights by A to B, or an agreement made after that date providing for a transfer to give effect to the entitlement or requirement in (b) above otherwise than by B. This provision reverses the Special Commissioners' decision, confirmed by the Court of Appeal in *HMRC v Bank of Ireland Britain Holdings Ltd* CA, [2008] STC 398 and *DCC Holdings (UK) Ltd v HMRC* [2008] EWHC 2429 (Ch), [2009] STC 77 (see **5.9 ANTI-AVOIDANCE**).

For transfers from A to B it is clarified that it is only the transfer from A to B and the transfer back to A that are not treated as related transactions.

In relation to agreements to sell securities, arrangements excluded from *ICTA 1988, s 730A* (as amended by *FA 2002, Sch 25 para 52*) (deemed payments of loan interest in the case of the sale and repurchase of securities, see **5.6 ANTI-AVOIDANCE**), by virtue of *subsection (8)* of that section, are *not* 'repo or stock-lending arrangements'.

The exclusion does not apply to any redemption or discharge of rights or liabilities under a loan relationship to which any repo or stock-lending arrangements relate. The substitution of any securities in any case involving a repo arrangement is to be treated for this purpose as if it were an initial transfer from A to B.

The exclusion does not affect the availability or otherwise of double tax relief under *TIOPA 2010, s 108*; *ICTA 1988, s 807A(2A)* (see **32.4 DOUBLE TAX RELIEF**).

[*CTA 2009, Sch 2, para 66; FA 1996, Sch 9 para 15 as originally enacted; FA 2002, Sch 25 para 32; FA 2003, Sch 38 paras 18, 19; F(No 2)A 2005, Sch 7 para 19; FA 2006, Sch 6 para 20; FA 2007, Sch 14 para 10; SI 2007 No 2483*].

Simon's Taxes. See **D1.759.**

Partnerships involving companies

[54.72] Where any of the partners in a firm (i.e. a partnership which carries on a trade or business) is a company, and a money debt is owed to or by the firm, no account is taken of debits or credits in relation to the money debt, or any loan relationship arising from it, in calculating the profits of the firm for corporation tax purposes. Each company partner is instead required to bring into account a share of those debits and credits as follows. The credits and debits are determined separately for each company partner as if the money debt were owed to or by the company for the purposes of its trade or business, and as if anything done by or in relation to the firm in connection with the money debt were done by or in relation to the company. The company must then bring into account a share of those debits and credits corresponding to its share in partnership profits.

Where the company's accounting date or functional currency differs from that of the partnership, HMRC consider that the company is not required to substitute its own accounting date or functional currency for that of the partnership in computing the company partner's credits and debits. (Revenue Tax Bulletin December 2002 pp 987–989).

Where a company partner uses fair value accounting for its interest in the partnership, it must use fair value accounting in determining those debits and credits.

Credits and debits relating to exchange gains or losses are generally included in the determination of credits and debits (as in **54.17** above) but may be excluded to the extent that they are recognised in the firm's statement of recognised gains or losses, statement of recognised income and expense, statement of changes in equity or statement of income and retained earnings, to the extent they are carried to and sustained by partnership reserves).

Where the firm holds a deeply discounted security (within the meaning of *ITTOIA 2005, s 430* — see **54.46** above) each partner is treated as beneficially entitled to a separate share of the security corresponding to their share in partnership profits.

Where a company partner is a debtor or creditor in relation to money lent by or to the firm, and the company controls the firm (see **54.32** above), there is deemed to be a connection between the company and any other partner companies which are treated under the above provisions as having a corresponding creditor or debtor relationship, and the connected companies rules apply accordingly (see **54.31** above). Control of the firm may for this purpose be by the company alone or by the company together with other company partners which it controls or is controlled by or which are under common control.

[*CTA 2009, ss 380–385, Sch 2 para 71; FA 1996, Sch 9 para 19; FA 2002, Sch 25 para 35; FA 2004, s 52, Sch 10 para 35*].

Miscellaneous provisions

Options etc.

[54.73] Where the amortised cost basis of accounting applies for an accounting period, and the question of an amount becoming due under a loan relationship after the end of the period (or of its amount or timing) depends on the exercise of an option by a party to the relationship, it is assumed that the option will be exercised in the manner which, as at the end of the period, appears most advantageous to that party (disregarding taxation). This applies equally where the option is exercisable by an associate of a party to the relationship (within **22.9 CLOSE COMPANIES**), and where a similar power is exercisable other than under an option.

[*CTA 2009, s 420; FA 1996, Sch 9 para 3*].

Distributions

[54.74] Except where, on or after 12 March 2008, the distribution arises as a result of or in connection with arrangements one of the main purposes of which is securing a tax advantage (within *CTA 2010, s 1139*; formerly *ICTA 1988, s 840ZA*), credits relating to any amounts treated as **DISTRIBUTIONS** (**31**) are excluded from these provisions, but this does not prevent them from being brought into charge to corporation tax for other purposes. Debits relating to any amounts treated as **DISTRIBUTIONS** (**31**) are excluded from these provisions, but this does not prevent them from being brought into charge to corporation tax for other purposes.

[*CTA 2009, s 465; FA 1996, Sch 9 para 1*].

Credits and debits relating to capital expenditure

[54.75] Debits or credits in respect of a loan relationship which, under generally accepted accounting practice, are allowed to be treated as amounts brought into account in determining the value of a fixed capital asset or project are to be brought into account as if they were treated as profit and loss items. However, no debit may be brought into account under these rules if it has been taken into account in determining a debit arising from any **INTANGIBLE ASSETS** (**48**) under *CTA 2009, Pt 8* (previously *FA 2002, Sch 29*). Where a debit is brought into account under this provision, no further debit will be allowed for the writing down of that debit attributable to the value of the fixed capital assets or project or for the amortisation or depreciation representing a writing off of the interest component of the asset.

[*CTA 2009, s 320; FA 1996, Sch 9 para 14; FA 2004, s 52, Sch 10 para 33*].

Credits and debits recognised in equity

[54.76] Where debits or credits in respect of a loan relationship are, under generally accepted accounting practice, recognised in equity or shareholders' funds but not in any of the company's statements of items brought into account in computing profits or losses for the period, they are to be brought into account as if they were treated as profit and loss items. (Such items may, for example, be interest treated for accounting purposes as a dividend on equity, as would happen where a debtor relationship is treated as being an equity instrument for accounting purposes.)

[*CTA 2009, s 321; FA 1996, Sch 9 para 14A; FA 2005, s 80, Sch 4 para 30*].

Life assurance policies and capital redemption contracts

[54.77] For accounting periods beginning before 1 April 2008, debits and credits relating to a life assurance policy (within the meaning of former *ICTA 1988, Pt 13 Ch 2*) are excluded from these provisions, but this does not prevent their being brought into charge to corporation tax for other purposes.

[*FA 1996, Sch 9 para 1A; F(No 2)A 2005, Sch 7 para 14; FA 2007, Sch 10 paras 6, 17; FA 2008, Sch 14 para 17; CTA 2009, Sch 1 para 674*].

Manufactured interest

[54.78] This provision applies where an amount is payable under any arrangements relating to the transfer of an asset representing a loan relationship, and that amount ('manufactured interest') is, or falls to be treated when paid as, representative of interest ('the real interest') under the relationship. For the purposes of the current provisions, the manufactured interest is treated as interest under a loan relationship, and as regards the company to whom the manufactured interest is payable, as if that relationship were the one under which the real interest is payable.

Where a company disposes of its right to receive a manufactured interest payment without disposing of its right to the underlying asset (for example where a company stock lends a creditor relationship and it disposes of its right to receive manufactured interest that is payable in respect of interest paid on the creditor relationship during the term of the stock loan) any credits arising as a result of the disposal are required to be brought into account in computing its loan relationship profits.

See **54.4** above for the determination of the trading or non-trading nature of the associated debits and credits.

The above applies equally to deemed manufactured interest payments under *CTA 2010, s 812(2)(3)(6)*, previously *ICTA 1988, s 736B(2)* or, for arrangements coming into force before 1 October 2007, *ICTA 1988, s 737A(5)* (deemed manufactured payments in the case of stock lending arrangements and sale and repurchase of securities).

Where a company is the borrower under a stock lending arrangement for the purposes of *CTA 2010, s 812(2), (3), (6)*, previously *ICTA 1988, s 736B(2)*, it may not bring debits into account for loan relationship purposes in respect of the representative payment which is treated as made under that provision (i.e. a deemed manufactured dividend). For the manufactured interest provisions generally, see **5.9 ANTI-AVOIDANCE**.

[*CTA 2009, ss 539–541; FA 1996, s 97; FA 2002, Sch 25 para 13; F(No 2)A 2005, Sch 7 para 11; FA 2007, Sch 14 para 16*].

Simon's Taxes. See **D1.745**.

Disguised interest

[54.79] This legislation was introduced by *FA 2009* with the aim of ensuring that the return on a transaction which is designed to produce an interest-like return and which has a tax avoidance purpose (see below) is taxed under the loan relationships legislation.

The legislation applies, subject to a number of exclusions (see below), where:

(a) a company is a party to an arrangement (to which it had become party on or after 22 April 2009) which produces a return for the company on any amount which is economically equivalent to interest (see below). An arrangement is defined as including any agreement, understanding, scheme, transaction or series of transactions (whether or not legally enforceable), other than one which constitutes a finance lease within the meaning of *CAA 2001, s 219; CTA 2009, s 486B(9)*; or

(b) two or more persons are party to an arrangement which produces a return which is economically equivalent to interest for the persons taken together but not for either of them individually. Where a company is a party to such arrangements its share of the return, determined on a just and reasonable basis, is treated as a profit arising from a loan relationship.

Note it is possible for a company that is not a party to an arrangement for a tax avoidance purpose to elect that the disguised interest legislation apply to the return. Such an election must be made no later than the time at which the arrangement begins to produce a return for the company and is irrevocable. No election may be made, however, where the arrangement would only be within the disguised interest legislation by virtue of *CTA 2009, s 486B(6)* (return arising to two or more persons — see (b) above). The purpose of this election is to enable a lender under a structured finance arrangement to elect to be taxed under this regime where it might otherwise be taxed on a greater amount than under the disguised interest rules.

[*CTA 2009, ss 486A–486E*].

Tax avoidance purpose

An arrangement will be seen as having a '*tax avoidance purpose*' if it is reasonable to assume that the main purpose or one of the main purposes of the company being a party to the arrangement is to obtain a relevant tax advantage. '*Obtain a relevant tax advantage*' means to secure that the return (or any part of it) is produced in such a way that its treatment for corporation tax purposes is more advantageous to the company than it would be if it were:

(a) charged to corporation tax as income of the company; or
(b) brought into account as income of the company for corporation tax purposes,

at the time at which the amounts would be brought into charge to tax under the disguised interest legislation.

This tax avoidance condition does not apply to a return produced for an excluded controlled foreign company (CFC). An excluded CFC is defined as a CFC whose profits are apportioned for the relevant accounting period in accordance with *ICTA 1988, s 752* (by virtue of *s 747(3)*), or for which an apportionment is avoided because the company is engaged in exempt activities. This is because HMRC consider it to be unclear as to whether a company that is not within the charge to corporation tax can have a main purpose of avoiding it.

[*CTA 2009, s 486D; Explanatory notes to Finance Bill 2009, Clause 48, Sch 24 para 27*].

Return that is economically equivalent to interest

A return will be treated as economically equivalent to interest if (and only if):

(a) it is reasonable to assume that it is a return by reference to the time value of that amount of money;
(b) it is at a rate reasonably comparable to what is (in all the circumstances) a commercial rate of interest; and
(c) at the time when the company becomes party to the arrangement, or if later, when the arrangement begins to produce a return for the company, there is no practical likelihood that the return will cease to be produced in accordance with the arrangement unless the person making the payment is prevented from producing it by reason of insolvency or otherwise.

Where this provision applies the debits and credits arising to the company in respect of the return, whether or not recognised in arriving at its accounting profit or loss for the period, have to be determined for the purposes of the loan relationships legislation using an amortised cost basis of accounting. The definition of debits and credits includes exchange gains and losses arising as a result of translating at different times the carrying value of the return or the amount by reference to which the return falls to be produced (i.e. the notional principal).

[*CTA 2009, s 486B*].

Exclusions

The disguised interest rules do not apply to the extent that the return arising to a company:

(a) is charged to, or is brought into account as, income of the company for corporation tax purposes, no later than the time when the amounts are brought into account under the disguised interest rules;

(b) would be included in computing the company's profits for the purposes of the derivative contracts legislation or the intangible fixed assets legislation, but for any exception relating to particular credits or debits. This exclusion does not prevent the disguised interest rules from applying where the profits or losses arising to a company on a derivative are treated as chargeable gains or allowable losses under *CTA 2009, s 641* (see **Simon's Taxes D1.883**);

(c) would be taken into account in computing the company's loan relationship profits under the loan relationship rules (in *CTA 2009, Pt 5*), otherwise than as a result of the disguised interest provisions, but for any exemption relating to particular debits or credits; or

(d) is from an arrangement which only involves relevant shares (see below).

[*CTA 2009, ss 486C, 486E*].

Relevant shares

The disguised interest legislation also does not apply for an accounting period (relevant accounting period) to an arrangement which produces a return for the company (holding company) if the arrangement only involves relevant shares (see below) held by the holding company throughout the relevant period (see below). This thus means that the return must be solely derived from the shares. Where the shares are combined with some other transaction, for example a derivative (e.g. an option or forward over the shares), the legislation is capable of applying.

An arrangement is regarded as only involving relevant shares if and only if the return produced reflects only an increase in the fair value of the shares. This is defined as an amount which the company would obtain from a knowledgeable and willing purchaser of the shares dealing at arm's length [*CTA 2009, s 486E(4)(a)*]. For these purposes there is an increase in the fair value of the shares even if the increase is realised by the payment of a distribution in respect of the shares.

The relevant period is defined as the period beginning with the later of the time when the company becomes a party to the arrangement and the time when the arrangement begins to produce a return for the company and ending with the earliest of the:

(a) end of the relevant accounting period (see above);
(b) time the company ceases to be party to the arrangement; and
(c) time when the arrangement ceases to produce a return for the company.

Shares are treated as relevant shares if, throughout the relevant period, they are:

(a) fully paid-up shares of a relevant company (see below);

(b) shares of a company, other than a relevant company, which would be accounted for by the issuer as a liability in accordance with generally accepted accounting practice and which produce for the holding company a return in relation to any amount which is economically equivalent to interest. The reason for this exclusion is because such shares could fall to be treated as if they were a loan relationship of the holding company by virtue of the shares accounted as liabilities rules.

For these purposes shares are treated as being fully paid-up if there are no actual or contingent obligations to meet unpaid calls on the shares or to make a contribution to the capital of the issuer which could affect the value of the shares.

A company is a relevant company if:

(a) it and the holding company are connected companies. The *CTA 2009, s 466* definition of connection applies for these purposes (i.e. one company controls the other or both companies are under the control of the same person);

(b) it is a relevant joint venture company. A company is a joint venture company for these purposes if the holding company is one of two persons who, taken together, control it, the holding company is a person which satisfies the 40% test in *ICTA 1988, s 755D(3)*, and the other person is a person who satisfies the 40% test in *ICTA 1988, s 755D(4)* (this requires that the other person has a holding of at least a 40% and not more than 55% in the joint venture company). The control test in *ICTA 1988, s 755D* applies for these purposes save that no rights and powers are attributed to a person by subsection *(6)(c)* or *(d)* of that section; or

(c) it is a relevant controlled foreign company. A company is a relevant controlled foreign company if any of its chargeable profits are apportioned to the holding company for the relevant accounting period in accordance with *ICTA 1988, s 752* (by virtue of *s 747(3)* of that Act) or are not apportioned because of *ICTA 1988, s 748(1)* (excluded activities) or *ICTA 1988, s 748(3)* (motive test).

[*CTA 2009, s 486E*].

Transitional provisions

Certain provisions were repealed with effect from 22 April 2009 following the introduction of the disguised interest legislation. Where a transaction was previously dealt with under these provisions and the company was treated as being party to an arrangement within the meaning of *CTA 2009, s 486B(9)* in respect of the transaction, it was treated as having become a party to an arrangement on that date. The disguised interest legislation only applied to the transaction, however, if the other necessary conditions were satisfied.

[*CTA 2009, s 547, Pt 6 Chs 7, 8; FA 2009, Sch 24 paras 8, 12, 13; Explanatory notes to Finance Bill 2009, Clause 48, Sch 24 para 89*].

Shares accounted for as liabilities — times after 22 April 2009

[54.80] From 22 April 2009, where certain conditions are satisfied a company (investing company) that holds shares in another company is required to treat the shares for tax purposes as if they were a creditor relationship. (A share is not defined other than that it excludes a share in a building society.) The *CTA 2009, s 476(1)* definition of a share only applies as regards the exclusion it contains for a share in a building society. [*CTA 2009, 521A(5)*].

Where the conditions are met, any distributions received by the investing company in respect of the share are not treated as distributions and thus have to be included in computing the profits arising in respect of the deemed creditor relationship. The provision which deems a distribution received in respect of such a share not to be a distribution for tax purposes does not prevent the dividend from being treated as a dividend for the purposes of determining whether the requirements of the CFC acceptable distribution policy have been satisfied.

Further, the investing company is not permitted to claim relief for any debit arising in respect of the share except in the case of a foreign exchange loss.

There is no requirement that the investing company should follow a particular accounting treatment in respect of the share.

[*CTA 2009, ss 521A–521F*].

Qualifying conditions

[54.81] Such treatment applies where the following conditions are satisfied:

(a) the share would be accounted for by the issuing company as a liability in accordance with generally accepted accounting practice. Note that this condition does not require that the issuing company actually accounts for the share as a liability;
(b) the share produces for the investing company a return on any amount which is economically equivalent to interest. This would cover, for example, a preference share which carries a dividend linked to a rate of interest or a fixed rate preference share;
(c) the issuing company and the investing company are not connected companies. The *CTA 2009, s 466* definition of connection applies;
(d) the share does not fall to be treated for the accounting period in question as if it were a creditor relationship of the investing company because of *CTA 2009, s 490* (holdings in OEICs, unit trusts and offshore funds treated as creditor relationships);
(e) the share is not an excepted share (see below); and
(f) the investing company holds the share for an unallowable purpose (see below).

The provisions of *CTA 2009, s 550(3)* (repos: ignoring effect on the borrower of sale of securities) do not apply for the purposes of the shares as liability provisions. [*CTA 2009, s 521A(5)*]. The result of this is that where a company sells shares under the terms of a repo it will not be treated as continuing to own the shares for the purposes of the shares as liabilities provisions. In such cases the return that the company receives from the repo of the shares might be taxable under the disguised interest provisions, where the necessary conditions are satisfied, as it will no longer be derived wholly from share ownership.

[*CTA 2009, ss 521B–521D; Explanatory Notes to Finance Bill 2009, Clause 48, Sch 24 para 52*].

Excepted shares

[54.82] A share will be treated as being an excepted share where it is a qualifying publicly-issued share or it is a share which mirrors a qualifying public issue.

[*CTA 2009, s 521D*].

Qualifying publicly-issued share

A share is treated as being a qualifying publicly-issued share if it was issued by a company as part of an issue of shares to persons not connected with the company and less than 10% of the shares in issue are held by the investing company or persons connected with it. The *CTA 2010, s 1122* definition of connection applies for these purposes. This is because this is the 'default' definition of connection for the purposes of the *CTA 2009*.

[*CTA 2009, s 521D(1), (2), Sch 4*].

Mirroring a public issue

A share is treated as mirroring a public issue where it is a first-level or a second-level mirroring share. The legislation refers to what is termed here as a first-level mirroring share as 'mirroring shares'.

A share is treated as a first-level mirroring share where the following conditions are satisfied:

(a) a company (company A) issues shares (the public issue) to persons not connected with the company;
(b) within seven days of that issue one or more other companies (companies BB) issue the first-level mirroring shares to company A on the same, or substantially the same, terms as the public issue;
(c) company A and companies BB are members of the same group relief group of companies. This is defined as a group of companies for the purposes of *CTA 2010, Pt 5 (group relief)*; and
(d) the total nominal value of the first level mirroring shares does not exceed the nominal value of the public issue.

A share is treated as a second-level mirroring share where:

(a) the share is issued within seven days of the public issue by one or more other companies (companies CC) to one or more of companies BB on the same, or substantially the same, terms as the public issue;
(b) company A, companies BB and companies CC are each members of the same group relief group of companies (within the meaning of *CTA 2010, Pt 5*); and
(c) the total nominal value of the second-level mirroring shares does not exceed the nominal value of the public issue.

The exceptions for first-level and second-level mirroring shares are a little unusual given that the shares as liability provisions do not apply where the investing company is connected with the issuing company for the purposes of *CTA 2009, s 466*. Under this definition one company is connected with the other where one company controls the other or both companies are under the control of the same company. The cases in which company A, companies BB and companies CC will be members of the same group relief group of companies and yet not connected with each other for the purposes of *CTA 2009, s 466* will be very rare. However, there is nothing which requires the first-level mirroring shares or the second-level mirroring shares to continue to be held by company A and companies BB respectively in order for such shares to be treated as being excepted in shares, and thus the exception will continue to apply where such shares are sold to unconnected companies.

The reason for the inclusion of an exception for first-level and second-level mirroring shares is because the shares as liability provisions were introduced as part of a consultation exercise and there was a request to preserve the provisions for first-level and second-level mirroring shares that were contained in the former *FA 1996, s 91D*.

[*CTA 2009, s 521D*].

Unallowable purposes

[54.83] An investing company will be treated as holding a share for an unallowable purpose if the main purpose or one of the main purposes for which it holds the share is to obtain a relevant tax advantage. (Note though that even if a share is not held for an unallowable purpose an investing company may elect for the shares as liabilities rules to apply in relation to the share.)

A relevant tax advantage is where the return produced by the share (or any part of it) is received in a way that means its treatment for corporation tax purposes is more advantageous to the investing company than it would be if the return were:

(a) charged to corporation tax as income of the investing company; or
(b) brought into account as income of the investing company for corporation tax purposes,

at the time when the amount would be brought into account for the purposes of *CTA 2009, s 521B* (i.e. the time that the return would be recognised were the investment in the share treated as an investment in a creditor loan relationship).

This provision does not apply if the investing company is an excluded controlled foreign company. A company will be an excluded controlled foreign company if any of its chargeable profits are apportioned for the accounting period in accordance with *ICTA 1988, s 752* (by virtue of *ICTA 1988, s 747(3)*) or are not so apportioned because of *ICTA 1988, s 748(1)*.

[*CTA 2009, s 521E*].

Beginning or ceasing to fall within the shares as liability provisions

[54.84] Where a share begins or ceases to fall within the shares as liability provisions, the investing company is treated for the purposes of the loan relationships legislation as having disposed of the share immediately before that time for a consideration equal to the notional carrying value of the shares at that time and as having immediately reacquired the share for the same consideration. The notional carrying value of the share is the value at which the share would have been carried in the company's accounts had a period of account ended immediately before the time that the share began or ceased to fall within the shares as liability provisions.

For capital gains purposes immediately before a share becomes subject to the shares as liability provisions the investing company is deemed to have disposed of it for a consideration equal to its notional carrying value and where a share ceases to become subject to the provisions the investing company is deemed to have acquired the share for its notional carrying value immediately before the shares ceased to be subject to the shares as liability provisions. The definition of notional carrying value is as set out above.

[*CTA 2009, s 521F; TCGA 1992, s 116B as amended by FA 2009, Sch 24 para 5*].

Transitional provisions

[54.85] Where the shares as loan relationship provisions formerly contained in *CTA 2009, Pt 6 Ch 7* applied to a share because it was redeemable, or only did not apply to a redeemable share because it was not designed to produce a return which equated in substance to the return on an investment of money at a commercial rate of interest, and *CTA 2009, s 521B* applied in relation to the share and the company with effect from 22 April 2009, the holder was deemed to have acquired the share for an amount equal to its notional carrying value on that date. Notional carrying value is defined as having the same meaning as in *CTA 2009, s 521F(2)* (as read with *s 521F(3); FA 2009, Sch 24 para 15(3))*. This is the value at which the share would have been carried in the company's accounts had a period of account ended immediately before 22 April 2009. Any difference between the old carrying value of the share for the purposes of the shares as loan relationship rules and the notional carrying value of the share at 22 April 2009 was treated as a tax nothing [*Explanatory Notes to Finance Bill 2009, Clause 48, Sch 24 para 96*]. In such cases *CTA 2009, s 521F* was not treated as applying by virtue of *CTA 2009, s 521B* coming into force.

[*CTA 2009, Sch 24 para 15*].

Shares treated as loan relationships – times before 22 April 2009

[54.86] The following provisions were repealed by FA 2009, Sch 24 para 8 with effect from 22 April 2009.

A share (other than a share in a building society) in one company (the 'issuing company') held by another company (the '*investing company*') was treated for an accounting period of the investing company as if it were rights under a creditor relationship of that company. Such treatment applied to that part of an accounting period during which the share was 'subject to outstanding third party obligations' and was an 'interest-like investment'.

Where this provision applied, distributions in respect of the share were treated as if they were not distributions (for distributions made before 9 October 2007, as if they were not distributions within former *ICTA 1988, s 209(2)(a)(b)* (see **31.2, 31.3 DISTRIBUTIONS**)), and the credits (and debits, but see below) to be brought into account under the loan relationship rules had to be determined on the basis of fair value accounting. For accounting periods ending on or after 12 March 2008 (and, for accounting periods beginning before that date, in respect only of debits on or after that date), no debits were permitted to be brought into account by the investing company in respect of the shares.

For this purpose, a share was 'subject to outstanding third party obligations' if it was subject to undischarged obligations ('*third party obligations*') to meet unpaid calls on it or to make a contribution to the capital of the issuing company that could affect the share's value and those obligations were obligations of a person other than the investing company. In relation to shares held by the company, a share was also '*subject to outstanding third party obligations*' if it was, or or might under any 'relevant arrangements' be, subject to third party obligations (as defined above) and those obligations could include obligations of the investing company which, under any 'relevant arrangements' could, or might be, discharged directly or indirectly by a person other than the investing company. '*Arrangements*' included any agreement or understanding (whether or not legally enforceable) and they were '*relevant*' if entered into at any time on or before the share was issued. In relation to shares held on or after 6 March 2007, 'shares' did not include shares in a building society.

A share was an '*interest-like investment*' if its nature was such that its fair value was likely to increase at a rate which represented a return on an investment of money at a commercial rate of interest and was unlikely (ignoring fluctuations resulting from exchange rate changes) to deviate to a substantial extent from that rate of increase. It was assumed for this purpose that any third party obligations would be met in the amounts and at the time at which they were due and that no transaction (or series of transactions) intended to cause the share not to be an interest-like investment would be entered into. In determining debits and credits for the purpose of these transactions, amounts were left out of account which would cause those assumptions not to be met.

A share was treated as continuing to be held by a company notwithstanding that it has been transferred to another person under a repo or stock lending arrangement or under a transaction treated as not involving a disposal by TCGA 1992, s 26 (transfer of asset by way of security).

[*CTA 2009, ss 522(4)(6), 523–525, 534(1)–(4); FA 1996, s 91A; F(No 2)A 2005, Sch 7 paras 10(2)(7), 13; FA 2006, Sch 6 para 13; FA 2007, Sch 5 para 12; FA 2008, Sch 22 para 8*].

Non-qualifying shares

[54.87] A share was also treated as rights under a creditor relationship for that part of an accounting period of an investing company during which the above provisions did not apply and the share was a 'non-qualifying share' and was not in any event treated as such rights under *CTA 2009, s 490* (previously *FA 1996, Sch 10 para 4* (holdings in unit trusts and offshore funds — see **54.99** below)). Where this provision applied, distributions in respect of the share were treated, during those times, as if they were not distributions (for distributions made before 9 October 2007, as if they were not distributions within *ICTA 1988, s 209(2)(a)(b)* (see **31.2, 31.3 DISTRIBUTIONS**)), and the debits and credits to be brought into account under the loan relationship rules had to be determined on the basis of fair value accounting.

For accounting periods ending on or after 12 March 2008 (and, for accounting periods beginning before that date, in respect only of debits on or after that date), no debits could be brought into account by the investing company in respect of the shares, except where condition (3) below applies.

A share was a 'non-qualifying share' if *CTA 2009, s 130* (previously *ICTA 1988, s 95*) did not apply to distributions in respect of it and if one or more of the conditions listed below was satisfied. Broadly, and subject to further conditions and exclusions, those conditions were as follows.

(1) The assets of the issuing company were of such a nature that the fair value of the share was likely to increase at a rate which represented a return on an investment of money at a commercial rate of interest and was unlikely to deviate to a substantial extent from that rate of increase (ignoring fluctuations resulting from exchange rate changes). This condition was not satisfied if the whole or substantially the whole by fair value of the assets of the issuing company were 'income producing' (as defined). It was assumed that no transaction (or series of transactions) intended to cause this condition not to be satisfied would be entered (or, on or after 12 March 2008 had been entered) into by any person (before 12 March 2008, by the investing company) and where the condition was satisfied, no credits could be brought into account in relation to any such transactions that would (apart from that assumption) cause the condition not to be satisfied.

(2) The share was 'redeemable' (as defined), if it was designed to produce a return which equated, in substance, to the return on an investment of money at a commercial rate of interest and was not an 'excepted share' (as defined).

(3) There was a scheme or arrangement (in relation to times on or after 12 March 2008, whether or not the investing company was a party to it) under which the share and one or more 'associated transactions' (as defined) were together designed to produce a return (in relation to times on or after 12 March 2008, for one or more persons) which equated, in substance, to the return on an investment of money at a commercial rate of interest. This condition was not satisfied if the share by itself was within either of the above conditions, or would have been but for falling within the income producing assets or excepted share exemptions from those conditions. For accounting periods ending on or after 12 March 2008 (and, for accounting periods beginning before that date, in respect only of debits on or after that date), where this condition was satisfied, the debits to be brought into account by the investing company could

not exceed the credits brought inot account in respect of the associated transactions under the derivative contracts rules (see **30 DERIVATIVE CONTRACTS LEGISLATION**).

Previously, debits and credits in relation to any such associated transaction were to be brought into account on a fair value basis by the investing company under the derivative contracts rules as if it were, or were a transaction in respect of, a derivative contract (if that was not in fact the case). The Treasury has the power to add, vary or remove conditions by regulations.

[*CTA 2009, ss 523, 526–533, 534(1)(5)–(7), Sch 2 paras 76, 77; FA 1996, ss 91B–91F; F(No 2)A 2005, Sch 7 paras 10(3)–(5)(7), 13; FA 2006, Sch 6 paras 13–15; FA 2007, Sch 5 para 13; Sch 22 paras 10, 12, 14, 15; FA 2008, Sch 22 paras 6, 13*].

Where either of the above provisions began to apply in the case of any shares, the investing company was deemed for chargeable gains purposes to have disposed of the share immediately before that time, and to have immediately reacquired it, at its fair value. Where at any time, either of the above provisions ceased to apply to a share, the investing company was deemed for chargeable gains purposes and for the purposes of the loan relationship provisions, to have disposed of the share immediately before that time, and to have immediately reacquired it, at its fair value.

[*CTA 2009, s 535, Sch 1 para 366; TCGA 1992, s 116B; FA 1996, s 91G; F(No 2)A 2005, Sch 7 para 10(6)*].

Payments in return for capital contribution to partnership

[54.88] The following provisions apply to partnership returns arising on or after 12 March 2008 and before 22 April 2009, when the provision was repealed by *FA 2009, Sch 21, para 8*.

Where a company was a party to 'relevant arrangements' under which a firm of which it was a member received or might become entitled to receive a capital contribution from any person, directly or indirectly and a sum of money or other asset was received, directly or indirectly, by that person or a person connected to that person, the return under the arrangements was treated as a profit from a loan relationship of the company. The credits to be brought into account had to be calculated on the amortised cost basis.

Where a company is a party to relevant arrangements under which it makes a capital contribution to a firm of which it is a member, the firm's profits are shared so that the company's share is less than it would be if profits were share in proportion to the total capital contributions of the members, and the company or a connected person is entitled to a greater share of the capital of the firm than it would otherwise be due, the return is to be treated as a profit on a loan relationship, calculated on the amortised cost basis.

Where the return under either of the above provisions is already included in corporation tax profits under other provisions, the charge under the above provisions is reduced on a just and reasonable basis.

'*Relevant arrangements*' are arrangements (including any scheme, agreement, understanding, transaction or series of transactions) designed to produce for the company a return equating to a return at a commercial rate of interest and which has as its purpose, or one of its main purposes, the securing of a tax advantage.

[*CTA 2009, ss 536–538; FA 1996, ss 91H, 91I; FA 2008, Sch 22 para 17*].

Loan relationships with embedded derivatives

[54.89] Special provisions apply to loan relationships with 'embedded derivatives'. This is where a company, in accordance with generally accepted accounting practice, splits the rights and liabilities under the loan relationship into those under the loan relationship (the 'host contract') and '*embedded derivatives*' which are those under one or more derivative financial instruments or equity instruments. In this case, the host contract will fall, for corporation tax purposes, within the loan relationship rules and the embedded derivatives within the derivative contracts rules under *CTA 2009, s 585* (see **30 DERIVATIVE CONTRACTS LEGISLATION**). The embedded derivatives are treated as having the character (be it an option, a future or a contract for differences) which the rights and liabilities would have if contained in a separate contract.

Election

[54.90] Where a company is not permitted to adopt split treatment for its loan relationships containing embedded derivatives ('*relevant assets*') because it still uses 'old UK GAAP' i.e. UK GAAP excluding FRS 26, but it would have been able to adopt such treatment had it been subject to international accounting standards or 'new UK GAAP', it can elect for the embedded derivative provisions to apply in relation to those assets.

The election is irrevocable and normally has effect in relation to all relevant assets held by the company including those subsequently acquired. It normally had to be made in writing to an HMRC officer by 31 December 2005. A later election was and, in certain cases, still is possible, if:

(a) the company did not hold relevant assets at the beginning of its first period of account beginning or after 1 January 2005, but subsequently acquires such assets, in which case it must elect within 90 days of acquiring its first relevant asset; or
(b) the company did not have a period of account beginning in 2005 but held relevant assets at the beginning of its first period of account beginning after the end of that year, in which case it had to elect within 90 days after the beginning of that period of account.

If the election is made after 31 December 2005 in accordance with (a) above (because of a first-time acquisition of relevant assets), the election has effect from the beginning of the period of account in which the first relevant asset is acquired. If made after 31 December 2005 in accordance with (b) above (because it does not have a period of account beginning in 2005), the election had effect from the beginning of the company's first period of account beginning on or after 1 January 2005.

Where such an election was (or is) made, *CTA 2009, ss 315–318; FA 1996, Sch 9 para 19A* (see **51.8** above under change of accounting policy) and the equivalent derivative contracts provision in *CTA 2009, ss 613–615* (previously *FA 2002, Sch 26 para 50A* (see **30.15 DERIVATIVE CONTRACTS LEGISLATION**)) apply from the date the election has effect. The effect is that, where the tax treatment of a relevant asset changes as a result of an election, any changes in value of a company's loan relationships or derivative contracts is taken into account as a debit or credit even though there has been no actual change in accounting policy.

An election made on or after 12 March 2008 did not apply to relevant assets to which the provisions below relating to loan relationships treated differently by a connected debtor and creditor applied (see **54.57**).

[*CTA 2009, ss 415–417, Sch 2 para 64; FA 1996, s 94A; FA 2004, s 52, Sch 10 para 13; FA 2005, Sch 4 para 28; F(No 2)A 2005, Sch 6 para 7; FA 2008, Sch 22 para 18*].

Gilt-edged securities

Index-linked

[54.91] Where a loan relationship is represented by an index-linked gilt-edged security, the debits and credits brought into account for this purpose must be determined using fair value accounting and an adjustment is to be made wherever the fair value of the security is to be found at two different times and there is a change in the retail price index or, for securities issued after 19 July 2011 relevant prices index (each hereafter referred to as RPI) between those times. The carrying value of the security is to be increased or decreased, as the case may be, at the earlier time by the same percentage as the percentage increase or reduction in the RPI between the earlier and later time. (Thus, any increase or reduction in value attributable to a change in the RPI is left out of account in computing the loan relationship debit or credit.)

The Treasury may by order disapply this provision, or specify a different basis of adjustment, in relation to any description of index-linked gilt (but not with retrospective effect).

Hedging

For increases in the RPI over periods beginning on or after 9 December 2009, where a company acquires index linked gilt-edged securities and the inflation risk is hedged, any increase in carrying value to give relief for the inflation gain will be reduced to the extent of the hedge. This provision prevents the investor from obtaining double relief for the inflationary gain. It applies where there is between two times:

(a) a 'relevant hedging scheme';
(b) an increase in RPI; and
(c) part or all of the 'index-linked capital return' is hedged.

A '*relevant hedging scheme*' is a scheme with the purpose, or one of the main purposes, of any party on entering the scheme is to hedge part or all of the indexed-linked capital return on the security.

The '*index-linked capital return*' is that part of the return which would increase the carrying value of the security and is attributable to the RPI.

The return is hedged if the pre-tax economic profit or loss by the company or group is unaffected by movements in the RPI.

A group is the investing company and all its associates. To be associated, one of five conditions must be met:

(i) the financial results of the companies must meet the consolidation requirement;
(ii) there must be a connection between the companies for the accounting period;
(iii) company A must have a major interest in B or B in A;
(iv) the financial results of A and a third company meet the consolidation requirement and at the relevant time the third company has a major interest in B;
(v) there is a connection between A and a third company and the third company has a major interest in B.

The consolidation requirement is met if consolidated accounts are required under *Companies Act 2006* or exemption applies.

There are transitional provisions in *FA 2010, Sch 14 para 9* which apply where the index-linked gilt was acquired before 9 December 2009 and the date the increase in RPI would be brought into account falls on or after that date.

[*CTA 2009, ss 400A, 400B, 400C; FA 2010, s 41, Sch 14*].

Strips

[54.92] Where a gilt is exchanged for strips of the same security, it is treated as redeemed at market value and the strips as acquired at that value in total, apportioned by reference to their own market values. Similarly where strips are consolidated into a gilt, each strip is treated as redeemed at market value and the gilt as acquired at the sum of those values. The Treasury may make regulations for determining market value for these purposes.

[*CTA 2009, s 401; FA 1996, s 95*].

Special rules for 5.5% Treasury Stock 2008/2012

[54.93] Where a loan relationship represented by these gilts is held otherwise than in the course of activities forming an integral part of a trade carried on by the company, debits and credits falling to be brought into account under the current provisions in respect of the relationship are confined to those relating to interest.

[*CTA 2009, Sch 2 para 69; FA 1996, ss 94, 95, 96*].

FOTRA securities

[54.94] A company which is the beneficial owner of a FOTRA security (within *CTA 2009, s 1280(1)*) must not bring into account for loan relationship purposes any amount relating to changes in the value of the security or any debit in respect of the loan relationship represented by the security (including expenses related to holding the security or any transaction concerning it. This provision applies only if the company would be exempt from corporation tax on the security under *CTA 2009, s 1279* (previously *FA 1996, s 154*).

[*CTA 2009, s 404; FA 1996, s 154(6)*].

Non-resident holders of certain war loan

[54.95] If a non-UK resident company carries on in the UK a business of banking, insurance or consisting of dealing in securities, special rules apply to restrict the amount of interest on money borrowed for business purposes brought into account as a debit. See *CTA 2009, s 405; ICTA 1988, s 475(1)–(5), (8), (9)*.

Simon's Taxes. See D1.758.

Collective investment schemes

[54.96] Special provisions apply in relation to such schemes. Broadly, these are as follows.

Investment trusts and venture capital trusts

[54.97] Any capital profits or losses arising to an investment trust or a venture capital trust from a creditor relationship must not be brought into account in determining loan relationship credits or debits. Capital profits or losses in this case are those which are accounted for through the capital column of the income statement in accordance with the relevant Statement of Recommended Practice (SORP) (or which would have been so carried had the relevant SORP been correctly applied). The relevant SORP is that relating to the Financial Statements of Investment Trust Companies issued by the Association of Investment Trust Companies in January 2003 and revised in December 2005 (as modified, amended or revised) or any subsequent SORP replacing it.

[*CTA 2009, ss 395, 396; FA 1996, Sch 10 paras 1–1B; FA 2004, s 52, Sch 10 para 38*].

See generally **53.1** INVESTMENT TRUSTS and **74** VENTURE CAPITAL TRUSTS.

Authorised unit trusts and open-ended investment companies

[54.98] 'Capital profits, gains or losses' arising to an authorised unit trust or an open-ended investment company on a creditor relationship must not be brought into account as loan relationship debits or credits. '*Capital profits, gains or losses*' in this case are those which, in preparing accounts in accordance with UK generally accepted accounting practice, fall to be dealt with in the statement of total return (under the heading of 'net gains/losses') in accordance with the relevant Statement of Recommended Practice (SORP). The relevant SORP in the case of an authorised unit trust or an open-ended investment company, is that relating to authorised investment funds, issued by the Investment Management Association in November 2008.

[*SI 2006 No 964, Regs 8, 12*].

See generally **52 INVESTMENT FUNDS**.

Corporate holdings in authorised unit trusts, open-ended insurance companies, and offshore funds

[54.99] Holdings of rights under a unit trust scheme, shares in an open-ended investment company or an interest in an offshore fund which fail to satisfy the 'qualifying investments test', are treated for the purposes of the current provisions as rights under creditor relationships, in relation to which a fair value basis of accounting must be used. Credits relating to distributions of an authorised unit trust or to distributions of an open-ended investment company, other than 'interest distributions' (as defined in *SI 2006 No 964, Reg 18(3)*) are excluded. There are special rules dealing with cases where a holding comes within these provisions.

Debits or credits are to be left out of account for these purposes in respect of an investment or a liability if the investment or liability was incurred, or any transaction or series of transactions was entered into in relation to the investment or liability, with a '*relevant avoidance intention*' (being the intention to eliminate or reduce the credits or creating or increasing the debits brought into account under these provisions). This rule applies to accounting periods ending on or after 6 March 2007 in the case of investments and in the case of liabilities to accounting periods ending on or after 9 May 2007. However, where the accounting period straddles those dates, only transactions on or after those dates are taken into account.

The '*qualifying investments test*' requires that not more than 60% of the market value of scheme or fund investments is represented by 'qualifying investments' (defined, broadly, as at **52.6 INVESTMENT FUNDS**).

[*CTA 2009, ss 490–497; FA 1996, Sch 10 paras 4–8; FA 2004, s 52, Sch 10 para 41; FA 2007, Sch 5 para 16; SI 1997 No 213; SI 2006 No 964, Regs 90, 95; SI 2006 No 981*].

Simon's Taxes. See **D1.765, D1.766, D1.774.**

Key points

[54.100] Points to consider are as follows.

Scope

1. The loan relationships legislation applies to loans and loan notes (including loan notes that are issued where there is no underlying loan, e.g. loan notes that are issued in exchange for shares as part of a corporate take over). It also covers interest and discount arising on money debts that are not loan relationships and most foreign exchange gains and losses arising on such money debts (although there are exceptions for non-deductible expenditure). See **54.2** and **54.3**.

2. The loan relationships legislation also applies to impairment losses arising in respect of debts owed in respect of a trade or a UK or overseas property business. The releases of the corresponding liabilities were also brought within the scope of the loan relationships legislation with effect from 22 April 2009. The effect is that where the debtor and creditor are connected, the creditor will be unable to obtain relief for any impairment provision or any loss arising if the debt is released but correspondingly the debtor company will not be liable to tax if the debt in question is released. See **54.27, 54.31, 54.32, 54.33, 54.34, 54.35, 54.36.**

Recognition of profits and loses

3. In general, profits and losses arising on:

(i) loan relationships; and
(ii) interest, discount and foreign exchange movements arising on other money debts,

are brought into account for tax purposes on the basis on which these are reflected in a company's accounts (including amounts taken to reserves, subject to exceptions for exchange movements on loan relationships — see below) in accordance with generally accepted accounting practice.

The definition of generally accepted accounting practice covers accounts prepared in accordance with international financial reporting standards, or UK generally accepted accounting practice including or excluding FRS 26. See **54.8**.

Matching

4. Where a company uses a debtor relationship to hedge an investment in a branch, or in shares in ships and aircraft, exchange movements arising on the loan relationship will be left out of account for tax purposes where they are taken to reserves in its accounts or where certain conditions specified by regulations are satisfied. Such deferred gains will typically be brought into account for tax purposes when the matched asset is disposed of. In the case of shares the matched exchange movement is included in arriving at the chargeable gain or allowable loss arising on the disposal of the shares and where the matched shares qualify for the substantial shareholding exemption (*TCGA 1992, Sch 7AC*), the matched gain or loss is not brought into account for tax purposes. See **54.17–54.23**.

Connected company rules

5. Where a company is connected with the other party to a loan relationship it is required to use an amortised cost basis of accounting for that loan relationship and where the loan relationship is a creditor relationship, the company is unable to obtain relief for any impairment losses or any losses arising from a release of all or part of the debt represented by the creditor relationship. Correspondingly, however, a debtor company is generally not liable to tax on the release of a debtor relationship that is a connected companies relationship.

Two companies will be treated as connected with each other where one company controls the other or both companies are under common control. The loan relationship definition of control tracks that of *CTA 2010, s 1124* (formerly *ICTA 1988, s 840*). See **54.32, 54.34, 54.35**.

6. An anti-avoidance provision applies to prevent groups of companies from buying back loan relationships standing at a discount in the market, or at a discount from unconnected lenders. Where the price at which the creditor relationship is purchased is less than the carrying value at which the loan relationship is carried in the debtor company's accounts, the debtor company is liable to tax on the difference, subject to limited exceptions. Where a repurchase falls within one of the exceptions and the debt is later released, in most cases the release will be treated as taxable. See **54.37–54.38**.

Interest paid to a connected person

7. A company is unable to obtain relief for interest on an accruals basis where the interest is payable to a connected person (an extended definition of connection applies) and the interest is not paid within 12 months of the end of the accounting period in which it accrued. This restriction will not apply where the connected creditor is within the charge to the loan relationships legislation in respect of the interest payment in question. See **54.43**.

8. In addition, for accounting periods beginning on or after 1 April 2009, the late paid interest rule, in general, will only apply in the case of interest payable to a company where the connected company is resident for tax purposes in a tax haven and is not within the charge to the loan relationships legislation (i.e. it is not operating UK through a UK permanent establishment). See **54.43**.

Similar restrictions apply in respect of the discount payable on relevant discounted securities and similar exceptions apply. See **54.46, 54.47**.

Intra-group transfers

9. Where profits and losses arising on a loan relationship are determined for tax purposes using an amortised cost basis of accounting it is possible for the loan relationship to be transferred at its carrying value to another company in the same *TCGA 1992* group that is within the charge to the loan relationships legislation in respect of the loan relationship that is transferred. The carrying value of the loan relationship is the value at which it would have been carried in the transferor's accounts had an accounting period ended immediately before the date of the transfer. See **54.58**.

10. A degrouping charge arises where the transferee company leaves the group within six years of the transfer and in such cases the transferee company is normally deemed to have disposed of the loan relationship at its market value immediately before the group, where this would give rise to a gain. See **54.61**.

11. Where a loss would arise in such circumstances no disposal is deemed to take place unless the loan relationship is being hedged with a derivative contract and a degrouping charge arises in respect of the derivative contract under the equivalent degrouping provisions of the derivative contracts legislation. In such cases the amount of the loss that can be brought into account for tax purposes is not restricted by reference to the amount of the gain arising on the derivative contract. See **54.61**.

Loans for unallowable purposes

12. The many anti-avoidance provisions include loan relationships for unallowable purposes. A company can be denied relief on a just and reasonable basis for any debits arising on a loan relationship or in respect of a related transaction (an acquisition or disposal, in whole or in part, of a loan relationship) to the extent that it is a party to the loan relationship at any time in an accounting period, or it enters into a related transaction for an unallowable purpose.

The definition of an unallowable purpose includes cases where the main purpose or one of the main purposes for the company being a party to the loan relationship or entering into the related transaction is to secure a tax advantage, whether for itself or any other person. See **54.52**.

55

Losses

Cross-references. See **39.2–39.18 GROUP RELIEF.**

Simon's Taxes. See **D1.11**.

See **17.3 CAPITAL GAINS** for the treatment of capital.

Introduction

[55.1] There are several ways of obtaining relief for losses of a company, depending on the source of them. The following table illustrates the various reliefs available:

Source of loss	Relief available			
	Current year	Carry back	Carry forward	Paragraph
Trading	y	y	y	**55.3, 55.4, 55.5**
UK Property	y	n	y	**55.7**

Source of loss	Relief available			
Overseas income	n	n	y	**55.8**
Miscellaneous income	y	n	y	**55.9**
Charges on income	n/a	n/a	n/a	**55.10**
Qualifying charitable donations	y	n	n	**55.10**

In addition, terminal loss relief may be available on cessation of trading, and under this losses may be carried back three years.

Loss relief must be claimed (with the exception of losses carried forward). Such claims must be made within two years of the end of the accounting period in which the loss was incurred (or such later period as Revenue and Customs may allow (**68 TIME LIMITS**)). The claim must normally be made in the company's corporation tax return.

[*CTA 2010, s 37(7) for trading losses; ICTA 1988, s 393A(10)*].

Losses eligible for relief

[55.2] A loss is not available for relief as a trading loss under **55.3** or **55.4** below unless:

(a) the trade is carried on in the exercise of functions conferred by or under any enactment (normally any public sector body); or
(b) for the accounting period in question, the trade was carried on on a commercial basis and with a view to the making of a profit either in the trade itself or in any larger undertaking of which it formed part.

A trade carried on so as to afford a 'reasonable expectation of profit' is treated as carried on with a view to making a profit. If there is a change in the manner of carrying on the trade in an accounting period, it is treated as having throughout that period been carried on in the same manner as at the end of that period.

[*CTA 2010, s 44; ICTA 1988, s 393A(3)(4); CTA 2009, Sch 1 para 111*].

These provisions are without prejudice to those in **55.22** below.

For the determination of the amount of losses see **66.8 RETURNS**.

Simon's Taxes. See **D1.1110**.

Trading losses — current year relief

[55.3] A company which 'carries on a trade' may claim that a loss incurred in that trade be set off against total profits (including chargeable gains) of the same accounting period. [*CTA 2010, s 37(1)(2)(3)(a); ICTA 1988, s 393A(1)(a)*]. The claim may also require that any unrelieved balance of the loss be carried back against total profits of the previous accounting period or periods so far as they fall (wholly or partly) within the period of 12 months ending with the start of the loss making period — see **55.4** below.

A trading loss is computed in the same way as trading income.

[*CTA 2009, s 47; CTA 2010, s 35(3); ICTA 1988, ss 393(7), 393A(9)(a)(b)*].

A company '*carries on a trade*' if it is within the charge to corporation tax in respect of that trade. 'Trade' includes, for this purpose, an office. [*CTA 2010, s 36(3)(4); ICTA 1988, ss 393(10), 393A(9)(c)*]. No claim under *CTA 2010, s 37* can, however, be made if in the loss-making accounting period the trade is carried on wholly outside the UK.

[*CTA 2010, s 37(5)(6); ICTA 1988, s 393A(3)*].

See also **55.2, 55.23** below for restrictions on this relief.

Note that *capital losses* cannot generally be set off against trading profits (but see **55.17** below regarding certain losses of investment companies on unquoted shares).

See **21.3 CLAIMS**. See also generally HMRC Company Taxation Manual, CTM04580 and CTM04590.

Simon's Taxes. See **D1.1102, D1.1104.**

Example

A Ltd is a trading company. Its results for the year ended 31 March 2012 show:

	£
Trading loss	(100,000)
Property income	30,000
Income from non-trading loan relationships	40,000
Chargeable gains	72,000
Management expenses	(20,000)
Qualifying charitable donations	(10,000)

The loss may be relieved as follows:

	£
Property income	30,000
Income from non-trading loan relationships	40,000
Chargeable gains	72,000
	142,000
Deduct Management expenses	(20,000)
	122,000
Deduct Trading loss	(100,000)
	22,000

Deduct Qualifying charitable donations	(10,000)
Taxable Total Profits	£12,000

Trading losses — carry-back relief

[55.4] Where a company incurs a trading loss in an accounting period and makes a claim to set the loss against other profits of that accounting period (see **55.3** above), the claim can also require that the balance of the loss not so relieved be carried back. Thus a claim for current year relief must be made first, where possible. [*CTA 2010, s 37(4)*].

The loss is then set against the profits (including chargeable gains) of preceding accounting periods falling wholly or partly within the period of twelve months immediately preceding the accounting period in which the loss is incurred. Profits of an accounting period beginning before, and ending within, that period are apportioned on a time basis. No relief is available for accounting periods ending earlier (but see below for the extension of the carry-back period in certain circumstances). The company must have been carrying on the same trade in the accounting period to which the loss is carried back, and must have done so not wholly within the UK.

The profits of each accounting period are treated as reduced by losses so carried back. Partial relief claims are not allowed, i.e. if carry-back of a loss is claimed, any part of the loss not relieved in the immediately preceding accounting period must be carried back to the period before that and so on, and losses arising in earlier accounting periods are relieved in priority to those of later periods.

If, for a single accounting period, losses of two or more different accounting periods are to be deducted under these provisions and those at **55.3** above, the deduction is made in the order in which the losses were made, earliest first.

The carry-back period is extended by virtue of *FA 2009, Sch 6* in the following cases.

- For a temporary period of two years (accounting periods ending after 23 November 2008 and before 24 November 2009 and ending after 23 November 2009 and before 24 November 2010) losses of those two twelve month periods may be set off against the total profits of the three years preceding the loss making period, up to a maximum of £50,000 in total for the accounting period(s) ending within each twelve month period. This is regardless of the number of accounting periods falling within each of those periods.
  Therefore, for example, if two or more loss making accounting periods ended after 23 November 2008 and before 24 November 2009, the total extended loss relief claims for those accounting periods together would be capped at £50,000. If the next accounting period ends after 23 November 2009 and before 24 November 2010 then a further £50,000 (maximum) of loss relief is available to be carried back three years in respect of that period.

If a loss-making accounting period falling within the above periods is less than 12 months, the £50,000 limit is pro-rated accordingly. Time apportionment is used to find the losses attributable to the specified period and the profits against which they may be set. The relief must be claimed in the company's corporation tax return or an amended return within two years of the end of the accounting period in which the loss being carried back arises.

It should be noted the extended carry back is in addition to the 12 month carry back rule described above. Therefore companies who do not use up their available losses in the relevant accounting periods under the general 12 month carry back rule (uncapped) will be able to carry back all or some of their remaining losses for a further two years (capped).

- A three year carry-back period applies to terminal losses (see **55.6** below).

See Example D below.

Excess qualifying charitable donations may not be carried back.

See **55.1** above for the time limits for making a claim.

[*CTA 2010, ss 37(3)(b)(4)(6)(8), 38, 40, 42, Sch 1 para 702, Sch 2 para 18; ICTA 1988, ss 393A(1)(b)(2)–(2C), 393B; FA 2009, s 23, Sch 6 para 3*].

See also **55.2** and **55.22** below.

Simon's Taxes. See **D1.1102, D1.1105**.

Trading losses — carry-forward relief

[55.5] Where a company which carries on a trade (see **55.3** above) suffers a loss in that trade in an accounting period, the default position is that those losses may be carried forward and set off against any 'profits of the trade' in succeeding accounting periods. So long as the company carries on the same trade, its trading profits from it are treated as reduced by the losses carried forward (or the balance of such losses not relieved in an earlier accounting period).

Prior to *CTA 2010*, pursuant to *ICTA 1988, s 393(9)*, when computing losses under these provisions, any excess charges on income incurred wholly and exclusively for the purposes of the trade would be treated as a trading expense (and could thus be carried forward). However, in practical terms, post the amendments to the definition of charges on income effective from 16 March 2005, 'trade' charges no longer existed (as such payments would be deductible as expenses of the trade). Therefore this provision was not re-written to *CTA 2010* as it was considered redundant.

Whether the same trade is being carried on in subsequent accounting periods is a question of fact with each situation being decided on its own facts.

For example, in the case of *Kawthar Consulting Ltd* before the Special Commissioners', a company's activities were described in its accounts as being:

- 'manufacturers, designers, importers, exporters and dealers in computers' for the years ended 31 December 1984 to 1987;
- 'manufacturers, designers, importers, exporters and dealers in computers and computer software' for the years from 1988 to 1997; and
- 'computer consultancy and the provision of management services' for the years from 1998 to 2001.

From 1987 to 1990 the company was mainly concerned with a large project for one client. After 1990, when the client went into administration, the company's turnover flagged until 1997 when another major contract was secured. (The project was run through another group company which provided the necessary software).

The company wanted to carry forward the losses arising in the earlier years to the 1998 accounting period, maintaining that it had throughout carried on the same trade, described as 'IT consultancy': it had never ceased trading nor changed from carrying on one trade to carrying on another.

It was held that there had been a change in the trade in the period after 1997 because:

- the involvement of the other group company constituted a major change in the manner in which company was carrying on its trading activities; and
- there had been an overall change in emphasis of activities towards consultancy services (as opposed to providing computer software etc.).

It was held, the earlier changes prior to 1997 simply amounted to organic developments in the nature of the activities over the years to 1997 and did not amount to a change in the trade of providing computer systems. *Kawthar Consulting Ltd v HMRC* [2005] SSCD 524 (SpC 477).

In *Rolls-Royce Motors Ltd*, a company (run as six divisions) ran into financial difficulties. As part of its recovery plan, the assets and undertakings of four of the divisions were transferred to a Government owned company, with the remaining two being transferred to a subsidiary of the original company. It was held that the subsidiary was not carrying on the same trade as the company before the transfer (as four of the six divisions were now in Government ownership) and therefore losses incurred before the transfer could not be offset against subsequent profits. *Rolls-Royce Motors Ltd v Bamford* Ch D 1976, 51 TC 319.

[*CTA 2010, s 45(1)–(4), Sch 2 para 17; ICTA 1988, s 393(1)*].

For this purpose, a loss is computed in the same way as trading income.

[*CTA 2009, s 47; CTA 2010, s 35(3); ICTA 1988, s 393(7)*].

See **55.2** above as regards determination of losses, and **39.5 GROUP RELIEF** for group relief interaction.

'*Profits of the trade*' means the profits of the trade which are chargeable to corporation tax. Where a loss is carried forward to a later accounting period the trading profits for which are insufficient to absorb it, interest and dividends which would be trading receipts but for having been otherwise subjected to tax (as in the case of banks, share dealers, and other companies carrying on financial business) are to be treated as profits of the trade.

[*CTA 2010, ss 45(5), 46; ICTA 1988, s 393(8); CTA 2009, Sch 1 para 110*].

It was held that for interest etc to constitute trading receipts it must arise from capital actively employed in the trade and, in a real and practical sense, at risk in the ordinary course of current trading. Interest etc. received on reserve funds was therefore excluded *Bank Line Ltd v CIR* CS 1974, 49 TC 307.

Similarly it was also held in another case that, when establishing whether interest etc constituted trading income, the crucial test was whether the investments were employed in the business in the year in question. The Court of Appeal, whose judgment was approved, considered decisive the facts that the liabilities against which the investments were provided were liabilities to third parties rather than customers, and that, in view of the long-term nature of the liabilities, the business could be carried on for a long period without maintaining a fund of investments at all. *Nuclear Electric plc v Bradley* HL 1996, 68 TC 670.

(HMRC Business Income Manual, BIM40801, 40805). For the general inclusion of trade interest in trading profits, see **54 LOAN RELATIONSHIPS**.

As to whether the successor into which the trade was hived down before sale to the eventual claimant was trading see *Barkers of Malton Ltd v HMRC* [2008] SSCD 884 (Sp C 689).

See **55.16** below for the carry forward of losses in a currency other than sterling where the company prepares its accounts in the foreign currency.

Simon's Taxes. See **D1.1102, D1.1106.**

Examples (A) Same year and carry forward

B Ltd has carried on the same trade for many years. The results for the years ended 31 January 2010, 2011 and 2012 are shown below.

	2010	2011	2012
	£	£	£
Trading profit/(loss)	(200,000)	100,000	50,000
Property income	15,000	10,000	20,000
Income from non-trading loan relationships	5,000	20,000	30,000
Chargeable gains	56,000	47,000	40,000
Management expenses	—	(90,000)	—

B Ltd may claim to set off the trading loss against other profits of the same accounting period. Assuming the claim is made (and that no claim is made to carry back the balance of the loss), the loss will be set off as follows.

		Loss memorandum
	£	£
Year ended 31 January 2010		
Trading loss		(200,000)
Property income	15,000	

Income from non-trading loan relationships	5,000	
Chargeable gains	56,000	
	76,000	
Deduct Other profits from trading loss	(76,000)	76,000
TTP	—	
		(124,000)
Year ended 31 January 2011		
Trading profits	100,000	
Deduct Loss brought forward	(100,000)	100,000
	—	(24,000)
Property income	10,000	
Income from non-trading loan relationships	20,000	
Chargeable gains	47,000	
	77,000	
Deduct Management charges (restricted)	(77,000)	
TTP	—	
		(24,000)
Management expenses carried forward £13,000		
Year ended 31 January 2012		
Trading income	50,000	
Deduct Loss brought forward	(24,000)	24,000
	26,000	
Property income	20,000	
Income from non-trading loan relationships	30,000	
Chargeable gains	40,000	
	116,000	
Deduct: management expenses	(13,000)	
TTP	£103,000	

(B) Same year and carry back

For the years ending 31 March 2011 and 31 March 2012, X Ltd has the following results.

	2011	2012
	£	£
Trading profit/(loss)	60,000	(200,000)

Property income	25,000	30,000
Income from non-trading loan relationships	15,000	10,000
Chargeable gains	15,000	45,000
Management expenses	(40,000)	(40,000)

The loss can be relieved as follows.

	£	Loss memorandum £
Year ended 31 March 2012		
Trading loss		(200,000)
Property income	30,000	
Income from non-trading loan relationships	10,000	
Chargeable gains	45,000	
	85,000	
Deduct Management expenses	(40,000)	
	45,000	
Deduct Trading loss	(45,000)	45,000
TTP	—	
		(155,000)
Year ended 31 December 2011		
Trading income	60,000	
Property income	25,000	
Income from non-trading loan relationships	15,000	
Chargeable gains	15,000	
	115,000	
Deduct Management expenses	(40,000)	
	75,000	
Deduct Loss carried back	(75,000)	75,000
TTP	—	
Loss carried forward		(£80,000)

(C) Accounting periods of different lengths

Y Ltd, which previously made up accounts to 31 December, changes its accounting date after the year ended 31 December 2010 to 30 September. Its results for the accounting periods to 31 December 2010, 30 September 2011 and 30 September 2012 are as follows.

	12 months 31.12.10	9 months 30.9.11	12 months 30.9.12
	£	£	£
Trading profit/(loss)	255,000	(90,000)	(420,000)
Income from non-trading loan relationships	25,000	30,000	—
Chargeable gains	40,000	—	20,000

Y Ltd makes all available loss relief claims so as to obtain relief against the earliest possible profits.

The computations are summarised as follows.

	12 months 31.12.10	9 months 30.9.11	12 months 30.9.12
	£	£	£
Trading income	255,000	—	—
Income from non-trading loan relationships	25,000	30,000	—
Chargeable gains	40,000	—	20,000
	320,000	30,000	20,000
Loss relief			
CTA 2010, s 37(3)(a)		(30,000)	(20,000)
CTA 2010, s 37(3)(b)	(140,000)		
TTP	£180,000	—	—

Loss memoranda

	9 months 30.9.11	12 months 30.9.12	Total
	£	£	£
Trading loss	90,000	420,000	510,000
Relieved against current year profits	(30,000)	(20,000)	(50,000)
Relieved by carry-back to y/e 31.12.10	(60,000)	(80,000)	(140,000)
Carried forward	Nil	£320,000	£320,000

Note

The 'specified period' for carry-back of the loss of the year ended 30 September 2012 is the twelve months from 1 October 2010 to 30 September 2011. Thus only one-quarter (£80,000) of the profits of the year ended 31 December 2010 are available for offset against the loss of the year ended 30 September 2012.

(D) Extended carry back of losses (FA 2009, Sch 6 para 3)

Y Ltd has income and losses as follows:

	£
Year 11 Trading income	80,000
Property income	20,000
Year 12 Trading income	12,000
Property income	20,000
Year 13 Trading loss	(100,000)
Property income	20,000
Year 14 Trading loss	(75,000)
Property income	20,000
Loss Memorandum	
Year 13	
(AP ends after 23.11.08 and before 24.11.09)	
Sideways loss relief *s 37(3)(a)* (property income)	20,000
Carry back one year *s 37(3)(b)* (Year 12)	32,000
Extended carry back *FA 2009, Sch 6* (Year 11)	48,000
	100,000
Year 14	
(AP ends after 23.11.09 and before 24.11.10)	
Sideways loss relief *s 37(3)(a)* (property income)	20,000
Extended carry back *FA 2009, Sch 6* (Year 11) — capped	50,000
	70,000
Unrelieved loss carry forward against future trading profits	5,000

Terminal losses — carry-back relief

[55.6] The relief described at **55.4** above (which permits the carry back of trading losses) also applies where a loss is incurred in the accounting period in which the trade ceases, except that losses incurred in the twelve months prior to cessation may be carried back to accounting periods ending within the three years preceding the start of the accounting period in which the loss is incurred (with losses of any accounting period falling partly within and partly outside that twelve-month period being apportioned on a time basis).

Where the final twelve months straddles two accounting periods this means the part of the terminal loss which arises in the earlier accounting period may be carried back to accounting periods which end more than three years prior to the start of the twelve month terminal loss period.

Claims to relief must be made within two years of the end of the accounting period in which the loss is incurred, or within such further period as HMRC may allow (for which see **55.1** above).

The enhanced carry back of losses does not apply if, when a company ceases to carry on a trade on or after 21 May 2009, any of the activities of the trade continue to be carried on by a person or persons not within the charge to corporation tax and the cessation of trade is part of a scheme or arrangement with a main purpose of securing the enhanced carry-back.

[*CTA 2010, ss 39, 41, Sch 2 para 20; ICTA 1988, s 393A; FA 2009, s 62*].

See also HMRC Manual CTM04520 and CTM04530.

Example

A Ltd ceased to trade on 31 July. Recent results were as follows:

	12 months to 30 Nov	12 months to 30 Nov	12 months to 30 Nov	12 months to 30 Nov	8 months to 31 July
	Year 1	Year 2	Year 3	Year 4	Year 5
	£	£	£	£	£
Trading result	19,500	15,000	10,000	(15,000)	(40,000)
Schedule A	1,125	1,125	1,250	600	—
Chargeable gain	—	7,000	—	—	2,500

The maximum amount of the loss which can be treated as a terminal loss is the loss for the 12 months to 31 July: Year 5, as follows:

	£
8 months to 31 July: Year 5	40,000
4 months to 30 November: Year 4 (4/12 × 15,000)	5,000
Available for terminal loss relief	45,000

However, part of the loss will be relieved against general profits of the current or previous accounting period, in this case, leaving a balance of £40,650 (see loss memo below) available for offset as a terminal loss.

The loss arising in the four months to 30 November: Year 4 which forms part of the terminal loss may be carried back to accounting periods ending within the three years preceding the start of this accounting period (1 December: Year 3). Thus this part of the terminal loss may be carried back to the period ending 30 November:Year 1. However, the loss should be set off against profits arising in later periods first (on a LIFO basis).

The terminal loss arising in the 8 month period to 31 July:Year 5 may be carried back to accounting periods preceding the start of this loss making period (1 December:Year 4). Thus this loss may be carried back to the accounting period ending 30 November:Year 2.

The earlier part of the terminal loss is used first as losses of earlier accounting periods are relieved before the losses of later periods.

Therefore, the losses will be relieved as follows:

	12 months to 30 Nov Year 1	12 months to 30 Nov Year 2	12 months to 30 Nov Year 3	12 months to 30 Nov Year 4	8 months to 31 July Year 5
	£	£	£	£	£
Trading result	19,500	15,000	10,000	—	—
Schedule A	1,125	1,125	1,250	600	—
Chargeable gain	—	7,000	—	—	2,500
	20,625	23,125	11,250	600	2,500
Less: Loss relief					
Current period				(600)	(2,500)
Carried back			(11,250)		
Terminal		(3,150)			
		(19,975)			
TTP	20,625	Nil	Nil	Nil	Nil

Loss memo		12 months to 30 Nov Year 4	8 months to 31 July Year 5
		£	£
Loss for period		15,000	40,000
Set against:	Profits of same period *s 37(3)(a)*	(600)	(2,500)
	Profits of previous period *s 37(3)(b)*	(11,250)	—
Balance available as terminal loss (total £40,650)		3,150	37,500
Terminal loss relief *s 39*		(3,150)	(19,975)
Unrelieved		Nil	19,975

In *Electronics Ltd v HM Inspector of Taxes* [2005] SSCD 512 (Sp C 476), a claim for terminal loss relief on the closure of two of the company's six divisions was denied on the basis that the trade of all six divisions was a single trade. The Special Commissioners considered the trade of all divisions to be too similar to be broken down into discrete categories and that the place of operational management was not decisive in determining whether there was more than one trade.

HMRC may allow a claim for carry-back of losses from the final period of account of a company which has collapsed despite no formal accounts having been prepared for the period if it is apparent from all the facts that the claimed losses will be significantly less than the losses actually suffered by the company, even after any possible adjustment of the computations for capital items, disallowable expenditure, balancing charges, etc. See HMRC Company Taxation Manual, CTM04570.

Simon's Taxes. See **D1.1102, D1.1105.**

Property business losses

UK property businesses

[55.7] Losses incurred in a property income business are automatically:

- set against total profits of the same accounting period. (Total profits means profits from any source, including chargeable gains); or
- carried forward, if they cannot be used against total profits. Such losses become a property income business loss of the subsequent period and are available for offset against total profits or further carried forward if not utilised, for so long as the company continues to carry on the property business. Relief is, however, denied for non-commercial losses in the same circumstances as apply in the case of trading losses — see **55.2** above.

There are no rules covering the interaction of property income business losses and trading losses carried forward. The order of offset will therefore be decided by the company and based on its individual circumstances.

Lettings treated as a trade under the provisions for UK furnished holiday lettings (see **62.6 PROPERTY INCOME**) are excluded from the company's UK property business for the purposes of the above provisions. Losses from such lettings are instead dealt with under the trade loss provisions (see **55.3** onwards above). However, pursuant to the changes in *FA 2011* the loss relief allowed for furnished holiday lettings under *CTA 2010* is restricted — the relief for losses against total profits (under *CTA 2010, ss 37–44*, and *ss 48–54*) is removed for accounting periods ending on or after 1 April 2011. Losses can be carried forward under *CTA 2010, s 45* and set against profits of the same trade.

[*CTA 2010, ss 62, 63, 65 (as amended by FA 2011); ICTA 1988, s 392A; CTA 2009, Sch 1 para 108*].

See also **51.6 INVESTMENT COMPANIES AND INVESTMENT BUSINESS** for the conversion of UK property business losses to management expenses where an investment company ceases to carry on a UK business, and also **51.9** for restrictions applying to property business losses on the change of ownership of an investment company or a company with investment business.

Overseas property businesses

Losses from overseas property businesses (see **62 PROPERTY INCOME**) are available for carry forward against future profits from the same business. This provision is, however, subject to the same commerciality test as applies to UK property business losses (see above). Before *CTA 2009* took effect, overseas property businesses were taxed and losses relievable under *Schedule D, Case V* (see **55.8** below), but this label has now been removed.

See also the provisions with regard to losses of an EEA furnished holiday lettings business which is treated as a trade and post *FA 2011* (new *CTA 2010, s 67A*) has similar restrictions as to trade loss relief as outlined for a UK furnished holiday lettings business.

[*CTA 2010, ss 66, 67, 67A (as inserted by FA 2011); ICTA 1988, s 392B; CTA 2009, Sch 1 para 109*].

See generally **62 PROPERTY INCOME.**

Overseas income losses

[55.8] Losses from overseas trades can only be carried forward and set against future profits of the same trade.

Relief is not available for losses arising on other overseas sources, apart from overseas property businesses — see **55.7** above.

Miscellaneous losses

[55.9] Losses on transactions within the charge to corporation tax under any of the miscellaneous income provisions listed at *CTA 2010, s 1173* (previously *ICTA 1988, s 834A*) may be set off against income from such transactions in the same or any subsequent accounting period. Such income is then treated as reduced by so much of the loss as has not been relieved in an earlier accounting period. Before *CTA 2009* took effect, such transactions were within *Schedule D, Case VI*, but that label has now been removed.

[*CTA 2010, s 1173; ICTA 1988, s 396; FA 2007, s 57; CTA 2009, Sch 1 para 112*].

Losses must be set against the first arising profits. No claims are required in this respect.

These provisions do not apply to losses in relation to:

- premiums, leases at an undervalue etc. (see **62.9–62.12**);
- certain exchange losses (see **30.30**); and
- miscellaneous profits of non-distributing offshore funds (for disposals on or after 1 April 2007).

Subject to any express provision to the contrary, the same rules apply in calculating miscellaneous losses as apply in calculating the corresponding miscellaneous income. [*CTA 2009, s 1306*].

Companies in partnership

Where tax in respect of any of the profits of a partnership of which a company is a member (and to which arrangements as outlined in **55.24** below apply) is chargeable on miscellaneous income, the company's share is treated as arising from a trade carried on by the partnership and any allowance under *CAA 2001, s 19* or *CAA 1990, s 61(1)* is treated as made in taxing that trade.

Restrictions are applicable to the loss relief available to a corporate limited partner or a corporate partner of an LLP. See further *CTA 2010, ss 55–61*, also **58.9** and **58.10** partnerships.

[*CAA 2001, Sch 2 para 21; CTA 2010, ss 55–61*].

Charges on income

[55.10] Prior to *CTA 2010*, pursuant to *ICTA 1988, s 393(9)*, where charges on income exceeded the profits of the accounting period in which they were paid, it was possible to treat them as a trading loss available for carry forward against trading income of subsequent accounting periods, where such charges had been incurred wholly and exclusively for the purposes of the trade — i.e. they were 'trade' charges. Where the company also had an actual trading loss to carry forward, this could be increased by the charges. No claim was required in this respect.

The maximum amount which could be utilised in this way was the lower of the:

- excess charges for the accounting period; and
- trade charges paid during the accounting period.

Any charges which could not be relieved in this way were lost.

However, in practical terms, 'trade' charges disappeared after the amendments made to *ICTA 1988, s 338A* with effect to payments made on or after 16 March 2005. Since then charges made wholly and exclusively for the purposes of a trade are deductible as expenses of the trade. Charges on income were thus limited to certain donations to charity.

On this basis the provisions of *ICTA 1988, s 393(9)* were considered redundant and were not replicated in the re-write process to *CTA 2010*. See further the explanatory note to *CTA 2010, s 45*.

Charges on income have been replaced by the provisions relating to 'qualifying charitable donations' which are found at *Part 6 CTA 2010* – Charitable Donations Relief (*CTA 2010, s 189 et seq.*). Any current year excess of donations over a company's taxable total profits cannot be carried back or forward and will be lost unless a claim for group relief can be made.

See further chapter **61 PROFIT COMPUTATIONS** at **61.11**. See also HMRC Manual CTM09010 and CTM09100.

Special situations

Company reconstructions

[55.11] The following provisions apply where, on a company ('the predecessor') ceasing to carry on a trade, another company ('the successor') begins to carry it on, and:

(a) on, or within two years after, the cessation, the trade is at least 75% 'owned' by the same persons as owned a similar interest within a year before the cessation; and
(b) throughout the periods referred to above, the trade is carried on by a company which is within the charge to tax in respect of it.

References to 'the trade' include any other trade comprising the activities of the original trade.

[*CTA 2010, ss 939–951; ICTA 1988, s 343(1)*].

'*Ownership*'. A trade carried on by two or more persons is treated as owned by them in the shares in which they are entitled to the profits.

A trade or an interest therein belonging to trustees (other than for charitable or public purposes) is treated as owned by the persons entitled to the trust's income for the time being.

A trade or an interest therein belonging to a company shall (if necessary to bring the provisions of *CTA 2010, Pt 22 Ch 1; ICTA 1988, s 343* into effect) be treated as owned by:

- the beneficial owners of the 'ordinary share capital' of the company in proportion to their holdings; or
- the company's 'parent company'; or
- the beneficial owners of the 'ordinary share capital' of the parent company in proportion to their holdings; or
- the person or body of persons controlling a corporate shareholder within the previous three categories.

'*Ordinary share capital*' is as defined in *CTA 2010, s 1119; ICTA 1988, s 832(1)*.

A '*parent company*' is one owning, directly or indirectly, 75% of the ordinary share capital of the company (determined in accordance with *CTA 2010, ss 1155–1157; ICTA 1988, s 838(5)–(10)*) and which is not also a subsidiary of a third company.

In determining for the purposes of (a) and (b) above to what extent a trade belongs to the same persons, persons who are 'relatives' and the persons from time to time entitled to the income under a trust are respectively treated as a single person. '*Relative*' means spouse, civil partner, ancestor, lineal descendant, brother or sister. There is no requirement that the interest of the members of a group of persons in the predecessor and successor companies should be in the same proportions, so long as the same persons meet the requisite 75% ownership test.

[*CTA 2010, ss 941–947; ICTA 1988, s 344; SI 2005 No 3229, Reg 66*].

Example 1

Mr Z is the beneficial owner of the whole of the ordinary share capital of X Ltd and Y Ltd. X Ltd transfers its trade to Y Ltd which then continues to carry on the trade; the succession rules at *CTA 2010, Pt 22 Ch 1* apply to the transfer.

Example 2

A Ltd and B Ltd are both 90% subsidiaries of a non-resident company, C Ltd; the succession rules at *CTA 2010, Pt 22 Ch 1* cover a transfer of trade by M Ltd to N Ltd.

Example 3

The ordinary share capitals of P Ltd and S Ltd are owned as follows:

	P Ltd	*S Ltd*
Mr A	40	30
Mr B	25	35
Mr C	10	5

Mrs C (C's wife)	–	10
Others	25	20
	100	100

The succession rules at *CTA 2010, Pt 22 Ch 1* cover the transfer of a trade from P Ltd to S Ltd, or vice versa. The differing interests of the persons controlling 75% of the ordinary share capital are not relevant, and Mr and Mrs C are treated as a single person.

The following modifications are made to the general loss relief provisions:

- the special reliefs for terminal losses (see **55.6** above) are not available to the predecessor. [*CTA 2010, s 944; ICTA 1988, s 343(4A)*];
- trading losses may be carried forward (see **55.5** above) against income arising from the same trade to the successor, as if there had been no succession;
- losses of the trade transferred arising in subsequent periods cannot be carried back to a period before the transfer of the trade.

Where the amount of the 'relevant liabilities' immediately before a transfer exceeds the open market value of 'relevant assets' at that time, the losses which may be carried forward are reduced or extinguished by the amount of that excess.

'*Relevant assets*' are;

- assets which were vested in the predecessor immediately before the transfer, and which were not transferred to the successor; and
- consideration given to the predecessor by the successor in respect of the change of company carrying on the trade (but the assumption by the successor of any liabilities of the predecessor is not treated as consideration for this purpose).

'*Relevant liabilities*' are liabilities outstanding and vested in the predecessor immediately before the transfer, and not transferred to the successor. However, the following are excluded:

- share capital;
- share premium account;
- reserves; or
- 'relevant loan stock' of the predecessor unless such liability arose on a conversion of a liability not representing any such item within one year before the transfer.

As an anti-avoidance measure, where a liability was transferred to the successor, but the creditor agreed to accept part payment in settlement of the whole, the balance of the liability is treated as not having been transferred to the successor.

Any assets or liabilities apportioned to a successor on a previous application of these provisions (see below) are excluded.

In a First Tier Tribunal case it was held that the successor company must assume legal responsibility for the liabilities of the predecessor, otherwise such liabilities will be taken as remaining with the predecessor, which will reduce the loss available to the successor company. In this instance the successor company had merely loaned the predecessor funds to discharge its liabilities, instead of assuming responsibility for them, and therefore the successor was not able to use the trading losses post the transfer of trade. *Houston Cox Interiors Ltd v HMRC* ([2010] UKFTT 510 (TC) TC00765 – 21 Oct 2010).

'*Relevant loan stock*' is any loan stock or similar security, secured or unsecured, but excluding any in respect of which, at the time the liability giving rise to it was incurred, the creditor was carrying on a trade of lending money. The amount of a liability representing relevant loan stock which is not a relevant liability, but which is secured on a relevant asset, is deducted from the value of the asset for the purposes of this provision.

[*CTA 2010, ss 944, 945; ICTA 1988, ss 343(3)(4), 344(5)–(12)*].

Capital allowances are given to, and balancing charges made on, the successor as if there had been no succession (and losses are calculated accordingly unless the successor is a 'dual resident investing company' (see **39.23 GROUP RELIEF**) and begins to carry on the trade after 31 March 1987. [*CTA 2010, s 948; ICTA 1988, s 343(2)*]. Where the trade is transferred during the currency of accounting periods of the companies concerned:

(i) writing-down allowances are calculated on the 'pool' at the end of the transferee's accounting period, and apportioned on a time basis between the periods in which each company carried on the trade;
(ii) annual investment allowance and first-year allowances are given to the company incurring the expenditure; and
(iii) balancing adjustments are made on the company carrying on the trade at the relevant time.

(CCAB Guidance Notes TR 500, 10 March 1983). See also HMRC Capital Allowances Manual, CA 15400.

An anti-avoidance measure, with effect for cessations on or after 22 November 2006, counters the use of reconstructions of companies carrying on a 'business of leasing plant and machinery' (see **5.27 ANTI-AVOIDANCE**) to avoid tax. Where the predecessor and successor companies carry on the business otherwise than in partnership, for capital allowances purposes, they are not treated as the same person under *CTA 2010, s 948; ICTA 1988, s 343(2)* unless the principal company of the group is the same before and after the change, or, from 21 March 2007, in the case of a consortium, the percentage of the successor held by the principal company is the same before and after the reconstruction. Where the parties are carrying on the leasing business in partnership, the predecessor has to stop trading on the date of transfer for *CTA 2010, s 948; ICTA 1988, s 343(2)* to apply. The effect of this is to ensure that the companies share the same principal company for the purposes of *FA 2006, Sch 10* (sale of lessor company carrying on business of leasing plant or machinery — see **5.27** *et seq.* **ANTI-AVOIDANCE**).

If *CTA 2010, s 948; ICTA 1988, s 343(2)* does not apply to a transfer, for capital allowances purposes there is deemed to be a disposal by the predecessor of the leasing assets at market value and an acquisition by the successor at that value on the date of cessation of the trade.

[*CTA 2010, s 950; ICTA 1988, s 343A; FA 2007 Sch 6, para 1*].

Repeated successions are each treated in accordance with the above provisions, provided that the conditions in (a) and (b) above are satisfied on each occasion.

Where the successor takes over part of the predecessor's trade, or where the activities to which it succeeds are carried on as part only of the successor's existing trade, the transferred activities are treated as a separate trade and receipts, expenses, etc. are apportioned as may be just. See *Falmer Jeans Ltd v Rodin* Ch D, 1990, 63 TC 55 for a case in which this provision was held to apply.

See also **55.12** and **55.13** below.

Simon's Taxes. See **D6.315–D6.332.**

Example

A Ltd and B Ltd are two wholly-owned subsidiaries of X Ltd. All are within the charge to corporation tax, although A Ltd has accumulated trading losses brought forward and unrelieved of £200,000 and has not paid tax for several years. As part of a group reorganisation, A Ltd's trade is transferred to B Ltd on 31 October 2011.

A Ltd's balance sheet immediately before the transfer is as follows.

	£		£
Share capital	100,000	Property	90,000
Debenture secured		Plant	20,000
on property	50,000	Stock	130,000
Group loan	10,000	Trade debtors	120,000
Trade creditors	300,000		
Bank overdraft	60,000		
	520,000		
Deficit on reserves	(160,000)		
	£360,000		£360,000

Book values represent the approximate open market values of assets. B Ltd takes over the stock and plant to continue the trade, paying £150,000 to A Ltd and taking over £15,000 of trade creditors relating to stock. A Ltd is to collect outstanding debts and pay remaining creditors.

A Ltd's 'relevant assets' are:

	£
Freehold property (£90,000 – £50,000)	40,000
Trade debtors	120,000
Consideration from B Ltd	150,000
	£310,000

A Ltd's 'relevant liabilities' are:

	£
Bank overdraft	60,000
Group loan	10,000
Trade creditors (£300,000 – £15,000)	285,000
	£355,000

Tax losses transferable with trade:
£200,000 – £(355,000 – 310,000) = £155,000

Privatisation

[55.12] BT plc is treated for all purposes of corporation tax as being the same person as British Telecommunications, to whose business it succeeded on privatisation, except that it is not regarded by virtue of the above provision alone as a nationalised undertaking within *TCGA 1992, s 170(12)*. Losses arising in the Post Office non-telecommunications business prior to their separation cannot be carried forward to the successor company.

Surplus ACT arising to the successor company on privatisation may not be carried back to a period before the transfer (*CIR v Aberdeen Milk Co Ltd* CS, 73 TC 563).

Predecessor company	**Reference**
British Telecommunications	*British Telecommunications Act 1981, s 82; Telecommunications Act 1984, s 72*
British Airways Board and the National Freight Corporation	*ICTA 1988, s 513 – now spent*
British Airports Authority	*British Airports Act 1986, s 77*
British Gas Corporation	*Gas Act 1986, s 60*
British Steel Corporation	*British Steel Act 1988, s 11*
General Practice Finance Corporation	*Health and Medicines Act 1988, s 6*
Statutory port undertakings	*Ports Act 1991, s 35*
National research development council and National enterprise Board	*British Technology Group Act 1991, s 12*
Milk marketing boards	*Agriculture Act 1993, Sch 2 Pt 1*
Northern Ireland Airports Ltd	*Finance Act 1996, s 203*
	Finance Act 1994, Sch 25
Atomic Energy Authority	*Atomic Energy Authority Act 1995, Sch 3*

Change in ownership of a company

[55.13] Special rules apply if there is a 'change in the ownership of a company' and:

(a) within any period of three years in which the change in ownership occurs there is a 'major change in the nature or conduct of a trade' carried on by the company; or
(b) the change in ownership occurs at any time after the scale of activities in a trade carried on by the company has become small or negligible and before any considerable revival in the trade.

[*CTA 2010, s 673(1)–(3); ICTA 1988, s 768(1)*].

There is a '*change in the ownership of a company*' if:

(i) a single person acquires as beneficial owner more than half the ordinary share capital (see *CTA 2010, s 1119*) of the company; or
(ii) two or more persons each acquire as beneficial owner a holding of at least 5% (or an addition to their existing holding sufficient to raise it to 5%) of the company's ordinary share capital, and the combined holdings exceed half that capital. Acquisitions by, and holdings of, **CONNECTED PERSONS** (**25**) are treated as a single acquisition or holding.

See, however, **39.27 GROUP RELIEF** for the interaction of these provisions and the demerger provisions of *CTA 2010, ss 1073–1099; ICTA 1988, ss 213–218.*

In comparing a person's holdings at any two dates, he is to be treated at the later date as having acquired whatever he did not hold at the earlier date, irrespective of intervening acquisitions and disposals. Comparisons are made in percentage terms throughout.

Acquisitions of shares on death are left out of account as is any gift which was unsolicited and made without regard to these provisions.

The date of any acquisition corresponds with the date of the contract of sale, or with the assignment of the benefit of that contract, or with the acquisition of the option to acquire, as the case may be.

Where the existence of extraordinary rights or powers renders ownership of the ordinary share capital an inappropriate test of change of ownership, holdings of all kinds, or of any particular kind, of share capital, voting power or any other special kind of power may be taken into account instead.

A change in the direct ownership of a company is ignored if, immediately before and after the change, it continues to be a 'qualifying 75% subsidiary' of the same company.

A '*qualifying 75% subsidiary*' is a '*75% subsidiary*' (defined under *CTA 2010, s 1154* by reference to direct or indirect ownership of at least 75% of ordinary share capital), with an additional requirement that the parent company would be beneficially entitled to at least 75% of any profits available for distribution to equity holders and of any assets so available on a winding-up (see **39.4 GROUP RELIEF**).

No event or situation preceding a change of ownership to which these provisions have applied is to be taken into account in ascertaining whether a subsequent change has taken place.

HMRC may consider that the ordinary share capital test is not appropriate where persons have extraordinary rights. In this situation, an alternative basis for quantifying ownership may be proposed.

For the interaction of these provisions and the demergers provisions see **39.27 GROUP RELIEF.**

[*CTA 2010, ss 719–721, 723–726; ICTA 1988, ss 768, 768A, 769*].

Major change

[55.14] A '*major change in the nature or conduct of a trade*' includes a major change in the type of property dealt in, or the services or facilities provided, in the trade, or in customers, outlets or markets, even if that change is the result of a gradual process which began outside the three-year period. A '*change*' for these purposes is to be decided by a qualitative test but in determining whether a change is '*major*' the change should not be viewed in isolation but a quantitative test of fact and degree should be applied (*Willis v Peeters Picture Frames Ltd* CA (NI) 1982, 56 TC 436). [*CTA 2010, s 673(4); ICTA 1988, s 768(4)*]. The cessation of a trade is unlikely to be regarded as a major change in the nature or conduct of the trade, although the events leading up to it may be so; the interposition of a holding company between a company and its shareholders usually represents a change in ownership, but does not represent a major change in the nature or conduct of a trade carried on by the company.

HMRC Statement of Practice, SP 10/91 (as revised) sets out other factors to which HMRC will have regard in considering whether there has been a major change in the nature or conduct of a trade or business. This applies for the purposes of these provisions and for the purposes of *CTA 2010, ss706–712; ICTA 1988, s 767A* (company purchase schemes, see **59.11 PAYMENT OF TAX**), *CTA 2010, ss 677–691* (change in ownership of investment companies, see **51.9 INVESTMENT COMPANIES AND INVESTMENT BUSINESS**), *TCGA 1992, Sch 7A* (restriction on pre-entry losses, see **38.14 GAINS AND LOSS BUYING**) and *SI 1999 No 358* (carry forward of shadow ACT, see **3.8 ADVANCE CORPORATION TAX — SHADOW ACT**).

These would include changes in factors such as location of the business premises, identity of suppliers, management or staff, methods of manufacture, or pricing or purchasing policies, in so far as they are indicative of a major change. It will not be regarded as a major change in the nature or conduct of a trade where all that has happened is that changes have been made to increase efficiency, or to keep pace with developing technology in the industry concerned or with developing management techniques, or to rationalise the product range by withdrawing unprofitable items and, possibly, replacing them with new items of a related kind. Although it is acknowledged that every case rests on its own facts, examples are cited where a change would *not* be regarded as major.

The following examples are cited by HMRC, although they do acknowledge that every case will be decided on its particular facts.

Major change	**No major change**
A company operating a dealership in saloon cars switches to operating a dealership in tractors (a major change in the type of property dealt in).	A company manufacturing kitchen fitments in three obsolescent factories moves production to one new factory (increasing efficiency).
A company owning a public house switches to operating a discotheque in the same, but converted, premises (a major change in the services or facilities provided).	A company manufacturing kitchen utensils replaces enamel with plastic, or a company manufacturing time pieces replaces mechanical with electronic components (keeping pace with developing technology).
A company fattening pigs for their owners switches to buying pigs for fattening and resale (a major change in the nature of the trade, being a change from providing a service to being a primary producer).	A company manufacturing both filament and fluorescent lamps (of which filament lamps form the greater part of the output) concentrates solely on filament lamps (a rationalisation of product range without a major change in the type of property dealt in).
A company switches from investing in quoted shares to investing in real property for rent (a change in the nature of investments held).	A company whose business consists of making and holding investments in UK quoted shares and securities makes changes to its portfolio of quoted shares and securities (not a change in the nature of investments held).

Where these provisions have to be considered in relation to the transfer of part of a trade which is to be treated as the transfer of a separate trade under *CTA 2010, s 951; ICTA 1988, s 343(8)* (see **55.11** above), SP 10/91 indicates that the transfer of the part-trade will not of itself be regarded as a major change in the nature or conduct of either the part-trade transferred or that retained. Instead, each of the trades (or the relevant part of a combined trade) after the transfer will be compared with the equivalent part of the combined trade before the transfer. In cases where the transfer occurs *after* the relevant change of ownership, however, it may be necessary to consider whether it involves a major change in the nature or conduct of the undivided trade as it subsisted at the date of the change in ownership, and in such cases it may be appropriate to regard the transfer as constituting a major change, depending on the surrounding circumstances. HMRC will not, however, take this point if there was no other major change in either the original trade, or the parts into which it was divided, in the relevant period.

Effect of provisions

[55.15] Where these provisions apply, no relief may be claimed under *CTA 2010, s 45* (previously *ICTA 1988, s 393*) against the income or other profits of an accounting period ending after the change of ownership for losses incurred in an accounting period beginning before the change. This provision applies equally to UK property business losses.

Relief may similarly not be claimed under *CTA 2010, ss 37, 42* (previously *ICTA 1988, s 393A(1)*) for a loss incurred in an accounting period ending after the change to be set against profits of an accounting period beginning before the change. For these purposes only, the accounting period in which the change takes place is treated as two separate accounting periods, ending with the date of the change and beginning with the following date respectively. The profits or losses of the whole period are apportioned to each on a time basis, or by such other method as is just and reasonable.

[*CTA 2010, s 674; ICTA 1988, ss 768(1)–(3), 768A*].

Where a pre-change of ownership loss includes unrelieved capital allowances, those capital allowances are treated as not having been given when calculating any balancing charges on an asset owned at the date of the change in ownership and sold later. (In determining whether a capital allowance could have been relieved it is to be assumed that relief would have been given for the capital allowance in priority to any loss.)

This provision is necessary because the cancellation of losses does not affect underlying computations of capital allowances. This is because the trade itself does not cease. Without this provision a company which, at the time of the change of ownership, owns assets on which capital allowances have been given could effectively be penalised twice by:

- disallowance of any unused capital allowances included in the losses disallowed; and
- a balancing charge when the assets are disposed of.

See CTM06430.

[*CTA 2010, s 675; ICTA 1988, s 768(6)(7)*].

Company reconstructions

Where the change in ownership takes place after a company reconstruction under *CTA 2010, s 944* (see **55.11** above), for the purposes of the restriction on carry-forward of relief under *CTA 2010, s 674(2)*, references to the trade in the above provisions *include* the trade as carried on by the predecessor, and relief for losses incurred before the company reconstruction are restricted in the same way as losses incurred after the company reconstruction.

[CTA *2010, s 676; ICTA 1988, s 768(5)*].

Assessment

As the operation of these provisions can depend on events occurring after the change of ownership, the time limit for making assessments is extended (where relevant) to six years after the latest relevant event (being an event occurring not later than three years after the change of ownership).

[*CTA 2010, s 727; ICTA 1988, s 768(8)*].

Powers to obtain information

HMRC may, by notice in writing, require any person who is the registered owner of shares, stock or securities of a company, to state whether he is the beneficial owner, and, if not, to supply the name and address of the person or persons on whose behalf he holds them.

[*CTA 2010, s 728; ICTA 1988, s 768(9)*].

Property business losses

Where either (a) or (b) above applies in relation to a company carrying on a UK property business or an overseas property business (see **62 PROPERTY INCOME**), so that the provisions described apply, or would apply, in relation to trading losses, a similar restriction applies to prevent property business losses (see **62 PROPERTY INCOME**) incurred before the change being set against profits arising after the change.

[*CTA 2010, ss 704, 705; ICTA 1988, ss 768D, 769; CTA 2009, Sch 1 para 223*].

General

These provisions are intended to prevent the purchase of companies with accumulated trading or property losses, in order to claim relief against the purchaser's trading profits and vice versa.

See also **3.8 ADVANCE CORPORATION TAX — SHADOW ACT, 51.9 INVESTMENT COMPANIES AND INVESTMENT BUSINESS** and **59.11 PAYMENT OF TAX.**

Simon's Taxes. See D1.1113.

Companies accounting in foreign currency

[55.16] There are provisions which aim to ensure that, where a company has had a functional currency other than sterling in a period in which a loss was incurred, or in a period against the profits of which a loss is to be relieved, the loss and the profits are translated at the same rate of exchange. The provisions apply to profits and losses arising in accounting periods commencing on or after 29 December 2007.

The general rule is that, in computing the profits or losses of a company which prepares accounts in a foreign currency, translation into sterling is to be made at:

- the average exchange rate for the accounting period concerned;
- at the appropriate spot rate; or
- on a just and reasonable basis derived from a number of spot rates.

See **36.7 FOREIGN CURRENCY**. This rule is subject to the provisions below.

[*CTA 2010, s 11; FA 1993, ss 92D, 92E(4); FA 2009, Sch 18, para 5*].

Where a loss has to be translated into its sterling equivalent in order to calculate a 'carried-back amount' (i.e. a trading loss carried back under *CTA 2010, s 37*, a deficit of an insurance company carried back under *CTA 2009, s 389(2)* or a non-trading loan relationship deficit carried back under *CTA 2009, s 459(1)(b)*), one of three rules applies.

- If the tax calculation currencies (i.e. the currencies used to calculate the company's profits or losses before translation into sterling) are the same in the accounting period of loss or deficit and the period to which the carried-back amount is to be carried back, the same rate of exchange is used as that required under *CTA 2009, s 11* to be used in calculating the profit against which the amount is to be set off.
- If the later tax calculation currency is not the same as that for the earlier period, and the earlier currency is sterling, the rate to be used is the spot exchange for the last day of the 'relevant accounting period'.
- If the two currencies are different and neither is sterling, the carried-back amount must be converted into the tax calculation currency for the earlier period at the spot rate of exchange for the last day of the relevant account period before being translated into sterling at the same rate as the profits against which the loss is to be set are required to be translated under *CTA 2009, s 11*.

For this purpose, the '*relevant accounting period*' is the most recent accounting period of the company before that in which the carried-back amount arises in which the tax calculation currency is the same as the tax calculation currency of the period to which the amount is to be carried back.

[*CTA 2010, ss 12, 17(2)(5); FA 1993, s 92DA; FA 2009, Sch 18*].

Where a UK resident company prepares its accounts in accordance with generally accepted accounting practice ('GAAP') in sterling or in another currency, but identifies its functional currency as sterling, a loss arises on a generally accepted accounting practice basis for corporation tax, which is to be a carried-back amount and the tax calculation currency for the period to which the loss is to be carried back is not sterling, the loss must first be translated into that earlier tax calculation currency at spot rate for the last day of the relevant accounting period before being translated into sterling at the rate required under *CTA 2010, s 11* to be used to convert the profits against which the loss is to be set.

[*CTA 2010, s 14; FA 1993, s 92DC; FA 2009, Sch 18*].

For 'carried-forward amounts', one of the following three rules for translation applies.

- Where the tax calculation currency is the same in the period in which the amount arises and the period to which it is carried forward, the amount must be translated at the same rate as applies under *CTA 2010, s 11* to the profits against which it is to be set off.
- Where the earlier tax calculation currency is not the same as the later currency and the later currency is sterling, the spot rate for the first day of the 'relevant accounting period' must be used.

- Where the earlier tax calculation currency is not the same as the later currency and the later currency is not sterling, the carried-forward amount must first be translated into the later currency at the spot rate of exchange for the first day of the relevant accounting period, and then into sterling at the same rate as that applied to the profits against which the amount is to be set off.

For this purpose, the '*relevant accounting period*' means the first accounting period after the period in which the carried-forward amount arose when the tax calculation currency became the tax calculation currency of the period to which the amount is to be carried forward.

'*Carried-forward amounts*' are trade losses carried forward under *CTA 2010, s 45*; UK property business losses carried forward under *CTA 2010, s 62(5)* or *s 63(3)*; overseas property losses carried forward under *CTA 2010, s 66(3)*; losses from miscellaneous transactions carried forward under *CTA 2010, s 91(6)*; expenses and other losses of insurance companies carried forward; non-trading loan relationship deficits carried forward under *CTA 2009, s 753(3)*; non-trading losses on intangible fixed assets carried forward under *CTA 2009, 753(3)*; expenses relating to patent income carried forward under *CTA 2009, s 925(3)*; and management expenses carried forward under *CTA 2009, s 1223*.

[*CTA 2010, ss 13, 17(3); FA 1993 s 92DB; FA 2009, Sch 18*].

For a UK resident company prepares its accounts in accordance with generally accepted accounting practice ('GAAP') in sterling or in another currency, but identifies its functional currency as sterling, the position is as follows. Where a loss arises on a generally accepted accounting practice basis for corporation tax, which is to be carried-forward and the tax calculation currency for the period to which the loss is to be carried forward is not sterling, then the loss must first be translated into that later tax calculation currency at spot rate for the first day of the relevant accounting period before being translated into sterling at the rate required under *CTA 2010, s 11* to be used to convert the profits against which the loss is to be set. [*CTA 2010, s 15; FA 1993, s 92DD; FA 2009, Sch 18*].

Losses on unlisted shares

[55.17] Certain companies may claim relief against income for losses arising on the disposal of unlisted shares for which they have 'subscribed' and which are ordinary share capital of 'qualifying trading companies'. To be eligible to claim relief, a company must meet the following conditions:

- it must have been an 'investment company' on the date of disposal;
- it must have been an investment company throughout the six years prior to the disposal or for a shorter period ending with disposal and has not before the beginning of that period been a 'qualifying trading company' or an 'excluded company'; and
- it must not have been associated with, or a member of the same group as, the 'qualifying trading company' during its ownership of the shares.

For this purpose, an '*investment company*' is a company whose business consists wholly or mainly in the making of investments and which derives the principal part of its income from the making of investments. 'Holding companies' of a 'trading group' are, however, excluded.

A '*holding company*' is a company whose business consists mainly in the holding of shares or securities of 51% subsidiaries.

A '*trading group*' is a 'group' (i.e. a company and its 51% subsidiaries) the business of the members of which, taken together, consists wholly or mainly in the carrying on of a trade or trades (disregarding any trade carried on by a subsidiary which is an excluded company or, as regards shares issued before 6 April 1998, which is non-UK resident).

Companies are '*associated*' where one controls the other or both are under common control, control being as defined in **22.6 CLOSE COMPANIES**.

A claim is available only if:

- the disposal is at arm's length; or
- the disposal is by way of a distribution in a dissolution or winding-up; or
- the value of the shares has become negligible and a claim to that effect made under *TCGA 1992, s 24(2)*; or
- the disposal consists of the entire loss, destruction, dissipation or extinction of an asset (within *TCGA 1992, s 24(1)*).

No relief is available where, under *TCGA 1992, s 137*, shares are deemed to have been disposed of on a share exchange or reorganisation, etc. within *TCGA 1992, ss 135* or *136*.

The allowable loss is as calculated for the purposes of corporation tax on chargeable gains. The normal rules for the substitution of market value for consideration apply (see *TCGA 1992, s 17*), but the allowable loss may not exceed the actual loss incurred.

[*CTA 2010, ss 68, 69, 90(1)(6); ICTA 1988, ss 573(1)(5), 575(1)(3), 576L(1)*].

The shares disposed of must be:

- unquoted at the time of issue;
- originally 'subscribed for' by the company and issued in consideration for money, or money's worth; and
- ordinary share capital.

A company '*subscribes for*' shares in another company if they are issued to it by the other company in consideration of money (or money's worth). If a company has subscribed for shares, it is treated as having subscribed for any bonus shares subsequently issued to it in respect of those shares, provided that the bonus shares are in the same company, of the same class and carry the same rights as the original shares. The bonus shares are treated as issued at the time the original shares were issued. For this purpose, shares are treated as being of the same class only if they would be so treated if they were listed in the UK and traded on the London Stock Exchange. [*CTA 2010, ss 73, 89, 90(1)(2); ICTA 1988, s 573(6)*].

Note that, before *CTA 2010* took effect, the legislation did not include the extension of these provisions to bonus shares. However, the extension was made in practice (see the Explanatory Notes to the 2009 Corporation Tax Bill, Annex 1 Change 12).

A '*qualifying trading company*' is defined as a company which:

(a) has carried on its business wholly or mainly in the UK throughout the period ending on the date of disposal and beginning with the incorporation of the company (or, if later, one year before the date on which the shares were issued);
(b) has met the gross asset condition immediately before and after the issue of the shares; and
(c) for a continuous period of six years ending on the date of disposal/date of cessation either:
- meets all the trading, control and independence conditions; or
- has ceased to meet the trading etc conditions in the three years before the date of disposal and has not, since the date of cessation been an excluded company (**53.23**), investment company (**48.1**), trading company or holding company of a trading group (**53.23**).

The six year period can be shorter, provided that before the start of the shorter period the company had not met the trading etc requirements or was not an excluded company.

[*CTA 2010, Conditions A–D, s 78*].

As to condition (a), in a case regarding share loss relief for individuals, *Professor Sir P Lachmann v HMRC (and related appeal)* [2010] UKFTT 560 (TC), TC00811, a couple claimed loss relief in respect of the disposal of shares in a Canadian company. HMRC rejected the claim on the grounds that what is now *ITA 2007, s 134* stipulated that the company must have 'carried on its business wholly or mainly in the United Kingdom'. The First-Tier Tribunal dismissed the couple's appeal against this decision.

As regards shares issued before 6 April 1998, a '*qualifying trading company*' is a company none of whose shares have been listed on a recognised stock exchange at any time in the period ending with the date of disposal of the shares and beginning with the incorporation of the company, or, if later, one year before the date on which the shares were subscribed for, and which:

(1) either (i) is a trading company on the date of the disposal, or (ii) has ceased to be a trading company within the previous three years and has not since that time been an investment company or an 'excluded company'; and
(2) either (i) has been a trading company for a continuous period of six years ending on the date of disposal of the shares or the time it ceased to be a trading company, or (ii) if shorter, a continuous period ending on that date or that time and had not before the beginning of that period been an excluded company or an investment company; and
(3) has been resident in the UK since incorporation until the date of disposal.

Securities on the Alternative Investment Market ('AIM') are treated as unlisted for these purposes. (Revenue Press Release 20 February 1995).

[*CTA 2010, ss 78, 90(1), Sch 2 para 28; ICTA 1988, ss 576(4)–(4B), 576A, 576L(1); ITA 2007, Sch 1 para 120, Sch 2 para 38*].

The conditions

[55.18] The conditions which must be met are as follows.

The trading condition

The company must either:

(i) exist wholly for the purpose of carrying on one or more 'qualifying trades' (see **28.7 CORPORATE VENTURING SCHEME**) (disregarding purposes having no significant effect on the extent of its activities); or

(ii) be a '*parent company*' (i.e. a company that has one or more 'qualifying subsidiaries' (as defined)) and the business of the '*group*' (i.e. the company and its qualifying subsidiaries) must not consist wholly or as to a substantial part in the carrying on of 'non-qualifying activities'.

Where the company intends that one or more other companies should become its qualifying subsidiaries with a view to their carrying on one or more qualifying trades, then, until any time after which the intention is abandoned, the company is treated as a parent company and those other companies are included in the group for the purposes of (ii) above.

For the purpose of (ii) above, the business of the group means what would be the business of the group if the activities of the group companies taken together were regarded as one business. Activities are for this purpose disregarded to the extent that they consist in:

- holding shares in or securities of any of the company's qualifying subsidiaries;
- making loans to another group company;
- holding and managing property used by a group company for the purposes of a qualifying trade or trades carried on by any group company;
- holding and managing property used by a group company for the purposes of research and development from which it is intended either that a qualifying trade to be carried on by a 'group company' will be derived or, for shares issued after 5 April 2007, a qualifying trade carried on or to be carried on by a group company will benefit. '*Group company*' includes, for this purpose, any existing or future company which will be a group company at any future time; or
- any activities that are not part of the company's main purpose.

Activities are similarly disregarded to the extent that they consist, in the case of a subsidiary whose main purpose is the carrying on of qualifying trade(s) and whose other purposes have no significant effect on the extent of its activities (other than in relation to incidental matters), in activities not in pursuance of its main purpose.

'*Non-qualifying activities*' are:

- excluded activities within **28.7 CORPORATE VENTURING SCHEME**; and
- non-trading activities (other than research and development (as defined)).

References in the definition of 'qualifying trade' and 'excluded activities' at **28.7 CORPORATE VENTURING SCHEME** to 'period B' are to be taken for the above purposes to refer to the continuous period mentioned in (b) above.

For the ascertainment of the purposes for which a company exists, see HMRC Venture Capital Schemes Manual VCM15070.

A company ceases to meet the trading requirement if, before the time that is relevant for the purposes of (a) above, a resolution is passed or an order is made for the winding-up of the company or if the company is dissolved without winding-up. This does not, however, apply if the winding-up is for genuine commercial reasons and not part of a scheme a main purpose of which is tax avoidance and the company continues, during the winding-up, to be a trading company. (Note that the continuation of trading condition now applies in relation to shares issued after 5 April 2001 but did originally apply up to and including 20 March 2000, after which a drafting error inadvertently altered the law.) For shares issued after 20 March 2000, a company does not cease to meet the trading requirement by reason of anything done as a consequence of its being in administration or receivership (both as defined by *ITA 2007, s 252*), provided everything so done and the entry into administration or receivership are for genuine commercial (and not tax avoidance) reasons. For shares issued after 16 March 2004, these provisions are extended to refer also to the winding-up, dissolution, administration or receivership of any of the company's subsidiaries.

[*CTA 2010, ss 79, 80, Sch 2 paras 29, 30, 43–49; ICTA 1988, ss 576B, 576C; ITA 2007, Sch 1 paras 122, 123; FA 2007, Sch 16 paras 11, 13, 14*].

The control and independence condition

The issuing company must not:

(I) control another company other than a qualifying subsidiary (as defined) or, for shares issued before 21 March 2000, have a 51% subsidiary other than a qualifying subsidiary, 'control' being construed in accordance with *CTA 2010, ss 450, 451* and being considered with or without connected persons within **25 CONNECTED PERSONS**;

(II) be a 51% subsidiary of another company or otherwise under the control of another company, 'control' being construed in accordance with *CTA 2010, s 1124* and again being considered with or without connected persons; or

(III) be capable of falling within (I) or (II) by virtue of any arrangements (as very broadly defined).

[*CTA 2010, s 81, Sch 2 para 31; ICTA 1988, s 576D; ITA 2007, Sch 1 para 124*].

The qualifying subsidiaries condition

The company must not have any subsidiaries other than qualifying subsidiaries (as defined).

[*CTA 2010, s 82, Sch 2 para 32; ICTA 1988, s 576E; ITA 2007, Sch 1 para 125*].

The property managing subsidiaries condition

For shares issued on or after 17 March 2004, any 'property managing subsidiary' (as defined) that the company has must be a 'qualifying 90% subsidiary' (as defined).

[*CTA 2010, s 83, Sch 2 paras 33, 41; ICTA 1988, s 576F; ITA 2007, Sch 1 para 126*].

The gross assets condition

The value of the company's gross assets must not exceed £7 million immediately before the issue of the shares in respect of which relief is claimed and must not exceed £8 million immediately afterwards. In relation to shares issued before 6 April 2006, these limits were £15 million and £16 million respectively; the higher limits continue to apply in relation to shares issued after 5 April 2006 to a person who subscribed for them before 22 March 2006. If the issuing company is a parent company, the gross assets test applies by reference to the aggregate gross assets of the company and all its qualifying subsidiaries (disregarding certain assets held by any such company which correspond to liabilities of another).

[*CTA 2010, s 84, Sch 2 para 34; ICTA 1988, s 576G; ITA 2007, Sch 1 para 127*].

The general approach of HMRC to the gross assets requirement is that the value of a company's gross assets is the sum of the value of all of the balance sheet assets. Where accounts are actually drawn up to a date immediately before or after the issue, the balance sheet values are taken provided that they reflect usual accounting standards and the company's normal accounting practice, consistently applied. Where accounts are not drawn up to such a date, such values will be taken from the most recent balance sheet, updated as precisely as is practicable on the basis of all the relevant information available to the company. Values so arrived at may need to be reviewed in the light of information contained in the accounts for the period in which the issue was made, and, if they were not available at the time of the issue, those for the preceding period, when they become available. The company's assets immediately before the issue do not include any advance payment received in respect of the issue. Where shares are issued partly paid, the right to the balance is an asset, and, notwithstanding the above, will be taken into account in valuing the assets immediately after the issue regardless of whether it is shown in the balance sheet. (HMRC SP 2/00).

The unquoted status condition

For shares issued on or after 7 March 2001, the company must be 'unquoted' at the time (the '*relevant time*') at which the shares are issued and no arrangements must then exist for it to cease to be unquoted. If, at the time of issue, arrangements exist for the company to become a wholly-owned subsidiary of a new holding company by means of a share exchange within the provisions below, no arrangements must exist for the new company to cease to be unquoted. A company is '*unquoted*' if none of its shares etc. are listed on a recognised stock exchange or on a foreign exchange designated for the purpose, or dealt in on the Unlisted Securities Market (now closed) or outside the UK by such means as may be designated for the purpose. Securities on the Alternative Investment Market ('AIM') are treated as unquoted for these purposes. (Revenue Press Release 20 February 1995). If the company is unquoted at the time of the share issue, it does not cease to be unquoted in relation to those shares solely because they are listed on an exchange which becomes a recognised stock exchange or is designated by an order made after the date of the issue (see HMRC Venture Capital Schemes Manual VCM15020).

[*CTA 2010, s 85, Sch 2 para 35; ICTA 1988, s 576H; ITA 2007, s 184(2), Sch 1 para 128; FA 2007, Sch 26 para 7*].

Treasury power to amend conditions

The Treasury may amend the above requirements by order.

[*CTA 2010, s 86, Sch 2 para 36; ICTA 1988, s 576I; ITA 2007, Sch 1 para 129*].

An '*excluded company*' is a company whose trade consists mainly of dealing in land, in commodities or futures or in shares, securities or other financial instruments (as regards shares issued before 6 April 1998 — dealing in shares, securities, land, trades or commodity futures) or which is not carried on a commercial basis with a reasonable expectation of profit, or a company which is the holding company of a group other than a trading group, or which is a building society (see **9 BUILDING SOCIETIES**) or a registered industrial and provident society (as defined). [*CTA 2010, s 90(1), Sch 2 para 40; ICTA 1988, s 576L(1)*].

Operation of and claims for relief

[55.19] Relief is given after calculating the loss (in accordance with the chargeable gains rules but is not offset against the total chargeable gains for the period). This loss is then deducted from the total income of the accounting period in which the loss arises in priority to expenses such as management expenses and charges on income, but after any CVS loss relief claim (**28 CORPORATE VENTURING SCHEME**).

If the loss cannot be fully utilised in this way, the excess may be carried back and set against income of the previous twelve months. Where an accounting period falls partly within the twelve month period, the loss can only be set against income attributable to the specified period (**53.6 INVESTMENT TRUSTS (MAINLY REITS)**) and therefore the profits of such an accounting period must be apportioned on a time basis. There is no facility to carry forward any element of the loss, and therefore if the loss cannot be utilised within the specified period, a claim should not be made.

Any earlier loss is relieved in priority to a later one.

Relief must be claimed within two years of the end of the accounting period in which the loss was incurred.

Where relief is claimed under these provisions, no relief may be claimed against chargeable gains in respect of the loss so relieved, but this does not preclude such relief for any part of the loss not relieved under these provisions.

[*CTA 2010, ss 70–72; ICTA 1988, s 573(2)–(4A); FA 2000, Sch 15 para 70*].

Limits on relief

Where a company claims relief under these provisions for a loss on the disposal of shares which form part of a 'section 104 holding' or a '1982 holding' (i.e. holdings of shares which are pooled for chargeable gains purposes) either at the time of the disposal or an earlier time, the relief is restricted to the sums that would have been allowable as deductions in computing the loss if the qualifying shares had not formed part of the holding.

Where the qualifying shares were acquired on the same day as other shares that are not capable of being qualifying shares (see below), so that under *TCGA 1992, s 105(1)(a)* all the shares are treated as acquired by a single transaction, the amount of relief is restricted to the sums that would have been allowable as deductions in computing the loss if the qualifying shares and the other shares were not so treated.

Where the qualifying shares, taken as a single asset, and other shares or debentures in the same company which are not capable of being qualifying shares, also taken as a single asset, are treated for chargeable gains purposes as the same asset under *TCGA 1992, s 127*, the relief is restricted to the sums that would have been allowable as deductions in computing the loss if the qualifying shares and the other shares or debentures were not to be treated as the same asset.

For these purposes, shares are not capable of being qualifying shares at any time if they were not acquired by subscription or if the gross assets condition would not be met if the shares were disposed of at that time. Additionally, for the purposes only of the 'same asset' restriction above, shares are not capable of being qualifying shares at any time if they are shares of a different class from the qualifying shares concerned.

[*CTA 2010, s 75; ICTA 1988, s 576(1)*].

Identification

[55.20] The following provisions apply to identify whether a disposal of shares forming part of a mixed holding (i.e. a 'holding' of shares including shares that are not capable of being qualifying shares and other shares) is a disposal of qualifying shares and, if so, to which of any qualifying shares acquired at different times the disposal relates. Except as noted below, the normal chargeable gains identification rules apply and where shares are thereby identified with the whole or any part of a *section 104* holding or a 1982 holding, they are further identified on a last in/first out (LIFO) basis. This does not apply where the holding includes shares issued on or after 1 April

2000 to which investment relief under the Corporate Venturing Scheme is attributable and which have been held continuously (see **28.2**, **28.20**(a) CORPORATE VENTURING SCHEME) by the company; the identification rules at **28.17** CORPORATE VENTURING SCHEME (generally first in/first out) apply instead.

Where the above rules cannot identify the shares disposed of, the identification is to be made on a just and reasonable basis.

A '*holding*' of shares for these purposes is any number of shares of the same class held by one company in the same capacity, growing or diminishing as shares of that class are acquired or disposed of. Shares comprised in a 'new holding' following a reorganisation to which *TCGA 1992, s 127* applies are treated as having been acquired when the original shares were acquired. Any shares held or disposed of by a nominee or bare trustee for a company are treated as held or disposed of by the company.

[*CTA 2010, ss 76, 77; ICTA 1988, s 576(1)–(1D); ITA 2007, Sch 1 para 120*].

Other situations

Anti-avoidance

[55.21] Any claim to relief will bring in the value shifting provisions to give a tax-free benefit (*TCGA 1992, s 30*).

The Finance Act 2011 introduces a targeted anti-avoidance rule for corporation tax that applies to disposals of share or securities, which will be found in new substituted provisions *TCGA 1992, ss 31–34*. The general value shifting rule in *s 30* will then no longer apply to disposals of shares or securities by companies, as the new provisions will take effect.

[*TCGA 1992, s 125A; ICTA 1988, s 576(2); ITA 2007, Sch 1 para 309; CTA 2010, Sch 1 para 231*].

Company reconstructions

On a **reorganisation** of share capital, new shares may be acquired in exchange for the original holding, and the general rule for capital gains tax purposes is that a disposal will not arise in these cases.

If the new shares are later sold, loss relief may be available if either:

- at the date of the reorganisation the old shares met all of the qualifying conditions; or
- the new shares were acquired for new consideration. Loss relief in this case will be restricted to the amount of that consideration used in the computation of the disposal of the new shares.

'*New consideration*' is money or money's worth excluding any surrender or alteration to the original shares (or rights attached thereto), and excluding the application of assets of the company or of distributions declared but not made out of those assets.

[*CTA 2010, s 74; ICTA 1988, ss 575(2), 576(5)*].

Share exchanges

Where, by means of an exchange of shares, all of the shares (the old shares) of a company (the old company) are acquired by a company (the new company) in which the only previously issued shares are subscriber shares, then, subject to the further conditions below being satisfied, the exchange is not regarded as involving a disposal of the old shares and an acquisition of the new company shares (the new shares). Where old shares held by a company were subscribed for by it, the new shares stand in the shoes of the old shares, e.g. as if they had been subscribed for and issued at the time the old shares were subscribed for and issued and as if any requirements under the above provisions met at any time before the exchange by the old company had been met at that time by the new company.

The further conditions are as follows.

- (a) The shares must be issued after 5 April 1998.
- (b) The consideration for the old shares must consist entirely of the issue of the new shares.
- (c) The consideration for old shares of each description must consist entirely of new shares of the 'corresponding description'.
- (d) New shares of each description must be issued to holders of old shares of the 'corresponding description' in respect of and in proportion to their holdings.
- (e) For new shares issued on or after 6 April 2007, the exchange of shares is not treated for chargeable gains purposes as involving a disposal of the old shares or an acquisition of the new shares by virtue of *TCGA 1992, s 127*.
- (f) For new shares issued before 6 April 2007, before the issue of the new shares, on the written application of either the old or new company, HMRC must have notified to that company their satisfaction that the exchange:
  - (i) is for genuine commercial reasons; and
  - (ii) does not form part of a scheme or arrangements to which *TCGA 1992, s 137(1) applies*.

HMRC may, within 30 days of an application, request further particulars, which must then be supplied within 30 days of the request (or such longer period as they may allow in any particular case).

For these purposes, old and new shares are of a '*corresponding description*' if, assuming they were shares in the same company, they would be of the same class and carry the same rights.

An exchange within these provisions, or arrangements for such an exchange do not breach the control and independence requirement above.

[*CTA 2010, ss 87, 88, Sch 2 para 37; ICTA 1988, ss 576J, 576K*].

Simon's Taxes. See **D1.1120.**

Example

Z Ltd has been an investment company since its incorporation in 1972. It is not part of a trading group and has no associated companies. It makes up accounts to 31 December. On 6 February 2011, Z Ltd disposed of part of its holding of shares in T Ltd for full market value. Z Ltd makes no global re-basing election under *TCGA 1992, s 35(5)*.

Details of disposal	
Contract date	6.2.11
Shares sold	2,000 Ord
Proceeds (after expenses)	£4,500

Z acquired its shares in T Ltd as follows.

				£
6.4.81 subscribed for	1,000	shares	cost (with expenses)	5,000
6.4.91 acquired	1,500	shares	cost (with expenses)	4,000
	2,500			£9,000

T Ltd shares were valued at £3 per share at 31 March 1982. T Ltd has been a UK resident trading company since 1980. Its shares are not quoted on a recognised stock exchange.

Z Ltd may claim that part of the loss incurred be set off against its income as follows.

Identification of the shares in the pool which are sold takes place on a last in, first out basis.

(i) Shares acquired 6.4.91 (not subscribed for)

	£
Proceeds of 1,500 shares	
$\frac{1,500}{2,000} \times £\ 4,500$	3,375
Cost of 1,500 shares	(4,000)
Capital loss *not* available for set-off against income	£(625)

(ii) Shares acquired 6.4.81 (subscribed for)

	Cost basis	31.3.82 value basis
	£	£
Proceeds of 500 shares		
$\frac{500}{2,000} \times £\ 4,500$	1,125	1,125
Cost of 500 shares	(2,500)	

31.3.82 value		(1,500)
	£(1,375)	£(375)
Capital loss available for set-off against income		£(375)

The loss of £375 is available primarily against income of the year ended 31 December 2011, with any balance being available against, broadly speaking, income of the 12 months ended 31 December 2010 (see **55.17** above).

Certain business activities

Farming and market gardening

[55.22] A loss incurred in any accounting period in a trade of farming or market gardening cannot be relieved against other income or gains or carried back if a loss, ignoring capital allowances, has been incurred in that period and in each accounting period falling wholly or partly within the five years up to the beginning of the accounting period in question.

This provision does not deny relief where:

(i) the farming, etc. is part of, and ancillary to, a larger trading undertaking; or
(ii) the farming, etc. activities in the year are carried on in a way which might reasonably be expected by a competent farmer to produce profits in the future and the activities in the preceding five years could not reasonably have been expected to become profitable until after the year under review; or
(iii) the trade was started or treated as started (see *CTA 2010, s 50*) during the preceding five years.

[*CTA 2010, ss 48–51; ICTA 1988, s 397; ITA 2007, Sch 1 para 74; CTA 2009, Sch 1 para 113*].

Simon's Taxes. See B5.175.

Leasing contracts for plant and machinery

[55.23] There is a restriction on the offset of 'losses incurred on a leasing contract' if:

- a company incurs capital expenditure on plant or machinery which it leases out to a third party;
- in the accounting period in which annual investment allowance (**11.15**) or first year allowances (**11.13**) are available (if at all), there are arrangements for either a successor company or a company connected with the first company, to take over all or part of the first company's obligations under the leasing contract.

The restriction operates by treating any 'losses incurred on a leasing contract' as if they arose on a separate 'leasing contract trade' and they are therefore only available for offset against future profits arising on the same leasing contract.

Anti-avoidance provisions restrict the offset of losses where there is a change in the ownership (or corporate partnership interest) of a company carrying on the business of leasing plant or machinery (**5.20**).

'*Losses incurred on a leasing contract*' (and profits arising) are computed, and are treated for relief purposes, as if the performance of the leasing contract constituted a separate trade, begun at the commencement of the letting. Loss relief is thus restricted to future profits on the leasing contract.

'*First-year allowance*' and '*annual investment allowance*' are as defined in *CAA 2001, Pt II* (or *CAA 1990, Pt II*). See **11.13 CAPITAL ALLOWANCES — PLANT AND MACHINERY: ELIGIBLE EXPENDITURE AND INITIAL ALLOWANCES.**

'*Successor company*' is as defined in **55.11** above or a company connected (see **25 CONNECTED PERSONS**) with the first company.

[*CTA 2010, s 53; ICTA 1988, s 395*].

Sale of lessors

For restriction of relief for losses in the case where there is a change in the ownership of a company carrying on a business of leasing plant or machinery, see **5.27** *et seq.* **ANTI-AVOIDANCE.**

Leasing partnerships

For restriction of relief for losses in the case where there is a change in the interest of a company in a business, carried on in partnership, of leasing plant or machinery, see **5.20** and **5.27 ANTI-AVOIDANCE.** For restrictions on the set-off against an individual's total income of certain losses arising from first-year allowances incurred by the individual in partnership with a company, see Tolley's Income Tax under Losses.

Simon's Taxes. See **D1.1111** and **D1.1112.**

Companies trading in partnership

[55.24] There is a restriction on loss relief where a company ('the partner company') is a member of a trading partnership and arrangements exist whereby another partner (or a person connected with him, see **25 CONNECTED PERSONS**) receives any payment or enjoys any benefit in money's worth in respect of the partner company's 'share in the profits or losses' of the partnership or whereby the partner company (or a person connected with it) receives any payment or enjoys any such benefit in respect of its share of losses (other than a payment for group relief, see **39.2–39.18 GROUP RELIEF**).

If the above conditions are satisfied for any accounting period, the company's share of partnership losses and qualifying charitable donations (see *CTA 2010, s 189; ICTA 1988, s 338*) may be set off only against its share of profits from the partnership's trade, and no other loss incurred by the company in that period may be set against such profits.

[*CTA 2010, ss 958–962; ICTA 1988, s 116; FA 1998, Sch 3 para 10*].

The company's '*share in the profits or losses*' of the partnership is determined under *CTA 2009, s 1262* (previously *ICTA 1988, s 114(2)*) (see **58.3 PARTNERSHIPS**).

See also **55.9, 55.23** above and **55.26** below and **58.9 PARTNERSHIPS**.

Dealings in commodity futures

[55.25] Special rules apply to **restrict loss relief** when a company deals in commodity futures, as follows:

Transaction	Restriction
Participates in a trade of dealing in commodity futures in partnership (where one of the partners is a company) and arrangements are made with the sole or main benefit being to reduce a tax liability by making a loss relief claim against general income of the current or previous year. [*CTA 2010, s 52(1)–(4)*. See Simon's Taxes. D1.1110.	Loss relief claim under *CTA 2010, s 37* is denied. If relief has already been given, it will be withdrawn by an assessment on overseas income or miscellaneous income.

Write-off of government investment

[55.26] Where any amount of Government investment in a company is written-off, an equal amount is set against the company's 'carry-forward losses' as at the end of the accounting period before that in which the investment was written-off, and against such losses of subsequent accounting periods until the amount written-off is extinguished.

[*CTA 2010, s 92; ICTA 1988, s 400(1)*].

This does not prevent a company from deducting a sum in calculating its profits, and in particular, expenditure is not treated as met by a public body for capital allowances or chargeable gains purposes by reason only that an amount of government investment has been written off.

[*CTA 2010, s 96(1)–(3); ICTA 1988, s 400(6)*].

'*Carry-forward losses*' at the end of an accounting period are any trading losses, losses from a property or overseas property business, management expenses, capital allowances or allowable capital losses available for carry-forward at the end of the period, and any unused qualifying charitable donations for the period.

[*CTA 2010, s 95(1); ICTA 1988, s 400(2); CTA 2009, Sch 1 para 116; SI 2004 No 2310, Art 13*].

The set-off is made against allowable capital losses of a period only after all other carry-forward losses of the period have been exhausted.

[*CTA 2010, s 95(4); ICTA 1988, s 400(3)*].

In determining the carry-forward losses at the end of the accounting period before that of the write-off, valid claims for group relief, or for relief of trading losses or capital allowances against profits generally and/or of earlier accounting periods, are effective provided that they are made before the write-off date. Such claims made on or after that date are ineffective until the amount written-off has been set off in full.

[*CTA 2010, s 95(2)(3); ICTA 1988, s 400(4)*].

Where the company concerned is a member of a group (i.e. a parent company and its 51% subsidiaries), the set-off for an accounting period may be made against carry-forward losses of any other company which is a group member at the end of the accounting period, any allocation between group companies being on a 'reasonable and just' basis.

[*CTA 2010, s 93; ICTA 1988, s 400(5)*].

An amount of Government investment in a company is treated as written off if:

(a) its liability to repay money lent out of public funds by a Minister of the Crown, the Scottish Ministers or a Northern Ireland department is extinguished; or
(b) any of its shares subscribed for out of public funds by a Minister etc. are cancelled; or
(c) any 'commencing capital debt' (i.e. any debt to a Minister etc. assumed as such under an enactment) is reduced otherwise than by being paid off; or
(d) any 'public dividend capital' (i.e. any amount paid by a Minister etc. under an enactment which so describes it or which corresponds with enactments relating to similar payments so described) is reduced otherwise than by being repaid.

The amount and date of the write-off are determined accordingly. No restriction is, however, made under these provisions if, and to the extent that, the amount written-off is replaced in some other form by money provided out of public funds by a Minister etc.

[*CTA 2010, s 94; ICTA 1988, s 400(7)–(10)*].

There is no write-off if the amount written off is replaced in some other form by money provided out of public funds by a Minister, etc. notwithstanding *CTA 2009, s 464(1)* (matters to be brought into account in the case of loan relationships only under the loan relationship provisions, see **54.2 LOAN RELATIONSHIPS**).

[*CTA 2010, s 96(4); ICTA 1988, s 400(9A); CTA 2009, Sch 1 para 116*].

These provisions apply in priority to the loan relationship rules.

[*CTA 2010, s 96(4)*].

Simon's Taxes. See D1.1114.

Double taxation

[55.27] Where:

- interest, dividends or royalties accrue to a non-resident company carrying on a business in the UK;
- which have been treated as tax-exempt under double taxation arrangements (*TIOPA 2010, s 2*);

then they are not to be excluded from trading income or profits of the business so as to give rise to losses to be set off against income or profits.

[*CTA 2010, s 54; ICTA 1988, s 808*].

Key points

[55.28] Points to consider are as follows.

- Losses arising from different sources of income are subject to different rules regarding utilisation, including the types of profits against which the losses may be offset, the periods in which they may be offset and the order in which they are required to be relieved. For example, only trading losses may be carried back to offset profits arising in the twelve months prior to the period in which the loss arose.
- Trading losses may generally only be carried back to relieve profits arising in the twelve months prior to the period in which the loss arose. However, this period has been extended to three years for trading losses arising in accounting periods ended after 23 November 2008 and before 24 November 2010 (as split into two twelve month periods). The maximum amount of losses that may be carried back under these provisions is £50,000 in total for accounting periods ending in each twelve month period, the losses may only be used to offset trading profits, and profits are relieved in later periods before earlier periods.
- Any qualifying charitable donations (previously 'charges on income') which cannot be offset against other income of the company arising in the same period or, in the event that the company is a member of a group, surrendered as group relief, will be lost as it is not possible to carry them forward for future offset.
- Where a company transfers part or all of its trade to another company within the same 75% ownership, any trading losses of the company are automatically transferred to the successor company. However, there is a restriction of the losses transferred to the extent that liabilities of the trade not transferred exceed the assets of the trade that are not transferred.

- Given the broad application of the loss restriction provisions on a change of ownership of a company (see **55.13**), in most cases it is unlikely that a purchaser would ascribe value to tax losses in the target company.
- Where a company has a functional currency other than sterling and seeks to offset losses arising against prior year or future profits, care is needed to ensure that the appropriate exchange rate is used to convert the losses into sterling (see **55.25**).
- Losses arising on a disposal of shares are generally treated as capital losses. However, with regard to an investment company, provided certain conditions are met as regards to the investing and investee company (see **55.17**), the investing company may be able to claim a deduction for the loss against income profits. A claim should only be made in respect of such part of any loss that can be used to shelter income profits arising in the period in which the loss arises, or in the prior twelve months, as any loss that cannot be so used cannot be carried forward.

56

Mutual Companies

Cross-references. See **9 BUILDING SOCIETIES**; **62.19**(b) **PROPERTY INCOME**; **75 VOLUNTARY ASSOCIATIONS.**

Simon's Taxes. See B1.436–B1.440, D7.508, D7.644.

Introduction

[56.1] A person cannot derive a taxable profit from trading with himself except in certain cases of self-supply by a trader of trading stock, see *FA 2008, s 37* which gives statutory effect to *Sharkey v Wernher* (1955) 36 TC 275, HL.

This principle is extended to a group of persons engaged in mutual activities of a trading nature, if there is:

- an identifiable 'fund' for the common purpose with complete identity between contributors; and
- participators in, the fund (the 'mutuality principle').

Transactions with non-members

[56.2] A body not liable to tax as regards transactions with members may nevertheless be treated as generating taxable trading income from transactions with non-members and is liable in the ordinary way on any investment etc. income. Whether the mutuality principle applies depends on the facts.

See *Liverpool Corn Trade Association Ltd v Monks* (1926) 10 TC 442 (trade association providing corn exchange etc. held to be trading and not 'mutual' — but see **71.67 TRADING EXPENSES AND DEDUCTIONS** for special arrangements available for trade associations); *English & Scottish Joint CWS Ltd v Assam Agricultural IT Commr* (1948) 27 ATC 332, PC (wholesale co-operative with two members held to be trading and not mutual — there was no 'common fund').

A members' club does not trade and is not liable on its surplus from the provision of facilities for members (*Eccentric Club Ltd* [1924] 1 KB 390, 12 TC 657, CA), but it is liable on the surplus attributable to non-members (*Carlisle & Silloth Golf Club v Smith* (1913) 6 TC 48, CA). For further cases, see Tolley's Income Tax under Mutual Trading.

Payments on liquidation etc.

[56.3] For distribution of assets by a mutual concern to a trading company, see **70.57** **TRADE PROFITS — INCOME AND SPECIFIC TRADES.**

Credit unions

[56.4] In making loans to its members or investing its surplus funds (e.g. by placing them on deposit), a credit union (within *Industrial and Provident Societies Act 1965* or *Credit Unions (Northern Ireland) Order 1985*) is not regarded as trading. No loan relationship credits are brought into account where a member of the union is the debtor under the loan relationship. Likewise, no debits are brought into account where a member is the creditor. Annual payments are not deductible in computing the profits of a trade carried on by a credit union.

[*CTA 2009, ss 40, 133, 397, 1319; ICTA 1988, s 487*].

Transfers of business

[56.5] The Treasury are given wide powers to regulate, by statutory instrument, the tax consequences of the transfer of a 'mutual society'. For this purpose a '*mutual society*' is defined as an incorporated building society, a registered friendly society or an industrial and provident society, registered or deemed to be registered.

[*FA 2009, s 124*].

Mutual life assurance companies

[56.6] Payments made to persons participating in the mutual activities of a company carrying on mutual life assurance business are not treated as **DISTRIBUTIONS (31)**.

[*ICTA 1988, s 490(2)*].

57

Offshore Funds

Simon's Taxes. See **B5.701–B5.727, B8.622–B8.640.**

Introduction

[57.1] The offshore funds legislation was updated in 2009 to provide more certainty for investors and funds, and to give funds the benefit of a less onerous procedure than the existing distribution regime. The new provisions involve permitting funds to have 'reporting fund' status whereby they report the income that has been rolled up to investors, who enter it on their tax return.

FA 2008, ss 41, 42, now *TIOPA 2010, Pt 8*, gave power to replace the 1984 regime (see below) for the taxation of offshore funds, through primary or secondary legislation. The new legislation came into force on 1 December 2009. Secondary legislation has been introduced in *SI 2009 No 3001* (amended by *SI 2009 No 3139*). Guidance was published by HMRC and can now be found within the new Offshore Funds Manual published in May 2010 (see www.hmrc.gov.uk/offshorefunds/new-manual.htm). In preparation for the new regime, a number of the existing provisions were repealed in *FA 2008* from 1 December 2009. In addition a new definition of offshore fund has been introduced in *TIOPA 2010*.

Both regimes do have a common purpose, in that they work by charging realisations of interests in offshore funds to tax as income rather than chargeable gains, unless the fund meets certain conditions: under the 1984 regime the fund needed to distribute sufficient income to be certified as a 'distributing' fund; under the 2009 regime the fund has certain reporting obligations to be met in order to be treated as a 'reporting' fund. Essentially, under either regime, meeting such obligations ensures capital gains treatment on a disposal of an interest in the fund by an investor.

Further amendments have been made to the new 2009 regime by the Offshore Funds (Tax) (Amendment) Regulations 2011 (*SI 2011 No 1211*) which came into force on 27 May 2011 and have effect for distributions made or treated as made on or after that date.

The 2009 regime

[57.2] *TIOPA 2010, Pt 8; FA 2008, ss 41, 42* (as was) and *SI 2009 No 3001* (as amended by *SI 2009 No 3139*, and *SI 2011 No 1211*) introduce a new regime for offshore funds, details of which are found below.

Where a fund satisfies the various conditions below as to the reporting of information to participators then they would be treated as a 'reporting fund'. Generally UK resident investors in these funds will be taxable on their share of the fund's reported income each year, irrespective of whether such income is actually distributed to them. Any gain or loss on disposal will be treated as a capital gain or loss. UK investors are able to then accumulate this taxed income within the fund.

For non-reporting funds, UK investors are chargeable to income or corporation tax on any distributions made to them. If the fund is transparent for income tax purposes then the investor will be chargeable to tax on the income in the underlying investments. The untaxed accumulated income and gains are treated as offshore income and a disposal of an interest in a non-reporting fund will give rise to a gain chargeable to income tax — an offshore income gain. This is the same treatment for non-distributing funds under the 1984 regime (see below).

HMRC's offshore funds manual provides detailed guidance on the new regime and can be found at: www.hmrc.gov.uk/offshorefunds/new-manual.htm.

Changes with effect from May 2011

[57.3] The amending regulations *SI 2011 No 1211* (which have effect from 27 May 2011) introduce changes to the following areas:

For Reporting Funds

- Changes in the calculation of reportable income to take account of equalisation arrangements.
- Adjustments to the calculation of reported income per unit for funds not applying equalisation, including transitional provisions so the new rules apply to reports made after the regulations come into force.
- Provision is made for a reporting fund to change its equalisation arrangements.
- The category of fund which is considered 'equivalent' to UK AIFs is being broadened and in addition, a change to the computation of reportable income allows the rules for transactions which are not considered to be trading to be applied.
- The 'Diversity of Ownership' rule will apply at sub-fund level and the changes will permit investors in a feeder fund to be considered when assessing the Master Fund.
- New simplified rules are introduced for calculating the reportable income of a transparent reporting fund.
- Changes to simplify compliance with the rules when computing reportable income for an index-tracking fund.
- Extended time limits for application and withdrawal.
- Clarification of the scope of reporting requirements.
- Changes to allow for continuity of reported income where *TCGA 1992, s 106A* applies to a disposal and acquisition covering the end of a reporting period.

All Offshore Funds

- A new exception from the offshore income gain tax charge is introduced for non-reporting funds invested mostly in unlisted trading companies.
- Corporate holders will look through fiscally transparent funds for the purposes of the loan relationship rules as these funds will be treated as outside of scope of such legislation.
- An extension to the transitional period to widen the ability to apply for distribution status, and to ensure that the regulations deal with earlier periods.

Definition of offshore fund, etc.

[57.4] A three part definition of 'offshore fund' is included at *TIOPA 2010, ss 355, 356*, to replace the definition in *FA 2009*. To be an '*offshore fund*' an entity must fall into one of the following categories:

(a) a mutual fund, constituted as a company (not including an LLP) resident outside the UK;

(b) a mutual fund where the property is held on trust for the participants and the trustees are not UK resident; or

(c) a mutual fund constituted by other arrangements that create co-ownership rights and are governed by the law of a territory outside the UK (but not including a trading or business partnership).

A '*mutual fund*' is an arrangement affecting any type of property, including money, provided that the purpose of the arrangements is to participate in the acquisition, holding, management or disposal of property or the receipt of income or other payments arising from property so held. Participants must not have day to day control of the management of the property (not including the right to be consulted or give directions) and a reasonable investor would be able to realise his investment for an amount calculated entirely or almost entirely by reference to the net asset value of the property or calculated by reference to an index of any description (the Treasury have power to amend this condition by statutory instrument).

This definition is subject to qualifications for umbrella arrangements and arrangements where there is more than one class of interest. In these cases, each part or class of the arrangements are to be looked at separately, and the umbrella or main arrangements are disregarded. Arrangements are not a mutual fund where they allow a participant to realise all or part of the investments for net asset value or in accordance with an index, or only to do so on a winding up and either the arrangement is not designed to wind up etc. on a specified date or one which is determinable or there is a definite time for winding up etc., the return is not designed to be equivalent to interest and:

- none of the assets are 'relevant income-producing assets'; or
- under the terms of the arrangements, the participants are not entitled to the income or other benefit from the assets or from the income from the assets; or under the terms of the arrangements, any income, net of reasonable expenses, must be paid or credited to the participants and any UK resident individual participant is chargeable to income tax on it.

A '*relevant income-producing asset*' is an asset which produces income which would be subject to UK income tax if it were held directly by an individual resident in the UK. Hedged assets are not relevant income producing assets if no income is expected to arise from the hedged asset or any product of the hedging.

These provisions may be amended by statutory instrument.

Where umbrella arrangements are in place, each part of the asset is treated as separate arrangements, and the umbrella arrangement is disregarded.

Where there is more than one class of arrangement, each class is treated separately and the main arrangements are disregarded.

'*Umbrella arrangements*' means arrangements providing for separate pooling of each participant's contributions and the profits or income attaching to them, out of which payments may be made.

There are also amendments in *FA 2009* to the capital gains treatment of offshore funds, which apply from 1 December 2009 for individuals, from 1 April 2010 for participant companies. Where a fund is neither a unit trust nor a company, it will be treated for capital gains purposes as if it were a company, and the participants' rights will be treated as if they were shares. There is a right to make an irrevocable election, in the corporation tax return or by amendment of a return, for this change to have applied from the accounting period beginning on or after 1 April 2003 or from any other accounting period commencing before a date to be appointed.

[*TIOPA 2010, ss 354–363; FA 2009, s 44, Sch 44. See further HMRC offshore funds manual OFM02000 et seq.*].

FA 2011, s 59 introduces a new provision with regard to the residence of an offshore fund which is an undertaking for collective investment in transferable securities ('UCITS') per the UCITS Directive 2009/65/EC. The UCITS IV directive provides that an investment fund authorised under the Directive may have a manager which is not resident in the same Member State as that in which the fund is established and regulated. *FA 2011* inserts a new *s 363A* into *TIOPA 2010* to treat certain offshore funds as not being resident in the UK, in cases where they might otherwise be resident by virtue of having a UK resident fund manager. Thus the offshore fund and their investors will not be subject to any tax consequences in the UK as a result of having a UK resident management company.

The new *s 363A* applies where: the offshore fund is a body corporate established in a Member State as an UCITS and is treated as resident in that State for the purposes of any tax imposed under that law on income; and where the body corporate would be treated as resident in the UK for the purposes of any enactment relating to income tax, corporation tax or capital gains tax; the fund will instead be treated as if it were not resident in the UK. In addition, if, under *TCGA 1992, ss 99* or *103A*, the offshore fund is treated as if it were a company, then for the purposes of *TCGA 1992*, the company is treated as neither resident nor ordinarily resident in the UK.

Reporting and non-reporting funds

Offshore funds are allocated into reporting and non-reporting funds (see **57.5** below). An investor will be taxed on its share of the income of an offshore fund, regardless of whether or not the income has been distributed or accumulated in the fund. The 2009 regime moves away from the 1984 regime's requirement to distribute in order to gain the capital gains exemption to a requirement that the offshore income fund's income be reported to UK investors so that they are taxed on their shares regardless of whether the income is actually distributed or not. (Under the 1984 provisions, the investor's liability to tax depended on a minimum 85% distribution of income by the fund.)

The application process is as detailed at **57.6** below.

An offshore fund is defined at *TIOPA 2010, ss 355, 356* and may take one of several forms e.g. a company with share capital, a unit trust or a contractual arrangement such as a Fonds Commun de Placement. Partnerships are specifically excluded from the definition of an offshore fund found at *TIOPA 2010, s 355(1)(c)* (mutual fund arrangements) and in addition limited liability partnerships (LLPs) are excluded from the definition of body corporate. However, it is notable that HMRC's guidance comments that this exclusion relates to UK LLPs; a LLP formed under the law of any other territory could still be an offshore fund if it is a body corporate (and opaque for capital gains purposes) and a mutual fund.

Other arrangements, e.g. certain unit trusts which are transparent for income tax but not capital gains tax, are within the definition of an offshore fund. In general, for corporation tax, the new regime takes effect for accounting periods ending on or after 1 December 2009 so far as it relates to corporation tax on income, and for disposals on or after 1 December 2009 for capital gains purposes.

There are, however, transitional provisions in *SI 2009 No 3001, Sch 1* which apply where an existing fund does not qualify as a reporting fund in various situations. There is guidance on *SI 2009 No 3001* in the new offshore funds manual at www.hmrc.gov.uk/offshorefunds/new-manual.htm. *SI 2009 No 3001* has been amended by *SI 2009 No 3139*. The changes in the latter statutory instrument take effect from the beginning of the new offshore fund regime i.e. 1 December 2009.

The amendments to the 2009 regulations applicable from 27 May 2011 contain provisions with regard to the transitional arrangements. *Sch 1 para 3* of the 2009 regulations is amended such that the fund or any person within *ICTA 1988, Sch 27, para 18(1)* (a person assessed to tax who would not have been so assessed if the fund had applied for distributing status) may apply to HMRC for an existing fund to become a distributing fund for the overlap period (which straddles 1 December 2009) and any earlier period, and also the succeeding year (where an application for the fund to be a reporting fund has not already been accepted). As amended, this does not apply to periods of account ending after 31st May 2012 (previously 2011).

Categories of funds

[57.5] Offshore funds are divided into two categories — reporting and non-reporting. A 'non-reporting fund' is any offshore fund which does not satisfy the conditions of a reporting fund. A 'reporting fund' is an offshore fund to which *SI 2009 No 3001, Pt 3* applies (see below). When an interest in a non-reporting fund is disposed of, any capital gain is taxed as income.

Reporting funds

[57.6] The manager of an eligible offshore fund (or prospective manager of a new fund) may make an application for the fund to be a reporting fund. The manager of a non-reporting fund may apply, provided that the fund is an eligible offshore fund, and has never been a reporting fund or has been such a fund but ceased to be such a fund by giving notice under *Reg 116* (i.e. where notice of termination is given).

The contents of an application are set out in *Reg 53*. Under the amended provisions a fund must apply for reporting status before the later of: the end of the first period of account for which reporting status is required; and the expiry of three months beginning with the first day on which interests are made available to UK resident investors. An application may be withdrawn at any time after the application has been made and before the end of 28 days after notice has been received from HMRC either accepting or rejecting the application; or at any later time before the end of the first reporting period. Previously the application would need to have been made in writing to HMRC within three months of the first day of the fund's first accounting period as a reporting fund.

HMRC are required to give notice of acceptance or of rejection of the application, or issue a request for further information. [*SI 2009 No 3001, Reg 54* and *SI 2009 No 3139, Reg 3*]. The applicant has a right of appeal against rejection. An appeal will normally be heard by the First-tier Tribunal. If an application is accepted, the fund becomes a reporting fund of the later of:

- the first day of the first period of account;
- the day on which the fund is established.

A reporting fund must make a report available (in one of four specified ways) to each participant for each reporting period within six months of the end of that period. *Regulation 92* gives the contents to be included in the report.

Computing reportable income

[57.7] A reporting fund needs to provide a computation of reportable income for a period of account, based on the 'total comprehensive income for the period' where international accounting standards are used, or the equivalent entries to this where it is not.

Thus, accounts must be prepared using either international accounting standards (IAS) or generally accepted accounting practice (GAAP). The basis to be used must be shown in the application for reporting status. If neither IAS nor an acceptable GAAP is being used then a statement must be provided showing which entries equate to 'total comprehensive income' per IAS, and what adjustments will be used to calculate the effective interest income and comparables required. Where there is a change in accounting policy, an adjustment is required. Where there is a change in accounting practice to GAAP, the fund must apply to give notice to HMRC that the accounts do not comply with IAS. If the new basis uses IAS, the fund must give notice to HMRC. HMRC must accept or reject the application within 28 days. If the application is rejected, there is a right of appeal to the Tribunal.

Adjustments to the income statement are required for:

- capital items;
- special classes of income e.g. group income from wholly-owned subsidiaries, income from other reporting funds, income from certain non-reporting funds, interest income computed in an unacceptable way;
- equalisation arrangementsoperated by the fund when a participator disposes of an interest in it;
- wholly-owned subsidiaries (95% or 100% subsidiaries), the receipts, expenditure, assets and liabilities of which are attributed to the fund;
- interests in other offshore funds — where a reporting fund (A) invests in another reporting fund (B) then the excess of income reported by B over what was distributed by B to A must be added to fund A's reportable income; where the investment is in a non-reporting fund then (if certain conditions are met) the fund undertakes its own calculation of the income from the non-reporting fund and includes this in its reportable income;

[*SI 2009 No 3001, Regs 62–72*].

Equalisation

Amendments have been made with effect from 27 May 2011 to the reportable income calculation with regard to equalisation.

Applications for reporting status should (per the amended *Reg 53*) state whether the fund is intending to operate equalisation arrangements (whether full or otherwise), and if not, whether the fund is intending to make income adjustments, or not, and if so whether such adjustments are on the basis of reported income or accounting income (giving further details where applicable).

Where the fund intends to make adjustments on the basis of accounting income then the difference between the amount of reported income per unit using this method, and the amount of reported income per unit as calculated on the basis of reported income, should be no more than 10%. If HMRC believe it will be more they will not accept the application. The manager can appeal such rejection within 42 days. The information above with regard to equalisation arrangements operated by funds, or income adjustments made, and the effect on reported income per unit, should be included in the report to participants.

A new *Reg 50A* is inserted giving the meaning of 'equalisation arrangements' and 'full equalisation arrangements'. A fund operates 'full equalisation arrangements' if the equalisation amount is included in the consideration for an initial purchase in a statement in writing to the participant making the acquisition, or it is included in the report to participants.

For funds operating equalisation arrangements: 'Equalisation amount' is now defined at amended *Reg 72(2)* as being that part of the acquisition price attributable to the undistributed income which has accrued to the fund in the period of account up to but not including the date of acquisition. When a person acquires an interest in the fund by initial purchase, then the reportable income must be increased by the equalisation amount. Where a participant disposes of their interest by redemption, then the reportable income must be reduced by an amount equal to that part of the redemption price that is attributable to the undistributed income that has accrued in the period up to but not including redemption.

For funds that do not operate equalisation arrangements: new *Regs 92A, 92B* and *92C*, are inserted into the 2009 regulations. These deal with the computation of reported income. Where the fund applies income adjustments on the basis of reported income the reported income per unit for a computation period is calculated by dividing the reported income of the fund for the period by the average number of units in the fund in issue during the period.

Where the fund applies income adjustments on the basis of accounting income, the reported income per unit for a reporting period is the product of the sum of the accounting income per unit for all computation periods in the reporting period ('AIU') and the reported income of the fund for the reporting period ('RI'), divided by the sum of accounting income for all the computation periods in the reporting period ('AI'). The computation period is as determined by the fund pursuant to certain rules (see *Reg 92C*). Where the difference in the amount of reported income per unit calculated using this method and the amount of reported income per unit using the reported income method (above) is, or is likely to be, more than 10% of the latter, then the fund must make income adjustments in that and future reporting periods on the basis of reported income, and the manager must give notice to HMRC of the change in method.

Where a participant has acquired an interest in a reporting fund by way of initial purchase and the fund operates full equalisation arrangements then the amount of any excess treated as additional distributions is reduced by the equalisation amount; similarly the amount of any actual distributions is treated as reduced by the amount by which the equalisation amount exceeds the excess. In the latter case the expenditure given for the acquisition of the interest (with regard to the position on disposal) shall be treated as reduced by the amount of the reduction in the actual distributions. [*New Reg 94A*].

There are transitional provisions with regard to funds which are reporting funds as at 27 May 2011. The manager of such a transitional fund must give the statements as to whether they intend to operate equalisation arrangements by a notice in writing to HMRC by 27 May 2012. A transitional fund will be treated as having operated equalisation arrangements, full equalisation arrangements or as not operating equalisation arrangements in accordance with that notice from the time that the fund first became a reporting fund for the purposes of any report made to participants after 27 May 2011. A manager of a transitional fund may also elect by notice that these equalisation provisions shall not apply in relation to a reporting period ending before 27 May 2011.

Where the requisite notice as to the fund's equalisation position is not given to HMRC, then the fund will be treated as not operating equalisation arrangements and as intending to make adjustments on the basis of reported income.

[*SI 2011 No 1211, Pt 2: Regs 4–17*].

Disposals

A charge to tax arises if a company disposes of an asset. An offshore income gain arises to the disposing company where either the asset is an interest in a non-reporting fund at the time of the disposal or the following are met:

- the reporting fund was previously a non-reporting fund;
- the interest was an interest in a non-reporting fund during some or all of the material period;
- an election was not prevented by *Reg 48(5)* (conversion of a non-reporting fund to a reporting fund);
- no election was made under *Reg 48(2)*.

Non-trading funds

Where the following two conditions are satisfied, a reporting fund is not treated as trading:

- the equivalence condition; and
- the diversity of ownership condition.

These provisions give certainty to these types of funds that transactions undertaken will be treated as disposals giving rise to capital gains as opposed to 'trading' profits (reportable income). See further the offshore funds manual OFM14500.

The '*equivalence condition*' requires the fund to meet two conditions throughout the period of account. These are that the fund is recognised by FSA under *Financial Services and Markets Act 2000, ss 264, 270* or *272* and that the fund is an Undertaking for Collective Investments in Transferrable Securities (UCITS) fund. The amendments to the 2009 regulations effective from 27 May 2011 include an additional category of fund which will be equivalent: a fund constituted in another EEA state which is authorised in that State to market to retail or professional investors and is required to limit its borrowing and exposure under derivative contracts and forward transactions to 100% of its net asset value.

[*SI 2011 No 1211, Reg 37*].

A '*diversely owned fund*' is one fulfilling the conditions in *SI 2009 No 3001, Regs 75* and *76*. The conditions per *Reg 75* are that throughout the period of account:

(A) the fund produces documents, available to investors and to HMRC, which contain:
   - a statement specifying the intended categories of investor;
   - an undertaking that interests in the fund will be widely available; and
   - an undertaking that interests in the fund will be marketed and made available per condition (C);

(B) the specification of the intended categories of investor do not have a limiting or deterrent effect, and, any other terms or conditions governing participation in the fund do not have a limiting or deterrent effect; and

(C) the interests in the fund must be marketed and made available: sufficiently widely to reach the intended categories of investors, and in a manner appropriate to attract those categories of investors; and a person who falls within one of the intended categories of investors can, upon request to the manager of this fund, obtain information about the fund and acquire units in it.

The changes effective from 27 May 2011 amend *Reg 75* to include in addition funds where an investor is: an offshore fund, an OEIC or an authorised unit trust scheme, ('the feeder fund'); with the same manager as the fund, and where the conditions A to C of *Reg 75* are met in relation to the fund when considering in addition the position with regard to the feeder fund, its documents and intended investors.

[*SI 2011 No 1211, Reg 38*].

The manager of an existing eligible offshore fund or the manager of a non-reporting fund may make an application to convert from a non-reporting to a non-trading reporting fund where the equivalence and diversity of ownership conditions are met. The procedure and when clearance may not be relied on are laid out in detail in *Regs 78* and *79* respectively. Where a diversely owned fund carries out an investment transaction (as defined in *Regs 81–89*) in an accounting period, the investment transaction is treated as a non-trading transaction.

Index tracking funds

Under the 2011 amendments to the 2009 regulations, where a reporting fund has an interest in a non-reporting fund, and:

- the aim of the fund's investment policy is to replicate the composition of a qualifying index;
- the main purpose of the investment in the non-reporting fund was to represent the composition of the qualifying index; and
- the capital and income of the fund replicate the returns of the investments comprised in the qualifying index;

then the adjustments identified at *SI 2009 No 3001, Regs 69–71* do not apply in respect of the interest in the non-reporting fund.

[*SI 2011 No 1211, Reg 35*].

Transparent funds

A new *Chapter 6A (Regs 89A–89E)* is inserted in the 2009 Regulations, effective from 27 May 2011, which deals with the reportable income for a transparent reporting fund.

A transparent fund must provide a computation of its reportable income for a period of account. This is comprised of:

- each of the separate sums of income for the period which fall within (a) or (b) of *Reg 11*, that is, income which would be chargeable on individual investors resident in the UK as 'relevant foreign income' under *ITTOIA 2005, s 830(2)*, such as trading income, property business income, interest, royalties, etc. (or where the income is from an asset is in the UK, would be so chargeable if the asset were not in the UK); and

- the adjustments made to those sums in accordance with the new regulations inserted at *89C–89E*.

The adjustments to be made include:

- where the transparent fund has invested in a reporting fund, the excess of the income reported by such fund in respect of its interest, over the amount distributed by the reporting fund (or its best estimate in the absence of a report from the reporting fund);
- where the transparent fund has invested in non-reporting funds (first case), the treatment above for investment in a reporting fund applies, if the following conditions apply:
  - (a) the transparent fund has access to the accounts of the non-reporting fund;
  - (b) the transparent fund has sufficient information to enable it to prepare a computation of reportable income for the non-reporting fund; and
  - (c) the transparent fund can reasonably expect to rely on continued access to the information:
- where the transparent fund has invested in non-reporting funds (second case), but the conditions in the first case (above) are not met, then the reportable income of the transparent fund shall include an amount equal to the increase in fair value of the interest in the non-reporting fund (as reduced by any decrease in fair value in an earlier period, under certain conditions).

A new *Reg 92D* is inserted for transparent reporting funds stating that the report to participants for a reporting period must contain sufficient information to enable those participants to meet their tax obligations in the UK with respect to their interest in the fund, and include a statement whether or not the fund remains a reporting fund at the date the fund makes the report available.

[*SI 2011 No 1211, Regs 21–27*].

Tax treatment of participants

[57.8] In a non-transparent fund, the excess of reported income over distributions is treated as additional distributions made to the participants in proportion to their rights, such distributions being made on the fund distribution date (see below). For a participant chargeable to corporation tax such distribution is exempt if an actual distribution would normally be treated as exempt, otherwise it will be chargeable to corporation tax under general principles.

Where the fund is transparent, any excess of reported income over the fund's income for the period is treated as additional (notional) income of the participants in proportion to their rights. The notional income is treated as a distribution to participants at the end of the reporting period on the 'fund distribution date'. The latter date is, where the fund reports to participants within six months of the end of the reporting period, the day the report is issued. In any other case, it is the last day of the reporting period.

Where the participant is chargeable to corporation tax, the notional distribution is exempt if an actual distribution would have been exempt. When a company disposes of an interest in the fund, any notional distributions on which it has borne tax is added to the acquisition costs for the purpose of calculating the chargeable gain or allowable loss.

The changes from 27 May 2011 include an amendment to *CTA 2009, s 490* with regard to offshore funds which are treated as creditor relationship rights. Where the fund is transparent then the holding will not be treated as falling within the *CTA 2009* provisions. Specifically *s 490(7)* is amended such that a holding in an offshore fund (including a unit trust which is also an offshore fund) is not treated as a creditor relationship if the income arising to the fund is treated as income of the company investor. Thus the loan relationship rules will apply directly with regard to the underlying assets of the fund, where relevant.

[*SI 2011 No 1211, Reg 45*].

Interaction with *TCGA 1992, s 106A*

With regard to the general provisions as to reported income, a new *para 3A* is inserted in *Reg 94* such that when a participant disposes of an interest in a reporting fund and *TCGA 1992, s 106A* (identification of securities for capital gains tax) applies to that disposal then the disposal is to be ignored when considering the calculation of the excess of reported income over distributed income and the participant treated as holding the interest at the end of the reporting period.

[*SI 2011 No 1211, Reg 40*].

Reporting fund becoming non-reporting fund

[57.9] Where a reporting fund becomes a non-reporting fund, the participant may elect to be treated as making a deemed disposal at the end of the fund's final period of account as a reporting fund and to acquire an interest in the non-reporting fund on the first day of that fund's first period of account.

Offshore income gains

[57.10] 'Offshore income gains' are treated as income of the company making the disposal for the accounting period in which the disposal is made.

However, no charge to tax under these provisions arises if any of the following apply:

- the interest in the fund falls within the loan relationship rules;
- the derivative contract rules apply to the interest in the fund;
- the intangible asset rules apply to the interest in the fund;

- the asset is a right under a policy of insurance;
- the interest in the fund is held as trading stock;
- the disposal is taken into account in computing trading profits;
- the asset is a loan which is not a 'participating loan';
- they are certain interests in 'transparent funds' (conditions apply);
- they are rights in an offshore fund acquired before 1 December 2009 and those rights did not constitute a material interest in an offshore fund on acquisition;
- they are offshore income gains of charitable trusts, which are exempt when the gains are applicable and applied for charitable purposes (but there is a deemed disposal if the charitable trust ceases).

[*SI 2009 No 3001, Regs 25–31*].

A reporting fund must provide details, to both HMRC and UK investors, of investors' shares of reported income. HMRC may require a fund to provide further information.

In most cases, if a fund has been a reporting fund throughout the period a UK investor has held the investment, any profit on disposal of the holding is taxed as a capital gain. However, this is subject to transitional provisions.

If the fund has been a non-reporting fund then any profit on disposal is charged to income as an offshore income gain.

Unlisted trading company exception: under the 2011 amendments to the 2009 regulations no liability to tax arises under *Reg 17* (charge to tax on participant disposing of an interest in a non-reporting fund) if:

- the disposal is a disposal of an interest in an offshore fund; and
- the sole or main purpose of the fund is to invest in qualifying companies;
- throughout the period starting with the date on which the interest was acquired and ending 12 months before the date of the disposal the fund met the investment condition (see below); and
- participants in the fund have access to, and are able to obtain copies of, sufficient information to demonstrate that the fund intends to dispose of any holdings of shares or securities as required to satisfy the investment condition.

The 'investment condition' is that at least 90% of the value of the assets of the fund consists of: direct or indirect holdings in qualifying companies; or holdings of shares or securities which are listed (on a recognised stock exchange or regulated market) and which the fund is going to dispose of as soon as reasonably practicable; or which the fund believes will cease to be listed (or admitted) within 12 months. Cash holdings are disregarded.

A '*qualifying company*' means a trading company or the holding company of a trading group or a trading subgroup, where: the shares of the company are not listed on a recognised stock exchange or admitted to trading on a regulated market; and the activities of the trading company or, in the case of a holding company, the activities of the members of the group or subgroup taken together, do not include to a substantial extent the carrying out of investment transactions undertaken in the course of a trade.

Reference is made to *TCGA 1992, Sch 7AC* (with regard to substantial shareholdings) for the definitions of 'qualifying company', 'trading company', 'trading group' and 'trading subgroup'.

[*SI 2011 No 1211, Reg 19*].

Computation of offshore income gains

[57.11] An offshore income gain is the 'basic gain' arising on a disposal.

The 'basic gain' is the gain computed using capital gains tax rules, but ignoring any corporation tax arising under the regulations or any indexation allowance available under capital gains tax rules and subject to the following:

- share for share exchange under *TCGA 1992, s 135*;
- share for share exchange under *TCGA 1992, s 135*;
- exchange of interests of different classes;
- earlier disposal to which no gain/no loss disposal applies;
- where there has been a previous no gain/no loss disposal;
- where a rollover relief claim or a claim for gift relief (check) for capital gains tax is made in respect of a transaction otherwise than at arm's length, the claims do not affect the computation of the basic gain;
- where the basic gain computation produces a loss, the basic gain is nil.

Reporting requirements

[57.12] A company must send or otherwise make available a report for each 'reporting period' to each participant. There are a number of methods of reporting (see *SI 2009 No 3001, Reg 90*).

A 'reporting period' is the same as the fund's period of account, where that is twelve months or less. Where the period of account exceeds twelve months, there are two reporting periods, the first being the first twelve months and the second the remainder. *Regulation 92* sets out the contents of the report.

A reporting fund must also provide HMRC with information for each period of account, within six months of the end of that account. The information required is: audited accounts; computation of reportable income; copy of participant's report; the reported income within each reporting period within the period of account; the amount distributed to participants; number of units in issue at the end of each reporting period falling within the period of account; the amount of reported income per such unit; a declaration that the fund has complied with its obligations under the regime (as per the application procedure) (see *Reg 106*).

Amendments to the 2009 regulations as from 27 May 2011 allow a reporting fund to provide unaudited accounts if HMRC are satisfied that it would be impossible or unreasonable to provide audited accounts and there is not reason to believe that the unaudited accounts cannot be relied upon for the purpose of calculating reportable income.

[*SI 2011 No 1211, Reg 41*].

Offshore income gains and capital gains

[57.13] The offshore income gain on disposal is deducted from consideration used in the capital gains disposal. However, where the disposal is a part disposal and apportionment is required, this rule does not apply. There are consequential adjustments to the calculation of rollover relief and in the case of reconstructions involving the exchange of shares or issue of securities.

Disposals of interest — capital gains implications

[57.14] A disposal of an interest in a reporting fund is a disposal for capital gains tax purposes and the accumulated undistributed income is taken into account as a cost of acquisition and disposal. Each undistributed amount is treated as incurred on the fund distribution date for the reporting period for which it is treated as a distribution.

Breaching the reporting fund requirements

[57.15] A breach may either be minor or serious. A minor breach is one:

- for which there is a reasonable excuse; or
- which is inadvertent and remedied as soon as reasonably possible.

Provided that, if the reporting fund corrects a minor breach without HMRC intervention (as defined in *Reg 108*), it is not regarded as a breach for these purposes. A serious breach is one which is designated as serious or which is not minor.

Leaving the reporting fund regime

[57.16] There are two ways of leaving the reporting fund regime:

- giving notice of termination;
- failing to comply with requirements.

Non-reporting funds

[57.17] Subject to transitional provisions and the exceptions above, there is a disposal of an interest in a non-reporting fund where there would be a capital gains tax disposal. However, where *TCGA 1992, ss 135, 136* would otherwise apply, the company is treated as disposing of an interest in a non-reporting fund for market value at the time of the exchange or deemed exchange.

If a participant disposes of an interest in a non-reporting fund then this will give rise to an offshore income gain which is charged to tax on income. There is similarly a charge to tax with regard to an offshore income gain where the asset disposed of is an interest in a reporting fund at the time of the disposal; the reporting fund was previously a non-reporting fund (which then applied for reporting status); the interest was in a non-reporting fund at the time of acquisition; the participant was not prevented from making an election to be treated as if they had disposed of their interest and reacquired it (see **57.18**); and no such election was made.

Where a disposal gives rise to an offshore income gain and is also a disposal for capital gains tax purposes, the amount of the offshore income gain is deducted from the consideration for capital gains purposes, except in the case of a part disposal where a fraction is applied before the deduction is made. Adjustments are also required where the disposal falls with *TCGA 1992, ss 135, 136 or 162*.

When a non-reporting fund which is a transparent fund has an interest in a reporting fund, it is taxed on its proportionate share of the reporting fund's income as if it were its miscellaneous income arising on the same date as the reporting funds excess is treated as made.

Conversion to a reporting fund

[57.18] Where an offshore fund stops being a non-reporting fund and becomes a reporting fund, a participant in the fund may make an election to be treated as disposing of its interest in the non-reporting fund on the disposal date (i.e. the final day of the last period of account before the fund becomes a reporting fund) and acquiring an interest in the reporting fund at the start of its first period of account. There must be a positive gain for this election to be available. A company must make the election in its corporation tax return for the accounting period that includes the disposal date.

A participant in a reporting fund when it becomes a non-reporting fund may elect to make a deemed disposal of the interest at the end of the reporting fund's final period and acquire an interest in a non-reporting fund at the start of that fund's first period of account. This election is conditional on the reporting fund having made a report to the participant for the final period. The deemed disposal and acquisition are treated as made for an amount equal to the net asset value of the participant's interest in the fund at the end of the period of account for which the fund's income is reported. The election should be included in the company participant corporation tax return for the accounting period in which the disposal falls.

Information requirements

[57.19] As highlighted at **57.12** above, *SI 2009 No 3001, Reg 106* lays down the information to be provided annually to HMRC within six months of the end of a period of account. In addition, HMRC may notify a fund to provide such information as they may require for the purpose. The fund must be given not less than 42 days to produce the information. See also **57.12** above with regard to the 2011 changes allowing a fund to provide unaudited accounts in certain circumstances.

The 1984 regime

[57.20] The following is the regime which operated before 1 December 2009.

Transitional rules

[57.21] An existing fund may apply to be treated as a distributing fund under the 1984 regime for the period of account overlapping 1 December 2009, and if successful may apply to continue to be treated as a distributing fund for the succeeding period of account, provided neither period of account ends on or after 31 May 2012.

A new fund established on or after 1 December 2009 under existing umbrella arrangements or arrangements with more than one class of interest may similarly apply to be a distributing fund in respect of a period of account with the same accounting date as the existing fund, if the existing fund is given distributor status.

Disposal of material interests in non-qualifying offshore funds

[57.22] The 1984 offshore fund regime applies to a disposal by any person of an asset:

(a) if, at the time of the disposal, the asset constitutes a 'material interest' in an 'offshore fund' (see **57.24** below) which is or has at any 'material time' been a 'non-qualifying offshore fund' (see **57.25** below); or

(b) if:
  (i) at the time of the disposal, the asset constitutes an interest in a UK resident company or in a unit trust scheme within *CTA 2010, s 621; ICTA 1988, s 469(7)* which has UK resident trustees; and
  (ii) at a 'material time' after 31 December 1984 the interest was a material interest in a 'non-qualifying offshore fund'. (For account periods (see **57.25** below) ending before 22 July 2004, this condition was that the company or unit trust was a 'non-qualifying offshore fund' and the asset constituted a 'material interest' in that fund.) For this purpose the provisions of *TCGA 1992, s 127*, equating original shares with a new holding on reorganisation, apply.

[*ICTA 1988, s 757(1); FA 1984, s 92(1); FA 2004, s 145, Sch 26 para 4(2)*].

A '*material time*' is any time after 31 December 1983 or, if later, the earliest date on which any 'relevant consideration' was given for the acquisition of the asset. '*Relevant consideration*' is that given by or on behalf of the person making the disposal or a predecessor in title which would be taken into account in determining any gain or loss on disposal under *TCGA 1992*. [*ICTA 1988, s 757(7)*].

With some modifications, a disposal occurs for offshore fund purposes if there would be a disposal under *TCGA 1992*. Death is an occasion of charge as the deceased is deemed to have made a disposal at market value, immediately before his death, of any asset which was or had at any time been a 'material interest' in a 'non-qualifying offshore fund'. In addition, neither *TCGA 1992, s 135* nor *s 136* will apply, and there will therefore be a disposal at market value, if an exchange or arrangement is effected in such a way that an interest in a 'non-qualifying offshore fund' is exchanged for an interest in a distributing fund. The same principle applies to exchanges of different classes of interest where they form separate funds in their own right (see **57.24** below). [*ICTA 1988, ss 757(2)–(6), 762A; FA 2004, s 145, Sch 26 paras 4(3)(4), 15(1)*].

A *Pt 5* transfer under *Proceeds of Crime Act 2002* (as in **10.13 CAPITAL ALLOWANCES — INTRODUCTION**) of an asset within (a) or (b) above is not treated as a disposal for offshore fund purposes where no compensating payment is made to the transferor. [*Proceeds of Crime Act 2002, Sch 10 paras 7, 10; CTA 2009, Sch 1 para 547*].

Offshore funds operating equalisation arrangements

[57.23] There are specific provisions to enable funds operating 'equalisation arrangements' to satisfy the 'distribution test' (see **57.26** below) which the nature of such funds might otherwise preclude. As a corollary, provision is also made to ensure that the 'accrued income' paid to outgoing investors as part of their capital payments is treated as income for tax purposes when the fund qualifies as a distributor.

Definition

For these purposes, an offshore fund operates '*equalisation arrangements*' where the first distribution paid to a person acquiring a 'material interest' by way of 'initial purchase' includes a payment which is a return of capital (debited to the fund's 'equalisation account') determined by reference to the income which had accrued to the fund in the period before that person's acquisition. An acquisition is by way of '*initial purchase*' if it is by way of direct purchase from the fund's managers in their capacity as such.

Where a sub-fund or class of interest is treated as a fund in its own right (see **57.24** below), this definition applies with appropriate modifications.

'Accrued income' chargeable to income tax — application of offshore fund rules

A disposal is one to which the offshore fund provisions apply, subject to exception below, if it is a disposal by any person of a 'material interest' in an 'offshore fund' operating equalisation arrangements where:

(i) the disposal proceeds are not a trading receipt; and
(ii) the fund *is not*, and *has not been*, at any material time (see above) a 'non-qualifying offshore fund' (see **57.25** below)

(i.e. the provisions apply also to *distributing* funds (see **57.26** below) with equalisation arrangements).

Capital gains tax rules for disposals apply as they do for other offshore fund disposals (see **57.1** above) with some variations. Death is not treated as a disposal in this context. In addition, *TCGA 1992, s 127* (reorganisations etc.) (including that section as applied by certain other *TCGA 1992* provisions) does not apply and there is a disposal at market value in such circumstances.

Exception

The offshore fund legislation does *not* apply as indicated above to a disposal where the fund's income for the period preceding the disposal is of such a nature that the part relating to the interest in question is in any event chargeable as mentioned at **57.27**(b) below on the person disposing of the interest (or would be so chargeable if residence/domicile/situation of assets requirements were met).

[*ICTA 1988, ss 757(2)(3), 758; FA 2004, s 145, Sch 26 para 5; SI 2004 No 2572, Reg 3*].

Material interests in offshore funds

[57.24] An **'offshore fund'** is a 'collective investment scheme' constituted by:

(a) a company resident outside the UK; or
(b) a unit trust scheme within *ICTA 1988, s 469(7)* which has non-UK resident trustees; or
(c) any other arrangements taking effect under overseas law which create rights in the nature of co-ownership under that law.

'Collective investment scheme' means, before 1 January 2007, as defined by *Financial Services and Markets Act 2000, s 235* and on or after 1 January 2007, any arrangements which are a collective investment scheme for the purposes of the *Financial Services and Markets Act 2000, Pt 17*, or would be if the words 'within a period appearing to him to be reasonable' were omitted from *s 236(3)(a)* of that Act. For account periods (see **57.25** below) ending on or after 22 July 2004, sub-funds of a main fund (the umbrella fund) and different classes of interest in a main fund constitute separate offshore funds. This allows the test for distributing status (see **57.26** below) to be applied to them independently. The offshore funds legislation is appropriately modified in its application to such sub-funds and classes of interest (see *SI 2004 No 2572*).

[*ICTA 1988, ss 756A–756C, 759(1)(1A); SI 2001 No 3629, Art 45; FA 2004, s 145, Sch 26 paras 3, 6(2); FA 2007, s 57(2)*].

A **'material interest'** is one which, when acquired, could reasonably be expected to be realisable (by any means, either in money or in asset form) within seven years for an amount reasonably approximate to its proportionate share of the market value of the fund's assets. For these purposes, an interest in an offshore fund which at any time is worth substantially more than its proportionate share of the fund's underlying assets is not to be regarded as so realisable. [*ICTA 1988, s 759(2)–(4)*]. If shares in a quoted overseas company have habitually been traded at or near net asset value, and an investor in these shares had a reasonable expectation, on acquisition, of a future sale at or near such value, those shares are likely to represent a 'material interest'. (HMRC Statement of Practice, SP 2/86).

Exceptions

The following are not material interests:

(i) interests in respect of loans etc. made in the ordinary course of banking business;

(ii) rights under insurance policies;
(iii) shares in a company resident outside the UK where:
 (a) the shares are held by a company and the holding is necessary or desirable for the maintenance and development of a trade carried on by the company, or by an associated company within *CTA 2010, s 449; ICTA 1988, s 416*; and
 (b) the shares confer at least 10% of the voting rights and, on winding-up, a right to at least 10% of the assets after discharging all prior liabilities; and
 (c) the shares are held by not more than ten persons and all confer both voting rights and a right to assets on winding-up; and
 (d) at the time of acquisition of the shares the company could reasonably expect to realise its interest for market value within seven years only by virtue of (I) an arrangement requiring the company's fellow participators to purchase its shares and/or (II) provisions of either the overseas company's constitution or an agreement between the participators regarding that company's winding-up.
(iv) interests in companies resident outside the UK at any time when the holder is entitled to have the company wound up and to receive in that event in the same capacity more than 50% of the assets after discharging all prior liabilities.

[*ICTA 1988, s 759(5)–(8)*].

HMRC have also indicated that normal commercial loans or other debt instruments entitling the lender to no more than a fixed return of principal on redemption, and which are not geared to the underlying asset value of the borrower's business, are not regarded as 'material interests'. (HMRC Statement of Practice, SP 2/86).

HMRC have issued an internet statement (www.hmrc.gov.uk/collective/def-offshore.htm) to clarify the effect of the change in the definition of an offshore fund in *FA 2007, s 57*.

'Market value' for the purposes of the offshore funds legislation is determined according to capital gains tax rules with necessary modifications of *TCGA 1992, s 272(5)* (market value in relation to rights in unit trust schemes) where appropriate. [*ICTA 1988, s 759(9)*].

Non-qualifying offshore funds

[57.25] An offshore fund is **'non-qualifying'** except during an 'account period' in respect of which it is certified by HMRC as a distributing fund pursuing a 'full distribution policy' (see **57.26** below). For these purposes, the first '*account period*' begins when the fund begins to carry on its activities or, if later, on 1 January 1984. An '*account period*' ends on the fund's accounting date or, if earlier, twelve months from the beginning of the period or on the fund's ceasing to carry on its activities. In addition, if the fund is a non-UK resident company, an '*account period*' ends when it becomes UK resident, and if the fund is a unit trust with non-UK resident trustees, it ends when those trustees become UK resident. Where a sub-fund or class of interest is treated as a fund in its own right (see **57.24** above), references to '*account period*' are to the account period of the main fund. [*ICTA 1988, s 760(1)(2)(8)–(10A); FA 1984, s 95(8); FA 2004, s 145, Sch 26 para 7(3)*].

Conditions for certification

The investment conditions for certification are significantly relaxed in relation to account periods ending on or after 22 July 2004. For earlier account periods, and subject to the modifications of conditions for certification in certain cases noted below, an offshore fund is not to be certified as a 'distributing fund' for any account period if, at any time in that period:

(a) more than 5% by value of the fund's assets consists of interests in other offshore funds (but see below); or
(b) more than 10% by value of the fund's assets consists of interests in a single company. For this purpose:
    (i) the value of an interest in a single company is determined as at the most recent occasion (in that account period or earlier) on which the fund acquired an interest in that company for money or money's worth. However an occasion is disregarded if it is one on which *TCGA 1992, s 127* (equation of original shares and new holding) applied, including that section as applied by later provisions of *TCGA 1992* (reorganisations, conversion of securities etc.), and on which no consideration is given for the interest other than the interest in the original holding;
    (ii) an interest is disregarded, except for determining the total value of the fund's assets, if it consists of a current or deposit account provided in the normal course of its banking business by a company whose business it is to provide such account facilities in any currency for members of the public and bodies corporate; and
    (iii) Government-owned national or supra-national bodies whose activities are directed not with a view to commercial profits, but to the exercise of a wider social or economic function, are not regarded as companies for this purpose (HMRC Statement of Practice, SP 2/86); or
(c) the fund's assets include more than 10% of the issued share capital, or any class of it, in any company; or
(d) there is more than one class of material interests (see **57.24** above) in the fund and, were each class and the assets represented by it in a separate offshore fund, each such separate fund does not pursue a 'full distribution policy'. For this purpose, interests held solely by persons involved in the management of the fund's assets are disregarded if they carry no right or expectation to participate in profits and no right to anything other than the return of the price paid on winding-up or redemption.

For account periods ending on or after 22 July 2004, all of the above conditions are removed apart from (a). It follows that the commentary below on inadvertent failures and modifications of conditions apply, in relation to such account periods, only to condition (a). As a transitional measure, sub-funds that constitute an offshore fund in their own right as a result of *FA*

2004 (see **57.24** above) may have regard to the investments of the main fund (the umbrella fund) in applying the test at (a) above for account periods ending between 22 July 2004 and 31 December 2005 inclusive.

Where HMRC are satisfied that an apparent failure to comply with any of (a)–(c) above occurred inadvertently and was remedied without unreasonable delay, that failure may be disregarded.

[*ICTA 1988, s 760(3)–(7), Sch 27 para 14; FA 2004, Sch 26 paras 13, 14(7), 17*].

Modifications of conditions for certification

The conditions for certification in (a)–(d) above are modified in certain cases.

(A) **Investments in second tier funds.** If offshore funds ('primary funds') would fail to meet the conditions in (a) to (c) above because of investments in other offshore funds (referred to below as 'second tier funds') which could themselves be certified as qualifying distributing funds (without any modification of the (a) to (c) conditions), then the primary funds' interests in the second tier funds are left out of account, except for determining the total value of the primary funds' assets, in establishing whether the primary funds are prevented by (a) to (c) above from being certified as distributing funds. In addition, where the above applies, if at any time in a primary fund's account period that fund's assets include an interest in another offshore fund or in any company and the qualifying second tier fund's assets also include an interest in that other fund or company, then the primary fund's interest is aggregated with its proportionate share of the second tier fund's interest in determining whether the primary fund is within the limits in (a) to (c) above. Its share of the second tier fund's interest is the proportion which the average value during its account period of its own holding of interests in the second tier fund bears to the average value during the period of all interests in the second tier fund. [*ICTA 1988, s 760(3), Sch 27 paras 6, 7, 9; FA 2004, Sch 26 para 14(2)(3)*].

(B) **Investments in trading companies.** Where the assets of an offshore fund include an interest in a company whose business is wholly the carrying on of trade(s) the limit of 10% of a fund's assets invested in a single company in (b) above is increased to 20% and the 10% limit on the proportion of a class of share in any company in (c) above is increased to allow holdings of less than 50%. For these purposes companies are excluded if their business consists to any extent of banking or money-lending or of dealing, including dealing by way of futures contracts and traded options, in commodities, currency, securities, debts or other assets of a financial nature. [*ICTA 1988, s 760(3), Sch 27 paras 4(2), 10; FA 2004, Sch 26 para 14(4); CTA 2009, Sch 1 para 289*]. Dealing in commodities, currency and financial assets incidental to the business of a company will be disregarded in determining whether the company is trading. (HMRC Statement of Practice, SP 2/86).

(C) **Wholly-owned subsidiaries.** Where an offshore fund has a wholly-owned subsidiary company, the receipts, expenditure, assets and liabilities of the fund and the subsidiary are aggregated so that the fund and the subsidiary are treated as one for the purposes of determining whether the fund is within the limits in (a) to (d) above. In the same way, the interest of the fund in the subsidiary and any distributions or other payments between the fund and the subsidiary are left out of account. A wholly-owned subsidiary is one owned either directly and beneficially by the fund, or directly by the trustees of the fund for the benefit of the fund, or, in the case of a fund within **57.24**(c) above, in some other equivalent manner. Where the subsidiary has only one class of issued share capital, ownership of at least 95% of that capital by the offshore fund constitutes the subsidiary a wholly-owned subsidiary for this purpose, and only a corresponding proportion of the subsidiary's receipts, expenditure, assets and liabilities are then aggregated with those of the offshore fund. [*ICTA 1988, s 760(3), Sch 27 para 11; FA 2004, Sch 26 para 14(5); SI 2004 No 2572, Reg 4(1)(6)*].

(D) **Subsidiary dealing and management companies.** The investment restriction in (c) above does not apply to so much of an offshore fund's assets as consists of share capital of a company which is either:

(1) a wholly-owned subsidiary of the fund (as defined in (C) above) whose sole function is dealing in material interests in the offshore fund for management and administrative purposes and which is not entitled to any distribution from the fund; or

(2) a subsidiary management company of the fund whose sole function is to provide the fund, or other funds with an interest in the company, with advisory services or administrative, management and related property holding services on arm's length commercial terms. For the purposes of determining whether a company is a subsidiary management company of a fund, that company and any wholly-owned subsidiary companies it may itself have are regarded as a single entity. [*ICTA 1988, s 760(3), Sch 27 para 12; FA 2004, Sch 26 para 14(6)*].

(E) **Disregard of certain investments.** Certain holdings which would otherwise fall within the restriction at (c) above are not taken into account for the purposes of that restriction. This applies where no more than 5% of the value of the offshore fund's assets consists of such holdings and of interests in other non-qualifying offshore funds. [*ICTA 1988, s 760(3), Sch 27 para 13; FA 2004, Sch 26 para 14(6)*].

The distribution test

[57.26] An offshore fund pursues a **'full distribution policy'** with respect to an account period if:

(a) a distribution is made for that account period or for some other period falling wholly or partly within that period; and

(b) subject to modifications below, the distribution represents at least 85% of the fund's income and not less than 85% of its 'UK equivalent profits' for that period; and

(c) the distribution is made during or within six months after the end of the account period (the six-month limit may be extended at HMRC's discretion); and

(d) the form of the distribution is such that if any part of it were received in the UK by a company or an individual resident there and did not form part of the profits of a trade, profession or vocation, it would be chargeable to:
- corporation tax on income from non-trading loan relationships in respect of income arising from securities or possessions out of the UK or on overseas income; or
- income tax under any of the provisions listed at *ITTOIA 2005, s 830(2)* (relevant foreign income — see Tolley's Income Tax under Foreign Income) (or, before 2005/06, under *Schedule D, Case IV* or *V*).

These conditions may equally be satisfied by any two or more distributions taken together. [*ICTA 1988, Sch 27 para 1(1); ITTOIA 2005, Sch 1 para 350(2); F(No 2)A 2005, s 23(2); CTA 2009, Sch 1 para 289*].

The basic conditions in (a) to (d) above are modified in certain cases (see **57.27** below).

A fund is treated as pursuing a full distribution policy for any account period in which there is no income and no 'UK equivalent profits', or for account periods ending after 28 November 1994 for which gross fund income does not exceed 1% of the average value of fund assets during the period, but it will not be so treated for any account period for which no accounts are prepared. [*ICTA 1988, Sch 27 para 1(2)(2A)(3)(3A); FA 1995, s 134(4)(9); SI 2004 No 2572, Reg 4(1)(2); CTA 2009, Sch 1 para 289*].

Non-UK legal restrictions

Where in an account period an offshore fund is subject to non-UK legal restrictions on making distributions by reason of an excess of losses over profits as computed according to the law in question, a deduction is allowed from the fund's income of any amount which cannot be distributed but which would otherwise form part of the fund's income for that account period. [*ICTA 1988, Sch 27 para 1(6)(7); SI 2004 No 2572, Reg 4(1)(2); CTA 2009, Sch 1 para 289*].

Apportionment of income and distributions between account periods

Where a period for which accounts are made up or for which a distribution is made covers the whole or part of two or more account periods of the fund, the income or distribution is apportioned on a time basis according to the number of days in each period. A distribution made out of specified income but not for a specified period is attributed to the account period in which the income arose. Where no period or income is specified, a distribution is treated as made for the last account period ending before the distribution. If the distribution made, or treated as made, for an account period exceeds the income of that period the excess is reallocated to previous periods, to later periods before earlier ones, until exhausted, unless the distribution was apportioned on a time basis as mentioned above in which case the excess is first reapportioned on a just and reasonable basis to the other account period(s). [*ICTA 1988, Sch 27 para 1(4)(5); CTA 2009, Sch 1 para 289*].

'UK equivalent profits' of an offshore fund are the total profits, excluding chargeable gains, on which, after allowing for any deductions available, corporation tax would be chargeable, assuming that:

(i) the offshore fund is a UK resident company in the account period in question, but in no other; and
(ii) the account period is an accounting period of that company; and
(iii) any dividends or distributions from a UK resident company are included.

The rules for **LOAN RELATIONSHIPS** (**54**) and derivative contracts (see **30 DERIVATIVE CONTRACTS LEGISLATION**) used to be disregarded for this purpose, and it was assumed that income tax, rather than corporation tax, rules applied, as they did for unauthorised unit trusts. However, for account periods ending on or after 22 July 2004, the corporation tax rules relating to creditor loan relationships and profits/losses from derivative contracts apply as if the fund were an authorised unit trust. This change in treatment does not apply to funds in existence on or before 22 July 2004 unless they elect for it to apply. Such an election, once made, is irrevocable. Where, in a case where no election has been made, a new sub-fund or class of interest is established *after* 22 July 2004 and is regarded as a separate offshore fund by virtue of **57.24** above, the change in treatment does not apply to the sub-fund or class either, so that they always take the same treatment as the 'parent' fund.

Any UK government securities or securities of foreign states which are exempt from tax (see **46.11 INCOME TAX IN RELATION TO A COMPANY**) must be brought into account in determining the fund's total profits.

Whether a fund is trading will turn on the particular facts, but in general a fund would not normally be regarded as trading in respect of relatively infrequent transactions, or where the intention was merely to hedge specific investments which were not associated with trading activities. (HMRC Statement of Practice, SP 2/86).

The deductions referred to above include a deduction equal to that allowed against a fund's income where non-UK legal restrictions prevent distribution (see above) and a deduction equal to any foreign capital tax allowed as a deduction in determining the fund's income for the account period in question.

Interest paid to a non-UK resident is deductible in the same way as if it were paid to a UK resident. UK income tax (whether suffered by deduction or by assessment) is available as a deduction. (HMRC Statement of Practice, SP 2/86).

[*ICTA 1988, Sch 27 para 5; FA 1996, Sch 10 para 3; FA 2002, Sch 26 para 35; FA 2004, s 145, Sch 26 paras 1, 2; SI 2004 No 2572, Regs 4(1)(5), 6, 7; ITTOIA 2005, Sch 1 para 350(4); CTA 2009, Sch 1 paras 58, 289; FA 2009, Sch 14 para 13*].

Modifications of distribution test

[57.27] The basic rules of the distribution test in **57.26**(a) to (d) above are modified in various circumstances.

(a) **Funds operating equalisation arrangements.** Where an offshore fund operates such arrangements (see **57.23** above) throughout an account period (see **57.25** above), an amount equal to any 'accrued income' which is part of the consideration for certain disposals in that period is treated as a distribution for the purposes of the distribution test. This applies to a disposal:

(i) which is a disposal of a material interest in the fund to either the fund or the fund managers in their capacity as such; and

(ii) which is one to which the offshore fund rules apply (whether or not by virtue of their application to disposals from distributing funds with equalisation arrangements — see **57.23** above), or which is one to which the rules would apply if the provisions regarding the non-application of *TCGA 1992, ss 127, 135* applied generally and not only for the purpose of determining whether a disposal from a distributing fund with equalisation arrangements is brought within the rules (see **57.23** above); and

(iii) which is not a disposal within the *exception* at **57.23** above (where the income of the fund is, or would be, chargeable to tax as overseas income in any event).

The '*accrued income*' referred to above is that part of the consideration which would be credited to the fund's equalisation account if the interest were resold to another person by way of 'initial purchase' (see **57.23** above) on the same day. However, there are provisions to ensure that this accrued income figure is reduced where the interest disposed of was acquired by way of initial purchase (by any person) after the beginning of the account period by reference to which the accrued income is calculated. In addition, where an offshore commodity dealing fund (see also (c) below) operates equalisation and there is a disposal within (i) to (iii) above, one half of the accrued income representing commodity profits is left out of account in determining what part of the disposal consideration represents accrued income.

For the purposes of the distribution test, the distribution which the fund is treated as making on a disposal is treated as being paid to the person disposing of his interest, in the income form required by **57.26**(d) above, out of the income of the fund for the account period of disposal. Where a distribution is made to the managers (in their capacity as such) of a fund operating equalisation arrangements it is disregarded for the purposes of the distribution test except to the extent that it relates to that part of the period for which the distribution is made during which the managers (in that capacity) held that interest.

[*ICTA 1988, Sch 27 paras 2, 4(4); SI 2004 No 2572, Reg 4(1)(3); CTA 2009, Sch 1 para 289*].

(b) **Funds with income taxable on investors.** Where sums forming part of the income of an offshore fund within **57.24**(b) or (c) above:

(i) are chargeable to corporation tax as non-trade profits (formerly under *Schedule D, Case III*) in respect of income arising from securities or possessions out of the UK or as foreign income (formerly under *Schedule D, Case V*) in the hands of the company (or would be so chargeable if the assets from which the income is derived were situated outside the UK where this is not, in fact, the case); or

(ii) are chargeable to income tax under any of the provisions listed at *ITTOIA 2005, s 830(2)* (relevant foreign income — see Tolley's Income Tax under Foreign Income) (or, before 2005/06, under *Schedule D, Case IV* or *V*) in the hands of an individual (with the same proviso as in (i) above); or

(iii) would be so chargeable if the company or individual were UK resident or if the individual were domiciled in the UK and both resident and ordinarily resident there,

any such sums which are not actually part of a distribution complying with the part of the distribution test in **57.26**(c) and (d) above are treated as distributions which do so comply made out of the income of which they are part and paid to the holders of the interests in question. [*ICTA 1988, Sch 27 para 3; ITTOIA 2005, Sch 1 para 350(3); F(No 2)A 2005, s 23(3)(4); CTA 2009, Sch 1 para 289*].

(c) **Funds with commodity dealing income.** Where an offshore fund's income includes commodity dealing profits, half of those profits are left out of account in determining the fund's income and UK equivalent profits for the purposes of the distribution test in **57.26**(b) above. '*Commodities*' are defined as tangible assets dealt with on a commodity exchange, excluding currency, securities, debts or other financial assets. '*Dealing*' includes dealing by way of futures contracts and traded options. Where the fund's income includes both commodity dealing profits and other income, its expenditure is apportioned on a just and reasonable basis and the non-commodity dealing business is treated as carried on by a separate company when determining what expenditure, if any, is deductible under *CTA 2009, s 1219; ICTA 1988, s 75* (management expenses, see **51 INVESTMENT COMPANIES AND INVESTMENT BUSINESS**). See also (a) above for position where a commodity dealing fund operates equalisation arrangements. [*ICTA 1988, Sch 27 para 4; CTA 2009, Sch 1 para 289; SI 2004 No 2572, Reg 4(1)(4)*].

(d) **Wholly-owned commodity dealing subsidiaries.** In a situation within **57.25**(C) above, the fund and the subsidiary dealing company are similarly treated as a single entity for the purposes of the distribution test. [*ICTA 1988, Sch 27 para 11; SI 2004 No 2572, Reg 4(1)(6)*].

(e) **Investments in second tier funds.** In a situation within **57.25**(A) above, the UK equivalent profits of the primary fund for the period are increased by its 'share' of the 'excess income' (if any) of the second tier fund in determining whether not less than 85% of the primary fund's UK equivalent profits are distributed. The '*excess income*' of the second tier fund is the amount by which its UK equivalent profits exceeds its distributions. There are provisions for apportioning excess income between periods on a time basis when the account periods of the primary and second tier funds do not coincide. The primary fund's '*share*' of the excess income is the proportion which the average value during its account period of its own holding of interests in the second tier fund bears to the average value of all interests in that fund. [*ICTA 1988, Sch 27 paras 6, 8, 9*].

Qualifying investments test

[57.28] When an offshore fund which fails to meet the qualifying investments test at any time in the relevant period, pays a dividend or manufactured overseas dividend on or after 22 April 2009, the dividend is treated as interest for tax purposes in the recipients' hands. This means that an individual recipient who is a higher rate taxpayer is liable to pay tax at 40% instead of 32.5%. The 'relevant period' is the 'relevant period of account of the offshore fund or the year ending on the last day of that period if longer and the 'relevant period of account' is the period of account ending before the dividend is paid where distributable profits at the end equal or exceed the dividend or the period in which the dividend is paid.

The 'qualifying investments test' is that the market value of the fund's qualifying investments exceeds 60% of the market value of all the assets of the fund (excluding cash awaiting investment). Qualifying investments are as defined in *CTA 2009, s 494*. See **54.96** loan relationships.

Certification procedure

Fund requesting certification

[57.29] Application for certification as a distributing fund for an account period must be made within six months of the end of that period and should be sent to the HMRC Offshore Funds Centre, 1st Floor, Concept House, 5 Young Street, Sheffield S1 4LB. The application must be accompanied by a copy of the fund's accounts covering or including the account period for which certification is sought and provision of the required information in relation to the account period in question will assist HMRC in its consideration of the application. For details of the information required see HMRC Offshore Funds Guide Manual at OSFG01050.

Where HMRC is satisfied that the necessary conditions are met it must certify the fund as a distribution fund for the period in respect of which application was made. HMRC must give written notice if, after application, it determines that no certificate should be issued. It must also give notice where it appears that the accounts or other information provided do not make full and accurate disclosure of all relevant matters, in which case any notice of certification previously given is void. The fund may appeal to the tribunal (formerly Special Commissioners) against HMRC decisions within 90 days. The tribunal has jurisdiction to review any decision of HMRC relevant to a ground of the appeal. [*ICTA 1988, Sch 27 paras 15, 16; SI 2004 No 2572, Reg 4(1)(7)*].

A list of offshore funds which have been granted UK distributor status is available on HMRC's website.

Investor requesting certification

No appeal may be brought against a tax assessment (see **57.30** below) on the grounds that a fund should have been certified as a distributing fund in respect of an account period. However, where a fund does not apply for certification, an investor, who is assessed to tax for which he would not be liable if the fund were certified, may by notice in writing require HMRC to take action with a view to determining whether the fund should be so certified.

If more than one request from an investor is received, HMRC is taken to have complied with each if it complies with one.

Broadly, the procedure is as follows.

(i) HMRC invites the fund to apply for certification. The time limit for application (see above) is then extended, if necessary, to 90 days from the date of HMRC's invitation.
(ii) If the fund does not then apply for certification HMRC must determine the question as if such application had been made having regard to any accounts or information provided by the investor.
(iii) If, after HMRC has determined that the fund should not be certified, other accounts or information are provided which were not previously available, they must reconsider their determination.
(iv) HMRC must notify the investor who requested them to take action of their decision.
(v) HMRC has wide powers enabling it to disclose to interested parties information regarding HMRC or tribunal decisions or details of any notice given to a fund regarding a lack of full and accurate disclosure of information (see above).

[*ICTA 1988, Sch 27 paras 17, 18, 20*].

Postponement of tax

There are provisions to enable an investor to apply for tax assessed to be postponed pending HMRC's determination of the question of certification. [*ICTA 1988, Sch 27 para 19*].

Charge to corporation tax of offshore gain

[57.30] Where a disposal to which the offshore fund rules apply (including a disposal of a holding in a distributing fund operating equalisation arrangements — see **57.23** above) gives rise to an 'offshore income gain', then subject to below, that gain is treated for all purposes as income arising to the investor at the time of disposal and is chargeable to corporation tax as miscellaneous income (formerly under *Schedule D, Case VI*) in the accounting period in which the disposal is made.

For HMRC practice as regards identification of part disposals out of mixed holdings where a non-qualifying offshore fund has subsequently obtained distributor status, please see HMRC Savings and Investment Manual SAIM6380.

The following provisions have effect in relation to corporation tax on offshore income gains as they have in relation to corporation tax on chargeable gains.

(a) *TCGA 1992, s 2* (persons chargeable).
(b) *TCGA 1992, s 10* (gains accruing to non-residents carrying on a trade in the UK through a branch or agency) except that assets need not be situated in the UK.
(c) *TCGA 1992, s 12* (foreign assets of UK resident or ordinarily resident persons with foreign domicile chargeable on remittance basis).

Charitable exemption applies similarly to that for capital gains (see **20.7 CHARITIES**).

Where a disposal to which the offshore fund rules apply is one of settled property, any offshore income gain will escape the tax charge provided that the general administration of the trust is ordinarily carried on outside the UK and a majority of the trustees are not resident or not ordinarily resident in the UK.

[*ICTA 1988, s 761; ITTOIA 2005, Sch 1 para 308; F(No 2)A 2005, s 23(1); CTA 2009, Sch 1 para 220*].

HMRC do not regard an offshore income gain as qualifying as eligible investment income for the purposes of investment trusts per *CTA 2010, s 1158; ICTA 1988, s 842*. This view was stated in HMRC Tax Bulletin October 2005 p 1242. The date from which it is effective has been postponed to 1 January 2008. (See HMRC internet statement dated 15 December 2006.)

Computation of offshore income gain

[57.31] The computation of the gain depends upon whether the disposal is of an interest in a non-qualifying fund (see **57.32** below) or of an interest involving an equalisation element (see **57.33** below).

Disposals of interests in non-qualifying funds

[57.32] A '*material disposal*' (one to which the offshore fund rules apply otherwise than by virtue of the provisions regarding distributing funds operating equalisation arrangements — see **57.23** above and **57.33** below) gives rise to an '*offshore income gain*' equal to the 'unindexed gain' or, if less, the 'post-1983 gain'.

Subject to the modifications to the capital gains tax rules mentioned in **57.1** above and to exceptions below, the '*unindexed gain*' is the gain calculated under capital gains tax rules without indexation allowance and without regard to any corporation tax charge arising under the offshore fund rules. The exceptions are as follows.

(a) Where there has been indexation on an earlier disposal on a no gain/no loss basis within *TCGA 1992, s 56(2)*, the unindexed gain on the material disposal is computed as if indexation had not been available on the earlier disposal and, subject to that, as if the earlier disposal had produced neither gain nor loss.

(b) If the material disposal forms part of a transfer to which *TCGA 1992, s 162* applies (rollover relief on transfer of business), the unindexed gain is computed without any deduction falling to be made under that section in computing a chargeable gain.

(c) Any claim for relief under *FA 1980, s 79* (relief for gifts) does not affect the computation of the unindexed gain on the disposal. (See now *TCGA 1992, s 67*.)

(d) In the case of an insurance company carrying on life assurance business, where a profit from overseas life assurance business, attributable to a material disposal, is taken into account in the computation under *ICTA*

1988, s 441, the unindexed gain, if any, accruing on disposal is computed as if *TCGA 1992, s 37(1)* did not apply. For accounting periods beginning before 1 January 1992, this applies equally where a profit arising from general annuity business attributable to a material disposal is taken into account (or would be but for the provisions relating to offshore income gains of insurance companies (see **57.34** below)) in the computation under *ICTA 1988, s 436*.

(e) Where the computation of the unindexed gain would otherwise produce a loss, the unindexed gain is treated as nil so that no loss can arise on a material disposal.

[*ICTA 1988, Sch 28 paras 1–3, 5; FA 1990, Sch 7 para 7; FA 1991, Sch 7 para 10*].

'Post-1983 gains'

A person making a material disposal who acquired, or is treated as having acquired, the interest in question in the offshore fund before 1 January 1984, is treated as having disposed of and immediately reacquired his interest at market value on that date. The offshore income gain from 1 January 1984 to the date of disposal is then calculated in the ordinary way. If the person making the material disposal acquired the interest in question by way of a deemed no gain/no loss disposal (other than those arising by virtue of the indexation provisions of *FA 1982, s 86(5), Sch 13*) any previous owner's acquisition of the interest is treated as his acquisition of it. [*ICTA 1988, Sch 28 para 4*].

Disposals involving an equalisation element

[57.33] A disposal is a '*disposal involving an equalisation element*' if it is a disposal to which the offshore fund rules apply by virtue of the provisions relating to distributing funds operating equalisation arrangements (see **57.23** above). Such a disposal gives rise to an '*offshore income gain*' of an amount equal, subject to below, to the 'equalisation element' relevant to the asset disposed of. [*ICTA 1988, Sch 28 para 6(1)(3); SI 2004 No 2572, Reg 5*].

The **'equalisation element'** is the amount which would be credited to the fund's equalisation account in respect of accrued income if, on the date of the disposal, the asset disposed of were acquired by another person by way of 'initial purchase' (see **57.23** above). However, where the person making the disposal acquired the asset in question after the beginning of the account period by reference to which the accrued income is calculated, or at or before the beginning of that period where that period began before and ended after 1 January 1984, there are provisions to ensure that the equalisation element is reduced to exclude any part which accrued prior to either 1 January 1984 or to the investor's period of ownership. Where any of the accrued income represents commodity dealing profits (within **57.27**(c) above) half of that income is left out of account in determining the equalisation element. [*ICTA 1988, Sch 28 para 6(2)(4)–(6); SI 2004 No 2572, Reg 5*].

'Part I gains'

Where the offshore income gain as computed above would exceed the 'Part I gain', the offshore income gain is reduced to the lower figure. If there is no 'Part I gain' there can be no offshore income gain. The '*Part I gain*' is, broadly, the amount which would be the offshore income gain on the disposal if the disposal were a 'material disposal' within **57.32** above (i.e. within *ICTA 1988, Sch 28 Pt I*) as modified by certain consequential amendments. [*ICTA 1988, Sch 28 paras 7, 8*].

Miscellaneous

Offshore income gains accruing to persons resident or domiciled abroad

[57.34] There are consequential provisions made in connection with gains accruing to certain non-resident investors in offshore funds which modify, for the purposes of the offshore fund legislation, provisions relating to:

(a) chargeable gains accruing to certain non-resident companies under *TCGA 1992, s 13*;
(b) gains of non-resident settlements under *TCGA 1992, ss 80–98*;
(c) avoidance of tax by the transfer of assets abroad under *ITA 2007, ss 716–735* (formerly *ICTA 1988, ss 739, 740)*.

To the extent that an offshore income gain is treated by virtue of (a) or (b) above as having accrued to any person resident or ordinarily resident in the UK, that gain is not deemed to be the income of any individual under *ITA 2007, ss 716–735* (formerly *ICTA 1988, s 739* or *s 740*) or any provision of *ITTOIA 2005, Pt 5 Ch 5*, previously *ICTA 1988, Pt XV* (settlements). [*ICTA 1988, s 762; ITTOIA 2005, Sch 1 para 309*].

Capital gains tax

There are provisions to prevent a double charge to tax when a disposal gives rise to both an offshore income gain and a chargeable gain for capital gains tax purposes.

Where an offshore income gain arises on a 'material disposal' within **57.32** above, that gain is deducted from the sum which would otherwise constitute the amount or value of the consideration in the calculation of the capital gain arising under *TCGA 1992* (on 'the 1992 Act disposal'), although the offshore gain is not to be taken into account in calculating the fraction under *TCGA 1992, s 42(2)* (part disposal).

Where the 1992 Act disposal forms part of a transfer within *TCGA 1992, s 162* (rollover relief on transfer of business wholly or partly for shares) then, in determining the amount of the deduction from the gain on the old assets, the offshore income gain is deducted from the value of the consideration received in exchange for the business.

Where an exchange of shares or securities constitutes a disposal of an interest in an offshore fund (see **57.1** and **57.23** above), the amount of any offshore income gain to which the disposal gives rise is treated as consideration for the new holding.

Where the offshore fund provisions apply to a disposal of an interest in a fund operating equalisation arrangements (see **57.23** above) and the disposal:

(a) is not to the fund or to its managers in their capacity as such; and

(b) gives rise to an offshore income gain in accordance with **57.33** above; and

(c) is followed subsequently by a distribution to either the person who made the disposal or to a person connected with him (within *CTA 2010, s 1122; ICTA 1988, s 839*, see **25 CONNECTED PERSONS**) and that distribution is referable to the asset disposed of,

then the subsequent distribution (or distributions) is (are) reduced by the amount of the offshore income gain.

[*ICTA 1988, s 763; FA 2004, s 145, Sch 26 para 15(2)*].

For disposals on or after 6 March 1998, exemption from capital gains tax under *TCGA 1992, s 76(1)* is disapplied where the disposal is of an interest in a trust which has at any time been an offshore trust, or where the interest disposed of originated in a trust which has at any time been an offshore trust. [*TCGA 1992, s 76(1A)(1B)(3); FA 1998, s 128*]. See Tolley's Capital Gains Tax under Offshore Settlements.

Example

[57.35]

R Ltd, is a UK resident company which draws up accounts to 31 March. It invests in non-qualifying offshore funds as follows.

(i)	ABC fund		£
	30.11.83	1,000 shares purchased at £10 per share	10,000
	1.1.84	Market value per share = £20	20,000
	1.4.10	On amalgamation with XYZ fund (an offshore fund which is not and has not been non-qualifying) the 1,000 original shares are exchanged for 2,000 new shares in XYZ which have a value of £15 per share	30,000
(ii)	DEF fund		£
	1.8.83	500 units purchased at £25 per unit	12,500
	1.1.84	Market value per unit = £20	10,000
	1.2.10	500 units sold for £40 per unit	20,000

R Ltd has offshore income gains and capital gains/losses in its accounting period ending 31 March 2009 as follows.

Offshore income gains

Disposal on 1.2.10 of 500 DEF units

	Post-1983 gain	Unindexed gain
	£	£
Disposal proceeds	20,000	20,000
Market value at 1.1.84	10,000	
Cost		12,500
	£10,000	£7,500

As the unindexed gain is less than the post-1983 gain, the offshore income gain chargeable as income is £7,500.

Disposal on 1.4.10 of 1,000 ABC shares

	Post-1983 gain	Unindexed gain
	£	£
Disposal consideration	30,000	30,000
Market value at 1.1.84	20,000	
Cost		10,000
	£10,000	£20,000

The offshore income gain chargeable as income is the £10,000 post-1983 gain as this is less than the unindexed gain.

Capital gains computation

Disposal on 1.2.10 of 500 DEF units

	£
Disposal proceeds	20,000
Offshore income gain	7,500
	12,500
Cost	12,500
Chargeable gain/allowable loss	Nil

Disposal on 1.4.10 of 1,000 ABC shares

There is no liability to corporation tax on capital gains as the share exchange is not treated as a disposal under *TCGA 1992, s 135* (exchange of securities for those in another company). See Tolley's Capital Gains Tax.

Note

(a) The £10,000 offshore income gain arising on the exchange of ABC shares for XYZ shares will be treated as part of the acquisition cost for capital gains purposes on a subsequent disposal of XYZ shares (see **57.34** above).

Key points

[57.36] Points to consider are as follows.

- Interests in offshore funds may give rise to a capital disposal in certain circumstances. If the fund does not qualify then the 'gain' is subject to income tax. Funds that do not qualify for capital treatment are often referred to as Roll-up Funds with any gain arising on the ultimate disposal of units in such funds being subject to income tax at the UK resident taxpayers top rate of tax, without any relief for underlying taxes suffered within the fund.
- The definition of a qualifying fund has changed since 2009. As a result of this change the tax treatment of UK taxpayers with interests in qualifying funds has also been amended such that an annual tax charge arises as well as a charge to capital gains tax on disposal.
- Under the old rules (the 1984 rules) it was a requirement that 85% of income be distributed to the 'shareholder'. If this test was satisfied the fund was qualifying and on the ultimate disposal of the units the gain was treated as a capital gain. Income tax was due on the income distributions received by the UK resident taxpayer.
- Since 2009 a qualifying fund (a 'reporting fund') now has to report its income to HMRC. Shareholders are subject to income tax on distributions received, but in addition they are also liable to income tax on their share of the reported undistributed income.
- The new 2009 regime was amended in 2011 and various changes were introduced, notably with regard to the operation of equalisation arrangements by reporting funds for new and departing investors.
- Where a UK resident taxpayer is subject to income tax on reported but undistributed income they can treat the 'deemed' distributions as additional costs of acquisition for capital gains tax purposes. This ensures that the taxpayer does not suffer double tax on the ultimate disposal of the units in the fund, as the element of growth that is represented by retained income in the fund is accounted for by these additional acquisition costs.
- Funds may fall in and out of qualification each year depending on their reporting status. However such changes in status will make the UK taxpayers reporting extremely complex.
- If a reporting fund becomes a non-reporting fund the 'shareholder' has the right to elect for a deemed disposal of their interest to crystallise the capital gain. Going forward they will subjected

to the income tax regime applicable to non-reporting funds such that a future actual disposal of their interest in the fund will give rise to an income gain subject to income tax at their top marginal rate of tax.

- If a non-reporting fund becomes a reporting fund then the 'shareholder' has the right to elect for a deemed disposal of their interest to crystallise an income gain. Going forward they will be subject to the normal income tax annual charge and a capital gain on ultimate disposal.
- On a practical level these new rules require detailed record keeping by the taxpayer in order to ensure that disposals of units in qualifying funds are not unduly overtaxed.

58

Partnerships

Cross-references. See also **54.72 LOAN RELATIONSHIPS; 55.24, 55.9 LOSSES.**

See HMRC Company Taxation Manual CTM36500 *et seq*.

Simon's Taxes. See B7.204, D7.1.

Introduction

[58.1] Companies can form partnerships with individuals, other companies and trustees. Persons carrying on a trade in partnership are referred to collectively as a '*firm*'. A '*company partnership*' is a partnership in which at least one partner is a company. A company member of a partnership is liable to pay corporation tax on its profits.

This chapter looks at the tax treatment of companies in partnership. Further guidance can be found in HMRC's Company Tax Manual at CTM36505ff. The legislation is contained in the main in *CTA 2009, Pt 17*. [*CTA 2009, s 1257*].

Tax treatment of a company partner's partnership profits and losses

Overview

[58.2] A company that is a member of a partnership is liable to pay corporation tax on its share of partnership profits whereas a partner who is an individual is charged to income tax on his or her share of partnership profits. The following paragraphs look at the tax treatment of a company partner's partnership profits and losses.

Trading profits and losses

[58.3] A partnership is not generally treated for corporation tax purposes as an entity which is separate and distinct from its members.

To assess the amount charged to corporation tax (if any) in respect of a company partner's share of partnership profits, the following approach is adopted.

Step 1 — compute profits of partnership as if the partnership were a company

For any accounting period (see below) of a partnership carrying on a trade for which there is at least one partner who is a UK resident company (a company partner), the trading profits or losses are computed for corporation tax purposes as if the partnership were a UK resident company.

Similarly, for any accounting period for which there is at least one partner who is a non-UK resident company, the profits or losses are similarly computed as if the partnership were a non-UK resident company. For such companies, the computation will cover only those profits in respect of which the company is within the charge to UK corporation tax, generally those arising from a permanent establishment within the UK.

Thus, two separate computations of profits/losses are needed if the partnership includes both resident and non-resident companies (and a third computation is needed if it also includes one or more individuals — see the corresponding chapter of Tolley's Income Tax). See also HMRC Company Taxation Manual CTM36510, 36520.

In computing the profit or loss for the accounting period in question, no account is taken of any losses for any other accounting period, e.g. losses brought forward. Any interest paid or other distribution made by the partnership is not regarded as a distribution, and may therefore be deductible in computing profits.

Step 2 — apportion profits (or losses) to company partner

The taxable profits or allowable losses of the partnership for the accounting period (as adjusted for corporation tax purposes) are apportioned in accordance with the partnership's profit-sharing arrangements during that accounting period (subject to **58.4** below). If the partnership pays charges on income, these are similarly apportioned by reference to the accounting period in which they are paid.

Step 3 — assess company partner to corporation tax on its share of partnership profits

The company partner is assessed to corporation tax on its share of the partnership profits. The share of partnership profits are treated as if they were a separate trade carried on by the company, distinct from any other trade that may be carried on alone by the company.

These rules apply equally where the partnership carries on a business other than a trade.

[*CTA 2009, ss 1256–1260, 1262; ICTA 1988, ss 111(1), 114, 115(4); ITTOIA 2005, Sch 1 para 92*].

Accounting periods

[58.4] In order to work out the company partner's share of partnership profits and losses, it is first necessary to work out the notional profits as if the partnership were a company. The profits are computed for an accounting period which is the period that would be an accounting period if the partnership were a company (see **2 ACCOUNTING PERIODS**).

For the purposes of the computation, the following assumptions are made as regards this notional company:

- the company is UK resident;
- it acquires a source of income when the trade begins to be carried on by a partnership that includes a company;
- it ceases to trade when the trade ceases to be carried on by a partnership that includes a company; and
- it ceases to trade and immediately afterwards starts to trade if there is a change of partners such that both before and after the change the partnership includes a company but no company that carried on the trade before the change continues to carry it on after the change.

It follows that changes of partners are disregarded for corporation tax purposes so long as a company that carried on the trade in partnership before the change continues to carry it on in partnership after the change.

For the sole purpose of determining, in relation to a company partner, the accounting periods by reference to which profits are to be calculated, the residence of the notional company at any time is taken to be the same as the company partner's.

If the accounting period of the partnership does not coincide with the company partner's own accounting period, the company's share of profit or loss must be apportioned between the company's accounting periods with which the partnership accounting period partially coincides.

[*CTA 2009, ss 1261, 1265*].

The company tax return of a company in a partnership is required to include details from the partnership return (for which see Tolley's Income Tax under Returns).

Simon's Taxes. See D7.102 *et seq.*

Example

X Ltd and Mr Brown have been in partnership for many years and share profits in the ratio 2:1. The partnership's trading results for the year ended 30 September 2010 are as follows.

	Trading profits	Capital allowances
	£	£
Year ended 30 September 2010	72,000	33,000

X Ltd's chargeable profits in respect of the partnership are as follows.

	£
Year ended 30.9.10	
Trading profits	48,000
Deduct Capital allowances	22,000
Chargeable profits	£26,000

Mr Brown's trading income for tax purposes is £13,000.

Note

Capital allowances are a deduction in arriving at profits for both income and corporation taxes.

Losses

[58.5] Partnership losses are computed in the same way as profits. Losses are then apportioned between the individual partners in accordance with the partnership profit-sharing arrangements. It is for each corporate partner to choose how to utilise its own share of losses and to make its own claim(s) for loss relief (see **55 LOSSES**).

Where the partnership as a whole makes a profit (as adjusted for tax purposes) but, after the allocation of prior shares (e.g. salaries and interest on capital) the result is that a company partner makes a loss, the loss-making partner cannot claim tax relief for its loss. Instead, the company is treated as making neither profit nor loss, and its 'loss' is reallocated to the profit-making partners in accordance with the profit sharing arrangements in proportion to the profits already allocated to them. The effect of this reallocation to reduce the profit-making partners' profits for tax purposes.

In the situation where *the partnership as a whole makes a profit*, the company partner's share (in accordance with the profit sharing ratios) is a profit but one of the other partner's makes a loss, that loss is reallocated to the partners showing a profit in accordance with the profit sharing arrangements. The effect of the reallocation is to reduce the profits for tax purposes of the company partner (and also any other partners who have made a profit). The formula at *CTA 2009, s 1263(3)* sets out the calculation of the company partner's profits in this situation where the loss of the loss-making partner is reallocated in accordance with the steps set out at *CTA 2009, s 1263(4)*.

In a case *where there is an overall partnership loss*, the aggregate losses allocated to loss-making partners cannot exceed the overall loss and no partner is taxed on a share of profit. Instead, a profit-making company partner is treated as making neither profit nor loss, and its 'profit' is reallocated to the loss-making partners inaccordance with the profit-sharing arrangements.

Likewise, if there is *an overall partnership loss*, the company partner's share is a loss, but the comparable amount for at least one other partner is a profit, the profits of the profit-making partners are reallocated to those showing a loss, thereby reducing the company partner's loss (and that of any other loss-making partners). The formula at *CTA 2009, s 1264(3)* sets out the calculation of the company's partner's loss in this situation. The profit of the profit-making partners is reallocated in accordance with the steps set out at *CTA 2009, s 1264(4)*.

These rules are based on long-established practice (see HMRC Business Income Manual BIM72245) and are given statutory effect for accounting periods ending on or after 1 April 2009.

[*CTA 2009, ss 1259(5), 1263, 1264; ICTA 1988, s 114(1)*].

Interest paid

[58.6] A payment of yearly interest chargeable to tax under *ITTOIA 2005* or *CTA 2009* (or previously under *Schedule D, Case III*) by a partnership of which a company is a member must be paid under deduction of income tax at the basic rate in force for the tax year in which the payment is made. Before 2008/09, the deduction was at the savings rate. [*ITA 2007, s 874; ICTA 1988, s 349(2); ITTOIA 2005, Sch 1 para 148(3); FA 2008, Sch 1 paras 26, 65*]. See, however, **46.2 INCOME TAX IN RELATION TO A COMPANY** for relief from deduction of tax from certain payments to companies within the charge to corporation tax and **46.5 INCOME TAX IN RELATION TO A COMPANY** for relief on certain payments made on or after 1 January 2004 between associated companies of different EU member states.

Partnership liabilities

[58.7] Partners are jointly and severally liable. Partnership liabilities include the whole of the income tax liability of the individual partners, notwithstanding that a company partner's profit share is liable only to corporation tax.

Special types of partnership

Members of non-UK resident partnership or partnerships controlled abroad

[58.8] Where a UK resident company is:

- a member of a partnership which is non-UK resident; or
- which carries on any trade or business the control and management of which is outside the UK,

any relief given under a doube taxation agreement relieving partnership income from UK corporation tax does not affect the UK tax liability of the UK-resident company in respects of its share of the partnership income. If the UK resident partner's share of income consists of or includes a share in a qualifying distribution made by a UK resident company, the partner is entitled to the share of the tax credit in respect of the distribution corresponding to its share of the distribution. For these purposes, the members of a partnership include any company which is entitled to a share of the income of the partnership.. Similar provisions apply to capital gains.

[*CTA 2009, s 1266, Sch 1 para 365; ICTA 1988, s 115(5)–(5C); TCGA 1992, s 59(2); ITTOIA 2005, Sch 1 paras 95, 431; FA 2008, s 58*].

Limited partnerships

[58.9] The amount of relief that is given for loss made by a company in a trade carried on by that company as a limited partner may be restricted in certain circumstances.

For these purposes, a '*limited partner*' is a company carrying on a trade:

(a) as a limited partner in a limited partnership registered under the *Limited Partnerships Act 1907*;
(b) as a general partner in a partnership, but which is not entitled to take part in the management of the trade, and which is entitled to have its liabilities for debts or obligations incurred for the trade discharged or reimbursed by some other person, in whole or beyond a certain limit; or
(c) who, under the law of any territory outside the UK, is not entitled to take part in the management of the trade, and is not liable beyond a certain limit for debts or obligations incurred for the trade.

The amount of relief is restricted if at any time in an accounting period the company carries on a trade as a limited partner and the company makes a loss in that trade in that period. The restriction operates by capping the relief given for the loss and any relief against total profits (under *CTA 2010, s 37*) or under group relief (under *CTA 2010, Pt 5*) for the accounting period in question, and for any other accounting period at any time in which the company carries on the trade as a limited partnerat the level of the company's 'contribution to the firm' at the end of the loss-making period. If the company ceases to carry on the partnership trade during that period, the restriction is applied by reference to the company's contribution to the firm at the time of the cessation.

If the partnership is carrying on more than one trade, relief given under *CTA 2010, s 37* or *Pt 5* given in respect of each trade is taken into account for the purposes of applying the restriction.

A company's '*contribution to the firm*' at any time is the aggregate of:

(A) capital contributed *less* any capital directly or indirectly withdrawn, any capital the company is or may be entitled to withdraw at any time it carries on the trade as a limited partner, and any capital which it is or may be entitled to require another person to reimburse to it; and

(B) any of the company's share of the profits of the trade to which the company is entitled but which have not been added to the partnership's capital or which the company has not received in money or money's worth.

[*CTA 2010, ss 56–58, Sch 2 para 23; ICTA 1988, ss 117, 118*].

Limited liability partnerships

[58.10] For corporation tax purposes, where a trade or other business is carried on by a limited liability partnership (an 'LLP') within *Limited Liability Partnerships Act 2000, s 1* with a view to profit, the activities of the LLP (i.e. anything it does) are treated as carried on in partnership by its members, rather than by the LLP as such. Consequently, anything done by or to the LLP for the purposes of, or in connection with, its activities is treated as done by to or in relation to the members as partners. Property of the LLP is treated as held by the members as partnership property.

This remains the case where an LLP no longer carries on any trade, profession or other business with a view to profit, if the cessation is only temporary and during a winding up following a permanent cessation, provided that the winding up did not occur for reasons wholly or in part connected with tax avoidance and it was no unreasonably prolonged. However, this rule ceases to apply on the appointment of a liquidator or (if earlier) on the making of a winding-up order by the court, or on the occurrence of any corresponding event under the law of a country or territory outside the UK.

Similar provisions apply for capital gains tax purposes (see *TCGA 1992, ss 59A, 156A* and *169A*). See Tolley's Capital Gains Tax under Partnerships and Hold-Over Reliefs.

Similar provisions to those at **58.9** above apply to restrict loss relief available to company members of LLPs. The restriction applies where a company carries on a trade as a member of a LLP at any time in an accounting period and the company makes a loss in that period. The sum of the relief and any relief under *CTA 2010, s 37* (against total profits) or under *CTA 2010, Pt 5* (group relief) in an accounting period during which the company carries on a trade as a member of a LLP is limited to the company's contribution to the LLP at the end of the loss-making period or, if the company ceases to carry on the trade as a member of the LLP during the period, at the time of cessation.

A member's contribution to the firm at any time (a 'relevant time') is the greater of the 'amount subscribed' by the member and the amount of its liability on a winding up (see below). The 'amount subscribed' by a member is the amount contributed to the LLP as capital, less so much of that amount (if any) as:

(a) it has previously, directly or indirectly, drawn out or received back;
(b) it so draws out or receives back during the five years beginning with the relevant time;
(c) it is or may be entitled so to draw out or receive back at any time when it is a member of the LLP; or
(d) it is or may be entitled to require another person to reimburse to it.

The amount of the liability of a member on a winding up is the amount which it is liable to contribute to the assets of the LLP in the event of its being wound up, and which it remains liable so to contribute for at least the period of five years beginning with the relevant time (or until the partnership is wound up if that happens before the end of that period).

Where as a result of the operation of the restriction, relief has not been given under *CTA 2010, s 37* or *Pt 5* for a loss made by the member company as a member of the LLP in a previous accounting period, the unrelieved loss is treated as having been relieved under *CTA 2010, s 37* or *Pt 5* in the current period for the purposes of determining the amount of the restriction, if any, for the current period. However, no account is taken on the unrelieved loss if it has been treated as being made under a previous period and as result relief would have been given under *CTA 2010, s 37* or *Pt 5* if claimed. Further, no account is taken of a loss for which relief has been given other than under *CTA 2010, s 59*.

[*CTA 2009, s 1273; CTA 2010, ss 59–61, Sch 2 para 24; ICTA 1988, ss 118ZA–118ZD; Limited Liability Partnerships Act 2000, s 10(1); ITTOIA 2005, Sch 1 para 97*].

Investment LLPs and property investment LLPs

[58.11] A number of tax exemptions for income and gains do not apply where the income and gains are received by a member of a 'property investment LLP', Interest relief under *ICTA 1988, s 362* (see Tolley's Income Tax under Interest Payable) is denied where the partnership is an 'investment LLP'.

An '*investment LLP*' is an LLP whose business consists wholly or mainly in the making of investments and the principal part of whose income is derived therefrom, and a '*property investment LLP*' is similarly defined by reference to investments in land. The status of an LLP in this respect is determined for each period for which partnership accounts are drawn up. [*ICTA 1988, s 842B*].

The following exemptions do not apply to property investment LLPs:

(a) *Pension funds, etc.*

(i) Exemptions under *ICTA 1988, ss 592(2), 608(2)(a), 613(4), 614(3)–(5), 620(6), 643(2)* (see **35.14 EXEMPT ORGANISATIONS** and Tolley's Income Tax under Personal Pension Schemes), including exemptions for related stock lending fees and income from related futures and options.

(ii) Corresponding exemption from the trusts rate of income tax under *ICTA 1988, s 686* (accumulation and discretionary trusts, see Tolley's Income Tax under Settlements). [*ITA 2007, s 492; ICTA 1988, s 686(6A)*].

(iii) Corresponding exemptions under *TCGA 1992, s 271(1)* (see **35.14 EXEMPT ORGANISATIONS**). [*TCGA 1992, s 271(12)*].

(b) *Friendly societies*. Exemption under *ICTA 1988, s 460* of profits from life and endowment business, or under *ICTA 1988, s 461* or *s 461B* of profits from other business of registered or incorporated societies. [*ICTA 1988, ss 460(2)(cb), 461(3A), 461B(2A)*]. See **37.3 FRIENDLY SOCIETIES**.

[*FA 2001, s 76, Sch 25*].

Anti-avoidance

Realisation of capital

[58.12] Anti-avoidance provisions apply where a company realises capital from a partnership on or after 17 March 2004 either by way of directly or indirectly receiving back any capital from the partnership or by disposing of all or part of its partnership interest on or after that date. The provisions were repealed with effect from 22 April 2009, having been superseded by the disguised interest provisions contained in *CTA 2009, Pt 6 Ch 2A* (as introduced by *FA 2009, s 48* and *Sch 24*) (See **5.10 ANTI-AVOIDANCE**).

The provisions applied where:

(a) the capital realised exceeds the company's contribution to the partnership (including any amount paid by the company to acquire an interest in the partnership but excluding any amount originally contributed by a person from whom the company acquired the partnership interest and any contributions made after the capital realisation);

(b) that excess results wholly or partly from an arrangement under which the profits of the partnership for any period (but excluding any profits derived from income arising before 17 March 2004 (such profits to be derived on a just and reasonable basis)) were not, or not fully, allocated to the company in accordance with its capital share; and

(c) had such profits been allocated to the company in accordance with its due share, some or all of them would have been chargeable to corporation tax.

The company was charged to tax on so much of the amount of:

(i) the excess of the realised capital over contributions (as in (a) above), that did not exceed

(ii) the amount by which the company's due share of allocated profits exceeded the amount allocated to it.

These provisions do not apply if and to the extent that the chargeable amount is taken into account in arriving at the former charge under *CTA 2009, ss 536–538; FA 1996, ss 91H or 91I* (see **54.86 LOAN RELATIONSHIPS**).

[*FA 2004, ss 131, 132; CTA 2009, Sch 1 para 572 (repealed by FA 2009 s 48 and Sch 24: see now CTA 2010, Pt 6 Chs 2A, 6A)*].

Interaction with chargeable gains

Where a company is chargeable to corporation tax as above on a receipt on or after 17 March 2004 and before 22 April 2009 from the disposal of all or part of it's partnership interest on or after that date (a '*section 131 disposal*') the amount subject to the *section 131 charge* will be taken into account in computing gains under the chargeable gains legislation (see **17.1 CAPITAL GAINS**) so as to avoid double taxation.

[*FA 2004, s 133 prior to repeal by FA 2009, s 48 and Sch 24 para 8(b)*].

Leasing partnerships

For restriction of relief for losses in the case where there is a change in the interest of a company in a business, carried on in partnership, of leasing plant or machinery, see **5.22** and **5.29 ANTI-AVOIDANCE.**

Administration

Returns and filing dates

[58.13] Where a partnership includes one or more companies and one or more individuals, the filing date of the partnership return cannot be earlier than the filing date for the individuals' personal returns and may be later depending on the companies' accounting periods.

Example

For example, a partnership between A, an individual, and B Ltd has an accounting date of 31 December. A would be required to include the partnership income for the year ended 31 December 2009 in his tax return 2009/10, last filing date 31 January 2011. B Ltd's accounting period is 31 July 2010, its corporation tax return being due on 31 May 2011. This is the date for filing the partnership returns.

The period of return will be the same as the tax year:

- where the partnership makes up accounts to 5 April;
- where there are no partnership accounts ending in the tax year; or
- for investment partnerships which do not carry on a trade or profession.

For periods beginning on or after 6 April 2007, the filing date cannot be earlier than the end of the period of nine months beginning at the end of the relevant period. The filing date for an electronic return cannot be earlier not be earlier than the first anniversary of the end of the relevant and at least three months after the date of the notice to file. Where a partnership consists wholly of companies, HMRC normally set the filing date on the same basis as partnerships with individual and company members.

Key points

[58.14] Points to consider are as follows.

- The starting point is to establish whether a partnership exists. The mere existence of a partnership agreement is not sufficient. The partners should be carrying on a business together with a view to making a profit.
- Where there is a corporate member in the partnership it is still treated as see through for tax purposes with the corporate being charged to corporation tax on its share of the profits. In determining its share of taxable profits the profits must be calculated in accordance with corporation tax principles.
- Where there are losses in an LLP the sideways relief which can be claimed by the corporate partner is restricted to the amount of the capital contribution. The contribution made to the LLP is made up of two parts: Part 1 — any amounts contributed to the LLP less any repayments (this includes repayments in the five years following the use of the loss). Also less amounts the partner is entitled to draw back while a member of the LLP. Part 2 — the amount of the company's liability on a winding up of the LLP where that is not part of the capital in Part 1. The liability on a winding up is the amount the company must contribute if the LLP is wound up and the company must remain liable to contribute it for a period of five years beginning with the time the loss is used.
- For corporates wishing to accelerate the use of losses terms should be included in the members' agreement to make the company liable on a winding up for an amount equal to the loss used.
- For other partnerships the losses are restricted to the capital plus the partner's share of profits. However the amounts unused as a result of the restriction are treated as being made in the current period so can be eligible for group relief.
- In addition, sideways loss relief for non-active individual partners is restricted to an annual maximum of £25,000.
- Where there are corporate members in a partnership the filing deadline will not always be 31 January.

59

Payment of Tax

Cross-references. See **3 ADVANCE CORPORATION TAX; 46 INCOME TAX IN RELATION TO A COMPANY; 49 INTEREST ON UNPAID TAX; 65.6 RESIDENCE.**

Introduction

[59.1] The dates for payment of tax differ for small and large companies within the UK tax regime. In addition there are provisions which allow for special arrangements to be entered into by groups of companies, and which also allow for tax to be recovered from other parties, in lieu of the company taxpayer.

This chapter considers these and other matters concerned with the payment of tax by a company, including enforcement procedures and recent developments such as managed payment plans.

Due dates for payment

[59.2] The general rules is that corporation tax is due and payable on the day following the expiry of nine months from the end of the accounting period, on the basis of the amount computed in the company tax return for the period (see **66.8 RETURNS**). This is subject to the instalment provisions described at **59.3** below, with regard to instalment payments for large companies.

Any excess over the tax payable of 'relevant amounts' stated in the company tax return is repaid.

'*Relevant amounts*' are corporation tax paid and not repaid, corporation tax refunds surrendered to the company intra-group (see **39.25 PAYMENTS AND COLLECTIONS OF TAX**), certain income tax suffered and **CONSTRUCTION INDUSTRY SCHEME** (**26**) deductions.

[*TMA 1970, s 59D*].

A company may claim repayment of corporation tax paid for an accounting period where the company's circumstances change so that it has grounds for believing that the amount paid exceeds its probable (although not yet finally established) liability. No claim may be made before the 'material date' in relation to the tax being the later of: the date the tax was paid or the date it became due and payable (see further **50.2 INTEREST ON OVERPAID TAX**).

If the tax is the subject of an outstanding appeal, the company may apply to the Tribunal for a determination of the amount to be repaid (and the application may be combined with a postponement application under *TMA 1970, s 55*, see **59.10** below). If the company tax return (see **66.4 RETURNS**) has not been made, **CONSTRUCTION INDUSTRY SCHEME** (**26**) deductions are ignored for these purposes.

[*TMA 1970, s 59DA*].

'Large' companies to which instalment payments apply are precluded from making a claim under *section 59DA* where a claim for repayment of instalment payments is made (see **59.3** below).

[*SI 1998 No 3175, Reg 6(8)*].

As regards due dates for payment of tax for **accounting periods ending before 1 July 1999**, i.e. before the introduction of self-assessment, see the 2005–06 and earlier editions of Tolley's Corporation Tax.

Instalment payments

[59.3] A system of quarterly accounting for corporation tax was phased in for 'large companies' from accounting periods ending on or after 1 July 1999 to accounting periods ending before 1 July 2002, the provisions described below operate for accounting periods ending on or after that date. Corporation tax for this purpose includes any liability under *CTA 2010, s 455* (previously *ICTA 1988, s 419*) — loans to participators (see **22.12 CLOSE COMPANIES**) or *s 747(4)(a)* (amounts apportioned in respect of controlled foreign companies, see **27.8 CONTROLLED FOREIGN COMPANIES**). [*TMA 1970, s 59E; CTA 2010, Sch 1 para 155(a); SI 1998 No 3175*].

The self-assessment company tax return (see **66.4 RETURNS**) requires the company to state whether it is liable to make instalment payments on account of its corporation tax liabilities. Although HMRC will at some stage check the position, initial payment applications, interest calculations, etc. will be based on the company's statement of its position. (HMRC Company Taxation Manual CTM92690). For entries required on form CT600, see Revenue Tax Bulletin April 2001 pp 831–833.

Large companies

A '*large company*', subject to the exclusions described below, is a company whose profits in any accounting period exceed the small profits rate upper limit (the 'upper relevant maximum amount' as was) in force at the end of the accounting period (see **67.3 SMALL PROFITS — REDUCED RATES**). This is currently £1,500,000 divided by one plus the number of 'associated companies' (if any) at any time in the period (see **67.4 SMALL PROFITS — REDUCED RATES**), proportionately reduced for periods of less than twelve months. Certain adjustments made in the case of insurance companies are, however, disregarded. A company is *not* large as respects an accounting period for which:

(a) its total corporation tax liability, reduced by any deductions under the **CONSTRUCTION INDUSTRY SCHEME (26)** from payments in the period, does not exceed £10,000 (£5,000 in relation to accounting periods ending before 1 July 2000), proportionately reduced for accounting periods of less than twelve months; or
(b) its profits do not exceed £10,000,000, provided that it was not a large company (disregarding the £10,000,000 exclusion) in the twelve months preceding the period.

As regards (b) above, the £10,000,000 limit is reduced in the same proportion as the upper limit for short accounting periods or where there are associated companies (see **67.3**, **67.4 SMALL PROFITS — REDUCED RATES**), except that the number of associated companies required to be taken into account is determined as at the end of the immediately preceding accounting period, or at the commencement of the accounting period concerned if there was no immediately preceding accounting period or there was a gap between the two accounting periods.

In addition, as regards (b) above, a company is treated as not having been large in the twelve months preceding the period in question where either:

(i) during any part of the twelve months it did not exist or did not have an accounting period; or
(ii) an accounting period during which it was not a large company (other than by virtue of (b) above) either falls within or ends in the twelve months.

'*Profits*' of an accounting period for these purposes are the assessable profits on which corporation tax finally falls to be charged for the period plus franked investment income ('FII') of the period other than any FII received from fellow group members (and distributions are treated as coming from within the group as within the meaning of *CTA 2010, s 32; ICTA 1988, s 13(7)*).

[*SI 1998 No 3175, Regs 2(2)(3), 3; SI 2000 No 892*].

Instalments

Amounts in respect of a large company's total corporation tax liability for an accounting period (as reduced by any deductions under the **CONSTRUCTION INDUSTRY SCHEME** (**26**) from payments in the period) become due and payable in up to four instalments as follows.

(1) The first instalment is due six months and thirteen days from the start of the accounting period, and the last instalment is due three months and fourteen days from the end of the accounting period, except that if the latter date precedes the former (i.e. where the accounting period is less than three months), a single instalment equal to the total corporation tax liability is due and payable on the latter date.

(2) Where there is a gap of more than three months between the two dates referred to in (1) above (i.e. where the accounting period is longer than six months), a second instalment is due and payable three months after the first, and if the gap exceeds six months, a third instalment is due and payable three months after the second. Thus for the year ending 31 December 2011, instalments will be due on 14 July 2011, 14 October 2011, 14 January 2012 and 14 April 2012.

Thus in the case of the year ending 31 December 2011 instanced at (2) above, the four instalments are each of one-quarter of the final corporation tax liability. For an accounting period of eight months ending 31 August 2011, instalments are due on 14 July 2011, 14 October 2011 and 14 December 2011, the first two being of three-eighths of the total corporation tax liability and the final one of the balance of one-quarter.

Where the company's estimate of the amount of its total corporation tax liability for the period is revised, subsequent instalment payments are recalculated accordingly, and top-up payments may be made at any time. The due and payable amount of each instalment for the purposes of interest on over- or under-payments (see below) is that based on the total corporation tax liability as returned by the company (or as determined by the inspector where the normal due date has passed).

[*SI 1998 No 3175, Reg 5*].

As regards estimation of quarterly payments, see HMRC guidance published on their website (at www.hmrc.gov.uk/ctsa/quarterly_payments.htm).

Although HMRC will send a reminder and payslip (Form CT608) to those companies which it appears likely will be required to make instalment payments, it is in any event the company's responsibility to make such payments if they are due. Since payments are processed automatically, it is important to ensure that the correct payslip is used or the correct reference quoted to prevent misallocation. (HMRC Company Taxation Manual CTM92550 and Revenue Tax Bulletins April 1999 p 646 and April 2001 p 833).

A *repayment* may be claimed where the company has grounds for believing that changed circumstances since an instalment or instalments were paid has rendered its earlier calculation of its total corporation tax liability excessive, so that the aggregate amount of the instalments paid exceeds what would have been payable by the date of the claim based on the new figure for that liability. Repayment of that excess may be claimed, and the claim must state the amount to be repaid and the grounds for the company's belief that its earlier calculation was excessive.

If an appeal against an assessment, or an amendment of a self-assessment, in respect of the total liability for the accounting period concerned is outstanding, the company may apply to the Tribunal for a determination of the amount to be repaid pending determination of the appeal. Such claims and applications are treated in the same way as appeals, and an application for determination of a repayment may be combined with an application for postponement of payment of tax under *TMA 1970, s 55* (see **59.10** below).

Alternatively, the provisions of *CTA 2010, s 963; FA 1989, s 102* (surrender of tax refund within group, see **39.25 PAYMENTS AND COLLECTIONS OF TAX**) are applied to allow the surrender of excess instalment payments intra-group.

A special anti-avoidance provision applies, in the period from 25 November 1997 to 29 June 2002, being the transitional period to the instalment regime, if a company changed its accounting date or entered in to arrangements or transactions which transferred profits intra-group. See earlier editions of Tolleys Corporation Tax.

[*SI 1998 No 3175, Regs 6, 9, 14; SI 1999 No 1929*].

Interest on unpaid instalments

Unpaid instalment payments (tax which is overdue) carry interest at a special rate from the instalment due date to the date of payment during the period until nine months after the end of the accounting period concerned (whereafter the normal interest rate provisions apply). The special rate is currently set at 1.5% p.a. whereas the normal overdue corporation tax interest rate is currently 3% p.a.. See **49.2 INTEREST ON OVERDUE TAX** for the rates. [*TMA 1970, s 87A* as amended by *CTA 2009, Sch 1 para 305*].

Interest on overpaid instalments

Similarly, excess payments in respect of instalments carry interest at a special rate (which also applies to early payments by companies not liable to pay by instalments) from the date the excess arises (but not earlier than the due date of the first instalment) until it is extinguished (but not later than nine months after the end of the accounting period concerned, from when the normal interest rate provisions apply). The special rate is currently set at 0.5% p.a., which is the same as the current rate applicable under self-assessment for normal overpaid corporation tax. See **50.2 INTEREST ON OVERPAID TAX** for the rates. [*ICTA 1988, s 826*].

Information etc. powers

HMRC have powers to require the production of a wide range of information and records relating to instalment payments once the filing date for the return for the accounting period (normally twelve months after the end of the period, see **66.9 RETURNS**) has passed. [*SI 1998 No 3175, Regs 10–12; as amended by SI 1999 No 1929, SI 2005 No 889*].

HMRC will seek to make use of these powers only where there are indications that a company may have deliberately or recklessly failed to comply with its instalment payment obligations, or fraudulently or negligently made a repayment claim (see HMRC Company Taxation Manual, CTM92770 and HMRC Enquiry Manual, EM8320).

Penalties

Where interest is charged on unpaid instalments as above, and the company, or a person acting on its behalf, either:

(I) deliberately or recklessly failed to make an instalment payment; or
(II) fraudulently or negligently made a claim for repayment of an excess amount of instalment payments,

the company is liable to a penalty of up to twice the amount of the interest. [*SI 1998 No 3175, Reg 13; TMA 1970, s 59E*]. HMRC will seek a penalty under these provisions only in the most serious cases involving flagrant abuse of the regulations (see HMRC Enquiry Manual EM8330, Revenue Tax Bulletin August 1999 pp 683, 684, and further guidance published on HMRC's website (at www.hmrc.gov.uk/ctsa/penpowers.htm).

Generally, penalties under *TMA 1970, s 98* apply for any failure to provide information, produce documents, etc. as required under these provisions.

Group payment arrangements

Any group of companies with instalment payment liabilities which wishes to do so may make arrangements with HMRC to account for corporation tax relating to accounting periods ending on or after 31 December 1999 on a group basis rather than company by company (see **39.24 PAYMENTS AND COLLECTIONS OF TAX**). This will enable profit forecasts to be made at group level and mitigate the interest differential on over- and under-paid tax.

[*TMA 1970, s 59F; FA 1998, s 36*].

Groups wishing to take part in such arrangements should contact the Group Payment Team at the appropriate Accounts Office (Shipley tel. 01274 539561 or Cumbernauld tel. 01236 783488). (HMRC Company Taxation Manual, CTM97410.)

Broadly, a nominated company may contract with HMRC to make instalment payments on behalf of group companies covered by the arrangements ('participating companies') on the due dates on the basis of the most recent forecast of group profits. Once all the participating companies have either filed their returns or had their corporation tax liabilities determined by HMRC (the 'closing date', which cannot be earlier than the normal due date nine months after the end of the accounting period), the nominated company will be issued with a notice showing what it has paid and the liability at the closing date. It will then be invited to make good any shortfall, or allocate it to any company whose liability it has reason to believe will decrease after the closing date, and to apportion payments to the participating companies. It may allocate any surplus to participating companies or require its repayment.

The arrangements need not apply to all group members, and separate arrangements may be entered into for different sub-sets within a group. Not all companies covered by the arrangements need be UK-resident, although the nominated company must be. All companies must have filed returns and paid the due tax in respect of their last but one accounting period. They must have a common accounting period (subject to special arrangements for companies joining the group and aligning their accounting date). There is provision for either the nominated company or HMRC to remove a company from the arrangements in specified circumstances where the rules regarding eligibility to enter the arrangements would no longer be met.

Any group wishing to take part in the arrangements must normally deliver its signed contract to the appropriate Accounts Office (as above) at least two months prior to the first instalment payment due date. All payments must be made by electronic funds transfer.

For detailed requirements, see HMRC Company Taxation Manual, CTM97400 *et seq* which also includes the group payment arrangement contract and the administrative and guidance notes. Guidance is also provided in Revenue Tax Bulletins April 1999 pp 647–650 and April 2001 pp 831–836. These include the entries required on return form CT600, the effect of arrangements on tax repayments and group surrenders thereof, the allocation of payments under an arrangement, the departure from a group of a participating company and the treatment of long periods of account.

Insurance companies and friendly societies

Special provision is made for the interest consequences of the set-off of a provisional repayment under *ICTA 1988, Sch 19AB* (see **37.3 FRIENDLY SOCIETIES**) against an instalment payment under the current provisions. [*SI 1998 No 3175, Reg 15*]. *Sch 19AB* was repealed in 2001. This paragraph does not apply in relation to an income tax deduction from a payment received after 30 September 2001, nor to tax credits in respect of distributions made on or after 6 April 2004.

Oil and gas companies

For accounting periods ending on or after 1 July 2005, corporation tax and supplementary charge on ring fence profits are excluded from the calculation of 'mainstream' corporation tax instalment payments and such profits are subject instead to a separate set of rules. Large companies will be required to pay ring fence profits in no more than three instalments. This does not affect any amounts treated as becoming due and payable before 1 July 2005. [*SI 1998 No 3175, Reg 5A*; *SI 2005 No 889*].

HMRC guidance

See generally HMRC Company Taxation Manual, CTM92500 *et seq*. See also Revenue Tax Bulletins April 1999 pp 645–650, February 2000 pp 723–726 and April 2001 pp 831–836 and HMRC publication CTSA/BK3 'A Modern System for Corporation Tax Payments'.

Simon's Taxes. See **A4.511, A4.607, A4.624, A4.633, A6.503, D1.1321, D1.1328–D1.1332.**

Payment

[59.4] As from 1 April 2011 all payments of corporation tax must be made electronically, see **59.20** below.

In euros

[59.5] Tax payments may be made in euro through automated banking systems, from euro accounts or (at certain locations) in euro bank notes (but not coins). Costs incurred in respect of a euro payment drawn on an overseas bank account will be borne by the taxpayer, but other administrative costs will not be passed on. The exchange rate used is the one in force when the payment is presented by the clearing bank. If the conversion rate used leaves a shortfall, the difference will have to be paid. If it results in an overpayment, any repayment arising will be made in sterling.

For payment by cheque see **49.7 INTEREST ON OVERDUE TAX** and for payment electronically see **59.20** and also **41.12 HMRC — ADMINISTRATION**.

Charges

[59.6] HMRC may provide by statutory instrument for a charge to be made for payments in a specified form (e.g. by credit card) where there is a cost to HMRC attached to that method of payment. HMRC is permitted to make a charge of 1.25% (0.91% before 14 December 2009) of the payment where it is made using a 'credit card' and is authorised by telephone. As from 1 April 2011 corporation tax must be paid electronically. Where a payment is made by credit card over the internet, the payment must include a charge of 1.4% (as from 1 April 2011 – 1.25% prior to this) of the tax paid. For this purpose, a 'credit card' is a card which is a credit-token falling within *Consumer Credit Act 1974, s 14(2)(b)* or would be such a credit-token were it to be given to an individual.

[*FA 2008, s 136; SI 2008 No 1948; SI 2008 No 2991; SI 2009 No 3073; SI 2011 No 711*].

Set-off

[59.7] With effect from 21 July 2008, for England, Wales and Northern Ireland, except in an insolvency (see below), where a company owes money to HMRC but is also due a repayment, the credit may be set off against the debit, subject to any right of HMRC to set the credit against any other sum. Any transfer of the right to the tax repayment due to the company is disregarded. Where, on or after 25 June 2008, there is such a transfer of a right to a repayment to another person, HMRC must use the power of set-off notwithstanding the transfer if they are obliged to do so under legislation in respect of the original creditor and may do so if they had the power of set-off had the creditor retained the right to the repayment.

HMRC have the right of set-off whether the tax in question became due before or after the transfer, but not if repayment has already been made. These provisions take priority where the transferee wishes to set off the repayment against tax due by him — i.e. the set-off against the original creditor's tax debt is effected first. Where the repayment is contingent on the original creditor making a claim, these set-off provisions apply only if a claim is made. References to sums payable to and by a person are to a sum to be paid, repaid or credited to that person. In determining the repayment to be set off, HMRC may make any deduction they could have made if the original creditor had retained the right to the repayment, including a deduction arising from any defence to a claim for the sum.

Following set-off, both HMRC and the original creditor are treated as having discharged their obligations up to the amount of the tax covered by the repayment. These set-off provisions take priority over those in any other legislation.

Where a company is insolvent, but a post-insolvency credit arises (i.e. after the insolvency procedure has commenced) the power of set-off may not be used by HMRC against pre-insolvency debits in relation to the person.

[*FA 2008, ss 130, 131, 133*].

Enforcement

[59.8] With effect from 21 July 2008 the previous HMRC powers of distraint are replaced. HMRC are empowered to use *Sch 12* of the *Tribunals, Courts and Enforcement Act 2007* to take control of a person's goods if there is non-payment of a sum due to them. This power is exercisable in England and Wales only.

In Scotland, the provisions of *FA 2008, s 128* and *Sch 43* apply as from 9 November 2009, whereby HMRC are given power to apply to the Sheriff Court for a summary warrant. An application must be accompanied by a certificate stating that:

(a) the sum has not been paid by any of the persons named;
(b) each person has been asked to pay the amount due by him; and
(c) at least 14 days, beginning with the date of the demand, has elapsed without payment being made.

The application must be signed by an officer of HMRC. The sum payable by each taxpayer must be stated.

This power does not apply to VAT, CIS or PAYE and NIC.

The Sheriff must grant a summary warrant which authorises HMRC to recover the amounts due by attachment, money attachment, earnings arrestment or arrestment and action of forthcoming or sale. Fees and outlays in connection with collection are payable by the taxpayer.

[*FA 2008, ss 127, 128, Sch 43; SI 2009 No 3024*].

Prior to the above coming into force, the Collector may distrain. [*TMA 1970, ss 61–64; FA 1989, ss 152–155*]. See also *Herbert Berry Associates Ltd v CIR* HL 1977, 52 TC 113. Where amount due (or any instalment) is less than £2,000, the Collector may within six months of due date take summary magistrates' court proceedings. The Collector may recover the tax by proceedings in the County Court. [*TMA 1970, ss 65, 66; FA 1984, s 57; SI 1989 No 1300; SI 1991 Nos 724, 1625*]. But for limitations in Scotland and Northern Ireland see *TMA 1970, ss 65(4), 66(3)(4), 67; FA 1976, s 58; FA 1995, s 156*, and for time limits for proceedings see *Mann v Cleaver* KB 1930, 15 TC 367 and *Lord Advocate v Butt* CS 1992, 64 TC 471. Unpaid tax (and arrears) may also be recovered (with full costs) as a Crown debt in the High Court. [*TMA 1970, s 68*]. The amount of an assessment which has become final cannot be re-opened in proceedings to collect the tax (*Pearlberg* CA 1953, 34 TC 57; *CIR v Soul* CA 1976, 51 TC 86), and it is not open to the taxpayer to raise the defence that the Revenue acted *ultra vires* in raising the assessment (*CIR v Aken* CA 1990, 63 TC 395).

County Court proceedings

[59.9] An officer of HMRC, or a person appointed by them, may conduct county court proceedings for recovery of any amount due to them. [*TMA 1970, s 66; CRCA 2005, s 25; FA 2008, s 137*].

A certificate from an officer of HMRC that an amount due to them is unpaid is sufficient evidence of the fact. Any document held out as such a certificate is treated as such until this assumption is disproved. [*CRCA 2005, s 25A; FA 2008, s 138*].

Payment of tax pending appeal

[59.10] Where there is an appeal against an amendment of a self-assessment, an assessment to corporation tax other than a self-assessment or an assessment to income tax on company payments (but excluding income tax accountable by quarterly etc. returns, see **49.8 INTEREST ON OVERDUE TAX**), the full amount charged will be due and payable (as if there had been no appeal) unless the appellant applies for payment of part of the tax assessed to be postponed.

The application must in the first instance be made in writing to HMRC within 30 days after the date of the issue of the notice of assessment, stating the amount of tax believed to be overcharged (and payment of which is to be postponed), and the grounds for that belief.

Application may be made outside the normal 30-day time limit if there is a change in circumstances giving grounds for belief that the appellant is overcharged. In HMRC's view, this condition requires a change in the circumstances in which the original decision not to apply for postponement was made, not just a change of mind, e.g. further accounts work indicating a substantially excessive assessment, or further reliefs becoming due. (Notes of CCAB meeting with Revenue on the 1982 Finance Bill TR 477, 22 June 1982.)

The appellant and an HMRC officer may agree the amount of tax to be postponed and written confirmation of such agreement shall be treated as if the tribunal had determined it. Failing such agreement an appeal can be made to the tribunal (within 30 days of HMRC's decision) to determine the amount, in the same way as an appeal.

Any tax which is the subject of such an application and which is not postponed by agreement or by the tribunal shall be due and payable as if charged by an assessment issued on the date of the tribunal's determination (or of written confirmation of the agreement with HMRC's officer) and against which no appeal is pending. If circumstances change, a further application may be made by either the appellant or HMRC's officer giving notice to the other to vary the amount postponed.

On determination of the appeal, any tax overpaid is repaid and any postponed tax then becoming collectable or not previously charged becomes due and payable as if charged under an assessment issued when the inspector issues to the appellant notice of the total amount payable.

[*TMA 1970, s 55; FA 1994, Sch 19 para 18; FA 1998, Sch 19 para 28; SI 1998 No 3173; SI 2009 No 56*].

See also **66.8 RETURNS.**

Simon's Taxes. See **A4.609, D1.1352.**

Recovery of tax from third parties

Change in ownership of company — corporation tax

[59.11] Where an HMRC officer considers that:

(a) there has been a change in ownership of a company (see **55.13 LOSSES**);
(b) any corporation tax assessed on the company for an accounting period beginning before the date of the change remains unpaid at any time after the '*relevant date*' (i.e. the date six months after the date of the corporation tax assessment); and
(c) any of the three conditions referred to below is fulfilled,

any of the following persons ('linked' to the company per *CTA 2010*) may be assessed and charged in the name of the company to an amount of corporation tax as below:

(i) any person who at any time during the '*relevant period*' (i.e. the period of three years before the change in ownership, but not so as to include any period before a previous change in ownership) had 'control' of the company; and

(ii) any company of which a person within (i) has at any time in the three years before the change in ownership had 'control'.

For this purpose, a person has '*control*' of a company if he exercises, is able to exercise, or is entitled to acquire direct or indirect control over the company's affairs. In particular, he has control if he possesses or is entitled to acquire 50% of the company's share capital, issued share capital or voting power. He also has control if he possesses or is entitled to acquire so much of the issued share capital as would give the right to receive the greater part of the company's income, were all that income distributed, or rights to the greater part of the company's assets in a distribution on a winding-up or in other circumstances. Future rights and rights of nominees are included.

There may be attributed to a person the rights and powers of any associate (see **22.9 CLOSE COMPANIES**) or associates of his, or of any company or companies controlled by him (with or without his associates), together with any nominee of such company or associate. However, the rights and powers of associates' associates and of companies controlled only by associates are disregarded. Where two or more persons together satisfy any of the conditions for control, control will only be imputed to each of them where they have acted together to put themselves in a position where they will in fact satisfy the condition in question.

The three alternative conditions referred to at (c) above are as follows.

(A) At any time during the three years before the change in ownership the activities of a trade or business of the company cease or the scale of those activities become small or negligible, and there is no significant revival of those activities before the change occurs.

(B) At any time after the change in ownership, but under arrangements made before that change, the activities of a trade or business of the company cease or the scale of those activities become small or negligible.

(C)

- (a) At any time during the six years beginning three years before the change in ownership, there is a 'major change in the nature or conduct of a trade or business' of the company;
- (b) assets of the company are transferred (including any disposal, letting or hiring of an asset, and any grant or transfer of any right, interest or licence in or over it, or the giving of any business facilities with respect to it) to a person within (i) above (or to a person connected with such a person within *CTA 2010, ss 1122, 1123; ICTA 1988, s 839*), or under arrangements which enable any of those assets (or assets representing those assets) to be transferred to such a person, during the three years before the change in ownership (or after the change but under arrangements made before the change); and
- (c) the major change in the nature or conduct of the trade or business of the company is attributable to the transfer(s) of the company's assets.

For the purposes of (C)(a) above, a '*major change in the nature or conduct of a trade or business*' includes:

- a major change in the type of property dealt in, or services or facilities provided;
- a major change in customers, outlets or markets;
- a change by which the company ceases to be a trading company (i.e. one whose business is wholly or mainly a trade or trades) and becomes an investment company (i.e. one whose business consists wholly or mainly in the making of investments and the principal part of whose income is derived from investments, but excluding a company whose business consists wholly or mainly in holding shares or securities of 90% subsidiaries which are trading companies);
- a change by which the company ceases to be an investment company and becomes a trading company; and
- if the company is an investment company, a major change in the nature of its investments.

A change includes a change achieved gradually through a series of transfers. See further HMRC Statement of Practice 10/91.

The tax charged in an assessment under these provisions must not exceed the amount of the tax which, at the time of the assessment, remains unpaid by the company, and the assessment is not out of time if made within three years of the final determination of the liability of the company for the accounting period concerned.

TMA 1970, s 87A (see **49.2** interest on overdue tax) applies in relation to tax so assessed by reference to the company's due and payable date. The tax (and any interest) paid is not an allowable deduction for any tax purposes, but the payer is entitled to recover an amount equal to the tax (and any interest) from the company. An amount so recovered (or received under an indemnity in this respect) is not chargeable to tax on the recipient. (Revenue Tax Bulletin April 1995 p 208).

Power to obtain information

HMRC may, by notice in writing, require any person who is the registered owner of shares, stock or securities of a company to state whether he is the beneficial owner thereof and, if not, to supply the name and address of the person(s) on whose behalf he holds them.

[*CTA 2010, ss 706–712, 716, 717, 728; ICTA 1988, ss 767A, 767B*].

See also **17.10, 17.11 CAPITAL GAINS; 18.11 PAYMENTS AND COLLECTIONS OF TAX; 29.1 DEGROUPING CHARGES** and **65.8 RESIDENCE.**

Change in ownership of company — postponed corporation tax

[59.12] Provisions supplementing the above deal with cases where a corporation tax liability has been postponed to a period commencing after a change in ownership within **55.13 LOSSES**.

Where an HMRC officer considers that there has been a change in the ownership of a company, and that any corporation tax for an accounting period ending on or after the change which has been assessed on that company or an 'associated' company remains unpaid at any time more than six months after it was assessed, then (subject to the further 'expectation' condition referred to below) any one of the persons listed below may be assessed and charged (in the name of the company in default) to an amount of corporation tax not exceeding the amount remaining unpaid. Such persons referred to as 'linked' to the company per the legislation found in *CTA 2010, s 713*.

Such an assessment is not out of time if made within three years of the date of final determination of the liability of the company in default for the accounting period for which the tax was assessed. INTEREST ON OVERDUE TAX (**49**) then runs by reference to the date of the original liability of that company.

A company is '*associated*' with another for these purposes if, at the time of the assessment (or at an earlier time before the change in ownership), it has control of or is controlled by the other or they are under common control. 'Control' is defined as for **59.11** above.

The 'expectation' condition

The further condition referred to above is that it would be reasonable (apart from these provisions) to infer, from either or both of the terms of any transactions entered into in connection with the change (for which see below) and the other circumstances of the change and of any such transactions, that at least one of those transactions was entered into by one or more of the parties to it on the assumption that a 'potential tax liability' would be unlikely to be met, or met in full, were it to arise.

A '*potential tax liability*' is a corporation tax liability which, in circumstances reasonably foreseeable at the time of change in ownership (or in circumstances the occurrence of which is something of which there was at that time a reasonably foreseeable risk), would or might arise from an assessment made, after the change in ownership, on the company transferred or an associated company, whether or not a particular associated company.

A transaction is for these purposes entered into in connection with a change in ownership if the change is effected by the transaction (with or without other transactions) or by other transactions forming part of the same series of transactions or scheme (by whomsoever entered into). A 'scheme' is any scheme, arrangements or understanding of any kind, and the cases in which transactions form part of a scheme or series include cases in which it would be reasonable to assume that one or more of them would not have been entered into independently of the other(s), or that if entered into independently it would not have taken the same form or been on the same terms.

Persons assessable

The persons who may be assessed and charged are any person 'linked' to the company, that is any person who at any time during the 'relevant period' before the change had control of the transferred company, and any company of which such a person has at any time had control within the period of three years before the change in ownership. The '*relevant period*' is the period of three years before the change in ownership, or if, during that three years, there was an earlier change in ownership of the transferred company, the period between those changes.

Tax paid under these provisions is not an allowable deduction for tax purposes, but the payer is entitled to recover an amount equal to the tax (and any interest thereon) from the transferred (or associated) company.

Before 1 April 2009, HMRC had specific powers to require any person (subject to certain exclusions) to supply (within not less than 30 days) specified documents and other particulars relating to liabilities which could arise under these provisions (but excluding documents etc. relating to the conduct of any pending tax appeal).

[*CTA 2010, ss 706–709, 713–718, 728; ICTA 1988, ss 767AA, 767B, 767C; FA 2008, Sch 36 para 81; SI 2009 No 404*].

Simon's Taxes. See **D6.463, D6.464.**

Recovery of tax payable by non-resident company

[59.13] Where corporation tax assessed on a non-UK resident company (i.e. in respect of UK branch profits) remains in whole or part unpaid six months after the due date, the following companies may be served notice by HMRC requiring them to pay the tax.

(1) Any company which was, at any time in the 'relevant period', a 51% subsidiary (by reference to ordinary share capital) of the non-resident company, or of which the non-resident company was a 51% subsidiary, or where both were 51% subsidiaries of a third company.

(2) Any company which was, at any time during the 'relevant period', a member of a consortium which owned (see **39.19 GROUP RELIEF**) the non-resident company at that time.

(3) Any company which was, at any time during the 'relevant period', a member of the same group (as for group relief purposes, see **39.3 GROUP RELIEF**) as a company which was at that time a member of a consortium which owned (see **39.19 GROUP RELIEF**) the non-resident company.

The '*relevant period*' is the period beginning twelve months before the start of the accounting period in question and ending when the unpaid tax first became payable.

The notice may require payment, within 30 days of service, of the overdue tax or (in the case of a company within either or both of (2) and (3) above but not within (1) above) of an appropriate proportion thereof (see *FA 2000, Sch 28 para 5*). A payment made in pursuance of a notice is not an allowable deduction in computing profits, but the paying company may recover the amount from the non-resident company. The notice must state the amount of the unpaid tax, the date it first became payable and the amount required to be paid by the recipient. For recovery and appeals purposes, it has effect as if it were a notice of assessment of an amount of tax due from the recipient. **INTEREST ON OVERDUE TAX (49)** runs from the original due date.

HMRC have three years from the date on which the liability of the non-resident company is finally determined (including a determination under *FA 1998, Sch 18 para 36* or *37* in the absence of a full return, see **66.27 RETURNS**) in which to serve notice under these provisions. In the case of a self-assessed liability, including one superseding a determination, the date of determination of the liability is taken as the last date on which notice of an enquiry into the return may be given (see **66.19 RETURNS**), or, if such notice is given, 30 days after the action which concludes the enquiry process (see **66.24 RETURNS**). In the case of a discovery assessment (see **7.3 ASSESSMENTS**), it is the due and payable date or (if there is an appeal against the assessment) the date the appeal is finally determined.

[*CTA 2010, ss 973–980; FA 2000, s 98, Sch 28*].

Simon's Taxes. See D2.245.

Recovery from officers of the company

[59.14] Tax which has fallen due may be recovered from the treasurer or acting treasurer (the 'proper officer') of a company which is not a body corporate or not incorporated under a UK enactment or by charter. That officer then has a right of reimbursement out of moneys coming into his hands on behalf of that company, and to be indemnified by the company for any balance. [*TMA 1970, s 108(2)(3)*].

Managed payment plans

[59.15] *FA 2009, s 111* (now *TMA 1970, ss 59G, 59H*) has been introduced as part of the exercise to tackle debt (see **59.21** below). The aim is to make payment easier by spreading the liability, where otherwise it would be due in one or two instalments, rather than to offer credit facilities. A company may enter a managed payment plan with HMRC in respect of its corporation tax liability. Plans are not available to 'large' companies paying their corporation tax in instalments or to a group of companies which has entered into a group payment arrangement.

The conditions for entering a plan are:

(a) it is agreed between the parties that payment in instalments will be acceptable;
(b) the instalments before the due date are balanced by the instalments after it;
(c) such other conditions imposed by HMRC by statutory instrument are met.

(b) is determined by adding up the time value of the instalments due before the due date and that for instalments falling due after the due date and comparing them. If they are equal, or approximately equal, the condition will be fulfilled. Time value is amount of instalment multiplied by the number of days between the due date of the instalment and the due date of the tax. No interest or penalties will be incurred on instalments made after the due date, provided they are paid in time under the plan. HMRC may make regulations by statutory instrument to determine when an amount is approximately equal to another. Different provision may be made for different cases.

The draft guidance indicated that a managed payment plan would allow corporation tax to be paid in equal monthly instalments over a 12 month period. The instalment dates would start six months before the tax due date and end six months after. Four conditions would need to be complied with:

- the company's self-assessment return must have been submitted for the year;
- all taxes previously due must have been paid;
- payments should be made by direct debit or standing order;
- payments should be made on the fifteenth day of each month.

This provision as inserted into *TMA 1970* by *TIOPA 2010* has effect for corporation tax for accounting periods ending on or after 1 April 2010. It was announced on 29 January 2010 on the HMRC website that their intention was for managed payment plans to be launched from April 2011. However, the details currently given by HMRC on their website on how to pay corporation tax do not provide information as to possible payment plans.

[*FA 2009, s 111; now relocated by TIOPA 2010 to TMA 1970, ss 59G, 59H*].

Special cases

Partnership liabilities

[59.16] See **58.7** partnerships.

Over-repayments

[59.17] Corporation tax over-repaid and not assessable under *FA 1998, Sch 18 para 41* may be assessed for that period as if it were unpaid tax. Any associated excess **INTEREST ON OVERPAID TAX** (**50**) may be included in the assessment. The time limit for such assessments is extended to the end of the accounting period following that of the repayment if it would otherwise be out of time, subject to the usual fraudulent or negligent conduct provisions. From a date to be appointed, the phrase 'subject to the usual fraudulent or negligent conduct provisions' is amended to 'subject to the provisions where loss of tax was brought about carelessly or deliberately by the taxpayer'.

Similar provisions apply to enable excess set-offs or payments of tax credit to be recovered, including any **INTEREST ON OVERPAID TAX** (**50**) in respect of tax credits.

Where the assessment is to recover a repayment of tax paid for an accounting period, or a repayment of tax on a payment received in an accounting period, the assessment is treated as being for that accounting period, and the sum assessed carries interest under *TMA 1970, s 87A* (see **49.2 INTEREST ON OVERDUE TAX**) from the date the repayment being recovered was made until payment.

These provisions also apply the discovery assessment rules of *FA 1998, Sch 18 paras 41–48* to recovery assessments, and extend the period during which assessments may be made to the completion of enquiries in certain cases. See **66.26 RETURNS.**

[*CTA 2010, ss 1110, 1111; ICTA 1988, s 252; FA 1998, Sch 3 para 21, Sch 18 paras 52, 53; FA 2008, Sch 39 para 3; CTA 2009, Sch 1 para 454 which amends FA 1998 Sch 18*].

Certificates of tax deposit

[59.18] Companies may make deposits, evidenced by Certificates of Tax Deposit, with HMRC for the subsequent payment of tax, and any liability met by the tendering of such a deposit (and accrued interest) is treated as paid on the normal due date, or on the date of the deposit if later. Petroleum royalties may also be paid in this way. The minimum initial deposit is £500 with minimum additions of £250 subject to a continuing minimum of £500. Certificates are obtainable from the office of any Collector of Taxes. Deposits of £100,000 or over must be made by direct remittance to the Bank of England.

However it should be noted that the taxes which can be paid using certificates of tax deposit are:

- Income Tax;
- Class 4 National Insurance contributions (NICs);
- Capital Gains Tax;
- Petroleum Revenue Tax;
- Petroleum Royalty;
- Inheritance Tax.

Certificates may not be purchased for use against corporation tax liabilities, income tax liabilities under PAYE or the construction industry tax deduction scheme, or VAT liabilities.

Interest, which is payable gross but taxable, will accrue for a maximum of six years from the date of deposit to the date of payment of tax (or, if earlier, the normal due date for payment of tax, i.e. disregarding the fact that the payment date may be later due to late issue of the assessment in question or to an appeal having been made against the assessment). A deposit may be withdrawn for cash at any time but will then receive a reduced rate of interest.

Where a certificate is used in settlement of a tax liability, interest at the higher rate up to the normal due date may be less than interest at the encashment rate up to the reckonable date. In such circumstances the taxpayer may instruct the Collector to calculate interest on the latter basis. The rates of interest, published by the Treasury, and calculated by reference to the rate on comparable investment with the Government, vary with the size and period of the deposit, and the rate payable on a deposit is adjusted to the current rate on each anniversary of the deposit.

Deposits are not transferable except in settlement of tax payable by the depositor's holding company, subsidiary company, or fellow-subsidiary.

Profits or gains on certificates of deposit issued after 31 March 1996 are chargeable to tax within the loan relationship provisions (see **54.3 LOAN RELATIONSHIPS**). See HMRC Inspector's Manual, IM4602.

For rates of interest, see Tolley's Income Tax under Certificates of Deposit. Information on current rates may be obtained from www.hmrc.gov.uk/payin ghmrc/cert-tax-deposit.htm.

Simon's Taxes. See **A4.635**.

Date of payment for interest purposes

[59.19] As to the date on which tax is treated as having been paid, see **49.7 INTEREST ON OVERDUE TAX.**

Payment electronically

[59.20] HMRC have exercised their power to require tax to be paid electronically. Corporation tax payments made on or after 1 April 2011 must be made electronically. If a payment is not made electronically, HMRC need not accept the payment.

[*FA 2007, s 94; SI 2009 No 3218*].

Future developments

[59.21] It has been announced that there will be a new method of paying tax — managed payment plans — and legislation was passed in *FA 2009* in this regard. On 29 January 2010 HMRC announced on their website that it was their intention to launch managed payment plans (MPPs) from April 2011.

Such a plan would be a voluntary agreement under which the tax due will be spread in instalments falling equally either side of the normal due date. Provided the taxpayer adheres to the plan, no interest, penalties or surcharges would arise. HMRC may refuse an MPP. See further **59.15** above.

[*FA 2009, s 111, per TIOPA 2010 relocated to TMA 1970, ss 59G, 59H*].

60

Penalties

Cross-references. See also **65.8 RESIDENCE** and **73.5 VALUE ADDED TAX.**

Simon's Taxes. See **A4.5, A6.602–A6.617, D1.1324.**

Introduction

[60.1] As a result of an overhaul of the penalty system for taxes, the Finance Acts of 2007, 2008 and 2009 have introduced a new penalty regime for corporation tax (and in addition for other UK taxes, including income tax, capital gains tax, VAT, inheritance tax, etc.). Most penalties are now behaviour-based, with the penalty actually charged based on whether the offence was careless, deliberate and not concealed or deliberate and concealed.

However, it should be noted that the new regime is being introduced in stages. Therefore whilst the new penalties apply to corporation tax with regard to failure to notify chargeability and submission of incorrect returns, matters such as late filing of returns continues to be dealt with under the old regime at the present time.

The provisions relating to fraudulent or negligent conduct no longer apply with the introduction of this new regime.

This chapter outlines the situations that will give rise to a penalty, the provisions with regard to mitigation that may apply, and possible recourse to a civil or criminal prosecution.

Situations giving rise to penalties

Incorrect returns

Behaviour-based penalties

[60.2] With effect for documents relating to accounting periods beginning on or after 1 April 2008 where the return is due on or after 1 April 2009, a new regime is introduced for penalties in respect of errors in company tax returns, claims for allowances, deductions or reliefs, other documents submitted to HMRC and in accounts forming the basis of a return.

The regime applies where an inaccuracy in the document provided leads to an underpayment of tax, over-repayment of tax or overstated statement of loss and where such an error was careless or deliberate. It is to be extended with effect from 1 April 2009 to errors in a taxpayer's document attributable to a third party who has supplied false information or withheld information.

The regime also applies where there is an understated assessment issued by HMRC for an accounting period beginning on or after 1 April 2008 and the taxpayer has not taken reasonable steps to notify them of the understatement within 30 days of the date of the under-assessment. In deciding whether or not reasonable steps were taken, HMRC will take into account what steps it would regard as reasonable, and whether the taxpayer knew or should have known about the understatement.

Behaviour-based penalties also apply with regard to a failure to notify HMRC that the company is within the charge to tax (see **60.5** below).

No penalty can be charged under the new regime in respect of any period for which a return is required before 1 April 2009.

It should be noted that *FA 2010* introduces changes to the behaviour-based penalties regime with regard to offshore income, as such penalties apply to income tax and CGT only. With regard to corporation tax the penalties are unchanged. The penalties are separated into three new categories, with categories 2 and 3 applying to income tax and CGT only. Corporation tax penalties are now classed as category 1 penalties, however the standard penalties described herein continue to apply to this category.

Quantum of penalties

The amount of penalties (related to the degree of culpability in terms of percentage of 'potential lost revenue') is as follows:

- careless – i.e. the taxpayer has not taken 'reasonable care' – 30%;
- deliberate but not concealed – i.e. no steps taken to conceal – 70%; and
- deliberate and concealed – 100%.

HMRC consider that what constitutes 'reasonable care' has to be viewed in the light of each person's abilities and circumstances. They do not expect the same level of knowledge or expertise from an unrepresented self-employed individual as from a large multinational company. They expect a higher degree of care to be taken over large and complex matters than simple straightforward ones. In HMRC's view, it is reasonable to expect a person encountering a transaction or other event with which they are not familiar to take care to check the correct tax treatment or to seek suitable advice. (HMRC Brief 19/2008).

Reasonable steps to inform HMRC of an inaccuracy would, in their view, include consulting with an accountant or agent to discuss the position so that they can inform HMRC, or contacting HMRC directly to discuss the inaccuracy (HMRC Guidance Note, 1 April 2008).

An inaccuracy in a document given to HMRC by the company that is neither careless nor deliberate when it is given, is to be treated as careless if the company discovered the inaccuracy later and fails to take reasonable steps to inform HMRC.

The definition of '*potential lost revenue*' is the amount of tax due or payable as a result of correcting the error. The calculation differs depending on whether there was a single error or there were multiple errors. In a straightforward case, the calculation follows from the definition.

Group relief is ignored in calculating potential lost revenue (although an inaccurate claim for relief may give rise to a penalty). Relief under *CTA 2010, s 458; previously ICTA 1988, s 419(4)* where a loan to a participator is repaid or written off is also ignored. For multiple errors, careless inaccuracies are taken as corrected before deliberate inaccuracies and any overstatements relating to the same period are taken into account. Such overstatements are set off firstly against understatements not liable to a penalty, then careless understatements, then deliberate but not concealed understatements and finally against deliberate and concealed understatements. Possible overpayments to be repaid to another person are not taken into account.

Where the error is in the quantum of a loss, and not all the loss has been set off in calculating a tax liability, the potential lost revenue is calculated as the total of the tax relating to the loss set off, plus 10% of the loss which was not so used. However, where there is no reasonable likelihood of the taxpayer using the loss, the potential lost revenue in respect of it is treated as nil. If the error has resulted in delaying a tax liability, the potential revenue lost is equivalent to 5% of the delayed tax for each year of delay.

Mitigation of penalties

Deductions from penalties are given for disclosure to HMRC. Disclosure must include telling HMRC about the inaccuracy, giving them reasonable help to quantify the tax lost and giving HMRC access to records. A 30% penalty may be reduced, or eliminated, where the taxpayer makes an unprompted disclosure and may be reduced to between 15% and 30% where he makes a prompted disclosure.

For a 70% penalty, an unprompted disclosure may allow HMRC to reduce the penalty to between 20% and 70% while for a prompted disclosure the penalty may be reduced to between 35% and 70%. For a 100% penalty, the reduction is from 30% to 100% and from 50% and 100% respectively for unprompted and prompted disclosures. In every case, HMRC decides on the reduction by considering the 'quality' of the disclosure (including timing, nature and extent). A disclosure is '*unprompted*' if it is made when the person making it has no reason to believe that HMRC has discovered or are about to discover the inaccuracy or under-assessment.

HMRC have the power to mitigate a penalty for special circumstances. Such special circumstances do not include ability to pay or the fact that the taxpayer's liability is compensated for by another taxpayer's overpayment. HMRC may suspend all or part of a penalty by giving the company notice in writing. The notice must state the part of the penalty to be suspended, the period of suspension (not more than two years) and the conditions with which the taxpayer company must comply. The penalty may only be suspended if the conditions would help the company to avoid further penalties for careless inaccuracies. The notice may state the action the company has to take and the timescale for this action. If, at the end of the period, the company can show that the conditions were complied with, the specified part or all the penalty may be cancelled, otherwise, the suspended part or all the penalty is payable. While a penalty is suspended, if the company becomes liable for another penalty, the suspended penalty becomes payable. HMRC issued a factsheet on 17 August 2009 entitled 'Compliance checks — suspending penalties for careless errors'. *STI 2009 p 2466.*

A penalty will be assessed, and the assessment will be treated like any other corporation tax assessment. Where there was an error in the return, the assessment must be issued within twelve months of the end of the appeal period for a return in respect of which the penalty was incurred or, if there is no such assessment, the date the error was corrected. Where there was an error in an assessment issued by HMRC, the assessment must be made within twelve months of the end of the appeal period for the amended assessment which corrected the understatement.

HMRC have the power to suspend all or part of a penalty for careless inaccuracy.

The taxpayer has a right of appeal to the tribunal.

Where HMRC think that a director or secretary of the taxpayer company was responsible for a deliberate error, that officer will be liable for a portion of the penalty which HMRC decides (which may be 100%) along with the company.

No penalty is due in respect of any error where the taxpayer has been convicted of an offence in respect of it.

Reduction for other penalty

The amount of a penalty in respect of a document relating to a particular tax year or accounting period is reduced by the amount of any other penalty or any interest charge determined by reference to the same tax liability. Where a penalty is imposed under these provisions and those at **49 INTEREST ON OVERDUE TAX** above in respect of the same inaccuracy, the aggregate of the penalties cannot exceed 100% of the potential lost revenue. No reduction is made for a tax-related penalty within **60.11** below.

Inaccuracy caused by a third party

A company is liable for a careless inaccuracy in a document where the inaccuracy was caused by a third party acting on the taxpayer company's behalf (e.g. a professional agent). However, where the taxpayer company satisfies HMRC that it took reasonable care to avoid the inaccuracy or unreasonable failure, the company is not liable. In looking at the degree of culpability (see above) a reference to the taxpayer company includes a reference to a third party acting on its behalf.

Where the taxpayer company is a member of a partnership, a co-partner may be liable to a penalty if the inaccuracy also affects the partner's tax liability. Potential lost revenue is to be calculated separately for each partner, the suspension rules will apply jointly to the company and its partner's penalty and a reference to the taxpayer company is to include a reference to the partner. The company has a right of appeal against the partner's penalty, in addition to its own rights of appeal.

Where the inaccuracy is caused by a person other than the taxpayer company and as a result a return or other specified document has a 'relevant inaccuracy', a penalty is payable by the person causing the inaccuracy if the inaccuracy was caused by the third party supplying the taxpayer with false information or withholding information from them with the intention that the document would be inaccurate.

For this purpose, a '*relevant inaccuracy*' is an inaccuracy which is, or which leads to:

(a) an understatement of a liability to tax;
(b) a false or inflated statement of loss; or
(c) a false or inflated claim to repayment of tax.

A penalty under this provision (which may be up to 100% of lost revenue) may be imposed on the third party in addition to any penalty under any provision in *FA 2007, Sch 24*. The amendments made to *Sch 24* by *FA 2008, Sch 40* generally take effect for return periods after 1 April 2009 where the return is due on or after 1 April 2010. However, *SI 2009 No 571* states that the start date for most provisions in Sch 40 is 1 April 2009, the later date being applicable only to certain pension schemes and indirect tax returns.

Powers to amend provisions

The Treasury may by order make any incidental, supplemental, consequential, transitional, transitory or saving provision in connection with these provisions.

[*FA 2007, s 97, Sch 24; FA 2008, Sch 40; SI 2008 No 568; SI 2009 No 56*].

Failure to notify coming within charge to corporation tax

[60.3] With effect for accounting periods beginning on or after 22 July 2004, a company (but not an unincorporated association or partnership) must give notice to HMRC of when its first accounting period begins (e.g. when the company starts its business) and of when any subsequent accounting period begins that does not follow on immediately from the end of a previous accounting period (see **66.2 RETURNS**). Failure to do so renders the company liable to penalties under *TMA 1970, s 98* of up to £300 for the initial failure and up to £60 per day for continuing failure thereafter or, for fraudulently or negligently giving an incorrect notice, up to £3,000 (see **60.9** below). See **60.13** below as regards 'reasonable excuse' for failure. [*FA 2004, s 55*].

From 1 April 2010, the penalty for non-compliance under *TMA 1970, s 98* is repealed. *FA 2008, Sch 41* updates the penalty regime for failure to notify chargeability under *FA 1998, Sch 18 para 2*.

[*FA 2008, s 123, Sch 41 para 25*].

Failure to notify chargeability

[60.4] A company chargeable to corporation tax which has not already made a company tax return for an accounting period, and has not received a notice requiring such a return (see **66.4 RETURNS**), must give notice of its chargeability to the inspector within twelve months from the end of the period.

Failure to do so under self-assessment renders the company liable to a penalty not exceeding so much of the tax payable for the period as remains unpaid twelve months after the end of the period, any relief deferred under *CTA 2010, s 458(5)* (previously *ICTA 1988, s 419(4A)*) in respect of the repayment, etc. of a loan to a participator (see **22.15 CLOSE COMPANIES**) being disregarded. From 1 April 2010, any penalty for non-compliance is charged under *FA 2008, Sch 41* (see below).

[*FA 1998, Sch 18 para 2; FA 2008, Sch 41 para 25; CTA 2010, Sch 1 para 297(3); SI 2009 No 511*].

Penalties for non-compliance from 1 April 2010

With effect from 1 April 2010, penalties for non-compliance with the above provisions have been brought within a unified penalty code for failures relating to a range of taxes. The code is described below, but only to the extent that it relates to the above provisions.

A person is not liable to a penalty for a failure in respect of which he has been convicted of an offence.

Amount of penalty

The amount of the penalty depends on whether or not the failure is deliberate and is subject to reduction as detailed below.

For a deliberate and concealed failure (i.e. where the failure was deliberate and the taxpayer made arrangements to conceal the situation giving rise to the obligation), the penalty is 100% of the 'potential lost revenue' (see below).

For deliberate but not concealed failure (i.e. where the failure was deliberate but the taxpayer did not make arrangements to conceal the situation giving rise to the obligation), the penalty is 70% of the potential lost revenue.

For any other case, the penalty is 30% of the potential lost revenue.

For corporation tax purposes, the '*potential lost revenue*' is equal to the amount of tax payable for the accounting period that, by reason of the failure, remains unpaid twelve months after the end of the period. Tax payable is computed disregarding any deferred relief arising from the repayment of loans made to close company participators. The fact that potential lost revenue may be balanced by a potential overpayment by another person is ignored, except to the extent that that person's tax liability is required or permitted to be adjusted by reference to the taxpayer's.

No penalty is due in relation to a failure that is not deliberate if the taxpayer satisfies HMRC or, on appeal, the tribunal, that there is a reasonable excuse for the failure. Insufficiency of funds is not a reasonable excuse for this purpose and neither is the taxpayer's reliance on another person to do anything, unless he took reasonable care to avoid the failure. If the taxpayer had a reasonable excuse, he is treated as continuing to have a reasonable excuse after the excuse has ceased if the failure is remedied without unreasonable delay.

Reduction for disclosure

A reduction in a penalty will be given where the taxpayer discloses a failure to notify. The penalty will be reduced to a percentage which reflects the quality of the disclosure and the amount of the reduction will depend on whether the disclosure is 'prompted' or 'unprompted'.

In the case of an unprompted disclosure, a 100% penalty may not be reduced to a percentage below 30%, and a 70% penalty may not be reduced to a percentage below 20%. A 30% penalty may be reduced to any percentage, including 0%, unless HMRC do not become aware of the failure until twelve months after the time tax first becomes unpaid by reason of the failure, in which case the penalty may not be reduced below 10%.

In the case of a prompted disclosure, a 100% penalty may not be reduced to a percentage below 50%, a 70% penalty may not be reduced to a percentage below 35%, and a 30% penalty may not be reduced to a percentage below 10% (20% where HMRC do not become aware of the failure until twelve months after the time tax first becomes unpaid by reason of the failure).

A person is treated as making a disclosure for these purposes only if he tells HMRC about the failure, gives them reasonable help in quantifying the tax unpaid and allows them access to records for the purpose of checking how much tax is unpaid. A disclosure is '*unprompted*' if made when the taxpayer has no reason to believe HMRC have discovered or are about to discover the failure. In all other cases, disclosures are '*prompted*'.

Reduction in special circumstances

HMRC can also reduce, stay or agree a compromise in relation to proceedings for a penalty if they think it right to do so because of special circumstances. Ability to pay and the fact that a potential loss of revenue from one taxpayer is balanced by a potential overpayment by another are not special circumstances for this purpose.

Reduction for other penalty or surcharge

The amount of a penalty in respect of a failure is reduced by the amount of any other penalty (see **49 INTEREST ON OVERDUE TAX**), the amount of which is determined by reference to the same tax liability. No reduction is made for a tax-related penalty within **60.11** below.

Agents

A person is liable to a penalty under the above provisions where the failure is by a person acting on his behalf. He is not, however, liable to a penalty in respect of anything done or omitted by his agent, if he satisfies HMRC or, on appeal, the tribunal, that he took reasonable care to avoid the failure.

Company officers

Where a company is liable to a penalty under the above provisions for a deliberate failure and the failure was attributable to a company 'officer', the officer as well as the company is liable to pay the penalty (but not so that HMRC can claim more than 100% of the penalty).

HMRC can pursue the officer for such part (including all) of the penalty as they specify by written notice. That portion of the penalty is treated as a penalty for the purpose of these provisions. A further notice may be issued specifying an additional portion of the penalty. In relation to a body corporate, a director, shadow director or secretary of the company is an '*officer*'; in any other case, a director, manager, secretary or any other person managing or purporting to manage any of the company's affairs is an '*officer*'.

[*FA 2008, s 123, Sch 41 paras 1, 5–7, 11–15, 20–24; CTA 2010, Sch 1 para 583*].

See **60.13** below as regards reasonable excuse for failure.

Simon's Taxes. See **A4.516, A6.202, D1.1302.**

Failure to make a return

[60.5] Whist the new regime is operational with regard to incorrect returns and failure to notify, as above, it is not yet applicable with regard to failure to make a return in respect of corporation tax. However, the new provisions are outlined below.

Thus, from a date to be appointed, a penalty for failing to make a corporation tax or CIS return or deliver any document before the filing date will be issued under *FA 2009, s 106, Sch 55*.

The penalties are as follows:

Returns filed late		Penalty
1 day		£100
3 months		HMRC can impose £10 per day (maximum 90 days)
6 months		Higher of 5% of tax liability and £300
12 months	Deliberate and concealed	up to 100% of tax liability or £300
	Deliberate and not concealed	up to 70% of tax liability or £300
	Other cases	up to 5% of tax liability or £300

After three months HMRC may decide that a daily penalty of £10 per day is payable and give notice accordingly of the date from which the penalty is due (the 'penalty date').

The '*penalty date*' is the day after the filing day (i.e. the first day on which liability to a penalty arises). The daily penalty may be charged for up to 90 days. Where the failure lasts for six months from the penalty date, a penalty of 5% of the tax liability which would have been shown on the return, or £300, if greater, will be charged. Where the default continues for a year, behaviour-based penalties (see table above) will be charged, but these may be reduced for prompted or unprompted disclosure, assistance and access. HMRC also have discretion to make a further reduction for 'special circumstances'.

'*Special circumstances*' do not include ability to pay or the fact that one taxpayer's liability is balanced by another taxpayer's overpayment. Reducing a penalty includes staying it and agreeing a compromise. Special rules apply to CIS returns and documents. Where a penalty is assessed before the return is made, HMRC are empowered to determine the amount of tax in respect of which a penalty should be charged. If a return is subsequently filed, the penalty must be re-assessed. Where the tax in question is in respect of a loan to a participator, no account is taken of subsequent repayment of the loan in assessing the penalty.

The company taxpayer has a right of appeal against a penalty notice, in the same way as it may appeal an assessment. A penalty will not arise if HMRC or (on appeal) a tribunal find that there has been reasonable excuse. Lack of funds, reliance on another party and the existence of a reasonable excuse in the past are not reasonable excuses. No penalty is charged where the failure or action giving rise to a penalty under *FA 2009, Sch 55* has lead to a criminal conviction.

It is the responsibility of HMRC to assess the penalty, notify the taxpayer of it and to give the period in respect of which the penalty is assessed. The due date for payment is 30 days after the notice is issued. An assessment of a penalty under *Sch 55* must be made on or before the end of two years from the filing date, or, if later the end of twelve months from the end of the appeal period for the assessment in respect of which the penalty arose and, where there is no assessment, twelve months from the date of ascertainment of a liability, or nil liability.

More than one penalty may be issued in respect of the same failure. However, where a penalty is charged other than under *FA 2009, Sch 55, Sch 56* in respect of the same liability to tax, it is deducted from the penalty due under these provisions. The Treasury is given wide powers to implement these provisions by statutory instrument.

[*FA 2009, s 106, Sch 55*].

Existing regime

Until the date to be appointed for the new penalty regime above to apply, a company which fails to make a return for any period, when required to do so by notice (see **66.7 RETURNS**), is liable to a penalty of £200 (£100 if the return is delivered within three months of the final day for delivery).

If the return period is one for which accounts are required under *Companies Act 2006* or *Companies Act 1985* (or NI equivalent), penalties do not apply provided that the return is delivered by the last day for delivery of those accounts.

The penalties are increased to £1,000 and £500 respectively for failure in relation to a return for an accounting period where a penalty under these provisions was incurred for each of the two immediately preceding accounting periods, and the company was within the charge to corporation tax for the whole of the three accounting periods. (See *Lessex Ltd v Spence* [2004] STC (SCD) 79 where three successive defaults straddled the introduction of the self-assessment system applying to accounting periods ending on or after 1 July 1999 and a drafting error in *FA 1998, Sch 18 para 17(3)* was not considered to prevent the higher penalty from applying.)

An additional penalty is imposed, where the return is still outstanding at the later of the end of the final day for delivery of the return and 18 months after the end of the return period. The additional penalty is 10% of the tax unpaid at the time the penalty arises if the return is delivered within two years after the end of the return period, otherwise 20%. The tax taken into account for this purpose under self-assessment is the tax payable for the return period, disregarding any relief deferred under *CTA 2010, s 458(5)* (previously *ICTA 1988, s 419(4A)*) in respect of the repayment, etc. of a loan to a participator, see **22.15 CLOSE COMPANIES**.

[*FA 2009, Sch 55; CTA 2010, Sch 1 para 723*].

By concession, automatic penalties are not charged provided that the return is received on or before the last business day within seven days following the filing date. (HMRC Extra-Statutory Concession, B46).

If, exceptionally, the company is unable to produce final figures for the return by the due date, it should make estimates to the best of its ability and alert the inspector to the basis on which the estimates are made. When the company can replace the estimates with accurate figures, or becomes aware that an estimate is no longer the best estimate, the inspector should be so informed without unreasonable delay. Provided these guidelines are followed, no late filing penalty (see above) or incorrect return penalty (see **60.7** below) should be imposed, provided in the latter case that neither fraud nor negligence was involved. The inclusion in a return of unreasonable estimates, while not invalidating the return, may render the company liable to incorrect return penalties. Any extension of the time limit for making a return under *TMA 1970, s 118(2)* (see **60.13** below) must be agreed with the inspector in advance. (HMRC Company Tax Manual, CTM10413).

See **60.13** below as regards reasonable excuse for failure.

With regard to timing and receipt of a return, in the recent case of *GV Cox Ltd v HMRC*, [2011] UKFTT 311 (TC), a company did not post its corporation tax return for the year ending 31 May 2009 until 27 August 2010. HMRC did not receive the return until 6 September 2010. HMRC imposed a penalty of £200 under *FA 1998, Sch 18 para 17(2)(b)*. The company appealed, contending that the return had been submitted within three months of the filing date, so that the penalty should only be £100 (under *FA 1998, Sch 18 para 17(2)(a)*). The First-tier Tribunal rejected this contention and dismissed the appeal, observing that the effect of *Sch 18 para 17(2)(a)* was that the penalty was only £100 provided that the return was delivered within three months of the filing date. Judge Brooks held that, since the return had not been posted until Friday 27 August 2010, and the following Monday had been a bank holiday, the company could not have a reasonable expectation that HMRC would receive the return by Tuesday 31 August 2010.

See Revenue Tax Bulletin October 2003 p 1064 regarding the automation of late filing penalties.

Simon's Taxes. See A4.507, A4.525, D1.1312.

Failure to pay on time

[60.6] The new penalty regime for late payment of tax applies to the late payment of PAYE, NIC and CIS payments from 6 April 2010. However, with regard to other taxes, such as corporation tax, the new regime will be implemented gradually.

Therefore, from a date to be appointed, where corporation tax is not paid before the filing date for the company tax return for the accounting period to which the tax relates, and no managed payment plan or deferral agreement is in force, a penalty of 5% of the tax due is payable under *FA 2009, Sch 56*. A further penalty of 5% is due if the amount is unpaid after three months and a further 5% if it is unpaid after nine months.

HMRC have the power to mitigate a penalty if there are 'special circumstances'. These do not include ability to pay or the fact that the amount due is balanced by an overpayment by another taxpayer.

Where a deferral agreement is entered into before the date the penalty is due, it does not become due unless the debtor company defaults on the agreement and HMRC issues a notice charging a penalty, the due date of which is the date of the notice.

Where a penalty arises under these provisions, HMRC must assess it and send notice to the taxpayer company stating the period in respect of which the penalty is assessed. The company has 30 days from the date the notice is issued to pay. The penalty assessed may be increased if it appears it was underestimated.

HMRC have until the later of two years from (normally) the due date of the tax subject to the penalty and last day of the year beginning with the end of the appeal period for the tax assessment, or, if there was no assessment, the date when the amount of tax is ascertained.

The taxpayer company may appeal against the assessment of a penalty or against its amount, in the same way as it could appeal an assessment to tax. The penalty is not required to be paid until the appeal is settled. A possible ground of appeal is 'reasonable excuse'. The following are not regarded as '*reasonable excuse*':

(a) unable to find the funds to meet the liability;
(b) reliance on a third party to take action, unless the company took reasonable care to avoid the default;
(c) where a reasonable excuse has ceased but the default has not been remedied without unreasonable delay.

Where a company has suffered a criminal conviction in respect of the default, a civil penalty under *FA 2009, Sch 56* is not charged.

[*FA 2009, s 107, Sch 56*].

Under the existing regime large companies are currently subject to a charge to interest arises where their quarterly instalment payments are not paid by the due dates (see **49 INTEREST ON OVERDUE TAX**). Where a charge to interest arises and the company (or a person acting on its behalf) has deliberately or recklessly failed to make the payment, a penalty is imposed not exceeding twice the amount of the interest charge.

A similar penalty is imposed where a fraudulent or negligent claim is made for repayment of an instalment payment.

[*TMA 1970, s 59E(4); SI 1998 No 3175, Reg 13*].

Negligence or fraud

[60.7] The provisions with regard to fraud or negligence are repealed with effect from the introduction of the penalty provisions under the new regime, as above.

Previously, the maximum penalty for negligently or fraudulently delivering, making, or submitting an incorrect return or claim for allowance or relief etc., or incorrect accounts, in addition to any tax actually chargeable, is the amount of tax underpaid, by reason of the incorrectness, for the accounting period(s) to which the return etc. relates.

See also **66.16 RETURNS**.

Accounts are deemed to have been submitted on behalf of a company unless it is shown that they were submitted without the company's consent or connivance.

[*FA 1998, Sch 18 paras 20, 89*].

Simon's Taxes. See **A4.510, A6.602, A6.703.**

[60.8] For the position if an agent is negligent or fraudulent, see *Mankowitz v Special Commrs* (1971) 46 TC 707 and cf *Clixby v Pountney* (1967) 44 TC 515. Assisting in, or inducing, the preparation or delivery of any information, return, accounts or other document known to be incorrect and to be, or to be likely to be, used for any tax purpose carries a maximum penalty of £3,000. [*TMA 1970, s 99; FA 1989, s 166*]. See also **60.18** below.

Failure to make other returns etc.

[60.9] Failure to render any return, certificate, statement or other document required under the provisions listed in the Table in *TMA 1970, s 98* carries a maximum penalty of £300, plus up to £60 for each day the failure continues after that penalty is imposed (but not for any day for which such a daily penalty has already been imposed).

The maximum penalty for fraudulently or negligently delivering any incorrect information etc. under any of these provisions is £3,000.

Penalties for failure to render information etc. required by notice cannot be imposed after the failure is rectified, and daily penalties can similarly not be imposed where the information etc. was required other than by notice. [*TMA 1970, s 98; FA 1989, s 164*].

Special penalties are imposed by regulation in relation to failure to make a return in accordance with provisions under the PAYE and **CONSTRUCTION INDUSTRY SCHEME (26)** regulations and under the mandatory PAYE e-filing regulations (see **41.12 HMRC — ADMINISTRATION**). [*TMA 1970, s 98A; FA 1989, s 165; SI 1993 No 744 (as amended by SI 2003 No 2494)*]. See also above with regard to the new regime and PAYE and CIS payments.

See **61.15 PROFIT COMPUTATIONS** as regards penalties under *TMA 1970, s 98B* in relation to European Economic Interest Groupings.

Failure to allow access to computer records renders a person liable to a £300 from 21 July 2008 (formerly £500) penalty. [*FA 2008, s 114; FA 1988, s 127*].

For unlawfully possessing or disposing of an exemption certificate relating to a sub-contractor in the construction industry, or making false statements relating thereto, the maximum penalty is £3,000 (a maximum fine of £5,000 applying before 1 August 1999). [*ICTA 1988, s 561(10)(11); FA 1995, Sch 27 para 3; FA 2004, s 72*].

See **60.13** below as regards reasonable excuse for failure.

Penalties for failure to keep records as required under *FA 1998, Sch 18 para 21* (see **66.18 RETURNS**) apply of up to £3,000. [*FA 1998, Sch 18 para 23*]. A penalty also applies of £50, plus a daily fine of up to £150 for continuing failure, for failure to provide documents as required under *FA 1998, Sch 18 para 27* (see **66.20 RETURNS**). [*FA 1998, Sch 18 para 29*].

Failure to disclose tax avoidance schemes

[60.10] Failure to notify HMRC of the notifiable proposals or notifiable arrangements, or failure to notify the client of the relevant scheme reference number under the provisions of *FA 2004, ss 308(1)(3), 309(1), 310, 312(1), 313A, 313B* (see **5.41 ANTI-AVOIDANCE**) will render the scheme promoter etc. liable to a penalty of up to £5,000. A further penalty or penalties will be imposed of up to £600 for each day on which the failure continues after the above penalty is imposed.

A penalty of the 'prescribed sum' is provided for failure to comply with *FA 2004, ss 313A, 313B* (pre-disclosure enquiry). The 'prescribed sum' is to be determined by regulation.

From 1 November 2008, the same penalties also apply for failure by a client to inform other parties to the arrangements of the reference number.

Parties to notifiable arrangements who fail to notify HMRC of the scheme reference number etc. under *FA 2004, s 313(1)* will be liable to a penalty of £100 in respect of each scheme to which the failure relates. The penalty will be increased for a second failure, occurring within three years from the date on which the first failure began, to £500 in respect of each scheme to which the failure relates (whether or not the same as the scheme to which the first failure relates). Any further such failures occurring within three years from the date on which the previous failure began, will result in a penalty of £1,000 in respect of each scheme to which the failure relates (whether or not the same as the schemes to which any of the previous failures relates).

Changes with effect from 1 January 2011

FA 2010, s 56 and *Sch 17* amend the provisions of *FA 2004* which require promoters and users of certain tax avoidance schemes to provide information about them to HMRC; and also *TMA 1970, s 98C*, with effect from 1 January 2011. In particular, *FA 2010* amends the definition of 'promoter' and the time at which the duty to disclose a scheme arises; requires promoters of notifiable schemes periodically to provide lists of clients; empowers HMRC to require intermediaries who are concerned in the marketing of a scheme, but who are not promoters, to identify the promoter; and substantially increases the penalties available to the tribunal where a scheme is not disclosed as required.

With regard to the penalties imposed by *TMA 1970, FA 2010, Sch 17 para 10(2)* amends *s 98C*.

The amendments add a new category to *s 98C(2)*, adding the new duties of promoters to provide client lists and of introducers to identify promoters to HMRC to the list of duties to which a penalty relates. The penalty in these cases is the existing single initial penalty not exceeding £5,000.

However, *s 98C(1)(a)* is also amended with regard to the failure to disclose a scheme (as identified at s *98C(2)(a)(b)* and *(c)*). The initial single penalty (of £5,000) for such a failure is replaced with an initial daily penalty not exceeding £600 for each day during the 'initial period', which is defined in new subsection *s 98C(2ZA)*.

The 'initial period' begins with the 'relevant day' and ends on the day the penalty is determined by the tribunal, or the day before the person complies with the duty in question, whichever is earlier. The 'relevant day' is defined in a table — in each case it is the day after the end of the period during which the person should have complied with the duty in question. Therefore the 'initial period' is the period of non-compliance beginning on the day after the deadline for complying, and ending when the penalty is determined, or when the person complies if earlier.

In determining the level of penalty for failure to disclose a scheme the tribunal is also, to take account of all relevant matters, including the need for the penalty to be an adequate deterrent, having regard in particular to:

(i) in the case of a promoter's failure to make a disclosure within the prescribed period, to the fees received or likely to have been received in connection with the scheme; and
(ii) in the case of a taxpayer's failure to make a disclosure within the prescribed period, to the tax advantage obtained or sought from the scheme.

New *s 98C(2ZC)* provides that where the daily penalty determined above appears inappropriately low, then the tribunal may increase the penalty to an amount, not exceeding £1 million.

HMRC may commence proceedings before the First-tier Tribunal for re-determination of a penalty where it appears that the 'relevant day' from which a penalty has been determined is incorrect. This may occur in cases where the tribunal has made an order under *FA 2004, s 306A* that a scheme be treated as notifiable.

The new provisions also allow the Treasury to vary by secondary legislation the amounts of both the proposed initial daily penalty of £600 and the possible increase of penalty to £1 million in s *98C(2ZC)*. Such regulations are subject to an affirmative resolution of the House of Commons.

The initial penalty for failure to comply with other duties (duties imposed by the disclosure regime other than disclosing the scheme) mentioned in *TMA 1970, s 98C(2)* remains unchanged.

These amendments have effect from 1 January 2011.

[*TMA 1970, s 98C; FA 2004, s 315(1); FA 2007, s 108(9); FA 2008, Sch 38 para 7; FA 2010, s 56, Sch 17; SI 2011 No 3019*].

Simon's Taxes. See **A7.235**.

Failure to comply with investigatory powers under FA 2008, Sch 36

[60.11] The penalties below apply to offences under the investigatory powers of *FA 2008, Sch 36* which applies from 1 April 2009.

Fixed and daily penalties

Where a person fails to comply with an information notice within *FA 2008, Sch 36 Pt 1* (see **43.4 HMRC INVESTIGATORY POWERS**) he is liable to a fixed penalty of £300 and, for each subsequent day of continuing failure, a further penalty not exceeding £60. For this purpose, failing to comply with a notice includes concealing, destroying or otherwise disposing of, or arranging for the concealment, destruction or disposal of, a document in breach of *FA 2008, Sch 36 paras 42, 43* (see **43.9 HMRC INVESTIGATORY POWERS**).

Where a person deliberately obstructs an HMRC officer in the course of an inspection of business premises under *FA 2008, Sch 36 Pt 2* (see **43.10 HMRC INVESTIGATORY POWERS**) which has been approved by the tribunal (see **6.31 APPEALS**) he is liable to a fixed penalty of £300 and, for each subsequent day of continuing obstruction, a further penalty not exceeding £60.

No penalty is due where a person fails to do anything required to be done within a limited time period if he does it within such further time as an HMRC officer allows. A person is not liable to a penalty if he satisfies HMRC or (on appeal) the tribunal that there is a reasonable excuse for the failure or obstruction. An insufficiency of funds is not a reasonable excuse for this purpose unless it is attributable to events outside the person's control. Where a person relies on another person to do anything, that is not a reasonable excuse unless the first person took reasonable care to avoid the failure or obstruction. Where a person has a reasonable excuse which ceases, he is treated as continuing to have a reasonable excuse if the failure is remedied or the obstruction stops without unreasonable delay.

The Treasury can make regulations amending the amounts of the above penalties.

[*FA 2008, s 113, Sch 36 paras 39–41, 44, 45*].

Tax-related penalty

The Upper Tribunal may impose a tax-related penalty where a person's failure or obstruction continues after a fixed penalty has been imposed under the above provisions. An HMRC officer must have reason to believe that the amount of tax that that person has paid, or is likely to pay, is significantly less than it would otherwise have been as a result of the failure or obstruction, and the officer must make an application to the Upper Tribunal before the end of the twelve months beginning with the 'relevant date'. In deciding the amount of the penalty (if any), the Upper Tribunal must have regard to the amount of tax which has not been, or is likely not to be, paid by the person.

The '*relevant date*' is the date on which the person became liable to the penalty. Where, however, the penalty is for a failure relating to an information notice against which a person can appeal, the relevant date is the later of the end of the period in which notice of such appeal could have been given and, where an appeal is made, the date on which the appeal is determined or withdrawn.

A tax-related penalty is in addition to the fixed penalty and any daily penalties under the above provisions.

[*FA 2008, Sch 36 para 50*].

A person is not liable to a penalty under any of the above provisions in respect of anything for which he has been convicted of an offence. [*FA 2008, Sch 36 para 52*].

Miscellaneous

Interest on penalties

[60.12] Penalties imposed under *FA 1998, Sch 18* in connection with the company tax return, carry interest calculated from the due date (broadly, 30 days after issue of a notice of determination by an officer of HMRC or immediately upon determination by Appeal Commissioners or judgment of the High Court — see **59.17** below) to the date of payment. [*TMA 1970, s 103A*]. Rates of interest on penalties are synonymous with those on unpaid tax — see **49.2 INTEREST ON OVERDUE TAX.**

Reasonable excuse for failure

[60.13] It is generally provided that a person is deemed not to have failed to do anything required to be done where there was a reasonable excuse for the failure and, if the reasonable excuse ceased, provided that the failure was remedied without unreasonable delay after the excuse had ceased. Similarly, a person is deemed not to have failed to do anything required to be done within a limited time if he did it within such further time as HMRC, or the Commissioners or Revenue officer concerned, may have allowed. [*TMA 1970, s 118(2)*].

In *Creedplan Ltd v Winter* [1995] STC (SCD) 352, the Special Commissioner, in confirming a penalty under *TMA 1970, s 94(1)(a)* (before its repeal on the introduction of self-assessment), considered that 'there is no reasonable excuse . . . for sending in a return which was less than was required' (but cf. *Akarimsons Ltd v Chapman* [1997] STC (SCD) 140 in which a penalty under *section 94(1)(b)* was quashed). See also *Steeden v Carver* [1999] STC (SCD) 283, in which reliance on HMRC's advice as to the practical extension of a deadline, unequivocally given, was held to be 'as reasonable an excuse as could be found'.

See HMRC Company Taxation Manual, CTM94140 for HMRC's approach to 'reasonable excuse'.

Procedure

[60.14] With regard to 'new regime' penalties, where a penalty is due and settlement of the case is not by way of contract settlement, HMRC must issue an assessment charging the penalty. A penalty assessment is treated as, and enforced as, an assessment to tax and must be issued within certain time limits, see further below. All HMRC decisions in relation to penalties are appealable to the Tribunal.

With regard to penalties under the old regime, the following applies.

Except in the case of:

(a) penalty proceedings instituted before the courts in cases of suspected fraud (see below);
(b) penalties imposed for failure to comply with Commissioners' precepts;

(c) penalties under:
  (i) *TMA 1970, s 93(1)(a)*,
  (ii) *TMA 1970, s 98(1)(i)* (see **60.9** above),
  (iii) *TMA 1970, s 98A(2)(a)(i)* (see **60.9** above), or
  (iv) *TMA 1970, s 98B(2)(a)* (see **60.9** above),
  (for which see further below),

an authorised officer of HMRC may make a determination imposing a penalty of an amount which he considers correct or appropriate.

The notice of determination must state the date of issue and the time within which an appeal can be made. It cannot be altered unless:

(i) there is an appeal (see below);
(ii) an authorised officer discovers that the penalty is or has become insufficient (in which case he may make a further determination); or
(iii) the penalty arises under *FA 1998, Sch 18 para 18(2)*, and an authorised officer subsequently discovers that the amount of tax is or has become excessive (in which case it is to be revised accordingly).

A penalty under these provisions is due 30 days after the date of issue of the notice of determination, and is treated as tax charged under an assessment and due and payable. [*TMA 1970, ss 100, 100A*].

Appeals

The general appeals provisions (see APPEALS (**6**)) apply to an appeal against a determination as if it were an appeal against an assessment to tax, and the tribunal is given broad specific powers to confirm, set aside or amend determinations.

Without prejudice to the general procedural rules in *TMA 1970, s 56*, an appeal against a determination lies to the Upper Tribunal. [*TMA 1970, s 100B; SI 2009 No 56*].

Proceedings before the First-tier Tribunal

For a penalty within (c) above, an authorised officer may commence proceedings before the First-tier Tribunal. The proceedings are by way of information in writing to the First-tier Tribunal, and upon summons issued by them to the defendant (or defender), and are heard and decided in a summary way. An appeal lies to the Upper Tribunal on a question of law or, by the defendant (defender), against the amount. The court can confirm, set aside or vary the determination as seems appropriate. The penalty is treated as tax charged in an assessment and due and payable.

[*TMA 1970, s 100C; SI 2009 No 56*].

Proceedings before court

If HMRC consider that liability arises from fraud by any person, proceedings can be brought in the High Court (or Court of Session). If the Court does not find fraud proved, it can nevertheless impose a penalty to which it considers the person liable.

[*TMA 1970, s 100D*].

General matters

Non-receipt of notice of the hearing at which the tribunal awarded penalties is not a ground of appeal to the courts. A mere denial of liability to penalties implies an intention by the taxpayer to set up a case in refutation, and details must be supplied.

Statements made or documents produced by or on behalf of a company are admissible evidence in proceedings against it, notwithstanding that reliance on HMRC's practice in cases of full disclosure may have induced it to make or produce them. For statements made, or documents produced, on or after 10 July 2003, the detailed provision is amended to reflect changes to the 'Hansard' procedure (for which see Tolley's Income Tax under Fraudulent or Negligent Conduct: Offers by taxpayer, 2009/2010 edition and prior). [*TMA 1970, s 105; FA 2003, s 206*].

Penalties must be paid before the end of the period of 30 days beginning with the day on which the notification of the penalty is issued.

An assessment of a penalty within **60.11** above must be made before the end of the twelve months beginning with the end of the 'appeal period' for the assessment of tax unpaid by reason of the failure or, where there is no such assessment, the date on which the amount of tax unpaid by reason of the failure is ascertained.

The imposition of penalties calculated as a percentage of unpaid tax was held to be in the nature of 'criminal' (rather than 'civil') proceedings for the purposes of the European Convention on Human Rights in *King v United Kingdom (Nos 1 & 2): 18881/02*, [2004] STC 911, ECHR.

For relevant cases, see Tolley's Income Tax and/or Tolley's Tax Cases.

Simon's Taxes. See **A4.520–A4.524**.

Mitigation or limitation of penalties

[60.15] The following mitigation rules do not apply to penalties under the new regime, per *FA 2007, Sch 24* or *FA 2008, Sch 41*. For the separate rules applicable to those penalties see the relevant paragraphs above.

HMRC may mitigate penalties before or after judgment [*TMA 1970, s 102*]. See Tolley's Tax Cases generally.

Where two or more tax-geared penalties relate to the same liability, the aggregate amount of the penalties is limited to the greater or greatest penalty applicable. [*TMA 1970, s 97A; FA 1998, Sch 18 para 90*].

Negotiated settlements

In the case of tax-based penalties where a maximum penalty of 100% is in strict law exigible, the inspector will start with the figure of 100% and then take the following factors into account in arriving at the penalty element which he will expect to be included in any offer in settlement of liabilities.

(a) Disclosure. A reduction of up to 20% (or 30% where there has been full voluntary disclosure), depending on how much information was provided, how soon, and how that contributed to settling the investigation.
(b) Co-operation. A reduction of up to 40%, depending upon a comparison of the extent of co-operation given in the investigation with the co-operation which the inspector believes would have been possible.
(c) Gravity. A reduction of up to 40%, depending upon the nature of the offence, how long it continued and the amounts involved.

(HMRC Pamphlet IR 160).

Contract settlements

In cases of fraudulent or negligent conduct (pre 1 April 2009), the taxpayer could be invited to offer a sum in full settlement of liability for tax, interest and penalties (a 'contract settlement') and such offers are often accepted by HMRC without assessment of all the tax. A binding agreement so made could not be repudiated afterwards by the taxpayer or his executors.

Contract settlements may also be used to bring an enquiry (or compliance check) to a close, instead of a closure notice.

See *CIR v Nuttall* (1989) 63 TC 148, CA, for confirmation of power to enter into such agreements. Amounts due under such an agreement which are unpaid may be pursued by an action for a debt, but the Crown does not rank as a preferential creditor in respect of the sums due (*Nuttall* above; *CIR v Woollen* [1992] STC 944, 65 TC 229, CA).

Simon's Taxes. See **A4.574**.

Delay

[60.16] In *King v UK (No 3)* (2004) 76 TC 699 it was found that an 'unreasonable delay' by HMRC in bringing penalty proceedings could infringe the taxpayer's human rights, even if there had also been delay by the taxpayer. The implications of the case extend to voluntary contract settlements as well as to formal penalty proceedings. See Special Criminal Investigation Manual, SCIG14320.

Time limits

[60.17] As noted above, with regard to 'new regime' penalties, where a penalty is due and settlement of the case is not by way of contract settlement, HMRC must issue an assessment charging the penalty. A penalty assessment is treated as, and enforced as, an assessment to tax and must be issued within certain time limits. The time limit for assessment of these penalties has been shortened compared to the previous regimes (see below) in recognition of the requirements of *HRA 1998, Sch 1 Art 6*.

The time limits under the new regime are:

(a) Incorrect returns — *FA 2007, Sch 24*:
   (i) If the penalty is payable under *FA 2007, Sch 24 para 1*, the assessment must be made within twelve months from the end of the appeal period for the decision correcting the inaccuracy. If there was no assessment, the twelve-month period runs from the date on which the inaccuracy was corrected.
   (ii) If the penalty is payable under *FA 2007, Sch 24 para 2*, the time is twelve months from the end of the appeal period for the amended assessment which corrected the understatement.

   [*FA 2007, Sch 24 para 13*].

(b) Failure to notify chargeability — *FA 2008, Sch 41*:
   (i) Where an assessment to recover the tax arising from the failure for the year in question has been issued, the penalty assessment must be made within 12 months of the earlier of: expiry of the thirty-day appeal period for the assessment of the unpaid tax; and the determination or withdrawal of an appeal against that assessment.
   (ii) Where such an assessment has not been issued, the penalty assessment must to be made within 12 months of the date that the amount of tax unpaid as a result of the failure is ascertained.

Further penalty assessments may be made in cases where the potential lost revenue increases after an initial penalty assessment has been made.

[*FA 2008, Sch 41 para 16*].

Otherwise, the time within which a penalty can be determined, or proceedings commenced, depends on the penalty, as follows.

(a) If the penalty is ascertainable by reference to tax payable, the time is the later of six years after the penalty was incurred and three years after the determination of the amount of the tax.
(b) If the penalty arises under *TMA 1970, s 99* (see **60.8** above), the time is 20 years after the date when it was incurred.
(c) In any other case, the time is six years from the time when the penalty was, or began to be, incurred.

[*TMA 1970, s 103*].

Final determination of tax

Provisional agreement of the amount due subject to the inspector's being satisfied with statements of assets, etc. is not final determination for these purposes (*Carco Accessories Ltd v CIR* (1985) 59 TC 45, Ct of Sess).

Simon's Taxes. See **A4.523**.

Failure to state tax credit etc.

[60.18] Failure to provide the required written statement of the amount of dividend or interest paid and the amount of the related tax credit etc. (see **31.17 DISTRIBUTIONS**) carries a penalty of £60 for each offence with a maximum of £600 in respect of any one distribution etc. [*ICTA 1988, ss 234(4), 234A(9); CTA 2010, s 1107*].

Liability under criminal law

[60.19] Most of HMRC's compliance work is dealt with using HMRC's civil powers which allow HMRC to make assessments and determinations (including with regard to penalties as above), carry out enquiries, obtain information and impose financial penalties where offences have been committed.

Under general law HMRC may institute criminal proceedings against taxpayers, their own servants and others. 'False statements to the prejudice of the Crown and public revenue' are criminal offences, (*R v Hudson* (1956) 36 TC 561) as they constitute a fraud on Crown and the public, which is indictable as a common law offence of cheating the public revenue.

HMRC can also institute criminal prosecutions for perjury or conspiracy. False statements in income tax returns, or for obtaining any allowance, reduction or repayment may involve liability to imprisonment for up to two years, under the *Perjury Act 1911, s 5*, for 'knowingly and wilfully' making materially false statements or returns for tax purposes. Also, in Scotland, summary proceedings may be taken under *TMA 1970, s 107*.

There is also a statutory offence where a person fraudulently evades income tax, and in a minority of cases HMRC will consider taking a criminal prosecution for evasion.

Since the merger of the Inland Revenue and HM Customs and Excise in April 2005, HMRC prosecutions have been conducted by the Revenue and Customs Prosecution Office (RCPO). The Director of RCPO is appointed by the Attorney General. The Director may institute and conduct criminal proceedings instituted in England and Wales relating to a criminal investigation by HMRC. The Director may also take over the conduct of such proceedings instituted by HMRC.

In April 2005, HMRC and RCPO entered into a memorandum of understanding with the Treasury and the Attorney General as to the conduct of criminal investigations and prosecutions by the two departments. Under this agreement, it was acknowledged that HMRC would retain:

(a) the responsibility for the conduct of criminal investigations (such responsibility being through Treasury Ministers who are accountable to Parliament); and
(b) policy responsibility for the criteria to be used in deciding whether alternatives to prosecution should be applied,

and that:

(c) the Director of RCPO would be accountable to Parliament via the Attorney General; and
(d) the RCPO's responsibility would be for the conduct of any criminal prosecution (including the decision whether or not to proceed with a particular case).

Changes brought in by *FA 2007* also allow HMRC officers certain powers under the *Police and Criminal Evidence Act 1984*.

See further the Memorandum of Understanding at: www.hmrc.gov.uk/about/memorandum-rcpo.htm.

With regard to HMRC policy on criminal investigations see also: www.hmrc.gov.uk/prosecutions/crim-inv-policy.htm.

With regard to criminal investigations and proceedings generally see further **Simon's Taxes A6.11** *et seq*.

61

Profit Computations

Cross references. See subjects dealt separately under **1.1** INTRODUCTION AND RATES OF TAX; **5** ANTI-AVOIDANCE; **10–16** on CAPITAL ALLOWANCES; **17** CAPITAL GAINS; **27** CONTROLLED FOREIGN COMPANIES; **30** DERIVATIVE CONTRACTS LEGISLATION; **32** DOUBLE TAX RELIEF; **36** FOREIGN EXCHANGE GAINS AND LOSSES; **39** GROUP RELIEF; **46** INCOME TAX IN RELATION TO A COMPANY; **48** INTANGIBLE ASSETS; **51** INVESTMENT COMPANIES AND INVESTMENT BUSINESS; **54** LOAN RELATIONSHIPS; **55** LOSSES; **62** PROPERTY INCOME; **64** RESEARCH AND DEVELOPMENT EXPENDITURE; **65.4** RESIDENCE; **70** TRADE PROFITS; **71** TRADING EXPENSES AND DEDUCTIONS; **72** TRANSFER PRICING.

Simon's Taxes. See D1.106, D1.3.

Introduction

[61.1] This chapter includes some worked examples referring to the detailed guidance elsewhere in the book. The purpose is to assist in understanding corporation tax principals and provide guidance as to layout. Also included in this chapter is guidance on the profits and sources of income that make up a company's taxable total profits (as profits chargeable to corporation tax are now referred to, post *CTA 2010*) and guidance on miscellaneous sources not covered elsewhere in the book.

Examples

[61.2]

The following examples illustrate various aspects of corporation tax computations, including computational profit adjustments, loss relief and group considerations.

Taxable Total Profits

[61.3]

A Ltd, incorporated on 1 June 2004, commences business on 1 January 2011. The accounts for the year ended 31 December 2011 show the following.

	£		£
Wages and salaries	178,400	Gross trading profit	2,274,760
Directors' remuneration	82,200	Income from property	8,000
Rent, rates and insurance	49,200	Government securities	340
Motor expenses	38,000	UK company dividends	1,500
Bad debts	8,200	Profit on sale of shares	64,000
Research and development	36,000		
General expenses	94,000		
Legal and professional costs	16,000		
Overdraft interest	6,000		
Debenture finance charges	3,500		
Audit and accountancy	16,000		
Depreciation of fixed assets	82,000		
Loss on sale of fixed assets	6,000		
Net profit	1,733,100		
	£2,348,600		£2,348,600

The following further information is available.

			£
(a)	Capital allowances for the year are:		
	Plant and machinery (including advertising sign)		48,000
	Research and development		24,000

			£
(b)	Bad debts consist of:		
	Trade debts written off		6,100
	Reserve created	— general	1,800
		— specific	300
			£8,200

(c) General expenses include:

		£
Advertising — erection of permanent sign (see (a) above)		1,050
Defalcations by junior staff		1,280
Entertaining	— small promotional gifts	1,400
	— customers	4,100
	— staff Christmas party	450
Gifts, donations	— wines, etc. on exhibition stand	800
	— trade protection society	250
	— Oxfam (within *CTA 2010, s 190*)	500
	— political party	500
Inducement to planning official		750
Interest on unpaid tax		500
New premises — rehabilitation costs		3,000
Share sale — commission and fees		1,500
VAT — penalty for late return		400

(d) The company qualifies as a small and medium-sized enterprise for the purpose of research and development expenditure. The £36,000 qualifies as 'relevant' expenditure (see **64 RESEARCH AND DEVELOPMENT**) of which £24,000 relates to the cost of a dedicated research employee and £8,000 to consumable items.

(e) Legal and professional costs consist of:

Company secretarial services	6,150
Debenture issue (see (f) below)	1,800
Debt collection	2,100
Industrial tribunal representation	750
Lease variation	1,000
Patent infringement claim work	3,400
Preparation of staff service agreements	800
	£16,000

(f) Debenture finance charges relate to £50,000 nominal stock issued on 1 January 2005 for trade finance at £96 per £100, carrying interest at 6.6% payable annually in arrears, for redemption 31 December 2014. The charge to profit and loss comprises interest of £3,300 and redemption reserve costs of £200 on a straight line basis. As these are arrived at under an amortised cost basis of accounting, the charges are allowable for tax purposes. The issue costs included in legal and professional costs (see (e) above) are also allowable.

The overdraft interest charge is similarly on an amortised cost basis and allowable.

The £340 Government securities credit relates to £9,000 4% Treasury Stock acquired in March 2009 at £9,080 with four years to redemption. It represents gross interest £360 less £20 premium amortisation charge on a straight line basis. It is thus properly chargeable as income from non-trading loan relationships. The interest was received on 7 March and 7 September.

(g) Chargeable gain on share sale 30 September 2011 £51,100.

(h) 26-year lease on new premises, at annual rent £22,500, purchased on 1 January 2005 at a premium of £200,000.

Cost of rehabilitation of premises to make suitable for trade use, between 1 January 2011 and 31 March 2011, £18,000.

Rates, etc. incurred before 1 January 2011, £20,000.

The computation for *year ended 31 December 2011* is as follows.

		£	£
Net profit			1,733,100
Add: Bad debts — general reserve (see **71.5**)		1,800	
Advertising — sign erection (note 1)		1,050	
Entertaining customers (see **71.41**)		4,100	
Gifts, donations (see **71.49**)	— wines, etc.	800	
	— Oxfam	500	
	— political party	500	
Inducement (note 2)		750	
Interest on unpaid tax (see **49.2**)		500	
New premises — rehabilitation costs (see **71.8**)		3,000	
Share sale commission and fees (note 3)		1,500	
VAT penalty (see **71.58**)		400	
Lease variation expenses		1,000	
Depreciation		82,000	
Loss on sale of fixed assets		6,000	103,900
			1,837,000
Less: Income from property (see **62**)		8,000	
Government securities (see **49.2**)		340	
Dividends received		1,500	
Profit on share sale		64,000	73,840
			1,763,160
Less: Plant and machinery allowances (see **11**)		48,000	
Research and development allowances (see **64**)		24,000	
Research and development relief (see **64**)		18,000	
Lease premium allowance (note 4)			
200,000 (1 − $^{25}/_{50}$) ÷ 26		3,846	
Pre-trading expenditure (rent and rates)(note 5)		110,000	203,846
			£1,559,314
Trading income			1,559,314
Income from property		8,000	
			8,000
Chargeable gain (see **17**)			51,100
Total profits			1,618,414
Less: Non-trading loan relationship debit (interest on unpaid tax £500 *less* interest on securities £340)			160
			1,618,254

	1,618,254
Less: Charitable donation	500
Taxable Total Profits (TTP)	£1,617,754
Tax chargeable:	
FY 2010 @ 28% on ¼ × 1,617,754 = 404,439	113,242.92
FY 2011 @ 26% on ¾ × 1,617,754 = 1,213,315	315,461.90
	£428,704.82

Notes

1. The costs of erecting the advertising sign is capital and has been included in calculating the capital allowances.

2. The inducement payment is a bribe and as such illegal see **71.52**.

3. The share sale commission and fees have been included in calculating the capital gain at (g).

4. The proportion of the lease premium allowable is calculated under *CTA 2009, ss 217–220* see **71.62**.

5. Pre-trading expenditure in the seven years before a company starts to carry on a trade is allowable, subject to conditions, under *CTA 2009, s 61* see **71.60**.

Small profits rate

[61.4]

Raven Ltd has the following results for the year to 31 March 2011:

	£
Adjusted trade profits	225,000
Loan relationship credit	11,000
UK property business	40,000
Dividend received	23,400

Raven has profits in the small profits marginal rate band (ie, above £300,000 but less than £1,500,000). (See **67 SMALL PROFITS — REDUCED RATES**).

	£
Trade profit	225,000
Loan relationship credit	11,000
UK property business	40,000
Profits chargeable to corporation tax	276,000
FII (23,400×100/90)	26,000
Augmented profits	302,000
CT liability:	
TTP × 28%	77,280

Less 7/400 × (1,500,000 – 302,000) × 276,000/302,000)	(19,160)
Corporation tax liability	58,120

Commencing to trade and short accounting periods

[61.5]

Warren Ltd, a new company was set up by its parent company on 1 February 2011. The company commenced trading on 1 March 2011. Its parent company also owns the entire share capital of another company.

Warren Ltd draws up accounts to 31 August 2011 which is also the accounting date for the other group companies.

The results for Warren Ltd are:

		£
Trading income		360,000
Bank interest		2,200
		362,200
Expenses		
Cost of sales	88,000	
Depreciation	17,500	
Employee costs	55,000	
Legal fees	5,000	
Entertaining	2,500	
Rent paid	45,000	
Profit per accounts		(213,000)
		149,200

Notes:

(1) The legal fees include £500 for share issue costs and £3,000 for a 45 year lease on the premises used by the company.

(2) The company is entitled to capital allowances of £125,000.

Warren Ltd comes within the charge to corporation tax when it commences to trade. A chargeable accounting period begins on 1 March 2011. This chargeable accounting period ends when the accounts end on 31 August 2011. (See **2 ACCOUNTING PERIODS**).

The computation for the period ended 31 August 2011 is as follows:

		£
Profit per the accounts		149,200
Less bank interest		(2,200)
		147,000
Add: Depreciation	17,500	
Legal fees (£500 + £3,000) (see **71.54**)	3,500	
Entertaining clients (see **71.41**)	2,500	23,500

Less capital allowances	125,000
Trade profit	45,500
Loan relationship credit	2,200
TTP	47,700

The chargeable accounting period is six months long and the company has two associated companies, thus the limits are:

Upper limit:	1,500,000/3 × 6/12	250,000
Lower limit:	300,000/3 × 6/12	50,000

The company has received no dividends and therefore augmented profits equal TTP. Warren Ltd's profits are therefore charged at the small profits rate.

Long accounting periods

[61.6]

Ward Plc acquired a 100% interest in a trading subsidiary, Connor Ltd on 1 December 2009. Ward Plc has a year end of 31 March.

Connor Ltd drew accounts annually to 31 October, but agreed to change its accounts date to match its parent. Accounts were therefore prepared for the period 1 November 2009 to 31 March 2011. The accounts showed the following:

		£
Trading income		288,000
Bank interest receivable		40,800
UK dividends receivable		3,800
		332,600
Less expenses		
Depreciation	10,000	
Entertaining clients	6,500	
Employee costs	91,000	
Office costs	27,000	
Gift aid donation	25,000	
Loss on sale of asset	3,000	162,500
Net profit for period		170,100

Notes to accounts:

1. A gift aid donation of £25,000 is paid annually on 3 October each year.

2. The loss arose on the sale of a photocopier in February 2011. Proceeds of sale were £1,000. The photocopier had originally cost £4,000.

3. The UK dividends received were as follows:

500 ICI Plc shares (17.8.10)	£2,000
200 Kingfisher Group Plc shares (2.1.11)	£1,800

On 25 February 2011, Connor Ltd sold the Kingfisher shares making a chargeable gain (after indexation) of £18,283. The holding in Kingfisher Group Plc represents less than 1% of the company's share capital.

4. The capital allowances pools at 1 November 2009 were as follows:

General pool	£12,000
Finance director's car (purchased in 2008)	£18,000

The only addition in the period was the purchase of a replacement photocopier for £3,179 in January 2011.

The 17 month accounting period is split for tax purposes into the 12 months to 31 October 2010 and the five months to 31 March 2011 as follows:

Profit per accounts		170,100
Add:		
Depreciation	10,000	
Client entertaining	6,500	
Gift aid	25,000	
Loss on sale of asset	3,000	
Less:		44,500
Bank interest	40,800	
UK dividends	3,800	
		(44,600)
Adjusted profits for 17 months		170,000
	Year end 31.10.10	5 months to 31.3.11
	£	£
Adjusted profits (12:5)	120,000	50,000
Less capital allowances (W1)	(5,400)	(5,146)
Trade profit	114,600	44,854
Loan relationship credit (12:5)	28,800	12,000
Capital gain	—	18,283
	143,400	75,137
Less charitable donations	(25,000)	—
TTP	118,400	75,137
FII (× 100/90)	2,222	2,000
Augmented profits	120,622	77,137
Limits		
£1,500,000/2	750,000	
£1,500,000/2 × 5/12		312,500
£300,000/2	150,000	
£300,000/2 × 5/12		62,500
Corporation tax liability:		
£118,400 @ 21%	24,864	
£75,137 @ 28%		21,038
Less marginal relief		

7/400 × (312,500–77,137) × 75,167/77,137		(4,012)		
Corporation tax liability	24,864	17,026		

Working 1; Capital allowances				
Year ended 31 October 2010	AIA @ 100%	General Pool	Car	Total
	£	£	£	£
TWDV B/fwd		12,000	18,000	
WDA @ 20%		(2,400)		2,400
WDA restricted			(3,000)	3,000
		9,600	15,000	5,400
5 Months to 31 March 2011				
TWDV B/fwd		9,600	15,000	
Addition:				
Photocopiers (1/10)	3,179			
AIA	(3,179)			3,179
Disposal (2/10)		(1,000)		
		8,600		
WDA @ 20% × 5/12		(717)		717
WDA 3,000 × 5/12			(1,250)	1,250
TWDV c/fwd		7,883	13,750	5,146
The AIA limit £100,000 × 5/12 = 41,667				

Trade losses

[61.7]

Katchi Ltd (not part of a group) has the following results.

	Trade profit / (loss)
Year ended 30 June 2007	30,000
Year ended 30 June 2008	70,000
Year ended 30 June 2009	30,000
Year ended 30 June 2010	(80,000)
Year ended 30 June 2011	(50,000)

Relief for the losses will be claimed as follows:

	Y/E 30.6.07	Y/E 30.6.08	Y/E 30.6.09	Y/E 30.6.10	Y/E 30.6.11
	£	£	£	£	£
Trade profit	30,000	70,000	30,000	Nil	Nil
Losses relief					
1 year carry back			(30,000)		
Extended carry back					

(from Y/E 30.6.10)		(50,000)			
PCTCT/ TTP	30,000	20,000	Nil	Nil	Nil

Loss memo	
Loss for year ended 30 June 2010	80,000
Less offset previous year	(30,000)
Less extended carry back to year ended 30 June 2008	(50,000)
Carry forward	Nil
Loss for year ended 30 June 2011	50,000
Less offset previous year	Nil
Carry forward	50,000

The loss of the year ended 30 June 2010 can be carried back 12 months under *CTA 2010, s 37(3)(b)* and in addition up to three years to a maximum of £50,000. The loss of the year ended 30 June 2011 can only be carried forward.

Group relief

[61.8]

D Ltd and E Ltd are wholly-owned subsidiaries of C Ltd, no other company being associated with any of them. Results for each for the year ended 31 December 2011 are as follows.

C Ltd	£
Trading profit (after capital allowances)	452,000
Chargeable gain on disposal	65,000
D Ltd	
Trading loss (after capital allowances)	87,000
Income chargeable on non-trading loan relationships	2,000
E Ltd	
Trading profit (after capital allowances)	118,000
Income from property	2,000

Ignoring group relief, the computation for each company is as follows.

C Ltd	
Total profits	£517,000

The upper limit for profits to be taxable at the small profits rate is £300,000 *divided by* 1 + the number of associated companies, i.e. £100,000. The limits for marginal relief are similarly reduced to profits between £100,000 and £500,000. C Ltd's profits are thus taxable in full at 28% / 26%.

Corporation tax liability:	
FY 2010 @ 28% on $\frac{1}{4}$ × 517,000 = 129,250	36,190
FY 2011 @ 28% on $\frac{3}{4}$ × 517,000 = 387,750	100,815
Corporation tax payable	£137,005
D Ltd	
Total profits	2,000
Less: Trading loss set against profits [*CTA 2010, s 37*]	2,000
Corporation tax liability	—
Trading loss unrelieved	85,000
Loss available for group relief	£85,000
E Ltd	
Total profits	£120,000

Since this is between the upper and lower limits for marginal small profits relief (see under C Ltd above), such relief is available.

Corporation tax liability:		
FY 2010 @ 28% on $\frac{1}{4}$ × 120,000 = 30,000	8,400	
Less: $\frac{7}{400}$ × (125,000 – 30,000)	1,662	
		6,738
FY 2011 @ 26% on $\frac{3}{4}$ × 120,000 = 90,000	23,400	
Less: $\frac{3}{200}$ × (375,000 – 90,000) =	4,275	
		19,125
Corporation tax payable		£25,863

If D Ltd surrenders its losses by group relief, £65,000 to C Ltd, £20,000 to E Ltd, the computations are as follows.

C Ltd	
Total profits	517,000
Less: Group relief	65,000

TTP		£452,000
Corporation tax liability:		
FY 2010 @ 28% on 1/4 × 452,000 = 113,000	31,640	
Less: 7/400 × (125,000 – 113,000)	210	
		31,430
FY 2011 @ 26% on 3/4 × 452,000 = 339,000	88,140	
Less: 3/200 × (375,000 – 339,000) =	540	
		87,600
Corporation tax payable		£119,030
D Ltd		
Losses available for group relief		85,000
Less: Losses surrendered		85,000
E Ltd		
Total profits		120,000
Less: Group relief		20,000
Profits chargeable to corporation tax		£100,000
Corporation tax liability:		
FY 2010 @ 21% on 1/4 × 100,000 = 25,000		5,250
FY 2011 @ 20% on 3/4 × 100,000 = 75,000		15,000
Corporation tax payable		£20,250

This gives the optimum group tax position, as any switch of group relief from C Ltd to E Ltd saves tax on E Ltd at 20% / 21%, whereas C Ltd's marginal tax rate is 27.5% / 29.75%. A switch of relief from E Ltd to C Ltd has no effect on the overall liability, as E Ltd would also be taxable at a marginal rate of 27.5% / 29.75% on its additional profits coming into charge.

Profits to be included

[61.9] '*Profits*' are defined as 'income and chargeable gains' [*CTA 2009, s 2(2); ICTA 1988, s 6(4)(a)*] and include:

- overseas profits of a UK resident company, whether remitted to the UK or not [*CTA 2009, s 2(2); ICTA 1988, s 70(1)*];
- profits arising in the winding-up of a company [*CTA 2009, s 6(2); ICTA 1988, s 8(2)*] (see **76 WINDING UP**);
- profits accruing to the company's benefit under any trust, or arising from a **PARTNERSHIP** (**58**), which would be chargeable if they accrued to the company directly [*CTA 2009, s 7; ICTA 1988, s 8(2)*]; and

- dividends or interest from **BUILDING SOCIETIES** (**9**).

Profits do not include dividends and any other **DISTRIBUTIONS** (**31**) from UK resident companies [*CTA 2009, s 1285; ICTA 1988, s 208*], from 1 July 2009 this is extended by *FA 2009, s 34* to also include most non UK dividends (see **31.15**) and profits accruing to the company in a fiduciary or representative capacity and in which it has no beneficial interest.

[*CTA 2009, s 6(1); ICTA 1988, s 8(2)*].

As regards certain directors' fees paid to other companies, see HMRC Extra Statutory Concession, A37.

For treatment of profits arising from underwriting business of a corporate member of Lloyd's, see *FA 1994, ss 219–230, Sch 21* (as amended).

Under *CTA 2009, s 8* corporation tax is calculated by reference to accounting periods. Prior to *CTA 2009*, corporation tax was assessed for periods of account. A '*period of account*' in relation to a trade or other business meant a period for which accounts are drawn up. [*ICTA 1988, s 832(1)*].

Corporation tax computations

[61.10] A company which is resident in the UK is chargeable to corporation tax in respect of all its profits wherever arising. A non resident company which carries on a trade in the UK through a permanent establishment is liable to corporation tax on the income and gains of the permanent establishment. Profits are computed *separately for each source* within the charge to corporation tax (see **1.1 INTRODUCTION** and **65.4 RESIDENCE**). Total profits are the aggregate of these sources including chargeable gains (after allowable losses) with the resulting total being known as taxable total profits (TTP) post *CTA 2010*, previously known as the profits chargeable to corporation tax (PCTCT) for the period. The main sources of income and reliefs are:

Source	Type	See
Trading income	Profits from a trade	**70 TRADE PROFITS — INCOME AND SPECIFIC TRADES** and **71 TRADING EXPENSES AND DEDUCTIONS**
Property income	Profits from letting UK and overseas property	**62 PROPERTY INCOME**
Loan relationships	Debits and credits arising from money debts	**54 LOAN RELATIONSHIPS**
Miscellaneous income	Sundry income	**61**
Chargeable gains	Capital gains and losses on disposals	**17 CAPITAL GAINS**, **18 CAPITAL GAINS — GROUPS** and **19 CAPITAL GAINS**

Source	Type	See
Management expenses	Expenses of companies with investment business	**51 INVESTMENT COMPANIES AND INVESTMENT BUSINESS**
Intangible assets	Receipts and expenditure in respect of intangible assets	**48 INTANGIBLE ASSETS**
Research and development relief	Relief for expenditure on R&D	**64 RESEARCH AND DEVELOPMENT EXPENDITURE**
Charitable donations relief	Previously known as charges on income, now mainly gift aid donations.	**20.12 CHARITIES** and **61.11**
Loss relief	Relief for losses	**55 LOSSES**

Accounting periods ending before 1 April 2009

Profits were still computed *separately for each source* within the charge to corporation tax. However they were traditionally computed under the income tax provisions applicable to income from that source as if the accounting period were a tax year, and in accordance with income tax law and practice (excluding provisions applicable solely to individuals, and subject to any special corporation tax provision, see below and **70 TRADE PROFITS — INCOME AND SPECIFIC TRADES** and **71 TRADING EXPENSES AND DEDUCTIONS**) for the tax year in which the accounting period ends, but on the basis of the actual income arising in the accounting period.

The repeal (by *CTA 2009*) of *ICTA 1988, s 9(1)* (which provided that income be computed for corporation tax purposes according to income tax principles) does not affect the relevance for corporation tax purposes of any case law that was relevant immediately before the repeal.

[*CTA 2009, Sch 2 para 11*].

From the mid-1990s the move was towards a separate computational regime for corporation tax, with special rules on, for example, interest (see **54 LOAN RELATIONSHIPS**), **INTANGIBLE ASSETS** (**48**) and **RESEARCH AND DEVELOPMENT** (**64**). The law relating to the taxation of 'trading income' (previously within *Schedules A, D* and *F* and the cases of *Schedule D*) was consolidated in *Income Tax (Trading and Other Income) Act 2005* (*ITTOIA 2005*) as part of the Tax Law Rewrite programme, and has effect for income tax purposes for 2005/06 and subsequent years and, for corporation tax purposes where relevant, for accounting periods ending after 5 April 2005. [*ITTOIA 2005, s 883(1)*]. For corporation tax purposes, income continued to be computed and assessments made under *Schedules A* and *D* and the Cases of *Schedule D*, as if they were still part of income tax law, and not under *ITTOIA 2005* until 31 March 2009. For accounting periods ending on or after 1 April 2009, *CTA 2009* applies to determine profits for corporation tax; *CTA 2009* abolished the *Schedule A, D* and *F* labels, though this is purely a cosmetic change.

[*ICTA 1988, ss 9, 836B; ITTOIA 2005, Sch 1 paras 7, 340*].

For accounting periods ending before 1 April 2009, *Schedule D, Case III* encompassed tax in respect of non-trading profits or gains from loan relationships (see **54.5 LOAN RELATIONSHIPS**), tax in respect of any annuity or other annual payment (not chargeable as property income) payable in respect of anything other than a loan relationship (wherever, and at whatever intervals, payable), and (where it does not fall within the loan relationship rules, see **54.3 LOAN RELATIONSHIPS**) any discount arising otherwise than in respect of a loan relationship.

[*ICTA 1988, s 18(3A); F(No 2)A 2005, Sch 7 para 12(9); Sch 11 Pt 2(8)*].

Income of a trade assessable under *Schedule D, Case V* was computed in accordance with the rules of *Schedule D, Case I*. [*ICTA 1988, s 70(2)*]. Income from an overseas property business assessable under *Schedule D, Case V* (see **62 PROPERTY INCOME**) was computed in accordance with the rules of *Schedule A*.

[*ICTA 1988, s 70A*].

See **70.16 TRADE PROFITS** for post-cessation receipts chargeable to tax under *Schedule D Case VI*.

As stated above, the *Schedule A* and *Schedule D* labels are now defunct.

See **36.9** *et seq*. **EXCHANGE GAINS AND LOSSES** as regards use of currencies other than sterling.

Subject to any express authorising provision, no deduction may be made in computing profits in respect of any dividends or other **DISTRIBUTIONS (31)**, nor in computing income from any source in respect of any charges on income now charitable donations relief (see **61.11** below). No deduction may be made in computing income from any source for corporation tax purposes in respect of interest (except under the **LOAN RELATIONSHIPS (54)** provisions) or losses from 'intangible fixed assets' (except under the **INTANGIBLE ASSETS (48)** provisions).

[*CTA 2009, s 1305, Sch 1 para 104; ICTA 1988, s 337A; previously ICTA 1988, ss 337(2), 337A; ICTA 1988, s 817; ITTOIA 2005, Sch 1 para 327*].

See, however, **61.11**–**61.13** below regarding allowance of 'charges on income' (now charitable donations). See also **61.14** *et seq*. below and **70 TRADE PROFITS** as regards special corporation tax computational provisions.

Total profits for the accounting period were arrived at by aggregating the amounts shown by these separate computations together with any chargeable gains for the period (less allowable losses).

Where income was chargeable to corporation tax under, or by virtue of, any of the provisions listed at *CTA 2010, s 1173(1)* previously *ICTA 1988, s 834A* (inserted by *CTA 2009, Sch 1 para 274* — income previously chargeable under *Schedule D, Case VI*) and any period for which accounts are drawn up (a '*period of account*') does not coincide with an accounting period, the profits or losses for the accounting period may, if necessary, be arrived at by apportioning the profits and losses of the relevant periods of account between accounting periods on a time basis, by reference to the number of days in the respective periods. [*CTA 2009, s 1307, Sch 2 para 143*]. Prior to *CTA 2009* (see **70 TRADE PROFITS**), the similar provisions in *ICTA 1988, s 72* applied to income within *Schedule D, Case VI* in the same way that they applied to *Cases I* and *II*.

See also **10 CAPITAL ALLOWANCES — INTRODUCTION** as to the means of making such allowances.

See **66.32 RETURNS** as regards rounding of tax computations.

Simon's Taxes. See **D1.302–D1.309**.

Charitable donations relief

Previously known as charges on income

[61.11] Qualifying donations to charities (see **20.12 CHARITIES**) notwithstanding the restrictions referred to below, and certain gifts of shares and securities to charities (see **20.17 CHARITIES**) to the extent they are not dividends or other distributions and are not deductible in computing income (see below), are under *CTA 2010* eligible for relief under charitable donations relief, previously known as charges on income (pre *CTA 2010*).

Charitable donations relief is deducted from the company's total profits for the period after any other relief but before group relief (*CTA 2010, s 189*). The general rule is that where the amount of the donation exceeds the company's taxable total profits for a period the excess cannot be carried back or forward. Instead the excess will be lost unless a claim for group relief can be made.

A company will make a qualifying payment for the purposes of *CTA 2010, s 191* if:

(1) the payment is a payment of a sum of money;
(2) the payment is not subject to a condition as to repayment;
(3) the company making the payment is not a charity, and
(4) the payment is not disqualified under:
    (a) *s 193* — an associated acquisition is made by the charity;
    (b) *s 194* — the payment is regarded as a distribution, or
    (c) *s 195* — benefits are associated with the payment. In this regard *FA 2011* has increased the limits with respect to the restrictions on benefits associated with the payments, the sum of the total values of the benefits should not be more than £2,500 for gifts made in an accounting period ending on or after 1 April 2011 (amended *CTA 2010, s 197(3)*).

The general rule is that charitable donations relief can only be claimed in respect of the period during which the payment or donation is made. However, special provision is made for companies which are wholly owned by a charity under *CTA 2010, s 199*.

Tainted charitable donations

The provisions of *FA 2011* introduce a new anti-avoidance rule at *Sch 3* with regard to charitable donations, with effect from 1 April 2011. The rule prevents the usual tax reliefs from applying where donors enter into arrangements to obtain a financial advantage from the charity in return for their donation.

The provisions are aimed at substantial donors to charities, dealt with for corporation tax purposes at *CTA 2010, ss 512–510*. A new *Pt 21C* (*ss 939A–939I*) is inserted into *CTA 2010*. The new rule is based on the purpose test and considers the reason why the donor or someone connected with them entered into arrangements with a charity. A tainted donation is thus one which satisfies all three of the following conditions:

(A) the donor or person connected with them enter into arrangements and it is reasonable to assume that the donations and the arrangements would not have been made independently of each other;

(B) the donor or person connected with them enter into arrangements with the main purpose (or one of the main purposes) of obtaining a financial advantage directly or indirectly from the charity;

(C) the donor is not a qualifying company that is wholly owned by a charity or a relevant housing provider linked with the charity which received the donation. This allows for wholly owned trading companies of charities, which generally donate their profits to the parent each year, and relevant housing providers, to be outside of scope of the rules.

Certain financial advantages are ignored: where the person who receives the advantage applies it for charitable purposes; those which fall within the exceptions under the gift aid scheme; and where the benefits are already taken into account in computing the relief due on gifts of shares, securities, real property, trading stock etc. to charities.

Where a tainted charitable donation has been made then corporation tax relief is denied to the donor. Where more than one donation forms part of the arrangement, none of the donations ('associated donations') are eligible for tax relief (regardless of whether they are tainted in their own right).

In addition, the legislation with regard to substantial donors is then to be repealed as from 1 April 2013.

[*CTA 2010, Pt 21C, ss 939A–939I*].

See further **20.10 CHARITIES** — transactions with substantial donors for more details.

Rules applying to charges on income prior to the introduction of charitable donations relief

Prior to the introduction of charitable donations relief in *CTA 2010*, relief for donations to charity were given under the provisions relating to charges on income.

The definition of what was classed as a charge on income had changed over time, and most recently, post 16 March 2005, charges on income were restricted to certain donations to charity including gifts of shares etc. to charity, per the definition found at *ICTA 1988, s 338A*.

No payment which was deductible in computing profits for the purposes of corporation tax would be treated as a charge on income. Thus expenses which were incurred wholly and exclusively for the purposes of the trade would be deductible as a trade expense, and therefore 'trade' charges on income (which prior to 16 March 2005 were afforded special treatment with regard to trade losses) essentially became redundant.

Similarly with regard to annuities and other annual payments — post 16 March 2005 such payments would, where applicable, be deducted from the relevant profit calculation as appropriate (for example, as a management expense).

Specifically excluded from charges on income were:

(i) any payment *to* a non-resident *unless* the paying company was UK resident, and either:
   (a) the company deducted, and accounted under *ICTA 1988, Sch 16* (see **46.2 INCOME TAX IN RELATION TO A COMPANY**) for, income tax under *ITA 2007, ss 449, 901, 903* (formerly *ICTA 1988, s 349)*, or
   (b) the payment was payable out of income chargeable under *Schedule D, Case V* (as was), or
   (c) for payments made after 31 March 2001, the person beneficially entitled to the interest was a company which carried on a trade in the UK through a permanent establishment (see **65.6 RESIDENCE**) and in computing whose 'chargeable profits' the payment falls to be brought into account; and

(ii) any payment *by* a non-resident company *unless* it is incurred wholly and exclusively for the purposes of a trade carried on (or to be carried on) in the UK through a permanent establishment (see **65.6 RESIDENCE**); and

(iii) any payment which is charged to capital, or is not ultimately borne by the company; and

(iv) any payment not made under a liability incurred for valuable and sufficient consideration (in relation to which an expected business advantage is not sufficient, see *Ball v National and Grindlays Bank Ltd* CA 1971, 47 TC 287); and

(v) any annual payment for non-taxable consideration or, if made on or after 2 December 2004, for dividends within *ICTA 1988, s 125* (see **5.36 ANTI-AVOIDANCE**).

As regards (i) above, a company is regarded as having deducted the full amount of income tax in cases where it deducts at a reduced rate, or makes no deduction, in accordance with a direction from HMRC International (see *SI 1970 No 488, Reg 6*).

[*ICTA 1988, ss 125(1), 338–338B (ICTA 1988, s 338(2)–(7) as originally enacted); FA 2005, s 91; F(No 2)A 2005, s 38(8)–(13); Sch 11 Pt 2; CTA 2009, s 1305, Sch 1 para 104*].

A sum is deductible in computing income when it is so deductible under the ordinary principles of commercial trading, whether or not it is actually so deducted (*Wilcock v Frigate Investments Ltd* Ch D 1981, 55 TC 530). For a case in which relief for interest paid under a circular arrangement was allowed, see *MacNiven v Westmoreland Investments Ltd* HL 2001, 73 TC 1.

Relief

Charges on income were deductible in the accounting period in which they were paid from company profits as reduced by all other reliefs except group relief (see **39.2 GROUP RELIEF**).

[*ICTA 1988, s 338* (*s 338(1) as originally enacted*); *FA 2002, Sch 30 para 1(2)*].

Annuities to former partners — pre 16 March 2005

Where a partnership business is incorporated, or a company takes over a partnership, and the agreement in either case refers to the company assuming responsibility for payment of an annuity to a former partner, then provided that the annuity is commercial in amount, the payment will not be prevented by (iii) above from being a charge on income. *CTA 2009, s 1301* formerly *ICTA 1988, s 125* (annual payments for non-taxable consideration, see **46.2**(a) **INCOME TAX IN RELATION TO A COMPANY**) is not in practice considered to apply to such payments in respect of a *bona fide* commercial transaction. (HMRC Company Taxation Manual, CTM09090).

Excess charges

Charges on income (provided that they were incurred wholly and exclusively for the purposes of a trade) were taken into account in computing losses to be carried forward and terminal losses, but not losses to be carried back. However, post 16 March 2005 the reference to such 'trade' charges became redundant and this provision was not replicated in *CTA 2010*. See further the explanatory note to *CTA 2010, s 45*. See **55.5–55.6 LOSSES.**

Simon's Taxes. See **D1.315–D1.321**.

Particular computational matters

[61.12] The following paragraphs refer to matters (in alphabetical order) relating to corporation tax, or of relevance to companies and not dealt with in the other chapters. See **70 TRADE PROFITS — INCOME AND SPECIFIC TRADES** and **71 TRADING EXPENSES AND DEDUCTIONS** for the computation of trading profits. See also **10 CAPITAL ALLOWANCES — INTRODUCTION; 30 DERIVATIVE CONTRACTS LEGISLATION; 36 FOREIGN EXCHANGE GAINS AND LOSSES; 48 INTANGIBLE ASSETS; 54 LOAN RELATIONSHIPS; 62 PROPERTY INCOME** and **64 RESEARCH AND DEVELOPMENT.**

Annual payments not otherwise charged

[61.13] There is a residual charge to corporation tax on income in respect of annual payments not charged to corporation tax under any other provision (other than any such payments not so charged only because of an exemption).

In determining whether payments are annual payments, the frequency with which they are made is irrelevant. [*CTA 2009, ss 976, 977; ICTA 1988, s 18(3)(3A); FA 1996, s 105, Sch 14 para 5*].

For accounting periods ending before 1 April 2009, annual payments not otherwise charged to corporation tax were chargeable under *Schedule D, Case III* if from a UK source, or *Schedule D, Case V* if from a non-UK source.

The phrase 'annual payment' derives its meaning from an extensive body of case law for which see Tolley's Tax Cases.

There is an exemption from the charge under these provisions where a payment is made by a person liable to pool betting duty in consequence of his receiving a reduction in that duty and is made in order to meet (directly or indirectly) capital expenditure incurred in improving spectator safety or comfort at a soccer ground. [*CTA 2009, s 978; FA 1990, s 126(1)(3); FA 1991, s 121(1)(3)*].

Contaminated or derelict land remediation expenditure

[61.14] Pursuant to the findings of the OTS with regard to their review of reliefs, and the government's response, it was announced in the 2011 Budget that the provisions in *CTA 2009, Pt 14* which provide tax relief for contaminated or derelict land remediation are to be abolished after 2012, following a period of consultation.

Capital expenditure

Relief is available under *CTA 2009, Pt 14* for capital expenditure incurred on or after 11 May 2001 which is 'qualifying land remediation expenditure' incurred by a company in respect of 'land' in the UK acquired by the company for the purposes of a trade or UK property business carried on by it (pre-trading expenses being ignored). '*Land*' is defined as 'any estate, interest or rights in or over land' and for these purposes, 'land' includes buildings (see HMRC Corporate Intangibles, Research & Development Manual, CIRD60130 and *Interpretation Act 1978, Sch 1*).

For expenditure incurred on or after 1 April 2009, the relief is also available where the land was in a derelict state (i.e. it is not in productive use and cannot be put into such use without the removal of buildings etc.). To qualify for the relief, the taxpayer must acquire a major interest in the land. A major interest is a freehold interest in the land or a leasehold interest which is either a grant or an assignment of a lease for a term of at least seven years.

The relief applies where, at the time of the acquisition, all or part of the land was in a contaminated or, on or after 1 April 2009, a derelict state *other than* wholly or partly as a result of the company's own actions or inaction (or the actions or inaction of a person with a 'relevant connection' to the company). Such expenditure is, if the company so elects by written notice, allowed as a deduction in computing the profits of the trade or business for the accounting period in which the expenditure was incurred (and may also attract the enhanced deduction described below). The election must specify the accounting period in respect of which it is made and must be made within two years after the end of that period. The relief does **not** apply to so much of the 'qualifying land remediation expenditure' as represents expenditure which has been allowed as a deduction for an earlier accounting period or in respect of which any capital allowance (see **CAPITAL ALLOWANCES — INTRODUCTION** (**10**)) have been, or may be, given.

See generally the HMRC Corporate Intangibles Research and Development Manual, CIRD60000 *et seq.*

'*Qualifying land remediation expenditure*' is expenditure meeting the following five conditions.

(a) It must be on land all or part of which is in a '*contaminated state*'. Before 1 April 2009, this means it is in such a condition, by reason of substances in, on or under it, that 'harm' is being caused (or there is a possibility of harm being caused) or '*pollution of controlled waters*' (i.e. the entry into 'controlled waters' of any poisonous, noxious or polluting matter or any solid waste matter) is being, or is likely to be, caused. For expenditure on or after 1 April 2009, land is in a '*contaminated state*' if something in, on or under the land is in such a condition that relevant harm is likely to be caused. However land is not contaminated by reason only of the presence in, on or under it of living organisms or decaying matter deriving from living organisms, air or water or anything other than the result of industrial activity, although this may be disapplied by statutory instrument. '*Harm*' in this context means:
    - (i) harm to the health of living organisms (an example of harm would be illness caused by asbestos);
    - (ii) interference with the ecological systems of which any living organisms form part;
    - (iii) offence to the senses of human beings; or
    - (iv) damage to property.

    For expenditure on or after 1 April 2009, '*relevant harm*' is defined as death, significant injury or damage to living organisms, significant pollution of controlled water, material adverse impact on the ecosystem or structural or other significant damage to buildings or other structures or interference with buildings or other structures that significantly compromises their use.

    SI 2009 No 2037 extends the relief to remedial expenditure to clear land of arsenic, arsenical compounds, radon or Japanese Knotweed. Only such part of a site as is contaminated by these items qualifies for relief.

    A nuclear site is not contaminated or derelict land for the purpose of this relief.

    '*Controlled waters*' are as under *Water Resources Act 1991, Pt III* or comparable Scottish or Northern Irish legislation. For expenditure incurred on or after 1 April 2009, HMRC accept that a 'substance' includes plants, e.g. Japanese Knotweed. Any cases open at 24 November 2008 will be settled on the basis of the revised guidance in HMRC Brief 62/2008.

The land must be in a contaminated state when acquired, or in the case of derelict land, be in such a state throughout the period beginning on the earlier of 1 April 1998 and the date the major interest was acquired. These requirements may be varied by statutory instrument.

(b) It must be on 'relevant land remediation' undertaken directly by the company or on its behalf. '*Relevant land remediation*' is the doing of any works, the carrying out of any operations or the taking of any steps in relation to the land (or adjoining or adjacent land), or any controlled waters affected by the state of that land, for the purpose of preventing or minimising, or remedying or mitigating the effects of, any harm, or any pollution of controlled waters, by reason of which the land is in a contaminated state, or restoring the land or waters to their former state. Preparatory activities are included provided that they are for the purpose of assessing the condition of the land or waters concerned and are connected to the remediation activities undertaken by the company or on its behalf. The removal of Japanese Knotweed to a landfill site is not relevant contaminated land remediation.

(c) It must be incurred on employee costs (see below) or on materials employed directly in the remediation or be 'qualifying expenditure on sub-contracted land remediation'.

(d) It must be expenditure which would not have been incurred had the land not been in a contaminated state. Any increase in expenditure by reason only of the land being in a contaminated state is treated as satisfying this condition, as is expenditure on works done, operations carried out or steps taken mainly for the purposes described in (b) above.

(e) No grant or subsidy may be received in respect of the expenditure, nor may it be met directly or indirectly by any person other than the company (any unallocated payment being allocated for this purpose in a just and reasonable manner).

As regards (c) above, employee costs include all employment income (other than benefits in kind), employer NICs and pension contributions paid to, or in respect of, directors or employees directly and actively engaged in the relevant land remediation in (b) above. If between 20% and 80% of a director's or employee's time is spent directly and actively so engaged, an appropriate proportion of costs related to him or her qualify. If less than 20% is so spent, none of the costs qualify, and if more than 80%, all of the costs qualify. (For expenditure incurred before 1 April 2004, employment costs include benefits in kind.) Staff providing support services (e.g. secretarial or administrative services) are not thereby treated as engaged in the activities they support.

The specified purposes for relevant derelict land remediation are the removal of post-tensioned concrete heavyweight construction, building foundations and machinery bases, reinforced concrete pilecaps, reinforced concrete basements, or redundant services which are located below the ground.

'*Qualifying expenditure on sub-contracted land remediation*' is expenditure consisting of payments made for sub-contracted land remediation work. Except where the company and the sub-contractor are connected persons (within *CTA 2010, s 1122* previously *ICTA 1988, s 839*), such payments qualify in full. Where the company and the sub-contractor are connected persons, then provided that, in accordance with generally accepted accounting practice (see **70.18** above), the whole of the sub-contractor payment and all of the sub-contractor's 'relevant expenditure' has been brought into account in determining the sub-contractor's profit or loss for a 'relevant period', the whole of the sub-contractor payment (up to the amount of the sub-contractor's 'relevant expenditure') qualifies. '*Relevant expenditure*' is expenditure on employee costs or materials (as under (c) above), not of a capital nature, which is incurred by the sub-contractor in carrying on, on behalf of the company, the activities to which the sub-contractor payment relates, and which satisfies (e) above. A '*relevant period*' is a period for which the sub-contractor draws up accounts and which ends not more than twelve months after the end of the period of account of the company in which, in accordance with generally accepted accounting practice (see **70.18** above), the sub-contractor payment is brought into account in determining the company's profit or loss. Any necessary apportionment of expenditure for these purposes is made on a just and reasonable basis.

A person has a '*relevant connection*' to a company if he is or was a 'connected person' within *CTA 2010, s 1122* previously *ICTA 1988, s 839* either when the action (or inaction) in question occurred, or when the land in question was acquired by the company, or at any time when the remediation work was undertaken.

[*CTA 2009, ss 1144–1148, 1170–1179; FA 2001, s 70, Sch 22 paras 2–11, 31; ITEPA 2003, Sch 6 para 258; FA 2004, Sch 17 para 7; FA 2009, Sch 7; SI 2009 No 2037*].

Land remediation relief

Where 'qualifying land remediation expenditure' (as above) is incurred by a company **on or after 1 April 2001** in respect of land in the UK acquired by the company for the purposes of a trade or UK property business carried on by it 'land remediation relief' is available for the accounting period in which that expenditure, being capital expenditure, is allowed as a deduction in computing profits of the trade or business under the land remediation relief provisions. No relief is available in respect of any part of the expenditure which qualifies for capital allowances. The relief applies where, at the time of the acquisition, all or part of the land was in a contaminated or derelict state *other than* wholly or partly as a result of the company's own actions or inaction (or the actions or inaction of a person with a relevant connection to the company, as above). Where the company, or a person connected with it, caused the contamination or dereliction. [*CTA 2009, ss 1147, 1150; FA 2001, s 70, Sch 22 para 12; FA 2009, Sch 7 para 11*].

The relief takes two forms.

(a) For any accounting period for which land remediation relief is available and in which the company is carrying on a trade or UK property business in computing profits from which qualifying land remediation expenditure is deductible (including capital expenditure allowed as a trade deduction as above), the company may claim relief for an additional 50% of that expenditure, i.e. for 150% of that expenditure in total. For contaminated land the land must be in a contaminated state at the time of acquisition and for derelict land the land must be have been derelict throughout the period beginning with the earlier of 1 April 1998 and the date of acquisition. Any capital expenditure allowed as a deduction in computing profits is not an allowable deduction for capital gains purposes under *TCGA 1992, s 39* as amended by *CTA 2010, Sch 1 para 229*. [*CTA 2009, s 1149; FA 2001, s 70, Sch 22 para 13; FA 2009, Sch 7 para 10*].

(b) For an accounting period in which the company has a 'qualifying land remediation loss', it may claim a 'land remediation tax credit' equal to 16% of the amount of that loss. The 16% figure is subject to revision by the Treasury by order. A '*qualifying land remediation loss*' arises for an accounting period in which the company is entitled to relief under (a) above and incurs a loss in the trade or UK property business concerned. The amount of the qualifying land remediation loss is so much of the trading or UK property business loss as is 'unrelieved' or, if less, 150% of the related qualifying land remediation expenditure. A trading or UK property business loss is '*unrelieved*' for this purpose to the extent that the loss has not and could not have been relieved by a claim under *CTA 2010, s 37* (previously *ICTA 1988, s 393A(1)(a)* or *s 392A(1)*); *CTA 2009, Sch 1 para 108* (against profits of the same period, see **55.3, 55.7 LOSSES**), and has not otherwise been relieved (including under *CTA 2010, s 37* (previously *ICTA 1988, s 393A(1)(b))* against profits of earlier periods, see **55.4 LOSSES**), and has not been surrendered under *CTA 2010, s 99* previously *ICTA 1988, s 403(1)* (group or consortium relief, see **39.2** *et seq.* **GROUP RELIEF**). Losses carried back or brought forward to the accounting period in question are disregarded for this purpose. The amount of the tax credit may be applied in discharging any liability of the company to corporation tax, or if PAYE and NIC payments are in arrears for the period to which the payment relates. Where the company's return is under enquiry, HMRC may make a provisional payment of such amount as they think fit.

Where tax credit is paid in respect of expenditure, it may not be taken into account in computing a gain or loss on disposal of the land to which it relates. The trading or UK property loss carried forward is reduced by the amount surrendered for tax credit. [*CTA 2009, ss 1151–1158; FA 2001, s 70, Sch 22 paras 14, 15; SI 2004 No 2310, Art 58*].

On receiving a claim for land remediation tax credit, HMRC will pay to the company the amount of the tax credit, and the amount of the company's trading or UK property business losses available to be carried forward from the period and will accordingly be reduced by the amount of the qualifying land remediation loss for the period (or by a corresponding proportion thereof where the amount of the tax credit claimed was less than 16% of the qualifying land remediation loss). Where a tax credit has been claimed in respect of a qualifying land remediation loss, the related qualifying land remediation expenditure is treated as non-allowable expenditure for capital gains tax purposes under *TCGA 1992, s 39*. [*CTA 2009, ss 1154, 1157, 1158; FA 2001, s 70, Sch 22 paras 16(1), 17, 19; SI 2004 No 2310, Art 59*].

The tax credit payment is not treated as income for any tax purposes, and (together with any interest paid with it, see below) may be applied to any corporation tax liability of the company. Where there is an enquiry into the company's tax return for the period (see **66.19 RETURNS**), payment need not be made until the enquiry is completed (although HMRC has discretion to make a payment on a provisional basis if they think fit). Similarly payment need not be made until all PAYE and NICs payments for payment periods (i.e. periods ending on the fifth day of each month for which liability to account for PAYE and NICs arises) ending in the accounting period have been made. [*CTA 2009, ss 1155; 1156; FA 2001, s 70, Sch 22 paras 16(2)–(5)*].

Claims and overpayments

As regards (b) above, a claim for payment of a land remediation tax credit must be made in a company tax return (or amended return) (see **66.4 RETURNS**) for the accounting period for which the credit is claimed, within one year of the filing date for that return (see **66.9 RETURNS**) or by such later time as HMRC may allow. It can similarly only be amended or withdrawn by amendment of the company tax return within the same time limit. It must specify the quantum of the amount claimed. Penalties not exceeding the excess credit claimed apply for fraudulent (deliberate) or negligent (careless) claims, and for failure to remedy other incorrect claims without unreasonable delay. See **60.2 PENALTIES** for the introduction of behaviour-based penalties. [*CTA 2009, s 1151; FA 1998, Sch 18 paras 10(2A), 83G–83L; FA 2001, Sch 23 paras 4, 6*]. For recovery of overpayments of land remediation tax credit, see **66.26 RETURNS**.

INTEREST ON OVERPAID TAX (50) applies to land remediation tax credit payments from the filing date (see **66.4 RETURNS**) for the company tax return for the accounting period for which the credit is claimed (or if later the date of receipt by HMRC of the return (or amended return) containing the claim) until payment. Such interest is recovered (as if it were **INTEREST ON UNPAID TAX (49)**) where there is a change in the tax credit payable resulting in an assessment (or amendment) to recover an amount of the credit (unless the change in the available credit results in a change in the company's corporation tax liability – see **50.2**(vi) **INTEREST ON OVERPAID TAX** – or is in whole or part to correct an HMRC error). [*ICTA 1988, s 826(1)(e)(3B)(8A)(8BA); FA 2001, Sch 23 para 3; CTA 2009, Sch 1 para 267; FA 2009, Sch 7*].

Anti-avoidance

Any transaction attributable to arrangements (including any scheme, agreement or understanding, whether or not legally enforceable) whose sole or main object is to enable a company to obtain a relief or payment under any of the above provisions to which it would not otherwise be entitled, or a greater relief or payment than that to which it would otherwise be entitled, is disregarded in determining the amount of any such relief or payment. [*CTA 2009, s 1169; FA 2001, Sch 22 para 29*].

Simon's Taxes. See D1.501–D1.517.

European economic interest groupings

[61.15] A European Economic Interest Grouping ('EEIG') within *Directive No 2137/85/EEC* (which applies to all EEIGs established within the European Economic Area), wherever it is registered, is regarded as acting as the agent of its members. Its activities are regarded as those of its members acting jointly, each member being regarded as having a share of EEIG property, rights and liabilities. The loan relationship rules have effect in relation to a grouping as if it were a partnership (in particular in the application of *CTA 2009, ss 380–385, 467, 472–474*, see **54.31, 54.43, 54.72 LOAN RELATIONSHIPS**). A person is regarded as acquiring or disposing of a share of the EEIG assets not only where there is an acquisition or disposal by the EEIG while he is a member but also where he becomes or ceases to be a member or there is a change in his share of EEIG property.

A member's share in EEIG property, rights or liabilities is that determined under the contract establishing the EEIG or, if there is no provision determining such shares, it will correspond to the profit share to which he is entitled under the provisions of the contract. If the contract makes no such provision, members are regarded as having equal shares.

Where the EEIG carries on a trade or profession, the members are regarded for the purposes of tax on income and gains as carrying on that trade or profession in partnership.

[*CTA 2010, s 990; ICTA 1988, s 510A; FA 2002, Sch 25 para 49; CTA 2009, Sch 1 para 176*].

Contributions to an EEIG from its members are not assessable on the EEIG, and the members are not assessable on distributions from the EEIG. (HMRC EEIGs Manual, EEIG34).

For the purposes of making assessments to income tax, corporation tax or capital gains tax on members of EEIGs (or of securing that members are so assessed), an inspector may, in the case of an EEIG which is registered, or has an establishment registered, in Great Britain or Northern Ireland, by notice require the EEIG to make a return containing such information as the notice may require, accompanied by such accounts and statements as the notice may require, within a specified time. In any other case, he may issue a similar notice to any UK resident member(s) of the EEIG (or if none is so resident, to any member(s)). Notices may differ from one period to another and by reference to the person on whom they are served or the description of EEIG to which they refer. Where a notice is given to an EEIG registered in Great Britain or Northern Ireland (or having an establishment registered there), the EEIG must act through a manager, except that if there is no manager who is an individual, the EEIG must act through an individual designated as a representative of the manager under the Directive. The return must in all cases include a declaration that, to the best of the maker's knowledge, it is correct and complete, and where the contract establishing the EEIG requires two or more managers to act jointly for the EEIG to be validly bound, the declaration must be given by the appropriate number of managers. [*TMA 1970, s 12A*].

A penalty not exceeding £300 (and £60 per day for continued failure) may be imposed in the case of failure to comply with a notice under the above provisions. The penalties are multiplied by the number of members of the EEIG at the time of the failure or at the end of the day for which a continuing penalty is imposed. No penalty may be imposed after the failure has been remedied, and if it is proved that there was no income or chargeable gain to be included in the return, the maximum penalty is £100. Fraudulent or negligent delivery of an incorrect return, etc. or of an incorrect declaration may result in a penalty not exceeding £3,000 for each member of the EEIG at the time of delivery, and the act or omission giving rise to the penalty is treated as the act or omission of each member of the EEIG for the purposes of extended time limits for assessments and consequential claims. [*TMA 1970, ss 36(4), 98B; FA 1998, Sch 18 para 91*].

Simon's Taxes. See **D4.501–D4.503.**

Foreign dividend coupons (sale of)

[61.16] The charge to corporation tax on income applies to income which is treated as arising from '*foreign holdings*' (i.e. shares outside the UK that are issued by or on behalf of a non-UK resident body of persons).

With regard to banks and persons dealing in coupons, income is treated as arising from such holdings in two cases:

(i) where a bank's office in the UK either pays over, or carries into an account, the proceeds of a sale or other realisation of 'dividend coupons' in respect of the holdings;
(ii) where proceeds arise from a sale of 'dividend coupons' in respect of the holdings to a person dealing in coupons in the UK and the seller is neither a bank (as defined) nor a dealer in coupons.

The provisions at (i) apply in any case where a bank's office is in the UK, whether or not the bank is resident in the UK. The provisions at (ii) apply in any case where a person is dealing in coupons in the UK whether or not that person is resident in the UK.

The amount of income treated as arising is the proceeds of sale or realisation. For accounting periods ending before 1 April 2009, the charge was under *Schedule D, Case V*. '*Dividend coupons*' means coupons (as defined) for dividends payable in respect of foreign holdings.

[*CTA 2009, ss 974, 975; ICTA 1988, s 18(3B)–(3E); FA 1996, Sch 7 para 4(3)*].

Income not otherwise charged

[61.17] There is a residual charge to corporation tax on income in relation to income not charged to corporation tax under any other provision. This does not apply to annual payments (for which see the similar residual charge at **61.13** above, income not charged to corporation tax because of an exemption (see, for example, below), and deemed income. [*CTA 2009, s 979; ICTA 1988, ss 9, 18(1)*].

Any gain arising in the course of dealing in financial futures or in traded or financial options, other than in the course of a trade, is dealt with under the chargeable gains rules and is not within the charge to corporation tax on income. [*CTA 2009, s 981; ICTA 1988, s 128(2)(3); TCGA 1992, s 143*].

Intellectual property

[61.18] For corporation tax purposes, expenditure and receipts in respect of intellectual property created or acquired from an unrelated party **on or after 1 April 2002** generally falls within the intangible assets regime. See in particular the commencement and transitional rules for that regime at **48.36 INTANGIBLE ASSETS**. The provisions below apply (subject to the transitional provisions) to expenditure on such assets not falling within that regime.

See **16.5** and **16.7 CAPITAL ALLOWANCES — MISCELLANEOUS** for allowances on capital expenditure in acquiring know-how and patent rights; **46.2** and **46.5 INCOME TAX IN RELATION TO A COMPANY** for patent royalties and other royalties paid to non-residents; **32.4 DOUBLE TAX RELIEF** for DTR treatment of royalties from abroad; **35.12 EXEMPT ORGANISATIONS** as regards research institution spin-out companies; **70.55, 70.57, 70.58 TRADE PROFITS — INCOME AND SPECIFIC TRADES** and **71.64 TRADING EXPENSES AND DEDUCTIONS** for trading receipts and expenses with regard to intellectual property.

Simon's Taxes. See B5.3.

Income from intellectual property

Subject to the exceptions noted below, the proceeds of disposal of know-how or for certain restrictive covenants relating to the disposal of know-how (whether or not legally enforceable) less expenditure wholly and exclusively incurred in acquiring the know-how are chargeable to corporation tax, provided they are not otherwise charged to tax. The exceptions are:

(a) the consideration is taken into account for capital allowance purposes;
(b) the consideration is taxed as trading income;
(c) the disposal is of goodwill and the capital sum is taxed as a part or whole disposal of a trade;
(d) the disposal is to a connected person.

Previously, trading etc. receipts, royalties, patent income and other income from 'intellectual property' was charged, on general principles (see **61.10** above), under miscellaneous income (previously *Schedule D, Case VI*) if from a UK source, or foreign income (*Case V* as was) if from a non-UK source. See also below for the spreading of patent royalties etc. over several tax years.

[*CTA 2009, ss 907–910*].

For income tax purposes for 2005/06 onwards, 'intellectual property' is specially chargeable to income tax under *ITTOIA 2005, Pt 5 Ch 2*. For these purposes, '*intellectual property*' is defined in *ITTOIA 2005, s 579* as:

(a) any patent, trade mark, registered design, copyright, design right or performer's or plant breeder's right;

(b) any rights under the law of any part of the UK which are similar to such rights;
(c) any rights under the law of any territory outside the UK which correspond or are similar to such rights; and
(d) any idea, information or technique not protected by a right within (a)–(c) above.

Intellectual property is similarly defined for corporation tax purposes under *FA 2000, Sch 20 para 7* in relation to **RESEARCH AND DEVELOPMENT EXPENDITURE** (**64.5**(3)) but otherwise definitions are provided only for:

- '*patent rights*', which means the right to do or authorise the doing of anything which would, but for the right, be an infringement of a patent. [*CTA 2009, s 912*; *ICTA 1988, s 533(1)*]; and
- '*know-how*', which means any industrial information or techniques likely to assist in manufacturing or processing goods or materials, in working a mine, oil-well or other source of mineral deposits (including searching for, discovery or testing of deposits or winning access thereto), or in carrying out any agricultural, forestry or fishing operations. A change restores a previous definition of mineral deposits. This change is expected to have no practical effect. [*CTA 2009, s 176, Sch 1 para 184*, *change 41 listed in Annex I to CTA 2009*; *ICTA 1988, s 533(7)*]. HMRC consider that it does not include information about marketing, packaging or distribution Revenue Tax Bulletin, August 1993 p 86).

Patent royalties may be subject to deduction of tax at source (see **46.2** and **46.5** **INCOME TAX IN RELATION TO A COMPANY**), as are other royalties paid to non-UK residents.

Patent income and expenses

It has been confirmed that a Patent Box regime will be introduced as from 1 April 2013. Proposals for the regime are under consultation throughout 2011, with draft legislation to be published in Autumn 2011. The regime will focus on patents, and not extend to other types of IP. The proposed rate of tax is to be 10% on net profits. Profits can arise from both patent royalty income and embedded income in the price of patented products. The proposals favour a formulaic approach to determination rather than using an arm's length approach per the OECD transfer pricing guidelines. It will apply to all patents first commercialised after 29 November 2010. In the meantime the existing regimes continue.

'*Patent income*' means any royalty or other sum paid in respect of the use of a patent or any amount on which corporation tax is payable in relation to (i) the sale of patent rights under *CTA 2009, ss 912, 918 or 1272; ICTA 1988, ss 524, 525* (see below) or (ii) balancing charges under the capital allowances code for patent rights (see **16.7 CAPITAL ALLOWANCES — MISCELLANEOUS**).

Relief can be claimed for expenses incurred by a company, otherwise than for the purposes of a trade, in connection with the grant, maintenance or extension of the term of a patent or in connection with a rejected or abandoned patent application, provided that, if the expenses had been incurred for the purposes of a trade, they would have been allowable in calculating the profits of that trade.

Where a claim is made, the expenses are deducted or set off against the company's 'patent income' for the accounting period in which they are incurred with any unallowed balance being carried forward indefinitely against patent income without further claim, so long as the company remains within the charge to corporation tax. For this purpose, '*patent income*' has the same meaning as above, but any **CAPITAL ALLOWANCES — MISCELLANEOUS** (**16.7**) must be deducted before relief is given for the expenses.

Where or to the extent that expenditure is funded by a grant or other contribution from a public body, or a contribution by a person other than the company, the company is not regarded as having incurred the expenditure for the purpose of the above provisions. The exception to this is that the company is treated as having incurred the expenditure if the contributor (assuming he is within the charge to tax) is not a public body and the expenditure is not eligible for capital allowances or for relief in arriving at the contributor's trading profits.

[*CTA 2009, ss 924, 927; ICTA 1988, ss 526, 528, 533(1); CAA 2001, Sch 2 para 46; ITTOIA 2005, Sch 1 paras 203, 205*].

Spreading of patent royalties

Where royalties are received, less tax, for user of a patent which comprises two or more complete years, the corporation tax liabilities are reducible, on application, to the total that would have been payable if the royalties had been paid by equal instalments (corresponding to the number of complete years concerned, but not exceeding six years) made at yearly intervals ending with the date of actual receipt. [*ICTA 1988, s 527; ITTOIA 2005, Sch 1 para 204*].

Sales of patent rights

Profits from sales of the whole or part of any patent rights (including receipts for rights for which a patent has not yet been granted), which consist wholly or partly of a capital sum, are chargeable to tax under miscellameous income previously *Schedule D Case VI*. The company is charged to tax if a UK resident or, if not UK resident, where the patent is a UK patent. If the company is non-UK resident, the charge does not apply if it is within the charge to corporation tax in respect of the sale proceeds.

In the case of a sale by a non-UK resident, the purchaser may have to deduct tax at source under *ITA 2007, s 901; ICTA 1988, s 349(1)* (see **46.2 INCOME TAX IN RELATION TO A COMPANY**) although this may be modified by double tax agreements.

References above to the sale of patent rights include the exchange of patent rights, and in the case of such an exchange, references above and below to the proceeds of sale and the price include the consideration for the exchange, and references to capital sums included in the proceeds include references to so much of the consideration for the exchange as would have been a capital sum if it had been a money payment. Where patent rights are acquired or disposed of together with other property, the acquisition costs or proceeds, as appropriate, must be apportioned on a just and reasonable basis.

Spreading provisions

In the case of a UK-resident company, the chargeable profits are spread equally over a period of six tax years, starting with the accounting period in which the proceeds are received. If the proceeds are received in instalments, each instalment is likewise spread over six tax years. The company may elect, by notice to an officer of HMRC, to disapply spreading, so that the profits (or instalments) are taxed in the accounting period in which they were received. The election must be made within two years after the end of the accounting period in which the profits or instalment were received.

Where the seller is a partnership and the sale is in the course of a trade carried on by the partnership, each amount chargeable to corporation tax under the above spreading provisions is chargeable on the partners for the time being carrying on the trade, unless there is a partnership change such that no corporate partner which carried on the trade before the change continues to do so afterwards. See *CTA 2009, s 1271(4)–(6)* (and, in the event of a subsequent cessation of the partnership trade, *CTA 2009, s 1272*) for the mechanics by which this is achieved. For accounting periods ending before 1 April 2009, these mechanics were not fully set out by statute but were generally applied in practice (see Change 89 listed in Annex 1 to the Explanatory Notes to *CTA 2009*).

Where a body corporate commences winding-up during the period over which the charge is spread in that period, no such election can be made and any charge arising under the spreading provisions becomes immediately chargeable in the accounting period in which winding-up commences.

The making of an election for spreading does not affect the amount of income tax to be deducted by the purchaser in the case of a sale by a non UK resident, and any adjustment required as a result of such an election is made by repayment of tax on a year by year basis.

Similar provision is made for companies not resident in the UK in receipt of a lump sum or instalments for the sale of patent rights. However the obligation to deduct income tax from the payment to the non-UK resident is not affected by the right to spread the tax charge or by the right to claim a deduction for expenditure on the patent rights. Any necessary adjustment is made by repayment of tax.

Licences

The acquisition of a licence in respect of a patent is treated for the purposes of the above provisions as a purchase of patent rights, and the grant of a licence is treated as a sale of part of such rights. Where, however, the licence is a licence to exercise the rights to the exclusion of all other persons (including the grantor) for the whole of the period until the rights come to an end, the grant is treated as a sale of the whole of the rights. The use in certain circumstances of an invention, which is the subject of a patent, by the Crown or a foreign government is treated as use under a licence.

The sale of a right to acquire future patent rights under a patent which has not yet been granted is treated as a sale and purchase of patent rights and, if the purchaser exercises the right to acquire the patent rights, the expenditure on the right to acquire is treated as part of the cost of the patent rights.

[*CTA 2009, ss 912–923, 1271, 1272; ICTA 1988, ss 524, 525, 533(1)–(6); ITTOIA 2005, Sch 1 paras 201, 202, 209*].

Disposal of know-how

Subject to the exceptions below, profits arising where consideration is received for the disposal of 'know-how' are chargeable to corporation tax as miscellaneous income (previously under *Schedule D Case VI*). Also included within the charge are profits arising where consideration is received for giving, or wholly or partly fulfilling, an undertaking (whether or not legally enforceable) which is given in connection with a disposal of know-how and which restricts or is designed to restrict any person's activities in any way. Sale of know-how includes exchange of know-how. Sale of know-how includes sale of know-how with other property. A sale is regarded as one bargain, even if the consideration specifies separate prices or that the deal comprises separate sales. The consideration and expenditure is allocated on a just and reasonable basis. Where the apportionment or allocation materially affects more than one taxpayer, the rules in *CAA 2001, s 563(2)–(6)* must be used to determine the allocation. The matter '*materially affects*' a taxpayer is it is material to the determination of his tax liability in any period.

Where the know-how disposed of has been used in a trade, and the disposal is part of the disposal of all or part of the trade, the consideration is treated for corporation tax purposes as a capital receipt for goodwill, subject to the exclusions below. If the purchaser is within the charge to corporation tax, the consideration paid is treated as a capital payment for goodwill, unless the trade was carried on wholly outside the UK before the transaction took place. If the seller is within the charge to corporation tax, it may, under *CTA 2009, s 178*, jointly elect with the purchaser within two years of the disposal not to apply these provisions. Where an election is made within the equivalent income tax provision (*ITTOIA 2005, s 194*) and the purchaser is within the charge to corporation tax, the parties are treated as also making an election under *CTA 2009, s 178*.

The charge does not apply if:

- the consideration is brought into account as a revenue receipt under general principles (see above under Income from intellectual property);
- the consideration is brought into account as a disposal value under the capital allowances know-how code — *CAA 2001, s 462* (see **16.5 CAPITAL ALLOWANCES — MISCELLANEOUS**);
- the consideration is treated as a trading receipt (see **70.55 TRADE PROFITS**);
- the consideration is received as part of the disposal of all or part of a trade and is treated as a capital receipt for goodwill under these provisions (see **70.55 TRADE PROFITS**); or

- the disposal is by way of a sale and the buyer is a body of persons (including a firm) over which the seller or buyer has control or the buyer and seller are both bodies of persons and another person has control over them both.

[*CTA 2009, ss 176–179, 928–931, Sch 1 paras 182–184; ICTA 1988, ss 531(4)–(8), 532; ITTOIA 2005, Sch 1 paras 207, 208*].

Life policies etc. held by companies

[61.19] The legislation described below does not apply for corporation tax purposes from 1 April 2008. In practice very few companies own life policies and annuity contracts and where they are used for investment, economically they resemble debt-like instruments and will therefore be taxed as such under the loan relationship legislation.

A gain arising under a policy, etc. held by or for a company is generally brought into charge to corporation tax under miscellaneous income (previously *Schedule D, Case VI*) (with a right of recovery against trustees where the policy, etc. was held in trust), but policies, etc. issued before 14 March 1989 are excluded. [*ICTA 1988, ss 546C(7)(b), 547(1)(b)(1A)(4)(8), 551A; ITTOIA 2005, Sch 1 para 216*]. Certain events which are excluded from the charge on individual policy holders are treated as chargeable events where, immediately before the event, the rights conferred by the policy were in the beneficial ownership of a company, or were held on trusts created, or as security for debt owed, by a company. [*ICTA 1988, s 540(5A)*]. *ICTA 1988, s 548* (which treats certain loans as giving rise to a partial surrender of rights under a policy) is also applied to policies issued after that date and held by or for companies. [*ICTA 1988, s 548(1)(3); ITTOIA 2005, Sch 1 para 218*]. Special provisions apply in relation to chargeable events in respect of 'qualifying endowment policies' (within *ICTA 1988, Sch 15 para 2*) held as security for a debt owed by the company. [*ICTA 1988, s 541(4A)–(5)*].

For these purposes, a policy made before 14 March 1989 is to be treated as made on or after that date if it is varied on or after that date so as to increase the benefits secured or to extend the term of the policy, and any exercise of rights conferred by the policy is to be regarded for this purpose as a variation. [*ICTA 1988, s 539(9)*].

For policies issued, varied or with a right exercised on or after 21 March 2007, an anti-avoidance provision countering the use of life assurance policies to shelter investment income is introduced. In calculating the gain on a chargeable event, the total of premiums paid is reduced by the total commission on the policy 'rebated' (as defined) or 'reinvested' (as defined). Policies to which the provisions apply must involve payment of commission (which includes any passing of value to or for the benefit of an intermediary or a person connected with him) that has, at any time, been rebated or re-reinvested.

The anti-avoidance provision applies if one of two conditions apply. The first is that the total amount paid under the policy (including lump sum payments, in the case of an annuity contract) paid in a 'relevant period' exceeded £100,000. The second is that the premiums on all policies exceed the threshold of £100,000 at some time when the taxable person held the policy.

The '*relevant period*' is either that beginning at the start of the tax year in which the chargeable event occurred and ending with that event or any of the three preceding tax years.

The threshold and the definition of 'the relevant period' may be amended by statutory instrument.

[*ICTA 1988, ss 548A, 548B*; *FA 2007, s 29*].

See generally Tolley's Income Tax under Life Assurance Policies.

Simon's Taxes. See **B8.641**.

Office (income from the holding of an)

[61.20] The charge to corporation tax on income applies to income from the holding of an office, computed in accordance with income tax law (in particular *ITEPA 2003, Pt 2* — see Tolley's Income Tax under Employment Income) for the tax year in which the company's accounting period ends. [*CTA 2009, s 969; ICTA 1988, s 9(1)(2)(3)(4); ITEPA 2003, s 5(3)*].

In computing such income, no deduction is allowed in respect of a debt owed to the company except:

- by way of 'impairment loss' (see **71.5 TRADING EXPENSES**); or
- so far as the debt is released wholly and exclusively for the purposes of the office as part of a 'statutory insolvency arrangement' (see **71.5 TRADING EXPENSES**).

This does not apply in relation to a debt falling with the regime for **LOAN RELATIONSHIPS** (**54**). For the purposes of these provisions, 'debt' includes an obligation or liability which falls to be met otherwise than by the payment of money.

[*CTA 2009, s 970; ICTA 1988, s 88D*].

Personal service companies and managed service companies

[61.21] There are provisions designed to deny opportunities for the avoidance of tax and Class 1 National Insurance Contributions by the use of intermediaries such as personal service companies. The rules (commonly known as IR35 after the Revenue Budget Press Release in 1999) apply where the worker would otherwise be an employee of the client or the income would be income from an office held by the worker.

As this is essentially an income tax and national insurance measure, the main coverage is in Tolley's Income Tax and Tolley's National Insurance Contributions.

A personal service company which is within IR35 will have to make an adjustment in its corporation tax computation. The deemed employment payment, and associated national insurance contributions, are treated as an allowable expense in computing the business profits (or losses) of the intermediary for the period of account in which the payment is made (but for no other period of account).

[*CTA 2009, s 139; FA 2000, Sch 12 para 17; ITEPA 2003, Sch 6 para 244(2)*].

Legislation is included in *FA 2007* to remove the tax saving opportunities offered by managed service companies (also known as composite companies). IR35 was not effective with these companies, therefore the legislation removes them from the IR35 regime entirely.

Instead, PAYE and Class 1 NICs will have to be deducted from the full amount of all payments or benefits provided to the workers. There is also provision to ensure that those workers are not more favourably treated than ordinary employees so far as travel and subsistence are concerned. To ensure companies do not close down and avoid the liabilities, powers are given to HMRC to recover the tax from all or any parties involved.

The provisions apply from 6 April 2007 for income tax and from 6 August 2007 for national insurance.

A managed service company which is within these rules will have to make an adjustment in its corporation tax computation. The deemed employment payment, and associated employer's national insurance contributions, are treated as an allowable expense in computing the business profits (or losses) of the company for the period of account in which the payment is made (but for no other period of account).

[*CTA 2009, s 141; FA 2007, Sch 3 para 10*].

As these are essentially an income tax and national insurance measure, the main coverage is in Tolley's Income Tax personal service companies etc.

Simon's Taxes. See **D6.823**.

Settlements

[61.22] Discretionary payments by trustees treated as income of the payee are taken as being net after tax at the rate applicable to trusts. [*CTA 2010, s 610*; *ICTA 1988, s 687*]. Where *s 687* applies to a payment made after 1 July 1997 to a company within the charge to corporation tax, other than a charity (within *CTA 2010, s 467*; *ICTA 1988, s 506(1)*) or a body treated as a charity under *CTA 2010, s 468*; *ICTA 1988, ss 507, 508*, the payment is disregarded for corporation tax purposes, and no credit is given, or repayment made, of the tax deducted. In the case of non-UK resident companies, this applies to so much (if any) of the payment as is comprised in the company's profits for corporation tax purposes [*F(No 2)A 1997, s 27*].

Mineral royalties

[61.23] Where in any accounting period a UK resident company is entitled to receive 'mineral royalties' under a 'mineral lease or agreement', only one-half of any such royalties receivable in the accounting period is treated as income for corporation tax purposes.

Management expenses available for set-off against those royalties, whether under the general rules for computing PROPERTY INCOME (**62**) or under the special rules (in **62.19** PROPERTY INCOME) for taxing a 'UK section 39(4) concern' (mines, quarries etc.), are similarly reduced by one-half.

For these purposes, '*mineral royalties*' means so much of any rent receivable under a 'mineral lease or agreement' as relates to the winning and working of 'minerals'. (See *CTA 2009, s 275* for an extended meaning of mineral royalties in NI.) '*Minerals*' means all minerals or substances in or under land which are ordinarily worked for removal, by either underground or surface working, but does not include water, peat, top-soil or vegetation. Coal is *not* excluded (*Bute v HMRC* (Sp C 637), [2008] SSCD 258). A '*mineral lease or agreement*' means a lease, profit à prendre, licence or other agreement conferring a right to win and work minerals in the UK; a contract for the sale or conveyance of minerals in or under land in the UK; or a grant of a right (other than an ancillary right) under *Mines (Working Facilities and Support) Act 1966, s 1*.

Where Betterment Levy (which was abolished after July 1970) was not chargeable on the grant of the lease, or any subsequent renewal, extension or variation of it, the other half of the royalties receivable is treated as a chargeable gain for purposes of corporation tax on chargeable gains.

Where, on the last disposition (before 23 July 1970) affecting the lease, Betterment Levy was chargeable under Case B (as defined by *Land Commission Act 1967, Pt III*) the chargeable gain, as above, is limited to a fraction (base value of that disposition/ consideration received) of one-half of the royalties received. After 5 April 1988, this limitation applies only if it applied to a chargeable period ending on or before that date. But if such a lease is renewed, extended or varied after 22 July 1970, one-half of any subsequent royalty receipt is treated as a chargeable gain.

Where payments under a mineral lease etc. relate both to the winning and working of minerals and to other matters, the part to be treated as mineral royalties for these purposes will be calculated under regulations made by HMRC. See *SI 1971 No 1035*.

These chargeable gains are assessable in full, without any deduction on account of expenditure incurred.

Terminal Losses

If the mineral lease comes to an end while the person entitled to receive the royalties still has an interest in the land, and an allowable loss would then arise to that person if the interest was sold for a price equal to its market value, the person may claim to be treated for corporation tax on capital gains purposes as if the interest had been sold, and immediately reacquired, at that price, the resultant loss being allowed, on election, either (a) against corporation tax on capital gains for the accounting period in which the lease expires, or (b) against chargeable gains, in respect of mineral royalties under the lease, in accounting periods falling within the previous 15 years. From a date to be determined by statutory instrument, a claim under this provision must be made within four years of the date of the event giving rise to the claim (previously six years).

[*CTA 2009, ss 135, 274–276; ICTA 1988, ss 121, 122; TCGA 1992, ss 201–203; ITTOIA 2005, Sch 1 paras 105, 106; FA 2008, Sch 39 para 29; CTA 2009, Sch 1 para 378*].

Further to the review by the OTS of redundant reliefs it was announced in the Budget 2011 that the relief in respect of mineral royalties is to be abolished in 2011–12 after a period of consultation. The consultation document confirms that the provisions under consideration are those in *CTA 2009, ss 135, 258, 273, ITTOIA 2005, ss 157, 319, 340, and TCGA 1992, ss 201–203*. Comments should be submitted to HMRC by 31 August 2011.

Simon's Taxes. See **B5.662, B5.663, C2.1111, D1.306.**

Woodlands

[61.24] Profits (and losses) from the commercial occupation of woodlands in the UK are ignored for corporation tax purposes. For this purpose, the occupation of woodlands is commercial if the woodlands are managed on a commercial basis and with a view to the realisation of profits. [*CTA 2009, s 980; FA 1988, Sch 6 paras 2(1), 3(2)*].

See **70.29**(h) **TRADE PROFITS** as regards short rotation coppice being treated as farming and not as woodlands.

In *Jaggers (trading as Shide Trees) v Ellis* Ch D 1997, 71 TC 164, land on which trees were planted and cultivated in a manner normally associated with Christmas tree production was held not to be woodland.

For the purpose of computing the profits of a trade of dealing in land, there is disregarded any part of the cost of purchasing UK woodlands in the course of the trade that is attributable to trees or saleable underwood growing on the land. If the woodlands are subsequently sold in the course of the trade and any of the trees and underwood are still growing, the amount disregarded on purchase is excluded from the sale proceeds. These rules do not apply if the purchase was under a pre-1 May 1963 contract. [*CTA 2009, s 134, Sch 2 para 29; ICTA 1988, s 99(1)*].

Simon's Taxes. See **B5.130.**

Corporation tax return

[61.25] It should be noted that all corporation tax returns for periods ending on or after 1 April 2010 to be submitted on or after 1 April 2011 must filed electronically. See **66.31 RETURNS** for the self-assessment return form (Form CT600).

62

Property Income

Cross references. See **15.2** *et seq.* CAPITAL ALLOWANCES — BUILDINGS for allowances available in respect of industrial buildings and **15.23** CAPITAL ALLOWANCES — BUILDINGS for flat conversion allowances.

Introduction

[62.1] Income tax was traditionally charged via a schedular system providing discrete rules for different types of income, with income from property being charged to tax under *Schedule A*. This regime, incorporating the concept of a 'Schedule A business' and including furnished lettings (previously chargeable under *Schedule D, Case VI*), was introduced by *FA 1995* for income tax purposes only and, with effect from 1 April 1998, the *Finance Act 1998* extended it to corporation tax with the necessary amendments and modifications.

Corporation tax was charged on rents etc. (see **62.2** below) less deductible expenses (see **62.4** below) with certain lease premiums also being taxable (see **62.9** below). Before 1 April 2009, assessments were made under Schedule A but this label was dropped in *CTA 2009* under the Tax Law Rewrite programme. However the principles regarding the calculation of profits under such a business remain broadly similar (however, see further below).

[*FA 1998, s 38, Sch 5*].

The law relating to the taxation of 'trading income' and 'property income' was rewritten in *Income Tax (Trading and Other Income) Act 2005* (*ITTOIA 2005*) as part of the Rewrite, and has effect for income tax purposes for 2005/06 and subsequent years and, for corporation tax purposes where relevant, for accounting periods ending after 5 April 2005. [*ITTOIA 2005, s 883(1)*].

For corporation tax purposes, property income continued to be computed and assessments made under *Schedule A* and not under *ITTOIA 2005* (see **61.10 PROFIT COMPUTATIONS**). However, as noted above, for accounting periods ending on or after 1 April 2009, *CTA 2009* applies with corporation tax no longer being charged under 'Schedule A'. See **70.2** for the transitional provisions where *CTA 2009* changes the law.

It can no longer be assumed that the coverage in Tolley's Income Tax of any particular type of receipt or deduction etc. relating to a 'property business' applies equally for corporation tax purposes and so all such matters are now dealt with in this chapter, which provides an outline of the calculation of profits applicable to a property business, chargeable to corporation tax.

As noted above, corporation tax is charged on rents etc. (see **62.2** below) less deductible expenses (see **62.4** below). Certain lease premiums etc. are also taxable (see **62.18** below).

Relevant definitions

Where this work refers simply to a '*property business*', then unless the context clearly suggests otherwise, it means either a UK property business or an overseas property business (see in both cases **62.2** below).

In this chapter, '*lease*' includes an agreement for a lease (in so far as the context permits) and any tenancy, but not a mortgage over the property.

'*Premises*' includes land. [*CTA 2009, s 291, Sch 1 para 13; ICTA 1988, s 24(1)*].

'*Land*' includes an estate or interest in land. Where the business is an overseas property business, the legislation is to be read so as to produce an effect most closely corresponding with that produced on a UK property. [*CTA 2009, s 290*].

CTA 2009, ss 287, 288 set out certain priority rules where a receipt or other credit item could be dealt with either as trading income or property income (*s 287*); or, either as property income within **62.19** below (electric-line wayleaves or mines, quarries etc.) or as other property income (*s 288*).

See **70.54** as regards the inclusion in trading profits of receipts from, and expenses of letting of, surplus business accommodation, which has been put on a statutory footing.

See **71.7** as regards the inclusion in trading profits of receipts and expenses in respect of tied premises (breweries etc), which would otherwise be brought into account in calculating profits of a property business.

[*CTA 2009, ss 287, 288, Change 5 in the Annex to the Corporation Tax Act 2009*].

Charge to tax

[62.2] Corporation tax is chargeable on the profits of a property business, whether it is a 'UK property business' or an 'overseas property business'.

See **62.4** below as regards the computation of the profits of a property business. The person liable to pay the tax is the person in receipt of, or entitled to, the profits.

For these purposes, a person's 'UK property business' consists of every business which he carries on for 'generating income from land' (see below) in the UK and any other transactions which he enters into for that purpose. A company's UK property business is separate from any property business carried on by a partnership of which it is a member. An 'overseas property business' is similarly defined.

Where this chapter refers simply to a 'property business' it means either a UK or an overseas property business (unless the context clearly suggests otherwise). Any reference to something being charged to tax as property income or within the charge to tax on property income is a reference to its having to be brought into account in computing the profits of a property business.

'*Generating income from land*' means exploiting an estate, interest or right in or over land as a source of rent or other receipts. Expenditure by a tenant on maintenance and repairs which the lease does not require him to carry out counts as rent in the landlord's hands. The reference above to 'any other transaction' brings into charge, for example, one-off or casual lettings. 'Other receipts' include:

- payments in respect of a licence to occupy or otherwise use land or in respect of the exercise of any other right over land; and
- rentcharges and any other annual payments reserved in respect of, or charged on or issuing out of, land.

For the above purposes, the following activities are *not* treated as carried on for generating income from land:

- farming or market gardening in the UK, which is instead treated as a trade — see **70.29**;
- any other *occupation* of land, but commercial occupation of land is treated as a trade (with the exception for woodlands) — see **70.2**; and
- activities for the purposes of a concern within *CTA 2009, s 39* (mines, quarries etc.) — see **70.56** and **66.14** below.

[*CTA 2009, ss 204–208, 1270(2)(3)*].

Receipts from furnished lettings in most cases are charged as income from a property business, unless the lettings fall within trading income and casual lettings.

Caravans and caravan sites

Receipts from furnished lettings also includes lettings from caravans which are at a fixed location.

However, if a company carries on material activities connected with the operation of a caravan site and those activities themselves constitute a trade or a part of a trade, the income and expenses of letting the caravans and/or pitches can be included in computing the profits of that trade instead of being treated as property income. This applies by statute for accounting periods ending on or after 1 April 2009 (*CTA 2009, s 43*) but previously applied by concession (see HMRC Extra Statutory Concession C36 (previously B29)). See **62.3** (B) below as regards furnished holiday lettings.

A '*caravan*' is defined in *CTA 2009, s 1314* as a structure designed or adapted for living in and which is capable of being moved or towed or transported on a motor vehicle or trailer or a motor vehicle designed or adapted for living in. Railway rolling stock on rails and tents are not included. The definition may include a structure of two sections, separately constructed but designed to be bolted together on site, even though it cannot be legally moved in its assembled condition. See change 96 listed in Annex IV to *CTA 2009*.

[*CTA 2009, ss 43, 213, Change 4 listed in Annex IV to CTA 2009*].

Exclusions

[62.3] The following items are excluded from the computation of property income for corporation tax purposes, as they are taxed under distinct regimes:

(i) interest payable, and other amounts falling within the loan relationships legislation in *CTA 2009, ss 292–439; FA 1996, Pt IV, Ch II* (see **54 LOAN RELATIONSHIPS**);
(ii) profits and losses on derivative contracts falling within *CTA 2009, ss 570–710; FA 2002, Sch 26* (see **30 DERIVATIVE CONTRACTS LEGISLATION**); and
(iii) foreign exchange gains and losses falling within (i) or (ii) above.

[*CTA 2009, s 211*].

In addition, property income does not include:

- profits from occupying land (e.g. from woodlands) (see **70.2 TRADE PROFITS — INCOME AND SPECIFIC TRADES**);
- profits chargeable to corporation tax as trading income from farming and market gardening (for which see **70.29 TRADE PROFITS — INCOME AND SPECIFIC TRADES**);
- profits chargeable to corporation tax as trading income from mining, quarrying and other such concerns (for which see **70.2 TRADE PROFITS — INCOME AND SPECIFIC TRADES**);
- trading receipts and expenses from tied premises (for which see **71.7 TRADING EXPENSES AND DEDUCTIONS**);
- rent charged to corporation tax as trading income in connection with mines, quarries, etc. [*CTA 2009, s 271; ICTA 1988, s 119; ITTOIA 2005, Sch 1 para 103*]; or

- rent charged to corporation tax as trading income in connection with electric line wayleaves (see **62.19** below).

The letting of all property in the UK by the same person is to be treated as a single business, except in the case of the following. (See **62.19** below for rental income from land outside the UK.) [*CTA 2009, s 205*].

(A) *Companies not resident in the UK.* In the case of a non-resident company trading in the UK through a permanent establishment (see **65.6 RESIDENCE**), a property business within the charge to corporation tax is treated as a separate business from any UK property business chargeable to income tax. [*ICTA 1988, s 15(1A) – not rewritten to CTA 2009 as considered unnecessary; ITTOIA 2005, Sch 1 para 8*]. See **65.5** *et seq.* **RESIDENCE.**

(B) *Furnished holiday lettings.* Income from the commercial letting of furnished holiday accommodation which does not amount to the carrying on of a trade is taxed as income from a property business. However, separate calculations are required of holiday letting profits and other profits for the purposes of capital allowances and loss relief. See **62.6** below. [*CTA 2009, s 269, ICTA 1988, s 15*].

Flat management companies

Residential service charges received by an occupier-controlled flat management company are normally received as capital by the landlord in his capacity as trustee. See **66.5 RETURNS** with regard to the concessional exemption from the requirement to deliver returns. See HMRC Property Income Manual, PIM1070. For a general article on the trust implications of flat management companies, service charge funds and sinking funds, see HMRC Tax Bulletin August 2000 pp 770–774.

Miscellaneous

Receipts from sales of turf have been held to be taxable as property income although they may alternatively be taxed as trading income (*Lowe v J W Ashmore Ltd* (1970) 46 TC 597); but receipts from sale of colliery dross bings were held to be capital (*Roberts (Inspector of Taxes) v Lord Belhaven and Stenton's Executors* (1925) 9 TC 501, 1925 SC 635, Ct of Sess). Sums received for licence to tip soil on land were held to be capital (*McClure v Petre* (1988) 61 TC 226). Note that these cases were decided under the pre-1 April 1998 regime, which differed in a number of material respects from the current rules.

Computing the profits of a property business

[62.4] The profits or losses of a property business are to be computed in accordance with the principles applicable to the computation of trading profits (see **70 TRADE PROFITS — INCOME AND SPECIFIC TRADES**). These include the fundamental rules that profits or losses be computed in accordance with generally accepted accounting practice (GAAP), that capital receipts and expenditure be excluded and that, subject to any specific rule to the contrary, expenditure is not deductible unless incurred wholly and exclusively for the purposes of the business.

Profits are calculated on an accruals basis rather than a cash basis.

Capital allowances are treated as deductions and balancing charges as receipts of the business and debits and credits in respect of intangible assets are treated similarly.

[*CTA 2009, ss 210, 212*].

As detailed in *CTA 2009, s 210* only the following specific trading income equivalents apply to the computation of property business profits or losses:

CTA 2009	Main pre-April 2009 provision	Brief description	See main coverage at
s 46	*FA 1998, s 42*	Use of generally accepted accounting practice	**70.19** TRADE PROFITS — INCOME AND SPECIFIC TRADES
s 47	*FA 1988, Sch 5 para 8*	Losses computed on same basis as profits	**55.3** LOSSES
s 48	*FA 1988, s 46*	Receipts and expenses	**71.2** TRADING EXPENSES AND DEDUCTION
s 52	*ICTA 1988, s 72*	Apportionment of profits and losses to accounting periods	**2.3** ACCOUNTING PERIODS
s 53	*ICTA 1988, s 74*	Capital expenditure non-deductible	**71.8** TRADING EXPENSES AND DEDUCTION
s 54	*ICTA 1988, s 74*	'Wholly and exclusively' rule for expenditure	**71.78** TRADING EXPENSES AND DEDUCTION
s 55	*ICTA 1988, s 88D*	Bad and doubtful debts	**71.5** TRADING EXPENSES AND DEDUCTION
ss 56–58B	*ICTA 1988, ss 578B*	Car or motor cycle hire	**71.9** TRADING EXPENSES AND DEDUCTION
s 59	*ICTA 1988, s 74*	Patent royalties paid	**70.58** TRADE PROFITS — INCOME AND SPECIFIC TRADES
s 61	*ICTA 1988, s 401*	Pre-trading expenses	**71.60** TRADING EXPENSES AND DEDUCTION
s 68	*ICTA 1988, s 74*	Replacement and alteration of trade tools	**71.8** TRADING EXPENSES AND DEDUCTION
s 69	*ICTA 1988, s 73*	Payments for restrictive undertakings	**71.22** TRADING EXPENSES AND DEDUCTIONS

ss 70, 71	*ICTA 1988, s 86*	Employees seconded to charities or educational bodies	**71.18** TRADING EXPENSES AND DEDUCTIONS
s 72	*ICTA 1988, s 86A*	Payroll deduction schemes: contributions to agent's administrative costs	**71.30** TRADING EXPENSES AND DEDUCTIONS
ss 73–75	*ICTA 1988, ss 588, 589A*	Counselling and retraining services for employees	**71.16** TRADING EXPENSES AND DEDUCTIONS
ss 76–81	*ICTA 1988, ss 579, 580*	Redundancy payments etc	**71.23** TRADING EXPENSES AND DEDUCTIONS
ss 82–86	*ICTA 1988, ss 79, 79B*	Contributions of local enterprise organisations or urban regeneration companies	**51.4** INVESTMENT COMPANIES AND INVESTMENT BUSINESS
ss 87, 88	*ICTA 1988, ss 82A, 82B*	Scientific research	**64** R&D EXPENDITURE
ss 89, 90	*ICTA 1988, s 83*	Expenditure in connection with patents, designs or trade marks	**70.58** TRADE PROFITS — INCOME AND SPECIFIC TRADES
s 91	*ICTA 1988, s 88*	Payments to Export Credits Guarantee Department	**70.57** TRADE PROFITS — INCOME AND SPECIFIC TRADES
s 92	*ICTA 1988, s 76A*	Levies under *FISMA 2000*	**51.4** INVESTMENT COMPANIES — MANAGEMENT EXPENSES
s 93	*ICTA 1988, s 71*	Capital receipts excluded from profits	**71.78** TRADING EXPENSES AND DEDUCTION
s 94	*ICTA 1988, s 94*	Debts incurred and later released	**70.22** TRADE PROFITS — INCOME AND SPECIFIC TRADES and **54** LOAN RELATIONSHIPS
s 101	*ICTA 1988, s 49*	Distribution of assets of mutual concerns	**31.22** DISTRIBUTIONS
s 102	*ICTA 1988, s 93*	Industrial development grants	**70.73** TRADE PROFITS — INCOME AND SPECIFIC TRADES
s 103	*ICTA 1988, s 74*	Sums recovered under insurance policies	**70.73** TRADE PROFITS — INCOME AND SPECIFIC TRADES
s 104	*ICTA 1988, s 76A*	Repayments under *FISMA 2000*	**51** INVESTMENT COMPANIES
s 108		Receipts of benefits by donor or connected persons	**71.49** TRADING EXPENSES AND DEDUCTION

s 131	*ICTA 1988, s 477(B)*	Incidental costs of issuing qualifying shares of Building Societies	**9.2 BUILDING SOCIETIES**
s 133	*ICTA 1988, s 487(3)*	Annual payments by a credit union	**56.4 MUTUAL COMPANIES**
ss 172–175	Annex 1 to Explanatory notes on the *Corporation Tax Act 2009*, change 40	Unremittable amounts	**71.74 TRADING EXPENSES AND DEDUCTION**

The following further provisions apply in calculating profits from a property business:

(i) the computational provisions relating to the charge on trading profits (see **70 TRADE PROFITS — INCOME AND SPECIFIC TRADES**) apply generally to the computation of profits from a property business as if the property business were a trade, except in the case of the treatment of premiums paid as a revenue expense under *CTA 2009, ss 62–67* (see **62.13** below) and the treatment of receipts and expenses relating to tied premises as those of a trade (see **71.7 TRADE PROFITS — INCOME AND SPECIFIC TRADES**);
(ii) the provisions relating to post-cessation receipts and expenses, etc.(see below);
(iii) the provisions for the treatment of a company commencing or ceasing to carry on a trade [*CTA 2009, s 41, Sch 1 para 519; ICTA 1988, s 337(1)*];
(iv) change of accounting basis (see **70.20 TRADE PROFITS — INCOME AND SPECIFIC TRADES**); and
(v) any rule permitting a deduction takes priority over a rule prohibiting a deduction, except in relation to car or motor cycle hire, unpaid remuneration, employee benefit contributions and crime-related payments. [*CTA 2009, s 214, Change 7 in the Explanatory Notes to the Corporation Tax Bill*].

In the case of *Kato Kagaku Co Ltd v Revenue and Customs Comrs* [2007] STC (SCD) 412 a deduction from property income was claimed for an indemnity payment paid in respect of a swap contract entered into in connection with obtaining finance for the purpose of purchasing the rented property. The appeal was allowed in part. The indemnity payment was a capital payment, but a deduction was available as the payment was an incidental cost of finance. However, no deduction was allowed in respect of that part of the payment which arose due to exchange rate fluctuations. The indemnity was not a premium.

CTA 2009, s 215 et seq.; ICTA 1988, s 34 et seq. continue to provide for the treatment of premiums on the grant of leases or subleases of less than 50 years. See further **62.9** with regard to the treatment of lease premiums etc.

[*CTA 2009, s 210, ICTA 1988, ss 21A, 21B; ITTOIA 2005, Sch 1 paras 12, 13; FA 2006, s 102(3)*].

Miscellaneous restrictions, use of cash basis etc.

The following provisions apply in calculating income from *any* source (thus including a property business):

- no deductions for employees' Class 1 NICs (see **71.21**);
- restriction of, or no deduction for business entertainment and gifts (see **71.41**);
- timing of deductions for employees' remuneration (see **71.28**);
- no deductions for illegal payments (see **71.52**);
- no deductions for tax penalties, interest and surcharges (see **71.58**); and
- restriction of deductions for annual payments (see **5.36 ANTI-AVOIDANCE**).

For a general article on what constitutes an allowable *repair* calculating the profits of a property business, see HMRC Tax Bulletin June 2002, pp 935, 936.

See also **61.14 PROFIT COMPUTATIONS** as regards reliefs for certain expenditure on remediation of contaminated land.

See generally the HMRC Property Income Manual.

In practice, a cash basis may be used instead of a full earnings basis (as required by generally accepted accounting practice) where gross annual receipts do not exceed £15,000, provided that it is used consistently and gives a reasonable overall result not substantially different from that produced on an earnings basis (see HMRC Property Income Manual, PIM1101).

Profits or losses on contracts taken out to hedge interest payments deductible in computing profits or losses of the property business will normally be taxed or relieved as receipts or deductions of that business. Such profits or losses would generally be computed on an accruals basis in accordance with normal accountancy practice. For corporation tax purposes where these fall within the loan relationship or derivative contracts rules then these will apply.

Similarly deposits paid to landlords by tenants or licensees will ordinarily be receipts of the business, to be recognised in accordance with generally accepted accountancy practice, normally by being deferred and matched with the related costs. Excess deposits which are refunded should be excluded from the business receipts. (See HMRC Property Income Manual, PIM1051 and PIM2105).

As regards allowable legal and professional and other costs, see HMRC Property Income Manual, PIM2200.

Apportionment of profits

Per the table above,*CTA 2009, s 210* provides that certain provisions applying to the computation of trading are to apply for the computation of a property business. These include *CTA 2009, s 52* which deals with apportionment etc.

of profits and losses to accounting periods. Where a period of account of a property business does not coincide with an accounting period, profits must be apportioned to accounting periods. This must normally be done by reference to the number of days in the periods concerned [*CTA 2009, s 52; ICTA 1988, ss 21A(2), 72; ITTOIA 2005, Sch 1 para 44*].

In practice, the company may choose any other method, e.g. months and part-months, if it is reasonable to do so and so long as the chosen method is applied consistently.

Change of accounting basis

If a company changes the basis on which it calculates profits from a property business, both bases being in accordance with the law or practice in the periods before and after the change respectively, the provisions dealing with change of basis for trading profits purpose broadly apply also to property income. (See **70.20 TRADE PROFITS — INCOME AND SPECIFIC TRADES.**)

A positive or negative adjustment is to be calculated as if the property business were a trade. Subject to the exception for depreciation adjustments (see below) in the former case (positive adjustment), the amount is treated as a receipt of the property business on the first day of the first period for which the new basis is used. In the case of a negative adjustment, the treatment is the same for a deduction as for a receipt. Where the adjustment affects the depreciation charge, the adjustment is not made until the asset is sold or written off. These provisions take effect for periods of account ending after 31 March 2009.

[*CTA 2009, ss 180–183, 261–262, 1267, 1269, Sch 2 para 51*].

Commencement and discontinuance

Where a company starts or ceases to be within the charge to corporation tax in respect of a property business, it is treated as starting or ceasing to carry on the business at that time.

[*CTA 2009, s 289; ICTA 1988, ss 110, 337(2); ITTOIA 2005, Sch 1 paras 90, 145*].

Post-cessation receipts

Corporation tax is charged on any 'post-cessation receipts' of a UK property business by adapting the rules applicable to trades under *CTA 2009, ss 188–201* (previously *ICTA 1988, ss 103–106, 110*) (see **70.16 TRADE PROFITS — INCOME AND SPECIFIC TRADES**) in suitably modified form.

A '*post-cessation receipt*' is a sum which is received after a company permanently ceases to carry on a UK property business and which arises from the carrying on of the business before cessation.

'*Cessation*' includes permanently ceasing the property business, ceasing to be within the charge to corporation tax or ceasing to be a partner in a continuing property business. Where a trade ceases on the sale of the right to receive property income, but the transferee does not carry on that business, the amount received is treated as a post-cessation receipt. If the transfer is not at arm's length, the amount brought into account is the value of the rights were the transfer at arm's length.

The charge for any accounting period is on the full amount of post-cessation receipts for that period. The charge does not apply in relation to an overseas property business.

[*CTA 2009, ss 249, 280–286; ICTA 1988, s 21B; ITTOIA 2005, s 353, 362, Sch 1, para 13*].

Deduction for energy-saving expenditure

From 8 July 2008, a deduction is available for expenditure on energy-saving items for a dwelling-house. The expenditure on equipment installed in the building, rather than in the individual dwelling-house, may be claimed, although it must be for a dwelling-house's benefit. The conditions for relief are:

(i) the company carries on a property business which consists of or includes a dwelling-house;
(ii) the property in question is used in the course of that business;
(iii) the expenditure is incurred before 1 April 2015;
(iv) the expenditure is incurred in acquiring and installing an energy-saving item in the dwelling house or the building containing it (e.g. a block of flats);
(v) a deduction is not prohibited on the grounds that the expenditure is not incurred wholly, exclusively and necessarily for the purposes of the property business;
(vi) the expenditure is capital in nature;
(vii) the expenditure is not incurred while the property is in the course of construction;
(viii) the company has an interest at the time the item is installed; and
(ix) it does not qualify for capital allowances.

No relief is available if the business is that of furnished holiday letting and the property in question was included in the accounting period in which the expenditure was incurred.

The maximum deduction per dwelling house is £1,500. Expenditure may be apportioned so as to give an amount qualifying for deduction and an ineligible amount. Apportionment may be necessary where more than one taxpayer is entitled to a deduction, where expenditure exceeds the maximum amount and where expenditure benefits more than one property. The definition of an 'energy-saving item' is hot water system insulation, draught proofing, solid wall insulation and floor insulation. [*SI 2007 No 3278*].

No deduction is granted if the property in question is used for a furnished holiday lettings business in the accounting period in which the expenditure is incurred. Expenditure on energy-saving items for a property will not qualify for relief to the extent it is not for the benefit of a dwelling-house i.e. if it benefits the property generally but not individual dwelling-houses. Pre-trading expenditure deemed to be incurred on the first day the company carries on the UK property business under *CTA 2009, s 61; ICTA 1988, s 401* does not qualify for a deduction unless it was incurred within the six months prior to commencement of the trade.

Wide powers are provided for determining the details of the relief by regulation.

[*CTA 2009, ss 251–253, Sch 2 para 50; ICTA 1988, ss 31ZA–ZC; FA 2007, s 17; SI 2007 No 945; SI 2007 No 831; SI 2008 No 1521*].

Integral features

Where capital allowances are available on expenditure on the repair or replacement of an integral feature, no relief is to be given for the same expenditure in computing the profits of the property business. (See **11.3 CAPITAL ALLOWANCES: PLANT AND MACHINERY — ELIGIBLE AND INITIAL ALLOWANCES**).

[*CTA 2009, s 263; CAA 2001, s 33A*].

Simon's Taxes. See B6.201–B6.203.

Furnished lettings

[62.5] Furnished lettings are taxable as, or as part of, a property business (and the computational rules at **62.4** above thus apply). See **62.6** below for special rules for furnished holiday lettings.

A '*furnished letting*' is a lease or other arrangement to which a company is party for 'generating income from land' (including a caravan or houseboat) and the person entitled to the use of the premises is also entitled to the use of furniture. Any consideration receivable for the use of furniture is chargeable as property income in the same way as rent (and expenditure incurred in providing furniture is treated accordingly). This does not apply to any amount taken into account in computing profits of a trade involving the making available of furniture for use in premises.

[*CTA 2009, ss 205, 207, 209, 248, 249; ICTA 1988, s 15(1)*].

Dependent on the nature of the lettings, including their frequency and the extent to which the landlord provides services, e.g. cleaning, laundry and meals, the letting may amount to a trade of providing serviced accommodation and be taxed as trading income rather than property income.

Alternatively, the provision of services may amount to a trade separate to the letting (cf. *Salisbury House Estate Ltd v Fry* (1930) 15 TC 266, HL). In *Gittos v Barclay* (1982) 55 TC 633, the letting of two villas in a holiday village was held not to amount to trading. A similar decision was reached in *Griffiths v Jackson*; *Griffiths v Pearman* (1982) 56 TC 583 in relation to the extensive letting of furnished rooms to students. Note that all the decisions cited were made before 1 April 1998 when non-trading furnished lettings were within *Schedule D, Case VI* rather than *Schedule A*.

Capital allowances are not due on plant or machinery let for use in a dwelling-house (see *CAA 2001, s 35* also **15.28 CAPITAL ALLOWANCES — BUILDINGS**) (but see **62.6** below as regards furnished holiday lettings). Furniture and furnishing may be dealt with on the renewals basis but an alternative HMRC concession is to allow as depreciation 10% of the rents received as reduced by any council tax and water rates or material payments for services borne by the landlord but which are normally a tenant's burden. Where the 10% deduction is allowed, no further deduction is given for the cost of renewing furniture or furnishings, nor for fixtures such as cookers, dishwashers or washing machines which, in unfurnished accommodation, the tenant would normally provide for himself. However, the cost of renewing fixtures which are an integral part of the building (e.g. baths, toilets, washbasins) may be claimed in addition, provided that they are revenue repairs to the fabric.

From 1 April 2011 this concession is given statutory effect under *CTA 2009, ss 248A–248C* per *SI 2011 No 1032*. A person or company carrying on a property business in a tax year or accounting period (for corporation tax) which includes a furnished letting of a dwelling house which is 'eligible' may make a 'wear and tear allowance election' for that tax year, or for that accounting period within two years of the end of the accounting period. A dwelling house is eligible in relation to a person if it contains (and that person, rather than the superior landlord, is responsible for ensuring it contains) sufficient furniture, furnishings and equipment for normal residential use.

Any different basis in use for a particular case prior to 1975/76 will not normally be disturbed (HMRC Extra Statutory Concession B47). See *Abidoye v Hennessey* [1979] STC 212.

If a trade of providing furniture for use in the premises is carried on and the company is assessed on the income as trading income, such treatment takes priority.

[*CTA 2009, s 248*].

Where a company carries on a furnished holiday letting business and other property businesses or transactions, separate computations are needed, with such allocations as are just and reasonable for each part where there are capital allowances claims or a loss claim.

[*CAA 2009, s 269*].

Simon's Taxes. See **B6.204.**

Furnished holiday lettings

[62.6] Over recent years there have been discussions as to the regime for furnished holiday lettings and consideration was given to withdrawing reliefs for such lettings. However, it was announced in the Budget of 22 June 2010 that the reliefs for furnished holiday lettings will not now be withdrawn. The existing arrangements under which the rules were extended to furnished lettings situated in the European Economic Area continued to apply for 2010/2011 and have been put onto a statutory footing by the *Finance Act 2011*, applicable for companies from 1 April 2011. Certain other changes have also been introduced to the regime which apply to accounting periods beginning on or after 1 April 2012.

Specifically, legislation has been introduced in the *Finance Act 2011 (s 52, Sch 14)* which amends the tax treatment of furnished holiday lettings as follows:

(a) furnished holiday lets in both the UK and the European Economic Area (EEA) will be eligible as qualifying furnished holiday lettings, for accounting periods beginning on or after 1 April 2011;

(b) the minimum period over which a qualifying property must be available for letting to the public in the relevant period will be increased from 140 days to 210 days in a year with effect for accounting period beginning on or after April 2012;

(c) the minimum period over which a qualifying property is actually let to the public in the relevant period will be increased from 70 days to 105 days in a year with effect for accounting periods beginning on or after April 2012;

(d) losses made in a qualifying UK or EEA furnished holiday lettings business may only be set against income from the same UK or EEA furnished holiday lettings business, with effect for accounting periods beginning on or after 1 April 2011; and

(e) a 'period of grace' is introduced to allow businesses that do not continue to meet the 'actually let' requirement for one or two years to elect to continue to qualify throughout that period, with effect for accounting periods beginning on or after 1 April 2010.

UK furnished holiday lettings business

In so far as a UK property business consists in the 'commercial letting' of 'furnished holiday accommodation' (a 'furnished holiday lettings business') for an accounting period, it is treated as a trade chargeable as trading income for the purposes of relief for losses under *CTA 2010, ICTA 1988, ss 392A–396; CTA 2009, Sch 1 paras 108, 112* (see **55 LOSSES**). However, pursuant to the changes in *FA 2011*, the loss relief allowed under *CTA 2010* is restricted – the relief for losses against total profits (under *CTA 2010, ss 37–44*, and *ss 48–54*) is removed for accounting periods ending on or after 1 April 2011. Losses can be carried forward under *CTA 2010, s 45* and set against profits of the same trade.

In addition, a furnished holiday lettings business is a qualifying activity for the purposes of capital allowances on plant and machinery (see **11.2 CAPITAL ALLOWANCES — PLANT AND MACHINERY: ELIGIBLE EXPENDITURE AND INITIAL ALLOWANCES**).

In contrast to furnished lettings generally, it is possible to claim capital allowances on plant or machinery provided for use in a dwelling-house, but the 10% wear and tear allowance in **62.5** above cannot be claimed as an alternative.

All commercial lettings of furnished holiday accommodation by a particular company (or partnership) are treated as a single trade or, for capital allowances purposes, as a single qualifying activity, separate from any other trade or other qualifying activity carried on by that company.

Where there is a letting of accommodation only part of which is holiday accommodation, such apportionments are to be made as are just and reasonable.

A loss may not be relieved both under this provision and under any other relieving provision.

EEA furnished holiday lettings business

The intention behind the changes in *FA 2011* is to formally put furnished holiday lettings elsewhere in the European Economic Area (EEA) on the same footing with regard to tax treatment as to a UK furnished holiday lettings business — provided the accommodation meets all the qualifying conditions. Thus, such a business will be treated as a trade for loss relief (new *CTA 2010, s 67A* — with similar restrictions as above for a UK business) and will benefit from capital allowances and certain capital gains provisions, similarly to a UK furnished holiday lettings business.

'*EEA furnished holiday lettings business*' is defined as an overseas property business so far as it consists of the commercial letting of furnished holiday accommodation in one or more EEA states. The EEA business requires separate calculations from any other overseas property business for capital allowance and loss relief purposes (see new *CTA 2009, s 269A* and new *CTA 2010, s 67A(4)*).

With regard to capital allowances, *FA 2011* inserts a new *s 13B* into *CAA 2001* which identifies four types of qualifying activity: an ordinary UK property business; a UK furnished holiday lettings business; an ordinary overseas property business; and an EEA furnished holiday lettings business.

Where plant and machinery is used in one of these businesses and is then used in another of these businesses (whilst ownership is maintained) then, with regard to the change to the second business, the owner is treated as having acquired the plant and machinery for its market value on the date it ceased to be used in the first business (as if this were different plant and machinery). Thus, the second business starts its pool with an amount of 'notional' expenditure on the plant and machinery. If the market value is greater than the actual expenditure then the notional amount is the actual expenditure.

In addition, *FA 2011* introduces changes to the capital gains provisions (a new *s 241A, TCGA 1992*) to allow an EEA furnished holiday lettings business to be treated as a trade for the purposes of the following sections of *TCGA 1992*: *ss 152–157* (roll-over relief); *s 165* (gifts relief); *s 169S* (entrepreneurs relief); *s 253* (relief for loans to traders); and *Sch 7AC* (substantial shareholdings exemption). The provisions do not apply to any part of a chargeable period during which the accommodation is neither let commercially nor available to be so let, unless this is caused by works of construction or repair. Where only part of the accommodation is holiday lets, the just and reasonable apportionments can be made.

The changes have effect for disposals made in accounting periods beginning on or after 1 April 2011, and claims made on or after 1 April 2011. With regard to the new *s 241A*, and the question as to whether a trade was being carried on in respect of the EEA furnished lettings business for the purposes of roll-over relief (etc, as above), this section is treated as having had effect on or after 1 January 1994 and so relates to an EEA business carried on in any period beginning on or after that date.

Relevant definitions

'*Commercial letting*' is letting (whether or not under a lease) on a commercial basis and with a view to the realisation of profits, and accommodation is let '*furnished*' if the tenant is entitled to use of the furniture. This applies to EEA lettings as well, by concession pursuant to the technical note issued by HMRC on 22 April 2009, by statute post-*FA 2011*. For a case in which the 'commercial letting' test was satisfied despite a significant excess of interest over letting income, see *Walls v Livesey* [1995] STC (SCD) 12, but see also *Brown v Richardson* [1997] STC (SCD) 233 in which the opposite conclusion was reached. See HMRC Tax Bulletin October 1997 pp 472, 473 for HMRC's view of the requirements in this respect.

'*Qualifying holiday accommodation*' is accommodation which:

(a) is available for commercial letting to the public generally as holiday accommodation for at least 140 days (210 days for accounting periods beginning on or after 1 April 2012) in the twelve-month period referred to below; and
(b) is so let for at least 70 (105 for accounting periods beginning on or after 1 April 2012) such days (NB. periods where the property is let for 'longer-term occupation' is not counted as a let of holiday accommodation);
(c) during the 'relevant period' not more than 155 days fall during periods of longer-term occupation.

'*Longer-term occupation*' is any period during which the property is in the same occupation for more than 31 consecutive days (other than due to abnormal circumstances).

This requirement represents a relaxation from the earlier provisions which required a period of seven months during which the property should not be under longer term occupation, which caused some confusion, as whilst it stated the seven months need not be continuous, it was unclear as to how the test should operate. This rule was therefore changed for income tax purposes by *ITTOIA 2005, s 325* and for corporation tax purposes by *CTA 2009, s 267*. Reference now being made to periods of 31 days up to a total of 155 days throughout the accounting period.

The words 'in the same occupation' refer to tenants and do not prevent relief being due where the owner himself occupies the property outside the holiday season (HMRC Property Income Manual PIM4110).

The '*relevant period*' referred to above is the accounting period in question, unless:

(1) the accommodation was not let by the company as furnished accommodation in the preceding accounting period, in which case the twelve-month period runs from the date such letting commenced in the accounting period in question; or
(2) the accommodation was let by the company as furnished accommodation in the preceding accounting period but is not so let in the succeeding accounting period, in which case the twelve-month period is the twelve months ending with the last day of accounting period in which letting ceased.

In satisfying the 70-day test in (b) above, averaging may be applied to the number of let days of any or all of the accommodation let by the company which either is 'holiday accommodation' or would be 'holiday accommodation' if it satisfied the 70-day test on its own. An election for averaging must be made within two years following the end of the accounting period in which the accommodation was let. It must specify the accommodation to be included in the averaging calculation; 'holiday accommodation' cannot be included in more than one averaging election for an accounting period. See below for an example of how averaging works.

Averaging is, strictly speaking, by reference to the number of let days in the accounting period rather than in the twelve-month period referred to above ('the relevant period'); however, this was illogical and *ITTOIA 2005, ss 324, 326* removed this anomaly for income tax purposes by referring to the average of the 'number of let days during the relevant period' — see Change 77 listed in Annex 1 to the Explanatory Notes to the Income Tax (Trading and Other Income) Bill. See also *CTA 2009, s 268*: reference change 52 listed in Annex 1 to the Explanatory Notes to *CTA 2009*. The changes in the regime brought in by *FA 2011* ensure that the averaging election is made separately for properties in the EEA and those in the UK (new *CTA 2009, s 268(7)*).

[*CTA 2009, ss 264–269, Sch 1 paras 171, 172; ICTA 1988, ss 503, 504; CAA 2001, ss 15–17; ITTOIA 2005, Sch 1 paras 195, 196, 526–528; CTA 2009, Sch 1 paras 172, 476, 477*].

The new period of grace introduced by *FA 2011* relates to business which do not meet the letting condition of 105 days (post–1 April 2012). A new *s 268A* is added to *CTA 2009* which allows for an election to be made to treat the property as continuing to qualify for up to two more later accounting periods, notwithstanding that it does not meet the letting condition in the later periods. The election must be made within two years from the end of the accounting period. An election must be made for the first year where the letting condition is not satisfied in order for an election for the second year to be made. This applies for accounting periods within *s 268A(1)* (the initial accounting period where the business does qualify) beginning on or after 1 April 2010. An election can only be made if an averaging election has not been made.

Furnished holiday accommodation may include caravans (HMRC Press Release 17 May 1984).

See Tolley's Income Tax under Property Income for the letting of furnished holiday accommodation treated as a trade for certain income tax purposes [*ICTA 1988, s 504A; ITTOIA 2005, Sch 1 para 197*]. See Tolley's Capital Gains Tax as regards relief from capital gains tax in respect of furnished holiday lettings.

See **62.19** below in relation to the foot and mouth outbreak.

Simon's Taxes. See **B6.401–B6.404, B9.110.**

Example

X Ltd owns and lets out furnished holiday cottages. None is ever let to the same person for more than 31 consecutive days. Three cottages have been owned for many years but Rose Cottage was acquired on 1 June 2011 (and first let on that day) while Ivy Cottage was sold on 30 June 2011 (and last let on that day).

In B Ltd's accounting period ending 31 March 2012, days available for letting and days let are as follows.

	Days available	Days let
Honeysuckle Cottage	180	160
Primrose Cottage	130	100
Bluebell Cottage	150	60
Rose Cottage	150	60
Ivy Cottage	30	5

Additional information

Rose Cottage was let for 30 days between 1 April and 31 May 2012.

Ivy Cottage was let for 50 days in the period 1 July 2010 to 31 March 2011 but was available for letting for 110 days in that period.

Qualification as 'furnished holiday accommodation'

Honeysuckle Cottage qualifies as it meets both the 140-day availability test and the 70-day letting test.

Primrose Cottage does *not* qualify although it is let for more than 70 days as it fails to satisfy the 140-day test. Averaging (see below) is only possible where it is the 70-day test which is not satisfied.

Bluebell Cottage does not qualify by itself as it fails the 70-day test. However it may be included in an averaging election.

Rose Cottage qualifies as furnished holiday accommodation. It was acquired on 1 June 2011 so qualification in the accounting period ending 31 March 2012 is determined by reference to the period of twelve months beginning on the day it was first let, in which it was let for a total of 90 days.

Ivy Cottage was sold on 30 June 2011 so qualification is determined by reference to the period from 1 July 2010 to 30 June 2011 (the last day of letting). It does not qualify by itself as it was let for only 55 days in this period but it may be included in an averaging election.

Averaging election for accounting period ending 31 March 2012

	Days let
Honeysuckle Cottage	160
Bluebell Cottage	60
Rose Cottage	90
Ivy Cottage	55

$$\frac{160 + 60 + 90 + 55}{4} = 91.25 \text{ days}$$

All four cottages included in the averaging election now qualify as furnished holiday accommodation as each is deemed to have been let for 91.25 days in the accounting period ending 31 March 2012.

If the average had been less than 70, the two cottages which qualify in any case could have been included in an averaging election together with one of the non-qualifying cottages (leaving the other as non-qualifying). If averaging three cottages still did not improve the position, an average of just two could be tried.

See **62.5** for position where a furnished holiday business is carried on and there is also another property business or transaction.

Distributions from REITs

[62.7] A distribution received from a Real Estate Investment Trust (REIT) by a shareholder within the charge to corporation tax is treated in the shareholder's hands as profits of a UK property business to the extent that it is paid out of the tax-exempt profits (including tax-exempt chargeable gains) of the REIT. [*CTA 2010, s 548*].

Deduction of tax at source

Generally, basic rate tax is deducted at source from distributions by the REIT; the shareholder remains liable for any excess liability, i.e. excess of the higher rate of tax over the basic rate (where the distribution is subject to income tax in the hands of the recipient). The distribution does not carry a tax credit. [*CTA 2010, s 548; ITA 2007, ss 973, 974*]. However *SI 2006 No 2867* allows for certain distributions to be made without deduction of tax at source, for example, distributions to companies resident in the UK and within the charge to UK corporation tax, or non UK resident companies carrying on a trade in the UK through a permanent establishment where such distribution is taken into account in computing the chargeable profits for UK corporation tax purposes (*para 7*).

A distribution made by a company that has ceased to be a REIT is subject to the above treatment to the extent that it is paid out of tax-exempt profits made while the company was a REIT.

Profits of a single property business

Distributions subject to this treatment (known as property income distributions or PIDs) are treated in the shareholder's hands as profits of a single business, regardless of the fact that they may come from different REITs or be received by the shareholder in different capacities. The single business is separate from any UK or overseas property business carried on by the shareholder. Thus the losses on other property business of a shareholder cannot be set off against PIDs from a REIT.

These rules apply to a corporate partner's share of any such distributions received by a partnership as if it were received by it as a direct shareholder.

[*CTA 2010, ss 548, 549*].

If the shareholder is non-UK resident, a distribution out of tax-exempt profits is again treated as profits of a UK property business, but this does not preclude its being dealt with under the relevant dividend article of a double tax agreement (Treasury Explanatory Notes to Finance Bill 2006). Such distributions are outside the non-resident landlords regime at **62.18** below.

The treatment above does not apply to distributions falling to be taken into account in computing the recipient's trading profits (see **70.66 TRADE PROFITS — INCOME AND SPECIFIC TRADES** under Dealers in securities).

The requirements concerning deduction of basic rate tax at source are set out at *ITA 2007, ss 973, 974* and in regulations (see *SI 2006 No 2867* as amended). These inter alia specify classes of shareholder to whom distributions out of tax-exempt profits can be made without deduction of tax (such as UK resident corporate shareholders, see further above), and require REITs to provide shareholders with deduction certificates containing specified information and also provide for returns and payment of tax deducted to HMRC.

There are rules to determine the extent to which a distribution of a REIT is made out of its tax-exempt profits. It is one of the conditions of tax-exempt status that at least 90% of the profits of a REIT's property rental business is paid out as dividends within a specified time (see **53.11 INVESTMENT TRUSTS** for how the distributions are attributed firstly to the tax-exempt profits and then to other profits).

REITs can offer investors a stock dividend as an alternative, or in combination with, a cash dividend, in meeting the 90% profit distribution requirements when made on or after 16 December 2010 (post *F(No3)A 2010.*

[*CTA 2010, Pt 12, ss 518 et seq*; *FA 2006, ss 121–123; CTA 2009, Sch 1 para 689*].

Holders of excessive rights

CTA 2010, ss 551–554 (previously under regulations to be made by the Treasury per *FA 2006, s114*) imposes a tax charge on a REIT if it makes a distribution to a shareholder with a 10% interest or more in the company or its dividends. The issue is that such a shareholder, if they were resident in a territory with an appropriate treaty, would be able to make a claim for a repayment of withholding tax deducted, thereby removing the REIT profits from the UK tax net.

Therefore provisions were introduced to counter this, now found at *CTA 2010, ss 551–554.* A tax penalty may be levied on the REIT if it pays out a dividend to any corporate shareholder resident in the UK, or a country with which the UK has a double tax agreement, with an entitlement to 10% or more of the dividends, share capital or voting rights in the company (referred to as 'holders of excessive rights'), unless reasonable specified steps are taken. Such reasonable steps are set out in the HMRC REIT Manual.

In addition, in order for a holder of excessive rights to receive a distribution without the REIT incurring such a tax charge, it would have to enter into a dividend strip or share repurchase arrangement. The manufactured dividend provisions as set out in *CTA 2010, ss 785, 786 (previously FA 2006, s 139)* deal with this latter case.

[*CTA 2010, ss 518 et seq, 785, 786; FA 2006, ss 107(9)(b), 114, 122(4)*].

See generally **53.3** *et seq.* **INVESTMENT TRUSTS.**

Treatment of losses

[62.8] The treatment of losses from both a UK and overseas property business are now dealt with under the provisions found in *CTA 2010, ss 62 et seq.*

Losses from a UK property business

Where a company carrying on a UK property business makes a loss in that business then it may be set off against the company's total profits for the same accounting period. Any unrelieved part of the loss may be treated as a UK property business loss of succeeding periods, for set-off against total profits of such periods, provided that the company continues to carry on the property business in the period concerned.

Where the company is a company with investment business (see **51.6 INVESTMENT COMPANIES AND INVESTMENT BUSINESS**), and the UK property business ceases, unrelieved losses can be carried forward and treated as excess management expenses in the subsequent and later periods, provided that the company continues to be a company with investment business. These reliefs are available only where the UK property business is carried on on a commercial basis or in the exercise of statutory functions (see **55.2 LOSSES**).

Lettings treated as a trade under the provisions for UK furnished holiday lettings (see **62.6 ABOVE**) are excluded from the company's UK property business for the purposes of the above provisions. Losses from such lettings are instead dealt with under the trade loss provisions (see **55 LOSSES**). The change to this loss relief for periods beginning on or after 1 April 2011 is detailed at **62.6** above.

[*CTA 2010, ss 62–65; ICTA 1988, s 392A; CTA 2009, Sch 1 para 108; SI 2004 No 2310, Art 12*].

Where a claim is made to set off a non-trade loan relationship deficit against the gross profits for the deficit period, that deficit is set off before relief for UK property business losses.

[*FA 1996, Sch 8 para 1*].

See **54.4 LOAN RELATIONSHIPS.**

Losses from an overseas property business

Losses from overseas property businesses are available for carry forward against future profits from the same business. This provision is, however, subject to the same commerciality test as applies to UK property business losses (see above). Before *CTA 2009* took effect, overseas property businesses were taxed and losses relievable under *Schedule D, Case V*, but this label has now been removed.

[*CTA 2010, ss 66, 67; ICTA 1988, s 392B; CTA 2009, Sch 1 para 109*].

Group relief

Group relief is available for UK property business losses excluding losses brought forward from earlier periods and losses incurred in a UK property business which was not carried on either on a commercial basis or in the exercise of statutory functions.

[*CTA 2010, ss 99(1)(e), 102; ICTA 1988, s 403; CTA 2009, Sch 1 para 118*]. See **39.5 GROUP RELIEF**.

Change of ownership of company

The carry forward of UK property business losses, and overseas property business losses, is restricted on the change of ownership of a company in a similar manner as applies to trading losses and excess management expenses.

[*CTA 2010, ss 683, 684, 700, 701, 704, 705; ICTA 1988, ss 768D, 769; CTA 2009, Sch 1 paras 108, 222, 223*]. See **51.9 INVESTMENT COMPANIES AND INVESTMENT BUSINESS, 55.13 LOSSES**.

Lease premiums etc.

[62.9] The provisions treating certain lease premiums and related items as property business profits for corporation tax purposes are found in *CTA 2009, ss 215–247*.

The types of receipt within these provisions are:

(a) premiums payable under a '*short lease*' (i.e. a lease with an effective duration of 50 years or less);

(b) work done by a tenant, treated as a lease premium, in addition to any actual premium.
The amount of the premium is the excess of the value of the landlord's interest immediately after the lease is entered into, over what it would have been had the lease not included the obligation to carry out work. 'Excepted work' is left out of account.
'*Excepted work*' is work which, if the landlord and not the tenant were obliged to carry it out, would be an allowable deduction in calculating the profits from the landlord's property business;

(c) payments for surrender of a lease;

(d) amounts received for assignment of a lease granted at an undervalue;

(e) sums payable instead of rent;

(f) sums payable for variation or waiver of terms of lease;

(g) sales with the right to reconveyance; and

(h) sale and lease back transactions where the term of the leaseback is 50 years or less and the sale price exceeds the total of any premium and the value of the right to receive conveyance of the reversion immediately after the lease begins. However, these provisions do not apply if the lease is granted and begins to run within one month of the sale.

(d)–(h) are anti-avoidance provisions.

Short-term lease — receipt of income

In the case of (a) above, if a premium is payable under a '*short-term lease*' (i.e. lease whose effective duration, see below, is 50 years or less), or under the terms on which such a lease is granted, the company to which it is due (whether or not the landlord) is treated as entering into a transaction for the purpose of generating income from land. An amount must be brought into account as a receipt in computing the profits of the property business which consists of or includes that transaction (see **70.17** above) for the tax year in which the lease is granted. The amount to be brought into account is:

$$P \times \frac{50 - Y}{50}$$

where:

P = the amount of the premium, and

Y = the number of *complete* periods of twelve months (*other than the first*) comprised in the effective duration of the lease.

> *Example*
>
> A Ltd grants a 14-year lease of premises for a premium of £50,000 in its accounting period ended 30 June 2011. The amount to be included as a receipt in computing the profits of its property business for that period is as follows.
>
> $$£50{,}000 \times \frac{50 - 13}{50} = £37{,}000$$

Note that these provisions refer to leases granted and not to leases assigned.

Duration of a lease

There are rules contained within *CTA 2009, ss 243–245, Sch 2 para 44 (see change 50 list in Annex 1 of the Explanatory Notes to CTA 2009; previously ICTA 1988, s 38*) for ascertaining the effective duration of a lease, which is not necessarily the same as its contractual duration. In particular, any rights the tenant has to extend the lease, or any entitlement of the tenant to a further lease of the same premises, may possibly be taken into account.

In this connection, *CTA 2009, s 245* gives HMRC the power to demand any information relevant to the duration of the lease. This has subsequently been repealed by *FA 2009* with the changes to the information gathering powers of HMRC.

A lease's term is not treated as ending later than a date which the terms of the lease etc. (including the amount of the premium) make it unlikely it will continue beyond.

Work carried out by tenant

If the terms on which a lease is granted oblige the tenant to carry out work on the premises (see (b) above) (other than work such as normal repairs or maintenance which, if incurred by the landlord, would be deductible expenditure in computing the profits of his property business), the lease is treated as requiring the payment of a premium (or additional premium) to the landlord of the amount by which the value of the landlord's interest increases as a result of the obligation.

Sum in lieu of rent

If the terms on which a lease is granted require the tenant to pay a sum in lieu of rent for a period (and that period is less than 50 years) the company to whom the sum is due (whether or not the landlord) is treated as if it were entitled to a premium equal to that sum.

CTA 2009 makes it explicit that this applies irrespective of the duration of the lease itself, and in particular whether or not it is a short-term lease, though HMRC have always taken that view in any case (see change 44 listed in Annex 1 to *CTA 2009*).

The charge to corporation tax is made for the accounting period in which the sum becomes payable. The value of Y in the above formula is the number of complete periods of twelve months (other than the first) comprised in the period in relation to which the sum is payable (but excluding any part of the period other than that in relation to which the sum is payable) and P becomes S, the sum payable instead of rent.

'*Premium*' is widely interpreted for the above purposes by *CTA 2009, ss 246, 247* and, in particular, includes payments to a person connected with the landlord (as in **25 CONNECTED PERSONS**).

See generally HMRC Property Income Manual PIM1200–1214.

Payment by instalments

Where any premium etc. is payable by instalments, the tax thereon may itself be paid by such instalments as HMRC may allow in the particular case; the tax instalment period cannot exceed eight years or, if less, the period during which the premium instalments are payable. See HMRC Property Income Manual PIM1220.

[*CTA 2009, ss 236, 243–247, Sch 1 para 13; Changes 43, 44, 45 listed in Annex 1 to the Explanatory Notes on CTA 2009; ICTA 1988, ss 24, 34, 38, 39(1); ITTOIA 2005, Sch 1 paras 17, 22*].

Capital gains tax

See Tolley's Capital Gains Tax for the treatment of chargeable gains arising from disposal by way of a lease.

Note particularly that the part of the premium chargeable to income tax is omitted from the computation of the chargeable gain.

Surrender under the terms of a lease

If, under the terms on which a short-term lease is granted, a sum becomes payable by the tenant as consideration for the surrender of the lease, consequences ensue as above as if that sum were a premium (and the calculation above would apply, suitably amended, see *CTA 2010, s 220*). See HMRC Property Income Manual PIM1214. [*CTA 2009, s 220; ICTA 1988, ss 34(1)(4)(6)(7A), 39(1); ITTOIA 2005, Sch 1 para 17*].

Variation or waiver of term of lease

If a sum becomes payable by a tenant otherwise than by way of rent as consideration for the variation or waiver of the terms of a lease, and the sum is due to the landlord or to a company connected with the landlord (within **25 CONNECTED PERSONS**) (and the period for which the variation or waiver has effect is 50 years or less) consequences ensue as above as if that sum were a premium (the calculation above would apply, suitably amended, see *CTA 2010, s 221*).

The charge to corporation tax is made for the accounting period in which the contract for the variation or waiver is entered into. The value of Y in the above formula is the number of complete periods of twelve months (other than the first) comprised in the period for which the variation or waiver has effect (but excluding any part of that period preceding the time at which the variation or waiver takes effect or falling after the time at which it ceases to have effect). Minor changes have been made to clarify certain provisions which were ambiguous in *ICTA 1988*.

[*CTA 2009, ss 215–221, Changes 46, 49 in Annex l to Explanatory Notes to CTA 2009; ICTA 1988, s 34(1)(5)(6)(7)(7A); ITTOIA 2005, Sch 1 para 17*].

CTA 2009 makes it explicit that this applies irrespective of the duration of the lease itself, and in particular whether or not it is a short-term lease, though HMRC have always taken that view in any case (see Change 44 in Annex 1 of the Explanatory Notes to the *CTA 2009*). See HMRC Property Income Manual PIM1216.

Simon's Taxes. See B6.3, B9.2.

Anti-avoidance — leases granted at undervalue etc.

[62.10] If a short-term lease (as in **62.9** above) was granted at an undervalue and is assigned at a profit, similar consequences ensue as in **62.9** above as regards the assignor as if the assignor had received a premium (except that the opportunity to pay the tax by instalments is not available).

The charge to corporation tax is made for the accounting period in which the consideration for the assignment becomes payable. The value of P in the formula in **62.9** above is the lesser of the profit on the assignment and the amount of the undervalue (adjusted to take account of any profits on earlier assignments of the same lease).

This does not apply in relation to a lease granted before 6 April 1963 or arising from a contract entered into before that date. If the landlord, a company which assigned the lease or the assignee provides HMRC with a statement showing that there is or may be an amount taxable under these provisions, the HMRC officer musts certify the accuracy of the statement provided that he is satisfied that it is accurate.

[*CTA 2009, ss 222, 223, 237; ICTA 1988, ss 35, 39(1); ITTOIA 2005, Sch 1 para 18*].

Anti-avoidance — sale of land with right to reconveyance

[62.11] If land is sold subject to terms requiring it to be reconveyed on a future date to the vendor or a person connected with the vendor (within **25 CONNECTED PERSONS**) for a price lower than the sale price, similar consequences ensue as in **62.9** above as regards the vendor as if the vendor had received a premium. *ITTOIA 2005* makes it explicit that this applies only if the period beginning with the sale and ending with the earliest date on which, under the said terms, the land could fall to be reconveyed is 50 years or less (see Change 72 listed in Annex 1 to the Income Tax (Trading and Other Income) Bill). The equivalent for corporation tax is in *CTA 2009, ss 224, 226* — see change 47 listed in Annex 1 to the Explanatory Notes to *CTA 2009*. The charge to corporation tax is made for the accounting period in which the sale occurs.

The value of P in the formula in **62.9** above is the excess of the sale price over the price at which the land is to be reconveyed. The value of Y is the number of complete periods of twelve months (other than the first) comprised in the period of 50 years or less referred to above.

Similar provisions apply (with appropriate modifications) if, instead of being reconveyed, the land is to be leased back to the vendor or to a person connected with the vendor. (They do not, however, apply if the lease is granted and begins to run within one month after the sale.) In this case, the sale price is compared to the total of (i) any premium payable for the lease and (ii) the value on the date of sale of the right to lease back the land.

If the date for the reconveyance (or leaseback) is not fixed under the terms of the sale and the reconveyance price (or the total of (i) and (ii) above) varies dependent upon that date, the price (or total) is taken to be the lowest possible under the terms of the sale. There is provision for any overpaid tax to be repaid if the actual date of reconveyance (or of the grant of the lease) turns out to be different to the date by reference to which the tax charge was calculated; a claim for repayment must be made (from a date to be determined by statutory order) within four years (six years before that date) after the reconveyance (or the grant of the lease).

[*CTA 2009, ss 224, 225, 238, 239, Sch 2 para 42; ICTA 1988, s 36; ITTOIA 2005, Sch 1 para 19; FA 2008, Sch 39 para 17*].

See HMRC Property Income Manual PIM1222, 1224, 1226. For the so-called 'treasury arrangement' to avoid a charge under these provisions where there is a genuine commercial reason for the owner of mineral-bearing land to sell with a right to repurchase, see HMRC Property Income Manual PIM1228. See **5.17**, **5.18** **ANTI-AVOIDANCE** for other provisions concerning the sale and leaseback of land.

Sub-leases etc.

[62.12] Relief is due with regard to these charges, where any of the charges at **62.9** above apply, or the charge on assignment at **62.10** above applies, and the grant of the lease in question is out of a 'taxed lease' (or a head lease) or, as the case may be, the assignment in question is of a 'taxed lease' (or a head lease).

A '*taxed lease*' is one in respect of which there has already been such a charge (or there would have been a charge but for the availability of this relief).

Thus, in broad terms, the relief applies where the taxable company is itself a tenant and its own landlord has received a premium or other taxable sum in respect of the same property.

The amount given by the formula in **62.9** above is reduced by the proportion of amount previously charged which the duration of the sub-lease bears to the duration of the head lease. The amount of the reduction can be found by the formula:

$$\frac{A \times LRP}{TRP}$$

where:

A = the amount given by the formula in **62.9** above in respect of the previous charge;

LRP = the length of the 'receipt period' of the receipt under calculation; and

TRP = the total 'receipt period' of the receipt by reference to which the previous charge was made.

The '*receipt period*' is:

- in the case of a premium (or similar sum) or a sum payable for the surrender of a lease, the effective duration of the lease (see **62.9** above);
- in the case of a sum payable in lieu of rent, the period for which it is payable;
- in the case of a sum payable for variation or waiver, the period for which the variation or waiver has effect; and
- in the case of an assignment, the effective duration of the lease remaining at the date of the assignment.

If the current charge is under **62.9** above and the sub-lease relates to only part of the premises subject to the head-lease, the relief is reduced proportionately on a just and reasonable basis.

Example

A Ltd grants a 14-year lease of premises to B Ltd for a premium of £50,000 in June 2011. The amount to be included as a receipt in computing the profits of A Ltd's property business in its accounting period ending 31 December 2011 is £37,000 as computed in the Example in **62.9** above.

After 4 years, i.e. in June 2015, B Ltd grants a 10-year sub-lease for which it receives a premium of £60,000. The amount to be included as a receipt in computing the profits of B Ltd's property business for its accounting period ending 31 December 2015 is as follows.

		£
Normal calculation	$£60{,}000 \times \frac{50-9}{50}$	49,200
Less relief as above	$\frac{£37{,}000 \times 10}{14}$	26,429
		£22,771

The relief is restricted to the 'unrelieved balance' of the value of A in the above formula ('A' being the previous charge).

The '*unrelieved balance*' is found by deducting the following from the value of A:

- any relief previously given under these provisions;
- any deductions allowed under **62.13** below; and
- any deductions allowed under *CTA 2009, ss 62–67* (deductions allowed where the land is used for the purposes of a trade etc. — see **70.62 TRADE PROFITS — INCOME AND SPECIFIC TRADES**),

so far as attributable to the charge to which A relates.

If there is more than one previous charge in relation to which there is an unrelieved balance, an amount of relief is computed separately for each previous charge and then aggregated, but the total relief cannot exceed the total of the unrelieved balances.

For these purposes, in a case where the previous charge resulted from the tenant's obligation to carry out work on the premises (see **62.9** above), the value of A in the above formula is recomputed as if that obligation had not included the carrying out of any work that results in expenditure qualifying for **CAPITAL ALLOWANCES (10)**.

If the relief would otherwise exceed the amount from which it is deductible, it is restricted to that amount.

[*CTA 2009, ss 66, 228, 229; ICTA 1988, s 37(1)–(3), (7)–(9), Sch 30 paras 2, 3 (repealed by CTA 2009, Sch 1 para 292); ITTOIA 2005, Sch 1 para 20*].

Periods pre and post 2005/06 and FY 2005

The above provisions applied equally for the purposes of income tax before 2005/06 and corporation tax before the financial year 2005.

For 2005/06 onwards, the income tax rules are in *ITTOIA 2005, ss 287–290* (the above narrative being largely based on these provisions) but the equivalent corporation tax rules remained in *ICTA 1988, s 37* (as amended by *ITTOIA 2005, Sch 1 para 20* from 1 April 2005) until April 2009 when the Corporation Tax Act came into force.

ITTOIA 2005, ss 296–298 and *CTA 2009, ss 227–233, Sch 2 para 39; ICTA 1988, s 37(2)*, seek to ensure that the two sets of rules interact, for example where the landlord is an individual and the tenant is a company. The tenant remains entitled to the above relief even though the previous charge, i.e. the charge on the landlord etc., is a charge to income tax rather than corporation tax.

Where there is a receipt of a *Schedule A* business or overseas property business for an accounting period ending before 1 April 2009 (a pre-commencement receipt), the lease is treated as a taxed lease and the amount of the pre-commencement receipt is treated as a taxed receipt.

[*CTA 2009, Sch 2 para 39, Change 48 listed in Annex l to the Explanatory Notes to CTA 2009*].

See generally HMRC Property Income Manual PIM2300–2340.

Other deductions available to tenant

[62.13] A tenant is allowed a deduction, in computing the profits of the tenant's property business, by reference to a premium etc. charged on the landlord. The deduction is available to a tenant under a 'taxed lease' (or head lease).

A '*taxed lease*' is a lease by reference to which any of the charges at **62.9** have arisen, or the charge on assignment at **62.10** above has arisen (or would have done so but for the availability of the relief at **62.12** above).

The deduction is available for any 'qualifying day' on which the whole or part of the premises subject to the taxed lease is either occupied by the tenant for the purposes of carrying on a property business or sub-let. It is given by treating an amount calculated as below as a revenue expense of the tenant's property business, but *not* so as to override any statutory rule governing deductible expenditure generally (see **62.4** above).

A '*qualifying day*' is a day that falls within the 'receipt period' (as defined in **62.12** above) of the receipt charged under **62.9** or **62.10** above).

The amount of the expense for *each* qualifying day is the amount given by the formula in **62.9** above in respect of the charge under **62.9** or **62.10** above divided by the number of days in its receipt period.

Examples

(A)

A Ltd grants a 14-year lease of premises to B Ltd for a premium of £50,000 on 1 June 2011. The amount to be included as a receipt in computing the profits of A Ltd's property business for its accounting period ending 31 December 2011 is £37,000 as computed in the Example in **62.9** above. B Ltd immediately sub-lets the premises but does not receive any premium.

The number of days in the 14-year receipt period is 5,113. The deduction due to B Ltd in calculating the profits of its property business for any one qualifying day is £37,000 divided by 5,113 = £7.24.

For the accounting period ending 31 December 2011, the available deduction is £7.24 × 214 (1.6.11 to 31.12.11) = £1,549.

If, however, the tenant is also entitled to relief under **62.12** above, the tenant is treated as incurring a revenue expense for a qualifying day only to the extent (if any) that the daily amount computed as above exceeds the daily amount of the relief under **62.12**.

(B)

The sub-letting in Example (A) above ceases in the accounting period ending 31 December 2014. On 1 January 2015, B Ltd again grants a sub-lease of the premises but this time for a period of 11 years at a premium of £70,000. The amount to be included as a receipt in computing the profits of B Ltd's property business for the year ending 31 December 2015 is as follows.

		£
Normal calculation as in **62.9**	$£70{,}000 \times \frac{50-10}{50}$	56,000
Less relief as **62.12**	$\frac{£37{,}000 \times 11}{14}$	29,071
		£26,929

The number of days in the 11-year receipt period of the sub-lease is 4,018. The daily amount of the relief given is therefore £29,071 divided by 4,018 = £7.24.

This equals the daily expense computed in Example (A); as there is no excess, B Ltd is not entitled to any deduction for a revenue expense under these provisions for any of the 4,018 qualifying days covered by the sub-lease.

Supposing B Ltd had been able to obtain a premium of only £30,000 for the 11-year sub-lease. The amount to be included as a receipt in computing the profits of B Ltd's property business for the year ending 31 December 2015 would then be as follows.

		£
Normal calculation as in **62.9**	$£30{,}000 \times \frac{50-10}{50}$	24,000

Less $\frac{£37{,}000 \times 11}{14} = £29{,}071$ *but restricted to*	24,000
	Nil

The daily amount of the relief given is now £24,000 divided by 4,018 = £5.97.

This is less than the daily expense of £7.24 computed in Example (A), the deficit being £1.27.

B Ltd would be entitled to a deduction of £1.27 as a revenue expense for each of the 4,018 qualifying days covered by the sub-lease.

If a sub-lease relates to only part of the premises covered by the main lease, the above rules are applied separately to the different parts of the premises, the premium under the main lease being apportioned between those parts on a just and reasonable basis.

If the premises subject to the taxed lease (or head lease) are used for the purposes of a trade instead of for those of a property business, very similar rules apply under *CTA 2009, ss 62–67*, with the deduction being given as an expense in computing the profits of the trade etc. See **70.62 TRADE PROFITS — INCOME AND SPECIFIC TRADES.**

The total of the deductions allowed under these provisions, any deductions allowed under *CTA 2009, ss 62–67* referred to above and any relief given under **62.12** above cannot exceed the amount charged under **62.9** or, where appropriate, **62.10** above.

[*CTA 2009, ss 231–235, change 13 listed in Annex 1 to CTA 2009; ICTA 1988, ss 37(4)–(6)(9), 37A, 39(1); ITTOIA 2005, Sch 1 paras 20, 21*].

Interaction pre and post 2005/06 and CTA 2009

Before 2005/06, the above provisions applied equally for the purposes of income tax and corporation tax.

For 2005/06 onwards, the income tax rules are in *ITTOIA 2005*. For accounting periods ending after 31 March 2009, the equivalent corporation tax rules are in *CTA 2009*.

ITTOIA 2005, ss 296–298 as amended by *CTA 2009, Sch 1 paras 623, 624* seeks to ensure that the two sets of rules interact, for example where the landlord is a company and the tenant is an individual. The tenant remains entitled to the above deduction even though the lease premium is charged to income tax rather than corporation tax.

Simon's Taxes. See **B6.310, B6.311, B9.221–B9.223, B6.309** *et seq.*

See generally HMRC Property Income Manual PIM2300–2340.

Reverse premiums

[62.14] There are provisions to ensure that reverse premiums are taxable as revenue receipts.

They apply in relation to any 'reverse premium' (which is broadly a payment made, or benefit provided, by a landlord to a prospective tenant as an inducement to enter into a lease).

Other than in cases where the transaction is entered into for the purposes of the recipient's trade, or prospective trade, a reverse premium is to be treated as a receipt of a UK property business or an overseas property business carried on by the recipient.

Unless the specific anti-avoidance provisions apply (i.e. the parties are connected and the arrangements are not such as would have been agreed at arm's length), it is understood that, normally, accounting principles require such a payment to be spread over the period of the lease, or, if shorter, the period to the first rent review.

[*CTA 2009, s 250*].

Information re leases

[62.15] Information, including consideration for their grant or assignment etc., may be required, subject to penalty for non-compliance, from present or former lessees or occupiers, or from agents managing property or receiving rents etc.

See generally the information gathering powers of HMRC under *FA 2008, Sch 36* applicable from 1 April 2009.

[*CTA 2009, s 245 (now repealed by FA 2009); TMA 1970, ss 19, 98; ITTOIA 1988, Sch 1 para 367*].

Rent factoring

Transactions entered into between 20 March 2000 – 6 June 2006

[62.16] Details of the provisions which apply to transactions entered into after 20 March 2000 and before 6 June 2006 which were repealed by *FA 2006, Sch 6 para 1* can be found in the 2010–11 and earlier copies of Tolley's Corporation Tax. The provisions were repealed as a consequence of the introduction of the wider anti-avoidance provisions as to rent factoring described at **5.15** ANTI-AVOIDANCE.

Capital gains

[62.17] Any UK property business consisting of the letting of furnished holiday accommodation is treated as a trade for the purposes of replacement of business assets relief, relief for loans to traders, retirement relief and substantial shareholdings exemption. Similarly with regard to an EEA furnished holiday lettings business. See **62.6** above and the changes brought in by *FA 2011* with regard to an EEA furnished holiday lettings business.

See **19 CAPITAL GAINS — SUBSTANTIAL SHAREHOLDINGS** and Tolley's Capital Gains Tax under Furnished Holiday Accommodation, Losses and Rollover Relief.

[*TGCA 1992, ss 241, 241A (as inserted by FA 2011); FA 2002, Sch 8 para 3; ITTOIA 2005, Sch 1 para 441; CTA 2009, Sch 1 para 380*].

Non-resident landlords scheme

[62.18] Where a landlord is non-UK resident and is chargeable on the profits of a UK property business under *ITTOIA 2005, Ch 2 Pt 3* or *CTA 2009, Ch 2 Pt 4*, then tax is payable on the profits of the business at the basic rate. Such tax is to be deducted at source by the agent for the property or, where there is no agent, the tenant.

The non-resident landlord is then required to submit a self assessment tax return for the tax year (being the income tax year) declaring the profits for the year so chargeable and settling up any tax to be paid, taking into account any tax deducted at source. But note further point (vi) below with regard to applications to HMRC for such rental payments to be made gross.

The regulations giving effect to these requirements provide broadly as follows.

(i) Letting agents who receive or have control over UK property income of a non-resident must operate the scheme.

(ii) Where there is no letting agent acting, tenants of a non-resident must operate the scheme.

(iii) Tenants who pay less than £100 per week do not have to operate the scheme unless asked to do so by HMRC.

(iv) Letting agents and tenants who have to operate the scheme must pay tax at the basic rate each quarter on the non-resident's UK property income less certain allowable expenses and deductions, and must give the non-resident an annual certificate showing details of tax deducted.

(v) Non-residents whose property income is subject to deduction of tax may set the tax deducted against their UK tax liability through their self-assessment.

(vi) Non-residents may apply to HMRC for approval to receive their UK property income without deduction of tax provided that:
 (a) their UK tax affairs are up to date;
 (b) they have never had any obligations in relation to UK tax; or
 (c) they do not expect to be liable to UK income tax,
 and that they undertake to comply with all their UK tax obligations in the future. An appeal may be made against refusal or withdrawal of approval.

The regulations also make provision for interest on unpaid tax and for payments on account under self-assessment, and set out details of the annual information requirements on those operating the scheme, and of other information to be supplied on request.

Penalties apply under *TMA 1970, s 98* for non-compliance with these return and information provisions.

[*ITA 2007, s 972, Sch 2 para 100; ICTA 1988, s 42A(4)–(7); SI 1995 No 2902; ITTOIA 2005, Sch 1 para 25*].

HMRC publish detailed guidance notes for those required to operate the scheme (see www.hmrc.gov.uk/cnr/nrl_guide_notes.pdf and www.hmrc.gov.uk/cnr/nr_landlords.htm).

Simon's Taxes. See **B6.217**, **B9.503**.

Miscellaneous provisions

Capital allowances on plant and machinery

[62.19] A property business is a qualifying activity for the purposes of such allowances under *CAA 2001, Pt 2* (see **11.2 CAPITAL ALLOWANCES: PLANT AND MACHINERY — ELIGIBLE EXPENDITURE AND INITIAL ALLOWANCES**).

Capital allowances were similarly available under *CAA 1990, Pt II* on plant or machinery as if the property business were a separate trade for which the item was provided (subject to further separation where there are furnished holiday lettings — see **62.6** above).

Allowances are thus given as expenses, and charges treated as receipts, of the business. Plant or machinery provided for use in a dwelling-house is excluded (with a just and reasonable apportionment of expenditure where such use is partial).

[*CAA 2001, ss 15, 16, 35; ITTOIA 2005, Sch 1 paras 526, 527, 533; CTA 2009, Sch 1 para 476, 477*].

Overseas property business

An 'overseas property business' is defined in the same way as a 'UK property business' (see **62.2** above) except that the source of the income is outside the UK. Before *CTA 2009* took effect, rental income from land situated outside the UK was chargeable under *Schedule D Case V*.

The overseas letting is treated as a separate business and the same computational rules (including the lease premium rules) apply in determining the receipts and expenses to be included in computing the profits of overseas property business as if the property were situated in the UK. Where a business falls within the property income provisions and those for trading income, the trading income provisions take priority.

[*CTA 2009, ss 206, 209; ICTA 1988, s 70A*].

The special rules governing the tax treatment of furnished holiday lettings do not apply to an overseas property business, save the rules with regard to an EEA furnished holiday lettings business, see **62.6** above. [*CTA 2009, s 210(2); ICTA 1988, s 70A(6)*].

Overseas property business losses may be carried forward and set off against overseas property business profits from the same business in subsequent accounting periods, provided that the business is carried on on a commercial basis or in the exercise of statutory functions.

[*CTA 2009, s 287, Sch 1 paras 296, 300, 453, change 55 listed in Annex l of the Explanatory Notes to CTA 2009; CTA 2009, Sch 1 para 109*].

Non-resident companies are within the charge to income tax (not corporation tax) in certain circumstances (see **65 RESIDENCE**).

Where a company starts or ceases an overseas property business or to be within the charge to corporation tax in respect of an overseas property business, it is treated as starting or ceasing to carry on the business at that time.

[*ICTA 1988, s 337(2); FA 2002, Sch 30 para 1; ITTOIA 2005, Sch 1 para 145*].

Mutual businesses

The normal exemption for mutual companies (**56 MUTUAL COMPANIES**) does not extend to property businesses, the transactions and relationships involved in mutual business being instead treated as if they were between persons between whom no relationship of mutuality existed. Any surplus is chargeable on the company to which the profits arise or which is entitled to the profits. (This does not affect the treatment of Co-operative Housing Associations — see **45 HOUSING ASSOCIATIONS**.)

[*CTA 2009, s 260; ICTA 1988, s 21C; ITTOIA 2005, Sch 1 para 14*].

Items apportioned on sale of land

If on a sale of land, receipts and outgoings due to be received or paid by the buyer are apportioned to the seller, then, in computing the profits of the seller's property business, the part apportioned to it is treated as being of the same nature, i.e. revenue or capital, as the transaction itself.

So, for example, if rent is receivable in arrears and the sale price includes an accrual for rent receivable up to date of sale, the amount of that accrual is income in the hands of the vendor and not capital.

[*CTA 2009, s 259; ICTA 1988, s 40; ITTOIA 2005, Sch 1 para 23*].

Sea walls

For allowances for expenditure on making sea walls, see *CTA 2009, ss 254–257; ICTA 1988, s 30*; *ITTOIA 2005, Sch 1 para 15* and *Hesketh v Bray* (1888) 2 TC 380.

Electric-line wayleaves

Where rent is receivable for a UK electric-line wayleave, it is chargeable to corporation tax as property income. If a company carries on a UK property business in relation to some or all of the land to which the wayleave relates and the business has other receipts for the accounting period in question, the rent receivable for the wayleave is brought into account as profits from a property business. Otherwise, it is taxed as a separate item; the charge is on the full amount of the profits arising in the accounting period.

Rent is receivable for a UK electric-line wayleave if it is receivable in respect of an easement enjoyed in the UK, which includes any right, privilege or benefit in, over or derived from land in connection with any electric, telegraph or telephone wire or cable, including supporting poles or pylons and related apparatus. All references above to 'rent' include any other receipt in the nature of rent.

[*CTA 2009, ss 277–279, 287, 288; ICTA 1988, s 120; ITTOIA 2005, Sch 1 para 104*].

If, however, a company carries on a trade, profession or vocation on some or all of the land to which the wayleave relates and, apart from rent receivable, or expenses incurred, in respect of the wayleave, no other receipts or expenses in respect of any of the land are included in computing the profits of any property business of the company, rent receivable, or expenses incurred, in respect of the wayleave may be brought into account, at the company's option, in computing the profits of the trade etc. instead of being charged as above.

For accounting periods ending on or after 1 April 2009 (and see **70 TRADE PROFITS — INCOME AND SPECIFIC TRADES**), this treatment differs to some extent from both the law and practice prevailing for earlier years (see Change 6 listed in Annex 1 to the Explanatory Notes to *CTA 2009*). It extends to certain wayleaves other than those described above and to wayleaves relating to land outside the UK which would otherwise be included in an overseas property business.

[*CTA 2009, s 45*].

Mines, quarries etc.

Profits of mines, quarries, gravel pits, sand pits, brickfields, ironworks, gas works, canals, railways, rights of fishing, rights of markets, fairs and tolls and like concerns (as specified in *ICTA 1988, s 55, rewritten to CTA 2009, s 39*) are computed and charged to corporation tax trading income where they are carried on on a commercial basis. (see **70.56 TRADE PROFITS — INCOME AND SPECIFIC TRADES**).

Where no trade is carried on, or the trade is not carried on by the owner of the mine etc. income other than mineral royalties is taxable as income of a property business. If a company lets the right to work mineral deposits in the UK and it pays an amount wholly and exclusively as management expenses in that period, a deduction for the paid amount is against income for the accounting period, subject to the reduction of one half mentioned below. If the rent is received in kind, it is chargeable in the same way as rent received in cash: this is a change from the previous treatment.

Prior to the commencement of *CTA 2009*, the management expenses had to be wholly, exclusively and necessarily incurred in order to qualify for relief. Where mineral royalties are received in respect of mines etc exploited on a commercial basis by someone other than the owner or not commercially worked, only one half of the income and one half of allowable expenses are brought into account. HMRC may by statutory instrument provide the extent to which rents are mineral royalties.

[*CTA 2009, ss 39, 258, 270–276, changes 53, 54 listed in Annex 1 to the Explanatory Notes to CTA 2009 ICTA 1988, s 119*].

Key points

[62.20] Points to consider are as follows.

- The furnished holiday letting rules have been amended by *FA 2011* with effect from April 2011. The position with regard to an EEA furnished holiday lettings business has been formalised. The eligibility thresholds have been made stricter as from 2012 and the utilisation of losses arising from the furnished holiday letting business has been restricted.
- Distributions of income and gains deriving from a REIT's property rental business are treated as property income in the hands of shareholders and are generally subject to a deduction of 20% tax at source. UK resident corporate shareholders can receive the distributions without suffering deduction at source. Where the REIT's shareholders are non-UK resident, the dividend article of any relevant tax treaty applies to the distribution and as a result, for shareholders that can benefit from tax treaties, the rate of withholding may be lower than 20%. In these cases, the REIT is still required to withhold tax at a rate of 20%. The shareholder may then make a claim to HMRC for a refund.
- Where a corporate shareholder holds 10% or more shares in a REIT, it may be possible to ensure that the shareholder is not treated as a 'holder of excessive rights' by fragmenting its holding across a number of sister subsidiaries, each holding less than 10%, provided the parent company itself does not hold any shares in the REIT.
- Care is needed when considering how unrelieved property losses for an accounting period can be utilised. It is not possible to carry back property losses to a prior period. Property losses can be set off against the company's total profits for the accounting period in which the loss arises. They may only be group relieved to the extent that current period property losses exceed current period profits of the surrendering company (i.e. profits before offset of losses (current year or brought forward), charges on income and management expenses).
- Property losses carried forward are treated as property losses arising in the subsequent period and may be offset against total profits arising in that period.
- If a company with both an investment business and a property business ceases to carry on its property business but continues to have investment business, any unrelieved property losses may be carried forward and treated as management expenses deductible in later periods.

- If a company with a property business ceases that business, any property losses will lapse unless the company also has an investment business (see above). In the event that the company has sold all of its properties, but fully intends to acquire further assets in the future, it may be possible to treat the dormant period as a temporary break in business, with the effect that the losses should be available for use on recommencement of that business. The question as to whether a property business has ceased is a question of fact.
- Given the broad application of the loss restriction provisions on a change of ownership of a company (see **62.8**), in most cases it is unlikely that a purchaser would ascribe value to tax losses in the target company.
- Lease premia receivable in respect of leases with a term of less than 50 years are treated as part income and part capital in the hands of the landlord. The shorter the term of the lease, the greater the proportion of the premium treated as income. A revenue tax deduction is available to the payer of the premium over the term of the lease for the element of the premium that is treated as income in the hands of the landlord, provided that the tenant remains in occupation (where the tenant is a trader) or the property is sub-let (where the tenant has a property business).
- Where the provisions of a lease do not provide for it to be surrendered in return for the payment of a premium, any such premium received for a surrender of the lease will be treated as a capital receipt in the hands of the landlord. This results in a beneficial tax treatment for landlords with capital losses or those that are non-UK resident.
- A reverse premium is generally treated as an income receipt in the hands of an incoming tenant. Consideration could be given to structuring the incentive as a contribution by the landlord to tenant's fixtures and fittings that qualify for capital allowances, in which case the tenant loses the right to claim capital allowances, but is not taxed on the contribution. The tax position for the landlord is also likely to be improved as the landlord will be able to claim capital allowances on the contribution made towards qualifying assets, rather than relief for the premium being deferred until the property is sold (since it will otherwise generally be treated as enhancement spend).
- Non-UK resident owners of UK property are subject to basic rate income tax, currently at 20%, on rental income less deductible expenses. These expenses include capital allowances and interest on loans to acquire the property and for working capital purposes for the rental business. Such owners are not subject to tax on gains from the sale of UK property. Unless the non-UK resident is registered under the Non-Resident Landlord Scheme, the tenants or letting agent are required to withhold tax at a rate of 20% from rental payments made to the non-UK resident owner.

63

Purchase by a Company of its Own Shares

Simon's Taxes. See D6.605–D6.618.

Introduction

[63.1] A company is permitted to repurchase its own shares from shareholders. This may be useful in providing an exit route for investors where an external buyer for shares is not available. A company can buy back its own shares out of:

- distributable profits; or
- proceeds from a new share issue.

Companies Act 2006, Pt 18 provides the authority for a company to buy back its own shares, subject to various conditions. Such a purchase would normally be classified as a **DISTRIBUTION (31)** for an individual shareholder, but for a corporate vendor would still be treated as capital. However, provided specific conditions are fulfilled, certain payments on the redemption, or re-purchase by a company of its own shares will not be treated as distributions for individuals.

Normally the repurchased shares are cancelled however, a company may purchase and hold its own shares (known as treasury shares). See **63.10**.

See **63.2** onwards below.

Payments not treated as distributions

[63.2] Provided the conditions below are satisfied, certain payments (and other items normally treated as distributions) made by a company for the purchase, redemption or repayment of its own shares are not treated as distributions. Such payments in the hands of the vendor are brought into account for capital gains purposes only (but see **70.64 TRADE PROFITS — INCOME AND SPECIFIC TRADES** as regards dealers in securities).

The conditions are that:

Condition A: the company is an unquoted trading company, or the unquoted holding company of a trading group; and either:

- the transaction is wholly or mainly to benefit a trade carried on by the company or any of its 75% subsidiaries; or
- the transaction does not form part of a scheme or arrangement, the main, or one of the main purposes of which are to give the owner access to profits without receiving a dividend or tax avoidance; and
- the vendor shareholder, or his nominee, must be UK resident and (for a seller who is an individual) ordinarily resident in the year in which the transaction is carried out, or

Condition B: the whole of the payment is applied by the recipient in meeting an inheritance tax liability.

See, however, **31.11 DISTRIBUTIONS** as regards certain subsequent bonus issues.

Where the purchase is treated as a distribution, see also **31.16 DISTRIBUTIONS** as regards capital gains consequences.

The conditions for non-distribution treatment of such payments are set out at **63.3, 63.4–63.6** below. Revenue Tax Bulletin February 1996 pp 280–282 contains a short article dealing with various matters which in HMRC's experience are sometimes overlooked or misunderstood.

Simon's Taxes. See **D6.605**.

Example

A Ltd, an unquoted trading company, is planning to re-purchase the shares of Mr X, a 20% shareholder, for £100,000. Mr X owns 30,000 ordinary shares in A Ltd which he acquired from a third party in September 2003 for £50,000. The third party subscribed for the shares at par for £30,000 in May 2001.

Income treatment:	£	Capital treatment:	£
Income tax:		Capital gains tax:	
Proceeds	100,000	Proceeds	100,000
Less: original subscription cost	(30,000)	Less: cost of shares	(50,000)
Taxable as a distribution	70,000	Capital gain	50,000
		Less: annual exemption	(10,100)
Tax on the distribution:		Taxable gain	39,900
£70,000 × 25% (assuming a 40% tax rate payer)	£17,500	Tax on the gain: £39,900 × 18%	£7,182
Capital loss	£		
Original subscription cost	30,000		
Less: price paid	(50,000)		

Capital loss	(20,000)

The tax under the capital route will be even lower if entrepreneurs' relief is available to Mr X. That would require Mr X to have been an officer or employee of the company throughout the year ending with the disposal.

Conditions to be satisfied by the company

[63.3] For the treatment in **63.2** above to apply, the following conditions must be satisfied.

- The company must be an 'unquoted company', i.e. neither the company, nor any company of which it is a '51% subsidiary' and must have any class of shares listed in the official list of a stock exchange. (Shares dealt in on the Stock Exchange Unlisted Securities Market were not treated as quoted, see HMRC Share Valuation Manual, SVM09060.) Securities on the Alternative Investment Market ('AIM') are similarly treated as unquoted for these purposes. (HMRC Share Valuation Manual, SVM09070.)
  A company is a '51% subsidiary' of another if more than 50% of its ordinary share capital is beneficially owned directly or indirectly by the other company. [*CTA 2010, s 1047; ICTA 1988, s 838*].
- The company must be either a 'trading company' or the 'holding company of a trading group' (for definitions, see **31.30 GROUP RELIEF**). For this purpose, 'trade' does not include dealing in shares, securities, land or futures.

[*CTA 2010, s 1033; ICTA 1988, ss 219(1), 229(1)*].

Simon's Taxes. See D6.610.

Conditions regarding the reason for the purchase

[63.4] Either Condition A or Condition B must be met to enable the payment etc. to qualify for the treatment as in **63.2** above. In addition, as a general condition, the consideration must be in money and must be paid immediately, i.e. instalment payment is not possible. (Revenue Tax Bulletin February 1996 p 281.)

Condition A — Payment made for the benefit of the trade

Where Condition B does not apply, the purchase etc. of the shares must be made wholly or mainly to benefit a trade carried on by the company or by any '75% subsidiary'; it must not form part of a scheme or arrangement the main, or one such, purpose of which is either the obtaining by the vendor of a share in the company's profits without receiving a dividend, or the avoidance of tax.

[*CTA 2010, s 1033; ICTA 1988, s 219(1)(a)*].

As regards whether a purchase etc. is for the benefit of the trade, HMRC have given their interpretation in HMRC Statement of Practice, SP 2/82. This emphasises that the purpose must be the benefit of a trade and not, for example, the benefit of the vending shareholder (although he will usually also benefit), or of some wider commercial purpose to which the payment etc. may be put, or of a non-trading activity of the trading company. Generally, the condition will be satisfied where (after taking into account any associate's interests) the vending shareholder is genuinely giving up his entire interest of all kinds in the company. Four examples are cited.

(1) The withdrawal of his investment by an outside shareholder providing equity finance.
(2) The retirement of the proprietor of a company to make way for new management.
(3) The death of a shareholder, on which his personal representatives or the beneficiaries do not wish to keep the shares.
(4) A disagreement over the management of the company.

In the last example, however, the condition would only be satisfied if the disagreement would, as will usually be the case, have an adverse effect on the running of the trade. It would not be satisfied if the disagreement were, for example, over whether the company should discontinue trading and become an investment company, and the vending shareholder advocated the continuance of trading.

It may happen that the company wants, but cannot afford, to buy out a shareholder completely. In these circumstances, it is acceptable for the repurchase to proceed and for the shareholder to lend part of the consideration back to the company immediately after the purchase. Where the shares are of high market value and the issued capital is relatively small, this could result in the shareholder continuing to be 'connected with' the company (see below). To prevent this, it is acceptable for the company to make a bonus issue to increase its issued capital before the repurchase. (Revenue Tax Bulletin February 1996 p 281).

Where a shareholder is only 'substantially reducing' his interest (see below), the only situations in which HMRC envisage the condition being satisfied are where a complete disinvestment is to be achieved in a number of transactions, or where a small shareholding (not exceeding 5% of issued share capital) is retained for sentimental reasons.

A company is a '75% *subsidiary*' of another if not less than 75% of its ordinary share capital is beneficially owned directly or indirectly by the other company.

[*CTA 2010, s 1154; ICTA 1988, s 838*].

Condition B — Discharge of inheritance tax liability

Substantially the whole of the payment etc. (apart from any sum applied in paying capital gains tax on the disposal) must be used to meet the payee's inheritance tax liability on a death, within two years of that death, being a liability he could not have met without undue hardship other than through the purchase etc. of the shares or the purchase etc. of its own shares by another company within **63.3** above.

[*CTA 2010, s 1033; ICTA 1988, s 219(1)(b)*].

The further conditions which must be satisfied (as above) are as follows.

Conditions to be satisfied by the vendor

[63.5] The vendor (and any nominee holder) must be:

- resident and (except for companies) ordinarily resident in the UK in the year of assessment of the purchase etc. The residence and ordinary residence of trustees is determined as under *TCGA 1992, s 69* (see Tolley's Capital Gains Tax under Settlements), and that of personal representatives follows that of the deceased immediately before his death [*CTA 2010, s 1034*]; and
- the vendor must have held the shares for the five years ending with the date of purchase. If he acquired them under a will or intestacy, or as a personal representative, ownership by the deceased person (and, in the former case, by his personal representative) counts as ownership by the vendor, and the qualifying period is reduced to three years.

Similarly, where the shares were transferred to the vendor by his spouse or civil partner living with him at the time of transfer, the spouse's or partner's ownership counts as ownership by the vendor provided that the transferor either is still his spouse or partner living with him or is deceased at the time of the purchase etc. Where identification of different holdings of shares of the same class is necessary, earlier acquisitions are taken into account before later ones, and previous disposals identified with later acquisitions before earlier ones, for this purpose.

[*CTA 2010, ss 1055, 1056*].

Except in the case of certain shares allotted as stock dividends and falling within *CTA 2010, ss 1049–1051*; *ICTA 1988, s 249* (see Tolley's Income Tax under Savings and Investment Income), the time of acquisition of shares acquired through a reorganisation of share capital or conversion of securities etc. is that determined under *TCGA 1992, Pt IV, Ch II* (i.e. generally the date of acquisition of the original shares) (see Tolley's Capital Gains Tax under Shares and Securities).

Other conditions to be satisfied

Required reduction in the vendor's interest

[63.6] The vendor's shareholding must be substantially reduced or eliminated by the purchase. Where associates of the vendor are shareholders and the associate owns shares immediately after the purchase, the combined shareholdings of the vendor and his associates must be substantially reduced. However, this condition is relaxed if the vendor has agreed to the purchase in order for another vendor to satisfy the substantial reduction condition.

'Associate' includes spouse or civil partner and minor children, and a broad range of relationships whereby an individual or company may be able to influence the actions of another, or to benefit from the co-ordination of their actions.

[*CTA 2010, ss 1059, 1060*].

A shareholding is 'substantially reduced' if the proportion of the company's issued share capital held by him immediately after the purchase does not exceed 75% of that immediately before the purchase.

It is not regarded as so reduced if the share of profits to which the vendor would be entitled (beneficially except in the case of trustees or personal representatives) on a distribution of available profits by the company immediately after the purchase etc. exceeds 75% of the corresponding share immediately before the purchase etc.

Profits available for distribution by a company are as defined in *Companies Act 1985, s 263* (broadly, accumulated realised profits not distributed or capitalised less accumulated realised losses not written off) plus £100 plus, where any person is entitled to periodic distributions calculated by reference to fixed rates or amounts, the amount required to make the maximum distribution to which he would be entitled for a year.

[*CTA 2010, ss 1037, 1038*].

Reduction of a vendor's interest in a group situation

If the company making the purchase etc. is, immediately before that purchase etc., a member of a 'group of companies', and, immediately after the purchase etc., either:

- the vendor owns shares in other group member(s); or
- still owns shares in the company making the purchase etc. *and* had immediately before the purchase owned shares in other group member(s),

then the vendor's holding must be substantially reduced in relation to his interest in the group as a whole, taken as the average of his proportionate holdings of the issued share capital of the company purchasing the shares and of all other group members in which he holds shares immediately before or after the purchase. This includes, for averaging purposes, companies in which he held shares immediately before or after the purchase but in which he holds no shares when the average is to be determined.

A 'group of companies' for this purpose is a company (not a 51% subsidiary of any other company) and its 51% subsidiaries, except that a company which ceased to be a 51% subsidiary of another before the time of purchase of the shares is treated as continuing to be such a subsidiary if at that time there were arrangements in existence under which it could again become such a subsidiary.

Where the whole or a significant part of the business first carried on within three years before the purchase etc. by an unquoted company (see **63.3** above), the 'successor company', was previously carried on by the company purchasing the shares (or by a member of the same group), the successor company and any company of which it is a 51% subsidiary are treated as being members of the same group as the company purchasing the shares.

Where an associate of the vendor owns shares in any company in the same group as the company purchasing the shares immediately before the purchase, the combined interests of vendor and associate(s) must satisfy the substantial reduction test.

[*CTA 2010, s 1039*].

Where a vendor is connected with the company following the purchase

The vendor must not, immediately after the purchase, be 'connected with' the company purchasing the shares or any company in the same group.

He is so 'connected with' a company if, together with his associates he directly or indirectly possesses or is (or will be) entitled to acquire:

- more than 30% of its voting power, its issued ordinary share capital, or its issued share capital and loan capital (i.e. any debt incurred by the company for money borrowed, for capital assets acquired, for any right to income created in its favour or for insufficient consideration); or
- rights enabling him to more than 30% of its assets *available for distribution to the company's equity holders* (see **39.4 GROUP RELIEF**),

or if he has 'control' of it.

'*Control*' for this purpose means the power of a person by shareholding or voting power (whether directly or through another company), or under Articles of Association, to secure that the company's affairs are conducted according to his wishes. [*CTA 2010, s 1124; ICTA 1988, s 840*]. An interest in loan capital acquired in the normal course of a money-lending business is disregarded provided the lender takes no part in the management or conduct of the company.

[*CTA 2010, s 1042*].

Rights of the vendor after the purchase

The purchase must not be part of a scheme or arrangement the likely result of which is the acquiring by the vendor of rights such that, had he had them immediately after the purchase the above conditions could not have been satisfied. Any transaction within one year of the purchase is deemed to be part of a scheme of which the purchase is also a part.

[*CTA 2010, ss 1034–1143; ICTA 1988, ss 219(1)(a), 220–229*].

For a case where the above conditions, in particular condition in **63.6** above, were not met, see the case of *Preston Meats Ltd v Hammond* [2005] SSCD 90.

Simon's Taxes. See **D6.610–D6.617**.

HMRC information powers

[63.7] Within 60 days of making a payment treated by the company as not being a distribution under the provisions at **63.2** to **63.6** above, the company must notify the inspector of the particulars of the payment, and why it is regarded as falling within those provisions. If within **63.4** above, any person connected with the company who knows of any scheme or arrangement within 'Rights of the vendor after the purchase' in **63.6** must give details thereof to the inspector within 60 days of his coming to know of both the payment etc. and the scheme etc.

If the inspector has reason to believe that a payment treated by the company as being within the above provisions may form part of a scheme which:

- is set up mainly to allow participation in the company's profits without receiving a dividend, or to avoid tax; or
- results in the vendor acquiring rights such that, had he had them immediately after the purchase the substantial reduction conditions could not have been satisfied,

he may require the company or any person connected with it to furnish him, within not less than 60 days, with a written declaration as to whether, according to information reasonably obtainable, any such scheme exists or has existed and with such other information reasonably required by him as the company or person can reasonably obtain.

Any person receiving a payment treated as falling within the above provisions, or on whose behalf such a payment is received, may be required to notify as to whether he received the payment on his own or another's behalf and, in the latter case, to supply the other person's name and address.

Penalty provisions (see Tolley's Income Tax under Penalties) apply to returns required as above.

[*CTA 2010, s 1046; ICTA 1988, s 226*].

Clearance procedure

[63.8] A company may apply in writing for clearance from HMRC that a proposed transaction falls or, as the case may be, does not fall within the provisions at **63.2** to **63.6** above. HMRC must notify its decision within 30 days of receiving the application or, if further particulars are requested, within 30 days of the furnishing of the last such particulars. Such particulars must be requested within 30 days of the application (or of the furnishing of particulars previously requested), and must be supplied by the company within 30 days (or such longer period as HMRC may allow). Failure to supply full and accurate information voids any clearance. [*CTA 2010, ss 1044, 1045; ICTA 1988, s 225*].

Applications for clearance should be addressed to Clearance and Counteraction Team, Anti-Avoidance Group Intelligence, First Floor, 22 Kingsway, London WC2B 6NR (or, if market-sensitive information is included, to Team Leader at that address). Applications may be faxed to 020-7438 4409 or emailed to reconstructions@hmrc.gsi.gov.uk (after advising Team Leader if market-sensitive information is included). Application may be made in a single letter to the same address for clearance under *CTA 2010, s 1044; ICTA 1988, s 225* and under any one or more of *CTA 2010, s 1075; ICTA 1988, s 215* (demergers, see **31.37 GROUP RELIEF**), *CTA 2010, s 748; ICTA 1988, s 707* (transactions in securities, see **5.2 ANTI-AVOIDANCE**), *TCGA 1992, s 138(1)* (share exchanges, see Tolley's Capital Gains Tax under Anti-Avoidance), *TCGA 1992, s 139(5)* (reconstructions involving the transfer of a business, see **17.11 CAPITAL GAINS**), *TCGA 1992, s 140B* (transfer of a UK trade between EU member states, see **17.14 CAPITAL GAINS**), *TCGA 1992, s 140D* (transfer of non-UK trade between EU member states, see **17.21 CAPITAL GAINS**) and *CTA 2009, s 832* (see **48.27 INTANGIBLE ASSETS**).

The application should state whether the purchase, etc. is regarded as falling within *CTA 2010, s 1033; ICTA 1988, s 219* (see **63.4**), and give details of any earlier clearance applications (by the company or by a fellow group member). If the purchase etc. is regarded as within *CTA 2010, s 1033(2); ICTA 1988, s 219(1)(a)*, (see **63.4** above) the application must be in writing and should include:

(i) the name, tax district and reference number, and status (e.g. whether a trading company, etc) of the purchasing (etc.) company, and confirmation that it is unquoted;
(ii) full details of any group of which it is a member, and of company and (if appropriate) group shareholdings;
(iii) details of the proposed share purchase and of any other transactions between the company and vendor at or about the same time, and confirmation that the purchase is permitted by the company's Articles;
(iv) full details of any prior transactions and of the reasons for, and the benefits expected from, the purchase, etc.;
(v) confirmation, with any necessary calculations, etc., that the other conditions outlined in **63.6** above are satisfied; and
(vi) the company's latest available balance sheet and profit and loss account (and, in the case of a member of a group, those of any fellow group members and, if appropriate, of the group as a whole) together with a note of any later relevant and material changes.

However, if the purchase is regarded as within *CTA 2010, s 1033(3); ICTA 1988, s 219(1)(b)*, (see **63.4** above). The application should include the information as at (i) to (iv) and (vi) above, together with full details of the inheritance tax liability concerned and of the circumstances in which 'undue hardship' would arise.

An application for clearance that a proposed purchase, etc. does not fall within the provisions at **63.2** to **63.6** above should give full details of the purchasing company and of the proposed purchaser and be accompanied by a statement of the grounds on which clearance is sought.

If all details are not fully and accurately disclosed, the clearance will be void.

(HMRC Statement of Practice, SP 2/82)

[*CTA 2010, ss 1044, 1045*].

Returns and information

[63.9] Within 60 days of a payment falling within *CTA 2010, s 1033* being made, the company must make a return to HMRC giving details of it and the circumstances under which the company regards the payment as within *s 1033*.

Where the payment is other than for inheritance tax purposes, a person connected with the company must notify HMRC within 60 days if he knows of any scheme or arrangement wholly or mainly for the avoidance of tax.

If a company treats a payment as within *s 1033*, HMRC may require the recipient of the payment to state whether it is a nominee. If so, the name and address of the name and address of the person for whom he is acting must be provided. Similar powers apply where that person in turn is acting for another person.

Simon's Taxes. See **D6.605**.

'Treasury shares'

[63.10] The tax consequences of the acquisition by a company with share capital of its own shares are set out above. However companies may purchase and *hold* their own shares. These shares are known as 'treasury shares'. In these circumstances:

(a) The acquisition by the company of its own shares is not treated as the acquisition of an asset.

(b) The company is not treated as a member of itself by reason of the acquisition or holding of its own shares.

(c) (Subject to (f) below) the company's issued share capital is treated as reduced by the nominal value of the shares acquired.

(d) (Subject to (f) below) such of those shares as are not cancelled on acquisition are treated as if they had been so cancelled.

(e) Any subsequent cancellation of the shares by the company is disregarded (and so is not treated as a disposal of an asset and does not give rise to an allowable capital loss).

(f) Where the shares are issued to the company as bonus shares, i.e. as paid up otherwise than by the receipt of 'new consideration' (within *CTA 2010, s 1115; ICTA 1988, s 254*, see **31.13 DISTRIBUTIONS**), (c) and (d) above do not apply, and the shares are treated as not having been issued.

(g) Where, disregarding (a)–(f) above, a company holds any of its own shares and issues bonus shares in respect of any of those shares, these provisions do not prevent the existing shares from being the company's holding for the purposes of *TCGA 1992, s 126* (company reorganisations etc., see Tolley's Capital Gains Tax under Shares and Securities), although this does not apply where *s 126* is applied in a modified form by virtue of any other enactment.

(h) Where a company disposes of its own shares and, but for (a)–(f) above, would be regarded as holding the shares immediately before the disposal, (d), (e) and (f) above cease to apply in relation to the shares disposed of (the '*relevant shares*'), and:

- (i) the relevant shares are treated as having been issued by the company as new shares to the acquirer at the time of the disposal (and not as having been disposed of by the company at that time);
- (ii) the acquirer is treated as having subscribed for the shares an amount equal to the amount or value of the consideration (if any) payable for the disposal;
- (iii) if the amount or value of that consideration does not exceed the nominal value of the shares, the share capital of those shares is to be treated for the purposes of *CTA, Pt 23; ICTA 1988, Pt 6* (company distributions, etc.) as if it were an amount equal to the amount or value of the consideration; and
- (iv) if the amount or value of that consideration exceeds their nominal value, the shares are treated as if they had been issued at a premium representing that excess.

(i) Where a company purchases its own shares and the price payable is a trading expense (i.e. the company is a share dealer), (a)–(g) above do not apply, and (h) above does not apply to the disposal by the company of any of the shares.

[*FA 2003, s 195; SI 2003 No 3077; CTA 2009, Sch 1 para 565*].

64

Research and Development Expenditure

Simon's Taxes. See **D1.4**.

Introduction

[64.1] Relief is available for expenditure of a revenue nature on 'research and development' ('R&D'). There are two schemes:

- the small and medium-sized enterprise (SME) scheme; and
- the large company scheme.

The nature and rate of relief therefore depends on whether or not the company is an SME.

For the reliefs available to SMEs, see **64.5**, **64.8** and **64.9** below and for the relief available to 'large companies', see **64.10** below. The relief for SMEs has been increased for FY 2011 with qualifying expenditure now receiving a 200% deduction, subject to EU state aid approval. The changes introduced by the *FA 2011* will apply to expenditure incurred after 1 April 2011, and will be brought into force by Treasury Order.

Additional reliefs are available along similar lines for expenditure incurred on or after 22 April 2003 on research and development relating to certain vaccines or medicines. See **64.11** below. The *FA 2011* has introduced changes, reducing the vaccine relief available for SMEs for FY 2011, such change will be brought into force by Treasury Order.

A company may be eligible for relief under more than one type of relief in respect of the same expenditure. For provisions relevant to two or more categories of relief, see **64.2** below. See **64.14** below for claims procedures.

For reliefs for research and development expenditure of a capital nature, see **16.12 CAPITAL ALLOWANCES — MISCELLANEOUS.**

[*CTA 2009, Pt 13; see previously FA 2002, ss 53–56 and Schs 12, 13*].

HMRC guidance

HMRC publish guidance on research and development corporation tax relief on their website. The guidance covers all aspects of the scheme and includes an interactive calculator for working out R&D relief for SMEs. The guidance is available at www.hmrc.gov.uk/ct/forms-rates/claims/randd.htm.

Proposals for Reform and new Patent Box

R&D tax credits

The Corporate Tax Reform proposals published 29 November 2010 included further details of the consultation process with regard to R&D tax credits and consideration of the proposals put forward by the Dyson report. The Dyson review has raised concerns that the schemes may not be sufficiently well targeted. It proposes re-focusing them on hi-tech companies, small businesses and new start-ups as well as improving the ease with which the R&D tax credit can be claimed. The current document makes it clear that the government does not intend to restrict credits. The document does put forward areas for consultation (comments by 22 February 2011): amending the definition of R&D; introducing a statutory definition of production; which costs are to be eligible for relief; should internal use software relief be limited or excluded; should the claims process be improved, by offering a pre-clearance procedure. With only ten claims a year on average for vaccine research relief it is asked whether this should be abolished and support for such research given through other mechanisms. The *FA 2011* introduces some changes with regard to the rate for R&D relief for SMEs and the rate with regard to vaccine research, subject to EU state aid approval.

Further to this first round of consultation the government proposes: to amend the proposals with regard to subcontractors; externally provided workers; introduce a voluntary advance assurance scheme (with a proposed pilot scheme to run). Further consultation is open on questions as to: the current Qualifying Indirect Activities relief; relief for 'routine' activities of subcontractors; removal of PAYE/NIC cap; and the definition of a 'going concern'. Comments are requested by 2 September 2011.

Patent Box

It has been confirmed that a Patent Box regime will be introduced as from 1 April 2013. Proposals for the regime are under consultation, with draft legislation to be published in Autumn 2011. The regime will focus on patents, and not extend to other types of IP. The proposed rate of tax is to be 10% on net profits. Profits can arise from both patent royalty income and embedded income in the price of patented products. The proposals favour a formulaic approach to determination rather than using an arm's length approach per the OECD transfer pricing guidelines. It will apply to all patents first commercialised after 29 November 2010. Further consultation will be undertaken during 2011.

Further to this first round of consultation, various policy options were developed. Stage 2 of the consultation (from 30 June 2011) is open until 2 September 2011, and requests comments on: the ownership and development criteria for qualifying patents; calculation of arm's length profits attributable to patents; calculation of the patent box profits; technical/practical issues regarding the computational tax deduction; transfer pricing and double tax relief issues; and the proposed phase-in approach for transitional period.

Meaning of research and development

[64.2] For the purpose of the relief, the term *'research and development'* (*'R&D'*) means activities treated as such under generally accepted accounting practice (see **70.18 TRADE PROFITS — INCOME AND SPECIFIC TRADES**) [*CTA 2009, s 1041; ICTA 1988, s 837A*]. The definition also includes activities specified by Treasury regulations made under *ITA 2007, s 1006*. However, oil and gas exploration and appraisal (within *ICTA 1988, s 837B*) are expressly excluded [*TA 1988, s 837A(6)*]. Reference should also be made to the 2004 DTI guidelines, as referred to by HMRC, with regard to the definition of R&D which develops the definition found in SSAP 13/IAS 38. These can be found at HMRC manual CIRD81900.

These guidelines can also be found in **Tolley's Yellow Tax Handbook**, book 2, Misc IX which contains the DTI guidelines.

Relevant research and development

'Relevant research and development' in relation to a company is research and development either related to a trade carried on by the company or from which it is intended that such a trade will be derived. Research and development which may lead to or facilitate an extension of the trade and (except in relation to vaccine research relief) of a medical nature which has a special relation to the welfare of the workers employed in the trade are specifically included. [*CTA 2009, s 1042; FA 2000, Sch 20 para 4; FA 2002, Sch 12 para 17, Sch 13 para 5(1)(2)*].

'Small or medium-sized enterprise (SME)'

[64.3] As noted above, the relief available depends on whether or not the company is an SME.

Commission Recommendation 2003/361/EC of 6 May 2003 sets limits defining a micro, small or medium-sized enterprise. An SME must not exceed the thresholds. These limits apply for accounting ending on or after 1 January 2005 but are overridden for the purposes of R&D relief in relation to expenditure incurred on or after 1 August 2008 by limits sets by Treasury regulations. The Treasury limits are higher and bring more companies within the scope of the SME scheme. The thresholds are as shown in the table below.

	Limits applying to expenditure incurred on of after 1 August 2008
Number of employees	500
Annual turnover	€100 million
Balance sheet value	€86 million

In determining whether a company qualifies as an SME, its employee and financial figures must be aggregated with 100% of the figures for any 'linked enterprise' and with the amount of the figures for any 'partner enterprise' situated immediately 'upstream' or 'downstream' from it, proportionate to the percentage interest in the capital or voting rights (whichever is greater).

A '*linked enterprise*' is widely defined by the *Recommendation* but broadly covers enterprises where one has a majority of the voting rights in the other, has the right to appoint or remove the majority of the management of the other and has the right to exercise a dominant influence over the other. '*Partner enterprises*' are enterprises, other than linked enterprises, one of which (the '*upstream enterprise*') holds (solely or jointly with one or more linked enterprises) at least 25% of the capital or voting rights of the other (the '*downstream enterprise*').

A company will not qualify as an SME if at least 25% of its capital or voting rights are controlled by one or more public bodies. A company will still qualify as an SME if the 25% threshold is reached or exceeded by enterprises which are public investment corporations, venture capital companies, institutional investors (including regional development funds), universities or non-profit research centres, autonomous local authorities with an annual budget of less than €10 million and fewer than 5,000 inhabitants, or groups of individuals with regular venture capital investment activity who invest equity capital in unquoted businesses ('business angels'), provided the total investment of those investors in the same enterprise is less than €1,250,000.

A company is not an SME until it has satisfied these criteria over two consecutive accounting periods, and similarly does not cease to be one until it has ceased to fulfil the criteria over two accounting periods. However, this condition is disregarded in determining whether a company qualifies as an SME in an accounting period in which the limits for the employee or financial figures are exceeded where the company on its own does not exceed the limits but would do so if its figures were added to those of a partner or linked enterprise and the partner or linked enterprise would on its own exceed the limits. In determining whether a company qualifies as an SME in its first accounting period ending on or after 1 January 2005, the above provisions are treated as applying to the immediately preceding accounting period.

[*CTA 2009, ss 1120, 1121, Sch 2 para 118; FA 2000, Sch 20 para 2; SI 2004 No 3267; SI 2005 No 3376; SI 2008 No 1880*].

For accounting periods ending before 1 January 2005, a '*small or medium-sized enterprise*' is as defined in *Commission Recommendation 96/280/EC* of 3 April 1996 (although the Treasury may substitute another definition by order). [*FA 2000, Sch 20 para 2*, as originally enacted]. This requires that the company, together with any other company in which it holds more than 25% of the capital or voting rights, has less than 250 employees and either or both of annual turnover not exceeding €40 million and annual balance sheet total not exceeding €27 million. A company the capital or voting rights in which are owned as to more than 25% by enterprises not themselves small or medium-sized enterprises is excluded *unless* either those enterprises are public investment corporations, venture capital companies or institutional investors not exercising individual or joint control over the company in question, or the company's capital is spread in such a way that it is not possible to determine by whom it is held, and the company declares that it can legitimately presume that it is not owned as to 25% or more by an enterprise or enterprises which are not small or medium-sized. A company is not a small or medium-sized enterprise until it has satisfied these criteria over two consecutive financial years, and similarly does not cease to be one until it has ceased to fulfil the criteria over two financial years.

'Large company'

[64.4] A '*large company*' is a company which does not qualify as a small or medium-sized enterprise (as above). [*CTA 2009, s 1122; FA 2002, Sch 12 para 2; SI 2005 No 3376*].

R&D relief for large companies is given by *CTA 2009, Pt 13 Ch 5* ('Chapter 5 relief') — see further **64.10** below.

An insurance company (within *ICTA 1988, Pt 12 Ch 1*) carrying on life assurance or annuity business which would otherwise qualify as an SME is instead treated as a 'large company' for the purposes of the current provisions. [*CTA 2009, s 1081; FA 2002, Sch 12 para 12*]. This does not, however, apply for the purposes of vaccine research after 18 July 2007. [*FA 2002, Sch 13 para 22; FA 2007, Sch 10 para 16(1)(10)*].

SME relief — R&D incurred by SME

Conditions for relief

[64.5] An SME (see **64.1** above) is entitled to R&D tax relief under *CTA 2009, Pt 13 Ch 2* ('*Chapter 2 relief*') as described at **64.6** below for an accounting period in which it has 'total qualifying R&D expenditure' of not less than £10,000 (proportionately reduced for accounting periods of less than 12 months). For accounting periods beginning before 27 September 2003 the limit was £25,000.

A company's '*total qualifying R&D expenditure*' for an accounting period is the total of:

- its 'qualifying Chapter 2 expenditure' (in-house direct and contracted out R&D, see below);
- its 'qualifying Chapter 3 expenditure' (R&D subcontracted to the SME, see **64.8** below); and
- its 'qualifying Chapter 4 expenditure' (subsidised and capped R&D, see **64.9** below)

that is deductible in the period.

For this purpose, expenditure is deductible in an accounting period if it is allowable as a deduction in computing for corporation tax purposes the profits of a trade for the period (disregarding the pre-trading expenditure rules at **71.60 TRADING EXPENSES AND DEDUCTIONS** — see also **64.6** below). Qualifying Chapter 2 expenditure is also deemed to be deductible in an accounting period if it would have been allowable as a deduction had the company then been carrying on a trade consisting of the activities in respect of which the expenditure was incurred.

[*CTA 2009, ss 1044(1)–(3)(5), 1045(1)–(3), 1050; FA 2000, Sch 20 paras 1, 14(1); FA 2003, Sch 31 paras 1–3; FA 2008, Sch 29 para 8*].

Qualifying Chapter 2 expenditure

'*Qualifying Chapter 2 expenditure*' consists of 'qualifying expenditure on in-house direct R&D development' and 'qualifying expenditure on contracted out R&D'. Before *CTA 2009* took effect, it was an explicit requirement that expenditure must not be capital expenditure. This requirement has not, however, been included in the rewritten provisions, as *CTA 2009, s 53* prohibits a trading deduction for capital expenditure in any event.

Expenditure incurred by a company is '*qualifying expenditure on in-house direct R&D*' if:

(1) it is:
   - incurred on 'staffing costs';
   - (from 27 September 2003) 'qualifying expenditure on externally provided workers';
   - (from 1 April 2004) incurred on computer software or 'consumable items' (before that date, consumable stores); or
   - (from 1 August 2008) incurred on 'relevant payments' to subjects of a 'clinical trial';

(2) it is attributable to relevant R&D (see **64.1** above) undertaken by the company itself;

(3) any 'intellectual property' created as a result of the R&D is or will be vested in the company (either alone or with others). *F(No 3)A 2010, s 13* amends the provisions of *CTA 2009* and removes the intellectual property condition with effect for expenditure incurred by a company in an accounting period ending on or after 9 December 2009;

(4) the expenditure is not incurred in carrying on activities contracted out to the company by any other person (and see HMRC CIRD Manual at 84250 for what is considered to be subcontracting); and

(5) it is not subsidised (see further **64.9** below for relief in respect of subsidised and capped R&D).

Qualifying expenditure on contracted out R&D

A company's '*qualifying expenditure on contracted out R&D*' is expenditure incurred by it in making the 'qualifying element' of a 'subcontractor payment'. The expenditure must be attributable to relevant R&D undertaken on behalf of the company and must meet conditions (3)–(5) above.

[*CTA 2009, ss 1051–1053, Sch 2 paras 122(1), 123(1), 124(1); FA 2000, Sch 20 para 3; FA 2003, Sch 31 paras 1, 4; FA 2004, s 141(2); FA 2006, Sch 2 paras 1, 2; SI 2005 No 123; SI 2008 No 1878, Art 3*].

Staffing costs

For the purposes of (1) above, '*staffing costs*' are all employment earnings (other than benefits in kind), amounts (other than benefits in kind) paid to employees in respect of expenses, employer NICs (and, for expenditure incurred on or after 1 August 2008, equivalent contributions under the legislation of an EEA State), and employer pension contributions. Staffing costs are attributable to relevant R&D (and therefore meet condition (2) above) if paid to, or in respect of, directors or employees directly and actively engaged in the relevant R&D.

For expenditure incurred on or after 27 September 2003, the appropriate proportion of the staffing cost is allowable where the director or employee is only partly directly and actively involved in relevant R&D. For expenditure incurred before that date, if between 20% and 80% of a director's or employee's time is spent directly and actively so engaged, an appropriate proportion of the related staffing costs qualify. If less than 20% is so spent, none qualify, and if more than 80% the whole of the costs qualify.

Staff providing support services (e.g. secretarial or administrative services) are not thereby treated as engaged in the activities they support, although ancillary staff employed in a dedicated R&D facility (e.g. technicians, maintenance, clerical and security staff) may qualify.

FA 2004 clarifies (for expenditure on or after 1 April 2004) that benefits in kind are not to be included in staff costs (their being included in the definition of earnings for expenditure incurred in accounting periods ending on or after 6 April 2003 by virtue of *ITEPA 2003*).

[*CTA 2009, ss 1123, 1124, Sch 2 paras 119, 120, 121(1)(3); FA 2000, Sch 20 para 5; ITEPA 2003, Sch 6 paras 242, 245; FA 2003, Sch 31 paras 1, 5; FA 2004, Sch 17 para 7; FA 2008, s 27; SI 2003 No 2497; SI 2008 No 1930, Art 2*].

Qualifying expenditure on externally provided workers

A company incurs expenditure on externally provided workers if it makes a payment (a '*staff provision payment*') to another person (the '*staff provider*') in respect of the supply to the company, by or through the staff provider, of the services of externally provided workers. A person is an '*externally provided worker*' in relation to the company if:

(a) he is an individual;
(b) he is not a director or employee of the company;
(c) he personally provides, or is under an obligation personally to provide, services to the company under the terms of a contract between him and the staff provider by or through whom the services are supplied;
(d) he is subject to (or to the right of) supervision, direction or control by the company as to the manner in which those services are provided;
(e) the provision of the services to the company does not constitute the carrying on of activities contracted out by the company.

Such expenditure is attributable to relevant R&D (and therefore meets condition (2) above) to the extent that the externally provided workers are directly and actively engaged in such R&D. Services supplied in support of such activities carried on by others (e.g. secretarial or administrative services) are excluded. Except where the company and the staff provider are, or elect to be treated as if they were, connected persons (see further below), 65% of such staff provision payments are '*qualifying expenditure on externally provided workers*' for the purpose of (1) above.

Special provision is made where the company and the staff provider are connected persons within *CTA 2010, s 1122; ICTA 1988, s 839*. Provided that, in accordance with generally accepted accounting practice (see **70.18 TRADE PROFITS — INCOME AND SPECIFIC TRADES**), the whole of the staff provision payment and all of the staff provider's 'relevant expenditure' has been brought into account in determining the staff provider's profit or loss for a 'relevant period', the whole of the staff provision payment (up to the amount of the staff provider's 'relevant expenditure') qualifies. Any necessary apportionment of expenditure for these purposes is made on a just and reasonable basis.

'*Relevant expenditure*' is expenditure incurred by the staff provider on providing the externally provided workers, which is not of a capital nature and which is incurred on staffing costs or 'agency workers' remuneration'. A '*relevant period*' is a period of account ending not more than twelve months after the end of the period of account of the company in which, in accordance with generally accepted accounting practice, the staff provision payment is brought into account in determining the company's profit or loss. '*Agency workers' remuneration*' is remuneration receivable by an externally provided worker which is not employment income of that worker except under *ITEPA 2003, Pt 2 Ch 7* (agency workers).

The company and the staff provider may in any case jointly and irrevocably elect to be treated as connected for these purposes in relation to all staff provision payments paid under the same contract or other arrangement, such election to be made by written notice to HMRC within two years after the end of the company accounting period in which the contract or arrangement is entered into.

[*CTA 2009, ss 1127–1132, Sch 2 para 123(1); FA 2000, Sch 20 paras 8A–8E; FA 2003, Sch 31 paras 1, 6; SI 2003 No 2497*].

Consumable items

'*Consumable items*' are defined as consumable or transformable materials including water, fuel and power. Computer software and consumer items are attributable to relevant R&D (and therefore meet condition (2) above) if they are employed directly in relevant R&D. An appropriate portion of the costs are allowed if the software or consumable items are only partly so employed. Software or consumable items employed in the provision of secretarial, administration or other support services, in the support of other activities, are not to be treated as directly employed in those activities. Expenditure incurred before 1 April 2004 is incurred on consumable stores if so treated in accordance with generally accepted accounting practice (see **70.18 PROFIT COMPUTATIONS**), and it is attributable to relevant R&D if the stores are directly employed in relevant R&D.

[*CTA 2009, ss 1125, 1126, Sch 2 para 122; FA 2000, Sch 20 para 6; FA 2004, s 141(1); SI 2005 No 123*].

Relevant payments to subjects in a clinical trial

'*Relevant payments*' to subjects in a '*clinical trial*' are payments to those participating in an investigation in human subjects undertaken in connection with the development of a health care treatment or procedure. [*CTA 2009, s 1140; FA 2000, Sch 20 para 6A; FA 2006, Sch 2 para 1; SI 2008 No 1878*].

For the purposes of (3) above, with regard to expenditure incurred in an accounting period ending before 9 December 2009, '*intellectual property*' means:

- any industrial information or techniques likely to assist in the manufacture or processing of goods or materials, the working of, or winning access to, mines, oil wells or other mineral deposits, or the carrying out of any agricultural, forestry or fishing operations; and
- any patent, trade mark, registered design, copyright, design right or plant breeders' right, and any corresponding or similar rights under the law of a country outside the UK.

[*CTA 2009, s 1139; FA 2000, Sch 20 para 7*].

For the purposes of (5) above, expenditure is subsidised if a State aid notified to and approved by the European Commission is or has been obtained in respect of all or part of it (or if such aid is or has been obtained for any other expenditure attributable to the same R&D project). To the extent that some other grant or subsidy is obtained in respect of expenditure, or it is otherwise met directly or indirectly by any person other than the company, it is similarly excluded. Aid, grants, etc. not allocated to particular expenditure are for this purpose allocated in a just and reasonable manner. R&D tax reliefs within this chapter are not State aid for this purpose. [*CTA 2009, s 1138; FA 2000, Sch 20 para 8*].

Subcontractor payment

A '*subcontractor payment*' is a payment by a company to another person (the '*subcontractor*') in respect of R&D contracted out by the company to that person. Except where the company and the subcontractor are, or elect to be treated as if they were, connected persons (see below), the '*qualifying element*' of such a payment is 65% of it.

Special provision is made where the company and the subcontractor are connected persons within *ICTA 1988, s 839*. Provided that, in accordance with generally accepted accounting practice (see **61 PROFIT COMPUTATIONS**), the whole of the subcontractor payment and all of the subcontractor's 'relevant expenditure' has been brought into account in determining the subcontractor's profit or loss for a 'relevant period', the whole of the subcontractor payment is the qualifying element (up to the amount of the subcontractor's 'relevant expenditure'). Any necessary apportionment of expenditure for these purposes is made on a just and reasonable basis.

'*Relevant expenditure*' is expenditure on staffing costs, or software or consumable items (or, before 1 April 2004, consumable stores), or (for expenditure incurred on or after 1 August 2008) payments to subjects of a clinical trial, or (for expenditure incurred on or after 27 September 2003) externally provided workers, not of a capital nature, which is incurred by the subcontractor in carrying on, on behalf of the company, the activities to which the subcontractor payment relates, and which satisfies (6) above. A '*relevant period*' is a period of account ending not more than twelve months after the end of the period of account of the company in which, in accordance with generally accepted accounting practice, the subcontractor payment is brought into account in determining the company's profit or loss.

The company and the subcontractor may in any case jointly and irrevocably elect to be treated as connected for these purposes in relation to all subcontractor payments paid under the same contract or other arrangement, such election to be made by written notice to HMRC within two years after the end of the company accounting period in which the contract or arrangement is entered into.

[*CTA 2009, ss 1133–1136, Sch 2 paras 122(1), 123(1), 124(1); FA 2000, Sch 20 paras 9–12; FA 2003, Sch 31 para 7; FA 2006, Sch 2 para 1; SI 2008 No 1878, Art 2*].

Reliefs

[64.6] The R&D reliefs available to an SME take the form of:

- an additional deduction in calculating the profits of the trade; or
- a deemed trading loss.

Additional deduction in calculating profits

A company is entitled to corporation tax relief for an accounting period if it meets each of the conditions A to D as set out below [*CTA 2009, s 1044*].

Condition A is that the company is an SME in the period.

Condition B is that the company meets the R&D threshold in the period (see below).

Condition C is that the company carries on a trade for the period.

Condition D is that the company has 'qualifying Chapter 2 expenditure' (see above) which is allowable as a deduction in calculating the profits of the trade for the period for corporation tax purposes.

The relief, which must be claimed, is given in the form of an additional deduction in calculating the profits of the trade for the period. The additional deduction is 100% of the qualifying Chapter 2 expenditure. [*FA 2011, s 43*]. For expenditure incurred before 1 April 2011 the additional deduction is 75%. However, this is subject to the cap on R&D aid (see **64.9**). The provisions of *FA 2011* are subject to state aid approval and will come into force by Treasury Order.

Deemed trading loss

As an alternative to claiming a deduction for pre-trading expenditure, a company can elect for the relief to be given in the form of a deemed trading loss. However, it should be noted that an election cannot be made if the company is not a going concern (see **64.6**). Where an election is made, relief for pre-trading expenditure is given in this way instead of as a deduction under *CTA 2009, s 61*.

For the company to be entitled to relief in this manner, it must meet conditions A, B and C below [*CTA 2009, s 1045*].

Condition A is that the company is an SME in the period.

Condition B is that the company meets the R&D threshold in the period (see below).

Condition C is that the company has incurred qualifying Chapter 2 expenditure which is not allowable as a deduction in calculating for corporation tax purposes the profits of a trade carried on by it at the time that the expenditure was incurred, but would have been so allowable had it been carrying on a trade consisting of the activities in respect of which the expenditure was incurred.

The relief takes the form of a trading loss equal to 200% (175% for expenditure incurred before 1 April 2011) of the qualifying R&D expenditure. [*FA 2011, s 43*].

Unless the company is entitled to relief under these provisions for the preceding period, the trading loss cannot be set against the profits of that period under *CTA 2010, ss 37(3)(b)* or *42*. However, if the company begins in the accounting period or a later period to carry on a trade and the trade is derived from the research and development activities in respect of which the relief was obtained, the loss can be carried forward and set against future trading profits (under *CTA 2010, s 45*) to the extent that relief has not otherwise been given for the loss and it has not been surrendered as group relief (*CTA 2010, Pt 5*).

Restrictions apply where tax credit is claimed (see **64.7**).

Where an election is made for relief to be given as a deemed trading loss, the election must specify the accounting period for which it is made. The election, which must be in writing, must be made within two years of the end of the accounting period to which it relates [*CTA 2009, s 1047*].

Going concern condition

Relief is only available as an additional deduction or as a deemed trading loss if the going concern condition is met [*CTA 2009, s 1046*]. For these purposes, a company is a going concern if:

- its latest accounts were published on a going concern basis; and
- there is nothing in the accounts to indicate that they were only published on a going concern basis because the company would receive relief as outlined above or for vaccine research (see **64.11**) or tax credits as described at **64.7**.

Restriction on consortium relief

Where relief is claimed for qualifying Chapter 2 expenditure, either as an additional deduction in computing profits or as deemed trading loss, and at any time during the period the company is owned by a consortium in respect of which at least one of the members is a large company (see **64.4**), relief obtained for the R&D expenditure can only be surrendered to a member of the consortium for the purposes of a consortium group relief claim (under *CTA 2010, ss 132, 133*) if that company is an SME.

R&D threshold

The ability to claim relief for qualifying Chapter 2 expenditure, both as an additional deduction or as a deemed trading loss, is contingent on the company meeting the R&D threshold for the period. The threshold is set by *CTA 2009, s 1050*.

The R&D threshold is met if the company's total qualifying R&D expenditure for the period is at least £10,000 if the accounting period is a period of twelve months; if the accounting period is a period of less than twelve months, the total qualifying R&D expenditure must be at least equal to the amount found by the formula:

X/365 × £10,000

Where X is the number of days in the accounting period.

For the purposes of determining the threshold, a company's total qualifying R&D expenditure is the sum of:

- its qualifying Chapter 2 expenditure (see **64.4**);
- its qualifying Chapter 3 expenditure (see **64.8**); and
- its qualifying Chapter 4 expenditure (see **64.9**)

which is deductible in the period.

In determining whether expenditure is deductible in an accounting period, the following rules apply:

- qualifying Chapter 2 expenditure is treated as deductible if it is allowed as a deduction in calculating for corporation tax purposes the profits of a trade carried on by the company (ignoring pre-trading expenses treated as being incurred on the first day of the trade under *CTA 2009*, *s 61*), or would be so allowable were the company carrying on a trade at the time that the expenditure was incurred consisting of the activities in respect of which the expenditure was incurred; and

- qualifying Chapter 3 expenditure and qualifying Chapter 4 expenditure is deductible in an accounting period if it is allowable in calculating for corporation tax purposes the profits for the period of a trade carried on by the company.

[*CTA 2009, ss 1044–1050*].

Tax credits

[64.7] A company is entitled to an R&D tax credit for an accounting period in which it has a 'Chapter 2 surrenderable loss'. The tax credit must be claimed, but can only be claimed if the company is a going concern (see below). Where a claim is made, HMRC must pay the company the amount of the credit.

The R&D cap (see **64.9**) is also in point.

Chapter 2 surrenderable loss

A company has a '*Chapter 2 surrenderable loss*' if in an accounting period it obtains an additional deduction under *CTA 2009, s 1045* (see **64.6**) and makes a trading loss for that period or has deemed loss under *CTA 2009, s 1045* (see **64.6**).

Where relief for qualifying Chapter 2 expenditure is obtained by means of an additional deduction, the Chapter 2 surrenderable loss is so much of the trading loss as is unrelieved or, if less, 200% of the qualifying Chapter 2 expenditure in respect of which the relief was obtained. [*FA 2011, s 43*]. For expenditure before 1 April 2011 this was 175%. As noted above, these *FA 2011* rate changes will be brought in by Treasury Order.

Where relief is given for pre-trading expenditure by means of a deemed loss, the surrenderable Chapter 2 loss is so much of that deemed loss as is unrelieved.

The amount of the trading loss that is unrelieved is the amount of the loss as reduced by:

- any relief that was or could have been obtained by making a claim to deduct the loss from the profits of the accounting period under *CTA 2010, s 37(3)(a)*; or
- any other relief obtained by the company in respect of the loss, including relief under *CTA 2010, ss 37(3)(b)* or *42* against losses of an earlier accounting period; and
- any loss surrendered to members of a group or consortium under *CTA 2010, Pt 5*.

In determining the unrelieved amount of the loss, no account is taken of losses carried forward from an earlier accounting period (under *CTA 2010, s 45*) or carried back from a later accounting period (under *CTA 2010, s 37(3)(b)*).

Going concern condition

A claim for an R&D tax credit can only be made by a company at a time when it is a going concern. A company is a going concern for these purposes if its latest published accounts were prepared on a going concern basis and nothing in those accounts indicates that they were only prepared on a going concern basis on the expectation that a company would receive relief for Chapter 2 qualifying expenditure for vaccine research or R&D credits.

Amount of tax credit

The R&D tax credit to which a company is entitled is the lower of:

- 12.5% of the Chapter 2 surrenderable loss for the period (14% with regard to expenditure incurred before 1 April 2011); and
- the total amount of the company's PAYE and NIC liabilities for payment periods ending in the accounting period.

The percentage of the surrenderable loss can be changed by Treasury order. For expenditure incurred before 1 August 2008, the relevant percentage was 16%. *FA 2011* has reduced this percentage from 14% to 12.5% for expenditure incurred on or after 1 April 2011, such change to be brought in by Treasury Order.

For the purposes of working out the R&D tax credit, the total amount of the company's PAYE and NIC liabilities for the period is sum of amount A and amount B.

Amount A is the amount of income tax that the company is required to account for under PAYE to HMRC for the payment period (disregarding any deduction that the company is required to make in respect of child tax credit or working tax credit).

Amount B is the amount of Class 1 National Insurance contributions that the company is required to account for to HMRC for the payment period (disregarding any deduction for payments of statutory sick pay, statutory maternity pay, statutory paternity pay or statutory adoption pay).

Example

SME Ltd has the following results for the year ended 31 March 2012:

Trading loss	£170,000
Qualifying R&D	£45,000
PAYE/NIC liability	£85,000

The surrenderable loss is the lower of:

(i) £170,000
(ii) £45,000 × 200% = £90,000

i.e. £90,000

The tax credit given will be the lower of:

(i) 12.5% × £90,000 = £11,250

(ii) £85,000 (the NIC/ PAYE liability)

i.e. £11,250.

This tax credit of £11,250 will either be used to reduce SME Ltd's tax bill, if it has other sources of income or will be received as a tax free refund.

The trading loss of the company carried forward is now:

£170,000 – £90,000 = £80,000

For expenditure of £45,000 the company has received a refund of £11,250 which equates to 25% (11,250/45,000) or 200% × 12.5% = 25%.

The current proposals for change to the R&D system would remove this restriction of the tax credit to the company's total PAYE and NIC liability. It is envisaged these amendments would come into force as from April 2012.

Payment of tax credit

A payment in respect of an R&D credit is not treated as income of the company for any tax purpose [*CTA 2009, s 1061*].

The R&D tax credit and any associated interest thereon may be applied in discharging any liability of the company to corporation tax [*CTA 2009, s 1060(2)*].

In the event that there is an enquiry by HMRC into the company's tax return for the accounting period, the R&D credit need not be paid by HMRC until the enquiries are complete, although a provisional payment can be made if the HMRC officer thinks fit. Likewise, no R&D credit need be paid if the company has outstanding PAYE and NIC liabilities for the period. PAYE and NIC liabilities are regarded as outstanding for the period if the company has not paid to HMRC any amount that it is required to pay under the PAYE regulations [*SI 2003 No 2682*] or in respect of Class 1 National Insurance contributions for any payment period ending in the accounting period.

Restriction on losses carried forward

Where a company claims an R&D credit for an accounting period, the amount of the loss that is available to carry forward for relief against future trading profits (under *CTA 2010, s 45*) is treated as reduced by the amount of the surrenderable loss for the period. This is the amount of the Chapter 2 surrenderable loss in respect of which the company claims an R&D tax credit for the period [*CTA 2009, s 1062*].

[*CTA 2009, ss 1054–1062*].

SME relief — R&D subcontracted to SME

Conditions for relief

[64.8] An SME (see **64.1** above), that meets certain conditions is entitled to an additional deduction in calculating the profits of the trade for corporation tax purposes. The deduction for R&D subcontracted to the SME is given under *CTA 2009, Pt 13 Ch 3* and is additional to any Chapter 2 relief (see **64.5** above).

The availability of relief is contingent on conditions A, B and C, as set out below, being met.

Condition A is that the company is an SME in the period.

Condition B is that the company meets the R&D threshold in the period.

Condition C is that the company has qualifying Chapter 3 expenditure, which is allowable as a deduction for corporation tax purposes in calculating the profits for the period of a trade carried out by the company.

The relief, which must be claimed, takes the form of an additional deduction in calculating the profits of the trade for the period. The amount of the additional deduction is 30% of the qualifying Chapter 3 expenditure.

R&D threshold

The R&D threshold for an accounting period is met if qualifying R&D expenditure for the accounting period is at least £10,000 where the accounting period is a period of twelve months. Where the accounting period is less than twelve months, the R&D threshold is found by applying the formula:

X/365 × £10,000, where X is the number of days in the accounting period.

Total R&D expenditure

A company's '*total qualifying R&D expenditure*' for an accounting period is the total of:

- its 'qualifying Chapter 2 expenditure' (see **64.5** above);
- its 'qualifying Chapter 3 expenditure' (see below); and
- its 'qualifying Chapter 4 expenditure' (see **64.9** below)

that is deductible in the period.

For this purpose, expenditure is deductible in an accounting period if it is allowable as a deduction in computing for corporation tax purposes the profits of a trade for the period (disregarding the pre-trading expenditure provisions of *CTA 2009, s 61* (previously *ICTA 1988, s 401*) — see **71.60 TRADING EXPENSES AND DEDUCTIONS**).

[*CTA 2009, ss 1063(1)–(3), 1064; FA 2002, Sch 12 para 7; FA 2003, s 168, Sch 31 paras 11–13*].

Qualifying Chapter 3 expenditure

'*Qualifying Chapter 3 expenditure*' is expenditure incurred by the SME that meets conditions A and B below.

Condition A is that the expenditure is incurred on R&D that is contracted out *to* it either by a large company or by any person otherwise than in the course of a trade, profession or vocation (the profits of which are chargeable under *CTA 2009* or *ITTOIA 2005*).

Condition B is that the expenditure is expenditure that falls into one of the following two categories.

(i) *Expenditure on subcontracted R&D directly undertaken by the SME itself in-house.* This must meet the following additional conditions:
   (a) it must be incurred on staffing costs, or software or consumable items (or, before 1 April 2004, consumable stores) or (from 1 April 2006) relevant payments to subjects of a clinical trial; or (from 9 April 2003) be qualifying expenditure on externally provided workers (for which see **64.5** above, except that the abolition of the 20% and 80% limits on part-qualifying remuneration applies from 9 April 2003 rather than 27 September 2003); and
   (b) it must be attributable to 'relevant R&D' in relation to the SME (for which see **64.1** above).

(ii) *Expenditure on subcontracted R&D not undertaken in-house.* This must meet the following additional conditions:
   (a) it must be incurred in making payments to a 'qualifying body', an individual or a firm (i.e. a trading partnership) of individuals in respect of R&D contracted out *by* the SME to the body, individual or firm concerned;
   (b) it must be attributable to relevant R&D in relation to the SME; and
   (c) the R&D must be directly undertaken on behalf of the SME by the body, individual or firm concerned.

For the purposes of (ii)(a) above, a '*qualifying body*' is:

- a charity within *CTA 2009, s 1319* (see **20 CHARITIES**);
- an 'institute of higher education' within *Further and Higher Education Act 1992* (or Scottish or NI equivalent);
- a scientific research organisation within *ICTA 1988, s 508* (see **35.12 EXEMPT ORGANISATIONS**);
- a health service body within *ICTA 1988, s 519A* (see **35.11 EXEMPT ORGANISATIONS**); or
- any other body prescribed, or of a description prescribed, for the purpose by Treasury regulation.

[*CTA 2009, ss 1065–1067, 1142, Sch 2 paras 122(1)(2), 123(2); FA 2002, Sch 12 paras 8–10, 18; FA 2003, s 168, Sch 31 para 14; FA 2004, s 141; FA 2006, s 28, Sch 2 para 2; SI 2006 No 959, Art 5*].

SME relief — subsidised and capped R&D expenditure

Conditions for relief

[64.9] For accounting periods beginning on or after 9 April 2003, an SME (see **64.1** above), in addition to any Chapter 2 relief (see **64.5** above) and Chapter 3 relief (see **64.8** above), is entitled to R&D tax relief under *CTA 2009, Pt 13 Ch 4* ('*Chapter 4 relief*') in respect of subsidised and capped expenditure on R&D (see below).

The relief, which is given as an additional deduction in calculating the profits of the trade for corporation tax purposes, is available where conditions A, B and C below are met.

Condition A is that the company is an SME (see **64.1**) for the period.

Condition B is that the company meets the R&D threshold for the period.

Condition C is that the company has expenditure that is either qualifying Chapter 4 expenditure or capped R&D expenditure which is allowable as a deduction in calculating, for corporation tax purposes, the profits for the period of a trade carried on by the company.

The relief, which must be claimed, is given as an additional deduction in calculating profits for corporation tax purposes. The amount of the additional deduction is 30% of the qualifying Chapter 4 expenditure and the capped R&D expenditure.

The R&D threshold is as for Chapter 3 relief as set out at **64.8** above.

Qualifying Chapter 4 expenditure

'*Qualifying Chapter 4 expenditure*' is expenditure that meets conditions A to E below.

Condition A is that the expenditure is subsidised (see below).

Condition B is that the expenditure is:

- incurred on staffing costs;
- incurred on software or consumable items;
- qualifying expenditure on externally provided workers;
- incurred on relevant payments to the subjects of a clinical trial.

For what constitutes expenditure of this nature, see **64.5** above.

Condition C is that the expenditure is attributable to relevant research and development undertaken by the company itself.

Condition D is that any intellectual property created as a result of the research and development to which the expenditure is attributable is, or will be, vested in the company (whether alone or with other persons).

Condition E is that the expenditure is not incurred by the company in carrying on activities which are contracted out to the company by any person.

Subsidised expenditure

For the purposes of the relief, a company's expenditure is treated as subsidised [*CTA 2009, s 1138*]:

- if a notified State aid is, or has been, obtained in respect of the whole or part of the expenditure or any other expenditure, whenever incurred, attributable to the same research and development project;
- to the extent that a grant or subsidy (other than a notified State aid) is obtained in respect of the expenditure;

- to the extent that it is otherwise met directly or indirectly by a person other than the company.

For these purposes, notified State aid is State aid notified to and approved by the European Commission. However, the definition excludes relief and R&D tax credits given under *CTA 2009, Pt 13*.

Subsidised qualifying expenditure on contracted out R&D

For the purposes of the relief, subsidised qualifying expenditure on contracted out research and development is expenditure that is incurred by it in making the qualifying element of a subcontractor payment (see **64.8**) and which meets conditions A to F below.

Condition A is that the expenditure is subsidised (see above).

Condition B is that the subcontractor is a qualifying body, an individual or a firm, each member of which is an individual.

Condition C is that the body, individual or firm undertakes the contracted out research and development itself.

Condition D is that the expenditure is attributable to relevant research and development in relation to the company.

Condition E is that any intellectual property created as a result of the research and development to which the expenditure is attributable is or will be vested in the company (whether alone or with other persons).

Condition F is that the expenditure is incurred by the company in carrying out activities that are contracted out to the company by any person.

Capped R&D expenditure

A company's '*capped R&D expenditure*' is any expenditure in respect of which the company cannot claim Chapter 2 relief as a result only of the cap on R&D relief at **64.9** above. The expenditure must not be qualifying Chapter 3 expenditure (see **64.8** above) but must be expenditure which would have been qualifying Chapter 5 expenditure (see **64.10** below) had the company been a large company throughout the accounting period in question.

[*CTA 2009, ss 1068–1073; FA 2002, Sch 12 paras 10A–10C, 11; FA 2003, Sch 31 paras 15–17; FA 2008, Sch 8 para 2, Sch 10 para 9; SI 2008 No 1928, Art* 2].

Relief for large companies

Conditions for relief

[64.10] A large company is a company which is not an SME (as defined at **64.5**). A large company is entitled to R&D tax relief under *CTA 2009, Pt 13 Ch 5* ('*Chapter 5 relief*') for an accounting period if it meets conditions A, B and C below.

Condition A is that the company is a large company throughout the period.

Condition B is that the company meets the R&D threshold for the period.

Condition C is that the company carries on a trade in the period.

The relief, which must be claimed, is given as an additional deduction in calculating the profits of the trade for the period. The amount of the additional deduction is 30% of the 'qualifying Chapter 5 expenditure' (see below) which is incurred by the company and which is allowable as a deduction in calculating for corporation tax purposes the profits of the trade for the period.

[*CTA 2009, s 1074*].

R&D threshold

A company meets the R&D threshold for the accounting period if qualifying Chapter 5 expenditure for the period is at least £10,000 if the accounting period is a period of twelve months. Where the accounting period is less than twelve months, the qualifying R&D threshold is X/365 × £10,000, where X is the number of days in the accounting period.

[*CTA 2009, s 1075*].

Qualifying Chapter 5 expenditure

'*Qualifying Chapter 5 expenditure*' is expenditure in one of the following three categories. Before *CTA 2009* took effect, it was an explicit requirement that expenditure within (A) or (B) below must not be capital expenditure. This requirement has not, however, been included in the rewritten provisions, as *CTA 2009, s 53* prohibits a trading deduction for capital expenditure in any event.

(A) *Qualifying expenditure on in-house direct R&D.* This must meet the following conditions:

- (i) it must be incurred on staffing costs, or software or consumable items (or, before 1 April 2004, consumable stores), or (from 1 April 2006) relevant payments to subjects of a clinical trial; or (from 9 April 2003) be qualifying expenditure on externally provided workers (for which see **64.5** above, except that the abolition of the 20% and 80% limits on part-qualifying remuneration applies from 9 April 2003 rather than 27 September 2003);
- (ii) it must be attributable (see **64.5** above) to 'relevant R&D' (see **64.1** above) undertaken by the company itself; and
- (iii) if it is incurred in carrying on activities contracted out *to* the company, they must be contracted out *by* either another large company or any person otherwise than in the course of a trade, profession or vocation, the profits of which are chargeable as trading profits under *CTA 2009* or *ITTOIA 2005*.

(B) *Qualifying expenditure on contracted out R&D.* This must meet the following conditions:

  - (i) it must be incurred in making payments to a 'qualifying body' (see **64.8** above), an individual or a firm of individuals in respect of R&D contracted out *by* the company to the body, individual or firm concerned;
  - (ii) the body, individual or firm concerned must undertake the contracted out R&D itself;
  - (iii) the expenditure must be attributable to relevant R&D in relation to the company; and
  - (iv) if the contracted out R&D is itself contracted out *to* the company, it must be contracted out *by* either another large company or any person otherwise than in the course of a trade, profession or vocation, the profits of which are chargeable as trading profits under *CTA 2009* or *ITTOIA 2005*.

- (C) *Qualifying expenditure on contributions to independent R&D*. This must meet the following conditions:
  - (i) it must be incurred in making payments to a qualifying body, an individual or a firm of individuals for the purpose of funding '*funded R&D*', i.e. R&D carried on by the body, individual or firm concerned;
  - (ii) the funded R&D must be relevant R&D in relation to the company;
  - (iii) the funded R&D must not be contracted out *to* the body, individual or firm concerned by any other person; and
  - (iv) if the payment is made to an individual, the company must not, at the time of the payment, be connected with the individual within *ICTA 1988, s 838* (see **25 CONNECTED PERSONS**), and if it is made to a firm (other than a 'qualifying body'), it must not at that time be so connected with any member of the firm.

[*CTA 2009, ss 1076–1079; FA 2002, Sch 12 paras 4–6; FA 2003, s 168, Sch 31 para 10; FA 2004, s 141; FA 2006, s 28, Sch 2 para 2; SI 2006 No 959*].

See *CTA 2009, s 1080* for special provisions applying to insurance companies.

Vaccine research

Introduction to vaccine relief

[64.11] Subject to the necessary conditions being met, relief is available (under *CTA 2009, Pt 13 Ch 7*) for expenditure incurred by companies on research and development relating to vaccine or medicine research. Relief is available to both SMEs and large companies. With regard to SMEs the rate of relief has been reduced for expenditure incurred on or after 1 April 2011 by *FA 2011, s 43*.

[*CTA 2009, s 1085*].

Conditions for relief

Subject to the cap on R&D aid, a company is entitled to tax relief as described below for an accounting period for which its 'qualifying Chapter 7 expenditure' is not less than £10,000 (proportionately reduced for accounting periods of less than twelve months). For accounting periods beginning before 27 September 2003, the limit was £25,000.

For this purpose, expenditure is incurred 'for an accounting period' if:

- in the case of an SME (see **64.1** above), it is allowable as a trade deduction for that period (disregarding the pre-trading expenditure rules at **71.60 TRADING EXPENSES AND DEDUCTIONS**) or would be so allowable if, at the time of the expenditure, the company had been carrying on a trade consisting of the activities in respect of which it was incurred; or
- in the case of a company which is not an SME, it is allowable as a trade deduction for that period (including pre-trading expenditure so deductible by virtue of *CTA 2009, s 61*).

[*CTA 2009, ss 1087(1)(3), 1092(1)(3), 1097, 1099, 1100, Sch 2 para 115; FA 2002, Sch 13 paras 1(1), 2(2)(3); FA 2003, Sch 31 paras 20, 21; SI 2003 No 2497*].

Insurance companies

Before 19 July 2007, there were special provisions for reliefs and tax credits for insurance companies, and corresponding arrangements for clawback of relief, in such cases. [*FA 2002, Sch 13 paras 23, 25, 27(1); FA 2007, Sch 10 paras 16(10), 17(2)*].

Qualifying Chapter 7 expenditure

'*Qualifying Chapter 7 expenditure*' consists of 'qualifying expenditure on in-house direct R&D', 'qualifying expenditure on contracted out R&D' and, for expenditure incurred before 1 August 2008, 'qualifying expenditure on contributions to independent R&D'. Before *CTA 2009* took effect, it was an explicit requirement that expenditure must not be capital expenditure. This requirement has not, however, been included in the rewritten provisions, as *CTA 2009, s 53* prohibits a trading deduction for capital expenditure in any event.

Expenditure by a company is '*qualifying expenditure on in-house direct R&D*' if it meets the following conditions:

(i) it must be attributable to 'qualifying R&D activity' undertaken by the company itself;
(ii) the qualifying R&D activity to which it is attributable must be 'relevant R&D' (see **64.1** above) in relation to the company;
(iii) it must be incurred on staffing costs, or software or consumable items (or, before 1 April 2004, consumable stores), or (from 1 August 2008) relevant payments to subjects of a clinical trial; or (from 27 September 2003) must be qualifying expenditure on externally provided workers (see **64.5** above);

(iv) it must not be incurred in carrying on activities the carrying on of which is contracted out *to* the company by any person; and
(v) it must not be subsidised (see **64.5** above).

R&D is for these purposes '*qualifying R&D activity*' if it relates to:

- vaccines or medicines for the prevention or treatment of tuberculosis or malaria;
- vaccines for the prevention of infection by human immunodeficiency virus; or
- vaccines or medicines for the prevention of the onset, or treatment, of acquired immune deficiency syndrome resulting from infection by human immunodeficiency virus in clades A, C, D or E (or such other clade(s) as may be prescribed by Treasury order).

The Treasury may also make provision by regulations further defining the permissible areas of research. The vaccines or medicines must be for use in humans.

See **64.5** above for when different types of expenditure are 'attributable' to R&D.

Expenditure by a company is '*qualifying expenditure on contracted out R&D*' if it meets the following conditions:

(a) it must be the 'qualifying element' of a 'subcontractor payment' (see below);
(b) it must be attributable to qualifying R&D activity undertaken by the subcontractor itself;
(c) the qualifying R&D activity to which it is attributable must be relevant R&D in relation to the company;
(d) it must not be subsidised.

As regards (b) above, a 'subcontractor payment' is defined as at **64.5** above. Where the subcontractor is a charity (see **20 CHARITIES**), a scientific research organisation within *ICTA 1988, s 508* (see **35.12 EXEMPT ORGANISATIONS**) or a university and the expenditure is incurred before 1 August 2008, the 'qualifying element' is the whole of the payment. Otherwise, the qualifying element is as stated at **64.5** above. Note that the normal time limit for giving notice of an election for connected persons treatment under *CTA 2009, s 1135* does not apply if the subcontractor is a charity, university or scientific research organisation provided that the notice is given before 1 August 2009.

A company's '*qualifying expenditure on contributions to independent R&D*' is expenditure meeting the following conditions:

- it must be incurred on payments made to a charity within *FA 2010, Sch 6 para 1; ITA 2007, s 519; ICTA 2010, s 467; ICTA 1988, s 506(1)* (see **20 CHARITIES**), a scientific research organisation within *CTA 2010, s 469; ICTA 1988, s 508* (see **35.12 EXEMPT ORGANISATIONS**) or a university, for the purpose of funding qualifying R&D activity carried on by the body concerned;
- that activity must be relevant R&D related to a trade carried on by the company.

[*CTA 2009, ss 1086, 1098, 1101, 1102, Sch 2 paras 117, 122(1)(2), 123(4), 124(5); FA 2002, Sch 13 paras 2(1), 3, 4, 6–12; FA 2003, Sch 31 paras 20, 22, 24; FA 2004, s 141(2); FA 2006, Sch 2 para 3; FA 2008, s 27; SI 2003 No 2497; SI 2005 No 123; SI 2008 No 1878, Art 2; SI 2008 No 1930, Art 2*].

Reliefs — SMEs

[64.12] Where an SME (see **64.1** above) qualifies for vaccine research relief, the following reliefs are available, subject to the going concern condition below.

(i) Where the company is carrying on a trade in an accounting period and it has qualifying Chapter 7 expenditure (see **64.11** above) which is for that period (see **64.11** above), the company can claim an additional deduction of 20% of that expenditure (i.e. giving a total deduction of 120% of the expenditure). For expenditure incurred before 1 April 2011 this was an extra 40%, giving a total deduction of 140%. As noted above, these changes brought in by *FA 2011, s 43* will come into force by Treasury Order.
This is in addition to any deduction also available for an SME under other R&D provisions, so it is possible for a SME to obtain an enhanced deduction of 200% for expenditure under Chapter 2, and also an additional 20% under the vaccine research provisions (giving an overall total of 220%).
For expenditure incurred before 1 August 2008, the additional deduction is 50% of the expenditure (i.e. a total deduction of 150%). For expenditure incurred before 1 April 2007, the additional deduction is 50% of so much of the expenditure as also gives rise to Chapter 2 relief and 150% of so much of the expenditure as does not do so. Expenditure taken into account in determining the amount of the deduction can include pre-trading expenditure which is unrelated to the trade carried on in the period (but which is nevertheless qualifying Chapter 7 expenditure for the period).
If the company is a 'larger SME' (see **64.1** above) and obtains an SME tax credit (see **64.6**(c) above) for the period, the additional deduction is restricted to 20% of so much of the qualifying Chapter 7 expenditure as does not qualify for Chapter 2 relief (see **64.5** above). For expenditure incurred before 1 April 2011 this additional deduction was 40%.
[*CTA 2009, ss 1087(1)(2)(4)–(7), 1089, 1090, Sch 2 paras 112(1)(3), 118; FA 2002, Sch 13 paras 14, 15A; FA 2007, ss 49, 50; FA 2008, Sch 8 para 3, Sch 9 para 2; SI 2008 No 1929, Art 2; SI 2008 No 1933, Art 2*].

(ii) Where, in an accounting period, a company which is not carrying on a trade incurs qualifying Chapter 7 expenditure which is *not* allowable as under (i) above, but which would have been so allowable had the company then been carrying on a trade consisting of the activities in respect of which the expenditure was incurred (i.e. where the company incurs pre-trading expenditure), the company may elect to be treated as having incurred a trading loss in the accounting period equal to **20%** (40% for expenditure incurred before 1 April 2011, 50% for expenditure incurred before 1 August 2008) of so much of the expenditure as also qualifies for Chapter 2 relief (see **64.5** above) and **120%** (140% for expenditure incurred before 1 April 2011, 150% for expenditure incurred before 1 August 2008) of so much of the expenditure as does not do so. For expenditure incurred before 1 April 2007, the loss is restricted to 50% of the expenditure only where Chapter 2 relief is actually obtained.

If the company is a 'larger SME' (see **64.1** above) and obtains an SME tax credit (see **64.6**(c) above) for the period, the deemed trading loss is restricted to 120% (140% for expenditure incurred before 1 April 2011) of so much of the expenditure as does not qualify for Chapter 2 relief.

As noted above, the changes applicable to expenditure from 1 April 2011 are brought in by *FA 2011, s 43*, which section will come into force by Treasury Order.

Relief for the loss may be claimed in the usual ways (see **55 LOSSES**). The pre-trading expenditure rules of *CTA 2009, s 61* (see **71.60 TRADING EXPENSES AND DEDUCTIONS**) do not then apply to treat the expenditure as incurred on the first day of trading. Such an election must be made in writing to HMRC, specifying the accounting period to which it relates, within two years after the end of that period.

The trading loss may not be carried back to an earlier accounting period under *CTA 2010, s 37(3)(b)* (see **55.4 LOSSES**) unless the company is entitled to relief under this provision for the earlier period. If and when the company begins, in the same or any subsequent accounting period, to carry on a trade derived from the R&D in relation to which the relief was obtained, the loss (to the extent not otherwise relieved or surrendered) is treated as if it were a trading loss brought forward to that period under *CTA 2010, s 45* (see **55.5 LOSSES**).

[*CTA 2009, ss 1092(1)(2)(4)–(9), 1093, 1095, 1096, Sch 2 paras 112(1)(3), 118; FA 2002, Sch 13 paras 15, 15A; FA 2007, ss 49, 50; FA 2008, Sch 8 para 3, Sch 9 para 2; CTA 2010, Sch 1 para 660; SI 2008 No 1929, Art 2; SI 2008 No 1933, Art 2*].

(iii) Where a company has a 'Chapter 7 surrenderable loss' for an accounting period, it may instead claim an 'R&D tax credit' equal to 16% of the amount of that loss. There is, however, a limit on the total of the tax credits under this provision and those under **64.6**(c) above, which must not exceed the company's total PAYE and Class 1 NICs liability for payment periods (i.e. periods ending on the fifth day of each month for which liability to account for PAYE and NICs arises) ending in the accounting period. The 16% figure is subject to revision by the Treasury by order. PAYE and Class 1 NICs liabilities are determined for this purpose disregarding any deduction in respect of child tax credit or working tax credit, and for Class 1 NICs, deductions in respect of statutory sick pay and statutory maternity pay are also disregarded.

A '*Chapter 7 surrenderable loss*' arises for an accounting period where either (i) above applies and the company incurs a trading loss in the accounting period in the trade concerned, or (ii) above applies and the company is thereby treated as incurring a trading loss.

Where (i) above applies, the amount of the surrenderable loss is the lower of so much of that trading loss as is 'unrelieved' and the sum of the total amount deductible under (i) above and so much of the company's qualifying Chapter 7 expenditure for the period as does not qualify for Chapter 2 relief. Where the company is a 'larger SME' (see **64.1** above), the amount of the surrenderable loss is the lower of the unrelieved part of the loss and 120% of so much of the company's qualifying Chapter 7 expenditure for the period as does not qualify for Chapter 2 relief. Where (ii) above applies, the amount of the surrenderable loss is so much of the trading loss as is unrelieved.

For expenditure incurred before 1 April 2007, the amount of the surrenderable loss is the lower of so much of the loss as is unrelieved and the total amount deductible under (i) or (ii) above, as the case may be.

A trading loss is '*unrelieved*' for this purpose to the extent that the loss has not and could not have been relieved by a claim under *CTA 2010, s 37(3)(a)* (against profits of the same period, see **55.3 LOSSES**), and has not otherwise been relieved (including under *CTA 2010, s 37(3)(b)* against profits of earlier periods, see **55.4 LOSSES**), has not been surrendered under *CTA 2010, Pt 5* (group or consortium relief, see **39.2** onwards **GROUP RELIEF**), and has not been surrendered for R&D tax credit as a Chapter 2 surrenderable loss (see **64.6** above). Losses carried back or brought forward to the accounting period in question are disregarded for this purpose.

See **64.14** below as regards claims for such tax credits. On such a claim, HMRC will pay to the company the amount of the tax credit, and the amount of the company's trading losses available to be carried forward from the period is accordingly reduced by the surrenderable loss for the period (or by a corresponding proportion thereof where the amount of the credit was less than 16% of the surrenderable loss). The payment is not treated as income for any tax purposes, and (together with any interest paid with it) may be applied to any corporation tax liability of the company. Where there is an enquiry into the company's tax return for the period (see **66.19 RETURNS**), payment need not be made until the enquiry is completed (although HMRC have discretion to make a payment on a provisional basis if they think fit). Similarly payment need not be made until all the relevant PAYE and NICs payments (as above) have been made.

[*CTA 2009, ss 1103–1105, 1107–1111; FA 2002, Sch 13 paras 16–18, 19, 20; FA 2007, ss 49, 50; FA 2008, Sch 8 para 3, Sch 9 para 2; CTA 2010, Sch 1 para 661; SI 2008 No 1880, Art 2; SI 2008 No 1929, Art 2; SI 2008 No 1933, Art 2*].

The above reliefs are subject to the cap on R&D aid at **64.9** above.

Going concern condition

If a claim under (i) or (iii) above, or an election under (ii) above, is made on or after 1 August 2008, it can only be made at a time when the company is a 'going concern'.

If a company ceases to be a going concern after a claim under (iii) above is made, it is treated as if it had not made the claim and as if there had been no payment of R&D tax credit to carry interest under *ICTA 1988, s 826*. This provision does not, however, apply to the extent that the claim relates to an amount that was paid or applied before the company ceased to be a going concern.

For this purpose, a company is a '*going concern*' if its latest 'published' accounts were prepared on a going concern basis, and the justification for this treatment was not solely that the company would receive R&D tax credits. '*Published*' has the same meaning as in *Companies Act 2006, s 436(2)*.

[*CTA 2009, ss 1094, 1106; FA 2002, Sch 13 para 18A; FA 2008, s 28, Sch 9 para 2; SI 2008 No 1929, Art 2*].

Reliefs — large companies

[64.13] Where a large company (see **64.1** above) is carrying on a trade in an accounting period and it has qualifying Chapter 7 expenditure (see **64.11** above) which is for that period (see **64.11** above), the company can claim a deduction, in computing the profits of that trade for:

- an additional **40%** (50% for expenditure incurred before 1 August 2008) of so much of the qualifying Chapter 7 expenditure for the period as is allowable as a deduction in computing the profits of that trade; and
- **140%** (150% for expenditure incurred before 1 August 2008) of so much of the qualifying Chapter 7 expenditure as is not so allowable.

The deduction is in addition to any other deduction in respect of the expenditure.

For claims made on or after 1 August 2008, a claim must include a declaration that the relief has enabled an increase in:

(a) the amount, scope or speed of the R&D undertaken by the company; or
(b) the company's expenditure on R&D.

The above relief is subject to the cap on R&D aid at **64.9** above.

[*CTA 2009, ss 1087(1)(2)(4)–(8), 1088, 1091, Sch 2 para 112(1)(3); FA 2002, Sch 13 para 21; FA 2008, s 30*].

Claims

[64.14] For accounting periods ending on or after 31 March 2006, a claim for R&D tax relief must be made in a company tax return (or amended return) (see **66.4 RETURNS**) for the accounting period for which the claim is made, within one year of the filing date for that return (see **66.9 RETURNS**) or by such later time as HMRC may allow. It can similarly only be amended or withdrawn by amendment of the company tax return within the same time limit. It must specify the quantum of the amount claimed.

For accounting periods ending before 31 March 2006, a claim for payment of an R&D tax credit (under **64.5**(c) or **64.12**(iii) above) must be made (amended or withdrawn) in a company tax return (or amended return) for the accounting period for which the credit is claimed within the same time limits. Claims for enhanced deductions could be made under the normal rules within six years from the end of the accounting period to which they related (see **15.1 CLAIMS**). Under transitional provisions, claims for enhanced deductions relating to accounting periods ending after 31 March 2002 and before 31 March 2006 must be made, amended or withdrawn at any time up to 31 March 2008 or by such later time as HMRC may allow.

Penalties apply in relation to incorrect claims (see **60.2 PENALTIES**).

[*FA 1998, Sch 18 paras 10(2)(2B)(3), 83A–83F, 83LA–83LE, 83M–83R; FA 2002, Sch 14 paras 2, 4; FA 2006, Sch 3 paras 2–11; FA 2008, Sch 40 para 21(f); CTA 2009, Sch 1 para 454(3)(7)(8)(10)(11)*].

For recovery of overpayments of tax credits, see **7.4 ASSESSMENTS**.

Late claims should be dealt with in accordance with HMRC Statement of Practice 5/01 (HMRC CIRD Manual 81800).

The minutes of the November 2010 R&D Consultative Committee meeting were published on 11 January 2011. Some notable points were made with regard to claims and online filing. HMRC clarified that online filing would make no changes to the responsibility of the company and its agents. Any claim for R&D relief should be made by completing and submitting a company tax return, or by amending a return already submitted. From 1 April 2011 new returns will be made online, and so will the R&D claim within such return.

However, it remains possible for a company to amend a company tax return in any form it sees fit, including amending a return to make a claim for R&D relief. This could be done by letter. In particular it will not be mandatory for amendments to company tax returns to be made online. Thus where a company has one agent dealing with its general CT affairs, and another dealing with its R&D claims, then the R&D agent can continue to submit the claim to R&D relief as an amendment of the company tax return in writing (so issues surrounding the implications of different agents using different software should not arise).

Key points

[64.15] Points to consider are as follows.

- In order to claim enhanced relief for R&D expenditure the company needs first of all to identify qualifying R&D projects. These are projects that extend the bounds of scientific or technological understanding within the wider relevant community, and not projects that seek to expand the company's own knowledge in the area concerned.
- Scientific or technological research must be carried out on a systematic basis by staff that have requisite knowledge and expertise.

- The development of a new product may involve a number of R&D projects that qualify for enhanced relief as well as projects that do not have sufficient innovation to qualify. However, it is possible that the development of a prototype can be regarded as an R&D project that can qualify for the enhanced relief.
- Only certain categories of expenditure can qualify for enhanced relief, principally staff costs and consumables. Subcontracted R&D costs are subject to special rules, and often only 65% of such costs can be used in a claim for enhanced relief.
- Proper presentation of a claim, including the provisions of all relevant information, is essential to maximise the chances of acceptance. HMRC are likely to ask for timesheets or similar time recording to establish what proportion of employment costs are eligible for the enhanced relief, by looking at the time spent on qualifying R&D projects.
- Capitalised revenue expenditure that falls within one of the allowable categories can be claimed when incurred, rather than when it is released to Profit & Loss Account.
- Capital expenditure in connection with R&D may qualify for 100% first year allowances.
- The rate of enhancement and some of the detailed rules vary dependent on whether the claimant company is a small or medium sized entity or a large entity. The rules for establishing the size of a company for this purpose are complex, based on the Commission Recommendation 2003/361/EC of 6 May 2003. Linked and partner enterprises must be taken into account to determine the size of a company, which gives rise to difficulties where, for example, the claimant company has a bank or venture capital fund as a shareholder. What may look like an SME could turn out to be large.
- A claim for relief by an SME will not be accepted if a company was not a going concern when the claim was made, or if it ceases to be a going concern before the claim is processed.
- It is possible to claim a repayment linked to enhanced R&D expenditure, but this is capped at the amount of PAYE and NIC paid by the company. Furthermore, this is only a preferred option if the company is unlikely to be able to use the enhanced relief as part of a loss relief claim, as the rate at which the refund is made is less than the small company rate of corporation tax.
- *FA 2011* has increased the deduction for R&D relief for SMEs to 200%, however, it has reduced the tax credit available for such companies to 12.5% and has also reduced the additional vaccine research deduction for SMEs from 40% to 20%. This is subject to EU state aid approval and will come into force by Treasury Order.

65

Residence

Cross-references. See **5.12, 5.13 ANTI-AVOIDANCE; 8.5 BANKS; 17.13, 17.48 CAPITAL GAINS; 27 CONTROLLED FOREIGN COMPANIES; 31.6 DISTRIBUTIONS; 32 DOUBLE TAX RELIEF; 36 EXCHANGE GAINS AND LOSSES; 39.23 GROUP RELIEF; 72 TRANSFER PRICING.** For special rules concerning disposals of certain interests in offshore funds, see **57 OFFSHORE FUNDS.**

Simon's Taxes. See D4.1.

Introduction

[65.1] The question of a company's residence is important in that it will determine the extent to which the company is within the charge to UK corporation tax. UK resident companies are taxable on their worldwide income. Non-resident companies will be chargeable to UK corporation tax only if they are carrying on a trade in the UK through a permanent establishment [*CTA 2009, s 5*]. Special rules apply to European Companies, see further below.

The residence of companies in the UK was historically decided by case law (based on the concept of management and control of the company) until legislation was introduced by the *Finance Act 1988* (now found within *CTA 2009*) which introduced a test of residence for tax purposes based on incorporation which took effect from 15 March 1988. Residence status for the purposes of a Double Tax Arrangement did not affect residence for UK tax purposes until provisions were introduced in this respect by the *Finance Act 1994* (see below).

This chapter considers the tests for residence within UK tax law, and includes an examination of the position of non-resident companies with UK permanent establishments, UK representatives of such non-resident companies, and migration of companies from the UK.

Residence

The incorporation test

[65.2] A company incorporated in the UK is regarded for the purposes of the *Corporation Tax Acts* as resident there, irrespective of any rule of law giving a different place of residence [*CTA 2009, s 14*].

Certain transitional provisions were enacted with regard to companies carrying on business before the commencement of *FA 1988*. Therefore this 'incorporation test' does not apply in the following circumstances:

(a) Where, immediately before 15 March 1988, a company was carrying on business and was not UK resident, having ceased to be so resident in pursuance of a Treasury consent given under *ICTA 1988, s 765* (or any predecessor legislation), and, where the consent was a general consent, the company was liable, by reason of domicile, residence or place of management, to tax on income in a territory outside the UK. If, after 14 March 1988, the company ceases to carry on business or, where the consent was a general consent, ceases to be taxable in a territory outside the UK, the incorporation test applies after that time (or after 14 March 1993 if later).

(b) Where a company which carried on business at any time before 15 March 1988 ceased to be UK resident after 14 March 1988 in pursuance of a Treasury consent, and immediately thereafter carried on business. If, after ceasing to be UK resident, the company at any time ceases to carry on business, the incorporation test applies after that time (or after 14 March 1993 if later).

(c) Where a company not within (a) above carried on business at any time before 15 March 1988, and was not UK resident immediately before that date, the incorporation test applies only after 14 March 1993.

(d) Where a company not within (b) above carried on business at any time before 15 March 1988, and ceases to be UK resident on or after that date in pursuance of a Treasury consent, the incorporation test applies only after 14 March 1993.

If a company within (a)–(d) above becomes UK resident at a time after 14 March 1988, the incorporation test applies to it after that time.

Residence for the purposes of (a)–(d) above is determined without reference to the incorporation test.
[*CTA 2009, s 14, Sch 2 paras 13–15; FA 1988, s 66(1), Sch 7*].

A company which is no longer carrying on any business, or is being wound up outside the UK, is treated as continuing to be resident in the UK if it was regarded as so resident immediately before it ceased business or any of its activities came under the control of the foreign equivalent of a liquidator. [*CTA 2009, s 15; FA 1988, s 66, (2)*].

HMRC International Manual INTM120040 and SP 1/90 clarifies HMRC's interpretation of three points in relation to the above rule:

(i) As regards whether a company is 'carrying on business' at a particular time, 'business' has a wider meaning than 'trade', and can include, for instance, the purchase of stock prior to trading, or the holding of investments (which could include the holding of shares in a subsidiary company, or a holding consisting of a single non-income producing investment). A company (e.g. a 'shelf' company) whose transactions have been limited to those formalities necessary to maintain its registration is not regarded as having carried on business. Where, in terms of the application of general case law to the question of residence (see **65.3** below), a company can demonstrate that it is or was resident outside the UK by reference to the place 'where its real business is carried on', it will have carried on business for the above purposes.

(ii) As regards the requirement under (a) that a company be taxable in a territory outside the UK, the liability must be to tax on income, so that liability to a flat rate fee or lump sum duty does not fulfil the test. It is, however, satisfied where the company is within the charge to tax, even though it may pay no tax because, for example, it makes losses or claims double taxation relief.

(iii) The exceptions granted to companies who have ceased to be resident in pursuance of a Treasury consent do not apply to companies who ceased to be resident without Treasury consent but who were subsequently informed by letter that no action would be taken against them.

Companies becoming resident under the above provisions are under an obligation to notify chargeability (see **60.4 PENALTIES**) where appropriate, whether or not notice has been served requiring a return (see **66.4 RETURNS**).

Interaction with Double Tax Arrangements

It is possible for a company to be treated as dual resident for tax purposes. For example, a company might be incorporated within the UK, and so be UK resident, but also resident outside the UK under the rule of law of a foreign territory. In such a case UK tax law states that the company continues to be treated as UK resident, save where the provisions of an applicable double tax arrangement are in point.

Double tax arrangements generally have a tie-breaker rule to resolve issues of dual residence of companies. Where a company which would otherwise be regarded as UK-resident (whether under *CTA 2009, s 14, 15, 16* or *17* or earlier equivalents or by virtue of some other rule of law), is regarded for the purposes of any double taxation arrangements under *TIOPA 2010, s 2, s 6; ICTA 1988, s 788* as resident in a territory outside the UK (and as not UK-resident), then it is treated for UK tax purposes as resident outside the UK and as not UK-resident.

See further Revenue Tax Bulletin December 1994 p 179 for a list of double tax agreements to which this is applicable. It is assumed for this purpose that the company has made a claim for relief under the arrangements, in consequence of which a decision falls to be made as to its residence status thereunder.

The above rules for determining the residence of companies, also applies for the purposes of *TMA 1970 and TCGA 1992*. [*TMA 1970, s 109A; CTA 2009, Sch 1 paras 308, 384*].

[*CTA 2009, s 18; FA 1994, s 249; F(No 2)A 2005, s 60(2)*].

See generally Revenue Tax Bulletin December 1994 pp 179–181 for the application in practice of the above rule and revenue manuals INTM 120070 and 120080. There is an exception in the case of the controlled foreign company provisions where such company would still be regarded as UK resident [*ICTA 1988, s 747(1B)*] — see further **27 CONTROLLED FOREIGN COMPANIES.**

European Companies (SEs)

An SE (a European Company — see **34.5 EUROPEAN UNION LEGISLATION**) which transfers its registered office to the UK on or after 1 April 2005 in accordance with *Council Regulation (EC) 2157/2001, Art 8* is regarded upon registration in the UK as resident in the UK for tax purposes. Notwithstanding that a different place of residence may be given by any rule of law, the SE is not considered resident in that place for UK corporation tax purposes.

Under these provisions the SE will not lose its UK residence status by reason only of a later transfer from the UK of its registered office. Identical rules apply to an SCE (European Co-operative Society) which transfers its registered office on or after 18 August 2006 in accordance with *Council Regulation (EC) 1435/2003, Art 7*. [*CTA 2009, ss 16, 17; FA 1988, s 66A; F(No 2)A 2005, s 60(1)(3); SI 2007 No 3186*]. These provisions are subject to *CTA 2009, s 18* above.

Note

For **DOUBLE TAX RELIEF (32)** purposes, the definition of residence will often be affected by the terms of the relevant agreement. For the circumstances in which HMRC will certify that a company is UK resident for the purposes of double tax agreements, see Revenue Tax Bulletin December 2002 pp 989–991.

Simon's Taxes. See **D4.102–D4.109** and also INTM 162031.

Central management and control

[65.3] There is no general statutory definition of residence, and before the enactment of the deeming provisions described in **65.2** above the courts had determined that a company resides where its real business is carried on, i.e. *where its central management and control actually abide*. This test was set down in the case of *De Beers Consolidated Mines Ltd v Howe* (1906) 5 TC 198, HL, which involved a company established, and operating its business, in South Africa but whose important affairs were controlled from the UK, where the majority of the directors resided.

This criterion continues to apply for companies incorporated outside the UK and for companies covered by the transitional provisions.

In the following cases, the company was held to be managed and controlled from, and hence resident in, the UK: *Calcutta Jute Mills Co Ltd v Nicholson Ex D* (1876) 1 TC 83 (UK company operating abroad but directors and shareholders meeting in UK); *New Zealand Shipping Co Ltd v Thew* (1922) 8 TC 208, HL (New Zealand company with New Zealand directors, but overall control lay with separate London board); *American Thread Co v Joyce* (1913) 6 TC 163, HL (UK company operating in USA with US directors in charge of current business, but overall control in London); *John Hood & Co Ltd v Magee* (1918) 7 TC 327 (company registered in both UK and USA, with the only director resident in USA, but general meetings and material trading activities in UK). But in *A-G v Alexander Ex D* (1874) LR 10 Ex 20, a foreign state bank with a UK branch was held resident abroad, notwithstanding that shareholders' meetings were held in London.

The case *Unit Construction Co Ltd v Bullock (Inspector of Taxes)* [1960] AC 351, [1959] 3 All ER 831, HL, involved companies operating in South Africa. The constitution of each company gave control to the board of directors who had to hold their meetings outside the UK. However, as a question of fact, it was found that real control was being exercised by the directors of the parent company in the UK, even though this was unconstitutional.

However see also *Untelrab Ltd v McGregor*; *Unigate Guernsey Ltd v McGregor* [1996] STC (SCD) 1, in which subsidiaries of a UK-resident parent were held to be resident where their boards met (in Bermuda) and their business was transacted, as they did 'function in giving effect to [the] parent's wishes', notwithstanding that they were 'complaisant to do [the parent company's] will'. The directors were able to show that whilst no request from the parent had to date been improper or unreasonable, if it had been it would have been refused — the directors would not have carried out directions from the parent if they considered that such instructions were to the subsidiary's detriment. The Special Commissioners also held that the burden of proving residence on an appeal lies on the Crown.

An important case is *Wood and another v Holden* [2006] STC 443, CA, in which a married couple who were resident in the UK entered into a sophisticated scheme involving non UK resident companies, with the aim of avoiding CGT on a share disposal by taking advantage of *TCGA 1992, s 171*. The Revenue issued assessments on the basis that *TCGA 1992, s 171* did not apply because the 'central management and control' of the Dutch company to which the shares were transferred was exercised in the UK, by or on behalf of the husband.

The Court of Appeal held that the company in question was resident in the Netherlands as contended by the taxpayers. It argued that, in determining where central management and control was exercised, a distinction had to be made 'between cases where control of the company is exercised through its own constitutional organs (the board of directors or the general meeting) and cases where the functions of those constitutional organs are "usurped" – in the sense that management and control is exercised independently of, or without regard to, those constitutional organs.'

In the former case, it was important to recognise whether outside advisors dictated or merely influenced the decisions to be taken. The fact that the board may not have taken due care and consideration in making their decisions was not considered relevant in establishing the place of management and control. It was further held that, in appealing against an adjustment to a self-assessment, although the statutory burden of proof falls on the taxpayer, if the taxpayer produces evidence which suggests the assessment is wrong, 'the evidential basis must pass to the Revenue'.

More recently HMRC were successful in arguing that a Dutch company was being managed and controlled in the UK, through a former director who had not, as a matter of fact, relinquished his involvement with the company — *Laerstate BV v HMRC* FTT (TC 162), [2009] SFTD 551. The First-Tier Tax Tribunal found that the relevant decisions in relation to the BV were primarily taken by one of its directors, Mr Bock, in the UK. Whilst the BV did hold board meetings outside the UK, Mr Bock was not in regular attendance, although he was the driving force behind the company. As a director he was authorised to represent the BV and create legally binding obligations, and the minutes of the board meetings provided little evidence that there was any real consideration of matters by the board.

Even after Mr Bock had resigned as a director he continued to wield his influence and the Tribunal concluded that throughout the relevant period the BV's 'course of business and trading' was being undertaken largely by Mr Bock, in the UK, through his extensive involvement in '... policy, strategic and management matters...' The case highlights the importance of factual evidence. In addition it is interesting to note that the Tribunal considered the Netherlands-UK treaty test of effective management, and held that on the facts such effective management also took place in the UK.

Statement of Practice SP 1/90

HMRC's approach to applying the basic test can be found in SP1/90. The first step is to ascertain whether the directors in fact themselves exercise central management and control; if so, to then determine where that central management and control is exercised (not necessarily where they meet); if not, to establish where and by whom it is exercised.

The concept of the place of central management and control is directed at the highest level of control of the company's business, rather than the place where the main business operations are to be found. This must always be a question of fact in any particular case, but the place of directors' meetings will usually be of significance if they are the medium through which central management and control is exercised. If, however, central management and control is in reality exercised by, for example, a single individual, the company's residence will be where that individual exercises his powers.

With regard to the particular problem of residence of a subsidiary, HMRC would not normally seek to impute to the subsidiary the residence of its parent unless the parent in effect usurps the functions of the Board of the subsidiary. Matters taken into account would include the extent to which the directors of the subsidiary take decisions on their own authority as to investment, production, marketing and procurement without reference to the parent (and see below).

In all cases, HMRC will seek to determine whether a major objective of the existence of any particular factors bearing on residence is the obtaining of tax benefits from residence or non-residence, and to establish the reality of the central management and control.

See **65.2** above as regards deemed residence for tax purposes of companies incorporated in the UK. Before 15 March 1988 under the general law, incorporation in the UK and compliance with the requirements of the *Companies Acts* did not in themselves render a company tax resident here. See *Egyptian Delta Land and Investment* Co *Ltd v Todd (Inspector of Taxes)* [1929] AC 1, 14 TC 119, HL, and cf *Eccott v Aramayo Francke Mines Ltd* (1925) 9 TC 445, HL. A company may be resident in more than one country. See *Swedish Central Railway Co Ltd v Thompson* (1925) 9 TC 342, HL, and for an authoritative discussion of dual residence, *Union Corporation Ltd v CIR* (1953) 34 TC 207, HL.

As regards companies in liquidation, the appointment of a UK liquidator of a non-UK resident company may result in the company's becoming UK resident. The exercise of central management and control remains, however, a question of fact, and if it is exercised overseas by the liquidator, or if the liquidator acts in accordance with the wishes of non-resident shareholders so that it is not in fact exercised in the UK, the company will not become UK resident.

A company may have a domicile (see *Gasque v CIR* (1940) 23 TC 210), but it would seem from the *Union Corporation* case above that, for a company, ordinary residence and residence are synonymous. Similar rules apply for ascertaining the residence of **PARTNERSHIPS** (**58**).

Note

For **DOUBLE TAX RELIEF** (**32**) purposes, the definition of residence will often be affected by the terms of the relevant agreement. For the circumstances in which HMRC will certify that a company is UK resident for the purposes of double tax agreements, see Revenue Tax Bulletin December 2002 pp 989–991 and also INTM162031.

See **39.23 GROUP RELIEF** as regards certain 'dual resident investing companies'.

Simon's Taxes. See **D4.104.**

Overseas income and chargeable gains

[65.4] A UK resident company is chargeable to corporation tax on its overseas profits, and income, whether remitted to the UK or not. [*ICTA 1988, s 70(1)* this rule is not specifically rewritten in *CTA 2009* but the law remains unchanged; by virtue of *CTA 2009, s 8*, a UK resident company is charged on the full amount of its profits].

Where control of a UK resident company's trade rests abroad, the trade is a foreign possession, income from which is overseas income (*Mitchell (Surveyor of Taxes) v Egyptian Hotels Ltd* [1915] AC 1022, 6 TC 542, HL).

Where overseas income cannot be remitted to the UK, by reason of the laws or executive action of the government, or the impossibility of obtaining foreign currency in the territory that could be transferred to the UK (and where the income has not been realised outside that territory for sterling or an unblocked currency) then that income may be disregarded if the company so claims before any assessment by reference to that income becomes final. On or before 31 March 2009, the taxpayer company was required to exercise reasonable endeavour to remit the income. [*Change 90 listed in Annex 1 to the Explanatory Notes to CTA 2009*].

The claim must be made within two years of the end of the accounting period in which the income arises.

No claim may be made under these provisions if an Export Credit Guarantee Department (ECGD) payment has been made in respect of it.

When the income ceases to be unremittable or an ECGD payment is made in respect of it, then the relief claimed above will be withdrawn, either in whole or in part. The income is valued as at the date it ceases to be unremittable or the ECGD payment is made, taking into account foreign taxes chargeable on it in the territory concerned. Disputes are to be settled by the tribunal. These withdrawal provisions do not apply if the income originally arose in an accounting period ending before 1 October 1993.

Where relief falls to be withdrawn, but the company has permanently ceased to carry on the trade or property business or the source of other income no longer belongs to it, the following applies:

- for trading income, the income is treated as a post-cessation receipt (see **70.16 TRADE PROFITS — INCOME AND SPECIFIC TRADES**); and
- for a property business, the income is treated as a post-cessation receipt of a UK property business (see **62.4 PROPERTY INCOME**).

If no claim is made under these provisions, unremittable income is valued at its normal sterling exchange rate, if available, and in other cases, the official rate of exchange of the territory in which the income arises.

A claim may be made under *CTA 2009, s 1275* for an accounting period ending after 31 March 2009, despite the income having arisen in an accounting period ending before 1 April 2009. Withdrawal of relief under *CTA 2009, s 1276* (where the conditions of *s 1276* are satisfied) applies despite the income having arisen in an accounting period ending before 1 April 2009, and the claim being made either under *ICTA 1988, s 584* or *CTA 2009, s 1275*.

[*CTA 2009, ss 1274–1278; Sch 2 paras 134,135; change 91 listed in Annex 1 of the Explanatory notes to CTA 2009; ICTA 1988, s 584; ITTOIA 2005, Sch 1 para 245; SI 2009 No 56*].

Where tax on overseas income or chargeable gains has been assessed, HMRC may allow that tax to remain uncollected, without payment of interest, if they are satisfied that the income etc. cannot be remitted due to government action in the country of origin and that it is otherwise reasonable to do so. Interest then ceases to run from the date on which HMRC were first in possession of information necessary to enable them to agree to deferment. If that date is three months or less from the due and payable date, no interest is payable. But where a demand is later made for payment of the deferred tax, interest is exigible if the tax is not paid within three months of that demand. [*TMA 1970, s 92*]. HMRC may defer collection indefinitely.

The *Finance Act 2011* contains a proposed exemption for the profits of foreign permanent establishments of UK resident companies. The provisions allow a company to elect for such profits not to be subject to UK corporation tax. See further **32.7 DOUBLE TAX RELIEF** for details of the draft legislation.

Non-resident companies

[65.5] A non-UK resident company is liable to corporation tax if it is carrying on a trade in the UK through a 'permanent establishment' there. See further **65.6** below for the profits in respect of which non-resident companies are liable to tax and for the liability of 'UK representatives'.

Provided that there is a non-discrimination clause in the relevant double tax treaty, an overseas company should be able to benefit from the reduced rates of corporation tax available for companies with small profits (governed by world-wide company profits) as if the overseas company were UK resident (see **67 SMALL PROFITS — REDUCED RATES**). Associated companies are taken into account wherever resident. (CCAB Guidance Notes TR 500, 10 March 1983). If there is no such clause in the applicable treaty then the main rate of corporation tax applies.

See Revenue Tax Bulletin August 1995 pp 237–239 as regards application of the arm's length principle in measuring the profits chargeable on a non-resident in respect of UK trading. See generally, HMRC International Manual, INTM260000 *et seq*.

Where a non-resident company suffers income tax by deduction at source on income which is also subject to corporation tax then the income tax is set off against the corporation tax chargeable. If the income tax exceeds the corporation tax liability for the relevant accounting period, repayment of the excess may be claimed.

[*CTA 2010, s 968; ICTA 1988, ss 7(5), 11(3); FA 1998, Sch 18 para 10*].

A non-resident company is not liable to UK income tax on its UK income which is chargeable to corporation tax as in **65.6** below. [*CTA 2009, s 3; ICTA 1988, s 6(2)(b)*]. It is liable to UK income tax on income from other sources in the UK (excluding income specifically exempt in the hands of a non-resident).

Where a non-resident company is within the charge to corporation tax in respect of one source of income and is assessable to income tax on another source of income, capital allowances related to each source are given against income from that source only according to the rules of the tax involved. [*CAA 2001, s 566*].

Where a company becomes UK resident during a year of assessment, it is liable to capital gains tax on gains arising during that year prior to its becoming resident. Similarly, on a company's ceasing to be UK resident during a year of assessment, it is liable to capital gains tax on gains arising during that year after it ceases to be resident. (HMRC Capital Gains Manual CG42360–42411).

Non-payment of tax. There are special arrangements for collection of corporation tax unpaid within six months of the due date where any part of the tax relates to a chargeable gain accruing to the company on a disposal **before**

1 April 2000. HMRC may seek to recover that tax (or part) within three years of its determination from any person who is, or in the twelve months before the disposal was, a controlling director of the company (or of a company controlling it) or a member of the same 51% group. [*TCGA 1992, s 191*]. See now **18.11 PAYMENTS AND COLLECTIONS OF TAX.**

See **27 CONTROLLED FOREIGN COMPANIES** as regards special rules applying to those with an interest in such companies. See **39.23 GROUP RELIEF** as regards certain 'dual resident investing companies'.

Simon's Taxes. See **D4.115–D4.126.**

The charge to corporation tax

[65.6] For accounting periods of a non-resident company beginning after 31 December 2002, a non-resident company is within the charge to corporation tax only if it carries on a business in the UK through a UK **permanent establishment.**

The profits within the charge to corporation tax are those which are attributable to the permanent establishment, as follows:

- trading income arising directly or indirectly through or from the establishment;
- income from property or rights used by, or held by or for, the establishment; or
- chargeable gains within *TCGA 1992, s 10B* from assets used for the permanent establishment or for the trade carried on by the company through it (see Tolley's Capital Gains Tax under Overseas Matters).

Per the provisions within the legislation (*CTA 2009, ss 5(2)(3), 19–32; previously ICTA 1988, ss 11, 11AA, Sch A1*) the profits attributable to the permanent establishment are determined as if the permanent establishment were a distinct and separate enterprise, engaged in the same or similar activities under the same or similar conditions, dealing wholly independently with the non-UK resident company (the '*separate enterprise principle*').

It is assumed for this purpose that the establishment has the same credit rating as the non-resident company and has such equity and loan capital as it could reasonably be expected to have in these circumstances. No deduction may be made for tax purposes for costs in excess of those that would have been incurred on those assumptions.

In accordance with the separate enterprise principle, transactions between the permanent establishment and any other part of the non-UK resident company are treated as taking place on arm's length terms. If the non-resident company supplies the establishment with goods or services, then if they are of a kind which the company supplies on arm's length terms to third parties in the ordinary course of its business, the separate enterprise principle is applied to the transactions; if not, the matter is dealt with as an expense incurred by the company for the purposes of the permanent establishment.

Expenses, including executive and general administrative expenses, incurred for the purposes of the permanent establishment, whether incurred in the UK or elsewhere and whether or not incurred or reimbursed by the establishment, are deductible, at the actual cost to the non-UK resident company, if they are of a kind that would have been deductible if incurred by a UK resident company.

There are prohibitions on deductions for certain payments in respect of intangible assets, and for certain payments of interest and other financing costs, where such payments are made by the permanent establishment to any other part of the non-UK resident company.

CTA 2009, ss 25–28 (previously *ICTA 1988, Sch A1 paras 7–10*) make special provision applicable only to non-UK resident banks. (See also HMRC Banking Manual at BAM32000 *et seq*.). HMRC may make special provision (by regulations) in relation to insurance companies (for which see *SI 2003 No 2714* in respect of the application of *CTA 2009, s 21(1)* (previously *ICTA 1988, s 11A(2)*).

[*CTA 2009, ss 5(2)(3), 19–32; ICTA 1988, ss 11, 11AA, Sch A1; FA 2003, s 149, Sch 25*].

The meaning of 'permanent establishment'

The definition of a 'permanent establishment' is found at *CTA 2010, Pt 24 Ch 2 (s 1141 et seq)*. A company has a '*permanent establishment*' in a territory if (and only if):

(a) it has a 'fixed place of business' there through which its business is wholly or partly carried on, or
(b) it has an agent acting on its behalf there and this agent has and habitually exercises there authority to do business on its behalf.

A '*fixed place of business*' includes a place of management; a branch; an office, factory or workshop; an installation or structure for the exploration of natural resources; a mine or quarry, oil or gas well or any other place of extraction of natural resources; and a building site or construction or installation project.

There are three specific exclusions in that a company is *not* regarded as having a permanent establishment in a territory by reason of the fact that:

(i) it carries on business there through an agent of independent status acting in the ordinary course of his business (and see below the conditions with regard to the 'independent status'); or
(ii) a fixed place of business is maintained there for the purpose of carrying on company activities, or such activities are carried on there for or on behalf of the company by an agent, and those activities are, in relation to the company's business as a whole, only of a 'preparatory or auxiliary character'; or
(iii) the company is party to **ALTERNATIVE FINANCE ARRANGEMENTS** (**4**) in relation to an arrangement giving rise to an alternative finance return under *CTA 2009, ss 511–513, Sch 1 para 653; ITA 2007 ss 564I, 564K or 564L; FA 2005, s 47 or FA 2005, s 49A*.

Reference to activities of a 'preparatory or auxiliary character' include:

- the use of facilities for the purpose of storage, display or delivery of goods or merchandise belonging to the company;
- the maintenance of a stock of goods or merchandise belonging to the company for that purpose or for the purpose of processing by another person; and
- purchasing goods or merchandise, or collecting information, for the company.

Agents of independent status

For accounting periods beginning after 31 December 2002, three particular types of agent are given specific exemptions under the legislation, which provide certain conditions to be met in order for such UK persons to be treated as independent agents in respect of services provided to non-resident companies: a broker; an investment manager and a Lloyd's member's agent or syndicate managing agent for the company.

The tests and conditions applicable with regard to these agents have been re-written to *CTA 2010*, as from 1 April 2010 (income tax year 2010/11) and the provisions of *FA 2003, Sch 26*, from which they derive, have been repealed. The *CTA 2010* provisions mirror those found in the earlier legislation, however, reference should be made to *FA 2003, Sch 26*, and any relevant provisions of *FA 1995* as applicable.

For the purpose of these rules, a person is regarded as carrying out a transaction on behalf of another where he undertakes it himself or gives instructions for it to be carried out by another person. A person is not regarded as acting in an independent capacity on behalf of a company unless the relationship between them (legal, financial and commercial) is between independent businesses dealing at arm's length.

Where the non-resident company is a corporate member of Lloyd's, a person who acts on behalf of the company in relation to a transaction in the course of its underwriting business is regarded as an independent agent acting in the ordinary course of his business if he acts as members' agent or as managing agent of the syndicate concerned.

The independent broker conditions

A *broker* is regarded as an agent of independent status in respect of a transaction carried out on behalf of a non-resident company only if each of the following conditions is met:

(a) at the time of the transaction he is carrying on the business of broker;
(b) the transaction is carried out in the ordinary course of that business;
(c) his remuneration in respect of the transaction is not less than is customary for that class of business; and
(d) he does not fall to be treated as a permanent establishment of the non-resident company in relation to any other transaction in the same accounting period.

The independent investment manager conditions

An *investment manager* is regarded as an agent of independent status in respect of an investment transaction carried out on behalf of a non-resident company only if (for accounting periods ending on or after 21 July 2008) each of the following conditions is met:

(a) he is carrying on the business of providing investment management services, at the time of the transaction;
(b) the transaction is carried out in the ordinary course of that business;
(c) he acts on behalf of the non-resident company in an independent capacity;
(d) he meets the requirements of the '20% rule' (see below);
(e) his remuneration in respect of the transaction is not less than is customary for that class of business.

For accounting periods ending before 21 July 2008 an investment manager had to meet all the conditions above and additionally not fall to be treated as a permanent establishment of the non-resident company in relation to any other transaction in the same accounting period.

An '*investment transaction*' is a transaction in shares or stock, in futures or options contracts (not relating to land), and includes financial swap transactions such as credit derivatives, and from 12 April 2007, includes transactions in Community tradable emissions allowances or transferable units under the Kyoto protocol. Certain types of transaction are excluded; these are contracts relating to land, contracts of insurance, and contracts made in the course of capital redemption business. Other transaction may be included as designated by way of regulations (from 21 July 2008).

The requirements of the '*20% rule*' are broadly that the interests of the investment manager and **CONNECTED PERSONS (25)** in the relevant disregarded income (i.e. profits, see below) of the non-resident company's investment transactions in a qualifying period do not, or are not intended to, amount to 20% or more, with special provisions applying in relation to the non-resident company's participation in collective investment schemes (see *CTA 2010, ss 1147, 1148, 1152; FA 2003, Sch 26 paras 4, 5*). If that intention is not fulfilled, the failure must be attributable to matters outside their control and must not result from a failure to take reasonable steps to mitigate the effect of such matters.

For accounting periods ending on or after 21 July 2008, where the 20% rule is not satisfied, the investment manager will still be regarded as an agent of independent status except in relation to relevant disregarded income in which he and connected persons have or have had any beneficial entitlement.

The *relevant disregarded income* means profits derived from transactions carried out by the investment manager on behalf of the non-resident company in respect of which the manager is *not* treated as a permanent establishment (other than under the requirements of the 20% rule). This was previously termed 'relevant excluded income' per *FA 2003, Sch 26*. This definition is important when the interaction with a possible income tax charge (see below) is being considered.

A qualifying period is the accounting period in which the transaction is carried out or a period of up to five years comprising two or more complete accounting periods including the one in which the transaction was carried out.

There are certain further requirements with regard to the application of the 20% rule to collective investment schemes, see further *CTA 2010, s 1149* (previously *FA 2003, Sch 26 para 5*).

[*CTA 2010, ss 1141–1153; FA 2003, ss 148, 152, Sch 26 paras 2–5; FA 2005, s 48(2); FA 2006, s 95(9); FA 2008, s 38, Sch 16 paras 3, 8, 9, 11, SI 2007 No 964*].

Assessment, collection and recovery of corporation tax

Obligations and liabilities in relation to corporation tax which are imposed on a non-resident company are also imposed on its 'UK representative'. This applies to the assessment, collection and recovery of tax, or of interest on tax.

A UK 'permanent establishment' (see above) through which the non-resident company carries on a trade is the company's '*UK representative*' in relation to the 'chargeable profits' attributable to that establishment (see above) and within the charge to corporation tax. The permanent establishment continues to be the UK representative even after it ceases to be a permanent establishment through which the company carries on a trade. It is treated as a person separate and distinct from the company for these purposes.

Either the company itself or its UK representative may satisfy any such obligation or liability, and the company is bound by the acts or omissions of its UK representative. Formal notices, demands, etc. must, where relevant, be given or notified to, or served on, the UK representative for these provisions to apply to it. The company is not bound by a mistake in information provided by its UK representative in pursuance of such an obligation unless it resulted from an act or omission of the company, or from one to which the company consented or in which it connived.

Similarly the UK representative is not by virtue of these provisions liable to be proceeded against for a criminal offence in relation to any of the above unless it committed the offence itself or consented to, or connived in, its commission.

[*CTA 2010, ss 969–972; FA 2003, s 150, CTA 2009, Sch 1 para 562*].

See also **Simon's Taxes D4.117** and **D4.121**. CTM34210 and 34220.

The charge to income tax

[65.7] A non-resident company is chargeable to income tax on income arising within the UK which is not chargeable to corporation tax. This can include rents (not connected with a permanent establishment) payable to a non-resident company. However, there is a limit to the liability to income tax of non-resident companies. The limit is linked with the provisions in respect of the activities of an independent broker or investment manager, and the conditions outlined above with regard to such independent persons apply equally here.

Limit on liability to income tax

The limit on the liability to income tax of non-resident companies is given by the sum of two amounts, which are termed 'Amount A' and 'Amount B'.

Amount A is the total of amounts deducted, or treated as deducted from 'disregarded company income' (see below) together with tax credits in respect of such income. Amount B is the non-resident company's liability to income tax for the tax year if disregarded company income were to be ignored.

'Disregarded company income' (prior to *ITA 2007* this was referred to as 'excluded income') is made up of the following:

(a) disregarded savings and investment income;
(b) disregarded annual payments;
(c) income on transactions through a broker in the UK provided the independent broker conditions are satisfied;
(d) income on transactions through an investment manager in the UK provided the independent investment manager conditions are satisfied.
(e) any other description of income which the Treasury designate by regulations.

The independent broker and independent investment manager conditions are those described in **65.5** above.

Note for accounting periods ending on or after 21 July 2008 income may still fall to be disregarded even if the independent investment manager conditions are not met. This rule will apply if an investment manager (who, for whatever reason, is not regarded as an 'agent of independent status') carries out one or more transactions on behalf of a non-resident company; and either:

(i) the investment transaction meets all the investment manager conditions (outlined above); or
(ii) the investment transaction meets all the those conditions with the exception of the 20% rule. Where the 20% rule is not satisfied, profits are to be disregarded only if they do not represent relevant excluded income in which the investment manager and connected persons have or have had any beneficial entitlement.

An EU company is not liable to income tax on interest and royalty payments from an associated UK company or from the UK permanent establishment of another EU company provided that certain conditions are satisfied with effect from 1 January 2004, when the provisions of *Directive 2003/49/EC* on interest and royatlites became effective under UK law.

For a non-resident company which does not undertake a business (including a trade, profession or vocation) in the UK the charge to income tax is therefore limited to that deducted at source.

[*FA 1995, ss 128, 129; FA 2003, s 151, Sch 27 paras 6, 7; ITTOIA 2005, Sch 1 paras 480, 622; ITA 2007, s 815 et seq, Sch 1 para 452*].

Assessment, collection and recovery of income tax

As noted above the charge to income tax for a non-resident company arises only in limited circumstances and is limited in scope.

Further to the changes implemented with regard to the taxation under corporation tax rules of permanent establishments of non resident companies per *FA 2003, s 148* (now found in *CTA 2009* and *CTA 2010*, above), the *FA 1995, s 126* was amended for accounting periods beginning on or after 31 December 2002 (by *FA 2003, Sch 27 para 4*). The UK representative provisions in respect of income tax do not apply to income tax chargeable on income of a company otherwise than as a trustee (*ITA 2007, s 835D* (as inserted by *TIOPA 2010*); *FA 1995, s 126(10)*).

The obligations and liabilities in relation to income tax which are imposed on a non-resident company ***as a trustee*** are also imposed on a branch or agency which is the company's 'UK representative' in relation to the amounts giving rise to the tax.

The following are, however, excluded from being a 'UK representative':

(1) an agent acting other than in the course of carrying on a regular agency for the company;
(2) a broker;
(3) an investment manager acting in an independent capacity through whom certain investment transactions (see *FA 1995, s 127(3)–(12)*) are carried out;
(4) a Lloyd's member's agent or syndicate managing agent for the company;
(5) any party to, or person acting for a non-resident person who is party to, **ALTERNATIVE FINANCE ARRANGEMENTS (4)** within *CTA 2009, s 504* (previously *FA 2005, s 47* (entered into on or after 6 April 2005) or within *FA 2005, s 49A* (entered into on or after 1 April 2006).

With regard to (2) and (3) reference should be made to the conditions for independent brokers and investment managers described above at **65.5**, which were derived from the original *FA 1995* and *FA 2003* provisions.

As regards (3) above, see further HMRC Statement of Practice 1/01 which clarifies the requirements for the exclusion to apply. This statement of practice examines further the conditions for the investment manager exemption to apply, and considers the nature of 'independence'. The original statement applied from February 2001. On 20 July 2007, a revised statement was issued. This applies from the date of issue, except where the non-resident or his investment manager needs to make changes to current circumstances or contractual arrangements in order to comply with the revised statement, in which case the original statement may be applied until 31 December 2009.

This applies to the assessment, collection and recovery of tax, or of interest on tax. Either the company itself or its 'UK representative' may satisfy such obligations and liabilities, and the company is bound by the acts or omissions of its 'UK representative'.

A person is, however, guilty of a criminal offence in relation to any of the above only where he committed the offence himself or consented to, or connived in, its commission.

Formal notices, etc., where relevant, must be notified to the 'UK representative' for these provisions to apply. The 'UK representative' is treated as a person separate and distinct from the company for these purposes.

[*FA 1995, ss 126, 127, Sch 23; FA 2003, Sch 27 paras 4, 5; ITTOIA 2005, Sch 1 para 479; FA 2005, s 48(3); FA 2006, s 95(10)*].

Simon's Taxes. See **D4.116–D4.124**.

The effect of double taxation agreements

Most double taxation agreements lay down rules to determine in which country a particular source of income is to be taxed, ie in the country in which the income arises or the country in which the recipient of the income is resident. Such rules take precedence over the internal tax legislation of the countries concerned. This means that a non-resident company cannot be required to pay tax in the UK in excess of that stipulated in the double taxation agreement, but subject to that may be taxed in accordance with the provisions outlined above.

Company becoming non-resident

[65.8] A company may cease to be UK resident, even if it is incorporated it the UK, if it changes its central management and control, or effective management, and the terms of an applicable double tax treaty apply such that the company is considered resident in the other contracting state.

There are various migration provisions that apply in such circumstances with regard to capital gains, loan relationships, derivative contracts, and intangible fixed assets. In essence these are anti-avoidance provisions and provide for a charge to tax to arise on migration, save in certain circumstances, such as where a permanent establishment of the company continues to exist in the UK post migration.

Chargeable gains

If, at any time (the '*relevant time*'), a company ceases to be resident in the UK, and does not cease to exist, then:

(a) it is deemed to dispose of, and immediately re-acquire, all its assets at their market value at that time, and
(b) rollover relief under *TCGA 1992, s 152* is not subsequently available by reference to disposals of old assets made before that time.

If at any later time the company carries on a trade in the UK through a permanent establishment (see **65.6** above — previously a branch or agency), (a) above does not apply to any assets which, immediately after the relevant time, are situated in the UK and are used in or for a trade, or are used or held for the permanent establishment. Similarly (b) above does not apply to new assets acquired after the relevant time which are so situated and used or held. For this purpose assets situated in the UK include various assets and rights relating to exploration or exploitation activities in the UK or designated areas of the sea within *TCGA 1992, s 276*.
[*TCGA 1992, s 185*].

If the deemed disposal in (a) above includes any '*foreign assets*' (i.e. assets situated, and used in or for a trade carried on, outside the UK), postponement of tax will be available, as described below, if:

(i) immediately after the relevant time the company was a 75% subsidiary of a company (the '*principal company*') which was resident in the UK (i.e. not less than 75% of its ordinary share capital was owned directly by the principal company); and
(ii) both companies so elect in writing within two years after that time.

Any excess of gains over losses arising on the foreign assets included in the deemed disposal is treated as a single chargeable gain not accruing to the company on that disposal. An equal amount (the '*postponed gain*') is instead treated as follows.

If, within six years after the relevant time, the company disposes of any assets (the '*relevant assets*') chargeable gains on which were taken into account in arriving at the postponed gain, a chargeable gain equal to the whole, or the 'appropriate proportion', of the postponed gain, so far as this has not already been treated as a chargeable gain under these provisions, is deemed to accrue to the principal company. The '*appropriate proportion*' is the proportion which the chargeable gain taken into account in arriving at the postponed gain in respect of the part of the relevant assets disposed of bears to the aggregate of the chargeable gains so taken into account in respect of the relevant assets held immediately before the time of the disposal.

If at any time:
(a) the company ceases to be a 75% subsidiary of the principal company on a disposal by the principal company of ordinary shares in it; or
(b) after the company otherwise ceases to be a 75% subsidiary, the principal company disposes of ordinary shares in it; or
(c) the principal company ceases to be resident in the UK,

a chargeable gain equal to so much of the postponed gain as has not previously been charged under these provisions is deemed to arise to the principal company.

If any part of the postponed gain becomes chargeable on the principal company, and the subsidiary has unrelieved capital losses, the companies may jointly elect, in writing within two years, for part or all of the losses to be set against the amount so chargeable.

[*TCGA 1992, s 187*].

Similar provisions in respect of a company ceasing to be UK resident apply with regard to loan relationships (*CTA 2009, s 333*), derivative contracts (*CTA 2009, s 609*) and intangible fixed assets (*CTA 2009, ss 859–862*).

Simon's Taxes. See **D4.131**.

Notification and arrangements to pay tax

[65.9] There are certain administrative requirements which must be fulfilled before the company ceases to be UK resident. Previously these were found in *FA 1988, ss 130–132*, which has been rewritten by *TIOPA 2010* to *TMA 1970, ss109B–109F*, for corporation tax purposes for accounting periods ending on or after 1 April 2010.

A company must, before ceasing to be resident in the UK, give to HMRC:

(a) notice of its intention to cease to be UK resident, specifying the time when it intends so to cease;
(b) a statement of the amount of tax which it considers payable for periods beginning before that time; and
(c) particulars of the arrangements which it proposes to make to secure payment of that tax.

It must also make arrangements to secure the payment of that tax, and the arrangements must be approved by HMRC. Guidance notes regarding the giving of notice and the making of arrangements have been published by HMRC. (HMRC Statement of Practice, SP 2/90 as revised).

Any reference to tax payable includes the following (and tax under corresponding earlier legislation):

(i) tax under PAYE regulations;
(ii) income tax payable under *ITA 2007, ss 946, 962* (previously *ICTA 1988, s 350(4)(a)*) (company payments which are not distributions, see **46.2 INCOME TAX IN RELATION TO A COMPANY** and **9.2 BUILDING SOCIETIES**);
(iii) income tax payable under *ITA 2007, ss 965–970* as amended by *CTA 2009, Sch 1 para 715*, previously *ICTA 1988, s 555* (entertainers and sportsmen);
(iv) any amount payable under *FA 2004, ss 61, 62* (previously *ICTA 1988, s 559(4)*) (see **26.3 CONSTRUCTION INDUSTRY SCHEME**);
(v) any amount payable under *TMA 1970, s 77C* (previously *FA 1973, Sch 15 para 4)* (territorial extension of charge to tax, see **65.12** below);
(vi) interest on tax within (i)–(v) (whether or not the tax is paid).

Any question as to the amount of tax payable is to be determined by the First Tier Tax Tribunal, or the Upper Tribunal as applicable. If any information provided by the company does not fully and accurately disclose all the material facts and considerations, any resulting approval is void. [*TMA 1970, ss 109B–109F*; *FA 1988, s 130*].

A person who is, or who is deemed to be, involved in a failure to comply with the foregoing provisions is liable to a penalty not exceeding the amount of unpaid tax for periods beginning before the failure occurred.

Any tax not paid within six months of becoming payable can, within the three years following determination of the amount, be recovered from a person who is, or who was so in the year before residence ceased, a member of the same group or a controlling director. See **18.2 CAPITAL GAINS — GROUPS** with regard to the definition of a group which applies also in the twelve-month period before residence ceases.

[*TMA 1970, ss 109B–109F; FA 1988, ss 130–132*].

Simon's Taxes. See **D4.131**.

Banks, insurance companies and dealers in securities

[65.10] In contrast to other non-resident companies, banks, insurance companies and dealers in securities which are non-resident but carrying on business in the UK are not exempt on income from overseas securities, stocks and shares by reason of non-residence.

Certain income such as that deriving from foreign state securities, foreign dividends and interest on quoted Eurobonds, are included in computing the profits and losses of the UK trade of the non resident company (notwithstanding that for other non residents such income would be exempt). [previously *ICTA 1988, s 48, s 123(4) and s 474 — see now the computation of profits of a permanent establishment per CTA 2009, ss 25–28*, and the application of the loan relationship provisions in such instances]. See also *Owen v Sassoon* (1950) 32 TC 101 in which funds deposited against default by a Lloyd's underwriter were held to be within the underwriters profits chargeable to tax.

See Tolley's Income Tax under Life Assurance Policies for special treatment of policies issued by non-UK resident companies outside the scope of UK tax.

Non-resident performers

[65.11] *ITA 2007, s 966* requires deduction of tax from certain payments and transfers to entertainers and sportsmen and women in relation to activities performed in the UK in a tax year for which the performer is non-UK resident.

That legislation also applies in some cases to payments made to a person other than the performer (typically to a company controlled by the performer). In those cases, the payments are generally treated as made instead to the performer. See Tolley's Income Tax under Non-Residents for full coverage.

Where a payment or transfer made to a company is treated as above as made to a performer, the company is treated for corporation tax purposes as if the payment or transfer had not been made to it.

[*CTA 2009, s 1309; ICTA 1988, s 556; SI 1987 No 530, Reg 7*].

United Kingdom

[65.12] The United Kingdom for tax purposes comprises England, Scotland, Wales and Northern Ireland. The Channel Islands (Jersey, Guernsey, Alderney, Sark, Herm and Jethou) and the Isle of Man are not included. Great Britain comprises England, Scotland and Wales only.

Territorial extension of tax area

The territorial sea of the UK is regarded as part of the UK for tax purposes. Earnings, profits and gains from exploration or exploitation activities in a designated area (under *Continental Shelf Act 1964, s 1(7)*) (and unlisted shares deriving most of their value from assets used for such activities) are treated as arising in the UK. Transfers of exploration or exploitation rights by a company not resident in the UK to a company which is so resident or which is resident in the same territory, are brought within the provisions relating to intra-group transfers. See **18 CAPITAL GAINS — GROUPS.**

A resident licence-holder under *Petroleum (Production) Act 1934* may be held accountable for the liability of a non-resident and may be required by the inspector to provide information concerning transactions with other persons and emoluments or other payments made. [*per TIOPA 2010, s 371 rewritten to TMA 1970, Pt 7A; CTA 2009, s 1313; ICTA 1988, s 830; FA 1973, s 38, Sch 15; TCGA 1992, s 276; ITEPA 2003, s 41; ITTOIA 2005, Sch 1 paras 335, 387, 388, CTA 2009, Sch 1 para 270*].

The case *Clark v Oceanic Contractors Incorporated* (1982) 56 TC 183, HL, considers the liability of a non-resident company engaged in exploration and exploitation activities to apply PAYE to its employees subject to tax on employment income,

For the liability to tax on profits or gains of non-resident lessors of mobile drilling rigs, vessels or equipment used in connection with exploration or exploitation activities, see HMRC Statement of Practice, SP 6/84.

Simon's Taxes. See A1.109.

Key points

[65.13] Points to consider are as follows.

- Most residence issues arise for UK tax purposes where a company is incorporated outside the UK and is intended to be resident outside the UK for tax purposes. The following bullet points may be used as an initial checklist to establish and maintain the non-UK residence of such a company.
  - (a) It is generally preferable for the board of directors to exercise central management and control of the company — i.e. taking its strategic and policy decisions.
  - (b) The board should comprise appropriately senior and competent individuals with relevant experience. Corporate directors should be avoided.
  - (c) UK resident individuals should not be directors of the company unless it is necessary. Such individuals should not comprise a majority of the board, be able to form a quorum for a board meeting or pass a resolution.
  - (d) Where the board is influenced by others in the UK, the level of influence must be kept in check to avoid assertions that the board's powers are being usurped by persons in the UK.
  - (e) A board meeting should be held at least once each calendar quarter. Board meetings should be held in person outside the UK. Participation in board meetings by telephone and

written resolutions of the board should be avoided, particularly if one or more of the directors are resident or present in the UK.

(f) Where possible, focus on a particular jurisdiction as the place of residence of the company rather than having board meetings in a variety of different jurisdictions. That jurisdiction should have appropriate infrastructure (i.e. an office and personnel) for the company and the company books should be kept there.

(g) The board should avoid delegating its strategic powers to persons who are based or tax resident in the UK.

(h) Keep good written records of board proceedings, including notes of where the meetings are held and minutes which reflect discussions at the meetings.

(i) Documents relating to key decisions should be executed outside the UK and correspondence to which the company is a party should clearly show the company's address outside the UK. Care should be taken to ensure that informal correspondence does not imply that persons in the UK have the power to make decisions on behalf of the company.

- Where it appears that a company incorporated outside the UK may be resident in the UK for UK tax purposes, the terms of any applicable double tax treaty should be reviewed. This may rule out UK residence and/or dual residence.
- Bear in mind that treaty residence tests may focus on the test of effective management; this concept is broader and focuses more on day-to-day management of the business than on strategic and policy decisions of the business.
- As well as the compliance burden suffered by dual resident companies, such companies are unable to claim the benefit of certain UK tax reliefs (for example, group relief and intra-group 'no gain/no loss' transfers for the purposes of corporation tax on chargeable gains).
- Although a company may not be tax resident in the UK, it may still be carrying on a business in the UK through a permanent establishment. Where this is the case, an analysis of the UK business should be carried out to establish whether it constitutes a trade, which will bring the company within the charge to corporation tax to the extent that profits are attributable to the UK trade.
- Where a non-UK resident company is trading in the UK through a UK permanent establishment, consider whether it would be prudent to establish a UK subsidiary to ring fence UK tax liabilities, perhaps further safeguard the non-UK residence of the

company and avoid complicated attribution of profits calculations.

66

Returns

Simon's Taxes. See **D1.1301–D1.1315**.

Introduction

[66.1] This chapter details the provisions with regard to returns to be made by a company. It provides an outline of the procedures for submission and amendment of such returns, an overview of the enquiry process, and the position when no return is delivered.

Penalties with regard to matters such as late submission of returns, or submission of incorrect returns are considered in brief, the full details in this regard can be found at **60 PENALTIES**.

Returns of profits etc.

[66.2] The company tax return must include a self-assessment by the company of its corporation tax liability on the basis of the information contained in the return, and taking account of reliefs or allowances claimed in the return. See **66.4** *et seq.* below.

HMRC has given advance notice that it will require all company tax returns delivered after 31 March 2011 for accounting periods ending after 31 March 2010 to be filed online using iXBRL. Filing may be completed by using commercial software or by using HMRC's own software.

Notification of coming within charge to corporation tax

With effect for accounting periods beginning on or after 22 July 2004, a company (but not an unincorporated association or partnership) must give notice to HMRC of when its first accounting period begins (e.g. when the company starts its business) and of when any subsequent accounting period begins that does not follow on immediately from the end of a previous accounting period (e.g. when the company restarts its business after a period of dormancy). The notice stating when the accounting period began must be given to any HMRC officer within three months after the beginning of the accounting period in question. It must be in writing and contain other information as prescribed by regulation.

The information required by *SI 2004 No 2502* includes the name, address of the registered office and registered number of the company, the nature and principal place of business, the accounting date, details of the directors, details of any former business taken over, details of the parent company if part of a group, and the date on which there was an obligation (if any) to operate PAYE. The penalty provisions of *TMA 1970, s 98* apply for failure to give such notice (up to £300 for the initial failure and up to £60 per day for continuing failure thereafter) or for fraudulently or negligently giving an incorrect notice (up to £3,000) (see **60.3 PENALTIES**). See **60.13 PENALTIES** as regards 'reasonable excuse' for failure.

From 1 April 2010, the penalty for non-compliance under *TMA 1970, s 98* is repealed. *FA 2008, Sch 41* updates the penalty regime for failure to notify chargeability under *FA 1998, Sch 18 para 2*.

[*FA 2004, s 55; FA 2008, s 123, Sch 41 para 25; SI 2004 No 2502*].

Notification of chargeability

[66.3] A company chargeable to corporation tax which has not already made a company tax return for an accounting period, and has not received a notice requiring such a return (see **66.4** below), must give notice of its chargeability to the inspector within twelve months from the end of the period. Failure to do so renders the company liable to a penalty not exceeding so much of the corporation tax chargeable on its profits for the period as remains unpaid twelve months after the end of the period (disregarding any relief deferred under *CTA 2010, s 458(5)* (previously *ICTA 1988, s 419(4A)*) in respect of the repayment, etc. of a loan to a participator, see **22.15 CLOSE COMPANIES**). [*FA 1998, Sch 18 para 2; CTA 2010, Sch 1 para 297(3)*].

From 1 April 2010 any penalty for failure to notify HMRC is charged under *FA 2008, Sch 41*. The amount of the penalty will depend on whether or not the failure is deliberate and is subject to reduction. For deliberate and concealed failure the penalty is 100% of the 'potential lost revenue'. For deliberate but not concealed failure the penalty is 70% of the potential lost revenue, and for any other case the penalty is 30% of the potential lost revenue.

These penalties are subject to further reduction, please see further **60 PENALTIES.**

[*FA 2008, s 123, Sch 41*].

See **60.13 PENALTIES** as regards mitigation of penalties and 'reasonable excuse' for failure.

Simon's Taxes. See **D1.1302.**

Self-assessment returns

[66.4] The Revenue published a detailed 'Guide to Corporation Tax Self-Assessment', a free copy of which was sent to tax agents in May 1999. Whilst it has been largely superseded by guidance material included in the HMRC manuals it is still available on the HMRC website (at www.hmrc.gov.uk/ctsa/ctsaguide.pdf) because it provides a useful summary of the CTSA legislation in *FA 1998, Sch 18*. Reference is made to it below where relevant.

See generally HMRC Company Taxation Manual, CTM90000 *et seq*.

If so required by notice (Form CT603), a company must make a 'company tax return' on a prescribed form (or an approved substitute) of such information, relevant to its corporation tax liabilities, as is reasonably required under the notice. Supporting accounts, statements and reports may similarly be required. A completed return form unaccompanied by the related accounts and computations does not satisfy the filing obligation (see HMRC Company Taxation Manual, CTM93090). Details of assets acquired on which chargeable gains or allowable losses may arise may also be required.

Filing electronically

Self-assessment corporation tax returns periods ending on or after 1 April 2010, filed on or after 1 April 2011 must be filed electronically in a format approved by HMRC, which is — iXBRL. See further **66.29** below.

[*SI 2009 No 321*].

Most company tax returns will be by companies resident in the UK throughout the return period, and required to prepare accounts under *Companies Act 2006 or 1985* (or NI equivalent) for a period consisting of, or including, the return period, and in such cases the accounts required are only those it is required to prepare under the *Companies Acts*, and any attachments required under the *Companies Acts* must also accompany the company tax return.

In *Slater Ltd v Beacontree General Commrs* (2001) 74 TC 471 (and also the subsequent case of *Slater Ltd v CIR* [2002] EWHC 2676 (Ch), [2004] STC 1342, [2002] All ER (D) 275 (Nov)), it was, however, held that that restriction on the accounts which may be required did not restrict the information which may be required in support of those accounts. In the case of a non-resident company trading through a UK permanent establishment (or branch or agency), the accounts required are (English language) trading and profit and loss accounts of both the company and the UK permanent establishment together with the balance sheet of the company and (if prepared) of the UK permanent establishment. Other companies are required to deliver the accounts they are required to prepare by law or under their constitution. (HMRC Company Taxation Manual, CTM93180).

HMRC point out in Working Together issue 27 – June 2007 that it is the full accounts which must accompany the CTSA return, not abbreviated accounts.

HMRC had adopted the practice that such accounts should be signed. However, in the recent case of *Codu Computer Ltd v HMRC* (TC01055) [2011] UKFTT 186 (TC), the First Tier Tribunal found that there was no legal justification for such practice. In Codu a company (C) submitted two CT returns. HMRC rejected the returns on the grounds that they were incomplete because the accounts and directors' report had not been signed. C subsequently submitted the returns online, after the prescribed filing dates. HMRC imposed penalties of £100 for each return under *FA 1998, Sch 18 para 17(2)*. C appealed, contending firstly that no penalty was due because it had originally submitted the returns within the statutory time limits (and alternatively that it had a reasonable excuse because it had not been aware that HMRC would reject the returns). The First-Tier Tribunal accepted C's first contention and allowed the appeal. Judge Staker held that 'in the absence of any evidence or authority having been submitted by HMRC in support of the contention that the appellant was required specifically to submit the relevant documents in signed format, the tribunal finds that HMRC have failed to discharge the burden of proving that the appellant did not submit valid returns within the applicable deadline'.

Forms CT603 are usually issued to all active companies between three and seven weeks after the end of the period specified in them, which is usually a period thought to be an accounting period of the company. In a continuing case this will be based on the company's history. In the case of a new, or newly active, company, it will be based on information provided by the company in Form CT41G (new company details), which is issued to all such companies. If the company does not reply to such enquiries, it is assumed that the first accounting period runs for twelve months from the date of incorporation (see **66.2** above on the duty to give notice on coming within charge to corporation tax). (Revenue Guide to Self-Assessment, paras 2.2, 2.3.1).

As regards dormant companies, Forms CT204 are sent at intervals of not more than five years to check whether the company has traded or carried on any other activity, received any income or disposed of any assets in the review period, and to enquire about its future intentions. (Revenue Guide to Self-Assessment, para 2.4). See below as regards discretionary treatment as dormant of certain members' clubs etc.

The company tax return form prescribed by HMRC under *TMA 1970, s 113(1)* is Form CT600, which, with the accompanying guidance notes, also explains the requirements as to accompanying accounts, statements and reports. See **66.31** below as regards layout of the return. Guidance on HMRC's main requirements for substitute forms is available from HMRC's Business Services. Form CT600 and guidance notes would normally be issued with the notice requiring a return, except where an agent acts for the company or the company is recorded as using an approved substitute version of the return form (see HMRC Company Taxation Manual, CTM93140). However no paper returns will be issued for corporation tax returns periods ending on or after 1 April 2010, filed on or after 1 April 2011, as these returns must be filed electronically in a iXBRL.

The return must include a declaration to the effect that, to the best of the knowledge of the person making it, it is correct and complete, and must be delivered (together with all the supplementary information, etc. required) by the 'filing date', i.e. the later of:

(a) twelve months after the end of the period to which it relates;
(b) twelve months after the end of the period of account in which falls the last day of the accounting period to which it relates (except that periods of account in excess of 18 months are treated as ending after 18 months for this purpose, thus the deadline is 30 months from the beginning of that period); and
(c) three months after service of the notice requiring the return,

(and see HMRC Company Taxation Manual, CTM93040 for detailed application of these dates).

[*FA 1998, Sch 18 paras 3, 4, 11, 13, 14; ITA 2007, Sch 1 para 385; SI 2008 No 954, Art 25(2); CTA 2009, Sch 1 para 454*].

Before making their returns, companies may ask their Tax Office (on Form CG34) to check their valuations used for capital gains purposes in completing their returns. (HMRC Share Valuation Manual, SVM24041). HMRC has issued guidance on the valuation of unquoted shares 'Apportioning the Price Paid for a Business Transferred as a Going Concern'. It may be accessed at www.hmrc.gov.uk/shareschemes/shares-valuation.htm. The paper has been rejected robustly by RICS and other bodies. See 'The goodwill game' by Chris Hart in 'Taxation' 2 April 2009.

A return is not 'delivered' to the inspector until it is received in the inspector's office. As regards (c) above, the date of service of the notice is the fourth working day after the date of posting unless the company proves otherwise. (HMRC Company Taxation Manual, CTM93040, CTM93080). HMRC usually issue an acknowledgement of receipt of every company tax return (HMRC Company Taxation Manual, CTM93270).

The notice requiring the return specifies the period to which it relates. A return is required for any accounting period which ends during or at the end of that period (separate returns being required if there is more than one such accounting period). If no accounting period ends during or at the end of the specified period, but there is an accounting period which commences during that period, then a return is required for the part of the specified period which falls before the start of that accounting period. If the company was outside the corporation tax charge throughout the specified period a return is required for the whole of the period. If none of the above applies, no return is required in response to the notice. [*FA 1998, Sch 18 para 5*].

In the absence of a return, HMRC have power to determine the corporation tax liability. [*FA 1998, s 117, Sch 18 paras 36–40; FA 2008, Sch 39 paras 38–40*].

Where the company carries on a trade, profession or business in partnership, the return must include its share of any income, loss, consideration, tax, credit or charge stated in the partnership return under *TMA 1970, s 12AB* for any period including, or including any part of, the company tax return period. [*FA 1998, Sch 18 para 12*].

See **34.5 EUROPEAN UNION LEGISLATION** regarding the application of the corporation tax provisions where a company ceases to be UK-resident in the course of the formation of an SE or where an SE becomes non-UK resident.

Simon's Taxes. See **D1.1308–D1.1315**.

Concessional exemption from requirement to deliver return

[66.5] Members' clubs and similar organisations that exist primarily for recreational and other non-commercial purposes may, at the inspector's discretion, be treated as dormant even though they receive small amounts of investment income. HMRC will write to the company proposing this treatment, and if a company has not had such a letter the treatment does not apply. If a concern to which the concessional treatment applies is sent a notice to file, it will still have to make a return, and it will be expected to give notice of chargeability (see **66.3** above) if there are changes to the types and level of its income, to its rules or constitution, or to the way its financial affairs are controlled, or if chargeable assets are likely to be disposed of.

The treatment applies where the annual corporation tax liability is not expected to exceed £100 and the club is run exclusively for the benefit of its own members. The dormant status will be subject to review at least every five years. The concessional treatment is not extended to:

(i) a privately owned club run by its members as a commercial enterprise for personal profit;
(ii) a housing association or registered social landlord (under *Housing Associations Act 1986*);
(iii) a trade association;
(iv) a thrift fund;
(v) a holiday club;

(vi) a friendly society; or
(vii) a company that is a subsidiary of, or wholly owned by, a charity.

For each year of dormancy, the body must have no anticipated allowable trading losses, no chargeable assets likely to be disposed of and no anticipated payments subject to deduction of tax at source.

The concessional treatment is also extended to non-profit-making property management companies which pay no dividends and make no other distributions of profit, *which nevertheless remain liable to income tax* if they receive investment income on sinking funds, etc. held in designated accounts. Generally, where the annual income is below £1,000 and is taxed at source, a return will not be required every year.

(HMRC Internet Statement 25 August 2006 (available at www.hmrc.gov.uk/ct/clubs-charities-agents/clubs.htm).)

Estimates

[66.6] Where, despite the company's best efforts, a figure cannot be finalised by the filing date, the company may make its best estimate of the figure, tell the inspector that the figure is estimated and say when a final figure is expected. Provided that the company has taken all reasonable steps, a return so completed is not incomplete. If the company subsequently becomes aware that the estimate is no longer a 'best estimate', or that it can be replaced by an accurate figure, this information should be sent to the inspector without unreasonable delay. If estimates are submitted which prove not to be reasonable, the return is not thereby rendered incomplete, although penalties may arise if the return was completed fraudulently or negligently (see **66.25** below). (HMRC Company Taxation Manual, CTM93280).

Failure to render return

[66.7] From a date to be appointed a penalty for failing to make a corporation tax return will be issued under *FA 2009, s 105, Sch 55 and 56 (as amended by F(No 3)A 2010)*. The new penalties are as detailed in **60 PENALTIES**. However, until such appointed date, the following provisions apply.

A company which fails to make a return for any period, when required to do so, is liable to a penalty of £200 (£100 if the return is delivered within three months of the final day for delivery). If the return period is one for which accounts are required under *Companies Act 2006, 1985* or NI equivalent (see above), penalties do not apply provided that the return is delivered by the last day for delivery of those accounts. Extensions granted by the Secretary of State for the delivery of *Companies Act* accounts are taken into account in this context, and in practice the disapplication of penalties also applies where the return period overlaps the *Companies Act* accounts period (see HMRC Company Taxation Manual, CTM93070 and CTM94100).

The penalties are increased to £1,000 and £500 respectively for failure in relation to a return for an accounting period where a penalty under these (or preceding) provisions was incurred for each of the two immediately preceding accounting periods, and the company was within the charge to corporation tax for the whole of the three accounting periods. An additional penalty is imposed where the return is still outstanding at the later of the end of the filing date and 18 months after the end of the return period. The additional penalty is 10% of the tax unpaid at the time the penalty arises if the return is delivered within two years after the end of the return period, otherwise 20%.

The tax taken into account for this purpose is the unpaid tax for the return period (disregarding any relief deferred under *CTA 2010, s 458(5)* (previously *ICTA 1988, s 419(4A)*) in respect of the repayment, etc. of a loan to a participator, see **22.15 CLOSE COMPANIES**). [*FA 1998, Sch 18 paras 17, 18, 19; CTA 2010, Sch 1 para 297(5)*].

By concession, automatic penalties are not charged provided that the return is received on or before the last business day within seven days following the filing date. (HMRC Extra-Statutory Concession, B46). With the start of mandatory e-filing for CT returns, and the existing mandatory e-filing of other returns, such as PAYE, it is considered that ESC B46 is now redundant and it no longer applies post 31 March 2011. See also **42 HMRC EXTRA STATUTORY CONCESSIONS.**

HMRC have issued guidance (11 March 2011) with regard to what would (and would not) be considered a reasonable excuse in respect of missing the filing date for online filing. They have indicated that, generally, a 'reasonable excuse' is when some unforeseeable and exceptional event beyond the taxpayer's control has prevented the taxpayer from filing their return on time. For example: a failure in HMRC's own computer system; the taxpayer's computer breaks down just before or during the preparation of the online return; or a serious illness has made the taxpayer incapable of filing their tax return. It is stressed that the above are just examples and that each case is unique and will be considered on its own merits.

HMRC will not accept an excuse where the taxpayer has not made a reasonable effort to meet the deadline. For example, the taxpayer: found the online system too complicated to follow; was let down by their accountant; forgot about the deadline; or did not try to re-submit their return on time once a problem with the IT system was put right.

Further details can be found at: www.hmrc.gov.uk/online/excuse-missed-deadline.htm.

Self-assessment and payment of tax

[66.8] The company tax return must include a self-assessment by the company of its corporation tax liability on the basis of the information contained in the return, and taking account of reliefs or allowances claimed in the return. For this purpose a return is regarded as a return for an accounting period if the period is so treated in the return and is not longer than twelve months, whether or not it is in fact an accounting period. The self-assessment is required even if no tax is payable or a repayment due.

The calculation proceeds in four steps.

- *Step 1* The corporation tax chargeable on the company's profits (including its share(s) of any partnership profits) is calculated by applying the applicable rate or rates of corporation tax to those profits for that period.
- *Step 2* Effect is given to any available set-offs or reliefs under:
  - (i) *CTA 2010, ss 19, 20 or 21*; *ICTA 1988, s 13(2)* or (for financial years 2000 to 2005) *s 13AA(2)* (marginal relief for companies with small profits, see **67.3 SMALL PROFITS — REDUCED RATES**);
  - (ii) *FA 2000, Sch 15 Pt V* (**CORPORATE VENTURING SCHEME (28)**);
  - (iii) *CTA 2010, Pt 7*; *FA 2002, Sch 16 Pt 5* (**COMMUNITY INVESTMENT TAX RELIEF (23)**);
  - (iv) any double tax relief under *TIOPA 2010, ss 2 and 6, or s 18(1)(b)(2); ICTA 1988, s 788* or *s 790* (double taxation relief, see **32.2, 32.3 DOUBLE TAX RELIEF**); or
  - (v) *ICTA 1988, s 239* – set off of ACT – *SI 1999 No 358* (surplus ACT under the shadow ACT system, see **3.5 ADVANCE CORPORATION TAX — SHADOW ACT**).
- *Step 3* Add any amounts assessable or chargeable as if they were corporation tax under: *CTA 2010, s 455* (previously *ICTA 1988, s 419(1)*) (loans to close company participators — see **22.12 CLOSE COMPANIES**); *CTA 2010, s 330(1)* in respect of ring fence trades; or *ICTA 1988, s 747(4)(a)* (see **27.8 CONTROLLED FOREIGN COMPANIES**), as reduced by any reliefs specific to those amounts.
- *Step 4* Deduct any amounts to be set off against the overall corporation tax liability under: *CTA 2010, ss 967, 968; ICTA 1988, s 7(2)* or *s 11(3)* (income tax borne by deduction, see **46.9 INCOME TAX IN RELATION TO A COMPANY, 65.5 RESIDENCE**); *ICTA 1988, ss 246N* or *246Q* (ACT paid in respect of foreign dividend income).

[*FA 1998, Sch 18 paras 7, 8; FA 2006, s 26(7)–(11); CTA 2010, Sch 1 para 297(4)*].

Subject to the instalment provisions applicable to 'large' companies (see below and **59.3 PAYMENT OF TAX**), corporation tax is due and payable on the day following the expiry of nine months from the end of the accounting period, on the basis of the amount computed (as above) in the company tax return for the period. Any excess over the tax payable of 'relevant amounts' stated in the company tax return is repaid.

'*Relevant amounts*' are corporation tax paid and not repaid, corporation tax refunds surrendered to the company intra-group (see **39.25 PAYMENTS AND COLLECTIONS OF TAX**), income tax as described in *Step 4* above (so far as not set off under that calculation) and **CONSTRUCTION INDUSTRY SCHEME (26)** deductions. [*TMA 1970, s 59D*]. Payment applications and reconciliations by HMRC relate to a single accounting period (without the issue of 'taxpayer statements' covering more than one chargeable period as under income tax self-assessment). (HMRC Company Taxation Manual, CTM97160).

A company may claim repayment of corporation tax paid for an accounting period where the company's circumstances change so that it has grounds for believing that the amount paid exceeds its probable (although not yet finally established) liability. The claim must state the amount the company considers has been overpaid and the grounds for believing the payment to have become excessive. No claim may be made before the 'material date' in relation to the tax (see **50.2 INTEREST ON OVERPAID TAX**). If the tax is the subject of an outstanding appeal, the company may apply to the tribunal for a determination of the amount to be repaid (and the application may be combined with a postponement application under *TMA 1970, s 55*, see **59.10 PAYMENT OF TAX**).

If the company tax return has not been made, **CONSTRUCTION INDUSTRY SCHEME** (**26**) deductions are ignored for these purposes. [*TMA 1970, s 59DA*]. 'Large' companies to which instalment payments apply are precluded from making a claim under *section 59DA* where a claim for repayment of instalment payments is made (see **59.3 PAYMENT OF TAX**). [*SI 1998 No 3175, Reg 6(8)*].

See generally **50.2 INTEREST ON OVERPAID TAX, 49.2 INTEREST ON OVERDUE TAX.**

The company tax return requires the company to state whether it is liable to make instalment payments on account of its corporation tax liabilities (see **59.3 PAYMENT OF TAX**). Although HMRC will at some stage check the position, initial payment applications, interest calculations, etc. will be based on the company's statement of its position. (HMRC Company Taxation Manual, CTM92550, CTM92690).

Losses, etc.

It should be noted that losses and other negative amounts also have to be included in the return and become final in the same way as the assessment itself, and are similarly subject to enquiry, although this would not apply to, for example, a loss in a self-assessment return brought forward from a pre-self-assessment period. The same figure must be used for a negative amount which becomes final in any other return affected by it. (HMRC Company Taxation Manual, CTM95440, CTM95430). The use of the figure in another return does not give HMRC an opportunity to enquire into the figure by means of an enquiry into that return (although this does not prevent an enquiry into the use of the negative amount in that return). (HMRC Company Taxation Manual, CTM04150).

Simon's Taxes. See **D1.1311, D1.1320.**

Amendments to returns

[66.9] The company may, by notice to HMRC within twelve months of the filing date (see above), amend its own return. A return made for the wrong period must be amended within twelve months of what would have been the final date for delivery of a return for the period if it had been an accounting period.

HMRC may, by notice to the company, amend the return to correct obvious errors or mistakes (including arithmetical errors and errors of principle, but *not* where any judgment as to the accuracy of figures in the return is involved) up to nine months after the date of delivery of the return (or after the date of the amendment if the correction relates to a company amendment).

From 1 April 2010 HMRC may also amend a return for anything else they have reason to believe is incorrect, in the light of information held by them. An HMRC correction is, however, of no effect if the company amends the return so as to reject the correction or, if the time limit for an amendment has passed, gives written notice rejecting it to the officer of HMRC by whom the notice of correction was issued within three months of the date of issue.

[*FA 1998, Sch 18 paras 15(1)(4), 16; FA 2008, s 119*].

Amendments to returns must be in such form, and accompanied by such information, etc., as HMRC may require. [*FA 1998, Sch 18 para 15(2)(3)*]. No official form is prescribed for this purpose, and amendments may be made using an unofficial form or by correspondence. (HMRC Company Taxation Manual, CTM93300).

Returns of income tax deducted by a company

[66.10] Returns must be made by reference to 'return periods'. A '*return period*' ends on 31 March, 30 June, 30 September and 31 December and at the end of a company's accounting period.

[*ICTA 1988, Sch 13 para 1, repealed by FA 1998, Sch 3 para 41*].

[*ICTA 1988, Sch 16; Schedule rewritten to ITA 2007, Pt 15 Chs 15, 16, 17*]. For details, see **46.8 INCOME TAX IN RELATION TO A COMPANY.**

Returns of non-qualifying distributions

[66.11] Where a company makes a non-qualifying distribution (see **31.17 DISTRIBUTIONS**) it must make a return to the inspector (a) within 14 days of the end of the accounting period in which the distribution is made or (b) if the distribution is not made in any accounting period, within 14 days of when it is made. The return must show particulars of the transaction, the name and address of the person(s) receiving the distribution and the amount or value received by each.

[*CTA 2010, ss 1101–1103; ICTA 1988, s 234(5)–(9)*].

Simon's Taxes. See D5.505.

Returns of qualifying distributions

[66.12] The recipient is entitled to ask the distributing company for a written statement showing the amount or value of the distribution and the amount of tax credit which attaches to it, irrespective or whether or not the recipient would be entitled to a tax credit. The right to this statement is distinct from the duty on the distributing company to provide a tax certificate to the recipient of the distribution.

[*CTA 2010, ss 1100, 1104*].

Returns of stock dividends issued

[66.13] Where a company issues stock dividends (see **31.14**(g) **DISTRIBUTIONS**), it must make a return to the inspector within 30 days of the end of the return period as specified in **66.10** above. The return must show the first date on which the company was required to issue the shares, particulars of terms of issue and the cash equivalent of the share capital in accordance with *ITTOIA 2005, s 412*. See Tolley's Income Tax under Savings and Investment Income.

[*CTA 2010, ss 1052, 1053; ICTA 1988, s 250; ITTOIA 2005, Sch 1 para 120*].

Simon's Taxes. See D5.506.

Returns of interest by bankers etc.

[66.14] On receipt of notice from an inspector, any person (including the National Savings Bank and a building society) paying or crediting interest, on money received or retained in the UK in the ordinary course of his business, must make a return for any specified year of assessment (ending not more than three years before the date of service of the notice). The return must show the name and address of the recipient, the gross amount of interest paid or credited and the amount (if any) of tax deducted. The payer may exclude from that return interest paid to a person who has so requested and has given written notice that the person beneficially entitled to the interest is a non-UK resident company. Similarly, where a declaration of non-ordinary residence has been given to the payer to enable interest to be paid gross (see **8.7 BANKS**, **9.3 BUILDING SOCIETIES**), and the person who made that declaration has so requested, the payer is not required to include interest paid, credited or received before 6 April 2001 in the return under this provision. Notices may be issued concerning different parts or branches of a business. HMRC have powers by statutory instrument to make regulations requiring further prescribed information with the return, or providing that prescribed information is *not* required, or requiring information and returns to be in prescribed form, or providing for inspection of books, documents, records, etc. [*TMA 1970, s 17; SI 1990 No 2231; SI 2001 Nos 404, 405*].

Returns may similarly be required from any other person paying interest or receiving it on behalf of others. [*TMA 1970, s 18; SI 2001 No 405*].

With effect for interest payments on or after 6 April 2001, *SI 2001 No 405* excludes a wide range of payments from the application of *TMA 1970, ss 17* and *18*. In particular, the automatic reporting of payments to non-residents applies only to interest paid to individuals. For guidance on the making of information returns under *TMA 1970, ss 17* and *18*, see HMRC's website (at www.hmrc.gov.uk/s17-s18guidance/index.htm). HMRC have issued revised specifications for returns for the reporting year beginning 6 April 2004.

With effect for payments on or after 6 April 2005, references to interest paid without deduction of income tax in *TMA 1970, ss 17* and *18* include references to alternative finance return under **ALTERNATIVE FINANCE ARRANGEMENTS** (**4**). This applies to alternative finance arrangements entered into on or after 6 April 2005 subject to commencement rules for arrangements entered into before that date where a profit share return is payable on or after that date. *CTA 2009, Sch 1 para 299* brings alternative financial return within the treatment of interest.

For accounting periods ending on or after 5 April 2007, in relation to building societies, references to interest include references to dividends, including distributions whether or not described as dividends.

[*CTA 2009, ss 501–521; FA 2005, s 56, Sch 2 para 2; CTA 2009, Sch 1 para 659*].

EU Directive on the Taxation of Savings

[66.15] *The Reporting of Savings Income Information Regulations 2003* (*SI 2003 No 3297* as amended) implement into UK law the EU Directive on the Taxation of Savings (*Directive 2003/48/EC*, 3 June 2003), designed to counter cross-border tax evasion by individuals on their savings income. The Directive, referred to as the Savings Directive or the Savings Tax Directive, came into effect on 1 July 2005. Under the Directive, prescribed UK paying agents, e.g. businesses and public bodies that pay savings income to, or collect savings income for, individuals resident elsewhere in the EU have to report details of the income and the payee to HMRC, who then passes on the information to the corresponding tax authority in the payee's country of residence. Similar information regarding UK-resident payees will flow in the opposite direction. (Austria, Belgium and Luxembourg have imposed, for a transitional period, a withholding tax as an alternative to exchanging information.)

The regulations prescribe the types of paying agent and payee within the scheme, the information required, the time limits for compliance and the penalties for non-compliance, and it provides for inspection of paying agents' records. For these purposes, '*savings income*' means interest (including premium bond winnings but not interest unrelated to a money debt or penalty charges for late payments), interest accrued or capitalised at the sale, refund or redemption of a money debt, and certain income distributed by or realised upon the sale, refund or redemption of shares or units in a collective investment fund (see **52.1 INVESTMENT FUNDS**). Treasury regulations may also implement any similar arrangements made with non-EU countries (see further below). For HMRC guidance on savings income reporting and other related items, see www.hmrc.gov.uk/esd-guidance/index.htm. Version 9 of the guidance was issued on 9 February 2011. See also Treasury Explanatory Notes to Finance Bill 2003, European Commission Press Release 4 June 2003, Revenue Press Releases 30 June 2003, 22 September 2003 and Revenue Internet Statement 19 December 2003.

The Savings Directive applies to all EU member states. The EU has concluded similar savings taxation agreements with Andorra, Liechtenstein, San Marino, Monaco and Switzerland. These territories apply a withholding tax and will exchange information at the request of tax authorities of EU member states in all criminal or civil cases of tax fraud etc. on a reciprocal basis.

Similar agreements have been concluded by individual EU member states with ten dependent and associated territories of the UK and the Netherlands (Anguilla, Aruba (*SI 2005 No 1458*), the British Virgin Islands (*SI 2005 No 1457*), the Cayman Islands, Gibraltar (*SI 2006 No 1453*), Guernsey (*SI 2005 No 1262*), the Isle of Man (*SI 2005 No 1263*), Jersey (*SI 2005 No 1261*), Montserrat (*SI 2005 No 1459*), the Netherlands Antilles (*SI 2005 No 1460*) and the Turks & Caicos Islands). The British Virgin Islands, Guernsey, the Isle of Man, Jersey, the Netherlands Antilles and the Turks and Caicos Islands are applying a withholding tax during the same transitional period as applies to Austria, Belgium and Luxembourg. The agreements with Anguilla, Aruba, the Cayman Islands and Montserrat provide for exchange of information. The agreements with Anguilla, Cayman Islands and Turks and Caicos Islands do not, for the time being, have a reciprocal effect, as the residents of those territories are not taxable on their savings income. As the UK and Gibraltar are not separate member states, the Directive does not apply between them (HMRC Internet Statement 5 July 2005), but a bilateral agreement was signed on 19 December 2005 between the UK and Gibraltar under which those territories will exchange information with each other and by virtue of which Gibraltar will operate a withholding tax during the above-mentioned transitional period.

Where, under the Savings Directive or equivalent arrangements made with non-EU member states, a withholding tax is levied as an alternative to exchanging information, relief is available for such withholding tax (termed 'special withholding tax') against UK income tax and capital gains tax liabilities or, to the extent that set-off is not possible, by repayment. As an alternative, application may be made to HMRC for a certificate which can be presented to a paying agent to enable savings income to be paid to the applicant without deduction of such withholding tax.

[*TIOPA 2010, Pt 3, ss 135–145*].

The possibility of widening the scope of the Savings Directive was mooted during the review of its operation in 2008. In addition, it was argued that the transitional period might have come to an end with the significant increase in the number of tax information exchange arrangements between the EU Member States and other third countries. These matters remain the subject of debate.

Simon's Taxes. See **A4.120**.

Returns of income from UK securities

[66.16] A person receiving income on behalf of, or by or through whom income is paid to, another person resident in the UK must, within 28 days (or such longer time as may be specified in the necessary notice) make a return giving details similar to those in **66.14** above. [*TMA 1970, s 24*].

Other returns

[66.17] For returns by employers, hoteliers, stockbrokers, partnerships etc. and in respect of fees, commissions and copyrights, see Tolley's Income Tax under Returns. For returns by companies purchasing own shares, see **63.3** PURCHASE BY A COMPANY OF ITS OWN SHARES. For returns of Eurobond interest payments, see **46.2**(b) INCOME TAX IN RELATION TO A COMPANY.

Record keeping

[66.18] Provision may be made by statutory instrument for the records to include 'supporting documents'.

A company which may be required to deliver a company tax return (see **66.4** above) for any period must preserve for at least six years after the end of that period the records required to enable it to make a complete and correct return for the period. HMRC may specify, in writing, an earlier date. This includes records and 'supporting documents' (e.g. accounts, books, deeds, contracts, vouchers and receipts) of all receipts and expenses, and the matters in respect of which they arise, and, in the case of a trade involving dealing in goods, of all trade sales and purchases. The obligation to keep records permits keeping them in any form or keeping the information in them in any form, subject to any exceptions specified by HMRC in writing. HMRC is given power to amend these provisions by statutory order, and different provisions may be made for different cases.

If the company is required by notice to deliver a return for the period, the records must be preserved until the later of the end of the six years and either:

(a) the date on which any enquiry into the return is completed (see **66.9** above); or
(b) if there is no enquiry, the date on which HMRC no longer have power to enquire into the return (see **66.19** below).

If the notice requiring the return is given after the expiry of the six years, the records which must be preserved are any which the company still has in its possession at the time the notice is given.

The duty to preserve records may generally be satisfied by the preservation of the information contained in them (e.g. in electronic form), and a copy of any document forming part of the records is admissible in evidence before the Commissioners to the same extent as the records themselves. This does not, however, apply to vouchers, certificates etc. which show tax credits or deductions at source of UK or foreign tax, e.g. dividend vouchers, interest vouchers (including those issued by banks and building societies), which must be preserved in their original form.

The maximum penalty for failure to preserve records as above is £3,000 in relation to any one accounting period. No penalty is incurred where the records not preserved are such as might have been needed only for the purposes of claims, elections or notices not included in the return, or where they are vouchers, certificates, etc. showing UK tax credits or deductions at source (e.g. dividend vouchers and interest certificates) and HMRC are satisfied that other documentary evidence supplied to them proves any facts they reasonably require to be proved and which the voucher, etc. would have proved. In practice, HMRC will seek such penalties only in the more serious cases where, for example, records have been destroyed deliberately to obstruct an enquiry or there has been a history of serious record-keeping failures (see HMRC Enquiry Manual, EM4650).

[*FA 1998, Sch 18 paras 21–23; FA 2008, s 115, Sch 37 paras 7–9*].

See generally, HMRC Enquiry Manual, EM1001 *et seq*. See Revenue Tax Bulletin October 1998, at pp 587–589 for an article on the general application in practice of the record-keeping requirement (and April 2002 pp 925, 926 for clarification of that article), and at pp 579, 580 on its application to transfer pricing matters. Both these extracts are reproduced in Appendix 2 to HMRC's Guide to Self-Assessment.

Recent guidance has been issued, on 21 February 2011, to assist small and medium sized businesses. Free tools for SMEs can be found on the HMRC website, in particular, with regard to record keeping the following links may assist:

www.hmrc.gov.uk/factsheet/record-keeping.pdf;

www.businesslink.gov.uk/recordkeepingcheck.

Simon's Taxes. See **D1.1304**.

Enquiries into returns

[66.19] For accounting periods ending after 31 March 2008, an enquiry must be opened within twelve months after the date the return was filed with HMRC unless the return was filed late, when the rules are unchanged (see below). Notice of intention to open an enquiry must first be given.

However, where the company is a member of a group (other than a small group), the enquiry window continues to run until twelve months from the filing date. A group is defined as 'a parent undertaking and its subsidiary undertaking' and a group broadly qualifies as 'small' for a year if two or more of the qualifying conditions are met in that year and the preceding financial year. The qualifying conditions are met by a group in a year in which it satisfies two or more of the following requirements (per *Companies Act 2006, s 383* as amended by *SI 2008 No 393*):

1 Aggregate turnover	Not more than £6.5 million net (or £7.8 million gross)
2 Aggregate balance sheet total	Not more than £3.26 million net (or £3.9 million gross)
3 Aggregate number of employees	Not more than 50

'Net' means after any set-offs and other adjustments made to eliminate group transactions and 'gross' means without those set-offs and other adjustments. A company may satisfy any relevant requirement on the basis of either the net or the gross figure.

For accounting periods ending on or before 31 March 2008, HMRC may enquire into a company tax return if they give notice of their intention to do so within twelve months after the filing date (see **66.4** above) or, if the return was delivered after that date, by the quarter day (31 January, 30 April, 31 July or 31 October) next following the first anniversary of the day on which the return was delivered. HMRC consider that notice is 'given' when the notice is issued, which, in the case of notice by post, means the date of posting (see HMRC Enquiry Manual, EM1506, EM1510, EM1525), but in a Special Commissioner's decision on the similar provisions for individual self-assessment, it was held that service of the notice is treated as effected at the time at which the letter would be delivered in the ordinary course of post, i.e. on the second working day after posting for first class mail or on the fourth working day after posting for second class mail (*Wing Hung Lai v Bale* [1999] STC (SCD) 238). It was held in the case of *R (oao Spring Salmon and Seafood Ltd) v CIR* [2004] STC 444, Ct of Sess, that a notice of enquiry made under *FA 1998, Sch 18 para 24* was not required to be made in writing.

An enquiry following an amendment to a return must be notified by the quarter day next following the first anniversary of the making of the amendment, and if it is given at a time when notice of an enquiry could no longer have been given had the return not been amended, is limited to matters to which the amendment relates or which are affected by it. (In practice, except where an amendment relates to or affects matters fundamental to the whole return, HMRC enquiries will normally be limited to the area of the return that was amended, regardless of whether a full enquiry would still be in time (see HMRC Enquiry Manual, EM1520)).

Only one notice of enquiry may be given in respect of a return, except one given in consequence of an amendment (or further amendment(s)) by the company of the return.

HMRC does not have to justify an enquiry, by stating dissatisfaction with the return or identifying particular aspects giving cause for concern, and will not give reasons (although they may identify particular areas on which the enquiry will focus). Enquiries will range from questioning simple errors not identified during initial processing of the return through to full in-depth reviews of companies' affairs, including the underlying records. Business documents and records will commonly be requested. Although random selection will play a part, most enquiry cases will continue to be selected on the basis of a judgment, informed by all the information in HMRC's possession, of the risk of tax loss. (HMRC Enquiry Manual, EM1050–EM1070, EM1503, EM1550–EM1581).

Large companies

Where it is practical to do so, HMRC will aim to open all enquiries into a group's returns by the 'group anniversary target'. The '*group anniversary target*' is twelve months after the last company files its return. However, while

HMRC say that enquiries will be opened as early as possible, if it is not possible to open an enquiry within the group anniversary target, they will continue to open them up to the statutory deadline (twelve months after the filing date). There will be liaison through customer relationship managers and customer managers. Where there is no agreement to meet the group anniversary target, the statutory deadline will apply. See www.hmrc.gov.uk/ctsa/enq-window.htm.

Conduct of enquiry

These powers are to be replaced by the unified powers at **43.3–43.11 HMRC INVESTIGATORY POWERS** under *FA 2008*, effective from 1 April 2009.

Code of Practice No 14 (updated in April 2003) covers all aspects of enquiries under self-assessment. It is given to companies concerned at the start of every enquiry (except that where a simple enquiry is expected to be settled by a brief exchange of correspondence and not to involve penalties, a single-page version of the Code is issued instead). The code can be found at: www.hmrc.gov.uk/pdfs/cop14.htm

When the time limit for opening an enquiry into a return has passed, HMRC can still ask questions about the return, but further action can only be taken in cases of fraudulent or negligent conduct (as was, now deliberate or careless action) or failure to disclose all relevant information (see **7.3 ASSESSMENTS**). (HMRC Enquiry Manual, EM1053, EM3250 *et seq.*).

Subject to the limitation referred to above in the case of enquiries into amendments to returns, an enquiry extends to anything contained (or required to be contained) in the return, including any claim or election and any amount that affects or may affect the tax liability of another accounting period or another company. If it appears to HMRC that the return is, or may be, for the wrong period, or has become for the wrong period as a result of a direction from HMRC under *CTA 2009, s 11* (previously *ICTA 1988, s 12(5A)*) (see **2.5 ACCOUNTING PERIODS**), the enquiry may extend to the period for which the return should have been made. A return is for this purpose made for the wrong period if either it is made for a period treated as, but not in fact, an accounting period, or it is made on the basis that there is no accounting period ending in or at the end of the period specified in the notice requiring the return but there is in fact such an accounting period. The time limits for notice of enquiry into a return for the wrong period are by reference to the date by which the return would have been required to be delivered had the period for which the return was made not been the wrong period.

For accounting periods beginning on or after 1 April 2004, an enquiry may also extend to consideration of whether to give a company, which is a medium-sized enterprise, a transfer pricing notice under *ITIOPA 2010, s168(1); ICTA 1988, Sch 28AA para 5C* (see **72.6 TRANSFER PRICING**). An enquiry may also extend to a notice under *TIOPA 2010, ss 81, 82; ICTA 1988, s 804ZA* in respect of schemes and arrangements designed to increase double taxation relief (as introduced, for payments of foreign tax on or after 16 March 2005, by *FA 2005, s 87* — see **5.35 ANTI-AVOIDANCE**) or to a notice under *F(No 2)A 2005, s 24* or *s 26* (amended by *CTA 2009, Sch 1 para 670*) in respect of tax arbitrage (see **5.46 ANTI-AVOIDANCE**) or *TCGA 1992, s 184G* or *s 184H* (avoidance utilising losses — see **17.4 CAPITAL GAINS**).

These provisions are amended to provide for extended time limits in the cases of non-annual accounting of general insurance business and of insurance companies and friendly societies with non-annual actuarial investigations.

[*FA 1998, Sch 18; paras 24–26, 85–87; FA 2004, s 37(2), Sch 5 para 10; FA 2005, s 88(3)(5); F(No 2)A 2005, s 29(1); Companies Act 2006, s 474(1); FA 2006, s 71(2); FA 2007, s 96; CTA 2009, Sch 1 para 454, 671*].

Where an enquiry remains open after expiry of the period within which a notice of enquiry may be issued solely because of an unagreed valuation for the purpose of computing chargeable gains of a company or other body within the charge to corporation tax, HMRC will not raise further enquiries into unrelated matters unless, had the enquiry already been completed, a discovery could have been made (see **7.3 ASSESSMENTS**). This does not inhibit HMRC from enquiring into matters relating to the valuation which were not raised on first reference. (HMRC Statement of Practice, SP 1/02).

In March 2002, the Revenue published a framework within which income tax self-assessment enquiries will be worked and to which professional advisers are encouraged to adhere. Particular topics covered are the opening enquiry letter, requests for and conduct of interviews and meetings, and requests for non-business bank and building society accounts (plus credit/charge/store card details). (Revenue 'Working Together' Bulletin No 8, March 2002). A similar framework, suitably adapted, applies to corporation tax self-assessment enquiries. See Revenue 'Working Together' Bulletin No 12, March 2003.

On 29 October 2007, HMRC announced on its website the commencement of a trial of a different approach to enquiries, to run from November 2007 to April 2008. This is known as the 'Openness and Early Dialogue' ('OED') approach. Under this approach, HMRC advises the taxpayer whether the enquiry is full or aspect and why it has been opened. At the start, HMRC agrees with the taxpayer a timescale for an initial meeting (or, in some cases, telephone call), production of information and documents, examination of records and discussion of findings. Where possible, all these take place on the same day. If a taxpayer decides not to attend a meeting, this does not, in itself, be seen as a lack of co-operation. After the first meeting, HMRC will review the records. There may then be a second meeting to allow the taxpayer to answer questions or voice concerns, followed by agreement about actions required, or closure of the enquiry. See www.hmrc.gov.uk/ctsa/openness-early-dialogue-enquiries.htm. HMRC have confirmed post the trials that the OED approach was seen as being effective in reducing the financial and emotional burden of a compliance check as well as reducing the time taken for such a check. Since 2008 HMRC have been implementing OED in many areas where compliance checks are undertaken. See further Tax Adviser (March 2010) 'Openness and Early Dialogue' Jayne Banner, HMRC.

Power to call for documents

[66.20] From 1 April 2009 this power has been replaced by the new information gathering powers found in *FA 2008, Sch 36 Pt 1* (see **43.4 HMRC INVESTIGATORY POWERS**).

After (or at the same time as) giving notice of an enquiry, HMRC may by notice require the company to produce such documents (including computer records, see below) in the company's possession or power, and such information in such form, as they may reasonably require for the purposes of the enquiry. The notice is not restricted to documents, etc. the company is obliged to keep (see **66.18** above), but may require other information such as a profit and loss account, a balance sheet or a detailed factual account of how an entry in a return is made up, so long as they are relevant to the purposes of the enquiry and are in the company's possession or power. (HMRC Enquiry Manual, EM1555, EM1560, EM2200 *et seq.*). (In *Slater Ltd v Beacontree General Commrs* (2001) 74 TC 471 (and also the subsequent case of *Slater Ltd v CIR* [2002] EWHC 2676 (Ch), [2004] STC 1342, [2002] All ER (D) 275 (Nov)), it was held that the exemptions conferred on companies by the *Companies Act 1985* on the accounts which may be required did not restrict the information which may be required in support of those accounts.)

The notice must specify a period of not less than 30 days (from the date of receipt of the notice see *Self-assessed v Inspector of Taxes* [1999] STC (SCD) 253) within which the documents, etc. are to be produced, although if the company has genuine difficulty in meeting the deadline, HMRC may be prepared to agree a revised time scale (HMRC Enquiry Manual, EM1580, EM2217, EM2250). For HMRC's powers regarding computer records see **43.18 HMRC INVESTIGATORY POWERS.**

Documents, etc. relating to the conduct of any pending appeal or referral (see below) of questions to the Special Commissioners by the company (i.e. those brought into existence as part of the preparation for presentation of the appeal or referral, see HMRC Enquiry Manual, EM2218) are excluded.

For a case on the scope of such a notice, see *Mother v Inspector of Taxes* [1999] STC (SCD) 279 (concerning the similar powers in *TMA 1970, s 19A* relating to individual self-assessment enquiries).

Photographic or other facsimile copies of documents may be produced, but HMRC may by notice require production for inspection of the originals within a specified time of not less than 30 days. HMRC may take copies of, or make extracts from, any document produced to them.

The company may appeal in writing against any such notice within 30 days of the notice being given. The appeal is heard and determined in the same way as an appeal against an assessment, and the tribunal is required to confirm the notice only in so far as the documents or information appear to them to be reasonably required for the purposes of the enquiry, and to set it aside in so far as that condition is not met, their decision being final and conclusive. To the extent that a notice is confirmed on appeal, it must be complied with within 30 days after determination of the appeal. Under the new provisions post 1 April 2009 any notice should be complied with within the time specified. In addition, with effect from 1 April 2009 there is no right of appeal against a notice to produce information or documents which form part of the company's statutory records. [*FA 2008, Sch 36 paras 29, 62*].

Under the new regime, the penalty for failure to comply with a notice is £300, previously the penalty for failure to comply with a notice was £50. In addition, for each day on which the failure continues, a further penalty of £60 (under the new regime) can be imposed. Prior to 1 April 2009 an additional daily penalty might be imposed, not exceeding £30 if the penalty is determined by an officer of HMRC under *TMA 1970, s 100* or £150 if it was determined by the Commissioners under *TMA 1970, s 100C* (see **60.14 PENALTIES** in particular with regard to the new unified penalty regime), subject to the normal right of appeal. No penalty may be imposed after the failure has been remedied.

No penalty can be imposed where it is genuinely impossible to comply with a notice, e.g. where the documents, etc. concerned do not exist. If such documents, etc. were required to be kept, a penalty, as under **66.18** above, may arise, but no penalty for failure to produce can arise. (Revenue Guide to Self-Assessment, paras 6.10.7, 6.10.8).

[*FA 1988, s 127; FA 1998, Sch 18 paras 27–29; FA 2001, Sch 29 para 38(4)*].

As noted above, the powers to obtain information from third parties under *TMA 1970, s 20 et seq.*, can now be found in *FA 2008, Sch 36*, see further **43 HMRC INVESTIGATORY POWERS**.

Amendments during enquiry

[66.21] If during the course of an enquiry HMRC form the opinion that the company's self-assessed tax is insufficient and that unless the assessment is immediately amended there is likely to be a loss of tax, they may by notice to the company amend its self-assessment to make good the deficiency. An appeal in writing may be made against such an amendment within 30 days of the notice, but will not be heard and determined before completion of the enquiry (although application for postponement may be made under *TMA 1970, s 55*, see **59.10 PAYMENT OF TAX**).

If the enquiry is limited to matters arising from an earlier amendment by the company of its self-assessment (as above), the notice may only apply to a deficiency attributable to that amendment. In practice, HMRC normally ask the company to make an additional payment on account to cover any deficiency identified during an enquiry, and only make an amendment as above where the company refuses to make such a payment and they believe that tax is at risk, e.g. where the company might dispose of its assets or go into liquidation (see HMRC Enquiry Manual, EM1936, EM1951).

If a company amends its return during an enquiry, the amendment does not restrict the scope of the enquiry, but may be taken into account in the enquiry. So far as the amendment affects the self-assessed tax, or any amount that affects or may affect the tax payable for another accounting period or by another company, it does not take effect until after the enquiry is completed (without prejudice to any claim for repayment of tax under *TMA 1970, s 59DA*, see **66.8** above).

On completion of the enquiry, if the conclusions in the closure notice (see below) state either that the amendment was not taken into account or that no amendment is required arising from the enquiry, the deferred amendment takes effect immediately. Otherwise, it is taken into account by the company in amending its return in accordance with the closure notice. From a date to be appointed, HMRC will have the power to amend the company's self-assessment at the end of an enquiry. In that case, the company's amendment will take effect as part of the amendments made by the closure notice.

In practice, if the closure notice states that no amendment of the return is required, HMRC will give effect to the company amendment, and if it states that the return should be amended in consequence of the enquiry, the suggested amendments will normally take account of the company amendment. Where it says that the amendment has not been taken into account, the company may, if it so wishes, include its own amendment with those it makes in accordance with the closure notice, although this gives HMRC the opportunity (as above) to make further enquiries into matters relating to or affected by that amendment. (See HMRC COTAX Manual under Enquiries/CTSA Enquiries/Taxpayer Amendments; Revenue Guide to Self-Assessment, para 6.12.6).

[*FA 1998, Sch 18 paras 30, 31; FA 2008, s 119(5)*].

Referral of questions to the tribunal

[66.22] For enquiries commencing on or after (or in progress on) 11 May 2001, any question arising in connection with the subject matter of the enquiry while it is in progress may be referred to the tribunal (formerly the Special Commissioners) for its determination.

Written notice of referral must be given to the tribunal jointly by HMRC and the company, specifying the question(s) being referred, and more than one such referral may be made during the course of an enquiry. Either side may withdraw the notice at any time up to the first hearing by the tribunal by written notice to the other party and to the tribunal.

While proceedings on such a referral are in progress, no closure notice may be given nor any application made for a closure direction (see below). Proceedings are for this purpose treated as still in progress until the question(s) is (are) determined by the tribunal and there is no further possibility of the determination(s) being varied or set aside (other than by virtue of an out-of-time appeal for which permission could be granted).

The tribunal's determination is binding on the parties as if it were a decision on a preliminary issue on an appeal (and similar rights of appeal against the determination apply), and must be taken into account by HMRC in reaching their conclusions on the enquiry.

[*FA 1998, Sch 18 paras 31A–31D; FA 2001, Sch 29 para 7; SI 2001 No 4024*].

Completion of enquiry

[66.23] An enquiry into a return is completed when a closure notice is issued by HMRC to the company stating their conclusions. If the return was for the wrong period, the notice must designate the accounting period for which a return should have been made. If there is more than one accounting period ending in or at the end of the period specified in the notice requiring a return, the closure notice may only designate the first of those accounting periods for which no return has been delivered. If there is then another period for which a return should have been made under the original notice, and which no other return by the company can be amended to refer to, the original notice is taken to require the company to deliver a return in respect of the outstanding period. The filing date for the return for that period is the later of the original filing date and the thirtieth day after it is finally determined that the outstanding return is required.

The company may apply to the tribunal for a direction that HMRC give a closure notice within a specified period. Any such application is heard and determined as if it were an appeal. The tribunal must give a direction unless they are satisfied that HMRC have reasonable grounds for not giving a closure notice within a specified period. Such a direction does not require HMRC to confirm that the company's return and self-assessment are correct, and the closure notice will include HMRC's conclusions based on the information available at the time of completion and representing what they believe to be the correct amounts to be included in the return on the basis of that information (see HMRC Enquiry Manual, EM5620, Revenue Guide to Self-Assessment para 6.14.6). See *Jade Palace Ltd v HMRC* [2006] STC (SCD) 419 in which such a direction was given.

Recent case law has reinforced the principle that enquiries should not be used as a method of obtaining information as to a third party's tax affairs. In *Estate 4 Ltd v HMRC* (TC01131) [2011] UKFTT 269 (TC), HMRC began an enquiry in December 2009 into a return submitted by a company (E), whose accounts showed a turnover of £187,000 and directors' salaries of £116,500. A meeting took place in May 2010, and the officer responsible for the enquiry formed the opinion that the salaries shown in E's accounts were insufficient to meet its directors' living expenses. E applied for a closure notice, contending that it had already supplied information about its own income and could not be required to provide information about its directors' personal affairs. The company considered that HMRC was using the enquiry as a 'bridge' to other issues unrelated to the tax affairs of the company itself. The First-Tier Tribunal agreed and granted the application. Judge Clark held that there was no basis for continuing to make further enquiries into the level of the remuneration.

[*FA 1998, Sch 18 paras 32, 33, 35*].

Amendment of return following completion

[66.24] From 1 April 2010 the closure notice must state either that no adjustment is required, or it must make the amendments required to the return and any other returns filed by the company and affected by the closure notice. Thus the return is directly amended by the closure notice.

Before that date, the company has 30 days following completion of an enquiry into a return to amend the return in accordance with the conclusions in the closure notice and, if the return was for the wrong period, to make it a return for the period designated in the notice, and to make such amendments of its other returns as may be required to give effect to those conclusions. Any time limit constraints are lifted for this purpose. If after the 30 days has elapsed HMRC are not satisfied that the return is correct and complete and for the appropriate period, and that amendments required to other returns have been made, they have a further 30 days to make such amendments as they consider necessary. An appeal may be made in writing within 30 days of notification to the company of any such amendment(s). [*FA 1998, Sch 18 para 34; FA 2008, s 119*].

Penalties

[66.25] The penalties regime has been overhauled, and new provisions apply per *FAs 2007, 2008* and *2009*. For accounting periods beginning on or after 1 April 2008 where the return is due on or after 1 April 2009 behaviour-based penalties have been introduced with regard to penalties for delivering incorrect returns, statements, declarations, accounts etc. See further **60.3 PENALTIES.**

Prior to this, the maximum penalty for:

(a) negligently or fraudulently delivering, or failing within a reasonable time to remedy, an incorrect return; or
(b) making any incorrect return, statement or declaration in connection with a claim for any allowance, deduction or relief; or
(c) submitting incorrect accounts,

in addition to any tax actually chargeable, is the amount of tax underpaid, by reason of the incorrectness, for the accounting period(s) to which the return etc. relates (disregarding any relief deferred under *ICTA 1988, s 419(4A) (now CTA 2010, s 455)* in respect of the repayment, etc. of a loan to a participator, see **22.15 CLOSE COMPANIES**). Accounts are deemed to have been submitted on behalf of a company unless it is shown that they were submitted without the company's consent or connivance.

Where more than one tax-geared penalty is incurred in relation to an accounting period, each penalty after the first is reduced so that the total penalties in relation to any particular part of the tax do not exceed the amount of the greatest penalty imposed in relation thereto. For an example, see HMRC Company Taxation Manual, CTM94240.

[*FA 1998, Sch 18 paras 20, 89, 90; ITA 2007, Sch 1 para 385*].

Contract settlements for all outstanding liabilities will continue to be available in appropriate cases, in particular where penalties are involved. (HMRC Enquiry Manual, EM6001).

Choice of income category

[66.26] There are provisions concerning enquiries into a return which includes amounts which may be taxed on more than one basis, i.e. UK trading income or overseas trading income, or (in relation to life assurance business) under Case I of Schedule D or on the 'I minus E' basis. HMRC have the right to determine (finally and conclusively) which method is to be used (the 'Crown option'). The powers to require production of documents, etc. under *FA 1998, Sch 18 paras 27–29* (see **66.20** above) apply equally for this purpose. These provisions are no longer needed following the abolition of schedules for corporation tax under *CTA 2009*. [*FA 1998, Sch 18 para 84; CTA 2009, Sch 1 para 454*].

Determinations where no return delivered

[66.27] If no return is delivered, in response to a notice requiring one, on or before the filing date for the return required by the notice (see **66.4** above) (or, if no such date can be ascertained, by the later of 18 months from the end of the period specified in the notice and three months from the date of service of the notice (which is assumed to be four working days after its issue), (see HMRC Company Taxation Manual, CTM95350)), HMRC have power to determine, to the best of their information and belief, the tax payable by the company for the accounting period or periods ending in or at the end of the period specified in the notice. They may also determine what those accounting periods are if they have insufficient information to identify the company's accounting periods.

Notice of a determination under these provisions must be served on the company, stating the date of issue, but no determination may be made more than three years (post 1 April 2010, previously five years) after the first day on which the power of determination could have been exercised. The determination is of no effect if the company shows that it has no accounting period ending in or at the end of the period specified in the notice requiring the return, or that it has delivered the return(s) for that accounting period or each of those accounting periods, or that no return is yet due for any such period. An effective determination is superseded where, before the expiry of three years (post 1 April 2010, previously five years) from the day on which the power of determination first became exercisable (or, if later, the expiry of twelve months from the date of the determination), the company delivers a return for an accounting period ending in or at the end of the period specified in the notice requiring a return. If there is more than one determination in relation to the notice concerned, the determination superseded is that for the period which is, or most closely approximates to, the period for which the return is made.

In practice HMRC normally review cases for determination 18 months after the end of what is assumed or believed to be the company's accounting period. If the filing date is believed to be later than that, they will wait until after the presumed filing date before making a determination. Where, for example, they believe there would be a risk of loss of tax if no immediate action was taken, or the absence of a return prevents a proper review of other companies in the same group, an earlier review may be made of the need for a determination. (HMRC Company Taxation Manual, CTM95340).

If a return is delivered, in response to a notice requiring one, for an accounting period ending in or at the end of the period specified in the notice, but it appears to HMRC that there is another ('outstanding') period so ending which is or may be an accounting period, they have power to determine, to the best of their information and belief, the corporation tax payable by the company for the outstanding period. The power becomes exercisable once the filing date for the outstanding period has passed without a return being delivered, or, if no such filing date can be ascertained, once the later of 30 months from the end of the period specified in the notice and three months from the date of service of the notice has passed without a return for the outstanding period being delivered.

Notice of a determination under these provisions must be served on the company, stating the date of issue, but no determination may be made more than three years, from 1 April 2010, formerly five years after the first day on which the power of determination could have been exercised. The determination is of no effect if the company shows that the outstanding period is not an accounting period or that it has delivered a return for that period. An effective determination is superseded where, before the expiry of three years, from 1 April 2010, formerly five years from the day on which the power of determination first became exercisable (or, if later, the expiry of twelve months from the date of the determination), the company delivers a further return for an accounting period ending in or at the end of the period specified in the notice requiring a return.

The power to make a determination in the circumstances described above includes power to determine any of the constituent amounts required to calculate the amount of tax payable. The notice of determination may be accompanied by a notice of any determination by HMRC of the due and payable dates under *TMA 1970, s 59D* or *s 59E* (see **59.2 PAYMENT OF TAX**). For enforcement purposes (i.e. payment, collection and recovery, interest, penalties, etc.) the determination has effect as if it were a self-assessment, and is treated as made for an accounting period where HMRC had insufficient information to determine whether a period was an accounting period (see above). Where any proceedings have been begun for the recovery of tax charged by a determination, and before the proceedings are concluded the determination is superseded (as above), the proceedings may be continued as if they were for the recovery of so much of the tax charged by the self-assessment as is due and payable but unpaid.

[*FA 1998, Sch 18 paras 36–40; FA 2001, Sch 29 para 17; FA 2008, Sch 39 paras 38–40*].

Simon's Taxes. See **A6.508–A6.509.**

Examples of return periods

(A)

[66.28]

Aquarius Ltd has always prepared its accounts to 31 October. In 2011, it changes its accounting date, preparing accounts for the nine months to 31 July 2011. On 31 January 2011, HMRC issue a notice specifying a return period of 1 November 2009 to 31 October 2010. On 31 January 2012, they issue a notice specifying a return period of 1 November 2010 to 31 October 2011.

In respect of the first-mentioned notice, Aquarius Ltd is required to make a return for the period 1.11.09 to 31.10.10.

In respect of the second of the above-mentioned notices, the company is required to make a return for the period 1.11.10 to 31.7.11.

(B)

Pisces Ltd has always prepared its accounts to 31 December. In 2011, it changes its accounting date, preparing accounts for the nine months to 30 September 2011. On 15 December 2011, HMRC issue a notice specifying a return period of 1 October 2010 to 30 September 2011.

Pisces Ltd is required to make returns both for the period 1.1.10 to 31.12.10 and for the period 1.1.11 to 30.9.11.

(C)

Aries Ltd has always prepared accounts to 31 October. After 2010, it changes its accounting date, preparing accounts for the fifteen months to 31 January 2012. On 21 August 2011, HMRC issue a notice specifying a return period of 1 November 2009 to 31 October 2010. On 31 January 2012, they issue a notice specifying a return period of 1 November 2010 to 31 October 2011.

In respect of the first-mentioned notice, Aries Ltd is required to make a return for the period 1.11.09 to 31.10.10 accompanied by accounts and tax computations for that period.

In respect of the second of the above-mentioned notices, the company is required to make a return for the accounting period 1.11.10 to 31.10.11 accompanied by accounts and tax computations for the period of account 1.11.10 to 31.1.12.

(D)

Taurus Ltd has always prepared accounts to 31 October. After 2010, it changes its accounting date, preparing accounts for the fifteen months to 31 January 2012. On 31 January 2011, HMRC issue a notice specifying a return period of 1 November 2009 to 31 October 2010. On 1 April 2011, they issue a notice specifying a return period of 1 November 2010 to 31 January 2011.

In respect of the first-mentioned notice, the position is as in (C) above.

In respect of the second of the above-mentioned notices, Taurus Ltd is not required to make a return, but should notify HMRC of the correct accounting dates and periods.

(E)

Gemini Ltd was incorporated on 1 July 2008 but remained dormant until 1 April 2010 when it began to trade. The first trading accounts were prepared for the year to 31 March 2011 and the company retains that accounting date. On 1 May 2012, HMRC issue notices specifying return periods of 1 July 2008 to 30 June 2009, 1 July 2009 to 30 June 2010, 1 July 2010 to 30 June 2011 and 1 July 2010 to 31 March 2012.

In respect of the notice for the period 1.7.08 to 30.6.09, Gemini Ltd is required to make a return for that period.

In respect of the notice for the period 1.7.09 to 30.6.10, the company is required to make a return for the period 1.7.09 to 31.3.10.

In respect of the notice for the period 1.7.10 to 30.6.11, the company is required to make a return for the period 1.4.10 to 31.3.11 accompanied by accounts and tax computations for that period.

In respect of the notice for the period 1.7.11 to 31.3.12, the company is required to make a return for the period 1.4.11 to 31.3.12 accompanied by accounts and tax computations for that period.

(F)

The final dates for the filing with HMRC of the returns in (A)–(E) above, and for the payment of corporation tax (assuming none of the companies concerned fall within the definition of a 'large company', see **59.3 PAYMENT OF TAX**), are as follows.

Return period	*Filing date*	*Payment date*
(A) above		
1.11.09 – 31.10.10	31.10.11	1.8.11
1.11.10 – 31.7.11	31.7.12	1.5.12
(B) above		
1.1.10 – 31.12.10	15.3.12	1.10.11
1.1.11 – 30.9.11	30.9.12	1.7.12
(C) above		
1.11.09 – 31.10.10	21.11.11	1.8.11
1.11.10 – 31.10.11	31.1.13	1.8.12
(D) above		
1.11.09 – 31.10.10	31.10.11	1.8.11
(E) above		
1.7.08 – 30.6.09	1.8.12	—
1.7.09 – 31.3.10	1.8.12	—
1.4.10 – 31.3.11	1.8.12	1.1.12
1.4.11 – 31.3.12	31.3.13	1.1.13

Notes

(a) The time allowed for filing returns is effectively extended to the time allowed under the *Companies Act 2006* if this would give a later filing date. This will not be so in the majority of cases.

(b) HMRC may grant an extension, on an application by the company, if satisfied that the company has a 'reasonable excuse' (see **60.13 PENALTIES**) for not being able to meet the filing date as above.

Electronic filing of tax returns etc.

[66.29] Companies, organisations paying corporation tax and their agents can use the HMRC corporation tax online service to send the Company Tax Return (CT600), supplementary pages A to J, and accounts and computations over the Internet. The returns can be submitted using the HMRC's free Online Tax Return — CT or an authorised third party software package. Details of software available are listed on the HMRC website. An online filing facility is similarly available for PAYE and certain other returns.

Returns for periods ending on 1 April 2010 or later must be delivered electronically on or after 1 April 2011. The method of filing must be approved by HMRC and they will set down standards of accuracy and completeness, which must be met. [*SI 2009 No 3218*]. The required format is iXBRL — see below.

Mandatory e-filing

Electronic filing for PAYE returns is mandatory from 2010/11 for all employers. See **41.12 HMRC — ADMINISTRATION**.

It will be mandatory to file online corporation tax returns (including accounts) for any accounting period ending after 31 March 2010 filed after 1 April 2011 using iXBRL. Unincorporated associations, clubs and charities not required to prepare accounts under the *Companies Act* can send the accounts (but not the return) in PDF format rather than iXBRL.

See http://www.hmrc.gov.uk/ct/ct-online/file-return/online.htm for information on how to arrange to file online using iXBRL and also: www.hmrc.gov.uk/ct/mandatory-online-filing.pdf.

iXBRL

[66.30] After 31 March 2011, all corporation tax returns, accounts and computations will have to be filed using iXBRL (inline XBRL) — this involves the application of computer readable tags to business data allowing it to be processed automatically by relevant software. In the run up to April 2011, HMRC have provided advice on data-tagging. Initially (until April 2013), partial tagging will be accepted for accounts and computations from those not intending to use iXBRL enabled software.

The package forming a company's corporation tax return will have to be filed in the following formats:

- company accounts (UK GAAP or IFRS) — iXBRL;
- corporation tax return (CT 600) — iXBRL;
- other supporting papers, claims and elections — PDF.

A guide to iXBRL can be found at: www.hmrc.gov.uk/ct/ct-online/file-return/xbrl-guide.pdf.

HMRC regularly updates its list of recognised commercial software for online filing, see:

www.hmrc.gov.uk/efiling/ctsoft_dev.htm.

Corporation tax return — structure

[66.31] The form of company tax return (see **66.4** above) specified by HMRC for accounting periods ending on or after 1 April 2008 is Form CT600 (2008) Version 2, which will be issued (together with the CT600 Guide (2008) Version 2) with Form CT603, the notice requiring a return. Returns to be submitted after 1 April 2011 must be submitted electronically and therefore no paper return will be issued for such accounting periods. The CT600 Guide (2010) provides assistance with completing the return. Additional or replacement copies may be obtained from HMRC's website (at www.hmrc.gov.uk/ctsa/returns.htm) or from the CTSA Orderline (tel. 0845–300 6555). The following supplementary pages can also be obtained online or supplied on request to the Orderline.

The new bank levy will be an amount assessable or chargeable as if it were corporation tax and will therefore need to be included in the Company Tax Return form, alongside the *ICTA 1988, s 747* CFC tax chargeable.

CT600A *Loans to participators by close companies*. This must be completed if the company is a close company and made loans to an individual participator, or associate of a participator, that remained outstanding at the end of the period. See **22.12** *et seq.* **CLOSE COMPANIES.**

CT600B *Controlled foreign companies*. This must be completed if the company had an interest of 25% or more in the period in a foreign company which was controlled from the UK. See **27 CONTROLLED FOREIGN COMPANIES.** See also HMRC International Manual, INTM214010–214040 as regards completion of these supplementary pages. Until the consultation has been completed, in addition the new Bank Levy.

CT600C *Group and consortium companies*. This must be completed if the company is claiming or surrendering any amounts under the group or consortium relief provisions or any eligible unrelieved foreign tax for the period. See **39.2** *et seq.* **GROUP RELIEF, 32.12 DOUBLE TAX RELIEF.**

CT600D	*Insurance companies and friendly societies*. This must be completed if, in the period, the company either made claims under *ICTA 1988, Sch 19AB* to provisional payments (including notional repayments in respect of tax on gilt interest), or entered into business which it treats as overseas life assurance business.
CT600E	*Charities and community amateur sports clubs*. This must be completed if the company is, in the period, a charity or community amateur sports club claiming exemption or partial exemption from tax. See **20 CHARITIES**.
CT600F	*Tonnage tax*. This must be completed where an election has been made for the alternative tonnage tax regime (see **70.76 TRADE PROFITS — INCOME AND SPECIFIC TRADES**).
CT600G	*Corporate venturing scheme*. This must be completed if the company is claiming relief under the **CORPORATE VENTURING SCHEME (28)**.
CT600H	*Cross-border royalties*. This must be completed if the company made cross-border royalty payments after 1 October 2002 without deduction of tax or under deduction of tax at a treaty-specified rate (see **46.2 INCOME TAX IN RELATION TO A COMPANY**).
CT600I	*Supplementary charge in respect of ring fence trades*. This must be completed if the company carried on a ring fence trade in a period beginning (or deemed to have begun) after 16 April 2002.
CT600J	*Disclosure of tax avoidance schemes*. This must be completed for notifiable arrangements on or after 18 March 2004 (see **5.41 ANTI AVOIDANCE**).

Form CT600 (2008) consists of an opening page requiring company information, a summary of the return information and information on completion of the return. There are then a number of sections as follows:

- Turnover.
- Income — this includes profits from loan relationships, overseas income, property business, intangible fixed assets, tonnage tax and other profits not included in turnover.
- Chargeable gains.
- Losses brought forward against certain investment income.
- Non-trading deficits brought forward on loan relationships or derivative contracts.
- Deductions and reliefs — this includes corporate venturing scheme losses, losses on unquoted shares, management expenses, certain interest distributions, property business losses, non-trading losses from loan relationships and intangible fixed assets, capital allowances, trading losses carried back from subsequent periods, charges and group relief.
- The figure of profits chargeable to corporation tax.
- Tax calculation, arriving at the figure of corporation tax chargeable.
- Tax reliefs and deductions including Corporate Venturing Scheme investment relief, Community investment relief, double tax relief and ACT.

- Calculation of tax outstanding or overpaid, arriving at the figure of tax payable.
- Tax reconciliation — including tax credits payable or receivable, ring fence corporation tax and supplementary charge in respect of ring fence trades, tax already paid or outstanding, tax overpaid or tax refunds surrendered to the company.
- Indicators, including whether the company falls within the quarterly instalment payments regime, is within a group payment arrangement, has written down or sold intangible assets or has made cross-border royalty payments.
- Research and development expenditure and land remediation enhanced expenditure.
- Information about capital allowances and balancing charges.
- Losses, deficits and excess amounts — the various types must be listed and group companies must show the maximum amounts available for surrender by group or consortium relief.
- Overpayments and repayments — this must be completed if a repayment claim is made.

The final section is a declaration by the signatory.

A four-page, shorter version of the return, CT600 (Short) (2008) Version 2 may be used by companies with simpler tax affairs and where the only supplementary pages required are CT600A, CT600E and CT600J.

Rounding of tax computations

[66.32] To reduce the compliance burden on large companies whose statutory accounts are produced in round thousands, HMRC are generally prepared to accept profit computations for tax purposes in figures rounded to the nearest £1,000 from single companies with an annual turnover of at least £5 million (including investment and estate income) in the accounts in question or in the preceding year, where rounding at least to that extent has been used in preparing the accounts. (Turnover of groups of companies is not aggregated for this purpose.) Companies should continue to state amounts of group relief or relief for losses from other accounting periods in the actual sums surrendered, brought forward or carried back.

Such computations must be accompanied by a certificate by the person preparing the computations stating the basis of rounding, and confirming that it is unbiased, has been applied consistently and produces a fair result for tax purposes. It must also give the program or software used where relevant), or, if there have been no changes from the previous year in these respects, confirming the unchanged basis.

The rounding may not extend to the tax payable or other relevant figures of tax. Rounding is not acceptable where it would impede the application of the legislation, or where recourse to the underlying records would normally be necessary to do the computation. Thus it is not acceptable e.g. in computations of chargeable gains (except in relation to the incidental costs of acquisition and disposal), in accrued income scheme computations, in computations of tax credit relief, in relation to the CFC exemption limit (see **27.11**(iv) **CONTROLLED FOREIGN COMPANIES**) or in certain capital allowance computations. The inspector may exceptionally insist that roundings are not used in other circumstances. (HMRC Statement of Practice, SP 15/93).

See generally **Simon's Taxes B2.106** as regards the form of accounts.

67

Small Profits — Reduced Rates

Cross-references. See **22.20 CLOSE COMPANIES; 52.5 INVESTMENT FUNDS; 53.1 INVESTMENT TRUSTS** and **65.5 RESIDENCE.**

Simon's Taxes. See D1.1202–D1.1211.

Introduction

[67.1] As mentioned in **1.1 INTRODUCTION AND RATES OF TAX,** a special reduced rate of corporation tax, known as the 'small profits rate', applies where a UK company has profits below a certain level, being £300,000 (see further below). The rate for such profits for financial year 2011 is 20%. Profits above this level are subject to corporation tax at a rate which gradually increases to the full rate of 26% (FY 2011), which applies for profits of £1,500,000 and above.

This chapter provides the details with regard to the taxation of these lower levels of profit, and the profits which fall within the limits for the change of corporation tax rates, together with calculations for the taxation of profits in each instance.

Small profits rate

[67.2] The 'small profits rate' applies to the 'taxable total profits' of a UK resident company for an accounting period if the company's 'augmented profits' for that period do not exceed a 'lower limit'. The small profits rate does not apply to close investment-holding companies — see **22.20 CLOSE COMPANIES.**

Where the accounting period concerned is of twelve months, the '*lower limit*' is normally £300,000. If, however, the company has one or more associated companies, this amount is in effect divided between them; thus if a company has two associated companies, then the 'lower limit' is divided by three, and becomes £100,000, see **67.4** below for the details. Where the accounting period is less then twelve months, the lower limit (after any reduction for associated companies) is proportionately reduced.

Different rates apply depending on whether or not the profits are 'ring fence profits'.

For profits other than ring fence profits, the small profits rate for the financial year 2011 is 20%. The rate for the financial years 2010, 2009 and 2008 was 21%; for 2007 it was 20%; and for 2006 it was 19%. The small profits rate for ring fence profits in each of those years is 19%.

[*FA 2011, s 6; FA 2010, s 3; CTA 2010, ss 3(3), 18, 24; ICTA 1988, s 13; FA 2005, s 11; FA 2006, s 25; FA 2007, s 3(1); FA 2008, s 7*].

A UK permanent establishment of a non-UK resident company may qualify for the small profits rate if it can claim the benefit of a non-discrimination clause in the relevant double taxation agreement. In this case, the relief is determined by reference to worldwide profits of the company and its associates wherever resident.

Taxable total profits

'*Taxable total profits*' are the profits for an accounting period on which corporation tax is chargeable (see **1 INTRODUCTION AND RATES OF TAX**).

See **53.2 INVESTMENT TRUSTS** for the exclusion from taxable total profits *for small companies rate purposes only* of certain housing investment profits (prior to the introduction of real estate investment trusts (see **53.3 INVESTMENT TRUSTS**) for accounting periods beginning on or after 1 January 2007).

Augmented profits

'*Augmented profits*' are the taxable total profits for the accounting period plus franked investment income received. There is, however, an exclusion for franked investment income received:

(a) from a '51% subsidiary' or from a fellow 51% subsidiary of a parent company; or
(b) from a 'trading company' or 'relevant holding company' that is a 'quasi-subsidiary' of the recipient company.

[*CTA 2010, s 32*].

A '*51% subsidiary*' is a body corporate more than 50% of the 'ordinary share capital' of which is beneficially owned directly or indirectly by another. Share capital owned indirectly through a company which holds it as trading stock is disregarded for this purpose. A company is not treated as a 51% subsidiary unless the parent company would be beneficially entitled to more than 50% of any profits available for distribution to equity holders and of any assets so available on a winding-up (see **39.4 GROUP RELIEF**). [*CTA 2010, ss 33, 1154*].

'*Ordinary share capital*' means all the issued share capital of the company except non-participating shares carrying a fixed-rate dividend, but 'issued share capital' does not include founder members' deposits in a company limited by guarantee (*South Shore Mutual Insurance Co Ltd v Blair (Inspector of Taxes)* [1999] STC (SCD) 296). [*CTA 2010, s 1119*].

A '*trading company*' is a company the business of which consists wholly or mainly of the carrying on of a trade or trades. A '*relevant holding company*' means a company the business of which consists wholly or mainly in holding shares or securities of trading companies which are its '*90% subsidiaries*' (i.e. in which it holds directly not less than 90% of the ordinary share capital). [*CTA 2010, s 33*].

A company is a '*quasi-subsidiary*' of the recipient company if it is owned by a consortium of which the recipient company is a member; it is not itself a '75% subsidiary' of any other company; and no arrangements exist under which it could become such a subsidiary. [*CTA 2010, s 32(3)*].

A company is owned by a consortium if at least 75% of its ordinary share capital is beneficially owned amongst them by two or more companies, each owning at least 5% and beneficially entitled to at least 5% of any profits available for distribution to equity holders and of any assets so available on a winding-up (see **39.4 GROUP RELIEF**). Such companies are the '*members of the consortium*'. A '*75% subsidiary*' is a body corporate not less than 75% of the ordinary share capital of which is owned directly or indirectly by another.

Ring fence profits

'*Ring fence profits*' are defined as any income from oil extraction activities or oil rights and capital gain under *TCGA 1992, s 197(3)* on disposal of an interest in an oil field or an asset used in oil extraction.

[*CTA 2010, ss 32, 33, 275, 276, 1119, 1154; ICTA 1988, ss 13(7)–(8AB), 13ZA, 247(1A)(8)–(9A), 502, 832(1), 838(1); FA 2007, s 3*].

Claims. Before *CTA 2010* took effect (see **70.2 TRADE PROFITS — INCOME AND SPECIFIC TRADES**), the small profits rate (or marginal relief, see **67.3** below) had to be claimed. In practice, a clear indication in the company's return, computation or accompanying correspondence that profits of the accounting period should be charged at the small companies rate (or attract marginal relief) was accepted as a valid claim. The claim should, however, have included a statement of the number (or absence) of associated companies in the period (see **67.4** below). (HMRC Company Tax Manual, CTM03670).

For accounting periods to which *CTA 2010* applies, the small profits rate and marginal relief apply automatically where the conditions are satisfied.

Pre-*CTA 2010* terminology

Note that, before *CTA 2010* took effect, the small profits rate was known as the 'small companies rate'. 'Taxable total profits' were referred to as 'basic profits' and 'augmented profits' as 'profits' for the purposes of applying the rate.

Details with regard to the financial years 2000 to 2005 and the 'corporation tax starting rate' (which applied to profits below £10,000), and the 'non corporate distribution rate', can be found in earlier versions of this annual.

Simon's Taxes. See **D1.1202**.

Marginal relief

[67.3] Where the 'augmented profits' of a UK resident company for an accounting period exceed a 'lower limit' but do not exceed an 'upper limit', corporation tax is chargeable on the 'taxable total profits' at the full rate (see **1.3 INTRODUCTION AND RATES OF TAX**) reduced by marginal relief. The effect of this is to charge tax at a gradually increasing rate between the two limits, up to the full rate of 26% which is charged when the upper limit is reached.

The relief does not apply to close investment-holding companies — see **22.20 CLOSE COMPANIES.**

The amount of the relief is:

$$\text{relief fraction} \times (\text{upper limit} - \text{augmented profits}) \times \frac{\text{taxable total profits}}{\text{augmented profits}}$$

'*Taxable total profits*' and '*augmented profits*' are as defined in **67.2** above. Where the accounting period concerned is of twelve months, the '*lower limit*' is normally £300,000 and the '*upper limit*' is £1,500,000.

If, however, the company has one or more associated companies, these amounts are in effect divided between them as highlighted in **67.2** above; thus the limits for a company with two associated companies will be divided by three becoming £100,000 (lower) and £500,000 (upper); see **67.4** below for the details. Where the accounting period is less then twelve months, the limits (after any reduction for associated companies) are proportionately reduced.

The relief fraction to be used is either the standard fraction or the ring fence fraction. Where the company has no ring fence profits (see **67.2** above) the standard fraction is used.

For the financial year 2011 it is $^{3}/_{200}$. For 2010, 2009 and 2008 the fraction is $^{7}/_{400}$; for 2007 it is $^{1}/_{40}$; and for 2006 it is $^{11}/_{400}$.

Where the company has only ring fence profits the ring fence fraction is used. It is $^{11}/_{400}$ for all of the financial years 2006 to 2011. Where a company has both ring fence and other profits, there are special rules for apportioning profits between those profits for marginal relief purposes.

The chargeable profits of an accounting period which overlaps the end of a financial year are, if necessary, apportioned between the two years.

See **67.2** above as regards claims for relief.

[*FA 2011, s 6; FA 2010 s 3; CTA 2010, ss 19–24; CTA 2009, s 8(5); ICTA 1988, ss 8(3), 13(2)(3)(6); FA 2005, s 11(b); FA 2006, s 25(b); FA 2007, s 3(2); FA 2008, s 7*].

Where a company has no franked investment income (i.e. where taxable total profits are the same as the augmented profits), an alternative method of calculation can be used. This is to apply the small profits rate up to the lower limit and marginal rate to the balance of profits. The marginal rate is 27.5% for the financial year 2011, 29.75% for the financial years 2010, 2009 and 2008, 32.5% for the financial year 2007, and 32.75% for financial year 2006.

If the profits consist entirely of ring fence profits, the marginal rate is, 32.75% for those financial years.

A UK permanent establishment of a non-UK resident company may qualify for the marginal relief if it can claim the benefit of a non-discrimination clause in the relevant double taxation agreement. In this case, the relief is determined by reference to worldwide profits of the company and its associates wherever resident.

Examples

(A)

In its accounting period 1 April 2011 to 31 March 2012, X Ltd, a trading company, has chargeable profits of £300,000, including chargeable gains of £40,000, and also has franked investment income of £75,000 (representing net distributions received of £67,500). X Ltd has no associated companies.

Thus for the purposes of the marginal relief calculation, the taxable total profits of X Ltd are £300,000 and the augmented profits are £375,000.

Corporation tax payable is calculated as follows.

	£
Corporation tax at full rate of 26% on £300,000	78,000
$\frac{3}{200} \times £(1{,}500{,}000 - 375{,}000) \times \frac{300{,}000}{375{,}000}$	13,500
Corporation tax payable	£64,500

(B)

In its accounting period 1 April 2011 to 31 March 2012, Y Ltd, a trading company, has chargeable profits of £375,000 including chargeable gains of £40,000, but has no franked investment income. Y Ltd has no associated companies. Thus the taxable total profits of Y Ltd are the same as the augmented profits.

Corporation tax payable is calculated as follows.

	£
Corporation tax at full rate of 26% on £375,000	97,500
$^3/_{200}$ × £(1,500,000 – 375,000)	16,875
Corporation tax payable	£80,625

An alternative method of calculation, where there is no franked investment income, is to apply small companies rate up to the small companies rate limit and marginal rate (27.5% for FY 2011) to the balance of profits. Thus:

		£
£300,000	at 20%	60,000
75,000	at 27.5%	20,625
£375,000		£80,625

(C)

In its accounting period 1 January 2011 to 31 December 2011, Z Ltd had chargeable profits of £540,000 and franked investment income of £60,000. Z Ltd had no associated companies during that period.

There has been a change in rate between the two years (FY 2010 and FY 2011), so an apportionment is needed between the profits falling into each financial year (which runs from 1 April to 31 March).

Corporation tax payable is calculated as follows.

		£	£
Augmented profits	=	£600,000	
Taxable total profits	=	£540,000	
Lower relevant maximum	=	£300,000	
Corporation tax at full rate			
£540,000 at 28% × 3/12		37,800	
£540,000 at 26% × 9/12		105,300	
Less marginal relief			143,100
7/400 × £(1,500,000 – 600,000) × 540/600 × 3/12		3,544	
3/200 × £(1,500,000 – 600,000) × 540/600 × 9/12		9,113	(12,657)
Corporation tax payable			£130,443

Associated companies

[67.4] As mentioned in **67.2** and **67.3** above, the lower and upper limits are reduced where a company has 'associated companies'. This is done by dividing the limit by one plus the number of associated companies which the company has in the accounting period. [*CTA 2010, s 24(3); ICTA 1988, s 13(3)(b)*].

HMRC issued a consultation paper on 29 October 2009 entitled: 'Simplification review: The associated company rules as they apply to the small companies' rate of corporation tax'. That paper examined the rules governing control of a company through the attribution of rights held by one or more associates of a shareholder. The results of this consultation are now found in *FA 2011*, which amends the definition of associated company as it relates to the attribution of such rights. See further the discussion of 'control' below.

[*FA 2011, s 55; CTA 2010, s 27*].

Meaning of 'associated company'

A company is an '*associated company*' of another at any time if one of the two has 'control' of the other or both are under the control of the same person or persons.

This includes non-UK resident companies — although only UK companies are subject to corporation tax, the existence of worldwide subsidiaries or holding companies will dilute the upper and lower limits.

An associated company is treated as associated even if it was associated for part of the accounting period only. This applies to each of two or more associated companies, even if they were associated for different parts of the accounting period.

Non-trading companies

However, an associated company which has not carried on any trade or business at any time in that accounting period (or the part when it was associated) is disregarded.

For this purpose, a non-trading 'passive company' which has one or more '51% subsidiaries' and which carries on a business of making investments is treated as not carrying on a business (and so is disregarded in the count of associated companies).

A company is a '*passive company*' if it has no assets other than shares in 51% subsidiaries; has no income other than dividends which are franked investment income; has no chargeable gains; incurs no management expenses and makes no qualifying charitable donations (see **20.12 CHARITIES**). If the company receives dividends in an accounting period it must itself pay dividends in that period of an amount at least equal to the dividends received.

A '*51% subsidiary*' is a body corporate more than 50% of the 'ordinary share capital' of which is beneficially owned directly or indirectly by another.

[*CTA 2010, s 26*].

Note that, before *CTA 2010* took effect, the exclusion of passive companies was an HMRC practice only (see SP 5/94).

In *Revenue and Customs Comrs v Salaried Persons Postal Loans Ltd* [2006] STC 1315, the High Court upheld the decision of the Special Commissioners that the company, whose sole activity was the continuation of the letting of former trading premises after it ceased to trade, was not carrying on a business. For a case in which a company whose sole activity was the receipt of bank deposit interest was held not to be carrying on any business, see *Jowett v O'Neill and Brennan Construction Ltd* (1998) 70 TC 566.

Similarly a company set up for the sole purpose of owning a holiday home used exclusively by its sole shareholder and his family was held not to be carrying on any business (*John M Harris (Design Partnership) Ltd v Lee (Inspector of Taxes)* [1997] STC (SCD) 240). See, however, *Land Management Ltd v Fox (Inspector of Taxes)* [2002] STC (SCD) 152, in which an associated company whose principal activity was as an investment company with income derived from a tenanted residential freehold property was held to be carrying on a business (and this applied also to three subsidiary financial activities).

For a case on the inclusion of non-UK resident members of a group in determining the number of associated companies for the purpose of calculating the upper and lower limits, see *Jansen Nielsen Pilkes Ltd v Tomlinson (Inspector of Taxes)* [2004] STC (SCD) 226, 6 ITLR 715.

Meaning of 'control'

'*Control*' is as defined in *CTA 2010, ss 450, 451* (previously *ICTA 1988, s 416*), see **22.6 CLOSE COMPANIES**. That definition is, however, modified as follows.

(a) With effect from 1 April 2008, a business partner of a person is not treated as an associate of that person unless certain tax planning 'arrangements' involving that person and the partner have at any time had effect on the taxpayer company or in connection with its formation. The effect of the arrangements must be to reduce the taxpayer company's corporation tax liability as a result of an increase in relief under the small profits rate or marginal relief provisions. '*Arrangements*' do not include any guarantee, security or charge given to or taken by a bank but otherwise includes any agreement, understanding, transaction or series of transaction (whether legally enforceable or not). As the small profits rate limits are reduced according to the number of associates in the accounting period or any part of it, this rule did not benefit companies in the accounting period straddling 1 April 2008. The Chartered Institute of Taxation ('CIOT') has obtained clarification from HMRC on dealing with prior years, to which this does not apply. Unless the case is selected for full enquiry, the existence of associated companies is relevant only where the tax at stake is significant.
HMRC indicated that they have asked Local Compliance to take a practical approach, and to pursue enquiries only in cases where it is possible to establish evidence of associated companies. At a meeting with HMRC, CIOT were advised that, whilst the legislation was not backdated, the practice for earlier years will be influenced by the new rules in most cases. It is understood that HMRC do not expect an agent to embark on fact-finding where it would not be reasonable for him to know of the business affairs of his fellow partners.
This section has been amended by *FA 2011*. For accounting periods ending on or after 1 April 2011, any reference to the position in respect of partners is included within the treatment of associates (see sub paragraph (e) below). Under these new provisions, where there is no substantial commercial interdependence between the companies then there is no attribution of rights and duties of an associate (including a partner).

[*CTA 2010, s 27*].

(b) Fixed rate preference shares (as defined) held by a company are ignored in determining if one company is under the control of another if the company holding the shares is not a close company, takes no part in the management or conduct of the issuing company or of its business, and subscribed for the shares in the ordinary course of a business which includes the provision of finance.
[*CTA 2010, s 28*].

(c) A company is not under the control of another company if the only connection (past or present) between the two is that one company is a loan creditor (within *CTA 2010, s 453*) of the other and either the creditor company is not a close company or the creditor relationship arose in the ordinary course of the creditor company's business. Likewise, where two companies are controlled by the same person which is a loan creditor of each company, that person's rights as loan creditor are ignored in determining whether the two companies are associated. There must be no other connection (past or present) between the two companies, and the loan creditor must either not be a close company or the creditor relationship with each company must arise in the ordinary course of the creditor's business.
[*CTA 2010, s 29*].

(d) Where two companies are controlled by the same person by virtue of rights or powers held in trust by that person, those rights or powers are ignored in determining whether the two companies are associated, where there is no other connection (past or present) between the two companies.
[*CTA 2010, s 30*].

(e) For accounting periods ending before 1 April 2011, HMRC will not seek to attribute to any person the rights and powers of relatives, other than those of his or her spouse or civil partner and minor children, except where there is substantial commercial interdependence between the companies concerned. Pursuant to *FA 2011*, for accounting periods ending on or after 1 April 2011, HMRC will not attribute the rights and duties of associates (as within *CTA, s 451* ('control': rights to be attributed) in determining whether two companies are associated, or not, when the relationship between the two companies is not one of substantial interdependence. Regulations will set out which factors should be taken into account to determine 'substantial interdependence'.

Note that, before *CTA 2010* took effect, subparagraphs (b)–(e) applied by concession only. Sub paragraph (e) has also been put onto a statutory footing by *FA 2011, s 55* for periods ending on or after 1 April 2011, which section also amends paragraph (a) above. See HMRC Extra-Statutory Concession, C9. A company can elect for the provisions of *FA 2011, s 55* which amend *CTA 2010, s 27* only to have effect on accounting periods commencing after 1 April 2011. Such election must be made within one year from the end of the accounting period to which it relates.

[*FA 2011, s 55; CTA 2010, ss 25–30, 1154(2); ICTA 1988, s 13(4)–(4C)(5); FA 2008, s 35*].

See HMRC Company Taxation Manual, CTM60250 for HMRC's view of control where companies are under the control of more than one person or group of persons. For two companies to be under the control of the same persons, an irreducible group of persons having control of one must be identical with an irreducible group of persons having control of the other (i.e. in neither case could any definition of control be satisfied if any one of them were excluded).

In *Gascoines Group Ltd v Inspector of Taxes and related appeals* [2004] STC 844, a company controlled by trustees of a trust was considered to be associated with other companies controlled by the settlor of that trust. The trustees were associates of the settlor by virtue of what is now *CTA 2010, s 448(1)(b)* (previously *ICTA 1988, s 417(3)(b)*) and therefore, the rights of the trustees were to be attributed to the settlor who was to be taken to have control over the company controlled by the trustees.

Information powers

HMRC have powers to obtain information from shareholders and companies issuing bearer securities in order to identify the beneficial owners of shares etc. for the purposes of the associated company provisions. [*CTA 2010, s 31; FA 1989, Sch 12 Pt I; SI 2009 No 2035, Sch para 25*].

Change to upper and lower limits

The marginal relief limits (the upper and lower limits highlighted above) have not changed since FY 1994. There was a provision in *FA 1994* at *s 86* which allowed for a company's accounting period to be split into two separate accounting periods where the upper and lower limits changed for the purposes of calculating the charge to tax. This section has been repealed by *CTA 2010*, as being no longer required. Were the upper and lower limits to be changed, then it is likely similar provisions would be implemented with regard to accounting periods which straddle financial years. [*CTA 2010, s 1181; FA 1994, s 86(3)*].

Simon's Taxes. See **D1.1204.**

Example

Y Ltd has profits, consisting wholly of income, of £320,000 for the 12-month accounting period ended 31 December 2008. It has three associated companies throughout the accounting period.

There is no change in the marginal relief limits. The change in the corporation tax rate and in the marginal relief fraction require that the profits be apportioned to the relevant financial years, see **1.1 INTRODUCTION AND RATES OF TAX**. The apportionment will apply to the marginal relief calculation as the marginal relief fraction used differs between financial years.

Y Ltd's corporation tax liability for the year ended 31 December 2008 is therefore calculated as follows.

With three associated companies, the upper limit is £1,500,000 divided by 4, which is £375,000.

	£	
FY 2010		
£80,000 at 28%	22,400	
Less $^{3}/_{12} \times {}^{7}/_{400} \times (375{,}000 - 320{,}000) =$	241	
	22,159	
FY 2011		
£240,000 at 26%	62,400	
Less $^{9}/_{12} \times {}^{3}/_{200} \times (375{,}000 - 320{,}000) =$	619	
	61,781	
		£
Total liability: FY 2010		22,159
FY 2011		61,781
		£83,940

Key points

[67.5] Points to consider are as follows.

- The small profits rate applies to UK resident companies where the profits do not exceed the lower limit — currently £300,000.
- The small profits rate cannot be applied to close investment holding companies. A common error is where a company rents a property to a connected company and the small profits rate is applied.
- Profits between the lower limit and the upper limit (currently £1,500,000) are charged at the full corporation tax rate but there is a reduction in tax for marginal relief. The effect of this is for every £1 over the lower rate the company pays an additional 27.50p in corporation tax.
- Where there are associated companies the lower and upper limits are divided equally between the active companies. A company which has not carried on any trade or business in the period can be disregarded.
- Each of the main rate of corporation tax, the marginal rate fraction, and the small profits rate of corporation tax, have changed in *FA 2011*, which will have an impact on the calculation of tax payable, in particular with regard to periods which straddle both FY 2010 and FY 2011.

- The provisions with regard to the starting rate (FY 2000 to FY 2005) and non corporate distribution rate (FY 2004 and FY 2005) can be found in earlier versions of this annual.

68

Statutory Bodies

Simon's Taxes. See B5.647, B8.418, D1.201, D1.203, D1.233, D1.234, D6.451.

Introduction

[68.1] For corporation tax purposes, many statutory bodies are treated as if they were companies, with the result that they are charged to corporation tax on their profits and gains.

However, special rules apply to certain statutory bodies. Including:

- marketing boards;
- harbour reorganisation schemes;
- local authorities; and
- the Nuclear Decommissioning Authority.

This chapter looks at the provisions specific to these bodies and also at treatment of statutory bodies generally. It also considers the position of a statutory corporation borrowing in a foreign currency.

Marketing Boards

[68.2] Certain statutory bodies are required by the Government to pay all or part of their trading surplus into a reserve fund. A statutory body whose objects include:

- marketing an agricultural product; or
- stabilising the price of an agricultural product,

and which is obliged by or under a government-approved scheme to pay all or part of any trading surplus into a reserve fund may deduct such payments in computing the profits of the trade carried on by them, provided that the reserve fund meets the conditions set out below.

The first condition is that no sum can be withdrawn from the fund without the authority of a Minister or Department.

The second condition is that if money has been paid to the body by a minister or department in connection with arrangements for maintaining guaranteed prices or in connection with the body's trading arrangements and that money is repayable to the Minister or department, sums standing to the credit of the fund are required to be applied in repaying the money.

The third condition is that the fund is reviewed by a Minister at fixed intervals and if it appears to the Minister that the fund exceeds what is reasonably required by the body, the excess is withdrawn.

Any withdrawal from the fund which is not required to be passed on to a Minister or Government Department, producers, or persons paying levies or duties, is treated as a trading receipt.

The definition of Minister was widened in the rewrite to *CTA 2009* to include Ministers of the Crown, Scottish Ministers, Welsh Ministers or a Minister of Northern Ireland, to take account of the devolved powers given to the national parliaments.

[*CTA 2009, ss 153–155, Sch 2 para 33; ICTA 1988, s 509*].

Harbour reorganisation schemes

[68.3] A harbour reorganisation scheme is defined as any statutory provision providing for the management by a harbour authority of any harbour or group of harbours in the UK.

Where, under such a scheme, the trade of a body corporate (other than a limited liability company) is transferred to a harbour authority, the trade is not treated as discontinued. The effect of this is that loss relief is given as if the transferor has continued to carry on the trade, allowing any losses to be carried forward and set against subsequent profits.

Further, capital allowances are calculated as if the trade had continued and transferee is entitled to the same reliefs from corporation tax on chargeable gains as if there had been no change.

If only part of the body corporate's trade is transferred and the transferor continues to carry on the remainder of the trade, then the above provisions apply to the transferred part and it is treated as if it had always been a separate trade. Similarly if the trade is transferred in parts to two or more harbour authorities and the transferor is dissolved — the parts are treated as separate trades to which these provisions apply.

[*CTA 2010, ss 991–995; ICTA 1988, s 518*].

Local authorities etc. and health service bodies

[68.4] Local authorities and health service bodies are exempt from corporation tax.

A '*local authority*' is any incorporated or unincorporated association:

- of which all the constituent members are local authorities, groups of local authorites or local authority associations; and
- which has as its object or primary object the protection and furtherance of the interests in general of local authorities or any description of local authorities.

A '*health service body*' is a body that is:

- a Strategic Health Authority or Health Authority;
- a Special Health Authority;
- a Primary Care Trust;
- a Local Health Board or Board;
- (in Wales) a National Health Service trust;
- an NHS foundation trust;
- (in Scotland) a Health Board or Special Health Board, the Common Services Agency for the Scottish Heath Service or a State Hospital Management Committee;
- in Northern Ireland, a special health and social services agency, a Health and Social Care trust, a Health and Social Services Board, or the Northern Ireland Central Services Agency;
- the Scottish Dental Practice Board; and
- the Public Health Laboratory Service Board.

The Treasury may also make an order that an NHS foundation trust is liable to corporation tax in relation to a specified activity, which appears to the Treasury to be of a commercial nature and such order is necessary to avoid any differences in treatment between such trust and any other commercial body undertaking the same or similar activity.

[*CTA 2010, ss 984, 985, 986, 987; ICTA 1988, ss 519, 519A, 842A; TCGA 1992, ss 271(3), 288(1); ITA 2007, Sch 1 para 340*].

See **35.11 EXEMPT ORGANISATIONS.**

Nuclear Decommissioning Authority

[68.5] The Nuclear Decommissioning Authority ('NDA') is exempt from tax on trading income arising or accruing to it or to an 'NDA company' from the carrying on of exempt activities. An '*NDA company*' is defined as a 'relevant site licensee' (as defined) or a company of which the ordinary share capital is owned directly or indirectly by the NDA.

Exempt activities are specified by regulation (for which see *SI 2005 No 644* which also provides further conditions to be satisfied by a site licensee for it to qualify as an NDA company). They are defined as the operation of designated facilities for the treatment, storage transportation or disposal of hazardous material, carried on for the purpose of thermal oxide reprocessing or mixed oxide manufacture at Sellafield in Cumbria.

[*Energy Act 2004, ss 27–30, 47, Sch 4, as amended by CTA 2010, Sch 1 para 434; FA 2006, ss 99, 100*].

Other statutory bodies

[68.6] Subject to the special provisions above and, where appropriate, to the Crown exemption (see **35.6 EXEMPT ORGANISATIONS**), statutory bodies are liable in the ordinary way to corporation tax on their income and capital gains. Whether their activities amount to trading depends on the facts.

There is a wealth of case law on the subject. See *Mersey Docks and Harbour Board v Lucas* HL 1883, 2 TC 25 (trading surplus held chargeable notwithstanding that it had to be applied in reducing debt), *Port of London Authority v CIR* CA 1920, 12 TC 122, and *Forth Conservancy Board cases*, HL 1928, 14 TC 709, and HL 1931, 16 TC 103 (liable under Schedule D Case VI on surplus from shipping dues) and *British Broadcasting Corporation v Johns* CA 1964, 41 TC 471 (liable on trading profits from publications etc. but not on rest of surplus; not entitled to Crown exemption). For further cases, see Tolley's Tax Cases.

Statutory corporation borrowing in foreign currency

[68.7] Interest on securities issued after 5 April 1982 by, or on a loan to, a local authority or a statutory corporation (as defined) in a currency other than sterling shall be paid without deduction of income tax and be exempt from income tax (but not corporation tax) in the hands of a non-UK resident beneficial owner of such securities or, in the case of a loan, in the hands of the non-UK resident person for the time being entitled to repayment or eventual repayment of the loan. Securities issued before 6 April 1982 in the currency of a country outside the scheduled territories at the time of issue were similarly treated.

[*ICTA 1988, s 581(4); ITTOIA 2005, ss 755, 756, Sch 1 paras 241, 242*].

Key points

[68.8] The key points are as follows:

- Subject to special provisions to the contrary, statutory bodies are taxable to corporation tax on their income and gains.
- Special provisions apply which amend the rules in relation to certain statutory bodies.
- Local authorities and health service bodies are exempt from tax.
- Payments by agricultural marketing boards into Government reserve funds are deducted in computing taxable profits.
- The cessation and commencement rules do not apply on the transfer of a trade under a harbour reorganisation scheme.
- Nuclear Decommissioning Authority is exempt from tax arising on trading income derived from exempt activities.

69

Time Limits

Introduction

[69.1] The general rule with regard to time limits for claims, elections etc. within the Taxes Acts was six years from the end of the accounting period to which the claim related, save where other time limits are prescribed within the legislation. However, as part of an attempt to reduce compliance costs it was decided to align time limits for making claims and elections across income tax, corporation tax, VAT, PAYE and NIC.

From 1 April 2010, *FA 2008, Sch 39, para 37–66* amends existing legislation and reduces the normal time limit for claims and elections to four years from the end of the accounting period to which they relate.

It follows that the time limit for accounting periods up to 31 March 2004 is 31 March 2010, the time limit for periods up to 31 March 2005 is 31 March 2010 (the day before the new law comes into force) and the time limit for periods ending up to 31 March 2006 is 31 March 2010. [*FA 1998, Sch 18 para 55; FA 2008, Sch 39 para 45, SI 2009 No 403*]. See also Tolley's Income Tax.

This chapter outlines the various significant time limits in respect of different provisions within UK tax law which are relevant for companies.

It should be noted that a number of time limits (particularly in relation to procedural matters) were revised following the introduction of self-assessment for accounting periods ending on or after 1 July 1999.

Simon's Taxes. See **A4.204, D1.1345.**

Accounting principles

[69.2] Limits with regard to certain accounting principles are as follows:

(a) *On a change of basis from realisation basis to mark to market basis*, election to spread the adjustment income equally over six periods of account beginning with the first period to which the new basis applies. Election to be made within twelve months after the end of the first accounting period to which the new basis applies. [*CTA 2009, s 186; FA 2002, Sch 22 para 9*]. See **70.20 TRADE PROFITS — INCOME AND SPECIFIC TRADES.**

(b) *On a change of accounting approach in calculating profits in compliance with UK GAAP (or international accounting standards if applicable)*, election to treat the 'UITF 40' adjustment as arising and charged in an accounting period rather than spreading it over three to six years. Election to be made within one year of the filing date of the company's tax return for the accounting period for which the election is made. [*FA 2006, Sch 15 para 13; CTA 2009, Sch 1 para 696*]. See **70.20 TRADE PROFITS — INCOME AND SPECIFIC TRADES.**

Appeals

[69.3] Limits with regard to appeals are as follows:

(a) Formal notice of appeal against an amendment to a corporation tax return following an enquiry or against an assessment which is not a self-assessment, must be lodged within **30 days** after the date of issue of the notice of amendment or assessment. See **6.1 APPEALS.**

(b) For appeals from the First-tier Tribunal to the Upper Tribunal, written applications must be made to the First-tier Tribunal within **56 days** of the later of: the tribunal sending out full written reasons for the decision; notification of amended reasons following a review of a decision; or, notification that the application to set aside a decision has been unsuccessful. Appeals from the Upper Tribunal to the Court of Appeal are governed by the *Civil Procedures Rules 1998 (SI 1998 No 3132)*. See **6.24, 6.34 APPEALS.**

(c) Appeals on a question of residence or domicile must be lodged within **three months** of receipt of written notice of HMRC's decision. See **21.9 CLAIMS.**

(d) Except as indicated above, appeals against amendments to claims etc. must be made within **30 days** of the receipt of the decision on a claim or of an amendment of a claim, as the case may be. See **21.9 CLAIMS.**

Capital allowances

[69.4] Certain claims relating to capital allowances are treated as follows:

(a) With regard to the Special Leasing provisions, claims for machinery or plant allowances to be set off against income other than that against which they are primarily given must be made within **two years** of the end of the accounting period for which the allowances are made. [*CAA 2001, s 260(6)*].

(b) With regard to Overseas Leasing in *CAA 2001, Ch 11*, a notice that machinery or plant on which allowances have been given has ceased, during the 'requisite period', to be used for a 'qualifying purpose' (no longer used for 'protected leasing') must be given within **three months** of the end of the accounting period in which the non-qualifying use takes place, or within **30 days** of the cessation's coming to the notice of the lessor, whichever is the later. A notice with regard to the provision of plant and machinery leased to joint lessees under the provisions of *s 116(1)* must be given within three months of the end of the accounting period in which the plant and machinery is first leased; or within 30 days of such use coming to the notice of the lessor. [*CAA 2001, ss 119, 120*].

See generally **10 CAPITAL ALLOWANCES — INTRODUCTION.**

Capital gains

[69.5] Time limits in respect of certain capital gains provisions are as follows:

(a) **Assets held on 6 April 1965.** An election for such assets to be valued at 6 April 1965 must be made within **two years** after the end of the accounting period in which the relevant disposal was made. [*TCGA 1992, Sch 2 para 17*]. For certain concessional treatment on a company's leaving a group see **29.1 DEGROUPING CHARGES.**

(b) **Assets held on 31 March 1982.** An irrevocable election for assets to be valued at 31 March 1982 must be made within **two years** of the end of the accounting period in which the first relevant disposal occurs (or such longer time as HMRC may allow).

(c) **Assets of negligible value.** A claim must be made within **two years** after the end of the accounting period in which the relevant date falls. See Tolley's Capital Gains Tax.

(d) **Groups of companies.** A company leaving a group remains liable for unpaid corporation tax on chargeable gains arising from the disposal of any asset formerly owned by that company while it was a member of the group where the disposal occurs within **twelve months** following its departure from the group. [*TCGA 1992, s 190*].

(e) **Know-how.** Joint election for so much of the consideration for the sale of know-how of a trade (or part of a trade) **not** to be treated as a payment for goodwill must be made within **two years** of the disposal. [*CTA 2009, s 178; ICTA 1988, s 531(3)*]. See **70.55 TRADE PROFITS — INCOME AND SPECIFIC TRADES.**

(f) **Residence.** An election for any part of the 'postponed gain' on cessation of residence which becomes chargeable to be offset by capital losses of the subsidiary concerned must be made within **two years** of the cessation of residence. See **65.8 RESIDENCE.**

(g) **Rollover relief** is only available if the acquisition of the new assets is made within **three years** after the disposal of the old or within **twelve months** before. See **18.8 CAPITAL GAINS — GROUPS.**

For further details of the above and other time limits, see Tolley's Capital Gains Tax under the appropriate heading.

Chargeability to tax

[69.6] A company chargeable to corporation tax for any accounting period which has not received notice requiring a return for that period must notify the inspector that it is so chargeable within **one year** of the end of that period. [*TMA 1970, s 10; FA 1988, s 121; FA 1998, Sch 18 para 2, Sch 19 para 1*].

Coming within charge to corporation tax

[69.7] A company must give notice to HMRC of when its first accounting period begins and of when any subsequent accounting period begins that does not follow on immediately from the end of a previous accounting period. The notice must be given within three months after the beginning of the accounting period in question. See **66.2 RETURNS.** [*FA 2004, s 55*].

Construction industry — tax deduction scheme

[69.8] The requirements are equivalent to those in **69.26**(a) and (b) below (except that the relevant form is SC 35).

[*SI 2005 No 2045*].

Contaminated land remediation expenditure

[69.9] Contaminated land remediation expenditure is treated as follows:

(a) Election for 'qualifying land remediation expenditure' of a capital nature to be allowed as a deduction from trade or property business profits must be made within **two years** after the end of the accounting period in respect of which it is made. [*CTA 2009, ss 1147, 1148; FA 2001, Sch 22 para 1(8)*].

(b) Claims for 'land remediation tax credit' must be included in the company tax return (or amended return) and must be made within **one year** of the filing date for that return or by such later time as HMRC may allow.

[*CTA 2009, s 1151; TMA 1970, ss 83G–83L*].

Controlled foreign companies

[69.10] Claims under *ICTA 1988, Sch 24 para 9*, for losses of certain periods to be taken into account in computing chargeable profits, are to be made within **20 months** after the end of the accounting period. The same applies to claims under *para 4* for certain deemed claims and elections to be disregarded in computing chargeable profits.

[*ICTA 1988, ss 747–756, Schs 24–26; FA 1998, Sch 17*].

See **27.9 CONTROLLED FOREIGN COMPANIES.**

Corporate venturing scheme

[69.11] Corporate venturing scheme is treated as follows:

(a) The compliance statement to the effect that shares qualify for the relief must be made by the issuing company within **two years** after the end of the accounting period in which the shares were issued (or, if later, by two years after the minimum trading period condition is satisfied). [*FA 2000, Sch 15 para 42(4)*]. See **28.4 CORPORATE VENTURING SCHEME.**

(b) Claims for set-off of allowable losses against income must be made within **two years** after the end of the accounting period in which the loss was incurred. [*FA 2000, Sch 15 para 68*]. See **28.20 CORPORATE VENTURING SCHEME.**

Double taxation

[69.12] Relief by way of credit for foreign tax in respect of any income must be claimed within four years (from 1 April 2010, before that date six years) after the end of the accounting period for which the income is chargeable or, if later, within one year after the end of the accounting period in which the foreign tax is paid. [*TIOPA 2010, s 19; ICTA 1988, s 806(1)(b)*].

For distributions made before 1 July 2009, a similar time limit applies to claims to utilise unrelieved foreign tax. [*ICTA 1988, ss 806G, 806M(7); FA 2008, Sch 39 paras 24–26*].

See **32.5 DOUBLE TAX RELIEF.**

Employees' remuneration

[69.13] For accounting periods ending before 1 April 2009, a claim for the computation for a period of account to be adjusted for employees' remuneration paid after the computation has been made, but within nine months after the end of the period, must be made within two years of the end of the period of account.

[*FA 1989, s 43(5); ITEPA 2003, Sch 6 para 157*].

See **71.28 TRADE PROFITS — INCOME AND SPECIFIC TRADES.** (For later accounting periods, such matters are dealt with by way of amendment to the tax return and the two-year limit no longer applies.)

Error or mistake

[69.14] Relief for an error or mistake in the corporation tax return must be claimed within four years (from 1 April 2010, **six years** before that date) after the end of the relevant accounting period.

[*TMA 1970, s 33; FA 1998, Sch 18 para 51, Sch 19 para 15; FA 2008, Sch 39 para 43*].

See **21.10 CLAIMS** and also **21.11.**

Film tax relief

[69.15] A claim for film tax relief must be made in a company tax return (or amended return) for the accounting period for which the claim is made, within one year of the filing date for that return or by such later time as HMRC may allow. It can similarly only be amended or withdrawn by amendment of the company tax return within the same time limit. See **70.31 TRADE PROFITS — INCOME AND SPECIFIC TRADES.** [*FA 1998, Sch 18 para 83W; FA 2006, Sch 5 para 29*].

Financial instruments and derivative contracts

[69.16] The provisions of *CTA 2009, Pt 7* apply with regard to derivative contracts in respect of accounting periods ending on or after 1 April 2009.

Claims with regard to financial instruments and derivative contracts (prior to 1 April 2009) are treated as follows:

(a) An election with respect to certain contracts held immediately before and on the first day of the first accounting period beginning on or after 1 October 2002, to treat a derivative contract as two separate contracts, must be made within two years of the end of the first accounting period beginning on or after that date. [*FA 2002, Sch 28 para 5(5)(6)*].

(b) Where an election under (a) above is made and the disposal of the contract gives rise to an allowable loss, an election for the loss to be treated as a non-trading loan relationship debit (see **54.4 LOAN RELATIONSHIPS**) must be made within **two years** following the end of the accounting period in which the company ceased to be a party to the contract. [*FA 2002, Sch 28 para 5(9)(10)*].

(c) Where the pre-*FA 2004* basis of computation applies, an election by a non-resident company to use (with respect to a UK branch) a mark to market accounting basis for some or all of its derivative contracts (such election being treated as also extended to the company's loan relationships under *FA 1996, s 86(3A)*) must be made within two years following the end of the first accounting period beginning on or after 1 October 2002 in which the company is party to the derivative contract eligible for election. [*FA 2002, Sch 26 para 19*].

(d) For accounting periods beginning before 1 October 2002, a claim for certain qualifying payments to be treated as having become irrecoverable in an accounting period must be made within **two years** of the end of the accounting period.

Group relief

[69.17] For the position under self-assessment, see *FA 1998, Sch 18 Pt VIII* and further **21.2 CLAIMS.**

Herd basis

[69.18] An election by a farming company for the herd basis must be made within **two years** of the end of the first accounting period during which a production herd of the class concerned was kept or in which compensation is received for compulsory slaughter. See **70.42 TRADE PROFITS — INCOME AND SPECIFIC TRADES.**

Housing associations

[69.19] Exemption from corporation tax on rents and chargeable gains must be claimed within two years of the end of the relevant accounting period. The same applies to self-build societies. See **45 HOUSING ASSOCIATIONS.**

Income tax

[69.20] Returns of income tax deducted from payments made by a company are due within **14 days** of the end of the return period. See **46 INCOME TAX IN RELATION TO A COMPANY.**

Intangible assets

[69.21] Intangible assets claims are treated as follows:

(a) An election to replace accounts depreciation with a fixed writing-down allowance must be made within **two years** after the end of the accounting period in which the asset was created or acquired. [*CTA 2009, s 730; FA 2002, Sch 29 para 10*]. See **48.5 INTANGIBLE ASSETS.**

(b) An election to exclude from the intangible assets provisions certain expenditure on computer software must be made within **two years** after the end of the accounting period in which the expenditure was incurred. [*CTA 2009, s 815; FA 2002, Sch 29 para 83*]. See **48.4 INTANGIBLE ASSETS.**

Loan relationships

[69.22] Relief for a non-trading deficit of an accounting period may be claimed by set-off against other profits of the period or by carry back within **two years** of the end of the accounting period (or within such longer time as HMRC may allow). A claim for part or all of the deficit to be excepted from being set against non-trading profits of the accounting period immediately following the deficit period and treated as a non-trading deficit of that period to be carried forward for offset against non-trading profits of succeeding accounting periods, must be made within **two years** of the end of that period. [*CTA 2009, ss 458–460; FA 1996, s 83, Sch 8 para 4; FA 2002, Sch 25 paras 3, 19*]. See **54.4 LOAN RELATIONSHIPS.**

Loans to participators

[69.23] The time limit for claiming repayment of tax paid on a loan by a close company to certain participators is **four years** after the end of the **financial year** in which the loan is repaid. See *CTA 2010, s 458(3)* and further **22.15 CLOSE COMPANIES.**

Over-repaid tax

[69.24] Assessments to recover tax over-repaid may, if otherwise out of time, be made up to the end of the accounting period following that of the repayment or, if later, within **three months** of the closure of an HMRC enquiry into a self-assessment return. [*FA 1998, Sch 18 para 53, Sch 19 para 13*].

Patents

[69.25] Patents are treated as follows:

(a) Where a company resident in the UK sells patent rights wholly or partly for a capital sum, and does not wish that sum to be spread over six years, an election to have the entire sum charged to tax for the accounting period in which it was received must be made within **two years** of the end of that period.

(b) A non-resident company selling UK patent rights wholly or partly for a capital sum may claim to have that sum spread over six years (and not treated as a single lump sum) within **two years** of the end of the accounting period in which it was received.

[*CTA 2009, ss 914, 916; ICTA 1988, ss 524, 525*].

See **61.18 PROFIT COMPUTATIONS**.

PAYE

[69.26] PAYE is treated as follows:

(a) Remittances must be made to the Collector within **14 days** after the end of the tax month (ending on the fifth of the calendar month) or in certain cases the tax quarter (ending on 5 July etc.). Where the payment is made by an approved method of electronic communication in respect of PAYE payments made after 5 April 2004, the time limit is extended to **17 days** in both cases. (See **41.12 HMRC — ADMINISTRATION**.) [*SI 2003 No 2682, Reg 69; formerly SI 1993 No 744, Regs 40, 41 (as amended by SI 2003 No 2494)*].

(b) End-of-year returns, deduction cards and Form P35 are due within **44 days** after the end of the tax year. [*SI 2003 No 2682, Reg 73; formerly SI 1993 No 744, Reg 43*].

Payment of tax

[69.27] Corporation tax is generally payable **nine months** after the end of the accounting period (subject to any requirement for instalment payment). See **59 PAYMENT OF TAX**.

Pre-trading expenditure

[69.28] An election for a pre-trading debit on a loan relationship to be deferred to the period in which the trade commences must be made within **two years** of the end of the accounting period in which the debit arose. [*CTA 2009, ss 330(1)–(3); ICTA 1988, s 401(1AB)*].

Research and development expenditure

[69.29] Research and development expenditure is treated as follows:

(a) A claim for R&D tax relief for an accounting period must be made, amended or withdrawn in the company tax return (or amended return) for which the claim is made, within **one year** of the filing date for that return (see **66.9 RETURNS**) or by such later time as HMRC may allow.

[*FA 1998, Sch 18 paras, 83A–83F, 83LA–83LE, 83M–83R; FA 2006, Sch 3; FA 2008, Sch 40 para 21; CTA 2009, Sch 1 para 454 (3)(7)(8)(10)(11)*].

(b) An election for 'connected person's treatment' to be applied to all sub-contractor payments made under the same contract or arrangement must be made within **two years** after the end of the accounting period in which the contract or arrangement is entered into.
[*CTA 2009, s 1131; CTA 2009, s 1135; FA 2000, Sch 20 para 11; FA 2002, Sch 13 para 10*].
The similar election in relation to staff provision payments must be made within a similar time limit.
[*FA 2000, Sch 20 para 8D(4); FA 2003, Sch 31 para 6*].

(c) An election for the alternative treatment of pre-trading expenditure in an accounting period must be made within **two years** after the end of the accounting period to which the election relates.
[*CTA 2009, s 1047; FA 2000, Sch 20 para 14(6); FA 2002, Sch 13 para 15(4)*].

See **64 RESEARCH AND DEVELOPMENT**.

Returns

[69.30] Returns time limits are as follows:

(a) Company tax returns must be made within **one year** of the end of the accounting period (or of the period of account in which falls the last day of the accounting period) or, if later, within **three months** of the date of the notice requiring the return. [*FA 1998, Sch 18 para 14*]. See **66.4 RETURNS**.

(b) *Non-qualifying distributions* must be returned within **14 days** of the end of the accounting period in which they were made or within **14 days** of their having been made (if they were not made in an accounting period).

(c) *Stock dividends* must be returned within **30 days** of the end of the return period.

See **66.10** *et seq*. **RETURNS** and **69.2** and **69.20** above.

Trading losses

[69.31] A claim for trading losses to be set off against profits of the same or an earlier accounting period must be made within **two years** of the end of the accounting period in which the losses were incurred, or within such further period as HMRC may allow.

[*CTA 2010, s 37(7); ICTA 1988, s 393A(10)*]. See **55 LOSSES**.

Trading stock

[69.32] On the discontinuance of a profession, an election for work in progress to be taken at cost may be made up to **two years** after the end of the accounting period in which the discontinuance occurs. [*Removed in the rewrite to CTA 2009, as companies do not carry on professions for corporation tax purposes; ICTA 1988, s 101(2A); ITTOIA 2005, Sch 1 para 80*].

See **71.66 TRADING EXPENSES AND DEDUCTIONS.**

Unlisted shares

[69.33] Claims for relief of losses on such shares by investment companies must be made within **two years** of the end of the accounting period in which the loss was incurred.

[*CTA 2010, ss 70, 71; ICTA 1988, s 573*]. See **55.17 LOSSES.**

Unremittable income

[69.34] A claim for unremittable income to be left out of account must be made within **two years** after the end of the accounting period in which the income arose.

[*CTA 2009, s 1275; ICTA 1988, s 584(6)*].

See **65.4 RESIDENCE.**

70

Trade Profits — Income and Specific Trades

Cross-references. See **5** ANTI-AVOIDANCE; **27** CONTROLLED FOREIGN COMPANIES; **32** DOUBLE TAX RELIEF; **39** GROUP RELIEF; **48** INTANGIBLE ASSETS; **51** INVESTMENT COMPANIES AND INVESTMENT BUSINESS; **55** LOSSES; **61** PROFIT COMPUTATIONS; **64** RESEARCH AND DEVELOPMENT EXPENDITURE; **65.4** RESIDENCE; **72** TRANSFER PRICING.

Introduction

[70.1] This chapter deals with the charge to corporation tax on trade profits. This includes examining what is a trade; when a trade commences/ceases; how trade profits are calculated and the tax treatment of various types of income. For ease of use, a separate chapter **71 TRADING EXPENSES AND DEDUCTIONS** deals with common trading expenses and deductions. This chapter also describes the tax treatment of certain specific types of trades such as films, herd basis, mines and quarries. As shown in the index above, trade income and specific trades are arranged in alphabetical order.

Charge to tax

[70.2] The *Corporation Tax Act 2009* deals with the computation of a company's trade profits for accounting periods ending on or after 1 April 2009. Corporation tax is charged on the profits of a trade [*CTA 2009, s 35*]. The profits of a trade must be calculated in accordance with generally accepted accounting practice, subject to any adjustment required for corporation tax purposes. Assuming a company's accounts have been prepared in accordance with GAAP, the starting point is therefore normally the profit/loss before tax as shown in the accounts. This is then adjusted as necessary, mainly for the items mentioned in this chapter and **71 TRADING EXPENSES AND DEDUCTIONS.**

CTA 2010, Sch 2 para 10 and *TIOPA 2010, Sch 9 para 10* made some minor changes to the pre-existing law on calculation of trading profits. Subject to the election below, where a period of account straddles 1 April 2010 and the consequences of an event or transaction are different from what they would have been before the change, the affected person may elect to restore the treatment of the transactions for corporation tax or income tax to which it had been before the change. Where the same event or transaction affects more than one person, the election by one is of no effect unless all elect. The election must be made for corporation tax purposes on or before the second anniversary of the end of the accounting period straddling 1 April.

See **2 ACCOUNTING PERIODS** for the interaction of accounting periods/periods of accounts compared to tax basis periods. Power is given to apportion profits or losses, on a time basis in proportion to the number of days in the respective periods, if required for the purposes of arriving at the profits or losses of an accounting period that does not coincide with a period of account. [*CTA 2009, s 52; ICTA 1988, s 72*]. This applies only where such time apportionment is necessary (see *Marshall Hus & Partners Ltd v Bolton* (1980) 55 TC 539) and only to the *extent* that it is necessary (see *Lyons v Kelly* [2002] STC (SCD) 455).

Accounting periods ending before 1 April 2009

The law relating to the taxation of 'trading income' (previously within *Schs A, D* and *F* and the cases of *Sch D*) was consolidated in *Income Tax (Trading and Other Income) Act 2005* (*ITTOIA 2005*) and *Corporation Tax Act 2009 (CTA 2009)* as part of the Tax Law Rewrite programme. The former had effect for income tax purposes for 2005/06 and subsequent years and, for corporation tax purposes where relevant, for accounting periods ending after 5 April 2005. [*ITTOIA 2005, s 883(1)*]. The latter has effect, for corporation tax for accounting periods ending on or after 1 April 2009, and for income tax and capital gains purposes for accounting periods ending on or after 1 April 2009.

Prior to *CTA 2009*, the charge was generally under *Sch D, Case I* [*ICTA 1988, s 18; ITTOIA Sch 1 para 9*]; trades carried on wholly abroad were 'possessions' within *Sch D Case V* but a business controlled from the UK was within Case 1 even if the day-to-day trading activities were carried on wholly abroad (see **65 RESIDENCE**). The *Sch D* labels were removed by *CTA 2009*.

Corporation tax was also charged (under *Sch D, Case II*) on the profits of a profession carried on by a company. The rewrite took the view that a company cannot carry on a profession; if a company is providing professional services it is carrying on a trade. (Similarly, a company cannot carry on a vocation.) See Change 2 listed in Annex 1 to the Explanatory Notes to *CTA 2009*; this change is expected to have no practical effect.

For further guidance on *Sch D* see 2009/10 and earlier versions of this book.

It can no longer be assumed that the coverage in Tolley's Income Tax of any particular type of trading receipt (or deduction etc.) applies equally for corporation tax purposes and so all such matters are now dealt with in this work.

Whether a trade carried on

[70.3] Trade 'includes any venture in the nature of trade' [*CTA 2010, s 1120*] (previously 'every trade, manufacture, adventure or concern in the nature of trade' [*ICTA 1988, s 832(1)*]). For a discussion on the *scope* of a trade, see HMRC Business Income Manual BIM21000–21040. Whether a trade is being carried on is normally a question of fact but a trade can be deemed to exist (or not exist) by statute. The following covers the consideration of whether an activity amounts to trading by a company but see Tolley's Income Tax under Trading Income in relation to trading by individuals or partnerships. See also **56 MUTUAL COMPANIES** and **68 STATUTORY BODIES**. Special types of activity are dealt with below in alphabetical order.

Simon's Taxes. See B1.4.

Avoidance schemes

[70.4] A line is drawn between transactions of a trading nature which remain trading even though entered into to secure tax advantages and transactions so remote from ordinary trading as to be explicable only as fiscal devices and hence not trading.

In *Ransom v Higgs and Kilmorie (Aldridge) Ltd v Dickinson etc.* (1974) 50 TC 1, HL, the taxpayers entered into complex arrangements to siphon development profits into the hands of trustees. They succeeded, the Crown failing to establish that, looked at as a whole, the arrangements constituted trading. In *Johnson v Jewitt* (1961) 40 TC 231, CA, an elaborate and artificial device to manufacture trading losses was held not to amount to trading, but see *Ensign Tankers (Leasing) Ltd v Stokes* (1992) 64 TC 617, HL, where the company's investment in two film production partnerships was entered into with a view to obtaining first-year capital allowances. See also *Black Nominees Ltd v Nicol* (1975) 50 TC 229 and *Newstead v Frost* (1980) 53 TC 525, HL. See generally **ANTI-AVOIDANCE (5)**.

Betting

[70.5] Betting by professional bookmakers is assessable (*Partridge v Mallandaine* (1886) 2 TC 179) even if carried on in an unlawful way (*Southern v A B* (1933) 18 TC 59)). Also exempt from CGT. [*TCGA 1992, s 51(1)*]. Receipts from newspaper articles based on betting system held assessable in *Graham v Arnott* (1941) 24 TC 157.

Lotteries and football pools promotion constitutes trading, but where a pool or small lottery is run by a supporters club or other society on terms that a specified part of the cost of the ticket is to be donated to a club or body within the purposes in *Lotteries and Amusements Act 1976, s 5(1)*, the donation element is not treated as a trading receipt (HMRC Statement of Practice, SP/C1). For further detail, see HMRC Business Income Manual BIM61600–61615. See **20.6 CHARITIES** as regards charitable lotteries.

Horse racing etc.

[70.6] Racing and selling the progeny of a brood mare was held to constitute trading in *Dawson v Counsell* (1938) 22 TC 149, CA. In *Norman v Evans* (1964) 42 TC 188 the share of prize monies for letting racehorses was held to be assessable (under the old *Sch D, Case VI*). Profits from stallion fees are assessable (assessments upheld under both old *Sch D, Case I* and *Case VI*) (*Malcolm v Lockhart* (1919) 7 TC 99, HL; *McLaughlin v Bailey* (1920) 7 TC 508; *Derby (Lord) v Bassom (Inspector of Taxes)* (1926) 10 TC 357, 135 LT 274; *Wernher v CIR* (1942) 29 TC 20; *Benson v Counsel (Inspector of Taxes)* (1942) 1 KB 364, [1942] 1 All ER 435) but wear and tear allowances (the forerunner of modern capital allowances on plant etc.) for stallions was refused in *Derby v Aylmer* (1915) 6 TC 665. Profits from greyhound breeding were held to be trading in *Hawes v Gardiner* (1957) 37 TC 671. 'Private' horse racing and training is not normally trading (cf *Sharkey v Wernher* (1955) 36 TC 275, HL).

Illegal trading

[70.7] Crime, e.g. burglary, is not trading but the profits of a commercial business are assessable notwithstanding the business may be carried on in an unlawful way, e.g. 'bootlegging' (*Canadian Minister of Finance v Smith* (1926) 5 ATC 621, PC, and cf *Lindsay Woodward & Hiscox v CIR* (1932) 18 TC 43, Ct of Sess), operating 'fruit machines' illegal at the time (*Mann v Nash* (1932) 16 TC 523), street bookmaking illegal at the time (*Southern v A B* (1933) 18

TC 59) and prostitution (*CIR v Aken* (1990) 63 TC 395, CA). But penalties for trading contrary to war-time regulations held not deductible (*CIR v E C Warnes & Co* (1919) 12 TC 227; *CIR v Alexander von Glehn & Co* (1920) 12 TC 232). See also **70.5** above. See **71 TRADING EXPENSES AND DEDUCTIONS** as regards prohibition on deduction of expenditure involving crime.

Simon's Taxes. See B1.420.

Income from land

[70.8] Rents and other income derived from the exploitation of proprietary interests in land are taxed as profits from a property business (see **62 PROPERTY INCOME**) and not treated as income derived from a trade. The leading case is *Salisbury House Estate Ltd v Fry* (1930) 15 TC 266, HL, and see also *Sywell Aerodrome Ltd v Croft* (1941) 24 TC 126, CA; *Webb v Conelee Properties Ltd* (1982) 56 TC 149. For relaxations to this rule, see **70.23** below (tied premises), **70.54** below (surplus business accommodation), **62.2 PROPERTY INCOME** (caravan sites) and **62.19 PROPERTY INCOME** (electric-line wayleaves). The commercial *occupation* of UK land with a view to realisation of profits is treated as the carrying on of a trade (though this does not apply to woodlands or if the land in question is being prepared for forestry purposes). [*CTA 2009, ss 37, 38; ICTA 1988, s 53(3)(4); ITTOIA 2005, Sch 1 para 32*]. See **70.29** below as regards farming and market gardening and **61.24 PROFIT COMPUTATIONS** for a general exemption for woodlands. **Mines, quarries etc**. Profits of mines, quarries, gravel pits, sand pits, brickfields, ironworks, gas works, canals, railways, rights of fishing, rights of markets, fairs and tolls and like concerns are computed and charged to corporation tax *as if* the concern were a trade, and losses are relieved as if it were a trade carried on in the UK. This applies only where the concern is not, in fact, a trade on first principles and is not treated as such under the commercial occupation rule above. [*CTA 2009, s 39; ICTA 1988, s 55; ITTOIA, Sch 1 para 33*]. As regards rent received in connection with such concerns, see **62.19 PROPERTY INCOME.**

Isolated or speculative transactions

[70.9] For property transactions and share dealing see **70.13** and **70.14** respectively.

Whether the surplus on the purchase and resale of assets, otherwise than in the course of an established commercial enterprise, is derived from an 'adventure or concern in the nature of trade' depends on the facts. Para 116 of the Final Report of the Royal Commission on the Taxation of Profits and Income (1955 HMSO Cmd. 9474) lists six 'badges of trade':

(i) the subject matter of the realisation;
(ii) length of period of ownership;
(iii) frequency or number of similar transactions;
(iv) supplementary work on assets sold;
(v) reason for sale;
(vi) motive.

Other relevant factors may be the degree of organisation, whether the taxpayer is or has been associated with a recognised business dealing in similar assets and how the purchases were financed. For a review of the factors to be considered, see *Marson v Morton* (1986) 59 TC 381.

Tax cases where found trading:

- *Martin v Lowry* (1926) 11 TC 297, HL (a leading case) — on a purchase and resale of war surplus linen;
- *CIR v Livingston* (1926) 11 TC 538, Ct of Sess — a purchase, conversion and resale of a ship;
- *Cape Brandy Syndicate v CIR* (1921) 12 TC 358, CA — transactions in brandy;
- *Lindsay Woodward* at **70.7** above — whisky;
- *P J McCall decd v CIR* (1923) 4 ATC 522; *CIR v Fraser* (1942) 24 TC 498, Ct of Sess — whisky in bond;
- *Pickford v Quirke* (1927) 13 TC 251, CA — 'turning over' cotton mills;
- *Edwards v Bairstow & Harrison* (1955) 36 TC 207, HL — purchase and resale of cotton spinning plant;
- *Rutledge v CIR* (1929) 14 TC 490, Ct of Sess — purchase and resale of toilet rolls.

Tax cases where found not trading:

- *Jenkinson v Freedland* (1961) 39 TC 636, CA — the Commissioners' finding that a profit on the purchase, repair and sale (to associated companies) of stills was not assessable, was upheld;
- *Kirkham v Williams* (1991) 64 TC 253, CA — the Commissioners' decision that the sale of a dwelling house built on land partly acquired for storage etc. was an adventure in the nature of trade was reversed in the CA.

Simon's Taxes. See B1.405–B1.407, B1.447.

Liquidators or receivers

[70.10] Whether a liquidator or receiver is continuing the company's trade or merely realising its assets as best he can, is a question of fact. For liquidators or receivers see *Armitage v Moore* (1900) 4 TC 199; *CIR v 'Old Bushmills' Distillery* (1927) 12 TC 1148; *CIR v Thompson* (1936) 20 TC 422; *Wilson Box v Brice* (1936) 20 TC 736, CA; *Baker v Cook* (1937) 21 TC 337.

Miscellaneous

[70.11] Assessments were upheld on a committee operating golf links owned by a Town Council (*Carnoustie Golf Course Committee v CIR* (1929) 14 TC 498, Ct of Sess); trustees under a private Act managing a recreation ground (*CIR v Stonehaven Recreation Ground Trustees* (1929) 15 TC 419, Ct of Sess); temporary joint coal merchanting (*Gardner and Bowring Hardy & Co v CIR* (1930) 15 TC 602, Ct of Sess); promotion of mining companies to exploit mines (*Murphy v Australian Machinery etc. Co Ltd* (1948) 30 TC 244, CA, and cf *Rhodesia Metals v Commr of Taxes* (1940) 19 ATC 472, PC); purchase and resale of amusement equipment (*Crole v Lloyd* (1950) 31 TC 338).

A company which made loans to another company to finance a trading venture was held not to be trading itself (*Stone & Temple Ltd v Waters*; *Astrawall (UK) Ltd v Waters* (1995) 67 TC 145).

The activities of the British Olympic Association (which included the raising of funds through commercial sponsorship and the exploitation of its logo, but many of which were non-commercial) were held as a whole to be uncommercial and not to constitute a trade (*British Olympic Association v Winter* [1995] STC (SCD) 85).

For whether *ostrich farming* (i.e. the ownership of ostriches which are looked after on the owner's behalf by others) amounts to trading, and for the consequences of such trading, see Revenue Tax Bulletin June 1996 pp 318, 319, issue 23.

See also *J Bolson & Son Ltd v Farrelly* (1953) 34 TC 161, CA (deals in vessels by company operating boat services held a separate adventure), and *Torbell Investments Ltd v Williams* (1986) 59 TC 357 (dormant company revived for purpose of acquiring certain loans held to have acquired them as trading stock). But a company formed to administer a holidays with pay scheme for the building etc. industry was held not trading (*Building & Civil Engineering etc Ltd v Clark* (1960) 39 TC 12). Assessments on profits from promoting a series of driving schools were upheld in *Leach v Pogson* (1962) 40 TC 585; in concluding that the profit from *first* sale was assessable, Commissioners were entitled to take into account the subsequent transactions.

Oil-related activities

[70.12] The carrying on of oil-related activities (i.e. oil extraction activities within *CTA 2010, s 272* for corporation tax or *TIOPA 2010, Sch 1* for income tax (previously *ICTA 1988, s 502(1)*) and any activities consisting of the acquisition, enjoyment or exploitation of oil rights) as part of a trade is treated for corporation tax purposes as a separate trade in itself. [*CTA 2010, ss 274, 279*].

Property transactions

[70.13] This part relates to transactions in land and buildings otherwise than in the course of an established business of property development, building etc. For HMRC's view, see HMRC Business Income Manual BIM60000–60165. For other sales of property see **70.61** below.

A line is drawn between realisations of property held as an investment or as a residence and transactions amounting to an adventure or concern in the nature of trade. The principles at **70.9** above apply suitably adapted.

In *Leeming v Jones* (1930) 15 TC 333, HL, an assessment on the acquisitions and disposal of options over rubber estates was confirmed by Commissioners. In a Supplementary Case the Commissioners found there had been no concern in the nature of the trade. The Court held there was no liability. Per Lawrence LJ 'in the case of an isolated transaction ... there is really no middle course open. It is either an adventure in the nature of trade, or else it is simply a case of sale and resale of property.' See also *Pearn v Miller* (1927) 11 TC 610.

Property transactions were held to be trading in:

- *Californian Copper Syndicate v Harris* (1904) 5 TC 159 — purchase of copper bearing land shortly afterwards resold;
- *Thew v South West Africa Co* (1924) 9 TC 141, CA — numerous sales of land acquired by concession for exploitation;
- *Cayzer, Irvine & Co v CIR* (1942) 24 TC 491, Ct of Sess — exploitation of landed estate acquired by shipping company;
- *Emro Investments v Aller* and *Lance Webb Estates v Aller* (1954) 35 TC 305 — profits carried to capital reserve on numerous purchases and sales;
- *Orchard Parks v Pogson* (1964) 42 TC 442 — land compulsorily purchased after development plan dropped;
- *Parkstone Estates v Blair* (1966) 43 TC 246 — industrial estate developed: land disposed of by sub-leases for premiums;
- *Eames v Stepnell Properties Ltd* (1966) 43 TC 678, CA — sale of land acquired from associated company while resale being negotiated. See also *Bath & West Counties Property Trust Ltd v Thomas* (1977) 52 TC 20.

Property transactions held to be non-trading in:

- *Hudson's Bay v Stevens* 1909, 5 TC 424, CA — numerous sales of land acquired under Royal Charter: contrast *South West Africa Co* above;
- *Tebrau (Johore) Rubber Syndicate v Farmer* (1910) 5 TC 658 — purchase and resale of rubber estates: contrast *Californian Copper* above.
- *Rand v Alberni Land Co Ltd* (1920) 7 TC 629 — sales of land held in trust were held not trading but contrast *Alabama Coal Iron Land v Mylam* (1926) 11 TC 232; *Balgownie Land Trust v CIR* (1929) 14 TC 684, Ct of Sess; *St Aubyn Estates v Strick* (1932) 17 TC 412; *Tempest Estates v Walmsley* (1975) 51 TC 305.
- *CIR v Hyndland Investment Co Ltd* (1929) 14 TC 694, Ct of Sess; *Glasgow Heritable Trust v CIR* (1954) 35 TC 196, Ct of Sess; *Lucy & Sunderland Ltd v Hunt* (1961) 40 TC 132 — sales of property after a period of letting held realisations of investments or not trading. Contrast held trading in *Rellim Ltd v Vise* (1951) 32 TC 254, CA (notwithstanding that company previously admitted as investment company); *CIR v Toll Property Co* (1952) 34 TC 13, Ct of Sess; *Forest Side Properties (Chingford) v CIR* (1961) 39 TC 665, 40 ATC 155, CA.
- *Simmons v CIR* (1980) 53 TC 461, HL (reversing Commissioners' decision) — sales by liquidator of property owned by companies following abandonment of plan for their public flotation held not trading.
- *Rosemoor Investments v Inspector of Taxes* [2002] STC (SCD) 325 — it was not open to the Commissioners to recharacterise as trading a complex transaction routed via an investment company subsidiary and structured to produce capital.
- In *Ms P Azam* [2011] UKFTT 50 (TC) the Tribunal found, on the balance of probabilities, that the appellant was not engaged in a trade in property. The appellant purchased eleven properties and although

she claimed that it had always been her intention to sell each of the properties within a period of six months of their purchase, she had in fact not sold any of them. She claimed she had to rent the properties as she was waiting for an improvement in the property market. However, notwithstanding this, she continued to buy properties and thus repeat her mistake. The Tribunal was therefore satisfied on the balance of probabilities that at the time of purchasing subsequent properties, she was aware that she would have to rent the properties for some years, and indeed this could even have been the intention from the outset. Furthermore, the nature of the appellant's activities in relation to the properties were consistent with those of a landlord.

Simon's Taxes. See **B1.406, B5.213, B5.216–B5.222.**

Share dealing

[70.14] Share dealing with the public is strictly controlled by the *Financial Services and Markets Act 2000*. This paragraph is concerned with share transactions entered into (generally through the Stock Exchange) by persons not authorised to deal under that Act and the question arises whether they amount to an adventure or concern in the nature of trade. The principles of **70.9** above apply suitably adapted. The prudent management of an investment portfolio may necessitate changes in the holdings but this is not normally trading. Stock Exchange speculation, particularly by individuals, may be quasi-gambling and not trading — see Pennycuick J in *Lewis Emanuel & Son Ltd v White* (1965) 42 TC 369 in which, reversing the Commissioners' finding, he held that the Stock Exchange losses of a fruit etc. merchanting company were from a separate trade of share dealing but observed that gambling by the company would have been *ultra vires*. Subsequent *Companies Act* changes have, however, removed any such restriction on the activities of most companies (see HMRC Inspector' Manual IM 129a). In *Cooper v C & J Clark Ltd* (1982) 54 TC 670, the losses of a manufacturing company on its sale of gilts, in which it had invested temporarily surplus cash, were allowed as a set-off against its general trading profits. An individual speculating in stocks and shares and commodity futures was held to be trading in *Wannell v Rothwell* (1996) 68 TC 719 (although loss relief was refused on the grounds that the trading was 'uncommercial', see **55.6**(a) **LOSSES**), but the opposite conclusion was reached in *Salt v Chamberlain* (1979) 53 TC 143.

For share dealing by investment companies see *Scottish Investment Trust Co v Forbes* (1893) 3 TC 231 and *Halefield Securities Ltd v Thorpe* (1967) 44 TC 154. For trading in secured loans, see *Torbell Investments Ltd v Williams* (1986) 59 TC 357.

For share sales connected with an existing business see **70.64** below.

Commencement or cessation

[70.15] Where a company starts or ceases to be within the charge to corporation tax in respect of a trade, it is treated as starting or permanently ceasing to carry on the trade at that time. [*CTA 2009, s 41*].

For a short article on the distinction between succession to a trade, extension of an existing trade and commencement of a new trade, see HMRC Tax Bulletin February 1996 pp 285, 286, issue 21. For an in-depth discussion, see HMRC Business Income Manual BIM70500–70690.

Simon's Taxes. See B1.6.

Post-cessation receipts

[70.16] Corporation tax is charged on 'post-cessation receipts' arising from a trade to the extent that they have not been brought into account in computing trading profits or the profits of a property business for any period and that they are not otherwise chargeable to tax. However, a post-cessation receipt is not within this charge if it is received by or on behalf of a non UK resident which is beneficially entitled to it and it represents income arising outside the UK or it derives from a trade carried on wholly outside the UK. The charge is made on the full amount of post-cessation receipts received in the accounting period subject to the allowable deductions set out below.

For these purposes, a '*post-cessation receipt*' is a sum which a company receives after permanently discontinuing a trade (including on a change of ownership which, under *CTA 2009, s 41; ICTA 1988, s 337(1)* (company beginning or ceasing to carry on a trade, see above), is treated as a permanent discontinuance) but which arises from the carrying on of the trade before cessation. Certain sums as below are specifically treated as being, or as not being (as the case may be), post-cessation receipts.

Where the trade is carried on in partnership, the person treated as permanently discontinuing the trade is the partner. Receipts within the legislation will include, *inter alia*, royalties and similar amounts which under decisions such as *Carson v Cheyney's Exor* (1958) 38 TC 240, HL, prior to the original legislation being enacted, had been held not to be taxable.

Debts

To the extent that a deduction has been made, in computing the profits of the trade, for an impaired loss or a release of liability (see **71.5 TRADING EXPENSES AND DEDUCTIONS**), any amount received after cessation in settlement of that debt is a post cessation receipt. If an amount owed *by* the trader is released, in whole or in part, after cessation, the amount released is a post-cessation receipt; this applies only if a trading deduction was allowed for the expense giving rise to the debt and does not apply if the release of the debt is part of a statutory insolvency arrangement (as defined in **71.5 TRADING EXPENSES AND DEDUCTIONS**).

Transfers of rights

If a company permanently ceases to carry on a trade and the right to receive a post-cessation receipt is transferred for value to another person (other than one who succeeds to the trade), the transferor is treated as receiving at that point a post-cessation receipt equal to the consideration for the transfer or, if the transfer is not at arm's length, the value of the rights transferred. The post-cessation receipts themselves are not then charged when received by the transferee. This paragraph is subject to the provision that a sum received for the transfer of trading stock on a cessation is not a post-cessation receipt if the stock has been brought into account in the accounts to cessation.

If, however, the right to receive any sums arising from the transferor's trade are transferred to a company which does succeed to the trade, then, to the extent (if any) that they were not brought into account in computing the transferor's profits for any pre-cessation period, those sums are treated as trading receipts of the transferee as and when received. They are not post-cessation receipts.

Allowable deductions

A deduction from post-cessation receipts is allowed for any loss, expense or debit or capital allowance that would have been deductible if the trade had not ceased, has not been relieved in any other way and which does not arise directly or indirectly from the cessation itself. A deduction may not be given more than once. In the case of a loss, relief is given against the first available post-cessation receipts, i.e. receipts for an earlier accounting period in priority to those for a later one, but not so as give relief for a loss against receipts charged for an accounting period before that in which the loss is made.

Election to carry back

For accounting periods ending on or after 1 April 2009 (and see **70.2** above), a company may elect to carry back a post-cessation receipt received in an accounting period beginning not later than six years after cessation of trade. See Change 42 listed in Annex 1 to the Explanatory Notes to *CTA 2009*. The election allows for the receipt to be taxed as if it had arisen on the date of cessation. The election must be made within two years after the end of the accounting period in which the amount is received. Where loss relief has been given for the year of cessation by carry-back from a later period, this relief is not disturbed by an election. The '*additional tax*' (i.e. the recalculated liability to corporation tax for the accounting period in which cessation occurred less what it would have been without the election) is payable for the accounting period in which the receipt is received; if previous elections under these provisions have been made, these are taken into account in arriving at the additional tax.

[*CTA 2009, ss 95, 188–201; ICTA 1988, ss 103, 104–106, 110; ITTOIA 2005, Sch 1 paras 82–90; FA 2005, Sch 4 para 5*].

Simon's Taxes. See **B2.8** *et seq.*

Case law

[70.17] Whether or not a company has commenced/ceased trading and, if so, the date, are questions of fact.

- Preliminary activities in setting up a business do not amount to trading (*Birmingham & District Cattle By-Products Co Ltd v CIR* (1919) 12 TC 92). Carrying on negotiations to enter into contracts which, when formed, constitute operational activity, does not amount to trading (*Mansell v Revenue and Customs Comrs* [2006] STC (SCD) 605).

- For whether the sale of a business can be effective for tax purposes before the vending agreement, see *Todd v Jones Bros Ltd* (1930) 15 TC 396 and contrast *Angel v Hollingworth & Co* (1958) 37 TC 714.
- 'Permanent discontinuance' does not mean a discontinuance which is everlasting (see *Ingram v Callaghan* (1968) 45 TC 151, CA) but a trade may continue notwithstanding a lengthy break in active trading (*Kirk & Randall Ltd v Dunn* (1924) 8 TC 663 but contrast *Goff v Osborne & Co (Sheffield) Ltd* (1953) 34 TC 441).
- The trade was held to have been continuous when the owner of a drifter continued to manage it after its war-time requisition (*Sutherland v CIR* (1918) 12 TC 63, Ct of Sess); when a flour miller and baker gave up a mill (*Bolands Ltd v Davis* (1925) 4 ATC 532); when a barrister took silk (*Seldon v Croom-Johnson* (1932) 16 TC 740); when a building partnership transferred construction activities to a company but retained building land and continued to sell land with houses built thereon by the company (*Watts v Hart* (1984) 58 TC 209).
- A new trade was held to have commenced when the vendor of a business retained the benefit of outstanding hire-purchase agreements (*Parker v Batty* (1941) 23 TC 739) and when the vendor of a business got commission on open contracts completed by the purchaser (*Southern v Cohen's Exors* (1940), 23 TC 566).

It is similarly a question of fact whether a trader expanding by taking over an existing business and operating it as a branch has succeeded to the trade. See e.g. *Bell v National Provincial Bank of England Ltd* (1903) 5 TC 1, CA (bank succeeded to trade of single-branch bank taken over); *Laycock v Freeman Hardy & Willis Ltd CA* (1938) 22 TC 288 (shoe retailer did not succeed to trade of manufacturing subsidiaries taken over); *Briton Ferry Steel Co Ltd v Barry* (1939) 23 TC 414, CA (steel manufacturer succeeded to trade of tinplate manufacturing subsidiaries taken over); and *Maidment v Kibby* (1993) 66 TC 137 (fish and chip shop proprietor did not succeed to trade of existing business taken over). See also *H & G Kinemas Ltd* (1933) 18 TC 116 (cinema company disposed of existing cinemas and opened new one, held to commence new trade).

Whether or not there has been a commencement etc. has arisen in a number of cases where the activities of a company have altered on e.g. a change of shareholdings or a group reconstruction or on its absorption of another trade or part trade. See:

- *Robroyston Brickworks Ltd v CIR* [1976] STC 329, 51 TC 230, Ct of Sess — trade of a brick-manufacturing company treated as continuous despite closure of works and their re-opening five months later, following the acquisition of its shares by another company, at different premises and with different staff;
- *Howden Boiler & Armaments Co Ltd v Stewart* (1924) 9 TC 205 — shell-making considered an extension of the existing business as boilermakers;
- *Gordon & Blair Ltd v CIR* (1962) 40 TC 358, Ct of Sess — brewing company treated as ceasing the trade of brewing and beginning a new trade of beer selling when it ceased brewing but continued to sell beer supplied to its specification by another company;

- *Cannon Industries Ltd v Edwards* (1965) 42 TC 625 — assembly of electric food mixers for retail sale treated as extension of existing trade of manufacture of gas cookers.

Calculation of trade profits

Generally accepted accounting practice

[70.18] There is a requirement (since 2002) for trading profits to be computed in accordance with 'generally accepted accounting practice' (GAAP) (see also **70.19** below). [*CTA 2009, s 46*]. GAAP is defined (by *FA 2004, s 50*) by reference to the practice adopted in UK company accounts that are drawn up to give a true and fair view. The requirement is subject to any adjustment required or authorised by law; see, for example, the prohibition at **71.8 TRADING EXPENSES AND DEDUCTIONS** on deducting capital expenditure. With effect for periods of account beginning on or after 1 January 2005, 'generally accepted accounting practice' also incorporates international accounting standards in cases where accounts are prepared in accordance with such standards; in all other cases, the expression is restricted to UK GAAP. [*CTA 2009, s 46; ICTA 1988, s 836A; FA 1988, s 42; FA 2004, s 50; FA 2005, s 80, Sch 4 paras 25, 49, 50*].

Where one company within a group of companies (as defined in *TCGA 1992, s 170(3)–(6)* — broadly, a parent and its 75% subsidiaries) prepares accounts in accordance with international accounting standards and another company in the same group prepares accounts in accordance with UK generally accepted accounting practice and, as a result, a tax advantage is gained in relation to a transaction or a series of transactions, the profits will be computed for tax purposes as though both companies prepared accounts in accordance with UK generally accepted accounting practice. '*Tax advantage*' is as defined in *CTA 2010, s 1139; ICTA 1988, s 709* (see **5.2 ANTI-AVOIDANCE**) and '*series of transactions*' is as defined by *TIOPA 2010, s 147*; *ICTA 1988, Sch 28AA* — see **72.2 TRANSFER PRICING.** [*CTA 2010, s 996; FA 2004, s 51; FA 2005, Sch 4 para 50*].

For HMRC's view on the relationship between accounting profits and taxable profits, see HMRC Business Income Manual BIM31000–31120 and for generally accepted accounting practice and accounting standards, see BIM31020–31070. Although superseded by the BIM manual see HMRC Tax Bulletins: December 1997 pp 485, 486 issue 32, February 1999 pp 623–625 issue 39, April 1999 pp 636–641 issue 40, December 1999 pp 707–709 issue 44, June 2001 pp 859, 860 issue 53.

See **70.19** below for the application of accounting principles generally, and **70.20** below for the tax treatment where there is, from one period of account of a trade etc. to the next, a 'change of basis' in computing trading profits. [*CTA 2009, ss 180–187, Sch 2 para 34; FA 2002, s 64, Sch 22; FA 2005, s 81*].

Application of accountancy principles

[70.19] Although *CTA 2009, s 49* requires profits to be computed in accordance with GAAP (see **70.18**), accountancy principles cannot, override established income tax principles (*Heather v P-E Consulting Group Ltd*

(1972) 48 TC 293, CA; *Willingale v International Commercial Bank Ltd* (1977) 52 TC 242, HL; but see *Threlfall v Jones* (1993) 66 TC 77, CA; *Johnston v Britannia Airways Ltd* (1994) 67 TC 99). See also *RTZ Oil & Gas Ltd v Elliss* (1987) 61 TC 132. Other examples include:

- *Meat Traders Ltd v Cushing* [1997] STC (SCD) 245 — a 'provision for a future operating loss', whose inclusion could not be said to have 'violated existing accounting principles', was disallowed).
- *Robertson v CIR* [1997] STC (SCD) 282 — regards timing of inclusion of insurance agents' advance commission.
- *Herbert Smith v Honour* (1999) 72 TC 130 — timing of deductions in respect of future rents under leases of premises ceasing to be used for business purposes, and Revenue Press Release 20 July 1999 for Revenue practice following that decision.

Per Sir Thomas Bingham MR in *Threlfall v Jones*: '... I find it hard to understand how any judge-made rule could override the application of a generally accepted rule of commercial accountancy which:

(a) applied to the situation in question;
(b) was not one of two or more rules applicable to the situation in question; and
(c) was not shown to be inconsistent with the true facts or otherwise inapt to determine the true profits or losses of the business'. FRS 18 now requires companies to choose accounting policies that are most appropriate to their particular circumstances (see Revenue Tax Bulletin April 2002 p 923 to 924, issue 58).

If an entity has correctly followed an International Accounting Standard or USA standard, which does not conflict with UK GAAP, including the requirements of FRS 18 (accounting policies), and this accurately reflects the facts, the accountancy treatment will comply with the requirement of *FA 1998, s 42* (HMRC Business Income Manual BIM31027). This pre-dates the widening of the term 'generally accepted accounting practice' to include international accounting standards where appropriate (see **70.18**).

In a more recent case, the First Tier Tribunal considered that accounts not prepared in accordance with GAAP which therefore understated the value of a trader's work in progress amounted to negligent conduct. In *L Smith v HMRC*, UT May 2011, FTC/47/2010, HMRC formed the opinion that the accounts submitted by a building contractor seriously understated the value of his work in progress, and issued discovery assessments. The taxpayer appealed. The First-Tier Tribunal stated that it was 'not impressed' by the evidence given by the taxpayer's accountant, who had stated that he had 'in general not included work in progress in the accounts'. The tribunal noted that this ignored the requirements of SSAP9 and FRS5, and held that this was negligent conduct, within *TMA 1970, s 29(4)* as then in force. The tribunal reviewed the evidence in detail and allowed the appeals in part. The Upper Tribunal dismissed the taxpayer's appeal against this decision. Arnold J held that the First-Tier Tribunal had been entitled to conclude that accounts did not comply with standard accounting practice; that income should have been brought into account; and that the accountant had been guilty of negligent conduct.

For HMRC's view on the relationship between accounting profits and taxable profits, see HMRC Business Income Manual BIM31000–31120 and BIM42215. For generally accepted accounting practice and accounting standards, see BIM31020–31070. For the timing of deductions where an expense is taken to the balance sheet rather than charged immediately against profits, i.e. *deferred revenue expenditure*, see HMRC Business Income Manual BIM42215, 42220. For *provisions*, see HMRC Business Income Manual BIM46500 *et seq.* and HMRC Press Release 20 July 1999, HMRC Business Income Manual BIM31000 onwards.

With regard to loan relationships and derivatives, *F(No2)A 2010* introduced anti-avoidance provisions aimed at schemes under which the profits arising to a company from a financial asset have been claimed to fall out of account for tax purposes as a result of the 'derecognition' in the accounts of a loan or derivative, effective for debits/ credits arising on or after 22 June 2010. See further **5.54** **ANTI-AVOIDANCE** – loan relationship 'derecognition' provisions.

Provisions have been introduced in *FA 2011* with regard to changes in leasing accounting standards which applies to any period in respect of which a change to leasing standard has effect on or after 1 January 2011. The changes ensure that a business which accounts for lease transactions using the new form of leasing accounting standard (currently proposed to be introduced during 2011) will be treated for tax purposes as if the changes to the accounting standard had not taken place. A change which is a change to UK GAAP will not come within these provisions, where the change permits a business to account for a lease in a manner equivalent to that provided for by IFRS for small and medium-sized entities. See further **71.46** **TRADING EXPENSES AND DEDUCTIONS** – finance leasing *FA 2011* provisions.

Adjustments on change of basis

[70.20] These provisions apply to changes of basis used by companies in preparing their accounts. They take effect for a change of basis only if the first day of the first period of account applying the new basis falls within an accounting period ending after 31 March 2009. Similar provisions applied before that date.

The tax adjustment described below is required where there is, from one period of account of a trade etc to the next, a 'relevant change of accounting approach' in computing trading profits or a change in the tax adjustments applied, and the bases adopted before and after the change accorded with the law or accepted practice applicable in relation to the respective periods of account. A '*relevant change of accounting approach*' for this purpose is:

(a) a change of accounting principle or practice which, in accordance with 'generally accepted accounting practice', gives rise to a prior period adjustment;
(b) with effect for periods of account beginning on or after 1 January 2005, a change from using UK generally accepted accounting practice to producing accounts based on international accounting standards.

A 'change in the tax adjustments applied' is one which:

(1) does not include a change made in order to comply with amending legislation not applicable to the previous period of account; but

(2) includes a change resulting from a change of view as to what is required or authorised by law or as to whether any adjustment is so required or authorised.

Subject to the special cases referred to below, the adjustment required is calculated as follows.

(i) Taxable receipts and allowable expenses of the trade etc. for periods of account before the change are determined on the old and new bases, and the net understatement of profits (or overstatement of losses) on the old basis compared with that on the new basis (a negative figure indicating a net overstatement of profits (or understatement of losses)).

(ii) That figure is then adjusted for any difference between the closing stock or work in progress for the last period of account before the change and the opening stock or work in progress for the first period of account after the change, also taking account of any change in the basis of calculating those amounts.

(iii) Finally an adjustment is made for depreciation to the extent that it was not the subject of an adjustment for corporation tax purposes in the last period of account before the change but would be the subject of such an adjustment on the new basis.

No further deduction is allowed for amounts taken into account in calculating the adjustment. A positive adjustment is treated as a receipt of the trade on the first day of the first period to use the new basis. A negative adjustment is treated as an expense of the trade arising on the first day of the first period of account for which the new basis is used.

Special rules modify the above in a number of cases.

(A) **Expenses spread over more than one period of account after the change** on the new basis which were brought into account before the change on the old basis are excluded from the calculation at (i) above, but may not be deducted for any period of account after the change.

(B) **Adjustment not required until asset realised or written off.** Where the change of basis results from a tax adjustment affecting the calculation of amounts relating to trading stock or depreciation, the adjustment required by is brought into account only when the asset concerned is realised or written off.

(C) **Change from realisation basis to mark to market,** i.e. from recognition of a profit or loss on an asset only when it is realised to bringing assets into account in each period of account at fair value. Any adjustment required by the above for an understatement of profit (or overstatement of loss) or under or overstatement of a expense in relation to an asset that is trading stock within *CTA 2009, s 163*, formerly *ICTA 1988, s 100* is not given effect until the period of account in which the value of the asset is realised. An election may, however, be made for the adjustment receipt to be spread equally over six periods of account beginning with the first period after the change. The election must be within twelve months after the end of the first accounting period to which the new basis applies. If the trade etc. is permanently discontinued before the whole of the adjustment charge has been brought into charge, the uncharged balance is charged as if it arose immediately before the discontinuance. Special provision is made for the application of this rule in the case of insurance business transfers.

Similar provisions applied to changes of accounting basis taking effect in periods of account ending on or after 1 August 2001 further to *FA 2002*. Adjustments relating to UITF 40 are dealt with in the following section, provisions for which were introduced in *FA 2006, Pt 2, paras 9–15*.

[*CTA 2009, ss 180–187, Sch 2 para 34; FA 2002, s 64, Sch 22; ITTOIA 2005, Sch 1 paras 576, 578; FA 2005, s 81; F(No 2)A 2005, Sch 6 para 1*].

Spreading of UITF 40 adjustment

A positive adjustment (as calculated under *CTA 2009, ss 180–187*) can be spread over three to six years (as set out below) where it arises from a change in accounting approach, in the first period of account ending on or after 22 June 2005, in calculating profits in compliance with UK GAAP (or international accounting standards if applicable), in particular SSAP 9 and Application Note G to FRS 5 as interpreted by Urgent Issue Task Force Abstract 40 ('UITF 40') issued by the Accounting Standards Board on 10 March 2005).

SSAP (Statement of Standard Accounting Practice) 9 relates to the accounting rules for 'Stocks and Long-Term Work in Progress' and Application Note G of FRS (Financial Reporting Standard) 5 (on 'Reporting the Substance of Transactions) relates to 'Revenue Recognition'. UITF 40 concerns the interaction between the Application Note and SSAP 9 and clarifies the principles governing the recognition of revenue in the accounts for work in progress in relation to contracts for services. Broadly, it indicates that revenue arising from services provided on an on-going basis should be accounted for as it arises. Where contracts for a single service are accounted for as a long-term contract (lasting more than one year or more than one accounting period) and the obligations under the contract are performed gradually over a period of time, revenue is to be recognised as the activity progresses based on the appropriate proportion of the fair value of the contract. If the consideration for services is contingent upon some future event, revenue is not to be recognised until that even occurs. This is in contrast to previous practice where the revenue was recognised when billed and it is thought this will give rise to large adjustments in some cases.

Where a positive adjustment arises as a result of the above change in accounting policy, the amount chargeable to tax in the first three accounting periods beginning with that in which the whole of the adjustment would otherwise arise, is to be equal to the lower of one-third of the original adjustment (as calculated above) and one-sixth of the 'business profits' for that period. If the whole of the original adjustment is not charged to tax in those three years, an amount is to be charged to tax in the fourth and fifth accounting periods equal to the lower of the amount remaining untaxed, one-third of the original adjustment and one-sixth of the 'business profits' for that period. Any amount still remaining untaxed is treated as arising, and is charged to tax in, the sixth accounting period. '*Business profits*' for this purpose are profits as calculated for corporation tax purposes excluding any adjustment for a change in accounting policy as above and any capital allowances or balancing charges.

Special rules apply in the case where an accounting period is less than one year in length as a result of a change in accounting date, the company entering into administration (under *CTA 2009, s 10)* or an insurance business transfer scheme (under *CTA 2009, s 10*). In this case, the one-third of the original adjustment is proportionally reduced for the short period. Where any of the accounting periods falling within six years following the change in accounting policy is a short period, the rules relating the fourth and fifth accounting periods apply to all accounting periods after the third period and before that in which the sixth anniversary of the change falls, and the rule above relating to the sixth accounting period applies to the accounting period in which that anniversary falls. If any amount remains untaxed and an accounting period comes to an end because the company ceases to be within the charge to corporation tax or winding-up proceedings (under *CTA 2009, s 10*) are commenced, the rule for the sixth accounting period applies in relation to that final period. If the company permanently ceases to carry on the business for any other reason, the charge is spread as above ignoring the alternative limit for one-sixth of the business profits for the period.

A company can elect for an amount up to the whole of the amount of the adjustment not previously charged to be treated as arising and charged in an accounting period rather than spreading it as above. The election must be made within one year of the filing date of the company's tax return for the accounting period for which the election is made. If such an election is made, any spreading calculations in subsequent periods are to be made as though the original adjustment is reduced by the amount in respect of which the election is made.

Partnerships

In the case of trades carried on by a company in partnership, the adjustment (as above) is calculated as if the partnership were a company resident in the UK. Each partner's share is determined according to the profit-sharing arrangements for the twelve months immediately before the first day of the first period of account for which the new basis was adopted. Changes in the members of a partnership are disregarded so long as a company carrying on the trade in partnership immediately beforehand continues to carry it on in partnership immediately afterwards (see **58.3 PARTNERSHIPS**). An election for spreading of an adjustment under (C) above, or under the rules for spreading the UITF 40 adjustment, must be made jointly by all persons who were partners in the afore-mentioned twelve-month period.

If the partnership ceases to carry on a business on the date of the change in policy the UITF 40 adjustment is to be divided among the members according to the profit-sharing arrangements in the twelve-month period immediately preceding the cessation. If the cessation occurs on or after the date of the change in policy but before the first anniversary of that date, the adjustment is to be divided according to the profit-sharing arrangements for the period between that date and the date of cessation. If the cessation occurs after the first anniversary of the date of the change in policy, the adjustment is to be divided according to the profit-sharing arrangements for the period between the immediately preceding anniversary of that date and the date of cessation. If a UITF 40 election is made after cessation, it must be made by each former partner separately.

The UITF spreading adjustments do not affect the loan relationship or derivative contracts rules applying to partnerships.

See HMRC Business Income Manual BIM74201–74270.

[*CTA 2009, ss 10, 1267–1269; ICTA 1988, s 114(1); FA 2006, Sch 15 paras 9–15; CTA 2009, Sch 1 para 696*].

See HMRC Business Income Manual BIM34000–34135, 74200–74275.

Tax treatment of income and specific types of trade

[70.21] The following paragraphs refer to matters of relevance to companies in computing trading profits. See **61 PROFIT COMPUTATIONS** for the general principles in computing profits chargeable to corporation tax. See also **10 CAPITAL ALLOWANCES — INTRODUCTION; 34 FOREIGN EXCHANGE GAINS AND LOSSES; 30 DERIVATIVE CONTRACTS LEGISLATION; 48 INTANGIBLE ASSETS; 54 LOAN RELATIONSHIPS; 62 PROPERTY INCOME; 64 RESEARCH AND DEVELOPMENT** and **71 TRADING EXPENSES AND DEDUCTIONS.**

See HMRC Business Income Manual BIM50000 et seq. for HMRC guidance on measuring the profits of a wide range of particular trades.

See **70.18** re the requirement to adhere to generally accepted accounting practice (GAAP), **70.19** above re the application of accountancy principles generally and **70.20** above re adjustments required on a change of basis.

The provisions for computing trading profits are in *CTA 2009, Pt 3* (previously in *ICTA 1988, ss 74–99*). It has been clarified that, wherever they appear in corporation tax legislation in the context of computing trading profits, the words 'receipts' and 'expenses' refer generally to items brought into account as credits or debits in computing those profits, and contain no implication that an amount has actually been received or paid. [*CTA 2009, s 48; FA 1998, s 46(1)*].

Bad debts — Recovery of impairment losses

[70.22] (The tax treatment of impairment provisions is dealt with at **71.5 TRADING EXPENSES AND DEDUCTIONS.**)

If a debt owed to a company by a trader is released (otherwise than as part of a statutory insolvency arrangement — see **71 TRADING EXPENSES AND DEDUCTIONS**), and the expense giving rise to the debt has been allowed as a deduction for corporation tax purposes, the amount released is treated as a trading receipt arising in the accounting period in which the release is effected. [*CTA 2009, s 94; ICTA 1988, s 94; ITTOIA 2005, Sch 1 para 73; FA 2005, Sch 4 para 4*]. For accounting periods starting before 1 January 2002, the Revenue interpreted the decision in *British Mexican Petroleum Co Ltd v Jackson* 16 TC 570, HL, as meaning that trade debts *not* released but nevertheless written back were not taxable; they now take the view that the 'true and fair view' requirement (see **70.19** above) requires such write-backs to be taxed, subject only to the exception provided for releases under statutory insolvency arrangements (Revenue Tax Bulletin December 2001 pp 901, 902, issue 56 and see now HMRC Business Income Manual BIM40265). See generally Business Income Manual BIM40201 *et seq*.

An anomaly arose where a trade debt was released by a creditor that was connected with the debtor company because the release of debts did not fall within the loan relationship rules for companies. This meant that the creditor was denied tax relief for the debt but the debtor was still charged to tax under *CTA 2009, s 94* unless the release was part of a statutory insolvency agreement. For times on or after 22 April 2009 where a company is a debtor in respect of a debt for the purposes of its trade, UK or overseas property business, the loss arising from the release of that debt falls to be dealt with under the loan relationships legislation. As a result, where the debtor and the creditor are connected the release is treated as tax free in the hands of the debtor [*CTA 2009, ss 479(2)(d), (3A), 481(3)(f), (4A) as inserted by FA 2009, s 42 with effect from 22 April 2009*].

For debt recoveries and releases after the cessation of a trade, see **70.16** above. Bad debt allowances are not applicable where the business is assessed on a cash basis (see Tolley's Income tax under Cash Basis). For VAT on bad debts, see **73.2 VALUE ADDED TAX.**

Where an asset accepted in satisfaction of a trading debt is of market value (as at the date of acceptance) less than the outstanding debt, the deficit may be allowed as a deduction, provided the trader agrees that, on a disposal of the asset, any excess of disposal proceeds over that value (up to the amount by which the debt exceeds that value) will be brought in as a trading receipt (such receipt being excluded from any chargeable gain computation on the disposal) (HMRC Business Income Manual BIM42735).

Breweries, distilleries, licensed premises

Tied premises

[70.23] Receipts in respect of 'tied premises' which would otherwise be brought into account in calculating profits of a property business (see **62.2 PROPERTY INCOME**) are instead brought into account as trading receipts. For treatment of expenses see **71 TRADING EXPENSES AND DEDUCTIONS**. Any necessary apportionment (e.g. where only part of the premises qualifies) is on a just and reasonable basis. '*Tied premises*' are premises through which goods supplied by a trader are sold or used by another person, where the trader has an estate or interest in the premises which he treats as property employed for trade purposes. [*CTA 2009, s 42; ICTA 1988, s 98; ITTOIA 2005, Sch 1 para 77*]. (*Note.* These rules are of general application, although of most common application in the licensed trade.)

Capital receipts

[70.24] In computing trading profits, capital receipts are not brought into account; this is made explicit for accounting periods ending on or after 1 April 2009 (and see **70.2** above) but was already a long-established principle. [*CTA 2009, s 93*].

As to the distinction between capital and income receipts, 'no part of our law of taxation presents such almost insoluble conundrums as the decision whether a receipt or outgoing is capital or income for tax purposes' (Lord Upjohn in *Regent Oil Co Ltd v Strick (Inspector of Taxes)* [1966] AC 295, [1965] 3 All ER 174, HL, qv for a comprehensive review of the law). A widely used test is the 'enduring benefit' one given by Viscount Cave in *British Insulated and Helsby Cables Ltd v Atherton (Inspector of Taxes)* [1926] AC 205, 10 TC 155, HL. For other cases involving expenses see **71 TRADING EXPENSES AND DEDUCTIONS.**

A gain or loss on the sale of a capital asset not included in trading profits is dealt with according to the provisions relating to capital gains tax. A sale of a fixed asset on which capital allowances have been claimed may result in a balancing charge or allowance, see **10 CAPITAL ALLOWANCES — INTRODUCTION.**

The revenue or capital nature of a payment is fixed at the time of its receipt (*Tapemaze Ltd v Melluish* (2000) 73 TC 167, following *Morley (Inspector of Taxes) v Tattersall* [1938] 3 All ER 296, 22 TC 51, CA).

For a brief note on HMRC's approach to challenging schemes or arrangements designed to turn income into capital (or capital expenditure into a revenue deduction), see Revenue Tax Bulletin June 1997 p 438, issue 29.

For HMRC's own guidance on capital *v* income, see HMRC Business Income Manual BIM35000–35910.

For case law on the difference between capital and revenue see **Simon's Taxes B2.202–B2.204** and **B2.306.**

Car or (before 1 April 2009) motor cycle hire rebate

[70.25] Where the rental payments for hiring a car (or motor cycle) have been restricted see **71.9 TRADING EXPENSES AND DEDUCTIONS**, any subsequent rental rebate (or debt release other than as part of a statutory insolvency arrangement — see **71.5 TRADING EXPENSES AND DEDUCTIONS**) is reduced for tax purposes in the same proportion as the hire charge restriction. For accounting periods ending on or after 1 April 2009 (and see **70.2** above), this treatment extends to amounts brought in as post-cessation receipts (see **70.16** above) after the trade has ceased.

Commission, cashbacks and discounts

[70.26] HMRC Statement of Practice SP 4/97 sets out HMRC's views on the tax treatment of commissions, cashbacks and discounts. The types of payment with which the Statement is concerned are as follows.

Commissions

Sums paid by the providers of goods, investments or services to agents or intermediaries as reward for the introduction of business, or in some cases paid directly by the provider to the customer. Sums paid to an agent or intermediary may be passed on to the customer or to some other person.

Cashbacks

Lump sums received by a customer as an inducement for entering into a transaction for the purchase of goods, investments or services and received as a direct consequence of having entered into that transaction. The payer may be either the provider or another party with an interest in ensuring that the transaction takes place.

Discounts, i.e. where the purchaser's obligation to pay for goods, investments or services is less than the full purchase price, other than as a result of commissions or cashbacks.

The Statement also deals with commissions or cashbacks which are netted off, or invested or otherwise applied for the benefit of the purchaser, or where extra value is added to the goods, investments or services supplied (e.g. the allocation of bonus units in an investment) (although in the case of the addition of value to investments this may represent a return on the investment, which is outside the scope of the Statement).

The Statement provides detailed guidance on the circumstances in which liability may arise either as trading income or as miscellaneous income on receipts of commission etc. It also considers deductibility of commission etc. passed on to customers.

Generally, ordinary retail arm's length customers will not be liable to income tax or capital gains tax. The Statement outlines the circumstances in which receipts are treated as tax-free, or payments qualify for tax relief, and contains an element of concession for those who, in the ordinary course of their business, earn commission relating to their own transactions. It contains a warning that the principles outlined may not be followed where tax avoidance schemes are involved, or where the arrangements for the commission etc. include an increase in the purchase price of the goods etc. involved. The tax treatment of the payer and the recipient are in all cases considered independently of one another.

For an article explaining the legal basis of this approach, see HMRC Business Income Manual BIM40655–40710.

Whilst SP 4/97 is couched in terms of *Sch D Cases I, II* and *VI*, which schedules no longer applies for corporation tax purposes post 1 April 2009, the principles relating to the nature of the income are still relevant.

See also BIM80125 with regard to the provisions in respect of miscellaneous income under *CTA 2009, Ch 8, Pt 10.*

Compensation, damages etc. — receipts

[70.27] Compensation and damages receipts are treated as follows:

(a) **Capital sums** (i.e. sums not taken into account in computing income) received as compensation for damage, injury, destruction or depreciation of assets are subject to corporation tax on capital gains [*TCGA 1992, s 22(1)*] (but this does not apply to compensation or damages to an individual for wrong or injury to his person or in his profession or vocation). [*TCGA 1992, s 51(2)*]. See Tolley's Capital Gains Tax.

(b) **Cancellation or variation of trading contracts and arrangements.** An important case is *Van den Berghs Ltd v Clark* (1935) 19 TC 390, HL, in which a receipt on the termination of a profit-sharing arrangement was held to be capital. The arrangement related to the whole structure of the recipient's trade, forming the fixed framework within which its circulating capital operated.

Compensation etc. receipts were also held to be capital in:

- *Sabine v Lookers Ltd* (1958) 38 TC 120, CA — varying car distributor's agreement;
- *British-Borneo Petroleum v Cropper* (1968) 45 TC 201 — cancelling a royalty agreement;
- *Barr Crombie & Co Ltd v CIR* (1945) 26 TC 406, Ct of Sess — terminating agreement as ship-managers.

Other relevant cases:

- *Consultant v Inspector of Taxes* [1999] STC (SCD) 63 — termination of profit participation agreement. Receipts held not to be capital.
- *Chibbett v Robinson & Sons* (1924) 9 TC 48 — a payment by the liquidator of a shipping company to its managers as authorised by the shareholders held not assessable.

Compensation etc. receipts on the cancellation of contracts receipts from which, if completed, would have been trading receipts are normally themselves trading receipts, to be credited in the computations for the period in which cancelled. See:

- *Short Bros Ltd v CIR* and *Sunderland Shipbuilding Co Ltd v CIR* (1927) 12 TC 955, CA — cancellation of order for ships;
- *CIR v Northfleet Coal Co* (1927) 12 TC 1102; *Jesse Robinson & Sons v CIR* (1929) 12 TC 1241 — cancellation of contracts for sale of goods etc.;
- *Greyhound Racing Assn v Cooper* (1936) 20 TC 373 — cancellation of agreement to hire greyhound track;
- *Shove v Dura Mfg Co Ltd* (1941) 23 TC 779 — cancellation of commission agreement.

Similarly compensation to a merchanting company on cancellation of a contract to supply goods to it was held a trading receipt (*Bush, Beach & Gent Ltd v Road* (1939) 22 TC 519). See also *United Steel v*

Cullington (No 1) (1939) 23 TC 71, CA; *Shadbolt v Salmon Estates* (1943) 25 TC 52; *Sommerfelds Ltd v Freeman* (1966) 44 TC 43; *Creed v H & M Levinson Ltd* (1981) 54 TC 477.

Compensation received on the termination of agencies is a trading receipt unless the agency, by reason of its relative size etc., is part of the 'fixed framework' (see *Van den Berghs* above) of the agent's business. See *Kelsall Parsons* (1938) 21 TC 608, Ct of Sess; *CIR v Fleming & Co* (1951) 33 TC 57, Ct of Sess; *CIR v David MacDonald & Co* (1955) 36 TC 388, Ct of Sess; *Wiseburgh v Domville* (1956) 36 TC 527, CA; *Fleming v Bellow Machine Co* (1965) 42 TC 308; *Elson v James G Johnston Ltd* (1965) 42 TC 545 (in all of which the compensation etc. was held to be a trading receipt). See also *Anglo-French Exploration Co Ltd v Clayson* (1956) 36 TC 545, CA.

For payments received on termination of building society agencies, see HMRC Capital Gains Tax Manual CG13050 *et seq*.

More recently, in *Countrywide Estate Agents FS Ltd v HMRC* (TC00557) [2010] UKFTT 263 (TC), a company carried on business as a financial intermediary and received 25,000,000 from a life insurance company in return for entering into an exclusivity agreement. In its corporation tax return, this was treated as a capital receipt. HMRC issued an amendment charging corporation tax on the basis that it was a trading receipt. On appeal, the First-Tier Tribunal applied the principles laid down in *British Dyestuffs Corporation (Blackley) Ltd v CIR*, CA 1924, 12 TC 586, and on the evidence that the taxpayer company had not disposed of 'anything in the nature of a capital asset', dismissed the appeal.

(c) **Compensation etc. relating to capital assets.** Compensation to a company making fireclay goods for refraining from working a fireclay bed under a railway line was held to be capital (*Glenboig Union Fireclay Co Ltd v CIR* (1922) 12 TC 427, HL, and cf *Thomas McGhie & Sons v BTC* (1962) 41 ATC 144 and *Bradbury v United Glass Bottle* (1959) 38 TC 369, CA), but compensation to a colliery from the Government for requisition of part of its mining area was held to be a trading receipt (*Waterloo Main Colliery v CIR (No 1)* (1947) 29 TC 235). Compensation to a shipping company for delay in the overhaul of a ship was held to be a trading receipt (*Burmah Steam Ship Co v CIR* (1930) 16 TC 67, Ct of Sess) as was compensation to a jetty owner for loss of its use after damage by a ship (*London & Thames Haven v Attwooll* (1966) 43 TC 491, CA) and compensation for the detention of a ship (*Ensign Shipping Co v CIR* (1928) 12 TC 1169, CA, but contrast *CIR v Francis West* (1950) 31 TC 402, Ct of Sess). Compensation to a company for temporary loss of use of part of a landfill site was held to be a trading receipt (*Able (UK) Ltd v Revenue and Customs Comrs* [2008] STC 136, CA).

For insurance recoveries see **70.53** below.

(d) **Compensation on compulsory acquisition etc.** Where compensation is paid for the acquisition of business property by an authority possessing powers of compulsory acquisition, any amounts included as compensation for temporary loss of profits or losses on trading stock or to reimburse revenue expenditure, such as removal expenses and interest, are treated as trading receipts. (See HMRC Statement of Practice, SP 8/79 and HMRC Business Income Bulletin BIM40115. This Statement of Practice was originally issued as consequence of *Stoke-on-Trent City Council v Wood Mitchell & Co Ltd* [1979] STC 197, CA.)

(e) **Other compensation etc. receipts.** Voluntary payments to an insurance broker on the loss of an important client company (made by its parent company) were held, approving *Chibbett v Robinson* and *Carnaby Harrower* (see (b) above), not to be assessable (*Simpson v John Reynolds & Co* (1975) 49 TC 693, CA) and similarly for voluntary payments from a brewer to a firm of caterers for the surrender of the leases of tied premises (*Murray v Goodhews* (1977) 52 TC 86, CA) but *ex gratia* payments to an estate agent who had not been given an agency he expected were held, on the facts, to be additional remuneration for work already done and assessable. (*McGowan v Brown & Cousins (Stuart Edwards)* (1977) 52 TC 8). A payment to a diamond broker under informal and non-binding arbitration as damages for the loss of a prospective client was held assessable (*Rolfe v Nagel* (1981) 55 TC 585, CA). Compensation for 'loss of profits' following the destruction of the premises of a business not recommenced was held to be of a revenue nature in *Lang v Rice* (1983) 57 TC 80. For compensation receipts relating to the terms on which business premises are tenanted, see **70.62** below.

For the treatment of compensation received by businesses as customers of e.g. utility companies for interruptions and other service deficiencies, see HMRC Business Income Manual BIM40101.

Damages awarded to a theatrical company for breach of a licence it had, were held to be assessable (*Vaughan v Parnell & Zeitlin* (1940) 23 TC 505) as was compensation received by a development company under legislation for restricting development (*Johnson v W S Try Ltd* (1946) 27 TC 167, CA). A retrospective award for a war-time requisition of trading stock was held to be a trading receipt of the year of requisition (*CIR v Newcastle Breweries Ltd* (1927) 12 TC 927, HL).

Embezzlement etc.

[70.28] Where defalcations of employees of a company were made good by the auditor, who admitted negligence, a refund was held to be a trading receipt for the year in which it was made (*Gray v Penrhyn* (1937) 21 TC 252). This should be contrasted with *North v Spencer's Exors* (1956) 36 TC 668, 35 ATC 264, where a lump sum award paid to a doctor was held to be income of his practice in the years to which the award related.

Farming and market gardening

[70.29] Farming or market gardening in the UK is treated for corporation tax purposes as trading. All the UK farming carried on by a particular company (other than as part of a different trade) is treated as a single trade. Farming carried on by a partnership in which a company is partner is, however, separate from any farming carried on by the partner company itself. This does not apply to the woodlands or to land being prepared for forestry use. *CTA 2010, s 1125* (and previously *CTA 2009, s 1317*) defines farming as 'the occupation of land wholly or mainly for the purposes of husbandry'. The earlier definition referred only to the occupation of farm land. Market gardening is defined as 'the occupation of land as a garden or nursery for the purpose of growing produce for sale'.

[*CTA 2009, ss 36, 1270(1); ICTA 1988, ss 53(1)(2), 832(1); ITTOIA 2005, Sch 1 para 32*]. See *Bispham v Eardiston Farming Co* (1962) 40 TC 322 and *Sargent v Eayrs* (1972) 48 TC 573. The matters listed below are of particular application to farming or (where relevant) market gardening.

(a) **Compensation for compulsory slaughter**. Where compensation is received for compulsory slaughter of animals to which the herd basis (see **70.43–70.52** below) does not and could not apply, any excess of the amount received over the book value or cost of those animals may, by concession, be excluded from the year of receipt and treated, by equal instalments, as profits of the next three years. (HMRC Extra Statutory Concession, B11). (In practice, the profit on an animal born in the year of slaughter is deemed to be 25% of the compensation received.) For a worked example of this spreading relief, see HMRC Business Income Manual BIM55185; see also Revenue Tax Bulletin October 2001 p 890 issue 55 as regards certain aspects of the concession, in particular with regard to its application during the 2001 foot and mouth outbreak.
Compensation paid under the BSE Suspects Scheme and the BSE Selective Cull (where the animal was born after 14 October 1990) is for compulsory slaughter, and for these purposes includes Selective Cull 'top-up' payments. Payments under the Calf Processing Scheme, the Over Thirty Month Scheme and the BSE Selective Cull where the animal was born before 15 October 1990 are *not* for compulsory slaughter. (HMRC Tax Bulletin February 1997 pp 396, 397 issue 27).

(b) **Foot and mouth outbreak**. For the special measures for the 2001 outbreak, see Revenue Tax Bulletin Special Edition May 2001 and Revenue Tax Bulletin October 2001 pp 890, 891. For the 2007 outbreak, see HMRC news release 8 August 2007.

(c) **Grants and subsidies**. As regards the time at which a receipt should be brought in for tax purposes the starting point is to identify the precise purpose of the grant or subsidy. A distinction should be drawn between grants to meet particular costs and those subsidising the sale proceeds of a specific crop. The former should reduce the costs in question (and if those costs are included in the closing stock valuation, the net cost should be used), whereas the latter should be recognised as income of the year in which the crop is sold. (Revenue Tax Bulletin February 1993 p 53 issue 6). A grant subsidising trading income generally is a trading receipt of the period when the entitlement to the grant was established, provided that it can be quantified with reasonable accuracy. As regards instalments of grant, the tax treatment should follow accounting practice, which provides that information available before accounts are completed and signed should be taken into account as regards those to which entitlement arose in the period of account. (Revenue Tax Bulletin February 1994 p 108 issue 10).

As regards animal grants and subsidies, these are generally recognised either at the end of the retention period or on receipt. Either of these bases will be accepted for tax purposes provided that it is consistently applied, as will any other basis which reflects generally accepted accounting practice provided that it does not conflict with tax law. A change of basis should be made only where the need for change outweighs the requirement for accounts to be prepared on a consistent basis, and will be dealt with in accordance with HMRC Statement of Practice SP 3/90 (see **71.66 TRADING EXPENSES AND DEDUCTIONS**). (Revenue Tax Bulletin December 1994 p 182 issue 14).

The following relate to specific types of farm support payment.

(i) *Advances under British Sugar Industry (Assistance) Act 1931*, linked with sugar production and prices, were held to be assessable as trading receipts (*Smart v Lincolnshire Sugar Co Ltd* (1937) 20 TC 643, HL).

(ii) *Arable area payments*. Payments under the 1992 scheme for land set aside may be treated as sales subsidies, and hence recognised when the crops are sold. Valuations based on 75% of market value should include the same proportion of the related arable area payments. (Revenue Tax Bulletin February 1994 p 109). See (v) below for specific comment on oilseed support payments.

(iii) *Dairy herd conversion scheme*. Grants for changing from dairying to meat production were held to be assessable as trading receipts (*White v G & M Davis* (1979) 52 TC 597; *CIR v Biggar* (1982) 56 TC 254, Ct of Sess).

(iv) *Flood rehabilitation grants* in excess of rehabilitation costs (admitted to be capital) were held to be capital receipts (*Watson v Samson Bros* (1959) 38 TC 346).

(v) *Oilseed support scheme*. Payments of aid under the 1992 scheme are a subsidy towards the selling price, and as such should be recognised as income at the time of sale. If the final amount is not known when the accounts are prepared, but it is reasonably certain that a further payment will be received, the tax computations should be kept open to admit the final figure. If a reasonable estimate is included in the accounts and the difference when the final amount is known has only a small effect on the overall tax liability, the inspector may agree to recognise the difference in arriving at profits of the following year. (Revenue Tax Bulletin February 1993 p 53 issue 6).

(vi) *Ploughing subsidies* were held to be assessable as trading receipts (*Higgs v Wrightson* (1944) 26 TC 73).

(d) **Milk Quotas**. Under EU regulations each member state was allocated a share of EU milk production, and this share is divided amongst producers. Thus a milk quota is the specific quantity of dairy product which a producer can produce without creating liability to pay a levy for over production. A milk quota is not an interest in land and cannot be transferred separately from the land. It is better seen as a licence which can be sold with freehold land, with certain tenancies, and which can be leased. Normally a milk quota is treated as a chargeable asset, separate and distinct from the land to which it relates. Disposal of milk quota is normally liable to capital gains tax, computed separately from any land which is being sold or being transferred at the same time.

(e) **Share farming.** HMRC consider that both parties to a share farming agreement based on the Country Landowners Association model may be considered to be carrying on a farming trade for tax purposes. In the case of the landowner, he must take an active part in the share farming venture, at least to the extent of concerning himself with details of farming policy and exercising his right to enter onto his land for some material purpose, even if only for the purposes of inspection and policy-making. (Country Landowners Association Press Release 19 December 1991).

(f) **Short rotation coppice.** This is a way of producing renewable fuel for certain power stations. The cultivation of 'short rotation coppice' (i.e. a perennial crop of tree species planted at high density, the stems of which are harvested above ground level at intervals of less than ten years) is treated for tax purposes as farming and not as forestry, so that UK land under such cultivation is farm or agricultural land and not woodlands (which is exempt from tax). [*FA 1995, s 154; ITTOIA 2005, Sch 1 para 481*]. For HMRC's view of the taxation implications of short rotation coppice, see HMRC Business Income Manual BIM55120. For the general exemption for woodlands, see **61.24 PROFIT COMPUTATIONS.**

(g) **Sugar beet outgoers scheme.** Receipts and payments derived from the disposal of contract tonneage entitlement under contracts between farmers and British Sugar are to be dealt with on revenue and not capital account, i.e. as taxable receipts and allowable deductions in computing profits. Payments for entitlement which are amortised in the accounts over the period for which the entitlement may reasonably be expected to be of value to the business are similarly allowed for tax purposes. (See Revenue Interpretation 236; HMRC Tax Bulletin October 2001 pp 891, 892 issue 55).

(h) **Trading profits.** Proceeds from the sale of trees (mostly willows planted by the taxpayer) were held to be farming receipts (*Elmes v Trembath* (1934) 19 TC 72), but no part of the cost of an orchard with nearly ripe fruit purchased by a fruit grower was an allowable deduction in computing his profits, which included receipts from the sale of the fruit (*CIR v Pilcher* (1949) 31 TC 314, CA). Proceeds from sales of turf were held to be trading receipts from farming (*Lowe v J W Ashmore Ltd* (1970) 46 TC 597).

(i) **Woodlands grants.** The Forestry Commission's Woodland Grant Scheme (WGS) provides grants for the establishment and maintenance of woodlands. These grants are not taxable. Where the woodland concerned is being established on agricultural land, WGS participants can also apply to join the Farm Woodland Premium Scheme (FWPS). This is administered by the Department for Environment, Food and

Rural Affairs (Defra) and provides annual payments of up to £300 per hectare for up to 15 years to the farmer to compensate for lost farming income as a result of converting the land to woodland. Because the annual payments are made in lieu of farming income, they must be included in trading profits and are chargeable to income tax. (Sources: Defra and HMRC Business Income Manual BIM55165).

For these and other aspects of farming taxation, see HMRC Business Income Manual BIM55000–55730, 73000–73190 and 75600–75650.

Films

[70.30] A new regime (the 'FA 2006 regime') for film production companies applies in relation to films that commence principal photography on or after 1 January 2007, or expenditure incurred on or after 31 March 2008 (whenever the film is made). Transitional provisions are included in *CTA 2009, Sch 2 paras 130, 131*.

The *FA 2006* regime (rewritten in *CTA 2009*) is as set out at **70.31–70.40** below.

[*CTA 2009, Sch 2 paras 128, 129, Sch 1 paras 679, 681; FA 2006, ss 46, 47, 53; SI 2006 No 3265; SI 2006 No 3399*].

The Treasury have wide powers to make provision, by order (approved by a resolution of the House of Commons), regarding the tax treatment of films which have commenced principal photography before 1 January 2007 but are not completed by 1 January 2007. [*CTA 2009, Sch 1 para 680, Sch 2 para 130; FA 2006, s 52*].

For background information see the consultation document 'The Reform of Film Tax Incentives: Promoting the Sustainable Production of Culturally British Films', published on 29 July 2005, available on the Treasury website (at www.hm-treasury.gov.uk). A summary of the new regime and partial draft guidance is set out on the HMRC website (at www.hmrc.gov.uk/films). For detailed coverage, with examples, of how the old rules were applied in practice, see HMRC Business Income Manual BIM56000–56725.

FA 2006 regime

Film tax relief

[70.31] Under the *FA 2006* regime (see **70.30** above for commencement provisions) corporation tax relief is available for expenditure on a 'film' that qualifies for relief. A '*film*' includes any record, however made, of a sequence of visual images that is capable of being used as a means of showing that sequence as a moving picture. Each part of a series of films is treated as a separate film, unless the films form a series of not more than 26 parts, have a combined playing time of not more than 26 hours and the series is a self-contained work or is a documentary series with a common theme.

A film is completed when it is in such a condition that copies can be taken and distributed for presentation to the general public.

[*CTA 2009, s 1181; SI 2006 No 3399*].

A film qualifies for relief if all the following conditions are met.

(A) The film must be 'intended' for '*theatrical release*' (i.e. release to the paying public at the commercial cinema with the intention of obtaining the significant proportion of earnings from the release). A film is '*intended*' for theatrical release throughout an accounting period if it is intended for release at the end of that period. If it is not intended for release at the end of an accounting period, the condition is treated as not being met throughout that accounting period or in any subsequent accounting period but this does not affect any earlier accounting period where the condition was met.

(B) The film must be a '*British*' film, i.e. certified by the Secretary of State under the *Films Act 1985, Sch 1A*. (See *CTA 2009, s 1197; FA 2006, Sch 5 paras 15–25; SI 2007 No 1050, Reg 10*).

(C) At least 25% of the 'core expenditure' on the film incurred by the 'film production company' (or in the case of a 'qualifying co-production', by the 'co-producers') must be on '*UK expenditure*' (goods or services used or consumed in the UK). Any apportionment between UK and non-UK expenditure is to be made on a fair and reasonable basis. '*Core expenditure*' is the 'production expenditure' on pre-production, principal photography and post production. '*Production expenditure*' is expenditure on the film-making activities in connection with the film which are the activities involved in the development, pre-production, principal photography and post production of the film. The term 'principal photography' can include the generation of computer images in the film.

There can be only one 'film production company' in relation to the film. A 'film production company' is widely defined for this purpose to ensure the company has an active involvement in the film production and that its participation is not restricted to the provision or arrangement of finance. A '*film production company*' in relation to a film is the company that (otherwise than in partnership):

- is responsible for the pre-production, principal photography and the post-production of the film and is actively engaged in planning and decision-making during these stages;
- is responsible for delivery of the completed film;
- directly negotiates, contracts and pays for rights, goods and services in relation to the film.

A company may elect out of the regime, i.e. not to be treated as a film production company. The election must be made in the company's corporation tax return (either in the original return or by amendment to the original return). Similarly, the election may be withdrawn only by amending its return for the period. The election applies to films commencing principal photography in the accounting period in respect of which the return containing the election was made or any subsequent accounting periods.

In the case of a '*qualifying co-production*' (a film treated as a national film in the UK by virtue of an agreement between the UK government and any other government, international organisation or authority) the film production company is a company that (otherwise than in partnership) is a co-producer and makes an effective creative, technical and artistic contribution to the film. A '*co-producer*' is a person who is a co-producer for the purposes of the qualifying co-production agreement. If there is more than one company that fits the description of a film production company in relation to a film, the company most directly engaged in the activities referred to is the film production company.

[*CTA 2009, ss 1180–1189, Sch 1 para 675; FA 1998, Sch 18 para 10*; *FA 2006, ss 31–36, 38–41; SI 2006 No 3265; SI 2006 No 3399; FA 2007, s 58*].

Computation of profits and gains

[70.32] In relation to films certified by the Secretary of State, under the *Films Act 1985, Sch 1 (as amended by CTA 2009, Sch 1 para 319)*, as British films for the purpose of film tax relief and intended for theatrical release at the time principal photography commences, the production activities of the film production company in relation to the film are treated as a trade separate from any of its other activities. Such trade, '*the separate film trade*' is treated as commencing when pre-production of the film begins or, if earlier, when any income from the film is received by the company.

'*Film-making activities*' means activities involved in the development, pre-production, principal photography and post-production of the film and includes computer generation of images. The Treasury may (by regulation) amend this definition. Expenditure incurred by the company on film-making activities in connection with the film or on activities with a view to exploiting the film ('*costs of the film*') is deductible as revenue expenditure subject to the normal restrictions under the Corporation Taxes Acts. Expenditure is treated as revenue if it would otherwise be regarded as capital by reason only of being incurred on the creation of the film. '*Income*' means any receipts by the company in connection with the making or exploitation of the film. For this purpose, capital receipts are treated as revenue. '*Income from the film*' includes receipts from the sale of the film or rights in it, royalties or other payments for use of the film or aspects of it, payments for rights to produce games or other merchandise, and receipts by way of a profit share agreement. Pre-trading expenditure is treated as having been incurred immediately after the company began the separate film trade. Estimates must be made at the balance sheet date for each period of account on a just and reasonable basis taking into account all relevant circumstances. If such expenditure has already been taken into account for other tax purposes, the company tax return must be amended accordingly (notwithstanding any limitation on the time within which an amendment may normally be made).

In determining the profit or loss for the first period of account, the costs of the film incurred in that period are brought into account as a debit and the proportion of estimated total income from the film treated as earned in the period is brought into account as a credit. For any subsequent period of account, the difference between the costs of the film incurred to date and the corresponding amount for the previous period is brought into account as a debit. Similarly, the difference between the proportion of estimated total income from the film treated as earned at the end of that period and the corresponding amount for the previous period is brought into account as a credit.

The proportion of estimated total income from the film treated as earned at the end of any period of account is determined by the formula C/T × I where C is the total costs incurred to date, T is the estimated total cost of the film and I is the estimated total income from the film. Estimates are to be made as at the balance sheet date for each period of account, on a fair and reasonable basis and considering all relevant circumstances.

Costs are treated as incurred when they are represented in the state of completion of the work in progress. Accordingly, payments in advance are to be ignored until work has been represented in the state of completion. Unpaid amounts are included in costs only if there is an unconditional obligation to pay them but if the obligation is linked to income being earned from the film, the costs can be included only when the appropriate amount of income is or has been taken into account.

No relief is available for expenditure for which relief has been given under the pre-*FA 2006* regime (which covers income tax as well as corporation tax).

[*CTA 2009, ss 1190–1200, Sch 1 para 675; FA 2006, s 37, Sch 4; SI 2006 No 3265; SI 2006 No 3399; SI 2007 No 1050, Reg 9*].

Enhanced relief

[70.33] Film tax relief is available for expenditure on a film that commences principal photography on or after 1 January 2007, qualifies for film tax relief (as above) and where a claim is made. The film production company can claim an enhanced deduction in respect of '*qualifying expenditure*' on the film, such expenditure being defined as 'core expenditure' (see above). The rate of enhancement is:

- 100% for a '*limited-budget film*' (one on which the core expenditure is £20 million or less, the expenditure being deemed equal to an arm's length amount in the case of transactions between **CONNECTED PERSONS (25)**); and
- 80% for any other film.

For the first period of account during which the trade is carried on, the additional deduction is the relevant enhancement rate above multiplied by the lower of:

- the amount of the qualifying UK expenditure; or
- 80% of the total amount of qualifying expenditure.

For any subsequent period of account the additional deduction is:

- the relevant enhancement rate above multiplied by the lower of the amount of the qualifying UK expenditure incurred to date or 80% of the total amount of qualifying expenditure incurred to date;

- less the amount of the additional deduction (or aggregate amount of additional deductions) given in the previous period (or periods).

Film tax credits

[70.34] A film production company may claim a film tax credit for an accounting period in which it has a '*surrenderable loss*' which is equal to the lower of the amount of the trading loss for that period and the 'available qualifying expenditure'. The credit is not treated as income for tax purposes. A credit can be claimed for the whole or part of a surrenderable loss surrendered in a period at the rate of:

- 25% for a limited-budget film (as defined above); and
- 20% for any other film.

The trading loss is accordingly reduced for any amount so surrendered.

For the first period of account during which the trade is carried on, the '*available qualifying expenditure*' is the lower of:

- the amount of the qualifying UK expenditure; or
- 80% of the total amount of qualifying expenditure.

For any subsequent period of account the '*available qualifying expenditure*' is:

- the lower of the amount of the qualifying UK expenditure incurred to date or 80% of the total amount of qualifying expenditure incurred to date;
- less the amount of the loss surrendered (or aggregate amounts surrendered) in the previous period (or periods).

In determining the amount of the available qualifying expenditure for tax credit purposes, no account is taken of costs still unpaid four months after the end of the period of account in question.

Where a company is entitled to a film tax credit and makes a claim, the credit will be paid by HMRC but any amount payable in respect of the credit or interest thereon may be applied in discharging the company's liability to corporation tax. HMRC need not pay the credits (or may pay as much as they think fit) until the completion of enquiries into the company's tax return. Nor need they pay the credits before the company has settled its liabilities in an accounting period for PAYE, Class 1 National Insurance contributions or tax for foreign entertainers under *ITA 2007, s 966*. Relief is denied to the extent it arises from artificially inflated claims (as defined).

Per the June 2010 budget announcement, legislation has been introduced in *F(No 3)A 2010* to amend the provisions on how a surrenderable loss is calculated for film tax relief claims. The provisions apply to accounting periods ending on or after 9 December 2009, and will be treated as always having had effect in relation to these claims. They aim to resolve an anomaly arising with regard to the credit that can be claimed where a film's production spans more than one accounting period thus they ensure that the amount of film tax relief available is the same regardless of the profile of the UK expenditure.

The provisions of *CTA 2009, s 1201* are amended as follows:

- the 'company's loss' for the period per *s 1201(2)(a)* becomes the 'company's available loss'; and
- a company's 'available loss' is now the company's loss for a film in an accounting period as well as any 'relevant unused loss' which is the available loss in the previous accounting period that has not already been surrendered, or carried forward and offset against profits arising in the later period for the same film.

Where the available qualifying expenditure on the film for the accounting period is less than the 'available loss' then the surrenderable amount is the qualifying expenditure.

[*CTA 2009, ss 1201, 1202, Sch 1 para 675; FA 2006, s 34, Sch 5 paras 1–14; SI 2006 No 3265; SI 2006 No 3399*].

Claims and overpayments

[70.35] A claim for film tax relief must be made in a company tax return (or amended return) (see **66.4, 66.9 RETURNS**) for the accounting period for which the claim is made, within one year of the filing date for that return or by such later time as HMRC may allow. It can similarly only be amended or withdrawn by amendment of the company tax return within the same time limit. It must specify the quantum of the amount claimed. Penalties not exceeding the excess credit claimed apply for deliberate (fraudulent) or careless (negligent) claims, and for failure to remedy an incorrect claim without unreasonable delay.

For the purposes of a claim to tax credit an amount unpaid four months after the end of the accounting period is not taken into account. There is an anti-avoidance provision which applies when a transaction is part of transactions for a 'disallowable purpose'. A '*disallowable purpose*' is one which aims to give the company an additional deduction or a higher tax credit.

[*CTA 2009, ss 1201–1205, Sch 1 para 455; FA 1998, Sch 18 paras 10(4), 83S–83X; FA 2006, Sch 5 paras 27–29*].

Late claims should be dealt with in accordance with Statement of Practice 5/01 (HMRC CIRD Manual 81800). For recovery of overpayments of film tax credit, see **7.4 ASSESSMENTS**.

HMRC has established a specialist unit to deal with film tax relief claims. The address is Manchester Film Tax Credit Unit, Albert Bridge House, 1 Bridge Street, Manchester, M60 9AF.

Entitlement to relief

[70.36] Entitlement to the above relief is further conditional on the film continuing to meet the requirements for certification as a 'British film', the minimum percentage on UK expenditure and status (where a claim is made on that basis) as a limited-budget film.

In the company's '*completion period*', in which the film is completed or abandoned, the company tax return for that period must state that the film has been completed or abandoned and be accompanied by:

- a final certificate (from the Secretary of State under the *Films Act 1985, Sch 1*) (such a certificate also having effect for previous periods). Without the certificate, or if the certificate is revoked, entitlement to relief is withdrawn for any period and the company tax return must be amended for any period for which relief was claimed. If the film is abandoned, the return may be accompanied by an interim certificate in which case the company would still be entitled to relief in that or any previous period;
- a final statement of the amount of core expenditure that is UK expenditure. If the condition for UK expenditure is not met, entitlement to relief is withdrawn for any period and the company tax return must be amended for any period for which relief was claimed; and
- in the case where relief is claimed on the basis that the film is a limited-budget film, a final statement of core expenditure on the film. If the return shows the film is not a limited-budget film (or, if the film is abandoned, it would not have been such a film if it were completed, having regard to the proportion of work completed), entitlement to the limited-budget film relief is withdrawn for any period and the company tax return must be amended for any period for which such relief was claimed.

In any earlier accounting period ('interim accounting period') of the company the company tax return must:

(i) be accompanied by an interim certificate (similarly from the Secretary of State under the *Films Act 1985, Sch 1*). If an interim certificate ceases to be in force or is revoked then, unless a final certificate is provided as above, entitlement to relief is withdrawn for any period for which relief depended on the certificate and the company tax return for any such period must be amended accordingly;

(ii) state the amount of planned core expenditure that is UK expenditure and that the UK expenditure condition will be met on completion of the film. If it subsequently appears that the UK expenditure condition will not be met, relief is withdrawn for any period for which its entitlement depended on such a statement and the company tax return for any such period must be amended accordingly; and

(iii) in the case where relief is claimed on the basis that the film is a limited-budget film, state the amount of planned core expenditure on the film and that the conditions for such expenditure will be met on completion of the film. If it subsequently appears that the condition will not be met, limited-budget relief is withdrawn for any period and the company tax return for any such period for which such relief has been claimed must be amended accordingly.

The normal time limits for amendments or assessments do not apply in this case.

[*CTA 2009, ss 1212–1216; FA 2006, Sch 5 paras 30–34*].

Confidentiality

[70.37] *CRMA 2005, s 18(1)* does not prevent HMRC disclosing information to the Secretary of State or the UK Film Council in relation certification of films as British films for the purposes of film tax relief. There are restrictions on whom such information disclosed can in turn be disclosed to and provisions for prosecution for wrongful disclosure.

[*CTA 2009, ss 1206, 1207*].

Losses

[70.38] In the accounting periods of the film production company before that in which the film is completed or abandoned, relief for a trading loss is available only to the extent that it can be carried forward under *CTA 2010, s 45* (previously *ICTA 1988, s 393(1)*) to be set against profits of the same trade in a later period. Any such loss as is not attributable to film tax relief is treated as a loss incurred in the period to which it is carried forward.

To the extent they are not attributable to film tax relief, losses in later periods may be set against the profits of the same or earlier period under *CTA 2010, s 37* (previously *ICTA 1988, s 393A*); *CTA 2009, Sch 1 para 111* or surrendered as group relief under *CTA 2010, s 99* (previously *ICTA 1988, s 403*); *CTA 2007, Sch 1 para 118*. The amount of a trading loss attributable to film tax relief is the total loss less the amount of the loss there would have been had there been no additional deduction for enhanced relief in that or in any earlier period. This does not apply to a loss to the extent it is carried forward or surrendered as a terminal loss (as below).

If a film production company ceases to carry on the trade, it can elect to surrender part or all of any remaining losses (which could otherwise be carried forward as above) to another of its trades in relation to a qualifying film. The loss would be treated as a loss brought forward by that other trade in the accounting period following that at the end of which the cessation takes place. Part or all of such a loss can also be surrendered to a trade in relation to a qualifying film of another company in the same group (for group relief purposes). That company may elect for the surrendered loss to be treated as a loss brought forward by it for set off against profits of its accounting period beginning after the cessation.

[*CTA 2010, ss 45, 37, 99; CTA 2009, ss 1208–1211, Sch 1 para 677; FA 2006, ss 43–45*].

Terminal loss relief

[70.39] A company may make a claim to have a loss, which would otherwise have been carried forward against income from the abandoned film, set against the profits from another film trade carried on by it.

A loss claim by a claimant (which is also a film production company) in respect of a terminal loss incurred by another group company must be included in the claimant company's corporation tax return for the accounting period of the claim, either when the return is filed or by amending the self assessment within the required time limit. The claim must state the surrendering company's name and the amount of relief, which must be quantifiable at the time the claim is made.

The claim must also give details of any group company not resident in the UK for tax purposes either in the surrendering company's accounting period of claim or the claimant's corresponding accounting period.

The amount available for surrender is calculated by taking the surrendering company's loss under *CTA 2009, s 1211* and deducting all amounts for which that company has given, and not withdrawn, notices of consent. There are rules to determine which claims and withdrawals are to be matched. (*SI 2007 No 678, Reg 7(4)* and *(5)*). The surrendering company's written consent ('notice of consent') is required to the claim, which must state:

(A) the surrendering company's name, tax reference and its accounting period to which the claim relates;
(B) the claimant company's name, tax reference and its accounting period to which the claim relates; and
(C) the amount of the terminal loss being surrendered.

A notice may not be amended, but can be withdrawn (by notice to the officer who had received the original notice of consent) and replaced. The notice of withdrawal must contain the consent of the surrendering company, unless the reason for the withdrawal is that the loss available for relief has been reduced. The surrendering company must also submit an amended corporation tax return or returns, if the return or returns for the periods in question have already been filed. If it does not do so, the notice is not effective.

A claim may be withdrawn until the latest of:

(a) a year from the claimant company's filing date for the accounting period of claim;
(b) where an enquiry has been opened, 30 days after the enquiry is closed;
(c) where a return is amended following an enquiry, 30 days after the amendment is issued; and
(d) where an amendment is appealed, 30 days after the appeal is settled,

but HMRC may agree to a later time limit.

There are provisions requiring the surrendering company to withdraw the notice or notices of consent where the amount available for surrender is reduced.

[*CTA 2009, s 1211; SI 2007 No 678*].

HMRC are given power to assess any other company which benefited from a loss relief claim where the tax due by the claimant company after a notice has been withdrawn remains unpaid six months after the surrendering companies time limit for claims, provided that the assessment must not be made more than two years after the time limit expires. The company so assessed has a right of recovery against the claimant company. [*SI 2007 No 678, Reg 14*]. There is also a power to assess where the relief given is found to be excessive. [*SI 2007 No 678, Reg 15*].

Treasury powers

[70.40] The Treasury have powers to make provision, by order (approved by a resolution of the House of Commons) to make various amendments. They may provide that certain activities are not film-making activities, amend the definition or vary the minimum percentage of UK expenditure, provide that particular sorts of expenditure are not qualifying expenditure or amend the percentage of qualifying expenditure used to calculate the enhanced deduction. They may also, by order, vary the way in which surrenders and claims of losses are made.

[*CTA 2009, ss 1183, 1198–1200, 1211; FA 2006, ss 33, 35, 41, 45, Sch 5 paras 3, 4*].

Gifts and donations received

[70.41] The fact that a receipt is gratuitous is not in itself a reason for its not being a trading receipt. See *Severne v Dadswell* (1954) 35 TC 649 (payments under war-time arrangements held trading receipts although *ex gratia*); *CIR v Falkirk Ice Rink* (1975) 51 TC 42, Ct of Sess (donation to ice rink from associated curling club held taxable); *Wing v O'Connell Supreme Court* [1927] IR 84 (gift to professional jockey on winning race taxable).

Cremation fees (often known as 'ash cash') assigned in advance, and paid directly, to a medical charity may escape liability to tax on miscellaneous income where the doctor entitled to them is not chargeable to tax on trading income, but liability to tax on trading income is not affected by such assignment. See HMRC Business Income Manual BIM54015.

Gifts to charities and educational establishments

A relief is available for certain gifts by trading companies for the purposes of a charity (within **20 CHARITIES**), any of the similar bodies listed in *CTA 2009, s 105(4)*, a 'designated educational establishment' or a registered community amateur sports club.

Where the gift is of an article manufactured by the company, or of a type sold by the company, in its trade, it is not required to bring in any amount as a trading receipt in respect of the disposal of the article.

For accounting periods ending before 1 April 2009 (and see **70.2** above), for gifts to educational establishments only:

- it was a requirement that the article would have been classified as plant or machinery if the establishment had incurred expenditure on it for the purposes of a trade carried on by it; and
- a claim was required if the relief was to apply; the claim had to be made within two years after the accounting period in which the gift was made and had to specify both the article and the educational establishment concerned.

Also for accounting periods ending before 1 April 2009, for gifts *other than* to educational establishments, the gift had to made *to* the charity etc. and not merely 'for the purpose' of it; the current wording is slightly less restrictive.

Where the gift is of an item of plant or machinery used in the course of the company's trade, its disposal value for capital allowances purposes (see **12.24 CAPITAL ALLOWANCES — PLANT AND MACHINERY: POOLING AND DISPOSALS**) is nil.

The value of any benefit received by the company or by a person connected with the company (within **25 CONNECTED PERSONS**), which is in any way attributable to the making of a gift for which relief has been given as above, must be brought into account as a trading receipt in the accounting period in which the benefit arises or, if the company has ceased to carry on the trade by then, as a post-cessation receipt (within **70.16** above). For accounting periods beginning before 1 April 2009 (and see **70.2** above), a benefit received after cessation of trading was charged under *Sch D, Case VI* and not as a post-cessation receipt.

See also **20.10 CHARITIES** — substantial donors, and **61.11 PROFITS COMPUTATIONS** — charitable donations relief, with respect to the position of substantial donors who receive benefits from a charity and the anti-avoidance provisions introduced in this regard by *FA 2011*.

'*Designated educational establishment*' means any educational establishment designated (or of a category designated) in regulations, broadly all UK universities, public or private schools and further and higher educational institutions (see *SI 1992 No 42* as amended by *SI 1993 No 561*).

[*CTA 2009, ss 105, 106, 108, Sch 2 paras 26, 27; 84; CAA 2001, s 63(2)–(4), Sch 2 paras 16, 17; ITTOIA 2005, Sch 1 paras 57, 58, 535*].

Gifts of medical supplies and equipment

Where, for humanitarian purposes, a company makes a gift from trading stock of medical supplies or medical equipment for human use, no amount is required to be brought into account for tax purposes in respect of the donated items as a trading receipt. Transportation, delivery or distribution costs incurred by the company in making the gift are deductible in computing trading profits for the accounting period in which those costs are incurred.

The value of any benefit received by the company or by a person connected with the company (within **25 CONNECTED PERSONS**) which is in any way attributable to a gift (or to ancillary costs) for which relief has been given as above must be brought into account as a trading receipt in the accounting period in which the benefit arises or, if the company has ceased to carry on the trade by then, as a post-cessation receipt (within **70.16** above). For accounting periods beginning before 1 April 2009 (and see **70.2** above), a benefit received after cessation of trading was charged under *Sch D, Case VI* and not as a post-cessation receipt.

The Treasury may by order exclude from the relief medical supplies or medical equipment of any specified description.

[*CTA 2009, ss 107, 108; FA 2002, s 55*].

No claim form or entry on the CT600 tax return is required for operation of this relief. For this and for the 'humanitarian purposes' requirement, and the broad scope of 'medical supplies and equipment', see the article on the operation of the scheme in the HMRC Tax Bulletin October 2002, pp 975–977 issue 61 & 62.

Simon's Taxes. See **B2.441, B2.442, D1.353**.

Herd basis

[70.42] See generally HMRC Business Income Manual BIM55501–55640.

Animals kept for the purposes of a trade

[70.43] Animals and other living creatures kept for the purposes of farming or similar trades (e.g. animal or fish breeding) are generally treated as trading stock (see **71.66 TRADING EXPENSES AND DEDUCTIONS**) unless:

- they are part of a herd in relation to which an election is made under *CTA 2009, s 109/122* (previously *ICTA 1988, s 97, Sch 5*) for the 'herd basis' to apply; or
- the animals etc. are kept wholly or mainly for the work they do in connection with the trade or for public exhibition or racing or other competitive purposes.

[*CTA 2009, ss 50, 109(1); ICTA 1988, s 97, Sch 5 paras 1, 7, 9(1)(2)(5); ITTOIA 2005, Sch 1 para 343*].

Once an election is made the animals in the herd from part of the farmer's fixed capital for tax purposes, much like plant and machinery (although the herd does not qualify for capital allowances). Animals etc. are exempt from capital gains tax as wasting assets within *TCGA 1992, s 45*.

Herd basis — definitions

[70.44] For the purposes of the herd basis rules, an '*animal*' means any living creature, a '*herd*' includes a flock and any other collection of animals, and a '*production herd*' means a herd of animals of the same species, irrespective of breed, kept by a farmer or other trader wholly or mainly for the saleable produce obtainable from the living animal, which includes the young of the animal and any other product obtainable from it without slaughtering it. The herd basis provisions apply equally to animals kept singly and to shares in animals.

Immature animals kept in a production herd are generally not regarded as part of the herd for these purposes, but if:

- the nature of the land on which the herd is kept is such that replacement animals have to be bred and reared on that land (e.g. acclimatised hill sheep);

- the immature animals in question are bred and maintained in the herd for the purpose of replacing animals in the herd;
- it is necessary to maintain the immature animals for that purpose,

the immature animals are regarded as part of the herd in so far as they are required to prevent a fall in numbers.

An immature animal which is not regarded as part of the herd is regarded as added to the herd when it reaches maturity. Female animals are treated as becoming mature when they produce their first young or, in the case of laying birds, when they first lay (but see below as regards temporary concession during the 2001 foot and mouth outbreak).

[*CTA 2009, ss 110, 111(5), 122; ICTA 1988, Sch 5 paras 8(1)–(5), 9(2)–(4); ITTOIA 2005, Sch 1 para 343*].

Herd basis elections

[70.45] An election for the herd basis to have effect must specify the class of production herd to which it relates and must be made not later than two years after the end of the first accounting period during the whole or part of which a production herd of the class specified was first kept by the company. The election is irrevocable, and has effect in relation to all the production herds of the class to which it relates, including any which the farmer has ceased to keep before making the election or starts to keep after making the election. The election cannot relate to more than one class of production herd, but separate elections can be made for different classes. Two or more production herds are of the same class if the animals kept in those herds are of the same species (irrespective of breed) and the saleable produce for which the herds are wholly or mainly kept is of the same kind. An election has effect for every accounting period in which the farmer carries on the trade and keeps a production herd of the relevant class.

If the farmer is a partnership of which the company is a member, it is the partnership that has the right to elect for the herd basis to apply. In this case, the election must be made not later than the first anniversary of 31 January following the tax year in which ends the first period of account during the whole or part of which a production herd of the class specified was first kept by the partnership. Where there is a change in the persons carrying on a trade in partnership, a further election is required if the herd basis is to continue to apply. This is given clear statutory effect by *CTA 2009* (see **70.2** above) but accords with HMRC's interpretation (in HMRC Business Income Manual BIM55610) of the earlier legislation. The further election must be made not later than the first anniversary of 31 January following the tax year in which ends the first period of account during the whole or part of which the 'new' firm keeps a production herd of the class to which the election relates.

[*CTA 2009, ss 111(2), 122, 1319; ICTA 1988, Sch 5 paras 2, 8(6); ITTOIA 2005, Sch 1 para 343*].

See below as regards a further opportunity to make an election in a case of compulsory slaughter.

Further assessments may be made for any accounting period as necessary, and repayments may be made (on a claim), to give effect to a herd basis election. [*CTA 2009, s 127; ICTA 1988, Sch 5 para 11; ITTOIA 2005, Sch 1 para 343*].

Five-year gap between keeping herds

[70.46] If a farmer has kept a production herd of a particular class, ceases to keep herds of that class for at least five years and then does so once more:

- any herd basis election previously made in relation to herds of that class ceases to have effect; but
- the farmer may make a further election by reference to the first accounting period (or period of account in the case of a partnership) in which the farmer again keeps a production herd of that class.

For accounting periods ending before 1 April 2009, the previous election did not automatically lapse but HMRC practice was to disregard it in these circumstances (see Change 32 listed in Annex 1 to the Explanatory Notes to *CTA 2009*).

[*CTA 2009, s 123; ICTA 1988, Sch 5 para 4; ITTOIA 2005, Sch 1 para 343*].

Consequences of herd basis election

[70.47] Where a herd basis election is in force, the animals in the herd are in effect treated as capital assets instead of as trading stock. The initial cost of the herd is not deductible in computing trading profits, and its value is not brought into account. No deduction is allowed for additions to the herd (as opposed to replacement animals — see below). If the additional animal was previously part of trading stock, a receipt must be brought into account equal to the cost of breeding it, or acquiring it, and rearing it to maturity. If it is not possible to ascertain actual costs of breeding and rearing, an alternative deemed cost method may be used (HMRC Business Income Manual BIM55410, 55530). [*CTA 2009, ss 112, 113; ICTA 1988, Sch 5 para 3(2)(3); ITTOIA 2005, Sch 1 para 343*].

Replacement animals

The replacement of an animal dying or ceasing to be a member of a herd gives rise to a trading receipt equal to the disposal proceeds (if any) of the animal replaced, and a trading deduction equal to the cost of the replacement animal (so far as not otherwise allowable) but limited to the cost of an animal of similar quality to that replaced (for which see Revenue Tax Bulletin October 2001 pp 890, 891). See below for meaning of disposal proceeds. Where the animal replaced was compulsorily slaughtered, and the replacement animal is of inferior quality, the trading receipt is restricted to the amount allowable as a deduction in respect of the new animal. [*CTA 2009, ss 111(3), 114, 115; ICTA 1988, Sch 5 para 3(4)–(6), (12); ITTOIA 2005, Sch 1 para 343*].

Whether a particular animal brought into the herd replaces an animal disposed of is a question of fact, requiring a direct connection between the disposal and the later addition rather than a simple restoration of numbers. As a practical matter, HMRC will accept that replacement treatment is appropriate where animals are brought into the herd within twelve months of the corresponding disposal. Where disposal and replacement are in different accounting periods, the overall profit or loss may either be brought in the first period and any necessary adjustment made in the second, or the profit or loss arising in the first period may be held over to the second period. Where the interval is more than twelve months, there is unlikely to be sufficient evidence to support the necessary connection where the new animal is bought in. Where animals are home bred, however, a longer interval may be reasonable where e.g. there is insufficient young stock to replace unexpected disposals. (See HMRC Business Income Manual BIM55520 and Revenue Tax Bulletin February 1997 p 396, issue 27).

Disposal of animals from the herd

[70.48] Where an animal is disposed of from the herd, any profit is brought into account as a trading receipt and any loss is deductible as an expense. This does not apply if the animal is replaced (for which see above) or on a disposal of the whole or a substantial part of the herd within a 12-month period (for which see below). The profit or loss is computed by reference to disposal proceeds and the cost of breeding the animal, or acquiring it, and rearing it to maturity. Market value is substituted for acquisition cost if the animal was acquired other than for valuable consideration. [*CTA 2009, s 116; ICTA 1988, Sch 5 para 3(10); ITTOIA 2005, Sch 1 para 343*]. For HMRC's interpretation of this provision, including a change of view on how the profit on such disposals is to be computed, see Revenue Tax Bulletin April 2003 pp 1024, 1025.

For the purposes of the herd basis rules, the disposal of an animal includes its death or destruction as well as its sale, and disposal proceeds include sale proceeds and, in the case of death or destruction, insurance or compensation money received and proceeds of carcass sales. [*CTA 2009, s 111(3)(4); ICTA 1988, Sch 5 para 3(12); ITTOIA 2005, Sch 1 para 343*].

On the disposal of the whole or a substantial part of the herd, either all at once or over a period of twelve months or less, any profit is not brought into account as a receipt and any loss is not deductible as an expense. (20% or more of the herd is regarded as a 'substantial' part of it (but this does not prevent a smaller percentage from being regarded as 'substantial' in any particular case); this has statutory effect for accounting periods ending on or after 1 April 2009, but reflects previous practice — see HMRC Business Income Manual BIM55525.) If, however, the disposal is of *the whole herd* and the farmer acquires, or starts to acquire, a new production herd of the same class within 5 years of the disposal, the following rules apply.

(i) The replacement rules above apply as if a number of animals, equal to the smaller of the number in the old herd and the number in the new, had been disposed of in the old herd and replaced in that herd. Disposal proceeds of any animal are brought into account when the 'replacement' animal is acquired.

(ii) If the number of animals in the new herd is smaller than that in the old by an insubstantial margin (i.e. normally less than 20% — see above), the difference is subject to the normal disposal rules in *CTA 2009, s 116* above.
(iii) If the number of animals in the new herd is smaller than that in the old by a substantial margin (i.e. normally 20% or more — see above), the difference is treated as a disposal of a substantial part of the herd.
(iv) If the number of animals in the new herd is greater than that in the old, the difference is treated as additions to the herd.

For accounting periods ending before 1 April 2009 (and see **70.2** above), these rules operated slightly differently — see Change 31 listed in Annex 1 to the Explanatory Notes to *CTA 2009*).

If the disposal is of *a substantial part of the herd* and the farmer acquires, or starts to acquire, a new production herd of the same class within 5 years of the disposal, the following rules apply.

(1) The replacement rules above apply insofar as the animals included in the part disposed of are replaced. Disposal proceeds of an animal included in the part sold are brought into account when the replacement animal is acquired.
(2) If some of the animals included in the part disposed of are not replaced, any profit on their disposal is not brought into account as a receipt and any loss is not deductible as an expense.

Where the disposal of all or a substantial part of a herd is for reasons wholly outside the farmer's control and a 'replacement' animal is of inferior quality to the old, the replacement rules above apply as they do when animals are slaughtered under a disease control order (whether or not that is indeed the case).

[*CTA 2009, ss 111(6), 117–121; ICTA 1988, Sch 5 para 3(7)–(9)(11); ITTOIA 2005, Sch 1 para 343*].

Elections following compulsory slaughter

[70.49] Where compensation is receivable in respect of the whole, or a substantial part (normally 20% or more), of a production herd slaughtered by order under animal diseases laws, the farmer may, notwithstanding the time limits above, elect for the herd basis to apply. The election must be made not later than two years after the end of the first accounting period in which the compensation falls (or would otherwise fall) to be taken into account as a trading receipt. The election has effect for that accounting period and each subsequent accounting period of account in which the farmer carries on the trade and keeps a production herd of that class. (There are appropriate modifications where the farmer is a partnership rather than a company.) [*CTA 2009, s 124; ICTA 1988, Sch 5 para 6; ITTOIA 2005, Sch 1 para 343*].

Compensation paid under the BSE Suspects Scheme and the BSE Selective Cull (where the animal was born after 14 October 1990) is for compulsory slaughter, and for these purposes includes Selective Cull 'top-up' payments.

Payments under the Calf Processing Scheme, the Over Thirty Month Scheme and the BSE Selective Cull where the animal was born before 15 October 1990 are *not* for compulsory slaughter. See Revenue Tax Bulletin February 1997 pp 396, 397, issue 27 for this and for the application of these provisions to BSE compensation generally. For compulsory slaughter in cases where the herd basis does not and could not apply, see **70.29**(a) above.

Anti-avoidance

[70.50] There are provisions for the prevention of avoidance of tax in the case of a non-arm's length transfer of all or part of a production herd where either transferor and transferee are bodies of persons under common control or the sole or main benefit of the transfer relates to its effect on a herd basis election. [*CTA 2009, s 125; ICTA 1988, Sch 5 para 5*].

Information etc.

[70.51] Where an election has effect, HMRC may by notice require the farmer to make returns of information as to the animals kept and their produce. [*CTA 2009, s 126; ICTA 1988, Sch 5 para 10*].

Foot and mouth outbreak 2001

[70.52] For the full range of measures, including acceptance of herd basis elections, in relation to the 2001 foot and mouth disease outbreak, see Revenue Tax Bulletin Special Edition May 2001 and Revenue Tax Bulletin October 2001 pp 890, 891. In particular, by concession, certain replacement animals slaughtered before giving birth may be regarded as having been mature notwithstanding *ICTA 1988, Sch 5 para 8(4)* (now *CTA 2009, s 111(5)*) (see above), and hence treated as having been part of the herd rather than trading stock (HMRC Extra Statutory Concession B56).

Simon's Taxes. See **B5.150–B5.154**.

Example

A farming company acquires a dairy herd and elects for the herd basis to apply. The movements in the herd and the tax treatment are as follows.

Year 1	No	Value
		£
Mature		
Bought @ £150	70	10,500
Bought in calves @ £180		
(Market value of calves £35)	5	900
Immature		
Bought @ £75	15	1,125

Year 1	**No**	**Value**
Herd Account		
Friesians	70	10,500
Friesians in calf (5 × £(180 – 35))	5	725
Closing balance	75	£11,225

Trading Account		£
Calves (5 × £35)	5	175
Immature Friesians	15	1,125
Debit to profit and loss account		£1,300

Year 2

	No	**Value** £
Mature		
Bought @ £185	15	2,775
Sold @ £200	10	2,000
Died	3	—
Immature		
Born	52	—
Matured @ 60% of market value of £200 (note (a))	12	1,440

Herd Account		£
Opening balance	75	11,225
Increase in herd		
Purchases	15	2,775
Transferred from trading stock	12	1,440
	27	4,215
Replacement cost £4,215 × 13/27	(13)	2,029
Non-replacement animals cost	14	2,186
Closing balance	89	£13,411

Trading Account	£
Sale of 10 mature cows replaced	(2,000)
Transfer to herd — 14 animals	(1,440)

Year 2

	£
Cost of 13 mature cows purchased to replace those sold/deceased ($^{13}/_{15}$ × £2,775)	2,405
Net credit to profit and loss account (note (b))	£(1,035)

Year 3

	No	Value £
Mature		
Jerseys bought @ £250	70	17,500
Friesians slaughtered @ £175 (market value £185)	52	9,100
Immature		
Friesians born	20	—
Matured		
Friesians @ 60% of market value of £190 (note (a))	15	1,710

Herd Account	No	£	£
Opening balance	89		13,411
Increase in herd			
Jerseys	18		4,500
52 Improvement Jerseys @		250	
less Market value of Friesians		185	
52 @		65	3,380
Transfer from trading stock			
Friesians	15		1,710
Closing balance	122		£23,001

Trading Account	£
Compensation	(9,100)
Transfer to herd	(1,710)
Purchase of replacements (note (c)) (52 × £185)	9,620
Net credit to profit and loss account	£(1,190)

Year 4

The farmer ceases dairy farming and sells the whole herd.

Year 4

		No	Value
			£
Mature			
Jerseys sold @ £320		70	22,400
Friesians sold @ £200		52	10,400
Immature			
Friesians sold @ £100		65	6,500
Herd Account			£
Opening balance		122	23,001
Friesians	52		
Jerseys	70		
Sales		(122)	(32,800)
Profit on sale (note (d))			£(9,799)
Trading Account			£
Sale of 65 immature Friesians			(6,500)
Credit to profit and loss account			£(6,500)

Notes

(a) The use of 60% of market value was originally by agreement between the National Farmers' Union and HMRC (see HMRC Business Economic Note 19: Farming — Stock Valuation for Income Tax purposes, at paragraph 7.2). Alternatively, the actual cost of breeding or purchase and rearing could be used.

(b) As the cost of rearing the 12 cows to maturity will already have been debited to the profit and loss account, no additional entry is required to reflect that cost. Due to the fact that the animals were in opening stock at valuation and will not be in closing stock, the trading account will in effect be debited with that valuation.

(c) The cost of the replacements is restricted to the cost of replacing like with like.

(d) Provided these animals are not replaced by a herd of the same class within five years the proceeds will be tax-free.

Insurance received

[70.53] Premiums paid for business purposes are normally allowable (see **71.53 TRADING EXPENSES AND DEDUCTIONS**) and any corresponding recoveries are normally trading receipts (or set off against trading expenses or capital, according to the nature of the policy). Where a deduction was allowed for a loss or expense and the company trader recovers a capital sum under an insurance policy or contract of indemnity in respect of that loss or expense, the sum must be brought into account, up to the amount of the deduction, as a trading receipt. [*CTA 2009, s 103, Sch 2 para 25*]. The legislation applicable for accounting periods ending before 1 April 2009 was very differently worded, but *CTA 2009, s 103* is said to reflect previous practice based on accountancy treatment (see Change 25 listed in Annex 1 to the Explanatory Notes to *CTA 2009*). Otherwise, if capital, the recovery may be taken into account, where appropriate, for the purposes of **CAPITAL ALLOWANCES — INTRODUCTION (10)** or **CAPITAL GAINS (17)**.

The whole of a recovery in respect of the destruction of trading stock was held to be a trading receipt of the year of destruction, notwithstanding that it exceeded the market value of the stock lost or not all the stock was replaced (*J Gliksten & Son Ltd v Green (Inspector of Taxes)* [1929] AC 381, 14 TC 364, HL; *Rownson Drew & Clydesdale Ltd v CIR* (1931) 16 TC 595). The total recovery under a loss of profits was held a trading receipt although in excess of the loss suffered (*R v British Columbia Fir & Cedar* (1932) 15 ATC 624, PC). See also *Mallandain Investments Ltd v Shadbolt* (1940) 23 TC 367. For recoveries under accidents to employees see *Gray & Co v Murphy* (1940) 23 TC 225; *Keir & Cawder Ltd v CIR* (1958) 38 TC 23, Ct of Sess. Where a shipping company insured against late delivery of ships being built for it, both premiums and recoveries held capital (*Crabb v Blue Star Line Ltd* (1961) 39 TC 482).

For premiums on policies insuring against death or critical illness of key employees see **71.53 TRADING EXPENSES AND DEDUCTIONS**.

Simon's Taxes. See **B2.211**.

Commissions

HMRC Statement of Practice SP 4/97 (see **70.26** above) deals widely with commissions, cashbacks and discounts.

See also *Robertson v CIR* [1997] STC (SCD) 282 as regards timing of inclusion of insurance agents' advance commission.

Investment income (including letting income)

[70.54] Investment income may be treated as a trading receipt where it is the fruit derived from a fund employed and risked in the business (see *Liverpool and London and Globe Insurance Co v Bennett* (1913) 6 TC 327, HL). This treatment is not confined to financial trades, but the making and holding of investments at interest must be an integral part of the trade. See *Nuclear Electric plc v Bradley* (1996) 68 TC 670, HL, in which (in refusing the company's claim that interest on investments to meet possible long term future liabilities was trading income) the crucial test was considered to be whether the investments were employed in the business (of producing electricity) in the accounting period in question. The Court of Appeal, whose judgment was approved, considered decisive the facts that the liabilities against which the investments were provided were liabilities to third parties, not to customers, and that, in view of the long-term nature of the liabilities, the business could be carried on for a long period without maintaining any fund of investments at all. See also *Bank Line Ltd v CIR* (below).

See **55.17 LOSSES** as regards relief available to investment companies for losses on shares subscribed for in certain unlisted trading companies.

Payments received in lieu of dividends in contango operations were held to be trading receipts in *Multipar Syndicate Ltd v Devitt* (1945) 26 TC 359; also co-operative society 'dividends' on trading purchases (*Pope v Beaumont* (1941) 24 TC 78). For interest received by underwriters on securities deposited with Lloyd's see *Owen v Sassoon* (1950) 32 TC 101 and for discount receivable on bills see *Willingale v International Commercial Bank Ltd* (1978) 52 TC 242, HL.

In *Rosemoor Investments v Insp of Taxes* [2002] STC (SCD) 325, it was decided that an investment company's participation in a property refinance scheme was by way of investment, not by way of trade. That case involved a complex transaction routed via an investment company subsidiary. The transaction was structured to produce capital. The main issue in the appeal was whether Rosemoor's participation in the transactions was by way of trade (as argued by HMRC) or by way of investment (as argued by Rosemoor). That issue raised the following points: whether the transaction was the provision of short-term finance by Rosemoor's parent company, for whom the transaction was a trading transaction; or, if the transaction was that of Rosemoor, whether its participation was by way of trade or investment. The Commissioners decided that, in reality, the transaction was not the provision of short-term finance by Rosemoor's parent company. The transaction was Rosemoor's, and having regard to the 'badges of trade' and considering the whole picture, it was clear Rosemoor had invested its money and was not dealing in land as a trade. Accordingly, the appeal was allowed.

In certain cases income received under deduction of tax was unable to be included in a trading assessment (*Sch D, Case I or II*) (cf. *F S Securities Ltd v CIR* (1964) 41 TC 666, HL; *Bucks v Bowers* (1969) 46 TC 267; *Bank Line Ltd v CIR* (1974) 49 TC 307, Ct of Sess), and nor, subject to the Crown option between Cases could income received gross from sources within *Sch D, Cases III, IV* or *V* (cf. *Northend v White & Leonard & Corbin Greener* (1975) 50 TC 121) and also from sources *explicitly* within *Sch D, Case VI*.

Rents receivable

Rents receivable and other letting income are within the charge to tax on property income as opposed to trading income (see **70.2** above).

If, however, a company lets **surplus business accommodation** and the conditions below are satisfied, it may choose to include the receipts and expenses of the letting in computing its trading profits instead of treating them as receipts and expenses of a property business. The conditions are that the let accommodation must be 'temporarily surplus to requirements', it must not be part of trading stock, it must be part of a building of which another part is used to carry on the trade, and the letting receipts must be relatively small. For these purposes, 'letting' includes a licence to occupy. Once the receipts and expenses of a letting are included in trading profits, all subsequent receipts and expenses of the letting must similarly be so included. This relaxation of the main rule above was previously applied by HMRC in practice (see Revenue Tax Bulletin February 1994 p 115, issue 10) but for corporation tax purposes it applies by statute for accounting periods ending on or after 1 April 2009. The statute additionally contains rules for determining whether or not accommodation is '*temporarily surplus to requirements*'. It must have been used for trading within the last three years or acquired within that period; the company must intend to use it for trading in future; and the letting itself must be for a term of no more than three years. The position is judged as at the beginning of a period of account. (See Change 5 listed in Annex 1 to the Explanatory Notes to *CTA 2009*). [*CTA 2009, s 44*].

See **62.2 PROPERTY INCOME** for a further relaxation of the main rule above, this time in relation to caravan site operators.

Know-how

[70.55] For corporation tax purposes, 'know-how' created or acquired from an unrelated party **on or after 1 April 2002** generally falls within the intangible assets regime. See in particular the commencement and transitional rules for that regime at **48.36 INTANGIBLE ASSETS**. The following applies where know-how does not fall within that regime.

'*Know-how*' is any industrial information and techniques likely to assist in (a) manufacturing or processing goods or materials, (b) working, or searching for etc., mineral deposits, or (c) agricultural, forestry or fishing operations. For capital allowances on purchases of know-how, see **16.5 CAPITAL ALLOWANCES — MISCELLANEOUS.**

Where know-how used in the vendor's trade is disposed of, with the trade thereafter continuing, the consideration received is treated as a trading receipt, except to the extent that it is brought into account as a disposal value for capital allowances purposes (see **16.5 CAPITAL ALLOWANCES — MISCELLANEOUS**). This does not apply to a sale between bodies of persons (which includes partnerships) under the same control.

If the know-how is disposed of as part of the disposal of all or part of the trade, both vendor and purchaser are treated for corporation tax purposes as if the consideration for the know-how were a payment for goodwill. They may, however, jointly elect to disapply this treatment (within two years of the disposal, and provided they are not bodies under common control), and it is disapplied in any event in relation to the purchaser if, prior to his acquiring it, the trade was carried on wholly outside the UK. In either case, the purchaser may then claim capital allowances on the expenditure (see **16.5**(iii) **CAPITAL ALLOWANCES — MISCELLANEOUS**).

Any consideration received for a restrictive covenant in connection with a disposal of know-how is treated as consideration received for the disposal of the know-how. An exchange of know-how is treated as a sale of know-how.

[*CTA 2009, ss 176–179, 907–910; Sch 1 paras 182–184; CAA 2001, Sch 2 para 48; ITTOIA 2005, Sch 1 paras 207, 209*].

For patents, see **70.58** below.

Simon's Taxes. See **B5.343–B5.348.**

Mines, quarries etc.

[70.56] A key issue with regard to the profits from this business is whether any expenditure is capital or revenue in nature, and there is a considerable body of case law that considers this in respect of various items of expenditure. See **14.1** *et seq.* **CAPITAL ALLOWANCES** for mining etc. expenditure allowable. The relevant legislation which applied before 1 April 1986 originated from 1945 and may therefore affect any pre-1945 decisions below. See also **61.23 PROFIT COMPUTATIONS** in respect of 'mineral royalties' under a lease, licence or agreement conferring a right to win and work minerals in the UK or under a sale or conveyance of such minerals.

The cost of sinking (*Coltness Iron Co v Black* (1881) 1 TC 287, HL), deepening (*Bonner v Basset Mines* (1912) 6 TC 146) or 'de-watering' (*United Collieries v CIR* (1929) 12 TC 1248, Ct of Sess) a pit is capital.

A lump sum paid at the end of a mining lease for surface damage was held capital (*Robert Addie & Sons v CIR* (1924) 8 TC 671, Ct of Sess) but not periodic payments during the currency of the lease based on acreage worked (*O'Grady v Bullcroft Main Collieries* (1932) 17 TC 93). *Bullcroft* was decided before the enactment of what was *ICTA 1988, s 119* and is now *CTA 2009, s 270* and rents and tonnage payments for the right to withdraw surface support are easements within *s 119* (*CIR v New Sharlston Collieries Co Ltd* [1937] 1 KB 583, [1937] 1 All ER 86, 21 TC 69), CA. For shortworkings, see *Broughton & Plas Power v Kirkpatrick* (1884) 2 TC 69; *CIR v Cranford Ironstone* (1942) 29 TC 113. Provision for the future costs of abandoning an oil field and of restoring hired equipment used therein to its original state held capital (*RTZ Oil and Gas Ltd v Elliss* (1987) 61 TC 132).

For HMRC's view of the treatment of payments by mining concerns to landowners for restoration for surface damage, see HMRC Business Income Manual BIM62025. In particular, a payment of compensation for ascertained past damage is allowable, as is a provision for such expenditure where made in accordance with generally accepted accounting practice and accurately quantified.

Purchase of unworked deposits by sand and gravel merchant held capital (*Stow Bardolph Gravel Co Ltd v Poole* (1954) 35 TC 459, CA) as was purchase of land with nitrate deposits by chemical manufacturer (*Alianza Co v Bell* (1905) 5 TC 172, HL) and payment by oil company for unwon oil in wells it took over (*Hughes v British Burmah Petroleum* (1932) 17 TC 286). See also *Golden Horse Shoe v Thurgood* (1933) 18 TC 280, CA (purchase of tailings for gold extraction, allowable), and *CIR v Broomhouse Brick* (1952) 34 TC 1, Ct of Sess (purchase of blaes for brick manufacture, allowable).

See generally HMRC Business Income Manual BIM62000–62085.

Production wells etc.

The costs of drilling the second and subsequent production wells in an area are not generally allowable. [*CTA 2009, s 137; ICTA 1988, s 91C; ITTOIA 2005, Sch 1 para 71*]. Although not specifically stated in the statute, this prohibition applies particularly to intangible drilling costs. For a discussion of this, see HMRC Oil Taxation Manual OT26237. Such costs may attract mineral extraction capital allowances (see **14.1** *et seq.* **CAPITAL ALLOWANCES — MINERAL EXTRACTION**).

Simon's Taxes. See **B5.651–B5.653.**

Miscellaneous receipts

[70.57] Card winnings of club proprietor, trading receipts (*Burdge v Pyne* (1968) 45 TC 320). For lotteries and football pools, see **70.5** above.

Mutual concerns, distribution of assets from

If a deduction has been allowed (in computing trading profits) for a payment to a corporate mutual concern for the purposes of its mutual business and the company receives a distribution in money or money's worth upon the winding-up or dissolution of the mutual concern, the amount or value received is a trading receipt. This applies only if the assets being distributed represent profits of the mutual concern. It does not apply to distributions of chargeable gains; this has statutory authority for accounting periods ending on or after 1 April 2009 (and see **70.2** above) and was apparently HMRC practice previously (see Change 24 listed in Annex 1 to the Explanatory Notes to *CTA 2009*). If the trade has ceased by the time of the distribution, the amount or value received is a post-cessation receipt (within **70.16** above); for accounting periods ending before 1 April 2009, such amount or value was chargeable under *Sch D, Case VI* and not treated as a post-cessation receipt. [*CTA 2009, s 101; ICTA 1988, s 491; ITTOIA 2005, Sch 1 para 189*]. See generally **56 MUTUAL COMPANIES.**

Overpayments received, due to errors by customers or their banks which the taxpayer neither caused nor facilitated, held not to be trading receipts (*Anise Ltd v Hammond* [2003] STC (SCD) 258).

Sales of assets

See *T Beynon & Co v Ogg* (1918) 7 TC 125(profits of colliery agent from deals in wagons held trading receipts); *Gloucester Railway Carriage v CIR* (1925) 12 TC 720, HL (sale by wagon manufacturer of wagons previously let, held trading receipts); *Bonner v Frood* (1934) 18 TC 488 (sale of rounds by credit trader, held trading receipts).

Timber purchases and sales

For purchases and sales of standing timber by timber merchants see *Murray v CIR* (1951) 32 TC 238, Ct of Sess; *McLellan, Rawson & Co v Newall* (1955) 36 TC 117; *Hood Barrs v CIR (No 2)* (1957) 37 TC 188, HL; *Hopwood v C N Spencer Ltd* (1964) 42 TC 169; *Russell v Hird and Mercer* (1983) 57 TC 127. For sales of trees by farmer see *Elmes v Trembath* (1934) 19 TC 72.

General

See also *Thompson v Magnesium Elektron* (1943) 26 TC 1, CA (payments based on purchases, held trading receipts); *British Commonwealth International Newsfilm v Mahany* (1962) 40 TC 550, HL (payments to meet operating expenses, trading receipts).

Simon's Taxes. See **B1.431.**

Patents

[70.58] For corporation tax purposes, expenditure and receipts in respect of intellectual property acquired or created **on or after 1 April 2002** falls within the intangible assets regime. See in particular the commencement and transitional rules for that regime at **48.36 INTANGIBLE ASSETS.**

Sums received on the sale of patent rights may, dependent on the facts, be trading receipts (*Rees Roturbo Development v Ducker* [1928] 1 KB 506, 13 TC 366, CA; *Brandwood v Banker* (1928) 14 TC 44; *CIR v Rustproof Metal Window* (1947) 29 TC 243, CA, and cf *Harry Ferguson (Motors) v CIR* (1951) 33 TC 15). Other sums are taxable under *CTA 2009, ss 912–920; ICTA 1988, s 524*, see **61.18 PROFIT COMPUTATIONS.**

Where a company held a patent for renovating car tyres, lump sums received by it under arrangements for giving the payer a *de facto* franchise in his area, were held to be capital receipts (*Margerison v Tyresoles Ltd* (1942) 25 TC 59).

For know-how and trade marks, see **70.55** and **71.71** respectively.

Simon's Taxes. See **B2.456, B5.310.**

Pooling of profits

[70.59] Where traders pool profits or act together in consortia but so as not to form **PARTNERSHIPS (62)** or trade jointly (cf *Gardner and Bowring Hardy v CIR* (1930) 15 TC 602, Ct of Sess; *Geo Hall & Son v Platt* (1954) 35 TC 440) each trader's share of the pooled profits will normally be treated as a receipt of his main trade and any payment under the arrangement by one trader to another will be deductible in computing his profits (*Moore v Stewarts & Lloyds Ltd* (1905) 6 TC 501, Ct of Sess, and cf *United Steel v Cullington (No 1)* (1939) 23 TC 71, CA). In *Utol Ltd v CIR* (1943) 25 TC 517 payments by one company to another under a profit sharing arrangement were held to be dividends payable less tax under the law then in force. For compensation received on the termination of a profit sharing arrangement see *Van den Berghs* at **70.27**(b) above.

For the tax treatment of consortium losses and relief, see **39 GROUP RELIEF.**

Private Finance Initiative ('PFI') projects

[70.60] For a series of articles on the tax aspects of PFI projects (dealing with the introduction by the public sector body of surplus land, or cash derived there from, with stamp duty considerations, with income arising from leases of fully serviced accommodation and with the scope of a PFI operator's trade), see Revenue Tax Bulletin April 1999 pp 642–645 issue 40, October 1999 pp 694–697 issue 43, August 2002 p 950 issue 60. See also HMRC Business Income Manual BIM64000–64405.

Property sales and other property receipts

[70.61] As to whether a trade of property dealing is carried on, see **70.13** above; for rents receivable, see **70.54** above. For builders and property developers generally, see HMRC Business Income Manual BIM51500–51665. The trade of furnished holiday lettings is considered at **62.6 PROPERTY INCOME.**

Sales of property by builders in special circumstances have been considered in a number of cases. Profits held trading receipts:

- *Spiers & Son v Ogden* (1932) 17 TC 117 — building activities extended;
- *Sharpless v Rees* (1940) 23 TC 361 — sale of land acquired for hobby abandoned for health reasons;
- *Shadford v H Fairweather & Co* (1966) 43 TC 291 — sale of site after development plan dropped;
- *Snell v Rosser, Thomas & Co* (1967) 44 TC 343 — sale of land surplus to requirements;
- *Bowie v Reg Dunn (Builders)* (1974) 49 TC 469 — sale of land acquired with business;
- *Smart v Lowndes* (1978) 52 TC 436 — sale of land in wife's name.

Sales of property built but let meanwhile held trading in *J & C Oliver v Farnsworth* (1956) 37 TC 51; *James Hobson & Sons v Newall* (1957) 37 TC 609; *W M Robb Ltd v Page* (1971) 47 TC 465 and this notwithstanding active building given up (*Speck v Morton* (1972) 48 TC 476; *Granville Building Co v Oxby* (1954) 35 TC 245). But in *Harvey v Caulcott* (1952) 33 TC 159 the sales were held realisations of investments and in *West v Phillips* (1958) 38 TC 203 some houses were treated as investments and others as trading stock. See also *Andrew v Taylor* (1965) 42 TC 557, CA. Sales of houses retained after business *transferred* held sales of investments in *Bradshaw v Blunden (No 1)* (1956) 36 TC 397; *Seaward v Varty* (1962) 40 TC 523, CA. See also *Hesketh Estates v Craddock* (1942) 25 TC 1 (profit on sale of brine baths held trading receipt of mixed business including land development).

For house sales subject to ground rents etc, see *CIR v John Emery & Sons* [1937] AC 91, 20 TC 213, HL; *B G Utting & Co Ltd v Hughes* (1940) 23 TC 174, HL; *McMillan v CIR* (1942) 24 TC 417, Ct of Sess; *Heather v Redfern & Sons* (1944) 26 TC 119. For ground rents (England) and feu duties (Scotland) there should be credited the lower of their market value and cost, the cost being taken as the proportion of the cost of the land and building in the ratio of the market value to the sum of the market value and the sale price. For ground annuals (Scotland) which are perpetual the realisable value is brought in. The right to receive the rent then becomes part of the fixed capital of the trade, whose subsequent sale is not taken into account for corporation tax purposes. Any premiums on the grant of leases are part of the sale proceeds.

Turf sales by a farmer were held to be farming receipts in *Lowe v J W Ashmore Ltd* (1970) 46 TC 597. For timber sales see **70.57** above.

A lump sum received by a property investment company in return for the assignment for a five-year term of a stream of rental income was held to be a capital receipt for part disposal of the company's interest (*CIR v John Lewis Properties plc* [2003] STC 117, CA), but see now **62.16 PROPERTY INCOME** as regards special rent factoring provisions.

Any excess of allowable deductions over rent received by a builder from property held as trading stock may be allowed as a trading expense (HMRC Business Income Manual BIM51555).

In *Rosemoor Investments v Insp of Taxes*, [2002] STC (SCD) 325, it was decided that an investment company's participation in a property refinance scheme was by way of investment, not by way of trade; for further details, see **70.54** investment income, above.

Annuities under *Agriculture Act 1967* for giving up (after attaining age of 55) uncommercial agricultural land are treated as earned income and receipts of grants under the same *Act* for the same reason are exempt from capital gains tax. [*TCGA 1992, s 249*].

Where sales of land etc., are capital, the profits on assets disposed of are liable to capital gains tax. But see also **5.16 ANTI-AVOIDANCE** for provisions affecting land or land development. [*CTA 2010, ss 815–833; ICTA 1988, s 776; CTA 2009, Sch 1 para 231*].

For transactions not at market value see **71.66 TRADING EXPENSES AND DEDUCTIONS.**

Simon's Taxes. See B.2 on transactions in land.

Rents etc. for business premises

Reverse premiums

[70.62] In *New Zealand Commissioner of Inland Revenue v Wattie and another* (1998) 72 TC 639, PC, a decision which has persuasive authority in the UK, it was held that a lump sum paid by a landlord to a prospective tenant as an inducement to enter into a lease at an above-market rental (generally known as a reverse premium) was a receipt of a capital nature. Legislation was introduced to counter this decision, and it applies in relation to any 'reverse premium' received broadly after 9 March 1999. For these purposes, a '*reverse premium*' is a payment or other benefit received by way of inducement in connection with a transaction (the '*property transaction*') entered into by the company or a person 'connected' with the company (see below), where:

(a) the property transaction is one under which the company or connected person becomes entitled to an estate or interest in, or a right in or over, land; and
(b) the payment (or other benefit) is made (or provided) by:

- (i) the person (the '*grantor*') by whom that estate, interest or right is granted, or was granted at an earlier time; or
- (ii) a person 'connected' with the grantor; or
- (iii) a nominee of (or a person acting on the directions of) the grantor or a person connected with the grantor.

As regards (b)(i) above, the use of the word 'grantor' means that the provisions do not apply when a freehold is conveyed. The most common occasion on which the provisions will apply will be a payment by a landlord as an inducement to a tenant to take a new lease, but they may apply where an existing tenant pays a new tenant an inducement to take over the remaining term of a lease if (and only if) (b)(ii) or (iii) applies to the existing tenant (Revenue Tax Bulletin December 1999 pp 711–713 issue 44).

For the purposes of these provisions, persons are '*connected*' with each other if they are connected within *CTA 2010, s 1122* (see **25 CONNECTED PERSONS**) at any time during the period when the 'property arrangements' are entered into. The '*property arrangements*' comprise the property transaction and any arrangements entered into in connection with it (whether earlier, simultaneously or later).

A reverse premium is treated as a receipt of a revenue nature. Where the property transaction is entered into by the recipient of the reverse premium for the purposes of a trade carried on (or to be carried on), the reverse premium must be taken into account in computing the trading profits. In any other case, the reverse premium is to be treated as a receipt of a UK property business, or (as the case may be) an overseas property business (see **62 PROPERTY INCOME**), carried on by the recipient.

It is understood that accountancy principles require the receipt to be brought into account by spreading over the period of the lease or, if shorter, to the first rent review. This treatment must normally be followed for tax purposes (see **70.19** above) but, as an anti-avoidance measure, is overridden where:

- (A) two or more parties to the property arrangements (see above) are connected persons (see above); and
- (B) the terms of the those arrangements differ significantly from those which, at that time and under prevailing market conditions, would be regarded as reasonable and normal between persons dealing at arm's length in the open market.

In such case, the full amount or value of the reverse premium must be brought into account in the period of account in which the property transaction (see above) is entered into or, where applicable, the first period of account of the trade which the recipient subsequently begins to carry on.

For accounting periods ending on or before 5 April 2005 or on or after 1 April 2009 none of these provisions apply where the person entering into the transaction is an individual and the property in question is, or will be, occupied by him as his only or main residence. Nor do they apply, for *any* accounting period, to the extent that the payment or benefit is consideration for the first leg of a sale and leaseback arrangement within **5.17** or **5.18 ANTI-AVOIDANCE**) or is taken into account under *CAA 2001, s 532* (contributions to expenditure) to reduce the recipient's expenditure qualifying for capital allowances (see **10.5 CAPITAL ALLOWANCES — INTRODUCTION**).

[*CTA 2009, ss 96–100, Sch 2 para 24; FA 1999, s 54, Sch 6; CAA 2001, Sch 2 para 104; SI 2004 No 2310, Sch para 51; ITTOIA 2005, Sch 1 para 509; CTA 2010, Sch 1 para 596*].

It will be seen that a reverse premium within the above provisions is not confined to a lump sum payment and that 'other benefit' may include, for example, a contribution to the tenant's costs or an assumption of the recipient's liabilities under an existing lease. 'Other benefit' must, however, represent money or something capable of being turned into money. It does not include a sum foregone or deferred by the provider, rather than actually expended, such as a rent free period. See the article in the Revenue Tax Bulletin December 1999 pp 711–713 issue 44, in particular in relation to the meeting of the tenant's costs.

For HMRC approach to these rules, see HMRC Business Income Manual BIM41050–BIM41145.

Simon's Taxes. See **B2.208, B2.447, B2.465, B6.205**.

General

[70.63] See **5.17 ANTI-AVOIDANCE** [*CTA 2010, ss 834–848*] regarding restrictions where there is a lease-back at a non-commercial rent and **5.18 ANTI-AVOIDANCE** [*CTA 2010, ss 849–862*] for taxation of capital sums received on certain lease-backs.

Simon's Taxes. See **B2.465**.

Shares and securities

[70.64] For whether a trade of 'share dealing' carried on see **70.14** above. For transactions not at market value see **71.66 TRADING EXPENSES AND DEDUCTIONS**.

Profits and losses on realisations of investments by a bank in the course of its business enter into its trade (*Case I*) profits (*Punjab Co-operative Bank v Lahore IT Commr* (1940) 19 ATC 533, PC, and see *Frasers (Glasgow) Bank v CIR* (1963) 40 TC 698, HL) and similarly for insurance companies (*Northern Assce Co v Russell* (1889) 2 TC 551; *General Reinsurance Co v Tomlinson* (1970) 48 TC 81 and contrast *CIR v Scottish Automobile* (1931) 16 TC 381, Ct of Sess). Profits/losses held capital in *Stott v Hoddinott* (1916) 7 TC 85 (investments acquired by architect to secure contracts); *Jacobs Young & Co v Harris* (1926) 11 TC 221 (shares held by merchanting company in subsidiary wound up); *Alliance & Dublin Consumers' Gas Co v Davis* (1926) 5 ATC 717 (investments of gas company earmarked for reserve fund). A profit by a property dealing company on the sale of shares acquired in connection with a property transaction was held a trading receipt (*Associated London Properties v Henriksen* (1944) 26 TC 46, CA) but contrast *Fundfarms Developments v Parsons* (1969) 45 TC 707 and see now **5 ANTI-AVOIDANCE**.

Shares allotted for mining concessions granted by company dealing in concessions held trading receipts at market value (*Gold Coast Selection Trust v Humphrey* (1948) 30 TC 209, HL). See also *Murphy v Australian Machinery & Investment Co* (1948) 30 TC 244, CA, and *Scottish & Canadian Investment Co v Easson* (1922) 8 TC 265, Ct of Sess.

For options, see *Varty v British South Africa Co* (1965) 42 TC 406, HL (no profits or loss until shares sold). See also *Walker v Cater Securities* (1974) 49 TC 625.

Conversion etc. of shares and securities held as circulating capital

[70.65] Where a new holding of shares or securities (as defined) is issued in exchange for an original holding a profit on sale of which would fall to be treated as part of trading profits of a banking, insurance or share dealing business, the transaction is treated as not involving any disposal of the original holding, the new holding being treated as the same asset as the original holding. This applies only to transactions which result in the new holding being equated with the original holding under *TCGA 1992, ss 132–136* (capital gains rollover in cases of conversion etc.) or *TCGA 1992, s 134* (compensation stock).

For accounting periods ending before 1 April 2009 (and see **70.2** above), the above rules applied only if the company was beneficially entitled to the shares or securities in question; this condition has been dropped (see Change 33 listed in Annex 1 to the Explanatory Notes to *CTA 2009*).

The above rules do not apply to shares or securities for which unrealised profits or losses (computed on a mark to market basis by reference to fair value) are brought into account in the period of account in which the transaction takes place. Where consideration is receivable in addition to the new holding, the above rule apply only to a proportion of the original holding, computed by reference to the market value of the new holding and the other consideration received.

[*CTA 2009, s 129, Sch 2 para 28; ICTA 1988, s 473; FA 2002, s 67; ITTOIA 2005, Sch 1 para 183*].

Dealers in securities etc.

[70.66] Any distribution by a UK-resident company (or payment representative of such a distribution) *received by* a company as a receipt of its trade is taken into account (exclusive of any tax credit) in computing trading profits. Accordingly the normal exemption from corporation tax of UK company distributions under *CTA 2009, s 1285(2)* (previously *ICTA 1988, s 208*) does not apply.

Any payment *made by* a trading company which is representative of a UK company distribution is allowed as a deduction in computing trading profits. Subject to *CTA 2010, s 799* (previously *ICTA 1988, Sch 23A para 7A*) in relation to manufactured payments under arrangements having an unallowable purpose — see **5.9 ANTI-AVOIDANCE**.

For accounting periods ending before 1 April 2009 (and see **70.2** above), these provisions were drafted so as to apply only to dealers in securities; it is likely that this will continue to be their main practical application (see Change 34 listed in Annex 1 to the Explanatory Notes to *CTA 2009*).

[*CTA 2009, s 130; ICTA 1988, s 95; FA 2003, Sch 43 Pt 3(6); FA 2004, s 137(2)(6); ITTOIA 2005, Sch 1 para 74*].

See **5.37 ANTI-AVOIDANCE** as regards arrangements to pass on the value of dividend tax credits.

For accounting periods beginning on or after 1 January 2005, in cases where, in accordance with generally accepted accounting practice (see **70.18** above), profits and losses on the sale of securities are calculated by reference to the fair value of the securities and taken to reserves rather than profit or loss account, they are nevertheless brought into account in computing trading profits. [*CTA 2009, s 128; ICTA 1988, s 472A; FA 2004, s 54(1)*].

The *Finance Act 2011* amends the treatment of gilts, so that gilt-edged securities whose return is calculated by reference to an index of prices published by the Office for National Statistics are taxed in the same way as gilt-edged securities linked to the retail price index. A new *s 399(4)* is inserted into *CTA 2009* which provides a new definition of index-linked gilt which refers to an index of prices published by the Statistics board. The change will apply to index-linked gilt-edged securities issued on or after the date of Royal Assent.

FISMA levies

[70.67] In computing the profits of a trade carried on by a company authorised for the purposes of *Financial Services and Markets Act 2000* ('FISMA'), a deduction is available for certain levies payable under that Act, so far as not otherwise deductible. A deduction is similarly available for sums paid by a company as a result of an award of costs under costs rules within the ambit of that Act. Certain repayments under that Act must be brought into account as a trading receipt. For accounting periods ending on or after 1 April 2009 (and see **70.2** above), a deduction is available for some levies and costs that would not previously have been deductible (see Change 22 listed in Annex 1 to the Explanatory Notes to *CTA 2009*). [*CTA 2009, ss 92, 104; ICTA 1988, s 76A; Financial Services and Markets Act 2000, s 411; SI 2001 Nos 3538, 3629*].

Extra return on new issues of securities

[70.68] Where:

(a) securities of a particular kind are issued (being the original issue of securities of that kind);
(b) new securities of the same kind are issued subsequently;
(c) a sum (the 'extra return') is payable by the issuer in respect of the new securities, to reflect the fact that interest is accruing on the old securities and calculated accordingly; and

(d) the issue price of the new securities includes an element (separately identified or not) representing payment for the extra return,

the extra return is treated for all tax purposes (except corporation tax) as a payment of interest, but the issuer is not entitled to tax relief, either as a deduction in computing profits or otherwise as a deduction or set-off, for the payment. [*ITA 2007, s 845*].

Euroconversion of shares

[70.69] Costs incurred in respect of the conversion of a trading company's shares or other securities from the currency of a State which has adopted the euro into euro (a 'euroconversion', see *SI 1998 No 3177, Reg 3*) which is effected solely by the issue of replacement shares and other securities are allowable as a trading deduction. In the case of a company with investment business (or, subject to special provisions, a company carrying on life assurance business), such costs are treated as management expenses (see **51.4 INVESTMENT COMPANIES AND INVESTMENT BUSINESS**). [*SI 1998 No 3177, Pt II; SI 2004 No 2310, Art 77; SI 2008 No 2647*].

General

[70.70] See also **5 ANTI-AVOIDANCE**, including transactions in securities to obtain tax advantage [*CTA 2010, s 731*].

For share transactions entered into to secure tax advantages see **70.4** above and for transactions in dividend-stripping before the enactment of existing legislation see Tolley's Tax Cases.

Sound recordings income

[70.71] Receipts from disposal of the original master version of the sound recording are treated as revenue receipts in the period of account (or if no accounts are made up, accounting period) in which they are received. An '*original master version*' is a master tape or master audio disc and the term '*sound recording*' does not include a film soundtrack. Such receipts can include amounts received from the disposal of any interest or rights in or over the original master version (including those created by the disposal), and insurance, compensation or similar money derived from the original master version.

See also **70.30** above with regard to films and the new regime for film tax relief applicable to companies for films commenced after 1 January 2007 (or any expenditure incurred after 31 March 2008).

[*CTA 2009, ss 150, 151, Sch 1 para 679; FA 2006, ss 48–50*].

Subscriptions and contributions

[70.72] For any receipts from trade and professional associations see **71.67 TRADING EXPENSES AND DEDUCTIONS.**

Subsidies, grants etc.

[70.73] For payments under the **Business Start-up scheme**, see Tolley's Income Tax under Trading Income (Subsidies, grants etc.). Where the business is run through a company, the payments are made to the individual as agent of the company and are treated as miscellaneous income of the company. (HMRC Business Income Manual BIM40400, 40405).

Farming support payments

See **70.29** above.

Fishing grants

For the tax treatment of decommissioning grants, laying-up grants, exploratory voyage grants and joint venture grants under *SI 1983 No 1883*, see HMRC Business Income Manual BIM57001.

Football pools promoters

See **71 TRADING EXPENSES AND DEDUCTIONS.**

Industrial development grants

Grants to a company under *Industrial Development Act 1982, s 7* or *s 8* (or corresponding NI legislation) are trading receipts, unless the grant is designated as made towards the cost of specified capital expenditure or as compensation for loss of capital assets or, is made towards the meeting of a corporation tax liability. [*CTA 2009, s 102; ICTA 1988, s 93; ITTOIA 2005, Sch 1 para* 72].

An earlier interest relief grant under *Industry Act 1972* was held to be assessable in *Burman v Thorn Domestic Appliances (Electrical) Ltd* (1981) 55 TC 493, as was a similar grant undifferentiated between revenue and capital in *Ryan v Crabtree Denims Ltd* (1987) 60 TC 183, applying *Gayjon Processes Ltd* (below) and distinguishing *Seaham Harbour* (below).

Research grant by trading company to medical practitioner held assessable (*Duff v Williamson* (1973) 49 TC 1). For research grants and fellowships generally, see HMRC Business Income Manual BIM65151.

Temporary employment subsidy was paid under *Employment and Training Act 1973, s 5* (as amended by *Employment Protection Act 1975, Sch 14 para* 2) as a flat-rate weekly payment or (in the textile, clothing and footwear industries) by way of reimbursement of payments made to workers on short time.

Such payments were held to be taxable as trading receipts in *Poulter v Gayjon Processes Ltd* (1985) 58 TC 350, distinguishing the grants made by the Unemployment Grants Committee in *Seaham Harbour* (below).

Unemployment grants

Subsidy to dock company (from Unemployment Grants Committee) for extension work to keep men in employment held, although the grant was made in terms of interest, not to be a 'trade receipt' for tax purposes (*Seaham Harbour v Crook* (1931) 16 TC 333, HL).

See **10.8 CAPITAL ALLOWANCES — INTRODUCTION** for effect of grants and subsidies on capital allowances.

Telecommunications rights

[70.74] See *CTA 2009, ss 892, 897; FA 2002, Sch 29 paras 127, 128* for application, in relation to telecommunications rights, of the special provisions for the taxation of **INTANGIBLE FIXED ASSETS** (**48**) which apply to assets acquired or created on or after 1 April 2002. (See in particular the commencement and transitional rules for that regime at **48.36**). The provisions below apply to rights acquired before that date.

Special rules applied in relation to licences granted under *Wireless Telegraphy Act 1949, s 1* as a result of bidding for such licences under *Wireless Telegraphy Act 1998, s 3* regulations, and to rights derived directly or indirectly there from. They also applied to indefeasible rights to use a telecommunications cable system ('IRUs') acquired after 20 March 2000, unless they were acquired from an 'associate' (within **22.9 CLOSE COMPANIES**) or an 'associated company' (within **22.10 CLOSE COMPANIES**) or, in relation to an individual, being a company of which that individual has control (within **22.6 CLOSE COMPANIES**) which acquired them on or before that date, and to derived rights.

Acquisition costs and disposal proceeds in respect of such rights which, in accordance with generally accepted accounting practice (see **70.19** above), may be taken into account in determining accounting profit or loss, and which are so taken into account in any relevant statutory accounts required under *Companies Act 2006, s 394* (or NI or foreign equivalent), are treated as being of a revenue nature in computing profits chargeable to corporation tax. This applies equally to costs of extension of attached rights or of cancellation or restriction of rights attached to derivative rights, and to receipts from cancellation or restriction of attached rights or from granting derivative rights or extensions of rights attached to derivative rights.

Similar treatment applies to amounts in respect of the revaluation of such rights provided that, in accordance with generally accepted accounting practice (see **70.19** above), they fall to be taken into account for accounting purposes, whether or not they may be so taken into account in determining profit or loss or are so taken into account in any relevant statutory accounts. The period of account for which such an amount is taken into account for tax purposes is that in which it is recognised for accounting purposes in accordance with generally accepted accounting practice.

Where the taxpayer company is a member of a group of companies (within *Companies Act 2006, s 474(1)* or NI or foreign equivalent) which is required to produce consolidated group accounts (within *Companies Act 2006 s 399* or NI or foreign equivalent), the company's accounting policies, and method of applying those policies, in respect of rights within these provisions must not be more cautious than that adopted in the group accounts. This applies in relation to each group of which the company is a member, if there is more than one.

[*ITTOIA 2005, ss 146–148; Sch 1 paras 517, 523; Sch 2 paras 39, 40*].

See generally HMRC Corporate Intangibles Research and Development Manual, CIRD70000 *et seq*. For an article giving HMRC's view on the interpretation of *FA 2000, Sch 23* (as replaced by *ITTOIA 2005, Pt 2 Ch 10*), see Revenue Tax Bulletin December 2000 pp 815–817, issue 50.

Tied petrol stations receipts

[70.75] For tied licensed premises see **70.23** above.

In the hands of the retailer, exclusivity payments from the oil companies were held to be capital, when in respect of capital expenditure incurred by the retailer (*CIR v Coia* (1959) 38 TC 334, Ct of Sess; *McLaren v Needham* (1960) 39 TC 37; *Walter W Saunders Ltd v Dixon* (1962) 40 TC 329; *McClymont v Glover (Inspector of Taxes)* [2004] STC (SCD) 54) but revenue, when in respect of repairs etc. (*McLaren v Needham* above) or sales promotion (*Evans v Wheatley* (1958) 38 TC 216) or where petrol sales were a relatively small part (some 30%) of the company's turnover (*Tanfield Ltd v Carr* [1999] STC (SCD) 213).

For a summary of HMRC's view of such arrangements, see HMRC Business Income Manual BIM40300.

Tonnage tax

[70.76] Tonnage tax is an alternative charge to corporation tax in respect of certain shipping profits. 'Qualifying companies', or groups of companies of which at least one member is a 'qualifying company', may elect for their corporation tax profits from the activities of 'qualifying ships' to be calculated by reference to the net tonnage of each of those ships, and for losses to be left out of account for corporation tax purposes. All 'qualifying companies' within a group must be taxed on the same basis. The regime was amended by *FA 2005* to implement the recommendations of the 'Post Implementation Review of Tonnage Tax', issued by the Revenue and Department of Transport in December 2004, and to ensure compliance with European Community guidelines on state aid to the maritime transport industry.

A '*qualifying company*' is a company within the charge to corporation tax which operates 'qualifying ships' which are strategically and commercially managed in the UK (for which see Revenue Tax Bulletin October 2000 p 787, issue 48). Certain temporary cessations from operating any 'qualifying ships' may be disregarded.

'*Qualifying ships*' are broadly ships carrying on certain activities which are of at least 100 tons gross tonnage, but excluding fishing and factory support vessels, pleasure craft, harbour and river ferries, offshore installations (within *CTA 2010, s 1132* or, for accounting periods ending before 1 April 2004, offshore installations such as fixed and floating oil rigs and platforms, floating production, storage and offtake vessels), existing dedicated shuttle tankers subject to the petroleum revenue tax regime, dredgers (other than, from 1 July

2005, certain 'qualifying dredgers' as defined), and any vessel whose main purpose is the provision of goods or services normally provided on land. Other types of vessel may be added to or removed from the excluded categories by Treasury order. The activities in which they must be engaged are transportation by sea, the provision of marine assistance or the provision of transport for services necessarily provided at sea. They may also, to a limited extent, include certain secondary and incidental activities (see *SI 2000 No 2303, Reg 3*). From broadly 1 July 2005, flagging rules apply for qualifying dredgers and tugs which must be registered in a member state to qualify for tonnage tax (or other state aids). Other ships may be registered under any flag but where the relevant conditions are met, operators bringing 'new' ships within tonnage tax will have to do so under a member state registration. Otherwise, ships can still qualify if they are re-registered to a Community flag within three months of first operation. A '*new*' ship for these purposes is, broadly, one which is brought within tonnage tax (in a financial year which is not excepted by Treasury Order) after the later of 1 July 2005 or the end of the first accounting period in which the company (or group) became a tonnage tax company but the financial years 2005, 2006 and 2007 are excepted (see *SI 2005 No 1480; SI 2006 No 333*; and *SI 2007 No 850*). HMRC have announced that financial year 2008 will not be excepted (see HMRC Brief 4/08).

Foreign dividends from non-UK resident shipping companies are (subject to conditions) also included in the profits covered by an election, as is any loan relationship credit (see **54.6 LOAN RELATIONSHIPS**), any derivative contract credit (or, for accounting periods beginning before 1 October 2002, any profit on an interest rate or currency contract (see **30.2**) or, for accounting periods beginning before 1 October 2002, any exchange gain which would otherwise be treated as trading income. Otherwise, investment income is excluded.

Profits within the tonnage tax regime are 'ring-fenced', with appropriate anti-avoidance measures to prevent exploitation of the regime, and there are similarly capital allowance 'ring-fencing' provisions (as amended by *FA 2005*) (see also *SI 2000 No 2303, regs 4–8* as regards machinery and plant written-down values on exit from the regime or on transfer to use for offshore activities). No chargeable gains will arise during the currency of the election in relation to assets used for the qualifying activities, and balancing charges (on the disposal of assets for which capital allowances had previously been given) will be phased out using a sliding scale.

Capital allowances to lessors leasing to companies within the tonnage tax regime are similarly 'ring-fenced' and restricted.

However, with regard to lessors, provisions have been introduced in the *Finance Act 2011, s 57* to equalise the capital writing down allowances for ships leased to a company which has elected into the tonnage tax regime, with assets held outside the regime. The measure will have effect for chargeable periods ending on or after 1 January 2011 and a lessor will be able to claim writing down allowances at the main rate for capital allowances (for ships which are not long life assets, otherwise at the special rate (10%) for long life assets), on the first £40 million of expenditure, and at the special rate (10%) on the second £40 million of expenditure. See also Tax Information and Impact Note (TIIN) 'Leasing into Tonnage Tax', 9 December 2010.

Special provisions apply to the chartering in of qualifying ships and joint charters and to the chartering out of short-term over-capacity. There are also special rules for offshore activities in the UK sector of the continental shelf, and for group mergers and demergers.

Companies participating in the tonnage tax regime must also meet a minimum training obligation (for which see also *SI 2000 No 2129* as amended).

For existing qualifying companies, the *election* initially had to be made within twelve months from 28 July 2000. If the company was not a qualifying company on that date, it may have been made up to twelve months after its first becoming a qualifying company. In the case of a group no member of which was a qualifying company on 28 July 2000, it may have been made within twelve months of a group company first becoming a qualifying company, provided that the group is not substantially the same as a group which at any earlier time had a member which was a qualifying company. The election generally had effect from the beginning of the accounting period in which it was made (or, where that accounting period began before 1 January 2000, from the beginning of the following accounting period), subject to earlier or later effect in certain cases with HMRC agreement.

The Treasury has, however, provided a further opportunity for an election into tonnage tax by *SI 2005 No 1449* which allows for an election to be made at any time during the period beginning on 1 July 2005 and ending on 31 December 2006. The election in relation to this further period generally has effect from the beginning of the accounting period in which it was made (or, where that accounting period began before 1 January 2005, from the beginning of the following accounting period), subject to earlier or later effect in certain cases with HMRC agreement.

Special provisions apply in relation to mergers and demergers.

The election normally remains in effect for ten years for so long as the company (or group) qualifies and is not excluded, and (subject to the training requirements having been met) may at any time be renewed (such renewal being treated in effect as a valid new election).

The election ceases to have effect where a withdrawal notice is given by the company (or group) during a period beginning on 7 April 2005 and ending on 31 March 2006 provided the election in respect of which the withdrawal notice is given was in force for the whole of the three-year period ending on 7 April 2005. The withdrawal notice has effect at the end of the accounting period preceding the first accounting period of the company to begin after 1 July 2005 and is subject to transitional provisions. The Treasury may provide further opportunities for the withdrawal of elections by statutory instrument.

There is provision for exit charges on a company leaving the tonnage tax regime, and a bar on re-entry to the regime within ten years.

The Treasury may make provision by regulations for the application of the above provisions to activities carried on by a company in partnership. See now *SI 2000 No 2303, Regs 8–13*.

[*FA 2000, s 82, Sch 22; CAA 2001, Sch 2 para 108; FA 2003, s 169, Sch 32; FA 2004, Sch 27 para 7, Sch 42 Pt 2(18); FA 2005, s 93, Sch 7; FA 2006, Sch 9 paras 8–10; SI 2005 No 1449; SI 2005 No 1480; CTA 2009, Sch 1 para 470*].

A very lengthy and detailed Statement of Practice, setting out administrative practice for the operation of the entire regime and structured in the same order as the legislation, is contained in HMRC Statement of Practice, SP 4/00. Draft legislation was published by HMRC in a technical note early in 2008, but the legislation was not included in *FA 2008*, and HMRC's technical note was withdrawn while EC obtains member states' views on some issues relating to tonnage tax.

Unclaimed balances

[70.77] Unclaimed balances for which a firm was liable to account were held not assessable despite their being distributed to partners (*Morley v Tattersall* (1938) 22 TC 51, CA). Such balances held by a pawnbroker are, however, assessable when claimants' rights expire (*Jay's, the Jewellers v CIR* (1947) 29 TC 274), and deposits on garments not collected were held trade receipts assessable when received (*Elson v Prices Tailors* (1962) 40 TC 671). The fact that trading receipts were subsequently, and correctly, treated for accountancy purposes as an element in a sale of fixed assets did not alter their nature for tax purposes (*Tapemaze Ltd v Melluish* (2000) 73 TC 167). In *Anise Ltd and ors v Hammond* [2003] STC (SCD) 258, it was decided that overpayments received from customers were not trading receipts of the taxpayer. The Special Commissioners decided that the issue to be determined was whether the overpayments were trading receipts at the time they were received. They found as a fact that the overpayments were not received as part of the trading activities of the companies and therefore the sums were not received as trading receipts.

See **71.5 TRADING EXPENSES AND DEDUCTIONS** for releases of debts owing.

Unremittable amounts

[70.78] See **71.75 TRADING EXPENSES AND DEDUCTIONS**.

Key points

[70.79] The two key points for this chapter in practice are often whether activities amount to a 'trade' and whether all income is assessable as part of a trade. Whether activities amount to trading is considered in detail at **70.3**. It is principally a question of fact but in the words of Lord Wilberforce 'trade cannot be precisely defined'. Case law provides a vast volume of factors to consider which are summarised above. In general it is necessary to look at all relevant factors, particular circumstances, characteristics indicative of trading and assess whether looked at as a whole the company's activities amount to a trade. For whether a source of income is assessable see below to find the detailed guidance above.

Source of income	**See above at**
Bad debt —recoveries	**70.22**
Capital receipts	**70.24**
Car hire rebates	**70.25**
Cash back	**70.26**
Commission	**70.26**
Compensation	**70.27**
Damages	**70.27**
Discounts	**70.26**
Donations received	**70.41**
Embezzlement	**70.28**
Farming compensation	**70.29**
Farming grants and subsidies	**70.29**
Farming support payments	**70.29**
Gifts received	**70.41**
Grants	**70.73**
Impairment losses — recoveries	**70.22**
Insurance received	**70.53**
Investment income	**70.54**
Letting income	**70.54**
Miscellaneous receipts	**70.57**
Patents income	**70.58**
Property sales	**70.61**
Rents received	**70.62**
Reverse premiums	**70.62**
Shares and securities	**70.64**
Sound recording income	**70.71**
Subscriptions	**70.72**
Subsidies	**70.73**
Unremittable amounts	**70.78**
Woodlands	**70.29**

71

Trading Expenses and Deductions

Cross-references. See **5** ANTI-AVOIDANCE; **27** CONTROLLED FOREIGN COMPANIES; **32** DOUBLE TAX RELIEF; **39** GROUP RELIEF; **48** INTANGIBLE ASSETS; **51** INVESTMENT COMPANIES AND INVESTMENT BUSINESS; **55** LOSSES; **61** PROFIT COMPUTATIONS; **64** RESEARCH AND DEVELOPMENT EXPENDITURE; **65.4** RESIDENCE; **70** TRADE PROFITS — INCOME AND SPECIFIC TRADES; **72** TRANSFER PRICING.

Introduction

[71.1] Companies are required to compute their trading profits as part of their charge to corporation tax (see **70.2** TRADE PROFITS — INCOME AND SPECIFIC TRADES). The starting point is often their accounts which are required to be prepared in accordance with GAAP (see **70.18** TRADE PROFITS — INCOME

AND SPECIFIC TRADES) however tax law takes precedence over accounting practice and can require adjustments for certain types of expenditure. This chapter covers common trading expenses and allowable deductions.

Two of the most fundamental rules in the calculation of taxable trade profits are whether items will be disallowed for tax purposes under the capital expenditure rule (**71.8**) or the wholly and exclusively rule (**71.78**).

This chapter concludes with a table that briefly summarises the tax treatment of items of expenditure in calculating trading profits. This is referenced to the detailed explanations below, statue and HMRC manuals.

Some less common deductions specific to particular trades or activities are covered in **70 TRADE PROFITS — INCOME AND SPECIFIC TRADES** such as herd basis, taxation of films, tonnage tax, know how, mines and quarries, pooling of profits, shares and securities, telecommunications rights and unclaimed balances etc.

Allowable deductions

[71.2] The following paragraphs refer to matters of relevance to companies in computing trading profits. See **61 PROFIT COMPUTATIONS** and **70 TRADE PROFITS — INCOME AND SPECIFIC TRADES** for the general principles in computing profits chargeable to corporation tax. See also **10 CAPITAL ALLOWANCES — INTRODUCTION, 34 FOREIGN EXCHANGE GAINS AND LOSSES, 30 DERIVATIVE CONTRACTS LEGISLATION, 48 INTANGIBLE ASSETS, 54 LOAN RELATIONSHIPS, 62 PROPERTY INCOME, 64 RESEARCH & DEVELOPMENT.**

See HMRC Business Income Manual BIM50000 et seq. for HMRC guidance on measuring the profits of a wide range of particular trades.

See **70.18 TRADE PROFITS — INCOME AND SPECIFIC TRADES** re the requirement to adhere to generally accepted accounting practice (GAAP), **70.19 TRADE PROFITS — INCOME AND SPECIFIC TRADES** re the application of accountancy principles generally and **70.20 TRADE PROFITS — INCOME AND SPECIFIC TRADES** re adjustments required on a change of basis.

The provisions for computing trading profits are in *CTA 2009, Pt 3* (previously in *ICTA 1988, ss 74–99*). It has been clarified that, wherever they appear in corporation tax legislation in the context of computing trading profits, the words 'receipts' and 'expenses' refer generally to items brought into account as credits or debits in computing those profits, and contain no implication that an amount has actually been received or paid. [*CTA 2009, s 48; FA 1998, s 46(1)*].

CTA 2009, s 51 introduces a rule for accounting periods ending on or after 1 April 2009 (and see **70.2 TRADE PROFITS — INCOME AND SPECIFIC TRADES**) which is intended to resolve any conflict between statutory rules prohibiting a deduction in computing trading profits and statutory rules permitting such a deduction. It does so by giving priority, with specified exceptions, to the rule permitting the deduction. In practice, such conflict will rarely occur. See Change 7 listed in Annex 1 to the Explanatory Notes to *CTA 2009*.

Advertising

[71.3] Expenditure generally is allowable (but not capital outlay such as fixed signs (but see *Leeds Permanent Building Society v Proctor* (1982) 56 TC 293), nor initial costs etc. of new business). Contribution to campaign for Sunday opening held allowable (*Rhymney Breweries* (1965) 42 TC 509). As to political campaign see *Tate & Lyle* (1954) 35 TC 367, HL, contrasted with *Boarland v Kramat Pulai* (1953) 35 TC 1. See HMRC Business Income Manual BIM42550–42565.

Application of profits

[71.4] A requirement that a trading surplus is to be applied in a particular way does not remove the trade from assessment (under old *Schedule D Case I*) (*Mersey Docks and Harbour Board v Lucas* (1883) 2 TC 25, HL) and applications of the profits under the requirement are not allowable deductions (*City of Dublin Steam Packet Co v O'Brien* (1912) 6 TC 101; *Hutchinson & Co v Turner* (1950) 31 TC 495; *Racecourse Betting Control Board v Young (Inspector of Taxes)* [1959] 3 All ER 215, [1959] 1 WLR 813, HL, and cf *Pondicherry Rly Co Ltd v Madras Income Tax Comrs* (1931) LR 58 Ind App 239, 10 ATC 365, PC; *Tata Hydro-Electric Agencies* (1937) 16 ATC 54, PC; *India Radio & Cable Communication* Co (1937) 16 ATC 333, PC).

For circumstances in which the profits of a trade may not accrue to the proprietor, see *Alongi v CIR* (1991) 64 TC 304, Ct of Sess.

Bad debts — impairment losses

[71.5] For the purposes of these provisions, '*debt*' includes an obligation or liability which may be met otherwise than by the payment of money. International Accounting Standards refer to debtors as receivables.

Under *CTA 2009, s 55* in the case of debts not falling with the regimes for LOAN RELATIONSHIPS (**54**), DERIVATIVE CONTRACTS (**30**) INTANGIBLE FIXED ASSETS (**48**), a deduction is allowed in respect of a debt owed to the company for:

(a) an impairment loss (previously known as 'bad' and 'doubtful debts'); or
(b) a debt release to the extent the debt is released wholly and exclusively for the purposes of that trade as part of a 'statutory insolvency arrangement'.

A '*statutory insolvency arrangement*' is defined in *ICTA 1988, s 834/ITTOIA 2005, s 259* as a voluntary arrangement under, or by virtue of, *Insolvency Act 1986* (or Scottish or NI equivalents) or a compromise or arrangement under *Companies Act 2006, s 895* (or NI equivalent) or any corresponding arrangement or compromise under, or by virtue of, the law of a non-UK jurisdiction.

[*CTA 2009, s 55; ICTA 1988, ss 74(1)(j), 88D, 89, 106(2); ITTOIA 2005, Sch 1 paras 45, 65, 85; FA 2005, s 80, Sch 4 paras 1, 2, 3, 8*].

For accounting periods ending on or after 1 April 2009 the above rules apply where a trade is treated as notionally discontinued (see **70.15 TRADE PROFITS — INCOME AND SPECIFIC TRADES**). For earlier periods, a similar but not identical relief used to apply to debts taken over by the successor. [*ICTA 1988, s 89*]. (See Change 8 listed in Annex 1 to the Explanatory Notes to *CTA 2009*).

For release of a debt owed to a company by a trader see **70.22 TRADE PROFITS — INCOME AND SPECIFIC TRADES.**

Please also refer to the provisions of *CTA 2009* outlined at **54.3 LOAN RELATIONSHIPS** with regard to the position of money debts not arising from the lending of money (per *CTA 2009* 'relevant non-lending relationships') where certain payments and receipts, whilst not arising from loan relationships, are nevertheless taxed under the loan relationship provisions.

The impairment loss for a period of account may reflect events after the balance sheet (IAS Statement of Financial Position) date in so far as they furnish additional evidence of conditions that existed at the balance sheet date. See Revenue Tax Bulletin August 1994 p 154 issue 12, which also outlines the evidence which inspectors (Officers) required in support of the allowance of a provision for bad debts. The change in terminology does not represent a change of law. It is not possible to employ hindsight to revisit a past computation of taxable profit so as to provide for a debt in a period of account in which there was no evidence that it would eventually prove to be bad (*Thompson v CIR* (Sp C 458)).

Where an asset accepted in satisfaction of a trading debt is of market value (as at the date of acceptance) less than the outstanding debt, the deficit may be allowed as a deduction, provided the trader agrees that, on a disposal of the asset, any excess of disposal proceeds over that value (up to the amount by which the debt exceeds that value) will be brought in as a trading receipt (such receipt being excluded from any chargeable gain computation on the disposal) (HMRC Business Income Manual BIM42735).

An impairment loss agreed under conditions of full disclosure cannot be withdrawn because of a subsequent change in the circumstances (*Anderton & Halstead Ltd v Birrell* (1931) 16 TC 200) but a loss for year 1 may be revised, upwards or downwards, in the year 2 computation by reference to the circumstances for year 2 and similarly for later years. The amount of the loss depends on the likelihood of recovery. This is a question of fact but the fact that the debtor is still in business is not itself a reason for refusing a loss (*Dinshaw v Bombay IT Commr* (1934) 13 ATC 284, PC). See also *Lock v Jones* (1941) 23 TC 749.

General impairment loss provisions, i.e. not relating to specific debts (receivables), are not deductible. However where there are a large number of comparatively small debts, making the 'valuation' of individual debts impracticable, HMRC will normally agree to an allowance in accordance with a formula based on the impairment loss experience of the business. Typical businesses are mail-order firms and firms with a large proportion of hire-purchase sales. Where hire-purchase is involved the formula may also cover the spread of the profit on hire-purchase sales. But no provision for the estimated cost of collecting future debt instalments is permissible (*Monthly Salaries Loan Co Ltd v Furlong* (1962) 40 TC 313).

Where a builder sold houses leaving part of the sale proceeds with Building Societies as collateral security for mortgages by the purchasers, it was held the amounts should be brought in at valuation when the houses were sold and if practicable and otherwise when released by the Building Society (*John Cronk & Sons Ltd v Harrison* (1936) 20 TC 612, HL, and cf *Chibbett v Harold Brookfield & Son Ltd* (1952) 33 TC 467, CA). A similar decision was reached in *Absalom v Talbot* (1944) 26 TC 166, HL, where amounts were left on loan to the purchasers. See also *Lock v Jones* above. The HL judgments in *Absalom v Talbot* are an important review of the treatment of trading debts.

The normal debt considered for an impairment loss is a debt for goods or services supplied or a debt in a business, such as banking or money-lending, which consists of advancing money (see e.g. *AB Bank v Inspector of Taxes* [2000] STC (SCD) 229). Losses on advances by a brewery company to its customers were allowed as on the evidence it habitually acted as banker for them in the course of its brewing business (*Reid's Brewery v Male* (1891) 3 TC 279). But losses on advances to clients by solicitors were refused as there was no evidence that they were money-lenders (*CIR v Hagart & Burn-Murdoch* (1929) 14 TC 433, HL; *Rutherford v CIR* (1939) 23 TC 8, Ct of Sess. See also *Bury & Walkers v Phillips* (1951) 32 TC 198 and contrast *Jennings v Barfield* (1962) 40 TC 365). An allowance was refused for an irrecoverable balance due from the managing director of a company as outside the company's trade (*Curtis v J & G Oldfield Ltd* (1925) 9 TC 319). See also *Roebank Printing Co Ltd v CIR* (1928) 13 TC 864, Ct of Sess.

Advances to finance or recoup the losses of subsidiary or associated companies are capital. Allowances were refused in *English Crown Spelter v Baker* (1908) 5 TC 327 and *Charles Marsden & Sons v CIR* (1919) 12 TC 217 for losses on advances to facilitate the supply of materials for the trade of the lender as were losses on an advance to a company under the same control (*Baker v Mabie Todd & Co Ltd* (1927) 13 TC 235), amounts written off in respect of the losses of a subsidiary (*Odhams Press Ltd v Cook* (1940) 23 TC 233, HL) and payments to meet the operating losses of a subsidiary (*Marshall Richards Machine Co Ltd v Jewitt* (1956) 36 TC 511). See also *CIR v Huntley & Palmers Ltd* (1928) 12 TC 1209; *Henderson v Meade-King Robinson & Co Ltd* (1938) 22 TC 97; and *Stone & Temple Ltd v Waters; Astrawall (UK) Ltd v Waters* (1995) 67 TC 145. (NB The loss of a subsidiary may be eligible for group relief — see **39.5 GROUP RELIEF**.)

Losses relating to trade debts with a subsidiary were, however, held allowable in *Sycamore plc and Maple Ltd v Fir* [1997] STC (SCD) 1.

Payments by the purchaser to discharge the unpaid liabilities of the vendor to preserve goodwill etc. allowed in *Cooke v Quick Shoe Repair Service* (1949) 30 TC 460.

See **71.74** below for relief for certain unremittable overseas debts of trades carried on at least partly in the UK.

Note

Loans made to a trader for the setting up or purposes of his trade and irrecoverable are in certain circumstances allowable as a loss for capital gains tax — see Tolley's Capital Gains Tax.

For losses under guarantees see **71.50** below.

For release of loans see **54 LOAN RELATIONSHIPS.**

See generally HMRC Business Income Manual BIM42700–42750.

Simon's Taxes. See **B2.410.**

Bank Levy

[71.6] The Bank Levy has been introduced by *FA 2011, s 72 Sch 19* to apply to periods ending on or after 1 January 201. The levy applies to: the consolidated balance sheet of UK banking groups and building societies; the aggregated subsidiary and branch balance sheets of foreign banks and banking groups operating in the UK; and the balance sheets of UK banks in non-banking groups. These institutions and groups will only be liable for the levy where their relevant aggregate liabilities amount to £20 billion or more and the levy will be charged as if it were an amount of corporation tax chargeable on the relevant entity, and all provisions applying to the collection and payment of corporation tax apply equally to it. The levy is not deductible for corporation tax purposes [*FA 2011, Sch 19 para 45*].

See further **8 BANKS.**

Breweries, distilleries, licensed premises

Tied premises

[71.7] Expenses in respect of 'tied premises' which would otherwise be brought into account in calculating profits of a property business (see **62.2 PROPERTY INCOME**) are instead brought into account as trading expenses. Any necessary apportionment (e.g. where rents etc. relate only in part to the tied premises or where only part of the premises qualifies) is on a just and reasonable basis. '*Tied premises*' are premises through which goods supplied by a trader are sold or used by another person, where the trader has an estate or interest in the premises which he treats as property employed for trade purposes. [*CTA 2009, s 42; ICTA 1988, s 98; ITTOIA 2005, Sch 1 para 77*]. (*Note*. These rules are of general application, although of most common application in the licensed trade.)

Case law

Repairs, rates, insurance premiums paid on behalf of tied tenants allowable (*Usher's Wiltshire Brewery v Bruce* (1914) 6 TC 399, HL) but not extra expenditure incurred to keep licensed houses open while undergoing rehabilitation (*Mann Crossman & Paulin Ltd v Compton* (1947) 28 TC 410) or compensation to a tenant displaced on a licence transfer (*Morse v Stedeford* (1934) 18 TC 457). For compensation paid on the termination of tenancies of tied houses, see *Watneys (London) Ltd v Pike* (1982) 57 TC 372. Losses on advances to 'customers and connections' held allowable (*Reid's Brewery v Male* (1891) 3 TC 279).

The expenses of an unsuccessful application for licences were held not allowable (*Southwell v Savill Bros* (1901) 4 TC 430 — it was conceded that expenses of successful applications are capital) nor expenses of applying for licence transfers (*Morse v Stedeford* above; *Pendleton v Mitchells & Butlers* (1968) 45 TC 341). Contributions by a brewer to a trade association to promote Sunday opening in Wales allowed in *Cooper v Rhymney Breweries* (1965) 42 TC 509. Compensation Fund levies deductible (*Smith v Lion Brewery* (1910) 5 TC 568, HL) but not monopoly value payments (*Kneeshaw v Albertolli* (1940) 23 TC 462; *Henriksen v Grafton Hotels Ltd* (1942) 24 TC 453, CA).

Damages paid to hotel guest injured by falling chimney held not allowable — see *Strong & Co v Woodifield* at **71.11** below. For accrued whisky storage rents see *Dailuaine-Talisker Distilleries v CIR* (1930) 15 TC 613, Ct of Sess; *CIR v Oban Distillery Co* (1932) 18 TC 33, Ct of Sess, and *CIR v Arthur Bell & Sons* (1932) 22 TC 315, Ct of Sess.

Where a brewery company ceased brewing but continued to sell beer brewed for it by another company it was held to have discontinued its old trade and commenced a new one (*Gordon & Blair Ltd v CIR* (1962) 40 TC 358, Ct of Sess).

Simon's Taxes. See **B5.611–B5.614**.

Capital expenditure

[71.8] In computing trading profits, no deduction is allowed for items of a capital nature unless it is specifically provided otherwise. [*CTA 2009, s 53; ICTA 1988, s 74(1)(f)(g)*]. This is made explicit for accounting periods ending on or after 1 April 2009 (and see **70.2 TRADE PROFITS — INCOME AND SPECIFIC TRADES**) but was already a long-established principle. [*CTA 2009, s 93*].

As to the distinction between capital and revenue expenditure and between capital and income receipts, 'no part of our law of taxation presents such almost insoluble conundrums as the decision whether a receipt or outgoing is capital or income for tax purposes' (Lord Upjohn in *Regent Oil Co Ltd v Strick (Inspector of Taxes)* [1966] AC 295, [1965] 3 All ER 174, HL, qv for a comprehensive review of the law). A widely used test is the 'enduring benefit' one given by Viscount Cave in *British Insulated and Helsby Cables Ltd v Atherton (Inspector of Taxes)* [1926] AC 205, 10 TC 155, HL. For recent reviews of the cases, see:

- *Lawson v Johnson Matthey plc* (1992) 65 TC 39, HL — cash injection into subsidiary deemed revenue expenditure.

- *Halifax plc v Davidson* [2000] STC (SCD) 251 — costs incurred by a building society on conversion to a public limited company were disallowed as capital expenditure to the extent that they related to payment of statutory cash bonuses to non-voting members of the society, but otherwise allowed.
- *Dass v Special Commissioner and others* [2006] EWHC 2491 (Ch), [2007] STC 187 — the High Court held that an examination fee under consideration was incurred 'with a view to bringing into existence an asset or advantage for the enduring benefit of a trade' and was attributable to capital.

It is by virtue of the rule in *CTA 2009, s 53* above that depreciation of fixed assets is not allowable in computing profits (see **10.1 CAPITAL ALLOWANCES — INTRODUCTION**) (*In re Robert Addie & Sons* CES 1875, 1 TC 1). Where the depreciation charge in the accounts was reduced by capitalising part of it and including that part in the balance sheet value of stock (i.e. as an overhead cost), it was held by the House of Lords that net depreciation (i.e. the amount after deduction of depreciation included in stock) had to be added back in arriving at taxable profits on the basis that if the profit or loss was arrived at by deducting the net figure, the gross figure could not be adjusted for in the tax computation. Accounting principles stated that the profit or loss for a period of account had to take into account only revenue and expenditure relating to that year. (*Revenue and Customs Comrs v William Grant & Sons Distillers Ltd; Small (Inspector of Taxes) v Mars UK Ltd* [2007] UKHL 15). Where there is a change in basis from that in accordance with HMRC's view prior to the HL decision in these cases to the basis accepted by HL, a catch-up adjustment (which may be positive or negative) will be needed by reference to depreciation added back in previous years for stock not yet sold. An error or mistake claim in respect of earlier years is not appropriate as the computations were agreed on the basis of practice current at the time. See Business Income Manual BIM33190.

No deduction is allowed for expenditure on the provision or replacement of integral features (whether capital or revenue) which qualifies for special rate capital allowances. [*CTA 2009, s 60; ICTA 1988, s 74(1)(da); FA 2008, s 73(3)*].

A gain or loss on the sale of a capital asset not included in trading profits is dealt with according to the provisions relating to capital gains tax. A sale of a fixed asset on which capital allowances have been claimed may result in a balancing charge or allowance, see **10 CAPITAL ALLOWANCES — INTRODUCTION**.

The revenue or capital nature of a payment is fixed at the time of its receipt (*Tapemaze Ltd v Melluish* (2000) 73 TC 167, following *Morley (Inspector of Taxes) v Tattersall* [1938] 3 All ER 296, 22 TC 51, CA).

For a brief note on HMRC's approach to challenging schemes or arrangements designed to turn income into capital (or capital expenditure into a revenue deduction), see Revenue Tax Bulletin June 1997 p 438, issue 29.

For HMRC's own guidance on capital *v* revenue, see HMRC Business Income Manual BIM35000–35910.

For case law on the difference between capital and revenue see **Simon's Taxes** B2.304–B2.309.

Car or (before 1 April 2009) motor cycle hire

[71.9] On or after 1 April 2009, where a car, not falling into one of the following categories is hired, the hire charges are restricted by 15%. The excepted categories are:

(a) a car first registered before 1 March 2001;
(b) a car with low CO2 omissions (not more than 160 gm per kilometre driven);
(c) an electrically propelled car; or
(d) a qualifying hire car.

(b) and (c) are defined as for capital allowances.

Under *CTA 2009, s 58A* (short term hiring in and long-term hiring out) the restriction in deductible hire charges does not apply if A or B applies:

(A) —
- (i) the hire period does not exceed 45 consecutive days; and
- (ii) the hire period and any linked period do not together exceed 45 days 'the sub-hire period',

or if:

(B) —
- (i) the company makes the car available to a customer for more than 45 days; or
- (ii) a car is so made available and the linked periods exceed 45 days.

Condition B does not apply if the customer is an employee of the taxpayer company, or connected with it and there must be no reciprocal arrangements. The exceptions do not apply if there is an avoidance motive. Where there is a sub-hire period, expenditure must be apportioned between it and the remainder of the period on a time basis. If the contract provides for a replacement car in the event of the original car being unavailable, both cars are treated as if they were the same car. Where connected persons (whether both or all companies or not) incur hire charges in respect of the same vehicle for the same period, and one or more of them incur the expenses under commercial arrangements, the provisions will apply only to the commercial lessee or by the first commercial lessee in a chain.

If the rental agreement separately identifies charges for costs such as maintenance, those costs are not subject to the 15% restriction. However, the lease costs subject to restriction do include any unrelievable VAT (normally 50%).

Where a company has incurred expenditure on hiring a car or motor cycle under an agreement entered into on or before 8 December 2008, and the hire period in question begins before 1 April 2010, it may make an irrevocable election. The effect of such an election is that none of the *FA 2009* changes has effect on the deduction for hire charges for the car or motor cycle. The election must be by notice to an officer of HMRC no later than two years after the end of the first chargeable period in which hire charges under the agreement were incurred.

[*FA 2009, s 30, Sch 11*].

Lease commenced before 1 April 2009

Where, before 1 April 2009, a 'car or motor cycle' of which the retail price when new (i.e. unused and not second-hand) exceeds £12,000 is hired for the purposes of a trade, the hire charge is reduced for tax purposes by multiplying it by the fraction.

(12,000 + RP) ÷ 2RP

where RP is the retail price when new. If the price paid for the car by the lessor when new is known, it can be used as the retail price when new, but otherwise the manufacturer's list price, net of any discount generally available but inclusive of extras and VAT, should be used (HMRC Business Income Manual BIM47717).

For this purpose, a '*car or motor cycle*' is a mechanically propelled road vehicle which is neither (1) of a construction primarily suited for the conveyance of goods or burden of any description nor (2) of a type not commonly used as a private vehicle and unsuitable for such use.

The restriction does *not* apply to cars or motor cycles used wholly or mainly for a trade of hire to, or carriage of, members of the public and satisfying the same conditions as apply for the similar exception at **12.15 CAPITAL ALLOWANCES**. As regards hire-purchase agreements (as defined) under which there is an option to purchase for a sum not more than 1% of the retail price when new, the finance charge element, which strictly falls within the definition of a hire charge, is also excluded from the restriction. For accounting periods ending on or after 1 April 2009 (and see **70.2 TRADE PROFITS — INCOME AND SPECIFIC TRADES**), this exclusion is extended to hire-purchase agreements under which there is no option to purchase, and it seems that this was previously applied by HMRC in practice (see Change 10 listed in Annex 1 to the Explanatory Notes to *CTA 2009*).

Also *excluded* from the restriction is expenditure incurred after 16 April 2002 on hiring cars (but *not* motorcycles) first registered after that date which are 'electrically-propelled' or have 'low carbon dioxide emissions' (for which see **12.15 CAPITAL ALLOWANCES**) for a period of hire beginning before 1 April 2013 under a contract entered into before that date. The reduction (referred to at **12.15**) from 120g/km to 110g/km in the maximum carbon dioxide emissions limit does not apply where the period of hire began before 1 April 2008 (even if it continues on and after that date) under a contract entered into before that date.

'Hire charges' for these purposes were held to include payments under a finance lease providing a revolving facility for the purchase of vehicles for use in a contract hire operation (*Lloyds UDT Finance Ltd and Another v Britax International GmBH and Another* (2002) 74 TC 662, CA).

Where the above restrictions have applied, any subsequent rental rebate (or debt release other than as part of a statutory insolvency arrangement — see **71.5** above) is reduced for tax purposes in the same proportion as the hire charge restriction. For accounting periods ending on or after 1 April 2009 (and see **70.2 TRADE PROFITS — INCOME AND SPECIFIC TRADES**), this treatment extends to amounts brought in as post-cessation receipts (see **70.16 TRADE PROFITS — INCOME AND SPECIFIC TRADES**) after the trade has ceased.)

[*CTA 2009, ss 56–58, Sch 2 paras 16, 17; ICTA 1988, ss 578A, 578B; CAA 2001, Sch 2 para 52, Sch 3 para 113; FA 2002, s 60; ITTOIA 2005, Sch 1 para 238; FA 2008, s 77(4)(6)*].

See HMRC Business Income Manual BIM47715–47720.

Cemeteries and crematoria

[71.10] In computing profits of a trade consisting of, or including, the carrying on of a cemetery or the carrying on of a crematorium (and, in connection therewith, the maintenance of memorial garden plots), a deduction as a trading expense for any period of account is allowed for:

- the capital cost of purchasing and preparing land (including cost of levelling, draining or otherwise making suitable) sold for interments or memorial garden plots *in that period*; and
- a *proportion* (based on the ratio of number of grave-spaces/garden plots sold in the period to that number plus those still available — see Example below) of 'residual capital expenditure'.

'*Residual capital expenditure*' is the total 'ancillary capital expenditure' incurred before the end of the period of account in question after subtracting (i) amounts previously deducted under these provisions, any sale, insurance or compensation receipts for assets representing ancillary capital expenditure and sold or destroyed, and (ii) certain expenditure before the basis period for the tax year 1954/55. '*Ancillary capital expenditure*' is capital expenditure incurred on any building or structure (other than a dwelling-house), or on the purchase or preparation of other land not suitable or adaptable for interments or garden plots, which is in the cemetery or memorial garden and is likely to have little or no value when the cemetery or garden is full; it also includes capital expenditure on the purchase or preparation of land taken up by said buildings and structures.

For these purposes, sales of land in a cemetery include sales of interment rights, and sales of land in a memorial garden include appropriations of part of the garden in return for dedication fees etc. Expenditure met by subsidies cannot be deducted as above (the detailed rules being similar to those at **10.2 CAPITAL ALLOWANCES — INTRODUCTION**).

Any change in the persons carrying on the trade is ignored; allowances continue as they would to the original trader, disregarding any purchase price paid in connection with the change itself.

[*CTA 2009, ss 146–149; ICTA 1988, s 91; CAA 2001, Sch 2 para 19; ITTOIA 2005, Sch 1 para 67*].

For the treatment of lump sums for grave maintenance etc., see HMRC Business Income Manual BIM52505, 52510. For the treatment of expenditure and receipts in connection with the provision of niches and memorials, see BIM52520, 52525.

As regards crematoria, see also *Bourne v Norwich Crematorium* (1967) 44 TC 164.

Simon's Taxes. See **B5.620.**

Example

GE Ltd, which operates a funeral service, owns a cemetery for which accounts to 31 December are prepared. The accounts to 31.12.11 reveal the following.

(i)	Cost of land representing 110 grave spaces sold in period	£3,400
(ii)	Number of grave spaces remaining	275
(iii)	Residual capital expenditure on buildings and other land unsuitable for interments	£18,250

The allowances available are		£
(a)	Item (i)	3,400
(b)	$\frac{110}{110+275} \times £18{,}250$	5,214

Note

(a) £8,614 will be allowed as a deduction in computing GE Ltd's trading profits for the period of account ending on 31 December 2011.

Compensation, damages etc. — payments

[71.11] For compensation and redundancy payments to directors or employees see **71.26** below. An important case is *Anglo-Persian Oil Co Ltd v Dale* (1931) 16 TC 253, CA, in which a substantial payment by a company for the cancellation of its principal agency, with ten years to run, was held to be allowable. It was not for a capital asset nor to get rid of an onerous contract (cf *Mallett (or Mallet) (Inspector of Taxes) v Staveley Coal and Iron Co Ltd* [1928] 2 KB 405, 13 TC 772, CA) but to enable it to rationalise its working arrangements. The decision was applied in *Croydon Hotel & Leisure Co Ltd v Bowen* [1996] STC (SCD) 466, in which a payment for the termination of a hotel management agreement was held to be allowable. See also *Vodafone Cellular Ltd v Shaw* (1997) 69 TC 376, CA (payment for release from onerous agreement), in which the principle underlying the decision in *Van den Berghs Ltd v Clark* (see **70.27 TRADE PROFITS — INCOME AND SPECIFIC TRADES** (b)) was applied, but cf *Tucker v Granada Motorway Services Ltd* (1979) 53 TC 92, HL, where a payment to modify the method of calculating the rent was held to be capital, and *Whitehead v Tubbs (Elastics) Ltd* (1983) 57 TC 472, CA, where a payment to alter the terms of a capital loan by removing borrowing restrictions on the borrower was held to be capital.

A payment by a shipping company for cancelling an order it had placed for a ship was held capital (*'Countess Warwick' SS Co Ltd v Ogg* (1924) 8 TC 652 and contrast *Devon Mutual Steamship Insce v Ogg* (1927) 13 TC 184). A payment to an associated company in return for its temporarily ceasing production held allowable (*Commr of Taxes v Nchanga Consolidated Copper Mines* (1964) 43 ATC 20, PC) as were statutory levies on a brewery for a Compensation Fund where a licence is not renewed (*Smith v Lion Brewery Co Ltd* (1910) 5 TC 568, HL) and a payment to secure the closure of a rival concern (*Walker v The Joint Credit Card Co Ltd* (1982) 55 TC 617). Payments by a steel company to secure the closure of railway steel works were held capital (*United Steels v Cullington (No 1)* (1939) 23 TC 71, CA) as were payments to safeguard against subsidence on a factory site (*Bradbury v United Glass Bottle Mfrs* (1959) 38 TC 369; compare *Glenboig Union Fireclay* at **70.27 TRADE PROFITS — INCOME AND SPECIFIC TRADES** (c) and a payment for cancelling electricity agreement on closure of a quarry (*CIR v William Sharp & Son* (1959) 38 TC 341, 38 ATC 18, Ct of Sess). For compensation paid on the termination of tied houses of breweries, see *Watneys (London) Ltd v Pike* (1982) 57 TC 372.

Where damages awarded by a Court against a solicitor were later compounded, the compounded amount (accepted as allowable) was held to be an expense of the year in which the Court award was made (*Simpson v Jones* (1968) 44 TC 599). See also *CIR v Hugh T Barrie Ltd* (1928) 12 TC 1223.

Damages paid by a brewery to a hotel guest injured by a falling chimney were held to have been incurred by it *qua* property owner and not *qua* trader and not deductible (*Strong & Co of Romsey Ltd v Woodifield* (1906) 5 TC 215, HL). Penalties for breach of war-time regulations and defence costs not allowed (*CIR v Warnes & Co* (1919) 12 TC 227, HL; *CIR v Alexander von Glehn & Co Ltd* (1920) 12 TC 232, CA), nor fines imposed by professional regulatory body (*McKnight v Sheppard* (1996) 71 TC 419), nor damages for breach of American 'anti-trust' law (*Cattermole v Borax & Chemicals Ltd* (1949) 31 TC 202). See also *G Scammell & Nephew v Rowles* (1939) 22 TC 479; *Fairrie v Hall* (1947) 28 TC 200; *Golder v Great Boulder Proprietary* (1952) 33 TC 75; *Knight v Parry* (1972) 48 TC 580; *Hammond Engineering v CIR* (1975) 50 TC 313.

Simon's Taxes. See **B2.417, B2.419, B2.455.**

Computer software

[71.12] Subject to the application of the **INTANGIBLE ASSETS (48)** regime, HMRC's views on the treatment of expenditure on computer software are summarised as follows.

Software acquired under licence

Regular payments akin to a rental are allowable revenue expenditure, the timing of deductions being governed by correct accountancy practice (see **70.19 TRADE PROFITS — INCOME AND SPECIFIC TRADES**). A lump sum payment is capital if the licence is of a sufficiently enduring nature to be considered a capital asset in the context of the licencee's trade, e.g. where it may be expected to function as a tool of the trade for several years. Equally the benefit may be transitory (and the expenditure revenue) even though the licence is for an indefinite period. Officers will in any event accept that expenditure is revenue expenditure where the software has a useful economic life of less than two years. Timing of the deduction in these circumstances will again depend on correct accountancy practice.

Where the licence is a capital asset, capital allowances are available.

Expenditure on a package containing both hardware and a licence to use software must be apportioned before the above principles are applied.

Software owned outright

The treatment of expenditure on such software (including any in-house costs) follows the same principles as are described above in relation to licensed software.

(HMRC Business Income Manual BIM35800 *et seq*).

For the treatment of expenditure on systems modification work relating to the Year 2000 problem and to EMU conversion, see Revenue Tax Bulletin April 1998 p 531 issue 34. Broadly, such work will always be a revenue matter unless it is carried out as part of a major new project instituting changes on such a scale as to be of a capital nature in relation to the business.

See HMRC Business Income Manual BIM35800–35865 for a detailed analysis of HMRC's views generally.

Contracts

[71.13] For compensation etc. on the cancellation or variation of contracts see **71.11** above and **70.27 TRADE PROFITS — INCOME AND SPECIFIC TRADES**. For work in progress under contracts see **71.66** below.

Where a taxpayer took over a coal merchanting business on the death of his father, an amount paid for the benefit of contracts between his father and suppliers was held capital (*John Smith & Son v Moore* (1921) 12 TC 266, HL, and see *City of London Contract Corpn v Styles* (1887) 2 TC 239, CA). The completion of outstanding contracts following a partnership dissolution (*Hillerns & Fowler v Murray* (1932) 17 TC 77, CA) and on a company going into liquidation (*Baker v Cook* (1937) 21 TC 337) held to be trading.

Where under a long-term contract goods were invoiced as delivered, the sale proceeds are receipts of the year of delivery (*J P Hall & Co Ltd v CIR* (1921) 12 TC 382, CA). If contract prices are varied retrospectively the resultant further sums are assessable or deductible for the years applicable to the sums at the original prices (*Frodingham Ironstone Mines Ltd v Stewart* (1932) 16 TC 728; *New Conveyor Co Ltd v Dodd* (1945) 27 TC 11). Compare *English Dairies Ltd v Phillips* (1927) 11 TC 597; *Isaac Holden & Sons Ltd v CIR* (1924) 12 TC 768 and contrast *Rownson Drew & Clydesdale Ltd v CIR* (1931) 16 TC 595.

Losses because of a fall in prices fixed under forward contracts etc. cannot be anticipated (*Edward Collins & Sons Ltd v CIR* (1924) 12 TC 773, Ct of Sess; *Whimster & Co v CIR* (1925) 12 TC 813, Ct of Sess) and cf *Wright Sutcliffe Ltd v CIR* (1929) 8 ATC 168, Ct of Sess; *J H Young & Co v CIR* (1926) 12 TC 827, 4 ATC 579, Ct of Sess; *CIR v Hugh T Barrie Ltd* (1928) 12 TC 1223.

Embezzlement etc.

[71.14] Losses allowed as deductions, but not misappropriation by partner or director. See *Bamford v ATA Advertising* (1972) 48 TC 359 and cf *Curtis v J & G Oldfield Ltd* (1925) 9 TC 319. Where defalcations were made good by the auditor who admitted negligence, a refund held to be a trading receipt for the year in which made (*Gray v Penrhyn* (1937) 21 TC 252).

See **71.52** below as regards prohibition on deduction of expenditure involving crime.

Employees (and directors) — benefits

[71.15] See **71.28** below as regards timing of benefits.

Counselling services etc.

[71.16] Expenditure on counselling and other outplacement services which falls within the earnings exemption of *ITEPA 2003, s 310* (see Tolley's Income Tax under Employment Income) is deductible in computing the profits of the employer company's trade. [*CTA 2009, ss 54, 73, 74; ICTA 1988, ss 589A, 589B; ITEPA 2003, Sch 6 paras 69, 70; ITTOIA 2005, Sch 1 para 251*].

Council tax

[71.17] An employer who pays the council tax for an employee will normally be able to claim a deduction for it. If such payments are also made on behalf of members of the employee's family, they too are deductible if they are part of the employee's remuneration package (which would normally mean they were paid under the contract of employment). (HMRC Business Income Manual BIM46820).

Employees seconded to charities or educational bodies

[71.18] If an employer seconds an employee temporarily to a charity (as defined for charitable companies in *CTA 2010, s 467* and other bodies in *ITA 2007, s 519*) — see **20 CHARITIES**), any expenditure of the employer which is attributable to the employment is deductible in computing the employer's profits to the extent to which it would have been deductible if the employee's services had continued to be available to the employer. This relief is extended to secondments to educational establishments (as defined and including education authorities, educational institutions maintained by such authorities, and certain other educational bodies). For accounting periods ending on or after 1 April 2009 (and see **70.2 TRADE PROFITS — INCOME AND SPECIFIC TRADES**), the expenditure is deductible whether or not it would have been deductible if the employee carried out the same duties for the employer as he does for the charity etc.; this is in line with earlier generally accepted practice (see Change 14 listed in Annex 1 to the Explanatory Notes to *CTA 2009*). [*CTA 2009, ss 70, 71; ICTA 1988, s 86; ITTOIA 2005, Sch 1 para 60*].

Interest on director's property loan

[71.19] Where interest is paid by a company on a loan (other than an overdraft) taken out by a director to purchase land (including buildings etc.) occupied rent-free by the company and used for business purposes, it is considered that the company can obtain relief as a trading expense for the interest in the normal way and that the payments would not normally constitute either remuneration or a benefit of the director. (See HMRC Business Income Manual BIM45755–45765.)

Key employee insurance

[71.20] Premiums on policies in favour of the employer insuring against death or critical illness of key employees are generally allowable, and the proceeds of any such policies are treated as trading receipts. However, in *Beauty Consultants Ltd v Inspector of Taxes* [2002] STC (SCD) 352, premiums on a policy insuring a company against the death of either of its controlling shareholder-directors were disallowed, in that the premiums benefited the shareholders personally by improving the value of their shares. In *Greycon Ltd v Klaentschi* [2003] STC (SCD) 370, it was held that the company's sole purpose in taking out key man policies was to meet a requirement of an agreement under which funding and other benefits were obtained from another company, that the policies had a capital purpose and that, consequently, the proceeds of those policies were not trading receipts. See generally HMRC Business Income Manual BIM45525, 45530.

National insurance contributions ('NICs')

[71.21] Secondary (i.e. employers') Class 1 NICs are deductible in computing profits. Relief is similarly available for Class 1A NICs (payable by an employer where benefits-in-kind are provided to employees) and for Class 1B NICs (payable in respect of PAYE settlement agreements — see Tolley's Income Tax under Pay As You Earn). No deduction is allowed for employees' Class 1 NICs for any corporation tax purposes. [*CTA 2009, s 1302; ICTA 1988, s 617(3)–(5); ITEPA 2003, Sch 6 para 87(3); ITTOIA 2005, Sch 1 para 262*].

Payments for restrictive undertakings

[71.22] Payments to employees for restrictive undertakings, falling to be treated as earnings of the employee under *ITEPA 2003, s 225*, are deductible in computing profits. [*CTA 2009, s 69; ITEPA 2003, Sch 6 para 155; ITTOIA 2005, Sch 1 para 402*].

Redundancy payments

[71.23] Redundancy payments, or other employer's payments, under *Employment Rights Act 1996* (or NI equivalent) are allowable. Rebates recoverable are trading receipts. [*CTA 2009, ss 76–78, 81; ITEPA 2003, s 309, Sch 6 paras 63, 64; ITTOIA 2005, Sch 1 para 239*].

Non-statutory redundancy and similar payments are normally deductible unless made on the cessation of trading (but see following paragraphs) (*CIR v Anglo-Brewing Co Ltd* (1925) 12 TC 803; *Godden v Wilson's Stores* (1962) 40 TC 161, CA; *Geo Peters & Co v Smith* (1963) 41 TC 264) or as part of the bargain for the sale of shares of the company carrying on the business (*Bassett Enterprise Ltd v Petty* (1938) 21 TC 730, CA; *James Snook & Co Ltd v Blasdale* (1952) 33 TC 244, CA). See also *Overy v Ashford Dunn & Co* (1933) 17 TC 497 and contrast *CIR v Patrick Thomson Ltd* (1956) 37 TC 145, Ct of Sess. A payment to secure the resignation of a life-director who had fallen out with his co-directors was allowed in *Mitchell v B W Noble Ltd* (1927) 11 TC 372, CA. See also *O'Keeffe v Southport Printers Ltd* (1984) 58 TC 88. For provisions for future leaving payments see **71.61**.

Payments in addition to the statutory payment made on cessation of trading are allowable deductions if they would have been allowable had there been no cessation. Allowance is up to three times the statutory payment. For these purposes, a partnership change is treated as a cessation unless a company carrying on the trade in partnership immediately before the change continues to carry it on in partnership after the change. [*CTA 2009, ss 79, 80; ITTOIA 2005, Sch 1 para 66*]. Relief is similarly given under *s 79* for such payments made on cessation of *part* of a trade; for accounting periods ending before 1 April 2009, this had no statutory authority but was applied in practice (HMRC SP 11/81).

A gratuitous payment made on partial cessation of a company's trade to a managing director who nevertheless continued thereafter to be a director was held non-deductible in *Relkobrook Ltd v Mapstone (Inspector of Taxes)* [2005] STC (SCD) 272, [2005] SWTI 158.

Relief under *CTA 2009, ss 76–81* above is given for the accounting period in which the payment is made (or, if paid after cessation, for the accounting period in which falls the last day on which the trade is carried on). Where, instead, relief is due under general principles, a provision for future payments may be allowed as a deduction for a period of account provided that:

(a) it appears in the commercial accounts in accordance with generally accepted accounting principles;
(b) it was accurately calculated (normally requiring the identification of the individual employees affected) using the degree of hindsight permitted by SSAP 17;
(c) a definite decision to proceed with the redundancies was taken during the period; and
(d) payment was made within nine months of the end of the period.

(HMRC Business Income Manual BIM47215).

See generally HMRC Business Income Manual BIM47200–47215.

Retirement and benevolent provisions

[71.24] See Tolley's Income Tax under Retirement Schemes and under Pension Provision for the tax treatment of such schemes generally. In particular with regard to the extensive changes introduced by *FA 2011* with regard to the pensions regime, effective from 6 April 2011. The deductibility of payments by the employer under such schemes is set out below.

Pension provisions after 5 April 2006

It should be noted that pursuant to the changes introduced by *FA 2011* the annual allowance is reduced from £255,000 to £50,000.

For accounting periods ending after 5 April 2006 in relation to contributions to registered pension schemes, contributions made by an employer are deductible in computing profits for the period of account in which they are made (subject to the spreading provisions below). The contributions must meet the normal conditions for expenditure deductible in computing trading profits, in particular the 'wholly and exclusively' rule (see **71.78**), but it is specifically provided that they are not treated as capital expenditure even if they would fall to be so treated under general principles.

Certain payments an employer may make to discharge his statutory obligations in relation to an under-funded defined benefits scheme are treated as contributions to the scheme for the above purposes and, if made after cessation of the employer's business, are treated as if made immediately before cessation. Otherwise, no sums other than contributions are deductible in connection with the cost of providing benefits under the employer pension scheme; this overrides any contrary rule that might apply under generally accepted accounting practice.

HMRC are empowered to make regulations (see *SI 2005 No 3458*) restricting the deductibility of contributions to a registered scheme in respect of an individual if the individual's benefits from the scheme are dependent on the non-payment of benefits from an employer pension scheme which is not a registered scheme or if the transfer value of the individual's rights under the registered scheme is reduced by virtue of benefits being payable out of the non-registered scheme.

Where the contributions paid by an employer in a period of account exceed 210% of the contributions paid in the previous period of account, relief for the excess contributions may fall to be spread over more than one period of account as follows. Firstly, identify the amount of current period contributions that exceeds 110% of previous period contributions (the '*relevant excess contributions*'). If this amount is less than £500,000, spreading does not apply. Otherwise, relief for the relevant excess contributions is spread over the current and following periods of account as follows.

Amount of relevant excess contributions	*Spread equally over*
£500,000 to £999,999 inclusive	2 periods of account
£1,000,000 to £1,999,999 inclusive	3 periods of account

Amount of relevant excess contributions	*Spread equally over*
£2,000,000 or more	4 periods of account

If the current and previous periods of account are unequal in length, the amount of the previous period contributions is adjusted proportionately in order to determine the excess (if any). Any contributions paid in the current period to fund cost of living increases in current pensions are disregarded in determining any excess, as are any contributions to fund a future service liability for employees joining the scheme in the current period. If the employer ceases business, such that some of the excess contributions would otherwise remain unrelieved, the otherwise unrelieved amount is relieved in the period of account which ends with the date of cessation or, at the employer's option, is apportioned on a daily basis over the whole of the spreading period up to the date of cessation.

Indirect contributions made on or after 10 October 2007

Where a pension contribution is made in a chargeable period and, in the next period, an indirect payment is made to a registered pension scheme by the employer on or after 10 October 2007 (and not under a contract entered into before 9 October 2007) and the 'avoidance condition' is satisfied, relief for the payment is spread (see below). A payment is within this provision if all of part of it is intended to enable the payment of pension contributions under the original or a substitute scheme by a person other than the employer. The employer is '*entitled*' to relief if he would be entitled to a deduction as a trading expense or as management expenses. The '*avoidance condition*' is that spreading of relief would apply had the payment been made by the employer under the original scheme and the purpose, or one of the purposes, of the arrangement was to avoid spreading the relief.

The effect of *FA 2004, s 199A* is to treat the 'relevant relief' as if it were paid by the employer, so that spreading of relief applies. The '*relevant relief*' is the relief to which the employer would be entitled in respect of the payment, or of that part of the payment intended to facilitate the payment of pension contributions. The payment may be to the original pension scheme, or to a '*substitute scheme*', which is any scheme to which there is a relevant transfer within two years ending with the day the payment is made or to which it is envisaged a transfer may or will be made after that day. A '*relevant transfer*' is a transfer of more than 30% of the aggregate of:

- where there is a relevant transfer within two years, the market value of the assets and money in the scheme immediately before the transfer; and
- where the transfer is envisaged, the market value of those assets and that money on the day the payment is made.

[*FA 2004, ss 196–200; FA 2005, Sch 10 para 39; ITTOIA 2005, Sch 1 paras 646–649; FA 2008, s 90; CTA 2009, Sch 1 para 573–577*].

See HMRC draft guidance on employers' contributions to registered pension schemes (available on their website at www.hmrc.gov.uk/practitioners/registe red-contributions.htm) to be published in the HMRC Business Income Manual at BIM46000 *et seq*.

Simon's Taxes. See B2.427, E7.507.

Pension provision before 6 April 2006

See 2009/10 and earlier editions of Tolley's Corporation Tax.

Training costs

[71.25] Costs incurred by an employer in respect of employee training are generally allowable as a trading expense. For HMRC view of the circumstances in which such relief may be prohibited (including training for those with a proprietary stake in the business), see HMRC Business Income Manual BIM47080.

Retraining course expenses paid or reimbursed by an employer and satisfying the conditions of the earnings exemption in *ITEPA 2003, s 311* (see Tolley's Income Tax under Employment Income) are deductible in computing the profits of the employer's trade (or as a management expense). Similar provisions relating to recovery of tax, information and penalties as apply in relation to the earnings exemption apply in relation to this deduction. For accounting periods ending before 1 April 2009 the condition for this relief was slightly different (see Change 16 listed in Annex 1 to the Explanatory Notes to *CTA 2009*). [*CTA 2009, ss 74, 75, Sch 2 para 139; ICTA 1988, s 588; ITEPA 2003, Sch 6 para 67; ITTOIA 2005, Sch 1 para 250*]. See **71.72** below as regards contributions to training and enterprise councils.

Employees (and directors) — remuneration

[71.26] **Bona fide remuneration** is normally deductible including bonuses (see **71.27** bank payroll tax), commissions, tax deducted under PAYE and the cost of board, lodging, uniforms and benefits provided. The deduction is for the remuneration etc. payable; future payments cannot be anticipated (*Albion Rovers Football Club v CIR* (1952) 33 TC 331, HL). The remuneration etc. must be shown to be wholly and exclusively for the purposes of the trade. In *Stott & Ingham v Trehearne* (1924) 9 TC 69 an increase in the rate of commission payable to the trader's sons was disallowed as not on a commercial footing. See also *Johnson Bros & Co v CIR* (1919) 12 TC 147, *Copeman v William Flood & Sons Ltd* (1940), 24 TC 53 and *Earlspring Properties Ltd v Guest* (1995) 67 TC 259, CA. Payments by a farming couple to their young children for help on the farm were disallowed in *Dollar v Lyon* (1981) 54 TC 459. For excessive payments to 'service company' see *Payne, Stone Fraser* at **71.56** below. For wife's wages see *Thompson v Bruce* (1927) 11 TC 607; *Moschi v Kelly* (1952) 33 TC 442, CA. The salary etc. of an employee for service in an overseas subsidiary was allowed in computing the profits of the parent in *Robinson v Scott Bader & Co Ltd* (1981) 54 TC 757, CA. The secondment was wholly and exclusively for the purposes of the parent's business, notwithstanding the benefit to the subsidiary's business.

Any excess of the market value over the par value of shares issued to employees at par is not deductible (*Lowry v Consolidated African Selection Trust Ltd* (1940) 23 TC 259, HL). For payments to trustees to acquire shares for the benefit of employees, see *Heather v P-E Consulting Group* (1972) 48 TC 293, CA, *Jeffs v Ringtons Ltd* (1985) 58 TC 680 and *E Bott Ltd v Price* (1985) 59 TC 437, and contrast *Rutter v Charles Sharpe & Co Ltd* (1979) 53 TC 163 and *Mawsley Machinery Ltd v Robinson* 1998] STC (SCD) 236. See also **71.32** below.

With regard to the disguised remuneration rules introduced by *FA 2011*, see further **71.31** below.

Simon's Taxes. See B2.421.

Bank payroll tax

[71.27] *FA 2010* introduced a new tax called the Bank Payroll Tax (BPT) payable by entities such as banks on relevant remuneration (broadly bonuses) during the period 9 December 2009 to 5 April 2010. Bank payroll tax is due for payment by 31 August 2010. Under *FA 2010, Sch 1 para 15*, BPT is not allowable in calculating profits or losses for corporation tax purposes (and income tax).

Timing of deductions

[71.28] In calculating trading profits for a period of account, no deduction is allowed for an amount charged in the accounts in respect of employees' remuneration unless it is paid no later than nine months after the end of the period of account. Remuneration paid at a later time (and otherwise deductible) is deductible for the period of account *in which* it is paid. For these purposes, 'remuneration' includes any amount which is, or falls to be treated as, earnings for income tax purposes, and includes remuneration of office holders as well as other employees. Remuneration is treated as paid when it falls to be treated for income tax purposes as received by the employee (see Tolley's Income Tax under Employment Income). These provisions apply whether the amount charged is in respect of particular employments or employments generally and apply equally to remuneration for which provision is made in the accounts with a view to its becoming employees' remuneration. Computations prepared before the end of the said nine-month period must be prepared on the basis that any still unpaid remuneration will not be paid before the expiry of that nine-month period and thus will not be deductible for the period of account in question. If, in fact, such remuneration *is* paid by the end of the nine-month period, then for accounting periods ending on or after 1 April 2009 the matter may be dealt with by way of amendment to the tax return; for earlier accounting periods, the computation could be adjusted, but only on a claim for that purpose being made to HMRC no later than two years after the end of the period of account in question.

These provisions apply in calculating income for corporation tax purposes from any source, e.g. PROPERTY INCOME (**62**), and not just trading profits.

[*CTA 2009, ss 1288, 1289, Sch 2 para 140; FA 1989, s 43; ITEPA 2003, Sch 6 para 157; FA 2003, Sch 24 paras 10(1), 11; FA 2004, Sch 17 para 4*].

Similar provisions apply in relation to companies with investment business and insurance companies. [*FA 1989, s 44; ITEPA 2003, Sch 6 para 158; FA 2003, Sch 24 para 10(1); SI 2004 No 2310, Sch para 42*].

Payments to an employee benefit trust were held to fall within these restrictions in *Dextra Accessories Ltd and Others v Macdonald* [2005] UKHL 47 (and see now below under Employee benefit contributions). See also *Sempra Metals Ltd v Revenue and Customs Comrs* [2008] STC 1062.

Employee benefit contributions

[71.29] See **71.31** below with regard to the disguised remuneration provisions introduced by *FA 2011*.

Legislation was introduced in *FA 2003* to counter perceived avoidance of tax and national insurance contributions (NICs) through the abuse of employee benefit trusts. It provides rules for the timing of deductions for 'employee benefit contributions'. To this extent, these rules replace the timing rules described above. They apply in relation to deductions otherwise allowable in computing profits of a company for periods ending after 26 November 2002 in respect of contributions made after that date.

For these purposes, an '*employee benefit contribution*' was originally defined as a payment of money, or the transfer of an asset, by the employer to a scheme manager (third party before 21 March 2007) (e.g. the trustees of an employee benefit trust) who is entitled or required, under the terms of an employee benefit scheme, to hold or use the money or asset to provide benefits to employees (including, with effect after 5 April 2006, former employees). With effect after 20 March 2007, this definition is extended so as also to include any other act (for example, a declaration of trust), or any omission, which results in property being held, or becoming capable of being used, under such a scheme or which increases the total net value of property already so held or capable.

A deduction is allowed only to the extent that, during the period in question or within nine months after the end of it, 'qualifying benefits' are provided, or 'qualifying expenses' are paid, out of the contributions. (If the employer's contribution is itself a qualifying benefit, it is sufficient that the contribution be made during the period or within those ensuing nine months.) Any amount thus disallowed remains available for deduction in any subsequent period during which it is used to provide qualifying benefits. For these purposes, qualifying benefits are treated as provided, and expenses are treated as paid, as far as possible out of employee benefit contributions, with no account being taken of any other receipts or expenses of the scheme manager (third party before 21 March 2007).

A '*qualifying benefit*' is a payment of money or transfer of assets (other than by way of loan) that gives rise to *both* a charge to tax on employment income and a charge to NICs (or would do so but for available exemptions for duties performed outside the UK) or is made in connection with termination of employment or (with effect after 5 April 2006) is made under an employer-financed retirement benefits scheme. Money benefits are treated for these purposes as provided at the time the money is treated as received (for which see Tolley's Income Tax under Employment Income).

'*Qualifying expenses*' are those expenses (if any) of the scheme manager (third party before to 21 March 2007) in operating the scheme that would have been deductible in computing profits if incurred by the employer. Where a qualifying benefit takes the form of the transfer of an asset, the amount provided is the aggregate of the amount that would otherwise be deductible by the employer (in a case where the scheme manager (or third party) acquired the asset from the employer) and the amount expended on the asset by the scheme manager (or third party). If, however, the amount charged to tax under *ITEPA 2003* (or which would be so charged if the duties of employment were performed in the UK) is lower than that aggregate, any amount deductible under these provisions at any time is limited to that lower amount; this rule is aimed at a situation where the asset falls in value after its acquisition by the third party but before its transfer to the employee (Treasury Explanatory Notes to Finance Bill 2003).

These restrictions do not apply to disallow deductions for consideration given for goods or services provided in the course of a trade or profession, contributions to a retirement benefits scheme, approved personal pension scheme, registered pension scheme, qualifying overseas pension scheme (if the employee is a relevant migrant member — see Tolley's Income Tax under Pension Provision for 2006/07 onwards) or accident benefit scheme (as defined). They also do not apply to any deductions that are allowable under **71.32–71.37** below (employee share acquisitions), **71.38** below (share incentive plans) or **71.39** below (qualifying employee share ownership trusts).

Computations prepared before the end of the said nine-month period must be prepared by reference to the facts at the time of computation. If any contributions are used for qualifying purposes after that time, but within the nine months, the computation may be adjusted accordingly (subject to the normal time limits for amending tax returns).

[*CTA 2009, ss 1290–1297, Sch 2 para 141; FA 2003, s 143, Sch 24; SI 2004 No 2310, Sch para 71; FA 2007, s 34(1)–(6)(13)*].

Payments to a trust the beneficiaries of which were members of employees' families were held to fall within these restrictions in *Sempra Metals Ltd v Revenue and Customs Comrs* [2008] STC (SCD) 1062.

Payroll deduction schemes — agents' expenses

[71.30] Voluntary contributions made by an employer company to assist an approved agent with its costs in managing a payroll deduction scheme on the employer's behalf are deductible in computing the profits of the employer's trade. [*CTA 2009, s 72; FA 1993, s 69; ITEPA 2003, Sch 6 para 13*].

Disguised remuneration rules

[71.31] Anti-avoidance provisions have been introduced in *FA 2011, s 26 Sch 2* in order to counter third party arrangements which allow an employee to enjoy the benefits of a sum of money or other assets provided but which at the same time are structured such that there is no legal right to such money or assets, thereby avoiding or deferring a charge to tax or national insurance. In particular the new legislation is aimed at the use of employee benefit trusts and employer funded unapproved retirement benefits schemes.

A new *Part 7A* is inserted into *ITEPA 2003* which set out the scope of the arrangements which are caught within the provisions, and also provides gateways, which are exclusions from the regime. The drafting of arrangements which prima facie fall within the new regime is wide, and includes any agreement, scheme, settlement, transaction, trust or understanding whether or not it is legally enforceable.

The exclusions then limit the operation of the anti-avoidance provisions by providing for safe harbours, under certain specified conditions, in respect of: steps taken under HMRC approved SIPs, SAYE schemes, CSOPs, EMI options and certain pension schemes; loans made on commercial terms; transactions undertaken in the ordinary course of business; loans and benefits provided as a package of benefits in the ordinary course of the business; earmarked deferred remuneration which will vest within 5 years post the award date; incentive schemes with awards based on the market value of the shares; share awards linked to an exit event; shares earmarked for unapproved option schemes; options linked to an exit event; unapproved options, restricted securities and certain other acquisitions of employment related securities; employee car ownership schemes; exempt employment income; registered pension scheme contributions; non-UK resident duties of non-resident employees; consideration given by the employee; and non-domiciles and the remittance basis.

The charge to tax on the employee is triggered by a 'relevant step' which it is reasonable to suppose is taken wholly, or partly, pursuant to the arrangements or in connection (directly or indirectly) with them. The relevant step must be undertaken by a relevant third person and falls into three broad categories: the allocation of money or assets; the vesting of money or assets; or the making available of assets. A relevant third person could be the employer or the employee (acting as trustees) or some other person (whether or not as trustee). Generally an employer providing a benefit to the employee would not be within scope (where no third person is involved). Reference to a corporate employer includes all the group companies, where there is no connection with tax avoidance arrangements. The tax charge is the value of the relevant step.

The legislation imposes an income tax and NIC charge at the time of the earliest relevant event which falls outside of the gateways. Both the tax and NIC should be paid under PAYE and must be paid by the employer unless the person providing the reward deducts such tax at source and accounts for it to HMRC. The PAYE should be calculated by reference to the 'best estimate which can reasonably be made' (see *Sch 2 para 3* which introduces *ITEPA 2003, s 695A*), and paid on the normal PAYE due date. Where the relevant step takes place before Royal Assent, the payment is treated as made on the 30th day after the Act receives Royal Assent.

Corporate tax deductions

The provisions with regard to deductions for corporate employers for employee benefit contributions found at *CTA 2009, Pt 20* are also amended. *CTA 2009, s 1291* is amended to widen the definition of 'employee benefit scheme' to include relevant arrangements caught under *ITEPA 2003, Pt 7A*. *CTA 2009, s 1292* defines a qualifying benefit and is amended to include payments or transfers within the charge to tax under *ITEPA 2003, Pt 7A*. *CTA 2009, s 1293* as to the timing of benefits is amended to include the provision of benefits by a chargeable relevant step — provided at the date employment starts, if the step is before such date, or on the date the chargeable step is undertaken. The amount of the benefit provided will be the sum of money received as earnings (where the payment is money) otherwise with regard to benefits under *Pt 7A*, it is the cost of the relevant step but so as not to exceed the amount charged under *ITEPA 2003* (or which would be so charged had not the employee been non-UK resident in any tax year).

The provisions of new *Pt 7A* and the amendments to *CTA 2009* have effect for relevant steps undertaken, and payments or transfers made, on or after 6 April 2011. For a detailed analysis of the new rules please refer to Tolley's Income Tax 2011/ 2012.

[*FA 2011, s 26 Sch 2*].

Employee share schemes

[71.32] As described at **71.33–71.37** below, corporation tax relief is available to a company (the 'employing company') where, by reason of an employment with that company (whether it is his own or another person's employment), a person either acquires shares or obtains an option in pursuance of which he acquires shares. 'Employment' for this purpose includes (after 15 April 2003) a former or a prospective employment, the holding of an office, and being a member of a company whose affairs are managed by its members. 'Shares' includes stock and an interest in shares or stock. Shares are acquired by a person when he acquires a beneficial interest in them. [*CTA 2009, ss 1002, 1003, Sch 2 para 110; FA 2003, Sch 22 paras 69, 71, Sch 23 paras 10(2), 17(2), 22(4), 22D(4), 26, 30; SI 2003 No 1997*].

See also the reference above to the new disguised remuneration rules introduced by *FA 2011*.

For the provisions of *ITEPA 2003* pertaining to the employee, see Tolley's Income Tax under Share-Related Employment Income and Exemptions.

Transitional

The above-mentioned provisions did not apply for accounting periods beginning before 1 January 2003. Relief is not available under these provisions to the extent that a deduction is available or has been made to any company in respect of expenses referable, directly or indirectly, to the provision of the same shares for an accounting period beginning before that date. [*CTA 2009, Sch 2 para 107; FA 2003, Sch 23 para 33*].

Transfer pricing

For an article on the interaction of these provisions with the transfer pricing rules (see **72 TRANSFER PRICING**), see Revenue Tax Bulletin February 2003 pp 1002–1007.

Relief if shares acquired

[71.33] Relief is available to a company (the '*employing company*') if shares are acquired by an employee or another person by reason of the employee's employment by the company and:

- the employment is in relation to a business (the '*qualifying business*') carried on by the employing company;
- the employing company is within the charge to corporation tax in relation to the profits of that business; and
- the conditions below relating to the shares acquired and the employee's income tax position are all met.

This relief is not available if the employing company is entitled to the relief at **71.34** below (relief if option obtained) in relation to the acquisition of the shares.

The conditions relating to the shares acquired are as follows.

(a) They must be irredeemable, ordinary, fully paid-up shares and either:
  (i) shares of a class listed on a recognised stock exchange (see **22.4 CLOSE COMPANIES**); or
  (ii) shares in a company not under the control (within *CTA 2010, s 1124*) of another company; or
  (iii) shares in a company under the control of a company whose shares are listed on a recognised stock exchange and which is neither a close company (see **22 CLOSE COMPANIES**) nor a company which would be a close company if it were UK resident.

(b) The company whose shares are acquired must be:
  (i) the employing company; or
  (ii) a company of which the employing company is a 51% subsidiary; or
  (iii) a company which is a member of a consortium which owns the employing company or a company within (ii) above; or
  (iv) a company which is a member of a consortium of which the employing company or a company within (ii) above is also a member, and is also a member of the same 'commercial association of companies' as another company owned by the consortium; or
  (v) a company which has a 51% subsidiary within (iv) above.

Conditions (b)(ii) to (iv) above must be met at the time the shares are acquired. As regards (b)(iii) and (iv), a company is a member of a consortium owning another company if it is one of five or fewer companies which between them beneficially own at least 75% of that company's ordinary share capital, with each of them so owning at least 10%. As regards (b)(iv), a '*commercial association of companies*' means a company together with such of its associated companies (within **22.10 CLOSE COMPANIES**) as carry on businesses that are of such a nature that the businesses of the company and those associated companies, taken together, may be reasonably considered to make up a single composite undertaking.

The condition relating to the employee's income tax position is that the employee is subject to an income tax charge under *ITEPA 2003* in relation to the acquisition of the shares. If, however, the shares are 'restricted shares' (see **71.35** below), the condition is instead that the employee either has earnings subject to an income tax charge under *ITEPA 2003, Pt 2* in respect of the acquisition or has no such earnings but will be subject to a charge by virtue of *ITEPA 2003, s 426* if a chargeable event occurs.

In either case, if the condition is not met but would have been met if, at all material times, the employee had been UK resident and ordinarily resident and the duties of the employment had been performed in the UK, the condition is treated as if met.

If the shares are acquired on or after 20 July 2005 and are not restricted shares, it is a further condition that *ITEPA 2003, s 446UA* does not apply in relation to the shares. (That section applies if the shares are acquired at less than market value and the arrangements under which the right or opportunity to acquire them was made available had as one of its main purposes the avoidance of tax or national insurance contributions.)

The amount and nature of the relief

If the shares are neither 'restricted shares' nor 'convertible shares' (see, respectively, **71.35** and **71.36** below), the amount of relief is equal to the excess of the market value of the shares at the time they are acquired over the total amount or value of any consideration given in respect of the acquisition, by whomsoever given, with just and reasonable apportionment of any consideration given only partly in respect of the acquisition. The consideration excludes the performance of any duties of, or in connection with, the employment.

If the shares are 'restricted shares', the amount of relief is equal to the amount chargeable as earnings of the employee as a result of the acquisition. If the shares are 'convertible shares', the amount of relief is similarly computed, except that in calculating earnings for this purpose the market value of the shares is determined as if they were not convertible shares (and disregarding *ITEPA 2003, s 437(2)* and *(3)* if the shares are acquired on or after 20 July 2005). If the shares are both restricted and convertible, the amount of relief is equal to the greater of the two amounts so given (or, if the two amounts are the same, that amount). See, respectively, **71.35** and **71.36** below for additional corporation tax relief in certain circumstances in cases involving restricted or convertible shares.

In any case, the relief is given by way of deduction in computing the profits of the qualifying business for corporation tax purposes for the accounting period in which the shares are acquired. If the company is one with investment business, then unless the qualifying business is a property business (in which case the foregoing applies), the amount of relief is treated as management expenses. The relief is scaled down on a just and reasonable basis if the employment relates to both a qualifying business and another business. The relief is apportioned between qualifying businesses on a just and reasonable basis if the employment relates to more than one such business.

Transitional

FA 2003, Sch 22 made significant changes to these provisions, all of which are incorporated in the above coverage. For the most part, these changes applied with effect on and after 1 September 2003 regardless of when the shares were acquired. However, the provisions relating to 'restricted shares' replaced provisions relating to shares 'subject to forfeiture' but not so as to affect restricted shares acquired before 16 April 2003. Thus, the above provisions do not apply to restricted shares acquired before that date. For the provisions as they stood previously, see *FA 2003, Sch 23* prior to its amendment by *FA 2003, Sch 22*.

[*CTA 2010, s 1124, Sch 1 para 665; CTA 2009, ss 1004–1013, Sch 2 paras 108, 109; FA 2003, Sch 22 paras 60, 68–70, Sch 23 paras 1–4, 6–10, 18–22, 22A–22D, 23, 28–30; F(No 2)A 2005, Sch 2 para 20; FA 2008, s 49(7), (8), (13); SI 2003 No 1997; SI 2004 No 2310, Sch para 69*].

Relief if option obtained

[71.34] Relief is available to a company (the '*employing company*') if:

- an option to acquire shares is obtained by an employee or another person by reason of the employee's employment by the company;
- the person who obtained the option ('*the recipient*') acquires shares pursuant to it;
- the employment is in relation to a business (the '*qualifying business*') carried on by the employing company;
- the employing company is within the charge to corporation tax in relation to the profits of that business; and
- the conditions below relating to the shares acquired and the employee's income tax position are all met.

If the recipient dies and the shares are subsequently acquired by someone else under the option, the relief continues to be available as if the recipient had lived and had acquired the shares.

The conditions relating to the shares acquired are similar to those at **71.33**(a) and (b) above, subject to:

- Conditions (b)(ii)–(iv) (in **71.33**) in being judged at the time the option is obtained rather than at the time the shares are acquired.
- Condition (b) (in **71.33**) is extended in that the shares can be shares in a 'qualifying successor company' (see below).
- Condition (a)(iii) (in **71.33**) was removed for company share option plans to counter avoidance by *FA 2010, s 39*. The change has effect for options granted over shares on or after 24 March 2010. Options granted before 24 March 2010 continue to qualify for the exemption from the charge to income tax in respect of the exercise of the option, provided the other requirements are met. Where a scheme's rules provide that a company may grant options under (a)(iii) (in **71.33**) the company has a six month transitional period to amend its scheme rules. Any options granted during the transitional period do not qualify for the exemption. If a scheme is not amended by 23 September 2010 HMRC may withdraw approval of the scheme.

The condition relating to the employee's income tax position is that the acquisition of the shares is a chargeable event under *ITEPA 2003, s 476* in relation to the employee (whether or not an amount counts as employment income because of that event). If this condition is not met but would have been met if, at all material times, the employee had been UK resident and ordinarily resident and the duties of the employment had been performed in the UK, the condition is treated as if met. If the shares are acquired pursuant to the option after the death of the employee, the condition is treated as met if it would have been met had the employee been still alive.

Takeovers

Where another company obtains control (within *CTA 2010, s 1124*) of a company whose shares are the subject of an option within these provisions, and the option holder and the acquiring company agree to roll over the rights into a new option relating to shares in a 'qualifying company' (the '*qualifying successor company*'), the new option stands in the shoes of the old as far as the application of the current provisions is concerned. A '*qualifying company*' is a company within any of **71.33**(b)(i) to (v) above, substituting references to the acquiring company for references to the employing company and judging conditions (b)(ii) to (iv) at the time the takeover occurs.

The amount and nature of the relief

If the shares are neither 'restricted shares' nor 'convertible shares' (see, respectively, **71.35** and **71.36** below), the amount of relief is equal to the excess of the market value of the shares at the time they are acquired over the total amount or value of any consideration given in respect of the obtaining of the option or the acquisition of the shares, by whomsoever given, with just and reasonable apportionment of any consideration given only partly in respect of these matters. The consideration excludes (i) the performance of any duties of, or in connection with, the employment and (ii) certain employer national insurance contributions which the employee may have elected to pay.

If the shares are 'restricted shares' or 'convertible shares', the amount of relief is equal to the amount that counts as employment income of the employee under *ITEPA 2003, s 476* or, if the option is a qualifying option under the Enterprise Management Incentive provisions, the amount that would have so counted apart from those provisions. In the case of convertible shares, the amount that counts as employment income is determined for this purpose as if the shares were not convertible shares (disregarding *ITEPA 2003, s 437(2)* and *(3)* if the shares are acquired on or after 20 July 2005). In either case, no account is taken if any relief due under *ITEPA 2003, s 481* or *482* (relief for certain national insurance contributions). No account is taken of the death of the employee before the shares are acquired, if such is the case. If the shares are both restricted and convertible, the amount of relief is equal to the greater of the two amounts so given (or, if the two amounts are the same, that amount). See, respectively, **71.35** and **71.36** below for additional corporation tax relief in certain circumstances in cases involving restricted or convertible shares.

In any case, the relief is given by way of deduction in computing the profits of the qualifying business for corporation tax purposes for the accounting period in which the shares are acquired. If the company is one with investment business, then unless the qualifying business is a property business (in which case the foregoing applies), the amount of relief is treated as management expenses. The relief is scaled down on a just and reasonable basis if the employment relates to both a qualifying business and another business. The relief is apportioned between qualifying businesses on a just and reasonable basis if the employment relates to more than one such business.

Transfer of business within a group

There is special provision for the relief to be given to a successor company (or companies) where, between the grant of the option, and the acquisition of the shares, the whole, or substantially the whole, of the qualifying business is transferred intra-group to the successor company (or companies). Companies are for this purpose members of the same group if one is a 51% subsidiary of the other or both are 51% subsidiaries of a third company.

Transitional

The same comments apply as in **71.33** above.

[*CTA 2010, s 1124; CTA 2009, ss 1004, 1005, 1014–1024, Sch 2 paras 108, 109; FA 2003, Sch 22 paras 60, 63–70, 72, Sch 23 paras 1–4, 12–17, 21, 22, 22A–22D, 23, 27–30; FA 2004, Sch 16 para 5; F(No 2)A 2005, Sch 2 para 20; FA 2006, s 93; FA 2008, s 49(7), (13); SI 2003 No 1997; SI 2004 No 2310, Sch para 70*].

Additional relief for restricted shares

[71.35] Shares are '*restricted shares*' if they are restricted securities (or a restricted interest in securities) within *ITEPA 2003, ss 423, 424 as amended*.

If relief is potentially available under **71.33** or **71.34** above on acquisition, relief is also available to the employing company on a subsequent chargeable event under *ITEPA 2003, s 426* in relation to the restricted shares or if *ITEPA 2003, Pt 7 Ch 2* ceases to apply to the shares because the employee dies. If *ITEPA 2003, s 426* does not apply but would have applied if, at all material times, the employee had been UK resident and ordinarily resident and the duties of the employment had been performed in the UK, the relief still applies. If the original acquisition was made pursuant to an option and, because of the death of the recipient of the option the shares were acquired by someone else, the additional relief applies as if the recipient were still alive and had acquired the shares.

The relief is given for the accounting period in which the chargeable event occurs or the employee dies, whichever is applicable. It is given in the same manner as in **71.33** and **71.34** above. The quantum of relief is given by *CTA 2009, s 1026(3), (4)* (chargeable events) or *CTA 2009, s 1027(3), (4)* (death of employee) or, for accounting periods ending before 1 April 2009, by *FA 2003, Sch 23 para 21(6)–(9) as amended*.

Provisions similar to those at **71.34** above apply on a transfer of the qualifying business within a group in the period between the acquisition of the shares or the obtaining of the option and the chargeable event or employee's death. These enable the additional relief to be given to the successor company (or companies).

Transitional

The same comments apply as in **71.33** above.

[*CTA 2009, ss 1004, 1005, 1025–1029, Sch 2 paras 108, 109; FA 2003, Sch 22 paras 59, 68, 70, 72; Sch 23 paras 4, 9, 13, 16, 19, 21, 22, 23, 27–30; FA 2004, Sch 16 para 5; F(No 2)A 2005, Sch 2 para 20; SI 2003 No 1997; SI 2004 No 2310, Sch paras 69, 70*].

Additional relief for convertible shares

[71.36] Shares are '*convertible shares*' if they are convertible securities (or an interest in convertible securities) within *ITEPA 2003, s 436 as amended.*

If relief is potentially available under **71.33** or **71.34** above on acquisition, relief is also available to the employing company on a subsequent 'chargeable event' or on a 'relief event'.

If there has been an acquisition of convertible securities that are not shares and relief would have been potentially available under **71.33** or **71.34** above if they had been shares and had satisfied the conditions relating to shares acquired, this 'additional' relief is nevertheless available.

For these purposes, '*chargeable event*' means an event that is a chargeable event under *ITEPA 2003, s 438* in relation to the convertible securities and is a conversion of the securities into shares satisfying the conditions in **71.33** or **71.34** above (whichever is applicable) relating to shares acquired (disregarding the extension to these conditions referred to in **71.34**).

A '*relief event*' is the first event to occur after the death of the employee that would have been a 'chargeable event' (as above) if the employee had lived.

If *ITEPA 2003, s 438* does not apply but would have applied if, at all material times, the employee had been UK resident and ordinarily resident and the duties of the employment had been performed in the UK, the relief still applies. If the original acquisition was made pursuant to an option and, because of the death of the recipient of the option the shares were acquired by someone else, the additional relief applies as if the recipient were still alive and had acquired the shares.

The relief is given for the accounting period in which the chargeable event occurs or the relief event occurs, whichever is applicable. It is given in the same manner as in **71.33** and **71.34** above. The quantum of relief is given by *CTA 2009, s 1033(3), (4)* (chargeable events) or *CTA 2009, s 1034(3), (4)* (relief events) or, for accounting periods ending before 1 April 2009, by *FA 2003, Sch 23 para 22C(6)–(8) as amended.*

Provisions similar to those at **71.34** above apply on a transfer of the qualifying business within a group in the period between the acquisition of the shares or the obtaining of the option and the chargeable event or relief event. These enable the additional relief to be given to the successor company (or companies).

Transitional

The same comments apply as in **71.33** above.

[*CTA 2009, ss 1004, 1005, 1030–1036, Sch 2 paras 108, 109; FA 2003, Sch 22 paras 59, 69, 70, 72; Sch 23 paras 4, 9, 13, 16, 22A–22D, 23, 27–30; FA 2004, Sch 16 para 5; SI 2003 No 1997; SI 2004 No 2310, Sch paras 69, 70*].

Relationship with other reliefs

[71.37] A deduction under *CTA 2009, ss 983–998* in relation to a share incentive plan (see **71.38** below) is given priority over relief under **71.33–71.36** above, and no relief is available under **71.33–71.36** in respect of shares in relation to which a deduction is allowable, or has been made, under **71.38**.

Where relief under **71.33–71.36** above is available (or would be available were it not for the further condition in **71.33** concerning *ITEPA 2003, s 446UA*), no other corporation tax deduction is allowed to any company in respect of expenses directly related to the provision of the shares, including any amount paid or payable by the employing company in respect of the employee's participation in an employee share scheme. However, this does *not* exclude relief for the expenses of setting up an employee share scheme under which the shares are acquired, or of meeting, or contributing to, its administration costs, or for costs of borrowing for the purposes of the scheme, or for fees, commission, stamp duty or similar incidental expenses of acquiring the shares.

[*CTA 2009, ss 1037, 1038; FA 2003, Sch 23 paras 24, 25; F(No 2)A 2005, Sch 2 para 20*].

Share incentive plans

[71.38] Subject to the exceptions below, the items at (a)–(d) below are allowable deductions in computing company trading profits in connection with an approved share incentive plan within *ITEPA 2003, Sch 2* (see Tolley's Income Tax under Share-Related Employment Income and Exemptions). If the company is carrying on a property business (as in **62 PROPERTY INCOME**), the items are similarly treated as allowable deductions in computing the profits. If the company is one with investment business (other than a property business) they are treated as management expenses.

(a) The market value (at time of acquisition by the plan trustees, and see below) of free and matching shares awarded to employees under the plan (the deduction being given *to the employer company* for the period of account in which the shares are awarded);
(b) Any excess of the market value (at time of acquisition by the plan trustees, and determined as for capital gains tax purposes) of partnership shares over the amounts paid by participating employees to acquire them (the deduction being given *to the employer company* for the period of account in which the shares are acquired on participants' behalf);
(c) Expenditure incurred by the company in establishing a plan (the deduction being given for the period of account in which the expenditure is incurred, unless HMRC approve the plan more than nine months after the end of that period, in which case the deduction is given for the period of account in which approval is given);

(d) Contributions by the company to the expenses of plan trustees in operating a plan, *excluding* expenses in acquiring shares (other than incidental costs such as fees, commission, stamp duty etc.) but *including* interest on money borrowed to acquire shares.

Once a deduction is made under (a) or (b) above, no other deduction (other than any within (c) or (d) above) may be made by the employer company or any associated company (as defined) in respect of the provision of the shares, and no deduction within (a) or (b) above may then be made by any other company in that respect. Once a deduction is made under (c) above, no other deduction may be made in respect of the costs of setting up the plan.

For the purposes of (a) above, market value is determined as for capital gains tax purposes, and, for the purposes of that determination (and also for those of (iii) below), shares acquired by the trustees on different days are deemed to be awarded under the plan on a first in/first out basis. In the case of a group plan (i.e. a plan established by a parent company and extending to one or more companies under its control), the total market value of the shares awarded is apportioned between the relevant employer companies by reference to the number of shares awarded to the employees of each company.

No deduction is allowed under (a) or (b) above:

(i) in respect of shares awarded to an individual whose earnings from the eligible employment are not, at the time of the award, taxable earnings (whether or not subject to the remittance basis as regards overseas earnings);
(ii) in respect of shares that are liable to depreciate substantially in value for reasons that do not apply generally to shares in the company;
(iii) if a deduction has been made (on whatever basis), by the company, or an associated company (as defined) in respect of providing the same shares for the plan trust or for another trust (whatever its nature or purpose); or
(iv) in respect of the subsequent award of shares previously forfeited by participants (such shares being treated as acquired by the trustees at time of forfeit for no consideration).

No deduction is allowed under (c) above if any employee acquires rights under the plan, or the trustees acquire any shares, before the plan receives HMRC approval. Subject to (d) above, no deduction is allowed for expenses in providing dividend shares.

On withdrawal of HMRC approval to a plan, HMRC may, by notice, direct that any deductions made under (a) or (b) above be withdrawn also, in which case the company is deemed to have received an amount equal to the aggregate deductions for the period of account in which HMRC notify withdrawal of approval. See Tolley's Income Tax under Share-Related Employment Income and Exemptions for right of appeal.

The notional receipt is treated as a receipt of the company's trade or property business if applicable. If the business has ceased, it is treated as a post-cessation receipt (see **70.16 TRADE PROFITS — INCOME AND SPECIFIC TRADES**); for accounting periods ending before 1 April 2009, this was not explicit — see

Change 76 listed in Annex 1 to the Explanatory Notes to *CTA 2009*. In any other case, it is treated as a receipt within the charge to corporation tax on income; for accounting periods ending before 1 April 2009, the charge was under *Schedule D, Case VI*.

A payment made by the employer company (after 5 April 2003) to the trustees sufficient to enable them to acquire (other than from a company) a significant block of shares (at least 10% of the employer company's ordinary share capital) normally (see below for anti-avoidance) attracts a deduction (in computing trading profits etc.) which, in contrast to the above, is not deferred until the shares are awarded to employees. The deduction normally falls to be given for the period of account in which falls the first anniversary of the date of acquisition, provided the 10% requirement is then met. The deduction will, however, be clawed back unless at least 30% of those shares are awarded within five years of acquisition by the trustees and all of the shares are awarded within ten years. On clawback, the company is deemed to have received an amount equal to the deduction at the time that HMRC direct that the deduction be withdrawn, the notional receipt being treated as above. If all the shares are subsequently awarded, the deduction is reinstated at that later time. An appropriate proportion of the original deduction is also subject to clawback if the plan terminates before all the shares have been awarded or if shares are awarded to an individual within (i) above. In the event of HMRC withdrawing their approval to the plan, the same provisions apply as above as regards potential withdrawal of deductions.

FA 2010, s 42 amends CTA 2009, s 989 for events taking place on or after 24 March 2010 to deny a deduction for a payment to trustees above where the main purpose or one of the main purposes was tax avoidance arrangements. Arrangements are widely defined to include arrangements, a scheme of any kind, whether or not legally enforceable involving a single transaction or two or more transactions.

[*FA 2010, s 42; CTA 2009, ss 983–998, Sch 2 paras 105, 106; ICTA 1988, s 85B, Sch 4AA; ITEPA 2003, Sch 2 paras 92, 94, Sch 6 paras 12, 109; SI 2004 No 2310, Sch para 35*].

Employee share ownership trusts

[71.39] Expenditure incurred in setting up a qualifying employee share ownership trust (QUEST) (within *FA 1989, Sch 5*) is deductible in computing the company's trading profits. If the company is carrying on a property business (as in **62 PROPERTY INCOME**), the expenditure is similarly deductible in computing the profits. If the company is one with investment business (other than a property business) the expenditure is treated as management expenses.

If the deed establishing the trust is executed more than nine months after the end of the period of account in which the expenditure is incurred, the deduction is made for the period of account in which the deed is executed. (In the case of a company with investment business (other than a property business) the expenditure is treated as referable to the accounting period in which the deed is executed.)

[*CTA 2009, s 1000; SI 2004 No 2310, Sch para 6*].

See Tolley's Income Tax under Qualifying Employee Share Ownership Trusts for the definition of a QUEST, for the charge on trustees and for certain information requirements relating to trustees. See Tolley's Capital Gains Tax under Shares and Securities for details of a limited rollover relief on sale of shares to the trustees of such a trust in *TCGA 1992, ss 227–235*.

Non-qualifying employee share ownership trusts

For the treatment of contributions to employee share ownership trusts not within the above provisions which are not capital expenditure on general principles but which are required under UITF 13 to be treated as giving rise to an asset in the employer's accounts, see Revenue Tax Bulletin February 1997 pp 399, 400 issue 27. Broadly, relief for the contributions is deferred until the rights in the shares are transferred to employees, although this would not prevent a deduction for a properly calculated provision reflecting employees' accruing entitlement to such benefits.

Approved share option schemes

[71.40] Expenditure on establishing an approved SAYE option scheme or CSOP scheme (see Tolley's Income Tax under Share-Related Employment Income and Exemptions) is deductible in computing the company's trading profits provided that no employee or director obtains rights under the scheme before it is approved. If the company is carrying on a property business (as in **62 PROPERTY INCOME**), the expenditure is similarly deductible in computing the profits. If the company is one with investment business (other than a property business) the expenditure is treated as management expenses.

If the scheme is approved more than nine months after the end of the period of account in which the expenditure is incurred, the deduction is made for the period of account in which the approval is given. (In the case of a company with investment business (other than a property business) the expenditure is treated as referable to the accounting period in which the approval is given.)

[*CTA 2009, s 999; ITEPA 2003, Sch 6 para 11; SI 2004 No 2310, Sch para 4*].

Entertainment and gifts

[71.41] Subject to the exceptions below, no deduction is allowed, in computing income from any source, for expenses incurred in providing entertainment (including hospitality of any kind) or gifts. This includes sums paid to or on behalf of an employee (including a director), or put at the employee's disposal, *exclusively* for meeting expenses incurred, or to be incurred, by the employee in providing the entertainment or gift. (See Tolley's Income Tax under Employment Income for the employee's position.) It also includes expenses incidental to providing entertainment or gifts.

Entertainment expenditure is not within the above prohibition if:

- the entertainment is of a kind which it is the company's business to provide and it is provided in the ordinary course of that business either for payment or free of charge for advertising purposes; or

- the entertainment is provided for the company's employees (except where such entertainment is incidental to the entertainment of non-employees).

Gifts are not within the above prohibition if:

- they are of an item which it is the company's business to provide and are made for advertising purposes; or
- they incorporate a conspicuous advertisement for the company *and* do not consist of food, drink, tobacco or a token or voucher exchangeable for goods *and* the cost to the company of all such gifts to the same person in the same accounting period does not exceed £50; or
- they are provided for the company's employees (except where such gifts are incidental to the providing of gifts for non-employees); or
- they are made to a charity or to either of the similar organisations specified in *CTA 2009, s 1300(5)*.

[*CTA 2009, ss 1298–1300; CAA 2001, Sch 2 para 51; ITEPA 2003, Sch 6 para 62; SI 2004 No 2310, Sch para 23; ITTOIA 2005, Sch 1 para 235*].

By Extra Statutory Concession, B7, other gifts are allowed as deductions provided that they are:

(i) wholly and exclusively for the purposes of the business;
(ii) made for the benefit of a body or association established for educational, cultural, religious, recreational or benevolent purposes which is local to the donor's business activities and not restricted to persons connected with the donor; and
(iii) reasonably small in relation to the scale of the donor's business In *Bourne & Hollingsworth v Ogden* (1929) 14 TC 349 an abnormally large donation was disallowed. See also **71.49** below.

Deductions were allowed for items provided in the ordinary course of a trade of providing entertainment (see *Fleming v Associated Newspapers Ltd* (1972) 48 TC 382, HL). See also the VAT cases of *C & E Commissioners v Shaklee International and Another CA*, [1981] STC 776 and *Celtic Football and Athletic Co Ltd v C & E Commissioners CS*, [1983] STC 470. There is also a restriction on capital allowances where plant or machinery is used to provide entertainment, with similar exceptions as above where relevant (see **11.1 CAPITAL ALLOWANCES — PLANT AND MACHINERY: ELIGIBLE EXPENDITURE AND INITIAL ALLOWANCES**).

For an article on the scope and application of these rules, see Revenue Tax Bulletin August 1999 pp 679–682 issue 42 as supplemented by Revenue Tax Bulletin February 2000 p 729 issue 45. For further comprehensive guidance on business entertainment, see HMRC Business Income Manual BIM45000–45090.

Farming and market gardening

[71.42] Farming or market gardening in the UK is treated for corporation tax purposes as trading. All the UK farming carried on by a particular company (other than as part of a different trade) is treated as a single trade. Farming carried on by a partnership in which a company is partner is, however, separate from any farming carried on by the partner company itself. This does not apply to the woodlands or to land being prepared for forestry use. [*CTA 2009, ss 36, 1270(1); ITTOIA 2005, Sch 1 para 32*]. See *Bispham v Eardiston Farming Co* (1962) 40 TC 322 and *Sargent v Eayrs* (1972) 48 TC 573. The matters listed below are of particular application to farming or (where relevant) market gardening.

(a) **Compensation for compulsory slaughter.** See **70.29 TRADE PROFITS — INCOME AND SPECIFIC TRADES.**

(b) **Drainage.** Where land is made re-available for cultivation by the restoration of drainage or by re-draining, the net expenditure incurred (after crediting any grants receivable) will be allowed as revenue expenditure in farm accounts provided it excludes (i) any substantial element of improvement (e.g. the substitution of tile drainage for mole drainage) and (ii) the capital element in cases in which the present owner is known to have acquired the land at a depressed price because of its swampy condition (HMRC Statement of Practice, SP 5/81).

(c) **Farmhouses.** The apportionment of the running costs of a farmhouse between business and private use should be based on the facts of the case for the year of account in question (HMRC Business Income Manual BIM55250).

(d) **Foot and mouth outbreak.** For the special measures for the 2001 outbreak, see Revenue Tax Bulletin Special Edition May 2001 and Revenue Tax Bulletin October 2001 pp 890, 891. For the 2007 outbreak, see HMRC news release 8 August 2007.

(e) **Grants and subsidies.** See **70.29 TRADE PROFITS — INCOME AND SPECIFIC TRADES.**

(f) **Milk. Superlevy.** HMRC's view is that superlevy is an allowable trading deduction, but that the purchase of additional quota to avoid superlevy does not give rise to a deduction for either the superlevy thus avoided or the sum which would have been paid to lease rather than purchase the additional quota. (HMRC Business Income Manual BIM55340 and BIM55315).

    Residuary Milk Marketing Board receipts. B Reserve Fund distributions and sums repaid to producers under the Rolling Fund arrangements on the flotation of Dairy Crest (in the latter case whether taken in cash or in shares) are income receipts of the trade. Any element of a B Reserve Fund payment described as interest may also be treated as a trade receipt. Post-cessation treatment (see **70.16 TRADE PROFITS — INCOME AND SPECIFIC TRADES**) will apply where appropriate. (HMRC Tax Bulletin August 1997 p 461 issue 30).

    Milk Marque Ltd shares. Bonus preference shares (or loan stock) issued in October 1998 to dairy farmers supplying the company form part of the trading receipts of the farmer, the appropriate measure of the income (and of the capital gains tax base cost) being the nominal value of the shares (HMRC Tax Bulletin August 1999 p 685 issue 42).

    For capital gains tax considerations generally, see Tolley's Capital Gains Tax under Assets and Rollover Relief.

(g) **Share farming.** See **70.29 TRADE PROFITS — INCOME AND SPECIFIC TRADES.**

(h) **Short rotation coppice.** See **70.29 TRADE PROFITS — INCOME AND SPECIFIC TRADES.**

(i) **Stock valuations.** See **70.42 TRADE PROFITS — INCOME AND SPECIFIC TRADES** for the herd basis, and, for trading stock generally, **71.66 TRADE PROFITS — INCOME AND SPECIFIC TRADES.** In general, livestock is treated as trading stock unless the herd basis applies, and home-bred animals may be valued, if there is no adequate record of cost, at 75% for sheep and pigs (60% for cattle) of open market value. Dead stock may be taken at 75% of market value.
Where an animal grant or subsidy for which application has been made has not been taken into account for a particular period but has been applied for, and that application materially affects the value of the animal, the grant or subsidy should be taken into account as a supplement to the market value when deemed cost is computed. Grants or subsidies applied for but not recognised as income in the period concerned should also be taken into account in arriving at net realisable value for stock valuation purposes. (HMRC Tax Bulletin December 1994 p 182 issue 14).

(j) **Subscriptions** to the **National Farmers Union** are allowable in full.

(k) **Sugar beet outgoers scheme.** See **70.29 TRADE PROFITS — INCOME AND SPECIFIC TRADES.**

(l) **Trading profits.** See trade profits **70.29 TRADE PROFITS — INCOME AND SPECIFIC TRADES.**

(m) **Woodlands grants.** See trade profits **70.29 TRADE PROFITS — INCOME AND SPECIFIC TRADES.**

For these and other aspects of farming taxation, see HMRC Business Income Manual BIM55000–55730, 73000–73190 and 75600–75650.

Finance leasing

Long funding leases of plant or machinery

[71.43] The rules on leasing of *plant or machinery* are reformed by *FA 2006, s 81, Sch 8* with effect from, broadly, 1 April 2006 (see **13.13 CAPITAL ALLOWANCES — PLANT AND MACHINERY: FIXTURES AND LEASING** for the detailed commencement and transitional provisions). For long funding leases (within **13.4**), the new regime grants entitlement to capital allowances to the lessee rather than to the lessor as previously. See also **71.55** below. It follows that the Statement of Practice described below can have no application to a long-funding lease of plant or machinery. The *CTA 2010, Pt 21* provisions at **71.44, 71.45** below are specifically disapplied in relation to such leases.

Statement of Practice

In relation to finance leases entered into after 11 April 1991, HMRC practice described below applies to rentals payable by a lessee under a finance lease, i.e. a lease which transfers substantially all the risks and rewards of ownership of an asset to the lessee while maintaining the lessor's legal ownership of the asset. The treatment of such rentals depends upon whether or not SSAP 21 (or IAS 17) has been applied. This practice has no implications for the tax treatment of rentals receivable by the lessor, nor for the availability of capital allowances to the lessor. (HMRC Statement of Practice, SP 3/91 and Revenue Press Release 11 April 1991).

Finance lease rentals are revenue payments for the use of the asset, and, both under normal accounting principles and for tax purposes, should be allocated to the periods of account for which the asset is leased in accordance with the accruals concept. Where there is an option for the lessee to continue to lease the asset after expiry of the primary period under the lease, regard should be had, in allocating rentals to periods of account, to the economic life of the asset and its likely period of use by the lessee, as well as to the primary period.

Under SSAP 21, the lessee is required to treat a finance lease as the acquisition of an asset subject to a loan, to be depreciated over its useful life, with rentals apportioned between a finance charge and a capital repayment element. This treatment does not, however, affect the tax treatment, which remains as described above.

Where SSAP 21 has not been applied, the lessee's accounting treatment of rental payments is normally accepted for tax purposes, provided that it is consistent with the principles described above. If not, computational adjustments are made to secure the proper spreading of the rental payments.

Where SSAP 21 has been applied, the finance charge element of the rental payments for a period of account is normally accepted as a revenue deduction for that period. In determining the appropriate proportion of the capital repayment element to be deducted for tax purposes, a properly computed commercial depreciation charge to profit and loss account will normally be accepted. Where, however, the depreciation charge is not so computed, the appropriate proportion for tax purposes will be determined in accordance with the principles described above.

For comment on the principles set out in SP 3/91, and on their application to particular arrangements, see Revenue Tax Bulletin February 1995 pp 189–193, issue 15. This considers in particular: sums paid before the asset comes into use; depreciation of leased assets (and the interaction with SSAP 21); long-life assets; termination adjustments; fixtures leases; and the interaction of SP 3/91 with statutory restrictions on relief for rental payments.

See generally HMRC Business Income Manual BIM61000–61075 (leasing: general) and BIM61100–61195 (finance leasing).

See also above under Long funding leases of plant or machinery.

General

See **13.5, 13.24 CAPITAL ALLOWANCES — PLANT AND MACHINERY: FIXTURES AND LEASING** for other finance lease capital allowance restrictions. It was held in *Caledonian Paper plc v CIR* [1998] STC (SCD) 129 that annual or semi-annual payments of commitment fees, guarantee fees and agency fees relating to guarantees required in relation to finance leasing arrangements were deductible in computing profits, but that a one-off management fee was not.

Finance leases — return in capital form

[71.44] *FA 1997, Sch 12 Pt I* applied from 26 November 1996 in relation to asset leasing arrangements which fall to be treated under generally accepted accounting practice (GAAP) (see **70.19 TRADE PROFITS — INCOME AND SPECIFIC TRADES**) as finance leases or loans, and whose effect is that some or all of the investment return is or may be in the form of a sum that is not rent and would not, apart from these provisions, be wholly taxed as lease rental. Those provisions are now in *CTA 2010, Pt 21 Ch 2 (ss 899–924)* and are referred to below as the Chapter 2 provisions. The principal purposes of the Chapter 2 provisions are to charge any person entitled to the lessor's interest to tax by reference to the income return for accounting purposes (taking into account the substance of the matter as a whole, e.g. as regards connected persons or groups of companies); and to recover reliefs etc. for capital and other expenditure as appropriate by reference to sums received which fall within the provisions.

The Chapter 2 provisions apply where an asset lease (as widely defined) is or has at any time been granted in the case of which the conditions at (a)–(e) below are or have been met at some time (the '*relevant time*') in a period of account of the current lessor. Where the conditions have been met at a relevant time, they are treated as continuing to be met unless and until the asset ceases to be leased under the lease or the lessor's interest is assigned to a person not connected with any of the following:

(i) the assignor,
(ii) any other person who was the lessor at some time before the assignment, and
(iii) any person who at some time after the assignment becomes the lessor under arrangements made by a person who was the lessor (or was connected with the lessor) at some time before the assignment.

A lease to which the Chapter 2 provisions cease to apply can come within those provisions again if the conditions for their application are again met.

For the purposes of these provisions generally, and those at **71.45** below, **25 CONNECTED PERSONS** applies initially to determine if persons are connected. But persons who are thus connected at any time in the 'relevant period' are then treated as being connected throughout that period. The '*relevant period*' runs from the earliest time at which any of the leasing arrangements were made to the time when the current lessor finally ceases to have an interest in the asset or any arrangements relating to it.

The Chapter 2 provisions do *not* apply if (or to the extent that), as regards the current lessor, the lease falls to be regarded as a long funding lease (within **13.5 CAPITAL ALLOWANCES — PLANT AND MACHINERY: FIXTURES AND LEASING**) of plant or machinery.

The conditions referred to above are as follows.

(a) At the 'relevant time' (see above), and in accordance with GAAP, the leasing arrangements fall to be treated as a finance lease or loan, and either:
    (i) the lessor (or a connected person) is the finance lessor in relation to the finance lease or loan; or

(ii) the lessor is a member of a group of companies for the purposes of whose consolidated accounts the finance lease or loan is treated as subsisting.

(b) under the leasing arrangements, there is or may be payable to the lessor (or to a connected person), a sum (a '*major lump sum*') that is not rent but falls to be treated, in accordance with GAAP, partly as a repayment of some or all of the investment in respect of the finance lease or loan and partly as a return on that investment.

(c) Not all of the part of the major lump sum which is treated as a return on the investment (as in (b) above) would, apart from these provisions, be brought into account for corporation tax purposes, as 'normal rent' (see below) from the lease for periods of account of the lessor, in accounting periods of the lessor ending with the 'relevant accounting period'. The '*relevant accounting period*' is the accounting period (or latest accounting period) consisting of or including all or part of the period of account in which the major lump sum is or may be payable under the arrangements.

(d) The period of account of the lessor in which the relevant time falls (or an earlier period during which he was the lessor) is one for which the 'accountancy rental earnings' in respect of the lease exceed the normal rent. The normal rent is determined by treating rent as accruing and falling due evenly over the period to which it relates (unless a payment falls due more than twelve months after any of the rent to which it relates is so treated as accruing).

(e) At the relevant time, either:

(i) arrangements exist under which the lessee (or a person connected with the lessee) may directly or indirectly acquire the leased asset (or an asset representing it — see *CTA 2010, s 934*) from the lessor (or a person connected with the lessor), and in connection with that acquisition the lessor (or connected person) may directly or indirectly receive a 'qualifying lump sum' from the lessee (or connected person); or

(ii) in the absence of such arrangements, it is in any event more likely that the acquisition and receipt described in (i) above will take place than that, before any such acquisition, the leased asset (or the asset representing it) will have been acquired in an open market sale by a person who is neither the lessor nor the lessee nor a person connected with either of them.

In (i) above, a '*qualifying lump sum*' is a sum which is not rent but at least part of which would be treated under GAAP as a return on investment in respect of a finance lease or loan.

For the purposes of the Chapter 2 provisions (and also the provisions at **71.45** below):

- a '*normal rent*' for a period of account of a lessor is the amount which (apart from these provisions) the lessor would bring in for corporation tax purposes in the period as rent arising from the lease;

- '*rental earnings*' for any period is the amount that falls for accounting purposes to be treated, in accordance with GAAP, as the gross return for that period on investment in respect of a finance lease or loan in respect of the leasing arrangements; and
- the '*accountancy rental earnings*' in respect of a lease for a period of account of the lessor is the greatest of the following amounts of rental earnings for that period in respect of the lease:
  (i) the rental earnings of the lessor;
  (ii) the rental earnings of any person connected with the lessor;
  (iii) the rental earnings for the purposes of consolidated group accounts of a group of which the lessor is a member.

  Where (ii) or (iii) applies and the lessor's period of account does not coincide with that of the connected person or the consolidated group accounts, amounts in the periods of account of the latter are apportioned as necessary by reference to the number of days in the common periods.

Current lessor to be taxed by reference to accountancy rental earnings. If for any period of account of the current lessor (L):

- the Chapter 2 provisions apply to the lease; and
- the accountancy rental earnings exceed the normal rent.

L is treated for corporation tax purposes as if in that period of account L had been entitled to, and there had arisen to L, rent from the lease of an amount equal to those accountancy rental earnings (instead of the normal rent). That rent is deemed to have accrued at an even rate throughout the period of account (or so much of the it as corresponds to the period for which the asset is leased).

Reduction of taxable rent by cumulative rental excesses

If a period of account of the current lessor is one in which the normal rent in respect of the lease exceeds the accountancy rental earnings, and there is a 'cumulative accountancy rental excess', the rent otherwise taxable for the period (the '*taxable rent*') is reduced by setting that excess against it. It cannot be reduced to less than the accountancy rental earnings.

There is an '*accountancy rental excess*' for a period if the period is one in which the current lessor is taxed by reference to accountancy rental earnings as above; it is the excess of the accountancy rental earnings over the normal rent. If, however, the taxable rent for that period is reduced by a 'cumulative normal rental excess' (see below), the accountancy rental excess for the period is limited to the excess (if any) of the accountancy rental earnings, reduced by the same amount as the taxable rent, over the normal rent. A '*cumulative accountancy rental excess*' is so much of the aggregate of accountancy rental excesses of previous periods of account as has not already been used, whether under these rules, the bad debt rules below or the rules below on disposals.

If a period of account of the current lessor is one in which the current lessor is taxed by reference to accountancy rental earnings, and there is a 'cumulative normal rental excess', the taxable rent is reduced by setting that excess against it. It cannot be reduced to less than the normal rent.

The '*normal rental excess*' for a period of account is the excess (if any) of normal rent over accountancy rental earnings. If, however, the taxable rent for that period is reduced by a cumulative accountancy rental excess (as above), the normal rental excess for the period is limited to the excess (if any) of the normal rent, reduced by the same amount as the taxable rent, over accountancy rental earnings. A '*cumulative normal rental excess*' is so much of the aggregate of normal rental excesses of previous periods of account as has not already been used, whether under these rules or the bad debt rules below.

Bad debts

Where accountancy rental earnings for a period of account are substituted for normal rent for corporation tax purposes (as above), and a 'bad debt deduction' in excess of the accountancy rental earnings falls to be made for the period, any cumulative accountancy rental excess for the period is reduced (but not below nil) by that excess. If the accountancy rental earnings do not exceed the normal rent, any bad debt deduction acts to reduce the amount of the normal rent against which a cumulative accountancy rental excess may be set, and the cumulative accountancy rental excess is reduced (but not below nil) by any excess of the bad debt deduction over the normal rent. There is provision for such reductions in the cumulative accountancy rental excess to be reversed in the event of subsequent bad debt recoveries or reinstatements. A '*bad debt deduction*', in relation to a period of account of the lessor, means the total of the deductions (if any) falling to be made for accounting purposes for that period by way of impairment loss in respect of rents from the lease of the asset.

There are similar provisions relating to the effect of bad debt deductions on cumulative normal rental excesses.

Effect of disposals

If the current lessor (or a connected person) disposes of its interest under the lease or the leased asset or an asset representing the leased asset (see *CTA 2010, s 934*), the Chapter 2 provisions have effect as if immediately before the disposal (or simultaneous such disposals) a period of account of the current lessor ended and another began.

In determining the amount of any chargeable gain on the disposal, the disposal consideration is reduced by setting against it any cumulative accountancy rental excess (as above) for the period of account in which the disposal occurs. *TCGA 1992, s 37* does not exclude any money or money's worth from the disposal consideration so far as it is represented by any cumulative accountancy rental excess set off under this rule (whether on the current disposal or previously). On a part disposal, the cumulative accountancy rental excess is apportioned in the same manner as the associated acquisition costs. Where there are simultaneous disposals, the cumulative accountancy rental excess is apportioned between them on a just and reasonable basis.

On an assignment of the current lessor's interest under the lease treated under *TCGA 1992* as a no gain/no loss disposal (see *TCGA 1992, s 288(3A)*), a period of account of the assignor is treated as ending, and a period of account of the assignee as beginning, with the assignment. Any unused cumulative accountancy rental excess or cumulative normal rental excess at the time of the assignment is transferred to the assignee.

Capital allowances etc.

Where an occasion occurs on which a major lump sum (as in (b) above) falls to be paid, there are provisions (see *CTA 2010, ss 917–922*) for the withdrawal of earlier reliefs for expenditure incurred by the current lessor in respect of the leased asset. This applies to capital allowances (**10**) and to reliefs for capital expenditure under **71.10** above (cemeteries and crematoria) and **71.76** below (waste disposal). Deductions allowed under *F(No 2)A 1992, ss 40B, 42* (films and sound recordings) are similarly withdrawn. The earlier reliefs are withdrawn either by the bringing in of a disposal value or by the imposition of a balancing charge or, in the case of expenditure allowed in respect of cemeteries etc., waste disposal or films etc., by the bringing in of a countervailing receipt. These provisions apply equally to capital allowances for contributors to capital expenditure under *CAA 2001, ss 537–542*.

Pre-existing schemes for which (a)–(e) above are first met after 26 November 1996

Where a lease of an asset forms part of a 'pre-existing scheme' (as below) for which conditions (a)–(e) above are first met after 26 November 1996, the Chapter 2 provisions apply as if a period of account of the current lessor ended and another began both immediately before and immediately after those conditions came to be met, i.e. as if there was a brief separate period of account during which they came to be met. Any cumulative accountancy rental excess which would have arisen for that period, had the conditions been met in relation to the lease at all times on or after 26 November 1996, is treated as so arising, and the current lessor is treated as if, at the end of the immediately preceding period, there had accrued an additional amount of rent equal to that excess. (That rent is, however, left out of account in determining normal rent for comparison with accountancy rental earnings, as above.) Similarly a cumulative normal rental excess which would have arisen on those assumptions is treated as having arisen in the period in which the conditions came to be met.

A lease of an asset forms part of a '*pre-existing scheme*' if a contract in writing for the lease was made before 26 November 1996 and either:

(i) no terms of the contract remained to be agreed on or after that date, and any conditions were met before that date; or
(ii) the requirements in (i) were met before the end of the period ending with the later of 31 January 1997 and the expiry of six months after the making of the contract, or within such further time as HMRC may have allowed in any particular case, and in its final form the contract does not differ materially from how it stood when originally made.

Post-25 November 1996 schemes to which Chapter 3 provisions applied first

If the Chapter 2 provisions come to apply to a lease to which the Chapter 3 provisions at **71.45** below applied immediately beforehand, the cumulative accountancy rental excess and the cumulative normal rental excess are determined as if the Chapter 2 provisions had applied throughout the period for which the Chapter 3 conditions in fact applied.

[*TIOPA 2010, Sch 3 para 7, CTA 2010, ss 895–924, 930–937, Sch 2 para 98; TCGA 1992, s 37A; FA 1997 Sch 12 paras 1–7, 9–14, 20–30; FA 2006, Sch 9 para 7(1)(2)(4); CTA 2009, Sch 1 para 448; SI 2008 No 954, Art 22*].

For HMRC's views on various points of interpretation regarding the Chapter 2 provisions, see HMRC Business Leasing Manual BLM70005 onwards.

Simon's Taxes. See **B3.340E, B5.416.**

Finance leases not within the above provisions

[71.45] *CTA 2010, Pt 21 Ch 3 (ss 925–929)* (the Chapter 3 provisions) apply to arrangements, not within the Chapter 2 provisions at **71.44** above, which involve the lease of an asset and would fall to be treated under generally accepted accounting practice (GAAP) as finance leases or loans. The Chapter 3 provisions were previously in *FA 1997, Sch 12 Pt II* and applied from 26 November 1996. The main purpose of the Chapter 3 provisions is to charge tax on amounts falling to be treated under GAAP as the income return on investment in respect of the finance lease or loan (taking into account the substance of the matter as a whole, e.g. as regards connected persons or groups of companies). The Chapter 3 provisions accordingly apply where:

- a lease of an asset is granted on or after 26 November 1996;
- the lease forms part of a post-25 November 1996 scheme (i.e. a scheme that is not a pre-existing scheme as defined in **71.44** above);
- condition (a) at **71.44** above (or its income tax equivalent) is met at some time on or after 26 November 1996 in a period of account of the current lessor; and
- the Chapter 2 provisions described at **71.44** above do not apply because not all of conditions (b)–(e) at **71.44** above (or their income tax equivalents) have been met at that time.

Where condition (a) at **71.44** above was met at some time on or after 26 November 1996, it is treated as continuing to be met until either the asset ceases to be leased under the lease or the lessor's interest is assigned to a person not connected with any of the following:

(i) the assignor;
(ii) any other person who was the lessor at some time before the assignment, and
(iii) any person who at some time after the assignment becomes the lessor under arrangements made by a person who was the lessor (or was connected with the lessor) at some time before the assignment.

A lease to which the Chapter 3 provisions cease to apply can come within those provisions again if the conditions for their application are again met.

If for any period of account of the current lessor (L):

- the Chapter 3 provisions apply to the lease, and
- the 'accountancy rental earnings' (**71.44** above) exceed the 'normal rent' (**71.44** above),

L is treated for corporation tax purposes as if in that period of account L had been entitled to, and there had arisen to L, rent from the lease of an amount equal to those accountancy rental earnings (instead of the normal rent). That rent is deemed to have accrued at an even rate throughout the period of account (or so much of the it as corresponds to the period for which the asset is leased).

The provisions at **71.44** above relating to reduction of taxable rent by cumulative rental excesses, bad debt relief and the effect of disposals apply equally for the purposes of the Chapter 3 provisions.

The Chapter 3 provisions do *not* apply if (or to the extent that), as regards the current lessor, the lease falls to be regarded as a long funding lease (within **13.5 CAPITAL ALLOWANCES — PLANT AND MACHINERY: FIXTURES AND LEASING**) of plant or machinery.

[*TIOPA 2010, Sch 3; CTA 2010, ss 925–937; FA 1997, Sch 12 paras 15–17, 20–30; FA 2006, Sch 9 para 7(1)(3)(4)*].

For HMRC's views on various points of interpretation regarding the Chapter 3 provisions, see HMRC Business Leasing Manual BLM74600 onwards.

Simon's Taxes. See **B5.416**.

Changes to leasing accounting standards

[71.46] Provisions are introduced by *FA 2011, s 53* to ensure that the existing tax rules that rely on the accounting treatment of lease transactions continue to operate as they currently do. Much of the corporation tax code for lease transactions is based on accounting definitions with regard to accounts prepared in accordance with UK GAAP, or IAS.

Fundamental changes are expected with regard to IAS during 2011, and also in respect of UK GAAP (possibly in 2013). This will have an effect on the operation of the existing tax rules. The provision introduced as *FA 2011, s 53* requires businesses which account for lease transactions to treat them, for the purposes of the Taxes Acts only, as if the changes to accounting standards had not taken place. This will apply to any business, whether as lessee, lessor, or both, that accounts for lease transactions using a lease accounting standard that is newly issued or changed on or after 1 January 2011. It should therefore not change the existing tax treatment of leases and will ensure that such treatment continues.

[*FA 2011, s 53*].

Flooding

[71.47] A helpline to assist those affected by the floods in 2007 was set up: the number is 0845 3000 157. Retrospective legislation was included in Finance Bill 2008 to permit HMRC to waive interest and surcharges on tax paid late due to floods. Discretionary powers were used not to collect such interest and surcharges until that time.

HMRC may also enter arrangements for the collection of taxes, suspend debt collection proceedings, defer compliance checks and investigations, and waive penalties for deadlines missed as a result of the flooding.

Franchising

[71.48] For companies acquiring and selling franchises after 31 March 2002, the intangible assets regime (see **48 INTANGIBLE ASSETS**) is likely to apply and takes precedence over the below.

Under a business system franchising agreement (i.e. an agreement under which the franchisor grants to the franchisee the right to distribute products or perform services using that system), there is generally an initial fee (payable in one sum or in instalments) and continuing, usually annual, fees.

The capital or revenue treatment of the initial fee depends on what it is for. To the extent that it is paid wholly or mainly for substantial rights of an enduring nature, to initiate or substantially extend a business, it is a capital payment (as are any related professional fees). (See **71.78** for general principles.) It is immaterial that the expenditure may prove abortive, and the treatment of the payment in the hands of the franchisor is irrelevant. However, where goods or services of a revenue nature are supplied at the outset (e.g. trading stock or staff training), HMRC will accept that an appropriate part of the initial fee is a revenue payment, provided that the sum claimed fairly represents such items, and that it is clear that the items are not separately charged for in the continuing fees. The costs of the franchisee's own initial training are not normally allowable.

The continuing fee payable by the franchisee is generally a revenue expense.

(HMRC Business Income Manual BIM57620).

See generally HMRC Business Income Manual BIM57600–57620.

Gifts and donations etc.

[71.49] See also **71.41** above (entertainment and gifts), **70.41** for gifts received, disposals of assets and inventory, and **20.12** for gift aid donations (*FA 2011, s 41* increases the limits with regard to the maximum value of benefits a charity can provide to an individual or a corporate donor from £500 to £2,500). Anti-avoidance legislation has been introduced by *FA 2011, s 27 Sch 3* with regard to tainted charity donations made by substantial donors to charities where arrangements are entered into to obtain benefits from such donations — see further **20.10 CHARITIES** — substantial donors.

In relation to *ex gratia* payments on the termination of long-standing business arrangements, a distinction is drawn between parting gifts as personal testimonials (not taxable as business receipts) and payments which, on the facts, can be seen as additional rewards for services already rendered or compensation for a loss of future profits (taxable). For cases see **70.27**(e) **TRADE PROFITS — INCOME AND SPECIFIC TRADES.**

A relief is available for certain gifts by trading companies for the purposes of a charity see **70.41** trade profits. Relief is also available for gifts for humanitarian purposes of medical supplies or medical equipment again see **71.49 TRADE PROFITS — INCOME AND SPECIFIC TRADES.**

An ordinary annual subscription by a trading company to a charity, made for the benefit of its employees, may be allowed as a trade expense where the availability of the charity to the employees can reasonably be regarded as a direct and valuable advantage to the employer's business and the amount is not unreasonably high (see *Bourne & Hollingsworth v Ogden* (1929) 14 TC 349). This would include reasonable annual subscriptions made to, for example, a general hospital in the locality of the employer's place of business, or to a trade charity maintained primarily for the benefit of employees in the type of trade in question. It can also include subscriptions made to charities of benefit to a specific category of the employees.

For donations of part of cost of ticket in football pools and lotteries, see **70.5 TRADE PROFITS — INCOME AND SPECIFIC TRADES.**

Simon's Taxes. See B2.441.

Guarantees

[71.50] Losses under guarantees of the indebtedness of another are analogous to impairment losses (see **71.5** above) and similar principles apply.

Cases where losses were allowed as a deduction include:

- *Jennings v Barfield* (1962) 40 TC 365 — to a solicitor under the guarantee of a client's overdraft.
- *Lunt v Wellesley* (1945) 27 TC 78 — to a film-writer under guarantee of loans to a film company with which he was associated.

Cases where losses were refused include

- *Milnes v J Beam Group Ltd* (1975) 50 TC 675 — a company under a guarantee of loans to an associated company with which it had close trading connections.
- *Redkite Ltd v Inspector of Taxes* [1996] STC (SCD) 501 — a guarantee of loans to a subsidiary.

Also see *Bolton v Halpern & Woolf* (1980) 53 TC 445, CA, and *Garforth v Tankard Carpets Ltd* (1980) 53 TC 342.

A loss by an asphalt contractor under a guarantee to an exhibition (for which he hoped but, in the event, failed to work) allowed (*Morley v Lawford & Co* (1928) 14 TC 229, CA). BIM45305.

Payments under guarantees made to a trader for the setting up or the purposes of the trade and irrecoverable are in certain circumstances allowable as a loss for corporation tax. From a date to be determined by statutory instrument, a claim under these provisions must be made not more than four years from the end of the accounting period in which it is made (previously six years). [*TCGA 1992, s 253; FA 2008, Sch 39 para 30; CTA 2009, Sch 1 para 382*]. BIM45301 See Tolley's Capital Gains Tax.

Hire-purchase

[71.51] Where assets are purchased under hire-purchase agreements, the charges (the excess of the hire-purchase price over the cash price, sometimes called interest but not true interest) are, appropriately spread, allowable deductions (*Darngavil Coal Co Ltd v Francis* (1913) 7 TC 1, Ct of Sess). See **71.5** for the bad debt etc. provisions of hire-purchase traders. For relief on capital element, see **13.24 CAPITAL ALLOWANCES — PLANT AND MACHINERY: FIXTURES AND LEASING.**

For whether goods sold under hire-purchase are trading stock, see *Lions Ltd v Gosford Furnishing Co Ltd & CIR* (1961) 40 TC 256, Ct of Sess, and cf *Drages Ltd v CIR* (1927) 46 TC 389.

See generally HMRC Business Income Manual BIM40550–40555 (hire-purchase receipts) and BIM45350–45365 (hire-purchase payments).

Simon's Taxes. See **B2.406, B5.640–B5.642.**

Illegal payments etc.

[71.52] In computing income from any source for corporation tax purposes, no deduction may be made in respect of expenditure incurred:

(a) in making a payment the making of which constitutes a criminal offence; or
(b) in making a payment outside the UK where the making of a corresponding payment in any part of the UK would constitute a criminal offence there (since 31 March 2002).

A deduction is similarly denied for any payment induced by a demand constituting blackmail or extortion. [*CTA 2009, s 1304; FA 2002, s 68; SI 2004 No 2310, Sch para 24; ITTOIA 2005, Sch 1 para 236*].

For a discussion of the circumstances in which the above may apply, see HMRC Business Income Manual BIM43100–43185.

Simon's Taxes. See **B2.420.**

Insurance paid

[71.53] Premiums for business purposes are normally allowable including insurance of assets, insurance against accidents to employees, insurance against loss of profits and premiums under mutual insurance schemes (cf. *Thomas v Richard Evans & Co* (1927) 11 TC 790, HL; for trade associations, see **71.67**).

For any recoveries on insurance policies see **70 TRADE PROFITS — INCOME AND SPECIFIC TRADES.**

Premiums on policies in favour of the employer insuring against death or critical illness of key employees are generally allowable, and the proceeds of any such policies trading receipts. However, in *Beauty Consultants Ltd v*

Inspector of Taxes [2002] STC (SCD) 352, premiums on a policy insuring a company against the death of either of its controlling shareholder-directors were not allowed as deductions; the 'dual purpose rule' at **71.78** applied, in that the premiums benefited the shareholders personally by improving the value of their shares. In *Greycon Ltd v Klaentschi* [2003] STC (SCD) 370, it was held that the company's sole purpose in taking out key man policies was to meet a requirement of an agreement under which funding and other benefits were obtained from another company, that the policies had a capital purpose and that, consequently, the proceeds were not trading receipts.

Legal and professional expenses

[71.54] The costs of forming a company are capital but in so far as they relate to loan capital may qualify for relief by virtue of *CTA 2009, s 61* (pre-trading expenditure — see **71.60** below).

The expenses of a company incorporated by charter in obtaining a variation of its charter etc. were allowed (*CIR v Carron Co* (1968) 45 TC 18, HL). See also *McGarry v Limerick Gas HC* [1932] IR 125 and contrast *A & G Moore & Co v Hare* (1914) 6 TC 572, Ct of Sess. In general, the costs of maintaining existing trading rights and assets are revenue expenses (*Southern v Borax Consolidated* (1940) 23 TC 597; *Bihar etc IT Commr v Maharaja of Dharbanga* (1941) 20 ATC 337, PC, and compare *Morgan v Tate & Lyle Ltd* (1954) 35 TC 367, HL). But the incidental costs of acquiring new assets etc. are part of their capital cost. The expenses of obtaining or renewing a lease of business premises are strictly capital but, in practice, the expenses of renewing leases under 50 years are generally deductible (although a proportionate disallowance may apply where a lease premium is involved — see HMRC Business Income Manual BIM46420). The cost of an unsuccessful application to vary a carrier's licence was disallowed (*Pyrah v Annis & Co* (1956) 37 TC 163, CA) as was the cost of an unsuccessful application for planning permission (*ECC Quarries Ltd v Watkis* (1975) 51 TC 153.

Legal expenses in defending charges brought by a professional regulatory body were allowed as deductions on the grounds that they were incurred to prevent suspension or expulsion and thus to protect the taxpayer's business (applying *Tate & Lyle Ltd* (above)), although the fines imposed were disallowed (see **71.11** above) (*McKnight v Sheppard* (1999) 71 TC 419, HL).

Costs incurred by a partner in connection with the dissolution of the partnership were disallowed in *C Connelly & Co v Wilbey* (1992) 65 TC 208.

The cost of tax appeals even though successful is not deductible (*Allen v Farquharson Bros & Co* (1932) 17 TC 59; *Smith's Potato Estates v Bolland* (1948) 30 TC 267, HL; *Rushden Heel Co v Keene* (1948) 30 TC 298, HL). Where an accountant etc. agrees the tax liabilities based on the accounts he prepares, normal annual fees are allowed as a deduction but not fees for a special review of settled years (*Worsley Brewery Co v CIR* (1932) 17 TC 349, CA).

In the case of *Market South West (Holdings) Ltd v HMRC*, UT May 2011, [2010] UKFTT 121 (TC), a company operated an indoor market at a site in Cornwall. The relevant planning permission only allowed it to trade at weekends. They applied for planning permission to trade on weekdays. The council granted planning permission to trade on ten weekdays. The company subsequently breached the terms of this permission. The council issued an enforcement notice, against which the company appealed. The QB dismissed this appeal. In its tax return, the company claimed a deduction for the legal and professional fees incurred in applying for planning permission and in appealing against the enforcement notice issued by the council. HMRC issued an amendment disallowing the deduction on the basis that this was capital expenditure. The First-Tier Tribunal dismissed the company's appeal but the Upper Tribunal remitted the case for rehearing. Judge Avery Jones held that 'there should be an apportionment on the analogy of expenditure on a building that is partly an improvement and partly repairs'.

Additional accountancy expenses incurred as a result of an 'in-depth' examination by HMRC of a particular year's accounts will normally be allowed as a deduction if the investigation does not result in an adjustment to the profits of any earlier year or in the imposition of interest or interest and penalties in relation to the current year. Where the investigation reveals discrepancies and additional liabilities for earlier years, or results in a settlement for the current year including interest (with or without penalties), the expenses will be disallowed. (HMRC Statement of Practice, SP 16/91). In its application to self-assessment enquiries, the Statement of Practice is reworded to make it clear that the prohibition on allowance of accountancy expenses applies only where the enquiry reveals negligent or fraudulent conduct (see Revenue Interpretation RI 192 and see Revenue Tax Bulletin October 1998 p 596 issue 37).

It is HMRC's view that premiums for a fee protection insurance policy, which entitles the policy holder to claim for the cost of accountancy fees incurred in negotiating additional tax liabilities resulting from negligent (careless) or fraudulent (deliberate) conduct, are not allowable. Even if the policy covers other risks as well, the premiums cannot be apportioned between allowable and non-allowable elements. (Revenue Tax Bulletin June 2003 p 1036). See BIM46452.

HMRC BIM46400

Simon's Taxes. See **B2.449.**

Long funding leases of plant or machinery

[71.55] The rules on leasing of plant and machinery were reformed by *FA 2006, s 81, Sch 8* with effect from, broadly, 1 April 2006, and are now in *CTA 2010, ss 359–381, Sch 2 paras 61–64*. For 'long funding leases', the current regime grants entitlement to capital allowances to the lessee rather than to the lessor as previously (see **13.5 CAPITAL ALLOWANCES — PLANT AND MACHINERY: FIXTURES AND LEASING**). There were corresponding changes to the tax treatment of lease rentals, to ensure that the lessor is no longer taxed on, and the lessee does not obtain a deduction for, the capital element of rentals (see below). The regime applies only to leases which are essentially financing transactions, known as '*funding leases*', comprising mainly finance leases but also some operating leases. Leases of less than five years' duration are excluded from the regime, as are pre-1 April 2006 leases. For transitional rules see 2009–10 and earlier versions of this book.

The coverage below considers firstly the lessor's position and then the lessee's. The provisions differ in each case according to whether the lease is a long funding operating lease or a long funding finance lease.

For an HMRC Technical Note published on 1 August 2006 on the long funding leasing rules, see www.hmrc.gov.uk/leasing/tech-note.pdf. See also HMRC Business Leasing Manual BLM40000 *et seq*.

The provisions with regard to the sale of lessors are amended by *FA 2011, s 32* and *Sch 6* to ensure that the legislation correctly identifies the appropriate companies and bring in a charge that accurately reflects the deferred tax position of the company. See further **5.27 ANTI-AVOIDANCE** in this regard.

As regards finance leases that fall outside the definition of a long funding lease or preceded its introduction, see **71.43–71.45** above.

Lessors

Long funding operating leases

For any period of account for the whole or any part of which the company is the lessor of plant or machinery under a 'long funding operating lease' (see **13.5 CAPITAL ALLOWANCES — PLANT AND MACHINERY: FIXTURES AND LEASING**), it is entitled to a deduction as follows in computing its profits (so as to compensate it for non-entitlement to capital allowances). Firstly, determine the 'starting value' in accordance with *CTA 2010, ss 364, 365* (previously *ICTA 1988, s 502E(4)(5)*). This varies depending on whether or not there has been any previous use of the plant or machinery by the lessor and on the nature of any such previous use. In the most straightforward case where the sole use has been leasing under the long funding operating lease, the starting value is equal to cost. Secondly, deduct from the starting value the amount that is expected (at the commencement of the term of the lease — see *CAA 2001, s 70YI(1)*) to be the 'residual value' of the plant or machinery (i.e. its estimated market value assuming a disposal at the end of the term of the lease, less the estimated costs of that disposal). This gives the expected gross reduction in value over the term of the lease. Next, time-apportion that figure between all periods of account that coincide wholly or partly with the term of the lease. The resulting figure for each period of account is the amount deductible for that period.

Where the lessor (as above) incurs additional capital expenditure on the plant or machinery that is not reflected in its market value at the commencement of the term of the lease, an additional deduction is due as follows. Determine the amount which, at the time the additional expenditure is incurred, is expected to be the residual value of the plant or machinery. Deduct the amount previously expected to be the residual value. If this produces a positive amount, determine how much of that amount is attributable to the additional expenditure. Next, deduct the attributable amount from the amount of the additional expenditure. This gives the expected reduction in value of the additional expenditure over the remainder of the term of the lease. Time-apportion that figure between all periods of account that coincide wholly or partly with the term of the lease and which end after the additional expenditure is incurred. The resulting figure for each such period of account is the additional amount deductible for that period.

In the period of account in which a long funding operating lease *terminates*, any profit arising to the lessor from the termination must be brought into account as trading income and any loss so arising must be brought into account as a revenue expense. The profit or loss is computed as follows.

(1) Determine the 'termination amount' (for which see **13.9 CAPITAL ALLOWANCES — PLANT AND MACHINERY: FIXTURES AND LEASING** under Lessors) and subtract from it any sums paid to the lessee that are calculated by reference to the 'termination value' (as defined by *CAA 2001, s 70YH*), e.g. lease rental refunds.
(2) Determine the 'starting value' as above and subtract from it all deductions (other than additional deductions) allowable as above to that same lessor up to the date of termination.
(3) If any additional capital expenditure has been incurred as above, determine the total amount thereof and subtract from it all additional deductions allowable as above to that same lessor up to the date of termination.
(4) If the total in (1) above exceeds the aggregate of the totals in (2) and (3), a profit arises equal to the excess.
(5) If the total in (1) above falls short of the aggregate of the totals in (2) and (3), a loss arises equal to the deficit.

In computing the lessor's profits for the period of account in which termination occurs, no trading deduction is allowed for any sums paid to the lessee that are calculated by reference to the 'termination value' (as these are brought into account in (1) above).

[*CTA 2010, ss 363–369, 381; ICTA 1988, ss 502E–502G, 502L(2)–(4); FA 2006, Sch 8 para 11*].

Long funding finance leases

For any period of account in which the company is the lessor of plant or machinery under a 'long funding finance lease' (see **13.5 CAPITAL ALLOWANCES — PLANT AND MACHINERY: FIXTURES AND LEASING**), the amount to be brought into account as his taxable income from the lease is the amount of the 'rental earnings' in respect of the lease. The '*rental earnings*' for any period is the amount that, in accordance with generally accepted accounting practice (GAAP), falls to be treated as the gross return on investment for that period in respect of the lease. If, in accordance with GAAP, the lease falls to be treated as a loan in the accounts in question, so much of the lease rentals as fall to be treated as interest are treated for these purposes as rental earnings. There is also provision for exceptional profits or losses (including capital items) arising from the lease to be brought into account for tax purposes, as trading income or as revenue expenditure, if they fall to be brought into account under GAAP in the period of account in question but otherwise than as part of the profits calculation.

Where the lease *terminates* and any sum calculated by reference to 'termination value' (as defined by *CAA 2001, s 70YH*) is paid to the lessee, e.g. lease rental refunds, no deduction is allowed for that sum in computing the lessor's trading profits, except to the extent (if any) that it is brought into account in determining rental earnings.

[*CTA 2010, ss 360–362, 381; ICTA 1988, ss 502B–502D, 502L(4); FA 2006, Sch 8 para 11*].

Anti-avoidance legislation disapplies *CTA 2010, ss 360–369* above where:

(a) expenditure incurred on the leased plant or machinery is (apart from anything in *CTA 2010, ss 360–369*) allowable as a deduction in computing the lessor's trading profits because the plant or machinery is held, or comes to be held, as trading stock; or
(b) the long funding lease is part of an arrangement, including one or more other transactions, entered into by the lessor a main purpose of which is to secure that, over the term of the lease, there is a substantial difference between the amounts brought into account under GAAP and the amounts brought into account in computing taxable profits, such difference being at least partly attributable to the application of any of *CTA 2010, ss 360–369*.

Sub-paragraph (a) above applies where the expenditure is incurred after 8 October 2007 or the lessor becomes entitled to a deduction as a result of plant or machinery forming part of the trading stock on or after that date. Sub-paragraph (b) above applies where the arrangement is entered into on or after that date.

There is also anti-avoidance legislation designed to counter a scheme involving a mismatch in the treatment of lease rentals under a head lease and a sub-lease of the same plant or machinery. Under a typical scheme, the head lease from A to B will not be a long funding lease from B's (the lessee's) point of view but the sub-lease from B to C will be a long funding lease from B's (the lessor's) point of view. The result is that B would be entitled to tax relief on the full amount of the lease rentals under the head lease (i.e. including the capital element) but would not be chargeable to tax on the capital element of the sub-lease rentals. The legislation seeks to ensure that B is taxed on the full amount of the sub-lease rentals by disapplying *CTA 2010, ss 360–369* above in these circumstances in relation to the sub-lease. It applies where the sub-lease is entered into after 12 December 2007. There are additional provisions to ensure that a sub-lease already in existence at the beginning of 13 December 2007 is taxed broadly as if it were not a long-funding lease as regards rentals relating to any time on or after that date.

Further anti-avoidance provisions are introduced by *FA 2011* with regard to long funding finance leases in response to a scheme disclosed to HMRC. The scheme includes arrangements which act as a guarantee but which also result in the lessee acquiring the asset from the lessor at the end of the lease. The effects are such that: the lessee is entitled to include the residual 'guaranteed' amount in calculating the expenditure at the start of the lease; and when the payment is made under the arrangement that payment then reduces the disposal value (under *s 70E*) and the payment falls to be treated as qualifying expenditure for capital allowance purposes for a second time.

To counter such a scheme provisions are introduced, applicable with regard to payments made on or after 9 March 2011, such that *CAA 2001, ss 70C, 70D* are amended to prevent any relief from being available in excess of cost.

See further **13.6, 13.7** and **13.9 PLANT AND MACHINERY — FIXTURES AND LEASING.**

[*FA 2011, s 33; CTA 2010, ss 370–375, Sch 2 paras 62, 63; ICTA 1988, s 502GA–GC; FA 2008, Sch 20 paras 9, 11*].

Film lessors

Legislation originally included in *FA 2009* disapplies *CTA 2010, ss 360–369* above where the subject of the long funding lease is a film. This has effect where the 'inception' (see *CAA 2001, s 70YI(1)*) of the lease is after 12 November 2008. In addition, there are changes to the treatment of a long funding finance lease of a film where its inception was on or before 12 November 2008 and rentals are due after that date and relate to time falling after that date. The lessor will be taxed on both the finance charge element of the rentals and so much of the capital element of the rentals as relates to the time falling after 12 November 2008; the other rules in *CTA 2010, ss 360–362* above are suitably modified. [*CTA 2010, s 376, Sch 2 para 64; ITTOIA 2005, s 502GD; FA 2009, Sch 33 paras 1, 3–9*].

Insurance companies

Special provisions applied for accounting periods beginning before 1 January 2008 to lessor companies carrying on life assurance business. The provisions ensured that the general apportionment rules in *ICTA 1988, s 432A* applied to net amounts of profits or losses arising from long funding leases and that the above provisions were ignored in taking receipts into account in a *Schedule D, Case I* computation. These special provisions were repealed in the light of more general amendments made to *s 432A* by *FA 2008, Sch 17 para 17*. [*ICTA 1988, s 502H; FA 2006, Sch 8 para 11; FA 2008, Sch 17 para 17(11)*].

Lessees

Long funding operating leases

In computing the profits of a company for any period of account in which it is the lessee of plant or machinery under a 'long funding operating lease' (see **13.5 CAPITAL ALLOWANCES — PLANT AND MACHINERY: FIXTURES AND LEASING**), the otherwise allowable deductions in respect of amounts payable under the lease must be reduced as follows.

Firstly, determine the 'starting value' in accordance with *CTA 2010, s 380* (previously *ICTA 1988, s 502K(4)(5)*). In the straightforward case where the sole use of the plant or machinery has been in a qualifying activity (within **11.1 CAPITAL ALLOWANCES — PLANT AND MACHINERY: ELIGIBLE EXPENDITURE AND INITIAL ALLOWANCES**) carried on by the lessee, the starting value is equal to the market value of the plant or machinery at the commencement (see *CAA 2001, s 70YI(1)*) of the term of the lease. Secondly, deduct from the starting value the amount that is expected (at the commencement of the term of the lease) to be the market value of the plant or machinery at the end of the term of the lease. This gives the expected gross reduction over the term of the lease. Next, time-apportion that figure between all periods of account that coincide wholly or partly with the term of the lease. The resulting figure for each period of account is the amount of the reduction for that period.

[*CTA 2010, ss 379–381; ICTA 1988, ss 502K, 502L; FA 2006, Sch 8 para 11*].

Long funding finance leases

In computing the profits of a company for any period of account in which it is the lessee of plant or machinery under a 'long funding finance lease' (see **13.5 CAPITAL ALLOWANCES — PLANT AND MACHINERY: FIXTURES AND LEASING**), the amount deducted in respect of amounts payable under the lease must not exceed the amount that, in accordance with GAAP, falls to be shown in the lessee's accounts as finance charges in respect of the lease. If, in accordance with GAAP, the lease falls to be accounted for as a loan, it is for this purpose treated as if it fell to be accounted for as a finance lease.

Where the lease *terminates* and a sum calculated by reference to 'termination value' (as defined by *CAA 2001, s 70YH*) is paid to the lessee, e.g. lease rental refunds, that sum is not brought into account in computing the lessee's profits for any period. (It is, however, brought into account in calculating the disposal value of the plant or machinery for capital allowances purposes — see **13.6 CAPITAL ALLOWANCES — PLANT AND MACHINERY: FIXTURES AND LEASING** under Lessees: Disposal events and values).

See also the comments above with regard to the anti-avoidance legislation introduced by *FA 2011* which prevent relief from being obtained for any leased assets in excess of cost, to counter a scheme which used guarantee arrangements to obtain deductions twice on the same expenditure on long funding finance leases.

See further **13.6**, **13.7** and **13.9 PLANT AND MACHINERY — FIXTURES AND LEASING.**

[*FA 2011, s 33; CTA 2010, ss 377, 378, 381; ICTA 1988, ss 502I, 502J, 502L(4); FA 2006, Sch 8 para 11*].

Miscellaneous expenses

[71.56] Export Credits Guarantee Department A deduction is allowed for amounts payable by a trading company to that Department under an agreement entered into by virtue of arrangements made under Export and *Investment Guarantees Act 1991, s 2* or with a view to entering into such an agreement. For accounting periods ending before 1 April 2009 (and see **70.2 TRADE PROFITS — INCOME AND SPECIFIC TRADES**), the deduction is for amounts paid rather than payable. [*CTA 2009, s 91; ICTA 1988, s 88; ITTOIA 2005, Sch 1 para 64*].

Distribution of assets from mutual concerns see **70.57 TRADE PROFITS — INCOME AND SPECIFIC TRADES.**

Reimbursements of capital expenditure spread over 30 years held capital as regards both payer and recipient (*Boyce v Whitwick Colliery* (1934) 18 TC 655, CA). For allowances from railway in respect of traffic on sidings paid for by trader see *Westcombe v Hadnock Quarries* (1931) 16 TC 137; *Legge v Flettons Ltd* (1939) 22 TC 455.

Excessive payments to **service company** of professional firm held not deductible (*Stephenson v Payne, Stone Fraser & Co* (1967) 44 TC 507).

For purchases and sales of standing timber see **70.57 TRADE PROFITS — INCOME AND SPECIFIC TRADES.**

Video tape rental

Relief for the cost of acquiring video tapes for hire may be obtained by way of either:

(i) capital allowances (provided the useful economic life is at least two years);
(ii) valuation basis (where the useful economic life is two years or less); or
(iii) renewals basis.

See Revenue Tax Bulletin October 1995 pp 254, 255 issue 19 for a discussion of each of these methods in this context. See also HMRC Business Income Manual BIM67200–67220.

See also *CIR v Pattison* (1959) 38 TC 617, Ct of Sess (weekly instalments for business, capital).

Patents

[71.57] For corporation tax purposes, expenditure and receipts in respect of intellectual property acquired or created **on or after 1 April 2002** falls within the intangible assets regime. See in particular the commencement and transitional rules for that regime at **48.36 INTANGIBLE ASSETS.**

Expenses (agent's charges, patent office fees etc.) are deductible if incurred in obtaining, for the purposes of a trade, the grant of a patent or the extension of its term. Expenses are also deductible in connection with a rejected or abandoned application for a patent made for the purposes of the trade. [*CTA 2009, s 89, Sch 2 para 22; ICTA 1988, s 83; ITTOIA 2005, Sch 1 para 56*].

For capital expenditure on the purchase of patent rights see **16.7 CAPITAL ALLOWANCES — MISCELLANEOUS.**

For sums received on the sale of patent rights see **70.58 TRADE PROFITS — INCOME AND SPECIFIC TRADES.**

Royalties and other sums paid for the use of patents are not deductible in computing trading profits. [*CTA 2009, s 59*]. For spreading of patent royalties received, see **61.18 PROFIT COMPUTATIONS.**

For know-how and trade marks, see **70.55** and **71.56** respectively.

Simon's Taxes. See B5.329 *et seq.*, B2.456.

Penalties, interest and surcharges

[71.58] Generally, tax penalties, interest and surcharges are not allowable deductions in computing profits for any corporation tax purpose. This applies to interest and certain penalties and surcharges in respect of late paid or unpaid or under-declared value added tax, insurance premium tax, landfill tax, climate change levy, aggregates levy, stamp duty land tax, excise duties, customs, excise or import duties, and income tax payable under the CONSTRUCTION INDUSTRY SCHEME (**26**); for a list of the specific charges to which this prohibition applies, see *CTA 2009, s 1303*. It does *not* apply to interest on late paid or unpaid corporation tax, which is dealt with under the loan relationships rules — see **49.2** INTEREST ON UNPAID TAX. [*CTA 2009, s 1303; FA 1994, s 18, Sch 7 para 31; FA 1996, Sch 5 para 40; FA 2000, Sch 7 para 4; FA 2001, s 49(3); FA 2003, s 40, Sch 18 para 3; FA 2004, s 71(3)*].

See also BIM45740 and 31610.

Post cessation receipts (allowable deductions from)

[71.59] A deduction from post-cessation receipts is allowed for any loss, expense or debit or capital allowance that would have been deductible if the trade had not ceased, has not been relieved in any other way and which does not arise directly or indirectly from the cessation itself. A deduction may not be given more than once. In the case of a loss, relief is given against the first available post-cessation receipts, i.e. receipts for an earlier accounting period in priority to those for a later one, but not so as give relief for a loss against receipts charged for an accounting period before that in which the loss is made.

Pre-trading expenditure

[71.60] The general rule is that trading expenditure is deductible when incurred and hence is not allowable if incurred before trading commenced (cf. *Birmingham & District Cattle By Products Ltd v CIR* (1919) 12 TC 92). The rule is modified for certain pre-trading capital expenditure, including scientific research expenditure and abortive exploration expenditure by mining concerns (see **10** CAPITAL ALLOWANCES — INTRODUCTION).

There is also a special relief for expenditure incurred by a company within the seven years before it commences to carry on a trade which, had it been incurred on the first day of trading, would have been deductible in computing the trading profit. The expenditure is treated as if it was incurred on the on the first day of trading and is thus deductible. Expenditure otherwise deductible, e.g. pre-trading purchases of stock or advance payments of rent, is not within this special relief.

See also **54.6** LOAN RELATIONSHIPS for the election available to treat pre-trading debits as trading debits of the accounting period in which the trade commences.

[*CTA 2009, s 61; ITTOIA 2005, Sch 1 para 172*].

The above provisions apply equally to a property business carried on by a company (see **62 PROPERTY INCOME**).

Provisions for contingent and future liabilities

[71.61] For forward contracts see **71.13** above.

Where a company is required under overseas legislation to make leaving payments to its employees, a provision in its accounts for its prospective liability is permissible if capable of sufficiently accurate calculation (*Owen v Southern Railway of Peru* [1957] AC 334, [1956] 2 All ER 728, HL). The allowance each year is the actual payments as adjusted for any variation between the opening and closing provisions but the deductible provision for the year in which the legislation was enacted may include an amount in respect of previous services of the employees (*CIR v Titaghur Jute Factory Ltd* CS 1978, 53 TC 675).

No deduction is normally permissible for future repairs or renewals (*Clayton v Newcastle-under-Lyme Corpn* QB 1888, 2 TC 416; *Naval Colliery Co Ltd v CIR* HL 1928, 12 TC 1017; *Peter Merchant Ltd v Stedeford* CA 1948, 30 TC 496). However, this rule is now subject to Financial Reporting Standard FRS 12 (see **71.63** below). No deduction is permissible for the future cost of collecting debts (*Monthly Salaries Loan Co v Furlong* Ch D 1962, 40 TC 313) or for future payments of damages in respect of accidents to employees unless liability has been admitted or established (*James Spencer & Co v CIR* CS 1950, 32 TC 111). See also *Albion Rovers Football Club v CIR* HL 1952, 33 TC 331 (wages deductible when paid). A provision for regular major overhaul work accrued due on aircraft engines was allowed in *Johnston v Britannia Airways Ltd* Ch D 1994, 67 TC 99 (but see Revenue Tax Bulletin February 1999 p 624 issue 39 and further below as regards changes in accounting practice superseding this decision).

For provisions by insurance companies for unexpired risks etc., see *Sun Insurance Office v Clark* HL 1912, 6 TC 59. For the liability of cemetery companies in receipt of lump sums for the future maintenance of graves, see *Paisley Cemetery Co v Reith* CES 1898, 4 TC 1 and *London Cemetery Co v Barnes* KB 1917, 7 TC 92.

A provision by a company engaged in the exploitation of a North Sea oil field, for anticipated future expenditure on the completion of the exploitation, in dismantling installations used and (as required under its licence) in 'cleaning up' the sea bed, was disallowed as capital when incurred in *RTZ Oil & Gas Ltd v Elliss* Ch D 1987, 61 TC 132.

See generally HMRC Business Income Manual BIM42201, 46500–46565. See also Revenue Press Release 20 July 1999, and FRS 12 and articles in the Revenue Tax Bulletin April 1999 pp 636–639 issue 40 and December 1999 pp 707–709 issue 44 commenting on its implications for the treatment of provisions in tax computations.

Simon's Taxes. See B2.504.

Rents etc. for business premises

[71.62] Rents paid for business premises are deductible in computing profits. For repairs, see **71.63** below. As regards rents receivable, see **70.54 TRADE PROFITS — INCOME AND SPECIFIC TRADES.**

Where premises partly used privately (e.g. shop with residential accommodation above), *CTA 2009, s 54* (for accounting periods ending on or after 1 April 2009) gives the specific power to apportion dual purpose expenditure; see **71.78** under the 'wholly and exclusively' rule and see the note on *s 54* in the Explanatory Notes to *CTA 2009*. For earlier periods *ICTA 1988, s 74(1)(c)* provided for the allowance of not more than two-thirds of the rent unless the circumstances justified a higher proportion. In practice, the allowance was normally two-thirds for retail businesses and, although not provided for in the legislation, rates and 'common' repairs were similarly apportioned. For this see *Wildbore v Luker* HC 1951, 33 TC 46. For allowance for use of home for business, see *Thomas v Ingram* Ch D 1979, 52 TC 428. See also *Mason v Tyson* Ch D 1980, 53 TC 333 (expenses of flat used occasionally to enable professional man to work late not allowed as a deduction).

Additional rent liability incurred to obtain the freehold reversion to premises already rented held capital (*Littlewoods Mail Order v McGregor* CA 1969, 45 TC 519 following *CIR v Land Securities* HL 1969, 45 TC 495), as were periodical payments to reimburse capital expenditure incurred by landlord (*Ainley v Edens* KB 1935, 19 TC 303) and payments based on production for grant of sisal estates (*Ralli Estates v East Africa IT Commr* PC 1961, 40 ATC 9). But payments for the use of a totalisator calculated by reference to its cost were allowed (*Racecourse Betting Control Board v Wild* KB 1938, 22 TC 182) as were rents subject to abatement dependent on profits (*Union Cold Storage v Adamson* HL 1931, 16 TC 293). For Scottish duplicands see *Dow v Merchiston Castle School* CS 1921, 8 TC 149. Rent paid by partnership to partner owning business premises allowed (*Heastie v Veitch & Co* CA 1933, 18 TC 305). For excessive payments to professional 'service company' see *Payne, Stone Fraser* at **71.56** above.

Property no longer required

Where premises became redundant or were closed down, continuing rents (less sub-letting receipts) were allowed as a deduction (*CIR v Falkirk Iron* CS 1933, 17 TC 625; *Hyett v Lennard* KB 1940, 23 TC 346) but not payments to secure the cancellation of leases no longer required (*Mallett v Staveley Coal & Iron* CA 1928, 13 TC 772 (the leading case here); *Cowcher v Richard Mills & Co* KB 1927, 13 TC 216; *Union Cold Storage v Ellerker* KB 1939, 22 TC 547; *Dain v Auto Speedways* Ch D 1959, 38 TC 525; *Bullrun Inc v Inspector of Taxes* (Sp C 248), [2000] SSCD 384). See also *West African Drug Co v Lilley* KB 1947, 28 TC 140. Where the rent of a motorway service station was calculated by reference to takings, a lump sum payment for the exclusion of tobacco duty from takings was held capital (*Tucker v Granada Motorway*

Services HL 1979, 53 TC 92), but, distinguishing *Granada Motorways*, an amount received by a company in respect of its agent's negligent failure to serve its landlord with counter-notice of a notice of an increase in its rent, was held to be a trading receipt in *Donald Fisher (Ealing) Ltd v Spencer* CA 1989, 63 TC 168. Rent for a building not required for occupation for business purposes but to control access to the lessee's works was held deductible (less sub-let rents) in *Allied Newspapers v Hindsley* CA 1937, 21 TC 422.

For allowance of a provision in respect of future rents under leases of premises ceasing to be used for business purposes, see *Herbert Smith v Honour* Ch D 1999, 72 TC 130. Following that decision, HMRC accept that there is no longer a tax rule which denies provisions for anticipated losses or expenses (see HMRC Press Release 20 July 1999). See the article in the HMRC Tax Bulletin December 1999 pp 707–709 issue 44 summarising HMRC's view.

Rates and council tax

Business rates are deductible in the same way as rent. Council tax may similarly be deducted where it is attributable to premises (or part) used for trade purposes. (Revenue Press Release 16 March 1993).

Premiums

Certain lease premiums etc. in relation to leases not exceeding 50 years are chargeable on the landlord to an extent which varies with the length of the lease (see **62.9 PROPERTY INCOME**). For any part of the 'relevant period' (as defined in *CTA 2009, s 228(6)* — generally the duration of the lease) during which the company occupies the premises for the purposes of a trade or (with certain limitations) deals with its interest therein as property employed for the purposes of a trade, the company is treated as incurring expenditure of a revenue nature. This is deductible in computing the company's trading profits, subject to any rule that might prohibit such deduction in a particular case (e.g. the 'wholly and exclusively' rule). For each day of the relevant period on which the above conditions are satisfied, the amount of additional rent treated as incurred is the amount which falls to be included in computing the landlord's property income divided by the total number of days in the relevant period. If only part of the leased land is used for trading purposes, the amount is proportionately reduced. The amount is also proportionately reduced to the extent, if any, to which the company is entitled to an allowance under *CAA 2001, s 403* (mineral asset expenditure — see **14.2 CAPITAL ALLOWANCES — MINERAL EXTRACTION**).

If the company itself grants a sublease out of the leased property at a taxable premium, it is treated as paying additional rent only to the extent, if any, that the daily amount computed above exceeds the daily reduction in its own taxable premium. For more detail of how this rule operates, see **62.12 PROPERTY INCOME**. If the sublease relates to only part of the premises covered by the main lease, the above rules are applied separately to the different parts of the premises, the premium under the main lease being apportioned between those parts on a just and reasonable basis.

The above rules apply whether the premium is chargeable to income tax or corporation tax in the hands of the landlord. For accounting periods ending on or after 1 April 2009 they also apply in relation to leases of property *outside* the UK where the landlord's property business is an overseas property business; see Change 12 listed in Annex 1 to the Explanatory Notes to the *CTA 2009*.

[*CTA 2009, ss 62–67, Sch 2 paras 18–20; CAA 2001, Sch 2 para 18; ITTOIA 2005, Sch 1 paras 62, 63*].

Otherwise, lease premiums are not deductible in computing trading profits (cf. *MacTaggart v Strump* CS 1925, 10 TC 17).

In the case of a company dealing in land, there is provision to prevent a lease premium or similar sum being taxed as both (i) a trading receipt and (ii) a receipt of a property business (as in **62.9** *et seq.* **PROPERTY INCOME**). This is achieved by reducing the amount at (i) by the amount at (ii). [*CTA 2009, s 136; ICTA 1988, s 99(2)(3)*].

Reverse premiums

See **70.62 TRADE PROFITS — INCOME AND SPECIFIC TRADES** for treatment of reverse premiums received.

The payment of a reverse premium by a company to achieve the assignment of a lease which had become disadvantageous (due to the company's failure to meet its obligations under a repairing covenant) was held to be on capital account (*Southern Counties Agricultural Trading Society Ltd v Blackler* (Sp C 198), [1999] SSCD 200). HMRC take the view that where a reverse premium is paid by a developer trading in property, it is deductible in computing his trading profits (Revenue Press Release 9 March 1999).

For HMRC approach to these rules, see HMRC Business Income Manual BIM41050–BIM41145.

Simon's Taxes. See B9.235.

General

See **5.17 ANTI-AVOIDANCE** [*CTA 2010, ss 834–848*] regarding restrictions where there is a lease-back at a non-commercial rent and **5.18 ANTI-AVOIDANCE** *CTA 2010, ss 849–862*] for taxation of capital sums received on certain lease-backs.

Simon's Taxes. See B2.465.

Repairs and renewals

General

[71.63] Expenditure held to be capital as described below may qualify for **CAPITAL ALLOWANCES (10)**. Any allowable expenditure is deductible in the period when incurred and not when the repairs etc. accrued (*Naval Colli-*

ery Co Ltd v CIR HL 1928, 12 TC 1017). Provisions for future repairs and renewals were held not allowable in *Clayton v Newcastle-under-Lyme Corpn* QB 1888, 2 TC 416 and *Peter Merchant Ltd v Stedeford* CA 1948, 30 TC 496, but see now **70.19 TRADE PROFITS — INCOME AND SPECIFIC TRADES**, and HMRC Business Income Manual BIM46515, 46901, for the wider current acceptance of the application of normal accountancy principles in this context. Hence a provision for regular major overhaul work accrued due on aircraft engines was allowed as a deduction in *Johnston v Britannia Airways Ltd* Ch D 1994, 67 TC 99 (but see Revenue Tax Bulletin February 1999 p 624 issue 39 as regards changes in accounting practice superseding this decision).

Business premises

The general rule is that expenditure on additions, alterations, expansions or improvements is capital but the cost of repairs, i.e. restoring a building to its original condition, is allowable. However, the use of modern materials in repairing an old building does not make the expenditure capital (*Conn v Robins Bros Ltd* Ch D 1966, 43 TC 266), and HMRC now consider that this applies to the replacement of single-glazed windows by double-glazed equivalents (see Revenue Tax Bulletin June 2002 p 936 issue 59). If the expenditure is capital, the estimated cost of 'notional repairs' obviated by the work is not allowable (see *Wm P Lawrie* and *Thomas Wilson (Keighley)* below).

HMRC now accept that provisions properly made under Financial Reporting Standard 12 are tax deductible except where there is an express rule to the contrary (e.g. provisions for capital expenditure). (Revenue Press Release 20 July 1999). FRS 12 imposes a requirement that for a provision to be allowable it must be a present obligation (either legal or constructive) as a result of a past event; it must be probable that a transfer of economic benefits will be required to settle the obligation; and it must be possible to make a reliable estimate of the amount of that obligation (effective for accounting periods ending after 22 March 1999). See Revenue Tax Bulletin April 1999 pp 636–639 issue 40 and December 1999 pp 707–709 issue 44. Previously *ICTA 1988, s 74(1)(d)* (repealed by *CTA 2009*) prohibited any deduction 'beyond the sum actually expended' for repairs of premises, and HMRC considered that this debarred any allowance for such provisions (see HMRC Business Income Manual BIM46901). A Revenue contention to this effect was rejected by the Special Commissioners in *Jenners Princes Street Edinburgh Ltd v CIR* (Sp C 166), [1998] SSCD 196. It should be noted that HMRC's view is that *Jenners* would have been decided differently if FRS 12 had been in operation at the time (see HMRC Business Income Manual BIM46550). (Following the *Jenners* decision, the phrase 'beyond the sum actually expended' serves no real purpose and is not repeated in *ITTOIA 2005 or CTA 2009*.)

Summary of cases

- *Fitzgerald v CIR Supreme Court (IFS)* 1925, 5 ATC 414; *Wm P Lawrie v CIR* CS 1952, 34 TC 20A — renewal of a building, i.e. a complete re-construction, is capital.
- *O'Grady v Bullcroft Main Collieries* KB 1932, 17 TC 93 — the cost of rebuilding a factory chimney was held capital.

- Contrast *Samuel Jones & Co v CIR* CS 1951, 32 TC 513 — where the chimney was an integral part of the building and allowed.
- *Wm P Lawrie* (above) and *Thos Wilson (Keighley) v Emmerson* Ch D 1960, 39 TC 360 — roof replacements.
- *Wynne-Jones v Bedale Auction Ltd* Ch D 1976, 51 TC 426 and *Brown v Burnley Football Co Ltd* Ch D 1980, 53 TC 357 — the replacement of the ring in a cattle auction mart and of a stand in a football ground were held not to be repairs respectively in which the problem is reviewed.
- *Avon Beach & Cafe v Stewart* HC 1950, 31 TC 487 — cost of barrier against coastal erosion held capital.
- *Phillips v Whieldon Sanitary Potteries* HC 1952, 33 TC 213 — replacing a canal embankment was capital.
- *Pitt v Castle Hill Warehousing* Ch D 1974, 49 TC 638 — building new access road was capital.
- *Auckland Gas Co Ltd v CIR* PC, [2000] STC 527 — involving the insertion of plastic pipes within dilapidated metal ones over substantial lengths of a gas pipe network, held to be capital.
- *Transco plc v Dyall* (Sp C 310), [2002] SSCD 199 — Auckland Gas was considered but distinguished in case involving the insertion of plastic pipes in cast iron ones on a selective basis that had not changed the character of the pipeline system as a whole.
- *Jackson v Laskers Home Furnishers* Ch D 1956, 37 TC 69 — where on taking a lease of dilapidated property the dilapidations were made good under a covenant in the lease, the cost was held disallowable as attributable to the previous use of the premises.
- *Constrast Odeon Associated Theatres Ltd v Jones* CA 1971, 48 TC 257 — where cinemas were acquired in a state of disrepair (but still fit for public showings) because of war-time restrictions on building work, the cost of the repairs was allowed.

In practice, expenditure on repairing and redecorating newly acquired premises is allowed unless abnormal (and likely to be reflected in the purchase price or rent payable). See generally HMRC Business Income Manual BIM46906.

Dilapidations of a repair nature on the termination of a lease are generally deductible.

For repairs to tied premises see **71.7**.

From 1 October 2004, *Disability Discrimination Act 1995* requires service providers to make 'reasonable adjustments' to their premises to tackle any physical features that prevent disabled people from using their services. Whilst this does not give rise to any substantive changes to pre-existing tax treatment, HMRC have published online some related guidance covering such matters as ramps, toilets and washing facilities, signs, hand rails, lighting, doors, lifts, steps and stairs, alterations to walls and floors, car parks and paths. See www.hmrc.gov.uk/specialist/disability-act-guidance.htm

Plant and other business assets etc.

The general rules for premises above apply to plant with the important modification that expenditure on the renewal of plant is allowed as a deduction as an alternative to capital allowances. For this see **13.24 CAPITAL ALLOWANCES — PLANT AND MACHINERY: FIXTURES AND LEASING.** Replacements and alterations of trade tools (meaning any implement, utensil or article) are allowable deductions notwithstanding the fact that the expenditure would otherwise be capital. [*CTA 2009, s 68; ICTA 1988, s 74(1)(d)*]. The cost of initial and additional tools is capital and not deductible but may well attract plant and machinery capital allowances (see **11.3 CAPITAL ALLOWANCES — PLANT AND MACHINERY: ELIGIBLE EXPENDITURE AND INITIAL ALLOWANCES**).

For repairs soon after the acquisition of an asset see *Law Shipping v CIR* CS 1923, 12 TC 621 and *CIR v Granite City SS Co* CS 1927, 13 TC 1 in which the cost of repairs to ships attributable to their use before acquisition, was held capital. But see *Odeon Associated Theatres* above in which *Law Shipping* was distinguished. See also *Bidwell v Gardiner* Ch D 1960, 39 TC 31 in which the replacement of the furnishings of a newly acquired hotel was held capital.

Expenditure on renewal of railway tracks was allowed in *Rhodesia Railways v Bechuanaland Collector* PC 1933, 12 ATC 223, distinguishing *Highland Railway v Balderston* CES 1889, 2 TC 485 in which held capital. Abnormal expenditure on dredging a channel to a shipyard was held capital in *Ounsworth v Vickers Ltd* KB 1915, 6 TC 671 but the cost to a Harbour Board of removing a wreck (*Whelan v Dover Harbour Board* CA 1934, 18 TC 555) and of renewing moorings (*In re King's Lynn Harbour* CES 1875, 1 TC 23) was allowed. For shop fittings see *Eastmans Ltd v Shaw* HL 1928, 14 TC 218; *Hyam v CIR* CS 1929, 14 TC 479. See also *Lothian Chemical v Rogers* CS 1926, 11 TC 508.

Assets held under an operating lease

A deduction may be allowed for a provision to cover future repairs of assets held under an operating lease which contains a repairing obligation (for example, tenants' repairing leases of property). The obligation, required under FRS 12 (see above), subsists from the signing of the lease. (HMRC Business Income Manual BIM46535). It is unlikely HMRC would have accepted such a deduction prior to the decision in *Jenners* above.

See generally HMRC Business Income Manual BIM46900–46970.

Simon's Taxes. See **B2.404, B2.409, B2.466.**

Research and development and scientific research

[71.64] For enhanced tax reliefs for research and development expenditure incurred from 1 April 2000, see **64 RESEARCH AND DEVELOPMENT EXPENDITURE.**

Revenue expenditure incurred by a company on 'research and development' related to its trade, whether undertaken directly or on its behalf, is allowable as a deduction in computing profits. Expenditure incurred in the acquisition of rights in, or arising out of, the research and development is excluded, but the allowable expenditure otherwise includes all expenditure incurred in, or providing facilities for, carrying it out. Research and development 'related' to a trade includes any which may lead to or facilitate an extension of the trade, or which is of a medical nature and has a special relation to the welfare of workers employed in the trade. These provisions apply equally to expenditure on oil and gas exploration and appraisal (within *CTA 2010, s 1134*).

For accounting periods beginning after 31 December 2004, HMRC expenditure by a company on research and development is not precluded from deduction under these provisions by reason only of the fact that it is brought into account in determining the value of an intangible asset, but there are rules to prevent double relief in respect of the same expenditure. See also **48.34 INTANGIBLE ASSETS.**

Scientific research associations

Relief is similarly given for any sum paid to an Association (in an accounting period of the Association beginning on or after 1 January 2008) within the exemption at **35.12 EXEMPT ORGANISATIONS** which has as its object the undertaking of research and development which may lead to or facilitate an extension of the class of trade to which the company's trade belongs.

Previously, relief was available for sums paid to a scientific research association in an accounting period of the association beginning before 1 January 2008. The association to which the sum was paid had to be approved by the Secretary of State and had to have as its object the undertaking of 'scientific research' 'related' to the class of trade concerned.

Relief is also given for any sum paid to an approved university, college research institute etc. to be used for 'scientific research' 'related' to that class of trade.

'*Scientific research*' means any activities in the fields of natural or applied science for the extension of knowledge. Scientific research 'related' to a class of trade includes any which may lead to or facilitate an extension of trades of that class, or which is of a medical nature and has a special relation to the welfare of workers employed in trades of that class. Any question as to what constitutes scientific research is to be referred by HMRC to the Secretary of State, whose decision is final.

[*CTA 2010, ss 1134, 1138, CTA 2009, ss 87, 88, 1308; ICTA 1988, ss 82A, 82B; FA 2004, s 53; SI 2004 No 3268; ITTOIA 2005, Sch 1 paras 54, 55; F(No 2)A 2005, s 15; SI 2007 No 3424*].

For *capital expenditure* on research and development, see **16.12 CAPITAL ALLOWANCES — MISCELLANEOUS.**

For the definition of 'research and development', see **64.1 RESEARCH AND DEVELOPMENT EXPENDITURE.**

Sound recordings expenses

[71.65] See **70.71 TRADE PROFITS — INCOME AND SPECIFIC TRADES** for sound recording income.

Expenditure on the production or acquisition of the 'original master version' of a sound recording (including any rights held or acquired in it) is treated as expenditure of a revenue nature. An '*original master version*' is a master tape or master audio disc and the term '*sound recording*' does not include a film soundtrack.

Where the company's trade consists of, or includes, the exploitation of original master versions of sound recordings and these are not trading stock of that trade, the expenditure which is incurred on the production or acquisition of the original master version of a sound recording is revenue expenditure (whether incurred as above or otherwise). It is allocated to periods of account (or if no accounts are made up, to accounting periods) using an 'income matching' rule. So much of the expenditure as is just and reasonable is allocated to the relevant period having regard to:

- the amount of the expenditure that remains unallocated at the beginning of the period;
- the proportion which the estimated value of the original master version realised in the period (by way of income or otherwise) bears to the sum of the value so realised and the estimated remaining value at the end of the period; and
- the need to bring the whole expenditure into account over the time during which the original master version is expected to be realised.

Additional amounts can be allocated to a period provided the amount so allocated does not exceed the value of the original master version realised in that period (by way of income or otherwise).

[*CTA 2009, ss 150, 151, Sch 1 para 679; FA 2006, ss 48–50*].

The above provisions put HMRC Extra Statutory Concession B54 on a statutory footing.

Simon's Taxes. See **D7.1206.**

Stock (inventory) and work in progress

[71.66] See generally HMRC Business Income Manual BIM33000–33630. Following the adoption for tax purposes of the 'true and fair view' accounting basis (subject to any statutory adjustment) for periods of account beginning after 6 April 1999 (see **70.19 TRADE PROFITS — INCOME AND SPECIFIC TRADES**), HMRC Statement of Practice SP 3/90 (to which references are made below) is generally superseded and is accordingly withdrawn. However, the principles drawn from that Statement continue to be relevant for subsequent accounting periods (except as referred to below).

Basis of valuation

The general rule has long been that stock is to be valued at the lower of cost and market value. Leading cases are *Minister of National Revenue v Anaconda American Brass Co* (1955) 34 ATC 330, PC, and *BSC Footwear v Ridgway* (1971) 47 TC 495, HL. Market value held to be replacement price for a merchant (*Brigg Neumann & Co v CIR* (1928) 12 TC 1191) and retail price for a retailer in *BSC Footwear* above (HMRC prepared to take price net of any selling commission). Stock may be valued partly at cost and partly at market value where lower (*CIR v Cock Russell & Co* (1949) 29 TC 387). The base stock method is not permissible (*Patrick v Broadstone Mills* (1953) 35 TC 44, CA) nor is 'LIFO' (*Anaconda American Brass* above). See also *Asia Mill Ltd v Ryan (Inspector of Taxes)* [1951] WN 390, 32 TC 275, HL. The cost should include as a minimum the cost of materials and direct labour but the accounts treatment of overheads is normally accepted (*Ostime (Inspector of Taxes) v Duple Motor Bodies Ltd* [1961] 2 All ER 167, [1961] 1 WLR 739, HL).

However, HMRC now take the view that any valuation of stock included in financial statements prepared in accordance with generally accepted accounting practice (see **70.19** trade profits — income and specific trades) should be accepted provided that:

- it reflects the correct application of the principles of normal accountancy;
- the method pays sufficient regard to the facts; and
- the basis does not violate the taxing statutes as interpreted by the courts.

(HMRC Business Income Manual BIM33115).

A mark to market basis of valuation, used mainly by financial institutions and commodity dealers and under which stock is valued at market value, may also be acceptable (HMRC Business Income Manual BIM33160).

The principal accounting standards governing stock/inventory are SSAP 9 and IAS 2.

For the use of formulae in computing stock provisions and write-downs, see HMRC Tax Bulletin December 1994 p 184 issue 14. Broadly, Officers will accept formulae which reflect a realistic appraisal of future income from the particular category of stock and which result in the stock being included at a reasonable estimate of net realisable value (under IAS now fair value less costs to sell). Where computations are accepted without enquiry, it is on the assumption that profits are arrived at in accordance with such principles.

For the treatment of depreciation taken into account in arriving at stock valuations, see HMRC Tax Bulletin June 2002 pp 936, 937 issue 59.

For motor dealer stock valuations, see HMRC Tax Bulletin August 1994 p 156 issue 12.

As regards valuation of professional work in progress, it is understood that the following principles are, in broad terms, currently accepted by HMRC:

(i) nothing should be included for partners' time;
(ii) direct employment costs of fee-earners and direct overheads applicable, such as secretarial salaries, stationery, telephone costs etc. should be included;

(iii) general production overheads for general office areas, conference rooms etc. should be excluded, whilst those for individual office areas directly applicable should be discounted by, say, 30% for non-productive time; and

(iv) contingent fees should be included.

(Taxation Vol 141, No 3654 p 126, 30 April 1998). For further guidance on valuation of professional work in progress, see the detailed note agreed between the HMRC and the ICAEW in HMRC Tax Bulletin December 1998 pp 607–615 issue 38.

Changes in basis of valuation

Where the stock was found to be grossly undervalued it was held that an assessment to rectify the closing undervaluation must be reduced by the opening undervaluation to bring out the true profits (*Bombay IT Commr v Ahmedabad New Cotton Mills Co* (1929) 9 ATC 574, PC). But where a company altered its method of dealing with accrued profits on long-term contracts and the closing work in progress in the year 1 accounts on the old basis was substantially below the opening figure in the year 2 accounts on the new basis, held, distinguishing *Ahmedabad*, the difference must be included in the year 2 profits (*Pearce v Woodall-Duckham Ltd* (1978) 51 TC 271, CA).

Where there is a change in the basis of valuation, the following practice is applied for tax purposes. If the bases of valuation both before and after the change are valid bases, the opening figure for the period of change must be the same as the closing figure for the preceding period. If the change is from an invalid basis to a valid one, the opening figure for the period of change must be arrived at on the same basis as the closing figure for that period, and liabilities for earlier years will be reviewed where it is possible to do so. (HMRC Statement of Practice, SP 3/90 and HMRC Business Income Manual BIM33199). See, however, *Woodall-Duckham Ltd* (above) as regards long-term contracts.

See **70.20** for spreading of the tax charge in relation to adjustments on a change of accounting basis arising from the interpretation of UITF 40.

Long-term contracts

HMRC accept that accurate provisions for foreseen losses on long-term contracts (e.g. in the construction industry) made in accordance with correct accounting practice are tax deductible. (Revenue Press Release 20 July 1999 and HMRC Business Income Manual BIM33025).

In *Symons v Weeks and Others* (1982) 56 TC 630, it was held that progress payments under the long-term contracts of a firm of architects did not fall to be brought into account for tax before the relevant contract was completed, notwithstanding that they exceeded the figure brought in for work in progress, calculated on the correct principles of commercial accounting.

See above for changes of basis.

Goods sold subject to reservation of title

Where the supplier of goods reserves the title in them until payment is made (as a protection should the buyer become insolvent) and meanwhile the goods are treated by both parties for accountancy purposes as having been sold/purchased, HMRC will follow the accounts treatment (HMRC Statement of Practice, B6). See Note A of Financial Reporting Standard No 5 and HMRC Business Income Manual BIM33375.

Goods on consignment stock are normally treated as stock in the hands of the supplier until disposed of by the consignee (e.g. sale or return) (HMRC Statement of Practice, B6).

For **forward contracts**, see **71.13** above.

Insurance recoveries

See **70.53 TRADE PROFITS — INCOME AND SPECIFIC TRADES.**

Trading stock acquired or disposed of other than in the course of trade

Trading stock in relation to a trade means anything that is sold in the ordinary course of a trade or would be sold if mature or complete. It does not include raw materials, services performed in the ordinary course of a trade or anything produced as a result of those services. The tax treatment of changes in trading stock on or after 12 March 2008 are put on a statutory basis, replacing case law (see below for the case law which previously established the correct tax treatment). These provisions cover the following.

(a) Trading stock appropriated by the trader for another purpose (e.g. his own consumption). In this case, market value is brought into account as a receipt on the date of appropriation and any actual consideration received for it is left out of account for corporation tax.

(b) An item owned by the trader otherwise than as trading stock is appropriated to trading stock. For corporation tax purposes, the cost (treated as incurred at the time it became trading stock) to be brought into account on the date the item became trading stock is open market value of the item on the day it became trading stock, any actual value passing being left out of account.

(c) Trading stock is disposed of otherwise then in the course of trade and (a) above does not apply. Market value at the date of disposal is brought into account as a receipt at the date of disposal and any actual consideration is left out of account.

(d) Trading stock is acquired other than in the course of a trade and (b) above does not apply, open market value on the date it became stock has to be brought into the accounts as a cost arising at the date of acquisition. Any consideration passing is left out of account.

However, in the cases of (c) and (d), where the transfer pricing rules apply, these take precedence (see **72 TRANSFER PRICING**).

For these purposes only, '*trading stock*' is defined as stock held for sale in the course of a trade, or partially completed or immature items which are intended for sale when complete or mature. It does not include materials used for manufacture etc, services carried out in the course of a trade or materials used in the performance of these services.

[*TIOPA 2010, s 147, CTA 2009, ss 156–161; FA 2008, s 37, Sch 15 paras 5–10; ICTA 1988, Sch 28AA*].

Prior to 12 March 2008

Where trading stock is disposed of otherwise than by way of trade, the realisable value is to be credited for tax purposes. This was established by *Sharkey v Wernher* (1955) 36 TC 275, HL, approving *Watson Bros v Hornby* (1942) 24 TC 506. It applies, *inter alia*, to goods taken out of stock by a retailer for his own use (see below). It was applied in *Petrotim Securities Ltd v Ayres* (1963) 41 TC 389, CA, to a disposal of shares at gross under-value as part of a tax avoidance scheme, but in *Ridge Securities Ltd v CIR* (1963) 44 TC 373, dealing with the other end of the same scheme, it was held that the same principle applied to acquisitions of trading stock otherwise than by way of trade, market price being substituted for the actual purchase price. But the principle is not applicable to sales or purchases by way of trade notwithstanding not at arm's length. Hence when a share dealing company acquired shares at substantial overvalue from an associated company, the claim by the Revenue for market value failed (*Craddock v Zevo Finance Co* (1946) 27 TC 267, HL), and when a property dealing company acquired property from its controlling shareholder at substantial undervalue, its claim to substitute market value failed (*Jacgilden (Weston Hall) v Castle* (1969) 45 TC 685). See also *Skinner v Berry Head Lands* (1970) 46 TC 377 and *Kilmorie (Aldridge) v Dickinson* (1974) 50 TC 1, HL.

Appropriations to trading stock of assets held in another capacity are generally treated as a disposal and reacquisition at market value. Where a chargeable gain or allowable loss would otherwise arise for capital gains tax purposes under *TCGA 1992, s 161(1)*, the company may elect for the market value to be reduced for these purposes by the amount of the chargeable gain (or increased by the amount of the allowable loss), the trading profits being computed accordingly and the appropriation being disregarded for capital gains tax purposes. The election must be made within two years after the end of the accounting period in which the asset is appropriated. [*TCGA 1992, s 161(3)(3A); CTA 2009, Sch 1 para 374*].

What constitutes stock

The 12 March 2008 provisions have their own definition of stock (see above). For other purposes, case law applies as follows. Greyhounds kept by greyhound racing company were not trading stock (*Abbot v Albion Greyhounds (Salford)* (1945) 26 TC 390). Payments by cigarette manufacturer for cropping trees (not owned by it) for leaves used in manufacture, held to be for materials (*Mohanlal Hargovind of Jubbulpore v IT Commr* (1949) 28 ATC 287, PC). For payments for unworked minerals, sand and gravel etc, (including tailings etc) by mines, quarries etc. see **70.56 TRADE PROFITS — INCOME AND SPECIFIC TRADES**. For payments for oil by oil companies, see *Hughes v British Burmah Petroleum* (1932) 17 TC 286; *CIR v Europa Oil (NZ) Ltd* [1971] AC 760, [1971] 2 WLR 55, PC; *Europa Oil (NZ) v New Zealand Commr* [1976] STC 37, PC. For timber see **71.56** above and *Coates v Holker Estates Co* (1961) 40 TC 75.

Valuation on cessation of trade

Unless the transfer pricing provisions apply (*TIOPA 2010, s 147; ICTA 1988, Sch 28AA*), trading stock at cessation must be valued as follows. These rules apply to partnerships, unless a company carrying on the trade in partnership immediately before the change continues to do so after the change. For these provisions, 'trading stock' means any property sold in the ordinary course of the trade, or which would be sold if mature or manufacture etc were complete, or materials used in such manufacture etc. Trading stock also includes services performed in the ordinary course of the trade which are wholly or partly completed at cessation and for which it would be reasonable to invoice were there no cessation (or where the services are partly completed, when they are fully completed) and any item produced and material used in the performance of the services. Sale or transfer of trading stock includes sale or transfer of any benefits accruing, or which might reasonably be expected to accrue, from those services.

(1) If the trading stock at cessation is sold to a person carrying on (or intending to carry on) a trade in the UK who can deduct the cost as an expense for corporation tax purposes, the stock is valued at the amount realised on the sale. If, however, the two parties to the sale are connected persons (defined more broadly than by *CTA 2010, s 1122 see below*), arm's length value is to be taken instead unless an election is made under *CTA 2009, s 167* (see below). (Neither rule applies to a transfer of farm animals where the anti-avoidance rules for the herd basis (at **70.52 TRADE PROFITS — INCOME AND SPECIFIC TRADES**) apply.) If the stock is sold with 'other assets', the amount realised is arrived at on a just and reasonable apportionment (since 24 July 2002); For the purposes of these rules, a 'sale' includes a transfer for valuable consideration, with related expressions then being defined accordingly. Where arm's length value exceeds both (i) actual sale price and (ii) 'acquisition value', connected persons may jointly elect to substitute the greater of (i) and (ii) for the arm's length value. The election must be made within two years after the end of the accounting period in which cessation occurred. '*Acquisition value*' for this purpose is the amount which would have been deductible in calculation profits assuming that the stock had been sold in the course of trade immediately before cessation for a price equal to the value determined on a sale between 'connected persons' (see below) and the accounting period began immediately before the sale.
For the purpose of these provisions, parties are 'connected' if any of the following are met:
   (a) they are connected under *CTA 2010, s 1122/ICTA 1988, s 839*;
   (b) one is a partnership and the other has a right to share in the partnership's profits;
   (c) one is a company and is controlled by the other;
   (d) both are partnerships and another party has a right to share in the income or assets of both of them; or
   (e) both are companies, or one is a partnership and the other a company and, in either case, another party has control over both of them.

The cost of the trading stock to the buyer is taken to be the value determined under the above rules (or the corresponding income tax rules) in relation to the seller.

Any question as to the application of these rules is to be determined by the Tribunal in the same way as an appeal. See *Bradshaw v Blunden (No 2)* (1960) 39 TC 73; *CIR v Barr (No 2)* (1955) 36 TC 455, Ct of Sess.

These rules are not applicable to woodlands managed on a commercial basis (*Coates v Holker Estates* above). For their application to 'hire-purchase debts' see *Lions Ltd v Gosford Furnishing Co Ltd & CIR* (1961) 40 TC 256, Ct of Sess. A contention by HMRC that the rules did not apply to a transfer of closing stock simultaneous to a cessation was rejected in *Moore v Mackenzie* (1971) 48 TC 196.

(2) In all cases not within (1) above, trading stock is to be valued at the price it would have realised if sold in the open market at the time of the cessation.

The above provisions are disapplied in relation to any trading stock if a transfer pricing adjustment (see **72 TRANSFER PRICING**) falls to be made in connection with any provision made or imposed in relation to that stock and having effect in connection with the cessation (from 1 April 2004).

Similar rules as above apply in relation to '*work in progress*' (as defined in *CTA 2009, s 163; ICTA 1988, s 101(3)*) on cessation of a profession, except that there is no special rule for a transfer of work in progress to a connected person. Additionally, an election is available to the effect that, in computing profits to the date of cessation, closing work in progress is valued at cost and any realised excess over cost is then treated as a post-cessation receipt (see **70.16 TRADE PROFITS — INCOME AND SPECIFIC TRADES**); the election must be made no later than two years after the end of the accounting period in which the cessation occurred.

[*CTA 2009, ss 162–171, change 39 listed in Annex 1 to the Explanatory Notes to CTA 2009; ICTA 1988, ss 100–102; FA 2002, ss 105(1), 106; FA 2004, ss 30(9), 37(1)(2), Sch 5 para 2; ITTOIA 2005, Sch 1 paras 79–81; SI 2009 No 56*].

Recovery of assets under Proceeds of Crime Act 2002, Pt 5

Where the transfer of trading stock is a *Pt 5* transfer under *Proceeds of Crime Act 2002* (as in **10.13 CAPITAL ALLOWANCES — INTRODUCTION**) and the stock is to be treated, as a result of the transfer, as if sold in the course of the trade, it is treated, for the purpose of computing taxable profits and notwithstanding *CTA 2009, ss 162–171; ICTA 1988, s 100* above (if applicable), as sold at cost price. [*Proceeds of Crime Act 2002, Sch 10 para 11; ITTOIA 2005, Sch 1 para 583(6)*].

Subscriptions and contributions

Trade and professional associations

[71.67] Ordinary annual subscriptions to local associations, including Chambers of Commerce, are normally allowed as deductions in computing profits. Subscriptions to larger associations are deductible, and receipts therefrom chargeable, if the association has entered into an arrangement with HMRC under which it is assessed on any surplus of receipts over allowable expenditure (the association should be asked). Most associations enter into the arrangement but if not the deduction is restricted to the proportion applied by the association for purposes such that it would have been deductible if so applied by the subscriber (*Lochgelly Iron & Coal Co Ltd v Crawford* (1913) 6 TC 267, Ct of Sess). For other cases see Tolley's Tax Cases. Subscriptions to the Economic League are not deductible (*Joseph L Thompson & Sons Ltd v Chamberlain* (1962) 40 TC 657).

By concession, the payment of an ordinary annual subscription to a local trade association by a non-member is not regarded as a gift, and is thus normally allowed as a deduction notwithstanding **71.49** above, provided it satisfies the 'wholly and exclusively' rule at **71.78** (HMRC Extra Statutory Concession, B7).

Contributions to mutual insurance associations are deductible even though used to create a reserve fund (*Thomas v Richard Evans & Co Ltd* (1927) 11 TC 790, HL). See also **56 MUTUAL COMPANIES**.

Local enterprise organisations

Expenditure incurred by a company in making any contribution (whether in cash or kind) to a 'local enterprise organisation' is specifically allowed as deduction in computing trading profits if it would not otherwise be deductible. If, however, in connection with the making of the contribution, the trader or a person connected with him (see **25 CONNECTED PERSONS**) receives (or is entitled to receive) a 'disqualifying benefit' of any kind, whether or not from the organisation itself, the value of the benefit is subtracted from the deduction otherwise available. Any such benefit received after such a deduction has been given is recovered by treating its value as a trading receipt for the period of account (before 2005/06, for the tax year) in which it is received. If received after the trade has permanently ceased, it is treated as a post-cessation receipt (within **70.16 TRADE PROFITS — INCOME AND SPECIFIC TRADES**); for accounting periods ending before 1 April 2009, it was treated as income within *Schedule D, Case VI* but not specifically as a post-cessation receipt. A '*disqualifying benefit*' is a benefit the expenses of obtaining which would not be deductible if incurred directly by the trader in an arm's length transaction.

For these purposes, a '*local enterprise organisation*' means any of the following.

- A local enterprise agency, i.e. a body for the time being approved as such by the relevant national authority (e.g. for England and NI, by the Secretary of State). Various conditions are prescribed for approval. In particular, the body's sole aim must be the promotion or encouragement of industrial and commercial activity or enterprise in a particular area of the UK, with particular reference to small businesses. If that is only one of its main aims, it must maintain a separate fund for the sole purpose of pursuing that aim and the above relief applies only to contributions to that fund. Also, the body must be precluded from transferring its income or profits to its members or its managers, other than as a reasonable return for goods, labour or services provided, money lent or premises occupied. Approval may be conditional and may be withdrawn retrospectively.

- A training and enterprise council, i.e. a body which has an agreement with the Secretary of State to act as such.
- A Scottish local enterprise company, i.e. a company which has an agreement with Scottish Enterprise or Highlands and Islands Enterprise to act as such.
- A business link organisation, i.e. a person authorised by the Secretary of State to use a trade mark designated for these purposes.

[*CTA 2009, ss 82–85, Sch 2 para 21; ICTA 1988, ss 79, 79A; FA 1990, s 76; FA 1994, s 145; FA 2000, s 88, Sch 40 Pt II(9); SI 2004 No 2310, Sch para 3; ITTOIA 2005, Sch 1 paras 48, 49*].

Urban regeneration companies

Identical provisions to those described above in relation to local enterprise organisations apply to a contribution made to an urban regeneration company designated as such by Treasury order. A body may be so designated only if its sole or main function is to co-ordinate the regeneration of a specific urban area in the UK in association with public and local authorities. Designation orders may be backdated by up to three months or, in the case of the first such order, to 1 April 2003. [*CTA 2009, ss 82, 86; ICTA 1988, s 79B; FA 2003, s 180; SI 2004 No 2310, Sch para 3; ITTOIA 2005, Sch 1 para 50*]. The first designations are made by *SI 2004 No 439*.

Subsidies, grants etc.

[71.68] See **70.73 TRADE PROFITS — INCOME AND SPECIFIC TRADES.**

Football pools promoters

If the company carrying on the trade is liable to pool betting duty, e.g. it is a football pools promoter and it makes a 'qualifying payment' in consequence of its receiving a reduction in duty, it is allowed a deduction for that payment in computing its trading profits. A '*qualifying payment*' is a payment to meet (directly or indirectly) capital expenditure incurred by any person in improving spectator safety or comfort at a soccer ground or a payment to trustees established mainly for the support of athletic sports or games but with power to support the arts. [*CTA 2009, s 138; FA 1990, s 126; FA 1991, s 121; ITTOIA 2005, Sch 1 paras 416, 418; CTA 2009, Sch 1 para 357*]. See also **10 CAPITAL ALLOWANCES — INTRODUCTION.**

Taxation

[71.69] Income tax and corporation tax are not deductible in computing profits (cf *Allen v Farquharson Bros & Co* (1932) 17 TC 59). Overseas taxes may be subject to **DOUBLE TAX RELIEF** (**32**) but any such tax not relieved by credit on overseas income included in the profits may generally be deducted [*TIOPA 2010, s 112; ICTA 1988, s 811*] but not on UK income, e.g. profits of UK branches (*CIR v Dowdall O'Mahoney & Co Ltd* (1952) 33 TC 259, HL). See BIM45901

In *Harrods (Buenos Aires) v Taylor-Gooby* (1964) 41 TC 450, CA, an annual capital tax imposed by the Argentine on foreign companies trading there was not a tax on the profits and was allowable.

As regards relief for national insurance contributions by employers in respect of employees, see **71.21** above.

For taxation appeals see **71.54** above. For VAT, see **73 VALUE ADDED TAX.**

Simon's Taxes. See B2.472.

Tied petrol stations payments

[71.70] For tied licensed premises see **71.7** above.

'Exclusivity payments' by petrol company to retailers undertaking to sell only its goods were allowed in computing its profits in *Bolam v Regent Oil Co Ltd* (1956) 37 TC 56 (payments for repairs carried out by retailer), *BP Australia Ltd* (1965) 44 ATC 312, PC (lump sums paid for sales promotion), and *Mobil Oil Australia Ltd* (1965) 44 ATC 323, PC, but held capital in *Regent Oil Co Ltd v Strick (Inspector of Taxes)* [1966] AC 295, [1965] 3 All ER 174, HL, where the payment took the form of a premium to the retailer for a lease of his premises (immediately sub-let to him).

Trade marks or designs

[71.71] Expenses are deductible if incurred in obtaining, for the purposes of a trade, the registration of a trade mark or design, the renewal of registration of a trade mark or the extension of the period for which the right in a registered design subsists. [*CTA 2009, s 90, Sch 2 para 22; Copyright, Designs and Patents Act 1988, Sch 7 para 36(1)(2); Trade Marks Act 1994, s 106(2), Sch 5; ITTOIA 2005, Sch 1 para 56*]. For corporation tax purposes expenditure and receipts in respect of intellectual property acquired or created **on or after 1 April 2002** falls within the intangible assets regime. See in particular the commencement and transitional rules for that regime at **48.36 INTANGIBLE ASSETS.**

Training

[71.72] Costs incurred by an employer in respect of employee training are generally allowable as a trade expense. See **71.25** above for this and as regards certain other allowable employee training costs, and **71.67** above as regards contributions to training and enterprise councils.

Transfer fees

[71.73] The accounting treatment of transfer fees paid by football or other sports clubs may be affected by either FRS 10 (issued 4.9.1997) or the FRS for Smaller Entities (issued 10.12.1998). Where a transfer fee is paid under a contract entered into before the beginning of the first accounting period for which either of those standards has effect, then unless the club elects to the contrary (within two years after the end of that accounting period), the tax treatment of the payment is not affected by anything in the standard. Any necessary adjustments to give effect to this provision may be made, notwithstanding any relevant time limits. [*FA 1999, s 63; ITTOIA 2005, Sch 1 para 506*].

Unremittable amounts

[71.74] Where a trade is carried on partly in the UK and partly overseas, so that liability to UK corporation tax arises on trading profits, amounts received or receivable overseas (e.g. from export sales) which cannot be brought to the UK because of foreign exchange restrictions would nevertheless fall to be included in computing profits. No relief would be available under *CTA 2009, ss 1274–1275*; (previously *ICTA 1988, s 584)* (unremittable overseas income — see **65.4 RESIDENCE**), because the overall profits of the trade do not arise outside the UK, or under *CTA 2009, ss 55, 970* in respect of impairment losses. A debt is not impaired or bad merely because it is unremittable. The provisions (which supercede HMRC Extra Statutory Concession C34) described below are designed to give relief in such circumstances. There are two minor changes to the provisions — see below and Change 40 listed in Annex 1 to the Explanatory Notes to the *CTA 2009*. They are not expected to have a material effect.

Where amounts cannot be remitted solely as a result of local foreign exchange control restrictions, relief may be claimed, provided that:

(a) an amount received by, or owed to, a trading company is included in arriving at the trading profit of the company;
(b) it is paid or owned outside the UK
(c) some or all of it is unremittable.

An amount received is unremittable if it cannot be received in the UK due to foreign exchange restrictions. An amount owed (e.g. a trade debt) is unremittable if it temporarily cannot be paid due to exchange control restrictions or it can be paid in the overseas territory but could not then be transferred to the UK only due to foreign exchange restrictions. '*Foreign exchange restrictions*' are imposed by the law of the other country where the amount is paid or owed, by executive action of its government or the impossibility of obtaining, in that country, currency which could be remitted.

The company may claim relief from corporation tax on the unremittable income. No claim may be made if the company has received an amount under the ECGD scheme in respect of it. A claim may be made for an accounting period ending after 31 March 2009, despite the income having arisen in an accounting period ending before 1 April 2009.

Relief is given for the amount in question by deducting it from profits but not so as to create a trading loss. Any excess of unremittable amounts over profits for any period of account is carried forward to the next period of account, aggregated with any unremittable amounts for that period, and used to reduce or extinguish trading profits for that period, and so on *ad infinitum*. If no trading profit has been made for a period of account, any unremittable amounts are similarly carried forward.

However, no such deduction is allowed to the extent that:

- the amount in question is used to finance expenditure or investment outside the UK or is otherwise applied outside the UK; or
- a deduction is allowed under *CTA 2009, s 1275*; or
- it is an amount owed and an insurance recovery is received in respect of it.

Relief is withdrawn for an unremittable amount or any part of it if, subsequently, the amount (or part) ceases to be unremittable or is exchanged for (or discharged by) a remittable amount, or is used to finance overseas expenditure etc., or an 'allowable provision for impairment loss' is made in respect of it, or, in the case of an amount owed, is the subject of an insurance recovery, or the amount or part of it is applied outside the UK or is exchanged for or discharged by a remittable amount. The amount (or part) is treated as a trading receipt for the period of account in which the said event occurs, but only to the extent it has been deducted from profits. An 'allowable provision for impairment loss is either a debit in respect of impairment or a financial asset is brought into account under the loan relationship provisions. See **54 LOAN RELATIONSHIPS.**

The changes from C34 are:

- ESC C34 required the relief to be claimed. A claim could be made until at least 12 months after the end of the period of account in which the amount in question was received or, as the case may be, the debt arose, and no claim could be made after the assessment became final and conclusive. No claim is necessary under *CTA 2009, s 173;*
- relief for a debt was denied to the extent that the debt was insured, regardless of the extent (if any) to which an insurance recovery was actually received.

These provisions also apply to unremittable bank interest in appropriate circumstances (see **8.4 BANKS**).

There are rights of appeal. For periods ending after 31 March 2009, the normal appeal rules will apply (in practice, to the new tribunals). For periods ending before that date, there is a right of appeal to the Special Commissioners. (Change 98 listed in Annex 1 of the Explanatory Notes to *CTA 2009*.)

[*CTA 2009, ss 172–175, 1274–1278*].

Valuation fees

[71.75] Property valuation fees incurred in order to comply with *Companies Act 2006* are allowable as trading or management expenses. (HMRC Statement of Practice, C10). It is understood that regular property valuation fees (other than in connection with property acquisitions or sales) are similarly allowable.

Waste disposal

[71.76] Expenditure on purchase and reclamation of tipping sites by a company carrying on a waste disposal business was held to be capital in *Rolfe v Wimpey Waste Management Ltd* (1989) 62 TC 399, CA, as were instalment payments for the right to deposit waste material in *CIR v Adam* (1928) 14 TC 34, Ct of Sess. See also *McClure v Petre* (1988) 61 TC 226, where the receipt of sum for licence to tip soil was also held to be capital.

Site preparation and restoration expenditure

A deduction is allowed as below in computing profits where a company incurs, in the course of a trade, 'site preparation expenditure' in relation to a 'waste disposal site', and, at the time when the company first deposits waste materials on the site in question, it holds a current 'waste disposal licence'. Expenditure incurred for trade purposes by a company about to carry on the trade is for this purpose treated as incurred on the first day of trading. The deduction is not available where the company incurring the expenditure recharges it to another person who holds the licence when first depositing waste (see HMRC Business Income Manual, BIM67440). For accounting periods ending before 1 April 2009, a claim for the deduction had to be made in the prescribed manner and HMRC could also require plans and other documents to verify it. For accounting periods ending on or after 1 April 2009, no such claim is required but any supporting documentation should still be retained in case of an HMRC enquiry into a return.

A '*waste disposal site*' is a site used (or to be used) for the disposal of waste materials by their deposit on the site, and in relation to such a site, '*site preparation expenditure*' is expenditure on preparing the site for the deposit of waste materials. This includes expenditure incurred before the relevant licence is granted, and in particular expenses associated with obtaining the licence itself (HMRC Business Income Manual, BIM67440 and BIM67445). A '*waste disposal licence*' is a disposal licence under *Control of Pollution Act 1974, Pt 1* (or NI equivalent), a waste management licence under *Environmental Protection Act 1990, Pt 2* (or NI equivalent), a permit under regulations under *Pollution Prevention and Control Act 1999, s 2* (or NI equivalent), an authorisation for the disposal of radioactive waste, or a nuclear site licence.

The deductible amount of site preparation expenditure for a period of account is the amount allocated to that period, which itself is given by the formula:

$$RE \times \frac{WD}{SV + WD}$$

where:

RE	=	residual expenditure (see below);
WD	=	volume of waste materials deposited on the site during the period; and
SV	=	volume of the site not used up for the deposit of waste materials at the end of the period.

The residual expenditure for a period of account is the site preparation expenditure incurred by the company at any time before and up to the end of that period, less any expenditure which either has been allowed as a trading deduction for a prior period or is capital expenditure qualifying for capital allowances. If the trade commenced before 6 April 1989, a proportion of the expenditure incurred before that date (OE) is excluded, such proportion being calculated by reference to the volume of materials deposited before that date (OWD) and the unused volume of the site immediately before that date (OSV). The reduction is the amount given by the formula:

$$OE \times \frac{OWD}{OSV + OWD}$$

On and after 21 March 2000, any site preparation expenditure incurred by a predecessor of the company is brought into account above as if it had been incurred by the company. For this purpose, a predecessor of the company is a person who, on or after that date, has ceased to carry on the trade carried on by the company or has ceased to carry on a trade so far as relating to the site in question and who, in either case, has transferred the whole of the site to the company (though not necessarily the same estate or interest in the site).

A company making a 'site restoration payment', in the course of carrying on a trade, may deduct the payment in computing profits for the period of account (i.e. a period for which an account is drawn up) in which the payment is made. A payment will not qualify for relief to the extent that it represents either expenditure allowed as a trading deduction for prior periods or capital expenditure qualifying for capital allowances.

A '*site restoration payment*' is a payment made:

(a) in connection with the restoration of a site (or part thereof); and
(b) in order to comply with any condition of a 'relevant licence', or any condition imposed on the grant of planning permission to use the site for the carrying out of 'waste disposal activities', or any term of a 'relevant planning obligation'.

'*Waste disposal activities*' are the collection, treatment, conversion and final depositing of waste materials, or any of those activities.

A 'relevant planning obligation' is defined by *CTA 2009, s 145(6)* by reference to *Town and Country Planning Act 1990* and Scottish and NI equivalents.

[*CTA 2009, ss 142–145, Sch 2 paras 30–32; ICTA 1988, ss 91A, 91B, 91BA; SI 2000 No 1973; ITTOIA 2005, Sch 1 paras 68–70*].

See generally HMRC Business Income Manual BIM67405–67520.

Leasing. See **71.44** above as regards restrictions on relief under the above provisions where finance leasing arrangements are involved.

Simon's Taxes. See **B2.478**.

Landfill tax

There is an increase in the rate of such tax from £56 to £64 per tonne for disposals after 1 April 2012 per *FA 2011, s 25*. HMRC's views on the deductibility of landfill tax in computing trading income are as follows.

Site operators

Treatment of landfill tax charged on to customers will follow the generally accepted accounting practice. As regards self-generated waste, landfill tax (net of any credit following a contribution to an environmental trust) will be allowed as a deduction so long as the other costs incurred in disposing of the waste are deductible.

Customers of site operators

The landfill tax element of the global charge does not need to be separately invoiced, and deductibility of the landfill tax element will follow that of the non-landfill tax element of the charge.

Environmental trust contributions

Site operators may obtain relief from landfill tax by making such contributions, the deductibility of which is to be determined in the circumstances of each particular case under the normal test of whether the expenditure is incurred wholly and exclusively for trade purposes. In the case of an unconnected trust engaged in projects of possible use to the operator, the payment would *prima facie* be deductible. If the operator has some degree of control over the trust, or the income of the trust is ultimately received by a person connected with the operator, it might be less clear that the payment was for the purposes of the operator's own trade. Similarly if the trust's objects were insufficiently related to the operator's trade, it might be considered that contributions were for a general philanthropic, and hence non-trade, purpose.

(HMRC Business Income Manual, BIM67525 and BIM67530).

Websites

[71.77] The cost of setting up a website is likely to be capital expenditure; the regular update costs are likely to be revenue expenses (see HMRC Business Income Manual BIM35870).

Wholly and exclusively rule

[71.78] For an expense to be deductible, it must, *inter alia*, have been incurred 'wholly and exclusively for the purposes of the trade'. For accounting periods ending on or after 1 April 2009 (and see **70.2 TRADE PROFITS** —

INCOME AND SPECIFIC TRADES), it is specifically provided that if an expense is incurred for a *dual purpose*, this rule does not prohibit a deduction for any *identifiable* part or *identifiable* proportion of the expense which is incurred wholly and exclusively for the purposes of the trade; but this simply reflects a long-established principle (see below). [*CTA 2009, s 54; ICTA 1988, s 74(1)(a)*].

For a review of the leading cases on the 'wholly and exclusively' rule, see *Harrods (Buenos Aires) Ltd v Taylor-Gooby* (1964) 41 TC 450, CA, and for a frequently quoted analysis of the words see *Bentleys, Stokes & Lowless v Beeson* (1952) 33 TC 491, CA. Following that case the dual purpose rule (now in *ITTOIA 2005, s 34*) has figured prominently in Court decisions. 'Dual expenditure is expenditure that is incurred for more than one reason. If one of the reasons is not for business purposes, the expenditure fails the statutory test and there is no provision that allows a "business" proportion' (HMRC Business Income Manual BIM37007). *However*, in practice, where an identifiable part or proportion of an expense has been laid out wholly and exclusively for the purposes of the trade, HMRC do not disallow that part or proportion on the grounds that the expense is not *as a whole* laid out wholly and exclusively for the purposes of the trade (BIM37007); and see now *CTA 2009, s 54* above. See Tolley's Income Tax under Trading Income.

A purely incidental consequence of a business expense does not, however, preclude its being wholly and exclusively for business purposes (HMRC Business Income Manual BIM37007, 37400). See, for example, *Robinson v Scott Bader Ltd*, **71.26** above.

It should be borne in mind that the trade for whose purposes the expenditure is incurred must be that in which the expense arose. For a successful appeal against a decision in favour of HMRC on this point, see *Vodafone Cellular Ltd v Shaw* (1997) 69 TC 376, CA.

Two recent cases examine the question of the incidental non-business benefit. In *McQueen v Revenue and Customs Comrs* [2007] STC (SCD) 457 the taxpayer was the proprietor of a coach business and was also an amateur rally driver. He decided to use motor rallying as a way of advertising his business. He purchased a new rally car for this purpose and competed in several events. He claimed capital allowances on the car and claimed related expenditure as advertising expenses. HMRC issued discovery assessments on the basis that the expenditure had not been wholly and exclusively incurred for the purposes of the business. The Special Commissioner decided that the taxpayer's expenditure on motor rallying was incurred for the purposes of promoting his coach business and getting the names and liveries into the public awareness. Although the taxpayer gained some personal satisfaction from competing in rallies, his preferred leisure activity was sailing rather than rallying, and the private satisfaction of success on the rally circuit was an incidental benefit of the expenditure, rather than its purpose.

This can be contrasted with the case *Protec International Ltd v HMRC* [2010] UKFTT 628 in which the company carried on business in the construction industry and claimed deductions for significant payments to another company (M) which took part in motor rallies. The appellant's controlling director was an experienced rally driver who had driven for M. The Tribunal distinguished the McQueen case on the basis that there was no evidence from the appellant of any preferred leisure activity other than rallying and no evidence before it upon which to conclude that the director's private satisfaction was an incidental benefit of the expenditure. The Tribunal found the demonstrable lack of formal commerciality in the transaction inferred non-trade purpose and therefore there was a duality of purpose in the expenditure.

For HMRC's own guidance on the 'wholly and exclusively' rule, see HMRC Business Income Manual BIM37000–38600.

Key points

[71.79] The table below contains a brief summary of the tax treatment of common expenses and deductions. Please refer to the sections above for full explanations of the relevant points.

Expenditure/ item	Tax treatment in calculating trading profits	Reference
Accountancy fees	Normal recurring legal and accountancy fees in preparing accounts and or agreeing tax liabilities are allowed. Accountancy costs relating to an enquiry are not allowable if enquiry reveals discrepancies resulting from negligent (careless) or fraudulent (deliberate) conduct.	**71.54** BIM46450
Acquisition of company; costs	Normally capital and hence disallowed.	**71.54** BIM46435
Advertising	Generally allowed provided not capital.	**71.3**
Asset in satisfaction of trading debt	Where MV less than outstanding debt, deficit may be allowed as deduction provided trader agrees that on disposal of asset any excess proceeds treated as trading receipt.	**71.5** BIM42735
Bad debts / impairment losses	Relief normally available for impairment losses and statutory insolvency arrangements.	**71.5** *CTA 2009, s 55*
Capital expenditure	Normally disallowed in calculating trading profits.	**71.8** *CTA 2009, s 53*

Expenditure/ item	**Tax treatment in calculating trading profits**	**Reference**
Car hire	Part of hire cost frequently disallowed. From 1.4.09 disallowance = 15% of hire cost although rules on type of car and length of hire.	**71.9** *CTA 2009, s 56*
Compensation and damages payments	Whether allowable depends upon the specific circumstances and whether capital or outside trading activities.	**71.11**
Computer hardware	Normally capital (see **10 CAPITAL ALLOWANCES — INTRODUCTION**). Where package consists of both hardware and licence HMRC accept apportionment.	**71.12** BIM35800
Computer software	Expenditure normally accepted as revenue (hence allowable) where useful economic life less than two years.	**71.12** BIM35815
Contributions to local enterprise organisations	Contributions in cash or kind normally allowed as a deduction in computing profits.	**71.67** *CTA 2009, s 82*
Crime related expenses	Not allowed for tax purposes.	**71.52** *CTA 2009, s 1304*
Embezzlement	Losses generally allowed as deductions but not misappropriations by directors.	**71.14**
Employee benefits	Generally allowable but see specific types of benefits discussed above. For employee benefit trusts see **71.29**. See also **71.31** and the provisions with regard to disguised remuneration introduced by *FA 2011* with regard to arrangements and steps undertaken after 6 April 2011.	**71.15–50 INTEREST ON OVERPAID TAX**

Expenditure/ item	Tax treatment in calculating trading profits	Reference
Employee remuneration	Remuneration meeting the wholly and exclusively test is normally allowable (bank payroll tax see **71.27**). Payments to connected parties can be disallowed where not commercial. Also see above regarding timing of deductions where paid later than nine months after end of period of account.	**71.26**
Employee share schemes	Corporation tax relief is specifically available for certain qualifying types of employee share schemes.	**71.32–71.40** *CTA 2009, Pt 11 and 12, s 983* onwards
Entertainment	Generally disallowed.	**71.41** *CTA 2009, s 1298*
Entertainment exceptions	Entertainment may be allowable where provision is part of company's trade and or where it relates to employees.	**71.41** *CTA 2009, s 1299*
Expenses not wholly & exclusively for trade purposes	Normally disallowed in calculating trading profits. However where for dual purposes it may be possible to apportion.	**71.78** *CTA 2009, s 54*
Fee protection insurance	Allowable only to extent costs insured against would themselves have been allowable. Premiums disallowed in full if cover negligent (careless) or fraudulent (deliberate) conduct.	**71.54** BIM46452
Finance leases	Finance lease rentals are normally revenue payments for the use of the asset and hence allowable. The accounting and tax treatment of finance leases can be different see above.	**71.43–71.45** HMRC Business Leasing Manual
Fines	Not normally deductible as not wholly and exclusively for purpose of trade.	**71.11** BIM42515

Expenditure/ item	Tax treatment in calculating trading profits	Reference
Fines (parking)	Tax treatment depends; if fine is the liability of the employee, the company can claim tax relief although the employee will be chargeable on the emolument; If company car and paid as registered owner the employee is not taxable on an emolument and company cannot claim tax relief in calculating its profits.	**71.11** BIM42515
Formation of company; costs	Normally capital and hence disallowed although costs relating to loan capital may qualify for relief.	**71.54** BIM46435
Gifts	Generally disallowed but four exceptions; where part of trade, advertisement (limits), to employees and to certain bodies (charities).	**71.41** *CTA 2009, s 1300*
Gift aid donations	Not allowed in calculating trading profits but see **20.12** for relief calculating total taxable profits. See also **20.10 CHARITIES** with regard to the *FA 2011* changes in respect of substantial donors.	**20.10, 20.12 CHARITIES**
Guarantees	After regard to the loan relationship rules, it is necessary to consider whether incurred 'wholly and exclusively' and or capital expenditure.	**71.50** BIM45301
Hire purchase	The payments made need to be split between revenue (allowable) and capital (see **10 CAPITAL ALLOWANCES — INTRODUCTION**).	**71.51**
Illegal payments	Not allowed for tax purposes.	**71.52** *CTA 2009, s 1304*
In house professional fees	In house professional fees not allowed where capital in character eg purchase and sale of capital assets.	**71.54** BIM46410

Expenditure/ item	Tax treatment in calculating trading profits	Reference
Insurance	Premiums for business purposes are normally allowable.	Policies with a dual purpose (benefit shareholders personally) disallowed. **71.53, 71.20** BIM45500 *Beauty Consultants Ltd v Inspector of Taxes* [2002] STC (SCD) 352
Interest on director's property loan	Allowable provided relevant conditions (see above) met.	**71.19** BIM45755
Key employee insurance	Polices insuring against death or critical illness of key employees generally allowable. See insurance above for case involving dual purpose.	**71.20**
Lease premiums	Not normally deductible as capital. However part of certain lease premiums are taxed on the landlord as income. That part can be deducted over the period of the lease in calculating trading profits.	**71.62** *CTA 2009, ss 217–220*
Legal and professional expenses	Not allowable if capital or excluded by statute.	**71.54** BIM46400
National Insurance Contributions	Employers' Class 1, 1A and 1B NIC contributions are allowable.	**71.21** *CTA 2009, s 1302*
Onerous contract	Expenditure on the cancellation of a trade agreement normally allowable unless circumstances capital.	**71.11** BIM38220
Onerous lease	Lump sum to vary terms held to be capital.	**71.62, 71.11** *Tucker v Granada Motorway Services Ltd* BIM46810
Overseas taxation	Relief may be obtained through double tax relief see 24 but any not relieved may generally be deducted.	**71.69** BIM45901

Expenditure/ item	Tax treatment in calculating trading profits	Reference
Patents	No deduction allowed for royalties paid for use of patents. Expenses incurred in obtaining grant of patent may be allowable.	**71.57**, **48.36 INTANGIBLE ASSETS** *CTA 2009, s 59*
Penalties interest surcharges	Generally not allowable. Interest on corporation tax paid late/early is dealt with under **49.2 LOAN RELATIONSHIPS** where it is included as an allowable debit/credit.	**71.58** BIM45740, BIM31610
Pre-trading expenditure	Expenditure incurred in the prior seven years which would have been deductible in computing profits if the trade had commenced is allowed.	**71.60** *CTA 2009, s 61*
Provisions	May be allowable if (1) it relates to allowable revenue not capital expenditure, (2) It is in accordance with UK GAAP and FRS 12, (3) it does not conflict with any statutory rule, and (4) it is estimated with sufficient accuracy.	**71.61** BIM46510
Renewal of trade tools	Although normally regarded as capital, renewal (as opposed to initial cost) of trade tools is specifically allowable.	**71.63** *CTA 2009, s 68* BIM46935
Rent business premises	Costs for rent, rates insurance and repairs normally allowable. For partial private use see above.	**71.62** BIM46801
Rent premises no longer required	Continuing rents have been allowed as a deduction but not payments to secure the cancellation of the lease.	**71.62** *CIR v Falkirk Iron CS* (1933) 17 TC 625 *Cowcher v Richard Milss and Co KB* (1927) 13 TC 216
Repairs	Provided revenue and not capital nature normally allowable. The distinction between revenue and capital (repairs vs improvements / replacement of entirety) can cause problems in practice see above.	**71.63** BIM46900

Expenditure/ item	Tax treatment in calculating trading profits	Reference
Research and development	Specific tax reliefs exist see **64 RESEARCH AND DEVELOPMENT.**	**64 RESEARCH AND DEVELOPMENT, 71.64**
Reverse premiums (rent)	Depends upon particular circumstances. For a developer trading in property normally allowable in other circumstances the payment may be capital.	**71.62** BIM41060
Stock / inventory / WIP	The cost of stock is allowed in accordance with GAAP. For the definitions, recognition and valuation of these items see above.	**71.66** BIM33000–33630
Subscriptions	To associations are normally allowable, see above regarding checking status of the association.	**71.67**
Tax appeals	Costs not allowable however see BIM46455 for VAT and business rate appeals.	**71.54**
Taxation	Income tax and corporation tax are not deductible in computing profits.	**71.69**
Trade marks	Deduction allowed for expenses incurred in registration, extension and or renewal of trade mark for the purpose of the company's trade.	**71.71 48 INTANGIBLE ASSETS,** *CTA 2009, s 90*
Unremittable (from overseas) amounts	Relief via a deduction from profits is available in certain circumstances.	**71.74**
Valuation fees	Those incurred to comply with *Companies Act 2006* are allowable.	**71.75**
Website	Depends on exact circumstances but the initial cost of creation is likely to be capital whilst subsequent updates revenue.	**71.77** BIM35870

Expenditure/ item	Tax treatment in calculating trading profits	Reference
Wholly and exclusively	To be deductible an expense needs to be incurred wholly and exclusively for the purpose of the trade. Where dual purpose may be possible to apportion.	**71.78**

72

Transfer Pricing

Cross-references. See **31.6 DISTRIBUTIONS; 41.12 HMRC ADMINISTRATION; 60.7–60.12 PENALTIES.**

Other sources. See the HMRC International Manual at INTM430000 *et seq.*

Simon's Taxes. See **B2.215, D2.6.**

Introduction

[72.1] Transfer pricing rules seek to stop companies from gaining an advantage in relation to tax by entering into transactions with connected parties using non-arm's length prices. They generally operate to reverse the benefits obtained from such transactions.

The scope of the transfer pricing requirements under UK legislation extend to both UK and cross-border transactions. Dormant companies (see **72.5** below) and small and medium-sized enterprises (see **72.6** below) will, in most circumstances, be exempt from applying the transfer pricing and thin capitalisation rules. Where an adjustment is required by the provisions to increase the profits of one party, the corresponding adjustment provisions (see **72.7** below) are extended so that the connected UK party can make a compensating reduction in their taxable profits, and new provisions allow for a 'balancing payment' to be made tax-free up to the amount of the compensating adjustment (see **72.8** below).

[*TIOPA 2010, Pt 4; ICTA 1988, Sch 28AA; FA 2004, ss 30–37, Sch 5; CTA 2009, Sch 1 para 291*].

See generally HMRC International Manual at INTM430000 onwards on a number of transfer pricing issues and at 542000 onwards on thin capitalisation. HMRC guidance on the provision of documentation stresses that a business would not be expected to carry out extensive research or incur significant costs in producing documentation where the amounts at stake would not generally be significant and where both parties to a transaction were subject to similar levels of taxation. Similarly, HMRC would only put resources into making transfer pricing enquiries where the amounts of tax at stake appeared to be large.

The European Commission has adopted a Code of Conduct on transfer pricing documentation to standardise the documentation that multinational companies of different member states must provide to their respective tax authorities on their pricing of cross-border intra-group transactions. (See the European Commission Press Release IP/06/850 of 28 June 2006).

TIOPA 2010 provides for the transfer pricing provisions to be read in a way consistent with the OECD transfer pricing guidelines and model taxation treaty, whether there is a treaty in force between the UK and any particular country or not.

The OECD has issued detailed Transfer Pricing Guidelines for Multinational Enterprises and Tax Administrations, with regard to the application of transfer pricing provisions, including detailed analysis of the appropriate methodologies for determining the arm's length price. These Guidelines have recently been updated, and re-issued, in July 2010. Chapters I–III have been substantially revised and the re-issued Guidelines contain new, more detailed guidance on how to perform the comparability analyses, on how to select the most appropriate transfer pricing method for a particular case and on how to apply the OECD approved methods in practice. A new chapter IX has been introduced, providing detailed guidance on the transfer pricing aspects of business restructurings.

[*TIOPA 2010, s 164*].

Basic rule

[72.2] The key concept behind transfer pricing rules is that parties who are connected should transact with each other as if they were independent persons. If they do not, and a tax advantage is obtained, then the tax authority has the power to adjust the tax return and put the parties back into the position they would have been in if they had interacted independently.

The basic rule therefore is:

- where a provision has been made other than at an arm's length price (i.e. the price which would apply to a transaction between independent persons);
- with regard to a transaction(s) between persons who are connected (per the legislation where one party is participating in the management or control of the other (see below)); and

- this gives rise to an advantage in relation to UK tax; then
- HMRC is able to make an adjustment (on the basis of what the outcome would have been had an arm's length price been used).

In more detail: *TIOPA 2010, Pt 4; ICTA 1988, Sch 28AA* – the UK transfer pricing legislation – applies where provision (the '*actual provision*') has been made or imposed as between two persons (the '*affected persons*') by means of a transaction or series of transactions, and at the time the provision was made or imposed 'the participation condition' was fulfilled.

The '*participation condition*' is that at the time of making or imposing the actual provision or within six months of the date when the actual condition was made or imposed either:

(a) one of the affected persons was directly or indirectly participating in the management, control or capital of the other; or
(b) there was a person or persons who was or were directly or indirectly participating in the management, control or capital of each of the affected persons and

at the time the condition was made or imposed either:

(i) one of the parties participated in the management, control or capital of the other, directly or indirectly; or
(ii) the same person or persons was or were directly or indirectly taking part in the management, control or capital of each affected person.

Subject to the exceptions below (see **72.5** and **72.6**), if the actual provision differs from the provision which would have been made at arm's length as between independent enterprises (or if no provision would have been so made) and confers a 'potential advantage' (see **72.4** below) in relation to UK taxation on one of the affected persons or (whether or not the same advantage) on each of them, the profits and losses (and certain items treated as losses) of the potentially advantaged person, or of each of them, are computed for tax purposes as if the arm's length provision had been made or imposed (or, as the case may be, no provision made) instead of the actual provision.

See also HMRC International Manual, INTM432040.

[*TIOPA 2010, ss 147–149*].

Definitions

'*Transactions*' *etc.* A 'transaction' for these purposes includes schemes or arrangements of any kind, understandings and mutual practices (whether or not legally enforceable), and a 'series' of transactions includes a number of transactions entered into in pursuance of, or in relation to, the same scheme or arrangement.

A series of transactions is not prevented from being regarded as the means by which provision has been made or imposed between two persons by solely because:

- there is no transaction in the series to which both those persons are parties; or

- one or more transactions to which neither of them is a party; or
- that the parties to any scheme or arrangement in pursuance of which the transactions are entered into do not include one or both of them.

[*TIOPA 2010, s 150*].

'Participation in management' etc. A person is for these purposes treated as directly participating in the management, control or capital of another person at a particular time if and only if (but subject to the provisions below on persons acting together in relation to financing arrangements), at that time, the other person is a body corporate or partnership which that person controls (within *CTA 2010, s 1124; ICTA 1988, s 840*, see **63.6 PURCHASE BY A COMPANY OF ITS OWN SHARES**).

[*TIOPA 2010, ss 148, 157, 158*].

Similarly indirect participation requires that the person either would be taken to be participating directly if certain rights and powers including future rights and powers, were attributed to him, or is one of a number of 'major participants' in the other person's enterprise.

[*TIOPA 2010, s 159(3)(4); ICTA 1988, Sch 28AA para 4(3)–(6)(10)–(12)*].

A person is a '*major participant*' in another person's enterprise when the other person (the 'subordinate') is a body corporate or partnership, and he is one of two persons who control (as above) the subordinate, each of whom has at least 40% of the holdings, etc. giving that control (again after attribution of certain rights and powers as above).

Persons acting together in relation to financing arrangements. The meaning of 'indirectly participating' above is extended by *TIOPA 2010, ss 161, 162; ICTA 1988, Sch 28AA para 4A* to include circumstances where a number of parties act together in relation to the 'financing arrangements' of a business and could collectively control the business.

(A) For the purposes of (a) above (determining whether one of the affected persons was participating in the management, etc. of another), a person ('X') is treated as indirectly participating in the management etc. of another ('Y') if:
  - the actual provision relates, to any extent, to financing arrangements for Y (where Y is a body corporate or partnership);
  - X and other persons acted together in relation to the arrangements; and
  - X would be taken to have control of Y if, at any 'relevant time', there were attributed to X the rights and powers of each of those other persons (taking into account any additional rights or powers that would be attributed to any person if *TIOPA 2010, s 157; ICTA 1988, Sch 28AA para 4* (see under '*Participation in management etc.*' above) applied in that person's case).

(B) For the purposes of (b) above (determining whether there was a person (or persons) participating in the management, etc. of each of the affected persons), the rule in (i) above applies where the financing arrangements are for one of the affected persons and X would be taken to have control of each of the affected persons.

It is immaterial whether the persons acting together did so at the time the actual provision is made or imposed or did so at some earlier time.

For these purposes, parties are '*connected*' with each other if one of them is an individual and the other is one of the following: the individual's spouse or civil partner; a relative of the individual or spouse or civil partner; or the spouse or civil partner of a relative. Also, two persons are connected if one is a trustee of a settlement and the other is a settlor of that trust or a person connected with him. For this purpose, '*relative*' means brother, sister, ancestor or lineal descendant.

[*TIOPA 2010, s 163*].

'*Financing arrangements*' are arrangements made for providing or guaranteeing, or otherwise in connection with, any debt, capital or other form of finance. A '*relevant time*' is any time when the persons were so acting together and also any time in the six months after they ceased to do so. Where the conditions in (a) or (b) above are satisfied by virtue only of the above rule, a transfer pricing adjustment can be required only to the extent that the actual provision relates to the financing arrangements in question.

By way of transitional protection for debt finance provided to a person under a contract entered into before 4 March 2005, the application of *ICTA 1998, Sch 28AA para 4A* (now *TIOPA 2010, ss 158, 161, 162*) in such a case is delayed until accounting periods beginning on or after 1 April 2007 or, if the contract is varied before that date, the date of the variation.

Accounting periods straddling 4 March 2005, 1 April 2007 or the date of a variation (as the case may be) are treated, for these purposes only, as two separate periods, the first ending with the day before whichever of those dates is relevant and the second beginning on that date. Profits and losses are computed accordingly for the two periods and then aggregated (so that the above rules cannot affect profits arising before the relevant date). An advance made on or after 4 March 2005 in accordance with terms agreed before that date, or a change in the applied interest rate in accordance with terms agreed before that date, are not regarded as variations to the contract for these purposes (see the HMRC website (at www.hmrc.gov.uk/international/transfe rpricing.pdf)).

By virtue of *TIOPA 2010, s 148; ICTA 1988, Sch 28AA para 4B*, to the extent that the actual provision relates to financing arrangements, the conditions at (a) and (b) above are to be judged not only at the time the provision is made or imposed but at all times within the following six months; so to this extent transfer pricing adjustments may be triggered by events occurring up to six months before the necessary relationship exists between the parties.

'*Transfer pricing guidelines*' means all the documents published by the OECD as part of their Transfer Pricing Guidelines for Multinational Enterprises and Tax Administrations.

The *Finance Act 2011* amends the above definition of the OECD Guidelines, to take account of the updated and re-issued version published by the OECD. *TIOPA 2010, s 164(4)(a)* and *(b)* are amended to refer specifically to the

Transfer Pricing Guidelines approved on 22 July 2010, or such other document approved and published by the OECD in place of that (or a later) version of the Guidelines. The amendment has effect for accounting periods beginning on or after 1 April 2011.

[*TIOPA 2010, s 164(4)*].

In *DSG Retail Ltd v HMRC* SpC [2009] STC (SCD) 397 a company selling electrical goods encouraged customers to take out a warranty, insured with an Isle of Man fellow subsidiary. The Special Commissioners found that the arrangement potentially gave the UK company a tax advantage and a transfer pricing adjustment was imposed using the profit-split methodology. This case highlights various issues such as: the use of comparables; the importance of the concept of bargaining power; the application of the profit split method; and the identification of a provision through a series of transactions. Further discussion of this case can be found at HMRC manuals: INTM 435090.

For more detail on the financing arrangements rules, see the HMRC website (at www.hmrc.gov.uk/international/transferpricing.pdf).

[*TIOPA 2010, ss 157–163; ICTA 1988, Sch 28AA paras 1, 3, 4, 4A, 4B, 14; F(No 2)A 2005, Sch 8 paras 1(1)–(4), 4; CTA 2009, Sch 1 para 291*].

Thin capitalisation

[72.3] A company is thinly capitalised when its level of debt far exceeds its equity. Generally, where a company is thinly capitalised HMRC may not allow a deduction for all the interest payments made with regard to the debt of the company, on the basis that such company would not have been able to borrow that level of funds from a third party when considering the independent position of such company.

HMRC are reluctant to provide arbitrary 'safe harbour' ratios with regard to the level of debt:equity or income cover, and they stress that each case is considered on its particular merits. Having noted that, previously it was generally considered a gearing below 1:1 and an income cover of at least 3:1 was an appropriate guide. However recent updated guidance on thin capitalisation issued by HMRC in March 2010 dismisses the idea of having 'safe harbour' ratios as too simplistic an approach. Instead the new guidance (throughout) sets out broad principles upon which HMRC will base its interpretation and application of the thin capitalisation provisions.

See also the provisions applicable to accounting periods beginning on or after 1 January 2010 with regard to the Worldwide Debt Cap (an integral part of the new rules with regard to the taxation of foreign profits — see further **40 GROUPS OF COMPANIES — FINANCING COSTS AND INCOME**).

The impact of the ECJ in this field should also be noted. The ECJ considered the UK's pre 2004 thin capitalisation provisions in the case of *Test Claimants in the Thin Cap GLO* (C-524/04) [2007] ECR I-2107, [2007] STC 906, ECJ. It held that a Member State's thin capitalisation legislation, which is only applied to interest payments to non-resident lenders, is a restriction on the freedom of establishment. However, such a restriction may be justified on the basis of the prevention of tax avoidance, so long as the provisions are proportionate to that aim, in that the legislation should: provide for the consideration of objective criteria to identify purely artificial arrangements; allow taxpayers to produce evidence as to the commercial justification for the transaction; and should only apply to the interest element which exceeded an arm's length amount. The ECJ remitted the case back to the UK courts to determine whether the UK legislation met these conditions.

The case was referred back to the Ch D and Henderson J reviewed the case in detail, delivering judgment in November 2009. It was held that, in addition to the arm's length test, there should be an additional test that examines whether there is a genuine commercial justification for the high level of debt — the thin cap rules could then be dis-applied in such a case. Both sides appealed.

On 18 February 2011 the CA allowed HMRC's appeal (by a 2 to 1 majority, with Arden LJ dissenting). Burnton LJ commented that it was difficult to reconcile the original 2007 ECJ judgment in this case with the later cases of *Oy AA* (C231-05) and *SGI v Belgium* (C-311/08). The CA went on to hold that the application of an arm's length test was appropriate and sufficient, and that these provisions were thus a proportionate measure to achieve the anti-avoidance objectives. An additional 'commercial purpose' test was not required for the UK legislation to be compliant with the EC Treaty (as was). As the transactions in question did not satisfy the arm's length test the thin cap legislation had been correctly applied to them.

It is likely the taxpayers will seek leave to appeal from the Supreme Court.

Provision in relation to securities

The transfer pricing rules apply to a provision which differs from an arm's length provision in relation to a 'security' issued by a company ('*the issuing company*') to another company ('*the lending company*'). In considering whether the provision is at arm's length, account is to be taken of all factors including whether, in the absence of a 'special relationship' (and whether or not it is the business of the lending company to make loans generally):

(a) the loan would have been provided at all;
(b) the amount would have been advanced; and
(c) the rate of interest or other terms of the loan would have been agreed.

A '*security*' can include a loan or advance of money, whether secured or not. A '*special relationship*' in this case means any relationship where the participation is met by the affected person.

In considering whether the provision is made at arm's length, no account is to be taken of any 'guarantee' (or inference drawn from a 'guarantee') provided by a company with which the issuing company has a 'participatory relationship', when determining:

(i) the appropriate level or extent of the issuing company's overall indebtedness;
(ii) whether the issuing company would have issued the security or whether the lending company would have advanced the loan or the particular amount of the loan; and

(iii) the rate of interest and other terms expected in such a transaction.

Where a guarantee (as widely defined) is given for the issue of a security, in looking at the arm's length position of the loan, the following must be taken into account:

(A) Whether the guarantee would have been given at all;
(B) the amount which would have been guaranteed in the absence of the special relationship; and
(C) the consideration for the guarantee and other terms which would have been agreed.

In considering whether the provision of the guarantee is at arm's length items (i), (ii) and (iii) above are also taken into account.

[*TIOPA 2010, ss 152–154*].

A company has a '*participatory relationship*' with another in this case where one of them is directly or indirectly participating in the management, control or capital of the other, or the same person or persons is or are directly or indirectly participating in the management, control or capital of each of them.

A '*guarantee*' in this case includes any surety, relationship, arrangement, connection or understanding (whether formal or informal), such that the lending company has a reasonable expectation that the loan will be repaid by the guarantor (or guarantors) in the event of default by the issuing company.

HMRC guidance and SP4/07

Clarification is provided by HMRC on the new thin capitalisation rules in HMRC International Manual at INTM542000 *et seq.* and in Statement of Practice SP 4/07.

The guidance with regard to thin capitalisation in the International Manual was updated by HMRC in March 2010. As each case is different and should be assessed on its own merits, the new guidance takes a more principles-based approach, by setting out the basics (such as terminology etc.) and then providing examples of structures and what would be considered key factors. There are some new areas covered in the updated guidance, such as:

- credit ratings and the use of synthetic credit rating tools which are used widely by practitioners (the focus ultimately being on the quality of information used);
- the impact of IFRS;
- private equity deals, and how the provisions should apply to typical PE funding arrangements;
- an increased commentary with regard to property lending, and third party research as to asset values (etc.);
- the updated treatment of Double Tax Treaty applications as being distinct from thin capitalisation issues (per SP 4/07 — the contents of which are essentially now included in the manual).

Under the heading of 'separate entity', it is explained that actual assets or liabilities such as shares in subsidiaries and intra-group loans are not to be disregarded when assessing the borrowing capacity of a company but that they should be taken into account to the same extent that they would be by an unconnected lender. Reference should be made to the chapter on Intra-group Funding in HMRC International Manual, with regard to thinning out see INTM508000 onwards, with regard to avoidance and arbitrage see INTM509010 onwards. This effectively means that all assets and liabilities in direct or indirect subsidiaries should be taken into account.

It goes on to explain that the repeal of the UK grouping rule in calculating an individual company's debt capacity does not in practice affect the UK sub-group as a whole because of the provisions for loan guarantees and in particular the compensating adjustment for guarantors (see **72.7** below).

HMRC have issued Statement of Practice 04/07 'Advance Thin Capitalisation Agreements' under the APA legislation. This includes a Model ATCA and a commentary thereon. Further guidance is available in the HMRC's International Manual, which now includes much of what is in SP 4/07. These agreements are issued on the authority of *TIOPA 2010, s 218 et seq; FA 1999, ss 85–87*.

In general, the form of the transactions is not disregarded, except where the economic substance differs from the form, in which case HMRC have power to disregard form. The issue with thin capitalisation is to avoid enterprises funding UK operations from abroad in a form leading to excessive interest payments overseas, so artificially depressing UK profits for corporation tax. If one party is controlled by the other, or both are controlled by the same person or persons, the legislation applies and the test is whether the terms of the financing arrangement are such as would have been entered into between parties negotiating at arm's length.

For various reasons, it is desirable for companies to have certainty on the treatment of such transactions earlier than if the normal self-assessment process were allowed to take its course. The ATCA process has therefore been widened to include those to whom the double tax treaty process would not be available. Any business – including a partnership – may make an application, provided it has entered or is to enter a transaction falling within *TIOPA 2010, Pt 4; ICTA 1988, Sch 28AA* (provision not at arm's length). Application is at the discretion of the business, but the process is intended for transactions having a significant commercial impact on its profits or losses. To improve efficiency, use of the model ATCA is encouraged. HMRC may give guidance on a specific application, and the Statement of Practice also indicates circumstances in which an application might be declined.

The scope of an application is flexible, covering for example a single company or a group. Normally the agreement will cover a term of three to five years, but a degree of retrospection is possible, and HMRC and the applicant may jointly agree to a 'roll-back' of the ATCA to amend a self-assessment return for an earlier period and to resolve transfer pricing issues therein — however, HMRC will not use hindsight in such an arrangement.

The application should fulfil the requirements of *TIOPA 2010, s 223; FA 1999, s 85(5)* and should contain the proposed terms of the ATCA. The approach will be less formal than that for APAs (under SP 3/99, now SP 2/10). Correspondence in electronic form is welcomed, unless the documentation is voluminous when hard copy or disc format may be more appropriate. Once negotiations are entered into, the guidance at INTM542000 *et seq* remains applicable. Either side may withdraw from the negotiation process before final agreement is reached. Correspondence regarding the ATCA process and applications for ATCAs should be addressed to the Transfer Pricing Team at Business International.

Once reached, the agreement is binding, unless its terms are broken so that it is revoked, nullified, revised or over-ridden by mutual agreement. It would include provision for monitoring and for revision should circumstances change.

Where an ATCA is due to expire and it is wished to continue on similar terms, a new agreement should be entered into, rather than an extension of the old agreement.

Where there is fraud or negligence in making a return using an ATCA or false or misleading information has been provided to HMRC in the ATCA process, *TIOPA 2010, s 226; FA 1999, s 86(5)* provides that the agreement is treated as if it had never been made, resulting in incorrect returns giving rise to penalties. A penalty of £10,000 is provided for under *TIOPA 2010, s 227; FA 1999, s 86(8)* where false or misleading information has been provided in connection with an ATCA application. In practice, where a tax-geared penalty is due, a fixed penalty under this subsection will be reduced so that the total penalties do not exceed the greatest of them.

There is a right of appeal against an addition to profits as the result of the revocation or cancellation of an ATCA.

ATCAs must be distinguished from applications for treaty clearance, in respect of which HMRC issued a guidance note (26 April 2007) and draft statement of practice giving details of changes to clearance procedures. See www.hmrc.gov.uk/cnr/clearance-processes.htm. Treaty applications for interest to be paid under deduction of tax under a DTA are made by non-UK residents while an application for an ATCA is made by a UK resident.

Guarantees etc.

Similar provisions apply where the actual provision is made or imposed by means of a series of transactions which include the issue of a 'security' (see above) by one of the affected persons and the provision of a 'guarantee' (see above) by the other affected person (see **72.2** above) (whether or not the issuing company and lending company are so connected).

The effect of the provisions is that the interest attributable to the excessive part of such a loan is disallowed as if the loan was received from a connected party. In considering whether the provision is at arm's length, account is to be taken of all factors including whether, in the absence of a 'special relationship' (see above) (and whether or not it is the business of the guarantor to make guarantees generally):

(A) the guarantee would have been provided at all;
(B) the particular amount would have been guaranteed; and

(C) the consideration for the guarantee or other terms would have been agreed.

No account is to be taken of any guarantee (or inference drawn from a guarantee) provided by a company with which the issuing company has a 'participatory relationship', when determining any of (i) to (iii) above.

HMRC has issued HMRC Brief 01/09 which took the form of FAQs on ATCAs. ATCAs will be dealt with by HMRC's Business International directorate with effect from 5 January 2009. The process is intended primarily to deal with ATCAs, but other issues e.g. imputation of interest on outward loans may be covered in the course of exploring the basis of an ATCA. Occasionally in the past the teams dealing with ATCAs have discussed the level of return appropriate to a group finance or treasury company. This may continue, subject to size, complexity etc. There are no criteria set down for ATCAs and none are planned.

Guidance may be issued at a future time if it would be constructive to do so e.g. because HMRC's resources are becoming over-stretched. ATCAs are not intended to be pre-transaction rulings. In most cases, the relevant transactions will have taken place but the request is made before the return in question filed. However, an application may be made when plans are well enough advanced so that there is every expectation that the transactions will go ahead. The FAQs give guidance as to how taxpayers might best present information to make the process as efficient as possible and to maximise the effectiveness of the case.

[*TIOPA 2010, ss 152–158; ICTA 1988, Sch 28AA paras 1A, 1B; FA 2004, ss 34, 37; CTA 2009, Sch 1 para 291*].

Potential advantage

[72.4] The actual provision confers a '*potential advantage*' on a person in relation to UK taxation where its effect, compared to that of the corresponding arm's length provision, would be a reduction in chargeable profits or increase in losses (or conversion of profits into losses) of that person for any chargeable period. In determining the chargeable profits or allowable losses for this purpose in the case of a non-UK resident company, no account is to be taken of any income on which the income tax charge is limited under *ITA 2007, s 813; FA 2003, s 151* (see **65.6 RESIDENCE**).

For distributions paid on or after 1 July 2009 (subject to transitional provisions) the provisions under *CTA 2010, s 1000(1)* which deem excessive interest to be a distribution are to be disregarded for the purposes of the calculations under *TIOPA 2010, s 155*; *ICTA 1988, Sch 28AA para 5*. Profits include income and losses includes reliefs for pre-trading expenses, carry forward of certain interest, non-trading deficits on loan relationships, excess of management expenses and group relief.

[*TIOPA 2010, ss 155, 156; ICTA 1988, Sch 28AA paras 5, 14; FA 2004, ss 30(2), 37*].

Exemption for dormant companies

[72.5] The transfer pricing provisions do not apply, when calculating the profits or losses for any chargeable period, to companies which:

(a) are dormant throughout the accounting period ending on 31 March 2004, or if there is no such accounting period, the three-month period ending on that date; and
(b) have continued to be dormant at all times since the end of that period apart from any transfer pricing adjustments.

For these purposes, '*dormant*' has the same meaning as in *Companies Act 2006, s 1169*.

[*TIOPA 2010, s 165; ICTA 1988, Sch 28AA para 5A; FA 2004, ss 31(3), 37*].

Exemption for small and medium-sized enterprises

[72.6] The transfer pricing provisions do not apply, when calculating the profits or losses for any chargeable period, to a company which is a small or medium-sized enterprise. Such companies are as defined in the Annex to the Commission Recommendation *2003/361/EC* of 6 May 2003 with the modifications set out in *TIOPA 2010, s 172; ICTA 1988, Sch 28AA para 5D*.

Broadly, a small enterprise is defined as a business with less than 50 employees and either turnover or assets of less than €10 million and a small or medium-sized enterprise as a business with less than 250 employees and either turnover of less than €50 million or assets of less than €43 million. Associated enterprises are taken into account in determining whether a company is a small or medium-sized enterprise.

Exceptions

The exemption will not apply where:

(a) a small or medium-sized enterprise elects for the exemption not to apply, such election being irrevocable;
(b) at the time the actual provision was made or imposed, the other affected person or a 'party to the relevant transaction' is resident and liable to tax in a 'non-qualifying territory' (whether or not also resident in a 'qualifying territory');
(c) as respects any provision made or imposed, HMRC gives notice (a '*transfer pricing notice*') to a medium-sized enterprise, which is the advantaged party, requiring that company to increase profits or reduce losses of that chargeable period on an arm's length basis.

[*TIOPA 2010, ss 167, 168*].

As regards (b) above, where the actual provision is or was imposed by means of a series of transactions, a '*party to a relevant transaction*' is or was a party to one or more of those transactions. A company is not considered liable to tax in a non-qualifying territory if the liability relates only to income sourced from that territory or capital situated there. A '*non-qualifying territory*' is a territory which is not a qualifying territory. A '*qualifying territory*' is defined as:

(i) the UK;
(ii) a territory with which the UK has a double tax treaty (under *TIOPA 2010, ss 2–6; ICTA 1988, s 788*) containing a non-discrimination article (see *TIOPA 2010, s 173; ICTA 1988, Sch 28AA para 5E*) unless that territory has been designated as non-qualifying in regulations made by the Treasury; or

(iii) a territory with which the UK has a double tax treaty (under *TIOPA 2010, ss 2–6; ICTA 1988, s 788*) and which is designated as qualifying in regulations made by the Treasury.

[*TIOPA 2010, s 173*].

Transfer pricing notices issued to medium-sized companies

As regards (c) above, a transfer pricing notice, which may only be given following a notice of enquiry, may specify that an arm's length adjustment is to be made in respect of a certain, or certain types of, provision or in respect of all provisions which would fall within the transfer pricing rules but for the above exemption. The recipient of a notice may appeal in writing to the officer of HMRC identified for the purpose in the transfer notice, within 30 days from the date the notice is given (see **6.1 APPEALS**) but only on the grounds that the company is a small rather than a medium-sized enterprise.

The company receiving the notice may amend the company tax return to which the notice relates at any time within 90 days of the date the notice was given, or if an appeal is made, the day on which the appeal is finally determined or abandoned. HMRC may issue a closure notice once the 90 days have elapsed, or if earlier, once the tax return has been amended for the purpose of complying with the notice.

Where a medium-sized company is not excepted from exemption under (a) or (b) above, there is no need for the company's tax return to take account of the transfer pricing rules. However, this does not prevent the company's tax return from becoming incorrect if a transfer pricing notice is issued and the return is not amended within the period of 90 days as noted above when it should have been amended.

[*TIOPA 2010, ss 169, 170, 171; ICTA 1988, Sch 28AA paras 5B–5E; FA 2004, ss 31(4), 37*].

Elimination of double counting

[72.7] Where a potential advantage is conferred (as above) on only one of the affected persons (the '*advantaged person*'), and the other person (the '*disadvantaged person*') is within the charge to corporation tax (or income tax) in respect of profits arising from the relevant activities, then (except as below) the disadvantaged person may claim application of the arm's length provision instead of the actual provision (over-riding any applicable time limits for the necessary adjustments).

Such a claim may only be made if the arm's length provision has similarly been applied in the case of the advantaged person (in his return or following a determination, see **72.10** below), and the computations in the case of each of them on that basis must be consistent.

[*TIOPA 2010, ss 174, 176*].

Special provisions apply where the transfer pricing adjustment relates to a security issued by an affected party that has been guaranteed by a participant. Specifically, where the conditions at **72.2**(a) and (b) above are satisfied only by virtue of *TIOPA 2010, ss 161, 162; ICTA 1988, Sch 28AA para 4A* (financing arrangements — see **72.2** above), no claim by the disadvantaged person can be made where the actual provision is provision in relation to a security issued by one of the affected persons and the security is guaranteed by a person with whom the issuer of the security has a 'participatory relationship'.

Appropriately modified versions of **72.2**(a) and (b) above, as extended by *para 4A*, apply to determine the existence or otherwise of a '*participatory relationship*'.

[*TIOPA 2010, s 175*].

Claims — time limits

The claim must be made within two years of the making of the return or the giving of the notice taking account of the determination, as the case may be, and a claim based on a return which is subsequently the subject of such a notice may be amended within two years of the giving of the notice. (These time limits may be extended in certain cases where HMRC fails to give proper notice to disadvantaged persons under *FA 1998, s 111(3)*.)

[*TIOPA 2010, s 177; ICTA 1988, Sch 28AA para 6; FA 2001, Sch 29 para 35; FA 2004, ss 30(3)–(5), 35, 37; F(No 2)A 2005, Sch 8 paras 1(5), 4*].

Transfers of trading stock etc. A special provision applies where trading stock (as defined in *CTA 2009, s 163* formerly *ICTA 1988, s 100(2)*) or work in progress in a trade is transferred between associated parties at other than an arm's length price, and a transfer pricing adjustment is applied in the case of the advantaged person. In that case, a compensating adjustment may be claimed (as above) in respect of closing trading stock or work in progress by the disadvantaged person in the accounting period ending on or after the last day of that of the advantaged person in which the stock transfer occurred.

[*TIOPA 2010, s 180; ICTA 1988, Sch 28AA para 6A; FA 2004, ss 32(2), 37*].

Controlled foreign companies

A special provision applies where a transfer pricing adjustment has been applied to the profits or losses of a controlled foreign company the profits of which fall to be wholly apportioned to, and taxable in, the UK by virtue of *ICTA 1988, s 747(3)(4)* (see **27 CONTROLLED FOREIGN COMPANIES**). In this case, the controlled foreign company is treated as an advantaged person such that a compensating adjustment may be claimed (as above) by the disadvantaged party or parties (and references above to an advantaged person include a reference to a controlled foreign company).

[*TIOPA 2010, s 179; ICTA 1988, Sch 28AA para 6B; FA 2004, s 32*].

Thin capitalisation

Where the thin capitalisation provisions in **72.3** above apply in accounting periods beginning on or after 1 April 2004 (and see **72.1** above for periods straddling that date), a compensating adjustment may be claimed (and the claim may be amended) by the disadvantaged person or by the advantaged person on behalf of the disadvantaged person.

Such a claim (a *s 182* claim) may be made before or after the arm's length provision has been applied in the case of the advantaged person (in his return or following a determination – see **72.10** below) but the claim must be consistent with that computation. If the claim is not consistent with the computation, it is treated as if it were amended to make it consistent, allowing for any required adjustments to be made (whether by discharge or repayment of tax, the making of assessments or otherwise).

In making a *s 182* claim before the transfer pricing provision is applied, the lending company is not treated as chargeable to tax on income from non-trading loan relationships with respect to so much of the interest that is subject to the transfer pricing adjustment (see '*Reciprocal treatment*' below). Thus the condition for deducting tax at source under *ITA 2007, Pt 15* (formerly *ICTA 1988, s 349(2)*) is not met. The borrowing company may pay such interest to a non-resident lender without deduction of tax at source.

Claims must be made or amended before the expiry of the time limits noted above and the provisions of *TMA 1970, Sch 1A* (claims made outside a return) apply for this purpose.

If a 'relevant notice' is given by any person, it takes account of a transfer-pricing determination and it appears to an HMRC officer that a person may be disadvantaged he must give the disadvantaged person a notice containing details of the determination. A '*relevant notice*' is a closure notice in respect of a corporation tax or partnership return, a notice of assessment or a notice of discovery assessment or determination. Where the officer issues the notice late, or does not issue a notice at all, so that the disadvantaged person is prejudiced then the Commissioners for HMRC may extend the time limit for making an amendment to a compensating adjustment claim under *TIOPA 2010, s 174*.

[*TIOPA 2010, ss 181–185, 190; ICTA 1988, Sch 28AA para 6C; FA 2004, s 35(3)*].

Thin capitalisation — guarantees

Where a transfer pricing adjustment to disallow interest follows from the provision of a guarantee (see **72.3** above), the guarantor company can claim a compensating adjustment as if it was the borrower (the 'issuing company') and had paid the interest subject to the disallowance. Amounts are brought into account in computing the guarantor company's profits and losses accordingly. Where there is more than one guarantor, the total amount claimed by way of a compensating adjustment must not exceed the amount of interest disallowed.

A claim can also be made by the issuing company on behalf of the guarantor company or companies. Where a claim is made by a guarantor and the lending company subsequently makes a claim for a compensating adjustment in respect of the same loan, the claim made by the lending company must be reduced to the extent of the claim made by the guarantor company.

A claim made by the guarantor company will not be allowed where the lending company has earlier made a compensating adjustment claim for the full amount of the interest disallowance. The provisions above relating to claims and time limits apply equally to claims made by a guarantor company or by the issuing company on behalf of the guarantor company.

[*TIOPA 2010, ss 191–194; ICTA 1988, Sch 28AA para 6D; FA 2004, s 35(3)*].

Reciprocal treatment

Where a transfer pricing adjustment applies to disallow interest and the lending company claims a compensating adjustment under either *TIOPA 2010, s 174* or *s 182*; *ICTA 1988, Sch 28AA para 6* or *6C*, the interest disallowed as a deduction for the borrower is correspondingly not treated as chargeable as income from non-trading loan relationships for the lending company.

The condition for deduction at source in *ITA 2007, Pt 15*; *ICTA 1988, s 349(2)* is therefore not met. Therefore where a *s 182* (*Sch 28AA para 6C*), claim is made (see above) the borrowing company can pay interest to a non-resident lender without deduction of tax at source.

[*TIOPA 2010, s 187; ICTA 1988, Sch 28AA para 6E; FA 2004, s 35(4); CTA 2009, Sch 1 para 291*].

Foreign taxation

Where a claim for a compensating adjustment is made, it is assumed, as respects any foreign tax credit which has been or may be given to the disadvantaged person, that that foreign tax does not include tax which would not be or have become payable if the arm's length provision had also been substituted for the purposes of that tax, and that the profits from the activities in relation to which the actual provision was made or imposed and in respect of which the tax credit relief arises are reduced to the same extent as they are treated as reduced by virtue of the claim.

Where the application of the arm's length provision in a computation following such a claim involves a reduction in the amount of any income, and that income also falls to be treated as reduced under *TIOPA 2010, s 112*; *ICTA 1988, s 811(1)* by an amount of foreign tax (where credit relief is not available), the former reduction is treated as made before the latter, and the deductible foreign tax excludes that paid on so much of the income as is represented by the amount of the former reduction.

Any adjustment to double tax reliefs as above may be given effect by set-off against any relief or repayment arising from the claim, and may be made without regard to any time limit on assessments or amendments.

[*TIOPA 2010, ss 188, 189; ICTA 1988, Sch 28AA para 7*].

Balancing payments

[72.8] Where a transfer pricing adjustment applies and there is only one advantaged company, the disadvantaged person is within the charge to income tax or corporation tax, and a claim for a compensating adjustment can be made by the disadvantaged company (see **72.7** above), the disadvantaged company may make a balancing payment to the advantaged company by reason of the transfer pricing adjustment.

Such balancing payments must not in aggregate exceed the amount of the available compensating adjustment. The payments shall not be taken into account when computing profits or losses for tax purposes or be regarded as distributions.

The '*available compensating adjustment*' is the difference between the profits and losses of the disadvantaged company computed on the basis of the actual provision and computed for the purposes of making the compensating adjustment under **72.7** above (taking profits as positive amounts and losses as negative amounts) and the profits and losses of the disadvantaged person as calculated for tax purposes on a claim under *TIOPA 2010, s 174*.

[*TIOPA 2010, ss 194–196; ICTA 1988, Sch 28AA para 7A; FA 2004, s 30(6); F(No 2)A 2005, Sch 11 Pt 2(7)*].

Balancing payments made by guarantors. Where a transfer pricing adjustment applies in the case of the advantaged company and a claim for a compensating adjustment can be made by a guarantor company (see **72.7** above), the guarantor company may make balancing payments to the issuing company (i.e. the borrower) by reason of the transfer pricing adjustment.

Provided such balancing payments do not in aggregate exceed the amount of the compensating adjustment, the payments shall not be taken into account for corporation tax purposes when computing profits or losses of the guarantor company (or companies) or of the issuing company, or be regarded as charges on income (see **61.11 PROFIT COMPUTATIONS**).

The compensating adjustment in this case is the total reductions in interest or other amounts payable under the security subject to the guarantee (and thus treated as paid by the guarantor).

[*TIOPA 2010, ss 197, 198; ICTA 1988, Sch 28AA para 7C; FA 2004, s 36(3); F(No 2)A 2005, Sch 11 Pt 2(7)*].

Election to pay tax instead of balancing payment — thin capitalisation

Where both parties are companies, special provisions apply where the actual provision subject to a claim for a compensating adjustment under **72.7** above, is a provision in relation to a security (the 'relevant security') (see **72.3** above on thin capitalisation). In that case, instead of making a balancing payment as above, the disadvantaged company may elect to assume responsibility for the additional tax liability in relation to an accounting period of the advantaged company where the additional liability results from the transfer pricing adjustment in relation to the relevant security (i.e. a disallowance of interest or other amounts).

The tax liability in this case would not be treated as a liability of and recoverable from the advantaged company but would instead be treated as a corporation tax liability of the disadvantaged company.

The disadvantaged company may only make such an election where:

(a) the actual provision relating to the security forms part of a capital market arrangement involving the issue of a capital market investment (as defined in the *Insolvency Act 1986, s 72B(1), Sch 2A paras 1–3*) of a total value of at least £50 million; and

(b) the securities representing the capital market investment are issued wholly or mainly to independent persons (not the disadvantaged company and not persons having a participatory relationship (as defined in **72.3** above) with any of the affected companies).

An election, which is irrevocable, must be made in the disadvantaged company's tax return (whether by amendment or otherwise) for the chargeable period in which the relevant security is issued and has effect for that period and all subsequent chargeable periods (i.e. the lifetime of the loan). For this purpose, securities issued in a chargeable period beginning before 1 April 2004 are treated as though issued in a chargeable period beginning on that date. HMRC may refuse to accept such an election but only after a notice of enquiry has been issued to the disadvantaged company in respect of the tax return containing the election.

The above provisions relating to an election to pay tax instead of a balancing payment apply equally, with necessary modifications, in cases where a transfer pricing is made in respect of third party loans subject to a guarantee provided by a connected company (see **72.3** above).

[*TIOPA 2010, ss 199–203; ICTA 1988, Sch 28AA paras 7B, 7D; FA 2004, s 36(2)(4)*].

Capital allowances and capital gains

[72.9] These provisions do not affect the computation of capital allowances or balancing charges under the *Capital Allowances Acts*, or of capital gains or allowable losses under *TCGA 1992*, and do not require any income or losses to be treated as on capital rather than revenue account. However, for accounting periods beginning on or after 1 April 2004, a compensating adjustment may affect the computation of such allowances, charges, gains or losses.

[*TIOPA 2010, ss 213, 214; ICTA 1988, Sch 28AA para 13; CAA 2001, Sch 2 para 68; FA 2004, ss 32(4), 37*].

Determinations requiring the sanction of HMRC

[72.10] A determination of an amount falling to be brought into account under these provisions requires HMRC sanction, except in certain cases where an agreement has been reached between HMRC and the person concerned (see *TIOPA 2010, s 208–211; FA 1998, s 110(5)–(7)*).

Where such a determination is made for the purposes of either:

(i) giving a closure notice; or
(ii) giving a notice amending a partnership statement or return; or
(iii) making a discovery assessment; and
(iv) the notice of the closure, amendment or discovery assessment is given to any person without the determination having been approved by HMRC (or without a copy of HMRC's approval having been served on that person at or before the time the notice was given),

then the closure or amendment notice or discovery assessment is deemed to have been given or made (and in the case of an assessment notified) as if the determination had not been taken into account.

The approval must apply specifically to the case in question and the amount determined, but may otherwise be given (either before or after the making of the determination) in any such form or manner as HMRC may determine. An appeal relating to a determination approved by HMRC may not question HMRC's approval except to the extent that the grounds for questioning the approval are the same as the grounds for questioning the determination itself.

[*TIOPA 2010, ss 208–211*; *FA 1998, s 110; FA 2001, Sch 29 para 38*].

For the requirement that HMRC give notice of determinations to persons who it appears to them may be 'disadvantaged persons' (as above) by reference to the subject matter of the determination, see *FA 1998, s 111* (as amended).

See also HMRC International Manual, INTM434010–434080.

Appeals

[72.11] An appeal against an amendment of a return, the refusal of a claim or a discovery assessment or determination involving the application of *TIOPA 2010, Pt 4; ICTA 1988, Sch 28AA* lies to the tribunal.

Where the appeal relates to any provision as between two persons each of whom falls within the charge to income or corporation tax in respect of profits arising from relevant activities, either person may be a party to the proceedings and is entitled to appear before and be heard by the tribunal, or to make written representations to them. The tribunal must determine that aspect of the appeal separately from any other, that separate determination being treated as made in an appeal to which each of those persons was a party.

[*TIOPA 2010, s 212; ICTA 1988, Sch 28AA para 12; FA 2004, s 30(8); SI 2009 No 56*].

Miscellaneous

[72.12] For accounting periods beginning on or after 1 October 2002, amounts brought into account in respect of exchange gains and losses relating to **LOAN RELATIONSHIPS (54)** or in respect of derivative contracts (see **30.1 DERIVATIVE CONTRACTS LEGISLATION**) are not subject to application of an arm's length provision as above, but this does not affect the application of *TIOPA 2010, Pt 4; ICTA 1988, Sch 28AA* for the purposes of *CTA 2009, ss 447, 449, 452*; *FA 1996, Sch 9 para 11A* (as amended by *FA 2007, Sch 5 para 14*) (see **54.49 LOAN RELATIONSHIPS**) or *CTA 2009, ss 694, 698*; *FA 2002, Sch 26 para 27* (see **30.30 DERIVATIVE CONTRACTS LEGISLATION**) in the case of contracts not entered into at arm's length.

[*CTA 2009, ss 447, 694; ICTA 1988, Sch 28AA para 8; FA 2002, Sch 23 para 21, Sch 27 para 15*].

There are also special provisions relating to transactions involving oil and gas [*TIOPA 2010, ss 205, 206*; *ICTA 1988, Sch 28AA paras 9, 10*] and to 'ring-fenced' oil and gas exploration activities amended for accounting periods beginning on or after 1 April 2004 (and see **72.1** above for periods straddling that date).

[*TIOPA 2010, ss 205, 206; ICTA 1988, Sch 28AA paras 9–11; FA 2004, s 30(7); ITTOIA 2005, Sch 1 para 351*].

The provisions apply to unit trust schemes (see **52.5 INVESTMENT FUNDS**) as if they were bodies corporate, with appropriate modification.

[*TIOPA 2010, s 207; ICTA 1988, Sch 28AA para 14(5); CTA 2009, Sch 1 para 291*].

Practical issues

Pre-transaction guidance

[72.13] Revenue Policy International, 100 Parliament Street, London SW1A 2BQ may be approached for pre-transaction guidance on the likely tax treatment in particular cases when financial arrangements are in the process of being put in place.

See Revenue Tax Bulletin October 1998 pp 579–582, 587, 588 for general guidance on the record-keeping required for self-assessment under the above provisions and on the application of the provisions to financial transactions and arrangements; December 1998 pp 603–605 for guidance on penalties under those provisions; April 2000 pp 740–742 for the practical implications of the new regime for non-UK resident landlords; and August 2002 pp 943–947 for guidance on the nature of the risk assessment carried out by HMRC before undertaking a transfer pricing enquiry and a suggested timetabling framework for such enquiries.

See also HMRC International Manual, INTM433020–433030 for guidance on record-keeping; INTM460000 *et seq.* for internal HMRC guidance on transfer pricing enquiries.

Enquiries

[72.14] HMRC have issued in June 2008 'Guidelines for the conduct of transfer pricing enquiries', which can be found at www.hmrc.gov.uk/large-business/guidelines-transfer-pricing.pdf.

Advance pricing agreements

[72.15] In accordance with an internet statement dated 26 April 2007, applications for treaty relief received by HMRC after 21 March 2007 are dealt with under a new system, based broadly on self-assessment criteria (process now, check later). (See www.hmrc.gov.uk/cnr/clearance-processes.htm and SP 4/07.) A clearance will be issued in response to every application where the criteria are met (these differ from treaty to treaty) — HMRC will not consider the transfer pricing implications (e.g, with regard to thin capitalisation in respect of interest payments etc.) at the time of the treaty relief application.

Where the criteria are not met, correspondence will be entered into by HMRC with the applicant. The detail of the application will be considered along with the risk assessment of the applicant's self-assessment return, and an enquiry opened at that time, if appropriate.

The taxpayer also has the option of entering into a thin capitalisation agreement (see SP 4/07 with regard to Advance Thin Capitalisation Agreements), but it is important it is made clear at the outset that the company is seeking such an agreement.

With regard to other transfer pricing issues, a taxpayer may apply to HMRC for an advance pricing agreement ('APA') (which will always be a written document), on a prospective basis, on the resolution of complex transfer pricing issues relating to any one or more of the following matters which fall, or might fall, to be determined.

(a) Where the taxpayer is not a company, the attribution of income to a branch or agency through which the taxpayer has been carrying on, or is proposing to carry on, a trade in the UK.
(b) Where the taxpayer is a company, the attribution of income to a permanent establishment (see **65.6 RESIDENCE**) through which the taxpayer has been carrying on, or is proposing to carry on, a trade in the UK.
(c) The attribution of income to any permanent establishment of the taxpayer (wherever situated) through which he has been carrying on, or is proposing to carry on, any business.
(d) The extent to which income which has arisen or which may arise to the taxpayer is to be taken for any purpose to be income arising outside the UK.
(e) The treatment for tax purposes of any provision operating between the taxpayer and any 'associate' of his. Persons are '*associates*' for this purpose if (as in **72.2**(a) and (b) above in relation to *TIOPA 2010, Pt 4; ICTA 1988, Sch 28AA*) one directly or indirectly participates, at the time of the making or imposition of the provision, in the management, control or capital of the other, or the same person or persons so participate in the management, control or capital of each of them (with further special provision in relation to sales of oil).
(f) The treatment for tax purposes of any provision operating between a 'ring fence trade' carried on by the taxpayer and any other activities the taxpayer carries on. A '*ring fence trade*' for this purpose is a trade which is treated as a separate trade under *CTA 2010, ss 274, 279; ICTA 1988, s 492(1)*, or would be so treated if a different trade were also carried on.

[*TIOPA 2010, ss 218, 219*].

The potential scope of an APA is flexible and it may relate to all the transfer pricing issues of the business in question, or it may be limited to one or more specific issues. However, thin capitalisation issues will generally be dealt with via a separate Advance Thin Capitalisation Agreement (see also **72.3** above).

The application must set out the taxpayer's understanding of what would, in their case, be the effect, in the absence of any agreement, of the provisions in relation to which clarification is sought, and in what respects clarification is required. They must also propose how the clarification might be effected in a manner consistent with that understanding.

Per SP 2/10 the APA may be unilateral, bilateral or multilateral, involving multiple jurisdictions (strictly complimentary bilateral APAs). Where a taxpayer is interested in applying for an APA it is recommended by HMRC that it is first contacted on an informal basis to discuss the taxpayer's plans before presenting a formal application — the 'expression of interest process'. This ensures unsuitable applications are taken no further and also allows HMRC to outline a realistic timetable for agreeing the APA.

Where HMRC and the taxpayer have entered into such an agreement (an 'advance pricing agreement' or 'APA') in relation to a chargeable period, then (except as below) any questions relating to those matters are, to the extent provided for in the APA, to be determined in accordance with the APA rather than by reference to the legislative provisions which would otherwise have applied.

However, per *TIOPA 2010, s 220(5)*, where the relevant matter falls within (e) or (f) above and not within (a), (b), (c) or (d) above, the only legislative provisions which can be displaced are those contained in *TIOPA 2010, Pt 4 (Transfer Pricing); ICTA 1988, Sch 28AA*.

Where an APA relating to a chargeable period beginning or ending before the date of the APA provides for the manner in which consequent adjustments are to be made, those adjustments are to be made in the manner provided for in the APA.

An APA does not, however, have effect in relation to the determination of any question which relates to:

(i) a time after the revocation of the APA by an officer of HMRC, in accordance with its terms;
(ii) a time after or in relation to which any provision of the APA has not been complied with, where the APA was conditional upon compliance with that provision; or
(iii) any matter as respects which any other essential conditions have not been, or are no longer, satisfied.

The APA must contain a declaration that it is made for the purposes of *TIOPA 2010, s 218; FA 1999, s 85*. It may be made on or after 27 July 1999 and may apply in relation to any chargeable period ending on or after that date (and this may include periods ending before the date of the APA). It is for HMRC to ensure that the APA is modified so as to be consistent with any double taxation arrangements.

Where the APA makes provision for its modification or revocation by HMRC, this may take effect from such time (including a time before the modification or revocation) as HMRC may determine.

An APA does not have effect if a time to which the matter under consideration relates falls after an HMRC officer has recorded the revocation of the agreement under its terms, or falls after a 'significant' provision has been breached, or where a key condition relating to that matter has not been met or is no longer met. A term is '*significant*' or is a '*key condition*' if it is a condition of the agreement having effect.

Any party to an APA must provide HMRC with all such reports and other information as he may be required to provide under the APA or by virtue of any request made by an officer of HMRC in accordance with its terms.

An APA is deemed never to have been made where, before it was made, the taxpayer fraudulently or negligently provided HMRC with false or misleading information in relation to the application for the APA or in connection with its preparation, and HMRC notifies the taxpayer that the APA is nullified by reason of the misrepresentation. A penalty not exceeding £10,000 may apply for so giving such false or misleading information.

For details about the application process see further SP 2/10.

[*TIOPA 2010, ss 218–230; FA 1999, ss 85, 86; ITTOIA 2005, Sch 1 para 508*].

Effect of APA on third parties

Where an APA has effect in relation to any provision between the taxpayer and another person, then in applying the transfer pricing rules under *TIOPA 2010, ss 174–178* and *188–189* (see above) to the other person, the arrangements set out in the APA similarly apply in determining any question as to:

(A) whether the taxpayer is a person on whom a potential advantage in relation to UK taxation is conferred by the actual provision; or
(B) what constitutes the arm's length provision in relation to the actual provision.

This is subject to any APA made between HMRC and the other person. The notice requirements of *FA 1998, s 111* are correspondingly amended.

[*TIOPA 2010, s 222; FA 1999, s 87*].

For a detailed explanation of how APAs are administered, see HMRC Statement of Practice, SP 2/10 and HMRC International Manual, INTM469000 *et seq*. The contact address for APA applications and other information is APA Co-Ordinator Ian Wood, Business International, 3rd Floor, 100 Parliament Street, London SW1A 2BQ or, where oil taxation is involved, Susan New, Large Business Service Oil & Gas (APAs), 3rd Floor, 22 Kingsway, London WCB 6NR.

See also Revenue Tax Bulletin October 1999 pp 697, 698 for a note on the scope of agreements, and for procedural guidance relating to bilateral agreements in the light of HMRC's experiences and observations in concluding agreements with treaty partners under double tax treaty mutual agreement procedures.

Transfer Pricing and Arbitration

SP 1/11

Transfer pricing, mutual agreement procedure and arbitration

[72.16] This statement of practice was issued on 15 February 2011. It describes HMRC's practice in relation to methods for reducing or preventing double taxation and supersedes Tax Bulletins 25 and 31. The statement examines the use of mutual agreement procedure (MAP) under a relevant UK Double Taxation Treaty and/or the EU Arbitration Convention and it also describes the UK's approach to the use of arbitration where MAP is unsuccessful.

Where a taxpayer wishes to invoke the MAP with regard to transfer pricing adjustments, either under the UK's tax treaties and/ or the Arbitration Convention, then details of the cases should be sent to the Business International Unit. Information requests in this regard should be addressed to Douglas Jones, HMRC Business International, 3rd Floor, 100 Parliament Street, London SW1A 2BQ.

The statement notes that the MAP found in most of the UK's tax treaties (and also within the Arbitration Convention, see further below) provide for the competent authorities of the relevant tax treaty partners to consult each other when a taxpayer enterprise claims that it is being taxed otherwise than in accordance with the convention, as a result of the actions of one or both of the relevant fiscal authorities.

It should be noted that the MAP is a process of consultation (not litigation) and the taxpayer is not a formal party to those consultations, although they may be invited to participate informally (at the tax authorities' discretion).

With regards to the UK there is no set form of presentation, UK taxpayers may present their cases in writing to HMRC. They should specify the year(s) concerned, the nature of the action giving rise, or expected to give rise, to taxation not in accordance with the convention, and the full names and addresses of the parties to which the MAP relates, including the UK enterprise's tax office and reference number.

The statement of practice highlights the fact that it is advantageous to present a case early to invoke MAP, because early action by the competent authority can sometimes help to ensure that unrelievable double taxation does not arise from the actions of one fiscal authority. For example, this could happen where the UK's treaty partner is adopting an inappropriate transfer pricing methodology during the course of an audit and the UK is able to persuade it to use the most appropriate methodology. As already noted, the taxpayer is not directly involved in the negotiations between the competent authorities but may participate indirectly through discussions with its domestic competent authority, or at the discretion of the parties.

HMRC does point out that the MAP is not an alternative to the normal enquiry process. The MAP considers how any double taxation of profits might be relieved but only once the quantum of profits has been established by a transfer pricing enquiry. Therefore the competent authorities will not conduct a transfer pricing enquiry as part of the MAP and MAP will not suspend or replace an enquiry.

In addition it is noted in the statement that the MAP does not provide a parallel avenue to the domestic appeals process. The UK follows the approach adopted by most countries and described in the Commentary to the OECD Model Tax Convention on *Article 25* (*para 76*). Under this approach a person cannot pursue simultaneously the MAP and domestic legal remedies. Therefore a case may be presented and accepted for MAP while the domestic remedies are still available. In such cases, the UK will generally require that the taxpayer agrees to the suspension of these domestic remedies until the MAP process is finished. If the taxpayer does not agree, the UK will delay the MAP until these domestic remedies are exhausted.

Where a solution or mutual agreement has been reached under the terms of a UK tax treaty, it will be given effect notwithstanding anything in any enactment, in accordance with *TIOPA 2010 s 124(2); ICTA 1988, s 815AA(2)*. Where normal time limits may have expired before a solution or mutual agreement is reached, a claim for relief consequential to that solution or mutual agreement, for example to losses, group relief, capital allowances etc., must be made within twelve months following the notification of the solution or mutual agreement per *TIOPA 2010, s 124(4); ICTA 1988, s 815AA(3)*.

It is notable that where a claim for relief is made in pursuance of an agreement or opinion reached under the Arbitration Convention, the normal time limits for claiming relief under the Taxes Acts do not apply so there is no time limit for claiming the appropriate relief (*TIOPA 2010, s 127(5); ICTA 1988, s 815B(3)*).

How the relief is granted by the UK authorities depends on the facts and circumstances of the particular case. Relief may be granted either by deduction against UK profits or by tax credit. Once the matter has been agreed by the competent authorities the UK taxpayer is invited to submit revised computations reflecting the agreed relief. The statement of practice does note that the UK tax authority does not accept that it is permissible for a taxpayer to make, unilaterally, an adjustment through its accounts and return to obtain corresponding relief for an adjustment which reduces its UK tax liability, either when self-assessing or in response to an adjustment imposed by another jurisdiction. The only avenue to relief is presentation of a case invoking MAP.

The statement then gives further details with regard to the position in respect of secondary adjustments and also refers to SP 2/10 with regard to APAs.

Arbitration Convention

The Convention (*90/463/EEC*) on the elimination of double taxation in connection with the adjustment of profits of associated enterprises required member states to adopt certain procedures and to follow the opinion of an advisory commission in certain cases of dispute relating to transfer pricing adjustments.

In its original form, the Arbitration Convention came into force for five years from 1 January 1995, and was extended to 31 December 2004 through the Extension Protocol published in 2000. The last of the 15 'old' EU states finally ratified the Extension Protocol in July 2004, meaning that the Convention has only been legally in force between these 15 states since that date. It will now automatically be extended every five years for a further five years, unless the signatory states decide otherwise (see Revenue Tax Bulletin August 1998 pp 575, 576).

TIOPA 2010, s 127; *ICTA 1988, s 815B* makes provision for domestic legislation and agreements to be over-ridden where necessary under the Convention, and *TIOPA 2010, ss 126, 128*; *ICTA 1988, s 816(2A)* and *FA 1989, s 182A* provide the necessary information powers and confidentiality requirements in relation to disclosures of information to an advisory commission. [*F(No 2)A 1992, s 51*]. See also the comments made above with regard to SP1/11, which outlines HMRC's approach to the use of the Convention.

Code of Conduct

The European Commission has adopted a proposal for a Code of Conduct to ensure a more effective and uniform application of the Convention by EU member states. The Code determines procedural rules covering time limits for dealing with complaints, arrangements concerning the advisory commission that must be established to deal with disputes concerning the elimination of double taxation following transfer-pricing adjustments, and the suspension of tax collection during the dispute resolution period. The Code has recently been revised and updated.

See the Official Journal C176 of 28/07/2006 and the revised code in Official Journal C322 of 30/12/2009.

Examples

(A)

[72.17]

A Ltd provides management and administrative services to a number of its wholly-owned subsidiaries. All companies in the group have accounting periods ending on 31 March and do not qualify as small or medium-sized enterprises for transfer pricing purposes.

For the accounting period ending 31 March 2012, A Ltd makes a charge for its management and administrative services to B Ltd of £450,000. Following an enquiry into A Ltd's return for that period, it is agreed that the arm's length value of the services to A Ltd was £600,000. An adjustment is accordingly made of £150,000 to increase A Ltd's taxable profits by that amount.

B Ltd can claim (within the required time limit, see **72.7** above) to apply a corresponding adjustment to reduce its taxable profits for the same period by £150,000 (increasing its deductible expenses to £600,000). B Ltd may also make a balancing payment to A Ltd of up to £150,000 without it being treated as a distribution or charge on income or otherwise taken into account for tax purposes.

(B)

On 1 April 2011, B Ltd is granted a loan of £5,000,000 at 6% interest p.a. from an unassociated bank. The loan is guaranteed by B Ltd's parent company, G plc. Both companies draw up accounts for the year ended 31 March and neither company qualifies as a small or medium-sized enterprise for transfer pricing purposes.

Following an enquiry into B Ltd's return for the accounting period ending 31 March 2012, HMRC successfully maintain that, in the absence of the guarantee from G plc, the bank would not have advanced more than £1,000,000 to B Ltd. Accordingly, an adjustment is made to increase B Ltd's profits for the period by £240,000 in disallowing the interest on £4,000,000 of the loan.

G plc could make a claim (or B Ltd could claim on its behalf) for a corresponding adjustment before or after the transfer pricing adjustment is made in B Ltd's return, or following the determination (but within the required time limit, see **72.7** above), so that it is treated as having paid the interest subject to the disallowance. Accordingly, provided the interest in G plc's case would not be subject to a transfer pricing adjustment, G plc could claim a deduction for £240,000 in respect of the interest paid by B Ltd.

G plc can make a balancing payment of up to £240,000 to B Ltd without it being treated as a distribution or charge on income or otherwise taken into account for tax purposes. Alternatively, where the conditions (a) and (b) in **72.8** above are met, G plc can elect to pay the tax liability in respect of the interest disallowed, of £64,400 (tax at 26%). In that case, B Ltd would not have to pay the tax liability arising in respect of the transfer pricing adjustment.

Key points

[72.18] Points to consider are as follows.

- Following the 2002 European Court judgment in the case of Lankhorst-Hohorst (C-324/00), where the ECJ concluded that the German thin capitalisation measures breached EU law, the UK transfer pricing rules were amended (by *FA 2004*) to ensure their non-discriminatory compliance with EU law. Transfer pricing regulations previously only applied where one party was outside the UK, however, the changes mean that the transfer pricing rules apply equally between UK and offshore connected entities as well as UK to UK connected entities. *ICTA 1988, Sch 28AA,* (as was) was also amended to include the UK's thin capitalisation rules.
- Where, as a result of a transfer pricing enquiry, UK to UK adjustments are made in one company's corporation tax computation, a corresponding adjustment can be reflected in the other company's tax computation. This means that for UK to UK adjustments the overall corporation tax liability within the group is unlikely to change but will merely be redistributed.
- Where the adjustment is between a UK and offshore entity then similar favourable adjustments do not arise. It may be possible to challenge this where the foreign entity is resident in a jurisdiction

with which the UK has a double tax treaty which contains an appropriate non-discrimination clause, but such a challenge would require an application to a fiscal court in that jurisdiction. Practically speaking, such a challenge would not be viable.

- Small and medium enterprises may largely be exempt from the transfer pricing rules, although such entities may be caught in certain circumstances where the listed exceptions apply. For the definition of small and medium reference needs to be made to EU Commissions Recommendation of 2003/361/EC as amended by the UK's taxing statutes.
- A common misconception is that the transfer pricing rules only apply to connected parties which either have a direct controlling relationship or are under common control. In reality, for transfer pricing purposes it is not necessary to have control. A 40% interest between the parties is sufficient to invoke the rules.
- If transactions are sufficiently large then HMRC will expect to see a thorough analysis of the pricing policy between connected parties. Such an analysis needs to be substantiated by appropriate documentation. The EU code of conduct on transfer pricing lays out the recommended documents needed.
- As noted above, the transfer pricing rules also cover thin capitalisation. Where a subsidiary is overly debt laden through connected party debt then the transfer pricing rules can reduce or disallow any interest expense claimed by the paying company. This is particularly the case where the interest payments are to a connected offshore lender.
- Although there is no safe-haven debt to equity ratio in UK tax law, practically speaking a maximum ratio of 3:1 is normally acceptable, although recent HMRC commentary in March 2010 states that they have moved away from considering such ratios, as they are too simplistic, and now take a principles based approach with regard to thin capitalisation. A ratio in excess of this may be challenged by HMRC but may be accepted if a commercial case can be substantiated based on the facts.
- HMRC may give a pre-transaction transfer pricing ruling in certain circumstances.
- To assist with the resolution of transfer pricing disputes HMRC have issued SP 1/11 which outlines their procedures using the mutual agreement procedure found at *Article 25* of a double tax treaty (per the OECD model) or using the EU Arbitration Convention.

73

Value Added Tax

See HMRC Business Income Manual BIM31500–31625 and, generally, Tolley's Value Added Tax.

Non-taxable persons

[73.1] VAT relating to expenditure deductible for corporation tax purposes is also deductible. Capital allowances on any such expenditure are based on the VAT-inclusive cost. See HMRC Statement of Practice, B1.

Taxable persons

[73.2] Income and expenditure are taken into account *exclusive* of VAT, and capital allowances are determined accordingly. However, capital allowances on motor cars are computed on the VAT-inclusive cost, as the VAT is not reclaimable. Entertainment expenses *disallowed* for corporation tax purposes include VAT. The full amount of a bad debt (i.e. including irrecoverable VAT) is allowed as a trading expense. See HMRC Statement of Practice, B1.

Partly-exempt persons

[73.3] Entertainment expenses and expenditure on motor cars are treated as in **73.2** above. Input VAT on items of expenditure constituting exempt output must be allocated to the categories of such expenditure. It will be treated for corporation tax purposes as part of that expenditure. HMRC is prepared to consider any 'reasonable arrangements' for allocation.

VAT unreclaimed due to the excessive cost of keeping the necessary records may be treated as part of the expenditure to which it relates for corporation tax purposes. See HMRC Statement of Practice, B1.

Pre-incorporation expenditure

[73.4] Regulations may be made to allow the deduction as input tax of VAT paid on goods acquired before incorporation and services supplied before that time for the business's benefit or in connection with its incorporation.

[*VATA 1994, s 24(6)(c)*].

Interest, penalties etc. and repayment supplement

[73.5] No deduction is allowed for corporation tax purposes in respect of any payment by way of VAT

(a) penalty under *VATA 1994, ss 60–70* or *FA 2003, s 25* or *s 26;*
(b) interest under *VATA 1994, s 74*; or
(c) surcharge under *VATA 1994, s 59*.

Similarly any VAT repayment supplement under *VATA 1994, s 79* is disregarded for corporation tax purposes.

[*CTA 2009, ss 1286, 1303; ICTA 1988, s 827*].

Flat rate scheme

[73.6] An optional VAT flat rate scheme is available to all businesses with a VAT-exclusive annual taxable turnover of up to £150,000 in the year of entry to the scheme. Prior to 1 April 2009 there was also a requirement that VAT-inclusive turnover, including the value of exempt supplies and other non-taxable income, should not exceed £187,500.

Where the company uses the flat-rate scheme, receipts and expenses to be taken into account are generally *inclusive* of normal output and input VAT (assuming the small business to be a non-taxable person), but the flat-rate VAT itself can either be deducted from turnover or treated as a separate expense and in either case is an allowable deduction for tax purposes. Any irrecoverable VAT on capital items forms part of their cost for the purposes of CAPITAL ALLOWANCES (**10**).

For HMRC's view as to how trading profits are to be computed by businesses adopting the scheme, see HMRC Business Income Manual BIM31585.

74

Venture Capital Trusts

Cross-references. See **30.47** DERIVATIVE CONTRACTS LEGISLATION; **54.96** LOAN RELATIONSHIPS.

Simon's Taxes. See C3.11, D8.2, E3.2, E3.2.

Introduction

[74.1] The venture capital trust scheme described at **74.2** and onwards was introduced in 1995 to encourage individuals to invest in unquoted trading companies through such trusts by providing reliefs for income tax and capital gains tax (see **74.25** and **74.26** below).

The Treasury has wide powers to make regulations governing all aspects of the reliefs applicable to venture capital trust investments, and for the requirements as regards returns, records and provision of information by the trust.

[*ITA 2007, ss 272, 284; ITTOIA 2005, Sch 1 para 477; FA 2007, Sch 16 para 21; SI 1995 No 1979; SI 1999 No 819*].

See generally HMRC Venture Capital Schemes Manual, VCM10000–17320, VCM60000 onwards and the guidance at www.hmrc.gov.uk/guidance/vct.htm.

For company reorganisations involving venture capital trusts, see **17.11 CAPITAL GAINS**. For the transfer of assets within a group of companies to a company which subsequently becomes a venture capital trust, see **29.8 DEGROUPING CHARGES.**

A centralised service is available for companies newly raising money under the venture capital trust scheme. All enquiries about whether a company meets the requirements should be made to Small Company Enterprise Centre, Ty Glas, Llanishen, Cardiff, CF14 5ZG (Tel. 029 2032 7400; fax 029 2032 7398; e-mail: enterprise.centre@ir.gsi.gov.uk).

This initial point of contact is supported by specialist HMRC units that deal with the corporation tax affairs, and the monitoring, of such companies as well as companies raising money under other types of venture capital scheme or granting options under enterprise management incentives. (Revenue Press Release 25 September 2000). The approval of venture capital trusts themselves is dealt with by HMRC (CTTG) (see **74.2** below).

Conditions for approval

[74.2] A '*venture capital trust*' ('VCT') is a company approved for this purpose by HMRC. The time from which an approval takes effect is specified in the approval, and may not be earlier than the time the application for approval was made.

[*ITA 2007, ss 259, 283*].

Except as detailed further below, approval may not be given unless HMRC are satisfied that the following conditions are met in relation to the most recent complete accounting period of the company and will be met in relation to the accounting period current at the time of the application for approval.

The conditions in more detail:

Close company condition

ITA 2007, s 259 states that the company must not be a close company, in other words it must not be under the control of five or fewer participators or any number of directors who are participators (*CTA 2010, Pt 10*). A company is not a close company if it is controlled by a company which is not a close company, or the public holds 35% or more of the voting share capital of the company and the shares have been subject to dealings on a recognised stock exchange in the preceding twelve months and those shares are listed on such an exchange. However if the voting power held by the principal members exceeds 85%, the public holding test threshold is disregarded and the company may be close.

The listing condition

Legislation contained in *F(No 3)A 2010, s 5* and *Sch 2* amended the requirement that shares be included in the official UK list. From 6 April 2011, the requirement is that they must be admitted to trading on a 'regulated market' as defined in Directive 2004/39/EC of the European Parliament and of the Council on Market in Financial Instruments. Prior to 6 April 2011, the requirement was that the shares had been listed in the Official UK List of the Stock Exchange.

The nature of income condition

The company's income (as defined) in the relevant period must be derived wholly or mainly from shares or 'securities'. HMRC's interpretation of wholly or mainly for the purposes of this test is that at least 70% of the VCT's income must be from shares and securities.

'*Securities*' for these purposes are deemed to include liabilities in respect of certain loans not repayable within five years, and any stocks or securities which are not re-purchasable or redeemable within five years of issue. Provided that the loan is made on normal commercial terms, HMRC will not regard a standard event of default clause in the loan agreement as disqualifying a loan from being a security for this purpose. If, however, the clause entitles the lender (or a third party) to exercise any action which would cause the borrower to default, the clause would not be regarded as 'standard'. (HMRC SP 8/95).

Income for this test is taken to be gross statutory income for tax purposes, hence UK dividends are included on a gross, receipts basis, as are overseas dividends received post 1 July 2009 (which are treated as franked investment income for this purpose). Income from loan relationships is on an accruals basis, in line with the accounts.

The obvious exclusions are bank interest, commissions and profits from futures and options contracts, however UK scrip dividends are also excluded. Overseas scrip dividends, by contrast may, in certain situations, constitute eligible investment income.

The income retention condition

An amount greater than 15% of its income (as defined) from shares and securities in the period must not be retained by the company.

Only dividends declared for the accounting period in question can be counted for the purposes of this test. Prior period dividends paid in the period in question cannot be counted. This test is relaxed in situations where the company is required to retain income by virtue of a restriction imposed by law, for example in cases where brought forward reserve levels are in deficit and all current period profits are required to make good that deficit. There is also no requirement to retain income where the distributable amount is below a de minimis threshold of £10,000. This threshold is proportionally reduced for a short accounting period. The relaxation does not apply if the distributable amount exceeds the amount restricted by law and the excess is more than the de minimis threshold of £10,000.

The 15% holding limit condition

No 'holding' in any company other than a VCT (or a company which could be a VCT but for the listing condition above) may represent more than 15% of the value of the company's investments at any time in those periods.

Where an addition is made to a holding, the entire holding is revalued to the market value at the time of the latest addition. A holding comprises shares or securities of one or more classes held in the same company and an addition only occurs where the company is liable to give consideration for further investments received. A payment to discharge a liability of the investee which increases the value of the holding will also constitute an addition, for example for partly-paid shares, where a second or subsequent instalment is paid.

'*Holding*' means the shares or securities of whatever class or classes held in any one company. Holdings in associated investee companies must be combined for the purposes of the test, including members of the VCT's own group (taken here to mean 51% subsidiaries) and money owed intra group will be treated as a security. Hence intra group transactions between the VCT and its subsidiaries will constitute an addition for the purposes of revaluing the group holding of the VCT for this test.

Where the VCT is a member of a partnership there are potential pitfalls in meeting the 15% holding limit condition. For the purposes of this condition the underlying holdings of the partnership will count towards the test and not the percentage stake in the partnership itself. Problems can arise for the VCT in obtaining sufficient information from the partnership in respect of its underlying holdings. Similarly in respect of the income retention test, the VCT must be able to determine accurately both the amount and the nature of the income arising to it in respect of its partnership holding for the period in question. Holdings in overseas partnership can also be problematic, in particular where the classification of income differs from that applicable in the UK.

See below for the value of the company's investments.

The 70% qualifying holdings condition

Throughout the accounting periods at least 70% (by value) of the company's investments must be represented by shares or securities in 'qualifying holdings'.

The requirements to be satisfied for a holding to be a qualifying holding fall into three groups:

- the form of the investment;
- the type of company invested in; and
- the way in which money raised is to be used.

These conditions are examined in detail below at **74.6** onwards.

With effect from 6 April 2007 for the purpose of this test and for the purpose of the 15% holding limit condition, the company's investments are to include all money in the company's possession and any sum owned to the company if the company has account-holder's rights over that sum. Examples would be bank accounts, whether interest bearing or not, and accounts held on the company's behalf by third parties such as solicitors or fund managers. However money held for example by the company as trustee for a third party would not usually be included in the company's investments for the purpose of the 70% test.

Where a VCT disposes of a qualifying holding on or after 6 April 2007, the disposal is disregarded for a period of six months for the purpose of the 70% qualifying holding condition under *ITA 2007, s 280A*.

Where this 70% qualifying holdings condition is breached inadvertently, and the position is corrected without delay after discovery, approval will in practice not be withdrawn on this account. Full details of any such inadvertent breach should be disclosed to HMRC as soon as it is discovered. It is not clear whether this practice continues after 6 April 2007. See also below under 'Withdrawal of approval' as regards the Treasury's power to make regulations.

On a second and subsequent issue of shares by an approved VCT, the 70% qualifying holdings condition and the 30% eligible shares condition below do not have to be met in relation to the money raised by such an issue, in the accounting period of that issue or any later accounting period ending no more than three years after the making of that issue.

See the 15% holding limit condition above for the meaning of 'the company's investments' and see below for the value of investments.

The 70% eligible shares condition

The proportion of the VCT's qualifying holdings which must be represented by holdings of 'eligible shares' was increased from 30% to 70% from 6 April 2011, and from the same date there is a new definition of eligible shares [*ITA 2007, s 285(3A)*]. Transitional provisions apply where shares in relevant companies were issued before 6 April 2011 or were acquired with money raised before 6 April 2011.

Eligible shares are ordinary share capital, carrying no present or future preferential rights to dividends or assets on a winding up and no present or future rights to redemption. The aim of this test is to ensure that the VCT takes an equity stake in small businesses, rather than merely providing them with finance.

Alternative requirements for the giving of approval

Where any of the above conditions are not met, approval may nevertheless be given where HMRC are satisfied as to the meeting of those conditions (and in some cases other conditions imposed by regulations) in certain future accounting periods.

[*ITA 2007, ss 274, 276, 277, 280, 280A, 285, Sch 2 paras 64, 66, 67; FA 2007, Sch 16 para 20, Sch 26 para 12(6); ITA 2007, s 275*].

Value of investments

The value of any investment for the purposes of the 15% holding limit condition, the 70% qualifying holdings condition and the 70% eligible shares condition above is the value when the investment was acquired. However, where it is added to by a further holding of an investment of the same description (otherwise than for no consideration), or a payment is made in discharge of any obligation attached to it which increases its value, the value of the investment is the value immediately after the most recent such addition or payment.

For this purpose, where, in connection with a 'scheme of reconstruction' (within *TCGA 1992, s 136*; previously a 'scheme of reconstruction or amalgamation'), a company issues shares or securities to persons holding shares or securities in another company in respect of, and in proportion to (or as nearly as may be in proportion to) such holdings, without the recipients' becoming liable for any consideration, the old and the new holdings are treated as the same.

Where:

(i) shares or securities in a company are exchanged for corresponding shares and securities in a new holding company; or
(ii) a VCT exercises conversion rights in respect of certain convertible shares and securities,

then, subject to detailed conditions (see *ITA 2007, ss 326–329*), the value of the new shares is taken to be the same as the value of the old shares when they were last valued for these purposes.

Where, under a company reorganisation or other arrangement:

- a VCT exchanges a qualifying holding for other shares or securities (with or without other consideration); and
- the exchange is for genuine commercial reasons and not part of a tax avoidance scheme or arrangements,

regulations provide a formula which values the new shares or securities by reference to the proportion of the value of the old shares or securities that the market value of the new shares or securities bears to the total consideration receivable. If no other consideration is receivable, the value of the new shares or securities is identical to that of the old shares or securities. The provisions extend to new shares or securities received in pursuance of an earn-out right conferred in exchange for a qualifying holding, in which case an election is available (under *Reg 10*) to modify the formula by effectively disregarding the earn-out right itself.

[*ITA 2007, ss 278, 279, Sch 2 para 65; SI 2002 No 2661*].

Withdrawal of approval

[74.3] Approval may be withdrawn where there are reasonable grounds for believing that either:

- the conditions for approval were not satisfied at the time the approval was given;
- in a case where HMRC were satisfied that a condition would be met in relation to any period, that condition has not been, or will not be, met in that period;

- in a case of provisional approval in relation to a second or further issue by an approved VCT, any additional condition included in the approval notice has not been met;
- in a case of full approval, or where provisional approval has become full, a condition was not, or will not be met in relation to the company's last or current accounting period; or
- in a case where there has been a further issue of ordinary shares, the conditions for approval will not be met in the first accounting period to which the relaxation, in respect of the additional funds, does not apply.

The withdrawal is effective from the time the company is notified of it, except that:

(1) where approval is given on HMRC being satisfied as to the meeting of the relevant conditions in future accounting periods, and is withdrawn before all six of the conditions above have been satisfied in relation to either a complete twelve-month accounting period or successive complete accounting periods constituting a continuous period of twelve months or more, the approval is deemed never to have been given; and

(2) for the purposes of relief for capital gains accruing to a VCT under *TCGA 1992, s 100* withdrawal may be effective from an earlier date, but not before the start of the accounting period in which the failure occurred (or is expected to occur).

An assessment as a consequence of the withdrawal of approval may, where otherwise out of time, be made within three years from the time the notice of the withdrawal was given.

For the detailed requirements as regards granting of approval, breach of conditions for and refusal (and withdrawal) of approval, and appeals procedures, see *SI 1995 No 1979, Pt II.*

Applications for approval should be made to:

Small Companies Enterprise Centre (Admin Team)
1st Floor
Ferrers House
Castle Meadow Road
Nottingham
NG2 1BB

[*ITA 2007, ss 281, 282*].

FA 2007 introduced provisions for the making of Treasury regulations to enable a VCT to apply to HMRC for a determination that they will not exercise, for a certain period, their power to withdraw approval by reason of a specified breach, including a future breach, of the above conditions (see *ITA 2007, s 284(1)(aa)(2)(3)*).

Mergers

[74.4] For mergers of two or more VCTs, regulations enable the merging VCTs to retain VCT status and provide for their investors, who continue as investors in the 'successor company', not to lose their tax reliefs. This treatment applies to two types of merger within *SI 2004 No 2199*:

(1) shares in one of the merging companies (company A) are issued to members of the other merging company (or companies) either in exchange for their shares in that other company (or companies) or by way of consideration for a transfer to company A of the whole or part of the business of that other company;
(2) shares in a company (company B), which is not one of the merging companies, are issued to members of the merging companies either in exchange for their shares in those companies or in consideration for the transfer to company B of the whole or part of the businesses of those companies.

Company A or, as appropriate, company B is the '*successor company*'.

For the regulations to apply, a merging company or the successor company must apply to HMRC for approval, and approval must be granted before the merger takes place. For the procedure for obtaining approval see *SI 2004 No 2199, Reg 10*. HMRC will not approve the merger unless they are satisfied that strict conditions are met, including that the merger is for *bona fide* commercial reasons and is not part of a scheme or arrangements with a tax avoidance purpose. For the detailed conditions, see *SI 2004 No 2199, Reg 9(3)*.

Where approval is obtained, the following apply:

- income tax investment relief within **74.25** below cannot be obtained in respect of any shares issued to effect the merger by the successor company, and such shares are ignored in determining whether the 'permitted maximum' has been exceeded;
- the nature of income, income retention, 70% qualifying holdings, 70% eligible shares and 15% holding limit conditions, and the provisions at **74.6** below apply to the successor company:
  (i) as if the property of the merging companies were vested in the successor company (so that transfers between a merging company and the successor company are disregarded);
  (ii) disregarding, in the hands of the successor company, any assets consisting in rights against, or shares or securities of, another company which is a merging company; and
  (iii) disregarding, in the hands of the successor company, the use of any money which, in the hands of another company which is a merging company, would have been disregarded under *ITA 2007, s 280(2)* (use of money raised by further issue of shares to be ignored for certain periods for the purposes of the 70% qualifying holdings and 70% eligible shares conditions — see above), for the same periods as are mentioned in that provision;
- a disposal by a merging company to the successor company after the merger of an asset held by the merging company immediately before, or in the period during which, the merger takes place is not prevented by *TCGA 1992, s 171(2)(cc)* (see **18.4 CAPITAL GAINS — GROUPS**) from being treated as a disposal at no gain/no loss;
- for the purposes of the income tax reliefs at **74.25** below and capital gains tax deferral relief at **74.26** below (see Tolley's Capital Gains Tax under Venture Capital Trusts):

(i) any share for share exchange or share for business transfer is not treated as a disposal of the 'old shares' or as a chargeable event for the purposes of deferral relief;

(ii) any other act (including the giving of relief) carried out, or failure to act, in relation to the old shares is treated as carried out, or omitted, in relation to the corresponding new shares;

(iii) references to the company in which the old shares were held are to be read as references to the successor company;

- for the purposes of capital gains tax relief on disposal (see Tolley's Capital Gains Tax under Venture Capital Trusts), if the successor company is not otherwise a VCT at the time the shares issued to effect the merger are acquired but is a VCT at the time of a subsequent disposal of the shares, it is treated as a VCT at and from the time of acquisition;
- where any of the qualifying holding requirements at **74.6** below (other than the qualifying subsidiaries requirement) were satisfied to any extent or for any period in relation to an investment held by a merging company immediately before the merger, they are treated as satisfied to the same extent or for the same period when held by the successor company, as if the two companies were the same company;
- for the purposes of the 15% test above and the qualifying subsidiaries requirement at **74.22** below, the period in which the merger takes place is disregarded and if as a result of the merger that test or requirement is no longer met, it is treated as met for a period of one year;
- for the purposes of the 70% qualifying holdings, 70% eligible shares and 15% holding limit conditions above and the proportion of eligible shares requirement at **74.11** below, the value of investments in the hands of the successor company immediately after the merger is taken to be their value when last valued before the merger in accordance with the rules governing those conditions and that requirement, unless there has been a transaction other than the merger as a result of which the investments would fall to be revalued; and
- where provisional approval of a merging company other than the successor company is withdrawn following the merger, the withdrawal takes effect from the time the company is notified of it (and the approval is not deemed never to have been given).

[*ITA 2007, ss 321–325; SI 2004 No 2199, Regs 1, 9–13*].

Winding-up

[74.5] Regulations enable a VCT commencing winding-up on or after 17 April 2002 to retain its VCT status during a 'prescribed winding-up period', thereby enabling investors' reliefs to continue for that period.

A VCT-in-liquidation can obtain this treatment:

- if it has been approved as a VCT continuously for at least three years ending with the commencement of the winding-up (five years where the VCT, having previously obtained approval, issues ordinary share capital between 6 April 2004 and 5 April 2006, without having done so before 6 April 2004); or

- where the winding-up is by court order, it is approved as a VCT immediately before the commencement.

The winding-up must be for *bona fide* commercial reasons and not part of tax avoidance arrangements and the VCT-in-liquidation must notify HMRC of the commencement. A VCT-in-liquidation which has been at any time a merger company (see above) other than a successor company does not qualify. The '*prescribed winding-up period*' for these purposes is the three years beginning with the commencement of the winding-up, but if the winding-up ends, the company ceases to be wound up or is dissolved, the period comes to an end on the earliest of those events.

Where the VCT-in-liquidation fulfils the above requirements, the following apply:

(I) For the purposes of the income tax relief on investments (see **74.25** below), the commencement of the winding-up does not affect the status of the VCT-in-liquidation as a VCT (i.e. the commencement itself is not treated as an event leading to the withdrawal of approval and the provisions for withdrawal of relief are not triggered by it).

(II) Gains accruing to the VCT-in-liquidation during the prescribed winding-up period on disposal of assets acquired before the commencement of the winding-up are not chargeable gains (and losses are not allowable losses).

(III) Capital gains tax relief on disposal of VCT shares (see **74.26** below) is available (provided that the other conditions for that relief are met) for disposals in the prescribed winding-up period as if the VCT-in-liquidation were a VCT. If, at the end of that period the VCT-in-liquidation still exists and the conditions for approval as a VCT (see above) are not then fulfilled, approval is treated, for the purposes of that relief, as withdrawn at that time.

[*SI 2004 No 2199, Regs 1–7*].

Simon's Taxes. See **D8.205–D8.212**.

Qualifying holdings

[74.6] A VCT's holding of shares or securities in a company is comprised in its '*qualifying holdings*' at any time if the shares or securities were first issued to the VCT, and have been held by it ever since, and the following 16 requirements are satisfied at that time.

If the requirements for the maximum qualifying investment, use of the money raised or relevant company to carry on the relevant qualifying activity requirements would be met by part of the money raised through the issue, and the holding is not otherwise capable of being treated as separate holdings, it is treated as two separate holdings.

These two holdings consist of:

(i) a holding from which that part of the money was raised; and

(ii) a holding from which the remainder was raised,

with the value being apportioned accordingly to each holding. In the case of the use of money raised requirement, this does not require an insignificant amount applied for other purposes to be treated as a separate holding.

[*ITA 2007, ss 286, 293(7)*].

Permanent establishment

[74.7] The requirement that the trade must be carried on wholly or mainly in the UK was replaced from 6 April 2011 with a requirement that the company must have a permanent establishment in the UK (*ITA 2007, s 286A*). A company has a permanent establishment in the UK if (and only if) either:

- it carries on business here wholly or partly through a 'fixed place of business'; or
- an agent in the UK has the authority to enter into contracts on behalf of the company and does so on a habitual basis.

[*ITA 2007, s 302A(2)*].

A fixed place of business is not exclusively defined and can include:

- a place of management;
- a branch;
- an office, factory or workshop;
- a mine, quarry, oil or gas well, or any other place where natural resources are extracted; and
- a building site, or construction or installation project.

[*ITA 2007, s 302A(3)*].

However, the company will not be treated as having a permanent establishment in the UK if the activities carried on here are merely of a 'preparatory or auxiliary character', having regard to the activities of the company as a whole. Again the definition of those activities is not exhaustive, but includes:

- facilities used by the company for the purposes of storage, display or delivery of its goods or merchandise;
- the maintenance of a stock of goods, etc. belonging to the company for those purposes or for the purpose of them being processed by another person;
- purchasing goods or merchandise or the collection of information for use by the company.

[*ITA 2007, s 302A(4)–(6)*].

A company is also not to be regarded as having a UK permanent establishment by reason of:

- it carrying on business here through an 'agent of independent status' (including a broker or general commission agent) who is acting in the ordinary course of his business, or;

- it controlling a company which is UK resident or which carries on business here, whether through a permanent establishment or some other means.

Financial health requirement

[74.8] In respect of shares issued on or after 6 April 2011, the requirement is that, at the time of the issue of the relevant holding, the company is not 'in difficulty'. This term is defined as meaning that it would be reasonable to assume that the relevant company would be regarded as in difficulty under the European Commission's Community Guidelines on State Aid for Rescuing and Restructuring Firms in Difficulty (2004/C 244/02) (*ITA 2007, s 286B*). These guidelines regard a firm as being 'in difficulty' where it is unable, whether through its own resources or with the funds which it is able to obtain from its owners/shareholders or creditors, to stem losses which, without outside intervention by the public authorities, will almost certainly condemn it to going out of business in the short or medium term.

Maximum qualifying investment requirement

[74.9] The maximum qualifying investment a VCT may make in an investee company is £1 million per relevant period. A relevant period is the period beginning with the earlier of 6 months before the issue of the relevant holding or the beginning of the tax year in which the issue of the holding took place and ending with the issue of the holding. However the £1 million amount is reduced proportionally if the investee or any of its qualifying subsidiaries is a member of a partnership or a party to a joint venture carrying on the qualifying trade, in which case the limit is divided by the number of companies involved in the partnership or joint venture. Any amount raised in excess of the maximum qualifying investment will not constitute a qualifying holding of the VCT.

[*ITA 2007, s 287, Sch 2 para 68*].

No guaranteed loan requirement

[74.10] The holding in question must not include any securities (as defined in **74.2** above) relating to a guaranteed loan. A security relates to a guaranteed loan if there are arrangements entitling the VCT to receive anything (directly or indirectly) from a 'third party' in the event of a failure by any person to comply with the terms of the security or the loan to which it relates. It does not matter whether or not the arrangements apply in all cases of a failure to comply or only in some such cases.

'*Third party*' means any person other than the investee company itself and, if it is a parent company that meets the trading requirement below, its subsidiaries. This condition applies for accounting periods (of the VCT) ending after 1 July 1997, but does not apply in the case of shares or securities acquired by the VCT by means of investing money raised by the issue before 2 July 1997 of shares or securities (or money derived from the investment of any such money raised).

[*ITA 2007, s 288, Sch 2 para 69*].

Proportion of eligible shares requirement

[74.11] Where the money used by the VCT for the investment was originally raised after 1 July 1997, that investment cannot be part of the VCT's qualifying holdings at any time unless at least 10% by value of the VCT's *total* holding of shares in and securities of the company consist of 'eligible shares' (as defined for the purposes of the 70% eligible shares condition at **74.2** above — broadly, ordinary, non-preferential, shares). For this purpose, the value of shares etc. at any time is taken to be their value immediately after the most recent of the events listed below, except that it cannot thereby be taken to be less than the amount of consideration given by the VCT for the shares etc. The said events are as follows.

- The acquisition of the shares or securities by the investing company.
- The acquisition by the investing company (other than for no consideration) of any other shares or securities of the relevant company which are of the same description as those already held.
- The making of any such payment in discharge (in whole or in part) of any obligation attached to the shares in or securities of the relevant company in a case where such discharge increases the value of the shares or securities.

[*ITA 2007, s 289, Sch 2 para 70*].

Trading requirement

[74.12] The company must either:

(a) exist wholly for the purpose of carrying on one or more 'qualifying trades' (disregarding any purpose having no significant effect on the extent of its activities); or

(b) be a '*parent company*' (i.e. a company that has one or more 'qualifying subsidiaries' — see the qualifying subsidiaries requirement below) and the business of the '*group*' (i.e. the company and its qualifying subsidiaries) must not consist wholly or as to a substantial part (i.e. broadly 20% — see HMRC Venture Capital Schemes Manual VCM17040) in the carrying on of 'non-qualifying activities'.

Where the company intends that one or more other companies should become its qualifying subsidiaries with a view to their carrying on one or more qualifying trades, then, until any time after which the intention is abandoned, the company is treated as a parent company and those other companies are included in the group for the purposes of (b) above.

For the purpose of (b) above, the business of the group means that which would be the business of the group if the activities of the group companies taken together were regarded as one business. Activities are for this purpose disregarded to the extent that they consist in:

(i) holding shares in or securities of any of the company's subsidiaries;
(ii) making loans to another group company;
(iii) holding and managing of property used by a group company for the purposes of one of more qualifying trades carried on by any group company; or
(iv) holding and managing of property used by a group company for the purposes of research and development from which it is intended either, that a qualifying trade to be carried on by a group company will be derived or that a qualifying trade carried on or to be carried on by a group company will benefit.

References above to a group company include references to any existing or future company which will be a group company at any future time.

Activities are similarly disregarded to the extent that they consist, in the case of a subsidiary whose main purpose is the carrying on of qualifying trade(s) and whose other purposes have no significant effect on the extent of its activities (other than in relation to incidental matters), in activities not in pursuance of its main purpose.

'*Non-qualifying activities*' are:

(I) excluded activities (as below); and
(II) non-trading activities.

[*ITA 2007, ss 290, 332, Sch 2 para 71; FA 2008, Sch 11 paras 8–13*].

A company does not cease to meet this requirement by reason only of anything done as a consequence of its being in administration or receivership (both as defined — see *ITA 2007, s 331*), provided everything so done and the making of the relevant order are for genuine commercial (and not tax avoidance) reasons. [*ITA 2007, s 292, Sch 2 para 73*].

Qualifying trade

[74.13] A trade is a 'qualifying trade' if:

(i) it is conducted on a commercial basis with a view to the realisation of profits; and
(ii) it does not consist wholly or to a substantial extent in the carrying on of 'excluded activities'.

For these purposes, 'trade' (except in relation to the trade mentioned in (l) below) does not include a venture in the nature of trade. '*Excluded activities*' are:

(a) dealing in land, commodities or futures, or in shares, securities or other financial instruments (see below);
(b) dealing in goods otherwise than in an ordinary trade of wholesale or retail distribution (see below);
(c) banking, insurance, money lending, debt factoring, hire-purchase financing or other financial activities;
(d) leasing or letting or receiving royalties or licence fees;

(e) providing legal or accountancy services (see below);
(f) property development;
(g) farming or market gardening;
(h) holding, managing or occupying woodlands, any other forestry activities or timber production;
(i) operating or managing hotels or comparable establishments (i.e. guest houses, hostels and other establishments whose main purpose is to offer overnight accommodation with or without catering) or property used as such;
(j) operating or managing nursing homes or residential care homes (both as defined) or property used as such;
(k) shipbuilding;
(l) producing coal;
(m) production of steel; and
(n) providing certain services to other businesses.

The exclusions at (l) to (n) above have effect in relation to holdings of shares and securities issued on or after 6 April 2008 other than holdings acquired by the VCT by means of investment of:

- money raised by the issue before 6 April 2008 of shares in or securities of the VCT; or
- money derived from the investment by the VCT of money so raised.

None of these excluded activities must be engaged in to a substantial degree (likely to be in excess of 20% as a rule of thumb) by the investee, judged by any measure (e.g. turnover or capital employed). (HMRC Venture Capital Schemes Manual VCM17040).

As regards exclusion (a), dealing in land includes cases where steps are taken, before selling the land, to make it more attractive to a purchaser; such steps might include the refurbishment of existing buildings. (HMRC Venture Capital Schemes Manual VCM17050).

As regards exclusion (b), a trade of wholesale distribution is a trade consisting of the offer of goods for sale either to persons for resale, or processing and resale, (which resale must be to members of the general public for their use or consumption) by them. A trade of retail distribution is a trade in which goods are offered or exposed for sale and sold to members of the general public for their use or consumption.

A trade is not an ordinary wholesale or retail trade if it consists, to a substantial extent, of dealing in goods collected or held as an investment (or of that and any other activity within (a)–(n) above), and a substantial proportion of such goods is held for a significantly longer period than would reasonably be expected for a vendor trying to dispose of them at market value.

As regards the application of exclusion (d) in relation to shares issued after 5 April 2000, a trade is not excluded from being a qualifying trade solely because at some time it consists, to a substantial extent, in the receiving of royalties or licence fees substantially attributable (in terms of value) to the exploitation of 'relevant intangible assets'.

A '*relevant intangible asset*' is an 'intangible asset' the whole or greater part of which (by value) has been created by the 'issuing company', or by a company which was a subsidiary of the issuing company at the time it created the whole or greater part (by value) of the asset. For this purpose only, an '*issuing company*' includes a company all of whose shares were acquired by the issuing company at a time when the only shares issued in the issuing company were subscriber shares, and the consideration for the acquisition consisted wholly in the issue of shares in the issuing company.

Also as regards exclusion (d), a trade will not be excluded by reason only of it consisting of letting ships (other than offshore installations) or pleasure crafts, provided that:

(i) the company beneficially owns all the ships it so lets;
(ii) every ship beneficially owned by the company is UK-registered;
(iii) the company is solely responsible for arranging the marketing of the services of its ships; and
(iv) in relation to every letting on charter, certain conditions as to length and terms of charter, and the arm's length character of the transaction, are fulfilled.

If any of (i)–(iv) above is not fulfilled in relation to certain lettings, the trade is not thereby excluded if those lettings and any other excluded activities taken together do not amount to a substantial part of the trade. As regards exclusion (e), the provision of the services of accountancy personnel is the provision of accountancy services (*Castleton Management Services Ltd v Kirkwood* (Sp C 276), [2001] STC (SCD) 95).

Exclusion (j) applies only if the person carrying on the activity in question has some legal interest in the property concerned or occupies that property.

'*Property development*', in exclusion (f), means the development of land by a company, which has (or has had at any time) an 'interest in the land' (as defined), with the sole or main object of realising a gain from the disposal of an interest in the developed land.

[*ITA 2007, ss 189, 192–199, 253, 257(3), Sch 1 para 483; FA 2007, Sch 16 paras 11(1)(7), 13, 14*].

The Treasury may, by statutory instrument, amend any of the above provisions. [*ITA 2007, s 200*].

The changes in the rules concerning the receipt of royalties and licence fees which apply in relation to EIS shares issued after 5 April 2000 also have effect for the purpose of determining whether shares or securities issued after that date are to be regarded as comprised in a VCT's qualifying holdings.

'Research and development' from which it is intended that a qualifying trade carried on 'wholly or mainly in the UK' will either be derived or, for shares issued to the VCT after 5 April 2007, benefit, is treated as the carrying on of a qualifying trade. Preparing to carry on such research and development does not, however, count as preparing to carry on a trade. '*Research and development*' has the meaning given by *ITA 2007, s 1006*.

[*ITA 2007, ss 300, 303–310, 313(5)–(7), Sch 2 paras 78, 81–85; FA 2007, Sch 16 para 12*].

In considering whether a trade is carried on 'wholly or mainly in the UK', the totality of the trade activities is taken into account. Regard will be had, for example, to where capital assets are held, where any purchasing, processing, manufacturing and selling is done, and where the company employees and other agents are engaged in its trading operations. For trades involving the provision of services, both the location of the activities giving rise to the services and the location where they are delivered will be relevant. No one factor is itself likely to be decisive in any particular case. A company may carry on some such activities outside the UK and yet satisfy the requirement, provided that the major part of them, that is over one-half of the aggregate of these activities, takes place within the UK. Thus relief is not excluded solely because a company's products or services are exported, or because its raw materials are imported, or because its raw materials or products are stored abroad. Similar principles apply in considering the trade(s) carried on by a company and its qualifying subsidiaries.

In the particular case of a ship chartering trade, the test is satisfied if all the charters are entered into in the UK and the provision of the crews and the management of the ships while under charter take place mainly in the UK. If these conditions are not met, the test may still be satisfied depending on all the relevant facts and circumstances of the case.

(HMRC SP 3/00).

Carrying on of a qualifying activity requirement

[74.14] In relation to shares or securities issued to the VCT after 16 March 2004, a 'qualifying company' (whether or not the same such company at all times) must, when the shares were issued to the VCT and at all times since, have been carrying on one of the following two '*qualifying activities*':

(A) carrying on a 'qualifying trade', 'wholly or mainly in the UK' (see the trading requirement above); or
(B) preparing to carry on a qualifying trade which, at the time the shares were issued, was intended to be carried on wholly or mainly in the UK.

The second of these conditions is, however, relevant only for a period of two years after the issue of the shares, by which time the intended trade must have been commenced by a 'qualifying company', and ceases to be relevant at any time within those two years after the intention is abandoned.

For these purposes, '*qualifying company*' means the relevant company itself or any 'qualifying 90% subsidiary' of that company. In determining the time at which a qualifying trade begins to be carried on by a 'qualifying 90% subsidiary', any carrying on of the trade by the qualifying 90% subsidiary before it became such a subsidiary is disregarded. A qualifying 90% subsidiary includes any existing or future company which will be a qualifying 90% subsidiary at any future time.

A company (the subsidiary) is a '*qualifying 90% subsidiary*' of the relevant company at any time when:

- the relevant company possesses at least 90% of both the issued share capital of, and the voting power in, the subsidiary;
- the relevant company would be beneficially entitled to at least 90% of the assets of the subsidiary available for distribution to equity holders on a winding-up or in any other circumstances;
- the relevant company is beneficially entitled to at least 90% of any profits of the subsidiary available for distribution to equity holders;
- no person other than the relevant company has control (within *ITA 2007, s 995* — see **25 CONNECTED PERSONS**) of the subsidiary; and
- no arrangements exist by virtue of which any of the above conditions would cease to be met.

For the above purposes, *CTA 2010, Pt 5 Ch 6* applies, with appropriate modifications, to determine the persons who are equity holders and the percentage of assets available to them.

A subsidiary does not cease to be a qualifying 90% subsidiary by reason only of it or any other company having commenced winding up or by reason only of anything done as a consequence of any such company being in administration or receivership, provided the winding-up, entry into administration or receivership (both as defined) or anything done as a consequence of its being in administration or receivership is for genuine commercial reasons and is not part of a tax avoidance scheme or arrangements.

Also, the listed conditions are not regarded as ceasing to be satisfied by reason only of arrangements being in existence for the disposal of the relevant company's interest in the subsidiary if the disposal is to be for genuine commercial reasons and is not to be part of a tax avoidance scheme or arrangements.

On or after 6 April 2007, a company (company A) is also a qualifying 90% subsidiary of the relevant company if:

- company A would be a qualifying 90% subsidiary of another company (company B) if that company were the relevant company and company B is a 'qualifying 100% subsidiary' of the relevant company; or
- company A is a qualifying 100% subsidiary of company B and company B is a qualifying 90% subsidiary of the relevant company.

No account is taken for this purpose of any control the relevant company may have of company A.

Maximum amount raised annually through risk capital schemes requirement

[74.15] Subject to the commencement provisions below, the total amount of 'relevant investments' in the relevant company and its subsidiaries in the year ending with the date of issue of the holding in question must not exceed £2 million. Investments in subsidiaries count towards the limit if the company concerned was a subsidiary of the relevant company at any time in the year, whether or not it was a subsidiary at the time of the investment. It is however proposed that, subject to EU approval, the *Finance Act 2012* will increase this limit to £10m, with effect from 6 April 2012.

A '*relevant investment*' in a company is made if:

(a) an investment of any kind in the company is made by a VCT; or
(b) the company issues shares (money having been subscribed for them) and provides HMRC with an Enterprise Investment Scheme ('EIS') compliance statement under *ITA 2007, s 205* or a Corporate Venturing Scheme ('CVS') compliance statement under *FA 2000, Sch 15 para 42* in respect of the shares.

Investments within (b) above are treated as made when the shares concerned are issued.

Where this requirement is not met as a consequence of the provision of an EIS or CVS compliance statement, it is treated as met throughout the period from the time of the issue of the relevant holding ending with the time the compliance statement was provided.

This requirement does not have to be satisfied in relation to an investment by the VCT of money raised by the issue of its shares or securities before 6 April 2007 or of money derived from the investment of such money.

An investment made by a VCT is not a relevant investment within (a) above if it is made before 6 April 2007 or if it is an investment of money raised by the issue of shares or securities of the VCT before that date or of money derived from the investment of such money.

[*ITA 2007, s 292A; FA 2007, Sch 16 paras 6, 8*].

Use of the money raised requirement

[74.16] The money raised by the issue of shares to the VCT must be employed *wholly* (disregarding insignificant amounts) for the purposes of the 'relevant qualifying activity'. For shares or securities issued on or after 22 April 2009, where two or more years have passed since commencement of trading, all the money raised must be applied wholly for the purpose of a relevant qualifying activity.

For issues prior to 22 April 2009, at any time within 12 months after the issue (or after the date of commencement of the qualifying trade where this is later than the date of issue) this condition is treated as satisfied if at least 80% of that money has been, or is intended to be, so employed. At any time within the following 12 months, the condition is treated as satisfied if at least 80% of that money *has been* so employed. For this purpose, a qualifying activity is a '*relevant qualifying activity*' if it was a qualifying activity at the time the shares were issued, or if it is a qualifying trade and preparing to carry it on was a qualifying activity at that time.

[*ITA 2007, s 293, Sch 2 para 74; FA 2009, s 27, Sch 8 paras 5, 9*].

Money whose retention can reasonably be regarded as necessary or advisable for financing current business requirements is regarded as employed for trade purposes (HMRC Venture Capital Schemes Manual VCM12080, 62150–62153).

In relation to buy-outs (and in particular management buy-outs), HMRC will usually accept that where a company is formed to acquire a trade, and the funds raised from the VCT are applied to that purchase, the requirement that the funds be employed for the purposes of the trade is satisfied. Where the company is formed to acquire another company and its trade, or a holding company and its trading subsidiaries, this represents an investment rather than employment for the purposes of the trade. However, HMRC will usually accept that the requirement is satisfied if the trade of the company, or all the activities of the holding company and its subsidiaries, are hived up to the acquiring company as soon as possible after the acquisition. In the case of a holding company and its subsidiaries, to the extent that the trades are not hived up, the holding cannot be a qualifying holding. (Revenue Tax Bulletin issue 18 (August 1995) www.hmrc.gov.uk/bulletins/tb18.htm).

Relevant company to carry on the relevant qualifying activity requirement

[74.17] In relation to shares or securities issued to the VCT **after 16 March** 2004, at all times after the issue of the holding, the relevant qualifying activity by reference to which the use of money raised requirement is satisfied must not be carried on by any person other than the relevant company or a 'qualifying 90% subsidiary'.

This requirement is not treated as not met merely because the trade in question is carried on by a person other than the relevant company or a qualifying subsidiary at any time after the issue of the shares and before the relevant company or a qualifying 90% subsidiary carries on the trade. The carrying on of the trade by a partnership of which the relevant company or a qualifying 90% subsidiary is a member, or by a joint venture to which any such company is a party, is permitted.

The requirement is also not regarded as failing to be met if, by reason only of a company being wound up or dissolved or being in administration or receivership (both as defined), the qualifying trade ceases to be carried on by the relevant company or a qualifying 90% subsidiary and is subsequently carried on by a person who has not been connected (within *ITA 2007, s 993* – see **25 CONNECTED PERSONS** – but with the modifications to the meaning of 'control' that apply for the purposes of the control and independence requirement below) with the relevant company at any time in the period beginning one year before the shares were issued. This let-out applies only if the winding-up, dissolution or entry into administration or receivership (and everything done as a consequence of the company being in administration or receivership) is for genuine commercial reasons and not part of a tax avoidance scheme or arrangements.

[*ITA 2007, s 294, Sch 2 para 75*].

Unquoted status requirement

[74.18] The relevant company must be an '*unquoted company*', i.e. none of its shares, stocks, debentures or other securities must be:

- listed on a recognised stock exchange;
- listed on a designated exchange in a country outside the UK; or
- dealt in outside the UK by such means as may be designated for the purpose by order.

Shares listed on the Alternative Investment Market ('AIM') of the Stock Exchange, or on the PLUS Quoted or PLUS Traded Markets, are treated as unquoted for these purposes. (HMRC Venture Capital Schemes Manual VCM15020).

If the relevant company ceases to be an unquoted company at a time when its shares are comprised in the qualifying holdings of the VCT, this requirement is treated as continuing to be met, in relation to shares or securities acquired before that time, for the following five years.

[*ITA 2007, s 295; FA 2007, Sch 26 para 12(7)*].

Control and independence requirement

[74.19] The company must not 'control' (with or without 'connected persons') any company other than a 'qualifying subsidiary' (see the qualifying subsidiaries requirement below), nor must another company (or another company and a person connected with it) control it. Neither must arrangements be in existence by virtue of which such control could arise. For these purposes, '*control*' is as under *CTA 2010, s 450*, except that possession of, or entitlement to acquire, fixed-rate preference shares (as defined) of the company which do not, for the time being, carry voting rights are disregarded, as is possession of, or entitlement to acquire, rights as a loan creditor of the company. '*Connected persons*' are as under *ITA 2007, s 993* (see **25 CONNECTED PERSONS**) except that the definition of 'control' therein is similarly modified. [*ITA 2007, ss 296, 313(4)–(7)*].

Gross assets requirement

[74.20] The value of the company's gross assets or, where the company is a parent company, the value of the 'group assets', must not have exceeded £7 million immediately before the issue or £8 million immediately thereafter. It is proposed that, subject to EU approval, these limits will be replaced by a single limit of £15m before the issue of the relevant share. This will apply in respect of shares issued on or after 6 April 2012.

'*Group assets*' are the gross assets of each of the members of the group, disregarding assets consisting in rights against, or shares in or securities of, another member of the group.

[*ITA 2007, s 297, Sch 2 para 76*].

The general approach of HMRC is that the value of a company's gross assets is the aggregate of the company's gross assets as shown in its balance sheet. Where accounts are actually drawn up to a date immediately before or after the issue, the balance sheet values are taken provided that they are in accordance with generally accepted accounting practice. Where accounts are not drawn up to such a date, such values will be taken from the most recent balance sheet, updated as precisely as is practicable taking into account all the relevant information available to the company. Values so arrived at may need to be reviewed in the light of information contained in the accounts for the period in which the issue was made, and, if they were not available at the time of the issue, those for the preceding period, when they become available.

The company's assets immediately before the issue do not include any advance payment received in respect of the issue. Where shares are issued partly paid, the right to the balance is an asset, and, notwithstanding the above, will be taken into account in valuing the assets immediately after the issue regardless of whether it is stated in the balance sheet. (HMRC SP 2/06).

Number of employees requirement

[74.21] The number of 'full-time equivalent employees' for the relevant company must be less than 50 at the time the holding is issued. If the company is a parent company, the sum of the full-time equivalent employees for it and each of its qualifying subsidiaries must be less than 50 at that time. It is proposed that, subject to EU approval, this limit will be raised to the equivalent of 250 full-time employees in respect of shares issued on or after 6 April 2012.

This requirement must be satisfied only in relation to holdings issued on or after 6 April 2007. It does not, however, have to be satisfied in relation to such holdings if they are acquired by the investment of money raised by the issue before 6 April 2007 of shares in or securities of the VCT or of money derived from the investment of such money.

A company's '*full-time equivalent employees*' for this purpose is the number of its full-time employees plus, for each employee who is not full-time, a just and reasonable fraction. Directors are counted as employees for this purpose, but employees on maternity or paternity leave and students on vocational training are excluded.

[*ITA 2007, s 297A; FA 2007, Sch 16 para 3(3)(5)–(7)*].

Qualifying subsidiaries requirement

[74.22] Any subsidiary that the relevant company has must be a 'qualifying subsidiary' of the company.

A subsidiary is a '*qualifying subsidiary*' of the relevant company if the following conditions are satisfied in relation to that subsidiary and every other subsidiary of the relevant company.

In relation to shares or securities issued to the VCT **after 16 March 2004**, the subsidiary must be a **51%** subsidiary (see *CTA 2010, s 1154*) of the relevant company and no person other than the relevant company or another of its subsidiaries may have control (within *CTA 2010, s 1124(1)–(3)* — see **25 CONNECTED PERSONS**) of the subsidiary. Furthermore, no arrangements may exist by virtue of which either of these conditions would cease to be satisfied. The conditions are not regarded as ceasing to be satisfied by reason only of the subsidiary or any other company in the process of being wound up or by reason only of anything done as a consequence of its being in administration or receivership, provided the winding-up, entry into administration or receivership or anything done as a consequence of its being in administration or receivership is for genuine commercial reasons and is not part of a tax avoidance scheme or arrangements.

The conditions above are not regarded as ceasing to be satisfied by reason only of arrangements being in existence for the disposal of the interest in the subsidiary held by the relevant company (or, as the case may be, by another of its subsidiaries) if the disposal is to be for genuine commercial reasons and is not part of a tax avoidance scheme or arrangements.

[*ITA 2007, ss 298, 302, 989, Sch 2 para 80*].

Property managing subsidiaries requirement

[74.23] In relation to shares or securities issued to the VCT **after 16 March 2004**, the company must not have a 'property managing subsidiary', which is not a 'qualifying 90% subsidiary' (see the carrying on of a qualifying activity requirement above) of the company.

A '*property managing subsidiary*' is a subsidiary whose business consists wholly or mainly in the holding or managing of 'land' or any property deriving its value from land' (as defined).

[*ITA 2007, s 299, Sch 2 para 77*].

Supplementary provisions

Winding up of the relevant company

[74.24] Where the relevant company is being wound up, none of the requirements listed at **74.2** above are regarded on that account as not being satisfied provided that they would be met apart from the winding up, and that the winding up is for genuine commercial reasons and is not part of a scheme or arrangement the main purpose of which is the avoidance of tax.

[*ITA 2007, s 312, Sch 2 para 86*].

Power to amend requirements

The Treasury have power by order to modify the trading requirement, the carrying on of a qualifying activity requirement and the qualifying subsidiaries requirement as they consider appropriate, and to substitute the sum referred to in the maximum qualifying investment requirement and the gross assets requirement above.

[*ITA 2007, s 311*].

Restructuring

Where shares or securities in a company are exchanged for corresponding shares and securities in a new holding company, then subject to detailed conditions, including HMRC approval, to the extent that any of the requirements listed below was satisfied in relation to the old shares, it will generally be taken to be satisfied in relation to the new shares. The consideration for the old shares must consist wholly of the issue of shares in the new company.

The requirements to which the above provision applies are:

- the maximum qualifying investment requirement;
- the proportion of eligible shares requirement;
- the trading requirement;
- the carrying on of a qualifying activity requirement;
- the use of the money raised requirement;
- the relevant company to carry on the relevant qualifying activity requirement;
- the control and independence requirement;
- the gross assets requirement; and
- the number of employees requirement.

[*ITA 2007, ss 326–328, Sch 2 para 87; FA 2007, Sch 16 para 3(4)*].

Conversion of shares

Where a VCT exercises conversion rights in respect of certain convertible shares and securities, then subject to detailed conditions, for the purposes of the requirements listed below, the conversion is treated as an exchange of new shares for old shares to which the restructuring provisions above apply. The requirements are:

- the maximum qualifying investment requirement;
- the proportion of eligible shares requirement;
- the carrying on of a qualifying activity requirement;
- the use of the money raised requirement;
- the relevant company to carry on the relevant qualifying activity requirement; and
- the gross assets requirement.

[*ITA 2007, s 329, Sch 2 para 87*].

Reorganisations etc.

Where, under a company reorganisation or other arrangement:

- a VCT exchanges a qualifying holding for other shares or securities (with or without other consideration); and
- the exchange is for genuine commercial reasons and not part of a tax avoidance scheme or arrangements,

the new shares or securities may be treated as being qualifying holdings for a specified period even if some or all of the requirements at **74.6** above are not otherwise satisfied. Regulations specify the circumstances in which, and conditions subject to which, they apply and which requirements are to be treated as met.

Where the new shares or securities are those of a different company than before and they do not meet any one or more of the above requirements (disregarding the maximum qualifying investment requirement and the use of the money raised requirement), those requirements are treated as met for, broadly, three years in the case of shares, or five years in the case of securities, reduced in either case to, broadly, two years where the company is not, or ceases to be, an unquoted company as in the unquoted status requirement above.

A formula is provided for valuing the new shares or securities for the purposes of the proportion of eligible shares requirement above. The provisions extend to new shares or securities received in pursuance of an earn-out right conferred in exchange for a qualifying holding, in which case an election is available (under *Reg 10*) to modify the said valuation formula by effectively disregarding the earn-out right itself.

[*ITA 2007, ss 330, 303–311, Sch 2 para 88; SI 2002 No 2661*].

Simon's Taxes. See **D8.223, D8.235–D8.237.**

Income tax reliefs

[74.25] Relief from income tax is granted in respect of both investments in VCT share issues (up to £200,000 for 2004–05 onwards, previously £100,000, in a year of assessment) and distributions from such trusts (in respect of shares acquired up to a 'permitted investment limit' in any year of assessment). The rate of relief for investments (given by deduction from the individual's income tax liability) is 30% in relation to shares issued on or after 6 April 2006 (40% for shares issued on or after 6 April 2004 and 20% for shares issued before that date).

[*ITTOIA 2005, Pt 6 Ch 5, Sch 1 paras 140, 346*].

See **74.4** and **74.5** above as regards mergers and winding-up of VCTs. For the detailed conditions for both reliefs, and for the circumstances in which investment relief is withdrawn, see Tolley's Income Tax under Venture Capital Trusts.

Simon's Taxes. See **E3.210–E3.213.**

Capital gains tax reliefs

[74.26] The capital gains of a VCT are not chargeable gains.

[*TCGA 1992, s 100(1)*].

In addition, individual investors in VCTs are entitled to two reliefs:

(a) on disposal of VCT shares (up to a 'annual permitted maximum' acquired in any year of assessment); and
(b) for shares issued before 6 April 2004, by deferral of chargeable gains on re-investment in VCT share issues (up to the income tax relief limit, see **74.25** above).

[*TCGA 1992, ss 151A, 151B, Sch 5C; FA 2004, Sch 19 paras 4–7; ITTOIA 2005, Sch 1 para 437*].

See **74.4** and **74.5** above as regards mergers and winding-up of VCTs. For the detailed conditions for these reliefs, and for relief on withdrawal of approval, see Tolley's Capital Gains Tax under Venture Capital Trusts. See also **Simon's Taxes C3.1103–C3.1113.**

75

Voluntary Associations

See **66.5 RETURNS** as regards tax returns by members' clubs and similar organisations. For the special treatment of certain societies, see **9 BUILDING SOCIETIES; 20 CHARITIES; 35 EXEMPT ORGANISATIONS; 37 FRIENDLY SOCIETIES; 45 HOUSING ASSOCIATIONS; 47 INDUSTRIAL AND PROVIDENT SOCIETIES** and **56 MUTUAL COMPANIES.** Generally, see HMRC guidance 'Unincorporated organisations and Corporation Tax' (http://www.hmrc.gov.uk/ct/clubs-charities-agents/clubs.htm). See *Worthing Rugby Football Club Trustees v CIR* [1987] 1 WLR 1057, [1987] STC 273, CA, and *Blackpool Marton Rotary Club v Martin* (1988) 62 TC 686. See also Revenue Tax Bulletin, issue 37 (October 1998): http://www.hmrc.gov.uk/bulletins/tb37.htm for HMRC's approach to such bodies with trivial liabilities.

Simon's Taxes. See **B1.440, B2.213, C1.211, D1.212.**

Introduction

[75.1] A club or society may be established as a company or as an unincorporated association of individuals. Whichever form it takes, it is liable to corporation tax on income (other than that generated from members e.g. membership fees or catering income from sales to members — this is why clubs insist that visitors become day members instead of taking a day ticket) and on capital gains. However, special rules apply to certain types of club, which in some cases offer a number of tax advantages.

This chapter covers the taxation treatment of the sports club, with particular focus on community amateur sports clubs. It also covers certain other commonly-found clubs and societies.

Community amateur sports clubs (CASCs)

[75.2] Community amateur sports clubs enjoy a number of tax advantages, including the ability to claim back tax on gift aid donations and relief on any corporation tax, income tax and capital gains tax paid. A club must register with HMRC for community amateur sports club (CASC) status. For details on how to register, see the HMRC website at http://www.hmrc.gov.uk/charities/casc/register.htm.

A club is entitled to be registered as a CASC if it is, and if it is required to be by its constitution, a club which (*CTA 2010, s 658; FA 2010, s 30, Sch 6 para 31*):

- is open to the whole community;
- is organised on an amateur basis;
- has as its main purpose the provision of facilities for, and the promotion of participation in, one or more eligible sports;
- meets the location condition; and
- meets the management condition.

Open to the whole community

A club is regarded as being '*open to the whole community*' if its membership is open to all without discrimination, its facilities are available to members without discrimination and any fees charged do not represent a significant obstacle to membership or to the use of the facilities [*CTA 2010, s 659*].

Amateur basis

A club is organised on an amateur basis if it is non-profit making, it provides members and their guests with the ordinary benefits of an amateur sports club and its constitution provides for any net assets on dissolution to be applied for approved sporting or charitable purposes. A club is '*non-profit making*' if any surplus or gains are required to be reinvested in the club and the distribution of assets to its members is prohibited (*CTA 2010, s 660*).

Ordinary benefits of an amateur sports club

The '*ordinary benefits of an amateur sports club*' include:

- the provision of sporting facilities;
- the reasonable provision of maintenance of club-owned sports equipment;
- the provision of suitably qualified coaches;
- the provision, or reimbursement, of the costs of coaching courses;
- the provision of insurance;
- the provision of medical treatment;
- reimbursement of reasonable travel expenses incurred by players and officials travelling to away matches;
- the reasonable provision of post-match refreshments; and
- the sale or supply of food and drink as a social benefit that arises indirectly from the sporting purposes of the club.

Sporting or charitable purposes

'*Sporting or charitable purposes*' include the purpose so the governing body of the eligible sport, the purposes of another registered club and the purposes of a charity.

An '*eligible sport*' is one designated as such by Treasury Order. The designated sports are those appearing on the list of activities recognised by the various National Sports Councils (which is available on the Sport England website at www.sportengland.org/about_us/recognised_sports.aspx). A list of registered clubs is published on HMRC's website (at www.hmrc.gov.uk/casc/clubs.htm). HMRC also handles deregistration or termination of registration (when the conditions are no longer complied with).

Location and management conditions

The '*location condition*' is met if the club is established in a member State or relevant territory and the facilities that it provides for eligible sports are located in a single member State or territory [*CTA 2010, s 661A; FA 2010, s 30, Sch 6 para 32*].

The '*management condition*' is met if the managers (i.e. persons having the general control and management of the administration of the club) are fit and proper persons to be managers of the club [*CTA 2010, s 661B; FA 2010, s 30, Sch 6 para 32*].

Registered clubs are entitled to certain tax exemptions (see below).

A club has a right of appeal against any decision by HMRC not to register it as a CASC or to deregister it [*CTA 2010, s 671*]. HMRC must notify the club on any decision to register it, refuse to register it or to cancel its registration as a CASC [*CTA 2010, s 670*].

Exemptions

Community amateur sports clubs enjoy a number of tax advantages including certain exemptions from tax.

Exemption for UK trading income

A club that is registered with HMRC as a CASC throughout an accounting period can claim for its UK trading income for the period to be exempt from corporation tax if conditions A and B below are met [*CTA 2010, s 662*].

Condition A is that the receipts that would otherwise be brought into account in calculating the club's UK trading income for the period do not exceed the relevant threshold. The relevant threshold is set at £30,000 for a twelve-month accounting period. It is proportionately reduced for periods of less than twelve months.

Condition B is that the whole of the UK trading income for the period is applied for a qualifying purpose.

Exemption for UK property income

A club that is registered with HMRC as a CASC throughout an accounting period may make a claim for its UK property income to be exempt from corporation tax if conditions A and B below are met [*CTA 2010, s 662*].

Condition A is that the receipts that would otherwise be brought into account in calculating the club's property income for the period do not exceed the relevant threshold. The relevant threshold for UK property income is set at £20,000 for a twelve-month period. This is proportionately reduced for accounting periods of less than twelve months.

Condition B is that all of the UK property income for that period is applied for qualifying purposes.

Exemption for interest and gift aid income

A club that is registered with HMRC as a CASC throughout an accounting period can make a claim for its interest income for the period and its gift aid income for the period to be exempt from corporation tax if the whole of that interest income and gift aid income is applied for charitable purposes [*CTA 2010, s 664*].

Exemption for chargeable gains

A club that is registered with HMRC as a CASC can make a claim for any gain that accrues not to be a chargeable gain (and therefore outside the charge to corporation tax on chargeable gains) provided that the whole of the gain is applied for charitable purposes. [*CTA 2010, s 665*].

Restrictions on exemptions

The availability of the above exemptions may be restricted in the event that the club incurs non-qualifying expenditure. The rules for restricting the exemptions are set out in *CTA 2010, ss 666–668*.

In the event that an asset ceases to be held for a qualifying purpose, the club is treated as disposing and immediately reacquiring the asset at the market value at the date on which it ceased to be used for a qualifying purpose. The resulting deemed gain does not benefit from the exemption for chargeable gains [*CTA 2010, s 669*].

[*CTA 2010, ss 658–671; FA 2002, s 58, Sch 18; FA 2004, s 56*].

Mutual trading — members' clubs

[75.3] A club established by its members for its own social and recreational purposes is not carrying on a trade and as such is not liable to tax on its surplus from the provision of facilities for members. Any surplus that arises if subscriptions exceed expenditure is treated as a surplus rather than as a trading profit. However, if the club provides services on a commercial basis to outsiders, such as visitors or temporary members, any surplus arising is taxable as trading income. See **56.1 MUTUAL COMPANIES**.

For HMRC's views on the circumstances in which a members' sports club's commercial activities can give rise to taxable trading profits (or to allowable trading losses), see HMRC's Business Income Manual, BIM24215.

VAT repayments

Repayments under *SI 1994 No 687* which are returned to members *pro rata* to the VAT originally paid by them do not give rise to a distribution for tax purposes. Interest on the repayments is chargeable to corporation tax, but other supplemental payments are not chargeable. See HMRC's Business Income Manual, BIM31610.

Holiday clubs and thrift funds

[75.4] Holiday clubs and thrift funds formed annually for the purpose of saving for holidays are regarded as being outside the scope of corporation tax.

Investment clubs

[75.5] An investment club comprises a group of people who have joined together to invest, primarily on the Stock Exchange. Members are entitled to a share of the income received on the investments and of the gains and losses on the disposal of any shares or other investments.

Each individual is assessed to capital gains tax on his share of the gains and losses. Gains can be measured either in accordance with rules agreed with HMRC for investment club purposes or under the usual rules. Under the former, the club adopts a standard agreement (on form 185) which allows each member to be assessed on a proportionate share of the club's income and gains. See HMRC Capital Gains Manual CG20620–CG20625.

Lotteries etc.

[75.6] Supporters of a sports club may raise fund for the club by running or promoting a lottery. Any lottery must comply with the terms of the *Lotteries and Amusements Act 1975*. The tax treatment of sports supporters' lotteries is set out in HMRC Statement of Practice C1. This provides that where a football pool or small lottery is run by the supporters of a club or other society on the basis that a stated percentage or fraction of the cost of each ticket will be given to the club, HMRC accept that the donation element can be excluded when computing for tax purposes the profits of the trade promoting the pool or lottery.

[HMRC Statement of Practice C1].

Dissolution

[75.7] An unincorporated association which sells its only fixed asset and closes down is liable to corporation tax on any chargeable gain arising by virtue of *CTA 2010, s 1118*.

Returns

[75.8] See **66.5 RETURNS** with regard to the concessional exemption from the requirement to deliver returns where the annual corporation tax liability is not expected to exceed £100.

Key points

[75.9] The key points are as follows:

- A club may be established as a company or unincorporated society and be liable to corporation tax on income generated other than by members.
- Special rules apply to certain types of clubs.
- Community amateur sports clubs (CASCs) enjoy a number of tax advantages, including exemption from tax on UK trading profits and UK property income (up to certain limits) and on interest and gift aid income and chargeable gains.
- The tax exemptions available to CASCs are contingent on certain conditions being met.
- To enjoy the tax advantages available to CASCs a club must be registered as a CASC with HMRC. CASCs must meet certain conditions.
- Clubs established by members for their own social and recreational purposes are not trading and as such are not liable to tax on any surplus of subscriptions over income. However any profit on commercial activities is taxable.
- Holiday clubs and thrift funds are outside the scope to tax.
- Members of investment clubs are taxed on income and gains arising from their investments. These may be computed according to normal rules or in accordance with a standard agreement with HMRC.
- Where a lottery is run to raise money for a sports club and a percentage of the ticket price is donated to the club, the donation element is excluded from the computation of profits for tax purposes.

76

Winding Up

Cross-reference. See **65.3 RESIDENCE.**

Simon's Taxes. See D6.7.

Introduction

[76.1] For most corporation tax purposes, the effect of passing of a resolution to wind up, filing a winding up petition or appointing an administrator is the same. However, there are some differences relating to beneficial ownership of assets and accounting periods.

On the commencement of a winding up, an accounting period ends and a new one commences. Thereafter an accounting period only ends on the expiration of twelve months from its beginning or by completion of the winding-up.

[*CTA 2009, s 12; ICTA 1988, s 12(7)*].

Where a company enters administration, an accounting period ends immediately before the administration commenced, and another begins immediately thereafter unless the company was being wound up at that time.

[*CTA 2009, s 10; ICTA 1988, s 12(7ZA); FA 2003, Sch 41 paras 1, 5*].

Liquidation

[76.2] Corporation tax is charged on the profits of a company arising in the winding-up in the financial year (i.e. a year to 31 March — see **1 INTRODUCTION AND RATES OF TAX**) in which the winding-up is completed (the final year) at the rate of corporation tax 'fixed' or 'proposed' for that year. If, however, the rate for the final year has not been proposed or fixed before the winding-up is completed, the rate fixed or proposed for the previous financial year (the penultimate year) applies for the final year. Where the winding-up commenced before the company's final year, the company's profits arising in the penultimate year are charged at the rates applicable to that year.

For the above purposes, the rate of corporation tax means the full rate or, if applicable, the small companies rate. A corporation tax rate is '*fixed*' if it is fixed by an Act passed before the completion of the winding-up. A rate is '*proposed*' if it is proposed by a Budget resolution.

[*CTA 2010, ss 626(2), 627, 628, 632; ICTA 1988, s 342(1)–(3)(7)(8)*].

An assessment on a company's profits for an accounting period falling after the commencement of the winding-up is not invalid because made before the end of the accounting period. The liquidator may determine beforehand an assumed date when the winding-up will be completed for the purpose of making an assessment for a period intended to end with the completion of the winding-up. A date so assumed will not alter the company's final and penultimate years, and if it falls short of the actual completion date, a new accounting period will commence from the assumed date and *CTA 2009, s 12(4)* (previously *ICTA 1988, s 12(7)*) (length of accounting period after commencement of winding-up, see **76.6** below) will apply as if that new accounting period began with the commencement of the winding-up.

[*CTA 2010, s 629; ICTA 1988, s 342(4)–(6); CTA 2009, Sch 1 para 105*].

In the company's final accounting period (i.e. the period ending with the completion of the winding-up), any income consisting of **INTEREST ON OVERPAID TAX** (**50**) is excluded from charge provided that it does not exceed £2,000.

[*CTA 2010, s 633; ICTA 1988, s 342(3A); CTA 2009, Sch 1 para 106*].

Corporation tax on chargeable gains is a 'necessary expense' of a winding-up within the meaning of *Companies Act 1985, s 560* (*Re Mesco Properties Ltd* CA 1979, 54 TC 238).

The Crown may set off a debt due from one Government Department to the company against a debt due to another Department (or other Departments) under *Bankruptcy Act 1914, s 312*. See *Re Cushla Ltd* Ch D, [1979] STC 615 which involved a VAT repayment and liabilities to HMRC and the DSS (now the Department for Work and Pensions).

Administration

[76.3] Where a company enters administration a new accounting period begins. An accounting period ends when it comes out of administration.

Corporation tax is charged on the profits arising in the administration in the financial year (i.e. a year to 31 March — see **1 INTRODUCTION AND RATES OF TAX**) in which the 'dissolution event' occurs (the 'final year') at the rate of corporation tax 'fixed' or 'proposed' for that year. If, however, the rate for the final year has not been proposed or fixed before the dissolution event, the rate fixed or proposed for the previous financial year (the penultimate year) applies for the final year.

The rate of corporation tax for these purposes means the full rate or, if applicable, the small companies rate. A corporation tax rate is '*fixed*' if it is fixed by an Act passed before the dissolution event. A rate is '*proposed*' if it is proposed by a Budget resolution.

The '*dissolution event*' is the sending by the administrator of a notice under *Insolvency Act 1986, Sch B1 para 84(1)* (company moving from administration to dissolution) or, if the company entered administration other than under that Act, anything else done for a like purpose.

An administrator's appointment is normally for twelve months, but this may be extended by six months by creditors or indefinitely by the court.

An assessment on a company's profits for an accounting period in which the company is in administration is not invalid because it is made before the end of the accounting period. In making an assessment after the company enters administration and before the dissolution event, the administrator may act on an assumption as to the date on which an accounting period will end by reason of the occurrence of the dissolution event. A date so assumed will not alter the company's final and penultimate years, and if it falls short of the actual date, a new accounting period will commence from the assumed date, and *CTA 2009, s 10(1)* (previously *ICTA 1988, s 12(3)*) (see **2.5 ACCOUNTING PERIODS**) will apply as if the company entered administration at the start of that new accounting period.

In the accounting period ending with the dissolution event, any **INTEREST ON OVERPAID TAX (50)** is excluded from charge provided that it does not exceed £2,000.

[*CTA 2010, ss 626(3)(4), 630–633; ICTA 1988, s 342A; CTA 2009, Sch 1 para 106*].

Effect on group relationship

[76.4] The passing of a resolution, or the making of an order, or any other act, for the winding-up of a company does not mean that a company (or any of its 75% subsidiaries) ceases to be a member of a group for the purpose of the capital gains provisions in *TCGA 1992, ss 171–181*, regarding which see **18.2 CAPITAL GAINS — GROUPS**. [*TCGA 1992, s 170(11)*]. For other group purposes, e.g. group relief, such acts bring about the end of the group relationship, although the making of an administration order would not of itself bring about such a change.

A company in administration does not lose beneficial ownership of its assets. However, where the company in administration is a subsidiary, there may no longer be a group relationship as the subsidiary is under the control of the administrator, not the parent company shareholders.

Release of debts

[76.5] The release does not give rise to a taxable receipt in the debtor company in relation to debts released as part of a statutory insolvency arrangement.

[*CTA 2009, s 94; ICTA 1988, s 94; FA 2005, s 80, Sch 4 paras 4, 8*].

The creditor will obtain relief for a debt so released, provided that it is released wholly and exclusively for trade purposes.

[*CTA 2009, s 55; ICTA 1988, s 74(1)(j)* (as originally enacted), *s 88D; FA 2005, Sch 4 para 2*].

Vesting of company's assets in liquidator

[76.6] The vesting of a company's assets in a liquidator is disregarded for capital gains purposes and all acts of the liquidator in relation to those assets are treated as acts of the company. [*TCGA 1992, s 8(6)*].

Expenses of winding-up

All expenses properly incurred in a voluntary winding-up, including the remuneration of the liquidator, are payable out of the company's assets in priority to all other claims.

[*Insolvency Act 1986, s 115*].

Insolvency Rules 1986, Rule 4.218(1) provides that expenses of a liquidation are to be paid out of the assets in the order of priority therein specified, subject to a discretionary power of the court under *Insolvency Act 1986, s 156* to vary the order where assets are insufficient to satisfy liabilities.

[*SI 1986 No 1925, Rules 4.218(1), 4.220*].

Included in the normal order of priority is the amount of any corporation tax on chargeable gains accruing on the realisation of any asset of the company. [*Rule 4.218(1)(p)*]. Notwithstanding the specific inclusion of corporation tax on chargeable gains, corporation tax chargeable on a company's post-liquidation profits is to be treated as a 'necessary disbursement' of the liquidator (within *Insolvency Rules 1986, Rule 4.218(1)(m)*), and thus as an expense requiring priority as above (*Re Toshoku Finance UK plc, Kahn and another v CIR* HL, [2002] STC 368). (See, however, **54.35 LOAN RELATIONSHIPS** for provisions which prevent liability arising in the particular circumstances of this case for accounting periods beginning on or after 1 October 2002.)

Profits arising in winding-up

[76.7] A company is chargeable to corporation tax on the profits arising in the winding-up of the company.

[*CTA 2009, s 6(2); ICTA 1988, s 8(2)*].

Cancellation of tax advantages

[76.8] See *ICTA 1988, ss 703–709*, as described at **5.2 ANTI-AVOIDANCE.**

Payment of tax

[76.9] Where a company is being wound up, is in administrative receivership or having its affairs, business and property managed by an administrator, the company is not required to file its self-assessment corporation tax return electronically.

[*SI 2009 No 3218*].

77

Finance Act 2011 Summary

[77.1] (Royal Assent 19 July 2011)

Finance Act 2011 Statutory reference	
s 4	Main rate for financial year 2011. From 1 April 2011 the corporation tax main rate will be 26% for profits other than for ring fenced profits. See **1.3 INTRODUCTION AND RATES OF TAX.**
s 5	**Charge and main rate for financial year 2012.** From 1 April 2012, the corporation tax main rate will still be 25% (30% for ring fenced profits). See **1.3 INTRODUCTION AND RATES OF TAX.**
s 6	**Small profits rates and fractions for financial year 2011.** The small profits rate will remain at 20% from 1 April 2011 (19% on ring fenced profits). The standard fraction is 3/200ths, the ring fence fraction is 11/400ths. See **1.3 INTRODUCTION AND RATES OF TAX; 67.2 SMALL PROFITS — REDUCED RATES.**
s 7	**Increase in the supplementary charge.** The supplementary charge is respect of ring fenced trades is increased from 20% to 32% for accounting periods beginning on or after 24 March 2011. See**1.2 INTRODUCTION AND RATES OF TAX.**
s 10	**Plant and machinery writing down allowance.** The main rate for capital allowances is reduced from 20% to 18% and the special rate is reduced from 10% to 8%, for new and unrelieved expenditure as from 1 April 2012. See **12 PLANT AND MACHINERY, 12.7 WRITING DOWN ALLOWANCES** and **12.9 SPECIAL RATE POOL.**
s 11	**Annual investment allowance.** The maximum amount of the annual investment allowance (AIA) is reduced from £100,000 to a new limit of £25,000. The increase has effect for expenditure incurred on or after 1 April 2012. See **11.15 CAPITAL ALLOWANCES — PLANT AND MACHINERY: ELIGIBLE EXPENDITURE AND INITIAL ALLOWANCES.**
s 12	**Short life assets.** The period over which an asset can receive short life asset treatment is increased from four years to eight years. This applies to expenditure incurred on or after 1 April 2011. See **12.22 CAPITAL ALLOWANCES — PLANT AND MACHINERY: SHORT LIFE ASSETS.**
s 25	**Landfill tax.** Increase in rate from £56 to £64 per tonne for disposals on or after 1 April 2012. See **71.76 TRADING EXPENSES AND DEDUCTIONS — WASTE DISPOSAL.**

s 26, Sch 2 **Employment income provided through third parties.** The legislation introduces new anti-avoidance rules with regards to the use of EBTs and EFURBs to avoid income tax and national insurance contributions (and circumvent the approved pension scheme limitations). See **71.29** **TRADING EXPENSES AND DEDUCTIONS** — employee benefit contributions and Tolley's Income Tax.

s 26, Sch 2 **Employment income provided through third parties.** The legislation introduces new anti-avoidance rules with regards to the use of EBTs and EFURBs to avoid income tax and national insurance contributions (and circumvent the approved pension scheme limitations). See **71.29** **TRADING EXPENSES AND DEDUCTIONS** — employee benefit contributions and Tolley's Income Tax.

s 27, Sch 3 **Tainted charity donations.** Anti-avoidance provisions have been introduced with regard to substantial donors to charity where arrangements are entered into to obtain benefits from such donations. See further **20.10 CHARITIES — SUBSTANTIAL DONORS** and **61.11 PROFIT COMPUTATIONS — CHARITABLE DONATIONS RELIEF.**

s 28, Sch 4 **Amounts not fully recognised for accounting purposes.** Anti-avoidance provisions are introduced which amend the rules for loan relationships and derivatives that apply to amounts that are not fully recognised for accounting purposes. As from 6 December 2010 derecognition in the accounts is overridden for tax purposes and any losses made are not allowable where a company is party to tax avoidance arrangements. See **5.55 ANTI-AVOIDANCE; 30 DERIVATIVE CONTRACTS LEGISLATION** and **54 LOAN RELATIONSHIPS.**

s 29 **Loan relationships involving connected debtor and creditor.** Anti-avoidance legislation at *CTA 2009, ss 418* and *419* is amended to ensure the legislation applies where a company connected with the creditor company is entitled to receive the shares issued, and also ensures that the legislation applies where one or more of the parties is a CFC. See **30 LOAN RELATIONSHIPS.**

s 30, Sch 5 **Group mismatch schemes.** This ensures that groups cannot use loan relationships or derivative contracts to reduce their tax liability purely as a result of asymmetries in the way different members. See **30 LOAN RELATIONSHIPS.**

s 31 **Companies ceasing to be member of group.** The degrouping rules for CGT groups of companies are amended to ensure that tax is not avoided by a series of transactions undertaken prior to disposal with the intention to escape the degrouping charge. See **18 CAPITAL GAINS — GROUPS.**

s 32, Sch 6 **Leasing business.** The sale of lessor provisions are amended to ensure that the legislation correctly identifies the appropriate companies and brings in a charge which accurately reflects the deferred tax position of the company. See **5.27 ANTI-AVOIDANCE.**

s 33	**Long funding finance leases.** In response to a disclosed scheme provisions have been introduced such that *CAA 2001, ss 70C* and *70D* are amended to prevent any relief from being available in excess of cost. See **13.6, 13.7** and **13.9 PLANT AND MACHINERY.**
s 34, Sch 7	**Investment companies.** Provisions are introduced to ensure that investment companies are not able to generate foreign exchange losses by changing their functional currency. See **51 INVESTMENT COMPANIES** and **36 FOREIGN CURRENCY.**
s 41	**Gift Aid.** The limits are increased for the maximum value of benefits a charity can provide to an individual or corporate donor from £500 to £2,500. See **20 CHARITIES.**
s 43	**Relief for R&D expenditure by SMEs.** The rate of R&D relief for SMEs is increased however, the additional deduction for R&D expenditure on drugs and vaccines is reduced. See **20 CHARITIES.**
s 44, Sch 9	**Value shifting.** Provisions are introduced to simplify the rules that apply where the capital gains proceeds on a disposal are reduced because the value of an asset has been reduced. See **18 CAPITAL GAINS — GROUPS.**
s 45, Sch 10	**Company ceasing to be a member of a group.** The rules with regard to degrouping charges for groups are simplified, with regard to capital gains and intangible fixed assets. See **18 CAPITAL GAINS — GROUPS** and **48 INTANGIBLE ASSETS.**
s 46, Sch 11	**Pre-entry losses.** The rules with regard to pre-entry losses are simplified, in particular the use of losses that arise after a company joins a group will no longer be restricted. See **18 CAPITAL GAINS — GROUPS.**
s 47, Sch 12	**CFCs.** Various interim changes are introduced to the CFC rules as a first step towards full reform in 2012. See **27 CONTROLLED FOREIGN COMPANIES.**
s 48, Sch 13	**Foreign permanent establishment profits.** An opt in exemption for foreign PE profits has been introduced as from Royal Assent. See **32 DOUBLE TAX RELIEF.**
s 49	**Meaning of investment trust.** The provision amends *CTA 2010* to provide a new definition of investment trust and to provide a power to the Treasury to make regulations about the circumstances in which applications for investment trust status may be approved. See **53 INVESTMENT TRUSTS.**
s 50	**Power to make provision about treatment of transactions.** A new *Chapter 3A* is inserted into *CTA 2010* to provide a power for the Treasury to make regulations as to the treatment of certain transactions of investment trusts. See **53 INVESTMENT TRUSTS.**
s 52, Sch 14	**Furnished holiday lettings.** The trading treatment of furnished holiday lettings is formally extended to EEA lettings; corporation tax loss relief against total profits is removed; and the length of days property must be available to let and actually let is extended. See **62 PROPERTY INCOME.**

s 53 **Changes to leasing accounting standards.** The changes introduced ensure that a business which accounts for lease transactions using the new form of leasing accounting standard (currently proposed to be introduced during 2011) will be treated for tax purposes as if the changes to the accounting standard had not taken place. See **70.19 TRADE PROFITS — APPLICATION OF ACCOUNTANCY PRINCIPLES** and **71.46 TRADE PROFITS — INCOME AND SPECIFIC TRADES.**

s 54 **Leasing companies — withdrawal of election.** The election out of qualifying change of ownership in *CTA 2010, s 398A* is withdrawn, and only applies before 23 March 2011. See **5.28 ANTI-AVOIDANCE.**

s 55 **Companies with small profits: associated companies.** The legislation is amended to ensure companies are not held to be associated through an attribution of rights, solely by virtue of relationships between individuals, but rather only where the level of commercial interdependence between the companies makes it appropriate to do so. See **67 SMALL PROFITS REDUCED RATES.**

s 57 **Tonnage tax — capital allowances.** Changes are made to equalise the position of ships leased to companies operating the tonnage tax regime with assets outside the regime. The rate on the first £40m of expenditure will be the main rate (for long life assets the special rate), and on the next £40m of expenditure the rate will be the special rate. See **70.76 TRADE PROFITS — TONNAGE TAX.**

s 58 **Transfer pricing — application of OECD principles.** The definition of 'guidelines' is amended to refer to the OECD July 2010 version. See **72 TRANSFER PRICING.**

s 59 **Offshore funds.** A new *s 363A* is inserted into *TIOPA 2010* so as to treat certain offshore funds as not resident in the UK where they might otherwise be so treated by virtue of having a UK resident fund manager. See **57 OFFSHORE FUNDS.**

s 60 **Index linked gilts.** The definition of index linked gilts is amended to include payments determined wholly or partly by reference to an index of prices published by the Statistics board. See **54 LOAN RELATIONSHIPS.**

ss 65–71 **Pensions changes.** See Tolley's Income Tax with regard to the changes to the pensions regime.

s 72, Sch 19 **Bank levy.** A new tax, the bank levy, is introduced which applies to periods of account ending on or after 1 January 2011. See **8 BANKS.**

s 86, Schs 23 and 24 **Data-gathering powers.** This section introduces *Sch 23* and *Sch 24* which provide information powers to HMRC for collecting data from certain third parties and amends HMRC's information and inspection powers at *FA 2008, Sch 36*. See **43 HMRC INVESTIGATORY POWERS.**

s 87, Sch 25 **Mutual assistance for recovering of taxes.** The schedule gives effect to the EU Directive 2010/24/EU on the mutual assistance of the recovery of claims relating to taxes, duties and other measures. See **43 HMRC INVESTIGATORY POWERS**.

78 Table of Statutes

References on the right-hand side of this table are to paragraphs.

79 Table of Statutory Instruments

Paragraph references printed in **bold** type indicate where the Statutory Instrument is set out in part or in full.

80 Table of Cases

This Table of Cases is referenced to paragraph numbers.

A

B

C

D

E

F

G

H

I

J

K

L

M

N

O

P

Q

R

S

T

U

V

Y

Yates (Inspector of Taxes) v GCA International Ltd [1991] STC 157, 64 TC 37 .... 32.2
Young v Duthie (Inspector of Taxes) (1969) 45 TC 624, 48 ATC 171, [1969] TR 167 .... 7.9; 43.20
Young (J H) & Co v CIR (1926) 12 TC 827, 4 ATC 579, 1926 SC 30, 1925 SLT 628, Ct of Sess 71.13
Yuill v Fletcher (Inspector of Taxes) [1984] STC 401, 58 TC 145, [1984] LS Gaz R 1604, CA 5.16
Yuill v Wilson (Inspector of Taxes) [1980] 3 All ER 7, [1980] 1 WLR 910, [1980] STC 460, 52 TC 674, 124 Sol Jo 528, HL 5.16

Decisions of the European Court of Justice are listed below numerically. These decisions are also included in the preceding alphabetical list.

106/77: Amministrazione delle Finanze dello Stato v Simmenthal SpA [1978] ECR 629, [1978] 3 CMLR 263, ECJ 34.2
8/81: Becker v Finanzamt Münster-Innenstadt [1982] ECR 53, [1982] 1 CMLR 499, ECJ 34.2
C-283/94: Denkavit Internationaal BV v Bundesamt für Finanzen [1996] ECR I-5063, [1996] STC 1445, ECJ 34.4
C-291/94: VITIC Amsterdam BV v Bundesamt für Finanzen [1996] ECR I-5063, [1996] STC 1445, ECJ 34.4
C-292/94: Voormeer BV v Bundesamt für Finanzen [1996] ECR I-5063, [1996] STC 1445, ECJ 34.4
C-28/95: Leur-Bloem v Inspecteur der Belastingdienst/Ondernemingen Amsterdam 2 [1998] QB 182, [1997] ECR I-4161, [1997] All ER (EC) 738, [1998] 2 WLR 27, [1998] 1 CMLR 157, [1997] STC 1205, ECJ 34.4
C-264/96: Imperial Chemical Industries plc v Colmer (Inspector of Taxes) [1998] ECR I-4695, [1998] All ER (EC) 585, [1999] 1 WLR 108, [1998] 3 CMLR 293, [1998] STC 874, ECJ; apld sub nom ICI plc v Colmer (Inspector of Taxes) [2000] 1 All ER 129, [1999] 1 WLR 2035, [2000] 1 CMLR 142, [1999] STC 1089, [1999] 46 LS Gaz R 40, 144 Sol Jo LB 7, HL 39.19
C-397/98: Metallgesellschaft Ltd v CIR [2001] Ch 620, [2001] ECR I-1727, [2001] All ER (EC) 496, [2001] 2 WLR 1497, [2001] 2 CMLR 700, [2001] STC 452, 3 ITLR 385, [2001] All ER (D) 96 (Mar), ECJ 3.1; 32.3
C-410/98: Hoechst AG v CIR [2001] Ch 620, [2001] ECR I-1727, [2001] All ER (EC) 496, [2001] 2 WLR 1497, [2001] 2 CMLR 700, [2001] STC 452, 3 ITLR 385, [2001] All ER (D) 96 (Mar), ECJ 3.1; 32.3
C-58/01: Oce van Grinten NV v CIR [2003] ECR I-9809, [2003] 3 CMLR 1104, [2003] STC 1248, 6 ITLR 137, [2003] All ER (D) 169 (Sep), ECJ 32.14
C-319/02: Manninen, Re [2005] Ch 236, [2004] ECR I-7477, [2005] All ER (EC) 465, [2005] 2 WLR 670, [2004] 3 CMLR 881, [2004] STC 1444, 7 ITLR 119, [2004] All ER (D) 42 (Sep), ECJ 31.26; 34.4
C-446/03: Marks & Spencer plc v Halsey (Inspector of Taxes) [2006] Ch 184, [2005] ECR I-10837, [2006] All ER (EC) 255, [2006] 2 WLR 250, [2006] STC 237, 8 ITLR 358, (2005) Times, 15 December, [2005] All ER (D) 174 (Dec), ECJ 39.2
C-196/04: Cadbury Schweppes plc v Revenue and Customs Comrs [2007] Ch 30, [2006] ECR I-7995, [2007] All ER (EC) 153, [2006] 3 WLR 890, [2007] 1 CMLR 43, [2006] STC 1908, 9 ITLR 89, (2006) Times, 20 September, [2006] All ER (D) 48 (Sep), ECJ 27.1; 27.6; 27.11
C-374/04: Test Claimants in Class IV of the ACT Group Litigation v CIR [2006] ECR I-11673, [2007] All ER (EC) 351, [2007] 1 CMLR 1111, [2007] STC 404, 9 ITLR 360, [2006] All ER (D) 157 (Dec), ECJ 32.3
C-446/04: Test Claimants in the FII Group Litigation v CIR [2006] ECR I-11753, [2007] 1 CMLR 1021, [2007] STC 326, 9 ITLR 426, [2006] All ER (D) 168 (Dec), ECJ 31.26

81 Index

This index is referenced to chapter and paragraph number.

B

D

F

G

H

I

J

O